CONCISE MAJOR 21ST-CENTURY WRITERS

CONCISE MAJOR 21ST- CENTURY WRITERS

A Selection of Sketches from
Contemporary Authors

Tracey L. Matthews, Project Editor

Volume 3: Gu-Ma

THOMSON
GALE™

Detroit • New York • San Francisco • New Haven, Conn. • Waterville, Maine • London • Munich

THOMSON
GALE

Concise Major 21st-Century Writers

Project Editor
Tracey L. Matthews

Editorial
Michelle Kazensky, Josh Kondek, Lisa Kumar, Julie Mellors, Joyce Nakamura, Mary Ruby

Composition and Electronic Capture
Carolyn A. Roney

Manufacturing
Rita Wimberley

Library of Congress Control Number: 2006929297

ISBN 0-7876-7539-3 (hardcover : set), ISBN 0-7876-7540-7 (v. 1), ISBN 0-7876-7541-5 (v. 2), ISBN 0-7876-7542-3 (v. 3), ISBN 0-7876-7543-1 (v. 4), ISBN 0-7876-7544-X (v. 5)

Printed in the United States of America
10 9 8 7 6 5 4 3 2 1

Contents

Introduction

Concise Major 21st-Century Writers (*CMTFCW*) is an abridgement of the 2004 eBook-only edition of Thomson Gale's *Major 21st-Century Writers* (*MTFCW*), a set based on Thomson Gale's award-winning *Contemporary Authors* series. *CMTFCW* provides students, educators, librarians, researchers, and general readers with a concise yet comprehensive source of biographical and bibliographical information on 700 of the most influential and studied authors at the turn of the twenty-first century as well as emerging authors whose literary significance is likely to increase in the coming decades.

CMTFCW includes sketches on approximately 700 authors who made writing literature their primary occupation and who have had at least part of their oeuvre published in English. Thus novelists, short story writers, nonfiction writers, poets, dramatists, genre writers, children's writers, and young adult writers of about sixty nationalities and ethnicities are represented. Selected sketches of authors that appeared in the 2004 edition of *MTFCW* are completely updated to include information on their lives and works through 2006. About thirty authors featured in *CMTFCW* are new to this set evidencing Thomson Gale's commitment to identifying emerging writers of recent eras and of many cultures.

How Authors Were Chosen for *CMTFCW*

The preliminary list of authors for *MTFCW* was sent to an advisory board of librarians, teaching professionals, and writers whose input resulted in informal inclusion criteria. In consultation with the editors, the list was narrowed to 700 authors for the concise edition plus criteria were established for adding authors. Criteria our editors used for adding authors not previously published in the last edition of *MTFCW* include:

- Authors who have won major awards

- Authors whose works are bestsellers

- Authors whose works are being incorporated into curricula and studied at the high school and/or college level

Broad Coverage in a Single Source

CMTFCW provides detailed biographical and bibliographical coverage of the most influential writers of our time, including:

- *Contemporary Literary Figures*: Mitch Albom, Sherman Alexie, Maya Angelou, Margaret Atwood, Dan Brown, Michael Chabon, J.M. Coetzee, Don DeLillo, Joan Didion, Dave Eggers, Gabriel Garcia Marquez, Nadine Gordimer, Khaled Hosseini, Toni Morrison, Joyce Carol Oates, Thomas Pynchon, J.K. Rowling, Salman Rushdie, Amy Tan, and John Updike, among many others.

- *Genre Writers*: Ray Bradbury, Tom Clancy, Philip K. Dick, Neil Gaiman, Sue Grafton, Dennis Lehane, Stephen King, Walter Mosley, Christopher Paolini, Anne Rice, Nora Roberts, Art Spiegelman, and Jane Yolen, among many others.

- *Novelists and Short Story Writers*: James Baldwin, Charles Baxter, Peter Carey, Carlos Fuentes, Graham Greene, Sebastian Junger, Sue Monk Kidd, John le Carré, Yann Martel, Rick Moody, Chuck Palahniuk, and Zadie Smith, among many others.

- *Dramatists*: Edward Albee, Samuel Beckett, Athol Fugard, Tony Kushner, David Mamet, Arthur Miller, Neil Simon, Tom Stoppard, Wendy Wasserstein, Alfred Uhry, Paula Vogel, and Tennessee Williams, among many others.

- *Poets*: Gwendolyn Brooks, Allen Ginsburg, Louise Glück, Jorie Graham, Seamus Heaney, Ted Kooser, Mary Oliver, Kenneth Rexroth, Adrienne Rich, Derek Walcott, and C.K. Williams, among many others.

How Entries Are Organized

Each *CMTFCW* biography begins with a series of rubrics that outlines the author's personal history, including information on the author's birth, death, family life, education, career, memberships, and awards. The *Writings* section lists a bibliography of the author's works along with the publisher and year published. The *Sidelights* section provides a biographical portrait of the author's development; information about the critical reception of the author's works; and revealing comments, often by the author, on personal interests, motivations, and thoughts on writing. The *Biographical/Critical Sources* section features a useful list of books, articles, and reviews about the author and his or her work. This section also includes citations for all material quoted in the *Sidelights* essay.

Other helpful sections include *Adaptations*, which lists the author's works that have been adapted by others into various media, including motion pictures, stage plays, and television or radio broadcasts, while the *Work in Progress* section lists titles or descriptions of works that are scheduled for publication by the author.

Using the Indexes

CMTFCW features a Nationality/Ethnicity index as well as a Subject/Genre index. More than sixty nations are represented in the Nationality/Ethnicity index, reflecting the international scope of this set and the multinational status of many authors. The Subject/Genre index covers over fifty genres and subject areas of fiction and nonfiction frequently referenced by educators and students, including social and political literature, environmental issues, and science fiction/science fantasy literature.

Citing *CMTFCW*

Students writing papers who wish to include references to information found in *CMTFCW* may cite sources in their bibliographies using the following format. Teachers adhering to other bibliographic formats may request that their students alter the citation below, which should only serve as a guide:

"Margaret Atwood." *Concise Major 21st-Century Writers*. Ed. Tracey L. Matthews. Detroit: Thomson Gale, 2006, pp. 214-223.

Comments Are Appreciated

CMTFCW is intended to serve as a useful reference tool for a wide audience, so your comments about this work are encouraged. Suggestions for authors to include in future editions of *CMTFCW* are also welcome. Send comments and suggestions to: *Concise Major 21st-Century Writers*, Thomson Gale, 27500 Drake Rd., Farmington Hills, MI 48331-3535; call at 1-248-699-4253; or fax at 1-248-699-8070.

Concise Major 21st-Century Writers
Advisory Board

In preparation for the first edition of *Major 20th-Century Writers* (MTCW), the editors of *Contemporary Authors* conducted a telephone survey of librarians and mailed a survey to more than 4,000 libraries to help determine the kind of reference resource the libraries wanted. Once it was clear that a comprehensive, yet affordable source of information on twentieth-century writers was needed to serve small and medium-sized libraries, a wide range of resources was consulted: national surveys of books taught in American high schools and universities; British secondary school syllabi; reference works such as the *New York Library Desk Reference, Reading Lists for College-Bound Students: The Books Most Recommended by America's Top Colleges, The List of Books, E.D. Hirsch's Cultural Legacy,* and volumes in Thomson Gale's Literacy Criticism and Dictionary of Literary Biography series. From these resources and with advice of an international advisory board, the author list for the first edition of MTCW was finalized, the sketches edited, and the volume published.

For the eBook edition of *Major 21st-Century Writers* (MTFCW), the editors compiled a preliminary author list based largely upon a list of authors included in the second print edition of MTCW with recommendations based on new inclusion criteria. This list was sent to an advisory board of librarians, authors, and teaching professionals in both the United States and Britain. In addition to vetting the submitted list, the advisors suggested other noteworthy writers. Recommendations made by the advisors ensure that authors from all nations and genres are represented.

Concise Major 21st-Century Writers (CMTFCW) is an abridgement of the eBook-only edition of MTFCW. The editors built upon the work of past advisors of the eBook edition to create a concise version and added authors who have earned increased recognition since the publication of MTFCW. The advisory board for MTFCW played a major role in shaping the author list for CMTFCW, and the editors wish to thank them for sharing their expertise. The twenty-seven member advisory board includes the following individuals:

- **Carl Antonucci,** Director of Library Services, Capital Community College, Hartford, Connecticut

- **Barbara Bibel,** Reference Librarian, Oakland Public Library, Oakland, California

- **Beverly A. Buciak,** Librarian, Brother Rice High School, Chicago, Illinois

- **Mary Ann Capan,** District Library Media Specialist, Sherrard Jr. Sr. High School, Sherrard, Illinois

- **Linda Carvell,** Head Librarian, Lancaster Country Day School, Lancaster, Pennsylvania

- **Anne Christensen,** Librarian II, Phoenix Public Library, Phoenix, Arizona

- **Peggy Curran,** Adult Services Librarian, Naperville Public Library, Naperville, Illinois

- **Eva M. Davis,** Youth Services Manager, Ann Arbor District Library, Ann Arbor, Michigan

- **Thomas Eertmoed,** Librarian, Illinois Central College, East Peoria, Illinois

- **Lucy K. Gardner,** Director, Howard Community College, Columbia, Maryland

- **Christine C. Godin,** Director of Learning Resources, Northwest Vista College, San Antonio, Texas

- **Francisca Goldsmith,** Senior Librarian, Berkeley Public Library, Berkeley, California

- **Nancy Guidry,** Reference Librarian, Bakersfield College, Bakersfield, California

- **Jack Hicks,** Administrative Librarian, Deerfield Public Library, Deerfield, Illinois

- **Charlie Jones,** School Library Media Specialist, Plymouth High School Library Media Center, Canton, Michigan

- **Carol M. Keeler,** Upper School Media Specialist, Detroit Country Day School, Beverly Hills, Michigan

- **Georgia Lomax,** Managing Librarian, King County Library System, Covington, Washington

- **Mary Jane Marden,** Librarian, M.M. Bennett Library, St. Petersburg College, Pinellas Park, Florida

- **Frances Moffett,** Materials Selector, Fairfax County Public Library, Chantilly, Virginia

- **Ruth Mormon,** Upper School Librarian, The Meadows School, Las Vegas, Nevada

- **Bonnie Morris,** Upper School Media Specialist, Minnehaha Academy, Minneapolis, Minneapolis

- **Nancy Pinkston,** English Teacher, Sherrard Jr. Sr. High School, Sherrard, Illinois

- **Robert Reginald,** Head of Technical Services and Collection Development, California State University, San Bernadino, California

- **Janet P. Sarratt,** Library Media Specialist, John E. Ewing Middle School, Gaffney, South Carolina

- **Brian Stableford,** 0.5 Lecturer in Creative Writing, University College, Winchester (formerly King Alfred's College), Reading, England

- **Stephen Weiner,** Director, Maynard Public Library, Maynard, Massachusetts

- **Hope Yelich,** Reference Librarian, College of William and Mary, Williamsburg, Virginia

Concise Major 21st-Century Writers

VOLUME 1: A-Cl

Abbey, Edward 1927-1989

Abe, Kobo 1924-1993

Achebe, Chinua 1930-

Ackroyd, Peter 1949-

Adams, Alice 1926-1999

Adams, Douglas 1952-2001

Affabee, Eric
  See Stine, R.L.

Aghill, Gordon
  See Silverberg, Robert

Albee, Edward 1928-

Albom, Mitch 1958-

Aldiss, Brian W. 1925-

Aldrich, Ann
  See Meaker, Marijane

Alegría, Claribel 1924-

Alexie, Sherman 1966-

Allan, John B.
  See Westlake, Donald E.

Allen, Paula Gunn 1939-

Allen, Roland
  See Ayckbourn, Alan

Allende, Isabel 1942-

Allison, Dorothy E. 1949-

Alvarez, A. 1929-

Alvarez, Julia 1950-

Amado, Jorge 1912-2001

Ambrose, Stephen E. 1936-2002

Amichai, Yehuda 1924-2000

Amis, Kingsley 1922-1995

Amis, Martin 1949-

Anand, Mulk Raj 1905-2004

Anaya, Rudolfo A. 1937-

Anderson, Laurie Halse 1961-

Anderson, Poul 1926-2001

Andrews, Elton V.
  See Pohl, Frederik

Angelou, Maya 1928-

Anouilh, Jean 1910-1987

Anthony, Peter
  See Shaffer, Peter

Anthony, Piers 1934-

Archer, Jeffrey 1940-

Archer, Lee
  See Ellison, Harlan

Ard, William
  See Jakes, John

Arenas, Reinaldo 1943-1990

Arias, Ron 1941-

Arnette, Robert
  See Silverberg, Robert

Aronson, Marc 1948-

Ashbery, John 1927-

Ashbless, William
  See Powers, Tim

Asimov, Isaac 1920-1992

Atwood, Margaret 1939-

Axton, David
  See Koontz, Dean R.

Ayckbourn, Alan 1939-

Bachman, Richard
  See King, Stephen

Bainbridge, Beryl 1934-

Baker, Nicholson 1957-

Baker, Russell 1925-

Baldacci, David 1960-

Baldwin, James 1924-1987

Ballard, J.G. 1930-

Bambara, Toni Cade 1939-1995

Banat, D.R.
  See Bradbury, Ray

Banks, Iain M. 1954-

Banks, Russell 1940-

Baraka, Amiri 1934-

Barclay, Bill
  See Moorcock, Michael

Barclay, William Ewert
  See Moorcock, Michael

Barker, Clive 1952-

Barnes, Julian 1946-

Baron, David
  See Pinter, Harold

Barrington, Michael
  See Moorcock, Michael

Barthelme, Donald 1931-1989

Bashevis, Isaac
  See Singer, Isaac Bashevis

Bass, Kingsley B., Jr.
  See Bullins, Ed

Baxter, Charles 1947-

Beagle, Peter S. 1939-

Beattie, Ann 1947-

Beauvoir, Simone de 1908-1986

Beckett, Samuel 1906-1989

Beldone, Phil "Cheech"
  See Ellison, Harlan

Bell, Madison Smartt 1957-

Bellow, Saul 1915-2005

Benchley, Peter 1940-2006

Benitez, Sandra 1941-

Berendt, John 1939-

Berger, Thomas 1924-

Berry, Jonas
  See Ashbery, John

Berry, Wendell 1934-

Bethlen, T.D.
  See Silverberg, Robert

Binchy, Maeve 1940-

Bird, Cordwainer
  See Ellison, Harlan

Birdwell, Cleo
  See DeLillo, Don

Blade, Alexander
  See Silverberg, Robert

Blais, Marie-Claire 1939-

Bliss, Frederick
  See Card, Orson Scott

Block, Francesca Lia 1962-

Bloom, Amy 1953-

Blount, Roy, Jr. 1941-

Blue, Zachary
  See Stine, R.L.

Blume, Judy 1938-

Bly, Robert 1926-

Boland, Eavan 1944-

Böll, Heinrich 1917-1985

Boot, William
  See Stoppard, Tom

Borges, Jorge Luis 1899-1986

Bowles, Paul 1910-1999

Box, Edgar
  See Vidal, Gore

Boyle, Mark
  See Kienzle, William X.

Boyle, T. Coraghessan 1948-

Brackett, Peter
  See Collins, Max Allan

Bradbury, Edward P.
  See Moorcock, Michael

Bradbury, Ray 1920-

Bradley, Marion Zimmer 1930-1999

Bragg, Rick 1959-

Brashares, Ann 1967-

Breslin, Jimmy 1930-

Brink, André 1935-

Brodsky, Iosif
Alexandrovich 1940-1996

Brodsky, Joseph
  See Brodsky, Iosif Alexandrovich

Brodsky, Yosif
  See Brodsky, Iosif Alexandrovich

Brookner, Anita 1928-

Brooks, Cleanth 1906-1994

Brooks, Gwendolyn 1917-2000

Brooks, Terry 1944-

Brown, Dan 1964-

Brown, Dee Alexander 1908-2002

Brown, Rita Mae 1944-

Brown, Sterling Allen 1901-1989

Brownmiller, Susan 1935-

Bruchac, Joseph, III 1942-

Bryan, Michael
  See Moore, Brian

Buckley, William F., Jr. 1925-

Buechner, Frederick 1926-

Bukowski, Charles 1920-1994

Bullins, Ed 1935-

Burke, Ralph
  See Silverberg, Robert

Burns, Tex
  See L'Amour, Louis

Busiek, Kurt

Bustos, F.
  See Borges, Jorge Luis

Butler, Octavia E. 1947-2006

Butler, Robert Olen 1945-

Byatt, A.S. 1936-

Cabrera Infante,
Guillermo 1929-2005

Cade, Toni
  See Bambara, Toni Cade

Cain, G.
  See Cabrera Infante, Guillermo

Caldwell, Erskine 1903-1987

Calisher, Hortense 1911-

Calvino, Italo 1923-1985

Camp, John 1944-

Campbell, Bebe Moore 1950-

Capote, Truman 1924-1984

Card, Orson Scott 1951-

Carey, Peter 1943-

Carroll, James P. 1943-

Carroll, Jonathan 1949-

Carruth, Hayden 1921-

Carter, Nick
  See Smith, Martin Cruz

Carver, Raymond 1938-1988

Cavallo, Evelyn
  See Spark, Muriel

Cela, Camilo José 1916-2002

Cela y Trulock, Camilo José
  See Cela, Camilo José

Cesaire, Aimé 1913-

Chabon, Michael 1963-

Chang, Iris 1968-2004

Chapman, Lee
  See Bradley, Marion Zimmer

Chapman, Walker
  See Silverberg, Robert

Charby, Jay
  See Ellison, Harlan

Chávez, Denise 1948-

Cheever, John 1912-1982

Chevalier, Tracy 1962-

Childress, Alice 1920-1994

Chomsky, Noam 1928-

Cisneros, Sandra 1954-

Cixous, Hélène 1937-

Clancy, Tom 1947-

Clark, Carol Higgins 1956-

Clark, Curt
  See Westlake, Donald E.

Clark, John Pepper
  See Clark Bekederemo, J.P.

Clark, Mary Higgins 1929-

Clark Bekederemo, J.P. 1935-

Clarke, Arthur C. 1917-

Clarke, Austin C. 1934-

Clavell, James 1925-1994

Cleary, Beverly 1916-

Clifton, Lucille 1936-

Clinton, Dirk
  See Silverberg, Robert

Clowes, Daniel 1961-

VOLUME 2: Co-Gr

Codrescu, Andrei 1946-

Coe, Tucker
  See Westlake, Donald E.

Coetzee, J.M. 1940-

Coffey, Brian
  See Koontz, Dean R.

Coleman, Emmett
  See Reed, Ishmael

Collins, Billy 1941-

Collins, Max Allan 1948-

Colvin, James
  See Moorcock, Michael

Condé, Maryse 1937-

Connell, Evan S., Jr. 1924-

Conroy, Pat 1945-

Cook, Roy
  See Silverberg, Robert

Cooper, J. California

Cooper, Susan 1935-

Coover, Robert 1932-

Cormier, Robert 1925-2000

Cornwell, Patricia 1956-

Corso, Gregory 1930-2001

Cortázar, Julio 1914-1984

Courtney, Robert
  See Ellison, Harlan

Cox, William Trevor
  See Trevor, William

Craig, A.A.
  See Anderson, Poul

Creeley, Robert 1926-2005

Crews, Harry 1935-

Crichton, Michael 1942-

Crowley, John 1942-

Crutcher, Chris 1946-

Cruz, Victor Hernández 1949-

Culver, Timothy J.
  See Westlake, Donald E.

Cunningham, E.V.
  See Fast, Howard

Cunningham, J. Morgan
  See Westlake, Donald E.

Cunningham, Michael 1952-

Curtis, Price
  See Ellison, Harlan

Cussler, Clive 1931-

Cutrate, Joe
  See Spiegelman, Art

Dahl, Roald 1916-1990

Dale, George E.
  See Asimov, Isaac

Danticat, Edwidge 1969-

Danziger, Paula 1944-2004

Davies, Robertson 1913-1995

Davis, B. Lynch
  See Borges, Jorge Luis

Deighton, Len 1929-

Delany, Samuel R. 1942-

DeLillo, Don 1936-

Demijohn, Thom
  See Disch, Thomas M.

Denis, Julio
  See Cortázar, Julio

Denmark, Harrison
  See Zelazny, Roger

dePaola, Tomie 1934-

Derrida, Jacques 1930-

Desai, Anita 1937-

DeWitt, Helen 1957-

Dexter, Colin 1930-

Dexter, John
  See Bradley, Marion Zimmer

Dexter, N.C.
  See Dexter, Colin

Dexter, Pete 1943-

Diamond, Jared 1937-

Dick, Philip K. 1928-1982

Didion, Joan 1934-

Dillard, Annie 1945-

Disch, Thomas M. 1940-

Disch, Tom
  See Disch, Thomas M.

Doctorow, E.L. 1931-

Domecq, H. Bustos
  See Borges, Jorge Luis

Domini, Rey
  See Lorde, Audre

Dorris, Michael 1945-1997

Douglas, Leonard
  See Bradbury, Ray

Douglas, Michael
  See Crichton, Michael

Dove, Rita 1952-

Doyle, John
  See Graves, Robert

Doyle, Roddy 1958-

Dr. A.
  See Asimov, Isaac

Dr. Seuss
  See Geisel, Theodor Seuss

Drabble, Margaret 1939-

Gibson, William 1948-

Gibson, William2 1914-

Gilchrist, Ellen 1935-

Ginsberg, Allen 1926-1997

Ginzburg, Natalia 1916-1991

Giovanni, Nikki 1943-

Glück, Louise 1943-

Godwin, Gail 1937-

Golden, Arthur 1956-

Golding, William 1911-1993

Goodkind, Terry 1948-

Gordimer, Nadine 1923-

Goryan, Sirak
    See Saroyan, William

Gottesman, S.D.
    See Pohl, Frederik

Gould, Stephen Jay 1941-2002

Goytisolo, Juan 1931-

Grafton, Sue 1940-

Graham, Jorie 1950-

Grant, Skeeter
    See Spiegelman, Art

Grass, Günter 1927-

Graves, Robert 1895-1985

Graves, Valerie
    See Bradley, Marion Zimmer

Gray, Alasdair 1934-

Gray, Francine du Plessix 1930-

Gray, Spalding 1941-2004

Greeley, Andrew M. 1928-

Green, Brian
    See Card, Orson Scott

Greene, Graham 1904-1991

Greer, Richard
    See Silverberg, Robert

Gregor, Lee
    See Pohl, Frederik

Grisham, John 1955-

Grumbach, Doris 1918-

VOLUME 3: Gu-Ma

Guest, Judith 1936-

Gump, P.Q.
    See Card, Orson Scott

Guterson, David 1956-

Haddon, Mark 1962-

Hailey, Arthur 1920-2004

Halberstam, David 1934-

Hall, Donald 1928-

Hall, Radclyffe 1886-1943

Hamilton, Franklin
    See Silverberg, Robert

Hamilton, Jane 1957-

Hamilton, Mollie
    See Kaye, M.M.

Hamilton, Virginia 1936-2002

Handke, Peter 1942-

Hardwick, Elizabeth 1916-

Hargrave, Leonie
    See Disch, Thomas M.

Harjo, Joy 1951-

Harris, E. Lynn 1957-

Harris, Robert 1957-

Harris, Thomas 1940-

Harson, Sley
    See Ellison, Harlan

Hart, Ellis
    See Ellison, Harlan

Harvey, Jack
    See Rankin, Ian

Hass, Robert 1941-

Havel, Vaclav 1936-

Hawkes, John 1925-1998

Hawking, S.W.
    See Hawking, Stephen W.

Hawking, Stephen W. 1942-

Haycraft, Anna
    See Ellis, Alice Thomas

Hayes, Al
    See Grisham, John

Hazzard, Shirley 1931-

Head, Bessie 1937-1986

Heaney, Seamus 1939-

Hébert, Anne 1916-2000

Hegi, Ursula 1946-

Heinlein, Robert A. 1907-1988

Heller, Joseph 1923-1999

Hellman, Lillian 1906-1984

Helprin, Mark 1947-

Hempel, Amy 1951-

Henley, Beth 1952-

Herbert, Frank 1920-1986

Hersey, John 1914-1993

Hiaasen, Carl 1953-

Highsmith, Patricia 1921-1995

Hijuelos, Oscar 1951-

Hill, John
    See Koontz, Dean R.

Hillenbrand, Laura 1967-

Hillerman, Tony 1925-

Hinojosa, Rolando 1929-

Hinton, S.E. 1950-

Hoban, Russell 1925-

Hochhuth, Rolf 1931-

Høeg, Peter 1957-

Hoffman, Alice 1952-

Hollander, Paul
  See Silverberg, Robert

Homes, A.M. 1961-

hooks, bell 1952-

Hosseini, Khaled 1965-

Houellebecq, Michel 1958-

Houston, Jeanne Wakatsuki 1934-

Howard, Maureen 1930-

Howard, Warren F.
  See Pohl, Frederik

Hoyle, Fred 1915-2001

Hubbell, Sue 1935-

Hudson, Jeffrey
  See Crichton, Michael

Hughes, Ted 1930-1998

Humes, Edward

Hwang, David Henry 1957-

Ionesco, Eugene 1912-1994

Irving, John 1942-

Isaacs, Susan 1943-

Isherwood, Christopher 1904-1986

Ishiguro, Kazuo 1954-

Ives, Morgan
  See Bradley, Marion Zimmer

Jakes, John 1932-

James, Mary
  See Meaker, Marijane

James, P.D. 1920-

James, Philip
  See Moorcock, Michael

Janowitz, Tama 1957-

Jarvis, E.K.
  See Ellison, Harlan

Jarvis, E.K.2
  See Silverberg, Robert

Jenkins, Jerry B. 1949-

Jhabvala, Ruth Prawer 1927-

Jiang, Ji-li 1954-

Jimenez, Francisco 1943-

Jin, Ha 1956-

Johnson, Adam 1967-

Johnson, Angela 1961-

Johnson, Charles 1948-

Jones, Diana Wynne 1934-

Jones, Edward P. 1950-

Jones, Gayl 1949-

Jones, LeRoi
  See Baraka, Amiri

Jong, Erica 1942-

Jorgensen, Ivar
  See Ellison, Harlan

Jorgenson, Ivar2
  See Silverberg, Robert

Judd, Cyril
  See Pohl, Frederik

Junger, Sebastian 1962-

Karageorge, Michael A.
  See Anderson, Poul

Karr, Mary 1955-

Kastel, Warren
  See Silverberg, Robert

Kaufman, Moises 1963-

Kavanagh, Dan
  See Barnes, Julian

Kaye, M.M. 1908-2004

Kaye, Mollie
  See Kaye, M.M.

Keillor, Garrison 1942-

Kelly, Lauren
  See Oates, Joyce Carol

Keneally, Thomas 1935-

Kennedy, William 1928-

Kennilworthy Whisp
  See Rowling, J.K.

Kerr, M.E.
  See Meater, Marijane

Kerry, Lois
  See Duncan, Lois

Kesey, Ken 1935-2001

Keyes, Daniel 1927-

Kidd, Sue Monk

Kienzle, William X. 1928-2001

Kincaid, Jamaica 1949-

King, Stephen 1947-

King, Steve
  See King, Stephen

Kingsolver, Barbara 1955-

Kingston, Maxine Hong 1940-

Kinnell, Galway 1927-

Kinsella, Thomas 1928-

Kinsella, W.P. 1935-

Kizer, Carolyn 1925-

Knight, Etheridge 1931-1991

Knowles, John 1926-2001

Knox, Calvin M.
  See Silverberg, Robert

Knye, Cassandra
  See Disch, Thomas M.

Koch, Kenneth 1925-2002

Kogawa, Joy 1935-

Kolb, Edward W. 1951-

Kolb, Rocky
  See Kolb, Edward W.

Koontz, Dean R. 1945-

Kooser, Ted 1939-

Kosinski, Jerzy 1933-1991

Kozol, Jonathan 1936-

Krakauer, Jon 1954-

Kumin, Maxine 1925-

Kundera, Milan 1929-

Kunitz, Stanley 1905-

Kushner, Tony 1956-

L'Amour, Louis 1908-1988

L'Engle, Madeleine 1918-

La Guma, Alex 1925-1985

Lahiri, Jhumpa 1967-

Lamb, Wally 1950-

Lange, John
  See Crichton, Michael

Laredo, Betty
  See Codrescu, Andrei

Laurence, Margaret 1926-1987

Lavond, Paul Dennis
  See Pohl, Frederik

Leavitt, David 1961-

le Carré, John 1931-

Lee, Don L.
    See Madhubuti, Haki R.

Lee, Harper 1926-

Lee, Stan 1922-

Le Guin, Ursula K. 1929-

Lehane, Dennis 1965-

Leonard, Elmore 1925-

LeSieg, Theo.
    See Geisel, Theodor Seuss

Lessing, Doris 1919-

Lester, Julius 1939-

Lethem, Jonathan 1964-

Levi, Primo 1919-1987

Levin, Ira 1929-

Levon, O.U.
    See Kesey, Ken

Leyner, Mark 1956-

Lindbergh, Anne Morrow 1906-2001

Lively, Penelope 1933-

Lodge, David 1935-

Logan, Jake
    See Smith, Martin Cruz

Long, David 1948-

Loos, Anita 1893-1981

Lorde, Audre 1934-1992

Louise, Heidi
    See Erdrich, Louise

Lowry, Lois 1937-

Lucas, Craig 1951-

Ludlum, Robert 1927-2001

Lynch, B. Suarez
    See Borges, Jorge Luis

M.T.F.
    See Porter, Katherine Anne

Macdonald, Anson
    See Heinlein, Robert A.

MacDonald, John D. 1916-1986

Mackay, Shena 1944-

MacKinnon, Catharine A. 1946-

MacLeish, Archibald 1892-1982

MacLeod, Alistair 1936-

Maddern, Al
    See Ellison, Harlan

Madhubuti, Haki R.

Maguire, Gregory 1954-

Mahfouz, Naguib 1911-

Mailer, Norman 1923-

Makine, Andreï 1957-

Malabaila, Damiano
    See Levi, Primo

Malamud, Bernard 1914-1986

Malcolm, Dan
    See Silverberg, Robert

Malouf, David 1934-

Mamet, David 1947-

Mara, Bernard
    See Moore, Brian

Marchbanks, Samuel
    See Davies, Robertson

Marías, Javier 1951-

Mariner, Scott
    See Pohl, Frederik

Markandaya, Kamala 1924-2004

Markham, Robert
    See Amis, Kingsley

Marshall, Allen
    See Westlake, Donald E.

Marshall, Paule 1929-

Martel, Yann 1963-

Martin, Webber
    See Silverberg, Robert

Mason, Bobbie Ann 1940-

Mason, Ernst
    See Pohl, Frederik

Mass, William
    See Gibson, William2

Massie, Robert K. 1929-

Mathabane, Mark 1960-

Matthiessen, Peter 1927-

Maupin, Armistead 1944-

Mayo, Jim
    See L'Amour, Louis

VOLUME 4: Mc-Sa

McBride, James 1957-

McCaffrey, Anne 1926-

McCall Smith, Alexander 1948-

McCann, Edson
    See Pohl, Frederik

McCarthy, Cormac 1933-

McCourt, Frank 1930-

McCreigh, James
    See Pohl, Frederik

McCullough, Colleen 1937-

McCullough, David 1933-

McDermott, Alice 1953-

McEwan, Ian 1948-

McGuane, Thomas 1939-

McInerney, Jay 1955-

McKie, Robin

McKinley, Robin 1952-

McLandress, Herschel
    See Galbraith, John Kenneth

McMillan, Terry 1951-

McMurtry, Larry 1936-

McNally, Terrence 1939-

McPhee, John 1931-

McPherson, James Alan 1943-

Meaker, M.J.
    See Meaker, Marijane

Meaker, Marijane 1927-

Mehta, Ved 1934-

Members, Mark
    See Powell, Anthony

Méndez, Miguel 1930-

Merchant, Paul
    See Ellison, Harlan

Merrill, James 1926-1995

Merriman, Alex
    See Silverberg, Robert

Merwin, W.S. 1927-

Michener, James A. 1907-1997

Miéville, China 1973-

Miller, Arthur 1915-

Millett, Kate 1934-

Millhauser, Steven 1943-

Milosz, Czeslaw 1911-2004

Min, Anchee 1957-

Mitchell, Clyde
    See Ellison, Harlan

Mitchell, Clyde2
    See Silverberg, Robert

Momaday, N. Scott 1934-

Monroe, Lyle
    See Heinlein, Robert A.

Moody, Anne 1940-

Moody, Rick 1961-

Moorcock, Michael 1939-

Moore, Alan 1953-

Moore, Brian 1921-1999

Moore, Lorrie
    See Moore, Marie Lorena

Moore, Marie Lorena 1957-

Mora, Pat 1942-

Morgan, Claire
    See Highsmith, Patricia

Mori, Kyoko 1957-

Morris, Mary McGarry 1943-

Morrison, Chloe Anthony Wofford
    See Morrison, Toni

Morrison, Toni 1931-

Morrow, James 1947-

Mortimer, John 1923-

Mosley, Walter 1952-

Motion, Andrew 1952-

Mowat, Farley 1921-

Mukherjee, Bharati 1940-

Munro, Alice 1931-

Murdoch, Iris 1919-1999

Murray, Albert L. 1916-

Myers, Walter Dean 1937-

Myers, Walter M.
    See Myers, Walter Dean

Nafisi, Azar 1950-

Naipaul, Shiva 1945-1985

Naipaul, V.S. 1932-

Narayan, R.K. 1906-2001

Naylor, Gloria 1950-

Nemerov, Howard 1920-1991

Newt Scamander
    See Rowling, J.K.

Ngugi, James T.
    See Ngugi wa Thiong'o

Ngugi wa Thiong'o 1938-

Nichols, John 1940-

Nichols, Leigh
    See Koontz, Dean R.

North, Anthony
    See Koontz, Dean R.

North, Milou
    See Dorris, Michael

North, Milou2
    See Erdrich, Louise

Nosille, Nabrah
    See Ellison, Harlan

Novak, Joseph
    See Kosinski, Jerzy

Nye, Naomi Shihab 1952-

O'Brian, E.G.
    See Clarke, Arthur C.

O'Brian, Patrick 1914-2000

O'Brien, Edna 1932-

O'Brien, Tim 1946-

O'Casey, Brenda
    See Ellis, Alice Thomas

O'Faolain, Sean 1900-1991

O'Flaherty, Liam 1896-1984

Oates, Joyce Carol 1938-

Oates, Stephen B. 1936-

Oe, Kenzaburo 1935-

Okri, Ben 1959-

Olds, Sharon 1942-

Oliver, Mary 1935-

Olsen, Tillie 1912-

Ondaatje, Michael 1943-

Osborne, David
    See Silverberg, Robert

Osborne, George
    See Silverberg, Robert

Osborne, John 1929-1994

Oz, Amos 1939-

Ozick, Cynthia 1928-

Packer, Vin
    See Meaker, Marijane

Paglia, Camille 1947-

Paige, Richard
    See Koontz, Dean R.

Pakenham, Antonia
    See Fraser, Antonia

Palahniuk, Chuck 1962-

Paley, Grace 1922-

Paolini, Christopher 1983-

Parfenie, Marie
    See Codrescu, Andrei

Park, Jordan
    See Pohl, Frederik

Parker, Bert
    See Ellison, Harlan

Parker, Robert B. 1932-

Parks, Gordon 1912-2006

Pasternak, Boris 1890-1960

Patchett, Ann 1963-

Paton, Alan 1903-1988

Patterson, James 1947-

Payne, Alan
    See Jakes, John

Paz, Octavio 1914-1998

Peretti, Frank E. 1951-

Petroski, Henry 1942-

Phillips, Caryl 1958-

Phillips, Jayne Anne 1952-

Phillips, Richard
    See Dick, Philip K.

Picoult, Jodi 1966-

Piercy, Marge 1936-

Piers, Robert
    See Anthony, Piers

Pinsky, Robert 1940-

Pinta, Harold
    See Pinter, Harold

Pinter, Harold 1930-

Plimpton, George 1927-2003

Pohl, Frederik 1919-

Porter, Katherine Anne 1890-1980

Potok, Chaim 1929-2002

Powell, Anthony 1905-2000

Powers, Richard 1957-

Powers, Tim 1952-

Pratchett, Terry 1948-

Price, Reynolds 1933-

Prose, Francine 1947-

Proulx, E. Annie 1935-

Puig, Manuel 1932-1990

Pullman, Philip 1946-

Pygge, Edward
    See Barnes, Julian

Pynchon, Thomas, Jr. 1937-

Quindlen, Anna 1953-

Quinn, Simon
    See Smith, Martin Cruz

Rampling, Anne
    See Rice, Anne

Rand, Ayn 1905-1982

Randall, Robert
    See Silverberg, Robert

Rankin, Ian 1960-

Rao, Raja 1909-

Ravenna, Michael
    See Welty, Eudora

Reed, Ishmael 1938-

Reid, Desmond
    See Moorcock, Michael

Rendell, Ruth 1930-

Rensie, Willis
    See Eisner, Will

Rexroth, Kenneth 1905-1982

Rice, Anne 1941-

Rich, Adrienne 1929-

Rich, Barbara
    See Graves, Robert

Richler, Mordecai 1931-2001

Ríos, Alberto 1952-

Rivers, Elfrida
    See Bradley, Marion Zimmer

Riverside, John
    See Heinlein, Robert A.

Robb, J.D.
    See Roberts, Nora

Robbe-Grillet, Alain 1922-

Robbins, Tom 1936-

Roberts, Nora 1950-

Robertson, Ellis
    See Ellison, Harlan

Robertson, Ellis2
    See Silverberg, Robert

Robinson, Kim Stanley 1952-

Robinson, Lloyd
    See Silverberg, Robert

Robinson, Marilynne 1944-

Rodman, Eric
    See Silverberg, Robert

Rodríguez, Luis J. 1954-

Rodriguez, Richard 1944-

Roquelaure, A.N.
    See Rice, Anne

Roth, Henry 1906-1995

Roth, Philip 1933-

Rowling, J.K. 1965-

Roy, Arundhati 1960-

Rule, Ann 1935-

Rushdie, Salman 1947-

Russo, Richard 1949-

Rybczynski, Witold 1943-

Ryder, Jonathan
    See Ludlum, Robert

Sábato, Ernesto 1911-

Sacco, Joe 1960-

Sacks, Oliver 1933-

Sagan, Carl 1934-1996

Salinger, J.D. 1919-

Salzman, Mark 1959-

Sanchez, Sonia 1934-

Sanders, Noah
    See Blount, Roy, Jr.

Sanders, Winston P.
    See Anderson, Poul

Sandford, John
    See Camp, John

Saroyan, William 1908-1981

Sarton, May 1912-1995

Sartre, Jean-Paul 1905-1980

Satterfield, Charles
    See Pohl, Frederik

Saunders, Caleb
    See Heinlein, Robert A.

VOLUME 5: Sc-Z

Schaeffer, Susan Fromberg 1941-

Schulz, Charles M. 1922-2000

Schwartz, Lynne Sharon 1939-

Scotland, Jay
   See Jakes, John

Sebastian, Lee
   See Silverberg, Robert

Sebold, Alice 1963-

Sedaris, David 1957-

Sendak, Maurice 1928-

Seth, Vikram 1952-

Shaara, Jeff 1952-

Shaara, Michael 1929-1988

Shackleton, C.C.
   See Aldiss, Brian W.

Shaffer, Peter 1926-

Shange, Ntozake 1948-

Shapiro, Karl Jay 1913-2000

Shepard, Sam 1943-

Shepherd, Michael
   See Ludlum, Robert

Shields, Carol 1935-2003

Shreve, Anita 1946-

Siddons, Anne Rivers 1936-

Silko, Leslie 1948-

Sillitoe, Alan 1928-

Silverberg, Robert 1935-

Silverstein, Shel 1932-1999

Simic, Charles 1938-

Simon, David 1960-

Simon, Neil 1927-

Simpson, Louis 1923-

Singer, Isaac
   See Singer, Isaac Bashevis

Singer, Isaac Bashevis 1904-1991

Škvorecký, Josef 1924-

Smiley, Jane 1949-

Smith, Martin
   See Smith, Martin Cruz

Smith, Martin Cruz 1942-

Smith, Rosamond
   See Oates, Joyce Carol

Smith, Wilbur 1933-

Smith, Zadie 1976-

Snicket, Lemony 1970-

Snodgrass, W.D. 1926-

Snyder, Gary 1930-

Solo, Jay
   See Ellison, Harlan

Solwoska, Mara
   See French, Marilyn

Solzhenitsyn, Aleksandr I. 1918-

Somers, Jane
   See Lessing, Doris

Sontag, Susan 1933-2004

Soto, Gary 1952-

Soyinka, Wole 1934-

Spark, Muriel 1918-

Sparks, Nicholas 1965-

Spaulding, Douglas
   See Bradbury, Ray

Spaulding, Leonard
   See Bradbury, Ray

Spencer, Leonard G.
   See Silverberg, Robert

Spender, Stephen 1909-1995

Spiegelman, Art 1948-

Spillane, Mickey 1918-

Stack, Andy
   See Rule, Ann

Stacy, Donald
   See Pohl, Frederik

Stancykowna
   See Szymborska, Wislawa

Stark, Richard
   See Westlake, Donald E.

Steel, Danielle 1947-

Steig, William 1907-

Steinem, Gloria 1934-

Steiner, George 1929-

Steiner, K. Leslie
   See Delany, Samuel R.

Stephenson, Neal 1959-

Sterling, Brett
   See Bradbury, Ray

Sterling, Bruce 1954-

Stine, Jovial Bob
   See Stine, R.L.

Stine, R.L. 1943-

Stone, Robert 1937-

Stone, Rosetta
   See Geisel, Theodor Seuss

Stoppard, Tom 1937-

Straub, Peter 1943-

Styron, William 1925-

Swenson, May 1919-1989

Swift, Graham 1949-

Swithen, John
   See King, Stephen

Symmes, Robert
   See Duncan, Robert

Syruc, J.
   See Milosz, Czeslaw

Szymborska, Wislawa 1923-

Talent Family, The
   See Sedaris, David

Talese, Gay 1932-

Tan, Amy 1952-

Tanner, William
   See Amis, Kingsley

Tartt, Donna 1964-

Taylor, Mildred D. 1943-

Tenneshaw, S.M.
   See Silverberg, Robert

Terkel, Studs 1912-

Theroux, Paul 1941-

Thomas, D.M. 1935-

Thomas, Joyce Carol 1938-

Thompson, Hunter S. 1937-2005

Thornton, Hall
  See Silverberg, Robert

Tiger, Derry
  See Ellison, Harlan

Tornimparte, Alessandra
  See Ginzburg, Natalia

Tremblay, Michel 1942-

Trevor, William 1928-

Trillin, Calvin 1935-

Trout, Kilgore
  See Farmer, Philip José

Turow, Scott 1949-

Tyler, Anne 1941-

Tyree, Omar

Uchida, Yoshiko 1921-1992

Uhry, Alfred 1936-

Uncle Shelby
  See Silverstein, Shel

Updike, John 1932-

Urban Griot
  See Tyree, Omar

Uris, Leon 1924-2003

Urmuz
  See Codrescu, Andrei

Vance, Gerald
  See Silverberg, Robert

Van Duyn, Mona 1921-2004

Vargas Llosa, Mario 1936-

Verdu, Matilde
  See Cela, Camilo José

Vidal, Gore 1925-

Vile, Curt
  See Moore, Alan

Vine, Barbara
  See Rendell, Ruth

Vizenor, Gerald Robert 1934-

Vogel, Paula A. 1951-

Voigt, Cynthia 1942-

Vollmann, William T. 1959-

Vonnegut, Kurt, Jr. 1922-

Vosce, Trudie
  See Ozick, Cynthia

Wakoski, Diane 1937-

Walcott, Derek 1930-

Walker, Alice 1944-

Walker, Margaret 1915-1998

Wallace, David Foster 1962-

Walley, Byron
  See Card, Orson Scott

Ware, Chris 1967-

Warren, Robert Penn 1905-1989

Warshofsky, Isaac
  See Singer, Isaac Bashevis

Wasserstein, Wendy 1950-2006

Watson, James D. 1928-

Watson, John H.
  See Farmer, Philip José

Watson, Larry 1947-

Watson, Richard F.
  See Silverberg, Robert

Ways, C.R.
  See Blount, Roy, Jr.

Weldon, Fay 1931-

Wells, Rebecca

Welty, Eudora 1909-2001

West, Edwin
  See Westlake, Donald E.

West, Owen
  See Koontz, Dean R.

West, Paul 1930-

Westlake, Donald E. 1933-

White, Edmund 1940-

Wideman, John Edgar 1941-

Wiesel, Elie 1928-

Wilbur, Richard 1921-

Williams, C.K. 1936-

Williams, Juan 1954-

Williams, Tennessee 1911-1983

Willis, Charles G.
  See Clarke, Arthur C.

Wilson, August 1945-2005

Wilson, Dirk
  See Pohl, Frederik

Wilson, Edward O. 1929-

Winterson, Jeanette 1959-

Wolf, Naomi 1962-

Wolfe, Gene 1931-

Wolfe, Tom 1931-

Wolff, Tobias 1945-

Woodiwiss, Kathleen E. 1939-

Woodson, Jacqueline 1964-

Wouk, Herman 1915-

Wright, Charles 1935-

Wright, Judith 1915-2000

Xingjian, Gao 1940-

Yolen, Jane 1939-

York, Simon
  See Heinlein, Robert A.

Zelazny, Roger 1937-1995

Zindel, Paul 1936-2003

Gu

GUEST, Judith 1936-
(Judith Ann Guest)

PERSONAL: Born March 29, 1936, in Detroit, MI; daughter of Harry Reginald (a businessman) and Marion Aline (Nesbit) Guest; married, August 22, 1958; husband's name, Larry (a data processing executive); children: Larry, John, Richard. *Education:* University of Michigan, B.A., 1958.

ADDRESSES: Home—4600 West 44th St., Edina, MN 55424. *Agent*—Patricia Karlan Agency, 3575 Cahvenga Blvd., Suite 210, Los Angeles, CA 90068; c/o Author Mail, Viking/Penguin, 375 Hudson St., New York, NY 10014.

CAREER: Writer. Employed as teacher in public grade schools in Royal Oak, MI, 1964, Birmingham, MI, 1969, and Troy, MI, 1975.

MEMBER: Authors Guild, Authors League of America, PEN American Center, Detroit Women Writers.

AWARDS, HONORS: Janet Heidinger Kafka Prize, University of Rochester, 1977, for *Ordinary People.*

WRITINGS:

Ordinary People (novel), Viking (New York, NY), 1976.

Second Heaven (novel), Viking (New York, NY), 1982.

The Mythic Family: An Essay, Milkweed Press (Minneapolis, MN), 1988.

(With Rebecca Hill) *Killing Time in St. Cloud* (novel), Delacorte (New York, NY), 1988.

Errands (novel), Ballantine (New York, NY), 1996.

Icewalk (essay), Minnesota Center for the Book Arts (Minneapolis, MN), 2001.

Also author of a screenplay adaptation of *Second Heaven* and of three short stories by Carol Bly, titled *Rachel River, Minnesota.* Contributor to periodicals, including *The Writer.*

ADAPTATIONS: Ordinary People was filmed by Paramount in 1980, directed by Robert Redford, starring Mary Tyler Moore, Donald Sutherland, Timothy Hutton, Judd Hirsch, and Elizabeth McGovern; a stage version was published by Dramatic Publishing in 1983. *Errands* was adapted for audiobook.

SIDELIGHTS: Judith Guest achieved startling success with her debut novel *Ordinary People,* and continued writing novels with similar themes. Contrary to custom, Guest sent the manuscript to Viking Press without a preceding letter of inquiry and without the usual plot synopsis and outline that many publishing houses require. The manuscript was read by an editorial assistant who liked it well enough to send Guest a note of encouragement and pass the story along to her superiors for a second reading. Months passed. Then, in the summer of 1975, when Guest was in the midst of moving from Michigan to Minnesota, came the word she had been waiting for: Viking would be "honored" to publish *Ordinary People,* the first unsolicited manuscript they had accepted in twenty-six years. Guest's book went on to become not only a best-selling novel—selected by four book clubs, serialized in *Redbook,* and sold to Ballantine for paperback rights for $635,000—but also an award-winning film that captured the 1980 Oscar for best movie of the year. Since that time, Guest has published several other novels, including the family stories *Second Heaven,* and *Errands,* and the mystery *Killing Time in St. Cloud.*

The story of a teenage boy's journey from the brink of suicide back to mental health, *Ordinary People* shows the way that unexpected tragedy can destroy even the most secure of families. Seventeen-year-old Conrad Jarrett, son of a well-to-do tax lawyer, appears to have everything: looks, brains, manners, and a good relationship with his family. But when he survives a boating accident that kills his older brother, Conrad sinks into a severe depression, losing touch with his parents, teachers, friends, and just about everyone else in the outside world. His attempt to kill himself by slashing his wrists awakens his father to the depth of his problems, but it also cuts Conrad off from his mother—a compulsive perfectionist who believes that his bloody suicide attempt was intended to punish her. With the help of his father and an understanding analyst, Conrad slowly regains his equilibrium. "Above all," commented *New York Review of Books* contributor Michael Wood, "he comes to accept his mother's apparent failure to forgive him for slashing his wrists, and his own failure to forgive her for not loving him more. It is true that she has now left his father, because he seemed to be cracking up under the strain of his concern for his son, but Conrad has learned 'that it is love, imperfect and unordered, that keeps them apart, even as it holds them somehow together.'"

"The form, the style of the novel dictate an ending more smooth than convincing," according to Melvin Maddocks in *Time.* "As a novelist who warns against the passion for safety and order that is no passion at all, Guest illustrates as well as describes the problem. She is neat and ordered, even at explaining that life is not neat and ordered." While *Newsweek*'s Walter Clemons thought that *Ordinary People* "solves a little too patly some of the problems it raises," he also allowed that "the feelings in the book are true and unforced. Guest has the valuable gift of making us like her characters; she has the rarer ability to move a toughened reviewer to tears." *Village Voice* contributor Irma Pascal Heldman also had high praise for the novel, writing that "Guest conveys with sensitivity a most private sense of life's personal experiences while respecting the reader's imagination and nurturing an aura of mystery. Without telling all, she illuminates the lives of 'ordinary people' with chilling insight."

Guest's insights into her male protagonist are particularly keen, according to several reviewers, including Lore Dickstein, who wrote in the *New York Times Book Review:* "Guest portrays Conrad not only as if she has lived with him on a daily basis—which I sense may be true—but as if she has gotten into his head. The dialogue Conrad has with himself, his psychiatrist, his friends, his family, all rings true with adolescent anxiety. This is the small, hard kernel of brilliance in the novel." But while acknowledging that Guest's male characters are well-defined, several reviewers believe that Beth, the mother, is not fully developed. "The mother's point of view, even though she is foremost in the men's lives, is barely articulated," wrote Dorothea D. Braginsky in *Psychology Today.* "We come to know her only in dialogue with her husband and son, and through their portrayals of her. For some reason Guest has given her no voice, no platform for expression. We never discover what conflicts, fears and aspirations exist behind her cool, controlled facade."

Guest herself expressed similar reservations about the character, telling a *Detroit News* contributor that Beth is "pretty enigmatic in the novel. The reader might have been puzzled by her." But Guest also believes that Mary Tyler Moore's portrayal of Beth Jarrett in the film adaptation of the novel did much to clarify the character. "[Mary Tyler Moore] just knocks me out," Guest told John Blades in a *Chicago Tribune* interview. "She's a terrific actress, a very complex person, and she brought a complexity to the character that I wish I'd gotten into the book. I fought with that character for a long time, trying to get her to reveal herself, and I finally said this is the best I can do. When I saw Mary in the movie, I felt like she'd done it for me."

Guest was also pleased with the movie's ending, which was more inconclusive than the book's ending. "The more things get left open-ended the better," Guest told Blades. "If you tie everything into a neat little bow, people walk out of the theater and never give it another thought. If there's ambiguity, people think about it and talk about it." She believes director Robert Redford's sensitive presentation "leaves the viewer to his own conclusions," which is how it should be.

In 1982 Guest published *Second Heaven,* a novel that shares many of its predecessor's concerns. "Again, a damaged adolescent boy stands at the center of the story; again, the extent of his wounds will not be immediately apparent," noted Peter S. Prescott in *Newsweek.* "Again, two adults with problems of their own attempt to save the boy from cooperating in his own destruction." In an interview with former *Detroit Free Press* book editor Barbara Holliday, Guest reflected on her fascination with what she calls this "crucial" period known as adolescence: "It's a period of time . . . where people are very vulnerable and often don't have much experience to draw on as far as human relationships go. At the same time they are making some pretty heavy decisions, not necessarily physical but psychological decisions about how they're going to relate to people and how they're going to shape their lives. It seems to me that if you don't have sane sensible people around you to help, there's great potential for making irrevocable mistakes."

The way that signals can be misinterpreted, leading to a breakdown in communication between people who may care deeply for one another, is a theme of both her novels and a topic she handles well, according to novelist Anne Tyler, who is also known for her ability to accurately portray human relationships. "[Guest] has a remarkable ability to show the unspoken in human relationships—the emotions either hidden or expressed so haltingly that they might as well be hidden, the heroic self-control that others may perceive as icy indifference," Tyler wrote in the *Detroit News.*

In *Second Heaven,* it is Gale Murray, abused son of a religiously fanatic father and an ineffectual mother, who hides his feelings behind a facade of apathy. After a brutal beating from his father, Gale runs away from home, seeking shelter with Catherine "Cat" Holzmann, a recently divorced parent with problems of her own. When Gale's father tries to have his son institutionalized, Cat enlists the aid of Mike Atwood, a disenchanted lawyer who is falling in love with Cat. He takes on the case, largely as a favor to her. According to Norma Rosen in the *New York Times Book Review,* "Cat and Michael must transcend their personal griefs and limits in order to reach out for this rescue. In saving another's life they are on the way to saving their own."

Because of the story's clear delineation of good versus evil and its melodramatic courtroom conclusion, *Second Heaven* struck some critics as contrived. "Everything in the book is so neat and polished; so precisely timed and calibrated," suggested *New York Times* reviewer Christopher Lehmann-Haupt, "the way the newly divorced people dovetail, conveniently providing a surrogate mother and a fatherly counselor for battered Gale Murray. . . . The reader continually gets the feeling that Mrs. Guest is working with plumb line and level and trowel to build her airtight perpendicular walls of plot development." Or, as Rosen puts it: "On the one hand there are the clear evils of control, rules, order. They are associated with inability to love, fanaticism,

brutality. Clutter and lack of organization are good. . . . Yet in the context of the author's antineatness and anti-control themes, the technique of the novel itself appears at times to be almost a subversion: the quick-march pace, the click-shot scenes, the sensible serviceable inner monologues unvaried in their rhythms."

While acknowledging the book's imperfections, Jonathan Yardley maintained in the *Washington Post* that "the virtues of *Second Heaven* are manifold, and far more consequential than its few flaws. . . . Neither contrivance nor familiarity can disguise the skill and, most particularly, the sensitivity with which Guest tells her story. She is an extraordinarily perceptive observer of the minutiae of domestic life, and she writes about them with humor and affection." Concluded *Tribune Books* contributor Harry Mark Petrakis: "By compassionately exploring the dilemmas in the lives of Michael, Catherine, and Gale, Judith Guest casts light on the problems we often endure in our own lives. That's what the art of storytelling and the craft of good writing are all about."

With *Errands* Guest continues to examine the contemporary American family with adolescent children in crisis, though this novel was based in fact. Guest was inspired by her own family history as recounted in a diary that told of her grandfather's premature death and the fate of his widow and five children in Detroit during the 1920s. As Guest told Joanne Kaufman of *People,* she did not simply want to base the story on her ancestors, who repressed their feelings. "I needed to make it my story. . . . I never heard about the sadness and anger you feel when you lose your father at age ten, as my father did," she said, adding, "I wanted to write a story to find out what it felt like."

Thus readers first meet the Browner family of *Errands,* a word that has the more serious connotation of "mission," as they begin their annual vacation. They are a likable, normal family except that Keith, the father, must begin chemotherapy as soon as they return. But the treatment is not successful; his wife, Annie, and three young children, Harry, Jimmy, and Julie, must carry on without him. Life without Keith is a struggle for each of them, and they are each in a state of crisis when Jimmy has a dangerous accident that almost blinds him. But Jimmy's accident requires them to support each other and begins the rebuilding process for this troubled family. The work caught the attention of reviewers. Writing in the *New York Times Book Review,* Meg Wolitzer admired the "natural cadences and rhythms" spoken by the children but suggested that the adults "never fully come to life" and that overall "the novel, while appealing, seems slightly sketchy and meditative." Although *Entertainment Weekly*'s Vanessa V. Friedman found the characters stock treatments and "unsympathetic" at that, others praised Guest's portrayal of family dynamics during a crisis. For example, *Booklist*'s Brad Hooper noted that "Guest is perfectly realistic in her depictions of family situations; her characters act and react with absolute credibility." And Sheila M. Riley of *Library Journal* declared *Errands* "true, touching, and highly recommended."

BIOGRAPHICAL AND CRITICAL SOURCES:

BOOKS

Contemporary Literary Criticism, Thomson Gale (Detroit), Volume 8, 1978; Volume 30, 1984.

Szabo, Victoria and Angela D. Jones, *The Uninvited Guest: Erasure of Women in Ordinary People,* Popular Press (Bowling Green, OH), 1996.

PERIODICALS

Billboard, January 18, 1997, Trudi Miller Rosenblum, review of *Errands* (audio version), p. 74.

Booklist, October 15, 1996, Brad Hooper, review of *Errands,* p. 379.

Chicago Tribune, November 4, 1980.

Detroit Free Press, October 7, 1982, review of *Second Heaven.*

Detroit News, September 26, 1982, review of *Second Heaven;* October 20, 1982, review of *Second Heaven.*

Entertainment Weekly, February 14, 1997, Vanessa V. Friedman, review of *Errands,* pp. 56-57.

Library Journal, May 1, 1976, Victoria K. Musmann, review of *Ordinary People,* p. 1142; July 1, 1982, Michele M. Leber, review of *Second Heaven,* p. 1344; April 15, 1983, "Lorain, Ohio, Public Library Invites Judith Guest for Tea," p. 786; October 15, 1996, Sheila M. Riley, review of *Errands,* p. 90; March 1, 1997, Carolyn Alexander and Mark Annichiarico, review of *Errands* (audio version), p. 118.

Ms., December, 1982, review of *Second Heaven.*

Newsweek, July 12, 1976, review of *Ordinary People;* October 4, 1982, review of *Second Heaven.*

New Yorker, July 19, 1976, review of *Ordinary People;* November 22, 1982, review of *Second Heaven.*

New York Review of Books, June 10, 1976, review of *Ordinary People.*

New York Times, July 16, 1976, review of *Ordinary People;* October 22, 1982, review of *Second Heaven;* January 12, 1997, Meg Wolitzer, "Ordinary Loss," review of *Errands,* p. 18.

New York Times Book Review, July 18, 1976, review of *Ordinary People;* October 3, 1982, review of *Second Heaven;* January 12, 1997, Meg Wolitzer, "Ordinary Loss," review of *Errands,* p. 18.

People, February 10, 1997, Joanne Kaufman, "Family Matters," review of *Errands,* p. 33.

Psychology Today, August, 1976, review of *Ordinary People.*

Publishers Weekly, April 19, 1976, review of *Ordinary People;* October 28, 1996, Sybil S. Steinberg, review of *Errands,* p. 56.

Redbook, January, 1997, Judy Koutsky, "Red Hot Books," review of *Errands,* p. G-4.

Saturday Review, May 15, 1976, review of *Ordinary People.*

School Library Journal, September, 1976, Jay Daly, review of *Ordinary People,* p. 143; December, 1982, Priscilla Johnson and Ron Brown, review of *Second Heaven,* p. 87; August, 1983, Hazel Rochman, "Bringing Boys Books Home," review of *Ordinary People,* pp. 26-27; July, 1997, Carol Clark, review of *Errands,* p. 116.

Sunday Times (London, England), February 16, 2003, Marianne Gray, review of *Ordinary People,* p. 29.

Time, July 19, 1976, review of *Ordinary People;* October 25, 1982, review of *Second Heaven.*

Tribune Books (Chicago, IL), October 3, 1982, review of *Second Heaven.*

Village Voice, July 19, 1976, review of *Ordinary People.*

Washington Post, September 22, 1982, review of *Second Heaven.*

Washington Post News Feed, February 24, 1997, Reeve Lindbergh, review of *Errands,* p. D4.

*   *   *

GUEST, Judith Ann
See GUEST, Judith

*   *   *

GUILLEMIN, Jacques
See SARTRE, Jean-Paul

GUMP, P.Q.
See CARD, Orson Scott

* * *

GUTERSON, David 1956-

PERSONAL: Born May 4, 1956, in Seattle, WA; son of Murray Bernard (a criminal defense attorney) and Shirley (Zak) Guterson; married Robin Ann Radwick, January 1, 1979; children: Taylor, Travis, Henry, Angelica. *Education:* University of Washington, B.A., 1978, M.A., 1982. *Hobbies and other interests:* Hiking, hunting.

ADDRESSES: Agent—Georges Borchardt, Inc., 136 East 57th St., New York, NY 10020.

CAREER: Writer. High school English teacher in Bainbridge Island, WA, 1984-94.

AWARDS, HONORS: PEN/Faulkner Award for Fiction, Folger Shakespeare Library, Barnes & Noble Discovery Award, and Pacific Northwest Booksellers Award, all 1995, all for *Snow Falling on Cedars.*

WRITINGS:

The Country ahead of Us, the Country Behind (stories), Harper (New York, NY), 1989.
Family Matters: Why Homeschooling Makes Sense, Harcourt Brace (New York, NY), 1992.
Snow Falling on Cedars, Harcourt Brace (San Diego, CA), 1994.
East of the Mountains, Harcourt Brace (San Diego, CA), 1999.
Our Lady of the Forest, Knopf (New York, NY), 2003.

Contributor to periodicals, including *Harper's, Sports Illustrated,* and *Gray's Sporting Journal.*

Snow Falling on Cedars has been translated into twenty-one languages.

ADAPTATIONS: Snow Falling on Cedars was adapted as a motion picture starring Max Von Sydow and Ethan Hawke, Universal, 2000, and as an audiobook by Random House Audiobooks, 1995. Selections from *The*
Country ahead of Us, the Country Behind were recorded by Random House Audiobooks (New York, NY), 1996. *East of the Mountains* was adapted as an audiobook, BDD Audio, 1999.

SIDELIGHTS: Although David Guterson made his literary debut in 1989 with the collection of short stories *The Country ahead of Us, the Country Behind,* it was not until his first novel, *Snow Falling on Cedars,* was published five years later that the world took notice of the clean-living English teacher from the Pacific Northwest. The debut novel, which recounts the trial of a Japanese man for the alleged killing of a Caucasian fisherman in 1954, became a phenomenal best-seller and winner of the prestigious PEN/Faulkner Award. It sold more than two million copies in the United States alone, was translated into twenty-one languages, and resulted in a motion picture of the same title, starring Ethan Hawke and Max Von Sydow. Guterson's subsequent novels, including *East of the Mountains* and *Our Lady of the Forest,* have further demonstrated the depth of his talent and his ongoing concern for addressing universal and timeless moral issues in his writing.

The son of a criminal defense attorney and a homemaker, Guterson and his two brothers and two sisters grew up on the north end of Seattle, Washington. Guterson spoke fondly of the region to Bill Donahue of *Book:* The woods nearby were like "Valhalla, the land of the giants. We'd go into them, my friends and I, and get completely lost. Or we'd eat blackberries and wander around with stains on our faces." He and his friends were also active in the Boy Scouts, though their popular name for the den was "Plastered Plums," which reflected their long hair and countercultural bent. Although as a child Guterson liked to read, he did not consider becoming a writer until his junior year of college, after he was inspired by the teacher of a short-story writing class. There his teacher "emphasized that stories really matter, that when people read stories they are transfigured by them. That spoke to me," the novelist told John DiConsiglio in an interview in *Literary Cavalcade.* One day Guterson "went to the library and after an hour of working on this story," he recalled to Donahue, "I thought 'This is fun.' And I knew that it was also meaningful, useful. I knew from my own life as a reader how powerful stories are—how they shape human values." During summers Guterson had worked with the Forest Service fire-fighting crew, and he at first planned to become a firefighter, but as his interest in writing grew, he decided to become an English teacher and writer because he felt the work of teaching would enrich his writing efforts.

Shortly after his wife, Robin, gave birth to the first of their four children, Guterson and his family moved to an old bungalow on Bainbridge Island in Puget Sound, which then was home to some 8,000 people, but by 2000 would boast an upscale population of 20,000. For a decade Guterson taught English at Bainbridge Island High School and wrote in the early mornings after walking his dog. Writing in an eclectically decorated study, Guterson was happy if he managed to write 250 words per day. This desire to pen *le mot juste,* he explained to Donahue, "goes back to 'In the beginning was the word.' We constitute our world using words, and the more accurate the words are, the more clarified the world is. Getting it right feels almost like a holy act."

Guterson's first published fiction is contained in *The Country ahead of Us, the Country Behind,* a collection of short stories; his first nonfiction work is *Family Matters: Why Homeschooling Makes Sense,* a profile of the homeschooling movement with a discussion of the impetus for its growth. The couple home-schooled their own four children, gradually transitioning them into the public schools. Guterson does not see home-schooling as right for everyone, but he believes that people should have the option.

He wrote his debut novel, *Snow Falling on Cedars,* over a decade, stopping midway to pen *Family Matters.* Among his inspirations for the novel were a photographic exhibit depicting the one-hundred-year history of the Japanese-American community of Bainbridge Island, including their deportation and internment in California camps during World War II. "I was quite moved by the photo exhibit, in particular by seeing in those photos the faces of people I knew, which gave history a real face, which made history come alive, which made history real," he told Bob Edwards in a radio interview published on the National Public Radio Web site. Another was Harper Lee's classic novel *To Kill a Mockingbird,* which Guterson presented each year to his high school students. One reason Guterson's novel required ten years to complete was his effort to maintain historical accuracy.

With much of its action taking place during the 1940s, *Snow Falling on Cedars* tells the story of Caucasian teen Ishmael's enduring love for a Japanese girl, Hatsue, on the fictional island of San Piedro in Puget Sound. The format of a later courtroom drama in which Hatsue's husband, Kabuo, is accused of murdering a Caucasian fisherman over a land dispute is the jumping off point for numerous omniscient flashbacks that tell a nuanced story of love in spite of prejudice, the intern-

ment of the Japanese, the horrors of World War II in the Pacific, and the recurrent struggle to do what is right. In the process, Ishmael comes to terms both with his losses and with his father's legacy of high moral standards.

By all accounts, Guterson's efforts paid off handsomely, bringing him fame and critical acclaim, and making him a millionaire through books sales and the sale of movie rights. Reviewers praised his characterizations, courtroom scenes, historical accuracy, and lyrical descriptions of the Pacific Northwest. *Time* reviewer Pico Iyer called the novel a "beautifully assured and full-bodied story" that is also "unusually lived in, focused and compassionate." Several critics voiced qualified praise, including Tom Deignan of the *World and I,* who wrote that while *Snow Falling on Cedars* is "often long-winded, . . . Guterson had a lush, rugged landscape and good old courtroom drama to serve as the book's sturdy spine." In the opinion of William Swanson, writing in *Minneapolis-St. Paul* magazine, Guterson "provides one of the most vividly realized physical settings this side of McCarthy's Tex-Mex landscapes. His development of the book's large cast is equally exhaustive, but not so effective." *Booklist* reviewer Dennis Dodge praised the novel as "compellingly suspenseful on each of its several levels."

After the success of *Snow Falling on Cedars,* Guterson felt some pressure to produce another best-selling literary novel: "When it comes time to sit down and write the next book, you're deathly afraid that you're not up to the task," he told Alden Mudge for *BookPage.* "That was certainly the case with me after *Snow Falling on Cedars.*"

By now Guterson had quit his teaching job to devote himself full-time to writing. When the once athletic writer began suffering from back trouble while still in his mid-thirties, he began to grapple with issues surrounding aging, and these thoughts led to his next work of fiction. *East of the Mountains* is an older man's tale, a mythic journey in the ancient concept of romance as quest. In it readers follow the story of retired physician and widower Ben, who, suffering from colon cancer, plans to commit suicide while on a hunting trip and make his death appear to be an accident. During his three-day journey to the semiarid steppe desert of eastern Washington State, Ben encounters challenges and meets strangers who make him reconsider both his grief and his choice to end his life. "Guterson's prose is spare and powerful," Tony Freemantle remarked of the 1999 novel in the *Houston Chronicle.*

Like *Snow Falling on Cedars, East of the Mountains* employs numerous flashbacks to add depth to the story line. Using this technique, Guterson "manages in a few words to paint a vivid picture of the physical and moral landscape through which Ben travels and, in a series of flashbacks seamlessly woven into the narrative, of the path through life he has already navigated," explained Freemantle. Instead of snow, the main symbolism in *East of the Mountains* pertains to apples, a famous produce crop for Washington state as well as a recurring symbol in literature, including King Arthur's legend, the Judeo-Christian story of the fall from grace, and the golden apple of Greek mythology's Trojan War.

The setting of *East of the Mountains* is a desert-like landscape that recalls the biblical tradition of the Christian hermits. "When Guterson is at his best, the story and the landscape nearly become one," wrote *New York Times Book Review* critic Robert Sullivan. The critic went on to praise the author's "smooth and pleasing and often sensual" prose and favorably compared his combination of story and setting to that of Wallace Stegner. For his part, Guterson explained to Mudge that in formulating his novels, he starts with a "love of place, which seeks expression, which wants to use me to express itself. . . . It's almost as if I'm compelled to sing these places."

While some critics found *East of the Mountains* less engaging than Guterson's debut novel, others recognized a development in the author's style. In *East of the Mountains* Guterson intentionally cultivated a leaner prose style because he believed it more in keeping with the novel's themes and subject matter. Calling Guterson a "prodigious storyteller," *Quadrant* reviewer Sarah Barnett noted: "Guterson words his pages sparsely, evoking emotions economically. He is able to weave a sort of eloquent beauty into suffering. The very humanness of loving and losing, the bittersweet sense of being parted from a soulmate, is captured on the pages of *East of the Mountains*." Bennett concluded, "Its simplicity makes it no less rich in the writing and no less rewarding in the reading" than *Snow Falling on Cedars*.

Continuing to explore the novel format, in 2003 Guterson published *Our Lady of the Forest*. The novel focuses on Ann, a runaway teenager, who is one of four main characters in the story. When the troubled teen has a vision of the Blessed Virgin Mary while picking mushrooms in a Pacific Northwest forest, her vision sets in motion a chain of events that transforms the area around North Fork, Washington, into an unflattering portrait of modern U.S. society. According to a *Kirkus Reviews* critic, *Our Lady of the Forest* is a "witty fable of faith, greed, purity, and hope" told in a manner that is "sharp

and incisive without a trace of cynicism or credulity." A *Publishers Weekly* reviewer predicted that the "gloominess of this uncompromising novel" might put off some readers, but that Guterson's story would conversely attract others because of its "intensity." In *Time* Iyer voiced appreciation for this gloom, seeing in it a return to the traditions of American fiction embodied in the works of Nathaniel Hawthorne and Ralph Waldo Emerson. *Our Lady of the Forest* presents "an unflinching picture of Hawthorne's descendants in the wake of [rock star] Kurt Cobain," Iyer noted. "More than that, it shows Guterson to be a serious and searching craftsman, very much in the American grain and determined to take himself further."

Guterson once commented: "I write because something inner and unconscious forces me to. That is the first compulsion. The second is one of ethical and moral duty. I feel responsible to tell stories that inspire readers to consider more deeply who they are." Although his life changed in a material sense as a result of the success of *Snow Falling on Cedars,* he has taken those changes in stride. His status as a well-known author "doesn't matter. It might be entertaining for my fifteen minutes, but I'm ephemeral," he told *Book* interviewer Donahue. "What lasts I hope, are my books. Stories will always matter—stories that present human beings in crisis, deciding how to confront their struggles, how to be fully human. Stories deliver us the heroes of the common people. Without them, we wouldn't have culture. We wouldn't know who we are."

BIOGRAPHICAL AND CRITICAL SOURCES:

BOOKS

Contemporary Novelists, 7th edition, St. James Press (Detroit, MI), 2001.

PERIODICALS

Antioch Review, winter, 2000, Carolyn Maddux, review of *East of the Mountains,* p. 116.
Atlanta Journal-Constitution, April 18, 1999, Diane Roberts, review of *East of the Mountains,* p. L11; May 30, 1999, Don O'Briant, "Seeds of 'Cedars': Guterson Deals with Fallout of Success," p. K12.
Book, May, 1999, review of *East of the Mountains,* p. 77; March-April, 2000, Bill Donahue, "Living in His Landscape, the Northwesterner Looks East of the Mountains with His New Novel"; November, 2000, p. 10.

Booklist, September 1, 1992, Denise Perry Donavin, review of *Family Matters: Why Homeschooling Makes Sense,* p. 14; August, 1994, Dennis Dodge, review of *Snow Falling on Cedars,* p. 2022; January 1, 1999, review of *East of the Mountains,* p. 792; June 1, 1999, review of *East of the Mountains,* p. 1797; September 15, 2000, Karen Harris, review of *Snow Falling on Cedars* (audio version), p. 262.

Books, summer, 1999, review of *East of the Mountains,* p. 20.

Christian Science Monitor, May 6, 1999, Kendra Nordin, review of *East of the Mountains,* p. 20.

Economist (United Kingdom), June 19, 1999, review of *East of the Mountains,* p. S14.

English Journal, October, 1997, Donna C. Neumann, review of *Snow Falling on Cedars,* p. 112; March, 1999, John Manear, review of *The Country ahead of Us, the Country Behind,* pp. 118-119.

Entertainment Weekly, December 29, 1995, Dave Karger, "David Guterson," p. 55; April 23, 1999, review of *East of the Mountains,* p. 56.

Gentleman's Quarterly, May, 1999, Thomas Mallon, review of *East of the Mountains,* pp. 112-115.

Globe and Mail (Toronto, Ontario, Canada), April 24, 1999, review of *East of the Mountains,* p. E4.

Guardian (London, England), June 2, 1999, Nick Wroe, review of *East of the Mountains,* p. T16.

Houston Chronicle (Houston, TX), May 16, 1999, Tony Freemantle, review of *East of the Mountains,* p. 22.

Hungry Mind Review, winter, 1999, review of *Snow Falling on Cedars,* p. 11.

Kirkus Reviews, January 15, 1999, review of *East of the Mountains,* p. 88; July 15, 2003, review of *Our Lady of the Forest,* p. 927.

Library Journal, July, 1989, Francis Poole, review of *The Country ahead of Us, the Country Behind,* p. 109; September 1, 1992, Hilma F. Cooper, review of *Family Matters,* p. 186; August, 1994, Sheila Riley, review of *Snow Falling on Cedars,* p. 129; February 15, 1999, review of *East of the Mountains,* p. 183; September 15, 2001, review of *Snow Falling on Cedars,* p. 140; June 1, 2003, Rebecca Stuhr, review of *Our Lady of the Forest,* p. 166.

Literary Cavalcade, January, 1998, John DiConsiglio, "Mountain Main" (interview), pp. 4-5.

Los Angeles Times, May 9, 1999, Jonathan Levi, review of *East of the Mountains,* p. 2; December 12, 1999, Patrick Goldstein, "*Snow Falling on Cedars* Was No Simple Screenplay," p. E1.

Maclean's, June 21, 1999, review of *East of the Mountains,* p. 52.

Minneapolis-St. Paul, April, 1996, William Swanson, "When 'Snow' Turns to Gold," pp. 30-32.

New Republic, February 8, 1993, Alan Wolfe, review of *Family Matters,* pp. 25-32.

Newsweek, December 18, 1995, Malcolm Jones, Jr., "*Snow* on Top," p. 72.

New Yorker, May 17, 1999, Joyce Carol Oates, "Off the Road: A Strange Journey through the Pacific Northwest," pp. 89-91.

New York Times, April 9, 1999, Michiko Kakutani, "Distracting Detours in the Hunt for a Final Exit," p. E47; December 22, 1999, Stephen Holden, "Prejudice Lingers in the Land of Mists," p. E5.

New York Times Book Review, September 3, 1989, Lois E. Nesbitt, review of *The Country ahead of Us, the Country Behind,* p. 14; October 16, 1994, Susan Kenney, review of *Snow Falling on Cedars,* p. 12; May 9, 1999, Robert Sullivan, review of *East of the Mountains,* p. 16.

New York Times Upfront, November 15, 1999, "No Snow in Texas," p. 7.

Observer (London, England), June 6, 1999, review of *East of the Mountains,* p. 11.

People, March 13, 1995, Joanne Kaufman, review of *Snow Falling on Cedars,* p. 31; March 4, 1996, Kim Hubbard, "Out of the Woods" (interview), pp. 89-90.

Publishers Weekly, May 26, 1989, Sybil Steinberg, review of *The Country ahead of Us, the Country Behind,* pp. 54-55; July 13, 1992, review of *Family Matters,* p. 42; August 1, 1994, review of *Snow Falling on Cedars,* p. 70; January 11, 1999, review of *East of the Mountains,* p. 51; April 5, 1999, John Blades, "David Guterson: Stoic of the Pacific Northwest," pp. 215-216; May 3, 1999, review of *East of the Mountains,* p. 35; July 28, 2003, review of *Our Lady of the Forest,* p. 75.

Quadrant, December, 1999, Sarah Barnett, review of *East of the Mountains,* p. 85+.

Spectator, May 8, 1999, Katie Grant, review of *East of the Mountains,* pp. 34-35.

Time, September 26, 1994, Pico Iyer, review of *Snow Falling on Cedars,* p. 79; April 26, 1999, review of *East of the Mountains,* p. 98; November 10, 2003, Pico Iyer, review of *Our Lady of the Forest,* p. 93.

Time Canada, May 3, 1999, Pico Iyer and Andrea Sachs, review of *East of the Mountains,* p. 57.

Times Literary Supplement, June 11, 1999, Bill Brown, review of *East of the Mountains,* p. 23.

Wall Street Journal, April 23, 1999, David Byers, review of *East of the Mountains,* p. W7.

Washington Post Book World, May 2, 1999, review of *East of the Mountains,* p. 3.

Woman's Journal, June, 1999, review of *East of the Mountains,* p. 16.

World and I, September, 1999, reviews of *East of the Mountains,* p. 242, and Tom Deignan, "A Farewell," p. 256.

ONLINE

BookPage, http://www.bookpage.com/ (May 10, 2003), Alden Mudge, "Guterson Offers a Moving Story of One Man's Final Pilgrimage."

National Public Radio Web Site, http://www.npr.org/ (January 3, 2002), Bob Edwards, transcript of *Morning Edition* interview with Guterson.

Printed Matter, http://www.dcn.ca.us/ (November 12, 1995), Elisabeth Sherwin, "New Writer Thanks Harper Lee for Leading the Way."

H

HADDON, Mark 1962-

PERSONAL: Born 1962, in Northampton, England; married Sos Eltis (an educator); children: Alfie. *Education:* Merton College, Oxford, B.A., 1981; Edinburgh University, M.A., 1984. *Hobbies and other interests:* Marathon canoeing, abstract painting.

ADDRESSES: Home—Oxford, England. *Agent*—c/o Author Mail, Doubleday, 1745 Broadway, New York, NY 10019.

CAREER: Author. During early career, assisted patients with multiple sclerosis and autism, and worked a variety of part-time jobs, including at a theater box office and in a mail order business; worked as an illustrator and cartoonist for periodicals, including cartoon strip "Men—A User's Guide"; creator of and writer for children's television series *Microsoap.*

AWARDS, HONORS: Smarties Prize shortlist, 1994, for *The Real Porky Philips;* Book Trust Teenage Prize, Whitbread Book of the Year, Art Seidenbaum Award for First Fiction, Commonwealth Writers Prize for best first book, all 2003, and Children's Fiction Prize from the *Guardian,* all for *The Curious Incident of the Dog in the Night-Time;* two British Academy of Film and Television Arts (BAFTA) awards and Best Children's Drama award from the Royal Television Society, all for *Microsoap.*

WRITINGS:

The Curious Incident of the Dog in the Night-Time (novel), Doubleday (New York, NY), 2003.

FOR CHILDREN

(And illustrator) *Gilbert's Gobstopper,* Hamish Hamilton (London, England), 1987, Dial Books for Young Readers (New York, NY), 1988.

(And illustrator) *Toni and the Tomato Soup,* Harcourt Brace (San Diego, CA), 1988.

A Narrow Escape for Princess Sharon, Hamish Hamilton (London, England), 1989.

Gridzbi Spudvetch!, Walker (New York, NY), 1993.

Titch Johnson, Almost World Champion, illustrated by Martin Brown, Walker (New York, NY), 1993.

(And illustrator) *The Real Porky Philips,* A & C Black (London, England), 1994.

Baby Dinosaurs at Home, Western Publishing (New York, NY), 1994.

Baby Dinosaurs at Playgroup, Western Publishing (New York, NY), 1994.

Baby Dinosaurs in the Garden, Western Publishing (New York, NY), 1994.

Baby Dinosaurs on Vacation, Western Publishing (New York, NY), 1994.

The Sea of Tranquility, illustrated by Christian Birmingham, Harcourt Brace (San Diego, CA), 1996.

(And illustrator) *Agent Z and the Penguin from Mars,* Red Fox (London, England), 1996.

(And illustrator) *Agent Z and the Masked Crusader,* Red Fox (London, England), 1996.

(And illustrator) *Agent Z Goes Wild,* Red Fox (London, England), 1999.

Secret Agent Handbook, illustrated by Sue Heap, Walker Books (New York, NY), 1999.

(And illustrator) *Agent Z and the Killer Bananas,* Red Fox (London, England), 2001.

The Ice Bear's Cave, illustrated by David Axtell, Picture Lions (London, England), 2002.

Ocean Star Express, illustrated by Peter Sutton, Picture Lions (London, England), 2002.

Also author of episodes for children's television series, including *Microsoap* and *Starstreet;* contributor to screenplay adaptation of *Fungus and the Bogeyman,* by Raymond Briggs. Contributor of illustrations and cartoons to periodicals, including *New Statesman, Spectator, Guardian, Sunday Telegraph,* and *Private Eye.*

ADAPTATIONS: The Curious Incident of the Dog in the Night-Time has been adapted as an audiobook by Recorded Books, 2003, and is also scheduled to be adapted as a film written and directed by Steve Kloves and coproduced by Brad Pitt.

WORK IN PROGRESS: An adult novel, tentatively titled *Blood and Scissors.*

SIDELIGHTS: British author Mark Haddon was enjoying a successful career writing and illustrating children's books, as well as writing for popular children's television shows such as *Microsoap* and *Starstreet* before he surprised even himself with his wildly acclaimed first novel, *The Curious Incident of the Dog in the Night-Time.* Ostensibly a quirky mystery novel about a teenager who investigates the murder of his neighbor's dog, the story gained the most attention for its narrative technique in which Haddon uses the viewpoint of an autistic boy named Christopher. Originally, as the author told Dave Weich in a *Powell's* interview, the idea of the story came from an image in his mind of a poodle that had been killed by a gardening implement. Haddon, who admittedly has a rather dark sense of humor at times, thought beginning a novel this way could be funny, but in order to make it work he would have to tell the incident from a unique viewpoint. "The dog came first," Haddon told Weich, "then the voice. Only after a few pages did I really start to ask, *Who does the voice belong to?* So Christopher came along, in fact, after the book had already got underway." It was a fortuitous decision that would lead Haddon to win a Whitbread prize, among other honors.

Even though the character of Christopher Boone, who suffers from a disorder known as Asperger's syndrome, is fifteen years old, Haddon originally intended the book to be for an adult audience. After having written over a dozen books for children over the years, he wanted to write about more complex themes. The resulting novel "was definitely for adults," he told Weich, "but maybe I should say more specifically: It was for myself. I've been writing for kids for a long time, and if you're writing for kids you're kind of writing for the kid you used to be at that age. . . . I felt a great sense of freedom with this book because I felt like I was writing it for me." In presenting the final manuscript to his agent, however, it was decided that it would be marketed to both an adult and a teenage audience.

The Curious Incident of the Dog in the Night-Time can be seen, in some ways, as an extension of Haddon's previous books for children, some of which contain a good dose of mystery and, often, humor. For example, his debut children's book, *Gilbert's Gobstopper,* is definitely meant to be humorous and, in its own way, have a touch of adventure. When Gilbert loses his jawbreaker, the reader is treated to a trip from the gobstopper's viewpoint as it travels through sewer pipes, enters the ocean, is found by a fisherman, and goes on ever-more surprising turns that include a trip into outer space. "This irreverent entertainment will tickle many a funnybone," asserted Carolyn Polese in a *School Library Journal* review.

Haddon also combines adventure and humor in his "Agent Z" series for children that includes *Agent Z and the Penguin from Mars, Agent Z and the Masked Crusader, Agent Z Goes Wild,* and *Agent Z and the Killer Bananas.* The Agent Z of the title actually refers to a group of three boys, including Jenks, Ben, and Barney, who assume the secret identity as part of their club. The boys get involved in one goofy adventure after another, such as the time they take advantage of Mr. Sidebottom's obsession with UFOs by concocting an alien plot using a penguin and some foil, or the time the boys make a mock movie about killer bananas. Reviewers generally had high praise for these books. *School Librarian* contributor Alicen Geddes-Ward, for one, called *Agent Z Meets the Masked Crusader* a "witty, tight and brilliantly funny book." Adrian Jackson, writing in *Books for Keeps,* similarly felt that *Agent Z and the Penguin from Mars* was "a real hoot of a story, wildly imagined."

But Haddon does not view children as mere material for humorous stories. Some of his children's books show a decidedly more sensitive side to youngsters, such as *The Real Porky Philips* and *Titch Johnson, Almost World Champion.* In a story that *Books for Keeps* critic Gill Roberts called "powerful, poignant and pertinent," *The Real Porky Philips* is about a young, sensitive, overweight boy who finds the courage to finally assert his real personality after he has to play the role of a genie in the school play. *Titch Johnson, Almost World Champion* has a similar theme about self-confidence. Here, Titch, who seems to not be good at anything except balancing forks on his nose, gains a better appreciation of himself after successfully organizing a fundraising event.

The rich world of dreams and imagination is explored in *The Sea of Tranquility* and *Ocean Star Express*. In the former, Haddon draws on his own childhood fascination with the achievement of mankind's first landing on the Moon in 1969. The boy in the tale has a picture of the solar system on his wall and fantasizes about what it would be like to be an astronaut. Combined with this storyline are facts about the actual landing, including interesting tidbits, for example, the footprints left there will remain for millions of years because of the lack of wind and rain on the Moon. Carolyn Boyd, writing in *School Librarian*, felt that "this book will appeal to those who remember the first moon landing and to young readers who will marvel at it." *Ocean Star Express*, by comparison, is not as grounded in reality. Here, a boy named Joe is becoming bored during his summer holiday when Mr. Robertson, the owner of the hotel where his family is staying, invites him to see his train set. No ordinary toy, apparently, the train takes Joe and the owner on a magical ride around the world in what a *Kirkus Reviews* contributor called a "sweet and simple story that young train enthusiasts will enjoy."

While Haddon received a good deal of praise for many of his children's books, including being shortlisted for the Smarties Prize for *The Real Porky Philips*, his *The Curious Incident of the Dog in the Night-Time* has brought him considerably more critical attention. It combines the humor, sensitivity, and adventure of his earlier books with a highly challenging narrative perspective that impressed many reviewers. The protagonist of the story, Christopher Boone, suffers from Asperger's syndrome, a type of autism that prevents him from being able to accurately perceive and interpret other people's emotions. While he possesses an extremely logical mind, he is dispassionate and unable to empathize with other people whose feelings he cannot comprehend. This makes Christopher both a very reliable narrator, because he is incapable of lying, and an unreliable one, because he cannot fully appreciate the motives behind other people's actions. Making the character even more complicated, Haddon gives Christopher other flaws, including an aversion to being touched, a hatred of the colors brown and yellow, and a sometimes uncontrollable bladder. On the other hand, Christopher is brilliant at math, loves puzzles, and has a photographic memory.

The novel is ostensibly being written by Christopher, whose school counselor has assigned him the task of writing a book as a type of therapy. Haddon becomes his character fully in the story, even numbering the chapters in prime number order rather than sequentially because of Christopher's fascination for prime numbers.

The story begins when Christopher discovers the dead poodle, Wellington. A great lover of dogs, as well as a fan of the Sherlock Holmes detective stories, he decides to find out who killed Wellington and why. The chapters then alternate between narratives of Christopher's progress in the investigation and chapters that include mathematical puzzles, charts, and other calculations the fifteen-year-old uses to try to reason out the information he has gathered. But as his investigation advances, the death of the poodle proves to be a knot that, when untied, reveals much more painful truths involving something terrible that happened between Christopher's parents and their neighbors and what really happened to his supposedly "dead" mother.

Critics appreciated the use of Christopher's dispassionate voice because it forces the author to obey the old writing caveat that authors should always "show and not tell" what is happening in the story. Furthermore, what interested many reviewers is that even though Christopher has autism, Haddon in no way makes this the theme of *The Curious Incident of the Dog in the Night-Time*. Indeed, the word "autism" is never even used. Instead, the novel might best be viewed as an examination of "the process of writing itself," as Daniel J. Glendening put it in *America's Intelligence Wire*. The story's point of view allows considerable latitude for reader interpretation, and indeed Haddon remarked to Weich that people he has talked to have had amazingly disparate reactions to his novel. "People have said to me that it's a desperately sad book and they wept most of the way through it," the author said. "Other people say it's charming and they kept laughing all the time. People say it has a sad ending; people say it has a happy ending. Because Christopher doesn't force the reader to think one thing and another, I get many different reactions."

Although Haddon has had some personal experience in the past working with autistic people, he has admitted doing very little formal research when creating the character of Christopher. While many critics had no problem buying into the author's portrayal of the boy's condition, one reviewer, Nicholas Barrow of the *Spectator*, found it highly flawed. Barrow considered Haddon's descriptions to be a "total exaggeration of a fifteen-year-old boy with Asperger's," objecting to the "cliché" of an autistic boy who is a math genius, noting that Christopher is unbelievable as a teenager because he never thinks even once about sex, and finding the boy's problem with incontinence inconsistent with Asperger's patients. In the end, Barrow found the portrayal of Christopher to be "patronising, inaccurate and not entertaining," and that "some people with Asperger's would be offended by this book." However, if one considers that Haddon's motive is not to discuss the issue of mental or emotional disabilities, but rather to experiment with literary perspective and create an interesting story, then one would fall into the more predominant camp that found Haddon's narrator absorbing. As one *Publishers Weekly* critic put it, "The novel brims with touching, ironic humor. The result is an eye-opening work in a unique and compelling literary voice." "In Christopher, Haddon has tapped into a unique, yet memorable voice that lingers well after the last page," Jennifer Fish added in the *Florida Times Union*. London *Independent* reviewer Nicholas Tucker concluded, "How Haddon achieves this most delicate of balances is a tribute to his skill as a successful cartoonist as well as novelist." And Glendening called *The Curious Incident of the Dog in the Night-Time* "modern writing at its finest."

BIOGRAPHICAL AND CRITICAL SOURCES:

PERIODICALS

America's Intelligence Wire, January 19, 2004, Daniel J. Glendening, "Author Mark Haddon Takes a Novel Approach to Autism."

Atlanta Journal-Constitution, June 29, 2003, John Freeman, "Whodunit Unveils Autistic Boy's Mind," p. D2; October 26, 2003, Greg Changnon, "Teen 'Rain Man' Confronts Canine and Other Mysteries," p. F3.

Book, January-February, 2003, Adam Langer, "The New Houdini: Mark Haddon," p. 43; July-August, 2003, Beth Kephart, "Little Sherlock," p. 76.

Booklist, April 1, 2003, Kristine Huntley, review of *The Curious Incident of the Dog in the Night-Time*, p. 1376; January 1, 2004, Mary McCay, review of *The Curious Incident of the Dog in the Night-Time*, p. 890.

Bookseller, January 24, 2003, "A Young Detective Obsessed by Detail," p. 29.

Books for Keeps, July, 1993, Adrian Jackson, review of *Gridzbi Spudvetch!*, p. 28; May, 1994, Steve Rosson, review of *The Real Porky Philips*, p. 8; July, 1995, Adrian Jackson, review of *Agent Z and the Penguin from Mars*, p. 12; September, 1995, Gill Roberts, review of *The Real Porky Philips*, p. 12.

Books for Your Children, summer, 1994, S. Williams, review of *The Real Porky Philips*, p. 13.

British Book News, March, 1988, Judith Elkin, review of *Gilbert's Gobstopper*, p. 13.

Daily Variety, August 2, 2002, Michael Fleming, "WB Looking 'Curious': Pitt, Grey Keen on Haddon Adventure Tale," p. 5.

Economist, May 24, 2003, "Great Expectations; New Fiction," p. 85.

Entertainment Weekly, June 20, 2003, Ken Tucker, review of *The Curious Incident of the Dog in the Night-Time*, p. 76.

Florida Times Union, August 31, 2003, Jennifer Fish, "It All Adds Up to Great Debut Novel: Tale's Hero an Autistic Math Genius," p. D4.

Growing Point, July, 1989, review of *Toni and the Tomato Soup*, p. 5197.

Independent (London, England), June 6, 2003, Nicholas Tucker, "Making Sense of an Abnormal Normality: *The Curious Incident of the Dog in the Night-Time*," p. 15.

Junior Bookshelf, June, 1993, review of *Gridzbi Spudvetch!*, p. 105; August, 1993, review of *Titch Johnson, Almost World Champion*, p. 135.

Kirkus Reviews, January 1, 2003, review of *Ocean Star Express*, p. 60; April 15, 2003, review of *The Curious Incident of the Dog in the Night-Time*, p. 557.

Kliatt, January, 2004, Jacqueline Edwards, review of *The Curious Incident of the Dog in the Night-Time* (audiobook), p. 44.

Knight Ridder/Tribune News Service, June 25, 2003, Marta Salij, review of *The Curious Incident of the Dog in the Night-Time*, p. K1715.

Library Journal, May 1, 2003, David Hellman, review of *The Curious Incident of the Dog in the Night-Time*, p. 155; January, 2004, Michael Adams, review of *The Curious Incident of the Dog in the Night-Time*, p. 184.

M2 Best Books, November 14, 2003, "Author Mark Haddon Set for Awards Hatrick"; January 26, 2004, "Haddon's Curious Tale Continues Its Unexpected Success"; January 28, 2004, "Haddon Claims Whitbread Book of the Year Prize."

Magpies, September, 1996, Margaret Philips, review of *The Sea of Tranquility*, p. 28.

Newsweek, September 8, 2003, David Noonan, "'Allowed to Be Odd': The Hero of a Best-selling New Novel Is a 15-Year-Old Boy with Autism—But That Label Never Appears in the Book," p. 50.

New York Times Book Review, June 15, 2003, Jay McInerney, "The Remains of the Dog," p. 5.

Publishers Weekly, May 13, 1988, Kimberly Olson Fakih and Diane Roback, review of *Gilbert's Gobstopper*, p. 273; April 25, 1994, review of *Baby Dinosaurs at Home*, *Baby Dinosaurs on Vacation*, *Baby Dinosaurs at Playgroup*, and *Baby Dinosaurs in the Garden*, p. 75; September 16, 1996, review of *The Sea of Tranquility*, p. 82; July 1, 2002, John F. Baker, "Obsessed by Sherlock Holmes," p. 14; April 7, 2003, review of *The Curious Incident of the Dog in the Night-Time*, p. 42.

Reading Teacher, October, 1989, review of *Gilbert's Gobstopper,* p. 56.

School Librarian, August, 1989, Joyce Banks, review of *A Narrow Escape for Princess Sharon,* p. 104; August, 1993, Julie Blaisdale, review of *Gridzbi Spudvetch!,* and Caroline Axon, review of *Titch Johnson, Almost World Champion,* p. 109; November, 1993, Alicen Geddes-Ward, review of *Agent Z Meets the Masked Crusader,* p. 155; February, 1997, Carolyn Boyd, review of *The Sea of Tranquility,* p. 19; August, 2001, review of *Agent Z and the Killer Bananas,* p. 136; summer, 2002, review of *Ocean Star Express,* pp. 74-75.

School Library Journal, September, 1988, Carolyn Polese, review of *Gilbert's Gobstopper,* p. 160; October, 1989, Susan H. Patron, review of *Toni and the Tomato Soup,* p. 84; September, 1994, Linda Wicher, review of *Baby Dinosaurs at Home, Baby Dinosaurs at Playgroup, Baby Dinosaurs in the Garden,* and *Baby Dinosaurs on Vacation,* p. 185; September, 1996, John Peters, review of *The Sea of Tranquility,* p. 178; October, 2003, Jackie Gropman, review of *The Curious Incident of the Dog in the Night-Time,* p. 207.

Spectator, May 17, 2003, Nicholas Barrow, "It Ain't Necessarily So," p. 65.

Star-Ledger (Newark, NJ), July 6, 2003, Deborah Jerome-Cohen, "From the Shadows, Words," p. 4.

WWD (Women's Wear Daily), August 7, 2003, Samantha Conti, "A Dog's Tale," p. 4.

ONLINE

MostlyFiction, http://www.mostlyfiction.com/ (August 3, 2003), Mary Whipple, review of *The Curious Incident of the Dog in the Night-Time.*

Powell's City of Books, http://www.powells.com/ (February 10, 2004), Dave Weich, "The Curiously Irresistible Literary Debut of Mark Haddon."

*   *   *

HAILEY, Arthur 1920-2004

PERSONAL: Born April 5, 1920, Luton, England; immigrated to Canada, 1947, naturalized citizen (retaining British citizenship), 1952; died of a stroke November 24, 2004, in the Bahamas; son of George Wellington (a factory worker) and Elsie Mary (Wright) Hailey; married Joan Fishwick, 1944 (divorced, 1950); married Sheila Dunlop, July 28, 1951; children: (first marriage) Roger, John, Mark; (second marriage) Jane, Steven,

Diane. *Education:* Attended elementary school in England. *Hobbies and other interests:* Travel, reading, music, boat handling, fishing.

CAREER: Office boy in London, England, 1934-39; Maclean-Hunter Publishing Co., Toronto, Ontario, assistant editor of *Bus and Truck Transport,* 1947-49, editor, 1949-53; Trailmobile Canada Ltd., Toronto, sales promotion manager, 1953-56; full-time writer, beginning 1956. *Military service:* Royal Air Force, pilot, 1939-47; served in Europe, the Middle East, and the Far East; became flight lieutenant; served as first editor of R.A.F. training magazine *Air Clues;* recipient of R.A.F. Air Efficiency Award.

MEMBER: Writers Guild of America, Authors League of America, Association of Canadian Television and Radio Artists (honorary life member), Lyford Cay Club (Bahamas).

AWARDS, HONORS: Gold medal of Canadian Council of Authors and Artists, 1956; Best Canadian Playwright Award, 1957 and 1958; Emmy Award nomination, c. 1957, for *No Deadly Medicine;* Doubleday Canadian Prize Novel Award, 1962, for *In High Places;* gold medal of Commonwealth Club of California, 1968, for *Airport.*

WRITINGS:

NOVELS

(With John Castle) *Flight into Danger* (based on *Zero Hour!,* Hailey's television play *Flight into Danger*), Souvenir Press (London), 1958, U.S. published as *Runway Zero Eight,* Doubleday, 1959.

The Final Diagnosis (based on his television play *No Deadly Medicine*), Doubleday, 1959.

In High Places, Doubleday, 1962.

Hotel, Doubleday, 1965.

Airport, Doubleday, 1968.

Wheels, Doubleday, 1971.

The Moneychangers, Doubleday, 1975.

Overload, Doubleday, 1979.

Strong Medicine, Doubleday, 1984.

The Evening News, Doubleday, 1990.

Detective, Crown (New York City), 1997.

OTHER

Flight into Danger (television play), CBC, 1956.

(With Hall Bartlett and John Champion) *Zero Hour!* (screenplay based on his television play *Flight into Danger*), Paramount, 1957.

Close-up on Writing for Television (collection of television plays), Doubleday, 1960.

Author of over twenty television plays, including *No Deadly Medicine,* 1957, and *Course for Collision,* 1962, produced programs, including *Westinghouse Studio One, Playhouse 90,* and *Kraft Theatre.*

All of Hailey's novels have appeared in foreign editions, and most have been published in forty languages.

ADAPTATIONS: Films based on Hailey's novels include *The Young Doctors,* based on *The Final Diagnosis,* United Artists, 1961; *Hotel,* Warner Bro., 1967; *Airport,* Universal, 1969; *Wheels,* Universal, 1977; *The Moneychangers,* Paramount, 1977; and *Overload.* In addition, the films *Airport 1975, Airport 1977,* and *Concorde-Airport 1979,* although not based on Hailey's work, were produced as sequels to the original *Airport.*

SIDELIGHTS: Arthur Hailey's career as a professional writer began in 1955 when, on a business flight across Canada, he began to fantasize about what might happen if both the pilot and copilot suddenly became incapacitated—leaving him, a rather rusty World War II fighter pilot, the only person able to land the plane. It took Hailey just six evenings and two weekends to turn the daydream into his first television play, *Flight into Danger.* Being unfamiliar with the conventions of television writing, he wrote the play in standard theatrical form without camera directions; and not knowing anyone in the TV industry, he simply mailed it to "Script Department, Canadian Broadcasting Corp." The play reached Nathan Cohen, script editor of CBC's *General Motors Theatre,* who ironically noticed it amidst countless other unsolicited scripts precisely because of the peculiar style in which it was written. The initial broadcast on April 7, 1956, drew rave reviews and extraordinary viewer response; it was subsequently presented on networks in the United States and Great Britain where it was equally well received. Since then, Hailey's success as a writer for television and especially as a novelist has been phenomenal. He has had six consecutive best sellers, and several major motion pictures have been based on his books.

Strangely it is Hailey's success that has caused the most discourse among critics. In an attempt to explain the author's ability to turn out consistent best-sellers, some reviewers accuse him of writing "formula" or "programmed" novels, and others say that he sets out to write books that will make good films. Joseph McLellan outlines the supposed Hailey formula: "Start with something large and complicated, a business or institution that touches the lives of large numbers of people and is not fully understood by the public. Ideally, the subject should have a touch of glamour and some element of risk in its routine activities. The writer takes the reader inside this subject, letting him see it from various points of view and tossing in an occasional little sermon on public responsibilities. Numerous characters are formed out of available material (cardboard will do nicely) and they are set in motion by a series of crises, small, medium, and large, which illustrate the nature and particularly the weaknesses of the activity that is the real subject (in a sense the real hero) of the book." And yet, if there is a formula that Hailey follows, it seems to have little effect on his readers who flock to the bookstores at the mere hint of a press release from his publisher. As Peter Andrews puts it: "Hailey's novels are such genuine publishing events that to criticize them is like putting the slug on the Rockettes. It's not going to change anything. No sooner is his contract inked than mighty lumberjacks start to make their axes ring. Paperback houses and book clubs fairly whimper to give him money while the work is still in progress, and Ross Hunter calls up the old actors' home to begin casting his next blockbuster. At the publication party itself the last deviled egg is still to be consumed when his book busts through on the best-seller list."

No doubt the formula accusations stem from certain characteristics that are evident in all of Hailey's writing: the meticulous attention to detail, the multiple plots and subplots, and his penchant for choosing as subjects monolithic structures (a hotel, an airport, the automobile industry) about which most people know little, but with which they are unquestionably fascinated. Hailey's ability to research a subject with unusual vigor and tenacity has resulted in a group of books that truly take the reader into the hearts of these otherwise unapproachable institutions. Patricia MacManus, in a review of *Hotel,* says that the book "undoubtedly covers every department in the curriculum of Cornell's School of Hotel Administration." And she feels that there are "enough intersecting story-lines to keep even the most plot-addicted readers scurrying to stay abreast of the multi-layered goings-on at the St. Gregory, the fictitious New Orleans hostelry of *Hotel.*" Robert Cromie writes that Hailey covers his subject in *Airport* with such great detail that the book is likely "to upset airline executives, managers of non-mythical airports, and perhaps the Federal agencies." Some of the sensitive areas include "the dangers inherent in too-short runways, the curtailing of power during the vital early stages of take-off as a sop to nearby homeowners, the possibility that the easy availability of insurance at every major field may encourage bomb-for-profit schemes, the frantic efficiency which *usually* prevails in the radar room as traffic is supervised, and even the airlines' pregnancy plan for unwed stewardesses." And Kenneth R. Clark of the *Chicago Tribune* finds Hailey's *Evening News,* a thriller about the inner workings of a network news bureau, to be a "breakneck tale" that is "right on the mark, right down to the tiniest nuances of office politics, internecine squabbling, journalistic scorn of authority, and the mechanics of covering late-breaking news."

If there can be said to be a formula or pattern to Hailey's work, it is the now-famous system he has developed in order to garner the vast quantity of detail and technical information with which he packs his books. He spends about a year researching his subject, six months reviewing notes and planning, and eighteen months writing. While researching *Hotel,* he read twenty-seven books about hotels and twelve on New Orleans. At the same time he collected numerous clippings from hotel trade publications as well as those sent to him by his agent and friends. He studied five large hotels in depth (including a six-week stay as a paying guest at an old hotel in New Orleans), and twenty-eight smaller ones. During his research for *Airport,* Hailey spent hours in the airports of New York, Los Angeles, Chicago, Washington, DC, Tampa, Toronto, Montreal, London, Paris, and Brussels, interviewing airport and airline employees and absorbing the atmosphere.

One facet of Hailey's craft that induces some agreement among the critics is his ability to weave an interesting tale. Frank Cameron, in an explanation of the author's rise to success, writes: "For one thing, no one has yet devised a satisfactory substitute for innate talent and Hailey is a born story teller. In this sense he is reminiscent of Somerset Maugham although without Maugham's urbanity of style. Hailey is Hailey. He has his own crisp style which has the twin virtues of economy and sustained suspense. A Hailey novel or a Hailey television play is meant to entertain. There is no emphasis on the introspective agonizing of any character. An obscure reference or bit of *avant-garde* rhetoric does not exist in his works. Moralizing he leaves to other writers unless he can weave it into his own story in ways that do not interrupt the plot and pace." Hailey told Patricia Farrell: "It is very obvious that people like reading facts as a background to fiction and this I try to do. It just seems that I happen to have the ability to do it, but I don't strive to be a proselytizer, a crusader, an educator, a consumer advocate; I'm none of those things. I'm a story teller and anything else is incidental."

BIOGRAPHICAL AND CRITICAL SOURCES:

BOOKS

Contemporary Literary Criticism, Volume 5, Thomson Gale (Detroit), 1976.

Dictionary of Literary Biography, Volume 88: *Canadian Writers, 1920-1959, Second Series,* Thomson Gale, 1989.

Dictionary of Literary Biography Yearbook, 1982, Thomson Gale, 1983.

Hailey, Sheila, *I Married a Bestseller,* Doubleday, 1978.

PERIODICALS

America, May 8, 1965; November 20, 1971.

American Way, July, 1975.

Best Sellers, February 15, 1965; April 1, 1968; October 15, 1971; April, 1975.

Booklist, March 1, 1965; April 15, 1968; November 15, 1971; April 15, 1975.

Books and Bookmen, May, 1965; September, 1975.

Book Week, January 24, 1965.

Book World, January 24, 1965; April 14, 1968.

Boston Globe, July 13, 1997.

Chicago Sunday Tribune, December 13, 1959.

Chicago Tribune, April 23, 1990.

Flying, May, 1968.

Kirkus Reviews, January 15, 1959; November 1, 1978.

Library Journal, March 1, 1962; March 1, 1968.

Miami Herald, June 1, 1975.

National Observer, April 1, 1968; November 6, 1971; May 3, 1975.

National Review, June 20, 1975.

New Republic, October 23, 1971.

New Statesman, July 4, 1975.

New Yorker, October 3, 1959; January 27, 1962.

New York Herald Tribune, October 18, 1959.

New York Times, April 5, 1959; April 20, 1968; July 28, 1975; December 18, 1978.

New York Times Book Review, September 20, 1959; February 21, 1965; April 7, 1968; September 19, 1971; May 18, 1975; February 11, 1979; June 22, 1997, p. 20.

Observer, May 2, 1965.

Publishers Weekly, October 30, 1975.

San Francisco Chronicle, April 19, 1959; December 13, 1959; February 4, 1962.

Saturday Evening Post, November, 1975.

Time, March 26, 1965; March 22, 1968; October 11, 1971; April 14, 1975.

Wall Street Journal, September 21, 1971; March 20, 1975.

Washington Post, July 25, 1969; March 23, 1975.

Washington Post Book World, March 23, 1975; January 15, 1979.

Writer's Digest, August, 1972.

OBITUARIES:

PERIODICALS

Chicago Tribune, November 26, 2004, section 3, p. 8.
New York Times, November 26, 2004, p. C10.
Times (London, England), November 27, 2004, p. 80.
Washington Post, November 27, 2004, p. B4.

ONLINE

New York Times Online, http://www.nytimes.com/ (November 26, 2004).

*   *   *

HALBERSTAM, David 1934-

PERSONAL: Born April 10, 1934, in New York, NY; son of Charles A. (a surgeon) and Blanche (a teacher; maiden name, Levy) Halberstam; married Elzbieta (an actress), June 13, 1965 (divorced, 1977); married Jean Sandness Butler, June 29, 1979; children: Julia. *Education:* Harvard University, B.A., 1955. *Hobbies and other interests:* Reading detective and suspense novels, watching late movies on television, fishing.

ADDRESSES: Home—New York, NY, and Nantucket, MA. *Agent*—Robert Solomon, 488 Madison Ave. New York, NY 10019.

CAREER: Daily Times Leader, West Point, MS, reporter, 1955-56; *Nashville Tennessean,* Nashville, TN, reporter, 1956-60; *New York Times,* New York, NY, staff writer, 1960-67, foreign correspondent in the Congo (now Zaire), 1961-62, Vietnam, 1962-63, Warsaw, Poland, 1965, and Paris, France, 1966; *Harper's,* New York, NY, contributing editor, 1967-71.

MEMBER: Society of American Historians, Adlai Stevenson Institute of International Affairs (fellow).

AWARDS, HONORS: Page One Award, Newspaper Guild of New York, 1962; George Polk Memorial Award, Long Island University, 1963; Louis M. Lyons Award, 1964; Pulitzer Prize, Columbia University, 1964, for international reporting; Overseas Press Club Award, 1973; Political Book Award, 1986, for *The Reckoning;* American Book Award, Before Columbus Foundation, 1988, for *The Reckoning;* Elijah Lovejoy Award, Colby College, 1997; Bob Considine Award from St. Bonaventure College, Robert Kennedy Award, and Robert Melcher Book Award from Unitarian Church, all 1999, all for *The Children;* various honorary degrees.

WRITINGS:

FICTION

The Noblest Roman, Houghton (Boston, MA), 1961.
(Editor) *Stephen Crane, Great Stories of Heroism and Adventure,* Platt (New York, NY), 1967.
One Very Hot Day (novel), Houghton (Boston, MA), 1968.

NONFICTION

The Making of a Quagmire: America and Vietnam During the Kennedy Era, Random House (New York, NY), 1965.
The Unfinished Odyssey of Robert Kennedy, Random House (New York, NY), 1969.
Ho, Random House (New York, NY), 1971.
The Best and the Brightest, Random House (New York, NY), 1972, reprinted with a new foreword by John McCain, Modern Library (New York, NY), 2001.
The Powers That Be, Knopf (New York, NY), 1979.
The Breaks of the Game, Knopf (New York, NY), 1981.
On a Very Hot Day, Warner Books (New York, NY), 1984.
The Amateurs: The Story of Four Young Men and Their Quest for an Olympic Gold Medal, Morrow (New York, NY), 1985.
The Reckoning, Morrow (New York, NY), 1986.

The Summer of '49, Morrow (New York, NY), 1989.

The Next Century, Morrow (New York, NY), 1991.

(Editor) *The Best American Sports Writing, 1991,* Houghton (Boston, MA), 1991.

·*The Fifties,* Villard (New York, NY), 1993.

October 1964, Villard (New York, NY), 1994.

(Editor) *The Kansas Century: One Hundred Years of Championship Jayhawk Basketball,* Andrews & McMeel (Kansas City, MO), 1997.

The Children, Random House (New York, NY), 1998.

(Editor) *The Best American Sports Writing of the Century,* Houghton (Boston, MA), 1999.

Playing for Keeps: Michael Jordan and the World He Made, Random House (New York, NY), 1999.

War in a Time of Peace: Bush, Clinton, and the Generals, Scribner (New York, NY), 2001.

(Author of text) *New York September 11: As Seen by Magnum Photographers,* PowerHouse Books (New York, NY), 2001.

Firehouse, Hyperion (New York, NY), 2002.

Teammates, Hyperion (New York, NY), 2003.

(Editor) *Defining a Nation: Our America and the Sources of Its Strength,* National Geographic (Washington, DC), 2003.

Contributor of articles to magazines, including *Atlantic Monthly, Esquire, Harper's Bazaar,* and *McCall's.* Columnist for ESPN.com.

WORK IN PROGRESS: A book on the Korean War and a book about the 1958 baseball championship series between the New York Giants and the Baltimore Colts, both for Hyperion.

SIDELIGHTS: David Halberstam's best-selling books are characterized by voluminous research and an anecdotal, novelistic narrative style. Although the subjects he tackles have ranged from the Japanese auto industry to rowers competing to enter the Olympic Games, Halberstam has consistently been attracted by the question of power and to those individuals who are able to influence events in the United States. Three of his best-known books, *The Best and the Brightest, The Powers That Be,* and *The Reckoning,* have been described collectively as a trilogy on power in America.

Beginning his career as a war correspondent and political reporter, Halberstam was assigned to South Vietnam by the *New York Times* in 1962, and his controversial articles often questioned the official version of events in the Vietnam War. In 1964 he was awarded a Pulitzer Prize for international reporting, and after that, he con-tinued to examine the war in a series of books and in many magazine articles. In *The Best and the Brightest,* Halberstam traces American entanglement in Vietnam and criticizes the leaders of the Kennedy and Johnson administrations for this involvement; he also offers biographical studies of the presidents themselves, and of McGeorge Bundy, then-Secretary of Defense Robert S. McNamara, then-Secretary of State Dean Rusk, economist Walt W. Rostow, General Maxwell Taylor, and General William C. Westmoreland.

In *The Powers That Be,* Halberstam makes the case that the media helped shape recent American politics and society through depictions of the histories of four news reporting giants: *Time,* Columbia Broadcasting System (CBS), the *Washington Post,* and the *Los Angeles Times.* Former CBS correspondent Daniel Schorr, reviewing the book for the *Progressive,* thought Halberstam showed himself to be squarely on the side of the reporters. Schorr observed, "The price of compelling narrative [in this book] is acceptance of the author's perspective. Halberstam's own experience and feeling inevitably color his story." In an article for *Time,* Paul Gray also commented on Halberstam's inclusion of personal feeling, remarking that Halberstam, despite his prodigious research, "listens selectively, and at times relentlessly forces his material in the direction he wants it to go. . . . [His] picture is educational but also highly interpretative."

In the *New Statesman* Godfrey Hodgson expressed disappointment that Halberstam restricted himself to only four opinion-makers. Despite this, Hodgson found Halberstam to be quite readable. "The sheer energy of his infatuation with what he calls power (and I would call influence) carries you along with him," wrote Hodgson. Although questioning the lack of analysis and explanation "of how these empires of the written and the spoken word are held together," the critic admitted that "I lay back, let the tide carry me down the river, took no notice of the mistakes floating past like flotsam, or of the interesting landscapes we were ignoring on the bank, and found myself enjoying it."

In *The Breaks of the Game* and *The Amateurs,* Halberstam turns his investigative reporting and characteristic narrative style to the world of sports. *The Breaks of the Game* examines the gritty world of professional basketball, and *The Amateurs* looks at top-level rowing among the four men's single sculls who competed for the right to represent the United States in the 1984 Olympics. Halberstam told a *New York Times Book Review* interviewer that he was upset by the televised 1984 Winter

Olympics because of the "hype" involved. He explained that he selected sculling as a subject precisely because the athletes had no expectations of fame or remuneration.

David Guy, writing in the *Chicago Tribune Book World,* characterized *The Amateurs* this way: "Halberstam has written a penetrating, fascinating and remarkably suspenseful narrative about one of the last truly non-professional sports in the country, amateur rowing, and in particular about rowing's most prestigious event, the single scull." *New York Times* reviewer Christopher Lehmann-Haupt noted that the subject of *The Amateurs* is "the psychology of competitive rowing. It's about the need to drive oneself through various levels of pain if one wants to win at sculling." As in some of his other work, Halberstam enlivens the story with biographical information, in this case offering the biographies of the four competitors. Critiquing the book for the *Washington Post Book World,* John Jerome noted, "In his usual fashion Halberstam interviews everyone, triangulates every opinion, gets incisive insights and hard judgments even from the oarsmen's mothers. The result is pure reporting on a level undreamt of elsewhere in sports."

With *The Reckoning,* the final volume in what many view as his trilogy on power in America, Halberstam discusses the history of two automobile makers—Ford in the United States and Nissan in Japan—from World War II to the mid-1980s. Halberstam selected the number-two auto company in each country as his subjects because this approach was journalistically more manageable than writing about the largest and most powerful automakers. John F. Baker, who interviewed Halberstam for *Publishers Weekly,* described the book as "a study of American arrogance and blindness and Japanese self-sacrifice and tenacity—and [it] is up-to-date enough to register the recent entry on the auto scene of Korea as an unlikely rival to Japan for the rich American market." Halberstam told Baker: "I like to think the book has value as an alarm clock, telling Americans there's something very out of sync with their society." *Washington Monthly* contributor James Fallows voiced a similar view: "*The Reckoning*'s importance is in helping to shake us out of our complacency."

The Reckoning "does more than scold, however," noted James Flanigan in the *Los Angeles Times Book Review.* He explained, "One of the book's strengths is its reporting on Japanese recent history, on how a devastated nation became an economic power." In the *New York Times,* Peter T. Kilborn related that "Halberstam spent five years at this enterprise, and it shows. For all that

has been written of the two countries' industrial competition, much of his work is new and telling." Famed economist John Kenneth Galbraith, writing in the *New York Times Book Review,* called Halberstam's research "formidable," and pointed out that the author persists beyond the exterior of the story: "He seeks out executives, workers and trade unionists and tells of their lives, aspirations, achievements, disappointments, failures and, especially as regards the managers at Ford, of their unending, vanity-inspired and functionally damaging bureaucratic jealousies and infighting."

Some reviewers, though, criticized Halberstam for the unattributed stories that he relates in making his case about the two automakers. Although Fallows praised *The Reckoning* as "a thorough and engrossing case study" and gave the book a largely positive review, he also thought that the revealing anecdotes and mini-biographies at the heart of Halberstam's work are judgments rather than "truth" and should be presented as such. Fallows likewise noted that "it would be fairer to give the reader some idea of the deduction, interpretation, and yes, guesswork that lie behind the stories." In Chicago's *Tribune Books,* Peter Collier registered a similar objection: "A nonfiction novelist at heart, Halberstam is somewhat cavalier about documentation. He includes a list of the people he interviewed for the book, but doesn't use footnotes. This is not a pedantic quibble: In a place like Detroit, where everyone has a private agenda and speaks with a sharpened tongue, it is valuable to know who is saying what about whom." But some commentators emphasized that Halberstam's writing style and the scope of his projects lend themselves to taking a distinct critical stance, whether it be to praise or to blame. Nevertheless, *Washington Post Book World* contributor Robert Kuttner declared, "Like Halberstam's other books, this one is a tour de force of reporting, synthesis and storytelling. Admirers of Halberstam will recognize the familiar formula; his critics will be freshly annoyed by it."

With *The Summer of '49* Halberstam once again took up the subject of professional sports, this time major league baseball. He portrays the 1949 American League pennant race, in which the Boston Red Sox suddenly overtook their arch-rivals, the New York Yankees, only to lose the championship in the final game of the season. The story is told through accounts of two opposing baseball heroes: Joe DiMaggio of the Yankees and Ted Williams of the Red Sox. Justin Kaplan, writing in the *New York Times Book Review,* described the book as "vigorous, altogether engrossing, loaded with dugout insight and wonderful vignettes." In addition to chronicling the pennant race, Halberstam identifies this season as a turning point in baseball—the time in which sport gave way to show business. As Thomas H. Kean noted in the *Wall Street Journal*, "In the days following World War II, baseball was, as Mr. Halberstam says, 'not so much a sport but a blinding national myth.' It was the way for the children of immigrants to escape and to excel." In summing up Halberstam's achievement, *Time* magazine's Martha Duffy wrote, "this new work may be his most appealing, mainly because it is quirky and informal, and the author leaves his moral fervor in the bat rack."

In *The Next Century,* a slim volume that examines America since Vietnam, Halberstam makes a case he has made before: Americans have ignored growing problems such as weakening educational standards and a decline in economic productivity to the detriment of the nation's future. Some critics have pointed out that the book's title is a misnomer since Halberstam examines the twentieth century in great detail, but never quite predicts what the next century will hold. Dan Tucker, reviewing the book in the *Chicago Tribune,* called *The Next Century* "an attempt to sort out the main forces at work on American society and the world, and to see in what directions they seem to be pushing us."

The *New York Times*' Lehmann-Haupt stated, "As one prominent Japanese he [Halberstam] talked to sees it, what America needs is some sort of shock to jar it 'out of its complacency, an event on the order of *Sputnik.*' 'The Next Century' is far from shock therapy. But by addressing readers intelligently instead of bludgeoning them with dire statistics, it catches the ear." Several critics praised Halberstam for resisting the temptation to blame Japan for its success. Bill Bradley, then a U.S. senator, commented in the *New York Times Book Review* that *The Next Century* "is one of the few books to recognize that the challenge facing the United States is not finding a scapegoat for our economic blunders but making the most of our physical and mental capabilities, improving our productivity in an open, democratic structure."

Halberstam examines the political, historical, and sociological perspective of the decade from 1950 to 1960 in his book *The Fifties.* He discusses events that run the gamut from the politics of the Eisenhower years to the success of the television series *I Love Lucy.* In a review for the *Washington Post,* Stephen Birmingham called *The Fifties* "absorbing" and credited Halberstam with "customary balance and thoroughness." But John Podhoretz, writing in the *Wall Street Journal,* pointed out

that Halberstam's anecdotes about the suburbanization of America and the rise of McDonald's are familiar ones, and he faulted Halberstam for cataloguing events rather than analyzing why the memory of this particular decade holds such appeal for Americans. Podhoretz wrote, "Mr. Halberstam is so intent on avoiding controversy that he cannot and will not take sides in the debate on the meaning of the decade he has written 800 pages about." *Chicago Tribune* reviewer Herbert Gold voiced a similar objection, but remarked favorably on those sections of the book that investigate less well-known events. Observed Gold: "Chapter 25, about the overthrow of Mossadegh and the installation of the Shah of Iran, has some bite because the story is less familiar. It's a nice and nasty interlude in which we find the aged Winston Churchill congratulating Kermit Roosevelt of the CIA on a well-managed coup."

Halberstam's *October 1964* finds the author returning to a memorable baseball season, this time the 1964 season in which the St. Louis Cardinals defeated the New York Yankees to win the World Series. Through colorful vignettes of the two teams' unusually articulate and influential players, Halberstam draws parallels between the events of the 1964 season and the groundbreaking social changes that were affecting every aspect of American culture at the time, from race relations to the contentious Vietnam War to the growing power of the media. In particular, Halberstam focuses on the racial issues that came into play during the season. While the Yankees had long been a dominant force, their aging, mostly white roster stood in stark contrast to that of the upstart Cardinals. Under the direction of cantankerous owner August Busch, the beer magnate, the Cardinals roster included many young black stars: Bob Gibson, Lou Brock, and Curt Flood. Halberstam points out that the integrated Cardinals team was free of racial strife; its victory in the World Series symbolized the sport's transformation from one focused on power and high-scoring innings to one featuring speed and aggressive base running.

Writing in the *Los Angeles Times Book Review*, Allen Barra remarked that "the overview afforded by 'October 1964' is splendid." *Washington Post Book World* contributor Frank Mankiewicz commented that "Halberstam describes the final game of the 1964 series accurately and so dramatically, I almost thought I had forgotten the ending." James E.B. Breslin, however, critiquing for the *New York Times Book Review,* compared *October 1964* unfavorably to *The Summer of '49,* noting that Halberstam "does not have the intimate emotional connection to the 1964 season that he did to 1949" and as a result "takes only a halfhearted swing at social history," instead concentrating on "individuals who transcend that history." Nevertheless, Breslin termed the book "engaging."

After writing *The Children,* an award-winning study of young people involved in the civil rights movement in the early 1960s, Halberstam returned to the subject of sports with *Playing for Keeps: Michael Jordan and the World He Made,* a biography of the man whom some observers consider the greatest pro basketball player ever. "Air Jordan" played for the Chicago Bulls from 1984 to 1999—with a brief detour to attempt a baseball career—and led the Bulls to multiple NBA championships. (He came out of retirement in 2001 to play with the Washington Wizards.) Halberstam chronicles the athlete's success on the basketball court, something due, the author says, not only to Jordan's great natural ability but also to his disciplined efforts; he also explores Jordan's rise as a media star with high-profile commercial endorsements, and seeks to explain Jordan's significance for basketball as a whole.

In the words of *New Statesman* contributor John Dugdale, "Jordan was a deus ex machina for a sport in a slump when he entered the professional ranks in 1984—so miraculously answering the dreams of hard-boiled businessmen that they could scarcely believe their luck; but also, David Halberstam suggests, himself benefitting as commodity and salesman by arriving just when the smart new NBA commissioner David Stern was revamping basketball's image." Jordan's brilliant playing, good looks, gentlemanly manner, and hard-to-resist charm—evident in his commercials for Nike shoes, McDonald's restaurants, and other consumer products—gave him a sterling public persona, but Halberstam shows there is more to the story, Dugdale and other critics observed. "Jordan emerges simple in essence and ambiguous in context," remarked L.S. Klepp in *Entertainment Weekly.* "The simple essence is his relentless will to be better than anyone else, to win and win with a vengeance. . . . But for all his devotion to the game, Jordan had a lot to do with the way it veered into tawdry entertainment." Klepp explained that Halberstam's "underlying theme" is that Jordan's role in popularizing pro basketball "didn't corrupt him but did corrupt the sport," and that his successors are unlikely to handle themselves with such grace as he did. Not that Jordan lacks faults: Dugdale reported, "His evident intelligence never extended to political issues"—he was "bewildered" by protests against Nike's use of child labor in developing countries.

Several other reviewers pointed out Halberstam's willingness to deal with all aspects, admirable and less so, of Jordan's character. "Jordan, as drawn by Halberstam,

is generous, loyal, thoughtful but flawed," related Ira Berkow in the *New York Times Book Review,* adding that "he is, Halberstam underscores, no Jackie Robinson, Muhammad Ali or Paul Robeson in the civil rights arena." Berkow praised Halberstam by saying, "He skillfully skirts hagiography and writes as credible reporter." *USA Today* writer Erik Brady noted that Halberstam's treatment of Jordan "is mostly admiring, though not entirely," and that "Jordan emerges in all his complexity, as do his lessers." Brady termed *Playing for Keeps* "a meticulously reported book," depicting Jordan and his teammates, coaches, and other associates "in revealing, delicious detail." Dugdale called the book "as ambitious and omnicompetent as its subject" and "much richer than a conventional sports biography." Berkow criticized the book for "an occasional excess of information regarding peripheral aspects of Jordan's life and lapses in which the language is less than carefully or thriftily wrought." He concluded, though, that "Halberstam overall has succeeded in lending perspective to the world Michael Jordan both made and inherited, as well as in portraying Michael Jordan the man and not the icon."

Halberstam left sports for international affairs with *War in a Time of Peace: Bush, Clinton, and the Generals.* This book examines U.S. foreign policy in the 1990s, as pursued by presidents George Bush and Bill Clinton. Following the breakup of the Soviet Union, the United States faced no opposing superpower but dealt with small wars around the world—in Iraq, Bosnia, Somalia, and other places. It was sometimes slow to intervene in these conflicts, though, and unsure of what constituted U.S. interests after the end of the cold war. *War in a Time of Peace* is designed as a companion to *The Best and the Brightest.* Many of the political and military leaders of the 1990s—of whom Halberstam provides detailed portrayals in the newer work—had been young adults during the Vietnam War; some had served in it, and it was a haunting memory.

"Still, Halberstam is smart enough to avoid concluding that the memory of Vietnam drove the major military decisions of the Clinton administration or, as it turned out in some cases, the nondecisions," observed Jane Perlez in the *New York Times Book Review. New York Times* reviewer Richard Bernstein noted that this memory "was a major element in the almost paralyzing caution" of Clinton and his advisers, "but it was far from the only factor. Among the others was the simple fact that George Bush's striking victory against Iraq in the gulf war did not give him much political lift at home, and for the Clinton administration, political lift at home was all important. Meanwhile, the calamity of the Somalia operation, which involved the loss of 18 soldiers in a grisly mob attack in 1993, cast a shadow over all future operations." Halberstam portrays the United States as "groping for a strategy, a vision of what it should do in a turbulent and unsettled post-cold war world to stabilize it at low cost," related *Nation* contributor Dusko Doder, and finally discovering, during the 1999 Kosovo conflict, "that things in the world could be changed by a minimum, casualty-free application of American air power."

Doder was not wholly convinced by Halberstam's endorsement of this means of warfare. "In making the argument for the use of air power, Halberstam presents a fuzzy account of the collapse of the Bosnian Serbs in 1995," Doder wrote, also maintaining that the book lacks "Halberstam's bone-deep knowledge and refined critical powers that gave his Vietnam book a firm spine of political argument. He does not know the Balkans; as a result, he brings little knowledge or insight gained firsthand." Doder added that in light of the terrorist attacks on the United States on September 11, 2001—which occurred after *War in a Time of Peace* went to press—and the subsequent war in Afghanistan, "the book's seductive concept that a war can be won by air power alone is now being put to a real test. . . . Given the short American political attention span, the air bombardments in the Balkans could be presented as victories even though they resolved none of the problems on the ground, where U.S. troops continue doing constabulary duty to keep peace in Bosnia and Kosovo. The war against terrorism is something of an entirely different magnitude, and it will engage our attention for a long time." To some other reviewers, though, Halberstam's book retained great relevance after September 11. "Now that foreign affairs have come home to the United States in the most crushing of ways," commented Perlez, "are [Americans] ready to read an account of foreign policy and its makers by one of the most astute writers in the trade? If they want to learn about the past decade, they should. If they want to think seriously about the future, they must." Bernstein granted that "the situation in Afghanistan is different, but it would be difficult to imagine a better, more detailed and informed account of how the country has handled its recent crises than Mr. Halberstam's new book." After the September 11 attacks, Halberstam came out with two books on the tragedy: *New York September 11: As Seen by Magnum Photographers,* a book of photos from the event accompanied by text by Halberstam, and *Firehouse,* which is the story of the valiant firefighters who died trying to save lives at the World Trade Center.

In *Defining a Nation: Our America and the Sources of Its Strengths,* Halberstam enlists thirty-six leading histo-

rians and writers to ask why our country "for all its flaws, for all the things I dissent from, remains so powerful a beacon to so many of the less favored of the world." He introduces essays by contributors like Walter Cronkite, Louis Auchincloss, Joan Didion, Anna Quindlen, and Anthony Lewis that define key issues and events that have shaped the American character, from Paul Revere's ride to Margaret Sanger's campaign for birth control. Halberstam explains that he chose immigration, innovation, and egalitarianism as his themes and focuses on the country's last 100 years because until the eve of World War I, America "was still growing in its body." Each contributor illuminates an aspect of America's uniqueness: for Richard Reeves it's the changes wrought by the GI Bill, for Julia Reed it's regional cooking, for Nick Kotz it's farming, for Bill Geist it's cars or, as he puts it, "freedom machines." Halberstam pens essays on inventor Henry Ford and the Civil Rights Movement, two of his favorite subjects.

Whether Halberstam is writing about basketball's Air Jordan or the U.S. military's air power, his books are often best-sellers, even when they receive mixed reviews from critics. His many readers seem to agree with James Fallows's judgment of *The Reckoning:* "Because the book is so richly detailed, so complete in its coverage, and so readable page-by-page and anecdote-by-anecdote, the complaints about it, which will come, need to take second place to its virtues."

BIOGRAPHICAL AND CRITICAL SOURCES:

BOOKS

Downie, Leonard, Jr., *The New Muckrakers: An Inside Look at America's Investigative Reporters,* New Republic Books (Washington, DC), 1976.

Dygert, James H., *The Investigative Journalist: Folk Heroes of a New Era,* Prentice-Hall (Englewood Cliffs, NJ), 1976.

Prochnau, William W., *Once upon a Distant War,* Times Books (New York, NY), 1995.

PERIODICALS

Business Week, October 8, 2001, "Not Halberstam's Best or Brightest," p. 18.

Chicago Tribune, September 27, 1987; February 25, 1991; June 20, 1993.

Chicago Tribune Book World, May 6, 1979; November 15, 1981; July 14, 1985.

Commentary, June, 1999, Joseph Epstein, "He Flew through the Air," p. 46; January, 2002, Jacob Heilbrunn, review of *War in a Time of Peace: Bush, Clinton, and the Generals,* p. 58.

Entertainment Weekly, February 5, 1999, L.S. Klepp, "The Air up There," p. 62.

Foreign Affairs, November-December 2001, Michael Hirsh, "America Adrift: Writing the History of the Post Cold Wars," p. 158.

Globe & Mail (Toronto, Ontario, Canada), December 13, 1986; February 16, 1991, p. C7.

Library Journal, October 1, 2001, James R. Holmes, review of *War in a Time of Peace,* p. 124.

Los Angeles Times Book Review, November 23, 1986, pp. 1, 13; March 31, 1991, p. 6; August 21, 1994, p. 4.

Nation, November 26, 2001, Dusko Doder, "Air Power Politics," p. 22.

National Review, November 5, 2001, Andrew J. Bacevich, "Fog of Wars," p. 62.

New Republic, December 3, 2001, Robert Kagan, "How We Unlearned the Art of War: When America Blinked," p. 29.

New Statesman, May 25, 1973; October 5, 1979; April 3, 2000, John Dugdale, "Fateful Tango," p. 58.

Newsweek, November 20, 1972; April 30, 1979; April 17, 1989.

New York Review of Books, January 25, 1973.

New York Times, April 25, 1979; June 17, 1979; July 18, 1985; October 20, 1986; April 18, 1987; February 11, 1991, p. C14; August 11, 1994, p. C18; January 19, 1999, Michiko Kakutani, "When He Shot, He Scored: Jordan the Man and Athlete," p. E1; October 10, 2001, Richard Bernstein, "A New and Cautious Age in American Intervention," p. E8.

New York Times Book Review, November 12, 1972; April 22, 1979; June 17, 1979; January 10, 1982; August 11, 1985; October 26, 1986, pp. 1, 57-58; May 7, 1989; February 17, 1991, p. 9; August 14, 1994, p. 9; January 31, 1999, Ira Berkow, "Looking Over Jordan," p. 11; September 30, 2001, Jane Perlez, "The 90's Wars," p. 8.

Progressive, January, 1973; July, 1979.

Publishers Weekly, December 11, 1978; October 17, 1986, pp. 44-45; February 14, 1994.

Time, April 30, 1979; November 2, 1981; July 29, 1985; May 22, 1989.

Tribune Books (Chicago), October 5, 1986, pp. 1, 3; April 2, 1989.

USA Today, December 2, 1999, Erik Brady, "'Keeps' Pumps Fresh Air into Jordan Profile."

Wall Street Journal, June 26, 1989; June 23, 1993.

Washington Monthly, April, 1987, pp. 39-45; September, 2001, Nicholas Thompson, review of *War in a Time of Peace: Bush, Clinton, and the Generals,* p. 41.

Washington Post, May 9, 1979; June 7, 1979; October 31, 1986.

Washington Post Book World, November 12, 1972; April 22, 1979; November 15, 1981; June 30, 1985, pp. 1, 8; October 19, 1986, pp. 1, 11; March 3, 1991, p. 11-12; May 23, 1993; August 21, 1994, p. 1.

*　　*　　*

HALL, Donald 1928-
(Donald Andrew Hall, Jr.)

PERSONAL: Born September 20, 1928, in New Haven, CT; son of Donald Andrew (a businessman) and Lucy (Wells) Hall; married Kirby Thompson, September 13, 1952 (divorced, 1969); married Jane Kenyon (a poet), April 17, 1972 (died, April 22, 1995); children: (first marriage) Andrew, Philippa. *Education:* Harvard University, B.A., 1951; Oxford University, B. Litt., 1953; attended Stanford University, 1953-54.

ADDRESSES: Home—Eagle Pond Farm, Danbury, NH 03230. *Agent*—Gerald McCauley Agency, Inc., Box 844, Katonah, NY 10536.

CAREER: Harvard University, Cambridge, MA, junior fellow in Society of Fellows, 1954-57; University of Michigan, Ann Arbor, 1957-75, began as assistant professor, became professor of English; full-time freelance writer, 1975—. Bennington College graduate Writing Seminars, poet-in-residence, 1993—. Broadcaster on British Broadcasting Corporation radio programs, 1959-80; host of *Poets Talking* (television interview series), 1974-75; has given poetry readings at colleges, universities, schools, and community centers.

MEMBER: PEN, American Academy and Institute of Arts and Letters.

AWARDS, HONORS: Newdigate Prize, Oxford University, 1952, for poem "Exile"; Lamont Poetry Prize, Academy of American Poets, 1955, for *Exiles and Marriages;* Edna St. Vincent Millay Award, Poetry Society of America, 1956; Guggenheim fellowship, 1963-64, 1972-73; *New York Times* Notable Children's Books citation, 1979, for *Ox-Cart Man;* Sarah Josepha Hale Award, 1983, for writings about New England; *Horn Book* Honor List, 1986, for *The Oxford Book of Children's Verse in America;* Lenore Marshall Prize, 1987, for *The Happy Man;* National Book Critics Circle

Award for poetry, and *Los Angeles Times* Book Prize in poetry, both 1989, both for *The One Day;* named poet Laureate of New Hampshire, 1984-89, 1995—; Associated Writing Programs Poetry Publication Award named in Hall's honor.

WRITINGS:

FOR CHILDREN

Andrew the Lion Farmer, illustrated by Jane Miller, F. Watts (New York, NY), 1959, illustrated by Ann Reason, Methuen (London, England), 1961.

Riddle Rat, illustrated by Mort Gerberg, Warne (London, England), 1977.

Ox-Cart Man, illustrated by Barbara Cooney, Viking (New York, NY), 1979.

The Man Who Lived Alone, illustrated by Mary Azarian, Godine (New York, NY), 1984.

(Editor) *The Oxford Book of Children's Verse in America,* Oxford University Press, 1985.

The Farm Summer 1942, illustrated by Barry Moser, Dial (New York, NY), 1994.

I Am the Dog, I Am the Cat, illustrated by Barry Moser, Dial (New York, NY), 1994.

Lucy's Christmas, illustrated by Michael McCurdy, Harcourt Brace (New York, NY), 1994.

Lucy's Summer, illustrated by Michael McCurdy, Harcourt Brace (New York, NY), 1995.

When Willard Met Babe Ruth, illustrated by Barry Moser, Harcourt Brace (New York, NY), 1996.

Old Home Day, illustrated by Emily Arnold McCully, Harcourt Brace, (New York, NY) 1996.

The Milkman's Boy, illustrated by Greg Shed, Walker (New York, NY), 1997.

POETRY

Fantasy Poets No. 4, Fantasy Press, 1952.

Exile, Fantasy Press, 1952.

To the Loud Wind and Other Poems, Pegasus, 1955.

Exiles and Marriages, Viking (New York, NY), 1955.

The Dark Houses, Viking (New York, NY), 1958.

A Roof of Tiger Lilies, Viking (New York, NY), 1964.

The Alligator Bride: Poems, New and Selected, Harper (New York, NY), 1969.

The Yellow Room: Love Poems, Harper (New York, NY), 1971.

The Gentleman's Alphabet Book (limericks), illustrated by Harvey Kornberg, Dutton (New York, NY), 1972.

The Town of Hill, Godine (New York, NY), 1975.

A Blue Wing Tilts at the Edge of the Sea: Selected Poems, 1964-1974, Secker & Warburg (London, England), 1975.

Kicking the Leaves, Harper (New York, NY), 1978.

The Toy Bone, BOA Editions, 1979.

Brief Lives: Seven Epigrams, William B. Ewart, 1983.

The Twelve Seasons, Deerfield Press, 1983.

Great Day in the Cow's House, illustrated with photographs by T.S. Bronson, Ives Street Press, 1984.

The Happy Man, Random House (New York, NY), 1986.

The One Day, Ticknor & Fields, 1988.

Old and New Poems, Ticknor & Fields, 1990.

The Museum of Clear Ideas, Ticknor & Fields, 1993.

The Old Life, Houghton Mifflin (Boston, MA), 1996.

Without, Houghton Mifflin (Boston, MA), 1998.

The Purpose of a Chair, Brooding Heron Press (Waldron Island, WA), 2000.

The Painted Bed, Houghton Mifflin (Boston, MA), 2002.

White Apples and the Taste of Stone: Poems, 1946-2006, Houghton Mifflin (Boston, MA), 2006.

Contributor of poetry to numerous periodicals, including the *New Yorker, New Republic, New Criterion, Kenyon Review, Iowa Review, Georgia Review, Ohio Review, Gettysburg Review, Nation,* and *Atlantic.*

PROSE

String Too Short to Be Saved: Recollections of Summers on a New England Farm (autobiography), illustrated by Mimi Korach, Viking (New York, NY), 1961, expanded edition, Godine (New York, NY), 1979.

Henry Moore: The Life and Work of a Great Sculptor, Harper (New York, NY), 1966.

As the Eye Moves: A Sculpture by Henry Moore, illustrated with photographs by David Finn, Abrams (New York, NY), 1970.

Marianne Moore: The Cage and the Animal, Pegasus, 1970.

The Pleasures of Poetry, Harper (New York, NY), 1971.

Writing Well, Little, Brown (New York, NY), 1974, 9th edition (with Sven Birkerts), HarperCollins (New York, NY), 1997.

(With others) *Playing Around: The Million-Dollar Infield Goes to Florida,* Little, Brown (Boston, MA), 1974.

(With Dock Ellis) *Dock Ellis in the Country of Baseball,* Coward (New York, NY), 1976.

Goatfoot Milktongue Twinbird: Interviews, Essays, and Notes on Poetry, 1970-76, University of Michigan Press (Ann Arbor, MI), 1978.

Remembering Poets: Reminiscences and Opinions— Dylan Thomas, Robert Frost, T.S. Eliot, Ezra Pound, Harper (New York, NY), 1978, revised edition published as *Their Ancient Glittering Eyes, Remembering Poets and More Poets,* Ticknor & Fields, 1992.

To Keep Moving: Essays, 1959-1969, Hobart & William Smith Colleges Press, 1980.

To Read Literature, Holt (New York, NY), 1980.

The Weather for Poetry: Essays, Reviews, and Notes on Poetry, 1977-1981, University of Michigan Press (Ann Arbor, MI), 1982.

Fathers Playing Catch with Sons: Essays on Sport (Mostly Baseball), North Point Press, 1985.

Seasons at Eagle Pond, illustrated by Thomas W. Nason, Ticknor & Fields, 1987.

Poetry and Ambition, University of Michigan Press (Ann Arbor, MI), 1988.

Here at Eagle Pond, illustrated by Thomas W. Nason, Ticknor & Fields, 1990.

Life Work, Beacon Press (Boston, MA), 1993.

Death to the Death of Poetry: Essays, Reviews, Notes, Interviews, University of Michigan Press (Ann Arbor, MI), 1994.

Principle Products of Portugal: Prose Pieces, Beacon Press (Boston, MA), 1995.

Willow Temple: New and Selected Stories, Houghton Mifflin (Boston, MA), 2003.

Breakfast Served Any Time All Day: Essays on Poetry New and Selected, University of Michigan Press (Ann Arbor, MI), 2003.

The Best Day the Worst Day: Life with Jane Kenyon (memoir), Houghton Mifflin (Boston, MA), 2005.

Contributor of short stories and articles to numerous periodicals, including the *New Yorker, Esquire, Atlantic, Playboy, Transatlantic Review,* and *American Scholar.* Author of afterword to Jane Kenyon's *Otherwise: New and Selected Poems.*

PLAYS

An Evening's Frost, first produced in Ann Arbor, MI; produced Off-Broadway, 1965.

Bread and Roses, produced in Ann Arbor, MI, 1975.

Ragged Mountain Elegies (produced in Peterborough, NH, 1983), revised version published as *The Bone Ring* (produced in New York, NY, 1986), Story Line, 1987.

EDITOR

The Harvard Advocate Anthology, Twayne (New York, NY), 1950.

(With Robert Pack and Louis Simpson) *The New Poets of England and America,* Meridian Books, 1957.

Whittier, Dell (New York, NY), 1961.

Contemporary American Poetry, Penguin (London England), 1962, Penguin (Baltimore, MD), 1963.

(With Robert Pack) *New Poets of England and America: Second Selection,* Meridian Books, 1962.

A Poetry Sampler, F. Watts (New York, NY), 1962.

(With Stephen Spender) *The Concise Encyclopedia of English and American Poets and Poetry,* Hawthorn, 1963.

(With Warren Taylor) *Poetry in English,* Macmillan (New York, NY), 1963.

A Choice of Whitman's Verse, Faber & Faber (London, England), 1968.

Man and Boy, F. Watts (New York, NY), 1968.

The Modern Stylists, Free Press (New York, NY), 1968.

American Poetry: An Introductory Anthology, Faber & Faber (London, England), 1969.

(With D.L. Emblem) *A Writer's Reader,* Little, Brown (New York, NY), 1969, 9th edition, Longman (New York, NY), 2002.

The Pleasures of Poetry, Harper (New York, NY), 1971.

The Oxford Book of American Literary Anecdotes, Oxford University Press (Oxford, England), 1981.

To Read Literature: Fiction, Poetry, Drama, Holt (New York, NY), 1981, 3rd edition, Harcourt (New York, NY), 1992.

Claims for Poetry, University of Michigan Press (Ann Arbor, MI), 1982.

To Read Poetry, Holt (New York, NY), 1982, revised edition published as *To Read a Poem,* Harcourt (New York, NY), 1992.

The Contemporary Essay, St. Martin's Press (New York, NY), 1984, 3rd edition, 1995.

To Read Fiction, Holt (New York, NY), 1987.

(With Pat Corrington Wykes) *Anecdotes of Modern Art: From Rousseau to Warhol,* Oxford University Press (New York, NY), 1990.

Andrew Marvell, *The Essential Marvell,* Ecco Press (New York, NY), 1991.

Edwin Arlington Robinson, *The Essential Robinson,* Ecco Press (New York, NY), 1993.

Oxford Illustrated Book of American Children's Poems, Oxford University Press (New York, NY), 1999.

Former poetry editor, *Paris Review.* Former member of editorial board, Wesleyan University Press poetry series; editor, University of Michigan "Poets on Poetry" series.

SIDELIGHTS: Considered one of the major American poets of his generation, Donald Hall's works explore a longing for the more bucolic past and reflect the poet's abiding reverence for nature. Although Hall gained an early success with his 1955 poetry collection *Exiles and Marriages,* his more recent poetry has generally been regarded as the best of his career. Often compared favorably with such writers as James Dickey, Robert Bly, and James Wright, Hall uses simple, direct language to evoke surrealistic imagery. In addition to his poetry, Hall has built a respected body of prose work that includes essays, short fiction, plays, and children's books. Hall, who lives on the New Hampshire farm he visited in summers as a boy, is also noted for the anthologies he has edited and is a popular teacher, speaker, and reader of his own poems.

Born in 1928, Hall grew up in Hamden, Connecticut, a child of the Great Depression of the 1930s, though not greatly affected by it. The Hall household was marked by a volatile father and a mother who was "steadier, maybe with more access to depths because there was less continual surface," as Hall explained in an essay for *Contemporary Authors Autobiography Series* (*CAAS*). "To her I owe my fires, to my father my tears. I owe them both for their reading." By age twelve, Hall had discovered the poet and short story writer Edgar Allan Poe: "I read Poe and my life changed," he remarked in *CAAS*. Another strong influence in Hall's early years was his maternal great-grandfather's farm in New Hampshire, where he spent many summers. The pull of nature became a compulsion in him so strong that decades later he bought that same farm and settled there as a full-time writer and poet.

Hall attended Philips Exeter Academy and despite early frustrations had his first poem published at age sixteen. He was a participant at the prestigious Bread Loaf Writer's Conference that same year. From Exeter, Hall went to Harvard University, where he attended class alongside other poets-in-training, among them Adrienne Rich, Robert Bly, Frank O'Hara, and John Ashbery; he also studied for a year with Archibald MacLeish. In his time at Oxford University, Hall became one of the few Americans to win the coveted Newdigate contest for his poem "Exile."

Returning to the United States, Hall spent three years at Harvard and there assembled *Exiles and Marriages,* a collection crafted in a tightly structured style on which Hall imposes rigid rhyme and meter. In 1957 he took a position as assistant professor of English at the University of Michigan, where he remained until 1975. During those years he wrote volumes of poetry and essays, but Hall had always contemplated returning to the rural paradise that he had found as a youth in New Hampshire. Finally he was in a position to make this a reality, and when his grandmother, who owned Eagle Pond Farm, passed away, he bought the farm, left teaching, and moved there with his second wife, poet Jane Kenyon. With one child in college at the time and another having not yet started, the move to New Hampshire was a risky one. Giving up the relative security of a tenured position at Michigan was a difficult decision, "but I did not hesitate, I did not doubt," Hall recalled in *CAAS.* "I panicked but I did not doubt." The collections *Kicking the Leaves* and *The Happy Man* reflect Hall's happiness at his return to the family farm, a place rich with memories and links to his past. Many of the poems explore and celebrate the continuity between generations, as the narrative voice in his poetry often reminisces about the past and anticipates the future.

Old and New Poems contains several traditional poems from earlier collections, as well as more innovative verses not previously published. Hall's well-known poem "Baseball," included in *The Museum of Clear Ideas,* is the poet's ode to the great American pastime and is structured around the sequence of a baseball game, with nine stanzas with nine lines each. Written following the 1995 death of his second wife to leukemia, *Without* reflects on the changes Kenyon's death made to his life. *The Painted Bed* finds Hall in another phase of the grieving process, the poems included showcasing the poet's "distinctive musical mark" and "exhibiting the terrible suffering of the bereaved with dignity and beauty," according to *Book* contributor Stephen Whited.

Reviewers have continued to praise Hall as the poet continues to challenge both himself and his readers while retaining a sense of tradition and the commonplace. Acclaim has been heaped, in particular, on the award-winning *The One Day,* with *Ploughshares* contributor Liam Rector dubbing it "an eloquent consummation of Modernism." *The One Day* consists of a single poem of 110 stanzas, divided into three sections. Each section presents a unique elderly narrative voice reflecting, in blank verse, upon the meaning of life while looking back on the past. In two of the three sections Hall alternates between male and female narrators.

In addition to his accomplishments as a poet, Hall is respected as an academic who, through writing, teaching, and lecturing, has made significant contributions to the study and craft of writing. As Rector explained, Hall "has lived deeply within the New England ethos of plain living and high thinking, and he has done so with a sense of humor and eros." In *Remembering Poets: Reminiscences and Opinions—Dylan Thomas, Robert Frost, T.S. Eliot, Ezra Pound,* a 1978 work that was expanded as *Their Ancient Glittering Eyes: Remembering Poets and More Poets,* Hall recounts his relationship with fellow poets such as T.S. Eliot, Ezra Pound, Dylan Thomas, and Robert Frost. His books on the craft of writing include *Writing Well*—in its ninth edition by 1997—and *Death to the Death of Poetry. Life Work* is Hall's memoir of the writing life and his tenure at Eagle Pond Farm, while his children's book *Ox-Cart Man* is one among several works that have established him in the field of children's literature. A fable on the cyclical nature of life, *Ox-Cart Man* expresses for readers "the sense that work defines us all, connects us with our world, and we are all rewarded . . . in measure of our effort," according to Kristi L. Thomas in *School Library Journal.*

Hall continues to live and work on his New Hampshire farm, a site that serves as both his abode and an inspiration for much of his work. Following his second wife's death in the spring of 1995, Hall appeared at several tributes to Kenyon's work and composed an afterword to a posthumous collection of her poetry, *Otherwise: New and Selected Poems.* In 2005, Hall published the memoir *The Best Day the Worst Day: Life with Jane Kenyon.* After initiating the book with his account of Kenyon's death, he then tells the story of their first meeting in 1969 at the University of Michigan. At the time, Kenyon was a student, and Hall a professor of literature. The couple, married for twenty-three years, had what a reviewer for *Publishers Weekly* referred to as, "an extraordinarily happy marriage between poets, blissful despite the difference in their ages. . . and her illness and chronic clinical depression." The couple lived and wrote side by side on their farm, pausing from their work to take walks and tend to their garden—the story of their "harmonious life," as a reviewer for *Kirkus Reviews* referred to it, is also a history of the treatments his wife had to undergo for leukemia. The same reviewer noted, "Hall depicts their kinship poignantly, sparing few details of human fragility and debilitation. The days of Kenyon's virtual imprisonment inside a sterile cell. . . reads like a scene in a death chamber." The reviewer for *Publishers Weekly* concluded that although Hall dealt with the topic of his wife's death in a collection of poems, "this heartfelt memoir should reach people who seldom read poetry."

BIOGRAPHICAL AND CRITICAL SOURCES:

BOOKS

Children's Books and Their Creators, edited by Anita Silvey, Houghton Mifflin (Boston, MA), 1995.

Contemporary Authors Autobiography Series, Volume 7, Thomson Gale (Detroit, MI), 1988, pp. 55-67.

Contemporary Literary Criticism, Thomson Gale (Detroit, MI), Volume 13, 1980, Volume 37, 1986, Volume 59, 1989.

Dictionary of Literary Biography, Volume 5: American Poets since World War II, Thomson Gale (Detroit, MI), 1980.

Hall, Donald, *Riddle Rat,* Warne (London, England), 1977.

Hall, Donald, *The Man Who Lived Alone,* Godine (New York, NY), 1984.

Hall, Donald, *I Am the Dog, I Am the Cat,* Dial (New York, NY), 1994.

Hall, Donald, *The Best Day the Worst Day: Life with Jane Kenyon,* Houghton Mifflin (Boston, MA), 2005.

PERIODICALS

Book, May-June, 2002, Stephen Whited, review of *The Painted Bed,* p. 85.

Booklist, March 15, 1996, Bill Ott, review of *When Willard Met Babe Ruth,* p. 1262; March 15, 2000, Gillian Engberg, review of *The Oxford Illustrated Book of American Children's Poems,* p. 1380; March 1, 2002, Ray Olson, review of *The Painted Bed,* p. 1079; April 15, 2003, Ellen Loughran, review of *Willow Temple: New and Selected Stories,* p. 1448.

Bulletin of the Center for Children's Books, February, 1980, Zena Sutherland, review of *Ox-Cart Man,* p. 110; July, 1994, Deborah Stevenson, review of *The Farm Summer 1942,* p. 358; October, 1994, Roger Sutton, review of *Lucy's Christmas,* pp. 48-49; December, 1994, Roger Sutton, review of *I Am the Dog, I Am the Cat,* p. 129.

Horn Book, February, 1982, Mary M. Burns, review of *Ox-Cart Man,* pp. 44-45; July-August, 1994, Nancy Vasilakis, review of *The Farm Summer 1942,* p. 441; September-October, 1994, Ann A. Flowers, review of *I Am the Dog, I Am the Cat,* p. 577; November-December, 1994, Elizabeth S. Watson, review of *Lucy's Christmas,* p. 711.

Junior Bookshelf, December, 1980, review of *Ox-Cart Man,* pp. 283-284.

Kirkus Reviews, August 15, 1994, review of *I Am the Dog, I Am the Cat,* p. 1129; October 15, 1994, review of *Lucy's Christmas,* pp. 1420-1421; November 1, 1984, review of *The Man Who Lived Alone,* p. 88; March 1, 1996, review of *When Willard Met Babe Ruth,* pp. 374-375; July 15, 1996, review of *Old Home Day,* p. 1048; March 15, 2003, review of *Willow Temple,* p. 416; March 15, 2005, review of *The Best Day the Worst Day,* p. 334.

Library Journal, April 15, 2003, review of *Willow Temple,* p. 128.

New York Times Book Review, January 13, 1985, Thomas Powers, review of *The Man Who Lived Alone,* p. 26.

Ploughshares, fall, 2001, Liam Rector, "About Donald Hall," p. 270.

Poetry, December, 2003, review of *Breakfast Served Any Time All Day,* p. 177; May, 2005, Vivian Gornick, "It's All In the Art," review of *The Best Day the Worst Day,* p. 161.

Publishers Weekly, June 13, 1977, review of *Riddle Rat,* p. 108; April 11, 1994, review of *The Farm Summer 1942,* p. 65; April 10, 1995, review of *Lucy's Summer,* p. 62; August 12, 1996, review of *Old Home Day,* p. 82; July 14, 1997, review of *The Milkman's Boy,* p. 83; February 25, 2002, review of *The Painted Bed,* p. 56; March 31, 2003, review of *Willow Temple,* p. 39; March 7, 2005, review of *The Best Day the Worst Day,* p. 57.

Quill and Quire, May, 1995, review of *Lucy's Summer,* p. 51.

School Library Journal, October, 1979, Kristi L. Thomas, review of *Ox-Cart Man,* p. 140; February, 1985, Anna Biagioni Hart, review of *The Man Who Lived Alone,* p. 64; January, 2000, Margaret Bush, review of *The Oxford Illustrated Book of American Children's Poems,* p. 121.

Sewanee Review, winter, 2000, review of *Without,* p. 6.

*   *   *

HALL, Donald Andrew, Jr.
See HALL, Donald

*   *   *

HALL, Marguerite Radclyffe
See HALL, Radclyffe

HALL, Radclyffe 1886-1943
(Marguerite Radclyffe Hall, Marguerite Radclyffe-Hall)

PERSONAL: Born 1886, in Bournemouth, Hampshire, England; died of cancer October 7, 1943, in London, England; companion of Ladye Mabel Batten, 1908-16; companion of Una Troubridge, 1916-43. *Education:* Attended King's College, London; educated in Germany. *Religion:* Catholic.

CAREER: Writer. Society for Psychical Research, council member, 1916-24.

AWARDS, HONORS: James Tait Black Memorial Prize, 1927; Femina-Vie Heureuse prize, 1927, for *Adam's Breed;* Eichelbergher Humane Award Gold Medal, c. 1926.

WRITINGS:

POETRY

'Twixt Earth and Stars: Poems, John and Edward Bumpus (London, England), 1906.

A Sheaf of Verses: Poems, John and Edward Bumpus (London, England), 1908.

Poems of the Past and Present, Chapman and Hall (London, England), 1910.

Songs of Three Counties, and Other Poems, Chapman and Hall (London, England), 1913.

The Forgotten Island, Chapman and Hall (London, England), 1915.

NOVELS

The Forge, Arrowsmith (London, England), 1924.

The Unlit Lamp, Cassell (London, England), 1924, reprinted with a new introduction by Zoe Fairbairns, Virago (London, England), 1981.

A Saturday Life, Arrowsmith, 1925, reprinted with a new introduction by Alison Hennegan, Penguin (New York, NY), 1989.

Adam's Breed, Cassell (London, England), 1926, reprinted with a new introduction by Alison Hennegan, Penguin (New York, NY), 1986.

The Well of Loneliness, J. Cape (London, England), 1928, reprinted with a new introduction by Alison Hennegan, Penguin (New York, NY), 1982, with a commentary by Havelock Ellis, Anchor Books (New York, NY), 1990.

The Master of the House, J. Cape (London, England), 1932.

The Sixth Beatitude, Heinemann (London, England), 1936.

OTHER

Policeman of the Land: A Political Satire, Sophistocles Press, 1928.

Miss Ogilvy Finds Herself (short stories), Heinemann (London, England), 1934.

Your John: The Love Letters of Radclyffe Hall, edited and with an introduction by Joanne Glasgow, New York University Press (New York, NY), 1997.

SIDELIGHTS: Radclyffe Hall is perhaps best known for her 1928 novel, *The Well of Loneliness,* one of the first modern literary works whose plot concerned a same-sex relationship between women. Despite its laudatory critical reception, Hall's book was the subject of a ban under Britain's Obscene Libel Act, but late-twentieth-century scholars have since reappraised it as one of the premiere fictional portrayals of contemporary gay and lesbian life, a sensitive work that helped open doors of cultural acceptance for later writers.

Hall was born into a wealthy family in Hampshire, England, in 1886. Raised as a boy by her emotionally unstable parents, she was known as "John" to her friends and found security and support in her maternal grandmother, who encouraged the young girl's creative gifts. After receiving a large inheritance at the age of seventeen, Hall attended King's College in London and spent a year abroad in Germany. An accomplished amateur musician, she often wrote lyrics to accompany her compositions, and at the urging of her grandmother published some of this writing as a volume of verse titled *'Twixt Earth and Stars* in 1906.

Following her book's publication, Hall became acquainted with Ladye Mabel Batten, a literary figure who subsequently became her companion and mentor. During the early years preceding World War I Hall produced several other volumes of poetry, including *A Sheaf of Verses* and *Songs of Three Counties, and Other Poems,* with have been considered noteworthy for their frank expressions of passion between women. In *Radclyffe Hall at the Well of Loneliness: A Sapphic Chronicle,* scholar Lovat Dickson wrote of the good influence Batten was on the shy Hall, encouraging her writing and remaining a steady companion. The critic noticed the improvement from Hall's debut to the publication of *A Sheaf of Verses,* remarking that "for the first time, with increasing confidence and power, the passion of those first years of their association is struck for all to hear." During this period Hall became a Catholic, like Batten, and her new faith grew to become an integral element in her subsequent works. Batten encouraged Hall to branch out into fiction, and the writer's first foray into this genre came with the 1924 publication of *The Forge.* By this time Hall was alone; Batten passed away in 1916, and the grieving Hall felt in part responsible, since she had developed a romantic interest in Batten's niece, Una Troubridge, prior to Batten's death.

The Unlit Lamp, Hall's second novel, also published in 1924, is seen by scholars as a thematic precursor to *The Well of Loneliness.* Much more subtle in its addressing of same-sex romance, the work's possibly scandalous subject matter was so restrained that it was hardly noted in contemporary reviews. The novel is the tale of a young Julia Ogden and her affection toward her tutor, Elizabeth Rodney. Ogden's increasing devotion to Rodney incenses her mother, and the conflict this presents in the Ogden family is the basis for the novel. The two younger women dream of leaving their small coastal town for London in order to pursue a university education, but the plans are continually waylaid due to financial considerations or the interference of the manipulative, emotionally needy Mrs. Ogden. Yet "the mother is no ogre," observed Stephen Brook in an essay on Hall for the *Spectator,* "which is why the portrait is so brilliant." Brook termed the novel "a powerful and detailed portrayal not just of Lesbian love, but of how the emotional needs of three flawed women are finally irreconcilable."

It had taken Hall two years to write *The Unlit Lamp,* and it took another two years before she found a publisher for it. "It is by the standards of the time a good first novel," wrote Dickson in *Radclyffe Hall at the Well of Loneliness,* "conveying with noticeable skill for a beginner subtleties in human relationships that could only have been observed by someone of acute sympathies."

Hall's next novel, *Adam's Breed,* follows a young man who is besieged by a collective guilt about the materialism of early twentieth-century society; it also reflects Hall's compassion for the welfare of animals. By this time Hall and Troubridge, the wife of a naval officer, had become involved in a long-term relationship. Troubridge, in her biography *The Life of Radclyffe Hall,* would write of her lover's compassion for animals and Hall's difficulty in accepting their often cruel treatment at the hands of humans, recalling that Hall "taught me to appreciate the rights of animals and conferred on me the painful privilege of the 'seeing eye,' until in the end I also could not fail to remark on the underfed or overloaded horse or ass, the chained and neglected dog, the untamed bird in the dirty, cruelly tiny cage." Gian-Luca, the protagonist of *Adam's Breed* is a young headwaiter of Italian descent who is sickened by the gorging he witnesses nightly among wealthy patrons of the restaurant; he is also acutely aware of the plight of animals he sees mistreated in everyday life. The pressure builds until Gian-Luca flees the city to live simply in the woods, but again becomes despondent when the pony he has befriended is captured for manual labor.

When *Adam's Breed* appeared in print, a *New York Times Book Review* contributor found both praiseworthy elements as well as some flaws, noting "the first part of the book moves along with a great deal of interest." However, the critic added, "the last part of the book degenerates into high-falutin' sentimentalism. . . . It seems predetermined and does not ring true."

Hall's landmark novel, *The Well of Loneliness,* appeared in print in 1928. The proclivities of its protagonist are explicit, and the passions depicted toward other female characters in the novel are also frank. Some details are autobiographical: the heroine's parents wished for a boy while the mother was expecting, and thus named the baby girl Stephen. As a young girl, Stephen develops a crush on one of the maids of the household, an incident which Dickson noted also took place in Hall's own youth. As a young girl, Stephen feels she is not like other young girls, and finds herself more drawn to masculine pursuits; like Hall, the protagonist is an accomplished equestrienne. As she enters young adulthood, she sees the folly of pursuing heterosexual relations, especially after a swain named Martin—with whom she feels only a brotherlike affinity—proclaims his love for her and she feels obligated to send him away. Stephen eventually becomes enmeshed in a quasi-relationship with a married woman in the small town in which they live; when Stephen's mother learns of the affair, she condemns her daughter harshly.

As *The Well of Loneliness* continues, Stephen enlists in a service corps for women when World War I breaks out and meets Mary, who is young, somewhat naive, and soon completely devoted to Stephen. The two return to Stephen's family estate, and their passion is not consummated quickly, "even though [Mary] makes no

secret of her desire for it," wrote Dickson in *Radclyffe Hall at the Well of Loneliness.* "The strain on both of them is intense. Although the language in which this protracted restraint is presented is novelettish, the sense of strain is vividly conveyed, and the reader sees some of the handicaps of perversion," Dickson explained.

When Martin returns and falls in love with Mary, Stephen relinquishes her paramour unto him, knowing that Mary "cannot stand the social isolation of her life with Stephen" and "would have grown bitter at the judgments Stephen has the strength to rise above," Jane Rule pointed out in *Lesbian Images.* It is this self-sacrifice that may have been what Hall wished to convey, that sexual "inverts," while not concerned with reproducing themselves for posterity, may indeed be of a higher spiritual and moral nature than non-inverts. Secondarily, Hall may have also chosen to portray those whom nature had made inverts as objects of compassion, because societal mores might never allow them to lead happy, fulfilling—and prejudice-free—lives. In the end, Stephen beseeches God to "Give us also the right to our existence."

After its publication in 1928, *The Well of Loneliness* was publicly condemned and a trial soon followed. Hall lost the case and the novel was banned in England; in a similar case in a New York court the obscenity charges were dropped. Critical reaction to the novel was mixed, and was often tied in with a defense of it due to the controversy. Leonard Woolf, part of the influential British literary circle known as the Bloomsbury Group and husband to novelist Virginia Woolf, commented in the *Nation and Athenaeum* that Hall's novel "is written with understanding and frankness, with sympathy and feeling," but charged that as a work of literary merit, it falls short. Woolf termed *The Well of Loneliness* "formless and therefore chaotic. . . . It is emotionally that the book loses way, and a sign of this is Miss Hall's use of language. At the beginning the language is alive; the style is not brilliant or beautiful, but it is quick and vivid. . . . But as the book goes on, life and emotion die out of the language, and Miss Hall drops into journalese or the tell-tale novelist's cliches when she wants to heighten the emotion."

Novelist and literary critic Rebecca West, one of Hall's contemporaries, also found fault artistically with the author's use of language, remarking in a review for *Bookman* that the novelist seems to be inciting a feeling of sentimentalism in the reader. Such pandering to popular taste, West claimed, made it hard to defend *The Well of Loneliness* on purely artistic merit in the courts. Conversely, in her book *The School of Femininity: A Book for and about Women as They Are Interpreted through Feminine Writers of Yesterday and Today,* Margaret Lawrence praised the author's "mystical sensitivity to tone. Her phrasing shows it. Her words are put down in relation to their sounds set against other sounds. She produces by this means a disturbing emotional effect." In the *International Journal of Sexology,* Clifford Allen also lauded *The Well of Loneliness,* granting that while its author "may have had faults in style . . . on no occasion did she indulge in dishonesty, never did she describe things falsely or cast a gloss over what was real. She never pretended that homosexuality led to other than unhappiness. It was her very honesty which led to her book's being banned."

Hall penned two other novels before ill health curtailed her writing in the years before her death. 1932's *The Master of the House* is the story of a man whose life paralleled that of Jesus Christ. Lawrence, writing in *The School of Femininity,* deemed this novel an appropriate companion to *The Well of Loneliness.* "While the heroine in the one book lives the life of a man within the body of a woman, the man in the other book lives the life of a Christ within the body of a mortal," Lawrence wrote. "Neither of them has any concern with normal experience. They should be kept together and read together. They are part of the same mysterious saga." Many elements of *The Master of the House* correspond to the life of Christ as presented in the Bible: Christophe is the son of a carpenter and his wife, Jouse and Marie; his cousin Jan, like John the Baptist, remains a confidant through adulthood. Hall set her updated version of the Biblical tale shortly before the outbreak of World War I, and the two men are sent to Palestine to defend that region against the Turkish army. There Christophe is ambushed, and his journey to death closely follows Christ's procession to the cross.

Dickson, writing in *Radclyffe Hall at the Well of Loneliness,* observed that Hall's attempt to retell the story of Christ in a modern atmosphere "diminishes the glory and the brightness that myth has attached to it. . . . One sees, looking at it from this distance, that the book in fact fails through over-earnestness, a mood antipathic to the time in the early thirties when it was published." L.A.G. Strong, critiquing the novel for the *Spectator* at the time of its publication, declared that while if divorced from the Biblical comparison the novel would hold up on its own, "by adding this weight of symbolism to it, [Hall] makes it totter dangerously."

Hall's seventh and final novel, *The Sixth Beatitude,* appeared in 1936. It is the story of a poor woman, Hannah Bullen, whose somewhat unconventional life—

unmarried, she is mother to two—in a small English seaside town is marked by poverty and strife within her immediate family. The title of the work refers to the Roman Catholic notion of purity of mind and chastity of heart, and Hall attempts to portray the goodness of her protagonist despite the squalor of her surroundings. A contemporary reviewer in the *Times Literary Supplement* noted that "Hall certainly conveys, without any special pleading or attitudinizing, the native richness of speech and character that can exist in a row of old hovels in an old town, the warmth that somehow makes the dirt, cold and bickering bearable." Gwen Leys, critiquing *The Sixth Beatitude* for the *New York Herald Tribune Books,* noted that the author's characterizations of the peripheral figures of Bullen's life "give this story its bite, its fight and its character," yet concluded that "Hall is relentlessly determined to be grim."

Hall died of cancer in 1943. Although *The Well of Loneliness* is often cited as a pivotal work of twentieth-century lesbian fiction, the rest of her novels and poetry have often been overshadowed by the scandal that followed her best-known title—yet they also evince many of the same themes and convictions important to her. "The work of Radclyffe Hall . . . is serious, profound and beautiful work, in no way doctrinaire, yet thoroughly indoctrinated," wrote Lawrence in an essay published in *The School of Femininity.* "Her emotion is still yet deep. She is like a quiet pool of great depth. She is ageless. . . . She is preoccupied with the mysteries, as the priestesses were, and she pities the human race as it passes them by for things that can be added up and multiplied and subtracted and divided."

BIOGRAPHICAL AND CRITICAL SOURCES:

BOOKS

Baker, Michael, *Our Three Selves: A Life of Radclyffe Hall,* Hamish Hamilton (London, England), 1985.

Castle, Terry, *Noel Coward and Radclyffe Hall: Kindred Spirits,* Columbia University Press (New York, NY), 1996.

Cline, Sally, *Radclyffe Hall: A Woman Called John,* Overlook Press (New York, NY), 1998.

Dickson, Lovat, *Radclyffe Hall at the Well of Loneliness: A Sapphic Chronicle,* Scribner (New York, NY), 1975.

Feminist Writers, St. James Press (Detroit, MI), 1996.

Gay and Lesbian Literature, St. James Press (Detroit, MI), 1994.

Glasgow, Joanne, editor and author of introduction, *Your John: The Love Letters of Radclyffe Hall*, New York University Press (New York, NY), 1997.

Lawrence, Margaret, *The School of Femininity: A Book for and about Women as They Are Interpreted through Feminine Writers of Yesterday and Today*, Frederick A. Stokes (New York, NY), 1936.

O'Rourke, Rebecca, *Reflecting on The Well of Loneliness*, Routledge (New York, NY), 1989.

Rule, Jane, *Lesbian Images*, Doubleday (New York, NY), 1975.

Troubridge, Una, *The Life of Radclyffe Hall*, Citadel Press (New York, NY), 1973.

Twentieth-Century Literary Criticism, Volume 12, Thomson Gale (Detroit, MI), 1984.

Twentieth-Century Romance and Historical Writers, 3rd edition, St. James Press (Detroit, MI), 1994.

PERIODICALS

Bookman, January, 1929.

Critical Survey, September, 2003, p. 23.

Herizons, Stacy Kauder, review of *The Well of Loneliness*, p. 40.

International Journal of Sexology, Volume 4, 1950.

Journal of Modern Literature, winter, 2003, p. 145.

Life and Letters, October, 1928, pp. 329-341.

Nation and Athenaeum, August 4, 1928, p. 593.

New Republic, September 18, 1929, pp. 132-133; November 25, 1985, p. 34.

New Statesman, September 13, 1968, pp. 321-322.

New York Herald Tribune Books, April 26, 1936, p. 10.

New York Times Book Review, May 23, 1926, pp. 9, 17.

Publishers Weekly, December 30, 1996, review of *Your John: The Love Letters of Radclyffe Hall*, p. 47.

Spectator, February 7, 1981, pp. 21-23.

Times Literary Supplement, April 18, 1936, p. 333.

Twentieth-Century Literature, winter, 1994, Adam Parkes, "Lesbianism, History, and Censorship," p. 434; fall, 2003, Laura Green "Hall of Mirrors: Radclyffe Hall's *The Well of Loneliness* and Modernist Fictions of Identity," p. 277.

*   *   *

HAMILTON, Franklin
See SILVERBERG, Robert

*   *   *

HAMILTON, Jane 1957-

PERSONAL: Born July 13, 1957, in Oak Park, IL; daughter of Allen B. and Ruth (Hubert) Hamilton; married Robert Willard (an orchard owner), June, 1982; children: two. *Education:* Carleton College, B.A., 1979.

ADDRESSES: Home—Rochester, WI. *Agent*—c/o Doubleday Publishers, 1540 Broadway, New York, NY 10036.

CAREER: Apple farmer, beginning c. 1979; freelance author, 1982—.

AWARDS, HONORS: Ernest Hemingway Foundation Award from PEN American Center, 1989, for *The Book of Ruth; Publishers Weekly* Best Book citation, *Chicago Tribune* Heartland Prize, and Orange Prize shortlist, all 1998, all for *The Short History of a Prince.*

WRITINGS:

The Book of Ruth (novel), Ticknor & Fields (New York, NY), 1988, published as *The Frogs Are Still Singing*, Collins (London, England), 1989.

The Guardian, T. Nelson Publishers (Nashville, TN), 1994.

A Map of the World (novel), Doubleday (New York, NY), 1994.

The Short History of a Prince, Random House (New York, NY), 1998.

Disobedience (novel), Doubleday (New York, NY), 2000.

Contributor of essays and reviews for periodicals and Web sites.

ADAPTATIONS: A Map of the World was adapted as an audiobook, Bantam Doubleday Dell, 1995, and produced as a film, 2000. *The Book of Ruth* was adapted as a film for Columbia Broadcasting System, Inc. (CBS)-TV, 2004.

SIDELIGHTS: Jane Hamilton spent most of her life in small towns in the Midwest. She was born in 1957 in Oak Park, Illinois, a birthplace she shares with writers Ernest Hemingway and Carol Shields. Hamilton's mother and grandmother were also writers, and, as Hamilton told *Publishers Weekly* contributor Sybil Steinberg, "I just assumed that if you were a girl-child you were supposed to grow up and write." After Hamilton graduated from Carleton College in Minnesota, she declined a position with a New York City publishing firm to work in an apple orchard in Wisconsin and eventually married one of the orchard's owners. However, Hamilton followed in her family tradition and put her experiences with rural, small-town living into critically acclaimed novels that include *The Book of Ruth* and *A Map of the World.*

Though Hamilton preserves the atmosphere of her native Midwest in her fiction, her stories are not autobiographical. Interviewed by Michael Schumacher for *Writer's Digest,* Hamilton confided: "My mother was horrified when she read [*The Book of Ruth*] . . . because she saw its having no relation to my life. She wondered how 'Sweet Jane' could come up with the squalid, squalid people." The "squalid people" Hamilton referred to include her protagonist and narrator, Ruth, who manages to find hope despite a loveless childhood and abandonment by her father; Ruth's mother, May, who is embittered by the loss of her first husband in World War II and who marries Ruth's father for reasons other than love; and Ruby, an emotionally disturbed man whom Ruth marries and brings to live in May's small house with disastrous results. The novel was inspired by a 1983 news story that profiled several Wisconsin men who killed their mothers-in-law. Hamilton told Schumacher, "I wanted to see if I could write about other people besides myself." Previously, her efforts at fiction fell into the category of autobiographical short stories.

The Book of Ruth was well received by critics. Richard Eder, reviewing the novel in the *Los Angeles Times,* compared its author to nineteenth-century novelist Charles Dickens, and observed: "There is no perspective, no breathing space between Ruth and her pain; between Ruth and those she lives among, each of whom is drawn in harsh and sometimes grotesque contrasts of dark and light." Eder further commented that "the real achievement of this first novel is not so much the blackness as the suggestion of resilience." Jay Parini, who hailed the work in the *Times Literary Supplement* by its British title of *The Frogs Are Still Singing,* termed Hamilton's debut "a well drawn, often tender portrait of a young woman caught in a situation of bleak cultural and material deprivation." Even more profuse in her praise was Suzanne Berne in *Belles Lettres,* who applauded what she felt to be "a breathtaking book, precise and beautiful in its language, full of sharp wisdom, and permeated by an appreciation of the world's ironies even in the midst of great pain." Judith Paterson in the *Washington Post Book World* lauded *The Book of Ruth* as "passionate and adroit" and concluded that it "asks one of literature's biggest questions: what is the meaning of human suffering? In the end, she gives the old answer—to expose the truth and teach forgiveness." Despite critical praise, *The Book of Ruth* did not draw wide attention until it chosen, seven years after publica-

tion, for talk-show host Oprah Winfrey's Book Club. In 2004, *The Book of Ruth* was produced as a made-for-television movie starring Christine Lahti, Nicholle Tom, and Evan Jones.

In Hamilton's 1994 effort, *A Map of the World,* she introduces protagonists Alice and Howard, a couple who move to a farming community in order to fulfill Howard's dream of being a dairy farmer. After six years' residence, they are still viewed by their neighbors as outsiders, not just because of their relative newness but for reasons including the fact that they once had an African American sporting dreadlocks as a house guest. Bill Kent stated in the *New York Times Book Review,* "after just a few pages . . . we know Alice Goodwin is going to get it, bad." *New York Times* critic Michiko Kakutani commented that *A Map of the World* "aspires to combine a melodramatic soap-opera plot with highly tuned literary writing, the pacing of a thriller with the psychological detail of a Bildungsroman." Although Kakutani felt that the resulting novel is "something of a mixed bag," she praised "the strengths of Ms. Hamilton's writing: her eye for the emotional detail, her expert manipulation of point of view, her ability to show us Alice's fears and delusions, her need for penance and her yearning for redemption." Similarly, John Skow in *Time* noted that *A Map of the World* "would be soap opera if the author were not unusually good at transforming acute, intuitive perceptions into sentences." He finished by calling the book "very good stuff by a novelist whose momentum seems unstoppable." Kent pointed out in the *New York Times Book Review* that "when it's working well, it lays out an exciting human drama against a setting so vividly realized that you can almost smell the loamy soil." Because of its rural setting, John Blades in the *Chicago Tribune* compared *A Map of the World* favorably with Jane Smiley's Pulitzer Prize-winning novel *A Thousand Acres,* and Laura Shapiro, discussing the book's horrific events in *Newsweek,* asserted that "there's nothing garish or manipulative about Hamilton's approach. . . . she is exploring them, not exploiting them. Her tone is beautifully controlled, her style calm and lucid." Shapiro concluded that Hamilton "proves . . . that she is one of our best."

The Short History of a Prince was described by a *Maclean's* reviewer as "a relatively placid tale" compared with the more blatantly painful themes in Hamilton's first two novels. The novel focuses on exdancer Walter McCloud during his move from Manhattan to Wisconsin where he takes a job as a high school teacher. "The narrative alternates between the adult Walter—witty, eccentric and emotionally adrift—to an adolescent Walter who is passionate about ballet and desperately in love with a male classmate," explained the *Maclean's* critic, adding that, "While the novel lacks the momentum of her earlier books, Hamilton's consummate skill makes Walter affecting and memorable." *Newsweek's* Laura Shapiro, dubbing the book "gentle and reflective," noted that Hamilton's "characters live with ordinary and sometimes extraordinary torment, yet her writing remains buoyant and her sensibility full of light." Shapiro praised in particular Hamilton's portrayal of her gay protagonist as "subtle, moving and utterly convincing." According to Steinberg in *Publishers Weekly*, Walter's "quiet suffering and endurance is faithful to the longings and insecurities of outsiders in society who take refuge in the spiritual solace of literature, dance and music."

Nancy Pearl, in the *Seattle Times*, said that *The Short History of a Prince* "is not without its flaws. As she did in *A Map of the World*, Hamilton insists on including too many unnecessary subplots, and it sometimes feels as though the book is going to sink under the weight of all that's happening." Ultimately, however, added Pearl, "Hamilton creates stories that are almost impossible to set aside." Lucy Ferriss, in the *St. Louis Post-Dispatch*, described the novel as "far more nuanced and powerful" than Hamilton's earlier fiction and a book "that wades into waters that are even more treacherous for literary fiction."

Disobedience looks back at the inner life of an adolescent boy from a perspective of a decade. Seventeen-year-old Henry Shaw sets up an e-mail account for his mother, Beth, only to accidentally find out that she is using it to communicate with a lover. Rather than backing away, Henry begins to eavesdrop on his mother's secret life. *Lancet* contributor Kirstie Archer found that "as the story unfolds it becomes clear that Henry's account of his father, and perhaps of the whole story, is unreliable. And here we find the underlying subject of the novel: the nature of truth and authenticity. How much of our perception of other people is the truth, and how much is an invention to suit our own needs?" Henry's sister, Elvira, also struggles with issues of authenticity when she prefers to be a boy in the Civil War re-enactments she and her father share an interest in. Revelation and exposure bring crises to the family, along with enlightenment. According to Liza Schwarzbaum in *Entertainment Weekly*, while "Elvira is a pip, a fabulous creation," *Disobedience* is Henry's story. "Henry's voice is exactly right: he's a thoughtful, intelligent boy whose hormones are sending him confusing messages, and whose tendency is to mock both parents with typical teen sardonic humor," wrote a *Pub-*

lishers Weekly critic. *Guardian* critic Julie Myerson was not so taken with *Disobedience*, and found Henry's obsession with his mother's affair "just too weird and worrying. You know it, I know it, even he . . . is beginning to know it. But it's just not clear whether the author knows it. There is nothing wrong with splattering a novel with all this Oedipal ooze if the author is willing to get in there, rummage around and explore it. But Hamilton seems bafflingly bent on passing her tale off as a mere insightful little vignette of teenage sensitivity and familial betrayal." However, the *Publishers Weekly* critic concluded: "Hamilton manages to grant psychological validity to all the members of this ordinary-seeming but emotionally distracted family" with "her tender evocation of both human fallibility and our ability to recover from heartbreaking choices."

BIOGRAPHICAL AND CRITICAL SOURCES:

PERIODICALS

Atlanta Journal-Constitution, April 2, 1998, section E, p. 5; October 22, 2000, section D, p. 4.
Austin American-Statesman, March 29, 1998, section D, p. 6; March 24, 2000, section E, p. 1; October 15, 2000, section L, p. 6.
Belles Lettres, fall, 1988, p. 13.
Bloomsbury Review, March-April, 1995, p. 15.
Book, November-December, 2000, interview with Hamilton.
Booklist, June 1, 1994, p. 1771; October 15, 1997, p. 424; January 1, 1998, p. 743; January 1, 1999, p. 778; August 2000, p. 2074; June 1, 2001, p. 1908.
Boston Herald, October 27, 2000, p. 40.
Chicago Tribune, June 6, 1994, John Blades, review of *A Map of the World,* section 5, p. 2.
Christian Century, May 24, 1995, p. 567.
Christian Science Monitor, June 3, 1994, p. 13; November 9, 2000, p. 18.
Daily Telegraph (London, England), February 17, 2001.
Entertainment Weekly, June 10, 1994, p. 61; March 21, 1997, p. 65; March 27, 1998, Lisa Schwarzbaum, review of *The Short History of a Prince,* p. 62; October 20, 2000, Lisa Schwarzbaum, review of *Disobedience,* p. 70.
Guardian (London, England), April 7, 2001, Julie Myerson, review of *Disobedience,* p. 10.
Independent (London, England), February 10, 1996, p. 11; August 1, 1998, p. 12.
Independent on Sunday (London, England), February 4, 2001, p. 48.

Lancet, March 24, 2001, Kirstie Archer, review of *Disobedience,* p. 968.

Library Journal, November 1, 1988, p. 109; May 15, 1994, p. 99; February 1, 1998, p. 110; May 15, 1998, p. 134; September 15, 2000, p. 112; February 1, 2001, p. 144.

Los Angeles Times, November 3, 1988, section 5, p. 12; January 5, 1994, Richard Eder, review of *A Map of the World,* p. 3; October 15, 2000, p. 11.

Maclean's, June 22, 1998, review of *The Story of a Prince,* p. 48; January 8, 2001, review of *Disobedience,* p. 45.

Midamerica, 2000, p. 119.

Milwaukee Journal Sentinel, January 14, 2000, section E, p. 3; October 8, 2000, p. 06.

Newsweek, June 13, 1994, Laura Shapiro, review of *A Map of the World,* p. 55; April 13, 1998, Laura Shapiro, review of *The Short History of a Prince,* p. 76.

New Yorker, August 15, 1994, p. 78.

New York Times, June 28, 1994, section C, p. 19; December 3, 1999, section B, pp. 24, section E, 24; October 19, 2000, section B, p. 9, sectin E, p. 9; April 30, 2004, Virginia Heffernan, review of *The Book of Ruth* (TV adaptation).

New York Times Book Review, March 12, 1989, p. 22; July 17, 1994, Bill Kent, review of *A Map of the World,* p. 726; April 26, 1998, p. 22; November 19, 2000, p. 9; July 22, 2001, p. 28.

NWSA Journal, spring, 1999, p. 21.

Observer (London, England), February 11, 2001, p. 15.

People, May 30, 1994, p. 30; April 6, 1998, p. 31; November 20, 2000, p. 57.

Publishers Weekly, September 16, 1988, Sybil Steinberg, review of *The Book of Ruth,* p. 62; April 4, 1994, review of *Map of the World,* p. 57; December 22, 1997, review of *The Short History of a Prince,* p. 36; February 2, 1998, Sybil Steinberg, interview, "Jane Hamilton: A Kinship with Society's Outcasts," p. 68; April 6, 1998, sound recording review, *The Short History of a Prince,* p. 34; February 7, 2000, John F. Baker, brief article, "New Novel from Hammond," p. 12; August 7, 2000, review of *Disobedience,* p. 72.

St. Louis Post-Dispatch, April 5, 1998, Lucy Ferriss, review of *A Map of the World,* section D, p. 6.

San Francisco Chronicle, March 29, 1998, p. 4.

School Library Journal, February 2001, p. 143.

Seattle Times, April 12, 1998, section M, p. 2; March 3, 2000, section F, p. 4; October 15, 2000, section M, p. 1.

Time, June 27, 1994, p. 75.

Times Literary Supplement, November 24, 1989, Jay Parini, review of *The Book of Ruth,* p. 1313; January 20, 1995, Jean Hanff Korelitz, review of *A Map of the World,* p. 20.

U.S. Catholic, May 1997, p. 46.

U.S. News and World Report, June 13, 1994, p. 82.

Variety, May 20, 1987, p. 102; July 15, 1987, p. 14; June 15, 1988, p. 13; April 19, 1989, p. 24; May 10, 1989, p. 27; February 7, 1990, p. 34.

Wall Street Journal, January 13, 1989, section A, pp. 9-10; July 5, 1994, section A, p. 8, 10; October 20, 2000, section W, p. 10.

Washington Post, October 19, 2000, section C, p. O2.

Washington Post Book World, February 5, 1989, Judith Paterson, review of *The Book of Ruth,* p. 6; May 29, 1994, Carol Shields, review of *A Map of the World,* p. 5.

Writer's Digest, October, 1990, Michael Schumacher, review of *The Book of Ruth,* pp. 28-29.

ONLINE

BookReporter, http://www.bookreporter.com/ (March 25, 2004), review of *Disobedience.*

OnMilwaukee, http://www.onmilwaukee.com/ (October 16, 2000), interview with Hamilton.

*   *   *

HAMILTON, Mollie
See KAYE, M.M.

*   *   *

HAMILTON, Virginia 1936-2002
(Virginia Esther Hamilton)

PERSONAL: Born March 12, 1936, in Yellow Springs, OH; died of breast cancer, February 19, 2002, in Dayton, OH; daughter of Kenneth James (a musician) and Etta Belle (Perry) Hamilton; married Arnold Adoff (an anthologist and poet), March 19, 1960; children: Leigh Hamilton, Jaime Levi. *Education:* Studied at Antioch College, 1952-55, Ohio State University, 1957-58, and New School for Social Research, 1958-60.

CAREER: Novelist and author of children's books.

AWARDS, HONORS: Notable Children's Book citation, American Library Association (ALA), 1967, and Nancy Block Memorial Award, Downtown Community School Awards Committee, New York, both for *Zeely;* Edgar

Allan Poe Award for best juvenile mystery, Mystery Writers of America, 1969, for *The House of Dies Drear;* Ohioana Literary Award, 1969; John Newbery Honor Book Award, American Library Association (ALA), 1971, for *The Planet of Junior Brown;* Lewis Carroll Shelf Award, *Boston Globe-Horn Book* Award, 1974, John Newbery Medal, ALA, and National Book Award, both 1975, and Gustav-Heinemann-Friedinspreis für Kinder und Lugendbucher, 1991, all for *M.C. Higgins, the Great;* John Newbery Honor Book Award, ALA, Coretta Scott King Award, ALA, *Boston Globe-Horn Book* Award, and American Book Award nomination, all 1983, all for *Sweet Whispers, Brother Rush; Horn Book* Fanfare Award in fiction, 1985, for *A Little Love;* Coretta Scott King Award, ALA, *New York Times* Best Illustrated Children's Book citation, Children's Book Bulletin Other Award, and *Horn Book* Honor List selection, all 1986, all for *The People Could Fly: American Black Folktales; Boston Globe-Horn Book* Award, 1988, and Coretta Scott King Award, ALA, 1989, both for *Anthony Burns: The Defeat and Triumph of a Fugitive Slave;* John Newbery Honor Book Award, ALA, 1989, for *In the Beginning: Creation Stories from around the World;* D.H.L., Bank Street College, 1990; Regina Medal for lifetime achievement, Catholic Library Association, 1990; U.S. nominee, Hans Christian Andersen Award, International Board on Books for Young People, 1992, for body of work; Laura Ingalls Wilder Award for lifetime achievement, ALA, 1995; MacArthur Foundation grant, 1995; Coretta Scott King Award, ALA, 1996, for *Her Stories;* LL.D., Wright State University; honorary doctorate, Ohio State University, Kent State University, 1996; an annual grant for graduate students at Kent State University College of Education and School of Library Science was created in Hamilton's name, 2004.

WRITINGS:

FICTION FOR CHILDREN

Zeely, illustrated by Symeon Shimin, Macmillan (New York, NY), 1967.

The House of Dies Drear, illustrated by Eros Keith, Macmillan (New York, NY), 1968.

The Time-Ago Tales of Jahdu, Macmillan (New York, NY), 1969.

The Planet of Junior Brown, Macmillan (New York, NY), 1971.

Time-Ago Lost: More Tales of Jahdu, illustrated by Ray Prather, Macmillan (New York, NY), 1973.

M.C. Higgins, the Great, Macmillan (New York, NY), 1974, published with teacher's guide by Lou Stanek, Dell (New York, NY), 1986, published with

short stories, poems, and memoirs by various writers, as *M.C. Higgins, the Great: With Connections,* Holt, Rinehart (Austin, TX), 1998.

Arilla Sun Down, Greenwillow (New York, NY), 1976.

Illusion and Reality, Library of Congress (Washington, DC), 1976.

Justice and Her Brothers (first novel in "Justice" trilogy), Greenwillow (New York, NY), 1978.

Jahdu, illustrated by Jerry Pinkney, Greenwillow (New York, NY), 1980.

Dustland (second novel in "Justice" trilogy), Greenwillow (New York, NY), 1980.

The Gathering (third novel in "Justice" trilogy), Greenwillow (New York, NY), 1981.

Sweet Whispers, Brother Rush, Philomel (New York, NY), 1982.

The Magical Adventures of Pretty Pearl, Harper (New York, NY), 1983.

Willie Bea and the Time the Martians Landed, Greenwillow (New York, NY), 1983.

A Little Love, Philomel (New York, NY), 1984.

Junius over Far, Harper (New York, NY), 1985.

The People Could Fly: American Black Folktales, illustrated by Leo and Diane Dillon, Knopf (New York, NY), 1985, published with cassette, 1987.

The Mystery of Drear House: The Conclusion of the Dies Drear Chronicle, Greenwillow (New York, NY), 1987.

A White Romance, Philomel (New York, NY), 1987.

In the Beginning: Creation Stories from around the World, Harcourt (San Diego, CA), 1988.

Anthony Burns: The Defeat and Triumph of a Fugitive Slave, Knopf (New York, NY), 1988.

Bells of Christmas, illustrated by Lambert Davis, Harcourt (San Diego, CA), 1989.

The Dark Way: Stories from the Spirit World, illustrated by Lambert Davis, Harcourt (San Diego, CA), 1990.

Cousins, Putnam (New York, NY), 1990.

The All-Jahdu Storybook, illustrated by Barry Moser, Harcourt (San Diego, CA), 1991.

Drylongso, illustrated by Jerry Pinkney, Harcourt, Brace (San Diego, CA), 1992.

Many Thousand Gone: African Americans from Slavery to Freedom, illustrated by Leo and Diane Dillon, Knopf (New York, NY), 1992.

Plain City, Blue Sky Press (New York, NY), 1993.

Her Stories: African-American Folktales, Fairy Tales, and True Tales, Scholastic (New York, NY), 1995.

Jaguarundi, Blue Sky Press (New York, NY), 1995.

When Birds Could Talk and Bats Could Sing: The Adventures of Bruh Sparrow, Sis Wren, and Their Friends, illustrated by Barry Moser, Blue Sky Press (New York, NY), 1995.

A Ring of Tricksters: Animal Tales from America, the West Indies, and Africa, Blue Sky Press (New York, NY), 1997.

Second Cousins, Scholastic (New York, NY), 1998.

Bluish: A Novel, Blue Sky Press (New York, NY), 1999.

The Girl Who Spun Gold, illustrated by Leo and Diane Dillon, Blue Sky Press (New York, NY), 2000.

Wee Winnie Witch's Skinny: An Original Scare Tale for Halloween, illustrated by Barry Moser, Blue Sky Press (New York, NY), 2001.

Time Pieces: The Book of Times, Blue Sky Press (New York, NY), 2002.

Bruh Rabbit and the Tar Baby Girl, illustrated by James Ransome, Blue Sky Press (New York, NY), 2003.

OTHER

W.E.B. Du Bois: A Biography (for children), Crowell (New York, NY), 1972.

Paul Robeson: The Life and Times of a Free Black Man (for children), Harper (New York, NY), 1974.

(Editor) W.E.B. Du Bois, *The Writings of W.E.B. Du Bois,* Crowell (New York, NY), 1975.

(Author of introduction) Martin Greenberg, editor, *The Newbery Award Reader,* Harcourt (New York, NY), 1984.

ADAPTATIONS: The House of Dies Drear was adapted for the Public Broadcasting Service series *Wonderworks* and released on videocassette, Public Media Video (Chicago, IL), 1984, and on audiocassette by Recorded Books (Frederick, MD), 1995. *The People Could Fly* was adapted for the *Reading Rainbow* television series. *M.C. Higgins, the Great* was released on audiodisc, Recorded Books (Frederick, MD), 1993. *The Planet of Junior Brown* was adapted as the film *Junior's Groove,* PIX Entertainment, 1999.

SIDELIGHTS: During a career that spanned more than three decades, Virginia Hamilton helped launch a new era in the portrayal of African Americans in children's literature, at the same time setting a new standard of quality in the genre. Not only have many of her works received awards such as the National Book Award, but her novel *M.C. Higgins, the Great* was the first work ever to win both the National Book Award and the Newbery Medal. Hamilton, winner of every major award in her field, including the 1995 Laura Ingalls Wilder Award for lifetime achievement, is widely recognized as a gifted and demanding storyteller. As Ethel L. Heins wrote in *Horn Book:* "Few writers of fiction

for young people are as daring, inventive, and challenging to read—or to review—as Virginia Hamilton. Frankly making demands on her readers, she nevertheless expresses herself in a style essentially simple and concise." Her "rare ability to combine storytelling with scholarly research allowed her to rescue and retell important narratives that would otherwise have remained lost," Bonnie Verbug added in an article for *Black Issues Book Review.*

Hamilton's vision was deeply influenced by her background. Her mother's side of the family was descended from a fugitive slave, Levi Perry, who settled in the Miami valley town of Yellow Springs, in southern Ohio. The Perry family grew and prospered by farming the rich Ohio soil. "I grew up within the warmth of loving aunts and uncles, all reluctant farmers but great storytellers," Hamilton once recalled in a *Horn Book* article by Lee Bennett Hopkins. "I remember the tales best of all. My own father, who was an outlander from Illinois, Iowa, and points west, was the finest of the storytellers besides being an exceptional mandolinist. Mother, too, could take a slice of fiction floating around the family and polish it into a saga."

While attending Antioch College on a scholarship, Hamilton majored in writing and composed short stories. One of her instructors liked her stories enough to encourage the young student to leave college and test her skills in New York City. Hamilton was eager to experience the excitement of city life, and so in 1955 she began spending her summers in New York, working as a bookkeeper. Later, she moved to the city permanently. "I don't have a clear recollection of the day I officially left home to go to New York," she once told an interviewer. "My plan was to find a cheap apartment, a part-time job, write and have a good time. And it all came together."

An important influence on the creation of *Zeely* came after Hamilton married poet and anthologist Arnold Adoff, whom she met not long after arriving in New York City. The two newlyweds traveled to Spain and then to northern Africa. "Going to Africa had been an enduring dream of Hamilton's," according to *Dictionary of Literary Biography* contributor Jane Ball, "and the land of dark-skinned people had 'a tremendous impression' on her . . . even though her stay was brief. The impact is apparent on her first book." According to John Rowe Townsend in his *A Sounding of Storytellers: New and Revised Essays on Contemporary Writers for Children, Zeely* exemplifies the type of writing Hamilton produced throughout her career: there "is not taint of racism in her books. . . . All through her work runs an awareness of black history, and particularly of black history in America. And there is a difference in the furniture of her writing mind from that of most of her white contemporaries: dream, myth, legend and ancient story can be sensed again and again in the background of naturalistically-described present-day events."

Zeely is the story of a young girl who calls herself Geeder as a means of escaping who she really is, Elizabeth Perry. Geeder is fascinated by Zeely, a tall, regal-looking woman she sees tending pigs on a farm, obsessively imagining her to be a Watusi queen. By the end of the tale, Zeely convinces Geeder she is nothing of the sort. *Horn Book Magazine* reviewer Rudine Sims Bishop sums up Geeder's story nicely: "Zeely sees in Geeder something of herself as a young girl, and helps her, through a couple of stories, to separate her fantasies from reality but at the same time to hold on to her 'most fine way of dreaming.'"

In Hamilton's "Jahdu" tales, including *The Time-Ago Tales of Jahdu, Time-Ago Lost: More Tales of Jahdu, Jahdu,* and *The All-Jahdu Storybook,* Hamilton took an approach that mimics the style of the traditional folktale. These works tell of the fantastic adventures of Jahdu and his "encounters [with] the allegorical figures Sweetdream, Nightmare, Trouble, Chameleon, and others," wrote Marilyn F. Apseloff in the *Dictionary of Literary Biography.* "These original tales have a timeless quality about them; in addition, they reveal racial pride, as Jahdu discovers in [*The Time-Ago Tales of Jahdu*] . . . that he is happiest when he becomes a part of a black family in Harlem." Similarly, in the collections *The People Could Fly: American Black Folktales, In the Beginning: Creation Stories from around the World,* and *The Dark Way: Stories from the Spirit World,* Hamilton retells old myths and folktales from her own black ancestry——as well as many other cultures—in an attempt to restore pride in this diverse and rich literary heritage.

One ethnic group in particular, Native Americans, influenced Hamilton's writing in books like the Edgar Award-winning *The House of Dies Drear.* "The references to Indians in her books," observed Apseloff, "are probably the result of two factors: Hamilton knew that many Shawnees lived in the Yellow Springs area originally, with Cherokees further south, and her grandmother claimed to be part American Indian." Despite this element in the story, however, *The House of Dies Drear* is a mystery novel centered on the history of the Underground Railroad, the route fugitive blacks took to escape slavery in the South before the U.S. Civil War. It "is a taut mystery, one which youngsters gulp down quickly and find hard to forget," attested Hopkins. Hamilton called *The House of Dies Drear* one of her favorite books, "I think, because it is so full of all the things I love: excitement, mystery, black history, the strong, black family. In it I tried to pay back all those wonderful relatives who gave me so much in the past."

Hamilton's *M.C. Higgins, the Great* emphasizes the importance of family. The story portrays the Higginses, a close-knit family that resides on Sarah's Mountain in southern Ohio. The mountain has special significance to the Higginses, for it has belonged to their family since M.C.'s great-grandmother Sarah, an escaped slave, settled there. The conflict in the story arises when a huge spoil heap, created by strip mining, threatens to engulf the family home. M.C. is torn between his love for his home and his concern for his family's safety, and he searches diligently for a solution that will allow him to preserve both. *M.C. Higgins, the Great* was highly praised by critics, including poet Nikki Giovanni, who wrote in the *New York Times Book Review:* "Once again Virginia Hamilton creates a world and invites us in. *M.C. Higgins, the Great* is not an adorable book, not a lived-happily-ever-after kind of story. It is warm, humane and hopeful and does what every book should do—creates characters with whom we can identify and for whom we care."

Hamilton chronicles slavery in both *Anthony Burns: The Defeat and Triumph of a Fugitive Slave* and *Many Thousand Gone: African Americans from Slavery to Freedom.* In *Anthony Burns* she relates the true story of an escaped slave who was captured and tried under the Fugitive Slave Act. The trial triggered riots and ended with Burns's return to his former owner. Hamilton based her account on court records, newspaper reports, biographies, and other primary sources. "Told in an appropriately restrained, unadorned style, incorporating verbatim the speeches of counsel for both sides, *Anthony Burns* is a work of simple, but noble, eloquence," praised Elizabeth Ward in the *Washington Post Book World.* A reviewer for *Children's Book Review Service* also found the work compelling and remarked, "Black history comes alive in this striking, gripping, personalized account."

Based on information found in nineteenth-century archives and oral histories, *Many Thousand Gone* contains biographical profiles of celebrated and obscure individuals that reveal their personal experiences with slavery. The stories included provide insight on slavery in America from the early 1600s to its abolishment in 1865 with the ratification of the Thirteenth Amendment to the Constitution. "All of these profiles drive home the sickening realities of slavery in a personal way," asserted David Haward Bain in the *New York Times Book Review,* the critic adding that "many also show how the experiences of individuals in the legal system worked in the larger struggle for freedom." Michael Dirda concluded in the *Washington Post Book World* that "as a kind of portrait gallery of the brave and resourceful, *Many Thousand Gone* deserves many thousand readers."

Throughout the 1990s Hamilton continued to pen works dealing with folklore and strong female characters. In the *New York Times Book Review* Veronica Chambers characterized Hamilton's *Her Stories: African-American Folktales, Fairy Tales, and True Tales* as "possibly the first collection of such folk literature to focus exclusively on African-American women and girls." Hamilton recasts stories dealing with animals, fairy tales, the supernatural, folkways, and true experiences that were passed down through oral history and in several African languages, as well as Spanish and English. "Hamilton's retellings of these stories strike a nice balance between dialect and accessibility, modernizing just enough to make the stories easily readable without sacrificing the flavor of the originals," credited Jennifer Howard in a *Washington Post Book World* review.

Another tale with a strong heroine is Hamilton's retelling of the European Rumplestiltskin tale as *The Girl Who Spun Gold. School Library Journal*'s Carol Ann Wilson dubbed the 2000 book "charming and visually stunning" as well as "humorous and, at times, scary," while both *Horn Book* reviewer Robert Strang and *Booklist* critic Hazel Rochman remarked on how well the tale sounds. It is told in "immediate, colloquial style, with a rhythm just right for reading aloud," Rochman noted.

In addition to the folktales focusing on human characters, Hamilton also published animal-centered tales as *Jaguarundi, When Birds Could Talk and Bats Could Sing: The Adventures of Bruh Sparrow, Sis Wren, and Their Friends,* and *A Ring of Tricksters: Animal Tales from America, the West Indies, and Africa.* She also penned several realistic novels set in contemporary times, among them *Cousins,* its sequel *Second Cousins,* and *Bluish. Cousins* tells the story of cousins Cammy and Patty Ann, who do not get along at day camp, while the sequel tells what happens when a family reunion brings two sophisticated New York cousins into the pic-

ture. *Bluish* follows the efforts of the new girl at a Manhattan magnet school, ten-year-old Dreenie, to make friends, which she does, with Natalie, who has leukemia. "Spare prose expresses each stage of the girls' friendship," commented a *Publishers Weekly* reviewer of *Bluish,* and Dreenie comes to accept Natalie—nicknamed Bluish for her pale skin and prominent veins—illness and all. A *Horn Book* reviewer found Hamilton's portrayal of the fifth graders' speech and behavior "right on target." Among those portrayed is the emotionally needy Tuli, whose characterization in the capable hands of Hamilton was called "funny," "touching," and one of the highlights of the novel by *Booklist*'s Rochman.

Hamilton's final novel, *Time Pieces: The Book of Times,* was completed shortly before the author succumbed to breast cancer. Published posthumously, it is semiautobiographical and weaves together her childhood experiences and the family tales that made up part of her heritage. In it discerning readers can see many of the nuggets of family history around which Hamilton built her long works; as *Booklist*'s Rochman predicted: "Her fans will also be fascinated to see the seeds of so many books here." The stories included in *Time Pieces* are set into the framework of a contemporary tale about a girl named Valena who likes to hear her family's stories. While a *Publishers Weekly* contributor called the contemporary-framed tale "sketchy" when contrasted with the richness of the family stories, in *School Library Journal* Lauralyn Persson praised the humor and suspense of the tales and the "simplicity and directness of the language," which qualities, she maintained, "serve the subject matter beautifully." In *Kirkus Reviews* a commentator concluded that *Time Pieces* "makes a loving, thoughtful addition" to Hamilton's "unique literary legacy."

BIOGRAPHICAL AND CRITICAL SOURCES:

BOOKS

Children's Literature Review, Thomson Gale (Detroit, MI), Volume 1, 1976, Volume 8, 1985, Volume 11, 1986, Volume 40, 1996.

Contemporary Literary Criticism, Volume 26, Thomson Gale (Detroit, MI), 1983.

Dictionary of Literary Biography, Thomson Gale (Detroit, MI), Volume 33: *Afro-American Fiction Writers after 1955,* 1984, Volume 52: *American Writers for Children since 1960: Fiction,* 1986.

Egoff, Sheila A., *Thursday's Child: Trends and Patterns in Contemporary Children's Literature,* American Library Association (Chicago, IL), 1981, pp. 31-65, 130-158.

Hamilton, Virginia, interview with Marguerite Feitlowitz in *Authors and Illustrators for Young Adults,* Volume 2, Thomson Gale (Detroit, MI), 1989.

Mikkelsen, Nina, *Virginia Hamilton,* Twayne (New York, NY), 1994.

St. James Guide to Young Adult Writers, 2nd edition, St. James Press (Detroit, MI), 1999.

Sims, Rudine, *Shadow and Substance: Afro-American Experience in Contemporary Children's Fiction,* National Council of Teachers of English, 1982, pp. 79-102.

Townsend, John Rowe, *A Sounding of Storytellers: New and Revised Essays on Contemporary Writers for Children,* Lippincott (Philadelphia, PA), 1979, pp. 97-108.

Wheeler, Jill C., *Virginia Hamilton,* Abdo & Daughters (Minneapolis, MN), 1997.

PERIODICALS

African American Review, spring, 1998, Roberta Seelinger Trites, "'I Double Ever Never Lie to My Chil'ren': Inside People in Virginia Hamilton's Narratives," pp. 146-156.

Best Sellers, January, 1983.

Black Issues Book Review, November, 1999, reviews of *Bluish* and *Bells of Christmas,* p. 72; September, 2000, Khafre Abif, review of *The Girl Who Spun Gold,* p. 80; July, 2001, review of *The Girl Who Spun Gold,* p. 74.

Book, January, 2001, Kathleen Odean, review of *The Girl Who Spun Gold,* p. 83.

Booklist, August, 1982, p. 1525; April 1, 1983, pp. 1034-1035; July, 1985, p. 1554; February 15, 1994, Ilene Cooper, review of *The Bells of Christmas,* p. 1095; April 1, 1994, p. 1464; December 15, 1994, p. 753; November 1, 1995, Hazel Rochman, review of *Her Stories,* p. 470; January 1, 1998, Julie Corsaro, review of *A Ring of Tricksters,* p. 802; September 15, 1999, Hazel Rochman, review of *Bluish,* p. 257; August, 2000, Hazel Rochman, review of *The Girl Who Spun Gold,* p. 2134; February 15, 2001, review of *The Girl Who Spun Gold,* p. 1152, and review of *Sweet Whispers, Brother Rush,* p. 1149; July, 2001, review of *The Girl Who Spun Gold,* p. 2011; December 15, 2002, Hazel Rochman, review of *Time Pieces: The Book of Times,* p. 761.

Book Report, March, 1999, review of *Second Cousins,* p. 57; November, 1999, review of *Bluish,* p. 61.

Bulletin of the Center for Children's Books, September, 1978, p. 9; March, 1981, p. 134; July-August, 1982, p. 207; November, 1983, pp. 50-51; April, 1985, p. 148; June, 1988; November, 1998, Janice M. Del Negro, review of *Second Cousins,* pp. 97-98; October, 1999, Janice M. Del Negro, review of *Bluish,* p. 54; December 15, 2002, Hazel Rochman, review of *Time Pieces: The Book of Times,* p. 761.

Catholic Library World, September, 1999, review of *A Ring of Tricksters,* p. 33.

Childhood Education, summer, 2003, Jeanie Burnett, review of *Time Pieces,* p. 245.

Children's Book Review Service, April, 1985, p. 97; July, 1988, review of *Anthony Burns,* p. 146; October, 1992, p. 22; March, 1995, p. 90; October, 1995, p. 22; March, 1996, p. 91; October, 1999, review of *Bluish,* p. 189.

Children's Bookwatch, December, 1999, review of *Bluish,* p. 4.

Children's Literature Association Quarterly, fall, 1982, pp. 45-48; winter, 1983, pp. 10-14, 25-27; spring, 1983, pp. 17-20; fall, 1986, pp. 134-142; winter, 1995-96, pp. 168-174.

Children's Literature in Education, winter, 1983; summer, 1987, pp. 67-75.

Christian Science Monitor, May 4, 1972, p. B5; March 12, 1979, p. B4; May 12, 1980, p. B9; March 2, 1984, p. B7; August 3, 1984.

Detroit Free Press, January 27, 2002, review of *Many Thousand Gone,* p. 5E.

Horn Book, October, 1968, p. 563; February, 1970; February, 1972; October, 1972, p. 476; December, 1972, Lee Bennett Hopkins, "Virginia Hamilton," pp. 563-569; June, 1973; October, 1974, pp. 143-144; April, 1975; August, 1975, pp. 344-348; December, 1976, p. 611; December, 1978, pp. 609-619; June, 1980, p. 305; October, 1982, pp. 505-506; March-April, 1983 p. 175; February, 1984, pp. 24-28; September-October, 1984, pp. 597-598; September-October, 1985, pp. 563-564; March-April, 1986, pp. 212-213; January-February, 1988, pp. 105-106; March-April, 1989, pp. 183-185; July-August, 1993, p. 437; September-October, 1993, p. 621; March-April, 1994, p. 204; July-August, 1995, pp. 436-445; September-October, 1996, Nancy Vasilakis, review of *When Birds Could Talk and Bats Could Sing,* p. 604; January-February, 1998, p. 83; January-February, 1999, p. 61; September-October, 2000, Robert Strang, review of *The Girl Who Spun Gold,* p. 586.

Instructor, January, 2001, Judy Freeman, "All You Need Is Love," p. 19; May, 2001, review of *The Girl Who Spun Gold,* p. 37.

Interracial Books for Children Bulletin, numbers 1 and 2, 1983, p. 32; number 5, 1984; Volume 15, number 5, 1984, pp. 17-18; Volume 16, number 4, 1985, p. 19.

Kirkus Reviews, July 1, 1974; October 15, 1980, pp. 1354-1355; April 1, 1983; October 1, 1985, pp. 1088-1089; March 1, 1996, p. 375; October 15, 1999, review of *Bluish,* p. 1643; November 1, 2002, review of *Time Pieces,* p. 1612.

Kliatt, July, 1999, review of *Plain City,* p. 4.

Language Arts, March, 2002, review of *The Girl Who Spun Gold,* p. 355.

Lion and the Unicorn, Volume 9, 1985, pp. 50-57; Volume 10, 1986, pp. 15-17.

Los Angeles Times Book Review, March 23, 1986; May 22, 1988, p. 11; December 17, 1989, p. 8; November 18, 1990, p. 8.

New York Times Book Review, October 13, 1968, p. 26; October 24, 1971, p. 8; September 22, 1974, p. 8; December 22, 1974, Nikki Giovanni, review of *M.C. Higgins, the Great,* p. 8; October 31, 1976, p. 39; December 17, 1978, p. 27; May 4, 1980, pp. 26, 28; September 27, 1981, p. 36; November 14, 1982, pp. 41, 56; September 4, 1983, p. 14; March 18, 1984, p. 31; April 17, 1985, p. 20; November 10, 1985, p. 38; November 8, 1987, p. 36; October 16, 1988, p. 46; November 13, 1988, p. 52; December 17, 1989, p. 29; November 11, 1990, p. 6; November 22, 1992, p. 34; February 21, 1993, David Haward Bain, review of *Many Thousand Gone,* p. 23; November 12, 1995, Veronica Chambers, review of *Her Stories,* p. 23; September 22, 1996, review of *When the Birds Could Talk and Bats Could Sing,* p. 28; April 19, 1998, review of *A Ring of Tricksters,* p. 32; February 11, 2001, Linda Villarosa, review of *The Girl Who Spun Gold,* p. 27.

Publishers Weekly, January 4, 1993, review of *Cousins,* p. 74; January 18, 1993, p. 470; February 6, 1995, review of *Plain City,* p. 86; February 19, 1996, p. 214; October 6, 1997, p. 59; April 20, 1998, p. 69; October 25, 1999, review of *Bluish,* p. 81; November 4, 2002, review of *Time Pieces,* p. 85.

Reading Teacher, February, 1999, review of *A Ring of Tricksters,* p. 498; May, 2001, review of *The Girl Who Spun Gold,* p. 832.

School Library Journal, December, 1968, pp. 53-54; September, 1971, p. 126; December, 1978, p. 60; March, 1980, p. 140; April, 1981, p. 140; April, 1983, p. 123; August, 1985, p. 97; December, 1994, Karen K. Radtke, review of *Jaguarundi,* p. 75; January, 1995, p. 70; February, 1996, pp. 70-71; December, 1996, p. 29; November, 1999, Katie O'Dell, review of *Bluish,* p. 158; September, 2000, Carol Ann Wilson, review of *The Girl Who Spun Gold,* p. 217; December, 2002, Lauralyn Persson, review of *Time Pieces,* p. 140.

Times (London, England), November 20, 1986.

Times Literary Supplement, May 23, 1975; July 11, 1975, p. 766; March 25, 1977, p. 359; September 19, 1980, p. 1024; November 20, 1981, p. 1362; August 30, 1985, p. 958; February 28, 1986, p. 230; October 30, 1987, p. 1205; November 20, 1987, p. 1286; July 29, 1988, p. 841.

Tribune Books (Chicago, IL), November 10, 1985, pp. 33-34; October 16, 1988, p. 9; November 13, 1988, p. 6; February 26, 1989, p. 8; November 11, 1990; February 14, 1993.

Voice of Youth Advocates, August, 1980, pp. 31-32; October, 1983, p. 215; June, 1985, p. 130; October, 1988, p. 201; February, 1994, Alice F. Stern, review of *Plain City,* p. 267; August, 1997, p. 173; February, 1999, Joyce Sparrow, review of *Second Cousins,* p. 434.

Washington Post Book World, June 25, 1967, p. 12; November 10, 1974; November 7, 1976, p. G7; November 11, 1979; September 14, 1980, p. 6; November 7, 1982, p. 14; November 10, 1985; July 10, 1988, p. 11; April 8, 1990, p. 8; November 4, 1990, p. 19; December 9, 1990, p. 14; February 14, 1993, Michael Dirda, review of *Many Thousand Gone,* p. 10; December 5, 1993, Elizabeth Ward, review of *In the Beginning,* pp. 21, 26; December 10, 1995, Jennifer Howard, review of *Her Stories,* p. 17.

OBITUARIES:

PERIODICALS

Black Issues Book Review, March-April, 2003, pp. 71-73.

Horn Book, May-June, 2002, pp. 366-367.

New York Times, February 20, 2002, p. 19.

*   *   *

HAMILTON, Virginia Esther
    See HAMILTON, Virginia

*   *   *

HANDKE, Peter 1942-

PERSONAL: Born December 6, 1942, in Griffen, Carinthia, Austria; son of Bruno (stepfather; an army sergeant) and Maria (Siutz) Handke; married Libgart Schwarz, 1966 (separated, 1972); children: Amina. *Education:* Attended a Jesuit seminary, and University of Graz, 1961-65.

ADDRESSES: Home—53 rue Cecille-Dinant, F-92140 Clamart, France. *Agent*—c/o Author Mail, Suhrkamp Verlag, Postfach 101945, 6001 9 Frankfurt am Main, Germany; c/o Kurt Bernheim, 792 Columbus Ave., New York, NY 10025.

CAREER: Dramatist, novelist, poet, essayist, and screenwriter, 1966—.

AWARDS, HONORS: Gerhart Hauptmann Prize, 1967; Schiller Prize, 1972; Büchner Prize, 1973 (returned, 1999); Kafka Prize, 1979 (refused); Salzburg Literature Prize, 1986.

WRITINGS:

NOVELS

Die Hornissen (title means "The Hornets"), Suhrkamp (Frankfurt, Germany), 1966.

Der Hausierer (title means "The Peddler"), Suhrkamp (Frankfurt, Germany), 1967.

Die Angst des Tormanns beim Elfmeter (also see below), Suhrkamp (Frankfurt, Germany), 1970, translated by Michael Roloff as *The Goalie's Anxiety at the Penalty Kick,* Farrar, Straus & Giroux (New York, NY), 1972.

Der kurze Brief zum langen Abschied, Suhrkamp (Frankfurt, Germany), 1972, translated by Ralph Manheim as *Short Letter, Long Farewell,* Farrar, Straus & Giroux (New York, NY), 1974.

Die Stunde der wahren Empfindung, Suhrkamp (Frankfurt, Germany), 1975, translated by Ralph Manheim as *A Moment of True Feeling,* Farrar, Straus & Giroux (New York, NY), 1977.

Die linkshändige Frau (also see below), Suhrkamp (Frankfurt, Germany), 1976, translated as *The Left-Handed Woman,* Farrar, Straus & Giroux (New York, NY), 1978.

Three by Peter Handke (contains *A Sorrow beyond Dreams, Short Letter, Long Farewell,* and *The Goalie's Anxiety at the Penalty Kick,*) Avon (New York, NY), 1977.

Langsame Heimkehr (novella), Suhrkamp (Frankfurt, Germany), 1979, translated by Ralph Manheim as "The Long Way Around," in *Slow Homecoming,* Farrar, Straus & Giroux (New York, NY), 1983.

Die Lehre der Sainte-Victoire (novella), Suhrkamp (Frankfurt, Germany), 1980, translated by Ralph Manheim as "The Lesson of Mont Sainte-Victoire," in *Slow Homecoming,* Farrar, Straus & Giroux (New York, NY), 1983.

Kindergeschichte (novella), Suhrkamp (Frankfurt, Germany), 1981, translated by Ralph Manheim as "Children's Stories" in *Slow Homecoming,* Farrar, Straus & Giroux (New York, NY), 1983.

Slow Homecoming, Farrar, Straus & Giroux (New York, NY), 1983.

Across (novella), translated by Ralph Manheim, Farrar, Straus & Giroux (New York, NY), 1986.

Die Wiederholung, Suhrkamp (Frankfurt, Germany), 1986, translated by Ralph Manheim as *Repetition,* Farrar, Straus & Giroux (New York, NY), 1988.

Nachmittag eines Schriftstellers, Suhrkamp (Frankfurt, Germany), 1987, translated by Ralph Manheim as *The Afternoon of a Writer,* Farrar, Straus & Giroux (New York, NY), 1989.

Die Abwesenheit: ein Marchen, Suhrkamp (Frankfurt, Germany), 1987, translated as *Absence,* Farrar, Straus & Giroux (New York, NY), 1990.

Das Spiel vom Fragen; oder, Die Reise zum Sonoren, Suhrkamp (Frankfurt, Germany), 1989, translated as *Voyage to the Sonorous Land; or, The Art of Asking and The Hour We Knew Nothing of Each Other,* Yale University Press (New Haven, CT), 1996.

Langsam im Schatten, Suhrkamp (Frankfurt, Germany), 1992.

Mein Jahr in der Niemandsbucht: Ein Marchen aus den neuen Zeiten, Suhrkamp (Frankfurt, Germany), 1994, translated by Krishna Winston as *My Year in the No-Man's-Bay,* Farrar, Straus & Giroux (New York, NY), 1998.

In einer dunklen Nacht ging ich aus meinem stillen Haus, Suhrkamp (Frankfurt, Germany), 1997, translated by Krishna Winston as *On a Dark Night I Left My Silent House,* Farrar, Straus & Giroux (New York, NY), 2000.

Der Bildverlust, oder, Durch die Sierra de Gredos, Suhrkamp (Frankfurt, Germany), 2002.

PLAYS

Publikumsbeschimpfung (produced in Frankfurt, 1966), published in *Publikumsbeschimpfung und andere Sprechstücke* (see below), translated by Michael Roloff as *Offending the Audience* in *Kaspar and Other Plays,* Farrar, Straus & Giroux (New York, NY), 1969.

Selbstbezichtigung (produced in Öberhausen, Germany, 1966), published in *Publikumsbeschimpfung und andere Sprechstücke* (see below), translated by Michael Roloff as *Self-Accusation* in *Kaspar and Other Plays,* Farrar, Straus & Giroux (New York, NY), 1969.

Publikumsbeschimpfung und andere Sprechstücke, Suhrkamp (Frankfurt, Germany), 1966, translated by Michael Roloff as *Kaspar and Other Plays,* Farrar, Straus & Giroux, 1969, published as *Offending the Audience,* Methuen (London, England), 1971.

Weissagung (produced in Öberhausen, Germany, 1966), published in *Publikumsbeschimpfung und andere Sprechstücke,* translated by Michael Roloff as *Prophecy* in *The Ride across Lake Constance and Other Plays,* Farrar, Straus & Giroux (New York, NY), 1976.

Hilferufe (produced in Stockholm, Sweden, 1967), published in *Deutsches Theater der Gegenwart 2,* 1967, translated by Michael Roloff as *Calling for Help* in *The Ride across Lake Constance and Other Plays,* Farrar, Straus & Giroux (New York, NY), 1976.

Kaspar (produced in Frankfurt, Germany, 1968), Suhrkamp (Frankfurt, Germany), 1968, translated by Michael Roloff (produced in New York, NY, 1973), published in *Kaspar and Other Plays* (Farrar, Strauss & Giroux (New York, NY), 1969, published separately, Methuen (London, England), 1972.

Das Mundel will Vormund sein (produced in Frankfurt, Germany, 1969), published in *Peter Handke,* Suhrkamp (Frankfurt, Germany), 1969, translated by Michael Roloff as *My Foot My Tutor* in *The Ride across Lake Constance and Other Plays* (Farrar, Straus & Giroux (New York, NY), 1976.

Quodlibet (produced in Basle, Switzerland, 1970), published in *Theater Heute,* March, 1970, translated by Michael Roloff in *The Ride across Lake Constance and Other Plays,* Farrar, Straus & Giroux (New York, NY), 1976.

Wind und Meer: 4 Hörspiele (title means "Wind and Sea: Four Radio Plays"), Suhrkamp (Frankfurt, Germany), 1970.

Chronik der laufenden Ereignisse (film scenario; title means "Chronicle of Current Events"), Suhrkamp (Frankfurt, Germany), 1971.

Der Ritt über den Bodensee (produced in Berlin, Germany, 1971), Suhrkamp (Frankfurt, Germany), 1971, translated by Michael Roloff as *The Ride across Lake Constance* (produced in New York, NY, 1972), published in *The Contemporary German Drama,* Equinox Books (New York, NY), 1972, published separately, Methuen (London, England), 1973.

Die Unvernünftigen sterben aus (produced in Zürich, Switzerland, 1974), Suhrkamp (Frankfurt, Germany), 1973, translated by Michael Roloff and Karl Weber as *They Are Dying Out,* Methuen (London, England), 1975.

The Ride across Lake Constance and Other Plays, Farrar, Straus & Giroux (New York, NY), 1976.

Das ende des Flanierens, Davidpresse, 1976.

(And director) *The Left-Handed Woman* (screenplay; adaptation of Handke's novel), 1978.

Über die Dörfer: Dramatisches (dramatic poem; produced in Salzburg, Austria, 1982), music by Walter Zimmermann, Suhrkamp (Frankfurt, Germany), 1981.

Die Geschichte des Bleistifts, Residenz Verlag (Salzburg, Austria), 1982.

Der Chinese des Schmerzes, Suhrkamp (Frankfurt, Germany), 1983.

Phantasien der Wiederholung, Suhrkamp (Frankfurt, Germany), 1983.

Aber ich lebe nur von den Zwischenreaumen, Ammann, 1987.

(With Wim Wenders) *Der Himmel über Berlin: ein Filmbuch* (screenplay), Suhrkamp (Frankfurt, Germany), 1987, translated as *Wings of Desire,* Orion, 1988.

Die Theaterstucke, Suhrkamp (Frankfurt, Germany), 1992.

Die Stunde da wir nichts voneinander wussten: Ein Schauspiel, Suhrkamp (Frankfurt, Germany), 1992.

Walk about the Village: A Dramatic Poem, Ariadne Press (Riverside, CA), 1996.

Zurüstungen für die Unsterblichkeit: ein Königsdrama, Suhrkamp (Frankfurt, Germany), 1997.

Die Fahrt im Einbaum; oder, Das Stück zum Fiolm vom Kreig (title means "Journey in a Canoe; or, The Play about the Film of the War"; produced in Vienna, Austria, 1999), translated by Scott Abbott, 2001.

Undertagblues: ein Stationendrama, Suhrkamp (Frankfurt, Germany), 2003.

POETRY

Die Innenwelt der Aussenwelt der Innenwelt, Suhrkamp (Frankfurt, Germany), 1969, portions translated by Michael Roloff as *The Innerworld of the Outerworld of the Innerworld,* Seabury Press (New York, NY), 1974.

Als das Wünschen noch geholfen hat, Suhrkamp (Frankfurt, Germany), 1974, translated by Michael Roloff as *Nonsense and Happiness,* Urizen Books (New York, NY), 1976.

Noch einmal für Thukydides, Residenz (Salzburg, Austria), 1990, translated by Tess Lewis as *Once Again for Thucydides,* New Directions (New York, NY), 1999.

OTHER

Begrüssung des Aufsichtsrats (experimental prose pieces; title means "Welcoming the Board of Directors"; also see below), Residenz (Salzburg, Austria), 1967.

(Compiler) *Der gewöhnliche Schrecken* (title means "The Ordinary Terror"), Residenz (Salzburg, Austria), 1969.

Peter Handke: Prosa, Gedichte, Theaterstücke, Hörspiel, Aufsätze (collected works) Suhrkamp (Frankfurt, Germany), 1969.

Deutsche Gedichte (title means "German Poems"), Euphorion-Verlag, 1969.

Ich bin ein Bewohner des Elfenbeinturms (essays; title means "I Live in an Ivory Tower"), Suhrkamp (Frankfurt, Germany), 1972.

Wunschloses Unglück (biography), Residenz Verlag, 1972, translated by Ralph Manheim as *A Sorrow beyond Dreams*, Farrar, Straus & Giroux (New York, NY), 1975, 3rd edition, with notes by Julie Wigmore, St. Martin's Press (New York, NY), 1993, introduction by Jeffrey Eugenides, New York Review of Books (New York, NY), 2002.

Stücke, Suhrkamp (Frankfurt, Germany), 1972.

Stücke 2, Suhrkamp (Frankfurt, Germany), 1973.

(Author of text) *Wiener Läden*, photographs by Didi Petrikat, Hanser (Munich, Germany), 1974.

Falsche Bewegung (film scenario; title means "False Move"), Suhrkamp (Frankfurt, Germany), 1975.

Das Gewicht der Welt: ein Journal, Residenz Verlag, 1977, translated by Ralph Manheim as *The Weight of the World*, Farrar, Straus & Giroux (New York, NY), 1984.

Gedicht an die Dauer, Suhrkamp (Frankfurt, Germany), 1986.

(Author of text) *Walter Pichler: Skupturen, Zeichnugne, Modelle* (exhibition catalogue), Die Galerie (Frankfurt am Main, Germany), 1987.

Versuch über die Mudigkeit (essay), Suhrkamp (Frankfurt, Germany), 1989, published in *The Jukebox, and Other Essays on Storytelling*, Farrar, Straus & Giroux (New York, NY), 1994.

Wiederholung (fairy tales), Collier (New York, NY), 1989.

Versuch über die Jukebox (essay), Suhrkamp (Frankfurt, Germany), 1990, translated in *The Jukebox, and Other Essays on Storytelling*, Farrar, Straus & Giroux (New York, NY), 1994.

Versuch über den gegluckten Tag (essay), Suhrkamp (Frankfurt, Germany), 1991, translated in *The Jukebox, and Other Essays on Storytelling*, Farrar, Straus & Giroux (New York, NY), 1994.

Abschied des Träumers vom Neunten Land (essay; title means "The Dreamer's Farewell from the Ninth Land"), Suhrkamp (Frankfurt, Germany), 1992.

Noch einmal vom Neuten Land, Gespräch mit Jöze Horvat, Wieser, 1993.

André Müller im Gespräch mit Peter Handke, Bibliothek der Provinz, 1993.

The Jukebox, and Other Essays on Storytelling, Farrar, Straus & Giroux (New York, NY), 1994.

Eine Winterliche Reise zu den Flüssen Donau, Save, Morawa, und Drina; oder, Gerechtingkeit für Serbien (essay; originally published in *Süddeutsche Zeitung*, January, 1996), Suhrkamp (Frankfurt, Germany), 1996, translated by Scott Abbott as *A Journey to the Rivers: Justice for Serbia*, Viking (New York, NY), 1997.

Sömmerlicher Nachtrag zu einer Winterlichte Reise (essay; title means "A Summer's Addendum to a Winter's Voyage"), Suhrkamp (Franfurt, Germany), 1996.

Am Felsfenster Morgens: und andere Ortszeiten 1982-1987, Residenz (Salzburg, Austria), 1998.

(With Lisl Ponger) *Ein Wortland: eine Reisse durch Kärnten, Slowenien, Friaul, Istrien und Dalmatien* (travel writing), Wiser (Klagenfurt), 1998.

Lucie im Wald mit den Dingsda: eine Geschichte, Suhrkamp (Frankfurt, Germany), 1999.

Unter Tränen fragend: nachträgliche Aufzeichnungen von zwei Jugoslawien-Durchquerungen im Krieg, März und April 1999 (title means "Notes after the Fact on Two Trips through Yugoslavia during the War, March and April 1999"), Suhrkamp (Frankfurt, Germany), 2000.

(With Dimitri Analis) *Milos Sobaic*, Différence (Paris, France), 2002.

Contributor to periodicals and newspapers, including *Süddeutsche Zeitung*.

ADAPTATIONS: *A Sorrow beyond Dreams* was dramatized as a monologue by Daniel Freudenberger, and staged at the Marymount Manhattan Theatre, 1977.

SIDELIGHTS: Described by *New York Times Book Review* contributor Lee Siegel as "a cross between Holden Caulfield and Bertolt Brecht," Austrian-born writer Peter Handke rose to prominence as a major figure in postmodern German literature during the 1970s and 1980s. A prolific writer of novels, plays, screenplays, poems, travel writing, and political reportage, Handke is highly respected as a stylistic innovator and as a chronicler of psychological alienation.

Nicholas Hern, in *Peter Handke: Theatre and Anti-Theatre,* joined other critics in suggesting that Handke's legal training may have been an important influence on his prose style. Hern pointed out that the majority of Handke's "plays and novels consist of a series of affirmative propositions each contained within one sentence. . . . The effect . . . is not unlike the series of clauses in a contract or will or statute-book, shorn of linking conjunctions. It is as if a state of affairs or a particular situation were being defined and constantly redefined until the final total definition permits of no mite of ambiguity." Handke's prose has reminded other readers of the propositions making up Ludwig Wittgenstein's *Tractatus Logico-Philosophicus;* the inquiries into language characteristic of both Wittgenstein and the French structuralists touch on themes that are central to Handke's work. Discussing his more strictly literary masters, Handke once said that American novelist William Faulkner remains the most important of all writers to him.

Handke's remarkable style was first displayed in the experimental prose pieces he wrote and published in magazines while still a university student, as well as in *Die Hornissen,* which reminded many reviewers of the French "new novel" of that era. *Die Hornissen,* which appeared in the spring of 1966, was generally well received, but its success was not what made Handke suddenly appear on the international literary scene. In April, 1966, he participated in the twenty-eighth convention of Group 47, an association of German writers that met in Princeton, New Jersey. On the last day of the conference Handke, then aged twenty-four, began what came to be called "Handke-Publicity." In his book, *Group 47,* Siegfried Mandel wrote: "Shaking his Beatle-mane, Handke . . . railed against what he had been listening to: impotent narrative; empty stretches of descriptive (instead of analytical) writing pleasing to the ears of the older critics; monotonous verbal litanies, regional and nature idyllicism, which lacked spirit and creativeness. The audience warmed up to the invective with cheers, and later even those whose work had been called idiotic, tasteless, and childish came over to congratulate the Group 47 debutant and to patch things up in brotherly fashion."

Handke's first play was a major hit when it was produced during a week of experimental new drama in Frankfurt. In *Publikumsbeschimpfung—Offending the Audience—*all the comfortable assumptions of bourgeois theater are called into question and the audience is systematically mocked and insulted. The play continued to remain popular with German theatregoers, as did Handke's other early *"sprechstücke"*—plays which in

various ways investigate the role of language in defining the individual's social identity.

The power of language is also the theme of *Kaspar,* Handke's first full-length play, which focuses on 1828 Nuremberg and the actual case of a sixteen-year-old boy who had apparently been confined all his life in a closet, and who was discovered physically full-grown but with the intellect of an infant. Kaspar Hauser's story intrigued a number of writers, and in Handke's play he is indoctrinated with conventional moral precepts in the process of being taught to speak. As Nicholas Hern put it, "the play is an abstract demonstration of the way an individual's individuality is stripped from him by society, specifically by limiting the expressive power of the language it teaches him." In Germany *Kaspar* was voted play of the year, and was regarded by many critics as one of the country's most important postwar dramas.

Handke has continued to write plays, for stage as well as for radio, television, and the screen. Discussing Handke's second full-length play, *The Ride across Lake Constance,* most critics thought the play dealt with the problems of communication, though in a baroque and bewildering fashion. Handke's approach fascinated reviewers, several of whom could make no sense of it at all. Hern wrote that in this play, "Handke has moved from a Wittgensteinian distrust of language to a Foucaultian distrust of what our society calls reason. His play is by no means surrealist in externals only: it parallels the surrealists' cardinal desire—the liberation of men's minds from the constraints of reason. Thus Handke continues to demonstrate that the consistently *anti*-theatrical stance which he has maintained throughout his dramatic writing can none the less lend concrete theatrical expression to abstract, philosophical ideas, thereby generating a new and valid form of theatre."

Meanwhile, Handke established a second reputation as one of the most important German novelists of his generation. His first success in this form was *The Goalie's Anxiety at the Penalty Kick,* which reflects the same preoccupations as do his plays. The partly autobiographical *Short Letter, Long Farewell,* about a young Austrian writer's haphazard journey across the United States to a dangerous meeting with his estranged wife, had a mixed but generally favorable reception. And there was little but praise for *A Sorrow beyond Dreams,* Handke's profoundly sensitive account of his mother's life, which ended in suicide. In the *New York Review of Books,* Michael Wood wrote that "Handke's objective tone is a defense against the potential flood of his feelings, of course, but it is also a act of piety, an expression of respect: this woman's bleak life is not to be made into 'literature.' . . . Handke's mother is important not because she is an especially vivid case but because she is not, because she is one of many."

In *The Afternoon of a Writer,* Handke explores a professional writer's feelings of alienation and anxiety. The protagonist of the work makes no deep connections with other people, choosing instead to withdraw into his writing. His greatest fear is that he will lose his gift of language and imagination—a loss that would leave him completely alienated from the world. Ursula Hegi found *The Afternoon of a Writer* "fascinating," and commented in the *Los Angeles Times Book Review* that "Handke's new novel poses interesting questions about the balance between the nature of solitude and the nature of writing." Anthony Vivis of the *Times Literary Supplement,* however, faulted the extreme minimalism of the work and implied an autobiographical connection between its protagonist and Handke; the novelist, Vivis asserted, "appears to fear the threat, rather than confront the challenge, of his creativity."

Handke's novel *Absence* also subverts the expectations of plot and character development that are met with more traditional novels. The book portrays the walking journey of four characters who are identified simply as "old man," "young woman," "gambler," and "soldier." Writing in the *New York Times Book Review,* Elizabeth Tallent commented: "The soldier is defined by his absence, the young woman by her narcissism, the old man by his profound detachment, the gambler by his inability to love. Yet none of them determines the direction of the tale, whose shape is, instead, that of a quest—one conjured from aimlessness." Also praising the novel, Michael Hofmann observed in the *Times Literary Supplement* that "The book is counter-psychological, magical, perception-led."

My Year in the No-Man's-Bay, a sequel to *The Afternoon of a Writer,* presents a protagonist named Gregor Keuschnig—called Gregor K., in what *New York Times Book Review* contributor Lee Siegel identified as a "jab at Kafka"—who is recalling the year of his artistic and spiritual transformation in a nondescript suburb of Paris. Yet Gregor is unable to focus on this particular year; each time he attempts it, he is distracted into telling other stories. "By the time he arrives at the novel's last section," wrote Siegel, "you realize that Gregor has collapsed all time together." Siegel found this structural device "breathtaking," but noted that the result is disappointing. "Rejecting character, plot and psychology as

mere fictions," the critic commented, Handke "relies on an ostentatious thematic framework that winds up being more implausible than any old-fashioned novelistic trick."

Handke uses the motif of the journey as a structuring device in *On a Dark Night I Left My Silent House.* In this novel, a middle-aged pharmacist from a small village near Salzburg is beaten by strangers he encounters on a wooded path. Unable to speak after the attack, he joins a pair of drifters on a long, indirect drive across Europe. The group eventually ends up in Spain, after which the pharmacist slowly hikes back to his village. When he arrives, he discovers that some things seem the same and others seem different. Keith Miller observed in a review for the *Times Literary Supplement* that this journey suggests several things, including medieval knightly quests, the attraction of Southern Europe to Germanic romantic thinkers, and even an allegory of contemporary Europe in the age of economic union. Noting that the book has the feel of a dream, Miller observed that "if the novel beguiles or engages, it is through its language rather than the usual questions of what happens to whom." *New York Times Book Review* contributor Kai Maristed also noted the intense interior focus of the book, concluding that "It is Peter Handke's loving gaze, honed by time and discipline, that shows readers the way out again into the world's prolific and astonishing strangeness." Claiming that Handke's pharmacist can be seen as "a kind of fictional blank slate for the writing of theory," *New York Times* reviewer Richard Bernstein found *On a Dark Night I Left My Silent House* filled with "disparate images . . . [that] all suggest the rich randomness of thought," and added that, though the novel's lack of plot is a weakness, "as an assemblage, these images have the capacity to haunt."

With *The Jukebox and Other Essays on Storytelling,* Handke presents "Essay on Tiredness," "Essay on the Jukebox," and "Essay on the Successful Day." As in Handke's fiction, the psyche of the writer and the seemingly mundane aspects of experience—such as boredom and tiredness—are of central interest. "Essay on the Jukebox," for example, says very little about jukeboxes and instead explores the creative processes of a writer who is preparing to write about jukeboxes. Sven Birkerts commented in the *New York Times Book Review* that, "Shuttling between fiction and essay, [Handke] is making what feels like a new form, a kind of associative philosophical meditation that both maps and manifests the movements of the mind." Critics emphasized Handke's rambling, digressive, idiosyncratic writing style, praising his dry humor and experimentalism, although some also noted that readers may find the work tedious.

Although his philosophical stance on a number of European matters has been considered controversial, Handke's refusal to use his plays and novels as vehicles for political propaganda was much criticized by German socialists. For Handke's part, he has maintained that literature and political commitment are incompatible: "It would be repugnant to me to twist my criticism of a social order into a story or to aestheticize it into a poem," he writes in one of his essays. "I find that the most atrocious mendacity: to manipulate one's commitment into a poem or to make literature out of it, instead of just saying it loud."

The novelist's caveat against mixing politics and writing does not extend to Handke's nonfiction works, and he is unabashedly political in his books of travel and reportage about the former Yugoslavia. In *A Journey to the Rivers: Justice for Serbia,* he expresses regret over the dissolution of the Yugoslav federation into separate countries and emphasizes the shared past of the various ethnic groups in the region. At the same time, he argues that the Western media portrayed Serbs in an unfair light during the late twentieth-century war in Bosnia. Most journalists, he writes, "confuse their role . . . with that of judge, or even demagogue, and . . . are just as nasty as the dogs of war on the battlefield," emphasizing "the sale of naked, randy, market-oriented facts, or bogus facts." This position, which some took to imply support for the regime of dictator Slobodan Milosovic, earned Handke some ill will within the European community, especially from those who supported the NATO bombing during the conflict. Reviewers, too, raised questions about Handke's position. In the *Time Literary Supplement,* Edward Timms acknowledged the impact of *A Journey to the Rivers,* yet commented that "it cannot be said that the book is entirely convincing. . . . [Handke] tends toward polemical generalization, while his counterbalancing narrative of his encounters in Serbia has an impressionistic subjectivity which at times verges on the sentimental."

For other critics, however, the book's subjectivity was seen as a plus. As Bernd Reinhardt explained in a *World Socialist Web site* article, "For Handke, the truth about the war is not one-dimensional," and he is intent on correcting what he considers to be serious media distortions. Indeed, though Handke has commented about keeping political content out of artistic works, he made the Bosnia War the subject of his play *Journey in a Canoe.* While noting the play's theme, Reinhardt pointed out that it contains "no trace of pro-Serbian sentiment."

Commenting on Handke's changing role from outspoken experimentalist to a more inward-looking, metaphysical approach, *World Literature Today* contributor Erich Wolfgang Skwara explained that the author's unwillingness to go along with social trends in favor of examining "what existence should and must be in order to allow for dignity" has caused his work to be rejected by many critics in Germany. Because of his outsider status, Handke's more recent works have "suffered unfair rejection and criticism—clearly not aimed at the always poetic and convincing texts but meant as a sort of 'revenge' against a poet who refuses to play along with established opinions."

BIOGRAPHICAL AND CRITICAL SOURCES:

BOOKS

Contemporary Literary Criticism, Thomson Gale (Detroit, MI), Volume 5, 1976, Volume 8, 1978, Volume 10, 1979, Volume 15, 1980, Volume 38, 1986.

DeMeritt, Linda C., *New Subjectivity and Prose Forms of Alienation: Peter Handke and Botho Strauss,* P. Lang (New York, NY), 1987.

Dictionary of Literary Biography, Volume 124: *Twentieth-Century German Dramatists, 1919-1992,* Thomson Gale (Detroit, MI), 1992.

Firda, Richard Arthur, *Peter Handke,* Twayne (New York, NY), 1993.

Hern, Nicholas, *Peter Handke: Theatre and Anti-Theatre,* Wolff, 1971.

Klinkowitz, Jerome, *Peter Handke and the Postmodern Transformation: The Goalie's Journey Home,* University of Missouri Press, 1983.

Linstead, Michael, *Outer World and Inner World: Socialisation and Emancipation in the Works of Peter Handke, 1964-1981,* P. Lang (New York, NY), 1988.

Mandel, Siegfried, *Group 47,* Southern Illinois University Press, 1973.

Perrarm, Garvin, *Peter Handke, The Dynamics of the Poetics and the Early Narrative Prose,* P. Lang (New York, NY), 1992.

Ran-Moseley, Faye, *The Tragicomic Passion: A History and Analysis of Tragicomedy and Tragicomic Characterization in Drama, Film, and Literature,* P. Lang (New York, NY), 1994.

Rischbieter, Henning, *Peter Handke,* Friedrich, 1972.

Schlueter, June, *The Plays and Novels of Peter Handke,* University of Pittsburgh Press (Pittsburgh, PA), 1981.

PERIODICALS

America, April 3, 1999, Robert E. Hosmer, Jr., review of *Once Again for Thucydides,* p. 23.

Booklist, January 1-15, 1997, p. 806; October 1, 2000, review of *On a Dark Night I Left My Silent House,* p. 322.

Chicago Tribune, December 1, 1989; December 15, 1989.

Drama Review, fall, 1970.

Economist, October 18, 1997, p. 14.

Kirkus Reviews, June 1, 1994, p. 753; November 1, 1996, p. 1581; November 1, 2000, review of *On a Dark Night I Left My Silent House,* p. 1517.

Library Journal, July, 1994, p. 93; January 1, 1997, p. 124; December, 2002, Ali Houissa, review of *A Sorrow beyond Dreams,* p. 127.

Los Angeles Times, May 22, 1985; June 25, 1986; May 20, 1988.

Los Angeles Times Book Review, July 16, 1989, p. 3.

Modern Drama, spring, 1995, p. 143; July, 1996, pp. 39-40; winter, 1996, p. 680.

Nation, December 4, 1989; January 12, 1997, p. 12.

New Leader, October 2, 1989.

New Republic, February 28, 1970; September 28, 1974; May 23, 1988.

New Statesman, August 5, 1988; July 13, 1990, p. 36; July 19, 1991, p. 38.

Newsweek, July 3, 1978.

New Yorker, December 25, 1989.

New York Review of Books, May 1, 1975; June 23, 1977; September 21, 2000, J.S. Marcus, reviews of *My Year in the No-Man's Bay, Repetition,* and *A Sorrow beyond Dreams,* pp. 80-81.

New York Times, January 30, 1977; March 22, 1971; June 17, 1978; January 25, 1980; April 2, 1980; July 12, 1984; June 25, 1986; April 29, 1988; August 28, 1989; September 3, 1989, p. 17; September 7, 1994, p. C17; March 18, 1996, p. A7; November 29, 2000, Richard Bernstein, review of *On a Dark Night I Left My Silent House.*

New York Times Book Review, May 21, 1972; September 15, 1974; April 27, 1975; July 31, 1977; June 18, 1978; July 22, 1984; August 4, 1985; July 17, 1986; August 7, 1988; June 17, 1990, p. 8; August 21, 1994, p. 10; April 6, 1997, p. 16; October 25, 1998, Lee Siegel, review of *My Year in the No-Man's-Bay;* December 17, 2000, Kai Maristed, review of *On a Dark Night I Left My Silent House,* p. 15.

Publishers Weekly, September 12, 1977; October 30, 2000, review of *On a Dark Night I Left My Silent House,* p. 45.

Review of Contemporary Fiction, summer, 2001, Michael Pinker, review of *On a Dark Night I Left My Silent House,* p. 163.

Süddeutsche Zeitung, May 14, 1999, interview with Handke.

Text und Kritik, no. 24, 1969 (Handke issue).

Time, May 9, 1988.

Times (London, England), May 15, 1972; November 13, 1973; December 9, 1973; April 3, 1980; July 25, 1985; August 4, 1988; July 8, 1989.

Times Literary Supplement, April 21, 1972; December 1, 1972; April 18, 1980; July 17, 1981; November 15, 1985; October 3, 1986; October 5, 1990; May 24, 1991; April 26, 1996, p. 29; April 26, 1996, Edward Timms, review of *Eine winterliche Reise zu den Flüssen Donau, Save, Morawa und Drina;* December 22, 2000, Keith Miller, review of *On a Dark Night I Left My Silent House.*

Tribune Books (Chicago, IL), July 3, 1988.

Wall Street Journal, June 3, 1999, John Reed, "Theater: In the Line of Balkan Fire," p. A24.

Washington Post Book World, July 28, 1985.

World Literature Today, spring, 1987, p. 284; spring, 1991, p. 301; autumn, 1992, p. 716; summer, 1993, p. 604; summer, 1995, p. 572; summer, 1997, p. 584; winter, 1997, p. 147; summer, 1999, review of *Am Felsfenster Morgens,* p. 523; autumn, 1999, review of *Die Fahrt im Einbaum,* p. 728; winter, 2001, Scott Abbott, review of *Unter Tränen fragend,* p. 78; April-June, 2003, Erich Wolfgang Skwara, review of *Der Bildverlust, oder Durch die Sierra de Gredos,* p. 77.

ONLINE

World Socialist Web Site, http://www.wsws.org/ (August 11, 1999), Bernd Reinhardt, "The Austrian Writer Peter Handke, European Public Opinion, and the War in Yugoslavia."

*   *   *

HANDLER, Daniel
   See SNICKET, Lemony

*   *   *

HARDWICK, Elizabeth 1916-
   (Elizabeth Bruce Hardwick)

PERSONAL: Born July 27, 1916, in Lexington, KY; daughter of Eugene Allen and Mary (Ramsey) Hardwick; married Robert Lowell (a poet), July 28, 1949 (divorced, 1972); children: Harriet. *Education:* University of Kentucky, A.B., 1938, M.A., 1939; Columbia University, graduate study, 1939-41.

ADDRESSES: Home—15 West 67th St., New York, NY 10023.

CAREER: Writer. Barnard College, New York, NY, adjunct associate professor of English.

MEMBER: American Academy and Institute of Arts and Letters.

AWARDS, HONORS: Guggenheim fellowship in fiction, 1948; George Jean Nathan Award for dramatic criticism (first woman recipient), 1966; National Academy and Institute of Arts and Letters award in literature, 1974; National Book Critics Circle Award nomination, 1980, for *Sleepless Nights;* Gold Medal for criticism, American Academy of Arts and Letters, 1993; Iva Sandrof Award for Lifetime Achievement in Publishing, National Book Critics Circle, 1995.

WRITINGS:

The Ghostly Lover (novel), Harcourt (New York, NY), 1945, reprinted, Ecco Press (New York, NY), 1989.
The Simple Truth (novel), Harcourt (New York, NY), 1955, reprinted, Ecco Press (New York, NY), 1982.
(Editor) *The Selected Letters of William James,* Farrar, Straus (New York, NY), 1960, reprinted, Anchor Books (New York, NY), 1993.
A View of My Own: Essays in Literature and Society, Farrar, Straus (New York, NY), 1962, reprinted, Ecco Press (New York, NY), 1982.
Seduction and Betrayal: Women and Literature (essays), Weidenfeld and Nicolson (London, England), 1974, New York Review of Books (New York, NY), 2001.
A New America?: Essays, Norton (New York, NY), 1978.
Sleepless Nights (novel), Random House (New York, NY), 1979, reprinted, New York Review of Books (New York, NY), 2001.
Bartleby in Manhattan and Other Essays, Weidenfeld and Nicolson (London, England), 1983, reprinted, Vintage Books (New York, NY), 1984.
(Editor, with Robert Atwan) *The Best American Essays 1986,* Ticknor & Fields (New York, NY), 1986.
Sight Readings: Essays on Writers, Biographies about Them, and Public Happenings Here and There, Random House (New York, NY), 1998.
American Fictions, Modern Library (New York, NY), 1999.
Herman Melville, Viking (New York, NY), 2000.

Work appears in numerous anthologies, including two volumes of *O. Henry Memorial Award Prize Stories* and six volumes of *The Best American Short Stories* series. Editor, "Rediscovered Fiction by American Women: A Personal Selection" series, Ayer, beginning 1977. Contributor to periodicals, including *Partisan Review, New Yorker, Yale Review,* and *Harper's.* Founder and advisory editor, *New York Review of Books.*

SIDELIGHTS: An accomplished essayist and novelist, Elizabeth Hardwick is known "primarily for brilliant literary and social criticism, which has graced the pages of many of the country's leading liberal journals, most notably the *Partisan Review* and the *New York Review of Books,*" according to Joseph J. Branin, writing in the *Dictionary of Literary Biography.* Hardwick began her literary career in 1945 with the novel *The Ghostly Lover,* which centers on one Marian Coleman. "Throughout the novel, Marian is presented as a profoundly lonely young person," noted Branin, adding that Hardwick's protagonist searches for intimacy in her personal relationships "but finds it impossible to break through the separateness of the characters in the novel." According to Carol Simpson Stern in *Contemporary Novelists, The Ghostly Lover* "offers telling glimpses into her life, the life of her restless parents, the hot, lazy days in the South, the grubby days studying in New York, and the dreams of the ghostly men who pursue her."

While *The Ghostly Lover* garnered mixed critical reaction, soon after its publication Hardwick was contacted by Philip Rahv, an editor of the avant-garde *Partisan Review,* who asked Hardwick to become a contributor. "She accepted the offer eagerly and thus began her long and successful career as a social and literary critic," Branin explained. As Hardwick's reputation as a writer grew, so did her fame outside the editorial offices. She married noted American poet Robert Lowell in 1949, a union that lasted until 1972, when Lowell divorced Hardwick to marry Irish author Caroline Blackwood. Lowell returned to America and to Hardwick in 1977, only a year before he died of heart failure. As Hardwick recalled to a *New York Times* reporter, Lowell was "the most extraordinary person I have ever known, like no one else—unplaceable, unaccountable."

Hardwick's second novel, *The Simple Truth,* tells the story of speculation and accusation surrounding a sensational murder trial. "Tightly plotted, probing the motives behind a frightful act, the novel examines the death of a beautiful college girl, Betty Jane Henderson, who died in her boyfriend's rooming-house, after hours," explained Stern. The murder trial serves as the focus of the book, and Hardwick views it "from numerous perspectives. . . . The truth about the act, late at night, in a rooming-house where two lovers frolicked and struggled, ultimately emerges, but equally as interesting is the picture of the psyches of the characters who become caught up in the trial."

The author's third novel, *Sleepless Nights,* "is a difficult work to classify," allowed Branin. Some critics have viewed the work as autobiographical because the story centers on a writer named Elizabeth, who grew up in Kentucky and moved to Manhattan. In the course of the story the narrator "remembers certain people and places from her past," as Branin explained adding that the narrator's "compassion for her old acquaintances and her careful observations as she brings these memories to life give the work its power and unity." "The autobiographical component of the novel is openly confronted, and handled effectively," added Stern. "Roaming like an insomniac from one recollection to another, the book continually surprises us with its fleeting memories of rooms we have all known, feelings we have felt, losses we have never remedied." Stern dubbed *Sleepless Nights* "a queer blend of autobiography and fiction. Hardwick's decision to create a persona with her own name heightens our sense of how life informs fiction. The Elizabeth of this book is very nearly the Elizabeth Hardwick who lives, the woman who is a career journalist, writer, reviewer. . . . The memories and imaginings of the persona curl about the lives of deprived souls, of which Elizabeth is one."

Perhaps more well known than her novels, Hardwick's essays and critical writings have earned her a substantial reputation. Her 1974 collection, *Seduction and Betrayal: Women and Literature,* caught the attention of several critics, including Rosemary Dinnage, who remarked in a *Times Literary Supplement* review that the book "is so original, so sly and strange, but the pleasure is embedded in the style, in the way [the author] flicks the English language around like a whip." Hardwick's concern in *Seduction and Betrayal,* according to Dinnage, "is to present her own angry and witty view of the sexes, and for this she has more scope with the fictional beings and the companions of writers than with the great creative women, for these less easily align themselves with the victims." Hardwick "is no handwringer," declared *Books and Bookmen* critic Jean Stubbs. "She is a literary surgeon, admirably equipped to expose the nerves." And in the opinion of Joan Didion, writing in the *New York Times Book Review,* "Perhaps no one has written more acutely and poignantly about the ways in which women compensate for their relative physiological inferiority."

By the time Hardwick's collection *Bartleby in Manhattan and Other Essays* was published, she was almost universally acclaimed as a major essayist, prompting *New York Times* reviewer Christopher Lehmann-Haupt to remark, "One is interested in anything that Elizabeth Hardwick writes. That is a given." For this volume of social and literary musings, however, Lehmann-Haupt had some reservations: "The subjects . . . give one a moment or two of pause. The atmosphere in the South during the civil rights movement of the 1960s? The significance of Martin Luther King, Jr. and of Lee Harvey Oswald and his family?" "It isn't so much that we've lost interest in these topics," the critic continued, "as that they've become as familiar to us by now as our fingers and our toes." Another reviewer found more to recommend in *Bartleby in Manhattan and Other Essays.* "Hardwick's [concerns] have two qualities that make her one of our finest critics: a heart that wants to be moved and a critical intelligence that refuses to indulge it," maintained *Los Angeles Times Book Review* critic Richard Eder. "Much that she deals with produces more disquiet in her than reward; she looks for values in the fiery writing of the '60s and the distanced writing of the '70s and finds them poor or limited. Our reward is the record of her search." "Whatever her subject," claimed novelist Anne Tyler, writing in *New Republic,* Hardwick "has a gift for coming up with descriptions so thoughtfully selected, so exactly right, that they strike the reader as inevitable." As Tyler also noted, "Mere aptitude of language, of course, is not sufficient. What makes *Bartleby in Manhattan* memorable is the sense of the author's firm character. 'Pull yourself together,' she says briskly to a racist who tells her he feels sick at the sight of an integrated crowd."

More of Hardwick's essays on literature have been collected as *American Fictions.* The subjects range from mid-twentieth-century poet Sylvia Plath to writer Truman Capote, from Norman Mailer to Edith Wharton. In "astute, informative, and engaging narratives," Hardwick explores the writers and their work, according to Julia Burch in *Library Journal.* Other critics also praised her unique blend of biography and incisive literary analysis, including a *Publishers Weekly* reviewer who concluded: "Hardwick's smart, eloquent discussions of important works of American fiction bear little resemblance to the normally arid field of literary criticism. Indeed, these fine essays are often as satisfying as the works and authors inspiring them."

In *Herman Melville* Hardwick offers a short but perceptive biography of one of America's greatest writers. The author of *Moby-Dick* was an intensely private man, with a life "barely public enough for any biographer to pin him down," in the words of a writer for *Publishers Weekly,* who concluded that, despite the lack of solid material, Hardwick is somehow "able to convey both the complexity of the man as well as the inherent impossibility of the biographer's task to fully elucidate the life of a multifarious individual." In twelve chapters, organized more along thematic than chronological lines, Hardwick examines Melville's successes and failures, his perennial financial troubles, his difficult family life, and his homoeroticism, as expressed in his writings and his profound friendship with another American writer, Nathaniel Hawthorne. The central focus of her book, however, is Melville's literature. Reviewing the book for *Salon.com,* Maria Russo concluded: "Perhaps Hardwick's most extraordinary achievement in *Herman Melville* is how she conveys a subtle understanding of Melville's heart and spirit while insisting that she wouldn't dare try to grasp them. We get a glimpse of great genius that's satisfying even as it leaves the mystery intact." A reviewer in the *Economist* writes, "Her readings of Melville are alive with detail and analysis—a surprising word here, a dying cadence there, the shapes and structure of plot and meaning—but she is above all conscious of the inexplicable in his work."

In 2001, the *New York Review of Books* published new editions of *Sleepless Nights* and *Seduction and Betrayal: Women and Literature* in a boxed set. "Both books are unforeseeably wonderful," enthused Gabriele Annan in a *Spectator* review, "funny and sad, penetrating as a scan and full of passages of such breathtaking perception and felicitous wording that it would be a luxury to be able to remember them verbatim for the rest of one's life." "Hardwick's writing is so masterly (and masterful)," added Doris Anderson in *Herizons,* "that it seems more sensible to quote than describe it." For many critics and readers Hardwick remains what *New Republic* contributor Joan Joffe Hall dubbed "the voice of tough-minded gentility." "She inspires confidence because she seems just like the reader," Hall added, "a shade smarter perhaps, able to turn the commonplace into revelation, talking in someone's living room with an earnest casualness beyond personality. It's the quality most of us aspire to."

BIOGRAPHICAL AND CRITICAL SOURCES:

BOOKS

Contemporary Literary Criticism, Volume 13, Thomson Gale (Detroit, MI), 1980.

Contemporary Novelists, 6th edition, St. James Press (Detroit, MI), 1996.

Dictionary of Literary Biography, Volume 6: *American Novelists since World War II,* Thomson Gale (Detroit, MI), 1980.

Ward, William S., *A Literary History of Kentucky,* University of Tennessee Press (Knoxville, TN), 1988.

PERIODICALS

American Book Review, March-April, 1985.

Antioch Review, fall, 1999, review of *American Fictions,* p. 575.

Atlantic, June, 1979.

Booklist, June 1, 1998, review of *Sight Readings: Essays on Writers, Biographies about Them, and Public Happenings Here and There,* p. 1706; June 1, 2000, Donna Seaman, review of *Herman Melville,* p. 1835.

Books and Bookmen, January, 1976.

Chicago Tribune, November 25, 1986.

Economist, August 26, 2000, review of *Herman Melville,* p. 73.

Entertainment Weekly, August 14, 1998, review of *Sight Readings,* p. 76.

Herizons, fall, 2002, Doris Anderson, review of *Seduction and Betrayal: Women and Literature,* p. 45.

Hudson Review, winter, 1974-1975.

Kirkus Reviews, June 1, 1998, review of *Sight Readings,* p. 793.

Library Journal, July, 1998, review of *Sight Readings,* p. 90; October 15, 1999, Julia Burch, review of *American Fictions,* p. 70; July, 2000, Henry L. Carrigan, review of *Herman Melville,* p. 91.

London Review of Books, November 17, 1983.

Los Angeles Times Book Review, May 29, 1983, Richard Eder, review of *Bartleby in Manhattan and Other Essays;* September 20, 1998, review of *Sight Readings,* p. 8.

Nation, June 14, 1975.

New Republic, May 25, 1974, Joan Joffe Hall, review of *Seduction and Betrayal;* June 20, 1983, Anne Tyler, review of *Bartleby in Manhattan and Other Essays.*

New Statesman, August 17, 1979.

Newsweek, June 17, 1974; May 30, 1983.

New York Review of Books, January 27, 1974; April 29, 1979; September 24, 1998, review of *Sight Readings,* p. 4; July 20, 2000, John Leonard, review of *Herman Melville,* p. 4.

New York Times, April 2, 1982; May 24, 1983; July 30, 2000, Erica Da Costa, review of *Herman Melville.*

New York Times Book Review, May 5, 1974, Joan Didion, review of *Seduction and Betrayal;* June 12, 1983, Christopher Lehmann-Haupt, review of

Bartleby in Manhattan and Other Essays; July 26, 1998, review of *Sight Readings,* p. 10; December 6, 1998, review of *Sight Readings,* p. 88.

Publishers Weekly, May 25, 1998, review of *Sight Readings,* p. 70; November 8, 1999, review of *American Fictions,* p. 56; May 29, 2000, review of *Herman Melville,* p. 62.

Sewanee Review, fall, 1984; January, 1999, review of *Sight Readings,* p. 114.

Spectator, December 29, 2001, Gabriele Annan, review of *Sleepless Nights* and *Seduction and Betrayal,* p. 34.

Times Literary Supplement, November 29, 1974, Rosemary Dinnage, review of *Seduction and Betrayal.*

Village Voice, May 7, 1979.

Washington Post Book World, May 12, 1974; May 29, 1983.

World Literature Today, spring, 1980.

ONLINE

KYLIT, http://www.arh.eku.edu/ (December 3, 2000), Melissa Turner, "Elizabeth Hardwick."

Salon.com, http://www.salon.com/ (July 26, 2000), Maria Russo, review of *Herman Melville.*

*   *   *

HARDWICK, Elizabeth Bruce
See HARDWICK, Elizabeth

*   *   *

HARGRAVE, Leonie
See DISCH, Thomas M.

*   *   *

HARJO, Joy 1951-

PERSONAL: Born May 9, 1951, in Tulsa, OK; daughter of Allen W. and Wynema (Baker) Foster; children: Phil, Rainy Dawn. *Education:* University of New Mexico, B.A., 1976; University of Iowa, M.F.A., 1978; attended Anthropology Film Center, Santa Fe, 1982. *Hobbies and other interests:* Performing on the saxophone with band Joy Harjo and Poetic Justice.

ADDRESSES: Home—1140-D, Alewa Dr., Honolulu, HI 96817. *E-mail*—katcvpoet@aol.com.

CAREER: Institute of American Indian Arts, Santa Fe, NM, instructor, 1978-79, 1983-84; Arizona State University, Tempe, lecturer in creative writing and poetry, 1980-81; University of Colorado, Boulder, assistant professor, 1985-88; University of Arizona, Tucson, associate professor, 1988-90; University of New Mexico, Albuquerque, professor, 1991-97. Visiting professor of creative writing at the University of Montana, 1985, at University of Hawaii at Manoa, 2003. Writer and consultant for Native American Public Broadcasting Consortium, National Indian Youth Council, and National Endowment for the Arts, all 1980-83. Member of steering committee of En'owkin Centre International School of Writing. Writer-in-residence at schools, including Navajo Community College, 1978; University of Alaska Prison Project, 1981; and Institute of Alaska Native Arts, 1984. Recordings with band, Joy Harjo and Poetic Justice, include *Furious Light,* 1986, *The Woman Who Fell from the Sky,* 1994, and *Letter from the End of the Twentieth Century,* 1997.

MEMBER: PEN (member of advisory board), PEN New Mexico (member of advisory board).

AWARDS, HONORS: Academy of American Poetry Award and University of New Mexico first-place poetry award, both 1976; National Endowment for the Arts fellow, 1978; named one of the Outstanding Young Women in America, 1978, 1984; first place in poetry, Santa Fe Festival for the Arts, 1980; Arizona Commission on the Arts Creative Writing fellow, 1989; American Indian Distinguished Achievement Award, 1990; Josephine Miles Award for excellence in literature, PEN Oakland, William Carlos Williams award, Poetry Society of America, and American Book Award, Before Columbus Foundation, all 1991, for *In Mad Love and War;* Wittner Bynner Poetry fellowship, 1994; Lifetime Achievement award, Native Writers' Circle of the Americas, 1995; Oklahoma Book Arts award, 1995, for *The Woman Who Fell from the Sky;* Delmore Schwartz Memorial award, and Mountains and Plains Booksellers' award, both 1995, both for *In Mad Love and War;* Bravo Award, Albuquerque Arts Alliance, 1996; New Mexico Governor's Award for excellence in the arts, 1997; Lila Wallace/*Reader's Digest* Fund Writers' Award, 1998; National Council on the Arts, presidential appointment, 1998; 1998 Outstanding Musical Achievement Award presented by The First Americans in the Arts Council; Honorary doctorate, St. Mary-in-the-Woods College, 1998; Charlotte Zolotow Award, Highly Commended Book, 2001, and Wordcraft Circle of Native Writers and Storytellers Writer of the Year Award, both for *The Good Luck Cat;* Arrell Gibson Award for Lifetime Achievement, Oklahoma Center for the Book, 2003; Oklahoma Book Award, 2003, for *How We Became Human.*

WRITINGS:

POETRY

The Last Song (chapbook; also see below), Puerto Del Sol Press (Las Cruces, NM), 1975.
What Moon Drove Me to This? (contains *The Last Song*), I. Reed Books (New York, NY), 1980.
She Had Some Horses, Thunder's Mouth Press (New York, NY), 1983.
Secrets from the Center of the World, illustrated by Steven Strom, University of Arizona Press (Tucson, AZ), 1989.
In Mad Love and War, Wesleyan University Press (Middletown, CT), 1990.
The Woman Who Fell from the Sky, Norton (New York, NY), 1994.
A Map to the Next World: Poetry and Tales, Norton (New York, NY), 2000.
How We Became Human: New and Selected Poems, 1975-2001, Norton (New York, NY), 2002.

OTHER

(Editor with Gloria Bird) *Reinventing the Enemy's Language: North American Native Women's Writing,* Norton (New York, NY), 1997.
The Good Luck Cat (children's fiction), illustrated by Paul Lee, Harcourt (San Diego, CA), 2000.

Also author of the film script *Origin of Apache Crown Dance,* Silver Cloud Video, 1985; coauthor of the film script *The Beginning,* Native American Broadcasting Consortium; author of television plays, including *We Are One, Uhonho,* 1984, *Maiden of Deception Pass,* 1985, *I Am Different from My Brother,* 1986, and *The Runaway,* 1986. Contributor to numerous anthologies and to several literary journals, including *Conditions, Beloit Poetry Journal, River Styx, Tyuoyi,* and *Y'Bird.*

WORK IN PROGRESS: A collection of personal essays.

SIDELIGHTS: Strongly influenced by her Muskogee Creek heritage, feminist and social concerns, and her background in the arts, Joy Harjo frequently incorporates Native American myths, symbols, and values into her writing. Her poetry additionally emphasizes the

Southwest landscape and the need for remembrance and transcendence. She once commented, "I feel strongly that I have a responsibility to all the sources that I am: to all past and future ancestors, to my home country, to all places that I touch down on and that are myself, to all voices, all women, all of my tribe, all people, all earth, and beyond that to all beginnings and endings. In a strange kind of sense [writing] frees me to believe in myself, to be able to speak, to have voice, because I have to; it is my survival." In answer to a question from Pam Kingsbury for the *Southern Scribe,* Harjo remarked, "I am most often defined by others as: Native American, feminist, western, southwestern, primarily. I define myself as a human writer, poet and musician, a Muskoke writer (etc.)—and I'm most definitely of the west, southwest, Oklahoma and now my path includes LA and Honolulu . . . it throws the definition, skews it. It would be easier to be seen, I believe, if I fit into an easy category, as in for instance: The New York School, the Black Mountain School, the Beats—or even as in more recently, the slam poets. But I don't."

Harjo's work is largely autobiographical, informed by her love of the natural world and her preoccupation with survival and the limitations of language. Her first volume of poetry was published in 1975 as a nine-poem chapbook titled *The Last Song.* These early compositions, mainly set in Oklahoma and New Mexico, reveal Harjo's remarkable power and insight, especially as evident in the title poem, "The Last Song," and in "3 AM." Harjo wrote in "3 AM" about an exasperating airport experience: "the attendant doesn't know / that third mesa / is a part of the center / of the world / and who are we just two indians / at three in the morning trying to find our way back home." Commenting on "3 AM" in *World Literature Today,* John Scarry wrote that the poem "is a work filled with ghosts from the Native American past, figures seen operating in an alien culture that is itself a victim of fragmentation. . . . Here the Albuquerque airport is both modern America's technology and moral nature—and both clearly have failed. Together they cannot get these Indians to their destination, a failure that stretches from our earliest history to the sleek desks of our most up-to-date airline offices."

What Moon Drove Me to This?, Harjo's first full-length volume of poetry, appeared four years later and includes the entire contents of *The Last Song.* "With this collection," C. Renee Field wrote in the *Dictionary of Literary Biography,* "Harjo continued to refine her ability to find and voice the deep spiritual truths underneath everyday experiences, especially for the Native American." In an interview with Laura Coltelli in *Winged Words: American Indian Writers Speak,* Harjo shares the creative process behind her poetry: "I begin with the seed of an emotion, a place, and then move from there. . . . I no longer see the poem as an ending point, perhaps more the end of a journey, an often long journey that can begin years earlier, say with the blur of the memory of the sun on someone's cheek, a certain smell, an ache, and will culminate years later in a poem, sifted through a point, a lake in my heart through which language must come."

The search for freedom and self-actualization considered central to Harjo's work, is particularly noted in her third book of poetry, *She Had Some Horses,* in which she frequently incorporates prayer-chants and animal imagery. For example, in "The Black Room," a poem about childhood rape, Harjo repeats the mantric line "She thought she woke up." In the title poem, "She Had Some Horses," one of Harjo's most highly regarded and anthologized poems, she describes the "horses" within a woman who struggles to reconcile contradictory personal feelings and experiences to achieve a sense of oneness. The poem concludes: "She had some horses she loved. / She had some horses she hated. / These were the same horse." As Field observed, "The horses are spirits, neither male nor female, and, through them, clear truths can be articulated." As Scarry noted, "Harjo is clearly a highly political and feminist Native American, but she is even more the poet of myth and the subconscious; her images and landscapes owe as much to the vast stretches of our hidden mind as they do to her native Southwest."

Nature is central to Harjo's works, as evident in her 1989 prose poetry collection *Secrets from the Center of the World.* Each poem in this volume is accompanied by a color photograph of the Southwest landscape, which, as Margaret Randall noted in *Women's Review of Books,* works to "create an evocative little gem, intensely personal, hauntingly universal." Offering praise for the volume in the *Village Voice,* Dan Bellm wrote, "*Secrets* is a rather unlikely experiment that turned into a satisfying and beautiful book. . . . As Harjo notes, the pictures 'emphasize the "not-separate" that is within and that moves harmoniously upon the landscape.'" According to Randall, "There is no alteration in these photographs, nor do the poems lack a word or possess one too many. Language and visual image are perfectly tuned and balanced, producing an experience in which neither illustrates the other but each needs its counterpart." Bellm similarly added, "The book's best poems enhance this play of scale and perspective, suggesting in very few words the relationship between a human life and millennial history."

Her best-known volume, the multiaward-winning *In Mad Love and War,* is more overtly concerned with

politics, tradition, remembrance, and the transformational aspects of poetry. In the first section, which relates various acts of violence, including the murder of an Indian leader as well as others' attempts to deny Harjo her heritage, Harjo explores the difficulties many Native Americans face in modern American society: "we have too many stories to carry on our backs like houses, we have struggled too long to let the monsters steal our sleep, sleep, go to sleep. But I never woke up. Dogs have been nipping at my heels since I learned to walk. I was taught to not dance for a rotten supper on the plates of my enemies. My mother taught me well." The second half of the book frequently emphasizes personal relationships and change.

"Harjo's range of emotion and imagery in this volume is truly remarkable," wrote Scarry. "She achieves intimacy and power in ways that send a reader to every part of the poetic spectrum for comparisons and for some frame of reference." In the poem "Autobiography," a mother describes to her daughter how God created humans to inhabit the earth. In another, "Javelina," Harjo invokes the strong voice of "one born of a blood who wrestled the whites for freedom, and I have since lived dangerously in a diminished system." Leslie Ullman noted in the *Kenyon Review,* "Like a magician, Harjo draws power from overwhelming circumstance and emotion by submitting to them, celebrating them, letting her voice and vision move in harmony with the ultimate laws of paradox and continual change." Commenting on "Javelina," Ullman added that Harjo's "stance is not so much that of a representative of a culture as it is the more generative one of a storyteller whose stories resurrect memory, myth, and private struggles that have been overlooked, and who thus restores vitality to the culture at large." Praising the volume in the *Prairie Schooner,* Kathleen West wrote, "*In Mad Love and War* has the power of beauty and prophecy and all the hope of love poised at its passionate beginning. It allows us to enter the place 'we haven't imagined' and allows us to imagine what we will do when we are there."

In 1994, Harjo followed *In Mad Love and War* with *The Woman Who Fell from the Sky,* another book of prose poetry. The title is based on an Iroquois myth about the descent of a female creator. As Frank Allen noted in *Library Journal,* Harjo is concerned with the vying forces of creation and destruction in contemporary society, embodied in such symbolism as wolves and northern lights contrasted with alcoholism and the Vietnam War. *Booklist* reviewer Pat Monaghan praised the poems as "stunning, mature, wholehearted, musical," and the collection together as a "brilliant, unforgettable book."

A Map to the Next World: Poetry and Tales includes a long introduction and much commentary with the poems. As a *Publishers Weekly* reviewer described, "A facing-page dialogue between poetry and prose, the absorbing long poem 'Returning from the Enemy,' attempts to reconcile memories of the poet's absent father with memories of her own children, of ancestors and of 'each trigger of grass:' 'We want to know if it's possible to separate and come back together, as the river licking the dock merges with the sea a few blocks away. / Long-legged birds negotiate the shore for food. / I am not as graceful as these souls.'"

How We Became Human: New and Selected Poems, 1975-2001, in the words of a *Publishers Weekly* reviewer, "show the remarkable progression of a writer determined to reconnect with her past and make sense of her present, drawing together the brutalities of contemporary reservation life with the beauty and sensibility of Native American culture and mythology." Including poems from every previous collection, *How We Became Human,* according to Pam Kingsbury of the *Library Journal,* "explores the role of the artist in society, the quest for love, the links among the arts, what constitutes family, and what it means to be human. Using the chant/myth/storytelling forms of her ancestors, she draws the reader into the awareness that 'one people is related to another.'" The same *Publishers Weekly* critic remarked that Harjo "contends that poetry is not only a way to save the sanity of those who have been oppressed to the point of madness, but that it is a tool to rebuild communities and, ultimately, change the world: 'All acts of kindness are lights in the war for justice.' Alive with compassion, pain and love, this book is unquestionably an act of kindness." Harjo is currently writing a book of stories that is half-memoir, half-fiction and working on a book project with Laguna Pueblo photographer Lee Marmon.

Harjo has also branched out into children's fiction with *The Good Luck Cat. School Library Journal* reviewer Joy Fleischhacker recommended the story of a cat that has outlived eight of its nine lives: "Harjo's text presents some striking images while still maintaining a believably childlike tone. The realistic acrylic paintings beautifully convey both action scenes (Woogie falling from a tree) and quiet moments (the hopeful girl placing her missing pet's bowl and toys on the back step). Lee has a knack for capturing the cat's agility and suppleness. Details woven into the story and pictures provide a glimpse of the protagonist's Native American heritage." A *Publishers Weekly* reviewer observed, "Harjo combines a childlike voice with a command of detail and imagery ('When I pet her she purrs as if she has a drum near her heart')."

In addition to her fictional works, Harjo has done much to popularize other Native American women writers. An interview with Laura Coltelli, published as *Spiral of Memory: Interviews: Joy Harjo,* appeared in 1997 and offers additional insight into the writer's background, art, and views on poetry. And in *Reinventing the Enemy's Language: North American Native Women's Writing,* Harjo presents a collection of stories that act to spur readers to social and political activism. The works, from such authors as Louise Erdrich and diarist Mary Brave Bird, present a new genre, according to *Progressive* contributor Mark Anthony Rolo, but rather than faddish, it is "a new sphere of storytelling, part of a larger hidden culture. These writers immunize us against the plague of marginalization. Their growing acceptance is a shift away from the Western literary canon. Perhaps this is the kind of politics Harjo and Bird should lobby for in the second volume of North American native women's writings."

Consistently praised for the depth and thematic concerns in her writings, Harjo has emerged as a major figure in contemporary American poetry. Sometimes, for taking a position on numerous political, social, economic, and humanitarian issues, she has received criticism for being overly "politically correct." But, as Field noted, "She does not tell her reader how to feel but simply tells the truth she sees. Harjo's poetry is not so much about 'correctness' as it is about continuance and survival." While Harjo's work is often set in the Southwest, emphasizes the plight of the individual, and reflects Creek values, myths, and beliefs, her oeuvre has universal relevance. Bellm asserted: "Harjo's work draws from the river of Native tradition, but it also swims freely in the currents of Anglo-American verse— feminist poetry of personal/political resistance, deep-image poetry of the unconscious, 'new-narrative' explorations of story and rhythm in prose-poem form." According to Field, "To read the poetry of Joy Harjo is to hear the voice of the earth, to see the landscape of time and timelessness, and, most important, to get a glimpse of people who struggle to understand, to know themselves, and to survive."

Paula Gunn Allen in *The Sacred Hoop* stated that Harjo's "thrust, in her work . . . is toward reconciliation of the polarities into an order that is harmonious, balanced, and whole." Harjo "articulates her certain understanding of the spherical unity of the universe, its essential 'spiritness,' . . . in her poetry" and, quoting her: "I have this image. It's not a generator, it's not a power plant. But it's like they have these different points in between. So it's a place, it's a poem, like a globular, like a circle with center points all over. And poems are like that. They have circuits."

Commenting on her writing as a means of survival, Harjo told Coltelli, "I don't believe I would be alive today if it hadn't been for writing. There were times when I was conscious of holding onto a pen and letting the words flow, painful and from the gut, to keep from letting go of it all. Now, this was when I was much younger, and full of self-hatred. Writing helped me give voice to turn around a terrible silence that was killing me. And on a larger level, if we, as Indian people, Indian women, keep silent, then we will disappear, at least in this level of reality." Field noted, "As Harjo has continued to refine her craft, her poems have become visions, answers to age-old questions, keys to understanding the complex nature of twentieth-century American life, and guides to the past and the future."

Harjo told *CA:* "I agree with Gide that most of what is created is beyond us, is from that source of utter creation, the Creator, or God. We are technicians here on Earth, but also co-creators. I'm still amazed. And I still say, after writing poetry for all this time, and now music, that ultimately humans have a small hand in it. We serve it. We have to put ourselves in the way of it, and get out of the way of ourselves. And we have to hone our craft so that the form in which we hold our poems, our songs in attracts the best.

"My particular road is not about taking established forms and developing them. I admire a finely constructed sonnet but I do not wish to work in that Euro-classical form. I honor that direction, but I am working to find my own place and one who is multicultural, multiracial. I am influenced by Muscogean forms, European and African forms, as well as others that have deeply moved me, say for instance, Navajo. When I began writing poetry as a painting major at the University of New Mexico, I was learning Navajo language. It influenced me deeply because intimate to the language were the shapes of the landscape, the history. I became aware of layers of meaning marked by sandhills, by the gestures of the earth.

"African-American influences in poetry and music have been critical to my development as a writer and musician. This is not something new. There is history and a relationship between Africans and Muscogean peoples begun in the southeastern U.S. We've influenced each other, yet this influence is rarely talked about. I can hear the African influence in our stomp dance music, and can hear Muscogean influence in jazz, the blues, and rock. It's all there.

"I have also taken up saxophone and perform professionally with my band. I am asked often about how music has informed my poetry, changed it. It's difficult to say exactly, except to acknowledge that of course it has all along. The first poetry I heard and recognized as pure poetry was the improvised line of a trumpet player on a jazz tune on the radio when I was four years old. That was it. I've been trying to get it right ever since. Sometimes I hear the origin of that line when I'm at the stomp grounds. One of these days I'll be able to sing it, write it." Harjo's interest in music has taken the form of combining poetry and song, poetry and saxophone, and she tours with her band, Poetic Justice.

BIOGRAPHICAL AND CRITICAL SOURCES:

BOOKS

Balassi, William, John F. Crawford, and Annie O. Eysturoy, editors, *This Is about Vision: Interviews with Southwestern Writers,* University of New Mexico Press (Albuquerque, NM), 1990.

Brogan, Jacqueline Vaught, and Cordelia Chavez Candelaria, editors, *Women Poets of the Americas: Toward a Pan-American Gathering,* University of Notre Dame Press (Notre Dame, IN), 1999.

Bruchac, Joseph, editor, *Survival This Way: Interviews with American Indian Poets,* University of Arizona Press (Tucson, AZ), 1987.

Bryan, Sharon, ed., *Where We Stand: Women Poets on Literary Tradition,* Norton (New York, NY), 1993.

Buelens, Gert, and Ernst Rudin, editors, *Deferring a Dream: Literary Sub-Versions of the American Columbiad,* Birkhauser (Boston, MA), 1994.

Coltelli, Laura, editor, *Winged Words: American Indian Writers Speak,* University of Nebraska Press (Lincoln, NE), 1990.

Coltelli, Laura, editor, *Native American Literatures.* SEU (Pisa, Italy), 1994.

Coltelli, Laura, editor, *The Spiral of Memory: Interviews: Joy Harjo,* University of Michigan Press (Ann Arbor, MI), 1996.

Contemporary Literary Criticism, Volume 83, Thomson Gale (Detroit, MI), 1994.

Contemporary Women Poets, St. James Press (Detroit, MI), 1997.

Dictionary of Literary Biography, Thomson Gale (Detroit, MI), Volume 120: *American Poets since World War II,* 1992, Volume 175: *Native American Writers of the United States,* 1997.

Gunn Allen, Paula, *The Sacred Hoop: Recovering the Feminine in American Indian Traditions,* Beacon Press (Boston, MA), 1986.

Harjo, Joy, *She Had Some Horses,* Thunder's Mouth Press (New York, NY), 1983.

Harjo, Joy, *In Mad Love and War,* Wesleyan University Press, 1990.

Hinton, Laura, and Cynthia Hogue, editors, *We Who Love to Be Astonished: Experimental Women's Writing and Performance Poetics,* University of Alabama Press (Tuscaloosa, AL), 2002.

Hobson, Geary, editor, *The Remembered Earth: An Anthology of Contemporary Native American Literature,* Red Earth, 1979.

Keller, Lynn, and Cristanne Miller, editors, *Feminist Measures: Soundings in Poetry and Theory,* University of Michigan Press (Ann Arbor, MI), 1994.

Norwood, Vera, and Janice Monk, editors, *The Desert Is No Lady: Southwestern Landscapes in Women's Writing and Art,* Yale University Press (New Haven, CT), 1987.

Pettit, Rhonda, *Joy Harjo,* Boise State University (Boise, ID), 1998.

Swann, Brian, and Arnold Krupat, editors, *I Tell You Now: Autobiographical Essays by Native American Writers,* University of Nebraska Press (Lincoln, NE), 1987.

PERIODICALS

Albuquerque Journal, February 7, 1997 p. E13; May 11, 1997, p. C9; September 15, 2002, p. F8.

Albuquerque Tribune, February 7, 1997, p. B4; January 21, 1998, p. C6.

American Book Review, April-May, 1991, pp. 10-11.

American Indian Quarterly, spring, 1983, p. 27; spring, 1991, p. 273; fall, 1992, p. 533; winter, 1995, p. 1; spring, 2000, p. 200.

American Studies International, June, 1997, p. 88.

Belles Lettres, summer, 1991, pp. 7-8; summer, 1994, p. 46.

Bloomsbury Review, March-April, 1996; November-December, 1997, p. 18.

Booklist, November 15, 1994, p. 573; June 1, 1997, p. 1649; February 1, 2000, p. 1005.

Boston Herald, April 10, 2003, p. 067.

Buffalo News (Buffalo, NY), October 4, 1998, p. G6.

Current Biography, August, 2001, p. 50.

ELF: Eclectic Literary Forum, fall, 1995, p. 44.

Guardian (London, England), October 18, 2003, p. 7.

Kenyon Review, spring, 1991, pp. 179-83; summer, 1993, pp. 57-66.

Legacy: A Journal of American Women Writers, 2002, p. 106.

Library Journal, October 15, 1994, p. 72; November 15, 1994, p. 70; June 1, 1997, p. 100; June 15, 2002, p. 70.

Los Angeles Times, February 10, 1989, section 5, pp. 1, 14-16.

MELUS, spring, 1989-90; fall, 1993, p. 41; summer, 1994, p. 35.

Ms., July-August, 1991; September-October, 1991, p. 73.

Native American Literatures: Forum, 1989, p. 185.

North Dakota Quarterly, spring, 1985, pp. 220-234.

Oregonian (Portland, OR), October 19, 1998.

Poetry, August, 1996, pp. 281-302.

Poets and Writers Magazine, 1993, p. 23.

Prairie Schooner, summer, 1992, pp. 128-132.

Progressive, December, 1997, p. 42.

PSA News: Newsletter of the Poetry Society of America, winter, 1993, p. 17.

Publishers Weekly, November 28, 1994, p. 54; November 28, 1994, p. 54; April 21, 1997, p. 57; January 10, 2000, p. 58; May 22, 2000, p. 92; June 17, 2002, p. 58.

Religion and Literature, spring, 1994, p. 57; summer, 2001, p. 59.

Rochester Democrat and Chronicle (Rochester, NY), March 29, 2000, p. 1c.

San Francisco Chronicle, September 7, 1997, p. 2.

School Library Journal, April, 2000, p. 106.

Small Press Review, March, 1983, p. 8.

Studies in American Indian Literatures: The Journal of the Association for the Study of American Indian Literatures, spring, 1994, p. 24; spring, 1995, p. 45.

Village Voice, April 2, 1991, p. 78.

Washington Post, August 20, 2000, p. X12.

Western American Literature, summer, 2000, p. 131.

Whole Earth Review, summer, 1995, p. 43; summer, 1998, p. 99.

wicazo sa review: A Journal of Native American Studies, 2000 p. 27.

Women's Review of Books, July, 1990, pp. 17-18.

World Literature Today, winter, 1991, pp. 167-168; spring, 1992, pp. 286-291.

ONLINE

PAL: Perspectives in American Literature—A Research and Reference Guide, http://www.csustan.edu/english/reuben/pal/chap10/harjo.html/ (March 10, 2004).

Poetry Magazine, http://www.poetrymagazine.com/ (March 3, 2003).

Southern Scribe, http://www.southernscribe.com/ (March 3, 2003), interview with Harjo.

OTHER

The Power of the Word (video), with Bill Moyers, PBS Video (Alexandria, VA), 1989.

HARRIS, E. Lynn 1957-

PERSONAL: Born 1957, in Flint, MI; son of Etta (an assembly worker) Harris. *Ethnicity:* "African American." *Education:* University of Arkansas, Fayetteville, B.A. (with honors), 1977; studied business at Southern Methodist University. *Religion:* Christian *Hobbies and other interests:* Arkansas Razorback fan.

ADDRESSES: Home—New York, NY, and Chicago, IL. *Agent*—c/o Author Mail, Doubleday, 1540 Broadway, New York, NY 10036.

CAREER: Corporate sales for IBM, AT&T, and Hewlett-Packard, 1977-90; author, 1990—.

AWARDS, HONORS: Novel of the Year prize, Blackboard African-American Bestsellers, Inc., 1996, for *Just as I Am;* National Association for the Advancement of Colored People Image Award nominee, 1997, and James Baldwin Award for Literary Excellence, both for *If This World Were Mine;* named *SBC Magazine* Brother of the Year in literature; Harlem Y. Mentor Award; BMAD (Gay Men of African Descent) Angel Award; Writers for Writers Award, Barnes & Noble, 2001; Blackboard Book Award for fiction, 2002, for *Any Way the Wind Blows.*

WRITINGS:

Invisible Life, Consortium Press (Atlanta, GA), 1991.
Just as I Am: A Novel, Doubleday (New York, NY), 1994.
And This Too Shall Pass, Doubleday (New York, NY), 1996.
If This World Were Mine, Doubleday (New York, NY), 1997.
Abide with Me, Doubleday (New York, NY), 1999.
Not a Day Goes By: A Novel, Doubleday (New York, NY), 2000.
(With others) *Got to Be Real: Four Original Love Stories,* New American Library (New York, NY), 2000.
Any Way the Wind Blows: A Novel, Doubleday (New York, NY), 2001.
A Love of My Own, Doubleday (New York, NY), 2002.
(Editor, with Marita Golden) *Gumbo: A Celebration of African-American Writing,* Harlem Moon (New York, NY), 2002.
What Becomes of the Brokenhearted: A Memoir, Doubleday (New York, NY), 2003.

Contributor to periodicals, including *American Visions, Brotherman, Essence,* and *Go the Way Your Blood Beats.*

WORK IN PROGRESS: A memoir tentatively titled *For Colored Boys Who've Considered Suicide When Being Gay Was Too Tough.* Also working on a young adult novel series titled "Diaries of a Light-skinned Colored Boy" and a screenplay for Warner Brothers, a remake of the 1976 movie *Sparkle.* In addition, three of Harris's books—*Invisible Life, Just as I Am,* and *Not a Day Goes By*—were considered for film adaptation.

SIDELIGHTS: E. Lynn Harris, a computer salesman-turned-novelist, used writing to help liberate him from a depression born of hiding his homosexuality. Successful but unhappy in his former technology job, Harris was lonely and became a heavy drinker. When he met noted author Maya Angelou at a business function in 1983, he confessed to the poet that he had a desire to write. She encouraged him to write every day, even if his output was only a single word. Eventually, Harris left his sales job and wrote a semi-autobiographical novel, *Invisible Life.* Although the book was initially rejected by several publishers, it eventually reached a large audience and Harris became an increasingly well-known name in African American fiction.

It took a great deal of determination to put *Invisible Life* into readers' hands. Harris decided to self-publish the novel, using his own savings and funds raised from AIDS organizations. But as he told a reviewer for *Publishers Weekly,* the hard work was yet to come: "I had over five thousand copies in rented office space. At the first book party we sold only forty-two, and I felt sick." The author filled the trunk of his car with books and began distributing them to black-owned bookstores in Atlanta; he also left copies in black beauty shops, asking that they be kept in the shops for patrons to read. Word of mouth finally created a demand for the book and stores began to order copies in greater numbers. Subsequently, *Essence* named *Invisible Life* one of its ten best books, and a story in the *Atlanta Constitution* led to a trade paperback publishing contract with Anchor Books.

Harris's first novel treats gay themes but attracted a wide audience, especially among black, female heterosexual readers. *Invisible Life* is the story of a black man, Raymond Tyler, who has a long-term relationship with a girl during high school and college. But in the senior year of his college career, Tyler becomes attracted to a man and enters a double life, dating women from whom he hides the fact of his bisexuality—or perhaps homosexuality. The novel details his experiences in gay bars, the impact of AIDS on his life, his relationship with a married man, and his own interest in having a family.

Harris continued Tyler's story in *Just as I Am,* in which Tyler's former girlfriend, Nicole, also serves as narrator. While Harris was credited for the book's depiction of gay life, several reviewers noted its lack of substance. A *Publishers Weekly* critic called it an "unappealing potboiler" and "more checklist than novel," while a reviewer for *Kirkus Reviews* dubbed the author's first two novels "saccharine treatments." David Ehrenstein, writing in the *Los Angeles Times Book Review,* commented that while the author deals with "potentially very serious material . . . Harris is barely up to the task of regurgitating the clichés of a previous generation of gay pulpsters." Commenting on Harris's readership, Ehrenstein noted that "the fascination many heterosexual women have for homosexual men has—finally—been revealed as a market ripe for the plucking."

Harris next began working on a nonfiction project, a memoir tentatively titled *For Colored Boys Who've Considered Suicide When Being Gay Was Too Tough,* a title reminiscent of Ntozake Shange's play *For Colored Girls Who Have Considered Suicide/When the Rainbow Is Enuf.* But he first returned to publishing with the novel *And This Too Shall Pass,* a story about young black professionals, male and female, gay and straight. Each of Harris's protagonists face different crises, including alcoholism, sexual orientation, and physical abuse. The plot revolves around a young NFL quarterback for a fictional Chicago team who is falsely accused of sexual assault by Mia, a young, black sportscaster. Other characters in the novel include Tamela, an attorney for a large Chicago law firm, and a gay sportswriter named Sean who ultimately falls for the football player. *Booklist* reviewer Charles Harmon liked the novel's characters, dialogue, and plot, and concluded that the book had "something to impress nearly any reader." A reviewer in *Publishers Weekly* found the novel "entertaining" and noted that "despite some stilted dialogue, this novel should broaden the author's readership."

Continuing with a slightly older group of black characters, Harris created *If This World Were Mine,* which contributor Rhonda Johnson called "an engrossing, fast-paced buppie *Big Chill*" in an *Entertainment Weekly* review. The four central characters, who are friends approaching the age of forty, meet regularly to share their journals. The meetings ultimately serve as more than a writing exchange; they provide a support group for a variety of troubles. A *Publishers Weekly* reviewer considered it to be "another involving tale" but added, "it's likely that many readers will long for more structure and dramatic payoff." Ray Olson commented in *Booklist* that *If This World Were Mine* is "more in the vein of Terry McMillan than of Toni Morrison."

In 2000 Harris's book *Not a Day Goes By* reached the number-two spot on the *New York Times* bestseller list. A reviewer for *Publishers Weekly* pointed out that this was nothing new for Harris. "Following a string of bestselling novels featuring plots that mix romance, deception, betrayal and bisexuality, Harris . . . scores again." In 2001 Harris published *Any Way the Wind Blows,* which, Theola S. Labbe, a *Publishers Weekly* reviewer, noted "picks up where . . . *Not a Day Goes By* left off, following the adventures of a macho sports agent who breaks the hearts of women and men. . . . As in previous works, the characters are generally African American, upwardly mobile, gay or bisexual and in search of love."

Some reviewers have criticized Harris's writing, stating that his plots sometimes read like predictable soap opera storylines. Many also see Harris's stories, as Labbe put it, "as a bit too pat." Some reviewers have expressed concern over the author's lightweight approach to serious topics such as AIDS and bisexuality. Harris responded to such concerns in his interview with Labbe: "Sometimes I can see their point. . . . I do take note, I do listen to criticism and I think I handle criticism pretty well."

In the 2002 novel *A Love of My Own,* Harris brings back Raymond Tyler as the novel's protagonist. Tyler becomes the CEO of *Bling Bling,* a hip-hop magazine, and meets Zola Denise Norwood, who is the magazine's editor-in-chief. She is also having an affair with the periodical's wealthy publisher, David McClinton. The new job requires Tyler to relocate to New York, a much-needed move since he has just ended a long-term relationship. As in Harris's novels, there is a heavy emphasis on relationships and sex, but the terrorist attacks on the World Trade Center of September 11 eventually prompt Tyler, Norwood, and others to reevaluate their lives. A *Publishers Weekly* contributor commented, "A more serious effort than Harris's previous works, this book is loaded with sensational goings-on and characters, both old and new, who will keep readers returning for more of the same." Denise Simone, writing in *Black Issues Book Review,* noted that "fans of Harris' work won't be disappointed."

After writing numerous novels, Harris turned to his own life for *What Becomes of the Brokenhearted: A Memoir,* published in 2003. In an interview with Elizabeth Millard of *Publishers Weekly,* Harris noted that he had originally set out to write a memoir when he ended up with his first novel. "Every time I gave a reading, people would ask me personal questions, and I saw that my readers were becoming much more interested in who I was. When I began to answer them and look back on my life, I realized there were some moments that made me who I am, and I wanted to share that." In the memoir, Harris delves into all the difficulties of his life, from his years of alcoholism and depression as he dealt with his homosexuality to finally attaining a successful lifestyle only to go broke and lose it all. He also discusses how he finally turned his life around and became a best-selling author. A *Publishers Weekly* contributor noted that readers "should appreciate the deep honesty with which he describes each stumble and fall." Adrian King, writing in *Lambda Book Review,* commented that she found Harris's fiction "more fulfilling" than his memoir, but also noted that *What Becomes of the Brokenhearted* "speaks directly to what Harris has repeatedly espoused in his previous eight novels—that love has many forms and we get from it what we put into it." *Booklist* contributor Whitney Scott predicted that fans of Harris's fiction will be "caught up in this engaging writer's engagingly told life story."

BIOGRAPHICAL AND CRITICAL SOURCES:

BOOKS

Contemporary Black Biography, Volume 12, Thomson Gale (Detroit, MI), 1996.

PERIODICALS

Advocate, March 8, 1994, p. 73; August 29, 2000, Austin Foxxe, review of *Not a Day Goes By,* p. 67.

American Visions, June, 1994, p. 30.

Atlanta Constitution, June 9, 1992, p. D1; January, 2001, Anthony Johnson, review of *Not a Day Goes By,* p. 23.

Black Issues Book Review, September, 2000, Kenneth E. Reeves, review of *Not a Day Goes By,* p. 21; May, 2001, Nikitta A. Foston, review of *Got to Be Real: Four Original Love Stories,* p. 19; July, 2001, Glenn Townes, review of *Any Way the Wind Blows,* p. 30; September-October, 2002, Denise Simone, review of *A Love of My Own,* p. 25; January-Febru-

ary, 2003, Zakia Carter, review of *Gumbo: An Anthology of African-American Writing,* p. 30; September-October, 2003, Curtis Stephen, review of *What Becomes of the Brokenhearted,* p. 52.

Booklist, February 15, 1994, Whitney Scott, review of *Just as I Am,* p. 1060; February 15, 1996, Charles Harmon, review of *And This Too Shall Pass,* p. 990; June 1, 1997, Ray Olson, review of *If This World Were Mine,* p. 1619; June 1, 2000, Whitney Scott, review of *Not a Day Goes By,* p. 1797; July, 2001, Vanessa Bush, review of *Any Way the Wind Blows,* p. 1950; December 15, 2002, Vanessa Bush, review of *Gumbo,* p. 726; July, 2003, Whitney Scott, review of *What Becomes of the Brokenhearted,* p. 1843.

Dallas Morning News, April 3, 1996, p. 1C.

Ebony, October, 2000, "Q&A with Best-selling Author E. Lynn Harris"; August, 2003, review of *What Becomes of the Brokenhearted,* p. 30.

Emerge, July/August, 1996, p. 77.

Entertainment Weekly, April 15, 1994, Michael E. Ross, review of *Invisible Life,* p. 55; August 22, 1997, Rhonda Johnson, review of *If This World Were Mine,* p. 129.

Essence, July, 1992, p. 42; April, 1996, p. 88; August, 2001, review of *Any Way the Wind Blows,* p. 64.

Gay and Lesbian Review Worldwide, January, 2001, Timothy Burton, review of *The Young and the Reckless,* p. 42.

Houston Chronicle, April 14, 1996, p. 20.

Kirkus Reviews, December 15, 1993, p. 1542.

Lambda Book Report, May, 1992, p. 48; March-April, 1994, Canaan Parker, review of *Just As I Am,* p. 20; May, 1994, p. 38; May, 1995, p. 39; December 2003, Adrian King, review of *What Becomes of the Brokenhearted,* p. 32.

Library Journal, February 1, 1994, p. 111; February 1, 1996, p. 98; June 15, 1996, p. 105; September 15, 1999, Catherine Swenson, review of *Abide with Me,* p. 128; March 1, 2000, review of *Not a Day Goes By,* p. S1; November 1, 2000, Ann Burns and Emily Joy Jones, review of *Got to Be Real: Four Original Love Stories,* p. 101; January, 2003, Ann Burns, review of *Gumbo,* p. 110.

Los Angeles Times Book Review, July 10, 1994, David Ehrenstein, review of *Just as I Am,* pp. 4, 10.

Newsweek, April 29, 1996, p. 79.

New York Times, March 17, 1996, p. A43.

People, April 15, 1995, p. 115; May 15, 1995, p. 115.

Progressive, January, 2001, Kate Clinton, review of *Abide with Me,* p. 36.

Publishers Weekly, December 6, 1993, pp. 29, 32; January 24, 1994, review of *Just As I Am,* p. 41; January 29, 1996, review of *And This Too Shall Pass,*

p. 84; March 4, 1996, p. 31; July 1, 1996, p. 56; July 28, 1997, review of *If This World Were Mine*, p. 55; April 19, 1999, Alissa Quart, "E. Lynn Harris: Tales of the Good Life," p. 44; June 26, 2000, review of *Not a Day Goes By*, p. 50; December 4, 2000, review of *Got to Be Real*, p. 53; June 25, 2001, review of *Any Way the Wind Blows*, p. 49; July 30, 2001, Theola S. Labbe, "E. Lynn Harris, Black, Male, out, and On Top," p. 53; July 29, 2002, review of *A Love of My Own*, p. 56; November 25, 2002, review of *Gumbo*, p. 42; June 16, 2003, review of *What Becomes of the Brokenhearted*, p. 61; June 16, 2003, Elizabeth Millard, "Writing to Find Some Kind of Peace of Mind" (interview), p. 62.

Tribune (Chicago, IL), December 5, 1994, p. C1.

USA Today, August 17, 1994, p. 7D; June 25, 2001, review of *Any Way the Wind Blows*, p. 49.

*   *   *

HARRIS, Robert 1957-
(Robert Dennis Harris)

PERSONAL: Born March 7, 1957, in Nottingham, England; son of Dennis Harris (a printer) and Audrey (Hardy) Harris; married Gillian Hornby (a journalist), 1988; children: Holly Miranda, Matilda Felicity, Charlie Robert Nicholas, Samuel Orlando Hornby. *Education:* Selwyn College, Cambridge, B.A. (with honors), 1978. *Politics:* "Supporter of the British Labour Party." *Hobbies and other interests:* Reading history, walking, fishing, listening to music.

ADDRESSES: Home—The Old Vicarage, Kintbury, Berkshire RG17 9TR, England.

CAREER: Writer. British Broadcasting Corporation (BBC-TV), London, England, researcher and film director for *Tonight, Nationwide,* and *Panorama,* 1978-81, reporter for *Newsnight,* 1981-85, and for *Panorama,* 1985-87; *Observer,* London, England, political editor, 1987-89; Thames TV, London, England, political reporter for *This Week,* 1988-89; *Sunday Times,* London, England, political columnist, 1989-92.

WRITINGS:

(With Jeremy Paxman) *A Higher Form of Killing: The Secret Story of Gas and Germ Warfare,* Chatto & Windus (London, England), 1982, published as *A*

Higher Form of Killing: The Secret Story of Chemical and Biological Warfare, Hill & Wang (New York, NY), 1982, reprinted under original title, Random House (New York, NY), 2002.

Gotcha!: The Media, the Government, and the Falklands Crisis, Faber & Faber (London, England), 1983.

The Making of Neil Kinnock, Faber & Faber (London, England), 1984.

Selling Hitler, Pantheon (New York, NY), 1986.

Good and Faithful Servant: The Unauthorized Biography of Bernard Ingham, Faber & Faber (London, England), 1990.

NOVELS

Fatherland, Random House (New York, NY), 1992.

Enigma, Random House (New York, NY), 1995.

Archangel, Hutchinson (London, England), 1998.

Pompeii, Random House (New York, NY), 2003.

Harris's work has been translated into several languages.

ADAPTATIONS: Fatherland was adapted as a TV movie for Home Box Office (HBO). *Archangel* has been adapted for audio cassette. *Enigma* was adapted as a film in 2001.

SIDELIGHTS: Robert Harris had written several books of nonfiction during the 1980s before the publication of his popular 1992 novel *Fatherland.* Constructed around the premise that Adolf Hitler led the Nazis to victory in World War II, with Germany defeating both Great Britain and the Soviet Union and fighting the United States to an uneasy deadlock, *Fatherland* became a bestseller, selling three million copies worldwide. Several of Harris's previous nonfiction works, such as *A Higher Form of Killing: The Secret Story of Chemical and Biological Warfare* and *Gotcha!: The Media, the Government, and the Falklands Crisis,* also deal with war and its repercussions. In *Selling Hitler* Harris details the 1983 hoax in which a counterfeiter claimed to have discovered the diaries of the dead Nazi leader.

A true account of the Hitler diary hoax, *Selling Hitler,* reveals the extent to which greed influenced the publishing industry to overlook the veracity of the (supposedly) newly discovered diaries in favor of their marketability. "One merit of Robert Harris's thorough and mordantly funny account of the diaries scandal in *Selling Hitler* is that he lets no one off the hook," commented *New York Times Book Review* critic James Markham. The diaries were originally obtained by a reporter for the German magazine *Stern;* according to Jonathan Alter in *Newsweek,* "Executives at *Stern*'s parent company, Gruner and Jahr, smelled money. Not wanting to see the bubble burst, *Stern* subjected the papers to only the most cursory handwriting examination." Markham noted in the *New York Times Book Review* that Harris presents "an unsettling portrait of the press baron, Rupert Murdoch, who aggressively bought up rights to the diaries for his corporation . . . and then nonchalantly dismissed their fraudulence with an unhappily memorable one-liner: 'After all, we are in the entertainment business.'" *New Statesman* reviewer Paul Hallam wrote that Harris tells this "sick saga . . . with skill and wit."

The first of Harris's novels, *Fatherland,* unfolds in docudrama style. The setting is 1964, on the eve of an important visit by the president of the United States, Joseph P. Kennedy, to the German Fuhrer, Adolf Hitler, in a Berlin which is now the site of the grandiose Great Hall (built to the specifications of Nazi architect Albert Speer, the building can accommodate 180,000 people). The Allies have lost World War II, the wartime British prime minister, Winston Churchill, is in exile in Canada, and Germany now controls all of Europe and a good part of the Soviet Union. Against this background a German police detective, Xavier March, investigates the murder of a Nazi party official and in the course of his probe unearths a terrible secret with wide-ranging implications. Pursued by the Gestapo, March attempts to publicize a crime of immeasurable dimensions—the systematic murder of millions of European Jews, whom the world believes to have been nonviolently relocated to the East. "March's inquiries jeopardize the crowning achievement of Hitler's three decades in office: world peace," commented Mark Horowitz in the *Los Angeles Times Book Review.* Coming at a time when the American president is making overtures to end the cold war with Germany, "revelations of a Holocaust would make appeasement impossible," Horowitz explained.

New York Times Book Review critic Newgate Callendar wrote that *Fatherland* is an "absorbing, expertly written novel. . . . [It] is a bleak book. But what concerns the author is the indestructibility of the human spirit, as exemplified by Xavier March." In *Time* John Skow stated that Harris's "brooding, brown-and-black setting of a victorious Nazi regime is believable and troubling, the stuff of long nights of little sleep." And in the *Los Angeles Times Book Review* Horowitz remarked that "*Fatherland* works fine as a sly and scary page-turner."

Harris followed *Fatherland* with his second novel, *Enigma.* Like its predecessor, *Enigma* is a World War II

thriller, this time set in a secret code-breaking headquarters in England. At the height of the war, brilliant-but-inexperienced researcher Thomas Jericho has managed to crack a Nazi code nicknamed Shark—but the marathon effort has led to his nervous breakdown. Before his recovery is complete, however, Jericho is called back to work on an even tougher Nazi code: Enigma, which is generated on new four-rotor encrypting machines. With a battalion of American warships about to lock horns with German U-boats, it is vital that the code be cracked in time to ensure an Allied victory. Complications further ensue when Jericho suspects his new love, Claire Romilly, of being a spy.

"The second novel is always the most difficult, especially after a big hit," wrote Clive Ponting in *New Statesman & Society.* The critic acknowledged Harris's sophomore effort as an "ultimately . . . formulaic thriller whose location cannot disguise its rather ordinary plot," though Ponting added that the author does provide "a good pace." John Skow in *Time* found more to like in *Enigma,* saying that the results of Harris's efforts to portray genius are "worthy and believable, if not luminous." And to a *Publishers Weekly* contributor, the novel is "a rare mix of cerebral and visceral thrills that features risky exploits complementing the exhilarating challenge [of] solving daunting puzzles within puzzles." Apart from being an international bestseller, *Enigma* was the subject of a BBC documentary on the making of a thriller.

The author is "at his best," wrote Skow, in his third novel, *Archangel.* In the "what-if" tradition of *Fatherland, Archangel* takes on modern Russian history, exploring the implications of a pro-Stalinist cult which discovers the long-lost son of the late dictator and seeks to bring the scion to power. Such a premise powers the novel's theme: "Scratch the surface of post-Soviet Russia," commented *New Statesman* contributor Kate Saunders, "and you will find unreconstructed, bloody-minded old commies." While this over-the-top plot could be the stuff of potboilers, Harris "makes you believe it as it's happening," in the words of *New York Times* writer Christopher Lehmann-Haupt. To Michael Specter of the *New York Times Book Review,* the author "has given those of us who retain some literary nostalgia for the Evil Empire exactly what we have been waiting for." "Building on accurate historical sense," noted *Booklist* contributor Gilbert Taylor, Harris describes would-be historical events compellingly enough to "[reward] readers with a thoroughly thrilling tale."

Harris's 2003 novel, *Pompeii,* spins a new twist on an old tale. According to a reviewer for the *Economist,* "Mr. Harris sticks to the *Enigma* formula of placing fictional characters . . . into an authentic setting." The book takes place in 79 A.D. in the Roman Empire two days before the eruption of Mount Vesuvius. The fictional protagonist, civil engineer Marcus Attilus Primus, is elected to investigate the water supply blockage to the aqueduct along the Bay of Naples. His findings lead him to believe bigger problems may be on the horizon and with the approval of his admiral, Attilus sails to Pompeii to get to the root of the problem, which lies at the base of Mount Vesuvius. Although readers are familiar with the tragic ending of this familiar tale, "the events are handled with a skill that kept me turning the pages," Jasper Griffin wrote in the *Spectator*. He concluded that "Harris has done his homework" in depicting the "picture of life" during ancient Rome. The *Economist* reviewer called *Pompeii*, "an engaging thriller with no small lesson for our own times."

BIOGRAPHICAL AND CRITICAL SOURCES:

PERIODICALS

Booklist, September 15, 1995, Gilbert Taylor, review of *Enigma,* p. 142; November 1, 1998, Gilbert Taylor, review of *Archangel,* p. 451; October 15, 2003, Kristine Huntley, review of *Pompeii,* p. 390.

Books, autumn, 1999, review of *Archangel,* p. 20.

Bookseller, May 23, 2003, "Death of a Boom Town: Robert Harris Exlpores the Final Hours of Pompeii," p. 30.

Economist (US), November 28, 1998, review of *Archangel,* p. 89; September 6, 2003, review of *Pompeii,* p. 76.

Entertainment Weekly, October 20, 1995, Michael Giltz, review of *Enigma,* p. 58; February 5, 1999, review of *Archangel,* p. 64; November 21, 2003, Jennifer Reese, "Blast from the Past: Robert Harris's Pompeii Vividly Imagines the Two Days before the Vesuvius Blew Its Top," p. 88.

Europe, March, 2000, Robert Guttman, review of *Archangel,* p. 36.

Guardian, September 5, 1995, Roy Ackerman, "First among Sequels," p. 12.

Kirkus Reviews, August 15, 1995, review of *Enigma,* p. 1130; November 1, 1998, review of *Archangel,* p. 1552; September 15, 2003, review of *Pompeii,* p. 1145.

Library Journal, October 1, 1995, Dawn Anderson, review of *Enigma,* p. 119; January, 1999, Roland Person, review of *Archangel,* p. 150; October 15, 2003, Jane Baird review of *Pompeii,* p. 98.

Los Angeles Times Book Review, July 5, 1992, Mark Horowitz, review of *Fatherland,* pp. 2, 9; February 1, 1999, review of *Archangel,* p. 9.

National Review, February 22, 1999, review of *Archangel,* p. 51.

New Statesman, May 1, 1987, Paul Hallam, review of *Selling Hitler;* October 16, 1998, Kate Saunders, review of *Archangel,* p. 57.

New Statesman & Society, Sept 1, 1995, Clive Ponting, review of *Enigma,* p. 33; September 15, 2003, Philip Kerr, review of *Pompeii,* p. 48.

Newsweek, May 26, 1986, Jonathan Alter, review of *Selling Hitler,* p. 70; February 1, 1999, review of *Archangel,* p. 66.

New York Review of Books, December 17, 1992, pp. 38-44.

New York Times, October 11, 1995, Alan Riding, "An Enigma Wrapped in a Mystery," p. C17; January 21, 1999, Christopher Lehmann-Haupt, review of *Archangel,* p. E9.

New York Times Book Review, April 13, 1986, James Markham, review of *Selling Hitler,* June 28, 1992, Newgate Callendar, review of *Fatherland,* pp. 11-12; p. 28; October 22, 1995, Peter Vansittart, review of *Enigma,* p. 46; February 14, 1999, Michael Specter, review of *Archangel,* p. 10.

Observer (London, England), February 13, 1983; June 9, 1996, review of *Enigma,* p. 16; September 27, 1998, review of *Archangel,* p. 14; October 3, 1999, review of *Archangel,* p. 16.

People, October 30, 1995, J.D. Reed, review of *Enigma,* p. 42.

Publishers Weekly, September 11, 1995, review of *Enigma,* p. 74; November 30, 1998, review of *Archangel,* p. 49; October 27, 2003, review of *Pompeii,* p. 45.

School Library Journal, June, 1996, Carol Beall, review of *Enigma,* p. 168.

Spectator, March 12, 1983, pp. 20-22; August 26, 1995, Kingsley Amis, review of *Enigma,* p. 26; September 26, 1998, Douglas Hurd, review of *Archangel,* p. 45; November 21, 1998, review of *Archangel,* p. 43; November 28, 1999, review of *Archangel,* p. 46; October 4, 2003, Jasper Griffin, "Fire from Heaven," p. 53.

Sunday Times (London, England), September 13, 1998, Norman Stone, "Stalin and Me, a Bit of a Thriller," p. N4.

Time, July 6, 1992, John Skow, review of *Fatherland,* pp. 75-76; October 23, 1995, John Skow, review of *Enigma,* p. 102; February 15, 1999, John Skow, review of *Archangel,* p. 80.

Times Educational Supplement, April 3, 1983, p. 27; July 19, 1996, review of *Enigma,* p. R6.

Times Literary Supplement, September 22, 1995, Keith Jeffrey, review of *Enigma,* p. 22; September 25, 1998, Richard Overy, review of *Archangel,* p. 21.

Tribune Books (Chicago, IL), November 19, 1995, review of *Enigma*, p. 6.

Virginia Quarterly Review, autumn, 1999, review of *Archangel*, p. 131.

Washington Post Book World, July 11, 1982, pp. 1-2; October 15, 1995, review of *Enigma*, p. 4.

* * *

HARRIS, Robert Dennis
See HARRIS, Robert

* * *

HARRIS, Thomas 1940(?)-

PERSONAL: Born c. 1940, in Jackson, MS; son of William Thomas (an electrical engineer and farmer) and Polly (a high-school teacher) Harris; children: Anne. *Education:* Baylor University, B.A., 1964.

ADDRESSES: Agent—c/o Author Mail, Random House, 201 E. 50th St., New York, NY 10022.

CAREER: Writer. Worked as a night police reporter for the Waco *News-Tribune,* Waco, TX; *Associated Press,* New York City, assistant editor, general assignment reporter, and night editor, 1968-74.

AWARDS, HONORS: Bram Stoker Award for Best Novel, Horror Writers Association and Anthony Award, all 1989, all for *Silence of the Lambs.*

WRITINGS:

Black Sunday, Putnam (New York, NY), 1975, reprinted, Dutton (New York, NY), 2000.

Red Dragon, Putnam (New York, NY), 1981, published as *Manhunter,* Bantam (New York, NY), 1986, reprinted as *Red Dragon,* Dutton (New York, NY), 2000.

The Silence of the Lambs, St. Martin's (New York, NY), 1988.

Hannibal, Delacorte (New York, NY), 1999.

ADAPTATIONS: Black Sunday was filmed by John Frankenheimer for Paramount, 1977; *Red Dragon* was filmed as *Manhunter* by Michael Mann for De Laurentiis Entertainment Group, 1986; *The Silence of the Lambs* was filmed by Jonathan Demme for Orion, 1991; *Hannibal* was filmed in 2001; *Red Dragon* was adapted for film a second time by director Brett Ratner and released by Universal Pictures, 2002. The author's works have also been adapted into audio books, including *Black Sunday,* BDD Audio, 2000, and *Hannibal,* Bantam Doubleday Dell, 1999.

SIDELIGHTS: Thomas Harris is known for his novels that combine detailed examination of police procedure with spellbinding suspense. Writing in the *St. James Guide to Horror, Ghost, and Gothic Writers,* S.T. Joshi noted that Harris's *Red Dragon* and *The Silence of the Lambs* "are certainly among the more successful works of popular fiction in recent years." An essayist for *Contemporary Southern Writers* found that all of Harris's novels "are crime-thrillers: fast-paced, intricately plotted, suspense-charged narratives fueled by the urgency of a countdown to catastrophe."

Much of Harris's personal history is cloaked in mystery. Having judiciously avoided interviews, Harris has made it difficult to find or confirm biographical information about him. He has also reportedly made it very clear to his friends, acquaintances, and even childhood neighbors that he would appreciate their restraint as well; fond as they are of their places in his inner circle, they have for the most part complied. Still, over the years some information has surfaced. Harris grew up in Rich, Mississippi, a small farming town, and was reportedly an outcast. His father went off to war and left his wife and young son to manage on their own and proved to be a less than adequate farmer after his return. Many of the difficulties of Harris's childhood are related in his books through the experiences of various characters, according to off-the-record accounts from people who knew his family. Stanley Gaines, Harris's best friend in high school and one of the few who has consented to an interview, told Meg Laughlin of the *Knight Ridder/ Tribune News Service* that "in high school, Tom blossomed. Sometimes, the things that make you an outcast as a kid make you cool when you get older." Whatever it was that Harris may have been trying to get back at the townsfolk for, several have acknowledged that he succeeded in the best possible way. As one Rich resident told Laughlin, "He left and got wealthy and famous." Another implied that however poorly Harris may have been treated as a youth, he is now the pride of his former hometown: "One of the things we love about Tom is that he is so gracious we know he has forgiven everyone."

While his childhood may have provided much of Harris's characterization and even story lines (serial killer and cannibal William Coyner did his deeds in nearby

Cleveland, Mississippi), many of the gruesome details came from his years as a journalist. After high school, Harris earned a bachelor's degree in English from Baylor University in Waco, Texas, and took a job as a night police reporter with the local newspaper. After several years, he screwed up his courage and set out for New York. "It took guts for a boy from Mississippi to go to the big city," Bob Sadler, Harris's former editor, told Laughlin. "You can be talented and be too afraid to do something about it. Tom wasn't." Harris left behind his old life in more ways than one: His wife, whom he had married while in college, and his daughter remained in Waco. In 1968 Harris found a job as an assistant editor with the Associated Press (AP) news service, again working the night shift and handling crime stories. A fellow reporter, Nicholas Pileggi, recalled to Cathleen McGuigan of *Newsweek* that Harris's demeanor did not portend his future works. "Tom was very quiet and cheery," Pileggi commented. "He did cover a lot of bloody stuff, but we all did." It was at this time that Harris began to develop his work ethic for extensive research, at the same time sating his thirst for knowledge. Those close to Harris mark a distinction between interest and obsession, however. "He has this imagination that's just unbridled," Walter Stovall, an old AP colleague, told McGuigan. "But it's not anything that roils around in his brain."

Harris's first book, *Black Sunday,* was conceived during his tenure with the AP. During slow periods, Harris and two colleagues passed the time by cooking up plots for novels; among these was the story that became *Black Sunday*. In the novel, Harris pits a crazed Vietnam veteran and a group of Arab extremists—who plan to bomb the Super Bowl stadium as a protest of the United States' support of Israel—against cunning FBI and Israeli agents whose mission is to stop them. The president of the United States is among the 100,000 spectators in the stadium, and all are unaware that the blimp flying overhead may attack them at any second. *Black Sunday* received mixed reviews from critics. Newgate Callendar of the *New York Times Book Review,* for example, found *Black Sunday* to be "written in a stolid, expository, unimaginative style," while L.W. Lindsay in the *Christian Science Monitor* labeled the book "a dud." But the critic for *Library Journal* was enthusiastic: "The action is up-to-date, . . . very violent . . . , and the plot is packed with business. Not a bit believable, but successful entertainment." In the *St. James Guide to Horror, Ghost, and Gothic Writers,* Joshi called *Black Sunday* "a mere potboiler" but admitted that one sequence, a psychological history of one of the terrorists, was quite interesting: "It is written in a clinical, almost emotionless manner, but it nevertheless provides

the necessary psychological motivation for the entire novel." John Frankenheimer's movie adaptation of the book also met with mixed critical reaction, but was well-liked by the movie-going public.

Harris's second effort was the bestseller *Red Dragon,* about Will Graham, an FBI agent searching for a deformed murderer who calls himself Red Dragon. Graham attempts "to hunt down [the] serial killer by adopting the mind-set of the criminal." This novel was more warmly received than *Black Sunday,* with a *New York Times* reviewer declaring that Harris's "depiction of police technology is comprehensive and compelling. . . . For all the gruesome nature of his subject, he writes with taste and with a high intelligence and verve." Critic Jospeh Amie, writing in the *Saturday Review,* observed: "The suspense is sustained by deft characterizations, fascinating crime-lab details, and a twisting plot, and understated prose," while *Newsweek*'s Jean Strouse deemed *Red Dragon* "gruesome, appalling, occasionally formulaic and mechanical," but "guaranteed to terrify and succeed." In the *New York Times Book Review* Thomas Fleming recommended the book for "those who like their flesh to crawl."

Harris produced *The Silence of the Lambs* in 1988. Like *Red Dragon, The Silence of the Lambs* deals with an FBI hunt for a serial killer. Utilizing some of the characters and themes of its predecessor, the novel presents the search through the eyes of female agent Clarice Starling. "It is a superlative mystery," exclaimed Douglas Winters in the *Washington Post Book World.* "Harris tells the story with the stunning and unflinching eye of the combat photographer . . . as remarkable as its predecessor in mingling the horror story with the police procedural." Christopher Lehmann-Haupt of the *New York Times* termed the novel "superb," adding that "Mr. Harris doesn't fool around or settle for trite effects. He goes straight for the viscera." Joshi ranked *The Silence of the Lambs* higher than *Red Dragon,* "in fullness of characterization, in intricacy of plot, and in cumulative suspense."

With *Silence of the Lambs,* Harris's reputation as well as his value as a commodity in the world of fiction writing were assured. The film version of *Silence of the Lambs,* directed by Jonathan Demme and starring Jodie Foster as Starling and Anthony Hopkins as a riveting Lecter, all of whom received Oscar Awards for their work, served to enhance Harris's reputation and left readers and moviegoers alike waiting breathlessly for the next installment. After heated sparring among New York's largest publishing houses, Harris accepted a contract for $5.25 million for his next two works. When he failed to produce a *Silence* sequel after several years, some observers questioned whether Delacorte had indeed gotten the bargain it had at first anticipated. Such doubts were laid to rest when, more than a decade later, Harris finally delivered.

Eleven years after *The Silence of the Lambs* enthralled critics and readers, Harris ended a long sabbatical by producing the psychological thriller *Hannibal*. "*Hannibal* is entirely different in tone from either *Silence* or *Manhunter,*" Stephen Hunter wrote in the *Washington Post*. "Where they were gritty, journalistically researched pieces that turned on, and demanded, reality in their making, *Hannibal* is more like an extremely grim fairy tale combined with a cookbook." In *Hannibal*, Harris revisits the mind of the cannibal with cultivated tastes whom *Denver Post* critic Tom Walker has declared "the best literary villain since Iago." In this third installment of the Lector trilogy, Harris introduces the character of Mason Verger, whose encounter with Lector has left him hideously disfigured. As he lies in a darkened room, attached to a respirator, Verger plots a vicious revenge and attempts to use FBI agent Clarice Starling, a character who featured prominently in *The Silence of the Lambs,* to bait the brilliant, elusive Lector. Harris addresses his central theme when he wrote in *Hannibal:* "Now that ceaseless exposure has calloused us to the lewd and the vulgar, it is instructive to see what still seems wicked to us. What still slaps the clammy flab of our submissive consciousness hard enough to get our attention?"

Critics were divided in their reception of *Hannibal*. *New York Times* critic Christopher Lehmann-Haupt observed that "Mr. Harris seems determined to top himself in monstrosity at any and all cost." The reviewer went on to note: "The result shades toward the stuff of comic books." Owen Gleiberman of *Entertainment Weekly* was another critic who found it difficult to take the novel seriously, commenting that *Hannibal* was Harris's "gaudiest, most lavishly over-the-top book yet . . . Hitchcock by way of the Marquis de Sade." Lehmann-Haupt did admit that "*Hannibal* remains full of wonderful touches, typical of Mr. Harris's grasp of arcane detail." Some critics criticized *Hannibal* for its gratuitous violence, and others felt that the book was somewhat less inventive than *The Silence of the Lambs*. A reviewer for the *Economist* noted that *Hannibal* "is less a sequel than a baroque variation, transposed in part to Italy, in which Lecter is more gourmet than cannibal." Stephen King, however, writing for the *New York Times,* praised Harris's work by placing it in a category of "novels that so bravely and cleverly erase the line between popular fiction and literature."

In an extensive review of *Hannibal* in the *Nation*, Annie Gottlieb delved into why readers are not only spellbound by the character of Hannibal Lecter but may actually even like him. The reviewer noted that she would have preferred for Harris to have kept Lecter more of an unknown entity than revealing more about the killer's life and youth in *Hannibal*. Nevertheless, Gottlieb noted that she "liked him a lot better than I thought I would." The critic went on to say that the reader's attraction is due, in part, to the fact that Lecter seems to go only after those who "pant after money, self-advancement or sensation," and concluded: "We love Hannibal Lecter because he's the part of us that's smart and sensitive and stylish enough to despise us. As we watch him and Clarice ride into the sunset, progenitors of a finer new species, or just aristocratic refugees from the ruin of the old, we might recall that Kafka wrote our epitaph: 'There is infinite hope, but not for us.'"

BIOGRAPHICAL AND CRITICAL SOURCES:

BOOKS

Contemporary Southern Writers, St. James Press (Detroit, MI), 1999.
Harris, Thomas, *Red Dragon,* Putnam (New York, NY), 1981, published as *Manhunter,* Bantam (New York, NY), 1986.
Harris, Thomas, *Hannibal,* Delacorte (New York, NY), 1999.
Magistrale, Tony, and Michael A. Morrison, editors, *A Dark Night's Dreaming: Contemporary American Horror Fiction,* University of South Carolina Press (Columbia, SC), 1996.
St. James Guide to Horror, Ghost, and Gothic Writers, St. James Press (Detroit, MI), 1998.

PERIODICALS

Advocate, August 31, 1999, review of *Hannibal,* p. 74.
Best Sellers, March 1, 1975.
Christian Science Monitor, January 10, 1975, p. 10.
Commonweal, Marcy 9, 2001, Richard Alleva, review of *Hannibal,* p. 23.
Critic, May/June, 1975.
Denver Post, June 13, 1999.
Economist, July 17, 1999, review of *Hannibal.*
Entertainment Weekly, May 7, 1999, p. 22; June 25, 1999, Owen Gleiberman, review of *Hannibal,* p. 123.

Journal of American Culture, spring, 1995, Joseph Grixti, "Consuming Cannibals: Psychopathic Killers as Archetypes and Cultural Icons."

Knight Ridder/Tribune News Service, June 10, 1999, p. K4078; August 4, 1999, p. K6478.

Library Journal, April 1, 1975; November 1, 1981; July, 1999, Mark Annichiarico, review of *Hannibal,* p. 131.

London Review of Books, July 29, 1999, p. 10-11.

Los Angeles Times Book Review, July 17, 1988.

Nation, July 27, 1999, Annie Gottlieb, "Free-Range Rude," review of *Hannibal,* p. 28.

National Review, July 12, 1999, p. 53.

New Statesman, June 21, 1999 Robert Winder, review of *Hannibal,* p. 44.

Newsweek, November 9, 1981; June 7, 1999, p. 72; June 21, 1999, Jeff Giles, review of *Hannibal,* p. 75.

New York Times, August 15, 1988; March 25, 1990; June 10, 1999; June 13, 1999.

New York Times Book Review, February 2, 1975, p. 14; November 15, 1981, p. 14.

Notes on Contemporary Literature, January, 1995, "Thomas Harris Issue."

People, April 12, 1999, p. 12.

Publishers Weekly, June 14, 1999, p. 46; June 14, 1999, review of *Hannibal,* p. 46; July 5, 1999, review of *Hannibal,* p. 34; June 12, 2000, Daisy Maryles, "High on Hannibal," p. 30.

Saturday Review, November, 1981.

Time, June 21, 1999, Paul Gray, review of *Hannibal,* p. 72.

Times (London, England), May 25, 1991.

Tribune Books (Chicago, IL), August 14, 1988.

Washington Post, July 18, 1999, Stephen Hunter, review of *Hannibal,* p. G1.

Washington Post Book World, August 21, 1988; May 21, 1989.

*   *   *

HARSON, Sley
  See ELLISON, Harlan

*   *   *

HART, Ellis
  See ELLISON, Harlan

*   *   *

HARVEY, Jack
  See RANKIN, Ian

HASS, Robert 1941-

PERSONAL: Surname rhymes with "grass"; born March 1, 1941, in San Francisco, CA; son of Fred (in business) and Helen (Dahling) Hass; married Earline Leif (a psychotherapist), September 1, 1962; married Brenda Hillman (a poet), 1995; children: (first marriage) Leif, Kristin, Luke. *Education:* St. Mary's College of California, B.A., 1963; Stanford University, M.A., 1965, Ph.D., 1971.

ADDRESSES: Home—576 Santa Barbara Rd., Berkeley, CA 94707. *Agent*—c/o Author Mail, Ecco Press, 26 West 17th St., New York, NY 10011.

CAREER: State University of New York at Buffalo, assistant professor, 1967-71; St. Mary's College of California, Moraga, professor of English, 1971-74, 1975-89; University of California, Berkeley, professor of English, 1989—. Visiting lecturer at University of Virginia, 1974, Goddard College, 1976, and Columbia University, 1982. Poet in residence, The Frost Place, Franconia, NH, 1978; U.S. Poet Laureate and poetry consultant to the Library of Congress, 1995-97.

AWARDS, HONORS: Woodrow Wilson fellow, 1963-64; Danforth fellow, 1963-67; Yale Series of Younger Poets Award from Yale University Press, 1972, for *Field Guide;* U.S.-Great Britain Bicentennial Exchange Fellow in the Arts, 1976-77; William Carlos Williams Award, 1979, for *Praise;* Guggenheim fellow, 1980; National Book Critics Circle Award in criticism, 1984, and Belles Lettres Award, Bay Area Book Reviewers Association, 1986, both for *Twentieth Century Pleasures: Prose on Poetry;* award of merit, American Academy of Arts and Letters, 1984; MacArthur Foundation grant, 1984; PEN award for translation, 1986; National Book Critics Circle Award in poetry, 1997, for *Sun under Wood.*

WRITINGS:

POETRY

Field Guide, Yale University Press (New Haven, CT), 1973, reprinted, with a new preface by the author, 1998.

Winter Morning in Charlottesville, Sceptre Press (Knotting, Bedfordshire, England), 1977.

Praise, Ecco Press (Hopewell, NJ), 1979.

(Contributor) *Phrases After Noon,* Frankfort Arts Foundation (Frankfort, KY), Larkspur Press (Monterey, KY), 1985.

The Apple Trees at Olema, Ecco Press (Hopewell, NJ) 1989.

Human Wishes, Ecco Press (Hopewell, NJ), 1989.

Sun Under Wood: New Poems, Ecco Press (Hopewell, NJ), 1996.

(Editor, with John Hollander, Carolyn Kizer, Nathaniel Mackey, and Marjorie Perloff) *American Poetry: The Twentieth Century,* two volumes, Library of America (New York, NY), 2000.

Contributor of poetry to various anthologies, including *The Young American Poets,* edited by Paul Carroll, Follett (New York, NY), 1968, and *Five American Poets,* Carcanet (Manchester, England), 1979.

TRANSLATOR

(With Robert Pinsky) Czeslaw Milosz, *The Separate Notebooks,* Ecco Press (Hopewell, NJ), 1983.

(With Milosz) Czeslaw Milosz, *Unattainable Earth,* Ecco Press (Hopewell, NJ), 1986.

(With Louis Iribarne and Peter Scott) Milosz, *Collected Poems, 1931-1987,* Ecco Press (Hopewell, NJ), 1988.

(With Milosz) Czeslaw Milosz, *Provinces,* Ecco Press (Hopewll, NJ) 1993.

(And editor and author of introduction) *The Essential Haiku: Versions of Basho, Buson, and Issa,* Ecco Press (Hopewell, NJ), 1994.

Czeslaw Milosz, *Road-side Dog,* Farrar, Straus and Giroux (New York, NY), 1998.

Czeslaw Milosz, *Treatise on Poetry,* Ecco Press/Harper Collins (New York, NY), 2001.

OTHER

Twentieth Century Pleasures: Prose on Poetry, Ecco Press (Hopewell, NJ), 1984.

(Editor) *Rock and Hawk: A Selection of Shorter Poems by Robinson Jeffers,* Random House (New York, NY), 1987.

(Co-editor with Bill Henderson and Jorie Graham) *The Pushcart Prize XII,* Pushcart (Wainscott, NY), 1987.

(Editor with Charles Simic) Tomaz Salamun, *Selected Poems* (translations from the Slovene), Ecco Press (Hopewell, NJ), 1988.

(Editor) Tomas Transtroemer, *Selected Poems of Tomas Transtroemer, 1954-1986,* translated by May Swenson and others, Ecco Press (Hopewell, NJ), 1989.

(Editor with Stephen Mitchell) *Into the Garden: A Wedding Anthology, Poetry and Prose on Love and Marriage,* HarperCollins (New York, NY), 1993.

(With Milosz) Czeslaw Milocz, *Facing the River: New Poems,* Ecco Press (Hopewell, NJ), 1995.

(Author of introduction) *Back Roads to Far Towns: Basho's Oku-No-Hosomichi,* translated by Cid Corman and Kamaike Susumu, with notes by the translators, illustrated by Hayakawa Ikutada, Ecco Press (Hopewell, NJ), 1996.

(Editor and author of commentary) *Poet's Choice: Poems for Everyday Life,* Ecco Press (Hopewell, NJ), 1998.

(Essayist) *California: Views by Robert Adams of the Los Angeles Basin, 1978-1983,* San Francisco: Mathew Marks Gallery and New York: Fraenkel Gallery, 2000.

(Editor, with Jessica Fisher) *The Addison Street Anthology: Berkeley's Poetry Walk,* Heyday Books (Berkeley, CA), 2004.

Weekly columnist for the *Washington Post,* featuring the work of famous and new poets.

SIDELIGHTS: Despite Robert Haas's success as a translator and critic, Forrest Gander declared in a *Dictionary of Literary Biography* essay that "it is for his own musical, descriptive, meditative poetry that Robert Hass is primarily recognized." Critics celebrate Hass's poetry for its clarity of expression, its conciseness, and its imagery, often drawn from everyday life. "Robert Hass," stated Carolyn Kizer in the *New York Times Book Review,* "is so intelligent that to read his poetry or prose, or to hear him speak, gives one an almost visceral pleasure." "Hass has noted his own affinity for Japanese haiku," Gander continued, "and his work similarly attends to the details of quotidian life with remarkable clarity." "Poetry," Hass tells interviewer David Remnick in the *Chicago Review,* "is a way of living . . . a human activity like baking bread or playing basketball."

With his first collection of poems, *Field Guide,* Hass won the 1973 Yale Series of Younger Poets Award and established himself as an important American poet. Many critics noted that Hass drew on his native California countryside and his background in Slavic studies to provide much of the imagery for the volume. "The poems in *Field Guide,*" wrote Gander, "are rich with Russian accents, aromas of ferny anise and uncorked wines, and references to plant and animal life: the green whelks and rock crabs, tanagers and Queen Anne's lace, sea spray and pepper trees of the Bay Area." "He is a fine poet," Michael Waters related in *Southwest Review,* "and his book is one of the very best to appear in a long time. . . . *Field Guide* is a means of naming things, of establishing an identity through one's surroundings, of translating the natural world into one's private history. This is a lot to accomplish, yet Robert Hass manages it with clarity and compassion." In the *Ontario Review* Linda W. Wagner commented that "*Field Guide* is an impressive first collection. . . . Hass's view of knowledge is convincing. As we read the sonorous and generally regular poems, we are aware that the poet has achieved his apparent tranquility by living close to the edge. . . . One can be reminded only of the best of Hemingway."

Hass confirmed his ability with *Praise,* his second volume of poems, which won the William Carlos Williams Award in 1979. "In many ways," Gander explained, "*Praise* addresses the problems implicit in the first book: Can the act of naming the world separate us from the world? How is it possible to bear grief, to accept death, and how can the spirit endure?" According to William Scammell in the *Times Literary Supplement,* these poems "unite freshness and wonder with a tough, inventive imagination." Writing in the *Chicago Review,* Ira Sadoff remarked that *Praise* "might even be the strongest collection of poems to come out in the late seventies." Sadoff noted that *Field Guide* "was intelligent and well-crafted; it tapped Hass's power of observation carefully and engagingly." Nevertheless, the reviewer had "reservations" about *Field Guide* that "stemmed from some sense of chilliness that seemed to pervade a number of poems, as if the poems were wrought by an intellect distant from its subject matter." Sadoff continued: "I have no such problems with *Praise.* . . . [It] marks Hass's arrival as an important, even pivotal, young poet."

Hollins Critic reviewer Robert Miklitsch expressed similar feelings about *Praise,* which he felt "marks the emergence of a major American poet. If his first book, *Field Guide,* . . . did not provoke such acclaim, the second book will." *Ontario Review* contributor Charles Molesworth, wrote that Hass is "slowly but convincingly becoming one of the best poets of his generation. . . . [*Praise*] is about language, its possibilities and its burdens, its rootedness in all we do and its flowering in all we hunger for and fear. . . . But the loving tentativeness, the need to see and to save, these are Hass's own gifts. He is that extremely rare person: a poet of fullness."

In 1984, Hass published *Twentieth Century Pleasures: Prose on Poetry,* a collection of previously published essays and reviews. In the volume, the author examines American writers (including Robert Lowell and James Wright) as well as European and Japanese poets. Many critics appreciated the book, honoring it with the 1984 National Book Critics Circle award, among others. "Mr. Hass's style balances conversational directness and eloquent complexity," noted *New York Times Book Review* contributor Anthony Libby. He concluded: "Mr. Hass believes that poetry is what defines the self, and it is his ability to describe that process that is the heart of this book's pleasure."

Since the publication of *Twentieth Century Pleasures,* Hass has continued to write both poetry and prose. In his third collection of poetry, *Human Wishes,* "Hass writes in tones ranging from intimate to sarcastic," commented Gander, "and he writes of incidents as various as fishing with children and driving a dead man through the rain." The collection "is a distinct joy to experience in this time when so many published works deal with violence, aberration, and alienation," declared Daisy Aldan in *World Literature Today.* "His elegant gleanings of essence, often impressionist in tone, make us aware once again that beauty and meaningful silence still exist." *Nation* critic Don Bogen explained that *Human Wishes* "reveals [Hass's] basic concerns: He is a student of desire, of what we want and how likely we are to get it." Bogen also noted, "In *Human Wishes,* Robert Hass captures both the brightness of the world and its vanishing."

Hass pays tribute to some of his non-Western mentors in *The Essential Haiku: Versions of Basho, Buson, and Issa,* translations of short works by the most famous seventeenth-and eighteenth-century masters of the short Japanese poem. And, as Andrew Rathmann suggested in a *Chicago Review* article, Hass deserves a great deal of credit for these translations. "The translations . . . must by anyone's standard be considered remarkable poetic achievements in themselves," wrote the reviewer, "comparable—in terms of sheer written fluency—to the best poems in his three previous books" of poems. Hass also succeeds at bringing a poetic form that has a long history of development in Japan to an American audience. As Mark Ford explained in the *New Republic,* the verse form known as *haiku* was developed in the nineteenth century from an older form named *hokku. Hokku* in turn was only part of a larger verse form known as *haikai,* which was practiced as a sort of game by several collaborating poets. Each of the three *haiku* masters (Basho, Buson, and Issa) used the short verse form to record commonplace images in an uncommon way.

"Hass's language is unflashy, his interpretations sensible and his pacing effective," Ford declared. The three chosen writers in Hass's book "demonstrate the ways in which great art may intensify and illuminate our engagements with the real, the experience of art."

In 1996, Hass published another collection of poems, *Sun under Wood*. The poems were well received by critics and the book earned the 1997 National Book Critics Circle Award. In the opinion of *Poetry* contributor David Baker "Hass's new volume contains many of his most important works to date, among them 'Faint Music,' 'Interrupted Meditation,' 'The Seventh Night,' and several brilliant longer poems, including 'English: An Ode' and 'Dragonflies Mating.'" For Gail Wronsky, writing in the *Antioch Review*, "'Forty Something' achieves a kind of perfect unification of form, tone, and story, and is a funny poem as well." The effect that Hass creates in these poems, according to Baker, is that "he is something of a buttoned-down [Allen] Ginsberg, emotionally and formally open, inclusive, enthusiastic, if considerably more ironic." He also demonstrates a sensitivity to and understanding of the people around him, both men and women. Wronsky maintained that "Hass has gone from brilliant poet to wise one with this collection, primarily because he has been listening to the female voices around him and within him. The poems in this book are large and wide and deep because of that particular exploration."

Not all critics were convinced that *Sun under Wood* represents Hass's best effort. Peter Davidson of the *Atlantic Monthly* found that these new poems do not compare favorably with those in previous collections. "The charm and modesty remain," he noted, "but these poems keep relaxing into the voice of an onlooker rather than taking on the energy of full participation—as though they came to the poet through a window, a filter, a screen of white noise and unscented air." Critic Dana Gioia attempted to identify what separates the better poems in *Sun under Wood* from the weaker ones. She wrote in the *Washington Post Book Review*, "When Hass's new poems succeed, they achieve a quiet sublimity enriched by introspection. When they go awry, they lose themselves in a mosquito swarm of amusing but academic *apercus*." Still, she conceded, "This risk is the price of Hass's originality." And, in the estimation of *Poetry* contributor David Baker, "All through *Sun under Wood*, Hass's ability to convert the comedic to sublime, the anecdotal to the metaphysical and ethical, the personal to the social, is remarkable." He concluded, "This book reaches a level of achievement Hass has not reached before. It is literary and messy, discursive and lyric. It is risky, large, and hugely compassionate."

From 1995 to 1997, Hass set aside his personal role as poet to take up the mantle of the nation's poet, serving as U.S. Poet Laureate and poetry consultant to the Library of Congress. Long a largely ceremonial position, the poet laureate has recently become far more of a public advocate for poets and their work, a potentially thankless task. Yet, as Michael Coffey reported in *Publishers Weekly*, "Being the frontman for a quaint art that barely has a profession tied to it unless it's called teaching—does not faze Hass. Rather, it is a task to which he has taken naturally. In fact, there may not be a better poet today working with such Catholic tastes, boundless energy and open aesthetics as Hass." In one sense, this new role was a logical extension of his personal, private work to a public arena. Sarah Pollock elaborated in *Mother Jones*, "Hass' tenure as poet laureate has been a more public expression of the lifelong concerns that inform his poetry: a close attention to the natural world, a sense of self developed in relation to the landscape, and acute awareness of both the pleasures and pains of being human."

The poet laureate position also heightened the political sensibilities of the poet and his work. Hass recognized early on that the political and business climate seemed to have little use for poetry and other arts. As Hass explained to Francis X. Clines in the *New York Times*, he came to realize that "Capitalism makes networks. It doesn't make communities. *Imagination* makes communities." Recognizing that capitalism and its networks held sway in political and business thought, Hass set out to infuse some imagination into the situation. He focused on promoting literacy. And, he told Clines, "I thought an interesting thing to do would be to go where poets don't go." He visited businesses, convincing some to support poetry contests for schoolchildren. He spoke to civic groups, praising their efforts to support education and trying to broaden their horizons. As a result, Clines observed, "He has shaped [the poet laureate position] to become more like a missionary drummer in the provinces of commerce than as a performing bard in celebrity coffeehouses." Because of these efforts, "Robert Hass is the most active Poet Laureate of the United States we've ever had," commented *Los Angeles Times Book Review* contributor Frances Mayes, "and he sets a standard for those who follow."

BIOGRAPHICAL AND CRITICAL SOURCES:

BOOKS

Claims for Poetry, University of Michigan Press (Ann Arbor, MI), 1982.

Contemporary Literary Criticism, Volume 18, Thomson Gale (Detroit, MI), 1981.

Contemporary Poets, sixth edition, St. James Press (Detroit, MI), 1996.

Dictionary of Literary Biography, Volume 105: *American Poets since World War II, Second Series,* Thomson Gale (Detroit, MI), 1991.

Poetry Criticism, Volume 16, Thomson Gale (Detroit, MI), 1997.

Proofs and Theories: Essays on Poetry, Ecco Press (Hopewll, NJ) 1994.

San Francisco Renaissance: Poetics and Community at Mid-Century, Cambridge University Press (New York, NY), 1989.

PERIODICALS

Antioch Review, summer, 1997, p. 380.

Atlantic Monthly, June, 1979, p. 93; March, 1997, p. 100.

Booklist, September 15, 1996, p. 205; March 1, 1998, p. 1086.

Boston Globe, September 24, 1989.

Chicago Review, winter, 1980, p. 133; spring, 1981, pp. 17-26; winter, 1983, p. 84; winter, 1997, p. 106.

Chicago Tribune, March 7, 1997, p. 2.

Harper's, May, 1979, p. 88.

Hollins Critic, February, 1980, Robert Miklitsch, p. 2.

Hudson Review, winter, 1973-1974, p. 717.

Iowa Review, fall, 1991, p. 126.

Library Journal, October 1, 1996, p. 82.

Los Angeles Times Book Review, November 18, 1984; April 13, 1997, p. G.

Mother Jones, March-April, 1997, p. 16.

Nation, May 19, 1979, p. 574; December 11, 1989, pp. 722-23.

New England Review, Volume 2, number 2, 1979, pp. 295-314.

New Republic, March 16, 1992, pp. 34-5; October 31, 1994, pp. 48-51.

New York Review of Books, November 7, 1985, pp. 53-60.

New York Times, December 9, 1996, p. A1.

New York Times Book Review, May 4, 1980, p. 15; March 3, 1985, p. 37; November 12, 1989, p. 63; April 27, 1997, p. 13.

Ontario Review, fall, 1974, p. 89; fall-winter, 1979-80, p. 91.

Parnassus, February, 1988, pp. 189-95.

Poetry, January, 1980, p. 229; March, 1985, pp. 345-48; January, 1993, pp. 223-26; August, 1997, p. 288.

Publishers Weekly, September 30, 1996, review of *Sun under Wood,* p. 82; October 28, 1996, p. 51; March 24, 1997, p. 25.

Raritan, summer, 1990, p. 126.

Southern Review, spring, 1996, p. 391.

Southwest Review, June, 1975, p. 307.

Studia Neophilologica, Volume 61, number 2, 1989, p. 193; Volume 63, number 2, 1991, p. 189.

Times Literary Supplement, May 28, 1982; March 15, 1985, p. 293.

Voice Literary Supplement, December, 1989, pp. 5-6.

Washington Post, March 19, 1997, p. D1.

Washington Post Book World, August 19, 1979, p. 8; January 26, 1997, p. 8.

World Literature Today, winter, 1985, p. 163; spring, 1990, p. 313.

ONLINE

American Poetry Review, http://members.aol.com/grace7623/haas.htm/ (August 21, 2004), Grace Cavalieri, interview with author, March, 1997.

Suite101.com, http://www.suite101.com/article.cfm/poetry_reviews/91240/ (August 21, 2004), Thadine Franciszkiewicz, "Robert Haas: Fresh Perspective of Poetry," April 24, 2002.

*   *   *

HAVEL, Vaclav 1936-

PERSONAL: Born October 5, 1936, in Prague, Czechoslovakia (now Czech Republic); son of Vaclav M. (a building contractor and restaurateur) and Bozena (Vavreckova) Havel; married Olga Splichalova, 1964 (died, January 27, 1996); married Dagmar Havlova, January 4, 1997. *Education:* Attended technical college, 1955-57, and Prague Academy of Art, 1962-67.

ADDRESSES: Agent—Aura Pont Agency, Radilcka 99, 150 00 Prague, Czech Republic.

CAREER: Playwright and politician. ABC Theatre, Prague, Czechoslovakia, stagehand, 1959-60; Theatre on the Balustrade, Prague, stagehand, 1960-61, assistant to artistic director, 1961-63, literary manager, 1963-68, resident playwright, 1968; imprisoned for dissent, 1977, 1979-83, and 1989; president of Czechoslovakia, 1989-92; president of Czech Republic, 1993-2003. *Military service:* Czech Army, 1957-59.

MEMBER: PEN (member of board of directors), Union of Writers (Czechoslovakia), Charter 77 (co-founder), Committee for the Defense of the Unjustly Persecuted (VONS).

AWARDS, HONORS: Austrian State Prize for European Literature, 1969; Obie awards, *Village Voice,* 1970, for *The Increased Difficulty of Concentration,* 1984, for *A Private View,* and, 1985-86, for *Largo Desolato;* Erasmus Prize, 1986; Los Angeles Drama Critics Circle Award, 1988, for *Largo Desolato;* German Booksellers Association prize, 1989; Olof Palme prize, 1989; Simon Bolívar prize, UNESCO, 1990; President's Award, PEN Center USA West, 1990; Charlemagne prize, Sonning prize, Averell Harriman Democracy Award, B'Nai Brith prize, Freedom Award, Raoul Wallenberg Human Rights Award, and International Book Award, all 1991; Onassis Prize Athinai, Order of White Eagle, and Golden Honorary Order of Freedom, all 1993; Indira Gandhi prize, Philadelphia Liberty Medal, and Jackson H. Ralston Prize in International Law, all 1994; Geuzenpenning, Catalonia international prize, and Future of Hope Award, all 1995; Order of the Bath and Virgin Mary's Land Cross, both 1996; Prix Special, International Association of Theatrical Critics (France), Statesman of the Year award (co-recipient with German President Roman Herzog), Institute for East-West Studies, J. William Fulbright prize, and Peace and Democracy award (Burma), all 1997; Compostela Group prize (Spain), 1998; First Decade award, *Gazeta Wyborcza* (Poland), Open Society prize (Hungary), and St. Adalbert Foundation prize (Slovakia), all 1999; Evelyn F. Burkey award, Authors Guild of America, Olympic Gate award, International Olympic Committee, Foundation Stätsbrugerlicher Stiftung, and Wild Geese award (Prague), all 2000. Recipient of honorary degrees from numerous institutions, including Columbia University, Hebrew University—Jerusalem, Lehigh University, University of Brussels, Harvard University, University of New South Wales, Trinity College—Dublin, and various universities in the Czech Republic.

WRITINGS:

PLAYS; IN ENGLISH TRANSLATION

Zahradni slavnost (also see below; first produced in Prague, Czechoslovakia, 1963), [Czechoslovakia], 1964, translation by Vera Blackwell published as *The Garden Party,* J. Cape (London, England), 1969.

Vyrozumeni (also see below; first produced in Prague, Czechoslovakia, 1965; produced Off-Broadway, 1968), Dilia, 1965, translation by Vera Blackwell published as *The Memorandum,* J. Cape (London, England), 1967.

Ztizena moznost soustredeni (first produced in Prague, Czechoslovakia, 1968; produced in New York, NY, 1969), Dilia, 1968, translation by Vera Blackwell published as *The Increased Difficulty of Concentration,* J. Cape (London, England), 1972.

Sorry: Two Plays (contains *Audience* and *Vernisaz;* also see below), translation by Vera Blackwell, Methuen (London, England), 1978.

A Private View (one-act plays; contains *Interview, A Private View,* and *The Protest;* translation by Vera Blackwell, produced in New York, NY, 1983, produced as *The Vanek Plays,* London, England, 1990), portions included in *The Vanek Plays: Four Authors, One Character,* translation by M. Pomichalek and A. Mozga, University of British Columbia Press (Vancouver, British Columbia, Canada), 1987.

Largo Desolato (produced in Bristol, England; translation by Marie Winn produced in New York, NY, 1986), translation by Tom Stoppard, Faber & Faber (Boston, MA), 1987.

Pokouseni (first produced in Vienna, Austria, 1985; produced by the Royal Shakespeare Company; translation by Marie Winn produced in New York, NY, 1989), translation by George Thiener, Faber & Faber (Boston, MA), 1988.

The Garden Party, and Other Plays, Grove Press (New York, NY), 1993.

Selected Plays, 1984-1987 (included *Largo Desolato* and *Temptation*), Faber & Faber (Boston, MA), 1988.

Redevelopment, translation by James Saunders, Faber & Faber (Boston, MA), 1994.

The Beggar's Opera, translation by Paul Wilson, Cornell University Press (Ithaca, NY), 2001.

Also author of *The Conspirators,* 1971, *The Mountain Hotel,* 1974, *Mistake,* and *The Guardian Angel;* author of adaptation of John Gay's 1765 work *The Beggar's Opera,* 1972. Contributor to anthologies, including *Three Eastern European Plays,* 1970.

IN CZECH

(With Ivan Vyskocil) *Autostop* (play; title means "Hitchhike"), first produced in Prague, Czechoslovakia, 1961.

Protokoly (anthology; title means "Protocols"; contains plays *Zahradni slavnost* and *Vyrozumeni,* two essays, and selected poems), introduction by Jan Grossman, Mlanda Fronta, 1966.

Hry 1970-1976 (plays; contains *Spiklenci, Zebracka Opera, Horsky Hotel, Audience,* and *Vernisaz*), Sixty-Eight Publishing House (Toronto, Ontario, Canada), 1977.

Pokouseni: Hra o deseti obrazech, Obrys/Kontur (Munich, Germany), 1986.

Dalkovy Vyslech: Rozhovor s Karlem Hvizdalou, Rozmluvy, 1986.

Asanace: Hra o peti jednanich, Obrys/Kontur, 1988.

Letni premitani, Odeon, 1991.

Sila bessilsnykh, Polifakt, 1991.

Hry: soubor her z let 1963-1988 (plays), Lidove noviny, 1992.

Vazeni obcane: projevy cervenec 1990-cervenec 1992, Lidove noviny, 1992.

Antikaody: Vaclav Havel, Odeon, 1993.

Deset dopiseu Olze (correspondence), Vybor dobre veule, 1997.

Hovory s Havly: Dalkove rozhovory s Vaclavem Havlem a s Ivanem M. Havlem, Zdenek Susa, 1999.

Havel's speeches were collected and published in annual editions, Paseka, 1992-1998.

OTHER

(With others) *The Power of the Powerless: Citizens against the State in Central Eastern Europe,* edited by John Keane, M.E. Sharpe (Armonk, NJ), 1985.

Vaclav Havel; or, Living in Truth (essay collection), edited by Jan Vladislav, Faber & Faber (Boston, MA), 1987.

Letters to Olga: June 1979 to September 1982 (correspondence), translated by Paul Wilson, Knopf (New York, NY), 1988.

Disturbing the Peace: A Conversation with Karel Hvizdala (interviews), translated by Paul Wilson, Knopf (New York, NY), 1990.

Open Letters: Selected Writings, edited by Paul Wilson, Knopf (New York, NY), 1991.

Summer Meditations (essays), translated by Paul Wilson, Knopf (New York, NY), 1992.

A Word about Words, Cooper Union (New York, NY), 1992.

The Art of the Impossible: Politics As Morality in Practice; Speeches and Writings, 1990-1996, translated by Paul Wilson and others, Knopf (New York, NY), 1997.

Responsibility, Safety, Stability: Vaclav Havel concerning NATO: Selected Speeches, Articles, and Interviews, 1990-1999, North Atlantic Treaty Organization, 1999.

(Author of introduction) Allen Ginsburg, *Spontaneous Mind: Selected Interviews, 1958-1996,* HarperCollins (New York, NY), 2001.

Also author of monograph on writer/painter Joseph Capek, 1963, and of *Slum Clearance,* 1987. Contributor to *New York Review of Books* and other periodicals.

Havel's writings have been translated into numerous languages.

ADAPTATIONS: Letters to Olga was set to music and performed by Petr Kotik and the S.E.M. Ensemble, 1989.

SIDELIGHTS: Vaclav Havel's unique career has led him from early praise as a promising dramatic talent to the presidency of a free Czechoslovakia. Havel enjoyed early success as a playwright in his home country, where his first three plays—*The Garden Party, The Memorandum,* and *The Increased Difficulty of Concentration*—were acclaimed for their inventive take on bureaucracy and its effects in creating a dehumanized society. After the Soviet invasion of 1968, however, Havel's works were banned and the dramatist himself became the target of government harassment and imprisonment for his outspokenness. Nevertheless, Havel's works found staging in the Western world, increasing his fame and leading *Tulane Drama Review* critic Henry Popkin to call Havel "the leading Czech dramatist since Karel Capek." In the meantime, Havel gained renown at home for his willingness to suffer government retribution in order to air his views on freedom and human rights. As a result, the sweeping changes that took place in Eastern Europe in late 1989 not only led to the reinstatement of Havel's plays on the Czech stage, but also to his election as president of Czechoslovakia, a position he held until February of 2003.

According to Popkin, Havel's first play, *The Garden Party,* "touches upon the discomforts endured by political bureaucracy as it makes its transition from Stalinism to an awkward and severely limited liberalism." The play concerns the career of Hugo Pludek, who, continually mouthing platitudes and political slogans, rises rapidly to control of the Office of Liquidation and the Office of Inauguration. The play focuses on efforts to dissolve the Office of Liquidation, which, however, can only dissolve itself—an impossibility since, once the process was begun, the office would no longer exist to finish the job. In the *Tulane Drama Review* Jan Grossman described *The Garden Party* as dominated by cliché: "Man does not use cliché, cliché uses man. Cliché is the hero, it causes, advances, and complicates the plot, determining human action, and deviating further and further from our given reality, creates its own." Marketa Goetz-Stankiewicz elaborated, noting in *The Silenced Theatre* that Havel's main concern in the play is "the power of language as a perpetuator of systems, a tool to influence man's mind and therefore one of the strongest (though secret) weapons of any system that wants to mould him."

The Memorandum also concerns the political power of language, in this instance the distortion of language by bureaucracy. Havel's second play revolves around Ptydepe, an artificial and incomprehensible language designed to make all office communication precise and unemotional. The fall and rise of an office manager as a result of his inability to use the new language constitutes the play's main action. A writer for the *Times Literary Supplement* commented: "In *The Garden Party* Havel showed us words dominating human beings: the phrase is the real hero of the piece, creating the situations and complicating them, directing human destinies instead of being their tool. In *Vyrozumeni*—to use the original Czech title of *The Memorandum*—man finds himself enmeshed not merely in a succession of phrases but in a whole language." As Grossman explained, "Man makes an artificial language which is intended to render communication perfect and objective, but which actually leads to constantly deepening alienation and disturbance in human relations."

Despite its treatment of serious issues and themes, *The Memorandum* is an amusing, entertaining play. Clive Barnes of the *New York Times*, for example, called it a "witty, funny and timely" political satire, while *Nation* critic Robert Hatch considered it a "bureaucratic burlesque." Havel's use of his invented language contributes to the comic and absurd aspects of the play. As Paul I. Trensky elaborated in the *Slavic and East European Journal*, "The scenes with the greatest force of absurd comedy are those in which Ptydepe is given voice directly." "The theory of the new languages discussed in the play is brilliantly worked out," Martin Esslin similarly stated in *The Theatre of the Absurd*. In addition, Esslin remarked, "Havel is a master of the ironical, inverted repetition, of almost identical phrases in different contexts."

After Havel was silenced by the Czech authorities, his *The Increased Difficulty of Concentration* was produced

in New York City by the Lincoln Center Repertory Theatre. The play depicts the attempts of philosopher Dr. Eduard Huml to deal with a series of challenges: the contrary demands of his wife and mistress; the dictation of a pedantic essay to a beautiful secretary; and his participation in an experiment that requires him to answer the questions of a temperamental computer. The form of the drama is variable; "chronology has been banished from the premises," observed *Washington Post* writer David Richards, so that "Havel's scenes follow one another with a blithe disregard for logic." Thus a character may exit and re-enter on opposite ends of the stage, and scenes fluctuate back and forth in time.

Cue reviewer Marilyn Stasio found the work a "potent satiric drama" that, "for all its ominous undertones, [is] an inescapably funny play." Mel Gussow in the *New York Times* judged the play to be "gentler" than *The Memorandum,* while a *Variety* critic considered it "a better play than Havel's earlier work, . . . with application beyond the border of eastern Europe." In his review for the *Nation,* Harold Clurman noted the play's importance for a Czech audience: "The speech that seems almost embarrassingly out of place with us, a speech in which the central character declares his conviction that the truth of life cannot be measured by computers or bureaucratic dictates but only by the motivations of the human heart, is what Havel meant his play to say. That is what gave it social force in his country. . . . Thus the play, a farce of no great subtlety, becomes something vital to the Czech citizen forever under the vigilant and evil eye—of who can say just what." But Richards suggested that *The Increased Difficulty of Concentration* is entertaining no matter who the audience, calling it "a decidedly unusual comedy, full of the slapstick invention and mishap that Havel obviously sees as a measure of our absurd world."

Although Havel received many invitations to work in the West after 1968, he chose to remain in Czechoslovakia, afraid that if he left he would not be allowed back in the country. Forbidden to work in the theater, he devoted much of his time to speaking out against government oppression. In 1969, for example, he visited steel mills in Ostrava and spoke to union members about workers and intellectuals cooperating to defend the freedoms gained in the spring of 1968. This led to government surveillance of the playwright and his family; and even members of his audience became victims of police reprisals, such as when his adaptation of *The Beggar's Opera* was produced by amateurs in 1975. In 1977 Havel became one of the three principal spokesmen for the Charter 77 manifesto, which charged the Czech government with human-and civil-rights violations and called for compliance with the provisions of the Helsinki Agreement. After joining with the artists, writers, intellectuals, and working people of the Charter 77 movement, Havel was arrested and imprisoned several times.

These experiences are reflected in many of Havel's later works, including the three "Vanek" plays, staged together as *A Private View* and *Largo Desolato*. The three short plays of *A Private View*, consisting of *Interview*, the title piece, and *The Protest*, "are linked both thematically and by the presence in each of a mild-mannered, steel-cored autobiographical character named Ferdinand Vanek, dissident artist and outsider in hopeless conflict with an oppressive social order," as Helen Dudar explained in the *New York Times*. The first play shows Vanek being offered favors by his factory foreman if he will inform on himself; the second brings the artist in contact with a bourgeois couple who refuse to understand his cause; and the third portrays Vanek's encounter with a fellow artist who uses convoluted logic to avoid signing a political protest. "In each of the plays we see how others react to [Vanek] . . . and to his martyrdom," commented Gussow, "how each wears his guilt as a badge of identity: the price of prosperity is the loss of humanity. Vanek has become a public conscience and his very presence is a 'living reproach' to those who are compromisers and cowards."

"All three plays suggest what their author has been publicly saying," stated London *Times* writer Benedict Nightingale: "that lies erode the human spirit, and honesty, once lost, will take time to recover." But while the plays point out this truth, they do so without preaching or being simplistic. As Nightingale observed, the play's "point is the stronger for Havel's unerring refusal to idealize his main character or to damn his less principled acquaintances." *A Private View* "reminds us of the importance of the artist as provocateur," concluded Gussow. "Despite his victimization, Havel has retained his comic equilibrium and his sense of injustice. Confronted by public and private absurdities, the artist clings to first principles: self-respect and an unquenchable morality."

In the award-winning *Largo Desolato*, Havel "has once again attempted to transmute the nightmare of totalitarian repression into bleak comedy of high linguistic absurdity," Frank Rich maintained in the *New York Times*. The protagonist, dissident writer Leopold Kopriva, is tormented both by government thugs who watch over and interrogate him and an assortment of friends, fans, and well-wishers who continually remind him of their

expectations for him. But while *Largo Desolato* deals with issues of the artistic conscience, it is also a comedy; Irving Wardle of the London *Times*, in his review of the Tom Stoppard translation, praised the play as "a wonderfully comic and unself-pitying piece of work: a notable instance of how adversity can sharpen the power of irony."

Havel also brings an ironic edge to *Temptation*, which transports the legend of Faust into a modern totalitarian society. Havel's Dr. Foustka is an institute scientist whose forbidden studies conjure the appearance of Fistula, a being who grants the doctor the ability to get ahead with the bureaucracy and with women. When Foustka's study is discovered, however, he begins a chain of deception that leads to a surprising twist. As with Havel's previous work, proposed Rich, in *Temptation* "even simple words (starting with 'morality') are inverted in meaning by a state that demands intellectual conformity and that governs by fear. It's Mr. Havel's incredible gift," Rich continued, that "he spins out the nightmare of repression in intricate verbal comedy to match that of Tom Stoppard." Nightingale likewise praised the playwright's verbal skill: "It says much for Havel's passion and skill that his satiric updating of the Faust legend remains so eloquent," the critic wrote, describing *Temptation* as "a study of the moral convolutions of the dissident in a corrupt society." "As in Havel's early work," concluded Wardle, "the shape is indestructibly elegant, full of ironic echoes and balanced repetitions which become funnier with every recurrence; and in which all the allegorical elements are progressively sharpened to a political cutting edge."

Although Havel's works involve bureaucratic situations and contain a political edge, there is a universality to his plays, according to critics. As Wardle commented, in such works as *Largo Desolato* "the brilliance of the piece is that it extends beyond its own country to the civil rights public at large." And because his plays deal with the dehumanization of man within the increasing mechanization of society, Havel has also been labeled an absurdist and, in fact, credited with bringing the absurdist method to Czechoslovakia. However, Grossman considered Havel's drama not absurd but "appellative": "His plays are inventive, artificial; but this quality has nothing to do with romantic fantasies or . . . unbridled insanity." The critic elaborated: "Havel's artificial structuring of the world is made up of real, even commonplace and banal, components, joined most reasonably into a whole."

Thus grounded in reality, Havel's plays remain decidedly allegorical; the protagonist of a Havel play is political bureaucracy itself, or a mechanism of bureaucracy which controls not only the characters, but also the plot and action of the play. For Havel, Grossman maintained, the mechanization of man is not just a theme, "but the central subject, from which his technique derived and on which it is focused." As a *Times Literary Supplement* reviewer similarly observed: "In his preoccupation with the logical and the illogical Havel is a second Lewis Carroll, except that many people in Prague who saw his plays came out laughing 'with a chill up their spine.' His theatre could be the theatre of the absurd but it is not: his central theme is mechanization and what it makes a man, but mechanization is a gimmick rather than an inescapable factor in progress (as Capek might have seen it). It is clear that Havel's master in ideas was Kafka and in expression Ionesco," the critic concluded. "His is something of a genius whose promise is even greater than his performance."

In 1975 Havel's adaptation of British playwright John Gay's *The Beggar's Opera* eluded censors for one memorable performance. Havel used the play to lambaste the communist regime, and the work brought down the wrath of authorities on the Czech playwright, forcing him out of the theater. In 2003 an English translation of Havel's version of *The Beggar's Opera* saw a stage revival in London and in book form. It differs from Gay's version in that Havel adopts a colloquial style, a comic tone, and includes original subplots that satirize collectivism and the loss of individuality under communism. As Ming-Ming Shen Kuo of *Library Journal* noted, even in the English version, the "political overtones remain sharp." Ian Shuttleworth of the *Financial Times* maintained that the work "brilliantly succeeds in being an indictment of the labyrinthine strategies of deception and the informant networks of the Communist state." Although the Czech people no longer suffer under communist rule, the play can be "read equally in a contemporary context of 'spin,'" Shuttleworth continued, "where everyone is repeatedly trying to justify even to themselves the unjustifiable, and self-interest is served by selling oneself out to the big boys. Goodbye dictatorship of the proletariat, hello global market."

Although he has been acclaimed for his dramatic works, Havel is also known for his development as a political philosopher; Toronto *Globe and Mail* contributor Peter C. Newman, for instance, called the writer "the most influential theorist on the nature of totalitarianism and dissent." During his censorship by the Czech government, Havel's ideas were often spread underground, and while in prison many of them found their way out in the form of Havel's letters to his wife. Published as *Let-*

ters to Olga, these correspondences provide "a rare opportunity for meditation that has been all too rare in the life of a profound philosopher," Roger Scruton remarked in the London *Times.* Similarly, *Disturbing the Peace: A Conversation with Karel Hvizdala* provides Havel with an opportunity to "provoke, enchant and illuminate," as Cameron Smith asserted in the Toronto *Globe and Mail.* This series of tape-recorded interviews from 1985 "is an excursion into humanity's great themes, as Havel himself encountered them—life, death, God, art, freedom, responsibility, courage, fear—by one of the grand figures of our time."

In *Disturbing the Peace* Havel notes the following of his country: "The idea that a writer is the conscience of his nation has its own logic and its own tradition here. For years, writers have stood in for politicians: they were renewers of the national community, maintainers of the national language, interpreters of the national will. This tradition has continued under totalitarian conditions, where it gains its own special coloring: the written word seems to have acquired a kind of heightened radioactivity—otherwise they wouldn't lock us up for it!" This tradition notwithstanding, Havel was frequently quoted as saying that he would rather be a playwright than a statesman.

Just as his plays "don't simply shrug and walk away" and "say that people and societies do have to make choices," as *Los Angeles Times* writer Dan Sullivan observed, throughout his life Havel has complied with what he has seen as his duty. As he was quoted by Henry Kamm in the *New York Times:* "I have repeatedly said my occupation is writer. . . . I have no political ambitions. I don't feel myself to be a professional politician. But I have always placed the public interest above my own. . . . And if, God help us, the situation develops in such a way that the only service that I could render my country would be to [accept public office], then of course I would do it." These circumstances arose during Czechoslovakia's political upheaval in 1989, when Havel emerged as the leader of the opposition to the Communist government. In a unanimous vote by Czechoslovakia's parliament, Havel was chosen to serve as president, and when free elections were held the following year he was reaffirmed as his country's leader.

The volume *Open Letters* collects various writings that showcase Havel's eloquence as a statesman, ranging from his first words of protest in 1965 to what Irving Howe in the *New York Times Book Review* called his "soberly triumphant" inaugural address of 1990. Havel's essays, noted Tony Judt in the *Times Literary Supplement,* "show a complex political and moral sensibility. They are written with wonderful clarity and directness; whatever posterity will say of Havel's plays, there can be no doubt that, as an author, he has a rare gift for metaphor and example." *Summer Meditations,* which includes writings from Havel's early years in public office, focuses mainly on the issue of morality in politics. Havel, commented Steven Lukes in the *Times Literary Supplement,* uses words "for uplift and exhortation: the President as Preacher. They are, needless to say, meditations far more articulate and intelligent than any other current world statesman is likely to produce." As quoted by Lukes, Havel writes that "politics is not essentially a disreputable business; and to the extent that it is, it is only disreputable people who make it so."

In 1997 Havel released *The Art of the Impossible: Politics As Morality in Practice,* a collection of speeches delivered between 1990 and 1996 as president first of Czechoslovakia and then the Czech Republic. George Stephanopoulos in the *Los Angeles Times Book Review* observed that these speeches address all the relevant questions facing modern European politics—NATO's future, European integration, East-West relations, as well as globalization—but "more interesting, and lasting, are Havel's meditations on the timeless questions of politics and philosophy: What is the nature of civic responsibility? When do the ends justify the means in state-craft? Can intellectuals serve with integrity in the political arena? Is it possible for people who hold political power to 'live in truth' and approach the ideal of 'politics as morality in practice?'" Noting the Czech president's silence regarding certain government policies in these speeches, Douglas A. Sylva in the *New York Times Book Review* pointed out that Havel "cares much more about what his people think and feel than how they should resolve specific political questions."

Critical reception to *The Art of the Impossible* called attention to the uniqueness Havel demonstrated in his role as president. Jean Bethke Elshtain, writing in *Commonweal,* saw Havel as struggling with the dichotomy of being both an intellectual and a politician as well as demonstrating a great concern for morality in politics: "Havel's great fear is that relinquishing a politics of high morality often leads to a politics of brute instrumentality; thus, he rejects politics that is simply 'the art of the possible.'" Preston Jones in *First Things* considered Havel's references to a transcendent force distinctive: "Yet that he speaks about such things openly, and not merely for political reasons, sets him apart from the great majority of the industrialized world's public officials." Stephanopoulos found that Havel's "words are a

sorely needed antidote to the grandiosity that infects so many who practice politics and the apathy that characterizes so many who live in our society but ignore the duties of citizenship."

After losing in the Czech Republic's parliamentary elections in 2003, Havel and his second wife, Czech actress Dagmar Veskrnova, retired to their home in the seaside town of Algarve, where he planned to write his memoirs.

BIOGRAPHICAL AND CRITICAL SOURCES:

BOOKS

Contemporary Literary Criticism, Thomson Gale, (Detroit, MI), Volume 25, 1983, Volume 58, 1990, Volume 65, 1991.

Czech Literature since 1956: A Symposium, edited by William E. Harkins and Paul I. Trensky, Bohemica (New York, NY), 1980, pp. 103-118.

Drama Criticism, Volume 6, Thomson Gale, (Detroit, MI) 1996.

Esslin, Martin, *The Theatre of the Absurd,* revised edition, Doubleday (New York, NY), 1969.

Esslin, Martin, *Reflections: Essays on Modern Theatre,* Doubleday (New York, NY), 1969.

Goetz-Stankiewicz, Marketa, *The Silenced Theatre: Czech Playwrights without a Stage,* University of Toronto Press (Toronto, Ontario, Canada), 1979.

Goetz-Stankiewicz, Marketa, and Phyllis Careys, editors, *Critical Essays on Vaclav Havel,* Hall (New York, NY), 1999.

Havel, Vaclav, *Disturbing the Peace: A Conversation with Karel Hvizdala,* translation by Paul Wilson, Knopf (New York, NY), 1990.

Havel, Vaclav, *Summer Meditations,* translation by Paul Wilson, Knopf (New York, NY), 1992.

Keane, John, *Vaclav Havel: A Political Tragedy in Six Acts,* Bloomsbury Press (London, England), 1999.

Kriseova, Eda, *Vaclav Havel: The Authorized Biography,* translation by Caleb Crain, St. Martin's Press (New York, NY), 1993.

Labyrinth of the Word: Truth and Representation in Czech Literature, Oldenbourg (Munich, Germany), 1995, pp. 144-157.

Matustik, Martin J., *Postnational Identity: Critical Theory and Existential Philosophy in Habemas, Kierkegaard, and Havel,* Guilford (New York, NY), 1993.

Simmons, Michael, *The Reluctant President: The Political Life of Vaclav Havel,* Methuen (London, England), 1991.

Symynkywicz, Jeffrey, *Vaclav Havel and the Velvet Revolution,* Dillon Press (New York, NY), 1995.

Twentieth-Century European Drama, edited by Brian Docherty, St. Martin's Press (New York, NY), 1994, pp. 172-182.

Vladislav, Jan, editor, *Vaclav Havel; or, Living in Truth,* Faber & Faber (London, England), 1987.

PERIODICALS

Back Stage, June 18, 1999, Karl Levett, review of *Largo Desolato,* p. 56.

Booklist, June 1, 2001, Jack Helbig, review of *The Beggar's Opera,* p. 1825.

Chicago Tribune, December 30, 1989; February 22, 1990.

Christianity and Literature, fall, 1994, Phyllis Carey, "Face to Face: Samuel Beckett and Vaclav Havel," pp. 43-57.

Commonweal, October 24, 1997, Jean Bethke Elshtain, "Philosopher President," pp. 23-24.

Cross Currents, Volume 10, 1991, Marketa Goetz-Stankiewicz, "Shall We Dance? Reflections on Vaclav Havel's Plays," pp. 213-222; summer, 1992, Phyllis Carey, "Living the Lies: Vaclav Havel's Drama," pp. 200-211; fall, 1997, Walter H. Capps, "Interpreting Vaclav Havel," pp. 301-316.

Cue, December 13, 1969.

Czechoslovak and Central European Journal, winter, 1991, Paul I. Trensky, "Vaclav Havel's 'Temptation Cycle,'" pp. 84-95.

Essays in Theatre, May, 1992, Michael L. Quinn, "Delirious Subjectivity: Four Scenes from Havel," pp. 117-132.

Financial Times, January 21, 2003, Ian Shuttleworth, "New Spin on Havel's Old Satire Theatre *The Beggar's Opera,*" p. 15.

First Things, December, 1998, p. 61.

Globe and Mail (Toronto, Ontario, Canada), April 30, 1988; October 28, 1989; December 30, 1989; January 6, 1990; June 23, 1990.

Humanist, May-June, 1994, p. 40; November-December, 1994, p. 39.

Insight on the News, August 8, 1994, p. 37.

Kenyon Review, spring, 1993, Robert Skloot, "Vaclav Havel: The Once and Future Playwright," pp. 223-231.

Library Journal, May 15, 2001, Ming-Ming Shen Kuo, review of *The Beggar's Opera,* p. 124.

Los Angeles Times, February 15, 1989; February 22, 1989; December 4, 1989; December 10, 1989; December 17, 1989; January 13, 1990; February 23, 1990.

Los Angeles Times Book Review, April 3, 1988; June 29, 1997, p. 11.

Maclean's, August 17, 1998, p. 52.

Modern Drama, March, 1984, M.C. Bradbrook, "Vaclav Havel's Second Wind," pp. 124-132; winter, 1997, Jude R. Meche, "Female Victims and the Male Protagonist in Vaclav Havel's Drama," pp. 468-476.

Nation, May 27, 1968; December 22, 1969.

New Statesman, July 22, 1994, p. 32.

Newsweek, July 18, 1994, p. 66.

New Yorker, May 18, 1968; February 17, 2003, David Remnick, "Exit Havel," p. 90.

New York Review of Books, August 4, 1977; March 22, 1979; August 15, 1991, Dana Emigerova and Lubos Beniak, "'Uncertain Strength': An Interview with Vaclav Havel," pp. 6, 8; September 24, 1992, George F. Kennan, review of *Summer Mediations,* pp. 3-4.

New York Times, May 6, 1968; October 22, 1969; December 5, 1969; December 14, 1969; November 20, 1983; November 21, 1983; March 23, 1986; March 26, 1986; March 31, 1988; February 5, 1989; April 9, 1989; December 8, 1989; December 17, 1989; December 18, 1989; December 23, 1989; December 30, 1989; January 12, 1990; January 13, 1990; June 27, 1990; May 26, 1991, Irving Howe, review of *Open Letters,* p. 5.

New York Times Book Review, May 8, 1988; May 26, 1991; June 7, 1992; August 3, 1997, p. 17; October 11, 1998, review of *The Art of the Impossible,* p. 32.

New York Times Magazine, October 25, 1987.

Observer Review, December 17, 1967.

Plays and Players, August, 1971.

Progressive, April, 1993, Erwin Knoll, review of *Open Letters, Summer Meditations,* and *Living in Truth,* pp. 40-43.

Prompt, number 12, 1968.

Representations summer, 1993, Martin Prochazka, "Prisoner's Predicament: Public Privacy in Havel's *Letters to Olga,*" pp. 126-154.

Sewanee Review, spring, 1992.

Slavic and East European Journal, spring, 1969, Paul I. Trensky, "Vaclav Havel and the Language of the Absurd," pp. 42-65.

Slavic and East European Performance, spring, 1992, M. Quinn, review of *Largo Desolato,* pp. 8-12; spring, 1996, Jarka Burian, "Vaclav Havel's Notable Encounters in His Early Theatrical Career," pp. 13-29.

Slavic Review, summer, 1992, Alfred Thomas, reviews of *The Vanek Plays* and *Living in Truth,* pp. 348-351.

Style, summer, 1991, Veronika Ambros, "Fictional World and Dramatic Text: Vaclav Havel's Descent and Ascent," pp. 310-319.

Thought, September, 1991, Phyllis Carey, "Contemporary World Drama 101: Vaclav Havel," pp. 317-328.

Time, June 14, 1968; July 25, 1969.

Times (London, England), October 15, 1986; February 12, 1987; May 2, 1987; April 27, 1988; February 29, 1989; March 4, 1989; February 17, 1990; March 7, 1990; June 8, 1990.

Times Literary Supplement, March 7, 1968; March 10, 1972; October 21, 1991; September 25, 1992.

Tulane Drama Review, spring, 1967.

Variety, December 17, 1969.

Washington Post, August 26, 1988; February 22, 1989; May 15, 1989; October 27, 1989; January 7, 1990; January 9, 1990; March 4, 1990.

Washington Post Book World, June 14, 1992.

World and I, August, 2001, Lesley Chamberlain, "Play It Again, Vaclav: The Wisdom of Havel's Plays," p. 76.

World Literature Today, summer, 1981, Marketa Goetz-Stankiewicz, "Vaclav Havel: A Writer for Today's Season," pp. 389-393; spring, 1991, Karen von Kunes, "The National Paradox: Czech Literature and the Gentle Revolution," pp. 327-240.

*   *   *

HAWKES, John 1925-1998
(John Clendennin Burne Hawkes, Jr.)

PERSONAL: Born August 17, 1925, in Stamford, CT; died of a stroke May 15, 1998, in Providence, RI; son of John Clendennin Burne and Helen (Ziefle) Hawkes; married Sophie Goode Tazewell, September 5, 1947; children: John Clendennin Burne III, Sophie Tazewell, Calvert Tazewell, Richard Urguhart. *Education:* Harvard University, A.B., 1949.

CAREER: Harvard University Press, Cambridge, MA, assistant to production manager, 1949-55; Harvard University, Cambridge, visiting lecturer, 1955-56, instructor in English, 1956-58; Brown University, Providence, RI, assistant professor, 1958-62, associate professor, 1962-67, professor of English, 1967-88, T.B. Stowell University Professor, beginning 1973, professor emeritus, beginning 1988. Visiting assistant professor of humanities, Massachusetts Institute of Technology, 1959; leader of novel workshop, Utah Writers' Conference, Salt Lake City, summer, 1962; special guest, Aspen Institute for Humanistic Studies, summer, 1962; staff member, Bread Loaf Writers' Conference, summer, 1963, writer in residence, University of Virginia, April, 1965; visiting professor of creative writing, Stanford University, 1966-67; visiting distinguished professor of creative writing, City College of the City University of New York, 1971-72. Member of panel on Educational Innovation, Washington, DC, 1966-67. *Military service:* American Field Service, 1944-45.

MEMBER: American Academy of Arts and Letters.

AWARDS, HONORS: Guggenheim fellowship, 1962-63; American Academy of Arts and Letters award, 1962; Ford Foundation fellowship in theater, 1964-65; Rockefeller Foundation grant, 1966; Prix du Meilleur Livre Étranger, 1973; Prix Medicis Étranger for best foreign novel translated into French, 1986, for *Adventures in the Alaskan Skin Trade.*

WRITINGS:

Fiasco Hall (poems), Harvard University Printing Office, 1949.

(Editor with Albert J. Guerard and others) *The Personal Voice: A Contemporary Prose Reader,* Lippincott (Philadelphia, PA), 1964.

Innocent Party: Four Short Plays (contains *The Questions,* first produced in Stanford, CA, January 13, 1966; produced by National Broadcasting Company (NBC-TV), 1967; produced Off-Broadway at Players Workshop, January 14, 1972; *The Wax Museum,* first produced in Boston, MA, April 28, 1966; produced Off-Broadway at Brooklyn Academy of Music, April 4, 1969; *The Undertaker,* first produced at Theatre Company of Boston, March 28, 1967; and *The Innocent Party,* first produced at Theatre Company of Boston, February, 1968; produced Off-Broadway at Brooklyn Academy of Music, April 4, 1969), New Directions (New York, NY), 1967.

(Editor with others) *The American Literary Anthology I: The First Annual Collection of the Best from the Literary Magazines,* Farrar, Straus (New York, NY), 1968.

Lunar Landscapes: Stories and Short Novels, 1949-1963 (includes *The Owl, The Goose on the Grave,* and *Charivari*), New Directions (New York, NY), 1969.

The Universal Fears, Lord John Press (Northridge, CA), 1978.

Humors of Blood & Skin: A John Hawkes Reader (autobiographical notes), introduction by William H. Gass, New Directions (New York, NY), 1984.

(With others) C.W. Tazewell, editor, *Hawkes Scrapbook: A New Taste in Literature,* W.S. Dawson (Virginia Beach, VA), 1990.

The Lime Twig; Second Skin; Travesty, Penguin (New York, NY), 1996.

NOVELS

The Cannibal, New Directions (New York, NY), 1949.

The Beetle Leg, New Directions (New York, NY), 1951.

The Goose on the Grave: Two Short Novels (contains *The Goose on the Grave* and *The Owl;* also see below), New Directions (New York, NY), 1954.

The Lime Twig, New Directions (New York, NY), 1961.

Second Skin, New Directions (New York, NY), 1964.

The Blood Oranges, New Directions (New York, NY), 1971.

Death, Sleep, and the Traveler, New Directions (New York, NY), 1974.

Travesty, New Directions (New York, NY), 1976.

The Owl, New Directions (New York, NY), 1977.

The Passion Artist, Harper (New York, NY), 1979.

Virginie: Her Two Lives, Harper (New York, NY), 1982.

Adventures in the Alaskan Skin Trade, Simon & Schuster (New York, NY), 1985.

Innocence in Extremis (novella), Burning Deck, 1985.

Whistlejacket, Weidenfeld & Nicolson (London, England), 1988, Dalkey Archive (Normal, IL), 1997.

Sweet William: A Novel of Old Horse, Simon & Schuster (New York, NY), 1993.

The Frog, Viking (New York, NY), 1996.

An Irish Eye, Viking (New York, NY), 1997.

OTHER

Contributor to anthologies, including *New Directions in Prose and Poetry II; The World of Black Humor: An Introductory Anthology of Selections and Criticism,* edited by Douglas M. Davis, 1967; *Write and Rewrite: A Story of the Creative Process,* edited by John Kuehl, 1967; *Flannery O'Connor,* edited by Robert E. Reiter; *The American Novel since World War II; Writers as Teachers, Teachers as Writers; Montpellier: Centre de'etude et de recherches sur les ecrivains du Sud sur Etats-Unis de L'Universite Paul Valery,* edited by Pierre Gault. Contributor of short stories, poems, articles, and reviews to periodicals, including *Audience, Voices: A Journal of Poetry, Sewanee Review, Massachusetts Review,* and *Tri-Quarterly.*

SIDELIGHTS: American Novelist John Hawkes has most often been characterized as an avant-garde writer. Hawkes's own declarations about his work and methods in an interview for *Wisconsin Studies in Contemporary Literature* support this assessment: "I began to write fiction on the assumption that the true enemies of the novel were plot, character, setting, and theme, and having once abandoned these familiar ways of thinking about fiction, totality of vision or structure was really all that remained. And structure—verbal and psychological coherence—is still my largest concern as a writer." Hawkes's rejection of traditional novelistic methods resulted in books critics have called nightmarish and dreamlike.

Hawkes's works have been attacked by critics who object to his unconventional methods. Alexander Klein, writing in the *New Republic,* contended that in *The Cannibal* "Hawkes presents a 'surrealistic novel' which manages for long stretches to make dullness and surrealism appear practically synonymous. Actually the book is a series of related images (some fresh and sharp) and fragmentary sketches (a few vividly effective), gimcracked together with a semblance of plot and allegory." In like manner, a *New Yorker* reviewer found that *The Lime Twig* "is struck through with bright flashes of emotion and imagery, but they do not compensate for the general murkiness of his prose, and they are not well enough balanced with the proportion and perspective that it very badly needs." In the *New York Times Book Review,* Jack Beatty called *Adventures in the Alaskan Skin Trade* "the most accomplished meaningless novel I have ever read."

Despite such criticism, critics have also found both method and purpose in the seeming madness of Hawkes's novels. Robert Scholes noted in his *The Fabulators* that "Hawkes means to use conscious thought and art to illuminate the unconscious, to show us things about ourselves which may be locked in our own unconscious minds, avoiding the scrutiny of our consciousness." In an interview with Scholes, Hawkes' once remarked about the nightmares evinced in his writing: "We can't deny the essential crippling that is everywhere in life. I don't advocate crippling; I'm an opponent of torture. I deplore the nightmare; I deplore terror; I happen to believe that it is only by traveling those dark tunnels, perhaps not literally but psychically, that one can learn in any sense what it means to be compassionate." "My fiction," Hawkes concluded in the interview, "is generally an evocation of the nightmare or terroristic universe in which sexuality is destroyed by law, by dictum, by human perversity, by contraption, and it is this destruction of human sexuality which I have attempted to portray and confront in order to be true to human fear and to human ruthlessness, but also in part to evoke its opposite, the moment of freedom from constriction, constraint, death."

In addition to discussing the psychological elements in his novels, Hawkes also commented on his concern with structure. "My novels are not highly plotted," he observed in *Wisconsin Studies,* "but they're elaborately structured." In his *Comic Terror: The Novels of John Hawkes,* Donald J. Greiner pointed out that "structure often holds the key to Hawkes's difficult fiction. . . . Structure in his work is based upon cross-references, parallels, and contrasts, rather than upon the development of plot and character. It is this technique that enriches the nightmarish overtones of the novels and gives them their poetic quality." Scholes also noted the novels' meticulously wrought structures; *The Lime Twig,* for example, "which seems so foggy and dreamlike, is actually as neatly put together as the electrical circuitry of the human nervous system." Scholes stressed the careful interweaving of recurring images and verbal patterns.

Whistlejacket is characteristic of Hawkes' works due to its reliance on structural and thematic parallels. On the surface the novel is a murder mystery; it details the lives of the Van Fleet family, which devotes itself to uppercrust hobbies and trying to hide its dirty secrets. Yet as Patrick McGrath noted in the *New York Times Book Review,* "Questions of representation, of the layers of meaning that come to light when surfaces are peeled back to expose the dark structures within, are central to *Whistlejacket.*" McGrath called the novel a "brilliantly sustained reflection on surface and depth, illusion and exposure, and the construction of meaning." Not all critics, however, praised the elaborate structures of Hawkes's writing. For John Clute in the *Washington Post Book World,* Hawkes's *Whistlejacket* is "like spindrift," written "in a style whose haste too often approaches the slovenly."

Hawkes described in a *Massachusetts Review* interview the centrality of visual images to his creative method: "I write out of a series of pictures that literally and actually do come to mind, but I've never seen them before. It is perfectly true that I don't know what they mean, but I feel and know that they have meaning. *The Cannibal* is probably the clearest example of this kind of absolute coherence of vision of anything I have written, when all the photographs do add together or come out of the same black pit."

Another element of Hawkes's work is its humor. As Greiner showed, many reviewers have been discon-

certed by Hawkes's "black humor" and the bleakness of his comedy, but other critics see the humor as a central, important part of the novels. Greiner, for instance, found that Hawkes "daringly mixes horror with humor, the grotesque with the heroic, creating a complex tone which some readers find hard to handle." The critic contended that Hawkes rejects traditional comedy, which usually aims to mock aberrant behavior and assert a "benevolent social norm." Hawkes's characters, "while they perform ridiculous acts and reveal absurd personal defects in the manner of traditional comedy, rarely discover their faults in time so as to be safely reestablished with society." In fact, Hawkes dismissed orthodox social norms. Fiction, he said, "should be an act of rebellion against all the constraints of the conventional pedestrian mentality around us. Surely it should destroy conventional morality."

While Hawkes spurns conventional morality, his "contemporary humor," Greiner argued, "maintains faith in the invulnerability of basic values: love, communication, sympathy. Given a world of fragmentation, self-destruction, and absurdity, Hawkes tries to meet the terrors with a saving attitude of laughter so as to defend and celebrate these permanent values." In his 1993 novel *Sweet William: A Novel of Old Horse,* for instance, Hawkes presents the story of a bright, stubborn pony who achieves fame and accolades as a young racer but whose mature years are spent as a stud and a racer in a decrepit stable. William's comfortable life as a horse is ruined by his own tantrums and pride, which cause him to injure the humans who care for him, but William remains unapologetic for his actions and disdainful of humans to the end.

A similar example of Hawkes's dark humor is his 1996 novel, *The Frog,* about a young French boy who swallows a frog, only to have the frog—which the boy names Armand—take up residence for good. Armand serves as a friend and companion to his host, even as his host is accused of madness and consigned to a sanatorium not once but twice in his life. In his *Massachusetts Review* interview, Hawkes insisted on his comic intentions: "I have always thought that my fictions, no matter how diabolical, were comic. I wanted to be very comic—but they have not been treated as comedy. They have been called 'black, obscene visions of the horror of life' and sometimes rejected as such, sometimes highly praised as such."

In addition to considering particular elements in his fiction, in his interview Hawkes examined the relationship between fiction and life: "I think that we read for joy, for pleasure, for excitement, for challenge. It would seem pretty obvious, however, that fiction is its own province. Fiction is a made thing—a manmade thing. It has its own beauties, its own structures, its own delights. Its only good is to please us and to relate to our essential growth. I don't see how we could live without it. It may be that the art of living is no more than to exercise the act of imagination in a more irrevocable way. It may be that to read a fiction is only to explore life's possibilities in a special way. I think that fiction and living are entirely separate and that the one could not exist without the other."

With *Humors of Blood & Skin: A John Hawkes Reader,* a collection of short stories and excerpts from his novels, critics took the opportunity to comment on the body of Hawkes's work. Writing in the *New York Times Book Review,* Arthur C. Danto concluded: "Hawkes has the power to do, gorgeously and as art, what most of us can at best do drably and as dream—transform incident into phantasm. For connoisseurs of this rare craft, the refined rewards are frequent and the pleasures subtle and the charms undeniable." In the volume's introduction, William H. Gass offers this assessment: "I hope that the book which you are holding now will provide . . . exhilaration, for these lines are alive as few in our literature are; it is a prose of great poetry; it is language linked like things in nature are—by life and by desire; it is exploratory without being in the least haphazard or confused. . . . [I]t shows me how writing should be written, and also how living should be lived. It is a prose that breathes what it sees."

BIOGRAPHICAL AND CRITICAL SOURCES:

BOOKS

Bellamy, Joe David, editor, *The New Fiction: Interviews with Innovative American Writers,* University of Illinois Press (Champaign, IL), 1974.

Busch, Frederick, *Hawkes: A Guide to His Works,* Syracuse University Press (Syracuse, NY), 1973.

Contemporary Literary Criticism, Thomson Gale (Detroit, MI), Volume 1, 1973, Volume 2, 1974, Volume 3, 1975, Volume 4, 1975, Volume 7, 1977, Volume 9, 1978, Volume 14, 1980, Volume 15, 1980, Volume 27, 1984, Volume 49, 1988.

Dictionary of Literary Biography, Thomson Gale (Detroit, MI), Volume 2: *American Novelists since World War II,* 1978, Volume 7: *Twentieth-Century American Dramatists,* 1981.

Dictionary of Literary Biography Yearbook: 1980, Thomson Gale (Detroit, MI), 1981.

Ferrari, Rita, *Innocence, Power, and the Novels of John Hawkes,* University of Pennsylvania Press (Philadelphia, PA), 1996.

Greiner, Donald J., *Comic Terror: The Novels of John Hawkes,* Memphis State University Press (Memphis, TN), 1973.

Hawkes, John, *Humors of Blood & Skin: A John Hawkes Reader,* introduction by William H. Gass, New Directions (New York, NY), 1984.

Hryciw, Carol A., *John Hawkes: An Annotated Bibliography,* Scarecrow (Metuchen, NJ), 1977.

Kuehl, John, *John Hawkes and the Craft of Conflict,* Rutgers University Press (Rutgers, NJ), 1975.

Laniel, Christine, editor, *Facing Texts: Encounters between Contemporary Writers and Critics,* Duke University Press (Durham, NC), 1988.

Littlejohn, David, *Interruptions,* Grossman, 1970.

Malin, Irving, *New American Gothic,* Southern Illinois University Press (Carbondale, IL), 1962.

Marx, Lesley, *Crystals out of Chaos: John Hawkes and the Shapes of Apocalypse,* Fairleigh Dickinson University Press (Rutherford, NJ), 1997.

Moore, Harry T., editor, *Contemporary American Novelists,* Southern Illinois University Press (Carbondale, IL), 1964.

Santore, Anthony C., and Michael Pocalyko, editors, *A John Hawkes Symposium: Design and Debris,* New Directions (New York, NY), 1977.

Scholes, Robert, *The Fabulators,* Oxford University Press (New York, NY), 1967.

Whelan, Michaele, *Navigating the Minefield: Hawke's Narratives of Perversion,* Peter Lang (New York, NY), 1998.

PERIODICALS

American Scholar, summer, 1965.

Audience, spring, 1960.

Book Week, September 26, 1965.

Chicago Tribune Book World, September 16, 1979.

Commonweal, July 2, 1954.

Contemporary Literature, Volume 2, number 3, 1970.

Critique, Volume 6, number 2, 1963; Volume 14, number 3, 1973.

Daedalus, spring, 1963.

Encounter, June, 1966.

Globe and Mail (Toronto, Ontario, Canada), September 17, 1988.

Harvard Advocate, March, 1950.

Kirkus Reviews, April 1, 1996, p. 468.

Kliatt, January, 1995, p. 8.

Life, September 19, 1969.

Listener, July 18, 1968; May 5, 1970.

Los Angeles Times Book Review, May 9, 1982.

Massachusetts Review, summer, 1966.

Mediterranean Review, winter, 1972.

Minnesota Review, winter, 1962.

Nation, September 2, 1961; November 16, 1985.

National Observer, June 19, 1971.

New Leader, December 12, 1960; October 30, 1961.

New Republic, March 27, 1950; November 10, 1979; November 18, 1985.

New Statesman, March 11, 1966; November 10, 1967; May 1, 1970.

Newsweek, April 3, 1967.

New Yorker, April 29, 1961.

New York Review of Books, July 13, 1967; June 10, 1982.

New York Times, September 15, 1971.

New York Times Book Review, May 14, 1961; May 29, 1966; September 19, 1971; April 21, 1974; March 28, 1976; September 16, 1979; June 27, 1982; November 25, 1984; September 29, 1985; November 25, 1985; August 7, 1988.

Publishers Weekly, April 15, 1996, p. 47.

Saturday Review, August 9, 1969; October 23, 1971.

Southwest Review, winter, 1965; October 23, 1971.

Time, February 6, 1950; September 24, 1979.

Times Literary Supplement, February 17, 1966; October 15, 1971; February 14, 1975; February 18, 1986; March 31, 1989.

Village Voice, April 10, 1969; May 23, 1974; September 3, 1979; May 18, 1982; September 17, 1985.

Washington Post, October 1, 1969.

Washington Post Book World, October 14, 1979; May 30, 1982, pp. 1-2; September 29, 1985; July 24, 1988, pp. 1, 7.

Wisconsin Studies in Contemporary Literature, summer, 1965.

*   *   *

HAWKES, John Clendennin Burne, Jr.
   See HAWKES, John

*   *   *

HAWKING, Stephen W. 1942-
   (S.W. Hawking, Stephen William Hawking)

PERSONAL: Born January 8, 1942, in Oxford, England; son of Frank (a research biologist) and E. Isobel (a secretary) Hawking; married Jane Wilde (a linguist), 1965, divorced, 1990; children: Robert, Lucy, Timothy. *Education:* Oxford University, B.A., 1962; Cambridge University, Ph.D., 1966.

ADDRESSES: Office—Department of Applied Mathematics and Theoretical Physics, Cambridge University, Silver St., Cambridge CB3 9EW, England.

CAREER: Theoretical physicist. Cambridge University, Cambridge, England, research fellow at Gonville and Caius College, 1965-69, member of Institute of Theoretical Astronomy, 1968-72, research assistant at Institute of Astronomy, 1972-73, research assistant in department of applied mathematics and theoretical physics, 1973-75, reader in gravitational physics, 1977-79, Lucasian Professor of Mathematics, 1979—. Fairchild Distinguished Scholar at California Institute of Technology, 1974-75.

MEMBER: Royal Society of London (fellow), Pontifical Academy of Sciences, American Academy of Arts and Sciences, American Philosophical Society, Royal Astronomical Society of Canada (honorary member).

AWARDS, HONORS: Eddington Medal, Royal Astronomical Society, 1975; Pius IX Gold Medal, Pontifical Academy of Sciences, 1975; Dannie Heinemann Prize for mathematical physics, American Physical Society and American Institute of Physics, 1976; William Hopkins Prize, Cambridge Philosophical Society, 1976; Maxwell Medal, Institute of Physics, 1976; Hughes Medal, Royal Society of London, 1976; honorary fellow of University College, Oxford, 1977; Albert Einstein Award, Lewis and Rosa Strauss Memorial Fund, 1978; Albert Einstein Medal, Albert Einstein Society (Bern, Switzerland), 1979; Franklin Medal, Franklin Institute, 1981; Commander of the British Empire, 1982; honorary fellow of Trinity Hall, Cambridge, 1984; Royal Astronomical Society Gold Medal, 1985; Paul Dirac Medal and Prize, Institute of Physics, 1987; Wolf Foundation Prize for physics, 1988; named a Companion of Honour on the Queen's Birthday Honours List, 1989; Britannica Award, 1989. Honorary degrees from various universities, including Oxford, 1978; Chicago, 1981; Leicester, Notre Dame, and Princeton, 1982; Newcastle and Leeds, 1987; and Tufts, Yale, and Cambridge, 1989.

WRITINGS:

A Brief History of Time: From the Big Bang to Black Holes, introduction by Carl Sagan, Bantam Books (New York, NY), 1988, updated and expanded tenth anniversary edition, 1998, published as *The Illustrated A Brief History of Time,* 1996.

Black Holes and Baby Universes and Other Essays, Bantam Books (New York, NY), 1993.

The Universe in a Nutshell, Bantam (New York, NY), 2001.

(With Kip S. Thorne, Igor Novikov, Timothy Ferris, and Alan Lightman) *The Future of Spacetime,* Norton (New York, NY), 2002.

On the Shoulders of Giants: The Great Works of Physics and Astronomy, Running Press (Philadelphia, PA), 2002.

The Theory of Everything: The Origin and Fate of the Universe, New Millennium Press (Beverly Hills, CA), 2002.

Also author and editor of many articles for scientific journals. *A Brief History of Time: From the Big Bang to Black Holes* has been translated into over thirty languages.

ACADEMIC WRITINGS; UNDER NAME S.W. HAWKING

(With G.F.R. Ellis) *The Large Scale Structure of Space-Time,* Cambridge University Press (Cambridge, England), 1973.

(Editor, with Werner Israel) *General Relativity: An Einstein Centenary Survey,* Cambridge University Press (Cambridge, England), 1979.

Is the End in Sight for Theoretical Physics? An Inaugural Lecture, Cambridge University Press (Cambridge, England), 1980.

(Editor, with M. Rocek) *Superspace and Supergravity: Proceedings of the Nuffield Workshop, Cambridge, June 16-July 12, 1980,* Cambridge University Press (Cambridge, England), 1981.

(Editor, with G.W. Gibbons and S.T.C. Siklos) *The Very Early Universe: Proceedings of the Nuffield Workshop, Cambridge, 21 June to 9 July 1982,* Cambridge University Press (Cambridge, England), 1983.

(Editor, with G.W. Gibbons and P.K. Townsend) *Supersymmetry and Its Applications: Superstrings, Anomalies, and Supergravity: Proceedings of a Workshop Supported by the Ralph Smith and Nuffield Foundations, Cambridge, 23 June to 14 July 1985,* Cambridge University Press (Cambridge, England), 1986.

(Editor, with Werner Israel) *Three Hundred Years of Gravitation,* Cambridge University Press (Cambridge, England), 1987.

(Editor, with G.W. Gibbons and T. Vachaspati) *The Formation and Evolution of Cosmic Strings; Proceedings of a Workshop supported by the SERC and held in Cambridge, 3-7 July, 1989,* Cambridge University Press (Cambridge, England), 1990.

The Nature of Space and Time, Princeton University Press (Cambridge, England), 1996.

ADAPTATIONS: Errol Morris directed a film version of *A Brief History of Time* for Anglia Television, 1991; *Black Holes and Baby Universes and Other Essays,* read by Simon Prebble, was adapted for audio cassette, Bantam, 1993; *A Brief History of Time* was adapted for audio cassette as part of the collection *Great Science Writers of the Decade,* Dove Audio (Beverly Hills, CA), 1995.

SIDELIGHTS: "Where did the universe come from, and where is it going? Did the universe have a beginning, and if so, what happened *before* then? What is the nature of time? Will it ever come to an end?" These are the questions that absorb physicist Stephen W. Hawking, questions posed in his best-selling book, *A Brief History of Time.* Queries such as these drive the scientist towards his goal of helping to create a "Theory of Everything" (known to physicists as "TOE," or the "Grand Unification Theory," or "GUT"). Hawking believes that such an all-encompassing explanation may be worked out within the lifetime of many of his readers.

Hawking made it to University College, Oxford, when he was seventeen years old. He wanted to study mathematics and physics, but his father wanted him to go into biology (the senior Hawking felt that teaching would be the only opportunity in his son's future if he studied math). So Hawking compromised, taking chemistry in addition to physics. In *Black Holes and Baby Universes and Other Essays,* Hawking noted that, though he is now a professor of mathematics, he had no "formal instruction in mathematics since I left St. Albans school. . . . I have had to pick up what mathematics I know as I went along." The problem with biology, Hawking felt, was that it was not an exact enough science, like physics or math. Besides, he wrote in *Black Holes and Baby Universes,* "it also had a rather low status at school. The brightest boys did mathematics and physics; the less bright did biology."

Hawking estimates he did about one thousand hours of work during his three years at Oxford, "an average of an hour a day," he told Gene Stone in *Stephen Hawking's a Brief History of Time: A Reader's Companion.* "I'm not proud of this lack of work, I'm just describing my attitude at the time, which I shared with most of my fellow students: an attitude of complete boredom and feeling that nothing was worth making an effort for." He didn't have many friends his first year or so; many of his classmates were older, having done national service before college. By his third year, though, Hawking was experiencing his happiest time at Oxford, discussing ideas and partying with friends, and rowing for the boat club.

When it came time to choose an academic specialty, Hawking was sure it would be physics, but his interests within physics lay in cosmology and elementary particles—the very large and the very small. He finally decided on cosmology, since that field was governed by Einstein's "General Theory of Relativity" (there was no comparable theory in elementary particles). Eventually, Hawking would pull these interests together again with his renowned theory about black holes.

Along with choosing his specialty came the sticky business of where to pursue that specialty. At Oxford, the program of study was set up so that the only examination was at the end of a student's three years of study. Hawking did not do well on his test, scoring on the borderline between a first and second class degree. This put him in the unenviable position of having to undergo an interview with the examiners so that they could decide which he should get. At one point in the interview, Hawking said in *Black Holes and Baby Universes,* "they asked my about my future plans. I replied that I wanted to do research. If they gave me a first, I would go to Cambridge. If I only got a second, I would stay in Oxford. They gave me a first."

Having earned his bachelor's degree from Oxford, Hawking went on to Cambridge to study for his doctorate. He took a break, however, to visit Iran with a friend. His mother recalled for Stone that while Hawking was there, a severe earthquake struck between Tehran and Tabriz. At the time, Hawking was riding a bus to Tabriz. Apparently, the ride was so bumpy that neither he nor his friend noticed the earthquake, and no one told them it had occurred. Hawking's family waited anxiously for three weeks to hear from him. "He had been ill well before" the trip, his mother recalled, but "when he finally came home he looked very much worse for wear."

During his last year at Oxford, Hawking remembered in *Black Holes and Baby Universes,* "I seemed to be getting clumsier, and I fell over once or twice for no apparent reason." While he was at Cambridge, his mother noticed his problems, and the family ended up at a spe-

cialist who put Hawking in the hospital for tests. He remembered, "They took a muscle sample from my arm, stuck electrodes into me, injected some radio-opaque fluid into my spine, and watched it going up and down with X-rays as they tilted the bed." The diagnosis was amyotrophic lateral sclerosis (ALS) or motor neuron disease, known in the United States as Lou Gehrig's disease (named after the New York Yankee player who died of the illness in 1941).

Hawking was given two and one-half years to live. He gradually lost the use of his body as it deteriorated. The long-term prognosis was grim: eventually, only his lungs and heart would work. His brain, however, would be totally unaffected to the end. At first, Hawking was extremely depressed. He spent a lot of time listening to classical music by Richard Wagner, a longtime family favorite, and sitting in his room. "But," he asserted in *Black Holes and Baby Universes,* "reports in magazine articles that I drank heavily are an exaggeration." He also remembers having troubling dreams at that time. A couple of them made a tremendous impact on his outlook: "I dreamt that I was going to be executed. I suddenly realized that there were a lot of worthwhile things I could do if I were reprieved. Another dream that I had several times was that I would sacrifice my life to save others."

Just before being diagnosed, Hawking met Jane Wilde at a New Year's party. The two fell in love and got engaged. The scientist told Kitty Ferguson, in *Stephen Hawking: Quest for a Theory of Everything,* that "the engagement changed my life. It gave me something to live for. It made me determined to live. Without the help that Jane has given I would not have been able to carry on, nor would I have had the will to do so."

After an engagement during which they commuted between London and Cambridge, the couple was married in July, 1965, after Hawking won his fellowship to work at Gonville and Caius College at Cambridge. They eventually found a house conveniently located near the Department of Applied Mathematics and Theoretical Physics, where Hawking would work. He lived by himself during the week, and Jane commuted on weekends to Cambridge until she finished her degree. Over the years, the Hawkings had three children—Robert, born in 1967; Lucy, born in 1970; and Timothy, born in 1979.

Hawking soon found that he needed a wheelchair to get around; he also required nursing care around the clock. When he contracted pneumonia in 1985, an operation was necessary to save his life; it also removed his voice. A computer programmer in California sent Hawking a program called Equalizer, which, Hawking said "allowed me to select words from a series of menus on the screen, by pressing a switch with my hand." When he has completed his statement, the computer attached to his wheelchair sends it to a speech synthesizer. "The only problem," said Hawking, "is that it gives me an American accent."

Before his impending marriage, Hawking realized he needed to finish his doctorate and get a job. He looked for a thesis topic. In Ferguson's *Stephen Hawking: Quest for a Theory of Everything,* Hawking said, "I started working hard for the first time in my life. To my surprise, I found I liked it. Maybe it is not really fair to call it work." His imagination was caught after reading Roger Penrose's ideas about collapsing stars that turn into black holes, or singularities (tiny but incredibly dense points of mass in spacetime from which not even light can escape due to the immense gravitational pull). Hawking asked: If stars gradually burn out and collapse under their own gravity into singularities, what happens if one looks back in time, to the beginning of the universe? What if the universe began as a singularity and then exploded in what is called the Big Bang?

Hawking worked with Penrose to prove that there must be a singularity in spacetime if general relativity is correct and the universe contains as much matter as scientists have observed. This bit of information was not completely well-received. Hawking said in *A Brief History of Time* that the opposition was "partly from the Russians because of their Marxist belief in scientific determinism [the idea that everything in the universe can be predicted], and partly from people who felt that the whole idea of singularities was repugnant and spoiled the beauty of Einstein's theory." Now, Hawking's theory is generally accepted; as he put it, "one cannot really argue with a mathematical theorem."

By the 1970s Hawking's work led him to study elementary particles in more depth, to see how they might contribute to an understanding of the cosmos. That study is now known as quantum mechanics, or the scientific theories dealing with the behavior of very small particles, such as photons and electrons, which make up larger particles, such as atoms. The basic rule of quantum mechanics is the uncertainty principle, formulated by the German physicist Werner Heisenberg. The uncertainty principle showed that some things in the universe just cannot be predicted—in particular, the behavior of small particles. Heisenberg found, and many research-

ers have since confirmed, that one can never know both the position and speed, or velocity, of a particle. Scientists can measure one but not the other at the same time. Hawking explained why in *Black Holes and Baby Universes:* "You had to use at least one packet, or quantum [of light] to try to measure the position of a particle. This packet of light would disturb the particle and cause it to move at a speed in some direction. The more accurately you wanted to measure the position of the particle, the greater the energy of the packet you would have to use and thus the more it would disturb the particle." The best scientists can do with these particles is to predict for them to be in a number of possible "quantum states" along the spacetime continuum.

In 1973, Hawking discovered that black holes appear to emit particles. In *A Brief History of Time,* he wrote that he was surprised and annoyed, but every time he redid the calculations, he came up with the same result. Knowing that nothing can escape from a black hole, Hawking theorized that what must be happening is that the particles come from the space just outside the event horizon (the boundary of a black hole).

At first, Hawking told only a few close colleagues about his discovery. But physicists around the world began checking his findings on their own and, when they reached the same conclusions, they agreed he was correct. Hawking told Stone that "Einstein never accepted quantum mechanics, because of its element of chance and uncertainty. He said, 'God does not play dice.' It seems that Einstein was doubly wrong. The quantum effects of black holes suggest that not only does God play dice, he sometimes throws them where they cannot be seen."

Hawking is not known as a particularly religious man, feeling that people were too insignificant in the grand expanse of the universe for a being such as God to care. Yet the subject of God comes up rather often in Hawking's writings and interviews. Tensions between science and the Roman Catholic church go back to Galileo's time. An experience of Hawking offers one example. He attended a cosmology conference at the Vatican in 1981 and gave a paper called "The Boundary Conditions of the Universe" in which he proposed that space and time in the universe were similar to the earth's surface—finite in area but without boundaries or edges. Pope John Paul II granted the conference participants an audience. In his interview for Stone, Hawking recalled that the Pope "told us that it was all right to study the evolution of the universe after the big bang, but we should not inquire into the big bang itself because that was the moment of creation and therefore the work of God." He continued, "I was glad then that he did not know that the subject of the talk I had just given at the conference was the possibility that spacetime was finite but had no boundary, which means that it had no beginning, no moment of creation."

Hawking has made a number of provocative comments about the impact the current state of physics might have on the existence of God. In the chapter called "The Origin and Fate of the Universe" in *A Brief History of Time,* Hawking theorized that "if the universe is really completely self-contained, having no boundary or edge, it would have neither beginning nor end: it would simply be. What place, then, for a creator?" Some of the physicist's most well-known queries conclude the book: "Why does the universe go to all the bother of existing? Is the unified theory so compelling that it brings about its own existence? Or does it need a creator, and, if so, does he have any other effect on the universe? And who created him?" Hawking continued that if a unified theory is found, everyone will "be able to take part in the discussion of the question of why it is that we and the universe exist. If we find the answer to that, it would be the ultimate triumph of human reason—for then we would know the mind of God."

Michael D. Lemonick, writing in *Time,* noted that many *Brief History* readers have the impression that Hawking is trying to disprove the existence of God. Hawking responded that "you don't need to appeal to God to set the initial conditions for the universe, but that doesn't prove there is no God—only that he acts through the laws of physics."

Though *A Brief History of Time* is certainly Hawking's most popular book, it was not his first. *The Large Scale Structure of Space-Time,* cowritten with G.F.R. Ellis, deals with classical cosmological theory and is filled with equations. But Hawking wanted to write a book that would be sold at airport newsstands. He chose to submit his manuscript to Bantam, a publisher specializing in popular books, because "I wanted to explain how far I felt we had come in our understanding of the universe: how we might be near finding a complete theory that would describe the universe and everything in it. . . . I wanted it to get to as many people as possible," as he said in *Black Holes and Baby Universes.* Toward that end, his editor advised him that every equation he put in the book would halve the sales. Hawking managed with only e=mc2.

In *A Brief History of Time,* Hawking gives an overview of the history of physics, relying heavily on pictorial diagrams and examples using everyday objects and ideas to explain the nature of spacetime and imaginary time (which Hawking now wishes he had explained more thoroughly), general relativity, the uncertainty principle and elementary particles, black holes, the origin and possible future of the universe. In the process, he discusses his own theories and ideas on black holes, Hawking Radiation, the Big Bang, and the still elusive "Theory of Everything."

Jeremy Bernstein, writing in the *New Yorker,* compared *A Brief History of Time* to Steven Weinberg's *The First Three Minutes.* One problem in the book, he said, is some inaccuracy in Hawking's account of physicist George Gamow's work—Gamow's 1948 paper was on "The Origin of Chemical Elements," not microwave radiation. But Bernstein also pointed out that "very few active scientists . . . actually take the trouble to read the papers of their early predecessors. A kind of folklore builds up which bears only a tangential relationship to reality." Martin Gardner spotted a couple of other historical errors in his *New York Review of Books* article. First, Newton believed in absolute time, not absolute space, and second, it was not Berkeley who believed that "'all material objects . . . are an illusion.'" In an aside, Gardner considered "The Origin and Fate of the Universe" chapter "the book's centerpiece." Taking the book as a whole, *Commentary* critic Jeffrey Marsh called it "a concise, firsthand account of current scientific thinking," and A.J. Ayer, writing in the *London Review of Books,* said that "Hawking gives a more lucid account than any that has yet come my way" of the complicated world of modern physics.

When producer Gordon Freeman and Hawking decided to make a film of *A Brief History of Time,* they went to Steven Spielberg for financing assistance. Errol Morris would direct, Gerald Peary would write the film, and Hawking would contribute to the narrative of the film and help edit the final product. The movie was filmed in a studio made to resemble Hawking's office in Cambridge. Writer Peary interviewed director Morris for *Interview.* When asked if Hawking disliked anything in the film, Morris replied that "he was always opposed to the chicken at the very beginning of the movie." Asked what brought Hawking the "most immediate pleasure" about the film, Morris said that "he thanked me for making his mother into a movie star."

In a review of the film, *Time's* Richard Schickel saw the "bottom line" as: "The real world and the theoretical universe of a physicist are explored with simplicity and elegance." The film is a series of short scenes focusing on Hawking, family members, Hawking, colleagues, old friends, Hawking—all having to do with Hawking's life and work in physics. Schickel writes that in watching the film "one begins to perceive a powerful analogy between Hawking's condition and the thrust of his thought. His disease seems to have affected him much as loss of energy affects a failing star."

After reviewing *Black Holes and Baby Universes,* critics who complained that the author did not reveal enough of himself in *A Brief History of Time* were not disappointed. The first three essays in the book are autobiographical. The last chapter is a transcript of Hawking's appearance on BBC's *Desert Island Discs* program in 1992. And in between are more essays on cosmology and quantum mechanics. A reviewer for *Publishers Weekly* said that Hawking "sheds light" on his personal life, and his "mind sparks in" the scientific essays that comprise the rest of the book. Michael D. Lemonick, writing in *Time,* quoted Hawking's answer to the question, "Why, when his days are already overcrowded with scientific meetings, lecture tours and the occasional sit-down with disabled kids, did he take the time to write a new book? 'I had to pay for my nurses.'"

In 1995, Hawking teamed up with Roger Penrose to write *The Nature of Space and Time.* The book contains lectures both professors delivered during the mid-1990s. Delving into quantum and gravitational theories, the book is, "although well done . . . not for the general reader," according to a reviewer for *Publishers Weekly.* *American Scientist* reviewer Arlen Anderson praised Hawking and Penrose, admitting that even though *The Nature of Space and Time* is a challenging read, "Hawking and Penrose chose to treat the audience's intelligence with respect and to give them a sincere taste of 'the real thing.'"

Hawking's 2001 book, *Universe in a Nutshell,* confused critics as much as it charmed them. Here, Hawking deals with the history of relativity, predicting the future, shaping time, and even individuals using time travel to wipe out bad genes from the pool. *Booklist* reviewer Brad Hooper praised Hawking for not "watering down his material condescending to his audience." Gregory Benford, who interviewed Hawking for *Reason,* noted that *Universe in a Nutshell* includes "friendly illustrations to help readers decipher such complex topics as superstring theory and the nature of time." Benford explained that translating equations into text is challenging and "pictures help enormously." A reviewer for *Scientific American* agreed that the illustrations "add illumination to the illuminating text." *American Scientist* reviewer Rocky Kolb described other methods Hawking used to assist readers in decoding the text. One such example is the independent nature of each chapter. Readers are able to jump around and read chapters that interest and skip more complex material. While Kolb admitted that *Universe in a Nutshell* is not easy reading, he commended Hawking's use of "broad brush [strokes], but even with the absence of details the reader is able to appreciate the grandeur of the landscape."

Hawking added personal anecdotes to *Universe in a Nutshell* and even touched on subjects not directly related to cosmology: evolution of intelligence and the future of mankind. An *M2 Best Books* reviewer praised Hawking for his ability to "make the unreachable available" and making *Universe in a Nutshell* "both rigorous and comprehensible." And Jeffrey Beall, writing for *Library Journal,* wrote that by infusing wit into his writing and not taking himself too seriously, Hawking helps "place our strange universe in a more human context."

BIOGRAPHICAL AND CRITICAL SOURCES:

BOOKS

Cole, Ron, *Stephen Hawking: Solving the Mysteries of the Universe,* Raintree Steck-Vaughn (Austin, TX), 1997.

Ferguson, Kitty, *Stephen Hawking: Quest for a Theory of Everything,* Bantam Books (New York, NY), 1992.

Filkin, David, *Stephen Hawking's Universe: The Cosmos Explained,* Basic Books (New York, NY), 1997.

Hawking, Stephen, *A Brief History of Time: From the Big Bang to Black Holes,* Bantam Books (New York, NY), 1988.

Hawking, Stephen, *Black Holes and Baby Universes and Other Essays,* Bantam Books (New York, NY), 1993.

Henderson, Harry, *Stephen Hawking,* Lucent Books (San Diego, CA), 1995.

McDaniel, Melissa, *Stephen Hawking: Revolutionary Physicist,* Chelsea House (New York, NY), 1994.

Sakurai, Gail, *Stephen Hawking: Understanding the Universe,* Children's Press (New York, NY), 1996.

Stone, Gene, *Stephen Hawking's A Brief History of Time: A Reader's Companion,* Bantam Books (New York, NY), 1992.

Strathern, Paul, *Hawking and Black Holes,* Anchor Books (New York, NY), 1998.

White, Michael, and John Gribbin, *Stephen Hawking: A Life in Science,* Dutton (New York, NY), 1992.

PERIODICALS

American Journal of Physics, July, 1997, Curt Cutler, review of *The Nature of Space and Time,* p. 676.

American Scientist, July-August, 1997, Arlen Anderson, review of *The Nature of Space and Time,* p. 377; March-April, 2002, Rocky Kolb, "Hawking's Brane New World," p. 182.

Astronomy, November, 1996, review of *The Nature of Space and Time,* p. 100.

Booklist, December 1, 2001, Brad Hooper, review of *The Universe in a Nutshell,* p. 616.

Choice, June, 1995, C.J. Meyers, review of *A Brief History of Time,* p. 1633; June, 1996, D. Park, review of *The Nature of Space and Time,* p. 1683.

Commentary, September, 1988, Jeffrey Marsh, review of *A Brief History of Time.*

Forbes, March 23, 1987, p. 142.

Interview, September, 1992.

Library Journal, February 15, 1996, Jack W. Weigel, review of *The Nature of Space and Time,* p. 172; January, 2002, Jeffrey Beall, review of *The Universe in a Nutshell,* p. 146.

London Review of Books, January 5, 1989, A.J. Ayer, review of *A Brief History of Time;* August 1, 1996 review of *The Nature of Space and Time,* p. 18.

M2 Best Books, January 7, 2002, review of *The Universe in a Nutshell.*

Mercury, May-June, 1997, Arno F. Granados, review of *The Nature of Space and Time,* p. 33.

Nature, January 25, 1996, review of *The Nature of Space and Time,* p. 309.

New Scientist, March 16, 1996, John Barrow, review of *The Nature of Space and Time,* p. 2021; November 17, 2001, David Lindley, "A Small Slice through Space," p. 56.

New Statesman, November 19, 2001, Bryan Appleyard, "King of Infinite Space," p. 52.

New Statesman & Society, June 24, 1988, p. 39.

Newsweek, June 13, 1988, p. 56.

New Yorker, June 6, 1988, Jeremy Bernstein, review of *A Brief History of Time,* p. 117.

New York Review of Books, June 16, 1988, Martin Gardner, review of *A Brief History of Time.*

People, September 11, 1989, p. 11.

Physics Today, July, 1996, John Preskill, review of *The Nature of Space and Time,* p. 18.

Publishers Weekly, November 1, 1993, p. 33; January 15, 1996, review of *The Nature of Space and Time,* p. 456; March 10, 1997, review of *The Large, the Small, and the Human Mind,* p. 59; November 19, 2001, Daisy Maryles and Dick Donahue, "A Mighty 'Universe,'" p. 21.

Reason, April, 2002, Gregory Benford, "Leaping the Abyss," p. 25.

Science, June 7, 1996, Robert M. Wald, review of *The Nature of Space and Time,* p. 1445; April 12, 2002, Marc Kamionkowski, review of *The Universe in a Nutshell,* p. 267.

Science and Society, summer, 1995, Derek Lovejoy, review of *A Brief History of Time,* p. 206.

Science News, May 18, 2002, review of *The Future of Spacetime,* p. 319.

Scientific American, March, 2002, review of *The Universe in a Nutshell,* p. 100.

Spectator, November 10, 2001, Robert Macfarlane, review of *The Universe in a Nutshell,* p. 80.

Time, February 8, 1988, p. 58; August 31, 1992; September 27, 1993; November 5, 2001, Michael D. Lemonick, "Beyond the Theoretical," p. 106.

Times Higher Education Supplement, March 15, 1996, Joseph Silk, review of *The Nature of Space and Time,* p. 24; February 1, 2002, Philip Anderson, "Einstein and the P-branes," p. 25.

*   *   *

HAWKING, Stephen William
   See HAWKING, Stephen W.

*   *   *

HAWKING, S.W.
   See HAWKING, Stephen W.

*   *   *

HAYCRAFT, Anna
   See ELLIS, Alice Thomas

*   *   *

HAYCRAFT, Anna Margaret
   See ELLIS, Alice Thomas

*   *   *

HAYES, Al
   See GRISHAM, John

HAZZARD, Shirley 1931-

PERSONAL: Born January 30, 1931, in Sydney, Australia; daughter of Reginald (a government official) and Catherine (Stein) Hazzard; married Francis Steegmuller (a novelist and biographer), December 22, 1963 (died, October, 1994). *Education:* Educated at Queenwood College, Sydney, Australia.

ADDRESSES: Home—200 East 66th St., New York, NY 10021. *Agent*—McIntosh & Otis, Inc., 475 5th Ave., New York, NY 10017.

CAREER: Writer. Worked for British Intelligence in Hong Kong (now China), 1947-48, and for British High Commissioner's Office, Wellington, New Zealand, 1949-50; United Nations, New York, NY, worked in general service category, Technical Assistance to Underdeveloped Countries, 1952-62, served in Italy, 1957. Boyer lecturer, Australia, 1984, 1988.

MEMBER: American Academy and Institute of Arts and Letters.

AWARDS, HONORS: U.S. National Institute of Arts and Letters award in literature, 1966; National Book Award nomination, National Book Foundation, 1971, and National Book Award for fiction, 2003, for *The Great Fire;* Guggenheim fellow, 1974; National Book Critics Circle Award, American Book Award nomination, and PEN/Faulkner Award nomination, all 1981, for *The Transit of Venus;* Miles Franklin Award, 2004, and Howells Medal for the most distinguished American novel published in five years' time, American Academy of Arts and Letters, 2005, for *The Great Fire.*

WRITINGS:

Cliffs of Fall, and Other Stories, Knopf (New York, NY), 1963, reprinted, Picador (New York, NY), 2004.
The Evening of the Holiday (novel), Knopf (New York, NY), 1966, reprinted, Picador (New York, NY), 2004.
People in Glass Houses: Portraits from Organization Life (interrelated stories), Knopf (New York, NY), 1967, reprinted, Picador: St. Martin's (New York, NY), 2004.
The Bay of Noon (novel), Atlantic-Little, Brown (Boston, MA), 1970, reprinted, Picador (New York, NY), 2003.

Defeat of an Ideal: A Study of the Self-Destruction of the United Nations (nonfiction), Atlantic-Little, Brown (Boston, MA), 1973.
The Transit of Venus (novel), Viking (New York, NY), 1980.
Coming of Age in Australia (lectures), Australian Broadcasting Corp. (Sydney, Australia), 1985.
Countenance of Truth: The United Nations and the Waldheim Case (nonfiction), Viking (New York, NY), 1990.
Greene on Capri: A Memoir, Farrar, Straus & Giroux (New York, NY), 2000.
The Great Fire (novel), Farrar, Straus & Giroux (New York, NY), 2003.

Work appears in anthologies, including several volumes of *Winter's Tales* and *O. Henry Prize Stories.* Contributor to periodicals, including the *New Yorker, Ladies' Home Journal,* and *McCall's.*

ADAPTATIONS: The Great Fire has been adapted as an audio book, Recorded Books, 2004.

SIDELIGHTS: Even before the publication of her best-selling novel *The Transit of Venus,* Shirley Hazzard's work met with critical approval. For example, Robie Macauley wrote in the *New York Times Book Review* that Hazzard's *The Bay of Noon* is "one of those rare novels that tries to address itself to the reader's intelligence rather than his nightmares. Its assumptions are fine and modest: That the reader will enjoy a sense of place if that place is drawn for him so perfectly that it seems to breathe, that the reader will understand a story based on the interactions of personality rather than mere violence, that the reader will take pleasure in a style that is consciously elegant and literary." "People in Glass Houses: Portraits from Organization Life," wrote Laurie Clancy in *Contemporary Novelists,* "is a brilliantly funny and scathing collection of eight inter-related stories concerning an unnamed 'organization' which is transparently the United Nations."

Regardless, it was with the release of *The Transit of Venus* that Hazzard gained a wider and more diverse readership. Writing in the *Chicago Tribune,* Lynne Sharon Schwartz remarked: "If the literary establishment were given to pageantry, [*The Transit of Venus*] ought to be welcomed with a flourish of trumpets. Last year John Gardner clamored for moral fiction: Here is a book that ventures confidently amid the abiding themes of truth, beauty, goodness, and love, and is informed, moreover, by stringent intelligence and lacerating irony. Hazzard spares no one, not even her reader." Clancy commented that "Hazzard's masterpiece and the basis of her reputation is undoubtedly *The Transit of Venus*." Clancy added: "The meticulous—sometimes almost too meticulous—craftsmanship of the novel and the elegance and subtle wit of the style are a delight and almost unique among contemporary Australian fiction writers."

Los Angeles Times critic Doris Grumbach wrote that she was very moved by *The Transit of Venus*. She felt that it "is an impressive, mature novel, full and satisfying, by a novelist whose earlier work—two novels and two collections of stories . . . did not prepare us for this book. Without fear of exaggeration I can say it is the richest fictional experience I have had in a long time, so sumptuous a repast that it may not be to every reader's taste."

Although characterization plays a vital role in all of her writings, Hazzard exhibits particular skill in this area in *The Transit of Venus*. Webster Schott pointed out in the *Washington Post:* "Her purpose is to reveal [the characters] in the act of living and to make their pleasure, anguish and confusion rise out of their personalities as they respond to change." Schott added: "All of *The Transit of Venus* is human movement, and seen from near the highest level art achieves."

John Leonard suggested in the *New York Times* that Hazzard's skill not only lies in her characterizations but in her literary style in general. "Miss Hazzard writes as well as Stendhal," Leonard remarked. "No matter the object—a feeling, a face, a room, the weather—it is stripped of its layers of paint, its clots of words, down to the original wood; oil is applied; grain appears, and a glow. Every epigram and apostrophe is earned. A powerful intelligence is playing with a knife. It is an intelligence that refuses to be deflected by ironies; irony isn't good enough."

The feature that several critics have identified as the underlying factor of Hazzard's skillful characterization and literary style is her sensitivity. Schott wrote: "Her perceptions of gesture, voice, attitude bespeak an omniscient understanding of human personality. The story she tells is, for the most part, so usual as to sound irrelevant. What she brings to it is virtually everything that story alone cannot tell about human lives." Similarly, Schwartz remarked that "*The Transit of Venus* evidences the wisdom of one not only well traveled but well acquainted with truth and falsehood in their numberless

guises. Interwoven with the story of Caro's and Grace's lives and loves are a devastating representation of British class structure, with barriers and loopholes clearly marked; an acerbic, satirical view of a governmental bureaucracy that scoops the marrow out of men and leaves them empty bone; a glimpse at underground activists struggling for fundamental political decencies in Latin America, as well as a survey of various modes of contemporary marriage."

After the publication of *The Transit of Venus* Hazzard released a collection of lectures, *Coming of Age in Australia,* as well as the nonfiction volume *Countenance of Truth: The United Nations and the Waldheim Case.* Then, after taking a ten-year break from publishing, she released her memoir *Greene on Capri.* In it, Hazzard relates the visits she and her husband made to the island of Capri in the Bay of Naples over the course of three decades. The book primarily focuses on some of the close friends they made there, including the noted writer Graham Greene, who was among many artists who lived in or traveled often to Capri. "Hazzard writes evenhandedly of their relationship with the sometimes volatile, contrary and often solitary Greene," wrote a *Publishers Weekly* contributor. The reviewer went on to note that the author's "precise prose beautifully captures the literary tone of the island." In addition, critics noted that the memoir has many interesting aspects. Robert Murray Davis, writing in *World Literature Today,* called the memoir "a curiously old-fashioned book," noting that it is not overly detailed or speculative like modern memoirs.

The Great Fire, Hazzard's first novel to be published since *The Transit of Venus,* was widely praised. The story takes place in Japan following World War II, where Aldred Leith, who fought for the British during the war, falls in love with a very young Australian woman still under the guardianship of her parents. The novel focuses on Leith's love for the girl and empathy for her dying brother. The story demonstrates that love is a type of redemption for Leith; following his horrible and emotionally deadening war experience, it allows him to once again feel fully part of the world. John Freeman, writing in *People,* commented that the author's "sentences twist, turn and fold delicately inward, capturing the way survivors . . . carefully ration emotions and memories."

Compared to her more famous novel, *The Great Fire,* has a "broader canvas" noted Anita Brookner in the *Spectator.* The characters in *The Great Fire* are set against the overwhelming backdrop that is the war. Indeed, Brookner stated: "This is a novel of high seriousness . . . . It is the time and place that remain the novel's salient features."

BIOGRAPHICAL AND CRITICAL SOURCES:

BOOKS

Contemporary Literary Criticism, Volume 18, Gale (Detroit, MI), 1981.

Contemporary Novelists, 6th edition, St. James Press (Detroit, MI), 1996.

Dictionary of Literary Biography Yearbook: 1982, Gale (Detroit, MI), 1983.

Geering, R.G., *Recent Fiction,* Oxford University Press (Melbourne, Australia), 1974.

Hazard, Shirley, *Greene on Capri: A Memoir,* Farrar, Straus & Giroux (New York, NY), 2000.

PERIODICALS

Antipodes, June, 2004, "*The Great Fire* by Shirley Hazzard. (2004 Miles Franklin Award)," p. 81.

Biography, fall, 2000, David Lodge, review of *Green on Capri,* p. 803.

Booklist, January 1, 2004, review of *The Great Fire,* p. 776.

Chicago Tribune, March 9, 1980, Lynne Sharon Schwartz, review of *The Transit of Venus.*

Library Journal, June 1, 2004, Michael Rogers, review of *The Bay of Noon,* p. 200; November 1, 2004, Michael Rogers, review of *People in Glass Houses,* p. 134.

Los Angeles Times, March 9, 1980, Doris Grumbach, review of *The Transit of Venus.*

New York Times, February 26, 1980, John Leonard, review of *The Transit of Venus.*

New York Times Book Review, April 5, 1970, Robie Macauley, review of *The Bay of Noon;* March 16, 1980, Gail Godwin, review of *The Transit of Venus,* p. 7; May 11, 1980, Michiko Kakutani, "Shirley Hazzard," p. 46; April 29, 1990, Paul Lewis, review of *Countentance of Truth: the United Nations and the Waldheim Case,* p. 13.

People, December 1, 2003, John Freeman, review of *The Great Fire,* p. 49.

Publishers Weekly, February 2, 1990, Genevieve Stuttaford, review of *Countenance of Truth,* p. 70; March 9, 1990, Wendy Smith, "Shirley Hazzard; in

Life as in Art, It's the Individual and the Truth that Matter Most to This Author," p. 48; January 3, 2000, review of *Green on Capri,* p. 65.

Spectator, November 15, 2003, Anita Brookner, review of *The Great Fire,* p. 60.

Washington Post, March 9, 1980, Webster Schott, review of *The Transit of Venus.*

World Literature Today, autumn, 2000, Robert Murray Davis, review of *Green on Capri,* p. 830.

*   *   *

HEAD, Bessie 1937-1986

PERSONAL: Born Bessie Amelia Emery, July 6, 1937, in Pietermaritzburg, South Africa; died of hepatitis April 17, 1986, in Botswana; married Harold Head (a journalist), September 1, 1961 (divorced); children: Howard. *Education:* Educated in South Africa as a primary teacher.

CAREER: Teacher in primary schools in South Africa and Botswana for four years; journalist at Drum Publications, Johannesburg, South Africa, for two years; writer. Represented Botswana at international writers conference at University of Iowa, 1977-78, and in Denmark, 1980.

AWARDS, HONORS: The Collector of Treasures and Other Botswana Village Tales was nominated for Jock Campbell Award for literature by new or unregarded talent from Africa or the Caribbean, *New Statesman,* 1978.

WRITINGS:

When Rain Clouds Gather (novel), Simon & Schuster (New York, NY), 1969.

Maru (novel), McCall, 1971.

A Question of Power (novel), Davis Poynter, 1973, Pantheon (New York, NY), 1974.

The Collector of Treasures and Other Botswana Village Tales (short stories), Heinemann (Portsmouth, NH), 1977.

Serowe: Village of the Rain Wind (historical chronicle), Heinemann (Portsmouth, NH), 1981.

A Bewitched Crossroad: An African Saga (historical chronicle), Donker (Craighall), 1984, Paragon House, 1986.

A Gesture of Belonging: Letters from Bessie Head, 1965-1979, edited by Randolph Vigne, Heinemann (Portsmouth, NH), 1990.

A Woman Alone: Autobiographical Writings, edited by Craig MacKenzie, Heinemann (Portsmouth, NH), 1990.

Tales of Tenderness and Power, Heinemann (Portsmouth, NH), 1990.

Life, adapted by Ivan Vladislaviac, illustrated by Renee Koch, Viva (Johannesburg, South Africa), 1993.

The Cardinals, with Meditations and Short Stories, David Philip (Cape Town, South Africa), 1993, Heinemann (Portsmouth, NH), 1996.

The Lovers, adapted by Ina Lawson, illustrated by Renee Koch, Viva (Johannesburg, South Africa), 1994.

Contributor to *Deep Cuts: Graphic Adaptations of Stories,* Maskew Miller Longman (Cape Town, South Africa), 1993; contributor to periodicals, including London *Times, Presence Africaine, New African,* and *Transition.*

SIDELIGHTS: "Unlike many exiled South African writers," wrote a London *Times* contributor, author Bessie Head "was able to root her life and her work anew in a country close to her tormented motherland." Born of racially mixed parentage in South Africa, Head lived and died in her adopted Botswana, the subject of much of her writing; in 1979, after fifteen years as part of a refugee community located at Bamangwato Development Farm, she was granted Botswanan citizenship. In *World Literature Written in English,* Betty McGinnis Fradkin described Head's meager existence after a particularly lean year: "There is no electricity yet. At night Bessie types by the light of six candles. Fruit trees and vegetables surround the house. Bessie makes guava jam to sell, and will sell vegetables when the garden is enlarged." Despite her impoverished circumstances, Head acknowledged to Fradkin that the regularity of her life in the refugee community brought her the peace of mind she sought: "In South Africa, all my life I lived in shattered little bits. All those shattered bits began to grow together here. . . . I have a peace against which all the turmoil is worked out!" "Her novels strike a special chord for the South African diaspora, though this does not imply that it is the only level at which they work or produce an impact as novels," observed Arthur Ravenscroft in *Aspects of South African Literature.* "They are strange, ambiguous, deeply personal books which initially do not seem to be 'political' in any ordinary sense of the word."

Head's racially mixed heritage profoundly influenced both her work and her life, for an element of exile as well as an abiding concern with discrimination, whatever its guise, permeate her writing. Noting in *Black Scholar* that Head "probably received more acclaim than any other black African woman novelist writing in English," Nancy Topping Bazin added that the author's works "reveal a great deal about the lives of African women and about the development of feminist perspectives." According to Bazin, Head's analysis of Africa's "patriarchal system and attitudes" enabled her to make connections between the discrimination she experienced personally from racism and sexism, and the root of oppression generally in the insecurity that compels one to feel superior to another. Head was "especially moving on the position of women, emerging painfully from the chrysalis of tribalist attitudes into a new evaluation of their relationship to men and their position in society," stated Mary Borg in a *New Statesman* review of Head's first novel, *When Rain Clouds Gather.* Considered "intelligent and moving" by a *Times Literary Supplement* contributor, the 1969 work was described by another as combining "a vivid account of village life in Botswana with the relationship between an Englishman and an embittered black South African who try to change the traditional farming methods of the community."

The black male flees South African apartheid only to experience discrimination from other blacks as a refugee in Botswana. For this novel, Head drew upon her own experience as part of a refugee community, which, as she once indicated in *World Literature Written in English,* had been "initially, extremely brutal and harsh." Head explained that she had not experienced oppression by the Botswanan government itself in any way, but because South African blacks had been "stripped bare of every human right," she was unaccustomed to witnessing "human ambition and greed . . . in a black form." Calling *When Rain Clouds Gather* "a tale of innocence and experience," Ravenscroft acknowledged that "there are moments of melodrama and excessive romanticism, but the real life of the novel is of creativity, resilience, reconstruction, fulfillment." Most of the major characters "are in one sense or another handicapped exiles, learning how to mend their lives," explained Ravenscroft, adding that "it is the vision behind their effortful embracing of exile that gives Bessie Head's first novel an unusual maturity." Ravenscroft found that in addition to the collective, cooperative enterprise that the village itself represents in *When Rain Clouds Gather,* it speaks to an essential concern of Head's writing by offering a solution for personal fulfillment: "Against a political background of self-indulgent, self-owning traditional chiefs and self-seeking, new politicians more interested in power than people, the village of Golema Mmidi is offered as a difficult alternative: not so much a rural utopia for the Africa of the future to aim at, as a means of personal and economic independence and interdependence, where the qualities that count are benign austerity, reverence for the lives of ordinary people (whether university-educated experts or illiterate villagers), and, above all, the ability to break out of the prison of selfhood without destroying individual privacy and integrity."

Head's second novel, *Maru,* is also set in a Botswanan village. According to Ravenscroft, though, in this book "workaday affairs form the framework for the real novel, which is a drama about inner conflict and peace of mind and soul." *Maru* is about the problems that accompany the arrival of the well-educated new teacher with whom two young chiefs fall in love. It is "about interior experience, about thinking, feeling, sensing, about control over rebellious lusts of the spirit," said Ravenscroft, who questioned whether or not "the two chief male characters . . . who are close, intimate friends until they become bitter antagonists, are indeed two separate fictional characters, or . . . symbolic extensions of contending character-traits within the same man?" Although the new teacher has been raised and educated by a missionary's wife, she belongs to the "lowliest and most despised group in Botswana, the bushmen," explained a London *Times* contributor. "Problems of caste and identity among black Africans are explored with sensitivity," remarked Martin Levin in the *New York Times Book Review.* Ravenscroft suggested that while *Maru* is more personal than Head's first novel, it is also more political, and he was "much impressed and moved by the power . . . in the vitality of the enterprise, which projects the personal and the political implications in such vivid, authentic parallels that one feels they are being closely held together."

Head's critically well-received third novel, *A Question of Power,* relates the story of a young woman who experiences a mental breakdown. In a *Listener* review, Elaine Feinstein observed that "the girl moves through a world dominated by strange figures of supernatural good and evil, in which she suffers torment and enchantment in turn: at last she reaches the point where she can reject the clamorous visions which beset her and assert that there is 'only one God and his name is Man.'" According to Bazin, Head once acknowledged in an interview with Lee Nichols in her *Conversations with African Writers: Interviews with Twenty-six African Authors* that *A Question of Power* is largely autobiographical. "Like Elizabeth, the protagonist in *A Question of Power,* Bessie Head was born in a South African mental hospital," explained Bazin. "Her mother, a wealthy, upper-class, white woman, was to spend the rest of her life there, because in an apartheid society, she had allowed herself to be made pregnant by a black stableman. Until age thirteen, Bessie Head, like Elizabeth, was raised by foster parents and then put in a mission orphanage." Paddy Kitchen pointed out in the *New Statesman,* though, that the novel merely "contains parallels and winnowings from life, not journalist records," adding that "the incredible part is the clarity of the terror that has been rescued from such private, muddled nightmares." Similarly, Ravenscroft discerned no "confusion of identity" between the character and her creator: "Head makes one realize often how close is the similarity between the most fevered creations of a deranged mind and the insanities of deranged societies." Lauded for the skill with which she recreats the hellish world of madness, Head was also credited by critics such as Jean Marquard in *London Magazine* with having written "the first metaphysical novel on the subject of nation and a national identity to come out of southern Africa." In his *The Novel in the Third World,* Charles R. Larson credited the importance of *A Question of Power* not just to the introspection of its author, but to her exploration of subjects hitherto "foreign to African fiction as a sub-division of the novel in the Third World: madness, sexuality, guilt." Noting that the protagonist's "Coloured classification, her orphan status at the mission, and her short-lived marriage" represent the origin of most of her guilt, Larson attributed these factors directly to "the South African policy of apartheid which treats people as something other than human beings." Further, Larson felt that Head intended the reader to consider all the "variations of power as the evils that thwart each individual's desire to be part of the human race, part of the brotherhood of man." *A Question of Power,* wrote Roberta Rubenstein in the *New Republic,* "succeeds as an intense, even mythic, dramatization of the mind's struggle for autonomy and as a symbolic protest against the political realities of South Africa." And in *Books Abroad,* Robert L. Berner considered it "a remarkable attempt to escape from the limitations of mere 'protest' literature in which Black South African writers so often find themselves." Berner recognized that Head could have "written an attack on the indignities of apartheid which have driven her into exile in Botswana," but instead chose to write a novel about the "response to injustice—first in madness and finally in a heroic struggle out of that madness into wholeness and wisdom." Ravenscroft perceived in *A Question of Power* "an intimate relationship between an individual character's private odyssey of the soul and public convulsions that range across the world and from one civilization to another," and deemed the novel "a work of striking virtuosity—an artistically shaped descent into the linked hells of madness and oppression, and a resolution that provides the hope of both internal and external reconciliation."

Critics have analyzed Head's first three novels, *When Rain Clouds Gather, Maru,* and *A Question of Power,* collectively in terms of their thematic concerns and progression. Suggesting that these three novels "deal in different ways with exile and oppression," Marquard noted that Head's "protagonists are outsiders, new arrivals who try to forge a life for themselves in a poor, under-populated third world country, where traditional and modern attitudes to soil and society are in conflict." Unlike other twentieth-century African writers who were also concerned with such familiar themes, said Marquard, Head "does not idealize the African past and . . . she resists facile polarities, emphasizing personal rather than political motives for tensions between victim and oppressor." Ravenscroft recognized "a steady progression from the first novel to the third into ever murkier depths of alienation from the currents of South African, and African, matters of politics and power." Similarly, Marquard detected an inward movement "from a social to a metaphysical treatment of human insecurities and in the last novel the problem of adaptation to a new world, or new schemes of values, is located in the mind of a single character." Ravenscroft posited that "it is precisely this journeying into the various characters' most secret interior recesses of mind and (we must not fight shy of the word) of soul, that gives the three novels a quite remarkable cohesion and makes them a sort of trilogy."

Considering *When Rain Clouds Gather, Maru,* and *A Question of Power* to be "progressive in their philosophical conclusion about the nature and source of racism," Cecil A. Abrahams suggested in *World Literature Written in English* that "ultimately, Head examines . . . sources of evil and, conversely, of potential goodness. The most obvious source is the sphere of political power and authority; it is clear that if the political institutions which decree and regulate the lives of the society are reformed or abolished a better or new society can be established." According to Ravenscroft, the elements of imprisonment and control provide thematic unity among the novels. Pointing to the "loneliness and despair of exile" in each of them, Ravenscroft found the resilience of their characters "even more remarkable," and concluded that "what the three novels do say very clearly is that whoever exercises political power, however laudable his aims, will trample upon the faces and limbs of ordinary people, and will lust in that trampling. That horrible obscenity mankind must recognize in its collective interior soul." And Head, said Ravenscroft, "refuses to look for the deceiving gleam that draws one to expect the dawn of liberation in the South, but accepts what the meagre, even parched, present offers."

Head's collection of short stories, *The Collector of Treasures and Other Botswana Village Tales,* which was considered for the *New Statesman*'s Jock Campbell Award, explores several aspects of African life, especially the position of women. Linking Head to the "village storyteller of the oral tradition," Michael Thorpe noted in *World Literature Today* that her stories are "rooted, folkloristic tales woven from the fabric of village life and intended to entertain and enlighten, not to engage the modern close critic." In the *Listener,* John Mellors related Head's statement that "she has 'romanticised and fictionalized' data provided by old men of the tribe whose memories are unreliable." In its yoking of present to past, the collection also reveals the inevitable friction between old ways and new. The world of Head's work "is not a simply modernizing world but one that seeks, come what may, to keep women in traditionally imprisoning holes and corners," said Valerie Cunningham in the *New Statesman.* "It's a world where whites not only force all blacks into an exile apart from humanity but where women are pushed further still into sexist exile." In *The Collector of Treasures and Other Botswana Village Tales,* added Cunningham, "Head puts a woman's as well as a black case in tales that both reach back into tribal legend and cut deep into modern Africa."

Head's *The Cardinals, with Meditations and Short Stories* contains a novella written prior to her exile, as well as seven short pieces set in South Africa. A *Publishers Weekly* reviewer remarked that the stories "read . . . like scattershot historical information mixed with outdated ideas" and that the introduction is "far more interesting than the work itself." The central novella concerns a woman named Mouse who was sold by her mother for five shillings when she was a child. Later, she perseveres to become a newspaper reporter, struggling in a male-dominated world and becoming involved with a man who, unbeknownst to either of them, is her father. Adele S. Newson remarked in *World Literature Today* that, "Drawing from the experiences of her South African existence, Head provides something of a poetic rendering of what it means to be a woman and a writer in the male-dominated, racist, and sexist South Africa of her formative years as a writer." In the *New York Times Book Review,* Scott Martelle noted that the book "bears the unpolished marks of an immature writer, particularly in long stretches of improbable dialogue. But the work overcomes these weaknesses to stand as a clearsighted snapshot of people trying to pursue their lives within a system that seeks to deny their existence."

Two books by Head—*Serowe: Village of the Rain Wind* and *A Bewitched Crossroad: An African Saga*—are categorized as historical chronicles and combine historical accounts with the folklore of the region. The collected interviews in *Serowe* focus on a time frame that spans the eras of Khama the Great (1875-1923) and Tshekedi Khama (1926-1959) through the Swaneng Project beginning in 1963 under Patrick Van Rensburg, a South African exile who worked to right the wrongs done by whites in that country. Larson, who considered "reading any book by Bessie Head . . . always a pleasure," added that *Serowe* "falls in a special category." Calling it a "quasi-sociological account," Larson described it as "part history, part anthology and folklore." "Its citizens give their testimonies, both personal and practical, in an unselfconscious way," added Paddy Kitchen in the *Listener,* "and Bessie Head—in true African style—orders the information so that, above all, it tells a story." *Serowe* is "a vivid portrait of a remarkable place . . . one wishes there were many more studies of its kind," remarked a *British Book News* contributor. Kitchen believed it to be "a story which readers will find themselves using as a text from which to meditate on many aspects of society." And discussing her book, *A Bewitched Crossroad,* which examines on a broader scope the African tribal wars in the early nineteenth century, Thorpe found that "in her moral history humane ideals displace ancestor-worship, and peace-loving strength displaces naked force." Questioned by Fradkin about the manner in which she worked, Head explained: "Every story or book starts with something just for myself. Then from that small me it becomes a panorama—the big view that has something for everyone."

Published posthumously, *Tales of Tenderness and Power* and *A Woman Alone: Autobiographical Writings* are companion collections of short pieces. The stories in *Tales of Tenderness and Power* date from the early 1960s, when Head lived in South Africa, to the 1980s, where she lived in Serowe. "Her stories are small descriptions of how traditions change over time, of how colonialism appears to the colonized, of chiefly justice and political corruption, of neighbors helping each other through famines and of villagers attacking deviants, of lovers and families," summarized Gay W. Seraman in the *Women's Review of Books,* while a *Publishers Weekly* reviewer found that the stories in *Tales of Tenderness and Power* "offer a rare insight into African history, culture and lore from a black perspective."

In the *Times Literary Supplement* Maya Jaggi declared that both collections "testify to Head's subtlety, versatility and prowess as a story-teller" and "are enriched by Head's distinctive vision, whether in their scornful exposure of corruption and abuses of power, or their epiphanic moments of generosity and tenderness." Ac-

cording to Charles Larson in the *Washington Post Book World,* the stories collected in *Tales of Tenderness* are "not only humane but genuinely hopeful about the human condition." But, he added, Head's memoir in *A Woman Alone* "reads like a horror tale, filled not only with the most appalling acts of inhumanity but also with one of the most agonizing accounts of loneliness one is likely to encounter." Jaggi characterized *A Woman Alone* as "brief, fragmentary and sometimes repetitive," yet called it a work that "builds a surprisingly coherent portrait of a sensitive, compassionate and talented writer transcending an onerous legacy. . . . These notes and sketches yield valuable insights into Head's views on politics, literature and feminism."

A Gesture of Belonging: Letters from Bessie Head, 1965-1979 provides further insight into Head and her works. The letters were addressed to editor Randolph Vigne, who puts them into a context by contributing explanatory notes regarding the author's circumstances and clarifying her references. Vigne shared Head's interests in political activism and journalism in Cape Town; she refers to him as "my papa" in many of the letters. "Of significant literary interest is the light the letters shed on the composition and reception of her works. Present also, however, is a disquieting strain of paranoia and contradictory responses," remarked A.A. Elder in *Choice.* Despite her concerns about the extent to which Vigne bowdlerized the letters, Arlene A. Elder maintained in *Callaloo* that *A Gesture of Belonging* "will help satisfy those clamoring for more biographical information about the writer as well as those hoping to put her works within the contexts of her own assessment of them and their relationship to the political and personal issues with which she was struggling as she composed them." Desiree Lewis concluded in *World Literature Today:* "Head's restless struggles both against and with available narratives, forms, and discourses were rarely univocal, linear, or intentional ones. Her lesser-known fiction encodes traces of her complex battle to construct identities beyond dominant fictions and to discover the conditions for her own creativity."

Through her writing, Head reinforced "the ideals of humility, love, truthfulness, freedom, and, of course, equality," wrote Bazin. By the time of her death she had achieved an international reputation and had begun to write her autobiography. Head endured much difficulty during her life; despite her rejection of South Africa as well as the hardships of her exiled existence, however, she emerged from the racist and sexist discrimination she both witnessed and experienced, to the affirmation she once explained to Fradkin represented the only two themes present in her writing—"that love is really good

. . . and . . . that it is important to be an ordinary person." She added, "More than anything I want to be noble." According to Kitchen, "a great deal has been written about black writers, but Bessie Head is surely one of the pioneers of brown literature—a literature that includes everybody."

BIOGRAPHICAL AND CRITICAL SOURCES:

BOOKS

Abrahams, Cecil, editor, *The Tragic Life: Bessie Head and Literature in Southern Africa,* Africa World Press (Trenton, NJ), 1990.

Black Literature Criticism, Thomson Gale (Detroit, MI), 1992.

Contemporary Literary Criticism, Thomson Gale (Detroit, MI), Volume 25, 1983, Volume 67, 1992.

Dictionary of Literary Biography, Volume 117: *Twentieth-Century Caribbean and Black African Writers, First Series,* Thomson Gale (Detroit, MI), 1992.

Eilersen, Gilliam Stead, *Bessie Head: Thunder behind Her Ears: Her Life and Writing,* Heinemann (Portsmouth, NH), 1996.

Heywood, Christopher, editor, *Aspects of South African Literature,* Heinemann (Portsmouth, NH), 1976.

Ibrahim, Humam, *Bessie Head: Subversive Identities in Exile,* University Press of Virginia (Charlottesville, VA), 1996.

Larson, Charles R., *The Novel in the Third World,* Inscape Publishers, 1976.

MacKenzie, Craig, and Cherry Clayton, editors, *Between the Lines: Interviews with Bessie Head, Sheila Roberts, Ellen Kuzwayo, Miriam Tlali,* National English Library Museum (Grahamstown, South Africa), 1989.

Nichols, Lee, editor, *Conversations with African Writers: Interviews with Twenty-six African Writers,* Voice of America (Washington, DC), 1981.

Olaussen, Maria, *Forceful Creation in Harsh Terrain: Place and Identity in Three Novels by Bessie Head,* Peter Lang (New York, NY), 1997.

Ola, Virginia, *The Life and Works of Bessie Head,* E. Mellen Press (Lewiston, NY), 1994.

Zell, Hans M., and others, *A New Reader's Guide to African Literature,* Holmes & Meier, 2nd edition, 1983.

PERIODICALS

Best Sellers, March 15, 1969.
Black Scholar, March-April, 1986.

Books Abroad, winter, 1975.
British Book News, November, 1981.
Callaloo, winter, 1993, p. 277.
Choice, July-August, 1991, p. 1788; December, 1991, p. 592.
Journal of Commonwealth Literature, Volume 21, number 1, 1986.
Kola, winter, 2000, Horace I. Goddard, "Liberation and Self-Understanding: A Study of Bessie Head's Female Characters," p. 53.
Listener, February 4, 1971; November 22, 1973; April 20, 1978; July 2, 1981.
London Magazine, December-January, 1978-1979.
Ms., January, 1987.
New Republic, April 27, 1974.
New Statesman, May 16, 1969; November 2, 1973; June 2, 1978.
New York Times Book Review, September 26, 1971; March 31, 1996.
Publishers Weekly, October 12, 1990, p. 56; January 1, 1996, p. 68.
Research in African Literatures, summer 1999, James M. Garrett, "Writing Community: Bessie Head and the Politics of Narrative," p. 122.
Times (London, England), May 1, 1986.
Times Literary Supplement, May 2, 1969; February 5, 1971; December 7, 1990, p. 1326.
Washington Post Book World, February 17, 1991, p. 4.
Women's Review of Books, January, 1991, p. 1.
World Literature Today, winter, 1982; summer, 1983; winter, 1983; winter, 1986; autumn, 1994, p. 869; winter, 1996, p. 73.
World Literature Written in English, Volume 17, number 1, 1978; Volume 17, number 2, 1978; Volume 18, number 1, 1979.

*   *   *

HEANEY, Seamus 1939-
(Seamus Justin Heaney)

PERSONAL: Born April 13, 1939, in County Derry, Northern Ireland; son of Patrick (a farmer) and Margaret Heaney; married Marie Devlin, 1965; children: Michael, Christopher, Catherine. *Education:* Attended St. Columb's College, Derry; Queen's University, Belfast, B.A. (first class honors), 1961, St. Joseph's College of Education, teacher's certificate, 1962.

ADDRESSES: Office—19 Strand Rd., Dublin 4, Ireland.

CAREER: Poet, translator, educator, and critic. Worked as secondary school teacher in Belfast, Northern Ireland, 1962-63; St. Joseph's College of Education, Belfast, lecturer, 1963-66; Queen's University, Belfast, lecturer in English, 1966-72; freelance writer, 1972-75; Carysfort College, Dublin, Ireland, lecturer, 1976-82; Harvard University, Cambridge, MA, visiting lecturer, 1979, visiting professor, 1982-86, Boylston Professor of Rhetoric and Oratory, 1986-96; Oxford University, Oxford, England, professor of poetry, 1990-94. Visiting lecturer, University of California—Berkeley, 1970-71. Has given numerous lectures and poetry readings at universities in England, Ireland, and the United States.

MEMBER: Irish Academy of Letters (Aosdana), Royal Dublin Society, American Academy of Arts and Letters (honorary foreign member), American Academy of Arts and Sciences.

AWARDS, HONORS: Eric Gregory Award, 1966, Cholmondeley Award, 1967, Somerset Maugham Award, 1968, and Geoffrey Faber Memorial Prize, 1968, all for *Death of a Naturalist;* Poetry Book Society Choice citation, 1969, for *Door into the Dark;* Irish Academy of Letters Award, 1971; writer-in-residence award, American Irish Foundation, and Denis Devlin Award, both 1973, both for *Wintering Out;* E.M. Forster Award, American Academy and Institute of Arts and Letters, 1975; W.H. Smith Award, Duff Cooper Memorial Prize, and Poetry Book Society Choice citation, all 1976, all for *North;* Bennett Award, *Hudson Review,* 1982; D.H. L., Fordham University, and Queen's University (Belfast, Ireland), both 1982, Harvard University, 1998, University of Wales, 1999, University of Birmingham, 2000, Rhodes University (South Africa), and University of East Anglia, both 2002, and University of Dundee, and University of London, both 2003; *Los Angeles Times* Book Prize nomination, 1984, and PEN Translation Prize for Poetry, 1985, both for *Sweeney Astray: A Version from the Irish;* Whitbread Award, 1987, for *The Haw Lantern,* and 1997, for *The Spirit Level;* Lannam Foundation Award, 1990; Premio Mondello (Palermo, Sicily), 1993; Nobel Prize for Literature, 1995; St. Louis Literary Award, 1998; *Irish Times* Award, 1999, for *Opened Ground;* Whitbread Award for poetry and book of the year, 1999, for *Beowulf;* Wilfred Owen Award for poetry, 2000; shortlisted for T.S. Eliot Prize, 2001, for *Electric Light;* Truman Capote Award for literary criticism, 2003, for *Finders Keepers;* made Commandeur de l'Ordre des Arts et Lettres, French Ministry of Culture.

WRITINGS:

POETRY COLLECTIONS

Death of a Naturalist, Oxford University Press (New York, NY), 1966.

Door into the Dark, Oxford University Press (New York, NY), 1969.

Wintering Out, Faber (London, England), 1972, Oxford University Press (New York, NY), 1973.

North, Faber (London, England), 1975, Oxford University Press (New York, NY), 1976.

Field Work, Farrar, Straus (New York, NY), 1979.

Poems: 1965-1975, Farrar, Straus (New York, NY), 1980.

(Adapter) *Sweeney Astray: A Version from the Irish,* Farrar, Straus (New York, NY), 1984, revised edition, with photographs by Rachel Giese, published as *Sweeney's Flight,* 1992.

Station Island, Farrar, Straus (New York, NY), 1984.

The Haw Lantern, Farrar, Straus (New York, NY), 1987.

New and Selected Poems, 1969-1987, Farrar, Straus (New York, NY), 1990, revised edition published as *Selected Poems, 1966-1987,* 1991.

Seeing Things: Poems, Farrar, Straus (New York, NY), 1991.

The Midnight Verdict, Gallery Books (Old Castle, County Meath, Ireland), 1993.

The Spirit Level, Farrar, Straus (New York, NY), 1996.

Opened Ground: Selected Poems, 1966-1996, Farrar, Straus (New York, NY), 1998.

Electric Light, Farrar, Straus (New York, NY), 2001.

Contributor to *101 Poems against War,* edited by Matthew Hollis and Paul Keegan, Faber and Faber (London, England), 2003.

POETRY CHAPBOOKS

Eleven Poems, Festival Publications (Belfast, Northern Ireland), 1965.

(With David Hammond and Michael Longley) *Room to Rhyme,* Arts Council of Northern Ireland, 1968.

A Lough Neagh Sequence, edited by Harry Chambers and Eric J. Morten, Phoenix Pamphlets Poets Press (Manchester, England), 1969.

Boy Driving His Father to Confession, Sceptre Press (Surrey, England), 1970.

Night Drive: Poems, Richard Gilbertson (Devon, England), 1970.

Land, Poem-of-the-Month Club, 1971.

Servant Boy, Red Hanrahan Press (Detroit, MI), 1971.

Stations, Ulsterman Publications (Belfast, Northern Ireland), 1975.

Bog Poems, Rainbow Press (London, England), 1975.

(With Derek Mahon) *In Their Element,* Arts Council of Northern Ireland, 1977.

After Summer, Deerfield Press, 1978.

Hedge School: Sonnets from Glanmore, Charles Seluzicki (Portland, OR), 1979.

Sweeney Praises the Trees, [New York, NY], 1981.

PROSE

The Fire i' the Flint: Reflections on the Poetry of Gerard Manley Hopkins, Oxford University Press (New York, NY), 1975.

Robert Lowell: A Memorial Address and Elegy, Faber (London, England), 1978.

Preoccupations: Selected Prose, 1968-1978, Farrar, Straus (New York, NY), 1980.

The Government of the Tongue: Selected Prose, 1978-1987, Farrar, Straus (New York, NY), 1988.

The Place of Writing, Scholars Press, 1989.

The Redress of Poetry, Farrar, Straus (New York, NY), 1995.

Crediting Poetry: The Nobel Lecture, Farrar, Straus (New York, NY), 1996.

Finders Keepers: Selected Prose, 1971-2001, Farrar, Straus (New York, NY), 2002.

EDITOR

(With Alan Brownjohn) *New Poems: 1970-1971,* Hutchinson (London, England), 1971.

Soundings: An Annual Anthology of New Irish Poetry, Blackstaff Press (Belfast, Northern Ireland), 1972.

Soundings II, Blackstaff Press (Belfast, Northern Ireland), 1974.

(With Ted Hughes) *The Rattle Bag: An Anthology of Poetry* (for children), Faber (London, England), 1982.

The Essential Wordsworth, Ecco Press (New York, NY), 1988.

(With Ted Hughes) *The School Bag,* Faber (London, England), 1997.

Yeats ("Poet to Poet series"), Faber (London, England), 2000.

Also editor of *The May Anthology of Oxford and Cambridge Poetry,* 1993.

OTHER

(With John Montague) *The Northern Muse* (sound recording), Claddagh Records, 1969.

The Cure at Troy: A Version of Sophocles' "Philoctetes" (drama; produced by Yale Repertory Theater, 1997, produced in Oxford, England, 1999), Farrar, Straus (New York, NY), 1991.

(Translator, with Stanislaw Baranczak) *Laments,* Farrar, Straus (New York, NY), 1995.

(With Joseph Brodsky and Derek Walcott) *Homage to Frost,* Farrar, Straus (New York, NY), 1996.

(Translator) *Beowulf: A New Verse Translation,* Farrar, Straus (New York, NY), 2000.

(Translator) Leos Janacek, *Diary of One Who Vanished: A Song Cycle,* Farrar, Straus (New York, NY), 2000.

(Author of introduction) Darcy O'Brien, *A Way of Life, Like Any Other,* New York Review Books, 2001.

(Translator) Sorley McLean, *Hallaig,* 2002.

(Translator) *The Midnight Verdict* (collection), Dufour, 2002.

(Author of introduction) David Thomson, *The People of the Sea: A Journey in Search of the Seal Legend,* Counterpoint, 2002.

(With Liam O'Flynn) *The Poet and the Piper* (audio), Claddagh Records, 2003.

(Author of introduction) Thomas Flanagan, *There You Are: Writing on Irish and American Literature and History,* edited by Christopher Cahill, New York Review Books, 2003.

(Translator) *The Burial at Thebes: A Version of Sophocles' "Antigone,"* Farrar, Straus (New York, NY), 2004.

Contributor to books, including *The Writers: A Sense of Ireland,* O'Brien Press (Dublin, Ireland), 1979; *Canopy: A Work for Voice and Light in Harvard Yard,* Harvard University Art Museums, 1997; *Healing Power: The Epic Poise—A Celebration of Ted Hughes,* edited by Nick Gammage, Faber, 1999; *For the Love of Ireland: A Literary Companion for Readers and Travelers,* Ballantine, 2001; and *Don't Ask Me What I Mean: Poets in Their Own Words,* Picador, 2003. Contributor of poetry and essays to periodicals, including *New Statesman, Listener, Guardian, Times Literary Supplement,* and *London Review of Books.*

Heaney's papers and letters are collected at Emory University, Atlanta, GA.

ADAPTATIONS: The film *Bye-Child,* directed by Bernard MacLaverty, is based on a poem by Heaney.

SIDELIGHTS: Nobel laureate Seamus Heaney has been widely recognized as a major poet of the twentieth century. A native of Northern Ireland and son of a cattle farmer, and a man who divides his time between his Dublin home and a teaching position at Harvard University, Heaney has attracted a readership on several continents and has won prestigious literary awards in England, Ireland, and the United States. As Blake Morrison noted in his work *Seamus Heaney,* the author is "that rare thing, a poet rated highly by critics and academics yet popular with 'the common reader.'" Part of Heaney's popularity stems from his subject matter—modern Northern Ireland, its farms and cities beset with civil strife, its natural culture and language overrun by English rule. *Washington Post Book World* contributor Marjorie Perloff suggested that Heaney is successful "because of his political position: the Catholic farm boy from County Derry transformed into the sensitive witness to and historian of the Irish troubles, as those troubles have shaped and altered individual lives." *New York Review of Books* essayist Richard Murphy described Heaney as "the poet who has shown the finest art in presenting a coherent vision of Ireland, past and present." Heaney's poetry was described by Robert Buttel in the *Concise Dictionary of British Literary Biography* as "manifestly regional and largely rural in subject matter and traditional in structure—a poetry that appears to be a deliberate step back into a premodernist world of William Wordsworth and John Clare and to represent a rejection of most contemporary poetic fashions."

Inevitably, Heaney has been compared with Irish poet William Butler Yeats; in fact, several critics called Heaney the greatest Irish poet since Yeats. However, *New York Review of Books* contributor Richard Ellmann once wrote: "After the heavily accented melodies of Yeats, and that poet's elegiac celebrations of imaginative glories, Seamus Heaney addresses his readers in a quite different key. He does not overwhelm his subjects; rather he allows them a certain freedom from him, and his sharp conjunctions with them leave their authority and his undiminished." Elizabeth Jennings made a similar observation in the *Spectator,* calling Heaney "an extremely Irish poet most especially in language, but he is not a poet in the Yeatsian mould; not for him high-mannered seriousness or intentional rhetoric. He is serious, of course, but it is the gravity which grows in his roots, not one which is obtrusive in the finished artefact."

Heaney once described himself in the *New York Times Book Review* as one of a group of Catholics in Northern Ireland who "emerged from a hidden, a buried life and entered the realm of education." This process began for Heaney at age eleven; that year he left the family farm to study on scholarship at a boarding school in Belfast.

Access to the world of English, Irish, and American letters—first at St. Columb's College and then at Queen's University, Belfast—was a pivotal experience for the poet, who was especially moved by artists who created poetry out of their local and native backgrounds—authors such as Ted Hughes, Patrick Kavanagh, and Robert Frost. Recalling his time in Belfast, Heaney once noted: "I learned that my local County Derry [childhood] experience, which I had considered archaic and irrelevant to 'the modern world' was to be trusted. They taught me that trust and helped me to articulate it." Searching his cultural roots, but also letting his literary education enrich his expression, Heaney began to craft "a poetry concerned with nature, the shocks and discoveries of childhood experience on a farm, the mythos of the locale—in short, a regional poetry," according to Robert Buttel in his book *Seamus Heaney.*

Heaney's sort of poetry, Buttel continued, was, in the early 1960s, "essentially a counter-poetry, decidedly not fashionable at the time. To write such poetry called for a measure of confidence if not outright defiance." According to Morrison, a "general spirit of reverence toward the past helped Heaney resolve some of his awkwardness about being a writer: he could serve his own community by preserving in literature its customs and crafts, yet simultaneously gain access to a larger community of letters." Indeed, Heaney's earliest poetry collections—*Death of a Naturalist* and *Door into the Dark*—evoke "a hard, mainly rural life with rare exactness," in the words of *Parnassus* contributor Michael Wood. Using descriptions of rural laborers and their tasks and contemplations of natural phenomena—filtered sometimes through childhood and sometimes through adulthood—Heaney seeks the self by way of the perceived experience, celebrating life force through earthly things. Buttel wrote in *Seamus Heaney:* "Augmenting the physical authenticity and the clean, decisive art of the best of the early poems, mainly the ones concerned with the impact of the recollected initiatory experiences of childhood and youth, is the human voice that speaks in them. At its most distinctive it is unpretentious, open, modest, and yet poised, aware." *Newsweek* correspondent Jack Kroll noted that in these first poems, Heaney "makes you see, hear, smell, taste this life, which in his words is not provincial, but parochial; provincialism hints at the minor or the mediocre, but all parishes, rural or urban, are equal as communities of the human spirit."

As a poet from the north of Ireland, Heaney often reflects in his work upon the "Troubles," the often-violent political struggles between some Northern Irish Protestants and their British allies and the militant Irish Republican Army and its supporters at home and abroad. The poet sought to weave the ongoing Irish conflict into a broader historical frame embracing the general human situation in the books *Wintering Out* and *North.* While some reviewers criticized Heaney for being an apologist and mythologizer, *New York Review of Books* correspondent Richard Murphy suggested that his poetry "is seriously attempting to purge our land of a terrible blood-guilt, and inwardly acknowledging our enslavement to a sacrificial myth. I think it may go a long way toward freeing us from the myth by portraying it in its true archaic shape and color, not disguising its brutality."

Morrison suggested that the role of political spokesman has never particularly suited Heaney. The author "has written poems directly about the Troubles as well as elegies for friends and acquaintances who have died in them; he has tried to discover a historical framework in which to interpret the current unrest; and he has taken on the mantle of public spokesman, someone looked to for comment and guidance," noted Morrison. "Yet he has also shown signs of deeply resenting this role, defending the right of poets to be private and apolitical, and questioning the extent to which poetry, however 'committed,' can influence the course of history." In the *New Boston Review,* Shaun O'Connell contended that even Heaney's most overtly political poems contain depths that subtly alter their meanings. "Those who see Seamus Heaney as a symbol of hope in a troubled land are not, of course, wrong to do so," O'Connell stated, "though they may be missing much of the undercutting complexities of his poetry, the backwash of ironies which make him as bleak as he is bright." Any claim to see Heaney as nonpolitical, however, is countered by the poet's ongoing involvement as fundraiser, supporter, representative, ally of peace and humanitarian causes and against torture and war.

After moving to Dublin, Heaney undertook the translation and adaptation of the Irish lyric poem *Buile Suibhne.* The work concerns an ancient king who, cursed by the church, is transformed into a mad birdman and forced to wander in the harsh and inhospitable countryside. Heaney's translation of the epic was published as *Sweeney Astray: A Version from the Irish.* In the *Dictionary of Literary Biography* Buttel contended that the poem "reveals a heartfelt affinity with the dispossessed king who responds with such acute sensitivity, poetic accuracy, and imaginative force to his landscape." *New York Times Book Review* contributor Brendan Kennelly also deemed the poem "a balanced statement about a tragically unbalanced mind. One feels that this balance, urbanely sustained, is the product of a

long, imaginative bond between Mr. Heaney and Sweeney." This bond is extended into Heaney's 1984 volume *Station Island,* where a series of poems titled "Sweeney Redivivus" take up Sweeney's voice once more. Buttel saw these poems as part of a larger theme in *Station Island;* namely, "a personal drama of guilt, lost innocence, and lost moral and religious certainty played against the redemptions of love, faith in the integrity of craft and of dedicated individuals, and ties with the universal forces operating in nature and history."

Reviewing *The Haw Lantern, Times Literary Supplement* reviewer Neil Corcoran felt that the poems included therein "have a very contemporary sense of how writing is elegy to experience." W.S. DiPiero imagined Heaney's intent in the *American Scholar:* "Whatever the occasion—childhood, farm life, politics and culture in Northern Ireland, other poets past and present— Heaney strikes time and again at the taproot of language, examining its genetic structures, trying to discover how it has served, in all its changes, as a culture bearer, a world to contain imaginations, at once a rhetorical weapon and nutriment of spirit. He writes of these matters with rare discrimination and resourcefulness, and a winning impatience with received wisdom." Heaney, declared Buttel, remains "in a long tradition of Irish writers who have flourished in the British literary scene, showing the Britons new possibilities for poetry in their mother tongue."

With the publication of *Selected Poems, 1966-1987,* Heaney marked the beginning of a new direction in his career. *Poetry* contributor William Logan commented of this new direction, "The younger Heaney wrote like a man possessed by demons, even when those demons were very literary demons; the older Heaney seems to wonder, bemusedly, what sort of demon he has become himself." In *Seeing Things* Heaney demonstrates even more clearly this shift in perspective. Jefferson Hunter, reviewing the book for the *Virginia Quarterly Review,* maintained that collection takes a more spiritual, less concrete approach. "Words like 'spirit' and 'pure,' as opposed to words like 'reek' and 'hock,' have never figured largely in Heaney's poetry," Hunter explained. In some poems in *Seeing Things* these words "create a new distanced perspective and indeed a new mood" in which "'things beyond measure' or 'things in the offing' or 'the longed-for' can sometimes be sensed, if never directly seen." Heaney also creates a direct link between himself and some of his ancient poetic predecessors, Hunter continued. "'The Golden Bough' translates the famous passage of *Aeneid* VI wherein the Sybil tells the hero what talisman he must carry on his trip to the underworld, while 'The Crossing' translates Dante's and Virgil's confrontation with the angry Charon in *Inferno III*."

The Spirit Level continues to explore themes of politics, humanism, and nature. "Heaney's latest collection is a moving and human book, one that includes in its composition a plea for hope, for innocence, for balance, and to seek eventually that 'bubble for the spirit level,'" wrote *World Literature Today* reviewer Sudeep Sen. Donna Seaman remarked in *Booklist:* "Heaney navigates skillfully from the personal to the universal, from life to death, seeking that precious equilibrium that only poetry can possess."

Regarding *Opened Ground: Selected Poems, 1966-1996,* *New York Times Book Review* commentator Edward Mendelson commented that, "With the prospect of decades of work ahead of him, Heaney has assembled a collection with a satisfying heft and more than enough variety of subject and style to delineate the shape of a long and constantly evolving career. It eloquently confirms his status as the most skillful and profound poet writing in English today." *New York Times* critic Michiko Kakutani claimed that the collection demonstrates "the consummate virtuosity of his work."

With *Electric Light,* according to an *Economist* reviewer, Heaney "returns to the pastoral," though the critic also pointed out, "More striking are recollections of the classical sources of pastoral, as he combines allusions to Homer and Virgil with sightseeing in Greece. The 'Eclogues' of Virgil, written in the aftermath of an era of civil war, provide a suggestive analogy. Mr Heaney translates them, alludes to them and . . . imitates them. . . . Much like Virgil's, they touch on new problems that peace may bring about." According to John Taylor in *Poetry,* Heaney "notably attempts, as an aging man, to re-experience childhood and early-adulthood perceptions in all their sensate fullness." Taylor felt that Heaney succeeds when "reminiscing verses are moving in this subtle, withheld way," but overall found the volume disappointingly uneven and containing "more exercises than deeply-felt memorials." In contrast, Paul Mariani, in an *America* review, found *Electric Light* "a Janus-faced book, elegiac" and "heartbreaking even." Mariani noted in particular Heaney's frequent elegies to other poets and artists, and called Heaney "one of the handful writing today who has mastered that form as well."

In the prose work *The Redress of Poetry,* according to James Longenbach in the *Nation,* "Heaney wants to think of poetry not only as something that intervenes in the world, redressing or correcting imbalances, but also as something that must be redressed—re-established, celebrated as itself." The book contains a selection of lectures the poet delivered at Oxford University on subjects ranging from Christopher Marlowe to Philip Larkin. *New York Times Book Review* contributor J.D. McClatchy called the lectures "a meditation on the uses of art and power, a fresh and astute defense of poetry against any attempt to reduce it to a relevant or useful commodity." However, in the *Times Literary Supplement,* John Bayley criticized Heaney for not providing fresh ideas about poetry, saying the book "gives the impression of being adjusted with courtly discretion to an audience who expect the familiar rather than the new." Bayley continued: "The poet as diplomat is an honourable and unusual role . . . but the critic exercising the same kind of function runs the risk of giving pleasure without surprise or illumination."

Heaney's *Finders Keepers: Selected Prose, 1971-2001* earned the Truman Capote Award for literary criticism, the largest annual prize for literary criticism in the English language. John Carey in the London *Sunday Times* proposed that Heaney's "is not just another book of literary criticism, nor even just a book about poetry by the greatest living poet. It is a record of Seamus Heaney's thirty-year struggle with the demon of doubt. The questions that afflict him are basic. What is the good of poetry? How can it contribute to society? Is it worth the dedication it demands?" As Patricia Monaghan noted in *Booklist,* "Not surprisingly for a poet from a war-wracked land, Heaney comes back again and again to the question of how poetry can matter against human savagery. Again and again, he concludes that beauty and the meaning it gives to life must matter."

In addition to writing poetry and criticism, Heaney has also served as a translator of other poets' work. His version of Sophocles' *Philoctetes* earned praise from critics when it was performed at the Yale Repertory Theater in 1998. His translation of the epic Anglo-Saxon poem *Beowulf* was considered groundbreaking because of the freedom he took in using modern language. Several reviewers noted that *Beowulf* has become something of a tired chestnut in the literary world, but credited Heaney with breathing new life into the ancient classic. Malcolm Jones in *Newsweek* stated: "Heaney's own poetic vernacular—muscular language so rich with the tones and smell of earth that you almost expect to find a few crumbs of dirt clinging to his lines—is the perfect match for the Beowulf poet's Anglo-Saxon. . . . As retooled by Heaney, *Beowulf* should easily be good for another millennium."

Heaney's *Beowulf* translation stirred up some controversy when in 2000 it was awarded the Whitbread Award, one of Great Britain's top literary honors. Stiff competition came in the form of a book in J.K. Rowling's "Harry Potter" novel series, and Rowling's supporters on the Whitbread judges' panel felt that as a translation, *Beowulf* was not eligible for consideration; others argued that the award should be given to a more fresh, modern work than *Beowulf*. On the other hand, Gary McKeone commented in the *Christian Science Monitor* that Heaney's translation has "true literary merit. This is translation at its potent best. . . . Heaney's subtle, luminous vernacular ignites the poem for a new generation of readers."

In an interview published in *Viewpoints: Poets in Conversation with John Haffenden*, Heaney offered some insight into his craftsmanship: "One thing I try to avoid ever saying at readings is '*my* poem'—because that sounds like a presumption. The poem *came, it came*. I didn't go and fetch it. To some extent you wait for it, you coax it in the door when it gets there. I prefer to think of myself as the host to the thing rather than a big-game hunter." Elsewhere in the same interview he commented: "You write books of poems because that is a fulfillment, a making; it's a making sense of your life and it gives achievement, but it also gives you a sense of growth."

BIOGRAPHICAL AND CRITICAL SOURCES:

BOOKS

Allen, Michael, editor. *Seamus Heaney*, St. Martin's Press (New York, NY), 1997.

Andrews, Elmer, editor, *The Poetry of Seamus Heaney: Essays, Articles, Reviews*, Columbia University Press (New York, NY), 2000.

Beckett, Sandra L., editor, *Transcending Boundaries: Writing for a Dual Audience of Children and Adults*, Garland (New York, NY), 1999.

Bemporad, J., *Seamus Heaney: Life and Works*, Books Inc. (London, England), 1999.

Booth, James, editor, *New Larkins for the Old: Critical Essays*, St. Martin's Press (New York, NY), 2000.

Brown, Terence, *Northern Voices: Poets from Ulster*, Rowman & Littlefield (Totowa, NJ), 1975.

Burris, Sydney, *The Poetry of Resistance*, Ohio University Press (Athens, OH), 1990.

Buttel, Robert, *Seamus Heaney*, Bucknell University Press (Cranbury, NJ), 1975.

Concise Dictionary of British Literary Biography: Contemporary Writers, 1960 to the Present, Thomson Gale (Detroit, MI), 1992.

Contemporary Literary Criticism, Thomson Gale (Detroit, MI), Volume 5, 1976, Volume 7, 1977, Volume 14, 1980, Volume 25, 1983, Volume 37, 1986, Volume 74, 1993, Volume 91, 1996.

Corcoran, Neil, *The Poetry of Seamus Heaney: A Critical Study*, Faber (London, England), 1998.

Curtis, Tony, editor, *The Art of Seamus Heaney*, Wolfhound Press (Dublin, Ireland), 1994.

Deane, Seamus, *Strange Country: Modernity and Nationhood in Irish Writing since 1790*, Clarendon Press (Oxford, England), 1997.

Dictionary of Literary Biography, Volume 40: *Poets of Great Britain and Ireland since 1960*, Thomson Gale (Detroit, MI), 1985.

Duffy, Edna, *The Subaltern Ulysses*, University of Minnesota Press, 1994.

Durkan, Michael J., *Seamus Heaney: A Reference Guide*, G.K. Hall (New York, NY), 1996.

Fenton, James, *The Strength of Poetry?*, Oxford University Press (New York, NY), 2001.

Garratt, Robert F., *Critical Essays on Seamus Heaney*, G.K. Hall (New York, NY), 1995.

Goodby, John, *Irish Poetry since 1950: From Stillness into History*, University Press (Manchester, England), 2000.

Harmon, Maurice, editor, *Image and Illusion: Anglo-Irish Literature and Its Contexts*, Wolfhound Press, 1979.

Hensen, Michael, and Annette Pankratz, editors, *The Aesthetics and Pragmatics of Violence*, Stutz (Passau, Germany), 2001.

Kerridge, Richard, and Neil Samuels, editors, *Writing the Environment: Ecocriticism and Literature*, Zed (London, England), 1998.

Kiberd, Declan, *Inventing Ireland: The Literature of the Modern Nation*, J. Cape (London, England), 1995.

Kirkland, Richard, *Literature and Culture in Northern Ireland since 1965: Moments of Danger*, Longman (London, England), 1996.

Kirkpatrick, Kathryn. *Border Crossings: Irish Women Writers and National Identities*, University of Alabama Press (Tuscaloosa, AL), 2000.

Longley, Edna, *Poetry in the Wars*, Bloodaxe (Newcastle on Tyne, England), 1986.

Mahoney, John L., editor, *Seeing into the Life of Things: Essays on Literature and Religious Experience*, Fordham University Press (New York, NY), 1998.

Malloy, Catharine, and Phyllis Carey, editors, *Seamus Heaney—The Shaping Spirit*, University of Delaware Press (Newark, NJ), 1996.

McGuinness, Arthur E., *Seamus Heaney: Poet and Critic,* P. Lang (New York, NY), 1994.

Molino, Michael R., *Questioning Tradition, Language, and Myth: The Poetry of Seamus Heaney,* Catholic University of America Press (New York, NY), 1994.

Morrison, Blake, *Seamus Heaney,* Methuen (London, England), 1982.

O'Brien, Eugene, *Seamus Heaney and the Place of Writing,* Florida University Press (Gainesville, FL), 2002.

O'Brien, Eugene, *Seamus Heaney: Creating Ireland of the Mind,* Liffey Press (Dublin, Ireland), 2003.

Parini, Jay, editor, *British Writers: Retrospective Supplement I,* Scribner (New York, NY), 2002.

Roberts, Neil, editor, *A Companion to Twentieth-Century Poetry,* Blackwell (Oxford, England), 2001.

Scott, Jamie S., and Paul Simpson-Housley, editors, *Mapping the Sacred: Religion, Geography, and Postcolonial Literatures,* Rodopi (Amsterdam, Netherlands), 2001.

Stewart, Bruce, editor, *That Other World,* Smythe (Gerrards Cross, England), 1998.

Thomas, Harry, editor, *Talking with Poets,* Handsel (New York, NY), 2002.

Tobin, Daniel, *Passage to the Center: Imagination and the Sacred in the Poetry of Seamus Heaney,* University Press of Kentucky (Lexington, KY), 1999.

Vendler, Helen, *Seamus Heaney,* Harvard University Press (Cambridge, MA), 1998.

Viewpoints: Poets in Conversation with John Haffenden, Faber (London, England), 1981.

Welch, Robert, *Changing States: Transformations in Modern Irish Writing,* Routledge (London, England), 1993.

Wills, Clair, *Improprieties: Politics and Sexuality in Northern Irish Poetry,* Oxford University Press (Oxford, England), 1993.

PERIODICALS

America, August 3, 1996, p. 24; March 29, 1997, p. 10; October 11, 1997, p. 8; December 20, 1997, p. 24; July 31, 1999, John F. Desmond, "Measures of a Poet," p. 24; July 31, 1999, p. 24; April 23, 2001, p. 25.

American Scholar, autumn, 1981.

Antioch Review, spring, 1993; spring, 1999, p. 246.

Ariel, October, 1998, p. 7.

Atlantis, June, 2001, p. 7.

Back Stage, December 19, 1997, review of *The Cure at Troy: A Version of Sophocles' "Philoctetes,"* p. 34.

Booklist, May 1, 1996, p. 1485; October 15, 1998, review of "Opened Ground," p. 388; February 15, 2000, Ray Olson, "A New Verse Translation," p. 1073; March 15, 2001, p. 1346; May 1, 2002, p. 1499.

Books for Keeps, September, 1997, p. 30.

Canadian Journal of Irish Studies, July, 1998, p. 51; December, 1998, p. 63.

Christian Scholar's Review, fall, 2001, p. 59.

Christian Science Monitor, April 22, 1999, Elizabeth Lund, "The Enticing Sounds of This Irishman's Verse," p. 20; February 3, 2000, Gary McKeone, "'Harry Potter' Falls to a Medieval Slayer," p. 1; April 13, 2000, p. 15; April 26, 2001, p. 19.

Classical and Modern Literature, spring, 1999, p. 243; fall, 2001, p. 71.

Commonweal, May 17, 1996, p. 10; November 6, 1998, p. 18; December 1, 2000, p. 22.

Contemporary Literature, winter, 1999, p. 627.

Contemporary Review, April, 2000, p. 206.

Critical Inquiry, spring, 1982.

Critical Quarterly, spring, 1974; spring, 1976.

Daily Telegraph (London, England), February 19, 2000, p. 116; March 31, 2001; April 13, 2002; May 5, 2003.

Dalhousie Review, autumn, 2000, p. 351.

Economist, September 12, 1998, review of *Opened Ground,* p. 14; November 20, 1999, "Translations of the Spirit," p. 101; June 23, 2001, p. 121.

Eire-Ireland, summer, 1978; winter, 1980; fall-winter, 2001, p. 7.

Encounter, November, 1975.

English, summer-autumn, 1997; summer, 1998, p. 111; summer, 2000, p. 143; summer, 2001, p. 149.

Essays in Criticism, April, 1998, p. 144.

Evening Standard, April 9, 2001, p. 47; April 8, 2002, p. 52.

Explicator, fall, 2002, p. 56.

Financial Times, March 21, 1998, p. 5; March 24, 2001, p. 4; March 30, 2002, p. 4; September 27, 2003, p. 26.

Globe and Mail (Toronto, Ontario, Canada), September 3, 1988.

Guardian (London, England), April 3, 1997, p. 9; October 9, 1999, p. 6; October 16, 1999, p. 10; October 18, 1999, p. 17; December 4, 1999, p. 11; January 19, 2000, p. 21; January 29, 2000, p. 3; September 30, 2000, p. 11; March 24, 2001, p. 12; April 7, 2001, p. 8; July 27, 2002, p. 21.

Harper's, March, 1981.

Harvard Review, fall, 1999, p. 74; fall, 2000, p. 12.

Independent (London, England), April 5, 1997, p. 7; December 1, 1997, p. 5; September 5, 1998, p. 17; September 8, 1998, p. 11; April 10, 1999, p. 5; October 2, 1999, p. 10; January 26, 2000, p. 5; January 29, 2000, p. 5; March 31, 2001, p. 10; June 16, 2001, p. 11; December 8, 2001, p. 9; February 19, 2003, p. 5; September 27, 2003, p. 33.

Independent on Sunday (London, England), April 6, 1997, p. 29; July 20, 1997, p. 32; November 9, 1997, p. 38; September 6, 1998, p. 10; March 21, 1999, p. 9; April 4, 1999, p. 11; October 10, 1999, p. 10; April 8, 2001, p. 46.

Irish Literary Supplement, fall, 1997, p. 14.

Irish Studies Review, spring, 1996; December, 2002, p. 303.

Irish Times (Dublin, Ireland), February 22, 2003, p. 61; April 12, 2003, p. 62; July 5, 2003, p. 57; July 12, 2003, p. 59; July 19, 2003, p. 55; August 2, 2003, p. 59; October 25, 2003, p. 55.

Irish University Review, spring-summer, 1998, pp. 56, 68; autumn-winter, 1999, p. 358.

Journal of Commonwealth and Postcolonial Studies, spring, 2000, p. 51.

Journal of Modern Literature, summer, 2000, pp. 471, 597; fall, 2001, p. 1.

Jouvert, fall, 1999, p. 40.

Kentucky Philological Review, March, 1998, p. 17.

Kenyon Review, winter, 2002, p. 160.

Kliatt, March, 1998, p. 57.

Library Journal, May 15, 1997, review of *The Spirit Level,* p. 120; September 1, 1997, review of *The Spirit Level,* p. 235; April 1, 1999, Barbara Hoffert, review of *Opened Ground,* p. 96; December, 1999, Thomas L. Cooksey, review of *Beowulf,* p. 132; August, 2000, p. 110; April 1, 2001, p. 104; April 1, 2002, p. 106; June 1, 2002, p. 155.

Listener, December 7, 1972; November 8, 1973; September 25, 1975; December 20-27, 1984.

Lit, October, 1999, pp. 149, 181.

Literature and Theology, March, 2003, p. 32.

London Review of Books, November 1-14, 1984; May 27, 1999, review of *Opened Ground,* p. 20.

Los Angeles Times, May 16, 1984; January 5, 1989; December 31, 2000, p. 6; April 22, 2001, p. 3.

Los Angeles Times Book Review, March 2, 1980; October 21, 1984; June 2, 1985; October 27, 1987; August 26, 1990; December 27, 1992.

Nation, November 10, 1979; December 4, 1995, p. 716; January 4, 1999, Jay Parini, review of *Opened Ground,* p. 25.

New Boston Review, August-September, 1980.

New Criterion, May, 2000, p. 31.

New Literary History, winter, 1999, p. 239.

New Republic, March 27, 1976; December 22, 1979; April 30, 1984; February 18, 1985; January 13, 1997, review of *Homage to Robert Frost,* p. 14;

February 28, 2000, Nicholas Howe, "Scullion-speak," p. 32.

New Statesman, April 25, 1997; September 18, 1998, review of *Opened Ground,* p. 54; April 15, 2001, p. 53.

Newsweek, February 2, 1981; April 15, 1985; February 28, 2000, Malcolm Jones, "'Beowulf' Brawling: A Classic Gets a Makeover," p. 68.

New Yorker, September 28, 1981; September 23, 1985; March 20, 2000, pp. 54, 56-66, 68, 79.

New York Review of Books, September 20, 1973; September 30, 1976; March 6, 1980; October 8, 1981; March 14, 1985; June 25, 1992; March 4, 1999, Fintan O'Toole, review of *Opened Ground,* p. 43; July 20, 2000, p. 18; November 29, 2001, p. 49; December 5, 2002, p. 54.

New York Times, April 22, 1979; January 11, 1985; November 24, 1998, Michiko Kakutani, review of *Opened Ground;* January 30, 1999, p. B11; January 20, 2000, Sarah Lyall, "Wizard vs. Dragon: A Close Contest, but the Fire-Breather Wins," p. A17; January 27, 2000, p. A27; February 22, 2000, Richard Eder, "Beowulf and Fate Meet in a Modern Poet's Lens," p. B8; March 20, 2000, Mel Gussow, "An Anglo-Saxon Chiller (with an Irish Touch)," p. B1; February 1, 2001, p. B3, E3; April 20, 2001, p. B37, E39; May 27, 2001, p. AR19; June 2, 2001, p. A15, B9; September 30, 2002, p. B3, E3.

New York Times Book Review, March 26, 1967; April 18, 1976; December 2, 1979; December 21, 1980; May 27, 1984; March 10, 1985; March 5, 1989; December 14, 1995, p. 15; June 1, 1997, p. 52; December 20, 1998, review of *Opened Ground,* p. 10; June 6, 1999, review of *Opened Ground,* p. 37; February 27, 2000, James Shapiro, "A Better 'Beowulf,'" p. 6; December 3, 2000, p. 9; April 8, 2001, p. 16; April 29, 2001, p. 22; June 3, 2001, p. 24; October 6, 2002, p. 33.

New York Times Magazine, March 13, 1983.

Nexos, July, 1999, p. 83.

Observer (London, England), March 23, 1997, p. 16; January 4, 1998, p. 15; September 6, 1998, review of *Opened Ground,* p. 17; November 7, 1999, p. 8; January 23, 2000, p. 11; September 10, 2000, p. 16; April 15, 2001, p. 15; April 7, 2002, p. 13.

Papers on Language and Literature, spring, 2001, p. 205.

Parnassus, spring-summer, 1974; fall-winter, 1977; fall-winter, 1979.

Partisan Review, number 3, 1986; fall, 1997, p. 674.

Philosophy and Literature, October, 2002, p. 405.

Poetry, June, 1992; December, 2000, p. 211; February, 2002, p. 296.

Princeton University Library Chronicle, spring, 1998, p. 559.

Publishers Weekly, April 29, 1996, p. 63; January 27, 1997, p. 14; November 2, 1998, review of *Opened Ground,* p. 74; February 7, 2000, Jana Riess, "Heaney Takes U.K.'s Whitbread Prize," p. 18; February 14, 2000, Judy Quinn, "Will Readers Cry 'Wulf'?," p. 86; February 21, 2000, review of *Beowulf,* p. 84; March 13, 2000, Daisy Maryles, "A Real Backlist Mover," p. 22; August 14, 2000, p. 349; September 4, 2000, p. 44; February 19, 2001, p. 87.

Saturday Review, July-August, 1985.

Sewanee Review, winter, 1976; April-June, 1998, p. 184.

South Carolina Review, fall, 1999, pp. 119, 132.

Southern Review, January, 1980; spring, 2000, p. 418; spring, 2002, p. 358.

Spectator, September 6, 1975; December 1, 1979; November 24, 1984; June 27, 1987; September 16, 1995, p. 39; September 5, 1998, review of *Opened Ground,* p. 36; April 6, 2002, p. 32.

Sunday Times (London, England), September 6, 1998, p. 7; October 3, 1999, p, 4; October 17, 1999, p. 41; February 6, 2000, p. 18; October 1, 2000, p. 46; December 10, 2000, p. 16; April 1, 2001, p. 35; April 14, 2002, p. 34; April 13, 2003, p. 49.

Symbiosis, April, 1999, p. 63; October, 2002, p. 133.

Time, March 19, 1984; February 25, 1985; October 16, 1995; March 20, 2000, Paul Gray, "There Be Dragons: Seamus Heaney's Stirring Translation of Beowulf Makes Waves on Both Shores of the Atlantic," p. 84.

Times (London, England), October 11, 1984; January 24, 1985; October 22, 1987; June 3, 1989; September 11, 1998, p. 21; October 29, 1998, p. 44; March 27, 1999, p. 16; September 23, 1999, p. 42; October 26, 1999, p. 50; May 20, 2000, p. 19; April 4, 2001, p. 15; April 17, 2002, p. 21; July 2, 2003, p. 2.

Times Educational Supplement, November 7, 1997, p. 2; September 11, 1998, review of *Opened Ground,* p. 11.

Times Literary Supplement, June 9, 1966; July 17, 1969; December 15, 1972; August 1, 1975; February 8, 1980; October 31, 1980; November 26, 1982; October 19, 1984; June 26, 1987; July 1-7, 1988; December 6, 1991; October 20, 1995, p. 9.

Tribune Books (Chicago, IL), April 19, 1981; September 9, 1984; November 8, 1987; November 25, 1990.

Twentieth Century Literature, fall, 2000, p. 269.

Twentieth-Century Studies, November, 1970.

U.S. News and World Report, March 20, 2000, Brendan I. Koerner, "Required Reading," p. 68.

Variety, May 4, 1998, Markland Taylor, review of "The Cure at Troy," p. 96.

Virginia Quarterly Review, autumn, 1992.

Wall Street Journal, April 2, 1999, review of *Opened Ground,* p. W6; February 24, 2000, Elizabeth Bukowski, "Seamus Heaney Tackles *Beowulf,*" p. A16; March 10, 2000, "Slaying Dragons," p. W17.

Washington Post Book World, January 6, 1980; January 25, 1981; May 20, 1984; January 27, 1985; August 19, 1990.

Washington Times, November 29, 1998, p. 6; February 6, 2000, p. 8; June 9, 2002, p. B08.

World Literature Today, summer, 1977; autumn, 1981; summer, 1983; autumn, 1996, p. 963; summer, 1999, p. 534; autumn, 2000, p. 247; winter, 2001, p. 119; winter, 2002, p. 110.

ONLINE

Biblio, http://www.biblio-india.com/ (November-December, 2000).

Interviews with Poets, http://www.interviews-with-poets.com/ (March 26, 2004).

*　　*　　*

HEANEY, Seamus Justin
　　See HEANEY, Seamus

*　　*　　*

HÉBERT, Anne 1916-2000

PERSONAL: Born August 1, 1916, in Sainte-Catherine-de-Fossambault, Quebec, Canada; died of cancer, January 22, 2000, in Quebec City, Quebec, Canada; daughter of Maurice-Lang (a literary critic) and Marguerite Marie (Tache) Hébert. *Education:* Attended College Saint-Coeur de Marie and College Notre Dame.

CAREER: Poet and novelist. Worked for Radio Canada, 1950-53, and for National Film Board, 1953-54, 1959-60.

MEMBER: Royal Society of Canada.

AWARDS, HONORS: Grants from Canadian government, 1954, Canadian Council of Arts, 1960 and 1961, Guggenheim Foundation, 1963, and Province of Quebec, 1965; Prix de la Province de Quebec, France

Canada prize, and Duvernay prize, all 1958, all for *Les Chambres de bois;* Molson Prize, 1967; French booksellers prize, 1971; Governor General award, 1975, for *Les Enfants du sabbat,* and 1992, for *L'Enfant charge de songes;* Grand Prix de Monaco, 1975; French Academy award, 1975; Prix David (Quebec), 1978; Prix Femina, 1982, for *Les Fous de bassan;* D.Litt., University of Toronto, 1967, University of Quebec, 1979, McGill University, 1980, University of Laval, and University of Laurentienne; Giller Prize finalist, 1999, for *Am I Disturbing You?*

WRITINGS:

POETRY

Les Songes en equilibre (title means "Dreams in Equilibrium"), Éditions de l'Arbre (Montreal, Quebec, Canada), 1942.

Le Tombeau des rois (also see below), Institut Litteraire du Quebec, 1953, translation by Peter Miller published as *The Tomb of the Kings,* Contact Press (Toronto, Ontario, Canada), 1967.

Poemes (includes *Le Tombeau des rois*), Éditions du Seuil (Montreal, Quebec, Canada), 1960, translation by Alan Brown published as *Poems,* Musson (Don Mills, Ontario, Canada), 1975.

Saint-Denys Garneau and Anne Hébert (selected poetry), translation by F.R. Scott, Klanak Press (Vancouver, British Columbia, Canada), 1962, revised edition, 1978.

Eve: Poems, translation by A. Poulin, Jr., Quarterly Review of Literature, 1980.

Selected Poems, translation by A. Poulin, BOA Editions (Brockport, NY), 1987.

Oeuvres poetiques: 1950-1990, Boreál (Montreal, Quebec, Canada), 1992.

Le Jour n'a d'egal que la nuit, Boreál (Montreal, Quebec, Canada), 1992, published as *Day Has No Equal but Night,* translation by A. Poulin, BOA Editions (Brockport, NY), 1994.

Poemes pour la main gauche, Boreál (Montreal, Quebec, Canada), 1997.

NOVELS

Les Chambres de bois, Éditions du Seuil (Montreal, Quebec, Canada), 1958, translation by Kathy Mezei published as *The Silent Rooms,* Musson (Don Mills, Ontario, Canada), 1974.

Kamouraska, Éditions du Seuil (Montreal, Quebec, Canada), 1970, translation by Norman Shapiro, Crown (New York, NY), 1973.

Les Enfants du sabbat, Éditions du Seuil (Montreal, Quebec, Canada), 1975, translation by Carol Dunlop-Hébert published as *Children of the Black Sabbath,* Crown (New York, NY), 1977.

Heloise, Éditions du Seuil (Montreal, Quebec, Canada), 1980, translation by Sheila Fischman, Stoddart (Toronto, Ontario, Canada), 1982.

Les Fous de bassan, Éditions du Seuil (Montreal, Quebec, Canada), 1982, translation by Sheila Fischman published as *In the Shadow of the Wind,* Stoddart (Toronto, Ontario, Canada), 1983.

Le Premier jardin, Éditions du Seuil (Montreal, Quebec, Canada), 1988, translation published as *The First Garden,* Anansi (Concord, Ontario, Canada), 1990.

L'Enfant charge de songes (title means "The Child Filled with Dreams"), Éditions du Seuil (Montreal, Quebec, Canada), 1992, translation published as *Burden of Dreams,* Anansi (Concord, Ontario, Canada), 1994.

Aurelien, Clara, Mademoiselle et le Lieutenant Anglais, translation by Sheila Fischman published as *Aurelien, Clara, Mademoiselle, and the English Lieutenant,* General Distribution Services, 1996.

Un Habit de lumiere, Éditions du Seuil (Montreal, Quebec, Canada), 1999, translation by Sheila Fischman published as *A Suit of Light,* Anansi (Toronto, Ontario, Canada), 2000.

OTHER

Le Torrent (short stories), Beauchemin, 1950, new edition published as *Le Torrent, suivi de deux nouvelles inedites,* Éditions HMH (Montreal, Quebec, Canada), 1963, translation by Gwendolyn Moore published as *The Torrent: Novellas and Short Stories,* Harvest House (Montreal, Quebec, Canada), 1973.

Les Invites au proces, le theatre du grand prix (radio play; produced by Radio-Canada, 1952), published in *Le Temps sauvage, La Merciere assassinee, Les Invites au proces: Theatre,* 1967.

(With others) *Trois de Quebec* (radio play), Radio-Canada, 1953.

Les Indes parmi nous (screenplay), National Film Board of Canada, 1954.

La Canne a peche (screenplay), National Film Board of Canada, 1959.

Saint-Denys Garneau (screenplay), National Film Board of Canada, 1960.

Le Temps sauvage (play; produced in Quebec, 1966), published in *Le Temps sauvage, La Merciere assassinee, Les Invites au proces: Theatre,* 1967.

Le Temps sauvage, La Merciere assassinee, Les Invites au proces: Theatre (plays), Éditions HMH, 1967.

(With F.R. Scott) *Dialogue sur la traduction,* edited by Jeanne Lapointe, Éditions HMH, 1970.

La Cage: L'Ile de la demoiselle (play), Boreál (Montreal, Quebec, Canada), 1990.

Est-ce que je te derange?, Éditions du Seuil (Montreal, Quebec, Canada), 1998, translation by Sheila Fischman published as *Am I Disturbing You?,* Anansi (Toronto, Ontario, Canada), 1998.

Also author of *Drole de mic-mac* and *Le Medecin du nord,* both 1954, and *Le Deficient mental,* 1960. Contributor of poems to literary journals.

SIDELIGHTS: French-Canadian poet and novelist Anne Hébert was acclaimed as one of her country's most distinguished literary stylists. Continuing from her first book of verse, 1942's *Les Songes en equilibre,* Hébert contributed novels, poems, and plays to the growing body of modern Canadian letters, winning the poet numerous awards for her work. Praised by critics for her originality, Hébert was particularly known for the novel *Kamouraska,* published in 1970, and the poetry cycle *Le Tombeau des rois,* translated as *The Tomb of the Kings* and first published in 1953.

Hébert was born in 1916 and raised in an intellectually stimulating environment. Her father, Maurice-Lang Hébert, was a distinguished literary critic; among his friends were some of the finest minds in Quebec. Due to a childhood illness Hébert was educated privately and spent most of her time at the family's country home in Sainte-Catherine-de-Fossambault. She began writing poetry in her adolescence with the advice and guidance of both her father and her cousin, poet Hector de Saint-Denys Garneau.

Unlike Saint-Denys Garneau, who remained in self-isolation until his death, Hébert emerged from the spiritual struggle described in her first two books of poetry. *Les Songes en equilibre,* her poetic debut, chronicles the experiences of a young woman who travels from carefree childhood to the renunciation of pleasure and the acceptance of a lonely life of spiritual and poetic duty. Hébert received strict Roman Catholic training as a child, and believed the obligation of a poet is to be a spiritual force in man's salvation.

In her second book of poetry, *The Tomb of the Kings,* Hébert reveals that the austere life she chose for herself had stifled her work. It is in this volume of her poetry that she emerges from a dark and deep spiritual struggle. Samuel Moon characterized *The Tomb of the Kings* as a work "closely unified by its constant introspection, by its atmosphere of profound melancholy, by its recurrent themes of a dead childhood, a living death cut off from love and beauty, suicide, the theme of introspection itself. Such a book would seem to be of more interest clinically than poetically, but the miracle occurs and these materials are transmuted by the remarkable force of Mlle. Hébert's imagery, the simplicity and directness of her diction, and the restrained lyric sound of her *vers libre.*"

Although known primarily as a poet, Hébert also wrote for the stage and television, and was the author of several published novels. Characteristic of her prose work is the theme of the inhibiting burden of the past, which binds any freedom for future actions. Many critics have noted that this theme is a French-Canadian phenomenon.

Hébert's first novel, *Les Chambres de bois,* appeared in 1958. Catherine, the novel's chief protagonist, is married to an artist who is repulsed by sex. She eventually abandons her husband for another man, and discovers happiness in this new relationship. According to an article in *Contemporary Literary Criticism, Les Chambres de bois* "was well received by critics who applauded Hébert's use of symbolist imagery." A contributor to *Books and Writers* commented that the "fantastic elements" found in *Les Chambres de bois* can also be found in Hébert's subsequent works.

Kamouraska, Hébert's second novel, was published seventeen years after *Les Chambres de bois,* and drew praise from both Canadian and U.S. critics. A *Choice* reviewer noted that the novel "conveys the same sense of mounting and almost unendurable excitement that one felt on first reading a Brontë novel—except that *Kamouraska* is modern in style and explicitness. The events are a stream-of-consciousness re-creation of a murder of passion that actually occurred in 1840. Hébert's poetic vision draws the thoughtful reader to be one with each of the frenzied characters." *Kamouraska* tells the story of Elisabeth d'Aulnieres, who conspires to slay her abusive spouse with the aid of her lover, Doctor George Nelson. Following the murder of Antoine Tassy, Nelson escapes to the United States, but Elisabeth is imprisoned for the crime. A *Canadian Forum* critic compared Hébert's "highly complex style and imagery" with that of writers Marcel Proust, Franz Kafka, and James Joyce, and stated that "the greatness of this work resides in the happy mixture of particularity and universality, unity and complexity, vitality and artistic originality, and, above all, in the way the author makes simplistic moral judgment of the characters impossible."

Mel Watkins in the *New York Times* called Hébert a "stylist of the first rank" in his review of *Children of the Black Sabbath,* a novel that deals with a young novice possessed by the devil. Watkins observed that Hébert "both complements and heightens this eerie, aphotic atmosphere with the verity and density of her minor characters and with the restrained elegance of her prose. The result is an impressionistic tale that moves smoothly. . . . The vitality of the prose, of itself, makes it one of the best of its kind." Suspense and atmosphere are keys to Hébert's later works, as well. *Heloise* recounts the tale of a Paris vampire, and *Les Fous de bassan* concerns the reactions of several people to a savage crime. For the latter work, Hébert received the Prix Femina, an award honoring novels penned by women.

Hébert's treatment of her characters in *Les Fous de bassan*—translated in 1984 as *In the Shadow of the Wind*—drastically departs from her previous books. While Hébert's other novels portray strong women who break down societal conventions, the cousins Nora and Olivia of *In the Shadow of the Wind* are at the mercy of their cruel cousin Stevens, and one is sexually abused by their uncle Reverend Jones. The story of the girls' murders is narrated at different times by Stevens, Reverend Jones, and Nora prior to her death as well as by Olivia thereafter. In the work, the cousins are depicted as "the source of temptation." As Lori Saint-Martin commented in *Women's Review of Books,* "Such a purely misogynistic vision is relatively rare today—especially among women writers. Coming from Anne Hébert, the turnaround is even more disturbing."

While such misogyny may have been a departure for Hébert, critics nonetheless praised *Les Fous de bassan.* A *Publishers Weekly* critic found the dark tale reminiscent of Edith Wharton's *Ethan Frome,* while C.D.B. Bryan in the *New York Times Book Review* termed it "haunting" and remarked that "The winds Anne Hébert stirs up in her readers' minds do not die down until long after the book has been closed." Despite such praise and receipt of the Prix Femina, the book was deemed flawed by Matthew Clark in *Quill and Quire:* "I find the language precious, the characterization thin, the situation conventionally Gothic, and the actions unmotivated."

Hébert's 1992 novel *L'Enfant charge de songes* received the Canadian Governor General Award for French fic-

tion. Its English title, *Burden of Dreams,* aptly describes the protagonists of the novel who, according to Bettina L. Knapp in *World Literature Today,* are never "described as flesh-and-blood beings." Anne Denoon in *Books in Canada* noted that from the novel's "very first page the reader is acutely conscious of entering a strange, unruly and disquieting world." Knapp praised the novelist's imaginative plot, exclaiming: "More than a first-class storyteller, Hébert fuses supernatural and natural domains, the collective with the individual." Stephen Smith in *Quill and Quire* found that "the overwhelming impression that Anne Hébert's plangent novel leaves is of blurred edges: it's an impressionistic landscape, a story filtered through fevered sleep."

After an absence of nearly twenty years, Hébert returned to poetry with the 1994 publication *Day Has No Equal but Night.* The volume includes both previously published work and unpublished work, "adding," according to contributor J. Warwick in *Choice,* "a new political dimension . . . but not eclipsing her intensely personal themes." Translator A. Poulin, Jr. chose to include the poet's original French, with its English translation on the facing page. While Poulin had served as translator for Hébert's *Selected Poems,* published in 1988, reviewers were mixed in their opinion of the translator's literal treatment of Hébert's words in this work, Judy Clarence in *Library Journal* calling Poulin's effort "clunky and cumbersome." Acknowledging the difficulty in translating Hébert's imaginative writing, Sarah Lawall in *World Literature Today* maintained that Poulin "offers fluent, readable, and usually literal translations that also emulate the form of the original *vers libre.* Still there are some instances where the word choice seems either mistaken or else inattentive to indications in the text." Despite the translation, reviewers continued to be fascinated by Hébert's work. Pat Monaghan, reviewing *Day Has No Equal but Night* in *Booklist,* lauded Hébert as "a visionary descendant" of French poet Arthur Rimbaud.

In 1999 Hébert's final novel, *Un Habit de lumiere,* was published. Bettina L. Knapp noted in a *World Literature Today* article that this work is "reminiscent of some of [Hébert's] . . . previous writing," such as *L'Enfant charge de songes* and *Les Fous de Bassan,* which are also filled with "deeply troubled and troubling beings." The story in *Un Habit de lumiere* revolves around the strong fantasy lives of three members of a Spanish family residing in Paris. Hébert examines the inner lives of Rose-Alba, Rose's husband, and their son, Miguel, contrasting each person's dream worlds with the stifling reality of their everyday lives. Knapp concluded by saying that *Un Habit de lumiere* presents "a pitiful world of. . . . pitifully predictable solutions."

Three years prior to her death from cancer in 2000, Hébert returned from Paris to spend her final years in her native Quebec. In a *Maclean's* article, Sheila Fischman, who translated seven of Hébert's novels, stated that the late writer "used the French language like something fine and rare; her style is . . . luminous and pure. Every word she used was necessary and right. . . . Hébert's great achievement will be part of our human experience as long as fine writing is admired and read."

After Hébert's death, Marie-Claire Blais wrote appreciatively of Hébert in *Time International:* Hébert "was a poet for whom the beauty of the world was a vast source of inspiration and delight. . . . For future generations of writers and poets who will come after her, this great artist will continue to be an exemplary model of courage and perseverance in the way that she approached the act of writing."

BIOGRAPHICAL AND CRITICAL SOURCES:

BOOKS

Contemporary Literary Criticism, Thomson Gale (Detroit, MI), Volume 4, 1975, Volume 13, 1980, Volume 29, 1984.
Contemporary Women Poets, St. James Press (Detroit, MI), 1997.
Contemporary World Writers, St. James Press (Detroit, MI), 1993.
Dictionary of Literary Biography, Volume 68: *Canadian Writers, 1920-1959, First Series,* Thomson Gale (Detroit, MI), 1988.
Knight, Kelton, *Anne Hébert: In Search of the First Garden,* P. Lang (New York, NY), 1995.
Lewis, Paula Gilbert, editor, *Traditionalism, Nationalism, and Feminism: Women Writers of Quebec,* Greenwood Press (Westport, CT), 1985.
Mitchell, Constantina, *Shaping the Novel: Textual Interplay in the Fiction of Malraux, Hébert, Modiano,* Berghahn Books (Providence, RI), 1995.
Russell, Delbert W., *Anne Hébert,* Twayne (New York, NY), 1983.

PERIODICALS

American Review of Canadian Studies, fall, 1987.
Booklist, January 15, 1991, p. 1045; September 1, 1993, p. 43; March 15, 1994, p. 1323.

Books in Canada, April, 1990, p. 47; February, 1995, p. 35.
Canadian Forum, November-December, 1973; December, 1999, Suzette Mayr, review of *Am I Disturbing You?,* pp. 42-44.
Canadian Literature, Volume 58, 1973; spring, 1981; summer, 1985; autumn, 1991, p. 175; summer, 1992, p. 187; spring, 1994, p. 110; summer, 2000, Eva-Marie Kroller, pp. 5-9.
Choice, September, 1973; September, 1994, p. 117.
Essays on Canadian Writing, Volume 12, 1978; summer, 1983.
French Review, May, 1986; December, 1988, p. 363; February, 1991, p. 451; December, 1999, Patrice J. Proulx, review of *Est-ce que je te derange?,* pp. 380-381; December, 2000, Douglas L. Boudreau, "Anglophone Presence in the Early Novels of Anne Hébert," pp. 308-319; December, 2000, Karin Egloff, review of *Un Habit de lumiere,* pp.398-399.
Journal of Canadian Fiction, Volume 2, number 1, 1972.
Library Journal, March 15, 1994, p. 74.
Los Angeles Times, January 26, 2000.
Modern Fiction Studies, summer, 1981.
New York Times, September 7, 1977.
New York Times Book Review, July 22, 1984, p. 7.
Poetry, June, 1968.
Publishers Weekly, May 18, 1984, p. 142; March 28, 1994, p. 91.
Quebec Studies, Volume 3, 1985; Volume 4, 1986; Volume 5, 1987; Volume 6, 1988; Volume 8, 1989.
Quill and Quire, November, 1983, p. 20; January, 1995, p. 35.
Studies in Canadian Literature, Volume 14, number 1, 1989.
Waves, spring, 1982.
Women's Review of Books, November, 1984.
World Literature Today, spring, 1993, p. 323; autumn, 1994, p. 781; winter, 2000, Bettina L. Knapp, review of *Un Habit de lumiere,* p. 104.
Yale French Studies, Volume 65, 1983.

ONLINE

Books and Writers, http://www.kirjasto.sci.fi/ (May 11, 2003).

OBITUARIES:

PERIODICALS

Los Angeles Times, January 26, 2000, p. A16.
Maclean's, February 7, 2000, p. 57.

New York Times, February 3, 2000, p. A23.
Time International, February 7, 2000, p. 56.

*　　*　　*

HEGI, Ursula 1946-

PERSONAL: Born May 23, 1946, in Düsseldorf, West Germany; came to the United States in 1965, naturalized citizen, 1970; daughter of Heinrich and Johanna (Maas) Koch; married Ernest Hegi (a management consultant), October 21, 1967 (divorced, 1984); companion to Gordon Gagliano (an architect); children: Eric, Adam. *Education:* University of New Hampshire, B.A., 1978, M.A., 1979.

ADDRESSES: Home—Nine Mile Falls, WA 99026. *Agent*—c/o Author Mail, Simon & Schuster, 1230 Avenue of the Americas, New York, NY 10020.

CAREER: University of New Hampshire, Durham, lecturer in English, beginning 1978; currently professor of fiction writing, Eastern Washington University. Participates in writing conferences; gives poetry and fiction readings. Serves on the board of National Book Critics Circle.

MEMBER: Associated Writing Programs.

AWARDS, HONORS: Nominee, PEN/Faulkner Award, 1994, for *Stones from the River.*

WRITINGS:

Intrusions (novel), Viking (New York, NY), 1981.
Unearned Pleasures and Other Stories, University of Idaho Press (Moscow, ID), 1988.
Floating in My Mother's Palm (novel), Poseidon Press (New York, NY), 1990.
Stones from the River, Poseidon Press (New York, NY), 1994.
Salt Dancers, Simon & Schuster (New York, NY), 1995.
Tearing the Silence: Being German in America, Simon & Schuster (New York, NY), 1997.
The Vision of Emma Blau, Simon & Schuster (New York, NY), 2000.
Hotel of the Saints: Stories, Simon & Schuster (New York, NY), 2001.

Trudi & Pia, Atheneum Books for Young Readers (New York, NY), 2003.
Sacred Time, Simon & Schuster (New York, NY), 2004.

Contributor to magazines, including *McCall's, Feminist Studies, Ms., Blue Buildings, Bradford Review,* and *Kayak.*

ADAPTATIONS: The Vision of Emma Blau was adapted for audio by Simon & Schuster Audio.

SIDELIGHTS: Ursula Hegi was born in Düsseldorf, Germany, in 1946, less than a year after the end of World War II. She immigrated to the United States at the age of eighteen, married, and raised two sons before beginning studies at the University of New Hampshire. In short stories, novels, and nonfiction, Hegi rehearses the pain of internal shame—shame that is the product not of what one has done but of what one is. Hegi's characters are, like herself, German Americans born in the immediate aftermath of World War II and surrounded by people directly or indirectly implicated in wartime atrocities who steadfastly refuse to speak about the war. Her first novel, *Intrusions,* is the author's only attempt to overlay a story with humor and a modernist technique. *Floating in My Mother's Palm,* her second novel, essentially tells the author's own story of growing up in the first generation after World War II, cushioned from knowledge of the part her parents and countrymen played in the atrocities of that war by their perfect silence on the subject but nonetheless attuned to the guilt and self-hatred she sees in the adults around her.

Reading more like a collection of interconnected stories than a traditional novel, *Floating in My Mother's Palm* is set in the fictional German town of Bergdorf, a place Hegi has returned to several times in her fiction. The interwoven lives of the villagers are the stuff of these stories, which "glow with the luminosity of Impressionist paintings," commented Sybil Steinberg in *Publishers Weekly.*

Among the secondary characters in *Floating in My Mother's Palm* is Trudi Montag, the town librarian, a dwarf who seems to know everyone's secrets. Trudi became the central character in Hegi's next novel, *Stones from the River,* a highly celebrated treatment of life in a German town just before and during the rise of Hitler. Because Trudi is a dwarf, the townspeople fail to treat her like a person and end up spilling their secrets in front of her as though she weren't there. During the war, Trudi is able to hide several Jews, in part because of this invisibility. Reviewers were quick to draw comparisons between Hegi's dwarf and another famous fictional dwarf living through the Nazi era in Germany, that created by Günter Grass in *The Tin Drum.* "For both authors [Hegi and Grass]," noted Victoria J. Barnett in the *Christian Century,* "the Third Reich is part of a continuum (for Hegi, of silence; for Grass, of moral chaos) that begins long before 1933 and is not broken after 1945. Further, they contend that the failure to deal honestly with the past ensures the continuance of moral corruption." Thus, the importance of telling stories, of Trudi's stories, whatever their partiality or intent, lies in breaking the silence. "Telling a story and living a life—this compelling novel makes us see how little difference there is between them," observed Bill Ott in *Booklist.* Likewise, *New York Times* contributor Suzanne Ruta remarked: "In [Trudi's] progress from malicious gossip to serene artist, she hints at the ambiguous roots of the writer's vocation."

Stones from the River earned a nomination for the PEN/Faulkner Award and was chosen for *Oprah's* talk show reading club. The novel was quickly followed by *Salt Dancers,* set in the author's adopted home of Washington State, where a forty-one-year-old woman decides to confront her abusive father in the hope of healing old wounds that might cause her to abuse her own unborn child. *Christian Century* contributor Sondra B. Willobee viewed *Salt Dancers* as a recovery novel, one in which the protagonist essentially travels the road from childhood injury through understanding to recovery. "Julia is distinguished from the heroines of other recovery novels by her awareness of her own cruelty and her willingness to understand the roots of her parents' pain," Willobee observed. Like Hegi's other protagonists, Julia learns the importance of moving out of the silence of memories and into the realm of stories. Returning home to confront her father, she realizes that she had forgotten a myriad of good times in her childhood, and along with new insights, she gains renewed relationships with her father, her estranged brother, and with the mother who had abandoned her years before.

For John Skow, who reviewed *Salt Dancers* for *Time,* Hegi's 1995 novel is too programmatic, too closely aligned to the recovery model, to be successful as fiction. The novel's conclusion is especially flawed, according to Skow: "This slack stuff is soap opera, and even a writer as gifted as Hegi can't dress it up as anything else." For other reviewers, Hegi's skills as a writer allowed her to overcome any flaws in her plot. *Booklist* reviewer Margaret Flanagan averred: "In achingly beautiful prose that exacts a huge emotional toll, the author

at once shatters and rebuilds the myth of the family unit." Similarly, a contributor to *Publishers Weekly* compared *Salt Dancers* favorably with Hegi's *Stones from the River* and *Floating in My Mother's Palm,* concluding: "There is both poignancy and suspense in Julia's journey through her past, and the surprises she encounters in herself as well as others lead to a healing resolution that has the open-ended feel of real life." And for Abby Frucht, who reviewed *Salt Dancers* for the *New York Times,* Hegi's novel compared favorably with other contemporary accounts of childhood abuse reckoned in adult terms by writers such as Kaye Gibbons, Dorothy Allison, and Mona Simpson: "Perhaps it is the peculiar authority of the narrative voice in Ursula Hegi's latest novel—its refusal either to sentimentalize or sensationalize, its insistence on undulating intuitively through the various part of the story—that makes *Salt Dancers* seem fresh."

Hegi turned to nonfiction with *Tearing the Silence: On Being German in America.* The book is based on the author's interviews with more than two hundred people who, like her, were born in Germany during or just after World War II and later immigrated to the United States. *Tearing the Silence* offers representative discourses on such *verboten* topics as racial prejudice and what these German Americans knew about their parents' involvement with Nazism. "The stories differ strikingly, but for the most part they share a common element: shame for the sins of their fathers," observed Sally Eckhoff for *Salon.com.* Although a *Publishers Weekly* reviewer proclaimed, "These are powerful portraits of survivors of Hitler's legacy," *Nation* contributor Amei Wallach complained that in choosing to write nonfiction, Hegi forfeits her best tools: she is "a novelist who knows perfectly how to tune nuance, charge scenes and beguile language. But at the very moment that she has chosen to write about the subject closest to her, her own story, she abandons what she's best at, on the wrongheaded assumption that fact is more convincing that fiction." Other critics felt differently, however. For example, Kay Meredith Dusheck contended in *Library Journal:* "This singular work is an important addition to a greater understanding of the Holocaust."

In *The Vision of Emma Blau,* Hegi returns to fiction and the fictional world of Burgdorf, Germany, with an epic story of a family of German immigrants whose lives are ruined by the obsession of one of its members. Near the turn of the twentieth century, Stefan Blau leaves his home town of Burgdorf to come to the East Coast of the United States. After arriving, he has a vision of a young girl dancing in a courtyard, and resolves to make that vision a reality by building the Wasserburg, a luxury hotel set on the banks of a lake in New Hampshire. His singular focus on attaining that goal leads him to neglect his family. After the death of his first two wives in childbirth, Stefan returns to Burgdorf to find a third wife. He returns to New Hampshire with Helene Montag, aunt of Trudie Montag, the librarian in *Stones from the River,* who appears briefly in *Floating in My Mother's Palm.* "This book started in my head long before I wrote *Stones,*" Hegi explained to an interviewer for *Publishers Weekly.* "I started it right after *Floating,* and when *Stones* crowded it aside, I had already begun to think about this boy who runs away from Germany to the United States."

Critical response to *The Vision of Emma Blau* was generally positive. In a review in the *Atlantic,* Phoebe-Lou Adams counted among the assets of the novel "a large cast of convincing Blaus, tenants, relatives back in Germany, and Winnipesaukee [New Hampshire] locals." Hegi's account of the family of German Americans in the 1950s was also remarked upon. "In *The Vision of Emma Blau,* [Hegi] tells a story whose scope is an entire century, one filled with insight into a family legacy of secrets, the difficulties of assimilation, intergenerational misunderstanding and half-truths grown unmanageable over time," observed Valerie Ryan in the *Seattle Times.* A contributor to *Publishers Weekly* similarly acknowledged "Hegi's gift for depicting family dynamics and sexual relationships, including the concealed sorrows and tensions that motivate behavior," adding, "but it is her larger perspective of a family's cultural roots that grants her novel distinction."

In *Sacred Time,* Hegi again shows her penchant for and ability to portray the complex dynamics of a large family. In this novel, she leaves Germany for the United States, following—for more than fifty years—the lives of a turbulent and chaotic yet charming Italian-American family living in the Bronx, New York. A reviewer for *Publishers Weekly* described the opening as "boisterously funny," but pointed out that the subsequent family tragedy creates a "moving if occasionally manipulative" novel. Beth E. Anderson, reviewing *Sacred Time* for *Library Journal,* commented that "Hegi puts her readers smack in the center of the psychological morass" while creating quirky characters that provide the reader with comic relief in what would otherwise be an unremittingly grim story. Caledonia Kearns, reviewing the book for the *Boston Globe,* wrote, "It is to Hegi's credit that she has created characters whose intensity and love for one another ring true."

BIOGRAPHICAL AND CRITICAL SOURCES:

BOOKS

Bauermeister, Erica, *Five Hundred Great Books by Women,* Penguin (New York, NY), 1994.

PERIODICALS

Atlantic, March, 2000, Phoebe-Lou Adams, review of *The Vision of Emma Blau,* p. 116.

Booklist, March 15, 1994, Bill Ott, review of *Stones from the River,* p. 1327; August, 1995, Margaret Flanagan, review of *Salt Dancers,* p. 1929; July, 1997, Mary Carroll, review of *Tearing the Silence,* p. 1793; November 15, 1999, Grace Fill, review of *The Vision of Emma Blau,* p. 580.

Boston Globe, May 23, 2004, Caledonia Kearns, review of *Sacred Time,* section L, p. 9.

Christian Century, August 10, 1994, Victoria J. Barnett, review of *Stones from the River,* p. 755; April 24, 1996, Sondra B. Willobee, review of *Salt Dancers,* p. 464.

Chronicle of Higher Education, December 7, 1994, Peter Monaghan, "A Writer Confronts Her German Ghosts," p. A6.

Entertainment Weekly, March 21, 1997, Lisa Schwarzbaum, review of *Stones from the River,* p. 65.

Glamour, March, 1994, Laura Mathews, review of *Stones from the River,* p. 156.

Kirkus Reviews, May 1, 1997, review of *Tearing the Silence.*

Library Journal, March 1, 1990, Mary Soete, review of *Floating in My Mother's Palm,* p. 116; January, 1994, Michael T. O'Pecko, review of *Stones from the River,* p. 160; July, 1995, Patricia Ross, review of *Salt Dancers,* p. 120; June 1, 1997, Kay Meredith Dusheck, review of *Tearing the Silence,* p. 122; December, 1999, Eleanor J. Bader, review of *The Vision of Emma Blau,* p. 186; December 2003, Beth E. Anderson, review of *Sacred Time,* p. 166.

Mother Jones, July-August, 1990, Georgia Brown, review of *Floating in My Mother's Palm,* p. 56.

Nation, July 28, 1997, Amei Wallach, review of *Tearing the Silence,* p. 31.

Newsweek, April 18, 1994, Laura Shapiro, review of *Stones from the River,* p. 63.

New York Times, March 18, 1990, Edward Hoagland, review of *Floating in My Mother's Palm,* section 7, p. 5; March 20, 1994, Suzanne Ruta, "The Secrets of a Small German Town"; August 27, 1995, Abby Frucht, "Like a Motherless Child"; August 17, 1997, Walter Reich, "Guilty Long Ago"; February 13, 2000, Diana Postlethwaite, review of *The Vision of Emma Blau.*

New York Times Book Review, March 20, 1994, Jon Elsen, "What Wasn't Taught in School," p. 2.

Publishers Weekly, January 5, 1990, Sybil Steinberg, review of *Floating in My Mother's Palm,* p. 62; January 17, 1994, review of *Stones from the River,* p. 400; March 14, 1994, Kitty Harmon, interview with Hegi, p. 52; May 22, 1995, review of *Salt Dancers,* p. 46; June 16, 1997, review of *Tearing the Silence,* p. 55; November 29, 1999, review of *The Vision of Emma Blau,* p. 51; October 6, 2003, review of *Sacred Time,* p. 57.

Seattle Times, February 6, 2000, Valerie Ryan, "An Insightful *Vision:* Ursula Hegi Continues to Write about Matters German."

Time, August 21, 1995, John Skow, review of *Salt Dancers,* p. 68.

USA Today, December 2, 1999, Jacqueline Blais, "*Stones* Breaks the Grip of Silence."

Wall Street Journal, April 8, 1997, Amy Gamerman, "Behind the Scenes at Oprah's Book Club," p. A20; February 4, 2000, Gabriella Stern, review of *The Vision of Emma Blau,* p. W8.

ONLINE

Barnes & Noble.com, http://www.barnesandnoble.com/ "Meet the Writers—Ursula Hegi," (August 20, 2004).

Salon.com, http://www.salon.com/ (June 30, 1997), Sally Eckhoff, review of *Tearing the Silence.*

*   *   *

HEINLEIN, Robert A. 1907-1988

(Robert Anson Heinlein, Anson Macdonald, Lyle Monroe, John Riverside, Caleb Saunders, Simon York)

PERSONAL: Surname rhymes with "fine line"; born July 7, 1907, in Butler, MO; died of heart failure May 8, 1988, in Carmel, CA; son of Rex Ivar (an accountant) and Bam (Lyle) Heinlein; married Leslyn McDonald (divorced, 1947); married Virginia Doris Gerstenfeld, October 21, 1948. *Education:* Attended University of Missouri, 1925; U.S. Naval Academy, graduate, 1929; University of California—Los Angeles, graduate study (physics and mathematics), 1934.

CAREER: Writer, 1939-88. Owner of Shively & Sophie Lodes silver mine, Silver Plume, CO, 1934-35; candidate for California State Assembly, 1938; worked as a real estate agent c. 1930s; aviation engineer at Naval Air Experimental Station, Philadelphia, PA, 1942-45; guest commentator during Apollo 11 lunar landing, Columbia Broadcasting System, 1969; James V. Forrestal

Lecturer, U.S. Naval Academy, 1973. *Military service:* U.S. Navy, commissioned ensign, 1929; became lieutenant, junior grade; retired due to physical disability, 1934.

AWARDS, HONORS: Guest of Honor, World Science Fiction Convention, 1941, 1961, 1976; Hugo Award, World Science Fiction Convention, 1956, for *Double Star,* 1960, for *Starship Troopers,* 1962, for *Stranger in a Strange Land,* and 1967, for *The Moon Is a Harsh Mistress;* Boys' Clubs of America Book Award, 1959; Sequoyah Children's Book Award, Oklahoma Library Association, 1961, for *Have Space Suit—Will Travel;* named best all-time author, *Locus* magazine readers' poll, 1973 and 1975; National Rare Blood Club Humanitarian Award, 1974; Nebula Award, Grand Master, Science Fiction and Fantasy Writers of America, 1975; Council of Community Blood Centers Award, 1977; American Association of Blood Banks Award, 1977; Inkpot Award, 1977; L.H.D., Eastern Michigan University, 1977; Distinguished Public Service Medal, National Aeronautics and Space Administration (NASA), 1988 (posthumously awarded), "in recognition of his meritorious service to the nation and mankind in advocating and promoting the exploration of space"; the Rhysling Award of the Science Fiction Poetry Association is named after a character in Heinlein's story "The Green Hills of Earth"; Tomorrow Starts Here Award, Delta Vee Society; numerous awards for work with blood drives.

WRITINGS:

SCIENCE FICTION NOVELS

Methuselah's Children (originally serialized in *Astounding Science Fiction,* July-September, 1941), Gnome Press (Hicksville, NY), 1958.

Beyond This Horizon (originally serialized under pseudonym Anson MacDonald in *Astounding Science Fiction,* April and May, 1942), Fantasy Press (Reading, PA), 1948, reprinted, Baen (Riverdale, NY), 2001.

Sixth Column, Gnome Press (Hicksville, NY), 1949, published as *The Day after Tomorrow,* New American Library (New York, NY), 1951.

Waldo [and] *Magic, Inc.* (also see below), Doubleday (New York, NY), 1950, published as *Waldo: Genius in Orbit,* Avon (New York, NY), 1958.

Universe, Dell (New York, NY), 1951, published as *Orphans of the Sky,* Gollancz (London, England), 1963.

The Puppet Masters (also see below; originally serialized in *Galaxy Science Fiction,* September-November, 1951), Doubleday (New York, NY), 1951.

Revolt in 2100, Shasta (Chicago, IL), 1953.

Double Star (originally serialized in *Astounding Science Fiction,* February-April, 1956), Doubleday (New York, NY), 1956.

The Door into Summer (originally serialized in *Magazine of Fantasy and Science Fiction,* October-December, 1956), Doubleday (New York, NY), 1957.

Starship Troopers (originally serialized as "Starship Soldier" in *Magazine of Fantasy and Science Fiction,* October and November, 1959), Putnam (New York, NY), 1959.

Stranger in a Strange Land, Putnam (New York, NY), 1961, revised and uncut edition with preface by wife Virginia Heinlein, 1990.

Glory Road (originally serialized in *Magazine of Fantasy and Science Fiction,* July-September, 1963), Putnam (New York, NY), 1963, reprinted, Tor Books (New York, NY), 2004.

Farnham's Freehold (originally serialized in *If,* July, August, and October, 1964), Putnam (New York, NY), 1964.

Three by Heinlein (contains *The Puppet Masters, Waldo,* and *Magic, Inc.*), Doubleday (New York, NY), 1965, published as *A Heinlein Triad,* Gollancz (London, England), 1966.

The Moon Is a Harsh Mistress (originally serialized in *If,* December, 1965, January-April, 1966), Putnam (New York, NY), 1966, reprinted, Tor Books (New York, NY), 1996.

A Robert Heinlein Omnibus, Sidgwick & Jackson (London, England), 1966.

I Will Fear No Evil (originally serialized in *Galaxy,* July, August, October, and December, 1970), Putnam (New York, NY), 1971.

Time Enough for Love: The Lives of Lazarus Long, Putnam (New York, NY), 1973.

The Notebooks of Lazarus Long (excerpted from *Time Enough for Love: The Lives of Lazarus Long*), Putnam (New York, NY), 1978, illuminated by D.F. Vassallo, Pomegranate Artbooks (San Francisco, CA), 1995.

The Number of the Beast, Fawcett (New York, NY), 1980.

Friday, Holt (New York, NY), 1982, reprinted, Ballantine (New York, NY), 1997.

Job: A Comedy of Justice, Ballantine (New York, NY), 1984.

The Cat Who Walks through Walls: A Comedy of Manners, Putnam (New York, NY), 1985.

To Sail beyond the Sunset: The Life and Loves of Maureen Johnson, Being the Memoirs of a Somewhat Irregular Lady, Putnam (New York, NY), 1987.

For Us, the Living: A Comedy of Customs, Scribner (New York, NY), 2004.

SCIENCE FICTION NOVELS; FOR YOUNG ADULTS

Rocket Ship Galileo (also see below), Scribner (New York, NY), 1947.

Space Cadet (also see below), Scribner (New York, NY), 1948.

Red Planet, Scribner (New York, NY), 1949, expanded with previously unpublished passages, Del Rey (New York, NY), 1989.

Farmer in the Sky (originally serialized as "Satellite Scout" in *Boy's Life,* August-November, 1950), Scribner (New York, NY), 1950.

Between Planets (originally serialized as "Planets in Combat" in *Blue Book,* September and October, 1951), Scribner (New York, NY), 1951.

The Rolling Stones (originally serialized as "Tramp Space Ship" in *Boy's Life,* September-December, 1952), Scribner (New York, NY), 1952, published as *Space Family Stone,* Gollancz (London, England), 1969.

Starman Jones, Scribner (New York, NY), 1953.

Star Beast (originally serialized as "The Star Lummox" in *Magazine of Fantasy and Science Fiction,* May-July, 1954), Scribner (New York, NY), 1954.

Tunnel in the Sky, Scribner (New York, NY), 1955, reprinted, Del Rey (New York, NY), 2003.

Time for the Stars, Scribner (New York, NY), 1956.

Citizen of the Galaxy (originally serialized in *Astounding Science Fiction,* September-December, 1957), Scribner (New York, NY), 1957.

Have Space Suit—Will Travel (originally serialized in *Magazine of Fantasy and Science Fiction,* August-October, 1958), Scribner (New York, NY), 1958, reprinted, Ballantine (New York, NY), 2003.

Podkayne of Mars: Her Life and Times (originally serialized in *Worlds of If,* November, 1962, January and March, 1963), Putnam (New York, NY), 1963, published as *Podkayne of Mars,* Baen (Riverdale, NY), 1993.

STORY COLLECTIONS

The Man Who Sold the Moon, Shasta (Chicago, IL), 1950, 3rd edition, 1953.

The Green Hills of Earth, Shasta (Chicago, IL), 1951.

Assignment in Eternity, Fantasy Press (Reading, PA), 1953.

The Menace from Earth, Gnome Press (Hicksville, NY), 1959.

The Unpleasant Profession of Jonathan Hoag, Gnome Press (Hicksville, NY), 1959, published as *6 x H,* Pyramid Publications (New York, NY), 1962.

The Worlds of Robert A. Heinlein, Ace Books (New York, NY), 1966.

The Past through Tomorrow: Future History Stories, Putnam (New York, NY), 1967.

The Best of Robert Heinlein, 1939-1959, two volumes, edited by Angus Wells, Sidgwick & Jackson (London, England), 1973.

Destination Moon, Gregg (Boston, MA), 1979.

Expanded Universe: The New Worlds of Robert A. Heinlein, Ace Books (New York, NY), 1980, reprinted, Baen (Riverdale, NY), 2004.

Requiem: New Collected Works by Robert A. Heinlein and Tributes to the Grand Master, edited by Yoji Kondo, Tom Doherty Associates (New York, NY), 1992.

The Fantasies of Robert A. Heinlein, Tor (New York, NY), 1999.

SCREENPLAYS

(With Rip Van Ronkel and James O' Hanlon) *Destination Moon* (based on *Rocket Ship Galileo;* produced and directed by George Pal/Eagle Lion, 1950), edited by David G. Hartwell, Gregg, 1979.

(With Jack Seaman) *Project Moonbase,* Galaxy Pictures/Lippert Productions, 1953.

OTHER

(Editor) *Tomorrow, the Stars,* Doubleday (New York, NY), 1952.

Grumbles from the Grave (collected correspondence), edited by Virginia Heinlein, Ballantine (New York, NY), 1989.

Take Back Your Government: A Practical Handbook for the Private Citizen Who Wants Democracy to Work (political commentary), with introduction by Jerry Pournelle, Baen (Riverdale, NY), 1992.

Tramp Royale (autobiographical fiction), Ace Books (New York, NY), 1992.

Also author of engineering report, *Test Procedures for Plastic Materials Intended for Structural and Semi-Structural Aircraft Uses,* 1944. Contributor to books, including *Of Worlds Beyond: The Science of Science Fiction,* edited by Lloyd Arthur Eshbach, Fantasy Press, 1947. Also contributor to anthologies and to the *Encyclopaedia Britannica.* Contributor of numerous short stories and articles, sometimes under pseudonyms Lyle Monroe, John Riverside, Caleb Saunders, and Simon York, to *Saturday Evening Post, Analog, Galaxy, Astounding Science Fiction,* and other publications.

The author's papers are archived at the University of California—Santa Cruz.

ADAPTATIONS: The television series *Tom Corbett: Space Cadet,* which aired from 1951-56, was based on Heinlein's novel *Space Cadet;* a military simulation board game was created based on *Starship Troopers; Starship Troopers* was released as an animated feature in Japan; *Red Planet* was adapted as a three-part cartoon miniseries, released as *Robert A. Heinlein's Red Planet; The Puppet Masters* was filmed in 1994, released as *Robert A. Heinlein's The Puppet Masters,* starring Donald Sutherland; *Starship Troopers* was filmed in 1996, directed by Paul Verhoeven; television, radio, and film rights to many of Heinlein's works have been sold.

SIDELIGHTS: "The one author who has raised science fiction from the gutter of pulp space opera . . . to the altitude of original and breathtaking concepts," Alfred Bester once wrote in *Publishers Weekly,* "is Robert A. Heinlein." Heinlein's influence in his field was so great that Alexei Panshin stated in his *Heinlein in Dimension: A Critical Analysis* that "the last twenty-five years of science fiction may even be taken in large part as an exploration by many writers of the possibilities inherent in Heinlein's techniques." Some critics compared Heinlein's influence on the genre to that of H.G. Wells. Writer Robert Silverberg, for example, wrote in a *Locus* obituary of Heinlein that like "no one else but H.G. Wells, he gave science fiction its definition," adding that Heinlein "utterly transformed our notions of how to tell a science fiction story, and the transformation has been a permanent and irreversible one."

Having been forced to abandon a military career because he suffered from tuberculosis, Heinlein began writing in the late 1930s as a way to make money to pay off a mortgage. He wrote his first novel, a time-travel tale called *For Us, the Living: A Comedy of Customs* in 1939, but it did not see publication until 2004. Still, he did begin to make a living from selling stories to science fiction magazines, and he not only paid off the mortgage but found his life's work.

During the 1940s Heinlein's work for science fiction magazines began building his reputation as a talented author. His influence began with this period and, as Panshin pointed out, derived from his "insistence in talking clearly, knowledgeably, and dramatically about the real world [which] destroyed forever the sweet, pure, wonderful innocence that science fiction once had. . . . In a sense, Heinlein may be said to have offered science fiction a road to adulthood." Speaking of this early work, Daniel Dickinson wrote in *Modern Fiction Studies* that Heinlein possessed "a vast knowledge of science, military affairs, and politics" which enabled him to write "stories that shimmered gemlike amid the vast mass of middling, amateurish tales that choked the pulp SF journals. Heinlein's influence was enormous; dozens of young writers strove to imitate his style, and editors refashioned their publications to reflect the new sense of sophistication Heinlein and a few others were bringing to the field." In a poll taken by *Astounding Science Fiction* magazine in 1953, eighteen top science fiction writers of the time cited Heinlein as the major influence on their work.

After working as an engineer during World War II, Heinlein returned to writing in the late 1940s. It was during this time that he moved from the genre magazines in which he had made his reputation to more mainstream periodicals, particularly the *Saturday Evening Post.* As *Dictionary of Literary Biography* contributor Joseph Patrouch wrote, "Heinlein was the first major science-fiction writer to break out of category and reach the larger general-fiction market, and therefore he was the first to start breaking down the walls that had isolated science fiction for so long."

Heinlein also began to publish novels for young people in the late 1940s. Dickinson called this work "a series of well-crafted novels that continue to attract readers both young and old." Theodore Sturgeon of the *Los Angeles Times Book Review* believed that Heinlein's "series of 'juveniles' had a great deal to do with raising that category from childish to what is now called YA—'Young adult.'" Several reviewers deemed Heinlein's ostensibly "juvenile" books to be better than much of what is marketed as adult science fiction. H.H. Holmes, for example, wrote in the *New York Herald Tribune Book Review* that "the nominally 'teen-age' science-fiction novels of Robert A. Heinlein stand so far apart from even their best competitors as to deserve a separate classification. These are no easy, adventurous, first-steps-to-space boys' books, but mature and complex novels, far above the level of most adult science fiction both in characterization and in scientific thought." "A Heinlein book," Villiers Gerson observed in the *New York Times Book Review,* "is still better than ninety-nine per cent of the science-fiction adventures produced every year." Heinlein's novels of this time have been reprinted and marketed to adult readers since their initial appearances.

In the 1950s Heinlein entered the field of television and motion pictures. His novel *Space Cadet* was adapted as the television program *Tom Corbett: Space Cadet.* He wrote the screenplay and served as technical advisor for the film *Destination Moon.* Heinlein also wrote an original television pilot, "Ring around the Moon," which was expanded without his approval by Jack Seaman into the screenplay for the film *Project Moonbase.* The 1956 movie *The Brain Eaters* was based on Heinlein's *The Puppet Masters,* also without his knowledge or approval, and in an out-of-court settlement, Heinlein received compensation and the right to demand that certain material be removed from the film.

In the late 1950s Heinlein turned away from his juvenile fiction and published the first of what became a string of controversial novels. *Starship Troopers,* the first of Heinlein's books to speculate not on future scientific changes, but on future societal changes, postulates a world run by military veterans. The novel's protagonist is an army infantryman. Military law takes precedent over civil law in this world, and military discipline is the norm. As Heinlein explained to Curt Suplee of the *Washington Post,* the society depicted in the novel is "a democracy in which the poll tax is putting in a term of voluntary service—which could be as a garbage collector." While some critics have seen *Starship Troopers* as having fascistic and militaristic tendencies, Dennis E. Showalter, assessing the book in *Extrapolation,* thought that while the pervasive military presence in the hypothetical society would "chill the heart of the civil libertarian," the novel is "neither militaristic nor fascist in the scholarly sense of these concepts." Despite the controversy, *Starship Troopers* became one of Heinlein's most popular novels. It won a Hugo Award and has remained in print for more than three decades.

Heinlein followed *Starship Troopers* with another controversial novel, this one quite different in its speculations about the future. *Stranger in a Strange Land* tells the story of Valentine Michael Smith, a Martian with psi powers who establishes a religious movement on Earth. Members of his Church of All Worlds practice group sex and live in small communes. *Stranger in a Strange Land* is perhaps Heinlein's best-known work. It has sold millions of copies, won a Hugo Award, created an intense cult following, and even inspired a real-life Church of All Worlds, founded by some devoted readers of the book.

Stranger in a Strange Land is, David N. Samuelson wrote in *Critical Encounters: Writers and Themes in Science Fiction,* "in some ways emblematic of the Sixties. . . . It fit the iconoclastic mood of the time, attacking human folly under several guises, especially in the person or persons of the Establishment: government, the military, organized religion. By many of its readers, too, it was taken to advocate a religion of love, and of incalculable power, which could revolutionize human affairs and bring about an apocalyptic change, presumably for the better." Robert Scholes and Eric S. Rabkin wrote in their *Science Fiction: History, Science, Vision* that "the values of the sixties could hardly have found a more congenial expression."

Heinlein once told *Chicago Tribune* interviewer R.A. Jelliffe that in *Stranger in a Strange Land* he intended to "examine every major axiom of the western culture, to question each axiom, throw doubt on it—and, if possible, to make the anti-thesis of each axiom appear a possible and perhaps desirable thing—rather than unthinkable." This ambitious attack caused a major upheaval in science fiction. *Stranger in a Strange Land*, Patrouch explained, "forced a reevaluation of what science fiction could be and do. As he had done immediately before World War II, Heinlein helped to reshape the genre and make it more significant and valuable than it had been."

In subsequent novels Heinlein continued to speculate on social changes of the future, dealing with such controversial subjects as group marriage and incest. In *The Moon Is a Harsh Mistress* lunar colonists practice a variety of marriage forms because of the shortage of women on the moon. Variations on group marriage are necessary. In *I Will Fear No Evil* an elderly, dying businessman has his brain transplanted into the body of a young woman. He then impregnates himself with his own sperm, previously stored in a sperm bank. *Time Enough for Love: The Lives of Lazarus Long* explores varieties of future incest through the immortal character Lazarus Long. Long rescues a young girl from a fire, raises her as his daughter, then marries her and has children. He also creates two female clones of himself with whom he has sex. In another episode, Lazarus travels back in time 2,000 years and has intercourse with his own mother. In these novels of the 1960s and 1970s, *Extrapolation* contributor Diane Parkin-Speer wrote, "a defense of unconventional sexual love is [Heinlein's] central theme. . . . The ideal sexual love relationship, first presented in *Stranger in a Strange Land*, is heterosexual, non-monogamous, and patriarchal, with an emphasis on procreation. The protagonists of the novels and their various sexual partners express unorthodox sexual views and have no inhibitions or guilt."

Beginning with his novel *Friday,* published in 1982, Heinlein tempered his social speculations by presenting them in the context of a science fiction adventure. The novel tells the story of Friday, a female "artificial person"—a genetically designed human—working for a government spy agency of the next century. In her interplanetary travels as a courier of secret documents, Friday enjoys sexual exploits with both men and women. But as an artificial person, she is insecure about herself and uneasy about the role she must play to pass in human society. When assassinations and terrorism rock the Earth, Friday must fight her way back home across several foreign countries. This journey becomes a symbolic quest for her own identity. Many critics welcomed the change in Heinlein's writing. Dickinson called it a "paean to tolerance that Heinlein sings through the Friday persona. . . . With this book, Heinlein once again pulled the rug out from under those who had him pegged." Sturgeon found *Friday* a "remarkable and most welcome book" that is "as joyous to read as it is provocative."

In *Job: A Comedy of Justice* and *The Cat Who Walks through Walls: A Comedy of Manners,* Heinlein continued to combine serious subject matter with rollicking interplanetary adventure. *Job* is a science fiction cover of the biblical story of a man who is tested by God. In this novel, Alex Hergensheimer shifts between alternate worlds without warning. These jarring disruptions force him to continually reassess himself and adapt his behavior to new and sometimes dangerous conditions. Gerald Jonas of the *New York Times Book Review*, while finding *Job* not as fine as earlier, "classic Heinlein," still described the book as "an exhilarating romp through the author's mental universe (or rather universes), with special emphasis on cultural relativism, dogmatic religion (treated with surprising sympathy) and the philosophical conundrum of solipsism. . . . Heinlein has chosen to confront head on the question posed by the original story: why do bad things happen to good people?" Although Sue Martin of the *Los Angeles Times Book Review* called *Job* "another dreadful wallow in the muddy fringe of a once-great, if not the greatest, SF imagination," Kelvin Johnston of the London *Observer* commented that Heinlein is a "veteran raconteur who couldn't bore you if he tried."

Evaluations of Heinlein's career often point out the polarized critical reaction to his work. Though Heinlein "set the tone for much of modern science fiction," as Jonas reported, and Sturgeon believed "his influence on science fiction has been immense," there are critics who have characterized him as right-wing or even fascist and, based on their reaction to his politics, denigrate the value of Heinlein's work. Heinlein's belief in self-reliance, liberty, individualism, and patriotism make him appear, Joseph D. Olander and Martin Harry Greenberg noted in their *Robert A. Heinlein,* "to adopt positions favored by the American political right." Writing in the *Detroit News,* Bud Foote defined Heinlein's political thought, which Foote saw as having stayed consistent since the 1950s, in this way: "The greatest thing to which a human can aspire is living free. Enslaving one's fellow-human physically, mentally or spiritually is the unforgivable sin; allowing oneself so to be enslaved is nearly as bad. Honorable people meet their obligations; there's no such thing as a free lunch. All systems are suspect; all forms of government are terrible, with rule by the majority low on the list." Suplee saw much of Heinlein's fiction as concerned with "how freedom of will and libertarian self-reliance can coexist with devotion to authority and love of country." Olander and Greenberg thought Heinlein's best work deals with "some of the perennial concerns of philosophy, such as the best form of government, whether and to what extent political utopias are possible, and the dimensions of power, liberty, equality, justice, and order."

Central to Heinlein's vision is the strong and independent hero found in much of his fiction. The Heinlein hero, Olander and Greenberg explained, "is always tough, just, relatively fearless when it counts, and endowed with extraordinary skills and physical prowess." Johnston described the typical Heinlein protagonist as a "lone male genius on the Last Frontier who prevails against any organized authority that dares to restrict his potential." Writing in his study *The Classic Years of Robert A. Heinlein,* George Edgar Slusser characterized Heinlein's protagonists as "elite" men born with inherently superior traits. "Heinlein's elite are not known by physical signs, nor do they bear the traditional hero's stamp," Slusser wrote. They possess "a common mental disposition: they believe in individual freedom, and are willing to band together to fight entangling bureaucracy and mass strictures."

"His was a fiction of ideas," commented a *National Review* contributor in an appreciation of Heinlein written shortly after the writer's death. John Christie, in an obituary of Heinlein for London's *Guardian,* observed that the author "used his work unhesitatingly as a vehicle for strongly-held values of American, libertarian individualism." Whether one might think these values, in expressing them through his work, Christie added, Heinlein became and remained "the pre-eminent figure of his generation" in science fiction. Christie predicted that Heinlein would have "successors, but few peers."

BIOGRAPHICAL AND CRITICAL SOURCES:

BOOKS

Aldiss, Brian W., *Billion Year Spree: The True History of Science Fiction,* Doubleday (New York, NY), 1973.

Atheling, William, Jr., *The Issue at Hand,* Advent, 1964.

Atheling, William, Jr., *More Issues at Hand,* Advent, 1970.

Clareson, Thomas D., editor, *Voices for the Future: Essays on Major Science Fiction Writers,* Volume 1, Bowling Green University (Bowling Green, OH), 1976.

Contemporary Literary Criticism, Thomson Gale (Detroit, MI), Volume 1, 1973, Volume 3, 1975, Volume 8, 1978, Volume 14, 1980, Volume 26, 1983, Volume 55, 1989.

Dictionary of Literary Biography, Volume 8: *Twentieth Century American Science Fiction Writers,* Thomson Gale (Detroit, MI), 1981.

Downing, Nancy Bailey, *A Robert A. Heinlein Cyclopedia: A Complete Guide to the People, Places, and Things in the Fiction of Robert A. Heinlein,* Borgo Press (San Bernardino, CA), 1996.

Olander, Joseph D., and Martin Harry Greenberg, editors, *Robert A. Heinlein,* Taplinger (New York, NY), 1978.

Panshin, Alexei, *Heinlein in Dimension: A Critical Analysis,* Advent, 1968.

Riley, Dick, editor, *Critical Encounters: Writers and Themes in Science Fiction,* Ungar (New York, NY), 1978.

Scholes, Robert, and Eric S. Rabkin, *Science Fiction: History, Science, Vision,* Oxford University Press, 1977.

Slusser, George Edgar, *The Classic Years of Robert A. Heinlein,* Borgo Press (San Bernardino, CA), 1977.

Slusser, George Edgar, and Robert Reginald, editors, *Yesterday or Tomorrow?: Questions of Vision in the Fiction of Robert A. Heinlein: A Festschrift in Memory of Pilgrim Award Winner, Dr. Thomas Dean Clareson (1926-1993),* Borgo Press (San Bernardino, CA), 1996.

Stephens, C. P., *A Checklist of Robert A. Heinlein,* Ultramarine Publishing Company, 1994.

Usher, Robin, *Self-Begetting, Self-Devouring: Jungian Archetypes in the Fiction of Robert A. Heinlein,* Borgo Press (San Bernardino, CA), 1996.

PERIODICALS

Analog, May, 1954; September, 1964.

Chicago Tribune, August 6, 1961.

Chicago Tribune Book World, August 17, 1980; January 7, 1984.

Christian Science Monitor, November 7, 1957.

Detroit News, July 25, 1982.

Entertainment Weekly, November 4, 1994, p. 49.

Extrapolation, December, 1970; May, 1975; spring, 1979; fall, 1979; fall, 1982; fall, 1990, p. 287.

Locus, May, 1989, p. 46; November, 1989, p. 23; January, 1991, p. 43.

Los Angeles Times, December 19, 1985.

Los Angeles Times Book Review, June 20, 1982; October 21, 1984; December 16, 1990, p. 10; December 23, 1990, p. 7; December 30, 1990, p. 10.

Magazine of Fantasy and Science Fiction, June, 1956; November, 1961; March, 1971; October, 1980.

Modern Fiction Studies, spring, 1986.

National Observer, November 16, 1970.

National Review, March 26, 1963; November 16, 1970; December 12, 1980.

New Statesman, July 30, 1965.

New Yorker, July 1, 1974.

New York Herald Tribune Book Review, November 28, 1954; November 13, 1955; November 18, 1956; May 12, 1962.

New York Times, March 3, 1957; August 22, 1973.

New York Times Book Review, October 23, 1949; November 14, 1954; December 29, 1957; December 14, 1958; January 31, 1960; March 23, 1975; August 24, 1980; September 14, 1980; July 4, 1982; November 11, 1984; December 22, 1985; December 9, 1990, p. 13.

Observer (London, England), December 23, 1984.

Publishers Weekly, July 2, 1973; June 28, 1993, p. 72; October 10, 1994, p. 13.

Punch, August 25, 1965; November 22, 1967.

Saturday Review, November 1, 1958.

Science Fiction Chronicle, September, 1988, p. 45.

Science Fiction Review, November, 1970.

SF Commentary, May, 1976.

Spectator, June 3, 1966; July 30, 1977.

Speculation, August, 1969.

Times Literary Supplement, October 16, 1969; December 11, 1970; April 2, 1971; June 14, 1974.

Washington Post, September 5, 1984.

Washington Post Book World, May 11, 1975; June 27, 1982; December 31, 1989, p. 4; December 30, 1990.

OBITUARIES:

PERIODICALS

Guardian (London, England), May 12, 1988.

National Review, June 10, 1988, p. 21.

Washington Post, May 10, 1988, p. B6.

HEINLEIN, Robert Anson
    See HEINLEIN, Robert A.

*   *   *

HELLER, Joseph 1923-1999

PERSONAL: Born May 1, 1923, in Brooklyn, NY; died of a heart attack, December 12, 1999, in East Hampton, CT; son of Isaac (a truck driver) and Lena Heller; married Shirley Held, September 3, 1945 (divorced); married Valerie Humphries, 1987; children: (first marriage) Erica Jill, Theodore Michael. *Education:* Attended University of Southern California; New York University, B.A., 1948; Columbia University, M.A., 1949; graduate study, Oxford University, 1949-50.

CAREER: Novelist. Pennsylvania State University, University Park, instructor in English, 1950-52; *Time,* New York, NY, advertising writer, 1952-56; *Look,* New York, NY, advertising writer, 1956-58; *McCall's,* New York, NY, promotion manager, 1958-61; former teacher of fiction and dramatic writing at Yale University and University of Pennsylvania; City College of the City University of New York, Distinguished Professor of English, until 1975; full-time writer, 1975—. Worked in the theater, movies, and television. *Military service:* U.S. Army Air Forces, World War II; served as B-25 wing bombardier; flew sixty missions; became first lieutenant.

MEMBER: Phi Beta Kappa.

AWARDS, HONORS: Fulbright scholar, 1949-50; National Institute of Arts and Letters grant in literature, 1963; Prix Interallie (France) and Prix Medicis Étranger (France), both 1985, both for *God Knows;* Thomas Cooper Medal, University of South Carolina, 1996.

WRITINGS:

Catch-22 (novel; also see below; portions originally published in *New World Writing,* 1955), Simon & Schuster (New York, NY), 1961.

Something Happened (novel; portions originally published in *Esquire,* September, 1966), Knopf (New York, NY), 1974.

Good as Gold (novel), Simon & Schuster (New York, NY), 1979.

God Knows (novel), Knopf (New York, NY), 1984.

(With Speed Vogal) *No Laughing Matter* (autobiography), Putnam (New York, NY), 1986.

Picture This, Putnam (New York, NY), 1988.

Closing Time, Simon & Schuster (New York, NY), 1994.

Now and Then: From Coney Island to Here, Franklin Library, 1998.

Portrait of an Artist, as an Old Man, Simon & Schuster (New York, NY), 2000.

Catch as Catch Can: The Collected Stories and Other Writings, Simon & Schuster (New York, NY), 2003.

Contributor to books, including *Nelson Algren's Own Book of Lonesome Monsters,* Lancer, 1960; contributor of short stories to periodicals, including *Atlantic Monthly, Esquire,* and *Cosmopolitan;* contributor of reviews to periodicals, including *New Republic.*

PLAYS

We Bombed in New Haven (two-act; first produced at Yale Repertory Theater, 1967, produced on Broadway, 1968), Knopf (New York, NY), 1968.

Catch-22: A Dramatization (one-act play; based on novel of same title; first produced in East Hampton, NY, 1971), Samuel French (New York, NY), 1971.

Clevinger's Trial (based on portion of *Catch-22;* produced in London, England, 1974), Samuel French (New York, NY), 1973.

SCREENPLAYS

(With David R. Schwartz) *Sex and the Single Girl* (based on the book by Helen Gurley Brown), Warner Bros., 1964.

(Uncredited) *Casino Royale* (based on the novel by Ian Fleming), Columbia Pictures, 1967.

(With Tom Waldman and Frank Waldman) *Dirty Dingus Magee* (based on the novel *The Ballad of Dingus Magee* by David Markson), Metro-Goldwyn-Mayer, 1970.

Also author, under pseudonym, of other television screenplays, c. 1960s. Contributor to *Of Men and Women* (television drama), American Broadcasting Companies, Inc., 1972.

ADAPTATIONS: Catch-22 was produced as a motion picture adapted by Buck Henry and directed by Mike Nichols, Paramount, 1970. *Now and Then: From Coney Island to Here* was adapted for audio cassette.

SIDELIGHTS: "There was only one catch . . . and that was Catch-22," Doc Daneeka informs Yossarian. As Yossarian, the lead bombardier of Joseph Heller's phenomenal first novel, soon learns, this one catch is enough to keep him at war indefinitely. After pleading with Doc Daneeka that he is too crazy to fly any more missions, Yossarian is introduced to Catch-22, a rule which stipulates that anyone rational enough to want to be grounded could not possibly be insane and therefore must return to his perilous duties. The novel *Catch-22* is built around the multifarious attempts of Captain John Yossarian to survive World War II, to escape the omnipresent logic of a regulation which somehow stays one step ahead of him.

At the time of its publication in 1961, Heller's antiwar novel met with modest sales and lukewarm reviews. But by the middle of its first decade, it became a favored text of the counterculture. *Catch-22* "came when we still cherished nice notions about WW II," Eliot Fremont-Smith recalled in the *Village Voice.* "Demolishing these, it released an irreverence that had, until then, dared not speak its name." With more than ten million copies in print by the end of the twentieth century, *Catch-22* became generally regarded as one of the most important novels of the postwar era. The title itself has become part of the language, and its "hero" Yossarian, according to Jack Schnedler of the *Newark Star-Ledger,* "has become the fictional talisman to an entire generation."

In the *New York Times Book Review,* Heller once cited three reasons for the success of *Catch-22:* "First, it's a great book. I've come to accept the verdict of the majority. Second, a whole new generation of readers is being introduced to it. . . . Third, and most important: Vietnam. Because this is the war I had in mind; a war fought without military provocation, a war in which the real enemy is no longer the other side but someone allegedly on your side. The ridiculous war I felt lurking in the future when I wrote the book." "There seems no denying that though Heller's macabre farce was written about a rarefied part of the raging war of the forties during the silent fifties," Josh Greenfeld wrote in a *New York Times Book Review* article, "it has all but become the chapbook of the sixties." Joseph Epstein likewise summarized in *Book World: Catch-22* "was a well-aimed bomb."

In *The Bright Book of Life,* Alfred Kazin found that "the theme of *Catch-22* . . . is the total craziness of war . . . and the struggle to survive of one man, Yossarian, who knows the difference between his sanity and the insanity of the system." After his commanding officer repeatedly raises the number of bombing missions required for discharge, Yossarian decides to "live forever or die in the attempt." "Yossarian's logic becomes so pure that everyone thinks him mad," Robert Brustein wrote in the *New Republic,* "for it is the logic of sheer survival, dedicated to keeping him alive in a world noisily clamoring for his annihilation." Brustein continued: "According to this logic, Yossarian is surrounded on all sides by hostile forces. . . . [He] feels a blind, electric rage against the Germans whenever they hurl flak at his easily penetrated plane; but he feels an equally profound hatred for those of his own countrymen who exercise an arbitrary power over his life."

"The urgent emotion in Heller's book is . . . every individual's sense of being directly in the line of fire," Kazin believed. In the *Dictionary of Literary Biography,* Inge Kutt viewed Pianosa, the fictional island in the Mediterranean Sea on which the novel is set, as a microcosm of "the postwar world which not only includes the Korean and Vietnam wars but also the modern mass society." "Heller's horrifying vision of service life in World War II is merely an illustration of the human condition itself," Jean E. Kennard asserted in *Mosaic.* "The world has no meaning but is simply there," and "man is a creature who seeks meaning," Kennard elaborated. "Reason and language, man's tools for discovering the meaning of his existence and describing his world, are useless."

Language, as presented in *Catch-22,* is more than useless; it is dangerous, a weapon employed by the authorities to enslave individuals in a world of institutionalized absurdity, a world where pilots lose their lives because their commanding officer wants to see prettier bombing patterns or his name in the *Saturday Evening Post.* Language, in the form of Catch-22, is the mechanism which transforms military doublethink into concrete reality, into commands which profoundly affect human life and death. Catch-22, as the novel states, is the rule "which specified that a concern for one's safety in the face of dangers that were real and immediate was the process of a rational mind. Or was crazy and could be grounded. All he had to do was ask; and as soon as he did, he would no longer be crazy and would have to fly more missions." As Jerry H. Bryant noted in his book *The Open Decision:* "Only the insane voluntarily continue to fly. This is an almost perfect catch because the law is in the definition of insanity. . . . The system is closed."

The acquiescence of men to language in *Catch-22,* Carol Pearson observed, is rooted in their failure to find any "transcendental comfort to explain suffering and to make life meaningful. . . . People react to meaninglessness by renouncing their humanity, becoming cogs in the machine. With no logical explanation to make suffering and death meaningful and acceptable, people renounce their power to think and retreat to a simpleminded respect for law and accepted 'truth.'" Writing in the *CEA Critic,* Pearson cited one of the book's many illustrations of this moral retreat: "The M.P.'s exemplify the overly law-abiding person who obeys law with no regard for humanity. They arrest Yossarian who is AWOL, but ignore the murdered girl on the street. By acting with pure rationality, like computers programmed only to enforce army regulations, they have become mechanical men." This incident, this "moment of epiphany," as Raymond M. Olderman described it in *Beyond the Waste Land,* symbolizes "much of the entire novel's warning—that in place of the humane, . . . we find the thunder of the marching boot, the destruction of the human, arrested by the growth of the military-economic institution."

In the novel, the character Milo Minderbinder is the personification of this military-economic system. An enterprising mess officer, Minderbinder creates a one-man international syndicate whose slogan, "What's good for MM Enterprises is good for the country," is used to justify a series of war-profiteering schemes. Minderbinder forms a private army of mercenaries available to the highest bidder, corners the market on food and makes enormous profits selling it back to army mess halls, and convinces the U.S. government that it must buy up his overstock of chocolate-coated cotton balls in the interest of national security. Milo's empire soon stretches across Europe and North Africa, and his ambitions culminate in one final economic boom. As Olderman observed: "The ultimate inversion comes when Milo bombs and strafes his own camp for the Germans, who pay their bills more promptly than some, and kills many Americans at an enormous profit. In the face of criticism, he reveals the overwhelming virtue of his profit." In the *Canadian Review of American Studies* Mike Franks concluded that "for Milo, contract, and the entire economic structure and ethical system it embodies and represents, is more sacred than human life."

"The military-economic institution rules, and the result is profit for some, but meaningless, inhuman parades for everyone else," Olderman wrote. Confronted with this "totally irrelevant and bureaucratic power that either tosses man to his death or stamps out his spirit," Yossarian must make a moral decision. Olderman surveyed Yossarian's alternatives: "He can be food for the cannon; he can make a deal with the system; or he can depart, deserting not the war with its implications of preserving political freedom, but abandoning a waste land, a dehumanized inverted, military-economic machine." As Bryant noted, "The only way that the circular justification of Catch-22 can be dealt with is by breaking out of the circle."

In the *Partisan Review,* Morris Dickstein commented: "The insanity of the system . . . breeds a defensive counter-insanity." Yossarian is "a protagonist caught up in the madness, who eventually steps outside it in a slightly mad way." Heller remarked in *Pages* that much of the humor in his novel arises out of his characters' attempts to escape, manipulate, and circumvent the logic of Catch-22. Before deserting, Yossarian tries to outwit Catch-22 in order to survive; he employs "caution, cowardice, defiance, subterfuge, stratagem, and subversion, through feigning illness, goofing off, and poisoning the company's food with laundry soap," Brustein wrote.

"Heller's comedy is his artistic response to his vision of transcendent evil, as if the escape route of laughter were the only recourse from a malignant world," Brustein stated. The novelist "is concerned with that thin boundary of the surreal, the borderline between hilarity and horror. . . . Heller often manages to heighten the macabre obscenity of war much more effectively through its gruesome comic aspects than if he had written realistic descriptions. And thus, the most delicate pressure is enough to send us over the line from farce to phantasmagoria." "Below its hilarity, so wild that it hurts, *Catch-22* is the strongest repudiation of our civilization, in fiction, to come out of World War II," Nelson Algren stated in the *Nation.*

Heller's subsequent novels continued this "war," extending the field of battle to governmental and corporate life. *Good as Gold,* Fremont-Smith noted in the *Village Voice,* is "touted . . . as doing for the White House what *Catch-22* did for the military," while the absurdity and alienation of the American business community is the focus of *Something Happened,* the story of Bob Slocum, a middle-level manager who describes himself as "one of those many people . . . who are without ambition already and have no hope."

In the *New Republic,* William Kennedy analyzed *Something Happened*'s restless protagonist: "Slocum is no true friend of anybody's. He is a woefully lost figure with a profound emptiness, a sad, absurd, vicious, grasping, climbing, womanizing, cowardly, sadistic, groveling, loving, yearning, anxious, fearful victim of the indecipherable, indescribable malady of being born

human." John W. Aldridge described Slocum as "a man raging in a vacuum." Writing in the *Saturday Review/ World,* Aldridge examined Slocum's plight: "He is haunted by the sense that at some time in the past something happened to him, something that he cannot remember but that changed him from a person who had aspirations for the future, who believed in himself and his work, who trusted others and was able to love, into the person he has since unaccountably become, a man who aspires to nothing, believes in nothing and no one, least of all himself, who no longer knows if he loves or is loved."

Slocum's loss of meaning is symbolized by the lost dreams of his youth. "As Yossarian kept flashing back to that primal, piteous scene in the B-25 where his mortally wounded comrade, Snowden, whimpered in his arms, so Slocum keeps thinking back, with impacted self-pity and regret, to the sweetly hot, teasing, slightly older girl in the insurance office where he worked after graduating from high school, whom he could never bring himself to 'go all the way' with," Edward Grossman wrote in *Commentary.* "He blew it," D. Keith Mano remarked in the *National Review,* "and this piddling missed opportunity comes to stand for loss in general. He makes you accompany him again and again, and again and again to the back staircase for a quiet feel that never matures." As Mano noted, "Slocum becomes semi-obsessed: telephones the insurance company to ascertain if his . . . girlfriend is still employed there, if *he* is still employed there. And he isn't." Instead, Slocum finds that this haunting figure of a girl, like his own spirit, has committed suicide.

In the *Atlantic Monthly,* Benjamin DeMott attributed Slocum's pain to the fact that "caring at levels deeper than these is beyond him." Melvin Maddocks pointed out that "it is not what has happened, but what has not happened to Slocum that constitutes his main problem." In a *Time* review, Maddocks described Slocum as "a weightless figure with no pull of gravity morally or emotionally" who can love only his nine-year-old son, and then only for "brief, affecting moments."

However much the circumstances of his life may conspire against Slocum, the real pressure is exerted from within. As Heller once commented in the *Newark Star-Ledger:* "All the threats to Bob Slocum are internal. His enemy is his own fear, his own anxiety." According to an *America* reviewer, "Heller has replaced the buzzing, booming world of an army at war with the claustrophobic universe of Bob Slocum's psyche, where all the complications, contradictions and absurdities are generated from within. . . . Like Yossarian, Slocum always feels trapped—by his wife, by his children, but mostly by himself." Slocum, who giggles inwardly at the thought of rape and glances over his shoulder for sodomists, confesses, "Things are going on inside me I cannot control and do not admire." "Within and without, his world is an unregenerate swamp of rack and ruin," Pearl K. Bell asserted in a *New Leader* review. "Pathologically disassociated from himself, Slocum is a chameleon, taking on the gestures and vocabularies of whichever colleague he is with; even his handwriting is a forgery, borrowed from a boyhood friend." This disassociation is more than a middle-age malaise; it is symptomatic of a deeper affliction, a crippling of the spirit that leaves Slocum barely enough strength to lament, "I wish I knew what to wish."

According to a *Playboy* critic, *Something Happened* "unleashed a fusillade of violently mixed reviews. . . . Nearly three quarters of the critics viewed Heller's looping, memory-tape narrative as a dazzling, if depressing, literary tour de force." Fremont-Smith, for instance, called *Something Happened* a "very fine, wrenchingly depressing" novel. "It gnaws at one, slowly and almost nuzzlingly at first, mercilessly toward the end. It hurts. It gives the willies." In his *New York Times Book Review* article, Kurt Vonnegut described the novel as "splendidly put together and hypnotic to read. It is as clear and hard-edged as a cut diamond." Melvin Maddocks, however, labeled Heller's second novel "a terrific letdown," while Grossman dubbed *Something Happened* "a painful mistake." He cited as a frequent criticism of the novel that Heller "indulges in overkill. When we have seen Bob Slocum suffer a failure of nerve (or a failure of common humanity) in a dozen different situations, we do not need to see him fail a dozen times more." Mano asserted that "you can start *Something Happened* on page 359, read through to the end, and still pass a multiple choice test in plot, character, style."

Heller's third novel "indicts a class of clerks," John Leonard wrote in the *New York Times*. *Good as Gold* is a fictional exposé of the absurd workings of the machinery of government, of a politics reduced to public relations, of a president who spends most of his first year in office penning *My Year in the White House,* of an administrative aide who mouths such wisdom as "Just tell the truth . . . even if you have to lie" and "This President doesn't want yes-men. What we want are independent men of integrity who will agree with all our decisions after we make them." Into this world stumbles Bruce Gold, a professor of English who is called to public service after writing a favorable review of the

Presidential book. Gold is rewarded for his kind words with a "spokesman" position but yearns for higher duty; specifically, he wants to be secretary of state, more specifically, he wants to be the first *real* Jewish secretary of state (Gold is convinced that Henry Kissinger, who prayed with Richard Nixon and "made war gladly," cannot possibly be Jewish). For his part, Gold chips in by coining such expressions as "You're boggling my mind" and "I don't know," phrases that enter the lexicon of the press conference and earn Gold the admiration of his superiors. As *Time*'s R.Z. Sheppard observed, Gold "is no stranger to double-think. A literary hustler whose interest in government is a sham, he does not even vote, a fact 'he could not publicly disclose without bringing blemish to the image he had constructed for himself as a radical moderate.'"

Good as Gold "is essentially about Jews, especially those like Gold, who wants to escape his identity while exploiting it, particularly by making a lot of money on a big book about Jews," Leonard Michaels commented in the *New York Times Book Review*. "Gold yearns to escape what he is so that he can become what he isn't, which is precisely what he hates. He nearly succeeds, nearly becomes a Washington non-Jewish Jew, a rich, powerful slave with a tall blonde wife." Gold, unlike other characters in the story, is very much aware of his moral degeneration; a passage from the book reads: "How much lower would he crawl to rise to the top? he asked himself with wretched self-reproval. Much, much lower, he answered in improving spirit, and felt purged of hypocrisy by the time he was ready for dinner."

In his *New York Times* article, Michaels elaborated on Gold's dilemma: "What is being proposed is that being brought up lower middle-class Jewish in this country means being humiliated by your own family; that you assimilate, by groveling, a vacuum and a lie; that you have masturbatory dreams of acquiring the power to exact revenge on the father who disdains you; that to acquire such power you will be willing to mortgage every morsel of your capacity for critical discrimination; that you lick the boots that specialize in stepping on you, and hate yourself in the morning."

Indeed, Heller's treatment of the "Jewish Experience in America"—particularly his attack on then-secretary of state Kissinger—aroused criticism, including accusations that *Good as Gold* was anti-Semitic. According to Sheppard, the book "is a savage, intemperately funny satire on the assimilation of the Jewish tradition of liberalism into the American main chance. It is a delicate subject, off-limits to non-Jews fearful of being thought anti-Semitic and unsettling to successful Jewish intellectuals whose views may have drifted to the right in middle age. Heller, who is neither a Gentile or a card-carrying intellectual, goes directly for the exposed nerve." In *Books and Bookmen,* Hayman pointed out that the Gentiles in Heller's satirical novel are "even more obnoxious" than the Jewish characters. "Both, fortunately, are extremely entertaining."

In the *New York Review of Books,* Thomas Edwards remarked that "*Good As Gold,* if hardly a perfect novel, is continuously alive, very funny, and finally coherent. . . . Like Heller's other novels, [it] is a book that takes large risks: it is sometimes rambling, occasionally self-indulgent, not always sure of the difference between humor and silliness. But this time the risks pay off. . . . Heller is among the novelists of the last two decades who matter." A *Hudson Review* contributor described it as a "big, ugly book," and Aram Bakshian, Jr. of the *National Review* called it "an embarrassing flop." Hayman found the novel flawed, but said that "nothing is unforgivable when a book makes you laugh out loud so often," and McPherson concluded: "When I didn't hate it, I loved it. Joseph Heller, of all people, would understand that." Finally, Mel Brooks in *Book World* rated *Good as Gold* "somewhere between *The Brothers Karamazov* and those dirty little books we used to read. . . . It's closer to *Karamazov.*"

Five years after publishing *Good as Gold,* Heller produced *God Knows,* a satiric novel whose tone has been likened to that of a stand-up comedy routine. The narrator of *God Knows* is the Old Testament's David—the killer of Goliath, poet and singer for biblical royalty, king of Israel, and father of the wise ruler Solomon—who is portrayed in the book as an idiot. Despite some critics' objections that the book lacks a unifying point, reviewers overwhelmingly proclaimed it, as did Stuart Evans in the London *Times,* "a very funny, very serious, very *good* novel." *Picture This,* published in 1988, is a reflection on such figures in Western history as Dutch painter Rembrandt, Greek philosophers Socrates and Plato, and several twentieth-century U.S. presidents. Similar in tone to *God Knows, Picture This* revels in anachronisms, mentioning the "freedom fighters" of the war between Athens and Sparta, for example, and "police actions" in the fifth century B.C. A few of the author's main themes, according to Richard Rayner of the London *Times,* are that "power and intellect are incompatible, that politicians wage disastrous wars for no good reason, . . . and that humanity learns nothing from its mistakes." Rayner added, though, that "Heller does all this in *Picture This* and gets away with it most of the time, for the simple reason that he is funny. . . .

He refuses to take institutions seriously; or rather, . . . he takes them *so* seriously they become hilarious."

While working on *God Knows* during the early 1980s, Heller was stricken with a nerve disease, Guillain-Barre syndrome, that left him paralyzed for several months. Though the author became too weak to move and almost too weak to breathe on his own, he eventually regained his strength and recovered from the often fatal disorder. After completing *God Knows,* Heller began writing his first memoir, *No Laughing Matter,* with Speed Vogel, a friend who helped him considerably during his illness. *No Laughing Matter* tells the story of Heller's convalescence and his friendship with Vogel in sections that are written alternately by the two men. Noting that Vogel's observations "provide comic relief to Mr. Heller's medical self-absorption," *New York Times* writer Christopher Lehmann-Haupt praised the book as both serious and comic. "It was indeed no laughing matter," Lehmann-Haupt observed. "And yet we do laugh, reading this account of his ordeal. We laugh because as well as being an astute observer of his suffering . . . Heller can be blackly funny about it." The reviewer added that "most of all, we laugh at the way Mr. Heller and his friends relate to each other. . . . [Their] interaction is not only richly amusing, it is positively cheering."

In 1994, thirty-four years after the publication of *Catch-22,* Heller published its sequel, *Closing Time.* The move astonished critics who felt a sequel was a gutsy undertaking considering the legendary status of the original novel. But *Closing Time* is not so much a sequel as it is a novel that involves a few of the characters from *Catch-22* in the 1990s. Those characters still have their quirks. John Yossarian still is in good health and still looking to be diagnosed with an ailment. Milo Minderbinder still runs MM Enterprises and has become a billionaire through questionable deals. The chaplain (renamed Albert Taylor Tapman) still is malleable. Of the characters carried over to *Closing Time,* Sammy Singer, a fainting unnamed gunner in *Catch-22,* has probably matured the most. A new protagonist is Giant Lew Rabinowitz, a childhood friend of Singer's who served in the infantry and succumbs to Hodgkin's disease during the course of the book.

About half of *Closing Time* is told in first-person narrative by Singer, Rabinowitz, and Rabinowitz's wife, Claire, after her husband's death. The second half of the book is told in the third person, referring to Yossarian. Employing black humor, Heller mixes sane tales with absurdities and phantasmagorias. The Port Authority

Bus Terminal serves as the farcical scene for many events. When Yossarian and a policeman explore the subbasements of the building, they enter a hell inhabited by dead family members and other personages, and Yossarian sees a younger self at the Coney Island Steeplechase Park. The upper level of the Bus Terminal crawls with absurdity too, as misfits of every stripe inhabit it. Yet Minderbinder picks up on Yossarian's suggestion and holds his son's wedding and reception at the Bus Terminal, shipping the riffraff to shelters in New Jersey and hiring actors, who do a more credible job playing their parts. Meanwhile, instead of going to the wedding, the president stays home to play computer games and accidentally deploys the U.S. missile arsenal and attack bombers.

Critics gave *Closing Time* generally favorable reviews. Writing in the *New York Times Book Review,* William H. Pritchard remarked, "Although *Closing Time* won't astonish readers with its inventive brilliance and surprise, . . . it contains a richness of narrative tone and of human feeling lacking in the earlier book." According to Mark Jackson of *Books,* Heller confronts "mortality, monumental literature, war and the decline of civilisation before this wonderful and unforgettable novel draws to a close." In Chicago's *Tribune Books,* John W. Aldridge characterized *Closing Time* as "a different, not better book than *Catch-22.*" While it lacks a "central dramatic element" and its black humor sometimes "seems gratuitous," "on the whole and considering the daunting precedent of *Catch-22* looming behind it, this is an impressive performance."

"*Catch as Catch Can: The Collected Stories and Other Writings* is a wonderful testament to the mystery of literary creativity and to how much it often owes to a combination of dogged effort and serendipity," wrote Sean McCann in a *Book* review of this posthumous collection of Heller's work. Many of the pieces included in this volume were written during the author's university studies. Other pieces are related to his most famous work, *Catch-22.* In a *Los Angeles Times Book Review* article, David L. Ulin noted that the title of the collection "plays on both the serendipitous nature of the contents and their connection to the author's most iconic effort." Although he felt that the pieces are "uninspired," *Catch as Catch Can* "does provide an interesting perspective on the author." *Library Journal* reviewer Edward B. St. John recommended this book as an addition to "most collections of postwar fiction." "Heller's *Catch as Catch Can* has some worthy entries," wrote Michael Upchurch of the *Knight Ridder/Tribune News Service,* citing in particular a reminiscence of Coney Island, as seen through the eyes of both the youthful and the ageing Heller.

Jeff Guinn of the *Knight Ridder/Tribune News Service* remarked that *Now and Then: From Coney Island to Here* "reflects the absolute best of Heller as writer and human being." This autobiography, published a year before the author's death in 1999, focuses on Heller's childhood on Coney Island and his experiences after World War II. "This nostalgic autobiography. . . . [is] not sentimental, but evocative," stated *Library Journal* reviewer Janice E. Braun. "The Coney Island scenes are the most vivid," added Jo Carr in a second *Library Journal* review. Daneet Steffens of *Entertainment Weekly* also praised the anecdotes about Coney Island. In a *People* article, Thomas Fields-Meyer mentioned that he appreciated the fact that Heller, unlike many writers, was able to pen a "memoir that dredges up [no] painful childhood traumas," instead focusing on "warmly recalled memories." A *Forbes* reviewer was delighted to encounter the actual people upon whom characters in *Catch-22* were based. Charles Glass concluded in the *New Statesman:* "You want to listen to the old man in the rocker . . . recalling unrelated incidents and people from childhood, because he is Joseph Heller. And Joseph Heller, one of the great postwar novelists, deserves respect."

Heller died of a heart attack in East Hampton, Connecticut, in 1999, and his last novel, *Portrait of an Artist, as an Old Man,* was published posthumously. Many critics viewed the book as autobiographical in nature, as it tells the story of an author who achieves literary success in his early years, and is thereafter considered a one-novel-wonder. The protagonist, Eugene Pota, is an author who experiences writer's block precisely at the point in his life when he would like to write just one more successful book before the end of his career.

Portrait of an Artist, as an Old Man "is a well-written, thoughtful and amusing depiction of a writer who . . . no longer has anything new to say yet still wants to say something," remarked *World Literature Today* critic Daniel Garrett. Robert L. McLaughlin, writing in the *Review of Contemporary Fiction,* felt that Heller penned "a smart, funny, bittersweet, personal novel . . . as a farewell gift" to the world of literature. "Although Heller clearly wanted to create a study of a soul in crisis. . . . it has only morbid interest," noted Stephen Amidon in a *Sunday Times* review of the novel, while *Book* reviewer Paul Evans praised Heller's ability to successfully describe every writer's ultimate dilemma. A *Publishers Weekly* writer considered the book to be "a pleasant reminder of the author's great charm and fluency." Donna Seaman of *Booklist* noted Heller's "impish pleasure in satirizing himself and literary ambition." "Though not a masterpiece, it has enough flashes of the old brilliance, the bawdy language and the caustic wit to enable him to end his literary career on an upbeat note," stated *Hindu* critic, M.S. Nagarajan.

In a *Knight Ridder/Tribune News Service* article written after Heller's death, Carolyn Alessio and Ron Grossman noted that Heller "was one of the few writers of this or any age to add a catch phrase to the English language." The writers concluded with comments that Heller made about his literary work: He "attributed his insights to lessons learned from the delicatessen philosophers of his Brooklyn youth. 'It gave me my literary voice,' he once said, 'a consistent one through my novels, that is divided, sentimental, sarcastic and critical.'"

BIOGRAPHICAL AND CRITICAL SOURCES:

BOOKS

A Dangerous Crossing, Southern Illinois University Press (De Kalb, IL), 1973.

Aichinger, Peter, *The American Soldier in Fiction, 1880-1963,* Iowa State University Press (Des Moines, IA), 1975.

American Novels of the Second World War, Mouton, 1969.

Authors and Artists for Young Adults, Volume 24, Thomson Gale (Detroit, MI), 1998.

Authors in the News, Volume 1, Thomson Gale (Detroit, MI), 1976.

Bergonzi, Bernard, *The Situation of the Novel,* University of Pittsburgh Press, 1970.

Bier, Jesse, *The Rise and Fall of American Humor,* Holt (New York, NY), 1968.

Bruccoli, Matthew J. and C.E. Frazer Clark, Jr., editors, *Pages: The World of Books, Writers, and Writing,* Thomson Gale (Detroit, MI), 1976.

Bryant, Jerry H., *The Open Decision: The Contemporary American Novel and Its Intellectual Background,* Free Press (New York, NY), 1970.

Burgess, Anthony, *The Novel Now: A Guide to Contemporary Fiction,* Norton (New York, NY), 1967.

Colmer, John, editor, *Approaches to the Novel,* Rigby (Adelaide, Australia), 1967.

Contemporary Literary Criticism, Thomson Gale (Detroit, MI), Volume 1, 1973, Volume 3, 1975, Volume 5, 1976, Volume 8, 1978, Volume 11, 1979, Volume 36, 1986, Volume 63, 1991.

Dictionary of Literary Biography, Thomson Gale (Detroit, MI), Volume 2: *American Novelists since World War II,* 1978, *Yearbook: 1980,* 1981, Volume 28: *Twentieth-Century American Jewish Fiction Writers,* 1984.

Encyclopedia of World Biography, 2nd edition, Volume 17, Thomson Gale (Detroit, MI), 1998.

Friedman, Bruce Jay, editor, *Black Humor,* Bantam (New York, NY), 1965.

Harris, Charles B., *Contemporary American Novelists of the Absurd,* College and University Press, 1971.

Harrison, Gilbert A., editor, *The Critic as Artist: Essays on Books, 1920-1970,* Liveright (New York, NY), 1972.

Hauck, Richard Boyd, *A Cheerful Nihilism: Confidence and the Absurd in American Humorous Fiction,* Indiana University Press, 1971.

Heller, Joseph, *Catch-22,* Simon & Schuster (New York, NY), 1961.

Heller, Joseph, *Something Happened,* Knopf (New York, NY), 1974.

Heller, Joseph, *Good as Gold,* Simon & Schuster (New York, NY), 1979.

Kazin, Alfred, *The Bright Book of Life: American Novelists and Storytellers from Hemingway to Mailer,* Little, Brown (Boston, MA), 1973.

Kiley, Frederick, and Walter McDonald, editors, *A Catch-22 Casebook,* Crowell (New York, NY), 1973.

Kostelanetz, Richard, editor, *On Contemporary Literature,* Avon (New York, NY), 1964.

Literary Horizons: A Quarter Century of American Fiction, New York University Press (New York, NY), 1970.

Littlejohn, David, *Interruptions,* Grossman, 1970.

Miller, James E., Jr., *Quests Surd and Absurd: Essays in American Literature,* University of Chicago Press (Chicago, IL), 1967.

Miller, Wayne Charles, *An Armed America, Its Face in Fiction: A History of the American Military Novel,* New York University Press (New York, NY), 1970.

Moore, Harry T., editor, *Contemporary American Novelists,* Southern Illinois University Press (De Kalb, IL), 1964.

Nagel, James, editor, *Critical Essays on Catch-22,* Dickenson, 1974.

Nelson, Gerald B., *Ten Versions of America,* Knopf (New York, NY), 1972.

Olderman, Raymond M., *Beyond the Waste Land: The American Novel in the Nineteen-Sixties,* Yale University Press (New Haven, CT), 1972.

Podhoretz, Norman, *Doings and Undoings: The Fifties and After in American Writing,* Farrar, Straus (New York, NY), 1964.

Potts, Stephen W., *From Here to Absurdity: The Moral Battlefields of Joseph Heller,* Borgo Press (San Bernardino, CA), 1995.

Richter, D. H., *Fable's End: Completeness and Closure in Rhetorical Fiction,* University of Chicago Press (Chicago, IL), 1974.

Scott, Nathan A., editor, *Adversity and Grace: Studies in Recent American Literature*, University of Chicago Press (Chicago, IL), 1968.

Scotto, Robert M., editor, *A Critical Edition of Catch-22*, Delta (New York, NY), 1973.

Tanner, Tony, *City of Words*, Harper (New York, NY), 1971.

Wallace, Ronald, *The Last Laugh*, University of Missouri Press, 1979.

Whitbread, Thomas B., editor, *Seven Contemporary Authors*, University of Texas Press (Austin, TX), 1966.

PERIODICALS

America, October 26, 1974; May 19, 1979.

American Heritage, June, 2001, review of *Something Happened*, p. 26.

Arizona Quarterly, winter, 1980.

Atlantic Monthly, January, 1962; October, 1974; March, 1979.

Book, September, 2000, Paul Evans, review of *Portrait of an Artist, as an Old Man*, p. 65; March-April, 2003, Sean McCann, review of *Catch as Catch Can: The Collected Stories and Other Writings*, pp. 71-72.

Book Digest, May, 1976.

Booklist, November 15, 1999, review of *Catch-22*, p. 601; May 1, 2000, Donna Seaman, review of *Portrait of an Artist, as an Old Man*, p. 1587.

Books, October, 1967; summer, 1995, p. 24; spring, 1998, review of *Now and Then*, p. 5.

Books and Bookmen, June, 1979.

Book Week, February 6, 1966.

Book World, October 6, 1974; March 11, 1979; December 9, 1979.

Canadian Review of American Studies, spring, 1976.

CEA Critic, November, 1974.

Chicago Tribune Book World, March 18, 1979.

Christian Science Monitor, October 9, 1974; March 28, 1979; April 9, 1979; October 4, 1994.

Commentary, November, 1974; June, 1979; February, 2000, Norman Podhoretz, "Looking Back at *Catch-22*," p. 32.

Commonweal, December 5, 1974; May 11, 1979.

Contemporary Literature, winter, 1998, Charlie Reilly, interview with Joseph Heller, p. 507.

Critique, Volume 5, number 2, 1962; Volume 7, number 2, 1964-65; Volume 9, number 2, 1967; Volume 22, number 2, 1970; Volume 17, number 1, 1975; Volume 18, number 3, 1977.

Detroit Free Press, March 18, 1979.

Entertainment Weekly, October 14, 1994, p. 53; March 6, 1998, Daneet Steffens, review of *Now and Then: From Coney Island to Here*, p. 74; June 20, 2001, review of *Portrait of an Artist, as an Old Man*, p. 61.

Forbes, March 9, 1998, review of *Now and Then*, p. S164.

Guardian (London, England), March 27, 1999, Diane Armstrong, interview with Heller, p. 22.

Harper's, March, 1979.

Hindu, pHNDU13092061, October 1, 2000.

Hudson Review, winter, 1979-80.

Insight on the News, November 7, 1994, p. 28.

Kirkus Reviews, January 1, 1998, review of *Now and Then*, p. 35; January 15, 2003, review of *Catch as Catch Can*, p. 113.

Knight Ridder/Tribune News Service, February 18, 1998, Jeff Guinn, review of *Now and Then*, p. K0932; December 14, 1999, p. K7920; June 21, 2000, Roger Moore, review of *Portrait of an Artist, as an Old Man*, p. K2527; March 26, 2003, Michael Upchurch, review of *Catch as Catch Can*, p. K3388.

Library Journal, March 15, 1998, Janice E. Braun, review of *Now and Then*, p. 65; June 1, 1999, Jo Carr, review of *Now and Then*, p. 207; February 15, 2003, Edward B. St. John, review of *Catch as Catch Can*, p. 139.

Life, January 1, 1968.

Listener, October 24, 1974; May 10, 1979.

London Review of Books, October 20, 1994, p.22.

Los Angeles Times Book Review, March 25, 1979; February 22, 1998, review of *Now and Then*, p. 9; March 30, 2003, David L. Ulin, review of *Catch as Catch Can*, p. R9.

Midstream, July, 2000, Sanford Pinsker, review of *Portrait of the Artist, as an Old Man*, p. 40.

Midwest Quarterly, winter, 1974.

Mosaic, fall, 1968; spring, 1971.

Motive, February, 1968.

Nation, November 4, 1961; October 19, 1974; June 16, 1979.

National Review, November 22, 1974; July 20, 1979.

Newark Star-Ledger, October 6, 1974.

New Leader, October 28, 1974; March 26, 1979.

New Republic, November 13, 1961; October 19, 1974; March 10, 1979.

New Statesman, October 25, 1974; October 7, 1994, p. 39; March 20, 1998, Charles Glass, review of *Now and Then*, p. 54.

Newsweek, October 14, 1974; December 30, 1974; March 12, 1979; October 3, 1994, p. 66; June 12, 2000, David Gates, review of *Portrait of an Artist, as an Old Man*, p. 74.

New York, September 30, 1974; September 12, 1994, p. 100.

New Yorker, December 9, 1961; November 25, 1974; April 16, 1979; October 10, 1994.

New York Review of Books, October 17, 1974; April 5, 1979; October 20, 1994, p. 20.

New York Times, October 23, 1961; December 3, 1967; December 7, 1967; June 19, 1970; October 1, 1974; March 5, 1979; September 19, 1984; February 13, 1986; September 1, 1988; February 24, 1998, Michiko Kakutani, review of *Now and Then,* p. E8; May 30, 2000, Michiko Kakutani, review of *Portrait of an Artist, as an Old Man,* p. B7.

New York Times Book Review, October 22, 1961; September 9, 1962; March 3, 1968; October 6, 1974; February 2, 1975; May 15, 1977; March 11, 1979; September 11, 1988; August 28, 1994, p. 3; September 25, 1994; February 15, 1998, Phillip Lopate, review of *Now and Then,* p. 32.

New York Times Sunday Magazine, March 4, 1979; January 12, 1986.

Observer (London, England), May 16, 1999, review of *Now and Then,* p. 14.

Paris Review, winter, 1974.

Partisan Review, Volume 43, number 2, 1976.

People, March 2, 1998, Thomas Fields-Meyer, review of *Now and Then,* p. 44.

Playboy, June, 1975; September, 1988.

Publishers Weekly, November 1, 1985; July 1, 1988; August 1, 1994; May 29, 2000, review of *Portrait of an Artist, as an Old Man,* p. 52.

Review of Contemporary Fiction, fall, 2000, Robert L. McLaughlin, review of *Portrait of an Artist, as an Old Man,* p. 144.

Rolling Stone, April 16, 1981.

San Francisco Chronicle, April 28, 1998, "Catch-22 Author Denies He Plagiarized," p. A2.

Saturday Review, October 14, 1961; August 31, 1968; February 6, 1971.

Saturday Review/World, October 19, 1974.

Spectator, June 15, 1962; October 26, 1974; May 5, 1979.

Stand, Volume 16, number 3, 1975.

Studies in the Novel, spring, 1971; spring, 1972.

Sunday Times (London, England), July 30, 2000, Stephen Amidon, review of *Portrait of an Artist, as an Old Man,* p. 46.

Time, October 27, 1961; February 1, 1963; June 15, 1970; October 14, 1974; March 12, 1979; October 3, 1994, p. 80.

Times (London, England), November 29, 1984; October 19, 1988; October 20, 1988; March 2, 2000, review of *Portrait of an Artist, as an Old Man,* p. 40.

Times Literary Supplement, October 25, 1974; March 20, 1998, review of *Now and Then,* p. 36; August 18, 2000, Lorna Sage, review of *Portrait of an Artist, as an Old Man,* p. 22.

Tribune Books (Chicago, IL), October 9, 1994, p. 1.

Twentieth Century Literature, January, 1967; October, 1973.

U.S. News and World Report, April 9, 1979.

Village Voice, March 5, 1979.

Vogue, January 1, 1963.

Wall Street Journal, June 9, 2000, Steve Barnes, review of *Portrait of an Artist, as an Old Man,* p. W9.

Washington Post, October 8, 1984; August 31, 1988; June 13, 2000, Steven Moore, review of *Portrait of an Artist, as an Old Man.*

World Literature Today, winter, 2001, Daniel Garrett, review of *Portrait of the Artist, as an Old Man,* p. 114.

Writer's Digest, March, 1987.

Yale Review, summer, 1975.

ONLINE

University of South Carolina Web site, http://www.sc.edu/ (May 11, 2003).

*   *   *

HELLMAN, Lillian 1906-1984
(Lillian Florence Hellman)

PERSONAL: Born June 20, 1906, in New Orleans, LA; died of cardiac arrest June 30, 1984, in Martha's Vineyard, MA; daughter of Max Bernard (a businessman) and Julia (Newhouse) Hellman; married Arthur Kober (a writer), December 30, 1925 (divorced, 1932). *Education:* Attended New York University, 1922-24, and Columbia University, 1924.

CAREER: Playwright and author. Horace Liveright, Inc. (publisher), New York, NY, manuscript reader, 1924-25; theatrical playreader in New York, NY, 1927-30; Metro-Goldwyn-Mayer, Hollywood, CA, scenario reader, 1930-31; returned to New York, NY, 1932, and worked as part-time playreader for producer Harold Shulman. Taught or conducted seminars in literature and writing at Yale University, 1966, and at Massachusetts Institute of Technology and Harvard University. Director of plays, including *Another Part of the Forest,* 1946, and *Montserrat,* 1949. Narrator, Marc Blitzstein Memorial Concert, New York, NY, 1964.

MEMBER: American Academy of Arts and Letters, American Academy of Arts and Sciences (fellow), Dramatists Guild (member of council), American Federation of Television and Radio Artists.

AWARDS, HONORS: New York Drama Critics Circle Award, 1941, for *Watch on the Rhine,* and 1960, for *Toys in the Attic;* Academy Award nominations for best screenplay, Academy of Motion Pictures Arts and Sciences, 1941, for *The Little Foxes,* and 1943, for *The North Star;* honorary M.A. from Tufts University, 1950; Antoinette Perry ("Tony") Award nominations, 1957, for best book of a musical, for *Candide* and 1960, for best play, for *Toys in the Attic;* Brandeis University Creative Arts Medal in Theater, 1960-61; LL.D. from Wheaton College, 1961, Douglass College of Rutgers University, Smith College, and New York University, all 1974, Franklin and Marshall College, 1975, and Columbia University, 1976; Gold Medal for drama, National Institute of Arts and Letters, 1964; National Book Award in Arts and Letters, 1970, for *An Unfinished Woman,* and nomination, 1974, for *Pentimento: A Book of Portraits;* elected to Theatre Hall of Fame, 1973; MacDowell Medal, 1976.

WRITINGS:

(Editor and author of introduction) Anton Chekhov, *Selected Letters,* Farrar, Straus (New York, NY), 1955, reprinted, 1984.

(Editor and author of introduction) Dashiell Hammett, *The Big Knockover* (selected stories and short novels), Random House (New York, NY), 1966, published as *The Dashiell Hammett Story Omnibus,* Cassell (London, England), 1966.

An Unfinished Woman (memoirs; also see below), Little, Brown (Boston, MA), 1969, reprinted, 1999.

Pentimento: A Book of Portraits (memoirs; also see below), Little, Brown (Boston, MA), 1973.

Scoundrel Time (memoirs; also see below), introduction by Garry Wills, Little, Brown (Boston, MA), 1976, reprinted, 2000.

Three (contains *An Unfinished Woman, Pentimento, Scoundrel Time,* and new commentaries by author), Little, Brown (Boston, MA), 1979.

Maybe: A Story (memoirs), Little, Brown (Boston, MA), 1980.

(With Peter S. Feibleman) *Eating Together: Recollections and Recipes,* Little, Brown (Boston, MA), 1984.

PLAYS

The Children's Hour (first produced in New York, NY, 1934; also see below), Knopf (New York, NY),

1934, reprinted, Dramatists Play Service (New York, NY), 1988.

Days to Come (first produced in New York, NY, 1936; also see below), Knopf (New York, NY), 1936.

The Little Foxes (three-act; first produced in New York, NY, 1939; also see below), Random House (New York, NY), 1939, reprinted, Viking (New York, NY), 1986.

Watch on the Rhine (three-act; first produced on Broadway, 1941; also see below), Random House (New York, NY), 1941, with foreword by Dorothy Parker, privately printed, 1942, reprinted, Dramatists Play Service (New York, NY), 1986.

Four Plays (contains *The Children's Hour, Days to Come, The Little Foxes,* and *Watch on the Rhine*), Random House (New York, NY), 1942.

The Searching Wind (two-act; first produced in New York, NY, 1944; also see below), Viking (New York, NY), 1944.

Another Part of the Forest (three-act; first produced in New York, NY, 1946; also see below), Viking (New York, NY), 1947, reprinted, 1973.

Montserrat (two-act; adapted from Emmanuel Robles's play; first produced in New York, NY, 1949; also see below), Dramatists Play Service (New York, NY), 1950.

The Autumn Garden (three-act; first produced in New York, NY, 1951; also see below), Little, Brown (Boston, MA), 1951.

The Lark (adapted from Jean Anouilh's play *L'alouette;* first produced on Broadway, 1955; also see below), Random House (New York, NY), 1956, acting edition, Dramatists Play Service (New York, NY), 1957.

(Author of book) Leonard Bernstein, *Candide: A Comic Opera Based on Voltaire's Satire* (first produced on Broadway, 1956; also see below), Random House (New York, NY), 1957.

Toys in the Attic (three-act; first produced off-Broadway, 1960; also see below), Random House (New York, NY), 1960.

Six Plays (contains *Another Part of the Forest, The Autumn Garden, The Children's Hour, Days to Come, The Little Foxes,* and *Watch on the Rhine*), Modern Library (New York, NY), 1960, with illustrations by Mark Bellerose, Franklin Library (Franklin Center, PA), 1978.

My Mother, My Father, and Me (adapted from Burt Blechman's novel *How Much?;* first produced on Broadway, 1963; also see below), Random House (New York, NY), 1963.

Collected Plays (contains *The Children's Hour, Days to Come, The Little Foxes, Watch on the Rhine, The Searching Wind, Another Part of the Forest, Mont-*

serrat, *The Autumn Garden, The Lark, Candide, Toys in the Attic,* and *My Mother, My Father, and Me*), Little, Brown (Boston, MA), 1972.

Also author of unpublished and unproduced play, *Dear Queen.*

SCREENPLAYS

(With Mordaunt Shairp) *Dark Angel,* United Artists, 1935.
These Three (based on *The Children's Hour*), United Artists, 1936.
Dead End, United Artists, 1937.
The Little Foxes (based on her play), RKO, 1941.
The North Star, a Motion Picture about Some Russian People (released for television broadcast as *Armored Attack*), introduction by Louis Kronenberger, RKO, 1943, Viking (New York, NY), 1943.
The Searching Wind, Paramount, 1946.
The Chase, Columbia, 1966.

OTHER

Pentimento: Memory as Distilled by Time (sound recording), Center for Cassette Studies, c. 1973.
Lillian Hellman: The Great Playwright Candidly Reflects on a Long Rich Life (sound recording), Center for Cassette Studies, c. 1977.
Conversations with Lillian Hellman, edited by Jackson R. Bryer, University Press of Mississippi (Jackson, MS), 1986.

Contributor of plays to anthologies, including *Four Contemporary American Plays,* Random House (New York, NY), 1961; *Six Modern American Plays,* Random House, 1966; and *A Treasury of the Theatre: Modern Drama from Oscar Wilde to Eugene Ionesco,* Simon & Schuster (New York, NY), 1967. Contributor of sketches to "Broadway Revue," produced in New York, NY, 1968; contributor of articles to *Collier's, New York Times, Travel and Leisure,* and other publications.

Hellman's manuscripts are collected at the University of Texas—Austin.

ADAPTATIONS: Marc Blitzstein adapted *The Little Foxes* as an opera, *Regina,* in 1949. *Another Part of the Forest* was filmed by Universal in 1948; *Toys in the Attic* was adapted for film by United Artists, 1963. Television adaptations include *Montserrat,* 1971, and *The Lark.* A section of Hellman's memoir *Pentimento* was adapted for the film *Julia,* 1977. In 1986, William Luce wrote a one-woman play, *Lillian,* based on Hellman's life; the production ran briefly in New York, NY. *An Unfinished Woman: A Memoir,* was made into an audio book, Books on Tape, 2003.

SIDELIGHTS: She has been called one of the most influential female playwrights of the twentieth century; the voice of social consciousness in American letters; the theatre's intellectual standard-bearer—and yet Lillian Hellman always prided herself on avoiding easy labels. At the time of her death in 1984, the author/playwright could claim more long-running Broadway dramas—five—than could renowned American writers like Tennessee Williams, Edward Albee, and Thornton Wilder.

Born in turn-of-the-twentieth century New Orleans to a struggling shoe merchant and his upper-middle-class wife, Hellman had the advantages of a solid education and a well-traveled childhood. By the early 1920s she had left college to work as a manuscript reader for a New York City publishing firm. For the ambitious Hellman, the benefits of working in publishing ran beyond five o'clock. "After working hours, [the publishers'] parties gave Hellman her firsthand acquaintance with the adventurous, often reckless life of the literary world of the 1920s," said Carol MacNicholas in a *Dictionary of Literary Biography* essay. "The bohemian life appealed to the young woman who was just advancing into her own twenties; she enjoyed the glamour of the writer's world and nurtured the impulse to find excitement in whatever she did."

For Hellman, that impulse led her into an early marriage to press agent Arthur Kober, and career jumps into playreading and book reviewing. Following her husband to Paris, Hellman made side trips to 1929 Germany, where the embryonic Nazi movement gave the woman her first exposure to anti-Semitism, a theme that would later emerge in her plays *Watch on the Rhine* and *The Searching Wind.* By 1930 the Kobers had moved to Hollywood, where Hellman read scripts for Metro-Goldwyn-Mayer and met the mystery novelist/screenwriter Dashiell Hammett.

Sensing that her marriage to Kober was failing, Hellman turned to Hammett, best known for the stylish suspense novel *The Thin Man* (some critics believe that Hammett based his suave detectives Nick and Nora

Charles on himself and Hellman), and he became her lover and mentor. Hammett encouraged Hellman's first produced play, *The Children's Hour*, in 1933; her earlier play, *Dear Queen*, was neither published nor produced. "A play about the way scandalmongering can ruin people's lives, [*The Children's Hour*] focuses on two young women, Karen Wright and Martha Dobie, who have set up a private boarding school," explained MacNicholas. "Their prospects for a happy and secure future are shattered when one of their pupils, Mary Tilford, a spoiled and vicious problem child, tells her grandmother, . . . a pillar of local society, about an abnormal sexual relationship between Karen and Martha." *The Children's Hour* caused a sensation in its time, not merely for its controversial subject matter—for a movie remake in 1936, a "safe" heterosexual triangle was substituted for the play's original theme—but also for its writer's obvious talent. "So far as sheer power and originality are concerned, [Hellman's] play is not merely the best of the year but the best of many years past," wrote J.W. Krutch in a *Nation* review.

With that success behind her, Hellman ushered in an era, from the late 1930s through the late 1940s, of classic dramas that helped shape a golden age of American theatre. Chief among them is *The Little Foxes*, perhaps the playwright's best known work. An excoriating look at the rivalries and disloyalty among a turn-of-the-twentieth century Southern family, the play explores how the wealthy Hubbard clan of New Orleans schemes to keep itself rich and powerful, at the expense of both outsiders and each other. In this tale, "William Marshall, a visiting Chicago businessman, has displayed a willingness to establish a local cotton mill to be controlled by the Hubbards if they can raise enough money to buy fifty-one percent of the new company," as MacNicholas explained. "An intense power struggle ensues, dividing the family into two camps: the powerful and cruel Hubbard siblings (Regina and her two brothers, Ben and Oscar), and those brought into the family by marriage (Horace, Regina's husband; Alexandra, their fair-minded daughter; and Birdie, Oscar's wife)." By the second act, added MacNicholas, every Hubbard is out for him-or herself.

The Little Foxes, both in its stage and film incarnations, was a popular and critical success. Some critics took its theme of greed as a parable for the rise of the industrial South; others saw the play as Hellman's look back at the turmoil within her own family. In 1946, seven years after *The Little Foxes* had premiered, Hellman produced what today is known as a "prequel": *Another Part of the Forest*, which takes a look at the Hubbard clan twenty years earlier than when audiences had first met

them. "Twenty years does not transport them to the age of innocence; their evil natures are already well cultivated," noted Richard Moody in his book *Lillian Hellman: Playwright*.

The mixed reviews of *Another Part of the Forest* focused on critics' speculation that Hellman had packed too much melodrama into the play. Moody found that the follow-up work did "not match the earlier play in concentrated power. [Hellman] has followed too many paths. If fewer crises had been packed into the two days [in which the story takes place], if the voices had been less strident, . . . [then the characters] might have become more fully realized, and our hearts might have become more committed." For all its structural faults, though, Moody called *Another Part of the Forest* "a strong and exciting play."

In between *The Little Foxes* and *Another Part of the Forest*, Hellman premiered the political drama *Watch on the Rhine*. This 1941 production focused on a Washington family and the war refugees they harbor. Among the boarders are a Romanian count, his American wife, and an anti-Nazi German. Fear and prejudice follow the characters, resulting in tragedy. Except "for those who suffered through the Hitler years," remarked Moody, "the fierce impact of the play in 1941 cannot be fully sensed. If it appears melodramatic now, it appeared melodramatic then, but with a difference: the world was boiling with melodrama. Cruelty and villainy were not figments of the playwright's imagination, and it was almost impossible for a writer to tell us anything we didn't already know or to dramatize atrocities more effectively than events had already dramatized them." Hellman "knew that her fiction must do more than demonstrate the strange and awful truth that screamed from the front pages of every daily paper," he added. Rosamond Gilder, writing in *Theatre Arts*, called *Watch on the Rhine* "more faulty in structure" than *The Children's Hour* and *The Little Foxes*, and also noted that Hellman, "whose hallmark has been an almost brutal cynicism, who has excelled in delineating mean, ruthless and predatory types," here indulges in "a tenderness, an emotionalism that borders on the sentimental."

The 1950s saw Hellman writing three play adaptations—*Montserrat*, *The Lark*, and the musical *Candide*—plus an original work, *The Autumn Garden*. It was not until 1960, however, that the playwright had her next important original drama produced. *Toys in the Attic* examines the psychological effects of sudden wealth on a poor family. One of Hellman's best plays, according to Moody, *Toys in the Attic* "achieves the magnitude and human revelation that have always been the mark of serious drama." The plot revolves around two sisters, Carrie and Anna Berniers, who have devoted their lives to their ne'er-do-well younger brother, Julian. They find that he has married a wealthy but neurotic woman, and when Julian returns home to visit, he brings his bride and virtual fistfuls of cash, which he distributes indiscriminately. "The sudden reversal of fortune is too shocking to accept, and Carrie is convinced that her brother has gone crazy," noted MacNicholas.

With *Toys in the Attic,* Hellman "picked up the sword of judgment many playwrights of the period [had] laid aside and [wielded] it with renewed vigor," said John Gassner in his book *Dramatic Soundings: Evaluations and Retractions Culled from Thirty Years of Dramatic Criticism.* Gassner also found that it is "the special merit of Lillian Hellman's work that dreadful things are done by the onstage characters out of affectionate possessiveness, rather than out of ingrained villainy. Although the author's corresponding view of life is ironic and is trenchantly expressed, there is no gloating over human misery, no horror-mongering, no traffic with sensationalism in *Toys in the Attic.*"

Toys in the Attic was Hellman's last major play. She produced one more drama, *My Mother, My Father, and Me,* an adaptation of Burt Blechman's novel *How Much?,* but it ran only briefly in 1963. From 1969 on, Hellman became well regarded for a quartet of books recounting events in her life. From the beginning of her public life, the writer's politics had been intertwined with her career. As MacNicholas pointed out, "The origins of [Hellman's] liberalism are traced to her childhood: on the one hand, she witnessed her mother's family increase their fortunes at the expense of Negroes; on the other, she admired the dignity and tough-mindedness of her black nurse Sophronia. Dashiell Hammett, of course, was a radical who shared and influenced much of her life in the 1930s and 1940s."

In Hellman's first book of memoirs, *An Unfinished Woman,* she takes an unconventional approach to traditional autobiography, as Moody explained. "Only in the first third of the book does she allow chronology to govern her narrative. After that she swings freely among her remembrances of places, times, and people—all intimately observed, all colored with some special personal involvement." However unconventional the memoir is, it nonetheless won the National Book Award in Arts and Letters in 1970.

The word "pentimento" describes a phenomenon in art wherein a painting fades to the point that one can see the rough sketches and previous drafts through the sur-

face of the finished work. The word also serves as the title of Hellman's second book of memoirs, a look at the friends and relations that fueled her adult years. This book garnered much critical notice, most notably for its sophisticated writing style. "It is now apparent that *An Unfinished Woman* was the beginning—a tryout, if you will, and more hesitant than arrogant—of a new career for Lillian Hellman," declared *New York* critic Eliot Fremont-Smith. *Pentimento: A Book of Portraits* "is its realization." Fremont-Smith also called the work one of "extraordinary richness and candor and self-perception, and triumph considering the courage such a book requires, a courage that lies . . . far deeper than one is usually inclined to accept."

Muriel Haynes, in a *Ms.* review, called *Pentimento* "a triumphant vindication of the stories the author threw away in her twenties because they were 'no good.' These complex, controlled narratives profit from the dramatist's instinct for climax and immediate, sharp characterization; but they have an emotional purity her plays have generally lacked." Less impressed was *London Magazine* reviewer Julian Symons, who said that the memoir "is not, as American reviewers have unwisely said, a marvel and a masterpiece and a book full of perceptions about human character. It is, rather, a collection of sketches of a fairly familiar kind, which blend real people known to history and Lillian Hellman . . . with people known only by their Christian names in the book, who may be real or partly fictionalized." By far the best known section of the book is "Julia," the story of Hellman's friendship during the 1930s with a rich young American woman working in the European underground against the Nazis. The story was adapted into the popular film *Julia* in 1977.

In the aftermath of *Pentimento,* as in her other books, Hellman was occasionally criticized for presenting her facts unreliably, "bending" the truth to support her views. Paul Johnson, in the *Spectator,* cited an article casting doubt whether "Julia" actually existed. "What [Boston University's Samuel McCracken] demonstrates, by dint of checking Thirties railway timetables, steamship passenger lists, and many other obscure sources, is that most of the facts Hellman provides about 'Julia's' movement and actions, and indeed her own, are not true." Johnson further suggested that what Hellman had been presenting all along is a left-wing apologia for World War II and the McCarthy era that followed.

Hellman, though no Stalinist, had in fact rebelled against the Cold-War communism investigations during the postwar era—in one of her most memorable lines, she informed the House Un-American Activities Committee (HUAC) during her questioning before that group in 1952, that she had no intention of cutting her conscience to fit that year's fashion. *Scoundrel Time* is based on the hour Hellman sat before the HUAC, as well as "what preceded the hearings, and what its consequences were," according to *Listener* critic David Hunt. Bruce Cook, in a *Saturday Review* article, called the work "a triumph of tone. No writer I know can match the eloquence of her ah-what-the-hell as she looks back over the whole sorry spectacle and tells with restraint and precision just what she sees." *Scoundrel Time,* in Maureen Howard's view, "is not a confessional book. Hellman has seldom told more than her work required." "Her stories are guarded and spare by design," Howard added in the *New York Times Book Review. Ms.* critic Vivian Gornick shared this view, calling *Scoundrel Time* "a valuable piece of work. The kind of work that stands alone, untouched, in the midst of foolish criticism and foolish praise alike."

Among the Hellman memoirs, her last work, *Maybe: A Story,* represents the most obvious tie between fact and fiction. *New Republic* critic Maggie Scarf called "monumental despair" the "true subject of *Maybe.* For Lillian Hellman has gone swimming in the waters of time and memory and found herself adrift in a vast sea of unreliability—the shore of solid information . . . seems to recede each time she believes she has the true details in sight." The narrative covers the life of Sarah Cameron, a longtime acquaintance of Hellman's. Robert Towers, in a *New York Times Book Review* article, commented that, "absorbing as this autobiographical material is, it does not compensate, in my opinion, for the emptiness at the heart of the book. Miss Hellman fails to bring Sarah Cameron into existence as even a remotely comprehensible woman. The evidence is so scattered, so inconsistent, so blurred by time and alcohol, that we are left with a wraith too insubstantial to evoke even a sense of mystery, much less to support a valid point about the ultimate unknowability of figures in our past."

To Gornick, writing in the *Village Voice,* Hellman's digressions into her past seem unworthy of the author's talent. "The association between Hellman and Sarah herself has no substance whatever; it's all fragments and fancy speculations and peripheral incidents and mysterious allusions that seem only to provide the writer with an excuse to call up once again Hammett and the drinking years, the aunts in New Orleans, making movies for Sam Goldwyn. The effort to surround Sarah with metaphoric meaning is strained and painfully obvious." Walter Clemons, in *Newsweek,* saw the inconsistencies

in *Maybe* in another way: "Her nonstory, for that is what her tale of Sarah turns out to be, is a tricky, nervy meditation on the fallibility of memory, the failure of attention, the casual aplomb of practiced liars, the shivery unpredictability of malice." Clemons also praised Hellman's sharp voice, given her advanced years and alcoholic history.

Maybe was Hellman's last major published work; a cookbook, cowritten with longtime friend Peter Feibleman, came out shortly after her June, 1984, death. The news of Hellman's passing brought out a string of testimonials from notable writers, including these words by *Newsweek*'s David Ansen: "In her 60s, looking back on her life in her memoirs, Hellman found her indelible voice. The gallery of portraits in *Pentimento*—especially 'Julia'—are unforgettable: whether they prove to be as much fiction as fact, as some have accused, cannot diminish their power and glamour. She may have called herself 'unfinished,' but a more appropriate title would have been 'An Unmellowed Woman.' . . . The Hellman anger arose from her clear-eyed view of social injustice and strong moral convictions, and she remained true to her passion throughout her rich and tumultuous life."

Decades after her death, Hellman's plays are still performed and the author herself remains a fascinating figure who continues to inspire scholarship and creativity. The 2001 musical *Imaginary Friends* focuses on Hellman's noted rivalry with fellow author Mary McCarthy. As noted by Hellman biographer William Wright in a *New York Times* article, "As a playwright, she had spent much of her life making up good stories. It was perhaps asking too much of her to abandon those skills in writing about her life and to switch abruptly to the tiresome confinements of truth. . . . However the falsehoods came about, they made her, for me and for others, even more interesting, if less admirable. Still, they have left a fog of mystery over her reputation that keeps us from letting her rest in peace, which of course is the last thing she would have wanted."

BIOGRAPHICAL AND CRITICAL SOURCES:

BOOKS

Adler, Jacob H., *Lillian Hellman,* Vaughn, 1969.
Authors in the News, Thomson Gale (Detroit, MI), Volume 1, 1976, Volume 2, 1976.
Contemporary Literary Criticism, Thomson Gale (Detroit, MI), Volume 2, 1974, Volume 4, 1975, Volume 8, 1978, Volume 14, 1980, Volume 18, 1981, Volume 33, 1985, Volume 44, 1987, Volume 52, 1989.

Dictionary of Literary Biography, Thomson Gale (Detroit, MI), Volume 7: *Twentieth-Century American Dramatists,* 1981.

Dictionary of Literary Biography Yearbook: 1984, Thomson Gale (Detroit, MI), 1985.

Falk, Doris V., *Lillian Hellman,* Ungar (New York, NY), 1978.

Gassner, John, *Dramatic Soundings: Evaluations and Retractions Culled from Thirty Years of Dramatic Criticism,* Crown (New York, NY), 1968.

Griffin, Alice, and Geraldine Thorsten, *Understanding Lillian Hellman,* University of South Carolina Press (Columbia, SC), 1998.

Lederer, Katherine, *Lillian Hellman,* Twayne (Boston, MA), 1979.

Mellen, Joan, *Hellman and Hammett: The Legendary Passion of Lillian Hellman and Dashiell Hammett,* HarperCollins (New York, NY), 1996.

Melnick, Ralph, *The Stolen Legacy of Anne Frank: Meyer Levin, Lillian Hellman, and the Staging of the Diary,* Yale University Press (New Haven, CT), 1997.

Moody, Richard, *Lillian Hellman: Playwright,* Bobbs-Merrill (Chicago, IL), 1972.

Turk, Ruth, *Lillian Hellman, Rebel Playwright,* Lerner (Minneapolis, MN), 1995.

Wright, William, *Lillian Hellman: The Image, the Woman,* Simon & Schuster (New York, NY), 1986.

PERIODICALS

Chicago Tribune, March 30, 1980.

Listener, November 18, 1986, David Hunt, review of *Scoundrel Time.*

London Magazine, August-September, 1974, Julian Symons, review of *Pentimento: A Book of Portraits.*

Ms., January, 1974, Muriel Haynes, review of review of *Pentimento;* August, 1976, Vivian Gornick, review of *Scoundrel Time.*

Nation, May 22, 1935, J.W. Krutch, review of *The Children's Hour.*

New Republic, August 2, 1980, Maggie Scarf, review of *Maybe: A Story;* August 13, 1984.

Newsweek, June 2, 1980, Walter Clemons, review of *Maybe.*

New York, September 17, 1973, Eliot Fremont-Smith, review of *Pentimento.*

New York Review of Books, June 10, 1976.

New York Times, November 13, 1980, August 26, 1984; November 3, 1996, William Wright, "Why Lillian Hellman Remains Fascinating," p. H9.

New York Times Book Review, September 23, 1973, April 25, 1976, Maureen Howard, review of *Scoundrel Time;* June 1, 1980, Robert Towers, review of *Maybe.*

Saturday Review, April 17, 1976, Bruce Cook, review of *Scoundrel Time.*

Spectator, July 14, 1984.

Theatre Arts, June, 1941, Rosamond Gilder, review of *Watch on the Rhine.*

Time, May 19, 1980.

Village Voice, May 19, 1980, Vivian Gornick, review of *Maybe.*

Washington Post, May 19, 1980.

OBITUARIES:

PERIODICALS

Chicago Tribune, July 1, 1984.

Los Angeles Times, July 1, 1984.

Newsweek, July 9, 1984.

New York Times, July 1, 1984.

Washington Post, July 1, 1984.

*   *   *

HELLMAN, Lillian Florence
See HELLMAN, Lillian

*   *   *

HELPRIN, Mark 1947-

PERSONAL: Born June 28, 1947, in New York, NY; son of Morris (a motion picture executive) and Eleanor (Lynn) Helprin; married Lisa Kennedy (a tax attorney and banker), June 28, 1980; children: Alexandra Morris, Olivia Kennedy. *Education:* Harvard University, A.B., 1969; A.M., 1972; postgraduate study at Magdalen College, Oxford, 1976-77. *Politics:* "Roosevelt Republican." *Religion:* Jewish.

ADDRESSES: Office—c/o Author Mail, Harcourt Brace Jovanovich, Inc., 15 East 26th St., New York, NY 10010.

CAREER: Writer. Hudson Institute, senior fellow; Harvard University, Cambridge, MA, former instructor. *Military service:* Israeli Infantry and Air Force, field security, 1972-73; British Merchant Navy.

MEMBER: American Academy in Rome.

AWARDS, HONORS: PEN/Faulkner Award, National Jewish Book Award, and American Book Award nomination, all 1982, all for *Ellis Island and Other Stories;* American Academy and Institute of Arts and Letters Prix de Rome, 1982; Guggenheim fellow, 1984; World Fantasy Award for Best Novella, World Fantasy Convention, 1997, for *A City in Winter: The Queen's Tale;* Mightier Pen Award, Center for Security Policy, 2001.

WRITINGS:

A Dove of the East and Other Stories, Knopf (New York, NY), 1975.

Refiner's Fire: The Life and Adventures of Marshall Pearl, a Foundling (novel), Knopf (New York, NY), 1977.

Ellis Island and Other Stories, Seymour Lawrence/ Delacorte (New York, NY), 1981.

Winter's Tale (novel), Harcourt (San Diego, CA), 1983.

Swan Lake (children's book), illustrated by Chris Van Allsburg, Houghton (Boston, MA), 1989.

A Soldier of the Great War (novel), Harcourt (New York, NY), 1991.

Memoir from Antproof Case (novel), Harcourt (New York, NY), 1995.

A City in Winter: The Queen's Tale, illustrated by Chris Van Allsburg, Viking (New York, NY), 1996.

The Veil of Snows, illustrated by Chris Van Allsburg, Viking (New York, NY), 1997.

The Pacific and Other Stories, Penguin (New York, NY), 2004.

Freddy and Fredericka, Penguin (New York, NY), 2005.

Editor, with Shannon Ravenel, of *The Best American Short Stories, 1988.* Contributor of numerous short stories and articles to periodicals, including *New Yorker, Esquire, New Criterion, National Review, Commentary, Weekly Standard,* and *New York Times Magazine;* contributing editor,*Wall Street Journal.*

SIDELIGHTS: Mark Helprin is a writer whose fiction is marked by language "more classical than conversational," observed Michiko Kakutani in the *New York Times,* and one who shapes his short stories and novels "less to show my place in the world than to praise the world around me." Explaining his artistic distance from the sparse, clean prose of writers such as American author Ernest Hemingway, Helprin told Jon D. Markman of the *Los Angeles Times,* "My models are the *Divine Comedy,* and the *Bible* and Shakespeare—where they use language to the fullest." Helprin's political concerns—he pursued Middle Eastern studies in graduate school and later served in the Israeli Infantry and Air Force—figure in his newspaper and magazine articles; his books, he has often said with little elaboration, are religious.

Majoring in English as an undergraduate at Harvard, Helprin wrote short stories and sent them to the *New Yorker* with no luck until 1969, when the magazine accepted two at the same time. These became part of his first book, *A Dove of the East and Other Stories,* in which critics have noted the author's grand depictions of nature as a source of strength and healing and his concern with characters who survive loss, particularly that of loved ones.

Some critics were impressed with the wide range of settings and the graceful prose exhibited in *A Dove of the East.* In the *Saturday Review* Dorothy Rabinowitz described Helprin's stories as "immensely readable," some "quite superb," writing that his "old-fashioned regard shines through all his characters' speeches, and his endorsement gives them eloquent tongues. Now and again the stories lapse into archness, and at times, too, their willed drama bears down too heavily. But these are small flaws in works so estimably full of talent and . . . of character." Amanda Heller, however, complained in the *Atlantic Monthly* that, as a result of Helprin's "dreamy, antique style," the stories' "sameness of tone" becomes monotonous. "It appears that Helprin is striving for loveliness above all else," Heller commented, "a tasteful but hardly compelling goal for a teller of tales."

Duncan Fallowell allowed in the *Spectator* that some selections from *A Dove of the East and Other Stories* are "unbeatably vague," but praised Helprin for "recognising the intrinsic majesty" of seemingly meaningless events, because, as Fallowell wrote, "he is also a seeker after truth. Bits of it are squittering out all over the place, sufficiently to fuse into a magnetic centre and make one recognise that the book is not written by a fool." Dan Wakefield, even more appreciative of Helprin's work, observed: "The quality that pervades these stories is love—love of men and women, love of landscapes and physical beauty, love of interior courage as well as the more easily obtainable outward strength. The author never treats his subjects with sentimentality but always with gentleness of a kind that is all too rare in our fiction and our lives."

Helprin's first novel, *Refiner's Fire: The Life and Adventures of Marshall Pearl, a Foundling,* further interested critics. A *New Yorker* reviewer found that Helprin describes the protagonist's boyhood "lyrically and gracefully" and proves himself to be "a writer of great depth and subtle humor." For Joyce Carol Oates the problem is "where to begin" in admiring a novel she described as a "daring, even reckless, sprawling and expansive and endlessly inventive 'picaresque' tale." She added: "At once we know we are in the presence of a storyteller of seemingly effortless and artless charm; and if the exuberant, extravagant plotting of the novel ever becomes tangled in its own fabulous inventions, and its prodigy of a hero ever comes to seem more allegorical than humanly 'real,' that storytelling command, that lovely voice is never lost."

With *Ellis Island and Other Stories* Helprin secured his place among contemporary writers, winning for this work a PEN/Faulkner Award, a National Jewish Book Award, and an American Book Award nomination—a rare feat for a collection of short stories. Though some critics, such as Anne Duchene in the *Times Literary Supplement,* found that Helprin's language sometimes overwhelms his intent, the greater critical response was laudatory. In the *Washington Post Book World,* Allen Wier called the collection "beautifully written and carefully structured. . . . His rich textures alone would be enough to delight a reader, but there is more: wonderful *stories,* richly plotted, inventive, moving without being sentimental, humorous without being cute." Harry Mark Petrakis stated in the *Chicago Tribune* that in *Ellis Island and Other Stories* Helprin "reveals range and insight whether he is writing of children or adults, of scholars, tailors, and lovers. His eye is precise and his spirit is compassionate, and when we finish the stories we have been rewarded, once more, with that astonishing catalyst of art." Reynolds Price, writing for the *New York Times Book Review,* cited as particularly memorable "The Schreuderspitze," in which a photographer who has lost his wife and son in a car accident risks his life to climb a mountain in an effort to regain his spirit; the first half of the title novella, and "North Light," which Price called "a brief and frankly autobiographical recollection of battle nerves among Israeli soldiers, a lean arc of voltage conveyed through tangible human conductors to instant effect."

Winter's Tale, Helprin's second novel, held a place on the *New York Times* bestseller list for four months despite mixed critical opinion. Seymour Krim, writing for *Washington Post Book World,* described the allegorical novel as "the most ambitious work [Helprin] . . . has yet attempted, a huge cyclorama" with a theme "no less than the resurrection of New York from a city of the damned to a place of universal justice and hope." In Krim's view, however, the novel reveals itself to be "a

self-willed fairy tale that even on its own terms refuses to convince." In the *Chicago Tribune Book World* Jonathan Brent called the book "a pastiche of cliches thinly disguised as fiction, a maddening welter of earnest platitudes excruciatingly dressed up as a search for the miraculous." In the opinion of *Newsweek*'s Peter S. Prescott, "Helprin fell into the fundamental error of assuming that fantasy can be vaguer than realistic fiction."

In the view of Benjamin de Mott of the *New York Times Book Review,* however, neither through the unique and compelling characters nor "merely by studying the touchstone passages in which description and narrative soar highest" can the reader "possess the work": "No, the heart of this book resides unquestionably in its moral energy, in the thousand original gestures, ruminations, . . . writing feats that summon its audience beyond the narrow limits of conventional vision, commanding us to see our time and place afresh." *Detroit News* reviewer Beaufort Cranford found that the book "fairly glows with poetry. Helprin's forte is a deft touch with description, and he has as distinct and spectacular a gift for words an anyone writing today." Further, Cranford noted, "Helprin's fearlessly understated humor shows his comfort with a narrative that in a less adroit grasp might seem too much like a fairy tale."

Openers contributor Ann Cunniff, who also caught the humor in *Winter's Tale,* praised "the beautiful, dreamlike quality" of some passages and Helprin's "frequent references to dreams." "All my life," Helprin explained to Cunniff, "I've allowed what I dream to influence me. My dreams are usually very intense and extremely detailed and always in the most beautiful colors. . . . Frequently, I will dream, and simply retrace that dream the day after when I write. It's just like planning ahead, only I do it when I'm unconscious."

In 1989 Helprin collaborated with illustrator Chris Van Allsburg on *Swan Lake.* Michael Dirda wrote in the *Washington Post Book World,* "The book is so attractive—in its story, illustrations and general design—that by comparison the original ballet almost looks too ethereal." In the *Chicago Tribune,* Michael Dorris raved, "This is one of those rare juvenile classics that will keep you awake to its conclusion . . . [and] will become, I predict, among those precious artifacts your grownup children will someday request for their own children." Helprin and Van Allsburg also combined their talents in 1996's *A City in Winter: The Queen's Tale* and 1997's *The Veil of Snows.*

In *A Soldier of the Great War,* which Shashi Tharoor described in the *Washington Post Book World* as "marvelously old-fashioned" and "a mammoth, elegiac, moving exegesis on love, beauty, the meaning of life and the meaninglessness of war," Helprin seemed to have transcended the criticism leveled at his earlier work. According to John Skow in *Time,* in this tale of the old Italian soldier Alessandro, Helprin has "simplified his language, though he still works up a good head of steam, and he has moderated his enthusiasm for phantasmagoric set pieces. He has also picked themes—war and loss, youth and age—that suit a large, elaborate style." Ted Solotaroff commented in the *Nation* that in *A Soldier of the Great War* Helprin takes "his penchant for life's heightened possibilities and transcendent meanings down into the vile trenches and nightmarish forests and jammed military prisons of the Italian sector of the war." Tharoor concluded: "Clearly a writer of great sensitivity, remarkable skill and capacious intellect, Helprin relishes telling stories in the grand manner, supplying details so complete as to leave the reader in no doubt about the texture of each place and the feelings of each character in it."

Helprin produced yet another expansive, picaresque novel with the mysteriously titled *Memoir from Antproof Case,* which was published in 1995. The story is the memoir of an elderly narrator who relates his fantastic and vivid life in a document he keeps locked inside an ant-proof case. While packing a pistol and hiding from his enemies in Brazil, the narrator describes his early life near New York City, his stay in a Swiss insane asylum, his involvement in World War II, his marriage to a wealthy heiress, and his employment with—and scheme to steal from—a powerful investment brokerage. While telling his life's story, the narrator divulges an odd obsession: the hatred of coffee, including the substance itself as well as the people who drink it. *Los Angeles Times Book Review* contributor Adam Begley described the novel thusly: "More odd mysteries than the anti-coffee mania await unraveling; lyrical passages brim with high-toned literary prose; broad comic riffs announce themselves with take-my-wife subtlety; and tall tales sprout magically at every turn, fed by a steady stream of flamboyant exaggeration."

Critics were positive in their appraisal of *Memoir from Antproof Case,* commending the author's trademark high-wire prose styling and his creation of another unusual, colorful, and rambling narrative. Terry Teachout, writing in the *Washington Post Book World,* called the novel "long, extravagant, daring, occasionally tedious but more often impressively compelling." Similarly, *New York Times Book Review* contributor Sven Birkerts remarked that the story "is rendered with great anecdotal charm and is embroidered throughout with vivid descriptions and delightful reflections." Not all reviewers' comments were positive; Begley, for instance, noted a "lurching Ping-Pong pattern" in the novel in which "suspense alternates with silliness," and Teachout declared that certain elements of *Memoir from Antproof Case* are "exasperating in the extreme." However, Teachout concluded, while "Helprin is a bit of a blowhard, . . . he is also one of the most ambitious novelists of our day."

In addition to his nine fictional works, Helprin wrote articles for the *Wall Street Journal* from 1985 to 2000. "Many people would probably be surprised to know that the same man who writes political commentary for the *Wall Street Journal* cites as his motto a line from Dante's *Inferno* that translates 'Love moved me, and makes me speak,'" remarked *American Enterprise* reviewer, John Meroney. Helprin also came to the political forefront in 1996, when word leaked out that he was the author of presidential candidate Bob Dole's strong resignation speech from the U.S. Senate. Meroney quoted from the speech: "I will run for President as a private citizen, a Kansan, an American, just a man." Dole's speech was "an unusually lyrical oration by the Kansas solon's dry standards," commented *Salon.com* contributor Mark Schapiro, who continued by noting that "Helprin's soaring words were widely credited with at least temporarily recharging Dole's languishing presidential campaign."

In 2001 Helprin was awarded the Mightier Pen Award by the Century for Security Policy. The Center's president and chief executive officer, Frank Gaffney, Jr., stated that Helprin is "one of the most important writers at work today." "Helprin's creative flair is tempered by intelligence, wisdom, and experience," noted John Elvin in *Insight on the News* in reference to Helprin's receipt of the Mightier Pen award.

BIOGRAPHICAL AND CRITICAL SOURCES:

BOOKS

Concise Dictionary of American Literary Biography Supplement: Modern Writers, 1900-1998, Thomson Gale (Detroit, MI), 1998.

Contemporary Literary Criticism, Thomson Gale (Detroit, MI), Volume 7, 1977, Volume 10, 1979, Volume 22, 1982, Volume 32, 1985.

Contemporary Novelists, 7th edition, St. James Press (Detroit, MI), 2001.

Dictionary of Literary Biography Yearbook: 1985, Thomson Gale (Detroit, MI), 1986.

Encyclopedia of American Literature, Continuum (New York, NY), 1999.

Modern American Literature, Thomson Gale (Detroit, MI), 1996.

PERIODICALS

American Enterprise, July, 2001, John Meroney, interview with Helprin, p. 14.

Atlantic Monthly, October, 1975.

Boston Globe, July 12, 1995, Michael Kenney, "Waging a War after All," p. 41.

Chicago Tribune, March 29, 1981; November 12, 1989.

Chicago Tribune Book World, March 29, 1981; October 9, 1983; October 23, 1988; November 12, 1989.

Commentary, June, 1981, pp. 62-66.

Detroit News, February, 23, 1982; March 14, 1982; October 9, 1983.

Globe and Mail (Toronto, Ontario, Canada), January 7, 1984; October 6, 1984.

Harper's, November, 1977.

Insight on the News, May 14, 2001, John Elvin, "A Mightier Pen for a Master Wordsmith," p. 35.

Los Angeles Times, November 8, 1984.

Los Angeles Times Book Review, September 25, 1983; May 5, 1991; May 14, 1995, p. 2.

Nation, June 10, 1991.

New Statesman, February 13, 1976.

Newsweek, September 19, 1983.

New Yorker, October 17, 1977.

New York Review of Books, February 23, 1978; August 15, 1991.

New York Times, January 30, 1981; March 5, 1981, Michiko Kakutani, "The Making of a Writer," p. 17; September 2, 1983.

New York Times Book Review, November 2, 1975; January 1, 1978; March 1, 1981; September 4, 1983; March 25, 1984; May 5, 1991, Thomas Keneally, review of *A Soldier of the Great War,* pp. 1-2; April 9, 1995, p. 3; January 4, 1998, review of *The Veil of Snows,* p. 20.

Openers, fall, 1984.

Publishers Weekly, February 13, 1981.

Saturday Review, September 20, 1975.

School Library Journal, February, 1999, review of *A City in Winter* (audiobook), p. 68; May, 1999, Tricia Finch, review of *Veil of Snows* (audiobook), p. 70.

Spectator, April 24, 1976.

Time, July 6, 1981; October 3, 1983; November 13, 1989; May 20, 1991.

Times Literary Supplement, March 13, 1981; November 25, 1983.

Tribune Books (Chicago, IL), June 9, 1996, p. 10.

Village Voice, May 28, 1991.

Washington Post Book World, February 22, 1981; September 25, 1983; November 5, 1989; May 5, 1991; March 26, 1995, p. 3.

ONLINE

Mark Helprin Bibliography, http://www.lib.ncsu.edu/staff/kamorgan/helprin-bib.html/ (May 11, 2003).

Salon.com, http://www.salon.com/ (August 14, 2003), Mark Schapiro, "Rewriting Bob Dole" (interview).

Wall Street Journal Online, http//www.wsj.com/ (August 9, 2000), "A Chat with Mark Helprin."

*   *   *

HEMPEL, Amy 1951-

PERSONAL: Born December 14, 1951, in Chicago, IL; daughter of Gardiner and Gloria Hempel. *Education:* Attended Whittier College, 1969-71, San Francisco State University, 1973-74, and Columbia University, 1981.

ADDRESSES: *Home*—New York, NY.

CAREER: Writer.

AWARDS, HONORS: Silver Medal, Commonwealth Club of California, 1986, for *Reasons to Live;* Pushcart Prize.

WRITINGS:

Reasons to Live (stories), Knopf (New York City), 1985.

At the Gates of the Animal Kingdom (stories), Knopf, 1990.

(Editor, compiler and contributor) *Unleashed: Poems by Writers' Dogs,* Crown (New York City), 1995.

Tumble Home: A Novella and Short Stories, Scribner (New York City), 1997.

The Dog of the Marriage: Stories, Scribner (New York, NY), 2005.

Works represented in anthologies, including *Best American Short Stories,* 1986, and *Norton Anthology of Short Fiction.* Contributor to periodicals, including *Vanity Fair, Harper's, Mother Jones, Triquarterly, Vogue, Interview,* and *New York Times Magazine;* contributing editor of *Vanity Fair,* 1985-86.

SIDELIGHTS: Amy Hempel has earned widespread distinction as the author of two acclaimed collections of short stories. Her first, *Reasons to Live,* is a rather brief volume of nearly one hundred thirty pages, yet it is comprised of fifteen tales. Critics have observed that these narratives, some numbering only one page in length, are written in an economical manner that nonetheless succeeds in conveying Hempel's quirky humor as well as her bleak worldview. Hempel's fictional realm is one of sadness and bittersweet consolations, and it is a world of natural catastrophe, automobile accidents, madness, and death. Among the more distinguished stories in *Reasons to Live* is "In the Cemetery Where Al Jolson Is Buried," where a woman desperately tries to distract her terminally ill friend by reciting various facts; "Tonight Is a Favor to Holly," which depicts the ironic existence of a woman devoted to what she calls "the beach life"; and "Nashville Gone to Ashes," about a veterinarian's widow who must take care of the animals she always resented in the wake of her husband's demise.

Upon its publication in 1985, *Reasons to Live* received attention as a provocative and disturbing story collection. Sheila Ballantyne, writing in the *New York Times Book Review,* declared that "at their best these stories are tough-minded, original and fully felt." Noting Hempel's minimalist technique, Ballantyne added, "In most of the stories that make up this collection, Amy Hempel has succeeded in revealing both the substance and intelligence beneath the surface of a spare, elliptical prose." More effusively, James Kaufmann reported in the *Washington Post* that "Hempel makes small and cryptic moments explode with suggestion." And *New York Times* critic Michiko Kakutani, who described *Reasons to Live* as a volume of "astringent" stories, affirmed that for Hempel "even the smallest act, the tiniest gesture. . . can be an act of courage." Kakutani also noted that Hempel portrays her characters "with charity and understanding."

In her next story collection, *At the Gates of the Animal Kingdom,* Hempel further refined her stylistically spare, narratively brief technique, thus prompting *New York Times Book Review* contributor Robert Towers to cast Hempel as a miniaturist rather than a minimalist. Hempel's fiction, Towers maintained, is marked "by an almost miraculous exactitude of observation and execution." Like the earlier book, *At the Gates of the Animal Kingdom* is concerned with people coping—or, at least, surviving—in a world of sadness and mayhem. "The Harvest," for instance, concerns a woman maimed in a motorcycle accident, and "The Day I Had Everything" relates the activities within an organization of women who lament the loss of loved ones and the unrelenting nature of physical decay. In still another tale, "Lead Us Not into Penn Station," a narrator merely relates a day's observations and events in New York City—a wino bleeds, a man recalls fornicating with a household appliance, a blind man enters a bank and orders a sandwich—and then expresses their cumulatively overwhelming nature.

At the Gates of the Animal Kingdom, which appeared in 1990, confirmed Hempel's stature as a unique storyteller. "The stories," Elizabeth Tallent wrote in the *Los Angeles Times Book Review,* "are . . . smartly observed, cryptically titled, the prose as tight as if it fears spilling a single drop." And Towers, in a *New York Times Book Review* assessment, lauded "the elegance and compactness" of Hempel's style and added, "What one cherishes in Amy Hempel are . . . her quirky sensibility and the beautifully honed verbal craft she brings to bear on the situations and themes that have attracted her amused and rueful eye." Towers acknowledged that Hempel manages to produce stories of both humor and sadness. He declared that in *At the Gates of the Animal Kingdom,* "The combination of comedy and loss is pervasive." Philip Gourevitch made a similar observation in the *Washington Post,* commenting that "it is Hempel's great achievement in these stories that she always maintains compassion and keeps the laugh lines coming."

Hempel's minimalist style was again showcased in her 1997 novella, *Tumble Home.* The slim volume, which also contained stories as short as one paragraph long, gained the attention of *New York Times* reviewer Elizabeth Gleick, who found that "each story is written as if assembled from fragments of conversations or snatches of melody."

Gleick singled out pieces such as "Weekend," which examined the group dynamics of families vacationing at the beach, as fiction that "has much in common with poetry. Using only a few phrases, [Hempel] succeeds in evoking a mood or . . . even an entire summer at the shore." In "Housewife," the tale of an unfaithful married woman is told in a single sentence, prompting critic

Claire Messud to declare in the *Washington Post Book World* that the author "unsettles our uncomfortable conceptions of 'story.'" (On the other hand, a *Kirkus Review* writer found the one-sentence story "just short and rather silly.")

The title novella of *Tumble Home* is a sort of free-association conversation in the form of a letter from young woman in a mental institution to the famous artist whom she may or may not have once met. In this longer work *Chicago Tribune* writer Andy Solomon found Hempel to be "at her most enigmatic and most lyrical." Solomon went on to note that "people attempting to find a plot in her fiction will be shocked. Even those attempting to find fiction in it will discover themselves in an exquisite but mysterious territory where, although the lines extend to the right margin, we sense ourselves in the presence of a poet."

Hempel moved from poetry-like fiction to poetry proper as editor of the 1995 collection *Unleashed: Poems by Writers' Dogs,* featuring works credited to the animal companions of such luminaries as Edward Albee, Maxine Kumin, John Irving, and Hempel herself. In Hempel's hands what "might have been nothing more than, well, doggerel—just another of those self-consciously cute cat and dog books that crowd the bookstore shelves" instead becomes "a summer treat, by turns endearingly funny and achingly tender," according to Polly Paddock in her *Chicago Tribune* review. Equally impressed was *New York Times* guest reviewer "Jacques," identified as the dog of novelist Daniel Pinkwater. While the critical canine noticed "a measure of contamination discernible in some of the selections, dogs talking about things no sensible [pooch] would ever think about," Jacques ultimately gave a paws-up to *Unleashed:* "I had a barking good time with this book. The compilers deserve to be given a croissant and have their ears scratched."

BIOGRAPHICAL AND CRITICAL SOURCES:

BOOKS

Contemporary Literary Criticism, Volume 39, Thomson Gale (Detroit), 1986.

PERIODICALS

Chicago Tribune, June 30, 1995; June 22, 1997.
Esquire, June, 1995, p. 44.
Kirkus Reviews, March 15, 1997.

Los Angeles Times, April 4, 1985.
Los Angeles Times Book Review, March 11, 1990, pp. 2, 11.
Newsweek, April 28, 1997, p. 78.
New York Times, April 13, 1985.
New York Times Book Review, April 28, 1985; March 11, 1990, p. 11; June 4, 1995; July 27, 1997.
People, September 25, 1995, p. 43.
Tribune Books (Chicago), April 29, 1990, p. 6.
Washington Post, March 8, 1990.
Washington Post Book World, May 7, 1985; April 13, 1997.

* * *

HENLEY, Beth
    See HENLEY, Elizabeth Becker

* * *

HENLEY, Elizabeth Becker 1952-
   (Beth Henley)

PERSONAL: Born May 8, 1952, in Jackson, MS; daughter of Charles Boyce (an attorney) and Elizabeth Josephine (an actress; maiden name, Becker) Henley. *Education:* Southern Methodist University, B.F.A., 1974; attended University of Illinois, 1975-76.

ADDRESSES: Home—Los Angeles, CA. *Agent*—Gilbert Parker, William Morris Agency, 1350 Avenue of the Americas, New York, NY 10019.

CAREER: Actress and playwright. Theatre Three, Dallas, TX, actress, 1972-73; Southern Methodist University, Directors Colloquium, Dallas, member of acting ensemble, 1973; Dallas Minority Repertory Theatre, teacher of creative dramatics, 1974-75; University of Illinois, Urbana, teacher of beginning acting, Lessac voice technique, and playwriting, 1975-76. Actress, Great American People Show, summer, 1976; producer, Loretta Theatre, a production company.

AWARDS, HONORS: Cowinner of Great American Playwriting Contest, Actor's Theatre of Louisville, 1978, Susan Smith Blackburn Award nomination, 1979, New York Drama Critics Circle Award for best new American play, from *Newsday,* 1981, Pulitzer Prize for drama, 1981, and Antoinette Perry ("Tony") Award nomination for best play, 1981, all for *Crimes of the Heart;* Academy Award nomination for best adapted screenplay, 1986, for movie version of *Crimes of the Heart.*

WRITINGS:

Am I Blue (one-act play; first produced in Dallas, Texas, at Southern Methodist University Margo Jones Theatre, 1973), Dramatists Play Service (New York, NY), 1982.

Crimes of the Heart (three-act play; first produced in Louisville, KY, 1979; produced on Broadway at John Golden Theatre, November 4, 1981; revived in New York, NY, 2001; also see below), Dramatists Play Service (New York, NY), 1981.

Morgan's Daughters (script for television pilot), Paramount, 1979.

The Miss Firecracker Contest (two-act play; first produced in Los Angeles, CA, 1980; produced off-Broadway at Manhattan Theatre Club, June, 1980; also see below), Dramatists Play Service (New York, NY), 1985.

The Wake of Jamey Foster (two-act play; first produced in Hartford, CT, 1982; produced on Broadway at Eugene O'Neill Theatre, October 14, 1982), Dramatists Play Service (New York, NY), 1985.

The Debutante Ball (play, first produced in Costa Mesa, CA, 1985), University Press of Mississippi (Jackson, MS), 1991.

(With Budge Threlkeld) *Survival Guides* (television script), Public Broadcasting System (Alexandria, VA), 1985.

Crimes of the Heart (screenplay; based on author's play of the same title), De Laurentiis Entertainment, 1986.

Nobody's Fool (screenplay), Island Pictures, 1986.

(With David Byrne and Stephen Tobolowsky) *True Stories* (screenplay), Warner Bros., 1986.

The Lucky Spot (play; first produced in Williamstown, MA, 1986; produced on Broadway at City Center Theatre, April, 1987), Dramatists Play Service (New York, NY), 1987.

Miss Firecracker (screenplay; based on her play), Corsair Pictures, 1988.

Abundance (play; produced in Los Angeles, CA, 1989), Dramatists Play Service (New York, NY), 1990.

Monologues for Women (play), Dramaline Publications (Rancho Mirage, CA), 1992.

(And director) *Control Freaks* (one-act play; produced in Los Angeles, CA, at Met Theater, 1993.

Beth Henley: Four Plays, Heinemann/Methuen (Portsmouth, NH), 1994.

L-Play (play), produced in Stockbridge, MA, 1996.

Come West with Me (screenplay; based on author's play *Abundance*), Twentieth Century-Fox, 1998.

Collected Plays, Volume I: *1980-1989,* Smith & Kraus (Lyme, NH), 2000.

Collected Plays, Volume II: *1990-1999,* Smith & Kraus (Lyme, NH), 2000.

Impossible Marriage (play), Dramatists Play Service (New York, NY), 1999.

Three Plays by Beth Henley, Dramatists Play Service (New York, NY), 2002.

Family Week (play), produced Off-Broadway, 2000.

Sisters of the Winter Madrigal (play), Dramatists Play Service (New York, NY), 2001.

Signature (play), Dramatists Play Service (New York, NY), 2003.

Revelers (play), Dramatists Play Service (New York, NY), 2003.

Ridiculous Fraud (play), produced at Sundance Institute Theatre Lab, Sundance, UT, 2004.

Tight Pants (play), produced in Los Angeles, CA, at the MET Theater, 2004.

SIDELIGHTS: Beth Henley is a member of the new breed of American playwrights dedicated to preserving regional voices on the stage. In Henley's case, her Mississippi upbringing provides the background for a host of Southern-accented plays, one of which, the black comedy *Crimes of the Heart,* went on to win her a Pulitzer Prize when she was twenty-nine years of age. Like many playwrights before her, Henley originally set her sights on being an actress, but ventured into writing after deciding there were not many good contemporary roles for Southern women. A graduate of Southern Methodist University, Henley got her first play produced there, a one-act work titled *Am I Blue.* In 1976, she moved to Los Angeles to live with actor/director Stephen Tobolowsky, with whom she would later collaborate on the screenplay *True Stories.* Three years later Henley submitted a three-act play to the Great American Play Contest sponsored by Actors Theatre of Louisville, Kentucky. Henley's play, *Crimes of the Heart,* won the contest and there began the first of its many successful stagings.

Set in Hazlehurst, Mississippi, a few years after Hurricane Camille, passed through the area, the story centers on three eccentric sisters who converge in the home of the youngest, Babe, after she has shot her well-to-do husband because, as Babe puts it, "I didn't like his looks." The other sisters include Meg, a would-be singer who has struck out in Hollywood; and Lenny, single and desperate at age thirty. These sisters, according to

Edith Oliver in a *New Yorker* review, the "walking wounded, who are in tears at one moment and giggling and hugging at the next, . . . are very much of the South, of Mississippi, and [novelist] Eudora Welty has prepared us for them." John Simon, reviewing the production for *New York* magazine, stated that "the play is an essence, *the* essence of provincial living." Simon further called *Crimes of the Heart* a "loving and teasing look back at deep-southern, small-town life, at the effect of constricted living and confined thinking on three different yet not wholly unalike sisters amid Chekhovian boredom in honeysuckle country, and, above all, at the sorely tried but resilient affection and loyalty of these sisters for one another."

Some critics took exception to Henley's use of ironic black humor in *Crimes of the Heart*. Michael Feingold, writing in the *Village Voice,* for instance, thought the playwright's attitude toward her three main characters, with its "pity and mockery aimed at them in laser-gun bursts," has "no organic connection and no deep roots. The play gives the impression of gossiping about its characters rather than presenting them, and [Henley's] voice, though both individual and skillful, is the voice of a small-town southern spinster yattering away on the phone, oozing pretended sympathy and real malice for her unfortunate subjects, and never at any point coming close to the truth of their lives." *New Leader* reviewer Leo Sauvage discovered "nothing enthralling in spending an evening with three badly adjusted, if not mentally retarded sisters, who are given free rein to exhibit their individual eccentricities," and dubbed Henley's humor "sick, not black."

Other reviewers saw more to value in Henley's work. *Crimes of the Heart* may be "overlong, occasionally cliched and annoyingly frivolous at moments," noted *Daily News* critic Don Nelson, "but Henley keeps intriguing us with a delightfully wacky humor plus a series of little mysteries played out by characters we can never dismiss as superficial on a set that absorbs us into their lives." "The physical modesty of her play belies the bounty of plot, peculiarity, and comedy within it," concluded *Saturday Review* writer Scot Haller of Henley's effort. "Like Flannery O'Connor, Henley creates ridiculous characters but doesn't ridicule them. Like Lanford Wilson, she examines ordinary people with extraordinary compassion. Treating the eccentricities of her characters with empathy, [Henley] manages to render strange turns of events not only believable but affecting."

Crimes of the Heart was nominated for a Tony award when first produced and subsequently adapted by its author into movie form, the screenplay of which was nominated for an Academy award. In a review of the movie adaptation for the *New Republic,* Stanley Kauffmann wrote, "Comic Beth Henley has adapted her play for the screen with careful balance. . . maintain[ing] the poise of her exceptionally good play. . . keep[ing] the braided deception and truth of the original." A review by Peter Travers for *People* was less flattering: "The seams in Henley's play . . . show up more glaringly when blown up to wide screen size," Travers maintained, adding that "Henley's saving grace is her antic humor." In 2001, a revival of *Crimes of the Heart* opened at the Second Stage Theater in New York City. The play starred Amy Ryan, Mary Catherine Garrison, and Enid Graham, and was directed by Garry Hynes.

Henley's screenplay *True Stories* takes a look at "the petty bourgeois customs, the media hype, the bloated vulgarities of American small-town life," according to Kauffmann in another review for the *New Republic.* In the film, director and cowriter David Byrne, the lead singer of the Talking Heads, serves as a tour guide to this mythical Texas town, driving around in a red convertible showing viewers the oh-so-local sites and scenery. According to Kauffmann, "The result has the shape, designed yet seemingly casual, of Monty Python scripts but very little of their incisive wit. . . . The catalog of cartoons along the way is trite and not often funny." A *People* critic called *True Stories* one of 1986's "most notable and offbeat films," and Henley, "one of the 25 Most Intriguing People of '86. . . . She earned her 1986 merit badge by wielding a wicked wit."

In other work for film in addition to *True Stories* and *Crimes of the Heart,* Henley adapted her play *The Miss Firecracker Contest* into a screenplay, and also wrote an original screenplay, *Nobody's Fool.* In *The Miss Firecracker Contest,* a ne'er-do-well young woman, Carnelle Scott, seeks to uplift her station in her small Mississippi town; in hopes of gaining respect she hopes to win the "Miss Firecracker" beauty contest, a rather cheesy local affair. To that end, Carnelle enlists other outcasts in her town to aid in her quest. As the play version opens, Carnelle is seen on a bare stage dressed in a leotard and draped in an American flag, tap-dancing and baton-twirling her way through the "Star-Spangled Banner." "Though [the playwright's] territory looks superficially like the contemporary American South," wrote *Time*'s Richard Schickel, "it is really a country of the mind: one of Tennessee Williams' provinces that has surrendered to a Chekhovian raiding party, perhaps. Her strength is a wild anecdotal inventiveness, but her people, lost in the ramshackle dreams and tumble-down ambitions with which she invests them, often seem to be metaphors waywardly adrift. They are blown this way and that by the gales of laughter they provoke, and they frequently fail to find a solid connection with clear and generally relevant meaning." Unfortunately for Henley, *The Miss Firecracker Contest* did not last long on the boards.

Nobody's Fool focuses on a frustrated young Arizona woman working as a waitress and trying to allow a new love into her life while living with the memories of a past one. According to Kauffmann, *Nobody's Fool* is "about helplessness and its counterfeit armor, about a young woman in the grip of a destructive sexual attraction who is ultimately saved by another lover—who may or may not turn out to be equally hurtful." In Kauffmann's words, the screenplay for *Nobody's Fool* is "authentic, unique [and] rounded." Henley "writes with a unique voice, quiet, comic, even whimsical, but with hidden venom." In an interview with Mark Lee for *Written By,* Henley said of *Nobody's Fool:* "It's very different to create something from scratch than having the great mercy of having source material. Over the years I've learned how to think more visually and let go of dialogue and visualize the movement of the film."

Henley's other screenplays, for both film and television, include the draft of the screenplay for the film version of Annie Proulx's novel *The Shipping News,* coauthoring the television script *Survival Guides* for public television, and penning the teleplay *Ruby McCullough,* based on a true story of a Southern black woman. Henley also wrote the script for the televison pilot *Morgan's Daughters,* served as a writer for the Public Broadcasting Service special *Trying Times,* and wrote a CBS television movie titled *Meant to Be,* that starred actors Ted Danson and Mary Steenburgen.

Other early plays by Henley include *The Wake of Jamey Foster, The Debutante Ball, The Lucky Spot, Monologues for Women,* and *L-Plays* which were produced at venues across the country, from New England and New York, to Chicago and California. More popular have been her longer works, among them *Impossible Marriage, Signature,* and *Sisters of the Winter Madrigal,* while other plays have been less successful. Keeping with her Southern theme, Henley sets *Impossible Marriage* in Savannah, Georgia, and relates the story of a young woman whose upcoming marriage is opposed by her older, and very pregnant, sister, as well as by others. A *TheaterMania.com* reviewer called *Impossible Marriage* "a surprisingly—for Henley, at least—upbeat family saga that served as a reminder of the power of her distinctive, theatrical voice," while in the *Long Island Business News,* Richard Scholem commented: "It's

impossible to keep a straight face watching Beth Henley's *Impossible Marriage.* . . . Its . . . bigger-than-life . . . characters are deliciously overwrought, over dramatic, over magnified and over the edge."

In *Signature,* another successful venture for Henley, the playwright takes a "high-tech, sci-fi, bizarrely futuristic look at Hollywood, where marriage is a career choice and everyone is desperate to make his or her mark on an indifferent world," according to Terri Roberts, in a review for *Back Stage West.* Citing a *New York Times* review, Roberts added that "Henley is on a word high. Those words dizzyingly play, collide, enlighten, ceaselessly question, and even give answers with wit and without avoidance." As Roberts quoted Henley herself, the playwright noted: "I was fascinated that Los Angeles is really about people who have come out here to make a signature, to make a mark, to not live and have a family and do a job and die in the place where they were born. . . . Everything seems so new and dangerous. . . . I like that notion for the play—that all these people are just on the edge and don't really know how to behave at all." In another *Back Stage West* review, Dany Margolies commented that the play's "characters range from unsettlingly slightly off-kilter personalities to the outrageously psychotic ones that seem comfortingly familiar."

Sisters of the Winter Madrigal is a one-act play that could have been longer, according to Laura Weinert in her review for *Back Stage West.* The play, Weinert asserted, seems to "yearn for expansion into [a] full-length play. . . . Rarely do we leave the theatre wishing the playwright had written more words." Henley's play, set in a rural town in a time long ago, focuses on two orphaned sisters, the town whore, and a betrothed cowhearder who is trying to wiggle out of a marriage in favor of a better offer. "One can't help but wonder what heights [the actors] might reach if [the play was] given an entire evening to fill and . . . able to build to more meaningful denouements," summarized the critic.

Diverting from her prominent theme of female bonding, Henley's *Ridiculous Fraud* is a comedy set in New Orleans about the relationship among three adult brothers, each trying to cope with the fact that their father is serving time for committing a "ridiculous fraud." Henley had the opportunity to develop this play, which was commissioned by the McCarter Theater Center of the Performing Arts in Princeton, New Jersey, at the Sundance Institute Theater Laboratory, in Sundance, Utah. *Tight Pants* is a one-act play exploring an erotic triangle. Daryl Miller, writing in the *Los Angeles Times,* noted in a review of the play's production that Henley's "deft writing is matched by spot-on acting and sharp directing." A contributor to the *Maestro Theatre* Web site called the farce "as odd as it is funny."

Many of Henley's plays have been incorporated into collections, including two volumes that together comprise much of her oeuvre, the two-volume *Collected Plays*. In a review for *Library Journal*, Thomas Luddy hailed the appearance of the work, noting that it "reveals a consistently excellent body of work from a distinctive voice of the American theater. . . . As this set reveals, Henley's most important contribution to the theater is her memorable gallery of women characters, which has kept her plays alive on stages across the country." Jack Helbig agreed, stating in *Booklist* that both volumes are "most welcome. . . . Henley wittily introduces each play and, as she does, sprinkles fascinating recollections of actors and directors involved in the premiere productions."

Henley's plays continue to be produced across the United States and internationally and have been translated into over ten languages. Her stage, movie, and television productions have starred a host of well-known actors, among them, Rosanna Arquette, Ted Danson, Holly Hunter, Diane Keaton, Jessica Lange, Carol Kane, Swoosie Kurtz, Laraine Newman, Tim Robbins, Sam Shepard, and Sissy Spacek. As actor Hunter told an online interviewer for *TheaterMania.com,* Henley "is an original observer. . . . And she is not really swayed by what other people think in terms of how she navigates her own life. . . . Beth keeps her unique point of view solidly intact."

In an interview with Mark Lee for *Written By*, Henley explained that in writing for both stage and film, she has had to bring different considerations to bear, particularly in adapting works from one medium to another. "The impulse of the theater will always be something about being there. And the fact that you can laugh and the person will react or not react. Or you can shout at them to stop, and they will hear you. The vitality of that is something I find overwhelming. Film is so different. I love that you can send that film out, and people can see it in countries that you've never been to, and you can touch people's hearts that can't get out of their village. They're being given a new perspective on the world. The influence of film is amazing. It can make your stories even more powerful."

BIOGRAPHICAL AND CRITICAL SOURCES:

BOOKS

Contemporary Literary Criticism, Thomson Gale (Detroit, MI), Volume 23, 1983.

Dictionary of Literary Biography Yearbook: 1986, Thomson Gale (Detroit, MI), 1987.

PERIODICALS

Back Stage, August 6, 1993, Rob Kendt, review of *Control Freaks,* p. 8.

Back Stage West, October 12, 2000, review of *Signature,* p. 18; July 19, 2001, Laura Weinert, review of *Sisters of the Winter Madrigal,* p. 12.

Booklist, June 1, 2000, Jack Helbig, review of *Collected Plays,* Volume I: *1980-1989* and *Collected Plays,* Volume II: *1990-1999,* p. 1836.

Chicago Sun-Times, April 28, 1989, Roger Ebert, review of *Miss Firecracker.*

Daily News (New York, NY), November 5, 1981.

Library Journal, October 15, 1991.

Long Island Business News, November 6, 1998, Benjamin Scholem, review of *Impossible Marriage,* p. 38.

Los Angeles Times, April 16, 1983; May 7, 2004, Daryl H. Miller, review of *Tight Pants.*

New Leader, November 30, 1981.

New Republic, November 10, 1986, Stanley Kauffmann, review of *True Stories,* p. 26; December 15, 1986, Stanley Kauffmann, review of *Nobody's Fool,* p. 22; February 2, 1987, Stanley Kauffmann, review of *Crimes of the Heart,* p. 26; December 17, 1990, Robert Brustein, review of *Abundance,* p. 28.

Newsday, August 27, 1996.

Newsweek, December 22, 1986; May 1, 1989.

New York, November 16, 1981; May 11, 1987; May 15, 1989; November 12, 1990.

New Yorker, January 12, 1981; May 11, 1987; May 29, 1989; November 12, 1990.

New York Times, June 8, 1979; December 22, 1980; February 15, 1981; April 14, 1981; June 10, 1981; June 11, 1981; October 25, 1981; November 5, 1981; December 28, 1981; April 14, 1982; May 28, 1984; November 2, 1986.

New York Times Magazine, May 1, 1983.

People, December 15, 1986, Peter Travers, review of *Crimes of the Heart* (movie), p. 12; December 22, 1986, "The 25 Most Intriguing People of '86," p. 91.

Playbill, July 5, 2004, Kenneth Jones, "Beth Henley, Joe Hortua, Tectonic Theatre, Stephen Dillane Work in 2004 Sundance Theatre Lab July 5-25."

Saturday Review, November, 1981; January, 1982.

Time, June 11, 1984; December 22, 1986; May 1, 1989.

Variety, May 10, 1989; August 9, 1993; April 17, 2000, Charles Isherwood, review of *Family Week,* p. 34.

Village Voice, November 18, 1981.

Washington Post, December 12, 1986.

Written By, June-July 2000, Mark Lee, interview with Henley.

ONLINE

Maestro Web site, http://www.maestro.ws/arts/ (April, 2004), "Beth Henley."

Met Theater Web site, http://www.7metshorts.com/ (July 31, 2004), review of *Tight Pants*.

TheaterMania.com, http://www.theatermania.com/ (April 11, 2000), Kathy Henderson, review of *Family Week*.

Univerity of Mississippi, Department of English Web site, http://www.olemiss.edu/depts/ english/ (July 29, 2004), "Beth Henley."

* * *

HERBERT, Frank 1920-1986
(Frank Patrick Herbert)

PERSONAL: Born October 8, 1920, in Tacoma, WA; died of complications following cancer surgery February 11 (some sources say February 12), 1986, in Madison, WI; son of Frank and Eileen Marie (McCarthy) Herbert; married Flora Parkinson, March, 1941 (divorced, 1945); married Beverly Ann Stuart, June 23, 1946; marriage ended; married third wife, Theresa; children: Penny (Mrs. D.R. Merritt), Brian Patrick, Bruce Calvin. *Education:* Attended University of Washington, 1946-47.

CAREER: Novelist. Reporter, photographer, and editor for west coast newspapers, including *Glendale Star* (CA), *Oregon Statesman, Seattle Star*, and *San Francisco Examiner*, 1939-69; educational writer, *Seattle Post-Intelligence*, Seattle, WA, 1969-72; lecturer in general and interdisciplinary studies, University of Washington, Seattle, 1970-72; consultant in social and ecological studies, Lincoln Foundation, and to countries of Vietnam and Pakistan, 1971; director and photographer of television show, *The Tillers*, 1973.

MEMBER: World without War Council (member of national council, 1970-73; member of Seattle council, 1972-86).

AWARDS, HONORS: Nebula Award, Science Fiction Writers of America, 1965, and Hugo Award, World Science Fiction Convention, 1966, both for *Dune;* Prix Apollo, 1978; Doctor of Humanities, Seattle University, 1980.

WRITINGS:

SCIENCE-FICTION NOVELS

The Dragon in the Sea (originally serialized in *Amazing Science Fiction* as *Under Pressure*), Doubleday (New York, NY), 1956, published as *Twenty-first Century Sub*, Avon (New York, NY), 1956, published as *Under Pressure*, Ballantine (New York, NY), 1974.

The Green Brain (originally serialized in *Amazing Stories*), Berkley Publishing (New York, NY), 1966.

Destination: Void (originally serialized in *Galaxy;* also see below), Berkley Publishing (New York, NY), 1966, revised edition, 1978.

The Eyes of Heisenberg (originally serialized in *Galaxy*), Berkley Publishing (New York, NY), 1966.

The Heaven Makers (originally serialized in *Amazing Stories*), Avon (New York, NY), 1968.

The Santaroga Barrier (originally serialized in *Amazing Stories*), Berkley Publishing (New York, NY), 1968.

Whipping Star (originally serialized in *If;* also see below), Berkley Publishing (New York, NY), 1970.

The God Makers (also see below), Berkley Publishing (New York, NY), 1971.

Hellstrom's Hive (based on the film *The Hellstrom Chronicle;* originally serialized in *Galaxy* as *Project 40*), Doubleday (New York, NY), 1973.

The Dosadi Experiment (sequel to *Whipping Star;* also see below), Berkley Publishing (New York, NY), 1977.

(With Bill Ransom) *The Jesus Incident* (also see below), Berkley Publishing (New York, NY), 1979.

Direct Descent, Ace Books (New York, NY), 1980.

Priests of Psi (also see below), Gollancz (London, England), 1980.

The White Plague, Putnam (New York, NY), 1982.

(With Bill Ransom) *The Lazarus Effect*, Putnam (New York, NY), 1983.

Worlds beyond Dune: The Best of Frank Herbert (contains *The Jesus Incident, Whipping Star, Destination: Void, The God Makers*, and *The Dosadi Experiment*), Berkley Publishing (New York, NY), 1987.

(With son, Brian Herbert) *Man of Two Worlds*, Ace Books (New York, NY), 1987.

(With Bill Ransom) *The Ascension Factor*, Ace Books (New York, NY), 1989.

"DUNE CHRONICLES" SERIES

Dune (originally serialized in *Analog;* also see below), Chilton, 1965, twenty-fifth anniversary edition, Ace Books (New York, NY), 1990.

Dune Messiah (originally serialized in *Galaxy;* also see below), Berkley Publishing (New York, NY), 1970.

Children of Dune (also see below), Berkley Publishing (New York, NY), 1976.

The Illustrated Dune, Berkley Publishing (New York, NY), 1978.

The Great Dune Trilogy (contains *Dune, Dune Messiah,* and *Children of Dune*), Gollancz (London, England), 1979.

God Emperor of Dune (excerpt appeared in *Playboy*), Berkley Publishing (New York, NY), 1981.

Heretics of Dune, Putnam (New York, NY), 1984.

Chapterhouse: Dune, Putnam (New York, NY), 1985.

House Atreides, Bantam (New York, NY), 1999.

House Harkonnen, Bantam (New York, NY), 2000.

House Corrino, Bantam (New York, NY), 2001.

Dune: The Machine Crusade, Tor (New York, NY), 2003.

SHORT STORIES

(With others) *Five Fates,* Doubleday (New York, NY), 1970.

The Worlds of Frank Herbert, Ace Books (New York, NY), 1970.

The Book of Frank Herbert, DAW Books (New York, NY), 1972.

The Best of Frank Herbert, Sphere Books (London, England), 1974.

The Priests of Psi, and Other Stories, Gollancz (London, England), 1980.

Eye ("Masterworks of Science Fiction and Fantasy" series), edited by Byron Preiss, illustrated by Jim Burns, Berkley Publishing (New York, NY), 1985.

OTHER

(Editor) *New World or No World* (interviews), Ace Books (New York, NY), 1970.

Soul Catcher (fiction), Berkley Publishing (New York, NY), 1972.

Threshold: The Blue Angels Experience (nonfiction), Ballantine (New York, NY), 1973.

(Editor with others) *Tomorrow, and Tomorrow, and Tomorrow,* Holt (New York, NY), 1974.

Sandworms of Dune (recording), Caedmon (London, England), 1978.

The Truths of Dune (recording), Caedmon (London, England), 1979.

The Battles of Dune (recording), Caedmon (London, England), 1979.

(With Max Barnard) *Without Me You're Nothing: The Essential Guide to Home Computers* (nonfiction), Simon & Schuster (New York, NY), 1981.

(Editor) *Nebula Awards Fifteen* (anthology), Harper (New York, NY), 1981.

The Dune Encyclopedia, edited by Willis E. McNelly, Putnam (New York, NY), 1984.

The Maker of Dune, edited by Timothy O'Reilly, Berkeley Publishing (New York, NY), 1987.

(Author of foreword) Bryan Brewer, editor, *Eclipse,* second edition, Earth View, 1991.

The Songs of Muad'Dib: The Poetry of Frank Herbert, edited by B. Herbert, Ace Books (New York, NY), 1992.

(With Sonny Detmer) *Ty: The Ty Detmer Story as told to Brenton Yorgason,* Bookcraft (Salt Lake City, UT), 1992.

Also author of *The Dune Coloring Book* (fourteen volumes), Putnam. Contributor of fiction to *Esquire, Galaxy, Amazing Stories, Analog,* and other magazines.

Dune has been translated into over fourteen languages.

ADAPTATIONS: Dune was adapted for the screen by David Lynch and filmed by Universal in 1984.

SIDELIGHTS: Frank Herbert is most often remembered as the creator of the tremendously popular "Dune Chronicles." The first volume, 1965's *Dune,* instantly placed him among such preeminent authors as J.R.R. Tolkien, C.S. Lewis, Robert Heinlein, and Isaac Asimov as a brilliant creator of imagined worlds. The novel first became a cult favorite and then a full-blown bestseller; it has never been out of print, selling tens of millions of copies and spawning five sequels and a film adaptation in the decades since it was first published. *Dune* is considered by many to be among the most influential novels in its genre, and is described by Robert A. Foster in the *Dictionary of Literary Biography* as "one of the unquestioned masterpieces of modern science fiction."

The popularity of *Dune* has been built around Herbert's portrayal of the desert planet Arrakis and its inhabitants—a portrayal which Joseph McClellan of the *Washington Post Book World* considered to be "more complete and deeply detailed than any author in the [science fiction] field had ever managed or attempted before." The novel takes place twenty-five centuries hence, when the known universe is controlled by two political powers, the Imperium and the Great Houses. These forces maintain a delicate and uneasy peace, occasionally punctuated by espionage, collusion, and infighting. The balance is further complicated by the presence of powerful independent organizations, such as the Spacing Guild and the cultish Bene Gesserit. As the novel opens, Duke Leto Atreides has been asked to abandon the throne of his home world of Caladan for that of Arrakis, known to its natives as Dune. This planet is a burning desert—quite unlike the watery paradise of Caladan—but is also the only source for the spice melange, an addictive narcotic which imparts to its user limited prescient abilities. The spice is highly valued by the Spacing Guild (whose navigators use the drug to help them traverse the cosmos), among others, making Arrakis a source of power to whoever controls it.

Leto takes his wife, Jessica, his son, Paul, and their entourage to Dune. Before they can assume control, however, they are ambushed by the forces of the Harkonnen family, arch rivals of House Atreides. Duke Leto is killed, but Paul and his mother escape to the desert wastes, where they encounter the indigenous people known as the Fremen. Years of living in the sands have forced the Fremen to adapt: they have constructed special suits to conserve and re-use their body's fluids; they have designed machinery to draw precious moisture from the atmosphere; and, most importantly, they have perfected methods by which melange can be harvested and distilled. The Fremen have learned the secret of the "spice cycle"—that the production of melange is intrinsic to the life cycle of Dune's most frightening creatures, the monstrous sandworms.

Paul and Jessica are introduced to the ways of Fremen culture. In a Fremen rite of passage, Paul ingests a near-lethal dose of spice, awakening within him the ability to see the future—and, to some extent, to alter it. He is hailed by the Fremen as their messiah, Muad'Dib. With them as his army, Paul struggles to wrest his father's usurped throne away from the Harkonnens; however, deep within the "network of probability" that makes up the future, Paul glimpses a terrible holy war drawing ever closer—a bloody jihad that he is destined to bring about.

While the plot of *Dune* is typical of heroic fantasy and science fiction, the world and culture of Arrakis set the novel apart from standard fare. Foster credited Herbert with establishing the science fiction tradition of "the invented-world novel, in which details of history, languages, customs, geography, and ecology . . . are combined with a rich complexity that pleases the reader by its verisimilitude and imaginative scope." While

New York Times reviewer John Leonard admitted that *Dune* was not the first science fiction novel to create a self-consistent and logical alien world—Tolkien had already done so with his "Lord of the Rings" trilogy, as had Lewis in his tales of Narnia—he considered Herbert's work to be more ambitious than that of his predecessors. "Tolkien and C.S. Lewis, with their ready-made Christian moralizing to fall back on, are not in Mr. Herbert's inventive league," Leonard wrote. "For *Dune,* [Herbert] dreamed up several complete religions, and alien ecology and technology, entire histories and cultures and black arts."

Lending an additional air of believability to the novel is Herbert's detailed account of Arrakis's ecosystem; for instance, Foster cited the spice cycle as "one of the best examples of true scientific imagination in science fiction." *Dune* represented the first time a fiction writer had addressed these issues so effectively, and the result was dramatic. Gerald Jonas explained in the *New York Times Book Review:* "So completely did Mr. Herbert work out the interactions of man and beast and geography and climate that [*Dune*] became the standard for a new subgenre of 'ecological' science fiction." As popularity of *Dune* rose, Herbert embarked on a lecture tour of college campuses, explaining how the environmental concerns of Dune's inhabitants were analogous to our own. In this way, he has often been credited as contributing to the birth of America's environmental movement. *America*'s Willis E. McNelly saw Herbert's message in the *Dune* novels as: "We need to understand what we are doing to our own environment . . . because some of the things we've done may already be beyond redemption with disastrous consequences for the earth and for human life."

Dune was soon followed by 1970's *Dune Messiah* and 1976's *Children of Dune*. These novels continued the account of Paul-Muad'Dib's rise to power, his attempts to unify Arrakis's people and to control its harsh climate, and the destructive results that follow. Paul's failure illustrates a motif that appears throughout Herbert's fiction: the false, or flawed, messiah. He elaborated in *Critical Encounters: Dune* "began with a concept: to do a long novel about the messianic convulsions which periodically inflict themselves on human societies. I had this theory that superheroes were disastrous for humans, that even if you postulated an infallible hero, the things this hero set in motion fell eventually into the hands of fallible mortals. What better way to destroy a civilization, a society or a race than to set people into the wild oscillations which follow their turning over their judgement and decision-making faculties to a superhero?" Herbert further commented in *Dream Makers:* "The bottom line in the *Dune* [series] is: beware of heroes. [It is] much better to rely on your own judgement, and your own mistakes."

At the end of *Children of Dune,* Paul has been replaced by his son, Leto II, as ruler of Arrakis and the Galactic Empire to which it belongs. A powerful prescient, Leto has guided his people down the "Golden Path" that will ultimately lead to three millennia of peace; furthermore, he has merged his body with larval sandtrout, and as they develop he will be transformed over thousands of years into a giant half-human, half-sandworm—the ultimate fusion of man and environment. Though he had planned to close his "Dune Chronicles" here, Herbert returned to Arrakis with *God Emperor of Dune, Heretics of Dune,* and *Chapterhouse: Dune.* While these later novels take place long after the rule of Paul-Muad'Dib, they continue to explore the themes first introduced in *Dune.* Although many critics echoed Leonard's complaint that "Frank Herbert should never have written a sequel to *Dune,* much less [five] of them," it is only when viewing the completed series that the importance of Herbert's work can be understood. As a writer for the *West Coast Review of Books* pointed out: "It's inevitable that sequels to a book as important as *Dune* would generate considerable controversy. The subjectivity of readers, measuring each new volume against their memory of the original, prevents them from properly appreciating the overall complexity and beauty of the series."

Later, many reviewers did begin to recognize the significance of Herbert's "Dune Chronicles." "In a very strict and limited way," commented Joseph M. Lenz in *Coordinates,* "the *Dune* books can be called classics. . . . I mean that they are classical, reminiscent of and belonging to a literary tradition that originates with Rome and *The Aeneid.*" Jonas cited Herbert's refusal to treat the science fiction genre lightly as a source of the series' power and popularity. "The conspiratorial characters of *Dune* deal only with issues of transcendent importance—the fate of mankind, the possibility of free will, the existence of evil," he pointed out. "The strength of [Herbert's] series comes from its utter seriousness. There is not a trace of irony, not a whiff of self-mocking doubt." Jonas continued: "Whatever else the characters in Herbert's books have to worry about, none suffers from that common malady of our day: a sense of meaninglessness. Virtually every page in the trilogy contains a sentence that hints at the momentousness of the events being described."

Foster observed that, "with its emphasis on intrigue, consciousness, supernormal mental powers, and the functional meaning of abstractions such as peace," most of the "action" in the *Dune* series takes place on an intellectual level. The contemplative nature of Herbert's fiction makes it an ideal forum for many of Herbert's philosophical beliefs, and nowhere are those beliefs better represented than in the "Dune Chronicles." "Herbert's work is informed by an evolving body of concepts to which the *Dune* [series] holds the key," claimed Timothy O'Reilly in *Frank Herbert.* Herbert's work "shows the possibilities for good and evil of factors present, but unnoticed, in our culture. He gives his readers ideals and dreams, but not as an excuse for avoiding the realities of the present. . . . Most of all, he offers a chance to practice in fiction the lessons that are increasingly demanded by our lives: how to live with the pressure of changing times." O'Reilly concluded: "The end result of all this art is a novel packed with ideas that cannot easily be shaken from the mind, but which is never overburdened by their weight."

By infusing his fiction with philosophical and theological discussion, Herbert successfully transcended the limitations common to the science fiction genre. "Although *Dune* possesses a broad popular appeal which is often denied to the 'highbrow' novel, it reveals itself to formal literary analysis as a subtle, complex, and carefully crafted work of art," maintained John Ower in *Extrapolation.* "It thus constitutes an eloquent comment on the increasing maturity of science fiction as a form." O'Reilly, too, saw *Dune* as a step in the evolution of the genre. He wrote in *Critical Encounters:* "When [a science fiction novel] reaches the subconscious levels . . . , as *Dune* so clearly does, it goes beyond being even a cautionary fable and becomes, in Herbert's own words, a 'training manual for consciousness.'" Because of the tremendous success of the "Dune Chronicles," it has been the tendency of some reviewers to dismiss Herbert's other works of short and long fiction as inferior. However, these works often reveal to the reader a number of motifs only hinted at in the *Dune* books. Three such works are *The Dragon in the Sea, Destination: Void,* and *The White Plague. The Dragon in the Sea* is set in the foreseeable future, near the end of the next world war. Because the superpowers have fought for sixteen years, they have nearly depleted their supplies of natural resources, and must send submarine wolf packs to steal crude oil from ocean wells. The action and dialogue take place entirely within the confines of a four-man "subtug," the Fenian Ram, whose crew acts as a microcosmic representation of the dangerous and paranoid world above the waves; as the tension in the subtug increases, each crew member must adapt to his environment or be destroyed by it. "The subtug crew responds to these pressures with adaptations which are insane when judged by outside standards," Foster notes, adding that "as Captain Sparrow explains, 'I'm nuts in a way which fits me perfectly to my world. That makes my world nuts and me normal. Not sane. Normal. Adapted.'"

Many critics considered *The Dragon in the Sea* to be vastly underrated, for it succeeds as both an action novel and a psychological thriller. "It all works," according to Foster, "because the conceptual unfolding is matched step by step in the action of the plot. The ideas never interrupt the action; they are tightly woven into it." J. Frances McComas, writing in the *New York Times Book Review,* felt that Herbert's account of a future war "comes very close to matching—in suspense, action and psychic strain—any chronicle of real war." The drama played out within the cramped space of the Fenian Ram is the same one Paul Atreides is forced to play out in the deserts of Arrakis: adapt or die. "All of Herbert's books portray and test the human ability to consciously adapt," contended O'Reilly. "He sets his characters in the most stressful situations imaginable [because] there is no test so powerfully able to bring out latent adaptability as one in which the stakes are survival."

The concept of forced adaptation was also the basis for Herbert's 1967 novel, *Destination: Void.* In the future, scientists are desperate to develop artificial intelligence, or thinking machines. In order to bring about this breakthrough, a series of spaceships are launched, each manned by a four-man skeleton crew. Unbeknownst to the crew, the ship has been designed to fail halfway into their long journey; the only way to ensure survival is to somehow raise the ship's computer to a level of human consciousness before the ship's systems fail. Each of the four crew members is expert in a single discipline—psychology, biology, chemistry, and computer science—and approaches the problem through that discipline; however, each one also represents an aspect of humanity—intelligence, sensation, intuition, and religious devotion—the sum of which are secretly fed to the computer. The computer learns from both the crew's methods and their emotions, and eventually evolves to full consciousness. It repairs itself and delivers the crew to a habitable planet; salvation does not come cheap, however, for the ship demands that it be worshiped as a savior.

David M. Miller, writing in his book *Frank Herbert,* called *Destination: Void* "an essay rather than an entertainment [wherein] the 'hero' is really the idea, and the novel is a 'lab-report.'" Patricia S. Warrick expressed a similar view in *The Cybernetic Imagination in Science*

Fiction, though she stressed the point that the novel "never sacrifices plot to philosophical discussion; it is uniquely successful in dramatizing the issues rather than merely talking about them." Though Miller admitted that *Destination: Void* resembles *The Dragon in the Sea* and *Dune* in that it explores the concept of growth through forced adaptation, "the reader may discover that it reveals some facets of Herbert's vision more explicitly" than his previous novels. Warrick concluded: "[*Destination: Void*] is a unique literary accomplishment."

In 1982's *The White Plague,* Herbert yet again explored the ability of humans to overcome incredible changes in their environment. Described by Jonas as "a brilliant, brooding meditation on the war between man's tendencies toward self-destruction and his instinct for self preservation," the novel tells the story of a biologist, John O'Neill, who is driven mad by the death of his wife and children, victims of an Irish Republican Army bomb. Bent on revenge, he develops a DNA-based plague virus that affects only females; when his demands are ignored by the government O'Neill unleashes his creation, killing hundreds of thousands of women and girls. Their world in a shambles, scientists and governments must unite to protect the surviving women and find a cure for the plague.

Although *Los Angeles Times Book Review* contributor Mark Rose called *The White Plague* "engaging entertainment, intriguing, wholly believable and even important," fellow critic Craig Shaw Gardner found certain flaws, particularly in Herbert's choice of narrator. Gardner commented in *Washington Post Book World:* "By writing most of the novel from the point of view of a mad man incapable of feeling . . . Herbert robs the reader of the opportunity for empathy, and the book falls flat." Still, *Fantasy Newsletter*'s William Coyle maintained that "the basic situation is vintage Herbert: catastrophe averted or mitigated by man's willingness to discard traditional behavior patterns."

Though Herbert will largely be remembered as the author of *Dune,* he left behind a greater legacy than of his fiction. "The commercial success of *Dune* paved the way for large advances, bigger printings, best-seller status, and heavy subsidiary sales for many other writers," explained McNelly. "Every member of the [Science Fiction Writers of America] owes Frank Herbert and *Dune* considerable gratitude." Don D'Ammassa, writing in the *Science Fiction Chronicle,* agreed that *Dune* opened the door for many other writers, for it "introduced science fiction to readers outside the normal science fiction spectrum." He concluded: "[Herbert's] departure deprives us of one of the most significant voices in the field, as well as one of the more talented writers."

BIOGRAPHICAL AND CRITICAL SOURCES:

BOOKS

Aldiss, Brian W., *Billion Year Spree: The True History of Science Fiction,* Doubleday (New York, NY), 1973.

Berger, Harold L., *Science Fiction and the New Dark Age,* Popular Press, 1976.

Contemporary Literary Criticism, Thomson Gale (Detroit, MI), Volume 12, 1980, Volume 23,1983, Volume 35,1985, Volume 44, 1987, Volume 85, 1995.

Dictionary of Literary Biography, Volume 8: Twentieth Century Science Fiction Writers, Thomson Gale (Detroit, MI), 1981.

McNelly, Willis E., *The Dune Encyclopedia,* Putnam (New York, NY), 1984.

Miller, David M., *Frank Herbert,* Starmont House, 1980.

O'Reilly, Timothy, *Frank Herbert,* Ungar (New York, NY), 1981.

Platt, Charles, *Dream Makers: The Uncommon People Who Write Science Fiction,* Berkley Publishing (New York, NY), 1980.

Riley, Dick, editor, *Critical Encounters: Writers and Themes in Science Fiction,* Ungar (New York, NY), 1978.

Scholes, Robert, *Structural Fabulation: An Essay on Fiction of the Future,* University of Notre Dame Press, 1975.

Scholes, Robert, and Eric S. Rabkin, *Science Fiction: History, Science, Vision,* Oxford University Press (New York, NY), 1977.

Slusser, George E., Eric S. Rabkin, and Robert Scholes, editors, *Coordinates: Placing Science Fiction and Fantasy,* Southern Illinois University Press (Carbondale, IL), 1983.

Warrick, Patricia S., *The Cybernetic Imagination in Science Fiction,* Massachusetts Institute of Technology Press (Cambridge, MA), 1980.

Yoke, Carl B., and Donald M. Hassler, editors, *Death and the Serpent: Immortality in Science Fiction and Fantasy,* Greenwood Press (Westport, MA), 1985.

PERIODICALS

Amazing Stories, July, 1956.
America, June 10, 1972; June 26, 1976.
Analog, July, 1956; April, 1966; June, 1970; August, 1981; February, 1984; September, 1984; August, 1985.
Booklist, May 1, 1976; July, 2003, Whitney Scott, review of *Dune,* p. 1908.
Commonweal, September 7, 1984, p. 475.
English Journal, February, 1974; March, 1994, p. 94.
Extrapolation, December, 1971; May, 1974; December, 1974; May, 1976; winter, 1983, pp. 340-355.
Fantasy Newsletter, November, 1982, p. 32.
Future Life, number 14, 1979.
Galaxy, April, 1966; September, 1976; August, 1977.
Library Journal, March 1, 1998, R. Kent Rasmussen, review of *Dune,* p. 142; October 15, 1999, Michael Rogers, review of *Dune,* p. 112.
Los Angeles Times, August 31, 1984.
Los Angeles Times Book Review, September 29, 1982, p. 2; August 28, 1983, p. 4; May 5, 1985, p. 7.
Maclean's, May 21, 1984, p. 62.
Magazine of Fantasy and Science Fiction, March, 1966; April, 1969; May, 1971; February, 1977.
National Observer, May 23, 1977.
Newsweek, April 30, 1984, p. 73.
New Worlds, October, 1966.
New York Times, September 2, 1977; June 1, 1979; April 27, 1981.
New York Times Book Review, March 11, 1956; September 8, 1974; August 1, 1976; November 27, 1977; May 17, 1981, p. 15; September 26, 1983, p. 15; June 10, 1984, p. 24; June 16, 1985, p. 18.
Observer (London, England), October 3, 1976.
Psychology Today, August, 1974.
School Library Journal, March, 1973.
Science Fiction & Fantasy Book Review, September, 1983, p. 30.
Science Fiction Chronicle, June, 1985, p. 42.
Science Fiction Review, August, 1970; August, 1979; November, 1983.
Science Fiction Studies, July, 1981, pp. 149-155.
Spectator, August 26, 1978; January 12, 1980.
Time, March 29, 1971; December 17, 1984, Richard Corliss, review of *Dune,* p. 99.
Times (London, England), November 7, 1984.
Times Literary Supplement, January 14, 1977.
Tribune Books (Chicago, IL), June 14, 1981; April 22, 1984, p. 11; June 30, 1985, p. 24.
Washington Post, December 14, 1984.
Washington Post Book World, May 9, 1976; May 24, 1981, p. 8; August 29, 1982, p. 7; May 26, 1985, p. 11; October 27, 1985, p. 17.
West Coast Review of Books, July-August, 1985, p. 28.

OBITUARIES:

PERIODICALS

AB Bookman's Weekly, March 24, 1986.

Chicago Tribune, February 14, 1986.
Detroit Free Press, February 13, 1986.
Detroit News, February 12, 1986.
Extrapolation, winter, 1986, pp. 352-355.
Fantasy Review, February, 1986, p. 6.
Los Angeles Times, February 13, 1986.
Newsweek, February 24, 1986.
New York Times, February 13, 1986.
Publishers Weekly, February 28, 1986.
Science Fiction Chronicle, April, 1986, p. 24.
Time, February 24, 1986.
Washington Post, February 13, 1986.

*   *   *

HERBERT, Frank Patrick
See HERBERT, Frank

*   *   *

HERSEY, John 1914-1993
(John Richard Hersey)

PERSONAL: Born June 17, 1914, in Tientsin, China; died March 23, 1993, in Key West, FL; son of Roscoe Monroe (a Y.M.C.A. secretary in China) and Grace (a missionary; maiden name Baird) Hersey; married Frances Ann Cannon, April 27, 1940 (divorced, February, 1958); married Barbara Day Addams Kaufman, June 2, 1958; children: (first marriage) Martin, John, Ann, Baird; (second marriage) Brook (daughter). *Education:* Yale University, B.A., 1936; attended Clare College, Cambridge, 1936-37. *Politics:* Democrat *Hobbies and other interests:* Sailing, gardening, fishing, reading.

CAREER: Writer. Private secretary, driver, and factotum for Sinclair Lewis, summer, 1937; writer, editor, and correspondent, *Time* magazine, 1937-44, correspondent in China and Japan, 1939, covered South Pacific warfare, 1942, correspondent in Mediterranean theater, including Sicilian campaign, 1943, and in Moscow, 1944-45; editor and correspondent for *Life* magazine, 1944-45; writer for *New Yorker* and other magazines, 1945-93; made trip to China and Japan for *Life* and *New Yorker,* 1945-46; fellow, Berkeley College, Yale University, 1950-65; master, Pierson College, Yale University, 1965-70, fellow, 1965-93; writer-in-residence, American Academy in Rome, 1970-71; lecturer, Yale University, 1971-75, professor, 1975-84, professor emeritus, 1984-93. Chair, Connecticut Volunteers for Stevenson, 1952; member of Adlai Stevenson's campaign staff, 1956. Editor and director of writers' co-operative magazine,

'47. Member of Westport (CT) School Study Council, 1945-50, of Westport Board of Education, 1950-52, of Yale University Council Committee on the Humanities, 1951-56, of Fairfield (CT) Citizens School Study Council, 1952-56, of National Citizens' Commission for the Public Schools, 1954-56; consultant, Fund for the Advancement of Education, 1954-56; chair, Connecticut Committee for the Gifted, 1954-57; member of Board of Trustees, Putney School, 1953-56; delegate to White House Conference on Education, 1955; trustee, National Citizens' Council for the Public Schools, 1956-58; member, visiting committee, Harvard Graduate School of Education, 1960-65; member, Loeb Theater Center, 1980-93; Yale University Council Committee on Yale College, member, 1959-61, chair, 1964-69; trustee, National Committee for Support of the Public Schools, 1962-68.

MEMBER: National Institute of Arts and Letters, American Academy of Arts and Letters (secretary, 1961-78, chancellor, 1981-84), American Academy of Arts and Sciences, Authors League of America (member of council, 1946-70, 1975-93, vice president, 1949-55, president, 1975-80), Authors Guild (member of council, 1946-93), PEN.

AWARDS, HONORS: Pulitzer Prize, 1945, for *A Bell for Adano;* Anisfield-Wolf Award, 1950, for *The Wall;* Daroff Memorial Fiction Award, Jewish Book Council of America, 1950, for *The Wall;* Sidney Hillman Foundation Award, 1951, for *The Wall;* Howland Medal, Yale University, 1952; National Association of Independent Schools Award, 1957, for *A Single Pebble;* Tuition Plan Award, 1961; Sarah Josepha Hale Award, 1963; named honorary fellow of Clare College, Cambridge University, 1967. Honorary degrees: M.A., Yale University, 1947; L.H.D., New School for Social Research, 1950, Syracuse University, 1983; LL.D., Washington and Jefferson College, 1950; D.H.L., Dropsie College, 1950; Litt.D., Wesleyan University, 1954, Bridgeport University, 1959, Clarkson College of Technology, 1972, University of New Haven, 1975, Yale University, 1984, Monmouth College, 1985, William and Mary College, 1987, Albertus Magnus College, 1988.

WRITINGS:

Men on Bataan, Knopf (New York, NY), 1942.
Into the Valley: A Skirmish of the Marines, Knopf (New York, NY), 1943, published as *Into the Valley: Marines at Guadalcanal,* University of Nebraska Press (Lincoln, NE), 2002.

Hiroshima (first published in *New Yorker,* August 31, 1946), Knopf (New York, NY), 1946, school edition, Oxford Book Co., 1948.

Here to Stay: Studies on Human Tenacity, Hamish Hamilton (London, England), 1962, Knopf (New York, NY), 1963.

The Algiers Motel Incident, Knopf (New York, NY), 1968, with an introduction by Thomas J. Sprague, Johns Hopkins University Press (Baltimore, MD), 1997.

(With others) *Robert Capa,* Paragraphic, 1969.

Letter to the Alumni, Knopf (New York, NY), 1970.

(Editor) *Ralph Ellison: A Collection of Critical Essays,* Prentice-Hall (Englewood Cliffs, NJ), 1973.

(Editor) *The Writer's Craft,* Knopf (New York, NY), 1974.

The President, Knopf (New York, NY), 1975.

Aspects of the Presidency: Truman and Ford in Office, Ticknor & Fields, 1980.

Blues, Knopf (New York, NY), 1987.

(Author of commentary) John Armour and Peter Wright, *Manzanar,* Times, 1988.

Life Sketches, Knopf (New York, NY), 1989.

Key West Tales (stories), Knopf (New York, NY), 1994.

Also author of *Fling and Other Stories,* 1990. Author of introduction to *Let Us Now Praise Famous Men,* by Walker Evans, Houghton Mifflin (New York, NY).

NOVELS

A Bell for Adano, Knopf (New York, NY), 1944, with new foreword by Hersey, Modern Library (New York, NY), 1946.

The Wall, Knopf (New York, NY), 1950.

The Marmot Drive, Knopf (New York, NY), 1953.

A Single Pebble, Knopf (New York, NY), 1956.

The War Lover, Knopf (New York, NY), 1959.

The Child Buyer, Knopf (New York, NY), 1960.

White Lotus, Knopf (New York, NY), 1965.

Too Far to Walk, Knopf (New York, NY), 1966.

Under the Eye of the Storm, Knopf (New York, NY), 1967.

The Conspiracy, Knopf (New York, NY), 1972.

My Petition for More Space, Knopf (New York, NY), 1974.

The Walnut Door, Knopf (New York, NY), 1977.

The Call: An American Missionary in China, Knopf (New York, NY), 1985.

Antonietta, Knopf (New York, NY), 1991.

ADAPTATIONS: A Bell for Adano was adapted as a stage play by Paul Osborn and first produced at the Cort Theater, New York, 1944, and filmed by Twentieth Century-Fox, 1945; *The Wall* was dramatized by Millard Lampell and first produced at the Billy Rose Theater, New York, 1960, and filmed for television by Columbia Broadcasting System, 1982; *The War Lover* was filmed by Columbia Pictures, 1962; *The Child Buyer* was adapted as a stage play by Paul Shyre and first produced at the University of Michigan Professional Theater Program, Ann Arbor, 1964.

SIDELIGHTS: In his article "The Novel of Contemporary History" published in the *Atlantic* in 1949, John Hersey stated: "Fiction is a clarifying agent. It makes truth plausible. Who had even a tenable theory about the Soviet purge trials until he had read Koestler's *Darkness at Noon?* Who understood the impact of Italian Fascism upon peasants, on the one hand, and upon thinking men, on the other, until he had read Silone's *Fontamara* and *Bread and Wine?* What is argued here is only this much: among all the means of communication now available, imaginative literature comes closer than any other to being able to give an impression of the truth."

This use of imaginative literature to present historical truth was one of Hersey's major concerns. His Pulitzer Prize-winning novel *A Bell for Adano* is set in an Italian village occupied by American troops during World War II; *The Wall* is set in the Jewish ghetto in Warsaw at the close of that war; and Hersey's nonfictional work *Hiroshima* uses fictional techniques to present its story of Japanese atom bomb survivors. "Hersey [has] dedicated himself to the goal of chronicling the events and issues of his time," Sam B. Girgus noted in the *Dictionary of Literary Biography.*

"Hersey is an impressive figure in contemporary American letters," wrote Nancy L. Huse in her study *The Survival Tales of John Hersey.* Huse finds in Hersey's work "a mind rebelling at the age's acceptance of nuclear weapons, the Holocaust, racism, and the annihilation of the individual in a technological society." This attitude "places Hersey as an intellectual contemporary of Bellow, Wright, Mailer and Agee," Huse argued. Similarly, Eva Hoffman, writing in the *New York Times,* noted that "it has been John Hersey's virtue as teacher and public figure . . . that, against all odds and the grain of the times, he has sustained the idea of writing as a moral mission." Jonathan Yardley, writing in the *Washington Post Book World,* found that "Hersey's decency is both transparent and transcendent. He cares about matters that deserve to be cared about, and he writes about them with palpable passion."

Although best known for his novels, Hersey was also an accomplished writer of short stories. He completed his final collection of stories, *Key West Tales,* shortly before his death in 1993. The collection, noted Alan Ryan in the *Washington Post Book World,* "confirms once again his mastery of the [short story] form." The fifteen stories are divided into two camps: seven are conventional stories dealing mostly with life in contemporary Key West, Florida; the other eight are short, italicized vignettes presenting Key West's history from the early 1800s to the 1950s. The contemporary stories cover such subjects as an English professor's battle with AIDS, a Cuban woman's first love, and a meeting between a young man and his mother, who gave him up for adoption when he was an infant. The historical vignettes, on the other hand, feature appearances by such famous residents of Key West as Ernest Hemingway, John James Audubon, and Harry S Truman. Reviewers praised Hersey's final effort for its lucid prose and wryly drawn characters. Writing in *World Literature Today,* Ronald Curran remarked that "One after the other, the cards in Hersey's Key West poker game amuse and delight." Likewise, Ryan commented that *Key West Tales* "has all the marks of a master who knows what readers want: a good story; characters who, but for the grace of God, might be us; and writing as bright and clear as ice." "This is the last of [Hersey's] work," concluded George Garrett in the *New York Times Book Review,* "and we can be sad about that, but still able to rejoice in the final bright gift he has given us."

BIOGRAPHICAL AND CRITICAL SOURCES:

BOOKS

Contemporary Literary Criticism, Thomson Gale (Detroit, MI), Volume 1, 1973, Volume 2, 1974, Volume 7, 1977, Volume 9, 1978, Volume 40, 1986, Volume 81, 1994.

Dictionary of Literary Biography, Volume 6: *American Novelists since World War II,* Thomson Gale (Detroit, MI), 1980.

Huse, Nancy Lyman, *John Hersey and James Agee: A Reference Guide,* G.K. Hall (New York, NY), 1978.

Huse, Nancy Lyman, *The Survival Tales of John Hersey,* Whitston, 1983.

Sanders, David, *John Hersey,* Twayne (Boston, MA), 1967.

Sanders, David, *John Hersey Revisited,* Twayne (Boston, MA), 1991.

PERIODICALS

Atlantic, November, 1949; April, 1966.
Book Week, September 26, 1965.

Commonweal, March 5, 1965.
Detroit Free Press, March 25, 1993, p. 6B.
Facts on File, April 1, 1993.
Life, March 18, 1966.
National Observer, February 8, 1965.
Newsweek, January 25, 1965; June 7, 1965.
New York Herald Tribune Book Review, August 29, 1946; March 5, 1950; August 20, 1950; June 3, 1956; September 25, 1960.
New York Times, April 22, 1985; March 25, 1993.
New York Times Book Review, February 6, 1944; February 26, 1950; June 10, 1956; September 25, 1960; January 19, 1965; February 28, 1966; May 10, 1987; May 19, 1991; February 13, 1994, p. 22.
Publishers Weekly, May 10, 1985.
Saturday Review, November 2, 1946; March 4, 1950; June 2, 1956; January 23, 1965.
Time, June 4, 1956; January 29, 1965; March 25, 1966.
Times Literary Supplement, December 7, 1946.
Tribune Books (Chicago, IL), March 13, 1994, p. 3.
Washington Post Book World, October 16, 1977; August 7, 1994, p. 6.
World Literature Today, autumn, 1994, p. 812.
Yale Review, winter, 1987.

OBITUARIES:

PERIODICALS

Detroit Free Press, March 25, 1993, p. 6B.

*   *   *

HERSEY, John Richard
See HERSEY, John

*   *   *

HIAASEN, Carl 1953-

PERSONAL: Born March 12, 1953, in Fort Lauderdale, FL; son of K. Odel (a lawyer) and Patricia (Moran) Hiaasen; married Constance Lyford (a registered nurse and attorney), November 12, 1970 (divorced, 1996); married, 1999; wife's name Fenia; children: (first marriage) Scott Andrew; (second marriage) Quinn. *Education:* Attended Emory University, 1970-72; University of Florida, B.S., 1974.

ADDRESSES: Office—Miami Herald, 1 Herald Plaza, Miami, FL 33101. *Agent*—Esther Newberg, International Creative Management, 40 West 57th St., New York, NY 10019.

CAREER: Writer. *Cocoa Today,* Cocoa, FL, reporter, 1974-76; *Miami Herald,* Miami, FL, reporter, 1976—, columnist, 1985—. Professor at Barry College, 1978-79.

MEMBER: Authors Guild, Authors League of America.

AWARDS, HONORS: National Headliners Award, distinguished service medallion from Sigma Delta Chi, public service first-place award from Florida Society of Newspaper Editors, Clarion Award, Women in Communications, Heywood Broun Award, Newspaper Guild, and finalist for Pulitzer Prize in public-service reporting, all 1980, all for newspaper series about dangerous doctors; Green Eyeshade Award from Sigma Delta Chi, first-place award for in-depth reporting, Florida Society of Newspaper Editors, grand prize for investigative reporting, Investigative Reporters and Editors, and finalist for Pulitzer Prize in special local reporting, all 1981, all for newspaper series on drug-smuggling industry in Key West; Silver Gavel Award, American Bar Association, 1982; Newbery honor book, American Library Association, 2003, and Rebecca Caudill Young Readers' Book Award, 2005, both for *Hoot;* Damon Runyon Award, 2003-2004.

WRITINGS:

NOVELS

(With William D. Montalbano) *Powder Burn,* Atheneum (New York, NY), 1981.
(With William D. Montalbano) *Trap Line,* Atheneum (New York, NY), 1982.
(With William D. Montalbano) *A Death in China,* Atheneum (New York, NY), 1984.
Tourist Season, Putnam (New York, NY), 1986.
Double Whammy, Putnam (New York, NY), 1987.
Skin Tight, Putnam (New York, NY), 1989.
Native Tongue, Knopf (New York, NY), 1991.
Strip Tease, Knopf (New York, NY), 1993.
Stormy Weather, Knopf (New York, NY), 1995.
Naked Came the Manatee, Putnam (New York, NY), 1996.
Lucky You, Knopf (New York, NY), 1997.
Sick Puppy, Knopf (New York, NY), 2000.
Basket Case, Knopf (New York, NY), 2002.
Hoot, Knopf (New York, NY), 2002.
Skinny Dip, Knopf (New York, NY), 2004.

OTHER

Team Rodent: How Disney Devours the World (nonfiction), Ballantine (New York, NY), 1998.
Kick Ass: Selected Columns of Carl Hiaasen, University Press of Florida (Gainesville, FL), 1999.
Paradise Screwed: Selected Columns of Carl Hiaasen, Putnam (New York, NY), 2001.

Also contributor to magazines and newspapers, including *Rolling Stone, Penthouse, Us, Playboy,* and *Esquire.*

ADAPTATIONS: Strip Tease was adapted as a motion picture, written and directed by Andrew Bergman, starring Demi Moore and Armand Assante, Castle Rock Entertainment, 1996.

SIDELIGHTS: As an award-winning investigative reporter for the *Miami Herald,* Carl Hiaasen has written about dangerous doctors, drug smuggling, and other serious crimes. His fictional works reflect his exposure to—and outrage over—Florida's social ills. A native of South Florida, Hiaasen has turned his righteous indignation into humorous satire in which heroes and villains alike exhibit farcical quirks and an attachment to creative forms of violence. The good guys are often eco-terrorists seeking to preserve the ever-dwindling plots of undeveloped land; the bad guys wallow in greed as they pursue the rape of the state. According to Joe Queenan in the *New York Times Book Review,* Hiaasen "has made a persuasive case that the most barbaric, ignorant and just plain awful people living in this country today reside, nay flourish, in the state of Florida." Desmond Ryan cited Hiaasen in the *Philadelphia Inquirer* for "his customary pungency, wit and flair," adding that the novelist "has a way of leaving the reprobates and sleazebags that infest the land of the hanging chad flattened like roadkill."

The son of an attorney, Hiaasen grew up with dual interests. He wanted to be a writer, but he also enjoyed the outdoors and especially savored Florida's unspoiled wilderness areas. He graduated from the University of Florida in 1974, and by 1976 had earned a position with the *Miami Herald* as a reporter. He soon became a member of the *Herald*'s investigative team, and he continues to write two columns a week that take aim at corruption in every level of government and business. Hiaasen began his fiction-writing career with coauthor William D. Montalbano and then struck out on his own with novels that "turn . . . journalistic experience to fictional advantage," in the words of *New York Times Book Review* contributor Herbert Mitgang. As Polly Paddock put it in the *Charlotte Observer,* "Underneath all Hiaasen's hijinks, there is the righteous indignation that marks both his journalistic and novelistic work. Hiaasen hates hypocrisy, pretension, corporate greed, political corruption and the rape of the environment. He won't let us forget that."

Tourist Season, a tongue-in-cheek account of terrorists who bully Miami tourists in order to depress the tourism industry, received considerable acclaim. *Chicago Tribune Book World* columnist Alice Cromie called the thriller "one of the most exciting novels of the season." Tony Hillerman noted in the *New York Times Book Review* that *Tourist Season* "is full of . . . quick, efficient, understated little sketches of the sort of subtle truth that leaves you grinning. In fact, Mr. Hiaasen leaves you grinning a lot." Regarding the book, Hiaasen once commented that "for inspiration, all I had to do was read the daily newspaper. Crime in Miami is so bizarre that no novelist's inventions could surpass true life."

In *Double Whammy* Hiaasen "comes up with a suitably manic plot, this time involving skullduggery on the bass-fishing circuit," said Kevin Moore in the *Chicago Tribune Book World.* R.J. Decker, a news photographer turned private eye, tangles with a host of bizarre characters, including a former governor of Florida who lives on roadkill and a murderer with the head of a pit bull attached to his arm. "The writing style is macabre-funny," noted Walter Walker in the *New York Times Book Review,* "and it delivers the plot's myriad twists and turns with breathtaking speed."

Greedy plastic surgeons, sensationalistic television personalities, and money-grubbing lawyers are the targets of *Skin Tight,* another fast-paced mix of satire and thriller. The hero, Mick Stranahan, a former Florida state investigator, is threatened by an old feud with a corrupt plastic surgeon suspected of murder. In self-defense, Stranahan keeps a trained barracuda under his stilt house. In one incident the barracuda eats the hand of a hit man trying to murder Stranahan, but the hit man gets a weed trimmer as a prosthesis—and then comes after Stranahan again. In the *New York Times Book Review,* Katherine Dunn observed that while the author's tone in *Skin Tight* holds no warmth towards its subjects (unlike *Tourist Season*) it is still fascinating and impressive. She added, "No one has ever designed funnier, more terrifying bad guys, or concocted odder ways of doing away with them."

Hiaasen's next novel, *Native Tongue,* garnered similar praise. The story is "a skillful, timely satire—a weird, wild, comic caper of ecological guerrilla warfare that bites as often as it laughs," wrote Richard Martins in the *Chicago Tribune Book World.* In the book, the fragile ecology of the Florida Keys is exploited and damaged by theme-park developers and environmental activists alike. According to Jack Viertel, writing in the *Los Angeles Times Book Review,* Hiaasen "might be termed a South Florida hybrid of Jonathan Swift, Randy Newman, and Elmore Leonard. . . . His novels are shot through with a kind of real passion that lurks beneath the manic prose—an urgent affection for his subject." Viertel concluded, "The ultimate enemy is always the same: overdevelopment of the last remaining wilderness in the state."

Strip Tease features a genuine heroine, Erin Grant, who resorts to nude dancing so that she can continue to finance the fight for custody of her daughter. Grant's ex-husband, the wheelchair-stealing Darrell, is one of the novel's many villains; others include a state congressman beholden to Florida's powerful sugar-growers. Writing in the *Times Literary Supplement,* Karl Miller remarked, "Hiaasen is against graft, exploitation, and the destruction of the environment. This is an ecologically green black comedy, in which men are scum and it is 'women's work,' according to Erin, to destroy them." In 1996 the novel was released as a motion picture starring Demi Moore.

In *Stormy Weather* Hiaasen uses the aftermath of a devastating hurricane to once again skewer the greedy and corrupt in South Florida. Characters include Edie Marsh, a con woman who has tried in vain to blackmail the Kennedys but who recognizes a new opportunity for enrichment when the hurricane blows through; an advertising executive who ends his honeymoon at Disneyland to venture to Miami to videotape the storm's damage; and a recurring Hiaasen bit player, the one-eyed former governor of Florida who now lives in the swamp, sustaining himself with roadkill. Chicago *Tribune Books* reviewer Gary Dretzka noted, "Hiaasen writes with the authority of a documentary filmmaker. . . . He displays no mercy for anyone perceived as being responsible for defiling his home environment." Calling *Stormy Weather* "caustic and comic," *Time* critic John Skow explained the author's use of villains in his literary formula: "turn over a rock and watch in glee and honest admiration as those little rascals squirm in the light."

An eco-terrorist with an anger-management problem serves as the hero in *Sick Puppy.* After seeking revenge on a litterbug, Twilly Spree discovers that the target of his revenge is also a big-time lobbyist involved in expediting the illegal sale of an untouched barrier island. Twilly kidnaps the man's dog and wife in the hope of using them as leverage to save the island. In the meantime, the lobbyist enlists the help of an unscrupulous developer and his sadistic sidekick to put an end to Twilly. A *Publishers Weekly* reviewer deemed the book "a devilishly funny caper" in which Hiaasen "shows himself to be a comic writer at the peak of his powers." Bill Ott observed in *Booklist* that "Hiaasen's brand of apocalyptic surrealism is nothing if not distinctive."

The publication of *Basket Case* marked a departure for Hiaasen. The novel is narrated in the first person by a principled journalist named Jack Tagger, and among the villains is the newspaper industry itself. Still, characteristic Hiaasen humor reigns. Tagger, an obituary writer, investigates the suspicious death of a former rock star, the lead singer of Jimmy and the Slut Puppies. Jimmy's silly lyrics are offered for the reader's perusal alongside Tagger's obsession with death and with the decline of serious reportage in newspapers. Ott in *Booklist* applauded Hiaasen for venturing beyond "his unique brand of apocalyptic surrealism" to produce "a rip-roaringly entertaining tale." *Orlando Sentinel* reviewer William McKeen declared that *Basket Case* "is what loyal readers have come to expect from the guy—an intelligent, funny, deeply moral book about the decline of Western Civilization." McKeen was particularly delighted with Tagger, declaring him "probably one of Hiaasen's most endearing fictional characters." In the *Fort Worth Star-Telegram,* Jeff Guinn concluded that *Basket Case* "proves two things about . . . Hiaasen: He was brave enough to venture beyond the sarcastic humor/ ecological themes that characterized his first eight novels, and he is a huge writing talent whose finest fiction may be yet to come."

In *Hoot* Hiaasen keep his characters dedicated to a higher cause, but this time Hiaasen's audience includes younger readers as he focuses on protagonists who are children. "My stepson, nephews and nieces are always bugging me about reading one of my books," the author was quoted as saying in *Book.* "Obviously, some of the language and adult situations went out the window, but I created the same sensibilities in my kid characters that my adult ones walk around with." *Hoot* tells the story of Roy Eberhardt, a middle-school student who moves into Coconut Cove with his family and tries to adjust to life in South Florida. Before long, he is dealing with a bully, a mysterious boy called Mullet Fingers, and a protest to stop a construction project that threatens the habitat of owls. Writing in the *School Library Journal,* Miranda Doyle found the novel "Entertaining but ulti-

mately not very memorable," while a *Publishers Weekly* contributor predicted that "Characteristically quirky characters and comic twists will surely gain the author new fans." Bill Ott, writing in *Booklist,* praised Hiaasen for letting "his inner kid run rampant" and added that the book "is full of offbeat humor, buffoonish yet charming supporting characters, and genuinely touching scene of children enjoying the wildness of nature."

For his novel *Skinny Dip,* Hiaasen once again writes for adults as he tells the tale of Chaz Perrone, an incompetent and greedy marine scientist who is helping a tycoon to illegally dump fertilizer into the Everglades. Perrone attempts to kill his wife, Joey, after she finds out about his illegal doings. But Joey survives and with the help of former cop Mick Stranahan begins to haunt and taunt her husband, in a comic romp that has its roots in the current events of the Sunshine State.

In addition to novels, Hiaasen has also published several volumes of his collected columns, as well as *Team Rodent: How Disney Devours the World,* a scathing critique of the Walt Disney Corporation. *Atlanta Journal-Constitution* writer Mike Williams observed that in his nonfiction, "Hiaasen wastes no time. He sets his tone to rapid-fire acerbic, squeezes off a few rounds to clear his muzzle, then goes on full automatic, like Rambo taking on the world." In the *Sarasota Herald Tribune* David Grimes remarked that "Reading a collection of Carl Hiaasen's newspaper columns reveals a frightening truth about his loopy novels: They're not that big an exaggeration." *Southern Cultures* reviewer David Zucchino maintained that when "Hiaasen opens fire . . . he is pitiless. He savages the men and institutions he believes are turning his beloved Miami and South Florida into a crass, violent, drug-soaked strip mall." A *Publishers Weekly* critic felt that Hiaasen "writes with an old-time columnist's sense of righteous rage and an utterly current and biting wit."

As to the aims Hiaasen holds for his fiction, the author once told *People* magazine: "All I ever ask of my main characters is that their hearts are in the right place, that when they step over the law it's for a higher cause." Discussing why he became an author, Hiassen told a contributor to the *Writer,* that he "enjoyed writing and getting a reaction" when he was very young. He added: "I think it's some sort of extension of being a class clown—that if you could write something and make somebody laugh, it was a good gig to have. I think there was an element of psychotherapy—it was a legal outlet for some of the ideas I was wanting to express as a kid."

BIOGRAPHICAL AND CRITICAL SOURCES:

PERIODICALS

Atlanta Journal-Constitution, June 14, 1998, Mike Williams, "Hiaasen Tackles 'Rodent' That Ate Florida," p. L11; January 2, 2000, Phil Kloer, "Hiaasen's 'Sick' Tale a Fun Ride," p. K12.

Book, September-October, 2002, "Kidding Around: Youth-Oriented Books by Adult Authors," p. 66.

Booklist, November 1, 1999, Bill Ott, review of *Sick Puppy,* p. 483; May 1, 2001, Bill Ott, "Hiaasen's People," p. 1704; September 15, 2001, David Pitt, review of *Paradise Screwed: Selected Columns of Carl Hiaasen,* p. 184; November 1, 2001, Bill Ott, review of *Basket Case,* p. 444; October 15, 2002, Bill Ott, review of *Hoot,* p. 405.

Charlotte Observer, January 16, 2002, Polly Paddock, review of *Basket Case.*

Chicago Tribune, January 23, 2002, Patrick T. Reardon, review of *Basket Case.*

Chicago Tribune Book World, March 16, 1986; January 31, 1988; September 10, 1989.

Detroit Free Press, May 4, 1986.

Entertainment Weekly, January 18, 2002, Bruce Fretts, "Sunny Delight," p. 72.

Fort Worth Star-Telegram, January 9, 2002, Jeff Guinn, review of *Basket Case.*

Gentleman's Quarterly, June, 1996, p. 92.

Globe and Mail (Toronto, Ontario, Canada), April 26, 1986.

Houston Chronicle, January 16, 2000, Jim Barlow, "Carl Hiaasen: The Kinky Friedman of Thriller Writers," p. 17.

Library Journal, June 15, 1981; March 15, 1986.

Los Angeles Times Book Review, April 29, 1984; October 13, 1991.

Maclean's, October 16, 1995, p. 79; January 17, 2002, Paula Friedman, review of *Basket Case,* p. 2.

New York Times, June 14, 1998, Deborah Stead, review of *Team Rodent: How Disney Devours the World,* p. B9; January 6, 2000, Christopher Lehmann-Haupt, "Lots of Bad-Natured Floridians and One Good-Natured Dog," p. B10; January 3, 2002, Janet Maslin, "An Obit Writer's Renewed Zest for Life," p. B13.

New York Times Book Review, January 10, 1982; February 13, 1983; June 24, 1984; March 16, 1986; March 6, 1988; October 15, 1989; September 3, 1995, p. 15; January 9, 2000, Joe Queenan, "Everything Is Rotten in the State of Florida," p. 10; March 25, 2001, Scott Veale, review of *Sick Puppy,* p. 28.

Orlando Sentinel, September 20, 1981; January 16, 2002, William McKeen, review of *Basket Case.*

People, May 15, 2000, Christina Cheakalos, "Hurricane Hiaasen," p. 139.

Philadelphia Inquirer, January 16, 2002, Desmond Ryan, review of *Basket Case.*

Playboy, October, 1995, p. 34.

Publishers Weekly, August 16, 1993; July 10, 1995, p. 44; October 25, 1999, review of *Kick Ass: Selected Columns of Carl Hiaasen,* p. 61; November 8, 1999, review of *Sick Puppy,* p. 49; November 12, 2001, review of *Basket Case,* p. 36; June 24, 2002, review of *Hoot,* p. 58.

Sarasota Herald Tribune, September 2, 2001, David Grimes, "More Florida Bad Guys in Carl Hiaasen Collection," p. E5.

School Library Journal, Miranda Doyle, review of *Hoot,* p. 188.

Southern Cultures, fall, 2000, David Zucchino, review of *Kick Ass,* p. 73.

Time, August 14, 1995, John Skow, review of *Stormy Weather,* p. 70.

Times Literary Supplement, November 5, 1993, p. 12; March 29, 1996, p. 14.

Tribune Books (Chicago, IL), September 1, 1991; July 10, 1994, p. 8; August 13, 1995, p. 5.

Vanity Fair, August, 1993.

Variety, July 13, 1998, Andrew Paxman, review of *Team Rodent,* p. 6.

Washington Post Book World, May 6, 1984; April 6, 1986.

Writer, June, 2003, "Carl Hiaasen (How I Write)," p. 66.

ONLINE

BookPage, http://www.bookpage.com/ (January 27, 2002), Jay Lee MacDonald, "Carl Hiaasen Takes a Bite out of Crimes against the Environment."

Carl Hiaasen's Home Page, http://www.carlhiaasen.com/ (April 7, 2004).

*   *   *

HIGHSMITH, Mary Patricia
See HIGHSMITH, Patricia

*   *   *

HIGHSMITH, Patricia 1921-1995
(Mary Patricia Highsmith, Claire Morgan)

PERSONAL: Born January 19, 1921, in Fort Worth, TX; died February 4, 1995, in Locarno, Switzerland; daughter of Jay Bernard Plangman and Mary (Coates)

Highsmith. *Education:* Barnard College, B.A., 1942. *Hobbies and other interests:* Drawing, painting, carpentering, snail watching, traveling by train.

CAREER: Writer, 1942-95.

MEMBER: Detection Club.

AWARDS, HONORS: Mystery Writers of America Scroll and Grand Prix de Litterature Policiere, both 1957, both for *The Talented Mr. Ripley;* Silver Dagger Award for best crime novel of the year, Crime Writers Association of England, 1964, for *The Two Faces of January;* Officer l'Ordre des Arts es des Lettres, 1990.

WRITINGS:

NOVELS

Strangers on a Train (also see below), Harper (New York, NY), 1950, reprinted, Norton (New York, NY), 2001.

(Under pseudonym Claire Morgan) *The Price of Salt,* Coward-McCann (New York, NY), 1952, published under name Patricia Highsmith as *Carol,* new afterword by Highsmith, Naiad Press (Tallahassee, FL), 1984.

The Blunderer (also see below), Coward-McCann (New York, NY), 1954, published as *Lament for a Lover,* Popular Library (New York, NY), 1956, reprinted under original title, Hamlyn (London, England), 1978, reprinted, Norton (New York, NY), 2001.

The Talented Mr. Ripley (also see below), Coward-McCann (New York, NY), 1955, reprinted, Norton (New York, NY), 2000.

Deep Water, Harper (New York, NY), 1957, reprinted, Norton (New York, NY), 2004.

A Game for the Living, Harper (New York, NY), 1958.

This Sweet Sickness (also see below), Harper (New York, NY), 1960, reprinted, Norton (New York, NY), 2002.

The Cry of the Owl, Harper (New York, NY), 1962.

The Two Faces of January, Doubleday (New York, NY), 1964.

The Glass Cell, Doubleday (New York, NY), 1964, reprinted, Norton (New York, NY), 2004.

The Story-Teller, Doubleday (New York, NY), 1965, published as *A Suspension of Mercy,* Heinemann (London, England), 1965, Norton (New York, NY), 2001.

Those Who Walk Away, Doubleday (New York, NY), 1967.

The Tremor of Forgery, Doubleday (New York, NY), 1969.

Ripley under Ground (also see below), Doubleday (New York, NY), 1970, reprinted, Norton (New York, NY), 1992.

A Dog's Ransom, Knopf (New York, NY), 1972.

Ripley's Game (also see below), Knopf (New York, NY), 1974, reprinted, Norton (New York, NY), 1993.

Edith's Diary, Simon & Schuster (New York, NY), 1977.

The Boy Who Followed Ripley, Crowell (New York, NY), 1980, reprinted, Norton (New York, NY), 1995.

People Who Knock on the Door, Heinemann (London, England), 1983, Mysterious Press (New York, NY), 1985, reprinted, Norton (New York, NY), 2001.

The Mysterious Mr. Ripley (contains *The Talented Mr. Ripley, Ripley under Ground,* and *Ripley's Game*), Penguin (New York, NY), 1985, reprinted, Norton (New York, NY), 1999.

Found in the Street, Heinemann (London, England), 1986, Atlantic Monthly Press (New York, NY), 1987.

Ripley under Water, Knopf (New York, NY), 1991.

Small G: A Summer Idyll, Bloomsbury (London, England), 1995.

SHORT STORIES

(With Doris Sanders) *Miranda the Panda Is on the Veranda* (juvenile), Coward-McCann (New York, NY), 1958.

The Snail-Watcher, and Other Stories, Doubleday (New York, NY), 1970, published as *Eleven: Short Stories,* Heinemann (London, England), 1970.

Little Tales of Misogyny (in German), Diogenes Verlag (Zurich, Switzerland), 1974, English-language edition, Heinemann (London, England), 1977, Mysterious Press (New York, NY), 1987, reprinted, Norton (New York, NY), 2002.

The Animal-Lover's Book of Beastly Murder (young adult), Heinemann (London, England), 1975, reprinted, Norton (New York, NY), 2002.

Slowly, Slowly in the Wind, Heinemann (London, England), 1979, Mysterious Press (New York, NY), 1987.

The Black House, David & Charles (New York, NY), 1979, published as *The Black House, and Other Stories,* Heinemann (London, England), 1981.

Mermaids on the Golf Course, and Other Stories, Heinemann (London, England), 1985, Mysterious Press (New York, NY), 1988, reprinted, Norton (New York, NY), 2003.

The Selected Stories of Patricia Highsmith, Norton (New York, NY), 2001.

Nothing That Meets the Eye: The Uncollected Stories of Patricia Highsmith, Norton (New York, NY), 2002.

OTHER

Plotting and Writing Suspense Fiction, Writers Inc. (Cincinnati, OH), 1966, enlarged and revised edition, St. Martin's Press (New York, NY), 1981.

Tales of Natural and Unnatural Catastrophes, Heinemann (London, England), 1987, Atlantic Monthly Press (Boston, MA), 1989.

Also author of material for television, including series *Alfred Hitchcock Presents.*

ADAPTATIONS: Strangers on a Train was adapted as a film, directed by Alfred Hitchcock, produced by Warner Bros., 1951, and also served as the basis for *Once You Kiss a Stranger,* Warner Bros., 1969; *The Talented Mr. Ripley* was filmed as *Purple Noon* by Times Film Corp., 1961 and under its own title, 1999; *The Blunderer* was filmed as *Le meurtrier,* 1963, and as *Enough Rope,* by Artixo Productions, 1966; *This Sweet Sickness* inspired the French film *Tell Her That I Love Her,* 1977; *Ripley's Game* was filmed as *The American Friend,* 1978, and under its own title, 2004. Many other novels by Highsmith were optioned for film.

SIDELIGHTS: The author of numerous short story collections and novels, including *Strangers on a Train* and *The Talented Mr. Ripley,* American-born fiction writer Patricia Highsmith enjoyed greater critical and commercial success in England, France, and Germany than in her native country. As Jeff Weinstein speculated in the *Voice Literary Supplement,* one reason for this is that Highsmith's books were "misplaced": relegated to the mystery and suspense shelves instead of being allowed to take their rightful place in the literature section. As far as her ardent admirers in the United States and abroad are concerned, Highsmith was more than just a superb crime novelist. In fact, declared Brigid Brophy in *Don't Never Forget: Collected Views and Reviews,* "there's the injustice. . . . As a novelist *tout court* [Highsmith is] excellent. . . . Highsmith and [Georges] Simenon are alone in writing books which transcend

the limits of the genre while staying strictly inside its rules: they alone have taken the crucial step from playing games to creating art."

The art in Highsmith's work springs from her skillful fusion of plot, characterization, and style, with the crime story serving primarily "as a means of revealing and examining her own deepest interests and obsessions," according to a *Times Literary Supplement* reviewer. Among her most common themes are the nature of guilt and the often symbiotic relationship that develops between two people—almost always men—who are at the same time fascinated and repelled by each other. Highsmith's works therefore "dig down very deeply into the roots of personality," wrote Julian Symons in *London Magazine,* exposing the dark side of people regarded by society as normal and good. Or, as Thomas Sutcliffe explained in the *Times Literary Supplement,* Highsmith wrote "not about what it feels like to be mad, but what it feels like to remain sane while committing the actions of a madman." Also in the *Times Literary Supplement,* James Campbell stated that "the conflict of good and evil—or rather, simple decency and ordinary badness—is at the heart of all Highsmith's novels, dramatized in the encounters between two characters, often in an exotic locale, where it is easier to lose one's moral bearings. Usually, we see events from the point of view of the innocent, the blind, as they stumble towards doom."

Highsmith's childhood prepared her for a fiction writer's solitary life. Her father, Jay Bernard Plangman, separated from her aloof mother, Mary Coates, four months before her birth, and Patricia met her father for the first time when she was age twelve. Plangman was a German American whose family was well-established in Texas, and her mother was of Scottish and Irish descent. Both of her parents were commercial artists. At first, Highsmith was cared for by her maternal grandmother, a hard-headed but jovial woman who treated her indulgently. When the young Highsmith was six, her mother married Stanley Highsmith, another artist, and the family relocated to New York City. Entering elementary school, Highsmith's pronounced Southern accent made communication with other students difficult. In addition, the Highsmith home was chaotic, and she acquired a bleak view of domesticity. Richard Corliss, writing in *Time,* commented on Highsmith's childhood: "If your father walked out before you were born and your mother says she tried to abort you by guzzling turpentine, you may grow up with a sour view of humanity."

Highsmith attended Barnard College and received her bachelor's degree in 1942. Her first stories, deemed too grotesque for the college magazine, deal with such topics as a homicidal nanny and a murderous son. "The Heroine," a short story, was published by *Harper's Bazaar* in 1946 when its author was twenty-four. She would continue to write short fiction throughout her lifetime, resulting in the published collections *Mermaids on the Golf Course*, *The Animal-Lover's Book of Beastly Murder*, and *Nothing That Meets the Eye: The Uncollected Stories of Patricia Highsmith*, the last which contains twenty-eight stories authored between 1938 and 1982. Commenting on Highsmith's short stories, *Library Journal* contributor Robert E. Brown noted that, apart from her novels, the story form "might be her best medium, riveting attention on her twists (plot and psychological), her use of language, and her experiments with viewpoint."

After graduation from Barnard, Highsmith found a job writing storylines for comic book series such as "Superman" and "Batman." The money she saved enabled Highsmith to visit Mexico, where she started her first novel, a meandering Gothic romance she never completed. After returning to New York and working in Bloomingdales for a short time—Highsmith's pseudonymly published lesbian romance-novel *The Price of Salt* fictionalizes this period of her life—she traveled to Europe in 1949 and wrote the manuscript *Strangers on a Train*. In this book, young Guy Haines meets Charles Bruno, a charming psychotic, on a train. Guy reluctantly becomes engaged in conversation with his fellow passenger, then foolishly reveals a resentment toward his wife. Bruno offers to kill Haines's wife if Haines will agree to murder Bruno's tyrannical father.

Such an entanglement between two men—one innocent but naive, the other intriguing and malevolent—became a recurring subject throughout Highsmith's body of work. Critical outrage over her characters' casual immorality also persisted, some describing her work as "sickening" and "nasty." However, soon after the book's publication, Alfred Hitchcock read *Strangers on a Train* and bought the film rights for $7,000. Highsmith promptly abandoned her job to become a full-time author.

Highsmith stayed in Europe for two years, sold short stories, and began another novel, *The Blunderer*. Her next book, *The Talented Mr. Ripley*, introduces suave Thomas Ripley, who murders a wealthy friend and then assumes his identity. A *New Yorker* reviewer called Ripley "one of the most repellent and fascinating characters to come along for quite a while." The character was Highsmith's personal favorite, and she wrote a number of sequels, *Ripley under Ground* and *Ripley under Water* among them.

In 1953 Highsmith embarked upon a nomadic existence in Europe, and she continued her wanderings in the United States toward the end of the 1950s. She loved to travel, using her experiences to enrich her books. In 1962 she moved to England and lived in a Suffolk village, then moved to France in 1967. At her death in 1995, Highsmith was living near Locarno, Switzerland, on Lake Miggiore.

Highsmith's preoccupations with guilt and contrasting personalities surfaced as early as *Strangers on a Train*. With the exception of the "Ripley" books, which focus on the activities of the opportunistic and amoral Tom Ripley, a man incapable of feeling guilt, these themes are at the heart of Highsmith's fiction.

According to Symons, Highsmith typically launched her stories with the kind of "trickily ingenious plot devices often used by very inferior writers." He hastened to add, however, that these serve only as starting points for the "profound and subtle studies of character that follow." As Burt Supree observed in the *Voice Literary Supplement*, most of Highsmith's characters—none of whom are "heroes" in the conventional sense—are likely to be "obsessive, unquestioning, humdrum men with no self-knowledge, no curiosity, and Byzantine fantasy-lives—respectable or criminal middle-class, middle-brow people of incredible shallowness. . . . Like lab animals, [they] come under careful scrutiny, but [Highsmith] doesn't care to analyze them or beg sympathy for them." According to an essayist for the *St. James Guide to Crime and Mystery Writers*, "Highsmith seems very dismissive of the emotional possibilities of innocence. Her characters are all surrounded by circumstantial evidence of their own guilt and complicity in crime, which the truly innocent haplessly internalise and which the truly guilty ignore. Highsmith's writing is thus profoundly ironic in its refusal to recognise the possibilities of justice, and it is appropriately aloof and distanced in its treatment of the moral issues raised." "I find the public passion for justice quite boring and artificial," Corliss quoted Highsmith as saying, "for neither life nor nature cares if justice is ever done or not."

Sutcliffe echoed this assessment of Highsmith's characters as basically sane people who commit apparently insane acts, usually while under considerable strain. "What she observes so truthfully is not the collapse of reason but its persistence in what it suits us to think of as inappropriate conditions," Sutcliffe assessed. He continued: "Even Ripley, the least scrupulous and likeable of her central characters, has motives for his actions, and though they are venal and vicious they are not irrational. Her suburban killers remain calculatingly evasive until the end. . . . They don't hear voices and they don't have fun. Indeed in the act of killing their attitude is one of dispassionate detachment, of a sustained attempt to rationalize the intolerable. . . . In all the books death is contingent and unsought, almost never meticulously planned and very rarely the focus for our moral indignation."

In the eyes of most critics, it is Highsmith's skill at depicting a character's slide into derangement or death that distinguishes her "in a field where imitative hacks and dull formula-mongers abound," remarked a *Times Literary Supplement* reviewer. Symons declared, "The quality that takes her books beyond the run of intelligent fiction is not [the] professional ability to order a plot and create a significant environment, but rather the intensity of feeling that she brings to the problems of her central figures. . . . From original ideas that are sometimes far-fetched or even trivial she proceeds with an imaginative power that makes the whole thing terrifyingly real." The world Highsmith creates for her characters has a "relentless, compulsive, mutedly ominous quality," asserted Hermione Lee in the London *Observer,* one that leaves the reader "in a perpetual state of anxiety and wariness."

The prose Highsmith uses to communicate a sense of chilling dread and almost claustrophobic desperation is flat and plain, devoid of jargon, cliches, and padding. Some critics have described it as reminiscent of a psychological case history: a detailed and dispassionate account of a life moving out of control. According to Reg Gadney in *London Magazine,* "It is a characteristic skill of Miss Highsmith to convey unease and apprehension with an understated narrative style and painstaking description of domestic practicalities. Her characters often seem to counterbalance their expectation of fear by entrenching themselves in domestic routines. . . . [Their] tenacious efforts . . . to keep hold of everyday reality and logic serve to heighten the menace and chaos." *New Statesman* reviewer Blake Morrison, in fact, believed Highsmith was "at her most macabre when most mundane."

Weinstein wrote that "the reader has no choice but to follow the work, nothing could go another way. You are trapped in the very ease of the reading. The result is like suffocation, losing breath or will." Orhan Pamuk, reviewing the "Ripley" books in the *Village Voice,* described the fascination: "To know that people really will be hurt bonds the reader, with an almost self-destructive joy, to Highsmith's novels. For the reader has already discovered that the banality and pettiness, which spread like an epidemic in every one of her books, are those of his own life. He might as well begin to loathe himself. We rediscover, in each novel, the vulnerability of our existence."

Symons identified several qualities in Highsmith's work that made the author, in his words, "such an interesting and unusual novelist." He particularly praised "the power with which her male characters are realized" as well as her ability to portray "what would seem to most people abnormal states of minds and ways of behavior." Symons continued: "The way in which all this is presented can be masterly in its choice of tone and phrase. [Highsmith's] opening sentences make a statement that is symbolically meaningful in relation to the whole book. . . . The setting is also chosen with great care. . . . [She seems to be making the point that] in surroundings that are sufficiently strange, men become uncertain of their personalities and question the reason for their own conduct in society." In short, remarked Symons, Highsmith's work is "as serious in its implications and as subtle in its approach as anything being done in the novel today."

Highsmith's final novel before her death in 1995 departs from her successful formula of suspense. *Small G: A Summer Idyll* features almost no mystery, death, or intrigue. Set in Zurich, Switzerland, the novel revolves around a group of characters who frequent Jacob's Bierstübe-Restaurant, known in gay travel-book parlance as a "small g": a place frequented by both straight and gay patrons. Rickie is a middle-aged gay man who is mourning his dead lover and coping with recent news that he is HIV-positive. He becomes friends with Luisa, a young woman stuck in the unpleasant employ of Renate, a crippled fashion designer who controls Luisa's life and actions. Eventually, Luisa inherits a fortune and gets away from Renate, while Rickie finds out that he is not HIV-positive after all. Many critics expressed disappointment with the novel, noting that Highsmith's trademark strengths are simply missing in this work. *New Statesman* reviewer Julie Wheelwright, for instance, noted that "the plot moves along pleasantly enough; but for a writer so skilled in creating suspense and insightful portraits, these qualities seem distinctly lacking in *Small G.* One wishes that, for her final novel, Highsmith had left a more lasting work than this light 'summer idyll.'" While praising the author's "limpid prose" and "deft characterization," *Times Literary Supplement* contributor James Campbell remarked that "if [*Small G*] can be read as a final utterance, Patricia Highsmith died having made peace with her demons. Good triumphed over bad. Too bad for her readers."

Highsmith "was a mean, cruel, hard, unlovable, unloving human being," publisher Otto Penzler once recalled to Daniel Fierman of *Entertainment Weekly*. "I could never penetrate how any human being could be that relentlessly ugly. . . . But her books? Brilliant." Fierman pointed out that, like so much of her fiction, Highsmith "was no picnic in real life."

Despite her sometimes cantankerous nature, Highsmith's reputation as a top-notch suspense writer remains secure. A *Times Literary Supplement* reviewer explained that "she is the crime writer who comes closest to giving crime writing a good name." And J.M. Edelstein in a *New Republic* article summed up: "Low-key is the word for Patricia Highsmith. . . . Low-key, subtle, and profound. It is amazing to me that she is not better known for she is superb and is a master of the suspense novel. . . . [The body of her work] should be among the classics of the genre." The essayist for the *St. James Guide to Crime and Mystery Writers* believed that Highsmith "dignified and complicated the forms of crime fiction. Her remarkable output is highly distinctive in its austerity of mood and in its dark brooding qualities. Her characterization and her construction of setting are more subtle and deft than that of any of her contemporaries."

BIOGRAPHICAL AND CRITICAL SOURCES:

BOOKS

Brophy, Brigid, *Don't Never Forget: Collected Views and Reviews,* Holt (New York, NY), 1966.

Contemporary Literary Criticism, Thomson Gale (Detroit, MI), Volume 2, 1974, Volume 4, 1975, Volume 14, 1980, Volume 42, 1987.

Harrison, Russell, *Patricia Highsmith,* Twayne (New York, NY), 1997.

Newsmakers 1995, Thomson Gale (Detroit, MI), 1995.

St. James Guide to Crime and Mystery Writers, 4th edition, St. James Press (Detroit, MI), 1996.

Symons, Julian, *Mortal Consequences: A History— From the Detective Story to the Crime Novel,* Harper (New York, NY), 1972.

Wilson, Andrew, *Beautiful Shadow: A Life of Patricia Highsmith,* Blooksbury (London, England), 2003, Bloomsbury USA (New York, NY), 2004.

PERIODICALS

Booklist, September 1, 2002, Frank Sennett, review of *Nothing That Meets the Eye: The Uncollected Stories of Patricia Highsmith,* p. 63.

Books & Bookmen, March, 1971; March, 1983.

Entertainment Weekly, February 11, 1994, p. 50; January 14, 2000, Daniel Fierman, "Mystery Girl: Deceased Mistress of Suspense Patricia Highsmith Is Finding New Fans with The Talented Mr. Ripley," p. 22; August 24, 2001, Mark Harris, "Strange Magic: Patricia Highsmith's Complex Yet Entrancing Crime Thrillers Find New Life Six Years after Her Death," p. 128.

Forbes, June 15, 1998, "A Dark View," p. 304.

Globe and Mail (Toronto, Ontario, Canada), January 21, 1984.

Journal of Popular Culture, February, 2004, William A. Cook, "*Ripley's Game* and *The American Friend:* A Modernist and Postmodernist Comparison," p. 399.

Kirkus Reviews, September 1, 2002, review of *Nothing That Meets the Eye,* p. 1268; April 1, 2004, review of *Small G: A Summer Idyll,* p. 287.

Library Journal, July, 2001, Edward B. St. John, review of *The Selected Stories of Patricia Highsmith,* p. 127; September 15, 2001, Lisa J. Cihlar, review of *Plotting and Writing Suspense Fiction,* p. 90; February 1, 2002, Michael Rogers, review of *People Who Knock on the Door* and *The Blunderer,* p. 138; October 1, 2002, Robert E. Brown, review of *Nothing That Meets the Eye,* p. 130.

Listener, July 9, 1970; February 17, 1983.

London Magazine, June, 1969; June-July, 1972.

Los Angeles Times Book Review, November 1, 1987; March 13, 1988; February 5, 1989; January 17, 1993.

New Republic, May 20, 1967; June 29, 1974; November 10, 2003, "The Ick Factor," p. 28.

New Statesman, May 31, 1963; February 26, 1965; October 29, 1965; January 25, 1969; March 30, 1979; October 2, 1981; March 17, 1995, p. 38.

Newsweek, July 4, 1977.

New Yorker, May 27, 1974.

New York Herald Tribune Books, February 7, 1960.

New York Review of Books, September 15, 1974; March 31, 1988, pp. 36-37; November 15, 2001, E.P. Sanders, review of *The Selected Stories of Patricia Highsmith,* p. 37.

New York Times Book Review, January 30, 1966; April 1, 1967; April 30, 1967; July 19, 1970; July 7, 1974; April 6, 1986; July 19, 1987; November 1, 1987; April 3, 1988; December 18, 1988; January 29, 1989; September 17, 1989; December 24, 1989; October 18, 1992.

Observer (London, England), February 12, 1967; January 19, 1969; July 12, 1970; January 9, 1983; March 12, 1995, p. 19.

Playboy, May, 1994, p. 34.

Publishers Weekly, November 2, 1992, pp. 46-47; February 23, 1998, Steven M. Zeitchik, "Highsmith

Gives $3M to Yaddo," p. 15; July 2, 2001, review of *The Selected Stories of Patricia Highsmith*, p. 49; August 6, 2001, "Mysteries of Writing," p. 81.

Punch, January 29, 1969; March 10, 1971; June 2, 1982.

Spectator, February 21, 1969; December 5, 1981; February 12, 1983; October 13, 1990, p. 33; December 7, 1991, p. 34; March 18, 1995, p. 34.

Time, December 27, 1999, Richard Corliss, "The Talented Ms. Highsmith: Ripley's Creator," p. 159.

Times (London, England), February 24, 1983; April 3, 1986.

Times Literary Supplement, June 1, 1967; September 24, 1971; April 25, 1980; October 2, 1981; February 4, 1983; September 27, 1985; April 18, 1986; December 6, 1987, p. 1227; October 4, 1991, p. 26; February 24, 1995, p. 32.

Tribune Books (Chicago, IL), October 4, 1992.

Village Voice, November 17, 1992.

Voice Literary Supplement, August, 1982.

Washington Post, June 28, 1980.

Washington Post Book World, September 15, 1985; October 6, 1985; October 18, 1992.

Washington Star-News, November 25, 1973.

OBITUARIES:

PERIODICALS

Los Angeles Times, February 5, 1995, p. A22.
New York Times, February 6, 1995, p. B8.
Times (London, England), February 6, 1995, p. 21.
Washington Post, February 6, 1995, p. B4.

*   *   *

HIJUELOS, Oscar 1951-

PERSONAL: Surname is pronounced "E-way-los"; born August 24, 1951, in New York, NY; son of Pascual (a hotel worker) and Magdalena (a homemaker; maiden name, Torrens) Hijuelos; divorced. *Ethnicity:* Hispanic *Education:* City College of the City University of New York, B.A., 1975, M.A., 1976. *Religion:* Catholic. *Hobbies and other interests:* Pen-and-ink drawing, old maps, turn-of-the-century books and graphics, playing musical instruments, jazz ("I absolutely despise modern rock and roll").

ADDRESSES: Home—211 West 106th St., New York, NY 10025. *Office*—Hofstra University, English Department, 1000 Fulton Ave., Hempstead, NY 11550.

CAREER: Transportation Display, Inc., Winston Network, New York, NY, advertising media traffic manager, 1977-84; writer, 1984—; Hofstra University, Hempstead, NY, professor of English, 1989—.

MEMBER: International PEN.

AWARDS, HONORS: Outstanding Writer citation from Pushcart Press, 1978, for story "Columbus Discovering America"; Oscar Cintas fiction-writing grant, 1978-79; Bread Loaf Writers Conference scholarship, 1980; fiction-writing grant from Creative Artists Programs Service, 1982, and Ingram Merrill Foundation, 1983; Fellowship for Creative Writers award, National Endowment for the Arts, and American Academy in Rome Fellowship in Literature, American Academy and Institute of Arts and Letters, both 1985, both for *Our House in the Last World;* National Book Award nomination, National Book Critics Circle Prize nomination, and Pulitzer Prize for fiction, all 1990, all for *The Mambo Kings Play Songs of Love.*

WRITINGS:

Our House in the Last World, Persea Books (New York, NY), 1983.

The Mambo Kings Play Songs of Love, Farrar, Straus (New York, NY), 1989.

(Designer) *Iguana Dreams: New Latino Fiction,* HarperPerennial, 1992.

The Fourteen Sisters of Emilio Montez O'Brien, Farrar, Straus (New York, NY), 1993.

(Author of introduction) Lori M. Calson, editor, *Cool Salsa: Bilingual Poems on Growing Up Latino in the United States,* Holt (New York, NY), 1994.

Mr. Ives' Christmas, HarperCollins (New York, NY), 1995.

(Author of introduction) Dorothy and Thomas Hoobler, *The Cuban American Family Album,* Oxford University Press (New York, NY), 1996.

Empress of the Splendid Season (novel), HarperCollins (New York, NY), 1999.

A Simple Habana Melody: From When the World Was Good, HarperCollins (New York, NY), 2002.

Work represented in anthology *Best of Pushcart Press III,* Pushcart, 1978.

ADAPTATIONS: The Mambo Kings Play Songs of Love was adapted as the film *The Mambo Kings* in 1992 and as a stage musical set for opening in 2005; *Empress of the Splendid Season* was adapted for audiobook, 1999; *A Simple Habana Melody: From When the World Was Good* was adapted for audiobook, 2002.

SIDELIGHTS: Award-winning novelist Oscar Hijuelos turns the characters and experiences of his Cuban-American heritage into fictional works that have won both critical and popular praise. As Marie Arana-Ward explained in the *Washington Post Book World,* "Once in a great while a novelist emerges who is remarkable not for the particulars of his prose but for the breadth of his soul, the depth of his humanity, and for the precision of his gauge on the rising sensibilities of his time. . . . Hijuelos is one of these."

Hijuelos once explained to *CA* that his first novel, *Our House in the Last World,* "traces the lives of a Cuban family who came to the United States in the 1940s and follows them to the death of the father and subsequent near collapse of the family. In many ways a realistic novel, *Our House in the Last World* also reflects certain Latin attributes that are usually termed 'surreal' or 'magical.' Although I am quite Americanized, my book focuses on many of my feelings about identity and my 'Cubanness.' I intended for my book to commemorate at least a few aspects of the Cuban psyche (as I know it)."

Reviewing *Our House in the Last World* for the *New York Times Book Review,* Edith Milton affirmed that Hijuelos is concerned "with questions of identity and perspective," especially those concerning family. Hijuelos is "especially eloquent," lauded *Cleveland Plain Dealer* critic Bob Halliday, "in describing the emotional storms" that transform the Santinio family of his novel as they "try to assimilate the rough realities of Spanish Harlem in terms of the values and personal identities they have inherited from their homeland." In an article for *American Literature,* Bridget M. Morgan stated: "Hijuelos compassionately depicts how each of the unequal participants in the American Dream is transformed by the process of assimilation." There is a "central tension," Milton explained, between the "lost, misremembered Eden [Cuba]" and the increasing squalor of the family's new life in their "last world"—New York. "Opportunity seems pure luck" to these well-intentioned immigrants, observed *Chicago Tribune Book World* reviewer Pat Aufderheide, and, in the absence of hope, each ultimately succumbs to the pressures that "work against the [American] dream of upward mobility." Hijuelos's "elegantly accessible style," Aufderheide stated, "combines innocence and insight" in creating the individual voices of his characters. Beyond that, noted the

reviewer, there is a "feel for the way fear . . . pervades" the Santinios' lives. The characters and the "sheer energy" of the narrative are the book's strengths. Milton concluded that Hijuelos "never loses the syntax of magic, which transforms even the unspeakable into a sort of beauty." Critic Roy Hoffman in the *Philadelphia Inquirer* called *Our House in the Last World* a "vibrant, bitter and successful" story and compared Hijuelos to an "urban poet" who creates a "colorful clarity of life." Halliday likewise deemed the book to be a "wonderfully vivid and compassionate" first novel.

It was Hijuelos's Pulitzer Prize-winning second novel, *The Mambo Kings Play Songs of Love,* that moved him to the first rank of American novelists. Telling the story of two brothers, Cesar and Nestor Castillo, who leave their native Cuba and make careers as singers in the Spanish Harlem of the 1950s, the novel traces the brothers' rise to an appearance on the *I Love Lucy* television show before fading away from public attention again, like the mambo dance their band played.

The Mambo Kings, Cathleen McGuigan explained in *Newsweek,* "isn't conventionally plotted; it slides back and forth in time and meanders into dreams and fantasies." The novel is comprised of the dreams and fantasies of Cesar Castillo at the end of his career when he lives in a run-down hotel called the Splendour and drinks away his days. McGuigan noted that Cesar "is a classic portrait of machismo: he's in closest touch with his feelings when they originate below the waist." But she acknowledged that "Hijuelos has a tender touch with his characters, and Cesar is more than a stereotype." Despite the novel's flaws, McGuigan found *The Mambo Kings Play Songs of Love* to be a "vibrant tragicomic novel." Joseph Coates in Chicago's *Tribune Books* found echoes of magical realism in the novel and felt that it "achieves the long backward look" of novels such as *One Hundred Years of Solitude,* "dealing as fully with the old worlds the migrants left as with the new ones they find." Writing in the *Washington Post Book World,* novelist Bob Shacochis also remarked upon Hijuelos's skilled contrasts between Cuban and American life, observing that "his *cu-bop* music scene gathers credibility as a grand metaphor for the splitting of a national family that took place [with the Cuban revolution] in 1959." Finally, Margo Jefferson of the *New York Times Book Review* observed that Hijuelos alternates "crisp narrative with opulent musings," achieving a "music of the heart."

Hijuelos's 1993 novel, *The Fourteen Sisters of Emilio Montez O'Brien,* takes a very different tack from its predecessor. Whereas *The Mambo Kings Play Songs of*

Love is told by one male narrator, *The Fourteen Sisters of Emilio Montez O'Brien* is told from a number of female viewpoints and spans several generations in the life of a Cuban-Irish family living in Pennsylvania. Writing in *Time,* Janice E. Simpson praised the novel's warmth, suggesting that reading it "is like leafing through the pages of a treasured family album," but lamented that "the fate of the sisters is determined and defined by their relationships with men." *American Literature*'s Bridget Morgan felt that Hijuelos's work "is a celebration, even in its darkest moments, of the strength of love and family." "Hijuelos . . . displays a poetic exuberance in *The Fourteen Sisters of Emilio Montez O'Brien,*" stated George R. McMurray, in a *World Literature Today* review. Jane Mendelsohn, writing in the *London Review of Books,* generally admired the way Hijuelos characterizes his female characters, observing that "the novel skillfully chronicles the lives" of all the sisters and that Margarita, in particular, is an embodiment of the "women's movement . . . in the 20th century." At the same time, Mendelsohn faulted the novel for its sentimentality and concluded that there is "nothing of the glorious flame which set *The Mambo Kings* on fire." Nick Hornby in the *Times Literary Supplement* called the novel "at all times readable and diverting," but found that its many characters bog down its pacing. In contrast, Arana-Ward praised the story for its celebration of "human diversity and its promise of vitality," as well as for its compelling characters, who "hold us captive until the very last page."

With the short novel *Mr. Ives' Christmas,* Hijuelos steps away from his trademark theme of ethnic identity. Edward Ives, the book's chief protagonist, is a foundling of unknown background who is raised by nuns in a New York City orphanage. After several years pass, he is adopted by a man who inspires in Edward a deep and lasting love for Catholicism. When Edward enters adulthood, he works for a Madison Avenue advertising agency and is quite successful in his profession. He marries a wonderful woman, Annie MacGuire, they have a healthy son, Robert, and a younger daughter. Their lives proceed for nearly two decades in a seemingly perfect, secure routine. This peace is shattered, however, a few days before one Christmas, when seventeen-year-old Robert is killed by a hoodlum. Edward's belief in God and the Catholic faith is deeply shaken by this meaningless murder and the book traces how he comes to terms with Robert's death. Writing in *Booklist* Donna Seaman called *Mr. Ives' Christmas* a "sad and enchanting novel . . . of giving and of grace." In a *New York Times* article, Jack Miles felt that the novel is Hijuelos's "deepest and . . . best."

Empress of the Splendid Season, published in 1999, features a young woman of aristocratic Cuban descent who is banished from her home when her father discovers her romantic involvement with an older man. Lydia leaves Cuba for New York City, where she meets and marries Raul, another Cuban immigrant. Raul supports Lydia and their two children, Rico and Alicia, by working as a waiter in two restaurants, until he suffers a nearly fatal heart attack. Lydia must then go to work, and as she is not fluent in English, she decides to hire herself out as a housekeeper. The novel reveals not only Lydia's daily work, but her relationship to her clients. There is one whom she particularly likes—-an international lawyer named Mr. Osprey, who intervenes in Rico's life when the boy is in trouble.

"While *Empress* does share similarities with Hijuelos's earlier work," wrote Joseph M. Viera in *American Writers,* "it nevertheless showcases the talents of a more mature, more seasoned author, as evidenced in the novel's compassionate narrative voice." London *Sunday Times* writer Phil Baker praised Hijuelos for his "lyrical . . . use of language" and his characterization of Lydia's inner life. "Hijuelos's achingly sweet novel captures beautifully the stateliness, strength and raw sensuality of Lydia España," said reviewer Barbara Mujica in an *Américas* article. Mujica concluded her review by saying: "Hijuelos transcends stereotypes and cliches, creating characters who speak to us on a profoundly human level."

Hijuelos introduces factual occurrences into his fictional rendition of *A Simple Habana Melody: From When the World Was Good.* Israel Levis's character is loosely based upon the life of Cuban composer Moises Simons, who brought the rumba rhythm to the United States with his 1930 song "The Peanut Vendor." In Levis's case, he writes a song called "Rosas Puras," basing it on a flower vendor's street call. His song becomes world famous due to a rendition by a Cuban songstress, Rita Valladares, whom Luis loves, unrequited, throughout his life. Hijuelos traces Levis's journeys from Cuba to Paris—where Cuban jazz musicians are highly welcome—to the Buchenwald concentration camp—he is mistaken for a Jew because of his relationship with a Jewish woman and because of his given name—and back to Cuba again.

Several reviewers commented on Hijuelos's novel. "This is a painfully sad novel about a sad man," wrote Mary Ann Horne in the *Orlando Sentinel.* She added, however, that "Hijuelos restrains his lyrical prose almost to the end of the book but sets it free as he sends Levis off to the afterlife." In the *Miami Herald* Fabiola Santiago commented: "*A Simple Habana Melody* is a love story to be enjoyed for its lyrical writing and desperately old-fashioned texture." Santiago found Valladares's character "too flatly portrayed," although she may have been "potentially more interesting . . . than Levis." "*Habana Melody* is . . . introspective, melancholy and sweetly elegiac," remarked Jerome Weeks in the *Dallas Morning News.*

New York Times critic Daniel Zalewski was less impressed by *A Simple Habana Melody.* The novel's "language . . . is consistently muted" in comparison to that of *The Mambo Kings Play Songs of Love,* Zalewski noted, continuing: "The result of all this linguistic tiptoeing is a melancholy, and sometimes wan, novel about the fruits and frustrations of repression." In a *St. Louis Post-Dispatch* review, Patricia Corrigan felt that Valladares's character is insufficiently developed to warrant Levis's attachment to her. She also questioned the insertion of a small incident when Levis seems attracted to the physical appearance of a man: "the references to homosexual tendencies read as though tacked on." Yet, Corrigan added, "As always, Hijuelos's powers of description are masterful, even lyrical, and occasionally droll, sometimes all at once."

"This heartbreaking novel laments lost love while it helps us remember how love felt when we were young," commented *Booklist*'s Bill Ott of *A Simple Habana Melody.* Allan Turner, writing in the *Houston Chronicle,* opined that "Hijuelos perhaps resolves his novel a bit too neatly," but noted, however, that the novel's "bittersweet strains will resonate long after the last page is turned." A *Publishers Weekly* reviewer felt that the author "triumphs in capturing the sights and sounds of Habana at the edge of modernity," while a *Kirkus* reviewer dubbed the book a "masterpiece of history, music, wonder and sorrow." Francine Prose stated in an *O* review that "*A Simple Habana Melody*keeps us enthralled, then lingers in our minds."

BIOGRAPHICAL AND CRITICAL SOURCES:

BOOKS

American Literature, Thomson Gale (Detroit, MI), 1999.

American Writers, Supplement VIII, Thomson Gale (Detroit, MI), 1998.

Contemporary Hispanic Biography Volume 1, Thomson Gale (Detroit, MI), 2002.

Contemporary Literary Criticism, Volume 65, Thomson Gale (Detroit, MI), 1990.

Contemporary Novelists, 7th edition, St. James Press (Detroit, MI), 2001.

Dictionary of Literary Biography, Volume 145: *Modern Latin-American Fiction Writers, Second Series,* Thomson Gale (Detroit, MI), 1994.

PERIODICALS

Américas, July, 1999, Barbara Mujica, review of *Empress of the Splendid Season,* p. 62.

Americas Review, Volume 22, number 1-2, pp. 274-276.

Bloomsbury Review, May, 1990, p. 5.

Book, May-June, 1999, Patrick Markee, "Oscar Hijuelos and the Old Neighborhood."

Booklist, October 1, 1995, Donna Seaman, review of *Mr. Ives' Christmas*; August, 1999, review of *The Mambo Kings Play Songs of Love,* p. 2024; May 1, 2002, Bill Ott, review of *A Simple Habana Melody: From When the World Was Good,* p. 1445; January 1, 2003, review of *A Simple Habana Melody,* p. 792.

Boston Globe, November 18, 1990, p. 21.

Chicago Tribune, August 9, 1990, p. 1; January 3, 1993; May 30, 1993, sec. 6, p. 5; December 24, 1996.

Chicago Tribune Book World, July 17, 1983.

Christian Century, May 22, 1996, p. 581.

Dallas Morning News, July 3, 2002, Jerome Weeks, review of *A Simple Habana Melody.*

Entertainment Weekly, March 19, 1993, p. 57.

Hispanic, June, 2002, Fabiola Santiago, review of *A Simple Habana Melody,* p. 58.

Horn Book, May-June, 1995, p. 316.

Houston Chronicle, March 6, 1999, Joan Ann Zuniga, review of *Empress of the Splendid Season,* p. 41; June 23, 2002, Allan Turner, review of *A Simple Habana Melody,* p. 16.

Insight on the News, October 23, 1989, p. 56.

Kirkus Reviews, March 15, 2002, review of *A Simple Habana Melody,* p. 359.

Library Journal, January, 1999, review of *Empress of the Splendid Season,* p. 150; April 1, 2002, review of *The Mambo Kings Play Songs of Love,* p. 168; May 1, 2002, review of *a Simple Habana Melody,* p. 133.

London Review of Books, September 23, 1993, p. 23.

Los Angeles Times, April 16, 1990, p. 1.

Los Angeles Times Book Review, September 3, 1989, p. 1; March 14, 1993, pp. 3, 8; March 7, 1999, review of *Empress of the Splendid Season,* p. 3.

Los Angeles Times Magazine, April 18, 1993, pp. 22-28, 54.

Miami Herald, May 29, 2002, Fabiola Santiago, review of *A Simple Habana Melody.*

New Republic, March 22, 1993, pp. 38-41.

New Statesman, December 15, 1995, p. 64.

Newsweek, August 21, 1989, p. 60.

New York, March 1, 1993, p. 46.

New Yorker, March 29, 1993, p. 107; August 21, 1995, pp. 126-127.

New York Times, September 11, 1989, p. C17; April 1, 1993, p. C17.

New York Times Book Review, May 15, 1983; August 27, 1989, pp. 1, 30; March 7, 1993, p. 6; December 3, 1995, Jack Miles, review of *Mr. Ives' Christmas,* p. 9; February 5, 1999, Michiko Kakutani, review of *Empress of the Splendid Season,* p. E45; February 21, 1999, Verlyn Klinkenborg, review of *Empress of the Splendid Season,* p. 5; June 23, 2002, Daniel Zalewski, review of *A Simple Habana Melody,* p. 11; July 7, 2002, review of *A Simple Habana Melody,* p. 18.

O, June, 2002, Francine Prose, review of *A Simple Habana Melody,* p. 155.

Observer (London, England), July 25, 1993, p. 53; February 21, 1999, review of *Empress of the Splendid Season,* p. 13; December 19, 1999, review of *Empress of the Splendid Season,* p. 14.

Orlando Sentinel, July 31, 2002, Mary Ann Horne, review of *A Simple Habana Melody.*

People, April 5, 1993, p. 26.

Philadelphia Inquirer, July 17, 1983.

Publishers Weekly, July 21, 1989, pp. 42, 44; February 1, 1999, review of *Empress of the Splendid Season,* p. 35; May 20, 2002, review of *A Simple Habana Melody,* p. 46.

St. Louis Post-Dispatch, June 16, 2002, Patricia Corrigan, review of *A Simple Habana Melody,* p. F10.

Spectator, February 27, 1999, review of *Empress of the Splendid Season,* p. 37.

Sunday Times (London, England), December 12, 1999, Phil Baker, review of *Empress of the Splendid Season,* p. 45.

Time, August 14, 1989, p. 68; March 29, 1993, pp. 63, 65; March 15, 1999, review of *Empress of the Splendid Season,* p. 92.

Times Literary Supplement, August 6, 1993, p. 19; February 19, 1999, Henry Hitchings, review of *Empress of the Splendid Season,* p. 22.

Tribune Books (Chicago, IL), August 13, 1989, p. 6; January 3, 1993, p. 6.

U.S. Catholic, May, 1996, p. 46.

Village Voice, May 1, 1990, p. 85.

Wall Street Journal, February 5, 1999, Wendy Bounds, review of *Empress of the Splendid Season,* p. W10.

Washington Post Book World, August 20, 1989; March 14, 1993, pp. 1, 10; January 31, 1999, review of *Empress of the Splendid Season,* p. 5.

World Literature Today, winter, 1994, George R. McMurray, review of *The Fourteen Sisters of Emilio Montez O'Brien,* p. 127.

* * *

HILL, John
See KOONTZ, Dean R.

* * *

HILLENBRAND, Laura 1967-

PERSONAL: Born 1967, in Fairfax, VA. *Education:* Kenyon College, Gambier, OH.

ADDRESSES: Agent—Tina Bennett, Janklow/Nesbit Associates, 445 Park Ave., New York, NY 10022.

CAREER: Contributing editor/writer, *Equus Magazine,* 1989—. Consultant for PBS documentary on Seabiscuit, 2002

AWARDS, HONORS: Eclipse Awards for magazine writing, 1998, 2001; Booksense Nonfiction Book of the Year, 2001, William Hill Sports Book of the Year, 2001, and National Book Critics Circle Award finalist, 2001, all for *Seabiscuit: An American Legend*; Los Angeles Book Prize finalist; second prize, Barnes & Noble Discover Award; finalist, Borders Original Voices Award.

WRITINGS:

Seabiscuit: An American Legend, Random House (New York, NY), 2001.

ADAPTATIONS: Laura Hillenbrand served as consultant on the Universal Studios movie based on the book, *Seabiscuit: An American Legend* (2003). An audiobook version of *Seabiscuit* was released by Random Audio-Books, 2001.

SIDELIGHTS: In her debut book, *Seabiscuit: An American Legend,* Laura Hillenbrand has written an exciting book that has already won the Triple Crown of publishing: runaway sales of a nonfiction sports book, nomination for the National Book Award Critics Circle Award, and a movie in production by Universal Studios.

The first paragraph of the preface sets the tone of the book. "In 1938, near the end of the decade of monumental turmoil, the year's number-one newsmaker was not Franklin Delano Roosevelt, Hitler, or Mussolini. It wasn't Pope Pius XI, nor was it Lou Gehrig, Howard Hughes, or Clark Gable. The subject of the most newspaper column inches in 1938 wasn't even a person. It was an undersized, crooked-legged racehorse named Seabiscuit. In the latter half of the Depression, Seabiscuit was nothing short of a cultural icon in America, enjoying adulation so intense and broad-based that it transcended sport."

The heroes in Seabiscuit's story include the burned-out, knobby-kneed racehorse; his jockeys, Red Pollard, down and out and half blind, and George Woolf, cool and cocky but doomed; the aging western trainer Tom Smith, and horseman Charles S. Howard, a Buick dealer and self-made man. Their story played out against the backdrop of the Great Depression. One in four breadwinners were unemployed, foreclosure was common, thousands were hungry. Spectator sports, radio programming, and movie theaters offered an escape and created instant celebrity, even for horses. Enamored of the rags-to-riches myth, Americans were quick to idolize those who exemplified it. Driven by hunger, hope, and heart, Seabiscuit and his crew lived the rags-to-riches dream.

Between 1935 and 1940, Seabiscuit traveled over 50,000 miles by train and was mobbed at every whistle stop. Jim Squires, reviewing the book for the *New York Times,* says that "as the most popular and most watched personality in the world, he was the 30's era equivalent of Elvis or the Beatles, and, as a sports attraction, could draw bigger crowds than Tiger Woods."

Charles Howard embodied the entrepreneurial spirit of the age. A one-time bicycle repairman, he became a millionaire selling "horseless carriages" to the western United States. He fell in love with racehorses and hired Tom Smith, a closed-mouthed old mustang breaker from the High Plains, as his trainer. It was Smith who saw something in this horse that had run seventeen races before he won. Small, mud-colored and knock-kneed, Charles Howard bought him at auction in 1936 for $8,000 and hired Red Pollard, a one eyed, over-the-hill boxer, as his jockey.

"Silent" Tom Smith set about transforming an animal everyone else called lazy, awkward, and hostile into a great racehorse. Even if no one from the Eastern establishment world of thoroughbreds had ever seen his frontier style of training, everyone agreed that the "Lone Plainsman," as Smith was called, could "talk horse." A newspaper reporter once quipped that "Tom Smith says almost nothing, constantly." Hillenbrand describes Smith, who'd trained rodeo horses and learned his craft from Plains Indians, "[as having] the ethereal quality of hoof prints in windblown snow."

Hillenbrand interviewed aging jockeys and horsemen to give the book plenty of local color. Racing scenes in California in the '30s and her characterization of Pollard and George Woolf were especially praised by the critics.

Pollard is remembered as the poet laureate of jockeys, known for his seemingly telepathic understanding of difficult horses and his love for Emerson's poetry. Hillenbrand's description of Pollard's tumble, which kept him out of a great match race, is especially good: "Jockeys say there is a small, bright sound when hooves clip against each other, a cheery portent of the wreck that is likely to follow . . . Pollard must have heard it. Fair Knightess' forelegs were kicked out from under her. Unable to catch herself, she pitched into a somersault at 40 miles per hour . . . Pollard went down with her, his helpless form following the line of her fall, over her back and neck and vanishing under her crashing body. She came down onto him with terrific force and skidded to a stop."

George Woolf was no less competitive as a jockey: In one race, recounts Hillenbrand, "The wire was looming overhead, and Ligaroti was lunging for the lead. Woolf could not move Seabiscuit up. With just a few yards to go, Woolf was frantic. . . . He had to move Ligaroti back. With twenty yards to go, Woolf tore his hand free, threw out his right arm and grabbed Ligaroti's bridle, just above the bit. Just as the wire passed overhead, he pulled back, lifting the horse's head up and to the left as Seabiscuit's head bobbed forward. Seabiscuit flew under the wire." As Jane Smiley wrote in the *Washington Post,* Hillenbrand's "effort shows in the details and the energy of her story; her historical figures, horses and people, live and breathe in a lively, lovely way."

All of America was listening to the long-awaited race between Seabiscuit and his arch rival, War Admiral. It was a classic match-up. Seabiscuit was the new West,

War Admiral represented the Eastern establishment. The country had waited for more than a year to see them race. In the climax of the book, Hillenbrand recounts "the greatest race in history," run at Pimlico Race Track in Maryland on November 1, 1938, with all the excitement of first class sports reporting.

That *Seabiscuit: An American Legend* was written at all is a story of courage all its own. In 1987, a virulent case of food poisoning left Hillenbrand bedridden for ten months, fighting fevers, chills, and profound exhaustion. Doctors could not make a definitive diagnosis: some thought she had contracted AIDS, others suspected multiple sclerosis. Since there was no clear diagnosis, some doctors, as well as some friends, thought it was merely psychosomatic. "I had difficulties with just about everyone taking it seriously at first," she said. Finally she was diagnosed with Chronic Fatigue Syndrome (CFS). Hillenbrand felt then—and still does now—that it is a ridiculous name for such a debilitating disease.

CFS is a disease that leaves many of its victims completely disabled and unable to take care of themselves. "This illness is to fatigue what a nuclear bomb is to a match," she says. "It's an absurd mischaracterization." In a *Washington Post* interview, Jennifer Frey wrote that "she is thirty-three years old and can't walk a block without becoming incredibly tired. Her morning shower exhausts her. Vertigo causes the words on the computer screen to dip and weave as she types."

"Random House editor Jon Karp once said that *Seabiscuit* is a metaphor for my life, and he's right," Hillenbrand commented. "The subjects that I've written about—the men and the horse—were radically different individuals, but the one thread that pulls through all of their lives and through the events that they live through together is the struggle between overwhelming hardship and the will to overcome it."

BIOGRAPHICAL AND CRITICAL SOURCES:

BOOKS

Hillenbrand, Laura, *Seabiscuit: An American Legend*, Random House, 2001.

PERIODICALS

Atlanta Journal-Constitution, May 3, 2001, Eleanor Ringel Gillespie, review of *Seabiscuit: An American Legend*, p. D4.

Booklist, September, 1, 2001, Bill Ott, review of *Seabiscuit*, p. 35; January 1, 2001, Dennis Dodge, review of *Seabiscuit*, p. 900.

Boston Herald, August 10, 2001, review of *Seabiscuit*, p. 42.

Business Week, March 26, 2001, review of *Seabiscuit*, p. 27.

Entertainment Weekly, March 26, 2001, review of *Seabiscuit*, p. 62.

Forbes, March 5, 2001, Mark Rotella, review of *Seabiscuit*, p. 116.

Guardian (London, England), August 4, 2001, Stephen Moss, review of *Seabiscuit*, p. 9.

Library Journal, April 1, 2001, Patsy E. Gray, review of *Seabiscuit*, p. 106.

London Review of Books, October 4, 2001, Marjorie Garber, review of *Seabiscuit*, p. 35.

Los Angeles Times, March 18, 2001, Susan Salter, review of *Seabiscuit*, p. 11; July 1, 2001, review of audio version of *Seabiscuit*.

New York Review of Books, July 19, 2001, Elizabeth Hardwick, review of *Seabiscuit*, p. 4.

New York Times, March 6, 2001, Michiko Katutani, "No Beauty, but They Had the Right Horse There," p. B7.

New York Times Book Review, March 11, 2001, Jim Squires, "Can Do! Once upon a Time There Was a Knock-kneed, Mud-colored Runt of a Horse. His Name Was Seabiscuit . . . ," p. 12.

Publishers Weekly, March 26, 2001, Daisy Maryles, review of *Seabiscuit*, p. 24; January 1, 2001, review of *Seabiscuit*, p. 75.

Sunday Telegraph (London, England), Max Davidson, review of *Seabiscuit*.

Time, April 2, 2001, Jesse Birnbaum, review of *Seabiscuit*, p. 72.

Times (London, England), Allan Mallinson, review of *Seabiscuit*, p. 15.

Times Literary Supplement, July 20, 2001, Alan Lee, review of *Seabiscuit*, p. 10.

US Weekly, May 7, 2001, Phoebe Hoban, review of *Seabiscuit*, p. 48; April 2, 2001, Sarah Goodyear, review of *Seabiscuit*, p. 74.

Wall Street Journal, March 9, 2001, Frederick C. Klein, review of *Seabiscuit*, p. W9.

Washington Post, March 9, 2001, Jennifer Frey, "Against the Odds: Laura Hillenbrand Surmounts Illness to Cross the Finish Line with 'Seabiscuit'," p. C01.

Washington Post Book World, March 18, 2001, Jane Smiley, "Track Star," p. T05.

ONLINE

Romance Reader, http://theromancereader.com/ (December 2, 2001), Cathy Sova, review of *Seabiscuit*.

HILLERMAN, Tony 1925-

PERSONAL: Born May 27, 1925; son of August Alfred (a farmer) and Lucy (Grove) Hillerman; married Marie Unzner, August 16, 1948; children: Anne, Janet, Anthony, Monica, Stephen, Daniel. *Education:* Attended Oklahoma State University, 1943; University of Oklahoma, B.A., 1946; University of New Mexico, M.A., 1966. *Politics:* Democrat *Religion:* Roman Catholic *Hobbies and other interests:* Trout fishing.

ADDRESSES: Home—Albuquerque, NM. *Agent*—c/o Author Mail, 7th Fl., HarperCollins Publishers, 10 E. 53rd St., New York, NY 10022.

CAREER: Borger News Herald, Borger, TX, reporter, 1948; *Morning Press- Constitution,* Lawton, OK, city editor, 1948-50; United Press International, Oklahoma City, OK, political reporter, 1950-52, Santa Fe, NM, bureau manager, 1952-54; *New Mexican,* Santa Fe, political reporter and executive editor, 1954-63; University of New Mexico, Albuquerque, associate professor, 1965-66, professor, 1966-85, chair of department, 1966-73, assistant to the president, 1975-80, professor emeritus of journalism, 1985—; writer. *Military service:* U.S. Army, 1943-45; received Silver Star, Bronze Star, and Purple Heart.

MEMBER: International Crime Writers Association, Mystery Writers of America (president, 1988), Albuquerque Press Club, Sigma Delta Chi, Phi Kappa Phi.

AWARDS, HONORS: Edgar Allan Poe Award, Mystery Writers of America, 1974, for *Dance Hall of the Dead;* Golden Spur award, Western Writers of America, 1987; Special Friend of Dineh award, Navajo Tribal Council, 1987; National Media Award, American Anthropological Association, 1990; Public Services Award, Department of the Interior, 1990; Arrell Gibson Lifetime Award, Oklahoma Center for the Book, 1991; Grandmaster Award, Mystery Writers of America, 1991; Ambassador award, Center for the Indian, 1992; Grand prix de litterature policiere; inducted into Oklahoma Hall of Fame, 1997; Jack D. Rittenhouse Award, Rocky Mountain Book Publishers Association, 1998; Agatha Award, 2001, for *Seldom Disappointed;* Malice Domestic Lifetime Achievement award, 2002; Robert Kirsch Award for lifetime achievement, *Los Angeles Times,* 2004; D.Litt., University of New Mexico, 1990, and Arizona State University, 1991.

WRITINGS:

MYSTERY NOVELS

The Blessing Way, Harper (New York, NY), 1970.

The Fly on the Wall, Harper (New York, NY), 1971.
Dance Hall of the Dead, Harper (New York, NY), 1973, reprinted, 2003.
Listening Woman, Harper (New York, NY), 1978.
People of Darkness, Harper (New York, NY), 1980.
The Dark Wind, Harper (New York, NY), 1982.
The Ghostway, Harper (New York, NY), 1984.
Skinwalkers, Harper (New York, NY), 1986.
A Thief of Time, Harper (New York, NY), 1988, ImPress (New York, NY), 2005.
Talking God, Harper (New York, NY), 1989.
Coyote Waits, Harper (New York, NY), 1990.
Sacred Clowns, HarperCollins (New York, NY), 1993.
The Fallen Man, HarperCollins (New York, NY), 1996.
The First Eagle, HarperCollins (New York, NY), 1998.
Hunting Badger, HarperCollins (New York, NY), 1999.
The Wailing Wind, HarperCollins (New York, NY), 2002.
The Sinister Pig, HarperCollins (New York, NY), 2003.
Skeleton Man, HarperCollins (New York, NY), 2004.
The Shape Shifter, HarperCollins (New York, NY), 2006.

COLLECTIONS

The Joe Leaphorn Mysteries, Harper (New York, NY), 1989.
The Jim Chee Mysteries, Harper (New York, NY), 1992.
Leaphorn and Chee: Three Classic Mysteries Featuring Lt. Joe Leaphorn and Officer Jim Chee, Harper (New York, NY), 1992.
The Leaphorn and Chee Novels, HarperCollins (New York, NY), 2005.
Leaphorn, Chee, and More, HarperCollins (New York, NY), 2005.

OTHER

The Boy Who Made Dragonfly: A Zuni Myth (juvenile), Harper (New York, NY), 1972.
The Great Taos Bank Robbery and Other Indian Country Affairs, University of New Mexico Press (Albuquerque, NM), 1973, published as *The Great Taos Bank Robbery: And Other True Stories of the Southwest,* Perennial (New York, NY), 2001.
(Editor) *The Spell of New Mexico,* University of New Mexico Press (Albuquerque, NM), 1984.
Indian Country: America's Sacred Land, illustrated with photographs by Bela Kalman, Northland Press (Flagstaff, AZ), 1987.

(Author of foreword) Erna Fergusson, *Dancing Gods: Indian Ceremonials of New Mexico and Arizona,* University of New Mexico Press (Albuquerque, NM), 1988.

Hillerman Country: A Journey through the Southwest with Tony Hillerman, illustrated with photographs by Barney Hillerman, HarperCollins (New York, NY), 1991.

(With Ernie Bulow) *Talking Mysteries: A Conversation with Tony Hillerman,* University of New Mexico Press (Albuquerque, NM), 1991.

(Editor) *Best of the West: An Anthology of Classic Writing from the American West,* HarperCollins (New York, NY), 1991.

(Author of foreword) Ernie Bulow, *Navajo Taboos,* Buffalo Medicine Books, 1991.

(Author of introduction) Howard Beyan, editor, *Robbers, Rogues, and Ruffians: True Tales of the Wild West,* Clear Light (New York, NY), 1991.

(With others) *The Perfect Murder: Five Great Mystery Writers Create the Perfect Crime,* Harper Prism (New York, NY), 1991.

New Mexico, Rio Grande, and Other Essays, illustrated with photographs by David Muench and Robert Reynolds, Graphic Arts Center, 1992.

(Editor) *The Mysterious West,* HarperCollins (New York, NY), 1994.

(Author of introduction), Robert Allen Rutland, *A Boyhood in the Dustbowl 1926-34,* University Press of Colorado (Boulder, CO), 1995.

Finding Moon (novel), HarperCollins (New York, NY), 1995.

(Editor, with Rosemary Herbert) *The Oxford Book of American Detective Stories,* Oxford University Press (New York, NY), 1996.

(Editor) *The Best American Mystery Stories of the Century,* Houghton Mifflin (Boston, MA), 2000.

Seldom Disappointed: A Memoir, HarperCollins (New York, NY), 2001.

Kilroy Was There: A GI's War in Photographs, photographs by Frank Kessler, Kent State University Press (Kent, OH), 2004.

(Editor, with Rosemary Herbert), *A New Omnibus of Crime,* Oxford University Press (New York, NY), 2005.

Contributor to books, including *Crime Lovers Casebook,* edited by Jerome Charyn, Signet (New York, NY), 1996; and also to periodicals, including *New Mexico Quarterly, National Geographic,* and *Reader's Digest.*

ADAPTATIONS: Many of Hillerman's mysteries have been recorded on audiocassette; the novel *Coyote Waits* was adapted for an episode the PBS series *American Mystery!*

SIDELIGHTS: A versatile novelist, Tony Hillerman "created the American Indian policier," according to critic Herbert Mitgang in the *New York Times,* and also "breaks out of the detective genre," as Daniel K. Muhlestein noted in the *Dictionary of Literary Biography.* Hillerman "is a writer of police procedurals who is less concerned with the identity of his villains than with their motivation," Muhlestein further commented. "Most mystery writers begin with plot. Hillerman begins with setting." Setting, for Hillerman, is the sprawling, arid, high plateau of the Southwest: the Four Corners region of Arizona, Utah, Colorado, and New Mexico that comprise Navajo country. Into this vast, empty space he sets his two protagonists, Jim Chee and Joe Leaphorn, detectives with the Navajo Tribal Police, who solve crimes using the most modern police methods as well as the most traditional of Navajo beliefs: a sense of *hozro,* or harmony. Hillerman has written more than a dozen Leaphorn-Chee mysteries, books that have garnered him awards ranging from the Mystery Writers of America to the Navajo Tribal Council's commendation to France's esteemed Grand prix de litterature policiere.

Hillerman's interest in the American Southwest is evident in both his popular mystery series and nonfiction works that explore the natural wonders of the region. A student of southwestern history and culture, Hillerman often draws his themes from the conflict between modern society and traditional Native American values and customs. The complex nature of this struggle is perhaps most evident in the author's works featuring Leaphorn and Chee, whose contrasting views about heritage and crime-fighting form an interesting backdrop to their criminal investigations. The intricate nature of Hillerman's plots, combined with detailed descriptions of people, places, and exotic rituals, has helped make his novels—from the first in the series, 1970's *The Blessing Way,* to the 1999 *Hunting Badger*—popular with readers and critics alike. Hillerman's novels are, as so many critics have observed, much more than mere police procedurals. His use of character and setting have pushed them beyond the bounds of the detective genre, a fact supported by their large sales in mainstream fiction.

Hillerman is no stranger to the world he portrays in his novels and nonfiction. Born on May 27, 1925, the youngest of three children of August Alfred and Lucy Grove Hillerman, he grew up in rural Oklahoma, where his parents farmed and ran a local store. Hillerman loved reading and books as a youth, and in those days before television and without even enough money for batteries for the radio, he also formed an appreciation for oral storytelling. He would listen to the men who gathered at his parents' store to tell stories and tall tales, and learned pacing, timing, and the importance of detail. Hillerman's youth was thus spent, as Muhlestein noted, "poor in money but rich in the tools of a future writer."

Hillerman also learned, according to Muhlestein, "what it meant to be an outsider," by attending a boarding school for Potawatomie Indian girls. Doubly removed because of both race and gender, Hillerman internalized this feeling of being an outsider, but also formed a deep and abiding respect for Indian ways and culture. As important as that message was, he also learned another: the significance of class in America. As a youngster Hillerman viewed himself as a country boy, one who got his haircuts at home, not at a barber shop. If the world were divided into urban and rural, he would opt for the latter.

After graduating from high school, Hillerman began college at Oklahoma State University, but then joined the army to fight in World War II. He took part in the D-Day landings, was wounded in Alsace, and earned a Silver Star, among other decorations. His letters home, which found their way into the hands of a journalist, were so detailed and spirited that the newspaperman convinced the young returning soldier to take up a career in writing.

Enrolling in journalism courses, Hillerman also worked part-time to support his education. It was in 1945, while driving a truckload of drilling pipe from Oklahoma to New Mexico, that he first encountered the Navajo and their reservation. The Navajos he first saw were engaged in a curing ceremony called the Enemy Way, during which a young Navajo fresh from service in the war, like Hillerman himself, was being cured of the foreign contamination and brought back into harmony with his own people. "When I met the Navajos I now so often write about," Hillerman recalled to Ernie Bulow in *Talking Mysteries,* "I recognized kindred spirits. Country boys. More of us. Folks among whom I felt at ease." In 1948, Hillerman graduated from the journalism program at the University of Oklahoma. He was also married that year to Marie Unzner; the couple would eventually have one child together and adopt five additional children.

Hillerman took several newspaper jobs in and around Oklahoma, Texas, and New Mexico before joining the staff of the Santa Fe *New Mexican* in 1954. He stayed with that paper until 1963, working at the end of his journalism career as executive editor. But he had a longing to become a novelist, and with the encouragement of his wife, left journalism behind to study writing, soon becoming a journalism professor at the University of New Mexico, where he remained until 1985. It was while he was a professor of journalism that he wrote his first novel, *The Blessing Way,* in which he introduces Joe Leaphorn, a fiftyish Navajo with the Tribal Police on the reservation. Leaphorn, however, was almost cut out of this manuscript at the urging of Hillerman's agent. Finally, an editor at Harper & Row wrote an enthusiastic critique of the manuscript, wanting Hillerman to increase Leaphorn's role, and the writer's first major protagonist was born.

In this debut novel, the motive for the murder of a young Navajo is witchcraft in the shape of a Navajo Wolf, akin to a werewolf. According to Geoff Sadler, a contributor for *Contemporary Popular Writers,* this novel "is a tense, exciting adventure that mixes espionage with witchcraft." Hillerman's second novel, *Fly on the Wall,* is a story of political corruption with a journalist serving as the chief investigator. Returning with his third novel to Navajo country, as he has remained with all but one more of his novels, Hillerman next sent his reserved, logical, and partially assimilated detective, Leaphorn, into Zuni country to investigate tribal rites in *The Dance Hall of the Dead.* This second "Leaphorn" novel, which earned its author the Edgar Allan Poe Award from the Mystery Writers of America, begins with the murder of Ernesto Cata, a Zuni boy who is in training for an important ceremonial role in his tribe. Suspicion falls on a Navajo boy, George Bowlegs, but when Bowlegs is in turn murdered, Leaphorn follows clues and his instinct to a white archaeologist who killed the boys to keep them from disclosing that he had been fudging finds at his excavation site. Hillerman's third "Leaphorn" novel, *Listening Woman,* finds the Navajo detective investigating two homicides and becoming trapped in an underground cavern with terrorists and their hostages. "The novel combines clever plotlines with sharp character insights and a taut, nailbiting payoff," wrote Sadler.

With *People of Darkness* Hillerman introduces a second major protagonist, Jim Chee, who, like Leaphorn, is a Navajo tribal officer, but who, unlike Leaphorn is more traditional, less experienced, younger, and more in flux. One major reason for creating Chee was that Hillerman had sold the television rights for his Leaphorn character; he also knew he needed a different kind of protagonist, someone younger and less sophisticated than Leaphorn. In this story, Chee, a part-time ceremonial singer who is also drawn to the white lifestyle and the possibility of a career in the FBI, investigates a burglary at a wealthy white man's house which leads to a thirty-year-old crime aboard an oil rig. Chee's second adventure, *The Dark Wind*, has the younger Navajo detective chasing criminals involved in a cocaine ring who have killed several Navajos. In *The Ghostway*, Chee is off to Los Angeles in pursuit of two Navajos who are stealing luxury cars. But when the thieves return to the reservation, one of them is killed in his uncle's hogan (dwelling). Chee's heritage comes to the fore when he discovers that whoever laid the young man out for burial neglected one of the ceremonies and was thus not really a Navajo. Such a connection with tradition might come in handy in Chee's work, but not in his love life, for it isolates him from his white schoolteacher lover who ultimately leaves the reservation. Reviewing *The Ghostway* in *Entertainment Weekly*, a contributor noted that you don't have to be "a regular at Tribal Policeman Jim Chee's pow-wows to dig *The Ghostway*, one of the freshest of Hillerman's whodunits."

After finishing *The Ghostway*, Hillerman bought back the rights to Joe Leaphorn, and in his next novel, *Skinwalkers*, he pairs the detective with Chee, as he has continued to do in succeeding titles. The two investigators act as foils to one another: Leaphorn the older, more mature and methodical detective, and Chee the more quixotic, impulsive loner. The Skinwalkers of the title are Navajo ghosts, and the novel, which starts out with a shotgun attack on Chee, has witchcraft at its very heart. Leaphorn helps the younger detective get to the bottom of this attack and others on the reservation. A Golden Spur Award winner, *Skinwalkers* is a "strong, neatly worked novel with a shocking climax," according to Sadler. Writing in *People*, Campbell Geeslin noted that Hillerman "packs his novels with compelling details of Navajo life and beautiful descriptive passages about the land and weather." Geeslin concluded, "Chee . . . is a perfect guide through Hillerman's effective, dreamlike world."

Skinwalkers was, according to Michael Neill in *People*, Hillerman's "commercial breakthrough," selling 40,000 copies in hardcover and 100,000 in paperback. Yet it was his next title, *A Thief of Time*, that secured him a place on the best-seller charts and propelled Hillerman to national attention. Beginning with a murder at an Anasazi historical site, the book features a psychopathic killer and more development of the relationship between Leaphorn and Chee. In this novel, Leaphorn has to cope with his wife's death as well as his own impending retirement. As Hillerman's main recurring char-

acters, Leaphorn and Chee serve a dual function. On one level, the officers act as guides into a world of traditions and customs unfamiliar to most readers; on another level, Hillerman's depiction of Leaphorn and Chee's day-to-day struggles—with bureaucratic red tape, discrimination, and intimate relationships—helps readers understand the difficulty of living in what amounts to two worlds with different, and often contradictory, sets of rules.

This culture clash is not always depicted in a negative light, however. In books such as *Listening Woman* and *The Ghostway*, Leaphorn and Chee use both standard police procedures and their special knowledge of tribal customs to solve a wide variety of baffling crimes. In *Listening Woman*, Leaphorn finds clues to a double murder in a group of ritual sand paintings. An oddly-performed death ceremony puts Chee on the trail of a missing girl and a killer in *The Ghostway*. Stolen pottery from a "lost" tribe becomes the focus of Leaphorn's investigation into artifact trafficking in *A Thief of Time*, a book that is at once "careful with the facts," and one that "transmutes knowledge into romance," as a contributor to *Time* magazine wrote. Karl G. Fredrikkson and Lilian Fredrikkson called *A Thief of Time* "probably Hillerman's best novel," in the *St. James Guide to Crime and Mystery Writers*, and they further noted, "History and tradition play integral parts in all Hillerman's novels and especially in this one." The Fredrikssons concluded that the main theme of all Hillerman's work "is the clash between the Navajo Way and the so-called American Way of Life, between tradition and the emptiness of modern society."

As with *Dance Hall of the Dead* and *A Thief of Time*, Hillerman's novel *Talking God* deals with anthropology. This time, both Chee and Leaphorn desert the reservation for Washington, DC, in search of missing Native American artifacts. "The plot," noted Louise Bernikow in a *Cosmopolitan* review, "comes to a crashing finale in the Smithsonian Institute, and the evil that has disturbed the spirits of the Navajo is laid to rest." Bernikow also commented that Hillerman's story "is complicated, emotional, and incredibly suspenseful." In *Coyote Waits*, an officer in the Navajo Tribal Police, Delbert Nez, is gunned down, and Leaphorn and Chee set out to find his killer. It looks as if a Navajo shaman might be responsible for the killing, until other suspects turn up, including a Vietnamese teacher. Behind it all lurks the mythic Navajo character representing chaos, the Coyote of the title. Phoebe-Lou Adams, writing in the *Atlantic*, felt the plot "is a humdinger even by the high Hillerman standard," while a writer for *Entertainment Weekly* dubbed it "sturdy work from an incorruptible craftsman." Reviewing the title in *People*, Neill concluded, "Hillerman's elevation into the best- seller ranks is a great justice of American popular writing. While his novels are mysteries, they are also exquisite explorations of human nature—with a great backdrop." Reviewing *Coyote Waits*, a contributor for *Publishers Weekly* commented, "Hillerman weaves an understated, powerful tale from strands of ancient Navajo mythology, modern greed and ambition, and above all, the sorrows and delights of characters."

In *Sacred Clowns*, the duo investigate the seemingly unrelated murders of a shop teacher at the mission school and a sacred clown dancer, a Hopi koshare. In this novel, Chee is increasingly attracted to the Navajo lawyer, Janet Pete, while Leaphorn considers a relationship with a linguistics professor. "Telling his story the Navajo way," wrote a contributor to *Publishers Weekly*, "Hillerman fully develops the background of the cases . . . so that the resolutions . . . ring true with gratifying inevitability." Gene Lyons, writing in *Entertainment Weekly*, noted that even "devoted readers . . . will find *Sacred Clowns* just a bit different from earlier books in the series." Lyons pointed to the essentially "comic" structure and tone of the novel.

One interesting aspect of Hillerman's novels is that his protagonists have not stayed rooted in time, but rather have developed and aged: Leaphorn has retired, yet keeps a hand in police affairs, while Chee begins to settle down. The pair took a hiatus in the mid-1990s while Hillerman turned his hand to various other projects, including *The Mysterious West* and another novel set in Vietnam, *Finding Moon*. Then in 1997, the duo returned with *The Fallen Man*. In this novel, mountaineers find a skeleton near the summit of Ship Rock in northwestern New Mexico. The skeleton in question turns out to be that of a member of a local white family who disappeared eleven years earlier. Leaphorn, who remembers the earlier disappearance, comes back into action, though Chee, now a lieutenant, at first bristles at his intrusion. Meantime also the romance between Chee and ambitious attorney Janet Pete, whom he is courting, takes twists and turns. "As always," noted a reviewer for *Publishers Weekly*, "Hillerman treats Indian tradition and modern troubles . . . with unsentimental respect, firmly rooting his mystery in the region's distinctive peoples and geography." Sikki Andur, writing in *Entertainment Weekly*, called this thirteenth novel "a scenic ride through a land where police are more worried about cattle rustling than dope dealing," and where "a cop who's been shot doesn't crave revenge—he wants harmony." *Booklist* reviewer Stephanie Zvirin commented, "As usual, Hillerman masterfully sets the scene, con-

veying contemporary culture and weaving in intriguing side plots to add depth to character and scene." Zvirin concluded that "with all Hillerman's stories, it's the oblique way" of getting to the end "that pulls [the reader] along."

The First Eagle, published in 1998, features another scientist who comes from outside to the "res," a theme found in several of Hillerman's books. This time it is a missing female biologist who has been tracking the Bubonic plague in the prairie dogs of the Southwest. Leaphorn is hired by the scientist's grandmother to find her; meanwhile Chee is investigating the bludgeon death of a Navajo Police officer at the site where the biologist was last seen. "Hillerman's trademark melding of Navajo tradition and modern culture is captured with crystal clarity in this tale of an ancient scourge's resurgence in today's word," noted a reviewer for *Publishers Weekly*. *Booklist* critic Zvirin felt that "Hillerman's respect and deep affection for his creations and their community" runs through all of the subplots and twists of action. *Hunting Badger*, published in 1999, was inspired by an actual manhunt in the Four Corners region in which the search for the killers was badly bungled by the FBI. In Hillerman's scenario, there is a robbery at an Ute casino, and the security officer there is killed in the process. Chee is drawn into the case along with Leaphorn. Reviews of this fifteenth book in the series were somewhat mixed. Wilda Williams, writing in *Library Journal*, felt that the novel "offers a paint-by-the-numbers plot with cardboard characters," but that "diehard fans will want this." However a reviewer for *Publishers Weekly* wrote that "Hillerman is in top form" with *Hunting Badger*, and *Booklist* critic Bill Ott dubbed *Hunting Badger* "a return to form for Hillerman." Ott concluded, "Nobody uses the power of myth to enrich crime fiction more effectively than Hillerman."

In *The Sinister Pig* readers are provided with "an intricate pattern of ingenious detective work, comic romance, tribal custom, and desert atmosphere" which provide "multifaceted reading pleasure" according to *Booklist* reviewer Connie Fletcher. The novel once again follows Hillerman's usual cast of characters as they try to solve a mystery involving a body discovered on Navajo land and its connection to billions of dollars owed to the Native Americans as oil royalties. Christine C. Menefee, reviewing the novel for *School Library Journal*, stated that readers "should enjoy the broader geographical and social canvas . . . in this tale of ordinary people unraveling knots of fraud and skullduggery."

In 2004, Hillerman continued his novels starring Leaphorn and Chee with *Skeleton Man*. In the story, the two Navajo Tribal Police members investigate the emergence of a stolen diamond. The diamond is one of many that initially disappeared when two planes collided in 1956 above the Grand Canyon, and the man carrying the jewel-filled briefcase was killed. The author creates "both a fascinating whodunit and a window into a rich culture that is foreign to many Americans," noted James Ireland Baker in *People*. Commenting on *Skeleton Man*, a *Publishers Weekly* reviewer concluded "Hillerman continues to shine as the best of the West."

That same year, Hillerman temporarily turned his attention away from novels to publish *Kilroy Was There: A GI's War in Photographs*. The book was created based on photographs from World War II taken by Frank Kessler, an Army Signal Corps cameraman. Hundreds of pictures were found stored in Kessler's attic after his death in 1990. Andrew J. Huebner, writing in *Journal of Popular Culture*, found the content "arresting," pointing out that the photos and words "represent the book's most significant contributions to popular understanding of World War II." "This book serves as a graphic bloody reminder of human ignorance and folly," stated Ray B. Browne in *Journal of American Culture*.

Hillerman has also been commended for his other nonfiction works and for anthologies that explore the natural beauty and unique history of the Southwest. In *New Mexico, Rio Grande, and Other Essays*, the author discusses a number of topics, including how geographical, political, and historical factors helped the Pueblo Indians thrive when many other tribes fell prey to conquering forces. In *The Mysterious West*, Hillerman as editor pulls together previously unpublished stories from writers such as J.A. Jance and Marcia Muller, while in *The Oxford Book of American Detective Stories* and *The Best American Stories of the Century* he shows his ties to the mystery genre are as strong as those to the Southwest. But in the final analysis, Hillerman is known for his Chee-Leaphorn books and their evocation of Navajo country. In these books, the author explores, as Muhlestein noted in *Dictionary of Literary Biography*, "the themes he cares about most deeply: the question of identity, the tension between the desire to assimilate and the need to retain native traditions, the shortcomings of Anglo justice, and the spiritual illness of white culture." As Fred Erisman commented in *Tony Hillerman*, "Leaphorn and Chee, as Navajos, give readers a sense of the demands of Southwestern life. In a larger sense, though, that they are Navajo is incidental; they are human as well as Navajo, and as they . . . grapple with the realities of their people, their place, and their time, their responsibilities help all readers to decipher the palimpsest of human life in all its complexity and all its majesty."

BIOGRAPHICAL AND CRITICAL SOURCES:

BOOKS

Bulow, Ernie, and Tony Hillerman, *Talking Mysteries: A Conversation with Tony Hillerman*, University of New Mexico Press (Albuqurerque, NM), 1991.

Contemporary Literary Criticism, Volume 62, Gale (Detroit, MI), 1990.

Contemporary Popular Writers, St. James Press (Detroit, MI), 1997.

Dictionary of Literary Biography, Volume 206: *Twentieth-Century American Western Writers, First Series*, Gale (Detroit, MI), 1999.

Erisman, Fred, *Tony Hillerman*, Boise State University, 1989.

Greenberg, Martin, editor, *The Tony Hillerman Companion: A Comprehensive Guide to His Life and Work*, HarperCollins (New York, NY), 1994.

Hillerman, Tony, *Seldom Disappointed: A Memoir*, HarperCollins (New York, NY), 2001.

Reilly, John M., *Tony Hillerman: A Critical Companion*, Greenwood Press (Westport, CT), 1996.

St. James Guide to Crime and Mystery Writers, 4th edition, St. James Press (Detroit, MI), 1996.

Sobol, John, *Tony Hillerman: A Public Life*, ECW Press, 1994.

PERIODICALS

Armchair Detective, fall, 1990, p. 426.

Atlantic, September, 1990, Phoebe- Lou Adams, review of *Coyote Waits*, p. 121; January, 1992, p. 115.

Booklist, October 1, 1994, p. 243; September 15, 1995, p. 116; March 1, 1996, p. 1125; November 1, 1996, Stephanie Zvirin, review of *The Fallen Man*, p. 459; October 15, 1997, p. 424; November 15, 1998, p. 604; June 1, 1999, p. 1853; July, 1999, Stephanie Zvirin, review of *The First Eagle*, p. 1829; April 1, 2000, p. 1437; May 1, 2000, Bill Ott, review of *Hunting Badger*, p. 1595; September 1, 2000, p. 144; May 1, 2003, Connie Fletcher, review of *The Sinister Pig*, p. 1547; September 15, 2004, Connie Fletcher, review of *Skeleton Man*, p. 179; October 15, 2005, Connie Fletcher, review of *A New Omnibus of Crime*, p. 33.

Cosmopolitan, June, 1989, Louise Bernikow, review of *Talking God*, p. 48.

Economist, August 14, 1993, pp. 83-84.

Entertainment Weekly, January 31, 1992, review of *Coyote Waits*, p. 54; April 3, 1992, review of *The Ghostway*, p. 47; September 17, 1993, Gene Lyons, review of *Sacred Clowns*, p. 82; November 3, 1995, p. 59; November 15, 1996, Sikki Andur, review of *The Fallen Man*.

Journal of American Culture, June, 2005, Ray B. Browne, review of *Kilroy Was There: A GI's War in Photographs*, p. 236.

Journal of Popular Culture, August, 2005, Andrew J. Huebner, review of *Kilroy Was There*, p. 972.

Kirkus Reviews, February 1, 1996, p. 179.

Library Journal, November 1, 1994, p. 77; March 1, 1996, p. 109; March 15, 1997, p. 102; July, 1998, p. 136; January, 1999, p. 184; November 15, 1999, Wilda Williams, review of *Hunting Badger*, p. 98; April 1, 2000, p. 150; Janurary 2004, Sandy Glover, review of *The Sinister Pig*, p. 186.

Los Angeles Times Book Review, January 21, 1990, p. 14; May 27, 1990, p. 10; December 16, 1990; November 17, 1991, p. 12; January 5, 1992, p. 9; October 3, 1993, p. 12.

New Yorker, August 23, 1993, p. 165.

New York Times, June 10, 1989, Herbert Mitgang, "Hillerman Adds Tribal Rites of Washington to the Navajos," p. 15; February 16, 2000, p. B2.

New York Times Book Review, December 23, 1990, p. 20; October 20, 1991, p. 36; February 2, 1992, p. 28; August 30, 1992, p. 14; October 17, 1993, p. 36; October 22, 1995, p. 29; November 21, 1999, p. 80.

People, February 9, 1987, Campbell Geeslin, review of *Skinwalkers*, p. 16; July 18, 1988, Michael Neill, "A Keen Observer in a World Not His Own," p. 85; August 27, 1990, Michael Neill, review of *Coyote Waits*, p. 22; December 6, 2004, James Ireland Baker, review of *Skeleton Man*, p. 55.

Publishers Weekly, October 24, 1980; May 11, 1990, review of *Coyote Waits*, p. 250; July 26, 1993, review of *Sacred Clowns*, p. 60; September 12, 1994, p. 85; September 4, 1995, p. 48; February 12, 1996, p. 63; October 21, 1996, review of *The Fallen Man*, p. 73; July 13, 1998, review of *The First Eagle*, p. 65; October 18, 1999, p. 74; November 22, 1999, p. 16; January 3, 2000, review of *Hunting Badger*, p. 40; March 6, 2000, p. 85; October 18, 2004, review of *Skeleton Man*, p. 50; September 5, 2005, review of *A New Omnibus of Crime*, p. 39.

Quadrant, July, 2000, p. 118.

School Library Journal, February, 1994, p. 136; March, 1995, p. 235; December 2003, Christine C. Menefee, review of *The Sinister Pig*, p. 176.

Time, July 4, 1988, review of *A Thief of Time*, p. 71.

Tribune Books (Chicago, IL), September 2, 1990; September 26, 1993, p. 6.

Wall Street Journal, August 13, 1998, p. A12.

Washington Post Book World, May 27, 1990, p. 12; July 26, 1992, p. 1; September 5, 1993, p. 4.

Writer's Digest, January, 2000, pp. 8-9.

ONLINE

Tony Hillerman Home Page, http://www.tonyhillerman books.com/ (March 7, 2006).

*   *   *

HINOJOSA, Rolando 1929-
(P. Galindo, Rolando R. Hinojosa-S., Rolando Hinojosa-Smith, Rolando R. Hinojosa-Smith, Rolando (R.) Hinojosa Smith)

PERSONAL: Born January 21, 1929, in Mercedes, TX; son of Manuel Guzman (a farmer) and Carrie Effie (a homemaker; maiden name, Smith) Hinojosa; married Patricia Mandley, September 1, 1963 (divorced, 1989); children: Clarissa Elizabeth, Karen Louise, Robert Huddleston. *Education:* University of Texas at Austin, B.S., 1953; New Mexico Highlands University, M.A., 1963; University of Illinois, Ph.D., 1969. *Politics:* Democrat. *Religion:* Catholic.

ADDRESSES: Office—Department of English, University of Texas at Austin, Austin, TX 78712. *E-mail*—RORRO@mail.utexas.edu.

CAREER: High school teacher in Brownsville, TX, 1954-56; Trinity University, San Antonio, TX, assistant professor of modern languages, 1968-70; Texas A & I University, Kingsville, associate professor of Spanish and chair of modern language department, 1970-74, dean of College of Arts and Sciences, 1974-76, vice president for academic affairs, 1976-77; University of Minnesota—Minneapolis, chair of department of Chicano studies, 1977-80, professor of Chicano studies and American studies, 1980-81; University of Texas at Austin, professor of English, 1981-85, E.C. Garwood Professor, 1985—, Mari Sabusawa Michener Chair, 1989-93. Consultant to Minneapolis Education Association, 1978-80, to U.S. Information Agency, 1980 and 1989, and to Texas Commission for the Arts and Humanities, 1981-82. Texas Center for Writers, University of Texas, Austin, 1989-93. *Military service:* U.S. Army 1946-49 and Army Reserves, ten years; became second lieutenant.

MEMBER: Modern Language Association (chair of Commission on Languages and Literature in Ethnic Studies, 1978-80), PEN, Academia de la Lengua Espanola en Norteamerica, Hispanic Society, Fellow Society of Spanish and Spanish American Studies (fellow), Texas Institute of Letters.

AWARDS, HONORS: Best in West Award for foreign language radio programming from the state of California, 1970-71; Quinto Sol Literary Award for best novel, 1972, for *Estampas del valle y otras obras;* Premio Casa de las Americas award for best novel, 1976, for *Klail City y sus alrededores;* Southwest Studies on Latin America award for best writing in the humanities, 1981, for *Mi querido Rafa;* distinguished alumnus award from University of Illinois College of Liberal Arts, 1988; Lifetime Achievement Award, Texas Institute of Letters, 1997; distinguished achievement award, University of Illinois, 1998; distinguished alumnus, Texas Southwest College, 1999.

WRITINGS:

NOVELS

Estampas del valle y otras obras (first novel in "Klail City Death Trip" series), Quinto Sol (Berkeley, CA), 1972, bilingual edition with translation by Gustavo Valadez and Jose Reyna published as *Sketches of the Valley and Other Works,* Justa Publications (Berkeley, CA), 1980, revised English language edition published as *The Valley,* Bilingual Press (Ypsilanti, MI), 1983.

Klail City y sus alrededores (second novel in "Klail City Death Trip" series), bilingual edition with translation by Rosaura Sanchez, Casa de las Americas, 1976, published under name Rolando R. Hinojosa-S. as *Generaciones y semblanzas* (title means "Biographies and Lineages"), Justa Publications (Berkeley, CA), 1977, translation by Hinojosa published as *Klail City,* Arte Publico Press (Houston, TX), 1987.

Korean Love Songs from Klail City Death Trip (novel in verse form; third in "Klail City Death Trip" series), illustrations by Rene Castro, Justa Publications (Berkeley, CA), 1978.

Claros varones de Belken (fourth novel in "Klail City Death Trip" series), Justa Publications (Berkeley, CA), 1981, bilingual edition with translation by Julia Cruz published as *Fair Gentlemen of Belken County,* Bilingual Press (Ypsilanti, MI), 1987.

Mi querido Rafa (fifth novel in "Klail City Death Trip" series), Arte Publico Press (Houston, TX), 1981, translation by Hinojosa published as *Dear Rafe,* 1985.

Rites and Witnesses (sixth novel in "Klail City Death Trip" series), Arte Publico Press (Houston, TX), 1982.

Partners in Crime, Arte Publico Press (Houston, TX), 1985.

Los amigos de Becky (seventh novel in "Klail City Death Trip" series), Arte Publico Press (Houston, TX), 1990, translation published as *Becky and Her Friends,* 1990.

The Useless Servants (eighth novel in "Klail City Death Trip" series), Arte Publico Press (Houston, TX), 1993.

El condado de Belken—Klail City, Editorial Bilingue, 1994.

Estampas del valle, Editorial Bilingue (Tempe, AZ), 1994.

Ask a Policeman, Arte Publico Press (Houston, TX), 1998.

OTHER

Generaciones, notas, y brechas/Generations, Notes, and Trails, (nonfiction; bilingual edition), translation by Fausto Avendano, Casa de las Americas (La Habana), 1978.

(Author of introduction) Carmen Tafolla, *Curandera,* M & A Editions, 1983.

(Contributor under name Rolando Hinojosa-Smith) Alan Pogue, *Agricultural Workers of the Rio Grande and Rio Bravo Valleys,* Center for Mexican American Studies, University of Texas at Austin (Austin, TX), 1984.

(Translator from the Spanish) Tomas Rivera, *This Migrant Earth,* Arte Publico Press (Houston, TX), 1985.

(Contributor) Jose David Saldivar, editor, *The Rolando Hinojosa Reader: Essays Historical and Critical,* Arte Publico Press (Houston, TX), 1985.

Valley: A Re-Creation in Narrative Prose of a Portfolio of Etchings, Engravings, Sketches, and Silhouettes by Various Artists in Various Styles, Bilingual Review Press (Tempe AZ), 1994.

Also author, under pseudonym P. Galindo, of *Mexican American Devil's Dictionary.* Work represented in anthologies, including *Festival de flor y canto: An Anthology of Chicano Literature,* edited by F.A. Cervantes, Juan Gomez-Quinones, and others, University of Southern California Press, 1976. Contributor of short stories, articles, and reviews to periodicals, including *Texas Monthly, Texas Humanist, Los Angeles Times,* and *Dallas Morning News.*

SIDELIGHTS: The first Chicano author to receive a major international literary award, Rolando Hinojosa won the prestigious Premio Casa de las Americas for *Klail City y sus alrededores* (*Klail City*), part of a series of novels known to English-speaking readers as "The Klail City Death Trip." Hinojosa's fiction, often infused with satire or subtle humor, is widely admired for its blending of diverse plot lines and narrative styles. The individual perspectives of many characters come together in his works to form a unique collective voice representative of the Chicano people. Hinojosa has also produced essays, poetry, and two detective novels titled *Partners in Crime* and *Ask a Policeman*.

Hinojosa was born in the Lower Rio Grande Valley in Texas. There his Chicano ancestors settled long before the United States annexed part of it. His Mexican American father fought in the Mexican Revolution, while his Anglo American mother maintained the family north of the border, and he was thus deeply influenced by both cultures. An avid reader during childhood, Hinojosa was raised speaking Spanish until he attended junior high school, where English was the primary spoken language. Like his grandmother, mother, and three of his four siblings, Hinojosa became a teacher; he has held several professorial posts and has also been active in academic administration and consulting work. Although he prefers to write in Spanish, Hinojosa has also translated his own books and written others in English.

Hinojosa entered the literary scene with the 1973 *Estampas del valle y otras obras*, which was translated as *Sketches of the Valley and Other Works*. The four-part novel consists of loosely connected sketches, narratives, monologues, and dialogues, offering a composite picture of Chicano life in the fictitious Belken County town of Klail City, Texas. The first part of *Estampas* introduces Jehu Malacara, a nine-year-old boy who is left to live with exploitative relatives after the deaths of his parents. Hinojosa synthesizes the portrait of Jehu's life through comic and satiric sketches and narratives of incidents and characters surrounding him. The second section is a collection of pieces about a murder presented through newspaper accounts, court documents, and testimonials from the defendant's relatives. A third segment, narrated by an omniscient storyteller, is a selection of sketches depicting people from various social groups in Klail City, while the fourth section introduces the series' other main character, Jehu's cousin Rafa Buenrostro. Also orphaned during childhood, Rafa narrates a succession of experiences and recollections of his life. Hinojosa later rewrote *Estampas del valle y otras obras* in English, publishing it as *The Valley* in 1983.

Hinojosa's aggregate portrait of the Spanish southwest continues in *Klail City y sus alrededores*, published in English as *Klail City*. Like its predecessor, *Klail City* is comprised of interwoven narratives, conversations, and anecdotes that portray fifty years in the town's collective life. Winner of the 1976 Premio Casa de las Americas, the book was cited for its "richness of imagery, the sensitive creation of dialogues, the collage-like structure based on a pattern of converging individual destinies, the masterful control of the temporal element and its testimonial value," according to Charles M. Tatum in *World Literature Today*. Introducing more than one hundred characters and developing further the portraits of Rafa and Jehu, *Klail City* prompted *Western American Literature* writer Lourdes Torres to praise Hinojosa for his "unusual talent for capturing the language and spirit of his subject matter."

Korean Love Songs from Klail City Death Trip and *Claros varones de Belken* are Hinojosa's third and fourth installments in the series. A novel comprised of several long poems originally written in English and published in 1978, *Korean Love Songs* presents protagonist Rafa Buenrostro's narration of his experiences as a soldier in the Korean War. In poems such as "Friendly Fire" and "Rafe," Hinojosa explores army life, grief, male friendships, discrimination, and the reality of death presented through dispassionate, often ironic descriptions of the atrocity of war. *Claros varones de Belken* (*Fair Gentlemen of Belken County*), released three years later, follows Jehu and Rafa as they narrate accounts of their experiences serving in the Korean War, attending the University of Texas at Austin, and beginning careers as high school teachers in Klail City. The book also includes the narratives of two more major characters, writer P. Galindo and local historian Esteban Echevarria, who comment on their own and others' circumstances. Expressing a favorable opinion of the book was *Los Angeles Times Book Review* writer Alejandro Morales, who concluded that "the scores of names and multiple narrators at first pose a challenge, but quickly the imagery, language and subtle folk humor of Belken County win the reader's favor."

Hinojosa continued the "Klail City Death Trip" series with *Mi querido Rafa*. Translated as *Dear Rafe*, the novel is divided into two parts and consists of letters and interviews. The first half of the work is written in epistolary style containing only letters from Jehu—now a successful bank officer—to his cousin Rafa. Between the novel's two parts, however, Jehu suddenly leaves his important position at the Klail City First National Bank, and in the second section, Galindo interviews twenty-one community members about possible reasons for Jehu's resignation. The two major characters are depicted through dialogue going on around and about them; the reader obtains a glimpse of Rafa's personality through Jehu's letters, and Jehu's life is sketched through the opinions of the townspeople. *San Francisco Review of Books* writer Arnold Williams compared the power of Hinojosa's fictional milieu, striking even in translation, to that of twentieth-century Jewish writer Isaac Bashevis Singer, noting that "Hinojosa is such a master of English that he captures the same intimacy and idiomatic word play in his re-creations."

After writing *Rites and Witnesses,* the sixth novel in the "Klail City Death Trip" series, Hinojosa turned to a conventional form of the novel with the 1985 *Partners in Crime,* a detective thriller about the murder of a Belken County district attorney and several Mexican nationals in a local bar. Detective squads from both sides of the border are called to investigate the case; clues lead to an established and powerful cocaine smuggling ring. Jehu and Rafa reappear in the novel as minor characters who nevertheless play important parts in the mystery's development. "Those who might mourn the ending of the ['Klail City Death Trip' series] and their narrative experimentation and look askance at Hinojosa's attempting such a predictable and recipe-oriented genre as the murder mystery need not worry," concluded Williams. "He can weave a social fabric that is interesting, surprising, realistic and still entertaining."

In *Becky and Her Friends* Hinojosa continues his attempt to capture the many voices of the Hispanic community. Twenty-six characters from previous novels in the "Klail City Death Trip" series (including Becky) are each given a chapter here to discuss Becky's divorce from Ira Escobar and her subsequent marriage to Jehu Malacara. Writing in *Western American Literature,* R.L. Streng noted that "the characters' voices are difficult to differentiate one from another, and since each character falls into a camp for or against Becky and her escapades, there is very little difference between what we hear from Lionel Villa and Viola Barragan in one camp or Elvira Navarrete and Ira Escobar in the other." Streng concluded that *Becky and Her Friends* "fails in its attempt to corral a variety of characters and establish a lively vocal forum. Instead, the novel is tedious and requires readers to wade through extensive and unnecessary redundancies. Other reviewers, however, praised the novel for its evocation of the American-Hispanic ethos, one that is simultaneously deeply traditional, Catholic, and superstitious."

Hinojosa extended the "Klail City Death Trip" series with *The Useless Servants,* a novel—unlike many others in the series—with only one narrative voice. A kind of novelization of his previous book of poems *Korean Love Songs from Klail City Death Trip, The Useless Servants* is the diary kept by Rafe Buenrostro when he was an infantryman in the U.S. Army during the Korean war. It is written very much in the manner of personal diaries, employing clipped phrases, few pronouns, and little explanation of the objects in the writer's daily routine—in this case, military jargon, acronyms, etc. Thematically, the book presents Rafe's experience of warfare and army life as a Hispanic-American. Critical reaction to the novel was mixed. B. Adler, writing in *Choice,* felt that the work "is curious in the lack of insight it demonstrates, its flatness overall, with no reaching toward even stylistic significance." Dismayed by Rafe's apparent detachment from his own experiences, Adler concluded: "Perhaps Hinojosa is trying to make a point about the essentially boring nature of the average human being, even when placed in an extraordinary situation such as war. The dilemma is how realistic to make dullness. Hinojosa is too successful here." On the other hand, while William Anthony Nericcio in *World Literature Toady* also found Hinojosa's use of military jargon and acronyms rather unrelenting, he lauded the author's allusions to Plato's *Republic,* stating that "Plato's cave fire and the Korean battlefield illuminate each other nicely." Nericcio also noted that *The Useless Servants* further enriches the thematic texture of its series, writing: "The studied effort at intertextual dialectics set up between volumes in the Klail City Death Trip Series is as dense and electric as some to be found in Faulkner's oeuvre."

Hinojosa once commented: "I enjoy writing, of course, but I enjoy the re-writing even more: four or five re-writings are not uncommon. Once finished, though, it's on to something else. At this date, every work done in Spanish has also been done in English with the exception of *Claros varones de Belken,* although I did work quite closely on the idiomatic expressions which I found to be at the heart of the telling of the story.

"I usually don't read reviews; articles by learned scholars, however, are something else. They've devoted much time and thought to their work, and it is only fair I read them and take them seriously. The articles come from France, Germany, Spain, and so on, as well as from the United States. I find them not only interesting but, at times, revelatory. I don't know how much I am influenced by them, but I'm sure I am, as much as I am influenced by a lifetime of reading. Scholars do keep one on one's toes, but not, obviously, at their mercy. Writing has allowed me to meet writers as diverse as Julio Cortazar, Ishmael Reed, Elena Poniatowski and George Lamming.

"My goal is to set down in fiction the history of the Lower Rio Grande Valley. . . . A German scholar, Wolfgang Karrer, from Osnabrueck University has a census of my characters; they number some one thousand. That makes me an Abraham of some sort.

"Personally and professionally, my life as a professor and as a writer inseparably combines vocation with avocation. My ability in both languages is most helpful, and thanks for this goes to my parents and to the place where I was raised.

"My main motivation (for writing) stems from a childhood need to express myself. The influences are so many and so diverse, I could not begin to name or list them all; a few, however, bear mentioning, Benito Perez Galdes; Anthony Powell, and Heinrich Boll.

"My writing begins with a half-formed idea that then takes off by itself. Sometimes, a stranger's passing comment may set off a train of thought that my or may not lead to a piece of writing.

"The inspiration comes from various places: A bicultural background, a sure knowledge of the history and myths of where I was born, the relating of official history and that which opposes it. I imagine my writing has changed, but I don't know to what degree. That, then is a matter for the critics.

"I don't think I've had or made changes in my writing; it happens that I've written three novels in fragmentary form, one in narrative verse, one consisting mainly of dialogues and monologues; there is also an epistolary novel. The two detective works are linear and both the English and Spanish versions of *Becky* (*Becky and Her Friends* and *Los Amigos de Becky*) consist of thirty-eight male and female voices, of all ages. There is also a first person novel in diary or log form. The many forms may appear as changes, however, I've chosen the different forms because I found them suitable for what I wanted to write at the time.

BIOGRAPHICAL AND CRITICAL SOURCES:

BOOKS

Bruce-Novoa, Juan, *Chicano Authors: Inquiry by Interview,* University of Texas Press (Austin, TX), 1980.

Dictionary of Literary Biography, Volume 82: *Chicano Writers,* First Series, Thomson Gale (Detroit, MI), 1989.

Lee, Joyce Glover, *Rolando Hinojosa and the American Dream,* University of North Texas Press (Denton, TX), 1997.

Saldivar, Jose David, editor, *The Rolando Hinojosa Reader: Essays Historical and Critical,* Arte Publico Press (Houston, TX), 1985.

Zilles, Klaus, *Rolando Hinojosa: A Reader's Guide,* University of New Mexico Press (Albuquerque, NM), 2001.

PERIODICALS

Choice, December 1993, B. Adler, review of *The Useless Servants.*

Hispania, September 1986.

Hispanic, September 1990, p. 48.

Los Angeles Times Book Review, April 12, 1987, Alejandro Morales, review of *Fair Gentlemen of Belken County;* October 10, 1993.

Publishers Weekly, November 28, 1986; July 12, 1993, review of *The Useless Servants,* p. 69.

San Francisco Review of Books, spring, 1985; fall/winter, 1985.

Western American Literature, fall, 1988, Lourdes Torres, review of *Klail City;* summer, 1991, R.L. Streng, review of *Becky and Her Friends.*

World Literature Today, summer, 1977, Charles M. Tatum, review of *Klail City y sus alrededores,;* summer, 1986; winter, 1995, William Anthony Nericcio, review of *The Useless Servants,* p. 139.

*   *   *

HINOJOSA-SMITH, Rolando
See HINOJOSA, Rolando

*   *   *

HINOJOSA-SMITH, Rolando R.
See HINOJOSA, Rolando

*   *   *

HINOJOSA-S., Rolando R.
See HINOJOSA, Rolando

HINTON, S.E. 1950-

PERSONAL: Born in 1950, in Tulsa, OK; married David E. Inhofe (in mail order business), September, 1970; children: Nicholas David. *Education:* University of Tulsa, B.S., 1970.

ADDRESSES: Home—Tulsa, OK.

CAREER: Writer. Consultant on film adaptations of her novels; minor acting roles in some film adaptations of her novels.

AWARDS, HONORS: New York Herald Tribune best teenage books citation, 1967, *Chicago Tribune Book World* Spring Book Festival Honor Book, 1967, *Media & Methods* Maxi Award, American Library Association (ALA) Best Young Adult Books citation, both 1975, and Massachusetts Children's Book Award, 1979, all for *The Outsiders;* ALA Best Books for Young Adults citation, 1971, *Chicago Tribune Book World* Spring Book Festival Award Honor Book, 1971, and Massachusetts Children's Book Award, 1978, all for *That Was Then, This Is Now;* ALA Best Books for Young Adults citation, 1975,*School Library Journal* Best Books of the Year citation, 1975, and Land of Enchantment Book Award, New Mexico Library Association, 1982, all for *Rumble Fish;* ALA Best Books for Young Adults citation, 1979, *School Library Journal* Best Books of the Year citation, 1979, New York Public Library Books for the Teen-Age citation, 1980, American Book Award nomination for children's paperback, 1981, Sue Hefly Award Honor Book, Louisiana Association of School Libraries, 1982, California Young Reader Medal nomination, California Reading Association, 1982, and Sue Hefly Award, 1983, all for *Tex;* Golden Archer Award, 1983; Recipient of first ALA Young Adult Services Division/*School Library Journal* Margaret A. Edwards Award, 1988, for body of work.

WRITINGS:

YOUNG ADULT NOVELS

The Outsiders, Viking (New York City), 1967.
That Was Then, This Is Now, illustrated by Hal Siegel, Viking, 1971.
Rumble Fish (also see below), Delacorte (New York City), 1975.
Tex, Delacorte, 1979.

Taming the Star Runner, Delacorte, 1988.
Hawkes Harbor, Tor (New York, NY), 2004.

OTHER

(With Francis Ford Coppola) *Rumble Fish* (screenplay; adapted from her novel), Universal, 1983.
Big David, Little David (for children), illustrated by Alan Daniel, Doubleday, 1995.
The Puppy Sister (for children), illustrated by Jacqueline Rogers, Delacorte, 1995.

ADAPTATIONS: Film adaptations of Hinton's novels include *Tex,* starring Matt Dillon, Walt Disney Productions, 1982; *The Outsiders,* starring C. Thomas Howell and Matt Dillon, Warner Bros., 1983; and *That Was Then, This Is Now,* starring Emilio Estevez and Craig Sheffer, Paramount, 1985. *The Outsiders* was adapted as a television series by Fox-TV, 1990. Current Affairs and Mark Twain Media adapted *The Outsiders* and *That Was Then, This Is Now* as filmstrips with cassettes, both 1978.*Rumble Fish* was adapted as a record and cassette, Viking, 1977.

SIDELIGHTS: Ponyboy. Greasers vs. Socs. For millions of fans around the world, these few words will instantly call up the world of *The Outsiders,* S.E. Hinton's classic novel about teen gangs and the troubled process of fitting in. Since publication of this first novel in 1967, "the world of young adult writing and publishing [has] never [been] the same," according to Jay Daly in the critical study, *Presenting S.E. Hinton.* Daly went on to note that "*The Outsiders* has become the most successful, and the most emulated, young adult book of all time." Ironically, this quiet revolution in book writing and publishing was wrought by a seventeen-year-old girl, who by all rights should have been one of the intended readers of the novel, not its author.

Hinton is credited with revolutionizing the young adult genre by portraying teenagers realistically rather than formulaically and by creating characters, settings, and dialogue that are representative of teenage life in America. *The Outsiders* was the first in her short but impressive list of books to feature troubled but sensitive male adolescents as protagonists. Hinton's subjects include social-class rivalry, poverty, alcoholism, drug addiction, and the cruelty teenagers often inflict on each other and on themselves. Film rights to all five of her novels have been acquired, and four have been adapted as major motion pictures.

Hinton was a high school sophomore at Tulsa's Will Rogers High School when she began writing *The Outsiders*. At the time she had not the slightest dream in the world that her manuscript would be published, let alone that it would sell millions of copies worldwide, spawn a motion picture, and start a trend in publishing toward gritty realism for younger readers. At the time, young Susie was simply working out private concerns. Firstly, she was reacting to divisions apparent in her own high school, and secondly, she was filling a void in subject matter that she herself wanted to read. At the time when Hinton began writing, young adult titles were mostly pure as corn and sweetly innocent; tales in which the major problem was which dress to wear to the prom or whether such-and-such a boy would be the date. "Into this sterile chiffon-and-orchids environment then came *The Outsiders*," observed Daly. "Nobody worries about the prom in *The Outsiders;* they're more concerned with just staying alive till June."

If Hinton turned the world of publishing upside down with her youthful title, its publication did the same for her life. As word of mouth slowly made the book a classic (it now has eight million copies in print), Hinton was attempting to develop a normal life, studying education at the University of Tulsa, marrying, and having a family. Writing block settled in and it was four years before her second title, *That Was Then, This Is Now,* came out, another edgy story of teen angst. Two further books were published in four-year intervals: *Rumble Fish* in 1975, and *Tex* in 1979. Then nearly a decade passed before publication of her fifth YA title, *Taming the Star Runner.* Since that time, Hinton has published two titles for younger readers. Small in output, Hinton has nonetheless made a major impact on children's literature, a fact confirmed by the 1988 presentation to her of the first annual Margaret A. Edwards Award for career achievement. Her books now have over ten million copies in print; four of her five YA titles have been filmed; and Hinton still receives bushels of mail from enthusiastic fans for all her books, but especially for *The Outsiders,* now over three decades old, but with a message that continues to speak across the generations.

Hinton was born in 1948, in Tulsa, Oklahoma, but little more is known about her early years, as Hinton herself is a very private person. Indeed, confusion reins around aspects of her life, such as her year of birth as well as her inspiration for beginning to write. What is known is that she grew up a voluntary tomboy in love with horses. That passion has not diminished over the years, and Hinton is still an avid horsewoman. She was able to use her horse lore in the novel, *Taming the Star Runner.* Hinton's tomboy status also brought her closer to

male friends than female. She identified more with active males than with the passive role females of the day were encouraged to project.

A self-confessed outsider as a youngster, Hinton did not belong to any one clique in school, but was friends with a wide variety of types. Along with horses Hinton also developed an early love of reading. "I started reading about the same time everyone else did," Hinton wrote in *Fourth Book of Junior Authors,* "and began to write a short time later. The major influence on my writing has been my reading. I read everything, including Comet cans and coffee labels." Her first writing efforts dealt with horses, and her stories were generally told from a boy's point of view. By the time she reached high school, she was ready to tackle a larger subject, namely the rivalry between two groups in the school, the "greasers" and the affluent "socs" (short for "socials").

In the wake of school shootings across the nation during the 1990s, all Americans have become more sensitive to the outsider groups at schools, to the cruel pecking orders established in the microcosm of schools. In Hinton's day, peer pressure was no less severe and oppressive. "I felt the greasers were getting knocked when they didn't deserve it," Hinton told an interviewer for *Seventeen* shortly after publication of her novel. "The custom for instance, of driving by a shabby boy and screaming 'Greaser!' at him always made me boil. But it was the cold-blooded beating of a friend of mine that gave me the idea of writing a book."

Hinton began the writing in her sophomore year, during the time her father, Grady P. Hinton, was diagnosed with a brain tumor. As Daly put it, "It is not something she talks about, but one gets the impression that his hospitalization, and the inevitable, unavoidable conclusion that his illness promised, were factors in her withdrawing into herself." While her mother spent more and more time at the hospital, Hinton spent more time in her room or at the dining room table working on her novel. "Susie was very close to her father," Hinton's mother told Yvonne Litchfield of the *Tulsa Daily World,* "and I noticed that the sicker he became the harder she worked." Hinton's father died in her junior year, about the time she completed her book.

Hinton worked through four drafts of her story before she was happy with it, but still she gave no thought to publication until the mother of one of her school friends—a professional children's writer—took a look at the manuscript. This reader immediately saw commercial possibilities for the book and urged Hinton to get in touch with her own New York agent. The Oklahoma teenager did just that, and the rest is publishing history.

Hinton's novel was, as Hinton myth has it, accepted for publication the night of her high school graduation, and it appeared in bookstores the spring of her freshman year at college at the University of Tulsa. As the book was written from the male perspective, Hinton's publisher, Viking, prompted her to adapt the more genderless author name of S.E. Hinton. Such a publication was an enormous gamble for a prestigious New York house, but Hinton's book was no overnight success. Slowly and by word of mouth sales grew and continued growing. Letters started arriving at the Hinton household from teenagers all over the country confessing that they never imagined somebody else felt like they did, that they were solaced by the fact that others felt like outsiders just as they did. It was soon apparent that Hinton had touched a raw nerve in American culture.

Hinton's novel deals with a matter of days in the lives of a small group of Tulsa teenagers, loosely modeled after Hinton's own classmates. The book begins and ends with the same lines: "When I stepped out into the bright sunlight from the darkness of the movie house, I had only two things on my mind: Paul Newman and a ride home." In fact the entire book is a composition that the narrator, Ponyboy Curtis, must complete for English class. Trailed home from the movie by a group of Socs (pronounced "soshes" for Socials), Ponyboy is jumped by these rivals, and is saved by his older brothers, Darry and Sodapop, along with other members of his gang, the greasers. These others include the tough guy, Dallas Winston, and the joker who carries a switchblade, Two-Bit Matthews.

Later that night, Ponyboy, Dallas, and another gang member, Johnny, sneak into the drive-in and meet up with two Socs girls, Cherry and Marcia. Confronted after the movie by more Socs, led by Bob Sheldon, their most dangerous fighter, Cherry avoids an altercation by leaving with the Socs. Ruminating about their situation in a vacant lot, Ponyboy and Johnny fall asleep and by the time Ponyboy gets home, he has a run-in with Darry, who has been waiting up for him. Orphaned, the three brothers take care of each other. But Ponyboy has had enough, and decides to run away. Heading off with Johnny, they get only as far as the park before Sheldon and the Socs meet up with them again. In the ensuing fight, Johnny kills Sheldon with a knife.

Heading out is not merely optional now, but vital. Dallas tells the duo of a church hideout in a nearby town, and for the next five days they hole up, reading *Gone with the Wind,* talking about the Robert Frost poem, "Nothing Gold Can Stay," appreciating sunsets and dawns, and munching on baloney sandwiches. When Dally, or Dallas, comes to visit, Johnny says he's through with running; he's going to turn himself in. On the way home, they go by the church and see that it is burning. Perhaps this is a result of the cigarettes they left inside, but whatever the cause they know that children are trapped inside. Without thinking, both Ponyboy and Johnny rush inside to save them. Though they rescue the children, Johnny is badly hurt when a timber falls on his back. Ponyboy and Dallas are also both badly burned.

Cast in the uncommon role of hero, Ponyboy goes to visit Johnny in critical condition at the hospital. Later that evening there is a big rumble between rival gangs, and even the injured Dallas shows up. Victorious, the greasers are jubilant, and Ponyboy and Dallas rush to the hospital to tell Johnny, only to discover him near death. With his dying words, Johnny tells Ponyboy to "Stay gold," referring to the Frost poem about youth and lost innocence. Johnny's death pushes the edgy Dallas over the line. He robs a grocery store and goes down in a hail of police bullets, an unloaded gun in his hands, his death a rather blindly foolish martyrdom.

Suffering from a concussion incurred at the big rumble, Ponyboy collapses, confined to bed for days. He gets it in his head that he killed Sheldon, not Johnny, and is set to confess at the hearing about the death, but he is acquitted before he has a chance to confess. He remains numb inside, until he discovers another exhortation from Johnny to stay gold, this time in a note left in their copy of *Gone with the Wind.* This breaks through to him and he picks up his pen to start his term paper, writing the first lines of the novel once again.

Critical reception of this publishing phenomenon was mostly laudatory; those with reservations mostly found the book erred on the side of over-sentimentality and cliched writing. "Can sincerity overcome cliches?" asked Thomas Fleming in the *New York Times Book Review.* Fleming answered his own question mostly in the positing: "In this book by a now 17-year-old author, it almost does the trick. By almost any standard, Miss Hinton's performance is impressive." Fleming's view was reflected by other reviewers, both then and now. Writing in *Horn Book,* Jane Manthorne called Hinton's work a "remarkable novel . . . a moving, credible view of the outsiders from inside." Lillian N. Gerhardt, reviewing the novel in *School Library Journal,* drew attention to the rare fact in juvenile novels of "confronting the class hostilities which have intensified since the Depression." Gerhardt noted that "Ponyboy . . . tells how it looks and feels from the wrong side of the tracks." Reviewing the book in *Atlantic Monthly,* Nat Hentoff lamented the sometimes "factitious" plot, but declared that Hinton, "with an astute ear and a lively sense of the restless rhythms of the young, also explores the tenacious loyalties on both sides of the class divide." Hentoff concluded that the book was so popular among the young "because it stimulates their own feelings and questionings about class and differing lifestyles." An English reviewer for the *Times Literary Supplement* cut to the chase when noting that it was largely irrelevant whether adult reviewers found the novel dull, contrived, over-sentimentalized, too violent, or just plain implausible. "Young readers will waive literary discrimination about a book of this kind and adopt Ponyboy as a kind of folk hero for both his exploits and his dialogue," the reviewer concluded.

In the event, this critic was dead on. Once word of mouth was established regarding the youth and gender of the writer of *The Outsiders,* sales continued to grow and grow. It was apparent that Hinton and Viking had struck an entirely untapped readership; young kids aching for their stories to be told from their point of view with their voice. Little matter that Hinton's supposed stark realism was really "mythic" as the critic Michael Malone pointed out in an extended piece on the author in *Nation.* "Far from strikingly realistic in literary form," Malone remarked, "[Hinton's] novels are romances, mythologizing the tragic beauty of violent youth. . . ." Malone and others have rightly pointed out that the vast majority of teenagers personally experience nothing close to the violence of Hinton's characters, nor do they suffer the vacuum of parental supervision of her Peter Pan-like cast of orphans and near orphans who must look after themselves or watch out that alcoholic, abusive parents do not do them harm.

Never mind, either, the fact of Hinton's sometimes "mawkish and ornate" prose, according to Malone, who noted that Ponyboy "fling[s] adjectives and archaic phrases ('Hence his name,' 'Heaven forbid') around like Barbara Cartland." Ponyboy, through whose eyes the action is viewed, describes characters with an elevated language that is often inappropriate to his spoken thought; he is also prone to quoting Frost. But never mind any of this; Ponyboy and his cast of friends and foes alike are romantic representations, not the viscerally realistic depictions they are usually labeled. Gene

Lyons, writing in *Newsweek,* got it right: "The appeal of Hinton's novels is obvious. . . . The narrator-hero of each is a tough-tender 14-to 16-year-old loner making his perilous way through a violent, caste-ridden world almost depopulated of grownups. 'It's a kid's fantasy not to have adults around,' says Hinton. While recklessness generally gets punished, her books are never moralistic—all manner of parental rules are broken with impunity."

Royalties from *The Outsiders* helped to finance Hinton's education at the University of Tulsa where she studied education and where she met her husband, David Inhofe. But for several years Hinton suffered from writer's block so severe that, as she told Carol Wallace in the *Daily News,* she "couldn't even write a letter." In an interview with Linda Plemons in the *University of Tulsa Annual,* Hinton confessed that "I couldn't write. I taught myself to type in the sixth grade, and I couldn't even type or use my typewriter to write a letter. Things were pretty bad because I also went to college and started reading good writers and I thought, 'Oh, no.' I read *The Outsiders* again when I was 20, and I thought it was the worst piece of trash I'd ever seen. I magnified all its faults."

Finally, after she decided that teaching was not for her, and with encouragement from Inhofe, Hinton sat down to write a second novel. Setting herself the goal of two pages a day, Hinton had, after a few months, a rough draft of the novel, *That Was Then, This Is Now.* Once again Hinton sets her action in the same Tulsa-like surroundings, and focuses on an orphan, Mark, who has lived with the narrator, Bryon, and Bryon's mother since his own parents killed each other in a fight. It is now over a year since the ending of *The Outsiders,* and the old gang and social rivalries are not as clear-cut as they once were. The days of hippies are at hand; drugs are part of the teen landscape. One of the characters, M&M, is a proto-hippy whose LSD overdose tips the balances between Bryon and Mark. No angel himself, Bryon turns in his foster brother for supplying M&M with drugs. There is gang violence aplenty, teens on the prowl and on their own—Ponyboy Curtis even makes an appearance. Overall the book is more disciplined than Hinton's first title, but as Daly and other critics pointed out, "it lacks something." For Daly, it was the inspirational "spark" missing that kept it from breathing true life as had *The Outsiders.*

Other reviewers, however, found Hinton's second novel a moving and heartfelt cry from yet another teenager in pain. For Michael Cart, writing in the *New York Times*

Books Review, Bryon's struggles with his future and with those he loves form the core of the book. "The phrase, 'if only' is perhaps the most bittersweet in the language," Cart noted, "and Miss Hinton uses it skillfully to underline her theme: growth can be a dangerous process." Though Cart had problems with Bryon's ultimate "life-denying self-pity," turning against his love and life, he concluded that Hinton created "a mature, disciplined novel, which excites a response in the reader. Whatever its faults, her book will be hard to forget." Reviewing the novel in *School Library Journal,* Brooke Anson remarked that the book was an "excellent, insightful mustering of the pressures on some teen-agers today, offering no slick solutions but not without hope, either." *Horn Book*'s Sheryl B. Andrews found that this "disturbing" and "sometimes ugly" book "will speak directly to a large number of teen-agers and does have a place in the understanding of today's cultural problems." Selected a Best Books for Young Adults in 1971, *That Was Then, This Is Now* confirmed Hinton as more than a one-book author.

Another four years passed between publication of *That Was Then, This Is Now* and Hinton's third novel, *Rumble Fish.* Hinton's narrator, Rusty-James, is another classic sensitive outsider type, who begins his narrative with the blunt declaration: "I was hanging out at Benny's, playing pool, when I heard Biff Wilcox was looking to kill me." Rusty-James's older brother, Motorcycle Boy, something of a Dallas Winston clone, meets a violent death in the novel, echoes of Dallas's demise in *The Outsiders.* And like Hinton's other novels, *Rumble Fish* takes place in compressed time, focusing on incidents which change the life of the narrator forever. Dubbed Hinton's "most ambitious" novel by Geoff Fox and George Walsh writing in *St. James Guide to Children's Writers,* the novel deals with Rusty-James's attempts to make some meaning of life after the passing of the gang conflicts that made his brother such a hero. Now, however, Motorcycle Boy is disenchanted, without hope, and virtually commits suicide, gunned down breaking into a pet store. By the end of the novel Rusty-James is left on his own, having lost his brother, his reputation, and his girl, and is without direction. As Jane Abramson noted in *School Library Journal,* "it is Rusty-James, emotionally burnt out at 14, who is the ultimate victim." Abramson concluded that the "[s]tylistically superb" *Rumble Fish* "packs a punch that will leave readers of any age reeling."

Some reviewers, such as Anita Silvey in *Horn Book,* found the novel unsatisfying and Hinton's further writing potential "unpromising." However, *Rumble Fish* did have admirers both in the United States and abroad. A *Publishers Weekly* contributor declared that "Ms. Hinton is a brilliant novelist," and Margery Fisher, writing in England's *Growing Point,* commented that "once more is the American urban scene in a book as uncompromising in its view of life as it is disciplined." While others complained of too blatant symbolism in the form of Motorcycle Boy and the fighting fish that give the book its title, Fisher concluded that "Of the three striking books by this young author, *Rumble Fish* seems the most carefully structured and the most probing." Exploring themes from aloneness to biological necessity, *Rumble Fish* tackles large questions in a small package. As Daly concluded about this third novel, "In the end we respond to *Rumble Fish* in a much deeper way than we do to *That Was Then, This Is Now.* It's an emotional, almost a physical response, as opposed to the more rational, intellectual reaction that the other book prompted." Daly went on to note that despite its defects in too-obvious symbolism, it "works as a novel. . . . And there is a name usually given to this kind of success. It is called art."

Hinton herself noted that she had been reading a lot about color symbolism and mythology when writing *Rumble Fish,* and that such concerns crept into the writing of the novel, especially in the character of Motorcycle Boy, the alienated, colorblind gang member looking for meaning. Hinton begins with character, as she has often noted in interviews, but in *Production Notes for Rumble Fish,* the screenplay of which she co-wrote with Francis Ford Coppola, she remarked that the novel "was a hard book to write because Rusty-James is a simple person, yet the Motorcycle Boy is the most complex character I've ever created. And Rusty-James sees him one way, which is not right, and I had to make that clear. . . . It's about over-identifying with something which you can never understand, which is what Rusty-James is doing. The Motorcycle Boy can't identify with anything."

The standard four years passed again before publication of Hinton's fourth title, *Tex,* which was, according to Daly, "Hinton's most successful effort" to date. Once again the reader is on familiar ground with near-orphan protagonists, and troubled youths. With *Tex,* however, Hinton opts for a more sensitive and perhaps less troubled narrator than before. Tex McCormick is, as Hinton noted in Delacorte Press's notes from the author, "perhaps the most childlike character I've ever done, but the one who makes the biggest strides toward maturity. I have to admit he's a favorite child." Of course this was several years before the birth of Hinton's own son, Nick.

Another fourteen-year-old lacking parental supervision, Tex has his older brother Mason to look after him while their father is on the rodeo circuit. A story of relationships, Hinton's fourth title focuses on the two teenagers at a time when Mason has had to sell off the family horses to pay bills, as no money has come from their father. This includes Tex's own horse, Negrito. Straining already strained relations between the brothers, this loss of a favored animal sets the plot in motion. Tex tries to run off and find the animal. Neither his friend Johnny nor Johnny's sister Jamie (the romantic attachment) is able to talk Tex out of it, but Mason drags him home in the pickup. Johnny and Tex are forever getting in trouble and things get rougher between Mason and Tex by the time the two brothers are kidnapped by a hitchhiker (Mark from *That Was Then, This Is Now,* who has busted out of jail). Tex's presence of mind saves them, but gets Mark, the hitchhiker, killed by the police. Notoriety at this brings the father home, but disappointment follows when he fails to track down Negrito as he promised. More trouble—in company with Johnny and then with a former friend of Mason's who now deals drugs—lands Tex in the hospital with a bullet wound. He learns that his real father was another rodeo rider, gets a visit from Johnny and Jamie, and once recovered and reconciled with Mason, convinces his older brother that he should go on to college as he's wanted to. Tex tells him he's lined up a job working with horses and can take care of himself.

"Hinton's style has matured since she exploded onto the YA scene in 1967," noted Marilyn Kaye in a *School Library Journal* review of *Tex.* Kaye felt that Hinton's "raw energy . . . has not been tamed—its been cultivated." The outcome, said Kaye, "is a fine, solidly constructed, and well-paced story." *Growing Point*'s Fisher once again had high praise for Hinton, concluding that "In this new book Susan Hinton has achieved that illusion of reality which any fiction writer aspires to and which few ever completely achieve."

Hinton's re-created reality was strong enough to lure Hollywood. Disney productions bought the rights to *Tex,* filming a faithful adaptation of the novel with young Matt Dillon in the lead role, and introducing actors Meg Tilly and Emilio Estevez. Shot in Tulsa, the movie production used Hinton as an advisor, introducing Dillon to her own horse, Toyota, which played the role of Negrito, and teaching the young actor how to ride. It was the beginning of a long and continuing friendship between Hinton and Dillon, who played in three of the four adaptations of her novels. The movie also started a trend of introducing young actors on their way up in her movies.

Next to get a film treatment was *The Outsiders,* though not from Disney this time but from Francis Ford Cop-

pola of *Godfather* fame. Somewhat operatic in its effect, the movie cast Dillon as Dallas Winston, and also starred such future luminaries as Patrick Swayze, Rob Lowe, Tom Cruise, and Estevez. Coppola also filmed *Rumble Fish,* shooting it in black and white to resonate with Motorcycle Boy's color blindness. Once again Dillon starred, with Micky Rourke as Motorcycle Boy. Dennis Hopper, Tom Waits, and Nicolas Cage rounded out the cast. The script was co-written by Hinton and Coppola. In both the Coppola adaptations, Hinton played bit parts as well as worked closely as an advisor during production. However, with the fourth movie adaptation, from a screenplay by Estevez and starring him, Hinton remained on the sidelines. Thus, within a few short years—from 1982 to 1985—all of Hinton's novels were turned into movies and her popularity was at an all-time high, with movie sales driving up book sales. Hinton had the added plus in that her experience with movies was a very positive one. "I really have had a wonderful time and made some very good friends," Hinton told Dave Smith of the *Los Angeles Times* regarding her work with Coppola. "Like a lot of authors, I'd heard the horror stories about how they buy the property and then want the author to disappear and not meddle around worrying about what they're doing to the book. But that didn't happen at all. They invited me in right from the start, and I helped with the screenplays."

Throughout the early 1980s, then, Hinton was busy with movie adaptations and with her son, born in 1983. It was not until 1988 that she brought out another novel, *Taming the Star Runner.* Earlier that year Hinton became the first recipient of the Young Adult Services Division/*School Library Journal* Author Achievement Award, otherwise known as the Margaret A. Edwards Award, for career achievement in YA literature. It had been nine years since publication of *Tex;* it was thus fitting that she would have a new title out after receiving such an award. Those first four books had a rough sort of unity to them: a portrayal of the difficult process of sorting through problems of alienation and belonging, with a kind of synthesis if not solution presented by the ending of *Tex.* In other words, that youthful furrow had been plowed, and Hinton was ready, it seemed, to move on to new acreage.

Taming the Star Runner, while dealing with some of the old themes, does set off in new directions. Hinton moves from first- to third-person narration in the story of fifteen-year-old Travis Harris who is sent off to his uncle's Oklahoma ranch in lieu of juvenile hall. He has nearly killed his stepfather with a fireplace poker, an attack not unprovoked by the abusive stepfather. What follows is the classic city boy-come-to-the-country motif. Unwillingly, Travis learns hard lessons on the ranch, but the change from urban to rural is not a Technicolor idyll. Travis arrives in the middle of his uncle's divorce, and the man is distant from him. He takes to hanging out at a barn on the property which is rented to Casey Kincaid, three years older than Travis and a horse trainer. She is in the process of taming the eponymous stallion, Star Runner. It is the relationship that grows between this unlikely pair that forms the heart of the book. Another major element—a tip of the hat to Hinton's own history—is the acceptance by a New York publisher of a book that young Travis has written. But there are no easy solutions: the stepfather refuses to give permission for publication, as he comes off less than noble in the pages of the manuscript. Finally Travis's mother stands up to the stepfather and signs permission for him. He has grown closer to Casey, as well as his uncle, but there are no completely happy endings for Hinton, either. Star Runner is killed in an electrical storm and Travis and his uncle are forced to move off the ranch to town, but he is now a published author and has made a real friend in Casey.

Reviews of the novel were largely positive. Nancy Vasilakis commented in *Horn Book* that it "has been generally agreed that no one can speak to the adolescent psyche the way S.E. Hinton can," and now with her fifth novel, Vasilakis felt that the author "hasn't lost her touch." In a lengthy critique in the *New York Times Book Review*, Patty Campbell noted that "Hinton has produced another story of a tough young Galahad in black T-shirt and leather jacket. The pattern is familiar, but her genius lies in that she has been able to give each of the five protagonists she has drawn from this mythic model a unique voice and a unique story." Campbell also commented on the "drive and the wry sweetness and authenticity" of the authorial voice, concluding that "S.E. Hinton continues to grow in strength as a young adult novelist." A *Kirkus Reviews* contributor also found much to praise in the novel, remarking that "Hinton continues to grow more reflective in her books, but her great understanding, not of what teenagers are but of what they can hope to be, is undiminished." Daly, in his critical study, *Presenting S.E. Hinton,* called this fifth novel "Hinton's most mature and accomplished work."

Since publication of *Taming the Star Runner,* Hinton's work has traveled light miles away from her cast of outsiders and bad boys. The year 1995 saw publication of two Hinton titles, both for younger readers. *Big David, Little David* is a picture book based on a joke she and her husband played on their son Nick when the boy was entering kindergarten. In the book, a boy named Nick wonders if a classmate who resembles his father and has the same name could possibly be the same person as his father. Another title inspired by her son is *The Puppy Sister,* about a sibling rivalry between a puppy and an only child, a situation complicated when the puppy slowly changes into a human sister.

After 20 years of publishing silence S.E. Hinton returns with *Hawkes Harbor.* Part adventure, part horror novel Hinton aims here for an adult audience. Beginning in the 1950's the story chronicles the exploits of orphan, Jamie Sommers. Raised by not so nice nuns he graduates to a life at sea. By the time he settles on the Delaware coast he has already survived death defying escapades including pirate battles, gun running, narrow escapes from shark attacks and rape accusations. Still no amount of rough living can prepare him for his meeting with Grenville Hawkes, a vampire Jamie unwittingly rouses and is subsequently bound to in everlasting servitude. The dynamic between Hawkes and Jamie is disturbing. It seems the vampire develops paternal feelings for his prey even paying for his hospitalization due to depression. Not surprisingly Jamie is haunted by aspects of his life, most acutely, his relationship to Hawkes. His therapy sessions are the method by which Hinton relays much information about Jamie's lurid past. Freed from the confines of the youth audience Hinton explores sexual situations and violent episodes in dark, sometimes comic detail.

Jennifer Mattson of *Booklist* felt the book will likely "appeal to vampire-lit groupies and curiosity seekers alike," but maintained the presence of vampire clichés, parody and sentimentality prevent Hinton from attaining her usual quality. However, a *Publisher's Weekly* reviewer compared the "basic elements" of *Hawkes Harbor* to her classic work, *The Outsiders,* further praising it as "a contemporary Treasure Island with a genre-bending twist."

Hinton has focused on family in recent years, and on her hobby of horseback riding. She is reportedly at work on another YA novel, though there are no indications whether or not she will return to her outsider themes. "I don't think I have a masterpiece in me," Hinton once told Smith in the *Los Angeles Times,* "but I do know I'm writing well in the area I choose to write in. I understand kids and I really like them. And I have a very good memory. I remember exactly what it was like to be a teenager that nobody listened to or paid attention to or wanted around."

BIOGRAPHICAL AND CRITICAL SOURCES:

BOOKS

Children's Literature Review, Thomson Gale (Detroit), Volume 3, 1978, Volume 23, 1991.
Contemporary Literary Criticism, Volume 30, Thomson Gale, 1984.
Daly, Jay, *Presenting S.E. Hinton,* Twayne, 1987.
Hinton, S. E., "Rumble Fish," *Production Notes,* No Weather Films, 1983.
St. James Guide to Young Adult Writers, St. James Press, 1999.
Stanek, Lou Willett, *A Teacher's Guide to the Paperback Editions of the Novels of S.E. Hinton,* Dell, 1980.

PERIODICALS

American Film, April, 1983.
Atlantic Monthly, December, 1967, Nat Hentoff, review of *The Outsiders.*
Booklist, April 1, 1994, p. 1463; October 15, 1994, p. 413; January 15, 1995, p. 936; June 1, 1995, p. 1760; August 2004, Jennifer Mattson, review of *Hawkes Harbor,* p. 1871.
Bulletin of the Center for Children's Books, February, 1995, p. 200; November, 1995, p. 92.
Daily News, September 26, 1982, Carol Wallace, "In Praise of Teenage Outcasts."
English Journal, September, 1989, p. 86.
Growing Point, May, 1976, Margery Fisher, review of *Rumble Fish,* p. 2894; May, 1980, Margery Fisher, review of *Tex,* pp. 3686-87.
Horn Book, August, 1967, Jane Manthorne, review of *The Outsiders,* p. 475; July-August, 1971, Sheryl B. Andrews, review of *That Was Then, This Is Now,* p. 338; November-December, 1975, Anita Silvey, review of *Rumble Fish,* p. 601; January-February, 1989, Nancy Vasilakis, review of *Taming the Star Runner,* pp. 78-79.
Kirkus Reviews, August 15, 1988, review of *Taming the Star Runner,* p. 1241.
Library Journal, June 15, 1971, Brooke Anson, review of *That Was Then, This Is Now,* p. 2138.
Los Angeles Times, July 15, 1982, Dave Smith, "Hinton, What Boys Are Made Of."
Nation, March 8, 1986, Michael Malone, "Tough Puppies," pp. 276-78, 280.
Newsweek, October 11, 1982, Gene Lyons, "On Tulsa's Mean Streets," pp. 105-106.
New York Times Book Review, May 7, 1967, Thomas Fleming, review of *The Outsiders,* sec. 2, pp. 10-12; August 27, 1967, pp. 26-29; August 8, 1971, Michael Cart, review of *That Was Then, This Is Now,* p. 8; April 2, 1989, Patty Campbell, review of *Taming the Star Runner,* p. 26; November 19, 1995, p. 37; November 16, 1997, p. 26.
Publishers Weekly, July 28, 1975, review of *Rumble Fish,* p. 122; December 12, 1994, p. 62; July 17, 1995, p. 230; July 28, 1997, p. 77; August 9, 2004, review of *Hawkes Harbor,* p. 230.
Quill & Quire, April, 1995, p. 37.
School Library Journal, May 15, 1967, Lillian N. Gerhardt, review of *The Outsiders,* pp. 2028-29; October, 1975, Jane Abramson, review of *Rumble Fish,* p. 106; November, 1979, Marilyn Kaye, review of *Tex,* p. 88; December, 1993, p. 70; April, 1995, p. 102; October, 1995, p. 104; May, 1996, p. 76.
Seventeen, October, 1967, "Face to Face with a Teen-Age Novelist."
Signal, May, 1980, pp. 120-22.
Times Literary Supplement, October 30, 1970, review of *The Outsiders.*
Tulsa Daily World, April 7, 1967, Yvonne Litchfield, "Her Book to Be Published Soon, But Tulsa Teen-Ager Keeps Cool," p. 20.
University of Tulsa Annual, 1983-84, Linda Plemons, "Author Laureate of Adolescent Fiction," p. 62.
Washington Post Book World, February 12, 1989.

OTHER

"S.E. Hinton: On Writing and *Tex,*" publicity release from Delacorte Press, winter, 1979/spring, 1980.

* * *

HOBAN, Russell 1925-
(Russell Conwell Hoban)

PERSONAL: Born February 4, 1925, in Lansdale, PA; son of Abram T. (an advertising manager for the *Jewish Daily Forward*) and Jeanette (Dimmerman) Hoban; married Lillian Aberman (an illustrator), January 31, 1944 (divorced, 1975); married Gundula Ahl (a bookseller), 1975; children: (first marriage) Phoebe, Abrom, Esme, Julia; (second marriage) Jachin Boaz, Wieland, Benjamin. *Education:* Attended Philadelphia Museum School of Industrial Art, 1941-43. *Hobbies and other interests:* Stones, short-wave listening.

ADDRESSES: Home and office—Fulham, London, England. *Agent*—David Higham Associates Ltd., 5-8 Lower John St., Golden Sq., London W1R 4HA, England.

CAREER: Artist and illustrator for magazine and advertising studios, New York, NY, 1945-51; Fletcher Smith Film Studio, New York, NY, story board artist and character designer, 1951; Batten, Barton, Durstine & Osborn, Inc., New York, NY, television art director, 1952-57; J. Walter Thompson Co., New York, NY, television art director, 1956; freelance illustrator for advertising agencies and magazines, including *Time, Life, Fortune, Saturday Evening Post,* and *True,* 1957-65; Doyle, Dane, Bembach, New York, NY, copywriter, 1965-67; novelist and author of children's books, beginning 1967. Art instructor at the Famous Artists Schools, Westport, CT, and School of Visual Arts, New York, NY. *Military service:* U.S. Army, Infantry, 1943-45; served in Italian campaign; earned the Bronze Star.

MEMBER: Authors Guild, Authors League of America, Society of Authors, PEN.

AWARDS, HONORS: American Library Association nomination for notable books, for *The Sorely Trying Day, The Mouse and His Child, How Tom Beat Captain Najork and His Hired Sportsmen,* and *Dinner at Alberta's;* Library of Congress Children's Book selection, 1964, for *Bread and Jam for Frances;* Boys' Club Junior Book Award, 1968, for *Charlie the Tramp;* *School Library Journal's* Best Books, 1971, Lewis Carroll Shelf Award and Christopher Award, both 1972, all for *Emmet Otter's Jug-Band Christmas;* Whitbread Literary Award, 1974, and International Board on Books for Young People Honor List, 1976, both for *How Tom Beat Captain Najork and His Hired Sportsmen;* John W. Campbell Memorial Award for the best science fiction novel of the year, Science Fiction Research Association, 1981, National Book Critics Circle nomination and Nebula Award nomination, 1982, all for *Riddley Walker;* Recognition of Merit, George G. Stone Center for Children's Books, 1982, for contributions to books for younger children.

WRITINGS:

CHILDREN'S NONFICTION

(Self-illustrated) *What Does It Do and How Does It Work?: Power Shovel, Dump Truck, and Other Heavy Machines,* Harper (New York, NY), 1959.
(Self-illustrated) *The Atomic Submarine: A Practice Combat Patrol under the Sea,* Harper (New York, NY), 1960.

CHILDREN'S FICTION

Bedtime for Frances, illustrated by Garth Williams, Harper (New York, NY), 1960, new edition, HarperTrophy (New York, NY), 1995.

Herman the Loser, illustrated by Lillian Hoban, Harper (New York, NY), 1961.
The Song in My Drum, illustrated by Lillian Hoban, Harper (New York, NY), 1961.
London Men and English Men, illustrated by Lillian Hoban, Harper (New York, NY), 1962.
(With Lillian Hoban) *Some Snow Said Hello,* Harper (New York, NY), 1963.
The Sorely Trying Day, illustrated by Lillian Hoban, Harper (New York, NY), 1964.
A Baby Sister for Frances, illustrated by Lillian Hoban, Harper (New York, NY), 1964, new edition, HarperTrophy (New York, NY), 1993.
Nothing to Do, illustrated by Lillian Hoban, Harper (New York, NY), 1964.
Bread and Jam for Frances, illustrated by Lillian Hoban, Harper (New York, NY), 1964, revised edition, HarperCollins (New York, NY), 1993.
Tom and the Two Handles, illustrated by Lillian Hoban, Harper (New York, NY), 1965.
The Story of Hester Mouse Who Became a Writer and Saved Most of Her Sisters and Brothers and Some of Her Aunts and Uncles from the Owl, illustrated by Lillian Hoban, Norton (New York, NY), 1965.
What Happened When Jack and Daisy Tried to Fool the Tooth Fairies, illustrated by Lillian Hoban, Scholastic (New York, NY), 1965.
Henry and the Monstrous Din, illustrated by Lillian Hoban, Harper (New York, NY), 1966.
The Little Brute Family, illustrated by Lillian Hoban, Macmillan (New York, NY), 1966, reprinted, Farrar, Straus and Giroux (New York, NY), 2002.
(With Lillian Hoban) *Save My Place,* Norton (New York, NY), 1967.
Charlie the Tramp, illustrated by Lillian Hoban, Four Winds (New York, NY), 1967, book and record, Scholastic (New York, NY), 1970.
The Mouse and His Child, illustrated by Lillian Hoban, Harper (New York, NY), 1967, new edition illustrated by David Small, 2001.
A Birthday for Frances, illustrated by Lillian Hoban, Harper (New York, NY), 1968, reprinted, HarperTrophy (New York, NY), 1994.
The Stone Doll of Sister Brute, illustrated by Lillian Hoban, Macmillan (New York, NY), 1968.
Harvey's Hideout, illustrated by Lillian Hoban, Parents' Magazine Press (New York, NY), 1969.
Best Friends for Frances, illustrated by Lillian Hoban, Harper (New York, NY), 1969, new illustrated edition, HarperCollins (New York, NY), 1994.
Ugly Bird, illustrated by Lillian Hoban, Macmillan (New York, NY), 1969.
The Mole Family's Christmas, illustrated by Lillian Hoban, Parents' Magazine Press (New York, NY), 1969.

A Bargain for Frances, illustrated by Lillian Hoban, Harper (New York, NY), 1970, reprinted, Harper-Festival (New York, NY), 1999.

Emmet Otter's Jug-Band Christmas, illustrated by Lillian Hoban, Parents' Magazine Press (New York, NY), 1971.

The Sea-Thing Child, illustrated by son, Abrom Hoban, Harper (New York, NY), 1972, new edition illustrated by Patrick Benson, Candlewick Press (Cambridge, MA), 1999.

Letitia Rabbit's String Song (Junior Literary Guild selection), illustrated by Mary Chalmers, Coward (New York, NY), 1973.

La Corona and the Tin Frog (originally published in *Puffin Annual,* 1974), illustrated by Nicola Bayley, J. Cape (London, England), 1978, Merrimack Book Service, 1981.

How Tom Beat Captain Najork and His Hired Sportsmen, illustrated by Quentin Blake, Atheneum (New York, NY), 1974.

Ten What?: A Mystery Counting Book, illustrated by Sylvie Selig, J. Cape (London, England), 1974, Scribner (New York, NY), 1975.

Crocodile and Pierrot: A See the Story Book, illustrated by Sylvie Selig, J. Cape (London, England), 1975, Scribner (New York, NY), 1977.

Dinner at Alberta's, illustrated by James Marshall, Crowell (New York, NY), 1975.

A Near Thing for Captain Najork, illustrated by Quentin Blake, J. Cape (London, England), 1975, Atheneum (New York, NY), 1976.

Arthur's New Power, illustrated by Byron Barton, Crowell (New York, NY), 1978.

The Twenty-Elephant Restaurant, illustrated by Emily Arnold McCully, Atheneum (New York, NY), 1978, illustrated by Quentin Blake, J. Cape (London, England), 1980.

The Dancing Tigers, illustrated by David Gentlemen, J. Cape (London, England), 1979, Merrimack Book Service, 1981.

Flat Cat, illustrated by Clive Scruton, Philomel (New York, NY), 1980.

Ace Dragon Ltd., illustrated by Quentin Blake, J. Cape (London, England), 1980, Merrimack Book Service, 1981.

They Came from Aargh!, illustrated by Colin McNaughton, Philomel (New York, NY), 1981.

The Serpent Tower, illustrated by David Scott, Methuen/Walker (London, England), 1981.

The Great Fruit Gum Robbery, illustrated by Colin McNaughton, Methuen (London, England), 1981, published as *The Great Gum Drop Robbery,* Philomel (New York, NY), 1982.

The Battle of Zormla, illustrated by Colin McNaughton, Philomel (New York, NY), 1982.

The Flight of Bembel Rudzuk, illustrated by Colin McNaughton, Philomel (New York, NY), 1982.

Big John Turkle, illustrated by Martin Baynton, Walker, 1983, Holt (New York, NY), 1984.

Jim Frog, illustrated by Martin Baynton, Walker, 1983, Holt (New York, NY), 1984.

Lavinia Bat, illustrated by Martin Baynton, Holt (New York, NY), 1984.

Charlie Meadows, illustrated by Martin Baynton, Holt (New York, NY), 1984.

The Rain Door, illustrated by Quentin Blake, J. Cape (London, England), 1986, HarperCollins (New York, NY), 1987.

The Marzipan Pig, illustrated by Quentin Blake, J. Cape (London, England), 1986.

Ponders, illustrated by Martin Baynton, Walker (London, England), 1988.

Monsters, illustrated by Quentin Blake, Scholastic (New York, NY), 1989.

Jim Hedgehog and the Lonesome Tower, illustrated by Betsy Lewin, Clarion Books (New York, NY), 1990.

Jim Hedgehog's Supernatural Christmas, illustrated by Betsy Lewin, Clarion Books (New York, NY), 1992.

M.O.L.E.: Much Overworked Little Earthmover, J. Cape (London, England), 1993.

The Court of the Winged Serpent, illustrated by Patrick Benson, Trafalgar Square (New York, NY), 1995.

Trokeville Way, Knopf (New York, NY), 1996.

Trouble on Thunder Mountain, illustrated by Quentin Blake, Orchard Books (New York, NY), 2000.

Jim's Lion, illustrated by Ian Andrew, Candlewick Press (Cambridge, MA), 2001.

CHILDREN'S VERSE

Goodnight, illustrated by Lillian Hoban, Norton (New York, NY), 1966.

The Pedaling Man, and Other Poems, illustrated by Lillian Hoban, Norton (New York, NY), 1968.

Egg Thoughts, and Other Frances Songs, illustrated by Lillian Hoban, Harper (New York, NY), 1972.

NOVELS

The Lion of Boaz-Jachin and Jachin-Boaz, Stein & Day (New York, NY), 1973.

Kleinzeit, Viking (New York, New York), 1974.

Turtle Diary, J. Cape (London, England), 1975, Random House (New York, NY), 1976.

Riddley Walker, J. Cape (London, England), 1980, Summit Books (New York, NY), 1981, expanded edition with new foreword, Indiana University Press (Bloomington, IN), 1998.

Pilgermann, Summit Books (New York, NY), 1983.

The Medusa Frequency, edited by Gary Fisketjohn, Atlantic Monthly (New York, NY), 1987.

Fremder, J. Cape (London, England), 1996.

Mr Rinyo-Clacton's Offer, J. Cape (London, England), 1998.

Amaryllis Night and Day, Bloomsbury (London, England), 2001.

Angelica's Grotto, Carroll & Graf (New York, NY), 2001.

Her Name Was Lola, Arcade (New York, NY), 2003.

Come Dance with Me, Bloomsbury (London, England), 2005.

Linger Awhile, Bloomsbury (London, England), 2006.

OTHER

(Illustrator) W.R. Burnett, *The Roar of the Crowd: Conversations with an Ex-Big-Leaguer,* C.N. Potter, 1964.

The Carrier Frequency (play), first produced in London, England, 1984.

Riddley Walker (stage adaptation of his novel), first produced in Manchester, England, 1986.

(Author of introduction) Wilhelm K. Grimm, *Household Tales,* illustrated by Mervyn Peake, Schocken, 1987.

A Russell Hoban Omnibus, Indiana University Press (Bloomington, IN), 1999.

Also author of *Come and Find Me* (television play), 1980. Contributor of articles to *Granta, Fiction Magazine,* and *Holiday.* Hoban's papers are included in the Kerlan Collection at the University of Minnesota.

ADAPTATIONS: *The Mouse and His Child* was made into a feature-length animated film by Fario-Lockhart-Sanrio Productions, 1977, and featured the voices of Cloris Leachman, Andy Devine, and Peter Ustinov (who also read an abridged version of the novel for a Caedmon recording in 1977); Glynis Johns recorded selections from *Bedtime for Frances, A Baby Sister for Frances, Bread and Jam for Frances,* and *A Birthday for Frances* in a sound recording entitled "Frances," as well as selections from *A Bargain for Frances, Best Friends for Frances,* and *Egg Thoughts, and Other Frances Songs* in a sound recording entitled "A Bargain for Frances and Other Stories," both by Caedmon in 1977; *Turtle Diary* was adapted for the screen by United British Artists/Brittanic in 1986, featuring a screenplay by Harold Pinter and starring Glenda Jackson and Ben Kingsley; *Riddley Walker* was staged by the Manchester Royal Exchange Theatre Company, 1986.

SIDELIGHTS: "Russell Hoban is a writer whose genius is expressed with equal brilliance in books both for children and for adults," wrote Alida Allison in *Dictionary of Literary Biography.* Largely self-educated, Hoban has moved masterfully from being an artist and illustrator to writing children's fables and adult allegorical fiction. Praising his "unerring ear for dialogue," his "memorable depiction of scenes," and his "wise and warm stories notable for delightful plots and originality of language," Allison considered Hoban to be "much more than just a clever and observant writer. His works are permeated with an honest, often painful, and always uncompromising urge toward self-identity." Noting that "this theme of identity becomes more apparent, more complex as Hoban's works have become longer and more penetrating," Allison stated, "Indeed, Hoban's writing has leaped and bounded—paralleling upheavals in his own life."

In an interview with Rhonda M. Bunbury in *Children's Literature in Education,* Hoban indicated that as a child he was "good with words and good with drawing. It just happened my parents more or less seized on the drawing and thought that I'd probably end up being a great painter. I did become an illustrator, but I think that the drawing formula was always a little bit poisoned by the expectations that were laid on me, while the writing was allowed to be my own thing." He wrote poetry and short stories in school, and won several prizes. Having attended the Philadelphia Museum School of Industrial Art, Hoban worked as a freelance illustrator before he began writing children's stories. He would drive throughout Connecticut, occasionally stopping at construction sites and sketching the machinery being used. A friend saw his work and suggested that it might make a good children's book; Hoban's first published work was about construction equipment—*What Does It Do and How Does It Work?: Power Shovel, Dump Truck, and Other Heavy Machines.*

Although Hoban has since originated several well-known characters in children's literature, including *Charlie the Tramp, Emmet Otter, The Mouse and his Child,* and *Manny Rat,* he is especially recognized for a series of bedtime books about an anthropomorphic badger named Frances. Reviewers generally concurred that these stories depict ordinary family life with much humor, wit, and style. Benjamin DeMott suggested in the *Atlantic Monthly* that "these books are unique, first, because the adults in their pages are usually humorous, precise of speech, and understandingly conversant with general life, and second, because the author confronts—not unfancifully but without kinky secret garden stuff—problems with which ordinary parents and children have to cope." *Bedtime for Frances,* for instance, concerns nighttime fears and is regarded by many as a classic in children's literature; and according to a *Saturday Review* contributor, "The exasperated humor of this book could only derive from actual parental experience, and no doubt parents will enjoy it."

"Hoban has established himself as a writer with a rare understanding of childhood (and parental) psychology, sensitively and humorously portrayed in familiar family situations," noted Allison. He and his first wife, Lillian, also an illustrator and author of books for children, collaborated on many successful works, including several in the Frances series. Allison added that although their work together was usually well-received, "there were pans as well as paeans." While some books have been faulted for "excessive coziness, for sentimentality, and for stereotyped male-female roles," Allison said that a more general criticism of their work together is that "it tends toward repetition." However, commenting in *Children and Books,* May Hill Arbuthnot and Zena Sutherland found that all of Hoban's stories about Frances show "affection for and understanding of children" as well as "contribute to a small child's understanding of himself, his relationships with other people, and the fulfillment of his emotional needs." Further, they said, "These characters are indeed ourselves in fur." Yet as a *Times Literary Supplement* contributor observed, "Excellent as [the Frances books] are, they give no hint that the author had in him such a blockbuster of a book as *The Mouse and His Child.*"

Revered in England as a modern children's classic, *The Mouse and His Child* was described in the *New York Times Book Review* by Barbara Wersba as a story about two wind-up toy mice who are discarded from a toyshop and are then "buffeted from place to place as they seek the lost paradise of their first home—a doll house—and their first 'family,' a toy elephant and seal." Ill-equipped for the baffling, threatening world into which they are tossed, the mouse and his child innocently confront the unknown and its inherent treachery and violence, as well as their own fears. The book explores not only the transience and inconstancy of life but also the struggle to persevere. "Helpless when they are not wound up, unable to stop when they *are,* [the

mice] are fated like all mechanical things to breakage, rust and disintegration as humans are to death," writes Margaret Blount in her *Animal Land: The Creatures of Children's Fiction.* "As an adult," said Blount, "it is impossible to read [the book] unmoved." Distressed, however, by the "continuing images of cruelty and decay," Penelope Farmer remarked in *Children's Literature in Education* that *The Mouse and His Child* is "like Beckett for children." But assessing whatever cruelty and decay there is in the novel as the "artful rendering of the facts of life," Allison affirmed, "If there is betrayal, there is also self-sacrifice. If there is loss, there is also love. If there is homelessness, there is also destination. The mouse child gets his family in the end; children's literature gets a masterpiece."

"Like the best of books, [*The Mouse and His Child*] is a book from which one can peel layer after layer of meaning," said the *Times Literary Supplement* contributor. Some critics, however, questioned the book's suitability for children. Hoban responded to these critics in an essay for *Books for Your Children:* "When I wrote [*The Mouse and His Child*] I didn't think it was [a children's book]. I was writing as much book as I was capable of at the time. No concessions were made in style or content. It was my first novel and . . . it was the fullest response I could make to being alive and in the world." Hoban indicated to Bunbury that the book has become his favorite book for children, the one that has given him the most satisfaction, "Though it may not be the best of my novels, it is the closest to my heart because of that." Believing the book reveals "an absolute respect for its subject—which means its readers as well," Isabel Quigley added in the *Spectator,* "I'm still not sure just who is going to read it but that hardly seems to matter. . . . It will last." Hoban felt that within its limitations, the book is suitable for children, though. "Its heroes and heroines found out what they were and it wasn't enough, so they found out how to be more," he says in his essay. "That's not a bad thought to be going with."

Nominated as the most distinguished book of fiction by the National Book Critics Circle and for the Nebula Award by the Science Fiction Writers of America, *Riddley Walker* imagines a world and civilization decades after a nuclear holocaust; the story of what remains is narrated in a fragmented, phonetical English by a twelve-year-old boy struggling to comprehend the past so that its magnificence might be recaptured. "Set in a remote future and composed in an English nobody ever spoke or wrote," wrote Benjamin DeMott in the *New York Times,* "this short, swiftly paced tale juxtaposes preliterate fable and Beckettian wit, Boschian monstrosities and a hero with Huck Finn's heart and charm, lighting by El Greco and jokes by Punch and Judy. It is a wrenchingly vivid report on the texture of life after Doomsday."

Detecting similarities in *Riddley Walker* to other contemporary works such as Anthony Burgess's *A Clockwork Orange,* John Gardner's *Grendel,* and the complete works of William Golding, DeMott believed that "in vision and execution, this is an exceptionally original work, and Russell Hoban is actually his own best source." *Riddley Walker* "is not 'like' anything," noted Victoria Glendinning in the *Listener.* As A. Alvarez observed in the *New York Review of Books,* Hoban has "transformed what might have been just another fantasy of the future into a novel of exceptional depth and originality."

Critically lauded and especially popular in England, *Riddley Walker* has been particularly commended for its inventive language, which Alvarez thought "reflects with extraordinary precision both the narrator's understanding and the desolate landscape he moves through." Reviewing the book in the *Washington Post Book World,* Michael Dirda commented that "what is marvelous in all this is the way Hoban makes us experience the uncanny familiarity of this world, while also making it a strange and animistic place, where words almost have a life of their own." "What Hoban has done," suggested Barbara A. Bannon in a *Publishers Weekly* interview with Hoban, "is to invent a world and a language to go with it, and in doing both he remains a storyteller, which is the most significant achievement of 'Riddley Walker.'"

Alvarez called *Riddley Walker* an "artistic tour de force in every possible way," but Natalie Maynor and Richard F. Patteson suggested in *Critique* that even more than that, it is "perhaps the most sophisticated work of fiction ever to speculate about man's future on earth and the implications for a potentially destructive technology." Eliot Fremont-Smith maintained in the *Village Voice* that "the reality of the human situation now is so horrendous and bizarre that to get a hold on it requires all our faculties, including the imaginative. We can't do it through plain fact and arms controllers' reasoning alone . . . [r]ead *Riddley,* too." Although Kelly Cherry referred to the novel in the *Chicago Tribune Book World* as a "philosophical essay in fictional drag," DeMott thought that Hoban's focus on what has been lost in civilization "summons the reader to dwell anew on that within civilization which is separate from, opposite to, power and its appurtenances, ravages, triumphs." *Ridley Walker,* said DeMott, is "haunting and fiercely imagined and—this matters most—intensely ponderable."

An American by birth but an Englishman at heart, Hoban has made his home in London for much of his adult life. In a 1998 *Pure Fiction Reviews* online interview with the author, John Forsyth declared that Hoban's enthusiasm for his adopted city "remains undiminished, decades after moving here . . . and that this affection places him in a whole tradition of English writing." As Hoban told Forsyth, "I came here because I was a great admirer of British ghost stories and supernatural stories. . . . I've been at great pains to have [my narrators] speak in an English manner, and to make their background a credible English background."

During the same interview Hoban revealed one more attraction of London—its subway system, the Underground. "I hate buses, you know; they never turn up, people rush ahead of you and all that," he elaborated. "At most Tube stations it tells you how long it's going to be till the next Wimbledon train or whatever. And then there's the perpetual nocturnal mood of the Underground; it never seems like daytime down there, it always seems like night. I'm a nocturnal kind of person, and I like to work at night."

The Underground plays a role in Hoban's 1998 adult novel, *Mr Rinyo-Clacton's Offer.* The story follows one Jonathan Fitch as he is approached in the Piccadilly Circus subway station by the title character, an eccentric aristocrat. The offer of the title is of the Faustian variety: Rinyo-Clacton offers Fitch a million pounds in exchange for his life in one year. "What kind of weirdo are you?," asks Fitch. "The kind with lots of money," is the reply. The book then goes on to examine the tragic circumstances that impel Fitch to consider the fateful deal.

For all their suspense, though, "in my books there aren't characters who are simply bad or simply good," Hoban told Fred Hauptfuhrer in *People.* "Nothing in life is that simple." Writing for adults has added both breadth and depth to Hoban's work; and as his work has grown in complexity, he has commented upon the process by which an idea evolves into a book. As he explained to Bannon: "There always seems to be something in my mind waiting to put something together with some primary thought I will encounter. It's like looking out of the window and listening to the radio at the same time. I am committed to what comes to me, however it links up."

Hoban's mind turned to questions about how humans perceive the world, time, and the reality of dreams with his next adult book. Writing in the *Economist* about Hoban's 2001 novel, *Amaryllis Night and Day,* a reviewer commented, "Readers without training in higher mathematics will need all the mental agility they can muster to follow him into the realm of pure geometry, which has inspired his . . . novel." The narrator is painter Peter Diggs, who meets a woman in his dreams named Amaryllis. Diggs eventually encounters the real-life Amaryllis, and the couple finds out that they share not only a dream life but also common real experiences and guilt. In addition to his strange relationship with Amaryllis, the narrator ponders the nature of labyrinths and Klein bottles (a type of glass that is twisted in a way that makes it difficult to distinguish the inside from the outside), which leads, as noted by James Hopkin in the *New Statesman,* "to meditations on the nature of time and perception." The *Economist* contributor found the novel's "characters stilted and the story contrived." Hopkin noted that Hoban's flaws in the novel were making the female characters too talented, beautiful, and irresistibly drawn to the narrator and said that "the mock-Hollywood happy ending is annoying, regardless of any ironic intent." Nevertheless, he also noted, "Yet Hoban has a gift for being almost inadvertently contemporary. He follows his own obsessions, but cannot help revealing aspects of a society that refuses to 'achieve grown-upness.'"

Hoban's next novel, *Angelica's Grotto,* is a dark, comic look at art connoisseur Harold Klein who wanders onto a pornographic Web site and ultimately an erotic odyssey. As noted by Christopher L. Reese in *World Literature Today,* the novel "explores a wide variety of issues and ideas, from dealing with old age to the relationships between art and pornography and between individuals and society." In his seventies, Klein has a strange problem in that the loss of his "inner voice" causes him to be totally uninhibited in all his utterances. When Klein meets the much younger Melissa Bottomley, the sex researcher who runs the Web porn site, they begin to act out their sexual fantasies. Reese found that the novel did not offer answers to the many questions it raises concerning "the individual concept of self and how it is created, and what we expect from art/pornography." Reese went on to note, "Overall, what Hoban has produced here is a comic piece of writing that considers several serious issues in a humorous light." A *Publishers Weekly* contributor commented, "Hoban . . . has fashioned an intensely conceived coda to the verities of desire and fulfillment—not to mention trust, honesty and pornography—and Klein is a sharp, funny and intelligent protagonist whom readers will find it hard not to like." Carrie Bissey, writing in *Booklist,* noted that "those willing to follow his [Hoban's] meandering thoughts will be rewarded by an intelligently bizarre novel."

Although focusing more on adult literature, Hoban has not forsaken his children's writings, such as his oversized picture book for older children called *Jim's Lion,* published in 2001. A story about an extremely sick boy who is worried about being anesthetized for an operation, the book describes Jim's relationship with South African nurse Bami and how she helps him face his fears. A *Publishers Weekly* contributor felt that the story was perhaps too frightening for children and commented that with "its complicated plot and its convoluted theme, this tale may perplex rather than soothe its intended audience." Cynthia Turnquest, writing in *Booklist,* called the book a "complex, touching story that will make a good springboard for discussing difficult questions about hospitalization and mortality." Faith Brautigan noted in *School Library Journal,* "Critically ill children, a population largely absent from the picture-book world, will now have a hero in Jim."

Hoban's adult novel *Her Name Was Lola* appeared on bookshelves in 2003. Once again, Hoban reveals his penchant for black comedy in a story about a struggling London writer named Max Lesser who has a series of successful children's books but is facing writer's block with his adult novel. Max soon meets two women and conducts a simultaneous affair with them. Lola, who Max declares to be his destined love, finds out about the other woman, Lula Mae, and leaves him. Lula Mae, a transplanted Texan who works in technology, eventually decides that Max is not the right man for her, even though she is carrying his child, and moves back to Texas. The story is told primarily in flashbacks as Max goes about trying to overcome his desolation at losing both women and being unable to finish his novel. Despite the fact that he felt that "Lola and Lula Mae aren't quite flesh and blood," Hugo Barnacle, writing in the *New Statesman,* noted, "Hoban apparently wants to see how much outrageous artifice and willful exposure of literary technique he can get away with while still working his magic on the reader. The answer is plenty. Far from being an arid exercise, the novel has great charm and grace." A *Publishers Weekly* contributor called the story a "quirky, tender tale" but noted that "some readers will enjoy the journey, while others will find that Hoban's form trumps his content." In a review in *Booklist,* Jennifer Baker stated that the novel was a "wonderfully funny, refreshing, and compelling love story."

BIOGRAPHICAL AND CRITICAL SOURCES:

BOOKS

Allison, Alida, editor, *Russell Hoban/Forty Years: Essays on His Writings for Children,* Garland Publishing (New York, NY), 2000.

Arbuthnot, May Hill, and Zena Sutherland, *Children and Books,* 4th edition, Scott, Foresman (Chicago, IL), 1972.

Blount, Margaret, *Animal Land: The Creatures of Children's Fiction,* Morrow (New York, NY), 1974.

Children's Literature Review, Volume 3, Thomson Gale (Detroit, MI), 1978.

Contemporary Literary Criticism, Thomson Gale (Detroit, MI), Volume 7, 1977, Volume 25, 1983.

Dictionary of Literary Biography, Volume 52: *American Writers for Children since 1960: Fiction,* Thomson Gale (Detroit, MI), 1986, pp. 192-202.

Hoban, Russell, *The Thorny Paradise: Writers on Writing for Children,* edited by Edward Blishen, Kestrel (Harmondsworth, England), 1975.

Hoban, Russell, *Mr Rinyo-Clacton's Offer,* J. Cape (London, England), 1998.

Twentieth-Century Children's Writers, 3rd edition, St. James Press (Detroit, MI), 1989.

Wilkie, Christine, *Through the Narrow Gate: The Mythological Consciousness of Russell Hoban,* Fairleigh Dickinson University Press (Rutherford, NJ), 1989.

PERIODICALS

American Artist, October, 1961.

Antioch Review, summer, 1982.

Atlantic Monthly, August, 1976, pp. 83-84; December, 1983.

Booklist, May 15, 2001, Carrie Bissey, review of *Angelica's Grotto,* p. 1731; January 1, 2002, Cynthia Turnquest, review of *Jim's Lion,* p. 865; June 1, 2004, Jennifer Baker, review of *Her Name Was Lola,* p. 1700.

Books for Your Children, winter, 1976, p. 3.

Chicago Tribune Book World, July 12, 1981, Kelly Cherry, review of *Riddley Walker.*

Children's Literature in Education, March, 1972; spring, 1976; fall, 1986, pp. 139-149.

Critique, fall, 1984.

Economist, January 27, 2001, review of *Amaryllis Night and Day,* p. 4.

Educational Foundation for Nuclear Science, June, 1982.

Encounter, June, 1981.

Globe and Mail (Toronto, Ontario, Canada), March 29, 1986.

Harper's, April, 1983.

Junior Bookshelf, July, 1963.

Library Journal, July, 2004, Robin Nesbitt, review of *Her Name Was Lola,* p. 70.

Listener, October 30, 1980, Victoria Glendinning, review of *Riddley Walker,* p. 589.

Los Angeles Times, February 14, 1986.

New Statesman, May 25, 1973; April 11, 1975; January 29, 2001, James Hopkin, review of *Amaryllis Night and Day,* p. 54; November 3, 2003, Hugo Barnacle, review of *Her Name Was Lola,* p. 55.

Newsweek, March 1, 1976; June 29, 1981; December 7, 1981; May 30, 1983; February 17, 1986.

New Yorker, March 22, 1976; July 20, 1981; August 8, 1983.

New York Review of Books, November 19, 1981, pp. 16-18.

New York Times, November 1, 1981; June 20, 1983; February 14, 1986.

New York Times Book Review, February 4, 1968; March 21, 1976; June 6, 1982; May 29, 1983; November 27, 1983.

Observer (London, England), March 13, 1983.

People, August 10, 1981.

Publishers Weekly, May 15, 1981, Barbara A. Bannon, interview with author; June 4, 2001, review of *Angelica's Grotto,* p. 57; November 12, 2001, review of *Jim's Lion,* p. 59; May 24, 2004, review of *Her Name Was Lola,* p. 42.

Saturday Review, May 7, 1960; May 1, 1976; December, 1981.

School Library Journal, January, 2002, Faith Brautigam, review of *Jim's Lion,* p. 101.

Spectator, May 16, 1969, pp. 654-655; April 5, 1975; March 12, 1983.

Time, February 16, 1976; June 22, 1981; May 16, 1983.

Times (London, England), January 7, 1982; March 24, 1983.

Times Literary Supplement, April 3, 1969, p. 357; March 16, 1973; March 29, 1974; October 31, 1980; March 7, 1986; April 3, 1987; September 4, 1987.

Village Voice, June 15, 1982, Eliot Fremont-Smith, review of *Riddley Walker.*

Washington Post, February 28, 1986.

Washington Post Book World, June 7, 1981, pp. 1, 14; June 27, 1982; May 29, 1983; July 12, 1987; October 14, 1990.

Wilton Bulletin, September 26, 1962.

World Literature Today, autumn, 2001, review of *Angelica's Grotto,* p. 162.

Pure Fiction Reviews, http://www.purefiction.com/ (October 2, 2001), interview with Russell Hoban.

* * *

HOBAN, Russell Conwell
See HOBAN, Russell

* * *

HOCHHUTH, Rolf 1931-

PERSONAL: Born April 1, 1931, in Eschwege, Germany; son of Walter (a shoe-factory owner and accountant) and Ilse (Holzapfel) Hochhuth; married Marianne Heinemann, June 29, 1957 (divorced, 1972); children: Martin, Friedrich. *Education:* Studied bookkeeping at a vocational school; attended universities of Marburg, Munich, and Heidelberg, 1952-55. *Religion:* German Evangelical Church

ADDRESSES: Home—P.O. Box 661, 4002 Basel, Switzerland.

CAREER: Acted as city-hall runner for first postwar mayor (his uncle) of Eschwege, Germany; C. Bertelsmann (publisher), Gütersloh, Westphalia, Germany, reader and editor, beginning 1955; Municipal Theatre, Basel, Switzerland, assistant director and playwright, 1963.

AWARDS, HONORS: Gerhart Hauptmann Preis, 1962, and Berliner Kunstpreis, 1963, both for *Der Stellvertreter;* Young Generation prize, 1963; Melcher prize, 1965; Basel Art prize, 1976; Stadt München und des Verbandes Bayerischer Verlager prize, 1980; Geschwister-Scholl prize, 1980; Lessing prize, 1981.

WRITINGS:

Der Stellvertreter: Schauspiel (play; produced in West Berlin at Volksbuehne Theatre, 1963; produced as *The Representative* by Royal Shakespeare Company, 1963; produced as *The Deputy* at Brooks Atkinson Theatre, New York, NY, 1964), foreword by Erwin Piscator, 1963, translation by Robert David MacDonald published as *The Representative,* Methuen (London, England), 1963, translation by Richard Winston and Clara Winston published as *The Deputy,* foreword by Albert Schweitzer, Grove (New York, NY), 1964, reprinted, Johns Hopkins University Press (Baltimore, MD), 1997.

Soldaten: Nekrolog auf Genf (play; produced in West Berlin at Volksbuehne Theatre, 1967; translation produced as *Soldiers* at Royal Alexandra Theater, Toronto, Ontario, Canada, 1968; produced in New York, NY, at Billy Rose Theatre, 1968), Rowohlt, 1967, translation by David MacDonald published as *Soldiers: An Obituary for Geneva,* Grove (New York, NY), 1968.

Guerillas: Tragoedie in fünf Akten (five-act play; produced in Stuttgart, West Germany, 1970), Rowohlt, 1970.

Krieg und Klassenkrieg (essays; title means "War and Class War"), foreword by Fritz J. Raddatz, Rowohlt, 1971.

Die Hebamme: Komoedie (play; title means "The Midwife"; produced in May, 1972), Rowohlt, 1971.

Lysistrate und die NATO (play; title means "Lysistrata and NATO"; produced, 1974), Rowohlt, 1973.

Zwischenspiel in Baden-Baden, Rowohlt, 1974.

Die Berliner Antigone: Prosa und Verse (novella; title means "The Berlin Antigone"), Rowohlt, 1975.

Tod eines Jaegers (play; title means "Death of a Hunter"), Rowohlt, 1976.

Eine Liebe in Deutschland (novel), Rowohlt, 1978.

Juristen: Drei Akte für sieben Spieler (play), Rowohlt, 1979.

Tell '38, Rowohlt, 1979, translated from the German, Little, Brown (Boston, MA), 1984.

Arztinnen: 5 Akte, Rowohlt, 1980.

A German Love Story (novel), translated by John Brownjohn, Little, Brown (Boston, MA), 1980.

Spitze des Eisbergs: Ein Reader, Rowohlt, 1982.

Rauber-Rede: 3 deutsche Vorwurfe. Schiller/Lessing/ Geschwister Scholl, Rowohlt, 1982.

Judith (play), produced in Glasgow, Scotland, at Citizens' Theatre, 1984.

Atlantik-Novelle: Erzahlungen und Gedichte (title means "Atlantic Novella"), Rowohlt, 1985.

Schwarze Segal: Essays und Gedichte, Rowohlt, 1986.

Tater und Denker: Profile und Probleme von Casar bis Junger: Essays, Deutsche Verlags-Anstahlt, 1987.

War hier Europa? Reden, Gedichte, Essays, Deutscher Taschenbuch Verlag, 1987.

Alan Turing: Erzahlung, Rowohlt, 1987.

Unbefleckte Empfangnis: Ein Kreidekreis (title means "Immaculate Conception: A Chalk Circle"), produced in Berlin, Germany, 1989.

Sommer 14: Ein Totentanz (title means "Summer 14"), produced in Vienna, Austria, at Akademietheater, 1990.

Alle Dramen (title means "All Dramas"), two volumes, Rowohlt, 1991.

Menzel: Maler des licts, Insel, 1991.

Von Syrakus aus gesehen, gedacht, erzeahlt, Volk & Welt (Berlin, Germany), 1991.

Tell gegen Hitler: Historische studien, Insel, 1992.

Wessis in Weimar: Szenen aus einem besetzten land, Volk & Welt (Berlin, Germany), 1993.

Julia oder der weg zur macht: Erzeahlung, Volk & Welt (Berlin, Germany), 1994.

Effis nacht: Monolog, Rowohlt, 1996.

Und Brecht sah das tragische nicht: Pleadoyers, Polimiken, Profile, Knesebeck, 1996.

(Coauthor) *The Deputy and Other Contemporary German Plays,* Continuum (New York, NY), 1999.

Hitlers Dr. Faust: Tragödie, Rowohlt, 2000.

Das Recht auf Arbeit; Nachtmusik: Zwei Dramen, Rowohlt, 2000.

Alle Erzählungen, Gedichte und Romane, Rowohlt, 2001.

Einspräche!: zur Geschichte, Politik und Literatur, Rowohlt, 2001.

Die Geburt der Tragëdie aus dem Krieg: Frankfurter Poetik-Vorlesungen, Rowohlt, 2001.

Mozart's Nachtmusik: Requiem for Three Characters in Two Scenes, translated and adapted by Robert David MacDonald, Oberon (London, England), 2001.

Zwischen Sylt und Wilhelmstrasse: Essays, Gedichte, Reden, Verlag Volk & Welt (Berlin, Germany), 2001.

McKinsey Kommt. Molieres Tartuffe: Zwei Theaterstücke, Deutscher Taschenbuch Verlag (Munich), 2003.

Nietzsches Spazierstock: Gedichte, Tragikomdie "Heil Hitler!," Prosa, Rowohlt, 2004.

EDITOR

Wilhelm Busch, *Saemtliche Werke, und eine Auswahl der Skizzen und Gemaelde,* Volume I, S. Mohn, 1959, Volume II, C. Bertelsmann, 1960.

Wilhelm Busch, *Lustige Streiche in Versen und Farben,* Ruetten & Loening, 1960.

Wilhelm Busch, *Saemtliche Bildergeschichten mit 3380 Zichnungen und Fachsimilies,* Ruetten & Leoning, 1961.

Liebe in unserer Zeit: Sechzehn Erzählungen (short story anthology), two volumes, Bertelsmann Lesering, 1961.

Theodor Storm, *Am grauen Meer,* Mosaik-Verlag, 1962.

Die grossen Meister: Deutsche Erzaehler des 20. Jahrhunderts (short story anthology), two volumes, Bertelsmann Lesering, 1964.

Des Lebens Uberfluss, R. Mohn, c. 1969.

Ruhm und Ehre, Bertelsmann, 1970.

Oscar Tellgmann, *Kaisers Zeiten: Bilder einer Epoche,* Herbig, 1973.

Also editor of Otto Flake's *Die Deutschen,* 1962, and Thomas Mann's *Dichter und Herrscher,* 1963.

OTHER

Author of plays *The Employer,* 1965, and *Anatomy of Revolution,* 1969.

ADAPTATIONS: Eine Liebe in Deutschland was adapted as the film *A Love in Germany,* starring Hanna Schygulla, directed by Andrzei Wajda, Triumph Films, 1984; *Der Stellvertreter* (*The Deputy,*) was adapted as the award-winning film *Amen,* directed by Constantin Costa-Gavras, Kino International, 2002.

SIDELIGHTS: Critics almost universally found that no previous post-World War II dramatic work shook the conscience of Europe as did Rolf Hochhuth's *The Deputy,* originally published in German as *Der Stellvertreter.* The impact was equated with that, in their times, of Emile Zola's letter "J'Accuse" and Erich Maria Remarque's novel *All Quiet on the Western Front.* It was propitious in timing, arriving on the scene shortly after Adolf Eichmann's war crimes trial and between sessions of the Second Vatican Council.

The thesis of Hochhuth's play is that Pope Pius XII should have spoken out more strongly and firmly than he did against the mass executions of the Jews during the Nazi period in Germany, especially against *die Endlösung*—the Final Solution. The dramatis personae are not for the most part, at least according to Hochhuth, actual historical people. The main protagonist, Jesuit Father Riccardo Fontana, is considered the most fictional character, although the writer was inspired in creating the role by the martyred Father Maximilian Kolbe—Prisoner Number 16670 in Auschwitz—and Bernhard Lichtenberg, prelate of St. Heldwig's Cathedral in Berlin; the work is dedicated to them.

Hochhuth has explained that he became interested in the subject on which he has written because, as a member of the young generation in Germany, he shared a great feeling of guilt about the past which he could not explain, but about which he felt he must seek to become informed. One of the books that stimulated him to begin work on the play was *The Final Solution*, by Gerald Reitlinger. After the death of Pope Pius XII, he spent three years in research preparation, three months in Rome, although secret Vatican archives were open to researchers only to the year 1846. Hochhuth also studied the Nuremburg Trial and Wehrmacht archives. A "Sidelights on History," composed of documentation and stage directions, was appended to the end of the published version of the play.

Complete performance of *The Deputy* would take six to eight hours; most actual performances last from two to three hours, and adaptations vary in different cities and languages. Hochhuth once commented that "the most comprehensive version was shown in Vienna, the shortest in Berlin, the most modern in Paris."

Demonstrations accompanied many performances of the play. Especially intense was the one at the Theatre Athenee in Paris, where protesters showered pamphlets on the audience, threw stench bombs, and even clambered onto the stage. On the Broadway premiere, about one hundred and fifty persons demonstrated outside the Brooks Atkinson Theater, including members of the American Nazi party who carried placards reading "Ban the Hate Show"; the doors of the theater were locked during intermission as a protective measure.

Producer and director Herman Shumlin reported that efforts were made to prevent presentation of *The Deputy* in the United States. Billy Rose withdrew his cooperation from the production. An interfaith group, however, headed by Edward Keating, editor of *Ramparts*—then a Roman Catholic paper for laymen—asked the public to regard the play with an open mind; Catholic reaction generally was more restrained than might have been expected, and, in some cases, contrite.

The play itself—its dramaturgy, blank verse and free rhythms—has not been considered by critics as exceptional. In fact, it has been described as old-fashioned, using late nineteenth-century techniques in weak German classical tradition. Hochhuth was, however, credited with recreating the flavor of Nazi jargon. A coincidental relationship between it and Johann von Schiller's *Don Carlos* was noted. It was also compared to Bertolt Brecht's *Heilige Johanne der Schlachthofe*.

Although critics tended to feel that *The Deputy* leaves a good bit to be desired artistically, most also saw other meaningful aspects to the work. As David Boroff wrote

in the *National Observer:* "Though it is both flawed and arguable, it has restored seriousness to the Broadway theater. Not since *Death of a Salesman* or *The Diary of Anne Frank* have audiences been so profoundly shaken." Walter Kerr, drama critic for the *New York Herald Tribune,* also thought that the work is deficient as a drama. But he, too, commented: "We are also left with the aftermath of *The Deputy,* making a clamor in the world which may, hopefully, become the equivalent of a call to prayer. Any virtues the work possesses are extra-theatrical. They may indeed become virtues."

The controversy that ensued over the production of Hochhuth's second play *Soldaten: Nekrolog auf Genf,* published in English as *The Soldiers,* was even greater that that surrounding his first. On April 24, 1967, against the protests of literary manager Kenneth Tynan and artistic director Laurence Olivier, who wanted the play performed, London's National Theatre decided that *The Soldiers* was unsuitable for production because it allegedly maligned certain notable Englishmen, principally Sir Winston Churchill. In the play, Hochhuth suggests that the death of General Wladyslaw Sikorski, the Polish exile leader during World War II, was not accidental but rather the result of the machinations of the British secret service and was, furthermore, the result of a plot about which Churchill had full knowledge. The Lord Chamberlain, Britain's theatrical censor at the time, suggested that he would allow the play to be publicly performed only if the relatives of the characters in the play gave their consent.

In 2002, French filmmaker Constantin Costa-Gavras, known for blending political content and high excitement, adapted *The Deputy* as the film *Amen,* in an effort to "explore the failure of Pope Pius XII to protest Hitler's extermination of the Jews during World War II," according to Joseph Cunneen in a review for *National Catholic Reporter.* But Cunneen found that "despite the urgency of its subject, the dialogue of *Amen* has little emotional power; its most suggestive images are the recurring shots of freight trains rolling through the German countryside. Making *Amen* as an English-language film may have been a shrewd commercial decision, but since most of the actors are not at home with the language, their words lack clarity and immediacy" and that like "*The Deputy,* which caused an international uproar when it appeared in 1963, *Amen* raises lots of still important questions, but somewhat softens the pope's failure by seeing it as part of a wider indifference to the Holocaust by those who knew what was going on."

BIOGRAPHICAL AND CRITICAL SOURCES:

BOOKS

Contemporary Literary Criticism, Thomson Gale (Detroit, MI), Volume 4, 1975, Volume 11, 1979, Volume 18, 1981.

Der Streit un Hochhuths "Stellvertreter," Basilius Presse, 1963.

Summa Inuria; oder, Durfte der Papst schweigen? Hochhuths "Stellvertreter" in der oeffentlichen Kritik, Rowohlt, 1963.

Taeni, Rainer, *Rolf Hochhuth,* translated by R.W. Last, Wolff, 1977.

Ward, M. E., *Rolf Hochhuth,* G.K. Hall (Boston, MA), 1977.

PERIODICALS

Catholic Insight, April, 2002, p. 23.

Chicago Tribune, January 30, 1985.

Christian Science Monitor, May 6, 1968; July 1, 1972.

Commentary, March, 1964.

Commonweal, February 28, 1964; March 20, 1964; May 31, 1968.

Detroit Free Press, March 29, 1964; September 24, 1967.

Globe and Mail (Toronto, Ontario, Canada), February 26, 1968.

Life, March 13, 1964; June 7, 1968.

Listener, October 12, 1967.

Los Angeles Times, November 15, 1984.

Los Angeles Times Book Review, June 22, 1980.

Midstream, April, 2001, p. 14.

Nation, March 16, 1964; May 20, 1968; August 25, 1969; August 17, 1970.

National Catholic Reporter, February 14, 2003, p. 15.

National Observer, March 2, 1964; March 4, 1968.

New Leader, March 16, 1964.

New Republic, March 14, 1964; December 10, 1984, p. 75.

New Statesman, October 4, 1963; July 22, 2002, p. 44.

Newsweek, March 2, 1964; March 11, 1968; January 20, 1969; June 1, 1970.

New Yorker, December 28, 1963; March 7, 1964; May 11, 1968.

New York Herald Tribune, February 27, 1964.

New York Review of Books, March 19, 1964.

New York Times, February 27, 1964; February 28, 1964; February 12, 1967; April 26, 1967; September 11, 1967; December 14, 1968; November 9, 1984; March 11, 1993; June 25, 1995.

New York Times Book Review, March 1, 1964.

New York Times Magazine, November 19, 1967.

Observer Review, October 15, 1967; May 12, 1968; October 27, 1968; December 15, 1968.

Saturday Evening Post, February 29, 1964.

Saturday Night, March, 1968.

Saturday Review, March 14, 1964.

Spectator, October 4, 1963; December 20, 1968.

Theatre Journal, March, 1994, p. 124.

Time, November 1, 1963; March 6, 1964; May 10, 1968.

Times (London, England), April 10, 1980; November 9, 1984; November 12, 1984; May 10, 1985; October 7, 1986.

Times Literary Supplement, May 28, 1970; May 2, 1980.

Transatlantic Review, autumn, 1968.

Tribune Books (Chicago, IL), June 15, 1980.

Village Voice, March 12, 1964.

Washington Post, January 19, 1969; May 3, 1972.

World Literature Today, spring, 1994, p. 365; summer-autumn, 2001, p. 186.

*   *   *

HØEG, Peter 1957-

PERSONAL: Born 1957, in Denmark; children: a daughter.

ADDRESSES: *Agent*—Nerete Ries, Monksgaard Rosinante, Norre Sogad 35, DK-1016 Copenhagen K., Denmark.

CAREER: Worked variously as an actor, dancer, drama teacher, and sailor; writer, 1983-.

WRITINGS:

Forestilling om det tyvende arhundrede (novel), Rosinante (Charlottenlund, Denmark), 1988, translation published as *The History of Danish Dreams,* Farrar, Straus (New York, NY), 1995.

Fortällinger om natten, Rosinante (Copenhagen, Denmark), 1990, translation published as *Tales of the Night* (short stories), Farrar, Straus (New York, NY), 1998.

Frøken Smillas fornemmelse for sne (novel; also see below), Rosinante (Copenhagen, Denmark), 1992, translation by Tiina Nunnally published as *Smilla's Sense of Snow,* Farrar, Straus (New York, NY), 1993.

De Maske Egnede (novel), Rosinante (Copenhagen, Denmark), 1993, translation by Barbara Haveland published as *Borderliners,* Farrar, Straus (New York, NY), 1994.

The Woman and the Ape, translation of *Kvinden og Aben* by Barbara Haveland, Farrar, Straus (New York, NY), 1996.

(Author of preface) Henrik Saxgren, *Point of View,* Aperture (New York, NY), 1998.

Tales of the Night, translated by Barbara Haveland, Farrar, Straus (New York, NY), 1998.

Smilla's Sense of Snow (screenplay), Fox/Searchlight, 1998.

Smilla's Sense of Snow has been translated into seventeen languages.

SIDELIGHTS: Danish author Peter Høeg gained critical acclaim for his 1992 novel *Frøken Smillas fornemmelse for sne,* translated into English as *Smilla's Sense of Snow.* Gaining an international following after the novel's publication in over thirty countries, Høeg has gained critical praise as well as comparison to such writers as Jules Verne, Jorge Luis Borges, John Le Carre, and Italo Calvino. Calling *Smilla's Sense of Snow* "one of the oddest and most beguiling journeys I've come across in contemporary fiction" in *New Republic,* contributor Brad Leithauser added that the novel extends far beyond the traditional limits of the genre, drawing on colonialism, Danish history, and the prejudicial attitudes toward Denmark's native Inuit culture. "Høeg understands just how Denmark and the Danish character are representative of a larger European attitude toward the non-European world," Jane Smiley explained in her review of the novel for *Washington Post Book World,* "and the remote and mysterious Inuit are representative of the destruction and transformation all non-European peoples have suffered at the hands of the most well-intentioned colonizers." Far more than a thriller, Høeg's novel brings to the fore the racial and cultural conflicts born of the colonialism of a century past, and their affect on modern society.

After a year on the bestseller list in Denmark, *Smilla's Sense of Snow* reached U.S. readers. The first of Høeg's novels to be translated into English, this thriller is told in the first person by Smilla Qaavigaaq Jaspersen, a thirty-seven-year-old, half-Inuit/half-Danish glaciologist who lives in Copenhagen. Smilla stumbles upon a conspiracy when she investigates the death of a neighbor boy who has fallen from the snow-covered roof of their apartment building. The intrigue eventually takes Smilla to Greenland in search of a mysterious and valuable object, which is also sought after by a host of minor characters.

Writing in *New Republic,* Leithauser noted that the plot of *Smilla's Sense of Snow* is typical of a thriller in its use of a small event leading to the discovery of a conspiracy. Such a plot, he remarked, "presents a monumental task to a writer bent on presenting it with artistic freshness." Leithauser commented that Høeg overcomes this obstacle "with great deftness. Everything in the story seems to build simultaneously." While calling the "sinuous turns of his story deeply engrossing," Richard Eder in *Los Angeles Times Book Review* faulted the work's ambiguous finale: "The book's only real weakness is an ending that doesn't live up to what has gone before and that fails to satisfy, not our emotional expectations, but our logical ones. It is not a matter of anti-climax . . . but of not quite making sense."

Other critics focused on character instead of plot in their appraisal of *Smilla's Sense of Snow.* The protagonist Smilla is a complex and erudite character whom *New York Times* reviewer Sarah Lyall described as "so fully and interestingly drawn that the book's plot almost become beside the point." Although in *New Republic* Leithauser criticized the archvillian as stereotypical, he called other, minor, characters "nothing short of dazzling."

"I'm fascinated by the ambiguity of Smilla, by the dichotomy between her two selves," Høeg told Lyall in *New York Times.* With her mixed ethnic heritage, Smilla can be seen as representing the native in the worldwide treatment of natives by imperial powers. Writing for *Washington Post Book World,* Jane Smiley labeled Høeg's insights into this war of cultures "first rate." According to Eder, who in *Los Angeles Times Book Review* called *Smilla's Sense of Snow* a "moving and suggestive book" and an "anti-colonial thriller," the novel's suspense lies in the development of its characters: "There is Smilla's character and that of half a dozen figures whom she encounters. There is the character of a process that has despoiled her Eskimo culture both of its adeptness and its sense of wonder within its own world, as it has done long before in the industrial world. In this respect, Høeg has written an artful and astonishing book." In *Washington Post Book World,* Smiley recommended *Smilla's Sense of Snow* as "a serious and absorbing novel of character and geography masquerading as a thriller."

Høeg's second novel to be translated into English is *Borderliners,* released in the United States in 1994. *Borderliners* focuses on the survival of three children at a strict Danish boarding school, and the novel is narrated by a teenager named Peter. At Peter's school, students' failure to conform to the authoritarian headmaster's standards symbolizes the artist's failure to conform in Danish society, with the consequence that both are banished to the lower rung of the class—or class system. Forming an alliance with two fellow boarders, Katarina and August—the latter a psychopathic child who has already murdered his parents—Peter sets out to subvert the extreme social experiment being conducted at the school. "Høeg's pervasive theme . . . is the abuse of children by the means that civilization—especially, perhaps, an enlightened Scandinavian civilization—has used to advance itself," observed Eder in *Los Angeles Times Book Review*. In the course of his investigations, Peter uncovers evidence of "some sort of Darwinian experiment," according to Michiko Kakutani in *New York Times*. "As evidence, [Peter] cites some disturbing incidents: a student's attempt to cut off his own tongue, the administration of sedatives to August, the concealment of student records."

"The well-crafted suspense, the emotions that strike unexpectedly and the intimate portrayal of Peter himself make this a forceful tale. The ending is especially charged," commented Laura Shapiro in *Newsweek*. In *Borderliners*, Eder pointed out in *Los Angeles Times Book Review*, "children stand for humanity's instinctive and unspoiled possibilities; by making them the victims, Høeg is able to distill the passionate rage that gives energy to his writing."

The History of Danish Dreams, released in English in 1995, is a translation of Høeg's first novel. The narrative encompasses four centuries and weaves the history of four families until they eventually mesh into one. Their story is described in a series of dreams— "dreams," in the words of *Los Angeles Times Book Review* contributor Jim Shepard, "because both grandiose aspiration and self-delusion are so central to the ways in which families and societies operate; dreams because of the book's pessimism concerning the likelihood of progressive change; and dreams because a history of dreams is, of course, by definition a sly critique of history itself." Høeg pens his novel in the style of magical realism and interweaves themes that will become characteristic of his later works: the representation of time, both physical and symbolic; social class; conflict between the individual and society; and mistreatment of children. *The History of Danish Dreams* is divided into three sections, with each section covering the lives of one generation of the families involved. The novelist stresses the absence of a vital "inner life" from generation to generation; children are locked into a cycle of mental isolation. In assessing *The History of Danish Dreams* Shepard wrote: "If the social criticism is at

times insistent, or unsubtle, the novel's gathering force—and its persistent return to the specifics of human suffering—ultimately grants such satire an affecting sadness." In *New Statesman*, Peter Whittaker was enthusiastic about Høeg's narrative, with its "subtle pleasures of character, language and sly wit." Comparing the novel to the works of Salman Rusdie and Gabriel García Márquez, he added that *The History of Danish Dreams* "heralds a writer who combines narrative scope and imaginative zest to breathtaking effect."

As in *Smilla's Sense of Snow*, the protagonist of Høeg's *The Woman and the Ape* is a female loner who stumbles upon forbidden scientific knowledge and risks her life in an effort to release it to the public. While *Smilla's Sense of Snow* remains rooted in the style of naturalism, despite its exotic aspects, *The Woman and the Ape* enters the realm of fantasy. The heroine, Madelene, a tippling trophy wife, finds a soul mate in a small talking ape whose captivity as a tamed and well-behaved helpmate and showpiece echoes her own. She rescues the ape from scientific experimentation and eventually the two enjoy a love affair. Going beyond the relationship between "civilized" and "primitive" man earlier explored in *Smilla's Sense of Snow*, Høeg examines the relationship between humans and animals—including the animal within. Discussing *The Woman and the Ape* in *Booklist*, a contributor called the novel "an anti-utopian fable in which civilization, the enemy, triumphs over disorder." Writing in *New York Times Book Review*, Joe Queenan compared Høeg to Ray Bradbury and lamented that "what starts out as a rather off-beat, enigmatic novel ends up in the entirely recognizable world of didactic science fiction." On the other hand, a contributor for *Kirkus Reviews* allowed that while the novel is "more than a little didactic in spots it was distinguished by enough wit and invention to redeem a dozen lesser books."

Høeg's first collection of short fiction, *Tales of the Night*, was not published in English until 1998, though it was written earlier than *Smilla's Sense of Snow* and *The Woman and the Ape*. The stories are all set on March 19, 1929, in the political and economic ferment of the time, and all are concerned with human love. Recounted in almost essay-style prose, they tend to explore one character, often a troubled genius whose worldview has collapsed. A *Booklist* reviewer maintained that the stories "read like entries from a writer's notebook, ideas and character sketches waiting to be molded into art . . . of interest to anyone curious about the evolution of a great writer." In *New York Times Book Review*, Jay Parini opined that in only one of the stories, "in Ignatio Rasker's decision to throw everything away for love, does Høeg live up to his full potential." Phoebe-Lou Adams, writing in *Atlantic,* was more impressed, describing the collection as "splendid stories and not to be missed by anyone who enjoys elegant writing and intellectual vigor."

BIOGRAPHICAL AND CRITICAL SOURCES:

BOOKS

Contemporary Literary Criticism, Volume 95, Thomson Gale (Detroit, MI), 1996.

PERIODICALS

Atlantic, December, 1994, p. 145; March, 1998, p. 118.

Booklist, October 1, 1996, p. 291; January 1, 1998.

Detroit Free Press, December 20, 1995, p. D4.

Kirkus Reviews, September 15, 1996.

London Review of Books, June 19, 1997, p. 21.

Los Angeles Times Book Review, September 26, 1993, Richard Eder, review of *Smilla's Sense of Snow,* pp. 2, 11; November 6, 1994, pp. 3, 11; December 24, 1995, pp. 2, 8.

Nation, November 20, 1995, John Leonard, "Children of the Panopticon," pp. 642-645.

New Republic, November 1, 1993, Brad Leithauser, review of *Smilla's Sense of Snow,* pp. 39-41; April 3, 1995, pp. 39-41.

New Statesman, September 3, 1993, John Williams, "Fire and Ice," p. 41; January 6, 1995, p. 37; January 5, 1996, Peter Whittaker, "Scintillating Sage," p. 41.

Newsweek, September 6, 1993, p. 54; November 28, 1994, p. 68.

New Yorker, September, 1993, Fernanda Eberstadt, "Northern Light," pp. 118-119.

New York Review of Books, November 18, 1992, Michael Meyer, "Danger: Thin Ice," p. 41.

New York Times, October 6, 1993, pp. C15, C20; November 29, 1994, p. B2.

New York Times Book Review, December 22, 1996, p. 8; March 1, 1998, p. 34.

Partisan Review, winter, 1994, pp. 80-85.

Publishers Weekly, October 4, 1993, p. 14.

Scandinavian Studies, winter, 1997, Mary Kay Norseng, review of *A House of Mourning,* pp. 52-83.

Time, November 6, 1995, p. 84.

Times Literary Supplement, September 17, 1993, p. 20; April 14, 1995, p. 20; November 28, 1997, p. 23.

Washington Post Book World, October 24, 1993, Jane Smiley, "In Distant Lands of Ice and Sun," pp. 1, 11; October 1, 1995, p. 4; April 26, 1998, Katherine Dunn, "In the Gothic Mode," p. 4.

*   *   *

HOFFMAN, Alice 1952-

PERSONAL: Born March 16, 1952, in New York, NY; married Tom Martin (a writer); children: Jake, Zack. *Education:* Adelphi University, B.A., 1973; Stanford University, M.A., 1975.

ADDRESSES: Home—Brookline, MA. *Agent*—c/o Author Mail, Little, Brown and Company, 1271 Avenue of the Americas, New York, NY 10020.

CAREER: Writer, 1975—.

AWARDS, HONORS: Mirelles fellow, Stanford University, 1975; Bread Loaf fellowship, summer, 1976; Notable Books of 1979 list, *Library Journal,* for *The Drowning Season.*

WRITINGS:

NOVELS

Property Of, Farrar, Straus (New York, NY), 1977.

The Drowning Season, Dutton (New York, NY), 1979.

Angel Landing, Putnam (New York, NY), 1980.

White Horses, Putnam (New York, NY), 1982.

Fortune's Daughter, Putnam (New York, NY), 1985.

Illumination Night, Putnam (New York, NY), 1987.

At Risk, Putnam (New York, NY), 1988.

Seventh Heaven, Putnam (New York, NY), 1990.

Turtle Moon, Berkley (New York, NY), 1993

Second Nature, Putnam (New York, NY), 1994.

Practical Magic, Putnam (New York, NY), 1995.

Here on Earth, Putnam (New York, NY), 1997.

The River King, Putnam (New York, NY), 2000.

Blue Diary, Putnam (New York, NY), 2001.

The Probable Future, Doubleday (New York, NY), 2003.

Blackbird House, Doubleday (New York, NY), 2004.

The Ice Queen, Little, Brown and Company (New York, NY), 2005.

FOR CHILDREN

Fireflies, illustrated by Wayne McLoughlin, Hyperion (New York, NY), 1997.

Horsefly, illustrated by Steve Johnson, Hyperion (New York, NY), 2000.

Aquamarine, Scholastic (New York, NY), 2001.

Indigo, Scholastic (New York, NY), 2002.

Green Angel, Scholastic (New York, NY), 2003.

(With Wolfe Martin) *Moondog,* illustrated by Yumi Heo, Scholastic (New York, NY), 2004.

The Foretelling, Little, Brown and Company (New York, NY), 2005.

Incantation, Little, Brown and Company (New York, NY), 2006.

Skylight Confessions, Little, Brown and Company (New York, NY), 2007.

OTHER

Independence Day (screenplay), Warner Bros., 1983.

Local Girls (short stories), Putnam (New York, NY), 1999.

Also author of other screenplays. Contributor of stories to *Ms., Redbook, Fiction, American Review,* and *Playgirl.*

ADAPTATIONS: *Practical Magic* was adapted by Robin Swicord, Akiva Goldsman, and Adam Brooks into a film directed by Griffin Dunne, starring Sandra Bullock, Nicole Kidman, and Aidan Quinn, and released by Warner Bros. in 1998; *Aquamarine* was made into a film directed by Elizabeth Allen, produced by Susan Cartsonis, and released by Twentieth Century Fox in 2006; a sound recording was produced of *Local Girls.*

SIDELIGHTS: Through the course of numerous novels, Alice Hoffman's work has been characterized by "a shimmering prose style, the fusing of fantasy and realism, [and] the preoccupation with the way the mythic weaves itself into the everyday," Alexandra Johnson summarized in the *Boston Review.* "Hoffman's narrative domain is the domestic, the daily. Yet her vision—and voice—are lyrical," the critic continues. "She is a writer whose prose style is often praised as painterly, and, indeed, Hoffman's fictional world is like a Vermeer: a beautifully crafted study of the interior life." Hoffman's characters "tend to be rebels and eccentrics," Stella Dong stated in a *Publishers Weekly* interview with the author. Hoffman explained that she writes about such people "because they're outsiders and to some extent, we all think of ourselves as outsiders. We're looking for that other person—man, woman, parent or child—who will make us whole." As the author once told *CA:* "I suppose my main concern is the search for identity and continuity, and the struggle inherent in that search."

The protagonist of Hoffman's first novel, *Property Of,* for instance, is an unnamed seventeen-year-old girl enamored of McKay, the leader of an urban gang involved in violence and drugs; the story of their year-long relationship is what *Times Literary Supplement* contributor Zachary Leader called "a sort of punk or pop-gothic *Jane Eyre.*" Despite the "harsh and gritty" quality of the world it portrays, *Property Of* is nevertheless "a remarkably envisioned novel, almost mythic in its cadences, hypnotic," Richard R. Lingeman observed in the *New York Times.* "McKay and the heroine are like tragic lovers in a courtly romance played out in candy stores, clubhouses and mean streets . . . . Hoffman imbues her juvenile delinquents with a romantic intensity that lifts them out of sociology." Edith Milton offered a similar assessment, commenting in the *Yale Review* that "the narrative is engrossing because Hoffman creates characters touched by legend." The critic further elaborated that Hoffman is able to balance "parody and sentiment, cutting her own flights of panting prose with acid self- mockery."

While the writing in *Property Of* "had speed, wit, and a mordant lyricism," Margo Jefferson remarked in *Ms.* that " *The Drowning Season* has extravagance and generosity as well." Tracing "a legacy of lovelessness from frozen White Russia to modern New York," as *Newsweek* contributor Jean Strouse described it, *The Drowning Season* follows Esther the White and Esther the Black, a grandmother and granddaughter who overcome a past of failed communication to slowly establish a relationship. Like Hoffman's first novel, *The Drowning Season* functions on two levels, as Susan Wood suggested in the *Washington Post:* "*The Drowning Season,* just as hypnotic and mythic in its language and rhythms, reverberates with situations and characters that suggest ancient myths and European folk tales and seems on one level to function as a symbolic, allegorical tale in a modern setting. Yet it is very much a novel about believable and imperfect human beings, as concrete and individualized as the family next door." Barry Siegel found Esther the White in particular "a truly compelling character," writing in the *Los Angeles Times Book Review* that while "she is the source of her family's malaise . . . Hoffman sees in her something much more complex than a villain." The critic concluded that Hoffman "is a superb writer who brings us to understand and to care about all her characters . . . . Hoffman at all times remains in control of her fine narrative."

Hoffman followed *The Drowning Season* with *Angel Landing,* a romance set near a nuclear power plant, and *White Horses,* the story of a young girl's obsession with her older brother. Teresa, the protagonist of *White Horses,* has been brought up hearing the family legend of the *Arias,* dangerous and beautiful young outlaws who carry women off to exciting lives; this legend led Teresa's mother into an unhappy marriage, and Teresa herself into an incestuous love for Silver, whom she sees as her ideal *Aria.* "Incest may be the most difficult theme for a novelist to undertake," stated *Newsweek* reviewer Peter S. Prescott, "yet Hoffman here makes it tolerable by the mythic mold in which she has cast her story." *New York Times Book Review* contributor Anne Tyler likewise saw a mythic dimension in the novel: "*White Horses* combines the concrete and the dreamlike. Its characters are people we think we recognize at first; but then on second thought we're not so sure." The critic continued, "There's an almost seamless transition from the real to the unreal, back and forth and back again." Stephanie Vaughn, however, faulted the novel's symbolism as "ask[ing] us to see an epic dimension that the story does not quite deliver," as she remarked in her *Washington Post* review. And while Tyler also thought that the novel is at times "burdened by the very musicality that was so appealing in the beginning," she admitted that "these are quibbles, and very minor quibbles at that. The overall impression is one of abundant life, masterfully orchestrated by the author." *White Horses,* Tyler concluded, "is a satisfying novel, at the same time mysterious and believable, and it marks a significant advance for Alice Hoffman."

While *Fortune's Daughter,* in the vein of Hoffman's earlier novels, "has the quality of folk tale—of amazing events calmly recounted," Perri Klass asserted in the *New York Times Book Review* that unlike *White Horses* it has "no . . . explicit myth. Instead, the sense of magic and elemental force arises from the central mystery of childbirth." Klass continued, "This novel's great strength lies in its two heroines, who both find themselves drawn, without plans, hopes or full understanding, into the inevitably mythological process of pregnancy and childbirth." Rae, pregnant with her first child, has just been deserted by the man for whom she left her home and traveled across a continent. Seeking reassurance, she finds Lila, a fortune teller who reads a child's death in Rae's tea leaves. Against Lila's wishes, Rae enlists the older woman's assistance with her pregnancy, evoking Lila's memories of the child she gave

up for adoption over twenty years ago. The result, observed Robin Hemley in the *Chicago Tribune Book World,* is "an elegant and evocative novel that conjures up a kind of modern-day female mythology."

Some critics, however, such as *Boston Review* contributor Patricia Meyer Spacks, felt the plot of *Fortune's Daughter* verges on "soap-opera sentimentalities." Nevertheless, they acknowledge, as Klass wrote, that "the peculiar offbeat humor keeps the narrative from drifting into melodrama." The critic elaborated, "It is in its juxtaposition of the mythic, the apocalyptic, with the resolutely ordinary, in its portrait of eccentric characters living in a very familiar world, that this novel finds its unique voice. It is beautifully and matter-of-factly told, and it leaves the reader with an almost bewildered sense that this primal mythological level does exist in everyday reality, and that there is no event, from the standard miracle of childbirth to the most bizarre magic imaginable, that cannot occur in a setting of familiar, everyday details."

"*Illumination Night,* Hoffman's sixth novel, is in many ways her most subtle," Johnson claimed, describing it as "a powerful if often disturbing look at the interior lives, domestic and emotional, of a young family and the teenage girl set on destroying them all." Andre and Vonny are a young couple concerned about their son's lack of growth and the tension in their marriage caused by the unwanted attentions of Jody, a neighboring sixteen-year-old, towards Andre. "This may sound like soap opera," *New York Times* critic Christopher Lehmann-Haupt declared, but Hoffman "has enough power of empathy to make her characters matter to us. Daringly mixing comedy with tragedy, and the quotidian with the fabulous, she has created a narrative that somehow makes myth out of the sticky complexities of contemporary marriage." Hoffman "has a penchant for finding a near-gothic strangeness and enchantment on the edges of everyday experience," Jack Sullivan likewise commented in the *Washington Post Book World.* Throughout the book "is the sure sense that magic and spirituality infuse our lives, and that this magic is as readily available to the poor as to the rich," *Los Angeles Times* critic Carolyn See similarly reported.

"Subtle touches here and there make this intelligent novel shine," Gwyneth Cravens maintained in the *New York Times Book Review.* "Ms. Hoffman knows how to tell a story in clear language and how to avoid subordinating the meanderings of temperament to logic or plot. The characters suddenly, and believably, change their behavior toward one another in the presence of the irrational." Other critics have also remarked on the quality of the author's characterizations. Lehmann-Haupt, for example, observed that "Hoffman writes so simply about human passions that her characters are branded onto one's memory," while London *Times* reviewer Philip Howard stated that Hoffman "hits bull's eyes on the incomprehensions between the young and the old, on the magic and pain of ordinary life." As Candice Russell noted in her *Chicago Tribune* review, the author's "omniscient voice . . . explores the underpinnings of her characters, who become increasingly connected and interdependent." Sullivan similarly praised Hoffman's narrative for its "unusually fluid form of subjectivity that becomes a kind of total omniscience . . . without breaking the rhythm of her prose or storyline. From a technical as well as emotional standpoint," the critic concluded, "this is an impressive, stirring performance."

With *At Risk,* the story of a young girl whose AIDS precipitates a family crisis, Hoffman "is mainstreaming a refined literary talent," *Time* writer R.Z. Sheppard recounted. By taking as her subject such a topical social concern, however, Hoffman has drawn criticism from some reviewers for letting the issue of AIDS overcome the story. *Washington Post* writer Jonathan Yardley, for example, contended that the novel "is very much wrought from material offered by the headlines, yet it fails to shape that material into anything approximating life." But Lehmann-Haupt believed that *At Risk* "does succeed in overcoming these obstacles [of topicality]. From its opening sentence, we know we are in a world that is specific and alive."

Because the issues in *At Risk* are more self-evident than in the author's other work, some reviewers have suggested that the novel does not contain as much of a "magical" element as do her other books. But *Newsweek* critic Laura Shapiro contended that "this wonderful book isn't markedly different in style or imagination from Hoffman's last novel." As Chicago *Tribune Books* contributor Michele Souda observed, the novel contains many "dark and bizarre experiences that remind us how much Hoffman has always trusted her characters' dreams and how well she has invented them." And, as the author explained to London *Times* writer Catherine Bennett, "part of the reason [for the diminished emphasis on magic] is that AIDS took the place of that, that was the inexplicable part of it. AIDS is like something you'd invent, it's bizarre, it's horrible, it's kind of like a spaceship—this disease just landing. I felt that anything else I was going to add was going to reduce it." The result, concluded Souda, is that Hoffman "has taken the nightmare of our time, stripped it of statistics and social rhetoric, and placed it in the raw center of family life."

In *Seventh Heaven* Hoffman returns again to the illusive quiet of suburbia, this time in 1959—the cusp of a new, noisier era. Into a seemingly idyllic New York community comes Nora Silk, a divorced woman whose unconventional manner disturbs the peaceful facade of the neighborhood. Nora is struggling to begin a new life and be a good mother to her children; she has little concern for what her neighbors think of her, giving her a freedom others resent. But as she gradually adjusts to her surroundings, so does the community begin to accept her and overcome their own inhibitions. "Hoffman is out to remind us that all those suburban stereotypes, creaky facades though they may often be, are propped up by some very real, and very basic, hopes and fears," Alida Becker remarked in the *New York Times Book Review*. The novel contains "many of the plot twists you'd expect from a late-fifties's melodrama," the critic continued, adding that "what's unexpected, though, is the wonderful blend of humor, shrewdness and compassion that Ms. Hoffman brings to these familiar scenes."

Detroit News contributor Alice Vachss likewise praised the author's writing: "Hoffman's usual abilities—her enchanting storytelling and her gift for interweaving magic and realism—are even more finely honed than in her previous novels." Hoffman's mystical elements are effectively incorporated into *Seventh Heaven,* according to some critics. As *People* reviewer Ralph Novak commented, the author "makes greater use of the supernatural—or the allure of the supernatural—without compromising her insight into human behavior." This insight is considerable, for "Hoffman has intuitive grasp of the thoughts and feelings that are masked by conventional behavior," a *Publishers Weekly* critic noted, commending in particular the author's "unerring understanding of people of nearly every age and across a broad social spectrum." *Seventh Heaven,* asserted Shapiro, "is one of the rare novels so abundant with life it seems to overflow its own pages . . . . Hoffman has always enjoyed a coterie of devoted fans, but her immensely winning novels deserve a much wider readership. *Seventh Heaven,* her eighth and best, confirms her place as one of the finest writers of her generation."

Turtle Moon and *Second Nature,* Hoffman's next two novels, again feature single women struggling to define life on their own terms. The novels are also infused with Hoffman's trademark use of magic and heightened realism. *Turtle Moon* is set in a sleepy Florida town with a large population of divorced women and follows the exploits of Bethany, a woman who has fled with her infant daughter from a child-custody fight; Lucy Rosen, a single mother; her son, Keith, a mean boy who bullies his peers and who steals at will; Julian Cash, an acerbic, taciturn policeman; and Julian's dog, Arrow, who shares his owner's temperament. The story revolves around the disappearance of Keith with Bethany's baby and the quest to solve a local murder. Reviewing the work in the *New York Times Book Review,* Frederick Busch averred that "Hoffman writes quite wonderfully about the magic in our lives and in the battered, indifferent world. I don't know that she's written better." *New York Times* daily reviewer Michiko Kakutani had a less enthusiastic view of the book, however, saying that it "showcases Hoffman's assurance as a writer, and her less admirable penchant for situating her characters in a slick, tricked-up plot that's decorated with pointlessly whimsical asides."

Second Nature is a tale about a wild man raised by wolves who brings love and joy to a lonely woman's suburban world. *New York Times Book Review* contributor Howard Frank Mosher called the novel "magical and daring" and commented that the book is written "with grace and beauty, making it at once [Hoffman's] richest and wisest, as well as her boldest, novel to date." Christopher Lehmann-Haupt, another critic for the daily *New York Times,* thought *Second Nature*'s premise about the conflict between nature and so-called civilization "familiar almost to the point of cliche," but liked some aspects of the story, "many of whose complications are richly ambiguous."

Hoffman's eleventh novel, *Practical Magic,* is set in a small Massachusetts town and features a matriarchal dynasty, the Owenses. Specifically, the novel focuses on two Owens sisters, Gillian and Sally, and the aunts who raise them. As children, Gillian and Sally sneak down from bed to listen as their aunts prescribe love potions for the town women. Determined not to suffer from any such lovesickness when they grow older, the girls take differing paths. Gillian becomes a promiscuous vagabond who never marries or has children, while dutiful Sally survives the death of her husband and subordinates her own desires to those of her daughters. Terming *Practical Magic* "a particularly arch and dexterous example of [Hoffman's] narrative powers," *Times Literary Supplement* reviewer Lorna Sage concluded that "Hoffman spins out the intrigue with show-off skill." Writing in the *New York Times Book Review,* Mark Childress noted that "Hoffman's trademark narrative voice is upbeat, breathless and rather bouncy. She creates vivid characters, she keeps things moving along, and she's not above using sleight of hand and prestidigitation to achieve her considerable effects."

Here on Earth deals with a married woman, March Murray, who becomes involved with an old lover, Hollis, when she comes back from California to her native Massachusetts for a funeral. It has echoes of Emily Bronte's *Wuthering Heights.* Hollis, for instance, resembles Bronte's dark, brooding Heathcliff. *New York Times Book Review* contributor Karen Karbo found it implausible that a smart, modern woman like March would resume a relationship with Hollis, and thought the course of their affair sadly predictable. "The madness of being madly in love is one of the most difficult subjects to write about convincingly," Karbo observed. "And you've got to give Hoffman points for trying. Unfortunately, just as March is too good for Hollis, Hoffman is too good for a story like this."

Local Girls is Hoffman's first collection of short stories, which are linked by their characters, members of a dysfunctional Long Island family, the Samuelsons. They follow the key character, Gretel, over roughly a decade of her life, beginning in her teen years. As she grows to womanhood, the intelligent, observant Gretel has to cope with troubles, including her parents' bitter divorce, her brother's drug addiction, and her mother's serious illness. Like many of Hoffman's other works, *Local Girls* has a strong element of female bonding— Gretel's best friend, Jill, and cousin Margot are her main sources of emotional support—and touches of magical realism. *Redbook* contributor Rose Martelli observed that Hoffman "turns [the Samuelsons'] trials into a celebration of family, revealing what it takes to brave real crises together." A *Publishers Weekly* reviewer noted that Hoffman's "disarming wit" keeps the tales from becoming depressing, adding, "she indicates that the human spirit can survive despite the cruel workings of fate." "These stories sometimes have a sketchy feel," noted *Library Journal* critic Barbara Hoffert. *New York Times Book Review* commentator Sarah Ferguson stated, "The stories suffer from a debilitating overlap when they're read as a collection. As in a soap opera, where any episode may be the viewer's first, background information is repeated and characters are reintroduced ad nauseam."

Hoffman again used interconnected stories in *Blackbird House,* a book in which the common bond of the stories is a Cape Cod farmhouse. For reviewer Ellen Shapiro, writing for *People,* this was problematic, "When all the dust settles, it is the house itself that emerges as the book's enduring—and inspiring—character." Other reviews, such as the one in *Publishers Weekly* praised the book: "Hoffman's lyrical prose weaves an undeniable spell."

The River King revolves around Haddan School, an exclusive preparatory academy in a picturesque small town in Massachusetts. The plot turns on an investigation into the death of a student named Gus Pierce, a "Holden Caulfield-like misfit," as *Entertainment Weekly* reviewer George Hodgman put it. Local police officer Abel Grey suspects that Gus's drowning was no accident or suicide, but murder, and in the course of his detective work he becomes attracted to photography teacher Betsy Chase, who is engaged to another Haddan faculty member. Meanwhile, Carlin Leander, a scholarship student who had befriended Gus, encounters what she believes to be his ghost. "The puzzle of the drowning helps propel Hoffman's at times meandering narrative, but she's more interested in the mysteries of love, the crimes of the heart," observed Nancy Pate in the *Orlando Sentinel*. A *Publishers Weekly* reviewer praised *The River King* as "a many-layered morality tale" and Hoffman as "an inventive author with a distinctive touch," while *Booklist* contributor Donna Seaman credited the author with "illuminating the power of emotion and the exquisite mysteries of life." Hodgman, however, was less impressed, finding some of the characters sketchily drawn, "basic romantic types," although he felt Hoffman "does a nice job of weaving together a meandering tapestry of plots." Amanda Fortini, writing in the *New York Times Book Review*, had a similar take, applauding Hoffman's "good old-fashioned storytelling" but deeming her characters "so numerous that she rarely has time to develop them beyond mere tag lines." *Library Journal* critic Reba Leiding deemed the novel a bit too atmospheric: "One wishes Hoffman had pared down the precious local descriptions and allowed the plot, which has some unexpected twists, to shine through." Pate, though, concluded that Hoffman "is a writer who can cast a spell."

In 2005, Hoffman published her next novel, *The Ice Queen*. At eight years old, the unnamed protagonist of the story wishes her mother dead during a fight, and to her horror, the wish comes true. She grows up unfeeling, with a heart made of what she imagines to be ice, until, as an adult, she is struck by lightning. She seeks out a fiery man who also survived a strike and the opposites fall passionately in love. "The characters interact with a crackle of electricity, and the book's payoffs are subtle and insightful, and while unexpected, not unearned," stated Charles De Lint in *Magazine of Fantasy and Science Fiction*. "Hoffman incorporates elements of fairy tales . . . , chaos theory, and magic realism," Sandy Freund wrote in *School Library Journal*. Amy Waldman called the language in the novel, "nothing less than stellar," and commented that "Hoffman reminds us how little distance there is between magic and mundane."

In the same year, Hoffman penned a young adult book, *The Foretelling*. In the story, Rain is a young girl who lives in a female-dominated Amazon community. She is shunned by her mother, the queen, because she is the product of rape. When her mother dies during the childbirth that she thought would bring her a new heir, Rain ascends to the throne and tries to protect the newborn son her mother left behind. "Many teens, particularly girls, will identify with Rain's self-doubt," noted Jennifer Mattson in *Booklist*. Claire Rosser, writing in *Kliatt*, stated that the story "holds the power of myth" and "examines what a society dominated by strong women would be like."

BIOGRAPHICAL AND CRITICAL SOURCES:

BOOKS

Contemporary Literary Criticism, Volume 51, Gale (Detroit, MI), 1989.

PERIODICALS

Belles Lettres, summer, 1992, p. 20.
Book, May-June 2003, Kristin Kloberdanz, review of *Green Angel*, p. 31; May-June 2003, Chris Bohjalian, "Girl Power," pp. 69- 71.
Booklist, March 15, 1999, Brad Hooper, review of *Local Girls*, January 1, 2000, review of *Local Girls*, p. 819; March 15, 2000, Mary McCay, review of *Local Girls, Practical Magic*, and *Angel Landing*, pp. 1396-1397; April 15, 2000, Donna Seaman, review of *The River King*, p. 1500; March 1, 2003, Donna Seaman, review of *The Probable Future*, pp. 1107-1108 April 15, 2003, Gillian Engberg, review of *Green Angel*, pp. 69-71; May 15, 2004, Donna Seaman, review of *Blackbird House*, p. 1519; June 1, 2004, Ilene Cooper, review of *Mondog*, pp. 1742-1743; July, 2005, Jennifer Mattson, review of *The Foretelling*, p. 1916.
Boston Review, September, 1985; October, 1987.
Chicago Tribune, August 31, 1987, Candice Russell, review of *Illumination Night*.
Chicago Tribune Book World, May 5, 1985, Robin Hemley, review of *Fortune's Daughter*.
Cosmopolitan, February, 1994.
Detroit News, September 5, 1990, Alice Vachss, review of *Seventh Heaven*.
Entertainment Weekly, October 23, 1998, review of film *Practical Magic*, p. 47; July 16, 1999, p. 62; August 4, 2000, George Hodgman, "Alice's Wonders," p. 78; June 27, 2003, Amy Feitelberg, "The Prob-

able Future: Anne Hoffman Mystical Fiction," p. 142; July 23, 2004, Henry Goldblatt, review of *Blackbird House,* p. 81.

Globe and Mail (Toronto, Ontario, Canada), August 25, 1990.

Horn Book, March- April, 2003, Lauren Adams, review of *Green Angel,* pp. 211-213.

Journal of Adolescent and Adult Literacy, November, 2003, Jean Boreen, review of *Green Angel,* pp. 271-273.

Kirkus Reviews, September 1, 1997, review of *Fireflies;* March 15, 2003, review of *The Probable Future,* p. 418; May 15, 2004, review of *Blackbird House,* p. 461; July 1, 2004, review of *Moondog,* p. 631.

Kliatt, July, 2003, Lesley S. J. Dr. Farmer, "Water Tales, two novels; Aquamarine and Indigo," p. 32; July, 2004, Janet Julian, review of *The Probable Future,* p. 19; September, 2005, Claire Rosser, review of *The Foretelling.*

Library Journal, May 15, 1999, Barbara Hoffert, review of *Local Girls,* p. 130; December, 1999, Rochelle Ratner, review of *Local Girls,* p. 205; April 1, 2000, Joyce Kessel, review of *Angel Landing,* p. 150; May 15, 2000, Reba Leidling, review of *The River King,* p. 124; March 15, 2003, Starr E. Smith, review of of *The Probable Future,* p. 114.

London Review of Books, August 6, 1992, p. 19.

Los Angeles Times, December 5, 1980; May 28, 1982; May 9, 1985; August 24, 1987; June 30, 1988.

Los Angeles Times Book Review, August 19, 1979; July 10, 1988; August 5, 1990; May 28, 1995, p. 1.

Magazine of Fantasy and Science Fiction, April, 1994; December, 1995, p. 46; October/November, 2005, Charles De Lint, review of *The Ice Queen,* p. 52.

Ms., August, 1979; May, 1982; June, 1985.

Nation, November 26, 1990.

Newsweek, May 23, 1977; April 12, 1982; August 1, 1988; August 20, 1990.

New Yorker, May 3, 1982; July 15, 1985; July 27, 1992; April 11, 1994.

New York Times, July 14, 1977; July 25, 1987; July 4, 1988; August 10, 1990; April 21, 1992, Michiko Kakutani, "Books of The Times: A Killer Strikes as Sea Turtles Fill the Streets"; February 10, 1994, Ruth Reichl, "At Home with Alice Hoffman: A Writer Set Free by Magic"; February 24, 1994, Christopher Lehmann-Haupt, "Books of The Times: A Wilderness Child Confronts Civilization," p. C19.

New York Times Book Review, July 15, 1979; November 9, 1980; March 28, 1982; March 24, 1985; August 9, 1987; July 17, 1988; August 5, 1990; April 26, 1992, Frederick Busch, "The Soul Is Part of the Action"; February 6, 1994, p. 13; June 25, 1995, p. 25; September 14, 1997, Karen Karbo, "Heathcliff Redux"; June 13, 1999, Sarah Ferguson, "Islanders," p. 31; July 16, 2000, Amanda Fortini, "The Spirit Moves Him."

Orlando Sentinel, August 2, 2000, Nancy Pate, review of *The River King.*

People, September 3, 1990; September 5, 1994, p. 34; July 3, 1995, p. 31; August 14, 2000; July 26, 2004, p. 47; August 11, 2003, p. 41; July 26, 2004, p. 47; May 9, 2005, Amy Waldman, review of *The Ice Queen,* p. 51.

Ploughshares, fall, 2003, Maryanne O'Hara, *About Alice Hoffman; a profile by Maryanne O'Hara,* pp. 194-198.

Publishers Weekly, April 12, 1985; June 1, 1990; February 3, 1992; November 29, 1993; January 2, 1995, p. 30; March 20, 1995, p. 40; April 22, 1996, p. 67; May 3, 1999, review of *Local Girls,* p. 1259; July 5, 1999, review of sound recording of *Local Girls,* p. 35; June 5, 2000, review of *The River King,* p. 71; July 31, 2000, Daisy Maryles, "Women, Women, Women," p. 21; August 14, 2000, review of *Horsefly,* p. 355; May 15, 2003, review of *The Probable Future,* p. 196; November 10, 2003, review of *Green Angel,* p. 37; June 21, 2004, review of *Blackbird House,* p. 42.

Redbook, July, 1999, Rose Martelli, "What Makes Families Strong?," p. G1.

School Library Journal, November, 1995, p. 138; July 2003, Pam Johnson, review of *The Probable Future,* p. 152; September, 2005, Sandy Freund, review of *The Ice Queen,* p. 244.

Time, July 18, 1988; August 6, 1990.

Times (London, England), November 28, 1985; October 1, 1987; October 1, 1988.

Times Literary Supplement, April 21, 1978; March 11, 1988; March 25, 1994, p. 21; July 5, 1996, p. 23.

Tribune Books (Chicago, IL), June 26, 1988; August 5, 1990; April 26, 1992, p. 6; February 20, 1994; August 6, 1995.

Vogue, July, 1992.

Washington Post, August 2, 1979; April 13, 1982; June 29, 1988, Jonathan Yardley, review of *At Risk.*

Washington Post Book World, December 21, 1980; August 2, 1987; June 4, 1995, p. 8.

Yale Review, winter, 1978, Edith Milton, review of *Property Of.*

ONLINE

Alice Hoffman Web site, http://www.alicehoffman.com/ (August 25, 2004).

BookBrowse.com, http://www.bookbrowse.com/ (August 25, 2004), "Alice Hoffman."

BookPage.com, http://www.bookpage.com/ (August 6, 2004), Ellen Kanner, "Making Believe: Alice Hoffman Takes Her Practical Magic to the River."

BookReporter.com, http://www.bookreporter.com/ (August 6, 2004), interview with Hoffman.

RomanceReader.com, http://www.romancereader.com/ (August 6, 2004), Susan Scribner, review of *Practical Magic.*

*   *   *

HOLLANDER, Paul
   See SILVERBERG, Robert

*   *   *

HOMES, A.M. 1961-
   (Amy Michael Homes)

PERSONAL: Born 1961, in Washington, DC; children: one daughter. *Education:* Attended American University; Sarah Lawrence College, B.A., 1985; University of Iowa, M.F.A., 1988.

ADDRESSES: Home—New York, NY. *Agent*—Wylie, Aitken and Stone, 250 West 57th St., Room 2106, New York, NY 10107.

CAREER: Writer. Held position at Columbia University, New York, NY, technical writing program, 1991; member of board of directors of Yaddo, Saratoga Springs, NY, and The Fine Arts Work Center, Provincetown, MA.

MEMBER: PEN.

AWARDS, HONORS: Benjamin Franklin Award; National Endowment for the Arts fellowship; New York Foundation for the Arts Artists fellowship; Center for Scholars and Writers fellowship, New York Public Library; Deutscher jugendliteraturpreis, 1993, for *Jack*; Guggenheim Foundation fellowship, 1998.

WRITINGS:

Jack (novel), Macmillan (New York, NY), 1989.
The Safety of Objects (stories), Norton (New York, NY), 1990.

In a Country of Mothers (novel), Knopf (New York, NY), 1993.
The End of Alice (novel), Scribner (New York, NY), 1996.
Appendix A: An Elaboration on the Novel "The End of Alice," Artspace Books (San Francisco, CA), 1996.
Music for Torching (novel), Rob Weisbach Books (New York, NY), 1999.
Things You Should Know: A Collection of Stories, HarperCollins (New York, NY), 2002.
Los Angeles: People, Places, and the Castle on the Hill, National Geographic (Washington, DC), 2002.

Author of artist's catalogs for Cecily Brown, Rachel Whiteread, Ken Probst, Gergory Crewdson, Carroll Dunham, and Todd Hido. Contributing editor to *Vanity Fair, Mirabella, Bomb,* and *Blind Spot.* Contributor to periodicals, including *Artforum, Harper's, New Yorker, Granta, New York Times,* and *Zoetrope.*

ADAPTATIONS: The Safety of Objects was adapted for film by Rose Troche and released by Metro-Goldwyn-Mayer in 2001.

SIDELIGHTS: A.M. Homes made her literary debut with *Jack,* a novel that follows an adolescent boy's emotionally painful progression into adulthood. Praised for its realistic portrayal of the average American teenager, the story is told from the point of view of the title character, who is in the midst of adjusting to his parents' recent divorce. An excerpt from the book relating the protagonist's anxiety about growing up appeared in Elizabeth Kastor's *Washington Post* article: "I'm stuck between things. I'm stuck between being a kid and being an adult. The things that kids do aren't really a whole lot of fun, but what adults do still seems too hard, and to be honest, boring as hell." Jack's ambivalence is soon intensified when he learns that his father is homosexual, and the boy subsequently becomes the victim of his classmates' insensitivity. "*Jack* is a story about prejudice and bias," Homes told Kastor. "Jack is this young, white male. He's never been exposed to any kind of prejudice." Both the discovery that his best friend's family is perhaps more dysfunctional than his own and a new friendship with a girl who also has a homosexual father help Jack to ultimately avoid feelings of self-despair. "Homes has given us a good youngster who in the end convincingly grows larger than his circumstances," wrote Crescent Dragonwagon in the *New York Times Book Review.* The reviewer also found that the author "handles the big subjects and adolescent passions subtly, deftly and with an appealing lack of melodrama."

In her next book, a collection of stories titled *The Safety of Objects,* Homes presents a cast of profoundly neurotic characters unable to cope with the tedium of life in middle-class America. Described as "vivid and disturbing" by Margaret Camp in the *Washington Post,* the narratives are concerned with what the reviewer termed "the dark harvest of our postmodern culture: a bunch of lonely, bored, angst-ridden, psycho adults and listless, alienated teenagers brimming with pubescent sexuality." In the story "Adults Alone," for example, a quintessential suburban couple spends ten days reveling in debauchery; they eat and drink to excess, watch pornographic videos, and smoke crack cocaine while the kids stay at their grandmother's house. And in "A Real Doll" a teenage boy has bizarre sexual encounters with his sister's vivified Barbie doll.

Camp assessed the collection as an "enthralling spiral into surrealist Hell," terming the stories "original and stiletto sharp." *Los Angeles Times Book Review* writer Amy Hempel wrote that the author "sustain[s] credibility by getting the details right," especially in "Looking for Johnny," which depicts the abduction of a nine-year-old boy, Erol. The narrative explores the psychological deficiencies of the kidnapper as well as the emotional trauma experienced by Erol when his captor finds him dull and returns the boy to his unsympathetic family. Hempel acknowledged that "there is not a misstep in this difficult story," and she labeled Homes "confident and consistent in her odd departures from life as we know it."

"The imagination that shapes A.M. Homes's fiction is exhilaratingly perverse," wrote *New York Times Book Review* contributor Maggie Paley. Homes's first adult novel, *In a Country of Mothers,* is ostensibly the story of Jody Goodman, a young college-bound woman seeking help from Dr. Claire Roth, a therapist who is old enough to be her mother. As therapy proceeds, however, the focus of the novel seems to move from Jody to Claire. Elaine Kendall explained in the *Los Angeles Times* that "Jody remains virtually unchanged by these meetings" while "Roth's interest in her patient progresses from unusual interest to downright obsession." Claire convinces herself that Jody is the long-lost daughter whom she handed over for adoption many years ago, a conviction based on the coincidence of Jody's date and place of birth. She steps over the threshold that transforms a therapist from an observer and counselor to an active participant in the patient's life. As the doctor's involvement escalates—from including Jody in Roth family outings to spying on the patient in Jody's own neighborhood—Claire is "ultimately . . . driven to the edge of madness," according to Kendall.

Some critics expressed disappointment with Homes's initial entry into adult fiction. *Belles Lettres* reviewer Bettina Berch referred to a novel "about a handful of self-obsessed people who make each other miserable for awhile." A *Kirkus Reviews* critic praised the novel's "snappy dialogue" and "transparently clear style," but decided that the novel's "strong premise has a weak follow-through." Carol Anshaw agreed, commenting in the *Chicago Tribune* that *In the Country of Mothers* fails to fulfill the promise "pulsing behind the type," but credited the author with "a fascinating story of the corruption of trust." Leigh Allison Wilson reported in the *Washington Post Book World,* however, that Homes succeeded in creating "portraits of good people gone terribly wrong, while at the same time offering visions of what might have been, what should have been." Wilson concluded, "A.M. Homes is a very dangerous writer. Danger for a reader of fiction is usually a safe place, the place of voyeurs and bystanders. Homes creates a much scarier place."

In her next novel, *The End of Alice,* Homes "takes us . . . with all the cunning and control of a brilliant lover . . . to places we dare not go alone," wrote Elizabeth Houghton in the *Los Angeles Times Book Review.* A young college woman, home for summer vacation, becomes sexually obsessed with a twelve-year-old boy. She explores her obsession directly, but also by corresponding with a convicted pedophile, sentenced to life in prison for molesting and eventually murdering a girl named Alice. In her letters, the narrator flirts with the convict, teasing him to revive his memories of Alice and to ponder how such warped events can happen. The memories, like the narrator's responses, grow sexually explicit and graphically pornographic, according to some critics. Jennifer Kornreich suggested in the *Women's Review of Books* that Homes's purpose may have been to achieve "the social . . . [benefit] of shock value" by "confronting people with ugliness . . . [to] force them to think." *Washington Post* reviewer Carolyn See wrote that "to use pornography as a teaching device may be fine for the writer, but the reader may feel put upon." Yet Houghton wrote, "It is easy to understand serious objection to the subject matter. But the writing takes flight from such an original departure point you find yourself transported high up above the noise, leaving judgment grounded." *New York Times Book Review* writer Daphne Merkin reported that the book's "underlying themes are more serious than prurient. *The End of Alice* is concerned with the fluid nature of identity, with the permeable boundaries that divide an overtly deranged consciousness from a smugly socialized one." Kornreich concluded, however, "Ultimately . . . Homes shies away from more questions than she confronts."

Homes returned to the characters she created in "Adults Alone" for her 1999 novel, *Music for Torching*. Paul and Elaine are no more mature than they were in the earlier short story, but their kids are older. The novel begins with them deliberately setting fire to their home after a barbecue accident, and follows each of them through tawdry affairs with neighbors and acquaintances. *Music for Torching* caused David Gates in *Newsweek* to compare Homes to John Cheever, but the critic stated that "Homes shows none of Cheever's nuanced ambivalence about leafy, loony suburbia and the annoyingly provincial, thwartedly poetic souls who live there; for her it's a zoo." L.S. Klepp in *Entertainment Weekly* noted that the novel's "effect is of rapid-fire satire bordering on bedroom farce—a caustic and giddy caricature of hollow, haywire suburbanites." *Review of Contemporary Fiction* writer Trey Strecker concluded that Homes "succeeds in showing that no one is 'normal' when we peer behind their white picket fences."

Three years later, Homes published another collection of short fiction, *Things You Should Know*. Reviewing the volume in *Newsweek*, Susannah Meadows praised "the force of Homes's storytelling," also remarking that, "enthralling and heartbreaking, most of these eleven pieces exemplify the fundamentals of great storytelling." Similarly, James O'Laughlin in *Booklist* noted the "remarkable range of dramas" included in *Things You Should Know*, as well as the "deft compactness" of the author's prose. *Library Journal* contributor Colleen Lougen described Homes's skill in the collection as "hypnotic," noting that it gives "the reader a peek into the exotic thoughts and worlds of people we do not normally meet in literature."

BIOGRAPHICAL AND CRITICAL SOURCES:

BOOKS

Homes, A. M., *Jack,* Macmillan (New York, NY), 1989.

PERIODICALS

Antioch Review, winter, 1994, p. 182.
Belles Lettres, fall, 1993, p. 42.
Booklist, May 15, 1999, Danise Hoover, review of *Music for Torching,* p. 1668; August, 2002, James O'Laughlin, review of *Things You Should Know: A Collection of Stories,* p. 1920.
Chicago Tribune, May 7, 1993.

Detroit Free Press, December 23, 1990.
Economist (US), July 5, 2003, Clare Boylan, review of *Things You Should Know,* p. 76.
Entertainment Weekly, June 11, 1999, L.S. Klepp, "Homes's Town: Following Up on Her Shocking Novel *The End of Alice,* A.M. Homes Takes on Suburban Angst and Marriage in *Music for Torching,*" p. 58.
Kirkus Reviews, March 1, 1993, p. 246; March 15, 1999, review of *Music for Torching,* p. 398; July 1, 2002, review of *Things You Should Know,* p. 905.
Lambda Book Report, July-August, 1999, Elizabeth Brownrigg, review of *Music for Torching,* pp. 14-15.
Library Journal, May 10, 1999, David Gates, review of *Music for Torching,* p. 79; August, 2002, Colleen Lougen, review *Things You Should Know,* p. 148.
London Review of Books, May 9, 1996, pp. 20-21.
Los Angeles Times, July 9, 1993, p. E5.
Los Angeles Times Book Review, October 28, 1990, p. 3; May 26, 1996, pp. 6-7; June 6, 1999, review of *Music for Torching,* p. 11.
New Statesman, January 1, 1999, Phil Whitaker, review of *Jack,* p. 49.
Newsweek, May 10, 1999, David Gates, "Burning Down the House," p. 79; September 2, 2002, Susannah Meadows, "Short Stories That Tell . . . Stories," p. 62.
New York Times Book Review, July 15, 1990, p. 24; May 23, 1993, p. 17; March 24, 1996, p. 14; May 30, 1999, Gary Krist, review of *Music for Torching,* p. 9.
Observer (London, England), December 13, 1998, review of *Jack,* p. 16; January 19, 2003, Zoe Green, review of *Los Angeles: People, Places, and the Castle on the Hill.*
Poets & Writers Magazine, July-August, 1999, Fran Gordon, review of *Music for Torching,* p. 24.
Publishers Weekly, March 15, 1993, p. 67; May 7, 1999, review of *Music for Torching,* p. 59; July 15, 2002, review of *Things You Should Know,* p. 52.
Review of Contemporary Fiction, fall, 1999, Trey Strecker, review of *Music for Torching,* p. 167; spring, 2003, Stacey Gottlieb, review of *Things You Should Know,* p. 149.
Times Literary Supplement, May 10, 1991, p. 20; September 3, 1999, Ali Sith, review of *Music for Torching,* p. 12.
Wall Street Journal, May 7, 1999, Garvirella Stern, review of *Music for Torching,* p. W9E.
Washington Post, September 24, 1990, p. B1; May 10, 1993, p. B2; May 3, 1996, p. D2.
Women's Review of Books, July, 1996, p. 45.

HOMES, Amy Michael
 See HOMES, A.M.

 *   *   *

hooks, bell 1952-
 [A pseudonym]
 (Gloria Jean Watkins)

PERSONAL: Born Gloria Jean Watkins, September 25, 1952, in Hopkinsville, KY; daughter of Veodis (a custodian) and Rosa Bell (a homemaker) Watkins. *Ethnicity:* Black *Education:* Stanford University, B.A. (English), 1973; University of Wisconsin, Madison, M.A. (English), 1976; University of California at Santa Cruz, Ph.D., 1983.

ADDRESSES: *Home*—New York, NY. *Office*— Department of Afro-American Studies, Yale University, New Haven, CT 06520.

CAREER: Social critic, educator, and writer. University of Southern California, Los Angeles, English instructor and senior lecturer in ethnic studies, 1976-79; taught various subjects at institutions, including San Francisco State University, during the early 1980s; Yale University, New Haven, CT, assistant professor of Afro-American studies and English, beginning c. 1985; Oberlin College, Oberlin, OH, associate professor of women's studies and American literature, 1988-94; City College of the City University of New York, distinguished professor of English, beginning 1994.

AWARDS, HONORS: American Book Award, Before Columbus Foundation, 1991, for *Yearning: Race, Gender, and Cultural Politics;* Writer's Award, Lila Wallace-*Reader's Digest,* 1994.

WRITINGS:

Ain't I a Woman: Black Women and Feminism, South End Press (Boston, MA), 1981.

Feminist Theory: From Margin to Center, South End Press (Boston, MA), 1984, 2nd edition, 1999.

Talking Back: Thinking Feminist, Thinking Black (essays), South End Press (Boston, MA), 1989.

Yearning: Race, Gender, and Cultural Politics, South End Press (Boston, MA), 1990.

(With Cornell West) *Breaking Bread: Insurgent Black Intellectual Life,* South End Press (Boston, MA), 1991.

A Woman's Mourning Song (poetry), Writers and Readers, 1992.

Black Looks: Race and Representation, South End Press (Boston, MA), 1992.

Sisters of the Yam: Black Women and Self Recovery, South End Press (Boston, MA), 1993, 2nd edition 2005.

Outlaw Culture: Resisting Representations (essays), Routledge (New York, NY), 1994, 2nd edition 2006.

Emma Amos: Changing the Subject: Paintings and Prints (catalog essay), Art in General (New York, NY), 1994.

Teaching to Transgress: Education As the Practice of Freedom, Routledge (New York, NY), 1994.

Killing Rage: Ending Racism, Holt (New York, NY), 1995.

Art on My Mind: Visual Politics (essays), Norton (New York, NY), 1995.

(Editor) *Gumbo YA YA: Anthology of Contemporary African-American Women Artists,* Midmarch Arts, 1995.

Bone Black: Memories of Girlhood, Holt (New York, NY), 1996.

Happy to Be Nappy (juvenile), illustrated by Chris Raschka, Hyperion (New York, NY), 1996.

Reel to Real: Race, Sex, and Class at the Movies, Routledge (New York, NY), 1996.

Wounds of Passion: A Writing Life, Holt (New York, NY), 1997.

Remembered Rapture: The Writer at Work, Holt (New York, NY), 1999.

All about Love: New Visions, Morrow (New York, NY), 2000.

Feminism Is for Everybody: Passionate Politics, South End Press (Cambridge, MA), 2000.

Where We Stand: Class Matters, Routledge (New York, NY), 2000.

Homemade Love (juvenile), Hyperion (New York, NY), 2001.

Salvation: Black People and Love, Morrow (New York, NY), 2001.

Be Boy Buzz (juvenile), Hyperion (New York, NY), 2002.

Communion: Female Search for Love, Morrow (New York, NY), 2002.

Rock My Soul: Black People and Self-Esteem, Atria Books (New York, NY), 2003.

We Real Cool: Black Men and Masculinity, Routledge (New York, NY), 2003.

Teaching Community: A Pedagogy of Hope, Routledge (New York, NY), 2003.

Skin Again (juvenile), illustrated by Chris Raschka, Hyperion (New York, NY), 2004.

The Will to Change: Men, Masculinity, and Love, Atria Books (New York, NY), 2004.

Also author of *And There We Wept* (chapbook of poems), 1978; *Black Is a Woman's Color* (part 1 of memoirs), c. 1996; and *Cat Island Woman* (part 2 of memoirs), c. 1996. Contributor to *Double Stitch: Black Women Write about Mothers and Daughters,* 1992; *Daughters of the Dust: The Making of an African-American Woman's Film,* 1992; *Felix Gonzales-Torres: Traveling,* 1994; and *Spoils of War: Women of Color, Culture, and Revolution,* 1998. Contributor of essays to periodicals, including *Utne Reader, Catalyst, Callaloo, Emerge,* and *Essence.*

SIDELIGHTS: bell hooks (cited in lowercase), has written prolifically about many social issues. Her work takes an approach that is at once analytical yet also impassioned and personal. She explores the ways that African-American culture, womanhood, feminism, the civil rights movement, and critical theory both clash and complement each other, in the world at large and in her personal life. She has challenged the feminist movement with being largely racist, and has frequently voiced her concern over the negative images of blacks perpetuated in the popular media. She has also written children's books and poetry, memoirs, and books dealing with the need for love and increased self-esteem among the members of the African-American community. "At her best she exhibits a command of various voices that range from subtle overlays of the personal and historical to a refreshing public forthrightness that stings," wrote P. Gabrielle Foreman in the *Women's Review of Books.* "Inevitably, a reader will cheer through one essay and scowl through another."

Born Gloria Jean Watkins, she grew up in rural Kentucky, in a small, segregated community with five sisters and one brother. Her father worked as a custodian for the U.S. Postal Service, and her mother worked as a domestic. hooks said that growing up in a family of strong women was extremely important to her, and she took her great-grandmother's name as a way of paying homage to the legacy of her female ancestors. She recalled in *Talking Back: Thinking Feminist, Thinking Black,* "I was a young girl buying bubble gum at the corner store when I first really heard the name bell hooks. I had just talked back to a grown person. Even now I can recall the surprised look, the mocking tones

that informed me I must be kin to bell hooks, a sharp-tongued woman, a woman who spoke her mind, a woman who was not afraid to talk back. I claimed this legacy of defiance, of will, of courage, affirming my link to female ancestors who were bold and daring in their speech."

hooks was drawn to literature and writing from an early age. Her scholastic achievement was such that she was able to attend Stanford University on scholarships. It was in college that she became aware of class differences and racism in a way she never had before. She found the campus environment much less liberal and open than she expected, and was surprised at the lack of attention paid to black women by the fledgling feminist movement. She perceived a lack of material about African-American women at the library, as well, which spurred her to begin writing her own books. Her first publication was the poetry chapbook *And There We Wept,* published in 1978.

After several years and numerous revisions, hooks published *Ain't I a Woman: Black Women and Feminism,* her first book of theory. In *Ain't I a Woman* she explains how racism pervades mainstream feminism and chides white women for ignoring blacks, while discussing how black women can find their place in feminism anyway. Using a feminist perspective, hooks chronicles the history of black women in America, from the slavery era through the 1970s, and posits the theory that African-American women were more strongly feminist in the nineteenth century than the twentieth. The work got a chilly reception, as many critics questioned hooks's methods of analysis and some of her assertions, such as her opinion that slavery was worse for women than for men. She has continued to develop similar themes in *Feminism, Feminist Theory: From Margin to Center,* and *Talking Back: Thinking Feminist, Thinking Black.*

In *Feminist Theory* hooks clearly states that the basic ills of the three "isms"—racism, classism, and sexism—have at their root the notion of domination. This kind of organization is opposed to a consensual/collectivist model which would eradicate the existing forces of control, manipulation, and domination, and thus redefine power throughout society. Being at the bottom of such a power structure, black women are naturally in the vanguard of liberation from the existing structure, by their very efforts at individual self-determination. They are not, however, recognized as such by mainstream feminist organizations, who see the world with the same hierarchical eyes as do white males, wanting merely to be in their positions. Real feminism, says hooks, should attack the whole hierarchical system. The paradigm is played out in hooks's book *Talking Back,* which contains twenty-three essays on different aspects of the black/feminist connection, varying from "writing autobiography, teaching women's literature, black homophobia, intimate violence, racist feminists, black porn, and politics at Yale," noted Beverly Miller in *Library Journal.*

hooks's first three works have sometimes been seen as taking on too many voices to deal with their complex, inflammatory issues. A reviewer for *Publishers Weekly,* for example, noted that "although the author makes perceptive and provocative observations, they are diminished by redundancy and weakened by her doctrinaire Marxist rhetoric." Patricia Bell-Scott, in the *Women's Review of Books,* admitted to reacting defensively to some arguments that run against the feminist grain, and pointed to the Marxist flavor as possibly irritating. "However," Bell-Scott continued, "we must keep in mind the author's goal, to enrich feminist discourse and 'to share in the work of making a liberatory ideology,' as we struggle with the uncomfortable issues she raises."

Although all of hooks's work contains self-examination, her fourth book, *Yearning: Race, Gender, and Cultural Politics,* seems to reassess all her efforts, as well as her various voices. In it she continues to broaden her cultural criticism, using more and more of the theoretical tools available to—and expected from—a cutting-edge, post-modern academic. Critics like P. Gabrielle Foreman find that central to this effort is the essay "Homeplace: A Site of Resistance," in which hooks once more returns home to find her "location" of strength, a sense of community in the households set up by black women. This "location" helps her to solidify her base point of view, even as she sets out to examine more of her overall culture, and a black woman's part in it, from more varied and theoretical perspectives. This might be the reason that critics, among them Foreman, see her often contradicting herself and taking on the white feminists' point of view. For Foreman, though, it is her "'intervention' into the politics of post-modern theory and practice that makes *Yearning* so timely and valuable." She tries, for example, to untangle the theories of "Otherness"—the position of outsiders within a culture—that have been primarily produced by insiders or white scholars. This includes their theorizing on "essentialism"—in this case the reality of racial groupings, and the politics of identity based on those groupings. This is a complicated question for hooks, since blacks can be affected by both sides of this dilemma.

The reassessment of hooks's "locations" as an African-American intellectual continue in *Breaking Bread: Insurgent Black Intellectual Life,* a dialogue with social critic and professor Cornel West. Their discussion ranges over the various crises of the black community, and how marketing to blacks, and depictions of blacks in the media, have contributed to those problems. This theme, which has threaded its way through her earlier work, is enlarged upon in *Black Looks: Race and Representation.* In its twelve chapters, she explores the implicit meaning of black images in phenomena such as advertising, Madonna's music videos, and the Anita Hill-Clarence Thomas hearings. Her most serious indictment of the media is that it further threatens the position of the black woman by selling black males a macho self-image. Widely greeted with approval for its groundbreaking breadth and theoretical rigor, *Black Looks* caused a *Library Journal* critic to remark, "hooks continues to produce some of the most challenging, insightful, and provocative writing on race and gender in the United States today."

In 1994 hooks published both *Teaching to Transgress: Education As the Practice of Freedom* and *Outlaw Culture: Resisting Representations.* Reviewing these books in the *New York Times Book Review,* Jerome Karabel noted that *Teaching to Transgress* is "often marred by a disconcerting reliance on pop psychology." However, Karabel concluded, each book allows readers "to confront the political undercurrents of life in America." " *Outlaw Culture: Resisting Representations* continues the investigation of the depiction of African Americans in modern culture that hooks explored in *Breaking Bread,*" noted Melissa L. Evans in *Feminist Writers.* "*Outlaw Culture* specifically focuses on cinematic, artistic, and musical representations of race, and is particularly interesting due to hooks's commentary on figures such as Madonna and gangster rap. Aside from cultural commentary, hooks also offers her commentary, critical as it is, on the 'new feminism' of figures such as Camille Paglia."

hooks recalls her own life in the books *Bone Black: Memories of Girlhood, Wounds of Passion: A Writing Life,* and *Remembered Rapture: The Writer at Work.* In *Bone Black* she relates the story of her youth in a traditional Southern working-class family. It is significant "both as a documentation of one black woman's girlhood and as a beautifully crafted narrative," decided Evelyn E. Shockley in her *African American Review* appraisal of the book. *Bone Black* was praised as "vivid" and "extraordinary" by Catherine Burt in *American Visions,* the critic adding that the book "reveals the events and experiences as well as the feelings, thoughts and dreams of a wise and sensitive girl as she sifts through the magical world around her and shapes her identity." *Bone Black* reveals much about the source of hooks's "forcefulness and candor," mused Donna Seaman in *Booklist,* and it does so in a book that is "lyrical, deeply moving, and brilliantly structured."

In *Wounds of Passion: A Writing Life* the author moves on to subjects such as poetry, feminism, sexuality, and a fifteen-year romantic relationship, telling her stories in a "consistently fresh and bravely honest voice," according to a *Publishers Weekly* writer. *Remembered Rapture: The Writer at Work* is a collection of twenty-two essays discussing spirituality and writing. The styles range from personal, reflective life memories to more highly structured, formal essays that reflect the author's experience as a university lecturer. As usual, hooks "emphasizes the importance of personal and political identity to writing," found a *Publishers Weekly* writer. "Her prose is clear and she presents her arguments with a confident passion. If her politics are predictable, hooks infuses the best of these essays with a personal tone that sheds warm light on this one particular writer's writing life."

hooks turns her attention to various aspects of love in books such as *All about Love: New Visions, Salvation: Black People and Love,* and *Communion: Female Search for Love.* In *All about Love* she suggests that the hatred encountered in the experience of racism and other oppressive relationships can be negated by the experience of profound love. She notes with distress the lack of belief in real love that is expressed by even very young children in contemporary times. Aleta Richards in the *Civil Rights Journal* stated that this book "teaches us how to find and keep love in a culture full of hatred." Richards remarked that while at first glace the book might seem to be a rather superficial pop-psychology manual, in fact, "it's an important book about the sociological implications of oppression and why it's hard to give and receive love in our highly individualized, Western culture."

In *Salvation* hooks again advocates for the increase of unselfish love. She identifies lack of love and trust as the root of many other social problems, particularly the collapse of communities. "Readers of every hue will benefit from hooks' piercing insights into the troubled state of our collective soul and find solace in her belief that 'love is our hope and salvation,'" commented Seaman in *Booklist. Communion* tackles problems unique to women, who are made to feel that their lovableness is based on their attractiveness and their service to oth-

ers. Women have made great strides in becoming socially empowered, but they are still questing for satisfying love, because society has conditioned men to think that withholding their emotions is a validation of their manhood. The author suggests that women may have to be creative in looking for love, pointing out the possibilities of same-sex love, romantic friendships, and "circles of love."

Low self-esteem, rooted in generations of slavery, has negatively affected the African-American spirit for years, hooks argues in *Rock My Soul: Black People and Self-Esteem.* She reflects on the successes and failures of efforts to build black pride in the past, and suggests pathways to a future in which African Americans can replace chronic emotional pain with healthy ways of thought. "To read her is to set out on the path toward healing," claimed Seaman in a *Booklist* review, while a *Publishers Weekly* writer concluded: "With each new book, hooks is deeply exploring the inner terrain of the black community, calling for a return to sound values, self-love and commonsense solutions while seeking new ways to cope with a modern world gone slightly mad."

In *We Real Cool: Black Men and Masculinity,* and the book's follow-up volume, *The Will to Change: Men, Masculinity, and Love,* hooks discusses the societal factors that define the identity of black men and how this identity shapes their relationships. hooks stated in *We Real Cool* that black men are taught to be aggressive and that hip-hop culture enforces this instruction. In addition, hooks argues that black men are rewarded for violent behavior because that behavior reinforces racial stereotypes. hooks's personal anecdotes to this effect, according to *Booklist* critic Vernon Ford, "reflect extraordinary insight into both our cultural frailties and our potential." And it is this potential that hooks turns to in *The Will to Change.* She notes that men must learn to love by looking to figures such as the Dalai Lama, and by seeking love, rather than solace, through sex. Although a *Publishers Weekly* reviewer felt that some of hooks's critiques were somewhat "retro," they also stated that the book itself is a "clarion call to the uncommitted to align themselves with visionary radical feminism."

BIOGRAPHICAL AND CRITICAL SOURCES:

BOOKS

Black Literature Criticism Supplement, Gale (Detroit, MI), 1999.

Black Writers, 2nd edition, Gale (Detroit, MI), 1994.

Contemporary Black Biography, Volume 5, Gale (Detroit, MI), 1994.

Contemporary Literary Criticism, Volume 94, Gale (Detroit, MI), 1996.

Dictionary of Literary Biography, Volume 246: *Twentieth-Century American Cultural Theorists,* Gale (Detroit, MI), 2001.

Encyclopedia of World Biography, 2nd edition, Gale (Detroit, MI), 1998.

Feminist Writers, St. James Press (Detroit, MI), 1996.

Newsmakers 2000, Gale (Detroit, MI), 2000.

Notable Black American Women, Book II, Gale (Detroit, MI), 1996.

The Schomburg Center Guide to Black Literature, Gale (Detroit, MI), 1996.

PERIODICALS

African American Review, fall, 1997, Evelyn E. Shockley, review of *Bone Black: Memories of Girlhood,* p. 552.

American Visions, April-May, 1997, Catherine Burt, review of *Bone Black,* p. 28.

Black Collegian, February, 1996, Mamie Webb Hixon, review of *Killing Rage: Ending Racism,* p. 11; October, 2002, Corinne Nelson, review of *Rock My Soul: Black People and Self-Esteem,* p. 126.

Black Enterprise, June, 1992, p. 23.

Black Issues Book Review, March, 2001, Angela Dodson, review of *Salvation: Black People and Love,* p. 64; March-April, 2002, Gary Dauphin, interview with hooks, p. 50; November-December, 2002, Evette Porter, review of *Be Boy Buzz,* p. 42.

Black Scholar, January, 1983, pp. 38, 46.

Booklist, June 1, 1995, Donna Seaman, review of *Art on My Mind: Visual Politics,* p. 1715; September 15, 1995, Bonnie Smothers, review of *Killing Rage,* p. 118; September 15, 1996, Donna Seaman, review of *Bone Black,* p. 189; September 15, 1997, Donna Seaman, review of *Wounds of Passion: A Writing Life,* p. 185; December 15, 1998, Donna Seaman, review of *Remembered Rapture: The Writer at Work,* p. 721; August, 1999, Hazel Rochman, review of *Happy to Be Nappy,* p. 2064; January 1, 2000, Donna Seaman, review of *All about Love,* p. 839; February 15, 2001, Donna Seaman, review of *Salvation,* p. 1098; February 15, 2002, Donna Seaman, review of *Communion: The Female Search for Love,* p. 1002; November 1, 2002, Hazel Rochman, review of *Be Boy Buzz,* p. 508; February 1, 2003, Donna Seaman, review of *Rock*

My Soul, p. 814, Gillian Engberg, review of *Homemade Love,* p. 1001; January 1, 2004, Vernon Ford, review of *We Real Cool: Black Men and Masculinity,* p. 58.

Bookwatch, July 1989, p. 4; September, 1992, p. 10.

Choice, April, 1982, p. 1141; July, 1985, p. 1703.

Chronicle of Higher Education, May 19, 1995.

Civil Rights Journal, fall, 2000, Aleta Richards, review of *All about Love,* p. 58.

Emerge, November, 1995, Lori S. Robinson, review of *Killing Rage,* p. 92; February, 2000, Meri Nana-Ama Danquah, review of *All about Love,* p. 108.

Essence, December, 1997, Martha Southgate, "Do We Need Kwanzaa?," p. 68; July, 1989, p. 20.

Horn Book, November/December, 2004, Susan Dove Lempke, review of *Skin Again,* p. 698.

Interview, October, 1995, Ingrid Sischy, interview with hooks, p. 122.

Kirkus Reviews, August 15, 2004, review of *Skin Again,* p. 807.

Library Journal, July, 1995, Ann Burns, review of *Killing Rage,* p. 107; October 1, 1997, Ann Burns, review of *Wounds of Passion,* p. 94; December 1, 1981, p. 178; March 15, 1985, p. 68; November 1, 1998, Ann Burns, review of *Remembered Rapture,* p. 81; December, 1988, p. 126; July, 1992, p. 109; July, 1993; November 1, 1999, Ann Burns, review of *All about Love,* p. 107; November 1, 2000, Ann Burns, review of *Where We Stand: Class Matters,* and *Salvation,* p. 104; February 15, 2002, Deborah Bigelow, review of *Communion,* p. 166; November 1, 2002, Ann Burns, review of *Rock My Soul,* p. 115; October 1, 2003, Scott Walter, review of *Teaching Community: A Pedagogy of Hope,* p. 92.

Ms., July, 1983, p. 24; October, 1985, p. 25; February-March, 2000, Pearl Cleage, review of *All about Love,* p. 84; December, 2000, Jocelyn L. Womac, review of *Feminism Is for Everybody: Passionate Politics,* p. 88.

Multicultural Review, April, 1992; March, 1993.

National Review, January 22, 2001, Maggie Gallagher, review of *Feminism Is for Everybody.*

New Directions for Women, January, 1992, p. 22.

New Statesman, October 22, 1982, p. 31; November 30, 1990, p. 39.

New York Review of Books, April 18, 1996, George M. Fredrickson, review of *Killing Rage,* p. 16.

New York Times Book Review, February 28, 1993; December 18, 1994; November 21, 1999, p. 58; January 30, 2000, Elise Harris, review of *All about Love,* p. 21.

Phylon, March, 1983, p. 85.

Political Science Quarterly, spring, 1983, p. 84.

Progressive, March, 1991, p. 42.

Publishers Weekly, June 26, 1995, review of *Art on My Mind,* p. 104; November 18, 1988, p. 72; November 22, 1991, p. 49; June 15, 1992, p. 95; July 17, 1995, review of *Killing Rage,* p. 211; August 5, 1996, review of *Bone Black,* p. 421; September 22, 1997, review of *Wounds of Passion,* p. 64; November 23, 1998, review of *Remembered Rapture,* p. 29; July 19, 1999, review of *Happy to Be Nappy,* p. 194; November 29, 1999, review of *All about Love,* p. 60; December 4, 2000, review of *Salvation,* p. 60; September 30, 2002, review of *Be Boy Buzz,* p. 71; November 18, 2002, review of *Homemade Love,* p. 59; November 25, 2002, Robert Fleming, interview with hooks, and review of *Rock My Soul,* p. 54; September 1, 2003, review of *Teaching Community,* p. 77; November 10, 2003, review of *We Real Cool,* p. 49; November 17, 2003, review of *The Will to Change: Men, Masculinity, and Love,* p. 58.

Queen's Quarterly, summer, 1990, p. 318.

Savoy, March, 2002, Catherine Kelly, review of *Communion,* p. 36.

School Library Journal, March, 1997, Dottie Kraft, review of *Bone Black,* p. 217; November, 1999, Karen James, review of *Happy to Be Nappy,* p. 120; December, 2002, Anna DeWind Walls, review of *Be Boy Buzz,* and Amy Lilien- Harper, review of *Homemade Love,* p. 97.

Sight and Sound, June, 1991, p. 36.

Signs, autumn, 1994.

Village Voice Literary Supplement, June, 1982, p. 10.

West Coast Review of Books, April, 1982, p. 51.

Women's Review of Books, February, 1985, p. 3; September, 1991, p. 12.

*   *   *

HOSSEINI, Khaled 1965-

PERSONAL: Born 1965, in Kabul, Afghanistan; immigrated to the United States, 1980. *Education:* Santa Clara University, B.A. (biology), 1988; University of San Diego, M.D., 1993. *Hobbies and other interests:* Soccer, racquetball, writing, involved in charities Paralyzed Vets of America and Aid the Afghan Children.

ADDRESSES: Office—The Permanente Medical Group, 555 Castro St., 3rd Fl., Mountain View, CA 94041. *E-mail*—khaled@khaledhosseini.com.

CAREER: Practicing physician specializing in internal medicine, 1996—; The Permanente Medical Group, Mountain View, CA, physician, 1999—.

AWARDS, HONORS: Original Voices Award, Borders Group, 2004, for *The Kite Runner.*

WRITINGS:

The Kite Runner, Riverhead Books (New York, NY), 2003.

ADAPTATIONS: The Kite Runner was adapted for audio (unabridged; eight cassettes), read by the author, Simon & Schuster, 2003.

SIDELIGHTS: Khaled Hosseini was born in Kabul, Afghanistan, the son of a diplomat father and teacher mother. In 1976 the family was relocated to Paris, France, where they remained until 1980 following the Soviet takeover of Afghanistan. They were then granted political asylum in the United States and moved to San Jose, California. Hosseini's parents left everything behind and relied on welfare until they were able to get back on their feet. Hosseini became a physician, but he had always loved to write. His debut novel, *The Kite Runner,* was called "painful, moving, remarkable" by *Library Journal* reviewer Michael Adams, who reviewed the audio version. In the book, Hosseini returns to the pre-Soviet Afghanistan of his childhood and relates his feelings for a servant who had lived in the household, a man who taught him to read and write. "Rather than settle for a coming-of-age or travails-of-immigrants story, Hosseini has folded them both into this searing spectacle of hard-won personal salvation," wrote a *Kirkus Reviews* critic. "All this, and a rich slice of Afghan culture too: irresistible."

The story spans four decades and is told by the protagonist, Amir, who as an adult is a writer living in California. His story goes back to his childhood in Kabul, when the quiet, motherless boy yearns for attention from his successful father, Bapa, but finds a friend in Hassan, the son of his father's servant. Amir resents sharing his father's affection with the loyal and talented Hassan, but when Amir wins a kite-flying contest, his father finally gives him the praise he craves. But in that single incident, he loses Hassan, who goes after a downed kite and is attacked and raped by Assef, the town bully. Because of his feelings of guilt for not helping his friend, Amir pushes Hassan away, even accusing of him of theft, and eventually, the family leaves the community.

The story then fast forwards to the adult Amir, who has fled Afghanistan during the Russian occupation, moved to the bay area of California, married a beautiful Afghan woman, and became a successful writer. His father has died of cancer, but in 2001 his father's partner, who knows the history of Amir and Hassan, calls from Pakistan. He tells Amir that Hassan and his wife have been executed by the Taliban, leaving their son, Sohrab. He suggests that Amir owes a debt to Hassan, and Amir agrees. He returns to find Sohrab in the custody of Assef, and it is then that he finally stands up to the man who had raped his friend.

Edward Hower wrote in the *New York Times Book Review* that "Hosseini's depiction of prerevolutionary Afghanistan is rich in warmth and humor but also tense with the friction between the nation's different ethnic groups." The critic added, "The novel's canvas turns dark when Hosseini describes the suffering of his country under the tyranny of the Taliban. . . . The final third of the book is full of haunting images." *School Library Journal* reviewer Penny Stevens called *The Kite Runner* a "beautifully written first novel." And a *Publishers Weekly* contributor called the novel "stunning," adding that "it is rare that a book is at once so timely and of such high literary quality."

BIOGRAPHICAL AND CRITICAL SOURCES:

PERIODICALS

Booklist, July, 2003, Kristine Huntley, review of *The Kite Runner,* p. 1864.

Kirkus Reviews, May 1, 2003, review of *The Kite Runner,* p. 630.

Kliatt, November, 2003, Nancy C. Chaplin, review of *The Kite Runner* (audiobook), p. 50.

Library Journal, April 15, 2003, Rebecca Stuhr, review of *The Kite Runner,* p. 122; November 15, 2003, Michael Adams, review of *The Kite Runner* (audio), p. 114.

New York Times Book Review, August 3, 2003, Edward Hower, review of *The Kite Runner,* p. 4.

Publishers Weekly, May 12, 2003, review of *The Kite Runner,* p. 43.

School Library Journal, November, 2003, Penny Stevens, review of *The Kite Runner,* p. 171.

Times (London, England), August 30, 2003, review of *The Kite Runner,* p. 17.

ONLINE

Khaled Hosseini Home Page, http://www.khaled hosseini.com/ (March 12, 2003).

Weekend Edition Sunday, http://www.npr.org/ (July 27, 2003), Liane Hansen, interview with Khaled Hosseini.

HOUELLEBECQ, Michel 1958-

PERSONAL: Born 1958.

ADDRESSES: Agent—c/o Author Mail, Librairie Artheme Fayard, 75, rue des Saints-Peres, 75279 Paris, Cedex 6, France. *E-mail*—michelhouellebecq@mac. com.

CAREER: Author. Former National Assembly computer programmer.

AWARDS, HONORS: Prix Flore, 1995, for *Extension du domaine de la lutte;* Prix Novembre, 1998, for *Les Particules Elementaires;* International IMPAC Dublin Literary Award, 2002, for *Atomised.*

WRITINGS:

H.P. Lovecraft: contre le monde, contre la vie, Editions du Rocher (Monaco), 1991, translation, with introduction by Stephen King, published as *H.P. Lovecraft: Against the World, Against Life,* Believer/ McSweeney's Books (New York, NY), 2005.

La Poursuite du bonheur: poemes, Editions de la Difference (Paris, France), 1991.

Rester vivant: methode, Editions de la Difference (Paris, France), 1991.

Extension du domaine de la lutte, Nadeau (Paris, France), 1994, translation by Paul Hammond published as *Whatever,* Serpent's Tail (London, England), 1999.

Le sens du combat, Flammarion (Paris, France), 1996.

Les Particules Elementaires, Flammarion (Paris, France), 1998, translation by Frank Wynne published as *The Elementary Particles,* Knopf (New York, NY), 2000, also published as *Atomised,* Heinemann (London, England), 2000.

Plateforme, Flammarion (Paris, France), 2001, translation by Frank Wynne published as *Platform: A Novel,* Knopf (New York, NY), 2003.

(Author of text) Michel Houellebecq, *Nudes* (photography), Harry N. Abrams (New York, NY), 2003.

Lanzarote, translated from French by Frank Wynne, William Heinemann (London, England), 2003.

La possibilite d'une ile, Fayard (London, England), 2005, translation by Gavin Bowd published as *The Possibility of an Island,* Knopf (New York, NY), 2006.

ADAPTATIONS: Film rights to *Les Particules Elementaires* have been sold.

SIDELIGHTS: Michel Houellebecq is a best-selling French author who has a growing English-speaking audience as his work is translated. His two well-known and controversial works, the 1994 short novel *Extension du domaine de la lutte* (published in 1999 as *Whatever*) and the novel *Les Particules Elementaires* (title means "Elementary Particles"), earned him a Prix Flore and a Prix Novembre respectively. In his works, Houellebecq relates his concerns regarding various societal problems, including those affecting the United States.

Houellebecq's *Extension du domaine de la lutte* is a story of alienation in the computer age. The unnamed narrator is a computer engineer without friends or purpose who withdraws rather than adapt to the world around him. He has had no romantic life since breaking up with his girlfriend two years earlier. Even more deprived than the narrator is Bernard, who is still seeking his first encounter. The two men are sent by their company on a consulting job. Bernard is described as having a very unattractive appearance, and the inappropriate advances he makes to several women are rejected. "That both men see women only in terms of their sexual features makes their impotence even more pathetic," wrote a *Publishers Weekly* reviewer. The more the narrator tries to define love, the less able he is to experience it. "The topic of sexual misery emerges, and the narrator interpolates two miniessays," wrote Maria Green, who reviewed the French version of the novel in *World Literature Today*. "The first deals with inequality, as pitiless on the sexual as on the economic level. The second is a virulent attack on psychoanalysis, another form of alienation."

The story has a tragic ending. The narrator has a nervous breakdown, and Bernard is killed in an automobile accident. While in a mental hospital, the narrator concludes that none of the patients are really ill—they are actually suffering from lack of physical contact. The narrator feels that, although technology keeps us informed and in touch, our lives are devoid of real interpersonal communication. In a *Booklist* review, Bonnie Johnston said, "Houellebecq captures precisely the cynical disillusionment of disaffected youth."

Houellebecq's novel *Les Particules Elementaires* sold over two hundred thousand copies in the four months following its publication. There are plans to produce a movie adaptation. An *Economist* reviewer said that the "remarkable best-seller is France's biggest literary sensation since Francoise Sagan, people are saying, or since Albert Camus even. It was not so much published as detonated in Paris . . . and the rows it provoked burst at once out of the review sections on to front pages." Houellebecq shows his contempt for the Socialist establishment that rose from the student protest movements, slams French universities for bowing to bureaucracy, and criticizes feminism.

The theme of *Les Particules Elementaires* (published in English as *The Elementary Particles* and as *Atomised*) claims that since 1968 sexual liberation and materialism have corrupted society, leading to despair and violence. Bruno and his half-brother Michel are the forty-something sons of a promiscuous and unloving mother. Bruno has failed at everything he has touched—marriage, fatherhood, writing, and teaching, and he "writes sadistic pornography," according to a reviewer writing in the *Economist*. Michel is a geneticist who despises humanity and envisions a world of engineered, sexless humans. The *Economist* contributor wrote that "the pairing of these two antiheroes—one literary and stuck in the past; the other scientific and future-mad—gives a clue to the book's ambition to be a novel of ideas." Adam Gopnik wrote in the *New Yorker* that the book "is less a novel than a kind of eighteenth-century *conte moral,* at once a narrative and a philosophical essay, in which an obsession with oral sex oscillates strangely with fatuous ideological posturing, as in a story by Sade or in the proceedings of an American congressional committee. It is obscene, hateful, pretentious, half educated, funny, ambitious, and oddly moving."

Bruno is obsessed by sex. He has his penis surgically enlarged, divorces his wife, and begins a relationship with a woman named Christine. During a group orgy, Christine's back is broken, and she then commits suicide. Bruno is institutionalized after going mad. Michel takes a position in Ireland to work in genetic research and creates a sexless and immortal humanoid. Gopnik wrote that "though the book's bitter tone and its readiness to say the unsayable recall Genet, and even Celine, its literary, dystopian feel brings it much closer to Burroughs (who anticipated the sexless clone years ago), or to J.G. Ballard." In spite of the book's disdain for American culture, Gopnik called this "a very 'American' book. If anything, Houellebecq envies the land of Bill Gates and Snoop Doggy Dogg for its nearness to the real infernal machines; the whole Western world is going straight to hell anyway, but at least Americans get the window seat." *Les Particules Elementaires* has been condemned for its language, scenes about masturbation, and antiliberal sentiments. Gopnik pointed out that what is termed liberalism in France is what is considered conservatism in the United States. "To the French left, 'liberalism' (or, as it is often called, 'wild' or 'savage' liberalism, a quaint and comic thought in American terms) has also come to mean, essentially, American civilization, in all its McDonald's, 'Friends,' and Exxon aspects." Being antiliberal in France means being for big government.

Gopnik concluded: "What is memorable in Houellebecq's book is not the pseudoscientific incantations, or the potted 'theories,' but the depth of feeling, the authentic disgust with *fin-de- siecle* liberal materialism. The scathing, sarcastic loathing for consumer society and its rituals—for women's magazines, gyms, night clubs, Club Med—gives real pathos to the book."

Houellebecq's 2001 book *Plateforme* was published in English as *Platform: A Novel* in 2003. The author tells the tale of Michel Renault, a disaffected Parisian bureaucrat who works for the Ministry of Culture and whose father has been murdered by a Muslim. Renault takes his inheritance, travels to Thailand with a tour group, and falls for a fellow tourist named Valerie. When the group returns to Paris, Michel and Valerie move in together and act out their sexual obsessions. Michel subsequently convinces Valerie, who works for a hotel chain, and her boss to turn various third-world hotels into sex resorts. A *Publishers Weekly* contributor noted that for Houellebecq hedonism is the only true thing of value in a culture that is spiritually bankrupt and, as a result, "only the sensations of the body have any worth—hence, the utopian value of sex tourism." As the novel progress, the plan appears to be going forward smoothly until one of the hotels is attacked by an Islamic terrorist group. The incident destroys Michel's love and ultimately his life. Calling *Platform* Houellebecq's "most controversial novel yet," *Harper's* contributor Cristina Nehring noted that "Houellebecq does, in fact, go after the big quarry, the big quandaries, the big issues of his age. But he goes after these issues in so individual and honest and blithely self-centered a way that it is almost impossible for him to offer a consistent statement about them." Nehring, who found the depiction of the constant coupling of the major characters to be "drab," also commented, "But if he is frequently incoherent in his general pronouncements, he is ingenious in his local insights. Houellebecq's fiction is full of jarringly honest microreflections; fascinating fragments, glittering shards that cut us to the quick." Richard Lacayo, writing in *Time,* noted that the author "has a gift for sleepy invective" and added, "But he's like a bad date—brimming with rank charm but few

useful judgments." A *Publishers Weekly* reviewer commented, "This is an important book, a rare must-read for anyone who wants to take the measure of contemporary European discontents."

In *Lanzarote* Houellebecq continues his exploration of the disillusioned and bored who find that the promises of materialism leave them empty. This time, the narrator seeks to dispel his ennui by going on a vacation trip to Lanzarote, part of the Canary Islands. He then meets two bisexual women and, in typical Houellebecq style, engages in vigorous sex with them. Another character, a Belgian police inspector, disdains such decadence but later becomes suspect in a pedophile scandal. In addition to writing the book, Houellebecq includes his own photographs of the island, which plays an important symbolic role in the novel. As pointed out by Philip Horne in the Manchester *Guardian,* "The doings of the Eurotourists take place against an alienating waste land, 'a barren desert' in which vast geologic forces dwarf human effort." *New Statesman* contributor Jason Cowley commented, "Lanzarote is a peculiar book. It is not quite an unconventional travelogue, nor is it fiction in any recognisable form. It reads more like random diary observations, or perhaps a long, hastily written e-mail to a close friend." Cowley also commented that readers should not expect realism in the author's works because "he is a programmatic writer, a thinker who begins with a thesis and ideas, and then seeks to dramatise them in a series of increasingly unreal situations. You read him, therefore, not to be drugged by narrative, but to be exhilarated by his insight into, and understanding of, the defining conflicts and tensions of the present."

In 2005, the English translation of Houellebecq's first book, *H.P. Lovecraft: contre le monde, contre la vie,* was published as *H.P. Lovecraft: Against the World, Against Life.* The analysis of cult writer Lovecraft and his work "provides a spirited introduction to an influential author" and a "perhaps overly kind portrait of Lovecraft the person," according to Jeff VanderMeer in *Review of Contemporary Fiction.* "Houellebecq's approach to Lovecraft is to play apologist for the man, while . . . providing astute analysis of the work," VanderMeer continued. Michel Basilieres wrote in *Globe & Mail:* "When Houellebecq offers his vision of what's really happening in Lovecraft's stories, he's virtually mapping out his own personal aesthetic." Basilieres concluded: "For admirers of either Lovecraft or Houellebecq, this book provides a necessary new take on what these authors are up to."

Houellebecq's next work was *La possibilite d'une ile,* or, *The Possibility of an Island.* In the novel, Daniel1 lives in a post-apocalyptic world of cloned, emotionless "neohumans." Cowley, again writing in *New Statesman,* noted that Houellebecq's "central characters . . . share a vision of humanity slouching towards oblivion and address the world in the same sardonic, bored and scabrous voice." *The Possibility of an Island* "is a surprising readable talk of a fascinating, if pathetic, universe defined by the malaise of modern western civilization," concluded Eric Pape in *Newsweek International.*

BIOGRAPHICAL AND CRITICAL SOURCES:

PERIODICALS

Booklist, January 1, 1999, Bonnie Johnston, review of *Extension du domaine de la lutte* (translated as *Whatever*), p. 832.
Economist, February 13, 1999, review of *Les Particules Elementaires* (translated as *The Elementary Particles*).
Entertainment Weekly, July 18, 2003, Troy Patterson, review of *Platform,* p. 80.
French Review, December, 1997, p. 316.
Globe & Mail (Toronto, Canada) July 2, 2005, Michel Basilieres, "Life? It's a Horror," p. D11.
Guardian, November 28, 1998, p. S10.
Harper's, August, 2003, Cristina Nehring, review of *Platform,* p. 75.
Independent, January 2, 1999, p.WR9.
Library Journal, July, 2003, Barbara Hoffert, review of *Platform,* p. 122.
New Statesman, July 28, 2003, Jason Cowley, review of *Lanzarote,* p. 37; November 7, 2005, Jason Cowley, "Existentialist Crisis," p. 54.
Newsweek International, October 17, 2005, Eric Pape, "A World Without Laughter: Houellebecq Sees a Future of Clones and Hedonists," p. 56.
New Yorker, December 28, 1998, Adam Gopnik, review of *Les Particules Elementaires* (translated as *The Elementary Particles*), pp. 61, 64-67; July 7, 2003, Julian Barrnes, review of *Platfrom,* p. 072.
People, August 25, 2003, review of *Platform,* p. 43.
Print, July-August, 2004, review of *Nude,* p. 28.
Publishers Weekly, November 23, 1998, review of *Extension du domaine de la lutte* (translated as *Whatever*), p. 58; June 9, 2003, review of *Platform,* p. 34.
Report, November 18, 2002, review of *Platform,* pp. 58- 59.
Review of Contemporary Fiction, Fall, 2005, review of *H.P. Lovecraft: Against the World, Against Life,* p. 149.

Time, July 14, 2003, Richard Lacayo, review of *Platform,* p. 72.
World Literature Today, summer, 1995, Maria Green, review of *Extension du domaine de la lutte,* p. 550.

ONLINE

Guardian (Manchester England), http://books.guardian.co.uk/ (August 9, 2003), Philip Horne, "Dust to Dust," review of *Lanzarote.*
Michel Houellebecq Home Page, http://homepage.mac.com/michelhouellebecq/ (March 7, 2006).

*   *   *

HOUSTON, Jeanne Toyo Wakatsuki
See HOUSTON, Jeanne Wakatsuki

*   *   *

HOUSTON, Jeanne Wakatsuki 1934-
(Jeanne Toyo Wakatsuki Houston)

PERSONAL: Born September 26, 1934, in CA; daughter of Ko (a fisherman) and Riku (Sugai) Wakatsuki; married James D. Houston (a writer), 1957; children: Corinne, Joshua, Gabrielle. *Ethnicity:* "Japanese American." *Education:* University of San Jose, B.A., 1956; also attended Sorbonne, University of Paris. *Politics:* Democrat. *Religion:* Buddhist. *Hobbies and other interests:* Swimming, dancing, film.

ADDRESSES: Home—2-1130 East Cliff Dr., Santa Cruz, CA 95062. *Agent*—Linda Allen Literary Agency, 1949 Green St. #5, San Francisco, CA 94123. *E-mail*—firehorsewoman@hotmail.com.

CAREER: Writer. Group worker and juvenile probation officer in San Mateo, CA, 1955-57. Writer-in-residence, Bellagio, Italy, 1995. Judge, Kiriyama Book Prize, 2002-04.

MEMBER: Writers Guild, Screen Writers Guild.

AWARDS, HONORS: Humanitas Prize, 1976, and Christopher Award, both for screenplay *Farewell to Manzanar;* award from National Women's Political Caucus; Wonder Woman Award, 1984; Hawaii International Film Festival award, 1989; U.S.-Japan creative arts fellowship, 1991-92; Santa Cruz Ethnic Arts Award of Recognition, 1992; honorary degree from DeAnza College, 1994; Rockefeller grant, 1995; Carey McWilliams Award, California Studies Association, 2000; Certificate of Commendation for Literature and History, California Senate, Legislature and City of Los Angeles, 2001; Japanese American of the Biennium 2002-04, Japanese-American Citizens League, 2004.

WRITINGS:

(With husband, James D. Houston) *Farewell to Manzanar: A True Story of Japanese-American Experience during and after the World War II Internment* (nonfiction; also see below), Houghton Mifflin (Boston, MA), 1973, reprinted, 2002.

(With James D. Houston and John Korty) *Farewell to Manzanar* (screenplay), Universal/MCA-TV, 1976.

(With Paul G. Hensler) *Don't Cry, It's Only Thunder* (nonfiction), Doubleday (New York, NY), 1984.

Beyond Manzanar: Views of Asian-American Womanhood (bound with *One Can Think about Life after the Fish Is in the Canoe, and Other Coastal Sketches,* by James. D. Houston), Capra Press (San Francisco, CA), 1985.

The Legend of Fire Horse Woman, Kensington Publishing (New York, NY), 2003.

Also author of teleplays *Barrio,* with James D. Houston, for National Broadcasting Co. (NBC); and *The Melting Pot,* with Houston, for Paramount Pictures.

Contributor of essays, articles and reviews to periodicals, including *Mother Jones, California, California Living, West, New England Review, San Francisco Review of Books, San Francisco Chronicle, Reader's Digest* (Japanese edition), *Der Spiegel, Dialogue, Los Angeles Times,* and *San Jose Mercury-News.* Work represented in numerous anthologies, including *Ethnic American Woman,* Kendell-Hunt, 1978; *Asian Americans: Social and Psychological Perspectives,* Science & Behavior Books, 1980; *Ethnic Lifestyles and Mental Health,* University of Oklahoma Press, 1980; *Common Ground,* Scott Foresman, 1982; *Crossing Cultures,* Macmillan, 1983; *Borzoi College Reader, American Childhoods,* Little, Brown, 1987; *Racism and Sexism,* St. Martins Press, 1988; *A Gathering of Flowers: Stories about Being Young in America,* Harper & Row, 1990; *American Mosaic,* Houghton Mifflin, 1991; *Listening to Ourselves,* Anchor Books, 1993; *Growing up Asian,* Morrow, 1993; *American Dragons,* HarperCollins, 1993; *Multitude: Cross-cultural Readings for Writers,*

McGraw-Hill, 1993; *Dreamers and Desperadoes,* Dell, 1993; *Under Western Eyes,* Anchor Books, 1995; *Where Coyotes Howl and the Wind Blows Free,* University of Nevada Press, 1997; *Literature and the Environment,* Longman, 1999; and *The Colors of Nature,* Milkweed Press, 2002.

SIDELIGHTS: With the publication of the memoir *Farewell to Manzanar,* Jeanne Wakatsuki Houston "became, quite unintentionally, a voice for a heretofore silent segment of society," according to a *Los Angeles Times* reporter. The book, which Houston coauthored with her husband, James D. Houston, describes the experience of Houston and her family as residents of an internment camp in Nevada wherein Japanese Americans were forcibly kept during World War II. Widely read, the book has sold more than a million copies since it was first published in 1973, and has been made into a film for television. In 2001 copies of the film were distributed to every public school and library in California as part of a curriculum focusing on history and civil rights.

Born in California, Houston was only seven years old when her family of first-and second-generation Japanese Americans was shipped to the Manzanar internment camp near the Sierra Nevada mountains. The Wakatsukis were one of the first families interned there and one of the last to be released. *Farewell to Manzanar* describes the indignities of the camp experience and the harmful effects it had on Houston's family, particularly her father. As a *New Yorker* critic observed, Ko Wakatsuki "was too old to bend with the humiliations of the camp. . . . His story is at the heart of this book, and his daughter tells it with great dignity." As Dorothy Rabinowitz wrote in the *Saturday Review,* "Houston and her husband have recorded a tale of many complexities in a straightforward manner, a tale remarkably lacking in either self-pity or solemnity." A *New York Times Book Review* critic concluded that *Farewell to Manzanar* is "a dramatic, telling account of one of the most reprehensible events in the history of America's treatment of its minorities."

Silenced by guilt and shame, Houston was thirty-seven years old before she felt comfortable articulating her feelings about the internment. As she later explained to a *Los Angeles Times* contributor, her experiences made her feel "sullied, like when you are a rape victim. . . . You feel you must have *done* something. You feel you are part of the act." *Farewell to Manzanar* was among the first works to publicize the story of Japanese Americans' internment. According to *Los Angeles Times* contributor Ajay Singh, almost a quarter century after its original publication it remains an "accessible and unsentimental work" that "shed light on a subject that had been largely ignored in popular histories." In 1998 the U.S. government formally apologized for interning 120,000 Japanese Americans during wartime.

Houston further explored the tribulations of post-World War II Asian-Americans in her 1985 book, *Beyond Manzanar: Views of Asian-American Womanhood.* Using a combination of essays and short fiction, she describes the difficulty she and other women have found in trying to assimilate with American culture while maintaining the traditions of their Japanese heritage. "Her descriptions of how she handles this challenge . . . constitute the book's most substantial assets," commented James W. Byrkit in *Western American Literature. Los Angeles Times Book Review* contributor Jonathan Kirsch, too, found the book a worthwhile endeavor. "Houston writes poignantly of the chasms of myth and expectation that must be spanned when a Japanese-American woman marries 'a blond Samurai,'" wrote Kirsch.

Houston has since gone on to publish several more books, among them *The Legend of Fire Horse Woman.* Although a novel, the book treads the same ground as *Farewell to Manzanar* in its focus on three generations of women living in a U.S. detention camp during World War II. In an interview for *Notable Asian-American Authors,* Houston discussed the difficulty she had fictionalizing the experience. When she wrote her first draft, she ended the book "just before World War II. I couldn't write any fictionalized accounts of the war, specifically about the camps. In the past, I could only write from my own memories, from the family's history. But more recently, I've written three short stories about fictionalized accounts of camp. So in the second draft of my novel, I plan to go beyond the war, to include the war and the camps." In an interview with Annie Nakao for the *San Francisco Chronicle,* Nakao explained that the book had taken Houston most of ten years to write, due to the difficulty in fictionalizing the experience. "It's like a sacred cow, the landmark communal experience of Japanese Americans," Houston explained to Nakao. "I didn't know if fictionalizing it would be offensive."

Despite her initial difficulties, much of the novel centers around Manzanar. Sayo, Hana, and Terri are three generations of Japanese-American women imprisoned at the internment camp. Sayo arrives in the United States in the early 1900s as the "Picture Bride" of the second son of a wealthy family from her home town in Japan. Sayo is lucky to be able to marry; she was born under the sign of the Fire Horse, an astrological sign extremely unlucky for women, as it means that they will have powerful, independent personalities. Sayo's role from the beginning is legendary; she does not accept conventions and follows her heart where it leads. With her husband, she has children, one of whom is Hana. When Hana grows into an adult, she marries a man who is abusive to her, but she is unable to find her voice and learn to stand up for herself. Terri, Hana's daughter, is a teenager when the three women are sent with their families to the camp; she is still finding her own identity, and she rebels against the norm by befriending a young soldier. Though the camp disempowers all those interned in it, each woman finds something of themselves during the experience. Discussing the novel with *Publishers Weekly* contributor Suzanne Mantell, Houston noted: "I wanted to write a book women would read and enjoy and identify but by the end would have learned something. I still believe in stories." Critics seemed to believe in the power of Houston's story as well; Barbara Langsam Shuman wrote in the *St. Louis Post-Dispatch,* "Houston's writing is lyrical, with vivid descriptive passages and characterizations that are both extraordinary and real." Hiromi Goto, in an article for the *Women's Review of Books,* noted that, while the women of the story seem only to discover more about themselves in relation to men, "Houston's characters are not victims who seek only to survive; they are women with agency who will not let history, political machinations, or social pressure dictate the courses of their lives."

According to Singh, Houston considers *Farewell to Manzanar* "not a sermon on political injustice nor an essay on the Constitution. It allows readers to enter the experience on the level of empathy." Yet the author's message is nevertheless clear. "For me to stand up here today and talk about injustice is freedom," she explained to a group of students, according to Sara Toth in the *St. Louis Post-Dispatch.* "We as Americans cannot forget the injustices of history."

BIOGRAPHICAL AND CRITICAL SOURCES:

BOOKS

Houston, Jeanne, and James D. Houston, *Farewell to Manzanar: A True Story of Japanese-American Experience during and after the World War II Internment,* Houghton Mifflin (Boston, MA), 1973, reprinted, 2002.
Notable Asian Americans, Thomson Gale (Detroit, MI), 1995.

PERIODICALS

Booklist, February 15, 1992, review of *Farewell to Manzanar,* p. 1100; April 15, 1992, review of *Farewell to Manzanar,* p. 1518; November 1, 1992, review of *Farewell to Manzanar,* p. 502; November 15, 2003, Kristine Huntley, review of *The Legend of Fire Horse Woman,* p. 575.

Book Report, January, 1994, review of *Farewell to Manzanar,* p. 25.

Library Journal, March 1, 1984, review of *Don't Cry, It's Only Thunder,* p. 484.

Los Angeles Times, November 15, 1984; November 6, 2001, Ajay Singh, "The Lessons of History," p. E1.

New Yorker, November 5, 1973.

New York Times Book Review, January 13, 1974.

Publishers Weekly, August 11, 2003, Suzanne Mantell, review of *The Legend of Fire Horse Woman,* p. 138; September 8, 2003, review of *The Legend of Fire Horse Woman,* p. 53.

St. Louis Post-Dispatch, April 15, 2002, Sara Toth, "Students Revel in Visit with Author of Readmore Novel, *Farewell to Manzanar,*" p. 3; November 16, 2003, Barbara Langsam Shuman, "The Truths of 'Manzanar' Turn into Lyrical Fiction," p. C12.

San Francisco Chronicle, December 14, 2003, Annie Nakao, "'Farewell to Manzanar' Author Returns to Internment Days in First Novel," p. E1.

San Francisco Review of Books, March, 1994, review of *Farewell to Manzanar,* p. 44.

Saturday Review, November 6, 1973.

Washington Post, February 27, 1984.

Women's Review of Books, July, 2004, Hiromi Goto, "Manzanar as Metaphor," p. 22.

*   *   *

HOWARD, Maureen 1930-

PERSONAL: Born June 28, 1930, Bridgeport, CT; daughter of William L. (a county detective) and Loretta (Burns) Kearns; married Daniel F. Howard (a professor of English), August 28, 1954 (divorced, 1967); married David J. Gordon (a professor), April 2, 1968 (divorced); married Mark Probst (a financial advisor and novelist); children: (first marriage) Loretta Howard. *Education:* Smith College, B.A., 1952. *Hobbies and other interests:* Gardening, cooking.

ADDRESSES: Home—New York, NY. *Agent*—Gloria Loomis, Watkins, Loomis Agency, 150 East 35th St., Ste. 530, New York, NY 10016.

CAREER: Author of novels, literary criticism, and book reviews; editor. Worked in publishing and advertising, 1952-54; University of California, Santa Barbara, lecturer in English and drama, 1968-69; New School for Social Research, New York, NY, lecturer in English and creative writing, 1967-68, 1970-71, 1974—; currently professor of writing, Columbia University, New York, NY; member of English Department Yale University, 1991—. Instructor at Amherst College and Brooklyn College.

AWARDS, HONORS: Guggenheim fellowship, 1967-68; fellow of Radcliffe Institute, 1967-68; National Book Critics Circle Award in general nonfiction, 1980, and American Book Award nomination in autobiography/biography, 1981, both for *Facts of Life;* PEN/Faulkner Award for Fiction nominations, 1983, for *Grace Abounding,* and 1987, for *Expensive Habits;* also for *Natural History;* Ingram Merrill fellow, National Endowment for the Arts, 1988; Literary Lion Award, New York Public Library, 1993; recipient of an Academy Award in Literature from the American Academy of Arts and Letters.

WRITINGS:

NOVELS

Not a Word about Nightingales, Atheneum (New York, NY), 1961.

Bridgeport Bus, Harcourt (New York, NY), 1966.

Before My Time, Little, Brown (Boston, MA), 1975.

Grace Abounding, Little, Brown (Boston, MA), 1982.

Expensive Habits, Summit Books (New York, NY), 1986.

(Coauthor) *Mrs. Dalloway,* Harcourt Brace (New York, NY), 1990.

Natural History, Norton (New York, NY), 1992.

A Lover's Almanac, Viking (New York, NY), 1998.

(Author of introduction) *Three Novels: "O Pioneers!," "The Song of the Lark," and "My Antonia,"* Carroll & Graf (New York, NY), 1998.

Big As Life: Three Tales for Spring (novellas), Viking (New York, NY), 2001.

The Silver Screen, Viking (New York, NY), 2004.

OTHER

(Editor) *Seven American Women Writers of the Twentieth Century,* University of Minnesota Press, 1977.

Facts of Life (autobiography), Little, Brown (Boston, MA), 1978, reprinted, with new afterword by the author, Penguin Books (New York, NY), 1999.

(Editor) *Contemporary American Essays*, Viking (New York, NY), 1984, published as *The Penguin Book of Contemporary American Essays*, Penguin Books (New York, NY), 1985.

(Coeditor) *Cabbage and Bones: An Anthology of Irish-American Women's Fiction*, Henry Holt, 1997.

Also author of a produced play and of screenplays. Works included in numerous anthologies, including *The Best American Short Stories, 1965*, edited by Martha Foley and David Burnett, Houghton Mifflin, 1965, and *Statements*, edited by Jonathan Baumbach, Braziller, 1975. Contributor to various periodicals, including *New York Times Book Review, New Republic, New Yorker, Hudson Review, Yale Review*, and *Vogue*.

SIDELIGHTS: Maureen Howard's literary talents are considered by many to be expansive. She is recognized as a thoroughly professional, perceptive, and sensitive literary critic and editor and a much-admired lecturer who shares her experience and thoughts on creative writing. Her novels are also praised for their clarity, linguistic precision, and character development. Peter S. Prescott declared in *Newsweek* that Howard is "a grand writer of English prose; she's witty and (a rarer quality in novelists) she's intelligent as well." Often compared to the writings of Henry James and Virginia Woolf, Howard's novels, in addition to her autobiography, have been described as brilliantly sensitive commentaries on contemporary American society.

Howard's first novel, *Not a Word about Nightingales*, portrays a family's unsuccessful attempt to achieve happiness and personal fulfillment. While on a research trip to Perugia, Italy, college professor Albert Sedgely discards his respected and secure middle-class life and family and decides to remain in the small village. After completely changing his priorities and his lifestyle, Sedgely takes a mistress and strives to find inner peace and happiness. Meanwhile, his wife sends their eighteen-year-old daughter, Rosemary, to convince Sedgely to return home. While Rosemary quickly becomes enchanted with the colorful Italian life, Sedgely becomes increasingly disenchanted. Back in the United States, Sedgely's wife is beginning to enjoy her newfound independence. Rosemary's attraction to her new lifestyle, too, is short-lived. Doris Grumbach explained in the *New York Times Book Review* that Howard's intent in *Not a Word about Nightingales* is to write "about the deadly continuity of the marital condition," a condition from which "there is no permanent exit, only acceptance and repetition of marriage's inexorable routine."

Not a Word about Nightingales perfectly highlights a recurring theme found in most of Howard's works of fiction—that the individual must accept the fact that the events that make up and shape his or her life are predetermined. While none of us can change our destiny, each one of us is free to grow, develop, and make choices within the limits our character allows. Remarked David M. Taylor in the *Directory of Literary Biography Yearbook: 1983*, Howard's protagonists "have limited control of their fates, but the exercise of will to effect change is championed rather than discouraged. It appears that the author believes that things will generally turn out badly, but the attempt at change is worthwhile."

In *Bridgeport Bus*, Howard's second novel, a major life change comes for thirty-five-year-old Mary Agnes Keely, an aspiring writer who after an argument with her stifling widowed mother leaves the home they both share and moves to New York City. Obtaining employment as a copywriter and showing real talent as a fledgling author, Mary Agnes takes in a troubled roommate, begins an affair with an advertising-agency artist, and keeps company with a group of Bohemian artists. Toward the end of the book, she finds herself pregnant and totally alone. While Elaine Ruben described *Bridgeport Bus* in the *New Republic* as "a funny, sad work some readers were fortunate to discover and then eager to pass on to friends," Daniel Stern wrote in the *Saturday Review*, "that such a diverse and sensitized imagination should exist in the captive body of an Irish Catholic spinster in fruitless rebellion against the paucity of experience to which she appears to be condemned is merely the cream of the irony." Stern continued that, by the time Howard's protagonist arrives at the "concluding insight that 'it was no great sin to be, at last, alone,' the reader has been rewarded for his attention in a thousand subtle but tangible ways."

Writing novels populated with solid characters such as Mary Agnes in *Bridgeport Bus* and other strong-willed women such as Laura Quinn in *Before My Time*, Maud Dowd in *Grace Abounding*, and Margaret Flood in *Expensive Habits*, in addition to the powerful cast found in her autobiography, *Facts of Life*, Howard is referred to by some critics as a "woman's writer." These reviewers remarked that her novels systematically revolve around women who are searching for their identity and their place within society's accepted boundaries. These female characters often work hard to grow and strive towards self-awareness, even against seemingly very difficult odds. A reviewer for the *Washington Post Book World* described Howard's novels as "meticulously observed and beautifully written short studies of women caught in the world of men, lost to themselves, and finding little meaning in what they do."

Most critics seemed to express a similar opinion to Paul Gray in his *Time* review of *Before My Time* when he commented that one of Howard's most identifiable and admired talents lies in her ability to successfully shape and structure the language in each of her books. This task is accomplished without distracting attention from her novel's other elements. "Certainly Miss Howard's stylistic virtuosity cannot be disputed," stated Pearl K. Bell in the *New Leader*. "Every inch of her prose . . . is trimmed and polished with meticulous skill." Sybil S. Steinberg of *Publishers Weekly* observed that the fact that "critics have generally praised Howard's impeccable command of language, her exact and tartly humorous prose, somewhat surprises [Howard.]" Howard explained to Steinberg: "Of course I am fascinated with language, but I don't think that is so unusual. I should think all writers who are serious about what they're doing *would* care a lot about language. I think it's very odd when I pick up a novel and see that language has not been honored or used well, or played with."

In her award-winning autobiography, *Facts of Life*, Howard recounts her life as the daughter of Irish-Catholic parents, a college professor's wife, and the experiences that have shaped her life. "Howard is a talented novelist who has never written anything so concentrated and properly disturbing as this memoir," stated Alfred Kazin in the *New Republic*. "The style is very, very bright; the other characters are wonderfully alive; the suffering and resentment out of which the book was written stick to it like a burr. . . . A painfully strong, good book." And Walter Clemons wrote in *Newsweek* that *Facts of Life* "is brief, witty and utterly original. Its candor and conspicuous reticences are exciting and puzzling. . . . It exemplifies Howard's unsettling combination of elegance and earthiness."

In her fourth novel, *Grace Abounding*, Howard follows the path of Maud Dowd's life beginning with her very colorless and spiritless existence as a forty-three-year-old widow and mother of a teenage daughter, Elizabeth. Maud spends much of her time spying on her neighbors—a pair of spinster sisters—and visiting her dying mother. Maud's life dramatically changes after her mother dies and, after ending a brief and dreadful relationship with an unworthy man, she moves to New York City to pursue vocal training for the talented Elizabeth. Maud remarries a successful and loving man, earns a Ph.D. in psychology, and becomes a children's therapist. Elizabeth, in turn, happily gives up her promising

singing career to marry and have children. Life for Maud is not entirely golden however, as she copes with the death of a three-year-old patient and wrestles with her own mortality.

Robert Dawidoff wrote in the *Los Angeles Times* that *Grace Abounding* "conveys a shrewd feeling for how life changes, how things affect and happen to people, how some stories have endings and meanings and some do not, staying, rather, unresolved in several memories—and how, where faith had best be, grace had better be." "It does give a sense of lives as they are really lived such as only a small minority of novelists in each generation can even or can even want to manage," remarked Noel Perrin in the *New York Times Book Review*. "Howard . . . is a writer to read. Here the sensibility. There the intelligence." Diane M. Ross commented in the *Chicago Tribune* that "meant to involve us in the irregular rhythms of particular lives, the structure of [*Grace Abounding*] allows for shifting points of view and for chronological gaps in the narrative. . . [*Grace Abounding*] depends upon an accumulation of detail and a pattering of scenes rather than a straightforward plot. . . . Howard crosscuts between characters and locations, and blithely elides large chunks of time. . . . Her details are epiphanies, and they range from the ridiculous to the graceful."

At the beginning of Howard's 1986 novel, *Expensive Habits*, seemingly successful and well-known writer Margaret Flood lies in a hospital room after learning she has a deteriorating heart disease. The forty-five-year-old returns to her Manhattan apartment and, through a sequence of flashback scenes, the reader sees Margaret's life as a continual series of episodes—many involving loyalty and betrayal—that leave her searching for her true identity and self-worth. Margaret hopes this search will bring her the peace and contentment she so desperately desires. Jonathan Yardley suggested in the *Washington Post Book World* that Howard's *Expensive Habits* "is a serious and accomplished piece of work . . . certainly a book rich in integrity and elegance, by a writer who matters." Nora Johnson of the *Los Angeles times Book Review* wrote: "Maureen Howard's fine fifth novel attempts more, and accomplishes more, than all the others, marking her steady progress toward the highest rank of American fiction writers. . . . It's dazzling to see how deftly she wields her author's tools." And Gray commented in *Time*: "The author smuggles more subjects into a book than its length seems to allow. . . . [Howard] has skills that do not comfortably translate into screaming paperback covers and megabuck reprints. She is one of those rare contemporaries whose work demands, and deserves, rereadings."

Natural History broke with the author's characteristic focus. Taking place in Connecticut's affluent Fairfield County, *Natural History* follows the Bray family whose patriarch, Billy Bray, is county detective. The aftermath of a murder investigation Bray undertakes in 1945 leaves the family shadowed by the murdered man's brother who seeks revenge for what he feels was a botched job by Bray in bringing his brother's killer to justice. Meanwhile, the Bray children, Cathy and James, grow up and leave Bridgeport for promising careers only to return in disillusionment. Critical of what he terms the novel's "unreadability," *Washington Post Book World* reviewer Noel Perrin contended that "the real character in this book is the city of Bridgeport [where the author was raised] and the author's purpose is to say goodbye. . . . That city has turned to slums and depression and homeless people in parks, and the book is a kind of wake." Also commenting on the novel's unconventionality, *Women's Review of Books* writer Gail Pool found *Natural History* to be "something of a stew. Though [Howard] juxtaposes strands of natural, social and personal history, patterns of American hopes and familiarities, she fails to weave these threads together into an enlightening or moving whole." *New Republic* reviewer Marc Robinson, however, praised Howard as "linguistically acrobatic, imaginatively daring," and maintained that "Howard's refreshing distrust of psychological consistency and ultimate 'meaning' informs . . . *Natural History*, making its emotional appeal indirect, unassuming, yet all the more satisfying once found."

A Lover's Almanac, described by Lorna Sage in the *New York Times Book Review* as a "strange bundle of a novel," tells the story of a Generation X couple who struggle with conventional impulses toward love and marriage on the eve of the millennium. An elderly couple also begin a romance, and the novel alternates between these parallel tales of lovers, with bits of wisdom from Benjamin Franklin, Thomas Edison, and many others thrown in, in the style of the *Old Farmer's Almanac*, leading Sage to call the novel "rich propaganda for whatever's real, though it looks fanciful on the surface." A *Kirkus Reviews* critic described this novel as a work "as expansive as an almanac, with a bit of everything in it," while a reviewer for *Booklist* asserted that Howard's improvisations on the almanac form, including bits of astrology and faux psychic predictions, explore "the often unexpected consequences of acts both creative and destructive."

In Howard's 2004 novel *The Silver Screen,* silent movie actress Isabel Maher must deal with the advent of the talkies and retires in Providence, Rhode Island, to care for her disabled husband and two children who, as they mature, have difficulty dealing with their mother's exotic past. Then, as they age themselves, they must deal with their mother's illness and death and the influence her life has had on theirs. While Ann H. Fisher commented in *Library Journal* that Howard's "prose is a bit languid and the story sometimes convoluted," a *Publishers Weekly* reviewer commented that Howard fleshes out the four primary characters "in lovely and precise prose and by the complexities of communication and disconnection." Donna Seaman, reviewing the novel for *Booklist,* stated: "*The Silver Screen* extends Howard's penetrating inquiry into love, art, and spirituality, and places her in accord with A.S. Byatt and Iris Murdoch."

BIOGRAPHICAL AND CRITICAL SOURCES:

BOOKS

Contemporary Literary Criticism, Thomson Gale (Detroit, MI), Volume 5, 1976, Volume 14, 1980, Volume 46, 1988.
Dictionary of Literary Biography Yearbook: 1983, Thomson Gale (Detroit, MI), 1984.

PERIODICALS

Booklist, September 1, 1997, review of *A Lover's Almanac;* May 15, 2004, Donna Seaman, review of *The Silver Screen,* p. 1580.
Chicago Tribune, November 14, 1982, Diane M. Ross, review of *Grace Abounding.*
Critics, February 1, 1979.
Harper's, November, 1978.
Kirkus Reviews, October 15, 1997, review of *A Lover's Almanac.*
Library Journal, June 15, 2004, Ann H. Fisher, review of *The Silver Screen,* p. 58.
Los Angeles Times, December 7, 1982, David Dawidoff, review of *Grace Abounding.*
Los Angeles Times Book Review, May 18, 1986.
Nation, December 21, 1992, p. 777.
New Leader, January 20, 1975, Pearl K. Bell, review of *Before My Time;* December 14, 1992, Hope Hale Davis, review of *Natural History,* p. 24.
New Republic, February 8, 1975, Alfred Kazin, review of *Facts of Life;* September 9, 1978, Elaine Ruben, review of *Bridgeport Bus;* October 4, 1982, Anne Tyler, review of *Grace Abounding,* p. 35; November 9, 1992, Marc Robinson, review of *Natural History,* p. 46.

Newsweek, January 20, 1975, Walter Clemons, review of *Facts of Life;* October 11, 1982, Peter S. Prescott, review of *Grace Abounding,* p. 109.

New York, June 19, 1995, p. 37.

New York Review of Books, December 3, 1992, p. 30.

New York Times, October 2, 1982, Anatole Broyard, review of *Grace Abounding,* p. 21; May 24, 1986, Michiko Kakutani, review of *Expensive Habits,* p. 11.

New York Times Book Review, January 19, 1975; September 26, 1982, Noel Perrin, review of *Grace Abounding,* p. 7; December 5, 1982, review of *Grace Abounding,* p. 40; June 8, 1986, Laurie Miller, review of *Careless about our Lives,* p. 9; October 18, 1992, Sean O'Casey, review of *Natural History,* p. 1; January 18, 1998, Lorna Sage, review of *A Lover's Almanac,* p. 6.

Partisan Review, Volume 56, number 1, 1987.

Publishers Weekly, August 24, 1992, review of *Natural History,* p. 58; May 17, 2004, review of *The Silver Screen,* p. 31.

Saturday Review, October 28, 1978, Daniel Stern, review of *Bridgeport Bus.*

Sewanee Review, winter, 1974-75.

Spectator, November 8, 1986.

Time, January 27, 1975, Paul Gray, review of *Before My Time;* May 26, 1986, Paul Gray, review of *Expensive Habits,* p. 78.

Washington Post Book World, October 10, 1982; May 11, 1986; November 22, 1992, p. 6.

Women's Review of Books, December 1992, Gail Pool, review of *Natural History,* p. 20.

*   *   *

HOWARD, Warren F.
See POHL, Frederik

*   *   *

HOYLE, Fred 1915-2001

PERSONAL: Born June 24, 1915, in Bingley, Yorkshire, England; died August 20, 2001, in Bournemouth, England; son of Ben and Mabel (Pickard) Hoyle; married Barbara Clark, December 28, 1939; children: Geoffrey, Elizabeth Jeanne (Mrs. N.J. Butler). *Education:* Emmanuel College, Cambridge, M.A., 1939.

CAREER: Cambridge University, Cambridge, England, research fellow of St. John's College, 1939-72, honorary fellow, beginning 1973, university lecturer in math-ematics, 1945-58, Plumian Professor of Theoretical Astronomy and Experimental Philosophy, 1958-73, director of Institute of Theoretical Astronomy, 1966-72. California Institute of Technology, visiting professor of astrophysics, 1953 and 1954, visiting professor of astronomy, 1956, Sherman Fairchild Distinguished Scholar, 1974-75; visiting professor of astronomy, then member of staff, Mount Wilson and Palomar Observatories in California, 1957-62; Royal Institution, London, England, professor of astronomy, 1969-72; Cornell University, Andrew D. White Professor-at-Large, 1972-78. Honorary research professor, University of Manchester, beginning 1972, and University of Cardiff, beginning 1975; honorary fellow, Emmanuel College, Cambridge, 1983. Senior exhibitioner of Royal Commission of the Exhibition of 1851, 1938; member of science research council, 1967-72. *Military service:* British Admiralty, wartime research, 1940-45.

MEMBER: Royal Astronomical Society (fellow; president, 1971-73), Royal Society (fellow; vice president, 1970-71), American Academy of Arts and Sciences (honorary member), American Philosophical Society, National Academy of Sciences (foreign associate), Royal Irish Academy (honorary member), Mark Twain Society (honorary member).

AWARDS, HONORS: Smith Prize, 1939; D.Sc. from University of East Anglia, 1967, University of Leeds, 1969, University of Bradford, 1975, and University of Newcastle, 1976; Gold Medal, Royal Astronomical Society, 1968; Kalinga Prize, 1968; Bruce Medal, Astronomical Society of the Pacific, 1970; knighted, 1972; Royal Medal, Royal Society, 1974; Dorothea Klumpke-Roberts Award, Astronomical Society of the Pacific, 1977; Karl Schwarzschild Medal, German Astronomical Society, 1992; Balzan Prize, 1994; Annenberg Award, American Astronomical Society, 1996, for astronomy education; Crafoord Prize, Swedish Academy, 1997; elected honorary fellow of Institute of Astronomy, Cambridge University.

WRITINGS:

NONFICTION

Some Recent Researches in Solar Physics, Cambridge University Press (Cambridge, England), 1949.

The Nature of the Universe, Harper (New York, NY), 1951, revised edition, 1960.

A Decade of Decision, Heinemann (London, England), 1953, published as *Man and Materialism,* Harper (New York, NY), 1956.

Frontiers of Astronomy, Heinemann (London, England), 1955, New American Library (New York, NY), 1957.

Astronomy, Doubleday (Garden City, NY), 1962.

Star Formation, Her Majesty's Statistical Office (London, England), 1963.

Contradiction in the Argument of Malthus, University of Hull (Hull, England), 1963.

Of Men and Galaxies, University of Washington Press (Seattle, WA), 1964.

Encounter with the Future, Trident, 1965.

Galaxies, Nuclei, and Quasars, Harper (New York, NY), 1965.

Man in the Universe, Columbia University Press (New York, NY), 1966.

From Stonehenge to Modern Cosmology, W.H. Freeman (New York, NY), 1972.

Copernicus, Harper (New York, NY), 1973.

The Relation of Physics and Cosmology, W.H. Freeman (New York, NY), 1973.

(With Jayant V. Narlikar) *Action-at-a-Distance in Physics and Cosmology,* W.H. Freeman (New York, NY), 1973.

Astronomy and Cosmology, W.H. Freeman (New York, NY), 1975.

Highlights in Astronomy, W.H. Freeman (New York, NY), 1975, published as *Astronomy Today,* Heinemann (London, England), 1975.

Ten Faces of the Universe, W.H. Freeman (New York, NY), 1977.

Stonehenge: A High Peak of Prehistoric Culture, W.H. Freeman (New York, NY), 1977.

Energy or Extinction?, Heinemann (London, England), 1977, second edition, 1980.

(With Chandra Wickramasinghe) *Lifecloud,* Harper (New York, NY), 1978.

The Cosmogony of the Solar System, Enslow (Hillsdale, NJ), 1978.

(With Chandra Wickramasinghe) *Diseases from Space,* Harper (New York, NY), 1979.

(With son, Geoffrey Hoyle) *Commonsense in Nuclear Energy,* Heinemann (London, England), 1979, W.H. Freeman (New York, NY), 1980.

(With Jayant V. Narlikar) *The Physics-Astronomy Frontier,* W.H. Freeman (New York, NY), 1980.

Steady-State Cosmology Re-Visited, Longwood (Dover, NH), 1980.

(With Chandra Wickramasinghe) *Space Travellers: The Bringers of Life,* Cardiff University Press (Cardiff, Wales), 1981.

The Quasar Controversy Resolved, Longwood (Dover, NH), 1981.

Facts and Dogmas in Cosmology and Elsewhere, Cambridge University Press (New York, NY), 1982.

Ice, New English Library (London, England), 1982.

(With Chandra Wickramasinghe) *Evolution from Space and Other Papers on the Origin of Life,* Enslow (Hillsdale, NJ), 1982, revised as *Evolution from Space: A Theory of Cosmic Creationism,* Simon & Schuster (New York, NY), 1984.

The Intelligent Universe: A New View of Creation and Evolution, Holt (New York, NY), 1983.

(With Chandra Wickramasinghe) *From Grains to Bacteria,* Longwood (Dover, NH), 1984.

(Editor, with Chandra Wickramasinghe) *Fundamental Studies and the Future of Science,* Cardiff University Press (Cardiff, Wales), 1984.

Living Comets, Longwood (Dover, NH), 1985.

(With Chandra Wickramasinghe and John Watkins) *Viruses from Space,* Cardiff University Press (Cardiff, Wales), 1986.

The Small World of Fred Hoyle (autobiography), M. Joseph (London, England), 1986.

(With Chandra Wickramasinghe) *Archaeopteryx, the Primordial Bird: A Case of Fossil Forgery,* Longwood (Dover, NH), 1987.

(With Chandra Wickramasinghe) *The Theory of Cosmic Grains,* Kluwer Academic Publishers (Dordrecht, Netherlands), 1991.

(With Chandra Wickramasinghe) *Our Place in the Cosmos,* J.M. Dent (London, England), 1993.

Home Is Where the Wind Blows (autobiography), University Science Books (Mill Valley, CA), 1994.

(With Jayant V. Narlikar) *Lectures on Cosmology and Action at a Distance Electrodynamics,* World Scientific (River Edge, NJ), 1996.

(With Chandra Wickramasinghe) *Life on Mars?: The Case for a Cosmic Heritage,* Clinical Press, 1997.

(Editor, with Chandra Wickramasinghe) *Astronomical Origins of Life: Steps toward Panspermia,* Kluwer Academic Publishers (Boston, MA), 1999.

Mathematics of Evolution, Acorn Enterprises, 1999.

(With G. Burbridge and Jayant V. Narlikar) *A Different Approach to Cosmology: From a Static Universe through the Big Bang toward Reality,* Cambridge University Press (New York, NY), 2000.

Author of pamphlets, including (with Chandra Wickramasinghe) *The Origin of Life,* 1980, *Why Neo-Darwinism Does Not Work,* 1982, and *Evolution from Space,* 1982, all published by Cardiff University Press (Cardiff, Wales). Contributor of numerous articles to scientific and professional journals.

SCIENCE FICTION

The Black Cloud, Harper (New York, NY), 1957.

Ossian's Ride, Harper (New York, NY), 1959.

(With John Elliott) *A for Andromeda,* Harper (New York, NY), 1962.

(With John Elliott) *Andromeda Breakthrough,* Harper (New York, NY), 1964.

October the First Is Too Late, Harper (New York, NY), 1966.

Element 79 (short stories), New American Library (New York, NY), 1967.

Comet Halley, St. Martin's Press (New York, NY), 1985.

SCIENCE FICTION; NOVELS; WITH SON, GEOFFREY HOYLE

Fifth Planet, Harper (New York, NY), 1963.

Rockets in Ursa Major, Harper (New York, NY), 1969.

Seven Steps to the Sun, Harper (New York, NY), 1970.

The Molecule Men: Two Short Novels, Harper (New York, NY), 1971.

The Inferno, Harper (New York, NY), 1973.

Into Deepest Space, Harper (New York, NY), 1974.

The Incandescent Ones, Harper (New York, NY), 1977.

The Westminster Disaster, Harper (New York, NY), 1978.

The Energy Pirate, illustrated by Martin Aitchison, Ladybird (Loughborough, England), 1982.

The Frozen Planet of Azuron, illustrated by Martin Aitchison, Ladybird (Loughborough, England), 1982.

The Giants of Universal Park, illustrated by Martin Aitchison, Ladybird (Loughborough, England), 1982.

The Planet of Death, illustrated by Martin Aitchison, Ladybird (Loughborough, England), 1982.

PLAYS

A Nightmare for Number Ten by James Warboys (three-act), Heinemann (London, England), 1953.

Rockets in Ursa Major (pantomime for children), produced in London, England, 1962.

Author of the opera libretto, *The Alchemy of Love.*

ADAPTATIONS: *A for Andromeda* was adapted for television, British Broadcasting Corp. (BBC), 1961; *Andromeda Breakthrough* was adapted for television, BBC, 1963.

SIDELIGHTS: Educator, astronomer, and author Fred Hoyle was internationally renowned for his theories on astronomy, cosmology, and evolution. Hoyle "published a string of books challenging first one and then another of the basic tenets of modern cosmology," explained John Durant in the *Times Literary Supplement.* In his 1951 book *The Nature of the Universe,* for example, Hoyle rejects the "Big Bang" theory of the origin of the universe in favor of the "Steady State" theory developed by him and his colleagues at Cambridge University. Ironically, although he never supported the "Big Bang," Hoyle gave it its name in a speech in which he derided the theory. *New York Times Magazine* correspondent Richard Powers called Hoyle "astronomy's most respected maverick outcast." Similarly, in a *Science* review of Hoyle's *A Different Approach to Cosmology: From a Static Universe through the Big Bang toward Reality,* David W. Hogg and Matias Zaldarriaga noted that the professor did the cosmological community "a great service by developing and defending a serious alternative to Big Bang models of cosmic origins."

Hoyle's fame as a scientist rests upon his work in the field of nucleogenesis: the study of the formation of chemical elements. With a partner, William Fowler, he conducted research that defeated the notion that all the elements were present in the primordial universe. It was when he ventured into the field of cosmology—the study of the origins of the universe—that Hoyle began to differ with the majority of scientific opinion. He proposed that the universe did not begin in a sudden event, but was rather formed through a process of steady-state creation.

Hoyle expounded upon his Steady State and other theories in *The Intelligent Universe: A New View of Creation and Evolution,* published in 1983. "Writing with the moral indignation of one who believes himself to be up against a conservative and conspiratorial establishment, and who consequently does not expect a fair hearing, Hoyle dismisses one piece of 'orthodox science' after another, replacing each with ingenious alternatives that pop up from page to page like so many rabbits out of a conjurer's hat," observed Durant. In *The Intelligent Universe,* Hoyle "presents both old and new evidence" for his Steady State theory, according to *Science Fiction Review* critic Gene Deweese, "and shows how the Big Bang has at least as many shortcomings and problems as the Steady State is supposed to have." Hoyle also advances an argument against nineteenth-century writer Charles Darwin's theory of evolution, claiming that "living organisms are too complex to have been produced by chance," to quote Durant. He suggested, instead, that "we owe our existence to another intelligence which created a structure for life as part of a deliberate plan," John R. Kalafut explained in *Best Sell-*

ers. Kalafut added, "In describing the attributes of an intelligence superior to ourselves, [Hoyle] admits that we may have to use the word forbidden in science, 'God.'" Durant found Hoyle's argument inadequate, however, stating that the chapter on Darwinism reads "more like the feeble meanderings of a latter-day fundamentalist than like the work of a major scientist." Kalafut, on the other hand, maintained that "this part of the book is extremely well done and the case against traditional evolution is argued most persuasively."

Hoyle and coauthor Chandra Wickramasinghe's 1979 book *Diseases from Space* introduces a similarly controversial theory. The authors hypothesize that viruses and bacteria fall into the atmosphere after being incubated in the interiors of comet heads, and that people become ill by breathing this infected air. They support their theory by stating that the spread of disease is frequently far too rapid to be attributable solely to person-to-person contact. Several reviewers expressed deep skepticism toward such a theory. One such critic, *Antioch Review* contributor Robert Bieri, wrote: "This is a fascinating, humorous, challenging book, but few biologists will buy the thesis."

In addition to his scientific works, Hoyle also authored over a dozen science-fiction novels, more than half of which were co-written with his son, Geoffrey Hoyle. Several critics have suggested that Hoyle's highly technical and scientific background enhances the credibility and appeal of his novels. For example, *Listener* reviewer Robert Garioch commented that *Seven Steps to the Sun* "is a remarkable story, well told, and too credible for comfort. . . . The science in *Seven Steps to the Sun* is correct, as a middle-aged reviewer may learn by consulting his 15-year-old son. The main interest, however, is in the anthropology. . . . It is not at all farfetched."

Hoyle was knighted in 1972 and received numerous prestigious honors for his work, including Sweden's 1997 Crafoord prize—an award akin to the Nobel, but awarded in fields not included in the Nobel balloting. He died at his home in England at the age of eighty-six. Richard Powers concluded of the scientist-writer: "Hoyle's relentlessly speculative, relentlessly human life was itself proof that new ideas are formed in the cracks between older, spreading ones. That process, like Hoyle's steady-state universe, seems indeed to go on without foreseeable end."

BIOGRAPHICAL AND CRITICAL SOURCES:

BOOKS

Encyclopedia of World Biography Supplement, Volume 18, Thomson Gale (Detroit, MI), 1998.

World of Scientific Discovery, 2nd edition, Thomson Gale (Detroit, MI), 1999.

PERIODICALS

Antioch Review, spring, 1981, Robert Bieri, review of *Diseases from Space*.

Best Sellers, April, 1984, John R. Kalafut, review of *The Intelligent Universe: A New View of Creation and Evolution*.

Books and Bookmen, December, 1979.

Books of the Times, September, 1980.

British Book News, September, 1986.

Evolution, August, 2000, J. Bruce Walsh, "No Light from the Black Cloud," pp. 1461-1462.

Listener, September 13, 1979, Robert Garioch, review of *Seven Steps to the Sun*.

Nature, May 22, 1997, David Hughes, "In Retrospect," p. 364; February 10, 2000, John Maynard Smith, review of *Mathematics of Evolution*, pp. 594-595.

New York Review of Books, October 23, 1980.

New York Times Book Review, April 29, 1984.

New York Times Magazine, December 30, 2001, Richard Powers, "Ba-Da Bang," p. 49.

Observer (London, England), August 10, 1986.

Physics Today, December, 2000, Mario Livio, review of *A Different Approach to Cosmology: From a Static Universe through the Big Bang towards Reality*, pp. 71-73.

Quarterly Review of Biology, June, 2001, Brian Charlesworth, review of *Mathematics of Evolution*, p. 234.

Science, December 15, 2000, David W. Hogg and Matias Zaldarriaga, review of *A Different Approach to Cosmology*, p. 2079.

Science Books and Films, March, 1981.

Science Fiction Review, February, 1986, Gene Deweese, review of *The Intelligent Universe*.

Sky & Telescope, April, 1998, Joshua Roth, review of *Life on Mars? The Case for a Cosmic Heritage*, pp. 68-69.

Spectator, August 23, 1986.

Sunday Telegraph (London, England), February 13, 2000.

Times Higher Education Supplement, September 22, 2000, Roger Blandford, review of *A Different Approach to Cosmology*, pp. 24-25.

Times Literary Supplement, February 10, 1978; December 9, 1983; July 13, 2001, Bernard Lovell, "Out of the Quagmire: Hubble, Hoyle, and the Origins of the Expanding Universe," pp. 3-4.

ONLINE

Bruce Medalists Web site, http://www.phys-astro.sonoma.edu/brucemedalists/ (January 28, 2002), "Fred Hoyle."

Cardiff University Web site, http://www.cf.ac.uk/maths/ (January 28, 2002), "Sir Fred Hoyle."

Panspermia.org, http://www.panspermia.org/ (July 5, 1996), Brig Klyce, "An Interview with Fred Hoyle."

OBITUARIES:

PERIODICALS

Astronomy, November, 2001, p. 32.
Independent, August 23, 2001, p. S6.
Physics Today, November, 2001, p. 75.

ONLINE

Space.com, http://www.space.com/scienceastronomy/ (January 28, 2002).

*   *   *

HUBBELL, Sue 1935-

PERSONAL: Born January 28, 1935, in Kalamazoo, MI; daughter of B. LeRoy (a landscape architect) and Marjorie (a homemaker; maiden name, Sparks) Gilbert; married Paul Hubbell (an engineer), October 31, 1955 (divorced, 1983); married Arne Sieverts (spokesperson for the U.S. Senate Foreign Relations committee), 1988; children: (first marriage) Brian; stepchildren: (second marriage) Michael, Lisa. *Education:* Attended Swarthmore College, 1952-54, and University of Michigan, 1954-55; University of Southern California, A.B., 1956, Drexel Institute, M.S., 1963.

ADDRESSES: Home—Missouri and Washington, DC. *Agent*—Liz Darhansoff, 1220 Park Ave., New York, NY 10128.

CAREER: The Book Shelf, Moorestown, NJ, manager, 1960-63; Trenton State College, Trenton, NJ, acquisitions librarian, 1963-67; elementary school librarian in Peacedale, RI, 1967-68; Brown University, Providence, RI, serials librarian, 1968-72; commercial beekeeper in Missouri, beginning 1973; writer, 1985—.

AWARDS, HONORS: Nomination for Walter Sullivan prize, 1991, for "Earthquake Fever" (magazine piece).

WRITINGS:

A Country Year: Living the Questions, illustrated by Lauren Jarrett, Random House (New York, NY), 1986.

A Book of Bees: . . . and How to Keep Them, illustrated by Sam Potthoff, Random House (New York, NY), 1988.

On This Hilltop, Ballantine (New York, NY), 1991.

Broadsides from the Other Orders: A Book of Bugs, illustrated by Dimitry Schidlovsky, Random House (New York, NY), 1993.

Far Flung Hubbell (collected essays and articles), Random House (New York, NY), 1995.

(Author of introduction) Rachel Carson, *The Edge of the Sea,* Houghton Mifflin (Boston, MA), 1998.

Waiting for Aphrodite: Journeys into the Time before Bones, Houghton Mifflin (Boston, MA), 1999.

Shrinking the Cat: Genetic Engineering before We Knew about Genes, illustrated by Liddy Hubbell, Houghton Mifflin (Boston, MA), 2001.

From Here to There and Back Again, University of Michigan Press (Ann Arbor, MI), 2004.

Contributor to magazines and newspapers, including *New Yorker, Smithsonian, New York Times Magazine, Time, Harper's, Sports Illustrated,* and *Discover.* Contributor to anthologies, including *Best Essays of the Year,* 1990.

Author's works have been translated into French and Japanese.

WORK IN PROGRESS: Research for a book on North Africa; magazine articles.

SIDELIGHTS: Writer and beekeeper Sue Hubbell's *A Country Year: Living the Questions* is a collection of forty-one essays describing Hubbell's reflections on life and her experiences with nature over the course of one year. Lauded by critics for her vivid descriptions of nature, Hubbell tells about her trips to her Missouri beehives in her thirty-year-old pickup truck and about making her own shingles in preparation for shingling a barn on her Ozark Mountain property. Doris Betts, writing in the *Los Angeles Times Book Review,* called *A Country Year* "a record of mysteries questioned, then embraced." According to Jeremiah Tax in *Sports Illustrated,* the essays in *A Country Year* "are filled with the wonders and surprise that the diligent, empathetic observer finds in the behavior of wild things." He added that "one's reaction when finishing many of the essays is likely to be an entrancement brought on by the softness and innocence of Hubbell's prose." Betts also praised Hubbell's writing, declaring that "like a pane of glass, her prose reveals without distortion or sentimentality." Dubbing the author a "sunny naturalist who writes stimulating prose," *Booklist* contributor Donna Seaman praised Hubbell's more recent book, *Waiting for Aphrodite: Journeys into the Time before Bones,* and noted that, "as philosophical as she is descriptive" in her nature writing, Hubbell brings to each of her works an "astute attention and fluid sense of wonder."

With *A Book of Bees: . . . and How to Keep Them* and *Broadsides from the Other Orders: A Book of Bugs,* Hubbell earned a reputation as "one of the two or three best writers-about-bugs now living," in the words of Noel Perrin, in the *Washington Post Book World.* *A Book of Bees* can be read as a primer in beekeeping: Hubbell educates readers on how hive frames are built to allow beekeepers get at the honey, how to calm angry bees, and how to peacefully integrate two warring colonies with just a piece of newspaper. But as David Quammen noted in the *New York Times Book Review,* even readers who have no interest in taking up beekeeping can appreciate her fascinating account of her mutually dependent relationship with the bees. "Strictly speaking," Hubbell admonishes in her book, "one never 'keeps' bees—one comes to terms with their wild nature."

The appeal of *Broadsides from the Other Orders,* according to Christopher Lehmann-Haupt in his *New York Times* review, is that while many writers would not be able to describe thirteen insect orders without falling into numbing repetition, Hubbell takes a refreshingly wide variety of approaches in her thirteen chapters. She goes to California to learn about the multi-million-dollar ladybug business; recounts the mating activities of camel crickets observed in her home terrarium; and explains the hundred-year history of humankind's attempts to eradicate the destructive gypsy moth. Lehmann-Haupt concluded that "given Ms. Hubbell's graceful prose and observant eye, she makes an excellent ambassador from [the insect] world to us."

In *Shrinking the Cat: Genetic Engineering before We Knew about Genes,* Hubbell discusses the largely controversial issue of genetic engineering, with some intriguing case studies. She clearly explains the effects of engineering efforts throughout the decades "in plain English, with no confusing scientific terminology to bore

or distract readers," according to Irwin Weintraub in *Library Journal.* Discussing such topics as silk worms, apples, and even the common housecat, Hubbell explains the dependency that has evolved alongside genetic engineering and some of the evolutional drawbacks that have come to pass. A reviewer for *Publishers Weekly* called Hubbell's *Shrinking the Cat* a "fresh and personalized take on genetics," while Gilbert Taylor commented in *Booklist* that the work is "An engaging synthesis of material that will appeal to Hubbell's well-established audience."

BIOGRAPHICAL AND CRITICAL SOURCES:

BOOKS

Hubbell, Sue, *A Book of Bees: . . . and How to Keep Them,* illustrated by Sam Potthoff, Random House (New York, NY), 1988.

PERIODICALS

Booklist, April 1, 1999, Donna Seaman, review of *Waiting for Aphrodite: Journeys into the Time before Bones,* p. 1373; September 15, 2001, Gilbert Taylor, review of *Shrinking the Cat: Genetic Engineering before We Knew about Genes,* p. 172.
Library Journal, October 15, 2001, Irwin Weintraub, review of *Shrinking the Cat,* p. 104.
Los Angeles Times Book Review, April 13, 1986.
New York Review of Books, February 16, 1989.
New York Times, June 24, 1993.
New York Times Book Review, April 13, 1986; October 30, 1988; July 11, 1993.
Publishers Weekly, September 10, 2001, review of *Shrinking the Cat,* p. 76.
Sports Illustrated, April 21, 1986.
Washington Post Book World, April 27, 1986; August 8, 1993.

*   *   *

HUDSON, Jeffrey
See CRICHTON, Michael

*   *   *

HUGHES, Edward James
See HUGHES, Ted

HUGHES, Ted 1930-1998
(Edward James Hughes)

PERSONAL: Born Edward James Hughes; August 17, 1930, in Mytholmroyd, West Yorkshire, England; died October 28, 1998, in Devon, England; son of William Henry (a carpenter) and Edith (Farrar) Hughes; married Sylvia Plath (a poet), 1956 (died, 1963); partner of Assia Wevill (died, 1969); married Carol Orchard, 1970; children: (first marriage) Frieda Rebecca, Nicholas Farrar; (with Wevill) Shura (daughter). *Education:* Pembroke College, Cambridge, B.A., 1954, M.A., 1959.

CAREER: Poet and educator. University of Massachusetts, Amherst, instructor, 1957-59. *Military service:* British Royal Air Force, 1948-50.

AWARDS, HONORS: First prize, Young Men's and Young Women's Hebrew Association Poetry Center contest, 1957, Guinness Poetry Award, 1958, for *The Hawk in the Rain;* Guggenheim fellowship, 1959-60; Somerset Maugham Award, 1960, Hawthornden Prize, 1961, and Abraham Wonsell Foundation awards, 1964-69, all for *Lupercal;* City of Florence International Poetry Prize, 1969, for *Wodwo;* Premio Internazionale Taormina, 1972; Queen's Medal for Poetry, 1974; *Season Songs* was a Children's Book Showcase title, 1976; Officer, Order of the British Empire, 1977; voted Britain's best poet by *New Poetry* readers, 1979; Signal Poetry awards, 1979, for *Moon-Bells and Other Poems,* 1981, for *Under the North Star,* and 1983, for *The Rattle Bag;* Royal Society of Literature Heinemann Award, 1980, for *Moortown;* runner-up for 1981 Neustadt International Prize for Literature; honorary doctorate degrees from Exeter College, 1982, Open University, 1983, Bradford College, 1984, and Pembroke College, 1986; named poet laureate of England, 1984; Kurt Maschler/Emil Award, National Book League (Great Britain), 1985, for *The Iron Man: A Story in Five Nights; Guardian* Award for children's fiction, 1985, for *What Is the Truth?: A Farmyard Fable for the Young;* honorary fellow, Pembroke College, Cambridge, 1986; Whitbread Award, 1997, for *Tales from Ovid;* Whitbread Prize for Poetry and Whitbread Book of the Year award, and Forward Prize, all 1998, all for *The Birthday Letters;* appointed to British Order of Merit, 1998.

WRITINGS:

POETRY

The Hawk in the Rain, Harper (New York, NY), 1957.
Pike, Gehenna Press (Northampton, MA), 1959.
Lupercal, Harper (New York, NY), 1960.
(With Thom Gunn) *Selected Poems,* Faber and Faber (London, England), 1962.
The Burning of the Brothel, Turret Books (London, England), 1966.
Recklings, Turret Books (London, England), 1966.
Scapegoats and Rabies: A Poem in Five Parts, Poet & Printer (Woodford Gree, Essex, England), 1967.
(With Ruth Fainlight and Alan Sillitoe) *Poems,* Rainbow Press (London, England), 1967, reprinted, 1971.
Animal Poems, Gilbertson (Crediton, Devon, England), 1967.
Gravestones, Exeter College of Art (Exeter, Devon, England), 1967, published as *Poems,* 1968.
I Said Goodbye to the Earth, Turret (London, England), 1969.
The Martyrdom of Bishop Farrer, Gilbertson (Crediton, Devon, England), 1970.
Crow: From the Life and Songs of the Crow, Faber and Faber (London, England), 1970, Harper (New York, NY), 1971, revised edition, Faber and Faber, 1972, reprinted, Harper (New York, NY), 1981.
Fighting for Jerusalem, Mid-NAG (Ashington, Northumberland, England), 1970.
A Crow Hymn, Sceptre Press (Frensham, Surrey, England), 1970.
A Few Crows, Rougemont Press (Exeter, Devon, England), 1970.
Amulet, privately printed, 1970.
Four Crow Poems, privately printed, 1970.
Autumn Song, illustrated by Nina Carroll, Steane (Kettering, Northamptonshire, England), 1971.
Crow Wakes: Poems, Poet & Printer (Woodford Gree, Essex, England), 1971.
In The Little Girl's Angel Gaze, Steam Press (London, England), 1972.
Selected Poems, 1957-1967, illustrated by Leonard Baskin, Faber and Faber (London, England), 1972, Harper (New York, NY), 1973.
Prometheus on His Crag: 21 Poems, illustrated by Leonard Baskin, Rainbow Press (London, England), 1973.
Cave Birds, Scolar Press (London, England), 1975, enlarged edition published as *Cave Birds: An Alchemical Drama,* illustrated by Leonard Baskin, Faber and Faber (London, England), 1978, Viking Press (New York, NY), 1979.
The Interrogator: A Titled Vulturess, Scolar Press (London, England), 1975.
Eclipse, Sceptre Press (Knotting, Bedfordshire, England), 1976.
Sunstruck, Sceptre Press (Knotting, Bedfordshire, England), 1977.

Chiasmadon, Charles Seluzicki (Baltimore, MD), 1977.

Guadete, Harper (New York, NY), 1977.

Orts, Rainbow Press (London, England), 1978.

Moortown Elegies, Rainbow Press (London, England), 1978.

A Solstice, Sceptre Press (Knotting, Bedfordshire, England), 1978.

Calder Valley Poems, Rainbow Press (London, England), 1978.

Adam and the Sacred Nine, Rainbow Press (London, England), 1979.

Henry Williamson: A Tribute, Rainbow Press (London, England), 1979.

Four Tales Told by an Idiot, Sceptre Press (Knotting, Bedfordshire, England), 1979.

Remains of Elmet: A Pennine Sequence, photographs by Fay Godwin, Rainbow Press (London, England), 1979, second revised edition published as *Elmet: Poems,* Faber and Faber (London, England), 1994.

In the Black Chapel (poster), Victoria and Albert Museum (London, England), 1979.

Moortown, Faber and Faber (London, England), 1979, Harper (New York, NY), 1980, portions published as *Moortown Diary,* Faber and Faber (London, England), 1989.

Sky-Furnace, painting by Roger Vick, Caricia Fine Arts (North Tawton, Devon, England), 1981.

A Primer of Birds: Poems, illustrated by Leonard Baskin, Gehenna Press (Lurley, Devon, England), 1981.

Selected Poems: 1957-1981, Faber and Faber (London, England), 1982, enlarged edition published as *New Selected Poems,* Harper (New York, NY), 1982, expanded edition published as *New Selected Poems, 1957-1994,* Faber and Faber (London, England), 1995.

River, photographs by Peter Keen, Faber and Faber (London, England), 1983, Harper (New York, NY), 1984.

Flowers and Insects: Some Birds and a Pair of Spiders, illustrated by Leonard Baskin, Alfred Knopf (New York, NY), 1986.

Tales of the Early World, Faber and Faber (London, England), 1988.

Wolfwatching, Faber and Faber (London, England), 1989.

Cappriccio, illustrated by Leonard Baskin, Gehenna Press (Searsmont, ME), 1990.

Rain-Charm for the Duchy and Other Laureate Poems, Faber and Faber (London, England), 1992.

The Birthday Letters, Farrar, Straus (New York, NY), 1998.

Lire Ted Hughes: New Selected Poems, 1957-1994 (in French and English), edited by Joanny Moulin, Du Temps (Paris, France), 1998.

Selected Poems, 1957-1994, Farrar, Straus (New York, NY), 2002.

Collected Poems, edited by Paul Keegan, Farrar, Straus (New York, NY), 2003.

Also author of broadsides *Woodpecker, Wolverine, Eagle, Mosquito, Tapir's Saga, Wolf-Watching, Mice Are Funny Little Creatures, Weasels at Work,* and *Fly Inspects,* Morrigu Press (North Tawton, Devon, England), 1979-83. Contributor to *All around the Year* by Michael Morpurgo, J. Murray, 1979.

PLAYS

The House of Aries (radio play), broadcast 1960.

The Calm, produced in Boston, MA, 1961.

A Houseful of Women (radio play), broadcast 1961.

The Wound (radio play; also see below), broadcast 1962, revised version produced in London, England, 1972.

Difficulties of a Bridegroom (radio play), broadcast 1963.

Epithalamium, produced in London, England, 1963.

Dogs (radio play), broadcast 1964.

The House of Donkeys (radio play), broadcast 1965.

The Coming of the Kings and Other Plays (juvenile; contains *Beauty and the Beast* [broadcast 1965; produced in London, England, 1971], *Sean, the Fool* [broadcast 1968; produced in London, 1971], *The Devil and the Cats* [broadcast 1968; produced in London, 1971], *The Coming of the Kings* [broadcast 1964; televised, 1967; produced in London, 1972], and *The Tiger's Bones* [broadcast 1965]), Faber and Faber (London, England), 1970, revised and expaned edition published as *The Tiger's Bones and Other Plays for Children,* illustrated by Alan E. Cober, Viking Press (New York, NY), 1975.

The Price of a Bride (juvenile radio play), broadcast 1966.

The Head of Gold (radio play), broadcast 1967.

(Adapter) *Seneca's Oedipus* (produced in London, England, 1968; produced in Los Angeles, CA, 1973; produced in New York, NY, 1977), Faber and Faber (London, England), 1969, Doubleday (New York, NY), 1972.

Orghast, produced in Persepolis, Iran, 1971.

Eat Crow, Rainbow Press (London, England), 1971.

The Iron Man (based on his book; televised 1972; also see below), Faber and Faber (London, England), 1973.

Orpheus (radio play; broadcast 1965), Dramatic Publishing, 1973.

The Pig Organ; or, Pork with Perfect Pitch (juvenile opera), music by Richard Blackford, produced in London, England, 1980.

JUVENILE

Meet My Folks! (verse), illustrated by George Adamson, Faber and Faber (London, England), 1961, Bobbs-Merrill (Indianapolis, IN), 1973, revised edition, Faber and Faber, 1987.

The Earth-Owl and Other Moon-People (verse), Faber and Faber (London, England), 1963, Atheneum (New York, NY), 1964, published as *Moon-Whales and Other Moon Poems,* illustrated by Leonard Baskin, Viking (New York, NY), 1976, revised edition published as *Moon Whales,* Faber and Faber, 1988.

How the Whale Became and Other Stories, Faber and Faber (London, England), 1963, revised edition, Atheneum (New York, NY), 1964, illustrated by Jackie Morris, Orchard Books (New York, NY), 2000.

Nessie, The Mannerless Monster (verse), illustrated by Gerald Rose, Faber and Faber (London, England), 1964, revised edition published as *Nessie the Monster,* illustrated by Jan Pyk, Bobbs-Merrill (Indianapolis, IN), 1974.

The Iron Giant: A Story in Five Nights, Harper (New York, NY), 1968, revised edition published as *The Iron Man: A Story in Five Nights,* Faber and Faber (London, England), 1968, revised edition, 1984, reprinted under original title, Knopf (New York, NY), 1999.

Five Autumn Songs for Children's Voices, illustrated by Phillida Gili, Gilbertson (Crediton, Devon, England), 1968.

Spring, Summer, Autumn, Winter, Rainbow Press (London, England), 1974, revised edition published as *Season Songs,* illustrated by Leonard Baskin, Viking Press (New York, NY), 1975, revised edition, Faber and Faber (London, England), 1987.

(And illustrator) *Earth-Moon,* Rainbow Press (London, England), 1976.

Moon-Bells and Other Poems, Chatto and Windus (London, England), 1978.

Under the North Star, illustrated by Leonard Baskin, Viking Press, (New York, NY), 1981.

(Editor, with Seamus Heaney) *The Rattle Bag: An Anthology of Poetry,* Faber and Faber (London, England), 1982.

What Is the Truth?: A Farmyard Fable for the Young, illustrated by R.J. Lloyd, Harper (New York, NY), 1984.

Ffangs the Vampire Bat and the Kiss of Truth, Faber and Faber (London, England), 1986.

The Cat and the Cuckoo: Collected Poems, Wykeham Press (Winchester, England), 1987, Roaring Brook Press (Brookfield, CT), 1988.

The Iron Woman, Dial (New York, NY), 1995.

The Mermaid's Purse, illustrated by Flora McDonnell, Knopf (New York, NY), 2000.

EDITOR

(With Patricia Beer and Vernon Scannell) *New Poems 1962,* Hutchinson (London, England), 1962.

(With Thom Gunn) *Five American Poets,* Faber and Faber (London, England), 1963.

Here Today, Hutchinson (London, England), 1963.

(With Alwyn Hughes) Sylvia Plath, *Ariel,* Faber and Faber (London, England), 1965, Harper (New York, NY), 1966.

(And author of introduction) Keith Douglas, *Selected Poems,* Faber and Faber (London, England), 1964, Chilmark Press (New York, NY), 1965.

Poetry in the Making: An Anthology of Poems and Programmes from "Listening and Writing," Faber and Faber (London, England), 1967, abridged edition published as *Poetry Is,* Doubleday (New York, NY), 1970.

(And author of introduction) Emily Dickinson, *A Choice of Emily Dickinson's Verse,* Faber and Faber (London, England), 1968.

(And translator, with Assia Gutmann) Yehuda Amichai, *Selected Poems,* Cape Goliard Press (London, England), 1968, revised edition published as *Poems,* Harper (New York, NY), 1969.

(And author of introduction) William Shakespeare, *With Fairest Flowers While Summer Lasts: Poems from Shakespeare* (also see below), Doubleday (New York, NY), 1971, published as *A Choice of Shakespeare's Verse,* Faber and Faber (London, England), 1971, introduction published as *Shakespeare's Poem,* Lexham Press (London, England), 1971.

Sylvia Plath, *Crossing the Waters: Transitional Poems,* Harper (New York, NY), 1971, published as *Crossing the Waters,* Faber and Faber (London, England), 1971.

Sylvia Plath, *Winter Trees,* Faber and Faber (London, England), 1971, Harper (New York, NY), 1972.

(And translator, with János Csokits) János Pilinszky, *Selected Poems,* Carcanet (Manchester, England), 1976.

(And author of introduction) Sylvia Plath, *Johnny Panic and the Bible of Dreams, and Other Prose Writings,* Faber and Faber (London, England), 1977, Harper (New York, NY), 1979.

(And translator, with Yehuda Amichai) Yehuda Amichai, *Amen,* Harper (New York, NY), 1977.

New Poetry 6, Hutchison (London, England), 1980.

(And author of introduction) Sylvia Plath, *The Collected Poems,* Harper (New York, NY), 1981.

(With Seamus Heaney) *Arvon Foundation Poetry Competition: 1980 Anthology,* Kilnhurst, 1982.

Sylvia Plath, *Sylvia Plath's Selected Poems,* Faber and Faber (London, England), 1985.

Winning Words (stories by children), Faber and Faber (London, England), 1991.

Dancer to God: Tributes to T.S. Eliot, Farrar, Straus (New York, NY), 1993.

Samuel Taylor Coleridge, *A Choice of Coleridge's Verse,* Faber and Faber (London, England), 1996.

(Consulting editor and author of foreword) Frances McCullough, editor, *The Journals of Sylvia Plath,* Dial (New York, NY), 1982, reprinted, Anchor Books (New York, NY), 1998.

OTHER

Wodwo (includes play, *The Wound*), Harper (New York, NY), 1967.

(Translator, with Assia Gutmann) Yehuda Amichai, *Selected Poems,* Cape Goliard Press (London, England), 1968, expanded edition published as *Poems,* Harper (New York, NY), 1970.

The Demon of Adachigahara (libretto), Oxford University Press (Oxford, England), 1969.

(With others) *Corgi Modern Poets in Focus I,* edited by Dannie Abse, Corgi (London, England), 1971.

(Adapter) *The Story of Vasco* (libretto; based on a play by Georges Schehade; produced in London, England, 1974), Oxford University Press (Oxford, England), 1974.

(Translator) Charles Simic and Mark Strand, editors, *Another Republic,* Ecco Press (New York, NY), 1977.

The Threshold (short story), Steam Press (London, England), 1979.

(Translator, with Yehuda Amichai) Yehuda Amichai, *Time,* Harper (New York, NY), 1979.

(Translator, with János Csokits) János Pilinszky, *The Desert of Love,* Anvil Press Poetry, 1988.

(Translator, with Harold Schimmel and Assia Gutmann) *The Early Books of Yehuda Amichai,* Sheep Meadow Press (Riverdale, NY), 1988.

Essential Shakespeare, Ecco Press (New York, NY), 1991.

Shakespeare and the Goddess of Complete Being, Farrar, Straus (New York, NY), 1992.

Winter Pollen: Occasional Prose (essays), edited by William Scammell, Faber and Faber (London, England), 1994, Picador USA (New York, NY), 1995.

The Dreamfighter, and Other Creation Tales (stories), Faber and Faber (London, England), 1995.

Difficulties of a Bridegroom: Collected Short Stories, Picador (New York, NY), 1995.

(Translator) Ovid, *Tales from Ovid,* Farrar, Straus (New York, NY), 1997.

(Translator) Aeschylus, *The Oresteia,* Farrar, Straus (New York, NY), 1999.

(Translator) Jean Racine, *Phèdre,* Farrar, Straus (New York, NY), 1999.

(Translator) Euripides, *Alcestis,* Farrar, Straus (New York, NY), 1999.

Contributor to numerous anthologies, including *Writers on Themselves,* BBC Publications, 1964. Contributor to periodicals, including *New Yorker, New York Review of Books,* and *Spectator.* Founding editor (with Daniel Weissbrot), *Modern Poetry in Translation,* 1964-71.

Hughes' papers are contained in a collection at Emory University.

ADAPTATIONS: The Iron Giant: A Story in Five Nights was adapted for film, 1999.

SIDELIGHTS: British author Ted Hughes's reputation as a poet of international stature was secured in the late 1950s with the publication of his first poetry collection, *The Hawk in the Rain.* According to *Dictionary of Literary Biography* contributor Robert B. Shaw, "Hughes's poetry signaled a dramatic departure from the prevailing modes of the period. The stereotypical poem of the time was determined not to risk too much: politely domestic in its subject matter, understated and mildly ironic in style. By contrast, Hughes marshaled a language of nearly Shakespearean resonance to explore themes which were mythic and elemental." Since that time, Hughes's poetry has fallen in and out of fashion with literary critics—he was excluded, for example, from an important anthology of British poetry published in the early 1980s—but his presence continued to be felt even after his death. Many critics point to his poetic works *Moortown* and *River* as marking a return to his former brilliance. His 1984 appointment as poet laureate of England assured Hughes's status as a major British poet of the twentieth century.

Usually written contrary to the prevailing style, Hughes's work has always been controversial. "Critics rarely harbor neutral feelings toward Hughes's poetry," observed Carol Bere in *Literary Review.* "He has been dismissed as a connoisseur of the habits of animals, his disgust with humanity barely disguised; labeled a 'voyeur of violence,' attacked for his generous choreographing of gore; and virtually written off as a cult poet. . . . Others admire him for the originality and command of his approach; the scope and complexity of his mythic enterprise; and the apparent ease and freshness with which he can vitalize a landscape, free of any mitigating sentimentality."

To read Hughes's poetry is to enter a world dominated by nature, especially by animals. This holds true for nearly all of his books, from *The Hawk in the Rain* to *Moortown,* an examination of life on a farm. Apparently, Hughes's love of animals was one of the catalysts in his decision to become a poet. According to London *Times* contributor Thomas Nye, Hughes once confessed "that he began writing poems in adolescence, when it dawned upon him that his earlier passion for hunting animals in his native Yorkshire ended either in the possession of a dead animal, or at best a trapped one. He wanted to capture not just live animals, but the aliveness of animals in their natural state: their wildness, their quiddity, the fox-ness of the fox and the crow-ness of the crow."

Hughes's apparent obsession with animals and nature in his poetry has incurred the disapproval of some critics. In *The Modern Poet: Essays from "The Review,"* Colin Falck wrote that the "real limitation of Hughes's animal poems is precisely that they conjure emotions without bringing us any nearer to understanding them. They borrow their impact from a complex of emotions that they do nothing to define, and in the end tell us nothing about the urban civilised human world that we read the poems in." Other commentators, however, saw Hughes's concentration on animals as his attempt to clarify his feelings on the human condition. "Stated in the broadest possible terms," noted Shaw, "Hughes's enterprise is to examine the isolated and precarious position of man in nature and man's chances of overcoming his alienation from the world around him. In pursuit of these interests Hughes focuses frequently (and often brilliantly) upon animals."

According to P.R. King in *Nine Contemporary Poets: A Critical Introduction,* Hughes's emphasis on wild creatures was not so much evidence of his concern for them as it was a clue to the importance the poet reserves for what animals symbolize in his work. Through animal imagery, Hughes exalted the instinctive power of nature that he found lacking in human society. "He sees in

them," King wrote, "the most clear manifestation of a life-force that is distinctly non-human or, rather, is non-rational in its source of power. Hughes observes in modern man a reluctance to acknowledge the deepest, instinctual sources of energy in his own being, an energy that is related to the elemental power circuit of the universe and to which animals are closer than man." King believed that Hughes's poetry written since 1970 "has moved on to express a sense of sterility and nihilism in modern man's response to life, a response which he connects with the dominance of man's rational, objective intellect at the expense of the life of emotions and imagination."

Hughes's best-known and most intriguing creation is an animal named Crow, who began appearing in his work in 1967 and eventually came to be the main character in several volumes of poetry, including *A Crow Hymn, Crow: From the Life and Songs of the Crow,* and *Crow Wakes.* In a *Time* review, Christopher Porterfield observed, "Crow is a sort of cosmic Kilroy. Alternately a witness, a demon, and a victim, he is in on everything from the creation to the ultimate nuclear holocaust. At various times he is minced, dismembered, rendered cataleptic, but always he bobs back. In his graceless, ignoble way, he is the lowest common denominator of the universal forces that obsess Hughes. He is a symbol of the essential survivor, of whatever endures, however battered." In *Ted Hughes,* Keith Sagar commented that in Crow he finds an "Everyman who will not acknowledge that everything he most hates and fears—the Black Beast—is within himself. Crow's world is unredeemable." *Newsweek*'s Jack Kroll called *Crow* "one of those rare books of poetry that have the public impact of a major novel or a piece of super-journalism," and summarized the effect of the character, noting that "in *Crow,* Ted Hughes has created one of the most powerful mythic presences in contemporary poetry."

Reviewers such as Richard Murphy and Sandra McPherson found Hughes at his best when he adhered to describing the natural world around him. In his *New York Review of Books* essay on the author, Murphy noted approvingly that in the progression of Hughes's career, "demons and mythical birds rightly give way to the real creatures of his imagination." In like fashion, in *American Poetry Review* McPherson found that "when Hughes leaves for the country and helps a halfborn calf in delivery and gets his boots muddy, he gives us rich energized poetry."

In a *Los Angeles Times Book Review* critique of *Moortown,* Peter Clothier noted, "The strength of the book is in the first group of raw poems, the 'Moortown' of the title." "The weight and power of the book come in the title sequence," observed *Times Literary Supplement* contributor Peter Scupham. Christopher Ricks in *New York Times Book Review* stated, "'Moortown' strikes me as one of [Hughes's] truest achievements in a very long time."

Moortown is a group of thirty-four poems that records Hughes's experiences working his Devonshire farm and culminates in a set of six pieces dedicated to the memory of his late father-in-law, Jack Orchard, who helped him run the farm. Filled with images of sheep and births of lambs and calves, the poems reveal Hughes as a tender observer of nature. The gentle, loving quality noted by critics gives way at times to brutal descriptions of the harsh realities of farm life. In one poem, for instance, Hughes describes a newborn lamb and its mother lying on the ground "face to face like two mortally wounded duelists." While Joseph Parisi noted in *Chicago Tribune Book World* that these poems show Hughes "at the height of his powers," McPherson explained that their strength comes from Hughes's respect for and intimate knowledge of his subject matter. "Hughes has to write out of love to make the most of his gifts," McPherson maintained. "His poems which grow from close contact with their subject have the real healing effect and are as healthy a poetry as is being written today."

Noting that four volumes of Hughes's poetry and three critical studies of his work appeared in the early 1980s, Murphy began a review of several of Hughes's poetical offerings with the proclamation, "Hughes is surviving." Hughes's survival as a poet seemed to rest on what McClatchy called his "capacity to change." Critics saw his works published during this period as turning points in his career, marking the author with a new sensibility that made him more that just an "animal poet." He used animals to express his insight into the enduring spirituality of nature. "Hughes' reputation rests on his very individual vision of the natural world," wrote *Listener* contributor Dick Davis. "He is popular for this very reason—he brings back to our suburban, centrally heated and, above all, *safe* lives reports from an authentic frontier of reality and the imagination. His poems speak to us of a world that is constantly true in a way that we know our temporary comforts cannot be."

Hughes was named poet laureate of England after the death of John Betjeman in 1984. Some of the poems he wrote thereafter are collected in *Rain-Charm for the Duchy and Other Laureate Poems.* Hilary Corke, writing in *Spectator,* commented that Hughes, who "had built his whole career on giving God's creation a thoroughly bad press," took on the laureateship "entirely seriously and energetically. This is the most traditional and royal-devoted laureate we have had for ages." "Where once a Hughes baby, or rather a giant windy abstract of a baby," Corke continued, "would be born to a giant windy abstract of a mother in a welter of ripping caverns, thrashing thighs, afterbirths, blood and all bodily juices, now we hear that 'Six Angels came, six bright Blessings / Hover above your fate.'" Corke concluded, "It is all very weird and wonderful." London *Observer* critic Andrew Motion wrote that "part of the purpose of these poems is to set aside the question 'Who they are about' and ask instead: 'What are they about?' The answer is the primitive idea of nationhood, and the national voice in poetry that Larkin identified. In every case and at nearly every opportunity, Hughes ignores all matters to do with individual character and goes instead for symbolic value." The poems, Motion concluded, "realise monarchy in terms of its natural kingdom. Instead of a family's voice, attitudes, and opinions we get a country's birds, beasts, and flowers."

Winter Pollen: Occasional Prose collects previously published reviews, prefaces, introductions, and other essays that covered a wide range of literary figures and issues. From discussions of the works of Thomas Wyatt, Laura Riding, Samuel Taylor Coleridge, T.S. Eliot, and his late wife Sylvia Plath, to reviews of Wilfred Owen, Isaac Bashevis Singer, and the drawings of Leonard Baskin, Hughes includes in his commentary enough aspects of his personal life that Peter Levi of *Spectator* wrote that there "are nearly all the essential pieces of an autobiography . . . scattered among the thirty years of essays in this book." Penelope Laurans wrote in *New York Times Book Review* that, "while [Hughes] sometimes seems disingenuous in his attempt to write in a disinterested way, at other times he succeeds in being so interesting and illuminating that nothing else seems to matter."

Hughes's *New and Selected Poems, 1957-1994* is an expanded edition of a 1982 work. Most critics felt that the best works in the book are those in which Hughes focused on nature, writing with, as a critic in the London *Observer* put it, "the unselfconscious power of witness." As has been said of his entire poetic oeuvre, the poems in which the metaphors are closely and organically related to a thing in nature are generally considered more successful than those manifestly about people.

Hughes was the author of a number of well-received translations, among them *Tales from Ovid. New York Times Book Review* contributor James Shapiro called

Hughes "well suited to his task. . . . For Hughes, poets whose work is enduring, like Ovid's, are particularly sensitive to the plate tectonics of historical change, especially the collision between a culture's skeptical, desacralizing impulses and the spiritual nature it would suppress or deny. Hughes's retelling of Ovid's 'Bacchus and Pentheus,' one of the most unnerving stories in *Tales from Ovid,* turns on just such a collision." Hughes selected for inclusion twenty-four of the more than 200 tales of *The Metamorphoses,* Shapiro noting that he discarded stories of marital devotion and homosexual love. In the first half Hughes concentrates on stories, said Shapiro, "that focus with great intensity on heterosexual desire, violence and transgression. Ovid's stories of seduction, incest, infanticide, rape, transsexuality, and the instability of identity speak directly to contemporary obsessions. . . . The second half . . . is dominated by the fate of those, like Pentheus, who refuse to accept the power of nature and the gods who personify it." Shapiro concluded that "this book brilliantly succeeds at bringing Ovid's passionate and disturbing stories to life." In reviewing *The Oresteia* in *New York Times Book Review,* Gary Wills wrote that "Aeschylus, the fifth-century B.C. Attic tragedian, is famous for his knottiness, his clotted images and riddling compound words. Ted Hughes . . . unties the knots and unpacks the compounded thoughts."

Although Hughes was considered one of the finest poets of the twentieth century, his poetic reputation was overshadowed by his marriage to fellow-poet Sylvia Plath, several of whose volumes of poetry he edited following her 1963 suicide. Hughes was also the executor of Plath's estate, and it was in the fulfillment of this post that he drew the ire of many in the literary community whose requests to quote from his late wife's works he rejected, and because he destroyed her final diary.

In the decade after her death, Plath was taken up by some as a symbol of suppressed female genius, and in this scenario Hughes was often cast as the villain. It did not help his case that the married woman for whom he left Plath killed herself and the daughter she had by Hughes in the same manner as had Plath. Subsequently, his readings were disrupted by cries of "murderer!" and his surname, which appears on Plath's gravestone, was repeatedly defaced. Hughes's unpopular decisions regarding Plath's writings, over which he had total control after her death, were often in service of his definition of privacy; he also refused to discuss his marriage to Plath following her death. Thus it was with great surprise that, in 1998, the literary world received Hughes's quite intimate portrait of Plath in the form of *The Birth-*

day Letters, a collection of prose poems covering every aspect of his relationship with his first wife.

As a reviewer for *Economist* noted: "Those who had been expecting a kiss-and-tell about Plath were disappointed. Restrained, oblique, symbolic, tender, by turns ghoulish and melodramatic, 'The Birthday Letters' draws a portrait of a young woman whose life, from first to last, seems to be engulfed by death." Katha Pollitt wrote in *New York Times Book Review* that Hughes's tone, "emotional, direct, regretful, entranced—pervades the book's strongest poems, which are quiet and thoughtful and conversational. Plath is always 'you'—as though an old man were leafing through an album with a ghost." Hughes wrote of the births of their children, their house in Devon, and other intimate memories in these poems. "The trouble is," said Pollitt, "if you added them all up, you'd have a twenty-page chapbook, instead of a volume of nearly 200 pages in which that intimate voice, insisting on its personal truth, is overwhelmed by others: ranting, self-justifying, rambling, flaccid, bombastic. . . . The more Hughes insists on his own good intentions and the inevitability of Plath's suicide, the less convincing he becomes."

Pollitt pointed out that some of the poems in *The Birthday Letters* have appeared in previous Hughes collections, and felt that although it is claimed that the eighty-eight poems were secretly written over twenty-five years, this is "an exaggeration: except for a handful in slant-rhymed quatrains, the poems are identical in style and perspective." Pollitt noted that in *The Birthday Letters* Hughes borrows from Plath's poems, and "frequently employs Plathian language. . . . But Plath's poetry is one of intense compression and musicality, its imagery complex and ambiguous, whereas *The Birthday Letters* is lax and digressive, the symbolism all on the surface, so these allusions, quotations, and re-renderings serve mostly to remind us of what a great poet she was."

Hughes died of cancer on October 28, 1998, in Devon, England. When *Collected Poems* was published in 2003 in celebration of his achievements, a reviewer for *Economist* called Hughes the "most important English poet of the post-war era." The book is the largest collection of poems in living memory, even though all his children's poems, translations, and verse dramas were not included. It does include, however, the controversial "The Birthday Letters" and a large number of previously uncollected poems—some reprinted for the first time—and spans four decades of his works. Donna Seaman, writing for *Booklist,* commented: "Hughes remains a controversial and compelling figure, one deserving of the serious attention this mammoth first collected edition of his poems demands."

BIOGRAPHICAL AND CRITICAL SOURCES:

BOOKS

Children's Literature Review, Volume 3, Thomson Gale (Detroit, MI), 1978.

Contemporary Literary Criticism, Thomson Gale (Detroit, MI), Volume 2, 1974, Volume 4, 1975, Volume 9, 1978, Volume 14, 1980, Volume 37, 1986.

Dictionary of Literary Biography, Thomson Gale (Detroit, MI), Volume 40: *Poets of Great Britain and Ireland since 1960, Part 1,* 1985, Volume 161: *British Children's Writers since 1960, First Series,* 1996.

Faas, Ekbert, *Ted Hughes: The Unaccommodated Universe,* Black Sparrow Press (Santa Barbara, CA), 1980.

Gifford, Terry, and Neil Roberts, *Ted Hughes: A Critical Study,* Faber and Faber (London, England), 1981.

Hamilton, Ian, editor, *The Modern Poet: Essays from "The Review,"* MacDonald (London, England), 1968.

King, P. R., *Nine Contemporary Poets: A Critical Introduction,* Methuen (London, England), 1979.

Malcolm, Janet, *The Silent Woman: Sylvia Plath & Ted Hughes,* Knopf (New York, NY), 1994.

Myers, Lucas, *Crow Steered/Bergs Appeared: A Memoir of Ted Hughes and Sylvia Plath,* Proctor's Hall Press (Sewanee, TN), 2001.

Newsmakers, 1999, Issue 2, Thomson Gale (Detroit, MI), 1999.

Sagar, Keith, *Ted Hughes,* Longman (London, England), 1972, enlarged as *The Art of Ted Hughes,* Cambridge University Press (Cambridge, England), 1978.

Sagar, Keith, *The Achievement of Ted Hughes,* Manchester University Press (Manchester, England), 1983.

Sagar, Keith, *The Challenge of Ted Hughes,* St. Martin's Press (New York, NY), 1994.

St. James Guide to Young Adult Writers, 2nd edition, St. James Press (Detroit, MI), 1999.

Tennant, Emma, *Sylvia and Ted,* Henry Holt (New York, NY), 2001.

PERIODICALS

Agenda, winter, 1994.

American Poetry Review, January-February, 1982; September, 1998, review of *The Birthday Letters,* p. 11.

Antioch Review, winter, 1999, review of *The Birthday Letters,* p. 117.

Booklist, February 15, 1998, review of *The Birthday Letters,* p. 946; March 15, 1999, review of *Tales from Ovid,* p. 1295; June 1, 1999, review of *The Oresteia,* p. 1770; November 15, 2003, Donna Seaman, review of *Collected Poems,* p. 565.

Bulletin of the Center for Children's Books, October, 1995.

Chicago Tribune, October 30, 1998, sec. 1, p. 13.

Chicago Tribune Book World, February 22, 1981, Joseph Parisi, review of *Moortown.*

Christian Science Monitor, March 11, 1998, review of *The Birthday Letters,* p. 14.

Commonweal, November 6, 1992.

Economist (U.S.), November 8, 2003, review of *Collected Poems,* p. 83.

Guardian (London, England), October 30, 1998, Katharine Viner and others, "Beneath the Passion, a Life Plagued by Demons," p. 4.

Independent, October 30, 1998, Boyd Tonkin, "The God of Granite Who Could Shatter Stones with Plain Words," p. 3, Lachlan Mackinnon, "Ted Hughes," p. 6.

Library Journal, May 15, 1993; February 15, 1998, review of *The Birthday Letters,* p. 145; review of *The Oresteia,* p. 110; June 1, 1999; December 2003, Ted Muratori, review of *Collected Poems,* p. 125.

Listener, January 12, 1984.

Literary Review, spring, 1981.

London Review of Books, February 19, 1998, review of *The Birthday Letters,* p. 8.

Los Angeles Times Book Review, August 10, 1980, Peter Clothier, review of *Moortown;* March 15, 1998, review of *The Birthday Letters,* p. 7.

Nation, April 20, 1998, review of *The Birthday Letters,* p. 25.

New England Review, fall, 1998, review of *The Birthday Letters,* p. 154.

New Republic, September 3, 1984; June 6, 1994, p. 34; March 30, 1998, review of *The Birthday Letters,* p. 30.

New Statesman, January 4, 1980.

New Statesman and Society, April 17, 1992; April 14, 1995, p. 45; January 30, 1998, review of *The Birthday Letters,* p. 45.

Newsweek, April 12, 1971, Jack Kroll, review of *Crow: From the Life and Songs of the Crow.*

New Yorker, August 23, 1993.

New York Review of Books, June 10, 1982; March 5, 1998, review of *The Birthday Letters,* p. 7.

New York Times Book Review, July 20, 1980, Christopher Ricks, review of *Moortown,* p. 13; April 21, 1991, William Logan, review of *Wolfwatching,* p. 22; January 7, 1996, Penelope Laurans, review of *Winter Pollen: Occasional Prose,* p. 21; October 13, 1996, Andy Solomon, review of *Difficulties of a Bridegroom: Collected Short Stories;* December 14, 1997, James Shapiro, "Sex and Violence in Latin Hexameter;" February 13, 1998, Michiko Kakutani, "A Portrait of Plath in Poetry for Its Own Sake," p. 43; March 1, 1998, Katha Pollitt, "Peering into the Bell Jar," p. 4; March 15, 1998, Carol Muske, review of *The Birthday Letters,* p. 5; May 31, 1998, review of *Tales from Ovid,* p. 24; January 24, 1999, Eavan Boland, "Ted Hughes: A Reconciliation," p. 31; September 5, 1999, Garry Wills, "After the Trojan Horse," p. 10.

Observer (London, England), June 14, 1992; March 5, 1995; February 1, 1998, review of *The Birthday Letters,* p. 15; December 6, 1998, review of *The Birthday Letters,* p. 15; May 2, 1999, review of *The Birthday Letters,* p. 14; May 15, 2001, Vanessa Thorpe, "Secret Passions of a Poet Laureate," p. 4.

Poetry, June, 1998, review of *The Birthday Letters* and *Tales from Ovid,* p. 154.

Publishers Weekly, July 17, 1995, p. 230; August 21, 1995, p. 56; February 2, 1998, review of *The Birthday Letters,* p. 75; May 31, 1999, review of *The Oresteia,* p. 89.

Quill and Quire, February, 1994, p. 40.

School Librarian, November, 1991, p. 144; August, 1993, p. 108; February, 1996, p. 28.

Sewanee Review, July, 1998, review of *Winter Pollen,* p. 69.

Spectator, June 20, 1992; March 12, 1994; March 18, 1995; January 31, 1998, review of *The Birthday Letters,* p. 42.

Time, April 5, 1971, Christopher Porterfield; February 16, 1998, review of *The Birthday Letters,* p. 101.

Times (London, England), January 8, 1987, April 8, 2000, James Bone, "Hughes Papers Reveal Devotion to Plath," p. 10; April 10, 2000, James Bone, "Plath Owed Her Success to Me, Says Hughes," p. 5, Erica Wagner, "At Last, Justice for Hughes," p. S6; May 15, 2001, Erica Wagner, "The Poet as Rock God," p. S2; October 30, 1998, Peter Stothard, "The Poet Laureate's Last Reading," p. 24.

Times Educational Supplement, January 30, 1998, review of *The Birthday Letters,* p. 12.

Times Literary Supplement, January 4, 1980; April 17, 1992; May 6, 1994; November 17, 1995; February 6, 1998, review of *The Birthday Letters,* p. 3; December 4, 1998, review of *The Birthday Letters.*

USA Today, October 29, 1998.

Washington Post Book World, November 22, 1992, Gary Taylor; March 8, 1998, Linda Pastan, "Scenes from a Marriage," p. 5; March 15, 1998, review of *Difficulties of a Bridegroom,* p. 12.

Women's Review of Books, June, 1998, review of *The Birthday Letters,* p. 8.

World Literature Today, spring, 1998, review of *Tales from Ovid,* p. 379; summer, 1998, review of *The Birthday Letters,* p. 621.

ONLINE

Academy of American Poets Web site, http://www.poets. org/ (April 12, 2004), "Ted Hughes."

OBITUARIES:

PERIODICALS

Los Angeles Times, October 30, 1998, pp. A1, A12.
New York Times, October 30, 1998, p. A1.
Washington Post, October 30, 1998, p. B6.

*   *   *

HUMES, Edward

PERSONAL: Born in Philadelphia, PA; married; children: one daughter. *Education:* Graduate of Hampshire College.

ADDRESSES: Home—Southern California. *Agent*—c/o Author Mail, Harcourt International, 6277 Sea Harbor Dr., Orlando, FL 32887. *E-mail*—contact@edward humes.com.

CAREER: Journalist and author. Reporter for *Texas Observer* magazine, *Pine Bluff Commercial, Tucson Citizen,* and *Orange County Register;* full-time author, 1989—. Consultant for CBS News' *Sixty Minutes;* columnist for *Buzz* magazine; writer-at-large for *Los Angeles Magazine,* beginning 2002.

AWARDS, HONORS: Pulitzer Prize for beat reporting, 1989; Best Book of the Year designation, Investigative Reporters and Editors of America, 1996, for *No Matter How Loud I Shout: A Year in the Life of Juvenile Court;* PEN Center USA Award for Nonfiction, 1997; best book designation, *Los Angeles Times,* and Edgar

Allan Poe Award nomination for nonfiction, Mystery Writers of America, both 1999, both for *Mean Justice: A Town's Terror, a Prosecutor's Power, a Betrayal of Innocence;* Edgar Allan Poe finalist for *Mississippi Mud: A True Story from a Corner of the Deep South;* journalism awards from Overseas Press Club, Associated Press Managing Editors, and California Newspaper Publishers Association.

WRITINGS:

Buried Secrets: A True Story of Serial Murder, Black Magic, and Drug-running on the U.S. Border, Dutton (New York, NY), 1991.
Good Cop, Bad Cop, 1992.
Murderer with a Badge: The Secret Life of a Rogue Cop, Dutton (New York, NY), 1992.
Mississippi Mud: A True Story from a Corner of the Deep South, Simon & Schuster (New York, NY), 1994.
No Matter How Loud I Shout: A Year in the Life of Juvenile Court, Simon & Schuster (New York, NY), 1996.
Mean Justice: A Town's Terror, a Prosecutor's Power, a Betrayal of Innocence, Simon & Schuster (New York, NY), 1999.
Baby ER: The Heroic Doctors and Nurses Who Perform Medicine's Tiniest Miracles, Simon & Schuster (New York, NY), 2000.
School of Dreams: Making the Grade at a Top American High School, Harcourt (Orlando, FL), 2003.

Contributor to periodicals, including *Los Angeles Times Sunday Magazine, Glamour, Los Angeles Magazine, Readers Digest, Oxford American,* and *California Lawyer.*

SIDELIGHTS: Pulitzer Prize-winning journalist and prize-winning author Edward Humes knew at the age of six he wanted to be a writer, and he has been writing ever since. Humes began his journalism career immediately out of college with the *Texas Observer* magazine, then, for the next ten years worked as a reporter for the *Pine Bluff Commercial* in Arkansas, for the *Tucson Citizen* in Arizona, and later for California's *Orange County Register.* "As a newspaper reporter, I gravitated toward stories that allowed me to dig behind the scenes and beneath the surface, looking for questions others hadn't asked or imagined," Humes noted on his Web site. "For me, the job amounted to this: license to find out the things I had always wanted to know, about anything and everything that interested, touched or outraged me."

When he left journalism to devote his time to writing nonfiction books, the time constraints of daily reporting were lifted; Humes suddenly found that instead of hours or days to construct a story, he had months and even years "to immerse myself in the inner workings of the places, characters and events I seek to understand and write about. I had found the greatest job I can imagine" he commented on his Web site.

Humes's books focus on true crime and narrative nonfiction. In the first genre, he takes a close look at and provides revealing exposés of ritualistic murders committed by a black-magic cult in *Buried Secrets: A True Story of Serial Murder, Black Magic, and Drug-Running on the U.S. Border;* uncovers the secret life of an otherwise mild-mannered traffic officer who arranged three contract killings in *Murderer with a Badge: The Secret Life of a Rogue Cop;* and delves into the mystery surrounding the shooting deaths of a leading couple in Biloxi, Mississippi in *Mississippi Mud: A True Story from a Corner of the Deep South.*

Mississippi Mud follows the quest of a murdered couple's adult daughter to investigate the circumstances of her parents' death. Living in a city described by a *Kirkus Reviews* critic as one "of both graceful antebellum mansions and a sleazy zone of strip joints, whorehouses, casinos and drug dens," Vince and Margaret Sherry—he was a circuit-court judge, she an anticorruption mayoral candidate—tangled with the so-called Dixie Mafia and both received death threats. In September of 1987 the couple was discovered shot to death in their home, but while overwhelming evidence indicated a mafia hit, Biloxi police "pursued the bizarre theory that the Sherry's son Eric had murdered his parents in a rage after discovering that he was adopted," according to the *Kirkus* critic. In detailing the events leading to the murders, Humes "wisely focused on [daughter Lynne Sherry Sposito's] tenacious refusal to let the investigation sink beneath the muddy swirl of graft," wrote *New York Times Book Review* contributor Margaret Maron. Maron went on to commend Humes for "lucid and unadorned prose" that "admirably suits this complex story of venality and betrayal."

In *No Matter How Loud I Shout: A Year in the Life of Juvenile Court* Humes stages an investigation into the juvenile justice system in Los Angeles, California, "which is about a step away from collapsing," observed *Washington Monthly* writer Patricia Cohen. Following a three-year study during which he also taught writing classes at a local juvenile hall, Humes profiled the cases of five children arrested for crimes ranging from gang warfare to murder. One subject, a fifteen-year-old from a middle-class home, shot and killed his employers for pocket money. He was arrested, but because the boy was nine days short of his sixteenth birthday, the longest sentence he could receive was eight years: "he will be set free at [age] twenty-five no matter what," Cohen pointed out. But another youth, age sixteen when he was forced to act as accomplice during a botched robbery, could have faced life in prison with no parole, even though he did not fire a gun.

Cohen described the characters in *No Matter How Loud I Shout* as reminiscent of those in a Michael Crichton thriller—from the dedicated prosecutor to the streetwise probation officer—while the "supporting cast is rounded out by an army of incompetent and insensitive bureaucrats, lawyers, and judges working in an underfunded and overwhelmed system." *Booklist* reviewer Kathleen Hughes noted that "the kids and their stories are both horrifying and pitiful," and cited the author's "unique insider's view" as a factor in the creation of "an important book with a message of great urgency."

Mean Justice: A Town's Terror, a Prosecutor's Power, a Betrayal of Innocence shows what happens when a city's quest for "justice served" contradicts the facts of the case. In Bakersfield, California, Patrick Dunn was arrested on suspicion of the murder of his wife, Sandy. The city of Bakersfield, Humes points out, has a history of collaring innocent people to stand trial in high-profile cases. In the Dunn case, the county sheriff and the district attorney "built a flimsy case . . . , ultimately concocting false information" to obtain a convictin, noted Michael Sawyer in *Library Journal. Mean Justice,* Sawyer continued, "hammers home the difficulty of proving one's innocence after being wrongly convicted." To *Booklist* critic David Pitt, the book demonstrates "miscarriages of justice so astonishing . . . readers might be inclined not to believe it if [the author] didn't document everything so carefully."

In *Baby ER: The Heroic Doctors and Nurses Who Perform Medicine's Tiniest Miracles* Humes writes about the year he spent visiting the neonatal intensive care unit (NICU) at Miller Children's Hospital in Long Beach, California. During this time, he observed eleven critically ill premature babies, seven who lived. Humes also writes from personal experience: his own daughter spent time in an NICU after developing a serious kidney infection. In his book, which a reviewer for *Newsweek* called "a moving account of life—and death— among the tiniest patients", Humes details the dedication and skill of the doctors and of the nurses in caring for these babies. He describes the relationships between parents and health professionals, technological advances that allow the doctors to perform complicated surgery on many of the babies, as well as the reasons for the rise in premature births.

Humes spent all of 2001 in Cerritos, California, at Whitney High School, one of the nation's most successful high schools, where the doors are open seven days a week, where drugs and discipline issues are relatively uncommon and taken very seriously, and where students consume copious amounts of caffeine so they can work virtually around the clock. While assisting seniors with college application essays, Humes immersed himself in the school's culture and subsequently wrote of his findings in *School of Dreams: Making the Grade at a Top American High School.* In this book, which a *Publishers Weekly* reviewer called a "well-written, informative study," Humes examines, among other aspects, what makes the school so sought after; families move to Cerritos from all over the world simply so their children have an opportunity attend Whitney. He also looks at the trade-offs involved in achieving such phenomenal academic standards and the price Whitney's students sometimes pay in the process. On his Web site, Humes notes that the students' greatest fear is "not living up to their families' stratospheric expectations," yet he finds Whitney High an "extraordinary community" with dedicated educators and students alike. He believes their experiences have much to teach the nation about what does and does not work in public education.

George Scott, reviewing the book for *Education News.-org,* commented that "Whitney High School is about superlative performance on The College Board's advanced placement testing program. . . . it is about producing students ready to compete in a global environment with the world's best students." Calling Humes' study "profound," Scott added that the author "extrapolates a simple behind-the-scenes concept of a storyteller describing an interesting place and interesting people into an extraordinarily layered focus on a full range of issues confronting America's public education system."

BIOGRAPHICAL AND CRITICAL SOURCES:

PERIODICALS

Booklist, March 15, 1996, Kathleen Hughes, review of *No Matter How Loud I Shout: A Year in the Life of Juvenile Court,* p. 1224; February 1, 1999, David

Pitt, review of *Mean Justice: A Town's Terror, a Prosecutor's Power, a Betrayal of Innocence*, p. 948; November 15, 2000, William Beatty, review of *Baby ER: The Heroic Doctors and Nurses Who Perform Medicine's Tiniest Miracles*, p. 597.

Economist, May 18, 1996, review of *No Matter How Loud I Shout*, p. S3.

Kirkus Reviews, January 1, 1996.

Library Journal, February 1, 1999, Michael Sawyer, review of *Mean Justice*, p. 108.

Los Angeles Times Book Review, April 28, 1991.

Newsweek, November 27, 2000, review of *Baby ER*, p. 84.

New York Times Book Review, February 7, 1993, Dennis J. Carroll, review of *Murder with a Badge: The Secret Life of a Rogue Cop*, p. 22; October 16, 1994, Margaret Maron, review of *Mississippi Mud: A True Story from a Corner of the Deep South*, p. 21; May 9, 1999, Laura Mansnerus, review of *Mean Justice*, p. 41; December 10, 2000, Frank T. Vertosick, Jr., review of *Baby ER*, p. 28.

Publishers Weekly, December 14, 1990, Genevieve Stuttaford, review of *Buried Secrets: A True Story of Serial Murder, Black Magic, and Drug-running on the U.S. Border*, p. 57; July 11, 1994, review of *Mississippi Mud*, p. 70; October 16, 2000, review of *Baby ER*, p. 60.

Washington Monthly, March, 1996, Patricia Cohen, review of *No Matter How Loud I Shout*, p. 58.

Washington Post Book World, February 17, 1999, p. 11.

ONLINE

EducationNews.org Web site, http://www.education news.org/ (August 27, 2003), review of *School of Dreams*.

Edward Humes Web site, http://www.edwardhumes. com/ (August 4, 2004).

*   *   *

HWANG, David Henry 1957-

PERSONAL: Surname pronounced "Wong"; born August 11, 1957, in Los Angeles, CA; son of Henry Yuan (a banker) and Dorothy Yu (a professor of piano; maiden name, Huang) Hwang; married Ophelia Y.M. Chong (an artist), September 21, 1985 (divorced, October, 1989); married Kathryn A. Layng (an actress), December 17, 1993; children: (second marriage) Noah, Eva. *Ethnicity:* "Asian American" *Education:* Stanford University, B.A., 1979; attended Yale University School of Drama, 1980-81. *Politics:* Democrat. *Hobbies and other interests:* Violin.

ADDRESSES: Home—New York, NY. *Agent*—William Craver, Authors and Artists Agency, 19 West 44th St., Suite 1000, New York, NY 10036; and Tory Metzger, Creative Artists Agency, 9830 Wilshire Blvd., Beverly Hills, CA 90212.

CAREER: Playwright; director of plays, including *A Song for a Nisei Fisherman*, 1980, *The Dream of Kitamura*, 1982, and *F.O.B.*, 1990; Asian American Theatre Center, San Francisco, CA, dramaturg, 1987—. Cofounder, Stanford Asian American Theatre Project; Theatre Communications Group, member of board of directors, 1987—. Menlo-Atherton High School, Menlo Park, CA, teacher of English and writing, 1980. Member of board of directors, President's Committee on the Arts and Humanities, 1994-2001; China Institute, 1993-2002; and Center for Arts and Culture, 1998-2000.

MEMBER: Writers Guild of America, Dramatists Guild (member of board of directors, 1988—), Young Playwrights, Inc., American Civil Liberties Union, PEN (member of board of directors, 1990—), Theatre Communications Group (vice president, 1999—), Phi Beta Kappa.

AWARDS, HONORS: Drama-Logue award, 1980, 1986, 1997; Obie Award for best play, *Village Voice*, 1981, for *F.O.B.*, and for best playwriting, 1997, for *Golden Child;* Drama Desk Award nomination, 1982, for *Family Devotions* and *The Dance and the Railroad;* CINE Golden Eagle, 1983, for television production *The Dance and the Railroad;* Rockefeller playwright-in-residence award and National Endowment for the Arts artistic associate fellowship, 1983-84; Guggenheim fellowship, 1984; National Endowment for the Arts, and New York State Council on the Arts fellowships, both 1985; Antoinette Perry "Tony" Award for best play, Outer Critics Circle Award for best Broadway play, John Gassner Award, and Drama Desk Award, all 1988, and Pulitzer Prize nomination, 1989, all for *M. Butterfly;* Los Angeles Drama Critics Award, 1991; Tony Award nomination for best play, and Outer Critics Circle Award nomination for best Broadway play, both 1998, both for *Golden Child;* Obie Award for playwriting, 1997; Tony Award nomination for Best Book of a Musical, 2003, for *Flower Drum Song;* honorary D.L., Columbia College, 1998.

WRITINGS:

PLAYS

F.O.B. (two-act; title means "Fresh off the Boat"; also see below), produced in Stanford, CA, 1978, produced off-Broadway, 1980.

The Dance and the Railroad (also see below; produced in New York, NY, 1981; produced off-Broadway, 1981), Dramatists Play Service (New York, NY), 1990.

Family Devotions (also see below), produced off-Broadway, 1981.

Sound and Beauty (two one-acts; includes *The House of Sleeping Beauties*, based on a novella by Yasunari Kawabata, and *The Sound of a Voice* [also see below]), produced off-Broadway, 1983.

F.O.B. [and] *The House of Sleeping Beauties*, Dramatists Play Service (New York, NY), 1983.

Broken Promises: Four Plays (contains *F.O.B., The Dance and the Railroad, Family Devotions,* and *The House of Sleeping Beauties*), Avon (New York, NY), 1983.

The Sound of a Voice, Dramatists Play Service (New York, NY), 1984.

Rich Relations (also see below), produced off-Broadway, 1986.

As the Crow Flies, produced in Los Angeles, CA, 1986.

Broken Promises (includes *The Dance and the Railroad* and *The House of Sleeping Beauties*), produced in London, England, 1987.

M. Butterfly (produced in Washington, DC, 1988; produced on Broadway, 1988; also see below), Plume (New York, NY), 1989.

One Thousand Airplanes on the Roof (musical; produced in New York, 1988), music by Philip Glass, Gibbs-Smith, 1989.

F.O.B. and Other Plays (includes *Rich Relations*), Plume (New York, NY), 1990.

The Voyage (opera), music by Philip Glass, produced in New York, NY, 1992.

Bondage (one-act; produced at the Humana Theatre Festival, 1992), in *The Best American Short Plays 1992-93*, Applause Theatre Book (New York, NY), 1993.

Face Value, produced in Boston, MA, 1993.

M. Butterfly (screenplay; based on his play), Warner Bros., 1993.

Golden Gate (screenplay), Samuel Goldwyn, 1994.

Golden Child, produced in New York, NY, 1996, produced on Broadway, 1998.

The Silver River (musical), music by Bright Sheng, produced in Santa Fe, NM, 1998, produced in New York, 2002.

(Adapter) Henrik Ibsen, *Peer Gynt,* produced in Providence, RI, 1998.

Trying to Find Chinatown: The Selected Plays of David Henry Hwang, Theatre Communications Group, 1999.

(Coauthor of book, with Robert Falls and Linda Woolverton) *Aïda* (rock musical), music by Elton John, lyrics by Tim Rice, produced on Broadway, 1999.

(Contributor) *The Square,* produced in New York, NY, 2001.

(Adaptor) *Flower Drum Song* (based on the musical by Oscar Hammerstein II and Richard Rodgers; produced in Los Angeles, CA, 2001; produced on Broadway, 2002), Theatre Communications Group (New York, NY), 2003.

(Adaptor with Neil LaBute) *Possession* (screenplay; based on the novel by A.S. Byatt), Warner Bros., 2002.

The Sound of a Voice (opera), music by Philip Glass, produced in Boston, 2003.

Ainadamar (opera), music by Osvaldo Golijov, produced at Tanglewood Festival, Lenox, MA, 2003.

(Adaptor) *Tibet Through the Red Box* (play; based on the book by Peter Sis), produced in Seattle, WA, 2004.

Also author, with Frederic Kimball, of teleplay *Blind Alleys,* 1985. Plays represented in anthologies, including *Between Worlds: Contemporary Asian-American Plays, New Plays USA 1, Best Plays of 1981-1982, Best Short Plays of 1982,* and *Best Plays of 1987-1988.*

SIDELIGHTS: Enjoying an unusually swift ascent to prominence on the American stage, David Henry Hwang gained widespread praise for his very first play in 1980 and went on to earn a Antoinette Perry—"Tony"—Award and a Pulitzer Prize nomination. Many of Hwang's plays refer to the experiences of Asian immigrants living in the United States and to East-West relations, leading some reviewers to pigeonhole him as an Asian author. Yet he has also written a science-fiction libretto, a cable television program on Middle East/Central American politics, and several non-Asian-themed plays. Hwang's Chinese-American heritage has been both "a minor detail, like having red hair," as he remarked in a *New York Times Magazine* interview, and the inspiration for most of his successful plays. Mingling Chinese influences with those of his birth country and in the process addressing wider concerns of race, gender, and culture, Hwang is "the first U.S. playwright to become an international phenomenon in a generation," according to William A. Henry III, writing in *Time.*

Hwang had just graduated from Stanford University when his first play, *F.O.B.*, was accepted for production at the prestigious National Playwrights Conference at Connecticut's O'Neill Theater Center in 1979; the following year producer Joseph Papp brought the play to New York's off-Broadway circuit where it won an Obie Award as the best new play of the season. First performed at Stanford, the drama focuses on Steve, a young Chinese immigrant "fresh off the boat," and the two Chinese-American students he meets in Los Angeles. The male student scorns Steve, preferring to renounce Steve's Chinese heritage; the woman tries to accommodate both traditions and becomes a pivot between the two men. Wrote Frank Rich in the *New York Times*, "The subject of the evening is a very old one: the price that minorities pay to assimilate in mainstream America. But David Henry Hwang . . . is too rambunctious to tell a familiar story in a tired way." One unusual aspect of *F.O.B.*, Rich noted, is a technical innovation: in the second act Hwang employs Chinese theatrical techniques to present his characters as figures from Chinese mythology. Rich also enjoyed the "comic verve" Hwang displays throughout and, while recognizing some flaws of construction and characterization in the work, asserted that the playwright "hits home far more often than he misses. . . . If West and East don't precisely meet in *F.O.B.*, they certainly fight each other to a fascinating standoff."

Hwang's next two plays, *The Dance and the Railroad* and *Family Devotions*, also focus on Chinese Americans. The first examines two nineteenth-century Chinese men working on the transcontinental railroad; the second looks at a well-established Chinese-American family of the twentieth century. Rich deemed *Railroad* "leaner" and "more accomplished" than *F.O.B.*, though similar to the earlier play in its mixture of American comedy and oriental technique and its interest in immigrant concerns. The play explores the confrontation between Ma, a new arrival to the United States, and Lone, who has been in America for two years. Sold into servitude by his parents after studying Chinese opera, Lone is a cynic who distances himself from the other laborers with daily dance sessions away from camp. Ma persuades Lone to teach him to dance, and during their workouts the two men explore their pasts and share their thoughts on the future. Judging the play "witty, poetic and affecting," Rich described Hwang as "a true original" with a "startling and far-ranging theatrical voice." *Family Devotions* also earned Rich's admiration, though the critic suggested that Hwang loses control of his plot near the play's end. The farcical drama hinges on the conflict between a wealthy, Americanized Chinese family of fanatical born-again Christians and

an austere, atheist uncle from Communist China who comes to visit. Rich and *New Yorker* critic Edith Oliver both judged *Family Devotions* among Hwang's funniest plays.

Departing from the Chinese-American angle, Hwang followed *Family Devotions* with a pair of stylized one-act plays set in Japan and jointly titled *Sound and Beauty*. *The House of Sleeping Beauties* reinvents a novella by Yasunari Kawabata, making Kawabata a character in a variation of his own story about a brothel of comatose virgins wherein elderly men sleep beside the drugged women as a means of accepting their own mortality. In Hwang's version, Kawabata visits the brothel to research a book, but becomes increasingly involved in the place and thoughts of his own mortality despite himself. The second play, *The Sound of a Voice*, pits a samurai warrior against a bewitching female hermit. Thinking she has the power to destroy men, the warrior plans to kill the hermit, but several weeks as her guest in the forest change his heart, with unexpected results. Writing in the *Los Angeles Times*, Dan Sullivan judged *The Sound of a Voice* "a skillfully ordered and beautifully written play" that combines the simplicity and mystery of folk tales with an insightful look at male and female psychology. Rich, reviewing both one-acts in the *New York Times*, found *The Sound of a Voice* flawed by overemphasized symbolism and both plays hobbled by Hwang's "efforts to duplicate the mood of Japanese literature and theater." Even so, admitted Rich, Hwang "is not standing still." The critic deemed *Sound and Beauty* "an earnest, considered experiment furthering an exceptional young writer's process of growth."

Hwang suffered his first critical failure with the 1986 play *Rich Relations*, characterized by Rich as "tired." Although not about Asian Americans, the play includes several elements characteristic of Hwang's earlier works: materialism and wealth, evangelical Christianity, and a family at odds. Noted Jeremy Gerard in the *New York Times Magazine*, "The playwright didn't disagree with the charge" that he was treading familiar ground. "*Rich Relations* was another attempt to write a spiritual farce," Hwang told Gerard. "It's about my family—except that they're not Asians." Ultimately the playwright found the flop liberating. As he related in a *Los Angeles Times* article, "I felt I'd done something I was pleased with and proud of—and everybody spat on it and I was still happy I did it. That gives you tremendous exhilaration, because the next time you want to pursue whatever it is you really want, it's not going to hurt that much if people don't like it."

Hwang bounced back from failure in 1988 with the popular *M. Butterfly*, based on a true story of a French diplomat and his Chinese lover, who turned out to be not only a spy but a man. Debuting in Washington, DC, and quickly moving on to Broadway, the play pleased audiences and many critics, earning a Pulitzer Prize nomination and a Tony Award. Surprised by such success, Hwang told *Los Angeles Times* interviewer Sylvie Drake that some of his play's appeal may derive from its use of Italian and Chinese opera music. Also, he said, "People associate a certain level of exoticism with the East; therefore they'll come to the theater to see this." Hwang decided to give audiences what they expected, "in spades, and at the same time try to subvert it by talking about exactly why it is that audiences are attracted to this material *at the time* that they are being attracted to it."

Hwang's strategy was to exploit parallels between the espionage incident and the Giacomo Puccini opera *Madama Butterfly,* which tells of a Japanese woman who falls in love with an European, is spurned, and commits suicide. In Hwang's play, the diplomat, Gallimard, represents Puccini's Westerner, Pinkerton; Gallimard's Butterfly is Song Liling, a Chinese opera diva/spy in drag who appears to fall in love with Gallimard. To Hwang, explained Rich, "a cultural icon like *Madama Butterfly* bequeaths the sexist and racist roles that burden Western men: Gallimard believes he can become 'a real man' only if he can exercise power over a beautiful and submissive woman, which is why he's so ripe to be duped by Song Liling's impersonation of a shrinking butterfly." Hwang's parallel includes a crucial twist: "At the beginning of the play," he asserted in a *Washington Post* interview, "the Frenchman sees himself as Pinkerton—he's found this beautiful Madame Butterfly in China. And by the end of the play he kind of realizes that it is he, the Frenchman, that has been sacrificed for love, that the spy was actually the Pinkerton who preyed on his love."

M. Butterfly drew both acclaim and criticism. Several reviewers applauded its ambition, richness, and drama, while others found its characterizations and plot twists unbelievable. Contrasting the work with other American plays, Rich observed that "instead of reducing the world to an easily digested cluster of sexual or familial relationships, Mr. Hwang cracks open a liaison to reveal a sweeping, universal meditation on two of the most heated conflicts—men versus women, East versus West—of this or any other time." In another *New York Times* review, however, John Gross judged *M. Butterfly* better as a personal tragedy than a wide-ranging play of ideas: calling it "a mess, intellectually speaking," Gross nonetheless admitted that "at its best it sweeps one up in a tense emotional drama." In the *New Yorker,* Edith

Oliver described the play as "funny, mysterious, and often beautiful" and labeled Hwang the most "audacious, imaginative, [and] gifted" young playwright in America.

Hwang's *Golden Child,* produced at the Joseph Papp Public Theater in 1996 and directed by James Lapine, begins in the back seat of a taxi when Andrew Kwong, a young Chinese American about to become a father, receives a visit from the ghost of his grandmother, Eng Ahn, who urges him to honor his ancestors and his origins. In a clever bit of theatrical sleight-of-hand, Kwong transforms into his grandfather, Eng Tieng-Bin, as Eng Ahn simultaneously becomes the child she once was. Most of the play takes place in a small Chinese village at the turn of the twentieth century. Within this milieu Hwang explores the disruption of feudal traditions as Tieng-Bin returns from abroad to his three wives with new ideas about marriage, education, and religion. Tieng-Bin sees Christianity as a route to a more modern world. His religious conversion has startling effects on the members of his household as each of his three wives struggles to come to terms with his spiritual and social reawakening. Ben Brantley, writing in the *New York Times,* found *Golden Child* less caustic than earlier plays like *Family Devotions,* writing that it "has the evenhandedness of a debate moderator who wants, above all, to be fair." Calling the play "likable, educational and, at times, very poignant," Brantley also added that "it's never able to generate much urgency." On the other hand, David Sterritt noted in the *Christian Science Monitor* that "while *Golden Child* is not likely to cause as much stir as Hwang's controversial *M. Butterfly* did . . . he [still] thoughtfully probes the topics he raises, weaving them into a domestic story that is increasingly melodramatic until enough destructive and self-destructive acts have occurred to match the music from *La Traviata* that provides the play's motifs." Sterritt also noted that the "play's most involving material clusters around issues of what it means to be born again in a spiritual sense . . . and a historical sense, as forward-thinking Chinese people look for ways of entering a new era dominated by Western values."

Hwang captivated stage audiences in 2001 with his updated adaptation of the 1958 Oscar Hammerstein II and Joseph Fields text of *Flower Drum Song.* C.Y. Lee, author of the novel, and the Rodgers and Hammerstein Organization gave Hwang permission to use his full artistic creativity in the reworking of this musical. "My original idea was to show both the cultural conflict and the closeness of the Chinese family. [That's hard to do] on stage, but David managed to simplify it. You really see the relationships and the love between these characters," praised Lee in a *USAToday.com* interview with

Elysa Gardner. In the same interview, Hwang remembered how some Asian Americans—himself included—were offended by certain stereotypes that appeared in the original libretto. He began to rethink his negative opinion after seeing a revival of *The King and I* on Broadway when he realized that "Rodgers and Hammerstein musicals are . . . more complex" than they might seem on first viewing.

In Hwang's adaptation he strengthens the female protagonist, Mei-Li, from a shy, mail-order bride to a feisty young woman fleeing China due to her father's problems with the Maoist regime. He changes the musical's setting to an old-style Chinese opera house in 1960's San Francisco that is run by a man whose son, Ta, transforms it into a Western-style nightclub when no opera is playing. Another alteration by Hwang is that some of the musical pieces appear at different points in the action than they did in the original musical.

The modernization of a classic musical earned a somewhat mixed response from theatre critics. "Hwang has made the show a richer, more nuanced exploration of the immigrant experience," asserted *Time* critic Richard Zoglin of *Flower Drum Song,* adding that "the show works because it doesn't condescend." "While it contains a workable premise and more assertive characters, the new book's themes are both clichéd and not terribly compelling," remarked *Hollywood Reporter* writer Frank Scheck. In a contrasting *Hollywood Reporter* review, Jay Reiner praised Hwang for his ability to revive "a flawed musical" from its "near-dead" status. Reiner admitted, however, that "there is a price to be paid for telling the story in this new way" with the consequence that Mei-Li and Ta's love story "sometimes gets lost in the shuffle and it's not always convincing." Judith Newmark noted in a review for *Knight Ridder/Tribune News Service:* "Hwang emphasizes respect for Chinese artistic tradition while [taking] a lighthearted, romantic look at assimilationist issues." In his *Variety* piece, Steven Oxman noted that Gordon Davidson, artistic director of the Center Theater Group in Los Angeles, felt that "the tension between the old and new is better realized . . . and therefore more affecting and more universal."

Hwang took the mixed critical response in stride. In a *Knight Ridder/Tribune News Service* article by Karen D'Souza he was quoted as saying: "I'm sure there will be extremists on both ends who will never like this project. There will be the Asian Americans who say that *Flower Drum* shouldn't be revived under any circumstances, and there will be the musical theater lovers who will dismiss this as a politically correct exercise. But you can't worry about expectations. You have to just do your work and roll the dice."

In a reflection of his versatility and willingness to overstep traditional boundaries, Hwang exercised his imagination in a different genre with his 1988 science-fiction collaboration with composer Philip Glass and scene designer Jerome Sirlin. Conceived and directed by Glass, *One Thousand Airplanes on the Roof* is a multimedia project in which Hwang's text served as a narrative framework for Glass's music and Sirlin's set and projection images. The play concerns a character who may have been kidnaped by visiting aliens. "She longs to discuss her experience, but knows her tale will be dismissed," explained Allan Kozinn in a *New York Times* review. "To appear sane, she has to deny it happened; but she fears that repressing this momentous experience will drive her crazy." The character's confusion and distress are illumined by ever-changing images of cities, grids, and stars projected on the set by Sirlin, whose work, according to *Washington Post* contributor Pamela Sommers, "steals the show." Sommers criticized Hwang's narrative as uneven, summarizing the evening as "intermittently compelling and disappointing . . . intriguing if perplexing." Kozinn, however, praised Hwang for his "rich, gripping monologue."

In another break from traditional theatre, in 1999 Hwang turned his considerable talents toward writing the book for the Disney-produced rock musical *Aïda,* in collaboration with Robert Falls and Linda Woolverton. With new music by Elton John and Tim Rice, the multi-award-winning musical retells the love story of Radames and Aïda. "Falls and Hwang have accented some universal resonance in the tale which gives the show necessary weight," wrote *Variety* reviewer Chris Jones of the 2000 Broadway production.

Moving from stage to screen, Hwang joined forces with Neil LaBute and Laura Jones to adapt *Possession,* a novel by A.S. Byatt that was awarded the Booker Prize, into a film. The storyline focuses upon romances occurring in parallel times and worlds: the Victorian Era and the present day. Two modern academics (portrayed by Aaron Eckhart and Gwyneth Paltrow) strive together to find a connection between the romantic lives of two Victorian poets, as unlikely as that connection might seem at first glance. *Possession* is a "witty, literate . . . mesmerizing . . . [and] devilishly clever screenplay," said Kirk Honeycutt in a *Hollywood Reporter* review.

"Hwang is a very clever and gifted playwright," acknowledged Jack Kroll of the playwright's career in *Newsweek.* Successful and praised at age twenty-three and the recipient of a coveted Tony award by age thirty, through his work for both stage and screen he continues to address universal issues through his imagination and vision, and has justifiably won a wide audience. "The main weakness of his writing," assessed Henry in *Time*, "is that its purpose often seems more political than literary, more attuned to social issues than to the private struggles of the human heart. The final scene of *M. Butterfly*, when the agony of one soul finally takes precedence over broad-ranging commentary, is among the most forceful in the history of the American theater. . . . If Hwang can again fuse politics and humanity, he has the potential to become the first important dramatist of American public life since Arthur Miller, and maybe the best of them all."

BIOGRAPHICAL AND CRITICAL SOURCES:

BOOKS

Asian-American Literature, Thomson Gale (Detroit, MI), 1999.
Contemporary Dramatists, 6th edition, St. James Press (Detroit, MI), 1999.
Contemporary Literary Criticism, Volume 55, Thomson Gale (Detroit, MI), 1989.
Contemporary Theatre, Film, and Television, Volume 5, Thomson Gale (Detroit, MI), 1988.
Dictionary of Literary Biography, Thomson Gale (Detroit, MI), 2000.
Encyclopedia of American Literature, Continuum (New York, NY), 1999.
Street, Douglas, *David Henry Hwang*, Boise State University Press, 1989.

PERIODICALS

Amerasia Journal, winter, 1994, p. 93.
Back Stage West, January 25, 2001, Charlene Baldridge, review of *F.O.B.*, p. 19.
Christian Science Monitor, November 29, 1996, p. 15.
Daily Variety, October 21, 2002, Robert Hofler, review of *Flower Drum Song*, pp. 1-2.
Hollywood Reporter, October 15, 2001, Jay Reiner, review of *Flower Drum Song*, pp. 6-7; August 9, 2002, Kirk Honeycutt, review of *Possession*, pp. 11-12; October 18, 2002, Frank Scheck, review of *Flower Drum Song*, pp. 15-16.
House and Garden, September, 1991, p. 72.
Journal of Dramatic Theory and Criticism, spring, 1991; fall, 1992.

Knight Ridder/Tribune News Service, October 12, 2001, Karen D'Souza, interview with Hwang, p. K7128; October 16, 2002, Judith Newmark, review of *Flower Drum Song*, p. K5257.
Literary Review, winter, 1999, Bonnie Lyons, interview with David Hwang, p. 230.
Los Angeles Times, February 19, 1986; March 26, 1988; June 7, 1988; October 30, 1988.
Modern Drama, March, 1990, pp. 59-66.
Nation, April 23, 1988, pp. 577-578.
New Republic, April 25, 1988, pp. 28-29; November 1, 1993, p. 72.
Newsweek, April 4, 1988, p. 75; October 26, 1992, p. 62.
New York, April 11, 1988, pp. 117-19; October 24, 1988, p. 145; October 26, 1992, p. 91; December 9, 1996, p. 76.
New Yorker, November 2, 1981; April 4, 1988, p. 72; October 11, 1993, p. 123; December 2, 1996, p. 121.
New York Times, June 10, 1980; March 31, 1981; July 12, 1981; October 19, 1981; November 7, 1983; April 22, 1986; February 25, 1988; March 21, 1988; March 25, 1988; April 10, 1988; May 22, 1988; June 5, 1988; September 24, 1988; November 23, 1988; December 11, 1988; December 16, 1988; May 20, 1990; November 10, 1996, p. H5; November 20, 1996, p. C20; November 21, 1996, p. B2; December 5, 1997, p. E2; March 24, 2000, Ben Brantley, review of *Aïda*, p. B26; October 14, 2001, Bernard Weinraub, review of *Flower Drum Song*, p. AR7.
New York Times Magazine, March 13, 1988.
People, January 9, 1984.
Rolling Stone, February 10, 1994, p. 52.
Theater, spring-summer, 1989, pp. 24-27.
Theatre Journal, March, 1990; December, 2002, Sun Hee Teresa Lee, review of *Flower Drum Song*, pp. 640-642.
Time, April 4, 1988, p. 74; August 14, 1989; October 26, 1992, p. 80; October 4, 1993, p. 85; October 28, 2002, Richard Zoglin, review of *Flower Drum Song*, p. 63.
Times (London, England), March 17, 1989; April 22, 1989.
Variety, December 13, 1999, Chris Jones, review of *Aïda*, p. 117; October 8, 2001, Steven Oxman, review of *Flower Drum Song*, p. 27; June 3, 2002, Robert Hofler, review of *Flower Drum Song*, p. A8.
Washington Post, February 10, 1988; December 10, 1988.

ONLINE

USAToday, http://www.usatoday.com/ (May 12, 2003), Elysa Gardner, interview with Hwang and C.Y. Lee.

I

IONESCO, Eugene 1912-1994

PERSONAL: Born November 26, 1912, in Slatina, Romania; became French citizen; died March 28, 1994, in Paris, France; son of Eugene (a lawyer) and Marie-Therese (Icard) Ionesco; married Rodica Burileanu, July 12, 1936; children: Marie-France. *Education:* Attended University of Bucharest; University of Paris, Sorbonne, licencie des letters, agrege des lettres.

CAREER: Professor of French in Romania, 1936-39; worked for publisher in France; full-time writer and painter.

MEMBER: Academie Française.

AWARDS, HONORS: Prix de la Critique, Tours Festival, 1959, for film *Monsieur Tete;* Officier des Arts et Lettres, 1961; Grand Prix Italia, 1963, for ballet version of *La leçon;* Grand Prix, Theatre de la Societe des Auteurs, 1966; Prix National du Theatre, 1969; Prix Litteraire (Monaco), 1969; Austrian Prize for European Literature, 1971; International Writers' fellow, Welsh Arts Council, 1973; Jerusalem Prize (Israel), 1973; Chevalier, French Legion of Honor, 1984; Ingersoll Prize: T.S. Eliot Award for Creative Writing, 1985.

WRITINGS:

PLAYS

Theatre (includes *La cantatrice chauve* [one-act; produced in Paris, France, 1950; produced as *The Bald Soprano* off-Broadway, 1958], *La leçon* [one-act; produced in Paris, 1951; produced as *The Lesson* off-Broadway, 1958], *Jacques, ou la soumission* [one-act; produced in Paris, 1955; produced as *Jack* off-Broadway, 1958], and *Le salon de l'automobile* [produced in Paris, 1953]), Arcanes (Paris, France), 1953.

Theatre, four volumes, Gallimard (Paris, France), Volume I (includes *La cantatrice chauve, La leçon, Jacques, ou la soumission, Les chaises* [one-act; produced in Paris, 1952; produced as *The Chairs* off-Broadway, 1958], *Victimes du devoir* [one-act; produced in Paris, 1953; produced as *Victims of Duty* off-Broadway, 1960], and *Amedée, ou comment s'en debarasser* [three-act; produced in Paris, 1954; produced as *Amedée, or How to Disentangle Yourself* in New York, NY, 1955]), 1954, new edition, 1970, Volume II (includes *L'impromptu de l'Alma, ou le cameleon du berger* [one-act; produced in Paris, 1956; produced as *Improvisation, or The Shepherd's Chameleon* off-Broadway, 1960], *Tueur sans gages* [three-act; produced in Paris, 1959; produced as *The Killer* in New York, NY, 1960], *Le nouveau locataire* [one-act; produced in Helsinki, Finland, 1955; produced as *The New Tenant* in New York, NY, 1960], *L'avenir est dans les oeufs* [one-act; produced in 1957], *Le Maitre* [produced in Paris, 1953; produced as *The Leader* in London, 1970], and *La jeune fille a marier* [produced in Paris, 1953; produced as *Maid to Marry* off-Broadway, 1970], 1958, new edition, 1970, Volume III (includes *Rhinoceros* [three-act; produced in Düsseldorf, 1959; produced in London, 1960; produced on Broadway, 1961], *Le pieton de l'air* [ballet-pantomime; produced in Paris, 1963; produced as *A Stroll in the Air* on Broadway, 1964], *Delire a deux* [one-act; produced in Paris, 1962], *Le tableau* [produced in Paris, 1955; produced as *The Painting* off-off-Broadway, 1969], *Scene a quatre* [produced in Spoleto, Italy, 1959; produced in New York, NY, 1970], *Les salutations* [produced in New York, NY, 1970], and *La Cholere*), 1963, Volume IV (includes *Le roi se meurt* [one-act; produced in Paris, 1962; produced as *Exit the King* in London, 1963; produced in Ann Arbor, MI, 1967], *La soif et la faim* [three-act; produced in Paris, 1966; produced as *Hunger and Thirst* in Stockbridge, MA, 1969], *La lacune* [produced in Paris, 1970; produced in New York, NY, 1970], *Le salon de l'automobile, L'oeuf dur, pour preparer un oeuf dur* [produced in New York, NY, 1970], *Le jeune homme a marier,* and *Apprendre a marcher* [ballet scenario; produced in Paris, 1960], 1966.

La niece-epouse (produced in Paris, France, 1953; produced as *The Niece-Wife* in London, England, 1971), in Richard N. Coe, *Ionesco: A Study of His Plays,* Methuen (London, England), 1971.

Les grandes chaleurs, produced in Paris, France, 1953.

Le connaissez-vous?, produced in Paris, France, 1953.

Le rhume onirique, produced in Paris, France, 1953.

Impromptu pour la Duchesse de Windsor, performed for Duke and Duchess of Windsor, 1957.

La leçon (also see below), published with Samuel Beckett's *Fin de partie,* (Paris, France) 1957, translated by Donald Watson as *The Lesson,* Samuel French (London, England), 1958.

The Chairs, translated by Donald Watson, Samuel French (London, England), 1958, revised edition, translated by Martin Crimp, Faber and Faber (London, England), 1997.

Plays, seven volumes, translated by Donald Watson, J. Calder (London, England), Volume I (includes *The Chairs, The Bald Prima Donna, The Lesson,* and *Jack, or Obedience*), 1958, translation by Donald M. Allen published as *Four Plays,* Grove (New York, NY), 1958, Volume II (includes *Amedée, or How to Get Rid of It, The New Tenant,* and *Victims of Duty*), 1961, translation by Allen, Grove, 1958, Volume III (includes *The Killer, Improvisation, or The Shepherd's Chameleon,* and *Maid to Marry*), 1962, Grove, 1960, Volume IV (includes *Rhinoceros, The Leader,* and *The Future Is in Eggs; or It Takes All Sorts to Make a World*), 1963, translation by Derek Prouse published as *Rhinoceros and Other Plays,* Grove, 1960, Volume V (includes *Exit the King, The Motor Show* [radio play], and *Foursome*), 1963, Volume VI (includes *A Stroll in the Air* and *Frenzy for Two*), 1965, Grove, 1968, Volume VII (includes *Hunger and Thirst, The Picture, Anger,* and *Salutations*), 1968, published as *Hunger and Thirst, and Other Plays,* Grove, 1969.

Le rhinoceros (three-act), Gallimard (Paris, France), 1959, edited by Reuben Y. Elliseon and Stowell C. Gooding, Holt (New York, NY), 1961, translation by Derek Prouse published as *Rhinoceros,* Samuel French (London, England), 1960.

(Coauthor) *Seven Capital Sins* (screenplay), Embassy, 1962.

La cantatrice chauve, published with *La leçon,* Gallimard (Paris, France), 1962, enlarged edition, 1964, translation by Donald Watson published as *The Bald Prima Donna: A Pseudo-Play,* Samuel French (London, England), 1961, Grove (New York, NY), 1965.

Le roi se meurt, Gallimard (Paris, France), 1963, translation by Donald Watson published as *Exit the King,* Grove (New York, NY), 1963.

Three Plays (includes *La cantatrice chauve, La leçon,* and *Les chaises*), edited by H.F. Brookes and C.E. Fraenkel, Heinemann (London, England), 1965.

La soif et la faim, [Paris, France], 1966.

Delire a deux, Gallimard (Paris, France), 1966.

Ches le docteur, Le cocotier en flammes, D'Isidione, Histoire des bandits, Il y eut e'abord, and *Leçons de française pour americains* (short plays), produced in New York, NY, 1970.

Jeux de massacre (one-act; produced in Düsseldorf, 1970; produced in Paris, France, 1970; produced as *Wipe-out Games* in Washington, DC, 1971), Gallimard (Paris, France), 1970, translation by Helen Gary Bishop published as *Killing Game,* Grove (New York, NY), 1974.

(And illustrator) *Victimes du devoir, and Une victime du devoir* (play and short story), edited by Vera Lee, Houghton (Boston, MA), 1972.

Macbett (adaptation of William Shakespeare's *Macbeth*), Gallimard (Paris, France), 1972.

Rhinoceros (screenplay; based on his play), 1973.

Ce formidable bordel!, Gallimard (Paris, France), translation by Gary Bishop published as *A Hell of a Mess,* Grove (New York, NY), 1975.

L'homme aux valises, Gallimard (Paris, France), 1975, adaptation by Israel Horovitz translated by Marie-France Ionesco as *Man with Bags,* Grove (New York, NY), 1977.

Voyages chez les morts ou themes et variations, Gallimard (Paris, France), 1981, translated by Barbara Wright as *Journeys among the Dead,* Calder (London, England), 1985.

Theatre complet, Gallimard (Paris, France), 1991.

OTHER

(Translator with G. Gabrin) Pavel Dan, *Le vieil Urcan,* Jean Vigneau (Paris, France), 1945.

Ionesco: Les rhinoceros au theatre (includes a short story and selections from his journal), R. Juilliard (Paris, France), 1960.

La photo du colonel (narratives; includes "Oriflamme," "La Photo du Colonel," "Le pieton de l'air," "Une victime du devoir," "Rhinoceros," "La vase," and "Printemps, 1939"), Gallimard (Paris, France), 1962, new edition, 1970, translations by Jean Stewart and John Russell published as *The Colonel's Photograph,* Faber (London, England), 1967, Grove (New York, NY), 1969.

Notes et contre-notes (essays and lectures), Gallimard (Paris, France), 1962, new edition, 1970, translation by Donald Watson published as *Notes and Counter-Notes,* Grove (New York, NY), 1964.

(Author of notes) Joan Miró, *Quelques fleurs pour des amis,* Societe Internationale d'Art (Paris, France), 1964.

Journal en miettes (autobiography), Mercure de France (Paris, France), 1967, translation by Jean Stewart published as *Fragments of a Journal,* Grove (New York, NY), 1968.

Story Number 1: For Children under Three Years of Age, illustrated by Etienne Delessert, translated by Calvin K. Towle, Harlin Quist (New York, NY), 1968.

Present passe, passe present (autobiography), Mercure de France, 1968, translation by Helen R. Lane published as *Present Past, Past Present,* Grove (New York, NY), 1971, reprinted, Da Capo (New York, NY), 1992.

(And illustrator) *Decouvertes* (essay), Skira (Geneva, Switzerland), 1969.

(With Michael Benamou) *Mise en train: Premiere année de français* (textbook), Macmillan (New York, NY), 1969.

(Author of script) Jan Lenica, *Monsieur Tete* (animated film), Bruckmann (Munich, Germany), 1970.

Story Number 2: For Children under Three Years of Age, illustrated by Etienne Delessert, Harlin Quist (New York, NY), 1970.

(Author of text) Gerard Schneider, *Catalogo* (exhibit catalogue), [Turin, Italy], 1970.

Story Number 3: For Children over Three Years of Age, illustrated by Philippe Corentin, translation by Ciba Vaughan, Harlin Quist (New York, NY), 1971.

(With Jean Delay) *Discours de reception d'Eugene Ionesco a l'Academie française et reponse de Jean Delay,* Gallimard (Paris, France), 1971.

Le solitaire, Gallimard (Paris, France), 1972, translation by Richard Seaver published as *The Hermit,* Viking (New York, NY), 1974.

(With Claude Bonnefoy) *Entre la vie et le reve,* Belfond (Paris, France), 1977.

Antidotes (essays), Gallimard (Paris, France), 1977.

Un homme en question (essays), Gallimard (Paris, France), 1979.

Variations sur un même theme, Gallimard (Paris, France), 1979.

Le blanc et le noir, Gallimard (Paris, France), 1985.

Non, Gallimard (Paris, France), 1986.

Viata grotesca si tragica a lui Victor Hugo: Hugoliade, translation from Romanian into French by Dragomir Costineanu and Marie-France Ionesco, Gallimard (Paris, France), 1982, translation from French into English by Yara Milos published as *Hugoliad: The Grotesque and Tragic Life of Victor Hugo,* Grove (New York, NY), 1987.

La quete intermittente (autobiography), Gallimard (Paris, France), 1988.

Ruptures de silence: rencontres avec Andre Coutin, Mercure de France (Paris, France), 1995.

Litterature roumaine: suivi de grosse chaleur, Fata Morgana (Saint-Clement-la-Riviere, France), 1998.

Work represented in anthologies and critical studies, including *Absurd Drama,* edited by Martin Esslin, and *New Directions,* edited by Alan Durrand. Contributor to periodicals, including *Lettres nouvelles, Lettres françaises, Encore, Figero, L'Express, Le Monde, Evergreen Review, Mademoiselle, Tulane Drama Review, Theatre Arts, Commentary, London Magazine,* and *Partisan Review.*

ADAPTATIONS: The New Tenant was filmed for Encyclopaedia Britannica Educational Corporation, 1975; *Delirium for Two* was filmed in Russian as *Bred Vdvoyom,* 1995.

SIDELIGHTS: Romanian-born French playwright Eugene Ionesco was one of the prominent voices of what is known as the Theatre of the Absurd, a movement of the 1950s and 1960s that blended surrealism with existential thought and vaudevillian clowning. Although he persistently discredited the label—preferring instead "theatre of derision"—Ionesco, along with fellow absurdists Samuel Beckett, Jean Genet, Arthur Adamov, and Edward Albee, wrote plays that were highly experimental for their time in which traditional plots, structures, and language were replaced with more fragmented, contradictory, and oftentimes nonsensical dialogue, images, and situations. His repeated use of black humor to capture the absurd essence of the human condition and its alienation, its inability to communicate, and its struggle to overcome modern society's destructive forces mark a distinctive trait in Ionesco's early plays, which are often considered his best.

Although labeled an absurdist, Ionesco considered himself a proponent of pataphysics—the science of imaginary solutions popularized by French playwright Alfred

Jarry in his *Ubu Roi*. In the pataphysical universe, "every event determines a law, a *particular* law," which, as Richard N. Coe asserted in *Ionesco: A Study of His Plays,* "is the same as saying there is no law, neither scientific, nor moral, nor aesthetic." Therefore, all things become equal, the sensical and the nonsensical alike. Man finds the nonsensical more preferable of the two because it allows him more freedom to think. This, then, is why Ionesco's plays appear to be nonsensical and absurd: in a world where there are no absolutes save truth, humans must invent such things as love, God, and goodness. The result for a playwright like Ionesco is to create the bizarre, the illogical, the nonrealistic because that is what humans find easiest to accept when they cannot agree to accept anything at all.

Though comic and seemingly without surface meaning, Ionesco's early plays often carry a biting social and political commentary, notwithstanding his repeated claims to be apolitical. Nowhere is this better exhibited than in his first two plays, *The Bald Soprano* and *The Lesson,* where his central theme is the absurdity of language and both its inability to provide us with competent tools for communication and its manipulative qualities which can turn it from a tool to a weapon. In *The Bald Soprano,* which Ionesco reportedly wrote because he wanted to learn English, viewers meet two couples: Mr. and Mrs. Smith, who speak in clichés and platitudes, and Mr. and Mrs. Martin, who appear at first as strangers at the Smiths' home but realize later that they share the same child and the same home. The dialogue among these four characters gradually disintegrates into nonsensical gibberish and finally into meaningless sounds, and the only change comes when in the end the two couples swap identities, and the play begins again where it started. Ionesco saw the play as an attack against the bourgeois and conformity.

In *The Lesson* a professor tutors his young female student in subjects ranging from basic math to complex philology. As the lesson progresses and the student, complaining of a toothache, fails to comprehend the professor's lengthy—and ultimately meaningless—diatribe on the functioning of language, he becomes increasingly agitated. The play reaches its climax when the professor, repeating the word "knife," stabs the girl to death. We soon discover she was the fortieth student he killed that day. Like *The Bald Soprano, The Lesson* ends where it begins, and the forty-first student is brought into the professor's chamber, presumably to face the same fate.

The cyclical endings of these early plays reflect a sense of hopelessness and a pessimistic view of the fate of humankind: history will always repeat itself no matter how horrible the event, no matter how widespread public disapproval is. Part of that hopelessness comes from the impotency of language, the most significant attribute/invention of human beings. How can we share thoughts, ideas, love, etc. if we ultimately cannot communicate with one another? Moreover, since language is so imprecise, it can also be misinterpreted and misused, especially upon those who take words at their face value alone. In *The Lesson,* for instance, when the maid discovers the professor has killed his fortieth student for the day, she tells him to wear a Nazi swastika armband so that no one will question what he has done. It is through this one action that the play takes on strong political overtones, marking the first of many criticisms Ionesco would level against the Nazis and the totalitarian regimes of his native Romania.

Ionesco's next two plays, *Jack, or The Submission* and *The Chairs,* are complementary in that the first play leads up to the beginning of a marriage and the second describes, in part, the ending of one. Again, both plays exploit the impotency of language to effectively communicate and the alienation of modern society. The title character of *Jack* is being coerced by his family—all members of which bear names that are variations of Jack—in finding a wife. They want offspring so that their race will be preserved. In the end, after a courtship that ends with a frenzied discussion where every noun is renamed "cat," Jack chooses Roberte II, a woman with three noses and nine fingers on one hand. Conversely, the Old Man and the Old Woman in *The Chairs* reflect the disintegration of a marriage. Throughout the play they bring in chairs for their several guests who will be attending a speech given by an Orator—a speech the Old Man has prepared as his final commentary on humanity. Gradually, they greet the invisible guests as they arrive, and the chairs—like many objects in Ionesco's plays—proliferate and begin to crowd the now-claustrophobic stage. At the end of *The Chairs,* the Orator, whom the Old Man has entrusted to deliver his message to the people, is able only to utter "the guttural sounds of a mute"; oral language has failed. When the Orator next attempts to communicate by writing an obscure word on the blackboard, its letters finally formulate the word "Adieu"—French for "good bye." Rosette C. Lamont, writing in *Ionesco's Imperatives: The Politics of Culture,* noted that *The Chairs* "is a twentieth century morality play which does not preach. The message of the play is an anti-message: speech, art, communication of any sort, are the illusions man needs while there is breath."

Ionesco gives many of his characters nondescript names, doing so to show how nonconformists are always at odds with a society that will repeatedly take the easiest path and conform. Ionesco does not focus on individual differences but rather on the basic identity of most people. Nowhere is this better illustrated than in a series of four plays Ionesco began writing in the late 1950s. Here he pursued his literary attack on the Nazis and the totalitarian regimes George Orwell criticized so well in *Animal Farm* and *1984*. These plays center on a man named Berenger, a modern-day Everyman, though Berenger is not the same character in each of the four plays. The first of these plays is *The Killer*, a Kafkaesque play where Berenger seeks out the Killer who is terrorizing the Radiant City because everyone, including the police and the city's totalitarian Architect/Doctor/Chief of Police proves incompetent. When Berenger confronts the Killer, he attempts to reason with him, but fails to offer any cogent argument as to why the Killer should not indiscriminately kill people. "The more he talks," Lamont contended, "the more reasons he finds for killing, or rather being killed. Though he is armed, Berenger knows that he, a humanist, will not be able to bring himself to shoot even an enemy who means to destroy him." He learns all too late that the Killer kills without reason. To rationalize with the irrational, Ionesco suggests here, is to fight a losing battle.

The second and certainly most famous of the Berenger plays is *Rhinoceros*, first produced in 1959. As the play opens, Berenger is conversing with his friend Jean when a rhinoceros charges by. Though dismissed at first as an oddity of nature, everyone gradually accepts the animals' presence and, by the play's end, even decides to become one themselves, leaving Berenger to contemplate whether he too should join the herd or not. In the final act, Berenger must fight not only rhinoceritis but his desire to join the herd with his fellows. When he decides in the end to fight them, he becomes a singular hero who challenges the mob mentality and mindless conformity. When we realize that the inspiration for this play came from Ionesco's reaction, as noted in his diary of 1940, to an antifascist friend's gradual acceptance of and ultimate conversion to Nazi fascism, the play takes on a much deeper, political meaning.

Although the next Berenger play, *A Stroll in the Air*, continues the attack against totalitarian regimes, Ionesco moves on to greater philosophical heights with the final Berenger play, *Exit the King*. This play addresses humankind's need to understand its own existence, its own mortality. Like King Lear or Hamlet in Shakespeare's great tragedies, Berenger asks, "Why was I born if it wasn't for ever?" Such metaphysics echo the existential musings of Jean-Paul Sartre and Albert Camus: the questioning of the meaning—or meaninglessness—of life. Having lived for over 500

years, and in that time invented steel, balloons, airplanes, the telephone, built Rome, New York, Paris, and Moscow, and wrote *The Iliad, The Odyssey,* and all of Shakespeare's tragedies, King Berenger is Everyman: his death is the death of all humanity; in his acceptance of his mortality are the seeds of our own metaphysical grapplings with life's inherent meaninglessness.

Ionesco wrote other successful plays in the 1950s and 1960s, including the 1952 radio play *Motor Show, Maid to Marry, The Leader,* and *Victim of Duty,* the latter another play about ruthless authoritarianism. Considered one of his best plays of this period is his first full-length play, *Amedée.* Drawn from a line in T.S. Eliot's poem *The Waste Land,* the play is about a couple's inability to confront their marital problems and to work through their pasts. In fact, Amedée and Madeleine have such difficulty in burying their troubled pasts—Madeleine's infidelity and Amedée's guilt for not having saved a drowning woman—that they remain at the forefront of the couple's present. Ionesco manifests this latent guilt in them by having the couple share their home with the corpse of Madeleine's lover, whom Amedée killed years before but never buried. Now, the couple work effortlessly to keep people and the police from entering their home, no easy task since the corpse is growing larger and larger each day until its physical presence literally fills the entire house. The corpse as metaphor for the growing distance between Amedée and Madeleine is an appropriate one for Ionesco, who relates the corpse to original sin and its growth to the passage of time. The dead body is a constant reminder of the couple's mutual sins, and its unabated growth reflects the mounting guilt they both must contend with for not having loved each other and for having tried to bury, instead of confront, their pasts.

Whether discouraged by the lack of *cause celebre* his later plays received, or feeling he had said in dramatic voice all he needed to say, Ionesco turned later in life to collecting and publishing nonfiction essays, lectures, addresses, criticism, and memoirs. *Fragments of a Journal* and *Present Past, Past Present,* his 1967 and 1968 autobiographies, confirmed his commitment to battle social and political oppression. *Antidotes,* a collection of essays that focus on the corruption of the so-called civilized world, appeared in 1977. The playwright's daughter, Marie-France Ionesco, translated her father's 1934 work *No,* a series of essays on Romanian culture, the demolition of Romanian literary idols, and the role of literature in life. A year later *Hugoliad* appeared, his youthful and scurrilous attack on French literary giant Victor Hugo, which Ionesco had also written during the 1930s. *The Intermittent Quest* is an eloquent and passionate tribute to the two women in Ionesco's life: his wife Rodica and his daughter Marie-France. He devoted most of his remaining years to painting and exhibiting his artwork and lithographs, and died in 1994.

Although Ionesco's plays were once considered avant garde, they have since been reviewed in a less-revolutionary light. However, many of his plays, especially *Rhinoceros,* are still performed and still hold relevance for postmodern audiences. As A.J. Esta noted in a theatre review of a 2002 performance of *Rhinoceros,* Ionesco's "vision of the futility of maintaining one's individuality in the face of conformity is as pertinent as today's headlines."

BIOGRAPHICAL AND CRITICAL SOURCES:

BOOKS

Bonnefoy, Claude, *Conversations with Eugene Ionesco,* translated by Jan Dawson, Faber (London, England), 1970, Holt (New York, NY), 1971.

Coe, Richard N., *Ionesco: A Study of His Plays,* Grove (New York, NY), 1961, revised and enlarged edition, Methuen (London, England), 1971.

Coll, Toby, editor, *Playwrights on Playwriting,* Hill & Wang (New York, NY), 1961.

Contemporary Literary Criticism, Thomson Gale (Detroit, MI), Volume 1, 1973, Volume 4, 1974, Volume 6, 1975, Volume 9, 1977, Volume 11, 1978, Volume 15, 1980, Volume 41, 1986, Volume 86, 1995.

Dobrez, Livio A. C., *The Existential and Its Exists: Literary and Philosophical Perspectives on the Works of Beckett, Ionesco, Genet, and Pinter,* Athlone (London, England,) 1986.

Duckworth, C., *Angels of Darkness,* Barnes & Noble (New York, NY), 1972.

Esslin, Martin, *The Theatre of the Absurd,* Doubleday (New York, NY), 1968.

Grossvogel, David I., *Four Playwrights and a Postscript: Brecht, Ionesco, Beckett, Genet,* Cornell University Press (Ithaca, NY), 1962.

Grossvogel, David I., *The Blasphemers,* Cornell University Press (Ithaca, NY), 1965.

Hayman, R., *Eugene Ionesco,* Heinemann (London, England), 1972.

Jacobson, J., and W.R. Mueller, *Ionesco and Genet,* Hill & Wang (New York, NY), 1968.

Kitchin, Laurence, *Mid-Century Drama,* Faber (London, England), 1960.

Kluback, William, and Michael Finkenthal, *The Clowns of the Agora: Conversations about Eugene Ionesco,* P. Lang (New York, NY), 1998.

Lamont, Rosette C., and Melvin J. Friedman, *The Two Faces of Ionesco,* Whitston (Troy, NY), 1978.

Lamont, Rosette C., *Ionesco's Imperatives: The Politics of Culture,* University of Michigan Press (Ann Arbor, MI), 1993.

Lane, Nancy, *Understanding Eugene Ionesco,* University of South Carolina Press (Columbia, SC), 1994.

Moore, Harry T., *French Literature since World War II,* Southern Illinois University Press (Urbana, IL), 1966.

Pronko, Leonard C., *Avant-Garde: The Experimental Theatre in France,* University of California Press (Berkeley, CA), 1962.

Pronko, Leonard C., *Eugene Ionesco,* Columbia University Press (New York, NY), 1965.

Southern, Terry, Richard Seaver, and Alexander Trocchi, editors, *Writers in Revolt,* Fell (New York, NY), 1963.

Wager, Walter, editor, *The Playwrights Speak,* Delacorte (New York, NY), 1967.

Wellworth, George, *Theatre of Protest and Paradox,* New York University Press (New York, NY), 1964.

Wulbern, J. H., *Brecht and Ionesco: Commitment in Context,* University of Illinois Press (Urbana, IL), 1971.

PERIODICALS

Back Stage, A.J. Esta, review of *Rhinoceros,* February 22, 2002, p. 19.

Boston Globe, November 30, 1989.

Chicago Tribune, March 26, 1980; December 8, 1985; July 25, 1986; March 26, 1987; April 19, 1987; September 16, 1987; August 7, 1989.

Los Angeles Times, November 4, 1987; February 7, 1988; February 16, 1988; February 17, 1988.

New Republic, February 15, 1988.

New York Times, March 12, 1980; June 12, 1987; June 15, 1988.

Times (London, England), January 17, 1987.

Times Literary Supplement, January 22, 1982; February 6, 1987; April 15, 1988.

Tribune Books (Chicago, IL), December 8, 1985.

Washington Post, January 30, 1989; November 8, 1989.

World Literature Today, autumn, 1978; spring, 1987.

OBITUARIES:

PERIODICALS

Knight Ridder/Tribune News Service, March 28, 1994, p. 0328K9259.

New York Times, March 29, 1994, p. A1.

IRVING, John 1942-
   (John Winslow Irving)

PERSONAL: Born March 2, 1942, in Exeter, NH; son of Colin F.N. (a teacher) and Frances (Winslow) Irving; married Shyla Leary, August 20, 1964 (divorced, 1981); married Janet Turnbull, June 6, 1987; children: (first marriage) Colin, Brendan, (second marriage) Everett. *Education:* University of New Hampshire, B.A. (cum laude), 1965; University of Iowa, M.F.A., 1967; additional study at University of Pittsburgh, 1961-62, and University of Vienna, 1963-64.

ADDRESSES: Home—Dorset, VT and Toronto, Ontario, Canada. *Agent*—c/o Random House Publicity, 1745 Broadway, New York, NY 10019.

CAREER: Novelist. Windham College, Putney, VT, assistant professor of English, 1967-69, 1970-72; University of Iowa, Iowa City, writer-in-residence, 1972-75; Mount Holyoke College, South Hadley, MA, assistant professor of English, 1975-78; Brandeis University, Waltham, MA, assistant professor of English, 1978-79. Teacher and reader at Bread Loaf Writers Conference, 1976. Phillips Exeter Academy, assistant wrestling coach, 1964-65; Northfield Mt. Hermon School, assistant wrestling coach, 1981-83; Fessenden School, assistant wrestling coach, 1984-86; Vermont Academy, head wrestling coach, 1987-89.

AWARDS, HONORS: Rockefeller Foundation grant, 1971-72; National Endowment for the Arts fellowship, 1974-75; Guggenheim fellow, 1976-77; *The World according to Garp* was nominated for a National Book Award in 1979 and won an American Book Award in 1980; named one of ten "Good Guys" honored for contributions furthering advancement of women, National Women's Political Caucus, 1988, for *The Cider House Rules;* Academy Award for screenplay based on material previously produced or published, 1999, for *The Cider House Rules.*

WRITINGS:

NOVELS, EXCEPT WHERE NOTED

Setting Free the Bears (also see below), Random House (New York, NY), 1969, Ballantine Trade (New York, NY) 2003.

The Water-Method Man (also see below), Random House (New York, NY), 1972.
The 158-Pound Marriage (also see below), Random House (New York, NY), 1974.
The World according to Garp, Dutton (New York, NY), 1978.
Three by Irving (contains *Setting Free the Bears, The Water- Method Man,* and *The 158-Pound Marriage*), Random House (New York, NY), 1980.
The Hotel New Hampshire, Dutton (New York, NY), 1981.
The Cider House Rules, Morrow (New York, NY), 1985.
A Prayer for Owen Meany, Morrow (New York, NY), 1989, Modern Library (New York, NY) 2002.
Son of the Circus, Random House (New York, NY), 1994.
Trying to Save Piggy Sneed, Arcade (New York, NY), 1996.
The Imaginary Girlfriend: A Memoir (autobiography), Random House (New York, NY), 1996.
A Widow for One Year, Random House (New York, NY), 1998.
The Cider House Rules: A Screenplay (produced by Miramax, 1999), Hyperion (New York, NY), 1999.
My Movie Business: A Memoir, Random House (New York, NY), 1999.
The Fourth Hand, Random House (New York, NY), 2001.
A Sound like Someone Trying Not to Make a Sound: A Story (children's fiction), illustrations by Tatjana Hauptmann, Random House (New York, NY), 2004.
Until I Find You, Random House (New York, NY), 2005.

Also contributor of short stories to *Esquire, New York Times Book Review, Playboy,* and other magazines; contributor of introduction to *Leah, New Hampshire: The Collected Stories of Thomas Williams,* Graywolf Press, 1993. Irving's manuscripts are collected at Phillips Exeter Academy in New Hampshire.

ADAPTATIONS: The World according to Garp was released as a film by Warner Brothers/Pan Arts in 1982 and starred Robin Williams, Glenn Close, and Mary Beth Hurt, and featured cameo performances by Irving and his sons; *The Pension Grillparzer,* based on portions of *The World according to Garp,* was adapted for the stage by director Mollie Bryce and produced in Hollyood, CA, 2004. *The Hotel New Hampshire* was released as a film by Orion Pictures in 1984 and starred Rob Lowe, Jodie Foster, and Beau Bridges; *The Cider*

House Rules was adapted for the stage by Peter Parnell and produced in Seattle, WA, 1996, and was again adapted for the stage by Tom Hulce and produced by the Dramatists Play Service in New York, NY, 2001; *Simon Birch,* based on Irving's *A Prayer for Owen Meany,* was released as a film by Buena Vista Pictures in 1998; *The Door in the Floor,* based on Irving's *A Widow for One Year,* was adapted into screenplay by Tod Williams and published by Ballantine, 2004, and the corresponding film was released by Focus Features in 2004. Irving's novels have been adapted as audiobooks by Random Audio.

WORK IN PROGRESS: A screenplay version of *The Fourth Hand,* for Miramax.

SIDELIGHTS: Novelist John Irving is praised as a storyteller with a fertile imagination and a penchant for meshing the comic and the tragic. Irving is perhaps best known for his critically acclaimed bestseller *The World according to Garp,* which sold more than three million copies in hardback and paperback following its 1978 publication. The novel achieved a cult status—complete with T-shirts proclaiming "I Believe in Garp"—and received serious critical attention, the two combining to propel the novel's author "into the front rank of America's young novelists," according to *Time* critic R.Z. Sheppard.

Though a contemporary novelist, Irving's concerns are traditional, a characteristic some critics have cited as distinguishing Irving's work from that of other contemporary fiction writers. *Dictionary of Literary Biography* contributor Hugh M. Ruppersburg, for example, wrote that "The concerns of Irving's novels are inherently contemporary. Yet often they bear little similarity to other recent fiction, for their author is more interested in affirming certain conventional values—art and the family, for instance—than in condemning the status quo or heralding the arrival of a new age.. . . What is needed, [Irving] seems to suggest, is a fusion of the compassion and common sense of the old with the egalitarian openmindedness of the new." Indeed, Irving's values are reflected in *The World according to Garp,* a work he described in *Washington Post Book World* as "an artfully disguised soap opera." "The difference is that I write well," Irving added, "that I construct a book with the art of construction in mind, that I use words intentionally and carefully. I mean to make you laugh, to make you cry; those are soap-opera intentions, all the way." A lengthy family saga, the novel focuses on nurse Jenny Fields, her illegitimate son, novelist T.S. Garp, and Garp's wife and two sons. *The World according to Garp* explicitly explores the violent side of contemporary life. Episodes involving rape, assassination, mutilation, and suicide abound, but these horrific scenes are always infused with comedy.

"A true romantic hero," according to *Village Voice* critic Eliot Fremont-Smith, Garp is obsessed with the perilousness of life and wants nothing more than to keep the world safe for his family and friends. Ironically then, Garp is the one who ultimately inflicts irreversible harm on his children, illustrating Irving's point that "the most protective and unconditionally loving parents can inflict the most appalling wounds on their children," explained Pearl K. Bell in *Commentary.* While Garp is obsessed with protecting his family and friends, his mother's obsession involves promoting her status as a "sexual suspect"—a woman who refuses to share either her life or her body with a man. Through her best-selling autobiography *A Sexual Suspect,* Jenny becomes a feminist leader. Her home evolves into a haven for a group of radical feminists, The Ellen James Society, whose members have cut out their tongues as a show of support for a young girl who was raped and similarly mutilated by her attackers. Both Garp and Jenny eventually are assassinated—she by an outraged anti-feminist convinced that Jenny's influence ruined his marriage and Garp by an Ellen Jamesian convinced he is an exploiter of women because of a novel he wrote about rape. Discussing these characters in a *Publishers Weekly* interview with Barbara A. Bannon, Irving remarked, "It mattered very fiercely to me that [Garp and Jenny] were people who would test your love of them by being the extremists they were. I always knew that as mother and son they would make the world angry at them."

Critics have noted that *The World according to Garp* demonstrates a timely sensitivity to women—an acknowledgment by Irving of the growing women's liberation movement of the late twentieth century—because it deals sympathetically with issues such as rape, feminism, and sexual roles. *Nation* contributor Michael Malone wrote, "With anger, chagrin and laughter, Irving anatomizes the inadequacies and injustices of traditional sex roles.. . . The force behind a memorable gallery of women characters—foremost among them, Garp's famous feminist mother and his English professor wife—is not empathy but deep frustrated sympathy." A similar opinion was expressed by *Ms.* contributor Lindsy Van Gelder, who admitted admiration for Irving's ability to explore "feminist issues from rape to sexual identity to Movement stardom. . . minus any Hey-I'm-a-man-but-I-really understand self-conscious fanfare."

Despite its fairytale-like qualities, Irving's *The Hotel New Hampshire* also explores adult issues like incest, terrorism, suicide, freakish deaths, and gang rape, all infused with the novelist's trademark macabre humor. A family saga in the tradition of *The World according to Garp, The Hotel New Hampshire* spans nearly four generations of the troubled Berry family. Headed by Win, a charming but irresponsible dreamer who is ultimately a failure at innkeeping, and Mary, who dies in the early stages of the novel, the Berry family includes five children: Franny, Frank, Egg, Lilly, and John, the narrator. While Egg perishes along with his mother, the remaining children are left to struggle through childhood and adolescence. Irving reflected on the Berry family in *New York: The Hotel New Hampshire* "takes a large number of people and says in every family we have a dreamer, a hero, a late bloomer, one who makes it very big, one who doesn't make it at all, one who never grows up, one who is the shit detector, the guide to practicality, and often you don't know who these people will be, watching them in their earlier years."

The Berrys, along with an array of subsidiary characters—human and animal—eventually inhabit three hotels: one in New Hampshire, one in Vienna, and one in Maine. According to Irving, the hotels are symbols for the passage from infancy to maturity. "The first hotel is the only real hotel in the story," stated Irving in *New York*. "It is childhood. The one in Vienna is a dark, foreign place, that phase called adolescence, when you begin leaving the house and finding out how frightening the world is.. . . The last one is no hotel at all.. . . It is a place to get well again, which is a process that has been going on throughout the novel."

Following such a phenomenally successful work, *The Hotel New Hampshire* naturally invited comparisons to its predecessor. "There is no question in my mind it's better than *The World according to Garp*," Irving maintained in *New York*. "It certainly is every bit as big a book, and it means much more. It's a more ambitious novel symbolically but with a different point of view, deliberately narrower." Irving nevertheless anticipated that critics would reject the novel; and, in fact, critics' opinions largely fulfilled Irving's dismal prediction. *Saturday Review* critic Scot Haller wrote that *The Hotel New Hampshire* "could not be mistaken for the work of any other writer, but unfortunately, it cannot be mistaken for Irving's best novel, either. It lacks the urgency of *Setting Free the Bears*, the bittersweet wit of *The 158-Pound Marriage*, the sly set- ups of *Garp*. The haphazardness that afflicts these characters' lives has seeped into the storytelling, too." *Time* critic R.Z. Sheppard offered the view that, unlike Garp's story, "John Berry's story is not resolved in violent, dramatic action, but in a quiet balancing of sorrow and hope. It is a dif-

ficult act, and it is not faultless. The dazzling characterizations and sense of American place in the first part of the novel tend to get scuffed in transit to Europe. There are tics and indulgences. But the book is redeemed by the healing properties of its conclusion. Like a burlesque *Tempest, Hotel New Hampshire* puts the ordinary world behind, evokes a richly allusive fantasy and returns to reality refreshed and strengthened."

Originally intended to be a saga of orphanage life in early twentieth-century Maine, Irving's sixth novel, *The Cider House Rules,* instead became a statement on abortion. The issue of abortion arose during Irving's research for the novel when he learned that abortion played a large role in orphanages at the time. Evoking the works of Victorian novelists such as Charles Dickens and Charlotte Brontë, Irving's *The Cider House Rules* is set in an orphanage in dreary St. Cloud, Maine, where the gentle, ether-addicted Dr. Larch and his saintly nurses preside lovingly over their orphans. Larch also provides illegal but safe abortions, and although he is painfully aware of the bleak existence many of the orphans endure, he does not encourage expectant mothers to abort. As he puts it, "I help them have what they want. An orphan or an abortion." One unadopted orphan in particular, Homer Wells, becomes Larch's spiritual son and protege. Larch schools Homer in birth and abortion procedures in the hope that Homer will one day succeed him at the orphanage. When Homer comes to believe that the fetus has a soul, however, he refuses to assist with abortions. A conflict ensues, and Homer seeks refuge at Ocean View apple orchard, located on the coast of Maine.

The book's title refers to the list of rules posted in Ocean View's cider house regarding migrant workers' behavior. Several critics acknowledged the significance of rules, both overt and covert, in the lives of the characters. Toronto *Globe & Mail* contributor Joy Fielding, for example, commented that *The Cider House Rules* "is all about rules; the rules we make and break; the rules we ignore; the rules we post for all to see; the invisible rules we create for ourselves to help us get through life; the absurdity of some of these rules and the hypocrisy of others, specifically our rules regarding abortion." *New York Times* reviewer Christopher Lehmann-Haupt similarly noted that Dr. Larch follows his own rules and that "the point—which is driven home with the sledgehammer effect that John Irving usually uses—is that there are always multiple sets of rules for a given society. Heroism lies in discovering the right ones, whether they are posted on the wall or carved with scalpels, and committing yourself to follow them no matter what."

Despite the multiplicity of rules and moral codes explored by Irving, critics tend to focus on abortion as the crucial issue of *The Cider House Rules*. They have expressed different opinions, however, concerning Irving's position on the abortion issue. *Time* critic Paul Gray commented that *The Cider House Rules* "is essentially about abortions and women's right to have them," and Susan Brownmiller described the work in *Chicago Tribune* as "a heartfelt, sometimes moving tract in support of abortion rights." *New York Times Book Review* contributor Benjamin DeMott offered this view: "The knowledge and sympathy directing Mr. Irving's exploration of the [abortion] issue are exceptional. Pertinent history, the specifics of surgical procedure, the irrecusable sorrow of guilt and humiliation, the needs and rights of children—their weight is palpable in these pages."

In his novel *A Prayer for Owen Meany,* which examines the good and evil—especially the capacity of each to be mistaken for the other—Irving's Christ-like hero knows his destiny, including the date and circumstances of his death. Small in size but large in spirit, Owen Meany has a distinctive but ineffable voice caused by a fixed larynx, and throughout the novel, Irving renders Owen's speech in upper case—suggested to him by the red letters in which Jesus's utterances appear in the New Testament. Believing that nothing in his life is accidental or purposeless, Owen professes himself an instrument of God, and his sacrifices result in the gradual conversion of his best friend, and the book's narrator, Johnny Wheelwright. "No one has ever done Christ in the way John Irving does Him in *A Prayer for Owen Meany,*" maintained Stephen King in his review of the novel for *Washington Post Book World.*

In a *Time* review, Sheppard pointed out that "anyone familiar with Irving's mastery of narrative technique, his dark humor and moral resolve also knows his fiction is cute like a fox." Sheppard suggested that, despite its theological underpinnings, *A Prayer for Owen Meany* "scarcely disguise[s] his indignation about the ways of the world," and actually represents "a fable of political predestination."

More bizarre characters and situations await readers of Irving's *A Son of the Circus.* Dr. Farrokkh Daruwalla is an Indian-born orthopedist who lives in Canada but makes periodic trips to India to work at a children's hospital, conduct genetic research on circus dwarfs, and write second-rate screenplays. As packed with characters and motifs that have come to be seen as characteristically Irving, *A Son of the Circus,* nevertheless disap-

pointed some reviewers. "The quirkiness with which the author customarily endows privileged characters is. . . scarce here," observed Webster Johnson in *Times Literary Supplement.* "In fact, Daruwalla and the rest incline towards the lacklustre; any colour derives chiefly from the compound incidents which entangle them." Bharati Mukherjee wrote in *Washington Post Book World* that the novel is Irving's "most daring and most vibrant. And though it is also his least satisfying, it has a heroic cheekiness.. . . But its very energy and outrageousness make it compete with rather than complement the tragic story of people.. . . Irving India-surfs himself into exhaustion until the subcontinent becomes, for the reader as well as for one of his characters, neither symbol nor place but a blur of alarming images."

Ruth Cole is the protagonist of *A Widow for One Year,* a novel that explores the nature of fiction writing through several of its characters. When the novel opens on Long Island in 1958, four-year-old Ruth witnesses the dissolution of her parents' marriage, which has suffered under the strain of the tragic death of the couple's teenage sons in a car accident before Ruth was born. Each of her parents drowns their pain in different ways; her father with women and alcohol, and her mother by turning their suburban home into a shrine for her dead sons. After Ruth's mother has an affair with her husband's teen-aged assistant, she abandons both her husband and daughter. Eddie O'Hare, the object of Ruth's mother's affections, looks back on the affair years later, writes a novel about the romance, and becomes part of Ruth's literary circle.

The second two sections of the book take place in the 1990s, where tragedy continues to follow Ruth. Now an adult, she finds her father in bed with her best friend, a betrayal that ultimately results in her father's suicide and a spiteful sexual encounter for Ruth that turns violent. She also becomes a famous author, loses her husband, writes a novel called *A Widow for One Year,* and becomes embroiled in the seamy side of Amsterdam during a book tour held where a serial killer is on the loose. Despite its complex plot, *A Widow for One Year* is, at its core, an exploration of writers and writing. The prominence of writers in the story, Michiko Kakutani explained in *New York Times,* is "to make some points about the ordering impulses of art and the imaginative transactions made by artists in grappling with the real world."

A Widow for One Year met with generally favorable reviews. Although Candia McWilliam described the novel in her *New Statesman* review as a book "in which too many women, alas, behave like men," she complimented Irving's "themes of bereavement and creativity, of love between young men and older women, of widowhood and human hope reborn." Kakutani noted that, while the novel is full of unbelievable coincidences and characters that border on caricature, Ruth is a "complex, conflicted woman" and Irving's "authoritative narrative steamrolls over the contrivances, implausibilities and antic excesses. . . to create an engaging and often affecting fable, a fairy tale that manages to be old-fashioned and modern all at once." William H. Pritchard, writing in *New York Times Book Review,* called *A Widow for One Year* one of Irving's best, commenting that "the writing is very much of the surface, strongly, sometimes even cruelly, outlined, unfriendly to ambiguity and vacillation, secure in its brisk dispositions of people and place."

In *The Fourth Hand* Irving's farcical tendencies are again at play. While a television reporter is on assignment covering a circus in India, his hand is eaten by a lion, the tragedy recorded on live television. The victim, Patrick Wallingford, is a handsome man, prone to affairs with women, who had cruised through life on his charm. Now he is known as the Lion Guy and, instead of attracting attractive women, he becomes a magnet for more offbeat characters. A recently widowed Green Bay, Wisconsin, woman, after her husband is killed in a freak accident, wants Patrick to have her husband's hand. In return, however, she requests visitation rights with the hand and the opportunity to be impregnated by Patrick. A deal is struck, and the anorexic and excrement-obsessed Dr. Zajac of Boston announces that he will perform the world's first hand transplant. Irving uses the character of Patrick to parody the empty world of television news broadcasting and the media's unending fascination with gruesome destruction. In the end, however, Irving turns the story into a tale of love's powers of redemption.

Recognizing Irving's trademark idiosyncratic characters and unlikely scenarios, along with his frequent themes of family and morality, several critics pointed out that *The Fourth Hand* treads ground that is too familiar. Paul Gray wrote in *Time* that the novel "offers the same mix of the macabre and the moral that Irving's army of admirers has come to expect" but maintained that the vapid Patrick cannot hold readers' interest. "Faced with a virtual cipher at the center of his tale, Irving works energetically to create distractions around the edges," Gray explained. Other critics had more appreciation for the novel's storyline. "Irving's worlds are ludicrous in the most appealing way and expertly sentimental at the same time," wrote Doug McClemont in *Library Jour-*

nal, "and his approachable language can be both musical and magical." Bonnie Schiedel, writing in *Chatelaine,* called *The Fourth Hand* "downright weird.. . . but also funny and bracingly original," while Caroline Moore in *Spectator* summarized the symbolism inherent in the novel's title: "It is the phantom 'fourth hand' of the imagination which. . . can bridge the gap between voyeurism and compassion, sensationalism and empathy."

Trying to Save Piggy Sneed collects Irving's non-novel works: memoirs, short stories, and homage pieces. "The Imaginary Girlfriend" details Irving's career as an amateur wrestler and coach and touches on his development as a writer, while other essays present homage to authors Günther Grass and Charles Dickens. The fiction section includes "Pension Grillparzer"—which originally appeared in *The World according to Garp*—and five other short stories. In *New York Times Book Review,* Sven Birkerts stated that *Trying to Save Piggy Sneed* "shows how one of our most widely read novelists fares in what he might consider a triathlon of lesser events. What we find, in this order, are disappointment, confirmations and surprises."

Because of their visual imagery and action, many of Irving's novels have been adapted for film, sometimes on the basis of the novelist's own screenplay. Irving's quest to adapt *The Cider House Rules* for film is the subject of *My Movie Business,* which was published in tandem with the film's release in 1999. The book also covers adaptations from Irving's other novels—even from scripts that he did not write—and his experience writing his first screenplay for *Setting Free the Bears.* Along the way, he elaborates on his pro-choice stance, the history of abortion in the United States, and his grandfather's career as an obstetrician.

As Irving explains in his book, in some ways, the story of *The Cider House Rules* encompasses all facets of the Hollywood movie industry. The film was thirteen years in the making. The script went through numerous revisions and directors came and went before Lasse Hallstrom signed on and the film was made. Along the way, Irving had to confront some harsh realities, notably trimming his first draft from nine hours down to a more theater-friendly two. This severe editorial surgery required leaving out many characters and subplots, but the novelist's efforts paid off when he won an Academy Award for best screenplay. "Irving comes off as a testy collaborator with a decidedly anemic view of the screenwriting process," Jonathan Bing maintained in *Variety.* However, Benjamin Svetkey wrote in *Entertainment*

Weekly that *My Movie Business* contains "sweetly personal moments" and would well-serve readers looking for "a charming, sublimely written technical primer" on the movie industry.

In 2004 Irving released the innovative story book *A Sound like Someone Trying Not to Make a Sound: A Story.* Originally told in his novel *A Widow for One Year,* the author adapted the children's story so that it could be published on its own. When the tale's main character, Tom, wakes up in the middle of the night having heard what he thinks is a monster near his bed, he attempts to wake his brother Tim; and when he is unsuccessful, Tom instead enlists his father's help in finding the source of the apparent terror. A *Kirkus Reviews* critic remarked that the tale is, "perfect for anyone who fears things that go bump in the night."

Until I Find You, published in 2005, is Irving's longest novel to date. Edward Nawotka, reviewing the book for *People,* observed that while it is the author's heaviest tome, "it's also the most intimate story he's ever told." The main character, Jack Burns, spends his life searching for his father. Burns's mother, Alice, a tattoo artist, leads him around the world during his childhood in an attempt to locate the boys' father, a Scottish organ player, but to no avail. As Burns grows older he picks up the search again, only to uncover dark truths. A reviewer for *Library Journal* noted that the novel is a "more contemplative journey than his previous works. . . requiring some patience and reflection."

Although he is not a prolific novelist, Irving remains highly popular with the reading public, as well as with moviegoers through his increasing activity as a screenwriter. Afforded the opportunity due to his stature within American letters, he regularly and publicly debates the nature and worth of novelists and their works. Long a proponent of character and plot driven fiction, Irving has been compared to such luminaries as Dickens and Henry James, both of whom had a similar preoccupation with the moral choices and failings of their characters. Making a similar comparison, Moore noted that "the greatest popular artists—from Dickens to Chaplin—are circus-lovers and showmen, with an unabashed streak of sentimentality and sensationalism. . . . Irving at his best, combining the grotesque, tragic and warm-hearted, has something of their quality."

BIOGRAPHICAL AND CRITICAL SOURCES:

BOOKS

Campbell, Josie P., *John Irving: A Critical Companion,* Greenwood Press (New York, NY), 1998.

Contemporary Literary Criticism, Gale (Detroit, MI), Volume 13, 1980, Volume 23, 1983, Volume 38, 1986, Volume 112, 1999.

Contemporary Novelists, 7th edition, St. James Press (Detroit, MI), 2001.

Contemporary Popular Writers, St. James Press (Detroit, MI), 1997.

Dictionary of Literary Biography, Volume 6: *American Novelists since World War II, Second Series,* Gale (Detroit, MI), 1980.

Dictionary of Literary Biography Yearbook: 1982, Gale (Detroit, MI), 1983.

Encyclopedia of World Literature in the Twentieth Century, St. James Press (Detroit, MI), 1999.

Harter, Carol C., *John Irving,* Twayne (New York, NY), 1986.

Irving, John, *The Cider House Rules,* Morrow (New York, NY), 1985.

Modern American Literature, 5th edition, St. James Press (Detroit, MI), 1999.

Reilly, Edward C., *Understanding John Irving,* University of South Carolina Press (Columbia, SC), 1993.

Runyon, Randolph, *Fowles/Irving/ Barthes: Canonical Variations on an Apocryphal Theme,* Ohio State University Press (Columbus, OH), 1981.

PERIODICALS

Book, July-August, 2001, interview with Irving.

Book-of-the-Month Club News, April, 1989, Phyllis Robinson, interview with Irving.

Chatelaine, August, 2001, Bonnie Schiedel, review of *The Fourth Hand,* p. 12.

Chicago Tribune, May 12, 1985, Susan Brownmiller, review of *The Cider House Rules.*

Christian Century, December 23, 1998, Christopher Bush, review of *A Widow for One Year,* p. 1253.

Commentary, September, 1978, Pearl K. Bell, review of *The World according to Garp.*

Entertainment Weekly, October 22, 1999, Benjamin Svetkey, review of *My Movie Business,* p. 79.

Globe & Mail (Toronto, Ontario, Canada), July 6, 1985, Joy Fielding, review of *The Cider House Rules.*

Kirkus Reviews, September 1, 2004, review of *A Sound like Someone Trying Not to Make a Sound: A Story,* p. 867.

Library Journal, June 1, 2001, Doug McClemont, review of *The Fourth Hand,* p. 216; July 1, 2005, review of *Until I Find You,* p. 68.

Ms., July, 1979, Lindsy Van Gelder, review of *The World according to Garp.*

Nation, June 10, 1978, Michael Malone, review of *The World according to Garp.*

New Statesman, May 22, 1998, Candia McWilliam, review of *A Widow for One Year,* p. 55.

New York, August 17, 1981, interview with Irving, pp. 29-32.

New York Times, May 20, 1985, Christopher Lehmann-Haupt, review of *The Cider House Rules;* May 1, 1998, Michiko Kakutani, "Randomness, Luck, and Fate, but Whew, No Bears," p. 51.

New York Times Book Review, May 26, 1985, Benjamin DeMott, review of *The Cider House Rules;* February 4, 1996, Sven Birkets, review of *Trying to Save Piggy Sneed,* p. 9; May 24, 1998, William H. Pritchard, "No Ideas! It's a Novel!," p. 7.

People, July 18, 2005, Edward Nawotka, review of *Until I Find You,* p. 49.

Publishers Weekly, April 24, 1978, Barbara A. Bannon, interview with Irving; September 3, 2001, review of *The Fourth Hand,* p. 30.

Saturday Review, September, 1981, Scot Haller, review of *The Hotel New Hampshire,* pp. 30-32.

School Library Journal, October 2004, Tana Elias, review of *A Sound like Someone Trying Not to Make a Sound,* p. 118.

Spectator, July 21, 2001, Caroline Moore, review of *The Fourth Hand,* p. 36.

Time, April 24, 1978, R.Z. Sheppard, review of *The World according to Garp;* August 31, 1981, R.Z. Sheppard, review of *The Hotel New Hampshire,* pp. 46-51; June 3, 1985, Paul Gray, review of *The Cider House Rules;* April 3, 1989, R.Z. Sheppard, review of *A Prayer for Owen Meany* p. 80; July 16, 2001, Paul Gray, "The Sound of One Hand Clapping: John Irving's New Novel Proves Disappointing," p. 72.

Times Literary Supplement, September 2, 1994, Webster Johnson, review of *A Son of the Circus,* p. 11.

Variety, March 6, 2000, Jonathan Bing, review of *My Movie Business,* p. 52.

Village Voice, May 22, 1978, Eliot Fremont-Smith, review of *The World according to Garp.*

Washington Post Book World, April 30, 1978, interview with Irving; March 5, 1989, Stephen King, review of *A Prayer for Owen Meany;* September 4, 1994, Bharati Mukherjee, review of *A Son of the Circus,* p. 5.

Writer, January, 2002, Dorman T. Schindler, "In High Gear: John Irving Is Writing More than Ever and Loving It," p. 28.

OTHER

Irving according to Irving (film), Landmark Media (Falls Church, VA), 2001.

IRVING, John Winslow
    See IRVING, John

*   *   *

ISAACS, Susan 1943-

PERSONAL: Born December 7, 1943, in Brooklyn, NY; daughter of Morton (an electrical engineer) and Helen (a homemaker; maiden name, Asher) Isaacs; married Elkan Abramowitz (an attorney), August 11, 1968; children: Andrew, Elizabeth. *Education:* Attended Queens College (now Queens College of the City University of New York). *Politics:* Democratic *Religion:* Jewish

ADDRESSES: Agent—c/o Owen Laster, William Morris Agency, 1325 Avenue of the Americas, New York, NY 10019.

CAREER: Novelist, essayist, and screenwriter. *Seventeen* magazine, New York, NY, 1966-70, began as assistant editor, became senior editor; freelance writer, 1970-76; political speech writer for Democratic candidates in Brooklyn and Queens, New York, and for president of the borough of Queens, New York, NY; movie producer.

MEMBER: International Association of Crime Writers, PEN (executive board member, 1993-97), Mystery Writers of America (national board member, chair of committee for freedom of speech, president, 2001), National Book Critics Circle, Creative Coalition, International Association of Crime Writers, Adams Round Table, American Society of Journalists and Authors, Adams Round Table, Poets & Writers (member of board of directors, 1994-99, Chairman, 1999—), Feminists for Free Expression, Queens College Foundation (trustee), Walt Whitman Birthplace Association (trustee), North Shore Child and Family Guidance Association (trustee), Nassau County Coalition against Domestic Violence Advisory Board.

AWARDS, HONORS: D.Litt., Dowling College, 1988; Queens College Barnes & Noble Writers for Writers Award, 1996; John Steinbeck Award, 1999.

WRITINGS:

NOVELS

Compromising Positions (also see below), Times Books (New York, NY), 1978.

Close Relations, Lippincott (Philadelphia, PA), 1980.
Almost Paradise, Harper (New York, NY), 1984.
Shining Through, Harper (New York, NY), 1988.
Magic Hour, HarperCollins (New York, NY), 1991.
After All These Years, HarperCollins (New York, NY), 1993.
Lily White, HarperCollins (New York, NY), 1996.
Red, White, and Blue, HarperCollins (New York, NY), 1998.
Long Time No See, HarperCollins (New York, NY), 2001.
Any Place I Hang My Hat, Scribner (New York, NY), 2004.

OTHER

Compromising Positions (screenplay; based on her novel of the same name), Paramount, 1985.
(And coproducer) *Hello Again* (screenplay), Buena Vista, 1987.
Brave Dames and Wimpettes: What Women Are Really Doing on Page and Screen, Ballantine (New York, NY), 1999.

Also contributor of reviews to newspapers, including *New York Times, Newsday, Washington Post,* and *Los Angeles Times.*

ADAPTATIONS: *Shining Through* was adapted for film by David Seltzer and released by Twentieth Century-Fox, 1992.

SIDELIGHTS: Susan Isaacs's popular and critically acclaimed novels feature a distinctive type of heroine. In her books, a *Time* reviewer summarized, "secretaries, housewives, the faceless masses of womanhood, all run into phone booths, change clothes, and come out like Cleopatra with the rectitude of Eleanor Roosevelt." This transformation begins when common people come in contact with uncommon events. Isaacs's characters confront murder, political intrigue, even World War II espionage. In spite of such daunting circumstances, the typical Isaacs protagonist displays an engaging sense of humor and a "can-do" attitude which ultimately prevails.

Isaacs achieved critical notice with her first novel, 1978's *Compromising Positions,* a book that *Chicago Tribune* contributor Clarence Petersen described as "the seeming result of an Erica Jong-Joan Rivers collaboration on a Nancy Drew mystery." The protagonist of the book is Judith Singer, a bored homemaker who seeks an outlet for her underemployed intelligence by playing detective after her periodontist is found murdered. Judith's list of suspects grows as she discovers that several of her neighbors—the attractive, upwardly mobile wives of successful men—had not only been seduced by the dentist, but were photographed in pornographic poses. While investigating the murder, Judith is romanced by a police officer, and then confronted by her dull but dutiful husband. In the end, she discovers a vital clue in the photographs that resolves the mystery. *Compromising Positions'* blend of humor, mystery, and a generous dash of sexual situations made it a bestseller. Critical response was also encouraging, though more reserved. *New York Times Book Review* contributor Jack Sullivan praised the novel's direction and humor, but criticized its lack of consistency. "What begins as a brilliant parody of suburban potboilers," Sullivan wrote, "ends by becoming one itself." A *Publishers Weekly* reviewer was more positive, noting that "the dialogue is ribald and wisecracking, the action fast and furious every step of the way."

Isaacs draws on her experience as a political speech writer in her second novel, *Close Relations.* The protagonist, Marcia Green, is a divorced woman working for a New York gubernatorial candidate. Against the backdrop of the campaign, Marcia becomes involved with two men—one Jewish and one Catholic—and her sexual encounters with each are treated in graphic detail. *Washington Post Book World* reviewer Susan Cheever noted Isaacs's refreshing portrayal of a female character who possesses "the kind of sexual appetites that have traditionally been a male prerogative—at least in literature." *Publishers Weekly* contributor Barbara A. Bannon was also impressed with *Close Relations,* emphasizing the book's "snappy dialogue yielding up laughs on every page, the love story tender and satisfying, the plot pulsing with adrenalin."

Isaacs's next effort, *Almost Paradise,* also turns on a love story, this one between Nick Cobleigh, member of a wealthy family and a successful actor, and Jane Heissenhuber, a lower-class woman who was raised by abusive parents. In a contemporary twist on the Cinderella story, poor Jane marries rich Nick, but they do not live happily ever after. Jane suffers from frigidity and agoraphobia; Nick has several extramarital affairs. The couple eventually separate, but are about to be reconciled when a sudden death brings the story to a close.

Almost Paradise received a cooler critical reaction than its Isaacs-penned predecessors. *Los Angeles Times Book Review* contributor Kenneth Atchity was particularly critical of the novel's conclusion, terming it a "shockingly happenstance, tragic ending." *New York Times* reviewer Michiko Kakutani also found fault with the book. "The characters not only speak in clichés," Kakutani wrote, "most of them *are* clichés." Other reviews were more favorable. Anna Shapiro, writing in the *New York Times Book Review,* found flaws in the novel but suggested that "one is reading too absorbedly to notice." Shapiro also praised Isaacs's pacing, emphasizing the author's ability to "keep the plot boiling."

For 1988's *Shining Through,* Isaacs moves away from her contemporary settings. Drawing readers back to World War II, she presents an intrigue that revolves around a secretary who becomes an American spy. This new subject matter challenged Isaacs, causing her to struggle with her portrayal of Linda Voss, the novel's protagonist. "She's not that easy to capture," Isaacs once explained. "There are enormous changes in the character; she goes from being a rather ordinary legal secretary to be something of a hero, having gotten involved in the war." In the course of her adventure, Linda, a Jew, puts herself at risk by posing as a cook in Nazi Germany; romance also figures in the saga as she tries to win the affections of her married boss. *New York Times Book Review* contributor Anne Tolstoi Wallach compared the book to films from the 1940s, "in which someone pretty much like us takes incredible risks for unimpeachable motives and wins just what *we* wanted." Wallach also applauded Isaacs's successful exploration of new subjects: "Like her girl-next-door heroines, she takes risks and her readers reap the rewards."

Having begun her literary career with the mystery *Compromising Positions,* Isaacs returned to familiar ground with her next effort, *Magic Hour.* Here the sleuth is Steve Brady, a Bridgehampton, Long Island, homicide detective and one of the few male protagonists to be found in Isaacs's work. Brady is a Vietnam veteran with a past record of abusing drugs and alcohol. Though he is engaged to be married, his plans undergo a sudden change when a movie producer is found murdered. In the course of the investigation, Brady falls for Bonnie, the victim's ex-wife and one of several suspects in the case. When the facts point to Bonnie as the murderer, Brady is forced to choose between his heart and his duty as a detective.

New York Times Book Review contributor Helen Dudar found that "it takes a while for the story to develop the kind of narrative drive a light novel of this sort wants." Despite this shortcoming, though, Dudar complimented Isaacs's "wicked eye for small, telling detail," and was impressed by the author's satiric portraits of affluent Long Island residents. Ultimately, Dudar found that reading *Magic Hour* "is like polishing off an entire box of chocolates. You know it can't be nourishing, but it *is* fun." Carolyn Banks, writing in the *Washington Post Book World,* was more enthusiastic, noting that "the plot is streamlined and the time-frame is short and the voice we hear is witty, and coming-right-at-us-real. . . . Isaacs never writes a *mere* mystery . . . but something more."

Isaacs continues her line of successful whodunits with *After All These Years.* The heroine, Rosie, is married to Richie, a recent millionaire due to his software company who has taken to being called Rick, among other affectations of his new wealth. Promptly after a lavish celebration of their silver wedding anniversary, Rick/Richie announces he is leaving Rosie for his beautiful—and younger—VP, Jessica. Later, however, Rosie finds Rick/Richie dead from a knife wound on her kitchen floor and, knowing herself to be the primary suspect—her fingerprints are on the knife—she sets out to find her husband's true killer. Although, as Barbara Raskin noted in the *New York Times Book Review,* "it's not hard to figure out who will win," the critic declared, "Still, you gotta laugh." Other reviewers also found *After All These Years* to be an enjoyable, if light, tale. "This is a good, fast, illogical read for the beach or plane; just don't ask questions. In a fairy tale, all things are possible," remarked Dorothy Uhnak in the *Washington Post Book World.* Taffy Cannon, contributor to the *Los Angeles Times Book Review,* found deeper meaning in the tale: *After All These Years* "could stand on its own as a credible mystery, but it's more than that. It seriously examines the plight of the discarded wife." Cannon concluded, however, that, "More to the point . . . it's pure fun and perfectly timed for summer reading."

In *Lily White* Isaacs combines elements of a murder mystery with a family history reminiscent of a therapy session. Lily White is a criminal defense lawyer in the suburb of Shorehaven, a far cry from her previous role in the Manhattan district attorney's office. She takes on the case of Norman, a con man accused of the murder of his latest victim. While chronicling Lily's efforts to find Norman innocent, Isaacs relates Lily's dysfunctional family history. Reviewers were mixed in their opinions of Isaacs's experiment. Calling it a "one-volume vacation reader," Elaine Kendall, writing for the *Los Angeles Times Book Review,* found "the route somewhat more circuitous than necessary." Jon Katz, contributing to the *New York Times Book Review,* lauded *Lily White* as "a big, fat, happy feast of a book," but noted, "the effect [of the two tales] is inevitably herky-jerky." *Time* reviewer John Skow was even more critical: "The flashback chapters [into Lily's family history] turn a tidy, well-told book into a fat, soggy one."

Isaacs breaks with her usual suspense novel format in *Red, White, and Blue*, a multigenerational tale of Jewish immigrants who strive for success in America. Though the book begins by chronicling the family's difficult early years in their adoptive country, it eventually develops a more romantic story line involving two characters who are distantly related. Lauren Miller is a reporter for a newspaper and Charlie Blair is an FBI agent. Both are investigating a white supremacy group in Wyoming, which quest leads to their meeting. Mary Frances Wilkens, reviewing the novel for *Booklist*, found that in *Red, White, and Blue* "Isaacs smoothly combines what could have been two different novels into one." Though a writer for *Publishers Weekly* praised Isaacs's research and considered her depictions of the white supremacist movement to be convincing, the critic felt that the book's "sappy" love story "overwhelms" the narrative. Wilkens, however, deemed the story "creative and exciting" and "superbly entertaining." Barbara E. Kemp agreed in her *Library Journal* review, writing that *Red, White, and Blue* "pose[s] . . . deeper questions about what it means to be an American."

In *Brave Dames and Wimpettes: What Women Are Really Doing on Page and Screen*, Isaacs examines how women are typically portrayed in television, film, and fiction. She finds that, as Laura Ellingson explained in a *Women and Language* review, "too many of the heroines offered up as icons for women are really wimpettes, whom we would be wise to reject rather than emulate. In contrast, too few brave dames provide inspiration and sound role models for women." Isaacs describes a wimpette as someone who is seemingly beautiful and strong, but is actually weak and is just trying to be what everyone else wants her to be. In contrast, a brave dame is a woman who is "passionate about something besides passion." Ellingson noted that "this book has several strengths to recommend it as a supplementary text for undergraduate courses," including the fact that "many of the examples are very recent, so students will have seen many of the movies and television programs and may identify with icons they feel are from their own generation." Yet other reviewers expressed less enthusiasm for the book. A critic for *Publishers Weekly* suggested that Isaacs's "foray into cultural criticism quickly turns into an object lesson on oversimplification" and concluded that "though no 'wimpette,' Isaacs fails to deliver deep insights or hardened convictions. She remains a popular entertainer at heart." Ell-

ingson, while observing that Isaacs "recognizes that cultural prescriptions for pleasing plots surround us from the very beginning of our lives," nonetheless finds merit in many depictions of women. "Isaacs's text," the critic concluded, "can be a great help in articulating what is good and bad about female characters in the media."

After twenty years and a multitude of events, Isaacs brings back the character from her debut novel in *Long Time No See*. The book brings readers up to speed on what has happened with Judith Singer over the past two decades, reintroducing some familiar characters while adding several new ones into the mix. The plot revolves around a "perfect housewife" who is reported missing following a trip to the store on Halloween. Eventually the body is discovered and that is where Judith steps in with enthusiasm. The book goes on to chronicle the list of suspects, which includes the victim's husband, Greg. In the end Judith solves the murder and ends the mystery.

A reviewer for *Publishers Weekly* wrote of *Long Time No See* that "the twenty years between Isaacs's best-selling *Compromising Positions* and this second book to feature amateur sleuth Judith Singer have not affected the author's talent for snappy dialogue and astringent assessments of cant and pretension," but added that "Judith's investigation, despite several clever twists, goes on too long, as does the murderer's bizarre confession." On the whole, though, the book and its protagonist enjoyed positive reviews, with Barbara Kemp writing in *Library Journal* that "the familiar mix of murder, humor, and wry social observation will delight [Isaacs's] many readers." *Booklist* reviewer Carrie Bissey added that "a gripping plot with skillfully rendered secondary characters and plenty of tart humor make this sequel every bit as entertaining as its predecessor."

Isaacs draws on her experience in politics to create Amy Lincoln, the protagonist of her thriller *Any Place I Hang My Hat*. As a reporter covering the campaign of the 2004 Democratic presidential nominee, Senator Thomas Bowles, Lincoln discovers that the senator has an illegitimate son. Rather than racing to the newsdesk with the scoop of the scandal, Amy is forced to confront her own past, "abandonment by her mother when she was only a baby, visitations to her father in prison, and being raised by her shoplifting grandmother," which ultimately creates the crux of the novel, her desire to help Freddy Carasco, the Senator's son, "reunite with his birth family," as Mary Frances Wilkens wrote in *Booklist*. Wilkens added that, "while Isaacs's plots often drift precariously close to cliché, she usually rights the ship with her keen sense of humor and character." A critic for *Publishers Weekly* concurred, noting that "the parade of lavishly and loopishly described secondary characters and gossipy New York scene-setting give the novel its zing."

In addition to her success as a novelist, Isaacs has also done well in transforming her tales for the screen. Her first exposure to the film industry came when she wrote the screenplay for *Compromising Positions*. Since that time she has written and coproduced a second movie, *Hello Again,* and has seen *Shining Through* adapted for the big screen. Whatever genre she is working in, Isaacs finds the writing process to be demanding but rewarding. She once explained: "There are always those days that you think you'd have been better off as a computer programmer, that you say to yourself, why am I doing this? I have no talent for it. Days when the prose is leaden, the work is lonely. . . . But most of the time, I enjoy it. It seems to me it's a legitimized way of telling yourself stories, and I guess very often I get that same thumb-sucking pleasure that a child gets from daydreaming. That part of it I like a lot."

BIOGRAPHICAL AND CRITICAL SOURCES:

BOOKS

Contemporary Literary Criticism, Volume 32, Thomson Gale (Detroit, MI), 1985.
Isaacs, Susan, *Brave Dames and Wimpettes: What Women Are Really Doing on Page and Screen,* Ballantine (New York, NY), 1999.

PERIODICALS

Bloomsbury Review, November, 1999, review of *Brave Dames and Wimpettes,* p. 19.
Booklist, May 1, 1996, p. 1469; September 15, 1998, Mary Frances Wilkens, review of *Red, White, and Blue,* p. 173; July, 2001, Carrie Bissey, review of *Long Time No See,* p. 1950; July, 2004, Mary Frances Wilkens, review of *Any Place I Hang My Hat.*
Books, June, 1997, review of *Lily White,* p. 19.
Chicago Tribune Book World, March 25, 1984; September 1, 1985; September 4, 1985.
Detroit News, November 9, 1980; March 18, 1984.

Entertainment Weekly, April 18, 1997, review of *Lily White,* p. 63; November 13, 1998, review of *Red, White, and Blue,* p. 70; February 5, 1999, review of *Brave Dames and Wimpettes,* p. 64.
Kirkus Reviews, September 15, 1998, review of *Red, White, and Blue,* p. 1313; December 15, 1998, review of *Brave Dames and Wimpettes,* p. 1776.
Kliatt, July, 1997, review of *Lily White,* p. 48; May, 1999, review of *Red, White, and Blue,* p. 63; July, 1999, review of *Brave Dames and Wimpettes,* p. 57; September, 1999, review of *Red, White, and Blue,* p. 58.
Ladies' Home Journal, September, 2001, Shana Aborn, "A Woman of Mystery" (interview), p. 38.
Library Journal, February 15, 1997, review of *Lily White,* p. 175; October 15, 1998, Barbara E. Kemp, review of *Red, White, and Blue,* p. 98; January, 1999, Melanie C. Duncan, review of *Red, White, and Blue,* p. 188; February 1, 2000, Laurie Selwyn, review of *Red, White, and Blue,* p. 133; August, 2001, Barbara E. Kemp, review of *Long Time No See,* p. 161.
Los Angeles Times, September 1, 1980; August 30, 1985.
Los Angeles Times Book Review, March 4, 1984, Kenneth Atchity, review of *Almost Paradise;* July 11, 1993, Taffy Cannon, review of *After All These Years,* p. 2; July 28, 1996, Elaine Kendall, review of *Lily White,* p. 4.
Newsweek, May 1, 1978.
New Yorker, May 15, 1978.
New York Times, February 1, 1984; August 30, 1985; September 30, 2001, Karen Karbo, "Nice Lawn!"
New York Times Book Review, April 30, 1978, Jack Sullivan, review of *Compromising Positions;* February 12, 1984, Anna Shapiro, review of *Almost Paradise;* September 11, 1988, Anne Tolstoi Wallach, review of *Shining Through,* p. 13; January 20, 1991, Helen Dudar, review of *Magic Hour,* p. 12; July 11, 1993, Barbara Raskin, review of *After All These Years,* p. 26; June 30, 1996, Jon Katz, review of *Lily White,* p. 19; April 13, 1997, review of *Lily White,* p. 32; December 20, 1998, Nora Krug, review of *Red, White, and Blue,* p. 18.
People, April 24, 1978; April 30, 1984.
Publishers Weekly, January 9, 1978; January 23, 1978; July 25, 1980; September 12, 1980; January 4, 1985; May 13, 1996, p. 54; September 7, 1998, review of *Red, White, and Blue,* p. 82; December 14, 1998, review of *Brave Dames and Wimpettes,* p. 68; February 1, 1999, review of *Brave Dames and Wimpettes,* p. 36; July 23, 2001, review of *Long Time No See,* p. 47; August 2, 2004, review of *Any Place I Hang My Hat.*

St. Louis Post-Dispatch, October 20, 1998, Sue Ann Wood, "Susan Isaacs Remains Serious in Her Latest Installment," p. D3.

Time, October 3, 1988; July 15, 1996, John Skow, review of *Lily White,* p. 68.

Times (London, England), April 3, 1997, Bronwen Maddox, "Carving a Career out of Murder, Betrayal, and Adultery," p. 21.

Times Literary Supplement, November 3, 1978.

Washington Post, September 3, 1985; November 8, 1998, Mike Musgrove, review of *Red, White, and Blue,* p. 4; September 2, 2001, Carolyn Banks, "Horsing Around," p. T10.

Washington Post Book World, August 31, 1980, Susan Cheever, review of *Close Relations;* February 12, 1984; January 27, 1991, Carolyn Banks, review of *Magic Hour,* p. 1; July 4, 1993, Dorothy Uhnak, review of *After All These Years,* p. 3; November 8, 1998, review of *Red, White, and Blue,* p. 4.

Women and Language, fall, 1999, Laura L. Ellingson, review of *Brave Dames and Wimpettes,* p. 37.

Writer, February, 1997, Lewis Burke Frumkes, "A Conversation with . . . Susan Isaacs" (interview), pp. 25-27.

ONLINE

Susan Isaacs Web site, http://www.susanisaacs.com/ (August 25, 2004).

*　　*　　*

ISHERWOOD, Christopher 1904-1986
(Christopher William Bradshaw Isherwood)

PERSONAL: Born August 26, 1904, in High Lane, Cheshire, England; immigrated to the United States, 1939, naturalized citizen, 1946; died of cancer, January 4, 1986, in Santa Monica, CA; son of Francis Edward (a military officer) and Kathleen (Machell-Smith) Isherwood; longtime companion of Don Bachardy (an artist). *Education:* Attended Repton School, 1919-22, and Corpus Christi College, Cambridge, 1924-25; King's College, University of London, medical student, 1928-29. *Politics:* Democrat. *Religion:* Vedantist. *Hobbies and other interests:* "I was a born film fan."

CAREER: Writer, 1926-86. Worked as a secretary to French violinist Andre Mangeot and his Music Society String Quartet, London, England, 1926-27; private tutor in London, 1926-27; went to Berlin, Germany, in 1929 to visit W.H. Auden, and stayed, on and off, for four years; taught English in Berlin, 1930-33; traveled throughout Europe, 1933-37; did film script work for Gaumont-British; went to China with Auden, 1938; dialogue writer for Metro-Goldwyn-Mayer, Hollywood, CA, 1940; worked with American Friends Service Committee, Haverford, PA, in a hostel for Central European refugees, 1941-42; resident student of Vedanta Society of Southern California, Hollywood, and coeditor with Swami Prabhavananda of the society's magazine, *Vedanta and the West,* 1943-45; traveled in South America, 1947-48; guest professor at Los Angeles State College (now California State University, Los Angeles) and at University of California, Santa Barbara, 1959-62; Regents Professor at University of California Los Angeles, 1965, and University of California, Riverside, 1966. *Exhibitions:* Huntington Library mounted an exhibition on Isherwood entitled "A Writer and His World," in 2004.

AWARDS, HONORS: Brandeis University creative arts award, 1974-75; PEN Body of Work Award, 1983; Common Wealth Award for distinguished service in literature, 1984.

WRITINGS:

NOVELS

All the Conspirators, Jonathan Cape (London, England), 1928, new edition, 1957, New Directions (New York, NY), 1958.

The Memorial: Portrait of a Family, Hogarth (London, England), 1932, New Directions (New York, NY), 1946.

The Last of Mr. Norris (also see below), William Morrow (New York, NY), 1935, published as *Mr. Norris Changes Trains,* Hogarth (London, England), 1935.

Sally Bowles (also see below), Hogarth (London, England), 1937.

Goodbye to Berlin (also see below), Random House (New York, NY), 1939.

Prater Violet, Random House (New York, NY), 1945.

The Berlin Stories (contains *The Last of Mr. Norris, Sally Bowles,* and *Goodbye to Berlin*), J. Laughlin (New York, NY), 1946, published as *The Berlin of Sally Bowles,* Hogarth (London, England), 1975.

The World in the Evening, Random House (New York, NY), 1954.

Down There on a Visit, Simon & Schuster (New York, NY), 1962.

A Single Man, Simon & Schuster (New York, NY), 1964.

A Meeting by the River (also see below), Simon & Schuster (New York, NY), 1967.

PLAYS

(With W.H. Auden) *The Dog beneath the Skin; or, Where Is Francis?* (three-act; produced in London, 1936; revised version produced in London, 1937), Random House (New York, NY), 1935.

(With W.H. Auden) *The Ascent of F6* (produced in London, 1937; produced in New York, 1939), Random House (New York, NY), 1937, 2nd edition, Faber & Faber (London, England), 1957.

(With W.H. Auden) *A Melodrama in Three Acts: On the Frontier* (produced in Cambridge, England, 1938; produced in London, 1939), Faber & Faber (London, England), 1938, published as *On the Frontier: A Melodrama in Three Acts,* Random House (New York, NY), 1939.

The Adventures of the Black Girl in Her Search for God (based on a George Bernard Shaw novella), produced in Los Angeles at Mark Taper Forum, March, 1969.

(With Don Bachardy) *A Meeting by the River* (based on Isherwood's novel), produced in Los Angeles at Mark Taper Forum, 1972, produced on Broadway at the Palace Theatre, March, 1979.

(With W.H. Auden) *Plays and Other Dramatic Writings, 1928-1938,* Faber & Faber (London, England), 1989.

SCREENPLAYS

(Author of scenario and dialogue with Margaret Kennedy) *Little Friend,* Gaumont-British, 1934.

(Contributor) *A Woman's Face,* Metro-Goldwyn-Mayer (Los Angeles, CA), 1941.

(With Robert Thoeren) *Rage in Heaven* (based on novel by James Hilton), Metro-Goldwyn-Mayer (Los Angeles, CA), 1941.

(Contributor) *Forever and a Day,* RKO (Los Angeles, CA), 1943.

(With Ladislas Fodor) *The Great Sinner,* Loew's, 1949.

Diane, Metro-Goldwyn-Mayer (Los Angeles, CA), 1955.

(With Terry Southern) *The Loved One* (based on the novel by Evelyn Waugh), Filmways, 1965.

(With Don Magner and Tony Richardson) *The Sailor from Gibraltar* (based on the novel by Marguerite Duras), Woodfall, 1967.

The Legend of Silent Night (television special; adapted from a story by Paul Gallico), broadcast by American Broadcasting Company (ABC-TV), 1969.

(With Don Bachardy) *Frankenstein: The True Story* (based on the novel by Mary Shelley; produced, 1972), Avon (New York, NY), 1973.

(With Aldous Huxley) *Jacob's Hands,* St. Martin's Press (New York, NY), 1998.

Also author of dialogue for other films. Also author, with Lesser Samuels, of original story for *Adventure in Baltimore,* RKO, 1949. Also author of scripts for television.

TRANSLATOR

Bertolt Brecht, *Penny for the Poor,* Hale (London, England), 1937, Hillman Curl (New York, NY), 1938, published as *Threepenny Novel,* Grove Press (New York, NY) 1956.

(With Swami Prabhavananda) *Bhagavad-Gita: The Song of God,* Rodd (Los Angeles, CA), 1944, published as *The Song of God: Bhagavad-Gita,* Harper & Row (New York, NY), 1951, 3rd edition, Vedanta Press (Los Angeles, CA), 1965.

(And editor, with Swami Prabhavananda) Shankara, *Crest-Jewel of Discrimination,* Vedanta Press (Los Angeles, CA), 1947.

(With Swami Prabhavananda and Frederick Manchester) *Upanishads: Breath of the Eternal,* Vedanta Press (Los Angeles, CA), 1947.

Charles Baudelaire, *Intimate Journals,* Rodd, 1947.

(And editor, with Swami Prabhavananda) *How to Know God: The Yoga Aphorisms of Patanjali,* Harper & Row (New York, NY), 1953.

OTHER

Lions and Shadows: An Education in the Twenties (autobiography), Hogarth (London, England), 1938, New Directions (New York, NY), 1947.

(With W.H. Auden) *Journey to a War,* Random House (New York, NY), 1939.

(Editor) *Vedanta for the Western World,* Rodd, 1945, published as *Vedanta and the West,* Harper & Row (New York, NY), 1951.

The Condor and the Cows: A South American Travel Diary, Random House (New York, NY), 1949.

(Editor) *Vedanta for Modern Man,* Harper & Row (New York, NY), 1951.

(Editor) *Great English Short Stories,* Dell (New York, NY), 1957.

An Approach to Vedanta, Vedanta Press (Los Angeles, CA), 1963.

Ramakrishna and His Disciples (biography), Simon & Schuster (New York, NY), 1965.

Exhumations: Stories, Articles, Verses, Simon & Schuster (New York, NY), 1966.

Essentials of Vedanta, Vedanta Press (Los Angeles, CA), 1969.

Kathleen and Frank (autobiography), Simon & Schuster (New York, NY), 1971.

Christopher and His Kind, 1929-1939 (autobiography), Farrar, Straus, & Giroux (New York, NY), 1976.

An Isherwood Selection, edited by Geoffrey Halson, Longman (London, England), 1979.

My Guru and His Disciple, Farrar, Straus, & Giroux (New York, NY), 1980.

(With Sylvain Mangeot) *People One Ought to Know* (poems), Doubleday (New York, NY), 1982.

October (autobiographical record of one month in Isherwood's life; with illustrations by Don Bachardy), limited edition, Twelvetrees Press (Los Angeles, CA), 1983.

(With Swami Gambhirananda) *History of the Ramakrishna Math and Mission,* Vedanta Press (Los Angeles, CA), 1983.

The Wishing Tree: Christopher Isherwood on Mystical Religion, edited by Robert Adjemian, Vedanta Press (Los Angeles, CA), 1987.

Where Joy Resides: A Christopher Isherwood Reader, edited by Don Bachardy and James P. White, Farrar, Straus, & Giroux (New York, NY), 1991.

(With Edward Upward) *The Mortmere Stories,* with images by Graham Crowley, Enitharmon Press (London, England), 1994.

Diaries, Volume One: 1939-1960, edited by Katherine Bucknell, Methuen (London, England), 1997.

The Repton Letters, edited by George Ramsden, Stone Trough Books (Settrington, York, England), 1997.

Lost Years: A Memoir, 1945-1951, edited by Katherine Bucknell, Harper & Row (New York, NY), 2000.

Contributor to books, including *The Complete Works of W.H. Auden,* Volume 1: *Plays and Other Dramatic Writings, 1928-1938,* 1990; and *The Faber Book of Gay Short Fiction,* 1991. Contributor to periodicals, including *Harper's Bazaar* and *Vogue.*

ADAPTATIONS: *The Berlin Stories* was adapted by John Van Druten as a play titled *I Am a Camera,* produced on Broadway in 1951, and published by Random House in 1952. *I Am a Camera* and *The Berlin Stories* were adapted by Joe Masteroff, John Kander, and Fred Ebb as the Broadway musical *Cabaret,* first produced in November, 1966. The screenplay for the movie version of *Cabaret,* written by Jay Presson Allen, was based on Isherwood's *The Berlin Stories,* and the film, directed by Bob Fosse and starring Liza Minnelli and Joel Grey, was released by Allied Artists in 1972.

SIDELIGHTS: Christopher Isherwood's career as a novelist, playwright, diarist, and teacher extended from the late 1920s through his death in 1986. During that era a sea change occurred in the acceptance of homosexuality in Western culture, and Isherwood is widely recognized as having made significant contributions to this trend. Best known for his *Berlin Stories,* from which the plays *I Am a Camera* and *Cabaret* were both adapted, Isherwood chronicled not only his own life but his minute observations of other people, places, and times as recorded in his letters and diaries. In *The Gay and Lesbian Review Worldwide,* Sara S. Hodson called Isherwood "indisputably one of the twentieth century's most important authors in English . . . one of the first self-consciously gay writers to be read extensively by a wider audience." Lewis Gannett in the *Gay and Lesbian Review* noted that Isherwood was an author who came to realize, "significant for both literature and the gay liberation movement, that his identity as a homosexual was inseparable from his identity as a writer. . . . He was living at ground zero of an emerging gay consciousness and was observing it closely."

According to Francis King in his study *Christopher Isherwood,* the British-born, Americanized Isherwood was a "suppose-if" writer. "For such novelists," King explained, "the process of creation begins with something that they themselves have either experienced or observed at close quarters. Taking this foundation of reality, they then proceed to build on it imaginatively by a series of 'suppose-ifs'. . . . When Isherwood has stayed closest to reality, . . . he has been at his best."

During a career spanning a host of genres, Isherwood transformed his life into an often bitingly comic fiction, using what David Daiches called "quietly savage deadpan observation." He was, according to Frank Kermode, "farcical about desperate matters . . . almost as if what mattered was their intrinsic comic value." Isherwood's unique view of the comic in art, a theory of "High Camp," is explained by a character in *The World in the Evening:* "True High Camp always has an underlying seriousness. You can't camp about something you don't take seriously. You're not making fun of it; you're making fun out of it. You're expressing what's basically serious to you in terms of fun and artifice and elegance. Baroque art is largely camp about religion. The Ballet is camp about love. . . . It's terribly hard to define. You have to meditate on it and feel it intuitively, like Lao-Tze's *Tao*."

"I believe in being a serious comic writer," Isherwood once said. "To me, everything is described in those terms. Not in the terms of the unredeemably tragic view of life, but at the same time, not in terms of screwball-ism. Nor in terms of saying, 'Oh, it's all lovely in the garden.' I think the full horror of life must be depicted, but in the end there should be a comedy which is beyond both comedy and tragedy. The thing Gerald Heard calls 'metacomedy'. . . . All I aspire to is to have something of this touch of 'metacomedy.' To give some description of life as it is lived now, and of what it has been like for me, personally, to have been alive."

While still at college in England, Isherwood began to write stories to his friend Edward Upward. The two young men created an entire imaginary village named Mortmere and set stories in this village. Most of their stories were horrific; titles included "The Horror in the Tower," "The Leviathan of the Urinals," and "The Railway Accident." As Upward recounted in the *Spectator*, Isherwood "would write a story and put it on the table in my sitting-room late at night when I was asleep in my bedroom and I would read it with delight at breakfast, and a morning or two later he would find a story by me on his table." In this way, the two budding writers encouraged and critiqued each other's work. In his later writing, Isherwood used much the same technique as he had in his "Mortmere" stories, often exaggerating real-life situations into a kind of comic fantasy.

Isherwood had great success with his Berlin books, *The Last of Mr. Norris* and *Goodbye to Berlin* (collected as *The Berlin Stories*), in which he fictionalized his stay in the pre-Nazi Berlin of the late 1920s and early 1930s. During this time, Isherwood lived with his German lover, Heinz, who was eventually arrested for his homosexuality, imprisoned, and then forced to join the German army. For his part, Isherwood correctly predicted that Nazi Germany would prove hostile to him, and he left before World War II began. In *The Last of Mr. Norris*, Isherwood's narrator is a William Bradshaw (Isherwood's two middle names), while in *Goodbye to Berlin* the narrator is named Christopher Isherwood. This matter-of-fact blend of fact and fiction reflected the naive, honest style Isherwood was seeking in these stories. In both books he uses the phrase "I am a camera" to indicate what he feels his role as narrator should be: a simple recording device.

Through passive, unengaged narrators, Isherwood successfully portrays the decadence of Weimar Germany in startling detail. As Claude J. Summers wrote in the *Dictionary of Literary Biography: British Novelists, 1930-1959*, "Isherwood evokes a mythic city of sexual and political excitement only to acknowledge the artificiality of myth in the harsh reality of loneliness and despair." Many reviewers praised Isherwood's unobtrusive writing style which, like the camera Isherwood claimed to be, allowed the reader to see what his narrator saw. "Isherwood's prose," Edmund Wilson noted in the *New Republic*, "is a perfect medium for his purpose. . . . The sentences all get you somewhere almost without your noticing that you are reading them; the similes always have point without ever obtruding themselves before the object. You seem to look right through Isherwood and to see what he sees." Similarly, David Garnett wrote in *New Statesman and Nation* that "the extraordinary effect of life which [Isherwood] achieves is due almost entirely to his power of expressing exactly his observations. Every detail seems true because each is the result of a sharp verbal focus in his mind."

Isherwood's comic touch is evident in *Mr. Norris Changes Trains*, which features the criminal adventures of Arthur Norris, an aging con man who befriends the naive William Bradshaw. Although morally bankrupt, Norris is irresistible to everyone he meets. Summers called him "among the most seductive comic figures in modern literature" and "both lovable and dangerous." B.R. Redman in the *Saturday Review of Literature* observed: "Astonishingly enough, one cannot dislike Arthur Norris. . . . Norris is soft and appealing. No, one does not dislike him. But it is possible, even easy to dislike the shadowy character of William Bradshaw. He is the repellent factor in the novel." Writing in *Books*, Terence Holliday found that "by touches so subtle as to be almost imperceptible in themselves, the delighted reader is made aware that there is rising before him that rarest phenomenon of the novelist's art—solid three-dimensional human character." As Michael de-la-Noy remarked in *Books and Bookmen*, "It was [Isherwood's] humor that very quickly raised his work above the level of mere confessional autobiography, that stamped it with a genius for comic characterisation in the mould of Evelyn Waugh."

Graham Greene, in an article for the *Dictionary of Literary Biography Yearbook: 1986*, described *The Last of Mr. Norris* as "a permanent landmark in the literature of our time." Summers called *Goodbye to Berlin* an "extraordinary achievement," later adding that it is "a book of haunting loneliness" and "a masterful study of an inhibited young man." Julian Symons concluded in the

Sunday Times that the Berlin stories "remain, and they capture a time, a place, and the people of a disintegrating society in a moving and masterly way. They are a unique achievement." Isherwood's Berlin stories were so popular that they were adapted first as the play *I Am a Camera,* then as the musical *Cabaret,* and finally as the film *Cabaret.* The stage and film versions of the story won a total of seven Tony Awards, a Grammy Award, and eight Academy Awards.

In later works, Isherwood continued to write about his own life in both fiction and nonfiction. James Atlas in the *New York Times* noted that Isherwood "devoted himself to chronicling his life more or less as it happens." A number of his many literary friends are featured as characters in these books. The poet Stephen Spender appears in Isherwood's *Lions and Shadows* as the character Stephen Savage. (Writing of the book in 1986, Spender claimed: "I have the feeling that Stephen Savage is more like the young Stephen Spender than I myself ever was.") Other *Lions and Shadows* characters were modeled after W.H. Auden and Edward Upward, while novelist Virginia Woolf appears in Isherwood's *The World in the Evening.* W. Somerset Maugham, in his novel *The Razor's Edge,* reversed this process, modeling the character of Larry after Isherwood, although Isherwood always denied the resemblance.

In the novel *A Single Man,* a study of a middle-aged homosexual in grief over the death of his longtime companion, Isherwood dealt with key concerns of his life, including spirituality and same-sex love. Set within the confines of a single day, the novel creates a portrait of George, the main character, going about the routine of his life in the face of tragedy. "Beautifully written in a style that alternates between poetic intensity and gentle irony, the book is a technical tour de force in which every nuance is perfectly controlled," Summers enthused. David Daiches in the *New York Times Book Review* found the novel to be "a sad, sly report on the predicament of the human animal," while Elizabeth Hardwick, writing in the *New York Review of Books,* called *A Single Man* "a sad book, with a biological melancholy running through it, a sense of relentless reduction, daily diminishment." Summers, however, saw the novel as culminating "in George's renewed commitment to life and in spiritual illumination." De-la-Noy judged *A Single Man* to be "not just [Isherwood's] masterpiece but one of the most remarkable novels of the twentieth century," and Summers considered it "among the most undervalued novels of our time."

In such nonfiction works as *Kathleen and Frank,* a remembrance of his parents, and *Christopher and His Kind,* an autobiography in which he first admitted his homosexuality, Isherwood wrote about his life in a novelistic fashion, detailing his childhood, his many years as a Hollywood screenwriter, and such matters as his affair with poet W.H. Auden, and his embrace of the Eastern philosophy of Swami Prabhavananda, a teacher of Vedanta. *Kathleen and Frank* combines Isherwood's mother's diaries with his own running commentary and remembrances. The biography begins with his parents' first meeting in the 1890s and proceeds until 1939, when Isherwood left England for America. The book ends with Isherwood's evaluation of his parents' impact upon his own personal development. Joseph Catinella in the *Saturday Review* praised Isherwood for his "novelist's eye for dramatic movement and detail" which produced "a splendid biography." W.H. Auden, writing in the *New York Review of Books,* claimed: "I cannot imagine any reader, whatever his social background and interests, not being enthralled by it."

In *Christopher and His Kind,* Isherwood describes his activities during the 1930s, looking back at that time and himself with a wry humor. Much new information about his life, previously unrevealed, is unveiled in the book, particularly Isherwood's sexual orientation and his various love relationships. "Invigorated and humanized by his commitment to gay liberation, the book is marred only by his tendency to devalue—in the interest of fact—some of his most brilliant fictional techniques in the Berlin stories," Summers commented. A *New Yorker* critic found the memoir to be written with "delicacy and wit," while Peter Stansky in the *New York Times Book Review* called the work "indispensable for admirers of this truly masterly writer." Lewis Gannett called *Christopher and His Kind* "in my opinion the finest gay autobiography ever written."

In addition to his work as a writer, Isherwood was known as a proponent of Hindu religious teachings, and this in turn informed his writing. His interest in Eastern philosophy began in 1939 when he first arrived in Los Angeles and met Swami Prabhavananda, a Hindu teacher. Prabhavananda's teachings emphasized a serene indifference to the things of the world, as well as a benevolent acceptance of homosexuality. From 1943 to 1945, Isherwood served as coeditor of the Hindu magazine *Vedanta and the West,* the official journal of Prabhavananda's Vedanta Society of Southern California. He also translated the *Bhagavad Gita,* a classic of the Hindu religion, while such books as *My Guru and His Disciple* and *An Approach to Vedanta* presented his own religious beliefs. Summers observed that all of Isherwood's later novels "illustrate the Vedantic belief that happiness lies in escape from the ego and in discovery of the *atman,* the impersonal God within man." Isherwood also became known as an outspoken advocate of homosexual rights, giving speeches and writing articles on the subject. His own relationship with painter Don Bachardy lasted from 1954 until Isherwood's death in 1986. John Boorman remarked in *American Film* that "of all the couples I got to know when I first started visiting Los Angeles more than twenty years ago, Christopher Isherwood and Don Bachardy had the only 'marriage' that survived."

Speaking at a forum in 1974, Isherwood declared that the goal of the gay rights movement should be "to be recognized as entirely natural and not to be questioned at all." British poet Stephen Spender declared in the *Observer* that Isherwood's involvement in gay rights "led to his becoming a kind of hero of the Gay community." After all, noted Felice Picano in the *Lambda Book Report,* Isherwood "accomplished nothing less than a complete coming out, decades before Stonewall, and years before such a thing was being done, or even wise to do."

Virtually all of Isherwood's writing, both fiction and nonfiction, was autobiographical in some way. His ability to create entertaining and meaningful work from the raw facts of his life experience—always rendered in a charming and insightful prose style—was what critics considered his unique talent, and the aspect of his writing that attracted the most praise from critics. King explained that the world Isherwood created was "a solipsistic circle: he himself [at] its centre, his perceptions its radii, his consciousness its circumference. What makes this world, admittedly confined, fascinating to the reader is the tone of voice—humane, totally truthful, ironic, benevolent—that its creator employ[ed] to describe it. It [was] chiefly this unique tone of voice that [gave] Isherwood his distinction as one of the most entertaining and likeable of novelists at work in the English language." Isherwood's unique tone also comes through in his travel writing, according to Thomas Dukes, a contributor to the *Dictionary of Literary Biography: British Travel Writers, 1910-1939.* "Like his best novels it includes astute, unsentimental observations about people and places situated in a particular time," the essayist observed. *Journey to a War,* which chronicles a visit to China in 1938, while the Sino-Japanese war raged and World War II was about to begin, and *The Condor and the Cows: A South American Travel Diary,* written in the late 1940s, "are valuable historical documents and illustrate Isherwood's talent for making his point through the meaningful anecdote," added Dukes. De-la-Noy described Isherwood as "a writer of genius, a brilliant entertainer and one of the finest prose stylists of his generation." According to

Summers, Isherwood "is increasingly recognized as one of the twentieth century's most insightful observers of the human condition."

The entries in *Diaries, Volume One: 1939-1960* cover the period from Isherwood's departure for America on January 19, 1939, with Auden until his fifty-sixth birthday, and they reflect the important matters in his life at the time, including his strict adherence to the Swami's teachings during the war years and his not entirely successful quest to lead a spiritually pure life; his personal relationships, including his longtime partnership with Bachardy and his busy social life in Hollywood; and his work. Alfred Corn wrote in the *Nation* that Isherwood's record is "intimate and compulsively readable," although not comprehensive: "You can see that sometimes Isherwood avoids writing when things have taken an embarrassing turn." *Times Literary Supplement* contributor Zachary Leader found that the tenor of the entries changed after Isherwood met Bachardy: "There are more jokes, though also more anxieties about health, appearance, fame. Bad habits quickly assert themselves, particularly a penchant for rage and resentment. . . . When the diaries ponder writing problems, the tone is the same for film or fiction: level, practical, realistic about audiences and their needs." *Time* reviewer Pico Iyer voiced a similar sentiment, noting that in the latter half of the book "more and more of his entries dwindle into local gossip and silly worries about his boyfriend and his weight." Corn, however, thought "the story of how [Isherwood and Bachardy] managed to overcome enormous differences—in age, nationality, experience and vocation—is touching." Also touching, but "a little exasperating," Corn commented, are the entries on Isherwood's religious pursuits: "Isherwood seems to be the only person not in on the secret that he wasn't cut out for seclusion and abstinence." Iyer concluded that "even at his weakest, he earns our trust with his entirely human cries of 'God, make me pure—but not just yet!'" Leader summed up the diaries by saying, "though not every entry is riveting, there is much here to ponder and praise, in the writing as well as in the life."

Bachardy, along with James P. White, anthologized selections from Isherwood's major works (including *Prater Violet* and the entirety of *A Single Man*) and essays for *Where Joy Resides: A Christopher Isherwood Reader.* In the *New Statesman & Society,* Robert Carver characterized the collection as "A Last Lover's anthology" subject to distortion, noting "what we get in this volume is very much the reconstructed American Gay Lib Vedanta Christopher." However, a *Washington Post Book World* critic praised the anthology, saying, "As always with Isherwood, the novels are a blend of autobiography and fiction, the writing is pellucid, and the artistry of the kind that conceals a high degree of art."

As the twentieth century closed, more Isherwood works were published: *Jacob's Hands,* an unproduced screenplay by Isherwood and Aldous Huxley that was discovered by actress Sharon Stone; and *Lost Years: A Memoir, 1945-1951,* Isherwood's reconstruction of events during a period when he did not maintain his customary detailed diaries. According to David Thomson, critiquing the latter volume for the *New York Times Book Review,* this was a time when, for Isherwood, "the stamina or self-awareness necessary for a journal dissolved in drink and promiscuity." Isherwood began putting together a retrospective of these years in the 1970s, and although he did not finish it, the book still provides important insights, in the opinion of some critics. Isherwood writes about himself in the third person, a device that "allows for greater analysis and intimacy" than one might find in a typical first-person memoir, commented Robert Plunket in the *Advocate.* Isherwood is also candid about his bouts of excessive drinking and his active sex life; he also details his practice of Hinduism, his work as a screenwriter, and his friendships with many figures in the arts, including Bertolt Brecht, E.M. Forster, Marlon Brando, and Georgia O'Keeffe. To Thomson, these mentions amount to mere name-dropping, and he was unimpressed with the book as a whole: "These are dazzlingly empty years more than they are lost ones. Their record here will do nothing for Isherwood and posterity." A *Publishers Weekly* critic, however, wrote of the book, "While it lacks the artfulness of the memoirs Isherwood chose to publish, it will nevertheless find grateful readers among those who care about his work." Plunket offered higher praise still, calling *Lost Years* "a book that anyone with even a passing interest in Isherwood or gay social history shouldn't miss."

In 2004, the Huntington Library mounted an exhibition called "Christopher Isherwood: A Writer and His World." The exhibition drew upon Isherwood's papers collected at the Huntington, as well as supplemental material provided by Don Bachardy and other sources, including the Margaret Herrick Library of the Academy of Motion Picture Arts and Sciences.

BIOGRAPHICAL AND CRITICAL SOURCES:

BOOKS

Berg, James, and Chris Freeman, editors, *Conversations with Christopher Isherwood,* University Press of Mississippi (Jackson, MS), 2001.

Berg, James, and Chris Freeman, editors, *The Isherwood Century: Essays on the Life and Work of Christopher Isherwood,* University of Wisconsin Press (Madison, WI), 2000.

Contemporary Literary Criticism, Thomson Gale (Detroit, MI), Volume 1, 1973, Volume 9, 1978, Volume 11, 1979, Volume 14, 1980, Volume 44, 1987.

Dictionary of Literary Biography, Thomson Gale (Detroit, MI), Volume 15: *British Novelists, 1930-1959,* 1983, Volume 95: *British Travel Writers, 1910-1939,* 1998.

Dictionary of Literary Biography Yearbook: 1986, Thomson Gale (Detroit, MI), 1987.

Ferres, Kay, *Christopher Isherwood: A World in Evening,* Borgo (San Bernardino, CA), 1994.

Finney, Brian, *Christopher Isherwood: A Critical Biography,* Oxford University Press (New York, NY), 1979.

Fryer, Jonathan, *Isherwood: A Biography of Christopher Isherwood,* New English Library (London, England), 1977, Doubleday (New York, NY), 1978.

Funk, Robert W., *Christopher Isherwood: A Reference Guide,* G.K. Hall (Boston, MA), 1979.

Heilbrun, Carolyn G., *Christopher Isherwood,* Columbia University Press (New York, NY), 1970.

Hynes, Samuel L., *The Auden Generation: Literature and Politics in England in the 1930s,* Bodley Head (London, England), 1976.

Isherwood, Christopher, *Christopher and His Kind,* Farrar, Straus & Giroux (New York, NY), 1976.

Isherwood, Christopher, *Diaries, Volume One: 1939-1960,* edited by Katherine Bucknell, Methuen (London, England), 1997.

Isherwood, Christopher, *Lost Years: A Memoir, 1945-1951,* edited by Katherine Bucknell, Harper & Row (New York, NY), 2000.

Isherwood, Christopher, *The World in the Evening,* Random House (New York, NY), 1954.

Izzo, David Garrett, *Christopher Isherwood: His Era, His Gang, and the Legacy of the Truly Strong Man,* University of South Carolina Press (Columbia, SC), 2001.

Kermode, Frank, *Puzzles and Epiphanies,* Chilmark (Washington, DC), 1962.

King, Francis, *Christopher Isherwood,* Longman (London, England), 1976.

Lehmann, John, *Christopher Isherwood: A Personal Memoir,* Holt (New York, NY), 1988.

Newquist, Roy, *Conversations,* Rand McNally (Chicago, IL), 1967.

Page, Norman, *Auden and Isherwood,* St. Martin's Press (New York, NY), 1997.

Parker, Peter, *Isherwood: A Life,* Picador (London, England), 2004, published as *Isherwood: A Life Revealed,* Random House, 2004.

Phelps, Gilbert, editor, *Living Writers,* Transatlantic (Albuquerque, NM), 1947.

Westby, Selmer, and Clayton M. Brown, *Christopher Isherwood: A Bibliography, 1923-1967,* California State College (Los Angeles, CA), 1968.

Wilde, Alan, *Christopher Isherwood,* Twayne (Boston, MA), 1971.

PERIODICALS

Advocate, March 12, 1991; March 4, 1997, review of *Diaries, Volume One,* p. 57; September 12, 2000, Robert Plunket, review of *Lost Years,* p. 63.

American Film, October, 1986, John Boorman, "Stranger in Paradise," pp. 53-57.

Antaeus, spring-summer, 1974, Daniel Halpern, "A Conversation with Christopher Isherwood," pp. 366-388.

Ariel: A Review of International English Literature, 1972.

Booklist, September 15, 2000, Brad Hooper, review of *Lost Years,* p. 203.

Books and Bookmen, March, 1986.

California Quarterly, winter-spring, 1977, Jeffrey Bailey, "Interview: Christopher Isherwood," pp. 87-96.

Contemporary Literature, winter, 1972, David P. Thomas, "Goodbye to Berlin: Refocusing Isherwood's Camera," pp. 44-52; autumn, 1975, Alan Wilde, "Language and Surface: Isherwood and the Thirties," pp. 478-491.

Critical Inquiry, March, 1975.

Encounter, August, 1954, Angus Wilson, "The New and Old Isherwood," pp. 62-68; November, 1962.

Gay and Lesbian Review, May, 2001, Lewis Gannett, "Time Regained," p. 35.

Gay and Lesbian Review Worldwide, July-August, 2004, Sara S. Hodson, "An Isherwood Treasure Trail," p. 22.

Journal of Modern Literature, February, 1976.

Lambda Book Report, January, 2001, Felice Picano, "Filling in the Blanks," p. 14.

London Magazine, June, 1961, Stanley Poss, "A Conversation on Tape," pp. 41-58; July, 1965, John Whitehead, "Isherwood at Sixty," pp. 90-100; April, 1968, Charles Higham, "Isherwood on Hollywood," pp. 31-38.

London Review of Books, January 26, 1995, review of *The Mortmere Stories,* p. 19; January 2, 1997, review of *Diaries, Volume One,* p. 32.

Los Angeles Times Book Review, May 5, 1991, p. 14; February 2, 1997, review of *Diaries, Volume One,* p. 6.

Modern Fiction Studies, winter, 1970.

Nation, February 10, 1997, Alfred Corn, review of *Diaries, Volume One,* p. 27.

New Republic, May 17, 1939; February 26, 1990.

New Review, August, 1975, Brian Finney, "Christopher Isherwood—A Profile," pp. 17-24.

New Statesman, October 3, 1986.

New Statesman and Nation, March 11, 1939.

New Statesman & Society, August 25, 1989; January 12, 1990.

New Yorker, December 27, 1976.

New York Review of Books, August 20, 1964; January 27, 1972, W.H. Auden, "The Diary of a Diary," pp. 19-20; February 20, 1997, review of *Diaries, Volume One,* p. 11.

New York Times, March 19, 1939; August 2, 1979; August 27, 1980.

New York Times Book Review, August 30, 1964; March 25, 1973; November 28, 1976; January 5, 1997, John Sturrock, "My Life Will Be What I Make of It," p. 6; March 28, 1999, p. 28; September 17, 2000, David Thomson, "Out of Film."

Observer, January 4, 1990, p. 45; November 10, 1996, review of *Diaries, Volume One,* p. 15.

Paris Review, spring, 1974, W.I. Scobie, "Art of Fiction: Interview," pp. 138-182.

Perspectives on Contemporary Literature, May, 1977.

Publishers Weekly, October 20, 1989; September 6, 1991; November 11, 1996, review of *Diaries, Volume One,* p. 63; July 27, 1998, review of *Jacob's Hands,* p. 53; August 21, 2000, review of *Lost Years,* p. 58.

Saturday Review, January 22, 1972.

Saturday Review of Literature, May 11, 1935.

Shenandoah, spring, 1965, George Wickes, "An Interview with Christopher Isherwood," pp. 22-52.

Sight and Sound, spring, 1986.

Spectator, March 1, 1935; March 3, 1939; January 18, 1986.

Time, January 13, 1997, Pico Iyer, review of *Diaries, Volume One,* p. 74.

Times Literary Supplement, September 10, 1964; November 3, 1995, p. 22; January 10, 1997, Zachary Leader, review of *Diaries, Volume One,* p. 5; May 15, 1998, p. 31.

Twentieth-Century Literature, October, 1976, Carolyn G. Heilbrun, "Christopher Isherwood: An Interview," pp. 253-263.

Washington Post Book World, April 28, 1991.

Washington Times, September 6, 1998, "'Micro-biography' of Two Men, One City," p. 6.

Yale Review, autumn, 1989.

ONLINE

Isherwood Century, http://www.theisherwoodcentury.
   org/ (August 25, 2004), essays and information
   about Isherwood.
Isherwood Foundation, http://www.isherwood
   foundation.org/ (August 25, 2004), foundation in
   honor of Isherwood.

OBITUARIES:

PERIODICALS

AB Bookman's Weekly, January 6, 1986.
Chicago Tribune, January 7, 1986.
Daily Variety, January 6, 1986.
Kenosha News, January 6, 1986.
Los Angeles Times, January 6, 1986.
Newsweek, January 20, 1986.
New York Times, January 6, 1986.
Observer, January 12, 1986.
Publishers Weekly, January 17, 1986.
Sunday Times (London), January 12, 1986.
Time, January 20, 1986.
Washington Post, January 6, 1986.

* * *

ISHERWOOD, Christopher William Bradshaw
   See ISHERWOOD, Christopher

* * *

ISHIGURO, Kazuo 1954-

PERSONAL: Born November 8, 1954, in Nagasaki, Japan; resident of Great Britain since 1960; son of Shizuo (a scientist) and Shizuko (a homemaker; maiden name, Michida) Ishiguro; married Lorna Anne MacDougall, May 9, 1986. *Education:* University of Kent, B.A. (with honors), 1978; University of East Anglia, M.A., 1980. *Hobbies and other interests:* Music, guitar, piano, cinema.

ADDRESSES: Office—c/o Author Mail, Faber and Faber, 3 Queen Square, London WC1N 3AU, England.

CAREER: Grouse beater for Queen Mother at Balmoral Castle, Aberdeen, Scotland, 1973; Renfrew Social Works Department, Renfrew, Scotland, community worker, 1976; West London Cyrenians Ltd., London, England, residential social worker, 1979-81; writer, 1982—.

AWARDS, HONORS: Winifred Holtby Award, Royal Society of Literature, 1983, for *A Pale View of Hills;* Whitbread Book of the Year Award, 1986, for *An Artist of the Floating World;* Booker Prize, 1989, for *The Remains of the Day;* Premio Scanno (Italy), 1995; Order of the British Empire for services to literature, 1995; honorary Litt.D., University of Kent, 1990, and University of East Anglia, 1995; *When We Were Orphans* shortlisted for Booker Prize, 2000.

WRITINGS:

A Pale View of Hills, Putnam (New York, NY), 1982.
An Artist of the Floating World, Putnam (New York, NY), 1986.
The Remains of the Day, Knopf (New York, NY), 1989.
The Unconsoled, Knopf (New York, NY), 1995.
When We Were Orphans, Knopf (New York, NY), 2001.
Never Let Me Go, Knopf (New York, NY), 2005.

Also contributor to *Introduction 7: Stories by New Writers,* Faber (London, England), 1981. Author of television film scripts, including *A Profile of Arthur J. Mason,* 1984, and *The Gourmet,* 1986. Contributor to literary journals, including *London Review of Books, Firebird, Bananas,* and *Harpers and Queen.*

ADAPTATIONS: The Remains of the Day was adapted into a feature film starring Anthony Hopkins and Emma Thompson by Merchant Ivory Productions, 1993. Ishiguro's unproduced screenplay *The Saddest Music in the World* was adapted by Guy Maddin and George Toles in 2004.

SIDELIGHTS: After his first three novels, Japanese-born Kazuo Ishiguro emerged as one of the foremost British writers of his generation. Ishiguro's novels commonly deal with issues of memory, self-deception, and codes of etiquette, leading his characters to a reevaluation or realization about the relative success or failure of their lives. His capture of the prestigious Booker Prize for his third novel, *The Remains of the Day,* confirmed the critical acclaim his work received. His fifth novel, *When We Were Orphans,* was also widely praised, and was shortlisted for the Booker Prize in 2000.

Ishiguro's highly acclaimed first novel, *A Pale View of Hills,* is narrated by Etsuko, a middle-aged Japanese woman living in England. The suicide of Etsuko's daughter, Keiko, awakens somber memories of the summer in the 1950s in war-ravaged Nagasaki when the child was born. Etsuko's thoughts and dreams turn particularly to Sachiko, a war widow whose unfortunate relationship with an American lover traumatizes her already troubled daughter, Mariko. Etsuko, too, will eventually embrace the West, and leave her Japanese husband to marry an English journalist. "Etsuko's memories, though they focus on her neighbor's sorrows and follies, clearly refer to herself as well," wrote Edith Milton in *New York Times Book Review.* "The lives of the two women run parallel, and Etsuko, like Sachiko, has raised a deeply disturbed daughter; like her, she has turned away from the strangling role of traditional Japanese housewife toward the West, where she has discovered freedom of a sort, but also an odd lack of depth, commitment, and continuity." Surrounded that summer by a new order that has shattered ancient ways, the two women choose the Western path of self-interest, compromising—to varying degrees—their delicate daughters. "In Etsuko's present life as much as in her past, she is circled by a chain of death which has its beginning in the war," suggested *New Statesman* reviewer James Campbell.

Reviewing *A Pale View of Hills* in *Spectator,* Francis King found the novel "typically Japanese in its compression, its reticence, and in its exclusion of all details not absolutely essential to its theme." While some reviewers agreed with *Times Literary Supplement* writer Paul Bailey that "at certain points I could have done with something as crude as a fact," others felt that Ishiguro's delicate layering of themes and images grants the narrative great evocative power. *A Pale View of Hills* "is a beautiful and dense novel, gliding from level to level of consciousness," remarked Jonathan Spence in *New Society.* "Ishiguro develops [his themes] with remarkable insight and skill," concurred Rosemary Roberts in *Los Angeles Times Book Review.* "They are described in controlled prose that more often hints than explains or tells. The effect evokes mystery and an aura of menace." King deemed the novel "a memorable and moving work, its elements of past and present, of Japan and England held together by a shimmering, all but invisible net of images linked to each other by filaments at once tenuous and immensely strong."

While *A Pale View of Hills* depicts the incineration of a culture and the disjointed lives of the displaced, Ishiguro's novel is not without optimism. Critics saw in the war survivors' tenacious struggle to resurrect some sort of life, however alien, great hope and human courage. "Sachiko and Etsuko become minor figures in a greater pattern of betrayal, infanticide and survival played out against the background of Nagasaki, itself the absolute

emblem of our genius for destruction," Milton continued. "In this book, where what is stated is often less important than what is left unsaid, those blanked-out days around the bomb's explosion become the paradigm of modern life. They are the ultimate qualities which the novel celebrates: the brilliance of our negative invention, and our infinite talent for living beyond annihilation as if we had forgotten it." Reiterated Roberts: "There is nobility in determination to press on with life even against daunting odds. Ishiguro has brilliantly captured this phoenixlike spirit; high praise to him."

In *An Artist of the Floating World* Ishiguro again explores Japan in transition. Set in a provincial Japanese town during 1949 and 1950, the story revolves around Masuji Ono, a painter who worked as an official artist and propagandist for the imperialist regime that propelled Japan into World War II. Knowing that his former ideals were errant does little to help Ono adjust to the bewildering Westernization that is going on all around him; nor does it quell his longings for the past, with its fervent patriotism, professional triumphs, and deep comradeship. "Ishiguro's insights . . . are finely balanced," wrote Anne Chisholm in *Times Literary Supplement.* "He shows how the old Japanese virtues of veneration for the Sensei (the teacher), or loyalty to the group, could be distorted and exploited; he allows deep reservations to surface about the wholesale Americanization of Japan in the aftermath of humiliation and defeat. Without asking us to condone Ono's or Japan's terrible mistakes, he suggests with sympathy some reasons why the mistakes were made."

Admiring how "Ishiguro unravels the old man's thoughts and feelings with exceptional delicacy," Chisholm determined that the story "is not only pleasurable to read but instructive, without being in the least didactic." "The old man's longings for his past become a universal lament for lost worlds," added the critic, who judged *An Artist of the Floating World* a "fine new novel."

In the opinion of Christopher Hitchens in *Nation,* Ishiguro's first two novels share a form in their "unmediated retrospective monologue." Hitchens cited their similar themes as well: "Each narrator has lived according to strict codes of etiquette and order; the ethos of actively and passively 'knowing one's place,' and adhering to protocol and precedent." Those same forms and themes shape the third novel, *The Remains of the Day,* which presents the narrative of Stevens, English butler to Lord Darlington of Darlington Hall. After more than thirty years of faithful service to the Lord, Stevens now finds himself in the employ of Mr. Farraday, a congenial American who has purchased the estate and keeps Stevens on as part of the colorful trappings. Farraday urges Stevens to take a motoring holiday through Cornwall. Concurrently, Stevens has received a letter from Miss Kenton (now Mrs. Benn), the exemplary housekeeper who had left Darlington Hall some twenty years before. Mrs. Benn's letter hints at unhappiness in her marriage and suggests a willingness to return to service at Darlington. Short of staff in the downsized estate, the ever-dutiful Stevens justifies his absence with the utilitarian purpose of hiring the former housekeeper.

As the journey proceeds and Stevens rambles about in Farraday's old Ford—taking eight days to go about one hundred miles—he reflects upon the people he meets, the countryside and, tellingly and ironically, his own life. At one point, Stevens proclaims the English landscape the most satisfying in the world precisely because of its lack of obvious drama or spectacle. This fondness to dampen the dramatic and spectacular and to fit in easily does, in fact, control his life. It is the reason he so thoroughly inhabits his role as butler. As he returns to the same memories again and again, the fog of self-deception lifts. One motoring mishap after another—a flat tire, overheated radiator—affords him the time and perspective he has never had. Meeting the ordinary people who actually suffered during the war, Stevens has difficulty admitting to his long service at Darlington. He begins to doubt the Lord's—and his own—judgment. The quiet tragedies of revelation continue as Stevens comes to realize what the perceptive reader has known all along: his proposed rendezvous with Mrs. Benn has more than a utilitarian purpose. She represents, in fact, his last chance to seize happiness in life.

Reviewing *The Remains of the Day* for the London *Observer,* Salman Rushdie noted: "Just below the understatement of the novel's surface is a turbulence as immense as it is slow." Drawing readers into its subtle complexities, the novel met with a highly favorable critical response. Galen Strawson, for example, praised the novel in *Times Literary Supplement,* writing that *The Remains of the Day* "is as strong as it is delicate, a very finely nuanced and at times humorous study of repression. . . . It is a strikingly original book, and beautifully made. . . . Stevens' . . . language creates a context which allows Kazuo Ishiguro to put a massive charge of pathos into a single unremarkable phrase." In *Chicago Tribune,* Joseph Coates described the novel as "an ineffably sad and beautiful piece of work—a tragedy in the form of a comedy of manners." He continued: "Rarely has the device of an unreliable narrator

worked such character revelation as it does here." Mark Kamine cited Ishiguro's technique in *New Leader:* "Usually the butler's feelings are hidden in painfully correct periphrasis, or refracted in dialogue spoken by other characters. . . . Few writers dare to say so little of what they mean as Ishiguro."

While many reviews of *The Remains of the Day* were favorable, this was not universally so. Writing for *New Statesman & Society,* Geoff Dyer wondered "if the whole idea of irony as a *narrative strategy* hasn't lost its usefulness." Dyer worried that Stevens's voice had been "*coaxed* in the interests of the larger ironic scheme of the novel." Comparing the novelist to Henry James, however, Hermione Lee defended Ishiguro's style in *New Republic:* "To accuse Ishiguro of costive, elegant minimalism is to miss the deep sadness, the boundless melancholy that opens out, like the 'deserts of vast eternity' his characters are reluctantly contemplating, under the immaculate surface."

Winning the Booker Prize for *The Remains of the Day* allowed Ishiguro "to break through the veil of expectations and constraints that both his success, and his readers' stubborn determination to take him absolutely literally, imposed," and "to try something wild and frightening that would prevent him from ever being taken as a realist again," according to Pico Iyer in a *Times Literary Supplement* review. Iyer noted that Ishiguro achieves this goal in his fourth novel, *The Unconsoled* "Even though every sentence and theme is recognizably [Ishiguro's]," noted Iyer, "he has written a book that passes on the bewilderment it seeks to portray."

The Unconsoled, much longer than Ishiguro's previous novels, details the journey of Ryder, a famous pianist, who finds himself in an unfamiliar town for a concert he does not remember arranging. Similar to the themes of his earlier books, Ishiguro again deals with codes of etiquette and order. "The book is in large part about assumptions and presumptions, about being put out and put upon—and about putting on a face of obliging acquiescence," stated Iyer. In one scene a hotel manager selfishly intent on making the pianist as comfortable as possible compels Ryder to change rooms, which in the end is an imposition rather than a kindness. *The Unconsoled* unfolds for the reader "a whole society that wonders if it has missed the point and missed the boat, and comes to see that perhaps, at some critical juncture, it was too timid, too accommodating, too dutiful to stand up for its real needs," added Iyer. He concluded: "*The Unconsoled* is a humane and grieving book, as well as one of the strangest novels in memory."

Indeed, *The Unconsoled* puzzled and irritated many reviewers. *Maclean's* contributor Guy Lawson noted that the book is built around "a clever idea: that music, no matter how unmelodic, represents a search for meaning in a confusing, contingent world," but complained that "Ishiguro . . . has written a book so plotless, so oblique, so difficult to read that the idea is lost in maddening digression after maddening digression." Several critics stressed the differences between *The Unconsoled* and Ishiguro's previous novels. *Commonweal's* Linda Simon speculated, "It may have been Ishiguro's aim to subvert the conventions of the novel as a way of underscoring his theme [of the difficulty of communication and connection], but the result is a book lacking the grace and precision that we have come to expect from a writer who, so amply in the past, has proved his intelligence, insight, and talents." A *Newsweek* reviewer added, "It's as if he got sick of reading about how compact his prose is—how he's the poet laureate of the unspoken and unexpressed—and suddenly retaliated with this dense snowstorm of words." In *New York Times,* Michiko Kakutani began by commenting on one of the similarities between *The Unconsoled* and *The Remains of the Day:* "Ryder and Stevens are actually mirror images of each other. Both are unreliable narrators whose fragmented, elliptical reminiscences will gradually expose their self-delusions. Both are willful professionals who hide behind the mask of their vocations. And both are cold, pragmatic men who have cut themselves off from reality and emotional commitment." Kakutani continued, "The biggest difference between the two men, it turns out, concerns the novels they star in. Where *The Remains of the Day* was a narrative tour de force attesting to Mr. Ishiguro's virtuosic control of the language, tone and character, *The Unconsoled* remains an awkward if admirably ambitious experiment weighed down by its own schematic structure."

The Unconsoled had its champions, though. In *New York Times Book Review,* Louis Menaud asserted that, "By the standards of *The Remains of the Day, The Unconsoled* can seem oblique, underpowered and, because of its length, slightly pretentious; but by the standards of *The Unconsoled, The Remains of the Day* is predictable and heavy-handed. If no one had ever heard of Kazuo Ishiguro, if he had never published a word before, it would have been much easier to see how singular the vision behind *The Unconsoled* really is." *Nation* commentator Charlotte Innes, noting that some critics found the book chaotic, contended that "far from being 'chaotic,' *The Unconsoled* is as tightly plotted as anything Ishiguro has written." She added, "*The Unconsoled* conveys the same bleak message as the rest of Ishiguro's much-praised work. Our self-deceptions are intol-

erable. Denial is a hedge against madness. . . . But his emphasis on the tremendous relief to be drawn from the complementary comforts of kindness and art suggest something more ambivalent here. . . . Music has no moral force. But the feeling it projects, like the lifegiving exuberance of Ishiguro's prose, is unmistakable."

When We Were Orphans offers a "fusion of Ishiguro's talents and techniques," including "the muffled misery and cool, clear prose" of *The Remains of the Day* and the "surreal paranoia" of *The Unconsoled,* according to *Time International* reviewer Elinor Shields. The novel begins in 1930, with its narrator, English detective Christopher Banks still haunted by the central mystery of his own life: the unexplained disappearance of his parents from their home in Shanghai when he was a child. His investigation finally takes him to Shanghai in the late 1930s, when the city is under attack from Japan. While chronicling Banks's pursuit of the truth behind his parents' vanishing, the story also gives us his remembrances of his youth in Shanghai, his education at prestigious British schools, and his rise to a position of prominence in detective work. The novel is at once a mystery, a work of historical fiction, and "a Freudian fairy tale about a painful transition to adulthood," Shields explained.

"The novel has its quiet successes," opined James Francken in a review of *When We Were Orphans* for *London Review of Books.* "The hand-me-down conventions of detective fiction are shown to be too neat. . . . And there are delicate comic details." But, the critic cautioned, "*When We Were Orphans* doesn't work as a detective novel. Banks's stilted narrative relies on the mystery of the unaccountable and the fear of the unexplained, but the danger never really becomes threatening: there is very little evil in the novel and not even much nastiness." Furthermore, he complained, Banks is "starchy" and "predictable." An *Economist* critic cited the novel's "story-telling strengths," but also commented on its inadequate characterization and "monotonous" dialogue. "The strongest impression is of nostalgia-soaked pastiche," the critic observed, a mix of "a novel of manners with a particular kind of detective novel." Shields, however, praised the work's "moments of unnerving suspense" and praised it as "a rich, satisfying read, clear yet complex." In *Publishers Weekly* a critic noted of *When We Were Orphans* that Ishiguro's novel "triumphs with the seductiveness of his prose and his ability to invigorate shadowy events with sinister implications."

In a profile by Susan Chira for *New York Times Book Review,* Ishiguro stated: "What I'm interested in is not the actual fact that my characters have done things they later regret. . . . I'm interested in how they come to terms with it." Ishiguro continued: "On the one hand there is a need for honesty, on the other hand a need to deceive themselves—to preserve a sense of dignity, some sort of self-respect. What I want to suggest is that some sort of dignity and self-respect does come from that sort of honesty."

BIOGRAPHICAL AND CRITICAL SOURCES:

BOOKS

Contemporary Literary Criticism, Volume 27, Thomson Gale (Detroit, MI), 1984.

Shaffer, Brian W., *Understanding Kazuo Ishiguro,* University of South Carolina Press (Columbia, SC), 1997.

PERIODICALS

Antioch Review, summer, 2001, Rosemary Hartigan, review of *When We Were Orphans,* p. 637.

Book, September, 2000, Helen M. Jerome, "An Artist of the World," p. 40.

Booklist, July, 2000, Brad Hooper, review of *When We Were Orphans,* p. 1974; April 1, 2001, Karen Harris, review of *When We Were Orphans,* p. 1490.

Chicago Tribune, October 1, 1989, p. 5.

Clio, spring, 2001, Cynthia F. Wong, interview with Ishiguro, p. 309.

Commonweal, March 22, 1996, Linda Simon, review of *The Unconsoled,* p. 25.

Comparative Literature, fall, 2001, Bruce Robbins, "Very Busy Just Now: Globalization and Harriedness in Ishiguro's 'The Unconsoled,'" p. 426.

Economist, May 6, 1995, p. 85; April 15, 2000, "New Novels," p. 12.

Encounter, June-July, 1982.

Harper's, October, 1995, p. 71; February, 1996, p. 30.

Library Journal, August, 2000, Barbara Hoffert, review of *When We Were Orphans,* p. 157.

London Review of Books, April 13, 2000, James Francken, "Something Fishy," p. 37.

Los Angeles Times, June 20, 1986.

Los Angeles Times Book Review, August 8, 1982; October 1, 1989; April 1, 1990; October 14, 1990.

Maclean's, May 22, 1995, Guy Lawson, review of *The Unconsoled,* p. 70.

Modern Fiction Studies, fall, 2002, John J. Su, "Refiguring National Character: The Remains of the British Estate Novel," p. 552.

Nation, June 11, 1990, p. 81; November 6, 1995, Charlotte Innes, review of *The Unconsoled,* p. 546.

New Leader, November 13, 1989, pp. 21-22; September, 2000, Tova Reich, review of *When We Were Orphans,* p. 42.

New Republic, January 22, 1990; November 6, 1995, p. 42.

New Society, May 13, 1982.

New Statesman, February 19, 1982; April 3, 2000, Phil Whittaker, "Return of the Native."

New Statesman & Society, May 26, 1989.

Newsweek, October 2, 1995, review of *The Unconsoled,* p. 92.

New Yorker, April 19, 1982; October 23, 1995, p. 90; September 11, 2000, Joan Acocella, review of *When We Were Orphans,* p. 95.

New York Review of Books, December 21, 1995, p. 17.

New York Times, October 17, 1995, Michiko Kakutani, "Books of the Times."

New York Times Book Review, May 9, 1982; June 8, 1986; October 8, 1989; October 15, 1995, Louis Menand, "Anxious in Dreamland," p. 7.

Observer (London, England), May 21, 1989, p. 53.

Publishers Weekly, July 3, 1995, review of *The Unconsoled,* p. 48; September 18, 1995, p. 105; July 10, 2000, review of *When We Were Orphans,* p. 41.

Sewanee Review, summer, 2001, Ben Howard, "A Civil Tongue: The Voice of Kazuo Ishiguro," p. 398.

Spectator, February 27, 1982.

Time, October 2, 1995, Paul Gray, review of *The Unconsoled,* p. 82.

Time International, April 24, 2000, Elinor Shields, "The End of Innocence," p. 65.

Times (London, England), February 18, 1982; February 28, 1983.

Times Literary Supplement, February 19, 1982; February 14, 1986; May 19, 1989; April 28, 1995.

World Literature Today, summer, 2000, Brian W. Shaffer, review of *When We Were Orphans,* p. 595.

Writer, May, 2001, Lewis Burke Frumkes, "Kazuo Ishiguro," p. 24.

Yale Review, April, 2001, Diana Postlethwaite, review of *When We Were Orphans,* p. 159.

ONLINE

January Magazine, http://www.januarymagazine.com/ (April 20, 2004), Linda Richards, interview with Ishiguro.

*   *   *

IVES, Morgan
See BRADLEY, Marion Zimmer

J

JAKES, John 1932-
(William Ard, John William Jakes, Alan Payne, Jay Scotland)

PERSONAL: Born March 31, 1932, in Chicago, IL; son of John Adrian (a Railway Express general manager) and Bertha (Retz) Jakes; married Rachel Ann Payne (a teacher), June 15, 1951; children: Andrea, Ellen, John Michael, Victoria. *Education:* DePauw University, A.B., 1953; Ohio State University, M.A., 1954. *Politics:* Independent. *Religion:* Protestant. *Hobbies and other interests:* Swimming, boating, acting and directing in community theater.

ADDRESSES: Agent—Rembar & Curtis, 19 W. 44th St., New York, NY 10036. *E-mail*—jjfiction@aol.com.

CAREER: Abbott Laboratories, North Chicago, IL, 1954-60, began as copywriter, became product promotion manager; Rumrill Co. (advertising agency), Rochester, NY, copywriter, 1960-61; freelance writer, 1961-65; Kircher Helton & Collet, Inc. (advertising agency), Dayton, OH, senior copywriter, 1965-68; Oppenheim, Herminghausen, Clarke, Inc. (advertising agency), Dayton, 1968-70, began as copy chief, became vice president; Dancer-Fitzgerald-Sample, Inc. (advertising agency), Dayton, creative director, 1970-71; freelance writer, 1971—. University of South Carolina, Columbia, Department of History, research fellow, 1989. DePauw University, Greencastle, IN, trustee.

MEMBER: Authors Guild, Authors League of America, Dramatists Guild, Science Fiction Writers of America, Western Writers of America, Century Association.

AWARDS, HONORS: LL.D., Wright State University, 1976; Litt.D., DePauw University, 1977; Porgie Award, 1977, for best books in a series; Ohioana Book Award for fiction, 1978, for "American Bicentennial" series; Friends of the Rochester Library Literary Award, 1983; Citizen-Celebrity Award for library advocacy, White House Conference on Libraries, 1995; Distinguished Alumni Award, Ohio State University, College of Humanities, 1995; Western Heritage Literature Award, National Cowboy Hall of Fame, 1995; D.H.L., Winthrop College, 1985, University of South Carolina, 1993, and Ohio State University, 1996; South Carolina Academy of Authors, 1996; Professional Achievement Award, Ohio State University Alumni Association, 1997; Career Achievement Award, South Carolina Humanities Association, 1998; Medal of the Thomas Cooper Society, University of South Carolina, 2002.

WRITINGS:

The Texans Ride North: The Story of the Cattle Trails (for children), John C. Winston (Philadelphia, PA), 1952.

Wear a Fast Gun, Arcadia House (New York, NY), 1956.

A Night for Treason, Bouregy & Curl (New York, NY), 1956.

(Under pseudonym Alan Payne) *Murder, He Says,* Ace Books (New York, NY), 1958.

(Under pseudonym Alan Payne) *This Will Slay You,* Ace Books (New York, NY), 1958.

The Devil Has Four Faces, Bouregy (New York, NY), 1959.

Johnny Havoc, Belmont Books (New York, NY), 1960.

(Under pseudonym William Ard) *Make Mine Mavis,* Monarch (Derby, CT), 1961.

(Under pseudonym William Ard) *And So to Bed,* Monarch (Derby, CT), 1962.

(Under pseudonym William Ard) *Give Me This Woman,* Monarch (Derby, CT), 1962.

Johnny Havoc Meets Zelda, Belmont Books (New York, NY), 1962, published as *Havoc for Sale,* Armchair Detective Library (New York, NY), 1990.

Johnny Havoc and the Doll Who Had "It," Belmont Books (New York, NY), 1963, published as *Holiday for Havoc,* Armchair Detective Library (New York, NY), 1991.

G.I. Girls, Monarch (Derby, CT), 1963.

Tiros: Weather Eye in Space, Messner (New York, NY), 1966.

When the Star Kings Die, Ace Books (New York, NY), 1967.

Great War Correspondents, Putnam (New York, NY), 1967.

Famous Firsts in Sports, Putnam (New York, NY), 1967.

Making It Big, Belmont Books (New York, NY), 1968, published as *Johnny Havoc and the Siren in Red,* Armchair Detective Library (New York, NY), 1991.

Great Women Reporters, Putnam (New York, NY), 1969.

Tonight We Steal the Stars (bound with *The Wagered World* by Laurence M. Janifer and S.J. Treibich), Ace Books (New York, NY), 1969.

The Hybrid, Paperback Library (New York, NY), 1969.

The Last Magicians, Signet (New York, NY), 1969.

Secrets of Stardeep, Westminster (Philadelphia, PA), 1969, published with *Time Gate* (also see below), New American Library (New York, NY), 1982.

The Planet Wizard, Ace Books (New York, NY), 1969.

The Asylum World, Paperback Library (New York, NY), 1969.

Mohawk: The Life of Joseph Brant, Crowell (New York, NY), 1969.

Black in Time, Paperback Library (New York, NY), 1970.

Six-Gun Planet, Paperback Library (New York, NY), 1970.

Mask of Chaos (bound with *The Star Virus* by Barrington T. Bayler), Ace Books (New York, NY), 1970.

Monte Cristo 99, Modern Library (New York, NY), 1970.

Master of the Dark Gate, Lancer Books (New York, NY), 1970.

Conquest of the Planet of the Apes (novelization of film of the same title), Award Books (New York, NY), 1972.

Time Gate, Westminster (Philadelphia, PA), 1972.

Witch of the Dark Gate, Lancer Books (New York, NY), 1972.

Mention My Name in Atlantis: Being, at Last, the True Account of the Calamitous Destruction of the Great Island Kingdom, Together with a Narrative of Its Wondrous Intercourses with a Superior Race of Other-Worldlings, As Transcribed from the Ms. of a Survivor, Hoptor the Vintner, for the Enlightenment of a Dubious Posterity, DAW Books (New York, NY), 1972.

On Wheels, Paperback Library (New York, NY), 1973.

The Best of John Jakes (science fiction), edited by Martin H. Greenberg and Joseph D. Olander, DAW Books (New York, NY), 1977.

The Bastard Photostory, Jove (New York, NY), 1980.

Susanna of the Alamo: A True Story (juvenile), Harcourt (New York, NY), 1986.

California Gold, Random House (New York, NY), 1989.

The Best Western Stories of John Jakes, edited by Martin Greenberg and Bill Pronzini, Ohio University Press (Athens, OH), 1991.

Homeland, Doubleday (New York, NY), 1993.

In the Big Country: The Best Western Stories of John Jakes, G.K. Hall (Thorndike, ME), 1993.

John Jakes' Mullkon Empire, Tekno Comix (Boca Raton, FL), 1995.

Great Stories of the American West, large print edition, G.K. Hall (Thorndike, ME), 1995.

American Dreams, Dutton (New York, NY), 1998.

On Secret Service (novel), Dutton (New York, NY), 2000.

The Bold Frontier, Signet (New York, NY), 2001.

Crime Time: Mystery and Suspense Stories, Five Star (Waterville, ME), 2001.

Charleston, Dutton (New York, NY), 2002.

Savannah; or, A Gift for Mr. Lincoln, Dutton (New York, NY), 2004.

"BRAK THE BARBARIAN" SERIES

Brak the Barbarian, Avon (New York, NY), 1968.

Brak the Barbarian versus the Sorceress, Paperback Library (New York, NY), 1969.

Brak versus the Mark of the Demons, Paperback Library (New York, NY), 1969.

Brak: When the Idols Walked, Pocket Books (New York, NY), 1978.

Fortunes of Brak, Dell (New York, NY), 1980.

"AMERICAN BICENTENNIAL" SERIES; ALSO PUBLISHED AS "KENT FAMILY CHRONICLES" SERIES

The Bastard (also see below), Pyramid (New York, NY), 1974, published in two volumes, Volume 1:

Fortune's Whirlwind, Volume 2: *To an Unknown Shore,* Corgi (London, England), 1975.

The Rebels (also see below), Pyramid (New York, NY), 1975.

The Seekers (also see below), Pyramid (New York, NY), 1975.

The Titans, Pyramid (New York, NY), 1976.

The Furies (also see below), Pyramid (New York, NY), 1976.

The Patriots (contains *The Bastard* and *The Rebels*), Landfall Press (Chicago, IL), 1976.

The Pioneers (contains *The Seekers* and *The Furies*), Landfall Press (Chicago, IL), 1976.

The Warriors, Pyramid (New York, NY), 1977.

The Lawless, Jove (New York, NY), 1978.

The Americans, Jove (New York, NY), 1980.

"NORTH AND SOUTH" TRILOGY

North and South, Harcourt (New York, NY), 1982.

Love and War, Harcourt (New York, NY), 1984.

Heaven and Hell, Harcourt (New York, NY), 1988.

PLAYS

(Author of lyrics) *Dracula, Baby* (musical comedy), Dramatic (Chicago, IL), 1970.

(Author of book and lyrics) *Wind in the Willows* (musical comedy), Performance (Elgin, IL), 1972.

A Spell of Evil (three-act melodrama), Performance (Elgin, IL), 1972.

Violence (two one-acts), Performance (Elgin, IL), 1972.

Stranger with Roses (one-act), Dramatic (Chicago, IL) 1972.

For I Am a Jealous People (adaptation of the story by Lester del Rey), Performance Publishing (Elgin, IL), 1972.

(Author of book and lyrics) *Gaslight Girl* (musical), Dramatic (Chicago, IL), 1973.

(Author of book and lyrics) *Pardon Me, Is This Planet Taken?* (musical), Dramatic (Chicago, IL), 1973.

(Author of book and lyrics) *Doctor, Doctor!* (musical), McAfee Music (New York, NY), 1973.

(Author of book and lyrics) *Shepherd Song* (musical), McAfee Music (New York, NY), 1974.

(Adapter) *Charles Dickens's A Christmas Carol,* Dramatic (Chicago, IL), 1997.

(Author of book and lyrics) *Great Expectations* (musical), produced by Arts Center of Coastal Carolina, 1999, National Alliance for Musical Theatre Festival, 2001.

UNDER PSEUDONYM JAY SCOTLAND

The Seventh Man, Bouregy (New York, NY), 1958, published under name John Jakes, Pinnacle (New York, NY), 1981.

I, Barbarian, Avon (New York, NY), 1959, published under name John Jakes, Pinnacle (New York, NY), 1979.

Strike the Black Flag, Ace Books (New York, NY), 1961.

Sir Scoundrel, Ace Books (New York, NY), 1962.

Veils of Salome, Avon (New York, NY), 1962, published under name John Jakes as *King's Crusader,* Pinnacle (New York, NY), 1976.

Arena, Ace Books (New York, NY), 1963.

Traitors' Legion, Ace Books (New York, NY), 1963, published under name John Jakes as *The Man from Cannae,* Pinnacle (New York, NY), 1977.

OTHER

(Editor, with Martin Harry Greenberg) *New Trails: Twenty-three Original Stories of the West from Western Writers of America,* Doubleday (Garden City, NY), 1994.

(Editor) *A Century of Great Western Stories,* Doherty/Forge (New York, NY), 2000.

Contributor of short stories to magazines.

Jakes's manuscripts are housed at the University of Wyoming, DePauw University, and the John Jakes Archive, Thomas Cooper Library, University of South Carolina, Columbia.

ADAPTATIONS: The Bastard, The Rebels, and *The Seekers* were adapted for television by Operation Prime Time and Universal Studios; *North and South* was filmed for television by ABC, 1985; *Love and War* was filmed for television by ABC, 1986; *Heaven and Hell* was filmed for television by ABC, 1995.

SIDELIGHTS: John Jakes was a prolific but obscure writer for some twenty years, until his "American Bicentennial" series of historical novels captured the public's imagination and made him famous. Jakes had published his first work while he was still a high school student, and throughout the 1950s and 1960s he turned out more than fifty books in various genres, including science fiction, mystery, children's literature, and suspense. Most of his early works were written in his spare time while he held down full-time positions in the advertising industry; the resounding success of the "American Bicentennial" series finally enabled him to devote himself to writing full time. Jakes has followed his landmark series with other best-selling novels based on American history, including *North and South, Love and War,* and *California Gold.*

While Jakes's books have been phenomenally popular, few critics have called his prose style anything more than workmanlike. The author himself harbors few pretensions. "Sue me for not being Flaubert," Jakes told *People* contributor Susan Schindehette. "I've given it the best shot I can." But Martin H. Greenberg and Walter Herrscher, writing in the *Dictionary of Literary Biography Yearbook: 1983,* praised Jakes as "a natural storyteller" whose body of work is consistently characterized by "attention to detail, careful plotting, epic sweep, and—where required, strong historical research." Discussing his early work, Greenberg and Herrscher stated: "Jakes was much more than simply a pedestrian science fiction writer. He did some outstanding work in this demanding popular genre, and his collection, *The Best of John Jakes,* contains excellent work, most notably the novella *Here Is Thy Sting,* which focuses on the meaning of death, and *The Sellers of the Dream,* a moving and devastating attack on our consumer society." Greenberg and Herrscher also praised Jakes's "Brak the Barbarian" series, which lampoons the "Sword and Sorcery" genre; his sci-fi/western *Six-Gun Planet;* and his futuristic novel *On Wheels,* which both men judge to be "a minor masterpiece of social speculation."

Whatever the merits of Jakes's early work, it brought him little recognition and only a modest secondary income. He felt he had bottomed out as a writer in 1973, when he accepted an assignment to write a novelization of the last film in the "Planet of the Apes" movie series. He remembers the job—which took him three weeks and earned him a quick fifteen hundred dollars—with bitterness. "When that *Planet of the Apes* thing came along, I said to [my wife], "I've been wasting the last twenty years." I finally began to think I couldn't cut it as a writer," he recalled in a *Publishers Weekly* interview with Robert Dahlin. Fortunately for Jakes, his fellow writer Don Moffitt had a higher opinion of his work.

Moffit had been approached by Lyle Kenyon Engel, a packager in the paperback trade industry, to write a series of historical novels for publication around the time of the bicentennial of the United States. The books would follow several generations of the fictional Kent family through the first hundred years of the country's history. Moffit was unavailable for the job, but he suggested that Engel review Jakes's early historical fiction, much of which had been published under the pseudonym Jay Scotland. These "solidly researched, well-plotted commercial novels with believable characters," as they are described in the *Dictionary of Literary Biography Yearbook: 1983,* convinced Engel that Jakes was the man to pen the Kent family chronicles.

The series was originally intended to total five books, but its success was so great that Engel was eager to extend Jakes's contract. Eight titles were eventually published, beginning with *The Bastard* in 1974 and concluding with *The Americans* in 1980. None of the titles sold less than 3.5 million copies, and the series as a whole has sold over fifty million copies. Marked by vivid plots and memorable, simply drawn characters, the saga takes readers through seven generations of the Kent family history. Engel would have continued the series for as long as it remained profitable, but after *The Americans,* Jakes rebelled. That act opened a professional rift between the two men, but Jakes stood firm in his decision. "I'll always be grateful to [Engel]," he explained in *Publishers Weekly,* "because he gave me the chance that made all the difference, but I believe in the theater principle. You should end something leaving the audience wanting more, rather than taking the television route where the story drags on and on week after week."

Following his triumph in the realm of paperback publishing, Jakes was approached by the Harcourt Brace Jovanovich publishing house to produce a trio of hardcover novels covering the Civil War era. The "North and South" trilogy—*North and South, Love and War,* and *Heaven and Hell*—intertwine fictional and real-life characters much as the "American Bicentennial" series does, and has proved to be as successful. The central characters are two men who, after becoming friends at West Point, find themselves enemies in war. Their descendants' adventures continue through the Reconstruction period and the taming of the American frontier. Rory Quirk, writing in the *Washington Post,* credited Jakes with creating "a graphic, fast-paced amalgam of good, evil, love, lust, war, violence and Americana." He further commented: "The imposition and ultimate failure of Reconstruction in the South covers some well-traveled ground but Jakes manages to resift the historical information, meld it with his fictional characters and produce an informative and nicely crafted narrative. . . . Jakes is particularly adept at capturing the splendid desolation of the untamed West, the mind-numbing isolation of duty with the frontier Army, and the unremitting brutality of the subjugation of the American Indian."

Jakes's 1993 novel *Homeland* captures another classic American scene: the European immigrant era around the turn of the twentieth century. The story's protagonist, Pauli Kroner, is fourteen years old in 1892 when he is sent by his ailing German aunt to live with relatives in Chicago. Renamed Paul Crown, the boy enters the prosperous household of his uncle Joe, who runs a brewery. While working at the brewery along with Joe's son, Joe Jr., Paul gains first-hand knowledge of the labor-management rifts that characterized the last decade of the nineteenth century. When a labor strike at the brewery results in a bombing that kills three workers, Joe Jr. is implicated. He runs away to the West coast; Uncle Joe blames Paul for assisting his son and banishes Paul from the house. The event provides Paul with the opportunity to seek work in a field he loves: photography. He begins working for a shady photographer and motion-picture camera innovator and eventually finds his way to Cuba during the Spanish-American War of 1898. There, while working on his photography, he meets many famous people, including Theodore Roosevelt. He also is reacquainted with his cousin, Joe Jr.

Jakes "is in top form in this book," remarked James Idema in a review of *Homeland* for Chicago's *Tribune Books*. Idema added that "from the start he makes everybody—fictitious and genuine—believable and maintains the plot at an entertaining boil." Writing in the *New York Times Book Review*, Frank Wilson called Jakes "a master of the ancient art of storytelling" and declared that the author "portrays Paul's world with an admirable combination of sympathy and detachment." And *Washington Post Book World* reviewer Bruce Cook concluded: "Jakes researches exhaustively. He writes acceptably. He is a master of an old-fashioned sort of novel that readers still enjoy."

In 1998 Jakes produced *American Dreams,* a sequel to *Homeland* that covers the years 1906 to 1917. The action revolves around Joe Crown, now a beer baron whose daughter, Fritzi, "defies her father to purse a dreadfully unsuccessful New York stage career," according to a *Publishers Weekly* reviewer. Fritzi's ambition takes her to Hollywood, where the film industry is in its infancy. *American Dreams* interweaves the fictional characters with such real-life figures as Charlie Chaplin and Thomas Edison. One character even matches wits with Kaiser Wilhelm. Eric Robbins of *Booklist* found that this book showcases Jakes's "pleasant storytelling style" and provides "a popular vehicle for readers who want tasty vignettes of the past."

Jakes marked his fiftieth year as a writer with the publication of *On Secret Service.* This novel explores a little-regarded aspect of the U.S. Civil War: the development of the U.S. Secret Service and its role following the assassination of President Abraham Lincoln. *Booklist*'s Brad Hooper found that in Jakes's hands Washington is found "brimming with as much espionage as a European capital during one of that continent's frequent internecine struggles." The author's historical research is "impeccable," according to Kelly Milner Halls in *Books,* the critic adding praise for the author's character development and singling out the secondary characters who propel the story line. To a *Publishers Weekly* contributor, *On Secret Service* shows Jakes as no less than "the foremost historical novelist of our national conflict."

Discussing his 2002 novel, *Charleston,* Jakes explained that it came about "from my fascination with much of the largely unknown history of the state where I've lived for the past twenty-five years. In the eighteenth and nineteenth centuries Charleston aristocrats controlled South Carolina, and South Carolina was a significant power in national affairs—sometimes beneficially, sometimes with a tragic result, notably the Civil War. The point I make about the book is this—in the years I've written about, roughly 1780 to Reconstruction, South Carolina history is American history in the fullest sense."

Published shortly after *Charleston, Savannah; or, A Gift for Mr. Lincoln* takes place during the winter of 1864 as the Civil War rages on. Union general William T. Sherman is making his way toward the coastline with his troops, along the way scooping up anything of economic value, burning towns, and leaving innocent civilians at the hands of the looters who follow in his wake. Jakes presents a story of "a charming widow and her young daughter, who are determined to prevent General Sherman from making Savannah a 'gift for Mr. Lincoln,'" according to *Library Journal* reviewer Barbara Hoffert. Jay Freeman of *Booklist* commented, "Although Jakes occasionally takes liberties with historical facts, he does recreate the spirit of the times, in the process telling a whopping good story," and creating "a fine work of popular historical fiction."

Discussing his work with Elizabeth Venant in the *Los Angeles Times*, Jakes explained that his early inspiration came from the swashbuckling adventure films of the 1930s and 1940s. "I have this gigantic cinemascope screen in my head," he commented. "I always see what I'm writing about in terms of the colors of the clothes, the weather, the sky." Responding to the charge that his work has little literary merit, Jakes stated: "There's an unfortunate lack in American letters. You have either very literary material or the trash end of the spectrum." He defends his own contribution to the reading public, saying: "One thing I'll never apologize for is my success. I paid my dues for twenty-five years. I worked my fingers down to the bone."

Viewing Jakes's career overall, Greenberg and Herrscher maintained that his "historical novels cannot be judged by usual literary standards. They are unabashedly fiction for the mass market, and it cannot be expected that they display the virtues of interpretive fiction. . . . Jakes's novels do not provide that main quality we expect from interpretive fiction: a sharper and deeper awareness of life, often in memorable prose. But Jakes has not claimed to be this kind of writer. In an afterword to *North and South* he says that his primary purpose is to entertain; and if a writer is to be judged solely on the success of his intentions, then John Jakes is without doubt one of the most successful and important writers in the history of commercial fiction."

BIOGRAPHICAL AND CRITICAL SOURCES:

BOOKS

Authors and Artists for Young Adults, Volume 32, Thomson Gale (Detroit, MI), 2000.

Contemporary Literary Criticism, Volume 29, Thomson Gale (Detroit, MI) 1984.

Contemporary Southern Writers, St. James Press (Detroit, MI), 1999.

Dictionary of Literary Biography Yearbook: 1983, Thomson Gale (Detroit, MI) 1984.

Hawkins, R., *The Kent Family Chronicles Encyclopedia,* Bantam (New York, NY) 1979.

Jones, Mary Ellen, *John Jakes: A Critical Companion,* Greenwood Press (Westport, CT), 1996.

St. James Guide to Science Fiction Writers, 4th edition, St. James Press (Detroit, MI), 1996.

PERIODICALS

Book, July-August, 2000, Kelly Milner Halls, review of *On Secret Service,* p. 78.

Booklist, May 1, 1998, Eric Robbins, review of *American Dreams,* p. 1477; March 15, 2000, Brad Hooper, review of *On Secret Service,* p. 1292; July, 2004, Jay Freeman, review of *Savannah; or, A Gift for Mr. Lincoln,* p. 1799.

Bookwatch, January, 1999, review of *Homeland* (audio version), p. 9.

Chicago Tribune Book World, February 21, 1982.

Christian Science Monitor, April 7, 1982, p. 17.

Detroit News, February 23, 1982.

Kirkus Reviews, May 15, 1998, review of *American Dreams,* p. 690.

KLIATT Young Adult Paperback Book Guide, January, 1999, review of *American Dreams* (audio version), p. 41; May, 1999, review of *Homeland* (audio version), p. 58.

Library Journal, November 1, 1998, Ray Vignovice, review of *American Dreams* (audio version), p. 137; July 1999, review of *North and South,* p. 53; March 15, 2000, Robert Conroy, review of *On Secret Service,* p. 127; June 1, 2004, Barbara Hoffert, review of *Savannah,* p. 101.

Los Angeles Times, September 18, 1989.

Los Angeles Times Book Review, March 21, 1982; December 2, 1984; September 27, 1987; August 20, 1989, p. 5.

New York Times, May 2, 1986.

New York Times Book Review, March 7, 1982, p. 24; October 8, 1989, p. 24; August 22, 1993, p. 14.

People, November 12, 1984, pp. 63-64; July 13, 1998, Erica Sanders, review of *American Dreams,* p. 47.

Publishers Weekly, April 5, 1976; November 30, 1984, pp. 99-100; October 3, 1994, p. 53; May 25, 1998, review of *American Dreams,* p. 64; February 28, 2000, review of *A Century of Great Western Stories,* p. 59; April 17, 2000, review of *On Secret Service,* p. 49.

School Library Journal, January, 1994, p. 144.

Tribune Books (Chicago, IL), July 18, 1993, p. 7.

Washington Post, March 7, 1976, p. F10; February 3, 1982, p. E3; February 28, 1982; November 3, 1984, p. 3.

Washington Post Book World, April 3, 1977; October 18, 1987; September 17, 1989; July 18, 1993, p. 1; January 8, 1995, p. 8.

Writer's Digest, February, 1998, Donald McKinney, "John Jakes: 'I'll Never Stop,'" p. 26.

ONLINE

John Jakes Home Page, http://www.johnjakes.com/ (August 19, 2004).

*   *   *

JAKES, John William
  See JAKES, John

*   *   *

JAMES, Mary
  See MEAKER, Marijane

JAMES, P.D. 1920-
[A pseudonym]
(Phyllis Dorothy James White)

PERSONAL: Born August 3, 1920, in Oxford, England; daughter of Sidney Victor (a tax officer) and Dorothy May Amelia (Hone) James; married Ernest Conner Bantry White (a medical practitioner), August 8, 1941 (died, 1964); children: Clare, Jane. *Education:* Attended Cambridge High School for Girls, 1931-37. *Religion:* Church of England. *Hobbies and other interests:* Exploring churches, walking by the sea.

ADDRESSES: Agent—Greene & Heaton Ltd., 37 Goldhawk Rd., London W12 8QQ, England.

CAREER: Festival Theatre, Cambridge, England, assistant stage manager prior to World War II; worked as a Red Cross nurse and at the Ministry of Food during World War II; North West Regional Hospital Board, London, England, became principal administrative assistant, 1949-68; Department of Home Affairs, London, England, principal administrative assistant in Police Department, 1968-72, and in Criminal Policy Department, 1972-79; full time writer, 1979—. Associate fellow, Downing College, Cambridge, 1986; British Broadcasting Corp. (BBC) general advisory council, 1987-88, member of Arts Council of Great Britain, 1988-92, and of British Council, 1988-93; governor, BBC, 1988-93. Magistrate, 1979-84.

MEMBER: Royal Society of Literature (fellow), Royal Society of Arts (fellow), Society of Authors (chair, 1985-87), Crime Writers Association, Detection Club, Institute of Hospital Administration (fellow).

AWARDS, HONORS: First prize, Crime Writers Association contest, 1967, for short story, "Moment of Power"; Order of the British Empire, 1983; created Life Peer of United Kingdom (Baroness James of Holland Park), 1991; Diamond Dagger Award, Crime Writers Association for services to crime writing; Silver Dagger Awards, Crime Writers Association, for *Shroud for a Nightingale* and *The Black Tower;* Edgar Award, Mystery Writers of America, for *Shroud for a Nightingale;* Scroll Award, Mystery Writers of America, for *An Unsuitable Job for a Woman;* Litt.D., University of Buckingham, 1992; Doctor of Literature, University of London, 1993.

WRITINGS:

MYSTERY NOVELS

Cover Her Face, Faber (London, England), 1962, Scribner (New York, NY), 1966.

A Mind to Murder, Faber (London, England), 1963, Scribner (New York, NY), 1967.
Unnatural Causes, Scribner (New York, NY), 1967.
Shroud for a Nightingale, Scribner (New York, NY), 1971.
An Unsuitable Job for a Woman, Faber (London, England), 1972, Scribner (New York, NY), 1973.
The Black Tower, Scribner (New York, NY), 1975.
Death of an Expert Witness, Scribner (New York, NY), 1977.
Innocent Blood, Scribner (New York, NY), 1980.
The Skull Beneath the Skin, Scribner (New York, NY), 1982.
A Taste for Death, Faber (London, England), 1985, Knopf (New York, NY), 1986.
Devices and Desires, Faber (London, England), 1989, Random House (New York, NY), 1990.
The Children of Men, Faber (London, England), 1992, Knopf (New York, NY), 1993.
Original Sin, Franklin Library (Franklin Center, PA), 1995, Knopf (New York, NY), 1995.
A Certain Justice, Knopf (New York, NY), 1997.
Death in Holy Orders, Knopf (New York, NY), 2001.
The Murder Room, Knopf (New York, NY), 2003.
The Lighthouse, Knopf (New York, NY), 2005.

OMNIBUS VOLUMES

Crime Times Three (includes *Cover Her Face, A Mind to Murder, and Shroud for a Nightingale*) Scribner (New York, NY), 1979.
Murder in Triplicate (includes *Unnatural Causes, An Unsuitable Job for a Woman,* and *The Black Tower*), Scribner (New York, NY), 1982.
Trilogy of Death, Scribner (New York, NY), 1984.
P.D. James: Three Complete Novels, Crown (New York, NY), 1987.
An Omnibus P.D. James (includes *Death of an Expert Witness, Innocent Blood,* and *An Unsuitable Job for a Woman*), Faber (London, England), 1990.
A Dalgliesh Trilogy (includes *The Black Tower, Death of an Expert Witness,* and *Shroud for a Nightingale*), Penguin/Faber (London, England), 1991.
In Murderous Company: Three Complete Novels Featuring Detectives Adam Dalgliesh and Cordelia Gray, Wings Books (New York, NY), 1992.

CONTRIBUTOR

Ellery Queen's Murder Menu, World Publishing (New York, NY), 1969.

Virginian Whitaker, editor, *Winter's Crimes 5,* Macmillan (London, England), 1973.

Ellery Queen's Masters of Mystery, Dial (New York, NY), 1975.

Hilary Watson, editor, *Winter's Crimes 8,* Macmillan (London, England), 1976.

Dilys Wynn, editor, *Murder Ink: The Mystery Reader's Companion,* Workman Publishing (New York, NY), 1977.

Crime Writers, BBC Publications (London, England), 1978.

Julian Symons, editor, *Verdict of Thirteen,* Harper (New York, NY), 1979.

George Hardinge, *Winter's Crimes 15,* St. Martin's Press (New York, NY), 1983.

OTHER

(With Thomas A. Critchley) *The Maul and the Pear Tree: The Ratcliffe Highway Murders, 1811,* Constable (London, England), 1971.

A Private Treason (play), first produced in the West End at the Palace Theatre, March 12, 1985.

(Author of foreword) *800 Years of Women's Letters,* Faber (Boston, MA), 1993.

Time to Be in Earnest: A Fragment of an Autobiography, Knopf (New York, NY), 2000.

James's work has been translated into several languages, including Japanese.

ADAPTATIONS: Cover Her Face, Unnatural Causes, The Black Tower, A Taste for Death, Devices and Desires, Death of an Expert Witness, and *Shroud for a Nightingale* have been adapted as television miniseries and broadcast by the Public Broadcasting System (PBS).

SIDELIGHTS: As P.D. James—a name she chose because it is short and gender-neutral—Phyllis Dorothy James White has established herself as one of England's most prominent mystery writers. Often ranked with such masters of the genre as Agatha Christie, Dorothy L. Sayers, and Margery Allingham, James is critically acclaimed for her ability to combine complex and puzzling plots with psychologically believable characters, particularly in her novels featuring Commander Adam Dalgliesh of Scotland Yard. Her "keen, cunning mind and a positively bloody imagination" make her "one of the finest and most successful mystery writers in the world," Peter Gorner wrote in the *Chicago Tribune.*

James began her writing career relatively late in life. When her husband returned from World War II suffering from severe mental illness, James needed to find a way to support her family. For nineteen years she worked as a hospital administrator and then, following her husband's death, entered the British Department of Home Affairs as a civil servant in the criminal department. Although she had wanted to write for many years, James was not able to devote time to this pursuit until the late 1950s. Then, as she told David Lehman and Tony Clifton in *Newsweek,* "I realized that if I didn't make the effort and settle down to begin that first book, eventually I would be saying to my grandchildren, 'Of course I really wanted to be a novelist.' There never was going to be a convenient time." While working in a hospital she began her first novel, *Cover Her Face.* Over a three-year period James wrote for two hours every morning before going to work, composing her story in longhand on notepaper, a method she still prefers. Once completed, the novel was accepted by the first publisher to whom it was sent. James's career as a mystery writer was launched. Since then, she has published over a dozen more mystery novels in addition to a novel about a twenty-first century dystopia, *The Children of Men,* and a work of nonfiction, *The Maul and the Pear Tree.* The latter book, written with Thomas A. Critchley, investigates a particularly gruesome murder committed in London in 1811. James has been a full-time writer since her retirement from government service in 1979.

Despite the difficulty of juggling two careers and her family responsibilities, James says she does not regret the long delay in becoming a full-time writer. "As a woman writer, I feel having a working life provided all sorts of experience that I wouldn't have got if I had just been living at home," she told Connie Lauerman in an interview for the *Chicago Tribune.* Her work as a hospital administrator and in the police and criminal policy departments has provided much of the background for her mystery novels, set in such places as a police forensic laboratory, a nurses' training school, and a home for the disabled.

There is an old-fashioned quality to James's mystery novels that puts them squarely in the tradition of classic English detective fiction, as practiced by Agatha Christie and other writers. The character of Adam Dalgliesh, Scotland Yard detective and published poet, for example, follows the familiar pattern of the gentleman detective popularized by such earlier writers as Dorothy L. Sayers and Ngaio Marsh. James's plots are puzzles which, she told Wayne Warga of the *Los Angeles Times,* follow the traditional formula. "You have a murder, which is a mystery," she explained. "There is a closed circle of suspects. . . . You have, in my case, a professional detective. He finds clues and information which, as he discovers them, are also available to the reader. And at the end of the story there is a credible and satisfactory resolution that the reader could have arrived at as well." James's style, too, commented Thomas Lask in the *New York Times*, "is what we think of as typically British. Her writing is ample, leisurely, and full of loving description of house and countryside." And like that of a number of other mystery writers, stated Norma Siebenheller in her study *P.D. James*, James's "work is literate, tightly constructed, and civilized. Her people are genteel and polite."

Yet, while conforming to many of the expectations of the genre, James goes beyond its limitations. For instance, where other writers have concentrated almost entirely on the puzzles in their books to the detriment of such things as characterization, James has not. Although she creates a puzzle for her readers, she focuses her attention on writing realistic mysteries with fully rounded characters. "The classic English mystery, as practiced by many of its female creators," Siebenheller explained, "is basically a puzzle-solving exercise. . . . One never gets over the feeling, when reading these books, that they are all make-believe. . . . James departs from that tradition. . . . The worlds she creates are peopled with varied and interesting characters whose actions spring from believable motivations and whose reactions are true to their complex personalities." As James told Carla Heffner in the *Washington Post,* her frequent comparison to Agatha Christie "amazes me. . . . Hers [is] the stereotype English crime novel which is set in the small English village where everyone knows their place. . . . I don't set my novels in that never-never land."

James's concern for realism is reflected in her creation of Adam Dalgliesh, a complex character who is, Siebenheller believed, "a far cry from the almost comical characters who served Christie and Sayers as sleuths." Dalgliesh is an introspective, serious figure—intensely devoted to solving the case at hand—who suppresses his personal feelings. His personality has been shaped by one tragic event many years before: the death of his wife and son during childbirth. It is this painful memory, and the essential chaos it implies, that has formed Dalgliesh's "vision of the world," as Erlene Hubly stated in *Clues*. Because of this memory, Dalgliesh is a "Byronic hero," Hubly argued, unable "to adjust to or accept society." Yet, because of his fear of chaos and death, he enforces the rules of society, convinced that they are all humanity has with which to create order. Dalgliesh

tries, wrote Hubly, "to bring order out of chaos: if he cannot stop death he can at least catch and punish those who inflict it on others."

While Dalgliesh is her most popular character, James's secondary characters are equally realistic. All of her books, Julian Symons noted in the *New York Times Book Review,* "are marked by powerful and sympathetic characterizations." Perhaps her most fully realized character after Dalgliesh is Cordelia Gray, a female private detective who appears in *An Unsuitable Job for a Woman* and *The Skull beneath the Skin*. As James related in the first of these two novels, Gray had a difficult childhood, being raised in a series of foster homes. Despite her past misfortunes, Gray is "a totally positive person," Siebenheller related. "Not only is she optimistic, capable, and clever, she is good-natured as well. . . . This is not to say Cordelia is a Pollyanna. She fully acknowledges the rougher edges of life." She and Dalgliesh enjoy a cordial rivalry whenever they meet on a murder case.

Many of James's other characters are from the respectable English middle class. Educated and humanistic, they find themselves "consumed by jealousy, hatred, lust, sexual fears, and ambition," Gorner stated. James explored her characters' labyrinthine emotional and psychological states with a penetrating and compassionate eye. Heffner, for example, sees James as someone "passionately curious about people and their peculiarities." Lask believed that James's work, despite its veneer of traditional English fiction, "is modern in the ambiguous makeup of her characters, their complex motives and the shrewd psychological touches of the relationship between the police and the criminals they pursue."

Moved by a deep moral concern, James sees mystery writing as an important expression of basic human values. Mystery novels, she told Heffner, "are like twentieth-century morality plays; the values are basic and unambiguous. Murder is wrong. In an age in which gratuitous violence and arbitrary death have become common, these values need no apology." The "corrosive, destructive aspect of crime," Siebenheller maintained, is one of James's major themes. She traces the effects of crime not only on the victim and criminal, but on their family and friends as well. James's concern is obvious, too, in the values she gives her characters. Comparing Adam Dalgliesh to James herself, Warga described him as "a man who is a realistic moralist much like his creator."

James moved away from her signature genre to a futuristic tale with *The Children of Men*, published in 1992.

The story is in the year 2021, after twenty-five years have passed during which humans have stopped bearing children as the result of a global disease. James examines the outcome through the eyes of Dr. Theodore Faron, an Oxford professor. Walter Wangerin, Jr., writing for the *New York Times Book Review,* compared the effort to James's crime novels and found that "in her other novels, the author's attention is upon the plot and these concerns [about the nature of humankind] appear only indirectly. But here Miss James makes these contemplations the very business of her book, and her view is Olympian." James Sallis, in the *Los Angeles Times Book Review,* viewed the novel "from first to last exceedingly well-wrought" but believed it falls short by making it a eulogy for a British culture that is long past. "James set out to provide a cosmic poem; considered for a while folding in the makings of a political novel; decided somewhere along the way to interpolate a religious fable; and ended up with a book that's none of these, but a kind of sympathy card for her own time and class." Peter Reading noted in the *Times Literary Supplement* that, "if this departure from James's usual genre is intended as a fable, its meaning is not readily communicated. However . . . her ability to create a well-paced plot ensures that her audience will find *The Children of Men* as exciting as her crime stories."

James "triumphantly [reverts] to original form," as Kate Kellaway noted in the London *Observer,* with her novel *Original Sin.* The story is set in a publishing company, where an elderly employee and part-time crime novelist, Esme Carling, is fired after thirty years at Peverell Press. Carling is later strangled with her most recent manuscript and her body dumped in the Thames. A reviewer for *Tangled Web* praised the author for her "impeccable style" in *Original Sin,* and noted that "the plot is clever and tight as always." The reviewer also praised James for taking the time to thoroughly explore the psychology of each character in depth, to cast suspicion on each, and to provide "a real challenge" to the reader trying to unravel the mystery.

In an interview with James, Kellaway asked her what she would do upon meeting the detective Dalgliesh, who returns in *Original Sin.* "If I met him I would say 'I did enjoy your last book of verse' and I wonder if he would then look at me very coolly," stated the author. Susannah Clapp remarked in the *Times Literary Supplement* that both James's moral "finger-wagging" as well as Dalgliesh's old-fashioned "rectitude and solemnity" extend the story unnecessarily. "By making Dalgliesh such a beacon not just of the law but of morality, spirituality and aesthetics, and by constantly hinting at the darkness of the age which laps him, she risks making

her own criminal world seem cosily dated." Clapp concluded, "There is never any danger of drivel, or difficulty with continuing to read P.D. James's novels—she always makes you want to go on—but they are least lively when most anxious to instruct."

Death in Holy Orders, published the year James celebrated her eightieth birthday, found her still at the top of her powers, according to numerous reviewers. The book utilizes all the classic elements of English mystery: an isolated setting, a collection of guests both welcome and unwelcome, and a shocking murder in a closed room. The setting in this case is a High Anglican theological college located on the coast of East Anglia. The place is a bastion of religious tradition; the victim is an archdeacon who wanted to close the college, believing it to be irrelevant to the modern world. The four resident priests all had good reason to dislike the archdeacon and all are under suspicion, as well as the rest of the staff and the three visitors who were there when the killing took place. Adam Dalgliesh is sent to investigate, and is forced to look deeply into his soul as well as the murder at hand. As *Christian Century* reviewer Trudy Bush related, "That James packs so much theological discussion and meaning into a suspenseful detective story, and manages sometimes to be very funny as well, makes her book remarkable. . . . This is a book very concerned with faith and with life's ultimate questions." Bush felt that the conclusion of the novel was somewhat "slack," yet added that nevertheless, "James here is writing at the top of her powers." She concluded that *Death in Holy Orders* is "a novel that, more than a murder mystery, is also a book about life's great mysteries." A reviewer for *Publishers Weekly* also praised the book for its "extraordinarily complex and nuanced plot" and the "masterful ease and conviction" with which the author presents her story.

The success of James's novels can be attributed to their popularity among two different audiences, Heffner explained: "The lovers of a good 'whodunit' who read her novels for their action and intricate plots; and the literary world that admires the books for their character and motivation." In the words of Christopher Lehmann-Haupt, writing in the *New York Times,* this wide acceptance has made James "one of the most esteemed practitioners of the [mystery] genre in the English-speaking world."

BIOGRAPHICAL AND CRITICAL SOURCES:

BOOKS

Concise Dictionary of British Literary Biography, Volume 8: *Contemporary Writers: 1960 to the Present,* Thomson Gale (Detroit, MI), 1992.

Contemporary Literary Criticism, Thomson Gale (Detroit, MI), Volume 18, 1981, pp. 272-277, Volume 46, 1988, pp. 204-211.

Dictionary of Literary Biography, Volume 87: *British Mystery and Thriller Writers since 1940, First Series,* Thomson Gale (Detroit, MI), 1989.

Encyclopedia of World Biography, second edition, Thomson Gale (Detroit, MI), 1998.

James, P.D., *An Unsuitable Job for a Woman,* Faber (London, England), 1972, Scribner (New York, NY), 1973.

Siebenheller, Norma, *P.D. James,* Ungar (New York, NY), 1981.

Wynn, Dilys, editor, *Murder Ink,* Workman Publishing (New York, NY), 1977.

Wynn, Dilys, editor, *Murderess Ink,* Workman Publishing (New York, NY), 1977.

PERIODICALS

Atlantic, June, 1980.
Booklist, April 15, 1999, review of *Original Sin,* p. 1457.
Chicago Tribune, June 10, 1980; November 6, 1986; November 16, 1986; February 4, 1990, pp. 1, 4.
Chicago Tribune Book World, May 18, 1980; September 19, 1982.
Christian Century, May 19, 1993, p. 561; July 4, 2001, Trudy Bush, review of *Death in Holy Orders,* p. 32.
Christian Science Monitor, June 25, 1980.
Clues, fall-winter, 1982; spring-summer, 1985.
Commonweal, April 23, 1993, p. 26.
Globe and Mail (Toronto), May 10, 1986; November 8, 1986; February 3, 1990, p. C8.
Kirkus Reviews, March 1, 2001, review of *Death in Holy Orders,* p. 296.
Kliatt, January, 1998, review of *A Certain Justice* (audio version), p. 42.
Library Journal, January, 1994, p. 184; September 1, 1995, p. 226; January, 1998, review of *A Certain Justice,* p. 55; February 1, 1998, review of *A Certain Justice* (audio version), p. 130; June 1, 1998, review of *A Certain Justice* (audio version), p. 184; March 15, 2001, Wilda Williams, review of *Death in Holy Orders,* p. 105.
Listener, June 5, 1975.
Los Angeles Times, June 6, 1980; November 6, 1986; January 21, 1987.
Los Angeles Times Book Review, June 22, 1980; November 30, 1986, p. 6; February 25, 1990, pp. 1, 11; April 4, 1993, p. 12.
Maclean's, June 30, 1980.

Ms., April, 1974; August, 1979.
National Catholic Reporter, May 28, 1993, p. 23.
New Republic, July 31, 1976; November 26, 1977.
New Statesman, September 25, 1992, p. 55; November 11, 1994, p. 37.
Newsweek, January 23, 1978; May 12, 1980; September 13, 1982; October 20, 1986, pp. 81-83; February 19, 1990, p. 66.
New Yorker, March 11, 1976; March 6, 1978; June 23, 1980; March 22, 1993, p. 111; January 19, 1998, review of *A Certain Justice,* p. 83.
New York Review of Books, July 17, 1980; April 26, 1990, p. 35; February 5, 1998, review of *A Certain Justice,* p. 19.
New York Times, December 11, 1977; July 18, 1979; February 8, 1980; April 27, 1980; May 7, 1980; March 11, 1986; October 5, 1986, Julian Symons, review of *A Taste for Death,* section 6, p. 48; October 23, 1986; January 25, 1990, p. C22; May 9, 1996, p. C20.
New York Times Book Review, July 24, 1966; January 16, 1972; April 22, 1973; November 23, 1975; April 27, 1980; September 12, 1982; April 6, 1986; November 2, 1986, p. 9; January 28, 1990, pp. 1, 31; April 26, 1990, p. 35; March 28, 1993, p. 23; April 2, 1995, p. 11.
New York Times Magazine, October 5, 1986.
Observer (London), October 16, 1994, p. 19; January 3, 1999, review of *A Certain Justice,* p. 14.
People Weekly, December 8, 1986; March 29, 1993, p. 23; February 13, 1995, p. 41.
Publishers Weekly, January 5, 1976, pp. 8-9; October 25, 1985; December 1, 1989, p. 48; March 19, 2001, review of *Death in Holy Orders,* p. 79.
School Library Journal, April, 1998, review of *A Certain Justice,* p. 158.
Spectator, December 23, 1972; June 12, 1976; September 19, 1992, p. 31.
Time, April 17, 1978; May 26, 1980; March 31, 1986; October 27, 1986, p. 98; March 1, 1993, p. 69.
Times (London), March 27, 1980; May 14, 1982; March 9, 1985; March 22, 1985; December 12, 1987.
Times Literary Supplement, October 22, 1971; December 13, 1974; March 21, 1980; October 29, 1982; June 27, 1986, p. 711; September 25, 1992, p. 26; October 21, 1994.
Tribune Books (Chicago), February 4, 1990.
Village Voice, December 15, 1975; December 18, 1978.
Voice Literary Supplement, October, 1982; April, 1990, p. 10.
Washington Post, April 30, 1980; November 10, 1986.
Washington Post Book World, April 15, 1977; April 27, 1980; September 19, 1982; April 20, 1986; November 9, 1986, pp. 5-6; January 21, 1990, p. 7.

ONLINE

Salon.com, http://www.salon.com/ (June 3, 2001), Jennifer Reese, interview with P.D. James.
Tangled Web, http://www.twbooks.co.uk/ (June 3, 2001), review of *Original Sin.*

* * *

JAMES, Philip
    See MOORCOCK, Michael

* * *

JANOWITZ, Tama 1957-

PERSONAL: Born April 12, 1957, in San Francisco, CA; daughter of Julian Frederick (a psychiatrist) and Phyllis (a poet and professor; maiden name, Winer) Janowitz; married Tim Hunt (curator of the Andy Warhol Foundation), 1992; children: Willow (adopted daughter). *Education:* Barnard College, B.A., 1977; Hollins College, M.A., 1979; postgraduate studies at Yale University School of Drama, 1980-81; Columbia University, M.F.A., 1985.

ADDRESSES: Agent—Amanda Urban, International Creative Management, 40 West 57th St., New York, NY 10019.

CAREER: Model with Vidal Sassoon (international hair salon) in London, England, and New York, NY, 1975-77; Kenyon and Eckhardt, Boston, MA, assistant art director, 1977-78; Fine Arts Work Center, Provincetown, MA, writer-in-residence, 1981-82; freelance journalist, 1985—. Appeared in film *Slaves of New York,* 1989; and in the first MTV "literary" video, *A Cannibal in Manhattan,* 1987. Member of board of directors, Barnard College Arts and Literature Committee, 1974-75.

MEMBER: Poets and Writers, Writers' Community (fellow, 1976), Associated Writing Program.

AWARDS, HONORS: Breadloaf Writers' Conference, 1975; Elizabeth Janeway Fiction Prize, 1976 and 1977; Amy Loveman Prize for poetry, 1977; Hollins College fellowship, 1978; National Endowment for the Arts grants, 1982 and 1986; Coordinating Council of Literary Magazines/General Electric Foundation award, 1984; Ludwig Vogelstein Foundation award, 1985; Alfred Hodder Fellow in the Humanities, Princeton University, 1986-87.

WRITINGS:

NOVELS

American Dad, Putnam (New York, NY), 1981.
A Cannibal in Manhattan, Crown (New York, NY), 1987.
The Male Cross-Dresser Support Group, Crown (New York, NY), 1992.
By the Shores of Gitchee Gumee, Crown (New York, NY), 1996.
A Certain Age, Doubleday (New York, NY), 1999.
Peyton Amberg, St. Martin's Press (New York, NY), 2003.

OTHER

Slaves of New York, Crown (New York, NY), 1986, Tri-Star, 1989.
Hear That? (children's fiction), SeaStar Books (New York, NY), 2001.
Area Code 212: New York Days, New York Nights (reminiscences), Bloomsbury (New York, NY), 2002.
Area Code 212: New York Days, New York Nights (essays), St. Martin's Press, (New York, NY), 2005.

Contributor to *Wanting a Child: Twenty-two Writers on Their Difficult but Mostly Successful Quests for Parenthood in a High-Tech Age,* edited by Jill Bialosky and Helen Schulman, Farrar, Straus & Giroux (New York, NY), 1999; and *Wonderful Town: New York Stories from "The New Yorker,"* edited by David Remnick, Random House (New York, NY), 2000. Contributor of short stories to magazines and periodicals, including *Paris Review, Mississippi Review,* and *Pawn Review.* Restaurant reviewer, *New York Press.* Contributor of articles to magazines, including *Rolling Stone* and *Mademoiselle.*

ADAPTATIONS: Slaves of New York was made into a movie starring Bernadette Peters and directed by Ismail Merchant and James Ivory, 1989.

SIDELIGHTS: Since the publication of her first novel, *American Dad,* at age twenty-three, author Tama Janowitz has captured media headlines, as much for her flamboyant and engaging personality and notoriety as friend to the late Andy Warhol as for her postmodernist fiction. A witty and sensitive observer of New York City's inner life, she has sometimes been taken to task—along with fellow novelists Bret Easton Ellis and Jay McInerney—for, as Terrence Rafferty commented in the *New Yorker,* "believing that the goal of their [literary] elders' activity was their celebrity . . . rather than their vision." Thomas De Pietro described the Janowitz "vision" in the *Hudson Review:* "Her rock-and-roll sensibility is new-wave and, although her characters prefer groups like Teenage Jesus and The Circle Jerks, she herself comes off like a literary Cyndi Lauper, a connoisseur of kitsch capable of being assimilated into the mainstream." Though often in interviews Janowitz offers a Marilyn Monroe-ish cluelessness, her incisive if indigestible observations on the dark underbelly of U.S. culture belie the pose.

Earl Przepasniak, the protagonist and narrator of Janowitz's debut novel, *American Dad,* is eleven years old when his parents divorce. Earl's father, a psychiatrist, is an amiable, self-absorbed, pot-smoking philanderer whose unrepressed behavior upsets and embarrasses the family. His mother, a poet, is killed halfway through the novel during a fight with her ex-husband over alimony payments. Earl's father is convicted of involuntary manslaughter—Earl testifies against him at the trial—and sentenced to ten-to-fifteen years in prison. With his mother dead and his father in jail, Earl decides to travel abroad and goes to London, where he pursues women and indulges in various other misadventures. Upon his return from Europe, Earl is, as several reviewers of *American Dad* observed, predictably wiser, and his enhanced sense of self leads to improved relations with his father.

Although Arnold Klein of the *Soho News* found *American Dad* "episodic and trivial," he noted that it has the "considerable virtue of being funny." Klein also appreciated Janowitz's depiction of Earl's psychiatrist father, which he called "an uncannily acute portrayal of a distinct social type." Garrett Epps stated in the *New Republic,* "There is not a false note in the presentation of this engaging villain." David Quammen, writing for the *New York Times Book Review,* lamented the untimely death of Earl's mother, whom he believed to be the novel's most well-drawn and endearing character. Echoing the reaction of several other reviewers, Quammen praised the novelist for her "fine comedic inventiveness, especially as applied in light dabs to character." According to Epps, Janowitz also has "a sharp eye for the things of this world . . . and her sensuous writing enlivens the book." Reviewers generally agreed that the

first half of *American Dad* is the stronger half, and the novel flounders, according to some, after Earl embarks on what one reviewer termed a European rite-of-passage trip. "Earl's adventures are mostly filler," wrote Epps, "[and they mar] what is otherwise one of the most impressive first novels I've read in a long time."

Slaves of New York, Janowitz's follow-up to *American Dad,* is a collection of twenty-two interconnected short stories—many of which originally appeared in the *New Yorker.* The stories center on Eleanor, a shy young jeweler who is financially bound to her boyfriend Stash—a self-proclaimed artist—because he has enough money to pay the rent. *Slaves* takes readers into the behind-the-scenes lives of Manhattan's bohemian elite: painters who adopt blood and ground-up bones as an artistic medium, pimps who contemplate the categorical imperative of philosopher Immanuel Kant, and a host of "couples" whose relationships are dictated by the lack of affordable housing in the Big Apple. "Janowitz writes about people who are not terribly nice," noted Victoria Radin in *New Statesman,* "with an underlying hopefulness that they'll get nicer; and she shows how little control they have over themselves or their lives without pitying or inflating them." While agreeing that *Slaves* is "resoundingly successful as a comedic look" at city dwellers, a reviewer for the *Los Angeles Times Book Review* also found that "pleasantly distracted by Janowitz's solid sense of humor, we don't notice that her characters' spiritual quest is largely for show." Indeed, the main criticism of *Slaves of New York* is that Janowitz's characters possess no depth: *Village Voice* reviewer Carol Ashnew termed them "permanent transients in a dress-up and play-act milieu full of style without the slightest pretense of substance." Despite (or because of?) the mixed critical response, Janowitz was asked to write the screenplay for a film version of *Slaves of New York,* which starred Bernadette Peters and was released in 1989.

After the popular success of *Slaves of New York,* its publisher, Crown, released a work of Janowitz juvenilia in an attempt to continue her momentum on the bestseller lists. A novel of the absurd and heavily indebted to the literature of the past, *A Cannibal in Manhattan* "begins as a travesty of *Robinson Crusoe,*" according to *Newsweek*'s David Lehman, and "borrows liberally from Evelyn Waugh's *Black Mischief,* broadly imitat[ing] the satire of *Candide.*" Unlike its predecessors, *A Cannibal in Manhattan* fared poorly with critics, who, as Rafferty noted in the *New Yorker,* had been fast becoming inured to the "death of the novel. . . . In more idealistic times, . . . the publication of . . . *A Cannibal in Manhattan* . . . might have been the occasion of panic in the streets of Morningside Heights, or for hastily convened symposia in *Partisan Review*." Taking place in the heart of the Big Apple, Janowitz's satire finds noble cannibal savage Mgungu Yabba Mgungu (even the unlikeliness of such a name coming from the South Pacific comments on the cosseted ignorance of the characters) plucked from his South Sea island home—where he had been living with three wives and assorted children and pigs—and transplanted to New York City by a society heiress playing part-time Peace Corps volunteer. Believing himself to have been selected to become her spouse, Mgungu attempts to fit in with his fiance's high-society friends, where, according to *Times Literary Supplement* reviewer Peter Reading, his activities serve "to accentuate the real absurdity, viciousness and debasement of the sophisticated civilization into which he is deposited." At the close of a dinner party after the couple's wedding, some so-called friends finally reveal to Mgungu that all his new bride really wanted was the recipe for a native hallucinogen and that it doesn't really matter now because his new wife has been freshly offered by underworld pals and served up as the main course at dinner. Some critics considered the cynical humor that redeemed *Slaves* to be unsuccessful in Janowitz's second novel. "Given the book's grisly central metaphor, the tone is shockingly light," observed Rafferty. "If we're really living in a country—or, at least, a city—of cannibals, shouldn't we be a little disturbed?"

Janowitz's same satiric voice "is instantly recognizable," Robert Plunket noted in a review of her next novel, *The Male Cross-Dresser Support Group* for the *New York Times Book Review*. Janowitz is, he stated, "precise, fearless, with the intuitive rhythm of someone who was born funny. . . . Most of all, it's great fun to see a first-rate comic mind tackle the important issues of the day—sexual identity, family values, the shocking behavior of rich WASP's with enormous trust funds." In this 1992 effort, readers are introduced to Pamela Trowel, a woman who lives a meaningless existence in a Manhattan apartment and supports herself with a mindless job selling advertising space for a low-budget hunting magazine until she encounters meaning in the form of a nine-year-old boy called Abdhul. She and the homeless waif become attached to each other and, after Pamela gets fired from her job, they decide to escape from New York rather than be separated by a city bureaucracy seemingly intent upon destroying supportive relationships between children and caring adults. The problem of sexual identity implied by the novel's title comes into play after Abdhul becomes lost; Pamela must adopt the identity of the popular "Paul" in order to discover his whereabouts. "In this postfeminist era,

when women still suffer from a lack of status and a lot of disillusionment, . . . Pamela is a kind of comic urban Everywoman," explained Susan Heeger in the *Los Angeles Times Book Review*. "But she's loyal and courageous," Heeger added, "and it's heartening to watch her find her way in the wilderness, despite all those who want to trample her." The author commented on the plight of her protagonist in the *Boston Globe,* telling interviewer Matthew Gilbert: "God knows the men don't come off well in this book, but the women are even worse. I mean women are so rotten to each other, particularly in New York. They're so competitive and back-stabbing and desperate."

In Janowitz's next novel, *By the Shores of Gitchee Gumee,* she broke away from her customary New York setting to write about life with the Slivenowiczes, a wacky, dysfunctional family living in a trailer on the outskirts of a tacky resort town in upstate New York. Their story involves the explosion of their home and their subsequent wanderings to Florida and Los Angeles. *Booklist* reviewer Donna Seaman approved of the "nimble, satisfyingly nasty, and wholly unexpected humor in [Janowitz's] newest novel." The book features Evangeline Slivenowicz, mother of five children by five different fathers. Her eldest daughter, Maud, functions as the story's narrator, one described by Seaman as "outrageously mercenary and amusingly foul-mouthed." The reviewer found the book audacious: "Who, in their wildest literary dreams, would ever have imagined the city cynic Janowitz parodying that most sentimental and overrated of American poets, Henry Wadsworth Longfellow?"

Not all critics shared Seaman's enthusiasm for *Gitchee Gumee,* however. Margot Mifflin in *Entertainment Weekly* found little appeal in the Slivenowiczes or their adventures, stating, "Janowitz seems to believe that a harebrained story starring irretrievably stupid characters constitutes parody. . . . Even judged by the sitcom standards it aspires to, *Gitchee Gumee* is pretty thin stuff." A *Publishers Weekly* reviewer was also unsatisfied with the book, calling it "painfully precious" and finding "equally awkward" the author's "arbitrary footnotes and haphazard allusions to, and quotations from, early American poetry. The dialogue and incidents dart rapid-fire at the reader as in a screwball comedy—but the screws here are loose, and what aims to be funny comes off as merely frantic."

Janowitz returned to her usual New York setting in her 1999 offering, *A Certain Age,* which the publishing world was already enthusiastically passing around in photocopy form before it appeared in public. The city's social climbers and their cocktail-party circuit are reexamined by the author, this time with the focus on an unmarried woman in her thirties and her ruthless quest for a wealthy, well-connected husband. Mark Lindquist of the *Seattle Times* highly recommended the new novel: "A few times a decade, at most, the right author mines the right territory at the right time, and that's what has happened here—*A Certain Age* is a brilliant Zeitgeist novel, smart and funny and fearless. A classic comeback." Lindquist remarked that "Janowitz has an empathy for her characters that distinguishes [the novel] from other postmodern fare." *Entertainment Weekly* reviewer A.J. Jacobs called *A Certain Age* "an homage to Edith Wharton's *House of Mirth*," but found that it fell far short of Wharton's work. The protagonist, Bridget Jones, is "one of the least likable characters in modern fiction history," stated Jacobs, making it hard to take 317 pages of reading about her. Elizabeth Gleick also found the book unappealing, noting in *Time:* "A hateful heroine and a catalog of her conspicuous consuming do not an amusing read make." A *People* reviewer was more pleased with the book, approving of its "knowing wink at a decaying demimonde." While allowing that "Janowitz's premise wears thin," the writer asserted that "her story amuses to the end." Emily Symon in the *Buffalo News* observed, "There's a great tradition of female writers who focus their powers of observation and description on the genteel brutality of upper class life; *A Certain Age* is simply the latest installment in a long-running serial," adding "Florence, seemingly absent the day they passed out heart and moral fiber, is a classic antihero—a semitragic end seems inevitable for her, though her story is told cleverly enough that it's possible to root for Florence in a wan, curious, halfhearted way" and finally, Janowitz is "still funny, which makes *A Certain Age* bearable in light of what it so surgically exposes about human female nature." Julie Lewis in a *Weekend Australian* interview noted, "A woman's status among the elite of New York is still based on who she [is] married to," and quoted Janowitz: "'I blame women for that. I blame women for sneering at other women when they are not paired off with somebody.'" Lewis added, "This feminism-free, super-wealthy class, [Janowitz] feels, is taking over her town. 'New York used to be the sort of city you could come to and still find a cheap apartment, get a job as a waitress, work in a coffee shop, pay the rent, go out at night and do performance art or paint. Now it's a city just for the very, very rich.'" It also seems that by the time she published *A Certain Age,* Janowitz's own life had veered away from that of her heroines'. The same year, she contributed to a book about the challenges of adopting children. She had met and married an Englishman who came to appraise Andy Warhol's possessions after his

death, they had adopted a Chinese baby, and Janowitz had begun writing comic restaurant reviews and (very sensible) parenting advice for magazines. She published the children's book *Hear That?* in 2001.

Janowitz's next novel, *Peyton Amberg,* both touched and impressed London *Guardian*'s Fay Weldon, who commented: "Madame Bovary, in the guise of Peyton Amberg, runs amok in Manhattan and is destroyed: that's the gist of this wonderful novel. It's not nice, mind you, not out of some well-behaved creative writing course the other side of the Atlantic, just glitteringly, angrily, ferociously accurate about the realities of the world." Weldon continued, "Janowitz allows her heroine no mercy, as the girl with the mad, abusive mother, 'hideous hippie hair sprouting from her head in various colours, like some terrible mutant dandelion', descends from the fantasy of happiness to the depths of degradation. . . . It is one of the funniest books I have read, and the bleakest." Peyton Amberg comes from a downwardly mobile Boston family, has married boringly, and become a travel agent, which gives her the room to have endless increasingly awful affairs in exotic places. The *New York Times*'s Mary Elizabeth Williams found that "Janowitz's harsh view of modern sex and her smooth way around the ugliest of encounters can make for vivid reading. She writes with brazen realism, but replaces Flaubert's poetic brutality with crude shocks." In the *Financial Times,* Lilian Pizzichinni commented, "as Janowitz herself has aged, so has her female lead and the result is a bleakness as compelling as was her youthful promise." "What is interesting here is that Janowitz has ditched the glamour to give us the dirt." Pizzichinni continued, "In a series of harrowing episodes Janowitz makes clear that Peyton's schizophrenic mother and absentee father contributed to her inability to connect, feel love or be possessed of a sense of worth. But Janowitz leavens the despair with a captivating ironic detachment: 'There were only another fifty years to get through before (Barry) died,' Peyton figures on her honeymoon. Meanwhile, she seeks out casual sex and new sensations to avoid the drudgery of married life."

Like her protagonist Earl in *American Dad,* Janowitz is the product of a broken marriage between a psychiatrist and a poet; critics noted that she interjects in the fictional lives of the characters she creates the ability to seek unusual ways of dealing with permissive parents or unstructured lifestyles. Several critics also noted parallels between Janowitz and Eleanor, the heroine of *Slaves of New York.* "Her story isn't as much mine as eighty of my girlfriends," Janowitz responded to Gini Sikes in an interview for *Mademoiselle.* "Just because I write that stuff doesn't mean it has anything to do with me." However, she also admitted to *CA* that an autobiographical element does run through her work. "I write about myself by pretending to be others," Janowitz once explained. "In my first novel I am a young boy trying to win his father's approval; in my second I am an elderly 'primitive' cannibal visiting 'civilized' New York City for the first time; and in [*Slaves of New York*] I am a young painter who is burdened with the weight of all of history, and is preoccupied with death and immortality."

In commenting on the "writing life," Janowitz has described the act of rising from bed as a daily struggle. "But generally the need to go to the bathroom and the desire for Wheat Chex forces me to get up," she quipped to *CA*. "Then there is the floor to be swept, and the thought that perchance on this day some mail will come. . . . This is not to say that I despise life. On the contrary, life is an overwhelming experience for me, so much so that getting out of bed becomes an Everest of Olympian proportions for me to climb. The glory of eating Wheat Chex is quite beyond belief. And then if I can actually drag myself to the typewriter and get some words down on paper, what joy I experience!

"For me, writing is overwhelmingly difficult, yet not so difficult, it seems, as actually having to go out and get a job. . . . Some people, sadly, are not meant to work, but I have learned this about myself at an early age. Certain people (though whom I cannot say) might feel that as a writer I should be working in order to collect experience; but it was Flannery O'Connor who said that each person has had enough experiences by the age of twenty to write for the rest of his or her life. Or something to that effect."

BIOGRAPHICAL AND CRITICAL SOURCES:

PERIODICALS

Baltimore News-American, May 24, 1981.

Baltimore Sun, June 7, 1981.

BELL: Belgian Essays on Language and Literature, 2002, p. 93.

Booklist, June 1, 1996, p. 1630; May 1, 1999, p. 1558.

Boston Globe, September 9, 1992, p. 69.

Boston Phoenix, May 12, 1981.

Buffalo News (Buffalo, NY), December 19, 1999, p. E6.

Childhood Education, fall, 2001, p. 50.

Daily Mail (London, England), August 29, 2003, p. 56.

Daily Telegraph (London, England), July 27, 2002; August 23, 2003.

Entertainment Weekly, September 13, 1996, p. 125; July 30, 1999, p. 64.

Evening Standard (London, England), July 15, 2002, p. 47.

Financial Times, July 20, 2002, p. 4; August 16, 2003, p. 33.

Fresno Bee (Fresno, CA), September 19, 1999, p. E3, interview with Janowitz.

Guardian (London, England), May 20, 2000, p. 11; September 6, 2003, p. 28.

Herald (Glasgow, Scotland), May 11, 2000, p. 22.

Horizon, June, 1981.

Houston Chronicle, April 4, 1981.

Hudson Review, autumn, 1986, p. 489.

Independent (London, England), July 17, 1999, p. 9; May 13, 2000, p. 11; May 27, 2000, p. 6; August 30, 2003, p. 25.

Independent on Sunday (London, England), October 27, 1996, p. 25; July 26, 1998, p. 27; July 3, 1999, p. 15; July 4, 1999, p. 5; July 18, 1999, p. 9; May 14, 2000, p. 48; September 7, 2003, p. 19.

Interview, August, 1981.

Irish Times (Dublin, Ireland), October 4, 2003, p. 61.

Kirkus Reviews, June 15, 1996.

Library Journal, July, 1996, p. 160; May 15, 1999, p. 126.

Listener, February 19, 1987, p. 36.

London Review of Books, February 5, 1987, pp. 12-13.

Los Angeles Times Book Review, April 26, 1987, p. 14; October 18, 1987, p. 10; September 13, 1992, p. 1; October 18, 1987, p. 10.

Mademoiselle, April, 1989, pp. 102, 104, 276.

Newark Star-Ledger, April 26, 1981.

New Republic, June 6, 1981; February 1, 1988, pp. 29-34.

New Statesman, February 27, 1987; March 4, 1988, p. 26.

Newsweek, September 7, 1987, p. 72.

New York Daily News, May 21, 1981.

New Yorker, October 26, 1987, pp. 142-146.

New York Times, October 19, 2003, p. ST11; October 26, 2003, p. 24.

New York Times Book Review, May 17, 1981; October 4, 1987, p. 12; August 20, 1992, p. 3; October 20, 1996, p. 13; August 8, 1999, p. 9; October 26, 2003, p. 24.

Observer (London, England), September 14, 2003, p. 6, interview with Janowitz.

Opera News, November, 1996, p. 26.

People, September 9, 1996, p. 38; July 19, 1999, p. 43.

Pittsburgh Press, July 20, 1981.

Publishers Weekly, June 17, 1996, p. 44; May 31, 1999, p. 62; April 16, 2001, p. 65; November 18, 2002, p. 14; September 1, 2003, p. 61; October 20, 2003, p. 51.

Rocky Mountain News (Denver, CO), August 15, 1999, p. 1E.

School Library Journal, June, 2001, p. 120.

Scotsman (Edinburgh, Scotland), July 29, 2000, p. 2, interview with Janowitz.

Seattle Times, August 5, 1999, p. G16.

Soho News, April 15, 1981.

Spectator, November 14, 1992, p. 39.

Springfield Republican, August 30, 1981.

Sunday Telegraph (Surrey Hills, Australia), November 24, 2002, p. T16.

Sunday Times (London, England), August 31, 2003, p. 52.

Tampa Tribune, August 8, 1999, p. 5.

Time, October 19, 1987, pp. 77-79; September 7, 1992, p. 69; August 2, 1999, p. 96.

Times (London, England), September 12, 2001, p. 17; June 29, 2002, p. 18; August 20, 2003, p. 9.

Times Literary Supplement, March 4-10, 1988, p. 245; July 2, 1999, p. 21.

Village Voice, August 5, 1986.

Wall Street Journal, July 22, 1986, p. 28; October 19, 1992, p. A12; July 30, 1999, p. W11.

Washington Post Book World, August 30, 1992, p. 2; October 20, 1996, p. 6.

Washington Times. August 29, 1999, p. 6.

Weekend Australian (Sydney, New South Wales, Australia), August 7, 1999, p. R10.

West Coast Review of Books, July, 1981.

ONLINE

Bold Type, http://www.randomhouse.com/boldtype/ (August 1999), Janowitz biography.

BookReporter, http://www.bookreporter.com/ (March 11, 2004), Joni Rendon, review of *Peyton Amberg.*

CityPaper, http://citypaper.net/ (July 22-29, 1999), Kristin Keith, review of *A Certain Age.*

EyeWeekly, http://www.eye.net/ (March 31, 1994), Elizabeth Mitchell, "Seeking That Tama-Friendly Audience."

Guardian Unlimited, http://books.guardian.co.uk/ (September 6, 2003), review of *Peyton Amberg.*

NewYork Metro, http://www.newyorkmetro.com/ (August 9, 1999), Vanessa Grigoriadis, review of *A Certain Age.*

*   *   *

JARVIS, E.K.
  See ELLISON, Harlan

JARVIS, E.K.
  See SILVERBERG, Robert

*   *   *

JENKINS, Jerry
  See JENKINS, Jerry B.

*   *   *

JENKINS, Jerry B. 1949-
  (Jerry Jenkins, Jerry Bruce Jenkins)

PERSONAL: Born September 23, 1949, in Kalamazoo, MI; son of Harry Phillip (a police chief) and Bonita Grace (Thompson) Jenkins; married Dianna Louise Whiteford, January 23, 1971; children: Dallas Lawrence, Chadwick Whiteford, Michael Bruce. *Education:* Attended Moody Bible Institute, 1967-68, Loop College, 1968, and William Rainey Harper College, 1968-70. *Politics:* Independent. *Religion:* "Jesus Christ." *Hobbies and other interests:* Photography, tournament table tennis, Scrabble club.

ADDRESSES: Home—Three-Son Acres, 40542 Cornell St. N, Zion, IL 60099. *Office*—820 North LaSalle Dr., Chicago, IL 60610.

CAREER: WMBI-FM-AM-Radio, Chicago, IL, night news editor, 1967-68; Day Publications, Mt. Prospect, IL, assistant sports editor, 1968-69; Des Plaines Publishing Co., Des Plaines, IL, sports editor, 1969-71; *Tri-City Herald,* Kennewick, WA, sportswriter, 1971; Scripture Press Publications, Wheaton, IL, associate editor, 1971-72, managing editor, 1972-73; Inspirational Radio-Television Guide, Chicago, IL, executive editor, 1973-74; *Moody Monthly* (magazine), Chicago, managing editor, 1974-75, editor, 1975-81, director, 1978-81; Moody Press, Chicago, director, 1981-83; Moody Bible Institute, Chicago, manager of Publishing Division, 1983-85, vice president of Publishing Branch, 1985-88, writer-in-residence, 1988—. Visiting lecturer in advanced journalism, Wheaton Graduate School, 1975.

MEMBER: Evangelical Press Association, Christian Booksellers Association, Evangelical Christian Publishers Association, U.S. Table Tennis Association.

AWARDS, HONORS: Novel of the Year nomination, *Campus Life* magazine, for *Margo;* Religion in Media Angel Award, for *Meaghan* and *Margo's Reunion;* Biography of the Year award, *Campus Life* magazine, 1980, for *Home Where I Belong;* Evangelical Christian Publishers Association Gold Medallion nomination, for *The Night the Giant Rolled Over* and *Rekindled: How to Keep the Warmth in Marriage.*

WRITINGS:

You CAN Get thru to Teens, Victor Books (Wheaton, IL), 1973.

Sammy Tippit: God's Love in Action, as Told to Jerry B. Jenkins, Broadman (Nashville, TN), 1973.

VBS Unlimited, Victor Books (Wheaton, IL), 1974.

(With Hank Aaron and Stan Baldwin) *Bad Henry,* Chilton (Radnor, PA), 1974.

The Story of the Christian Booksellers Association, Nelson (Nashville, TN), 1974.

(With Pat Williams) *The Gingerbread Man: Pat Williams Then and Now,* Lippincott (Philadelphia, PA), 1974.

Stuff It: The Story of Dick Motta, Toughest Little Coach in the NBA, Chilton (Radnor, PA), 1975.

(With Sammy Tippit) *Three behind the Curtain,* Whitaker House (New Kensington, PA), 1975.

(With Paul Anderson) *The World's Strongest Man,* Victor Books (Wheaton, IL), 1975, expanded edition published as *A Greater Strength,* Revell (Old Tappan, NJ), 1990.

(With Madeline Manning Jackson) *Running for Jesus,* Word (Dallas, TX), 1977.

(With Walter Payton) *Sweetness,* Contemporary Books (Chicago, IL), 1978.

(With Sammy Tippit) *You, Me, He,* Victor Books (Wheaton, IL), 1978.

(With B.J. Thomas) *Home Where I Belong,* Word (Dallas, TX), 1978.

Light on the Heavy: A Simple Guide to Understanding Bible Doctrines, Victor Books (Wheaton, IL), 1978.

(With Sammy Tippit) *Reproduced by Permission of the Author,* Victor Books (Wheaton, IL), 1979.

The Luis Palau Story, Revell (Old Tappan, NJ), 1980.

The Night the Giant Rolled Over, Word (Dallas, TX), 1981.

(With Pat Williams) *The Power within You,* Westminster (Philadelphia, PA), 1983.

(With Robert Flood) *Teaching the Word, Reaching the World,* Moody (Chicago, IL), 1985.

(With Pat Williams) *Rekindled: How to Keep the Warmth in Marriage,* Revell (Old Tappan, NJ), 1985.

(With Meadowlark Lemon) *Meadowlark,* Nelson (Nashville, TN), 1987.

(With Pat Williams and Jill Williams) *Kindling: Daily Devotions for Busy Couples,* Nelson (Nashville, TN), 1987.

The Operative (novel), Harper & Row (New York, NY), 1987.

A Generous Impulse: The Story of George Sweeting, Moody (Chicago, IL), 1987.

Carry Me: Christine Wyrtzen's Discoveries on the Journey into God's Arms, as Told to Jerry B. Jenkins, Moody (Chicago, IL), 1988.

(With Larry and Diane Mayfield) *Baby Mayfield,* Moody (Chicago, IL), 1989.

(With Deanna McClary) *Commitment to Love,* Nelson (Nashville, TN), 1989.

(With Orel Hershiser) *Out of the Blue,* Wolgemuth & Hyatt (Brentwood, TN), 1989.

Hedges: Loving Your Marriage Enough to Protect It, Wolgemuth & Hyatt (Brentwood, TN), 1989, expanded edition, Moody (Chicago, IL), 1993.

(With Pat Williams and Jill Williams) *Just Between Us,* Revell (Tarrytown, NY), 1991.

(With Joe J. Gibbs) *Joe Gibbs: Fourth and One,* Nelson (Nashville, TN), 1991.

Twelve Things I Want My Kids to Remember Forever, Moody (Chicago, IL), 1991.

The Rookie (novel), Wolgemuth & Hyatt (Brentwood, TN), 1991.

(With Nolan Ryan) *Miracle Man: Nolan Ryan, the Autobiography,* Word (Dallas, TX), 1992.

(With William Gaither) *I Almost Missed the Sunset: My Perspectives on Life and Music,* Nelson (Nashville, TN), 1992.

The Deacon's Woman and Other Portraits (fiction), Moody (Chicago, IL), 1992.

(Editor) *Families: Practical Advice from More than Fifty Experts,* Moody (Chicago, IL), 1993.

(With George J. Thompson) *Verbal Judo: The Gentle Art of Persuasion,* Morrow (New York, NY), 1993.

Winning at Losing, Moody (Chicago, IL), 1993.

Life Flies When You're Having Fun, Victor Books (Wheaton, IL), 1993.

(With Sammy Tippit) *No Matter What the Cost: An Autobiography,* Nelson (Nashville, TN), 1993.

As You Leave Home: Parting Thoughts from a Loving Parent, Focus on the Family (Colorado Springs, CO), 1993.

(With Gary Almy and Carol Tharp Almy) *Addicted Recovery,* Harvest House (Eugene, OR), 1994.

Still the One: Tender Thoughts from a Loving Spouse, Focus on the Family (Colorado Springs, CO), 1995.

And Then Came You: The Hopes and Dreams of Loving Parents, Focus on the Family (Colorado Springs, CO), 1996.

The Neighborhood's Scariest Woman, ("Toby Andrews and the Junior Deputies" series), Moody (Chicago, IL), 1996.

The East Side Bullies ("Toby Andrews and the Junior Deputies" series), Moody (Chicago, IL), 1996.

(With Brett Butler) *Field of Hope: An Inspiring Autobiography of a Lifetime of Overcoming Odds,* Nelson (Nashville, TN), 1997.

(With William Gaither) *Homecoming: The Story of Southern Gospel Music through the Eyes of Its Best-Loved Performers,* Zondervan (Grand Rapids, MI), 1997.

'Twas the Night Before, Viking (New York, NY), 1998.

Though None Go with Me (novel), Zondervan (Grand Rapids, MI), 2000.

Hometown Legend, Warner Books (New York, NY), 2001.

(With Tim F. LaHaye) *Perhaps Today: Living Every Day in the Light of Christ's Return,* Tyndale House (Wheaton, IL), 2001.

The Youngest Hero, Warner Books (New York, NY), 2002.

"MARGO MYSTERY" SERIES

Margo, Jeremy Books, 1979, published as *The Woman at the Window,* Nelson (Nashville, TN), 1991.

Karlyn, Moody (Chicago, IL), 1980, published as *The Daylight Intruder,* Nelson, (Nashville, TN), 1991.

Hilary, Moody (Chicago, IL), 1980, published as *Murder behind Bars,* Nelson (Nashville, TN), 1991.

Paige, Moody (Chicago, IL), 1981, published as *The Meeting at Midnight,* Nelson (Nashville, TN), 1991.

Allyson, Moody (Chicago, IL), 1981, published as *The Silence Is Broken,* Nelson (Nashville, TN), 1991.

Erin, Moody (Chicago, IL), 1982, published as *Gold Medal Murder,* Nelson (Nashville, TN), 1991.

Shannon, Moody (Chicago, IL), 1982, published as *Thank You, Good-Bye,* Nelson (Nashville, TN), 1991.

Lindsey, Moody (Chicago, IL), 1983, published as *Dying to Come Home,* Nelson (Nashville, TN), 1991.

Meaghan, Moody (Chicago, IL), 1983.

Janell, Moody (Chicago, IL), 1983.

Courtney, Moody (Chicago, IL), 1983.

Lyssa, Moody (Chicago, IL), 1984.

Margo's Reunion, Moody (Chicago, IL), 1984.

"JENNIFER GREY MYSTERY" SERIES

Heartbeat, Victor Books (Wheaton, IL), 1983.

Three Days in Winter, Victor Books (Wheaton, IL), 1983.

Too Late to Tell, Victor Books (Wheaton, IL), 1983.

Gateway, Victor Books (Wheaton, IL), 1983.

The Calling, Victor Books (Wheaton, IL), 1984.

Veiled Threat, Victor Books (Wheaton, IL), 1984.

"THE BRADFORD FAMILY ADVENTURE" SERIES

Daniel's Big Surprise, Standard Publishing (Cincinnati, OH), 1984.

Two Runaways, Standard Publishing (Cincinnati, OH), 1984.

The Clubhouse Mystery, Standard Publishing (Cincinnati, OH), 1984.

The Kidnapping, Standard Publishing (Cincinnati, OH), 1984.

Marty's Secret, Standard Publishing (Cincinnati, OH), 1985.

Blizzard!, Standard Publishing (Cincinnati, OH), 1985.

Fourteen Days to Midnight, Standard Publishing (Cincinnati, OH), 1985.

Good Sport/Bad Sport, Standard Publishing (Cincinnati, OH), 1985.

In Deep Water, Standard Publishing (Cincinnati, OH), 1986.

Mystery at Raider Stadium, Standard Publishing (Cincinnati, OH), 1986.

Daniel's Big Decision, Standard Publishing (Cincinnati, OH), 1986.

Before the Judge, Standard Publishing (Cincinnati, OH), 1986.

"DALLAS O'NEIL AND THE BAKER STREET SPORTS CLUB" SERIES

The Secret Baseball Challenge, Moody (Chicago, IL), 1986.

The Scary Basketball Player, Moody (Chicago, IL), 1986.

The Mysterious Football Team, Moody (Chicago, IL), 1986.

The Weird Soccer Match, Moody (Chicago, IL), 1986.

The Strange Swimming Coach, Moody (Chicago, IL), 1986.

The Bizarre Hockey Tournament, Moody (Chicago, IL), 1986.

The Silent Track Star, Moody (Chicago, IL), 1986.

The Angry Gymnast, Moody (Chicago, IL), 1986.

Mystery of the Phony Murder, Moody (Chicago, IL), 1989.

Mystery of the Skinny Sophomore, Moody (Chicago, IL), 1989.

"TARA CHADWICK" SERIES

Time to Tell, Moody (Chicago, IL), 1990.
Operation Cemetery, Moody (Chicago, IL), 1990.
Scattered Flowers, Moody (Chicago, IL), 1990.
Springtime Discovery, Moody (Chicago, IL), 1990.

"LEFT BEHIND" SERIES, WITH TIM F. LAHAYE

Left Behind: A Novel of the Earth's Last Days, Tyndale
   House (Wheaton, IL), 1995.
*Tribulation Force: The Continuing Drama of Those Left
   Behind,* Tyndale House (Wheaton, IL), 1996.
Nicolae: The Rise of Antichrist, Tyndale House
   (Wheaton, IL), 1997.
Soul Harvest: The World Takes Sides, Tyndale House
   (Wheaton, IL), 1998.
Apollyon: The Destroyer Is Unleashed, Tyndale House
   (Wheaton, IL), 1999.
Assassins: The Great Tribulation Unfolds, Tyndale
   House (Wheaton, IL), 1999.
The Indwelling: The Beast Takes Possession, Tyndale
   House (Wheaton, IL), 2000.
Desecration: Antichrist Takes the Throne, Tyndale
   House (Wheaton, IL), 2001.
The Mark: The Beast Rules the World, Tyndale House
   (Wheaton, IL), 2001.
The Remnant: On the Brink of Armageddon, Tyndale
   House (Wheaton, IL), 2002.
Armageddon, Tyndale House (Wheaton, IL), 2003.
Glorious Reappearing: The End of Days, Tyndale
   House (Wheaton, IL), 2004.

"GLOBAL AIR TROUBLESHOOTERS" SERIES

Terror in Branco Grande, Multnomah Books (Sisters,
   OR), 1996.
Disaster in the Yukon, Multnomah Books (Sisters, OR),
   1996.
Crash at Cannibal Valley, Multnomah Books (Sisters,
   OR), 1996.

"LEFT BEHIND—THE KIDS" SERIES; WITH TIM F. LAHAYE

The Vanishings, Tyndale House (Wheaton, IL), 1998.
Second Chance, Tyndale House (Wheaton, IL), 1998.
Through the Flames, Tyndale House (Wheaton, IL),
   1998.
Facing the Future, Tyndale House (Wheaton, IL), 1998.

(And with Chris Fabry) *The Underground,* Tyndale
   House (Wheaton, IL), 1999.
Nicolae High, Tyndale House (Wheaton, IL), 1999.
(And with Chris Fabry) *Death Strike,* Tyndale House
   (Wheaton, IL), 2000.
(And with Chris Fabry) *Busted!,* Tyndale House
   (Wheaton, IL), 2000.

OTHER

Also author of *Off the Map,* 1991. Contributor to periodicals, including *Moody Monthly, Power, Contact,
Coronet, Saturday Evening Post,* and *Campus Life.*

*ADAPTATIONS: Left Behind: A Novel of the Earth's
Last Days* was adapted for a feature film by Cloud Ten
Pictures, 2001. Books in the "Left Behind" series have
been adapted to audio cassette, interactive computer
games, mugs, T-shirts, and other marketing
merchandise.

WORK IN PROGRESS: A prequel and sequel, volumes
thirteen and fourteen, to the "Left Behind" series.

SIDELIGHTS: Jerry B. Jenkins is the author of over
one hundred titles, most of them religious and inspirational works. The best known of these are the dozen
titles of the "Left Behind" series, penned with Tim F.
LaHaye. With over sixty-two million copies of that series in print, the Jenkins-LaHaye team is, according to
Newsweek's David Gates, "arguably, the most successful literary partnership of all time." Gates further noted
that "their Biblical techno-thrillers about the end of the
world are currently outselling Stephen King, John Grisham, and every other pop novelist in America." The
books in the hugely popular series are "old-time religion with a sci-fi sensibility," wrote Gates; they combine "the ultimate certainty the Bible offers with the
entertainment-culture conventions of rock-jawed heroism and slam-bang special effects." Yet Jenkins continues to describe himself in interviews as "the most famous writer no one's ever heard of." Part of the reason
for this lack of name recognition is the fact that over
seventy per cent of the sales of the "Left Behind" series
are from the South and Midwest, only six percent from
the urban Northeast. A full eighty-five per cent of the
readership of the series terms themselves "born again"
Christians. As Gates put it, the typical buyer of the
books is a "forty-four-year-old born-again Christian
woman, married with kids, living in the South."

A native of Michigan, Jenkins worked as a journalist
and publishing executive before turning to authorship in
the 1970s. He wrote in a variety of nonfiction genres,

but all his books were grounded in his evangelical Christian faith. The author also earned a reputation as the writing talent behind celebrity memoirs; his "as told to" autobiographies include those of sports heroes Henry Aaron, Orel Hershiser, and Brett Butler. But Jenkins told a *Marriage Partnership* interviewer, "fiction was always my first love. I wrote nonfiction to pay the bills, in the hopes that the fiction would hit."

The fiction did hit—first with a set of youth-oriented mysteries, then with the debut of the "Left Behind" books. The books were conceived by LaHaye, a well-known evangelical minister who left the pulpit in 1981 to devote time to writing and politics. According to a *People* article by Thomas Fields-Meyer, LaHaye was inspired to storytelling during his travel days: "Sitting on airplanes and watching the pilots," he commented to Fields-Meyer, "I'd think to myself, 'What if the Rapture occurred on an airplane'?" LaHaye searched for three years for someone to shape his idea into a novel, and fellow evangelical Jenkins was his selection. Though nearly twenty-five years apart in age, the two were comfortable working together. "It's like a father-son thing," Jenkins said in *People*. Jenkins is the author of the novels; LaHaye serves as consultant for prophetic accuracy.

In 1995 *Left Behind* was published by Tyndale House. True to LaHaye's vision, the novel opens on an airplane en route to London. Pilot Rayford Steele, who is contemplating an extramarital affair with flight attendant Hattie Durham, is surprised when Hattie bursts into the cockpit with startling news: several of the passengers have disappeared in an instant, leaving only their clothes and other possessions piled on their seats. Making an emergency landing in his hometown of Chicago, Rayford returns home to find his wife and son, both recently born-again Christians, vanished as well. The conclusion: Christian true-believers have been spirited to heaven (the Rapture) while those back on Earth are faced with the biblical prophesy of war and pestilence leading to the Apocalypse, as heralded by the rise of the Antichrist.

Among those "left behind" is crusading journalist Cameron "Buck" Williams, who takes on the story for his magazine. His investigation leads to a charismatic Romanian politician, Nicolae Carpathia, who quickly rises to power by advocating a one-world government. Nicolae, appointed secretary general of the United Nations, has the power to control all but the unsaved; he reconstructs the nations of the Earth as the Global Community and plans to reign supreme over the world. When it

becomes apparent that Nicolae is the Antichrist incarnate, it is up to Rayford, Buck, and their band of believers, who dub themselves the Tribulation Force, to defend their world. As the last line of *Left Behind* puts it, the rebels' task was clear: "their goal was nothing less than to stand and fight the enemies of God during the seven most chaotic years the planet would ever see."

Left Behind was followed by a steady stream of sequels, one every six months, all advancing the Apocalyptic plot. While few mainstream critics praised the stylistic aspects of the novels, many acknowledged that Jenkins's tales had value as thought-provoking page-turners. "I found [the first novel] rattling good reading, professionally terse yet fluid," commented J.C. Furnas of *American Scholar*. "Suppose the late Ian Fleming [of James Bond fame] had got End-Times religion and built on it a portentous Scripture-based epic in 007 style, only with a certain paucity of toothsome women." While *Atlantic Monthly* reviewer Joseph Gross noted Jenkins' reliance on easy characterization—"everyone in the books is above average. The characters' brains and physical beauty are sometimes described with clumsy cultural references"—*National Review* contributor Matthew Scully had a different view. He thought Jenkins had "a gift for plot and dialogue" which would serve the author well through the book series.

Some criticism of the "Left Behind" books focused on the way non-evangelicals were portrayed. "The authors' perception of the Jews as a great people gone wrong streaks the books with a queasy, forced amiability teetering on contempt," stated *Commonweal* writer Richard Alleva. The Catholic church "takes its lumps, too," Alleva continued. "The latest pope is raptured, but that is because he had stirred up controversy in the church with a new doctrine that seemed to coincide more with the 'heresy' of Martin Luther than with historic orthodoxy." "Catholics' chances of making the Rapture are slim," noted Teresa Malcolm in a *National Catholic Reporter* piece, but in her opinion the saving of the fictional pope reflected that "overt anti-Catholicism was deliberately toned down to give the novels a wider appeal."

But the books' severest barbs are aimed at the United Nations, "which practically hands itself over to the Antichrist and becomes the arm of his will," according to Alleva. "And what is his will? A world government, a world capital called New Babylon, a world army, and a world religion—all the usual suspects placed at the service of Satan's minion. In a country like ours, where fear of centralization and government interference has led to bombings, mass slaughter, and the creation of various thug militia-groups, how could the 'Left Behind' series fail?"

The timing of a tale about the Rapture coincided with the end-of-the-millennium mood in the United States. Worldwide political unrest and "Y2K" technological concerns fueled the interest in end-times literature, and the "Left Behind" series played into that interest. Jenkins and LaHaye's books, promotional items and Web site have drawn massive attention, leading a *Publishers Weekly* editor to tell *People*'s Fields-Meyer that the stories comprise "the most successful Christian-fiction series ever." "Left Behind is truly newsmaking stuff," remarked Alleva. Still, Jenkins maintains that money is not the primary force propelling the series, even though it has been reported that each author has earned over fifty million dollars on the series. "Neither [LaHaye] nor I grew up in families where success was defined by money," he said in the *Marriage Partnership* interview. His ministry, he said, was always more important. And he takes pleasure in writing the novels: "Discovering what happens is as much fun for me as it is for readers. I don't kill my characters off; I find them dead."

Any thought that the "Left Behind" series was simply a manifestation of millennial fever was put to rest with the continued success of the series after the year 2000. And with the terrorist attacks of 2001 in New York and Washington, and the ensuing war in Iraq, many of the fans of the series felt that the world in fact was entering the last days as prophesied in the Book of Revelation. The series came to its final volume—though a prequel and sequel are planned—with volume twelve, *Glorious Reappearing: The End of Days,* in which Jesus reappears. That book sold over two million copies even before its publication date.

It has been noted, especially with the George W. Bush White House, that the series functions not just as fiction but also as a subtle form of propaganda for the conservative Christian interpretation of the Bible. According to Gates, "The many critics of the series see a resonance between its apocalyptic scenario and the born-again President Bush's apocalyptic rhetoric and confrontational Mid East policies." These same critics see a LaHaye's far-right political agenda in topics in the books such as the United Nations acting as an evil institution. Other criticism continues to come from Christians themselves who "find the books more interested in God's wrath than God's love—as well as scripturally questionable," as Gates further observed. Critics also point to the "pedestrian writing and . . . gruesome violence" in the books, as Malcolm Jones pointed out in *Newsweek.* According to Jones, "Characterization is minimal and when Christ isn't spouting Scripture, he sounds like a traffic cop."

Yet detractors aside, the success of the series is its own justification. As Melani McAlister commented in a *Nation* article on the "Left Behind" franchise, "The astonishing success of the . . . series suggests that the conservative obsession with biblical prophecy is increasingly shaping our secular reality." Responding to critics of the vengeful God presented in their books, however, Jenkins noted to Gates that he and LaHaye read the Bible with this interpretation and "we sort of have a responsibility to tell what it seems to say to us." Speaking with David D. Kirkpatrick of the *New York Times,* Jenkins also acknowledged that his warrior, judgmental, vengeful Jesus "might not please everyone." However, Jenkins concluded, "that is the way it is in the Bible."

BIOGRAPHICAL AND CRITICAL SOURCES:

PERIODICALS

American Scholar, winter, 2000, J.C. Furnas, "Millennial Sideshow," p. 87.
Atlantic Monthly, January, 2000, Joseph Gross, "The Trials of Tribulation," p. 122.
Booklist, February 1, 1992, review of *Off the Map,* p. 1005; November 1, 1995, John Mort, review of *Left Behind: A Novel of the Earth's Last Days,* p. 455; October 1, 1996, John Mort, review of *Tribulation Force: The Continuing Drama of Those Left Behind,* p. 304; March 1, 1997, John Mort, review of *The Rookie,* p. 1111; July, 1997, John Mort, review of *Nicolae: The Rise of Antichrist,* p. 1775, Ray Olson, review of *Homecoming: The Story of Southern Gospel Music through the Eyes of Its Best-Loved Performers,* p. 1788; June 1, 1998, John Mort, review of *Soul Harvest: The World Takes Sides,* p. 1669; October 15, 1998, Toni Hyde, review of *'Twas the Night Before,* p. 374; February 1, 1999, John Mort, review of *Apollyon: The Destroyer Is Unleashed,* p. 940; August, 1999, John Mort, review of *Assassins: The Great Tribulation Unfolds,* p. 1987; January 1, 2000, John Mort, review of *Though None Go with Me,* p. 874; December 15, 2000, Bonnie Smothers, review of *The Mark: The Beast Rules the World,* p. 763; July, 2001, John Mort, review of *Hometown Legend,*

p. 1951, Jeanette Larson, review of *The Indwelling: The Beast Takes Possession,* p. 2029; November 15, 2001, Judy Morrissey, review of *The Vanishings,* p. 591.

Christianity Today, September 1, 1997, Michael Maudlin, review of *Left Behind,* p. 22.

Christian Reader, September, 2000, review of *The Indwelling,* p. 7; November, 2000, review of *The Mark,* p. 6.

Commonweal, January 12, 2001, Richard Alleva, "Beam Me Up: A Repackaged Apocalypse," p. 17.

Electronic News, November 28, 1994, Grace Zisk, review of *Verbal Judo: The Gentle Art of Persuasion,* p. 34.

Free Inquiry, spring, 2001, Edmund Cohen, "Turner Diaries Lite," p. 58.

Insight on the News, August 26, 2002, Sheila R. Cherry, "Tour Guides to the Tribulation," pp. 36-39.

Kirkus Reviews, December 1, 1991, review of *Off the Map,* p. 1514; September 15, 1998, review of *'Twas the Night Before,* p. 1330.

Library Journal, June 1, 1996, Henry Carrigan, Jr., review of *Left Behind,* p. 92; September 1, 1996, Henry Carrigan, Jr., review of *Tribulation Force,* p. 164; October 1, 1997, Michael Colby, review of *Homecoming,* p. 84; June 1, 1998, Melissa Hudak, review of *Soul Harvest,* p. 94; November 1, 1998, review of *'Twas the Night Before,* p. 127; May 15, 1999, Melissa Hudak, review of *Left Behind,* p. 147; September 1, 1999, Melanie Duncan, review of *Assassins,* p. 172; November 1, 2000, Melanie Duncan, review of *The Mark,* p. 62.

Los Angeles Times Magazine, April 25, 2004, Nancy Shepherdson, "Waiting for Godot; the Bible Foretold It," p. 16.

Marriage Partnership, fall, 2000, review of *The Indwelling,* p. S4; summer, 2000, "Riding the Wave," p. S1; fall, 2001, review of *Desecration: Antichrist Takes the Throne,* p. S4; spring, 2002, review of *Desecration,* p. S4.

Nation, September 22, 2003, Melani McAlister, "An Empire of Their Own," p. 31.

National Catholic Reporter, June 15, 2001, Teresa Malcolm, "Fearful Faith in End Times Novel," p. 13.

National Review, December 21, 1998, Matthew Scully, "Apocalypse Soon," p. 62.

Newsweek, April 12, 2004, Malcolm Jones, "The Twelfth Book of Revelation," p. 60; May 24, 2004, David Gates, "Religion: The Pop Prophets," p. 44.

New York Review of Books, October 12, 1989, Wilfred Sheed, review of *Out of the Blue,* p. 49.

New York Times, February 11, 2002, David D. Kirkpatrick, "A Best-Selling Formula in Religious Thrillers," p. C2; March 29, 2004, David D. Kirkpatrick, "In the Twelfth Book of Best-Selling Series, Jesus Returns," p. A1; April 4, 2004, David D. Kirkpatrick, "The Return of the Warrior Jesus," p. D1.

New York Times Book Review, June 4, 1989, Charles Salzberg, review of *Out of the Blue,* p. 23.

People, December 14, 1998, Thomas Fields-Meyer, "In Heaven's Name," p. 139.

Publishers Weekly, September 14, 1998, review of *'Twas the Night Before,* p. 50; November 15, 1999, review of *Though None Go with Me,* p. 56; November 13, 2000, review of *The Mark,* p. 88; May 7, 2001, Cindy Crosby, "Left Behind Fuels Growth at Tyndale House," p. 18; July 16, 2001, review of *Hometown Legend,* p. 156; August 20, 2001, Daisy Maryles and Dick Donahue, "Making a Mark," p. 23; April 21, 2003, Daisy Maryles and Dick Donahue, "Armageddon Has Arrived," p. 16.

Today's Christian Woman, November, 2000, "Five Minutes with Jerry B. Jenkins," p. 78; March, 2001, "Down the Fiction Aisle," p. S4; September, 2001, review of *Desecration,* p. S4.

Voice of Youth Advocates, December, 1991, review of *The Rookie,* p. 312.

Wall Street Journal, July 14, 2000, Susan Lee, "Something of a Revelation," p. W11.

West Coast Review of Books, February, 1991, review of *The Rookie,* p. 7.

ONLINE

Official Jerry Jenkins Web site, http://www.jerryjenkins.com/ (March 15, 2002).

*   *   *

JENKINS, Jerry Bruce
See JENKINS, Jerry B.

*   *   *

JHABVALA, Ruth Prawer 1927-

PERSONAL: Born May 7, 1927, in Cologne, Germany; immigrated to England, 1939; naturalized British citizen, 1948; naturalized U.S. citizen, 1986; daughter of Marcus (owner of a clothing business) and Eleonora (Cohn) Prawer; married Cyrus S.H. Jhabvala (an architect), 1951; children: Renana, Ava, Firoza. *Education:* Queen Mary College, London, M.A., 1951.

ADDRESSES: *Home and office*—400 East 52nd St., New York, NY 10022. *Agent*—Rand Holston, Creative Artists Agency, 9830 Wilshire Blvd., Beverly Hills, CA 90212.

CAREER: Novelist and author of screenplays. Producer of documentary film *Courtesans of Bombay,* New Yorker, 1982.

MEMBER: Royal Society of Literature (fellow), Authors Guild, Authors League of America, Writers Guild of America.

AWARDS, HONORS: Booker McConnell Prize for Fiction, British Book Trust, 1975, for *Heat and Dust;* Guggenheim fellow, 1976; Neil Gunn International fellow, 1979; British Academy of Film and Television Arts (BAFTA) Award for best screenplay, 1983, for *Heat and Dust;* Literary Lion award, New York Public Library, 1983; MacArthur Foundation fellow, 1984-89; Writers Guild of America Award for best adapted screenplay, and Academy Award for best screenplay adaption, both 1986, and BAFTA Award nomination for best adapted screenplay, 1987, all for *A Room with a View;* New York Film Critics Award for best screenplay, 1990, for *Mr. and Mrs. Bridge;* Academy Award for best screenplay adaption, BAFTA Award nomination for best adapted screenplay, Writers Guild of America Award nomination for best screenplay based on material previously produced or published, and Golden Globe Award nomination for best screenplay—motion picture, all 1993, all for *Howards End;* Academy Award nomination for best writing—screenplay based on material from another medium, BAFTA Award nomination for best adapted screenplay, Writers Guild of America Award nomination for best screenplay based on material previously produced or published, and Golden Globe Award nomination for best screenplay—motion picture, all 1994, all for *The Remains of the Day;* Laurel Award for Screen Writing Achievement, Writers Guild of America, 1994; D.Litt. London University; L.H.D. Hebrew Union; D.Arts, Bard; BAFTA fellowship, 2002; NBC Screenwriters Tribute, 2003; Nantucket Film Festival honors, 2003; O. Henry Prize, 2005, for the short story "Refuge in London".

WRITINGS:

FICTION

To Whom She Will, Allen & Unwin (London, England), 1955, published as *Amrita,* Norton (New York, NY), 1956.

The Nature of Passion, Allen & Unwin (London, England), 1956.

Esmond in India, Allen & Unwin (London, England), 1957.

The Householder (also see below), Norton (New York, NY), 1960.

Get Ready for Battle, J. Murray (London, England), 1962.

Like Birds, Like Fishes, and Other Stories, J. Murray (London, England), 1963.

A Backward Place, Norton (New York, NY), 1965.

A Stronger Climate: Nine Stories, J. Murray (London, England), 1968.

An Experience of India (stories), J. Murray (London, England), 1971.

A New Dominion, J. Murray (London, England), 1972, published as *Travelers,* Harper (New York, NY), 1973.

Heat and Dust (also see below), J. Murray (London, England), 1975.

How I Became a Holy Mother, and Other Stories, J. Murray (London, England), 1975.

In Search of Love and Beauty, Morrow (New York, NY), 1983.

Out of India: Selected Stories, Morrow (New York, NY), 1986.

Three Continents, Morrow (New York, NY), 1987.

Poet and Dancer, Doubleday (New York, NY), 1993.

Shards of Memory, Doubleday (New York, NY), 1995.

East into Upper East: Plain Tales from New York and New Delhi (stories), Counterpoint Press (New York, NY), 1998.

My Nine Lives (fictionalized autobiography), J. Murray (London, England), 2004.

SCREENPLAYS

The Householder (based on her novel), Royal, 1963.

(With James Ivory) *Shakespeare Wallah* (produced by Merchant-Ivory Productions, 1966), Grove, 1973.

(With James Ivory) *The Guru,* Twentieth Century-Fox, 1968.

(With James Ivory) *Bombay Talkie,* Merchant-Ivory Productions, 1970.

Autobiography of a Princess (Cinema V, 1975), published in *Autobiography of a Princess: Also Being the Adventures of an American Film Director in the Land of the Maharajas,* Harper (New York, NY), 1975.

Roseland, Merchant-Ivory Productions, 1977.

Hullabaloo over Georgie and Bonnie's Pictures, Contemporary, 1978.

(With James Ivory) *The Europeans* (based on the novel by Henry James), Levitt-Pickman, 1979.

Jane Austen in Manhattan, Contemporary, 1980.

(With James Ivory) *Quartet* (based on the novel by Jean Rhys), Lyric International/New World, 1981.

Heat and Dust (based on her novel), Merchant-Ivory Productions, 1983.

The Bostonians (based on the novel by Henry James), Merchant-Ivory Productions, 1984.

The Courtesans of Bombay, Channel 4, England/New Yorker Films, 1985.

A Room with a View (based on the novel by E.M. Forster), Merchant-Ivory Productions, 1986.

(With John Schlesinger) *Madame Sousatzka* (based on the novel by Bernice Rubens), Universal, 1988.

Mr. and Mrs. Bridge (based on the novels *Mrs. Bridge* and *Mr. Bridge* by Evan S. O'Connell), Miramax, 1990.

Howards End (based on the novel by E.M. Forster), Merchant-Ivory Productions, 1992.

The Remains of the Day (based on the novel by Kazuo Ishiguro), Merchant-Ivory Productions, 1993.

Jefferson in Paris, Merchant-Ivory Productions, 1995.

Surviving Picasso, Merchant-Ivory Productions, 1997.

(With James Ivory) *A Soldier's Daughter Never Cries* (based on the novel by Kaylie Jones), October Films, 1998.

The Golden Bowl (based on the novel by Henry James), Miramax, 2000.

Le Divorce (based on the novel by Diane Johnson) Fox Searchlight, 2003.

OTHER

A Call from the East (play), produced in New York, NY, 1981.

Contributor of short stories to periodicals, including *New Yorker, Encounter, Kenyon Review, Yale Review, Zoetrope,* and *New Statesman.* Work represented in anthologies, including *Penguin Modern Stories 2,* Penguin, 1972.

SIDELIGHTS: Although Ruth Prawer Jhabvala has long been celebrated in Europe and India—the home of her husband—for her quality fiction and screenplays, it was not until she won an Academy Award for her screenplay adaptation of E.M. Forster's *A Room with a View* that she began attracting widespread attention in the United States for her work. As a German who became a British subject and lived in India for twenty-four years before moving to New York City, Jhabvala brings a unique perspective to her novels and stories of East-West conflict. "With a cool, ironic eye and a feeling for social nuance," asserted Bernard Weinraub in a *New York Times Magazine* article, Jhabvala has "developed a series of themes—families battered by change in present-day India, the timeless European fascination with the subcontinent—that were probably both incomprehensible and inconsequential to readers who were not intrigued with India in the first place. And yet," continued the critic, "as Mrs. Jhabvala's work darkened and turned more melancholy, as her detachment grew chilling in her later work, critics began to notice that the writer's India had become as universal as Faulkner's Yoknapatawpha and Chekhov's czarist Russia." "Like Jane Austen," noted *Saturday Review* contributor Katha Pollitt, Jhabvala "treats satirically and intimately a world in which conventions are precisely defined and widely accepted, even by those who are most harmed by them."

Jhabvala has led a rather unconventional life. She and her family narrowly escaped Nazi persecution as Jews, fleeing to safety in England in 1939. All her father's relatives died in the Holocaust. Ten years after the family's flight into exile she met the man who became her husband, architect Cyrus S.H. Jhabvala. After their marriage, the couple left Europe to live in newly independent India. "I was twenty-four," Jhabvala stated in an interview with David Streitfeld in the *Washington Post Book World,* "and just at the age when one really starts to write seriously. There was so much subject matter for me. I hardly finished a book before I started a new one. I was so full of energy, I immediately wrote as if I were an Indian, from inside." Yet, she wanted it understood she could not be known as an Indian writer. "I wasn't even really anything when I was in India, because I was a foreigner there. People are always asking where my roots are, and I say I don't have any."

Since the appearance of her first work in 1955, *Amrita* —published in Great Britain as *To Whom She Will*— Jhabvala has frequently been compared to British writer Jane Austen due to her cutting portrayals of the foibles of the Indian middle-class. In *Amrita,* commented Nancy Wilson Ross in the *New York Herald Tribune Book Review,* Jhabvala "has written a fresh and witty novel about modern India. It is not necessary to know anything about the customs and habits of . . . New Delhi—the setting of Mrs. Jhabvala's lively comedy of manners—to enjoy her ironic social commentary." In agreement, Anuradha Vittachi wrote in the *New Internationalist:* "Jhabvala has been praised as India's Dickens, her novels compared to Forster's *A Passage to India,* as India's answer to Thackeray's *Vanity Fair.*" "One might reasonably suppose from all this that Ruth Jhabvala is Indian," Vittachi continued. "In fact, the literary comparisons she attracts—Dickens, Forster, Thackeray—give a better clue to her background." In a *Times Literary Supplement* review of *A Backward Place,* the critic maintained that while Jhabvala "has not the sustained brilliance that Jane Austen often rises to . . . all the same her many excellent qualities are nearly all Austenish ones, and they make her a most interesting and satisfactory writer." Observed J.F. Muehl in his *Saturday Review* appraisal of Jhabvala's debut novel, the comparison to Austen "is not only just; it is inevitable."

Although Jhabvala secured her reputation as one of the foremost modern writers about India after the publication of her award-winning novel *Heat and Dust,* she was finding it difficult both to remain in and write about her adopted country. Vittachi explained that Jhabvala, like her character Judy in *A Backward Place,* "promptly fell in love with India's sensuousness after the greyness of wartime England," but that eventually, in Jhabvala's words, "'To have to look at this terrible abyss of poverty and chaos all the time' was too painful." Increasingly, critics began observing ambivalence toward India in Jhabvala's writing, a change evident in her retrospective collection of stories, *Out of India. New York Times* reviewer Michiko Kakutani, for example, commented that, "bit by bit, . . . the stories in *Out of India* darken, grow denser and more ambiguous. In choosing narrative strategies that are increasingly ambitious," explained the reviewer, "Jhabvala gradually moves beyond the tidy formulations of the comedy of manners, and a strain of melancholy also begins to creep into her writing."

Village Voice contributor Vivian Gornick similarly discerned "oppressiveness" in Jhabvala's writing, and speculated that the author was "driven to separate herself from India." The critic believed that this need undermined Jhabvala's work: "That drive deprives her of empathy and, inevitably, it deprives her characters of full humanness." In contrast, Paul Gray claimed in his *Time* review that the stories in *Out of India* "do not demystify India; they pay the place tributes of empathy and grace." "Reading [these stories] is like watching a scene through an exceptionally clear telescope," stated Rumer Godden in the *New York Times Book Review.* This distance, however, "does not take away from the stories sureness of touch," Godden continued. "They have a beginning, middle and end, but fused so subtly we drift into them—and are immediately at home—and drift out again."

Some of Jhabvala's more mature fiction, while eschewing the familiar Indian setting, explores her usual themes, such as the search for spiritual fulfillment. *Three Continents,* for example, relates the story of nineteen-year-old twins Michael and Harriet Wishwell, heirs to a large fortune, who are drawn to the promises of a trio of supposed spiritual philosophers. The twins become obsessed with the Rawul, his consort the Rani, and their "adopted son" Crishi, and turn over control of their lives and fortune to the swindlers. "In its geographical scope, its large and far-flung cast and its relentless scrutiny of both sexual and intellectual thralldom," maintained Laura Shapiro in *Newsweek, Three Continents* "is Jhabvala's most ambitious and impressive work." *Los Angeles Times* reviewer Elaine Kendall similarly called the novel "perhaps [Jhabvala's] most ambitious work," remarking that it "not only confronts" issues from her previous work "directly but in a more contemporary context."

Poet and Dancer, like *Three Continents,* is a non-Indian novel; it is, in fact, set in New York. Jhabvala told Streitfeld that the novel was inspired by the story of a double suicide, two sisters who killed themselves without any perceptible reason. "I was wondering how this could have happened—it was a very dark deed, a dark relationship," she stated. The relationship as Jhabvala depicts it is between two cousins, Angel and Lara. Angel, a poet, has lived her entire life in New York City, while Lara, a dancer, has travelled all over the world. "As the reader might expect," stated Claire Messud in the *Times Literary Supplement,* "Angel, to whom Lara appears an exotic and precious butterfly, devotes herself adoringly to her cousin; but Lara proves dangerous and ultimately mad, and the result of their closeness is their mutual destruction." Some critics expressed puzzlement over Angel's fascination with Lara, who, some felt, is depicted very unsympathetically. "There's something lacking in this small, well-made novel," declared *New Statesman* reviewer Wendy Brandmark, "some moral centre, some emotional touchstone. . . . We do not know why we should care about these characters and their destructive search for the perfect life, the perfect art, the perfect love."

In *Shards of Memory* Jhabvala "once again addresses the themes of family and history through the premise of a set of old papers," wrote Molly E. Rauch in the *Nation.* The novel follows successive generations of a family who follow the charismatic spiritual guru known only as "the Master." The interweaving of multiple memories within in the narrative, according to *Booklist* critic Ilene Cooper, is what makes the novel "intensely personal." But, Cooper argued, the "beguiling" structure of the book is not its only positive aspect: "At the forefront are the characters, and here Jhabvala has outdone herself." Critics laud Jhabvala's narrative skill in handling the ways each character was affected or touched by the Master. "Jhabvala handles this highly sophisticated, complicated story with sinuous skill," praised a *Publishers Weekly* critic.

Jhabvala followed *Shards of Memory* with a collection of short fiction titled *East into Upper East: Plain Tales from New York and New Delhi*. The stories, some of which were originally published in the *New Yorker,* were written over the span of twenty years. In these stories, noted a *Publishers Weekly* reviewer, Jhabvala "depicts characters struggling to reconcile dependency and accommodation in their relationships." A *Library Journal* critic lauded Jhabvala's "expert observation and unique insight," while Deborah Mason, in the *New York Times Book Review* claimed that the collection "reaffirms" Jhabvala "as a spell-binding urban fabulist." Jhabvala's 2004 novel, *My Nine Lives,* is a work of autobiographical fiction.

While Jhabvala has been a consistent force on the literary scene, she is also a member of the longest producer-director-writer partnership in film history. With Ismail Merchant and James Ivory, she has helped create numerous movies that, while not necessarily hits at the box office, have been praised by critics for their consistent literary quality. The Jhabvala/Merchant/Ivory association dates to 1963, when Ivory and Merchant telephoned the author, then living in India, and asked her to write a screenplay from her fourth novel *The Householder.* "That gave me the opportunity I otherwise would never have had," Jhabvala told Streitfeld. "I was so lucky. Merchant and Ivory are like a shield for me. I don't have to bother with the things that are so gruesome for other screenwriters, like story conferences." It is also true that Jhabvala influences the subjects chosen for the films. *International Herald Tribune* contributor Mary Blume explained, "Whatever the period, [Ivory] says their films present certain themes." As Ivory told Blume in the interview, "Where Ruth Jhabvala's concerned, again and again we've had women in the hands of very dubious men and how they strike out and somehow succeed. I think we tell these stories over and over again, no matter when they're set."

Although the author was initially reluctant to attempt screenplays, critic Yasmine Gooneratne maintained that the dramatic qualities necessary for films have always been present in Jhabvala's work. Writing in *World Literature Written in English,* Gooneratne stated that the author's early novels have "the tight structure of stage plays, and even [contain] casts of characters. The process by which the comparative simplicities of satiric drama yield to the complexity of ironic fiction is hastened, it would appear, through her experience of working repeatedly within the narrow limits of a screenplay." The critic cited the film-like structure of *Heat and Dust* as an example, and added that, "despite the fact that Mrs. Jhabvala's increasing technical skill as a writer of screenplays has helped her to devise ways and means to make the cinema screen yield workable equivalents for her established fictional techniques, it is probable that her artistry as a fiction-writer still outstrips her achievement as a writer for film. So rapid has her development been, however," Gooneratne continued, "that this is unlikely to be the case for very long." As Jhabvala herself told *Guardian* reviewer Philip Horne, in adapting literary classics to film "fidelity is not the first thing. . . . the theme and the feel of the characters—the ambience and their relationships—that is what you try and [capture] but never, never literally."

About *The Bostonians,* the 1984 adaptation of Henry James's novel, Vincent Canby of the *New York Times* remarked that "it's now apparent" that the trio has "enriched and refined their individual talents to the point where they have now made what must be one of their best films" to date. In 1986's *A Rooom with a View* director Ivory and screenwriter Jhabvala take "Forster's 1908 novel and preserved its wit, irony and brilliant observation of character," stated Lawrence O'Toole in *Maclean's.* "And they never allow its theme—the importance of choosing passion over propriety—to escape their grasp." Calling the film "an exceptionally faithful, ebullient screen equivalent to a literary work that lesser talents would embalm," Canby noted that, "maybe more important than anything else" in the film "is the narrative tone." He explained that Ivory and Jhabvala "have somehow found a voice for the film not unlike that of Forster, who tells the story of *A Room with a View* with as much genuine concern as astonished amusement. That's quite an achievement."

For their next film, *Mr. and Mrs. Bridge,* Jhabvala, Merchant, and Ivory focus on the foibles of the American, rather than the English, upper-middle class. Jhabvala's version of Evan S. Connell's two novels "is not social satire as much as a melancholy, delicate and gently funny look at the ordinariness of American life," declared Richard A. Blake in *America.* "In her adaptation, Jhabvala has tried to balance highlights of the Bridges' lives with dailiness," Stanley Kauffmann stated in the *New Republic,* "though inevitably there's less of the non-dramatic in the film than in the novels." The end result, Blake concluded, "is a charming, elegant and literate film, beautifully embellished by finely balanced, sensitive ensemble acting."

Despite the acclaim accorded the Merchant-Ivory-Jhabvala productions, as *Newsweek* contributor David Ansen noted, "there were always detractors who dismissed their works as enervated 'Masterpiece Theatre' gentility." This dichotomy is especially evident in the diversity of critical commentary that greeted the collaborators' version of Forster's *Howards End.* Reviewing this film—which brought Jhabvala her second Academy Award—in the *National Review,* John Simon termed the movie "inept," while Anne Billson stated in the *New Statesman and Society:* "If *Howards End* is supposed to be an indictment of snobbery and greed, it fails, because it revels in the snobbish and greedy way of life." "The qualities of such illustrated English Lit are not cinematic, but are those of the Edwardian theme park," Billson continued. "This film should be bought up by the National Trust, though it doesn't need to be preserved. It has already been pickled in the formaldehyde of nostalgia." *New Yorker* contributor Terrence Rafferty found the film well done, but added that "those of us who love Forster might miss the sense of strain, the awkward human beauty of his artistic failure."

In the opinion of *Commonweal* contributor Richard Alleva, Jhabvala, Merchant, and Ivory actually improve on author Kazuo Ishiguro's novel *The Remains of the Day* in adapting it to film. Alleva pointed out that Ishiguro, by seeing his story about a butler whose sense of self-worth rests wholly on his usefulness to his employer only through the butler's eyes, makes the novel "predictable." "It's a stunt," Alleva contended, "and you soon learn the mechanics of the stunt." But Jhabvala's "film adaptation is not a stunt, just a good movie," the reviewer continued, because it takes the story away from the butler-only point of view and presents the plot in a linear fashion. "The stoic poignancy of the title, *The Remains of the Day,*" Alleva concluded, "is more fully earned by the movie than by the book." Simon enjoyed the film as well, stating that " *The Remains of the Day* will long remain in your memory as a portrait of heroic futility, heartbreaking fatuity, and purblind doggedness, as they become the downfall of a society, an empire, and, worst of all, a single human soul."

Jhabvala's screenplay for Merchant-Ivory's *Surviving Picasso* is loosely based on Arianna Huffington's 1989 biography of the Spanish painter. The film follows the ten-year relationship between Picasso and Françoise Gilot, a young ingenue the painter met in Nazi-occupied Paris in 1943. Jhabvala's script is less concerned with the artistic muse inspiring Picasso's works than it is on the artist's love of life and how it influenced his imagination. Perhaps because of its subject, the film received mixed reviews. Bruce Williamson for *Playboy* found it

"an elegant, uncompromising" look at a man who was "a cruel, self-serving womanizer." John Simon in the *National Review,* on the other hand, maintained that the film sacrifices Picasso's passion on the altar of middle-brow civility. Labeling Jhabvala and Ivory "two old routiners," Simon observed that they "have by now achieved a certain slickness and fluency, but without the spark of inspiration that makes the whole world kin." Adams Mars-Jones in the London *Independent* wrote, on the other hand, that *Surviving Picasso,* "is the least Merchant Ivory-ish film to be made by that team for many years. For once, they are recreating not order but turmoil, and a man who demanded stability from the women who loved him, but then slipped away from those settled arrangements himself." Mars-Jones continued: "Françoise was almost half a century younger than Picasso, and seems to have walked into her life with him with her eyes wide shut. Her complaint essentially is that he was meant to be as wholly transformed by her as she was by him. The film shows that he almost was—that he was able to suspend some of his exploitative patterns." Noting that *Surviving Picasso* "ends with a montage of the work that Picasso was making during this period, perhaps with a view to rehabilitating the artist after indulging the man so little," the critic concluded that, ultimately, "a more complicated picture has emerged, of a monster without power except what his victims gave him, and a woman who found the thread out of that labyrinth."

The trio next took on Henry James's last novel, *The Golden Bowl.* Gary Arnold in the *Washington Times* commented that "Jhabvala's crisp scenario remedies the novelist's prolix tendencies while taking minor liberties with the time frame," while Susan Stark in the *Detroit News* felt the production "is, in some ways, the most complex and impressive of the three films" Merchant-Ivory based on James's work. Part of the reason for this, Stark wrote, is the novel's reach into both past and future. It is mainly set in the early twentieth century and features a complicated and complicating relationship between four people: an impoverished French prince, a wealthy American coal baron, his daughter, Maggie, and her best friend, Charlotte, a penniless American who had already been lovers with the prince and resumes her relationship after her marriage to Maggie's father. Jhabvala succeeds "wondrously well" in reshaping a complex and demanding novel as a script, Stark maintained, concluding: "To viewers who have come to see Ivory's signature as a guarantee of intelligence, visual splendor and reflective rue, *The Golden Bowl* is bliss. To those accustomed to hot, loud and fast at the movies, however, this film requires a period of serious adjustment."

New York Observer contributor Andrew Sarris acknowledged, "That the film came out as well as it did, considering that the novel is perhaps James's greatest, densest and most exquisitely articulated work, is itself little short of a miracle." One of the failures of the film, Sarris observed, is the ending, in which, rather than closing, as does the book, with "Maggie and the Prince in a troubled embrace," viewers see Charlotte and her husband arriving with all their art treasures in the United States. Sarris commented, "Certainly, Adam's art treasures and his dreams of a magnificent museum in an 'American city' are there in James's novel, and one can make of these dreams what one will, but the heart of the drama is the ultimate triumph of Maggie over Charlotte, at whatever cost." He surmised that Ivory and Jhabvala were uncomfortable with the bent of the novel: that it is money and not love that makes the world go round. A *New York Post* critic judged *The Golden Bowl* "the best Merchant-Ivory film in years" and "a surprisingly dramatic and forceful tale of love and adultery."

A film set in contemporary Paris, *Le Divorce,* fared relatively poorly with critics following its 2002 release. While some critics found it trite and shallow, Jonathan Romney in London's *Independent on Sunday* advised filmgoers not to "switch channels" because "there's something going on here." The tension in this film is set up between the United States and France. The French are depicted as "flighty on the one hand, impeccably classy on the other: the aristos shock the Americans by their blithe chatter about adultery," Romney explained. The Americans, on the other hand, "are gauche, impressionable, awkwardly attuned to the nuances of European culture." "Yet *Le Divorce* always contrives to move some way beyond the stereotypes, to provide some unexpected shading," the critic concluded. "In a key scene, Isabel and Yves watch TV, flipping between culture channel Arte, a prolix talk show in which Edgar suavely spouts his anti-abortion views, and *The Simpsons* dubbed into French. Yves expresses his horror that France is being swamped by American product, but can't stop watching the show anyway, while Isabel comments, 'How weird to be culturally threatened by a cartoon.' Where you might expect such patrician filmmakers to treat *The Simpsons* as some sort of lowbrow horror, they use it as a springboard for a discussion of cultural anxiety."

In some ways, Jhabvala has said, the two forms of writing—fiction and screenplays—enhance each other, though as she told Horne, "I started off and still am primarily a novelist, and not a screenwriter." "I certainly don't think I could write screenplays very well if I didn't, most of the time, work at creating characters and

dialogue and situations of my own in my fiction," she told Nancy Wilson Ross. "Then whatever I've accumulated of experience in that, I bring to the screenplays. And in writing novels you also get a certain feel for structure which you have to have in constructing a screenplay. But I also think the screenwriting has definitely influenced my fiction. For instance, I think you can see it in *Heat and Dust,* and in *In Search of Love and Beauty* in the way I've juggled scenes and time sequences around. That's something I learned in films."

While compared to well-known writers early in her career, Jhabvala has gone on to achieve a prominent literary standing with her consistently excellent work. "How does one know when one is in the grip of art, of a literary power?" asked Rabinowitz in the *New York Times Book Review.* "One feels, amongst other things, the force of personality behind the cadence of each line, the sensibility behind the twist of the syllable. One feels the texture of the unspoken, the very accents of a writer's reticence." Jhabvala, maintained the critic, "seems to come naturally by a good deal of that reticence." Godden similarly praised the author for her original voice, and added that in Jhabvala's many novels, screenplays, and short stories "I could wager there is not in any of them one shoddy line or unnecessary word, a standard few writers achieve. Each book," Godden continued, "has her hallmark of balance, subtlety, wry humor and beauty." And Weinraub, in assessing Jhabvala's reputation in the literary community, quoted the late novelist C.P. Snow: "Someone once said that the definition of the highest art is that one should feel that life is this and not otherwise. I do not know of a writer living who gives that feeling with more unqualified certainty than Mrs. Jhabvala."

BIOGRAPHICAL AND CRITICAL SOURCES:

BOOKS

Acheson, James, editor, *The British and Irish Novel since 1960,* St. Martin's Press (New York, NY), 1991.

Agarwal, Ramlal G. *Ruth Prawer Jhabvala: A Study of Her Fiction,* Envoy (New York, NY), 1990.

Ayyappa Paniker, K., editor, *Indian English Literature since Independence,* Indian Association for English Studies (New Delhi, India), 1991.

Brinker-Gabler, Gisela, and Sidonie Smith, editors, *Writing New Identities: Gender, Nation, and Immigration in Contemporary Europe,* University of Minnesota Press (Minneapolis, MN), 1997.

Chadha, Ramesh, *Cross-cultural Interaction in Indian English Fiction: An Analysis of the Novels of Ruth Jhabvala and Kamala Markandaya,* National Book Organisation (New Delhi, India), 1988.

Chakravarti, Aruna, *Ruth Prawer Jhabvala: A Study in Empathy and Exile,* BR Publishing (Delhi, India), 1998.

Contemporary Literary Criticism, Thomson Gale (Detroit, MI), Volume 4, 1975, Volume 8, 1978, Volume 29, 1984, Volume 94, 1997.

Dictionary of Literary Biography, Volume 194: *British Novelists since 1960, Second Series,* Thomson Gale (Detroit, MI), 1998.

Gooneratne, Yasmine, *Silence, Exile, and Cunning: The Fiction of Ruth Prawer Jhabvala,* Orient Longman (New Delhi, India), 1983.

Jain, Jasbir, and Amina Amin, editors, *Margins of Erasure: Purdah in the Subcontinental Novel in English,* Sterling (New Delhi, India), 1995.

Jha, Rekha, *The Novels of Kamala Markandaya and Ruth Jhabvala: A Study in East-West Encounter,* Prestige Books (New Delhi, India), 1990.

Kessler-Harris, Alice, and William McBrien, editors, *Faith of a (Woman) Writer,* Greenwood Press (Westport, CT), 1988.

Kundu, Rama, editor, *Indian Writing in English,* Volume I, Atlantic (New Delhi, India), 2003.

Pritchett, V. S., *The Tale Bearers: Literary Essays,* Random House (New York, NY), 1980.

Roberts, Sheila, and Yvonne Pacheco Tevis, editors, *Still the Frame Holds: Essays on Women Poets and Writers,* Borgo Press (San Bernardino, CA), 1993.

Ross, Robert L., editor, *International Literature in English: Essays on the Major Writers,* Garland (New York, NY), 1991.

Shepherd, Ronald, *Ruth Prawer Jhabvala in India: The Jewish Connection,* Chanakya, 1994.

Sucher, Laurie, *The Fiction of Ruth Prawer Jhabvala,* St. Martin's Press (New York, NY), 1988.

Werlock, Abby H. P., editor, *British Women Writing Fiction,* University of Alabama Press (Tuscaloosa, AL), 2000.

PERIODICALS

Albany Times Union, August 22, 2003.

America, March 2, 1991, p. 242; May 13, 1995, p. 24.

Ariel, July, 1986, p. 103; July, 1989, p. 19.

Booklist, September 1, 1995, p. 40; October 15, 1995, p. 421; September 15, 1998, p. 200.

Canadian Review of Comparative Literature, September, 1996, p. 803.

Christian Science Monitor, December 7, 1990, p. 13; March 19, 1993, p. 14; April 4, 1995, p. 13; August 8, 2003, p. 15.

Commonweal, December 17, 1993, pp. 14-16; May 19, 1995; October 23, 1998, p. 18.

Detroit News, May 25, 2001, p. 3.

Entertainment Weekly, April 7, 1995, p. 61; September 15, 1995, p. 116; September 27, 1996; August 15, 2003, p. 51.

Essays in Criticism, April, 1986, p. 142.

Financial Times, January 18, 1999, p. 17.

Globe and Mail (Toronto, Ontario, Canada), July 26, 1986; October 17, 1987.

Guardian (London, England), October 27, 2000, p. 8; August 11, 2002, p. 8; May 2, 2003, p. 23.

Independent (London, England), December 27, 1996, p. 15; October 9, 1998, p. 17; October 17, 1998, p. 16.

Independent on Sunday (London, England), September 27, 1998, p. 11; September 21, 2003.

International Herald Tribune, November 1, 1997, Mary Blume, "Merchant Ivory on Growing up in France."

Library Journal, October 1, 1995, p. 120; October 1, 1998, p. 138.

Literary Criterion, June, 1992, p. 133.

Los Angeles Times, November 9, 1983; September 4, 1987; April 27, 2001, p. F2.

Los Angeles Times Book Review, April 12, 1992, p. 14; March 14, 1993, p. 3; November 28, 1993, p. MAG30.

Maclean's, March 31, 1986; April 10, 1995, p. 51.

Modern Fiction Studies, winter, 1984; spring, 1994, p. 85.

Nation, September 11, 1995, p. 244.

National Catholic Reporter, May 11, 2001, p. 17.

National Review, December 13, 1993, pp. 61-63; May 1, 1995, p. 84; November 11, 1996, p. 59.

New Criterion, December, 1987, p. 5.

New Internationalist, January, 1983.

New Literature Review, 1988, p. 11.

New Republic, December 24, 1990, p. 26; April 24, 1995, p. 30.

New Statesman, October 31, 1975; April 15, 1983.

New Statesman and Society, May 29, 1992, pp. 32-33; April 9, 1993, p. 56.

Newsweek, April 19, 1976; March 10, 1986; August 24, 1987; March 16, 1992, p. 66.

New Yorker, May 4, 1992, pp. 74-76; March 22, 1993, p. 106; May 7, 2001, p. 101.

New York Herald Tribune Book Review, January 15, 1956.

New York Observer, April 30, 2001, p. 19; August 4, 2003, p. 21.

New York Post, April 27, 2001, p. 47; August 8, 2003, p. 45.

New York Review of Books, July 15, 1976; October 31, 1996, p. 14.

New York Times, August 30, 1973; July 19, 1983; September 15, 1983; August 2, 1984; August 5, 1984; April 5, 1985, p. C26; May 13, 1985, pp. 17, C17; March 7, 1986; April 3, 1986, pp. 17; May 17, 1986, pp. 12, 15; July 5, 1986; August 6, 1987, p. 21; September 17, 1987, p. C16; October 14, 1988, p. 22; March 8, 1992, p. H15; March 23, 1993, p. B4; November 5, 1993, p. B1; July 3, 1994, p. H9; March 21, 1997, p. B27; September 18, 1998, p. E12; April 27, 2001, p. B10.

New York Times Book Review, January 15, 1956; February 2, 1969; July 8, 1973; April 4, 1976; June 12, 1983; May 25, 1986, p. 1, 20; August 2, 1987, p. 28; August 23, 1987, p. 3; March 28, 1993, pp. 13, 106; September 17, 1995, p. 12; November 29, 1998, p. 20.

New York Times Magazine, September 11, 1983.

Observer (London, England), September 21, 2003.

People, March 17, 1986; September 28, 1987; April 10, 1995, p. 15; October 7, 1996.

Playboy, November, 1996.

Publishers Weekly, June 6, 1986; July 17, 1995, p. 217; August 31, 1998, p. 48; August 11, 2003, p. 118.

Rolling Stone, October 3, 1996, p. 77; May 10, 2001, p. 94.

San Francisco Chronicle, May 18, 2001, p. C3; August 8, 2003, p. D1.

Saturday Review, January 14, 1956; March 1, 1969; April 3, 1976; October 30, 1976.

Spectator, April 23, 1983; October 24, 1987; April 24, 1993, p. 28; July 15, 1995, p. 33; October 10, 1998, p. 43.

Studies in Short Fiction, winter, 1996, p. 43.

Sunday Independent (Ireland), September 21, 2003.

Sunday Telegraph (London, England), March 3, 2002, p. 7.

Sunday Times (London, England), October 25, 1998, p. 15; October 14, 2001, p. 19.

Time, May 12, 1986; October 6, 1986; April 10, 1995, p. 82.

Times (London, England), February 4, 1983; April 14, 1983; October 15, 1987; November 12, 1998, p. 43; August 6, 2003, p. 20.

Times Literary Supplement, May 20, 1965; November 7, 1975; April 15, 1983; April 24, 1987; November 13, 1987; April 16, 1993, p. 20.

Tribune Books (Chicago, IL), February 28, 1993, p. 6.

Twentieth Century Literature, July, 1969, p. 81.

Variety, October 28, 1996, p. 54; May 22, 2000, p. 24.

Village Voice, August 2, 1983; May 8, 1986; September 30, 1986.

Wall Street Journal, June 19, 1990, pp. A18, A22; March 12, 1992, pp. A11, A10; February 23, 1993, pp. A16, A18; April 6, 1995, p. A12; August 24, 1995, p. A14.

Washington Post, October 7, 1983; September 22, 1984; April 5, 1986; November 7, 1993, p. G4.

Washington Post Book World, September 12, 1976; September 18, 1983; May 25, 1986; February 21, 1993, p. 9; March 28, 1993, p. 15.

Washington Times, September 25, 1998, p. 17; May 18, 2001, p. 6.

World Literature Written in English, April, 1978, p. 219; November, 1979, p. 368; spring, 1992, p. 55.

ONLINE

Cambridge News Online, http://www.cambridge-news.co.uk/ (April 13, 2002).

International Herald Tribune, http://www.iht.com/ (November 1, 1997).

Washington Diplomat, http://www.washdiplomat.com/ (March, 2003).

*   *   *

JIANG, Ji-li 1954-

PERSONAL: Name is pronounced "Gee-lee Chiang"; born February 3, 1954, in Shanghai, China; daughter of Xi-reng (an actor) and Ying (in sales; maiden name, Chen) Jiang. *Education:* Attended Shanghai Teachers' College, 1978-80, and Shanghai University, 1980-84; University of Hawaii at Manoa, B.A., 1987.

ADDRESSES: Home—4 Commodore Dr., No. 444, Emeryville, CA 94608. *E-mail*—jjiang8888\@aol.com.

CAREER: Aston Hotels and Resorts, Honolulu, HI, corporate operations analyst, 1987-92; University Health System, Chicago, IL, budgeting director, 1995-96; East West Exchange, Inc., Emeryville, CA, founder and president.

MEMBER: American Chinese Zhi-Qing Association, American Chinese Intellectuals Association, PEN American Center West, Northern California Children's Bookseller's Association, South Bay Area Reading Council.

AWARDS, HONORS: Red Scarf Girl was awarded a Notable Children's Trade Book in the Field of Social Studies citation, National Council for the Social Studies, Books in the Middle: Outstanding Titles of 1997, *Voice of Youth Advocates,* Books for Youth Editors' Choice, American Library Association Booklist, Best Books of 1997 designation, *Publishers Weekly;* Nonfiction Honor List designation, *Voice of Youth Advocates,* and Book Links Lasting Connections Citation, American Library Association, all 1997; Children's Literature Award, California Bay Area Book Reviewers Association, Book of Distinction, *River Bank Review,* Parents' Choice Gold Award and Story Book Award, Judy Lopez Memorial Award, Notable Children's Book, Best Book for Young Adults, all 1998; and Pennsylvania Young Readers' Choice Award, 1999-2000.

WRITINGS:

Red Scarf Girl: A Memoir of the Cultural Revolution, HarperCollins (New York, NY), 1997.
Magical Monkey King: Mischief in Heaven, HarperCollins (New York, NY), 2004.

WORK IN PROGRESS: Research on "the differences and conflict between the East and West, in terms of culture, custom, philosophy, value, et cetera."

SIDELIGHTS: Red Scarf Girl is Ji-li Jiang's autobiographical account of her very difficult adolescence during Chairman Mao Tse Tung's 1966 Cultural Revolution in China. A talented girl with a seemingly bright future, Jiang embraced the revolutionary ideals of her day, until the movement degenerated into a witch hunt for anyone "tainted" by capitalism. Because Jiang's paternal grandfather was a wealthy landowner, her entire family faced severe persecution. "Jiang describes in terrifying detail the ordeals of her family and those like them, including unauthorized search and seizure, persecution, arrest and torture, hunger, and public humiliation," noted Janice M. Del Negro in a *Bulletin of the Center for Children's Books* review of Jiang's memoir. Roger Sutton, reviewing the work for *Horn Book,* called *Red Scarf Girl* "a rare personal glimpse of the upheaval China suffered during the 1960s" and added that "the child's point of view is firmly maintained" and the "conflict between political and family expectations is well portrayed." *School Library Journal* contributor John Philbrook praised the book as "a page-turner" and as "excellent discussion material," asserting that Jiang's "the writing style is lively and the events often have a heart-pounding quality about them." Similarly, Kat Kan, writing in *Voice of Youth Advocates,* contended that Jiang's "compelling story makes history come alive for teens, much as Anne Frank's diary has done for decades."

In the *Magical Monkey King: Mischief in Heaven,* Jiang retells a classic Chinese trickster story about a monkey who, part Earth and part Heaven, finds a new home for his threatened family while attempting to trick Jade Emperor and other powerful creatures. "It takes Buddha himself to rein Monkey in and lock him up until he learns from his mistakes," noted Denise Wilms in a *Booklist* review of Jiang's retelling. In *Kirkus Reviews* a contributor noted, "Clever, arrogant, far longer on appetite than attention span, Monkey makes an engaging antihero whose acquaintance young readers . . . will be glad to make."

Raised in a creative and affluent household, Jiang once commented: "When I was a little girl, I dreamed of being an actress. During the Cultural Revolution, although my talent was praised, I was turned down again and again for professional art troupes because of my family's political background. In 1976 the Cultural Revolution ended. New policies were supposed to be implemented. For the first time I might have a chance at achieving my dream, and I was excited. I sent in my application to the Shanghai Drama Institute and waited for the audition. Then I received a letter saying that my district had denied my participation again. I was in despair. I was making plastic flowers in a very small factory and earning seventy cents per day in Chinese currency, equivalent to about twenty-five cents in the United States. This [was] . . . my last chance, since the next year I would be too old to enter the program.

"Time passed, and I moved to America. My first year in Honolulu, I lived with an American family. They were very interested in my life in China. Using my very limited English, I shared some of my stories with them. One day I got a present from them, a copy of *The Diary of Anne Frank.* Inside they wrote: 'In the hope that some day we will read *The Diary of Ji-li Jiang.'. . . .* Not long after I started to work for a hotel chain, one of my co-workers asked me, 'Ji-li, how come you don't have bound feet?' I was shocked: this was like asking 'how come you don't wear a corset?' I realized then how little some Americans knew about China and the Chinese people. I made up my mind to write my story at once. We had experienced a holocaust, too. Few people knew about it. So finally I started writing my story."

Jiang has continued to promote understanding of her native country by founding her own company, East West

Exchange, Inc., which promotes and facilitates cultural exchange. "I believe it is very important to increase understanding between the east and the west," the author noted, adding that, on a personal level, it has been "very rewarding to bridge the gap between China and western countries."

BIOGRAPHICAL AND CRITICAL SOURCES:

PERIODICALS

ALAN Review, winter, 1998.
Booklist, October 1, 1997, p. 331; April 15, 2002, p. 1397.
Bulletin of the Center for Children's Books, February, 1998, p. 206.
Horn Book, January-February, 1998, p. 76.
Instructor, October, 1997, p. 48.
Kirkus Reviews, September 1, 1997, p. 1391; April 15, 2002, p. 571
Publishers Weekly, July 28, 1997, p. 75; November 10, 1997, p. 28.
School Library Journal, December, 1997, p. 139.
Voice of Youth Advocates, February, 1998, p. 365; June, 1998, p. 145.

ONLINE

Ji-li Jiang Web site, http://www.jilijiang.com/ (August 24, 2004).

*   *   *

JIMENEZ, Francisco 1943-

PERSONAL: Born June 29, 1943, in San Pedro, Tlaquepaque, Mexico; immigrated to United States, 1947, naturalized citizen, 1965; son of Francisco (a farm laborer) and Maria (a cannery worker; maiden name, Hernandez) Gonzalez Jimenez; married Laura Catherine Facchini (a teacher), 1968; children: Francisco Andres, Miguel Antonio, Tomas Roberto. *Ethnicity:* "Latino/Mexican-American." *Education:* University of Santa Clara, B.A., 1966; Columbia University, M.A., 1969, Ph.D., 1972; attended Harvard University, 1989. *Politics:* Democrat. *Religion:* Roman Catholic.

ADDRESSES: Home—624 Enos Ct., Santa Clara, CA 95051. *Office*—Department of Modern Languages and Literatures, University of Santa Clara, Santa Clara, CA 95053; fax: 408-554-4887. *E-mail*—fjimenez@mailer.scu.edu.

CAREER: Columbia University, New York, NY, instructor, 1971-72, assistant professor of Spanish, 1973; University of Santa Clara, Santa Clara, CA, assistant professor, 1973-77, associate professor, 1977-81, professor of modern languages and literature, 1981—, member of board of trustees of the university, 1981-87; director of Division of arts and humanities, 1981-90, director of Mexico summer study program at Universidad Nacional Autonoma de Mexico, 1984—, Phil and Bobbie Sanfilippo Professor, 1986—, associate vice president for academic affairs, 1990-94. Visiting professor at Universidad Nacional Autonoma de Mexico, summer, 1987, 1997; lectured at California State University—Bakersfield, San Diego State University, California State College (now University), Dominguez Hills, Stanford University, University of Texas—Austin, Harvard University, University of Notre Dame, Graduate Theological Union, and Wellesley College. Director of Institute of Poverty and Conscience, 1985; member of board of directors of Far West Laboratory for Educational Research and Development, 1988-94. California State Commission for Teacher Preparation and Licensing, vice chairman, 1976-77, chairman, 1977-79; member of board of directors of Circulo Artistico y Literario, 1980-90; vice chair of California State Humanities Council, 1987-91; member of Western Association Accrediting Commission for Senior Colleges and Universities (WASC), 1989-95, board of directors, 1992-95; member of bilingual advisory board of California Student Aid Commission, 1995; consultant to WNET-TV; member of board of trustees of Archbishop Mitty High School, 1995—.

MEMBER: Modern Language Association of America (member of Delegate Assembly, 1989-92), American Association of Teachers of Spanish and Portuguese, Hispanic Institute of the United States, National Chicano Council on Higher Education, National Association on Chicano Studies, Institute of Latin American Studies, American Association for Higher Education, Asociacion Latino Americana de Bellas Artes (member of board of directors, 1979—), Pacific Coast Council of Latin American Studies (member of board of governors, 1977-79), Association of California Teachers of Foreign Languages, Raza Administrators and Counselors in Higher Education.

AWARDS, HONORS: Woodrow Wilson fellow, 1966, faculty development grant, 1983; National Defense Foreign Language fellow, 1968-69, 1969-70, and 1970-71; Ford Foundation grant, 1969; annual award, *Arizona Quarterly,* 1973, for short story "The Circuit"; Distinguished Leadership in Education Award, California Teachers Association, 1979; teaching grant, Santa Clara

University Services Award, 1983; award for "dedicated and continuous service in education," Association of Mexican American Educators, 1986; Resolution of Commendation, California State Legislature and California State Commission on Teacher Credentialing, both 1986; Americas Award, 1997; College of Arts and Sciences Dave Logathetti Award for Excellence in Teaching, 1997; Teacher of the Year, for Santa Clara County, 1998; California State Assembly Certificate of Recognition, for outstanding achievement of meritorious nature benefitting students of Clara County, 1998; Professor Cedric Busette Memorial Award, for outstanding contributions to ethnic studies, 1998; Dia del maestro: Teacher of the Year Award (university category), Santa Clara County, 1998; SCU Faculty Senate Professor Award, 1998; Smithsonian Notable Book for Children, Smithsonian Institute, 1998, and Parents' Choice Recommended Award, 1999, both for *La Mariposa;* Jane Addams Honor Book Award, John and Patricia Beatty Award, California Library Association, and *Boston Globe-Horn Book* Award, all 1998, Smithsonian Notable Book for Children designation, and Book for the Teen-Age designation, New York Public Library, both 1999, and FOCAL Award, Los Angeles Public Library System, 2001, all for *The Circuit: Stories from the Life of a Migrant Child;* Key to the City of Long Beach for contributions to education, Mayor of Long Beach, 1999; Plate of Bounty, U.S. State Department of Education, 1999; Popular Paperback for Young Adults, American Library Association, 2000; Local Hispanic Hero in the San Francisco Bay Area, Telemundo KSTS-48 and Estereo Sol 98.9 FM, 2001; Cooperative Children's Book Center Choice, Cuffie Award for best treatment of a social issue, *Publishers Weekly,* Notable Children's Book, American Library Association, and *Americas* Commendment List, all 2001, all for *The Christmas Gift;* Pura Belpré Award Honor Book designation, 2002, for *Breaking Through;* named U.S. Professor of the Year, CASE/Carnegie Foundation, 2002.

WRITINGS:

Episodios nacionales de Victoriano Salado Alvarez (title means "National Episodes of Victoriano Salado Alvarez"), translated from the original English by Nicolas Pizarro Suarez, Editorial Diana (Mexico City, Mexico), 1974.

Chicano Literature: Sources and Themes, Bilingual Press (Jamaica, NY), 1974.

(With Gary D. Keller) *Viva la lengua! A Contemporary Reader* (title means "Long Live Language"), Harcourt (New York, NY), 1975, second edition, with Rose Marie Beebe, 1987.

(With Gary D. Keller and Nancy A. Sebastiani) *Spanish Here and Now,* Harcourt (New York, NY), 1978.

(Editor) *Identification and Analysis of Chicano Literature,* Bilingual Press (Jamaica, NY), 1978.

(Editor, with Gary D. Keller) *Hispanics in the United States: An Anthology of Creative Literature,* Bilingual Press (Jamaica, NY), Volume 1, 1980, Volume 2, 1982.

Mosaico de la vida: Prosa chicana, cubana, y puertorriquena (title means "Mosaic of Life: Chicano, Cuban, and Puerto Rican Prose"), Harcourt (New York, NY), 1981, second edition, 1987.

Poverty and Social Justice: Critical Perspectives, Bilingual Press (Jamaica, NY), 1987.

Work represented in anthologies, including *Perspectivas: Temas de hoy y de siempre,* edited by Mary Ellen Kiddle and Brenda Wegmann, Holt (New York, NY), 1974, second edition, 1978; *Purpose in Literature,* edited by Edmund J. Farrell, Ruth S. Cohen, and others, Scott, Foresman, 1979; *Fronteras,* edited by Nancy Levy-Konesky and others, Holt, 1989; *Mexican American Literature,* edited by Charles Tatum, Harcourt (New York, NY), 1990; and *Points of View: An Anthology of Short Stories,* edited by James Moffett, Mentor, 1995. Contributor to *Dictionary of Mexican-American History;* contributor of articles, stories, and reviews to periodicals, including *Arizona Quarterly, American Hispanist, Owl, Bilingual Review, Tiempo, Riversedge, California History, Los Angeles Times Book Review,* and *Hispania.* Member of editorial advisory board of the series "Studies in the Language and Literature of United States Hispaños," Bilingual Press. Cofounder and West-Coast editor of *Bilingual Review/La Revista Bilingue.*

Author's works have been published in Spanish translation.

FOR CHILDREN

The Circuit: Stories from the Life of a Migrant Child (for young adults), University of New Mexico Press (Albuquerque, NM), 1997.

La Mariposa (title means "The Butterfly"), Houghton Mifflin (Boston, MA), 1998.

Christmas Gift/El regalo de Navidad, illustrated by Claire B. Cotts, Houghton Mifflin (Boston, MA), 2000.

Breaking Through (for young adults), Houghton Mifflin (Boston, MA), 2001.

ADAPTATIONS: The Circuit and *Breaking Through* were both adapted as audiobooks, read by Robert Romirez, Recorded Books, 2001 and 2003, respectively.

WORK IN PROGRESS: La correspondencia de Victoriano Salado Alvarez; research on the Mexican-American oral tradition; a Spanish translation of *Breaking Through,* to be published by Houghton Mifflin; a third novel under contract with Houghton Mifflin.

SIDELIGHTS: A former illegal immigrant migrant worker, Francisco Jimenez returned to the United States as a young teen and has gone on to earn advanced college degrees and a career as a respected educator and author. Crediting his education at a Jesuit college for much of his success, Jimenez told an interviewer for *Migration World:* "Any successes attributed to anyone are the result of many people in our lives, caring about each other and supporting us." In an effort to help others in achieving their own success, Jimenez has authored several inspiring books for young children and teens, among them *La Mariposa, The Circuit: Stories from the Life of a Migrant Child,* and *Breaking Through,* all of which draw from the author's personal experiences as the member of a migrant farm family.

In *La Mariposa* Jimenez introduces young readers to a first grader whose education is made more difficult by the fact that he does not speak English. Moreover, Francisco begins school in January, well after the rest of the students in his first-grade class have become settled in their new experience, learned the routine, and made fast friends. A dreamer with a talent for drawing, the boy eventually wins the respect of his classmates, despite several setbacks, in this bilingual English-Spanish picture book, based on the author's own experiences failing the first grade.

The Circuit: Stories from the Life of a Migrant Child expands on the problems faced by the young boy in *La Mariposa:* balancing the desire for education with the need to help one's family earn a living in the fields, the language barrier, and poverty. The protagonist of these stories is Panchito, whose home has been a succession of migrant camps and schools, and who longs for a teacher who will help him catch up to other students his age. As *Horn Book* reviewer Hazel Rochman noted of the award-winning effort, in *The Circuit* Jimenez avoids "sermonizing" in favor of compelling descriptions of "the physicalness of the back-breaking work, the yearning for education, for place." One story in *The Circuit* was adapted and published separately as *The Christmas Gift/El regalo de Navidad,* a picture book that explores the true meaning of the holiday season by depicting a Christmas spent in the migrant camps. Noting that the tales collected in *The Circuit* realistically portray the lives of the thousands of Mexican Americans for whom "the American dream never comes to fruition," *Library Journal* contributor M. Otero-Boisvert added that Jimenez lifts "the story up from the mundane" through his depiction of "the strong bonds of love that hold this family together."

Jimenez continues his focus on children by addressing older readers in *Breaking Through,* a sequel to *The Circuit* that finds Panchito—now grown and called Frankie—facing increasing responsibilities as a teen whose father is frustrated over his inability to provide for his family. Fortunately, the family is now able to stay in one place, and jobs picking strawberries before and after school are gradually replaced by less-arduous office cleaning work. While noting that *Breaking Through* is not as "taut" as Jimenez' first volume, Rochman wrote that the author "writes with simplicity about a harsh world seldom seen in children's books," and his young protagonist "celebrates his Mexican roots even as he learns to be an American." Roger Sutton added in *Horn Book* that while the story's protagonist is "remarkably well behaved, . . . one never senses over-neatening by the author; rather, his truth to his teenaged self demonstrates a respect that embraces the reader as well."

Jimenez once commented with regard to his writing for young people: "My primary goal . . . is to fill the need for cultural and human understanding, between the United States and Mexico in particular. I write in both English and Spanish. The language I use is determined by what period in my life I write about. Since Spanish was the dominant language during my childhood, I generally write about those experiences in Spanish. My scholarly research has been published in both English and Spanish. Because I am bilingual and bicultural, I can move in and out of both American and Mexican cultures with ease; therefore, I have been able to write stories in both languages. I consider that a privilege."

BIOGRAPHICAL AND CRITICAL SOURCES:

BOOKS

Cassidy, Jack, and other editors, *Follow the Wind,* Scribner (New York, NY), 1987.

Meier, Matt S., *Mexican-American Biographies,* Greenwood Publishing Group (Westport, CT), 1988.

Meier, Matt S., *Notable Latino Americans: A Biographical Dictionary,* Greenwood Publishing Group (New York, NY), 1997.

PERIODICALS

America, December 21, 2001, Allen Figueroa Deck, review of *Breaking Through,* p. 22.

Booklist, December 1, 1997, Hazel Rochman, review of *The Circuit: Stories from the Life of a Migrant Child,* p. 619; March 1, 1999, Annie Ayres, review of *La Mariposa,* p. 1220; September 1, 2000, Hazel Rochman, review of *The Christmas Gift/El regalo de Navidad,* p. 132; September 1, 2001, Hazel Rochman, review of *Breaking Through,* p. 109; November 1, 2001, Gillian Engberg, review of *Breaking Through,* p. 478; January 1, 2002, review of *Breaking Through,* p. 765.

California Today, October 19, 1980.

El Observador, November 20, 1997.

Hispano, December 26, 1977; February 19, 1979; October 8, 1986.

Horn Book, September-October, 1998, p. 532; January, 1999, Hazel Rochman, review of *The Circuit,* and Jimenez' award acceptance speech, p. 49; January, 2000, p. 61; November-December, 2001, Roger Sutton, review of *Breaking Through,* p. 772.

KLIATT, January, 2004, Sunnie Grant, review of *Breaking Through,* p. 52.

La Oferta Review, June 17, 1998.

Library Journal, June 1, 2001, M. Otero-Boisvert, review of *The Circuit,* p. 55.

Miami Herald, October 12, 2001.

Migration World, September-October, 1995, Loretta Penahich, "Former Illegal Migrant Worker Gains University Honors," p. 43; November 4, 1995.

Publishers Weekly, October 5, 1998, review of *La Mariposa,* p. 90; November 15, 1999, p. 68; September 25, 2000, Elizabeth Deveroux, review of *The Christmas Gift/El regalo de Navidad,* p. 72; August 27, 2001, "Breaking Through Chronicles," p. 86.

Sacramento Bee, March 20, 1999.

San Francisco Chronicle, December 25, 1997.

San Jose Mercury News, April 18, 1993.

Santa Maria Times, October 23, 1997.

School Library Journal, October, 2000, review of *The Christmas Gift/El regalo de Navidad,* p. 60; September, 2001, Carol A. Edwards, review of *Breaking Through,* p. 225; October, 2003, Barbara Wysocki, review of *Breaking Through* (audio version), p. 93.

Semanario Azteca, November 3, 1986.

West Magazine, April 5, 1998.

World Literature Today, winter, 1981; spring, 1983.

Writing, February-March, 2001.

ONLINE

Francisco Jimenez Home Page, http://www.fajimenez.com/ (August 5, 2004).

Santa Clara University Web site, http://www.scu.edu/ (August 5, 2004), "Francisco Jimenez."

Tolerance.org, http://tolerance.org/ (August 5, 2004), Jeff Sapp, "Summer Reading: Books by Francisco Jimenez."

Unitarian Universalist Association Web site, http://www.uua.org/ (August 5, 2004), Rev. Keith Kron, book discussion guide for *The Circuit: Stories from the Life of a Migrant Child.*

*   *   *

JIN, Ha 1956-
   (Xuefei Jin)

PERSONAL: Born February 21, 1956, in Liaoning, China; son of Danlin (an officer) and Yuanfen (a worker; maiden name, Zhao) Jin; married Lisah Bian, July 6, 1982; children: Wen. *Education:* Heilongjian g University, B.A., 1981; Shangdong University, M.A., 1984; Brandeis University, Ph.D., 1992.

ADDRESSES: Office—Department of English, Callaway Memorial Center, 302 North Callaway, Emory University, Atlanta, GA 30322; fax: 404-727-2605. *Agent*—Christina Ward, P.O. Box 515, North Scituate, MA 02060.

CAREER: Emory University, Atlanta, GA, assistant professor of creative writing, 1993-2002; Boston University, 2002—. *Military service:* Chinese People's Army, 1987-95.

AWARDS, HONORS: Three Pushcart Prizes for fiction; prize from *Kenyon Review;* Agni Best Fiction Prize; PEN Hemingway Award for first fiction, 1998, for *Ocean of Words;* Flannery O'Connor Award, 1998, and 34th Georgia Author of the Year Awards for *Under the Red Flag;* National Book Award, 1999, and PEN/Faulkner Award for Fiction, 2000, both for *Waiting;* Townsend Prize for Fiction for *The Bridegroom.*

WRITINGS:

Between Silences: A Voice from China (poems), University of Chicago Press (Chicago, IL), 1990.

Facing Shadows (poems), Hanging Loose Press (Brooklyn, NY), 1996.

Ocean of Words: Army Stories, Zoland Books (Cambridge, MA), 1996, Vintage (New York, NY), 1998.

Under the Red Flag (stories), University of Georgia Press (Athens, GA), 1997, Zoland Books (Cambridge, MA), 1999.

In the Pond (novel), Zoland Books (Cambridge, MA), 1998.

Waiting (novel), Pantheon (New York, NY), 1999.

Quiet Desperation (stories), Pantheon (New York, NY), 2000.

The Bridegroom (stories), Pantheon (New York, NY), 2000.

Wreckage (poetry), Hanging Loose (Brooklyn, NY), 2001.

The Crazed, Pantheon (New York, NY), 2002.

War Trash, Pantheon (New York, NY), 2004.

ADAPTATIONS: Waiting has been adapted by Brilliance for audiotape and is being produced as a film.

WORK IN PROGRESS: Man to Be: Country Stories, short fiction.

SIDELIGHTS: In 1986 thirty-year-old Ha Jin came to the U.S. on a student visa from his native China to begin working on a Ph.D. in English at Brandeis University in Waltham, Massachusetts. His dissertation was on high Modernist poets Pound, Eliot, Auden, and Yeats because, as he told Dave Weich of *Powell's City of Books,* "Those four have poems which are related to Chinese texts and poems that reference the culture. My dissertation was aimed at a Chinese job market. I planned to return to China." Jin and his wife decided to stay in the U.S. after seeing what happened at Tiananmen Square on television. Before taking his degree in 1992, Jin had already published his first book of poems in English, *Between Silences.* The next year he began teaching at Emory University in Atlanta, Georgia, and another book of poetry, *Facing Shadows,* appeared a few years later in 1996. As Weich pointed out, it wasn't an easy beginning: "Taking odd jobs (a night watchman, a busboy) until eventually his publishing success convinced Emory University to hire him to teach and write, Jin was arguably one of the most prolific literary writers of the nineties." In the next three years Jin published two story collections and two novels, all written in English, all set in the People's Republic of China. Jin's work has received nearly universal acclaim from American critics and garnered numerous awards.

Jin's second collection of stories, *Under the Red Flag,* won the Flannery O'Connor Award for Short Fiction. The book is set in a rural town, Dismount Fort, during the Cultural Revolution that swept across China in 1966. This was a time when fanatical beliefs gained sway and those who did not embrace them were often persecuted. In what Paul Gray of *Time* singled out as the best story in the book, "Winds and Clouds over a Funeral," a communist official is torn between conflicting loyalties. His mother's last request upon her death bed was that she not be cremated. However, it is the official policy of the Communist Party that all dead bodies should be cremated in order to conserve arable land. In another story, the Communist Party has arrested a woman accused of being a whore and are planning a public humiliation and punishment for her. A young boy, the narrator of the story, looks forward to the event. In another, a man castrates himself to gain admission to the Communist Party. Gray noted: "Ha Jin is not a preachy author. He offers his characters choices that are incompatible and potentially destructive and then dispassionately records what they do next." Frank Caso of *Booklist* found *Under the Red Flag* to be a "powerful" collection, but also remarked "there is . . . an undisguised cynicism, in . . . many of the . . . tales, that the truth must first be shaped to a political purpose." A *Publishers Weekly* reviewer though, stating of Jin that "sometimes his allegories are too simple," maintained that the stories are used by Jin "to explore larger themes about human relationships and the effect of government on individual lives."

Jin's first novel, *In the Pond,* is the tale of a talented artist, Shao Bin, who must spend his time working at a fertilizer plant to support his family. After being assigned inferior housing, Bin protests by drawing a series of cartoons that criticize his supervisors at work, the villains of the story. After a series of conflicts with the supervisors, spurred on by more cartoons, Bin eventually receives a promotion to the propaganda office. A writer reviewing *In the Pond* for *Publishers Weekly* found that Jin "offers a wise and funny first novel that gathers meticulously observed images into a seething yet restrained tale of social injustice in modern China." The reviewer also applauded the complexity of the book's characters, such as the supervisors, and concluded by stating that the novel goes beyond its setting of Communist China to "engagingly illustrat[e] a universal conundrum."

A National Book and PEN/Faulkner Award winner, *Waiting,* which Jin told Weich was based on a true story, generated considerable critical attention. "[A] deliciously comic novel . . . [told] . . . in an impeccably deadpan manner," exclaimed Gray, again writing in *Time*. One *Publishers Weekly* reviewer deemed *Waiting* "quiet but absorbing . . . powerful," while another remarked that besides its "affecting love story," *Waiting* "presents a trenchant picture of Chinese life under communism." According to Shirley N. Quan of *Library Journal:* "This touching story about love, honor, duty, and family speaks feelingly to readers on matters of the heart." The plot of *Waiting* centers on three individuals: Lin, a medical student who later becomes a doctor; Shuyu, the woman his ailing parents force him to marry so they will have someone to care for them; and Manna Wu, a nurse with whom Lin falls in love. According to communist law, a couple must be separated for eighteen years before they can legally divorce. The novel covers twenty years, including the eighteen during which Lin and Manna maintain their relationship but decide to wait until they can marry before they will consummate it. Assessing the strengths and weaknesses of the book for *Entertainment Weekly,* Megan Harlan stated: "Jin overexplains the story's background. But the lengthy finale . . . resounds with elegant irony." Francine Prose of the *New York Times Book Review* noted: "Character is fate, or at least some part of fate, and Ha Jin's achievement is to reveal the ways in which character and society conspire."

Since the success of *Waiting,* Jin has produced two volumes of short stories, one of poetry, and another novel, *The Crazed.* Of the 2002 novel, *Commonweal*'s Valerie Sayers found, "In an age when so many critics have declared the death of literary realism, Ha Jin's depiction of real absurdity and absurd reality is a good argument against realism's premature burial." Neil Freudenberger in the *New Yorker* commented, "Ha Jin explores an intimate subject with a surgeon's combination of detachment and depth." Sayers added, *"The Crazed . . .* is also a compelling read, more directly political than *Waiting,* more focused on an inevitable plot march that will end in Tiananmen Square." The narrator is a young man, Jian Wan, studying for his Ph.D. exams and waiting to marry the daughter of his professor, Dr. Yang. The professor, however, suffers a stroke and while Jian and another student wait in the hospital for his wife to arrive home from a trip to Tibet, Yang raves and sings in hallucinations that take him wandering back to days of persecution during the Cultural Revolution, to sexual liaisons, and to his early ambitions. He also talks about spiritual matters. As Freudenberger noted, "Professor Yang slowly goes mad—conducting imaginary conversations, spilling his own secrets, and giving his student an education he's not sure he wants." Sayers considered

"many of the professor's monologues and spoken dreams, which are designed to unveil his biography as well as to move the plot along . . . ridiculously contrived in dramatic terms, yet their language is so direct that they remain strangely compelling." Yang's words move Jian to abandon his studies and join the students marching on Tiananmen Square. "The novel's climax is utterly realistic and utterly involving—its movement out of the sickroom and into the streets of Beijing provides just the right change of perception and scale," Sayers concluded.

The *Spectator*'s Jonathan Mirsky, however, found the novel plodding. He experienced Yang's ranting and singing, the slow unfolding of Jian's understanding through the confusing and hazy words of his professor as frustrating: "None of this is clear and after a while one ceases to care. The sordid dreariness, petty politicking and general hopelessness of Chinese academic life are well shown, but without a story it palls." Patrick Ness in the London *Daily Telegraph* maintained, "For these potentially incendiary materials, Ha Jin has adopted a curiously grey, meditative style. The pace is slow, and the prose tends toward the obvious ('I felt confused and upset'), draining colour and drama from the story." Mark Schechner of the *Buffalo News* suggested that Jin, in "the least subtle" of his books, may be using the "hoariest cliche of socialist writing, the general strike, and use it against the keepers of socialist myth. Only instead of the people triumphant, we have the carnage of Tiananmen and a baffled hero." But many critics, while they also had difficulty with linguistic and timing aspects of the work, held that the "hyperrealism" and attention to detail that Jin employed, together with the interest of the story and the movement to action at the end of the novel combined to create another compelling work. As Sarah A. Smith wrote in the *Guardian,* "At first glance Ha Jin appears to have lost some of his lightness of touch. There is a depressing, communism-by-numbers feel about the way he drops background detail into the plot," but, she continued, "Ha Jin's talent is narrative, however, and when he has dispensed with scene-setting *The Crazed* becomes a compelling book." She concluded, "If this novel fails to live up to the promise of its predecessor, it is perhaps because it falls prey to the problem that faces much diaspora literature—the need to explain the motherland, rather than just to write. But this shouldn't overshadow what Ha Jin has achieved in his tragi-comic portrayal of Yang and the naive Jian. This novelist has a fine sense of the human scale of history and an eye for the absurd."

Irene Wanner of the *Seattle Times* credited the success of Jin's work to its "skill, compassion and enlightening aspects." Gray felt Jin's success is in part due to the "accident of his birth." Having been born in another country, Gray explained, Jin was "protected from the homogenizing and potentially trivializing influences that afflict so many U.S.-born aspiring authors." However, Gray concluded that although "exotic subject matter" has helped Jin's career, his "narrative talent proves victorious."

Jin once told *CA:* "Because I failed to do something else, writing in English became my means of survival, of spending or wasting my life, of retrieving losses, mine and those of others. Because my life has been a constant struggle, I feel close in my heart to the great Russian masters, including Chekhov, Gogol, and Babel. As for poetry, some ancient Chinese influences are Tu Fu, Li Po, and Po Chu-I.

"Since I teach full time, my writing process has been adapted to my teaching. When I have a large piece of time, I write drafts of stories, or a draft of a novel, which I revise and edit when I teach. Each draft is revised thirty times before it is finished.

"If I am inspired, it is from within. Very often I feel that the stories have been inside me for a long time, and that I am no more than an instrument for their manifestation. As for the subject matter, I guess we are compelled to write about what has hurt us most."

Asked by Weich whether he would eventually write about the immigrant experience, Jin answered, "I haven't returned to China since I've been here. China is distant. I don't know what contemporary Chinese life is like now. I follow the news, but I don't have the mature sensation—I can't hear the noise, I can't smell the place. I'm not attached to it anymore. What's meaningful to me is the immigrant experience, the American life." The most important work of immigrant literature for him was Nabokov's *Pnin,* which, as he said, "deals with the question of language, and I think that's at the core of the immigrant experience: how to learn the language—or give up learning the language!—but without the absolute mastery of the language, which is impossible for an immigrant. Your life is always affected by the insufficiency."

BIOGRAPHICAL AND CRITICAL SOURCES:

PERIODICALS

Associated Press, October 1, 2003.
Atlanta Journal-Constitution, January 10, 1999, p. L11; October 31, 1999, p. L15; June 23, 2000, p. E5; October 8, 2000, p. D3; October 27, 2002, p. Q4.

Australian (Sydney, New South Wales, Australia), July 3, 2000, p. 013.
Booklist, November 1, 1997, Frank Caso, review of Under the Red Flag, p. 454; September 15, 2000, p. 216; April 1, 2002, p. 1314; September 1, 2002, p. 6; January 1, 2003, p. 792; March 15, 2003, p. 1338.
Boston Herald, November 17, 2002, p. 065.
Buffalo News (Buffalo, NY), December 8, 2002, p. F6.
Capital Times (Madison, WI), January 28, 2000, p. 9A; September 28, 2001, p. 9A; January 3, 2003, p. 11A.
Chicago Tribune Books, December 24, 1996, p. 6.
Christian Science Monitor, November 2, 2000, p. 21.
Commonweal, February 14, 2003, p. 17.
Courier-Mail (Brisbane, Australia), April 1, 2000, p. W09.
Daily Telegraph (London, England), January 6, 2001; May 12, 2001; October 19, 2002; September 27, 2003, p. 12.
Daily Telegraph (Surry Hills, Australia), June 10, 2000, p116.
Denver Post, October 27, 2002, p. EE-02.
Entertainment Weekly, October 29, 1999, Megan Harlan, review of Waiting, p. 106; December 3, 1999, Lori Tharps and Clarissa Cruz, "Between the Lines," p. 93; November 15, 2002, p. 140.
Guardian (London, England), October 7, 2000, p. 11; November 30, 2002, p. 27; October 04, 2003.
Herald (Glasgow, Scotland), June 22, 2000, p. 18.
Herald Sun (Melbourne, Australia), November 20, 1999, p. 023; June 3, 2000, p. W18.
Hindu, February 2, 2003.
Houston Chronicle (Houston, TX), December 5, 1999, p. 15; September 17, 2000, p. 24; December 17, 2000, p. 14; November 10, 2002, p. 18.
Independent (London, England), May 27, 2000, p. 10; October 10, 2003.
Indianapolis Star, November 28, 1999, p. D06; October 18, 2003, p. A15.
Knight Ridder/Tribune News Service, November 13, 2002, p. K4516.
Library Journal, October 15, 1999, Shirley N. Quan, review of Waiting, p. 105; September 1, 2000, p. 254; June 1, 2001, p. 170; September 15, 2002, p. 91.
Los Angeles Times, June 6, 2000, p. A1; June 24, 2000, p. A4; October 3, 2000, p. E-3; October 11, 2000, p. E-3.
Milwaukee Journal Sentinel, November 14, 1999, p. 8E; June 23, 2000, p. 08; October 8, 2000, p. 06.
New Straits Times, October 1 2003, p. 6.
Newsweek International, November 29, 1999, p.73.
New Yorker, November 4, 2002.

New York Review of Books, March 23, 2000, p. 29; March 13, 2003, p. 25.

New York Times, November 19, 1999, p. B44; June 24, 2000, p. A17, B9; October 21, 2002, p. B7.

New York Times Book Review, June 2, 1996, p. 21; January 11, 1998; January 31, 1999, p. 16; October 24, 1999, p. 9; October 22, 2000, p. 9; September 30, 2001, p. 24; October 27, 2002, p. 7.

New York Times Magazine, February 6, 2000, p. 38.

Plain Dealer (Cleveland, OH), November 2, 2002, p. E1.

Progressive, March, 2000, John McNally, review of *Waiting,* p. 44.

Publishers Weekly, February 26, 1996, review of *Ocean of Words: Army Stories,* p. 98; October 3, 1997, review of *Under the Red Flag,* p. 58; October 12, 1998, review of *In the Pond,* p. 58; August 23, 1999, review of *Waiting,* p. 42; November 1, 1999, review of *Waiting,* p. 46; March 20, 2000, p. 20; September 4, 2000, p. 81; June 4, 2001, p. 78; July 9, 2001, p. 13; September 30, 2002, p. 47.

Rocky Mountain News (Denver, CO), October 25, 2002, p. 26D.

St. Louis Post-Dispatch, October 31, 1999, p. F12.

St. Petersburg Times (St. Petersburg, FL), June 23, 2000, p. 10A; November 10, 2002, p. 4D.

Seattle Post-Intelligencer, November 18, 1999, p. D6.

Seattle Times, October 31, 1999, Irene Wanner, review of *Waiting;* November 18, 1999, p. A9; June 23, 2000, p. E3; October 15, 2000, p. M14; November 3, 2002, p. K12.

Spectator, June 3, 2000, p. 42; September 21, 2002, p. 45.

Star-Ledger (Newark, NJ), April 16, 2000, p. 005.

Star Tribune (Minneapolis, MN), January 24, 2000, p. 01E; November 10, 2002, p. 15F.

Sunday Mail (Brisbane, Australia), July 9, 2000, p. 023.

Sunday Times (London, England), June 24, 2001, p. 48.

Tampa Tribune, November 10, 2002, p. 4.

Time, December 1, 1997, Paul Gray, review of *Under the Red Flag,* p. 94; November 8, 1999, Paul Gray, "Divorce, Chinese-Style," p. 144.

Times (London, England), June 14, 2000, p. 19; December 16, 2000, p. 6; May 2, 2001, p. 15; January 26, 2002, p. 14; October 5, 2002, p. 15; November 2, 2002, p. 16.

Virginian Pilot, January 14, 2001, p. E3.

Wall Street Journal, October 22, 1999, p. W8; October 27, 2000, p. W12.

Washington Post, October 6, 2000, p. C03.

Washington Times, May 15, 2000, p. 8; December 15, 2002, p. B06.

Weekend Australian (Sydney, Australia), May 27, 2000, p. R13.

Winston-Salem Journal (Winston-Salem, NC), June 11, 2000, p. A20; January 26, 2003, p. A20.

World and I, May, 2000, p. 247.

World Englishes: Journal of English As an International and Intranational Language, July, 2002, p. 305.

World Literature Today, autumn, 1997, Timothy C. Wong, review of *Ocean of Words: Army Stories,* p. 862; autumn, 1997, K.C. Leung, review of *Facing Shadows,* p. 861; spring, 1998, Fatima Wu, review of *Under the Red Flag,* p. 454; spring, 1999, Jeffrey C. Kinkley, review of *In the Pond,* p. 389.

ONLINE

AsianWeek, http://www.asianweek.com/ (December 16, 1999), interview with Ha Jin.

AsiaSource, http://www.asiasource.org/ (November 17, 2000), interview with Ha Jin.

Austin Chronicle, http://www.austinchronicle.com/ (November 10, 2000), article on Ha Jin.

Boldtype, http://www.randomhouse.com/ (December 1999), "Ha Jin."

Book, http://www.bookmagazine.com/ (January, 2000), "Ha Jin of America,"

BookReporter, http://www.bookreporter.com/ (October 13, 2000), interview with Ha Jin.

BostonReview, http://www.bostonreview.net/ (August, 1988), "Ha Jin."

DesiJournal, http://www.desijournal.com/ (October 26, 2002), review of *The Crazed.*

Emory Magazine, http://www.emory.edu/ (spring, 1998), "Ha Jin."

MostlyFiction, http://mostlyfiction.com/ (October 12, 2002), review of *The Crazed.*

Powell's City of Books, http://www.powells.com/ (February 2, 2000), Dave Weich, interview with Ha Jin.

World and I, http://www.worldandi.com/ (May, 2000), review of *Waiting.*

*　　　*　　　*

JIN, Xuefei
See JIN, Ha

*　　　*　　　*

JOHNSON, Adam 1967-

PERSONAL: Born July 12, 1967, in SD; married Stephanie Harrell, 2000; children: James Geronimo, Jupiter. *Education:* Arizona State University, B.A., 1992; McNeese State University, M.A., M.F.A., 1996; Florida State University, Ph.D., 2001.

ADDRESSES: Home—San Francisco, CA. *Office*—English Department, Stanford University, Stanford, CA 94305. *E-mail*—adamjohn@stanford.edu.

CAREER: Educator and author. Stanford University, Stanford, CA, Jones Lecturer in creative writing and fiction, 2001—.

AWARDS, HONORS: Wallace Stegner Fellowship, Stanford University, 2001; California Book Award, 2003, for *Parasites Like Us.*

WRITINGS:

Emporium (short stories), Viking (New York, NY), 2002.
Parasites Like Us (novel), Viking (New York, NY), 2003.

Also contributor of short stories to numerous publications, including *Paris Review, Esquire,* and *Harper's.*

WORK IN PROGRESS: A novel set in contemporary Los Angeles.

SIDELIGHTS: In an interview for *Barnes & Noble. com,* author Adam Johnson admitted that he began writing creatively "by mistake." While attempting to sign up for a poetry course during college, he accidentally enrolled in a fiction class. "Immediately I knew writing was for me—suddenly my penchant for daydreaming, exaggerating, and lying all became useful and constructive, and I never looked back." Since then, Johnson has earned his Ph.D. from Florida State University, landed a lectureship in creative writing and fiction at Stanford University, and has begun publishing his fiction.

Among the stories in Johnson's first effort, *Emporium,* are "Trauma Plate," featuring the owners of a mom-and-pop bullet-proof vest rental shop; "Your Own Backyard," a story about a police officer turned zoo security guard who begins to notice his son's disturbing obsession with guns and desensitization to violence; and "Teen Sniper," which focuses on a fifteen-year-old sniper whose job is to shoot and kill disgruntled corporate employees. A reviewer for the *New Yorker* noted that the stories in *Emporium* capture "the loneliness of youth, the failure of parents, and the yearning for connection." A *Publishers Weekly* contributor commented, "Each of these unusual, skillful stories exhibits a fierce talent, showcasing Johnson's quirky humor and slicing insight." *Booklist* reviewer James O'Laughlin determined that "Johnson's is a distinctive new fictional sensibility," and a *Kirkus Reviews* critic observed that "Johnson's unique premises, hybrids of realism and allegory, blends of pedestrian, pop, and the bizarre, create unnerving moods."

Johnson followed *Emporium* with his first novel, *Parasites Like Us,* in which, according to a *Publishers Weekly* reviewer, "an archeological find sets off an apocalyptic epidemic." The book features archeology professor Hank Hannah and his two graduate students, Trudy and Eggers, who discover an ancient burial site of the prehistoric Clovis people and unwittingly release a deadly plague on the world. Writing for the *Magazine of Fantasy and Science Fiction,* Elizabeth Hand termed Johnson's work "the novelistic equivalent of a long drunken whacked-out binge with your closest, smartest, craziest friend." Michele Leber, writing in *Booklist,* depicted *Parasites Like Us* as a "weird but masterfully written debut novel" full of "inventiveness, black humor, and penetrating insight."

In his interview with *Barnes & Noble.com,* Johnson offered this advice to aspiring writers: "Find a mentor. . . . They have a lot to teach and share if you're willing to seek them out. Be humble, think of writing as a lifelong process of learning, and your audience will come."

BIOGRAPHICAL AND CRITICAL SOURCES:

PERIODICALS

Book, May-June, 2002, Kevin Greenberg, review of *Emporium,* p. 84; September-October, 2003, Kevin Greenberg, review of *Parasites Like Us,* p. 91.
Booklist, March 15, 2002, James O'Laughlin, review of *Emporium,* p. 1212; August, 2003, Michele Leber, review of *Parasites Like Us,* p. 1953.
Esquire, September, 2003, "Two More Books for Your Shelf," review of *Parasites Like Us,* p. 66.
Kirkus Reviews, February 1, 2002, review of *Emporium,* p. 127; June 15, 2003, review of *Parasites Like Us,* p. 826.
Magazine of Fantasy and Science Fiction, March, 2004, Elizabeth Hand, review of *Parasites Like Us,* p. 34.
New Yorker, April 22, 2002, "Briefly Noted," review of *Emporium,* p. 201.

Publishers Weekly, February 11, 2002, review of *Emporium,* p. 158; June 23, 2003, review of *Parasites Like Us,* p. 44.

ONLINE

Barnes & Noble.com, http://www.barnesandnoble.com/ (January 10, 2006), "Meet the Writers: Adam Johnson."

KQED Web site, http://www.kqed.org/ (January 10, 2006), "The Writers' Block: Adam Johnson."

Stanford Daily/Intermission, http://daily.stanford.edu/ (November 14, 2003), Anthony Ha, "*Intermission* Interviews Adam Johnson: Johnson Discusses His First Novel *Parasites Like Us.*"

Stanford University Web site, http://www.stanford.edu/ (January 10, 2006), "English Department Faculty."

*   *   *

JOHNSON, Angela 1961-

PERSONAL: Born June 18, 1961, in Tuskegee, AL; daughter of Arthur (an autoworker) and Truzetta (an accountant; maiden name, Hall) Johnson. *Education:* Attended Kent State University. *Politics:* Democrat

ADDRESSES: Home—Kent, OH. *Agent*—c/o Author Mail, Orchard Books, 387 Park Ave. S, New York, NY 10016.

CAREER: Volunteers in Service to America (VISTA), Ravenna, OH, child development worker, 1981-82; freelance writer of children's books, 1989—.

MEMBER: Authors Guild, Authors League of America.

AWARDS, HONORS: Best Books, *School Library Journal,* 1989, for *Tell Me a Story, Mama;* Ezra Jack Keats New Writer Award, United States Board on Books for Young People, 1991; Coretta Scott King Honor Book, American Library Association Social Responsibilities Round Table, 1991, for *When I Am Old with You;* Editor's Choice, *Booklist,* Best Books, *School Library Journal,* and Coretta Scott King Author Award, all for *Toning the Sweep;* Coretta Scott King Author Award, 1998, for *Heaven;* Coretta Scott King Honor Book citation, 1998, for *The Other Side: Shorter Poems;* MacArthur Foundation "genius grant," 2003.

WRITINGS:

CHILDREN'S BOOKS

Tell Me a Story, Mama, illustrated by David Soman, Orchard Books (New York, NY), 1989.

Do Like Kyla, illustrated by James Ransome, Orchard Books (New York, NY), 1990.

When I Am Old with You, illustrated by David Soman, Orchard Books (New York, NY), 1990.

One of Three, illustrated by David Soman, Orchard Books (New York, NY), 1991.

The Leaving Morning, illustrated by David Soman, Orchard Books (New York, NY), 1992.

The Girl Who Wore Snakes, illustrated by James Ransome, Orchard Books (New York, NY), 1993.

Julius, illustrated by Dav Pilkey, Orchard Books (New York, NY), 1993.

Toning the Sweep: A Novel, Orchard Books (New York, NY), 1993.

Joshua by the Sea, illustrated by Rhonda Mitchell, Orchard Books (New York, NY), 1994.

Joshua's Night Whispers, illustrated by Rhonda Mitchell, Orchard Books (New York, NY), 1994.

Mama Bird, Baby Birds, illustrated by Rhonda Mitchell, Orchard Books (New York, NY), 1994.

Rain Feet, illustrated by Rhonda Mitchell, Orchard Books (New York, NY), 1994.

Humming Whispers, Orchard Books (New York, NY), 1995.

Shoes Like Miss Alice's, illustrated by Ken Page, Orchard Books (New York, NY), 1995.

The Aunt in Our House, illustrated by David Soman, Orchard Books (New York, NY), 1996.

The Rolling Store, illustrated by Peter Catalanotto, Orchard Books (New York, NY), 1997.

Daddy Calls Me Man, illustrated by Rhonda Mitchell, Orchard Books (New York, NY), 1997.

Songs of Faith, Orchard Books (New York, NY), 1998.

Heaven, Simon & Schuster (New York, NY), 1998.

The Other Side: Shorter Poems, Orchard Books (New York, NY), 1998.

Maniac Monkeys on Magnolia Street, illustrated by John Ward, Random House (New York, NY), 1999.

The Wedding, illustrated by David Soman, Orchard Books (New York, NY), 1999.

Those Building Men, illustrated by Mike Benny, Scholastic (New York, NY), 1999.

Down the Winding Road, illustrated by Shane W. Evans, DK Ink, 2000.

Gone from Home: Short Takes (stories), Dell (New York, NY), 2001.

When Mules Flew on Magnolia Street, Alfred A. Knopf (New York, NY), 2001.

Rain Feet, illustrated by Rhonda Mitchell, Orchard Books (New York, NY), 2001.

Running Back to Ludie, Orchard Books (New York, NY), 2002.

Looking for Red, Simon & Schuster (New York, NY), 2002.

A Cool Moonlight, Dial Books (New York, NY), 2003.

The First Part Last, Simon & Schuster (New York, NY), 2003.

I Dream of Trains, illustrated by Loren Long, Simon & Schuster (New York, NY), 2003.

Just Like Josh Gibson, illustrated by Beth Peck, Simon & Schuster (New York, NY), 2003.

Violet's Music, illustrated by Laura Huliska-Beith, Dial Books (New York, NY), 2004.

Bird, Dial Books (New York, NY), 2004.

A Sweet Smell of Roses, illustrated by Eric Velasquez, Simon & Schuster Books for Young Readers (New York, NY), 2005.

Lily Brown's Paintings, paintings by E.B. Lewis, Orchard Books (New York, NY), 2006.

Contributor to several anthologies, including *Gone from Home: Short Takes,* DK Publishing, 1998, *In Daddy's Arms I Am Tall,* Simon & Schuster (New York, NY), 2003; and *Tripping Over the Lunch Lady,* Puffin (New York, NY), 2006.

ADAPTATIONS: Humming Whispers was recorded on audio cassette and released by Recorded Books, 1997.

SIDELIGHTS: Angela Johnson is the winner of a 2003 MacArthur Foundation "genius grant," a half-million-dollar prize awarded to a select few individuals in the arts and sciences who are thought to be making unique contributions to the betterment of society. In Johnson's case the award recognizes her ability to craft sensitive children's books about African-American family life and the wider issues of growing up in the modern world.

Johnson first drew the attention of critics through her picture books presenting warm portraits of African-American children and their relationship to parents, grandparents, siblings, and friends. Many reviewers have pointed out, however, that Johnson's stories capture emotions and experiences that are familiar to young readers of all cultures. Her books for and about older children tackle difficult issues such as divorce, the death of a sibling, and chronic illness with emphasis on learn-ing to survive and thrive such devastating events. "Johnson is a master at representing human nature in various guises at different levels," asserted *Twentieth-Century Children's Writers* contributor Lucille H. Gregory. Gregory also noted a "high consistency" in Johnson's books, a commendation underscored by Rudine Sims Bishop in *Horn Book,* who maintained that all of Johnson's works "feature charming first-person narrators." Bishop went on to note: "The characters are distinct individuals, but their emotions are ones shared across cultures."

Reaching a wide audience is exactly what Johnson strives for in her writing. As she once commented: "In high school I wrote punk poetry that went with my razor blade necklace. At that point in my life my writing was personal and angry. I didn't want anyone to like it. I didn't want to be in the school literary magazine, or to be praised for something that I really didn't want understood. Of course, ten years later, I hope that my writing is universal and speaks to everyone who reads it. I still have the necklace, though."

Many of Johnson's books for children feature young black protagonists narrating events that are common to children their age. In *Tell Me a Story, Mama,* which Rudine Sims Bishop called an "impressive debut" in *Horn Book,* a little girl asks her mother for a familiar bedtime story and ends up doing most of the storytelling herself as she reminds her mother of each favorite part. *Horn Book* contributor Maria Salvadore, one of a number of commentators offering a favorable assessment of Johnson's first book, observed: "By providing a glimpse of one African-American family, Johnson has validated other families' experiences, regardless of racial or ethnic background."

In subsequent works Johnson has continued to feature characters whose lives are enriched by familial affection and reassurance. In *Do Like Kyla,* a young narrator describes how she imitates her older sister all day long. But when it's time for bed, the young girl revels in the fact that "Kyla does like me." *When I Am Old with You* spotlights a boy who describes to his grandfather the things they will do together when the boy catches up to him in age. The young narrator of *One of Three* relates the fun she has being one of three sisters, as well as the frustration of not being able to join in some of the things her older siblings do. Reviewing *One of Three,* a *Publishers Weekly* contributor praised Johnson for her "perceptive and understated text," while Karen James, writing in *School Library Journal,* admired the way Johnson captured "the underlying love and strength of positive family relationships."

Unusual pets join the young protagonists in *The Girl Who Wore Snakes* and *Julius.* In the former, Ali's strong interest in snakes, which she wears as jewelry, surprises everyone in her family except her snake- loving aunt. *Julius,* illustrated by Dav Pilkey, features a young girl named Maya who receives Julius, an Alaskan pig, from her grandfather. Together, Maya and Julius teach each other new tricks and enjoy a variety of adventures. Betsy Hearne, writing in the *Bulletin of the Center for Children's Books,* called *Julius* a "gleeful celebration of silliness."

In 1993, Johnson published her first work for older children, *Toning the Sweep.* In this novel, fourteen-year-old Emily participates in the final days of her cancer-stricken grandmother's life by videotaping the ailing woman as she visits with friends, recalling stories of the past. "Full of subtle nuance, the novel is overlaid with meaning about the connections of family and the power of friendship," maintained *School Library Journal* contributor Ellen Fader. Writing in *Booklist* Quraysh Ali lauded the work, asserting: "With ingenuity and grace, Johnson captures the innocence, the vulnerability, and the love of human interaction as well as the melancholy, the self-discovery, and the introspection of adolescence." Mary M. Burns in *Horn Book* cited for special note "the skill with which the author moves between times past and times present without sacrificing her main story line or diluting the emotional impact."

Humming Whispers, another young adult work, tells the story of Sophie, an aspiring dancer who becomes worried that she is developing the schizophrenia that afflicts her older sister. Hazel Rochman characterized the novel in *Booklist* as "a bleak contemporary story of suffering, lit with the hope of people who take care of each other in the storm." *School Library Journal* contributor Carol Schene observed that while "there are no easy answers" for the characters in the book, "the frailty and strength of the human spirit" displayed by each one makes the story memorable. Elizabeth Bush, writing in the *Bulletin of the Center for Children's Books,* stated that the author "ably demonstrates the pervasive effects of mental illness on an entire family." A *Kirkus Reviews* contributor praised the way Johnson "carefully and richly fleshes out the characters."

Johnson returned to picture books with *Shoes Like Miss Alice's* and *The Rolling Store.* In the former work, Sara is hesitant about being with a new babysitter. Her fears are quickly dispelled, however, and a bond is formed when Miss Alice changes into a different pair of shoes for each special activity they do together. "Tucked in the tale is a nice message about being open to new people walking into your life," noted *Booklist* contributor Ilene Cooper. In *The Rolling Store,* a young black girl tells her white friend a family story about a general store on wheels that used to serve her grandfather's rural community when he was a boy. With help from the visiting grandfather, the girls create their own mobile store out of a small red wagon. "Johnson's family story has a certain nostalgic appeal," noted *Bulletin of the Center for Children's Books* editor Janice M. Del Negro. *Booklist* contributor Stephanie Zvirin deemed *The Rolling Store* "a sweet, upbeat story."

The author drew particularly favorable reviews for her novel *Heaven.* Fourteen-year-old Marley is the beloved only child in a happy family—until, by accident, she discovers that her parents are actually her uncle and aunt, and her real father is an itinerant "uncle" she hardly knows. This revelation leads Marley to investigate exactly what constitutes a family unit and how her identity is shaped by those who love her. Praising the book for its "plain, lyrical writing," *Booklist* contributor Hazel Rochman commented that the author "makes us see the power of loving kindness."

Johnson has also written collections of poems and has contributed to poetry anthologies. One of her best known poetry books is *The Other Side: Shorter Poems.* This work was inspired by the fact that her grandmother's hometown of Shorter, Alabama, was razed for redevelopment. During a nostalgic trip to the small town, Johnson wrote about her memories of growing up there. Nancy Vasilakis in *Horn Book* called *The Other Side* an "intriguing collection" and a "captivating narrative," while a *Publishers Weekly* contributor noted that the book offers "an unforgettable view of an insightful young woman growing up in the South."

Not all of Johnson's novels are so serious in tone. *Maniac Monkeys on Magnolia Street* and its sequel *When Mules Flew on Magnolia Street* introduce Charlie, a youngster who must adjust to new friends and new surroundings after moving to Magnolia Street. Told from Charlie's point of view, the two stories reveal how the youngster adapts to new situations by being "open to the small wonders around her," to quote Helen Rosenberg in *Booklist.* In her *Booklist* review of *When Mules Flew on Magnolia Street,* Denise Wilms likewise praised the "small slices of life" that Johnson serves to early readers.

Difficult family situations inform the novels *Running Back to Ludie* and *Looking for Red.* In *Running Back to Ludie,* a teenaged narrator explores her mixed emotions as she prepares to meet the mother who abandoned her to live in the woods. Joanna Rudge Long in *Horn Book* commented that the free verse style of the work helps to highlight the young person's feelings of rejection and reconciliation. "Johnson's exploration of the process is subtle and beautifully wrought," the critic commented. *Looking for Red* offers a more straightforward narrative with a dark secret at its core. Red's sister Mike is still reeling from grief in the wake of his disappearance, and she receives small solace from Red's equally traumatized friends. Only as the story proceeds does the reader realize that Mike and Red's friends share some of the responsibility for his accidental death. "The strength of this story is the accurate portrayal of the surreal nature of grief laden with guilt," observed Jean Gaffney in *School Library Journal.* In *Horn Book,* Joanna Rudge Long praised the "luminous ease" with which Johnson depicts the characters, "both their estrangement from reality and their eventual return toward it."

A Cool Moonlight tells the story of Lila, a child stricken with xeroderma pigmentosum, a rare over- sensitivity to sunlight. Forced to live a nocturnal lifestyle, Lila takes solace in imaginary friends until her ninth birthday, when she comes to terms with her individuality. Once again in *Horn Book* Joanna Rudge Long commended the novel, particularly for Johnson's "deft touches that make this spare portrait so effective."

Readers first met Bobby, the hero of *The First Part Last,* in *Heaven.* In *The First Part Last,* Johnson spins the story of Bobby's unexpected teenage parenthood, how it compromises his ambitions to be an artist but in return offers him the opportunity to love his infant daughter and connect with his parents. The responsibility for a helpless infant is scary—and at times frustrating—but Bobby is sustained by his fond memories of the past and moments of enjoyment in the present. A *Publishers Weekly* contributor liked the way Johnson "skillfully relates the hope in the midst of pain."

Johnson is still creating at least one new picture book per year. One successful title is *I Dream of Trains,* a poignant look at engineer Casey Jones through the eyes of a fictional black field worker. A young boy toiling in the heat lives for the moment when the mighty engine roars by and dreams of the day when he will board a train and leave the hard work behind. He is bolstered in his fantasy by the knowledge that some of those who work with the mighty Casey Jones are black men. In *Black Issues Book Review* Suzanne Rust wrote: "Bold and provocative in prose, picture and content," *I Dream of Trains* is "a work worthy of any contemporary collection."

Johnson's stories *Just Like Josh Gibson* and *Violet's Music* are both tales of triumph—triumph motivated, in these cases, by a love of baseball and of music, respectively. *Just Like Josh Gibson,* illustrated by Beth Peck, is a grandmother's story of her youthful dreams of playing baseball with the boys in the 1940's. One of her biggest heroes was the Negro Basebal League's Josh Gibson, who never got a chance to play on the then all-white major league teams. Grandma, however, relates that, unlike her hero, one day she did get her chance to play. *Childhood Education* contributor Julie Lavalle commented: "This heartwarming story is a poignant tribute." In *Violet's Music,* Johnson tells of Violet's love of music, which far outshines that of all her kindergarten classmates. As time passes and Violet grows older, she learns to play the guitar and eventually meets other musicians in a park and forms a band. Gillian Engberg, writing in *Booklist,* commented on the author's avoidance of using clichéd characters and noted "the story's cheerful energy and beat."

Johnson next wrote about death and giving in *Bird.* The serious topics are approached by telling the story from the point of view of a bird. The narrator, aptly named Bird, speaks of two boys she knows, one who died and whose heart was donated for transplantation and the other the boy who received the heart. A *Publishers Weekly* contributor who reviewed the book called it "a quiet, affecting story." Johnson continued to address serious topics and, upon working with illustrator Eric Velasquez to produce the large picture book *A Sweet Smell of Roses,* Johnson returned to the topic of civil rights. The story in *A Sweet Smell of Roses* centers around two young sisters and their attempt to join a Civil Rights march and listen to a speech by Dr. Martin Luther King. Hazel Rochman, writing in *Booklist,* noted that the "first-person narrative draws on the language of the struggle." In a review of the book for *School Library Journal,* a contributor wrote: "The lyrical text and realistic charcoal illustrations vividly portray the participants' experiences and emotions."

Since 1989, Johnson has published one or more books per year and continues to write at a steady pace. The author once remarked: "I don't believe the magic of listening to Wilma Mitchell read us stories after lunch will ever be repeated for me. Book people came to life. They sat beside me in Maple Grove School. That is when I knew. I asked for a diary that year and have not stopped writing. My family, especially my grandfather and father, are storytellers and those spoken words sit beside me too." As a "genius grant" recipient, Johnson will be awarded one-hundred- thousand dollars each year through 2008.

BIOGRAPHICAL AND CRITICAL SOURCES:

BOOKS

Children's Literature Review, Volume 33, Gale (Detroit, MI), 1994, pp. 93- 96.
Twentieth-Century Children's Writers, 4th edition, St. James (Detroit, MI), 1995, pp. 493- 494.

PERIODICALS

Black Issues Book Review, July-August, 2003, Suzanne Rust, review of I Dream of Trains, p. 65.
Booklist, April 1, 1993, Quraysh Ali, review of Toning the Sweep, p. 1432; February 15, 1995, Hazel Rochman, review of Humming Whispers, p. 1072; March 15, 1995, Ilene Cooper, review of Shoes Like Miss Alice's, p. 1334; February 15, 1997, Stephanie Zvirin, review of The Rolling Store, p. 1026; September 15, 1998, Hazel Rochman, review of Heaven, p. 219; November 15, 1998, Helen Rosenberg, review of The Other Side: Shorter Poems, p. 579; January 1, 1999, Helen Rosenberg, review of Maniac Monkeys on Magnolia Street, p. 878; February 15, 2000, Michael Cart, review of Down the Winding Road, p. 1118; November 15, 2000, Anna Rich, review of Heaven, p. 657; January 1, 2001, Denise Wilms, review of When Mules Flew on Magnolia Street, p. 960; February 15, 2001, Henrietta M. Smith, review of Rain Feet, p. 1161; January 1, 2002, review of Running Back to Ludie, p. 858; September 1, 2003, Hazel Rochman, review of The First Part Last, p. 122; October 1, 2003, Carolyn Phelan, review of A Cool Moonlight, p. 324; October 1, 2003, Gillian Engberg, review of I Dream of Trains, p. 328; March 15, 2004, Gillian Engberg, review of Violet's Music, p. 1308; February 1, 2005, Hazel Rochman, review of A Sweet Smell of Roses, p. 978.
Bulletin of the Center for Children's Books, May, 1993, Betsy Hearne, review of Julius, p. 284; April, 1995, Elizabeth Bush, review of Humming Whispers, p. 278; May, 1997, Janice M. Del Negro, review of The Rolling Store, pp. 325- 326.
Childhood Education, winter, 2004, Julie Lavalle, review of Just Like Josh Gibson, p. 107.
Horn Book, September- October, 1992, Rudine Sims Bishop, "Books from Parallel Cultures: New African-American Voices," p. 620; March-April, 1993, Ellen Fader, review of Julius, pp. 196-197; September-October, 1993, Mary M. Burns, review of Toning the Sweep, p. 603; March-April, 1995,

Maria Salvadore, "Making Sense of Our World," p. 229; November, 1998, Nancy Vasilakis, review of The Other Side, p. 750; November-December, 2001, Joanna Rudge Long, review of Running Back to Ludie, p. 766; July-August, 2002, Joanna Rudge Long, review of Looking for Red, p. 463; September-October, 2003, Joanna Rudge Long, review of A Cool Moonlight, p. 611.
Kirkus Reviews, April 1, 1995, review of Humming Whispers, p. 470.
New York Times Book Review, November 16, 2003, Marsha Wilson Chall, "One-Track Minds," p. 24.
Publishers Weekly, August 9, 1991, review of One of Three, p. 56; August 3, 1998, review of Heaven, p. 86; November 16, 1998, review of The Other Side, p. 76; November 23, 1998, review of Maniac Monkeys on Magnolia Street, p. 67; March 22, 1999, review of The Wedding, p. 91; March 6, 2000, review of Down the Winding Road, p. 109; May 27, 2002, review of Looking for Red, p. 60; June 16, 2003, review of The First Part Last, p. 73; October 20, 2003, review of I Dream of Trains, p. 53, and A Cool Moonlight, p. 55; May 16, 2005, review of A Cool Moonlight, p. 65; January 16, 2006, review of Bird, p. 67.
School Library Journal, October, 1991, Karen James, review of One of Three, p. 98; April, 1993, Ellen Fader, review of Toning the Sweep, p. 140; April, 1995, Carol Schene, review of Humming Whispers, p. 154; January, 2001, Maria B. Salvadore, review of When Mules Flew on Magnolia Street, p. 101; March, 2001, Susan Helper, review of Those Building Men, p. 236; October 22, 2001, review of Running Back to Ludie, p. 77; December, 2001, Nina Lindsay, review of Running Back to Ludie, p. 164; July, 2002, Jean Gaffney, review of Looking for Red, p. 120; September, 2003, Maria B. Salvadore, review of A Cool Moonlight, p. 215; October, 2003, Catherine Threadgill, review of I Dream of Trains, p. 126; October, 2005, review of A Sweet Smell of Roses, p. S27.

*   *   *

JOHNSON, Charles 1948-
(Charles Richard Johnson)

PERSONAL: Born April 23, 1948, in Evanston, IL; son of Benjamin Lee and Ruby Elizabeth (Jackson) Johnson; married Joan New (an elementary school teacher), June, 1970; children: Malik, Elizabeth. Ethnicity: Black. Education: Southern Illinois University, B.A., 1971, M.A., 1973; postgraduate work at State

University of New York at Stony Brook, 1973-76. *Religion:* Buddhist.

ADDRESSES: Office—Department of English, University of Washington, Seattle, WA 98105.

CAREER: Writer, cartoonist, and educator. *Chicago Tribune,* Chicago, IL, cartoonist and reporter, 1969-70; *St. Louis Proud,* St. Louis, MO, member of art staff, 1971-72; University of Washington, Seattle, assistant professor, 1976-79, associate professor, 1979-82, professor of English (Pollock Professor for Excellence in English, the University's first endowed chair in writing), 1982—. Director of Associated Writing Programs Awards Series in Short Fiction, 1979-81, member of board of directors, 1983—.

AWARDS, HONORS: Named journalism alumnus of the year by Southern Illinois University, 1981; Governors Award for Literature from State of Washington, 1983, for *Oxherding Tale;* Callaloo Creative Writing Award, 1983, for short story "Popper's Disease"; citation in *Pushcart Prize*'s Outstanding Writers section, 1984, for story "China"; Prix Jeunesse Award for the screenplay *Booker,* 1985; National Book Award, 1990, for *Middle Passage*; MacArthur Foundation Fellow, 1998; Honorary Ph.D., State University of New York at Stony Brook, 1999; Pacific Northwest Writers Association Achievement Award, 2001.

WRITINGS:

NOVELS

Faith and the Good Thing, Viking (New York, NY), 1974, reprinted, Simon & Schuster (New York, NY), 2001.
Oxherding Tale, Indiana University Press (Bloomington, IN), 1982.
Middle Passage, Macmillan (New York, NY), 1990.
Dreamer, Scribner (New York, NY), 1998.

CARTOON COLLECTIONS

Black Humor (self-illustrated), Johnson Publishing, 1970.
Half-Past Nation Time (self-illustrated), Aware Press, 1972.

Contributor of cartoons to periodicals, including *Ebony, Chicago Tribune, Jet, Black World,* and *Players.*

TELEVISION SCRIPTS

1970–1980 *Charlie's Pad* (fifty-two-part series on cartooning), PBS.
Charlie Smith and the Fritter Tree, PBS "Visions" series, 1978.
(With John Alman) *Booker,* PBS, 1983.

Contributor of scripts to numerous television series, including *Up and Coming,* PBS, 1981, and *Y.E.S., Inc.,* PBS, 1983.

OTHER

The Sorcerer's Apprentice (short stories), Atheneum (New York, NY), 1986.
Being and Race: Black Writing since 1970, Indiana University Press (Bloomington, IN), 1988.
Pieces of Eight, Discovery Press (Los Angeles, CA), 1989.
(Author of foreword) *Rites of Passage: Stories about Growing up by Black Writers from around the World,* Hyperion (New York, NY), 1993.
(Author of introduction) *On Writers and Writing,* Addison-Wesley (Reading, MA), 1994.
(Coeditor) *Black Men Speaking,* Indiana University Press (Bloomington, IN), 1997.
(Author of foreword) *Northwest Passages,* Bruce Barcott, Sasquatch Press (Seattle, WA), 1997.
(Coauthor) *Africans in America: America's Journey through Slavery,* Harcourt Brace (San Diego, CA), 1998.
(Coauthor) *I Call Myself an Artist: Writings by and about Charles Johnson,* Indiana University Press (Bloomington, IN), 1999.
(Author of foreword) *A Treasury of North American Folktales,* Norton (New York, NY), 1999.
(Editor, with Yuval Taylor) *I Was Born a Slave: An Anthology of Classic Slave Narratives,* Volume 1: *1772-1849,* Payback (Edinburgh, Scotland), 1999.
(Coauthor) *King: The Photobiography of Martin Luther King, Jr.,* Viking (New York, NY), 2000.
(With Jean Toomer and Rudolph P. Byrd) *Essentials,* LPC Group (Chicago, IL), 2001.
(Editor, with Max Rodriguez and Carol Taylor) *Sacred Fire: The QBR 100 Essential Black Books,* John Wiley (New York, NY), 2000.

Soulcatcher and Other Stories, Harcourt (San Diego, CA), 2001.

(Author of introduction) *Uncle Tom's Cabin,* (150th Anniversary Edition), Oxford University Press (New York, NY), 2002.

(Author of foreword) Fredrik Stromberg, *Black Images in the Comics: A Visual History,* Fantagraphics Books 2003.

Turning the Wheel: Essays on Buddhism and Writing, Scribner (New York, NY), 2003.

Dr. King's Refrigerator: And Other Bedtime Stories, Scribner (New York, NY), 2005.

Contributor to *Thor's Hammer: Essays on John Gardner,* edited by Jeff Henderson, Arkansas Philological Association, 1986. Work represented in anthologies, including *Best American Short Stories, 1982,* edited by John Gardner and Shannon Ravenel, Houghton Mifflin (Boston, MA), 1982. Contributor of short stories and essays to periodicals, including *Mother Jones, Callaloo, Choice, Indiana Review, Nimrod, Intro 10, Obsidian,* and *North American Review.* Fiction editor of *Seattle Review,* 1978—.

A special collection of Johnson's papers is held at the University of Delaware Library.

ADAPTATIONS: Middle Passage, Africans in America, and *Dreamer* have been adapted for audio cassette; John Singleton/ Warner Bros. bought the film rights for *Middle Passage* in 1997.

SIDELIGHTS: "Charles Johnson has enriched contemporary American fiction as few young writers can," observed *Village Voice* critic Stanley Crouch, adding that "it is difficult to imagine that such a talented artist will forever miss the big time." A graduate of Southern Illinois University, Johnson studied with the late author John Gardner, under whose guidance he wrote *Faith and the Good Thing.* Though Johnson had written six "apprentice" novels (the second of which became *Middle Passage*) prior to his association with Gardner, *Faith* was the first to be accepted for publication. Johnson once commented that he shares "Gardner's concern with 'moral fiction'" and believes in the "necessity of young (and old) writers working toward becoming technicians of language and literary form."

Faith and the Good Thing met with an enthusiastic response from critics such as Garrett Epps of *Washington Post Book World,* who judged it "a brilliant first novel" and commended its author as "one of this country's most interesting and inventive younger writers." Roger Sale, writing in the *Sewanee Review,* had similar praise. He commented: "Johnson, it is clear, is a writer, and if he works too hard at it at times, or if he seems a little too pleased with it at other times, he is twenty-six, and with prose and confidence like his, he can do anything."

The book is a complex, often humorous, folktale account of Faith Cross, a Southern black girl traveling to Chicago in search of life's "Good Thing," which she has learned of from her dying mother. In her quest, noted *Time*'s John Skrow, Faith "seeks guidance from a swamp witch, a withered and warty old necromancer with one green and one yellow eye," who "spouts philosophy as if she were Hegel." Skrow deemed the work a "wry comment on the tension felt by a black intellectual," and Annie Gottlieb of the *New York Times Book Review* called *Faith and the Good Thing* a "strange and often wonderful hybrid—an ebullient philosophical novel in the form of a folktale-cum-black-girl's odyssey." She noted that the novel's "magic falls flat" on occasion, "when the mix . . . is too thick with academic in-jokes and erudite references," but she added that "fortunately, such moments are overwhelmed by the poetry and wisdom of the book." In conclusion, Gottlieb found the novel "flawed yet still fabulous."

Johnson once described his second novel, *Oxherding Tale,* as "a modern, comic, philosophical slave narrative—a kind of dramatization of the famous 'Ten Oxherding Pictures' of Zen artist Kakuan-Shien," which represent the progressive search of a young herdsman for his rebellious ox, a symbol for his self. The author added that the novel's style "blends the eighteenth-century English novel with the Eastern parable."

Like his first novel, Johnson's *Oxherding Tale* received widespread critical acclaim. It details the coming of age of Andrew Hawkins, a young slave in the pre-Civil War South. Andrew is conceived when, after much drinking, plantation owner Jonathan Polkinghorne convinces his black servant, George Hawkins, to swap wives with him for the evening. Unaware that the man sharing her bed is not her husband, Anna Polkinghorne makes love with George and consequently becomes pregnant with Andrew. After the child is born Anna rejects him as a constant reminder of her humiliation, and he is taken in by George's wife, Mattie. Though he is raised in slave quarters, Andrew receives many privileges, including an education from an eccentric tutor who teaches him about Eastern mysticism, socialism, and the philosophies of Plato, Schopenhauer, and Hegel. In an interview with Rob Trucks of *TriQuarterly,* Johnson pointed out that

Oxherding Tale, which he said was very special for him, "threw a lot of people because they didn't know what to do with this book. They didn't understand it. People seem to think ideologically, very often, about Black art, and they have presuppositions in their mind, and all kinds of sociological clichés." He wrote the nonfiction work *Being and Race* to try and bridge this kind of gap in understanding.

Writing in *Literature, Fiction, and the Arts Review*, Florella Orowan called Andrew "a man with no social place, caught between the slave world and free white society but, like the hapless hero Tom Jones, he gains from his ambiguous existence the timeless advantage of the Outsider's omniscience and chimerism: he can assume whatever identity is appropriate to the situation." *Oxherding Tale* accompanies its hero on a series of adventures that include an exotic sexual initiation, an encounter with the pleasures of opium, escape from the plantation, "passing" as white, and eluding a telepathic bounty hunter called the Soulcatcher. As Michael S. Weaver observed in *Gargoyle*, Andrew "lives his way to freedom through a succession of sudden enlightenments. . . . Each experience is another layer of insight into human nature" that has "a touch of Johnson's ripe capacity for laughter." The book's climax, noted Crouch, is "remarkable for its brutality and humble tenderness; Andrew must dive into the briar patch of his identity and risk destruction in order to express his humanity."

Weaver admitted that "at times *Oxherding Tale* reads like a philosophical tract, and may have been more adequately billed as Thus Spake Andrew Hawkins." But he concluded that the novel "is nonetheless an entertaining display of Johnson's working knowledge of the opportunities for wisdom afforded by the interplay between West and East, Black and White, man and woman, feeling and knowing—all of them seeming contradictions." According to Crouch, the novel is successful "because Johnson skillfully avoids melodramatic platitudes while creating suspense and comedy, pathos and nostalgia. In the process, he invents a fresh set of variations on questions about race, sex, and freedom."

In the short-story collection *The Sorcerer's Apprentice*, Johnson continues to examine spiritual, mystical, and philosophical matters through the essentially realistic filter of historical African-American experience. Magic, however, particularly African voodoo practices, plays an essential role in most of the stories, lending these tales an element of the fantastic "without," as Michael Ventura noted in the *New York Times Book Review*,

"getting lost in fantasy." Johnson's overriding concern in this volume is with transcending the self, examining the importance of, and terror involved in, surrendering to nonrational forces. For example, in the title story, an older former slave in South Carolina—the Sorcerer—tries unsuccessfully to pass his abilities on to a young man born in freedom. He laments the fact that the youth has become too American, too rational, to accept African magic. Johnson writes that "magic did not reside in ratiocination, education, or will. Skill was of no service. . . . God or creation, or the universe—it had several names—had to *seize* you, *use* you, as the Sorcerer said, because it needed a womb, shake you down, speak through you until the pain pearled into a beautiful spell that snapped the world back together." Ventura concluded that "Mr. Johnson's spell of a book comes on with the authority of a classic."

In 1990, Johnson's literary stature was officially recognized when he won the National Book Award for his novel *Middle Passage*. Set in 1830, the story concerns the newly freed slave Rutherford Calhoun, an ardent womanizer, an admitted liar, and a thief who runs from New Orleans ahead of bill collectors and away from an ill-fated romance. He stows away on a ship, the Republic, that is setting out on a round-trip voyage to Africa where it will fill its hold with slaves. As the novel progresses, the ship's captain is revealed to be a kind of mad genius, the crew is shown to be comprised of a variety of unsavory sea-going types, and the slaves who are eventually transported are—like the Sorcerer in *The Sorcerer's Apprentice*—members of the (fictional) Allmuseri tribe of wizards. *Middle Passage*, like much of Johnson's fiction, relates the many aspects of the African-American experience through a fantastically tinted literary realism. Writing in *African American Review*, Daniel M. Scott III concluded of *Middle Passage*: "As Johnson sings the world, he searches experience and perception for the roots of reality and the doorways to transformation. Writing, understood as a mode of thought, *is* the middle passage, between what has been and what will be, between the word and the world." In answer to Trucks's question, "What do you think the protagonists of your first three novels—Faith Cross (*Faith and the Good Thing*), Andrew Hawkins (*Oxherding Tale*), and Rutherford Calhoun (*Middle Passage*)— have in common?" Johnson replied, "All those characters are seekers, questers (and adventurers). Fredrick T. Griffiths, the critic, rightly calls them 'phenomenological pilgrims.' He's so right—my characters are adventurers of ideas, truth-seekers (and thus have the philosophical impulse, even when they're not trained philosophers), and hunger for wisdom."

It is not to be wondered at, then, that Johnson's next novel, the *Dreamer*, is set during Dr. Martin Luther

King's 1966 Chicago campaign. Johnson, who has been a teacher for almost half his life, says that he enjoys doing research for his novels, relating to Trucks that "when I wrote *Oxherding Tale,* I speed-read every book on slavery in the State University of New York at Stony Brook's library, just because I wanted to immerse myself in that, in all the slave narratives. I spent six years just reading stuff on the sea, reading literature on the sea for *Middle Passage,* everything from Appolonius to *Voyage of Argo* forward to Conrad. All of Melville I looked at again, nautical dictionaries. Everything about the sea, because I didn't know that stuff." So, of course, "Dreamer embodies a great deal of history and biography." Johnson continued, "All of '92 I just was reading King. I was going off to do promotion for *Middle Passage,* lectures and stuff, and I would take the King books with me, so it was all going on continuously. I was accumulating. . . . sort of gathering things . . . on the Civil Rights movement. Letting all of that stuff come together until I was ready to write, and the first thing I was ready to write was the Prologue."

Calling the novel a "gospel," Johnson said of King, "He really was a philosopher. In the past, you know, I might have a problem I'm writing about and I'd ask, What would Kant have to say about this or What would Hegel say?, but now it's pretty easy for me to say, What would King say about this? I have a sense now," a statement that solves the question John Seymour of the *Nation* asked: "How does Johnson do it? How does he handle, with insight and sympathy, the Reverend Doctor's torment over the value of the risks he takes for the Movement's sake? Or the cost in time missed with his wife and children?"

Dreamer focuses on the last few months of King's life. As Seymour described, "It is the summer of 1966. More to the point, it is one of those long, hot summers that leave a trail of smoldering ashes, shattered nerves and broken lives in cities throughout the decade. A sad but dauntless Martin Luther King, Jr. is marooned in Chicago, struggling to forge strategy for social transcendence as all around him sirens roar, windows explode, contradictions surface, hope dies." In the midst of the violence, a man who looks so like him as to be a double is brought to his room and offers to stand in for him in dangerous situations. King tells his friends to take to a safe house Chaym Smith and teach him about the Movement. The complicated relationship in which more than physical appearances elide between the two men proceeds through the book, without satisfying the reader with neatly tied-up ends.

Seymour commented that Johnson grabs hold of situations where he can explore "the various ways one can

be. Not just be black or white or even American. Just be." "In engaging King's ghost," Seymour continued, "Johnson sets himself up for more ferocious versions of the tut-tuts he caught in some quarters for his antic spins on slave narratives. He raises the stakes in *Dreamer* not only by presuming to enter the mind and heart of a martyred icon but by imposing a Prince-and-the-Pauper thriller motif to explore what it meant—still means—to lead, to follow, to seek a path to freedom."

Continuing his search for like answers, *The Soulcatcher and Other Stories* was published in 2001. Judy Lightfoot in the *Seattle Times* described it as a peaceful work, despite the fact that it is about experiences under slavery: "Johnson's tales vary widely in technique. Characters are black and white, male and female, old and young, mute and eloquent, enslaved and elite; and the genres include dramatic monologues, personal letters, diary entries, and traditional omniscient storytelling. Yet something gently draws this diversity into harmony. It might be called a spirit of good will—a curious phrase, perhaps, for a book about slavery. But although Johnson faces history's horrors squarely, and his characters have righteously indignant moments, his book transcends indignation and blame."

Aside from the fiction, Johnson has coedited and coauthored several works, including *Black Men Speaking,* a volume of voices from all walks of life, *Africans in America: America's Journey through Slavery, I Call Myself an Artist: Writings by and about Charles Johnson,* and *King: The Photobiography of Martin Luther King, Jr.* James R. Kuhlman in *Library Journal* described Johnson's 2003 book, *Turning the Wheel: Essays on Buddhism and Writing,* as "an uncommon and useful overview of black American involvement in Buddhism." Although *Seattle Times* reviewer Kari Wergeland experienced the essays as scattered over a wider terrain and somewhat heavyhanded and uneven, she did conclude, "However, Johnson is a true renaissance man. His judicious knowledge of philosophy, history, literature, science, and other disciplines shines through all of his essays. He is a compassionate critic, and his pieces on novels such as Harriet Beecher Stowe's *Uncle Tom's Cabin,* Ralph Ellison's *Invisible Man* (a masterpiece which should get more attention in our universities), and Sinclair Lewis's *Kingsblood Royal* offer plenty of grist for the mill."

Johnson told *CA:* "As a writer I am committed to the development of what one might call a genuinely systematic philosophical black American literature, a body of work that explores classical problems and metaphysical questions against the background of black American life. Specifically, my philosophical style is phenomenology, the discipline of Edmund Husserl, but I also have a deep personal interest in the entire continuum of Asian philosophy from the Vedas to Zen, and this perspective inevitably colors my fiction to some degree.

"I have been a martial artist since the age nineteen and a practicing Buddhist since about 1980. So one might also say that in fiction I attempt to interface Eastern and Western philosophical traditions, always with the hope that some new perception of experience—especially 'black experience'—will emerge from these meditations."

BIOGRAPHICAL AND CRITICAL SOURCES:

BOOKS

Byrd, Rudolph P., editor, *I Call Myself an Artist: Writings by and about Charles Johnson*, Indiana University Press (Bloomington, IN), 1999.

Clark, Keith, editor, *Contemporary Black Men's Fiction and Drama*, University of Illinois Press (Urbana, IL), 2001.

Collier, Gordon, and Frank Schulze-Engler, editors, *Crabtracks: Progress and Process in Teaching the New Literatures in English*, Rodopi (Amsterdam, Netherlands), 2002.

Contemporary Authors Autobiography Series, Volume 18, Thomson Gale (Detroit, MI), 1994.

Contemporary Literary Criticism, Thomson Gale (Detroit, MI), Volume 7, 1977, Volume 51, 1988, Volume 65, 1991.

Cope, Kevin L., and Anna Battigelli, editors, *1650-1850: Ideas, Aesthetics, and Inquiries in the Early Modern Era*, AMS (New York, NY), 2003.

Dictionary of Literary Biography, Volume 33: *Afro-American Fiction Writers after 1955*, Thomson Gale (Detroit, MI), 1984.

Fabre, Genevieve, editor, *Parcours identitaires*, Presses de la Sorbonne Nouvelle (Paris, France), 1993.

Gates, Henry Louis, Jr., and Carl Pedersen, editors, *Black Imagination and "The Middle Passage,"* Oxford University Press (Oxford, England), 1999.

Hakutani, Yoshinobu, and Robert Butler, editors, *The City in African-American Literature*, Fairleigh Dickinson University Press (Madison, NJ), 1995.

Karrer, Wolfgang, and Barbara Puschmann-Nalenz, editors, *The African-American Short Story, 1970-1990*, Wissenschaftlicher (Trier, Germany), 1993.

Little, Jonathan, *Charles Johnson's Spiritual Imagination*, University of Missouri Press (Columbia, MO), 1997.

Nash, William R., *Charles Johnson's Fiction*, University of Illinois Press (Urbana, IL), 2002.

Rushdy, Ashraf H. A., *Neo-Slave Narratives: Studies in the Social Logic of a Literary Form*, Oxford University Press (New York, NY), 1999.

Stovall, Linny, editor, *Sex, Family, Tribe*, Blue Heron (Hillsboro, OR), 1992.

Travis, Molly Abel, *Reading Cultures: The Construction of Readers in the Twentieth Century*, Southern Illinois University Press (Carbondale, IL), 1998.

PERIODICALS

African-American Review, fall, 1992, p. 373; spring, 1995, p. 109; winter, 1995, pp. 631, 645, 657; winter, 1996, special issue; fall, 1999, pp. 401, 417; spring, 2003, p. 105.

American Quarterly, September, 1997, p. 531.

American Review, winter, 1996, p. 527.

Arizona Quarterly: A Journal of American Literature, Culture, and Theory, summer, 1994, p. 73.

Black American Literature, winter, 1991, p. 689.

Black Issues Book Review, January, 2001, p. 43.

Black Issues in Higher Education, October 30, 1997, p. 28.

Booklist, March 15, 1993, p. 1364; July, 1997, p. 1782; September 1, 1998, p. 3; January 1, 1999, p. 900; June 1, 1999, p. 1857; November 1, 2000, p. 499; March 1, 2001, p. 1226.

Brick, spring, 2002, p. 133.

Callaloo, October, 1978; fall, 1999, p. 1028; spring, 2003, p. 504.

Christian Science Monitor, October 15, 1998, p. B7.

Chronicle of Higher Education, January 16, 1991, p. A3.

College English, November, 1997, p. 753.

College Language Association Journal, June, 1978; September, 1986, p. 1.

Commonweal, December 2, 1994.

Comparatist: Journal of the Southern Comparative Literature Association, May, 2002, p. 121.

Contemporary Literature, summer, 1993, p. 159; spring, 2001, p. 160.

CR: The New Centennial Review, winter, 2001, p. 67.

Current Biography, September, 1991, p. 26.

Ebony, June, 2001, p. 23.

Essence, April, 1991, p. 36; January, 2001, p. 64.

Financial Times, September 26, 1998, p. 8.

Forbes, March 16, 1992, p. S26.

Gargoyle, June, 1978.

Grand Rapids Press (Grand Rapids, MI), November 4, 2003, p. B1.

Hemingway Review, 1999, p. 114.

Houston Chronicle (Houston, TX), June 7, 1998, p. 22.

Independent (London, England), October 10, 1998, p. 14.

Independent on Sunday (London, England), October 25, 1998, p. 11; May 2, 1999, p. 13; July 11, 1999, p. 12.

Jet, December 17, 1990, p. 28; November 29, 1999, p. 20.

Journal of African-American and African Arts and Letters, summer, 1997, p. 531.

Kentucky Philological Review, 1991, p. 27.

Kliatt, March, 1995.

Library Journal, May 1, 1990, p. 112; October 1, 1991, p. 159; July 1997, p. 109; April 1, 1998, p. 122; September 15, 1998, pp. 90, 128; November 1, 2000, p. 100; January 1, 2001, p. 130; April 15, 2001, p. 134; June 1, 2003, p. 120.

Literature, Fiction, and the Arts Review, June 30, 1983; January 22, 1995.

Los Angeles Times Book Review, June 24, 1990.

Massachusetts Review: A Quarterly of Literature, the Arts and Public Affairs, summer, 2001, p. 253.

Narrative, October, 1994, p. 179.

Nation, September 13, 1986, p. 226; April 27 1998, p. 27.

New England Review, spring, 1998, p. 49.

New Republic, December 24, 1990, p. 26.

New Yorker, December 20, 1982.

New York Review of Books, January 17, 1991, p. 3.

New York Times, November 28, 1990, pp. B1, C13; November 29, 1990, p. C22; January 2, 1991, pp. B1, C9; April 5, 1998; April 8, 1998, pp. B9, E11; July 1, 1990; June 15, 2003, p. 14.

New York Times Book Review, January 12, 1975; January 9, 1983; February 5, 1986; March 30, 1986, p. 7; July 1, 1990, p. 8; April 5, 1998, p. 14; October 18, 1998, p. 28; June 15, 2003, p. 14.

Olympian (Olympia, WA), June 10, 2001, p. D2.

People, January 14, 1991, p. 73; December 11, 2000, p. 55.

Popular Photography, April, 2001, p. 74.

Postscript: Publication of the Philological Association of the Carolinas, 1994, p. 1.

Publishers Weekly, April 6, 1990, p. 103; December 14, 1990, p. 14; April 12, 1991, p. 24; February 28, 1994, p. 65; January 13, 1997, p. 24; February 23, 1998, p. 50; September 21, 1998, p. 62.

Representations, spring, 1997, p. 24.

San Francisco Chronicle, April 19, 1998, p. 1.

School Library Journal, October, 1988, p. 176; August, 1994, p. 105; June, 1999, p. 80; April 2001, p. 173.

Seattle Post-Intelligencer (Seattle, WA), May 30, 2003, p. 25.

Seattle Times, March 29, 1998, p. M1; April 5, 1998, p. M2; 25 March, 2001, p. E12; June 22, 2003, p. K14.

Sewanee Review, January, 1975.

Shakespeare Survey: An Annual Survey of Shakespeare Studies and Production, 1998, p. 45.

Soundings: An Interdisciplinary Journal, winter, 1997, p. 607.

Studies in American Fiction, autumn, 1991, p. 141; spring, 1997, p. 81.

Sycamore: A Journal of American Culture, spring, 1997, p. 19.

Time, January 6, 1975.

Times Literary Supplement (London, England), January 6, 1984.

TriQuarterly, winter-summer, 2000, p. 537.

U.S. News & World Report, December 10, 1990, p. 21.

Village Voice, July 19, 1984.

Washington Post Book World, December 15, 1982; February 16, 1986; December 4, 1990, p. D1; December 13, 1990, p. A23; 24 August, 1997; April 11, 1998, p. B1; November 8, 1998, p. 1.

ONLINE

African-American Literature Book Club, http://aalbc.com/ (March 12, 2004), "Charles Johnson."

Columns, University of Washington Alumni Magazine, http://www.washington.edu/ (June, 1999), "Charles Johnson."

University of Washington Showcase, http://www.washington.edu/ (March 12, 2004), "Charles Johnson: National Book Award Winner."

* * *

JOHNSON, Charles Richard
See JOHNSON, Charles

* * *

JOHNSON, Marguerite Annie
See ANGELOU, Maya

* * *

JONES, Diana Wynne 1934-

PERSONAL: Born August 16, 1934, in London, England; daughter of Richard Aneurin (an educator) and Marjorie (an educator; maiden name, Jackson) Jones; married John A. Burrow (a university professor), December 23, 1956; children: Richard, Michael, Colin. Education: St. Anne's College, Oxford, B.A., 1956.

ADDRESSES: Home—9, The Polygon, Clifton, Bristol B58 4PW, England. *Agent*—Laura Cecil, 17 Alwyne Villas, London N1 2HG, England.

CAREER: Writer, 1965—.

AWARDS, HONORS: Guardian Award, 1977, for *Charmed Life; Boston Globe-Horn Book* Honor Book Award, 1984, for *Archer's Goon; Horn Book* Honor List, 1984, for *Fire and Hemlock; Horn Book* Fanfare List, 1987, for *Howl's Moving Castle;* Mythopoeic Children's Fantasy Award, 1996, for *The Crown of Dalemark,* and 1999, for *Dark Lord of Derkholm.*

WRITINGS:

ADULT FICTION

Changeover, Macmillan (London, England), 1970.
A Sudden Wild Magic, Morrow (New York, NY), 1993.

JUVENILE FICTION

Wilkins' Tooth, Macmillan (London, England), 1973, published as *Witch's Business,* Dutton (New York, NY), 1974.
The Ogre Downstairs, Macmillan (London, England), 1974.
Eight Days of Luke, Macmillan (London, England), 1974.
Dogsbody, Greenwillow (New York, NY), 1977.
Power of Three, Greenwillow (New York, NY), 1978.
Who Got Rid of Angus Flint?, illustrated by John Sewell, Evans Brothers (London, England), 1978.
The Four Grannies, illustrated by Thelma Lambert, Hamish Hamilton (London, England), 1980.
The Homeward Bounders, Greenwillow (New York, NY), 1981.
The Skiver's Guide, illustrated by Chris Winn, Knight Books (London, England), 1984.
Warlock at the Wheel and Other Stories, Greenwillow (New York, NY), 1984.
Archer's Goon, (also see below), Greenwillow (New York, NY), 1984.
Fire and Hemlock, Greenwillow (New York, NY), 1985.

Howl's Moving Castle, Greenwillow (New York, NY), 1986.
A Tale of Time City, Greenwillow (New York, NY), 1987.
Castle in the Air, Greenwillow (New York, NY), 1990.
Chair Person, illustrated by Glenys Ambrus, Puffin Books (New York, NY), 1991.
Black Maria, Methuen (London, England), 1991, published as *Aunt Maria,* Greenwillow (New York, NY), 1991.
A Sudden Wild Magic, Morrow (New York, NY), 1992.
Yes, Dear, illustrated by Graham Philpot, Greenwillow (New York, NY), 1992.
Hexwood, Greenwillow (New York, NY), 1993.
The Book of Changes, Douglas & McIntyre (Toronto, Ontario, Canada), 1994, Orchard Books (New York, NY), 1995.
The Time of the Ghost, Greenwillow (New York, NY), 1996.
Stopping for a Spell, Puffin Books (New York, NY), 1996.
Minor Arcana, Gollancz (London, England), 1996.
The Tough Guide to Fantasyland, Vista (London, England), 1996.
Dark Lord of Derkholm, Greenwillow (New York, NY), 1998.
Deep Secret, Tor (New York, NY), 1999.
Believing Is Seeing: Seven Stories, illustrated by Nenad Jakesevic, Greenwillow (New York, NY), 1999.
Year of the Griffin, Greenwillow (New York, NY), 2000.
Witch's Business, Greenwillow (New York, NY), 2002.
The Merlin Conspiracy, Greenwillow (New York, NY), 2003.
Wild Robert, Greenwillow (New York, NY), 2003.
Unexpected Magic: Collected Stories, Greenwillow (New York, NY), 2004.
Conrad's Fate, Greenwillow (New York, NY), 2005.

"CHRESTOMANCI" CYCLE; JUVENILES

Charmed Life, Macmillan (London, England), 1977, Greenwillow (New York, NY), 1979.
The Magicians of Caprona (also see below), Greenwillow (New York, NY), 1980.
Witch Week (also see below), Greenwillow (New York, NY), 1982.
The Lives of Christopher Chant (also see below), Greenwillow (New York, NY), 1988.
Chronicles of Chrestomanci (contains *Charmed Life, The Magicians of Caprona, Witch Week,* and *The Lives of Christopher Chant,* HarperCollins (New York, NY), 2001.
Mixed Magics: Four Tales of Chrestomanci, Greenwillow (New York, NY), 2001.

"DALEMARK" CYCLE; JUVENILES

Cart and Cwidder, Macmillan (London, England), 1975, Atheneum (New York, NY), 1977, reprinted, HarperTrophy (New York, NY), 2001.

Drowned Ammet, Macmillan (London, England), 1977, Atheneum (New York, NY), 1978, reprinted, HarperTrophy (New York, NY), 2001.

The Spellcoats, Atheneum (New York, NY), 1979, reprinted, HarperTrophy (New York, NY), 2001.

The Crown of Dalemark, Greenwillow (New York, NY), 1995, reprinted, HarperTrophy (New York, NY), 2001.

JUVENILE PLAYS

The Batterpool Business, first produced in London at Arts Theatre, October, 1968.

The King's Things, first produced in London at Arts Theatre, February, 1970.

The Terrible Fisk Machine, first produced in London at Arts Theatre, January, 1971.

Archer's Goon (adapted from Jones's juvenile book of the same title), first produced on BBC, 1992.

Contributor to books, including The Cat-Flap and the Apple Pie, W.H. Allen (London, England), 1979; Hecate's Cauldron, DAW Books (New York, NY), 1981; Hundreds and Hundreds, Puffin Books (New York, NY), 1984; Dragons and Dreams, Harper (New York, NY), 1986; Guardian Angels, Viking Kestrel (London, England), 1987; (and editor) Fantasy Stories, NESFA, 1995; Everard's Ride (miscellany), NESFA, 1995; (and editor) Hidden Turnings, Greenwillow (New York, NY).

SIDELIGHTS: Diana Wynne Jones, best known for her "Chrestomanci" cycle of novels, creates works that straddle the line between fantasy and science fiction. Her fans on both sides of the Atlantic include many adults who may have read her earlier works as teens. Jones, influenced by Norse, Greek, and Welsh myth, and by an earlier generation of fantasy writers, has created both stand-alone and series fantasies that innovatively mingle magic and realism. Jane Yolen in the Washington Post Book World called Jones "one of those English wonders who can combine wit with wisdom. Her sense of humor weaves in and out of the most absurd plots and twists around outrageous situations with a deftness any vaudevillian would envy." Booklist contributor Michael Cart wrote: "To my mind, Diana Wynne Jones is one of the greatest living fantasists; that the knee of every book lover does not bow at the sound of her name has always puzzled me." Cart added that Jones is "a master of the unexpected and never fails to surprise. . . . Her powers of imagination are quite breathtaking, while her ability to create strange, quirky, offbeat, mind-tickling worlds is absolutely astonishing."

Jones as a child endured the outbreak of World War II and her parents' indifference to her. Beginning at age five, she moved frequently with her sisters and her mother, and even after the family settled in rural Essex in 1943 she was neglected and expected to care for her younger siblings. Her father doled out one book a year for the girls to share, and Jones was desperate to read more even though she suffered from dyslexia. At age eight she said she wanted to become a writer, although her family trivialized her ambitions.

After Jones married and had her own children, and the quality of the juvenile fiction she read to her sons disappointed her, she started writing her own stories and novels for children. Two of her early titles, Wilkins' Tooth and The Ogre Downstairs set the themes and tones of her later works. In both stories, intrepid youngsters must tangle with the supernatural and survive by wit and teamwork. Donna R. White wrote in Dictionary of Literary Biography: "An immensely funny book, The Ogre Downstairs also explores two of Jones's pervading themes: displacement and alienation."

Jones's neglected childhood inspired her plots, heroes and heroines. A St. James Guide to Young Adult Writers contributor said the typical Jones protagonist "is likely to grow up among magical folk, often in an alternative world where history ran differently, or a secondary fantasy world, but this hero/ine feels inadequate because s/he does not appear to have magic powers. Using his/her own resources to cope with the problems magic is causing, at the climax a crisis reveals that our hero/ine does truly possess magic powers, sometimes superior to the others, and certainly unique. . . . Jones's books may be classified as domestic fantasy, as magic disrupts ordinary life, sometimes combined with high fantasy, as gods and goddesses become involved." White wrote that in Jones's imagined worlds, "fathers are usually ineffective, selfish, neglectful, unloving parents. Mothers, while portrayed as negatively as fathers, often ignore their children's needs to pursue their own desires."

The Homeward Bounders, which reflects Jones's originality, is a novel in which "she postulates a fantasy war game that applies to all worlds and times," Sarah Hayes wrote in the *Times Literary Supplement*. The book, a fantasy novel with science fiction elements, "contains terror, humor, adventure, everyday problems of survival and references to mythical characters," added *Times Literary Supplement* contributor Judith Elkin. The story follows the adventures of Jamie, a teenager who accidentally witnesses how the worlds are run while randomly moving among them. Although he makes friends, including the Flying Dutchman, Ahasuerus the Wandering Jew, Prometheus chained to a rock, and several children, he cannot return home unless by accident.

The "Chrestomanci" works are set in a world where the government licenses and supervises magic. The handsome enchanter, Chrestomanci, is the recurring character in a series of loosely related stories, including *Charmed Life, The Lives of Christopher Chant, The Magicians of Caprona,* and *Witch Week*. In each of the four novels the central characters must identify their own talents and learn to make use of them—and of course, some of that talent is put to evil use, leading to conflict. A *St. James Guide to Fantasy Writers* essayist wrote: "That Jones manages to make civil servants interesting to the younger reader is a testimony to her skill; that she does this by boring her young heroes and heroines reinforces this." A *Publishers Weekly* reviewer praised the "exuberant momentum" of the Chrestomanci cycle.

The "Dalemark" series is a darker and more conventional fantasy, set in its own world. The titles *Cart and Cwidder, Drowned Ammett, The Spellcoats,* and *The Crown of Dalemark* are linked, but not chronologically. Some critics, however, have said this series seems intended for an older audience, as it proves "full of moral uncertainties but retaining the strong sense of adventure and tension," according to the *St. James Guide to Fantasy Writers* contributor.

Jones's many stand-alone novels reflect her comfort in both fantasy and science fiction. An essayist for the *St. James Guide to Science Fiction Writers* observed: "Given the fact . . . that the author herself dislikes genre categories, it should come as no surprise that many of her books deal with themes which, depending on whose eyes they're seen through, would count as science fiction, and a good half dozen of her novels have overt science fictional ideas." Still, the reviewer noted the prevailing theme: "Many of her characters, children and teenagers, through the course of the novel, learn more about their place in their world, or find a new and more appropriate place." Popular titles such as *Sirius, Archer's Goon, A Sudden Wild Magic* and *Hex-*

wood present otherworldly, sometimes intergalactic, communities as a means to explore social, emotional, and political conventions in the modern world. The *St. James* essayist concluded: "I like to think that for Wynne Jones, science fiction and fantasy are merely two convenient and arbitrary points on a continuum of fiction writing and that she writes as she wishes, and leaves it to others to decide. That would certainly be in keeping with the free literary spirit which pervades these . . . novels."

White concluded: "By reworking her own childhood emotions and experiences, Diana Wynne Jones has created lively, original fantasies built on a foundation of psychological realism. Her neglected young heroes always find personal strength and are usually left in the care of at least one loving adult. Because Jones writes for her own entertainment (and for that of the literature-starved child she once was), she is able to amuse her readers as well, even while challenging them to keep up with her fast-paced, convoluted plots."

In *The Merlin Conspiracy* Arianrhod (Roddy) is a young girl who meets Nick during a magical journey. Mark McCann, on the Web site of Australia's *Sydney Morning Herald,* called the book "a generous serve of pluriversal adventure and rejigged English mythology."

Jones told *CA:* "When I write for children, my first aim is to make a story—as amusing and exciting as possible—such as I wished I could have read as a child. My second aim is equally important. It is to give children—without presuming to instruct them—the benefit of my greater experience. I like to explore the private terrors and troubles which beset children, because they can thereby be shown they are not unique in misery. Children create about a third of their misery themselves. The other two-thirds is [sic] caused by adults—inconsiderate, mysterious, and often downright frightening adults. I put adults like this in my stories, in some firmly contemporary situation beset with very real problems, and explore the implications by means of magic and old myths. What I am after is an exciting—and exacting—wisdom, in which contemporary life and potent myth are intricately involved and superimposed. I would like children to discover that potent old truths are as much part of everyone's daily life as are—say—the days of the week."

BIOGRAPHICAL AND CRITICAL SOURCES:

BOOKS

Authors and Artists for Young Adults, Thomson Gale (Detroit, MI), 1989.

Dictionary of Literary Biography, Volume 161: *British Children's Writers since 1960,* Thomson Gale (Detroit, MI), 1996, pp. 225-232.

Holtze, Sally Holmes, editor, *Fifth Book of Junior Authors,* Wilson (New York, NY), pp. 166-167.

Reading for the Love of It: Best Books for Young Readers, Prentice-Hall (Englewood Cliffs, NJ), 1987.

St. James Guide to Fantasy Writers, St. James (Detroit, MI), 1996.

St. James Guide to Science Fiction Writers, 4th edition, St. James (Detroit, MI), 1996.

St. James Guide to Young Adult Writers, 2nd edition, St. James (Detroit, MI), 1999.

PERIODICALS

Booklist, October 15, 1984, p. 300; June 1, 1986, p. 1455; April 15, 1987, p. 1274; October 1, 1988, p. 320; January 1, 1990, p. 906; March 15, 1991, p. 1503; January 15, 1992, p. 873; March 15, 1992, pp. 1364, 1372; June 1, 1994, p. 1803; April 15, 2001, Michael Cart, "Fantasy Is Flourishing," p. 1546.

Book Window, spring, 1978.

British Book News Children's Books, winter, 1987, Fiona Lafferty, "Realms of Fantasy: An Interview with Diana Wynne Jones," pp. 2-5.

Bulletin of the Center for Children's Books, July-August, 1975.

Chicago Tribune Book World, November 4, 1982.

Globe and Mail (Toronto), July 12, 1986.

Growing Point, May, 1974; April, 1975; October, 1975; December, 1975; March, 1978; May, 1981; January, 1982; November, 1982; March, 1986, p. 4580; March, 1987, p. 4772; September, 1990, p. 5395; September, 1991, p. 5584.

Horn Book, August, 1980; January, 1985, p. 58; May, 1986, p. 331; March, 1988, p. 208; March, 1991, p. 206; May, 1994, p. 345; May, 2001, review of *Mixed Magics: Four Tales of Chrestomanci,* p. 327.

Junior Bookshelf, August 1979; August, 1980; October, 1981; February, 1982; December, 1982; February, 1986, p. 42; October, 1987, p. 235; October, 1990, p. 245; April, 1994, p. 69.

Los Angeles Times, January 31, 1987; September, 1990, p. 37.

New Statesman, May 24, 1974; May 20, 1977; October 10, 1986, p. 30.

New York Times Book Review, May 5, 1974; April 19, 1992, p. 16.

Observer, November 25, 1984, p. 27; December 1, 1985, p. 20; December 13, 1987, p. 22.

Publishers Weekly, February 22, 1991, Kit Alderdice, "Diana Wynne Jones," pp. 201-202; October 19, 1998, review of *Dark Lord of Derkholm,* p. 82; October 16, 2000, review of *Year of the Griffin,* p. 77; April 23, 2001, review of *Mixed Magics,* p. 79; "For Diana Wynne Jones Fans," p. 79.

School Librarian, June, 1978; December, 1982.

School Library Journal, April, 1974; April, 1978; September, 1988, p. 184; April, 1991, p. 141; October, 1991, p. 142; March, 1994, p. 236; July, 2001, Patricia A. Dollisch, review of *Mixed Magics,* p. 110.

Spectator, June 30, 1979.

Times (London), May 1, 1986.

Times Educational Supplement, November 18, 1977; November 30, 1979; April 18, 1980; November 23, 1984, p. 38; October 24, 1986, p. 24; February 5, 1988, p. 58; November 9, 1990, p. R11; November 8, 1991, p. 38.

Times Literary Supplement, March 12, 1970; April 6, 1973; July 5, 1974; April 4, 1975; July 11, 1975; April 2, 1976; March 25, 1977; April 7, 1978; March 28, 1980; September 19, 1980; March 25, 1981; March 27, 1981; November 20, 1981; July 23, 1982; October 19, 1984; November 29, 1985; January 31, 1986; December 12, 1986; November 20-26, 1987; July 12, 1991, p. 20.

Use of English, summer, 1983, Gillian Spraggs, "True Dreams: The Fantasy Fiction of Diana Wynne Jones," pp. 17-22.

U.S. News and World Report, November 29, 1999, Holly J. Morris, "Mad about Harry? Try Diana," p. 80.

Washington Post Book World, May 13, 1984; May 12, 1985; May 11, 1986; June 14, 1987; November 8, 1987; February 11, 1990, p. 12; May 13, 1990, p. 18; May 12, 1991, p. 14; May 8, 1994, pp. 17, 19.

World of Children's Books, spring, 1978.

ONLINE

Sydney Morning Herald Web site, http://www.smh.com.au/ (May 24, 2003), Mark McCann, review of *The Merlin Conspiracy.*

*　　　*　　　*

JONES, Edward P. 1950-

PERSONAL: Born October 5, 1950. *Education:* Attended College of the Holy Cross, Worcester, MA, and University of Virginia.

ADDRESSES: *Home*—4300 Old Dominion Drive, No. 914, Arlington, VA 22207.

CAREER: Fiction writer. Columnist for *Tax Notes.*

AWARDS, HONORS: National Book Award finalist, and Ernest Hemingway Foundation/PEN Award, both 1992, both for *Lost in the City;* Lannan Foundation Literary Award and fellowship, 2003; National Book Award nomination for fiction, 2003, and National Book Critics Circle award, and Pulitzer Prize for fiction, both 2004, all for *The Known World;* O. Henry Prize, 2005, for the short story "A Rich Man."

WRITINGS:

Lost in the City (short stories), photographs by Amos Chan, Morrow (New York, NY), 1992.
The Known World, Amistad (New York, NY), 2003.

Contributor of short fiction to periodicals, including the *New Yorker.*

SIDELIGHTS: Called "a poignant and promising first effort" by *Publishers Weekly,* Edward P. Jones's first book, *Lost in the City,* was greeted with critical and popular acclaim. The work was nominated for the 1992 National Book Award, an honor last granted to a short-story collection six years earlier. The appeal of the fourteen-story collection lies in the realness of the people and the experiences that Jones presents. Each of the stories profiles African-American life in Washington, DC. The characters are all lost in the nation's capital, some literally, others figuratively. They are black working-class men and women who struggle to preserve their families, communities, neighborhoods, and themselves amid drugs, violence, divorce, and other crises. Jones's assortment of characters include a mother whose son buys her a new home with drug money, a husband who repeatedly stabs his wife as their children sleep, and a girl who watches her pigeons fly from her home after their cages are destroyed by rats. They are all stories that "affirm humanity as only good literature can," remarked Michael Harris in the *Los Angeles Times Book Review.* "There's no secret to it, or only the final, most elusive secret: Jones has near-perfect pitch for people. . . . Whoever they are, he reveals them to us from the inside out."

Washington Post writer Mary Ann French noted that in *Lost in the City* Jones "creates sympathy through understanding—a sadly needed service that is too sel-

dom performed." *Washington Post Book World* reviewer Jonathan Yardley commented that the assembled stories are set in the 1950s, 1960s, and 1970s, "so there is little sense of the drug-and-crime haunted place that the inner city has become." Nevertheless, Yardley added, "danger and death are never far in the background." While the stories usually convey a sense of hope despite some bleak settings and horrible events, "Jones is no sentimentalist," according to the critic. Rather, he is "a lucid, appealing writer. He puts on no airs, tells his stories matter-of-factly and forthrightly, yet his prose is distinctive and carries more weight than first impressions might suggest."

The Known World, Jones's first novel and second published book, generated even more critical acclaim than his short-story collection. In 2004 the work won the Pulitzer Prize and the National Book Critics Circle award for fiction, both on the heels of a National Book Award for fiction nomination in 2003. *The Known World* begins with the antebellum story of African-American Henry Townsend, a farmer, bootmaker, and former slave. Townsend, an intelligent man with a fondness for John Milton's *Paradise Lost,* has taken an unusual adviser: William Robbins, a powerful man residing in Manchester County, Virginia. Under Robbins's guidance, Townsend rises economically to become a landowner and, ironically, a slave owner. When he dies, his widow, Caldonia, cannot carry on alone and things at the Townsend plantation begin to deteriorate: slaves run off in the night, and families with once-strong bonds start to turn on one another. Outside the farm, everything else, in other words, "the known world," is falling apart, too: free black people are sold into slavery and rumors of slave rebellions circulate widely, setting white families on edge and destroying their trust in the blacks who have worked for them for years.

According to Champ Clark, writing in *People,* readers of *The Known World* "will be rewarded many times over by Jones's masterful ability to convey even the most despicable aspects of the nation's history with humanity and poetic language." In *Booklist,* Vanessa Bush described the novel as "a profoundly beautiful and insightful look at American slavery and human nature." "Jones moves back and forth in time," she explained, "making the reader omniscient, knowing what will eventually befall the characters despite their best and worst efforts, their aspirations and their moral failings." *Newsweek* reviewer Susannah Meadows was less enthusiastic about the novel, writing that while "The human mystery that drives the narrative is the question of how a freed man could own another, . . . Jones never quite solves the puzzle of Henry's odd spiritual kinship with his former master." Mark Harris, reviewing the book for *Entertainment Weekly,* cited the "difficulty and occasional randomness of Jones's storytelling." This "doesn't seem accidental," Harris maintained. Jones "is writing about a landscape in which families, identities, and the very notion of self can be destroyed in the course of a casual business transaction—and he doesn't want you to get too comfortable tracing a single life across a tidy narrative line."

In an interview with Robert Fleming of *Publishers Weekly,* Jones explained his use of a dispassionate voice when describing the brutal episodes that take place in *The Known World* by noting that he wanted "to highlight the inhumanity of the whole situation of slavery." "I didn't want to preach," he added. "It was my goal to be objective, to not put a lot of emotion into this, to show it all in a matter-of-fact manner. But still I knew I was singing to the choir. In a case like this, you don't raise your voice, you just state the case and that is more than enough."

Sarah Anne Johnson, in an interview with Jones for the *Writer,* asked the author where he found his inspiration for *The Known World.* "You just wake up one morning with some image or some words in your head, and you go from there," Jones replied. "The first thing that set me off with *The Known World* was the image of Henry Townsend on his deathbed in the first few pages. You have to figure out how he got to be in the bed and who's in the room with him. Then you branch out further and further until finally you have all the pages that are in the book right now."

Despite praising Jones's award-winning novel, several critics have noted that *The Known World* is not an easy read. A contributor to *Kirkus Reviews* described the first hundred pages as "daunting," saying, "The reader struggles to sort out initially quickly glimpsed characters and absorb Jones's handling of historical background information." But then the novel gains "overpowering momentum," the critic added, and becomes "a harrowing tale that scarcely ever raises its voice." "By focusing on an African-American slaveholder," Edward B. St. John noted in *Library Journal,* "Jones forcefully demonstrates how institutionalized slavery jeopardized all levels of civilized society so that no one was really free." The novel, St. John continued, is "a fascinating look at a painful theme." "Everyone in *The Known World* exhibits good, bad, and every other shade of humanity inside their actions," added Carroll Parrott Blue in *Black Issues Book Review.* "Jones uses his hardwon mastery of craft to gently entice us to stare directly into the face of our universally human quest for freedom."

BIOGRAPHICAL AND CRITICAL SOURCES:

BOOKS

Contemporary Literary Criticism, Yearbook 1992, Volume 76, Thomson Gale (Detroit, MI), 1992.

PERIODICALS

Black Issues Book Review, November-December, 2003, Carroll Parrott Blue, review of *The Known World,* p. 50.
Booklist, September 15, 2003, Vanessa Bush, review of *The Known World,* p. 211.
Entertainment Weekly, August 22, 2003, Mark Harris, review of *The Known World,* p. 134.
Kirkus Reviews, July 15, 2003, review of *The Known World,* p. 928.
Library Journal, August, 2003, Edward B. St. John, review of *The Known World,* p. 131.
Los Angeles Times Book Review, July 12, 1992, p. 6.
Newsweek, September 8, 2003, Susannah Meadows, review of *The Known World,* p. 57.
New York Times, June 11, 1992, p. C18; August 23, 1992, section 7, p. 16.
People, September 29, 2003, Champ Clark, review of *The Known World,* p. 45.
Publishers Weekly, March 23, 1992, p. 59; August 11, 2003, Robert Fleming, interview with Jones, p. 254.
Washington Post, July 22, 1992, pp. G1, G4; October 6, 1992, p. B4.
Washington Post Book World, June 21, 1992, p. 3.
Writer, August, 2004, Sarah Anne Johnson, interview with Jones, p. 20.

*   *   *

JONES, Everett LeRoi
　　See BARAKA, Amiri

*   *   *

JONES, Gayl 1949-

PERSONAL: Born November 23, 1949, in Lexington, KY; daughter of Franklin (a cook) and Lucille (Wilson) Jones; married Bob Higgins (later took the name Bob Jones; deceased). *Education:* Connecticut College, B.A., 1971; Brown University, M.A., 1973, D.A., 1975.

ADDRESSES: Home—Lexington, KY. *Agent*—c/o Author Mail, Beacon Press, 25 Beacon St., Boston, MA 02108.

CAREER: University of Michigan, Ann Arbor, 1975-83, began as assistant professor, became professor of English; writer.

MEMBER: Authors Guild, Authors League of America.

AWARDS, HONORS: Award for best original production in the New England region, American College Theatre Festival, 1973, for *Chile Woman;* grants from Shubert Foundation, 1973-74, Southern Fellowship Foundation, 1973-75, and Rhode Island Council on the Arts, 1974-75; fellowships from Yaddo, 1974, National Endowment of the Arts, 1976, and Michigan Society of Fellows, 1977-79; Howard Foundation award, 1975; Fiction Award from *Mademoiselle,* 1975; Henry Russell Award, University of Michigan, 1981; National Book Award nomination, 1998, for *The Healing.*

WRITINGS:

Chile Woman (play), Shubert Foundation (New York, NY), 1974.
Corregidora (novel), Random House (New York, NY), 1975.
Eva's Man (novel), Random House (New York, NY), 1976.
White Rat (short stories), Random House (New York, NY), 1977.
Song for Anninho (poetry), Lotus Press (Detroit, MI), 1981, reprinted, Beacon Press (Boston, MA), 1999.
The Hermit-Woman (poetry), Lotus Press (Detroit, MI), 1983.
Xarque and Other Poems, Lotus Press (Detroit, MI), 1985.
Liberating Voices: Oral Tradition in African American Literature (criticism), Harvard University Press (Cambridge, MA), 1991.
The Healing (novel), Beacon Press (Boston, MA), 1998.
Mosquito (novel), Beacon Press (Boston, MA), 1999.

Contributor to anthologies, including *Confirmation,* 1983, *Chants of Saints, Keeping the Faith, Midnight Birds,* and *Soulscript.* Contributor to periodicals, including *Massachusetts Review.*

WORK IN PROGRESS: Research on sixteenth-and seventeenth-century Brazil and on settlements of escaped slaves, such as Palmares.

SIDELIGHTS: Gayl Jones's novels *Corregidora* and *Eva's Man,* in addition to many of the stories in her collection *White Rat,* offer stark, often brutal accounts of black women whose psyches reflect the ravages of accumulated sexual and racial exploitation. In *Corregidora* Jones reveals the tormented life of a woman whose female forebears—at the hands of one man—endured a cycle of slavery, prostitution, and incest over three generations. *Eva's Man* explores the deranged mind of a woman institutionalized for poisoning and sexually mutilating a male acquaintance. And in "Asylum," a story from *White Rat,* a young woman is confined to a mental hospital for a series of bizarre actions that, in her mind, protests a society she sees as bent on her personal violation. "The abuse of women and its psychological results fascinate Gayl Jones, who uses these recurring themes to magnify the absurdity and the obscenity of racism and sexism in everyday life," commented Jerry W. Ward, Jr., in *Black Women Writers (1950-1980): A Critical Evaluation.* "Her novels and short fictions invite readers to explore the interior of caged personalities, men and women driven to extremes." Keith Byerman elaborated in the *Dictionary of Literary Biography.*: "Jones creates worlds radically different from those of 'normal' experience and of storytelling convention. Her tales are gothic in the sense of dealing with madness, sexuality, and violence, but they do not follow in the Edgar Allan Poe tradition of focusing on private obsession and irrationality. Though her narrators are close to if not over the boundaries of sanity, the experiences they record reveal clearly that society acts out its own obsessions often violently."

Corregidora, Jones's first novel, explores the psychological effects of slavery and sexual abuse on a modern black woman. Ursa Corregidora, a blues singer from Kentucky, descends from a line of women who are the progeny, by incest, of a Portuguese slaveholder named Corregidora—the father of both Ursa's mother and grandmother. "All of the women, including the great-granddaughter Ursa, keep the name Corregidora as a reminder of the depredations of the slave system and of the rapacious natures of men," Byerman explained in the *Dictionary of Literary Biography.* "The story is passed from generation to generation of women, along with the admonition to 'produce generations' to keep alive the tale of evil." Partly as a result of this history, Ursa becomes involved in abusive relationships with men. The novel itself springs from an incident of violence. After being thrown down a flight of stairs by her first husband and physically injured so that she cannot bear children, Ursa "discharges her obligation to the memory of Corregidora by speaking [the] book," noted John Updike in the *New Yorker*. The novel emerges as Ursa's struggle to reconcile her heritage with her present life. *Corregidora* "persuasively fuses black history, or the mythic consciousness that must do for black history, with the emotional nuances of contemporary black life," Updike continued. "The book's innermost action . . . is Ursa's attempt to transcend a nightmare black consciousness and waken to her own female, maimed humanity."

Corregidora was described as a novel of unusual power and impact. "No black American novel since Richard Wright's *Native Son* in 1940," wrote Ivan Webster in *Time,* "has so skillfully traced psychic wounds to a sexual source." Darryl Pinckney in *New Republic* called *Corregidora* "a small, fiercely concentrated story, harsh and perfectly told. . . . Original, superbly imagined, nothing about the book was simple or easily digested. Out of the worn themes of miscegenation and diminishment, Gayl Jones *excavated* the disturbingly buried damage of racism." Critics particularly noted Jones's treatment of sexual detail and its illumination of the central character. "One of the book's merits," according to Updike, "is the ease with which it assumes the writer's right to sexual specifics, and its willingness to explore exactly how our sexual and emotional behavior is warped within the matrix of family and race." In the book's final scene, Ursa comes to a reconciliation with her first husband, Mutt, by envisioning an ambivalent sexual relationship between her great-grandmother and the slavemaster Corregidora. *Corregidora* is a novel "filled with sexual and spiritual pain," wrote Margo Jefferson in *Newsweek;* "hatred, love and desire wear the same face, and humor is blues-bitter. . . . Jones's language is subtle and sinewy, and her imagination sure."

Jones's second novel, *Eva's Man,* continues her exploration into the psychological effects of brutality, yet presents a character who suffers greater devastation. Eva Medina Canada, incarcerated for the murder and mutilation of a male acquaintance, narrates a personal history that depicts the damaging influences of a sexually aggressive and hostile society. Updike described in the *New Yorker* the exploitative world that has shaped the mentally deranged Eva: "Evil permeates the erotic education of Eva Canada, as it progresses from Popsicle-stick violations to the witnessing of her mother's adultery and a growing awareness of the whores and 'queen bees' in the slum world around her, and on to her own reluctant initiation through encounters in buses and in bars, where a man with no thumb monoto-

nously propositions her. The evil that emanates from men becomes hers." In a narrative that is fragmented and disjointed, Eva gives no concrete motive for the crime committed; furthermore, she neither shows remorse nor any signs of rehabilitation. More experimental than *Corregidora, Eva's Man* displays "a sharpened starkness, a power of ellipsis that leaves ever darker gaps between its flashes of rhythmic, sensuously exact dialogue and visible symbol," according to Updike. John Leonard noted in the *New York Times* that "not a word is wasted" in Eva's narrative. "It seems, in fact, as if Eva doesn't have enough words, as if she were trying to use the words she has to make a poem, a semblance of order, and fails of insufficiency." Leonard concluded that *Eva's Man* may be one of the most unpleasant novels of the season. It is also one of the most accomplished."

Eva's Man was praised for its emotional impact, yet some reviewers found the character of Eva extreme or inaccessible. June Jordan in the *New York Times Book Review* called *Eva's Man* "the blues that lost control. This is the rhythmic, monotone lamentation of one woman, Eva Medina, who is nobody I have ever known." Jordan explained that "Jones delivers her story in a strictly controlled, circular form that is wrapped, around and around with ambivalence. Unerringly, her writing creates the tension of a problem unresolved." In the end, however, Jordan found that the fragmented details of Eva's story "do not mesh into illumination." On the other hand, some reviewers regarded the gaps in *Eva's Man* as appropriate and integral to its meaning. Pinckney in the *New Republic* called the novel "a tale of madness; one exacerbated if not caused by frustration, accumulated grievances" and commented on aspects that contribute to this effect: "Structurally unsettled, more scattered than *Corregidora, Eva's Man* is extremely remote, more troubling in its hallucinations. . . .The personal exploitation that causes Eva's desperation is hard to appreciate. Her rage seems never to find its proper object, except, possibly, in her last extreme act." Updike likewise held that the novel accurately portrays Eva's deranged state, yet he pointed out that Jones's characterization skills are not at their peak. "Jones apparently wishes to show us a female heart frozen into rage by deprivation, but the worry arises, as it did not in *Corregidora,* that the characters are dehumanized as much by her artistic vision as by their circumstances."

Jordan raised a concern in *New York Times Book Review* that the inconclusiveness of *Eva's Man* harbors a potentially damaging feature. "There is the very real, upsetting accomplishment of Gayl Jones in this, her second novel: sinister misinformation about women—about women, in general, about black women in particular." Jones commented in *Black Women Writers (1950-1980)* on the predicament faced in portraying negative characters: "To deal with such a character as Eva becomes problematic in the way that 'Trueblood' becomes problematic in [Ralph Ellison's] *Invisible Man.* It raises the questions of possibility. Should a Black writer ignore such characters, refuse to enter 'such territory' because of the 'negative image' and because such characters can be misused politically by others, or should one try to reclaim such complex, contradictory characters as well as try to reclaim the idea of the 'heroic image'?" Jones elaborated in an interview with Claudia Tate for *Black Women Writers at Work:* "'Positive race images' are fine as long as they're very complex and interesting personalities. Right now I'm not sure how to reconcile the various things that interest me with 'positive race images.' It's important to be able to work with a range of personalities, as well as with a range within one personality. For instance, how would one reconcile an interest in neurosis or insanity with positive race image?"

Although Jones's subject matter is often charged and intense, a number of critics have praised a particular restraint she manages in her narratives. Regarding *Corregidora*, Updike remarked, "Our retrospective impression of *Corregidora* is of a big territory—the Afro-American psyche—rather thinly and stabbingly populated by ideas personae, hints. Yet that such a small book could seem so big speaks well for the generous spirit of the author, unpolemical where there has been much polemic, exploratory where rhetoric and outrage tend to block the path." Similarly, Jones maintains an authorial distance in her fiction which, in turn, makes for believable and gripping characters. In the *Dictionary of Literary Biography,* Byerman commented, "The authority of [Jones's] depiction of the world is enhanced by [her] refusal to intrude upon or judge her narrators. She remains outside the story, leaving the reader with none of the usual markers of a narrator's reliability. She gives these characters the speech of their religion, which, by locating them in time and space, makes it even more difficult to easily dismiss them; the way they speak has authenticity, which carries over to what they tell. The results are profoundly disturbing tales of repression, manipulation, and suffering." Reviewers have also noted Jones's ability to innovatively incorporate Afro-American speech patterns into her work. In *Black Women Writers (1950-1980),* Melvin Dixon noted that "Gayl Jones has figured among the best of contemporary Afro-American writers who have used Black speech as a major aesthetic device in their works. Like Alice

Walker, Toni Morrison, Sherley Williams, Toni Cade Bambara, and such male writers as Ernest Gaines and Ishmael Reed, Jones uses the rhythm and structure of spoken language to develop authentic characters and to establish new possibilities for dramatic conflict within the text and between readers and the text itself." In her interview with Tate in *Black Women Writers at Work,* Jones remarked on the importance of storytelling traditions to her work: "At the time I was writing *Corregidora* and *Eva's Man* I was particularly interested—and continue to be interested—in oral traditions of storytelling—Afro-American and others, in which there is always the consciousness and importance of the hearer, even in the interior monologues where the storyteller becomes her own hearer. That consciousness or self-consciousness actually determines my selection of significant events."

In 1977 Jones published a collection of short stories called *White Rat.* A number of critics noted the presence of Jones's typical thematic concerns, yet also felt that her shorter fiction did not allow enough room for character development. Diane Johnson commented in the *New York Review of Books* that the stories in *White Rat* "were written in some cases earlier than her novels, so they confirm one's sense of her direction and preoccupations: sex is violation, and violence is the principal dynamic of human relationships." Mel Watkins wrote about Jones's short fiction in the *New York Times:* "The focus throughout is on desolate, forsaken characters struggling to exact some snippet of gratification from their lives. . . . Although her prose here is as starkly arresting and indelible as in her novels, except for the longer stories such as 'Jeveta' and 'The Women,' these tales are simply doleful vignettes—slices of life so beveled that they seem distorted." While Jones's writing often emphasizes a tormented side of life—especially regarding male-female relationships—it also raises the possibility for more positive interactions. Jones pointed out in the Tate interview that "there seems to be a growing understanding—working itself out especially in *Corregidora*—of what is required in order to be genuinely tender. Perhaps brutality enables one to recognize what tenderness is." Some critics have found ambivalence at the core of Jones's fiction. Dixon wrote that "Redemption . . . is most likely to occur when the resolution of conflict is forged in the same vocabulary as the tensions which precipitated it. This dual nature of language makes it appear brutally indifferent, for it contains the source and the resolution of conflicts." Dixon also noted, "What Jones is after is the words and deeds that finally break the sexual bondage men and women impose upon each other."

In 1991, Jones published her first book of literary criticism, *Liberating Voices: Oral Tradition in African*

American Literature. Here Jones argues that all literatures, not just African-American, develop in relation to and must come to terms with their own culture's oral storytelling practices. With this point in mind, she compares the poetry, short fiction, and novels of African-American authors—including Paul Laurence Dunbar, Jean Toomer, Zora Neale Hurston, Ralph Ellison, Amiri Baraka, Alice Walker, Langston Hughes, and Toni Morrison—with the works of longstanding canonical authors from a wide variety of historical eras and cultures, from Chaucer and Cervantes to Joyce. M. Giulia Fabi, in *American Literature*, called this a "daring and insightful study."

In 1998, Jones's first novel in twenty years was published and garnered a National Book Award nomination. In *The Healing*, Jones chooses to tell the story of Harlan Jane Eagleton backwards, "a feat accomplished with deceptive ease," noted Veronica Chambers in *Newsweek*. "Each section of the story happens further back in the past until we end at the beginning of the tale." Although the reader first sees Eagleton as a faith healer, Eagleton's life soon unfolds in reverse as the stories of her stints as the manager of an unbearable woman rock star, a beautician, and a racetrack gambler unfold until the reader arrives at the beginning of Eagleton's life. "And oh, what a beginning it is—surprising, romantic and wholly satisfying," wrote Chambers. A *Publishers Weekly* contributor commented, "From the opening pages we know we're in the presence of a masterly writer whose life experiences have sharpened her edges rather than softened them." Dianna Moeller, writing in *Library Journal*, commented, "Jones, who has created her own tradition of writing as oral storytelling, presents a powerful and unforgettable, story of transformation and hope."

In her 1999 follow-up novel, *Mosquito*, Jones tells the tale of Nadine Jane Johnson, an African-American truck driver nicknamed "Mosquito." As she drives around the Texas border, Mosquito expounds upon a variety of topics, from border towns to cactus to, as noted by Eleanor J. Bader in *Library Journal*, "theories about family, gender, imperialism, love, race, and platonic relationships." As the story progresses, Mosquito finds a pregnant woman hiding in her truck and becomes involved the a new type of "underground railroad," which serves as a sanctuary to Mexican immigrants. Bader commented, "By turns exhausting and exhilarating, *Mosquito* is a stunning glimpse into one woman's search for her place in the cosmos." Tamala M. Edwards, writing in *Time*, was disturbed by the novel's "muddled tangents" but noted, "Still, in rare moments, Jones' virtuosity grins up at us." A *Publishers Weekly*

contributor commented, "Here . . . Jones has written a powerfully hopeful 'jazz novel'; improvisations, repetitions and syncopies round out the free-form genius of her fractured tale."

BIOGRAPHICAL AND CRITICAL SOURCES:

BOOKS

Contemporary Black Biography, Volume 37, Thomson Gale (Detroit, MI), 2003.
Contemporary Literary Criticism, Thomson Gale (Detroit, MI), Volume 6, 1976, Volume 9, 1978.
Contemporary Novelists, 7th edition, St. James Press (Detroit, MI), 2001.
Coser, Stelamaris, *Bridging the Americas: The Literature of Paula Marshall, Toni Morrison, and Gayl Jones*, Temple University Press (Philadelphia, PA), 1995.
Dictionary of Literary Biography, Volume 33: *Afro-American Fiction Writers after 1955*, Thomson Gale (Detroit, MI), 1984.
Evans, Mari, editor, *Black Women Writers (1950-1980): A Critical Evaluation*, Anchor Press/Doubleday (Garden City, NY), 1984.
Robinson, Sally, *Engendering the Subject: Gender and Self-Representation in Contemporary Women's Fiction*, State University of New York Press (Albany, NY), 1991.
Tate, Claudia, editor, *Black Women Writers at Work*, Continuum (New York, NY), 1986.

PERIODICALS

African American Review, winter, 1994, p. 559; spring, 1994, p. 141; summer, 1994, p. 223; summer, 2000, Candice M. Jenkins, review of *The Healing*, p. 365, Laurie Champion, review of *Mosquito*, p. 366.
American Literature, June, 1993, M. Giulia Fabi, review of *Liberating Voices: Oral Traditions in African American Literature* and *The Healing*.
Artforum International, March, 1998, Jacqueline Woodson, review of *The Healing*, p. S24.
Belles Lettres, summer, 1992.
Black World, February, 1976.
Booklist, February 1, 1998, review of *The Healing*, p. 899.
Book World, February 22, 1987.
Canadian Literature, winter, 1992.
Choice, November, 1991.
College Literature, February, 1992.

Comparative Literature Studies, summer, 1999, Bernard W. Bell, reviews of *Liberating Voices: Oral Traditions in African American Literature* and *The Healing,* p. 247.

Esquire, December, 1976.

Essence, February, 1998, Lise Funderburg, review of *The Healing,* p. 76.

Guardian, November 16, 1998, Michael Ellison, review of *The Healing,* p. T8.

Journal of American Folklore, winter, 1993.

Kliatt, spring, 1986.

Library Journal, December, 1997, Dianna Moeller, review of *The Healing,* p. 152; January, 1999, Eleanor J. Bader, review of *Mosquito,* p. 152.

Literary Quarterly, May 15, 1975.

Massachusetts Review, winter, 1977.

Michigan Quarterly Review, spring, 2001, Arlene R. Keizer, review of *Mosquito,* p. 431.

Modern Fiction Studies, fall, 1993, p. 825.

Nation, May 25, 1998, Jill Nelson, review of *The Healing,* p. 30.

National Review, April 14, 1978.

New Republic, June 28, 1975; June 19, 1976.

Newsweek, May 19, 1975; April 12, 1976; February 16, 1998, Veronica Chambers, review of *The Healing,* p. 68.

New Yorker, August 18, 1975; August 9, 1976.

New York Review of Books, November 10, 1977, Diane Johnson, review of *White Rat.*

New York Times, April 30, 1976; December 28, 1977.

New York Times Book Review, May 25, 1975; May 16, 1976; March 15, 1987; May 10, 1998, Valerie Sayers, review of *The Healing,* p. 28.

Publishers Weekly, January 19, 1998, review of *The Healing,* p. 76; November 23, 1998, review of *Mosquito,* p. 57.

Time, June 16, 1975, Ivan Webster, review of *Corregidora;* February 8, 1999, review of *Mosquito,* p. 72

Times (London, England), April 1, 2000, Scott Bradfield, review of *The Healing,* p. 22, February 8, 1999, Tamala M. Edwards, review of *Mosquito,* p. 72.

Washington Post, October 21, 1977.

Women's Review of Books, March, 1998, Judith Grossman, review of *The Healing,* p. 15, March, 1999, Deborah McDowell, review of *Mosquito,* p. 9.

Yale Review, autumn, 1976.

ONLINE

Voices from the Gaps, http://voices.cla.umn.edu/ (August 2, 2003), "Gayl Jones."

JONES, LeRoi
   See BARAKA, Amiri

*   *   *

JONG, Erica 1942-

PERSONAL: Born March 26, 1942, in New York, NY; daughter of Seymour (an importer) and Eda (a painter and designer; maiden name, Mirsky) Mann; married Michael Werthman (divorced, 1965), married Allan Jong (a child psychiatrist), 1966 (divorced, September 16, 1975); married Jonathan Fast (a writer), December, 1977 (divorced, January, 1983); married Kenneth David Burrows (a lawyer), August 5, 1989; children: (third marriage) Molly Miranda. *Education:* Attended High School of Music and Art, New York, NY; Barnard College, B.A., 1963; Columbia University, M.A., 1965; postgraduate study at Columbia School of Fine Arts, 1969-70. *Politics:* "Left-leaning feminist." *Religion:* "Devout pagan."

ADDRESSES: Office—425 Park Ave., New York, NY 10022-3506; fax: 212-421-5279. *Agent*—Ed Victor, 6 Bayley St., Bedford Sq., London WC1, England. *E-mail*—queryjongleur@rcn.com.

CAREER: Writer and lecturer. City College of the City University of New York, lecturer in English, 1964-65 and 1969-70; University of Maryland, Overseas Division, Heidelberg, West Germany (now Germany), lecturer in English, 1966-69; instructor in English, Manhattan Community College, 1969-70; YM/YWCA Poetry Center, New York City, instructor in poetry, 1971-73; Bread Loaf Writers Conference, instructor, 1981, and Salzburg Seminar, instructor, 1993. Judge in fiction, National Book Award, 1995. Member, New York State Council on the Arts, 1972-74.

MEMBER: PEN, Authors League of America, Authors Guild (president, 1991-93), Dramatists Guild of America, Writers Guild of America, Poetry Society of America, National Writers Union (member of advisory board), Poets and Writers, Phi Beta Kappa.

AWARDS, HONORS: American Academy of Poets Award, George Weldwood Murray fellow, Barnard College, both 1963; Woodrow Wilson fellow, Columbia University, 1964; New York State Council on the Arts grant, 1971; Borestone Mountain Award in poetry, 1971; Bess Hokin prize, *Poetry* magazine, 1971; Madeline Sadin Award, *New York Quarterly,* 1972; Alice Faye di Castagnolia Award, Poetry Society of America, 1972; Creative Artists Public Service award, 1973, for *Half-Lives;* National Endowment for the Arts fellowship, 1973-74; Welsh College of Music and Drama, honorary fellow, 1994; International Sigmund Freud prize, 1979.

WRITINGS:

NOVELS

Fear of Flying, Holt (New York, NY), 1973.
How to Save Your Own Life, Holt (New York, NY), 1977.
Fanny, Being the True History of the Adventures of Fanny Hackabout-Jones, New American Library (New York, NY), 1980.
Parachutes and Kisses, New American Library (New York, NY), 1984.
Serenissima: A Novel of Venice, Houghton (Boston, MA), 1987, published as *Shylock's Daughter,* HarperCollins (New York, NY), 1995.
Any Woman's Blues, Harper (New York, NY), 1990.
Megan's Two Houses: A Story of Adjustment, Dove Kids (West Hollywood, CA), 1996.
Inventing Memory: A Novel of Mothers and Daughters, HarperCollins (New York, NY), 1997.
Sappho's Leap, W.W. Norton (New York, NY), 2003.

POETRY

Fruits and Vegetables, Holt (New York, NY), 1971.
Half-Lives, Holt (New York, NY), 1973.
Loveroot, Holt (New York, NY), 1975.
Here Comes, and Other Poems, New American Library (New York, NY), 1975.
The Poetry of Erica Jong (three volumes), Holt (New York, NY), 1976.
Selected Poetry, Granada (London, England), 1977.
The Poetry Suit, Konglomerati Press (Gulfport, FL), 1978.
At the Edge of the Body, Holt (New York, NY), 1979.
Ordinary Miracles: New Poems, New American Library (New York, NY), 1983.
Becoming Light: New and Selected Poems, HarperCollins (New York, NY), 1991.

OTHER

Fear of Flying (sound recording; includes selections from poetry and from the novel of the same title), Spoken Arts, 1976.

(Contributor) *Four Visions of America,* Capra Press (Santa Barbara, CA), 1977.
Witches (miscellany), illustrated by Joseph A. Smith, Abrams (New York, NY), 1981.
Megan's Book of Divorce: A Kid's Book for Adults, illustrated by Freya Tanz, New American Library (New York, NY), 1984.
Serenissima (sound recording of the novel of the same title), Brilliance Corp./Houghton (New York, NY), 1987.
Becoming Light (sound recording of the book of the same title), Dove Audio (Beverly Hills, CA.), 1992.
The Devil at Large: Erica Jong on Henry Miller, Turtle Bay (New York, NY), 1993.
Fear of Fifty: A Midlife Memoir, HarperCollins (New York, NY), 1994.
Zipless: Songs of Abandon from the Erotic Poetry of Erica Jong, 1995.
(Editor) *In Their Own Voices: A Century of Recorded Poetry* (sound recording), Rhino Records, 1998.
What Do Women Want?: Bread, Roses, Sex, Power, HarperCollins (New York, NY), 1998.

Also author of introduction to edition of Vladimir Nabokov's *Lolita,* 1988; author, with Jonathan Fast, of screenplay *Love al Dente.* Contributor of poems and articles to numerous newspapers and periodicals, including *Esquire, Ladies' Home Journal, Los Angeles Times, Ms., Nation, New Republic, New York, New Yorker, New York Times Book Review, Poetry,* and *Vogue.*

SIDELIGHTS: Best known as the author of the 1973 best-selling novel *Fear of Flying,* Erica Jong has received critical attention for her frank and unabashed portrayal of female sexuality. Despite Jong's literary output in the areas of poetry and social criticism, *Interview* contributor Karen Burke noted that "her fame from the enormous success of *Fear of Flying* has overshadowed these accomplishments." Recounting one woman's escapades during her search for sexual realization, *Fear of Flying* won its author "a special place in woman's literary history" in the opinion of *Ms.* reviewer Karen Fitzgerald. "Jong was the first woman to write in such a daring and humorous way about sex," Fitzgerald explained. "She popularized the idea of a woman's ultimate sexual fantasy . . . sex for the sake of sex."

Jong's poetry is written in the confessional mode, the "crazed exposure of the American ego," according to Douglas Dunn in *Encounter.* Dunn noted the similarity of Jong's verse to the work of confessional poets such as Sylvia Plath and Anne Sexton, who wrote extensively on existential despair and the relations between men and women—and who each ultimately committed suicide. Unlike such literary predecessors, Jong chooses to affirm life; according to Benjamin Franklin V in *Dictionary of Literary Biography,* her work is "generally positive and optimistic about the human condition." John Ditsky, writing for *Ontario Review,* explained that Jong is "a Sexton determined to survive"; he sees the influence of sensualist poet Walt Whitman in her verse. Above all, said Franklin, "her own work illustrates women's victory and that, instead of flaunting their success and subduing men, women and men should work together and bolster each other."

Fear of Flying protagonist Isadora Zelda White Stollerman Wing—a poet and writer like her creator—is a woman "unblushingly preoccupied with her own libido," according to Elizabeth Peer of *Newsweek. Fear of Flying* recounts Isadora's adventures in search of the ideal sexual experience. While accompanying her Chinese-American Freudian analyst husband to a congress of psychoanalysts in Vienna, she meets Adrian Goodlove, an English analyst and self-proclaimed free spirit. Goodlove coaxes Wing to leave her husband and run off with him on an existential holiday across Europe where they can gratify their sexual appetites without guilt and remorse. In the course of this sensual odyssey, Isadora realizes that Adrian, who had epitomized sex-for-the-sake-of-sex, is in fact impotent, and no source of good love at all. As Carol Johnson wrote in *Dictionary of Literary Biography,* Isadora finds Adrian's "promised 'liberation' to be simply a new style of confinement." After two weeks he deserts Isadora to keep a planned rendezvous with his own family and she returns to her husband unrepentant, if unfulfilled.

While sex plays a major role in *Fear of Flying,* it is only one of the novel's main focuses. Johnson remarked that the story "revolves around themes of feminism and guilt, creativity and sex," and indeed, Jong told *Interview*'s Burke that *Fear of Flying* is "not an endorsement of promiscuity at all. It [is] about a young woman growing up and finding her own independence and finding the right to think her own thoughts, to fantasize." Emily Toth pointed out in *Dictionary of Literary Biography* that "*Fear of Flying* is essentially a literary novel, a bildungsroman with strong parallels to the *Odyssey,* Dante's *Inferno,* and the myths of Daedalus and Icarus." Parts of the book may be regarded as satirical: Johnson stated that Jong's most erotic scenes "are parodies of contemporary pornography, her liberated woman [is] openly thwarted and unfulfilled." Other aspects of the novel, according to an *Atlantic* contributor, include a "diatribe against marriage—against the dread dullness of habitual, connubial sex, against the paucity of means of reconciling the desire for freedom and the need for closeness, against childbearing," and a search for personal creativity.

Critical reaction to *Fear of Flying* has varied. John Updike noted in *New Yorker* that Jong's work possesses "class and sass, brightness and bite." He compared the author to Chaucer and her protagonist to the Wife of Bath in the *Canterbury Tales,* and found parallels between *Fear of Flying* and both J.D. Salinger's *Catcher in the Rye* and Philip Roth's *Portnoy's Complaint.* Christopher Lehmann-Haupt of *New York Times* praised Jong's characterization of Isadora, saying, "I can't remember ever before feeling quite so free to identify my own feelings with those of a female protagonist." He concluded that "Isadora Wing, with her unfettered yearnings for sexual satisfaction and her touching struggle for identity and self-confidence, is really more of a person than a woman (which isn't to deny in the least Mrs. Jong's underlying point that it's harder to become a person if you're a woman than it is if you're a man)." In a *New York Times* appraisal, novelist Henry Miller compared *Fear of Flying* to his own *Tropic of Cancer*—only "not as bitter and much funnier"—and predicted that "this book will make literary history, that because of it women are going to find their own voice and give us great sagas of sex, life, joy, and adventure."

Isadora's story is continued in *How to Save Your Own Life.* Now a successful author of the very daring and explicit novel *Candida Confesses,* she strikes out on her own after her husband confesses to an affair with another woman early in their marriage. "Despite herb tea and sympathy" from various female friends, said Isa Kapp in *Washington Post Book World,* "her frame of mind is gloomy." Her sexual experiments continue, Kapp added, and include "a Lesbian episode justified as research, and an orgy itemized like the instructions for stuffing a holiday turkey." Isadora leaves her husband and travels to California to visit a movie producer interested in filming her book. There she meets and falls in love with Josh Ace, an aspiring screenwriter some years younger than herself. Convinced that she has found her ideal man, she prepares to settle down. *New York Review of Books* contributor Diane Johnson praised *How to Save Your Own Life* as "a plain, wholesome American story, containing as it does that peculiarly American and purely literary substance Fulfillment, [the] modern equivalent of fairy gold." However, in *New York Times Book Review,* John Leonard found the novel lacking in the "energy and irreverence of *Fear of Flying. . . .* Whereas the author of *Fear of Flying* was looking inside her own head, shuffling her fantasies, and with a manic gusto playing out her hand, the author of *How to Save Your Own Life* is looking over her shoulder, afraid that the critics might be gaining on her."

Some seven years later Isadora's latest romance sours; now almost forty and the mother of a three-year-old girl, she is deserted by Josh. Jong's 1984 novel *Parachutes and Kisses* tells of Isadora's attempt to cope with the pressures and problems of being a single mother, of approaching middle age, and of supporting a household on a writer's income. "It is about having it all in the 1980s," Jong explained to Gil Pyrah of the London *Times*. "Isadora exemplified the 1970s woman and now, in the 1980s, we are trying to be single parents, breadwinners, and feminine at the same time." In the course of her journey toward self-realization, Jong's heroine tours Russia, characteristically encountering a number of sexual adventures on the way. She eventually finds contentment of sorts with a young actor named Bean in the novel, which *Washington Post Book World* reviewer Grace Lichtenstein noted "is funny and searching enough to suggest that *How to Save Your Own Life* was Jong's sophomoric jinx."

Any Woman's Blues, which Jong published in 1990, is linked to the author's previous three novels in that it is presented in an introduction by a fictitious literary scholar as a manuscript left behind by Isadora Wing after she boards an airplane headed for the South Pacific and mysteriously disappears. "I knew I wanted to write a fable of a woman living in the Reagan era of excess and greed and avarice," Jong explained to Lynn Van Matre of *Chicago Tribune* in describing the novel, "an artist at the height of her powers who is hopelessly addicted to a younger man and goes through all the different states of change to get free." Protagonist Leila Sand is a wealthy and successful artist who is obsessed by her unfaithful and manipulative young lover. Focusing on Sand's codependence upon male attention, *Any Woman's Blues* follows Sand's downward spiral into alcoholism, sexual depravity, and drug abuse, coming up for air as she gains a spiritual strength that enables her to take control of her life. By the end of the story, Sand emerges as has Isadora before her: a more self-assured, emotionally integrated, focused person. "Co-dependency is just a trendy term for being a well-socialized woman," Jong explained to Josh Getlin in *Los Angeles Times*. "We're all trained to put other people's needs before our own. We're trained to be validated by what our husbands, children, and lovers think of us. It's not uniquely feminine, but it's considered normal in women, whereas in men it's considered a disease."

In 1994 Jong published *Fear of Fifty: A Midlife Memoir,* described by Lynn Freed in *Washington Post Book World* as "a funny, pungent, and highly entertaining memoir of her growing up, her men, her marriages, her motherhood, her writing, her successes and her failures on all fronts. And she has done so . . . with all her customary candor." The autobiography draws from the drama of the artist's own life, which has caused some critics to comment on the newsworthy Jong's obvious inability to either totally empathize with or reflect a global midlife female consciousness. Several critics have also noted the author's continued defense and reiteration of the sexually liberated attitudes embodied over twenty years earlier in *Fear of Flying*. "Two decades is a long time to go on playing the naughty girl who can sling dirty words and sleep around just like the guys," stated reviewer Nancy Mairs in *New York Times Book Review*. "What might have been outre at age thirty seems passe at age fifty." However, *Fear of Fifty* has been praised for its engaging style: what Roberta Rubenstein lauded in *Chicago Tribune* as a "funny, wise, candid, poignant, brash, painful, soul-baring, occasionally moralistic, but never dull memoir."

Jong's 2003 novel, *Sappho's Leap,* offers a "highly imaginative, sexy, and shrewd interpretation of the life of the first known woman poet, Sappho, who lived on the island of Lesbos 2,600 years ago and wrote and performed poems of indelible candor and eroticism," wrote Donna Seaman in *Booklist*. Sappho, the seventh-century B.C. Greek poet of sensual and sexual verse, is considered by some an early symbol of feminism. Beginning with her teenage years, the book traces Sappho through affairs with both sexes, arranged marriages, intellectual victories, and conversations with the gods. She has an affair with handsome singer Alcaeus who fathers her daughter, Cleis, even though he prefers boys to women. Then, a marriage to a foul and corpulent merchant creates dilemmas for Sappho, but she manages to avoid any consummation. In the end, the book proffers the premise that the seventh-century B.C. Greek poet Sappho did not commit suicide by leaping into the sea, propelled by unrequited love as legend would have it, but instead lived a rich and eventful life of travel, intellectual pursuits, and sexual escapades.

"The result is a vivid and entertaining portrait, but it's so juicily overwritten that one can't help but cringe," remarked Barbara Hoffert in *Library Journal*. Penelope Mesic, writing in *Book* also stated that the book was overwrought. "At least Sappho's frequent, explicit sexual encounters keep the reader turning the pages," wrote a *Publishers Weekly* reviewer. Lorna Koski, writing in *Women's Wear Daily,* concluded that *Sappho's Leap* is "a rollicking, imaginative recreation of her life, times, and writing," with a number of authentic historical figures included in the mix.

In her work, Jong, "creates an energetic, garrulous, witty, and tender verse, both erudite and earthy, about the conflict between sexuality and inhibiting intelligence, about death (and one's impulse both toward and away from suicide), the problems of sexual and creative energy (both consuming and propelling), and the hunger for love, knowledge, and connecting," observed an essayist in *Contemporary Novelists*. "Although she has aligned herself with the feminist movement, her poetry goes beyond the dilemma of being a woman in a male-dominated world, or for that matter, a Jew in an urban culture, to the ubiquitous need for human completeness in a fiercely hostile social and cosmic world."

Within each of Jong's fictional works are "women who are in an ambiguous position, philosophically confused, emotionally overwrought," according to Burke, who maintained that the author uses these women to create "a realistic collage of the woman's situation today." Jong agreed, describing the void she attempted to fill in literature about women to Burke in *Interview:* "Nobody was writing honestly about women and the variousness of their experience." What was missing from the American literary scene, she concluded, was "a thinking woman who also had a sexual life," a woman who could be as heroic as any man. As Peer has observed, Jong's protagonists make it clear "that women and men are less different than literature has led us to believe. With a courage that ranges from deeply serious to devil-may-care, Jong . . . [has] stripped off the pretty masks that women traditionally wear, exposing them as vulgar, lecherous and greedy, frightened and flawed—in short, as bewilderingly human. Sort of like men." For the author, writing such works has been a process of personal self-exposure as well. "It's a very profound self-analysis. It's like meditation," Jong confided to Dana Micucci of *Chicago Tribune.* "I try to tell a certain truth about the interior of my life and other women's lives. If you're writing the kinds of books I write, you come out a changed person."

BIOGRAPHICAL AND CRITICAL SOURCES:

BOOKS

Burstein, Janet Handler, *Writing Mothers, Writing Daughters: Tracing the Maternal in Stories by American Jewish Women,* University of Illinois Press (Urbana, IL), 1996.

Chapple, Steve, and David Talbot, *Burning Desires: Sex in America. A Report from the Field,* Signet (New York, NY), 1990.

Charney, Maurice, *Sexual Fiction,* Methuen (London, England), 1981.

Contemporary Literary Criticism, Thomson Gale (Detroit, MI), Volume 4, 1975, Volume 6, 1976, Volume 8, 1978, Volume 18, 1981, Volume 85, 1994.

Contemporary Novelists, 7th edition, St. James Press (Detroit, MI), 2001.

Cooper-Clark, Diana, *Interviews with Contemporary Novelists,* Macmillan (London, England), 1986.

Dictionary of Literary Biography, Thomson Gale (Detroit, MI), Volume 2: *American Novelists since World War II,* 1978, Volume 5: *American Poets since World War II,* 1980, Volume 28: *Twentieth-Century Jewish-American Fiction Writers,* 1984.

Friedman, Edward H., *The Antiheroine's Voice: Narrative Discourse and Transformations of the Picaresque,* University of Missouri Press (Columbia, MO), 1987.

Greene, Gayle, *Changing the Story: Feminist Fiction and the Tradition,* Indiana University Press (Bloomington, IN), 1991.

Modern American Literature, Volume 2, St. James Press (Detroit, MI), 1999.

Ostriker, Alicia Susan, *Stealing the Language: The Emergence of Women's Poetry in America,* Beacon Press (Boston, MA), 1986.

Packard, William, *The Craft of Poetry: Interviews from the New York Quarterly,* Doubleday (New York, NY), 1974.

Parini, Jay, editor in chief, *American Writers,* Supplement 5, Charles Scribner's Sons (New York, NY), 2000.

Suleiman, Susan Rubin, editor, *The Female Body in Western Culture: Contemporary Perspectives,* Harvard University Press (Cambridge, MA), 1985.

Templin, Charlotte, *Daughters of Valor: Contemporary Jewish American Women Writers,* University of Delaware Press (Newark, DE), 1997.

Templin, Charlotte, *Feminism and the Politics of Literary Reputation: The Example of Erica Jong,* University of Kansas Press (Lawrence, KS), 1995.

Templin, Charlotte, editor, *Conversations with Erica Jong,* University Press of Mississippi (Jackson, MS), 2002.

Todd, Janet, *Women Writers Talking,* Holmes and Meier (New York, NY), 1983.

Walden, Daniel, editor, *Twentieth-Century American-Jewish Fiction Writers,* Thomson Gale (Detroit, MI), 1984.

PERIODICALS

American Spectator, March, 1981, Joshua Gilder, review of *Fanny,* pp. 36-37.

Atlantic, December, 1973, Benjamin DeMott, "Couple Trouble: Mod and Trad," pp. 122-127; April, 1977; November, 1981.

Australian Women's Book Review, September, 1990, Julie Ann Ruth, "Isadora and Fanny, Jessica, and Erica: The Feminist Discourse of Erica Jong."

Book, May-June 2003, Penelope Mesic, review of *Sappho's Leap,* pp. 83-85.

Booklist, November 15, 1999, Bonnie Smothers, Brad Hooper, Kristine Huntley, review of *Fear of Flying,* p. 601; March 1, 2003, Donna Seaman, review of *Sappho's Leap,* p. 1107.

Boston Review, March-April 1992, Charlotte Temple, "The Mispronounced Poet: An Interview with Erica Jong," pp. 5-8, 23, 29.

Centennial Review, summer, 1987, Robert J. Butler, "The Woman Writer as American Picaro: Patterns of Movement in the Novels of Erica Jong," pp. 308-329.

Chicago Sun-Times, July 31, 1997, Susy Schultz, "Jong's Zipping Along," p. 33.

Chicago Tribune, April 25, 1990, Lynn Van Matre, "Every Woman's Blues: Erica Jong Shows Why Every Book 'Should Be a Healing Experience,'" p. 8; April 25, 1993, sec. 6, p. 3; July 31, 1994, sec. 14, p. 3; August 18, 1994, sec. 5, pp. 1-2.

Chicago Tribune Magazine, December 12, 1982.

Christian Science Monitor, October 24, 1984, Merle Rubin, "Diving into the Shallows of Narcissism," review of *Parachutes and Kisses,* pp. 21-22.

Columbia Forum, winter, 1975, Elaine Showalter and Carol Smith, "An Interview with Erica Jong," pp. 12-17.

Commentary, December, 1974, Jane Larkin Crain, "Feminist Fiction," review of *Fear of Flying,* pp. 58-62.

Detroit Free Press, May 17, 1987.

Economist, November 15, 1997, p. 14.

Elle, January, 1990, Margaret Cezair Thompson, review of *Any Woman's Blues,* p. 69.

Encounter, July, 1974; December, 1974.

Feminist Studies, spring, 1998, Molly Hite, "Writing and Reading—The Body: Female Sexuality and Recent Feminist Fiction," pp. 121-142.

Globe and Mail (Toronto, Ontario, Canada), November 24, 1984; November 21, 1987.

Harper's Bazaar, August, 1984.

Hudson Review, autumn, 1990, William M. Pritchard, "Novel Reports," review of *Any Woman's Blues,* pp. 489-498.

International Journal of Women's Studies, May-June, 1978, Joan Reardon, "*Fear of Flying:* Developing the Feminist Novel," pp. 306-320.

Interview, July, 1987, Karen Burke, interview with Erica Jong, pp. 95-96.

Kirkus Reviews, March 1, 2003, review of *Sappho's Leap,* p. 336.

Library Journal, September 1, 1994, p. 202; June 1, 1997, p. 148; July, 2000, Michael Rogers, review of *Witches,* p. 148; April 1, 2003, Barbara Hoffert, review of *Sappho's Leap,* p. 129.

Listener, August 23, 1990, Helen Burth, review of *Any Woman's Blues,* p. 28.

Los Angeles Times, November 4, 1981; May 16, 1987; May 18, 1987; January 22, 1990, pp. E1-2.

Los Angeles Times Book Review, March 20, 1977, Craig Fisher, "Fear of Flying Heroine Flies a New Flight Plan," review of *How to Save Your Own Life,* p. 112; August 17, 1980; June 24, 1984; November 11, 1984; August 21, 1994, pp. 2, 10.

Maclean's, August 21, 1978, Philip Fleishman, interview with Erica Jong, pp. 4-6.

Ms., November, 1980; July, 1981; July, 1986; June, 1987.

National Review, May 24, 1974, Patricia S. Coyne, "Women's Lit," review of *Fear of Flying,* p. 604; April 29, 1977, D. Keith Mano, "The Authoress as Aphid," review of *How to Save Your Own Life,* p. 498.

New Republic, February 2, 1974; September 20, 1980.

New Review, May, 1974.

New Statesman, April 19, 1974, Paul Theroux, "Hapless Organ," p. 554; January 1, 1999, Claire Rayner, review of *What Do Women Want? Bread, Roses, Sex, Power,* pp. 48-49.

Newsweek, November 12, 1973; May 5, 1975; March 28, 1977; November 5, 1984.

New York, June 9, 1975, Alfred Kazin, "The Writer as Sexual Show-off; or, Making Press Agents Unnecessary," pp. 36-40; July 18, 1994, Amy Virshup, "For Mature Audiences Only," pp. 40-47.

New Yorker, December 17, 1973, John Updike, "Jong Love," pp. 149-153; April 4, 1977; October 13, 1980; November 19, 1984.

New York Now, September 10, 1998, Wayne Robbins, "Flying High Again," pp. 17, 48.

New York Review of Books, March 21, 1974; April 28, 1977; November 6, 1980, Clive James, "Fannikin's Cunnikin," review of *Fanny,* p. 25.

New York Times, August 25, 1973; November 6, 1973; September 7, 1974, Henry Miller and Erica Jong, "Two Writers in Praise of Rabelais and Each Other," p. 27; June 11, 1975; March 11, 1977, Christopher Lehmann-Haupt, review of *How to Save Your Own Life,* p. C25; August 4, 1980; August 28, 1980; March 8, 1984; October 10, 1984; September 20, 1996.

New York Times Book Review, August 12, 1973; November 11, 1973; September 7, 1975; March 20,

1977; March 5, 1978; September 2, 1979; August 17, 1980; April 12, 1981; October 31, 1982; July 1, 1984; October 21, 1984; April 19, 1987, Michael Malone, review of *Serenissima*, p. 12; June 5, 1988; January 28, 1990, Benjamin Demott, review of *Any Woman's Blues*, p. 13; February 14, 1993, p. 10; July 24, 1994, p. 6; July 20, 1997, p. 17.

Novel, winter, 1987, James Mandrell, "Questions of Genre and Gender: Contemporary American Versions of the Feminine Picaresque," pp. 149-170.

Observer (London, England), January 31, 1999, review of *What Do Women Want?*, p. 11.

Observer Review, April 21, 1974, Martin Amis, "Isadora's Complaint," review of *Fear of Flying*, p. 37.

Ontario Review, fall-winter, 1975-76.

Parnassus, spring-summer, 1974, Margaret Atwood, pp. 98, 104.

People, May 25, 1987; September 12, 1994, p. 77.

Playboy, September, 1975, Gretchen McNeese, interview with Erica Jong.

Poetry, March, 1974.

Publishers Weekly, February 14, 1977; January 4, 1985; February 22, 1985; June 13, 1994, p. 22; July 4, 1994, p. 48; July 22, 1996, p. 240; May 5, 1997, p. 193; June 3, 2002, John F. Baker, "Jong's Sappho Novel for Norton," review of *Sappho's Leap*, p. 16; April 28, 2003, review of *Sappho's Leap*, pp. 47-48.

Review of Contemporary Fiction, fall, 1993, pp. 242-243.

Revue Française d'Etudes Americaines, November, 1986, Rolande Diot, "Sexus, Nexus, and Taboos versus Female Humor," p. 11.

Rice University Studies, winter, 1978, Jane Chance Nitzsche, "'Isadora Icarus': The Mythic Unity of Erica Jong's *Fear of Flying*," pp. 89-100.

Saturday Review, December 18, 1971; April 30, 1977; August, 1980, Anthony Burgess, review of *Fanny*, pp. 54-55; November, 1981; December, 1981.

Spare Rib, July, 1977, Rozsika Parker and Eleanor Stephens, interview with Erica Jong, pp. 15-17.

Spectator, September 3, 1994, p. 37.

Time, February 5, 1975, Christopher Lehmann-Haupt, "The Loves of Isadora," pp. 69-70; March 14, 1977; June 22, 1987.

Time Out, September 10, 1998, Gia Kourlas, "From Fear to Eternity: Twenty-five Years after *Fear of Flying*, Erica Jong Wonders What Do Women Want?" (interview), p. 208.

Times (London, England), November 27, 1980, Stuart Evans, review of *Fanny*, p. 14; November 2, 1984, Gill Pyrah, "Erica Tries a Parachute" (interview), p 11.

Times Literary Supplement, April 27, 1973; July 26, 1974; May 6, 1977; October 24, 1980; September 18, 1987, Valentine Cunningham, review of *Serenissima*, p. 1025; June 23, 1993, pp. 4-5; October 7, 1994, Wendy Steiner, review of *Fear of Fifty: A Midlife Memoir*, p. 44; March 19, 1999, Mary Margaret McCabe, review of *What do Women Want?*, p. 4.

Toronto Star, November 2, 1997, Judy Stoffman, "Portnoy, Stop Your Complaining. Writer Erica Jong Fights Stereotypes of Jewish Women," p. C4.

Tribune Books (Chicago, IL), June 10, 1979; August 10, 1980; April 5, 1981; October 14, 1984; April 5, 1987; April 25, 1990, pp. 11-13; July 31, 1994, p. 3.

University of Dayton Review, winter, 1986-1986, Francis Baumli, "Erica Jong Revisited, or No Wonder We Men Had Trouble Understanding Feminism," pp. 17-20.

Village Voice Literary Supplement, November 22, 1973, Molly Haskell, review of *Fear of Flying*, p. 27.

Virginia Quarterly Review, summer, 1979.

Viva, September, 1977, interview with Erica Jong.

Wall Street Journal, November 21, 1984, Anita Susan Grossman, "Sorry, Jong Number Three," review of *Parachutes and Kisses*, p. 28.

Washington Post, July 27, 1994, pp. 1, 12.

Washington Post Book World, December 19, 1971; July 6, 1975; March 20, 1977; August 17, 1980, Judith Martin, review of *Fanny*, p. 4; October 21, 1984; April 19, 1987, Joan Aiken, review of *Serenissima*, pp. 4-5; June 6, 1993, pp. 4-5; July 31, 1994, p. 5.

Women's Review of Books, November, 1994, Isabelle de Courtivron, review of *Fear of Fifty: A Midlife Memoir*, pp. 15-16.

Women's Wear Daily, May 14, 2003, Lorna Koski, review of *Sappho's Leap*, p. 20.

Writer's Digest, John Kern, "Erica: Being the True History of Isadora Wing, Fanny Hackabout-Jones, and Erica Jong" (interview), pp. 20-25.

ONLINE

Erica Jong Home Page, http://www.ericajong.com/ (November 13, 2003).

*   *   *

JORGENSEN, Ivar
  See ELLISON, Harlan

*   *   *

JORGENSON, Ivar
  See SILVERBERG, Robert

JUDD, Cyril
See POHL, Frederik

*   *   *

JUNGER, Sebastian 1962-

PERSONAL: Born January 17, 1962, in Boston, MA; son of Miguel (a physicist) and Ellen (an artist; maiden name, Sinclair) Junger. *Education:* Concord Academy, graduated 1980; Wesleyan University, B.A., 1984. *Politics:* Democrat. *Religion:* Atheist.

ADDRESSES: *Home*—88 E. 3rd, Unit 7, New York, NY 10003. *Office*—83 Rivington St., Apt. 3C, New York, NY 10002.

CAREER: Freelance writer.

WRITINGS:

The Perfect Storm: A True Story of Men against the Sea, Norton (New York, NY), 1997.
Frontline Diaries: Into the Forbidden Zone (documentary film), National Geographic Channel, 2001.
Fire, Norton (New York, NY), 2001.
A Death in Belmont, Norton (New York, NY), 2006.

Contributor to periodicals, including *Men's Journal, Outside, American Heritage,* and *New York Times Magazine.*

ADAPTATIONS: *The Perfect Storm* was produced as an audiobook (read by Stanley Tucci) and released by Random House Audio, 1997; *The Perfect Storm* was also adapted for film and released by Warner Brothers, 2000; *Fire* was produced as an audiobook, 2002.

SIDELIGHTS: With his first book, *The Perfect Storm,* Sebastian Junger quickly established himself as a bestselling writer of literary nonfiction, combining the journalist's clarity and eye for detail with the novelist's sense of narrative and drama. *The Perfect Storm* tells the story of a commercial swordfishing boat caught in the grip of a killer storm. The *Andrea Gail,* out of Gloucester, Massachusetts, was fishing the Great Banks of the North Atlantic in October, 1991, when the convergence of three storms from north, south, and west created a tempest of unmatched severity—in meteoro-

logical terms, a "perfect storm." Buffeted by one-hundred-foot waves and winds in excess of eighty-five m.p.h., the seventy-two-foot vessel was destroyed and her crew drowned. Drawing on interviews, radio dialogues, court depositions, and various other sources, Junger depicts a New England fishing community and the dangerous lives of the fishermen with gritty realism, and even recreates what the final harrowing hours of the *Andrea Gail* must have been like. The author also recounts tales of the storm's survivors, including Air National Guard rescue workers forced to abandon their helicopter and ride out the storm at sea.

In addition to exploring the human interest of the events surrounding the sinking of the *Andrea Gail,* Junger offers a great deal of historical and technical information on such topics as the commercial swordfishing industry, the formation of storms, fluid mechanics, naval architecture, and the experience of drowning. Junger's method of fusing large bodies of factual material with the elements of high drama left him open to criticism from a number of perspectives. *New York Observer* critic Warren St. John pointed to what he considered to be errors and omissions in *The Perfect Storm,* accusing the author of distorting the record to make a better story. Junger himself, on the other hand, feared the book would hold little interest for readers more concerned with plot and action than historical accuracy. "I didn't want to invent dialogue or fictionalize or do any of the stuff that readers love," he explained in an interview with Ellen Barry in the *Boston Phoenix.* "I was sure I was condemned to write a journalistically interesting book that just wouldn't fly. It would be too heavy. The topic is too weird and idiosyncratic. It's all the things that kill books."

Nonetheless, *The Perfect Storm* became a best- seller, with movie and paperback rights selling for hefty sums. Junger's desire to write about the fishermen's fate stemmed from having witnessed the 1991 storm first-hand and from having prior experience working a dangerous job, as a high-climber for tree-removal companies. The same love of adventure drew him to a writing career. "I write because it thrills me," he once told *CA.* "I write journalism—not fiction—because it thrusts me out there into the world and I'm so awed by what I find." Junger, who credits Barry Lopez, Joan Didion, Pete Matthiessen, Norman Maclean, and Michael Herr as his primary literary influences, continues to work as a freelance contributor to magazines. "I sit down in the morning with a cup of coffee, edit what I wrote the day before, start in on the next section, stop writing, go running and have lunch, take a nap on the floor (so I don't sleep too long), get up and write for another couple of hours and then go out to a bar and play pool or sit there and just think about what I wrote that day. If it went well I'll have a cigarette, too."

After the publication of *A Perfect Storm,* Junger traveled with Iranian photographer, Reza, into Afghanistan in order to meet Ahmad Shah Massoud, a Taliban resistance leader. The result of their journey was a documentary entitled *Frontline Diaries: Into the Forbidden Zone.* "I'd always wanted to make the pilgrimage into [his] territory to do a profile of him," Junger stated in a *NationalGeographic* online article by Ted Chamberlain. Both journalists spent a month in Afghanistan as guests of the Northern Alliance leader, Massoud, and "visited a refugee camp inhabited by thousands of Afghans who had fled the Taliban regime." *Los Angeles Times* writer Hugh Hart commented that "surreal touches abound" in *Frontline Diaries,* a documentary which "offers sobering footage detailing the hazards of war, Afghan-style." *Hollywood Reporter* contributor Marilyn Moss called it a "fascinating, well-documented and well-mounted look" at the ongoing struggle in Afghanistan. She also noted the "first-rate journalism" that permeates the documentary.

"Junger is an excellent storyteller . . . .[and] observer," said Justin Marozzi in a London *Sunday Telegraph* review of *Fire,* Junger's second book, which is a compilation of previously published magazine articles. Only the first two pieces are actually devoted to firefighting and the personalities engaged in controlling a forceful blaze in the canyons of Idaho. Other articles feature Kashmir terrorists, the war in Kosovo, the last person who harpoons whales by hand, and Ahmed Shah Massoud, the Afghan resistance fighter—and subject of the documentary, *Frontline Diaries*—who was assassinated in September, 2001.

"The essays are short, punchy, full of fascinating factual research and altogether very readable," remarked *New Republic* contributor David Thomson. Thomson's chief criticism of the work was what he viewed as a quality of over-simplification present in Junger's work. *Book* reviewer Chris Barsanti noted that the stories in *Fire* "are marked with a generous humanity and sharpness of eye." Iain Finlayson of the London *Times*wrote that the author's work "is frontline reporting of the highest order from the dangerous, blade-sharp edge of things." "[Junger's] stories . . . hold our interest" even when they are no longer present in the daily news, stated Anthony Brandt in *National Geographic Adventure.* "The jewel [of the book] is the profile of Massoud," wrote a *Business Week* reviewer. In a *Booklist*

article, Joanne Wilkinson commented that the book's "topics are compelling." *Library Journal*contributor Rachel Collins observed the author's "unfailing eye for detail" and for the fact that Junger tries to write his articles in such a way that he includes as many different perspectives as he possibly can. "The prose is clean and hard," said *Guardian*reviewer Steven Poole. London *Sunday Telegraph* critic Marozzi praised Junger's writing style in these words: "He understands, as too many of his colleagues do not, that his surroundings . . . are of more interest to the reader than his reactions to them."

BIOGRAPHICAL AND CRITICAL SOURCES:

PERIODICALS

Book, December 1, 1999, review of audiobook version of *The Perfect Storm: A True Story of Men against the Sea,* p. 718; November-December 2001, Chris Barsanti, review of *Fire,* p. 70.

Booklist, September 1, 2001, Joanne Wilkinson, review of *Fire,* p. 22; March 15, 2002, review of audiobook version of *Fire,* p. 1270.

BookPage, October, 2001, review of *Fire,* p. 2.

Business Week, October 22, 2001, review of *Fire,* p. 22E4.

Detroit Free Press, November 4, 2001, review of *Fire,* p. 4E.

Entertainment Weekly, July 14, 2000, Owen Gleiberman, review of the movie version of *The Perfect Storm,* p. 51; September 28, 2001, review of *Fire,* p. 68.

Globe and Mail (Toronto, Ontario, Canada), October 13, 2001, review of *Fire,* p. D12.

Guardian (London, England), October 19, 2002, Steven Poole, review of *Fire,*p. 30.

Harper's, November, 2001, review of *Fire,* p. 73.

Hollywood Reporter, September 25, 2001, Marilyn Moss, review of *Frontline Diaries: Into the Forbidden Zone,* p. 15.

Kirkus Reviews, August 1, 2001, review of *Fire,* p. 1092.

Kliatt Young Adult Paperback Book Guide, May, 1999, review of *The Perfect Storm,* p. 68.

Library Journal, September 1, 2001, Rachel Collins, review of *Fire,* p. 220; April 1, 2002, Mark Pumphrey, review of audiobook version of *Fire,* p. 160.

Los Angeles Times, September 24, 2001, Hugh Hart, review of *Frontline Diaries,* p. F-11.

National Geographic Adventure, November-December, 2001, Anthony Brandt, review of *Fire,* p. 59.

CONCISE MAJOR 21ST-CENTURY WRITERS

New Republic, November 5, 2001, David Thomson, review of *Fire,* p. 35.

New Yorker, August 11, 1997, p. 79.

New York Observer, August, 1997.

New York Review of Books, December 20, 2001, William McNeill, review of *Fire,* p. 86.

New York Times, October 6, 2001, Caryn James, review of *Frontline Diaries,* p. A13; October 17, 2001, Michiko Kakutani, review of Fire.

New York Times Book Review, June 18, 1997, p. 8; September 29, 2002, Scott Veale, review of *Fire,* p. 32; October 14, 2001, Paula Friedman, review of *Fire,* p. 28.

People, November 5, 2001, review of *Fire,* p. 52.

Publishers Weekly, April 7, 1997, p. 83; September 24, 2001, review of *Fire,* p. 79; September 24, 2001, interview with Sebastian Junger, p. 80.

Sunday Telegraph (London, England), November 11, 2001, Justin Marozzi, review of *Fire.*

Time, July 3, 2000, Richard Corliss, review of the movie version of *The Perfect Storm,* p. 56.

Times (London, England), November 14, 2001, Iain Finlayson, review of *Fire,* p. 12.

Times Literary Supplement, July 18, 1997, p. 8.

Underwater Naturalist, January, 1999, review of *The Perfect Storm,* p. 46.

Us Weekly, July 24, 2000, Oliver Jones, p. 54.

Washington Post, October 12, 2001, Carolyn See, review of *Fire,* p. C04.

Yankee, September, 2000, Robert Pushkar, review of *The Perfect Storm,* pp.66-75.

ONLINE

Boston Phoenix Online, http://www.bostonphoenix.com/ (October 11, 2001), Tamara Wieder, interview with Sebastian Junger.

Literati Web site, http://literati.net/ (May 12, 2003), reviews of *Fire* and *The Perfect Storm.*

National Geographic Web site, http://www.national geographic.com/ (May 12, 2003), Ted Chamberlain, review of *Frontline Diaries.*

K

KARAGEORGE, Michael A.
See ANDERSON, Poul

*   *   *

KARR, Mary 1955-

PERSONAL: Born January, 1955, in TX; daughter of J.P. (an oil refinery worker) and Charlie Marie (an artist and business owner; maiden name, Moore) Karr; married (divorced, c. 1992); children: Devereux Milburn.

ADDRESSES: Office—Department of English, 401 Hall of Languages, Syracuse University, Syracuse, NY 13244. Agent—Amanda Urban, International Creative Management, 40 West 57th St., New York, NY 10019.

CAREER: Writer. Syracuse University, Syracuse, NY, Peck Professor of English. Assistant professor at various institutions, including Tuft University, Emerson College, Harvard University, and Sarah Lawrence College.

AWARDS, HONORS: Mrs. Giles Whiting Writers Award, 1989; fellowship from Mary Ingraham Bunting Institute of Radcliffe College; PEN/Martha Albrand Award, and Carr P. Collins Prize from Texas Institute of Letters, both 1996, and New York Public Library Award, all for The Liar's Club: A Memoir; Best Book citation, Entertainment Weekly, Us, and Amazon.com, 2000, for Cherry; Guggenheim fellowship for poetry, 2004; two-time winner of Pushcart Prize in poetry and essay; state arts grants from Minnesota and Massachusetts; National Endowment of the Arts fellow.

WRITINGS:

Abacus (poetry), Wesleyan University Press (Middletown, CT), 1987.
The Devil's Tour (poetry), New Directions (New York, NY), 1993.
The Liars' Club: A Memoir, Viking (New York, NY), 1995.
Viper Rum: With the Afterword "Against Decoration," New Directions (New York, NY), 1998.
Cherry: A Memoir, Viking (New York, NY), 2000.

Also author of introduction to the new Modern Library edition of T.S. Eliot's The Wasteland. Contributor to periodicals, including Esquire, New Yorker, New York Times, Harper's Bazaar, Allure, Poetry, Parnassus, Ploughshares, Granta, Vogue, American Poetry Review, and Columbia.

SIDELIGHTS: In The Liars' Club: A Memoir, poet and essayist Mary Karr recreates and reflects on her rugged and often traumatic childhood in an industrial town in East Texas. Karr chose not to reveal the name of her home town but refers to it in her book by the fictional name of Leechfield. The work focuses primarily on events that took place between 1961 and 1963, when Karr was seven and eight years old, and the book contains the author's adult musings on her past and her family. In the course of the work, Karr describes mental illness, violence, neglect, and substance abuse. Her mother suffered from mental instability. Her father was a heavy drinker and a storyteller, an oil refinery worker who spent his leisure time at what many women in the small town called the "liars' club," the back room of the local bait shop, where men gathered to socialize and spin yarns. Jonathan Yardley, reviewing the book for the *Washington Post Book World,* called *The Liars' Club* "a beauty" and "a great pleasure to read." Louisa Ermelino described the work in *People* as "astonishing," and Michiko Kakutani in the *New York Times* lauded it as "extraordinary" and "one of the most dazzling and moving memoirs to come along in years." Molly Ivins, in her review for *Nation,* called the book "quite simply wonderful."

Reviewers have praised Karr's particular use of language, especially her command of East Texas colloquialisms, but also the poetic quality of her prose. "Her most powerful tool is her language, which she wields with the virtuosity of both a lyric poet and an earthy, down-home Texan," maintained Kakutani, who added, "It's a skill used . . . in the service of a wonderfully unsentimental vision that redeems the past even as it recaptures it on paper." According to Cyra McFadden in the *Los Angeles Times Book Review,* Karr "has a flawless ear for the salty, folksy East Texas dialect that she learned at her daddy's knee. . . . The language of *The Liars' Club* crackles with energy and wit." Asserted Elizabeth Young in a review for *New Statesman and Society,* "The book's rhythm is deceptively oral, seemingly circuitous when it is tightly structured. One's attention never flags. Karr's control of the drawling East Texas demotic . . . is spectacular." Wrote Ivins: "I have always claimed that being a literate Texan is like being bilingual, and Mary Karr is a perfect example of that bilingualism. She can switch from Yeats to Coonass without a pause, from down-home similes about dog shit to Ezra Pound. . . . To have a poet's precision of language and a poet's gift for understanding emotion and a poet's insight into people applied to one of the roughest, toughest, ugliest places in America is an astounding event."

Karr's use of humor is another aspect of her work often lauded by critics. "This is such a captivating book, at once hilarious and heartfelt, that you don't have to believe every word to love it," stated McFadden of the *Liars' Club.* "The way some people are born with perfect pitch, Karr . . . is blessed with a sense of humor that allows her to see whatever happens to her, good, bad or terrible, as just one more example of chaos theory at work." Sheila Ballantyne, writing in the *New York Times Book Review,* found a sense of anguish behind Karr's artistic achievement. "At times," the critic wrote, "it feels as if the book itself were trying to decide whether it can reasonably contain all that [Karr] needs to discover, and all that she needs to let go in order to become her own creation. . . . Not the least of her assets in this quest is her haunting, often exquisite phrasing of

states of being and qualities of mind that resonate long after a page is turned. . . . In the end, it is her toughness of spirit, as well as her poetry, her language, her very voice, that are the agents of rebirth that accompany her on this difficult, hard-earned journey." *The Liars' Club* spent nearly sixty weeks on the bestseller lists and sold more than half million copies in the United States.

In an interview for *Beatrice,* Karr was asked by Ron Hogan if she was surprised at the success of *The Liars' Club.* Karr responded: "I didn't believe it. My publishers were guardedly optimistic, but it seemed insane to me that they even thought they were going to earn back any of the money they'd given me. I was actually trying to talk them into doing a lower print run because I had this terrible feeling that they'd given me this money I could buy a used Toyota with and they were going to print all these copies they'd have to pulp and . . . they'd be mad. You know, if you've been a poet for 20 years in America, don't expect anybody to read anything you write." Shortly thereafter, however, the book had sold more than half a million copies.

The book's sequel, *Cherry,* deals with Karr's adolescence in the same small Texas town. The project proved difficult, Karr told *Publishers Weekly,* partly because "there's no language for talking about female adolescence. . . . I had to invent it; I wrote 500 pages and threw them away before I started approaching a voice that I thought was true." Another problem was the limitation of memory—with tongue-in-cheek, Karr has said that she was so immersed in drugs during that time that she can't remember what happened. Nevertheless, her narrative captures the simultaneously self-centered and insecure world of teenage girls as they experience falling in love and a yearning for independence from family and home town.

In the *New York Times Book Review,* Sara Mosle wrote that "If *The Liars' Club* succeeded partly because of its riveting particularity, *Cherry* succeeds because of its universality. The first book is about one harrowing childhood, the second about every adolescence. Karr's talent doesn't depend on the specifics of her autobiography. She can turn even the most mundane events—a first kiss, an altercation with a school principal—into gorgeous prose." Kakutani likewise commented that Karr "proves herself as fluent in evoking the common ground of adolescence as she did in limning her anomalous girlhood. . . . As she did in *The Liars' Club,* Ms. Karr combines a poet's lyricism and a Texan's down-home vernacular with her natural storytelling gift. Some of her stories are nostalgic for a vanished time and place; some are scathing in their evocation of an insular world; some are just plain funny." *Entertainment Weekly* correspondent Lisa Schwarzbaum wrote that "In this remembrance of blooming, Karr continues to set the literary standard for making the personal universal."

At age eleven, in the only journal Karr ever kept, she wrote that she wanted to publish books, "one-half poetry and one-half autobiography." Although she is better known for her memoirs, it was as a poet that she first established herself in the literary community. Her first volume of poetry, *Abacus,* was characterized by *New England Review* contributor Richard Katrovas as "among other things, a book of passionate friendship," treating women's issues and other personal concerns. Katrovas elaborated: "The sadness that films Mary Karr's vision seems not at all the milky sadness of melancholy, for she convincingly portrays a courage not to submit to her own darkness, acknowledging the terrors of a random universe and that the only stays against those terrors are soulfully construed meanings, the games we invent for the sake of private, fleeting, order." Karr's second poetry collection, *The Devil's Tour,* was also lauded by critics who again noted her ability to avoid excessive sentimentality and melodrama in her poems about the human condition. In his review in *Poetry,* David Barber asserted: "Avowedly unsentimental, Karr doesn't overcompensate by striking exaggerated poses of disabused wisdom or affecting mandarin disdain for the muddle of human relations. . . . Hers are the measured lamentations of a writer who will always side with the painful certitude over the wishful thought."

Critics once again praised Karr's particular use of language in her poetry. A *Publishers Weekly* contributor noted Karr's "delicate and meticulous control of detail" in *The Devil's Tour,* and *Library Journal* contributor Ellen Kaufman characterized the poems in *The Devil's Tour* as "movingly adept," applauding Karr's ability to write "natural-sounding formal meter." This blend of evocative language and emotional tone drew particular notice from Leslie Ullman in a *Poetry* review of the daring collection, *Viper Rum.* Ullman declared: "Karr's third collection probes, without sentimentality or loss of vitality, autobiographical material she has handled in previous collections and in her celebrated memoir, *The Liars' Club.*" Kaufman, in *Library Journal,* maintained that the work in *Viper Rum* is "confessional writing that conjures up the physical world." Ullman contended that the poems in *Viper Rum* "affirm human gestures towards life by highlighting them as gestures. . . . Karr peers beyond illusions of safety and is energized by the shadows out there, the persistent and unanswerable questions."

Reflecting upon her aspirations as an author, Karr told an interviewer for *Publishers Weekly:* "Public readings and the oral tradition [are] important to me. An aesthetic experience is fine, but unless someone is infused with feeling from a work of art, it's totally without conviction. My idea of art is, you write something that makes people feel so strongly that they get some conviction about who they want to be or what they want to do. It's morally useful not in a political way, but it makes your heart bigger; it's emotionally and spiritually empowering."

BIOGRAPHICAL AND CRITICAL SOURCES:

PERIODICALS

Entertainment Weekly, October 13, 2000, Lisa Schwarzbaum, "Teen Spirited," p. 72.

Library Journal, May 1, 1993, Ellen Kaufman, review of *The Devil's Tour,* pp. 88, 90; September 15, 1995, p. 84; July, 1998, Ellen Kaufman, review of *Viper Rum,* p. 93.

Los Angeles Times Book Review, July 16, 1995, Cyra McFadden, review of *The Liars' Club: A Memoir,* pp. 1, 12.

Nation, July 3, 1995, Molly Ivins, review of *The Liars' Club,* p. 21.

New England Review, spring, 1989, Richard Katrovas, review of *Abacus,* pp. 340-350.

New Statesman and Society, October 20, 1995, Elizabeth Young, review of *The Liars' Club,* pp. 39-40.

Newsweek, October 2, 2000, Malcolm Jones, "Bobby Socks, Hard Knocks: Mary Karr Takes on Teens," p. 74.

New York Review of Books, November 2, 2000, Joyce Carol Oates, review of *Cherry,* p. 30.

New York Times, May 26, 1995, Michiko Kakutani, review of *The Liars' Club,* p. C28; June 27, 1995, Dinita Smith, "Gritty Book Sets Prudence Aside," Karr discusses *The Liars' Club,* pp. B1, B4; September 26, 2000, Michiko Kakutani, "The Carefully Examined American Life, Continued."

New York Times Book Review, July 9, 1995, Sheila Ballantyne, review of *The Liars' Club,* p. 8; October 22, 2000, Sara Mosle, "Highway out of Town," p. 10.

People, July 17, 1995, Louisa Ermelino, review of *The Liars' Club,* p. 28.

Poetry, June 1994, David Barber, review of *The Devil's Tour,* pp. 164-167; February, 1999, Leslie Ullman, review of *Viper Rum,* p. 314.

Publishers Weekly, March 15, 1993, review of *The Devils' Tour,* p. 81; March 30, 1998, review of *Viper Rum,* p. 78; August 28, 2000, review of *Cherry,* p. 62; October 2, 2000, Wendy Smith, "Mary Karr: A Life Saved by Stories," p. 52.

Texas Monthly, October, 2000, Don Graham, "The Pits," p. 70.

Time, October 23, 2000, Paul Gray, "Texas Teen: A New Memoir from the Author of *The Liar's Club,*" p. C89.

Washington Post Book World, June 18, 1995, Jonathan Yardley, review of *The Liars' Club,* p. 3.

ONLINE

Beatrice Web site, http://www.beatrice.com/interviews/karr/ (August 4, 2004), Ron Hogan, "Everybody Thinks the Title Is Ironic, but I Mean It Completely Sincerely" (interview with Karr).

BookPage.com, http://www.bookpage.com/ (October 18, 2000), Ellen Kanner, "Mary Karr: Remembering the Agonies and Ecstasies of Adolescence."

Salon.com, http://www.salon.com/ (May 25, 1997), Dwight Garner, "A Scrappy Little Beast: Mary Karr Talks about the Ongoing Success of *The Liars' Club,* the Memoir Backlash and Settling Scores"; (August 4, 1998), Stephanie Zacharek, review of *Viper Rum.*

*   *   *

KASTEL, Warren
  See SILVERBERG, Robert

*   *   *

KAUFMAN, Moises 1963-

PERSONAL: Born November 21, 1963, in Venezuela.

ADDRESSES: Office—Tectonic Theater Project, 204 West 84th Street, New York, NY 10024. *E-mail*—info@thelecturebureau.com.

CAREER: Tectonic Theater Project, New York, NY, founder, artistic director; 42nd Street Collective, directing teacher. Director of plays, including *I Am My Own Wife, Women in Beckett, In the Winter of Cities, The Nest,* and *Marlowe's Eyes.*

MEMBER: Thespis.

AWARDS, HONORS: Lucille Lortel Award for Best Play, Outer Critics Circle Award for Best Off-Broadway Play, Garland Award for Best Play, Carbonell Award for Best Play, Circle Award for Direction, Bay Area Theater Critics, GLAAD Media Award for New York Theater, and Joe A. Callaway Award for Direction, Society of Stage Directors and Choreographers, all for *Gross Indecency;* Artist of the Year, Casa del Artista, 1999; Guggenheim fellowship in playwriting, 2002; Obie for Best Director, 2004; Tony nomination for Best Director, 2004.

WRITINGS:

Gross Indecency: The Three Trials of Oscar Wilde, Vintage Books (New York, NY), 1998.

The Laramie Project, Vintage Books (New York, NY), 2001.

ADAPTATIONS: The Laramie Project was adapted for film for HBO.

SIDELIGHTS: Moises Kaufman is a playwright, director, and founder of the Tectonic Theater Project. In his first published book, *Gross Indecency: The Three Trials of Oscar Wilde,* Kaufman tells the story of well-known British playwright Oscar Wilde's trials, resulting from his homosexuality. In 1895 Wilde was arrested, went through three trials, and was imprisoned for two years for what was called the gross indecency of sodomy. When he was released from prison he was shunned by many in his community and died shortly after. *Time* contributor Richard Zoglin called the book "A surprise success." *Gross Indecency* "rivals the best work of the season," observed Greg Evans in a *Variety* review.

The Laramie Project, a play by Kaufman that was later adapted as an Home Box Office (HBO) film, is set in Laramie, Wyoming. It is an re-enactment of interviews Kaufman and the members of Tectonic Theater Project conducted with the people of Laramie a month after twenty-one-year-old gay student Matthew Shepard was murdered in 1998 by two local men. *Hollywood Reporter* contributor Kirk Honeycutt concluded, "*The Laramie Project* achieves an intimacy that is heartfelt and deeply unsettling." *Backstage.com* contributor Victor Gluck called *The Laramie Project* "the most ambitious and powerful new American play of the past year."

BIOGRAPHICAL AND CRITICAL SOURCES:

PERIODICALS

Advocate, March 3, 1998, Luis Alfaro, "Oscar in America," p. 62; August 14, 2001, "Moises Kaufman," p. 81.
American Theatre, November, 1997, Jesse McKinley, "As Far as He Could Go," p. 24.
Back Stage, September 30, 1994, Dan Isaac, review of *The Nest,* p. 44; March 3, 2000, Sandra C. Dillard, "Denver," p. 44; June 2, 2000, Victor Gluck, review of *The Laramie Project,* p. 56; February 2, 2001, Sandra C. Dillard, "Denver," p. 49.
Back Stage West, June 14, 2001, Jean Schiffman, "Audience Rating," p. 6; August 16, 2001, Charlene Baldridge, review of *The Laramie Project,* p. 16.
Booklist, September 1, 2001, Jack Helbig, review of *The Laramie Project,* p. 43.
Daily Variety, January 14, 2002, Dennis Harvey, review of *The Laramie Project,* p. 13; March 11, 2002, Bill Higgins, Lily Oei, "High Drama from HBO," p. 35.
Gay & Lesbian Review Worldwide, fall, 2000, Allen Ellenzweig, "Current Event Theater," p. 64.
Hollywood Reporter, January 14, 2002, Kirk Honeycutt, review of *The Laramie Project,* p. 20; March 14, 2002, "Moises Kaufman Has Signed with ICMW," p. 24.
Lambda Book Report, January, 2002, Krandall Kraus, "Reality TV Comes to the Stage," p. 23.
Library Journal, September 1, 2001, Howard Miller, review of *The Laramie Project,* p. 179.
Nation, July 28, 1997, Laurie Stone, review of *Gross Indecency: The Three Trials of Oscar Wilde,* p. 34.
New Leader, June 2, 1997, Stefan Kanfer, review of *Gross Indecency,* p. 22.
New Republic, July 7, 1997, Robert Brustein, review of *Gross Indecency,* p. 28; June 19, 2000, Robert Brustein, "On Theater—The Staged Documentary," p. 29.
New Yorker, June 9, 2003, John Lahr, review of *I Am My Own Wife,* p. 106.
New York Times, November 22, 1991, Mel Gussow, "Listen to the Women of Beckett," p. C17; May 28, 2003, Bruce Weber, review of *I Am My Own Wife,* p. E1.
School Library Journal, November, 2001, Emily Lloyd, review of *The Laramie Project,* p. 194.
Time, June 16, 1997, Richard Zoglin, review of *Gross Indecency,* p. 75.
Variety, June 9, 1997, Greg Evans, review of *Gross Indecency,* p. 88; May 22, 2000, Charles Isherwood, review of *The Laramie Project,* p. 37; January 14, 2002, Dennis Harvey, review of *The Laramie Project,* p. 49.

ONLINE

HBO Web site, http://www.hbo.com/ (June 4, 2002), "Moises Kaufman Writer/Director"; review of *The Laramie Project.*
Tectonic Theater Project, Inc., http://www.tectonictheaterproject.org/ (June 4, 2002).
Time Online, http://www.time.com/ (June 4, 2002), "Q & A: Moises Kaufman."

*   *   *

KAVANAGH, Dan
See BARNES, Julian

*   *   *

KAYE, Mary Margaret
See KAYE, M.M.

*   *   *

KAYE, M.M. 1908-2004
(Mollie Hamilton, Mary Margaret Kaye, Mollie Kaye)

PERSONAL: Born August 21, 1908, in Simla, India; died January 29, 2004, in Lavenham, England; married Godfrey John Hamilton (an army officer), 1942 (died, 1985); children: Carolyn. *Education:* Attended schools in England.

CAREER: Writer and painter.

MEMBER: Royal Society of London (fellow).

WRITINGS:

HISTORICAL NOVELS

Shadow of the Moon, Messner (New York, NY), 1956, expanded edition, St. Martin's Press (New York, NY), 1979.

Trade Wind, Coward, McCann (New York, NY), 1963, revised edition, St. Martin's Press (New York, NY), 1981.

The Far Pavilions, St. Martin's Press (New York, NY), 1978.

MYSTERIES

Six Bars at Seven, Hutchinson (London, England), 1940.

Death Walked in Kashmir, Staples Press (London, England), 1953, published as *Death in Kashmir,* St. Martin's Press (New York, NY), 1984.

Death Walked in Berlin, Staples Press (London, England), 1955, published as *Death in Berlin,* St. Martin's Press (New York, NY), 1983.

Death Walked in Cyprus, Staples Press (London, England), 1956, published as *Death in Cyprus,* St. Martin's Press (New York, NY), 1984.

Later Than You Think, Longman (London, England), 1958, published under pseudonym Mollie Hamilton, Coward, McCann (New York, NY), 1959, published as *It's Later Than You Think,* World (Manchester, England), 1960, published as *Death in Kenya,* St. Martin's Press (New York, NY), 1983.

House of Shade, Coward, McCann (New York, NY), 1959, published as *Death in Zanzibar,* St. Martin's Press (New York, NY), 1983.

Night on the Island, Longman (London, England), 1960, published as *Death in the Andamans,* St. Martin's Press (New York, NY), 1985.

Three Complete Novels (contains *Death in Kenya, Death in Zanzibar,* and *Death in Cyprus),* Wings Books (New York, NY), 1994.

CHILDREN'S BOOKS; UNDER PSEUDONYM MOLLIE KAYE

(And illustrator) *The Animals' Vacation,* New York Graphic Society (New York, NY), 1964.

(And illustrator) *The Ordinary Princess,* Kestrel (London, England), 1980, Doubleday (New York, NY), 1984.

Thistledown, Quartet (London, England), 1982.

Also author of "Potter Pinner" series, including *Potter Pinner Meadow,* illustrated by Margaret Tempest, *Black Bramble Wood, Willow Witches Brook,* and *Gold Gorse Common,*) Collins (London, England), 1937-1945.

OTHER

(Illustrator and adaptor) *The Far Pavilions Picture Book,* Bantam (New York, NY), 1979.

(Editor) Emily Bayley and Thomas Metcalf, *The Golden Calm: An English Lady's Life in Moghul Delhi,* Viking (New York, NY), 1980.

(Editor) Rudyard Kipling, *Moon of Other Days: M.M. Kaye's Kipling: Favourite Verses,* Hodder & Stoughton (London, England), 1988, Salem House (Scranton, PA), 1989.

(Editor and author of foreword) Rudyard Kipling, *Picking Up Gold and Silver: Stories,* St. Martin's Press (New York, NY), 1989, published as *Picking Up Gold and Silver: A Selection of Kipling's Short Stories,* Macmillan (London, England), 1989.

(Author of foreword) Rudyard Kipling, *The Complete Verse,* Kyle Cathie (London, England), 1990.

The Sun in the Morning: My Early Years in India and England, St. Martin's Press (New York, NY), 1990.

Golden Afternoon (autobiography), Viking (London, England), 1997, St. Martin's Press (New York, NY), 1998.

Enchanted Evening (autobiography), Viking (New York, NY), 1999.

Also author of *Strange Island,* published by Thacker. Author of radio play *England Wakes,* 1941.

ADAPTATIONS: *The Far Pavilions* was produced as a miniseries by Home Box Office in 1984.

SIDELIGHTS: In 1978 British writer M.M. Kaye made publishing history with her novel *The Far Pavilions,* an historical romance set in nineteenth-century India. Previously a successful author of children's books and mysteries, Kaye set these genres aside to concentrate on this historical romance novel, and after fourteen years and a grueling battle against cancer, she finished the book, which has since been compared to *Gone with the Wind* and other classics of the genre. The book ultimately sold over fifteen million copies in sixteen languages and was adapted for a series of television films.

The Far Pavilions gives readers a detailed look at life in colonial India. It is a subject on which Kaye was well qualified to write, for she was born in Simla, India, into a British family that had already lived in that country for two generations. Although she was educated in England, Kaye returned to India after her schooling and married a British army officer. While she was thus a part of the ruling class in colonial India, Kaye was especially praised for creating an even-handed portrayal of both the native Indians and the English colonists. Brigitte Weeks wrote in the *Washington Post Book World* that *The Far Pavilions* is so powerful, its "readers . . . cannot ever feel quite the same about either the Indian subcontinent or the decrepit history of the British Empire."

The Far Pavilions has been compared to, among other books, Rudyard Kipling's *Kim*. Like Kipling's novel, Kaye's book features a young British boy, Ash, who is orphaned, then raised as an Indian and a Hindu. Ash is sent to live with aristocratic relatives in England when his parentage is finally revealed. Later, he returns to India as a soldier and finds himself torn between his two heritages. While some critics dismiss Kaye's plot as standard romantic-adventure fare, others praise her for skillfully combining Ash's adventures with an accurate historical account of the events between the Indian Mutiny and the Second Afghan War. Furthermore, emphasized *Spectator* contributor Francis King, Kaye possessed a "gift for narrative"; he found *The Far Pavilions* "absorbing" in spite of its more than nine hundred pages. A *New Yorker* writer concurred that Kaye was "a topnotch storyteller and historian," proving these skills in *The Far Pavillions* as she "holds the reader in thrall."

Most critics have pointed to Kaye's comprehensive vision of nineteenth-century India as the key to her novel's success. As *Times Literary Supplement* reviewer Theon Wilkinson explained: Kaye "writes with the conviction that events must be told in their fullness or not at all, that ever[y] facet of information touching the characters must be embraced; and *The Far Pavilions* is a great oriental pot-pourri from which nothing is left out: Indian lullabies; regimental bawdy songs; regimental history, wars and campaigns; weddings; funerals; poisonous plants—a tribute to much painstaking research, some drawn from original diaries and journals. . . . The length of the book is a challenge but the effort is rewarded." And Rahul Singh wrote in *Punch*, "There is none of the romantic sentimentality that saw India as a country of snake charmers and bejewelled princes, with the faithful Gunga Din thrown in. Nor the view of it as one vast, multiplying, putrefying sewer for which there was no possible hope. Ms. Kaye sees India as many Indians do, and for this one must applaud her."

Before publishing *The Far Pavilions*, Kaye had written two other books that are similar in theme. *Shadow of the Moon* dramatizes the events of the Indian Mutiny of 1857 through the story of an orphaned Anglo-Spanish heiress sent to India to marry a man she does not know but to whom she has been betrothed since childhood. *Trade Wind* is set in Zanzibar instead of India, but like *Shadow of the Moon* and *The Far Pavilions*, it exam-

ines two cultures in conflict while telling the exciting story of a young abolitionist from Massachusetts who is kidnaped by a handsome slave trader when she travels to Zanzibar. Neither book was particularly successful when first published, but when reissued after the publication of *The Far Pavilions*, both *Shadow of the Moon* and *Trade Wind* became best-sellers. Like *The Far Pavilions*, they have been praised for their fine descriptions of exotic settings.

Reviewing *Shadow of the Moon* for the *New York Herald Tribune*, David Tilden stated that the book is "filled with excitement and suspense, but the story of India itself will have even greater fascination for many readers [because] . . . Kaye pictures its welter of races, religions, ideals and superstitions; its fragrances and stench, beauty and horror." While also praising Kaye's portrait of India and its history, Nicholas Shrimpton in the *New Statesman* found some of the novelist's characterizations wanting, particularly with regard to the hero of the book, Alex Winter. According to Shrimpton: "When his [Alex's] mighty brain isn't predicting the next hundred years of Indian history, his mighty body is wrestling with sharks or saving the Raj single-handed. If you can tolerate a bionic tailor's dummy for a hero, however, the local colour is terrific." In marked contrast, Walter Shapiro, reviewing *Trade Wind* for the *Washington Post Book World*, had no problem with Kaye's characterizations, or anything else about the book. While granting that its story line might seem conventional, he felt that *Trade Wind* "transcends such easy labels as romance or exotic historical novel. It is a sophisticated treat for those traditional readers who favor good writing, subtle character development, clever plotting and a slightly ironic narrative tone."

Assessing *The Far Pavilions*, *Shadow of the Moon*, and *Trade Wind* for *Twentieth-Century Romance and Historical Writers*, Pamela Cleaver stated: "All three books are long and move at a stately pace. . . . descriptions are graphic and lyrical, the characters lively and well drawn. . . . the final outcome of these romances is predictable, the twists and turns of the plot are not. The writing is of a high quality and the books are extremely enjoyable." Cleaver further advised recommended the books for readers who "want to be immersed in the sights, sounds, and scents of the gorgeous East, to understand the thoughts of mid-Victorian men and women, [and] to enjoy lush, melodramatic romance against a background of authentic history."

Though overshadowed by the success of her historical fiction, Kaye's mystery novels comprised a significant portion of her creative output. Overall critical response to her mysteries in large part paralleled the response to her historicals: universal acclaim for the physical and social environments she crafted, and a more mixed response with regard to her plots and characterizations. *Later Than You Think* —published in the United States as *Death in Kenya*—takes place in Kenya shortly after the Mau-Mau uprising. Anthony Boucher, writing in the *New York Times,* described the novel as "a perfectly conventional whodunit of the feminine persuasion . . . redeemed by its setting." Likewise, a reviewer for the *Times Literary Supplement* felt that Kaye's imagination in the book was more taken with the "Kenya scene and the love-interest . . . than . . . the detective-work necessitated by the plot." Reviewing *House of Shade*— released in the United States as *Death in Zanzibar*—for the *Spectator,* Christopher Pym echoed such sentiments. He described the book as a "long, and long-drawn-out murder story distinguished by its Zanzibar setting . . . with some of the appeal of a good travel brochure."

Kaye also enjoyed considerable success with the three-part publication of her memoirs. *The Sun in the Morning: My Early Years in India and England* was published in 1990, followed by *Golden Afternoon* in 1997, and *Enchanted Evening* in 1999. Several reviewers cautioned that Kaye's memoirs are hardly a representative picture of life in India during the Raj. Her story is highly personal and she does not reflect on the political issues of the day. A *Contemporary Review* writer called *The Sun in the Morning* "a pleasant tale of an India that never was—except as an elderly lady recalls a privileged childhood, and as the passing of the years dims all discordant notes. . . . Kaye can—though rarely— add a touch of acid. But for the most part this is 'roses everywhere,' a tale of sugar and spice and all things sweet-scented." *Publishers Weekly* reviewer Genevieve Stuttaford concurred that *The Sun in the Morning* is "written with gushing, romantic enthusiasm," but nonetheless found much to recommend the "kaleidoscopic story of a long-lost innocence just before and after World War I." Kaye's glowing memories of India stand in sharp contrast to the grim picture she paints of her exile to England. *The Sun in the Morning* ends with the family anticipating a return to India. Kaye's young adult years there are related in *Golden Afternoon,* which also details the Kaye's sojourn in China. Raleigh Trevelyan, a writer for the *Times Literary Supplement,* advised that "the book ends with a promise to return to her beloved India: the subject, one hopes, of volume three of these memoirs."

Kaye's promise was kept with *Enchanted Evening,* which takes up her story in 1932 when Kaye was in her early twenties, and ends with her engagement in the 1940s. David Pitt, writing in *Booklist,* felt that while it might help to read the first two volumes of Kaye's autobiography before taking on this third title, it was not essential. "Kaye is such a good storyteller," Pitt wrote, "and her memories are so rich in detail, that the individual volumes of her saga can stand on their own." *Library Journal*'s Carol A. McAllister also had praise for this third installation of memoir, noting that Kaye's "affection for India is apparent in her lush, detailed descriptions of the country's natural beauty." And a reviewer for *Publishers Weekly,* while conceding that Kaye's memories of British imperialism "often seem remote, decadent, and even unjust," also found that "readers who enjoy tales about the halcyon days of the British Empire will be charmed." Kaye died in England in 2004 at the age of ninety-five. At the time of her death, she was busy collaborating on a musical adaptation of one of her novels.

BIOGRAPHICAL AND CRITICAL SOURCES:

BOOKS

Contemporary Literary Criticism, Volume 28, Thomson Gale (Detroit, MI), 1984.
Twentieth-Century Romance and Historical Writers, St. James Press (Detroit, MI), 1994.

PERIODICALS

Booklist, December 15, 2000, David Pitt, review of *Enchanted Evening,* p. 780.
Chapter One, May-June, 1979.
Christian Science Monitor, November 13, 1978.
Contemporary Review, February, 1991, review of *The Sun in the Morning: My Early Years in India and England,* p. 112.
Cosmopolitan, December,1 980, Jane Clapperton, review of *The Golden Calm: An English Lady's Life in Moghul Delhi,* p. 20; August, 1981, Jane Clapperton, review of *Trade Wind,* p. 24; June, 1984, Carol E. Rinzler, review of *Death in Cyprus,* p. 54.
Detroit News, October 7, 1979.
Economist, December 26, 1981, review of *Thistledown,* p. 106.
Horn Book, November, 1984, Nancy C. Hammond, review of *The Ordinary Princess,* p. 758.
Library Journal, June 15, 1981, review of *Trade Wind,* p. 1322; April 1, 1983, review of *Death in Zanzibar,* p. 761; October 1, 1990, V. Louise Saylor, review of *The Sun in the Morning,* p. 96; May 15,

1991, Jeffrey R. Luttrell, review of *Rudyard Kipling: The Complete Verse*, p. 83; December, 2000, Carol A. McAllister, review of *Enchanted Evening*, p. 132.

Los Angeles Magazine, September, 1981, Mark Wheeler, review of *Trade Wind*, p. 259.

Los Angeles Times, November 2, 1980; October 9 1984; May 23, 1986.

Maclean's, September 24, 1979.

National Review, May 16, 1980, Christina Steadman, review of *Shadow of the Moon*, p. 616.

New Statesman, October 1, 1979; October 12, 1979; November 14, 1980, Rosemary Stones, review of *The Ordinary Princess*, p. 20.

Newsweek, September 11, 1978.

New York, April 23, 1984, John Leonard, review of *The Far Pavilions*, p. 91.

New Yorker, October 9, 1978; September 24, 1979; March 2, 1981, review of *The Golden Calm*, p. 126; July 27, 1981, review of *Trade Wind*, p. 86.

New York Herald Tribune Book Review, September 1, 1957; September 20, 1959.

New York Times, October 26, 1958, p. 57; December 3, 1978; March 25, 1979.

New York Times Book Review, November 18, 1979; August 31, 1980, review of *Shadow of the Moon*, p. 19; March 4, 1984, review of *Death in Zanzibar*, p. 34; December 16, 1984, Richard Smith, review of *Death in Kashmir*, p. 26; August 25, 1985, Miriam Berkley, review of *Death in Berlin*, p. 16; August 17, 1990, Genevieve Stuttaford, review of *The Sun in the Morning*, p. 57; September 30, 1990, Geoffrey C. Ward, review of *The Sun in the Morning*, p. 14.

Parents' Magazine, November, 1984, Alice Siegel, review of *The Ordinary Princess*, p. 56.

People, November 20, 1978; May 16, 1983, review of *Death in Zanzibar*, p. 16.

Publishers Weekly, June 25, 1979; August 15, 1980, review of *The Golden Calm*, p. 49; May 8, 1981, Barbara A. Bannon, review of *Trade Wind*, p. 249; June 3, 1983, review of *Death in Kenya*, p. 64; August 3, 1984, review of *Death in Kashmir*, p. 55; April 26, 1985, Sybil Steinberg, review of *Death in Berlin*, p. 69; April 4, 1986, Sybil Steinberg, review of *Death in the Andamans*, p. 52; August 17, 1990, review of *The Sun in the Morning*, p. 57; October 25, 1999, p. 55; November 27, 2000, review of *Enchanted Evening*, p. 66.

Punch, November 14, 1979, Rahul Singh, review of *The Far Pavilions*.

School Library Journal, March, 1985, Linda Amers-Boman, review of *The Ordinary Princess*, p. 168.

Sewanee Review, summer, 1980.

Spectator, April 12, 1957; July 24, 1959, p. 118; September 9, 1978, Francis King, review of *The Far Pavilions*.

Teen, December, 1980, Linda E. Watson, review of *Shadow of the Moon*, p. 45.

Time, April 16, 1984, Richard Stengel, review of *The Far Pavilions*, p. 70.

Times Literary Supplement (London, England), April 19, 1957; August 22, 1958, p. 469; September 22, 1978, November 21, 1980; March 26, 1982; December 19, 1997, Raleigh Trevelyan, review of *Golden Afternoon*, p. 23.

Washington Post, September 11, 1979; April 21, 1984.

Washington Post Book World, September 10, 1978; July 12, 1981, Walter Shapiro, review of *Trade Wind*; November 11, 1984.

OBITUARIES:

PERIODICALS

Europe Intelligence Wire, February 6, 2004.

Guardian, February 4, 2004, p. 25.

Independent, February 5, 2004, p. 18.

Time (London, England), February 16, 2004, p. 23.

*   *   *

KAYE, Mollie
   See KAYE, M.M.

*   *   *

KEILLOR, Garrison 1942-
(Gary Edward Keillor)

PERSONAL: Born Gary Edward Keillor, August 7, 1942, in Anoka, MN; son of John Philip (a railway mail clerk and carpenter) and Grace Ruth (a homemaker; maiden name, Denham) Keillor; married Mary C. Guntzel, September 1, 1965 (divorced, May, 1976); married Ulla Skaerved (a social worker), December 29, 1985 (divorced); married; wife's name Jenny; children: (first marriage) Jason, (third marriage) a daughter. *Education:* University of Minnesota, B.A., 1966, graduate study, 1966-68. *Politics:* Democrat. *Religion:* Plymouth Brethren.

ADDRESSES: Office—c/o A Prairie Home Companion, Minnesota Public Radio New Media, 45 East 7th St., Saint Paul, MN 55101. *Agent*—American Humor Institute, 80 Eighth Ave., No. 1216, New York, NY 10011.

CAREER: Writer. KUOM-Radio, Minneapolis, MN, staff announcer, 1963-68; Minnesota Public Radio, St. Paul, MN, producer and announcer, 1971-74, host and principal writer for weekly program *A Prairie Home Companion,* 1974-87 and 1993—; host of *Garrison Keillor's American Radio Company of the Air,* 1989-1993.

AWARDS, HONORS: George Foster Peabody Broadcasting Award, 1980, for *A Prairie Home Companion;* Edward R. Murrow Award from Corporation for Public Broadcasting, 1985, for service to public radio; *Los Angeles Times* Book Award nomination, 1986, for *Lake Wobegon Days;* Grammy Award for best nonmusical recording, 1987, for *Lake Wobegon Days;* Ace Award, 1988; Best Music and Entertainment Host Award, 1988; Gold Medal for spoken English, American Academy of Arts and Letters, 1990; inducted into Museum of Broadcast Communications and Radio Hall of Fame, 1994; National Humanities Medal, National Endowment for the Humanities, 1999; Berliner Morgenpost Readers' Prize, Berlin Film Festival, for *A Prairie Home Companion.*

WRITINGS:

G.K. the DJ, Minnesota Public Radio, 1977.

The Selected Verse of Margaret Haskins Durber, Minnesota Public Radio, 1979.

Happy to Be Here: Stories and Comic Pieces, Atheneum (New York, NY), 1982, expanded edition, Penguin (New York, NY), 1983.

Lake Wobegon Days (novel), Viking (New York, NY), 1985.

Leaving Home: A Collection of Lake Wobegon Stories, Viking (New York, NY), 1987.

We Are Still Married: Stories and Letters, Viking (New York, NY), 1989.

WLT: A Radio Romance, Viking (New York, NY), 1991.

The Book of Guys, Viking (New York, NY), 1993.

Cat, You Better Come Home, illustrated by Steve Johnson, Viking (New York, NY), 1995.

The Old Man Who Loved Cheese, illustrated by Anne Wilsdorf, Little, Brown (Boston, MA), 1996.

Wobegon Boy, Viking (New York, NY), 1997.

(Editor, with Katrina Kenison) *The Best American Short Stories: 1998,* Houghton (Boston, MA), 1998.

Me: By Jimmy (Big Boy) Valente, Governor of Minnesota. As Told to Garrison Keillor, Viking (New York, NY), 1999.

(Coauthor) *Minnesota Days: Our Heritage in Stories, Art, and Photos,* Voyageur (Stillwater, MN), 1999.

In Search of Lake Wobegon, with photographs by Richard Olsenius, Viking (New York, NY), 2001.

Lake Wobegon Summer 1956, Viking (New York, NY), 2001.

(Editor and author of introduction) *Good Poems* (anthology), Viking (New York, NY), 2002.

Love Me, Viking (New York, NY), 2003.

A Prairie Home Companion (screenplay), 2005.

Contributor of articles and stories to periodicals, including *New Yorker, Harper's* and *Atlantic Monthly.*

RECORDINGS

A Prairie Home Companion Anniversary Album, Minnesota Public Radio, 1980.

The Family Radio, Minnesota Public Radio, 1982.

News from Lake Wobegon, Minnesota Public Radio, 1982.

Prairie Home Companion Tourists, Minnesota Public Radio, 1983.

Ten Years on the Prairie: A Prairie Home Companion 10th Anniversary, Minnesota Public Radio, 1984.

Gospel Birds and Other Stories of Lake Wobegon, Minnesota Public Radio, 1985.

A Prairie Home Companion: The Final Performance, Minnesota Public Radio, 1987.

More News from Lake Wobegon, Minnesota Public Radio, 1988.

Lake Wobegon Loyalty Days: A Recital for Mixed Baritone and Orchestra, Minnesota Public Radio, 1989.

Local Man Moves to City, Highbridge, 1991.

(With Frederica von Stade) *Songs of the Cat,* Highbridge, 1991.

Keillor has also recorded his book *Lake Wobegon Days.*

SIDELIGHTS: Born on August 7, 1942, in Anoka, Minnesota, Garrison Keillor was the third of six children born into a conservative religious family. His father, John Philip, worked as a railroad clerk and carpenter to support his family. Gary, however, had his eye on a literary career from a young age. In fact, at the age of thirteen, he started calling himself "Garrison" for professional reasons. His single-minded focus and hard work would pay off in later years as he became a household name.

With the words "It's been a quiet week in Lake Wobegon, my hometown," radio humorist and author Keillor introduced his monologue on his long-running Minnesota Public Radio program, *A Prairie Home Companion.* The stories he told over the air, based partly on his memories of growing up in semi-rural Anoka, Minnesota, were among the highlights of the live-broadcast show—an eclectic mixture of comedy and music (including bluegrass, blues, ethnic folk, choral, gospel, opera, and yodeling)—which reached an audience of about four million listeners per week by the time it went off the air in 1987. It reached a great many more people in its last year when the Disney Channel obtained cable television broadcasting rights.

As principal writer and host of the show, Keillor also revealed his humor in the commercials he wrote for the sponsors of his program, including Ralph's Pretty Good Grocery ("If you can't find it at Ralph's, you can probably get along without it"), Bertha's Kitty Boutique ("For persons who care about cats"), the Chatterbox Cafe ("Where the coffeepot is always on, which is why it always tastes that way"), Bob's Bank ("Neither a borrower nor a lender be; so save at the sign of the sock"), the Sidetrack Tap ("Don't sleep at our bar; we don't drink in your bed"), and especially those Powdermilk Biscuits ("Heavens, they're tasty") that "give shy persons the strength to get up and do what needs to be done."

Many critics place Keillor in the tradition of such American humorists as Ring Lardner, James Thurber, and Mark Twain. Like Twain, who gained a reputation traveling on the American lecture circuit in the last years of the nineteenth and first years of the twentieth century, Keillor's audience originally came from his live performances. Roy Blount, Jr., writing in the *New York Times Book Review* about *A Prairie Home Companion,* stated that it was "impossible to describe. Everyone I have met who has heard it has either been dumbfounded by it, or addicted to it, or both." "The same is true of Keillor's prose," Blount continued, referring to a series of pieces written for the *New Yorker* and collected in *Happy to Be Here: Stories and Comic Pieces.* However, "many of these pieces," wrote Peter A. Scholl in the *Dictionary of Literary Biography Yearbook: 1987,* "show the witty and urbane Keillor rather than the wistful, wandering storyteller in exile from Lake Wobegon, where 'smart doesn't count for very much.'"

In 1985, the publication of *Lake Wobegon Days* brought Keillor's small town to national prominence. Beginning with the first explorations of the French traders in the eighteenth century, Keillor goes on to describe the town's history up to the present day. But Lake Wobe-

gon is, according to Mary T. Schmich in the *Chicago Tribune,* "a town that lies not on any map but somewhere along the border of his imagination and his memory." Keillor described it in *Lake Wobegon Days:* "Bleakly typical of the prairie, Lake Wobegon has its origins in the utopian vision of nineteenth-century New England Transcendentalists, but now is populated mainly by Norwegians and Germans. . . . The lake itself, blue-green and sparkling in the brassy summer sun and neighbored by the warm-colored marsh grasses of a wildlife-teeming slough, is the town's main attraction, though the view is spoiled somewhat by a large grain elevator by the railroad track."

Lake Wobegon, in Keillor's stories, becomes a sort of American Everytown, "the ideal American place to come from," wrote Scholl. "One of the attributes of home in Keillor's work is evanescence. . . . Dozens of his stories concern flight from Lake Wobegon, and the title of his radio show gains ironic force with the realization that it was adapted from the Prairie Home Lutheran cemetery in Moorhead, Minnesota; we are permanently at home only when we are gone." Yet "the wonderful thing about Keillor's tone in detailing life as it is lived in Lake Wobegon is not derived from his pathos knowing he can never go home again," Scholl continued. "He refuses to emphasize his status as exile in the novel [*Lake Wobegon Days*]. The wonder flows from his understanding that the complicated person he has become . . . is truly no step up from the guy down in the Sidetrack Tap he might have been had he never left home in the first place."

Keillor left *A Prairie Home Companion* in June of 1987, deciding that he needed more time to devote to his writing, and, suggested Schmich, to escape the unwanted fame that dogged his heels in Minnesota. His next book, *Leaving Home,* consisted of edited versions of his monologues from the last months of the show, many of them about people leaving Lake Wobegon. "Every once in a while," declared Richard F. Shepard in the *New York Times,* "the author slips into a poetic mood and you know he is saying goodbye to a world that was, a goodbye he makes clear as he goes along." The book, Shepard concluded, "says what it has to say with a rare, dry humor that is in what we like to believe is the very best American tradition." "His humor," Scholl stated, "is sustained by his comic faith, which like Powdermilk Biscuits, helps readers and listeners 'get up and do what needs to be done.'"

Keillor lived briefly in Denmark with his Danish wife Ulla Skaerved, then returned to the United States and set up a residence in New York City. In 1989, he began a new radio program, *Garrison Keillor's American Radio Company of the Air*. Although one of his later books, *We Are Still Married*, mostly reprints pieces that appeared originally in the *New Yorker*, he has not yet exhausted his stories about the denizens of his quiet hometown. "In some hidden chamber of our hearts," wrote David Black in *Rolling Stone*, "most of us, no matter where we live, are citizens of Lake Wobegon," the place where, according to Keillor, "all the women are strong, all the men are good-looking, and all the children are above average."

Keillor made another foray into the world of novel writing with his 1992 release, *WLT: A Radio Romance*. The book is about Ray and Roy Soderbjerg, two brothers who establish a radio station during the glory days of radio in 1926. They bumble through their new enterprise, booking acts small and smaller as they explore the frontier of radio broadcasting. Acts such as the Shepherd Boys (a gospel group), Lily Dale (a wheelchair-bound woman with a seductive voice), and the Shoe Shine Boys (a folk group) compete with radio melodramas like *Adventures in Homemaking* and *Noontime Jubilee*. Brother Ray is a lecherous man who chases after any female who comes within his realm, whereas Roy craves the country life. The station "adopts" boy broadcaster Francis With, whose parents have either died or gone mad, and he is molded into the ubiquitous announcer Frank White, who becomes the station's top draw. The novel chronicles decades of the station's rise until television becomes the draw of the day.

The novel shows the appeal of radio during its golden days, the struggling personalities involved, the backstage hijinks, and the listeners' loyalties. Critical reaction to the book was mixed. Anne Bernays, writing in the *New York Times Book Review*, claimed that the work, unusual for the man so known for his humor, "is a much darker book than one would expect. . . . Mr. Keillor's famous grin now covers a grimace." She related that this undertone is one of her main problems with the work: "Funny and energetic as *WLT* is, the book's subtext of what can only be described as disappointment disappoints. I ended up wishing Mr. Keillor had let me laugh more; he still has the humorist's singular and worthy touch." Elizabeth Beverly of *Commonweal* criticized Keillor's style in writing the book, claiming that the chapters are too short and choppy: "They seriously hinder his ability to tell a story from the inside. There's not enough room to move, not enough time to fill in background information." Beverly concluded that "Keillor the novelist doesn't know what he wants. He cannot hear what he wants. He is learning to work in a me-

dium which, in this case, has resisted him. This novel is a failed venture, but bespeaks a great hope." While Michael Ratcliffe, writing in the London *Observer*, remarked that Keillor's novel is "very funny," he found fault with its structure, claiming that it is "not really a novel at all. Keillor is an intensive miniaturist, but he is driving a stretched limo here. . . . *Radio Romance* is like a brilliant bedding plant: it flowers as floribundantly as promised in the photograph, but puts down no roots to grow."

Keillor's next work was a book of short stories and vignettes called *The Book of Guys*. A comic spinoff of the work of Robert Bly, the Minnesota poet who wrote bestselling works about male bonding in the wilderness, *The Book of Guys* tracks the struggles with manhood experienced by such diverse protagonists as Dionysius and Buddy the Leper. Roy Bradley, Boy Broadcaster, for example, hails from the tongue-twisting village Piscacatawamaquoddymoggin, and his tale is as much one of a broken heart as of his radio vocation. Lonesome Shorty, a cowboy who takes to collecting china, ends up in conflict over how his hobby has created conflict in his previously conventional life. "Keillor puts on the mantle of guyness, with its repeating pattern of male bonding and rugged manly embraces, and camps around in it," commented Susan Jeffreys of *New Statesman & Society*.

Jeffreys claimed that the book "is the best thing he has done since *Lake Wobegon Days;* maybe even better." Lisa Zeidner praised the work in the *New York Times Book Review*, calling it "an endearingly acerbic collection." Zeidner, however, found that Keillor is not necessarily at his peak when he is pointing out the differences between the sexes: "The most substantial tales aren't really about manhood at all, but about the arbitrariness and absurdity of modern success, especially in show business," she commented. "He drags his heroes through the mud of contemporary culture and teaches them the essential tongue-in-cheek Lake Wobegon lesson . . . 'not to imagine we *are* someone but to be content being who we are.'"

The novel *Wobegon Boy* is the third of Keillor's Lake Wobegon books. The story follows John Tollefson as he leaves Lake Wobegon and takes a job at a radio station at a college in upstate New York. John's life is complicated as he enters into a partnership to open a restaurant, falls in love and gets married, experiences the death of his father, and is forced to resign from the station before finally pulling himself together. Julian Ferraro, commenting in the *Times Literary Supplement*, observed that this novel follows its Lake Wobegon predecessors in that "an intelligent, sensitive, liberal-arts-educated son of an insular community in the Midwest breaks free and lives a relatively sophisticated, cosmopolitan life on the East Coast, without ever being able fully to shed the vestiges of the values and attitudes of his home town."

Wobegon Boy's critical reception reflects Keillor's reputation as a storyteller. Ferraro found that "Keillor is . . . at his best as an energetic storyteller, and it is the various comic interludes—the 'dozens of stories of shame and degradation'—that provide the book's most entertaining moments." Reviewing the novel in the *Washington Post Book World,* Michael Kernan revealed: "Though I can't get enough of the Keillor stories on tape, I find his written version of the same material much less effective." Alex Heard in the *New York Times Book Review,* referring to Keillor's earlier book *Lake Wobegon Days* as a "part novel, part supercasual" hybrid, argued that "this time the hybrid, while often sharp and funny, doesn't work as well . . . mainly because Keillor is trying to make Tollefson . . . a three-dimensional character—as opposed to the 2-D vehicles for comic experiences and observations that populate Lake Wobegon. That's admirable, but it creates a slippery situation that sometimes squirts out of Keillor's hands." Kernan concluded with the view that Keillor "appears to ramble on for pages about this and that, entertaining us but not moving us, and then suddenly, at the very end, he pulls everything together and gives meaning and brightness to all that has gone before."

The novel *Lake Wobegon Summer 1956* tells of fourteen-year-old Gary trying to come to terms with his life in rural Minnesota, his sexual yearning, a job as the local newspaper's sportswriter, and his family's religious beliefs. "There is a good deal of *Catcher in the Rye* here: the lonely teenager who sees everything with an x-ray and dyspeptic eye," Jonathan Mirsky noted in the *Spectator.* "But it is less soft-centred and, to use Holden Caulfield's favourite word, less 'phony' than Salinger's too-admired book." Don McLeese in *Book* found that "Keillor's eye for evocative detail and penchant for parody give the novel the breezy charm of a summer reverie." Caroline Hallsworth, reviewing the novel in *Library Journal,* concluded: "Keillor's wry vignettes of Gary's summer of change and turmoil are laced with his trademark self-deprecating humor."

In the 2003 autobiographical novel *Love Me,* Larry Wyler leaves Minnesota and his sweetheart for New York City, hoping to become a famous writer. For a time he seems successful both at writing and womanizing, but his success lasts only a short time, and Wyler is soon brought low. He returns to Minnesota and a job as an advice columnist, giving out words of comfort under the pseudonym Mr. Blue.

Besides his adult fiction, Keillor has also written two books for children, *Cat, You Better Come Home* and *The Old Man Who Loved Cheese,* both of which feature his trademark sense of the absurd. In *Cat, You Better Come Home,* Keillor fictionalizes the life of a feline who wants more than she gets in her own house, so she runs away to a life of show business, only to return broken down to the man who loves her. *The Old Man Who Loved Cheese* features Wallace P. Flynn, a man whose love for the dairy product causes him to lose his wife and his family. However, after he realizes that the joys of human companionship are much more satisfying than his favorite food, he gives it up and his life is restored.

In 1999 Keillor was awarded the National Humanities Medal and was honored at a White House dinner hosted by President Bill Clinton. In July of 2001, Keillor underwent heart surgery at the Mayo Clinic in Rochester, Minnesota. He made a full recovery and continued to broadcast his show and write.

"Keillor's most lasting fame," according to an essayist for *Contemporary Popular Writers,* "will likely center around the *Prairie Home Companion.* With this radio show, Keillor has made a lasting contribution to the literary world, the art of story-telling, public broadcasting, and American culture in general by reviving in the 1980s and 1990s the pre-television tradition of gathering around the radio to listen to variety shows, comedies, and dramas. In this way, Keillor has answered the public's need for old-fashioned, wholesome, family-style entertainment, as well as for nostalgia for a simpler time and a less complicated lifestyle."

BIOGRAPHICAL AND CRITICAL SOURCES:

BOOKS

Contemporary Literary Criticism, Volume 40, Thomson Gale (Detroit, MI), 1986.

Contemporary Popular Writers, St. James Press (Detroit, MI), 1997.

Dictionary of Literary Biography Yearbook: 1987, Thomson Gale (Detroit, MI), 1988.

Encyclopedia of World Biography Supplement, Volume 22, Thomson Gale (Detroit, MI), 2002.

Keillor, Garrison, *Lake Wobegon Days,* Viking (New York, NY), 1985.

Lee, Judith Yaross, *Garrison Keillor: A Voice of America,* University Press of Mississippi (Jackson, MS), 1991.

PERIODICALS

Atlantic, October 8, 1997, Katie Bolick, "It's Just Work."

Book, September, 2001, Don McLeese, reviews of *Lake Wobegon Summer 1956* and *In Search of Lake Wobegon,* p. 80.

Booklist, June 1 and 15, 1996, p. 1732; January 1, 2003, review of *Good Poems,* p. 791.

Chicago Tribune, March 15, 1987.

Chicago Tribune Book World, January 24, 1982.

Children's Book Review Service, June, 1995, p. 124; July, 1996, p. 147.

Christian Century, July 21-28, 1982; November 13, 1985; March 22, 2003, "Wobegon Poets: A Prairie Poem Companion," p. 20.

Commonweal, April 10, 1992, p. 26.

Country Journal, January, 1982.

Detroit Free Press, September 8, 1985.

Detroit News, September 1, 1985.

Esquire, May, 1982.

Irish Times, March 7, 1998.

Kirkus Reviews, April 1, 1996, p. 532.

Library Journal, September 1, 2001, Caroline Hallsworth, review of *Lake Wobegon Summer 1956,* p. 234; March 1, 2003, Rochelle Ratner, review of *Good Poems* (audiobook), p. 136.

National Review, December 8, 1997; April 19, 1999.

New Statesman & Society, January 14, 1994, p. 40.

New York Times, October 31, 1982; August 20, 1985; October 31, 1985; October 21, 1987; August 26, 2001.

New York Times Book Review, February 28, 1982; August 25, 1985; November 10, 1991, p. 24; December 12, 1993, p. 13; May 21, 1995, p. 20; October 26, 1997, p. 14; March 28, 1999, p. 8.

Observer (London, England), January 19, 1992, p. 53; December 3, 1995, p. 16.

Publishers Weekly, September 13, 1985; May 8, 1995, p. 294; April 1, 1996, p. 74.

Rolling Stone, July 23, 1981.

Saturday Review, May-June, 1983.

School Library Journal, July, 1995, p. 78; May, 1996, p. 93; March, 2003, Sheila Shoup, review of *Good Poems,* p. 261.

Seattle Post-Intelligencer, October 7, 1999.

Spectator, November 24, 2001, Jonathan Mirsky, review of *Lake Wobegon Summer 1956,* p. 54.

Time, November 9, 1981; February 1, 1982; September 2, 1985; November 4, 1985; November 22, 1993, p. 82; December 11, 1995, p. 77.

Times Literary Supplement, February 27, 1998, p. 21.

Utne Reader, September-October, 2001, Karen Olson, "The News . . . As Seen from Lake Wobegon," p. 92.

Washington Post, August 23, 1989; July 9, 2001; July 15, 2001.

Washington Post Book World, January 18, 1982; November 28, 1993, p. 1; November 30, 1997, p.1.

Yale Review, January, 1993, p. 148.

ONLINE

Minnesota Author Biographies Project, http://people.mnhs.org/ (June 11, 2003).

Prairie Home Companion Web site, http://phc.mpr.org/ (June 11, 2003).

Prime Time Online, http://www.rny.com/ (November 13, 2001), Jeff Baenen, "Garrison Keillor Spins More Tales from Lake Wobegon."

*   *   *

KEILLOR, Gary Edward
See KEILLOR, Garrison

*   *   *

KELLY, Lauren
See OATES, Joyce Carol

*   *   *

KENEALLY, Thomas 1935-
(Thomas Michael Keneally)

PERSONAL: Born October 7, 1935, in Sydney, Australia; son of Edmund Thomas and Elsie Margaret (Coyle) Keneally; married Judith Martin, August 15, 1965; children: Margaret Ann, Jane Rebecca. *Education:* Attended St. Patrick's College, New South Wales.

ADDRESSES: Agent—Curtis Brown, P.O. Box 19, Paddington, New South Wales 2021, Australia.

CAREER: Writer and journalist. Trained for priesthood (never ordained); high school teacher in Sydney, Australia, 1960-64; University of New England, New South Wales, Australia, lecturer in drama, 1968-70; New York University, New York, NY, Inaugural Berg Professor, 1988; University of California, Irvine, School of Writing, visiting professor, 1985, distinguished professor 1991-95. Member of Australia-China Council, 1978-88; Australian Constitutional Committee, advisor, 1985-88; Literary Arts Board of Australia, member, 1985-88; Australian Republican Movement, chair, 1991-93, director, 1994—. Actor in films, including *The Devil's Playground,* 1976, and *The Chant of Jimmie Blacksmith,* 1978. *Military service:* Served in Australian Citizens Military Forces.

MEMBER: Australian Society of Authors (chair, 1987-90), National Book Council of Australia (president, 1985-90), PEN, Royal Society of Literature (fellow), American Academy of Arts and Sciences (fellow).

AWARDS, HONORS: Commonwealth Literary Fund fellowship, 1966, 1968, 1972; Miles Franklin Award, 1968, 1969; Captain Cook Bi-Centenary Prize, 1970; Heinemann Award, Royal Society of Literature, 1973, for *The Chant of Jimmie Blacksmith;* notable book citation, American Library Association, 1980, for *Confederates;* Booker McConnell Prize for Fiction, and fiction prize, *Los Angeles Times,* both 1982, both for *Schindler's List;* named Officer, Order of Australia, 1983.

WRITINGS:

NOVELS

The Place at Whitton, Cassell (London, England), 1964, Walker & Co. (New York, NY), 1965.
The Fear, Cassell (London, England), 1965.
Bring Larks and Heroes, Cassell (Melbourne, Australia), 1967, Viking Press (New York, NY), 1968.
Three Cheers for the Paraclete, Angus & Robertson (London, England), 1968, Viking Press (New York, NY), 1969.
The Survivor, Angus & Robertson (London, England), 1969, Viking Press (New York, NY), 1970.
A Dutiful Daughter, Viking Press (New York, NY), 1971.
The Chant of Jimmie Blacksmith, Viking Press (New York, NY), 1972.
Blood Red, Sister Rose: A Novel of the Maid of Orleans, Viking Press (New York, NY), 1974, published as *Blood Red, Sister Rose,* Collins (London, England), 1974.

Gossip from the Forest, Collins (London, England), 1975, Harcourt Brace (New York, NY), 1976.
Moses the Lawgiver, Harper (New York, NY), 1975.
Season in Purgatory, Collins (London, England), 1976, Harcourt Brace (New York, NY), 1977.
A Victim of the Aurora, Collins (London, England), 1977, Harcourt Brace (New York, NY), 1978.
Ned Kelly and the City of the Bees (juvenile), J. Cape (London, England), 1978, Penguin (New York, NY), 1980.
Passenger, Harcourt Brace (New York, NY), 1979.
Confederates, Collins (London, England), 1979, Harper (New York, NY), 1980.
The Cut-Rate Kingdom, Wildcat Press (Sydney, Australia), 1980.
Bullie's House, Currency Press (Sydney, Australia), 1981.
Schindler's List, Simon & Schuster (New York, NY), 1982, published as *Schindler's Ark,* Hodder & Stoughton (London, England), 1982.
A Family Madness, Hodder & Stoughton, 1985, Simon & Schuster (New York, NY), 1986.
The Playmaker, Simon & Schuster (New York, NY), 1987.
To Asmara: A Novel of Africa, Warner Books (New York, NY), 1989, published as *Towards Asmara,* Hodder & Stoughton (London, England), 1989.
By the Line, University of Queensland Press (St. Lucia), 1989.
Flying Hero Class, Warner Books (New York, NY), 1991.
Woman of the Inner Sea, Hodder & Stoughton (London, England), 1992; Doubleday (Garden City, NY), 1993.
Jacko the Great Intruder, Hodder & Stoughton (London, England), 1994.
A River Town, Nan A. Talese (New York, NY), 1995.
Bettany's Book, Bantam (New York, NY), 1999, hardcover edition, Doubleday (Sydney, Australia), 2000.
An Angel in Australia, Doubleday (Sydney, Australia), 2002.
Office of Innocence, Nan A. Talese (New York, NY), 2003.
The Tyrant's Novel, Nan A. Talese (New York, NY), 2004.

NONFICTION

Outback, photographs by Gary Hansen and Mark Lang, Hodder & Stoughton (London, England and Sydney, Australia), 1983, Rand McNally (Chicago, IL), 1984.

(With Patsy Adam-Smith and Robyn Davidson) *Australia: Beyond the Dreamtime,* BBC Publications (London, England), 1987, Facts on File (New York, NY), 1989.

With Yellow Shoes, Prentice-Hall (Tappan, NJ), 1992.

Now and in Time to Be: Ireland & the Irish, Norton (New York, NY), 1992.

The Place Where Souls Are Born: A Journey into the Southwest, Simon & Schuster (New York, NY), 1992, published as *The Place Where Souls Are Born: A Journey into the American Southwest,* Hodder & Stoughton (London, England), 1992.

Memoirs from a Young Republic, Heinemann (London, England), 1993.

Homebush Boy: A Memoir, Heinemann (London, England), 1995.

The Great Shame: A Story of the Irish in the Old World and the New, Random House (Milsons Point, New South Wales, Australia), 1998, published as *The Great Shame: And the Triumph of the Irish in the English-Speaking World,* Nan A. Talese (New York, NY), 1999.

American Scoundrel: The Life of the Notorious Civil War General Dan Sickles, Nan A. Talese (New York, NY), 2002, published in England as *American Scoundrel: Love, War and Politics in Civil War America,* Chatto and Windus (London, England), 2002.

Abraham Lincoln ("Penguin Lives" series), Lipper/Viking (New York, NY), 2003.

PLAYS

Halloran's Little Boat (produced in Sydney, 1966), published in *Penguin Australian Drama 2,* Penguin (Melbourne, Australia), 1975.

Childermass, produced in Sydney, 1968.

An Awful Rose, produced in Sydney, 1972.

Bullie's House, (produced in Sydney, 1980; New Haven, CT, 1985), Currency Press (Sydney, Australia), 1981.

Writing for television, including *Essington* (play), 1974; *The World's Wrong End* (play), 1981; and *Australia* (series), 1987; contributor to screenplays, including *The Priest,* 1973, and *Silver City,* 1985; and to periodicals, including *New York Times Book Review.*

Keneally's manuscripts are collected at the Mitchell Library, Sydney, and the Australian National Library, Canberra.

ADAPTATIONS: *Schindler's List* was adapted for film by Steven Zaillian for Amblin Entertainment, 1993.

SIDELIGHTS: Well known for his novel *Schindler's List,* which served as the basis for an award-winning motion picture in 1993, Thomas Keneally has become one of Australia's most distinguished authors. In works characterized by their sensitivity to style, their objectivity, their suspense, and diversity, this "honest workman"—as Raymond Sokolev calls Keneally in *New York Times*—has explored subjects as diverse as the history of his native Australia and war-torn Ethiopia.

While discussions of Keneally often emphasize his years spent as a seminary student, only one of his novels focuses directly on the subject. In *Three Cheers for the Paraclete,* his protagonist is a "doubting priest," Father James Maitland, who "runs afoul of the local taboos" in a Sydney seminary. As in many of his novels, Keneally presents his characters objectively and compassionately; priests and bishops are seen in the fullness of their humanity. Richard Sullivan wrote in *Washington Post Book World,* "Though this admirably sustained novel makes it clear that some structures are too rigid, that the Church is not unflawed in its members, both clerical and lay, and that more windows need opening, at the same time it reveals with fine objectivity that it is human beings who are at fault, each in his own way, Maitland as much as any."

A similar example of Keneally's desire for objectivity is evident in his account of the St. Joan of Arc story, *Blood Red, Sister Rose.* Bruce Cook of *Washington Post Book World* claimed Keneally's "intent, in fact, seems to be to reduce her and her legend to recognizably human dimensions." Placing Keneally's Joan of Arc in a historical perspective, *Time*'s Melvin Maddocks saw her standing between the "Joan-too-spiritual" of the original legend and the "Joan-too-earthy" of George Bernard Shaw. She is "less spectacular than the first two but decidedly more convincing and perhaps, at last, more moving."

Perhaps Keneally's most ambitious historical novel is *Confederates,* set during the American Civil War and told from a Southern perspective. The book has no central character, but rather focuses on a group of characters who are involved in the preparations for the Second Battle of Antietam, fought in 1862. Keneally "keeps his canvas as vast as possible," wrote John Higgins in *Times Literary Supplement,* "and his concern is as much with the conscripts as with the captains; the volunteers get just as large a show as the likes of Robert E. Lee and Stonewall Jackson."

Several critics found that Keneally's portrayal of the American South is surprisingly realistic. Jeffrey Burke of *New York Times Book Review,* for example, wrote that it "is almost necessary to remind oneself that the author is Australian, so naturally, intrinsically Southern is the narrative voice." Robert Ostermann of *Detroit News* stated that Keneally's account of the Second Battle of Antietam "deserves comparison . . . to Tolstoy's rendering of the Russian defeat and retreat at Borodino and to Hemingway's of the retreat from Caporetto in *Farewell to Arms,*" and added that "the fact that this massive, absorbing narrative is the work of an Australian—not a Southerner, not even a native American—testifies even further to the stature of his achievement."

With the publication of *Schindler's List,* published in England as *Schindler's Ark,* Keneally found himself embroiled in a controversy over whether his book was fiction or nonfiction, an important point since the book was nominated for England's prestigious Booker McConnell Prize for fiction. Although the story of Oskar Schindler, a German industrialist during World War II who saved the Jews assigned to work in his factory from Nazi gas chambers, is historical truth, Keneally wrote the book as a novel. "The craft of the novelist," Keneally explained in the London *Times,* "is the only craft to which I can lay claim, and . . . the novel's techniques seem suited for a character of such ambiguity and magnitude as Oskar [Schindler.]" After deliberation, the judges deemed the work a novel and awarded it the Booker Prize in 1982.

The controversy over *Schindler's List* is understandable. As Richard F. Shepard pointed out in *New York Times,* the real-life story of Oskar Schindler "is indeed stranger than fiction." The owner of a German armaments factory staffed with forced Jewish laborers from nearby concentration camps, Schindler made a fortune during the war by supplying the German army with war materials. But when the Nazi regime decided to solve the "Jewish question" through mass extermination of Jewish prisoners, Schindler acted to save as many of his workers as possible. He convinced the local S.S. chief to allow him to house his Jewish workers in a compound built on his factory grounds rather than at a concentration camp "so that their labor [could] be more fully exploited," as Schindler explained it. Through the use of bribes and favors, Schindler worked to reunite his workers with their families, provided them with adequate food and medical care, and even managed to get a particularly murderous S.S. officer transferred to the Russian front. When the Russian army threatened to capture the area of southern Poland where Schindler's factory was located—and the German army made plans to execute the Jewish workers before retreating—Schindler moved his company and his workers to safety in German-held Czechoslovakia. By the end of the war, Schindler had some thirteen hundred Jewish workers under his protection—far more than he needed to operate his factory—and had spent his entire fortune on bribes and favors.

Critical reaction to *Schindler's List* was generally favorable. Keneally, wrote Christopher Lehmann-Haupt in *New York Times,* "does not attempt to analyze in detail whatever made Oskar Schindler tick," which the reviewer found "a little disconcerting, considering the novelistic technique he employs to tell his story. But this restraint increases the book's narrative integrity. Because the story doesn't try to do what it can't honestly do, we trust all the more what it does do." Jonathan Yardley of *Washington Post Book World* felt that the book's major flaw is "the author's insistence on employing devices of the 'new' journalism. . . . But *Schindler's List* has about it a strong, persuasive air of authenticity, and as an act of homage it is a most emphatic and powerful document." Phillip Howard of the London *Times* agreed, saying that "the book is a brilliantly detailed piece of historical reporting. It is moving, it is powerful, it is gripping."

In *A Family Madness,* Keneally again returns to World War II, this time exploring its repercussions upon later generations. The book was inspired by a real-life tragedy in Sydney during the summer of 1984, in which a family of five willingly ended their lives. The author's rugby-playing protagonist, Terry Delaney, goes to work for a security firm owned by a Byelorussian named Rudi Kabbel. Haunted by traumatic memories of his childhood in Russia during the war and his father's wartime journals, which reveal countless horrors inflicted upon his family, Kabbel is mentally unstable. When Delaney, who is married, falls in love with Kabbel's daughter and fathers her child, the Kabbel family closes ranks—not only against Delaney but against the world. As Blake Morrison explained in the London *Observer,* "They sell up the business, surround themselves with heavy weaponry, and wait for the new dawn."

Writing in *Times Literary Supplement,* Michael Wood said, *A Family Madness* conveys the idea that "even here, in this comfort-loaded and forward-looking Australia, history will get you one way or another." Wood praised the novel, calling it "an ambitious and successful book that makes connections we need to think about." John Sutherland of *London Review of Books,* lauded the novel as "better than its applauded predecessor [*Schindler's List*]" and noted that the nobility of the characters makes a genuine claim on the reader. However, in a review for *New York Times Book Review,* Robert Towers criticized Keneally's characterization, writing that "the lack of an adequately realized psychological dimension" in the character of Rudi Kabbel "is . . . crippling to the novel's aspirations."

With the publication of *To Asmara,* as with *Schindler's List,* Keneally found himself once again accused of writing, not a novel, but an impassioned journalistic tribute. A fictionalized portrayal of the brutal African guerilla warfare of the 1980s, *To Asmara* focuses on the Eritrean Peoples Liberation Front's struggle to break free from an Ethiopia dominated by tyrants. Assisted by Russian military aid, the Ethiopian army was permitted to commit a form of genocide against the Eritreans, in the course of which Ethiopian troops destroyed the beautiful ancient city of Asmara.

Protagonist and narrator Tim Darcy is an Australian freelance journalist on "loose assignment" from the London *Times,* "one of those tentative, self-despising dreamers drawn to the empty quarters and violent margins of the West's known world," according to Robert Stone in *New York Times Book Review.* Stone had high praise for both the character of Darcy and the novel as a whole: "Not since *For Whom the Bell Tolls* has a book of such sophistication, the work of a major international novelist, spoken out so unambiguously on behalf of an armed struggle." In contrast, Andrew Jaffe, reviewing the book for *Los Angeles Times Book Review,* took issue with Keneally's advocacy of the Eritrean cause. Jaffe wrote, "The nobility of the rebels shouldn't be the concern of the novelist. His job is to sketch an intriguing story against an exotic backdrop. Keneally forgot to leave his commitment to the cause behind in Port Sudan."

Keneally uncharacteristically moves away from the sweeping panoramas of his earlier fiction and limits the action to the confines of one airplane in *Flying Hero Class.* Frank McCloud, tour manager for a troupe of Australian aboriginal dancers, finds himself involved in a hijacking on a flight from New York to Frankfurt following the troupe's performance. Describing *Flying Hero Class* as a "thoughtful and exciting novel," Richard Lipez pointed out in *Washington Post Book World*

that Keneally examines with ease two complex issues: the issue of Israeli security versus Palestinian justice and the issue of the territorial rights of the Australian aboriginal tribe versus U.S. and international mining interests. Although finding some fault with the novel, Edward Hower of *New York Times Book Review* shared Lipez's positive opinion. "Keneally's people are fascinating, and so are the ideas his plot generates, making the hijacking a metaphor for the complex relationship between the West and the third world peoples deprived of land and dignity," Hower stated, ending his review with the conclusion that "*Flying Hero Class* gives original insights into the way one man learns to reclaim responsibility for his own fate."

With *Woman of the Inner Sea,* Keneally returns to his native Australian turf and bases his plot on a real-life incident. In the work, Kate Gaffney-Kozinski, wife of a wealthy construction-empire scion, loses her husband to another woman, and her two precious children to the fire that levels the family's expensive beach home near Sydney. In an effort to forget, Kate boards a train for the interior. The place Kate chooses for her "self-annihilation" is Myambagh, a town built on the hard, flat rock of what was once an immense inland sea. Donna Rifkind, in *Los Angeles Times Book Review,* wrote that the Australian outback, "with its miles of empty red earth, stringybark and eucalyptus, savage storms and eccentric wildlife, represents more than just external landscape . . . the fluid unpredictability of the land also mirrors Kate's transformation."

In commending the novel, Rifkind wrote that in "the tragedy of her dead children and her subsequent pilgrimage, Kate represents a nation on a perpetual search for reinvention, a nation hardened by countless histories of hunger, tough luck and untimely death." Susan Fromberg Schaeffer echoed Rifkind's praise in *New York Times Book Review,* commenting that "*Woman of the Inner Sea* succeeds on many fronts. It is a picaresque and often hilarious adventure story, recounting one woman's unforgettable if improbable travels. It is a series of love stories . . . and it is a mystery story as well. But the novel is also very much an exploration of ethics."

Drawing on his family background again, Keneally's novel *River Town* is based on his Irish grandparents' immigration to Australia. In *River Town,* Keneally relates the experiences of a turn-of-the-century Irishman, Tim Shea, who immigrates to Australia when he tires of the confining mores of his own country. While happy to be rid of the restraints he experienced in Ireland, Tim discovers through a series of adverse events many of the same problems with the social conventions of the Australian frontier. In his new hometown of Kempsey, New South Wales, Tim becomes a community hero when he rescues two children from a cart accident. Shortly after, he finds himself being ostracized by the same community for his opposition to the Boer War—a position which ends in near economic disaster for Tim and his family when town members boycott his general store. As unfortunate events continue to plague Tim, he uncovers more of the very same social conventions he had hoped to leave behind in Ireland.

In general, critics were impressed with *River Town.* "This is truly a compassionate novel, full of vividly portrayed outcasts," wrote reviewer David Willis McCullough in *New York Times Book Review,* noting the characters are "outsiders in a nation of outsiders who are only beginning to define themselves in their new home, people who thought that 'if they traveled 12,000 miles, they might outrun original sin.'" Also finding the novel full of compassion and featuring a well-depicted historical background, a *Publishers Weekly* contributor concluded that "the story is haunting because it is both commonplace and universal. Keneally looks clearly at moral rot, but he is cautiously optimistic about the survival of good people and the uplifting heritage they bequeath." "Keneally has marvelous descriptive powers," said *Detroit News* reviewer Barbara Holiday, who praised the author's ability to "[bring] the community alive." Holiday summarized, "Keneally has written an absorbing homespun account of ordinary people who are heroic in spite of themselves."

While reviews of his fiction have been generally favorable, several of Keneally's works of nonfiction have been received with less enthusiasm. In *Now and in Time to Be: Ireland and the Irish,* for example, the author attempts to describe the land of his grandparents. In *New York Times Book Review* Katharine Weber wrote that "dazzled by his adventure" in Ireland, Keneally fails to discern what is significant and what is not. Peter Conrad, reviewing Keneally's study of Australian independence, titled *Memoirs from a Young Republic,* for *Observer,* Peter Conrad cited the author's carelessness, writing that, "Grammar and syntax frequently slump out of control." Many critics would agree that the novel is Keneally's forté. His impressive body of fiction, as Schaffer wrote in *New York Times Book Review,* "makes convincing the very serious belief that each of us has a necessary place—and that our most important task is to find it."

Keneally's later nonfiction works received considerable praise, however. *The Great Shame: A Story of the Irish* in the Old World and the New, published in the United States as *The Great Shame: And the Triumph of the Irish in the English-Speaking World,* was praised by Mary Elizabeth Williams in a review for *Salon.com.* Williams considered the book compelling because of "the smoothness with which the author moves around the globe. Observing both the rooted and the scattered, he shows not just how the outside world affected the Irish, but also how the Irish changed the world." Williams called Keneally's "greatest gift . . . his flair for molding real events into memorable narratives, in the smart turns of phrase that draw the reader into the action."

One of the figures in *The Great Shame* gets his own book with *American Scoundrel: The Life of the Notorious Civil War General Dan Sickles. Times Literary Supplement* reviewer Benjamin Markovits called Sickles "a characteristic object of Keneally's curiosity, a man, like Oskar Schindler, who exhibited the often uneasy relation between public and private virtues. Sickles, again like Schindler, excelled at the particulars of political life, at details and connections—like Keneally himself, whose talents as a writer reflect the qualities that draw him to his subjects."

Biographies of Abraham Lincoln abound, but in Keneally's *Abraham Lincoln* he touches on undocumented moments, and as *New York Times Book Review* contributor David Walton noted, "the droll and unusual image." Walton called this an "excellent brief biography." A *Kirkus Reviews* contributor called Keneally's look at Lincoln "so fresh that one wishes only that the 'Penguin Lives' format afforded Keneally room to say more about this iconic leader. Exemplary and illuminating, even for readers well-versed in Lincolniana."

BIOGRAPHICAL AND CRITICAL SOURCES:

BOOKS

Contemporary Literary Criticism, Thomson Gale (Detroit, MI), Volume 27, 1984, pp. 231-234, Volume 43, 1987, pp. 229-237, Volume 117, 1999, pp. 207-252.
Contemporary Novelists, St. James Press (Detroit, MI), 2001.
Encyclopedia of World Literature in the Twentieth Century, St. James Press (Detroit, MI), 1999.
Keneally, Thomas, *Three Cheers for the Paraclete,* Angus & Robertson (London, England), 1968, Viking Press (New York, NY), 1969.

Keneally, Thomas, *Homebush Boy: A Memoir,* Heinemann (London, England), 1995.

Pierce, Peter, *Australian Melodramas: Thomas Keneally's Fiction,* University of Queensland Press (Queensland, Australia), 1995.

Quartermaine, Peter, *Thomas Keneally,* Edward Arnold (London, England), 1992.

PERIODICALS

Chicago Tribune Book World, December 20, 1980; November 14, 1982.

Detroit News, September 28, 1980; November 21, 1982; May 21, 1995, p. 8J.

Kirkus Reviews, March 15, 1971; July 1, 1972; February 1, 1976; November 1, 1976; November 1, 2002, review of *Abraham Lincoln,* p. 1591.

Library Journal, February 15, 1995, pp. 122-124; March 1, 1997, p. 87.

London Review of Books, November 7, 1985, John Sutherland, review of *A Family Madness,* pp. 24-26.

Los Angeles Times Book Review, October 15, 1989, pp. 2, 13; May 16, 1993, p. 7.

Nation, November 6, 1972.

National Review, April 29, 1977.

New Statesman, September 1, 1972; October 26, 1973; October 11, 1974; September 19, 1975; September 3, 1976; September 9, 1978; January 19, 1979; November 2, 1979; September 29, 1985; September 12, 1993.

Newsweek, April 19, 1976; February 7, 1977; June 18, 1979.

New Yorker, February 10, 1975; August 23, 1976; May 23, 1977; May 8, 1978; May 19, 1986, pp. 118-19.

New York Times, April 4, 1970; September 9, 1972; October 18, 1982; November 22, 1982.

New York Times Book Review, September 27, 1970; September 12, 1971; January 16, 1972; August 27, 1972; December 3, 1972; February 9, 1975; April 11, 1976; February 27, 1977; October 14, 1977; March 26, 1978; July 8, 1979; October 5, 1980; September 20, 1987, pp. 7, 9; October 1, 1989, pp. 1, 42; April 7, 1991, p. 9; April 26, 1992, p. 12; April 18, 1993, p. 9; March 16, 1986; April 19, 1992; April 26, 1992, p. 22; May 14, 1995, p. 12; April 14, 2002, Kevin Baker, review of *American Scoundrel: Love, War and Politics in Civil War America,* p. 11; January 19, 2003, David Walton, review of *Abraham Lincoln,* p. 21.

Observer (London, England), April 25, 1971; September 10, 1971; November 24, 1974; September 21, 1975; December 14, 1975; September 5, 1976; September 4, 1977; January 21, 1979; October 21,

1979; September 29, 1985, p. 23; September 6, 1987, p. 25; March 10, 1991, p. 60; July 19, 1992, p. 58; September 12, 1993, p. 53.

Publishers Weekly, January 18, 1983, p. 447; August 7, 1987, p. 434; January 6, 1992, p. 60; January 30, 1995, p. 84; April 3, 1995, p. 40.

Spectator, March 1, 1968; November 25, 1972; September 7, 1974; November 15, 1975; September 4, 1976; September 3, 1977.

Time, May 15, 1995, Melvin Maddocks, review of *Blood Red, Sister Rose: A Novel of the Maid of Orleans,* p. 80.

Times (London, England), August 16, 1968; June 7, 1971; August 28, 1972; February 10, 1975; March 7, 1981; October 20, 1982; October 21, 1982.

Times Literary Supplement, May 7, 1970; April 23, 1971; September 15, 1972; October 26, 1973; October 11, 1974; September 19, 1975; September 3, 1976; October 14, 1977; November 2, 1979; November 23, 1979; October 18, 1985, p. 1169; October 20, 1989, p. 1147; January 29, 1993, p. 28; March 18, 1994, p. 13; May 24, 2002, Benjamin Markovits, review of *American Scoundrel.*

Washington Post Book World, April 27, 1969; April 19, 1970; August 29, 1971; August 13, 1972; January 26, 1975; February 20, 1977; March 26, 1978; August 31, 1980; October 4, 1981; October 20, 1982; March 24, 1991, p. 8.

West Coast Review of Books, July, 1978.

World Literature Today, winter, 1977; autumn, 1978; spring, 1980; autumn, 1996, p. 1025.

ONLINE

Salon.com, http://www.salon.com/ (September 13, 1999), Mary Elizabeth Williams, review of *The Great Shame: And the Triumph of the Irish in the English-speaking World.*

*   *   *

KENEALLY, Thomas Michael
See KENEALLY, Thomas

*   *   *

KENNEDY, William 1928-

PERSONAL: Born January 16, 1928, in Albany, NY; son of William J. (a deputy sheriff) and Mary Elizabeth (a secretary; maiden name, MacDonald) Kennedy; married Ana Daisy (Dana) Sosa (a former actress and dancer), January 31, 1957; children: Dana Elizabeth, Katherine Anne, Brendan Christopher. *Education:* Siena College, B.A., 1949.

ADDRESSES: Home—R.D. 3, Box 508, Averill Park, NY 12018. *Office*—Department of English, State University of New York at Albany, 1400 Washington Ave., Albany, NY 12222; NYS Writers Institute, Washington Avenue, Albany, NY 12222-0001. *Agent*—Liz Darhansoff, 1220 Park Ave., New York, NY 10028.

CAREER: Post Star, Glen Falls, NY, assistant sports editor and columnist, 1949-50; *Times-Union,* Albany, NY, reporter, 1952-56, special writer, 1963-70, and film critic, 1968-70; *Puerto Rico World Journal,* San Juan, assistant managing editor and columnist, 1956; Miami *Herald,* Miami, FL, reporter, 1957; correspondent for Time-Life publications in Puerto Rico, and reporter for Dorvillier (business) newsletter and Knight Newspapers, 1957-59; *Star,* San Juan, Puerto Rico, founding managing editor, 1959-61; full-time fiction writer, 1961-63; book editor of *Look* magazine, 1971; State University of New York at Albany, lecturer, 1974-82, New York State Writers Institute, founder and professor of English, 1983—. Writers Institute at Albany, founder, 1983, director, 1984—. Visiting professor of English, Cornell University, 1982-83. Cofounder, Cinema 750 film society, Rennselaer, NY, 1968-70; organizing moderator for series of forums on the humanities, sponsored by the National Endowment for the Humanities, New York State Library, and Albany Public Library. Panelist, New York State Council on the Arts, 1980-83. American Academy of Arts and Letters, member, beginning in 1993. *Military service:* U.S. Army, 1950-52; served as sports editor and columnist for Army newspapers; became sergeant.

MEMBER: Writers Guild of America, PEN, American Academy of Arts and Letters.

AWARDS, HONORS: Award for reporting, Puerto Rican Civic Association (Miami, FL), 1957; Page One Award, Newspaper Guild, 1965, for reporting; *Times-Union* won the New York State Publishers Award for Community Service, 1965, on the basis of several of Kennedy's articles on Albany's slums; National Association for the Advancement of Colored People award, 1965, for reporting; Writer of the Year Award, Friends of the Albany Public Library, 1975; National Endowment for the Arts fellowship, 1981; MacArthur Foundation fellowship, 1983; National Book Critics Circle Award, 1983, and Pulitzer Prize for fiction, 1984, both for *Ironweed;*

New York State Governor's Arts Award, 1984; honored by citizens of Albany and the State University of New York at Albany with "William Kennedy's Albany" celebration, September 6-9, 1984; Before Columbus Foundation American Book Award, 1985, for *O Albany!;* Brandeis University Creative Arts Award, 1986; L.H.D., Russell Sage College, 1980, Rensselaer Polytechnic Institute, 1987, Fordham University, 1992, and Trinity College, 1992; Litt.D., Siena College, 1984, and College of St. Rose, 1985; Commander, Order of Arts and Letters (France), 1993; PEN/Faulkner Award nomination, 2003, for *Roscoe.*

WRITINGS:

The Ink Truck (novel), Dial (New York, NY), 1969.
Legs (novel), Coward (New York, NY), 1975.
Billy Phelan's Greatest Game (novel), Viking (New York, NY), 1978.
Getting It All, Saving It All: Some Notes by an Extremist, New York State Governor's Conference on Libraries, 1978.
Ironweed (novel), Viking (New York, NY), 1983.
O Albany!: An Urban Tapestry (nonfiction), Viking (New York, NY), 1983, published as *O Albany! Improbable City of Political Wizards, Fearless Ethnics, Spectacular Aristocrats, Splendid Nobodies, and Underrated Scoundrels,* Penguin, 1985.
(With son, Brendan Kennedy) *Charley Malarkey and the Belly Button Machine* (juvenile), Atlantic Monthly Press (New York, NY), 1986.
(With Francis Coppola and Mario Puzo) *The Cotton Club,* St. Martin's Press (New York, NY), 1986.
(Author of introduction) *The Making of Ironweed,* Penguin Books, 1988.
Quinn's Book, Viking (New York, NY), 1988.
Very Old Bones, Viking (New York, NY), 1992.
Riding the Yellow Trolley Car: Selected Nonfiction, Viking (New York, NY), 1994.
(With Brendan Kennedy) *Charlie Malarkey and the Singing Moose* (juvenile), Viking (New York, NY), 1994.
The Flaming Corsage (novel), Viking (New York, NY), 1996.
The Albany Trilogy (contains *Legs, Billy Phelan's Greatest Game,* and *Ironweed*), Penguin (New York, NY), 1996.
(With Mary Lynch Kennedy and Hadley M. Smith) *Writing in the Disciplines: A Reader for Writers,* Prentice Hall (Englewood Cliffs, NJ), 1996.
Conversations with William Kennedy, edited by Neila C. Seshachari, University Press of Mississippi (Jackson, MS), 1997.
Roscoe (novel), Viking (New York, NY), 2002.

Contributor to books, including *Gabriel García Màrquez* (criticism), Taurus Ediciones, 1982; and *The Capitol in Albany,* Aperture, 1985. Contributor of articles, interviews, and reviews to periodicals, including *New York Times Magazine, National Observer, New York Times Book Review,Washington Post Book World, New Republic,* and *Look.*

SCREENPLAYS

(With Francis Ford Coppola) *The Cotton Club,* Orion Pictures, 1984.
Ironweed (based on Kennedy's novel), Tri-Star Pictures, 1987.

Also author of screenplay *Legs* for Gene Kirkwood and *Billy Phelan's Greatest Game* for Pepper-Prince Company.

SIDELIGHTS: Novels by Irish-American writer William Kennedy did not receive much critical attention when they first appeared. He was known primarily as a respected and versatile journalist who had worked for Albany, New York's *Times-Union,* the Miami *Herald,* and San Juan, Puerto Rico's *Star. Columbia Journalism Review* writer Michael Robertson cited former editor William J. Dorvillier's comment that Kennedy was "one of the best complete journalists—as reporter, editor, whatever—that I've known in sixty years in the business." But when Kennedy's 1983 novel *Ironweed* won the Pulitzer Prize, his fiction was given new life and three early novels were reissued and became bestsellers. Hollywood also took note; director Francis Ford Coppola enlisted Kennedy to write the screenplay for *The Cotton Club,* and he also wrote screen versions of his three other books.

O Albany!, written before *Ironweed*'s spectacular reception secured long-overdue literary recognition for Kennedy, is based in part upon a series of articles Kennedy wrote about city neighborhoods for the *Times-Union* in the mid-1960s. *Publishers Weekly* reviewer Joseph Barbato maintained that the essays in *O Albany!* provide readers with a "nonfiction delineation of Kennedy's imaginative source—an upstate city of politicians and hoodlums, of gambling dens and ethnic neighborhoods, which for all its isolation remains, he insists 'as various as the American psyche' and rich in stories and characters." Christopher Lehmann-Haupt agreed in the *New York Times* that "even more absorbing than the detail and the enthusiasm is the raw material of Mr. Kennedy's fiction, present on every page [of the essays]. Even if one doesn't give a damn for Albany, it is always interesting to watch the author's imagination at play in the city and its history, for one is witnessing the first steps in a novelist's creative process." As Kennedy explains in his introduction to the work, "I write this book not as a booster of Albany, which I am, nor as an apologist for the city, which I sometimes am, but rather as a person whose imagination has become fused with a single place, and in that place finds all the elements that a man ever needs for the life of the soul."

Legs, Billy Phelan's Greatest Game, and *Ironweed* are all set in the Albany of the 1930s. Margaret Croyden stated in the *New York Times Magazine* that the books "are inexorably linked to [Kennedy's] native city . . . during the Depression years, when Albany was a wide-open city, run by Irish bosses and their corrupt political machine. This sense of place gives Kennedy's work a rich texture, a deep sense of authenticity." Susan Chira of the *New York Times* added that Albany, "often dismissed by outsiders as provincial and drab, lives in Mr. Kennedy's acclaimed fiction as a raucous town that symbolizes all that was glorious and corrupt, generous and sordid in the America of the 20s and 30s."

The Ink Truck is a novel about an Albany newspaper strike featuring a main character described by *Time* reviewer R.Z. Sheppard as "a columnist named Bailey, a highly sexed free spirit with a loud checkered sports jacket, a long green scarf and a chip on his shoulder as big as the state capitol." "It is my hope," Kennedy told *Library Journal* in 1969, that *The Ink Truck* "will stand as an analgesic inspiration to all weird men of good will and rotten luck everywhere." The novel, Sheppard related, culminates in "a poignant conclusion, yet it does not show Kennedy at his full spellbinding power. Much of the book is inspired blarney, fun to read and probably fun to write."

This political landscape dominates Kennedy's novels. Kennedy wrote in *O Albany!* that "it was a common Albany syndrome for children to grow up obsessed with being a Democrat. Your identity was fixed by both religion and politics, but from the political hierarchy came the way of life: the job, the perpetuation of the job, the dole when there was no job, the loan when there was no dole, the security of the neighborhood, the new street-light, the new sidewalk, the right to run your bar after hours or to open a cardgame on the sneak. These things came to you not by right of citizenship. Republicans had no such rights. They came to you because you gave allegiance to Dan O'Connell and his party."

Kennedy's knowledge of Albany's political machinery is firsthand. A Toronto *Globe and Mail* reporter indicated that Kennedy's "father sold pies, cut hair, worked in a foundry, wrote illegal numbers, ran political errands for the Democratic ward heelers, and was rewarded by the Machine by being made a deputy sheriff." And, as Croyden explained, William Sr. "often took his son with him to political clubs and gambling joints where young Bill Kennedy, with his eye and ear for detail and for the tone and temper of Irish-Americans, listened and watched and remembered." Kennedy, wrote Doris Grumbach in the *Saturday Review*, "knows every bar, hotel, store, bowling alley, pool hall, and whorehouse that ever opened in North Albany. He knows where the Irish had their picnics and parties—and what went on at them; where their churches were; where they bet on horses, played the numbers, and bet on poker. He can re-create with absolute accuracy the city conversations."

One of the few Kennedy novels that does not rely heavily on firsthand experience is *Legs,* for which he did extensive research on the gangster era. *Legs,* according to *Washington Post* reviewer Curt Suplee , is a "fictional biography" of Jack "Legs" Diamond, the "vicious" Irish-American gangster-bootlegger "who in 1931 was finally shot to death" at an Albany rooming house. Kennedy's novel chronicles "Legs' attempts to smuggle heroin, his buying of politicians, judges and cops," and his womanizing, related W.T. Lhamon in the *New Republic.* A bully and a torturer who frequently betrayed associates, Diamond made many enemies. Several attempts were made on his life, and to many people, he seemed unkillable. Though vicious, Diamond was also a glamorous figure. *Listener* critic Tony Aspler indicated that writer F. Scott Fitzgerald met the gangster on a transatlantic crossing in 1926, and in the words of *Times Literary Supplement* writer Philip French, Diamond "may have been the model" for Fitzgerald's character Jay Gatsby. Legs Diamond, pointed out Suplee, "evolved into a national obsession, a godsend for copyshort newsmen, a mesmerizing topic in tavern or tearoom. Yet profoundly evil."

Kennedy's second novel in the "Albany" cycle, *Billy Phelan's Greatest Game,* explores the same territory. As *Newsweek* reviewer Peter S. Prescott related, "The year is 1938, the time is almost always after dark, and the characters . . . are constantly reminded of times further past, of the floods and strikes, the scandals and murders of a quarter century before." The plot of the novel is related by reporter Martin Daugherty. Through his eyes, wrote Suplee, "we watch Billy—a pool shark, bowling ace and saloon-wise hustler with a pitilessly rigid code of ethics—prowl among Albany's night-town denizens. But when kidnappers abduct the sole child of an omnipotent clan (patterned on the family of the late Dan O'Connell, of Albany's Democratic machine), Billy is pushed to turn informer, and faces competing claims of conscience."

Billy Phelan's Greatest Game received a smattering of mildly favorable critical attention, as did *Legs,* but did not sell particularly well; all three of the author's earlier novels sold only a few thousand copies. The first one hundred pages of *Ironweed*—detailing the story of Billy's father who left the family when Billy was nine—were originally accepted by Viking, but the book later lost the marketing backing it needed. In 1979 Kennedy agreed it would be best to submit the novel elsewhere. It was rejected twelve more times, and the author was disillusioned—past fifty and in debt—when Saul Bellow wrote Viking, admonishing them for slighting Kennedy's talent and asking them to reconsider their decision not to publish *Ironweed.* Viking heeded Bellow's letter, in which the Nobel Prize-winner referred to Kennedy's "Albany" novels, calling them "a distinguished group of books."

By itself, *Ironweed* did not appear to be a good publishing risk. The subject matter is relentlessly downbeat. *Ironweed* portrays "the world of the down-and-outer, the man who drifts by the windows of boarding houses and diners with a slouch hat and a brain whose most vivid images are twenty years old," noted *Detroit News* critic James F. Veseley. Prior to publication, editors took issue with the book's unconventional use of language. *New York Review of Books* critic Robert Towers wrote that, in *Ironweed,* Kennedy "largely abandons the rather breezy, quasi-journalistic narrative voice of his previous fiction and resorts to a more poetically charged, often surrealistic use of language as he re-creates the experiences and mental states of an alcoholic bum." As Kennedy told a Toronto *Globe and Mail* reporter, "They . . . objected that the book was overwritten, they didn't understand what I was doing in terms of language, they felt that no bum would ever talk like Francis does, or think like he does, that they thought of him only as a bum. They didn't understand that what I was striving for was to talk about the central eloquence of every human being. We all have this unutterable eloquence, and the closest you can get to it is to make it utterable at some point, in some way that separates it from the conscious level of life."

The figures in *Ironweed* are drawn from portraits Kennedy gathered for a nonfiction study of the street people of Albany, called *Lemon Weed.* Rejected by publishers, *Lemon Weed,* a collection of interviews with the homeless, was set aside while Kennedy worked on *Billy Phelan's Greatest Game.* After concentrating on its main character, Francis Phelan, the author decided to reshape the *Lemon Weed* material using the fictional Francis's point of view. Thus, "the specifics in *Ironweed*—the traction strike, professional baseball, Irish immigrant experiences, a vast Irish cemetery, an Irish neighborhood, the Erie Canal and so forth—are the elements of life in Albany," Kennedy told Croyden. "Some people say that *Ironweed* might have had any setting, and perhaps this is true. But the values that emerged are peculiar to my own town and to my own time and would not be the same in a smaller city, or a metropolis, or a city that was not Irish, or wasn't large enough to support a skid row."

Ironweed, "which refers to a tough-stemmed member of the sunflower family," according to Lehmann-Haupt, "recounts a few days in the life of an Albany skid-row bum, a former major-league third-baseman with a talent for running, particularly running away, although his ambition now, at the height of the Depression, has been scaled down to the task of getting through the next twenty minutes or so." Once Phelan ran from Albany after he threw a rock at a scab and killed him during a trolley strike, setting off a riot, but he was later in the habit of leaving the town and his family to play in the leagues every baseball season. When he accidentally dropped his newborn son—breaking his neck and killing him—while attempting to change the child's diapers, Francis ran from town and abandoned his family for good.

Now Phelan is back in Albany after twenty-two years, as Towers noted, "lurching around the missions and flophouses of the city's South End." On a cold Halloween night and the following All Saints' Day in 1938, the weekend of Orson Welles's *War of the Worlds* broadcast, Phelan "encounters the ghosts of his friends, relatives, and murder victims, who shout at him on buses, appear in saloons wearing corsages, talk with him from their graves in St. Agnes's cemetery," related Mark Caldwell in the *Voice Literary Supplement.*

Kennedy's next novel, *Quinn's Book,* set in pre-Civil War Albany, begins another cycle centered on residents of New York's capitol city. In the beginning, pre-teen narrator Daniel Quinn witnesses a spectacular drowning accident on the banks of the Hudson River followed by a deviant sexual act in which a whore, presumed drowned, miraculously revives. It is also his first meeting with "Maud the wondrous," a girl he saves from

drowning, who becomes the love of his life. "The end is a whirl of events that include sketches of high life in Saratoga and accounts of horse races, boxing matches and a draft riot," Richard Eder related in the *Los Angeles Times Book Review.* He continued, "Daniel shocks a fashionable audience with a bitterly realistic account of his Civil War experiences. Hillegond is savagely murdered; her murderer is killed by two owls jointly and mysteriously controlled by Maud and a magical platter owned by Daniel. The two lovers are lushly and definitively reunited." With these events, said Eder, *Quinn's Book* "elevates portions or approximations of New York history—Dutch, English, Irish—into legend."

Most reviews of *Quinn's Book* were favorable. Although George Garrett, writing in Chicago's *Tribune Books,* called *Quinn's Book* "one of the most bloody and violent novels" he has read, the gore is necessary to tell the whole truth about life in Albany, the critic added. In this regard, Garrett elaborated, the author's "integrity is unflinching. Yet this is, too, a profoundly funny and joyous story, as abundant with living energy as any novel you are likely to read this year or for a long time to come." Some readers feel that the idiomatic language Kennedy uses to evoke a past era sometimes misses the mark; however, countered T. Coraghessan Boyle in the *New York Times Book Review,* "The language of *Quinn's Book* rises above occasional lapses, and Quinn, as the book progresses, becomes increasingly eloquent, dropping the convoluted syntax in favor of a cleaner, more contemporary line. And if the history sometimes overwhelms the story, it is always fascinating. . . . Kennedy does indeed have the power to peer into the past, to breathe life into it and make it indispensable, and Quinn's battle to control his destiny and win Maud is by turns grim, amusing and deeply moving. In an era when so much of our fiction is content to accomplish so little, *Quinn's Book* is a revelation. Large-minded, ardent, alive on every page with its author's passion for his place and the events that made it, it is a novel to savor." Concluded Toronto *Globe and Mail* reviewer H.J. Kirchhoff, "This is historical fiction suffused with mysticism and myth. . . . *Quinn's Book* is superlative fiction."

In *The Flaming Corsage,* another contribution to the "Albany saga," Kennedy covers the twenty-eight years between 1884 and 1912, concentrating on the marriage between Edward Daugherty, an Irish-American playwright, and Katrina, the daughter of a patrician family that traces its roots back to English Puritan revolutionary Oliver Cromwell. In *The Flaming Corsage,* Kennedy dramatizes the conflict between Irish immigrants and the culture they struggled to adopt. Michael Gorra, writing for the *New York Times,* noted that "[never] before have we seen so clearly the degree to which Mr. Kennedy is not only a regional writer but an ethnic one. In the past, almost all his characters have been Irish Catholics, but here that's underlined by Edward's pursuit of the Episcopalian Katrina, a pursuit that offers a fuller sense of the society against which Irish America is defined." James B. Denigan, writing in *America,* called *The Flaming Corsage* "a complex, subtly sequenced novel that, in a florid tapestry of linguistic virtuosity, buttonholes readers with a compelling tale of guile, shame and conflict. In his novels, with their physical strength and vitality, obsession with capricious success and faith in a willful democracy hell-bent on denying class identity, Kennedy reconfirms that Albany is indeed a microcosm of America." Some critics, like Gorra, found *The Flaming Corsage* to be "less than the sum of its parts." The critic concluded, however, that narrative requirements of novel cycles are complex, and qualifies his criticism of Kennedy's latest effort: "It adds little to the Albany cycle as a whole; but neither, and despite my reservations, does it seriously detract from Mr. Kennedy's achievement."

Kennedy's fascination with Albany continues in his seventh novel, *Roscoe.* Although a fictional story about Roscoe Conway, a Democratic party boss immediately after World War II, *Roscoe,* like many of Kennedy's "Albany" novels, has a factual basis. "Most of the characters are based on real historical figures, the leaders of Albany's infamous O'Connell political machine," Sandy English explained in an online review of the novel for the World Socialist Web site. English lamented that it is difficult to "distinguish Kennedy's voice from Roscoe's, . . . at times it is not clear whether the sentiments are the protagonist's or the author's." Noting Kennedy's talent for portraying Irish Americans who, while "self-destructive and melancholic, . . . are also wildly comic and vibrantly alive," David W. Madden added in his *Review of Contemporary Fiction* appraisal that in *Roscoe* the author "has created a rich tapestry of mid-twentieth-century America . . . home to schemers and swindlers, crooked politicians and charming rogues, the America often unacknowledged in the euphoria of the war years." Calling *Roscoe* the "most overtly political novel in Kennedy's Albany cycle," *Book* reviewer Don McCleese added that the novel eschews formal conventions for vitality. "As the author approaches his mid-seventies," the critic explained, "he plainly has plenty on his mind and little patience with formalistic conventions. . . . Kennedy is less concerned with dotting 'i's and crossing 't's than with letting the reader know how things really work—in Albany, on earth, in heaven."

BIOGRAPHICAL AND CRITICAL SOURCES:

BOOKS

Contemporary Literary Criticism, Thomson Gale (Detroit, MI), Volume 6, 1976, Volume 28, 1984, Volume 34, 1985, Volume 53, 1989.

McCaffery, Larry, and Sinda Gregory, *Alive and Writing: Interviews with American Authors of the 1980s,* University of Illinois Press (Champaign, IL), 1987.

Reilly, Edward C., *William Kennedy,* Twayne (New York, NY), 1991.

Van Dover, J. K., *Understanding William Kennedy,* University of South Carolina Press (Columbia, SC), 1991.

PERIODICALS

America, May 19, 1984; November 21, 1992, p. 410; January 29, 1994, James E. Rocks, review of *Riding the Yellow Trolley Car,* p. 29; September 14, 1996, p. 28.

Book, January-February, 2002, Don McCleese, review of *Roscoe,* p. 64.

Booklist, January 1, 2003, review of *Roscoe,* p. 792.

Chicago Tribune, January 23, 1983.

Christianity Today, May 13, 1988, p. 63.

Classical and Modern Literature, summer, 1988, pp. 247-63.

Commonweal, October 13, 1978; September 9, 1983; May 20, 1988, p. 308; May 19, 1989, p. 298; May 22, 1992, p. 28; September 13, 1996, Daniel M. Murtaugh, review of *The Flaming Corsage,* p. 36.

Critique, spring, 1986, pp. 167-184.

Detroit News, January 30, 1983; February 26, 1984.

Economist, March 2, 2002, review of *Roscoe.*

Entertainment Weekly, April 24, 1992, p. 60; July 9, 1993, p. 45; June 17, 1994, p. 66.

Esquire, March, 1985.

Gentlemen's Quarterly, June, 1993, p. 47.

Globe and Mail (Toronto, Ontario, Canada), September 1, 1984; December 15, 1984; May 21, 1988.

Hudson Review, summer, 1983.

Library Journal, October 1, 1969; April 15, 1996, p. 122; September 1, 1996, p. 228.

Listener, May 6, 1976.

Los Angeles Times, December 14, 1984.

Los Angeles Times Book Review, December 26, 1982; September 23, 1984; May 22, 1988.

New Republic, May 24, 1975; February 14, 1983; June 27, 1988, p. 41.

New Statesman & Society, June 17, 1988, p. 44.

Newsweek, June 23, 1975; May 8, 1978; January 31, 1983; February 6, 1984; May 9, 1988, p. 72.

New York, May 23, 1988, p. 93.

New Yorker, February 7, 1983; January 11, 1988, p. 78; April 27, 1992, p. 106; January 21, 2002, review of *Roscoe,* p. 83.

New York Review of Books, March 31, 1983; August 13, 1992, p. 54.

New York Times, January 10, 1983; September 17, 1983; December 23, 1983; September 22, 1984; March 12, 1987; July 19, 1987; September 18, 1987; December 13, 1987; May 16, 1988; May 2, 1996, pp. B5, C19.

New York Times Book Review, January 23, 1983; November 13, 1983; January 1, 1984; September 30, 1984; October 2, 1986; January 25, 1987, p. 3; May 22, 1988, p. 1; May 20, 1990, p. 1; May 10, 1992, p. 1; May 16, 1993, p. 11; May 19, 1996, p. 7; May 4, 1997, p. 32; June 1, 1997, p. 52.

New York Times Magazine, August 26, 1984.

Observer (London, England), October 20, 1969.

Paris Review, fall, 1989, pp. 35-59.

People, December 24, 1984; January 18, 1988; May 25, 1992, p. 31; June 24, 1996, p. 29.

Playboy, June, 1988, p. 22.

Poets & Writers, March-April, 1994, pp. 42-49.

Publishers Weekly, December 9, 1983; May 18, 1988, p. 71; February 3, 1992, p. 62; March 15, 1993, p. 76; June 6, 1994, p. 64; March 4, 1996, p. 52; March 17, 1997, p. 81.

Review of Contemporary Fiction, summer, 2002, David W. Madden, review of *Roscoe,* p. 227.

Rolling Stone, September 30, 1993, p. 18.

Saturday Review, April 29, 1978.

Time, January 24, 1983; October 1, 1984; December 17, 1984; May 16, 1988, p. 92; April 27, 1992, p. 68; May 13, 1996, p. 92.

Times Literary Supplement, October 5, 1984.

Tribune Books (Chicago, IL), May 8, 1988.

Twentieth Century Literature, spring, 1999, Brock Clarke, "'A Hostile Decade': The Sixties and Self-Criticism in William Kennedy's Early Prose," p. 1.

Voice Literary Supplement, February, 1983; October, 1984.

Washington Post, October 5, 1969; May 18, 1975; December 28, 1983.

Washington Post Book World, January 16, 1983; January 29, 1984; October 14, 1984; May 8, 1988.

World Literature Today, summer, 1994, Marvin J. La-Hood, review of *Riding the Yellow Trolley Car,* p. 580; spring, 1997, Marvin J. LaHood, review of *The Flaming Corsage,* p. 386.

ONLINE

World Socialist Web site, http://www.wsws.org/ (January, 2004), Sandy English, review of *Roscoe.*

*   *   *

KENNILWORTHY WHISP
See ROWLING, J.K.

*   *   *

KERR, M.E.
See MEAKER, Marijane

*   *   *

KERRY, Lois
See DUNCAN, Lois

*   *   *

KESEY, Ken 1935-2001
(Ken Elton Kesey, O.U. Levon, a joint pseudonym)

PERSONAL: Born September 17, 1935, in La Junta, CO; died from complications following surgery for liver cancer, November 10, 2001, in Eugene, OR; son of Fred A. and Geneva (Smith) Kesey; married (Norma) Faye Haxby, May 20, 1956; children: Shannon A., Zane C., Jed M. (deceased), Sunshine M. *Education:* University of Oregon, B.A., 1957; Stanford University, graduate study, 1958-61, 1963.

CAREER: Novelist, artist, and farmer. Night attendant in psychiatric ward, Veterans Administration Hospital, Menlo Park, CA, 1961; Intrepid Trips, Inc. (motion picture company), president, 1964; *Spit in the Ocean* (magazine), editor, beginning 1974; University of Oregon, instructor in novel-writing, beginning 1990.

AWARDS, HONORS: Woodrow Wilson fellowship; Saxton Fund fellowship, 1959; Distinguished Service award, State of Oregon, 1978; Robert Kirsh Award, *Los Angeles Times,* 1991, for lifetime of work.

WRITINGS:

One Flew over the Cuckoo's Nest (novel), Viking (New York, NY), 1962, 40th anniversary edition, illustrated and with new introduction by Kesey, 2002.

Sometimes a Great Notion (novel), Viking (New York, NY), 1964.

(Contributor) *The Last Whole Earth Catalog: Access to Tools,* Portola Institute, 1971.

(Editor, with Paul Krassner, and contributor) *The Last Supplement to the Whole Earth Catalog,* Portola Institute, 1971.

(Compiler and contributor) *Kesey's Garage Sale* (interviews and articles, including "An Impolite Interview with Ken Kesey," and screenplay "O'Tools from My Chest"), introduction by Arthur Miller, Viking (New York, NY), 1973.

(Author of introduction) Paul Krassner, editor, *Best of "The Realist": The Sixties' Most Outrageously Irreverent Magazine,* Running Press, 1984.

Demon Box (essays, poetry, and stories, including "The Day after Superman Died," "Good Friday," "Finding Doctor Fung," "Run into the Great Wall," and "The Search for the Secret Pyramid"), Viking (New York, NY), 1986.

Little Tricker the Squirrel Meets Big Double the Bear (juvenile), illustrations by Barry Moser, Penguin (New York, NY), 1988.

(Under joint pseudonym O.U. Levon [anagram for "University of Oregon novel"] with others, and author of introduction) *Caverns* (mystery novel), Penguin (New York, NY), 1989.

The Further Inquiry (autobiographical screenplay), photographs by Ron Bevirt, Viking (New York, NY), 1990.

The Sea Lion (juvenile), Viking (New York, NY), 1991.

Sailor Song, Viking (New York, NY), 1992.

Last Go Round, Viking (New York, NY), 1994.

Kesey's Jail Journal: Cut the M Loose, Viking (New York, NY), 2003.

Also author of unpublished novels, "End of Autumn" and "Zoo," and of "Seven Prayers by Grandma Whittier," an unfinished novel serialized 1974-81 in *Spit in the Ocean.* Work included in anthologies, including *Stanford Short Stories 1962,* edited by Wallace Stegner and Richard Scowcroft, Stanford University Press, 1962. Contributor of articles to periodicals, including *Esquire, Rolling Stone,* and *Oui.*

A collection of Kesey's manuscripts is housed at the University of Oregon.

ADAPTATIONS: *One Flew over the Cuckoo's Nest* was adapted for the stage by Dale Wasserman and produced on Broadway, 1963, revived in 1971 and 2001, and published as *One Flew over the Cuckoo's Nest: A Play in Three Acts,* S. French (New York, NY), 1970, new edition with criticism, edited by John C. Pratt, 1973, revised edition, 1974; adapted for film by United Artists, 1975; and adapted for audiobook, 1998. *Sometimes a Great Notion* was adapted for film by Universal, 1972.

SIDELIGHTS: Ken Kesey, a writer and cultural hero of the mid-twentieth-century's so-called psychic frontier, is best known for his widely read novel *One Flew over the Cuckoo's Nest* and the insightful contemporary novel *Sometimes a Great Notion.* Kesey's works are set in California and Oregon, two locations representing two facets of Kesey's experience that provided the major tensions in his works. Oregon represents traditional rural family values and self-reliance inherited from Baptist pioneer stock; California is associated with the countercultural revolution in which Kesey played an important role during his lifetime. Therefore Kesey's name is often associated with the American West Coast and the hippie movement that centered itself there during the 1960s. Though he eventually adopted a more critical stance in regard to the alternative lifestyle he once championed, Kesey's later works remain haunted by fond references to the uninhibited life he enjoyed as a member of the Merry Pranksters, a group that traveled America in a bus when experimental drug use was at its peak. His novels, plays, screenplays, and essays express the author's intrepid quest for heightened consciousness in which he explored magic, hypnotism, mind-altering or psychoactive drugs, the occult, Eastern religions, and esoteric philosophies. His works also carry forward the American literary traditions of the Transcendentalists and the Beats as well as the frontier humor and vernacular style established by nineteenth-century humorist and novelist Mark Twain.

Kesey was born and raised "a hard-shell Baptist" in Colorado and Oregon, he once told Linda Gaboriau in a *Crawdaddy* interview. He accompanied his father on many hunting and fishing trips in the Pacific Northwest and developed a deep respect for nature. His love of the outdoors was matched by his fascination with extraordinary experience. He studied theatrical magic and learned to perform illusions. "I . . . did shows all through high school and in college," he once told Gaboriau. "I went from this into ventriloquism (and even had a show on TV), and from ventriloquism into hypnotism. And from hypnotism into dope. But it's always been the same trip, the same kind of search."

After high school Kesey auditioned for film roles in Hollywood before entering the University of Oregon in Eugene, where he majored in speech and communications and gained experience in acting and writing for radio and television. An active athlete during both high school and college, he won a scholarship as an outstanding college wrestler. Each of Kesey's interests figure largely in his works. Hunting and fishing are strategically important events in the two major works that established his literary reputation. His characters are physically strong and ready to compete against overwhelming pressure to conform to standards or submit to authorities that oppose their well-being. His style incorporates techniques borrowed from theatre and film such as flashbacks, fade-outs, and jump cuts, and he evidences a familiarity with the conventions of horror films and popular Westerns.

Kesey married his high school sweetheart, Faye Haxby, while at the University of Oregon, and moved to California where he enrolled in Stanford University's creative writing program. There he met Wallace Stegner, Richard Scowcroft, Malcolm Cowley, and Frank O'Connor—writers who were also literary critics—as well as fellow students Wendell Berry, Larry McMurtry, and Robert Stone. He also encountered the cultural radicalism then developing in Perry Lane, a section of Stanford patterned after the haven of the Beat movement in San Francisco's North Beach. According to *Free You* contributor Vie Lovell, to whom Kesey dedicated *One Flew over the Cuckoo's Nest,* the Perry Lane group "pioneered what have since become the hallmarks of hippie culture: LSD and other psychedelics too numerous to mention, body painting, light shows and mixed media presentations, total aestheticism, be-ins, exotic costumes, strobe lights, sexual mayhem, freakouts and the deification of psychoticism, eastern mysticism, and the rebirth of hair."

When Lovell suggested Kesey take part in the drug experiments being conducted at the Veterans Administration Hospital at Menlo Park, he accepted. There he was paid to ingest various psychoactive drugs and report on their effects. This experience, together with his experiences as an aide at the V.A. Hospital, led Kesey to write *One Flew over the Cuckoo's Nest.*

One Flew over the Cuckoo's Nest is a celebration of the resilience of the human spirit as seen in the characteristically American resistance to corrupt authority. The novel tells how Randle Patrick McMurphy, a cocky, fast-talking inmate of a prison farm who has had himself committed to a mental hospital to avoid work, creates upheaval in the ward that is so efficiently and repressively directed by Nurse Ratched. His self-confidence and irrepressible sense of humor inspire the passive, dehumanized patients to rebel against Ratched

and the "Combine" of society she represents. McMurphy ultimately sacrifices himself in the process of teaching his fellow patients the saving lessons of laughter and self-reliance.

Contemporary audiences reacted positively to Kesey's novel. In the early 1960s *One Flew over the Cuckoo's Nest* presented a critique of an American society that had been portrayed in the 1950s as a lonely crowd of organization men who could achieve affluence only through strict conformity. That critique continued to suit the mood of the 1970s and 1980s because larger themes were also involved: the modern technological world as necessarily divorced from nature; contemporary society as repressive; authority as mechanical and destructive; and contemporary man as weak, frightened, and sexless, a victim of rational but loveless forces beyond his control. The novel's message—that people need to get back in touch with their world, to open doors of perception, to enjoy spontaneous sensuous experience, and to resist the manipulative forces of a technological society—was particularly appealing to the young. By the 1970s it was the contemporary novel most frequently used in college courses.

American audiences have appreciated the work in its incarnations as play, novel, and film. The stage version by Dale Wasserman appeared on Broadway with Kirk Douglas starring as McMurphy in 1963 and was revived in 1971, and again in 2001 when it was produced by Chicago's Steppenwolf theater company and starred actor Gary Sinise. The film version, directed by Milos Forman and starring Jack Nicholson, was a box office hit and won six Academy Awards in 1975.

Kesey's novel has been analyzed by critics beyond the literary realm due to the breadth of subjects, issues, and disciplines it includes. In *Lex et Scientia,* the official journal of the International Academy of Law and Science, Ralph Porzio described *One Flew over the Cuckoo's Nest* as "a cornucopia of source material from disciplines so numerous and varied as to challenge the mind and imagination." Porzio observed that it touches upon psychology, psychiatry, medicine, literature, human relations, drama, art, cosmology, law, religion, American culture, and folk culture through a kaleidoscopic blend of tragedy, pathos, and humor. A partial list of topics that show up in various analyses of the book include: patterns of romance, patterns of comedy, patterns of tragedy, black humor, the absurd, the hero in modern dress, the comic Christ, folk and western heroes, the fool as mentor, the Grail Knight, attitudes toward sex, abdication of masculinity, the politics of laughter, mechanistic and totemistic symbols, the comic strip, the ritualistic father-figure, and the psychopathic savior.

Ronald Wallace, writing in *The Last Laugh: Form and Affirmation in the Contemporary American Comic Novel,* connected the novel directly to Kesey's early interest in comic books by pointing out that its main characters are drawn from ancient conventions of comedy. Wallace perceived in Nurse Ratched and McMurphy respectively the *aiazon*—the boastful, deluded fool—and the *eiron*—the witty self-deprecator who defeats his opponent by hiding his skill and intelligence. Furthermore, Wallace saw McMurphy as a "Dionysian Lord of Misrule" who "presides over a comic fertility ritual and restores instinctual life to the patients." In a *Critique* review, Terry G. Sherwood noticed the balance between comic strip conventions and those belonging to the serious novel, since the work's major confrontation is between good and evil. *Journal of Narrative Technique* reviewer Michael Boardman pointed out the novel's power as a classic tragedy because it portrays a character opposed by forces from within himself as well as from others. The conflict between Ratched and McMurphy becomes a struggle between McMurphy's need for freedom as an individual and his need to survive in a hostile environment by conforming to oppressive standards. The conventions of the Western novel with its characters, colloquialisms, and frontier values are also present in *One Flew over the Cuckoo's Nest,* observed Richard Blessing in *Journal of Popular Culture.* Blessing wrote, "Essentially, the McMurphy who enters the ward is a frontier hero, an anachronistic paragon of rugged individualism, relentless energy, capitalistic shrewdness, virile coarseness and productive strength. He is Huck Finn with muscles, Natty Bumppo with pubic hair. He is the descendant of the pioneer who continually fled civilization and its feminizing and gentling influence."

While many reviewers saw much to learn from the book, the brand of individualism and freedom presented in McMurphy's behavior approaches anarchy too closely for others. The mayhem he raises by throwing plates and butter at walls, shouting obscenities, breaking windows, sneaking prostitutes into the ward, and stealing boats, claimed Bruce E. Wallis in *Cithara,* is not a foundation for lasting sanity and self-esteem beyond reproach. The best opposition to society's more repressive forces, Wallis maintained, may not, after all, be man's sexual and nonrational capacities.

Some critics were alarmed by the novel's portrayal of women. Leslie Horst noted in *Lex et Scientia* that Kesey's depiction of Nurse Ratched is demeaning; in fact,

"considerable hatred of women is justified in the logic of the novel. The plot demands that the dreadful women who break the rules men have made for them become the targets of the reader's wrath." Viewing the novel primarily from the aspect of gender, Robert Forrey in *Modern Fiction Studies* claimed that "the premise of the novel is that women ensnare, emasculate, and, in some cases, crucify men." On the other hand, Wallace contended that there is no misogyny intended in Kesey's reversal of traditionally assigned gender-appropriate roles, which Wallace related to all comic literature "from Aristophanes to Erica Jong." Boardman suggested that Ratched is not meant to represent womankind, but to be the incarnation of evil required by the novel's dramatic action. In *The Art of Grit: Ken Kesey's Fiction,* M. Gilbert Porter reported Kesey's comment that any good story needs a villain that is truly recognizably evil if the writer is to fulfill his ethical purpose, that of standing "between the public and evil. . . . The good writer in [Kesey's] opinion is a person of 'power' and character who guards faithfully that axis of human choice."

In his book *Ken Kesey,* Barry Leeds commented that Kesey's second novel, *Sometimes a Great Notion,* is superior to *One Flew over the Cuckoo's Nest* because it is "a far more artistically impressive work on several levels. In terms of structure, point of view, theme, it is more ambitious, more experimental, and ultimately more successful." *Sometimes a Great Notion* reflects Kesey's Oregon background and the concerns of the upper Northwest region. The title refers to the folk-song refrain "Sometimes it seems a great notion / to jump in the river and drown," and signals one of the book's themes: the relatively high suicide rate in the Wakonda logging town and others like it. In the novel independent loggers Hank and Leland Stamper are at odds with their union-dominated community and with each other. After Hank becomes involved with his Ivy-league-educated half-brother's mother in a sexual relationship, Leland seeks revenge by seducing Hank's wife. The novel approaches these events from a variety of points of view to reveal what the brothers learn from each other.

Like William Faulkner, Kesey comments on the subjectivity of perception by using the cinematic device of multiple perspectives. To make the medium of fiction more fit for his purpose, he liberates himself from the chronological order used in most conventional novels. He also employs conscious authorial intrusion. Innovative use of italics, capital letters, and parentheses help him replicate in print the confusion, moral bankruptcy, and future shock his characters face.

In many ways, the conflict between the Stamper brothers corresponds to Kesey's own inner conflicts. During his college years, the conflict between his down-home athletic nature and his more artistic and intellectual side became more obvious. He could socialize with both intellectuals and more active groups, but they did not usually find each other mutually acceptable. The brothers in *Sometimes a Great Notion* embody these conflicting impulses. As he once explained to Gordon Lish in a *Genesis West* interview: "I want to find out which side of me really is: the woodsy, logger side—complete with homespun homilies and crackerbarrel corniness, a valid side of me that I like—or its opposition. The two Stamper brothers in the novel are each one of the ways I think I am."

In 1963, as Kesey was finishing *Sometimes a Great Notion,* a developer forced the evacuation of Perry Lane, and the Keseys moved to La Honda where he continued as a leader of the psychedelic movement. For the next few years he set aside his writing and sought an alternative with Neal Cassady and other kindred spirits in a group called the Merry Pranksters. His curiosity about altered states of consciousness stimulated by the experiments at the V.A. Hospital, Kesey continued his experimental drug use with the group at La Honda. Evolving from private parties to public parties to large-scale public events, the groups' "acid-tests" introduced light shows, psychedelic art, mixed-media presentations, and acid rock music to the growing hippie culture.

Headed for the New York World's Fair and the events surrounding the publication of *Sometimes a Great Notion,* the Pranksters crossed the country in a 1939 International Harvester bus decorated with bright colors applied at random. Kesey's accounts of those days appear in *Kesey's Garage Sale, Demon Box,* and *The Further Inquiry.*

Critics have referred to *Kesey's Garage Sale* as the book in which the destructive potential of drugs caught up with the author. It contains his screenplay "Over the Border," based on his 1967 flight to Mexico to avoid prosecution for marijuana possession. After witnessing the squalor and anti-American sentiments of small Mexican towns, and after his son survived a close brush with death, Kesey returned to California to serve a short sentence at the San Mateo County Jail and the San Mateo Sheriff's Honor Camp. Afterward, he moved to a farm in Pleasant Hill, Oregon, near Eugene. Many fans sought him out at the farm, looking for drug experiences or a place to live, and numbered in the hundreds each week during the 1970s. *Demon Box,* Kesey's 1986 collection of shorter works written in the '70s and '80s, reflects on both his pleasant and unpleasant experiences in the counterculture.

The Further Inquiry, Kesey's 1990 retrospective on the Merry Prankster years, examines the 1960s and 1970s from a more mature perspective. Structured as a mock trial, the screenplay pits a prosecutor named Chest against the testimony of the various Pranksters. Dierdre English observed in *New York Times Book Review* that, for the author, "the Pranksters were not pioneers but 'unsettlers,' and their destination was no destination. And one not need blame LSD and marijuana for the sins of heroin and cocaine to admit that the acid revolution did leave some dead Indians behind." In this trial, Kesey "is at once confessing to the damage done and asking for equal consideration of the righteous fun the Pranksters wreaked," English explained. "Uptight America was in desperate need of what they provided: an astoundingly successful communal exorcism of the stifling spirits of the 50s' conformity. In the current cultural atmosphere, a new puritanism about sex, drugs and rebellious play, it would be liberating to quaff a hit of what the Pranksters had—their all-out excitement, spontaneity and spoofing. But some of their ideas of fun no longer amuse." English concluded that the group is only partly acquitted by this defense, especially when compared to other accounts of their activities such as Paul Perry's *On the Bus: The Complete Guide to the Legendary Trip of Ken Kesey and the Merry Pranksters and the Birth of the Counterculture.*

Taking experimental literary risks in the 1980s, Kesey wrote the children's book *Little Trickler the Squirrel Meets Big Double the Bear.* In this story, as in his other books, good conquers evil in the form of a little squirrel who decides to stop the bullying of a local tyrant. He also worked with thirteen creative-writing graduate students to write *Caverns,* a mystery novel, leaving it to the students to see that it was published. The novel begins in 1934 when an itinerant evangelist named Loach discovers a cave decorated with archetypical "drawings that will challenge conventional ideas about American archaeology and Western religion," Alfred Bendixen related in *New York Times Book Review.* The story follows Loach from his discovery of the cave, to the murder of a photographer and a subsequent prison term, and finally to his quest to rediscover the cave, accompanied by an archaeologist, a reporter, a priest, two mediums, and a large cast of motley characters. Bendixen added, "The book is probably best described as a partly successful attempt to fuse the adventures of Indiana Jones with the cosmic spirit and multiple perspectives of 'The Canterbury Tales.'" However, Madison Smartt

Bell commented in *Voice Literary Supplement* "The result less resembles *The Canterbury Tales* than an uneven day at the Mingus Jazz Workshop. It's fun to isolate the solos; Kesey's seem the strongest, probably because they are the most recognizable. . . . Most scenes and characters are slightly overdrawn, giving the book a cartoon quality which is nonetheless appealing—it has the same amiably sarcastic relation to the junk adventure novels of the '30s and '40s that the Indiana Jones movies have to old serials. At the same time there are some moving and revealing moments." Bendixen observed that the novel is weakened by the lack of a unified authorial voice, its large cast of mostly unsympathetic characters, and its emphasis on plot and comic misadventures, yet it succeeds in being "a revolutionary model for the teaching of creative writing" by "reminding us . . . that the novel requires an individual voice, fully realized characters and a clear sense of time and place."

Working on the *Caverns* group project helped break the writer's block Kesey encountered half-way through his novel *Sailor Song,* a result of the tragic death of his son Jed in 1984. He finished the novel nine years later, making it his first adult novel in two decades. *Sailor Song* features trademark Kesey zaniness, especially in the details surrounding the plot. It takes place a few years in the future, where most of the ecological disasters that were predicted to happen during the 1980s actually do. There is global warming, nuclear pollution in the oceans, high rates of cancer, and drug addiction. The story is set in the run-down Alaskan fishing village of Kuinak, where residents as diverse as refugees, travelers, and DEAPS—Descendants of Early Aboriginal Peoples—try to make a comfortable home in an increasingly uncomfortable world. Ike Sallas, the hero of the novel, is a former crop duster who, when his daughter died of an ecologically based illness, took revenge on the world by dumping fertilizers on state fairs and other places where people congregated. After being caught he became a middle-class hero. Years later, living in Kuinak, he still inspires admiration among the natives. Enter Nicholas Levertov, an albino Hollywood movie producer, who stalks into this relatively untouched paradise scouting for a location to shoot his next movie. However, as Levertov soon makes clear, he intends to change Kuinak forever by turning it into a tourist attraction. The citizenry of the village go berserk, with some residents wanting the money to be gained by complying with Levertov's desires and others wanting the village to remain untouched.

Critical reception to Kesey's novel was mixed. "*Sailor Song* does not make one single particle of sense," complained *New York Times Book Review* critic Donald E.

Westlake, who dubbed the book "a long-awaited return, maybe too long," for Kesey. Westlake criticized the structure of the book and concluded that "the novel, having been incoherent from the beginning, turns apocalyptic at the end, which doesn't in any way help." Roger Rosenblatt, writing in *New Republic,* also had complaints about *Sailor Song.* "Kesey could have been a pretty good writer-writer, but chose instead to be a culture-writer. . . . Style to the culture-writer is not writing, but a kind of animated macho typing." Rosenblatt averred that "the new novel is plotless and idealess and pointless in its overflow of parables, anecdotes and caricatures. . . . His writing screams its own insecurity." Yet critic Joe Chidley in *Maclean's* had a different view of *Sailor Song,* praising Kesey's eccentric world and noting that the author's "patient development of a world about to self-destruct is fascinating. And he successfully weaves a moving and mature love story into the complicated tale." Chidley argued that with *Sailor Song* Kesey "proves that despite the long hiatus, he is still in full control of the narrative form" and shows himself to be a "prodigious talent that has been absent for far too long."

In a departure from much of his work, Kesey explores the world of the dime-novel western with his 1994 book *Last Go Round,* written with friend Ken Babbs and based on a story Kesey's father told about the 1911 Pendleton Round Up, where an African-American bronco rider, an older Native American, and a young boy from Tennessee battled to win the title of World Champion All Round Cowboy of the West. Kesey used this story as inspiration, creating his novel out of an amalgam of facts and his own imagination. Jackson Sundown, the Native American, manages to retain his dignity whether he is drinking or not. Johnathan E. Lee Spain is the naïve young Tennessean and the story's narrator, and George Fletcher is the African-American bronco rider. Kesey throws these characters together into a variety of adventures, all for one less-than-lofty goal: to win the silver saddle, and also manages to inject a 1990s race sensitivity into a novel of an earlier time.

Janet Burroway, writing in *New York Times Book Review,* claimed that with *Last Go Round* the authors "produced a pulp-thin plot . . . together with an excess of episode, inflated atmosphere and wonders of prowess, just what's demanded in the formula for the original dime westerns." She believed that the novel shows great promise but hoped Kesey's future efforts would be more focused: "we cheer him back on the bronc, hoping this is not the absolute Last Go Round. But neither does this novel win the silver saddle." Dick Roraback summed up the novel in *Los Angeles Times Book Review* by calling it "Entertaining. Wacky. Sometimes Sappy." Unfortunately for Burroway, *Last Go Round* was true to its title: it was Kesey's last work of fiction.

Though Kesey's works are few in number, they are considered significant additions to that body of writing that seeks to explore and extend the limits of the human spirit. His fiction displays a distinctive blending of a unique American tradition: As an extension of the Beat movement it reflects the concerns and attitudes of American Transcendentalists such as Ralph Waldo Emerson, Henry David Thoreau, and Walt Whitman. Kesey's approach to cherished American traditions and values is original and engaging, and his humor grows naturally out of the situations and idioms of his characters. He displays a skill for creating the revealing anecdote and readily perceives both the rational and more complex sides of human nature, giving his characters the spiritual depth necessary to fully represent themes of freedom and the moral responsibilities of creativity. His innovative fictional technique and self-criticism are notable. Furthermore, in keeping with Kesey's oft-cited declaration that he would "rather live a novel than write one," his personal quests made him an influential leader in culture as well as literature.

Kesey died of complications from surgery for liver cancer on November 10, 2001, shortly before the republication of his classic *One Flew over the Cuckoo's Nest.* For this fortieth anniversary edition, Kesey added a new introduction and twenty-five drawings he made during the period when he worked in a mental institution.

Following Kesey's death, various writers paid homage to him, citing ways in which Kesey had influenced both them and culture as a whole. A *People* writer said that Kesey's mantra that "It is possible to be different without being a threat" was one he followed throughout his life. In *Entertainment Weekly* Chris Nashawaty spoke of how he once sat next to Kesey during a meal at the Sundance Film Festival, and Kesey spoke of his long and interesting life to the young journalist. When Nashawaty entertained Kesey with a description of the beauty of the starry constellations that could be seen in the Sahara Desert, Kesey wished to write down the exact location of the place so that he might include it in "his list of wonders yet to discover."

BIOGRAPHICAL AND CRITICAL SOURCES:

BOOKS

Acton, Jay, Alan Le Mond, and Parker Hodges, *Mug Shots: Who's Who in the New Earth,* World Publishing, 1972.

Allen, Mary, *The Necessary Blankness: Women in Major American Fiction of the Sixties,* University of Illinois Press (Champaign, IL), 1976.

Billingsley, Ronald G., *The Artistry of Ken Kesey,* University of Oregon (Eugene, OR), 1971.

Concise Dictionary of American Literary Biography, 1968-1988, Thomson Gale (Detroit, MI), 1989.

Contemporary Literary Criticism, Thomson Gale (Detroit, MI), Volume 1, 1973, Volume 3, 1975, Volume 6, 1976, Volume 11, 1979, Volume 46, 1987, Volume 64, 1991.

Cook, Bruce, *The Beat Generation,* Scribner (New York, NY), 1971.

Dictionary of Literary Biography, Thomson Gale (Detroit, MI), Volume 2: *American Novelists since World War II,* 1978, Volume 16: *The Beats: Literary Bohemians in Postwar America,* 1983.

Harris, Charles B., *Contemporary American Novelists of the Absurd,* College & University Press, 1971.

Kesey, Ken, *One Flew over the Cuckoo's Nest,* Viking (New York, NY), 1962, 40th anniversary edition, 2002.

Kesey, Ken, *Kesey's Garage Sale,* Viking (New York, NY), 1973.

Kesey, Ken, *Sometimes a Great Notion,* Viking (New York, NY), 1964.

Kesey, Ken, *The Further Inquiry,* Viking (New York, NY), 1990.

Krassner, Paul, *How a Satirical Editor Became a Yippie Conspirator in Ten Easy Years,* Putnam (New York, NY), 1971.

Labin, Suzanne, *Hippies, Drugs, and Promiscuity,* Arlington House, 1972.

Leeds, Barry H., *Ken Kesey,* F. Ungar (New York, NY), 1981.

Perry, Paul, *On the Bus: The Complete Guide to the Legendary Trip of Ken Kesey and the Merry Pranksters and the Birth of the Counterculture,* Thunder's Mouth Press (New York, NY), 1990.

Porter, M. Gilbert, *The Art of Grit: Ken Kesey's Fiction,* University of Missouri Press (Columbia, MO), 1982.

Wallace, Ronald, *The Last Laugh: Form and Affirmation in the Contemporary American Comic Novel,* University of Missouri Press (Columbia, MO), 1971.

Wolfe, Tom, *The Electric Kool-Aid Acid Test,* Farrar, Straus (New York, NY), 1968.

PERIODICALS

Annals of the American Academy of Political and Social Science, Volume 376, 1968.

CEA Critic, Volume 37, 1975.

Children's Book Review Service, winter, 1992, p. 71.

Cithara, Volume 12, 1972.

Crawdaddy, Volume 29, 1972.

Critique, Volume 5, 1962; Volume 13, 1971.

Free You, Volume 2, 1968.

Genesis West, fall, 1963.

Harper's, August, 1994, p. 22.

Inc., August, 2001, review of *Sometimes a Great Notion,* p. 91.

Journal of American Studies, Volume 5, 1971.

Journal of Narrative Technique, Volume 9, 1979, Michael Boardman, review of *One Flew Over the Cuckoo's Nest.*

Journal of Popular Culture, winter, 1971, Richard Blessing, review of *One Flew Over the Cuckoo's Nest.*

Kirkus Reviews, May 15, 1994, p. 651.

Kliatt, September, 1998, review of *One Flew over the Cuckoo's Nest* (audiobook), p. 62.

Lex et Scientia, Volume 13, issues 1-2, 1977.

Library Journal, April 15, 1998, review of *One Flew over the Cuckoo's Nest* (audiobook), p. 134; February 1, 2002, Michael Rogers, p. 138.

Los Angeles Times Book Review, August 31, 1986; September 18, 1994, Dick Roraback, review of *Last Go Round,* p. 6.

Maclean's, September 7, 1992, Joe Chidley, review of *Sailor Song,* p. 50.

Modern Fiction Studies, Volume 19, 1973; Volume 21, 1975.

Nation, February 23, 1974.

New Republic, October 26, 1992.

New Statesman, October 10, 1986.

New Yorker, April 21, 1962; December 1, 1975.

New York Herald Tribune, February 25, 1962; July 27, 1964; August 2, 1964.

New York Review of Books, September 10, 1964.

New York Times, July 27, 1964; January 18, 1966; March 12, 1966; October 21, 1966; August 4, 1986; July 7, 1994, p. C18.

New York Times Book Review, February 4, 1962; August 2, 1964; August 18, 1968; October 7, 1973; August 4, 1986; September 14, 1986; December 31, 1989; January 21, 1990; December 9, 1990; August 23, 1992, p. 5; July 10, 1994, p. 11.

Northwest Review, spring, 1963; spring, 1977.

Observer, July 25, 1993, p. 25.

People, March 22, 1976.

Publishers Weekly, April 25, 1994, p. 53; August 1, 1994, p. 28.

Rocky Mountain Review, Volume 43, number 1, 1989.

Rolling Stone, March 7, 1970; September 27, 1973; July 18, 1974; October 5, 1989.

School Library Journal, November, 1991, p. 101.

Time, February 16, 1962; July 24, 1964; February 12, 1965; September 8, 1986.

Times Literary Supplement, February 24, 1966; February 25, 1972.

Voice Literary Supplement, February 2, 1990, Madison Smartt Bell, review of *Caverns.*

Washington Post, June 9, 1974.

Washington Post Book World, August 10, 1986; July 9, 1995, p. 12.

Western American Literature, Volume 9, 1974; Volume 10, 1975; Volume 22, 1987.

Whole Earth Review, spring, 2002, review of *One Flew over the Cuckoo's Nest,* p. 81.

Wisconsin Studies in Contemporary Literature, Volume 5, 1964; Volume 7, 1966.

ONLINE

Books and Writers, http://www.kirjasto.sci.fi/ (May 12, 2003).

OBITUARIES:

PERIODICALS

Book, March-April, 2002, David Bowman, pp. 34-35.

Entertainment Weekly, November 23, 2001, Chris Nashawaty, p. 16.

Los Angeles Times, November 11, 2001, p. A1.

New York Times, November 11, 2001, p. A34.

People, November 26, 2001, p. 156.

Time, November 19, 2001, p. 27.

Times (London, England), November 12, 2001, p. 19.

Washington Post, November 11, 2001, p. C6.

*   *   *

KESEY, Ken Elton
    See KESEY, Ken

*   *   *

KEYES, Daniel 1927-

PERSONAL: Born August 9, 1927, in Brooklyn, NY; son of William and Betty (Alicke) Keyes; married Aurea Vazquez (a fashion stylist, photographer, and artist), October 14, 1952; children: Hillary Ann, Leslie Joan. *Education:* Studied pre-med for one year at New York

University; Brooklyn College (now Brooklyn College of the City University of New York), A.B. (psychology), 1950, A.M., 1961; attended a postgraduate course taught by psychiatrist Kurt Goldstein at the City College of New York.

ADDRESSES: Agent—Marcy Posner, William Morris Agency, 1325 Avenue of the Americas, New York, NY 10019.

CAREER: Stadium Publishing Co., New York City, associate fiction editor, 1950-52; Fenko & Keyes Photography, Inc., New York City, co-owner, 1953; high school teacher of English, Brooklyn, NY, 1954-55, 1957-62; Wayne State University, Detroit, MI, instructor in English, 1962-66; Ohio University, Athens, lecturer, 1966-72, professor of English and Creative Writing, 1972—, director of creative writing center, 1973-74, 1977-78. Supervising producer of television movie *The Mad Housers,* 1990. *Military service:* U.S. Maritime Service, senior assistant purser, June, 1945-December, 1946.

MEMBER: PEN, Societe des Auteurs et Compositeurs Dramatiques, Authors Guild, Authors League of America, Dramatists Guild (full voting member), Mystery Writers of America, MacDowell Colony Fellows.

AWARDS, HONORS: Hugo Award, World Science Fiction Convention, 1959, for "Flowers for Algernon" (short story); Nebula Award, Science Fiction Writers of America, 1966, for *Flowers for Algernon* (novel); fellow, Yaddo artist colony, 1967; fellow, MacDowell artist colony, 1967; special award, Mystery Writers of America, 1981, for *The Minds of Billy Milligan;* Kurd Lasswitz Award for best book by a foreign author, 1986, for *Die Leben des Billy Milligan,* the German translation of *The Minds of Billy Milligan;* Edgar Allan Poe Award nomination, Mystery Writers of America, 1986, for *Unveiling Claudia: A True Story of a Serial Murder;* individual artists fellowship, Ohio Arts Council, 1986-87; Baker Fund Award, Ohio University, 1986; Award of Honor, Distinguished Alumnus Brooklyn College, 1988.

WRITINGS:

FICTION

Flowers for Algernon (novel), Harcourt (New York City), 1966, Modern Classics Edition, 1995, Creative Paperbacks (Mankato, MN), 2000.

The Touch (novel), Harcourt, 1968, published in England as *The Contaminated Man,* Mayflower (London), 1973.

The Fifth Sally (novel), Houghton (Boston), 1980.

Daniel Keyes Collected Stories, Hayakawa (Tokyo), 1993.

Daniel Keyes Reader, Hayakawa, 1994.

NONFICTION

The Minds of Billy Milligan (Book-of-the-Month Club selection), Random House, 1981, revised edition, with afterword, Bantam (New York City), 1982.

Unveiling Claudia: A True Story of a Serial Murder, Bantam, 1986.

The Milligan Wars (sequel to *The Minds of Billy Milligan;* also known as *The Milligan Wars: A True-Story Sequel*), Hayakawa, 1993, Bantam, 1996.

Algernon, Charlie and I: A Writer's Journey, Challcrest Press Books (Boca Raton, FL), 2000.

Author of short stories, including "Flowers for Algernon." Also contributor to numerous anthologies, including *Ten Top Stories,* edited by David A. Sohn, Bantam, 1964. Contributor of fiction to periodicals. Associate editor, *Marvel Science Fiction,* 1951.

"The Daniel Keyes Collection," a repository of papers and manuscripts, is housed at the Alden Library, Ohio University, Athens, OH.

ADAPTATIONS: Television play "The Two Worlds of Charlie Gordon," based on the short story "Flowers for Algernon," CBS Playhouse, February 22, 1961; feature film *Charly,* based on the novel *Flowers for Algernon,* starring Cliff Robertson, winner of an Academy Award for this role, Cinerama, 1968; two-act play *Flowers for Algernon,* adapted by David Rogers, Dramatic Publishing, 1969; dramatic musical *Charlie and Algernon,* first produced at Citadel Theater, Alberta, Canada, December 21, 1978, produced at Queens Theater, London, England, June 14, 1979, first produced in the United States at Terrace Theater, Kennedy Center, Washington, DC, March 8, 1980, produced on Broadway at Helen Hayes Theater, September 4, 1980; other adaptations of *Flowers for Algernon* include: French stage play, first produced at Theater Espace Massalia, Marseille, France, October 11, 1982; Irish radio monodrama, first broadcast by Radio Telefis Eireann, Dublin, Ireland, October 25, 1983; Australian stage-play, produced by Jigsaw Theater Company, March, 1984; Polish stage play, adapted by Jerzy Gudejka, first produced at W. Horzyca Memorial Theater of Torun, Torun, Poland, March 3, 1985; Japanese stage play, first produced at Kinokuniya Theater, Tokyo, Japan, January 20, 1987; and a radio play, Czechoslovak Radio Prague, 1988.

SIDELIGHTS: The author of several works focusing on psychological themes, Daniel Keyes told *CA* that he is "fascinated by the complexities of the human mind." Keyes is perhaps best known for his novel *Flowers for Algernon,* the story of Charlie, a mentally retarded man who is transformed into a genius by psychosurgery, only to eventually regress. *Flowers for Algernon,* which originally appeared as a short story in the *Magazine of Fantasy and Science Fiction,* is viewed by a *Times Literary Supplement* contributor as "a good example of that kind of science fiction which uses a persuasive hypothesis to explore emotional and moral issues. . . ." The reviewer continues that Keyes's ideas and speculations on the relationship between maturity and intelligence make *Flowers for Algernon* "a far more intelligent book than the vast majority of 'straight' novels. . . . Charlie's hopeless knowledge that he is destined to end in a home for the feeble-minded, a moron who knows that he is a moron, is painful, and Mr. Keyes has the technical equipment to prevent us from shrugging off the pain."

Two of Keyes's works, *The Fifth Sally* and *The Minds of Billy Milligan,* deal with the subject of multiple personalities and are dramatic recreations of factual cases. The title character of *The Fifth Sally* is Sally Porter, a woman who harbors four personalities that embody her emotional states: Nola, an intellectual artist; Derry, a free-spirited tomboy; Bella, a promiscuous woman; and Jinx, a murderous personality. The novel examines the efforts of Sally and her doctor to fuse the four beings into one complete person. "This is an intriguing story," wrote Mel Gilden in the *Los Angeles Times,* "but the reader is able to remain an observer rather than becoming emotionally involved. . . . Despite the intellectual distance maintained between Sally and reader, the book will reward almost anyone who reads it."

The Minds of Billy Milligan is based on the case of Billy Milligan, who was arrested on rape charges in Ohio in 1977 and who later became the first person in U.S. history to be acquitted of a major felony by reason of a multiple personality disorder. At the time of his arrest, Billy Milligan was found to possess no fewer than twenty-four personalities—three of them female—with ages ranging from three to twenty-four years old. Among Milligan's dominant personalities were Arthur,

an Englishman in charge of all the others; Ragen, a violent Yugoslav who acted as physical protector; and Adalana, a nineteen-year-old lesbian who confessed to instituting the three rapes with which Milligan was charged. According to Keyes, these personalities, along with all the rest, would share "the spot"—control of Milligan's consciousness—whenever their distinctive qualities were needed.

The circumstances under which Keyes was contracted to write Milligan's story proved unusual: It was only after several of Milligan's selves read *Flowers for Algernon* that they agreed among themselves to work with the author. In *The Minds of Billy Milligan,* Keyes writes of a personality known as "The Teacher." The Teacher kept the memory of all the other beings in Milligan and provided much of the book's background information. Through the different personas, the author describes the life of a young man who had suffered years of mental and physical abuse at the hands of his stepfather, and how Milligan had sought solace and protection from the various people existing in him. After Milligan was arrested and sent to a correctional institution for observation, debate surfaced as to how to best classify his mental state. According to Robert Coles in the *New York Times Book Review,* "Keyes makes quite evident in *The Minds of Billy Milligan,* [that] historical tensions within the [medical] profession have yet to be resolved, and have, in fact, been given new expression in this instance. . . ." While the prosecuting attorneys insisted that Milligan be jailed, doctors and psychologists in Ohio debated the location and terms of such a patient's incarceration. "When he was found 'insane,'" Coles continues, "the arguments did not by any means abate. Was he a 'sociopath'—a liar, an impostor? . . . Was he a severely disturbed and dangerous 'psychotic' who required careful watching, lots of medication, maybe a course or two of electric shock treatment?"

Coles ultimately commended Keyes for telling "this complicated story well. It reads like a play: Billy's 'personalities' come onstage, leave to be replaced by others and then reappear." Peter Gorner found this distracting; in a *Chicago Tribune* review of the book, he stated that the author "interviews everybody, reconstructs, flashes back, and confuses the story in a chatty, conversational style. The alter egos seem to dance before our eyes like a stroboscope." However, in the opinion of David Johnston in the *Los Angeles Times,* "telling the stories of twenty-four different personalities would be a difficult task for any writer. To tell of two dozen personalities in one human body is an extremely complex task. Keyes, on balance, carries it off quite well. While it shortchanges the reader by limiting explanation of motives almost exclusively to Milligan's personalities, [*The Minds of Billy Milligan*] is nonetheless a fascinating work." Finally, *Washington Post Book World,* reviewer Joseph McLellan pointed out that "complexity is . . . the keynote of the Billy phenomenon and equally of its treatment by Daniel Keyes. The challenge of first unearthing this story . . . and then telling it intelligibly was a daunting one. He has carried it off brilliantly, bringing to the assignment not only a fine clarity but a special warmth, and empathy for the victim of circumstances and mental failings that made *Flowers for Algernon* one of the most memorable novels of the 1960s."

As in his two previous works, Keyes unravels the bizarre incidents in a mentally ill person's life in *Unveiling Claudia: A True Story of a Serial Murder.* Claudia Elaine Yasko, having known both the victims and the murderers in three Ohio killings in the late 1970s, fantasized herself as the murderer. She confessed to the homicides in 1978 but the charges were dropped once the real killers were accidentally discovered. Keyes's book records the incidents and attempts to explain why Yasko knew so much about the killings. Gregor A. Preston wrote in the *Library Journal:* "while not as intriguing as Billy Milligan, this is a masterfully told, absorbing story."

BIOGRAPHICAL AND CRITICAL SOURCES:

BOOKS

Scholes, Robert, *Structural Fabulation,* University of Notre Dame Press (Notre Dame, IN), 1975.

PERIODICALS

Chicago Tribune, November 11, 1981.
Library Journal, July, 1986.
Los Angeles Times, December 12, 1980.
Los Angeles Times Book Review, January 3, 1982.
New York Times Book Review, November 15, 1981; August 24, 1986.
Saturday Review, March 26, 1966.
Times Literary Supplement, July 21, 1966.
Voice Literary Supplement, October, 1981.
Washington Post Book World, November 29, 1981.

ONLINE

Daniel Keyes Homepage, http://in.flite.net/~dkeyes/index.html/ (November 29, 1999).

KIDD, Sue Monk

PERSONAL: Born in Sylvester, GA; married Sandy Kidd (a marriage and individual counselor); children: Bob, Ann. *Education:* Texas Christian University, B.S., 1970; graduate study at Emory University. *Hobbies and other interests:* Reading, kayaking.

ADDRESSES: Home—Charleston, SC. *Agent*—c/o Author Mail, Viking Press, 375 Hudson St., New York, NY 10014.

CAREER: Author and nurse. Previously employed as a nurse, St. Joseph's Hospital, Fort Worth, TX, and instructor in nursing, Medical College of Georgia. Teacher of creative writing, speaker, and lecturer; Phoebe Pember House, Charleston, SC, writer in residence; Poets & Writers, Inc., board of advisors.

AWARDS, HONORS: Katherine Anne Porter Second Prize in Fiction, Nimrod/ Hardman Awards, 1993; fellowship in literature, South Carolina Arts Commission, 1993-94; South Carolina fiction project winner, South Carolina Arts Commission/*Charleston Post and Courier,* 1993, 1995, 1997; Isak Dinesen Creative Nonfiction Award, 1994; "100 Distinguished Stories" citation, *American Short Stories,* 1994, for "The Secret Life of Bees," and 1996, for "In the Graveyard of Afterbirth"; named to the South Carolina Readers Circuit, 1994, 1995, 1996; Bread Loaf scholar in fiction, Bread Loaf Writers Conference, 1995; participant in Exchange Program in Fiction for South Carolina, Poets & Writers, 1996; nominee for Orange Prize for excellence in women's fiction, 2002, Book of the Year award, Southeast Booksellers Association, 2003, Literature to Life award, American Place Theatre, New York, NY, 2004, and Book of the Year award (paperback), Book Sense, 2004, all for *The Secret Life of Bees.*

WRITINGS:

God's Joyful Surprise (nonfiction), Harper San Francisco (San Francisco, CA), 1988.
When the Heart Waits (nonfiction), Harper San Francisco (San Francisco, CA), 1990.
The Dance of the Dissident Daughter: A Journey from the Christian Tradition to the Sacred Feminine (nonfiction), Harper San Francisco (San Francisco, CA), 1996.
The Secret Life of Bees (novel), Viking (New York, NY), 2001.
The Mermaid Chair (novel), Viking (New York, NY), 2005.

Also author of *Love's Hidden Blessings,* a collection of essays. Contributor of short stories to *Best American Short Stories.* Contributor to periodicals, including *Readers Digest, Atlanta Journal- Constitution,* and *Anima.* Contributing editor, *Guideposts.*

ADAPTATIONS: The Secret Life of Bees has been adapted for the stage and produced at the American Place Theater, New York, NY; and has been optioned for screen adaptation by Focus Films. Unabridged versions of *The Secret Life of Bees* have been adapted for audiocassette and CD, read by Jenna Lamia, High-Bridge Audio, 2002, and for audiocassette, read by Karen White, Books on Tape, 2002; *The Mermaid Chair* has also been adapted as an audiobook.

SIDELIGHTS: Sue Monk Kidd became interested in writing when she was a child. "My desire to become a writer was born," she explained in her biography on her Home Page, "while listening to my father ply us with tales about mules who went through cafeteria lines and a petulant boy named Chewing Gum Bum." She wrote throughout her childhood, but at the age of sixteen stopped writing completely until long after she graduated from Texas Christian University with a nursing degree. "The only time I really doubted my career choice," she recalled in her biography, "was when my English professor said to me, and I quote, 'For the love of God, why are you a nursing major? You are a born writer.'" Kidd went on to work as a nurse and later as a nursing instructor.

In her thirties, Kidd nurtured her lifelong interest in spirituality with a serious study of Western religion and theology before turning to psychology and mythology. It was during this period that she returned to writing and published essays that grew out of her spiritual journey. She described her first book, *God's Joyful Surprise,* as "a spiritual memoir which chronicled my early experiences with contemplative Christian spirituality." She followed that book with *When the Heart Waits,* which portrays the psychological and spiritual transformation she later experienced. When her spiritual explorations took her into feminist theology in her forties, Kidd captured that experience in *The Dance of the Dissident Daughter.* "The book found a huge audience of women," she recounted in her biography, "and their response to it was astonishingly passionate."

But even as she was gaining recognition for her feminist religious studies, Kidd still held on to her childhood love for stories. She seriously studied the craft of

fiction in various courses and conferences before starting her first novel in 1997. Three years later, *The Secret Life of Bees* was sold for publication.

Set in South Carolina in 1964, *The Secret Life of Bees* is the story of fourteen-year-old Lily, who has been raised by her abusive father and their black servant, Rosaleen. When Lily was only four years old her mother was killed. Her father blames Lily for his wife's death. Lily and Rosaleen run away from her abusive father and the police, who have beaten Rosaleen for trying to vote. Not knowing where to go, they head for Tiburon, South Carolina, the words on the back of the cross Lily's mother wore. In Tiburon they find Black Madonna Honey, an apiary run by three black sisters—August, June, and May—who allow Lily and Rosaleen to stay with them. There Lily is happy. She learns much about bees, and finds out what really happened to her mother. A writer for *Publishers Weekly* noted that the book "features a hive's worth of appealing female characters, an offbeat plot and a lovely style." In what he called a "sweeping debut novel" in his *Library Journal* review, David A. Berona pointed out that "the stunning metaphors and realistic characters are so poignant that they will bring tears to your eyes." Beth Kephart, reviewing the book for *Book* magazine, observed: "Goodness—what it is, what it looks like, who bestows it—is the frame within which this book is masterfully hung, the organizing principle behind this intimate, unpretentious, and unsentimental work."

The Mermaid Chair, Kidd's follow-up to her successful first novel, tells the story of Jessie Sullivan, a middle-aged housewife and part-time artist who is drawn back to her childhood home after receiving some disturbing news about her estranged mother. Leaving behind her loyal, though slightly controlling, husband, Hugh, Jessie ventures back to tiny Egret Island, located off the coast of South Carolina. Upon her return, Jessie finds that her extraordinarily devout mother, Nelle, has cut off her finger for reasons unknown. Jessie suspects her mother's descent into madness may have something to do with her father's tragic death over thirty-three years ago, for which Jessie has always blamed herself. Her quest for answers leads Jessie to the local monastery where even more mysteries await her. Here she finds a strange chair fashioned with the image of a saint who was once a mermaid, as well as a young monk, Brother Thomas, who is on the verge of taking his final vows. In him, Jessie finds a passion she thought was lost and she begins to feel a reawakening of her emotions, her sensuality, and her artistic vision. The secrets of the past collide with the uncertainties of the present in what a writer for *Publishers Weekly* described as an "emotionally rich novel, full of sultry, magical descriptions of life in the South." In her review for *Entertainment Weekly*, Jennifer Reese called this effort by Kidd "a goopy follow up" to her best selling debut, *The Secret Life of Bees*. Conversely, while reviewing Kidd's novel for *Time*, Lev Grossman pointed out that the author's "writing is so smart and sharp, she gives new life to old midlife crises, and she draws connections from the feminine to the divine to the erotic that a lesser writer wouldn't see, and might not have the guts to follow."

BIOGRAPHICAL AND CRITICAL SOURCES:

PERIODICALS

Book, January- February, 2002, Beth Kephart, "Sweet as Honey."

Booklist, December 1, 2001, Kristine Huntley, review of *The Secret Life of Bees,* p. 628; February 15, 2005, Kristine Huntley, review of *The Mermaid Chair,* p. 1036.

Book World, April 10, 2005, Donna Rifkind, review of *The Mermaid Chair,* p. 6.

Entertainment Weekly, April 1, 2005, Jennifer Reese, review of *The Mermaid Chair,* p. 75.

Kirkus Reviews, October 15, 2001, review of *The Secret Life of Bees,* p. 1447; February 1, 2005, review of *The Mermaid Chair,* p. 140.

Library Journal, Henry Carrigan, Jr., review of *The Dance of the Dissident Daughter: A Journey from the Christian Tradition to the Sacred Feminine,* p. 100; December, 2001, David A. Berona, review of *The Secret Life of Bees,* p. 173.

Los Angeles Times, March 24, 2002, Susan Salter Reynolds, review of *The Secret Life of Bees,* p. R15.

New York Times Book Review, March 31, 2002, review of *The Secret Life of Bees,* p. 17; May 22, 2005, Dana Kennedy, review of *The Mermaid Chair,* p. 24.

Publishers Weekly, March 1, 1991, William Griffin, review of *Love's Hidden Blessings,* p. 43; April 22, 1996, review of *The Dance of the Dissident Daughter,* p. 65; August 6, 2001, Lucinda Dyer, "Sue Monk Kid: *The Secret Life of Bees,* " p. 49; November 12, 2001, review of *The Secret Life of Bees,* p. 33; February 21, 2005, review of *The Mermaid Chair,* p. 155; March 28, 2005, Marcia Ford, "Sue Monk Kidd: Monk Kidd's Monk," p. S16; April 4, 2005, Bob Summer, "Sue Monk Kidd: Monk Kidd's Monk," p. 39.

Time, April 4, 2005, Lev Grossman, "Sex and the Sacred: A Bittersweet Novel of Midlife Crisis and Forbidden Love from the Author of *The Secret Life of Bees*," p. 69.

Washington Post, January 13, 2002, review of *The Secret Life of Bees,* p. T05.

ONLINE

Sue Monk Kidd Home Page, http://www.suemonkkidd.com/ (August 12, 2005).

*   *   *

KIENZLE, William X. 1928-2001
(Mark Boyle, William Xavier Kienzle)

PERSONAL: Born September 11, 1928, in Detroit, MI; died of a heart attack, December 28, 2001, in West Bloomfield, MI; son of Alphonzo and Mary Louise (Boyle) Kienzle; married Javan Herman Andrews (an editor and researcher), November 29, 1974. *Education:* Sacred Heart Seminary College, Detroit, B.A., 1950; also attended St. John's Seminary, 1950-54, and University of Detroit, 1968. *Politics:* Independent. *Religion:* Roman Catholic.

CAREER: Ordained Roman Catholic priest, 1954; Roman Catholic Archdiocese of Detroit, Detroit, MI, archdiocesan priest in five parishes, 1954-74; *Michigan Catholic,* editor-in-chief, 1962-74; *MPLS Magazine,* Minneapolis, MN, editor-in-chief, 1974-77; Western Michigan University, Kalamazoo, associate director of Center for Contemplative Studies, 1977-78; University of Dallas, Irving, TX, director of Center for Contemplative Studies, 1978-79; writer, 1979-2001.

MEMBER: International Association of Crime Writers, Authors Guild, Authors League of America.

AWARDS, HONORS: Michigan Knights of Columbus journalism award, 1963, for general excellence; honorable mention from Catholic Press Association, 1974, for editorial writing.

WRITINGS:

MYSTERY NOVELS

The Rosary Murders, Andrews McMeel (Kansas City, MO), 1979.

Death Wears a Red Hat, Andrews McMeel (Kansas City, MO), 1980.

Mind over Murder, Andrews McMeel (Kansas City, MO), 1981.

Assault with Intent, Andrews McMeel (Kansas City, MO), 1982.

Shadow of Death, Andrews McMeel (Kansas City, MO), 1983.

Kill and Tell, Andrews McMeel (Kansas City, MO), 1984.

Sudden Death, Andrews, McMeel & Parker (Kansas City, MO), 1985.

Deathbed, Andrews, McMeel & Parker (Kansas City, MO), 1986.

Deadline for a Critic, Andrews, McMeel & Parker (Kansas City, MO), 1987.

Marked for Murder, Andrews McMeel (Kansas City, MO), 1988.

Eminence, Andrews McMeel (Kansas City, MO), 1989.

Masquerade, Andrews McMeel (Kansas City, MO), 1990.

Chameleon, Andrews McMeel (Kansas City, MO), 1991.

Body Count, Andrews McMeel (Kansas City, MO), 1992.

Dead Wrong, Andrews McMeel (Kansas City, MO), 1993.

Bishop as Pawn, Andrews McMeel (Kansas City, MO), 1994.

Call No Man Father, Andrews McMeel (Kansas City, MO), 1995.

Requiem for Moses, Andrews McMeel (Kansas City, MO), 1996.

The Man Who Loved God, Andrews McMeel (Kansas City, MO), 1997.

The Greatest Evil, Andrews McMeel (Kansas City, MO), 1998.

No Greater Love, Andrews McMeel (Kansas City, MO), 1999.

Till Death, Andrews McMeel (Kansas City, MO), 2000.

The Sacrifice, Andrews McMeel (Kansas City, MO), 2001.

The Gathering, Andrews McMeel (Kansas City, MO), 2002.

Author of *Campaign Capers* (play; produced in Detroit, MI), 1960. Contributor, under pseudonym Mark Boyle, to *MPLS Magazine.* Contributor to *Homicide Host Presents,* Write Way, 1996.

ADAPTATIONS: The Rosary Murders was adapted as a motion picture starring Donald Sutherland, Take One Productions, 1987.

SIDELIGHTS: After leaving the priesthood in 1974, William X. Kienzle "exchanged his pulpit for a typewriter," as Bill Dunn explained it in *Publishers Weekly,* and began writing the tales that made him a best-selling mystery author. The twenty years Kienzle spent in the priesthood provided the raw material for his popular series involving Father Robert Koesler, an amateur sleuth and sharply defined priest who resembles his creator in several ways. "The fictitious Father Koesler divides his time between his pastoral duties within the Detroit archdiocese and his journalistic duties as an editor of the area's Catholic newspaper, just as Kienzle spent his time during the 1960's," *Detroit News Magazine* writer Andrea Wojack noted.

Despite these similarities, Wojack did not envision Koesler as Kienzle in disguise. Rather, she saw him as a product of both Kienzle's background, in "the tradition of clerical detectives in fiction, like G.K. Chesterton's Father Brown and Harry Kemelman's Rabbi Small." Andrew M. Greeley similarly observed in the *Los Angeles Times Book Review:* "Kienzle is the Harry Kemelman of Catholicism, and his priest detective, Robert Koesler . . . is the Detroit response to Rabbi Small." The critic added: "I am not suggesting that Kienzle is consciously imitating Kemelman—though there would be nothing wrong with such imitation. Rather I am arguing that religio-ethnic subcultures are fertile seedbeds for mystery stories. Kienzle's sensitivity to the pathos and foolishness, shallow fads and rigid ideologies, mindless nonsense and deep faith of the contemporary Catholic scene compares favorably with Kemelman's vivid description of suburban Jewish life."

A native of Detroit, Kienzle also used the city and its Catholic parishes as a backdrop for his fiction, reportedly drawing many of his characters from people he knew. "Kienzle's portrayals of various priests obviously are an insider's (or ex-insider's) work," a *Detroit News* contributor commented. "He seems accurate, yet relaxed, in his depictions of the clergy, and his genuine affection for many of them far outruns any tendency toward satiric thrust." In addition, Father Koesler's solutions rely on his knowledge of the Church and its workings; in *Eminence,* for example, "Koesler's command of ecclesiastical detail is full and fascinating," *Los Angeles Times Book Review* critic Charles Champlin stated, and "the uses of Latin and points of Canon law are significant clues."

Despite Kienzle's assertion that his novels were, as Dunn reported, "first of all thrillers," many critics have found a deeper meaning in his work. In his review of

Mind over Murder, for example, *Detroit Free Press* contributor Neal Shine observed: "There has always been the sense that there's as much message as mystery in Kienzle's books. Kienzle is a former Detroit priest whose feelings about some of the ways in which the Catholic Church deports itself can hardly be called ambivalent. In *Mind over Murder* he goes to the heart of the matter for a lot of Catholics—marriage and the Church. The people with the clearest motives for rubbing out the monsignor are those who have run up against his incredibly inflexible rulings on marriage." *Chicago Tribune* writer Peter Gorner likewise remarked that in *Deadline for a Critic,* "Kienzle addresses serious modern issues"; nevertheless, the author also "stops to digress and tell us his wonderful stories." The critic concluded that "Kienzle's books are more small morality plays than classic mysteries. He always is welcomed to my shelves."

Although Kienzle included philosophical inquiries and religious asides in his books, many critics contended that his primary strength lied in the development of the mystery. In *Kill and Tell,* for example, "we're back to basics with a fascinating cast of three-dimensional characters who *act* like people caught up in a baffling case, a protagonist in Father Koesler who is both wry and intelligent, and an honest-to-badness murder at a tension-filled cocktail party that is truly puzzling," Don G. Campbell recounted in the *Los Angeles Times Book Review.* *Best Sellers* contributor Tony Bednarczyk likewise asserted that in *The Rosary Murders,* which he called a "well paced, tightly written novel," the author "creates well defined characters that inhabit his story rather than decorate it." "*The Rosary Murders* quickly established Father Koesler as among the most likable and authentic of all recent sleuths and gave his wise and compassionate creator a mid-life career and a new pulpit," Gorner concluded. "Since then, few mystery series have been more cozy and persuasive."

Other installments in the series include finding Father Koesler and his cohorts in the press and the police department in the midst of a plot involving a Mafia hitman who has confessed to murdering a priest in *Body Count;* investigating a thirty-year-old murder in *Dead Wrong;* and working to find the killers of several priests in advance of a visit by the pope in *Call No Man Father.* As always, Kienzle peppered his plot with numerous anecdotes from his own experience as a priest and set the stories in Detroit. "Kienzle's novels are longer and more leisurely than most mysteries, more discursive, and with shorter episodic scenes than in tightly plotted action stories of confrontation and violence," noted Jane Gottschalk in *Crime and Mystery Writers.*

"But in the bizarre plots," the critic added, "the sharp delineation of even the most minor characters (with more warts than beauty spots), and the sophisticated urbanity of the telling make them first-rate literate reading."

Reviewing Kienzle's twentieth entry in the "Father Koesler" series, *The Greatest Evil,* Melissa Hudak remarked in *Library Journal:* "Although billed as a mystery, Kienzle's latest offering is more a historical view of the Catholic Church's changing attitudes." About to retire as pastor of St. Joseph's Parish in Detroit, Father Koesler is enthusiastic about the man he has picked to replace him, Father Zachary Tully. However, Tully has doubts about taking the position because he would be under the authority of Auxiliary Bishop Vincent Delvecchio, a man known for his ultraconservative and authoritarian views. In the course of explaining to Tully the bishop's progression from an idealistic young seminarian to the rigid man he has become, Koesler stumbles upon a mystery. He begins to believe that the changes in Delvecchio may relate to his involvement in the death of a family member, a death that was supposedly from natural causes, but which Koesler now suspects could have been murder. Hudak recommended *The Greatest Evil* for its "fascinating insight" into the Catholic Church, but added that some Kienzle fans might be disappointed because the mystery element of the novel becomes secondary and discussion predominates over action.

A retired Father Koesler, now in his seventies, appears in *No Greater Love.* Although he has stepped down as pastor, Koesler is still helping out at St. Joseph's, where changing social values are fostering dissatisfaction and turmoil. Two women members of the congregation are lobbying to become priests. Another overzealous member wants his son to become a priest, despite the son's misgivings, and attempts to enlist Koesler's aid to indoctrinate the boy. Other issues that surface in the course of the narrative include "folk" masses, an aging priesthood, and the decrease in students graduating from the nearby seminary. The various conflicts eventually lead to a murder Koesler must unravel. A *Publishers Weekly* critic, praising Kienzle's "well-conceived characters," went on to observe: "The plot . . . plays itself out neither as a whodunit or a whydunit, but as a tragedy and morality play that develops slowly and inevitably to a violent climax."

Kienzle's first "Father Koesler" outing of the new millennium, *Till Death,* was viewed by a writer for *Publishers Weekly* as a marked departure from the mystery genre. The plot of the novel centers around the St. Ursula Survivor's Club, which Koesler established years earlier to help heal the psychological wounds of both priests and nuns who had served under the tyrannical Father Angelico. Two members of the club, Father Rick Casserly and Lillian Neidermier, the latter a lay principal of a Catholic school, are carrying on a secret love affair. Another member of the club, Dora Ricardo, a nun who has become a reporter, also develops a romantic interest in Father Casserly. The *Publishers Weekly* writer remarked that "Kienzle's characters usually serve didactic purposes, and here they demonstrate changes in love and marriage and the clergy. Unfortunately, these figures lack the substance to lift the story to tragedy."

In *The Sacrifice,* an Episcopal priest, Father George Wheatley, has decided he wants to convert to Catholicism. His proposed conversion is opposed by his son Ron, also an Episcopal priest, his daughter, Alice, and assorted members of the Catholic Church. When an explosion at the altar kills a priest, Wheatley and Father Koesler must identify and track down the murderer. Thematically, the novel explores the differences between Episcopalians, Anglicans, and Roman Catholics, and once again deals with the controversy of whether or not priests should be allowed to marry. Rex E. Klett of *Library Journal* labeled *The Sacrifice* "a potboiler" and criticized it for "a tedious exposition, argumentative and/or didactic digressions, and cheap narrative tricks." However, a critic for *Publishers Weekly* had a very different reaction, stating that while the "Father Koesler" series showed signs of age, *The Sacrifice* "is a refreshingly strong entry." The final volume in the series, *The Gathering,* was published in 2002, only months after its author's death.

BIOGRAPHICAL AND CRITICAL SOURCES:

BOOKS

Contemporary Authors Autobiography Series, Volume 1, Thomson Gale (Detroit, MI), 1984.
Contemporary Literary Criticism, Volume 25, Thomson Gale (Detroit, MI), 1983.
St. James Guide to Crime and Mystery Writers, St. James Press (Detroit, MI), 1996.

PERIODICALS

Best Sellers, July, 1979.

Booklist, April 15, 1992, p. 1506; May 1, 1995, p. 1555; April 15, 1998, Margaret Flanagan, review of *The Greatest Evil,* p. 1386.
Chicago Tribune, May 29, 1985; April 8, 1987; May 3, 1989.
Chicago Tribune Book World, July 11, 1982.
Detroit Free Press, February 22, 1980; April 26, 1981.
Detroit News, July 15, 1979; April 5, 1981.
Detroit News Magazine, March 16, 1980.
Library Journal, May 1, 1987; April 1, 1989; June 1, 1998, Melissa Hudak, review of *The Greatest Evil,* p. 94; April 1, 2001, Rex E. Klett, review of *The Sacrifice,* p. 137.
Los Angeles Times, April 24, 1981; May 7, 1987.
Los Angeles Times Book Review, June 22, 1980; May 23, 1982; August 5, 1984; May 7, 1987; April 9, 1989; April 11, 1993, p. 8.
Michigan Magazine, August 11, 1985.
National Catholic Reporter, July 15, 1988; May 26, 1995, p. 25.
New York Times Book Review, June 15, 1980; June 21, 1981; May 23, 1982; May 20, 1990.
Publishers Weekly, April 18, 1980; March 11, 1988; February 3, 1989; March 9, 1990; March 15, 1991; March 2, 1992, p. 52; March 8, 1993, p. 70; March 21, 1994; March 6, 1995, p. 63; March 18, 1996, p. 61; March 22, 1999, review of *No Greater Love,* p. 73; March 13, 2000, review of *Till Death,* p. 66; February 12, 2001, review of *The Sacrifice,* p. 187; April 1, 2002, review of *The Gathering,* p. 56.
Rapport, Volume 16, number 6, 1992, p. 21.
Tribune Books (Chicago, IL), November 7, 1993, p. 10.

OBITUARIES:

PERIODICALS

Chicago Tribune, January 5, 2002, section 1, p. 17.
Detroit Free Press, December 31, 2001.
Detroit News, January 1, 2002, p. A7.
Los Angeles Times, January 2, 2002, p. B9.
M2 Best Books, January 4, 2002.
Washington Post, January 2, 2002, p. B7.

* * *

KIENZLE, William Xavier
See KIENZLE, William X.

KINCAID, Jamaica 1949-

PERSONAL: Born Elaine Potter Richardson, May 25, 1949, in St. Johns, Antigua; daughter of a carpenter/cabinet maker and Annie Richardson; married Allen Shawn (a composer and professor); children: Annie Shawn, Harold. *Education:* Studied photography at New School for Social Research (now New School University); attended Franconia College. *Religion:* Jewish.

ADDRESSES: Home—P.O. Box 822, North Bennington, VT 05257.

CAREER: Writer. *New Yorker,* New York, NY, staff writer, 1976-95. Visiting professor, Harvard University, Cambridge, MA.

AWARDS, HONORS: Morton Dauwen Zabel Award, American Academy and Institute of Arts and Letters, 1983, for *At the Bottom of the River;* honorary degrees from Williams College and Long Island College, both 1991, and Colgate University, Amherst College, and Bard College; Lila Wallace-*Reader's Digest* Fund annual writer's award, 1992; National Book Critics Circle Award finalist for fiction, PEN Faulkner Award finalist, and *Boston Book Review* Fisk Fiction Prize, all 1997, all for *The Autobiography of My Mother;* National Book Award nomination, 1997, for *My Brother.*

WRITINGS:

At the Bottom of the River (short stories), Farrar, Straus (New York, NY), 1983.

Annie John (novel), Farrar, Straus (New York, NY), 1985.

Annie, Gwen, Lilly, Pam, and Tulip ("Artists and Writers" series), lithographs by Eric Fischl, Library Fellows of the Whitney Museum of American Art (New York, NY), 1986.

A Small Place (essays), Farrar, Straus (New York, NY), 1988.

Lucy (novel), Farrar, Straus (New York, NY), 1990.

The Autobiography of My Mother (novel), Farrar, Straus (New York, NY), 1995.

My Brother, Farrar, Straus (New York, NY), 1997.

(Author of introduction) *Generations of Women: In Their Own Words,* photographs by Mariana Cook, Chronicle Books (San Francisco, CA), 1998.

(Editor and author of introduction) *My Favorite Plant: Writers and Gardeners on the Plants They Love,* Farrar, Straus (New York, NY), 1998.

Poetics of Place (essay), photographs by Lynn Geesaman, Umbrage (New York, NY), 1998.

My Garden (Book) (essay), Farrar, Straus (New York, NY), 1999.

Talk Stories (essays), Farrar, Straus (New York, NY), 2000.

Mr. Potter, Farrar, Straus (New York, NY), 2002.

Contributor to books, including *Snapshots: Twentieth-Century Mother-Daughter Fiction,* D. Godine (Boston, MA), 2000; and *Whispers from the Cotton Tree Root: Caribbean Fabulist Fiction,* Invisible Cities Press (Montpelier, VT), 2000. Contributor to periodicals, including *New Yorker* and *Architectural Digest.* Recordings include *Jamaica Kincaid Interview with Kay Bonetti,* American Audio Prose Library (Columbia, MO), 1991; *Jamaica Kincaid Reads Annie John (The Red Girl Section), At the Bottom of the River (Girl and My Mother Sections), and Lucy,* American Audio Prose Library, 1991; and *Jamaica Kincaid Reading Her Short Story At the Bottom of the River,* Library of Congress Archive of Recorded Poetry and Literature, 1995.

SIDELIGHTS: Jamaica Kincaid gained wide acclaim with her first two works, *At the Bottom of the River* and *Annie John.* In these and other books about life on the Caribbean island of Antigua, where she was born, Kincaid employs a highly poetic literary style celebrated for its rhythms, imagery, characterization, and elliptic narration. As Ike Onwordi wrote in *Times Literary Supplement:* "Kincaid uses language that is poetic without affectation. She has a deft eye for salient detail while avoiding heavy symbolism and diverting exotica. The result captures powerfully the essence of vulnerability."

In an interview with Leslie Garis for *New York Times Magazine,* Kincaid noted of her island childhood, "Everyone thought I had a way with words, but it came out as a sharp tongue. No one expected anything from me at all. Had I just sunk in the cracks it would not have been noted. I would have been lucky to be a secretary somewhere." When she was seventeen years of age, Kincaid, whose given name was Elaine Potter Richardson, left the rural island to become an *au pair* in New York City. By the time she returned to Antigua almost twenty years later, she had become a successful writer for *New Yorker* magazine under her chosen name.

In her first collection of stories, *At the Bottom of the River,* Kincaid shows an imposing capacity for detailing life's mundane aspects. This characteristic of her writing is readily evident in the oft-cited tale "Girl," which consists almost entirely of a mother's orders to her daughter: "Wash the white clothes on Monday and put them on the stone heap; wash the color clothes on Tuesday and put them on the clothesline to dry; don't walk barehead in the hot sun; cook pumpkin fritters in very hot sweet oil . . . ; on Sundays try to walk like a lady, and not like the slued you are so bent on becoming." Anne Tyler, in a review for *New Republic,* declared that this passage provides "the clearest idea of the book's general tone; for Jamaica Kincaid scrutinizes various particles of our world so closely and so solemnly that they begin to take on a nearly mystical importance." "The Letter from Home," also from *At the Bottom of the River,* serves as further illustration of Kincaid's style of repetition and her penchant for the mundane. In this tale a character recounts her daily chores in such a manner that the story resembles an incantation: "I milked the cows, I churned the butter, I stored the cheese, I baked the bread, I brewed the tea," Kincaid begins. In *Ms.,* Suzanne Freeman cited this tale as evidence that Kincaid's style is "akin to hymn-singing or maybe even chanting." Freeman added that Kincaid's "singsong style" produces "images that are as sweet and mysterious as the secrets that children whisper in your ear."

With the publication of *At the Bottom of the River* Kincaid was hailed as an important new voice in American fiction. Edith Milton wrote in *New York Times Book Review* that Kincaid's tales "have all the force of illumination, and even prophetic power." David Leavitt noted in *Village Voice* that the author's stories move "with grace and ease from the mundane to the enormous," and added that "Kincaid's particular skill lies in her ability to articulate the internal workings of a potent imagination without sacrificing the rich details of the external world on which that imagination thrives." Doris Grumbach expressed similar praise in her review for *Washington Post Book World* by declaring that the world of Kincaid's narrators "hovers between fantasy and reality." Kincaid's prose "results not so much in stories as in states of consciousness," Grumbach noted, adding that the author's style, particularly its emphasis on repetition, intensifies "the feelings of poetic jubilation Kincaid has . . . for all life."

This exuberance for life is also evident in Kincaid's second book, *Annie John,* which contains interrelated stories about a girl's maturation in Antigua. In *Annie John* the title character evolves from a young girl to an aspiring nurse and from innocent to realist: she experiences her first menstruation, buries a friend, gradually establishes a life independent of her mother, and over-

comes a serious illness. She is ultimately torn by her pursuit of a career outside her life in Antigua, and Kincaid renders that feeling so incisively that, as Elaine Kendall noted in her review for *Los Angeles Times,* "you can almost believe Kincaid invented ambivalence." Critically acclaimed as a coming-of-age novel, *Annie John* was praised by a number of reviewers for expressing qualities of growing up that transcend geographical locations. Noting the book's vivid "recollections of childhood," Paula Bonnell remarked in *Boston Herald* that *Annie John* "conveys the mysterious power and intensity of childhood attachments to mother, father and friends, and the adolescent beginnings of separation from them." Susan Kenney, writing in *New York Times Book Review,* noted Annie John's ambivalence about leaving behind her life in Antigua and declared that such ambivalence is "an inevitable and unavoidable result of growing up." Kenney concluded that Kincaid's story is "so touching and familiar . . . so inevitable [that] it could be happening to any of us, anywhere, any time, any place. And that's exactly the book's strength, its wisdom, and its truth."

Kincaid's novel *Lucy* is a first-person narrative in which the nineteen-year-old title character not only expresses feelings of rage, but struggles with separation from her homeland and especially her mother. Lucy is a young woman from Antigua who comes to an unnamed American city to work as an *au pair.* She is employed by a wealthy, white couple, Mariah and Lewis, to take care of their four young daughters. In *Washington Post Book World,* Susanna Moore commented: "Lucy is unworldly. She has never seen snow or been in an elevator. . . . Written in the first person, [the novel] is Lucy's story of the year of her journey—away from her mother, away from home, away from the island and into the world." Richard Eder mused in *Los Angeles Times Book Review* that Lucy's "anger . . . is an instrument of discovery, not destruction. It is lucid and cool, but by no means unsparing." The novel ends with Lucy writing in a journal given to her by Mariah, the woman for whom she works, and weeping over the very first line: "'I wish I could love someone so much that I would die from it.' And then as I looked at this sentence a great wave of shame came over me and I wept and wept so much that the tears fell on the page and caused all the words to become one great blur."

In a discussion of *Lucy,* Derek Walcott commented in *New York Times Magazine* about Kincaid's identification with issues that thread through all people's lives: "That relationship of mother and daughter—today she loves her mother, tomorrow she hates her, then she admires her—that is so true to life, without any artificiality, that it describes parental and filial love in a way that has never been done before. [Kincaid's] work is so full of spiritual contradictions clarified that it's extremely profound and courageous." Thulani Davis, writing in *New York Times Book Review,* called Kincaid "a marvelous writer whose descriptions are richly detailed; her sentences turn and surprise even in the bare context she has created, in which there are few colors, sights or smells and the moments of intimacy and confrontation take place in the wings, or just after the door closes. . . . Lucy is a delicate, careful observer, but her rage prevents her from reveling in the deliciousness of a moment. At her happiest, she simply says, 'Life isn't so bad after all.'"

The Autobiography of My Mother follows Kincaid's two previous fictional efforts in its West Indies setting and vivid, poetic prose. The book's narrator, Xuela, is an elderly woman who recounts her difficult life, beginning with the death of her mother at Xuela's birth. In what reviewers have termed a chilling, unsparing tone, Xuela describes her childhood abuse at the hands of a stepmother; the corruption of her father, a policeman; and her decision to abort her unborn child after she realizes the baby is intended for its father and his barren wife. At the end of the novel, the narrator calls her account a story of the mother she never knew, of her unborn baby, and of "the voices that should have come out of me, the faces I never allowed to form, the eyes I never allowed to see me," as quoted by Dale Peck in *London Review of Books.*

As with the author's earlier works, *The Autobiography of My Mother* received significant critical praise, especially for Kincaid's lyrical writing style. "Kincaid has written a truly ugly meditation on life in some of the most beautiful prose we are likely to find in contemporary fiction," averred Cathleen Schine in *New York Times Book Review. Maclean's* reviewer Diane Turbide concurred, noting, "Kincaid employs an almost incantatory tone, using repetition and unusual syntax to give the book a hypnotic rhythm." Several reviewers commented that the author's striking prose is not matched by the novel's thematic development. Schine noted, "There is . . . something dull and unconvincing about Xuela's anguish." According to Peck, "The prose is lovely . . . and . . . distinctly, beautifully American, yet the sentiments expressed by the words themselves are trite, falsely universalising, and often just muddled." In contrast, *Time* reviewer John Skow stated of *The Autobiography of My Mother:* "The reward here, as always with Kincaid's work, is the reading of her clear, bitter prose."

Comparing Kincaid's work to that of Toni Morrison and Wole Soyinka, Henry Louis Gates, Jr., told Emily Listfield in *Harper's Bazaar* that "There is a self-contained world which they [each] explore with great detail. Not to chart the existence of that world, but to show that human emotions manifest themselves everywhere." Gates cited as an important contribution by Kincaid that "she never feels the necessity of claiming the existence of a black world or a female sensibility. She assumes them both. I think it's a distinct departure that she's making, and I think that more and more black American writers will assume their world the way that she does. So that we can get beyond the large theme of racism and get to the deeper themes of how black people love and cry and live and die. Which, after all, is what art is all about."

In *Mr. Potter* Kincaid spins a story about an illiterate chauffer who fathers numerous children with various women and abandons them all. The idea is based on Kincaid's own profligate father, showing the author once again blurring the lines between truth and fiction in her novels. As Donna Seaman noted in *Booklist,* "Kincaid cares little about the distinction between fiction and nonfiction since all of her incantatory yet thorny works are insistently self-referential." In an interview with Kim McLarin for *Black Issues Book Review,* Kincaid said the idea came to her while she was thinking about her mother. "The more I thought of her life," Kincaid told McLarin, "and how it was that I grew up without knowing this person that she loathed and who was my father, the more I wanted to write this book. Here was a person she absolutely detested. She never introduced me to him and he never had any interest in me. Although when I became a well-known [author], he came to visit me. When he found me not interested in the idea of his being my dad, he actually disinherited me. It's in his will."

A native Antiguan of African descent, the fictional Mr. Potter leads a predictable and unimaginative life. The book's narrator is one of his many illegitimate children, but Potter has no emotional connection to her and little attachment to anything else in his life. The narrator perseveres, however, in conjuring a connection with her past by bringing her father's life into some type of focus. A *Publishers Weekly* contributor noted that, "As in her previous books, Kincaid has exquisite control over her narrator's deep-seated rage, which drives the story but never overpowers it and is tempered by a clear-eyed sympathy." Lyle D. Rosdahl, writing in *Library Journal,* called *Mr. Potter* "vivid and affecting reading." In a review for *Book,* Paul Evans called the novel "astonishing and baffling, infuriating and gorgeous." Rosdahl also noted that the main character is almost entirely unsympathetic but added that Kincaid manages "to summon up in us a genuine pathos for the man and, more so, his daughter. The author does this with word torrents that build and crest, plunging us mercilessly into the emptiness of Potter's life."

With her memoir *My Brother*, Kincaid recounts the last years of life of her brother, Devon Drew, who died of AIDS in January of 1996 at the age of thirty-three. Kincaid left the island of Antigua when her brother was age three; when she returns they are strangers to each other, and she only learns of his bisexuality after his death. Kincaid reveals that during the period in which she bought medication for him, her brother was still engaging in unprotected sex. The reader also learns that her brother was a drug addict and that he had served time in prison for his involvement in a murder. While *My Brother* provides a portrait of the author's sibling, it also explores Kincaid's own reactions to her brother's life and death. The book also returns to ground made familiar in Kincaid's novels, offering another look at Antigua, which the author describes in *My Brother* as homophobic, and revisiting her problematic relationship with her mother.

As with the author's previous works, reviewers pointed to her distinctive writing style. Anna Quindlen in *New York Times Book Review* noted that Kincaid's "endless incantatory sentences [are] a contrast to the simple words and images—a tower built of small bricks." Even though she pointed out that "the unadorned, often flat style of Kincaid's prose can occasionally feel perfunctory," Quindlen argued that "its great advantage is that within the simple setting the observations glow." Regarding the memoir's narrative structure, Gay Wachman in *Nation* maintained that "the lucid, assertive, deceptively simple voice takes its time in fleshing out the figures of the memoir, both in their present and in the past, circling around Devon and the multiple meanings of his life, illness and death." Referring to "the measured and limpid simplicity of her prose," Deborah E. McDowell in *Women's Review of Books* linked *My Brother* to earlier works by the author in declaring that "despite the grimness of her work, few writers have made the aesthetics of death and darkness more luminous than has Jamaica Kincaid."

In addition to her autobiographical fiction and nonfiction, Kincaid has produced several books on gardening. As the editor and author of introduction of *My Favorite Plant: Writers and Gardeners on the Plants They Love*, she creates an "enchanting. . . . fascinating compilation," according to *Booklist* contributor Brad Hooper. *My Favorite Plant* contains "thirty-five brief essays and

poems" and is, judged a *Publishers Weekly* critic, "often beautiful, though some of its parts are not as radiant as others, and a few have yet to blossom."

Published in 1999, *My Garden (Book)* consists of a "personable and brightly descriptive, if somewhat rambling, book-length essay" that "shuttles constantly and with ease between the practical, technical difficulties of gardening and . . . larger meanings," observed a writer for *Publishers Weekly*. Alice Joyce, writing in *Booklist*, added that "Kincaid's views extend beyond the musings found in your usual garden journal." The author pairs "smart-mouth observations" with "intriguing autobiographical tidbits." Noting that Kincaid's "personality pervades the writing" in *My Garden (Book)*, Daniel Starr remarked in *Library Journal* that the author "may be crank, but she is always entertaining." Kincaid reveals "her love-hate relationship with gardening" in this "robust hybrid of memoir and gardener's journal," stated Megan Harlan in an *Entertainment Weekly* assessment of *My Garden (Book)*.

Kincaid's *Talk Stories* collects several "Talk of the Town" essays she wrote for the New Yorker from 1978 to 1983. The pieces were written before she became a well-known writer, and only one of them had her byline when published in the magazine. Nancy P. Shires, writing in *Library Journal*, noted, "The hallmarks of her style are seen developing here: the close observation of the mundane, use of repetition, lyrical and rhythmic qualities, elliptical narration, and ambivalence, experimentation, and humor." The "Talk of the Town" pieces cover a wide range of topics, befitting the diverse city that it focuses on, from New York City's West Indian-American Day carnival to the haunts of the rich and famous. A *Publishers Weekly* contributor called the book "an astounding display of early literary skill and youthful daring," while Donna Seaman, writing in *Booklist*, called the volume "Great fun to read" and "a literary feast of dishes both salty and sweet, bracing and voluptuous."

BIOGRAPHICAL AND CRITICAL SOURCES:

BOOKS

Black Literature Criticism, Volume 2, Thomson Gale (Detroit, MI), 1991.

Bloom, Harold, editor, *Jamaica Kincaid*, Chelsea House (Philadelphia, PA), 1998.

Contemporary Literary Criticism, Thomson Gale (Detroit, MI), Volume 43, 1987, Volume 68, 1991.

Cudjoe, Selwyn R., editor, *Caribbean Women Writers: Essays from the First International Conference,* Callaloo (Wellesley, MA), 1990.

Ferguson, Moira, *Jamaica Kincaid: Where the Land Meets the Body,* University Press of Virginia (Charlottesville, VA), 1994.

Kincaid, Jamaica, *At the Bottom of the River,* Farrar, Straus (New York, NY), 1983.

Kincaid, Jamaica, *Lucy,* Farrar, Straus (New York, NY), 1990.

Kincaid, Jamaica, *The Autobiography of My Mother,* Farrar, Straus (New York, NY), 1995.

Simmons, Diane, *Jamaica Kincaid,* Macmillan (New York, NY), 1994.

PERIODICALS

Advertising Age, February 12, 1996, p. 19.

Advocate, December 9, 1997, p. 82.

American Visions, April, 1991, p. 36.

Atlantic, May, 1985, p. 104.

Black Issues Book Review, March, 2001, Robert Fleming, review of *Talk Stories,* p. 67; July-August, 2002, Kim McLarin, review of *Mr. Potter,* p. 34.

Book, May-June, 2002, Paul Evans, review of *Mr. Potter,* p. 72.

Booklist, November 1, 1995, p. 449; December 1, 1995, p. 587; January 1, 1996, p. 868; September 1, 1997, p. 5; August, 1998, p. 1946; May 1, 1999, p. 1571; September 15, 1999, p. 210; November 15, 2000, Donna Seaman, review of *Talk Stories,* p. 586; March 1, 2002, Donna Seaman, review of *Mr. Potter,* p. 1052.

Boston Herald, March 31, 1985, Paula Bonnell, review of *Annie John.*

Christian Science Monitor, April 5, 1985.

CLA Journal, March, 2000, K.B. Conal Byrne, "Under English, Obeah English: Jamaica Kincaid's New Language," pp. 276-277.

Commonweal, November 4, 1988, p. 602.

Emerge, March, 1996, p. 60; November, 1997, p. 100.

Entertainment Weekly, February 9, 1996, p. 49; January 17, 1997, p. 59; November 7, 1997, p. 80; December 3, 1999, p. 94.

Essence, May, 1991, p. 86; March, 1996, p. 98; May, 2001, "First Person Singular" (interview), p. 108.

Harper's Bazaar, October, 1990, p. 82; January, 1996, p. 66; April, 1996, p. 28.

Hudson Review, autumn, 1996, p. 483.

Interview, October, 1997, p. 94.

Library Journal, April 1, 1985, p. 158; January, 1986, p. 48; July, 1988, p. 88; December 1, 1989, p. 118; November 1, 1990, p. 125; February 15, 1995,

p. 196; October 15, 1995, p. 61; January, 1996, p. 142; June 15, 1996, p. 105; October 1, 1997, p. 94; January 1998, p. 164; October 1, 1999, p. 125; October 15, 2000, Nancy P. Shires, review of *Talk Stories,* p. 70; April 1, 2002, Lyle D. Rosdahl, review of *Mr. Potter,* p. 140.

Listener, January 10, 1985.

London Review of Books, February 6, 1997, Dale Peck, review of *The Autobiography of My Mother,* p. 25.

Los Angeles Times, April 25, 1985, Elaine Kendall, review of *Annie John.*

Los Angeles Times Book Review, October 21, 1990.

Maclean's, May 20, 1985, p. 61; April 8, 1996, p. 72.

Mother Jones, September-October, 1997, p. 28.

Ms., January, 1984, p. 15; April, 1985, p. 14; January-February 1986, p. 90.

Nation, June 15, 1985, p. 748; February 18, 1991, p. 207; February 5, 1996, p. 23; November 3, 1997, p. 43.

Natural History, May, 1999, p. 16.

New Republic, December 31, 1983, Anne Tyler, review of *At the Bottom of the River.*

New Statesman, September 7, 1984, p. 33; September 20, 1985, p. 30; October 11, 1996, p. 45.

New Statesman & Society, October 7, 1988, p. 40.

Newsweek, October 1, 1990, p. 68; January, 1996, p. 62.

New York, January 22, 1996, p. 52.

New Yorker, December 17, 1990, p. 122.

New York Times Book Review, January 15, 1984, p. 22; April 7, 1985, p. 6; May 25, 1986, p. 24; December 7, 1986, p. 82; July 10, 1988, p. 19; October 28, 1990, p. 11; December 2, 1990, p. 16; February 4, 1996, p. 5; October 19, 1997, p. 7; December 5, 1999, p. 10; May 12, 2002, Sophie Harrison, review of *Mr. Potter,* p. 7.

New York Times Magazine, October 7, 1990, p. 42.

People, September 26, 1988, p. 37; November 5, 1990, p. 40; February 19, 1996, p. 27; October 20, 1997, p. 46; December 15, 1997, p. 109; January 24, 2000, p. 41; June 24, 2002, review of *Mr. Potter,* p. 394.

Publishers Weekly, October 14, 1983, p. 45; February 15, 1985, p. 86; August 17, 1990, p. 50; October 2, 1995, p. 67; October 9, 1995, p. 75; January 1, 1996, p. 54; April 1, 1996, p. 38; August 4, 1997, p. 53; August 31, 1998, p. 57; December 6, 1999, p. 67; December 13, 1999, p. 46; January 15, 2001, review of *Talk Stories,* p. 61; March 11, 2002, review of *Mr. Potter,* p. 49.

Saturday Review, June, 1985, p. 68.

School Library Journal, September, 1985, p. 154.

Time, February 5, 1996, p. 71; November 10, 1997, p. 108.

Times Literary Supplement, November 29, 1985; September 20, 1996, p. 22.

Village Voice, January 17, 1984.

Virginia Quarterly Review, summer, 1985.

Vogue, December, 1983, p. 62.

Voice Literary Supplement, April, 1985; February, 1996, p. 11.

Washington Post, April 2, 1985.

Washington Post Book World, October 7, 1990, Doris Grumbach, review of *At the Bottom of the River.*

Women's Review of Books, January, 1998, Deborah E. McDowell, review of *My Brother,* p. 1.

World Literature Today, autumn, 1985.

ONLINE

Salon.com, http://www.salon.com/ (April 9, 2004), Dwight Garner, interview with Kincaid.

*   *   *

KING, Stephen 1947-

(Richard Bachman, Eleanor Druse, Stephen Edwin King, Steve King, John Swithen)

PERSONAL: Born September 21, 1947, in Portland, ME; son of Donald (a merchant sailor) and Nellie Ruth (Pillsbury) King; married Tabitha Jane Spruce (a novelist), January 2, 1971; children: Naomi Rachel, Joseph Hill, Owen Phillip. *Education:* University of Maine at Orono, B.Sc., 1970. *Politics:* Democrat *Hobbies and other interests:* Reading (mostly fiction), jigsaw puzzles, playing the guitar ("I'm terrible and so try to bore no one but myself"), movies, bowling.

ADDRESSES: Agent—Arthur Greene, 101 Park Ave., New York, NY 10178.

CAREER: Writer. Has worked as a janitor, a laborer in an industrial laundry, and in a knitting mill. Hampden Academy (high school), Hampden, ME, English teacher, 1971-73; University of Maine, Orono, writer-in- residence, 1978-79. Owner, Philtrum Press (publishing house), and WZON-AM (rock 'n' roll radio station), Bangor, ME. Has made cameo appearances in films, including *Knightriders,* 1981, *Creepshow,* 1982, *Maximum Overdrive,* 1986, *Pet Sematary,* 1989, and *The Stand,* 1994; has also appeared in American Express credit card television commercial. Served as judge

for 1977 World Fantasy Awards, 1978. Participated in radio honor panel with George A. Romero, Peter Straub, and Ira Levin, moderated by Dick Cavett, WNET, 1980.

MEMBER: Authors Guild, Authors League of America, Screen Artists Guild, Screen Writers of America, Writers Guild.

AWARDS, HONORS: Carrie named to *School Library Journal*'s Book List, 1975; World Fantasy Award nominations, 1976, for *Salem's Lot,* 1979, for *The Stand* and *Night Shift,* 1980, for *The Dead Zone,* 1981, for "The Mist," and 1983, for "The Breathing Method: A Winter's Tale," in *Different Seasons;* Hugo Award nomination, World Science Fiction Society, and Nebula Award nomination, Science Fiction Writers of America, both 1978, both for *The Shining;* Balrog Awards, second place in best novel category, for *The Stand,* and second place in best collection category for *Night Shift,* both 1979; named to the American Library Association's list of best books for young adults, 1979, for *The Long Walk,* and 1981, for *Firestarter;* World Fantasy Award, 1980, for contributions to the field, and 1982, for story "Do the Dead Sing?"; Career Alumni Award, University of Maine at Orono, 1981; Nebula Award nomination, Science Fiction Writers of America, 1981, for story "The Way Station"; special British Fantasy Award for outstanding contribution to the genre, British Fantasy Society, 1982, for *Cujo;* Hugo Award, World Science Fiction Convention, 1982, for *Stephen King's Danse Macabre;* named Best Fiction Writer of the Year, *Us Magazine,* 1982; Locus Award for best collection, Locus Publications, 1986, for *Stephen King's Skeleton Crew;* Bram Stoker Award for Best Novel, Horror Writers Association, 1988, for *Misery;* Bram Stoker Award for Best Collection, 1991, for *Four Past Midnight;* World Fantasy award for short story, 1995, for *The Man in the Black Suit;* Bram Stoker Award for Best Novelette, Horror Writers Association, 1996, for *Lunch at the Gotham Cafe;* O. Henry Award, 1996, for "The Man in the Black Suit"; Bram Stoker Award for Best Novel, 1997, for *The Green Mile,* and 1999, for *Bag of Bones;* Bram Stoker Award nomination (with Peter Straub), 2001, for *Black House;* Medal for Distinguished Contribution to American Letters, National Book Award, 2003; *The Stand* was voted one of the nation's 100 best-loved novels by the British public as part of the BBC's The Big Read, 2003; Bram Stoker Award nomination, 2004, for *The Dark Tower VII;* Lifetime Achievement Award, World Fantasy Awards, 2004; Quill Book Award in the sports category, for *Faithful: Two Die-Hard Boston Red Sox Fans Chronicle the Historic 2004 Season,* 2005.

WRITINGS:

NOVELS

Carrie: A Novel of a Girl with a Frightening Power (also see below), Doubleday (New York, NY), 1974, movie edition published as *Carrie*, New American Library/Times Mirror (New York, NY), 1975, published in a limited edition with introduction by Tabitha King, Plume (New York, NY), 1991.

Salem's Lot (also see below), Doubleday (New York, NY), 1975, television edition, New American Library (New York, NY), 1979, published in a limited edition with introduction by Clive Barker, Plume (New York, NY), 1991.

The Shining (also see below), Doubleday (New York, NY), 1977, movie edition, New American Library (New York, NY), 1980, published in a limited edition with introduction by Ken Follett, Plume (New York, NY), 1991.

The Stand (also see below), Doubleday (New York, NY), 1978, enlarged and expanded edition published as *The Stand: The Complete and Uncut Edition*, Doubleday (New York, NY), 1990.

The Dead Zone (also see below), Viking (New York, NY), 1979, movie edition published as *The Dead Zone: Movie Tie-In*, New American Library (New York, NY), 1980.

Firestarter (also see below), Viking (New York, NY), 1980, with afterword by King, 1981, published in a limited, aluminum-coated, asbestos-cloth edition, Phantasia Press (Huntington Woods, MI), 1980.

Cujo (also see below), Viking (New York, NY), 1981, published in limited edition, Mysterious Press (New York, NY), 1981.

Pet Sematary (also see below), Doubleday (New York, NY), 1983.

Christine (also see below), Viking (New York, NY), 1983, published in a limited edition, illustrated by Stephen Gervais, Donald M. Grant (Hampton Falls, NH), 1983.

(With Peter Straub) *The Talisman*, Viking Press/Putnam (New York, NY), 1984, published in a limited two-volume edition, Donald M. Grant (Hampton Falls, NH), 1984.

The Eyes of the Dragon (young adult), limited edition, illustrated by Kenneth R. Linkhauser, Philtrum Press, 1984, new edition, illustrated by David Palladini, Viking (New York, NY), 1987.

It (also see below), limited German edition published as *Es,* Heyne (Munich), 1986, Viking (New York, NY), 1986.

Misery (also see below), Viking (New York, NY), 1987.

The Tommyknockers (also see below), Putnam (New York, NY), 1987.

The Dark Half (also see below), Viking (New York, NY), 1989.

Needful Things (also see below), Viking (New York, NY), 1991.

Gerald's Game, Viking (New York, NY), 1992.

Dolores Claiborne (also see below), Viking (New York, NY), 1993.

Insomnia, Viking (New York, NY), 1994.

Rose Madder, Viking (New York, NY), 1995.

The Green Mile (serialized novel), Signet (New York, NY), Chapter 1, "The Two Dead Girls" (also see below), Chapter 2, "The Mouse on the Mile," Chapter 3, "Coffey's Hands," Chapter 4, "The Bad Death of Eduard Delacroix," Chapter 5, "Night Journey," Chapter 6, "Coffey on the Mile," March-August, 1996, published as *The Green Mile: A Novel in Six Parts,* Plume (New York, NY), 1997.

Desperation, Viking (New York, NY), 1996.

(And author of foreword) *The Two Dead Girls,* Signet (New York, NY), 1996.

Bag of Bones, Viking (New York, NY), 1998.

Hearts in Atlantis, G.K. Hall (Thorndike, ME), 1999.

The Girl Who Loved Tom Gordon, Scribner (New York, NY), 1999.

Dreamcatcher, Simon & Schuster (New York, NY), 2001.

(With Peter Straub) *Black House* (sequel to *The Talisman*), Random House (New York, NY), 2001.

(Editor) Ridley Pearson, *The Diary of Ellen Rimbauer: My Life As Rose Red,* Hyperion (New York, NY), 2001.

From a Buick 8, Scribner (New York, NY), 2002.

(Under name Eleanor Druse) *The Journals of Eleanor Druse: My Investigation of the Kingdom Hospital Incident,* Hyperion (New York, NY), 2004.

Cell, Scribner (New York, NY), 2006.

Also author of early unpublished novels "Sword in the Darkness" (also referred to as "Babylon Here"), "The Cannibals," and "Blaze," a reworking of John Steinbeck's *Of Mice and Men.*

"THE DARK TOWER" SERIES

The Dark Tower: The Gunslinger (also see below), Amereon (New York, NY), 1976, published as *The Gunslinger,* New American Library (New York, NY), 1988, published in limited edition, illustrated by Michael Whelan, Donald M. Grant (Hampton Falls, NH), 1982, 2nd limited edition, 1984, revised and expanded edition, Viking (New York, NY), 2003.

The Dark Tower II: The Drawing of the Three (also see below), illustrated by Phil Hale, New American Library (New York, NY), 1989.

The Dark Tower III: The Waste Lands (also see below), illustrated by Ned Dameron, Donald M. Grant (Hampton Falls, NH), 1991.

The Dark Tower Trilogy: The Gunslinger; The Drawing of the Three; The Waste Lands (box set), New American Library (New York, NY), 1993.

The Dark Tower IV: Wizard and Glass, Plume (New York, NY), 1997.

The Dark Tower V: Wolves of the Calla, Plume (New York, NY), 2003.

The Dark Tower VI: The Songs of Susannah, Donald M. Grant (Hampton Falls, NH), 2004.

The Dark Tower VII, Scribner (New York, NY), 2004.

NOVELS; UNDER PSEUDONYM RICHARD BACHMAN

Rage (also see below), New American Library/Signet (New York, NY), 1977.

The Long Walk (also see below), New American Library/Signet (New York, NY), 1979.

Roadwork: A Novel of the First Energy Crisis (also see below) New American Library/ Signet (New York, NY), 1981.

The Running Man (also see below), New American Library/Signet (New York, NY), 1982.

Thinner, New American Library (New York, NY), 1984.

The Regulators, Dutton (New York, NY), 1996.

SHORT FICTION

(Under name Steve King) *The Star Invaders* (privately printed stories), Triad/ Gaslight Books (Durham, ME), 1964.

Night Shift (story collection; also see below), introduction by John D. MacDonald, Doubleday (New York, NY), 1978, published as *Night Shift: Excursions into Horror,* New American Library/Signet (New York, NY), 1979.

Different Seasons (novellas; contains *Rita Hayworth and the Shawshank Redemption: Hope Springs Eternal* [also see below]; *Apt Pupil: Summer of Corruption*; *The Body: Fall from Innocence*; and *The Breathing Method: A Winter's Tale*), Viking (New York, NY), 1982.

Cycle of the Werewolf (novella; also see below), illustrated by Berni Wrightson, limited portfolio edition published with "Berni Wrightson: An Appreciation," Land of Enchantment (Westland, MI), 1983, enlarged edition including King's screenplay adaptation published as *Stephen King's Silver Bullet,* New American Library/Signet (New York, NY), 1985.

Stephen King's Skeleton Crew (story collection), illustrated by J. K. Potter, Viking (New York, NY), 1985, limited edition, Scream Press, 1985.

My Pretty Pony, illustrated by Barbara Kruger, Knopf (New York, NY), 1989, limited edition, Library Fellows of New York's Whitney Museum of American Art, 1989.

Four Past Midnight (contains "The Langoliers," "Secret Window, Secret Garden," "The Library Policeman," and "The Sun Dog"; also see below), Viking (New York, NY), 1990.

Nightmares and Dreamscapes, Viking (New York, NY), 1993.

Lunch at the Gotham Cafe, published in *Dark Love: Twenty-two All Original Tales of Lust and Obsession,* edited by Nancy Collins, Edward E. Kramer, and Martin Harry Greenberg, ROC (New York, NY), 1995.

Everything's Eventual: 14 Dark Tales, Scribner (New York, NY), 2002.

Also author of short stories "Slade" (a western), "The Man in the Black Suit," 1996, and, under pseudonym John Swithen, "The Fifth Quarter." Contributor of short story "Squad D" to Harlan Ellison's *The Last Dangerous Visions;* contributor of short story "Autopsy Room Four" to *Robert Bloch's Psychos,* edited by Robert Bloch. Also contributor to anthologies and collections, including *The Year's Finest Fantasy,* edited by Terry Carr, Putnam (New York, NY), 1978; *Shadows,* edited by Charles L. Grant, Doubleday (New York, NY), Volume 1, 1978, Volume 4, 1981; *New Terrors,* edited by Ramsey Campbell, Pocket Books (New York, NY), 1982; *World Fantasy Convention 1983,* edited by Robert Weinberg, Weird Tales, 1983; *The Writer's Handbook,* edited by Sylvia K. Burack, Writer (Boston, MA), 1984; *The Dark Descent,* edited by David G. Hartwell, Doherty Associates, 1987; *Prime Evil: New Stories by the Masters of Modern Horror,* by Douglas E. Winter, New American Library (New York, NY), 1988; and *Dark Visions,* Gollancz (London, England), 1989.

SCREENPLAYS

Stephen King's Creep Show: A George A. Romero Film (based on King's stories "Father's Day," "The Lonesome Death of Jordy Verrill" [previously published as "Weeds"], "The Crate," and "They're Creeping Up on You"; released by Warner Bros. as *Creepshow,* 1982), illustrated by Berni Wrightson and Michele Wrightson, New American Library (New York, NY), 1982.

Cat's Eye (based on King's stories "Quitters, Inc.," "The Ledge," and "The General"), Metro Goldwyn-Mayer/United Artists, 1984.

Stephen King's Silver Bullet (based on and published with King's novella *Cycle of the Werewolf;* released by Paramount Pictures/Dino de Laurentiis's North Carolina Film Corp., 1985), illustrated by Berni Wrightson, New American Library/Signet (New York, NY), 1985.

(And director) *Maximum Overdrive* (based on King's stories "The Mangler," "Trucks," and "The Lawnmower Man"; released by Dino de Laurentiis's North Carolina Film Corp., 1986), New American Library (New York, NY), 1986.

Pet Sematary (based on King's novel of the same title), Laurel Production, 1989.

Stephen King's Sleepwalkers, Columbia, 1992.

(Author of introduction) Frank Darabont, *The Shawshank Redemption: The Shooting Script,* Newmarket Press (New York, NY), 1996.

Storm of the Century (also see below), Pocket Books (New York, NY), 1999.

(Author of introductions with William Goldman and Lawrence Kasdan) William Goldman and Lawrence Kasdan, *Dreamcatcher: The Shooting Script,* Newmarket Press (New York, NY), 2003.

TELEPLAYS

Stephen King's Golden Years, CBS-TV, 1991.

(And executive producer) *Stephen King's The Stand* (based on King's novel *The Stand*), ABC-TV, 1994.

(With Chris Carter) *Chinga,* (episode of *The X-Files,*) Fox-TV, 1998.

Storm of the Century, ABC-TV, 1999.

Rose Red (also see below), ABC-TV, 2001.

Stephen King's Kingdom Hospital, ABC-TV, 2004.

Desperation, USA, c. 2004.

Also author of *Battleground* (based on short story of same title; optioned by Martin Poll Productions for NBC-TV), and "Sorry, Right Number," for television series *Tales from the Dark Side,* 1987.

RECORDINGS

The Dark Tower: The Gunslinger, New American Library (New York, NY), 1988.

The Dark Tower II: The Drawing of the Three, New American Library (New York, NY), 1989.

The Dark Tower III: The Waste Lands, Penguin-HighBridge Audio (St. Paul, MN), 1991.

Needful Things, Penguin-HighBridge Audio (St. Paul, MN), 1991.

OMNIBUS EDITIONS

Stephen King (contains *The Shining, Salem's Lot, Night Shift,* and *Carrie*), W.S. Heinemann/Octopus Books (London, England), 1981.

(And author of introduction) *The Bachman Books: Four Early Novels* (contains *Rage, The Long Walk, Roadwork,* and *The Running Man*), New American Library (New York, NY), 1985.

Another Quarter Mile: Poetry, Dorrance (Philadelphia, PA), 1979.

Stephen King's Danse Macabre (nonfiction), Everest House (New York, NY), 1981.

The Plant (privately published episodes of a comic horror novel in progress), Philtrum Press (Bangor, ME), Part 1, 1982, Part 2, 1983, Part 3, 1985.

Black Magic and Music: A Novelist's Perspective on Bangor (pamphlet), Bangor Historical Society (Bangor, ME), 1983.

Dolan's Cadillac, Lord John Press (Northridge, CA), 1989.

Stephen King (contains *Desperation* and *The Regulators*) Signet (New York, NY), 1997.

Stephen King's Latest (contains *Dolores Claiborne, Insomnia* and *Rose Madder*) Signet (New York, NY), 1997.

OTHER

Nightmares in the Sky: Gargoyles and Grotesques (nonfiction), photographs by F. Stop FitzGerald, Viking (New York, NY), 1988.

On Writing: A Memoir of the Craft, Scribner (New York, NY), 2000.

(With Stewart O'Nan) *Faithful: Two Die-Hard Boston Red Sox Fans Chronicle the Historic 2004 Season,* Scribner (New York, NY), 2004.

The Colorado Kid, Hard Case Crime (New York, NY), 2004.

Author of e-book *The Plant,* self-published first two chapters on his Web site (www.stephenking.com), August, 2000; also published a short story, "Riding the Bullet," as an e-book, March, 2000. Author of weekly column "King's Garbage Truck" for *Maine Campus,* 1969-70, and of monthly book review column for *Adelina,* 1980. Contributor of short fiction and poetry to numerous magazines, including *Art, Castle Rock: The Stephen King Newsletter, Cavalier, Comics Review, Cosmopolitan, Ellery Queen's Mystery Magazine, Fantasy and Science Fiction, Gallery, Great Stories from Twilight Zone Magazine, Heavy Metal, Ladies' Home Journal, Magazine of Fantasy and Science Fiction, Maine, Maine Review, Marshroots,* Marvel comics, *Moth, Omni, Onan, Playboy, Redbook, Reflections, Rolling Stone, Science-Fiction Digest, Startling Mystery Stories, Terrors, Twilight Zone Magazine, Ubris, Whisper,* and *Yankee.* Contributor of book reviews to the *New York Times Book Review.*

Most of King's papers are housed in the special collection of the Folger Library at the University of Maine at Orono.

ADAPTATIONS: Many of King's novels have been adapted for the screen. *Carrie* was produced as a motion picture in 1976 by Paul Monash for United Artists, screenplay by Lawrence D. Cohen, directed by Brian De Palma, featuring Sissy Spacek and Piper Laurie, and was also produced as a Broadway musical in 1988 by Cohen and Michael Gore, developed in England by the Royal Shakespeare Company, featuring Betty Buckley; *Salem's Lot* was produced as a television miniseries in 1979 by Warner Brothers, teleplay by Paul Monash, featuring David Soul and James Mason, and was adapted for the cable channel TNT in 2004, with a teleplay by Peter Filardi and direction by Mikael Salomon; *The Shining* was filmed in 1980 by Warner Brothers/ Hawks Films, screenplay by director Stanley Kubrick and Diane Johnson, starring Jack Nicholson and Shelley Duvall, and it was filmed for television in 1997 by Warner Brothers, directed by Mick Garris, starring Rebecca De Mornay, Steven Weber, Courtland Mead, and Melvin Van Peebles; *Cujo* was filmed in 1983 by Warner Communications/Taft Entertainment, screenplay by Don Carlos Dunaway and Lauren Currier, featuring Dee Wallace and Danny Pintauro; *The Dead Zone* was filmed in 1983 by Paramount Pictures, screenplay by Jeffrey Boam, starring Christopher Walken; was adapted as a cable television series starring Anthony Michael Hall by USA Network, beginning 2002; *Christine* was filmed in 1983 by Columbia Pictures, screenplay by Bill Phillips; *Firestarter* was produced in 1984 by Frank Capra, Jr., for Universal Pictures in association with Dino de Laurentiis, screenplay by Stanley Mann, featuring David Keith and Drew Barrymore; *Stand by Me* (based on King's novella *The Body*) was filmed in 1986 by Columbia Pictures, screenplay by

Raynold Gideon and Bruce A. Evans, directed by Rob Reiner; *The Running Man* was filmed in 1987 by Taft Entertainment/Barish Productions, screenplay by Steven E. de Souza, starring Arnold Schwarzenegger; *Misery* was produced in 1990 by Columbia, directed by Reiner, screenplay by William Goldman, starring James Caan and Kathy Bates; *Graveyard Shift* was filmed in 1990 by Paramount, directed by Ralph S. Singleton, adapted by John Esposito; *Stephen King's It* (based on King's novel *It*) was filmed as a television miniseries by ABC-TV in 1990; *The Dark Half* was filmed in 1993 by Orion, written and directed by George A. Romero, featuring Timothy Hutton and Amy Madigan; *Needful Things* was filmed in 1993 by Columbia/Castle Rock, adapted by W. D. Richter and Lawrence Cohen, directed by Fraser C. Heston, starring Max Von Sydow, Ed Harris, Bonnie Bedelia, and Amanda Plummer; *The Tommyknockers* was filmed as a television miniseries by ABC-TV in 1993; *The Shawshank Redemption,* based on King's novella *Rita Hayworth and Shawshank Redemption: Hope Springs Eternal,* was filmed in 1994 by Columbia, written and directed by Frank Darabont, featuring Tim Robbins and Morgan Freeman; *Dolores Claiborne* was filmed in 1995 by Columbia; *Thinner* was filmed by Paramount in 1996, directed by Dom Holland, starring Robert John Burke, Joe Mantegna, Lucinda Jenney, and Michael Constantine; *Night Flier* was filmed by New Amsterdam Entertainment/Stardust International/Medusa Film in 1997, directed by Mark Pavia, starring Miguel Ferrer, Julie Entwisle, Dan Monahan, and Michael H. Moss; *Apt Pupil* was filmed in 1998 by TriStar Pictures, directed by Bryan Singer, starring David Schwimmer, Ian McKellen, and Brad Renfro; *The Green Mile* was filmed in 1999 by Castle Rock, directed by Frank Darabont, who also wrote the screenplay, starring Tom Hanks; *Hearts in Atlantis* was filmed in 2001 by Castle Rock, directed by Scott Hicks, screenplay written by William Goldman, starring Anthony Hopkins; *Dreamcatcher* was released in 2003 by Warner Brothers and Castle Rock Entertainment and was directed by Lawrence Kasdan, written by William Goldman, starring Morgan Freeman. Several of King's short stories have also been adapted for the screen, including *The Boogeyman,* filmed by Tantalus in 1982 and 1984 in association with the New York University School of Undergraduate Film, screenplay by producer-director Jeffrey C. Schiro; *The Woman in the Room,* filmed in 1983 by Darkwoods, screenplay by director Frank Darabont, broadcast on public television in Los Angeles, 1985 (released with *The Boogeyman* on video-cassette as *Two Mini-Features from Stephen King's Nightshift Collection* by Granite Entertainment Group, 1985); *Children of the Corn,* produced in 1984 by Donald P. Borchers and Terrence Kirby for New World Pictures, screenplay by George Goldsmith; *The Word*

Processor (based on King's "The Word Processor of the Gods"), produced by Romero and Richard Rubenstein for Laurel Productions, 1984, teleplay by Michael Dowell, broadcast November 19, 1985, on *Tales from the Darkside* series and released on videocassette by Laurel Entertainment, 1985; *Gramma,* filmed by CBS-TV in 1985, teleplay by Harlan Ellison, broadcast February 14, 1986, on *The Twilight Zone* series; *Creepshow 2* (based on "The Raft" and two unpublished stories by King, "Old Chief Wood'nhead" and "The Hitchhiker"), was filmed in 1987 by New World Pictures, screenplay by Romero; *Sometimes They Come Back,* filmed by CBS-TV in 1987; "The Cat from Hell" is included in a three-segment anthology film titled *Tales from the Darkside—The Movie,* produced by Laurel Productions, 1990; *The Lawnmower Man,* written by director Brett Leonard and Gimel Everett for New Line Cinema, 1992; *The Mangler,* filmed by New Line Cinema, 1995; and *The Langoliers,* filmed as a television mini-series by ABC-TV in 1995; the short fiction "Secret Window, Secret Garden" was adapted into the film *Secret Window,* distributed by Columbia Pictures, written and directed by David Koepp; 2004; the short story "All That You Love Will Be Carried Away" from the collection *Everything's Eventual* has been adapted and made into a short film by James Renner; film rights to the short story "1408" from the collection *Everything's Eventual* has been optioned by Dimension Films. *From a Buick 8* has been optioned by Chesapeake Films.

WORK IN PROGRESS: A series of original graphic novels based on the "Dark Tower" series, for Marvel.

SIDELIGHTS: "With Stephen King," mused Chelsea Quinn Yarbro in *Fear Itself: The Horror Fiction of Stephen King,* "you never have to ask 'Who's afraid of the big bad wolf?'—You are. And he knows it." Throughout a prolific array of novels, short stories, and screen work in which elements of horror, fantasy, science fiction, and humor meld, King deftly arouses fear from dormancy. The breadth and durability of his popularity alone evince his mastery as a compelling storyteller. "Nothing is as unstoppable as one of King's furies, except perhaps King's word processor," remarked Gil Schwartz in *People,* which selected King as one of twenty individuals who had defined the decade of the Eighties. And although the critical reception of his work has not necessarily matched its sweeping success with readers, colleagues and several critics alike discern within it a substantial and enduring literary legitimacy. In *American Film,* for instance, Darrell Ewing and Dennis Meyers called him "the chronicler of contemporary America's dreams, desires, and fears."

While striking a deep and responsive chord within its readers, the genre of horror is frequently trivialized by critics who tend to regard it, when at all, less seriously than mainstream fiction. In an interview with Charles Platt in *Dream Makers: The Uncommon Men and Women Who Write Science Fiction,* King suspected that "most of the critics who review popular fiction have no understanding of it as a whole." Regarding the "propensity of a small but influential element of the literary establishment to ghettoize horror and fantasy and instantly relegate them beyond the pale of so-called serious literature," King told Eric Norden in a *Playboy* interview, "I'm sure those critics' nineteenth-century precursors would have contemptuously dismissed [Edgar Allan] Poe as the great American hack." But as King contends in "The Horror Writer and the Ten Bears," his foreword to *Kingdom of Fear:* "Horror isn't a hack market now, and never was. The genre is one of the most delicate known to man, and it must be handled with great care and more than a little love." Furthermore, in a panel discussion at the 1984 World Fantasy Convention in Ottawa, reprinted in *Bare Bones: Conversations on Terror with Stephen King,* he predicted that horror writers "might actually have a serious place in American literature in a hundred years or so."

King's ability to comprehend "the attraction of fantastic horror to the denizen of the late twentieth century," according to Deborah L. Notkin in *Fear Itself,* partially accounts for his unrivaled popularity in the genre. But what distinguishes him is the way in which he transforms the ordinary into the horrific. Pointing out in the *Atlantic Monthly* that horror frequently represents "the symbolic depiction of our common experience," Lloyd Rose observed that "King takes ordinary emotional situations—marital stress, infidelity, peer-group-acceptance worries—and translates them into violent tales of vampires and ghosts. He writes supernatural soap operas." But to Gary Williams Crawford in *Discovering Stephen King,* King is "a uniquely sensitive author" within the Gothic literary tradition, which he described as "essentially a literature of nightmare, a conflict between waking life and the darkness within the human mind." Perpetuating the legacy of Edgar Allan Poe, Nathaniel Hawthorne, Herman Melville, Henry James, and H. P. Lovecraft, "King is heir to the American Gothic tradition in that he has placed his horrors in contemporary settings and has depicted the struggle of an American culture to face the horrors within it," explained Crawford, and because "he has shown the nightmare of our idealistic civilization." Observing that children suspend their disbelief easily, King argued in his *Danse Macabre* that, ironically, they are actually "better able to deal with fantasy and terror *on its own terms* than their elders are." In an interview for *High Times,* for instance, he marveled at the resilience of a child's mind and the inexplicable, yet seemingly harmless, attraction of children to nightmare-inducing stories: "We start kids off on things like 'Hansel and Gretel,' which features child abandonment, kidnapping, attempted murder, forcible detention, cannibalism, and finally murder by cremation. And the kids love it." Adults are capable of distinguishing between fantasy and reality, but in the process of growing up, laments King in *Danse Macabre,* they develop "a good case of mental tunnel vision and a gradual ossification of the imaginative faculty"; thus, he perceives the task of the fantasy or horror writer as enabling one to become "for a little while, a child again." In *Time* King discussed the prolonged obsession with childhood that his generation has had. "We went on playing for a long time, almost feverishly," he recalled. "I write for that buried child in us, but I'm writing for the grown-up too. I want grown-ups to look at the child long enough to be able to give him up."

The empowerment of estranged young people is a theme that recurs throughout King's fiction. "If Stephen King's kids have one thing in common," declared young-adult novelist Robert Cormier in the *Washington Post Book World,* "it's the fact that they all are losers. In a way, all children are losers, of course—how can they be winners with that terrifying adult world stacked against them?" His first novel, *Carrie,* is about a persecuted teenaged girl. "The novel examines female power," stated *Dictionary of Literary Biography* contributor Carol Senf, "for Carrie gains her telekinetic abilities with her first menstruation." "It is," Senf concluded, "a compelling character study of a persecuted teenager who finally uses her powers to turn the table on her persecutors. The result is a violent explosion that destroys the mother who had taught her self-hatred and the high-school peers who had made her a scapegoat." An alienated teenaged boy is the main character in King's *Christine,* and *Rage* features Charlie Decker, a young man who tells the story of his descent into madness and murder. In *The Shining* and *Firestarter,* Danny Torrance and Charlie McGee are alienated not from their families—they have loving, if sometimes weak, parents—but through the powers they possess and by those who want to manipulate them: evil supernatural forces in *The Shining,* the U.S. Government in *Firestarter.* Children also figure prominently, although not always as victims, in *Salem's Lot, The Tommyknockers, Pet Sematary, The Eyes of the Dragon,* and *The Talisman.*

King's most explicit examination of alienation in childhood, however, comes in the novel *It.* The eponymous IT is a creature that feeds on children—on their bodies and on their emotions, especially fear. IT lives in the sewers of Derry, Maine, having arrived there ages ago from outer space, and emerges about every twenty-seven years in search of victims. "*It* begins, demonically enough, in 1957," explained *New York Review of Books* contributor Thomas R. Edwards, "when a six-year-old boy has his arm torn off by what appears to be a circus clown lurking down a storm drain . . . . King organizes the tale as two parallel stories, one tracing the activities of seven unprepossessing fifth- graders—'The Losers' Club'—who discovered and fought the horror in 1958, the other describing their return to Derry in 1985 when the cycle resumes." The surviving members of the Losers' Club return to Derry to confront IT and defeat IT once and for all. The only things that appears to hurt IT are faith, humor, and childlike courage. "Only brave and imaginative children, or adults who learn to remember and honor their childish selves," Edwards concluded, "can hope to foil It, as the Losers finally do in 1985."

"*It* involves the guilts and innocences of childhood and the difficulty for adults of recapturing them," Christopher Lehmann-Haupt stated in the *New York Times.* "*It* questions the difference between necessity and free will. *It* also concerns the evil that has haunted America from time to time in the forms of crime, racial and religious bigotry, economic hardship, labor strife and industrial pollution." The evil takes shape among Derry's adults and older children, especially the bullies who terrorize the members of the Losers' Club.

Not surprisingly, throughout most of King's adolescence, the written word afforded a powerful diversion. "Writing has always been it for me," King indicated in a panel discussion at the 1984 World Fantasy Convention in Ottawa, reprinted in *Bare Bones.* Science fiction and adventure stories comprised his first literary efforts. Having written his first story at the age of seven, King began submitting short fiction to magazines at twelve, and published his first story at eighteen. In high school, he authored a small, satiric newspaper titled "The Village Vomit"; and in college he penned a popular and eclectic series of columns called "King's Garbage Truck." He also started writing the novels he eventually published under the pseudonymous ruse of Richard Bachman—novels that focus more on elements of human alienation and brutality than supernatural horror. After graduation, King supplemented his teaching salary through various odd jobs and by submitting stories to men's magazines. Searching for a form of his own, and responding to a friend's challenge to break out of the machismo mold of his short fiction, King wrote what he described to Abe Peck in *Rolling Stone College Papers* as "a parable of women's consciousness." Retrieving the discarded manuscript from the trash, though, King's wife, Tabitha, who is a writer herself, suggested that he ought to expand it. And because King completed the first draft of *Carrie* at the time William Peter Blatty's *The Exorcist* and Thomas Tryon's *The Other* were being published, the novel was marketed as horror fiction, and the genre had found its juggernaut. Or, as Don Herron put it in *Fear Itself*, "Like a mountain, King is there."

"Stephen King has made a dent in the national consciousness in a way no other horror writer has, at least during his own lifetime," stated Alan Warren in *Discovering Stephen King*. "He is a genuine phenomenon." A newsletter—"Castle Rock"—has been published since 1985 to keep his ever-increasing number of fans well informed; and Book-of-the-Month Club has been reissuing all of his best-sellers as the Stephen King Library collection. In his preface to *Fear Itself*, "On Becoming a Brand Name," King described the process as a fissional one in that a "writer produces a series of books which ricochet back and forth between hardcover and softcover at an ever increasing speed." Resorting to a pseudonym to get even more work into print accelerated the process for King; but according to Stephen P. Brown in *Kingdom of Fear*, although the ploy was not entirely "a vehicle for King to move his earliest work out of the trunk," it certainly triggered myriad speculations about, as well as hunts for, other possible pseudonyms he may also have used. In his essay "Why I Was Bachman" in *The Bachman Books: Four Early Novels by Stephen King*, King recalled that he simply considered it a good idea at the time, especially since he wanted to try to publish something without the attendant commotion that a Stephen King title would have unavoidably generated. Also, his publisher believed that he had already saturated the market. King's prodigious literary output and multimillion-dollar contracts, though, have generated critical challenges to the inherent worth of his fiction. Deducing that he has been somehow compromised by commercial success, some critics imply that he writes simply to fulfill contractual obligations. But as King told Norden, "Money really has nothing to do with it one way or the other. I love writing the things I write, and I wouldn't and 'couldn't' do anything else."

King writes daily, exempting only Christmas, the Fourth of July, and his birthday. He likes to work on two things simultaneously, beginning his day early with a two-or three-mile walk: "What I'm working on in the morning is what I'm *working* on," he said in a panel discussion at the 1980 World Fantasy Convention in Baltimore, reprinted in *Bare Bones*. He devotes his afternoon hours to rewriting. And according to his *Playboy* interview,

while he is not particular about working conditions, he is about his output. Despite chronic headaches, occasional insomnia, and even a fear of writer's block, he produces six pages daily; "And that's like engraved in stone," he told Joyce Lynch Dewes Moore in *Mystery*.

Aware that "people want to be scared," as he related to Abe Peck in a *Rolling Stone College Papers* interview, and truly delighted to be able to accommodate them, King rejects the criticism that he preys on the fears of others. As he explained to Jack Matthews in a *Detroit Free Press* interview, some people simply avoid his books just as those who are afraid of speed and heights, especially in tandem, shun roller coasters. And that, he declared to Paul Janeczko in *English Journal*, is precisely what he believes he owes his readers—"a good ride on the roller coaster." Regarding what he finds to be an essential reassurance that underlies and impels the genre itself, King remarked in *Danse Macabre* that "beneath its fangs and fright wig" horror fiction is really quite conservative. Comparing horror fiction with the morality plays of the late middle ages, for instance, he believes that its primary function is "to reaffirm the virtues of the norm by showing us what awful things happen to people who venture into taboo lands." Also, there is the solace in knowing "when the lights go down in the theatre or when we open the book that the evildoers will almost certainly be punished, and measure will be returned for measure." But King admitted to Norden that despite all the discussion by writers generally about "horror's providing a socially and psychologically useful catharsis for people's fears and aggressions, the brutal fact of the matter is that we're still in the business of public executions."

"Death is a significant element in nearly all horror fiction," wrote Michael A. Morrison in *Fantasy Review*, "and it permeates King's novels and short stories." Noting in *Danse Macabre* that a universal fear with which each of us must personally struggle is "the fear of dying," King explained to Bob Spitz in a *Penthouse* magazine interview that "everybody goes out to horror movies, reads horror novels—and it's almost as though we're trying to preview the end." But he submitted that "if the horror story is our rehearsal for death, then its strict moralities make it also a reaffirmation of life and good will and simple imagination—just one more pipeline to the infinite." While he believes that horror is "one of the ways we walk our imagination," as he told Matthews, he does worry about the prospect of a mentally unstable reader patterning behavior after some fictional brutality. Remarking that "evil is basically stupid and unimaginative and doesn't need creative inspiration from me or anybody else," King told Norden, for instance, that "despite knowing all that rationally, I have to admit that it is unsettling to feel that I could be linked in any way, however tenuous, to somebody else's murder."

An example of King's ability to "pour new wine from old bottles" is his experimentation with narrative structure. In *It, Carrie,* and *The Stand,* declared Tony Magistrale in the study *Landscape of Fear: Stephen King's American Gothic,* King explores story forms—"stream of consciousness, interior monologues, multiple narrators, and a juggling of time sequences—in order to draw the reader into a direct and thorough involvement with the characters and events of the tale." Both *The Dark Half* and *Misery,* according to George Stade in the *New York Times Book Review,* are "parable[s] in chiller form of the popular writer's relation to his audience." In *Gerald's Game*'s Jessie Burlingame has lost her husband to heart failure. He "has died after handcuffing her to the bed at their summer home," Senf explained in the *Dictionary of Literary Biography,* "and Jessie must face her life, including the memory that her father had sexually abused her, and her fears alone." *Dolores Claiborne* is the story of a woman suspected of murdering her employer, a crusty old miser named Vera Donovan. Dolores maintains her innocence, but she freely confesses that she murdered her husband thirty years previously when she caught him molesting their daughter.

"There are a series of dovetailing, but unobtrusive, connections," stated *Locus* contributor Edward Bryant, "linking the two novels and both Jessie and Dolores." Like *It,* both *Gerald's Game* and *Dolores Claiborne* are set in the town of Derry, Maine. They are also both psychological portraits of older women who have been subjected to sexual abuse. *Dolores Claiborne* differs from *Gerald's Game,* however, because it uses fewer of the traditional trappings of horror fiction, and it is related entirely from the viewpoint of the title character. *Dolores Claiborne* "is, essentially, a dramatic monologue," stated Kit Reed in the *Washington Post Book World,* "in which the speaker addresses other people in the room, answers questions and completes a narrative in actual time." "All but the last page is one long quote from Dolores Claiborne," asserted a *Rapport* reviewer. "King has taken horror literature out of the closet and has injected new life into familiar genres," Senf concluded. "He is not afraid to mix those genres in fresh ways to produce novels that examine contemporary American culture."

Insomnia, King's 1994 novel, continues the example set by *Gerald's Game* and *Dolores Claiborne.* It is also set in Derry, and its protagonist is an elderly man named Ralph Roberts, a retired salesman, newly widowed and suffering severely from insomnia. Ralph begins to see people in a new way: their auras become visible to him. "Ralph finds himself a man in a classic situation, a mortal in conflict with the fates—literally," declared *Locus* reviewer Bryant. "How much self-determination does he really possess? And how much is he acted upon?" Ralph also finds himself in conflict with his neighbor Ed Deepeneau, a conservative Christian and antiabortion activist who beats his wife and has taken up a crusade against a visiting feminist speaker. "There are some truly haunting scenes in the book about wife abuse and fanaticism, as well as touching observations about growing old, but they're quickly consumed by more predictable sensationalism," remarked Chris Bohjalian in the *New York Times Book Review.* "In a world teeming with timeless, omnipotent entities," declared novelist Kinky Friedman in the *Washington Post Book World,* "King has provided Ralph Roberts, that ancient vulnerable, white- haired widower, with the ultimate weapon, the power of the human spirit."

King delighted his readers and astounded his critics by issuing three new major novels in 1996: *Desperation, The Regulators*—under the pseudonym Richard Bachman—and *The Green Mile,* the last a Depression-era prison novel serialized in six installments. A *Publishers Weekly* reviewer said that "if the publishing industry named a Person of the Year, this year's winner would be Stephen King." The critic noted that, with *Desperation,* "King again proves himself the premier literary barometer of our cultural clime." Released on the same day from two different publishers, *Desperation* and *The Regulators* have interlocking characters and plots; each works as a kind of distorted mirror image of the other. In *Desperation,* which many critics agree is the better book, a group of strangers drive into Desperation, Nevada, where they encounter a malign spirit (Tak) in the body of police officer Collie Entragian. The survivors of this apocalyptic novel are few, but include David Carver, an eleven-year-old boy who talks to God, and John Edward Marinville, an alcoholic novelist. Robert Polito, writing for the *New York Times,* noted that "King's peculiar knack as a novelist is to strip away much of the complexity and nearly all of the art from a terrifying vision of an unknowable universe ruled by a limited, perhaps evil God and insinuate that Gnosticism into the rituals and commodities of everyday America." Polito admired King's capacity to tap into the collective unconscious of America at the end of the millennium but regretted that "the recurrent silliness shrugs off the horror and the social anger." Mark Harris, writing for *Entertainment Weekly,* however, remarked that King "hasn't been this intent on scaring readers—or been this successful at it—since *The Stand*," noting that "King has always been pop fiction's most compassionate sadist." In *Desperation*, King grapples with the nature of God, but Polito claimed that the "bromide" that "God is Love" can't dispel the novel's dark and cruel vision of the universe. King recorded the audio version of *Desperation* himself.

While *The Regulators* received little critical praise, King's experiment in serialization with *The Green Mile* captured the imagination of both readers and critics. An *Entertainment Weekly* reviewer called it a novel "that's as hauntingly touching as it is just plain haunted," and a *New York Times* contributor claimed that in spite of "the striking circumstances of its serial publication," the novel "manages to sustain the notes of visceral wonder and indelible horror that keep eluding the Tak books." Set in the Deep South in 1932, *The Green Mile* —a prison expression for death row—begins with the death of twin girls and the conviction of John Coffey for their murder. Block superintendent Paul Edgecombe, who narrates the story years later from his nursing home in Georgia, slowly unfolds the story of the mysterious Coffey, a man with no past and with a gift for healing.

King's next major novel, *Bag of Bones*, appeared in 1998. This tale of a writer struggling with both grief for his dead wife and writer's block while living in a haunted cabin met with a great deal of acclaim from critics. Also acclaimed was the following year's *Hearts in Atlantis*, which Tom De Haven described in *Entertainment Weekly* as "a novel in five stories, with players sometimes migrating from one story to the next." De Haven went on to note that "there's more heartbreak than horror in these pages, and a doomy aura that's more generational than occult." He also reported that the "last two stories are drenched in sadness, mortality, regret, and finally absolution," concluding that *Hearts in Atlantis* "is wonderful fiction." Similarly, Ray Olson praised the volume in *Booklist* as "a rich, engaging, deeply moving generational epic." *The Girl Who Loved Tom Gordon* also saw print in 1999. This novel, short by King's standards, centers on a nine-year-old girl from a broken home who gets lost in a forest for two weeks. She has her radio with her, and survives her ordeal by listening to Boston Red Sox games and imagining conversations with her hero, Red Sox relief pitcher Tom Gordon.

While these books were making their way to readers, however, King suffered a serious health challenge. On June 19, 1999, he was struck by a van while walking alongside a road near his home, sustaining injuries to his spine, hip, ribs, and right leg. One of his broken ribs punctured a lung, and he nearly died. He began a slow progress towards recovery, cheered by countless cards and letters from his fans. During his recovery, he began experimenting with publishing his fiction electronically. In August, 2000, King self-published the first two installments of his e-book *The Plant* on his Web site. Pricing the installments at one dollar each, King promised to publish additional chapters if at least 75 percent of those who download the first two installments paid for them. King also published a short story, "Riding the Bullet," in March, only distributed as an e-book publication in a number of formats. This tale was eventually reprinted in the 2002 collection *Everything's Eventual: 14 Dark Tales.*

King had also begun work on a writer's manual before his accident, and the result, 2000's *On Writing: A Memoir of the Craft,* sold more copies in its first printing than any previous book about writing. In addition to King's advice on crafting fiction, however, the book includes a great deal of autobiographical material. The author chronicles his childhood, his rise to fame, his struggles with addiction, and the horrific accident that almost ended his life. "King's writing about his own alcoholism and cocaine abuse," noted John Mark Eberhart in the Kansas City *Star,* "is among the best and most honest prose of his career." Similarly, Jack Harville reported in the Charlotte *Observer* that "the closing piece describes King's accident and rehabilitation. The description is harrowing, and the rehab involves both physical and emotional recovery. It is beautifully told in a narrative style that would have gained Strunk and White's approval." Some of the novels King has published since the beginning of the twenty-first century, including *Dreamcatcher* and *From a Buick 8,* have brought strong comparisons from critics with his earlier novels; in these specific cases, *It* and *Christine,* respectively. These books, however, were followed by an announcement King made in 2002 that he is planning to retire from publishing. In an interview with Chris Nashawaty in *Entertainment Weekly,* King clarified, "First of all, I'd never stop writing because I don't know what I'd do between nine and one every day. But I'd stop publishing. I don't need the money." Yet *Dreamcatcher* and *From a Buick 8* have garnered praise from reviewers as well. Rene Rodriguez in the *Miami Herald* maintained that " *Dreamcatcher* marks [King's] bracing return to all- out horror, complete with trademark grisly gross-outs, a panoramic cast of deftly drawn characters and a climactic race against time, with the fate of the planet hanging in the balance." Salem Macknee in the Charlotte *Observer,* noting surface similarities between *From a Buick 8* and *Christine,* assured readers that "this strange counterfeit of a Buick Roadmaster is no rerun. Stephen King has once again created an original, a monster never seen before, with its own frightful fingerprint."

King also received a great deal of praise for *Everything's Eventual*. Among other stories, the collection includes a few that he previously published in the *New Yorker*. Notable among these is "The Man in the Black Suit," which won the 1996 O. Henry Award for best short story and brought King comparisons with great nineteenth-century American fiction writer Nathaniel Hawthorne. "As a whole," concluded Rodriguez in another *Miami Herald* review, " *Everything's Eventual* makes a perfect showcase for all of King's strengths: His uncanny talent for creating vivid, fully realized characters in a few strokes, his ability to mine horror out of the mundane, . . . and his knack for leavening even the most preposterous contraptions with genuine, universal emotions."

Although he does not necessarily feel that he has been treated unfairly by the critics, King has described what it is like to witness the written word turned into filmed images that are less than generously received by reviewers. "Whenever I publish a book, I feel like a trapper caught by the Iroquois," he told Peck in *Rolling Stone College Papers*. "They're all lined up with tomahawks, and the idea is to run through with your head down, and everybody gets to take a swing . . . . Finally, you get out the other side and you're bleeding and bruised, and *then* it gets turned into a movie, and you're there in front of the same line and everybody's got their tomahawks out again." Nevertheless, in his essay "Why I Was Bachman," he readily admitted that he really has little to complain about: "I'm still married to the same woman, my kids are healthy and bright, and I'm being well paid for doing something I love." And despite the financial security and recognition, or perhaps because of its intrinsic responsibility, King strives to improve at his craft. "It's getting later and I want to get better, because you only get so many chances to do good work," he stated in a panel discussion at the 1984 World Fantasy Convention in Ottawa. "There's no justification not to at least try to do good work when you make the money."

According to Warren in *Discovering Stephen King,* there is absolutely nothing to suggest that success has been detrimental to King: "As a novelist, King has been remarkably consistent." Noting, for instance, that "for generations it was given that brevity was the soul of horror, that the ideal format for the tale of terror was the short story," Warren pointed out that "King was among the first to challenge that concept, writing not just successful novels of horror, but long novels." Moreover, said Warren, "his novels have gotten longer." King once quipped in the *Chicago Tribune Magazine* that his "philosophy has always been take a good thing and beat it 'til it don't move no more." Although some critics fault him for overwriting, Warren suggested that "the sheer scope and ambitious nature of his storytelling demands a broad canvas." Referring to this as "the very pushiness of his technique," the *New York Times'* Lehmann-Haupt similarly contended that "the more he exasperates us by overpreparing, the more effectively his preparations eventually pay off."

Influenced by the naturalistic novels of writers such as Theodore Dreiser and Frank Norris, King confessed to Janeczko that his personal outlook for the world's future is somewhat bleak. On the other hand, one of the things he finds most comforting in his own work is an element of optimism. "In almost all cases, I've begun with a premise that was really black," he said in a panel discussion at the 1980 World Fantasy Convention in Baltimore, reprinted in *Bare Bones*. "And a more pleasant resolution has forced itself upon that structure." But as Andrew M. Greeley maintained in *Kingdom of Fear:* "Unlike some other horror writers who lack his talents and sensitivity, Stephen King never ends his stories with any cheap or easy hope. People are badly hurt, they suffer and some of them die, but others survive the struggle and manage to grow. The powers of evil have not yet done them in." According to Notkin, though, the reassurance King brings to his own readers derives from a basic esteem for humanity itself: "For whether he is writing about vampires, about the death of 99 percent of the population, or about innocent little girls with the power to break the earth in half, King never stops emphasizing his essential liking for people."

"There's unmistakable genius in Stephen King," admitted Walter Kendrick in the *Village Voice,* adding that he writes "with such fierce conviction, such blind and brutal power, that no matter how hard you fight—and needless to say, I fought—he's irresistible." The less reserved critical affirmations of King's work extend from expressions of pragmatism to those of metaphor. Lehmann-Haupt, for example, a self-professed King addict, offered his evaluation of King's potential versus his accomplishments as a writer of horror fiction: "Once again, as I edged myself nervously toward the climax of one of his thrillers, I found myself considering what Stephen King could accomplish if he would only put his storytelling talents to serious use. And then I had to ask myself: if Mr. King's aim in writing . . . was not entirely serious by some standard that I was vaguely invoking, then why, somebody please tell me, was I holding on to his book so hard that my knuckles had begun to turn white?" Douglas E. Winter assessed King's contribution to the genre in his study *Stephen King: The Art of Darkness* this way: "Death, destruction, and destiny await us all at the end of the journey—in life as in horror fiction. And the writer of horror stories serves as the boatman who ferries people across that Reach known as the River Styx . . . . In the horror fiction of Stephen King, we can embark upon the night journey, make the descent down the dark hole, cross that narrowing Reach, and return again in safety to the surface—to the near shore of the river of death. For our boatman has a master's hand."

While King has played with the idea of giving up publishing his writings, his legion of fans continues to be delighted that the idea has not yet become a reality. In 2004, under the pseudonym of Eleanor Druse, King published *The Journals of Eleanor Druse: My Investigation of the Kingdom Hospital Incident.* He has also continued with his "Dark Tower" series (the illustrated novels featuring Roland the gunslinger) with the publication of *The Dark Tower V: Wolves of the Calla* in 2003. The book was published more than five years after the publication of the previous installment in the series, *The Dark Tower IV: Wizard and Glass.* King also completed the final two installments of the series in 2004, including *The Dark Tower VI: The Songs of Susannah* and *The Dark Tower VII: The Dark Tower.* In a surprise for fans, King introduced himself as a character in the sixth installment, which a *Publishers Weekly* reviewer called a "gutsy move" and commented, "that way there's no denying the ingenuity with which King paints a candid picture of himself."

In 2004, King varied a bit from his usual formula to write, in conjunction with Stewart O'Nan, a nonfiction book about one of his great loves, the Boston Red Sox. When the two authors began keeping diaries of every team-related moment in the year, *Faithful: Two Diehard Boston Red Sox Fans Chronicle the Historic 2004 Season* was originally expected to be the story of yet another disappointing season for fans of the seemingly cursed team. Instead the Red Sox won the World Series that season for the first time in eighty-six years.

With *Cell,* a 2006 novel that *Booklist* contributor Ray Olson considered "the most suspenseful, fastest-paced book King has ever written," the author uses cell phone signals as a source for inducing zombie-like violence in the majority of the population. A *Publishers Weekly* re-

viewer found "King's imagining . . . rich," and the dialogue "jaunty and witty" in this novel that borrows technique from Richard Matheson and George A. Romero, the horror legends to whom the book is dedicated. Olson concludes that with the publication of *Cell,* "King blasts any notion that he's exhausted or dissipated his enormous talent."

BIOGRAPHICAL AND CRITICAL SOURCES:

BOOKS

Badley, Linda, *Writing Horror and the Body: The Fiction of Stephen King, Clive Barker and Anne Rice,* Greenwood Press (Westport, CT), 1996.

Beahm, George W., *The Stephen King Story,* revised and updated edition, Andrews & McMeel (Kansas City, MO), 1992.

Beahm, George W., editor, *The Stephen King Companion,* Andrews & McMeel (Kansas City, MO), 1989.

Blue, Tyson, *Observations from the Terminator: Thoughts on Stephen King and Other Modern Masters of Horror Fiction,* Borgo Press (San Bernardino, CA), 1995.

Collings, Michael R., *Stephen King As Richard Bachman,* Starmont House (Mercer Island, WA), 1985.

Collings, Michael R., *The Works of Stephen King: An Annotated Bibliography and Guide,* edited by Boden Clarke, Borgo Press (San Bernardino, CA), 1993.

Collings, Michael R., *Scaring Us to Death: The Impact of Stephen King on Popular Culture,* 2nd edition, Borgo Press (San Bernardino, CA), 1995.

Contemporary Literary Criticism, Gale (Detroit, MI), Volume 12, 1980, Volume 26, 1983, Volume 37, 1985, Volume 61, 1990.

Davis, Jonathan P., *Stephen King's America,* Bowling Green State University Popular Press (Bowling Green, OH), 1994.

Dictionary of Literary Biography, Volume 143: *American Novelists since World War II, Third Series,* Gale (Detroit, MI), 1994.

Dictionary of Literary Biography Yearbook: 1980, Gale (Detroit, MI), 1981.

Docherty, Brian, editor, *American Horror Fiction: From Brockden Brown to Stephen King,* St. Martin's Press (New York, NY), 1990.

Hoppenstand, Gary, and Ray B. Browne, editors, *The Gothic World of Stephen King: Landscape of Nightmares,* Bowling Green State University Popular Press (Bowling Green, OH), 1987.

Keyishian, Amy, and Marjorie Keyishian, *Stephen King,* Chelsea House (Philadelphia, PA), 1995.

King, Stephen, *Stephen King's Danse Macabre* (nonfiction), Everest House (New York, NY), 1981.

King, Stephen, *The Bachman Books: Four Early Novels,* New American Library (New York, NY), 1985.

Magistrale, Tony, editor, *Landscape of Fear: Stephen King's American Gothic,* Bowling Green State University Popular Press (Bowling Green, OH), 1988.

Magistrale, Tony, editor, *A Casebook on "The Stand,"* Starmont House (Mercer Island, WA), 1992.

Magistrale, Tony, editor, *The Dark Descent: Essays Defining Stephen King's Horrorscape,* Greenwood Press (Westport, CT), 1992.

Magistrale, Tony, *Stephen King: The Second Decade—"Danse Macabre" to "The Dark Half,"* Twayne (New York, NY), 1992.

Platt, Charles, *Dream Makers: The Uncommon Men and Women Who Write Science Fiction,* Berkley (New York, NY), 1983.

Russell, Sharon A., *Stephen King: A Critical Companion,* Greenwood Press (Westport, CT), 1996.

Saidman, Anne, *Stephen King, Master of Horror,* Lerner Publications (Minneapolis, MN), 1992.

Schweitzer, Darrell, editor, *Discovering Stephen King,* Starmont House (Mercer Island, WA), 1985.

Short Story Criticism, Volume 17, Gale (Detroit, MI), 1995.

Underwood, Tim, and Chuck Miller, editors, *Fear Itself: The Horror Fiction of Stephen King,* Underwood-Miller, 1982.

Underwood, Tim, and Chuck Miller, editors, *Kingdom of Fear: The World of Stephen King,* Underwood-Miller, 1986.

Underwood, Tim, and Chuck Miller, editors, *Bare Bones: Conversations on Terror with Stephen King,* McGraw-Hill (New York, NY), 1988.

Underwood, Tim, and Chuck Miller, editors, *Feast of Fear: Conversations with Stephen King,* Carroll & Graf (New York, NY), 1992.

Underwood, Tim, and Chuck Miller, editors, *Fear Itself: The Early Works of Stephen King,* foreword by King, introduction by Peter Straub, afterword by George A. Romero, Underwood-Miller, 1993.

Winter, Douglas E., *Stephen King: The Art of Darkness,* New American Library (New York, NY), 1984.

PERIODICALS

American Film, June, 1986, article by Darrell Ewing and Dennis Meyers.

Atlantic Monthly, September, 1986.

Book, November-December, Chris Barsanti, review of *The Dark Tower V: Wolves of the Calla,* p. 75.

Booklist, July, 1999, Ray Olson, review of *Hearts in Atlantis,* p. 1893; May 1, 2004, Ray Olson, review of *The Dark Tower V: Song of Susannah,* p. 1483; September 1, 2004, Ray Olson, review of *The Dark Tower VII: The Dark Tower,* p. 6; January 1, 2006, Ray Olson, review of *Cell,* p. 24.

Boston Globe, October 10, 1980; April 15, 1990, p. A1; May 16, 1990, p. 73; July 15, 1990, p. 71; September 11, 1990, p. 61; October 31, 1990, p. 25; November 17, 1990, p. 12; December 5, 1990, p. 73; July 16, 1991, p. 56; September 28, 1991, p. 9; November 22, 1991, p. 1; August 21, 1992, p. 21; August 30, 1992, p. 14; May 8, 1993, p. 21; May 24, 1993, p. 43; October 16, 1994, p. 14; May 13, 1995, p. 21.

Chicago Tribune, August 26, 1990, p. 3; October 29, 1990, p. 5; November 16, 1990, p. 1; November 30, 1990, p. C29; June 29, 1992, p. 3; November 18, 1992, p. 3; November 7, 1993, p. 9; October 26, 1994, p. 1; May 14, 1995, p. 5.

Chicago Tribune Magazine, October 27, 1985.

Christian Science Monitor, January 22, 1990, p. 13.

Detroit Free Press, November 12, 1982, Jack Matthes, interview with author.

Detroit News, September 26, 1979.

English Journal, January, 1979; February, 1980; January, 1983; December, 1983; December, 1984.

Entertainment Weekly, October 14, 1994, pp. 52-53; June 16, 1995, p. 54; March 22, 1996, p. 63; April 26, 1996, p. 49; May 31, 1996, p. 53; June 28, 1996, p. 98; August 2, 1996, p. 53; September 6, 1996, p. 67; October 4, 1996, p. 54; October 18, 1996, p. 75; December 27, 1996, p. 28; February 7, 1997, p. 111; April 11, 1997, p. 17; April 25, 1997, p. 52; November 28, 1997, p. 41; September 17, 1999, Tom De Haven, "King of *Hearts:* He May Be the Master of Horror, but Stephen King Is Also Adept at Capturing Everyday America. In *Hearts in Atlantis,* His Take on the 60s, including the Effects of Vietnam, Is Scarily Accurate," p.72; September 27, 2002, Chris Nashawaty, "Stephen King Quits," p. 20; June 25, 2004, Gregory Kirschling, review of *The Dark Tower V: Song of Susannah,* p. 172.

Esquire, November, 1984.

Fantasy Review, January, 1984, Michael A. Morrison.

Film Journal, April 12, 1982.

High Times, January, 1981; June, 1981.

Library Journal, March 1, 2004, Kristen L. Smith, review of *The Dark Tower V: Wolves of the Calla,* p. 126; May 15, 2004, Nancy McNicol, review of *The Dark Tower V: Song of Susannah,* p. 115; September 15, 2004, Nancy McNicol, review of *The*

Dark Tower VII: The Dark Tower, p.49; September 15, 2005, Nancy McNicol, review of *The Colorado Kid,* p. 60.

Locus, September, 1992, pp. 21- 22, 67; November, 1992, pp. 19, 21; February, 1994, p. 39; October, 1994, pp. 27, 29.

Los Angeles Times, April 23, 1978; December 10, 1978; August 26, 1979; September 28, 1980; May 10, 1981; September 6, 1981; May 8, 1983; November 20, 1983; November 18, 1984; August 25, 1985; March 9, 1990, p. F16; October 29, 1990, p. F9; November 18, 1990, p. F6; November 30, 1990, p. F1; July 16, 1991, p. F1; May 28, 1992, p. E7; April 16, 1995, p. 28; November 7, 1997, p. D4.

Los Angeles Times Book Review, August 29, 1982; July 15, 1990, p. 12; June 9, 1991, p. 6; April 23, 1995, p. 14.

Maclean's, August 11, 1986.

Miami Herald, March 21, 2001, Rene Rodriguez, review of *Dreamcatcher;* March 27, 2002, Rene Rodriguez, review of *Everything's Eventual.*

Midwest Quarterly, spring, 2004, Tom Hansen, "Diabolical Dreaming in Stephen King's 'The Man in the Black Suit,'" p. 290.

Mystery, March, 1981.

New Republic, February 21, 1981.

New Statesman, September 15, 1995, p. 33.

Newsweek, August 31, 1981; May 2, 1983.

New Yorker, January 15, 1979; September 30, 1996, p. 78.

New York Review of Books, October 19, 1995, p. 54.

New York Times, March 1, 1977; August 14, 1981; August 11, 1982; April 12, 1983; October 21, 1983; November 8, 1984; June 11, 1985; April 4, 1987; January 25, 1988; June 17, 1990, p. 13; October 27, 1990, p. A12; November 16, 1990, p. C38; December 2, 1990, p. 19; June 3, 1991, p. C14; July 14, 1991, p. 25; October 2, 1991, p. C23; June 29, 1992, p. C13; November 16, 1992, p. C15; March 15, 1993, p. D6; June 27, 1993, p. 23; September 17, 1993, p. B8; April 24, 1995, p. C12; May 12, 1995, p. D18; June 26, 1995, p. C16; November 11, 1995, p. 39; April 7, 1996, p. E2; August 5, 1996, p. D7; October 26, 1996, 15; April 25, 1997, p. D22; October 27, 1997, p. C1; November 5, 1997, p. E3; November 7, 1997, pp. A30, D10; February 6, 1998, p. B10.

New York Times Book Review, May 26, 1974; October 24, 1976; February 20, 1977; March 26, 1978; February 4, 1979; September 23, 1979; May 11, 1980; May 10, 1981; September 27, 1981; August 29, 1982; April 3, 1983; November 6, 1983; November 4, 1984; June 9, 1985; February 22, 1987; December 6, 1987; May 13, 1990, p. 3; September 2,

1990, p. 21; September 29, 1991, pp. 13-14; August 16, 1992, p. 3; December 27, 1992, p. 15; October 24, 1993, p. 22; October 30, 1994, p. 24; March 24, 1995, p. C14; July 2, 1995, p. 11; October 20, 1996, p. 16.

New York Times Magazine, May 11, 1980.

Observer (Charlotte, NC), October 4, 2000, Jack Harville, review of *On Writing: A Memoir of the Craft;* Salem Macknee, review of *From a Buick 8.*

Observer (London, England), October 1, 1995, p. 15.

Penthouse, April, 1982, Bob Spitz, interview with author.

People, March 7, 1977; December 29, 1980; January 5, 1981; May 18, 1981; January 28, 1985; fall, 1989; April 1, 1996, p. 38; October 7, 1996, p. 32; October 21, 1996, p. 16; April 28, 1997, p. 15; January 19, 1998, p. 45.

Playboy, June, 1983, interview with author.

Publishers Weekly, January 17, 1977; May 11, 1984; March 13, 1996, p. 26; April 1, 1996, p. 22; May 13, 1996, p. 26; June 24, 1996, p. 43; August 5, 1996, p. 292; August 26, 1996, p. 34; September 9, 1996, p. 27; October 7, 1996, p. 20; April 7, 1997, p. 52; July 14, 1997, p. 65; October 27, 1997, p. 21; November 10, 1997, p. 10; April 19, 2004, review of *The Dark Tower VI: Song of Susannah,* p. 37; August 15, 2005, Orson Scott Card, review of *The Colorado Kid,* p. 40; January 2, 2006, review of *Cell,* p. 37.

Rapport, Volume 17, number 3, p. 20.

Rolling Stone College Papers, winter, 1980; winter, 1983.

Saturday Review, September, 1981; November, 1984.

Science Fiction Chronicle, December, 1995; June, 1997, p. 43.

Star (Kansas City, MO), October 4, 2000, John Mark Eberhart, review of *On Writing.*

Time, August 30, 1982; July 1, 1985; October 6, 1986; December 7, 1992, p. 81; September 2, 1996, p. 60.

Tribune Books (Chicago, IL) June 8, 1980.

Village Voice, April 29, 1981; October 23, 1984; March 3, 1987.

Voice Literary Supplement, September, 1982; November, 1985.

Wall Street Journal, July 7, 1992, p. B2; October 5, 1992, p. B3; November 7, 1997, p. B8.

Washington Post, August 26, 1979; April 9, 1985; May 8, 1987; October 29, 1990, p. B8; July 16, 1991, p. B1; April 13, 1992, p. C7; May 21, 1993, p. 16; May 27, 1993, p. D9; May 14, 1995, p. G1.

Washington Post Book World, May 26, 1974; October 1, 1978; August 26, 1980; April 12, 1981; August 22, 1982; March 23, 1983; October 2, 1983; November 13, 1983; June 16, 1985; August 26, 1990,

p. 9; September 29, 1991, p. 9; October 31, 1991, p. C7; July 19, 1992, p. 7; December 13, 1992, p. 5; October 10, 1993, p. 4; October 9, 1994, p. 4; March 6, 1995, p. D6.

ONLINE

Stephen King Web site, http://www.stephenking.com/ (June 28, 2002).

*   *   *

KING, Stephen Edwin
    See KING, Stephen

*   *   *

KING, Steve
    See KING, Stephen

*   *   *

KINGSOLVER, Barbara 1955-

PERSONAL: Born April 8, 1955, in Annapolis, MD; daughter of Wendell R. (a physician) and Virginia (a homemaker; maiden name, Henry) Kingsolver; married Joseph Hoffmann (a chemist), April 15, 1985 (divorced); married Steven Hopp; children: (first marriage) Camille; (second marriage) Lily. *Education:* DePauw University, B.A. (magna cum laude), 1977; University of Arizona, M.S., 1981, and additional graduate study. *Politics:* "Human rights activist." *Religion:* "Pantheist." *Hobbies and other interests:* Music, hiking, gardening, parenthood.

ADDRESSES: Agent—Frances Goldin, 57 East Eleventh St., New York, NY 10003.

CAREER: University of Arizona, Tucson, research assistant in department of physiology, 1977-79, technical writer in office of arid lands studies, 1981-85; freelance journalist, 1985-87; writer, 1987—.

MEMBER: Amnesty International, National Writers Union, National TV Turnoff, Environmental Defense, PEN West, Phi Beta Kappa, Heifer International, Green Empowerment.

AWARDS, HONORS: Feature-writing award, Arizona Press Club, 1986; American Library Association awards, 1988, for *The Bean Trees,* and 1990, for *Homeland;* citation of accomplishment from United Nations National Council of Women, 1989; PEN fiction prize and Edward Abbey Ecofiction Award, both 1991, both for *Animal Dreams;* Woodrow Wilson Foundation/Lila Wallace fellow, 1992-93; D.Litt., DePauw University, 1994; Book Sense Book of the Year Award, 2000, for *The Poisonwood Bible;* National Humanities Medal, 2000.

WRITINGS:

The Bean Trees (novel), HarperCollins (New York, NY), 1988.

Homeland and Other Stories (includes "Homeland," "Islands on the Moon," "Quality Time," "Covered Bridges," "Rose-Johnny," and "Why I Am a Danger to the Public"), HarperCollins (New York, NY), 1989.

Holding the Line: Women in the Great Arizona Mine Strike of 1983 (nonfiction), ILR Press (Ithaca, NY), 1989, with new introduction, 1996.

Animal Dreams (novel), HarperCollins (New York, NY), 1990.

Another America/Otra America (poetry), Seal Press (Seal Beach, CA), 1992, 2nd expanded edition, 1998.

Pigs in Heaven (novel) HarperCollins (New York, NY), 1993.

High Tide in Tucson: Essays from Now or Never, HarperCollins (New York, NY), 1995.

The Poisonwood Bible: A Novel, HarperFlamingo (New York, NY), 1998.

(Author of foreword) Joseph Barbato and Lisa Weinerman Horak, editors, *Off the Beaten Path: Stories Place,* Nature Conservancy (Arlington, VA), 1998.

Prodigal Summer, HarperCollins (New York, NY), 2000.

(Editor, with Katrina Kenison, and author of introduction) *The Best American Short Stories, 2001,* Houghton Mifflin (Boston, MA), 2001.

Small Wonder (essays), illustrated by Paul Mirocha, HarperCollins (New York, NY), 2002.

Last Stand: America's Virgin Lands (nonfiction), photographs by Annie Griffiths Belt, National Geographic Society (Washington, DC), 2002.

(Author of foreword) Norman Wirzhar, editor, *The Essential Agrarian Reader,* University Press of Kentucky (Lexington, KY), 2003.

Contributor to anthologies, including *New Stories from the South: The Year's Best, 1988,* edited by S. Ravenel, Algonquin Books (Chapel Hill, NC), 1988; *New Writ-*

ers of the Purple Sage: An Anthology of Recent Western Writing, edited by Russell Martin, Penguin (New York, NY), 1992; The Single Mother's Companion: Essays and Stories by Women, edited by Marsha R. Leslie, Seal Press (Seattle, WA), 1994; Mid-life Confidential: The Rock Bottom Remainders, edited by Dave Marsh, Viking (New York, NY), 1994; Journeys, edited by PEN-Faulkner Foundation, Quill & Bush (Rockville, MD), 1994; Heart of the Land: Essays on Last Great Places, edited by Joseph Barbato, Pantheon (New York, NY), 1994; I've Always Meant to Tell You: Letters to Our Mothers, edited by Constance Warlow, Pocket Books (New York, NY), 1997; and Intimate Nature: The Bond between Women and Animals, edited by Linda Hogan, D. Metzger, and B. Peterson, Ballantine (New York, NY), 1998. Contributor of fiction, nonfiction, and poetry to numerous periodicals, including Calyx, Cosmopolitan, Heresies, Mademoiselle, McCall's, New Mexico Humanities Review, Redbook, Sojourner, Tucson Weekly, Virginia Quarterly Review, Progressive, and Smithsonian. Reviewer for New York Times Book Review and Los Angeles Times Book Review.

ADAPTATIONS: Most of Kingsolver's novels have been adapted as audiobooks.

SIDELIGHTS: Best-selling author Barbara Kingsolver infuses her writings with a strong sense of family, relationships, and community. Kingsolver draws her characters from middle America—the shop owners, the unemployed, the displaced, the homeless, the mothers and children struggling to survive—and depicts how, by banding together, these seemingly forgotten people can thrive. As a firm believer in human dignity and worth, Kingsolver fills her works with themes of inspiration, love, strength, and endurance. Many critics have applauded her tenderness toward her characters and praise her insight into human nature, political repression, and ecological imperatives. In New York Times, Janet Maslin cited Kingsolver for her "sweet, ennobling enthusiasm for every natural phenomenon" as well as for an "overarching wisdom and passion."

Kingsolver's first novel, The Bean Trees, was published to an enthusiastic critical reception in 1988. The novel focuses on the relationships among a group of women and is narrated by Taylor Greer, a young, strong-willed Kentucky woman who leaves her homeland in search of a better life. During her westward travel, Taylor unexpectedly becomes the caretaker of a withdrawn two-year-old Cherokee girl named Turtle. Eventually the two settle in Arizona, where they find "an odd but dedicated 'family' in Tucson," the author once explained.

Included in this clan are Lou Ann Ruiz, a dejected mother whose husband has just left her, and Mattie, a warmhearted widow who runs the Jesus Is Lord Used Tires company. According to the author, "a new comprehension of responsibility" motivates Taylor to help Mattie shelter refugees from politically turbulent Central America.

Critics responded enthusiastically to The Bean Trees, noting the novel's sensitivity, humor, and lyricism. The Bean Trees "is as richly connected as a fine poem, but reads like realism," commented Jack Butler in New York Times Book Review. "From the very first page, Kingsolver's characters tug at the heart and soul," Karen FitzGerald noted in Ms. that "It is the growing strength of their relationships . . . that gives the novel its energy and appeal." And Margaret Randall in Women's Review of Books called The Bean Trees "a story propelled by a marvelous ear, a fast-moving humor and the powerful undercurrent of human struggle."

Favorable critical reviews also attended Kingsolver's next work, Homeland and Other Stories. Comprised of twelve short stories, Homeland relates stirring tales of individuals—mainly women—who struggle to find homes for themselves. Reviewers especially praised the title story, which reveals an aged Indian woman's disillusionment when she sees that her beloved Cherokee homeland has been transformed into a tourist trap. Another tale, "Islands on the Moon," shows how a mother and daughter—both single and pregnant—reconcile after years of estrangement. Among the distinctive characters that fill the remaining stories in the collection are a reformed thief striving for an honest living, a resilient union activist, a middle-class wife engaging in a secret affair, and a poor girl who befriends an outcast. Critics applauded Kingsolver's poetic language, her realistic portrayals of human nature, and her genuinely engaging tales. "Of the twelve stories in this first collection," remarked Russell Banks in New York Times Book Review, "all are interesting and most are extraordinarily fine." Chicago Tribune reviewer Bill Mahin called Kingsolver "an extraordinary storyteller."

While completing Homeland and Other Stories Kingsolver also completed Holding the Line: Women in the Great Arizona Mine Strike of 1983, a nonfiction book tracing the role of women during the Phelps Dodge Copper Company labor conflict. A year later, she returned to fiction with Animal Dreams, a novel that follows the growth of Codi Noline, an insecure woman who returns to her agricultural hometown of Grace, Arizona, after a fourteen-year absence. Characters' personal conflicts coupled with political struggles form the core of the novel. Codi finds her native community less than ideal: she faces grief, bigotry, disease, and environmental pollution and, through letters from her activist sister, learns of the political brutalities of Central America. Critics called the novel compassionate, humorous, and inspiring and praised Kingsolver's ability to mix commentary on political, social, racial, and personal turmoil. "*Animal Dreams* belongs to a new fiction of relationship, aesthetically rich and of great political and spiritual significance and power," wrote Ursula K. Le Guin in *Washington Post Book World*. "This is a sweet book, full of bitter pain; a beautiful weaving of the light and the dark." *Animal Dreams* is "a complex, passionate, bravely challenging book," maintained Melissa Pritchard in Chicago's *Tribune Books*, the critic going on to call Kingsolver "a writer of rare ambition and unequivocal talent."

In 1993 Kingsolver published *Pigs in Heaven*, a sequel to *The Bean Trees* that takes place three years after Taylor illegally adopts Turtle. In a strange turn of events, Turtle sees a man fall into the spillway of the Hoover Dam during a family vacation. Because of Turtle's insistence, Taylor sees to it that the man is rescued. The two become local heroes and are invited to appear on *Oprah Winfrey Show*. This newfound fame turns out to have unexpected consequences, however, as Cherokee lawyer Annawake Fourkiller sees the show and decides to investigate Taylor's adoption of Turtle. Threatened with losing her daughter, Taylor flees Arizona, beginning a difficult journey of economic struggle and emotional turbulence. Eventually, Taylor's mother Alice joins the pair in their flight, bringing her own wry perspective on life and undergoing her own personal journey.

Travis Silcox, writing in *Belles Lettres*, noted that, "despite its action, the novel suffers from a midpoint flatness." However, he praised Kingsolver's talent for characterization, adding that her "supporting characters enrich the story." Reviewer Wendy Smith likewise commended the novel, concluding in *Washington Post Book World* that "like all of Kingsolver's fiction, *Pigs in Heaven* fulfills the longings of the head and the heart with an inimitable blend of challenging ideas, vibrant characters and prose that sings. . . . It seems there's nothing she can't do." Karen Karbo averred in *New York Times Book Review* that Kingsolver's grip on the material she is writing is both skillful and satisfying: "As the novel progresses, she somehow manages to maintain her political views without sacrificing the complexity of her characters' predicaments." Karbo concluded that Kingsolver is "possessed of an extrava-

gantly gifted narrative voice, she blends a fierce and abiding moral vision with benevolent, concise humor. Her medicine is meant for the head, the heart and the soul—and it goes down dangerously, blissfully, easily."

While Kingsolver's early novels are typically intimate domestic dramas, 1998's *The Poisonwood Bible* is something quite different: a penetrating exploration of one American family's troubled sojourn in Africa. The novel's sweeping scope and its portrayal of African politics during the cold war marked a thematic departure for the author. It also proved to be a bestseller. In the wake of Kingsolver's success with *The Poisonwood Bible, Nation* contributor John Leonard heralded the writer as "at last our very own [Doris] Lessing and our very own [Nadine] Gordimer, and she is, as one of her characters said of another in an earlier novel, 'beautiful beyond the speed of light.'"

With *The Poisonwood Bible*, Kingsolver established a prominent place in American letters. The epic tale introduces the Price family—father Nathan, an evangelical missionary, his wife Orleanna, and their four daughters. The story begins as the family arrives in the Congo—now Zaire—as missionaries, and events are related from the point of view of Orleanna and the four young girls. Quickly it becomes apparent that Nathan Price is a violent fanatic whose mispronunciation of the local language only serves to alienate the African villagers. The Price women struggle against starvation, sickness, and predatory ants while Nathan sinks further and further into zealous madness. His bumbling serves to indict American behavior in Africa in a microcosm, but Kingsolver also explores the violent American intervention in Congolese affairs during the Eisenhower era and the role that intervention played in destabilizing an emerging nation. According to Verlyn Klinkenborg in *New York Times Book Review, The Poisonwood Bible* is "a story about the loss of one faith and the discovery of another. . . . Ultimately a novel of character, a narrative shaped by keen-eyed women contemplating themselves and one another and a village whose familiarity it takes a tragedy to discover."

Kingsolver animates *The Poisonwood Bible* with recollections of time she herself spent in the Belgian Congo, several years later than the 1963 setting of her novel. To quote Michiko Kakutani in *New York Times,* the "powerful . . . book is actually an old-fashioned nineteenth-century novel, a Hawthornian tale of sin and redemption and the 'dark necessity' of history." Kakutani added that the tale grapples with "social injustice, with the intersection of public events with private concerns and the competing claims of community and individual will." In *Nation,* Leonard likewise called *The Poisonwood Bible* "a magnificent fiction and a ferocious bill of indictment. . . . As in the keyed chords of a Baroque sonata, movements of the personal, the political, the historical and even the biological contrast and correspond. As in a Bach cantata, the choral stanza, the recitatives and the da capo arias harmonize. And a magical-realist forest sings itself to live forever."

Though the majority of reviewers applauded Kingsolver for her work in *The Poisonwood Bible,* there were a few dissenters. *Christianity Today* correspondent Tim Stafford maintained that Kingsolver "offers a cartoonish story of idiot missionaries and shady CIA operatives destroying the delicate fabric of the Congo, like bulldozers scraping their way through the forest jungle." Critics who were not won over by the novel were rare, however. More reflective of the majority view, a *Publishers Weekly* critic described the book as "a compelling family saga, a sobering picture of the horrors of fanatic fundamentalism and an insightful view of an exploited country." In *Booklist,* Donna Seaman commended *The Poisonwood Bible* as an "extraordinarily dramatic and forthright novel. . . a measureless saga of hubris and deliverance." A *Time* reviewer felt that the author's female characters "carry a story that moves through its first half like a river in flood." And in *Progressive,* Ruth Conniff praised Kingsolver for "writing a moving book that makes [political] ideas both personal and timely. Kingsolver is a terrific fiction writer."

Prodigal Summer is similar to Kingsolver's earlier novels in its sense of place and its more intimate scope. Three story lines gradually converge as residents of southern Appalachia respond in various ways to the wealth of nature surrounding them. According to Jennifer Schuessler in *New York Times Book Review,* readers of *Animal Dreams* and *The Bean Trees* "will find themselves back on familiar, well-cleared ground of plucky heroines, liberal politics and vivid descriptions of the natural world."

The three segments of *Prodigal Summer* introduce Deanna Wolfe, a wildlife biologist who seeks to protect a clan of coyotes from a poacher who eventually becomes her lover. Another segment is devoted to the predicament of Lusa Maluf Landowski Widener, a Palestinian-Jewish hybrid housewife who must stake a claim to her piece of Appalachia after her husband dies. The final segment introduces a pair of feuding neighbors, traditional farmer Garnett Walker and his organic opponent Nannie Rawley, whose search for common

ground ends in unstated affection for one another. Gradually the three separate plots weave together toward an ending that affirms the power of nature. Maslin, in her *New York Times* review of *Prodigal Summer,* deemed the work "an improbably appealing book with the feeling of a nice stay inside a terrarium." A *Publishers Weekly* reviewer also felt that readers would respond "to the sympathy with which [Kingsolver] reflects the difficult lives of people struggling on the hard edge of poverty." Michael Tyrell, writing in *Us,* suggested that, despite some passages that read like "overzealous lectures on ecology," *Prodigal Summer* excels in its "spirited, captivating heroine."

Kingsolver's 1992 book *Another America/Otra America* proved to be somewhat of a departure. Composed of original poetry, it also includes Spanish translations of her poems within the same volume. Reviewer Lorraine Elena Roses, commenting in *Women's Review of Books* on the presence of the translations, stated that "it's clear from the outset that Kingsolver feels a deep connection to the Spanish-speaking lands that begin before the Rio Grande and stretch all the way to the windswept limits of Tierra del Fuego." Kingsolver's poems explore her feelings about Latino human rights activists, Latin American victimization, and North American prejudices. *School Library Journal* contributor Deanna Kuhn called the book a "powerful collection." While praising Kingsolver's technical skill, Roses questioned whether "lyrical poetry [can] bear the weight of politics," but concluded that Kingsolver's poems "will appeal primarily to those who seek to commemorate and mark political occasions."

In *High Tide in Tucson,* published in 1995, Kingsolver offers opinions on a myriad of topics, from motherhood to the effect of the Gulf War. A *Kirkus Reviews* critic, while finding fault with the author's "hit-or-miss musings" and "smarmy self-reflections," commended Kingsolver's facility with nature writing. A second essay collection, *Small Wonder,* collects twenty-three essays on a variety of topics. While many essays were published previously, the book includes three written in collaboration with Kingsolver's husband, Steven Hopp. Subject matter ranges from the Columbine High School, Colorado, shootings to television, the homeless, and the difficulties of writing about sex. Judith Bromberg pointed out in *National Catholic Reporter* that *Small Wonder* came about after Kingsolver was asked to respond to the September 11, 2001 terrorist attack on the United States. She wrote five responsive essays in one month, all of which are included in this collection. Bromberg noted that, whether written before or after September 11, the essays "reflect [the event's] enormous reality and either draw meaning from it or attempt to lend some clarity to it." Piers Moore Ede commented in *Earth Island Journal* that Kingsolver's essays serve as "compelling, provocative . . . meditations" on how the event changed the world, and commended the author for having the courage to suggest that the attacks were perhaps a political protest against the "American Way."

Kingsolver has described herself as "a writer of the working class" who views her art as a daily job. "My idea of a pre-writing ritual is getting the kids on the bus and sitting down," she said in a *Book Page* online interview. Elsewhere in the same interview she outlined her goals as an author. "I'm extremely interested in cultural difference, in social and political history, and the sparks that fly when people with different ways of looking at the world come together and need to reconcile or move through or celebrate those differences," she said. "All that precisely describes everything I've ever written."

As an extension of her belief in literary fiction as a force for social change, Kingsolver has established and funded the Bellwether Prize. Awarded biennially, the prize consists of a $25,000 cash payment and guaranteed publication for a novel manuscript by an author who has not previously been widely published. The goal of the Bellwether Prize is to promote writing, reading, and publication of literary fiction that addresses issues of social justice and the impact of culture and politics on human relationships.

BIOGRAPHICAL AND CRITICAL SOURCES:

BOOKS

Contemporary Literary Criticism, Volume 55, Thomson Gale (Detroit, MI), 1989.

PERIODICALS

African Business, March, 1999, Christy Nevin, review of *The Poisonwood Bible,* p. 56.
Belles Lettres, fall, 1993, Travis Silcox, review of *Pigs in Heaven,* pp. 4, 42.
Bloomsbury Review, November-December, 1990.
Booklist, February 15, 1992, p. 1083; August, 1998, Donna Seaman, review of *The Poisonwood Bible,* p. 1922.

Chicago Tribune, May 18, 1988; June 23, 1989; July 11, 1993, p. 3.
Christianity Today, January 11, 1999, Tim Stafford, review of *The Poisonwood Bible,* p. 88.
Cosmopolitan, March, 1988.
Courier Journal (Louisville, KY), April 24, 1988.
Earth Island Journal, winter, 2002, Piers Moore Ede, review of *Small Wonder,* p. 45.
English Journal, January, 1994.
Entertainment Weekly, November 5, 1999, Rebecca Ascher-Walsh, "Kingsolver for a Day," p. 75.
Kirkus Reviews, August 1, 1995, p. 1080.
Los Angeles Times, April 3, 1988; April 24, 1988.
Los Angeles Times Book Review, July 16, 1989, September 9, 1990; July 4, 1993, pp. 2, 8.
Ms., April, 1988, Karen Fitzgerald, review of *The Bean Trees.*
Nation, January 11, 1999, John Leonard, review of *The Poisonwood Bible,* p. 28.
National Catholic Reporter, March 19, 1999, Judith Bromberg, review of *The Poisonwood Bible,* p. 13; Judith Bromberg, review of *Small Wonders,* p. 30.
New Republic, March 22, 1999, Lee Siegel, "Sweet and Low: The Poisonwood Bible," p. 30.
New Statesman, December 10, 1993.
Newsweek, July 12, 1993.
New Yorker, April 4, 1988.
New York Times, October 16, 1998, Michiko Kakutani, "No Ice Cream Cones in a Heart of Darkness;" November 2, 2000, Janet Maslin, "Three Story Lines United by the Fecundity of Nature."
New York Times Book Review, April 10, 1988, p. 15; June 5, 1988; June 11, 1989; January 7, 1990; September 2, 1990; June 27, 1993, p. 59; October 15, 1995, p. 21; October 18, 1998, Verlyn Klinkenborg, "Going Native;" November 5, 2000, Jennifer Schuessler, "Men, Women and Coyotes."
Progressive, February, 1996, p. 33; December, 1998, Ruth Conniff, review of *The Poisonwood Bible,* p. 39.
Publishers Weekly, August 31, 1990, p. 46; January 27, 1992, p. 93; August 7, 1995, p. 449; August 10, 1998, review of *The Poisonwood Bible,* p. 366; October 2, 2000, review of *Prodigal Summer,* p. 57.
San Francisco Chronicle, March 6, 1988.
School Library Journal, August, 1992, p. 192; November, 1993; February, 1996, p. 134.
Time, September 24, 1990; November 9, 1998, review of *The Poisonwood Bible,* p. 113.
Tribune Books (Chicago, IL), August 26, 1990, Melissa Pritchard, review of *Animal Dreams.*
Us, October 30, 2000, Michael Tyrell, review of *Prodigal Summer,* p. 49.
USA Today, October 11, 1990.

Utne Reader, July-August, 1993.

Washington Post Book World, September 2, 1990; June 13, 1995, p. 3; October 8, 1995, p. 13.

Women's Review of Books, May, 1988, Margaret Randall, review of *The Bean Trees;* July, 1992, Lorraine Elena Roses, review of *Another America/Otra America,* p. 42.

ONLINE

Barbara Kingsolver Home Page, http://www.kingsolver.com/ (April 12, 2004).

Book Page, http://www.bookpage.com/ (April 12, 2004), Ellen Kanner, "Barbara Kingsolver Turns to Her Past to Understand the Present" (interview).

KYLit Web site, http://www.english.eku.edu/services/kylit/ (December 5, 1994), George Brosi, "Barbara Kingsolver."

NewsHour Online, http://www.pbs.org/newshour/ (November 24, 1995), David Gergen, interview with Kingsolver.

Salon.com, http://www.salon.com/ (December 16, 1995), "Lit Chat with Barbara Kingsolver."

*   *   *

KINGSTON, Maxine Hong 1940-
(Maxine Ting Ting Hong Kingston)

PERSONAL: Born October 27, 1940, in Stockton, CA; daughter of Tom (a scholar, manager of a gambling house, and laundry worker) and Ying Lan (a practitioner of medicine and midwifery, field hand, and laundry worker; maiden name, Chew) Hong; married Earll Kingston (an actor), November 23, 1962; children: Joseph Lawrence Chung Mei. *Education:* University of California, Berkeley, A.B., 1962, teaching certificate, 1965.

ADDRESSES: Office—University of California, Department of English, 322 Wheeler Hall, Berkeley, CA 94720. *Agent*—c/o Author Mail, Alfred A. Knopf, Inc., 1745 Broadway, New York, NY 10019.

CAREER: Writer. Sunset High School, Hayward, CA, teacher of English and mathematics, 1965-67; Kahuku High School, Kahuku, HI, teacher of English, 1967; Kahaluu Drop-in School, Kahaluu, HI, teacher, 1968; Honolulu Business College, Honolulu, HI, teacher of English as a second language, 1969; Kailua High School, Kailua, HI, teacher of language arts, 1969;

Mid-Pacific Institute, Honolulu, HI, teacher of language arts, 1970-77; University of Hawaii, Honolulu, visiting associate professor of English, beginning 1977; Eastern Michigan University, Ypsilanti, Thelma McCandless Professor, 1986; University of California, Berkeley, Chancellor's Distinguished Professor, 1990—.

AWARDS, HONORS: General nonfiction award, National Book Critics Circle, 1976, for *The Woman Warrior: Memoirs of a Girlhood among Ghosts; Mademoiselle* magazine award, 1977; Anisfield-Wolf Race Relations Award, 1978; *The Woman Warrior* was named one of the top ten nonfiction works of the decade by *Time* magazine, 1979; National Education Association writing fellow, 1980; named Living Treasure of Hawaii, 1980; *China Men* was named to the American Library Association Notable Books list, 1980; National Endowment for the Arts Writers Award, 1980 and 1982; American Book Award for general nonfiction, 1981, for *China Men;* Stockton (CA) Arts Commission Award, 1981; Guggenheim fellow, 1981; Hawaii Award for Literature, 1982; Hawaii Writers Award, 1983; PEN West Award in fiction for *Tripmaster Monkey: His Fake Book,* 1989; California Governor's Art Award, 1989; Major Book Collection Award, Brandeis University National Women's Committee, 1990; American Academy and Institute of Arts and Letters, 1990; inducted into the American Academy of Arts and Sciences, 1992; National Humanities Medal, 1997. Honorary degrees from Eastern Michigan University, 1988, Colby College, 1990, Brandeis University, 1991, University of Massachusetts, 1991, and Starr King School for the Ministry, 1992.

WRITINGS:

The Woman Warrior: Memoirs of a Girlhood among Ghosts (also see below), Knopf (New York, NY), 1976.

China Men (also see below), Knopf (New York, NY), 1980.

Hawai'i One Summer (essays), Meadow Press (San Francisco, CA), 1987.

Through the Black Curtain (contains excerpts from *The Woman Warrior, China Men,* and *Tripmaster Monkey*), Friends of the Bancroft Library, University of California (Berkeley, CA), 1987.

Tripmaster Monkey: His Fake Book (novel; also see below), Knopf (New York, NY), 1988.

Conversations with Maxine Hong Kingston, edited by Paul Skenazy and Tera Martin, University Press of Mississippi (Jackson, MS), 1998.

(Editor, with Jack Hicks, James D. Houston, and Al Young) *The Literature of California, Volume 1: Native American Beginnings to 1945,* University of California Press (Berkeley, CA), 2000.

To Be the Poet (lectures and poems), Harvard University Press (Cambridge, MA), 2002.

The Fifth Book of Peace (novel), Knopf (New York, NY), 2003.

Contributor to books, including *Your Reading,* edited by Jerry Walker, National Council of Teachers of English, 1975. Contributor of stories and articles to periodicals, including *New York Times Magazine, Ms., New Yorker, New West, New Dawn, American Heritage,* and *Washington Post. The Woman Warrior* and *Tripmaster Monkey* have been published in Chinese.

ADAPTATIONS: The Woman Warrior was adapted into a play by Sharon Ott and produced at the Berkeley Repertory Theatre, 1994.

SIDELIGHTS: Maxine Hong Kingston "blends myth, legend, history, and autobiography into a genre of her own invention," wrote Susan Currier in *Dictionary of Literary Biography Yearbook: 1980.* Kingston's books *The Woman Warrior: Memoirs of a Girlhood among Ghosts* and *China Men* are classified as nonfiction, but, according to Anne Tyler in *New Republic,* "in a deeper sense, they are fiction at its best—novels, fairytales, epic poems." Both books are based on the history and myth imparted to Kingston by members of her family and other Chinese-American "story-talkers" who lived in her childhood community in Stockton, California. "The result," noted *Contemporary Novelists* contributor Sanford Pinsker, "is a species of magical realism, one that continually hovers between fact and the imagination, between what was and what might have been."

Pinsker added that "the confusion of actuality and invention may be worth quarreling about, but what matters finally are the stories themselves—and they are quite good. Indeed, one would be hard-pressed to think of books that detail the joys and pains of growing up within a strictly defined ethnic community that could match Kingston's sentence for sentence, paragraph for paragraph, page for page. She is, quite simply, a marvelous writer." *The Woman Warrior* and *China Men,* he said, "remind us that what James Joyce, an Irishman on the other side of the world, set out to accomplish when his protagonist set off to forge on the smithy of his soul 'the uncreated conscience of my race' can also happen when a young Chinese-American writer sets out to discover who she is amid the rich tapestry of memory and the imagination."

Currier described *The Woman Warrior* as "a personal work, an effort to reconcile American and Chinese female identities." Primarily a memoir of Kingston's childhood, *The Woman Warrior* also concerns itself with the lives of other women in her family, as embellished or imagined by the author. According to *Washington Post* critic Henry Allen, "in a wild mix of myth, memory, history and a lucidity which verges on the eerie," Kingston describes "their experiences as women, as Chinese coming to America and as Americans." "Its companion volume, *China Men . . .* attempts a broader synthesis," said Currier, "dealing with male Chinese 'sojourners' in North America and Hawaii, but it is inextricably tied to the autobiographical interests of *The Woman Warrior.*" Kingston's mother dominates *The Woman Warrior* while her father is the focus of *China Men.* "In both books," Currier commented, "additional characters flesh out the social, political, and cultural history Kingston introduces." *China Men* also includes the fictionalized histories of several members of Kingston's family and the community in which she grew up.

Harper's critic Frances Taliaferro remarked that the books' "titles plainly speak their ostensible subjects, female and male; just as plainly the books must be read together. Though I have no inherited command of the terms yin and yang, it seems to me that like those opposing principles the two books form one whole, for the shaping imagination is indivisible." Kingston told *New York Times Book Review* critic Timothy Pfaff that she considers the two works "one big book. I was writing them more or less simultaneously. The final chapter in *China Men* began as a short story that I was working on before I even started *The Woman Warrior.*"

Many of the stories included in *The Woman Warrior* are reconstructed from those Kingston's mother related to her as "lessons 'to grow up on,'" wrote Currier. Kingston's mother, referred to as Brave Orchid in the book, married her father in China, before he immigrated to New York City. For fifteen years he worked in a laundry and sent part of the money he earned back to China, enabling Brave Orchid to study for certifications in medicine and midwifery, which eventually provided her with a good income and respect in what *Ms.* critic Sara Blackburn called "a starving society where girl children were a despised and useless commodity." She came to the United States when her husband sent for her, having to give up her medical practice to work for the benefit of her family as a laundress and field hand. Her first two children had died in China while she was alone, but within her first year in the United States, at the age of forty-five, she gave birth to Maxine in Stockton, where the family later settled.

Maxine was named after a lucky blonde American gamester in a gambling parlor her father managed. The first of her mother's six American-born children, she grew up surrounded not only by the ghosts of the ancestors and characters who peopled her mother's tales, but also by Americans who, as "foreigners," were considered "ghosts" by her mother. And, according to *New York Times Book Review* critic Jane Kramer, the young Maxine, "in a country full of ghosts, is already a half-ghost to her mother." Kingston's memoir, described by *Time* critic Paul Gray as "drenched in alienation," is also characterized by ambiguity, since, as he points out, it "haunts a region somewhere between autobiography and fiction." It is difficult to distinguish whether the narrator of the book's stories "is literally Maxine Hong Kingston," Gray commented. "Art has intervened here. The stories may or may not be transcripts of actual experience."

Kingston turns to the men of her family in *China Men,* a book that also "span[s] two continents and several generations," according to Currier. *New York Times* reviewer John Leonard commented that it is "framed, on the one hand, by a wedding and a funeral, and, on the other, by the birth of boys. . . . In between is sheer magic: poetry, parable, nightmare, the terror and exhilaration of physical labor, the songs of survival, the voices of the dead, the feel of wood and blood, the smell of flowers and wounds. History meets sensuality." In *China Men,* wrote Allen, Kingston "describes the men slaving for a dollar a week building sugar plantations; smuggling themselves into America in packing crates; building the railroads; adopting new names, such as Edison, Roosevelt and Worldster." Although women are not prominent as characters in *China Men,* Kingston told Pfaff, "There still are women who take the role of storyteller. The women are not centerstage, but without the female storyteller, I couldn't have gotten into some of the stories."

In order to "understand the men with whom she is connected," Kingston adopts many of the same techniques she used in *The Woman Warrior,* indicated *New York Times* critic Mary Gordon, "the blend of myth, legend and history, the fevered voice, relentless as a truth-seeking child's." She begins with the story of her father, who has trained as a scholar in China, and, according to Gray, "is subject to black moods and bitterness over his low estate" during much of Maxine's childhood. Perhaps in reflection of his heritage, "his angriest curses vilify women's bodies," wrote Gray. "The girl both understands and is bewildered." But, since her father was not a "story-talker" like Brave Orchid, and was silent about his past, Kingston must "piece together the few facts she has and invent the rest," Gordon wrote. *Newsweek* critic Jean Strouse commented that "in a dreamlike mix of memory and desire, she tries out versions of her father's life, weaving them through her narrative." Not only does the author recreate his life in China and provide five different versions of how he entered the United States; she also widely separates the story of "the father from China" from that of the man she knew and refers to as "the American father."

In Kingston's tale, "the father from China" found his skills in calligraphy and poetry useless in the United States. After immigrating, he became part-owner of a laundry in New York City, wrote Frederick Wakeman, Jr. in *New York Review of Books,* "along with three other China Men who spend their salaries on $200 suits, dime-a-dance girls, motorcycles, and flying lessons." Kingston follows this account of idyllic bachelor existence with an ancient Chinese ghost story about a beautiful spirit woman who, wrote Wakeman, "beguiles a handsome traveler until he loses nearly all memory of his family back home." Eventually, the man is "released from her spell" and returns to his wife. "In the same way," pointed out Wakeman, "the father from China turns away from the lure of his three high-living friends, and puts the temptations of bachelorhood behind him after his wife joins him in New York." But, according to Kingston, soon after Brave Orchid arrived in the United States and weaned her husband away from his companions—she cooked the men elaborate meals and insisted they keep the Chinese holidays—the partners cheated the father from China out of his share of the business. The couple then left for California where "the American father" had to struggle to support his family.

The book, commented Strouse, "is about a great deal more than sexual warfare, however. It tells of emigration, persecution, work, endurance, ritual, change, loss and the eternal invention of the new." In a later section of the book, Kingston presents the story of the father she knew in Stockton, and she ends *China Men* with characters of her own generation, relating the tale of a brother's tour of duty in Vietnam and his attempts to locate relatives in Hong Kong. Rounding out the book are the highly representative, embellished histories of earlier China Men who preceded her father to America. She tells of a great-grandfather who traveled to Hawaii to clear the land and work on a sugar plantation. The overseers forbade talking, she relates, and Gordon maintained that "nowhere is Mrs. Kingston's technique—the close focus, the fascination with the details of survival strategies, the repetitive fixated tone—more successful than in her description of the plantation workers' talking into the earth in defiance of the silence imposed upon them by white bosses. The men dig holes and shout their longings, their frustrations, down the hole to China, frightening their overseers, who leave them alone." "The poignancy of that moment is the fruit of stunning historical reconstruction coupled with the imagination of a novelist," Gray indicated.

Throughout the rest of the work, Kingston often blends history with pure fantasy. "What makes the book more than nonfiction," wrote Anne Tyler in *New Republic,* "are its subtle shifts between the concrete and the mythical." *Washington Post Book World* critic Edmund White commented that "by delving into her own girlhood memories, by listening to the tall tales her Chinese immigrant parents told her . . . by researching the past in books and by daydreaming her way into other lives, the author has stitched together a unique document so brightly colored that it seems to be embroidery sewn in brilliant silk threads, a picture of fabulous dragons sinuously coiling around real people, a mandarin square of triumph and privation, of memorable fact and still more vivid fancy." Kingston, he indicated, has "freely woven fairy tales into her recital of facts and rendered her account magical." As Tyler commented, "Edges blur; the dividing line passes unnoticed. We accept one fact and then the next, and then suddenly we find ourselves believing in the fantastic. Is it true that when one of the brothers was born, a white Christmas card flew into the room like a dove?"

In her imaginative fervor, Kingston often alters and even popularizes classical Chinese myths. Although, in general, Wakeman found *China Men* praiseworthy, he wrote that "as Kingston herself has admitted, many of the myths she describes are largely her own reconstructions. Often, they are only remotely connected with the original Chinese legends they invoke; and sometimes they are only spurious folklore, a kind of self-indulgent fantasy that blends extravagant personal imagery with appropriately *voelkisch* themes." He added that "precisely because the myths are usually so consciously contrived, her pieces of distant China lore often seem jejune and even inauthentic—especially to readers who know a little bit about the original high culture which Kingston claims as her birthright."

However, Kingston wrote that, as a sinologist, Wakeman "is a scholar on what he calls the 'high tradition,' and so he sees me as one who doesn't get it right, and who takes liberties with it. In actuality, I am writing in the peasant talk-story Cantonese tradition ('low,' if you will), which is the heritage of Chinese Americans. Chinese Americans have changed the stories, but Mr. Wakeman compares our new stories to the ancient, scholarly ones from the old country, and finds them somehow inauthentic." Furthermore, claimed Gordon, "the straight myth and the straight history are far less compelling than the mixture [Kingston] creates." As Kingston told Pfaff, "I have come to feel that the myths that have been handed down from the past are not something that we should be working toward, so I try to deal with them quickly—get them over with—and then return to a realistic kind of present. This time I'm leaving it to my readers to figure out how the myths and the modern stories connect. Like me, and I'm assuming like other people, the characters in the book have to figure out how what they've been told connects—or doesn't connect—with what they experience." "This sort of resurrection," concluded Wakeman, "is an important way for Kingston to establish a link between her present Americanness and the China of her ancestor's past. The myths—which by their very nature mediate the irreconcilable—initially make it possible for her to rediscover an otherwise lost China, and then summoning it, lay that spirit to rest."

Kingston's first outright novel, *Tripmaster Monkey: His Fake Book,* presents Chinese history and myth with a wild humor through the character of Wittman Ah Sing, a young Chinese-American in 1960s San Francisco whose philosophy of life calls for doing as one pleases whatever the consequences. His life is not without frustration, though, as white Americans fail to accept him fully—even though he is a fifth-generation American, "as American as Jack Kerouac or James Baldwin or Allen Ginsberg, as American as Walt Whitman, 'the poet that his father tried to name him after,'" noted LeAnne Schreiber in the *New York Times Book Review.* But he also is an incarnation of the mythical Monkey King. "Like Monkey, the trickster saint of Chinese legend who helped bring Buddha's teachings to China, Wittman will bring China to America," Schreiber explained, and he means to do so by staging a massive theatrical production. Herbert Gold, in his review for Chicago's *Tribune Books,* believed that the novel "blends the kind of magic realism familiar to readers of Latin American fiction with the hard-edged black humor of flower-epoch comic writers and performers—a little bit of Lenny Bruce and a whole lot of Gabriel Garcia Marquez. Kingston's energy, talent and unique perspective make an odd dish work, like some sort of hefty Chinese *nouvelle maxi-cuisine* stew." Schreiber noted that "Wittman is at times compelling, touching, wildly imaginative, and yet he made me long for another voice. . . . Except in occasional descriptive passages, I cannot hear the precise, sinewy, and, yes, let's admit it, beautiful voice of the author above the racket of her creation." Writing in the *New Republic,* Anne Tyler allowed that Wittman occasionally "wear[s] us out with his exuberance," but she noted that he and his story hold the reader's interest thanks to "the tiny, meticulously catalogued details that fill his quieter moments." She summed up *Tripmaster Monkey* as "a great, huge sprawling beast of a novel, over 400 pages densely packed with [Wittman's] rantings and ravings and pranks and high jinks. . . . That Wittman is Chinese gives his story depth and particularity. That he's American lends his narrative style a certain slangy insouciance. That he's Chinese-American, with the self-perceived outsider's edgy angle of vision, makes for a novel of satisfying complexity and bite and verve."

In *To Be the Poet,* which is based on Kingston's 2000 William E. Massey Lectures at Harvard University, the author presents a book about her decision and desire to become a poet or, at the very least, to lead the life of a poet. "Prose is tremendously hard work," Kingston told Lori Tsang in an interview for *Women's Review of Books.* "Just once in a while I want the happy life of a poet." In the book, Kingston recounts how she gathered advice from other poets and writers and goes on to talk about her past and how she is attempting to live like a poet. The book also includes some of Kingston's poetry. Noting that *To Be the Poet* reads "like short diaries," *Publishers Weekly* contributor Michael Scharf remarked that devotees will appreciate Kingston's versification of the story of the Woman Warrior Mu Lan "even as they await her return to other forms." Writing in *Library Journal,* Ron Ratliff commented, "What results is irreverent, serious, and playful but always instructive."

Despite her professed desire to focus more on poetry, Kingston had been working for more than a decade on a sequel to her novel *Tripmaster Monkey.* Calling the book *The Fourth Book of Peace,* Kingston drew her inspiration from a Chinese legend about Three Books of Peace. As the legend goes, the books discussed how humans could live in peace but were destroyed by fire. Ironically, Kingston had been working on the book for two years when a fire destroyed her home in 1991 and the only copy of the manuscript while Kingston was away attending her father's funeral. As a result, Kingston had to begin again, and she ended up producing a much different book than a traditional novel. "Kingston writes in a panoply of languages: American, Chinese, poetry, dreams, mythos, song, history, hallucination, meditation, tragedy—all are invoked in this complex stream-of-consciousness memoir," wrote a *Publishers Weekly* contributor of Kingston's reworked book, called *The Fifth Book of Peace.* Kingston divides the book into four sections. The opening section, "Fire," describes Kingston's experience of returning from her father's funeral only to find her manuscript destroyed. In "Paper," Kingston recounts the Chinese legend about the Three Books of Peace as her inspiration to write the book that was lost. In the third section, "Water," the author reconstructs her lost novel as she tells the story of *Tripmaster Monkey* character Wittman Ah Sing and his wife, Tana, as they flee to Hawaii as part of Sing's plan to evade the draft during the Vietnam War. The final section, "Earth," recounts Kingston's real-life efforts at conducting writing workshops for Vietnam and other war veterans.

Writing in *Entertainment Weekly,* reviewer Rebecca Ascher-Walsh remarked that the book "is thoughtful and passionate, but ultimately the gamble of mixed modes of storytelling doesn't pay off." *New York Times Book Review* contributor Polly Shulman commented that Kingston does not repeat her past success in combining fiction with memory, as she fails "to integrate the sections of the new book." On the other hand, a *Publishers Weekly* contributor praised the book and the book's thematic focus on why people can't live in peace instead of war. Referring to a passage in the book in which Kingston's mother visits her in a dream and asks what she has been doing to educate America, the reviewer remarked, "This is vintage Kingston: agent provocateur, she once again follows her mother's dictate 'to educate the world.'"

BIOGRAPHICAL AND CRITICAL SOURCES:

BOOKS

Contemporary Literary Criticism, Thomson Gale (Detroit, MI), Volume 12, 1980, Volume 19, 1981, Volume 58, 1990.

Contemporary Novelists, St. James Press (Detroit, MI), 1996.

Dictionary of Literary Biography, Volume 173: *American Novelists since World War II, Fifth Series,* Thomson Gale (Detroit, MI), 1996.

Dictionary of Literary Biography Yearbook: 1980, Thomson Gale (Detroit, MI), 1981.

Feng, Pin-chia, *The Female Bildungsroman by Toni Morrison and Maxine Hong Kingston: A Postmodern Reading,* Peter Lang (New York, NY), 1998.

Gao, Yan, *A Metaphorical Strategy: A Study of Maxine Hong Kingston's Creative Use of Chinese Sources,* Peter Lang (New York, NY), 1996.

Ho, Wendy, *In Her Mother's House: The Politics of Asian-American Mother-Daughter Writing*, Alta-Mira Press (Walnut Creek, CA), 1999.

Ludwig, Sami, *Concrete Language: Intercultural Communication in Maxine Hong Kingston's "The Woman Warrior" and Ishmael Reed's "Mumbo Jumbo,"* Peter Lang (New York, NY), 1996.

Rainwater, Catherine, and William J. Scheick, *Contemporary American Women Writers: Narrative Strategies,* University Press of Kentucky (Lexington, KY), 1985.

Simmons, Diane, *Maxine Hong Kingston,* Twayne (New York, NY), 1999.

Skandera-Tromblay, Laura, editor, *Critical Essays on Maxine Hong Kingston,* G.K. Hall (New York, NY), 1998.

Skenazy, Paul, and Tera Martin, editors, *Conversations with Maxine Hong Kingston,* University Press of Mississippi (Jackson, MS), 1998.

Smith, Jeanne Rosier, *Writing Tricksters,* University of California Press (Berkeley, CA), 1997.

Smith, Sidonie, *A Poetics of Women's Autobiography: Marginality and the Fictions of Self-Representation,* Indiana University Press (Bloomington, IN), 1987.

Wong, Sau-ling Cynthia, *Maxine Hong Kingston's "The Woman Warrior": A Casebook,* Oxford University Press (New York, NY), 1999.

PERIODICALS

Chicago Sun-Times, September 28, 2003, Stephen J. Lyons, review of *The Fifth Book of Peace,* p. 15.

Entertainment Weekly, September 12, 2003, Rebecca Ascher-Walsh, review of *The Fifth Book of Peace,* p. 159.

Harper's, August, 1980, Frances Taliaferro, review of *China Men,* p. 76

Library Journal, September 1, 1998, Kitty Chen Dean, review of *Conversations with Maxine Hong Kingston,* pp. 180-181; October 1, 2002, Ron Ratliff, review of *The Fifth Book of Peace,* p. 94.

Los Angeles Times, January 7, 2001, Thomas Sanchez, review of *The Literature of California, Volume 1: Native American Beginnings to 1945,* p. BR1; October 19, 2003, Michael Frank, review of *The Fifth Book of Peace,* p. R10.

Ms., January, 1977, Sara Blackburn, review of *The Woman Warrior: Memoirs of a Girlhood among Ghosts.*

New Republic, April 17, 1989, Anne Tyler, "Manic Monologue," pp. 44-46.

Newsweek, June 16, 1980, Jean Strouse, review of *China Men,* p. 88.

New York Review of Books, August 14, 1980, Frederick Wakeman, Jr., review of *China Men,* p. 42.

New York Times, June 3, 1980, John Leonard, review of *China Men,* p. C9; June 15, 1980, Mary Gordon, review of *China Men,* p. 1.

New York Times Book Review, November 7, 1976, Jane Kramer, review of *The Woman Warrior: Memoirs of a Girlhood among Ghosts*; June 15, 1980, Timothy Pfaff, "Talk with Mrs. Kingston," p. 1; April 23, 1989, LeAnne Schreiber, review of *Tripmaster Monkey: His Fake Book,* p. 9; February 14, 1999, Sandra L. Mardenfeld, review of *Hawai'i One Summer,* p. 21; September 28, 2003, Polly Shulman, review of *The Fifth Book of Peace,* p. 8.

People, October 6, 2003, V.R. Peterson, review of *The Fifth Book of Peace,* p. 58.

Publishers Weekly, August 19, 2002, Michael Scharf, review of *To Be the Poet,* p. 82; June 23, 2003, review of *The Fifth Book of Peace,* p. 53.

Time, December 6, 1976, Paul Gray, review of *The Woman Warrior;* June 30, 1980, Paul Gray, review of *China Men,* p. 76; May 1, 1989, p. 70.

Tribune Books (Chicago, IL), April 16, 1989, Herbert Gold, review of *Tripmaster Monkey,* pp. 1, 10.

Virginia Quarterly Review, summer, 2001, David Wyatt, review of *The Literature of California, Volume 1,* pp. 537-541.

Washington Post, June 26, 1980, Henry Allen, review of *China Men.*

Washington Post Book World, June 22, 1980, Edmund White, review of *China Men.*

Women's Review of Books, July, 2002, Lori Tsang, "From Warrior to Poet: Maxine Hong Kingston Talks to Lori Tsang," p. 6.

ONLINE

University of North Carolina Penbroke, http://www.uncp.edu/ (November 26, 2003), "Maxine Hong Kingston."

Women in Modern Literature, http://www.llcc.cc.il.us/womencen/womenslit/Kingston.htm/ (November 26, 2003), biography of Maxine Hong Kingston.

OTHER

Interview: Maxine Hong Kingston Discusses Her Latest Work, "The Fifth Book of Peace" (transcript of National Public Radio *All Things Considered* interview), September 24, 2003.

Interview: Maxine Hong Kingston Discusses Her New Book, "To Be the Poet" (transcript of National Public Radio *Weekend Edition* interview), September 22, 2002.

Maxine Hong Kingston Interview with Kay Bonetti, sound recording, American Audio Prose Library (Columbia, MO).

*   *   *

KINGSTON, Maxine Ting Ting Hong
    See KINGSTON, Maxine Hong

*   *   *

KINNELL, Galway 1927-

PERSONAL: Born February 1, 1927, in Providence RI; son of James Scott and Elizabeth (Mills) Kinnell; married Ines Delgado de Torres; children: Maud, Fergus, Natasha. *Education:* Princeton University, A.B. (summa cum laude), 1948; University of Rochester, M.A., 1949.

ADDRESSES: Home—Sheffield, VT 05866; 432 Hudson St., New York, NY 10014. *Office*—New York University, Department of English, New York, NY 10003.

CAREER: Poet and translator, 1949—. Alfred University, Alfred, NY, instructor in English, 1949-51; University of Chicago, Chicago, IL, supervisor of liberal arts program at downtown campus, 1951-55; University of Grenoble, Grenoble, France, American lecturer, 1956-57; University of Nice, Nice, France, lecturer in summer session, 1957; University of Iran, Teheran, Iran, Fulbright lecturer, 1959-60; Columbia University, New York, NY, adjunct associate professor, 1972, adjunct professor, 1974, 1976; University of Hawaii at Manoa, Honolulu, Citizens' Professor, 1979-81; New York University, New York, NY, director of writing program, 1981-84, Samuel F.B. Morse Professor of Arts and Sciences, Erich Maria Remarque Professor of Creative Writing. Poet-in-residence, Juniata College, 1964; Reed College, 1966-67; Colorado State University, 1968; University of Washington, 1968; University of California—Irvine, 1968-69; University of Iowa, 1970; and Holy Cross College, 1977. Resident writer, Deya Institute (Mallorca, Spain), 1969-70. Visiting professor, Queens College of the City University of New York, 1971; Pittsburgh Poetry Forum, 1971; Brandeis University, 1974; Skidmore College, 1975; and University of Delaware, 1978. Visiting poet, Sarah Lawrence College,

1972-78; Princeton University, 1976; and University of Hawaii. Visiting writer, Macquarie University (Sydney, Australia), 1979. Director, Squaw Valley Community of Writers, 1979—. Field worker for Congress of Racial Equality (CORE), 1963. Recorded poetry to sound and video cassette, including *Galway Kinnell Reading His Poems with Comment in New York City* (audio cassette), 1959; *Poetry Breaks I, Galway Kinnell,* (video cassette), 1988; and *Galway Kinnell and Sharon Olds Reading Their Poems in the Montpelier Room* (audio cassette), 1996. Chancellor, Academy of American Poets, 2001—. Advisory Board Member, Red Hen Press (Granada Hills, CA). *Military service:* U.S. Navy, 1944-46.

MEMBER: PEN, National Academy and Institute of Arts and Letters, Corporation of Yaddo.

AWARDS, HONORS: Ford grant, 1955; Fulbright scholarship, 1955-56; Guggenheim fellowships, 1961-62, 1974-75; National Institute of Arts and Letters grant, 1962; Longview Foundation award, 1962; Rockefeller Foundation grants, 1962-63, 1968; Bess Hokin Prize, 1965, and Eunice Tietjens Prize, 1966, both from *Poetry* magazine; Cecil Hemley Poetry Prize from Ohio University Press, 1968, for translation of Yves Bonnefoy's work; special mention by judges of National Book Awards for poetry, 1969, for *Body Rags;* Ingram Merrill Foundation award, 1969; Amy Lowell traveling fellowship, 1969-70; National Endowment for the Arts grant, 1969-70; Brandeis University Creative Arts Award, 1969; Shelley Prize, Poetry Society of America, 1974; Medal of Merit, National Institute of Arts and Letters, 1975; London Translation Prize, 1979; National Book Award for poetry (co-recipient) and Pulitzer Prize for Poetry, both 1983, both for *Selected Poems;* National Book Award for poetry finalist, 1996, for *Imperfect Thirst;* MacArthur fellow, 1984; National Book Critics Circle Award, 1986, for *The Past;* appointed Vermont State Poet, 1989-93.

WRITINGS:

POETRY

What a Kingdom It Was, Houghton (Boston, MA), 1960, revised, 2002.
Flower Herding on Mount Monadnock, Houghton (Boston, MA), 1964, revised, 2002.
Body Rags (also see below), Houghton (Boston, MA), 1968.

Poems of Night, Rapp & Carroll (London, England), 1968.

The Hen Flower, Scepter Press (Frensham, England), 1969.

First Poems: 1946-1954, Perishable Press (Mt. Horeb, WI), 1970.

The Shoes of Wandering, Perishable Press (Mt. Horeb, WI), 1971.

The Book of Nightmares, Houghton (Boston, MA), 1971.

The Avenue bearing the Initial of Christ into the New World: Poems 1946-1964, Houghton (Boston, MA), 1974, revised, 2002.

St. Francis and the Snow, Ravine Press (Chicago, IL), 1976.

Three Poems, Phoenix Book Shop (New York, NY), 1976.

Fergus Falling, Janus Press (Newark, VT), 1979.

There Are Things I Tell to No One (single poem), Nadja (New York, NY), 1979.

Two Poems, Janus Press (Newark, VT), 1979.

Mortal Acts, Mortal Words (also see below), Houghton (Boston, MA), 1980.

The Last Hiding Place of Snow, Red Ozier (New York, NY), 1980.

Selected Poems, Houghton (Boston, MA), 1982.

The Fundamental Project of Technology (single poem; also see below), Ewert (Concord, NH), 1983.

The Geese, Janus Press (Newark, VT), 1985.

The Seekonk Woods, with photographs by Lotte Jacobi, Janus Press (Newark, VT), 1985.

The Past (includes *The Fundamental Project of Technology; also see below),* Houghton (Boston, MA), 1985.

When One Has Lived a Long Time Alone, Knopf (New York, NY), 1990.

Three Books (includes *Body Rags, Mortal Acts, Mortal Words,* and *The Past),* Houghton (Boston, MA), 1993.

Imperfect Thirst, Houghton (Boston, MA), 1994.

A New Selected Poems, Houghton Mifflin (Boston, MA), 2001.

Also author of poem *When the Towers Fell,* 2002; poems have been anthologized in *Contemporary American Poetry,* Penguin (New York, NY), 1962; *Where Is Vietnam?: American Poets Respond,* Doubleday (New York, NY), 1967; Scott Walker, editor, *Buying Time,* Graywolf Press (Minneapolis, MN), 1985; Robert Hass, editor, *Best American Poetry of 2001,* Scribner (New York, NY), 2001; and *Pocket Book of Modern Verse.* Contributor of poetry to numerous journals and periodicals, including *New Yorker, Hudson Review, Poetry, Nation, Choice, Harper's,* and *New World Writing.*

TRANSLATOR

Rene Hardy, *Bitter Victory,* Doubleday (New York, NY), 1956.

Henri Lehmann, *Pre-Columbian Ceramics,* Viking (New York, NY), 1962.

The Poems of François Villon, New American Library (New York, NY), 1965, new edition, University Press of New England (Hanover, NH), 1982.

Yves Bonnefoy, *On the Motion and Immobility of Douve,* Ohio University Press (Athens, OH), 1968, reprinted, Bloodaxe Books (Newcastle upon Tyne, England), 1992.

Yvan Goll, *Lackawanna Elegy,* Sumac Press, 1970.

(With Richard Revear) Yves Bonnefoy, *Early Poems,* Ohio University Press (Athens, OH), 1991.

(With Hannah Liebmann) Rainer Maria Rilke, *The Essential Rilke,* Ecco Press (New York, NY), 1999.

OTHER

Thoughts Occasioned by the Most Insignificant of All Human Events (essay; first published in *Pleasures of Learning,* 1958), Ewert (Concord, NH), 1982.

Black Light (novel), Houghton (Boston, MA), 1966, revised edition, North Point Press (San Francisco, CA), 1980.

The Poetics of the Physical World (lecture), Colorado State University, 1969.

Walking down the Stairs: Selections from Interviews, University of Michigan Press (Ann Arbor, MI), 1978.

How the Alligator Missed Breakfast (juvenile), illustrated by Lynn Munsinger, Houghton (Boston, MA), 1982.

Remarks on Accepting the American Book Award, Ewert (Concord, NH), 1984.

(Author of postscript) Paul Zweig, *Eternity's Woods,* Wesleyan University Press (Middletown, CT), 1985.

(Editor and author of introduction) Walt Whitman, *The Essential Whitman,* Ecco Press (New York, NY), 1987.

Poetry Breaks I, Galway Kinnell, (video reading), Leita Hagemann and WGBH Educational Foundation (Boston, MA), 1988.

SIDELIGHTS: Galway Kinnell is an award-winning poet whose work over four decades has sought to establish the significance of life through daily human experience: the poetic, the cosmic, the social, the cultural, and the individual. *New York Times Book Review* essayist

Morris Dickstein called Kinnell "one of the true master poets of his generation and a writer whose career exemplifies some of what is best in contemporary poetry." Dickstein added: "There are few others writing today in whose work we feel so strongly the full human presence." Robert Langbaum observed in the *American Poetry Review* that Kinnell, "at a time when so many poets are content to be skillful and trivial, speaks with a big voice about the whole of life." As Al Haley noted of Kinnell on the *Abiline University* Web site, "His poetry is understandable, and at the same time amazingly lyrical, energetic, and inventive. He has lived long enough to have produced a significant body of work that makes a lasting contribution to American poetry."

According to Charles Frazier in the *Dictionary of Literary Biography,* Kinnell's poetry "has been devoted to a remarkably consistent, though by no means limited, range of concerns. The subjects and themes to which he has returned again and again are the relation of the self to violence, transience, and death; the power of wilderness and wildness; and the primitive underpinnings of existence that are disguised by the superstructure of civilization. Kinnell's approach to these topics is by way of an intense concentration on physical objects, on the constant impingement of the other-than-human on our lives." *Hudson Review* contributor Vernon Young wrote: "By turn and with level facility, Kinnell is a poet of the landscape, a poet of soliloquy, a poet of the city's underside and a poet who speaks for thieves, pushcart vendors and lumberjacks with an unforced simulation of the vernacular."

The theme of death's inevitability permeates Kinnell's poetry as he seeks to derive understanding of the total life experience. To Charles Molesworth, writing in *Encyclopedia of World Literature in the Twentieth Century,* Kinnell's early poems "revolved around questions of suffering and death, using an essentially religious consciousness to question the human condition. Yet the religious fervor of the poetry never inhibited a full acceptance of the secular notions of pleasure and joy." Frazier contended that much of the poet's work "is a ritual filled with the dual awareness of the regrettability and the necessity of death." Kinnell's verse is sometimes harsh and violent—and sometimes bleak—but at the core is the notion that, as death looms, one must live with great intensity. *Partisan Review* essayist Alan Helms stated: "Kinnell's willed choice and his one necessity are to explore the confusion of a life beyond salvation, a death beyond redemption. The result is often compelling reading." In the *Washington Post Book World,* Robert Hass offered a similar assessment. "It is increasingly clear," Hass concluded, "that Kinnell's ambition all along has been to hold death up to life, as if he had it by the scruff of the neck, and to keep it there until he has extracted a blessing from it."

Kinnell often uses fire as a key image to signify cyclical phenomena: consumption by flame leads to death, which in turn allows rebirth. According to Richard Howard in his *Alone with America: Essays on the Art of Poetry in the United States since 1950,* Kinnell's poetry "is an Ordeal by Fire. . . . It is fire—in its constant transformations, its endless resurrection—which is reality, for Kinnell. . . . The agony of that knowledge—the knowledge or at least the conviction that all must be consumed in order to be reborn, must be reduced to ash in order to be redeemed—gives Galway Kinnell's poetry its astonishing resonance." In *The Fierce Embrace: A Study of Contemporary American Poetry,* Molesworth concluded: "The persistence of fire and death imagery throughout Kinnell's poetry forces us to disregard, or at least to minimize, the habitual expectation of ironic distance that we bring to much modern poetry. His obviously attempts to be a poetry of immersion into experience rather than of suspension above it."

To further illustrate his themes, Kinnell chooses earthy, natural elements: animals, blood, stars, skeletons, insects. Jerome McGann suggested in the *Chicago Review* that Kinnell finds solace in the regenerative power of nature, evident in even the least promising situations. In Kinnell, said McGann, "we see that the idea of paradise gets reborn in the cultivation of waste places. . . . Life is found in death, fountains in deserts, gain in loss, spring in winter, light in darkness. All these matters are the recurrent subjects of Kinnell's verse."

Kinnell does not think of himself as a "nature poet," per se, however. In an interview with Daniela Gioseffi for *Hayden's Ferry Review,* he noted: "I don't recognize the distinction between nature poetry and, what would be the other thing? Human civilization poetry? We are creatures of the earth who build our elaborate cities and beavers are creatures of the earth who build their elaborate lodges and canal operations and dams, just as we do. The human is unique in that it's taken over, but that's no reason to say that the human is of a different kind, a kind created in the image of some god while all the others are created in the image of mere lumps of dirt. . . . Poems about other creatures may have political and social implications for us."

Indeed, Kinnell achieved major recognition with the publication *Body Rags,* a collection that contains some of his best-known animal poems, in which the author explores himself through the subjective experiences of a fly, a crow, a porcupine, and a bear. In "The Bear," for instance, Kinnell "seeks entrance into a primitive state of identification with the nonhuman," according to Frazier. In *Modern Poetry Studies,* John Hobbs related how "The Bear" originated: "Speaking of the origins of 'The Bear' in an interview Kinnell said, 'I guess I had just read [e. e. cummings'] poem on Olaf. . . . And then I remembered this bear story, how the bear's shit was infused with blood, so that the hunter by eating the bear's excrement was actually nourished by what the bear's wound infused into it.'" The poem extrapolates the incident and follows the hunter as his identity merges with that of the bear he stalks. Hobbs added: "To the question of a conflict between the sacredness of all life and killing the bear, we can see that the hunter slowly becomes the bear, even after its death. . . . In a sense, the hunter hunts and kills himself."

Kinnell weaves this kind of pointedly unlovely imagery into many of his poems in order to present a balanced depiction of life. The author told the *Los Angeles Times:* "I've tried to carry my poetry as far as I could, to dwell on the ugly as fully, as far, and as long, as I could stomach it. Probably more than most poets I have included in my work the unpleasant because I think if you are ever going to find any kind of truth to poetry it has to be based on all of experience rather than on a narrow segment of cheerful events." *New Statesman* reviewer Alan Brownjohn praised the "precise, Roethke-ish sense of the natural processes," he saw in *Body Rags.* In a review for *Nation,* John Logan predicted that with the publication of *Body Rags,* "we can single out Kinnell as one of the few consummate masters in poetry."

Like his contemporaries, Kinnell "has attempted to develop the poetic explorations of Robert Lowell and Theodore Roethke in order to learn how the breakthroughs of these poets could form a basis for a poetry that served the needs of the final third of the twentieth century," stated a contributor to *Contemporary Poets.* "His own innovations have led [Kinnell] to abandon the intricate, allusive, and sometimes dense structures that characterized works of the school of [T. S.] Eliot and [Ezra] Pound. His poems have avoided studied ambiguity, and he has risked directness of address, precision of imagery, and experiments with surrealistic situations and images."

Yet Kinnell's verse does pay homage to numerous great poets, including Pound, Eliot, Robert Frost, William Carlos Williams, William Black, cummings, and Low-

ell. Critics most often compare his work to that of Walt Whitman, however, because of its transcendental philosophy and personal intensity, and Kinnell himself edited *The Essential Whitman.* As Robert Langbaum observed in *American Poetry Review:* "Like the romantic poets to whose tradition he belongs, Kinnell tries to pull an immortality out of our mortality." In *Western Humanities Review,* Molesworth noted a poetic legacy in Kinnell's writing from Pound, Blake, and Whitman. Yet the critic also perceived an ultimate difference from these poets in terms of Kinnell's poetic direction, claiming: "Kinnell became a shamanist, rather than a historicist, of the imagination." In seeing Whitman as the primary influence on Kinnell, Frazier wrote: "In developing his sense of the potentiality of free verse to correspond not to some external pattern but to what he calls 'the rhythm of what's being said,' Kinnell points most often to Walt Whitman. . . . Whitmanesque roughness and colloquiality make themselves felt not only in the longer, looser poems, . . . but also in the shorter, more personal lyrics."

His pushcart vendors, lumberjacks, animal images, and surrealism notwithstanding, Kinnell's is an intensely personal poetry, mining his own experiences of love, fatherhood, anxiety, joy, and spirituality. Said Kinnell of his work in his Gioseffi interview, "Self-knowledge is always helpful to our well being—but if we divide humankind into the good and the bad—and put ourselves among the good and others among the bad or poor slobs, we can never write truthful poetry. It's all false, if based on that erroneous premise—that we are the pure poet and the stupid rabble is all to blame. No doubt some people are morally better or worse than some others, but it is necessary to see that there's no absolute classification. . . . Knowing that what we call evil in others also exists in ourselves makes it more possible to write something that has authenticity."

Yet as Stephen Yenser noted in the *Yale Review,* Kinnell's best work is "a poetry that, however personal in its references, continually expands into larger statements." These "larger statements" surfaced early for Kinnell, taking advantage of opportunities to work for the civil rights movement, "instead of merely stewing about it," as he told Gioseffi, and to protest the Vietnam War.

Kinnell was born and raised in Rhode Island. He began to study poetry seriously as a teenager at the Wilbraham Academy in Massachusetts, and he continued his studies at Princeton University. There he came under the influence of his roommate, W.S. Merwin—who introduced him to the work of William Butler Yeats—and the poet Charles G. Bell, who recognized and encouraged his talent. After graduating from Princeton with highest honors, he received his master's degree from the University of Rochester and embarked on a teaching career that would carry him to France, Spain, Hawaii, and Iran. Soon after publishing his first book of poems, *What a Kingdom It Was,* Kinnell realized he could be more productive outside the academic environment. For much of the early 1960s he worked odd jobs, and, for a time, helped to register Southern black voters with the Congress of Racial Equality (CORE), because, as he told Gioseffi, he found it "unbearable to live in a segregated society."

All his experiences—world travel, city life, harassment as a member of CORE and an anti-Vietnam war demonstrator—eventually found expression in his poetry, and critics were quick to observe the immediacy and impact of his voice. The *Dictionary of Literary Biography* essayist quoted Ralph Mills, who noted that Kinnell's early writings signaled "decisive changes in the mood and character of American poetry as it departed from the witty, pseudo-mythic verse, apparently written to critical prescription, of the 1950s to arrive at the more authentic, liberated work of the 1960s." As Kinnell told Gioseffi, "There's this thing about political poems—one must learn something from them, learn something about the political event, and if possible in the best poems, about oneself as well."

Other well-known Kinnell works include *The Book of Nightmares,* published in 1971, and *The Avenue bearing the Initial of Christ into the New World: Poems 1946-1964.* In a review of the latter work, Williamson asserted that the title poem "is still arguably as good as anything [Kinnell] has written." The critic added that the work, which explores life on Avenue C in New York City's Lower East Side, "reminds one of Crane and early Lowell in its sonority, but more of [T.S. Eliot's] 'The Waste Land'—if, indeed of anything in literature in its ability to include a seething cauldron of urban sensations, of randomness and ugliness, yet hold its own poetic shape." James Atlas of *Poetry* offered a similar opinion of Eliot's influence on the work: *The Avenue bearing the Initial of Christ into the New World* "is one of the most vivid legacies of [*The Waste Land*] in English, building its immense rhetorical power from the materials of several dialects, litanies of place, and a profound sense of the spiritual disintegration that Eliot divined in modern urban life. And, like Eliot's, Kinnell's is a religious poem. . . . Since it is impossible to isolate any single passage from the magnificent sprawl of this poem, I can only suggest its importance by

stressing that my comparison of it to [*The Waste Land*] was intended to be less an arbitrary reference than an effort to estimate the poem's durable achievement."

Comparing *The Book of Nightmares* to *Body Rags,* Marjorie Perloff found the latter work "somewhat uneven. . . . As in his earlier poems," she commented in *Contemporary Literature,* "Kinnell uses images of nature in its most elemental forms . . . to discover the deeper instincts of the submerges self." To Langbaum, however, *The Book of Nightmares* "emerges as one of the best long poems of recent years. . . . [It] is, like so many poems, autobiographical and confessional." Langbaum cited Kinnell's use of free verse, adding: "but he universalizes his experience through an imagery that connects it with cosmic process." The critic concluded that "even with its weak spots, its few lapses in intensity, *The Book of Nightmares* is major poetry." *Western Humanities Review* correspondent Fred Moramarco, described *The Book of Nightmares* as "simply a stunning work, rich in its imagery, haunting in its rhythms, evocative and terrifyingly accurate in its insights."

While the poems in the more recent *Mortal Acts, Mortal Words* and *The Past* maintain the balance and intensity of *The Book of Nightmares,* some critics discerned a change in Kinnell's orientation. As Michiko Kakutani of the *New York Times* observed: "Human mortality, as ever, [remains] Mr. Kinnell's great subject, but one [senses] that his perspective has begun to shift. Whereas the earlier works focused on the skull beneath the skin," or the hidden horror of life, "the later ones dwell, however tentatively, on the undying spirit, on the possibility that death may mean not mere extinction, but a reconciliation with the universe's great ebb and flow." *Times Literary Supplement* contributor Mark Ford found the poems in *The Past* "more relaxed and meditative, less obsessively physical," with a "growing awareness of the domestic that has begun to infiltrate Kinnell's poetry in recent years."

Selected Poems, for which Kinnell won the Pulitzer Prize and was cowinner of the National Book Award in 1983, is, to quote Dickstein, "more than a good introduction to Galway Kinnell's work. It is a full scale dossier." The collection, published in 1982, contains works from every period in the poet's career and was released just shortly before he won a prestigious MacArthur foundation grant. In his review of the book, Hass concluded that Kinnell is "widely read by the young who read poetry. If this were a different culture, he would simply be widely read. . . . The common reader—the one who reads at night or on the beach for pleasure and instruction and diversion—who wants to sample the poetry being written in [his] part of the twentieth century could do very well beginning with Galway Kinnell's *Selected Poems*."

Subsequently, Kinnell has published *When One Has Lived a Long Time Alone*, a collection of poems that closely examines loneliness. In the sequence of eleven poems that gives the book its title, each poem consists of thirteen lines and begins and ends with the words "when one has lived a long time alone." Noted Anthony Thwaite in the *Washington Post:* "I was glad to see Kinnell showing not only a sense of humor, something he has shown flickeringly before, but—in 'Oatmeal'—a fully-fledged sense of the marvelously ridiculous." Richard Calhoun took a more serious approach to *When One Has Lived a Long Time Alone*, writing in *Reference Guide to American Literature* that this collection specifies "the need for love, or at least for the presence of another creature, any creature, to negate loneliness. More than lonely immersion of self into nature is now required; lovers, friends, some kind of companionship, as well as the order and form that song and poems bring into life, all are now integral."

In *Imperfect Thirst* Kinnell reasserts his position as a latter-day romantic. As David Baker wrote in *Poetry:* "Kinnell's gift has always been to mediate between the visible, substantial world and the inutterably spiritual or mystical, and his approach in his greatest poems, like 'The Bear,' 'The Last River,' or any of the *Nightmares,* requires giving over the body's self to the regions of mystery and otherness he identifies in 'There Are Things I Tell to No One': 'I believe, / rather, in a music of grace / that we hear, sometimes, playing to us / from the other side of happiness.'" The volume is symmetrically structured in five sections containing five poems each, and Thomas M. Disch maintained in the *Hudson Review* that it offers further evidence that "among contemporary poets few can rival Galway Kinnell for sheer amiability."

A New Selected Poems, a retrospective collection, focuses on the poetry of the 1960s and 1970s, eras when, according to a *Publishers Weekly* contributor, Kinnell's poetry "typically [developed] . . . numbered sections full of dark imagery." Bernard Dick, in *World Literature Today,* noted the inclusion of the eleven related poems from *When One Has Lived a Long Time Alone* as the "real triumph" of this collection, saying that "never has loneliness been so seductive, so strangely inviting, so desirable, and at the same time so horrifying." Of Kinnell's later poetry, Ned Balbo, writing in *Antioch*

Review, characterized them as "more relaxed and idiomatic, more apt to very tone, and frequently erotic." Balbo pointed to "Last Gods" as an example, saying that in this verse Kinnell "discovers the sacred element in a sexual encounter."

"It strikes me that Kinnell's is an utterly healthy poetry," noted Susan B. Weston in the *Iowa Review.* "It is healthy precisely because it confronts horrors—drunks dying of cirrhosis; war and destruction; the communal nightmare of a failing culture; the individual nightmare of the failure of love—along with all that is lovely and loving. These facets of the single gem, the human condition, are examined with a jeweler's sense not only of their beauty but also of their dimension. . . . Kinnell's gift is a cursed awareness of time—not just of individual mortality but of geological time that lends special poignance to even the most hostile of human encounters." In the *Boston Review,* Richard Tillinghast commented that Kinnell's work "is proof that poems can still be written, and written movingly and convincingly, on those subjects that in any age fascinate, quicken, disturb, confound, and sadden the hearts of men and women: eros, the family, mortality, the life of the spirit, war, the life of nations. . . . [Kinnell] always meets existence head-on, without evasion or wishful thinking. When Kinnell is at the top of his form, there is no better poet writing in America."

One topic Kinnell faced head-on was the tragedy of September 11, 2001, in his poem, *When the Towers Fell.* As he told Alice Quinn in an interview for the *New Yorker Online,* which published the work: "I wanted to make my account true to my own feelings, but I also felt I should protect the [victims'] families from any tendencies I might have to depict things in extreme ways. I didn't feel constrained so much as wary of going too far. At the same time, I believe that a poem that goes too far is ipso facto preferable to one that falls short." Said Quinn of *When the Towers Fell:* "The poem has a definite dramatic structure. Each section rises to a crescendo, a sort of fearful apprehension that will be confirmed. And there's a tentative, probing, investigative quality to the way it moves forward, seeking and searching." Responding to Quinn's comments about the qualities of this poem, Kinnell noted, "They were not the result of art but of my struggle to visualize and to understand. I wrote the poem in sections, and I tried to put these sections, or moments, into a clear narrative order, so that I wouldn't have to spell out the connectives between them and could focus entirely on the moments themselves."

In an interview with Elizabeth Lund for the *Christian Science Monitor Online,* Kinnell noted: "It's the poet's job to figure out what's happening within oneself, to figure out the connection between the self and the world, and to get it down in words that have a certain shape, that have a chance of lasting." But the terrorist attacks were "so huge that it [was] difficult to write about them directly." "Kinnell fans have long loved his work for its intelligence and honesty, his keen eye for detail, and the subtle connections between people and their environment," Lund added. "There is an authenticity, a humanity to his work that few of his contemporaries can match. . . . Kinnell never seems to lose his center, or his compassion. He can make almost any situation, any loss, resonate. Indeed, much of his work leaves the reader with a delicious ache, a sense of wanting to look once more at whatever scene is passing."

BIOGRAPHICAL AND CRITICAL SOURCES:

BOOKS

Calhoun, Richard James, *Galway Kinnell,* Macmillan (New York, NY), 1992.

Cambon, Glauco, *Recent American Poetry,* University of Minnesota (Minneapolis, MN), 1962.

Contemporary Literary Criticism, Thomson Gale (Detroit, MI), Volume 1, 1973, Volume 2, 1974, Volume 3, 1975, Volume 5, 1976, Volume 13, 1980, Volume 29, 1984.

Contemporary Poets, seventh edition, St. James Press (Detroit, MI), 2001.

Dickey, James, *Babel to Byzantium,* Farrar, Straus (New York, NY), 1956, new edition, 1968.

Dictionary of Literary Biography, Volume 5: *American Poets since World War II,* Thomson Gale (Detroit, MI), 1980.

Dictionary of Literary Biography Yearbook, 1987, Thomson Gale (Detroit, MI), 1988.

Encyclopedia of World Literature in the Twentieth Century, Volume 2, St. James Press (Detroit, MI), 1999.

Galway Kinnell: A Bibliography and Index of His Published Works and Criticism of Them, Frederick W. Crumb Memorial Library, State University College (Potsdam, NY), 1968.

Guimond, James, *Seeing and Healing: The Poetry of Galway Kinnell,* Associated Faculty Press (Gaithersburg, MD), 1988.

Howard, Richard, *Alone with America: Essays on the Art of Poetry in the United States since 1950,* Atheneum (New York, NY), 1965, new edition, 1969.

Kinnell, Galway, *Walking down the Stairs: Selections from Interviews,* University of Michigan Press (Ann Arbor, MI), 1978.

Mills, Ralph, *Cry of the Human: Essays on Contemporary American Poetry,* University of Illinois Press (Champaign, IL), 1975.

Modern American Literature, fifth edition, St. James Press (Detroit, MI), 1999.

Molesworth, Charles, *The Fierce Embrace: A Study of Contemporary American Poetry,* University of Missouri Press (Columbia, MO), 1979.

Nelson, Howard, editor, *On the Poetry of Galway Kinnell: The Wages of Dying,* University of Michigan Press (Ann Arbor, MI), 1987.

Poulin, A., Jr., editor, *Contemporary American Poetry,* Houghton (New York, NY), 1985.

Reference Guide to American Literature, fourth edition, St. James Press (Detroit, MI), 2000.

Shaw, Robert B., editor, *American Poetry since 1960: Some Critical Perspectives,* Dufour (Chester Springs, PA), 1974.

Thurley, Geoffrey, *The American Moment: American Poetry in Mid-Century,* St. Martin's Press (New York, NY), 1977.

Tuten, Nancy L., editor, *Critical Essays on Galway Kinnell,* G.K. Hall (New York, NY), 1996.

Zimmerman, Lee, *Intricate and Simple Things: The Poetry of Galway Kinnell,* University of Illinois Press (Champaign, IL), 1987.

PERIODICALS

American Book Review, March, 1987.

American Poetry Review, March-April, 1979.

Antioch Review, winter, 2001, Ned Balbo, review of *A New Selected Poems,* p. 121.

Atlantic, February, 1972.

Beloit Poetry Journal, spring, 1968; fall-winter, 1971-72.

Boston Review, February, 1983.

Carleton Miscellany, spring-summer, 1972.

Chicago Review, Volume 25, number 1, 1973; Volume 27, number 1, 1975.

Chicago Tribune Book World, June 8, 1980; February 2, 1986.

Commonweal, November 4, 1960; December 24, 1971; August 15, 1986.

Contemporary Literature, winter, 1973, Marjorie Perloff, review of *The Book of Nightmares;* autumn, 1979.

Explicator, April, 1975.

Hayden's Ferry Review, fall-winter, 2002-03, Daniela Gioseffi, interview with Kinnell.

Hudson Review, summer, 1968; autumn, 1971; winter, 1974-75; spring, 1986; summer, 1995.

Iowa Review, winter, 1979.

Kenyon Review, summer, 1986.

Literary Review, spring, 1981.

Los Angeles Times, June 16, 1983.

Massachusetts Review, summer, 1984.

Modern Poetry Studies, winter, 1974; number 11, 1982.

Nation, September 16, 1968, John Logan, review of *Body Rags,* p. 244.

New Republic, July 27, 1974; August 3, 1974.

New Statesman, September 12, 1969, Alan Brownjohn, review of *Body Rags,* p. 347.

New York Times, September 1, 1971; November 2, 1985; August 21, 1989.

New York Times Book Review, July 5, 1964; February 18, 1968; November 21, 1971; January 12, 1975; June 22, 1980; September 19, 1982; March 2, 1986.

Parnassus, fall-winter, 1974; annual, 1980.

Partisan Review, winter, 1967; Volume XLIV, number 2, 1977.

Perspective, spring, 1968.

Poetry, February, 1961; February, 1967; November, 1972; February, 1975; July, 1991, p. 217; April, 1996, p. 33.

Princeton University Library Chronicle, autumn, 1963.

Publishers Weekly, September 26, 1994, p. 57; December 5, 1994, p. 56; March 6, 2000, review of *A New Selected Poems,* p. 106.

Shenandoah, fall, 1973.

Times Literary Supplement, September 21, 1969; March 1, 1985; November 6, 1987; November 12, 1987.

Tribune Books (Chicago, IL), February 3, 1991.

Village Voice, April 1, 1986.

Virginia Quarterly Review, autumn, 1995, p. 656.

Washington Post Book World, September 5, 1982; January 5, 1986; December 30, 1990.

Western Humanities Review, spring, 1972; summer, 1973.

World Literature Today, autumn, 2000, Bernard Dick, review of *A New Selected Poems,* p. 819.

Yale Review, autumn, 1968; October, 1980.

ONLINE

Abilene Christian University Web site, http://www.acu.edu/events/news/ (January 23, 2003),"Pulitzer Prize-Winning Poet to Read in Major Literary Event."

Christian Science Monitor Online, http://www.csmonitor.com/ (October 25, 2001), Elizabeth Lund "Galway Kinnell Searches for the Real Beauty."

Cortland Review Online, http://www.cortlandreview.com/ (June 13, 2002), Daniela Gioseffi, interview with Kinnell.

New Yorker Online, http://www.newyorker.com/ (August 3, 2004), Alice Quinn, "Writing for the Dead, an Interview with Galway Kinnell."

Rambles.net, http://www.rambles.net/ (June 13, 2002), Daina Savage, review of *Imperfect Thirst.*

Salon.com, http://www.salon.com (August 5, 2002).

University of Illinois Department of English Web site, http://www.english.uiuc.edu/maps/poets/ (August 3, 2004) "Modern American Poetry, Galway Kinnell."

*　　*　　*

KINSELLA, Thomas 1928-

PERSONAL: Surname accented on first syllable; born May 4, 1928, in Dublin, Ireland; son of John Paul (a trade unionist and brewery worker) and Agnes (Casserly) Kinsella; married Eleanor Walsh, December 28, 1955; children: Sara, John, Mary. *Education:* University College, Dublin, diploma in public administration, 1949.

ADDRESSES: Home—Killalane, Laragh, County Wicklow, Ireland. *Office*—English Department, Temple University, Philadelphia, PA 19103, and Peppercanister Press, 47 Percy Ln., Dublin 4, Ireland.

CAREER: Poet. Irish Civil Service, Dublin, Ireland, Land Commission, junior executive officer, 1946-50, Department of Finance, administrative officer, 1950-60, assistant principal officer, 1960-65; Southern Illinois University at Carbondale, poet-in-residence, 1965-67, professor of English, 1967-70; Temple University, Philadelphia, PA, professor of English, 1970-90, founding director, Temple-in-Dublin Irish Tradition program, 1976—. Founding director, Peppercanister Press, Dublin, 1972—; director, Dolmen Press Ltd. and Cuala Press Ltd., Dublin. Artistic director, Lyric Players Theatre, Belfast, Ireland.

MEMBER: Irish Academy of Letters.

AWARDS, HONORS: Guinness Poetry Award, 1958, for *Another September;* Irish Arts Council Triennial Book Award, 1961, for *Poems and Translations;* Denis Devlin Memorial Award, 1964-66, for *Wormwood,* 1967-69, for *Nightwalker and Other Poems,* and 1988 and 1994; Guggenheim fellowships, 1968-69, 1971-72; Before Columbus Foundation award, 1983; D.Litt., National University of Ireland, 1984. *Another September* and *Downstream* were Poetry Book Society choices.

WRITINGS:

POETRY

The Starlit Eye, Dolmen Press (Dublin, Ireland), 1952.
Three Legendary Sonnets, Dolmen Press (Dublin, Ireland), 1952.
Per Imaginem, Dolmen Press (Dublin, Ireland), 1953.
The Death of a Queen, Dolmen Press (Dublin, Ireland), 1956.
Poems, Dolmen Press (Dublin, Ireland), 1956.
Another September, Dolmen Press (Dublin, Ireland), 1958, revised edition, 1962.
Moralities, Dolmen Press (Dublin, Ireland), 1960.
Poems and Translations, Atheneum (New York, NY), 1961.
(With John Montague and Richard Murphy) *Three Irish Poets,* Dolmen Press (Dublin, Ireland), 1961.
Downstream, Dolmen Press (Dublin, Ireland), 1962.
Wormwood, Dolmen Press (Dublin, Ireland), 1966.
Nightwalker and Other Poems, Dolmen Press (Dublin, Ireland), 1967.
(With Douglas Livingstone and Anne Sexton) *Poems,* Oxford University Press (New York, NY), 1968.
Nightwalker and Other Poems, Dolmen Press (Dublin, Ireland), 1968, Knopf (New York, NY), 1969.
Tear, Pym-Randall (Cambridge, MA), 1969.
Finistere, Dolmen Press (Dublin, Ireland), 1971.
Notes from the Land of the Dead: Poems, Cuala Press (Dublin, Ireland), 1972, published as *Notes from the Land of the Dead and Other Poems,* Knopf (New York, NY), 1973.
Butcher's Dozen: A Lesson for the Octave of Widgery, Peppercanister (Dublin, Ireland), 1972, revised edition, 1992.
A Selected Life, Peppercanister (Dublin, Ireland), 1972.
Vertical Man: A Sequel to A Selected Life, Peppercanister (Dublin, Ireland), 1973.
The Good Fight: A Poem for the Tenth Anniversary of the Death of John F. Kennedy, Peppercanister (Dublin, Ireland), 1973.
New Poems, 1973, Dolmen Press (Dublin, Ireland), 1973.
Selected Poems, 1956-1968, Dolmen Press (Dublin, Ireland), 1973.
One (also see below), Peppercanister (Dublin, Ireland), 1974.
A Technical Supplement, Peppercanister (Dublin, Ireland), 1975.
Song of the Night and Other Poems, Peppercanister (Dublin, Ireland), 1978.
The Messenger, Peppercanister (Dublin, Ireland), 1978.

Poems, 1956-1973, Wake Forest University Press, 1979.
Peppercanister Poems, 1972-1978 (also see below), Wake Forest University Press (Winston-Salem, NC), 1979.
Fifteen Dead (also see below), Dufour (Dublin, Ireland), 1979.
One and Other Poems, Dolmen Press (Dublin, Ireland), 1979.
Poems, 1956-76, Dolmen Press (Dublin, Ireland), 1980.
One Fond Embrace, Deerfield Press (Hatfield, MA), 1981.
Songs of the Psyche, Peppercanister (Dublin, Ireland), 1985.
Her Vertical Smile, Peppercanister (Dublin, Ireland), 1985.
Out of Ireland, Peppercanister (Dublin, Ireland), 1987.
St. Catherine's Clock, Peppercanister (Dublin, Ireland), 1987.
Blood and Family, Oxford University Press (New York, NY), 1989.
Personal Places, Dedalus (Dublin, Ireland), 1990.
Poems from Centre City, Dedalus (Dublin, Ireland), 1990.
Open Court, Peppercanister (Dublin, Ireland), 1991.
Madonna and Other Poems, Peppercanister (Dublin, Ireland), 1991.
Collected Poems, 1956-1994, Oxford University Press (New York, NY), 1996.
The Pen Shop, Dufour Editions (Chester Springs, PA), 1997.
The Familiar, Dufour Editions (Chester Springs, PA), 1999.
Godhead, Dufour Editions (Chester Springs, PA), 1999.
Citizen of the World, Dufour Editions (Chester Springs, PA), 2000.
Littlebody, Dufour Editions (Chester Springs, PA), 2000.

TRANSLATOR FROM THE GAELIC

The Breastplate of Saint Patrick, Dolmen Press (Dublin, Ireland), 1954, published as *Faeth Fiada: The Breastplate of Saint Patrick,* 1957.
Longes Mac n-Usnig, Being the Exile and Death of the Sons of Usnech, Dolmen Press (Dublin, Ireland), 1954.
Thirty Three Triads, Dolmen Press (Dublin, Ireland), 1955.
The Tain, Dolmen Press (Dublin, Ireland), 1969, Oxford University Press (New York, NY), 1970, reprinted, 1985.

(With Sean O'Tuama) Sean O'Tuama, editor, *An Duanaire—An Irish Anthology: Poems of the Dispossessed, 1600-1900,* Dolmen Press (Dublin, Ireland), 1980, University of Pennsylvania Press (Philadelphia, PA), 1981.

OTHER

(Contributing editor) *The Dolmen Miscellany of Irish Writing,* Dolmen Press (Dublin, Ireland), 1962.

(With W.B. Yeats) *Davis, Mangan, Ferguson?: Tradition and the Irish Writer* (essays), Dolmen Press (Dublin, Ireland), 1970.

(Editor) Austin Clarke, *Selected Poems,* Wake Forest University Press (Winston-Salem, NC), 1976.

(Editor) Sean O'Riada, *Our Musical Heritage* (lectures on Irish traditional music), Gael-Linn, 1981.

(Editor and translator from the Gaelic) *The New Oxford Book of Irish Verse,* Oxford University Press (New York, NY), 1986.

(With John Montague and Brendan Kennelly) *Myth, History, and Literary Tradition,* Dundalk Arts (Dundalk, Ireland), 1989.

The Dual Tradition: An Essay on Poetry and Politics in Ireland, Carcanet (Manchester, England), 1995.

Also contributor of poetry to *Six Irish Poets,* edited by Robin Skelton, Oxford University Press (New York, NY), 1962. Recorded *Patrick Galvin and Thomas Kinsella Reading Their Poems* (sound cassette), 1980.

SIDELIGHTS: In a *New York Times Book Review* article, Calvin Bedient maintained that Thomas Kinsella "can hardly write a worthless poem." He is "probably the most accomplished, fluent, and ambitious Irish poet of the younger generation," according to *New York Times Book Review* critic John Montague, while *Dictionary of Literary Biography* essayist Thomas H. Jackson judged that Kinsella's "technical virtuosity and the profound originality of his subject matter set him apart from his contemporaries." He "seems to me to have the most distinctive voice of his generation in Ireland, though it is also the most versatile and the most sensitive to 'outside' influences," M.L. Rosenthal indicated in *The New Poets: American and British Poetry since World War II.*

Kinsella has described himself as coming from "a typical Dublin family," Jackson reported. His father, a longtime socialist, was a member of the Labour Party and the Left Book Club, and by means of a series of grants

and scholarships Kinsella pursued a science degree at University College in Dublin, where he ultimately obtained a diploma in public administration. He entered the Irish civil service in 1946, but, with the encouragement of his wife in particular, also pursued his craft. During those early years, he met Liam Miller, founder of Dolmen Press, who published several of Kinsella's works; later, Kinsella became a director of the press. He also established an important friendship at that time with Sean O'Riada, a musician described by a *Times Literary Supplement* critic as "the most distinguished of modern Irish composers," who became, in Jackson's words, "a much-loved participant in [Kinsella's] growing intellectual life. O'Riada expressed in his life as much as in his music what seems to be a current Irish ambition in the arts—namely, to contain the world in the capacious and elegant vessel of the Irish imagination and tradition," explained the *Times Literary Supplement* critic.

Kinsella, too, "has explored Irish themes more and more in his later verse," wrote Jackson, "but only in terms of exploring his own consciousness and consciousness in general." His poems since 1956, Kinsella once commented have been "almost entirely lyrical—have dealt with love, death and the artistic act; with persons and relationships, places and objects, seen against the world's processes of growth, maturing and extinction." By the time he wrote *Nightwalker and Other Poems,* which was first published in 1968, he had become "more and more concerned—in longer poems—with questions of value and order, seeing the human function (in so far as it is not simply to survive the ignominies of existence) as the eliciting of order from experience— the detection of the significant substance of the individual and common past and its translation imaginatively, scientifically, bodily, into an increasingly coherent and capacious entity; or the attempt to do this, to the point of failure." A *Times Literary Supplement* reviewer characterized Kinsella's earlier poems as "on the whole less distraughtly introspective than [his more] recent work" but indicated that "they display the same fine knack of delving deeply into self-communion while staying nervously responsive to an actual world."

"All Kinsella's finest [early] poems are written in partial forfeiture to the inevitable destruction of life and pleasure," Calvin Bedient stated in *Eight Contemporary Poets.* The theme of his first major collection *Another September,* according to Jackson, "is order, the fruit of art, which in Kinsella's view is one major form of the mind's stance against mutability and corruption." Most of the poems in that volume, particularly "Baggot Street Deserta," confront "with stoic acceptance the grim fact of loss as a chief keynote of life," Jackson commented. In Kinsella's eyes "life is a tide of loss, disorder, and corruption, and the poetic impulse is an impulse to stem that tide, to place form where time leaves disorder and pain." Kinsella's collection *Downstream,* which includes five poems published earlier as *Moralities,* also conveys a "preoccupation with the passing of time—change as dying, change as birth—that has marked Kinsella's poetic mind from very early on," noted Jackson.

In *Downstream* Kinsella "turns more to the things people actually do in and with their lives. That many of the poems' titles refer to jobs, types of people, and life choices signals the linkage of the temporal and the abstract, the deeply buried and the visibly lived." This volume includes the "earliest of Kinsella's journey poems," pointed out Jackson, including "A Country Walk" and "Downstream." And in the opinion of John D. Engle in *Parnassus,* these are Kinsella's "most lasting early poems."

Beginning with *Downstream* and continuing with the short sequence *Wormwood* and the cumulative *Nightwalker and Other Poems,* "Kinsella emerged as a master not of slick verse but more saddened, more naked, more groping—of a poetry of subdued but unrelenting power," Bedient stated. "Here surfaced a poetry that, if almost completely without a surprising use of words, all being toned to a grave consistency, has yet the eloquence of a restrained sorrow, a sorrow so lived-in that it seems inevitable. With its sensitive density of mood, its unself-conscious manner, there is nothing in this poetry for other poets to imitate. Its great quality is the modesty and precision of its seriousness."

The poem "Nightwalker" itself is "a long nocturnal meditation on Ireland past and present, on the poet's consciousness as a source of order amid decay and betrayal," Jackson related. In the view of Dennis Paoli, writing in *Encyclopedia of World Literature in the Twentieth Century,* through the *Nightwalker* collection Kinsella laments "the near destruction of the Irish language in the [eighteenth century] and satirizes its institutionalization in the [twentieth]."

The culminating entry in *Nightwalker and Other Poems,* "Phoenix Park," is a journey poem described by Jackson as "an ambitious composition that shows how far the poet has come since his earliest work. The title is the name of Dublin's largest park, but it bears connotation of the phoenix itself, the bird that rises from the ashes of its own cremation to live another millennium."

John Montague, writing in *New York Times Book Review,* referred to the poem as the poet's "farewell to Ireland, in the shape of a drive with his wife along the Liffey [River], as well as an extension of the theme of married love." The poet and his wife, who are about to leave Dublin, drive past "various places meaningful to them," according to Jackson, and "the poet recalls their significance or associations . . . ; he reviews symbolic moments of his life, where he partook of possibilities which his children came to pursue or re-enact."

Modern travel poems like these face "a solitary consciousness towards place and time yet do not, as it were, sit still, are not even ostensibly at rest, but move through the world, continually stimulated to new observations, reactions, associations," Bedient observed. "Cast through space, these poems bring a flutter to the tentativeness of consciousness, which they heighten. They ride on motion the way, and at the same time as, the mind floats on duration. . . . They say that life is only here and now, and fleeting, a thing that cannot stand still," Bedient explained, "and more, that space is as unfathomably deep as time, in time's body, but at least outside ourselves, both mercifully and cruelly outside. The poems increase the sense of exposure to existence as actual travel renews and magnifies the sensation of living."

As the couple in "Phoenix Park" pass by familiar landmarks, Jackson reported, "the lovers' marriage is seen as a powerful form which overcomes loss and the chaos of life. Their love is 'the one positive dream' to which the speaker of 'Phoenix Park' refers as the exception to the fact that 'There's a fever now that eats everything.' . . . He expatiates on the implications of their love as evincing the 'laws of order,' on their love as ordeal, a continual wounding and healing, and a continual growing, and arrives at a sense of existence as a necessary ordeal—when we think we have attained some abstract 'ultimate,' living must end."

After the publication of *Nightwalker and Other Poems,* Kinsella left the civil service to enter academic life and become a full-time writer. He also set up Peppercanister Press at his home in Dublin, primarily to publish limited editions of his works in progress. *Butcher's Dozen: A Lesson for the Octave of Widgery,* the press's first publication, was described by M.L. Rosenthal in the *New York Times Book Review* as a "rough-hewn, deliberately populist dream-visionary poem" on the 1972 shooting-down of thirteen demonstrators in Derry by British troopers and the investigation that followed. But, according to Edna Longley in the *Times Literary*

Supplement, "despite these latent social and political contours," Kinsella's writing "overwhelmingly takes the traditional form of self-searching. (It is a deeper question whether the extreme isolation of his poetic persona owes more to culture than to idiosyncrasy.)"

Butcher's Dozen was revised in 1992 to mark the twentieth anniversary of the slayings. In 1999 *Explicator* critic Neville Newman revisited the poem and found that "phantoms represent the dead civilians and address a variety of national and cultural issues." In the poem, the bitter irony Kinsella uses to describe the attack takes the form of a satire on the children's rhyme "Tom, Tom the Farmer's Son." "The pig of the children's verse becomes the acronym by which the armored personnel carriers of the type deployed against the protesters are known," noted Newman. A reference to a "hooligan" running away puns on the Irish surname Houlihan, reflecting "the way that a long-established anti-Irish bias on the part of the British has passed into day-to-day language." And Kinsella's poetic assessment of the official investigation—which failed to prove that the Irish protesters were armed at the time they were killed—provides "observation that a life was lost for nothing more than 'throwing stones,'" as Newman quoted Kinsella, and "emphasizes the overreaction of the British to the incident."

Kinsella once explained that his poetry of this time begins to involve a turning "downward into the psyche toward origin and myth," and that it is "set toward some kind of individuation." The theme of his next major work, *Notes from the Land of the Dead and Other Poems,* according to a *Times Literary Supplement* critic, "is the spiritual journey from despair and desolation, 'nightnothing,' to a painful self-renewal." The poems in this work abandon syntax, Jackson commented, "because they have left the world to which syntax is relevant and moved to the world of dream, phantasm, and myth, the world in short of psychic exploration."

The volume includes an untitled prologue that Jackson described "as a mystical version of a Kinsellan wandering poem [which] recounts the speaker's descent into a psychic underworld, a reversion to the embryo stage." And "the low point of coherent consciousness in this exploration is [the poem] 'All Is Emptiness and Must Spin,'" related Jackson. John D. Engle explained in *Parnassus* that in *Notes from the Land of the Dead and Other Poems,* "Kinsella heads down, a quest hero, into the past and subconscious; he would retrieve the scary flotsam of memory, a dying old harpy of a grandmother or, perhaps, obsessive shadowplays drawn from a childhood reading of the *Book of Invasions,* Ireland's ancient and wild Genesis. After the confusing bobs and weaves of something like a plot, he bears back his prize: a new awareness, at once modest and enough to change one's life."

Discussing *Notes from the Land of the Dead and Other Poems* in the *New York Times Book Review,* Bedient found Kinsella's style "an almost constant pleasure," but also complained that, here, "Ireland's best living poet has brooded himself to pieces." Vernon Young mentioned in *Parnassus* the fact that, for many years, Kinsella translated "The Tain," an eighth-century Irish epic, "and in that translation you can find both the savage emblems and the bleak outlook of the independent poems [in *Notes from the Land of the Dead and Other Poems*]: as if the repetitive sanguinary deeds of the epic (to my mind a monotonously vindictive chronicle without a tremor of mercy or grace) had been used to compound the lethal evidence of mindless struggle forecast by the origin of the species."

However, Engle remarked that "the poetry of *Notes* is not as extravagantly disheveled as it occasionally seems, and what comes dressed as nihilism turns out to be something else." Kinsella was influenced by Jung, according to Jackson, and "where the earlier work was so concerned with the idea of suffering and pain as the motives of growth, the ordeal as a linear meeting of successive tests, these new poems take up the Jungian idea of a creative union of opposites. The ordeal of suffering and growth becomes the more comprehensive rhythm of destruction and creation, decay and regeneration, death and birth."

Kinsella continues in the same thematic direction with *Peppercanister Poems, 1972-1978,* which, along with the poem "Butcher's Dozen," includes meditations on the deaths of Kinsella's father and his friend, Sean O'Riada, and, according to Jackson, several poems "dealing with the poet's family history and himself as artist." And in an eight-poem sequence "One," Engle commented, Kinsella "plunges again through the crust of appearance into this region of process and origin. The eight poems send his thoughts again into a hoard of personal and common memory, back to his own childhood and further still to merge with those of Ireland's first wave of settlers. . . . This is Jung country."

"Jung and Kinsella's idea that creation and destruction, love and hate, life and death are interinvolved is an attempt to reclaim the wholeness of existence, not to deny its beauty," Jackson commented. "The poems here actually enact that stance: out of the death of a friend, of a father, or political matters comes poetry before our very eyes. Nor is being rooted in the prerational the same as being confined to it." Kinsella, Engle indicated, "is at home now in darkness, the secret shadows where we create and were created. If he invites us into a world that at times proves too elaborately personal, if he tries to do too much with his poems, these are generous blunders. They shouldn't obscure the fact that Kinsella is a serious poet of invention and honesty." Rosenthal concluded that "he is among the true poets, not only of Ireland but among all who write in English in our day."

Blood and Family is a collection of five of Kinsella's pamphlets, originally published by his own Peppercanister Press. The sections (originally pamphlets) of the book, which "include a sequence about the poet's childhood, a homage to Mahler, and an elegy for . . . Sean O'Riada, find their orders in disorder," noted William Logan in the *New York Times Book Review.* Noting the popularity of younger Irish poets, Logan continued, "Mr. Kinsella can still entertain the tragic possibilities, and his powerful recollective passions serve as an affront to a present that can only serve the past. His new poems are his darkest, and the least vulnerable to easy understanding." Kieran Quinlan, writing for *World Literature Today,* also commented on the complexity of the work, concluding, "This is difficult poetry that will offer only to some its hard-won satisfactions."

Personal Places and *Poems from Centre City,* both published in 1990, "extend and enrich" the poet's "focal emphasis on the most immediate and vivid data of concrete personal experience," found Tom Halpin in his review for the *Irish Literary Supplement.* To Halpin "the former deals with endings and beginnings, the dislocations inseparable from any attempt at continuity," while *Poems from Centre City* focuses on Kinsella's life in Dublin, including his writing mentors and family memories. Of *Poems from Centre City,* Elizabeth Gaffney stated in the *New York Times Book Review* that "the visions of Ireland in this idiosyncratic, melancholy collection ultimately cohere around the suggestion that another path might have permitted fulfillment of greater passion," while *Times Literary Supplement* contributor Steven Matthews felt that "the concentrated, vigorous, passionate sense of loss and betrayal in this book promises a revelatory renewal beyond the limits of our foul ascending city." Adam Thorpe, writing in the *Listener,* praised both volumes as "worth their weight in gold," finding them "both harrowing and uplifting." Halpin concluded, "In *Personal Places* and *Poems from Centre City* the surefooted control of Kinsella's voice—a var-

iegated blend of sorrow, compassion, love, anger and humor—earns at the end of each sequence its right to affirm and celebrate, however paradoxically but with no hint of irony, the capacity of poetry to face the worst within and without, and more than weather it in the process of imaginative transformation."

In *The Dual Tradition: An Essay on Poetry and Politics in Ireland,* Kinsella examines the concept that "Literature in Ireland is not divided but dual, and to consider either of its parts in isolation from the other is to diminish both," as Patricia Craig wrote in the *Times Literary Supplement.* This refers in part to "the hidden Ireland," or the Ireland unknown to the non-Irish speaker. Kinsella, like Yeats, writes about this "hidden Ireland," but is not a Gaelic speaker. According to Carol Rumens in the *New Statesman & Society,* Kinsella had examined this personal divide in his 1966 composition for the Modern Language Association, but she found that "his prose [in *The Dual Tradition*] carries little of that earlier energy and conviction." "He offers a politically sensitized historic overview that nevertheless reflects a poet's primary concerns," felt Rosenthal, this time writing for *Ploughshares.* In a review for *World Literature Today,* William Pratt recommended *The Dual Tradition* to "any reader who is not Irish, since it makes distinctions that are exclusively ethnic, unrelated to artistic merit." Craig concluded that the book adds up to "a succinct history of poetry in Ireland, in Irish and English—a brisk run through the centuries."

As the twentieth century drew to a close, Kinsella produced the 1997 collection *The Pen Shop* and followed that with such *fin-de-siècle* works as *The Familiar, Godhead,* and *Citizen of the World. The Pen Shop* finds the poet on a "leisurely stroll though Dublin," according to Pratt of *World Literature Today,* where Kinsella writes of such places as the O'Connell Bridge, Bewley's Oriental Café, and the titular Pen Shop. Pratt found all this "evocative of [James] Joyce's Dublin," particularly in Kinsella's mixing of reality and fantasy. But the reviewer also wondered if Kinsella had deliberately set out to produce poems Pratt characterized as "slight." In the critic's view, "Kinsella seems to be frittering away his talents in trivialities at this late point in his career." "Slight," though, was hardly the word David Lloyd used to describe the 2001 collection, *Citizen of the World.* Indeed, "this is [poetry] that doesn't pander to the reader," wrote Lloyd. "Few people or places are identified beyond the briefest phrase, few situations fleshed out, or social or historical contexts illuminated." The title piece is a portrait of the English novelist Oliver Goldsmith, using a quote from the writer to explore the theme of a mind "not at ease."

The poetry of Kinsella, as George O'Brien summed up in the *Reference Guide to English Literature,* "is a commitment to negotiate the leap of artistic faith which alone can overcome the abyss of unjustifiable unknowing that is the mortal lot." O'Brien singled out Kinsella's "composed and graceful suspension" and concluded that his "anti-romantic conception of poetry, which entails giving tongue to darkness rather than to fire, identifies Kinsella as a crucial reviser of the Irish poetic tradition and a major figure in the problematic history of poetry in English during the postwar years."

BIOGRAPHICAL AND CRITICAL SOURCES:

BOOKS

Badin, Donatella Abbate, *Thomas Kinsella,* Twayne, 1996.

Bedient, Calvin, *Eight Contemporary Poets,* Oxford University Press (New York, NY), 1974.

Contemporary Literary Criticism, Thomson Gale (Detroit, MI), Volume 4, 1975, Volume 19, 1981.

Dictionary of Literary Biography, Volume 27: *Poets of Great Britain and Ireland, 1945-1960,* Thomson Gale (Detroit, MI), 1984.

Dunn, Douglas, editor, *Two Decades of Irish Writing,* Dufour, 1975.

Encyclopedia of World Literature in the Twentieth Century, St. James Press (Detroit, MI), 1999, pp. 639-640.

Harmon, Maurice, *The Poetry of Thomas Kinsella: "With Darkness for a Nest,"* Wolfhound Press, 1974.

Jackson, Thomas H., *The Whole Matter: The Poetic Evolution of Thomas Kinsella,* Syracuse University Press (Syracuse, NY), 1995.

John, Brian, *Reading the Ground: The Poetry of Thomas Kinsella,* Catholic University of America Press, 1996.

Kersnowski, Frank L., *The Outsiders: Poets of Contemporary Ireland,* Texas Christian University Press, 1975.

Kinsella, Thomas, *Nightwalker and Other Poems,* Knopf (New York, NY), 1969.

Kinsella, Thomas, *Notes from the Land of the Dead and Other Poems,* Knopf (New York, NY), 1973.

Orr, Peter, editor, *The Poet Speaks: Interviews with Contemporary Poets,* Routledge, 1966.

Reference Guide to English Literature, second edition, St. James Press (Detroit, MI), 1991, pp. 817-818.

Rosenthal, M. L., *The New Poets: American and British Poetry since World War II,* Oxford University Press (New York, NY), 1967.

Rosenthal, M. L., *Poetry and the Common Life,* Oxford University Press (New York, NY), 1974.

Viewpoints: Poets in Conversation with John Haffenden, Faber, 1981.

PERIODICALS

Agenda, autumn, 1997, review of *The Pen Shop,* p. 191.

America, March 16, 1974; March 18, 1995, review of *Poems from Centre City,* p. 30.

Books in Canada, June, 1988, review of *Notes from the Land of the Dead,* p. 4.

Choice, February, 1996.

Commonweal, June 6, 1980.

Eire-Ireland, number 2, 1967; spring, 1968, p. 108; summer, 1979, pp. 80-82.

Explicator, spring, 1999, Neville Newman, "Kinsella's 'Butcher's Dozen,'" p. 173.

Genre, winter, 1979.

Hollins Critic, October, 1968, John Rees Moore, review of *Nightwalker,* pp. 11-12.

Hudson Review, winter, 1968-69; spring, 1996, review of *Poems from Centre City,* p. 170.

Irish Literary Supplement, fall, 1988, review of *St. Catherine's Clock* and *Out of Ireland,* p 34; fall, 1990, Tom Halpin, review of *Poems from Centre City* and *Personal Places,* p. 19; spring, 1998, review of *The Dual Tradition: An Essay on Poetry and Politics in Ireland,* p. 13.

Kirkus Reviews, November 15, 1999, review of *Godhead* and *The Familiar,* p. 1773.

Kliatt Young Adult Paperback Book Guide, January, 1990, review of *The New Oxford Book of Irish Verse,* p. 27.

Listener, July 5, 1990, Adam Thorpe, review of *Poems from Centre City* and *Personal Places.*

Literary Review, winter, 1979, pp. 139-140.

Nation, June 5, 1972.

New Statesman, November 9, 1973; January 16, 1987, review of *Poems, 1956-1973,* p. 30.

New Statesman & Society, December 23, 1988, review of *Blood and Family,* p. 36; June 2, 1995, Carol Rumens, review of *The Dual Tradition,* p. 46.

New York Times Book Review, August 18, 1968; June 16, 1974; February 24, 1980; May 28, 1989, William Logan, review of *Blood and Family,* p. 24; December 24, 1995, p. 11; December 31, 1995, Elizabeth Gaffney, review of *Poems from Centre City,* p. 11.

Parnassus, spring-summer, 1975; spring, 1981.

Ploughshares, fall, 1996, M.L. Rosenthal, review of *The Dual Tradition,* p. 243.

Poetry, January, 1975.

Publishers Weekly, June 18, 2001, review of *Citizen of the World,* p. 78.

Shenandoah, summer, 1998, review of *Collected Poems, 1956-1994,* p. 116.

Stand, spring, 1990, review of *One Fond Embrace* and *Blood and Family,* p. 14; autumn, 1995, review of *Poems from Centre City,* p. 72.

Times Literary Supplement, October 5, 1967; December 18, 1969; December 8, 1972; August 17, 1973; November 23, 1973; December 19, 1980; May 30, 1986, review of *Songs of the Psyche* and *Her Vertical Smile,* p. 585; September 13, 1991, Steven Matthews, review of *Poems from Centre City* and *Personal Places,* p. 26; July 3, 1992, review of *Open Court,* p. 28; August 27, 1993, review of *Butcher's Dozen: A Lesson for the Octave of Widgery,* p. 12; June 17, 1994, review of *Poems from Centre City,* p. 28; September 13, 1996, p. 26; January 26, 1996, Patricia Craig, review of *The Dual Tradition,* p. 26.

Village Voice, March 14, 1974.

World Literature Today, winter, 1991, review of *Blood and Family,* p. 123; autumn, 1996, William Pratt, review of *The Dual Tradition,* p. 967; winter, 1998, William Pratt, review of *The Pen Shop,* p. 147; summer, 1998, Kieran Quinlan, review of *Collected Poems, 1956-1994,* p. 622; winter, 2002, David Lloyd, review of *Citizen of the World,* p. 153.

Yale Review, spring, 1962, Thom Gunn, review of *Poems and Translations,* pp. 486-487.

*   *   *

KINSELLA, William Patrick
  See KINSELLA, W.P.

*   *   *

KINSELLA, W.P. 1935-
  (William Patrick Kinsella)

PERSONAL: Born May 25, 1935, in Edmonton, Alberta, Canada; son of John Matthew (a contractor) and Olive Mary (a printer; maiden name, Elliot) Kinsella; married Myrna Salls, December 28, 1957 (divorced, 1963); married Mildred Irene Clay, September 10, 1965 (divorced, 1978); married Ann Ilene Knight (a writer), December 30, 1978 (divorced, 1997); married Barbara L. Turner, March 2, 1999; children: (first marriage) Shannon, Lyndsey, Erin. *Education:* University of Victoria, B.A., 1974; University of Iowa, M.F.A., 1978. *Religion:* Atheist.

ADDRESSES: Home—15325 19-A Ave., White Rock, British Columbia V4A 8S4, Canada; Box 2162, Blaine, WA 98230-2162. *Office*—P.O. Box 3067, Sumas, WA 98295-3067; and 9442 Nowell, Chilliwack, British Columbia V2P 4X7, Canada. *Agent*—Nancy Colbert, 55 Avenue Rd., Toronto, Ontario M5R 3L2, Canada.

CAREER: Government of Alberta, Edmonton, Canada, clerk, 1954-56; Retail Credit Co., Edmonton, Alberta, Canada, manager, 1956-61; City of Edmonton, Alberta, Canada, account executive, 1961-67; Caesar's Italian Village (restaurant), Victoria, British Columbia, Canada, owner, 1967-72; student and taxicab driver in Victoria, 1974-76; University of Iowa, Iowa City, instructor, 1976-78; University of Calgary, Calgary, Alberta, Canada, assistant professor of English and creative writing, 1978-83; author, 1983—.

MEMBER: American Amateur Press Association, Society of American Baseball Researchers, American Atheists, Enoch Emery Society.

AWARDS, HONORS: Award from Canadian Fiction, 1976, for story "Illianna Comes Home"; honorable mention in *Best American Short Stories 1980,* for "Fiona the First"; Houghton Mifflin Literary fellowship, 1982, Books in Canada First Novel Award, 1983, and Canadian Authors Association prize, 1983, all for *Shoeless Joe*; Writers Guild of Alberta O'Hagan novel medal, 1984, for *The Moccasin Telegraph*; Alberta Achievement Award for Excellence in Literature; Stephen Leacock Medal for Humor, 1987, for *The Fencepost Chronicles*; Author of the Year Award, Canadian Booksellers Association, 1987; Laurentian University, Ontario, Canada, D.Litt., 1990; University of Victoria, D.Litt, 1991; decorated, Order of Canada, 1994.

WRITINGS:

Dance Me Outside (stories), Oberon Press (Ottawa, Ontario, Canada), 1977, published as *Dance Me Outside: More Tales from the Ermineskin Reserve,* David Godine (Boston, MA), 1986.

Scars: Stories, Oberon Press (Ottawa, Ontario, Canada), 1978.

Shoeless Joe Jackson Comes to Iowa (stories), Oberon Press (Ottawa, Ontario, Canada), 1980, Southern Methodist University Press (Dallas, TX), 1993.

Born Indian, Oberon Press (Ottawa, Ontario, Canada), 1981.

Shoeless Joe (novel; based on title story in *Shoeless Joe Jackson Comes to Iowa*), Houghton Mifflin (Boston, MA), 1982.

The Ballad of the Public Trustee (chapbook), Standard Editions (Vancouver, British Columbia, Canada), 1982.

The Moccasin Telegraph (stories), Penguin Canada (Toronto, Ontario, Canada), 1983, published as *The Moccasin Telegraph and Other Indian Tales*, David Godine (Boston, MA), 1984, published as *The Moccasin Telegraph and Other Stories*, Penguin Books (New York, NY), 1985.

The Thrill of the Grass (chapbook), Standard Editions (Vancouver, British Columbia, Canada), 1984, new edition with additional stories, Penguin Books (New York, NY), 1984.

The Alligator Report (stories), Coffee House Press (Minneapolis, MN), 1985.

The Iowa Baseball Confederacy (novel), Houghton Mifflin (Boston, MA), 1986.

Five Stories (stories), illustrations by Carel Moiseiwitsch, Tanks (Vancouver, British Columbia, Canada), 1986.

The Fencepost Chronicles (stories), Totem Press (Don Mills, Ontario, Canada), 1986, Houghton Mifflin (Boston, MA), 1987.

Red Wolf, Red Wolf (stories), Collins (Toronto, Ontario, Canada), 1987.

The Further Adventures of Slugger McBatt: Baseball Stories by W.P. Kinsella, Collins (Toronto, Ontario, Canada), 1987, Houghton Mifflin (Boston, MA), 1988, reprinted as *Go the Distance,* Southern Methodist University Press (Dallas, Texas), 1995.

(With wife, Ann Knight) *The Rainbow Warehouse* (poetry), Pottersfield Press (East Lawrencetown, Nova Scotia, Canada), 1989.

Two Spirits Soar: The Art of Allen Sapp: The Inspiration of Allan Godor (art book), Stoddart (Toronto, Ontario, Canada), 1990.

The Miss Hobbema Pageant, HarperCollins (Toronto, Ontario, Canada), 1990.

The First and Last Annual Six Towns Area Old Timers' Baseball Game, wood engravings by Gaylord Schanilec, Coffee House Press (Minneapolis, MN), 1991.

Box Socials (novel), HarperCollins (Toronto, Ontario, Canada), 1992, Ballantine (New York, NY), 1993.

(With Furman Bisher and Dave Perkins) *A Series for the World: Baseball's First International Fall Classic,* Woodford Press (San Francisco, CA), 1992.

The Dixon Cornbelt League, and Other Baseball Stories, HarperCollins (Toronto, Ontario, Canada), 1993, HarperCollins (New York, NY), 1995.

Even at This Distance, Pottersfield Press (East Lawrencetown, Nova Scotia, Canada), 1994.

Brother Frank's Gospel Hour (stories), HarperCollins (Toronto, Ontario, Canada), 1994, Southern Methodist University Press (Dallas, TX), 1996.

(Author of introduction) Peter Williams, *When the Giants Were Giants: Bill Terry and the Golden Age of New York Baseball* (stories), Algonquin Books of Chapel Hill (Chapel Hill, NC), 1994.

The Winter Helen Dropped By (novel), HarperCollins (Toronto, Ontario, Canada), 1995.

If Wishes Were Horses, HarperCollins (Toronto, Ontario, Canada), 1996.

Magic Time, Doubleday Canada (Toronto, Ontario, Canada), 1998, Voyageur Press (Stillwater, MN), 2001.

The Silas Stories, HarperCollins (Toronto, Ontario, Canada), 1998.

The Secret of the Northern Lights, Thistledown Press (Saskatoon, Saskatchewan, Canada), 1998.

Japanese Baseball, and Other Stories, Thistledown Press (Saskatoon, Saskatchewan, Canada), 2000.

(Editor, contributor, and author of introduction) *Baseball Fantastic: Stories,* Quarry Press (Kingston, Ontario, Canada), 2000.

Contributor to *Ergo!: The Bumbershoot Literary Magazine,* edited by Judith Roche, Bumbershoot, 1991, and to numerous anthologies. Also author of foreword to *Hummers, Knucklers, and Slow Curves: Contemporary Baseball Poems,* edited by Don Johnson, University of Illinois Press (Champaign, IL), 1991.

ADAPTATIONS: Shoeless Joe was adapted and produced as the motion picture *Field of Dreams,* released in 1989 by Universal; *Shoeless Joe* was also optioned for musical-stage adaptation by Dreamfields Ltd.; *Dance Me Outside* was produced as a motion picture by Norman Jewison in 1995; *The Iowa Baseball Confederacy* was adapted for sound recording by New Letters, 1986; "Lieberman in Love" in *Red Wolf, Red Wolf* was adapted and produced as a short film by Christine Lahti for Chanticleer Films; *The Dixon Cornbelt League* was optioned for motion picture by Sony/TriStar.

SIDELIGHTS: Canadian author W.P. Kinsella has won an international readership with his imaginative fiction. Some of Kinsella's short stories follow the daily escapades of characters living on a Cree Indian reservation, while some of his longer works, including *Shoeless Joe* and *The Iowa Baseball Confederacy,* mix magic and the mundane in epic baseball encounters. A determined writer who published his first story collection at the age of forty-two, Kinsella has won numerous awards, and his books have been adapted into successful films, such as *Field of Dreams.*

A Cree Indian named Silas Ermineskin brought Kinsella his first literary recognition, beginning in 1974. Ermineskin was the most prominent member of a large cast of characters Kinsella created in a series of stories based on a government reservation for the Cree people. Kinsella portrayed this life in nearly one hundred stories, collected in *Dance Me Outside, Scars, Born Indian,* and *The Moccasin Telegraph.* Both Canadian and U.S. critics expressed admiration for what Kinsella accomplished in these tales. *Prairie Schooner* contributor Frances W. Kaye noted, "W.P. Kinsella is not an Indian, a fact that would not be extraordinary were it not for the stories Kinsella writes about . . . a Cree World. Kinsella's Indians are counterculture figures in the sense that their lives counter the predominant culture of North America, but there is none of the worshipfully inaccurate portrayal of 'the Indians' that has appeared from Fenimore Cooper through Gary Snyder." In *Wascana Review,* George Woodcock likewise cited Kinsella for an approach that "restores proportion and brings an artistic authenticity to the portrayal of contemporary Indian life which we have encountered rarely in recent years." Anthony Brennan offered a similar assessment in *Fiddlehead,* writing that *Dance Me Outside* "is all the more refreshing because it quite consciously eschews ersatz heroics and any kind of nostalgic, mythopoeic reflections on a technicolor golden age."

In 1980 Kinsella published *Shoeless Joe Jackson Comes to Iowa,* a collection of short pieces set in Iowa, urban Canada, and San Francisco. The title story also was selected to appear in an anthology titled *Aurora: New Canadian Writing 1979.* An editor at Houghton Mifflin saw Kinsella's contribution to *Aurora* and contacted the author about expanding the story into a novel. "It was something that hadn't occurred to me at all," Kinsella recalled in *Publishers Weekly.* "I told [the editor], 'I've never written anything longer than 25 pages, but if you want to work with me, I'll try it.'" Much to Kinsella's surprise, the editor agreed. Kinsella set to work expanding "Shoeless Joe Jackson Comes to Iowa," but he decided instead to leave the story intact as the first chapter and build on the plot with a variety of other material. "I enjoyed doing it very much," he said. "They were such wonderful characters I'd created, and I liked being audacious in another way. I put in no sex, no violence, no obscenity, none of that stuff that sells. I wanted to write a book for imaginative readers, an affirmative statement about life."

Shoeless Joe, a novel-length baseball fable set on an Iowa farm, won Kinsella the Houghton Mifflin Literary fellowship in 1982. The story follows a character named Ray Kinsella in his attempts to summon the spirits of the tarnished 1919 Chicago White Sox by building a ballpark in his cornfield. Among the ghostly players lured to Kinsella's perfectly mowed grass is Shoeless Joe Jackson, the White Sox star player who fell in scandal when it was revealed that his team threw the World Series. As the story progresses, the same mysterious loudspeaker voice that suggested construction of the ballpark says, "Ease his pain," and Ray Kinsella sets off to kidnap author J.D. Salinger for a visit to Fenway Park. The novel blends baseball lore with legend and historical figures with fictional characters. "I've mixed in so much, I'm not sure what's real and what's not," Kinsella told *Publishers Weekly,* "but as long as you can convince people you know what you're talking about, it doesn't matter. If you're convincing, they'll believe it."

Kinsella cemented his reputation as a writer of literary merit with *Shoeless Joe.* According to *Los Angeles Times* critic Alan Cheuse, the work "stands as fictional homage to our national pastime, with resonances so American that the book may be grounds for abolishing our northern border." *Detroit News* writer Ben Brown explained, "What we have here is a gentle, unselfconscious fantasy balanced perilously in the air above an Iowa cornfield. It's a balancing act sustained by the absolutely fearless, sentimentality-risking honesty of the author. And it doesn't hurt a bit that he's a master of the language. . . . This is an utterly beautiful piece of work." *Christian Science Monitor* contributor Maggie Lewis stated, "The descriptions of landscape are poetic, and the baseball details will warm fans' hearts and not get in the way of mere fantasy lovers. This book would make great reading on a summer vacation. In fact, this book *is* a summer vacation." But *Washington Post* critic Jonathan Yardley wrote, *Shoeless Joe* "is a book of quite unbelievable self-indulgence, a rambling exercise the only discernible point of which seems to be to demonstrate, ad infinitum and ad nauseam, what a wonderful fellow is its narrator/author."

Kinsella continued to express his fascination with baseball in his 1986 novel, *The Iowa Baseball Confederacy.* Jonathan Webb described the work in *Quill & Quire:* "*The Iowa Baseball Confederacy* contains bigger magic, larger and more spectacular effects, than anything attempted in *Shoeless Joe.* Kinsella is striving for grander meaning: the reconciliation of immovable forces—love and darker emotions—on conflicting courses." Time travel and a ballgame that lasts in excess of 2,600 innings are two of the supernatural events in the story; characters as diverse as Teddy Roosevelt and Leonardo da Vinci make cameo appearances. Chicago *Tribune Books* contributor Gerald Nemanic wrote: "Freighted with mythical machinery, *The Iowa Baseball Confederacy* requires the leavening of some sprightly prose. Kinsella is equal to it. His love for baseball is evident in the lyrical descriptions of the game."

Toronto *Globe and Mail* reviewer William French suggested that Kinsella lifts baseball to a higher plane in his novels. The author, French noted, is "attracted as much to the metaphysical aspects as the physical, intrigued by how baseball transcends time and place and runs like a subterranean stream of consciousness through the past century or so of American history. . . . His baseball novels are animated by a lighthearted wit and bubbling imagination, a respect for mystery and magic." "To be obsessed with baseball is to be touched by grace in Kinsella's universe," wrote Webb, "and a state of grace gives access to magic." Webb felt that in *The Iowa Baseball Confederacy*, Kinsella fails to persuade the reader to go along with his magic. French likewise stated: "In the end [of the novel], Kinsella's various themes don't quite connect. But it hardly matters; we're able to admire the audacity of Kinsella's vision and the sheen of his prose without worrying too much about his ultimate meaning." *Los Angeles Times Book Review* contributor Roger Kahn called *The Iowa Baseball Confederacy* "fun and lyric and poignant."

Although baseball surfaces as a theme in Kinsella's 1991 novel, *Box Socials,* the work primarily revolves around the young narrator, Jamie O'Day, and the quirky characters who live in and around 1940s Fark—a small town near Edmonton, Alberta, Canada. Filled with "crackpots bizarre enough to put [American humorist] Garrison Keillor to shame," commented Joyce R. Slater in Chicago *Tribune Books, Box Socials* features such individuals as Little Wasyl Podolanchuk, one of the only Ukrainian dwarfs in the province; teenaged Truckbox Al McClintock, who once batted against Hall of Fame pitcher Bob Feller; and bachelor Earl J. Rasmussen, who lives in the hills with 600 sheep and delights in belting out "Casey at the Bat" at whim. Reviewers noted that *Box Socials* is essentially a coming-of-age tale about the curious and wide-eyed Jamie, who learns about sex by listening in on the women who gab with his mother, and who attends his first box social and bids on poor, downtrodden Bertha Sigurdson's lunch, even though Velvet Bozniak paid him to bid on hers. "The 'little box social' turns out to be a humdinger," Fannie Flagg stated in the *New York Times Book Review,* "if you've never been to a box social, go to this one. Along with a lot of laughs, we are given a touching and sensitive portrayal of the love, sometimes happy, sometimes heartbreaking, between young men and young women, and experience the pangs of first

love through Jamie's eyes." Other reviewers praised Kinsella's leisurely narrative style. Patrick Goldstein in the *Los Angeles Times Book Review* remarked that *Box Socials* is "a delightful comic ramble, written in a quirky, digressive style that reads like a cross between [American avant-garde writer] Gertrude Stein and [American cartoonist] Al Capp." "If long-winded, seemingly pointless stories make you anxious," pointed out Slater, "Kinsella's not your man. If you're patient enough to stay for the payoff, if you're an admirer of the perfect wry phrase buried in verbiage, he will give you more than your money's worth."

Kinsella once again mixed magic and baseball in his 1993 work, *The Dixon Cornbelt League and Other Baseball Stories.* In this collection of nine stories, Kinsella uses mysticism and conflict to explore human nature. Supernatural events permeate many of the tales: "The Baseball Wolf" shows what happens when a shortstop transforms into a wolf in order to revive his fading career; in "The Fadeaway," even death cannot stop pitcher Christy Mathewson from relaying pitching tips to the Cleveland Indians through a dugout phone. Stephen Smith of *Quill & Quire* noticed the lack of "baseball activity" in *The Dixon Cornbelt League* and instructed the reader to "choose your own baseball imagery" when judging the stories. The story "Eggs" takes on a more realistic and serious topic. "Eggs" is an account of a pitcher's premature retirement due to the loss of his ability to throw a fastball. The pitcher's aspiration to return to baseball is unsupported by his wife and his unhappiness grows. *Publishers Weekly* critic Sybil S. Steinberg appreciated Kinsella's stories because they "read like lightning" and present "fascinating scenarios," yet she felt Kinsella does not fully satisfy his readers, does not offer enough substance or depth in the characters and their stories. Drew Limsky expressed a similar viewpoint in the *Washington Post Book World,* writing that "although Kinsella's voice is frequently winning even after he's run out of ideas, some of the entries are so slight they barely qualify as stories; they seem to belong to some lesser genre—tales or anecdotes, perhaps."

Kinsella has also produced short fiction on a variety of themes. *The Alligator Report,* published in 1985, contains stories that pay homage to surrealist Richard Brautigan, one of Kinsella's favorite authors. In a *Village Voice* review, Jodi Daynard wrote, "Kinsella's new stories replace humor with wit, regional dialect with high prose. . . . He uses surrealism most effectively to highlight the delicate balance between solitude and alienation, not to achieve a comic effect. . . . These are images that resonate—not comic ones, alas, but stirring, not woolly-wild, but urban gothic." *New York Times Book Review* contributor Harry Marten noted that in *The Alligator Report* Kinsella continued "to define a world in which magic and reality combine to make us laugh and think about the perceptions we take for granted."

In his 1994 book of short stories, *Brother Frank's Gospel Hour,* Kinsella revisits the inhabitants of Hobbema, Alberta. Two familiar inhabitants include Silas Ermineskin, a Cree writer, and his comical partner Frank Fencepost. The humorous pair return in the short story "Bull," a lighthearted rendering of an artificial insemination case in the Alberta Supreme Court. The other stories in *Brother Frank* cover a range of topics. "Rain Birds" looks at the results of corporate farming on nature; the reality of child abuse is explored in "Dream Catcher"; a boy ascertains the parallels between the sexes in "Ice Man"; and in "Brother Frank's Gospel Hour" comedy turns a staid gospel show upside down. Critical reaction to *Brother Frank* was predominantly positive. Scott Anderson of *Quill & Quire* credited Kinsella for his "understanding of human foibles" and his revelry in "the inventiveness of the human spirit in adversity."

Kinsella took a break from writing about America's favorite pastime in his 1995 novel, *The Winter Helen Dropped By.* Set in a small town in Alberta, Canada, Kinsella's four-part novel depicts one year during the Great Depression through the eyes of eleven-year-old Jamie O'Day, the narrator of *Box Socials.* "Every story is about sex or death, or sometimes both," begins O'Day as he takes readers through a steady succession of marriages, funerals, pregnancies, and the like. In the novel's first section, an Indian woman arrives at the O'Day's farmhouse in the middle of a blizzard. Another section finds a local widow in the midst of wedding preparations while small-town gossip threatens to muffle the celebration. And Jamie views his parents through childish eyes in "Rosemary's Winter," which Paul J. Robichaud praised in his *Quill & Quire* review as "the strongest section of the novel." Heavy with child, Jamie's mother has to get to town, but the creek has flooded. Her dreamer husband's solution to the dilemma is to construct a sailboat, which in his creative vision he sees as a "wheelless windwagon." While noting that Kinsella sometimes affects a too-down-home air, Robichaud added that *The Winter Helen Dropped By* "affords the reader a glimpse into a world that no longer exists, and provides considerable laughter and feeling while doing so."

Kinsella's literary alter ego, Ray Kinsella, and Gideon Clarke, a character from *The Iowa Baseball Confed-*

eracy, both return in the novel *If Wishes Were Horses,* published in 1996. Their role in this book is to listen to the strange tale of Joe McCoy, a washed-up pitcher who is on the run from the FBI after committing some crimes, including kidnapping. Joe believes that his wrongdoings have been prompted by unseen forces controlling him, and that he has another life more real than the one he has been living through. *Maclean's* reviewer Brian Bethune remarked: "In Kinsella's hands McCoy's colliding lives and ever more hallucinatory situation propel an absorbing story of longing and regret, in which the hero can taste and smell experiences that never happened. It is also very funny."

Kinsella suffered personal troubles in the late 1990s. He became embroiled in a legal case with Evelyn Lau, a writer and former romantic companion of Kinsella's, over a tell-all article she wrote and published detailing their relationship. While engaged in this case, in 1997 Kinsella was struck by a car and suffered the loss of his senses of smell and taste. He also claimed that, although doctors failed to prove a medical reason, injuries suffered in the accident had deprived him of his ability to write creatively. He did publish *Magic Time* in 1998, a novel he had begun six years earlier but never finished to his satisfaction. 'It's far from my best work, but if anybody wants to publish anything. . . . It's like playing baseball: if you get an at-bat, you take what you can,' Kinsella told Stephen Smith in *Saturday Night.* A *Publishers Weekly* reviewer called it "a warmhearted, homespun novel by the award-winning author." The plot takes in the trials and tribulations of a student athlete who ends up in what may be a beautifully disguised prison, and the book "satisfies with its endearing characters and baseball lore," concluded the reviewer.

BIOGRAPHICAL AND CRITICAL SOURCES:

BOOKS

Contemporary Authors Autobiography Series, Volume 7, Thomson Gale (Detroit, MI), 1988.
Contemporary Literary Criticism, Thomson Gale (Detroit, MI), Volume 27, 1984, Volume 43, 1987.
Contemporary Novelists, St. James Press (Detroit, MI), 2001.
Contemporary Popular Writers, St. James Press (Detroit, MI), 1997.
St. James Guide to Fantasy Writers, St. James Press (Detroit, MI), 1996.

PERIODICALS

Booklist, January 15, 1995, Dennis Dodge, review of *The Dixon Cornbelt League and Other Baseball*

Stories, p. 895; March 15, 1995, Ted Hipple, review of the sound recording of *The Iowa Baseball Confederacy,* p. 1343.

Books in Canada, October, 1981; February, 1984; November, 1984; October, 1993, pp. 41-42; September, 1994, pp. 38-39; October, 1995, pp. 45-46.

Canadian Literature, summer, 1982; autumn, 1995, pp. 149-50.

Christian Science Monitor, July 9, 1982.

Detroit Free Press, May 4, 1986.

Detroit News, May 2, 1982; May 16, 1982.

Explicator, spring, 1995, Clarence Jenkins, "Kinsella's *Shoeless Joe,*" p. 179.

Fiddlehead, fall, 1977; spring, 1981.

Globe and Mail (Toronto, Ontario, Canada), November 17, 1984; April 27, 1985; April 12, 1986.

Library Journal, February 1, 1982; November 1, 1990, p. 125; March 1, 1993, p. 85.

Los Angeles Times, August 26, 1982.

Los Angeles Times Book Review, May 23, 1982; July 6, 1986; March 29, 1992, p. 6.

Maclean's, May 11, 1981; April 19, 1982; July 23, 1984; May 1, 1989, p. 66; November 11, 1991, Victor Dwyer, review of *Box Socials,* p. 90; July 12, 1993, pp. 60-61; December 16, 1996, Brian Bethune, review of *If Wishes Were Horses,* p. 69; March 16, 1998, "From Love Story to Lawsuit," p. 12.

National Review, October 24, 1986, Mike Shannon, review of *The Iowa Baseball Confederacy,* p. 60.

Newsweek, August 23, 1982.

New York Review of Books, November 5, 192, pp. 41-45.

New York Times Book Review, July 25, 1982; September 2, 1984; January 5, 1986; April 20, 1986; May 19, 1991, p. 36; March 1, 1992, p. 29; July 12, 1992, p. 33; December 19, 1993, p. 14.

Prairie Schooner, spring, 1979.

Publishers Weekly, April 16, 1982; October 19, 1990, Penny Kaganoff, review of *Red Wolf, Red Wolf,* p. 53; March 2, 1992, review of *Box Socials,* p. 48; September 27, 1993, review of *Shoeless Joe Jackson Comes to Iowa,* p. 58; December 5, 1994, review of *The Dixon Cornbelt League,* pp. 65-66; February 13, 1995, p. 18; October 29, 2001, review of *Magic Time,* p. 36.

Quill & Quire, June, 1982; September, 1984; April, 1986; December, 1991, p. 17; June, 1993, p. 27; July, 1994, p. 94; September, 1995, p. 68.

Saturday Night, August, 1986, pp. 45-47; September, 1999, Stephen Smith, "A Loss for Words," p. 14.

Seattle Times, May 6, 1999, "*Shoeless Joe* Author Files B.C. Suit," p. B2.

Tribune Books (Chicago, IL), April 25, 1982; March 30, 1986; May 3, 1992, p. 6.

Village Voice, December 4, 1984; April 1, 1986.

Wascana Review, fall, 1976.

Washington Post, March 31, 1982.

Washington Post Book World, March 30, 1995, p. 4.

*   *   *

KITTEL, Frederick August
See WILSON, August

*   *   *

KIZER, Carolyn 1925-
(Carolyn Ashley Kizer)

PERSONAL: Born December 10, 1925, in Spokane, WA; daughter of Benjamin Hamilton (a lawyer and planner) and Mabel (a biologist and professor; maiden name, Ashley) Kizer; married Charles Stimson Bullitt, January 16, 1948 (divorced, 1954); married John Marshall Woodbridge (an architect and planner), April 11, 1975; children: (first marriage) Ashley Ann, Scott, Jill Hamilton. *Education:* Sarah Lawrence College, B.A., 1945; graduate study at Columbia University, 1945-46, and University of Washington, 1946-47; studied poetry with Theodore Roethke, University of Washington, Seattle, 1953-54. *Politics:* Independent. *Religion:* Episcopalian.

ADDRESSES: Home—19772 Eighth St. E, Sonoma, CA 95476; Paris, France.

CAREER: Poet, educator, and critic. *Poetry Northwest,* Seattle, WA, founder and editor, 1959-65; National Endowment for the Arts, Washington, DC, first director of literary programs, 1966-70; University of North Carolina at Chapel Hill, poet-in-residence, 1970-74; Ohio University, Athens, McGuffey Lecturer and poet-in-residence, 1975; Iowa Writer's Workshop, University of Iowa, Iowa City, professor of poetry, 1976; University of Maryland, College Park, professor, 1976-77; Stanford University, Stanford, CA, professor of poetry, spring, 1986; Princeton University, Princeton, NJ, senior fellow in the humanities, fall, 1986; Fannie Hurst Professor of Literature at Washington University, St. Louis, MO, 1971; lecturer at Barnard College, spring, 1972; acting director of graduate writing program at Columbia University, 1972; visiting professor of writing, University of Arizona, Tucson, 1989, 1990, and

University of California—Davis, 1991; Coal Royalty Chair, University of Alabama, 1995. Participant in International Poetry Festivals, London, England, 1960, 1970, Yugoslavia, 1969, 1970, Pakistan, 1969, Rotterdam, Netherlands, 1970, Knokke-le-Zut, Belgium, 1970, Bordeaux, 1992, Dublin, 1993, and Glasgow, 1994. Volunteer worker for American Friends Service Committee, 1960; specialist in literature for U.S. State Department in Pakistan, 1964-65; director of literary programs for the National Endowment for the Arts; poet-in-residence at the University of North Carolina and Ohio University. Member of founding board of directors of Seattle Community Psychiatric Clinic.

MEMBER: International PEN, Amnesty International, Association of Literary Magazines of America (founding member), Poetry Society of America, Poets and Writers, Academy of American Poets (chancellor), American Civil Liberties Union.

AWARDS, HONORS: Masefield Prize, Poetry Society of America, 1983; Washington State Governors Award, and San Francisco Arts Commission award, both 1984, both for *Mermaids in the Basement: Poems for Women*; award in literature, American Academy and Institute of Arts and Letters, 1985; Pulitzer Prize in poetry, 1985, for *Yin: New Poems*; Frost Medal, Poetry Society of America, Theodore Roethke Memorial Foundation Poetry Award, and President's Medal, Eastern Washington University, all 1988; D.Litt., Whitman College, 1986, St. Andrew's College, 1989, Mills College, 1990, and Washington State University, 1991.

WRITINGS:

POETRY

Poems, Portland Art Museum (Portland, OR), 1959.
The Ungrateful Garden, Indiana University Press (Bloomington, IN)), 1961.
Knock upon Silence, Doubleday (New York, NY), 1965.
Midnight Was My Cry: New and Selected Poems, Doubleday (New York, NY), 1971.
Mermaids in the Basement: Poems for Women, Copper Canyon Press (Port Townsend, WA), 1984.
Yin: New Poems (contains selections from *Mermaids in the Basement*), BOA Editions (Brockport, NY), 1984.
The Nearness of You: Poems for Men, Copper Canyon Press (Port Townsend, WA), 1986.

Harping On: Poems 1985-1995, Copper Canyon Press (Port Townsend, WA), 1996.
Cool, Calm, & Collected: Poems 1960-2000, Copper Canyon Press (Port Townsend, WA), 2000.
Pro Femina: A Poem, University of Missouri Press (Kansas City, MO), 2000.
(Coeditor) *American Poetry: The Twentieth Century*, Library of America (New York, NY), 2000.

OTHER

(Editor, with Elaine Dallman and Barbara Gelpi) *Woman Poet—The West*, Women-in-Literature (Reno, NV), 1980.
(Editor) Robertson Peterson, *Leaving Taos*, Harper (New York, NY), 1981.
(Editor) Muriel Weston, *Primitive Places*, Owl Creek Press (Seattle, WA), 1987.
(Translator) *Carrying Over* (poetry), Copper Canyon Press (Port Townsend, WA), 1988.
(Editor) *The Essential John Clare*, Ecco Press (Hopewell, NJ), 1992.
Proses: Essays on Poems & Poets, Copper Canyon Press (Port Townsend, WA), 1993.
(Editor) *One Hundred Great Poems by Women*, Ecco Press (Hopewell, NJ), 1995.
Picking and Choosing: Essays on Prose, Eastern Washington University Press (Cheney, WA), 1995.
(Compiler and author of introduction) Jeffrey Greene, *American Spiritualists*, Northeastern University Press (Boston, MA), 1998.

Contributor to numerous anthologies, including *New Poems by American Poets*, Ballantine (New York, NY), 1957; *New Poets of England and America*, Meridian Publishing (Salinas, CA), 1962; *Anthology of Modern Poetry*, Hutchinson (London, England), 1963; *Erotic Poetry*, Random House (New York, NY), 1963; and *New Modern Poetry*, Macmillan (New York, NY), 1967.

Translator of *Sept versants, sept syllables* (title means "Seven Sides, Seven Syllables"). Also contributor to various periodicals, including *Poetry, New Yorker, Kenyon Review, Spectator, Paris Review, Shenandoah, Antaeus, Grand Street*, and *Poetry East*.

SIDELIGHTS: Although Carolyn Kizer's poetry collections are not vast in number, they bear witness to her much-praised meticulousness and versatility. Critics noted although that Kizer's subject matter has changed over the years, the caliber of her art has remained high.

In 1985 her collection *Yin: New Poems*—twelve years in the making—won the Pulitzer Prize in poetry. Kizer is "a writer to treasure," maintained Elizabeth B. House in a *Dictionary of Literary Biography* essay. "She has created poetry that will endure. . . . Faced with the human inevitability of loss and destruction, Kizer, in both poetry and life, celebrates the joys of art, friendship, family, and good works. Undoubtedly, she has earned a secure niche in American letters."

"Like some people, Carolyn Kizer is many people," noted *Washington Post* reviewer Meryle Secrest. Kizer received her B.A. degree from Sarah Lawrence College in 1945 and then went on to do graduate work at both Columbia University and the University of Washington. During the mid-1950s, she studied poetry at the University of Washington under the tutelage of Theodore Roethke. According to *American Women Writers*, Kizer believes that it was "her study of the craft with Theodore Roethke at the University of Washington in the early 1950s that finally turned her into a self-assured poet." Later, Kizer cofounded the prestigious Seattle-based *Poetry Northwest*, a journal she edited from its inception in 1959 until 1965. In 1964 Kizer went to Pakistan as a U.S. State Department specialist and taught at various institutions, including the distinguished Kinnaird College for Women. Among her other activities, Kizer was the first director of literary programs for the newly created National Endowment for the Arts in 1966, a position she held until 1970. As literary director, she promoted programs to aid struggling writers and literary journals, and she worked to have poetry read aloud in inner city schools. In addition to teaching and lecturing nationwide, Kizer has translated Urdu, Chinese, and Japanese poetry. According to Kizer, "What is so marvelous about living today is that it is possible to extend, like a flower, spreading petals in all directions," recorded Secrest.

House claimed that, as a poet, Kizer deals equally well with subjects that have often been treated by women and those that have not. "Tensions between humans and nature, civilization and chaos," are topics no more and no less congenial to her than are love affairs, children, and women's rights. According to House, in Kizer's first two poetry collections, *The Ungrateful Garden* and *Knock upon Silence*, the poet employs grotesque imagery—"lice cozily snuggling in a captured bat's wing, carrion birds devouring the last pulp of hell-bound bodies," and other unsettling topics—but the poet is not fearful of femininity and sentimentality. Sometime in the past, Roethke composed a list of common complaints made against women poets that included such things as lack of sense of humor, narrow range of subject matter, lamenting the lot of women, and refusing to face up to existence. In *Alone with America: Essays on the Art of Poetry in the United States since 1950,* Richard Howard maintained that Kizer has first incurred and then overcome these complaints. "She does not fear—indeed she *wants*—to do all the things Roethke says women are blamed for, and indeed I think she does do them. . . . But doing them or not, being *determined* to do them makes her a different kind of poet from the one who manages to avoid the traps of his condition, and gives her a different kind of success," noted Howard.

The Ungrateful Garden, Kizer's first major collection, appeared in 1961. Devoted in large part to the examination of people's relationships to nature, it is a candid work, according to *Saturday Review* critic Robert D. Spector. Because "candor is hardly ever gentle, her shocking images are brutal," the critic continued. Kizer "abuses adult vanity by setting it alongside a child's ability to endure the removal of an eye. Pretensions to immortality are reduced to rubbish by 'Beer cans on headstones, eggshells in the [cemetery] grass.'" In the title poem and in one of her better-known pieces, "The Great Blue Heron," Kizer presents her belief that nature has no malevolence toward man, that the two simply exist side by side. In "The Great Blue Heron," according to House, "the heron is a harbinger of death, but [Kizer] never suggests that the bird is evil. As part of nature, he merely reflects the cycle of life and death that time imposes on all living creatures."

In *The Ungrateful Garden,* House also observed Kizer emphasizing the distance between humans and nature, and also the perils of modern governments quashing individual identity. Kizer demonstrates that a reprieve from the terrors of nature and government can be found in human relationships, and especially in poetry. In the poem "From an Artist's House," for example, the poet celebrates the unchanging nature of verse. On the whole, D.J. Enright of the *New Statesman* feels there are "some remarkably good things in this strong-tasting collection, thick with catastrophes and fortitude."

Whereas *Poetry* critic William Dickey considered *The Ungrateful Garden* to showcase a poet "more concerned with the manner of [her poems'] expression than with the material to be expressed," *Saturday Review* contributor Richard Moore commented that Kizer's third poetry collection, *Knock upon Silence,* contains relaxed meters and simple diction: "There are no verbal fireworks, no fancy displays." As with much of Kizer's poetry, an Eastern influence is present in *Knock upon Si-*

lence, with its calm, cool, sensitive verse. The collection consists of two long poems—"A Month in Summer" and "Pro Femina"—a section called "Chinese Imitations," and several translations of the eighth-century Chinese poet Tu Fu. "She's at the top of her form, which is to say, devastating in her observations of the human animal," wrote Gene Baro in the New York Times Book Review. "How true, one thinks, when this poet writes about feminine sensibility or about love."

Of the two longer poems included in Knock upon Silence, "A Month in Summer" received mixed reviews. This diary of love gone sour, which contains both prose segments and occasional haiku, is viewed by Moore as the "weakest part of [Kizer's] book. . . . It is moving in places, witty in others; but there is also a tendency to be straggling and repetitive." In contrast, Bewley cited this piece as "the heart and triumph" of Knock upon Silence: "It manages to compress within a very few pages alive with self-irony and submerged humor, more than most good novelists can encompass in a volume."

The other long selection in Knock upon Silence, "Pro Femina," is comprised of three conversational poems that discuss the role of the liberated woman in the modern world, particularly the woman writer. "Pro Femina" is a satiric piece keenly aware of the fact that women still confront obstacles related to their gender: "Keeping our heads and our pride while remaining unmarried; / And if wedded, kill guilt in its tracks when we stack up the dishes / And defect to the typewriter."

Kizer turns, in part, to different matters in her collection Midnight Was My Cry: New and Selected Poems, which contains several previously published poems and sixteen new ones. Though she remains dedicated to meter and Eastern restraint—"the poet's mind continually judges, restrains, makes passion control itself," wrote Eric Mottram in Parnassus—her newer poems express an interest in the social and political problems of the contemporary world, especially those of the 1960s. These poems center on antisegregation sit-ins, the Vietnam conflict, and the assassination of Senator Robert Kennedy. For Poetry contributor Richard Howard, Kizer has "reinforced her canon by some dozen first-rate poems, observant, solicitous, lithe."

Catching the literary world a little by surprise, Kizer published two poetry volumes in 1984, Mermaids in the Basement: Poems for Women and Yin: New Poems. Mermaids in the Basement received minor critical attention, perhaps because it contains several poems from her pre-

vious collections, including "A Month in Summer" and "Pro Femina," the latter one of her best-known poems satirizing as it does liberated women writers by mimicking the hexameter used by the ancient misogynist poet Juvenal. According to Patricia Hampl in the New York Times Book Review, "the craft for which . . . Kizer is known serves her well in [the poem] 'Thrall'; a remarkable compression allows her to review the entire disappointing history of her relationship with her father. . . . There is a great effort toward humor in these poems. But the tone is uneven; the humor, as well as the outrage, seems arch at times." Yin, in contrast, received a favorable critical reception from the outset, winning the Pulitzer Prize for poetry in 1985. "One could never say with certainty what 'a Carolyn Kizer poem' was—until now. . . . Now we know a Kizer poem is brave, witty, passionate, and not easily forgotten," contended Poetry critic Robert Phillips.

The word "yin" is Chinese for the feminine principle, and many of the poems in this award-winning collection focus on feminine perceptions and creativity. In her joint review of Mermaids in the Basement and Yin, Hampl considered the prose memoir in Yin titled "A Muse" to be "a real find. . . . This piece, about . . . Kizer's extraordinary mother, is not only a fascinating portrait, but a model of detachment and self-revelation." "A Muse" examined Kizer's childhood feelings about the ambitions her mother had for her: "The poet describes a . . . mama smothering her precocious offspring with encouragement. . . . Only with the woman's death does the speaker's serious life as an artist begin," assessed Joel Conarroe in the Washington Post Book World. In addition, "Semele Recycled" is considered an imaginative treat with its description of a modern-day Semele symbolically torn apart at the sight of her lover and then made whole again.

Probably the most admired piece in the Yin collection is the poem "Fanny." Written in Roman hexameter, this 224-line poem is the proposed diary of Robert Louis Stevenson's wife, Frances (Fanny), as she nurses her husband during the last years of his life. Remarked Kizer in Penelope Moffet's Los Angeles Times review: "'Fanny' is about what happens to women who are the surrogate of gifted men. Women who look after the great writers, whether mothers, sisters, wives, or daughters. What they do with their creativity, because they can't engage in open or active competition. I think 'Fanny' [is] a political poem, if you consider feminism a political issue, as I do." In addition, Conarroe claimed "Fanny" is "Keatsian in the sensuousness of its imagery, the laughing of its odors and textures. Kizer gives a shattering sense of a woman's sacrifice and isolation while communicating vividly the terrible beauty of the woman's obsession with her husband's health." Whereas Suzanne Juhasz in *Library Journal* considered *Yin* a "mixed bag, or blessing," most reviewers agree with Phillips that *Yin* "is a marvelous book."

Kizer's *The Nearness of You* serves as a "companion piece" to *Mermaids in the Basement*, as it is a collection of poetry on men. According to Charles Libby in the *New York Times Book Review*, the collection "shows evidence that writing about the other sex involves different struggles than writing about one's own. Despite many local triumphs, the new collection is in many ways less striking, technically and psychologically more self-conscious [than *Mermaids in the Basement*]." In *Contemporary Women Poets*, essayist John Montague noted, with relief, "In an era when a shrill feminism threatens to tilt the scales of past injustice, Kizer's view of the sexual universe contains polarity without hostility." Meanwhile Diane Wakoski, appraising *The Nearness of You* for the *Women's Review of Books*, found the work somewhat uneven, but concluded, "What this book convinces me of, finally, is that Carolyn Kizer is a poet of occasion, of person and personality. When she becomes historical or formal, when she attempts either love-lyrics or story poems, she is mediocre at best. . . . But as the ambassador of goodwill in the poetry world . . . as the woman longing for a family of artists and intellectuals who will replace the one she lost in growing up and leaving her father—yes, yes, yes. Believable, strong, someone who deserves to be remembered."

Kizer's subsequent collection, *Harping On: Poems 1985-1995*, was not published until 1996. Christine Stenstrom, writing for *Library Journal*, noted that Kizer's "political poems satisfy less than those vividly recalling parents and friends in small masterpieces of verse narrative." In *Publishers Weekly*, a critic described Kizer's voice in the book as "distinctly irreverent," her politics "left-leaning," and noted of her poetry that "Kizer employs everything from slanted rhymes to venerable forms like the villanelle and pantoum with a chatty grace that makes the intricacy of her structures all but invisible." Commenting on the satire that wires its way throughout the poems in *Harping On*, *New Leader* reviewer Phoebe Pettingell maintained that while the poet comes across as a "clever, tough-minded, and erudite" harpy "exercising her slashing wit on herself as often as others," the poetry scene of the 1990s "needs her voice, whether hectoring, prophesying, seducing, or informing, to raise our consciousness with the eloquence of her subtle lyrics."

Kizer's essays and criticism have been gathered in several volumes, including 1994's *Proses: Essays on Poems and Poets*. Kate Fitzsimmons, reviewing the book for the *San Francisco Review of Books*, found Kizer's writing to be engaging. "The joy Kizer experiences in reading other poets is infectious," Fitzsimmons concluded. "Whether she is writing about the lives of poets or their poetry, her enthusiasm for their work is evident, nearly tactile." While Doris Lynch in *Library Journal* praised the effort, a *Publishers Weekly* reviewer was less impressed, commenting that if the book had been written by a more-obscure writer, "it would fade quickly into blessed obscurity."

Antioch Review critic Carol Moldaw called Kizer's *Cool, Calm & Collected: Poems 1960-2000*, "consistently and fearlessly irreverent," and noted that Kizer uses "wit and irony to drive her points home." She added that "almost all of her poems have points, the way roses have thorns." Moldaw continued, "Kizer's poetic voice is one of the most engagingly warm human voices we have, and it would be a mistake to take this enormous, if hard to define, feat for granted. While in her poems from the 50s, Kizer has already begun to stake out the territory she will later make her own . . . and by the 60s she is already writing 'Chinese Imitations,'" but "it is in the 70s and 80s that you feel her hit her stride." Robert Phillips of the *Houston Chronicle* noted that *Cool, Calm & Collected* appears in Kizer's seventy-fifth year and that it "ranks among her best." He observed that one of Kizer's greatest strengths is her use of mythology. "Rather than dragging out the usual versions of the familiar tales, she goes the sources of the myths with surprising results," he explained.

Writing in *Booklist* Ray Olson observed that "Kizer's four decades of work demonstrate a highly skilled and witty formal poet who yet has been an avant-gardist thematically. Well before many others, she adopted the personae of goddesses in poems that remain more feminine and more feminist than many poems published yesterday." In the same publication, Patricia Monaghan reflected that Kizer "has produced dozens of tender, passionate poems of age and loss. . . . The stately power of her verse has never failed her."

Although the more pointed aspects of her verse are often couched in sarcasm and stylistic intricacy, Kizer considers herself a political poet. As she remarked to Moffet: "Because I do not feel that [it] is a steady undercurrent, just as feminism is, there are these parallel streams that I hope infuse everything that I do. And I find that stream getting more and more strong in my work. But I don't ever want to be hortatory or propagandistic." With regard to the quantity of poetic output—Kizer is not known for being especially prolific herself—she had this to say to inexperienced poets: "I think a lot of younger poets get terrible anxiety that they'll be forgotten if they don't have a book all the time. Well, maybe they will be forgotten, but if they're any good they'll come back."

In an interview with Allan Jalon for the *Los Angeles Times*, Kizer explained her writing style: "I'm not a formalist, not a confessional poet, not strictly a free-verse poet." Jalon described Kizer as, "Tough without being cold, sometimes satirical (she's a great admirer of Alexander Pope)," and noted that "her work expresses a wordly largeness that repeatedly focuses on the points at which lives meet. 'That's my subject,'" concluded Kizer. "No matter how brief an encounter you have with anybody, you both change."

BIOGRAPHICAL AND CRITICAL SOURCES:

BOOKS

Contemporary Authors Autobiography Series, Volume 5, Thomson Gale (Detroit, MI)), 1987.
Contemporary Literary Criticism, Thomson Gale (Detroit, MI), Volume 15, 1980, Volume 39, 1986.
Contemporary Women Poets, St. James Press (Detroit, MI), 1997.
Dictionary of Literary Biography, Volume 169: *American Poets since World War II, Fifth Series,* Thomson Gale (Detroit, MI), 1996.
Encyclopedia of American Literature, Continuum (New York, NY), 1999.
Howard, Richard, *Alone with America: Essays on the Art of Poetry in the United States since 1950,* Atheneum (New York, NY), 1969.
Kizer, Carolyn, *The Ungrateful Garden,* Indiana University Press (Bloomington, IN), 1961.
Kizer, Carolyn, *Knock upon Silence,* Doubleday (New York, NY), 1965.
Malkoff, Karl, *Crowell's Handbook of Contemporary American Poetry,* Crowell (New York, NY), 1973.
Rigsbee, David, editor, *An Answering Music: On the Poetry of Carolyn Kizer,* Ford-Brown (Boston, MA), 1990.

PERIODICALS

Antioch Review, winter, 2002, Carol Moldaw, review of *Cool, Calm & Collected: Poems, 1960-2000,* p. 166.
Approach, spring, 1966.
Booklist, November 1, 2000, Patricia Monoghan, review of *Cool, Calm & Collected,* p. 513; March 15, 2001, Ray Olson, review of *Cool, Calm & Collected,* p. 1349.
Hollins Critic, June, 1997.
Houston Chronicle, December 24, 2000, Robert Phillips, "Two Modern Masters: Collected Poems of Kizer, Kunitz, Prove Luminary Works," p. 13.
Hudson Review, spring, 1972; summer, 1985, pp. 327-340; summer, 2001, R.S. Gwynn, *Cool, Calm & Collected,* p. 341.
Library Journal, July, 1984; November 1, 1993, p. 93; July, 1996, p. 120; April 1, 2000, Daniel L. Guillory, review of *American Poetry: The Twentieth Century,* p. 105.
Los Angeles Times, January 13, 1985; March 5, 2001, Allan M. Jalon, "Everything, Forever, Everything Is Changed; A Glimpse of Einstein, the Bombing of Hiroshima, the Plight of Women; Moments Are Blazing Images in Carolyn Kizer's Poetry."
Michigan Quarterly Review, John Taylor, "Cool? Calm? Collected? A Meditation of Carolyn Kizer's Poetry," p. 162-173.
New Leader, February 254, 1997, p. 14.
New Statesman, August 31, 1962.
New York Review of Books, March 31, 1966; September 21, 2000, Brad Leithauser, review of *American Poetry,* pp. 70-74.
New York Times Book Review, March 26, 1967; November 25, 1984; March 22, 1987, p. 23; December 17, 2000, Melanie Rehak, "Freedom and Poetry," p. 23; April 2, 2000, William H. Pritchard, "Eliot, Frost, Ma Rainey, and the Rest," p. 10.
Paris Review, spring, 2000, Barbara Thompson, "Carolyn Kizer: The Art of Poetry," pp. 344-346.
Parnassus, fall-winter, 1972.
Poetry, November, 1961; July, 1966; August, 1972; March, 1985; November, 1985.
Prairie Schooner, fall, 1964.
Publishers Weekly, October 18, 1993, p. 70; August 26, 1996, p. 94; September 18, 2000, review of *Cool, Calm, & Collected,* p. 105.
San Francisco Chronicle, March 30, 2002, "Milosz, Straight Win California Book Awards," p. D5.
San Francisco Review of Books, October-November, 1994, p. 20.
Saturday Review, July 22, 1961; December 25, 1965.
Shenandoah, winter, 1966.
Tri-Quarterly, fall, 1966.
Village Voice, November 5, 1996.
Washington Post, February 6, 1968.
Washington Post Book World, August 5, 1984; February 1, 1987, p. 6.

Women's Review of Books, September, 1987, p. 6.
World Literature Today, summer, 1997.

ONLINE

Academy of American Poets Web site, http://www.poets.
org/poets/ (May 13, 2003), "Carolyn Kizer."
St. Martin's Press Web site, http://www.bedford
stmartins.com/ (May 13, 2003), "Carolyn Kizer."

* * *

KIZER, Carolyn Ashley
   ### See KIZER, Carolyn

* * *

KNIGHT, Etheridge 1931(?)-1991

PERSONAL: Born April 19, 1931 (one source says c. 1934), in Corinth, MS, USA; died of lung cancer, March 10, 1991, in Indianapolis, IN, USA; son of Bushie and Belzora (Cozart) Knight; married Sonia Sanchez (divorced); married Mary Ann McAnally, June 11, 1973 (divorced); married Charlene Blackburn; children: (second marriage) Mary Tandiwe, Etheridge Bambata; (third marriage) Isaac Bushie; (stepchildren) Morani Sanchez, Mongou Sanchez, Anita Sanchez. *Education:* Attended high school for two years; self-educated at "various prisons, jails." *Politics:* "Freedom." *Religion:* "Freedom."

CAREER: Poet. Writer-in-residence, University of Pittsburgh, Pittsburgh, PA, 1968-69, and University of Hartford, Hartford, CT, 1969-70; Lincoln University, Jefferson City, MO, poet-in-residence, 1972. Inmate at Indiana State Prison, Michigan City, 1960-68. *Military service:* U.S. Army, 1947-51, served in Guam, Hawaii, and Korea; became medical technician.

AWARDS, HONORS: National Endowment for the Arts grants, 1972 and 1980; National Book Award and Pulitzer Prize nominations, both 1973, for *Belly Song and Other Poems;* Self-development through the Arts grant, for local workshops, 1974; Guggenheim fellowship, 1974; American Book Award, Before Columbus Foundation, 1987, for *The Essential Etheridge Knight;* Shelly Award, Poetry Society of America.

WRITINGS:

(Contributor) *For Malcolm,* Broadside Press (Detroit, MI), 1967.

Poems from Prison, preface by Gwendolyn Brooks, Broadside Press (Detroit, MI), 1968.
(With others) *Voce Negre dal Carcere* (anthology), [Laterza, Italy], 1968, original English edition published as *Black Voices from Prison,* introduction by Roberto Giammanco, Pathfinder Press (New York, NY), 1970.
A Poem for Brother/Man (after His Recovery from an O.D.), Broadside Press (Detroit, MI), 1972.
Belly Song and Other Poems, Broadside Press (Detroit, MI), 1973.
Born of a Woman: New and Selected Poems, Houghton Mifflin (Boston, MA), 1980.
The Essential Etheridge Knight, University of Pittsburgh Press (Pittsburgh, PA), 1986.
Donald Hall and Etheridge Knight Reading Their Own Poems, (sound recording), Library of Congress (Washington, D.C.), 1986.

Ethheridge Knight, (sound recording), poems read by the author and broadcast on the radio program *New Letters on the Air,* 1986.

Work represented in many anthologies, including *Norton Anthology of American Poets, Black Poets, A Broadside Treasury, Broadside Poet, Dices and Black Bones,* and *A Comprehensive Anthology of Black Poets.* Contributor of poems and articles to many magazines and journals, including *Black Digest, Essence, Motive, American Report* and *American Poetry.* Poetry editor, *Motive,* 1969-71; contributing editor, *New Letters,* 1974.

SIDELIGHTS: Etheridge Knight began writing poetry while an inmate at the Indiana State Prison and published his first collection, *Poems from Prison* in 1968. "His work was hailed by black writers and critics as another excellent example of the powerful truth of blackness in art," wrote Shirley Lumpkin in the *Dictionary of Literary Biography.* "His work became important in African American poetry and poetics and in the strain of Anglo-American poetry descended from Walt Whitman." Knight attained recognition as a major poet, earning both Pulitzer Prize and National Book Award nominations for *Belly Song and Other Poems* as well as the acclaim of such fellow practitioners as Gwendolyn Brooks, Robert Bly, and Galway Kinnell.

When Knight entered prison, he was already an accomplished reciter of "toasts"—long, memorized, narrative poems, often in rhymed couplets, in which "sexual exploits, drug activities, and violent aggressive conflicts involving a cast of familiar folk . . . are related . . . using street slang, drug and other specialized argot, and often obscenities," explained Lumpkin. Toast-reciting at Indiana State Prison not only refined Knight's expertise in this traditional African American art form but also, according to Lumpkin, gave him a sense of identity and an understanding of the possibilities of poetry. "Since toast-telling brought him into genuine communion with others, he felt that poetry could simultaneously show him who he was and connect him with other people." In an article for the *Detroit Free Press* about Dudley Randall, the founder of Broadside Press, Suzanne Dolezal indicated that Randall was impressed with Knight and visited him frequently at the prison: "In a small room reserved for consultations with death row inmates, with iron doors slamming and prisoners shouting in the background, Randall convinced a hesitant Knight of his talent." And, said Dolezal, Randall felt that because Knight was from the streets, "He may be a deeper poet than many of the others because he has felt more anguish."

Much of Knight's prison poetry, according to Patricia Liggins Hill in *Black American Literature Forum,* focused on imprisonment as a form of contemporary enslavement and looks for ways in which one can be free despite incarceration. Time and space are significant in the concept of imprisonment, and Hill indicated that "specifically, what Knight relies on for his prison poetry are various temporal/spatial elements which allow him to merge his personal consciousness with the consciousness of Black people." Hill believed that this merging of consciousness "sets him apart from the other new Black poets . . . [who] see themselves as poets/priests. . . . Knight sees himself as being one with Black people." Randall observed in *Broadside Memories: Poets I Have Known* that "Knight does not objure rime like many contemporary poets. He says the average Black man in the streets defines poetry as something that rimes, and Knight appeals to the folk by riming." Randall also noted that while Knight's poetry was "influenced by the folk," it was also "prized by other poets."

Knight's *Born of a Woman: New and Selected Poems* included work from *Poems from Prison, Black Voices from Prison* and *Belly Song and Other Poems.* Although David Pinckney stated in *Parnassus* that the "new poems do not indicate much artistic growth," a *Virginia Quarterly Review* contributor wrote that Knight "has distinguished his voice and craftsmanship among contemporary poets, and he deserves a large, serious audience for his work." Moreover, H. Bruce Franklin sug-

gested in the *Village Voice* that with *Born of a Woman*, "Knight has finally attained recognition as a major poet." Further, Franklin credited Knight's leadership "in developing a powerful literary mode based on the rhythms of black street talk, blues, ballads, and 'toasts.'"

Reviewing *Born of a Woman* for *Black American Literature Forum* Hill described Knight as a "masterful blues singer, a singer whose life has been 'full of trouble' and thus whose songs resound a variety of blues moods, feelings, and experiences and later take on the specific form of a blues musical composition." Lumpkin suggested that an "awareness of the significance of form governed Knight's arrangement of the poems in the volume as well as his revisions. . . . He put them in clusters or groupings under titles which are musical variations on the book's essential theme—life inside and outside prison." Calling this structure a "jazz composition mode," Lumpkin also noted that it was once used by Langston Hughes in an arrangement of his poetry. Craig Werner observed in *Obsidian: Black Literature in Review:* "Technically, Knight merges musical rhythms with traditional metrical devices, reflecting the assertion of an Afro-American cultural identity within a Euro-American context. Thematically, he denies that the figures of the singer . . . and the warrior . . . are or can be separate." Lumpkin found that "despite the pain and evil described and attacked, a celebration and an affirmation of life run through the volume." And in the *Los Angeles Times Book Review*, Peter Clothier considered the poems to be "tools for self-discovery and discovery of the world—a loud announcement of the truths they pry loose."

Lumpkin pointed out that "some critics find Knight's use of . . . [language] objectionable and unpoetic and think he does not use verse forms well," and some believed that he "maintains an outmoded, strident black power rhetoric from the 1960s." However, Lumpkin concluded: "Those with reservations and those who admire his work all agree . . . upon his vital language and the range of his subject matter. They all agree that he brings a needed freshness to poetry, particularly in his extraordinary ability to move an audience. . . . A number of poets . . . consider him a major Afro-American poet because of his human subject matter, his combination of traditional techniques with an expertise in using rhythmic and oral speech patterns, and his ability to feel and to project his feelings into a poetic structure that moves others."

Knight once commented that he believed a definition of art and aesthetics assumes that "every man is the master of his own destiny and comes to grips with the society by his own efforts. The 'true' artist is supposed to examine his own experience of this process as a reflection of his self, his ego." Knight felt "white society denies art, because art unifies rather than separates; it brings people together instead of alienating them." He commented that the Western/European aesthetic dictates that "the artist speak only of the beautiful (himself and what *he sees*); his task is to edify the listener, to make him see *beauty* of the world." Rather, he believed, Black artists must stay away from this because "the red of this aesthetic rose got its color from the blood of black slaves, exterminated Indians, napalmed Vietnamese children." According to Knight, the black artist must "perceive and conceptualize the collective aspirations, the collective vision of black people, and through his art form give back to the people the truth that he has gotten from them. He must sing to them of their own deeds, and misdeeds."

In 1992, a play titled *And Now My Soul Can Sing!,* written by Knight's sister, Eunice Knight-Bowens and presented by The Etheridge Knight Festival of the Arts and the Indiana Historical Society, was staged in Indianapolis, Indiana. The play, described by a writer for the Indianapolis *Recorder* as a "creative, humanistic, artistic, educational, entertaining and historical docudrama" chronicles the obstacles Knight was faced with and overcame during his life.

BIOGRAPHICAL AND CRITICAL SOURCES:

BOOKS

Contemporary Literary Criticism, Volume 40, Thomson Gale (Detroit, MI), 1986.
Dictionary of Literary Biography, Volume 41: *Afro-American Poets since 1955,* Thomson Gale (Detroit, MI), 1985.
Randall, Dudley, *Broadside Memories: Poets I Have Known,* Broadside Press (Detroit, MI), 1975.

PERIODICALS

Black American Literature Forum, fall, 1980; summer, 1981, Patricia Liggins Hill, review of *Born of a Woman: New and Selected Poems.*
Black World, September, 1970; September, 1974.
Detroit Free Press, April 11, 1982, Suzanne Dolezal.
Hollins Critic, December, 1981.
Los Angeles Times Book Review, August 10, 1980, Peter Clothier, review of *Born of a Woman.*
Negro Digest, January, 1968; July, 1968.
Obsidian, summer and winter, 1981, Craig Werner, review of *Born of a Woman.*
Parnassus, spring-summer, 1981, David Pinckney, reviw of *Born of a Woman.*
Recorder, (Indianapolis, IN), "Voice of Poet Etheridge Knight Heard in Life's Song," section C, p. 3.
Village Voice, July 27, 1982, H. Bruce Franklin, review of *Born of a Woman.*
Virginia Quarterly Review, winter, 1981.

OBITUARIES:

PERIODICALS

New York Times, March 14, 1991, Gerald C. Fraser, "Elderidge Knight Is Dead at 57; Began Writing Poems in Prison," section D, p. 24.

*   *   *

KNOWLES, John 1926-2001

PERSONAL: Born September 16, 1926, in Fairmont, WV; died following a short illness November 29, 2001, near Fort Lauderdale, FL; son of James Myron and Mary Beatrice (Shea) Knowles. *Education:* Graduate of Phillips Exeter Academy, 1945; Yale University, B.A., 1949.

CAREER: Hartford Courant, Hartford, CT, reporter, 1950-52; freelance writer, 1952-56; *Holiday,* associate editor, 1956-60; full-time writer, beginning 1960. Writer-in-residence at University of North Carolina at Chapel Hill, 1963-64, and Princeton University, 1968-69. Taught creative writing at Florida Atlantic University, beginning c. 1986.

AWARDS, HONORS: Rosenthal Award from National Institute of Arts and Letters, and William Faulkner Foundation Award, both 1960, for *A Separate Peace.*

WRITINGS:

A Separate Peace (novel), Macmillan (New York, NY), 1960, reprinted, Rinehart and Winston (Austin, TX), 2000.
Morning in Antibes (novel), Macmillan (New York, NY), 1962.

Double Vision: American Thoughts Abroad (travel), Macmillan (New York, NY), 1964.

Indian Summer (novel), Random House (New York, NY), 1966.

Phineas (short stories), Random House (New York, NY), 1968.

The Paragon (novel), Random House (New York, NY), 1971.

Spreading Fires (novel), Random House (New York, NY), 1974.

A Vein of Riches (novel), Little, Brown (Boston, MA), 1978.

Peace Breaks Out (novel), Holt (New York, NY), 1981.

A Stolen Past (novel), Holt (New York, NY), 1983.

The Private Life of Axie Reed (novel), Dutton, 1986.

Backcasts: Memories and Recollections of Seventy Years as a Sportsman (memoir), Wilderness Adventure Books, 1993.

ADAPTATIONS: A Separate Peace was adapted as a film by Paramount Pictures in 1972, and was recorded as an audiobook, Audio Bookshelf, 2002.

SIDELIGHTS: John Knowles is an acclaimed American novelist whose first—and most famous—novel, *A Separate Peace,* received both the Faulkner Foundation Prize and the Rosenthal Award of the National Institute of Arts and Letters. *A Separate Peace* is Knowles' most lyrical work, describing in rich, evocative language the idyllic lives of school boys during the first years of American involvement in World War II. The plot is deceptively simple. The narrator, Gene Forrester, and his friend, Phineas (Finny), are both students at Devon, an Eastern seaboard private school much like Exeter, which Knowles attended. Gene is the more conscientious student of the two, and Phineas the more athletically and socially gifted. Though their bond is a strong one, it eventually suffers from competition. Gene, growing increasingly resentful of Phineas's popularity, finally causes him crippling injury by pushing him from a tree. A kangaroo court session ensues, with Gene accused of deliberately injuring Phineas, who leaves suddenly, again injures himself, and dies during surgery.

From this episode, Gene eventually accepts the necessity of exploring himself based upon his admission of guilt. Jay L. Halio, writing about *A Separate Peace* in *Studies in Short Fiction,* observed that "the prevailing attitude seems to be that before man can be redeemed back into social life, he must first come to terms with himself." The setting and plot of *A Separate Peace* play upon a series of contrasts between negative and positive elements, the combination of which stresses the need to tolerate, understand, and integrate radically opposing perceptions and experiences. The school itself stands between two rivers, the Devon and the Naguamsett, one pure and fresh, the other ugly and dirty. As James Ellis concluded in the *English Journal,* the Devon symbolizes Eden, a place of joy and happiness, while the Naguamsett indicates a landscape destroyed by personal greed and callousness toward the environment. The winds of war, blowing just beyond the lives of the boys, and the battle between Gene and Phineas encapsulated Knowles' twin purposes: to both explore the competing sides of an individual's personality and to imply that the conflict of nations is an extension of self-conflict and the antipathy one person feels toward another.

These internal and external conflicts result from fear, whether based on hatred, inadequacy, exposure, or rejection. This view of life as a battle between two opposing selves, persons, or camps—the solution being acceptance and love of others—is the most dominant theme in Knowles' fiction. It first appears in *A Separate Peace,* but it is never far from the center of his subsequent works.

Published twenty-two years after *A Separate Peace,* Knowles' *Peace Breaks Out* promised to "take its place alongside the earlier books as a fine novel," Dick Abrahamson maintained in the *English Journal.* Knowles' second Devon School novel takes place in 1945, and its main character and center of consciousness is Pete Hallam, a young teacher of history and physical education who has returned from World War II. Hallam has not only been wounded, captured, and incarcerated in a prison camp, but has also been abandoned by his wife. Because of the traumas he has suffered, he is not always articulate and tends to be somewhat cynical in his attempt to retreat into the past. Although also essentially romantic in nature, he has lost the ability to love, and he returns to Devon to lay the past to rest and to regain some sense of love and compassion.

At Devon the innocence Hallam remembers from his days as a student is now missing. Schoolboys, too, have been affected by the war—or perhaps Pete has simply matured enough through his own suffering to recognize the flaws in human nature. The conflict that helps Pete to understand himself is between two bright, articulate, and bitter students, Hochschwender and Wexford, who "hated each other. But also and simultaneously they seemed to hate something about themselves. There was a curious, fundamental similarity between them which made their mutual aversion almost incendiary." Bright and insecure, Hochschwender riles the other students with his outrageous statements about German superiority and his denial of the atrocities of World War II. Motivated in part by his insignificant Wisconsin background, his obviously Germanic name, and his fears of rejection, Hockschwender primarily assumes this position to test the tolerance of others, believing that under the surface of American liberalism is a strong strain of intolerance and bigotry. He is correct, and he himself becomes the target of that bigotry.

A second group of Knowles' novels—*Indian Summer, A Stolen Past,* and *The Paragon*— deals with Wexford-like characters who have power and authority generated by money, which becomes a substitute for human warmth and sexual expression. The forum for this exploration is no longer Devon but Yale University and its immediate environs. All three novels depend upon the mutually reinforcing opposition between the rich and the middle class, the quest for money and the desire for a good life, and excessive rationality and healthy sexuality.

Second only to *A Separate Peace* in critical acclaim, Knowles' *Indian Summer* concerns Cleet Kinsolving and his gradual realization of the emptiness of wealth and position. The spontaneous, impulsive, and intuitive Cleet, grandson of an Indian woman, contrasts with the more controlled, rational, spoiled, and mercantile Neil Reardon. Unlike many of Knowles' characters, Cleet understands himself: to "roll out his life full force" meant "to be strong, to be happy, to be physically tired at night, to land sex at one and the same time, to be proud of himself." When Cleet follows his native instincts, he feels complete and satisfied; when he becomes trapped in the rationalist-mercantile pursuits of others, he nearly destroys himself. Related to this view of the self is the perception of place. The Midwest and West are equated with personal freedom and lack of social restraint; Connecticut and the East are equated with acquisitiveness, self-denial, and atrophying social conventions.

After his discharge from the Army Air Force in 1946, Cleet takes a job in Kansas, working for a small crop-dusting firm and living in a tiny motel cabin. This Thoreau-like existence under the "vaults and domes of sky" emphasizes a simple, natural life, undiminished by material possessions. Here, in the midwest, Cleet's feelings and senses—his sight, hearing, taste, and sexuality—are at their finest. What Cleet fears most is the entrapment symbolized by the East. The appearance in Kansas of his childhood friend, Neil Reardon, realizes those fears. Cleet, in accepting Neil's offer of a

$200-per-week job in Cleet's home town of Wetherford, sells himself out to the Eastern establishment. Neil embodies the lust for acquisition, and he uses emotional attachments, generosity, loyalty, and philanthropy for his own ends so that they become deception, bribery, ambition, and willfulness. His marriage is empty, and his books and lectures merely hide his fear of failure. Even his desire to have a son is born of fear, and is in reality a need to ensure material immortality against an uncertain future.

Although the fictional narrator of Knowles' 1983 novel *A Stolen Past* has also been born in the East (Maryland) and educated there (at Devon and Yale), he has been no more faithful to it than Cleet. As a mature adult recalling his college experiences, Allan Prieston is realistic, knowing that he can never totally recapture the past; but he is also philosophical, understanding that the past will take its toll unless fully recognized and incorporated. A writer, Allan attempts to find his own literary voice and separate himself from his formative influences, notably mentor Reeves Lockhart. Allan recalls Reeves as an exceptional teacher, but in dignifying Reeve's memory, Allan failed to understand the loneliness, alcoholism, and crippling perfectionism that also plagued this teacher. By coming to terms with Reeves's weaknesses, however, Allan is better able to deal with his own limitations and feelings of inadequacy so that he can finally affirm himself as a "mischievous, conniving rascal and a cheat: a writer."

Whereas Allan's friendship with Reeves represents the possibilities and limitations of the mentor-student relationship, his friendship with Greg Trouvenskoy addresses peer admiration. Initially Allan idolizes Greg's maturity, good looks, popularity with men and women, and background. The son of noble Russians who escaped the Bolshevik revolution, Greg conveys a sense of wealth and prestige, punctuated by the family's possession of the wonderful Militsa diamond, their sole remaining treasure from the grand days in St. Petersburg. Handsome and elegant, full of wonderful stories of the Romanoffs and other Russian figures, Greg's parents fulfill Allan's every exotic impulse. They also make him aware of the weaknesses of the aristocratic, feudal system, for they have been dispossessed and are now U.S. citizens and New Deal Democrats. They have survived because they have the inner resources to make the transition from wealth and power to more average social positions.

In *The Paragon* main character Louis Colfax learns that individual people and events together create history. Of a family that had been rich in the nineteenth century,

Louis grows up with few material advantages and is surrounded by family members who are psychologically and socially damaged—passive, pious, repressive, oppressive, and alcoholic. Louis feels himself psychologically impaired by his environment. In his many despairing moments he withdraws and hopes to put an end to the cycle of biological and environmental determinism. In the end, he recognizes that his problems have been determined not only by his bizarre family but also by his own independent character and actions.

In *The Paragon* Knowles suggests that each person and culture has a repressed side referred to as "the animal inside the human." Indeed, in talking with his fiancée Charlotte Mills, Louis says, "I love you too much, like a man *and* like a woman. . . . I think I'm a lesbian." He believes she has her masculine side, just as he has his feminine side, and that both must be recognized and embraced. Knowles implies that all human beings have these opposing characteristics, one often suppressing another and destroying the balanced personality, and he suggests that this is even true of institutions and nations. Juxtaposed against male institutional power in *The Paragon* is the power of nature. The image of an Hawaiian volcano represents for Louis all of nature's raw power: "This was the ultimate, uncontrollable force on earth. No fence could stop it, no wall, no channel. No will could stop it, no bomb." *The Paragon,* then, pits the masculine against the feminine, the rational against the emotional, and the institutional against the natural.

Despite *The Paragon*'s complexity, critics have not been altogether appreciative of the book. Jonathan Yardley stated in the *New Republic* that he liked the novel but found it derivative of *A Separate Peace* and inherently false in tone. James Aronson in the *Antioch Review* agreed: "the dialogue is faked and stagey, the characters are stereotyped, the parallels between 1950 and 1970 are tritely obvious, and the shape of the novel is curiously disjointed." However, Webster Schott in the *New York Times Book Review,* found much to admire, especially in the conception of the protagonist: "the title is important. It's not 'A Paragon.' It's 'The Paragon.' And Knowles's model or pattern of perfection for youth and manhood is a seeking, nonconforming, erratically brilliant and socially maladjusted college student. For Knowles the perfect model must be less than perfect. Not an irony. A moral position."

In *A Vein of Riches* Knowles presents his strongest indictment of the rich by sympathetically portraying West Virginia miners who struck against rapacious coal bar-

ons between 1918 and 1921. The Catherwood family—Clarkson, Minnie, and Lyle—represent the attitudes of other mine-owner families towards the laboring classes and their own family affairs. The first part of the book primarily centers on the Catherwoods' views of the strikers, black servants, and the economy; the second, on the family's increasing financial difficulties and their problems in discovering personal fulfillment and meaning. In their personal roles and attitudes to others, the Catherwoods become a microcosm of the ownership class-what the strikers call "bloated capitalists" and "economic royalists." Shortsighted and greedy, they do not have the ability to manage the mines and guarantee prosperity and calm in both good times and bad.

Morning in Antibes, the first of Knowles' Mediterranean novels, treats class conflict, marital issues, and international relations. Here the setting is Juan-les-Pins on the Riviera, the playground of the rich from America—Nicholas and Liliane Bodine and Jimmy Smoot; France—Marc, Constance, and Titou de la Croie; and elsewhere. In contrast to the rich, those who work on the Riviera—the restaurateurs and servants, even the transvestites who participate in nightclub acts—are faced with arduous work schedules, little money, and the scorn of their patrons.

Also set in Southern France, *Spreading Fires* is a gothic tale of insanity and guilt, and in it Knowles explores deeply seated sexual attitudes. The book's protagonist is Brendan Lucas, a well-heeled American diplomat who rents a spacious villa overlooking the Mediterranean near Cannes. This area exudes sexuality in "the musky air, the sticky sea, the sensuous food, the sensual wine." Although Brendan does not overtly share in that pervasive spirit, he has, as Christopher Lehmann-Haupt put it in the *New York Times* "unresolved Oedipal rage" and homosexual anxieties. The conflict between sexuality and repression serves as the central issue of the book. For Knowles, sexual emotion is a side of the self that must be recognized.

Though best known for his novels, Knowles also produced *Phineas,* a collection of stories about adolescent boys and young men reaching a greater understanding of life. James P. Degman of the *Kenyon Review* admired Knowles' dramatization of the torments of sensitive and intelligent adolescents, particularly in the stories "Phineas," "A Turn with the Sun," and "Summer Street." An early version of the scene from *A Separate Peace* in which the narrator causes Finny to fall from a tree, "Phineas" focuses upon the narrator's attempts at confession and reconciliation. "A Turn with the Sun," set like "Phineas" at the Devon School, portrays an alienated young protagonist whose beautiful dive into a cold river ironically consolidates his relationship with his comrades and brings on his death. "Summer Street," in which a young boy copes with his anxieties about the birth of a sister, treats the development of imagination-both the quality of wonder and enchantment, as well as the fear of the unknown. Some people, Knowles implies in his story, have little imagination and will be mired in their environment; others suppress their imagination and lose access to a rich world; still others have this talent but need to foster and channel it so that it does not prove an instrument of evasion.

Conflicting personality traits, genders, and ways of functioning infuse all of Knowles' fictional work, as well as his nonfiction book, *Double Vision: American Thoughts Abroad*. In this travel account, Knowles shares with readers his impressions of Arab spontaneity and Greek hospitality, but he also criticizes the United States' puritanical Protestant habits, repressed sexuality, tendency toward violence in its cities, and unfair distribution of jobs and wealth. Knowles' own personal apprehensions and fear about the strangeness of Arab culture, its "paralyzed battlefield," raises another theme: the American fear of other cultures. This fear of the unknown, the strangeness of other people, is, the author implies, deeply human, but especially characteristic of Americans. Yet Knowles was not altogether negative about the United States and its ideals. In his book he expresses appreciation for American directness and honesty, the great energy of its people, and the security of governmental stability. He ends his book with the hope that that the United States would, with time, create a civilization in harmony with nature, one that would stress tolerance and equal rights for African Americans and women.

Knowles once noted that *A Separate Peace* was rather an albatross; in the eyes of critics as well as, perhaps, his own, nothing he produced ever equaled it. However, he also recognized that the novel, published so early in his career, allowed him to do as he wished the rest of his life. His final novel, *The Private Life of Axie Reed*, was published in 1986. His final published work, the memoir *Backcasts: Memories and Recollections of Seventy Years as a Sportsman*, was published seven years later, in 1993.

BIOGRAPHICAL AND CRITICAL SOURCES:

BOOKS

Bryant, Hallman Bell, *A Separate Peace: The War Within*, 1990.

Contemporary Literary Criticism, Thomson Gale (Detroit), Volume 1, 1973, Volume 4, 1975, Volume 10, 1979.

Dictionary of Literary Biography, Volume 6: *American Novelists since World War II,* Thomson Gale (Detroit, MI), 1980.

PERIODICALS

American Film, July-August, 1987, pp. 36-41.
Booklist, February 15, 1992, p. 1119.
Book Week, July 24, 1966.
Clearing House, September, 1973.
Commonweal, December 9, 1960.
English Journal, April, 1969; December, 1969.
Esquire, April, 1988, pp. 174-181.
Harper's, July, 1966.
Life, August 5, 1966.
Los Angeles Times, April 2, 1981; May 2, 1986; August 27, 1986.
Los Angeles Times Book Review, August 28, 1983.
Manchester Guardian, May 1, 1959.
New Statesman, May 2, 1959.
Newsweek, April 20, 1981.
New York Times, February 3, 1978; April 16, 1986.
New York Times Book Review, February 7, 1960; August 14, 1966; June 4, 1978; March 22, 1981; October 17, 1982; October 30, 1983; May 11, 1986.
Saturday Review, August 13, 1966.
Time, April 6, 1981.
Times Literary Supplement, May 1, 1959; August 31, 1984.
Tribune Books (Chicago, IL), March 29, 1981.
Washington Post Book World, March 15, 1981.

OBITUARIES:

PERIODICALS

Chicago Tribune, December 1, 2001, sec. 1, p. 23; December 2, 2001, sec. 4, p. 9.
Los Angeles Times, December 1, 2001, p. B20.
New York Times, December 1, 2001, p. A25.
Times (London, England), December 21, 2001.
U.S. News & World Report, December 10, 2001, p. 6.
Washington Post, December 1, 2001, p. B7.

*   *   *

KNOX, Calvin M.
See SILVERBERG, Robert

KNYE, Cassandra
    See DISCH, Thomas M.

*   *   *

KOCH, Kenneth 1925-2002

PERSONAL: Surname is pronounced "coke"; born February 27, 1925, in Cincinnati, OH; died of leukemia, July 6, 2002, in New York, NY; son of Stuart J. and Lillian Amy (Loth) Koch; married Mary Janice Elwood, June 12, 1954 (died, 1981); married Karen Culler, December 29, 1994; children: Katherine. *Education:* Harvard University, A.B., 1948; Columbia University, M.A., 1953, Ph.D., 1959.

CAREER: Rutgers University, Newark, NJ, lecturer, 1953-58; Brooklyn College (now of the City University of New York), Brooklyn, NY, lecturer, 1957-59; Columbia University, New York, NY, assistant professor, 1959-66, associate professor, 1966-71, professor of English and comparative literature, beginning 1971. Director of Poetry Workshop at New School for Social Research (now New School University), 1958-66. Exhibitions of Koch's collaborative work were held at the Ipswich Museum, England, 1993, at the Tibor de Nagy Gallery, New York, NY, 1994, and at Guild Hall, East Hampton, NY, 2000. *Military service:* U.S. Army, 1943-46.

MEMBER: American Academy of Arts and Letters.

AWARDS, HONORS: Fulbright fellow, 1950-51, 1978, and 1982; Guggenheim fellow, 1960-61; grant from National Endowment for the Arts, 1966; Ingram Merrill Foundation fellow, 1969; Harbison Award, 1970, for teaching; Frank O'Hara Prize, 1973, for *Poetry;* Christopher Book Award and Ohioana Book Award, both 1974, both for *Rose, Where Did You Get That Red?;* National Institute of Arts and Letters award, 1976; Award of Merit for Poetry, American Academy and Institute of Arts and Letters, 1986; National Book Critics Circle nomination, 1988, for *One Thousand Avant-garde Plays;* Bollingen Prize, Yale University, 1995; Rebekah Johnson Bobbitt National Prize for Poetry, Library of Congress, 1996, for *One Train: Poems;* named chevalier, Ordre des Arts et des Lettres (France), 1999; National Book Award finalist, 2000, for *New Address;* Levinson Prize, *Poetry,* 2000.

WRITINGS:

POETRY

Poems, Tibor de Nagy Gallery (New York, NY), 1953.

Ko; or, A Season on Earth (also see below), Grove (New York, NY), 1959.

Permanently, Tiber Press, 1960.

Thank You and Other Poems, Grove (New York, NY), 1962.

Poems from 1952 and 1953 (limited edition), Black Sparrow Press (Santa Barbara, CA), 1968.

The Pleasures of Peace and Other Poems, Grove (New York, NY), 1969.

When the Sun Tries to Go On, Black Sparrow Press (Santa Barbara, CA), 1969.

Sleeping with Women (limited edition), Black Sparrow Press (Santa Barbara, CA), 1969.

The Art of Love, Random House (New York, NY), 1975.

The Duplications (also see below), Random House (New York, NY), 1977.

The Burning Mystery of Anna in 1951, Random House (New York, NY), 1979.

Days and Nights, Random House (New York, NY), 1982.

Selected Poems, 1950-1982, Random House (New York, NY), 1985.

On the Edge, Viking (New York, NY), 1986.

Seasons on Earth (includes *Ko; or, A Season on Earth* and *The Duplications*), Penguin (New York, NY), 1987.

Selected Poems, Carcanet (Manchester, England), 1991.

One Train: Poems, Knopf (New York, NY).

On the Great Atlantic Rainway: Selected Poems, 1950-1988, Knopf (New York, NY), 1994.

Straits: Poems, Knopf (New York, NY), 1998.

New Addresses: Poems, Knopf (New York, NY), 2000.

Sun Out: Selected Poems, 1952-54, Knopf (New York, NY), 2002.

A Possible World, Knopf (New York, NY), 2002.

FICTION

(With Alex Katz) *Interlocking Lives,* Kulchur Foundation (New York, NY), 1970.

The Red Robins (also see below), Random House (New York, NY), 1975.

Hotel Lambosa and Other Stories, Coffee House Press (Minneapolis, MN), 1993.

NONFICTION

Wishes, Lies, and Dreams: Teaching Children to Write Poetry, Chelsea House (New York, NY), 1970.

Rose, Where Did You Get That Red?: Teaching Great Poetry to Children, Random House (New York, NY), 1973.

I Never Told Anybody: Teaching Poetry Writing in a Nursing Home, Random House (New York, NY), 1977, revised edition, Teachers and Writers Collaborative (New York, NY), 1997.

(With Kate Farrell) *Sleeping on the Wing: An Anthology of Modern Poetry, with Essays on Reading and Writing,* Random House (New York, NY), 1981.

(With Kate Farrell) *Talking to the Sun: An Illustrated Anthology of Poems for Young People,* Metropolitan Museum of Art/Holt (New York, NY), 1985.

The Art of Poetry (literary criticism), University of Michigan Press (Ann Arbor, MI), 1996.

Making Your Own Days: The Pleasures of Reading and Writing Poetry, Scribner (New York, NY), 1998.

Koch's works have been translated into French and Italian.

PLAYS

Little Red Riding Hood, produced in New York, NY, 1953.

Bertha (also see below), produced in New York, NY, 1959; produced as an opera, music by Ned Rorem, 1971.

Pericles (also see below), produced off-Broadway, 1960.

The Election (also see below), produced in New York, NY, 1960.

George Washington Crossing the Delaware (also see below), produced off-Broadway, 1962.

The Construction of Boston (also see below), produced off-Broadway, 1962; produced in Boston as an opera, music by Scott Wheeler, 1990–91.

Guinevere; or, The Death of the Kangaroo (also see below), produced in New York, NY, 1964.

The Tinguely Machine Mystery; or, The Love Suicides at Kaluka (also see below), produced in New York, NY, 1965.

The Moon Balloon (also see below), produced in New York's Central Park, 1969.

The Artist (opera; based on poem of the same title), music by Paul Reif), produced in New York, NY, 1972.

A Little Light, produced in Amagansett, NY, 1972.

The Gold Standard (also see below), produced in New York, NY, 1975.

Rooster Redivivus, produced in Garnerville, NY, 1975.

The Red Robins (based on novel of the same title; produced in New York, NY, 1978), Theatre Arts, 1979.

The New Diana, produced in New York, NY, 1984.

A Change of Hearts (opera; also see below), produced in New York, NY, 1985.

Popeye among the Polar Bears, produced in New York, NY, 1986.

(With composer Marcello Panni) *The Banquet,* produced in Bremen, Germany, 1998.

OMNIBUS VOLUMES; PLAYS

Bertha and Other Plays (also see below; includes *Bertha, Pericles, George Washington Crossing the Delaware, The Construction of Boston, The Return of Yellowmay, The Revolt of the Giant Animals, The Building of Florence, Angelica, The Merry Stones, The Academic Murders, Easter, The Lost Feed, Mexico, Coil Supreme, The Gold Standard,* and *Guinevere; or, The Death of the Kangaroo*), Grove (New York, NY), 1966.

A Change of Hearts: Plays, Films, and Other Dramatic Works, 1951-1971 (also see below; contains *Bertha and Other Plays, A Change of Hearts, The Tinguely Machine Mystery; or, The Love Suicides at Kaluka, The Moon Balloon, E. Kology, Without Kinship, Youth, The Enchantment,* and the film scripts *Because, The Color Game, Mountains and Electricity, Sheep Harbor, Oval Gold, Moby Dick, L'école normale, The Cemetery, The Scotty Dog,* and *The Apple*), Random House (New York, NY), 1973.

One Thousand Avant-garde Plays (produced in New York, NY, 1987), Knopf (New York, NY), 1988.

The Gold Standard: A Book of Plays, Knopf (New York, NY), 1996.

OTHER

(Editor, with others, and author of introduction) Joseph Ceravolo, *The Green Lake Is Awake: Selected Poems,* Coffee House Press (Minneapolis, MN), 1994.

Contributor to *Penguin Modern Poets 24,* Penguin, 1974; contributor of fiction, poetry, and plays to magazines, including *Art and Literature, Locus Solus, Poetry, Raritan, Grand Street,* and *New York Review of Books.* Member of editorial board of *Locus Solus,* 1960-62.

ADAPTATIONS: The Art of Love was adapted for stage by Mike Nussbaum and produced in Chicago, IL, 1976.

SIDELIGHTS: Prize-winning author Kenneth Koch published numerous collections of poetry, avant-garde plays, and short fiction while also serving as one of the nation's best-known creative writing teachers during a career that spanned over five decades. Associated with the New York School of poetry for most of his career, Koch used surrealism, satire, irony, and an element of surprise in many of his poems. However, "his satires are more than mere jokes," explained Roberta Berke in her *Bounds out of Bounds: A Compass for Recent American and British Poetry:* "They have a serious purpose of literary and social criticism." Koch explored an assortment of emotions in his poetry, but in an era seemingly dedicated to deep seriousness he refused to relinquish lightness or a sense of humor. According to Phoebe Pettingell in *New Leader,* Koch's works "convey his perennial freshness in at least two senses of that word: novelty and cheekiness. He has a subtle grasp of the nuances of language as well as a gift for hilarious parody, and behind his casual, friendly manner there is formidable technique and learning."

During his career, Koch was called "the funniest serious poet we have," by David Lehman in *Newsweek.* Although Peter Stitt maintained in *Georgia Review* that the author's "greatest commitment as a poet is to not making very much sense, to not taking things very seriously," other critics contend that Koch's poetry has an underlying seriousness and have praised his imagination and originality. Koch's "playfulness, in tone and technique, has often caused him to be underrated," stated *Salmagundi* contributor Paul Zweig. "But it is just his great capacity for humor, based on so much more than mere irony, that makes him important. He has reclaimed the humorous for serious writers of poetry and for that we are in his debt." David Lehman, in his book *The Last Avant-garde,* commented that Koch "had the misfortune to be a protean comic genius at the moment when the lyric poem [was] the be-all and end-all of verse and [was] mistakenly held to be incompatible with the spirit of comedy."

Koch himself once addressed the idea of comic poetry in an interview with Jordan Davis, published in Koch's *The Art of Poetry.* "Some readers think of a poem as a sort of ceremony—a funeral, a wedding—where anything comic is out of order. They expect certain feelings to be touched on in certain conventional ways. Dissociation, even obscurity, may be tolerated, but only as long as the tone remains solemn or sad enough." Koch continued, "There may be a perfectly serious poem, a good poem . . . and some other person writes a parody of it and one line of the parody may have more truth than the whole original poem, or at least be freer to

reach the intoxicating heights that sometimes seem where truth is from."

Koch is credited as being one of the founders of the New York School of poetry, which came into existence in the 1950s. At the time, the poets who were working within the "school"—including John Ashbery, Frank O'Hara, and Koch, among others—hardly considered themselves trend-setters. The name "New York School" was coined for them by Donald Allen for an anthology he was editing in the late 1950s, and it suggested a spirit of novelty and experimentation that well suited its young practitioners. "The so-called New York School assembled its own outsider identity from some of the same sources as the Beats: an urban male savvy, sometimes inflected with Jewish and gay sensibilities, and an openness to avant-garde work in other media," explained Christopher Benfey in *New Republic.* According to Benfey, Koch was "a conspicuous member of the New York School, often chronicling its exploits and mourning its losses." *Dictionary of Literary Biography* contributor Michael Adams observed that Koch "characterized the New York School style as 'anti-traditional, opposed to certain heavy uses of irony and symbolism.'" Adams also quoted Koch as saying, "I think we may have been more conscious than many poets of the surface of the poem, and what was going on while we were writing and how we were using words."

Like other poets of the New York School, Koch used stream-of-consciousness in his writing and stressed the importance of the present moment and the ordinary. In his essay in *Comic Relief: Humor in Contemporary American Literature,* John Vernon pointed out that Koch, "like most poets of the New York school, . . . often spices his poems with references to pop culture, deliberate clichés, archaisms, or both academic and romantic phrases and words." Pettingell, for one, concluded that these pop references and personal asides notwithstanding, Koch's work continues to stand the test of time quite well. "Today, Robert Lowell and Allen Ginsberg are looking pretty hoary to the students of Generation X, and Eliot seems as remote as the late Victorian authors," the critic maintained. "The joke is that those bards of the passing scene, Ashbery and Koch, continue to flourish. Indeed, today they appear to exemplify the tenets of postmodernism."

Koch's first book of poetry, titled simply *Poems,* first sparked the critical debate over the seriousness of his work. Finding the book "tasteless, futile, noisy and *dull,*" Harry Roskolenko further contended in *Poetry* that "Koch writes lazy verse and is precious and puerile." This negative review prompted a rebuttal from writer Frank O'Hara, who asserted in *Poetry* that Koch "has the other poetic gift: vivacity and go, originality of perception and intoxication with life. Most important of all, he is not *dull.*" *Washington Post Book World* contributor Michael Lally agreed, claiming that "Koch's work is always entertaining and usually enlightening." The poems in Koch's debut work cover a diversity of subjects; F.W. Dupee claimed in *New York Review of Books* that "Koch is fond of making poetry out of poetry-resistant stuff. Locks, lipsticks, business letterheads, walnuts, lunch and fudge attract him; so do examples of inept slang, silly sentiment, brutal behavior and stereotyped exotica and erotica." Employing the bizarre humor of surrealism and the techniques of abstract expressionism, Koch crafted poems that emphasize form and sound. The words Koch selects to present his subjects surge together "like an express train of exuberant sounds," observed *Poetry* contributor David Lehman, adding that "the poet takes a great deal of delight in the sounds of words and his consciousness of them; he splashes them like paint on a page with enthusiastic puns, internal rhymes, titles of books, names of friends . . . and seems surprised as we are at the often witty outcome."

Koch seemed to thrive on the intensity in writing a new poem, and many of his verses deal with the poetic imagination and the act of creation. *Poetry* contributor Paul Carroll explained: "Koch celebrates that splendid faculty with which men make poetry. His poems embody the poetic imagination as it rejoices in the ebullience of its health and freedom, its fecundity, its capacity for endless invention, its dear, outlandish ability to transform everyday, pragmatic reality into an Oz or a tea-party at the March Hare's house, its potency in, possibly, achieving a bit of immortality as a result of having brought forth some children of the soul." In the title poem in *The Pleasures of Peace and Other Poems*, Koch presents this theme of the creative mind at work through Giorgio Finogle and another poet. Both poets are writing a poem about the pleasures of peace, and thus find themselves competing against one another. This is but one example of the author's "celebration of the excitement of the imagination as it begins to create," according to Carroll.

In *The Art of Love*, Koch's "voice is unperturbed, offering serene and careless advice on the arts of love and poetry for those who have ears and can hear," explained Paul Wilner in *Village Voice*. Writing in *Poetry*, J.D. McClatchy referred to the book as an "erotic romp," and Wilner further described it as "updating Ovid by reinventing the alphabet of emotion." Zweig added that

Koch's "humor has an edge of satire; his ebullient absurdity slides into an original form of social and cultural criticism, as in 'The Artist' and 'Fresh Air,' both enormously funny epics about the impossibility of art." In the poem "The Art of Love," Koch parodies several advice-giving documents and tries to "enable both poet and reader to distance feelings, ideas, experiences, so as to perceive them strangely, freshly, as if they were rare or even alien curiosities, *objets d'art,* perhaps, in some great Bloomingdale's of the imagination," asserted Sandra M. Gilbert in *Poetry*. The drawback to this form of presentation is that detachment can filter in. *Shenandoah* contributor Conrad Hilberry observed, for instance, that Koch's verse, "like pop art, present great simplicity but maintain so much ironic distance that they make the ordinary reader uneasy." However, Aram Saroyan maintained in *New York Times Book Review* that the poems in *The Art of Love* embody "the ability to move the reader, plain but beautiful language that should appeal to a wide audience, a general graciousness of spirit that has long been an unremarked-on hallmark of Koch's writing, and last but not least, outright wisdom."

"Every book of poems by . . . Koch seems to be a new beginning, a starting over, a trying-out of new voices, styles and idioms," observed John Boening in his *World Literature Today* review of *Days and Nights*. This collection contains a wide variety of poems, in which, explained Mark Hillringhouse in *American Book Review*, "Koch has paid more attention to physical detail and places his emotions directly and concretely into the poem." The poems encompass such subjects as love, aging, loneliness, the past, and the future. One of the pieces, "To Janice," is "moving, intimate, smiling, tender, touching and inventive," according to Boening, who added that it alone "is worth the price of the book." And the title poem, "Days and Nights," is phrased in such a way so as to evoke "a whole spectrum of emotions; from lost time to old friends, to travels and defeats to fears of writing itself," asserted Hillringhouse. "Koch sets out to explore a new landscape that is honest to the act of writing and to the process of the imagination."

On the Edge consists of two lengthy poems, "Impressions of Africa" and "On the Edge," the second being "more ambitious, ranging widely over the facts and fiction of . . . Koch's life," in the words of *New York Times Book Review* correspondent John Ash. The poem moves back and forth between past and present, according to Denis Donoghue in *Commonweal*, with "memories and currencies of sentiment jostling one another within the strong propriety of the cadence." *Washington*

Post Book World contributor Peter Davison viewed the allusions the poem relies on as "calculated to exclude outsiders, to make the non-belonger feel stupid, to make the reader ransack for a footnote." Ash, however, viewed the book as taking "great risks," and claimed that "we cannot do better" than appraise the work according to Koch's "own demanding criteria, set out in his 'Art of Poetry.' Does it astonish? Is it sufficiently modern? Is it written in his own voice? Is it devoid of 'literary, "kiss-me-I'm-poetical" junk'? Is it 'serious without being solemn, fresh without being cold'? The answer, in all cases, must be affirmative."

The poem "Seasons on Earth" and two of Koch's previously published comic epics, "Ko; or, A Season on Earth" and "The Duplications," comprise *Seasons on Earth.* The book provides readers with "a poetic memoir that glances back at the time during which he wrote the earlier poems, a genre at which Koch's discursive talents have proved particularly masterful," explained Gary Lenhart in *American Book Review.* Lenhart added that the title poem continues the mastery of the narrative, "but new urgencies threaten to move the poet away from the strict adherence to form characteristic of the earlier poems." Adams described *Ko; or A Season on Earth* as "a comic epic modeled partially after Byron's *Don Juan* and Ariosto's *Orlando Furioso*" that "details the misadventures of a group of outlandish characters who flit about from continent to continent, reality to unreality." Among other things, the poem relates the story of Ko, a Japanese college student who comes to the United States to play baseball. Lenhart says that the poem "is bursting with the exuberance of a sensuous young poet impatient with the literary world."

In *Washington Post Book World,* Terence Winch regarded "The Duplications" as "something of a nonsense epic whose seriousness lies more in the demonstration of Koch's impressive technical skill than in the narrative itself." There are many "duplications" in the poem, maintained Winch, but the most important ones are the rhymes. And although the poem is a narrative, Winch also suggested that the way in which Koch's mind works and the language he uses deserve more attention than the actual story. His "work is important for its singularity as for its exuberant invention, inspired fluency, and histrionic imagination," concluded Lenhart.

Koch's mature works increasingly demonstrated the poet's willingness to experiment in a variety of forms. In 1994 he released two poetry collections, following his 1993 volume of short-short stories. All three books earned significant critical response, with the poetry col-

lections cited as factors in awarding Koch the Bollingen Prize. In a review of Koch's work in Chicago's *Tribune Books* Paul Hoover hailed the poet as "an extravagant improviser, natural formalist and borscht-belt comedian. His poems have daring, ease and sprezzatura; they are formally accomplished without pomposity." Hoover cited the collection *On the Great Atlantic Rainway* for displaying Koch as "a poet of intimacy and size, lyricism and intelligence. Because his work is light-hearted, it has been accused of triviality. Yet in poems like his hilarious polemic, 'Fresh Air,' Koch shows the fiercely moral nature of the true satirist."

In *Straights* Koch contributes not only poems but prose and even a fugue; still, the poems on themes of aging, seasonal change and "the loss of the sacred in everyday life" most accurately characterize the volume. *Straits* was viewed as a somewhat mixed bag, according to *Poetry* reviewer Ben Howard, although Koch's most successful entries feature a "sophisticated wit and stylistic panache," both of which "illuminate their subjects." Noting an autobiographical bent in the collection, a *Publishers Weekly* contributor remarked upon perceiving "glimpses of the man behind the curtain" in the collection.

Koch reaches even deeper into his own life for the stuff of *New Addresses* and *A Possible World.* Autobiographical in focus, the two collections would prove to be Koch's last gift to readers; he was by now engaged in the battle against leukemia that would ultimately end his life in July of 2002. A *Publishers Weekly* reviewer, praising *New Addresses* as the poet's finest work to date, discussed with Koch its autobiographical elements. "One poem led to another," Koch explained. Examining his life as it revealed itself in the poems of *New Addresses,* the poet also came to terms with a pivotal moment in his life: his military service during World War II. "I'd never really been able to write [about the war] because it's like being psychotic to be in a war. You're walking around with a gun . . . and they shoot you!" However, from a distanced perspective, the mature poet found that treating the war as a character, like any other person, "enabled me to get some of the feelings back, like the crazy idea that I couldn't be killed because I had to write." Containing "Bel Canto," "Variations on Home and Abroad," and "A Memoir," as well as a number of short verses expressing the author's love of travel, *A Possible World* "displays Koch's verve and light touch," according to a *Publishers Weekly* contributor, although the overall mood of the collection "is unmistakably colored by requiem."

Koch also wrote many short plays that critics have praised for equal measures of parody, satire, and irony.

As Koch once commented in his interview with Davis, "I like plays that are astounding in some way—that make convincing what is unusual and even, seemingly, impossible." Denis Donoghue suggested in a *New York Review of Books* essay that in *Bertha and Other Plays*, "Koch implies in his smiling way that nothing is too silly to be said or sung, provided we know exactly how silly it is." In *New York Review of Books*, Stephen Spender described the plays in *A Change of Hearts: Plays, Films, and Other Dramatic Works, 1951-1971* as being "written in a variety of styles, parodying other styles." Koch is extremely inventive, concluded Spender, "and has the funniness which comes out of exuberant vitality."

Koch's *One Thousand Avant-garde Plays* described as "a pure act of poetic invention" by David Lehman in *Washington Post Book World*. The cast of characters in these plays includes Lord Byron, Bozo, Olive Oyl, a Chinese cook, Little Red Riding Hood, Watteau, and hippopotami. "These brief plays are not fragments but full-blown dramas distilled to the action at the heart of each," asserted Lehman, concluding that "one can only applaud [Koch's] insistence on making plays that are at once intelligent and entertaining."

In an online interview with John Tranter for *Jacket,* Koch once praised "the genius in contemporary theatre. Most of the genius . . . seems to be in the directors. I'm not sure I can tell genius in an actor; there seems to be some there too. But the texts of contemporary plays I've seen have not seemed to me to be of the same quality—most of them—as that of the work of the best directors."

Aside from writing poetry, Koch also devoted his time to teaching poetry to children and to the elderly. In 1968 he began his experiment with children at P.S. 61, a New York City elementary school. His *Wishes, Lies, and Dreams: Teaching Children to Write Poetry* describes how writing became exciting for these students and includes some of the student poetry that resulted from Koch's instruction. *Saturday Review* contributor Herbert Kohl considered the work "perhaps the best book I have read portraying the joy and excitement young people experience when writing in a happy place where people care about their work."

Although the students in Koch's class wrote some exceptional poetry, Koch didn't stop there. As John Gardner explained in *New York Times Book Review* that because "the children themselves felt a need for something

more. Koch's response was to shift the experiment to 'teaching great poetry to children,' thus broadening the tradition available to them." The record of this experiment and its tremendous results is *Rose, Where Did You Get That Red?: Teaching Great Poetry to Children*. Koch also worked with the residents of Manhattan's American Nursing Home, and *I Never Told Anybody: Teaching Poetry Writing in a Nursing Home* was the result. As well as collecting his students' poems, the book presents what a *Time* reviewer described as a "highly readable account of how he coaxed his students along." At first unresponsive, the elderly and infirm students learned "to summon and repeat words joyfully, to exaggerate enthusiastically, to celebrate contrasts, to become immersed in nature, to imagine all sorts of places, to put themselves into many different kinds of shoes," wrote Robert Coles in *New York Times Book Review.*

"I seem to go on being influenced, and encouraged, by what I read," Koch once noted of his work as a poet. For his part, Koch also served as an influence to the writers who have followed in his wake. "Koch's poetry remains an underrated treasure, arousing discipleship and high ardor wherever the spirit of the New York school is strong and ignored wherever not," Lehman noted in his book. Bernard F. Dick in *World Literature Today* observed that the author's body of work depicts "a poet's progress, beginning with self-conscious experimentation in the usual way of finding a voice and ending with a voice as distinctive and resonant as the ones that echo through the poetry." Dick added that Koch's poems "attest to a creative power and its gradual refinement, as life and art, the playful and the profound."

BIOGRAPHICAL AND CRITICAL SOURCES:

BOOKS

Berke, Roberta, *Bounds out of Bounds: A Compass for Recent American and British Poetry,* Oxford University Press (Oxford, England), 1981.
Chevalier, Tracy, editor, *Contemporary Poets,* St. James Press (Detroit, MI), 1991.
Cohen, Sarah Blacher, editor, *Comic Relief: Humor in Contemporary American Literature,* University of Illinois Press (Champaign, IL), 1978.
Contemporary Dramatists, 6th edition, St. James Press (Detroit, MI), 1999.
Contemporary Literary Criticism, Thomson Gale (Detroit, MI), Volume 5, 1976, Volume 8, 1978, Volume 44, 1987.

Contemporary Poets, 7th edition, St. James Press (Detroit, MI), 2001.

Dictionary of Literary Biography, Volume 5: *American Poets since World War II,* Thomson Gale (Detroit, MI), 1980.

Diggory, Terence, and Stephen Paul Miller, *The Scene of My Selves: New Work on New York School Poets,* National Poetry Foundation, 2001.

Dupee, F. W., *"The King of Cats" and Other Remarks on Writers and Writing,* Farrar, Straus (New York, NY), 1965.

Howard, Richard, *Alone with America: Essays on the Art of Poetry in the United States,* Atheneum (New York, NY), 1969.

John Ashbery and Kenneth Koch: A Conversation, Interview Press, 1965.

Koch, Kenneth, *The Art of Love,* Random House (New York, NY), 1975.

Koch, Kenneth, *New Addresses: Poems,* Knopf (New York, NY), 2000.

Lehman, David, *The Last Avant-garde,* Doubleday (New York, NY), 1998.

PERIODICALS

American Book Review, May, 1984, Mark Hillringhouse, review of *Days and Nights;* November-December, 1986; May, 1989, Gary Lenhart, review of *Seasons on Earth;* February, 1994, pp. 12, 19.

American Poetry Review, November-December, 1995, review of *On the Great Atlantic Rainway* and *One Train.*

Booklist, May 15, 1993, p. 1674; October 1, 2002, Donna Seaman, "A Poet's Fond Farewell," p. 296.

Commonweal, November 29, 1985, Dennis Donoghue, review of *On the Edge.*

Comparative Literature Studies, June, 1980.

Georgia Review, fall, 1985, Peter Stitt.

New Leader, January 30, 1995, Phoebe Pettingell, pp. 14-15.

New Republic, August 2, 1969; March 13, 1995, Christopher Benfey, pp. 39-42.

Newsweek, September 16, 1985, David Lehman.

New York Review of Books, May, 1963, F.W. Dupee, review of *Poems;* October 20, 1966, Denis Donoghue, review of *Bertha and Other Plays;* September 20, 1973, Stephen Spender, review of *A Change of Hearts;* August 14, 1980; April 8, 1993, p. 36; January 16, 2003, Charles Simic, review of *Sun Out: Selected Poems, 1952-1954,* p. 13.

New York Times, November 21, 1970; April 10, 1977; January 19, 1978; January 12, 1979; February 7, 1995.

New York Times Book Review, February 11, 1968; December 23, 1973, John Gardner, review of *Rose, Where Did You Get So Red?;* September 28, 1975, Aram Saroyan, review of *The Art of Love;* April 10, 1977, Robert Coles, review of *I Never Told Anybody;* April 20, 1986, John Ash, review of *On the Edge;* June 4, 2000, Ken Tucker, "You Talking to Me?"

Poetry, March, 1955, Harry Roskolenko, review of *Poems;* June, 1955, Frank O'Hara, review of *Poems;* September, 1969; November, 1971; August, 1976, J.D. McClatchy, *The Art of Love;* August, 1978; April, 2000, Ben Howard, review of *Straits,* p. 32.

Publishers Weekly, April 5, 1993, p. 71; May 30, 1994, p. 45; April 27, 1998, review of *Straits,* p. 17; March 27, 2000, review of *New Addresses,* p. 71; September 23, 2002, review of *A Possible World* and *Sun Out,* p. 68.

Review of Contemporary Fiction, fall, 1993, pp. 221-22.

Sagetrieb, spring, 1993, p. 131.

Salmagundi, spring-summer, 1973.

Saturday Review, March 20, 1971, Herbert Kohl, review of *Wishes, Lies, and Dreams.*

Shenandoah, spring, 1978, Conrad Hilberry, review of *The Art of Love.*

Studies in Short Fiction, winter, 1995, pp. 102-105.

Time, April 4, 1977, review of *I Never Told Anybody.*

Times Literary Supplement, February 20, 1987.

Tribune Books (Chicago, IL), July 9, 1995, Paul Hoover, p. 6.

Village Voice, May 18, 1972; December 20, 1973; November 24, 1975, Paul Wilner, review of *The Art of Love.*

Washington Post Book World, August 3, 1975; April 17, 1977; January 12, 1986; April 13, 1986; August 28, 1988, Terence Winch, review of *Seasons on Earth;* January 1, 1995, David Lehman, review of *One Thousand Avant-garde Plays,* p. 8.

World Literature Today, winter, 1984, John Boening, review of *Days and Nights;* winter, 1994, Bernard F. Dick, review of *Hotel Lambosa and Other Stories,* p. 142; autumn, 1995, pp. 800-801.

Yale Review, July, 1985.

ONLINE

Jacket Online, http://www.jacket.zip.com/ (March 17, 1989), John Tranter, "Very Rapid Acceleration: An Interview with Kenneth Koch."

OBITUARIES:

PERIODICALS

Los Angeles Times, July 9, 2002, p. B10.

New York Times, July 8, 2002, p. A16.
Times (London, England), July 29, 2002.

ONLINE

International Herald Tribune Online, http://www.iht.com/ (July 9, 2002).

*   *   *

KOGAWA, Joy 1935-
(Joy Nozomi Kogawa)

PERSONAL: Born June 6, 1935, in Vancouver, British Columbia, Canada; daughter of Gordon Goichi (a minister) and Lois (a kindergarten teacher; maiden name, Yao) Nakayama; married David Kogawa, May 2, 1957 (divorced, 1968); children: Gordon, Deidre. *Education:* University of Alberta, 1954; Anglican Women's Training College, 1956; Conservatory of Music, 1956; University of Saskatchewan, 1968.

ADDRESSES: Home—845 Semlin Dr., Vancouver, British Columbia V5L 4J6, Canada.

CAREER: Office of the Prime Minister, Ottawa, Ontario, staff writer, 1974-76; freelance writer, 1976—; University of Ottawa, Ottawa, Ontario, Canada, writer-in-residence, 1978.

MEMBER: League of Canadian Poets, Writers Union of Canada, Order of Canada, 1986.

AWARDS, HONORS: Books in Canada First Novel Award, 1981, Canadian Authors Association Book of the Year Award, Before Columbus Foundation American Book Award, and American Library Association notable book citation, all 1982, all for *Obasan;* Periodical Distributors Best Paperback Fiction Award, 1983.

WRITINGS:

NOVELS

Obasan (novel), Lester and Orphen Dennys (Toronto, Ontario, Canada), 1981, David Godine (New York, NY), 1982.

Naomi's Road (juvenile fiction), Oxford University Press (Toronto, Ontario, Canada), 1986.
Itsuka (sequel to *Obasan*), Viking Canada (Toronto, Ontario, Canada), 1992, Anchor (New York, NY), 1994.
The Rain Ascends, Knopf (Toronto, Ontario, Canada), 1995.

POETRY

The Splintered Moon, University of New Brunswick (St. Johns, New Brunswick, Canada), 1967.
A Choice of Dreams, McClelland & Stewart (Toronto, Ontario, Canada), 1974.
Jericho Road, McClelland & Stewart (Toronto, Ontario, Canada), 1977.
Woman in the Woods, Mosaic Press (Oakville, Ontario, Canada), 1985.
A Song of Lilith, illustrated by Lilian Broca, Polestar (Vancouver, British Columbia, Canada), 2000.
A Garden of Anchors: Selected Poems, Mosaic Press (Oakville, Ontario, Canada), 2003.

Contributor to *Canadian Forum, West Coast Review, Queen's Quarterly, Quarry, Prism International,* and *Chicago Review.*

ADAPTATIONS: A Song of Lilith was adapted for the stage under the direction of Kristine Bogyo and produced in Toronto, Hamilton, and Vancouver, 2001.

SIDELIGHTS: Canadian author Joy Kogawa is best known for the novel *Obasan,* a fictionalization of her own experiences as a Japanese Canadian during World War II. Like *Obasan*'s narrator, Kogawa was torn from her family by government officials and exiled into a detention camp in the Canadian wilderness. She published her first book of poetry, *The Splintered Moon,* in 1967. After two follow-up volumes, she received national acclaim for *Obasan.* With *Obasan,* noted Gurleen Grewal in *Feminist Writers,* "Kogawa proved herself to be among the finest of feminist-humanist writers." In a review of Kogawa's poetry collection *A Song of Lilith* for *Canadian Woman Studies,* Shelagh Wilkinson praised the same quality, noting that "It is not very often that we find a feminist text that fulfills our need to celebrate the lost heroes of woman-centred myths [and] read epic poetry that gives us new insights into the strength of stories that have been abandoned through patriarchal selective vision." *A Song of Lilith,* maintained Wilkinson, is such a book.

Before turning to fiction, Kogawa was a "seasoned poet," explained Grewal. Gary Willis wrote in *Studies in Canadian Literature,* that her first three volumes of poetry are filled with "lyric verse" and poems that often "express feelings that emerge from a narrative context that is only partly defined." A poem from Kogawa's third collection, *Jericho Road,* for example, centers on "a striking surrealistic image" that never makes clear who the protagonist's enemies are. Kogawa explained to Janice Williamson in *Sounding Differences: Conversations with Seventeen Canadian Women Writers* that her poems often arise out of her dreams: "The practice of poetry. . . is the sweeping out of debris between the conscious and the unconscious." Grewal maintained that, in "fiction too, her endeavor is the same. Through protagonists Naomi Nakane's recollection of her painful childhood, *Obasan* lays bare the inter-generational pain of Japanese Canadians affected by the Canadian government's relocation and internment of its citizens during World War II."

Obasan was the first Canadian novel to deal with the internment of its citizens of Japanese heritage. The novel focuses on thirty-year-old Naomi. As children, she and her brother Stephen were separated from their loving parents during World War II. Their mother, visiting relatives in Japan, was not allowed to return to Canada, and their father was shipped to a labor camp, while Naomi and Stephen were sent to a frontier town along with their Uncle Isamu and Aunt Obasan. Tragically, their parents never returned, leaving the children to be raised by their aunt and uncle in a house filled with silence. One of the mysteries of Naomi's childhood involved her new family's yearly pilgrimages. As a child, she would continually ask, "Why do we come here every year?"; as an adult she has lost the ability to communicate. As Kogawa writes, Naomi is a victim of "the silence that will not speak." *Obasan* explores Naomi's search for the answer to her childhood question and shows her long-awaited acknowledgment of what Grewal termed "life's imperative to heal."

At the beginning of *Obasan* Naomi's uncle has just died; according to Erika Gottleib in *Canadian Literature,* the bulk of the novel "takes shape as a mourner's meditation during a wake, a framework well suited to the novel's central metaphor of a spiritual journey." Urged by her Aunt Emily, an activist seeking justice for internment victims, Naomi relives her past, thus enabling her to learn about the secrets long held by her family. She reviews documents about the Japanese internment to understand what happened to her family. At the end of the novel, Naomi learns the truth: that her mother suffered and died in Nagasaki, a victim of the U.S. bombing that leveled that city as World War II neared its end. Through her examination of the past and her examination of the truth, Naomi is at last free and learns to speak again.

Throughout the course of the novel, Naomi realizes her estrangement from mainstream Canadian society, as well as from traditional Japanese culture. Kogawa explores the differences between these two groups. As Willis noted of the novel, *Obasan* is "expressive of a sensibility that wishes to define, in relation to each other, Japanese and Canadian ways of seeing, and even to combine these divergent perceptions in an integrated and distinctive vision." In one scene, Naomi muses on carpentry: "There is a fundamental difference in Japanese workmanship—to pull with control rather than push with force." The contrast between the "restrained" Japanese and the "forceful" Canadians is also apparent in the difference between the *Issei*—those Japanese born in Japan—and the *Nisei*—those children born abroad of Japanese parents, as represented by Naomi's two aunts. Neither of their models works for Naomi who "like Kogawa," explained Willis, "has roots in both traditions." By the end of her own exploration, "Naomi blends a Japanese attention to silence with a Western attention to words. Indeed, it is this blending that gives rise to the distinctive beauties and subtleties of *Obasan.*"

Kogawa further enriches her text with documentation of mid-twentieth-century Canadian history. *Obasan* ends with the widely ignored memorandum sent by the Co-operative Committee on Japanese Canadians to the Canadian government in 1946, pointing out that the deportation of Japanese Canadians was "wrong and indefensible" and "an adoption of the methods of Nazism." Kogawa also includes among Aunt Emily's diaries and notes "a series of chilling nonfictional official papers and newspaper accounts," pointed out Edmund M. White in *Los Angeles Times Book Review.* These elements serve to emphasize what White described as the "systematic outrages inflicted by the Canadian government on its own citizens," actions that "echo the Nazi treatment of the Jews." Edith Milton opined in *New York Times Book Review* that *Obasan* "grows into a quietly appalling statement about how much hatred can cost when it is turned into a bureaucratic principle." White also drew comparisions between Kogawa's novel and *The Diary of Anne Frank* "in its purity of vision under the stress of social outrage."

The political implications of *Obasan* have been commented on by many critics, including Grewal who wrote that "this beautifully crafted novel with is moving resonances has done invaluable service to its varied readers. It has opened necessary dialogue; it has healed." Yet, *Obasan* always remains, according to Milton, "a tour de force, a deeply felt novel, brilliantly poetic in its sensibility." Willis noted that the message of Kogawa's poetry is more fully realized in *Obasan*, "an imaginative triumph over the forces that militate against expression of our inmost feelings." White pointed out that the novel has "a magical ability to convey suffering and privation, inhumanity and racial prejudice, without losing in any way joy in life and in the poetic imagination."

Out of *Obasan* came the novel *Itsuka*, as well as *Naomi's Road*, a version of the story for children. While *Itsuka* is generally thought of as a sequel to *Obasan*, Sandra Martin maintained in *Quill and Quire* that "Kogawa is not so much writing a sequel as reclaiming themes and characters" from *Obasan*. In *Itsuka*, Naomi goes to Toronto, gets a job at with a multicultural journal, and takes her first lover, Father Cedric, a French Canadian priest. With Cedric's help, she turns to activism in her desire to win redress for the victims of Canada's internment policies. In *Itsuka*, the political and erotic plots become intertwined. The book, using a similar technique as *Obasan*, closes with an apology from the Canadian government, in which it admits to instituting policies "influenced by discriminatory attitudes" toward Japanese Canadians and also to its own "unjust" actions.

Grewal maintained that *Itsuka* allows "the reader to witness Naomi's growth and personal fulfillment" and that it "openly bears the message of hope and trust implicit in *Obasan*." Yet, Martin compared *Itsuka* unfavorably to the first novel, finding that "Kogawa seems too close to the partisan squabbling that accompanies any such [political] movement. She hasn't yet absorbed the facts and translated them into fiction." Janice Kulyk Keefer, writing in *Books in Canada*, also admited to "a certain disappointment" with the book, one centering on "the absence in *Itsuka* of the kind of poetically charged language and intensity of perception that give *Obasan* its extraordinary power and beauty." Still, Keefer concluded that "it would be wrong to fault *Itsuka* for not being *Obasan Revisited*." "What Kogawa has done in her new novel is to move into a different kind of imaginative territory," the critic explained, "exposing the politics of multiculturalism that has in may ways abetted rather than eradicated the racism that she presents as an institutionalized aspect of Canadian life."

Like her fictional character Naomi, Kogawa has increasingly turned her attention to political work on behalf of Japanese-Canadian citizens. Although she

penned the novel *The Rain Ascends* in 1995, her writing has centered more on verse since publishing *Obasan* and *Itsuka*. The "insight" contained in her verse collection *Woman in the Woods*, according to *Books in Canada* reviewer Frank Manley, "is enlightening," due to the author's ability to convey her "passion for life" and her poems' "ability to say volumes with only a few words." These attributes have been cited by other reviewers as characteristic of much of Kogawa's verse. Wrote Martin, "Through her poetry, her sublime novel *Obasan*, her children's story *Naomi's Road*, and . . . *Itsuka*, Kogawa has written poignantly about how innocent and loyal Japanese Canadians were stripped of their home and their possessions, interned, and dispersed." Grewal perceived a more universal message in Kogawa's work: an emphasis on "compassion and arduous work of healing."

BIOGRAPHICAL AND CRITICAL SOURCES:

BOOKS

Cheung, King-Kok, *Articulate Silences: Hisaye Yamamoto, Maxine Hong Kingston, Joy Kogawa,* Cornell University Press (Ithaca, NY), 1993.
Contemporary Literary Criticism, Volume 78, Thomson Gale (Detroit, MI), 1994.
Feminist Writers, St. James Press (Detroit, MI), 1996.
Hogan, Robert, and others, editors, *Memory and Cultural Politics: New Essays in American Ethnic Literatures,* North Eastern University Press (Boston, MA), 1996.
James, William Closson, *Locations of the Sacred: Essays on Religion, Literature, and Canadian Culture,* Wilfrid Laurier University Press (Waterloo, Ontario, Canada), 1998.
Kreiswirth, Martin, and Mark A. Cheetham, editors, *Theory between the Disciplines: Authority/Vision/Politics,* University of Michigan Press (Ann Arbor, MI), 1990, pp. 213-229.
Ling, Amy, and others, editors, *Reading the Literatures of Asian America,* Temple University Press (Philadelphia, PA), 1992.
Pearlman, Mickey, editor, *Canadian Women Writing Fiction,* University Press of Mississippi (Jackson, MS), 1993.
Williamson, Janice, *Sounding Differences: Conversations with Seventeen Canadian Women Writers,* University of Toronto Press (Toronto, Ontario, Canada), 1993.

PERIODICALS

Booklist, January 1, 1994, p. 806.

Books in Canada, May, 1986, pp. 43-44; April, 1992, p. 35.

Canadian Ethnic Studies Journal, summer, 2002, Cherry Clayton, interview with Kogawa, p. 106.

Canadian Forum, February, 1982, pp. 39-40; December, 1992, p. 38.

Canadian Literature, summer, 1986, pp. 34-53; spring, 1988, pp. 58-66, 68-82; winter, 1990, pp. 41-57; autumn, 2002, Ian Rae, "Reconsidering Lilith," pp. 162-163.

Canadian Woman Studies, spring-summer, Shelagh Wilkinson, review of *A Song of Lilith,* p. 218.

Feminist Studies, summer, 1990, pp. 288-312.

Frontiers, January, 2003, Christina Tourino, "Ethnic Reproductions and the Amniotic Deep: Joy Kogawa's *Obasan,*" p. 134.

Herizons, December-February, 2000, p. 8.

Kunapipi, Volume 16, number 1, 1994.

Los Angeles Times Book Review, July 11, 1982, Edmund M. White, review of *Obasan,* p. 3.

Melus, fall, 1985, pp. 33-42.

Modern Fiction Studies, summer, 2002, p. 362.

Mosaic, spring, 1988, pp. 215-226.

New York Times Book Review, September 5, 1982; March 13, 1994, p. 18.

Quill and Quire, March, 1992, Sandra Martin, review of *Itsuka,* p. 57.

Semeia, spring-summer, 2002, Tat-siong Benny Liew, interview with Kogawa, p. 195.

Studies in Canadian Literature, Volume 12, number 2, 1987, pp. 239-249; 2001 (annual), Guy Beauregard, "After *Obasan:* Kogawa Criticism and Its Futures," pp. 5-22.

*   *   *

KOGAWA, Joy Nozomi
See KOGAWA, Joy

*   *   *

KOLB, Edward W. 1951-
(Edward William Kolb, Rocky Kolb)

PERSONAL: Born October 2, 1951, in New Orleans, LA; son of Edward William and Dorothy(Beaeman) Kolb; married Adrienne Margaret Wild, March 30, 1972; children: Karen, Jeffrey, Christine. *Education:* University of New Orleans, B.S. (physics), 1973; University of Texas, Ph.D. (physics), 1978.

ADDRESSES: Office—Department of Astronomy and Astrophysics, Enrico Fermi Institute, University of Chicago, 5640 South Ellis Ave., Chicago, IL 60637. *E-mail*—rocky@oddjob.uchicago.edu.

CAREER: Physicist and educator. Los Alamos National Laboratory, Los Alamos, NM, J. Robert Oppenheimer research fellow, 1980-81; Theoretical Astrophysics Group, Fermi National Accelerator Laboratory, Batavia, IL, deputy group leader, 1981-83, group head and scientist grade I, 1983, scientist grade II, 1984-90, and scientist grade III, 1991-93, 1998, 2001, then member and scientist grade III, 1994-98, 2001—; Enrico Fermi Institute, University of Chicago, Chicago, IL, professor of astronomy and astrophysics, 1983—. Visiting professor at University of California, Santa Barbara, 1981, 1992; University of Rome, 1987, 1988, 1990; University of Michigan, 1987; University of Sussex, 1990; CERN, Paris, France, 2001-02; and University of Texas, Austin, 2003. Has appeared in television programs, and in the IMAX film *The Cosmic Voyage.*

MEMBER: International Astronomical Union, American Physical Society (member of executive committee of division of astrophysics, 1993-95; division councilor of executive council, 2002-05), American Astronomical Society.

AWARDS, HONORS: Fellow, American Physical Society, 1984; Quantrell Award for Excellence in Undergraduate Teaching, University of Chicago, 1993; Eugene M. Emme Astronautical Literature Award, 1996; George Marx Medal, Hungarian Academy of Science, 2002; fellow, American Academy of Arts and Sciences, 2002; Örsted Medal, American Association of Physics Teachers, 2003.

WRITINGS:

(Editor, with others) *Inner Space—Outer Space: The Interface between Cosmology and Particle Physics,* University of Chicago Press (Chicago, IL), 1986.

(Editor, with Michael S. Turner) *The Early Universe—Reprints* (textbook), Addison-Wesley (Redwood City, CA), 1988.

(With Michael S. Turner) *The Early Universe* (textbook), Addison-Wesley (Redwood City, CA), 1990.

(Under name Rocky Kolb) *Blind Watchers of the Sky: The People and Ideas That Shaped Our View of the Universe,* Addison-Wesley (Reading, MA), 1996.

Contributor of articles to professional journals. Member of advisory board, *Astronomy.*

SIDELIGHTS: Astrophysicist and educator Edward W. "Rocky" Kolb literally "wrote the book" on particle physics and cosmology with help from scientific colleague and coauthor Michael S. Turner; their 1990 work The Early Universe is considered the standard college text in that advanced field of physics. Teaching and lecturing on the subject of physics at universities around the world, Kolb has also devoted much of his time to speaking on his favorite subject before general audiences as well as participating in workshops geared for science teachers and gifted high-school physics students.

Kolb and Turner are colleagues at the Fermi National Accelerator Laboratory where they cofounded the lab's Theoretical Astrophysics Group in 1981. As William H. Press explained in Astronomy, "Only dimly suspected [in the early 1980s] . . . , it is now taken as fact by most cosmologists and particle physicists that the gross nature of the universe today, both its chemical composition and its aggregate structure, was determined at very early times by processes whose study we would now conventionally assign to nuclear physics and high energy particle physics." Kolb and Turner were leaders in this new field of particle astrophysics, and their The Early Universe "is able not merely to summarize the field but to crystallize it," according to Press. The 1990 book summarizes the findings of previous scientists with regard to Hubble expansion, cosmic microwaves, and various galactic rotation curves, and also reviews the process of expansion known as the "big bang," with its attendant thermodynamic aspects. From here Kolb and Turner extend their discussion into modern particle theory as well as cosmological phase transitions and other mathematically complex studies. To supplement their text and provide scientific background information for readers who might otherwise not have access to such materials, the coauthors collected other relevant literature in the field and published it as The Early Universe—Reprints.

While The Early Universe would likely prove too daunting for the average reader, Kolb's Blind Watchers of the Sky brings the history of astronomy and cosmology down to the grasp of even the generalist. In what Astronomy critic Lew Phelps dubbed a "witty and fascinating tour" of the study of the heavens, Kolb presents the panorama of scientific discovery through profiles of the individuals who made those discoveries: Tycho Brahe, Copernicus, Johannes Kepler, Albert Einstein, Isaac Newton, and Edwin Hubble among others. As the author notes throughout his history, each scientist broke with tradition in interpreting their scientific observa-

tions in a new way, yet all were bound by misguided perceptions of their generations as well; in Brahe's case, as Phelps noted, the scientist's "observation of a supernova shattered the notion that the sky was immutable, yet he adhered to an Earth-centered model of the universe." Kolb traces the intellectual path, characterized by such fits and starts, and colors it with "relevant anecdotes drawn from art, music philosophy, history," as well as his well-honed sense of humor, Phelps added, noting appreciatively that Kolb provides a detailed bibliography and confines higher-level math to a single, inessential chapter. In Booklist, Gilbert Taylor also praised Blind Watchers of the Sky—the title is taken from a comment by Brahe to his detractors: "Oh thick wits. Oh blind watchers of the sky."—noting that Kolb's "bright style and flashing humor" enhances the author's "elucidating" work.

BIOGRAPHICAL AND CRITICAL SOURCES:

PERIODICALS

Astronomy, October, 1996, Lew Phelps, review of Blind Watchers of the Sky, p. 98; June, 2001, Rex Graham, "Deep-Dish Cosmologists," p. 44.
Booklist, March 15, 1996, Gilbert Taylor, review of Blind Watchers of the Sky, p. 1229.
Science, January 16, 1987, P.J.E. Peebles, review of Inner Space—Outer Space: The Interface between Cosmology and Particle Physics, p. 372; August 17, 1990, William H. Press, review of The Early Universe, p. 808.

ONLINE

Rocky Kolb Home Page, http://home.fnal.gov/~rocky/ (August 27, 2004).

*   *   *

KOLB, Edward William
  See KOLB, Edward W.

*   *   *

KOLB, Rocky
  See KOLB, Edward W.

KOONTZ, Dean R. 1945-

(David Axton, Brian Coffey, Deanna Dwyer, K.R. Dwyer, John Hill, Dean Ray Koontz, Leigh Nichols, Anthony North, Richard Paige, Owen West)

PERSONAL: Born July 9, 1945, in Everett, PA; son of Ray and Florence Koontz; married Gerda Ann Cerra, October 15, 1966.

ADDRESSES: Agent—Robert Gottlieb, Trident Media Group, 488 Madison Ave., 17th Floor, New York, NY 10022.

CAREER: Teacher-counselor with Appalachian Poverty Program, 1966-67; high school English teacher, 1967-69; writer, 1969—.

AWARDS, HONORS: Atlantic Monthly college creative writing award, 1966, for story "The Kittens"; Hugo Award nomination, World Science Fiction Convention, 1971, for novella *Beastchild;* Litt.D., Shippensburg State College, 1989; Bram Stoker Award nomination, Horror Writers Association, 2004, for *Robot Santa: The Further Adventures of Santa's Twin.*

WRITINGS:

NOVELS, EXCEPT AS INDICATED

Star Quest, Ace Books (New York, NY), 1968.
The Fall of the Dream Machine, Ace Books (New York, NY), 1969.
Fear That Man, Ace Books (New York, NY), 1969.
Anti-Man, Paperback Library (New York, NY), 1970.
Beastchild, Lancer Books (New York, NY), 1970.
Dark of the Woods, Ace Books (New York, NY), 1970.
The Dark Symphony, Lancer Books (New York, NY), 1970.
Hell's Gate, Lancer Books (New York, NY), 1970.
The Crimson Witch, Curtis Books (New York, NY), 1971.
A Darkness in My Soul, DAW Books (New York, NY), 1972.
The Flesh in the Furnace, Bantam (New York, NY), 1972.
Starblood, Lancer Books (New York, NY), 1972.
Time Thieves, Ace Books (New York, NY), 1972.
Warlock, Lancer Books (New York, NY), 1972.

A Werewolf among Us, Ballantine (New York, NY), 1973.
Hanging On, M. Evans (New York, NY), 1973.
The Haunted Earth, Lancer Books (New York, NY), 1973.
Demon Seed, Bantam (New York, NY), 1973.
(Under pseudonym Anthony North) *Strike Deep,* Dial (New York, NY), 1974.
After the Last Race, Atheneum (New York, NY), 1974.
Nightmare Journey, Putnam (New York, NY), 1975.
(Under pseudonym John Hill) *The Long Sleep,* Popular Library (New York, NY), 1975.
Night Chills, Atheneum (New York, NY), 1976.
(Under pseudonym David Axton) *Prison of Ice,* Lippincott (Philadelphia, PA), 1976, revised edition under name Dean R. Koontz published as *Icebound* (also see below), Ballantine (New York, NY), 1995.
The Vision (also see below), Putnam (New York, NY), 1977.
Whispers (also see below), Putnam (New York, NY), 1980.
Phantoms (also see below), Putnam (New York, NY), 1983.
Darkfall (also see below), Berkley (New York, NY), 1984, published as *Darkness Comes,* W. H. Allen (London, England), 1984.
Twilight Eyes, Land of Enchantment (Westland, MI), 1985.
(Under pseudonym Richard Paige) *The Door to December,* New American Library (New York, NY), 1985.
Strangers (also see below), Putnam (New York, NY), 1986.
Watchers (also see below), Putnam (New York, NY), 1987, reprinted, Berkley Books (New York, NY), 2003.
Lightning (also see below), Putnam (New York, NY), 1988, reprinted, Berkley Books (New York, NY), 2003.
Midnight, Putnam (New York, NY), 1989, reprinted, Berkley Books (New York, NY), 2004.
The Bad Place (also see below), Putnam (New York, NY), 1990.
Cold Fire (also see below), Putnam (New York, NY), 1991.
Three Complete Novels: Dean R. Koontz: The Servants of Twilight; Darkfall; Phantoms, Wings Books (New York, NY), 1991.
Hideaway (also see below), Putnam (New York, NY), 1992.
Dragon Tears (also see below), Berkley (New York, NY), 1992, also published in a limited edition, Putnam (New York, NY), 1993.
Dean R. Koontz: A New Collection (contains *Watchers, Whispers,* and *Shattered* [originally published under

pseudonym K. R. Dwyer; also see below]), Wings Books (New York, NY), 1992.

Mr. Murder (also see below), Putnam (New York, NY), 1993.

Winter Moon, Ballantine (New York, NY), 1993.

Three Complete Novels: Lightning; The Face of Fear; The Vision (The Face of Fear originally published under pseudonym Brian Coffey), Putnam (New York, NY), 1993.

Three Complete Novels: Dean Koontz: Strangers; The Voice of the Night; The Mask (The Voice of the Night originally published under pseudonym Brian Coffey; *The Mask* originally published under pseudonym Owen West), Putnam (New York, NY), 1994.

Dark Rivers of the Heart (also see below), Knopf (New York, NY), 1994.

Strange Highways (also see below), Warner Books (New York, NY), 1995.

Intensity (also see below), Knopf (New York, NY), 1995.

TickTock, Ballantine (New York, NY), 1996.

Three Complete Novels (contains *The House of Thunder, Shadowfires,* and *Midnight*), Putnam (New York, NY), 1996.

Santa's Twin, illustrated by Phil Parks, HarperPrism (New York, NY), 1996.

(Author of text) David Robinson, *Beautiful Death: Art of the Cemetery,* Penguin Studio (New York, NY), 1996.

Sole Survivor: A Novel, Ballantine (New York, NY), 1997.

Fear Nothing, Bantam (New York, NY), 1998.

Seize the Night (sequel to *Fear Nothing),* Bantam Doubleday Dell (New York, NY), 1999.

False Memory, Bantam (New York, NY), 2000.

From the Corner of His Eye, Bantam (New York, NY), 2000.

The Book of Counted Sorrows (e-book), bn.com, 2001.

One Door Away from Heaven, Bantam (New York, NY), 2002.

By the Light of the Moon, Bantam (New York, NY), 2003.

The Face, Bantam (New York, NY), 2003.

Odd Thomas, Bantam (New York, NY), 2004.

Robot Santa: The Further Adventures of Santa's Twin, HarperCollins (New York, NY), 2004.

The Taking, Bantam Books (New York, NY), 2004.

(With Kevin J. Anderson) *Dean Koontz's Frankenstein: Book one, Prodigal Son,* Bantam Books (New York, NY), 2005.

Velocity, Bantam Books (New York, NY), 2005.

Forever Odd, Bantam Books (New York, NY), 2005.

UNDER PSEUDONYM BRIAN COFFEY

Blood Risk, Bobbs- Merrill (Indianapolis, IN), 1973.

Surrounded, Bobbs- Merrill (Indianapolis, IN), 1974.

The Wall of Masks, Bobbs-Merrill (Indianapolis, IN), 1975.

The Face of Fear, Bobbs-Merrill (Indianapolis, IN), 1977.

The Voice of the Night, Doubleday (New York, NY), 1981.

Also author of script for *CHiPS* television series, 1978.

UNDER PSEUDONYM DEANNA DWYER

The Demon Child, Lancer Books (New York, NY), 1971.

Legacy of Terror, Lancer Books (New York, NY), 1971.

Children of the Storm, Lancer Books (New York, NY), 1972.

The Dark of Summer, Lancer Books (New York, NY), 1972.

Dance with the Devil, Lancer Books (New York, NY), 1973.

UNDER PSEUDONYM K. R. DWYER

Chase (also see below), Random House (New York, NY), 1972.

Shattered (also see below), Random House (New York, NY), 1973.

Dragonfly, Random House (New York, NY), 1975.

UNDER PSEUDONYM LEIGH NICHOLS

The Key to Midnight, Pocket Books (New York, NY), 1979.

The Eyes of Darkness, Pocket Books (New York, NY), 1981.

The House of Thunder, Pocket Books (New York, NY), 1982.

Twilight, Pocket Books, 1984, revised edition under name Dean R. Koontz published as *The Servants of Twilight,* Berkley (New York, NY), 1990.

Shadowfires, Avon (New York, NY), 1987.

UNDER PSEUDONYM OWEN WEST

(With wife, Gerda Koontz) *The Pig Society* (nonfiction), Aware Press (Granada Hills, CA), 1970.

(With Gerda Koontz) *The Underground Lifestyles Handbook,* Aware Press (Granada Hills, CA), 1970.

Soft Come the Dragons (story collection), Ace Books (New York, NY), 1970.

Writing Popular Fiction, Writer's Digest (Cincinnati, OH), 1973.

The Funhouse (novelization of screenplay), Jove (New York, NY), 1980.

The Mask, Jove (New York, NY), 1981.

How to Write Best-Selling Fiction, Writer's Digest (Cincinnati, OH), 1981.

OTHER

(Editor) *Life Is Good: Lessons in Joyful Living,* Yorkville Press (New York, NY), 2004.

(Editor) *Christmas Is Good: Trixie Treats and Holiday Wisdom,* Yorkville Press (New York, NY), 2006.

Contributor to books, including *Infinity 3,* edited by Robert Haskins, Lancer Books, 1972; *Again, Dangerous Visions,* edited by Harlan Ellison, Doubleday, 1972; *Final Stage,* edited by Edward L. Ferman and Barry N. Malzberg, Charterhouse, 1974; *Night Visions IV,* Dark Harvest, 1987; *Stalkers: All New Tales of Terror and Suspense,* edited by Ed Gorman and Martin H. Greenberg, illustrated by Paul Sonju, Dark Harvest, 1989; and *Night Visions VI: The Bone Yard,* Berkley, 1991.

ADAPTATIONS: Demon Seed was filmed by Metro-Goldwyn-Mayer/ Warner Bros., 1977; *Shattered* was filmed by Warner Bros., 1977; *Watchers* was filmed by Universal, 1988; *Hideaway* was filmed by Tri-Star, starring Jeff Goldblum, 1994; *Mr. Murder* was filmed by Patchett Kaufman Entertainment and Elephant Walk Entertainment, 1999. Many of Koontz's works were recorded unabridged on audiocassette, including *Cold Fire, Hideaway,* and *The Bad Place,* Reader's Chair (Hollister, CA), 1991; *Mr. Murder* and *Dragon Tears,* Simon and Schuster Audio; *Dark Rivers of the Heart, Icebound,* and *Intensity,* Random House Audio; and *Strange Highways* and *Chase,* Warner Audio.

SIDELIGHTS: Dean R. Koontz is one of popular fiction's most successful novelists. Originally a science fiction writer, Koontz branched out from the genre in 1972, focusing mainly on suspense fiction. His novels, many of which have been bestsellers, are known for tightly constructed plots and rich characters—often combining elements of horror, science fiction, suspense, and romance.

While a prolific writer early in his career, with regard to sales and mainstream popular success, Koontz's breakthrough was his 1980 novel *Whispers.* According to Michael A. Morrison in *Sudden Fear: The Horror and Dark Suspense Fiction of Dean R. Koontz, Whispers* seems at first to be "a simple genre novel of the psychopathic-madman- assaults-woman variety." The novel revolves around Bruno Frye and his obsession with Hilary Thomas, a Hollywood screenwriter. But, Morrison argues, the parallels between the two characters become evident: "Both are victims of parental abuse, and both carry deep-seated neuroses as a consequence. Indeed, all the main figures of Koontz's novel reflect the constricting influence of childhood on adult life—the sins of the fathers and mothers." Elizabeth Massie, also a contributor to *Sudden Fear,* pointed out that Hilary emerges as a much stronger character than she initially appears after surviving the second attack and apparently killing Frye. For Massie, this "allow[s] the story to take off flying. It allows the tale to spend the majority of its energy with . . . Frye, which it is well advised to do. Having seen Hilary in action against Frye, the reader can know that, regardless of peril, Hilary will put up the good fight." Morrison concluded that Frye ranks "as one of the most original psychological aberrations in horror fiction."

Critical reaction to *Whispers* was mixed. A *Publishers Weekly* reviewer argued that readers will need "strong stomachs to tolerate the overheated scenes of rape and mayhem." While the reviewer praised Koontz's portrait of Frye, it was also noted that the mystery is too easy to solve because the author gives too many clues. *Library Journal* contributor Rex E. Klett viewed Koontz edging "dangerously close to a ruinous occultism" with *Whispers,* but also found the novel a smooth read. Denis Pitts, reviewing the novel in *Punch,* called *Whispers* a "superior crime read." Pitts advises: "*Whispers* is not a book to be read by women of a nervous disposition living alone in a country house. Or men, come to think of it."

Strangers, published in 1986, is the story of a group of people connected only by a weekend each spent at a motel in Nevada two years prior—a weekend none of them remember. The characters begin to experience nightmares, unusual, intense fears, and even supernormal powers, driving each toward uncovering the mystery and conspiracy that joins them all. Deborah Kirk, writing in the *New York Times Book Review,* found some of the characters unconvincing but concluded that *Strangers* is "an engaging, often chilling, book," while *Library Journal* contributor Eric W. Johnson dubbed the novel an "almost unbearably suspenseful page-turner." A *Booklist* reviewer deemed Koontz a "true master," and found *Strangers* "a rich brew of gothic horror and science fiction, filled with delectable turns of the imagination."

Dark Rivers of the Heart, published in 1994, is a suspense thriller and political parable revolving around Spencer Grant, an ex-policeman who "confronts a maniacally fascistic secret government agency, an underground web of computer espionage and his own hideous past," summarized Curt Suplee in the *Washington Post Book World.* As Edward Bryant noted in *Locus,* Spencer has ample paramilitary and cyberspace navigational skills himself, which "is lucky, since the bad guys are *so* bad and so well-equipped with high- tech surveillance gadgets and weaponry." Spencer becomes involved with Valerie Keene, a waitress and computer hacker, and finds that federal agents are soon pursuing them both. Suplee commented that this familiar ground, in which "boy can't get girl until the nefarious father/superego figures are adequately purged," is offset by Koontz's narrative, which is replete with "so much novelty and so many odd asides, new characters and screwball sub themes that there's a fresh surprise on virtually every page." Suplee argued that readers may be put off by Koontz's implausible character motivations and "uneconomical" prose style, but concluded that, with regard to "narrative pace and incessant invention, Koontz delivers." Bryant viewed *Dark Rivers* as reflecting Koontz's trust in his readers, finding that the narrative "flows better than many of Koontz's other recent novels because the characters spend less time explaining important issues to each other at length," and in conclusion called the novel "enormously entertaining."

The prolific Koontz published two works in 1995, *Strange Highways* and *Intensity,* the former a collection of short stories, novellas, and two novel-length pieces. A *Publishers Weekly* reviewer argued that a few of the stories in *Strange Highways* are "slight, but none is a failure," and concluded that Koontz's collection is "well crafted and imaginative." Brad Hooper commented in *Booklist* that Koontz's "legion of fans won't be let down." Koontz's best-selling novel *Intensity* is the story of Chyna Shepherd, a psychology student who must combat Edgler Vess, a killer obsessed with intensity of sensation, be it pleasure or pain. Colin Harrison, in a *New York Times Book Review* piece on *Intensity,* lamented that, despite Koontz's "gift for gruesome storytelling," his villain, Vess, is a pop-culture cliché. A *Publishers Weekly* reviewer, however, found *Intensity* "masterful, if ultimately predictable," and lauded Koontz's racing narrative, calling it a contender for the most "viscerally exciting thriller of the year."

In the 1997 work *Sole Survivor,* readers are introduced to former crime reporter Joe Carpenter, a man devastated by the death of his wife and two children in a plane crash. Unemployed and living on insurance money, Carpenter is reduced to derelict status. Then why, Carpenter wonders, does he appear to be under surveillance? The plot thickens when Carpenter encounters a strange woman while visiting the graves of his family. The woman claims to be a survivor of the airplane crash, although there were officially no survivors. Carpenter sets out to unravel the mystery and find out what brought the plane down. In the course of his investigations, he comes upon strange suicides, an esoteric cult, and a cover-up that is much more far reaching than the plane crash. Reviewing *Sole Survivor* for the *New York Times Book Review,* Charles Salzburg dubbed Koontz "a master of his trade." Although faulting the novelist's prose style as excessively flowery and his "paranoid perspective" as "often unbelievable and downright annoying," Salzburg nevertheless concludes that Koontz "does know how to tell an exciting story."

Two of Koontz's novels from the late 1990s, *Fear Nothing* and *Seize the Night,* have the same protagonist and setting. Poet-surfer Christopher Snow lives in the California beach town of Moonlight Bay. Born with a genetic mutation that makes him sensitive to light, Snow can go outside only after dark. In *Fear Nothing,* Snow discovers that the body of his recently deceased father has vanished and been replaced by that of a murdered hitchhiker. With the help of his dog, a Labrador mix named Orson, his surfer-friend Bobby, and local disc jockey Sasha, Snow tries to get to the bottom of things and recover his father's corpse. Commenting on the book in the *New York Times Book Review,* Maggie Garb characterized *Fear Nothing* as an "overwrought narrative," maintaining that Koontz's detective trio "seem more like the stuff of adolescent fantasy than fully believable sleuths." Garb also criticized Koontz's "surfer lingo and literary pretension," as detrimental to the suspense of the book.

In *Seize the Night* Snow makes his second appearance. A reviewer for *Entertainment Weekly* describes the novel as "either an utterly zany thriller or the first really cool young-adult novel of 1999 . . . or Koontz without tears, sadism, or even much bloodshed." The actions starts when seven children are abducted from their homes. Snow is soon on the trail of the kidnappers along with his friends, which now include, in addition to Sasha and Bobbie, a mind-reading cat and a biker. The chase takes them to a supposedly abandoned military base, Fort Wyvern, where genetic experiments are being conducted. Among the strange, mutated creatures

Snow and his cohorts uncover are wormlike creatures that can devour just about anything. At one point Snow becomes trapped by a malfunctioning "temporal locator" that sends him both into the future and the past. An *Entertainment Weekly* reviewer noted that *Seize the Night* is "that holy-cow kind of novel—park your brains, don't ask why, tighten your seat belt." David Walton, writing in the *New York Times Book Review*, characterized the novel as "a bros-and-brew backslapper in which characters refer to Coleridge and T.S. Eliot as often as to genetic mutation."

A *Publishers Weekly* reviewer states of *False Memory* that "Koontz offers a standalone that's less thematically ambitious but more viscerally exciting" than the "Snow" novels that preceeded it. *False Memory* is the story of a woman who suffers from the mental disorder of autophobia, or fear of self. Marty Rhodes, successful at work and in her marriage, takes her agoraphobic friend Susan to therapy sessions with psychiatrist Mark Ahriman twice each week. Suddenly, Marty begins to develop a fear that she will inflict harm upon herself or her loved ones. Meanwhile, Marty's husband, Dusty, a painting contractor, finds himself having to save his half-brother Skeet from making a suicidal leap off a rooftop. After Dusty places Skeet in rehab, he returns home to find that Marty has removed all the sharp objects from the house. Soon Dusty begins to develop signs of paranoia. There are no coincidences here: all four of the novel's disturbed protagonists are victims of psychiatrist Mark Ahriman, who has used hypnosis to control their lives. Ray Olsen of *Booklist* called *False Memory* "a tale that is remarkably engaging, despite having so many pages and so little plot." Jeff Ayers expressed a similar viewpoint in *Library Journal* when he suggests that the book "could have been trimmed by 200 pages and not lost any impact. Still, the characters are rich, and the main story compelling." A *Publishers Weekly* reviewer commented that with "the amazing fertility of its prose, the novel feels like one of Koontz's earlier tales, with a simple core plot, strong everyman heroes (plus one deliciously malevolent villain) and pacing that starts at a gallop and gets only faster."

In *The Taking* Koontz offers up a "gripping, bloodcurdling, thought-provoking parable," according to Ray Olsen in *Booklist*. Novelist Molly Sloan and her husband are at their home in the San Bernardino Mountains in California, when everything starts to come apart. In addition to a mysterious glowing acid raid, the power is off, but somehow appliances run and clocks start spinning out of control. Before long the couple realizes that the country is under attack by a malevolent alien race. "Mixing a hair-raising plot with masterly story

telling and a subtle network of well-placed literary allusions, this deservedly popular author has written a tour de force," stated Nancy McNicol in *Library Journal*, while a reviewer for *Publishers Weekly* commented that "Koontz remains one of the most fascinating of contemporary popular novelists," with *The Taking* marking "an important effort, but not his best, though its sincerity and passion can't be denied."

Velocity, published in 2005, is "a stripped-down exploration of the dark side of the soul, set to a pace that barely allows readers to catch their breaths," observed Charles De Lint in *The Magazine of Fantasy and Science Fiction*. The novel follows the story of Billy Wiles, a bartender who finds himself receiving a series of notes offering impossible choices that become more and more personal. *School Library Journal* contributor Susan Salpini labeled Billy "an average man pushed to his limits by an implacable foe," and De Lint found that the book "explores the dark depths to which we can be pushed," and is effective, as are most of Koontz's works, at making the reader feel uncomfortable and drawn in at the same time.

Koontz's fictional characters are often pitted against unspeakable evil and amazing odds but nonetheless emerge victorious. Concerning this optimism Koontz once commented: "For all its faults, I find the human species—and Western culture—to be primarily noble, honorable, and admirable. In an age when doomsayers are to be heard in every corner of the land, I find great hope in our species and in the future we will surely make for ourselves. I have no patience whatsoever for misanthropic fiction, of which there is too much these days. In fact, that is one reason why I do not wish to have the 'horror novel' label applied to my books even when it is sometimes accurate; too many current horror novels are misanthropic, senselessly bleak, and I do not wish to be lumped with them. I am no Pollyanna, by any means, but I think we live in a time of marvels, not a time of disaster, and I believe we can solve every problem that confronts us if we keep our perspective and our freedom. Very little if any great and long-lasting fiction has been misanthropic. I strongly believe that, in addition to entertaining, it is the function of fiction to explore the way we live, reinforce our noble traits, and suggest ways to improve the world where we can."

BIOGRAPHICAL AND CRITICAL SOURCES:

BOOKS

Kotker, Joan G., *Dean Koontz: A Critical Companion*, Greenwood Press (Westport, CT), 1996.

Munster, Bill, editor, *Sudden Fear: The Horror and Dark Suspense Fiction of Dean R. Koontz,* Starmont House (Mercer Island, WA), 1988.

Munster, Bill, *Discovering Dean Koontz: Essays on America's Best-Selling Writer of Suspense and Horror Fiction,* Borgo Press (San Bernardino, CA), 1998.

Ramsland, Katherine M., *Dean Koontz: A Writer's Biography,* HarperPrism (New York, NY), 1997.

PERIODICALS

Analog, January, 1984.

Armchair Detective, summer, 1995, p. 329.

Booklist, March 1, 1986, p. 914; April 15, 1995, p. 1452; December 15, 1999, Ray Olsen, review of *False Memory,* p. 739; May 1, 2004, Ray Olsen, review of *The Taking,* p. 1483; November 15, 2005, Ray Olson, review of *Forever Odd,* p. 6.

Entertainment Weekly, January 12, 1996, p. 50; January 15, 1999, "'Night' Stalker," p. 56.

Library Journal, May 15, 1980, p. 1187; April 15, 1986, p. 95; January, 2000, Jeff Ayers, review of *False Memory,* p. 160; April 15, 2004, Kristen L. Smith, review of *The Face,* p. 146; June 15, 2004, Nancy McNicol, review of *The Taking,* p. 58.

Locus, February, 1989, p. 21; March, 1992, p. 62; September, 1994, p. 29; October, 1994, p. 21; December, 1994, p. 58; January, 1995, p. 49; February, 1995, p. 39.

Los Angeles Times, March 12, 1986.

Los Angeles Times Book Review, January 31, 1988; January 21, 1990; November 13, 1994, p. 14; May 21, 1995, p. 10.

Magazine of Fantasy and Science Fiction, December, 2005, Charles De Lint, review of *Velocity,* p. 35.

New York Times Book Review, January 12, 1975; February 29, 1976; May 22, 1977; September 11, 1977; June 15, 1986, p. 20; November 13, 1994, p. 58; February 25, 1996, p. 9; April 20, 1997, Charles Salzberg, review of *Sole Survivor;* February 8, 1998, Maggie Garb, review of *Fear Nothing;* February 7, 1999, David Walton, review of *Seize the Night.*

Observer (London, England), February 12, 1995, p. 22.

People, April 13, 1987; April 24, 1989; January 19, 2004, Rob Taub, review of *Odd Thomas,* p. 45.

Publishers Weekly, April 4, 1980, p. 61; March 7, 1986, p. 82; December 18, 1987; December 19, 1994, p. 52; April 24, 1995, p. 60; November 6, 1995, p. 81; February 5, 1996, p. 41; December 13, 1999, review of *False Memory,* p. 67; May 10, 2004, review of *The Taking,* p. 37.

Punch, July 15, 1981, p. 109.

Rapport, April, 1994, p. 27.

School Library Journal, May, 2004, Katherine Fitch, review of *Odd Thomas,* p. 175; September, 2005, Susan Salpini, review of *Velocity,* p. 244.

Science Fiction and Fantasy Book Review, October, 1983, pp. 25-26.

Science Fiction Chronicle, March, 1995, p. 39.

Time, January 8, 1996.

Times Literary Supplement, September 11, 1981.

Tribune Books (Chicago, IL), April 12, 1981.

Washington Post Book World, December 11, 1994, p. 8.

ONLINE

Bookreporter.com, http://www.bookreporter.com/ (March 2, 2001), "Author Profile: Dean Koontz."

Random House Web Site, www.randomhouse.com/ (August 2, 2004), "Dean Koontz: The Official Web Site."

*   *   *

KOONTZ, Dean Ray
   See KOONTZ, Dean R.

*   *   *

KOOSER, Ted 1939-
   (Theodore Kooser)

PERSONAL: Born April, 1939, in Ames, IA; son of Theodore, Sr. (a merchant) and Vera (Moser) Kooser; married Diana Tressler (a teacher), November 17, 1962 (divorced); married Kathleen Rutledge (an editor), September 24, 1977; children: (first marriage) Jeffrey Charles. *Ethnicity:* "German-American." *Education:* Iowa State University, B.S., 1962; University of Nebraska, M.A., 1968. *Politics:* Democrat. *Religion:* Unitarian-Universalist. *Hobbies and other interests:* Painting, drawing.

ADDRESSES: Home—1820 Branched Oak Rd., Garland, NE 68360-9303. *Office*—214 Andrews Hall, University of Nebraska, Lincoln, NE 68588-0333. *E-mail*—kr84428@navix.net.

CAREER: Writer. Bankers Life Nebraska (insurance firm), Lincoln, underwriter, beginning 1964; New Business, Lincoln, second vice president, 1972; Lincoln

Benefit Life Co., Lincoln, underwriter, 1973-84, second vice president for marketing, 1984-92, vice president for public relations, 1992-99. University of Nebraska, Lincoln, adjunct professor of writing, 1970-95, visiting professor, beginning 2000. Narrator of a sound recording of his work, *Out of the Ordinary* (lecture and poetry), 2005.

MEMBER: Academy of American Poets, Poetry Society of America, Society of Midland Authors.

AWARDS, HONORS: John H. Vreeland Award for creative writing, 1964; National Endowment for the Arts fellowships, 1976, 1984; Society of Midland Authors Prize, 1980, for *Sure Signs;* Stanley Kunitz Prize, 1984; Nebraska Book Award for poetry, 2001, for *Winter Morning Walks: 100 Postcards to Jim Harrison;* citation for "best book written by a Midwestern writer," Friends of American Writers, and Gold Award for Autobiography, *ForeWord* magazine, both 2002, for *Local Wonders: Seasons in the Bohemian Alps;* named U.S. poet laureate and consultant in poetry, Library of Congress, 2004-05; Pulitzer Prize for poetry, Columbia University, 2005, for *Delights and Shadows: Poems;* also received Pushcart Prize, James Boatwright Prize, and Merit Award from the Nebraska Arts Council.

WRITINGS:

UNDER NAME TED KOOSER; POETRY, EXCEPT AS NOTED

Official Entry Blank, University of Nebraska Press (Lincoln, NE), 1969.

Grass County, Windflower (Lincoln, NE), 1971.

Twenty Poems, Best Cellar Press (Crete, NE), 1973.

A Local Habitation and a Name, Solo Press (San Luis Obispo, CA), 1974.

Not Coming to Be Barked At, Pentagram Press (Milwaukee, WI), 1976.

Hatcher (illustrated fiction), Windflower (Lincoln, NE), 1978.

Old Marriage and New: Poems, Cold Mountain Press (Austin, TX), 1978.

Sure Signs: New and Selected Poems, University of Pittsburgh Press (Pittsburgh, PA), 1980.

(With William Kloefkorn) *Cottonwood County,* Windflower (Lincoln, NE), 1980.

(Editor) *The Windflower Home Almanac of Poetry,* Windflower, 1980.

On Common Ground: The Poetry of William Kloefkorn, Ted Kooser, Greg Kuzma, and Don Welch, Sandhills Press (Lewiston, ID), 1983.

One World at a Time, University of Pittsburgh Press (Pittsburgh, PA), 1985.

The Blizzard Voices, Bieler (Minneapolis, MN), 1986.

Weather Central, University of Pittsburgh Press (Pittsburgh, PA), 1994.

Winter Morning Walks: 100 Postcards to Jim Harrison, Carnegie-Mellon University Press (Pittsburgh, PA), 2001.

Local Wonders: Seasons in the Bohemian Alps (essays), University of Nebraska Press (Lincoln, NE), 2002.

(With Jim Harrison) *Braided Creek: A Conversation in Poetry,* Copper Canyon Press (Port Townsend, WA), 2003.

Delights and Shadows: Poems, Copper Canyon Press (Port Townsend, WA), 2004.

Flying at Night: Poems 1965-1985, University of Pittsburgh Press (Pittsburgh, PA), 2005.

The Poetry Home Repair Manual: Practical Advice for Beginning Poets (essays), University of Nebraska Press (Lincoln, NE), 2005.

(With Steve Cox) *Writing Brave and Free: Encouraging Words for People Who Want to Start Writing,* University of Nebraska Press (Lincoln, NE), 2006.

Poetry appeared in numerous magazines and literary reviews, including the *New Yorker, American Poetry Review, Poetry, Hudson Review, Kansas Quarterly, Kenyon Review, Antioch Review, Prairie Schooner, Atlantic Monthly,* and *Shenandoah.*

SIDELIGHTS: Although he spent thirty-five years in the insurance business, Ted Kooser remained committed to writing and has authored several books of poetry. He is considered by some critics to be among the best poets of his generation. "I don't know why this news hasn't been more widely trumpeted," wrote David Mason in the *Prairie Schooner.* "Perhaps it is because he has usually written brief, lucid poems while prominent critics fawn over poets who sprawl among their allusions." Mason also noted that in his collections Kooser "has mostly made short poems about perception itself, the signs of human habitation, the uncertainty of human knowledge and accomplishment."

Kooser began writing in his late teens and took a position teaching high school after graduating from Iowa State University in 1962. He soon enrolled in the graduate writing program at the University of Nebraska and worked as a graduate reader until he essentially flunked out a year later. In an interview on the *Barnes and Noble* Web site, Kooser said that he was "a completely undisciplined scholar."

Realizing that he had to make a living, Kooser took an entry-level job with an insurance company in Nebraska. He would remain in the industry until 1999. Throughout his insurance career, Kooser kept on writing, usually from about five-thirty to seven o'clock each morning before he went to the office. "I never saw myself as an insurance executive, but rather as a writer in need of a paying job," Kooser said in the *Barnes and Noble* interview.

In the late 1990s, Kooser developed cancer and essentially gave up both his job and writing. When he began to write again, Kooser would paste his daily poems on postcards he sent in correspondence with his friend and fellow writer Jim Harrison. The result was the 2001 collection of poems called *Winter Morning Walks: 100 Postcards to Jim Harrison.* Addressing both playful and serious poems, Kooser for the most part avoids talking directly about his illness in the collection. Rather, he refers to disease and the possibility of dying in metaphors focusing on the countryside around his Nebraska home, where he took long walks for inspiration.

"Kooser is one of the best makers of metaphor alive in the country, and for this alone he deserves honor," wrote Mason in a review of *Winter Morning Walks* for *Prairie Schooner.* Mason also noted, "Kooser has often argued against the knee-jerk narcissism of poetry, and here he rarely dwells on his autobiography, though we can sense his personality by the quality of his observations." John Taylor, writing in *Poetry,* noted that "a rare quality distinguishes *Winter Morning Walks.*"

Kooser strayed from poetry with his next book, a collection of essays titled *Local Wonders: Seasons in the Bohemian Alps.* Once again, Kooser zeroes in on the place he calls home. Just outside of Garland, Nebraska, the community is facetiously referred to as the "Bohemian Alps." The essays cover one year, or four seasons, in the author's life. Although Kooser reflects on his younger days—as when he recalls his grandmother's cooking—the essays focus largely on the details of his current life and surroundings, such as the essay about an old-fashioned outhouse that sits on his rural property. In a contribution to *Writer,* Kate Flaherty said, "Kooser's meditations on life in southeastern Nebraska are as meticulous and exquisite as his many collections of poetry, and his quiet reticence and dry humor are refreshing in this age of spill-it-all memoirs."

For *Braided Creek: A Conversation in Poetry* Kooser teamed up with his friend Harrison to publish their correspondence consisting of entirely short poems written to each other while Kooser was recovering from cancer. Writing in *Poetry,* contributor Ray Olson noted that "wit and wisdom" are the mainstay of these correspondences. Olson added, "Their conversation always repays eavesdropping."

As for Kooser, he returned to teaching poetry and nonfiction at the University of Nebraska, and he continues to write. "I waste very little time anymore," he said an interview for the University of Nebraska English Department newsletter.

Although sometimes classified as a "regional" writer because of his focus on the Midwest and Nebraska, Kooser has a different view of his work. He once told *CA:* "I work with all subject matter and in all forms. Most of my work reflects my interest in my surroundings here on the Great Plains, but I do not consider myself to be a regionalist writer."

Commenting on his writing, Kooser also told *CA:* "I wrote poetry from the time I was quite young and got serious about it as a teenager. The first poets I read have remained strong influences: Edward Arlington Robinson, Robert Frost, May Swenson, John Crowe Robinson, and others. The biggest influence on my writing today is growing older."

"I am often surprised by which poems magazine editors like, as opposed to those I think are my best work. My favorite book is *Weather Central,* but I am fond of *Delights and Shadows.*"

"I write for other people with the hope that I can help them to see the wonderful things within their everyday experiences. In short, I want to show people how interesting the ordinary world can be if you pay attention."

When Kooser was named America's national poet laureate in 2004, the honor coincided with the publication of *Flying at Night: Poems 1965-1985,* a collection of his previously published poetry. At the time of his recognition as poet laureate by the Library of Congress, the self-effacing poet was by no means a household name. Of *Flying at Night, New York Times Book Review* contributor Brad Leithauser wrote, "This is good, honest work," a tribute to the Midwest that the poet calls home. Though Kooser maintains that composing regional poetry has not been his primary aim, Leithauser observed that "Kooser has been memorializing a vanishing world." *Library Journal* reviewer Louis Mc-

Kee wrote: "Kooser's pure American voice and clear-eyed observation are a refreshing treat after the cynical, skeptical poetry from the . . . coasts."

The Poetry Home Repair Manual: Practical Advice for Beginning Poets is less a how-to manual than a collection of essays about poetry and poets, "a treatise of aesthetics under the guise of a textbook" as David Mason described it in the *Weekly Standard.* He added: "Kooser is out to rescue populism from its blunter forms, and his book is not without sophistication." Kooser does offer specific guidelines for writing poetry, Patricia Monaghan reported in her *Booklist* review, one of which is "to focus on the work of poetry rather than on the idea of being a poet."

BIOGRAPHICAL AND CRITICAL SOURCES:

PERIODICALS

Booklist, April 1, 2003, Ray Olson, review of *Braided Creek: A Conversation in Poetry,* p. 1367; February 15, 2005, Patricia Monaghan, review of *The Poetry Home Repair Manual: Practical Advice for Beginning Poets,* p. 1052.

Library Journal, April 15, 2005, Louis McKee, review of *Flying at Night: Poems 1965-1985,* p. 90.

New York Times Book Review, August 7, 2005, Brad Leithauser, review of *Flying at Night,* p. 15.

Poetry, February, 2002, John Taylor, review of *Winter Morning Walks: 100 Postcards to Jim Harrison,* p. 295.

Prairie Schooner, fall, 2002, David Mason, review of *Winter Morning Walks,* p. 187.

Weekly Standard, February 14, 2005, David Mason, review of *The Poetry Home Repair Manual,* p. 38.

Writer, November, 2002, Kate Flaherty, review of *Local Wonders: Seasons in the Bohemian Alps,* p. 56.

ONLINE

Barnes and Noble Web site, http://www.barnesandnoble. com/writers/ (November 3, 2003), "Ted Kooser."

University of Nebraska Web Site, Department of English Newsletter, http://www.unl.edu/englishhtml/news/ (March 29, 2002), Janet Carlson, "Profiles."

*   *   *

KOOSER, Theodore
See KOOSER, Ted

KOSINSKI, Jerzy 1933-1991
(Jerzy Nikodem Kosinski, Joseph Novak)

PERSONAL: Born June 14, 1933, in Lodz, Poland; came to United States, 1957, naturalized citizen, 1965; committed suicide, May 3 (one source says May 4), 1991, in New York, NY; son of Mieczyslaw (a classicist) and Elzbieta (a concert pianist; maiden name, Liniecka) Kosinski; married Mary Hayward Weir (an art collector), 1962 (died, 1968); married Katherina von Fraunhofer (an advertising executive), 1987. *Education:* University of Lodz, B.A., 1950, M.A. (history), 1953, M.A. (political science), 1955; Ph.D. candidate in sociology at Polish Academy of Sciences, 1955-57, and at Columbia University, 1958-63; graduate study at New School for Social Research, 1962-66.

CAREER: Writer and photographer. Ski instructor in Zakopane, Poland, winters, 1950-56; assistant professor (aspirant) of sociology, Polish Academy of Sciences, Warsaw, 1955-57; researcher at Lomonosov University, Moscow, 1957; variously employed as a paint scraper on excursion-line boats, a truck driver, chauffeur, and cinema projectionist; Center for Advanced Studies, Wesleyan University, resident fellow in English, 1967-68; Council of Humanities, Princeton University, visiting lecturer in English and resident senior fellow, 1969-70; Yale University, professor of English and resident fellow of Davenport College and School of Drama, 1970-73, fellow of Timothy Dwight College, 1986-91. Actor in films, including (as Grigory Zinoviev) *Reds,* Paramount, 1981. *Exhibitions:* One-man photographic exhibitions at the State's Crooked Circle Gallery, Warsaw, Poland, 1957, and elsewhere around the world.

MEMBER: International League for Human Rights (director, 1973-79), PEN (president, 1973-75), National Writers Club, Authors Guild, Authors League of America, American Federation of Television and Radio Artists, American Civil Liberties Union (chair of artists and writers committee), Screen Actors Guild, Century Association.

AWARDS, HONORS: Ford Foundation fellowship, 1958-60; Prix du Meilleur Livre Étranger (France), 1966, for *The Painted Bird;* Guggenheim fellowship in creative writing, 1967-68; National Book Award, 1969, for *Steps;* National Institute of Arts and Letters/ American Academy of Arts and Letters award in literature, 1970; John Golden fellowship in playwriting, 1970-72; Brith Sholom Humanitarian Freedom Award, 1974; American Civil Liberties Union First Amendment

Award, 1978; best screenplay of the year awards from Writers Guild of America, 1979, and British Academy of Film and Television Arts, 1981, both for *Being There;* Polonia Media National Achievement Perspectives Award, 1980; Spertus College of Judaica International Award, 1982; L.H.D. from Albion College, 1988, State University of New York, 1989; Harry Edmonds Life Achievement Award, International House, 1990.

WRITINGS:

FICTION

The Painted Bird, Houghton Mifflin (Boston, MA), 1965, expanded edition, Modern Library (New York, NY), 1970, revised 10th anniversary edition, with an introduction by the author, Houghton Mifflin, 1976, reprinted, Transaction Publishers (New Brunswick, NJ), 2000.

Steps, Random House (New York, NY), 1968, reprinted, Grove Press (New York, NY), 1997.

Being There (also see below), Harcourt (New York, NY), 1971, reprinted, Grove Press (New York, NY), 1999.

The Devil Tree, Harcourt (New York, NY), 1973, revised and expanded edition, St. Martin's Press (New York, NY), 1981, reprinted, Grove Press (New York, NY), 2003.

Cockpit, Houghton Mifflin (Boston, MA), 1975, reprinted, Arcade Publishing (New York, NY), 1989.

Blind Date, Houghton Mifflin (Boston, MA), 1977, reprinted, Grove Press (New York, NY), 1997.

Passion Play (also see below), St. Martin's Press (New York, NY), 1979, reprinted, Grove Press (New York, NY), 1998.

Pinball, Bantam Books (New York, NY), 1982; reprinted, Grove Press (New York, NY), 1996.

The Hermit of 69th Street: The Working Papers of Norbert Kosky, Henry Holt (New York, NY), 1988.

SCREENPLAYS

Being There (based on Kosinski's novel; Lorimar/United Artists, 1979), Scientia-Factum (New York, NY), 1977.

Passion Play (based on Kosinski's novel), Scientia-Factum (New York, NY), 1982.

NONFICTION

(Under pseudonym Joseph Novak) *The Future Is Ours, Comrade: Conversations with the Russians,* Doubleday (New York, NY), 1960.

(Under pseudonym Joseph Novak) *No Third Path: A Study of Collective Behavior,* Doubleday (New York, NY), 1962.

(Editor) *Socjologia Amerykanska: Wybor Prac, 1950-1960* (title means "American Sociology: Translations of Selected Works, 1950-1960"), Polish Institute of Arts and Sciences (New York, NY), 1962.

Notes of the Author on "The Painted Bird," Scientia-Factum (New York, NY), 1965.

The Art of the Self: Essays a propos "Steps," Scientia-Factum (New York, NY), 1968.

Passing By: Selected Essays, 1962-1991, Random House (New York, NY), 1992.

Conversations with Jerzy Kosinski, edited by Tom Teicholz, University Press of Mississippi (Jackson, MS), 1993.

Also author of *Dokumenty walki o Czlowieka: Wspomnienia Proletariatczykow* (title means "Documents concerning the Struggle of Man: The Reminiscences of the Members of 'Proletariat'") and *Program Rewolucji Jakoba Jaworskiego* (title means "The Program of the People's Revolution of Jakob Jaworski"), 1954-55.

Kosinski's books have been translated into numerous languages, including German, French, Italian, and Spanish.

SIDELIGHTS: A controversial novelist, Jerzy Kosinski first stunned the literary world in 1965 with *The Painted Bird,* a graphic account of an abandoned child's odyssey through war-torn Eastern Europe that some critics consider the best piece of literature to emerge from World War II. Kosinski's second novel, *Steps,* was equally successful and won a National Book Award in 1969. Other novels, all part of an elaborate fictional cycle, followed; though Kosinski labeled them fiction, his books parallel his real-life experiences, earning their author a reputation as a writer who mingles art and life.

The only child of Jewish intellectuals, Kosinski enjoyed a sheltered childhood until he was six years old. Then Hitler invaded Poland, disrupting the young boy's family and irrevocably altering the course his life would take. As Jews, Kosinski's parents were forced into hiding, and eventually their son was entrusted to a stranger's care. Though he was soon placed with a foster mother, she died within two months of his arrival, and, until the end of the war when he was reunited with his parents, young Kosinski wandered from one remote peasant village to another, living by his wits. By the time he was nine years of age, Kosinski had been so traumatized by his experience that he was struck mute. "Once I regained my speech after the war, the trauma began," he told Barbara Leaming of *Penthouse.* "The Stalinist [system in Poland] went after me, asking questions I didn't want to hear, demanding answers I would not give."

When the State refused to grant him and his family permission to immigrate to the West, Kosinski used the deceptive techniques he had mastered as a runaway to plot his escape. He was twenty-four and a doctoral student at the Polish Academy of Sciences in Warsaw when he undertook an elaborate and dangerous ruse. Inventing four academicians in four different branches of learning, Kosinski contrived to have his fictional associates sponsor him for a research project in the United States. It took him over two years to obtain the passport and the necessary travel documents, but by the winter of 1957, he was ready. He arrived in New York City a few days before Christmas, friendless, penniless, and with only a rudimentary knowledge of the spoken American idiom.

After his arrival, Kosinski became an American success story. Quickly mastering the language, he enrolled in a Ph.D. program, launched a writing career, and married the rich widow of an American steel baron. A prize-winning photographer, Kosinski was also an amateur athlete and, according to a writer for *New York Times Magazine,* "a polo-playing pet of the jet set." In 1981 he added a film role to his list of accomplishments, earning critical praise for his portrayal of the Soviet bureaucrat Grigory Zinoviev in Warren Beatty's film *Reds.* Despite the tremendous diversity that characterized both his personal and professional life, Kosinski remained deeply committed to writing: "Fiction is the center of my life," he once told Margaria Fichtner in a *Chicago Tribune* interview. "Anything I do revolves around what I write and what I write very often revolves around what I do."

To gather material, Kosinski frequently prowled the streets of New York and other cities, sometimes traveling in disguise. "I like to go out at night," he told Ron Base in *Washington Post.* "I like to see strange things, meet strange people, see people at their most abandoned. I like people who are driven. The sense of who they are is far greater."

Though Kosinski cloaked these experiences under a fictive mask, critics have said the autobiographical elements of his writing are unmistakable. "Mostly, in his novels," wrote Barbara Gelb in *New York Times Magazine,* "he describes actual events as a newspaper reporter would, altering details only slightly to fictionalize them." *Detroit News* staff writer Ben Brown agreed, delineating the following similarities between Kosinski and his characters: "Like the boy wanderer in *The Painted Bird,* Kosinski was an abandoned child, wandering alone through the rural villages of Eastern Europe during World War II. Like the emigrant photographer-social scientist in *Cockpit,* Kosinski, also a photographer-social scientist, escaped from [Poland] by creating a hole in the post-Stalinist bureaucracy through which he could slide to freedom in the West. By view of his marriage . . . Kosinski was surrounded by the kind of vast inherited wealth he gave Jonathan Wahlen in *The Devil Tree.* And like Fabian in . . . *Passion Play* [1979] . . . Kosinski is an expert horseman [and] an avid polo player." In fact, according to Base, Kosinski "never strays far from his own life in order to discover his novels' protagonists, and given the life he leads, who can blame him? Everything including his past and present seems calculated to yield a novel every three years or so."

Some critics believed it was not calculation, but necessity which motivated Kosinski's pen. Indeed, Kosinski, writing in *Notes of the Author on "The Painted Bird"* reinforced this point of view: "We fit experiences into molds which simplify, shape and give them an acceptable emotional clarity. *The remembered event becomes a fiction, a structure made to accommodate certain feelings.* If there were not these structures, art would be too personal for the artist to create, much less for the audience to grasp. *There is no art which is reality; rather, art is the using of symbols by which an otherwise unstateable subjective reality is made manifest.*"

The "subjective reality" that is "made manifest" in Kosinski's fiction is the ability of the individual to survive. "The whole didactic point of my novels is how you redeem yourself if you are pressed or threatened by the chances of daily life, how you see yourself as a romantic character when you are grotesque, a failure," Kosinski once told Ben Brown in a *Detroit News* interview. Though the theme is recurrent, Kosinski approaches it differently in each book, as Lawrence Cunningham explained in *America:* "At times, as in *The Painted Bird,* the individual is the victim of society, while in *Cockpit,* a Kafkaesque secret agent named Tarden wages a one-man war against the whole of society and those members of it who epitomize the brutality of that society. In *Being There* . . . the hero of the novel betrays the whole of American society not because of his power or viciousness, but because of his simplicity, naiveté and sheer ignorance of how the culture game is played." Notwithstanding these differences, Cunningham believed the novels share the same moral ambivalence: "In Kosinski's . . . universe there is, at the same time, grand moral testimony to the worth of the individual and a curious shrinking from the common bonds of trusting humanity. . . . Kosinski is a survivor. If his experience has not permitted him to teach us much about human relationships, it has been, nonetheless, a vade mecum [or manual] of making it in this very tough world."

And what makes this "alien world" of Kosinski's so frightening, according to Elizabeth Stone, is the sharp chill of recognition it causes the reader to feel. "In the lives of Kosinski's characters, there is something of ourselves," Stone wrote in *Psychology Today*. "Kosinski's novels pierce the social skin and go deeper. They are all accounts of the self in extreme psychological peril, and they make sense the way dreams make sense. . . . the novels recreate the aura of nightmare paranoia, rouse fears of psychic petrification, depersonalization, engulfment. . . . His characters chronicle not only what, at its worst, the world is like, but also what, at *our* worst, it feels like."

Not surprisingly, the survival techniques his characters employ are similar to tactics Kosinski himself once used. One such technique, according to Stone, is giving voice to experience, as the nameless protagonist of *The Painted Bird* does when he regains his speech. Another is the ability to cultivate invisibility and turn it into an advantage—which Kosinski did when he traveled in disguise and which Levanter of *Blind Date* does when he rapes a girl from behind, thus preventing her from identifying him. Though Kosinski said repeatedly that he never saw himself as a victim, critics have maintained that his characters—and even Kosinski himself—are obsessed with revenge. While he preferred to view revenge as a "defense rather than an obsession," Kosinski did not disagree. "My characters often defend themselves against entrapments by oppressive societies," he once told Leaming. "I see revenge as the last vestige of the eminently threatened self. . . . Revenge can be a positive force—the victim's final dignity."

In Kosinski's case, retaliation for injustices suffered under the Communist system came with the publication of his first book, a nonfiction collection of essays. Described by Gelb as "a strongly anti-communist tract," *The Future Is Ours, Comrade: Conversations with the Russians* became an instant best seller and was serialized by *Saturday Evening Post* and *Reader's Digest*.

Like his subsequent *No Third Path: A Study of Collective Behavior*, it was published in book form pseudonymously. "I didn't think my spoken English was good enough to publicly defend my sociological methods, my ethics and philosophy," the author later explained, "so I published it under the pen name Joseph Novak." Kosinski offered as explanation for the Novak pseudonym to *Washington Post Book World* interviewer Daniel J. Cahill: "When you're a student you're supposed to read serious books—not publish them. The pen name allowed me to conduct my studies uninterrupted by the controversy that my books triggered among my fellow students and professors. A side benefit of a pen name is that it allows you to recommend your own books, to those who don't know you've written them, as the very best on the subject—without ever feeling immodest."

One of the people who read *The Future Is Ours, Comrade* was Mary Weir, the affluent, thirty-one-year-old widow of steel magnate Ernest Weir. Weir, who read the book shortly after a trip to Russia, agreed so wholeheartedly with Kosinski's observations that she wrote him a fan letter. Kosinski, in a characteristic blending of fact and fiction, fictionalizes what followed in his novel *Pinball*. "Long ago," says Domostroy—one of the novel's protagonists and an obvious stand-in for Kosinski—"when I had received enough fan letters to know how similar they all were, I received one unusual one. The writer, a woman, said she knew me only from my work, . . . but her analysis . . . was so acute, as were her perceptions of . . . the undercurrents of my life, . . . that I was flat-out enthralled." The couple arranged a meeting, and ultimately married in 1962.

In his interview with Cahill Kosinski once described how his marriage to Weir enhanced his art: "During my marriage, I had often thought that it was Stendhal or F. Scott Fitzgerald, both preoccupied with wealth they did not have, who deserved to have had my experience" of an affluent lifestyle. Desiring to write fiction, he considered using his newly found understanding of a lifestyle immersed in luxury, but decided against it. "During my marriage I was too much a part of Mary's world to extract from it the nucleus of what I saw, of what I felt . . . ," he told Cahill. "So instead, I decided to write my first novel *The Painted Bird* about a homeless boy in war-torn Eastern Europe, an existence I've known but also one that was shared by millions of Europeans, yet was foreign to Mary and our American friends. The novel was my gift to Mary, and to her world."

Although *The Painted Bird* initiated Kosinski's career as a novelist, the years surrounding its release were full of personal tragedy as the author watched Weir die of an incurable illness in 1968. "In a curious way," wrote Base in *Washington Post,* "her death provided him with the ultimate freedom. Now he could draw on all the possibilities of his life without worrying about embarrassing wives and children." Though he did pursue these themes in a number of later books, his next novel is similar in setting and theme to *The Painted Bird.* "The protagonist-narrator of *Steps* is alternately the dark-complected boy of Kosinski's first novel . . . and that same boy as an adult," observed William Plummer in *Village Voice.* A series of seemingly unconnected, and often brutal, episodes, the book, according to Stanley Kauffmann in *New Republic,* "is a piercing view of [Kosinski's] past as part of the world's present. For me, the title does not signify progress from one place to another or from one state to another, but simply action about experience: steps taken to accommodate experience and continuing reality to the possibility of remaining alive. . . . The book says finally: 'Hell. Horror. Lust. Cruelty. Ego. But *my* hell and horror and lust and cruelty and ego. Life is—just possibly—worth living if we can imagine it better and imagine it worse.'"

While *Steps* won a National Book Award in 1969, its author sensed that the attitude of the publishing world toward literature was changing. His assessment was perhaps correct: when a young reporter retyped *Steps* and submitted it under a different name as an experiment, he found that it went unrecognized and rejected by every major publishing house—including the one that had originally released it.

From the time it was first published *Steps* aroused controversy. While critics generally agreed that the book is beautifully written, several reviewers, including Geoffrey Wolff in *New Leader,* questioned its morality: "Kosinski's power and talent are not in doubt. I can think of few writers who are able to so persuasively describe an event, set a scene, communicate an emotion. Nonetheless, the use he has set his power to is in doubt. His purpose is serious, I am sure, but he misreads our tolerance. He has created what never was on land or sea and arrogantly expects us to take his creations, his self-consuming octopus, his other monsters, as emblems." Echoing this sentiment, Robert Alter wrote in *New York Times Book Review* that *Steps* "is scarcely a novel at all but rather a series of discontinuous erotic jottings, sometimes brutal, generally deficient in feeling, and finally repetitious." According to *New York Times* reviewer Christopher Lehmann-Haupt, the problem is not just what Kosinski wrote, but how he wrote it: "Lacking a sense of the language, and thus lacking any style of his own, the author gropes for any passable cliché. It is just what happens in bad pornography."

Kosinski bridled at such comparisons. "Pornography views sex as physical, not spiritual," he told Leaming. "It does to sex what totalitarianism does to politics: it reduces it to a single dimension. But for me, as for all my fictional characters, sex is a spiritual force, a core of their being, indeed, the pro-creative basis for self-definition." Those critics who found his heavy doses of sex and violence gratuitous did not understand, he declared, what he was trying to do. "I am astonished again and again at how superficially people read books," he once told Ben Brown of *Detroit News.* "I know what I write. I know why I do it the way that I do it. There's no greater sense of responsibility than (my own). But I have a certain vision of literature I will not sacrifice for sentimental critics brought up on *Fiddler on the Roof.*"

As Arnost Lustig wrote in *Washington Post Book World:* "Kosinski develops his own style and technique, trying to avoid the classical plot and trying not to get lost in a limitless and chaotic jungle without beginning, middle and end. His style is in harmony with his need to express new things about our life and the world we do live in, to express the inexpressible."

A perfectionist, Kosinski wrote slowly and rewrote extensively. He rewrote his 1979 novel *Passion Play* almost a dozen times, and then further altered it in three different sets of galleys and two page proofs, where he condensed the text by one-third. Above his ten percent publisher's allowance, Kosinski had to bear the cost of such corrections. He did not, however, complain. "When I face the galley-proofs I feel as though my whole life was at stake on every page and that a messy paragraph could mess up my whole life from now on," he told Cahill. "As I have no children, no family, no relatives, no business or estate to speak of, my books are my only *spiritual* accomplishment, my life's most private frame of reference, and I would gladly pay all I earn to make it my best."

In the June 22, 1982 issue of *Village Voice* Geoffrey Stokes and Eliot Fremont-Smith challenged Kosinski's ethics and his role as the sole creative force behind his books. The journalists' allegations covered a broad spectrum, ranging from complaints of Kosinski lying about his past, to Kosinski having his first two books written and financed by the Central Intelligence Agency. The most serious accusations, however, concerned Kosinski's open but unacknowledged dependence on freelance editors during the revision process of his novels, including *Passion Play* and *Pinball.*

Several publishing-house editors came to Kosinski's defense, and in *Publishers Weekly* editor Les Pockell dismissed the charges as "totally ludicrous," explaining that Kosinski retained people to copyedit because he was "obsessive" about his writing. But perhaps the strongest reaction to *Village Voice* charges came from Kosinski himself. He told the newspaper that "Not a single comma, not a single word is not mine—and not the mere presence of the word but the reasons why as well. This goes for manuscript, middle drafts, final draft, and every f—ing galley—first page proofs, second and third, hardcover editions and paperback editions." Nonetheless, the controversy took its toll; as Kosinski told a *Washington Post Book World* reporter: "Like any other assassination, the damage has been done."

Tragically, in May of 1991, just under a decade after *Village Voice* controversy, Kosinski committed suicide, apparently discouraged by failing health and his inability to continue writing.

BIOGRAPHICAL AND CRITICAL SOURCES:

BOOKS

Aldridge, John Watson, editor, *The Devil in the Fire: Retrospective Essays on American Literature and Culture, 1951-71,* Harper's Magazine Press (New York, NY), 1972.

Bellamy, Joe D., editor, *The New Fiction: Interviews with Innovative American Writers,* University of Illinois Press (Champaign, IL), 1974.

Cahill, Daniel, *The Fiction of Jerzy Kosinski,* Iowa State University Press (Ames, IA), 1982.

Contemporary Literary Criticism, Thomson Gale (Detroit, MI), Volume I, 1973, Volume II, 1974, Volume III, 1975, Volume VI, 1976, Volume X, 1979, Volume XV, 1980.

Hicks, Jack, *In the Singer's Temple: The Romance of Terror and Jerzy Kosinski,* University of North Carolina Press (Chapel Hill, NC), 1981.

Klinkowitz, Jerome, *Literary Disruptions: The Making of a Post-Contemporary American Fiction,* University of Illinois Press (Champaign, IL), 1975.

Kosinski, Jerzy, *Notes of the Author on "The Painted Bird,"* Scientia-Factum (New York, NY), 1965.

Langer, Lawrence L., *Holocaust and the Literary Imagination,* Yale University Press (New Haven, CT), 1975.

Lavers, Norman, *Jerzy Kosinski,* G.K. Hall (Boston, MA), 1982.

Lupack, Barbara Tepa, editor, *Critical Essays on Jerzy Kosinski,* G.K. Hall (Boston, MA), 1998.

Plimpton, George, editor, *Writers at Work: The "Paris Review" Interviews,* Volume V, Penguin Putnam (New York, NY), 1981.

Salska, Agnieszka, and Marek Jedlianski, editors, *Jerzy Kosinski: Man and Work at the Crossroads of Cultures,* Uniwersytetu Lodzkiego (Lodz, Poland), 1997.

Sherwin, Byron L., *Jerzy Kosinski: Literary Alarmclock,* Cabala Press (Chicago, IL), 1982.

Sloan, James Park, *Jerzy Kosinski: A Biography,* Dutton (New York, NY), 1996.

Tiefenthaler, Sepp, *Jerzy Kosinski,* Bouvier Publishers (Bonn, DE), 1980.

PERIODICALS

America, November 11, 1978, Lawrence Cunningham.

American Photographer, June, 1980.

Centennial Review, winter, 1972.

Chicago, March, 1996, p. 35.

Chicago Review, summer, 1980.

Chicago Tribune, January 19, 1980, Margarita Fichtner, interview with Kosinski.

Christian Science Monitor, March 1, 1979.

Commentary, June, 1966.

Commonweal, July 1, 1966.

Critique, Volume XXII, number 2, 1981.

Denver Post, February 11, 1973; September 7, 1979.

Denver Quarterly, autumn, 1969; spring, 1971; winter, 1973.

Detroit News, October 7, 1979, Ben Brown, interview with Kosinski.

Fiction International, fall, 1973.

Guardian (Manchester, England), October 21, 1960; June 25, 1973.

Harper's, October, 1965; March, 1969.

Listener, May 8, 1969.

Los Angeles Times Calendar Magazine, April 22, 1973; August 1, 1982.

Media & Methods, April, 1975.

Nation, November 29, 1965.

National Review, February 8, 1966.

New Leader, October 7, 1968, Geoffrey Wolff, review of *Steps.*

New Republic, October 26, 1968; June 26, 1971.

New Statesman, October 22, 1960.

Newsweek, April 26, 1971; February 19, 1973; September 10, 1979; December 7, 1981.

New Yorker, October 10, 1994, p. 46.

New York Post, August 21, 1969; February 19, 1973.

New York Review of Books, February 27, 1969.

New York Times, December 12, 1966; September 13, 1979; February 25, 1982; November 7, 1982.

New York Times Book Review, May 22, 1960; October 31, 1965; October 20, 1968; February 11, 1973; August 10, 1975; October 21, 1979.

New York Times Magazine, February 21, 1982, Barbara Gelb.

North American Review, spring, 1973; March, 1980.

Paris Review, summer, 1972.

Penthouse, July, 1982, Barbara Leaming, interview with Kosinski.

Philadelphia Inquirer, February 18, 1973; February 21, 1982.

Polo, December, 1979.

Psychology Today, December, 1977, Elizabeth Stone.

Publishers Weekly, April 26, 1971; July 9, 1982.

San Francisco Review of Books, March, 1978.

Saturday Review, November 13, 1965; April 17, 1971; April 24, 1971; March 11, 1972.

Third Press Review, September-October, 1975.

Time, October 18, 1968; April 26, 1971; October 31, 1977; September 17, 1979; December 7, 1981; May 13, 1991, p. 55.

Times (London, England), March 10, 1982.

Times Literary Supplement, May 19, 1966.

U.S. News and World Report, January 8, 1979.

Village Voice, August 11, 1975; October 31, 1977; June 22, 1982, July 6, 1982.

Washington Post, August 30, 1971; March 25, 1973; November 27, 1977; September 16, 1979; February 4, 1980; February 21, 1982; April 5, 1989.

Washington Post Book World, November 27, 1977; September 16, 1979; February 21, 1982; July 11, 1982; July 10, 1988, p. 1; May 19, 1991, p. 15.

OBITUARIES:

PERIODICALS

Chicago Tribune, May 5, 1991.

Globe and Mail (Toronto, Ontatio, Canada), May 4, 1991.

Los Angeles Times, May 4, 1991.

Newsweek, May 13, 1991, p. 72.

New York Times, May 4, 1991.

Times (London), May 6, 1991.

Vanity Fair, October, 1991, p. 202.

Washington Post, May 4, 1991.

*   *   *

KOSINSKI, Jerzy Nikodem
   See KOSINSKI, Jerzy

KOZOL, Jonathan 1936-

PERSONAL: Born September 5, 1936, in Boston, MA; son of Harry (a psychiatrist) and Ruth (a psychiatric social worker; maiden name, Massell) Kozol; married briefly during the 1970s. *Education:* Harvard University, B.A. (summa cum laude), 1958; graduate study, Magdalen College, Oxford University, 1958-59. *Politics:* Independent. *Religion:* Jewish.

ADDRESSES: Home—P.O.Box 145, Byfield, MA 01922. *Agent*—Lynn Nesbit, Janklow & Nesbit, 445 Park Ave., New York, NY 10022.

CAREER: Writer. Elementary school teacher in Boston, MA, 1964-65, and in Newton, MA, 1966-68; Storefront Learning Center (alternative school), Boston, educational director and teacher of secondary level English, 1968-71; Center for Intercultural Documentation Institute, Cuernavaca, Mexico, instructor in alternatives in education, 1969, 1970, and 1974; South Boston High School, Boston, remedial writing and reading instructor, 1979; former director of National Literacy Coalition, Boston. Visiting instructor, Yale University, 1969, University of Massachusetts—Amherst, 1978-79, and Trinity College, Hartford, CT, 1980; visiting lecturer in literature and education at hundreds of colleges and universities, 1971-2001, including Antioch University, Vassar College, University of Wisconsin, University of Minnesota, Brown University, Boston University, Columbia University, Harvard University, and Princeton University. Trustee, New School for Children, Roxbury, MA. Consultant to U.S. Office of Economic Opportunity, 1965 and 1966, Pima County Board of Education, Tucson, AZ, 1974, Chicago Board of Education, 1975, Maryland State Penitentiary, Baltimore, MD, 1979, Connecticut Board of Education, Hartford, 1980, Rhode Island Board of Education, Providence, 1980, Cleveland Foundation, 1980—, Cleveland Public Library, 1980—, Edmonton Public Schools, Vancouver School Board, Syracuse University, University of Massachusetts, and others. Correspondent, *Los Angeles Times* and *USA Today,* 1982-83; reporter-at-large, *New Yorker,* 1988.

MEMBER: PEN, Fellowship of Reconciliation, Association of American Rhodes Scholars, National Coalition for the Homeless, National Coalition of Education Activists.

AWARDS, HONORS: Rhodes Scholar, 1958-59; Olympia Award, 1962; Sexton fellowship in creative writing, Harper & Row, 1962; National Book Award, 1968, for

Death at an Early Age: The Destruction of the Hearts and Minds of Negro Children in the Boston Public Schools; Guggenheim fellow, 1970 and 1984; Field Foundation fellow, 1972; Ford Foundation fellow, 1974; Rockefeller fellow, 1978 and 1983; Robert F. Kennedy Book Award, 1988; Conscience in Media Award, American Society of Journalists and Authors, 1988; Christopher Award, 1988, for *Rachel and Her Children: Homeless Families in America;* New England Book Award, and National Book Critics Circle Award finalist, both 1992, both for *Savage Inequalities: Children in America's Schools;* Anisfield-Wolf Book Award, for *Amazing Grace;* Christopher Award, for *Ordinary Resurrections.*

WRITINGS:

NONFICTION

Death at an Early Age: The Destruction of the Hearts and Minds of Negro Children in the Boston Public Schools, Houghton (Boston, MA), 1967, revised edition, New American Library (New York, NY), 1985.
Free Schools, Houghton (Boston, MA), 1972, revised edition published as *Alternative Schools: A Guide for Educators and Parents,* Continuum (New York, NY), 1982.
The Night Is Dark and I Am Far from Home, Houghton (Boston, MA), 1975, revised edition, Touchstone (New York, NY), 1990.
Children of the Revolution, Delacorte (New York, NY), 1978.
Prisoners of Silence: Breaking the Bonds of Adult Illiteracy in the United States, Continuum (New York, NY), 1979.
On Being a Teacher, Continuum (New York, NY), 1981.
Illiterate America, Anchor/Doubleday (New York, NY), 1985.
Rachel and Her Children: Homeless Families in America, Crown (New York, NY), 1988.
Savage Inequalities: Children in America's Schools, Crown (New York, NY), 1991.
Amazing Grace: The Lives of Children and the Conscience of a Nation, Crown (New York, NY), 1995.
Ordinary Resurrections: Children in the Years of Hope, Crown (New York, NY), 2000.

OTHER

(Author of foreword) Wendy E. Mouradian, editor, *Children Our Future: Ethics, Health Policy,*

Medical/Dental Care for Children (April 3-4, 1998 proceedings in Seattle, Washington), Washington State Department of Health (Seattle, WA), 1998.
(With Deborah Heier) *Will Standards Save Public Education?* Beacon Press (Boston, MA), 2000.

Contributor of essays to the *New York Times Book Review* and *Los Angeles Times,* 1970-2001, and to other periodicals, including *Atlantic, New York Times Magazine, Harvard Educational Review, Psychology Today, Saturday Review of Literature, Time, English Record, Nation, Newsweek, New Yorker, Harper's,* and *Washington Post;* contributor of guest editorials to *Saturday Evening Post* and *Look;* contributor of fiction to *Prairie Schooner* and *Esquire.* Book critic, *Life, New York Times, Washington Post,* and *Boston Globe,* 1970-93.

SIDELIGHTS: Jonathan Kozol is a well-known activist and writer who has focused his writings and efforts on ending illiteracy, improving the economic conditions of the poverty-stricken, and pricking the consciences of affluent Americans. Since his early account of teaching at an inner-city public school was published as *Death at an Early Age: The Destruction of the Hearts and Minds of Negro Children in the Boston Public Schools,* many of his writings have pertained to his career as a public school advocate and educator and his experience as an activist on education issues. In *Free Schools,* he recounted his experiences in setting up an alternative school in Boston. *Illiterate America,* a seminal work due to Kozol's exploration of illiteracy, draws on the author's background as a grass-roots organizer to outline his proposal for dealing with the problem of illiteracy in the United States.

In *Rachel and Her Children: Homeless Families in America,* Kozol shifted his focus slightly, looking closely at homeless families living in a shelter in New York City, but in 1991 he returned to education, pointing out in *Savage Inequalities: Children in America's Schools* the gross inequalities in school quality from community to community. With *Amazing Grace: The Lives of Children and the Conscience of a Nation* and *Ordinary Resurrections: Children in the Years of Hope,* Kozol put a human face on the conditions experienced by residents of Mott Haven, the poorest neighborhood in New York City.

Speaking to Paul Galloway of the *Chicago Tribune* about his interest in education, Kozol recounted his privileged childhood; attending a prep school, Harvard, and later Oxford University as a Rhodes Scholar; and then living in poor neighborhoods in Paris while he wrote a novel. He returned to the United States in 1963, somewhat confused about his next step, but planning to get a doctorate and teach English in a university. By chance, in 1964, he learned of a need for tutors in a summer program in Roxbury, and he volunteered. As Galloway reported, "He found that he loved teaching; he loved being with children. In September [1964] he became a teacher in the Boston school system."

Death at an Early Age, Kozol's first book, and winner of the National Book Award in 1968, is in large part a product of its times. Written several years before the integration of Boston public schools, much of the book relates to concerns that arose out of the desegregation debate that was taking shape while Kozol taught, as well as to civil rights conflicts that were transpiring in the South during the mid-1960s. The book documents the repressive teaching methods Kozol's colleagues used, techniques he believed were designed to reinforce a system that would keep the children separate and unequal.

Some reviewers found Kozol's work was open to criticism. As Charles R. Moyer stated in *Carleton Miscellany,* the author's "rather romantic primitivism blinds Mr. Kozol to his own brand of condescension which prevents him from ever seeing the black children in any role other than that of innocent victims." And Kozol's descriptions of "white teachers and agents of the system (with the possible exception of himself) are stereotyped and totally negative," Elizabeth M. Eddy maintained in the *Harvard Educational Review.* "In contrast, there is no unsympathetic sketch of a Negro child or adult."

Others, however, viewed *Death at an Early Age* as providing a public service. Kozol's book "eloquently describes the consequences of this system for both child and teacher, and Kozol himself is a dramatic example of the way in which the teacher is often discouraged from initiating creative learning activities in the classroom," Eddy reported, noting that "in addition, the book presents insightful material relevant to the pathological adaptations made by many teachers who remain in the slum school rather than moving elsewhere."

Free Schools provided parents and teachers dissatisfied with public schools with information on how to create and sustain an independent school for alternative urban education. Kozol explained not only about how to raise funds for a free school, but also how to become partially self-supporting. In addition, he included information on how to find a building and handle the building code harassment he argued was often selectively reserved for such institutions. Finally, Kozol explored the various options alternative schools have in deciding how to establish a governing structure.

Richard Poirier related in the *New York Times Book Review* that "the very form of the book—a kind of manual with advice on how to find a building, how to raise the money, recruit a faculty, set up a curriculum, with lists of contacts and leads—proves that difficulties can indeed be the seed of practical achievement rather than frustration, that anger can be transformed into energy." Jeffrey Lant in the *Southwest Review* found that *Free Schools* is a "potpourri of idiosyncratic views, a book in which Kozol unburdened himself of much of the built-up tension and anxiety which had come as a result of the conflicting pressures involved in establishing his school." And "the book convincingly suggests that a school only becomes 'free' when it creates around it a community of conscience about [immediate] and other injustices and the will to struggle against them," according to Poirier.

Washington Post Book World's Neil Postman believed *Illiterate America* to be Kozol's "best book since *Death at an Early Age.*" Kozol first investigated the problem of illiteracy in his report on the results of the 1961 Cuban literacy campaign, *Children of the Revolution,* which he followed with *Prisoners of Silence: Breaking the Bonds of Adult Illiteracy in the United States.* Postman indicated that "whereas his more recent work has been burdened by an excess of moral indignation, here Kozol allows the outrages of illiteracy to speak for themselves. He guides us through the 'hard facts' of the problem with the discipline and sureness of one who has spent seven years studying the figures."

It is in the government's interest to address the problem of illiteracy, Kozol believes, since illiterates are not only excluded from a multiplicity of benefits, both small and large, which are taken for granted by most Americans, but may also be unproductive and responsible for a large number of industrial accidents. And "the figures Kozol offers from official sources are staggering," according to Peter S. Prescott in *Newsweek.* As Kozol stated, one third of all Americans are completely or partially illiterate.

In his book Kozol praised several existing literacy programs by booksellers, libraries, and other groups as a good beginning, but he criticized others. Too many current literacy efforts are uninspired and unproductive, Kozol contended, particularly in their selection of curriculum material and methods of recruitment, and many are simply inconveniently located. He also found fault with some programs solely on philosophical grounds; he objected especially to the U.S. Army's program and to those of other groups that help the student reach short-term reading goals within the context of gaining high-tech employment skills but do not stress the humanities, political awareness, and the importance of critical thinking. Although Kozol regards the ability to read as a hard survival skill, needed by the citizen in order to perform a myriad of functions in his everyday existence, "we need above all else," he wrote *Illiterate America,* "to do away with the idea of literacy as training for domestication, contrived to fill existent or imagined lower level job slots and consumer roles, and search instead for instruments of moral leverage strong enough to scrutinize those roles and to examine the political determinants of subjugation: examine, study, stand back, and reflect upon their purpose and, by virtue of reflection and examination, first to denounce and finally to transform."

Reviewers were not without criticism for *Illiterate America.* The tone of Kozol's book is angry, according to a *New York Times* critic, but the reviewer remarked that "the kernel of [the author's] message is worth rescuing from the tide of his vehemence." Furthermore, maintained Glen Macnow in the *Detroit Free Press,* "in an age of self-serving conservatism," Kozol "is fighting for the ignored and forgotten." And, as Murphy concluded, "a polemic such as Mr. Kozol's serves a function. His enthusiasm renews our energies for the struggle before us, and gives welcome support to those committed to the notion that universal literacy and education are necessary for living a richer, better informed life."In the opinion of *Mother Jones* reviewer Barbara Ehrenreich, "to read *Illiterate America* is both to know what literacy is for and to understand why it can never be merely 'functional.' If it is a sin to read with pleasure about other people's illiteracy, then . . . the only cure, I am afraid, is to act on [the author's] proposal, and spread the power of the word."

Kozol's next work was inspired by his experiences researching his previous books. Shortly before Christmas of 1985, Kozol spent an evening at the Hotel Martinique in New York, which was serving four hundred of the city's homeless families, including 1,400 children, as a temporary shelter. There he began to talk with some of the residents, and returned many times in the course of writing *Rachel and Her Children.* Sam Roberts commented on the book in the *New York Times:*

"Individually, the voices of the pseudonymous Rachel and other residents of the Martinique are unsettling. Taken together, they represent a searing indictment of a society that has largely chosen to look the other way, to neglect a natural confluence of compassion and enlightened self-interest, and of people in government who may have done their best but whose best too often has not been good enough."

William J. Drummond, writing in Chicago's *Tribune Books,* declared that "Kozol's major achievement in *Rachel and Her Children* is to dispel the media-fashioned stereotype of the homeless and force the reader to look into their faces and listen to their voices." Teresa Funiciello, in the *Nation,* saw Kozol's method in another light. Though she believed Kozol "effectively uses the homeless to describe their own plight," she asserted that "he falls into the same trap that he warns others against: He can't quite hear what they are saying. He refuses to rely on them for prescriptive measures, instead choosing to derive political definitions primarily from the professional 'advocates.'" *New York Times* reviewer Christopher Lehmann-Haupt complained that, although Kozol "successfully humanizes his subject" and "even rises to an occasional pitch of eloquence," "there is something distinctly irritating and occasionally even infuriating about the tone of voice in which Mr. Kozol presumes to lecture us."

Kozol returned to the classroom in *Savage Inequalities.* "This is a painful book to read, alternately suffusing the reader with rage and sorrow," remarked Stan Persky in the Toronto *Globe and Mail.* Andrew Hacker described it in the *New York Times Book Review* as "an impassioned book, laced with anger and indignation, about how our public education system scorns so many of our children." In *Savage Inequalities,* Kozol examined several inner-city schools, beginning in East St. Louis, Illinois, and found the buildings dirty, deteriorating, crowded by the large numbers of students forced to use them, and physically unsafe. These schools also suffered from a scarcity of books, equipment, and teachers. They ran on a much smaller budget than those of such affluent schools as New Trier High in Winnetka, Illinois, and Rye, outside New York City, which he presents, among others, in contrast to the inner-city schools. It is no surprise that a further difference between the two kinds of schools is student population: in most of the inner-city ones, it is predominantly poor and black or Hispanic, while in the suburban institutions it is composed largely of white or Asian children from high-income families.

Publishers Weekly devoted its September 27, 1991 cover to an open letter to President George Bush urging him to read *Savage Inequalities.* Describing the book as "startling and disturbing," the editors noted that it tells "the story of two nations that are separate and unequal in their educational facilities" largely due to the "inequitable distribution of public funds." "The issue is not likely to disappear," Ruth Sidel stated in the *Nation,* but she believed that "the publication of *Savage Inequalities* will insure that the injustice and incredible short-sightedness of American educational policy are vividly and compassionately brought to the forefront of the public's consciousness and the agenda of policymakers." While acknowledging Kozol's argument that "better-off Americans . . . 'do not want poor children to be harmed; they simply want the best for their own children,'" *Time* contributor Emily Mitchell noted that "anyone who has seen the shameful disparities between public schools in rich and poor areas, or who has read Kozol's vivid account, will find it difficult to deny that the differences in funding make a mockery of the nation's ideal."

During the 1990s, curiosity led Kozol down a new path, one both challenging and rewarding. "I hadn't planned to write this book," he recalled of *Amazing Grace* to Lonnie Harp of *Education Week.* "I simply got on the train one day in midtown Manhattan because I'd been told of an Episcopal church where children were given a safe sanctuary, and I wanted to see it. In a matter of days, I became friends with people and just started writing what I was feeling and what they were saying." Many visits and mountains of yellow legal pads later, Kozol published the work, in which he again confronted the troubling questions of poverty and race in America.

Amazing Grace is Kozol's account of time spent in Mott Haven, a desperately poor neighborhood in the South Bronx of New York City. Perhaps the poorest urban neighborhood in all of the United States, Mott Haven's list of woes includes high rates of heroin users, AIDS sufferers, homicides, and unemployment. The city's residents, mostly black and Hispanic, are forced to contend with nightmarish housing conditions, substandard city services, and a deficient educational system. As in his previous books, Kozol reported these conditions with a mixture of rage and resignation, questioning how a city—and a nation—of such vast resources can allow such conditions to exist. After relating anecdote after anecdote of children living in miserable circumstances and adults with little hope of improving their lives, Kozol admitted "that the sense of human ruin on a vast scale becomes unmistakable," to quote *Nation* reviewer Kai Erikson.

Critics commended Kozol's achievement in making visible the sad characteristics of life in Mott Haven. Writing in the *Washington Post Book World,* Marie Arana-Ward called Kozol's text "a powerful book that lays bare what is surely the ugliest truth about us: that there are pockets of hell in our inner cities, and that even as an entire sector of America is condemned to burn in them, we insist on looking the other way." Erikson recommended it for "its calm power, its sensitivity and its almost painful clarity." "Kozol's job is to sound alarms and to put human faces in terrains that we know primarily from a numbing array of numbers and facts. This he does beautifully," she added.

Some reviewers, while conceding the power of Kozol's account, stated that the author seems to have become less hopeful about the possibility of change than in his previous books. "Like most of Mr. Kozol's writing, *Amazing Grace* is passionate and poignant. But in places it also seems jaded and languid, as if Mr. Kozol were becoming tired of shouting, of exposing this country's often cold treatment of its downtrodden," remarked Alex Kotlowitz in the *New York Times Book Review.* Similarly, Chicago *Tribune Books* reviewer Micaela di Leonardo noted "a new, exhausted, demoralized more in this account." Indeed, Kozol has long been frustrated by the stubbornness of social problems, or rather society's lack of true commitment to solving them. "I write because I want to make something different in the world," Kozol told Harp. About *Amazing Grace,* he continued, "This time, I want to raise the stakes and say the question here is not whether we know what the problem is or whether we have the strategy to deal with it or the money to deal with it. Those aren't really the questions. The question is whether we want to be one society or two. Until that is dealt with, nothing else will be solved, and all the rest—the reports and charity and pilot programs—will be pretense." In Harp's view, "This time around, Jonathan Kozol is shooting straight for the soul."

Another critic faulted Kozol for perceived errors of omission. In *Commentary* Sol Stern complained that some of Kozol's statistics (such as the murder rate) are outdated and that he ignored the success of students at Catholic elementary schools in the neighborhood or the construction of low-income housing in the area by a private group. Nevertheless, as Erikson pointed out, "Among the many virtues of Jonathan Kozol's strong and often beautiful book is that we cannot forget for even an instant that the poor are of our kind and live but a moment away." In that context, concluded Arana-Ward, "[Kozol's] book is as good as a blessing."

In 2000, Kozol's *Ordinary Resurrections: Children in the Years of Hope* was released. In this work he presented New York City's South Bronx through a different perspective, a less strident and more "hope"-filled outlook—that of the area's children. Exposing complex beliefs and a range of emotions, *Ordinary Resurrections: Children in the Years of Hope* presents the life and leadership seen in their peer-groups, home, schools, and religious institutions. Readers are also shown in following some of these children for more than six years how Kozol has been affected by what his subjects have given him. Daniel LeDuc, in a review for the *Philadelphia Inquirer*, noted that *Ordinary Resurrections* evinces "less anger—but no less passion" and is "a sobering reminder that not everyone is breathlessly tracking the stock market." "I wanted this book to be a very gentle book," Kozol told Mark Feeney of the *Boston Globe*. "I got sick of angry polemic. . . . So I tried to subdue my voice. I thought it would be unworthy of the children's sweetness if I wrote in a strident tone." While acknowledging the problems these children face and will likely face later in life, Kozol explained: "The spiritual strengths of the children and the dedication of their teachers in the public schools were decisive factors here [in the book's overall hopeful tone]. The schools are still unequal, and the medical and social inequalities these children face are still grotesque and shameful. But I've focused here on younger kids before they have been damaged by the cruelties of life. Their innocence and energy renewed my sense of hope."

BIOGRAPHICAL AND CRITICAL SOURCES:

BOOKS

Contemporary Literary Criticism, Volume 17, Thomson Gale (Detroit, MI), 1981.

Kozol, Jonathan, *Illiterate America*, Anchor/Doubleday (New York, NY), 1985.

Kozol, Jonathan, *Amazing Grace: The Lives of Children and the Conscience of a Nation*, Crown, 1995.

PERIODICALS

America, April 5, 1980.

Antioch Review, winter, 1977.

Best Sellers, August 15, 1972; June, 1981.

Booklist, March 15, 2000, Mary Carroll, review of *Ordinary Resurrections: Children in the Years of Hope*, p. 1291.

Boston Globe, May 17, 2000, Mark Feeney, "The Gentlest Angry Man," pp. C1, C6.

Carleton Miscellany, winter, 1969, Charles R. Moyer, review of *Death at an Early Age*.

Chicago Sunday Tribune, August 16, 1959.

Chicago Tribune, February 15, 1988.

Christianity Today, June 12, 2000, Lauren Winner, "Suffer the Children," (Interview), p. 94.

Christian Science Monitor, December 10, 1959; October 5, 1967; July 5, 2000, "At the Heart of No Ordinary Crusade."

Commentary, March, 1996, Sol Stern, review of *Amazing Grace*, pp. 70-72.

Commonweal, October 8, 1976; April 24, 1981.

Detroit Free Press, March 31, 1985, Glen Macnow, review of *Illiterate America*.

Education Week, October 11, 1995, Lonnie Harp, "Soul Searching," pp. 25-31.

Globe and Mail (Toronto, Ontario, Canada), February 27, 1988; November 23, 1991, p. C8.

Harvard Educational Review, spring, 1968, Elizabeth M. Eddy, review of *Death at an Early Age*.

Journal of Black Studies, January, 1998, Iris J. Creasy, "A New View of an Old Problem."

Journal Record, October 4, 2002.

Kirkus Reviews, August 1, 1975.

Library Journal, July, 2000, Jack Forman, review of *Ordinary Resurrections: Children in the Years of Hope*, p. 112.

Los Angeles Times Book Review, June 1, 1980; December 26, 1982; March 17, 1985; February 7, 1988, p. 1; October 6, 1991, p. 2.

Midwest Quarterly, spring, 1998, Adonna Zordel Helmig, review of *Amazing Grace*, pp. 360-361.

Mother Jones, April, 1985, Barbara Ehrenreich, review of *Illiterate America*.

Nation, October 28, 1978; April 2, 1988, pp. 465-474; November 18, 1991, pp. 620-622; November 20, 1995, Kai Erikson, review of *Amazing Grace*, pp. 616-619, 622.

New Republic, June 24, 1972; December 23, 1981; February 3, 1992, p. 43; June 17, 1996, Sara Mosle, review of *Amazing Grace*, pp. 27-29.

Newsweek, March 11, 1985; February 1, 1988, p. 55; May 22, 2000, Ellis Cose, "Bearing Witness in the Twilight: On a Journey to One of America's Poorest Neighborhoods, Jonathan Kozol Finds Both Bleakness and Beauty," p. 66.

New Yorker, October 18, 1958; March 16, 1968; October 27, 1975.

New York Herald Tribune, August 16, 1959.

New York Review of Books, December 21, 1967; February 16, 1989, pp. 24-27.

New York Times, August 16, 1959; March 21, 1985; January 25, 1988; January 28, 1988; October 15, 1995, Alex Kotlowitz, "Young and Poor."

New York Times Book Review, October 1, 1967; March 5, 1972; November 2, 1975; May 4, 1980; August

9, 1981; April 14, 1985; January 31, 1988, p. 7; October 6, 1991, p. 7; October 15, 1995, Alex Kotlowitz, review of *Amazing Grace,* p. 26.

Philadelphia Inquirer, May 14, 2000, Daniel LeDuc, review of *Ordinary Resurrections.*

Plough, January, 1996, Christopher Zimmerman, "A Conversation with Jonathan Kozol," pp. 1-7.

Publishers Weekly, September 27, 1991; March 20, 2000, review of *Ordinary Resurrections,* p. 77; May 15, 2000, Sally Lodge, "Quiet Times for a Crusader," p. 82; March 19, 2001, p. 96.

San Francisco Chronicle, August 19, 1959.

Saturday Review, October 11, 1958; September 5, 1959.

School Administrator, November, 2000, Paul Houston, "A Conversation With Kozol," p. 16.

School Library Journal, August, 2000, Jane S. Drabkin, review of *Ordinary Resurrections: Children in the Years of Hope,* p. 214.

Sojourners, September, 2000, Sara Wenger Shenk, review of *Ordinary Resurrections: Children in the Years of Hope,* p. 56.

Southwest Review, winter, 1977, Jeffrey Lant, review of *Free Schools.*

Theology Today, April, 1996, Robert Coles, review of *Amazing Grace.*

Tikkun, November-December, 1995, Ruth Sidel, review of *Amazing Grace,* pp. 76-77; July, 2000, Michael Nagler, review of *Ordinary Resurrections: Children in the Years of Hope,* p. 80.

Time, February 8, 1988, p. 74; October 14, 1991, pp. 60-61.

Times Literary Supplement, November 20, 1959.

Tribune Books (Chicago, IL), January 24, 1988, pp. 1, 9; October 13, 1991, p. 5; November 12, 1995, p. 7.

U.S. Catholic, October, 2000, "Still Separate and Unequal," (interview), p. 18.

Village Voice, December 1, 1975.

Washington Post, June 1, 2000, Megan Rosenfeld, "The Peace of Children," pp. C1-C2.

Washington Post Book World, November 19, 1978; March 16, 1980; June 14, 1981; March 31, 1985; June 2, 1985; January 31, 1988, pp. 1, 3; October 20, 1991, pp. 3, 7; October 22, 1995, p. 1.

*   *   *

KRAKAUER, Jon 1954-

PERSONAL: Born 1954, in Oregon; married. *Education:* Hampshire College, bachelor's degree, 1976. *Hobbies and other interests:* Mountain climbing.

ADDRESSES: Office—c/o Author Mail, Doubleday Broadway Group, 1540 Broadway, New York, NY 10036.

CAREER: Journalist. Worked variously as a carpenter and salmon fisherman, c. 1970s; freelance writer, 1983—; Everest '96 Memorial Fund, founder. Member of board, American Himalayan Foundation, and Alex Lowe Charitable Foundation.

AWARDS, HONORS: National Magazine Award, 1997; Walter Sullivan Allen Award, American Geophysical Union, 1997, for excellence in science journalism; *Time* book of the year designation, *New York Times* best books of the year designation, and National Book Critics Circle Award finalist, all 1997, and Pulitzer Prize finalist in general nonfiction, 1998, all for *Into Thin Air;* Academy Award in Literature, American Academy of Arts and Letters, 1999; *Los Angeles Times* Book Award nomination, 2003, for *Under the Banner of Heaven: A Story of Violent Faith.*

WRITINGS:

Eiger Dreams: Ventures among Men and Mountains (essay collection), Lyons and Burford (New York, NY), 1990.

(Photographer) *Iceland: Land of the Sagas,* (travelogue), text by David Roberts, Abrams (New York, NY), 1990.

(Author of foreword) David Roberts, *The Mountain of My Fear,* Mountaineers Books, 1991.

Into the Wild (nonfiction), Villard (New York, NY), 1996.

(Author of foreword) David Roberts, *Escape Routes: Further Adventure Writings,* Mountaineers Books, 1997.

Into Thin Air: A Personal Account of the Mount Everest Disaster, Villard (New York, NY), 1998.

(With David F. Breashears) *High Exposure: An Enduring Passion for Everest and Unforgiving Places,* Simon & Schuster (New York, NY), 2000.

(Author of introduction) Jamling Tenzing Norgay, with Broughton Coburn, *Touching My Father's Soul: A Sherpa's Journey to the Top of Everest,* HarperSanFrancisco (San Francisco, CA), 2001.

(Author of preface) Valerian Albanov, *In the Land of White Death: An Epic Story of Survival in the Siberian Arctic,* introduction by David Roberts, Random House (New York, NY), 2001.

Under the Banner of Heaven: A Story of Violent Faith, Doubleday (New York, NY), 2003.

Contributor of articles to periodicals, including *Smithsonian, EO, Architectural Digest, Rolling Stone, Time, Washington Post, New York Times,* and *National Geographic.* Contributing editor to *Outside* magazine.

Into Thin Air has been translated into over twenty languages.

EDITOR; *"MODERN LIBRARY EXPLORATION" SERIES*

Roland Huntford, *The Last Place on Earth: Scott and Amundsen's Race to the South Pole,* revised edition, Random House (New York, NY), 1999.

Gaston Rebuffat, *Starlight and Storm: The Conquest for the Great North Faces of the Alps,* Random House (New York, NY), 1999.

Francis Parkman, *La Salle and the Discovery of the Great West,* Random House (New York, NY), 1999.

Tim Severin, *The Brendan Voyage,* Random House (New York, NY), 2000.

Chauncey Loomis, *Weird and Tragic Shores,* Random House (New York, NY), 2000.

Robert Dunn, *The Shameless Diary of an Explorer,* Random House (New York, NY), 2001.

ADAPTATIONS: *Into Thin Air* has been recorded as an audiobook, read by the author, BDD Audio, 1997, and was adapted as a television film, 1998.

SIDELIGHTS: Best known as the author of the gripping 1997 book *Into Thin Air: A Personal Account of the Mt. Everest Disaster,* which describes a mountaineering tragedy, Jon Krakauer is a journalist and nonfiction author whose award-winning writings on mountain climbing and other sports combine the knowledge of the insider with the writer's sense of dramatic and well-timed storytelling. Critics have recommended the author's first book-length publication, *Eiger Dreams: Ventures among Men and Mountains,* a collection of essays on mountain climbing, for armchair adventurers, novices, and experienced climbers alike, praising its thrilling subject matter and Krakauer's unpretentious prose style. Krakauer's second book, *Into the Wild,* reconstructs the last days of Christopher McCandless, a young man who gave away all his possessions and traveled to the Alaskan wilderness only to die of starvation in an abandoned bus. Drawing on numerous interviews, Krakauer paints a touching picture of the troubled young man, while also attempting to understand the motivations for McCandless's trip to one of nature's most forbidding landscapes.

Eiger Dreams is a collection of twelve essays, several featuring famous eccentrics of the mountain-climbing set—including John Gill, who climbs boulders, and the Burgess twins, who, without an income, manage to travel the world climbing its most challenging peaks—while others center on the mountains themselves. The Eiger of the title is a fiercely difficult mountain in Switzerland that the author attempted and failed to climb, providing one of the occasional moments of humor in these adventure-filled pages. "Krakauer conveys well the formidable, even terrifying aspects of the sport," emphasized a reviewer for *Kirkus Reviews.* Tim Cahill, critic for the *New York Times Book Review,* singled out the author's avoidance of the clichés of "conquering" mountain peaks, and the trite epiphanies that occur there: "There is a beauty in his mountains beyond that expressed in conventional sermons. His reverence is earned, and it's entirely genuine."

Krakauer's *Into the Wild,* is the nonfiction account of the life and death of McCandless. A brilliant young man from a loving and prosperous family, McCandless abandoned his upper-middle-class existence to live the simple unencumbered life of a wanderer, influenced by the example of earlier American writers such as Henry David Thoreau and Jack London. In April of 1992 he hitchhiked to Alaska, carrying with him only a bag of rice, a .22-gauge shotgun, and some books. A few months later the young man's corpse was discovered alongside a desperate note in which he begged to be saved. Although McCandless's death was greeted with a mixture of derision and apathy by Alaskans, who pointed to the arrogance inherent in his ill-equipped and untutored attempt to live off the land, Krakauer manages to make his subject sympathetic, according to several reviewers. "The more we learn about him, the more mysterious McCandless becomes, and the more intriguing," wrote Thomas McNamee in the *New York Times Book Review.* Christopher Lehmann-Haupt similarly remarked in his review of *Into the Wild* for the *New York Times* that Krakauer mitigates the reader's desire to condemn McCandless by presenting him through the eyes of those who encountered him. The people Krakauer interviewed emphasize "how particularly intelligent, unusual and just plain likable this young man was," Lehmann-Haupt wrote, the critic also commenting favorably on Krakauer's apt placing of McCandless's quest in the context of other spiritual daredevils and sons of dominating, successful fathers. In this context, Krakauer reveals his own survival of an adolescent trek up Devils Thumb, a treacherous mountain on the Alaska-British Columbia border. Although McNamee complained that the author too-readily dismisses the possibility that McCandless's actions were at least partly the result of mental instability, he concluded that while the young man's "life and his death may have been meaningless, absurd, even reprehensible, but by the end of *Into the Wild,* you care for him deeply." Similarly, Lehmann-Haupt maintained that "Krakauer has taken the tale of a kook who went into the woods, and made of it a heart-rending drama of human yearning."

In Krakauer's most well-known work, *Into Thin Air,* he relives a 1996 guided climb up Mt. Everest in which he was participating in while on assignment for *Outside* magazine. First summitted in 1953 by Sir Edmund Hillary, Mount Everest by the mid-1990s had become the site of numerous commercial expedition tours where paid guides would lead amateur climbers able to pay the price. Investigating the safety practices of such ventures, and an experienced climber himself—although not at Everest's 29,028-foot altitude—forty-three-year-old Krakauer joined the small group of men and woman and their leaders, two ultra-experienced mountaineers, in their trip up to the summit. From base camp the group stopped at four intermediate camps staged along their route to Everest's highest altitude, each stay designed to allow their bodies to adapt to the depleted air pressure and oxygen levels that gradually weaken and befuddled weary mountaineers. Such conditions attack even experienced climbers; as *Entertainment Weekly* contributor Mark Harris noted, "there is no adjusting: Leave aside the blinding headaches, the gastrointestinal brutalities, the frozen fingers that frigid winds can produce, and the far more deadly possibilities of pulmonary or cerebral edema, and a climber will still face hypoxia, the oxygen deprivation that can reduce his judgment to that of a slow child just when he needs his adult wits most." As Krakauer later realized, it was hypoxia that, when a rogue storm hit Mount Everest, caused those attempting to scale the final, highly exposed region of the mountain to react poorly; when the storm clouds cleared eight people—including the two expedition leaders—were left dead, the author fortunate he was not among them.

"As an inquiry into the outer limits of human strength and into the inner turmoil of survivor's guilt, Krakauer's narrative leaves a reader virtually breathless," noted *Booklist* reviewer Gilbert Taylor. In *Newsweek* Jerry Adler wrote that *Into Thin Air* is "remarkable for its clear-eyed refusal to give the reader even a token reason for ever going above sea level." In addition to refraining from romanticizing the tragedy, Krakauer attempts to place responsibility judiciously, following what Adler described as "the disaster-book convention that the ghastly denouement must be the result of a series of small missteps, each seemingly innocuous." Not-

ing that Krakauer's book "offers readers the emotional immediacy of a survivor's testament as well as the precision, detail, and quest for accuracy of a great piece of journalism," Harris added that, "as the full horror of Krakauer's trop unfolds, it is impossible to finish this book unmoved and impossible to forget for a moment that its author would have given anything not to have written it."

Several years after his Mount Everest experiences Krakauer attempted another daunting project: to unearth the truth behind the headlines regarding a 1984 murder of Brenda Lafferty and her infant daughter at the hands of Brenda's Mormon brother-in-law. "Part *In Cold Blood,* part historical-theological muckraking," in the opinion of *Book* contributor Paul Evans, Krakauer's 2003 work *Under the Banner of Heaven: A Story of Violent Faith* "courts controversy in assessing not only the astonishing success of the Mormon faith . . . but also the history of violence that underscores it." Raised in a heavily Mormon community in Colorado, Krakauer adds to his familiarity of the Church of the Latter Day Saints by exploring the fundamentalist branch of this religion, a branch officially banned in 1890 due to its advocacy of polygamy. As Jennifer Reese explained in *Entertainment Weekly,* Mormon fundamentalists practice "a harsh, decentralized faith" that has over 30,000 adherents "in scattered pockets throughout the western U.S., Mexico, and Canada." Noting that *Under the Banner of Heaven* "is a departure from Krakauer's . . . macho page-turners about misadventures in the wilderness," Reese maintained that "it is every bit as engrossing." While cautioning that the author attempts to take on too much—mixing in everything from the history of Mormonism to the Elizabeth Smart kidnaping of 2002—Reese dubbed the book "rambling, unsettling, and impossible to put down." A *Publishers Weekly* reviewer noted in particular Krakauer's efforts, despite his own agnosticism, to condemn to broadly: while he "poses some striking questions about the close-minded, closed-door policies of the [Mormon] region," the reviewer wrote, Krakauer also "demonstrates that most nonfundamentalist Mormons are community oriented, industrious and law-abiding."

BIOGRAPHICAL AND CRITICAL SOURCES:

PERIODICALS

Book, July-August, 2003, Paul Evans, review of *Under the Banner of Heaven: A Story of Violent Faith,* p. 71.

Booklist, April 1, 1997, Gilbert Taylor, review of *Into Thin Air,* p. 1276; July, 2003, review of *Under the Banner of Heaven,* p. 1844.

Economist, September 6, 1997, review of *Into Thin Air,* p. 17.

Entertainment Weekly, May 2, 1997, Mark Harris, review of *Into Thin Air,* p. 50; August 1, 2003, Jennifer Reese, review of *Under the Banner of Heaven,* p. 81.

Kirkus Reviews, February 1, 1990, p. 159.

Library Journal, April 1, 1997, review of *Into Thin Air,* p. 117; June 15, 2003, Rachel Collins, review of *Under the Banner of Heaven,* p. 88.

Los Angeles Times Book Review, September 3, 1995, p. 9.

New Statesman, August 22, 1997, Peter Gillman, review of *Into Thin Air,* p. 44.

Newsweek, April 21, 1997, Jerry Adler, review of *Into Thin Air,* p. 76.

New York Times, January 4, 1996, p. C17.

New York Times Book Review, June 10, 1990, p. 48; March 3, 1996, p. 29.

People, February 12, 1996, p. 35.

Publishers Weekly, February 2, 1990, p. 73; October 19, 1990, p. 44; November 6, 1995, p. 76; March 17, 1997, review of *Into Thin Air,* p. 63; June 30, 2003, review of *Under the Banner of Heaven,* p. 72.

School Library Journal, May 2004, Vicki Reutter, review of *Into Thin Air,* p. 66.

Sports Illustrated, May 12, 1997, review of *Into Thin Air,* p. 18.

Time, April 21, 1997, John Skow, review of *Into Thin Air,* p. 123; July 21, 2003, Lev Grossman, review of *Under the Banner of Heaven,* p. 62.

USA Today Magazine, March, 2004, Gerald F. Kreyche, review of *Under the Banner of Heaven,* p. 81.

*   *   *

KUMIN, Maxine 1925-
(Maxine Winokur Kumin)

PERSONAL: Born June 6, 1925, in Philadelphia, PA; daughter of Peter (a pawnbroker) and Doll (Simon) Winokur; married Victor Montwid Kumin (an engineering consultant), June 29, 1946; children: Jane Simon, Judith Montwid, Daniel David. *Education:* Radcliffe College, A.B., 1946, M.A., 1948.

ADDRESSES: Home—40 Harriman Lane, Warner, NH 03278. *Agent*—Curtis Brown, 10 Astor Place, New York, NY 10003.

CAREER: Poet, children's author, and fiction writer. Tufts University, Medford, MA, instructor, 1958-61, lecturer in English, 1965-68; Radcliffe College, Cambridge, MA, scholar of Radcliffe Institute for Independent Study (now called The Bunting Institute), 1961-63. University of Massachusetts—Amherst, visiting lecturer in English, 1973; Columbia University, New York, NY, adjunct professor of writing, 1975; Brandeis University, Waltham, MA, Fannie Hurst Professor of Literature, 1975; Princeton University, Princeton, NJ, visiting senior fellow and lecturer, 1977; Washington University, St. Louis, MO, Fannie Hurst Professor of Literature, 1977; Randolph-Macon Woman's College, Lynchburg, VA, Carolyn Wilkerson Bell Visiting Scholar, 1978; Woodrow Wilson Visiting Fellow, 1979; Princeton University, visiting lecturer, 1979, 1981-82; Bucknell University, Lewisburg, PA, poet-in-residence, 1983; Massachusetts Institute of Technology, Cambridge, MA, visiting professor, 1984; Atlantic Center for the Arts, New Smyrna Beach, FL, master artist, 1984; University of Miami, Miami, FL, visiting professor, 1995; Pitzer College, Claremont, CA, visiting professor, 1996; Davidson College, Davidson, NC, McGee Professor of Writing, 1997; Florida International University, Miami, visiting professor, 1998-99. Member of staff, Bread Loaf Writers' Conference, 1969-71, 1973, 1975, 1977, and Sewanee Writers' Conference, 1993-94. Traveled with the United States Information Agency's Arts America Tour, 1983. Poetry consultant to Library of Congress, 1981-82. Elector, The Poet's Corner, Cathedral of St. John the Divine, 1990—; Chancellor, Academy of American Poets, 1995—.

MEMBER: Poetry Society of America, PEN, Authors Guild, Writers Union, Radcliffe Alumnae Association.

AWARDS, HONORS: Lowell Mason Palmer Award, 1960; National Endowment for the Arts grant, 1966; National Council on the Arts and Humanities fellow, 1967-68; William Marion Reedy Award, 1968; Eunice Tietjens Memorial Prize, *Poetry,* 1972; Pulitzer Prize for poetry, 1973, for *Up Country: Poems of New England;* Borestone Mountain Award, 1976; Radcliffe College Alumnae Recognition Award, 1978; Woodrow Wilson fellowship, 1979-80, 1991-93; American Academy and Institute of Arts and Letters award, 1980, for excellence in literature; Academy of American Poets fellowship, 1985; Levison award, *Poetry,* 1986; named Poet Laureate of the state of New Hampshire, 1989-94; Sarah Joseph Hale Award, Richards Library (Newport, NH), 1992; Poets' Prize, 1994, and Aiken Taylor Poetry Prize, 1995, both for *Looking for Luck;* Harvard Graduate School of Arts and Sciences Centennial Award, 1996; D.H.L., Centre College, 1976, Davis and Elkins

College, 1977, Regis College, 1979, New England College, 1982, Claremont Graduate School, 1983, University of New Hampshire, 1984, and Keene State College, 1995.

WRITINGS:

POETRY

Halfway, Holt (New York, NY), 1961.

The Privilege, Harper (New York, NY), 1965.

The Nightmare Factory, Harper (New York, NY), 1970.

Up Country: Poems of New England, New and Selected, illustrated by Barbara Swan, Harper (New York, NY), 1972.

House, Bridge, Fountain, Gate, Viking (New York, NY), 1975.

Progress Report (sound recording), Watershed, 1976.

The Retrieval System, Viking (New York, NY), 1978.

Our Ground Time Here Will Be Brief: New and Selected Poems, Viking (New York, NY), 1982.

Closing the Ring: Selected Poems, Press of Appletree Alley, Bucknell University (Lewisburg, PA), 1984.

The Long Approach, Viking (New York, NY), 1985.

Nurture, Viking Penguin (New York, NY), 1989.

Looking for Luck, W.W. Norton (New York, NY), 1992.

Connecting the Dots: Poems, W.W. Norton (New York, NY), 1996.

Selected Poems, 1960-1990, W.W. Norton (New York, NY), 1997.

The Long Marriage, W.W. Norton (New York, NY), 2001.

Bringing Together: Uncollected Early Poems, 1958-1988, W.W. Norton (New York, NY), 2003.

Jack and Other New Poems, W.W. Norton (New York, NY), 2005.

FICTION

Through Dooms of Love (novel), Harper (New York, NY), 1965, published as *A Daughter and Her Loves,* Gollancz (London, England), 1965.

The Passions of Uxport (novel), Harper (New York, NY), 1968.

The Abduction (novel), Harper (New York, NY), 1971.

The Designated Heir (novel), Viking (New York, NY), 1974.

Why Can't We Live Together Like Civilized Human Beings? (short stories), Viking (New York, NY), 1982.

Quit Monks or Die! (mystery novel), Story Line (Ashland, OR), 1999.

FOR CHILDREN

Sebastian and the Dragon, Putnam (New York, NY), 1960.

Spring Things, Putnam (New York, NY), 1961.

A Summer Story, Putnam (New York, NY), 1961.

Follow the Fall, Putnam (New York, NY), 1961.

A Winter Friend, Putnam (New York, NY), 1961.

Mittens in May, Putnam (New York, NY), 1962.

No One Writes a Letter to the Snail, Putnam (New York, NY), 1962.

(With Anne Sexton) *Eggs of Things,* Putnam (New York, NY), 1963.

Archibald the Traveling Poodle, Putnam (New York, NY), 1963.

(With Anne Sexton) *More Eggs of Things,* Putnam (New York, NY), 1964.

Speedy Digs Downside Up, Putnam (New York, NY), 1964.

The Beach before Breakfast, Putnam (New York, NY), 1964.

Paul Bunyan, Putnam (New York, NY), 1966.

Faraway Farm, W.W. Norton (New York, NY), 1967.

The Wonderful Babies of 1809 and Other Years, Putnam (New York, NY), 1968.

When Grandmother Was Young, Putnam (New York, NY), 1969.

When Mother Was Young, Putnam (New York, NY), 1970.

When Great-Grandmother Was Young, illustrated by Don Almquist, Putnam (New York, NY), 1971.

(With Anne Sexton) *Joey and the Birthday Present,* illustrated by Evaline Ness, McGraw-Hill (New York, NY), 1971.

(With Anne Sexton) *The Wizard's Tears,* McGraw-Hill (New York, NY), 1975.

What Color Is Caesar?, illustrated by Evaline Ness, McGraw-Hill (New York, NY), 1978.

The Microscope, illustrated by Arnold Lobel, Harper (New York, NY), 1984.

Mites to Mastodons: A Book of Animal Poems, Small and Large, illustrated by Pamela Zagarenski, edited by Liz Rosenberg, Houghton Mifflin (Boston, MA), 2006.

OTHER

(Author of introduction) Carole Oles, *The Loneliness Factor,* Texas Tech University Press (Lubbock, TX), 1979.

To Make a Prairie: Essays on Poets, Poetry, and Country Living, University of Michigan Press (Ann Arbor, MI), 1980.

(Editor) William Carpenter, *Rain,* Northeastern University Press (Boston, MA), 1985.

In Deep: Country Essays, Viking (New York, NY), 1987.

Women, Animals, and Vegetables: Essays and Stories, W.W. Norton (New York, NY), 1994.

Diane Ackerman and Maxine Kumin Reading from Their Work (sound recording), Archive of Recorded Poetry and Literature, Library of Congress (Washington, DC), 1994.

Always Beginning: Essays on a Life in Poetry, Copper Canyon (Port Townsend, WA), 2000.

Inside the Halo and Beyond: The Anatomy of a Recovery, W.W. Norton (New York, NY), 2000.

(Editor, with Deborah Brown and Annie Finch) *Lofty Dogmas: Poets on Poetics,* University of Arkansas Press (Fayetteville, AR), 2005.

Former columnist, *Writer.* Contributor of poetry to *New Yorker, Atlantic, Poetry, Saturday Review,* and other periodicals. Kumin's manuscripts are held at the Bienecke Library, Yale University.

SIDELIGHTS: Even though the awards she has received for her work have included the prestigious Pulitzer Prize, Maxine Kumin's works have yet to be the subject of serious study by academics. A former poetry consultant for the Library of Congress and a staff member of the Bread Loaf Writers' Conference, Kumin has remained active in teaching and writing during a career that has spanned over three decades. Despite the necessity of traveling away from home to lecture at schools and universities around the United States, Kumin has retained close ties with her farmhouse in rural New Hampshire; in an interview with Joan Norris published in *Crazy Horse,* the poet disclosed, "Practically all of [my poems] have come out of this geography and this state of mind."

Kumin is often referred to as a regional pastoral poet as her verse is deeply rooted to her native New England. "I have been twitted with the epithet 'Roberta Frost,' which is not a bad thing to be," Kumin told interviewer Karla Hammond in the *Western Humanities Review.* In other efforts to classify her work, critics have also described her as a transcendentalist, like Henry David Thoreau, or a confessional poet, like Kumin's friend and coauthor, the late Anne Sexton. But *New York Times* reviewer Michiko Kakutani found her most like Galway Kinnell, since both are "concerned with human mortality, with the love shared between parents and their children, with the seasonal patterns of nature and the possibility of retrieving and preserving the past." In many

ways, critics also point out, Kumin is not like other poets. "In a period when most contemporary poetry reflects a chaotic and meaningless universe, Kumin is one of a handful of poets who insist upon order," Susan Ludvigson elaborated in the *Dictionary of Literary Biography.* Whatever her link to other poets may be, Philip Booth maintained in the *American Poetry Review* that "what is remarkable . . . is the extent to which poets like Maxine Kumin can survive and outdistance both their peers and themselves by increasingly trusting those elements of their work which are most strongly individual." For Kumin, Booth noted, these elements include "the dailiness of farm life and farm death."

Her "well-made poems and stories are two ways of coming at the same immemorial preoccupations: aging and mortality," wrote Clara Claiborne Park in the *Nation,* and deemed Kumin's work "the fiction and poetry of maturity." Her poems are also mature for another reason: Kumin did not begin to write and publish until mid-life, though she had shown an inclination to write poetry much earlier. During high school, she wrote what she considered to be very poor poetry of a late adolescent. And later, as a freshman at Radcliffe, Kumin presented a sheaf of poems to the instructor for his comments. Kumin told Norris, "He had written on the front: 'Say it with flowers, but for God's sake don't try to write poems.' That just closed me off. I didn't try to write another poem for about six years." By that time she had become the wife of an engineer, the mother of three children, a resident of a Boston suburb, and was acutely miserable. When Kumin began writing again as a kind of therapy, she at last found encouragement in workshops at the Boston Center for Adult Education.

The poems Kumin began to compose during the early period in her writing career recall her childhood in a home on a hill "between a convent and a madhouse." In these poems, wrote Ludvigson, Kumin displays "an early mastery of technique" and "deals skillfully with subjects that she continues to explore throughout her career: religious and cultural identity, the fragility of human life, loss and the ever-present threat of loss, the relation of man to nature." Many of these early works were collected in Kumin's first book of poems, *Halfway,* which was published in 1961 when she was thirty-six. Another outgrowth of the Boston workshops Kumin attended was her friendship with Anne Sexton. Both homemakers with children when they began their literary careers, they wrote four children's books together and in general contributed to each other's development. "Maxine, a Radcliffe graduate, possessed a technical expertise and an analytical detachment that balanced Anne's mercurial brilliance," explained Linda Gray

Sexton and Lois Ames, editors of *Anne Sexton: A Self-Portrait in Letters.* The two poets "often communicated daily, by letter if separated by oceans, otherwise by telephone. They supervised each other's poetry and prose, 'workshopping' line by line for hours." Consequently, critics tried to trace a strong mutual influence, but both poets denied one. Ludvigson noted, "In a 1974 interview in *Women's Studies,* each claimed she never tampered with the other's voice, and each offered, according to Sexton, 'to think how to shape, how to make better, but not, how to make like me.'" Nonetheless, there were some significant exchanges. As Kumin related in the chapter she contributed to *Anne Sexton: The Artist and Her Critics,* Sexton had written several poems based on fairy tales that later became part of her Pulitzer Prize-winning book, *Transformations.* Sexton "had no thought of a collection at first," said Kumin. "I urged and bullied her to go on after the first few poems to think in terms of a whole book of them." Kumin also suggested the title. "We had been talking about the way many contemporary poets translated from languages they did not themselves read, but used trots or had the poems filtered through an interpreter, and that these poems were *adaptations.* It struck me then that Anne's poems about the fairy tales went one step further and were *transformations.*" Sexton reciprocated by suggesting the title for the book that was to become Kumin's Pulitzer Prize winner. "In that same conversation Annie was urging me to collect the 'pastoral' poems I'd written, and I said, 'but what would I call it?' and she said, '*Up Country,* of course.'"

"It is the tie between Kumin and Sexton that fascinates many readers," Ludvigson noted, and the public's interest peaked when Sexton committed suicide in 1974. . . . Yet, despite her connection to Sexton, Kumin's work shows little signs of being included in the confessional school. Rather, observed Monroe K. Spears in the *Washington Post Book World,* "much of her poetry throughout is openly autobiographical, and the reader becomes acquainted with her family. . . , her Frostian New Hampshire neighbor Henry Manley, . . . and so on." The "loss of the parent" and the "relinquishment of the child" are two central themes Kumin identified in a lecture on her work given at Princeton in 1977 and reprinted in *To Make a Prairie: Essays on Poets, Poetry, and Country Living.* Booth explained the presence of these themes in Kumin's 1978 book, *The Retrieval System,* by noting that the poet "is familiar (in every sense) with how one's parents depart toward death at nearly the same time one's children leave to find lives of their own. Inevitable as such desertions may be, their coincidence . . . is the shock which these seismographic poems record and try to re-

cover from." Booth believed Kumin's poems "amply show that suffering doesn't require confession to validate pain," and that her "mode is memorial rather than confessional."

"Transcendental" is another label sometimes applied to Kumin but in a modified sense; while Kumin's poetry may call up images of Thoreau and "insist on man's affinity with the natural world," Ludvigson noted that it falls short of suggesting the "merging of the self with nature" that transcendentalism requires. Joyce Carol Oates wrote in the *New York Times Book Review* that Kumin's 1972 work *Up Country* "acknowledges its debt to Thoreau" but provides "a sharp-edged, unflinching and occasionally nightmarish subjectivity exasperatingly absent in Thoreau." Ludvigson suggested that "her unsentimental relationship with nature . . . allows Kumin to write poems . . . which are ostensibly 'about' the necessary killing of woodchucks and mysterious tracks in the snow, but which chill us with her portrayal of man's capacity for brutality." Brad Crenshaw considered it "a major plus" that Kumin "is not much addicted to transcendental escapes." Rather, as he elaborated in a *Parnassus* review of 1982's *Our Ground Time Here Will Be Brief: New and Selected Poems,* "the voice of the poems is that of a strong woman. In an unforgiving environment, Kumin neither flinches at the strenuous physical labors that comprise her usual responsibilities, nor quails before her emotional disappointments. She's mentally tough. Her poetry records how she stands up to the disasters of weather, disease, difficult births and lamentable deaths, and how she's confident she'll remain standing until the very end."

Whereas critics debate Kumin's similarity to Thoreau, they unanimously recognize how her work resembles that of Robert Frost. The works of both poets show a close attention to the details of New England rural life. The poet told Hammond, "I particularly observe things in nature because they interest me, but I don't think of it as observing. What I'm always after is to get the facts: to be true to the actuality." Attention to nature provides Kumin with images well-suited to her themes of loss and survival. Oates explained, "Any group of poems that deals with nature is more or less committed to the honoring of cycles, the birth/death/birth wheel, the phenomenon of creatures giving way to creatures." Booth expressed a similar opinion when he commented: "The distinctive nature of Maxine Kumin's present poems derives from the primary fact that she lives in, and writes from, a world where constant (if partial) recovery of what's 'lost' is as sure as the procession of the equinoxes, or as familiar as mucking-out the horses' daily dung."

Kumin's preference for traditional verse forms is also what causes critics to liken her to Frost. Not only is there an order "to be discovered . . . in the natural world," she told Martha George Meek in a *Massachusetts Review* interview, "there is also an order that a human can impose on the chaos of his emotions and the chaos of events." Kumin achieves this order by structuring her poetry, controlling the most emotional subjects by fitting them to exacting patterns of syllable count and rhyme. As she told Hammond, "The harder—that is, the more psychically difficult—the poem is to write, the more likely I am to choose a difficult pattern to pound it into. This is true because, paradoxically, the difficulty frees me to be more honest and more direct."

When Kumin finds she has more to say than a poem's structure will accommodate, she approaches her subject again in fiction. "I tend to steal from myself," she said in an interview published in *To Make a Prairie*. "The compass of the poem is so small and so demanding, you have to be so selective, and there are so many things that get left out that you feel cheated. So you take all those things . . . and they get into fiction." Comparing Kumin's work in both genres, *Tribune Books* contributor Catherine Petroski commented, "Kumin's practice of poetry buttresses her practice of short fiction: The turns of phrase and points of view come from a poet, not a recorder of events. Similarly, the concerns of fiction—the chains of cause and effect, the explorations of character, the sense of scene—have much to do with the power of Kumin's best poems." Spears summed up his review by commenting: "One of the pleasures of reading Kumin is to see the same experience appear differently in the different forms of poems, stories, and novels."

If there is one experience that Kumin confronts in all her works, it is loss. The poet talked about her obsession with mortality in the conclusion of a *Country Journal* article in which she reflected on the death of a foal: "A horse-friend from New York state writes me her condolences. She too has lost not one foal, but twin Thoroughbreds. . . . According to some astrological prognosticatory chart, we are both sixes on the scale. Sixes, Mary Beth writes, practice all their lives to die well, 'act as Morticians of All Life and hold private burying rituals in their hearts.'" Accordingly, Kumin wrote, she believes "very strongly that poetry is essentially elegiac in its nature, and that all poems are in one sense or another elegies." She explained to Hammond, "Love poems, particularly, are elegies because if we were not informed with a sense of dying we wouldn't be moved to write love poems."

"Kumin writes as well as ever in her customary modes," Robert B. Shaw said in *Poetry* of *The Long Approach,*

Kumin's eighth book of poems. Many critics concurred with Shaw's assessment, yet some criticized those poems that examine such world problems as pollution, religious persecution, nuclear holocaust, and famine. These poems "are aimed resolutely outward," wrote *Washington Post Book World* contributor Wendy Lesser, who believed that Kumin's "issue" poems "founder on their opinion making." Holly Prado, writing in the *Los Angeles Times Book Review,* similarly said that the poet "doesn't arrive at her best work until . . . she arrives at her farm in New Hampshire." In this part of the book, Kumin "reverts . . . to what is close, ordinary, . . . [upon] which she can meditate with X-ray gaze," Harold Beaver explained in the *New York Times Book Review.* In his analysis of *The Long Approach* in *Poetry,* Shaw suggested: "If Kumin wishes to venture into public terrain, perhaps her voice, which is essentially private, needs to adjust itself to the new and very different demands she is now placing on it. This will no doubt take some time. It can be assumed, at any rate, that a poet of her intelligence stands an even chance of solving the problems involved."

Of *Nurture,* Kumin's next collection of poems, *New York Times Book Review* contributor Carol Muske remarked, "Maxine Kumin sounds weary . . . and with good reason. These poems are exhaustive in their sorrow: they are predominantly short, brutal elegies for the natural world." The poems in this 1989 collection reflect the author's trademark environmental consciousness and her anger at the devastation wrought by humans on the natural world; Diane Wakoski, writing in the *Women's Review of Books,* criticized these poems as "bitter, overstated, trivial." But Wakoski praised the more personal poems in the collection, noting that in these pieces "the goddess voice and stance returns." Kumin's 1992 verse collection, *Looking for Luck,* leaves behind some of the bitterness and anger apparent in her previous collection in exchange for "cheerful, chatty bulletins from the New Hampshire farm where she gardens and raises horses," commented Lisa Zeidner in the *New York Times Book Review.* And in her 1996 work, *Connecting the Dots: Poems,* the poet similarly "reexamines the familiar materials of her previous books with her far-ranging eye and technical skill," according to Fay Weldon, who reviewed the volume in the *Boston Book Review.* As with other Kumin collections, some criticism arose regarding the insubstantial theme and tone of some of the poems included in these volumes. "Sometimes the emotions seem too politely underplayed," declared Zeidner. However, reviewers commended Kumin's better poetry, praising her "linguistic brilliance and formal excellence," in the words of Weldon. Weldon concluded that Kumin "commands the nuances and music of rhyme and slant- rhyme as powerfully as any living poet."

In 1997, Kumin published *Selected Poems, 1960- 1990.* Extending from her first volume, *Halfway,* through 1989's *Nurture, Selected Poems* was praised by Judy Clarence in *Library Journal* for allowing the reader the opportunity to "move slowly, meanderingly, deliciously through the stages of Kumin's poetic life." Noting that the poet's "unsentimental affinity for animals has been her divining rod for locating and observing the natural world's seemingly inexhaustible beauty and mankind's terrifying willingness to destroy it," a *Publishers Weekly* reviewer praised the collection for illustrating this through Kumin's "plain style," "surprising imagery . . . and recurring reflections." Praising Kumin's collection for its accessibility by the average reader, Richard Tillinghast commented in his review for the *New York Times Book Review* that "her poems bracingly remind us of several enduring virtues valued by anyone who reads verse for pleasure. . . . She has the versatility to build an orderly, measured structure in rhyme and meter, or to adopt the easier virtues of free verse for a more transient, informal effect." Furthermore, the critic maintained, Kumin's poems are *about* something; they tell a story that carries the reader into the world Kumin creates and leads to a satisfying conclusion.

Kumin followed *Selected Poems* with *The Long Marriage,* which celebrates her five-decade marriage to her husband, their life together in New Hampshire, and nature. Donna Seaman, writing in *Booklist,* stated that Kumin's observations are "crisp" and added that "Kumin moves surefootedly" in her work. *New York Times Book Review* contributor Megan Harland similarly called Kumin's observations "earthy" and "practical," and she declared that "Kumin's tonal clarity is transformative."

Kumin's 1994 prose collection, *Women, Animals, and Vegetables,* offers insight into the author's pastoral life on her farm in New Hampshire. In essays and short stories, she "describes the pleasures of raising and riding horses, of gardening and mushrooming, of learning how in the country 'things have a way of balancing out,'" explained Christopher Merrill in the *Los Angeles Times Book Review.* Anne Raver, writing in the *New York Times Book Review,* averred that some of the material in the book pales in comparison to Kumin's poetry, which covers many of the same themes and issues "more brilliantly." She continued, "It is a Pulitzer Prize-winning poet's misfortune, perhaps, to be judged harshly by the standards she herself has set." But Merrill concluded of the collection: "This is a book many readers will find companionable."

Kumin's fifteenth poetry collection, *Jack and Other New Poems,* "serves up a startling refreshment . . . a bracing mix of persona poems, elegies, and lyric narratives, the stuff of biting paradox and stark self-appraisal," noted Elaine Sexton in *Prairie Schooner.* Sexton went on to observe that "in this collection, every poem is a portrait of the poet's fierce hold on life." The book features a collection of simply worded poems, each written in the voice of a different type of person, from a rapist to a hospice worker, to someone looking back on history. *Booklist* contributor Donna Seaman found the work to be a group of "well-turned, neatly well balanced poems" and a "radiant testimony to life attentively witnessed and cherished."

In 1999 Kumin published a mystery novel reflecting her commitment and concern for animals. *Quit Monks or Die!* is an unusual tale centering around the disappearance of a pair of monkeys at a testing lab and a murder of the lab director. A reviewer for *Publishers Weekly* called the plot for *Quit Monks or Die!* a "masterpiece of construction" and declared the book "one of the best mysteries of the year." *New York Times Book Review* critic Laura Jamison commented that Kumin's character sketches were "effective" and that she is "a capable stylist." And while Jamison was disappointed in the mystery's outcome, she commended Kumin for her "highly original prose" and was captivated by "her provocative analysis of human nature."

When Kumin was seventy-three she suffered an accident while preparing a horse for competition. In the accident, she broke her neck and received serious internal injuries, injuries that kill ninety-five percent of those who receive similar ones. She was able to make a successful recovery, however, and her book *Inside the Halo and Beyond: The Anatomy of a Recovery* describes her convalescence. Anne Roiphe, writing for the *New York Times Book Review,* described the language Kumin used in *Inside the Halo and Beyond* as "precise and spare." As her poetry deals with everyday life, so does the book. Roiphe noted that although Kumin is a poet, this book "is rarely poetic in the usual sense of heightened metaphor or compacted image." She did not write an autobiographical tell-all, but simply wrote about the specific experience of her time in recovery and people and feelings she encountered along the way. Roiphe likened the tenet "to a dignified prayer of thanks" that resonates "wisdom while announcing a triumph of body and soul." A reviewer for *Publishers Weekly* commented, however, that the book was "uneven and overlong," but believed that Kumin's fans would find *Inside the Halo and Beyond* "irresistible."

The same year that *Inside the Halo and Beyond* was released, Kumin also published *Always Beginning: Es-*

says on a Life in Poetry, a collection of essays and poems describing Kumin's daily life as a poet. She includes interviews, diary entries, and keynote addresses, as well as poetry. A reviewer for *Publishers Weekly* called Kumin's life as presented "wonderful[ly] poetic." Although *New York Times Book Review* reviewer Sunil Iyengar was less impressed, calling the book "bland" and "haphazard," *Library Journal* contributor Doris Lynch asserted that the essays encapsulate "a kind of grace."

Reviewing Kumin's multidecade career, Booth commented that the poet "has simply gotten better and better at what she has always been good at: a resonant language, an autobiographical immediacy, unsystematized intelligence, and radical compassion. One does not learn compassion without having suffered." Crenshaw noted that "Americans traditionally have preferred their women poets to be depressed and victimized," but he claimed that Kumin's "posture regarding despair" sets her apart from "the sweet innocents who have been driven to insane passions and flamboyant destructions." And Wakoski wrote in *Contemporary Women Poets*: "The one thing that is clear throughout [Kumin's] substantial body of work is that she believes survival is possible, if only through the proper use of the imagination to retrieve those things which are loved well enough."

BIOGRAPHICAL AND CRITICAL SOURCES:

BOOKS

Authors in the News, Volume 2, Thomson Gale (Detroit, MI), 1976.

Contemporary Literary Criticism, Thomson Gale (Detroit, MI), Volume 5, 1976, Volume 13, 1980, Volume 28, 1984.

Contemporary Women Poets, St. James Press (Detroit, MI), 1997.

Dictionary of Literary Biography, Volume 5: *American Poets since World War II*, Thomson Gale (Detroit, MI), 1980.

Grosholz, Emily, *Telling the Barn Swallow: Poets on the Poetry of Maxine Kumin*, University Press of New England (Boston, MA), 1997.

Kumin, Maxine, *Halfway*, Holt (New York, NY), 1961.

Kumin, Maxine, *To Make a Prairie: Essays on Poets, Poetry, and Country Living*, University of Michigan Press (Ann Arbor, MI), 1980.

McClatchy, J.D., editor, *Anne Sexton: The Artist and Her Critics*, Indiana University Press (Bloomington, IN), 1978.

Sexton, Anne, Linda Gray, and Lois Ames, editors, *Anne Sexton: A Self-Portrait in Letters*, Houghton Mifflin (New York, NY), 1977.

PERIODICALS

America, February 28, 1976.

American Poetry Review, March, 1976; November, 1978.

Atlantic, October, 1971.

Belles Lettres, fall, 1992, p. 51.

Booklist, August, 1999, Donna Seaman and Emily Melton, review of *Quit Monks or Die!*, p. 2035; May 1, 2000, Donna Seaman, review of *Inside the Halo and Beyond: The Anatomy of a Recovery* and *Always Beginning: Essays on a Life in Poetry*, p. 1639; November 15, 2001, Donna Seaman, review of *The Long Marriage*, p. 542; January 1, 2005, Donna Seaman, review of *Jack and Other New Poems*, p. 804.

Boston Book Review, July 1, 1996, Fay Weldon, review of *Connecting the Dots: Poems*.

Boston Herald, April 30, 2000, Elizabeth Hand, "Pain Purged on *Journey;* Kumin Heals from Horse Accident," p. O62; May 18, 2000, Stephanie Schorow, "Inside the *Halo* Justice," p. O59.

Choice, January, 1966.

Christian Science Monitor, August 9, 1961; February 28, 1973.

Country Journal, spring, 1979, article by Maxine Kumin.

Crazy Horse, summer, 1975, Joan Norris, interview with Maxine Kumin.

Hudson Review, summer, 2001, R. S. Gwynn, review of *Always Beginning*, p. 341.

Kirkus Reviews, May 1, 1994, p. 609; July, 1999, Margaret A. Smith, review of *Quit Monks or Die!*, p. 142; August 1, 1999, review of *Quit Monks or Die!*, p. 1176.

Library Journal, June 15, 1997, Judy Clarence, review of *Selected Poems, 1960-1990*, p. 74; July, 1999, review of *Quit Monks or Die!*, p. 142; June 1, 2000, Doris Lynch, review of *Always Beginning*, p. 124; September 1, 2001, Judy Clarence, review of *The Long Marriage*, p. 184; May 15, 2003, Diane Scharper, review of *Bringing Together: Uncollected Early Poems, 1958-88*, p. 93.

Los Angeles Times Book Review, June 13, 1982; December 1, 1985; June 26, 1988, p. 14; November 6, 1994, p. 13.

Massachusetts Review, spring, 1975, Martha George Meek.

Nation, July 24, 1982, Clara Claiborne Park, review of *Why Can't We Live Together Like Civilized Human Beings?,* p. 89.

New Leader, January 22, 1973.

New Letters, summer, 2000, Jeffrey S. Cramer, "Peaceable Island," p. 61.

New Republic, August 10, 1974.

New Yorker, December 4, 1971.

New York Times, June 26, 1974, review by Michiko Kakutani.

New York Times Book Review, March 28, 1965; May 5, 1968; November 19, 1972; June 23, 1974; September 7, 1975; April 23, 1978; August 8, 1982, Alicia Ostriker, review of *Our Ground Time Here Will Be Brief: New and Selected Poems,* p. 10; March 2, 1986, Harold Beaver, review of *The Long Approach,* p. 14; August 30, 1987, Adrienne S. Barnes, review of *In Deep: Country Essays,* p. 21; November 5, 1989, Carol Muske, review of *Nurture,* p. 32; March 21, 1993, Lisa Zeider, review of *Looking for Luck,* p. 14; August 28, 1994, Anne Raver, review of *Women, Animals, and Vegetables: Essays and Stories,* p. 12; August 3, 1997, Richard Tillinghast, review of *Selected Poems, 1960-1990,* p. 10; September 26, 1999, Laura Jamison, review of *Quit Monks or Die!,* p. 15; July 30, 2000, Anne Roiphe, review of *Inside the Halo and Beyond,* p. 15; September 3, 2000, Sunil Iyengar, review of *Always Beginning,* p. 15; December 9, 2001, Megan Harlan, review of *The Long Marriage,* p. 33.

Parnassus, spring-summer, 1973; spring, 1985, Brad Crenshaw, review of *Our Ground Time Here Will Be Brief.*

Poetry, January, 1979; April, 1990, p. 48; November, 1992; June, 1999, p. 181.

Prairie Schooner, spring, 1976; fall, 2005, Elaine Sexton, review of *Jack and Other New Poems,* p. 175.

Publishers Weekly, May 30, 1994, review of *Women, Animals, and Vegetables,* p. 41; June 3, 1996, review of *Connecting the Dots,* p. 73; January 6, 1997, "Telling the Barnswallow: Poets on the Poetry of Maxine Kumin," p. 58; April 28, 1997, review of *Selected Poems, 1960-1990,* p. 70; August 23, 1999, review of *Quit Monks or Die!,* p. 50; May 15, 2000, review of *Inside the Halo and Beyond,* p. 100; August 14, 2000, review of *Always Beginning,* p. 349; August 27, 2001, review of *The Long Marriage,* p. 75.

Saturday Review, May 6, 1961; December 25, 1965; May 9, 1970; March 25, 1972.

Sewanee Review, spring, 1974; winter, 1995, p. 141.

Shenandoah, spring, 1976.

Smithsonian, November, 1987.

Times Literary Supplement, May 9, 1975.

Tribune Books August 29, 1982; February 2, 1986; July 9, 1989, p. 6.

Village Voice, September 5, 1974; July 20, 1982.

Virginia Quarterly Review, spring, 1971.

Washington Post, May 6, 1980.

Washington Post Book World, May 5, 1968; October 10, 1971; June 22, 1982; February 2, 1986; November 22, 1992, p. 8.

Western Humanities Review, spring, 1979, Karla Hammond, interview with Maxine Kumin.

Women's Review of Books, October, 1989, Diane Wakowski, review of *Nurture,* p. 20; April, 2001, Judith Barrington, review of *Always Beginning* and *Inside the Halo and Beyond,* p. 6.

Yale Review, autumn, 1968.

ONLINE

Atlantic Unbound, http://www.theatlantic.com/ (February 2, 2002), Erin Rogers, "The Art of Living."

*   *   *

KUMIN, Maxine Winokur
See KUMIN, Maxine

*   *   *

KUNDERA, Milan 1929-

PERSONAL: Born April 1, 1929, in Brno, Czechoslovakia (now Czech Republic); immigrated to France, 1975; naturalized French citizen, 1981; son of Ludvik (a pianist and musicologist) and Milada (Janosikova) Kundera; married Vera Hrabankova, September 30, 1967. *Education:* Studied music under Paul Haas and Vaclav Kapral; attended Charles University (Prague, Czechoslovakia), and Film Faculty, Academy of Music and Dramatic Arts (Prague, Czechoslovakia), 1956.

ADDRESSES: Office—c/o École des Hautes Etudes, 54 Boulevard Raspail, 75006 Paris, France.

CAREER: Writer. Worked as a laborer and jazz pianist in provincial Czechoslovakia; Film Faculty, Academy of Music and Dramatic Arts, Prague, Czechoslovakia, assistant professor, 1958-69; Université de Rennes II, Rennes, France, invited professor of comparative literature, 1975-79; École des Hautes Etudes, Paris, France, professor, 1980—.

MEMBER: Czechoslovak Writers Union (member of central committee, 1963-69), American Academy of Arts and Letters.

AWARDS, HONORS: Klement Lukes Prize, 1963, for *Majitele klicu;* Czechoslovak Writers Union prize, 1968, for *Zert;* Czechoslovak Writers' Publishing House prize, 1969, for *Smesne lasky;* Prix Medicis, 1973, for *La vie est ailleurs;* Premio Letterario Mondello, 1978, for *The Farewell Party;* Commonwealth Award for distinguished service in literature, 1981; Prix Europa for literature; honorary doctorate, University of Michigan, 1983; *Los Angeles Times* Book Prize for fiction, 1984, for *The Unbearable Lightness of Being;* Jerusalem Prize for Literature on the Freedom of Man in Society, 1985; finalist for Ritz Paris Hemingway Award, 1985; Academie Française critics prize, 1987; Nelly Sachs prize, 1987; Osterichischeve state prize, 1987; *Independent* Award for foreign fiction, 1991; Jaroslav-Seifert Prize, 1994, for *Immortality;* Czech Medal of Merit, 1995; Herder Prize, University of Vienna, 2000.

WRITINGS:

NOVELS

Zert, Ceskoslovensky Spisovatel (Prague, Czechoslovakia), 1967, translation by David Hamblyn and Oliver Stallybrass published as *The Joke,* Coward (New York, NY), 1969, new translation by Michael Henry Heim with author's preface, Harper (New York, NY), 1982, definitive English edition revised by Kundera, HarperCollins (New York, NY), 1992.

La vie est ailleurs (French translation of the original Czech manuscript *Zivot je jinde*), Gallimard (Paris, France), 1973, translation from the original Czech manuscript by Peter Kussi published as *Life Is Elsewhere,* Knopf (New York, NY), 1974, Czech edition published by Sixty-Eight Publishers (Toronto, Ontario, Canada), 1979, definitive English edition revised by Kundera, Penguin, 1986, translation from the French by Aaron Asher, HarperPerennial (New York, NY), 1999.

La valse aux adieux (French translation of the original Czech manuscript *Valcik na rozloucenou*), Gallimard (Paris, France), 1976, translation by Peter Kussi published as *The Farewell Party,* Knopf (New York, NY), 1976, Czech editions published by Sixty-Eight Publishers (Toronto, Ontario, Canada), 1979, and Atlantis (Brno, Czech Republic), 1997), new translation by Aaron Asher based

on Kundera's revised French translation published as *Farewell Waltz: A Novel,* HarperCollins (New York, NY), 1998.

Le livre du rire et de l'oubli (French translation of the original Czech manuscript *Kniha smichu a zapomneni*), Gallimard (Paris, France), 1979, translation from the original Czech manuscript by Michael Henry Heim published as *The Book of Laughter and Forgetting,* Knopf (New York, NY), 1980, published with an interview with Kundera by Philip Roth, Penguin Books (New York, NY), 1981, new translation by Aaron Asher, HarperPerennial (New York, NY), 1996.

L'insoutenable l'egerete de l'etre (French translation of the original Czech manuscript *Nesnesitelna lehkost byti*), Gallimard (Paris France), 1984, translation from the original Czech by Michael Henry Heim published as *The Unbearable Lightness of Being,* Harper (New York, NY), 1984, Czech edition published by Sixty-Eight Publishers (Toronto, Ontario, Canada), 1985).

L'immortalite (French translation of the original Czech manuscript *Nesmrtelnost*), Gallimard (Paris, France), 1990, translation from the original Czech by Peter Kussi published as *Immortality,* Grove Weidenfeld (New York, NY), 1991, Czech edition published by Atlantis (Brno, Czech Republic), 1993).

La lnteur: roman, Gallimard (Paris, France), 1995, translation from the original French by Linda Asher published as *Slowness: A Novel,* HarperCollins (New York, NY), 1996.

L'identite: roman, Gallimard (Paris, France), 1997, translation from the original French by Asher published as *Identity: A Novel,* HarperFlamingo (New York, NY), 1998.

Ignorance, translation from the original French by Linda Asher, HarperCollins (New York, NY), 2002.

OTHER

Clovek zahrada sira (poetry; title means "Man: A Broad Garden"), Ceskoslovensky Spisovatel, 1953.

Posledni maj (poetry; title means "The Last May"), Ceskoslovensky Spisovatel, 1955, revised edition, 1963.

Monology (poetry; title means "Monologues"), Ceskoslovensky Spisovatel, 1957, revised edition, 1964.

Umeni romanu: cesta Vladislava Vancury za velkou epikou (critical study of writer Vladislav Vancura; title means "The Art of the Novel: Vladislav Vancura's Road in Search of the Great Epic"), Ceskoslovensky Spisovatel, 1961, revised edition, HarperPerennial (New York, NY), 2000.

Majitele klicu (play; title means "The Owners of the Keys"; first produced in Prague, Czechoslovakia, at National Theatre, April, 1962), Orbis, 1962.

Smesne lasky: tri melancholicke anekdoty (short stories; title means "Laughable Loves: Three Melancholy Anecdotes"), Ceskoslovensky Spisovatel, 1963.

Druhy sesit smesnych lasek (short stories; title means "The Second Notebook of Laughable Loves"; also see below), Ceskoslovensky Spisovatel, 1965.

Dve usi dve svatby (play; title means "Two Ears and Two Weddings"), Dilia (Prague, Czechoslovakia), 1968.

Treti sesit smesnych lasek (short stories; title means "The Third Notebook of Laughable Loves"), Ceskoslovensky Spisovatel, 1968.

(With Jaromil Jires) *The Joke* (screenplay; based on Kundera's novel *Zert*), directed by Jaromil Jires, Smida-Fikar—Studio de Cinema de Barrandov, 1968.

Ptakovina (two-act play; title means "Cock-a-Doodle-Do"), first produced in Liberec, Czechoslovakia, at Divadlo F.X. Saldy, January, 1968.

Smesne lasky (selection by Kundera of eight of the short stories previously published in *Smesne lasky: tri melancholicke anekdoty, Druhy sesit smesnych lasek,* and *Treti sesit smesnych lasek*), Ceskoslovensky Spisovatel, 1970, translation by Suzanne Rappaport of seven of these stories (based on Kundera's selection for the French edition *Risibles amours,* Gallimard [Paris, France], 1970) with introduction by Philip Roth published as *Laughable Loves,* Knopf (New York, NY), 1974, definitive English edition revised by Kundera and translated by Suzanne Rappaport, Penguin (New York, NY), 1987.

Jacques et son maitre: Hommage à Denis Diderot (three-act play; French translation of the original Czech manuscript *Jakub a jeho pan: pocta Denisi Diderotovi;* first produced in Paris, France, at Theatre des Maturins, 1981), published with an introduction by the author, Gallimard (Paris, France), 1981, translation from the original Czech by Michael Henry Heim published as *Jacques and His Master: An Homage to Diderot in Three Acts* (produced in Cambridge, MA, at American Repertory Theatre, January, 1985), Harper (New York, NY), 1985, translation by Simon Callow produced as *Jacques and His Master* in Toronto, Canada, at Free Theatre, May 14, 1987, Czech edition published by Atlantis (Brno, Czechoslovakia), 1992.

L'art du roman: essai, Gallimard (Paris, France), 1986, translation from the original French by Linda Asher published as *The Art of the Novel,* Grove (New York, NY), 1988.

Les Testaments trahis (essay), Gallimard (Paris, France), 1993, translation from the original French by Asher published as *Testaments Betrayed: An Essay in Nine Parts,* HarperCollins (New York, NY), 1995.

Contributor to periodicals, including translated articles and essays, to *New York Times Book Review, New York Review of Books, Harper'sReview of Contemporary Fiction, Times Literary Supplement, Cross Currents, New Yorker,* and *New Republic.* Member of editorial board of *Literarni noviny,* 1963-67 and 1968, and of *Literarni listy,* 1968-69.

Kundera's works have been translated into numerous languages, including German, Dutch, Danish, Norwegian, Swedish, Finnish, Portuguese, Spanish, Italian, Serbian, Slovene, Greek, Turkish, Hebrew, and Japanese.

ADAPTATIONS: The Unbearable Lightness of Being was adapted for film, written by Philip Kaufman and Jean-Claude Carriere, directed by Kaufman, and released by Orion, 1988.

SIDELIGHTS: Milan Kundera, a Czech-born novelist now living in France, "is one of the finest and most consistently interesting novelists in Europe and America," wrote Richard Locke in the *Washington Post Book World.* Writing from experience, Kundera "has brought Eastern Europe to the attention of the Western reading public, and he has done so with insights that are universal in their appeal," noted Olga Carlisle in the *New York Times Magazine.* His novels, according to David Lodge in the *Times Literary Supplement,* investigate "with a bold combination of abstraction, sensuality and wit, the problematic interrelationship of sex, love, death and the ultimate mystery of being itself."

Kundera began writing his first novel, *Zert (The Joke),* in 1962 during a time of political turmoil. He submitted it to a Prague publisher in December 1965, but they would not publish it because it was "diametrically opposed to the official ideology," Kundera explained in the preface to the 1982 edition of *The Joke.* But Kundera had held firm against the demands of government censors, and, finally, in 1967 the novel was published, unchanged. "Three editions of *The Joke* appeared in quick succession and incredibly large printings, and each sold out in a matter of days," the author recalled. During the enlightened Prague Spring of 1968, a time when Czechoslovakia was rediscovering its cultural freedom and writers were held in high esteem, Milan Kundera was one of the major literary figures of the day.

Within four months, however, Czechoslovakia was invaded by troops from the Soviet Union, Poland, East Germany, Hungary, and Bulgaria. During the next few years, Kundera's books were removed from libraries and bookstores, his plays were banned, and he lost his job and his right to work and publish in Czechoslovakia. At first, he was also forbidden to travel in the West, but finally in 1975 he was permitted to accept a teaching position in Rennes, France. Four years later, after the publication of *Le livre du rire et de l'oubli* (*The Book of Laughter and Forgetting*), the Czechoslovak government revoked his citizenship. Silenced in Czechoslovakia immediately after the invasion, Kundera became a writer without an audience. He did write two novels that were published in translation abroad, but not until he had settled in France did he feel at home with this new audience.

While growing up in Czechoslovakia, Kundera witnessed the dismemberment of a young republic by Nazis in search of *lebensraum*, or living space. He also witnessed the postwar political purges. Then, in the rise of Communism, he had found the promise of better times; but the promise was broken after the Communist coup of 1948. "I was nineteen," he wrote in the *New York Times Book Review*. "I learned about fanaticism, dogmatism, and political trials through bitter experience; I learned what it meant to be intoxicated by power, be repudiated by power, feel guilty in the face of power and revolt against it." Twenty years later, he saw another promise crushed, this time by invading Soviet tanks.

As a writer, Kundera is fascinated by the individual's struggle against power, and this conflict emerges as a central theme of his novels. Power—sterile, serious, focused on the future—dominates his public world and strives to rob the individual of authority, understanding, and history, absorbing him into "the people." Kundera believes that the small world of intimate life is the only refuge available. As he told Philip Roth in the *Village Voice*, "Intimate life [is] understood as one's personal secret, as something valuable, inviolable, the basis of one's originality." Here, to a small degree, the individual can attempt to exercise his freedom and react against the state. Through eroticism, humor, and memory, Kundera's characters make their stand in the face of power. By setting in opposition eroticism and sterility, humor and seriousness, memory and forgetting, Kundera "discovers" the variations of his central theme.

The dangers of a world lacking a sense of humor are evident in *The Joke*. Having missed an opportunity to cultivate his desire for Marketa because of her choice to attend a Party training session, Ludvik responds to her enthusiastic letters with a spiteful joke, written on a postcard: "Optimism is the opium of the people! A healthy atmosphere stinks of stupidity! Long live Trotsky!" But members of the power structure have no appreciation of jokes. His comrades learn of the card and expel him from the Party and the university. He is banished to work the provincial coal mines. Years later, his revenge, an "erotic power play, is thwarted, and turns into yet another joke at his expense," wrote Roth in *Reading Myself and Others*.

In *The Book of Laughter and Forgetting,* Kundera presents the image of poet Paul Eluard dancing in a circle lifted aloft by a girl laughing the laughter of angels. In 1950, Eluard was called upon by Dada-founding poet Andre Breton to help save their mutual friend Zavis Kalandra from hanging. (Kalandra, a Prague surrealist, had been accused by the Stalinists of betraying the people.) "But Eluard was too busy dancing in the gigantic ring encircling Paris, Moscow, Warsaw, Prague, Sofia, and Athens, encircling all the socialist countries and all the Communist parties of the world; too busy reciting his beautiful poems about joy and brotherhood," Kundera writes in his novel. As a poet himself during this period, Kundera told Antonin J. Liehm in *The Politics of Culture,* "I got a close look at poets who adorned things that weren't worth it, and am still able to remember vividly this state of passionate lyrical enthusiasm which, getting drunk on its frenzy, is unable to see the real world through its own grandiose haze." In Czechoslovakia, where poetry is the preferred literary form, he added, "on the other side of the wall behind which people were jailed and tormented, Gullibility, Ignorance, Childishness, and Enthusiasm blithely promenaded in the sun." "Milan Kundera," noted Neal Ascherson in the *New York Review of Books,* "who made his own transition from poetry to novel-writing, is one of the deadliest exponents of the argument that [there] have been too many poets, too few novelists: too much romantic narcissism and too little sober illustration of what is within the capacity of the human animal and what is not."

The Book of Laughter and Forgetting was published five years after Kundera's flight to France. Because of this, some critics viewed his work in the context of exile literature. In Elaine Kendall's estimation, "*The Book of Laughter and Forgetting* is a model of the exile's novel: bittersweet and sardonic but somehow neither corrosive nor sentimental." She added in her *Los Ange-*

les Times review that "Kundera deals in the gradual erosions of totalitarianism: the petty indignities, the constant discomforts and the everyday disillusions."

The book "calls itself a novel," wrote John Leonard in the *New York Times,* "although it is part fairy tale, part literary criticism, part political tract, part musicology and part autobiography. It can call itself whatever it wants to, because the whole is genius." Norman Podhoretz related his response to the book in an open letter to Kundera printed in *Commentary:* "What compelled me most when I first opened [it] was not its form or its aesthetic character but its intellectual force, the astonishing intelligence controlling and suffusing every line." *New York Review of Books* contributor Robert M. Adams spotlighted Kundera's control when he noted, "Again and again, in this artfully artless book an act or gesture turns imperceptibly into its exact opposite—a circle of unity into a circle of exclusion, playful children into cruel monsters, a funeral into a farce, freedom into lockstep, nudity into a disguise, laughter into sadism, poetry into political machinery, artificial innocence into cynical exploitation. These subtle transformations and unemphasized points of distant correspondence are the special privileges of a meticulously crafted fiction." Concluded Adams, "That a book which combines so delicately dry wit and a deep sense of humanity should cause the author to be deprived of his citizenship is one more of the acute ironies of our time."

First published in French as *L'insoutenable l'egerete de l'etre, The Unbearable Lightness of Being* focuses on the connected lives of two couples—Tomas and Tereza, and Franz and Sabina. Set in Czechoslovakia around the time of the Russian invasion, this work is often considered an examination of the hardships and limitations that can result from commitment and the meaninglessness of life without such responsibility. In his review of *The Unbearable Lightness of Being* in the *Times Literary Supplement,* David Lodge described the relationship between the intimate concerns of the individual and the larger concerns of politics in Kundera's world, saying that "although the characters' lives are shaped by political events, they are not determined by them. Tereza and Tomas return to Czechoslovakia for emotional, not ideological reasons. He refuses to retract his article not as a courageous act of political defiance, but more out of bloody-mindedness and complicated feelings about his son, who is involved in the dissident movement." As Richard Eder observed in the *Los Angeles Times,* "For the most part, *The Unbearable Lightness of Being* succeeds remarkably in joining a series of provocative and troubling speculations about human existence to charac-

ters that charm and move us." He added, "Kundera leads us captivatingly into the bleakness of our days." "Often witty, sometimes terrifying and always profound, Kundera brings genuine wisdom to his novels at a time when many of his fellow practitioners of the craft aspire only to cleverness," concluded Ian Pearson in *Maclean's.*

Published in English in 1988 as *The Art of the Novel, L'art du roman: essai* contains three essays, two interviews, Kundera's acceptance speech for the Jerusalem prize, and the definitions of sixty-three words Kundera believes are frequently mistranslated. In the essays Kundera traces the development of the European novel. Although most critics praise Kundera's belief that the novel is a "sequence of discoveries," they also accuse him of being arrogant and ethnocentric for his failure to consider any works by non-European or women writers. Terrence Rafferty, in the *New Yorker,* noted that "Kundera's polemical fervor in *The Art of the Novel* annoys us, as American readers, because we feel defensive, excluded from the transcendent 'idea of the novel' that for him seems simply to have been there for the taking." Kundera states in the work, "Need I stress that I intend no theoretical statement at all, and that the entire book is simply a practitioner's confession? Every novelist's work contains an implicit vision of the history of the novel, an idea of what the novel is: I have tried to express here the idea of the novel that is inherent in my own novels." Kundera continues his exploration of the novel in his *Testaments Betrayed: An Essay in Nine Parts,* which traces the evolution of the novel from Francois Rabelais to Franz Kafka and relates literature to music.

Kundera's novel *Immortality,* originally published as *L'immortalite,* is his first to be set in France. In this work, Kundera examines how media manipulation, popular culture, and capitalist technocracy have developed into instruments of propaganda that distort mankind's perception of reality. In addition to discussing the love triangles between Agnes, her husband Paul, and Agnes's sister, Laura, *Immortality* contains episodes from the lives of such literary figures as Johann Wolfgang von Goethe and Ernest Hemingway. While Kundera has consistently won praise for juxtaposing fictitious and biographical elements and simultaneously exploring recurring themes, some critics faulted *Immortality* for its disjointed plot and episodic characterizations. Jonathan Yardley, writing in the *Washington Post Book World,* noted that while "*Immortality* is ingenious, witty, provocative, and formidably intelligent," it, unlike the best of Kundera's earlier novels, "is all talk and no story." D.M. Thomas, however, wrote in the *New*

York Times Book Review, "*Immortality* is certainly a daunting novel: almost devoid of the good-natured or ill-tempered bustle of ordinary humanity . . . and yet the novel fascinates."

First appearing in French as *La lnteur: roman,* Kundera's 1996 novel, *Slowness,* ostensibly concerns "the failure of our speed-obsessed age to appreciate the delights of slowness (in lovemaking, in travel, in the rituals of daily life)," commented Michiko Kakutani in the *New York Times.* But, she continued, *Slowness* "is really concerned with the storytelling process itself, with the means by which the facts of real life are turned into fiction, the means by which people sell one version of themselves to the world, to friends, to lovers and to political rivals." Like other Kundera novels, *Slowness* does not employ a traditional narrative structure, juxtaposing different stories and characters connected by a central theme. Fredric Koeppel, in the *Detroit News,* commented that "Kundera carries his tangled tales off with wisdom, sweetness and wit that permeate each word and sentence." Kakutani claimed that, in Kundera's earlier works, humor and sex were "wonderfully anarchic," but in *Slowness,* his "humor has turned sour: it's no longer a gesture of liberation; it's become a symptom of weariness and cynicism." Koeppel offered a different opinion, however, finding that "Kundera handles his material with a lightness which, far from being unbearable, sparkles with the deftness of a magician shuffling cards for our delectation and mystification."

Another of Kundera's novels with a one-word title, *Ignorance,* is set in 1989, and it finds two middle-aged émigrés, Irena and Josef, meeting after many years as they make their way back to Prague, she from Paris and he from Denmark, after nearly thirty years in exile. Irena remembers Josef as the young man who tried to seduce her decades ago, an event that is destined to be repeated, and Josef, who has no memory of the incident, pretends that he does remember her. The story opens with Irena being urged by her friend Sylvie to go home, and she agrees to return with her lover Gustaf, a Swede who has a business in Prague. Josef is returning because it was the wish of his now-deceased wife, and becomes excited about the idea of having sex with Irena, who sees him as a possible escape from Gustaf and her family. Other characters include Milada, a former girlfriend of Josef, and Irena's sexy mother, who ends up bedding Gustaf. James Wood reviewed *Ignorance* in *New Republic,* commenting that "some of their encounters are mildly comic, and the book ends, in the familiar Kundera fashion, with a wild and supposedly comic erotic reckoning. Around these slim sketchy, al-

most hypothetical scenes, a witty essayistic voice theorizes: about the etymology of the word 'nostalgia,' about Odysseus returning from long exile to Ithaca, about the modest but passionate nationalism of the Czech people." The *Spectator*'s Robert Edric wrote that *Ignorance* "explores the concepts of émigré longing, of nostalgia, homesickness, and the reinvention of the lives of people caught up in events beyond their control. As in all of Kundera's work, there can never be any doubt that the narrator of events is Kundera himself, and that, in a Beckettian sense, the teller and the tale are indivisible, meaningless, one without the other."

Since losing his Czech home, audience, and citizenship, Kundera has found each in France. He told Roth in the *Village Voice* that "the years in France have been the best years of my life." Moreover, as Edmund White commented in the *Nation,* "Kundera—despite his irony, his abiding suspicion of any cant, any uniformity of opinion and especially of kitsch—is currently the favored spokesman for the uneasy conscience of the French intellectual." But Kundera understands the laughable nature of fame. He said in the *Village Voice* interview: "When I was a little boy in short pants I dreamed about a miraculous ointment that would make me invisible. Then I became an adult, began to write, and wanted to be successful. Now I'm successful and would like to have the ointment that would make me invisible."

BIOGRAPHICAL AND CRITICAL SOURCES:

BOOKS

Aji, Aron, editor, *Milan Kundera and the Art of Fiction: Critical Essays,* Garland Publishing (New York, NY), 1992.

Banerjee, Maria Nemcove, *Terminal Paradox: The Novels of Milan Kundera,* Grove (New York, NY), 1990.

Contemporary Literary Criticism, Thomson Gale (Detroit, MI), Volume 4, 1975, Volume 9, 1978, Volume 19, 1981, Volume 32, 1985, Volume 68, 1991, Volume 115, 1999, Volume 135, 2001.

Dictionary of Literary Biography, Volume 232: *Twentieth-Century Eastern European Writers, Third Series,* Thomson Gale (Detroit, MI), 2001.

Dolezel, Lubomir, *Narrative Modes in Czech Literature,* University of Toronto Press (Toronto, Ontario, Canada), 1973.

French, A., *Czech Writers and Politics, 1945-1969,* East European Monographs, 1982.

Encyclopedia of World Literature in the Twentieth Century, Volume 2, St. James Press (Detroit, MI), 1999, pp. 678-679.

Goetz-Stankiewicz, Marketa, *The Silenced Theatre: Czech Playwrights without a Stage,* University of Toronto Press (Toronto, Ontario, Canada), 1979.

Gopinathan Pillai, C., *The Political Novels of Milan Kundera and O.V. Vijayan: A Comparative Study,* Prestige, 1996.

Kundera, Milan, *Laughable Loves,* translation by Suzanne Rappaport with introduction by Philip Roth, Knopf (New York, NY), 1974.

Kundera, Milan, *The Book of Laughter and Forgetting,* translation by Michael Henry Heim published with an interview with the author by Philip Roth, Penguin Books (New York, NY), 1981.

Kundera, Milan, *The Joke,* translation by Michael Henry Heim with author's preface, Harper (New York, NY), 1982.

Liehm, Antonin J., *The Politics of Culture,* translation from the Czech by Peter Kussi, Grove (New York, NY), 1972.

Misurella, Fred, *Understanding Milan Kundera: Public Events, Private Affairs,* University of South Carolina Press (Columbia, SC), 1993.

O'Brien, John, *Milan Kundera and Feminism: Dangerous Intersections,* St. Martin's (New York, NY), 1995.

Petro, Peter, editor, *Critical Essays on Milan Kundera,* Twayne, 1999.

Porter, Robert, *Milan Kundera: A Voice from Central Europe,* Arkona (Denmark), 1981.

Roth, Philip, *Reading Myself and Others,* Farrar, Straus (New York, NY), 1975.

South Slavic and Eastern European Writers, Thomson Gale (Detroit, MI), 2000.

Trensky, Paul I., *Czech Drama since World War II,* M.E. Sharpe, 1978.

Zeman, Z.A. B., *Prague Spring,* Hill & Wang (New York, NY), 1969.

PERIODICALS

Book, September-October, 2002, Tom Leclair, review of *Ignorance,* p. 75.

Commentary, December, 1980; October, 1984.

Commonweal, May 18, 1984; June 2, 1989, pp. 339-341.

Contemporary Literature, fall, 1990, pp. 281-299.

Critical Quarterly, spring-summer, 1984.

Detroit News, July 20, 1996, p. D30.

Dissent, winter, 1983.

Globe and Mail (Toronto, Ontario, Canada), April 28, 1984.

Hudson Review, winter, 1995, p. 616.

Library Journal, October 15, 2002, Christopher Tinney, review of *Ignorance,* p. 94.

London Review of Books, December 4, 1986, pp. 10, 12; June 13, 1991, pp. 13-14.

Los Angeles Times, January 5, 1981; May 2, 1984.

Maclean's, May 14, 1984.

Nation, August 28, 1967; November 6, 1967; August 26, 1968; September 18, 1976; October 2, 1976; May 12, 1984; June 10, 1991, pp. 770-775.

National Review, March 20, 1981; January 21, 1983.

New Criterion, January, 1986, pp. 5-13.

New Republic, May 18, 1968; September 6, 1975; February 14, 1983; July 29, 1991, pp. 36-39; December 23, 2002, James Wood, review of *Ignorance,* p. 33.

New Statesman, November 4, 2002, Hugo Barnacle, review of *Ignorance,* p. 52.

Newsweek, July 29, 1974; November 24, 1980; November 8, 1982; April 30, 1984; February 4, 1985; November 11, 2002, Andrew Nagorski, review of *Ignorance,* p. 70.

New Yorker, May 16, 1988, pp. 110, 113-118.

New York Review of Books, May 21, 1970; August 8, 1974; September 16, 1976, February 5, 1981; May 10, 1984.

New York Times, November 6, 1980; January 18, 1982; April 2, 1984; December 17, 1992, p. C18; September 21, 1995; May 14, 1996, p. B2.

New York Times Book Review, January 11, 1970; July 28, 1974; September 5, 1976; November 30, 1980; October 24, 1982; April 29, 1984; January 6, 1985; April 28, 1991, p. 7; October 6, 2002, Maureen Howard, review of *Ignorance,* p. 38.

New York Times Magazine, May 19, 1985.

Paris Review, summer, 1984.

Partisan Review, Volume 11, 1985; Volume 17, 1985.

Publishers Weekly, July 24, 1995, p. 54; August 26, 2002, review of *Ignorance,* p. 38.

Review of Contemporary Fiction (issue devoted to Kundera and Zulfikar Ghose), summer, 1989.

Salmagundi (issue devoted to Kundera), winter, 1987.

San Francisco Review, spring, 1991, pp. 6, 12.

Saturday Review, December 20, 1969.

Spectator, June 10, 1978; February 13, 1982; June 23, 1984; November 22, 1986, pp. 38-39; October 19, 2002, Robert Edric, review of *Ignorance,* p. 50.

Time, August 5, 1974.

Times (London, England), February 17, 1983; May 24, 1984.

Times Literary Supplement, October 30, 1969; March 3, 1978; July 21, 1978; February 5, 1982; May 25, 1984; January 16, 1987, p. 55; May 17, 1991, p. 17.

Village Voice, December 24, 1980; November 23, 1982; June 26, 1984; March 29, 1988, p. 70.
Voice Literary Supplement, November, 1983.
Washington Post, November 22, 1980.
Washington Post Book World, December 19, 1982; April 22, 1984; May 5, 1991, p. 3.
World Literature Today, spring, 1983.

*   *   *

KUNITZ, Stanley 1905-
(Stanley Jasspon Kunitz)

PERSONAL: Born July 29, 1905, in Worcester, MA; son of Solomon Z. (a manufacturer) and Yetta Helen (Jasspon) Kunitz; married Helen Pearce, 1930 (divorced, 1937); married Eleanor Evans, November 21, 1939 (divorced, 1958); married Elise Asher (an artist), June 21, 1958; children: (second marriage) Gretchen. *Education:* Harvard University, A.B. (summa cum laude), 1926, A.M., 1927.

ADDRESSES: Home—37 West 12th St., New York, NY 10011-8502.

CAREER: Poet. *Wilson Library Bulletin*, New York City, editor, 1928-43; Bennington College, Bennington, VT, English faculty, 1946-49; Potsdam State Teachers College (now State University of New York College at Potsdam), Potsdam, NY, professor of English, 1949-50; New School for Social Research (now New School University), New York City, lecturer in English, 1950-57; Poetry Center, Young Men's Hebrew Association (YMHA), New York City, with poetry workshop, 1958-62; Columbia University, New York City, lecturer, 1963-66, adjunct professor of writing in School of the Arts, 1967-85. Member of staff of writing division, Fine Arts Work Center, Provincetown, MA, 1968—. Fellow, Yale University, 1969—; visiting senior fellow, Council of the Humanities, and Old Dominion Fellow in creative writing, Princeton University, 1978-79. Director of seminar, Potsdam Summer Workshop in Creative Arts, 1949-53; poet-in-residence, University of Washington, 1955-56, Queens College (now Queens College of the City University of New York), 1956-57, Brandeis University, 1958-59, and Princeton University, 1979. Danforth Visiting Lecturer at colleges and universities in the United States, 1961-63; visiting professor, Yale University, 1972, and Rutgers University, 1974. Lectured and gave poetry readings under cultural exchange program in USSR and Poland, 1967, in Senegal and Ghana, 1976, and in Israel and Egypt, 1980. Library of Congress, Washington, DC, consultant on poetry, 1974-76, honorary consultant in American letters, 1976-83. *Military service:* U.S. Army, Air Transport Command, 1943-45; became staff sergeant.

MEMBER: American Academy and Institute of Arts and Letters (secretary, 1985-88), Academy of American Poets (chancellor, 1970—), Poets House (founding president, 1985-90), Phi Beta Kappa.

AWARDS, HONORS: Garrison Medal for poetry, Harvard University, 1926; Oscar Blumenthal Prize, 1941; Guggenheim fellowship, 1945-46; Amy Lowell traveling fellowship, 1953-54; Levinson Prize, *Poetry* magazine, 1956; *Saturday Review* award, 1957; Harriet Monroe Poetry Award, University of Chicago, 1958; Ford Foundation grant, 1958-59; National Institute of Arts and Letters award, 1959; Pulitzer Prize, 1959, for *Selected Poems, 1928-1958;* Brandeis University creative arts award medal, 1964; Academy of American Poets fellowship, 1968; New England Poetry Club Golden Rose Trophy, 1970; American Library Association notable book citation, 1979, for *The Poems of Stanley Kunitz, 1928-1978;* Lenore Marshall Award for Poetry, 1980; National Endowment for the Arts senior fellowship, 1984; Bollingen Prize in Poetry, Yale University Library, 1987; Walt Whitman Award citation of merit, with designation as State Poet of New York, 1987; Montgomery Fellow, Dartmouth College, 1991; Centennial medal, Harvard University, 1992; National Medal of Arts, 1993; National Book Award, 1995, for *Passing Through: Later Poems, New and Selected;* Shelley Memorial Award, 1995; Courage of Conscience Award, 1998; Frost Medal, 1998; Jewish Cultural Achievement Award, 2000; named Poet Laureate of the United States, 2000. Litt.D., Clark University, 1961, Anna Maria College, 1977; L.H.D., Worcester State College, 1980, SUNY-Brockport, 1987, and Emerson College, 2001.

WRITINGS:

POETRY

Intellectual Things, Doubleday, Doran (New York, NY), 1930.
Passport to the War: A Selection of Poems, Holt (New York, NY), 1944.
Selected Poems, 1928-1958, Little, Brown (Boston, MA), 1958.

The Testing-Tree: Poems, Little, Brown (Boston, MA), 1971.

The Terrible Threshold: Selected Poems, 1940-70, Secker & Warburg (London, England), 1974.

The Coat without a Seam: Sixty Poems, 1930-1972, Gehenna Press (Northampton, MA), 1974.

The Lincoln Relics, Graywolf Press (Townsend, WA), 1978.

The Poems of Stanley Kunitz: 1928-1978, Little, Brown (Boston, MA), 1979.

The Wellfleet Whale and Companion Poems, Sheep Meadow Press (Riverdale-on-Hudson, NY), 1983.

Next-to-Last Things: New Poems and Essays, Little, Brown (Boston, MA), 1985.

Passing Through: Later Poems, New and Selected, Norton (New York, NY), 1995.

The Collected Poems, Norton (New York, NY), 2000.

(With Genine Lentine) *The Wild Braid: A Poet Reflects on a Century in the Garden,* Norton (New York, NY), 2005.

NONFICTION

(Translator with Max Hayward) *Poems of Anna Akhmatova,* Little, Brown (Boston, MA), 1973.

(Translator) Andrei Voznesensky, *Story under Full Sail,* Doubleday (New York, NY), 1974.

Robert Lowell: Poet of Terribilita, Pierpont Morgan Library (New York, NY), 1974.

A Kind of Order, a Kind of Folly: Essays and Conversations, Little, Brown (Boston, MA), 1975.

Interviews and Encounters with Stanley Kunitz, edited by Stanley Moss, Sheep Meadow Press (Riverdale-on-Hudson, NY), 1993.

Also contributor of translations to: Andrei Voznesensky, *Antiworlds,* Basic Books (New York, NY), 1966; Voznesensky, *Antiworlds* [and] *The Fifth Ace,* Anchor Books (New York, NY), 1967; and Yevgeny Yevtushenko, *Stolen Apples,* Doubleday (Garden City, NY), 1971.

EDITOR

Living Authors: A Book of Biographies, H.W. Wilson (New York, NY), 1931.

(With Howard Haycraft) *Authors Today and Yesterday: A Companion Volume to "Living Authors,"* H.W. Wilson (New York, NY), 1933.

(With Howard Haycraft) *The Junior Book of Authors: An Introduction to the Lives of Writers and Illustrators for Younger Readers,* H.W. Wilson (New York, NY), 1934, second revised edition, 1951.

(With Howard Haycraft) *British Authors of the Nineteenth Century,* H.W. Wilson (New York, NY), 1936.

(With Howard Haycraft) *American Authors, 1600-1900: A Biographical Dictionary of American Literature,* H.W. Wilson (New York, NY), 1938, 8th edition, 1971.

(With Howard Haycraft) *Twentieth-Century Authors: A Biographical Dictionary,* H.W. Wilson (New York, NY), 1942, first supplement, 1955.

(With Howard Haycraft) *British Authors before 1800: A Biographical Dictionary,* H.W. Wilson (New York, NY), 1952.

Poems of John Keats, Crowell (New York, NY), 1964.

(With Vineta Colby) *European Authors, 1000-1900: A Biographical Dictionary of European Literature,* H.W. Wilson (New York, NY), 1967.

(Editor and author of introduction) Ivan Drach, *Orchard Lamps,* Sheep Meadow Press (Riverdale-on-Hudson, NY), 1978.

Selections: University and College Poetry Prizes, 1973-78, Academy of American Poets, 1980.

(Author of introduction) *The Essential Blake,* Ecco Press (New York, NY), 1987.

(Editor, author of introduction, translator; with Max Hayward) *Poems of Akhmatova/Izbrannye stikhi,* Houghton Mifflin (Boston, MA), 1997.

(Editor, with David Ignatow) *The Wild Card: Selected Poems, Early and Late,* by Karl Shapiro, University of Illinois Press (Champaign, IL), 1998.

CONTRIBUTOR

War Poets: An Anthology of the War Poetry of the Twentieth Century, edited by Oscar Williams, John Day (New York, NY), 1945.

The Criterion Book of Modern American Verse, edited by W.H. Auden, Criterion, 1956.

How Does a Poem Mean?, edited by John Ciardi, Houghton Mifflin (Boston, MA), 1959.

John Fischer and Robert B. Silvers, editors, *Writing in America,* Rutgers University Press (New Brunswick, NJ), 1960.

Modern American Poetry, edited by Louis Untermeyer, Harcourt (New York, NY), 1962.

American Lyric Poems: From Colonial Times to the Present, edited by Elder Olson, Appleton (New York, NY), 1964.

Anthony J. Ostroff, editor, *The Contemporary Poet as Artist and Critic,* Little, Brown (Boston, MA), 1964.

Vineta Colby, editor, *American Culture in the Sixties,* H.W. Wilson (New York, NY), 1964.

The Distinctive Voice, edited by William J. Martz, Scott, Foresman (New York, NY), 1966.

Where Is Vietnam?: American Poets Respond, edited by Walter Lowenfels, Doubleday-Anchor (New York, NY), 1967.

Robert Lowell and others, editors, *Randall Jarrell, 1914-1965,* Farrar, Straus (New York, NY), 1967.

Norton Anthology of Modern Poetry, edited by Richard Ellmann and Robert O'Clair, W.W. Norton (New York, NY), 1973.

Fifty Years of American Poetry: Anniversary Volume for the Academy of American Poets, Abrams (New York, NY), 1984.

Contemporary American Poetry, edited by A. Poulin, Jr., Houghton Mifflin (Boston, MA), 4th edition, 1985.

Contributor to periodicals, including *Atlantic, New Republic, New Yorker, Antaeus, New York Review of Books, American Poetry Review,* and *Harper's.* General editor, "Yale Series of Younger Poets," Yale University Press (New Haven, CT), 1969-77.

SIDELIGHTS: Stanley Kunitz became the tenth Poet Laureate of the United States in the autumn of 2000. Kunitz was ninety-five years old at the time, still actively publishing and promoting poetry to new generations of readers. In the *New York Times Book Review,* Robert Campbell noted that Kunitz's selection as poet laureate—the highest literary honor in America— "affirms his stature as perhaps the most distinguished living American poet." *Atlantic Monthly* contributor David Barber likewise cited Kunitz as "not only one of the most widely admired figures in contemporary poetry but also, rarer still, a true ambassador for his art." Barber felt that Kunitz, having "continued to write poems of a startling richness at an advanced age . . . has arguably saved his best for last. . . . The venerable doyen of American poetry is still a poet in his prime."

Having published books throughout the greater part of the twentieth century, Kunitz has exerted a subtle but steady influence on such major poets as Theodore Roethke, W.H. Auden, and Robert Lowell. Through his teaching he has provided encouragement to hundreds of younger poets as well. His output has been modest but enduring: since 1930, he has published only a dozen volumes of poetry. "I think that explains why I am able to continue as a poet into my late years," Kunitz once explained in *Publishers Weekly.* "If I hadn't had an urgent impulse, if the poem didn't seem to me terribly important, I never wanted to write it and didn't. And that's persisted." While the complexity of Kunitz's ini-

tial works delayed critical attention, in 1959, he received a Pulitzer Prize for his third poetry collection, *Selected Poems, 1928-1958.* Since then, he has earned a high reputation for "work with a lifetime steeped in it," to quote Barber.

Some critics suggested that Kunitz's poetry has steadily increased in quality in the most recent decades. As *Virginia Quarterly Review* contributor Jay Parini observed: "The restraints of [Kunitz's] art combine with a fierce dedication to clarity and intellectual grace to assure him of a place among the essential poets of his generation, which includes Roethke, Lowell, Auden, and Eberhart." This place was confirmed in 1995, when Kunitz was honored with the National Book Award for *Passing Through: The Later Poems, New and Selected,* and again in 2000, when he assumed the mantle of poet laureate.

Kunitz's early poetry collections, *Intellectual Things* and *Passport to the War: A Selection of Poems,* earned him a reputation as an intellectual poet. Reflecting their author's admiration for English metaphysical poets like John Donne and George Herbert, the intricate metaphorical verses in these collections were recognized more for their craft than their substance. Thus, they were somewhat slow to garner widespread critical attention. "In my youth, as might be expected, I had little knowledge of the world to draw on," Kunitz once explained to *CA.* "But I had fallen in love with language and was excited by ideas, including the idea of being a poet. Early poetry is much more likely to be abstract because of the poverty of experience."

In his assessment of Kunitz's early work, Barber declared that the poems were "dense, fiercely wrought, intricately figured—and for their day rather beyond the pale. They gave the impression of owing more to the metaphysicals than to the moderns and of being nourished on a Yeatsian diet of eroticized mysticism. Formally accomplished, they were nonetheless humming with a cathartic energy that set them apart from the dominant strains of American lyric poetry."

Kunitz followed his Pulitzer Prize-winning *Selected Poems, 1928-1958,* with *The Testing-Tree: Poems,* a collection in which the author "ruthlessly prods wounds," according to Stanley Moss in the *Nation.* "His primordial curse is the suicide of his father before his birth. The poems take us into the sacred woods and houses of his 66 years, illuminate the images that have haunted him. . . . [Kunitz] searches for secret reality and the meaning of the unknown father. He moves from the known to the unknown to the unknowable—not necessarily in that order." And Robert Lowell commented in the *New York Times Book Review*: "One reads [*The Testing-Tree*] from cover to cover with the ease of reading good prose fiction. . . . I don't know of another in prose or verse that gives in a few pages the impression of a large autobiography." Discussing the self-revelatory nature of his work, Kunitz once told *CA*: "By its nature poetry is an intimate medium, . . . Perhaps that's why it is so dangerously seductive to the creative spirit. The transformation of individual experience—the transpersonalization of the persona, if you will—is work that the imagination has to do, its obligatory task. One of the problems with so much of what was called, in the '60s, confessional poetry was that it relied excessively on the exploitation of self, on the shock effect of raw experience. My conviction is that poetry is a legendary, not an anecdotal, art."

Published in 1971, *The Testing-Tree* was perceived by critics as a significant stylistic departure for its author. Lowell, for example, commented in the *New York Times Book Review* that the two volumes "are landmarks of the old and the new style. The smoke has blown off. The old Delphic voice has learned to speak 'words that cats and dogs can understand.'" *Dictionary of Literary Biography* contributor Marie Henault concurred: "*The Testing-Tree* [reveals] a new, freer poetry, looser forms, shorter lines, lowercase line beginnings. . . . Overall the Kunitz of this book is a 'new' Kunitz, one who has grown and changed in the thirteen years since *Selected Poems*." Gregory Orr offered this view in *American Poetry Review*: "There *is* a stylistic shift, but more deeply than that there is a fundamental shift in Kunitz's relation to the world and to his life."

Asked to comment on this stylistic shift in *Publishers Weekly*, Kunitz noted that his early poems "were very intricate, dense and formal. . . . They were written in conventional metrics and had a very strong beat to the line. . . . In my late poems I've learned to depend on a simplicity that seems almost nonpoetic on the surface, but has reverberations within that keep it intense and alive. . . . I think that as a young poet I looked for what Keats called 'a fine excess,' but as an old poet I look for spareness and rigor and a world of compassion." If Kunitz's earlier poems were often intricately woven, intellectual, lyricized allegories about the transcendence of physical limitations, his later work can be seen as an emotive acceptance of those limitations.

While Kunitz's style has changed, his themes have not. One of Kunitz's most pervasive themes concerns the simultaneity of life and death. "It's the way things are: death and life inextricably bound to each other," he once explained to *CA*. "One of my feelings about working the land [as a gardener] is that I am celebrating a ritual of death and resurrection. Every spring I feel that. I am never closer to the miraculous than when I am grubbing in the soil." He once revealed in the *New York Times*: "The deepest thing I know is that I am living and dying at once, and my conviction is to report that dialogue. It is a rather terrifying thought that is at the root of much of my poetry." Other themes concern "rebirth, the quest, and the night journey (or descent into the underworld)," explained the poet in *Poetry*.

Kunitz's willingness to explore such serious themes has prompted critics to applaud his courage, and to describe him as a risk taker. Analyzing one of Kunitz's better-known poems, "King of the River," from *The Testing-Tree*, *New York Times Book Review* contributor Robert B. Shaw wrote: "Kunitz's willingness to risk bombast, platitude or bathos in his contemplation of what he calls 'mystery' is evident in [this poem]. Mystery—of the self, of time, of change and fate—is not facilely dispelled but approached with imaginative awe in his work; in our rationalistic century this is swimming against the stream. This is a form of artistic heroism; and when Kunitz's scorning of safety meshes firmly with his technical skills, the outcome is poetry of unusual power and depth." Mary Oliver similarly observed in *Kenyon Review* that "what is revealed, then, is courage. Not the courage of words only, but the intellectual courage that insists on the truth, which is never simple."

Kunitz reveals within his works an optimism that is apparent in *Next-to-Last Things: New Poems and Essays*, his celebration of rural life published in 1985. A collection of twelve poems, several prose essays, and an interview from the *Paris Review*, *Next-to-Last-Things* reflects the poet's love of nature, acts of conscience, and the loneliness that comes from both age and creativity. *New York Times Book Review* contributor R.W. Flint observed: "The sharp and seasoned good humor Stanley Kunitz brings to the poems, essays, interviews and aphorisms in *Next-to-Last Things* is a tonic in our literary life. . . . Paradox and complication entice him, and he now cheerfully discusses a body of poetry, his own, that he rightly finds to have been 'essentially dark and grieving—elegiac.'"

In *Next-to-Last Things*, critics found that both Kunitz's perception of the themes of life and death and his style had undergone further transitions. *Chicago Tribune Book World* contributor James Idema noted that Kunitz's poetry had become yet more austere: "The poems that open the book are leaner than those from the early and middle years, narrower on their pages. . . . Some of them are serene and melancholy, as you might expect. Most reflect the sky-and-weather environment of his Provincetown summer home, where he is most comfortable confronting 'the great simplicities.' But the best ones are full of action and vivid imagery."

Passing Through: The Later Poems, New and Selected encapsulates much of Kunitz's later oeuvre and includes nine new works of poetry. "The Wellfleet Whale," a nature poem that speaks to a finback whale run aground, is accompanied by "Touch Me," wherein the artist characteristically contemplates an earthbound immortality. The collection, which earned its ninety-year-old author the National Book Award for poetry, is considered to possess an assured poetic voice and a heightened vision, sensitive to subtleties and nuances of life filled with meaning. "In youth, poems come to you out of the blue," Kunitz told Mary B.W. Tabor in the *New York Times.* "They're delivered at your doorstep like the morning news. But at this age," he added, "one has to dig."

Barber felt that, in *Passing Through,* "one enters the presence of an indomitable elder spirit writing with alertness, tenacity, and finesse, still immersed in the life of the senses and persisting in the search for fugitive essences. Neither resigned nor becalmed, Kunitz's . . . poems are by turns contemplative, confiding, mythic, and elegiac. If they have the measured and worldly tone that befits an old master, they also have the ardent and questing air of one whose capacity for artless wonder seems inexhaustible."

Although Kunitz's style has changed over his seven decades as a poet, his methods have not. A notebook and a pen render a sketch; many late nights over a manual typewriter result in a finished poem. What he does not find satisfactory, he destroys. "I don't want my bad poems to be published after I'm not around to check them," he told Tabor.

"I don't try to preordain the form of a poem," Kunitz once revealed to *CA,* discussing his personal experience of the poetic craft. "There's a good deal of automatism in the beginning, as I try to give the poem its head. Most of all I am looking for a distinctive rhythm. . . . I want the poem to grow out of its own materials, to develop organically." The organic quality of a poem is of primary importance to Kunitz. "I write my poems for the ear," he explained. "In fact, my method of writing a poem is to say it. The pitch and tempo and tonalities of a poem are elements of its organic life. A poem is as much a voice as it is a system of verbal signs. I realize that ultimately the poet departs from the scene, and the poems that he abandons to the printed page must speak for themselves. But I can't help wondering about the influence on posterity of the technical revolution that will enable them to see and hear, on film and tape, the poets of our century. Suppose we had videotapes of Keats reading his ode 'To Autumn' or Blake declaiming 'The Marriage of Heaven and Hell'!"

Kunitz's 100th birthday on July 29, 2005, was marked by celebrations in New York and Provincetown, Massachusetts, along with W.W. Norton's publication of *The Wild Braid: A Poet Reflects on a Century in the Garden,* co-written with Genine Lentine.

BIOGRAPHICAL AND CRITICAL SOURCES:

BOOKS

A Celebration for Stanley Kunitz on His Eightieth Birthday, Sheep Meadow Press (Riverdale-on-Hudson, NY), 1986.

Contemporary Literary Criticism, Thomson Gale (Detroit, MI), Volume 6, 1976, Volume 11, 1979, Volume 14, 1980.

Dictionary of Literary Biography, Volume 48:*American Poets, 1880-1945, Second Series,* Thomson Gale (Detroit, MI), 1986.

Henault, Marie, *Stanley Kunitz,* Twayne (New York, NY), 1980.

Hungerford, Edward, editor, *Poets in Progress,* Northwestern University Press (Chicago, IL), 1962, revised edition, 1967.

Kunitz, Stanley, *Interviews and Encounters with Stanley Kunitz,* Sheep Meadow Press (Riverdale-on-Hudson, NY), 1993.

Mills, Ralph J., Jr., *Contemporary American Poetry,* Random House (New York, NY), 1965.

Orr, Gregory, *Stanley Kunitz: An Introduction to the Poetry,* Columbia University Press (New York, NY), 1985.

Ostroff, Anthony J., editor, *The Contemporary Poet as a Critic and Artist,* Little, Brown (Boston, MA), 1964.

Rodman, Selden, *Tongues of Fallen Angels,* New Directions (Newton, NJ), 1974.

Rosenthal, M. L., *The Modern Poets: A Critical Introduction,* Oxford University Press (New York, NY), 1960.

PERIODICALS

American Poetry Review, March/April, 1976; July, 1980; September-October, 1985.

Atlantic Monthly, June, 1996, David Barber, "A Visionary Poet at Ninety."

Boston Review, December 2000-January 2001, p. 53.

Chicago Tribune Book World, December 22, 1985.

Contemporary Literature, winter, 1974.

Harper's, February, 1986.

Houston Chronicle, December 24, 2000.

Iowa Review, spring, 1974.

Kenyon Review, summer, 1986, pp. 113-35.

Los Angeles Times Book Review, September 24, 2000, p. 3.

Nation, September 20, 1971.

New Yorker, October 16, 1995, p. 50.

New York Quarterly, fall, 1970.

New York Review of Books, November 22, 1979.

New York Times, July 7, 1979; March 11, 1987; August 29, 1993, sec. 9, p. 3; November 30, 1995, p. B1, C18; August 2, 2000, Dinitia Smith, "The Laureate Distilled, to an Eau de Vie," p. B1.

New York Times Book Review, November 11, 1965; March 21, 1971; July 22, 1979; April 6, 1986, p. 11; October 1, 2000, Robert Campbell, "God, Man, and Whale," p. 16.

Paris Review, spring, 1982.

People Weekly, October 30, 2000, p. 159.

Poetry, September, 1980.

Prairie Schooner, summer, 1980.

Publishers Weekly, December 20, 1985; November 20, 1995, pp. 17, 20; July 31, 2000, review of *Collected Poems,* p. 89.

San Francisco Examiner, October 4, 2000.

Saturday Review, September 27, 1958; December 18, 1971.

Sewanee Review, winter, 1988, pp. 137-49.

Times Literary Supplement, May 30, 1980.

USA Today, October 12, 2000, p. 15A.

Virginia Quarterly Review, spring, 1980.

Washington Post, May 12, 1987; July 29, 2000.

Washington Post Book World, September 30, 1979.

Yale Literary Magazine, May, 1968.

Yale Review, autumn, 1971.

OTHER

CNN.com, http://www.cnn.com/ (August 1, 2000), "Stanley Kunitz Named U.S. Poet Laureate."

KUNITZ, Stanley Jasspon
See KUNITZ, Stanley

*   *   *

KUSHNER, Tony 1956-

PERSONAL: Born July 16, 1956, in New York, NY. *Education:* Columbia University, B.A., 1978; New York University, M.F.A., 1984.

ADDRESSES: Office—Walter Kerr Theatre, 225 West 48th St., New York, NY 10036. *Agent*—Joyce Ketay Agency, 1501 Broadway, Ste. 1908, New York, NY 10036.

CAREER: United Nations Plaza Hotel, New York, NY, switchboard operator, 1979-85; St. Louis Repertory Theatre, St. Louis, MO, assistant director, 1985-86; New York Theatre Workshop, New York, artistic director, 1987-88; Theatre Communication Group, New York, director of literary services, 1990-91; Juilliard School of Drama, New York, playwright-in-residence, 1990-92. Guest artist at New York University Graduate Theatre Program, Yale University, and Princeton University, beginning 1989.

MEMBER: AIDS Coalition to Unleash Power (ACT UP), American Academy of Arts and Letters.

AWARDS, HONORS: Directing fellowship, National Endowment for the Arts, 1985, 1987, and 1993; Princess Grace Award, 1986; playwriting fellowship, New York State Council for the Arts, 1987; John Whiting Award, Arts Council of Great Britain, 1990; Kennedy Center/American Express Fund for New American Plays Awards, 1990 and 1992; Kesserling Award, National Arts Club, 1992; Will Glickman playwriting prize, 1992; London *Evening Standard*Award, 1992; Pulitzer Prize for drama, Antoinette Perry Award ("Tony") for best play, and New York Drama Critics Circle Award for Best New Play, all 1993, all for *Millennium Approaches,* Part One of *Angels in America;* American Academy of Arts and Letters Award, 1994; Tony Award for best play, 1994, for *Perestroika,* Part Two of *Angels in America;* Lambda Literary Award, Drama, 1994, for *Angels in America;* Lambda Literary Award, Lesbian and Gay Drama, 1996, for *Thinking about the Longstanding Problems of Virtue and Happiness: Essays, a Play, Two Poems, and a Prayer; Village Voice* Obie Award, 2002, for *Homebody/Kabul;* Emmy

Award for Writing for a Miniseries, Movie or Dramatic Special for "Angels in America" (HBO), 2004; inducted into the American Academy of Arts and Letters, 2005.

WRITINGS:

PLAYS

Yes, Yes, No, No (juvenile; produced in St. Louis, MO, 1985), published in *Plays in Process*, 1987.

Stella (adapted from the play by Johann Wolfgang von Goethe), produced in New York, NY, 1987.

A Bright Room Called Day (produced in San Francisco, CA, 1987), Broadway Play Publishing, 1991.

Hydriotaphia, produced in New York, NY, 1987.

The Illusion (adapted from Pierre Corneille's play *L'Illusion comique*; produced in New York, NY, 1988, revised version produced in Hartford, CT, 1990), Broadway Play Publishing, 1991.

(With Ariel Dorfman) *Widows* (adapted from a book by Ariel Dorfman), produced in Los Angeles, CA, 1991.

Angels in America: A Gay Fantasia on National Themes, Part One: *Millennium Approaches* (produced in San Francisco, 1991), Hern, 1992, Part Two: *Perestroika,* produced in New York, NY, 1992.

A Bright Room Called Day, Theatre Communications Group (New York, NY), 1994.

Angels in America: A Gay Fantasia on National Themes Theatre Communications Group (New York, NY), 1995 (includes both parts; produced as two-part television film on Home Box Office, 2003),.

Slavs! Thinking about the Longstanding Problems of Virtue and Happiness, Theatre Communications Group (New York, NY), 1995.

A Dybbuk; or, Between Two Worlds (adapted from Joachim Neugroschel's translation of the original play by S. Ansky; produced in New York, NY, at Joseph Papp Public Theater, 1997), Theatre Communications Group (New York, NY), 1997.

The Good Person of Szechuan (adapted from the original play by Bertolt Brecht), Arcade, 1997.

(With Eric Bogosian and others) *Love's Fire: Seven New Plays Inspired by Seven Shakespearean Sonnets*, Morrow (New York, NY), 1998.

Henry Box Brown, or the Mirror of Slavery, performed at Royal National Theatre, London, 1998.

Homebody/ Kabul, (produced in New York, NY, 2001), Theatre Communications Group (New York, NY), 2002.

Caroline or Change (musical), produced in New York, NY, at Joseph Papp Public Theater, 2002.

OTHER

A Meditation from Angels in America, HarperSanFrancisco (San Francisco, CA), 1994.

Tony Kushner in Conversation, edited by Robert Vorlicky, University of Michigan Press (Ann Arbor, MI), 1997.

Death and Taxes: Hydriotaphia, and Other Plays, Theatre Communications Group (New York, NY), 2000.

Brundibar, illustrated by Maurice Sendak, Michael di Capua/Hyperion Books for Children (New York, NY), 2002.

Kushner also wrote the screenplay for the television movie adaptation of *Angels in America.*

ADAPTATIONS: Angels in America was adapted for a television movie produced by HBO, 2003, and as an English-language opera that premiered at the Theatre du Chatelet in Paris, 2004.

SIDELIGHTS: Playwright Tony Kushner took the theater world by storm in the early 1990s with his epic drama, *Angels in America: A Gay Fantasia on National Themes.* A seven-hour play in two separate parts, *Millennium Approaches* and *Perestroika*, *Angels in America* explores in uncompromising terms what it was like to be gay and affected by AIDS (acquired immunodeficiency syndrome) during the 1980s and 1990s. Despite its grim subject matter and open attacks on the administration of former U.S. President Ronald Reagan, the play has proved quite popular with mainstream audiences from Broadway to Los Angeles and London. It has also won great acclaim from drama critics, garnering both the Pulitzer Prize for drama and two Antoinette Perry ("Tony") awards for best play in 1993 and 1994.

Kushner was born in New York City in 1956, but his parents, who were classical musicians, moved to Lake Charles, Louisiana, shortly after his birth. His parents encouraged Kushner and his siblings to explore literature and the arts; the children were given a dollar whenever they had memorized a poem to recite. His mother was also an actress, and Kushner confided to Susan Cheever in the *New York Times* that "that's the major reason I went into the theater. I saw some of her performances when I was four or five years old and they were so powerful. I had vivid dreams afterwards." Kushner realized he was different from most other children in yet another significant way, however. "I have fairly clear memories of being gay since I was six," the play-wright told Richard Stayton in the *Los Angeles Times*. "I knew that I felt slightly different than most of the boys I was growing up with. By the time I was eleven there was no doubt. But I was completely in the closet."

He continued to keep his sexuality a secret throughout his undergraduate years at Columbia University, during which time he underwent psychotherapy trying to become heterosexual, even though his therapist told him at the beginning of treatment that psychotherapy did not change people's sexual orientation. Kushner eventually accepted this and "came out," meaning he told his family and friends that he was gay.

Kushner's early plays, however, did not focus on gay themes. *A Bright Room Called Day,* perhaps the best-known of his pre-*Angels* works, concerns a group of liberal-minded acquaintances in the Weimar Republic of Germany, just before the establishment of Adolf Hitler's Nazi regime. M. Elizabeth Osborn described the plot in *Contemporary Dramatists,* saying, this "circle of friends disintegrates under the pressures of Hitler's rise to power, one after another forced into hiding or exile until just one woman, Agnes, is left cowering in her apartment." This main story is entwined, however, with the commentary of Zillah Katz, a contemporary young American woman, who draws parallels—sometimes extreme—between Hitler's regime and the administrations of U.S. Presidents Ronald Reagan and George Bush, Sr. Osborn quoted Kushner as explaining that he continues to rewrite Zillah's lines because he "will cheerfully supply new material, drawing appropriate parallels between contemporary and historical monsters and their monstrous acts, regardless of how superficially outrageous such comparisons may seem. To refuse to compare is to rob history of its power to inform present action."

When *A Bright Room Called Day* was performed in New York City in 1991, it received less than enthusiastic reviews. A somewhat neutral Gerald Weales in *Commonweal* labeled it "ambitious," but observed that he felt it was "a more despairing play than it probably intended to be." Less ambiguous was the response of Frank Rich in the *New York Times,* who took exception to Kushner's linking of Nazi Germany with the United States during the 1980s. "Is the time ever right for a political work in which the National Socialism of the Third Reich is trivialized by being equated with the 'national senility' of the Reagan era?" he demanded. Rich also called the work "fatuous"and "an early front-

runner for the most infuriating play of 1991." *A Bright Room Called Day* did, however, impress Oskar Eustis, then artistic director of the Eureka Theater in San Francisco, California. He commissioned Kushner to write a comic play for his theater. This was the play that would become *Angels in America,* though the Eureka would no longer exist by the time the entire play was ready for production.

Though *Angels in America* is filled with many different characters, it is meant to be performed by eight persons who each play several roles. In *Millennium Approaches,* the story focuses on two couples—two gay men named Louis and Prior dealing with Prior's AIDS, and Harper and Joe, a nominally straight couple—although the married Mormon man, Joe, is trying to suppress his secret homosexuality. Also central to the play is the figure of lawyer Roy Cohn—based on the real Cohn who helped Senator Joseph McCarthy persecute suspected communists during the 1950s. Cohn also persecuted gays, although he himself was a closet homosexual and died of AIDS. The play's Cohn, whom Joe works for, is true to the somewhat rapacious image of the historical figure. Lloyd Rose in the *Washington Post* explained that "Cohn is clearly meant to be the Devil of the piece: the man who lies to himself, who abuses his power, who has sacrificed his moral self for success. Yet the play jolts with energy whenever he's onstage, because his self-hatred turns splendidly and splenetically outward. . . . Cohn rages against the definitions society would force on him. He destroys his own soul in satanic spite, and he goes down raging and in flames." In one scene, for example, after his doctor has told him that he has AIDS, Cohn declaims against labels: "They tell you one thing and one thing only: where does an individual so identified fit in the food chain, in the pecking order? Not ideology, or sexual taste, but something much simpler: clout. . . . Now to someone who does not understand this, homosexual is what I am because I have sex with men. But really this is wrong. Homosexuals are not men who sleep with other men. Homosexuals are men who in fifteen years of trying cannot get a pissant antidiscrimination bill through City Council. Homosexuals are men who know nobody and who nobody knows. Who have zero clout. Does this sound like me, Henry?"

Yet, while "the play is a political call to arms for the age of AIDS," as Rich noted in the *New York Times,* "it is no polemic." Critics of *Millennium Approaches* in its various performances greeted it with high praise. Rich himself first reviewed the London staging of *Angels in America's* first part, and at that time hailed it in the *New York Times* as "a searching and radical rethinking of the whole esthetic of American political drama in which far-flung hallucinations, explicit sexual encounters and camp humor are given as much weight as erudite ideological argument." John Lahr in the *New Yorker* noted that Kushner, "with immense good humor and accessible characters . . . honors the gay community by telling a story that sets its concerns in the larger historical context of American political life."

Millennium Approaches takes its name from the sense of apocalypse the character Prior feels while dealing with his deadly disease. At the end, an angel descends dramatically to visit him, and he is declared a prophet, temporarily, at least, saved from death by AIDS. *Perestroika,* by contrast, is a somewhat quieter piece, getting its title from the Russian word ex-Soviet leader Mikhail Gorbachev used for his proposals for "restructuring"economic and social policies. As Lahr reported, *Perestroika* "is the messier but more interesting of the two plays, skillfully steering its characters from the sins of separation in the eighties to a new sense of community in the embattled nineties." In the second part of *Angels,* the glorious being that visited Prior at the end of the first part turns out to represent stasis or death, and Prior decides to reject it. Cohn dies, but this does not prevent his ghost from reappearing later in the play—in the role of God's lawyer, no less. The comedy of *Millennium* continues; in *Perestroika,* according to Lahr, "Kushner uses laughter carefully, to deflate the maudlin and to build a complex tapestry of ironic emotion."Lahr concluded that Kushner's work is "a victory . . . for the transforming power of the imagination to turn devastation into beauty."

In 1995 Kushner wrote and produced what he terms a "coda" to *Angels in America, Slavs! Thinking about the Longstanding Problems of Virtue and Happiness,* which Christopher Hawthorne of *Salon.com* called "a compact, quirky exploration of the collapse of the Soviet Union and the ruin, both philosophical and environmental, left in its wake." *Slavs!* resembles the *Angels in America* plays because, according to Kushner in an interview with Andrea Bernstein of *Mother Jones,* the play proceeds from the problem that if you do not know where you are heading, it is difficult to move or make choices. In *Slavs!,* the character Prelapsarianov, "the world's oldest living Bolshevik," asks, "How are we to proceed without theory? Is it enough to reject the past, is it wise to move forward in this blind fashion? . . . You who live in this sour little age cannot imagine the sheer grandeur of the prospect we gazed upon."*Slavs!,* Kushner told *Mother Jones,* answers the conundrum of whether we make history or are made by history by arguing that socialists need to stop looking to the past for

an appropriate antecedent upon which to model the present revolutionary response. Kushner also remarked that in the United States it is easier to come out as a gay man than it is as a socialist. Reviews of *Slavs!* were somewhat lukewarm, and Kushner suspects it is because "people have been promised over and over by the media . . . that we don't have to think about these issues" anymore.

Continuing Kushner's search for how the past informs people's present choices and shapes the choices they make about the future is his play, *A Dybbuk; or Between Two Worlds,*an adaptation of S. Ansky's 1920 Yiddish play. *A Dybbuk* concerns the marriage of a young woman, Leah, the daughter of a wealthy man who has broken off negotiations with three prospective husbands because he is displeased with the financial terms of the engagements. A poor Yeshiva student loves Leah, and she secretly returns his passion. When the father announces that he has finally settled on an appropriate husband for Leah, the student, Khonen, turns to dark spiritual forces to prevent the marriage. Khonen returns as a dybbuk, a spirit that takes possession of Leah's body. When the father turns to a Hasidic rabbi for assistance, he finds himself under judgment. It seems that long ago, the father promised Leah to Khonen, but greed for a wealthy match had blinded him to Leah's fate. In the end, he pays for his transgression by donating half his wealth to the poor. Commenting on the play in *Variety,* Charles Isherwood suggested that the play's central truth "is the idea that even the smallest, most unintended immoral act can have profound social and even metaphysical consequences."

Writing in *New York* magazine, John Simon observed, "In *A Dybbuk* . . . Kushner's adaptation of S. Ansky's old chestnut, the work comes funnily, furiously, crochetily alive, as it links the two worlds of the living and the dead, the musty past and the lively present." Isherwood further commented, "The strange flavor of the play defies easy description," but overall he commended the closing speech and the ways in which the play finds connections with the evil of the Holocaust. Ben Brantley of the *New York Times*noted that there are "lovely touches" throughout the production, "not least the hauntingly atmospheric music of the Klezmatics." Brantley lamented the play's "analytical detachment," but found that "Kushner and Neugroschel have imbued much of their adaptation's language with an exquisite sense of poetry."

Homebody/Kabul, Kushner's play about Afghanistan, opens with an hour-long monologue by a British housewife on the meaning of life, the universe, and everything in it, and the remaining two hours and forty minutes are taken up with a murder committed in Kabul. The first hour, in which the woman reveals her empty marriage and encounter with an Afghan shopkeeper, has been performed by itself. James Reston, Jr. wrote in *American Theatre*that "the Homebody's confrontation with the terrible emptiness of her life leads to her disappearance. The playwright has her act on her romance, even if it means going to an unimaginably awful place, where she can take on the burqua, submit to a husband as his second or third wife, devote herself, unthinking like a teenager in a madrassa, to committing the entire Koran to memory. She acts on romance, and she sticks to it. She has rejected the values of her home, of her life, of her society, of the West. In the act is the whiff of metaphysical treason."

Toby Young reviewed the play in the *Spectator,* saying that the central focus "is the clash between the militant fundamentalism of the East and the moribund humanism of the West, yet it also touches on other, equally big subjects, such as the limits of scientific knowledge and the roles played by language and history in exacerbating international conflicts."

Robert Brustein noted in the *New Republic* that the play opened in December, 2000, prior to the attack on the World Trade Towers on September 11, 2001, after which Brustein felt it "was crying out for revision." Brustein felt that although the play is set in 1998, "it is now impossible to imagine these Western characters circulating among the Taliban without thinking of abductions, corpses, bomb craters, detention camps, and the recent terrorist attacks." He continued, "On second thought, instead of trying to update his play, Kushner might better have employed his energies trying to find some unity for it, or at least settling on what it was supposed to be about in the first place. I say this with profound respect for Kushner's talents. He is one of the very few dramatists now writing whose works are contributions to literature as well as to theater."

BIOGRAPHICAL AND CRITICAL SOURCES:

BOOKS

American Writers, Supplement IX, Scribner (New York, NY), 2001, pp. 131-149.

Completely Queer: The Gay and Lesbian Encyclopedia, Holt (New York, NY), 1998.

Contemporary Dramatists, St. James Press (Detroit, MI), 1999.

Contemporary Literary Criticism, Volume 81, Thomson Gale (Detroit, MI), 1994.

Dictionary of Literary Biography, Volume 228: *Twentieth-Century American Dramatists,* Thomson Gale (Detroit, MI), pp. 144-160.

Drama Criticism, Volume 10, Thomson Gale (Detroit, MI), pp. 212-283.

Drama for Students, Volume 5, Thomson Gale (Detroit, MI), 1999, pp. 1-33.

Geis, Deborah R., and Steven F. Kruger, *Approaching the Millennium: Essays on "Angels in America,"* University of Michigan Press (Ann Arbor, MI), 1997.

Savran, David, *Speaking on Stage: Interviews with Contemporary American Playwrights,* University of Alabama Press (Tuscaloosa, AL), 1996.

Vorlicky, Robert, editor, *Tony Kushner in Conversation,* University of Michigan Press (Ann Arbor, MI), 1997.

PERIODICALS

Advocate, November 17, 1992; December 14, 1993; December 28, 1993; February 5, 2002, Don Shewey, review of *Homebody/Kabul,* p. 49.

America, May 29, 1993; March 5, 1994, p. 12.

American Theatre, April, 1999, "Tony Kushner in Conversation," p. 45; September, 2000, Irene Oppenheim, "Shedding More Light on *Bright Room,*" p. 75; March, 2002, James Reston, Jr., review of *Homebody/Kabul,* p. 28.

Back Stage, January 28, 1994, Irene Backalenick, review of *The Illusion,* p. 60; January 11, 2002, David A. Rosenberg, review of *Homebody/Kabul,* p. 43.

Back Stage West, September 21, 2001, John Angell Grant, review of *The Illusion,* p. 24.

Booklist, September 1, 1993; April 15, 1994; January, 1, 1995, review of *A Bright Room Called Day,* p. 795; April 1, 1995, p. 1372; July, 1998, Ray Olson, review of *A Dybbuk* pp. 1851-1874.

Chicago, September, 1994, p. 37.

Chicago Tribune, May 5, 1993.

Choice, September, 1994, review of *Angels in America,* p. 198.

Chronicle of Higher Education, September 14, 1994, review of *Millennium Approaches,* p. A63.

Commentary, January, 1995, p. 51.

Commonweal, February 22, 1991, p. 132; July 16, 1993.

Daily Variety, August 27, 2002, Robert L. Daniels, review of *The Illusion,* p. 12.

Detroit News, June 1, 1993, p. 3D.

Economist, February 22, 1992; December 4, 1993.

Entertainment Weekly, November 26, 1993.

Europe Intelligence Wire, October 14, 2002, review of *Angels in America.*

Interview, February, 1994.

Lambda Book Report, May, 1994, review of *Angels in America,* p. 24; January, 1995, review of *A Bright Room Called Day,* p. 47.

Library Journal, July, 1994, review of *Angels in America,* p. 94; January, 1998, "Tony Kushner in Conversation," p. 101; September 15, 1999, review of *Refugees in an Age of Genocide,* p. 99.

London Review of Books, August 18, 1994, review of *The Jewish Heritage in British History,* p. 23.

Los Angeles Times Book Review, April 24, 1994, review of *Angels in America,* p. 12.

Los Angeles Times, May 13, 1990, pp. 45-46, 48; May 6, 1993, pp. F1, F7; December 24, 1995, review of *Slavs! Thinking about the Longstanding Problems of Virtue and Happiness,* p. 11.

Mother Jones, July-August, 1995, p. 59.

Nation, March 18, 1991; February 22, 1993; July 4, 1994; February 6, 1995, p. 177.

National Review, June 7, 1993; January 24, 1994, p. 71.

New Leader, June 14, 1993; December 13, 1993.

New Republic, May 24, 1993; June 14, 1993; December 27, 1993, p. 25; January 30, 1995, p. 30; March 18, 2002, Robert Brustein, review of *Homebody/Kabul,* p. 27.

Newsweek, May 10, 1993; May 17, 1993; December 6, 1993, p. 83; June 27, 1994, p. 46; December 17, 2001, Marc Peyser, review of *Homebody/Kabul,* p. 68.

New York, January 21, 1991; April 12, 1993; May 17, 1993; December 6, 1993, p. 130; April 4, 1994, p. 74; January 31, 1994, p. 69; December 1, 1997, p. 110.

New Yorker, November 23, 1992, pp. 126-130; May 31, 1993; June 21, 1993; December 13, 1993, p. 129; January 9, 1995, p. 85.

New York Times, January 18, 1990; January 8, 1991, p. C11, C14; March 5, 1992, C1, C21; September 13, 1992; April 14, 1993, p. B6; May 5, 1993; June 7, 1993; November 21, 1993; December 4, 1994; November 17, 1997, p. B2, B5; November 23, 1997, p. AR20; March 1, 1998.

New York Times Magazine, April 25, 1993, pp. 29-30, 48, 56.

Publishers Weekly, June 26, 1995, review of *Slavs!,* p. 105.

Spectator, June 1, 2002, Toby Young, review of *Homebody/Kabul,* p. 48.

Time, November 23, 1992; May 17, 1993; December 6, 1993.

Translation Review Supplement, December, 1999, review of *A Dybbuk,* p. 35.

Vanity Fair, March, 1993.

Variety, January 17, 1990; January 14, 1991; July 29, 1991; August 12, 1991; November 16, 1992; May 10, 1993; December 6, 1993; January 24, 1994; May 9, 1994; August 8, 1994; October 17, 1994; October 31, 1994; December 19, 1994, p. 86; February 27, 1995, p. 83; March 6, 1995, p. 71; November 18, 1997; September 2, 2002, Robert L. Daniels, review of *The Illusion,* p. 33.

Village Voice December 7, 1993; April 18, 1995.

Vogue, November, 1992.

Wall Street Journal, November 26, 1997, p. A12.

Washington Post, November 7, 1992, pp. G1, G4; May 5, 1993, B1, B10.

World Literature Today, winter, 1995, review of *Angels in America,* p. 144; summer, 1996, review of *Slavs!,* p. 695.

ONLINE

Metro Active Stage, http://www.metroactive.com/ (February 11, 2003), "Earth Angel: Tony Kushner Speaks on Art and Politics."

Playbill Web site, http://www.playbill.com/ (October 23, 2003), "Kushner's *Angels in America* Film Debuts in Two Parts on HBO, December 7 and 14."

Salon.com, http://www.salon.com/ (September, 1997), Christopher Hawthorne, review of *Slavs!.*

Steven Barclay Agency Web site, http://www.barclayagency.com/ (February 11, 2003), "Tony Kushner."

L

L'AMOUR, Louis 1908-1988
(Tex Burns, a house pseudonym, Jim Mayo)

PERSONAL: Born March 28, 1908, in Jamestown, ND; died June 10, 1988, of lung cancer in Los Angeles, CA; son of Louis Charles (a veterinarian and farm-machinery salesman) and Emily (Dearborn) LaMoore; married Katherine Elizabeth Adams, February 19, 1956; children: Beau Dearborn, Angelique Gabrielle. *Education:* Self-educated.

CAREER: Author and lecturer. Held numerous jobs, including positions as longshoreman, lumberjack, miner, elephant handler, hay shocker, boxer, flume builder, and fruit picker. Lecturer at many universities including University of Oklahoma, Baylor University, University of Southern California, and University of Redlands. *Military service:* U.S. Army, 1942-46; became first lieutenant.

MEMBER: Writers Guild of America (West), Western Writers of America, Academy of Motion Picture Arts and Sciences, American Siam Society, California Writers Guild, California Academy of Sciences.

AWARDS, HONORS: Western Writers of America Award-Novel, 1969, for *Down the Long Hills;* LL.D., Jamestown College, 1972; Theodore Roosevelt Rough Rider Award, North Dakota, 1972; National Book Award, 1980, for *Bendigo Shafter;* Buffalo Bill Award, 1981; LL.D., University of LaVerne and North Dakota State University, both in 1981; Distinguished Newsboy Award, 1981; National Genealogical Society Award, 1981; Congressional Gold Medal, 1983; Presidential Medal of Freedom, 1984; LL.D., Pepperdine University, 1984.

WRITINGS:

NOVELS

Westward the Tide, World's Work (Surrey, England), 1950, reprinted, Bantam (New York, NY), 1984.

Hondo (expanded version of his story, "The Gift of Cochise"; also see below), Gold Medal (Greenwich, CT), 1953, reprinted with introduction by Michael T. Marsden, Gregg (Boston, MA), 1978, original reprinted, Bantam (New York, NY), 1985.

Crossfire Trail (also see below), Ace Books (New York, NY), 1954, reprinted with introduction by Kieth Jarrod, Gregg (Boston, MA), 1980, original reprinted, Bantam (New York, NY), 1985.

Kilkenny (also see below), Ace Books (New York, NY), 1954, reprinted with introduction by Wesley Laing, Gregg (Boston, MA), 1980, original reprinted, Bantam (New York, NY), 1984.

Heller with a Gun (also see below), Gold Medal (Greenwich, CT), 1954, reprinted, Bantam (New York, NY), 1985.

To Tame a Land, Fawcett (Boston, MA), 1955, reprinted, Bantam (New York, NY), 1985.

Guns of the Timberlands, Jason (New York, NY), 1955, reprinted, Bantam (New York, NY), 1985.

The Burning Hills, Jason (New York, NY), 1956, reprinted, Bantam (New York, NY), 1985.

Silver Canyon (expanded version of his story, "Riders of the Dawn"), Avalon (New York, NY), 1956, reprinted, Bantam (New York, NY), 1981.

Last Stand at Papago Wells (also see below), Gold Medal (Greenwich, CT), 1957, reprinted, Bantam (New York, NY), 1986.

The Tall Stranger (also see below), Fawcett (Boston, MA), 1957, reprinted, Bantam (New York, NY), 1986.

Sitka, Appleton (New York, NY), 1957, reprinted, Bantam (New York, NY), 1986.

Radigan, Bantam (New York, NY), 1958, reprinted, 1986.

The First Fast Draw (also see below), Bantam (New York, NY), 1959, reprinted, G.K. Hall (Boston, MA), 1989.

Taggart, Bantam (New York, NY), 1959, reprinted, Bantam (New York, NY), 1982.

Flint, Bantam (New York, NY), 1960, reprinted, 1985.

Shalako, Bantam (New York, NY), 1962, reprinted, 1985.

Killoe (also see below), Bantam (New York, NY), 1962, reprinted, 1986.

High Lonesome, Bantam (New York, NY), 1962, reprinted, 1982.

How the West Was Won (based on the screenplay by James R. Webb), Bantam (New York, NY), 1963, reprinted, Thorndike (Waterville, ME), 1988.

Fallon, Bantam (New York, NY), 1963, reprinted, 1982.

Catlow, Bantam (New York, NY), 1963, reprinted, 1984.

Dark Canyon, Bantam (New York, NY), 1963, reprinted, 1985.

Hanging Woman Creek, Bantam (New York, NY), 1964, reprinted, 1984.

Kiowa Trail (also see below), Bantam (New York, NY), 1965.

The High Graders, Bantam (New York, NY), 1965, reprinted, 1989.

The Key-Lock Man (also see below), Bantam (New York, NY), 1965, reprinted, 1986.

Kid Rodelo, Bantam (New York, NY), 1966, reprinted, 1986.

Kilrone, Bantam (New York, NY), 1966, reprinted, 1981.

The Broken Gun, Bantam (New York, NY), 1966, reprinted, 1984.

Matagorda, Bantam (New York, NY), 1967, reprinted, 1985.

Down the Long Hills, Bantam (New York, NY), 1968, reprinted, 1984.

Chancy, Bantam (New York, NY), 1968, reprinted, 1984.

Conagher, Bantam (New York, NY), 1969, reprinted, 1982.

The Empty Land, Bantam (New York, NY), 1969, reprinted, 1985.

The Man Called Noon, Bantam (New York, NY), 1970, reprinted, 1985.

Reilly's Luck, Bantam (New York, NY), 1970, reprinted, 1985.

Brionne, Bantam (New York, NY), 1971, reprinted, 1989.

Under the Sweetwater Rim, Bantam (New York, NY), 1971.

Tucker, Bantam (New York, NY), 1971.

Callaghen, Bantam (New York, NY), 1972.

The Quick and the Dead, Bantam (New York, NY), 1973, revised edition, 1979.

The Man from Skibbereen, G.K. Hall (Boston, MA), 1973.

The Californios, Saturday Review Press (New York, NY), 1974.

The Rider of Lost Creek (based on one of his short stories), Bantam (New York, NY), 1976.

Where the Long Grass Blows, Bantam (New York, NY), 1976.

The Mountain Valley War (based on one of his short stories), Bantam (New York, NY), 1978.

Bendigo Shafter, Dutton (New York, NY), 1978.

The Iron Marshall, Bantam (New York, NY), 1979.

The Proving Trail, Bantam (New York, NY), 1979.

Lonely on the Mountain, Bantam (New York, NY), 1980.

Comstock Lode, Bantam (New York, NY), 1981.

The Cherokee Trail, Bantam (New York, NY), 1982.

The Shadow Riders, Bantam (New York, NY), 1982.

The Lonesome Gods, Bantam (New York, NY), 1983.

Son of a Wanted Man, Bantam (New York, NY), 1984.

The Walking Drum, Bantam (New York, NY), 1984.

Passin' Through, Bantam (New York, NY), 1985.

Last of the Breed, Bantam (New York, NY), 1986.

West of the Pilot Range, Bantam (New York, NY), 1986.

A Trail to the West, Bantam (New York, NY), 1986.

The Haunted Mesa, Bantam (New York, NY), 1987.

"SACKETT FAMILY" SERIES; NOVELS

The Daybreakers, Bantam (New York, NY), 1960, reprinted, 1984.

Sackett, Bantam (New York, NY), 1961, reprinted, 1984.

Lando, Bantam (New York, NY), 1962, reprinted, 1985.

Mojave Crossing, Bantam (New York, NY), 1964, reprinted, 1985.

The Sackett Brand, Bantam (New York, NY), 1965, reprinted, 1985.

Mustang Man, Bantam (New York, NY), 1966, reprinted, 1986.

The Sky-Liners, Bantam (New York, NY), 1967, reprinted, Thorndike (Waterville, ME), 1986.

The Lonely Men, Bantam (New York, NY), 1969, reprinted, Bantam (New York, NY), 1984.

Galloway, Bantam (New York, NY), 1970.

Ride the Dark Trail, Bantam (New York, NY), 1972, reprinted, 1986.

Treasure Mountain, Bantam (New York, NY), 1972.

Sackett's Land, Saturday Review Press (New York, NY), 1974.

To the Far Blue Mountains, Dutton (New York, NY), 1976.

Sackett's Gold, Bantam (New York, NY), 1977.

The Warrior's Path, Bantam (New York, NY), 1980.

Ride the River, Bantam (New York, NY), 1983.

Jubal Sackett, Bantam (New York, NY), 1985.

"THE CHANTRYS" SERIES; NOVELS

North to the Rails, Bantam (New York, NY), 1971.

The Ferguson Rifle, Bantam (New York, NY), 1973.

Over on the Dry Side, Saturday Review Press (New York, NY), 1975.

Borden Chantry, Bantam (New York, NY), 1977.

Fair Blows the Wind, Bantam (New York, NY), 1978.

"THE TALONS" SERIES; NOVELS

Rivers West, Saturday Review Press (New York, NY), 1974, reprinted, Dutton (New York, NY), 1989.

The Man from the Broken Hills, Bantam (New York, NY), 1975.

Milo Talon, Bantam (New York, NY), 1981.

PUBLISHED UNDER HOUSE PSEUDONYM TEX BURNS: "HOPALONG CASSIDY" SERIES; NOVELS

Hopalong Cassidy and the Riders of High Rock, Doubleday (Garden City, NY), 1951, Aeonian (Leyden, MA), 1974.

Hopalong Cassidy and the Rustlers of West Fork, Doubleday (Garden City, NY), 1951, reprinted, Aeonian (Leyden, MA), 1976.

Hopalong Cassidy and the Trail to Seven Pines, Doubleday (Garden City, NY), 1951, reprinted, Aeonian (Leyden, MA), 1976.

Hopalong Cassidy: Trouble Shooter, Doubleday (Garden City, NY), 1952, Aeonian (Leyden, MA), 1976.

ORIGINALLY PUBLISHED UNDER PSEUDONYM JIM MAYO; REPRINTED UNDER AUTHOR'S REAL NAME; NOVELS

Showdown at Yellow Butte (also see below), Ace Books (New York, NY), 1954, reprinted with introduction by Scott R. McMillan, Gregg (Boston, MA), 1980, original reprinted, Bantam (New York, NY), 1983.

Utah Blaine (also see below), Ace Books (New York, NY), 1954, reprinted with introduction by Wayne C. Lee, Gregg (Boston, MA), 1980, original reprinted, Bantam (New York, NY), 1984.

OMNIBUS VOLUMES

Kiowa Trail [and] *Killoe,* Ulverscroft (Leicester, England), 1979.

The First Fast Draw [and] *The Key-Lock Man,* Ulverscroft (Leicester, England), 1979.

Four Complete Novels (includes *The Tall Stranger, Kilkenny, Hondo,* and *Showdown at Yellow Butte*), Avenal Books (New York, NY), 1980.

Five Complete Novels (includes *Crossfire Trail, Utah Blaine, Heller with a Gun, Last Stand at Papago Wells,* and *To Tame a Land*), Avenal Books (New York, NY), 1981.

L'Amour Westerns (four volumes), Gregg (Boston, MA), 1981.

SHORT STORIES

War Party, Bantam (New York, NY), 1975.

Yondering, Bantam (New York, NY), 1980.

The Strong Shall Live, Bantam (New York, NY), 1980.

Buckskin Run, Bantam (New York, NY), 1981.

Law of the Desert Born, Bantam (New York, NY), 1983.

Bowdrie, Bantam (New York, NY), 1983.

The Hills of Homicide, Bantam (New York, NY), 1984.

Bowdrie's Law, Bantam (New York, NY), 1984.

Riding for the Brand, Bantam (New York, NY), 1986.

Dutchman's Flat, Bantam (New York, NY), 1986.

The Trail to Crazy Man, Bantam (New York, NY), 1986.

The Rider of the Ruby Hills, Bantam (New York, NY), 1986.

Night over the Solomons, Bantam (New York, NY), 1986.

West from Singapore, Bantam (New York, NY), 1987.

Lonigan, Bantam (New York, NY), 1988.

Long Ride Home, Bantam (New York, NY), 1989.

The Outlaws of Mesquite, Bantam (New York, NY), 1991.

Valley of the Sun: Frontier Stories, Bantam (New York City), 1995.

West of Dodge: Frontier Stories, Bantam (New York City), 1996.

End of the Drive, Bantam (New York, NY), 1997.

Monumental Rock, Bantam (New York, NY), 1998.

Beyond the Great Snow Mountain, Bantam (New York, NY), 1999.

Off the Mangrove Coast, Bantam (New York, NY), 2000.

May There Be a Road, Bantam (New York, NY), 2001.

With These Hands, Bantam (New York, NY), 2002.

From These Listening Hills, Bantam (New York, NY), 2003.

The Collected Short Stories of Louis L'Amour: The Frontier Stories, Volume 1, Bantam (New York, NY), 2003.

SCREENPLAYS

(With Frank J. Gill, Jr., and Jack Natteford) *East of Sumatra,* 1953.

(With George Van Marter and Franklin Coen) *Four Guns to the Border,* 1954.

(With Tom Hubbard and Fred Eggers) *Treasure of the Ruby Hills,* 1955.

(With Herb Meadow and Don Martin) *Stranger on Horseback,* 1955.

(With Jack Natteford) *Kid Rodelo,* 1966.

OTHER

Smoke from this Altar (poetry), Lusk (Oklahoma City, OK), 1939.

Frontier (essays), photographs by David Muench, Bantam (New York, NY), 1984.

The Sackett Companion: A Personal Guide to the Sackett Novels (nonfiction), Bantam (New York, NY), 1988.

A Trail of Memories: The Quotations of Louis L'Amour (excerpts from L'Amour's fiction), compiled by daughter, Angelique L'Amour, Bantam (New York, NY), 1988.

The Education of a Wandering Man (autobiography), Bantam (New York, NY), 1989.

Off the Mangrove Coast, Bantam (New York, NY), 2001.

Also author of *Man Riding West,* Carroll & Graf.

Also author of filmscripts and more than sixty-five television scripts. Contributor of more than four hundred short stories and articles to more than eighty magazines in the United States and abroad, including *Argosy, Collier's,* and *Saturday Evening Post.*

ADAPTATIONS: More than forty-five of L'Amour's novels and short stories have been adapted into feature films and television movies, including *Hondo,* Warner Bros., 1953, *East of Sumatra,* Universal, 1953, *Four Guns to the Border,* Universal, 1954, *Treasure of the Ruby Hills,* Allied Artists, 1955, *Kilkenny,* Columbia, 1956, *The Burning Hills,* Warner Bros., 1956, *Utah Blaine,* Columbia, 1956, *Walk Tall,* Allied Artists, 1957, *Last Stand at Papago Wells,* Columbia, 1958, *Heller with Pink Tights* (based on his *Heller with a Gun*), Paramount, 1960, *Guns of the Timberlands,* Warner Bros., 1960, *Taggart,* Universal, 1964, *Kid Rodelo,* Paramount, 1966, *Shalako,* Cinerama Releasing Corp., 1968, *Catlow,* Metro-Goldwyn-Mayer, 1971, *The Broken Gun,* Warner Bros., 1972, *The Man Called Noon,* Scotia-Barber, 1973, *Down the Long Hills,* Disney Channel, 1986, and *The Quick and the Dead,* Home Box Office, 1987; the "Sackett Family" series was made into a television miniseries, *The Sacketts.* Many of L'Amour's novels and short stories have been adapted for presentation on audio cassettes, including *Riding for the Brand* (adapted from a short story from *Riding for the Brand*), Bantam, 1987, *Bowdrie Passes Through,* (adapted from a short story from *Bowdrie*), Bantam, 1988, *Keep Travelin' Rider* (adapted from a short story from *Dutchman's Flat*), Bantam, 1988, and *One for the Mojave Kid* (adapted from a short story from *Dutchman's Flat*), Bantam, 1988.

SIDELIGHTS: Dubbed the "Paul Bunyan of American letters" by a contributor for *People,* Western writer Louis L'Amour was a "legend of excess." At his death in 1988 he had written ninety novels and twenty short-story collections, in addition to screenplays, essays, and books of poetry. When describing someone like L'Amour it was necessary to use terms as wide and grand as the West about which he wrote. He sold more books than nearly every other contemporary novelist. He wrote more million-copy bestsellers than any other American fiction writer. He was the only novelist in this nation's history to be granted either of the country's highest honors—the Congressional Gold Medal and the Presidential Medal of Freedom—and L'Amour received them both. When he died, nearly two hundred million copies of his books were in print. A contributor for *St. James Encyclopedia of Popular Culture* explained part of the attraction of L'Amour's books: "Decidedly outside the genteel traditions of the Eastern publishing establishment, L'Amour's works are noted for their spare prose, rugged situations, unambiguous morality, and colorful casts of straight-shooting characters who tamed the American frontier West with grit and determination."

L'Amour's achievements, including the prestigious National Book Award in 1980 for *Bendigo Shafter,* were even more remarkable when one considered the obstacles that he overcame to achieve popularity. He had no formal education, spent much of his youth wandering from job to job, and was over forty by the time he published his first novel. Among his first published books were some volumes of poetry and stories about the Far East. "I also wrote some sport stories, some detective stories, and some Western stories. It so happens that the Westerns caught on and there was a big demand for them. I grew up in the West, of course, and loved it, but I never really intended to write Westerns at all," L'Amour told *CA*. After he started publishing his work, his novels were often not even reviewed by critics. As Ned Smith of *American Way* noted, L'Amour suffered the same fate as the majority of Western writers who found themselves "largely greeted with indifference . . . by the critics." James Barron, writing in the *New York Times,* cited L'Amour's comment that explained how he felt about being labeled a writer of "Westerns": "If you write a book about a bygone period that lies east of the Mississippi River, then it's a historical novel. . . . If it's west of the Mississippi, it's a western, a different category. There's no sense to it."

L'Amour ignored criticism or—lack of it—and decided to do what hardly anyone had ever done before, make a living as a Western writer. L'Amour's determination to persevere led to increased critical interest in his work; the literary establishment eventually could no longer continue to disregard such a popular writer. *Newsweek* contributor Charles Leerhsen noted that as L'Amour entered his fourth decade as a novelist "the critics back East [were] finally reviewing his work—and praising his unpretentious, lean-as-a-grass-fed-steer style."

Some critics maintained that L'Amour's style was the key to his appeal. They applauded his ability to write quick-paced action novels filled with accurate descriptions of the Old West—or whatever other locale in which his protagonists found themselves. "Probably the biggest reason for L'Amour's success . . . ," wrote Ben Yagoda in *Esquire,* was "his attention to authenticity and detail. . . . His books are full of geographical and historical information."

Because of what *People* contributor Joseph Pilcher called L'Amour's "painstaking respect for detail," a typical L'Amour novel often seemed to contain as many factual elements as fictional ones. Writing in *Arizona and the West* about L'Amour's novel, *Lando,* Michael T. Marsden noted that in that book alone the writer "instruct[ed] his readers on the historical and cultural importance of Madeira wine, the nature of longhorn cattle,

the Great Hurricane of 1844, and the several cultural functions of a Western saloon, all the while providing them with an entertaining romance." In other L'Amour works readers learned such things as how native Americans made moccasins, how to pan for gold, and the finer points of Elizabethan decor.

Some critics felt that all the factual material in L'Amour's novels detracted from their narrative continuity. They also felt that L'Amour's energies might have been better spent developing his characters or varying his plots rather than on research. *New York Times Book Review* contributor Richard Nalley, for example, wrote: "There is wonderful information [in L'Amour's novel, *The Walking Drum,*] . . . but the author's historical research is presented textbook style, in great, undigested chunks. Although the adventure plot is at times gripping, the uneasy integration of Mathurin [the protagonist] with his surroundings prevents the reader from being entirely swept up in the romance."

In *Western American Literature* John D. Nesbitt observed a similar flaw in L'Amour's *Over on the Dry Side.* According to Nesbitt, in the novel "entertaining narrative effect is lost in favor of flat introduction of historical details and moral speeches." Despite such criticism, L'Amour had an enormous following of readers. In the *Lone Star Review* Steve Berner wrote: "It [was], in fact, pointless to discuss the merits or weaknesses of L'Amour's writings . . . since it [had] little or no effect on either author or his public." According to the *Washington Post*'s Richard Pearson, despite what he called "plots [that] could be predictable" and a technique of narrating that was "wooden," L'Amour was a skilled story teller. L'Amour's agent, C. Stuart Applebaum, observed in a *Detroit News* interview: "For many of his readers, he was the living embodiment of the frontier because of the authenticity of his stories and characters. His readers felt L'Amour walked the land his characters had walked. That was one of the major reasons of his enduring popularity."

L'Amour identified himself as a storyteller in the tradition of Geoffrey Chaucer (fourteenth-century author of *The Canterbury Tales*). Barron cited L'Amour's comment, "I don't travel and tell stories, because that's not the way these days. . . . But I write my books to be read aloud and I think of myself in that oral tradition."

One story that L'Amour seemed not to want to stop telling was the story of the Sackett family, continued in more than a dozen novels. These books explore the lives of the two branches of the Sackett clan and, to a lesser extent, two other frontier families, the Chantrys and the Talons, across three hundred years of history. In a *North Dakota Quarterly* article, Marsden commented that L'Amour's "formal family groupings may well constitute the most ambitious and complex attempt to date to create a Faulknerian series of interrelated characters and events in the popular Western tradition."

The publication of L'Amour's 1984 novel, *The Walking Drum,* caused a stir in literary circles because L'Amour had written a saga of medieval life in Europe instead of a Western. Apparently L'Amour's change of locale did not intimidate his readers, for the book appeared on the *New York Times* hardcover bestseller list five days before its official publication date. In *People* L'Amour explained to Pilcher that he was irritated that most books about the twelfth century dealt only with the Crusades and so, the novelist "decided to tell a swashbuckling adventure story about the period which would also show the history of the times—how people lived and how they worked."

According to *Los Angeles Times* writer Garry Abrams, L'Amour saw the publication of this non-Western novel as "a turning point" in his development as a writer. "From now on, he said, he want[ed] to concentrate less on promotion and more on 'improving my writing. I know how to write and I write fairly well. But you can never learn enough about writing.'" L'Amour concentrated on his writing by branching out in several directions. In 1987, he published *The Haunted Mesa,* which *Washington Post Book World* contributor Tony Hillerman referred to as "part western, part adventure, [and] part fantasy." He wrote *The Sackett Companion: A Personal Guide to the Sackett Novels,* which includes a Sackett family tree as well as background information on the sources behind the novels in the series, and completed his long-planned autobiography, *The Education of a Wandering Man.*

Explaining his approach to fiction writing to Clarence Petersen in the *Chicago Tribune,* L'Amour remarked: "A reader of my books expects to get an entertaining story, and he expects a little bit more. I've got to give him something of the real quality of the West, and I can do that because I'm a storyteller, and I don't have to imagine what happened in the Old West—I know what happened." Descended from pioneers who fought with the Sioux Indians and in the Civil War, L'Amour spent much of his early life traveling the West, working alongside the cattlemen and homesteaders who knew the most about the local history.

L'Amour's informers included one of his employers, a man who had been raised as an Apache Indian, who taught him much about the Indian experience of the American West. The novelist's characters also know much about Indian life, but the claims of their own culture exert a stronger hold. Pearson observed in the *Washington Post,* "Though Mr. L'Amour was often faulted by critics for cardboard, simplistic characters, his western heroes often fought an inner struggle against admiration for the Indian and his way of life on one hand and the need to advance 'civilization' on the other. His were often stories of culture in conflict." The title character of *Bendigo Shafter* describes the conflict felt by many of L'Amour's frontier heroes: "I could have lived the Indian way and loved it. I could feel their spirits move upon the air, hear them in the still forest and the chuckling water of the mountain streams, but other voices were calling me, too, the voices of my own people and their ways. For it was our way to go onward; to go forward and to try to shape our world into something that would make our lives easier, even if more complicated."

L'Amour wrote three novels a year for his publisher for more than thirty years. Even so, by the late 1980s, he had come nowhere near to exhausting the store of research he had gathered as a connoisseur of historical details. At the time of his death in 1988, he had developed outlines for fifty more novels. A year before he died, L'Amour noted: "There's a lot of Western material out there that's very fresh. And the Western novel is not dying, it's doing very well. It's selling every place but in the movies. . . . There seem to be some misconceptions about me and my type of writing, which have been perpetuated by several articles that weren't written too well. . . . Too often people start with a cliched idea of a Western writer. That automatically eliminates an awful lot of things that interest me. There's no difference in the Western novel and any other novel, as I said earlier. A Western starts with a beginning and it goes to an end. It's a story about people, and that's the important thing to always remember. Every story is about people—people against the canvas of their times."

The material was so plentiful, in fact, that more than a dozen new L'Amour short story volumes have been published since his death, several of which reached best-seller status. Reviewing the 2003 anthology, *The Collected Short Stories of Louis L'Amour: The Frontier Stories, Volume 1,* Wes Lukowsky of *Booklist* summed up not only the stories of that collection, but also the entire oeuvre of this American original: "L'Amour wrote about the big themes—love, courage, loyalty, honor—but he grounded them firmly in the context of daily struggles in an unforgiving land." L'Amour was, as the *People* contributor noted, "a magnificent chronicler of the American epic, Homer on the range."

BIOGRAPHICAL AND CRITICAL SOURCES:

BOOKS

Authors in the News, Volume 2, Thomson Gale (Detroit, MI), 1976.
Contemporary Literary Criticism, Volume 25, Thomson Gale (Detroit, MI), 1983.
Contemporary Popular Writers, St. James Press (Detroit, MI), 1997.
Dictionary of Literary Biography Yearbook: 1980, Thomson Gale (Detroit, MI), 1981.
Hall, Halbert W. with Boden Clarke, *The Work of Louis L'Amour: An Annotated Bibliography & Guide,* Borgo Press (San Bernadino, CA), 1995.
L'Amour, Louis, *Bendigo Shafter,* Dutton (New York, NY), 1978.
Pilkington, William T., editor, *Critical Essays on the Western American Novel,* G.K. Hall (Boston, MA), 1980.
St. James Encyclopedia of Popular Culture, St. James Press (Detroit, MI), 2000.

PERIODICALS

American Way, April, 1976.
Arizona and the West, autumn, 1978.
Book, May-June, 2002, Michael Phillips, review of *With These Hands,* p. 78.
Booklist, March 15, 1994, p. 1302; May 1, 1997, Wes Lukowsky, review of *End of the Drive,* p. 1480; June 1, 1998, Wes Lukowsky, review of *Monument Rock,* p. 1725; April 1, 1999, Budd Arthur, review of *Beyond the Great Snow Mountains,* p. 1385; March 15, 2000, Budd Arthur, review of *Off the Mangrove Coast,* p. 1328; May 1, 2001, Wes Lukowsky, review of *May There Be a Road,* p. 1666; April 15, 2002, Wes Lukowsky, review of *With These Hands,* p. 1383; April 1, 2003, Wes Lukowsky, review of *From the Listening Hills,* p. 1378; September 15, 2003, Wes Lukowsky, review of *The Collected Short Stories of Louis L'Amour,* p. 210.
Chicago Tribune, June 5, 1984; June 23, 1985; February 25, 1987.
Chicago Tribune Book World, September 9, 1984.
Detroit News, March 31, 1978; June 30, 1985.

Entertainment Weekly, May 4, 2001, Karen Valby, "Tome Raiders," p. 20.
Esquire, March 13, 1979.
Globe and Mail (Toronto, Canada), May 19, 1984; October 17, 1987.
Kirkus Reviews, February 15, 2002, review of *With These Hands,* p. 211; March 1, 2003, review of *From the Listening Hills,* p. 337; August 1, 2003, review of *The Collected Short Stories of Louis L'Amour,* p. 993.
Library Journal, March 1, 2000, review of *Off the Mangrove Coast,* p. 82; October 1, 2003, Ken St. Andre, review of *The Collected Short Stories of Louis L'Amour,* p. 119.
Lone Star Review, May, 1981.
Los Angeles Times, July 9, 1983; May 30, 1984; August 3, 1986; November 17, 1989.
Los Angeles Times Book Review, March 20, 1983; August 25, 1985; April 3, 1986; August 3, 1986.
Newsweek, November 10, 1975; July 14, 1986.
New Yorker, May 16, 1983.
New York Times, October 21, 1971; September 23, 1983.
New York Times Book Review, November 24, 1974; April 6, 1975; November 30, 1975; January 2, 1977; March 22, 1981; April 24, 1983; July 1, 1984; June 2, 1985; July 6, 1986.
North Dakota Quarterly, summer, 1978.
People, June 9, 1975; July 23, 1984.
Playboy, January, 1994, p. 41.
Publishers Weekly, October 8, 1973; November 27, 1978; November 4, 1978; May 5, 1997, review of *End of the Drive,* p. 198; March 2, 1998, review of *Monument Rock,* p. 57; June 29, 1998, Daisy Maryles, "Monumental Longevity," p. 19; May 8, 1999, review of *Beyond the Great Snow Mountains,* p. 46; March 13, 2000, review of *Off the Mangrove Coast,* p. 61; April 9, 2001, review of *May There Be a Road,* p. 49; April 8, 2002, review of *With These Hands,* p. 206; April 7, 2003, review of *From the Listening Hills,* p. 44.
Southwest Review, winter, 1984.
Time, April 29, 1974; December 1, 1980; August 19, 1985; July 21, 1986; August 4, 1986.
Times Literary Supplement, August 26, 1977.
Us, July 25, 1978.
USA Weekend, May 30-June 1, 1986.
Washington Post, March 20, 1981; June 23, 1983; November 30, 1989.
Washington Post Book World, December 12, 1976; March 1, 1981; April 17, 1983; December 2, 1984; June 16, 1985; July 6, 1986; June 14, 1987.
West Coast Review of Books, November, 1978.
Western American Literature, May, 1978; February, 1982.

ONLINE

Official Louis L'Amour Web site, http://www.louis
lamour.com/ (August 30, 2004).

OBITUARIES:

PERIODICALS

Chicago Tribune, June 19, 1988.
Detroit News, June 13, 1988.
Los Angeles Times, June 13, 1988.
New York Times, June 13, 1988.
People, June 27, 1988, "Louis L'Amour, the Best-
    Selling Bard of the Wild, Wild West, Dies at 80,
    but His 101 Books Will Live On."
Time, June 27, 1988, p. 54.
Times (London), June 14, 1988.
Washington Post, June 13, 1988.

*   *   *

L'ENGLE, Madeleine 1918-
(Madeleine Camp Franklin L'Engle)

PERSONAL: Surname pronounced "Leng-*el*"; born
Madeleine L'Engle Camp, November 29, 1918, in New
York, NY; daughter of Charles Wadsworth (a foreign
correspondent and author) and Madeleine (a pianist;
maiden name, Barnett) Camp; married Hugh Franklin
(an actor), January 26, 1946 (died, September, 1986);
children: Josephine (Mrs. Alan W. Jones), Maria (Mrs.
John Rooney), Bion. *Education:* Smith College, A.B.
(with honors), 1941; attended New School for Social
Research (now New School University), 1941-42; Columbia University, graduate study, 1960-61. *Politics:*
"New England." *Religion:* Anglican.

ADDRESSES: Home—924 West End Ave., New York,
NY 10025; Crosswicks, Goshen, CT 06756. *Agent*—
Robert Lescher, 155 East 71st St., New York, NY
10021.

CAREER: Writer. Active career in theater, 1941-47;
teacher with Committee for Refugee Education during
World War II; St. Hilda's and St. Hugh's School, Morningside Heights, NY, teacher, 1960-66; Cathedral of St.
John the Divine, New York, NY, librarian, 1966—. University of Indiana, Bloomington, IN, member of sum-

mer faculty, 1965-66, 1971; writer-in-residence, Ohio
State University, Columbus, OH, 1970, and University
of Rochester, Rochester, New York, 1972. Lecturer.

MEMBER: Authors Guild (president), Authors League
of America, PEN.

AWARDS, HONORS: And Both Were Young was named
one of the Ten Best Books of the Year, *New York Times,*
1949; Newbery Medal, American Library Association,
1963, Hans Christian Andersen Award runner-up, 1964,
Sequoyah Children's Book Award, Oklahoma State Department of Education, and Lewis Carroll Shelf Award,
all 1965, all for *A Wrinkle in Time; Book World* Spring
Book Festival Honor Book, and *School Library Journal*
Best Books of the Year selection, both 1968, both for
The Young Unicorns; Austrian State Literary Prize,
1969, for *The Moon by Night;* University of Southern
Mississippi Silver Medallion, 1978, for outstanding
contribution to the field of children's literature; American Book Award for paperback fiction, 1980, for *A
Swiftly Tilting Planet;* Smith Medal, 1980; Newbery
Honor Book, 1981, for *A Ring of Endless Light;* Books
for the Teen Age selections, New York Public Library,
1981, for *A Ring of Endless Light,* and 1982, for *Camilla;* Sophie Award, 1984; Regina Medal, Catholic Library Association, 1984; Adolescent Literature Assembly Award for Outstanding Contribution to Adolescent
Literature, National Council of Teachers of English, and
ALAN Award, both 1986; Kerlan Award, 1990; World
Fantasy Award, 1997, for lifetime achievement; Margaret A. Edwards Award, 1998, for lifetime achievement
in young adult literature; numerous honorary degrees.

WRITINGS:

The Small Rain: A Novel, Vanguard (New York, NY),
    1945, published as *Prelude,* 1968, new edition pub-
    lished under original title, Farrar, Straus (New
    York, NY), 1984.
Ilsa, Vanguard (New York, NY), 1946.
And Both Were Young, Lothrop (New York, NY), 1949,
    reprinted, Delacorte (New York, NY), 1983.
Camilla Dickinson, Simon & Schuster (New York,
    NY), 1951, published as *Camilla,* Crowell (New
    York, NY), 1965, reprinted, Delacorte (New York,
    NY), 1981.
A Winter's Love, Lippincott (Philadelphia, PA), 1957,
    reprinted, Ballantine (New York, NY), 1983.
The Arm of the Starfish, Farrar, Straus (New York, NY),
    1965.
The Love Letters, Farrar, Straus (New York, NY), 1966.

Lines Scribbled on an Envelope, and Other Poems, Farrar, Straus (New York, NY), 1969.

Dance in the Desert, illustrated by Symeon Shimin, Farrar, Straus (New York, NY), 1969.

Intergalactic P.S.3, Children's Book Council (New York, NY), 1970.

The Other Side of the Sun, Farrar, Straus (New York, NY), 1971.

Everyday Prayers, illustrated by Lucille Butel, Morehouse (New York, NY), 1974.

Prayers for Sunday, illustrated by Lizzie Napoli, Morehouse (New York, NY), 1974.

Dragons in the Waters (sequel to *The Arm of the Starfish*), Farrar, Straus (New York, NY), 1976.

(Editor, with William B. Green) *Spirit and Light: Essays in Historical Theology,* Seabury Press (New York, NY), 1976.

The Weather of the Heart (poetry), Harold Shaw (Wheaton, IL), 1978.

Ladder of Angels: Scenes from the Bible Illustrated by the Children of the World, Seabury Press (New York, NY), 1979.

Walking on Water: Reflections on Faith and Art (poetry), Harold Shaw (Wheaton, IL), 1980.

The Anti-Muffins, illustrated by Gloria Ortiz, Pilgrim (New York, NY), 1981.

The Sphinx at Dawn: Two Stories, illustrated by Vivian Berger, Harper (New York, NY), 1982.

A Severed Wasp (sequel to *A Small Rain*), Farrar, Straus (New York, NY), 1982.

And It Was Good: Reflections on Beginnings, Harold Shaw (Wheaton, IL), 1983.

A House like a Lotus (sequel to *The Arm of the Starfish*), Farrar, Straus (New York, NY), 1984.

Dare to Be Creative, Library of Congress (Washington, DC), 1984.

(With Avery Brooke) *Trailing Clouds of Glory: Spiritual Values in Children's Books,* Westminster (Louisville, KY), 1985.

A Stone for a Pillow: Journeys with Jacob, Harold Shaw (Wheaton, IL), 1986.

A Cry like a Bell (poetry), Harold Shaw (Wheaton, IL), 1987.

An Acceptable Time, Farrar, Straus (New York, NY), 1989.

Sold into Egypt: Joseph's Journey into Human Being, Harold Shaw (Wheaton, IL), 1989.

The Glorious Impossible, Simon & Schuster (New York, NY), 1990.

Certain Women, Farrar, Straus (New York, NY), 1992.

The Rock That Is Higher: Story as Truth, Harold Shaw (Wheaton, IL), 1993.

Anytime Prayers, Harold Shaw (Wheaton, IL), 1994.

Troubling a Star, Farrar, Straus (New York, NY), 1994.

Glimpses of Grace: Daily Thoughts and Reflections, collected by Carol Chase, Harper (San Francisco, CA), 1996.

A Live Coal in the Sea, Farrar, Straus (New York, NY), 1996.

Penguins and Golden Calves: Icons and Idols, Harold Shaw (Wheaton, IL), 1996, reissued as *Penguins and Golden Calves: Icons and Idols in Antartica and Other Unexpected Places,* Harold Shaw (Wheaton, IL), 2003.

(With Luci Shaw) *Wintersong: Seasonal Readings,* Harold Shaw (Wheaton, IL), 1996.

(With Luci Shaw) *Friends for the Journey: Two Extraordinary Women Celebrate Friendships Made and Sustained through the Seasons of Life,* Vine Books/Servant Publications (Ann Arbor, MI), 1997.

Bright Evening Star: Mystery of the Incarnation, Harold Shaw (Wheaton, IL), 1997.

Mothers and Daughters, Harold Shaw (Wheaton, IL), 1997.

Miracle on 10th Street and Other Christmas Writings, Harold Shaw (Wheaton, IL), 1998.

My Own Small Place: Developing the Writing Life, Harold Shaw (Wheaton, IL), 1998.

Mothers and Sons, Harold Shaw (Wheaton, IL), 1999.

(With Luci Shaw) *A Prayerbook for Spiritual Friends,* Augsburg (Minneapolis, MN), 1999.

The Other Dog, illustrated by Christine Davenier, Sea-Star Books (New York, NY), 2001.

Madeleine L'Engle Herself: Reflections on a Writing Life, collected by Carol Chase, WaterBrook Press (Colorado Springs, CO), 2001.

The Genesis Trilogy (contains *And It Was Good: Reflections on Beginnings, A Stone for a Pillow: Journeys with Jacob,* and *Sold into Egypt: Joseph's Journey into Human Being*), WaterBrook Press (Colorado Springs, CO), 2001.

"AUSTIN FAMILY" SERIES

Meet the Austins, illustrated by Gillian Willett, Vanguard (New York, NY), 1960.

The Moon by Night, Farrar, Straus (New York, NY), 1963.

The Twenty-four Days before Christmas: An Austin Family Story, illustrated by Inga, Farrar, Straus (New York, NY), 1964, illustrated by Joe De Velasco, Harold Shaw (Wheaton, IL), 1984.

The Young Unicorns, Farrar, Straus (New York, NY), 1968.

A Ring of Endless Light, Farrar, Straus (New York, NY), 1980.

Troubling a Star, Farrar, Straus (New York, NY), 1987.

A Full House: An Austin Family Christmas, Harold Shaw (Wheaton, IL), 1999.

"TIME FANTASY" SERIES

A Wrinkle in Time, Farrar, Straus (New York, NY), 1962.

A Wind in the Door, Farrar, Straus (New York, NY), 1973.

A Swiftly Tilting Planet, Farrar, Straus (New York, NY), 1978.

Many Waters, Farrar, Straus (New York, NY), 1986.

An Acceptable Time, Farrar Straus (New York, NY), 1996.

"CROSSWICKS JOURNALS"; AUTOBIOGRAPHY

A Circle of Quiet, Farrar, Straus (New York, NY), 1972.

The Summer of the Great-Grandmother, Farrar, Straus (New York, NY), 1974.

The Irrational Season, Seabury Press (New York, NY), 1977.

Two-Part Invention: The Story of a Marriage, Farrar, Straus (New York, NY), 1988.

PLAYS

Eighteen Washington Square, South: A Comedy in One Act (first produced in Northhampton, MA, 1940), Baker (New York, NY), 1944.

(With Robert Hartung) *How Now Brown Cow,* first produced in New York, NY, 1949.

The Journey with Jonah (one-act; first produced in New York, NY, 1970), illustrated by Leonard Everett Fisher, Farrar, Straus (New York, NY), 1967.

OTHER

Contributor of articles, stories, and poems to periodicals, including *McCall's, Christian Century, Commonweal, Christianity Today,* and *Mademoiselle.* Contributor to *Origins of Story: On Writing for Children,* edited by Barbara Harrison, Simon & Schuster, and *Watch for the Light: Reading for Advent and Christmas,* Plough Publishing, 2001. Author of foreword to *She Said Yes: The Unlikely Martyrdom of Cassie Bernall,* Plough Publishing, 1999.

Collections of L'Engle's manuscripts are housed at Wheaton College, at the Kerlan Collection of the University of Minnesota, and at the De Grummond Collection of the University of Southern Mississippi.

ADAPTATIONS: A Wrinkle in Time was recorded by Newbery Award Records, 1972, adapted as a filmstrip with cassette by Miller-Brody, 1974, and adapted for a four-part mini-series for ABC, 2004; *A Wind in the Door* was recorded and adapted as a filmstrip with cassette by Miller-Brody; *Camilla* was recorded as a cassette by Listening Library; *A Ring of Endless Light* was recorded, adapted as a filmstrip with cassette by Random House, and adapted for television on the Disney Channel, 2002. *And Both Were Young, The Arm of the Starfish, Meet the Austins, The Moon by Night, A Wrinkle in Time,* and *The Young Unicorns* have been adapted into Braille; *The Arm of the Starfish, Camilla, Dragons in the Waters, A Wind in the Door,* and *A Wrinkle in Time* have been adapted into talking books; *The Summer of the Great-Grandmother* is also available on cassette.

SIDELIGHTS: Madeleine L'Engle is a writer who resists easy classification. She has successfully published plays, poems, essays, autobiographies, and novels for both children and adults. She is probably best known for her "Time Fantasy" series of children's books: *A Wrinkle in Time, A Wind in the Door, A Swiftly Tilting Planet, Many Waters,* and *An Acceptable Time.* These novels combine elements of science fiction and fantasy with L'Engle's constant themes of family love and moral responsibility.

As the daughter of a respected journalist and a gifted pianist, L'Engle was surrounded by creative people from birth. She wrote her first stories at the age of five. She was an only child; in her autobiographies she writes of how much she enjoyed her solitude and of the rich fantasy life she created for herself amid her relatively affluent surroundings. As she wrote in *The Summer of the Great-Grandmother:* "[My mother] was almost forty when I was born. . . . Once she and Father had had their long-awaited baby, I became a bone of contention between them. They disagreed completely on how I ought to be brought up. Father wanted a strict English childhood for me, and this is more or less what I got— nanny, governesses, supper on a tray in the nursery, dancing lessons, music lessons, skating lessons, art lessons."

Her father's failing health sent her parents to Switzerland and young Madeleine to a series of boarding schools, where she found herself very unpopular because of her shy, introspective ways. "I learned," L'Engle recounted in *The Summer of the Great-Grandmother,* "to put on protective coloring in order to survive in an atmosphere which was alien; and I learned to concentrate. Because I was never alone . . . I learned to shut out the sound of the school and listen to the story or poem I was writing when I should have been doing schoolwork. The result of this early lesson in concentration is that I can write anywhere."

These unpleasant boarding school memories were the ones L'Engle transformed into her first published novel, written in the first years after her graduation from Smith College. The novel, titled *The Small Rain,* features Katherine Forrester, a boarding-school student who finds solace in her music and becomes increasingly dedicated to her art. *The Small Rain* thus featured "one of L'Engle's predominant themes: that an artist must constantly discipline herself; otherwise her talent will become dissipated and she will never achieve her greatest potential," commented Marygail G. Parker in *Dictionary of Literary Biography.*

After publishing several books in the late 1940s, L'Engle's career as a writer was postponed in favor of raising her own family. During the 1950s she and her husband operated a general store in rural Connecticut. L'Engle still wrote stories in her spare time, but these were invariably rejected by magazines. As she recounted in *A Circle of Quiet:* "During the long drag of years before our youngest child went to school, my love for my family and my need to write were in acute conflict. The problem was really that I put two things first. My husband and children came first. So did my writing." On her fortieth birthday, in 1958, discouraged by several years of rejections, she renounced writing completely, but found that she was unable to stop. She explained, "I had to write. I had no choice in the matter. It was not up to me to say I would stop, because I could not. It didn't matter how small or inadequate [was] my talent. If I never had another book published, and it was very clear to me that this was a real possibility, I still had to go on writing." Soon thereafter, things began to change for the author, and her writing began to sell again.

Selling *A Wrinkle in Time,* however, proved a challenge. The juvenile novel was rejected by twenty-six publishers in two years. Reasons given vary. The book was neither science fiction nor fantasy, impossible to pigeonhole. "Most objections," L'Engle recalled in an interview with *Children's Literature in Education,* "were that it would not be able to find an audience, that it was too difficult for children." Speaking to Michael J. Far-

rell in *National Catholic Reporter,* L'Engle commented that *A Wrinkle in Time* "was written in the terms of a modern world in which children know about brainwashing and the corruption of evil. It's based on Einstein's theory of relativity and Planck's quantum theory. It's good, solid science, but also it's good, solid theology. My rebuttal to the German theologians [who] attack God with their intellect on the assumption that the finite can comprehend the infinite, and I don't think that's possible."

The book was finally accepted by an editor at Farrar, Straus. "He had read my first book, *The Small Rain,* liked it, and asked if I had any other manuscripts," L'Engle recalled for *More Books by More People.* "I gave him *Wrinkle* and told him, 'Here's a book nobody likes.' He read it and two weeks later I signed the contract. The editors told me not to be disappointed if it doesn't do well and that they were publishing it because they loved it." The public loved the book too. *A Wrinkle in Time* won the Newbery Medal in 1963, the Lewis Carroll Shelf Award in 1965, and was a runner-up for the Hans Christian Andersen Award in 1964.

Speaking with Roy Newquist in his *Conversations,* L'Engle recalled winning the Newbery Medal: "The telephone rang. It was long distance, and an impossible connection. I couldn't hear anything. The operator told me to hang up and she'd try again. The long-distance phone ringing unexpectedly always makes me nervous: is something wrong with one of the grandparents? The phone rang again, and still the connection was full of static and roaring, so the operator told me to hang up and she'd try once more. This time I could barely hear a voice: 'This is Ruth Gagliardo, of the Newbery Caldecott committee.' There was a pause, and she asked, 'Can you hear me?' 'Yes, I can hear you.' Then she told me that *Wrinkle* had won the medal. My response was an inarticulate squawk; Ruth told me later that it was a special pleasure to her to have me *that* excited."

In *A Wrinkle in Time,* Meg Murry must use time travel and extrasensory perception to rescue her father, a gifted scientist, from the evil forces that hold him prisoner on another planet. To release him, Meg must learn the power of love. Writing in *A Critical History of Children's Literature,* Ruth Hill Viguers called *A Wrinkle in Time* a "book that combines devices of fairy tales, overtones of fantasy, the philosophy of great lives, the visions of science, and the warmth of a good family story. . . . It is an exuberant book, original, vital, exciting. Funny ideas, fearful images, amazing characters, and beautiful concepts sweep through it. And it is full of truth."

According to L'Engle, writing *A Wrinkle in Time* was a mysterious process. "A writer of fantasy, fairy tale, or myth," she explained in *Horn Book*, "must inevitably discover that he is not writing out of his own knowledge or experience, but out of something both deeper and wider. I think that fantasy must possess the author and simply use him. I know that this is true of *A Wrinkle in Time*. I can't possibly tell you how I came to write it. It was simply a book I had to write. I had no choice. And it was only *after* it was written that I realized what some of it meant."

In his book *A Sense of Story: Essays on Contemporary Writers for Children*, John Rowe Townsend examined the themes in L'Engle's work: "L'Engle's main themes are the clash of good and evil, the difficulty and necessity of deciding which is which and of committing oneself, the search for fulfillment and self-knowledge. These themes are determined by what the author *is*; and she is a practising and active Christian. Many writers' religious beliefs appear immaterial to their work; Miss L'Engle's are crucial." Townsend saw a mystical dimension to *A Wrinkle in Time*. In that book, he wrote, "the clash of good and evil is at a cosmic level. Much of the action is concerned with the rescue by the heroine Meg and her friend Calvin O'Keefe of Meg's father and brother, prisoners of a great brain called IT which controls the lives of a zombie population on a planet called Camazotz. Here evil is obviously the reduction of people to a mindless mass, while good is individuality, art and love. It is the sheer power of love which enables Meg to triumph over IT, for love is the force that she has and IT has not."

L'Engle has gone on to write several more books featuring the characters introduced in *A Wrinkle in Time*, creating the "Time Fantasy" series. In each of these books, she further develops the theme of love as a weapon against darkness. Although the series has been criticized as too convoluted for young readers, and some reviewers have found the Murry family to be a trifle unbelievable and elitist, most critics praise the series for its willingness to take risks. Michele Murray, writing in *New York Times Book Review*, claimed that "L'Engle mixes classical theology, contemporary family life, and futuristic science fiction to make a completely convincing tale." Speaking of *A Wind in the Door*, *School Library Journal* contributor Margaret A. Dorsey asserted: "Complex and rich in mystical religious insights, this is breathtaking entertainment."

L'Engle's ability to entertain is evident in her popularity with readers. *A Wrinkle in Time* has continued to be one of the best-selling children's books of all time, but

it has also gained a reputation as one of the most banned books, accused by some as providing an inaccurate portrayal of the deity. However, reviewing a year 2000 reprint of the ever-popular title, Patrick McCormick, writing in *U.S. Catholic,* felt that "this is a story that mixes mystery, science, and theology while offering a prescription of compassion and uncommon sense."

In 1998 L'Engle received the Margaret A. Edwards Award honoring her lifetime's work. In particular she was cited for the "Austin Family" series. "L'Engle tells stories that uniquely blend scientific principles and the quest for higher meaning," said Edwards Award Committee chair Jeri Baker, quoted on the American Library Association Web site. "Basic to her philosophy of writing is the belief that 'story' helps individuals live courageously and creatively." Asked about the evolution of the science fiction and fantasy genre, L'Engle told *Booklist* contributor Sally Estes, "I think right now it's in a state of transition—just as the whole planet is, as we head toward another millennium. We're just going to be different; things are changing. Computer chips are changing a lot of things. We're getting more and more used to living in an electronic world, and I think fantasy is probably the best way to reflect what that means to our lives."

In 2001 L'Engle published her first picture book, *The Other Dog,* a poodle's account of the arrival of a new "dog" in the family. In this case, the poodle belongs to the L'Engle family, and the new arrival—which is fed on demand, does its business in something called a diaper, and is not forced to go outside for a walk in all sorts of weather—is actually a baby. Our poodle narrator, Touche, however, does not yet realize this. *Booklist*'s Ilene Cooper called the picture book a "delightful offering" and further commented that young readers "who get the joke that Touche misses, will find this very funny." Starr LaTronica, writing in *School Library Journal,* called *The Other Dog* a "whimsical look at sibling rivalry from a canine point of view." A contributor for *Publishers Weekly* dubbed the picture book an "impish, tongue-in-cheek memoir," concluding that any family "with a cosseted dog and a new baby will feel this is written just for them."

In addition to her long career as a children's book writer, L'Engle has published both adult novels and nonfiction. Her nonfiction books explore family relationships as well as religious and metaphysical subjects. *Mothers and Daughters,* produced in collaboration with her adopted daughter, is an "homage to the relationship between mothers and daughters," according to a reviewer for *Publishers Weekly.* A compilation of short prose extracts, prayers, and quotations from her earlier works, *Mothers and Daughters* explores the "ebb and flow" of such relationships, according to the writer from *Publishers Weekly.* In *Bright Evening Star,* L'Engle "offers a set of poetic meditations on the meaning and mystery of the incarnation of God in Jesus," according to a contributor for *Publishers Weekly.* The same writer concluded, "While there is nothing very theologically profound about L'Engle's meditations, her sparkling prose and ability to tell a good story about the nature of faith make the book worthwhile." Indeed, in all of L'Engle's writing, the element of religion and faith is important if not central to the story. In an interview with Dee Dee Risher of the *Other Side,* L'Engle commented, "I didn't have a Damascus-road experience. I just wandered along in the world of literature and allowed myself to see stories more and more as proof [of Christianity]. Some stories we have heard so often we've forgotten what they mean." Speaking with Charlie LeDuff of *New York Times,* L'Engle remarked, "I'm lightly Episcopalian, but I thrive on the mystery. I don't particularly want to understand that mystery."

BIOGRAPHICAL AND CRITICAL SOURCES:

BOOKS

Authors and Artists for Young Adults, Volume 28, Thomson Gale (Detroit, MI), 1999.

Authors in the News, Volume 2, Thomson Gale (Detroit, MI), 1976.

Beacham's Encyclopedia of Popular Fiction, Beacham Publishing (Osprey, FL), Volume 2, 1996, Volume 8, 1996.

Beacham's Guide to Literature for Young Adults, Beacham Publishing (Osprey, FL), Volume 2, 1990, Volume 4, 1990, Volume 5, 1991, Volume 7, 1994.

Characters in Young Adult Literature, Thomson Gale (Detroit, MI), 1997.

Chase, Carole F., *Madeleine L'Engle, Suncatcher: Spiritual Vision of a Storyteller,* LuraMedia (San Diego, CA), 1995.

Children's Literature Review, Thomson Gale (Detroit, MI), Volume 1, 1976, Volume 14, 1988.

Contemporary Literary Criticism, Volume 12, Thomson Gale (Detroit, MI), 1980.

Dictionary of Literary Biography, Volume 52: *American Writers for Children since 1960: Fiction,* Thomson Gale (Detroit, MI), 1986.

Encyclopedia of World Biography Supplement, Volume 18, Thomson Gale (Detroit, MI), 1998.

Hopkins, Lee Bennett, *More Books by More People,* Citation (New York, NY), 1974.

Huck, Charlotte S., *Children's Literature in the Elementary School,* 3rd edition, Holt (New York, NY), 1976.

Karolides, Nicholas J., editor, *Censored Books, II: Critical Viewpoints, 1985-2000,* Scarecrow Press (Lanham, MD), 2002.

L'Engle, Madeleine, *A Circle of Quiet,* Farrar, Straus (New York, NY), 1972.

L'Engle, Madeleine, *The Summer of the Great-Grandmother,* Farrar, Straus (New York, NY), 1974.

Meigs, Cornelia, editor, *A Critical History of Children's Literature,* Macmillan (New York, NY), revised edition, 1969.

Newquist, Roy, *Conversations,* Rand McNally (New York, NY), 1967.

Norton, Donna E., *Through the Eyes of a Child: An Introduction to Children's Literature,* 2nd edition, Merrill Publishing (Indianapolis, IN), 1987.

St. James Guide to Children's Writers, 5th edition, St. James Press (Detroit, MI), 1998.

St. James Guide to Science Fiction Writers, 4th edition, St. James Press (Detroit, MI), 1996.

St. James Guide to Young Adult Writers, 2nd edition, St. James Press (Detroit, MI), 1998.

Shaw, Luci, editor, *The Swiftly Tilting Worlds of Madeleine L'Engle: Essays in Her Honor,* Shaw (Wheaton, IL), 1998.

Townsend, John Rowe, *A Sense of Story: Essays on Contemporary Writers for Children,* Lippincott (Philadelphia, PA), 1971.

Viguers, Ruth Hill, *Margin for Surprise: About Books, Children, and Librarians,* Little, Brown (Boston, MA), 1964.

Wytenbroek, J. R., with Roger C. Schlobin, *Nothing Is Ordinary: The Extraordinary Vision of Madeleine L'Engle,* Borgo Press (San Bernardino, CA), 1995.

PERIODICALS

America, October 2, 1993; March 16, 1996, p. 19.

Booklist, September 1, 1992, p. 4; April 15, 1994, p. 1547; August, 1994, p. 2039; May 1, 1996, p. 1488; May 15, 1996, p. 1604; March 15, 1997, p. 1253; May 15, 1998, pp. 1620-1621; March 1, 2001, Ilene Cooper, review of *The Other Dog,* p. 1287.

Book Report, November-December, 1994, Sister Mary Veronica, "Madeleine L'Engle," pp. 24-28.

Children's Literature in Education, winter, 1975, Ruth Rausen, "An Interview with Madeleine L'Engle;" summer, 1976, pp. 96-102; winter, 1983, pp. 195-203; spring, 1987, pp. 34-44.

Christian Century, April 6, 1977, p. 321; November 20, 1985, p. 1067.

Christianity Today, June 8, 1979.

Christian Science Monitor, May 12, 1980, Brad Owens, "L'Engle: A Voice for 'Love and Commitment,'" p. B8; February 4, 1993, p. 13; December 13, 1994, p. 11.

Horn Book, August, 1963, Madeleine L'Engle, "The Expanding Universe;" December, 1983.

Language Arts, October, 1977, pp. 812-816; February, 1993, "L'Engle Speaks of How Stories Capture Human Truths and Give People the Courage to Live," p. 137.

Library Journal, May 1, 1996, p. 100.

Lion and the Unicorn, fall, 1977, pp. 25-39.

Los Angeles Times, August 7, 1983; September 26, 1985; October 12, 1992, p. E1.

Ms., July-August, 1987.

National Catholic Reporter, June 20, 1986, Michael J. Farrell, "Madeleine L'Engle: In Search of Where Lion and Lamb Abide."

New Yorker, April 12, 2004, Cynthia Zarin, "The Story-teller," p. 60.

New York Times, June 1, 1991, p. 9; March 15, 2001, Charlie LeDuff, "Busier than Ever at 82, and Yes, Still Writing," p. B2.

New York Times Book Review, July 8, 1973, Michele Murray, review of *A Wind in the Door,* p. 8; June 15, 1980, review of *The Young Unicorns,* p. 31; June 29, 1980, review of *The Arm of the Starfish,* p. 35; January 11, 1981, review of *A Ring of Endless Light,* p. 29; November 30, 1986, review of *Many Waters,* p. 40; December 18, 1988, Dan Wakefield, review of *Two-Part Invention: The Story of a Marriage,* p. 35.

Other Side, March-April, 1998, Dee Dee Risher, "Listening to the Story," pp. 36-39; March-April, 1998, pp. 40-42.

PEN Newsletter, September, 1988, p. 18.

People, November 28, 1994, p. 47.

Publishers Weekly, July 13, 1990, p. 55; August 3, 1992, p. 58; July 4, 1994, p. 65; March 25, 1996, p. 60; May 13, 1996, p. 68; February 24, 1997, review of *Mothers and Daughters,* p. 76; September 15, 1997, review of *Bright Evening Star,* p. 70; October 18, 1999, p. 85; February 12, 2001, review of *The Other Dog,* p. 212.

School Library Journal, May, 1973, Margaret A. Dorsey, review of *A Wind in the Door,* p. 81; May, 1990, p. 66; November, 1990, p. 128; March, 1994, p. 183; June, 1995, pp. 60, 71; May, 2001, Starr LaTronica, review of *The Other Dog,* p. 126.

U.S. Catholic, August, 2000, Patrick McCormick, review of *A Wrinkle in Time,* p. 46.

Writer's Digest, April, 1992, Shel Horowitz, "The Story of Truth and Fact," p. 6.

ONLINE

American Library Association Web site, http://www.ala. org/ (April 22, 2004), "Madeleine L'Engle."

Madeleine L'Engle Home Page, http://www.madeleine lengle.com/ (April 22, 2004).

Madeleine L'Engle Workshop Web site, http://www. madeleinelengle.org/ (April 22, 2004).

*   *   *

L'ENGLE, Madeleine Camp Franklin
See L'ENGLE, Madeleine

*   *   *

LA GUMA, Alex 1925-1985
(Justin Alexander La Guma)

PERSONAL: Born February 20, 1925, Cape Town, South Africa; immigrated to London, England, 1966; died October 11, 1985, in Havana, Cuba; son of Jimmy and Wilhelmina (Alexander) La Guma; married Blanche Valerie Herman (an office manager and former midwife), November 13, 1954; children: Eugene, Bartholomew. *Education:* Cape Technical College, student, 1941-42, correspondence student, 1965; London School of Journalism, correspondence student.

CAREER: New Age (weekly newspaper), Cape Town, South Africa, staff journalist, 1955-62; free-lance writer and journalist, 1962-85. Member of African National Congress, 1955-85. Member of editorial board, Afro-Asian Writers Bureau, 1965-85.

MEMBER: Afro-Asian Writers Association (deputy secretary-general, 1973-85).

AWARDS, HONORS: Afro-Asian Lotus Award for literature, 1969.

WRITINGS:

NOVELS

And a Threefold Cord, Seven Seas Publishers (East Berlin, East Germany), 1964.

The Stone Country, Seven Seas Publishers (East Berlin, East Germany), 1967, Heinemann (London, England), 1974.

In the Fog of the Season's End, Heinemann (London, England), 1972, Third Press, 1973.

Time of the Butcherbird, Heinemann (London, England), 1979.

Memories of Home: The Writings of Alex La Guma, Africa World Press (Trenton, NJ), 1991.

(With Can Themba and Bessie Head) *Deep Cuts: Graphic Adaptations of Stories,* Maskew Miller Longman (Cape Town, South Africa), 1993.

OTHER

A Walk in the Night (novelette), Mbari Publications (Ibadan, Nigeria), 1962, expanded as *A Walk in the Night and Other Stories* (includes "The Gladiators," "At the Portagee's," "The Lemon Orchard," "A Matter of Taste," "Tattoo Marks and Nails," and "Blankets"), Northwestern University Press, 1967.

(Editor) *Apartheid: A Collection of Writings on South African Racism by South Africans,* International Publishers, 1971.

A Soviet Journey (travel), Progress Publishers (Moscow, USSR), 1978.

Jimmy La Guma: A Biography, Friends of the South African Library (Cape Town, South Africa), 1997.

Contributor of short stories to anthologies, including *Quartet: New Voices from South Africa* (includes "Nocturne" [originally published as "Etude"], "A Glass of Wine," and "Out of Darkness"), edited by Richard Rive, Crown, 1963, new edition, Heinemann, 1968; *Modern African Stories,* edited by Ellis Ayitey Komey and Ezekiel Mphahlele, Faber, 1964; *African Writing Today,* edited by Mphahlele, Penguin, 1967; *Africa in Prose,* edited by O.R. Dathorne and Willfried Feuser, Penguin, 1969; *Modern African Stories* (includes "Coffee for the Road"), edited by Charles R. Larson, Collins, 1971.

Contributor of short stories to magazines, including *Black Orpheus* and *Africa South.*

SIDELIGHTS: Until his death in 1985, fiction writer Alex La Guma was among South Africa's most noted anti-apartheid activists, combining autobiographical elements with pointed criticism of his country's treatment of native blacks within his novels and short fiction. Imprisoned in the early 1960s for his continued vocal opposition to the South African government's racist poli-

cies, La Guma began a self-imposed exile in London, England in 1966, remaining there until 1979 when he moved to Cuba. Among his novels are *And a Threefold Cord* and the critically acclaimed *In the Fog of the Season's End,* both of which were banned in South Africa during their author's lifetime.

La Guma's active opposition to the South African government's racist policies permeates his fiction as it did his life. Growing up in an impoverished black neighborhood, he was aware of the social and economic inequities that surrounded him through the work of his father, a local politician. A member of the Cape Town district Communist Party until it went underground in 1950, La Guma attended technical college for a year and then worked for a time on the staff of the leftist newspaper *New Age.* He came to the government's notice in 1955, when he helped draw up the Freedom Charter, a declaration of rights; in 1956, he and over 150 others were accused of treason; in 1961 he was arrested for helping to organize a strike and was subsequently imprisoned.

Various acts passed by the South African government kept La Guma either in prison or under twenty-four-hour house arrest for some years, including time in solitary confinement. La Guma spent this time writing; he composed the novel *And a Threefold Cord* while he was under house arrest in the early 1960s. He left South Africa in 1966 and moved to London where he remained until 1979, writing and working as a journalist. At the time of his death, La Guma was serving as the African National Congress representative to Cuba and working on his autobiography and his sixth novel.

Much of La Guma's work treats the situations and problems he encountered in his native Cape Town and which fueled his journalism career. The short novel *A Walk in the Night* "concerns the social, economic, and political purpose of the colored community" in Cape Town, according to *Dictionary of Literary Biography* essayist Cecil A. Abrahams. La Guma tells the story of Michael Adonis, a factory worker who has just lost his job because he talked back to his white supervisor. Frustrated, Michael commits a senseless crime; he kills the decrepit old ex-actor Doughty. Intertwined with Michael's fate are the lives of Raalt, a white constable on duty in the district where the murder is committed, and Willieboy, a malingerer and occasional criminal. The novelette, said Shatto Arthur Gakwandi in his *The Novel and Contemporary Experience in Africa,* avoids "being a sermon of despair [while also evading] advocating sentimental solutions to the problems that it portrays. Without pathos, it creates a powerful impression of that rhythm of violence which characterizes South African life." Gakwandi concluded: "All these characters are victims of a system that denies them the facility of living in harmony with fellow human beings and their frustrations find release in acts of violence against weaker members of their society."

In 1964's *And a Threefold Cord,* La Guma again examines his native Cape Town, particularly the slum that serves as the novel's setting. Winter has begun, bringing with it rain and illness and discomfort to slum residents like the Pauls family, who live in a cardboard shack woefully inadequate in keeping out the rain. Slum life is portrayed in all its squalor, as prostitution, alcoholism, violence, famine, joblessness, and sickness are an accepted part of daily life. La Guma's protagonists can be distinguished by their ability to perceive the inadequacies of their situation; "He distinguishes consistently between those who live parasitically off the slum people, and those whose work [in communities outside the slum] has given them a wider conception and extended standards of comparison," according to *Journal of Commonwealth Literature* contributor David Rabkin. *And a Threefold Cord,* which was completed during one of its author's imprisonments, was published in Berlin and did not achieve the widespread distribution of some of his more recent works.

In *The Stone Country,* which La Guma released in 1967, the author includes perceptions of the South African jail system he had by now become very familiar with. The title refers to the stone-walled world of prison, and the hierarchical social system, racial segregation, and acceptance of brutality toward blacks make the prison a microcosm of South Africa as a whole. Enter new inmate George Adams, who embodies the dignity of the free man, confident in his basic rights. Adams's treatment at the hands of a prison guard named Fatso causes him to slowly realize that, as Abrahams noted, "rights may exist but they are ignored. . . .[in] a world of survival of the fittest." Gradually, Adams is made aware that in prison, as in South Africa, "to exist one must either become a bully or find alternative means of survival that are not any more honorable."

La Guma's 1979 novel *Time of the Butcherbird* would be his last published novel. Written while its author was in self-imposed exile from his native land, the novel's title reflects La Guma's belief that the hour of South Africa's moral transition would soon be at hand. The butcherbird, common in areas where livestock are housed, preys on disease-carrying ticks and is therefore

hailed as a bringer of good luck and renewed health. The history of an Afrikaaner family—a counterpoint to the profiles of impoverished blacks that appear in La Guma's work—is represented through the character of Meulen, a racist landowner participating in a government-sanctioned effort to remove blacks from their homelands and apportion those lands among "deserving" whites. Meulen, then, is the parasite that threatens the country, and through his ultimate—and completely justifiable—death at the hand of a black agitator, the country finds itself rid of yet another destructive element threatening its health. Because of the novel's heavy use of symbolism and history, rather than action and current events, "readers have not shown the same enthusiasm for it" as they have other books by La Guma, according to Abrahams.

In the Fog of the Season's End remains La Guma's most highly praised work of fiction, as well as the one that reflects most on the author's own life. The protagonists, Elias and Beukes, are committed members of the resistance movement and are being hunted by the police for their activism against the oppressive white government. During a raid by the secret police, Elias is captured and eventually tortured to death, while Beukes escapes with a gunshot wound. Containing descriptions of acts of graphic violence done to blacks by whites, the novel also reflects La Guma's belief that the fight against apartheid would not be suppressed by such tactics. The power of La Guma's writing led John Updike, writing for the *New Yorker,* to say of *In the Fog of the Season's End* that it "delivers, through its portrait of a few hunted blacks attempting to subvert the brutal regime of apartheid, a social protest reminiscent, in its closely detailed texture and level indignation, of Dreiser and Zola."

Jimmy La Guma: A Biography is a warm recollection that Alex La Guma wrote of his father in the early 1960s, although it was not published until 1997. A youthful orphan, James La Guma spent most of his life as a political organizer and member of the South African Communist Party. This little book sheds some light on how and why the Soviet Union served as inspiration for much of the political left in repressive South Africa. In his review for the *Journal of African History,* Alf Stadler wrote: "Something of an oddity, this little book provides a lively footnote in the history of South Africa's left." Several of Alex La Guma's books have been translated into Russian and other languages, and portions have been included in numerous anthologies.

BIOGRAPHICAL AND CRITICAL SOURCES:

BOOKS

Abrahams, Cecil A., *Alex La Guma,* Twayne, 1985.

Asein, Samuel O., *Alex La Guma: The Man and His Work,* Heinemann (London, England), 1987.

Contemporary Literary Criticism, Volume 19, Thomson Gale (Detroit, MI), 1981.

Dictionary of Literary Biography, Volume 117: *Twentieth-Century Caribbean and Black African Writers, First Series,* Thomson Gale (Detroit, MI), 1988.

Duerden, Dennis, and Cosmo Pieterse, editors, *African Writers Talking: A Collection of Interviews,* Heinemann (London, England), 1972.

Encyclopedia of World Literature in the Twentieth Century, Volume 3, revised edition, Ungar, 1983.

Gakwandi, Shatto Arthur, *The Novel and Contemporary Experience in Africa,* Africana Publishing, 1977.

Moore, Gerald, *Twelve African Writers,* Indiana University Press, 1980.

Mphahlele, Ezekiel, *African Image,* Praeger, 1962.

Wanjala, C. L., *Standpoints on African Literature,* East African Literature Bureau, Nairobi, Kenya, 1973.

Zell, Hans M., and others, *A New Reader's Guide to African Literature,* 2nd revised and expanded edition, Holmes & Meier, 1983.

PERIODICALS

Black Scholar, July/August, 1986.

Busara, Volume 8, number 1, 1976.

Freedomways, Volume 25, number 3, 1985.

Journal of African History, October 1999, Alf Stadler, review of *Jimmy La Guma: A Biography,* p. 518.

Journal of Commonwealth Literature, June, 1973, pp. 54-61.

Journal of the New African Literature and the Arts, numbers 9-10, 1974, pp. 5-11.

New Statesman, January 29, 1965; November 3, 1972.

New Yorker, January 21, 1974, pp. 84-94.

Phylon, March, 1978, pp. 74-86.

Sechaba (London), February, 1971.

Times (London), November 23, 1985.

Times Literary Supplement, January 21, 1965, p. 52; October 20, 1972.

World Literature Today, winter, 1980.

World Literature Written in English, spring, 1981, pp. 5-16.

*   *   *

LA GUMA, Justin Alexander
See LA GUMA, Alex

LAHIRI, Jhumpa 1967-

PERSONAL: Born 1967, in London, England; daughter of a librarian and a teacher; married Alberto Vourvoulias (a journalist), January 15, 2001; children: Octavio. *Education:* Barnard College, B.A.; Boston University, M.A. (English), M.A. (creative writing), M.A. (comparative literature and the arts), Ph.D. (Renaissance studies).

ADDRESSES: Home—New York, NY. *Agent*—c/o Author Mail, Houghton Mifflin, 222 Berkeley St., Boston, MA 02116-3764.

CAREER: Writer.

AWARDS, HONORS: O. Henry Award, 1999, for "Interpreter of Maladies"; Pulitzer Prize for Fiction, 2000, for *Interpreter of Maladies;* shortlisted for M.F.K. Fisher Distinguished Writing Award, James Beard Foundation, 2001; Transatlantic Review Award, Henfield Foundation; fiction prize, *Louisville Review;* fellow, Fine Arts Work Centre, Provincetown; named one of the twenty best young writers in America by the *New Yorker.*

WRITINGS:

Interpreter of Maladies, Houghton Mifflin (Boston, MA), 1999.

(Author of introduction) Xavier Zimbardo, *India Holy Song* (photography collection), Rizzoli (New York, NY), 2000.

The Namesake, Houghton Mifflin (Boston, MA), 2003.

ADAPTATIONS: "A Temporary Matter," one of the stories from *Interpreter of Maladies,* was adapted for a film directed by Mira Nair.

SIDELIGHTS: London-born writer Jhumpa Lahiri, the daughter of Bengali parents, has spent considerable time with her extended family in Calcutta, India. This locale serves as the setting for three of the nine stories in her debut collection, *Interpreter of Maladies,* which won the Pulitzer Prize for fiction in 2000. The stories in the collection, three of which had already appeared in the *New Yorker,* deal with such themes as marital problems, experiences of Indian immigrants to the United States, and translations of not only language, but experience. *Newsweek* reviewer Laura Shapiro wrote that Lahiri "writes such direct, translucent prose you almost forget you're reading." Caleb Crain wrote in the *New York Times Book Review* that Lahiri's collection "features marriages that have been arranged, rushed into, betrayed, invaded, and exhausted. Her subject is not love's failure, however, but the opportunity that an artful spouse (like an artful writer) can make of failure—the rebirth possible in a relationship when you discover how little of the other person you know. In Lahiri's sympathetic tales, the pang of disappointment turns into a sudden hunger to know more."

The stories in *Interpreter of Maladies* include the title story, which earned an O. Henry Award in 1999, as well as "A Temporary Matter," which was adapted as a film by Indian filmmaker Mira Nair, and "This Blessed House," among others. "This Blessed House" is the story of Indian newlyweds Twinkle and Sanjeev, who are at odds over Twinkle's laid-back habits and her fascination with the Christian knickknacks left by the previous homeowners. They include a Nativity snow globe, a paint-by-number picture of the wise men, and a Virgin Mary lawn ornament. Crain wrote that Lahiri "is not out to convert Hindus here, nor is she indulging in sarcasm at the expense of sincere belief. But not even religion is sacred to her writerly interest in the power of a childlike sympathy, going where it ought not go."

Other stories featured in the collection include "When Mr. Pirzada Came to Dine," the story of ten-year-old Lilia who learns about the politics and hardships of India from a family friend; "Third and Final Continent," which tells of a librarian putting together the basics in his rented room in anticipation of the arrival of his wife; and "Mrs. Sen," the story of a lonely Indian wife trying to make do in the United States. She wears her beautiful saris as she prepares fresh fish which reminds her of her native Calcutta. She is sustained by aerograms from her family, who envy her, and the little boy she cares for, who learns what it's like to be isolated and lonely. In an interview in *Newsweek,* Lahiri told Vibhuti Patel that Mrs. Sen is based on her mother, who babysat in their home. "I saw her one way," she explained, "but imagined that an American child may see her differently, reacting with curiosity, fascination, or fear to the things I took for granted."

Because Lahiri was not born in India, her stories set in India have been criticized by some reviewers as inauthentic and stereotypical. *Time International* reviewer Nisid Hajari wrote that two of the stories set in Calcutta "survive on little more than smoothness. . . . The reader is lulled by Lahiri's rhythmic sentences and, for her Western audiences, no doubt by the Indian setting.

Lahiri hits her stride closer to home—on the uncertain ground of the immigrant." Other reviewers, however, have offered Lahiri nothing but praise. A *Publishers Weekly* reviewer wrote, "Lahiri's touch in these nine tales is delicate, but her observations remain damningly accurate, and her bittersweet stories are unhampered by nostalgia." Hajari, too, offered praise, saying, "The whole is assured and powerful, and it is perhaps not too harsh a criticism to say that readers should look forward to Lahiri's second book." Prema Srinivasan, writing for *Hindu,* called *Interpreter of Maladies* "eminently readable," and noted that its author "talks about universal maladies in detail, with a touch of humour and sometimes with irony which is never misplaced." In a *New York Times Book Review* article, Michiko Kakutani called *Interpreter of Maladies* an "accomplished collection. . . . Ms. Lahiri chronicles her characters' lives with both objectivity and compassion while charting the emotional temperature of their lives with tactile precision. She is a writer of uncommon elegance and poise, and with *Interpreter of Maladies* she has made a precocious debut."

Lahiri's much-praised debut into the world of fiction led to a lot of speculation surrounding the appearance of her second effort, a novel titled *The Namesake. The Namesake* deals with identity, the importance of names, and the effect the immigrant experience has on family ties. Gogol Ganguli finds himself saddled with a pet name, rather than a proper Bengali first name. Since he does not find out the significance of his name and its connection to a major incident in his father's life until he is older, the name seems empty to him. Gogol too feels somehow incomplete, and this feeling adds to his confusion and insecurity as an outsider trapped between two cultures: that of India, his parents' homeland, and that of the United States, his country of birth. While Gogol's parents followed the conventions of an arranged marriage, their son does not hold his family's cultural heritage in that high a regard, and wants more than his parents seem to have. Gogol's inner turmoil is also reflected in his unsuccessful romantic relationships. It is not until Lahiri's dissatisfied young protagonist comes to understand who his parents are that things begin to come together for him.

A contributor to *Time* magazine praised Lahiri's *The Namesake* as "delicate, moving," as did *Women's Review of Books* critic Mendira Sen, who wrote that this "beautifully crafted and elegantly written novel will speak to many." In the *Antioch Review,* Ed Peaco noted that, despite the lack of action on the part of the novel's fictional protagonist, "Lahiri's delicate details and soft rhetorical touch create an absorbing reading experience in which characters become friends in the sense that we can rely on them for wit, insight, and affirmation." Praising the author for her "spare, lyrical prose," *Herizons* contributor Irene D'Souza added that *The Namesake* is a "wondrous, gentle book" whose major strength is that it "demystifies a culture that often finds itself at odds with the majority."

BIOGRAPHICAL AND CRITICAL SOURCES:

PERIODICALS

Antioch Review, summer, 2004, Ed Peaco, review of *The Namesake,* p. 581.

Book, September-October, 2003, pp. 52, 77.

Booklist, June 1, 2003, Donna Seaman, review of *The Namesake,* p. 123; November 15, 2003, Donna Seaman, "Voices of India," p. 574.

Entertainment Weekly, April 28, 2000, p. 100; September 19, 2003, Gregory Kirschling, review of *The Namesake,* p. 40; September 19, 2003, Jennifer Reese, "A Name to Remember," p. 88.

Esquire, October, 2000, Sean Flynn, "Jhumpa Lahiri," p. 172.

Explicator, summer, 2001, Simon Lewis, review of *Interpreter of Maladies,* p. 219; winter, 2004, Jennifer Bess, review of *Interpreter of Maladies,* p. 125.

Herizons, summer, 2001, Irene D'Souza, review of *Interpreter of Maladies,* p. 32; summer, 2004, Irene D'Souza, review of *The Namesake,* p. 36.

Hindu, April 12, 2000, "Pulitzer for Jhumpa Lahiri"; February 5, 2001, "Beyond Bengal and Boston."

Kenyon Review, summer, 2004, David H. Lynn, "Virtue of Ambition," p. 160.

Kirkus Reviews, June 1, 2003, review of *The Namesake,* p. 773.

Library Journal, July, 2003, Starr E. Smith, review of *The Namesake,* p. 123.

Nation, October 23, 2004, David Bromwich, "The Man without Qualities," p. 36.

New Leader, September-October, 2003, Benjamin Austen, "In the Shadow of Gogol," p. 86.

Newsweek, July 19, 1999, Laura Shapiro, "India Calling: The Diaspora's New Star," p. 67; August 25, 2003, Barbara Kantrowitz, review of *The Namesake,* p. 61.

Newsweek International, September 20, 1999, Vibhuti Patel, "Maladies of Belonging."

New York Times, April 11, 2000, Felicity Barringer, "Author's First Book Wins Pulitzer for Fiction"; September 28, 2003, Stephen Metcalf, "Out of the Overcoat," p. 11.

New York Times Book Review, July 11, 1999, p. 11; August 6, 1999.

Publishers Weekly, April 19, 1999, review of *Interpreter of Maladies,* p. 59; July 26, 1999, p. 20; July 7, 2003, Edward Nawotka, interview with Lahiri, p. 49; September 15, 2003, Daisy Maryles, "See Jhumpa Jump," p. 17.

Spectator, January 17, 2004, Lee Langley, "Cola versus Curry," p. 39.

Time International, September 13, 1999, Nisid Hajari, "The Promising Land," p. 49.

Times of India, April 16, 2000, Ratnottama Sengupta, "Mira Nair to Film Jhumpa Lahiri Story."

Town and Country, January, 2004, p. 55.

Washington Post Book World, September 14, 2003, Christopher Tilghman, review of *The Namesake,* p. 10.

Women's Review of Books, March, 2004, Mendira Sen, "Names and Nicknames," p. 9.

World and I, January, 2004, Linda Simon, review of *The Namesake,* p. 230.

ONLINE

Bookbrowse.com, http://www.bookbrowse.com/ (August 3, 2004), "A Conversation with Jhumpa Lahiri."

Houghton Mifflin Web site, http://www.houghtonmifflinbooks.com/ (August 3, 2004).

PBS Web site, http://www.pbs.org/ (August 3, 2004), Elizabeth Farnsworth, interview with Lahiri.

PIF Magazine Online, http://www.pif.com/ (August 3, 2004), Arun Aguiar, interview with Lahiri.

*   *   *

LAMB, Wally 1950-
(Walter Lamb)

PERSONAL: Born October 17, 1950, in Norwich, CT; son of Walter A. (a utility superintendent) and Anna (a homemaker; maiden name, Pedace) Lamb; married Christine Grabarek (a high school teacher), July 1, 1978; children: Jared, Justin, Teddy. *Education:* University of Connecticut, B.A., 1972, M.A., 1977; Vermont College, M.F.A., 1984. *Politics:* "Left of center." *Religion:* "Questioning Catholic." *Hobbies and other interests:* Racquetball, running, rock and roll.

ADDRESSES: Office—P.O. Box 795 Willimantic, CT 06226.

CAREER: Norwich Free Academy, Norwich, CT, English teacher, 1972-88, writing center director, 1988-98; University of Connecticut, Storrs, CT, associate professor of creative writing, 1997-99; writer. Fresh Air Fund, host parent, 1982—; member of the board of directors of the public library in Willimantic, CT, 1988-96.

MEMBER: Poets & Writers, National Education Association, Phi Beta Kappa, Authors Guild, Writers Guild Of America, Connecticut Citizens Action Group.

AWARDS, HONORS: Literature grant, Connecticut Commission on the Arts visiting artist, 1987—; Governor's Arts Award from State of Connecticut, 1998; Teacher of the Year, Norwich Free Academy, 1989; William Peden Prize in fiction, University of Missouri, and Pushcart Prize, both 1990, both for short story "Astronauts"; national winner, Thanks to Teachers Excellence Award, 1990; fellowship from National Endowment for the Arts, 1993; Friends of the Library U.S.A. Reader's Choice Award, 1998; New England Book Award, 1999; Kenneth Johnson Memorial Book Award, 1999; Writers for Writers Award, 2002.

WRITINGS:

(Editor) *Always Begin Where You Are* (poetry textbook), McGraw (New York, NY), 1979.
(As Wally Lamb) *She's Come Undone* (novel), Pocket Books (New York, NY), 1992.
(As Wally Lamb) *I Know This Much Is True* (novel), HarperCollins (New York, NY), 1998.
(Editor) *Couldn't Keep It to Myself: Testimonies from Our Imprisoned Sisters,* Harpercollins (New York, NY), 2003.

Work represented in several anthologies, including *Streetsongs: New Voices in Fiction,* Longstreet Press, 1990; *Pushcart Prize XV: Best of the Small Presses, 1990-91,* edited by Bill Henderson, Pushcart Press (Wainscott, NY), 1990; and *Best of the Missouri Review, 1978-1990,* University of Missouri Press (Columbia, MO), 1991.

ADAPTATIONS: She's Come Undone (screenplay also written by Wally Lamb), Warner Brothers, 2001; *I Know This Much Is True* has been purchased by Twentieth-Century-Fox.

SIDELIGHTS: Connecticut author Wally Lamb is only the second writer to have two novels chosen to the nationally popular Oprah Book Club. His debut novel, *She's Come Undone,* was chosen as a notable work by television talk-show host Oprah Winfrey in 1997, and his follow-up work, *I Know This Much Is True,* earned the same honor in 1998, resulting in two bestsellers for the author. Both books present unsparing portraits of troubled people in troubled families. On the Web site *Teenreads.com,* a reviewer observed of Lamb's characters: "Interesting, temperamental, emotional human beings attach themselves to us like barnacles on the bottom of a ship. Characters that engage us—have us laughing, crying, hoping and praying for them as they stumble through life—trying to make sense of it all." *New York Times Book Review* correspondent Karen Karbo noted that Lamb "clearly aims to be a modern-day Dostoyevsky with a pop sensibility. In his view, it's not just the present that's the pits, that gives you nightmares and ruins your chances for happiness, it's also the ghosts of dysfunctional family members and your nonrelationship with a mocking, sadistic God, whom you still turn to in times of trouble—which is all the time."

She's Come Undone offers a humorous and poignant account of one woman's struggle to overcome a lifetime of unfortunate circumstances. "This is a tragicomic tale of a quirky, loveable, smart-mouthed survivor," wrote Susan Larson in the New Orleans *Times-Picayune.* Larson added that "this big, warm, embracing book is filled with a generous love and understanding of women." The book is narrated by Dolores Price, who reflects on the important events in her life. As Lamb once explained to *CA,* the use of a female narrator was not a conscious choice on his part. "The focal character of my novel . . . came to me initially as a voice inside my head," the author said, "an unnamed, self-deprecating woman joking about her recently failed marriage. As I began to invent a life around the voice, I had no idea that I was starting a novel or that the story would take me eight-and-a-half years to complete."

Dolores's story begins when she is a child. She endures her parents' failing marriage for several unhappy years before a divorce lands her mother in a state mental hospital and sends Dolores to live with her grandmother. The child's time there is also far from happy; she receives little comfort from her distant grandmother and is later raped by a neighbor. By the time she leaves for college, Dolores has become obese and withdrawn. Her fixation on her roommate's boyfriend, Dante Davis, offers little hope of satisfaction, and she eventually attempts to take her own life. Dolores, following in her mother's footsteps, winds up in a mental hospital. But unlike her mother, Dolores uses the experience as a means of reinventing herself. She loses weight, hatches a plan to win Dante's heart, and upon her release, she makes this dream a reality. Further misfortune awaits her after she is married, but Dolores proves herself a durable survivor who is able to carry on.

Though *She's Come Undone* is loaded with potentially grim material, critics have praised Lamb's use of comedy to lighten the story. Hilma Wolitzer, reviewing the novel in the *New York Times Book Review,* found that "its pleasures lie primarily in its lively narrative and biting humor," and the critic also characterized *She's Come Undone* as "an ambitious, often stirring and hilarious book." While Wolitzer did note several "excesses" regarding the inclusion of "topical plot turns" such as AIDS, abortion, and infertility, she found Dolores an engaging character who holds the reader's attention. "Excess is tolerable," Wolitzer wrote, when "characters are . . . endearing to the reader, as Dolores Price is, even in her most self-deprecatory moments."

The publication of *She's Come Undone* came eleven years after Lamb's literary career got off to a memorable start. Lamb once told *CA,* "I began writing fiction on Memorial Day, 1981, the morning our first child was born. After an 'all-nighter' in the delivery room, my wife and baby son were sleeping, and I ran home to grab a quick shower. I don't pretend to understand the chemical or psychological mix of adrenalin, exhaustion, and shower water which produced for me that morning the first fictional voice I ever heard: that of a wiseguy teenager complaining about his summer job as an ice cream vendor. By instinct, I jumped out of the shower, ran naked down the hallway, and scrawled on a piece of paper what the voice had said. About a month later— after I'd become proficient with diaper pins and carseat buckles—the jotted note resurfaced and I began what became my first story, 'Mister Softee,' which was published in *Northeast* magazine three years later."

Though the publication of *She's Come Undone* established Lamb as a professional writer, he continued to teach high school and college classes in Connecticut and was the recipient of teaching awards for his writing workshops. He found that the two pursuits—writing and teaching—often complement one another. "My work as a writer has altered the way I teach," he once explained to *CA.* "During my first years in the classroom, I taught writing by assigning topics and due dates and then evaluating my students' efforts, penning copious marginal comments about what each writer *might* have done to make the work more effective. My students, who rightfully assumed that their papers were, at that point, *faits accompli,* usually skipped the comments and flipped immediately to the grade. As I committed myself increasingly to fiction writing, I began to see that the most meaningful assignments come from the writer herself or himself and that feedback is helpful when the writing is ongoing, not after it's finished. With that in mind—and with the endorsement of the school administration—I designed and implemented the [Norwich Free]Academy's writing center. At the center, students are empowered by their own creative instincts and function both as creators and critics of writing— their own and others'. Teachers are trained to facilitate rather than dictate and are encouraged to write alongside their students and to submit their work to the critical process."

Five years elapsed between the publication of *She's Come Undone* and the citation from Winfrey that catapulted it to bestseller status. In the meantime Lamb published another novel, *I Know This Much Is True,* which was also chosen by Winfrey for her book club, thus assuring its status as a bestseller. The lengthy family saga is primarily narrated by Dominick Birdsey, whose twin brother, Thomas, commits an act of self-mutilation in the throes of paranoid schizophrenia. As Dominick tries to secure humane hospitalization for Thomas, he must also come to terms with the crib death of his baby daughter, the breakup of his marriage, and a family legacy of violence, depression, and damaging secrets. Karbo declared that the 900-page novel "never grapples with anything less than life's biggest questions."

In the *Washington Post Book World,* Mary Kay Zuravleff described *I Know This Much Is True* as "a torrential, encyclopedic saga of a troubled family." Zuravleff further commented: "Lamb's talent is such that he's able to describe Dominick's noble intentions alongside the resentment, embarrassment and fear that thwart those intentions." To quote an *Entertainment Weekly* reviewer, the novel "is about squarely facing your demons— which in Dominick's case means confronting pride, cruelty, selfishness, and guilt—and then changing your life." The reviewer felt that the book transforms one blue-collar New England family "into mythic world archetypes." A *Publishers Weekly* contributor maintained that the multi-generational story "largely succeeds in its ambitious reach." The contributor concluded that Lamb "creates a nuanced picture of a flawed but decent man," as well as "a fully developed and triumphantly resolved exploration of one man's suffering and redemption."

Lamb's interest in the work of other contemporary artists has helped him better understand the themes in his own writing. "Writers whose work I reread and study include Anne Tyler, Andre Dubus, John Edgar Wideman, J.M. Coetze, Junot Diaz, Margaret Atwood, John Updike, Toni Morrison, Harper Lee, Alice Walker, Gabriel Garcia Marquez, Flannery O'Connor, and Joseph Campbell," Lamb once explained. "These writers shake me up—disturb me in honest ways that allow me to hold onto hope. My fiction is equally informed by other media: the evocative lyrics of Laurie Anderson, Bruce Springsteen, and John Prine; the unexpected juxtaposition of artists Pablo Picasso and Rene-Francois-Ghislain Magritte; the edgy comedy of John Leguizamo, Tracey Ullman, and collaborators Lily Tomlin and Jane Wagner. For better or worse, television also fuels my work. I watch TV with a wary eye, acknowledging its influence without ever trusting it. I'm most responsive to artists who juggle three balls in the air: hope, pain, and humor. I aim for just such a juggling act in my own fiction."

The presence of conflicting emotions runs through many facets of Lamb's life, and it has proved a driving force in his writing. "As a father and teacher, I'm both hopeful and afraid," he once told *CA,* "and I think my stories reflect this. My three callings—fathering, teaching, and fiction writing—are Siamese triplets joined at the head and heart, impossible to separate. I write because complacency disturbs me in the face of the world's pain and because sometimes voices other than my own talk inside my head. I recognize these as gifts and follow."

BIOGRAPHICAL AND CRITICAL SOURCES:

BOOKS

Newsmakers 1999, no. 1, Thomson Gale (Detroit, MI), 1999.

PERIODICALS

Christianity Today, December 7, 1998, Susan Wise Bauer, "Oprah's Misery Index," p. 70.
Entertainment Weekly, June 19, 1998, "Brother's Keeper," p. 66.
Kirkus Reviews, May 1, 1998, review of *I Know This Much Is True.*
New York Times Book Review, August 23, 1992; June 14, 1998, Karen Karbo, "A Brother's Keeper," p. 15.
Publishers Weekly, May 4, 1998, review of *I Know This Much Is True,* p. 204.

Time, June 15, 1998, Elizabeth Gleick, "I Know This Much," p. 81.
Times-Picayune (New Orleans, LA), July 28, 1992.
Washington Post Book World, July 5, 1998, Mary Kay Zuravleff, "Brotherly Love and Family Madness," p. 1.
Writer, October, 1998, Lewis Burke Frumkes, "A Conversation with . . . Wally Lamb," p. 15.

ONLINE

Teenreads, http://www.teenreads.com/authors/ (March 6, 2001), "Author Profile: Wally Lamb."

*   *   *

LAMB, Walter
    See LAMB, Wally

*   *   *

LANGE, John
    See CRICHTON, Michael

*   *   *

LAREDO, Betty
    See CODRESCU, Andrei

*   *   *

LAURENCE, Jean Margaret Wemyss
    See LAURENCE, Margaret

*   *   *

LAURENCE, Margaret 1926-1987
    (Jean Margaret Wemyss Laurence)

PERSONAL: Born July 18, 1926, in Neepawa, Manitoba, Canada; died of cancer, January 5 (some sources say January 6), 1987, in Lakefield, Ontario, Canada; buried in Lakefield, Ontario, Canada; daughter of Robert Harrison (a lawyer) and Verna Jean (Simpson) Wemyss; married John Fergus Laurence (a civil engineer), 1947 (divorced, 1969); children: Jocelyn, David. *Education:* University of Manitoba, B.A., 1947.

CAREER: Writer. Worked as a reporter with the *Winnipeg Citizen;* writer-in-residence at University of Toronto, 1969-70, and University of Western Ontario, 1973; Trent University, Peterborough, Ontario, writer-in-residence, 1974, chancellor, 1981-83.

MEMBER: Royal Society of Canada (fellow).

AWARDS, HONORS: First Novel Award, Beta Sigma Phi, 1961; President's Medal, University of Western Ontario, 1961, 1962, and 1964, for best Canadian short stories; Governor General's Literary Award in fiction, 1966, for *A Jest of God,* and 1975; senior fellowships from Canada Council, 1967 and 1971; honorary fellow of United College, University of Winnipeg, 1967; Companion of Order of Canada, 1971; Governor General's Literary Award, Fiction, 1974, for *The Diviners;* Molson Prize, 1975; B'nai B'rith award, 1976; Periodical Distributors award, 1977; City of Toronto award, 1978; writer of the year award from Canadian Booksellers Association, 1981; Banff Centre award, 1983; numerous honorary degrees from institutions including Trent, Carleton, Brandon, Mount Allison, Simon Fraser, Queen's, McMaster, and Dalhousie universities and universities of Winnipeg, Toronto, and Western Ontario.

WRITINGS:

(Editor) *A Tree for Poverty* (Somali poetry and prose), Eagle Press (Nairobi), 1954; reprinted, McMaster University Library Press (Hamilton, Ontario, Canada), 1970.
This Side Jordan (novel), St. Martin's Press (New York, NY), 1960.
The Prophet's Camel Bell, Macmillan (London, England), 1963, published as *New Wind in a Dry Land,* Knopf (New York, NY), 1964.
The Tomorrow-Tamer, and Other Stories (short stories), Knopf (New York, NY), 1964; reprinted, McClelland & Steward (Toronto, Canada), 1993.
The Stone Angel (novel), Knopf (New York, NY), 1964.
A Jest of God (novel), Knopf (New York, NY), 1966, published as *Rachel, Rachel,* Popular Library, 1968, published as *Now I Lay Me Down,* Panther, 1968; reprinted, with afterword by Margaret Atwood, University of Chicago Press (Chicago, IL) 1993.
Long Drums and Cannons: Nigerian Dramatists and Novelists 1952-1966, Macmillan, 1968; edited and with introduction by Nora Foster Stovel, University of Alberta Press (Edmonton, Alberta, Canada), 2003.
The Fire-Dwellers (novel), Knopf (New York, NY), 1969; reprinted, University of Chicago Press (Chicago, IL), 1993.

A Bird in the House (short stories), Knopf (New York, NY), 1970; reprinted, University of Chicago Press (Chicago, IL), 1993.
Jason's Quest (for children), Knopf (New York, NY), 1970.
The Diviners (novel), Knopf (New York, NY), 1974, with afterword by Margaret Atwood, University of Chicago Press (Chicago, IL), 1993.
Heart of a Stranger (essays), McClelland & Stewart (Toronto, Ontario, Canada), 1976, edited and with an introduction by Nora Foster Stovel, University of Alberta Press (Edmonton, Alberta, Canada), 2003.
Six Darn Cows (for children), J. Lorimer (Toronto, Ontario, Canada), 1979.
The Olden Days Coat (for children), McClelland & Stewart (Toronto, Canada), 1979, reprinted, Tundra Books (Plattsburgh, NY), 1998.
The Christmas Birthday Story (for children), Knopf (New York, NY), 1980.
Dance on the Earth: A Memoir, McClelland & Stewart (Toronto, Ontario, Canada), 1989.
Margaret and Al: Margaret Laurence-Al Purdy. A Friendship in Letters, edited by John Lennox, McClelland & Stewart (Toronto, Ontario, Canada), 1993.
A Very Large Soul: Selected Letters from Margaret Laurence to Canadian Writers, edited by Andy Wainwright, Cormorant Books (Ontario, Canada), 1995.
Selected Letters of Margaret Laurence and Adele Wiseman, edited by John Lennox and Ruth Panofsky, University of Toronto Press (Toronto, Ontario, Canada), 1997.
Embryo Words: Margaret Laurence's Early Writings, edited by Nora Foster Stovel, Juvenilia Press (Edmonton, Alberta, Canada), 1997.

Contributor of short stories to *Story, Prism, Queen's Quarterly, Saturday Evening Post,* and *Post Stories: 1962.* Her holographs and notes are housed in the Margaret Laurence Archives at McMaster's University.

ADAPTATIONS: The Jest of God was adapted as the film "Rachel, Rachel," starring Joanne Woodward and directed by Paul Newman, Warner Bros., 1968 Sound recording adaptations include *Jason's Quest* Library Services Branch, (Vancouver, B.C., Canada), 1977, and *New Wind in a Dry Land* by CNIB (Toronto, Canada), 1979. Several works have been adapted as videorecordings, including *To Set the House in Order* Magic Lanterns Communication (Oakville, Ontario, Canada), in 1985 and *The Olden Days Coat,* by Magic Lantern Communications (Oakville, Ontario, Canada), in 1986.

The Stone Angel was adapted as a play by James W. Nichol, Playwrights Canada Press (Toronto, Canada), 1991. *The Diviners* was adapted as a two-and-a-half-hour television special by Credo Group (Winnipeg, Canada) and Columbia Broadcasting System, Inc., 1993.

SIDELIGHTS: Though she was not a prolific writer, Margaret Laurence's fiction made her "more profoundly admired than any other Canadian novelist of her generation," according to Toronto *Globe and Mail* critic William French. Often set in the fictional Canadian small town of Manawaka, her novels and short stories earned praise for their compassion and realism and the skill with which they were told. They also aroused controversy—religious fundamentalists attempted to have one novel, *The Diviners,* banned from schools because it contained explicit descriptions of an abortion and a sexual affair. Laurence frequently explored the predicaments of women in society, and some of her characters were recognized as early feminists. Reviewers judged her work a powerful influence on Canadian writing; in an *Atlantic* review of *The Fire-Dwellers* one writer deemed her "the best fiction writer in the Dominion and one of the best in the hemisphere."

Non-Canadian subjects also appeared in Laurence's works. *The Prophet's Camel Bell* is an account of her experiences while living for two years in the Haud desert of Somaliland (now Somalia) with her husband, sharing the hardships and privations of desert life with their Somali workers. West Africa serves as the setting for the stories in *The Tomorrow-Tamer* and the source of the literature Laurence discussed in *Long Drums and Cannons: Nigerian Novelists and Dramatists 1952-1966.* In addition, Laurence wrote short stories, some of which were published in periodicals such as *Queen's Quarterly* and the *Saturday Evening Post.* She also edited and translated *A Tree for Poverty: Somali Poetry and Prose* and wrote books for children.

In collaboration with her daughter, Laurence completed *Dance on the Earth: A Memoir* shortly before her death. Published posthumously in 1989, the memoir details the important influence of three women in Laurence's life: her mother, who died when Margaret was four; her aunt, who later married Laurence's father and thus became her step-mother; and her mother-in-law, who provided emotional support when Laurence's marriage to husband John ended. The work also contains Laurence's reminiscences about her own motherhood and reveals her passionate dislike of war, nuclear weapons, corrupters of the environment, and racism. However, as several critics noted, the memoir includes little about Laurence's attitude toward her writing, especially the reasons for the diminished output after she completed *The Diviners,* which is probably her most-enduring work. Writing in *Maclean's,* Morton Ritts noted the "preachy, mawkishly poetic and unforthcoming" character of parts of *Dance on the Earth* and remarked that "the rich complexity that typifies Laurence's best fiction is largely missing" from the work. *Canadian Literature* reviewer Colin Nicholson, while admitting that he "was left wanting more," commented that "the cadence of a distinctive voice is heard on page after page, by turns relaxed and chatty, moved and emotional, angry and impassioned, but overall celebratory and grateful, and sometimes very funny." Enid Delgatty Rutland wrote in *Queen's Quarterly,* "Despite the limitations in, and deficiencies of, the *Memoir,* a transparent reading of the work reveals beliefs, attitudes, values, and commitments that are fundamental to an understanding of Laurence, as a woman and an artist."

Several volumes of Laurence's letters have also been published since her death, including *A Very Large Soul: Selected Letters from Margaret Laurence to Canadian Writers* and *Margaret and Al: Margaret Laurence-Al Purdy. A Friendship in Letters.* George Woodcock, writing in *Canadian Literature,* called the latter volume a "remarkable and perhaps great book." After *Long Drums and Canoes* was reprinted in 2003, Wendy Griswold praised the publisher's decision to do so in her review for *Research in African Literatures.* She commented: "While literary critics are thick on the ground, the chance to see one master novelist analyze the craft of other writers is rare. And the fact that this analysis took place over thirty years ago yet continues to reward readers gives Long Drums and Canons historical as well as critical interest. . . . Although Laurence recognized that she was no literary critic and apologized for her lack of theory, in fact her perceptive-yet-straightforward observations offer an unusually lucid introduction to the first generation of Nigerian novelists and dramatists in English." Griswold noted that just as Laurence finished her manuscript in 1967, Nigeria broke apart, and a long and bloody war began with Biafra. Although the book was published in 1968, Laurence herself considered it irrelevant in light of the situation; the book was never released in Canada where, according to Griswold, Laurence's reputation would have won it the attention it deserves. Noting that Laurence's book has stood the test of time, Griswold said: "The only thing she was totally wrong about was the irrelevance of her book."

BIOGRAPHICAL AND CRITICAL SOURCES:

BOOKS

Contemporary Literary Criticism, Thomson Gale (Detroit, MI), Volume 3, 1975, Volume 6, 1976, Volume 13, 1980, Volume 50, 1988, Volume 62, 1990.

Dictionary of Literary Biography, Volume 53: *Canadian Writers since 1960, First Series,* Thomson Gale (Detroit, MI), 1986.

Hind-Smith, Joan, *Three Voices: The Lives of Margaret Laurence, Gabrielle Roy, and Frederick Philip Grove,* Clarke Irwin (Toronto, Ontario, Canada), 1975.

Irvine, Lorna, *Critical Spaces: Margaret Laurence and Janet Frame,* Camden House (Rochester, NY), 1995.

Kirkwood, Hilda, *Between the Lines,* Oberon Press (Ottawa, Canada), 1994.

Morley, Patricia, *Margaret Laurence,* Twayne (Boston, MA), 1981.

Thomas, Clara, *Margaret Laurence,* McClelland & Stewart (Toronto, Ontario, Canada), 1969.

Thomas, Clara, *The Manawaka World of Margaret Laurence,* McClelland & Stewart (Toronto, Ontario, Canada), 1975.

Verduyn, Christi, editor, *Margaret Laurence: An Appreciation,* Broadview Press (Toronto, Ontario, Canada), 1988.

Woodcock, George, editor, *A Place to Stand On: Essays by and about Margaret Laurence,* NeWest Press (Edmonton, Alberta, Canada), 1983.

PERIODICALS

Atlantic, June, 1969, March, 1970.

Canadian Forum, February, 1969, September, 1970.

Canadian Literature, spring, 1993, Colin Nicholson, review of *Dance on Earth: A Memoir,* p. 181; spring, 1994, George Woodcock, review of *Margaret and Al: Margaret Laurence-Al Purdy. A Friendship in Letters,* p. 102.

Chicago Tribune Book World, December 7, 1980.

Christian Science Monitor, June 12, 1969, March 26, 1970.

Fiddlehead, Number 80, 1969.

Globe and Mail (Toronto, Ontario, Canada), December 14, 1985, January 10, 1987, March 5, 1988, November 4, 1989.

Maclean's, May 14, 1979; October 23, 1989, Morton Ritts, review of *A Diviner's Life,,* p. 70.

New York Times Book Review, April 19, 1970.

Queen's Quarterly, spring, 1991, Enid Delgatty Rutland, review of *Dance on the Earth: A Memoir,* p. 216.

Saturday Night, May, 1969.

World Literature Today, winter, 1982.

OBITUARIES:

PERIODICALS

Globe and Mail (Toronto, Ontario, Canada), January 10, 1987.

Los Angeles Times, January 17, 1987.

Maclean's, January 19, 1987.

New York Times, January 7, 1987.

Publishers Weekly, February 20, 1987.

Times (London, England), January 7, 1987.

Washington Post, January 7, 1987.

* * *

LAVOND, Paul Dennis
See POHL, Frederik

* * *

LEAVITT, David 1961-

PERSONAL: Born June 23, 1961, in Pittsburgh, PA; son of Harold Jack (a professor) and Gloria (a homemaker; maiden name, Rosenthal) Leavitt. *Education:* Yale University, B.A., 1983.

ADDRESSES: Office—Department of English, University of Florida, 4008 Turlington Hall, P.O. Box 117310, Gainesville, FL 32611-7310. *E-mail*—dleavitt\@ufl.edu.

CAREER: Writer. Viking-Penguin, New York, NY, reader and editorial assistant, 1983-84; taught at Princeton University; University of Florida, Gainesville, professor of creative writing, 2000—.

MEMBER: PEN, Authors Guild, Authors League of America, Phi Beta Kappa.

AWARDS, HONORS: Willets Prize for fiction, Yale University, 1982, for "Territory"; O. Henry Award, 1984, for "Counting Months"; nomination for best fiction, National Book Critics Circle, 1984, and PEN/

Faulkner Award for best fiction, PEN, 1985, both for *Family Dancing;* National Endowment for the Arts grant, 1985; Visiting Foreign Writer, Institute of Catalan Letters, Barcelona, Spain, 1989; Guggenheim fellow, 1990; Literary Lion, New York Public Library.

WRITINGS:

Family Dancing (short stories), Knopf (New York, NY), 1984.

The Lost Language of Cranes (novel), Knopf (New York, NY), 1986.

Equal Affections (novel), Weidenfeld & Nicolson (London, England), 1989.

A Place I've Never Been (short stories), Viking (New York, NY), 1990.

While England Sleeps (novel), Viking (New York, NY), 1993, reprinted with a new preface by the author, Houghton Mifflin (Boston, MA), 1995.

(Editor, with Mark Mitchell) *Penguin Book of Gay Short Stories,* Viking (New York, NY), 1994.

(With Mark Mitchell) *Italian Pleasures,* Chronicle Books (San Francisco, CA), 1996.

Arkansas: Three Novellas (includes "The Term Paper Artist," "The Wooden Anniversary," and "Saturn Street"), Houghton Mifflin (Boston, MA), 1997.

(Editor and author of introduction, with Mark Mitchell) *Pages Passed from Hand to Hand: The Hidden Tradition of Homosexual Literature in English from 1748 to 1914,* Houghton Mifflin (Boston, MA), 1997.

The Page Turner (novel), Houghton Mifflin (Boston, MA), 1998.

Martin Bauman; or, A Sure Thing (novel), Houghton Mifflin (Boston, MA), 2000.

(Editor and author of introduction, with Mark Mitchell) E.M. Forster, *Selected Stories,* Penguin (New York, NY), 2001.

(With Mark Mitchell) *In Maremma: Life and a House in Southern Tuscany,* Counterpoint (Washington, DC), 2001.

The Marble Quilt (stories), Houghton Mifflin (Boston, MA), 2001.

Florence, a Delicate Case, Bloomsbury (New York, NY), 2002.

Collected Stories, Bloomsbury (New York, NY), 2003.

The Body of Jonah Boyd (novel), Bloomsbury (New York, NY), 2004.

Contributor to periodicals, including *Esquire, Harper's, New Yorker, New York Times Book Review, New York Times Magazine,* and *Village Voice.*

ADAPTATIONS: The Lost Language of Cranes was adapted for film by the British Broadcasting Corp. (BBC), 1991. *The Page Turner* was adapted for film by Spanish director Ventura Pons, as *Food of Love,* 2002.

SIDELIGHTS: Lauded for his insightful and empathetic characterizations, author David Leavitt has gained recognition as as one of the leaders of the gay literature movement in the United States. According to Daniel J. Murtaugh in the *Dictionary of Literary Biography,* "While Leavitt has converted the experiences of gay men and women into a matter of interest for the mainstream reader, he remains one of the most poignant and subjective tellers of what it means to be gay and how a gay person survives in a world of family, education, or business not necessarily receptive to sexual difference." Leavitt published his first story, "Territory," in the *New Yorker* at the age of twenty-one. The story of a mother and her homosexual son, it was the first of its kind to be published in that magazine, and it created "a small stir in the city's more conservative circles," according to an *Interview* writer. Leavitt also published pieces in other periodicals, including *Esquire* and *Harper's,* and in 1984 published his first book, a collection of short stories titled *Family Dancing.*

Family Dancing showcases Leavitt's insights into some of the more offbeat, troubling aspects of domestic life. Among the stories noted by critics are "Radiation," about a slowly dying cancer victim, "Out Here," which concerns sibling guilt, and "Aliens," in which a young girl believes herself to be an extraterrestrial creature. "Territory" is included in this collection, and several other works in the volume also address homosexual concerns, including "Dedicated," and "Out Here," in which one of the characters is a lesbian.

Family Dancing earned acclaim as an impressive debut volume. *Newsweek's* David Lehman, hailing the 1980s boom in short-story writing, called Leavitt's book "a first collection of unusual finesse," and Michiko Kakutani wrote in the *New York Times* that *Family Dancing* is "an astonishing collection" with "the power to move us with the blush of truth." In a review for the *Washington Post,* Dennis Drabelle praised Leavitt as "remarkably gifted," and reserved particular commendation for his tales of homosexuality. Leavitt, Drabelle contended, "captures the deep-rooted tensions between adult gays and their families and the efforts of childless gays to carve out families among their peers." Drabelle concluded that Leavitt's insights had "only just been tapped."

Leavitt devotes his first novel, *The Lost Language of Cranes,* to an in-depth depiction of homosexual life.

While the main character's romantic experiences are rather typical—he falls in love, loses his lover, and finds a more suitable mate—a subplot involving the protagonist's father delves into traumas specific to homosexuality. The father is a married man who spends Sunday afternoons indulging in his passion for patronizing pornography theaters. After learning that his son is a homosexual, he too makes his own difficult confession.

The Lost Language of Cranes chronicles more than just the elements of a homosexual life, however. It also addresses more universal issues regarding love and traces the hope, pain, ecstasy, and suffering that are all a part of romantic involvement. Other issues explored in the novel include the notion of family life, as Leavitt delineates the tensions and disappointments of the family as it is altered by the son's and the father's revelations. In addition, the anguish of the wife and mother is also evoked through her increased withdrawal from familial crises. Her disappointment, together with the father's anguish and the son's alternately exhilarating and crushing experiences with love, adds another dimension to Leavitt's work.

The Lost Language of Cranes garnered much critical acclaim. Susan Wood wrote in the *Washington Post* that Leavitt's novel "has much to recommend it," and Philip Lopate noted in the *New York Times Book Review* that the book is "readable and literate." An enthusiastic reviewer for Chicago's *Tribune Books* described the novel as "well-written and frankly interesting," and added that "Leavitt's style is compelling, and the subject matter . . . is equally elucidative." Similarly, Dorothy Allison wrote in the *Village Voice* that "Leavitt catches beautifully the terror and passion of new love" and shows a profound understanding of love's "tentativeness." She further declared that *The Lost Language of Cranes* "places David Leavitt firmly among the best young authors of his generation," and concluded that his novel gave her "new hope for modern fiction."

Critics of *The Lost Language of Cranes* were especially impressed with Leavitt's skill in portraying compelling characters and his ability to evoke the tension and turmoil, as well as the fulfillment and ecstasy, of love. The reviewer for *Tribune Books* declared that Leavitt "opens up the gay world to readers" and added that the narrative is "mature, quick-paced and fascinating." Likewise, Allison wrote that the novel's various characters are "so fully realized" that she found herself "tense with fear for each of them." Allison commended Leavitt for his artistry in evincing such a response from readers. "It is

David Leavitt's strength that he could inspire that kind of fear in me and win me back when his characters did not find true love or happiness," Allison noted. "At every moment I believed in them, and these days that is so rare as to suggest genius."

Leavitt's second novel, *Equal Affections,* which *Listener* reviewer John Lahr called a "tale of the extraordinariness of ordinary family suffering," centers around Louise Cooper, who is dying of cancer, and the members of her family who must deal with this reality. Louise's husband, Nat, is a computer visionary whose visions have never amounted to much. Her son Danny is a gay lawyer living in bland, immaculate monogamy in the suburbs with Walter, who has not fully committed to the relationship. Daughter April is a famous folk singer who "discovers" her true lesbian nature and turns her singing to feminist issues. Louise's bitterness over lost opportunities, her crisis of faith, and her impending death color her interactions with her husband and family. As Louise's twenty-year bout with cancer draws to a close, the family deals with this strain as well as their individual problems: Nat is having an affair with another woman, Danny endures Walter's Internet philandering, and April is artificially inseminated with donor sperm from a culturally aware San Francisco homosexual.

Equal Affections received mixed reviews. Acknowledging her disappointment in Leavitt's first novel, *The Lost Language of Cranes,* Beverly Lowry wrote in the *New York Times Book Review* that, in contrast, *Equal Affections* "does not compromise itself with easy answers. It is a gritty, passionate novel that should settle the question of David Leavitt's abilities. . . . He has the talent for a lifelong career." Lahr called the novel "adroit," while a *New York* writer found it to be "limp, dreary business." *Washington Post Book World* contributor Alan Hollinghurst praised Leavitt's characterizations, but observed that the "emotional drama . . . is distinctly soggy. Leavitt's characters are notoriously lachrymose, but here there's really too much tearful sentiment, spunky goodness and curtain-line corniness: this is a sleepie that turns into a weepie." London *Observer* correspondent Candia McWilliam was more enthusiastic, terming *Equal Affections* an "attentive, unsparing book."

In Leavitt's second collection of short stories, *A Place I've Never Been,* most of his tales focus on gay characters dealing with relationships. "When You Grow to Adultery" finds the protagonist leaving an old lover for a new one, and in "My Marriage to Vengeance," a lesbian character's former lover marries a man. In the title story, a woman finally realizes that her gay friend Nathan is too wrapped up in his own self-pity to contribute to their friendship. A mother tests the limits of her AIDS-stricken son's waning strength in "Gravity," and a heterosexual couple who have lost their respective spouses to cancer begin an affair in "Spouse Night."

Many critics praised *A Place I've Never Been.* Charles Solomon in the *Los Angeles Times Book Review* called Leavitt's writing "fine, polished prose that is refreshingly free of the drip-dry nihilism of his Brat Pack contemporaries." James N. Baker declared in *Newsweek* that Leavitt "is not an oracle nor is he a groundbreaker. . . . He remains what he has always been: a writer of conventional stories who casts an incisive, ironic eye on families and lovers, loyalty and betrayal." Reviewer Harriet Waugh wrote in the *Spectator:* "Short stories, unlike novels, have to be perfect. *A Place I've Never Been* . . . very nearly is." In her *New York Times Book Review* piece on the work, Wendy Martin called *A Place I've Never Been* a "fine new collection of short fiction," and Clifford Chase described Leavitt's short fiction as "at once wrenching and satisfying" in his review for the *Village Voice Literary Supplement.*

Leavitt's third novel, *While England Sleeps,* is set in the 1930s against the backdrop of the Spanish Civil War, and follows the love story between Brian Botsford, a literary aristocrat, and Edward Phelan, a lower-class ticket-taker on the London Underground. Brian ends the affair, and in an attempt to deny his homosexuality marries a woman whom his wealthy aunt thinks is suitable. Distraught, Edward joins the fight in Spain, but he soon deserts the military and lands in prison. Brian follows his lover to Spain and secures Edward's release, but Edward dies of typhoid on the voyage home.

While England Sleeps borrowed a segment of its plot from British poet Stephen Spender's 1948 autobiography, *World within World,* a fact first revealed by Bernard Knox in his review for the *Washington Post.* Leavitt admitted using an episode from Spender's life as a springboard for his novel and wrote in the *New York Times Magazine* that he had initially included an acknowledgment to Spender, "but had been advised by an in-house lawyer at Viking to omit the reference." He also defended his book on the basis that it is an historical novel and maintained that it "diverged from Spender's account in many more ways than it converged with it." Spender brought suit in London against Leavitt for

copyright infringement. Viking agreed to withdraw the book until Leavitt revised the manuscript according to some seventeen points cited in the Spender suit; once this had been done, however, Viking declined to publish the revised version. However, in the fall of 1995, Houghton Mifflin released the new version with an added preface by Leavitt that addresses the book's legal controversy.

Despite the controversy, the *Los Angeles Times* shortlisted *While England Sleeps* for its fiction prize after it had been withdrawn from its initial publication, and *While England Sleeps* continued to receive much publicity from reviewers. In a *New York Times* review, Christopher Lehmann-Haupt lauded Leavitt's authentic portrayal of the prewar European era and his depiction of the region's divergent social classes. In the scenes that take place in Spain, Lehmann-Haupt added, "the theme of sexual deception is chillingly replicated in the way the Communist leaders treat their followers." Lehmann-Haupt concluded that *While England Sleeps* should be credited for climbing "out of its preoccupation with sex and [making] a significant comment on the political issues of its time." Conversely, Jeremy Treglown noted in the *Times Literary Supplement* that "style is one thing about which Spender hasn't complained, yet the book's main offence lies in its novelettishness." D.T. Max observed in the *Los Angeles Times Book Review:* "A careful reading of *World within World* shows Spender's charge of plagiarism to be over the top—all the novel's words seem Leavitt's own—but a charge of laziness would be far harder to disprove, and the knowledge of it mars an otherwise graceful, romantic novel."

In his next foray into short fiction, *Arkansas: Three Novellas,* Leavitt once again explores issues of gay love and life, this time mixing directly autobiographical elements into the work. In "The Term Paper Artist," a young writer—named David Leavitt—tries to break through a case of writer's block caused by an accusation of plagiarism by an English poet. In an interview with Celestine Bohlen in the *New York Times,* Leavitt described his intent with this novella: "It is so common to write autobiographical fiction in which your own experience is thinly disguised. I thought it could be very interesting to do the opposite with a story where even a tiny amount of research into my life would prove it did not happen . . . and thereby turn the convention inside out." The volume's other two novellas, "The Wooden Anniversary" and "Saturn Street," both deal with characters whose lovers have died and who are struggling with moving on with their lives. "The Wooden Anniversary" is set in Italy, where Leavitt himself now lives.

Although *Arkansas* received some favorable critical reception, *New York Times* reviewer Michiko Kakutani termed the work "disappointing," criticizing the author's handling of sexual events as "repetitious, tiresome and sophomoric" and noting that "this sort of adolescent writing is unworthy of the richly talented Mr. Leavitt."

The Marble Quilt, published in 2001, reestablished Leavitt's critical standing as an author of short fiction, even as he experimented with "different formats and styles," according to *Booklist* reviewer Michael Spinella. "The Infection Scene" balances a story about the petulant Lord Alfred "Bosie" Douglas, young lover to nineteenth-century writer Oscar Wilde and later that same man's downfall, with a modern-day tragedy about AIDS; "The Black Box" finds two men drawn together as one mourns the recent loss of a lover in a tragic plane crash; and "The List" follows the gossip-ridden e-mail dialogue among a group of gay academics. The title story, about a murdered man whose life, as narrated by his former boyfriend during a police inquiry, is shown to be rife with contradictions, "is infused with an anger that exists . . . just below its dense writerliness," noted a *Publishers Weekly* contributor, adding that in *The Marble Quilt* Leavitt "achieves an electric narrative energy."

Leavitt's 1998 novel, *The Page Turner,* deals with the dual themes of love and ambition. Aspiring concert pianist Paul Porterfield, the book's narrator, is given the chance to turn pages for renowned artist Richard Kennington during a concert in California. The two men meet a few months later in Italy and begin a brief affair that is halted by Kennington's loyalty to a longtime partner and by Paul's realization that his talent does not equal Kennington's. The book also explores Paul's milieu in New York City and his mother's struggle to come to terms with the dissolution of her marriage. In her *New York Times* review of the book, Kakutani maintained that the novel "represents something of a rediscovery of the methods and ambitions of *Family Dancing.* It is by no means a perfect novel . . . but . . . it intermittently shimmers with the magical talent that first announced itself a decade and a half ago." Elizabeth Gleick also praised *The Page Turner* in the *New York Times Book Review* as "a perfectly enjoyable read" and "a portrait of the aspiring artist as a young man." Gleick continued: "Love and striving for selfhood may be inseparable, but in this novel the author achieves clarity, even flashes of poetry, only when grappling with the turning points in an artistic life."

The "artistic life" also informs *Martin Bauman; or, A Sure Thing,* Leavitt's *roman à clef* about the New York publishing world. The central character of this novel, Martin Bauman, is a youthful prodigy who publishes a groundbreaking short story with gay themes in an important literary magazine—and who thereafter has to struggle with his disillusion at the venality of the publishing business and with the dire predictions of his demanding college instructor, Stanley Flint. *Martin Bauman* "gives every appearance of being an extended, merciless excoriation of Leavitt's younger self—depicted here as a boy with a propensity for cheating on exams, a coddled yet chronically needy child-man not above betraying the people he loves when they prove insufficiently forthcoming with their reassurance," wrote Laura Miller in the *New York Times Book Review.* Miller added: "The pettiness of writers is so disheartening because, at its best, the experience of reading is so sublime; naturally, we expect better of the people who can engineer such a miracle. That Leavitt depicts his own generation of 'hot' young writers as not just preoccupied with reputation but also apparently indifferent to the alchemy of reading itself may be the most damning thing of all." A *Publishers Weekly* reviewer felt that the New York literary scene "is given a sound drubbing in this comedy of egos and coming-of-age tale. . . . Readers hip to the New York book biz will be tickled throughout by Leavitt's thinly veiled satiric references to various literary institutions." Kakutani, writing in the *New York Times,* found the book to be "as poignant and funny an account of literary apprenticeship as that found in the opening pages of William Styron's *Sophie's Choice.*"

In *The Body of Jonah Boyd* Judith "Denny" Denham reflects on a significant Thanksgiving dinner, thirty years before, at the house of her then employer/lover and his family. Sometime throughout the evening one of the members of the party, novelist Jonah Boyd, irretrievably misplaces his most recent manuscript, setting him off on a path of despair. "Leavitt drops you into this family, allows you to muck around in its glorious dysfunction, and then extracts you in an ingenious way," explained Henry Goldblatt in a review for *Entertainment Weekly.* Marc Kloszewski in *Library Journal* commented that *The Body of Jonah Boyd* is a "generally breezy and humorous book whose charms outweigh any flaws; many readers will enjoy it," while Ray Olson of *Booklist* acknowledged, "Followers of Leavitt's career may note that his nemesis, plagiarism, figures in here, while homosexuality, formerly prevalent in his fiction, does not, and conclude that this is his best novel."

In addition to his own writing, Leavitt has edited several well-received works with his companion, Mark Mitchell. The *Penguin Book of Gay Short Stories,* for instance, consists of pieces that focus on gay men and includes a wide variety of writers, both contemporary and historical, among them Larry Kramer, D.H. Lawrence, Graham Greene, Christopher Isherwood, Edna O'Brien, and James Purdy. Writing in the *New Statesman & Society,* Richard Canning bemoaned the omission of non-American and non-English writers as well as pre-1900 writers, questioning the inclusion of pieces that seem at odds with the authors' stated criteria. "Leavitt's preference for 'self-contained, autonomous works' rather than novel extracts is shelved for particular favourites." Nonetheless, Canning recommended the anthology as "no less comprehensive than any work subject to such criteria could be." Peter Parker in the *Observer* similarly questioned the scope of the pieces included, noting that the volume reflects Leavitt's own writing terrain—conservative, mainstream, "suburban-sensitive"—at the expense of angrier or more explicitly sexual literature. But Peter Parker, while admitting some reservations about inclusion criteria in his *Times Literary Supplement* review, commended Leavitt and Mitchell for choosing "so many stories of such high literary quality."

Leavitt and Mitchell also edited *Pages Passed from Hand to Hand: The Hidden Tradition of Homosexual Literature in English from 1748 to 1914.* The anthology includes excerpts from novels, stories, and obscure manuscripts that depict gay passion, sometimes in veiled form due to cultural taboos and censorship. According to Robert Dawidoff in the *Advocate,* the pieces, though of other eras and in some cases previously unknown to readers, "are often hauntingly familiar, partly because they have been incorporated into the gay literature we know but also because they concern the same uncomfortable and confused feelings gays experience even now." Dawidoff concluded that the book "belongs in every gay library. . . . It is like a time capsule, carefully secreted in the cornerstone of our gay foundation and now restored to us as a reminder and a treasure."

Leavitt's success has made him one of the few mainstream writers whose work deals primarily with homosexual themes. As Martin explained in the *New York Times Book Review:* "Leavitt has the wonderful ability to lead the reader to examine heterosexist assumptions without becoming polemical. In prose that is often spare and carefully honed, he sensitizes us to the daily difficulties of homosexual life—of negotiating public spaces, for example, where holding hands or a simple embrace becomes problematic." She added: "Leavitt's insight and empathy serve . . . to enlighten, to make us realize that human sexuality is a continuum of possibilities that encompasses the subtle as well as the sensational."

BIOGRAPHICAL AND CRITICAL SOURCES:

BOOKS

Contemporary Literary Criticism, Volume 34, Thomson Gale (Detroit, MI), 1985.
Dictionary of Literary Biography, Volume 130: *American Short Story Writers since World War II,* Thomson Gale (Detroit, MI), 1993.

PERIODICALS

Advocate, October 19, 1993, pp. 51-55; December 28, 1993, p. 76; February 17, 1998, Robert Dawidoff, review of *Pages Passed from Hand to Hand: The Hidden Tradition of Homosexual Literature in English from 1748 to 1914,* p. 53; March 31, 1998, Robert L. Pela, review of *The Page Turner,* p. 74.
Booklist, February 15, 1998, Ray Olson, review of *The Page Turner,* p. 982; August, 2000, Donna Seaman, review of *Martin Bauman; or, A Sure Thing,* p. 2074; September 2, 2001, Michael Spinella, review of *The Marble Quilt,* p. 51; April 1, 2004, Ray Olson, review of *The Body of Jonah Boyd,* p. 1348.
Entertainment Weekly, April 30, 2004, Henry Goldblatt, review of *The Body of Jonah Boyd,* p. 171.
Esquire, May, 1985.
Harper's, April, 1986.
Interview, March, 1985.
Kirkus Reviews, February 15, 1998, review of *The Page Turner.*
Library Journal, June 1, 1995; February 1, 1998, David Azzolina, review of *Pages Passed from Hand to Hand,* p. 86; February 15, 1998, Roger W. Durbin, review of *The Page Turner,* p. 170; September 1, 2000, Brian Kenney, review of *Martin Bauman; or, A Sure Thing,* p. 250; July, 2001, review of *The Marble Quilt,* p. 128; May 1, 2004, Marc Kloszewski, review of *The Body of Jonah Boyd,* p. 140.
Listener, June 15, 1989, John Lahr, review of *Equal Affections,* p. 25.
London Review of Books, May 23, 1991, pp. 22-23.
Los Angeles Times Book Review, March 5, 1989, p. 6; August 4, 1991, p. 1991; October 3, 1993, pp. 3, 12.
National Review, December 27, 1993, p. 72.
New Republic, April 6, 1998, Denis Donoghue, review of *Pages Passed from Hand to Hand,* p. 36.
New Statesman & Society, November 12, 1993, p. 38; March 11, 1994, p. 41.

Newsweek, January 14, 1985; February 13, 1989, p. 78; September 3, 1990, p. 66; November 8, 1993, p. 81.

New York, January 30, 1989; October 18, 1993, pp. 139-140.

New York Times, October 30, 1984; October 14, 1993, p. C20; February 20, 1994, p. D14; February 25, 1997, p. B1; March 11, 1997, p. B2; March 27, 1998, Michiko Kakutani, "Ambition, Manipulation and a Misguided Mother"; September 29, 2000, Michiko Kakutani, "The Writing Life: Never Unexamined, Often Nasty."

New York Times Book Review, September 2, 1984; October 5, 1986; February 12, 1989, p. 7; August 26, 1990, p. 11; October 3, 1993, p. 14; September 4, 1994, p. 10; April 26, 1998, Elizabeth Gleick, "On the Other Side of Arrival"; October 8, 2000, Laura Miller, "Who's Who?"

New York Times Magazine, July 9, 1989, pp. 28-32; April 3, 1994, p. 36.

Observer (London, England), May 28, 1989, p. 46; February 6, 1994, p. 21.

Partisan Review, winter, 1994, pp. 80-95.

Publishers Weekly, August 24, 1990, pp. 47-48; February 21, 1994; February 2, 1998, review of *The Page Turner,* p. 79; August 7, 2000, review of *Martin Bauman; or, A Sure Thing,* p. 74; July 30, 2001, review of *The Marble Quilt,* p. 56.

Spectator, March 9, 1991, Harriet Waugh, review of *A Place I've Never Been,* p. 28.

Time, November 8, 1993, p. 27.

Times Literary Supplement, June 9-15, 1989, p. 634; October 29, 1993, p. 20; February 4, 1994, p. 20.

Tribune Books (Chicago, IL), September 21, 1986.

Village Voice, October 14, 1986, Dorothy Allison, review of *The Lost Language of Cranes.*

Village Voice Literary Supplement, December, 1990, Clifford Chase, review of *A Place I've Never Been,* pp. 10-11.

Washington Post, November 19, 1984; March 2, 1985; October 7, 1986; February 17, 1994, p. A1.

Washington Post Book World, January 22, 1989, p. 4; October 7, 1990, p. 7; September 12, 1993, p. 5.

ONLINE

PureFiction.com, http://www.purefiction.com/ (December 12, 2000), interview with Leavitt.

*   *   *

le CARRÉ, John 1931-
(David John Moore Cornwell, John Le Carre)

PERSONAL: Born October 19, 1931, in Poole, Dorsetshire, England; son of Ronald Thomas Archibald and Olive (Glassy) Cornwell; married Alison Ann Veronica Sharp, November 27, 1954 (divorced, 1971); married Valerie Jane Eustace, 1972; children: (first marriage) Simon, Stephen, Timothy; (second marriage) Nicholas. *Education:* Attended Bern University, Switzerland, 1948-49; Lincoln College, Oxford, B.A. (with honors), 1956.

ADDRESSES: Home—London, England, and Cornwall, England. *Agent*—Bruce Hunter, David Higham Ltd., 5-8 Lower John St., Golden Sq., London W1R 4HA, England.

CAREER: Writer. Millfield Junior School, Glastonbury, Somerset, England, teacher, 1954-55; Eton College, Buckinghamshire, England, tutor, 1956-58; British Foreign Office, second secretary in Bonn, West Germany (now Germany), 1960-63, consul in Hamburg, West Germany (now Germany), 1963-64. *Military service:* British Army Intelligence Corps, beginning 1949.

AWARDS, HONORS: Gold Dagger, Crime Writers Association, 1963, Somerset Maugham Award, 1964, and Edgar Allan Poe Award, Mystery Writers of America, 1965, all for *The Spy Who Came in from the Cold;* James Tait Black Memorial Prize, 1977, and Gold Dagger award, 1978, both for *The Honourable Schoolboy;* Gold Dagger award, 1980; honorary fellow, Lincoln College, Oxford, 1984; Grand Master Award, Mystery Writers of America, 1986; Malparte prize, 1987; Diamond Dagger award, Crime Writers Association, 1988; Dagger of Daggers award, Crime Writers Association, 2005, for *The Spy Who Came in from the Cold.* Honorary doctorates, University of Exeter, 1990, University of St. Andrews, 1996, University of Southampton, 1997, and University of Bath, 1998.

WRITINGS:

NOVELS

Call for the Dead, Gollancz (London, England), 1960, published as *The Deadly Affair,* Penguin (New York, NY), 1966.

A Murder of Quality, Gollancz (London, England), 1962.

The Spy Who Came in from the Cold (also see below), Gollancz (London, England), 1963, Coward, McCann (New York, NY), 1964.

The Incongruous Spy: Two Novels of Suspense (contains *Call for the Dead* and *A Murder of Quality*), Walker (London, England), 1964.

The Looking Glass War (also see below), Coward, Mc-Cann (New York, NY), 1965.

A Small Town in Germany (also see below), Coward, McCann (New York, NY), 1968.

The Naive and Sentimental Lover, Knopf (New York, NY), 1971.

Tinker, Tailor, Soldier, Spy, Knopf (New York, NY), 1974.

The Honourable Schoolboy, Knopf (New York, NY), 1977.

Smiley's People, Knopf (New York, NY), 1980.

The Quest for Karla (contains *Tinker, Tailor, Soldier, Spy, The Honourable Schoolboy,* and *Smiley's People*), Knopf (New York, NY), 1982.

Three Complete Novels (contains *The Spy Who Came in from the Cold, A Small Town in Germany,* and *The Looking Glass War*), Avenel Books (New York, NY), 1983.

The Little Drummer Girl, Knopf (New York, NY), 1983.

A Perfect Spy, Knopf (New York, NY), 1986.

The Russia House, Knopf (New York, NY), 1989.

The Secret Pilgrim, Knopf (New York, NY), 1991.

The Night Manager, Knopf (New York, NY), 1993.

Our Game, Knopf (New York, NY), 1995.

John Le Carre: Three Complete Novels (includes *Tinker, Tailor, Soldier, Spy, The Honourable Schoolboy,* and *Smiley's People*), Wings (Avenel, NY), 1995.

The Tailor of Panama (also see below), Knopf (New York, NY), 1996.

Single & Single, Scribner (New York, NY), 1999.

The Constant Gardener, Scribner (New York, NY), 2001.

Absolute Friends, Little, Brown (New York, NY), 2003.

OTHER

Dare I Weep, Dare I Mourn (teleplay), produced on *Stage 66,* American Broadcasting Corp., 1966.

(With John Hopkins) *Smiley's People* (teleplay; based on his novel), British Broadcasting Corp., 1982.

The Clandestine Muse, Seluzicki (Portland, OR), 1986.

(With Gareth H. Davies) *Vanishing England,* Salem House, 1987.

The Tailor of Panama (screenplay; based on his novel), Columbia Pictures, 2001.

Contributor to periodicals, including *Saturday Evening Post.* Le Carré's books have been translated into thirty languages.

ADAPTATIONS: *The Spy Who Came in from the Cold* was filmed by Paramount, 1965; *Call for the Dead* was filmed as *The Deadly Affair* by Columbia, 1967; *The Looking Glass War* was filmed by Columbia, 1970; *Tinker, Tailor, Soldier, Spy* was filmed for television by the BBC, 1980; *The Little Drummer Girl* was filmed by Warner Brothers; *A Perfect Spy* was a seven-hour BBC-TV series and was shown on public television's *Masterpiece Theatre;* a film version of *The Russia House,* written by Tom Stoppard, directed by Fred Schepisi, and starring Sean Connery and Michelle Pfeiffer, was released in 1990; *A Murder of Quality* was produced for television by the BBC, 1991; *The Constant Gardener* was adapted for film and released by Focus Features in 2005. Many of le Carré's novels have been produced as audio cassettes;

SIDELIGHTS: The novels of John le Carré, who was born David John Moore Cornwell, depict the clandestine world of cold war espionage as a morally ambiguous realm where treachery, deceit, fear, and betrayal are the norm. The atmosphere in a le Carré novel, wrote a reviewer for the *Times Literary Supplement,* is one of "grubby realism and moral squalor, the frazzled, fatigued sensitivity of decent men obliged to betray or kill others no worse than themselves." Le Carré has used his fiction to dramatize what he sees as the moral bankruptcy of the cold war. In an open letter published in *Encounter,* le Carré wrote: "There is no victory and no virtue in the cold war, only a condition of human illness and a political misery." Leonard Downie, Jr. quoted le Carré in a *Washington Post* article as saying, "We are in the process of doing things in defense of our society which may very well produce a society which is not worth defending." It is this paradox, and the moral ambiguity which accompanies it, that informs le Carré's espionage novels and makes them, many critics believe, among the finest works of their genre. le Carré's novels are believed by some critics to have raised the entire espionage genre to a more respectable and serious level of literature. Joseph McClellan wrote in the *Washington Post Book World,* "The espionage novel has become a characteristic expression of our time . . . and John le Carré is one of the handful of writers who have made it so." George Grella stated in the *New Republic,* "More than any other writer, [le Carré] has established the spy as an appropriate figure and espionage as an appropriate activity for our time, providing both symbol and metaphor to explain contemporary history."

Speaking of the relationship between his life and writings to Fred Hauptfuhrer of *People,* le Carré revealed: "If I write knowledgeably about gothic conspiracies, it's because I had knowledge of them from earliest childhood." In several published interviews, le Carré has spoken of his personal life and how the business dealings and political ambitions of his father colored his own views of the world. Because his father often found himself in legal or financial trouble due to his sometimes questionable business deals, the family found itself, le Carré told Miriam Gross of the *Chicago Tribune Magazine,* "often living in the style of millionaire paupers. . . . And so we arrived in educated, middle-class society feeling almost like spies, knowing that we had no social hinterland, that we had a great deal to conceal and a lot of pretending to do." In an interview with Melvyn Bragg in the *New York Times Book Review,* le Carré stated: "From early on, I was extremely secretive and began to think that I was, so to speak, born into occupied territory." He told *Newsweek* that "there is a correlation, I suppose, between the secret life of my father and the secret life I entered at a formative age." Le Carré fictionalized his relationship with his father in the 1986 novel *A Perfect Spy.*

Le Carré was one of Ronald and Olive Cornwell's two sons. His father owned racehorses, declared bankruptcy on a few occasions, and was once jailed for insurance fraud. When the author was five, his mother, Olive, left the family when she became involved with one of her husband's associates. Both David and his brother, Tony, who were quite close as children, lived with their grandparents for a time. Le Carré was sent to a rigorous boarding school in England, which he disliked, and was then allowed to go to Switzerland, where he entered the University of Berne at the age of sixteen. When he did his National Service, he was sent to join the British Army Intelligence Corps because of his language skills.

Only in later years was le Carré more forthcoming about this part of his life. He admitted to working for "M.I." ("military intelligence," also known as "the Service") off and on from the late 1940s to the early 1960s. While still with the British Army, le Carré was posted to Vienna, Austria, which remained occupied by British, American, and Soviet forces in the decade following World War II. The arrangement made Vienna an epicenter that concealed the clashing ideologies of cold war politics, and in his work there le Carré became acquainted with the men and women who would provide the basis for his fictional characters. After his military stint ended, le Carré joined M.I.5, Britain's domestic intelligence-gathering service agency, an association he denied for several years after he became a best-selling author.

Le Carré married in 1954, and ostensibly left the service to teach school in Glastonbury. He began degree studies at Oxford University, and here allegedly infil-trated left-leaning political groups on campus on behalf of M.I.5. He quit once again, and became assistant master at Eton College in 1956, but disliked it heartily, in a repeat of his own experience at another of England's famed public schools. He attempted to support himself and a growing family by becoming a freelance illustrator, but once again returned to M.I.5 in London. He was transferred to M.I.6, the foreign intelligence service, in 1960, and was sent overseas. His cover was a job as an embassy secretary or political consul, in places such as Bonn and Hamburg.

Le Carré began writing espionage fiction during this time, and the nature of his M.I. job required him to use a pen name. From the outset, reviewers assumed that the intimate knowledge he displayed of the workings of the British government's espionage bureaucracy could only have come from someone with firsthand experience. "Le Carré's contribution to the fiction of espionage," wrote Anthony Burgess in the *New York Times Book Review,* "has its roots in the truth of how a spy system works. . . . The people who run Intelligence totally lack glamour, their service is short of money, [and] they are up against the crassness of politicians. Their men in the field are frightened, make blunders, grow sick of a trade in which the opposed sides too often seem to interpenetrate and wear the same face." Geoffrey Stokes, writing in the *Village Voice,* claimed that in le Carré's novels, "bureaucracy [is] transformed into poetry." "John le Carré," the pseudonym the author chose, was partly taken from the French term for "the square." "I've told so many lies about where I got the name from," Downie quoted le Carré as explaining, "but I really don't remember. The one time I did the celebrity circuit in America, I was reduced to inventing the fiction that I'd been riding on a bus to the foreign office and abstracted the name from a shoeshop. But that was simply because I couldn't convince anybody it came from nowhere."

Although the source for his pseudonym is now forgotten, the initial inspiration for le Carré's fiction is easily found. It comes from the sensational disclosures in the 1950s that several high-ranking members of the British Secret Service and Foreign Office were actually Soviet agents. These deep-penetration agents, called "moles," had infiltrated the British espionage establishment during World War II and had, over a period of years, risen to extremely sensitive positions. Of the several spies discovered, the most highly placed was Kim Philby, a man generally acknowledged to be the greatest traitor in British history. Philby had been in charge of British counter-intelligence against the Soviet Union while secretly working for the Soviets, and was responsible for betraying hundreds of British agents and sending them to their deaths. These real-life espionage revelations caught the interest of the British reading public, and such books as Ian Fleming's "James Bond" spy series became best-sellers. Le Carré, too, because of his own intelligence work, was intrigued and disturbed by the discovery of traitors in the British Secret Service. Grella stated that le Carré has an "obsession with the relationship between love and betrayal" and has consistently explored this theme in all of his fiction.

Le Carré wrote his first two novels, *Call for the Dead* and *A Murder of Quality,* while working for the British Foreign Office, first in London and then in Bonn. At that time the German capital was a center for intelligence operations. Le Carré told Gross, "You couldn't have been [in Germany] at that period without being aware of the shadow of an enormous intelligence apparatus." Le Carré introduced George Smiley, an intelligence agent featured in many of his later novels, in *Call for the Dead.* Smiley is an "improbable spy master," wrote Richard W. Noland in *Clues.* "Short, fat and of a quiet disposition, he appeared to spend a lot of money on really bad clothes, which hung about his squat frame like skin on a shrunken toad," Noland quoted from *Call for the Dead.* Though physically unimposing, Smiley is a brilliant espionage agent who has served in the British Secret Service for more than thirty years. In *Call for the Dead,* Smiley investigates the suicide of a Foreign Office clerk who had just been given a security clearance. In *A Murder of Quality* he tracks down the murderer of a schoolmaster's wife.

It was not until the publication of *The Spy Who Came in from the Cold* in 1963 that le Carré's work attracted widespread critical and popular acclaim. An immediate worldwide best-seller—the book has sold over twenty million copies since it first appeared—*The Spy Who Came in from the Cold* enabled le Carré to leave his position with the Foreign Office to write full time. He told Nicholas Wapshott of the London *Times:* "I had said to my accountant, if my assets reach 20,000 pounds, would you let me know? . . . When he told me I had reached that amount, with *The Spy Who Came in from the Cold,* it was a great relief. . . . I gave in my resignation." The novel tells the story of Alec Leamas, a fifty-year-old British intelligence agent who wishes to retire from active duty and "come in from the cold," as he describes it. He is persuaded to take on one last assignment before leaving the Secret Service: a pretended defection behind the Iron Curtain to give false information to the East Germans implicating one of their high-ranking intelligence officers as a British agent. It is thought that the officer will then be impris-

oned, thereby removing him from effective espionage work against the British. Leamas's real mission, and the treachery of his superiors, only gradually becomes clear to him as the plot unfolds.

Le Carré's pessimism about East-West relations is clearly evident in *The Spy Who Came in from the Cold,* where both sides in the cold war conflict are depicted as amoral and murderous. Noland, describing the situation as related in *Spy,* observed, "The bureaucracies of East and West wage the Cold War by one simple rule—operational convenience. . . . In the name of operational convenience and alliances of expediency, any and all human values—including love and life itself—are expendable." A *Times Literary Supplement* critic wrote that le Carré puts forth the ideas that "the spy is generally a weak man, the tool of bureaucrats who are neither scrupulous nor particularly efficient, and that there is nothing to choose between 'us' and 'them' in an ethical sense." This is underlined when Leamas and his girlfriend are pitted against the intelligence agencies of both Britain and East Germany, "the two apparently opposed organizations on one side and helpless human beings . . . on the other," Julian Symons wrote in *Mortal Consequences: A History from the Detective Story to the Crime Novel.* Symons called *The Spy Who Came in from the Cold* the best of le Carré's novels because "the story is most bitterly and clearly told, the lesson of human degradation involved in spying most faithfully read."

Many of the qualities in le Carré's writing that are most praised by critics were first displayed in *The Spy Who Came in from the Cold.* One of these is an authenticity and realism not usually found in espionage fiction. Anthony Boucher commented in the *New York Times Book Review,* "Here is a book a light year removed from the sometimes entertaining trivia which have (in the guise of spy novels) cluttered the publishers' lists." A reviewer for the *Times Literary Supplement* believed that, in *The Spy Who Came in from the Cold,* "the technicalities of [spy] network organization carry a stamp of authenticity seldom found in stories of this nature," although the critic decried the "basically sensational" subject matter.

To make his work seem as authentic as possible, le Carré introduces a number of slang terms peculiar to the espionage underworld. Words like "mole," borrowed from the Soviet KGB, and "circus," a nickname for the British Secret Service, are used throughout the book. Some of these terms are actual espionage jargon, but many were invented by le Carré himself. Le Carré told

Gross, "I thought it very important to give the reader the illusion of entering the secret world, and to that end I invented jargon that would be graphic and at the same time mysterious. Some people find it irritating. I rather like it." Le Carré, Downie reported, "borrowed 'mole' from the KGB and is pleased that it has quickly become part of the real spy language of the West."

The critical praise heaped on *The Spy Who Came in from the Cold* has continued with each succeeding espionage novel le Carré has published. *The Looking Glass War*, for example, was described by Hughes as "a superb spy story, unflawed, a bitter, cruel, dispassionate—yet passionate—study of an unimportant piece of espionage and the unimportant little men who are involved in it." A group of British agents mount an operation into East Germany that is doomed to failure under present political conditions, a fact which the agents refuse to see. Symons argued in the *New Review* that in both *The Spy Who Came in from the Cold* and *The Looking Glass War* betrayal is the primary theme. In the first, an agent is betrayed in order to further the career of a more highly placed agent. In the second, an entire operation is abandoned and the people involved in it are left to die. It is possible, Symons wrote, "to see espionage activities as brave and patriotic . . . and yet to view them also as basically disgusting, outrages to the human personality. From such a point of view these two books seem to say an ultimate word about the nature of spying."

Le Carré draws heavily upon his time at the British Foreign Office in writing *A Small Town in Germany,* a novel set in Bonn, West Germany. The novel relates the story of a British diplomat who disappears with very sensitive documents which may damage Britain's chances of joining the Common Market. Speaking of the novel in a *Nation* review, John Gliedman stated that le Carré "has long been a master of the essential machinery of the spy and detective novel. He has also shown himself to be a sensitive observer of character and manner, within the limits of the genre. But nothing which has come before quite prepares us for the literary distinction of this effort—the quality of its prose, the complexity of its construction, the cunning of some of its dialogue. . . . *A Small Town in Germany* is that rarest of all things in contemporary fiction—good art which is also popular art." Robert Ostermann, writing in *National Observer,* agreed that *A Small Town in Germany* is better than le Carré's previous fiction. He called it "broader in scope and more confidently crafted; tuned with exquisite fineness to the sliding nuances of its characters; shot through with the physical presence of Bonn . . . and conveyed in a tough, precise prose that matches the novel's mordant tone down to the smallest metaphor."

Tinker, Tailor, Soldier, Spy begins a loosely connected trilogy in which George Smiley is pitted against the Russian master spy "Karla." Writing in *Newsweek,* Alexis Gelber and Edward Behr reported that "with *Tinker, Tailor, Soldier, Spy* and Smiley, [le Carré] hit his stride." *Tinker, Tailor, Soldier, Spy* is a fictionalized treatment of the Kim Philby spy case in which Smiley goes after a Soviet mole in British intelligence, a mole placed and directed by Karla. The novel's structure "derives from the action of Smiley's search," wrote Noland, adding that Smiley "must pursue his man through the maze of official documents." Knowing the mole must be a highly placed agent, Smiley goes back through the records of intelligence operations, seeking a pattern of failure which might be attributed to the machinations of a particular agent. His investigation finally becomes, Noland believed, "a moral search . . . a quest for some kind of truth about England."

As in previous novels, le Carré examines the ramifications of betrayal, but this time in greater depth. The mole Smiley uncovers has not only betrayed his country and friends, but has seduced Smiley's wife as well. The critic for the *Times Literary Supplement* saw a "moral dilemma" at the center of the book: "Smiley gets his man. In doing so he removes from another man his last illusions about friendship, loyalty and love, and he himself is left drained in much the same way. It is a sombre and tragic theme, memorably presented." Similarly, Richard Locke wrote in the *New York Times Book Review* of the "interlocking themes of sexual and political betrayal" to be found in the book. Writing in *Clues,* Holly Beth King saw a deeper significance to the novel's title, which is derived from a children's nursery rhyme, a "whole intricately woven set of relationships between adults and children, between innocence and disillusionment, between loyalty and betrayal that gives the novel's title a deeper resonance."

Although the complexity of *Tinker, Tailor, Soldier, Spy* was praised by many critics, Pearl K. Bell opined in the *New Leader* that "it is myopic and unjust to link le Carré with high art." Bell believed that a more correct evaluation of le Carré will place him as "a master craftsman of ingeniously plotted suspense, weaving astoundingly intricate fantasies of discovery, stealth, surprise, duplicity, and final exposure." Similarly, Locke found that "le Carré belongs to the select company of such spy and detective story writers as Arthur Conan Doyle and Graham Greene in England, and Dashiell Hammett, James M. Cain, Raymond Chandler, and Ross Macdonald in America. There are those who read crime and espionage books for the plot and those who read them for the atmosphere. . . . le Carré's books . . . offer plenty for both kinds of readers." Bell concluded that le Carré is "unarguably the most brilliantly imaginative practitioner of the [espionage] genre today." Writing in *Newsweek,* Peter S. Prescott defined what he felt sets le Carré's espionage fiction apart from many other works in the genre: "Le Carré's work is above all plausible, rooted not in extravagant fantasies of the cold war but in the realities of the bureaucratic rivalry summoned up through vapors of nostalgia and bitterness, in understated pessimism, in images of attenuation and grinding down." In *Tinker, Tailor, Soldier, Spy,* Stokes argued, "Smiley is merely the protagonist; bureaucracy itself is the hero. . . . Without the structure bureaucracy imposes on the random accumulation of facts that assail us on a daily basis, there is indeed only 'perpetual chaos.'"

Smiley's running battle with Karla continues in *The Honourable Schoolboy,* a novel set in Hong Kong, where British intelligence is investigating a prosperous businessman who seems to be working for the Soviets. Several critics point out a similarity between le Carré's novel and Joseph Conrad's novel *Lord Jim.* The character of Jerry Westerby, a British intelligence officer and friend of Smiley, is very similar to that of Conrad's character Jim. Noland stated, "Le Carré obviously has Conrad's romantic protagonist in mind in his portrait of Westerby and in many of the events of the story." According to David Ansen in *Newsweek,* this "huge and hugely engrossing new thriller . . . keeps opening out, like a Conrad adventure, into ever-widening pools of moral and emotional complexity."

Again concerned with one of Karla's moles, this one working inside Communist China, *The Honourable Schoolboy* traces Smiley's diligent efforts to discover and capture the agent for the West. As in previous le Carré novels, *The Honourable Schoolboy* depicts an agent, this time Westerby, who is at odds with the amorality of espionage work and who, because of his belief in human values, loses his life in the course of an espionage operation. "The point, surely, is that such romantic heroism is not very useful in the world of Cold War espionage," wrote Noland. "It is difficult not to overpraise [*The Honourable Schoolboy*]," Mollie Panter-Downes wrote in her *New Yorker* review. Although finding the novel too long, the plot "essentially thin," and le Carré's "fondness for stylistic mocking" awkward, Panter-Downes nonetheless praised *The Honourable Schoolboy.* "It has a compelling pace," she stated, "a depth beyond its genre, a feeling for even the least of its characters, a horrifying vision of the doomed and embattled Southeast Asian left in the wake of the Vietnam War, and a dozen set pieces—following, fleeing, interrogating—that are awesomely fine."

Not all critics were as impressed with the novel. Louis Finger, writing in the *New Statesman,* believed that "the things that are wrong with le Carré, at the level of seriousness he no doubt feels he's aimed for here, totally debilitate the book's appeal as a run-of-the-mill espionage yarn." Responding to critics who classify le Carré's work as literature, Clive James in the *New York Review of Books* stated that "raising le Carré to the plane of literature has helped rob him of his more enviable role as a popular writer who could take you unawares."

Le Carré brings his trilogy to a close with *Smiley's People,* the last confrontation between George Smiley and master spy Karla. No longer content to thwart Karla's agents, Smiley works in this novel to force Karla himself to defect to the West. This operation is done off the record because the British Secret Service, due to political pressure, cannot engage in an offensive intelligence operation. It becomes instead a personal mission involving the retired Smiley and the friends and espionage contacts he has gathered over the years. "Smiley and his people," Noland stated, "carry it out by personal choice and commitment, not for the British (or American) establishment. The whole operation is a victory for personal human loyalty and skill."

Despite the success of the operation, there is an ambiguity about it which brings into question the morality of espionage. "Smiley and his people are fighting for decency," wrote Michael Wood in the *New York Times Book Review,* "but there is more blood on their hands than they or anyone else care to contemplate." Julian Moynihan clarified this in the *New Republic:* "We know that Smiley has ruined many lives, some innocent, in his tenacious pursuit of Karla. . . . and we just don't believe that the dirty tricks of one side are OK because they were ordered up by a decent little English guy with a disarming name." "If this is the end of the Smiley stories . . . it is an appropriately ambiguous conclusion to a series that has dealt splendidly in ambiguities from the beginning," concluded Joseph McClellan in the *Washington Post Book World.*

In *Smiley's People,* Tom Buckley stated in *Quest/80,* "Le Carré has done what no sensible person would have thought possible. He has written a novel at least as good as, and in some respects better than, his masterpiece, *The Spy Who Came in from the Cold.*" Jonathan Yardley agreed in the *Washington Post,* calling it "the best of the le Carré's novels." Yardley went on to evaluate le Carré's achievement as a writer by stating that he "has produced a body of work that is notable for technical brilliance, depth, and consistency of themes, and absolute verisimilitude."

In *The Little Drummer Girl* le Carré turns to a different world arena for his setting: the Middle East refugee camps of the Palestinians. Anatole Broyard in the *New York Times* said, "It is as if Mr. le Carré has had enough of British politics, as if he feels that neither Britain nor the Soviet Union is at the hot center of things anymore." Le Carré had originally planned to write a Smiley story set in the Middle East, but could not find a convincing plot for his character. Because the espionage activity in this novel is of an active and open variety, there is more action in *The Little Drummer Girl* than is usual for a le Carré novel. There is also a female protagonist, le Carré's first, who is recruited by the Israelis to infiltrate a Palestinian terrorist group and set up its leader for assassination. "The Israelis triumph in the novel," William F. Buckley, Jr. wrote in the *National Review,* "even as they do in life. But Mr. le Carré is careful to even up the moral odds. . . . He permits the Palestinian point to be made with rare and convincing eloquence." Writing in *Esquire,* Martin Cruz Smith gave the opinion that *The Little Drummer Girl* is "the most balanced novel about Jews and Arabs, outrage for outrage and tear for tear, I've read." Gelber and Behr wrote, "Without condoning terrorism, the book makes the reasons for it understandable—perhaps the first popular novel to do so."

Because of his insistence on looking at both sides in the Middle East conflict as having valid reasons for waging war, many critics believed le Carré succeeded in accurately presenting the situation in its complexity. It is through the character of Charlie, an actress recruited by the Israelis for the mission, that le Carré presents the arguments of both the Arabs and Jews. Charlie is first converted to the Israeli position by Israeli Intelligence and then, in order to play the part of a Palestinian sympathizer convincingly, she is indoctrinated in the Palestinian position. "In the course of the story," Hope Hale Davis stated in the *New Leader,* "we have a chance, with Charlie, to become passionately partisan on one side and then the other, and also—with less risk to the psyche than Charlie suffers—both sides at once." According to Mark Abley, writing in *Maclean's,* le Carré "is resigned to the fact that neither side will be pleased by his controversial new novel." This is because le Carré portrays both sides as amoral killers, much the way he portrays both sides in the cold war. le Carré told *Newsweek:* "There was no way of telling the story attractively unless one accepted certain premises—that terrible things were being done to the Jews. I began with the traditional Jewish hero looking for a Palestinian 'baddie.' Once into the narrative, the reader, I believed, would be prepared to consider more ambiguous moral preoccupations."

Some reviewers view le Carré as an apologist for the Palestine Liberation Organization (PLO), and *The Little Drummer Girl* as lacking the moral ambiguity that characterized his earlier books. "Here, one might have thought, is an ideal subject for moral ambiguity," David Pryce-Jones wrote in the *New Republic.* "Le Carré finds it clear-cut. To him, the Palestinians are good, the Israelis bad." In their review of the book for *Chronicles of Culture,* Rael Jean Isaac and Erich Isaac acknowledged that le Carré does introduce the kind of moral ambiguities and correspondences between adversaries that he uses in other novels, "but these suggestions of ambiguity and correspondence are deceptive, for le Carré sets Israel up as the villain of this novel. . . . Le Carré employs meretricious techniques to make Israel appear guilty of the vicious practices that the PLO has made famous."

In his novels since *The Little Drummer Girl,* le Carré spins plots that reflect the dissolution of the former Soviet Union, the end of the cold war, and the continued violence in the Middle East, while also continuing to portray flawed protagonists caught up in sinister circumstances. In *The Russia House,* which is set in a decaying Soviet Union, an aging publisher is recruited by British Intelligence to secure a top-secret manuscript from a Soviet engineer. After falling in love with the engineer's former girlfriend, however, the publisher must use his wits to keep himself and the woman alive while British and American spies pursue national interests not concerned with such individual freedoms. *The Night Manager,* on the other hand, leaves behind cold war settings altogether, as a hotel manager in Switzerland struggles against international arms dealers who are funded by wealthy British businessmen. *Our Game,* which is set in the warring republics of the former Soviet Union—Ossetia, Ingushetia, and Chechnya—features a troubled central character caught up in sociopolitical forces beyond his control, and *Absolute Friends* follows two spies and their involvement in the Iraq war in the wake of the September 11, 2001, terrorist bombings in the United States. Noting in particular the author's inclusion of politics in *Absolute Friends, Entertainment Weekly* contributor Mark Harris explained that le Carré's subject matter has always been the battle between "human frailty and geopolitical dogma." Praising the author for penning "coolheaded spy fiction at the height of the Cold War and then redefining the genre after it ended," Harris added that le Carré's anger at the U.S. involvement in the Iraq war is embedded in a story "told with bracing vigor and clarity; his people are vibrantly alive; his understanding of the world has rarely been keener."

Harris's claim that le Carré redefined the spy novel following the end of the cold war is substantiated by the imaginative plots the author has devised since the early 1990s, many of which move the intrigue from battling nation states to "the depredations of international arms merchants and the impact of predatory drug manufacturers on the Third World," according to a *Publishers Weekly* reviewer. In *The Tailor of Panama,* published in 1996, le Carré explores his characteristic terrain of spy games and intrigue, but this time against the unusual tropical backdrop of Panama. Harry Pendel, a clothes tailor to the powerful and wealthy of Panama, is coerced into spying for British Intelligence in the midst of a plot to undo the Panama Treaty that will give control of the Panama Canal back to Panama in 1999. Although he does his duty by supplying information to his British recruiter, Pendel finds his life and the lives of his family in jeopardy, in part because of the falsehoods he makes up to embellish his information. Writing in the *New York Times,* Michiko Kakutani praised le Carré's refined storytelling prowess and his "colorful and deft" depiction of Panama. Kakutani, however, averred that the author is less successful in creating a plausible story line. *Times Literary Supplement* reviewer Frederic Raphael concurred, remarking that le Carré "does not seem to finish his button-holes, or fashion his concealed pockets, with quite the old finesse." Still, Kakutani noted, "the result is a riotous, readable novel."

Le Carré's *Single and Single,* has been compared by some reviewers to *A Perfect Spy* because both feature a conflicted father-son relationship that have echoes in the author's personal life. Le Carré's father, who died in the mid-1970s, attempted to enrich himself through his son's notoriety. He called himself "Ron le Carré," and was able to obtain lavish dinners and hotel suites on the strength of the name. He often asked his son for money, and once tried to estimate the sum total, with interest, had all of le Carré's private-school tuition money been invested instead of used. Le Carré, however, dryly noted that his father had never paid the tuition bills anyway.

Oliver Single has a similarly troubled relationship with his notorious father, Tiger. The elder Single is a bon vivant venture capitalist in London, whose firm, Single & Single, launders money for a Russian-organized crime ring. He is determined that Oliver take over the business, but Oliver is plagued by moral doubts and, after an airport epiphany, "defects" at Heathrow Airport and tells a customs agent about the business. Tiger escapes a jail term, while Oliver is given a new identity and retires to the countryside to become a magician. The story is revealed in flashback, for *Single & Single* opens with the murder of the firm's former legal counsel in Turkey, one of the ramifications of Oliver's betrayal. The Russians are determined to kill Tiger as well, and Oliver joins authorities in the battle to break up the mob and save his father's life in the process. *Maclean's* writer Anthony Wilson-Smith called it "arguably the best of le Carré's five books this decade. Its musings over morality, pitch-perfect dialogue and easy command of diverse geography and characters show why le Carré is one of the finest novelists in any field."

Other reviews were similarly enthusiastic about the novel. "The opening sequence, in which Tiger's lawyer surreally describes his own assassination on a Turkish hilltop by mobsters seeking to avenge their undoing, is perhaps the most chilling passage Le Carré has ever written," noted a *Business Week* reviewer. *Washington Monthly* contributor David Ignatius particularly liked one of the lead characters, customs agent Nat Brock, and likened him to the memorable George Smiley. Ignatius granted that outwardly the fictional characters possess no similarities, but found other attributes in common. "He is a gray man, with a world-weariness so profound that the reader senses immediately that Brock has gazed into the very bottom of the abyss," Ignatius noted. "You have the feeling with Brock, just as with Smiley, that he knows how the story will end before it begins."

The Constant Gardener employed a similar backdrop of international intrigue in le Carré's tale of a rapacious pharmaceutical giant. The legitimate corporation is secretly testing a new miracle drug that, when officially released on the world market, portends massive profits. But Dypraxa, a cure for tuberculosis, possesses some deadly flaws, as clandestine research trials underway in Africa reveal—and the company is desperate to keep the true nature of Dypraxa a secret. In Kenya, Tessa Quayle, the beautiful young wife of a British diplomat, learns about the research trials, but her threat to alert the media and authorities to the pharmaceutical company's activities results in her murder. Her bereaved husband, Justin, takes up Tessa's cause in his search to find her killer.

A contributor to *Business Week* praised *The Constant Gardener* as a story "about the human capacity for transformation. Through Justin, the political themes are elevated to questions of loyalty, integrity, and personal sovereignty in a world that rewards betrayal, venality, and the abdication of moral responsibility." A *Publishers Weekly* reviewer also praised the veteran author's talents, writing that "Le Carré's manifold skills at scene-setting and creating a range of fearsomely convincing English characters, from the bluffly absurd to the irredeemably corrupt, are at their smooth peak here." In the

National Review, Anthony Lejeune paid similar tribute to the writer, noting that his novels "are impressive because he is an excellent craftsman, writing clear, classic prose and constructing his intricate plots so that they fit together like well-carpentered marquetry."

BIOGRAPHICAL AND CRITICAL SOURCES:

BOOKS

Aronoff, Myron J., *The Spy Novels of John le Carre: Balancing Ethics and Politics,* St. Martin's Press (New York, NY), 2001.

Barley, Tony, *Taking Sides: The Fiction of John le Carre,* Open University Press, 1986.

Bestsellers 89, Issue 4, Thomson Gale (Detroit, MI), 1989.

Contemporary Literary Criticism, Thomson Gale (Detroit, MI), Volume 3, 1975, Volume 5, 1976, Volume 9, 1978, Volume 15, 1980, Volume 28, 1984.

Contemporary Popular Writers, St. James Press (Detroit, MI), 1997.

Dictionary of Literary Biography, Volume 87: *British Mystery and Thriller Writers since 1940, First Series,* Thomson Gale (Detroit, MI), 1989.

Encyclopedia of World Biography, 2nd edition, Thomson Gale (Detroit, MI), 1998.

Harper, Ralph, *The World of the Thriller,* Press of Case Western University (Cleveland, OH), 1969.

Homberger, Eric, *John le Carre,* Ungar (New York, NY), 1985.

Monaghan, David, *The Novels of John le Carre: The Art of Survival,* Blackwell (Oxford, England), 1985.

Monaghan, David, *Smiley's Circus: A Guide to the Secret World of John le Carre,* Orbis (London, England), 1986.

Newsmakers 2000, Thomson Gale (Detroit, MI), 2000.

Palmer, Jerry, *Thrillers: Genesis and Structure of a Popular Genre,* St. Martin's Press (New York, NY), 1979.

Symons, Julian, *Mortal Consequences: A History from the Detective Story to the Crime Novel,* Harper (New York, NY), 1972.

Wolfe, Peter, *Corridors of Deceit: The World of John le Carre,* Bowling Green University Popular Press (Bowling Green, OH), 1987.

PERIODICALS

Armchair Detective, spring, 1980.

Booklist, December 15, 1998, Bill Ott, review of *Single & Single,* p. 707; June 1, 2001, Ted Hipple, review of *The Tailor of Panama,* p. 1908; December 1, 2003, Bill Ott, review of *Absolute Friends,* p. 626.

Book Week, January 26, 1964.

Business Week, March 15, 1999, "Rough Russians," p. 14E6; December 25, 2000, "Le Carre Takes on a New Evil Empire," p. 30.

Chicago Tribune, June 19, 1989.

Chicago Tribune Book World, March 6, 1983.

Chicago Tribune Magazine, March 23, 1980.

Christian Science Monitor, January 14, 1980.

Chronicles of Culture, August, 1983.

Clues, fall-winter, 1980; fall-winter, 1982.

Commentary, June, 1983.

Detroit News, August 29, 1982.

Economist, July 1, 1989, p. 75; January 6, 2001, review of *The Constant Gardener,* p. 5.

Encounter, May, 1996, "To Russia, with Greetings: An Open Letter to the Moscow *Literary Gazette,*" pp. 3-6

Entertainment Weekly, January 16, 2004, Mark Harris, review of *Absolute Friends,* p. 73.

Esquire, April, 1983.

Globe and Mail (Toronto, Ontario, Canada), June 10, 1989.

Harper, January, 1964; November, 1965; December, 1968.

Kirkus Reviews, November 1, 2000, review of *The Constant Gardener,* p. 1508; November 15, 2003, review of *Absolute Friends,* p. 1332.

Library Journal, February 1, 1999, A.J. Anderson, review of *Single & Single,* p. 121; December, 2000, David Dodd, review of *The Constant Gardener,* p. 189; May 15, 2001, John Hiett, review of *The Constant Gardener* and *The Tailor of Panama* (audio versions), p. 180; January, 2004, David Wright, review of *Absolute Friends,* p. 157.

Life, February 28, 1964.

Listener, July 4, 1974.

Los Angeles Times, May 31, 1989; October 16, 1989.

Los Angeles Times Book Review, June 18, 1989.

Maclean's, March 7, 1983; April 5, 1999, Anthony Wilson-Smith, "The le Carre File: A Celebrated Author's Painful Childhood Is the Catalyst for His Writing," p. 54.

Nation, December 30, 1968.

National Catholic Reporter, June 1, 2001, John Olinger, review of *The Constant Gardener,* p. 12.

National Observer, October 28, 1968.

National Review, March 13, 1983; March 22, 1999, Anthony Lejeune, "Daddy Dearest," p. 51.

New Leader, June 24, 1974; March 7, 1983; November, 2000, Walter Goodman, review of *The Constant Gardener,* p. 41.

New Republic, July 31, 1976; January 19, 1980; April 18, 1983; August 21, 1989, p. 30; August 9, 1993.

New Review, July, 1974.

New Statesman, July 12, 1974; September 23, 1977; February 5, 1999, Jason Cowley, "John le Carre," p. 18; January 8, 2001, John Dugdale, review of *The Constant Gardner,* p. 41.

Newsweek, October 28, 1968; June 17, 1974; September 26, 1977; March 7, 1983; June 5, 1989, p. 52; July 5, 1993; p. 54; March 1, 1999, "The Spy Who Came Into Some Money," p. 69.

New York, December 24, 1979; October 25, 1982.

New Yorker, October 3, 1977; August 23, 1993; p. 165.

New York Review of Books, October 27, 1977; February 7, 1980; April 14, 1983; September 28, 1989, p. 9; March 28, 1991; p. 8; August 12, 1993; p. 20.

New York Times, January 28, 1969; September 22, 1977; February 25, 1983; May 18, 1989, p. C28; December 1, 1991; July 8, 1993; October 18, 1996, p. B16; March 21, 1999, Michael Lewis, "Spying with Interest."

New York Times Book Review, January 12, 1964; June 5, 1965; March 11, 1966; January 27, 1967; June 30, 1974; September 25, 1977; January 6, 1980; March 13, 1983; June 7, 1987, p. 34; May 21, 1989, p. 3; January 6, 1991, p. 3; June 27, 1993.

New York Times Magazine, September 8, 1974.

People, August 19, 1974; September 13, 1993, p. 63; January 26, 2004, Sean Daly, review of *Absolute Friends,* p. 43.

Publishers Weekly, September 19, 1977; December 14, 1998, review of *Single & Single,* p. 54; February 1, 1999, review of *Single & Single,* p. 35; November 13, 2000, review of *The Constant Gardener,* p. 85; May 7, 2001, review of *The Tailor of Panama* (audio version), p. 48; November 24, 2003, review of *Absolute Friends,* p. 40.

Quest/80, January, 1980.

Salmagundi, summer, 1970.

Saturday Review, July 24, 1965.

Spectator, July 6, 1974.

Time, January 17, 1964; May 29, 1964; September 29, 1980; January 14, 1991, p. 61.

Times (London, England), September 6, 1982; June 24, 1989.

Times Literary Supplement, September 13, 1963; June 24, 1965; September 24, 1971; July 19, 1974; September 9, 1977; August 4, 1989; October 18, 1996, p. 22.

Tribune Books (Chicago, IL), May 21, 1989.

U.S. News and World Report, June 19, 1989, p. 59.

Village Voice, October 24, 1977; January 14, 1980.

Washington Monthly, May, 1999, David Ignatius, "Spy for a New Millennium," p. 48.

Washington Post, September 29, 1980; November 29, 1982; May 25, 1989; October 14, 1989.

Washington Post Book World, December 8, 1974; December 23, 1979; June 4, 1989.

Yale Review, January, 1994, p. 150.

ONLINE

John le Carre Home Page, http://www.johnlecarre.com/ (February 25, 2003).

*   *   *

LE CARRE, John
   See le CARRÉ, John

*   *   *

LEE, Don L.
   See MADHUBUTI, Haki R.

*   *   *

LEE, Harper 1926-
   (Nelle Harper Lee)

PERSONAL: Born April 28, 1926, in Monroeville, AL; daughter of Amasa Coleman (a lawyer) and Frances (Finch) Lee. *Education:* Attended Huntington College, 1944-45, and University of Alabama, 1945-49; also attended Oxford University. *Politics:* Republican. *Religion:* Methodist. *Hobbies and other interests:* Golf, music.

ADDRESSES: Home—Monroeville, AL. *Office*—c/o J.B. Lippincott Company, East Washington Square, Philadelphia, PA 19105. *Agent*—McIntosh & Otis, 353 Lexington Ave. 15th Fl., New York, NY 10016.

CAREER: Writer. Airline reservation clerk with Eastern Air Lines and British Overseas Airways, New York, NY, c. 1950s. Member, National Council on the Arts, 1966-72.

AWARDS, HONORS: Pulitzer Prize, Alabama Library Association award, and Brotherhood Award of National Conference of Christians and Jews, all 1961, *Best Sellers'* Paperback of the Year Award, 1962, and Alabama Humanities Award, 2002, all for *To Kill a Mockingbird.*

WRITINGS:

To Kill a Mockingbird, Lippincott (Philadelphia, PA), 1960.

Contributor to *Vogue* and *McCall's.*

To Kill a Mockingbird has been translated into ten languages.

ADAPTATIONS: *To Kill a Mockingbird* was filmed by Universal in 1962 and adapted as a London stage play by Christopher Sergel in 1987.

SIDELIGHTS: With the enormous popular and critical success of her novel *To Kill a Mockingbird,* Harper Lee established herself as a leading figure in American literature. Although she has not published any new fiction in the past four decades, Lee's reputation is secure. According to Dorothy Jewell Altman in *Dictionary of Literary Biography, To Kill a Mockingbird,* "a regional novel with a universal message, combines popular appeal with literary excellence, assuring Harper Lee's place in American letters."

To Kill a Mockingbird is narrated by six-year-old Jean Finch, nicknamed "Scout," who, along with her older brother Jem, watch as their father, an attorney in Maycomb, Alabama, defends Tom Robinson, a black man accused of raping a white woman, Mayella Ewell, daughter of Bob Ewell. During the three years of the trial, the two children come to an understanding of prejudice as their father stands his ground in defending a man he believes to be innocent. Scout and Jem are taunted by classmates and neighbors who object to the idea of a white man defending a black man, and the situation intensifies until Robinson is threatened with lynching; he is only saved by Jem and Scout's innocent intervention. At the trial, the jury finds Robinson guilty, even though Atticus proves he cannot possibly have committed the crime. Despite this truth and all his hard work, Atticus can't break through Maycomb's deeply entrenched racial prejudice that "*all* Negroes lie, that *all* Negroes are basically immoral beings, that *all* Negro men are not to be trusted around . . . [white] women." Told with "a rare blend of wit and compassion," according to a *Booklist* critic, the novel moves "unconcernedly and irresistibly back and forth between being sentimental, tough, melodramatic, acute, and funny," wrote a *New Yorker* reviewer.

One of the novel's subplots revolves around attempts by the two siblings and their friend Dill Harris to draw out Arthur "Boo" Radley, a local recluse who has remained hidden in the Radley home since his teenage years, when he was arrested for a prank and then released into his father's stern custody. Locked in the house, a victim of his father's religious notions and misplaced family pride, Radley eventually becomes a victim of the town's prejudice, and is feared by both adults and children. The children's wild ideas about the unseen Boo—that he eats raw squirrels and wanders the town by night—reflect the town's misconceptions about race. Dill, who is fascinated with Boo, convinces Jem and Scout that they should try and entice Boo to come out of his house so they can see him. Boo responds to this attention, secretly leaving gifts for the children in a hollow tree, mending Jem's pants when he tears them while climbing over the Radleys' fence to spy, and covering Scout with a blanket when she stands out in the cold watching a neighbor's house burn in a fire. In the end, Boo saves Scout from being killed when Bob Ewell, drunk and murderous, tries to kill her in order to exact vengeance on her father.

When Boo is revealed as a benefactor to the children, they must reconsider their preconceptions about him. "One of the most interesting features of *Mockingbird,*" writes William T. Going in his collection *Essays on Alabama Literature,* "is the skill with which Miss Lee weaves these two struggles about childhood and the law together into one thematic idea." "The achievement of Harper Lee," Edgar H. Schuster argued in the *English Journal,* "is not that she has written another novel about race prejudice, but rather that she has placed race prejudice in a perspective which allows us to see it as an aspect of a larger thing; as something that arises from phantom contacts, from fear and lack of knowledge; and finally as something that disappears with the kind of knowledge or 'education' that one gains through learning what people are really like when you 'finally see them.'"

Although the storyline of the novel appears to be simple, the book presents several opposing pairs of themes: ignorance versus knowledge, cowardice versus heroism, guilt versus innocence, and prejudice versus tolerance. The town's entrenched ignorance is contrasted with the education the children gain by following their innate instinct for truth and justice, and their accurate observations of the adults around them, particularly Atticus, who always tells them the truth. Atticus's clarity and courage is sharply contrasted with Bob Ewell's cowardice and bullying. Atticus tells Scout what true courage is, using the example of a neighbor who defeated her addiction to morphine: rather than being "a man with a gun in his hand," courage is "when you're licked before you begin but you begin anyway and you see it through no matter what." Atticus embodies this definition of courage when he defends Tom Robinson, a case he knows he will probably lose. Innocence and guilt are sharply contrasted when the most innocent characters in the book—Tom Robinson and Boo Radley—are judged guilty by society.

Throughout the book, Lee draws on the symbol of the mockingbird, which she associates with Boo Radley and Tom Robinson. This bird, which sings almost continuously, represents innocence and joy; the children's neighbor, Miss Maudie, tells them that it's a sin to kill one. Another symbolic moment occurs when an unusual snowstorm blankets Maycomb in white, and Jem builds a snowman over a base layer of mud. When the snowman melts, the mud is revealed. In one day, the snowman has gone from the black color of the underlying mud to white, and back to black, revealing how superficial skin color really is.

Lee drew upon her own childhood experiences as the daughter of a lawyer in Alabama to create the fictional events in *To Kill a Mockingbird.* Together with her brother and their childhood friend Truman Capote, Lee enjoyed many of the small-town adventures depicted in the novel; Capote would later base a character in his first novel, *Other Voices, Other Rooms,* on Lee. Scout's troubles in school—she is so far advanced in reading that she finds her school work boring—reflects Lee's own childhood boredom with grade school. Lee's older sister, Sook, a recluse who rarely left the family house, shares many of the qualities exhibited by the character Boo. Lee's father, Amasa Coleman, served in the Alabama State Legislature from 1927 to 1939, and was the model for Atticus Finch. "Although Lee stressed that *To Kill a Mockingbird* is not autobiographical," explained Altman, "she commented that a writer 'should write about what he [sic] knows and write truthfully.' The time period and setting of the novel obviously originated in the author's experience."

Lee began her writing career after leaving college in 1950 just before completing her law studies. While supporting herself in New York City as an airline reservation clerk, she sought the advice of a literary agent about her work. The agent advised her to expand one of the short stories she had written into the novel which became *To Kill a Mockingbird.* The process of writing the novel took several years. During this time Lee quit working, lived in a cold-water flat and was supported by friends who believed in her work. In 1957 she approached the publishing firm of Lippincott with the manuscript. Although editors criticized the novel's structure, which they felt read like a series of short stories strung together, they saw promise in the book and encouraged Lee to rewrite it. By 1960, with the help of Lippincott editor Tay Hohoff, *To Kill a Mockingbird* was finished.

The book was an immediate popular success, being selected by two major book clubs, the Literary Guild and the Book-of-the-Month Club, and condensed in *Reader's Digest.* In addition, the book won the Pulitzer Prize and several other awards. However, critical response to the novel was initially mixed. It was only with the success of the film adaptation in 1962—a winner of two Academy Awards and starring Gregory Peck and Mary Badham—that many critics took a second look at *To Kill a Mockingbird.* Initial reviews had sometimes highlighted the novel's melodramatic qualities or the unlikely nature of the story being narrated by a child of six. Phoebe Adams in *Atlantic,* for example, found the story "frankly and completely impossible, being told in the first person by a six-year-old girl with the prose style of a well-educated adult." Granville Hicks wrote in *Saturday Review* that "Lee's problem has been to tell the story she wants to tell and yet to stay within the consciousness of a child, and she hasn't consistently solved it." Later critics were more generous with the novel, citing Lee's storytelling abilities and creation of a believable small-town setting. As R.A. Dave wrote in *Indian Studies in American Fiction,* Lee "is a remarkable storyteller. The reader just glides through the novel abounding in humour and pathos, hopes and fears, love and hatred, humanity and brutality. . . . We hardly feel any tension between the novelist's creativity and social criticism [while] the tale of heroic struggle lingers in our memory as an unforgettable experience." He also wrote that Lee created "an epic canvas against which is enacted a movingly human drama of the jostling worlds—of children and adults, of innocence and experience, of kindness and cruelty, of love and hatred, of humor and pathos, and above all of appearance and reality—all taking the reader to the root of human behavior."

Despite these later critics' comments and the book's popular success, no book-length study of the work was published until Claudia Durst Johnson's *To Kill a Mockingbird: Threatening Boundaries* appeared in 1994. Johnson wrote, "Some of the most interesting criticism of the novel, and certainly the largest volume of commentary on the novel, has been done by legal rather than literary scholars." Teresa Goodwin Phelps wrote in

Alabama Law Review that "While the novel depicts change in one facet of law and society, it reinforces the status quo in other troubling aspects." These aspects include its casual attitude toward the sexual abuse of Mayella Ewell by her father, as well as its condescending view of poor whites.

Since its initial appearance in 1960, *To Kill a Mockingbird* has been a continuing favorite with high school and college students. But, aside from a few short articles for magazines, Lee has published no new work in over thirty-five years. The reason for this extended silence remains a matter of speculation. Lee has avoided making public comments about her life or her work, although reports at the time *To Kill a Mockingbird* was published described her as a slow, methodical writer who rewrote constantly. When pressed for personal information, Lee has used humor to protect her privacy, describing her political affiliation as "Whig," and saying that she believes "in Catholic emancipation and the repeal of the Corn Laws" and commenting that her favorite fan letter was one that accused her of not taking the rape of white women seriously: "Why is it that you young Jewish authors seek to whitewash the situation?" She responded with a clever letter, signing it "Harper Levy."

Lee has counted among her favorite authors Charles Lamb, Robert Louis Stevenson, Jane Austen, and Thomas Love Peacock, as well as various religious writers of the nineteenth century. As Lee once commented: "Writing is the hardest thing in the world. . . . but writing is the only thing that has made me completely happy."

Despite her love of writing, continuing to work after publishing *To Kill a Mockingbird* proved to be somewhat intimidating for Lee. She began a second novel in 1961, writing from noon until early evening, and revising so extensively that she produced only one or two pages per day, but never presented this work for publication. In the early 1960s she penned several short essays and an article titled "Love—In Other Words" for popular magazines. However, Lee retired from literary activity by mid-decade. Despite the fact that its author's renown rests on a single book, *To Kill a Mockingbird* retains its place in the American literary canon. In more recent years Lee has divided her time between New York City and her hometown of Monroeville, Alabama, where her sister, Alice Lee, practices as an attorney.

BIOGRAPHICAL AND CRITICAL SOURCES:

BOOKS

Contemporary Literary Criticism, Thomson Gale (Detroit, MI), Volume 12, 1980, Volume 60, 1990.

Dictionary of Literary Biography, Volume 6: *American Novelists since World War II,* Thomson Gale (Detroit, MI), 1980.

Going, William T., *Essays on Alabama Literature,* University of Alabama Press (Tuscaloosa, AL), 1975, pp. 9-31.

Johnson, Claudia Durst, *To Kill a Mockingbird: Threatening Boundaries,* Twayne (New York, NY), 1994.

Johnson, Claudia Durst, *Understanding "To Kill a Mockingbird": A Student Casebook to Issues, Sources, and Historic Documents,* Greenwood Press (Westport, CT), 1994.

Moates, Marianne M., *A Bridge of Childhood: Truman Capote's Southern Years,* Holt (New York, NY), 1989.

Naik, M. K., S.K. Desai, and S. Mokashi, editors, *Indian Studies in American Fiction,* Macmillan (New York, NY), 1974, pp. 211-323.

Sundquist, Eric J., *The South As an American Problem,* University of Georgia Press (Athens, GA), 1995.

PERIODICALS

Alabama Law Review, winter, 1974, Monroe Freedman, "Atticus Finch—Right and Wrong;" Teresa Godwin Phelps, winter, 1994, "The Margins of Maycomb: A Rereading of *To Kill a Mockingbird.*"

Alabama Review, April, 1973, Fred Erisman, "The Romantic Regionalism of Harper Lee," pp. 122-136.

America, May 11, 1991, pp. 509-511.

Atlanta Constitution, May 25, 1993, p. A11.

Atlanta Journal & Constitution, May 29, 1988, p. A2; August 26, 1990, p. M1.

Atlantic, August, 1960, Phoebe Adams, review of *To Kill a Mockingbird,* pp. 98-99.

Booklist, September 1, 1960; September 15, 1997, review of *To Kill a Mockingbird,* p. 250.

Chicago Sunday Tribune, July 17, 1960, p. 1.

Christian Science Monitor, October 3, 1961, Joseph Deitch, "Harper Lee: Novelist of the South," p. 6; September 11, 1997.

Commonweal, December 9, 1960, p. 289.

English Journal, October, 1963, pp. 506-511; December, 1964, pp. 656-661.

Harper's, September, 1999, review of *To Kill a Mockingbird,* p. 76.

Item, March 3, 1991, p. 24.

Kliatt, July, 1998, review of *To Kill a Mockingbird,* p. 47.

Library Journal, February 15, 1998, review of *To Kill a Mockingbird,* p. 114.

New Statesman, October 15, 1960, p. 580.

Newsweek, January 9, 1961, "Mocking Bird Call," p. 83.

New Yorker, September 10, 1960.

New York Herald Tribune, May 3, 1961, p. 16.

New York Herald Tribune Book Review, July 10, 1960, p. 5.

New York Times, June 6, 1993, p. 1.

New York Times Book Review, July 10, 1960, pp. 5, 18; April 8, 1962.

Philosophy and Literature, April, 2001, review of *To Kill a Mockingbird,* p. 127.

Phylon, June, 1961.

Saturday Review, July 23, 1960, pp. 15-16.

Southern Cultures, winter, 1995, Robert O. Stephens, "The Law and the Code in Harper Lee's *To Kill a Mockingbird.*"

Spectator, February 24, 1996, review of *To Kill a Mockingbird,* p. 36.

Times Literary Supplement, October 28, 1960.

USA Today, November 5, 1990, p. A3.

Vogue, April 15, 1961, Harper Lee, "Love—In Other Words," pp. 64-65.

Washington Post, August 17, 1990, p. C2.

Washington Post Book World, May 5, 1996, review of *To Kill a Mockingbird,* p. 17.

*   *   *

LEE, Nelle Harper
See LEE, Harper

*   *   *

LEE, Stan 1922-
(Stanley Martin Lieber)

PERSONAL: Born Stanley Martin Lieber, December 28, 1922, in New York, NY; name legally changed; son of Jack (a dress cutter) and Celia (Solomon) Lieber; married Joan Clayton Boocock, December 5, 1947; children: Joan C., Jan (deceased). *Education:* Attended high school in New York, NY.

ADDRESSES: Home—Los Angeles, CA. *Office*—Marvel Enterprises, 10 East 40th St., New York, NY 10016.

CAREER: Comic-book writer, editor, publishing executive, and film and television producer. Timely Comics (then Atlas Comics; now Marvel Comics), New York, NY, editorial assistant and copywriter, 1939-42, editor,

1942-72, publisher and editorial director, 1972—; associated with Marvel Productions, Los Angeles, CA. Adjunct professor of popular culture at Bowling Green State University; gives lectures on college campuses. Film appearances include as a hot dog vendor in *X-Men,* Twentieth Century-Fox, 2000; as a bystander in Times Square in *Spider-Man,* Columbia, 2002; as himself in *Mallrats,* Gramercy, 1995; and in shorts and cameo appearances. Narrator and voice-over actor for animated series based on Marvel Comics, including *Spider-Man and His Amazing Friends,* NBC, 1981; *The Incredible Hulk,* NBC, 1982; *The Fantastic Four,* syndicated, 1994; *Iron Man,* syndicated, 1994; and *Spider-Man,* Fox, 1994. Film and television producer; executive producer on films such as *Captain America,* Columbia, 1991; *Blade,* New Line Cinema, 1998; *X-Men,* 2000; and *Spider-Man,* 2002. Executive producer of television series, including *Biker Mice from Mars,* syndicated, 1993; *Silver Surfer,* Fox, 1998; *The Avengers,* Fox, 1999; and *X-Men: Evolution,* WB, 2000. His character Stripperella debuted in an animated feature, 2003. *Military service:* U.S. Army, 1942-45; became sergeant.

MEMBER: American Federation of Television and Radio Artists, National Academy of Television Arts and Sciences, National Cartoonists Society, Academy of Comic Book Arts (founder and president), Friars Club.

AWARDS, HONORS: Six Alley awards, 1963-68; award from Society for Comic Art Research and Preservation, 1968; Eureka Award, *Il Targa* (Milan, Italy), 1970, for world's best comic writing; annual award from Popular Culture Association, 1974; publisher of the year award from Periodical and Book Association of America, 1978; award from Academy of Comic Book Arts; honorary degree from Bowling Green State University.

WRITINGS:

(With John Buscema) *How to Draw Comics the Marvel Way,* Simon & Schuster (New York, NY), 1978.

Dunn's Conundrum (novel), Harper & Row (New York, NY), 1985.

The GOD Project (novel), Grove & Weidenfeld (New York, NY), 1990.

(With George Mair) *Excelsior! The Amazing Life of Stan Lee* (autobiography), Simon & Schuster (New York, NY), 2002.

COMIC BOOKS AND GRAPHIC NOVELS

The Mighty Thor, illustrated by Jack Kirby, Lancer Books (New York, NY), 1966.

Spider-Man Collector's Album, illustrated by Steve Ditko, Lancer Books (New York, NY), 1966.

Origins of Marvel Comics, Simon & Schuster (New York, NY), 1974.

Son of Origins of Marvel Comics, Simon & Schuster (New York, NY), 1975.

Bring on the Bad Guys: Origins of Marvel Villains, Simon & Schuster (New York, NY), 1976.

The Superhero Women, Simon & Schuster (New York, NY), 1977.

The Best of Spidey Super Stories, Simon & Schuster (New York, NY), 1978.

(With John Buscema) *How to Draw Comics the Marvel Way,* Simon & Schuster (New York, NY), 1978.

The Incredible Hulk, Simon & Schuster (New York, NY), 1978.

The Silver Surfer, illustrated by Jack Kirby, Simon & Schuster (New York, NY), 1978.

Marvel's Greatest Superhero Battles, Simon & Schuster (New York, NY), 1978.

Doctor Strange, Simon & Schuster (New York, NY), 1979.

The Fantastic Four, Simon & Schuster (New York, NY), 1979.

Captain America, Simon & Schuster (New York, NY), 1979.

Stan Lee Presents the Best of the Worst, Harper (New York, NY), 1979.

Complete Adventures of Spider-Man, Simon & Schuster (New York, NY), 1979.

(Presenter) *The Uncanny X-Men,* Marvel Comics (New York, NY), 1984.

The Best of Spider-Man, Ballantine Books (New York, NY), 1986.

Marvel Masterworks Presents Amazing Spider-Man (originally published as *The Amazing Spider-Man,* numbers 1-10), illustrated by Steve Ditko, Marvel Comics (New York, NY), 1987.

Marvel Masterworks Presents The X-Men (originally published as *The Uncanny X-Men* numbers 1-10), illustrated by Jack Kirby, Marvel Comics (New York, NY), 1987.

Monster Masterworks, Marvel Entertainment Group (New York, NY), 1989.

Silver Surfer: Judgment Day, illustrated by John Buscema, Marvel Comics (New York, NY), 1988.

The Enslavers ("Silver Surfer" graphic novel) Marvel Comics (New York, NY), 1990.

Marvel Masterworks Presents the Silver Surfer, illustrated by John Buscema, Marvel Comics (New York, NY), 1991.

Marvel Masterworks Presents Thor, illustrated by Jack Kirby, Marvel Comics (New York, NY), 1991.

Marvel Masterworks Presents Daredevil (originally published as *Dardevil, the Man without Fear,* numbers 1-10), illustrated by Wally Wood, Marvel Comics (New York, NY), 1991.

Marvel Masterworks Presents Doctor Strange (originally published as *Strange Tales,* numbers 110-111, 114-141), illustrated by Steve Ditko, Marvel Comics (New York, NY), 1992.

Marvel Masterworks Presents Iron Man (originally published as *Tales of Suspense,* numbers 39-50), illustrated by Don Heck, Marvel Comics (New York, NY), 1992.

Captain America, the Movie!, Marvel Comics (New York, NY), 1992.

The First Startling Saga of the Silver Surfer: The Coming of Galactus!, illustrated by Jack Kirby and Joe Sinnott, Marvel Comics (New York, NY), 1992.

Just Imagine Stan Lee Creating the DC Universe (includes *Just Imagine Stan Lee's Batman,* illustrated by Joe Kubert, *Just Imagine Stan Lee's Wonder Woman,* illustrated by Jim Lee, *Just Imagine Stan Lee's Superman,* illustrated by John Buscema, *Just Imagine Stan Lee's Green Lantern,* illustrated by Dave Gibbons, *Just Imagine Stan Lee's Aquaman,* illustrated by Scott McDaniel, (with Michael Uslan) *Just Imagine Stan Lee's JLA,* illustrated by Jerry Ordway, and *Just Imagine Stan Lee's The Flash,* illustrated by Kevin Maguire), DC Comics (New York, NY), 2002.

EDITOR

The Ultimate Spider-Man, Byron Preiss Multimedia (New York, NY) 1994.

The Ultimate Silver Surfer, Byron Preiss Multimedia (New York, NY) 1995.

The Ultimate Super-Villains, Byron Preiss Multimedia (New York, NY) 1996.

The Ultimate X-Men, Byron Preiss Multimedia (New York, NY) 1996.

(With Kurt Busiek) *Untold Tales of Spider-Man,* Byron Preiss Multimedia (New York, NY) 1997.

(With Peter David) *The Ultimate Hulk,* Byron Preiss Multimedia (New York, NY) 1998.

X-Men Legends, illustrated by Mike Zeck, Berkley Books (New York, NY), 2000.

Author of syndicated comic strips, including *My Friend Irma,* 1952, *Mrs. Lyons' Cubs,* 1957-58, *Willie Lumpkin,* 1960, *The Incredible Hulk,* and *Spider-Man.* Also editor of television scripts.

ADAPTATIONS: Included among the many media adaptations of Stan Lee's work are *The Incredible Hulk,* a television series broadcast by Columbia Broadcasting

System (CBS-TV), and a number of television specials featuring Spider-Man, Doctor Strange, and Captain America, broadcast by CBS-TV. Major motion pictures involving Lee's creations and cocreations include *X-Men, Spider-Man, Daredevil,* and *Hulk.*

SIDELIGHTS: Stan Lee is the cocreator of many of Marvel Comic's most popular superheroes, including Spider-Man, the Hulk, Daredevil, the X-Men, Iron Man, and the Fantastic Four. "Lee's metamorphosis from bespectacled kid in the Bronx to living symbol of a billion-dollar entertainment empire is every bit as impressive as any superhero origin story," wrote L.D. Meagher on the *CNN* Web site. As a youth, Lee was an avid reader, deeply immersed in the world of books and words. He was strongly influenced by swashbuckling actor Errol Flynn, as well as literary heroes such as Tom Swift, the Hardy Boys, and boy detective Poppy Ott. These characters kept Lee immersed in prose fiction and the fantasies spun out with the written word. Fueled by the desire to be a great novelist, Lee began writing early in life, winning the *New York Herald Tribune* essay contest three times in a row while in his early teens. At age seventeen, Lee—then known as Stanley Lieber—accepted a job with Timely Comics, owned by cousin-in-law Martin Goodman. Lee started with menial office chores and some proofreading for the company's line of comics. Within a year, however, Lee was doing some writing for Timely—his first published writing in comics was, ironically, a two-page text piece that appeared in *Captain America,* Number 3. He signed the piece "Stan Lee," reserving his real name for use on the serious works of literature he expected to write once he finished his stint in comics. "Circumstances conspired against him," stated a writer in *St. James Encyclopedia of Popular Culture.*

In the early 1940s, Lee found himself writing whatever material that Timely Comics' chief employees, editor/writer Joe Simon and artist/writer Jack Kirby, didn't have time for, according to an essayist in *Authors and Artists for Young Adults.* When Simon and Kirby left to work for rival DC Comics and begin forging stellar reputations for themselves in comics, both singly and as a team, Lee inherited their entire workload. At age twenty, Lee became the editor and main writer of a major comic-book publisher. Over the next two decades, Lee wrote prolifically, almost superheroically, in a wide range of genres, from westerns to romances, horror to science fiction, and perhaps most significantly, superheroes and costumed adventurers.

By the late 1950s and early 1960s, comics were in a protracted slump, near death and barely limping onward. The industry had suffered a tremendous blow in the 1950s with accusations by psychologist Frederic Wertham that comics were responsible for, among other things, juvenile delinquency. Wertham's views, codified in the book *Seduction of the Innocent,* were taken seriously, and senate hearings were held on the matter. Combined with difficulties with distributors, the once-robust comics industry seemed doomed. Publishers were trying different ways to revive interest in their books. Superheroes, minor figures compared to the popular horror and science fiction comics of the 1950s, were again getting some play in the comics' pages. In 1960, Atlas (formerly Timely) publisher Goodman noticed the success of the "Justice League of America," or "JLA," a team book published by rival DC. Goodman suggested to Lee that he create a superhero team along the lines of the JLA. Lee, by then "tired of following trends and cranking out hack work," took a gamble on his wife's advice, remarked the writer in *St. James Encyclopedia of Popular Culture.* Lee's wife advised him to write the book however he wanted; at best, Goodman would like it, and at worst, he'd fire Lee, which would allow Lee to leave the industry as he'd been planning. In response, Lee created *The Fantastic Four,* which appeared in 1961 and became the keystone of what would eventually be known as The Marvel Universe and a publishing epoch called The Marvel Age of Comics.

Other titles quickly followed the successful *Fantastic Four.* In collaboration with artist Jack Kirby, Lee was cocreator of characters such as the Incredible Hulk, the X-Men, and the Mighty Thor. In 1962, Lee and artist Steve Ditko created the Amazing Spider-Man. Appearing in *Amazing Fantasy,* Number 15, the final issue of a comic featuring predominantly science fiction and twist-ending fantasy stories, Spider-Man was well received and remained consistently popular from the feature's inception. Lee and Kirby began fleshing out The Fantastic Four, a team of four superheroes who argued, sulked, and fought among themselves more like a family than a group of colleagues—indeed, Sue Storm (the Invisible Girl) and Johnny Storm (the Human Torch) were siblings; Reed Richards (Mr. Fantastic) would eventually wed Sue; and Ben Grimm (the Thing) was a close friend of Reed's. "In collaboration with Jack Kirby, Lee made 'The Fantastic Four' grander, wackier, and at the same time, more human than anything the competition was producing," wrote the *St. James Encyclopedia of Popular Culture* essayist. "Most of the grandeur came from the imagination and pencil of Jack Kirby, but the humanity and sense of fun came from the dialogue and captions written by Stan Lee." Throughout the 1960s, Marvel's characters evolved and took on a greater sophistication as The Marvel Age of Comics unfolded. "The Marvel Age brought its own sensibility and vernacular expressed by characters who developed through their adventures instead of merely bouncing over tall buildings in a single bound from one escapade to the next," wrote Frank Houston on the *Salon.com* Web site.

Frequently credited with having revolutionized the comic-book industry, Lee created characters who appeal not only to the traditional adolescent comic-book audience, but also to college students. In *Quest,* Lee offered this explanation of the broad appeal of his work: "For the younger reader, there were colorful costumes, action, excitement, fantasy, and bigger-than-life adventures. For the newly proselytized older reader, we offered unexpectedly sophisticated plots and subplots, a college-level vocabulary, satire, science fiction, and as many philosophical and sociological concepts as we could devise."

Among the "sociological concepts" or social problems that Spider-Man comics have dealt with over the years are drug abuse, pollution, and racial injustice. "From 1967 to 1973, Spider-Man addressed himself to every important issue confronting American Society," wrote Salvatore Mondello in his essay on Spider-Man for the *Journal of Popular Culture.* "Once contemporary issues were discussed, 'The Amazing Spider-Man' became a subtle persuader, fashioning and reflecting public and popular attitudes under the rubric of entertainment." It was during this period that Spider-Man's popularity on college campuses blossomed. "In an era demanding relevance," Mondello noted, "few magazines were more typical or current than Lee's comic book."

Critics provide several explanations for the popular appeal of Lee's comic-book characters. One oft-cited explanation is that each of Lee's heroes, in addition to having a variety of superpowers, has flaws—human failings with which readers can identify. Peter Parker, a postgraduate science student whose encounter with a radioactive spider left him with spider-like superpowers, is one example. As Spider-Man, Parker uses his web-spinning powers to fight such villains as the Cyclone, Doctor Octopus, the Kingpin, and the Lizard. An impressive superhero, Parker is nonetheless a pitiable character who suffers from financial worries, dandruff, and an overprotective aunt. "Sure, he's a superhero," Lee admitted in *Quest.* "Sure, he's a regular one-man army. Sure, he's practically indestructible. But you're a lot better off. You seem to handle life's little vicissitudes far better than he can. Even though he's a living legend, you can feel superior to him. Now, how can you help but love a guy like that?" Though comics

have long been considered part of the children's demographic, Lee avoided focusing on any particular age group. "When I was at Marvel, in all honesty, I tried to write stories that would interest me," Lee said in an interview for *Brandweek.* "I'd say, what would I like to read? Then I'd try to write them clearly enough so that a youngster could enjoy and appreciate and understand the story, and I tried to write them intelligently enough so that an older person would enjoy it, too." Lee's work helped spark the revolution in thinking that comic books were not simply a children's entertainment medium, a renaissance that persists today with the increasingly popular form of graphic novels and consistent adult interest in traditional-form comic books.

The audience for Lee's comic books eventually grew to include college students and professors. Several colleges now offer courses on popular culture that feature many of Lee's characters, and Lee himself discusses his creations in lectures on college campuses. He is recognized by colleagues and literary critics alike for his significant contributions to the comic-book industry and to the comic book as an art form. According to Jeanette Kahn, publisher of *Superman* comic books, among others, at DC Comics, Lee is "the living superhero for the American comic industry."

With collaborator George Mair, Lee presented an autobiographical account of his life and industry history in *Excelsior! The Amazing Life of Stan Lee.* The book's title is based on one of the many catchphrases Lee used in his bombastic work for Marvel Comics. He would often conclude text pieces or his "Stan's Soapbox" editorial feature with the word "Excelsior!" as a combination of signature statement, rousing cheer, and exhortation to his readers to bigger and better things—though few probably knew that Lee had adopted the word because it sounded noble and dignified, and that excelsior was actually a type of packing material. In the book, Lee traces his career from the early days of comics in the 1940s to his height as the living embodiment of Marvel Comics. The Stan Lee persona is evident throughout the book, observed Stephen Weiner in *Library Journal.* The narrative "tone is warm, straight-talking, and simultaneously confident and insecure—the same traits with which Lee imbued his superheroes."

A detailed critical biography of Lee appeared in 2003. *Stan Lee and the Rise and Fall of the American Comic Book,* by Jordan Raphael and Tom Spurgeon, provides a detailed examination of Lee's development as a writer, his role in the creation of Marvel comics and in the comic-book renaissance of the early 1960s, and his place in the inexorable decline of the industry throughout the 1990s. Both Raphael and Spurgeon are well-steeped in the history and current state of the comic industry as both fans and serious journalists in the comics field, and their work is "an earnest, well-researched portrait of Marvel's mostly beloved living icon," wrote Richard Pachter on the *Miami Herald* Web site. Along with the positive side of Lee's long tenure in the industry, the authors also dissect the darker elements, including assertions that Lee has long accepted more credit for the creation of the early Marvel characters than he was due, at the expense of artist collaborators such as Jack Kirby and Steve Ditko. Raphael and Spurgeon "give Lee his due for shepherding Marvel Comics to the apex of the industry," Meagher wrote on the *CNN* Web site. "They also deflate some of the claims Lee, his fans, and his company have made about the role he played in giving birth to some of Marvel's iconic characters." Still, "the authors make an unimpeachable case for [Lee's] accomplishments as an editor, packager, production manager, and promoter," Pachter remarked, roles that "may have had more significance than the actual comics" in the company's growth as it outstripped rival publishers such as DC Comics.

Lee continues to be active in the print and video entertainment industry. In 2001, Lee formed his own production company, POW! Entertainment, which has secured deals with a number of companies for both children's entertainment features and programs for older viewers. POW! (at first glance a tribute to stereotypical comic-book sound effects, but which Lee says stands for Purveyors of Wonder) focuses on movies, television shows, and animation, according to an interview with Lee on the *GameNow* Web site. Lee was signed by video game producer Activision in late 2003 to work on games based on Marvel Comics characters. In July, 2003, Lee's character Stripperella debuted in an animated feature on TNN, later to be known as SpikeTV. With the tagline "Stripper by night, superhero by later night," the show follows the adventures of Erotica Jones, a stripper turned do-gooder who combats crime with fighting moves direct from the brass pole and with clever gadgets concealed in skimpy clothing and cosmetic cases. The show courts the adult male audience sought by SpikeTV with its double entendres, ribald storylines, and abundant animation of the female form. Although the character may be considered a bit of a departure from Lee's usual wholesome super characters, it is a parody rather than a straightforward drama, "a funny spoof of superheroes," wrote Shawn McKenzie on the *Entertain Your Brain!* Web site. Heavy with "pop-culture references, celebrity voices, and music-video pyrotechnics," the show provides a look at what might happen if Stan Lee "went to work for MTV," wrote Hal Erickson on the MSN Web site.

Lee's post-Marvel undertakings have not all been successful. An experiment in creating online comics ended in failure for Lee when one of his partners in Stan Lee Media was hit with criminal charges and the company failed. Bankruptcy proceedings at Marvel Comics resulted in contract difficulties for Lee—he had been under perpetual contract with the company he helped build, but Marvel's financial problems let Lee out of his exclusive deal. Eventually, Lee also sued over compensation from some of the highly successful Marvel-based films that have appeared since *Blade* and *X-Men* blazed onto the screen. But these setbacks came to be little more than the type of temporary defeat that Lee consistently used to create drama for his characters. He continues to write, produce, and create in the field that he has embraced for more than six decades.

Lee's quirky, soul-searching superheroes have entertained generations of avid readers, sparked nascent imaginations, increased vocabularies and reading abilities, and inspired philosophical contemplation of deceptively simple concepts such as "with great power comes great responsibility." In comics, "Lee's career is basically 'a meditation on the potential of the most damaged individuals to transcend the self-destructive society in which they operate,'" wrote the essayist in *Authors and Artists for Young Adults*. "For this new generation of superheroes, the super power itself is one element of their angst. In creating such a cast of unwilling heroes, Lee and company also revamped the idea of what constitutes heroism in America."

BIOGRAPHICAL AND CRITICAL SOURCES:

BOOKS

Authors and Artists for Young Adults, Volume 49, Thomson Gale (Detroit, MI), 2003.
Berger, Arthur Asa, *The Comic-Stripped American,* Walker (New York, NY), 1973.
Contemporary Literary Criticism, Volume 17, Thomson Gale (Detroit, MI), 1981.
Harvey, Robert C., *The Art of the Comic Book,* University Press of Mississippi (Jackson, MS), 1996.
Jones, Gerard, and Will Jacobs, *The Great Comic Book Heroes,* Prima Publishing (Rocklin, CA), 1997.
Kraft, David Anthony, *Captain America: The Secret Story of Marvel's Star-Spangled Super Hero,* Children's Press (Chicago, IL), 1981.

Kraft, David Anthony, *The Fantastic Four: The Secret Story of Marvel's Cosmic Quartet,* Children's Press (Chicago, IL), 1981.

Kraft, David Anthony, *The Incredible Hulk: The Secret Story of Marvel's Gamma-Powered Goliath,* Children's Press (Chicago, IL), 1981.

Lee, Stan, and George Mair *Excelsior! The Amazing Life of Stan Lee* (autobiography), Simon & Schuster (New York, NY), 2002.

Raphael, Jordan, and Tom Spurgeon, *Stan Lee and the Rise and Fall of the American Comic Book,* Chicago Review Press (Chicago, IL), 2003.

St. James Encyclopedia of Popular Culture, St. James Press (Detroit, MI), 2000.

PERIODICALS

AdWeek, May 1, 2000, Steve Pond, "Marvel Comics' Master Creates New Heroes for the Web," p. 30.

Best Sellers, March, 1985, review of *Dunn's Conundrum,* p. 454.

Booklist, February 1, 1990, review of *Marvel Masterworks Presents Amazing Spider-Man,* p. 1080; November 1, 1995, Carl Hays, review of *The Ultimate Silver Surfer,* p. 458; November 1, 1995, review of *The Ultimate Silver Surfer,* p. 461.

Books & Bookmen, review of *Dunn's Conundrum,* p. 30.

Bookwatch, January, 1996, review of *The Ultimate Silver Surfer,* p. 1.

Brandweek, May 1, 2002, Steve Pond, interview with Stan Lee.

Comic Book Marketplace, July, 1993, Bob Brodsky, "Maestro of the Marvel Mythos," pp. 28-54.

Entertainment Weekly, May 24, 2002, Marc Bernardin, review of *Excelsior! The Amazing Life of Stan Lee,* p. 90.

Independent (London, England), June 27, 2002, "How I Got Here: Stan Lee, Creator of Spider-Man," p. 15; July 1, 2002, Charles Shaar, "The Monday Book: The Amazing Life of Mr. Marvel by His Biggest Fan," p. 12.

Industry Standard, March 19, 2001, Laura Rich, "The Trials of a Comic-Book Hero," p. 45.

Interview, October, 1991, Henry Cabot Beck, "The Amazing Stan Lee," pp. 110-111.

Journal of Popular Culture, summer, 1976; fall, 1994, "Cultural and Mythical Aspects of a Superhero: The Silver Surfer, 1969-1970," pp. 203-213.

Kirkus Reviews, October 15, 1984, review of *Dunn's Conundrum,* p. 977; November 15, 1989, review of *The GOD Project,* p. 148; October 15, 1994, review of *The Ultimate Spider-Man,* p. 1366.

Library Journal, December, 1984, review of *Dunn's Conundrum,* p. 2298; January, 1990, review of *The GOD Project,* p. 148; December, 1994, review of *The Ultimate Spider-Man,* p. 139; October 15, 1995, review of *The Ultimate Silver Surfer,* p. 91; May 15, 2002, Stephen Weiner, review of *Excelsior!,* p. 93.

Listener, July 18, 1935, review of *Dunn's Conundrum,* p. 29.

Locus, January, 1995, review of *The Ultimate Spider-Man,* p. 50.

New Republic, July 19, 1975.

New Statesman, April 19, 1985, review of *Dunn's Conundrum,* p. 109.

New York Times, December 31, 1979; October 21, 1999, Frank Houston, "Creator of Fantastic Four Is Ready to Spin More Tales On-Line," p. D8; May 3, 2002, Peter M. Nichols, "How Spidey Was Hatched," p. E3.

New York Times Book Review, September 5, 1976; November 18, 1979; April 7, 1985, review of *Dunn's Conundrum,* p. 90; January 14, 1990, review of *The GOD Project,* p. 23.

Observer (London, England), April 14, 1985, review of *Dunn's Conundrum,* p. 23.

People, January 29, 1979.

Publishers Weekly, January 4, 1985, review of *Dunn's Conundrum,* p. 60; November 8, 1985, review of *Dunn's Conundrum,* p. 59; November 24, 1989, review of *The GOD Project,* p. 59; October 11, 1993, review of *How to Draw Comics the Marvel Way,* p. 56; October 11, 1993, review of the "Marvel Masterworks" series, p. 56; October 22, 2001, review of *The Alien Factor,* p. 54.

Quest, July-August, 1977.

Rolling Stone, September 16, 1971.

San Francisco Review of Books, March, 1995, review of *The Best of the World's Worst,* p. 36.

School Library Journal, May, 1996, Karen Sokoll, review of *The Ultimate Spider-Man,* p. 148; May, 2002, James O. Cahill, review of *The Alien Factor,* pp. 179-180.

Science Fiction Chronicle, June, 1995, review of *The Ultimate Spider-Man,* p. 38; May, 1996, review of *The Ultimate Silver Surfer,* p. 61; April, 2002, review of *Five Decades of the X-Men,* p. 50.

Tampa Tribune, March 8, 2002, "Caught Up Again by Hero Spider-Man," p. 1.

Time, February 5, 1979; February 14, 2000, "Look Up on the Net! It's . . . Cyber Comics: Stan Lee Takes *The 7th Portal* and Backstreet Boys On-Line," p. 76.

Tribune Books (Chicago, IL), February 18, 1990, review of *The GOD Project,* p. 7.

USA Today, January 4, 1985, review of *Dunn's Conundrum,* p. 3D.

Variety, September 17, 1986, Tom Bierbaum, "Stan Lee's Imperfect Heroes Lifted Marvel to Top of Heap," pp. 81-82.

Video Business, April 22, 2002, Lawrence Lerman, "Along Came a Spider-Man," p. 24.

Village Voice, December 23, 1974; December 15, 1975; December 13, 1976.

Voice of Youth Advocates, June, 1985, review of *Dunn's Conundrum,* p. 132; October, 1995, review of *The Ultimate Spider-Man,* p. 207; April, 1997, review of *The Ultimate X-Men,* p. 48.

Wall Street Journal, August 23, 1999, Colleen DeBaise, "Spider-Man Creator Takes Comics to the Web," p. B6F.

Washington Post, February 4, 1992, Richard Harrington, "Stan Lee: Caught in Spidey's Web," p. D1.

World & I, review of *The Silver Surfer,* p. 435.

ONLINE

Animation World Web site, http://www.awn.com/ (July, 1997), Michael Goodman, "Stan Lee: Comic Guru."

CNN.com, http://www.cnn.com/ (May 4, 2002), "Stan Lee: 'Insectman' Just Didn't Sound Right," interview with Stan Lee; (October 8, 2003), L.D. Meagher, "New Biography Offers Context for Marvel Comics King," review of *Stan Lee and the Rise and Fall of the American Comic Book.*

Entertain Your Brain! Web site, http://www.entertainyourbrain.com/ (July 4, 2003), review of *Stripperella.*

GameNow Web site, http://www.gamenowmag.com/ (October 1, 2003), "Call Me Stan," interview with Stan Lee.

Green Man Review On-Line, http://www.greenmanreview.com/ (November 7, 2003), Michael M. Jones, review of *Stan Lee and the Rise and Fall of the American Comic Book.*

IGN FilmForce Web site, http://www.filmforce.igm.com/ (June 26, 2000), Kenneth Plume, "Interview with Stan Lee"; (April 20, 2002), Kenneth Plume, "Nuff Said—An Interview with Stan Lee."

Lambiek, http://www.lambiek.net/ (November 7, 2003), biography of Stan Lee.

L.A. Weekly On-Line, http://www.laweekly.com/ (January 4-10, 2002), Jonathan Vankin, "The Neurotic Superhero: Stan Lee and His Human Marvels."

Miami Herald On-Line http://www.miamiherald.com/ (September 1, 2003), Richard Pachter, "Comic-Book Industry Comes to Life in Authors' Hands," review of *Stan Lee and the Rise and Fall of the American Comic Book.*

MSN, http://entertainment.msn.com/ (November 7, 2003), review of *Stripperella.*

Onion A.V. Club, http: //www.theonionavclub.com/ (June 20, 2001), Tasha Robinson, "Stan Lee."

Salon.com, http://www.salon.com/ (August 17, 1999), Frank Houston, "Brilliant Careers: Stan Lee."

Spiderman Insider Web site, http://www.spidermaninsider.com/ (November 7, 2003), biography of Stan Lee.

Stan Lee and the Rise and Fall of the American Comic Book Web site, http://www.stanleebook.com/ (November 7, 2003).

*   *   *

Le GUIN, Ursula K. 1929-
(Ursula Kroeber Le Guin)

PERSONAL: Surname pronounced "luh-gwin" born October 21, 1929, in Berkeley, CA; daughter of Alfred L. (an anthropologist) and Theodora Covel Brown (a writer; maiden name, Kracaw) Kroeber; married Charles Alfred Le Guin (an historian), December 22, 1953; children: Elisabeth, Caroline, Theodore. *Education:* Radcliffe College, A.B., 1951; Columbia University, A.M., 1952.

ADDRESSES: Agent—Virginia Kidd, P.O. Box 278, Milford, PA 18337; and c/o Matthew Bialer, William Morris Agency, 1350 Avenue of the Americas, New York, NY 10019-4702.

CAREER: Writer. Part-time instructor in French at Mercer University, 1954-55, and University of Idaho, 1956; Emory University, department secretary, 1955; visiting lecturer and writer-in-residence at various locations, including Pacific University, Portland State University, University of California, San Diego, University of Reading, Kenyon College, Tulane University, and First Australian Workshop in Speculative Fiction. Guest of honor at science fiction conventions, including World Science Fiction Convention, 1975. Creative consultant for Public Broadcasting Service television production *The Lathe of Heaven,* 1979.

MEMBER: Authors League of America, Writers Guild, PEN, Science Fiction Research Association, Science Fiction and Fantasy Writers of America, Science Fiction

Poetry Association, Writers Guild West, Amnesty International of the USA, National Abortion Rights Action League, National Organization for Women, Nature Conservancy, Planned Parenthood Federation of America, Women's International League for Peace and Freedom, Phi Beta Kappa.

AWARDS, HONORS: Fulbright fellowship, 1953; *Boston Globe-Horn Book* Award, 1968, Lewis Carroll Shelf Award, 1979; Nebula Award nomination for best novelette, Science Fiction Writers of America (now Science Fiction and Fantasy Writers of America), 1969, for "Nine Lives"; Nebula Award and Hugo Award, International Science Fiction Association, both for best novel, 1970, for *The Left Hand of Darkness;* Nebula Award nomination, 1971, and Hugo Award nomination, and *Locus* Award, both 1973, all for best novel, all for *The Lathe of Heaven;* Newbery Silver Medal Award, and finalist for National Book Award for Children's Literature, both 1972, both for *The Tombs of Atuan;* National Book Award for Children's Books, 1973, for *The Farthest Shore;* Nebula Award nomination, 1972, and Hugo Award, 1973, both for best novella, both for *The Word for World Is Forest;* Hugo Award for best short story, 1974, for "The Ones Who Walk away from Omelas"; American Library Association's Best Young Adult Books citation, 1974, Hugo Award, Nebula Award, and Jupiter Award, all for best novel, 1975, and Jules Verne Award, 1975, all for *The Dispossessed: An Ambiguous Utopia;* Nebula Award, and Jupiter Award, both for best short story, 1975, both for "The Day before the Revolution"; Nebula Award nomination for best novelette, 1975, for "The New Atlantis," 1979, for "The Pathways of Desire," 1988, for *Buffalo Gals, Won't You Come out Tonight,* and 1990, for "The Shobies' Story"; Nebula Award nomination for best novelette, and Jupiter Award, both 1976, both for "The Diary of the Rose"; Prix Lectures-Jeunesse, 1987, for *Very Far away from Anywhere Else;* Gandalf Award (Grand Master of Fantasy) nomination, 1978, and award, 1979; D.Litt., Bucknell University, 1978, and Lawrence University, 1979; D.H.L., Lewis and Clark College, 1983, and Occidental College, 1985; *Locus* Award, 1984, for *The Compass Rose;* American Book Award nomination, 1985, and Janet Heidinger Kafka Prize for Fiction, University of Rochester English Department and Writer's Workshop, 1986, both for *Always Coming Home;* Hugo Award for Best Novelette, World Science Fiction Society, and World Fantasy Convention Award for Best Novella, both 1988, both for *Buffalo Gals, Won't You Come out Tonight;* Nebula Award for best novel, 1991, for *Tehanu;* Nebula Award nomination for best novelette, 1994, and James Tiptree, Jr. Award, 1995, both for "The Matter of Seggri"; Nebula Award nomination for

best novella, 1994, and Sturgeon Award, both for *Forgiveness Day;* Nebula Award for best novelette, 1996, for *Solitude;* Life Achievement award, World Fantasy Convention, 1995; James Tiptree, Jr. Award, 1997, for "Mountain Ways"; Mythopoeic Fantasy Award in Adult Literature finalist, World Fantasy Award for best novel, and Nebula Award nomination for best novel, all 2002, all for *The Other Wind;* named Nebula Award Grand Master, 2002; Hugo Award nomination for best novelette, 2003, for "The Wild Girls"; Margaret A. Edwards Award, YALSA, 2004.

WRITINGS:

NOVELS (EXCEPT AS INDICATED)

Rocannon's World (bound with *The Kar-Chee Reign* by Avram Davidson; also see below), Ace Books (New York, NY), 1966.

Planet of Exile (bound with *Mankind under the Lease* by Thomas M. Disch; also see below), Ace Books (New York, NY), 1966.

City of Illusions (also see below), Ace Books (New York, NY), 1967.

Three Hainish Novels (contains *Rocannon's World, Planet of Exile,* and *City of Illusions*), Doubleday (New York, NY), 1967, published as *Worlds of Exile and Illusion,* Orb, 1996.

A Wizard of Earthsea (also see below), illustrated by Ruth Robbins, Parnassus Press (Berkeley, CA), 1968.

The Left Hand of Darkness, Walker (New York, NY), 1969, with new afterword and appendixes by Le Guin, 1994.

The Tombs of Atuan (sequel to *A Wizard of Earthsea;* also see below), illustrated by Gail Garraty, Atheneum (New York, NY), 1971.

The Lathe of Heaven (also see below), Scribner (New York, NY), 1971.

The Farthest Shore (sequel to *The Tombs of Atuan;* also see below), illustrated by Gail Garraty, Atheneum (New York, NY), 1972.

The Dispossessed: An Ambiguous Utopia, Harper (New York, NY), 1974, reprinted, Perennial Classics (New York, NY), 2003.

Very Far Away from Anywhere Else, Atheneum (New York, NY), 1976, published as *A Very Long Way from Anywhere Else,* Gollancz (London, England), 1976, reprinted under original title, Harcourt (Orlando, FL), 2004.

Earthsea (contains *A Wizard of Earthsea, The Tombs of Atuan,* and *The Farthest Shore*), Gollancz (London, England), 1977, published as *The Earthsea Trilogy,* Penguin (London, England), 1979.

Malafrena, Putnam (New York, NY), 1979.

The Beginning Place, Harper (New York, NY), 1980, published as *Threshold,* Gollancz (London, England), 1980.

The Eye of the Heron, and Other Stories (includes novella originally published in *Millennial Women;* also see below), Panther (London, England), 1980, Harper (New York, NY), 1983.

The Visionary: The Life Story of Flicker of the Serpentine (bound with *Wonders Hidden: Audubon's Early Years,* by Scott Russell Sanders), Capra (Santa Barbara, CA), 1984.

Always Coming Home (includes audiocassette of "Music and Poetry of the Kesh," with music by Todd Barton; also see below), illustrated by Margaret Chodos, Harper (New York, NY), 1985, published without audiocassette, Bantam (New York, NY), 1987.

Tehanu: The Last Book of Earthsea (sequel to *The Farthest Shore*), Atheneum (New York, NY), 1990.

(Reteller)*Lao Tzu: Tao Te Ching: A Book about the Way and the Power of the Way,* English translation by J.P. Seaton, Shambhala (Boston, MA), 1997.

Steering the Craft: Exercises and Discussions on Story Writing for the Lone Navigator or the Mutinous Crew (nonfiction), Eighth Mountain Press, 1998.

The Telling, Harcourt (New York, NY), 2000.

The Other Wind (sequel to *Tehanu*), Harcourt (New York, NY), 2001.

Tales from Earthsea, Harcourt (New York, NY), 2001.

FOR CHILDREN

Solomon Leviathan's 931st Trip around the World (originally published in *Puffin's Pleasures*), illustrated by Alicia Austin, Puffin (London, England), 1976, Cheap Street (New Castle, VA), 1983.

Leese Webster, illustrated by James Brunsman, Atheneum (New York, NY), 1979.

The Adventures of Cobbler's Rune, illustrated by Alicia Austin, Cheap Street (New Castle, VA), 1982.

Adventures in Kroy, Cheap Street (New Castle, VA), 1982.

A Visit from Dr. Katz (picture book), illustrated by Ann Barrow, Atheneum (New York, NY), 1988, published as *Dr. Katz,* Collins (London, England), 1988.

Catwings, illustrated by S.D. Schindler, Orchard Books (New York, NY), 1988.

Catwings Return, illustrated by S.D. Schindler, Orchard Books (New York, NY), 1989.

Fire and Stone, Atheneum (New York, NY), 1989.

Fish Soup, illustrated by Patrick Wynne, Atheneum (New York, NY), 1992.

A Ride on the Red Mare's Back, illustrated by Julie Downing, Orchard Books (New York, NY), 1992.

Buffalo Gals, Won't You Come out Tonight, illustrated by Susan Seddon Boulet, Pomegranate Artbooks (San Francisco, CA), 1994.

Wonderful Alexander and the Catwings, illustrated by S.D. Schindler, Orchard Books (New York, NY), 1994.

Jane On Her Own, illustrations by S.D. Schindler, Orchard Books (New York, NY), 2001.

Tom Mouse, illustrated by Julie Downing, Roaring Brook Press, 2002.

Gifts (young adult novel), Harcourt (Orlando, FL), 2004.

OTHER

Wild Angels (collection of early works), Capra, 1975.

(With mother, Theodora K. Quinn) *Tillai and Tylissos,* Red Bull, 1979.

The Word for World Is Forest (novella; originally published in *Again, Dangerous Visions;* also see below), Berkley (New York, NY), 1972.

From Elfland to Poughkeepsie (lecture), introduction by Vonda N. McIntyre, Pendragon Press (Portland, OR), 1973.

The Wind's Twelve Quarters: Short Stories, Harper (New York, NY), 1975.

Dreams Must Explain Themselves (critical essays), Algol Press (New York, NY), 1975.

(With Gene Wolfe and James Tiptree, Jr.) *The New Atlantis and Other Novellas of Science Fiction,* edited by Robert Silverberg, Hawthorn Books (New York, NY), 1975.

Orsinian Tales (short stories), Harper (New York, NY), 1976.

The Water Is Wide (short story), Pendragon Press (Portland, OR), 1976.

(With others) *The Altered I: An Encounter with Science Fiction* (includes Le Guin's play *No Use to Talk to Me*), edited by Lee Harding, Norstrilia Press (Melbourne, Australia), 1976.

(Editor) *Nebula Award Stories 11,* Gollancz (London, England), 1976, Harper (New York, NY), 1977.

The Language of the Night: Essays on Fantasy and Science Fiction (critical essays), edited by Susan Wood, Putnam (New York, NY), 1979, revised edition, edited by Le Guin, Women's Press, 1989.

(Editor, with Virginia Kidd) *Interfaces: An Anthology of Speculative Fiction,* Ace Books (New York, NY), 1980.

(Editor, with Virginia Kidd) *Edges: Thirteen New Tales from the Borderlands of the Imagination,* Pocket Books (New York, NY), 1980.

Torrey Pines Reserve (broadsheet), Lord John (Northridge, CA), 1980.

Hard Words, and Other Poems, Harper (New York, NY), 1981.

Gwilan's Harp, Lord John (Northridge, CA), 1981.

The Compass Rose (short stories), Harper (New York, NY), 1982.

(With artist Henk Pander) *In the Red Zone,* Lord John (Northridge, CA), 1983.

King Dog: A Screenplay (bound with *Dostoevsky: The Screenplay,* by Raymond Carver and Tess Gallagher), Capra, 1985.

(With Todd Barton) *Music and Poetry of the Kesh* (audiocassette), Valley Productions, 1985.

(With David Bedford) *Rigel Nine: An Audio Opera* (recording), Charisma, 1985.

(With composer Elinor Armer) *Uses of Music in Uttermost Parts* (music and text), first performed in San Francisco, CA, 1986.

Buffalo Gals and Other Animal Presences (short stories and poems), Capra, 1987, published as *Buffalo Gals,* Gollancz (London, England), 1990.

Wild Oats and Fireweed, Harper (New York, NY), 1988.

Dancing at the Edge of the World: Thoughts on Words, Women, Places (essays), Grove (New York, NY), 1989.

The Way the Water's Going: Images of the Northern California Coastal Range, photographs by Ernest Waugh and Alan Nicolson, Harper (New York, NY), 1989.

Searoad: Chronicles of Klatsand (short stories), HarperCollins (New York, NY), 1991.

Myth and Archetype in Science Fiction, Pulphouse, 1991.

Talk about Writing, Pulphouse, 1991.

Blue Moon over Thurman Street, photographs by Roger Dorband, NewSage Press (Portland, OR), 1993.

Earthsea Revisioned (lecture), Children's Literature New England (Cambridge, MA), 1993.

The Ones Who Walk away from Omelas (short story), Creative Education (Mankato, MN), 1993.

(Editor with Brian Attebery) *The Norton Book of Science Fiction: North American Science Fiction, 1960-1990,* Norton (New York, NY), 1993.

Going Out with Peacocks and Other Poems, HarperPerennial (New York, NY), 1994.

A Fisherman of the Inland Sea: Science Fiction Stories, HarperPrism (New York, NY), 1994.

Four Ways to Forgiveness (contains "Betrayals," "Forgiveness Day," "A Man of the People," and "A Woman's Liberation"), HarperPrism (New York, NY), 1995.

Unlocking the Air: And Other Stories (includes "Standing Ground," "Poacher," "Half Past Four," and "Limberlost"), HarperCollins (New York, NY), 1996.

(With Diana Bellessi) *The Twins, The Dream–Two Voices,* Arte Publico Press, 1996.

The Birthday of the World and Other Stories, HarperCollins (New York, NY), 2002.

Changing Planes (short stories), illustrated by Eric Beddows, Harcourt (New York, NY), 2003.

(Translator) Angélica Gorodischer, *Kalpa Imperial: The Greatest Empire That Never Was,* Small Beer Press (Northampton, MA), 2003.

The Wave in the Mind: Talks and Essays on the Writer, the Reader, and the Imagination, Shambhala (Boston, MA), 2004.

(Editor and author of introduction) *Selected Stories of H.G. Wells,* Modern Library (New York, NY), 2004.

Author of postcard short story, *Post Card Partnership,* 1975, and *Sword & Sorcery Annual,* 1975. "The Matter of Seggri" published in *Nebula Awards 30,* Harcourt, 1996. Author of novelette "The Wild Girls." Contributor to anthologies, including *Orbit 5,* 1969, *World's Best Science Fiction,* 1970, *The Best Science Fiction of the Year No. 5,* 1976, and *The Norton Anthology of Short Fiction,* 1978. Contributor of short stories, novellas, essays, and reviews to numerous science fiction, scholarly, and popular periodicals, including *Amazing Science Fiction, Science-Fiction Studies, New Yorker, Antaeus, Parabola, New Republic, Redbook, Playgirl, Playboy, New Yorker, Western Humanities Review, Yale Review,* and *Omni.*

ADAPTATIONS: The Lathe of Heaven was adapted for television by Public Broadcasting Service, 1979, and by Alan Sharp for A & E, 2002; *The Tombs of Atuan* was adapted as a filmstrip with record or audiocassette by Newbery Award Records, 1980; "The Ones Who Walk away from Omelas" was performed as a drama with dance and music at the Portland Civic Theatre, 1981.

WORK IN PROGRESS: Translator for Gabriela Mistral's *Gabriela Mistral: Selected Poems,* for University of New Mexico Press.

SIDELIGHTS: Critics have often found it difficult to classify the works of American author Ursula K. Le Guin: while some consider her writing science fiction or fantasy, Le Guin herself discounts any narrow genre categorizations. As she once explained, "some of my fiction is 'science fiction,' some of it is 'fantasy,' some of it is 'realist,' and some of it is 'magical realism.'" Le Guin has also written several volumes of poetry and essays. "A significant amount of science fiction has been profoundly thoughtful about the situation of contemporary humanity in the light of its possible futures and its imaginable alternatives," writes Derek de Solla Price in *New Republic,* adding that, "In recent years, no [writer] inside the field of science fiction or outside of it [has] done more to create a modern conscience than . . . Le Guin." Critics have distinguished Le Guin's work from other twentieth-century futurists such as George Orwell and Aldous Huxley, however. According to George Edgar Slusser in his *The Farthest Shores of Ursula Le Guin,* the author's "social analysis is acute, but its purpose is not indignation or reform. She has no social program, offers no panaceas." A *Cambridge Review* contributor described Le Guin as "an elegant, but not a light writer: not to be trifled with. Superficially, her work charms because it has all the glitter of high intelligence and efficiency."

Le Guin was born in Berkeley, California, to prominent anthropologist Alfred Kroeber and writer Theodora Kroeber. She studied Renaissance history as a graduate student at Columbia University and, after obtaining her master's degree, married history professor Charles Le Guin. In addition to introducing her to history and anthropology, Le Guin's formative environment gave her a perspective on religion different from that of many Americans. As she once told an interviewer, "My father was a cultural relativist. . . . I was brought up in an unreligious household; there was no religious practice of any kind. There was also no feeling that any religion was better than another, or worse; they just weren't part of our life."

Le Guin began her writing career with short fiction, and her first short story, "An die Musik," appeared in *Western Humanities Review* in 1961. A later story, "The Dowry of Angyar," which was published in *Amazing Science Fiction* in 1964, provided the impetus for Le Guin's first novel, *Rocannon's World.* "I always wanted to write, and I always knew it would be hard to make a living at it," she explained to *Boston Globe* contributor Maureen Dezell. "I was very arrogant and wanted to be free to write what I wanted to write and see if I could get it published on my own terms. I did, eventually. But it took a long time." Le Guin has been rewarded for her persistence and her vision on numerous occasions, winning the prestigious Nebula and Hugo awards for her short works, including the novella *The Word for World Is Forest* and "The Ones Who Walk away from Omelas."

The Word for World is Forest and the short story "The Ones Who Walked away from Omelas" introduce the themes that Le Guin threads throughout her fiction. *The Word for World Is Forest* looks at the use of force levied against an alien people, and many have interpreted it as a reflection on the U.S. intervention in Vietnam during the 1960s and early 1970s. "At the same time," cautioned Ian Watson in *Science-Fiction Studies,* "the obvious Vietnam analogy should not blind one to other relevant contemporary analogies—the genocide of the Guyaki Indians of Paraguay, or the genocide and deforestation along the Trans-Amazon Highway in Brazil, or even the general destruction of rainforest habitats from Indonesia to Costa Rica. Le Guin's story is multi-applicable—and multi-faceted."

"The Ones Who Walk away from Omelas" explains the necessity of individual morality. The society of Omelas is one of utopian happiness based on the unhappiness of a single scapegoat, who suffers for the entire community. According to Shoshana Knapp in *Journal of Narrative Technique,* in this short story "the world created is unfit for human habitation. The bargain on which it rests violates not only decency but logic. . . . To choose between torturing a child and destroying one's society (which includes other children) is a diabolical choice, not a human one."

Le Guin first began to receive extensive critical and popular attention with her "Earthsea" novels, which include *A Wizard of Earthsea, The Tombs of Atuan, The Farthest Shore, Tehanu,* and *The Other Wind.* The "Earthsea" series, considered by Le Guin to be among her best work, displays a holistic conception of the universe. As Robert Scholes suggested in *Hollins Critic,* "What Earthsea represents, through its world of islands and waterways, is the universe as a dynamic, balanced system . . . which include[s] a role for magic and for powers other than human, but only as aspects of the great Balance or Equilibrium, which is the order of this cosmos. Where C.S. Lewis worked out of a specifically Christian set of values, Ursula Le Guin works not with a theology but with an ecology, a cosmology, a reverence for the universe as a self-regulating structure." The theme of equilibrium between opposing forces works on several levels within the series. On the most immediate and recognizable level is the integration of man with himself. In *A Wizard of Earthsea* it is the young mage, or wizard, Ged who undertakes the journey to maturity and self-knowledge; in *The Tombs of Atuan* it is the girl-priestess, Tenar; and in *The Farthest Shore* it is the young prince Arran, accompanying Ged on a search for the source of an evil spreading through Earthsea. Writing in *Ursula K. Le Guin,* Margaret P. Esmonde suggested that "all of these journeys symbolize the journey every human being must make, one through pain and fear, aided only by trust in the goodness of man, hand holding hand, to the acceptance of mortality."

While Le Guin began her "Earthsea" saga intending to write only a trilogy, eighteen years after the publication of *The Farthest Shore,* a National Book Award-winner in 1973, she surprised and pleased fans with *Tehanu.* The story continues the stories of Ged and Tenar, who are now old, as their now-quiet lives become enmeshed with that of a little girl, Therru, who has been raped and burned but survives. "The astonishing clearsightedness of *Tehanu,*" explained Robin McKinley in *New York Times Book Review,* "is in its recognition of the necessary and life-giving contributions of female magic—sometimes disguised as domesticity." Although Dirda saw the novel as "meditative, somber, even talky," he acknowledged that it "builds to a climax of almost pornographic horror, nearly too shocking for its supposedly young adult pages." "The first three books lay out the answer to the problem of evil with some confidence (lack of balance)," related Meredith Tax in *Village Voice*; "this one asks, like Gertrude Stein on her deathbed, 'What is the question?'"

"Two Le Guin novels of unquestionably high standing, even among readers who generally do not care for science fiction, are *The Left Hand of Darkness* and *The Dispossessed: An Ambiguous Utopia,*" according to *Modern Fiction Studies* contributor Keith N. Hull. "In these novels Le Guin . . . describes herself as writing science fiction based on 'social science, psychology, anthropology [and] history,'" the critic added, noting that the result "is an emphasis on culture" rather than science and technology. *The Left Hand of Darkness* explores the themes of sexual identity, incest, xenophobia, fidelity, and betrayal in a tale of an Earth ambassador, Genly Ai, who is sent to the planet of Gethen, whose inhabitants are androgynous. Through his relationship with a native, Estraven, Ai gains understanding both of the consequences of his fixed sexual orientation and of Gethenian life. As in many of her works, Le Guin incorporates a social message in her science-fiction tale. Scholes maintained that "the great power of the book comes from the way it interweaves all its levels and combines all its voices and values into an ordered, balanced, whole."

In *The Dispossessed* Le Guin's protagonist is an alien in a strange culture; the physicist Shevek, however, is also at odds with his home planet's values. He is de-

voted to the spread of knowledge, but the development of his theories will inevitably bring his isolated colonial planet and its mother-planet into contact, although the two cultures bitterly oppose one another. Brian Attebery, in *Dictionary of Literary Biography,* described the novel's form as "slow, sober, down-to-earth. The writing verges on pure naturalistic reporting, except that the places being written about do not exist on Earth." Attebery praised *The Dispossessed* as "fuller than any other of [Le Guin's] stories in character and in social and political interplay."

A prolific writer, Le Guin's imagination, intellect, and wide-ranging knowledge has allowed her to vary her characters and settings widely. In addition, her novels and short fiction draws readers to different planets and different eras. While some of her novels, like the "Earthsea" books, transport readers from the known universe and the familiar, others adhere to somewhat more familiar spatial and temporal structures, or are at least set within the parameters of human history. The works which form Le Guin's "Hainish Cycle," for example—*Rocannon's World, Planet of Exile, City of Illusions, The Left Hand of Darkness,* and *The Dispossessed,* as well as numerous short stories—are bound by a common historical context: their characters and cultures originated with a race called the Hain, whose history encompasses Earth.

Another book which features a recognizable fictional terrain is *Always Coming Home,* which concerns a people known as the Kesh, who reside in northern California in the wake of nuclear war. The format moves between poetry and prose and includes stories, legends, and "autobiography;" the book was originally published with an audiocassette of Kesh music. Brian D. Johnson in *Maclean's* described *Always Coming Home* as "an 'archaeological dig' into the distant future—a search for 'shards of the broken pot at the end of the rainbow.'" Samuel R. Delany, writing in *New York Times Book Review,* praises the work, noting that, "With high invention and deep intelligence, *Always Coming Home* presents, in alternating narratives, poems and expositions, Ursula K. Le Guin's most consistently lyric and luminous book in a career adorned with some of the most precise and passionate prose in the service of a major imaginative vision." H.J. Kirchhoff in the Toronto *Globe and Mail* praised Le Guin's world-building, and wrote that in *Always Coming Home* the author "has created an entire culture, not just a cast of characters—an impressive achievement from an impressive writer."

Searoad: Chronicles of Klatsand and *Changing Planes* are two of several of Le Guin's collections of short fiction. Set in the Oregon town of Klatsand, *Searoad* follows the outwardly unremarkable lives of its inhabitants. "In understated stories that ask the reader not to pity their marginal characters but to respect their courage," explained Yvonne Fraticelli in *Women's Review of Books,* "Le Guin summons up a host of visionaries, dreamers and solitaries." Reviewing the work for *Belles Lettres,* Juli Duncan asserted that while "the stories are uneven," "each is perfectly tailored to its characters." *Searoad* represents a notable achievement for Le Guin, in the opinion of Patricia Dubrava Keuning in *Bloomsbury Review,* who maintained that *Searoad* is "Le Guin's first purely mainstream book of fiction, and with it, she has accomplished squarely what few writers succeed in doing: She has liberated herself from the genre pigeonhole." Even more liberating is *Changing Planes,* an "unusual travelogue" that presents sixteen stories conjuring up sixteen different modes of interplanetary travel, all united by Le Guin's "dispassion, wry humor, and . . . keen eye," according to *Booklist* contributor Sally Estes. While *Changing Planes* serves as light airport reading, it also is enriched by Le Guin's analytical nature; according to a *Kirkus* reviewer her "unconventional premises are more often than not shaped into entrancing, provocative narratives."

Le Guin's excursions into the world of children's fiction have included *Solomon Leviathan's 931st Trip around the World, Catwings,* and *Catwings Return.* In *Catwings,* four flying cats—Harriet, James, Thelma and Roger—escape city dangers to live in the country, where they are adopted by two children. *A Ride on the Red Mare's Back,* a book for younger children, looks at the issue of avoidance of responsibility. In it, a young girl learns that her little brother has been taken by trolls, and she goes out alone to rescue him, taking only a toy red horse, a warm scarf, knitting needles and yarn, and a bit of bread. Once she locates the boy in the trolls' castle, she finds that he has changed: he now wants to become a troll. "The boy's desire is an old one," Michael Dirda explained in *Washington Post Book World:* "Is it better to be a happy pig or an unhappy Socrates? Most of us don't get the chance to be quite either." Dirda went on to praise *A Ride on the Red Mare's Back* as "indisputably suspenseful, thought-provoking, and beautifully illustrated."

In addition to fiction, Le Guin has authored numerous nonfiction works, among them essays, poetry, and criticism. *Dancing at the Edge of the World: Thoughts on Words, Women, Places* collects several of her essays, addresses, and reviews, creating what *Los Angeles Times Book Review* critic Nancy Mairs described as "a trove of delights: insightful, impassioned, sometimes lyrical, often funny." Le Guin's shorter works also expand readers' understanding of the author's fiction; as Mairs explained, *Dancing at the Edge of the World* provides "insight into the writer at work." Elizabeth Hand, writing in *Washington Post Book World,* maintained that the selections shows Le Guin "at her best: insightful, funny, sharp, occasionally tendentious and nearly always provocative."

Another collection of nonfiction, *The Wave in the Mind: Talks and Essays on the Writer, the Reader, and the Imagination* focuses on the writer's craft as Le Guin has performed it, and also contains critical commentary on such writers as Samuel Clemens (Mark Twain) and Jorge Luis Borges. Praising Le Guin's commentary as "incisive," *Library Journal* contributor Carolyn M. Craft noted that in revealing prose that encompasses the author's recollections of family, reflects upon her personal values, and explores her opinions, the author "engages and challenges her readers' minds and values while . . . modeling good prose style." Hailing *The Wave in the Mind* as a "piquant, morally lucid, and enlivening volume," Donna Seaman added in her *Booklist* review that Le Guin, in addition to being a widely heralded fiction writer, "is also a forthright, incisive, and funny essayist."

BIOGRAPHICAL AND CRITICAL SOURCES:

BOOKS

Authors and Artists for Young Adults, Volume 9, Thomson Gale (Detroit, MI), 1992.

Bittner, James, *Approaches to the Fiction of Ursula K. Le Guin,* UMI Research Press (Ann Arbor, MI), 1984.

Bucknall, Barbara J., *Ursula K. Le Guin,* Ungar (New York, NY), 1981.

Children's Literature Review, Thomson Gale (Detroit, MI), Volume 3, 1978; Volume 28, 1992.

Cogell, Elizabeth Cummins, *Ursula K. Le Guin: A Primary and Secondary Bibliography,* G.K. Hall (Boston, MA), 1983.

Cogell, Elizabeth Cummins, *Understanding Ursula K. Le Guin,* University of South Carolina Press (Columbia, SC), 1990.

Concise Dictionary of American Literary Biography: Broadening Views, 1968-1988, Thomson Gale (Detroit, MI), 1989.

Contemporary Authors New Revision Series, Volume 52, Thomson Gale (Detroit, MI), 1996.

Contemporary Literary Criticism, Thomson Gale (Detroit, MI), Volume 8, 1978, Volume 13, 1980, Volume 22, 1982, Volume 45, 1987, Volume 71, 1992.

Contemporary Novelists, sixth edition, St. James Press (Detroit, MI), 1996, pp. 602-5.

Cummins, Elizabeth, *Understanding Ursula K. Le Guin,* University of South Carolina Press (Columbia, SC), 1990.

Dictionary of Literary Biography, Thomson Gale (Detroit, MI), Volume 8: *Twentieth-Century American Science Fiction Writers,* 1981, Volume 52: *American Writers for Children since 1960: Fiction,* 1986.

Jones, Libby Falk, and Sarah Webster Goodwin, *Feminism, Utopia, and Narrative,* University of Tennessee Press, 1990.

Keulen, Margarete, *Radical Imagination: Feminist Conceptions of the Future in Ursula Le Guin, Marge Piercy, and Sally Miller Gearhart,* Peter Lang (New York, NY), 1991.

Reference Guide to Short Fiction, St. James Press (Detroit, MI), 1993.

Reginald, Robert, and George Edgar Slusser, editors, *Zephyr and Boreas: Winds of Change in the Fiction of Ursula K. Le Guin: A Festschrift in Memory of Pilgrim Award Winner, Marjorie Hope Nicolson,* Borgo Press (San Bernardino, CA), 1996.

Reid, Suzanne Elizabeth, *Ursula K. Le Guin,* Twayne (New York, NY), 1997.

St. James Guide to Science Fiction Writers, St. James Press (Detroit, MI), 1996.

Short Story Criticism, Volume 12, Thomson Gale (Detroit, MI), 1993, pp. 205-52.

Slusser, George Edgar, *Between Two Worlds: The Literary Dilemma of Ursula K. Le Guin,* 2nd edition, Borgo Press (San Bernardino, CA), 1995.

Slusser, George Edgar, *The Farthest Shores of Ursula K. Le Guin,* Borgo Press (San Bernadino, CA), 1976.

Spivack, Charlotte, *Ursula K. Le Guin,* Twayne (Boston, MA), 1984.

Twentieth-Century Children's Writers, third edition, St. James Press (Detroit, MI), 1989, pp. 569-571.

Twentieth-Century Young Adult Writers, St. James Press (Detroit, MI), 1994.

Wayne, Kathryn Ross, *Redefining Moral Education: Life, Le Guin, and Language,* Austin & Winfield, 1994.

PERIODICALS

Analog Science Fiction/Science Fact, February, 1985, pp. 183-184; January, 1996, p. 273.

Atlantic, October, 1995, p. 129.

Belles Lettres, spring, 1992, pp. 53-54; spring, 1994, pp. 27-28.

Bloomsbury Review, June, 1992, pp. 9, 22.

Booklist, February 1, 1999, review of *Jane on Her Own,* p. 974; March 15, 1999, Ray Olson, review of *Sixty Odd,* p. 1277; March 1, 2001, Sally Estes, review of *Tales from Earthsea,* p. 1233; June 1, 2001, Sally Estes, review of *The Other Wind,* p. 1798; January 1, 2002, Sally Estes, review of *The Birthday of the World and Other Stories,* p. 776; April 15, 2003, Sally Estes, review of *Changing Planes,* p. 1428; February 1, 2004, Donna Seaman, review of *The Wave in the Mind: Talks and Essays on the Writer, the Reader, and the Imagination,* p. 942.

Book Report, March-April, 1989.

Boston Globe, July 13, 1994, Maureen Dezell, interview with Le Guin, p. 65.

Economist, December 22, 2001, review of *The Other Wind,* p. 117.

Extrapolation, December, 1976, pp. 28-41; May, 1977, pp. 131-141; fall, 1980, pp. 197-208; fall, 1995, p. 244; winter, 1996, p. 302; summer, 1997, p. 110; winter, 2000, p. 228; spring, 2001, p. 27; winter, 2001, p. 303.

Globe and Mail (Toronto, Ontario, Canada), December 7, 1985, H.J. Kirchoff, review of *Always Coming Home.*

Hollins Critic, April, 1974, Robert Scholes.

Horn Book, May-June, 2002, Susan P. Bloom, review of *Tom Mouse,* p. 316.

Journal of Narrative Technique, winter, 1985, Shoshana Knapp, review of "The Ones Who Walk away from Omelas," pp. 75-81.

Kenyon Review, summer, 1995, p. 192.

Kirkus Reviews, January 1, 2002, review of *The Birthday of the World and Other Stories,* p. 22; February 15, 2002, review of *Tom Mouse,* p. 260; May 1, 2003, review of *Changing Planes,* p. 633.

Kliatt, January, 2002, Lesley S.J. Farmer, review of *The Telling,* p. 18; July, 2002, Bette D. Ammon, review of *Tales from Earthsea,* p. 31.

Library Journal, July, 2001, Jackie Cassada, review of *The Other Wind,* p. 130; March 15, 2002, Jackie Cassada, review of *The Birthday of the World and Other Stories,* p. 112; March 15, 2004, Carolyn M. Craft, review of *The Wave in the Mind,* p. 76.

Locus, October, 1994, pp. 17, 19.

Los Angeles Times, September 5, 1982.

Los Angeles Times Book Review, September 5, 1982; March 5, 1989.

Maclean's, November 4, 1985, Brian D. Johnson, review of *Always Coming Home.*

Modern Fiction Studies, spring, 1986, Keith N. Hull, pp. 65-74.

Mosaic, December, 1996, p. 101; September, 1997, p. 59.

Ms., March-April, 1996, p. 88.

New Republic, February 7, 1976; October 30, 1976.

New York Review of Books, October 2, 1975, pp. 3-7; September 26, 2002, Margaret Atwood, review of *The Birthday of the World and Other Stories,* p. 23.

New York Times Book Review, September 29, 1985; November 13, 1988; May 20, 1990, p. 38; October 15, 1995; March 3, 1996, p. 10; May 12, 1996, p. 27.

Parabola, spring, 1998, pp. 19, 94; fall, 1999, Pamela Uschuk, review of *Sixty Odd,* p. 107.

Publishers Weekly, September, 1995, p. 32; August 7, 2000, review of *The Telling,* p. 79; August 13, 2001, review of *The Other Wind,* p. 290; January 14, 2002, review of *The Birthday of the World and Other Stories,* p. 45; April 14, 2003, review of *Changing Planes,* p. 45.

School Library Journal, April, 1996, p. 168; May, 2002, Kathie Meizner, review of *Tom Mouse,* p. 120.

Science Fiction Chronicle, December, 1995.

Science Fiction Review, spring, 1983, p. 41.

Science-Fiction Studies, spring, 1974, pp. 164-173; March, 1975, pp. 67-75; November, 1975, pp. 231-37; March, 1976; November, 1978, pp. 215-242; March, 1987, pp. 34-43; July, 1994, pp. 164-172.

Times Literary Supplement, April 6, 1973; June 3-9, 1988; March 11, 1994, p. 24.

Utopian Studies, winter, 2001, p. 56.

Village Voice, February 25, 1986, Meredith Tax, review of *Tehanu.*

Voice of Youth Advocates, April, 1991, pp. 14-16, 18.

Washington Post, October 31, 1993, p. 8.

Washington Post Book World, October 6, 1985; January 29, 1989; February 25, 1990; August 9, 1992, p. 11.

Women's Review of Books, July, 1992, Yvonne Fraticelli, review of *Searoad: Chronicles of Klatsand,* pp. 29-30; November, 2003, Susanna J. Sturgis, review of *Changing Planes,* p. 15.

*   *   *

LE GUIN, Ursula Kroeber
    See LE GUIN, Ursula K.

*   *   *

LEHANE, Dennis 1965-

PERSONAL: Born August 4, 1965, in Dorchester, MA; son of Michael (a foreman) and Ann (a school cafeteria worker) Lehane; married, 1999; wife's name, Sheila. *Ethnicity:* Caucasian. *Education:* Eckerd College, B.A.S., 1988; Florida International University, M.F.A., 1993. *Politics:* "Relatively apolitical." *Hobbies and other interests:* Directing films.

ADDRESSES: Agent—Ann Rittenberg, Ann Rittenberg Literary Agency, 1201 Broadway, Suite 708, New York, NY 10001.

CAREER: Writer. Therapeutic counselor for mentally handicapped, emotionally disturbed children, 1986-91; Florida International University, Miami, instructor in English, 1991-93; Ritz-Carlton Hotel, Boston, MA, chauffeur, 1993-95.

AWARDS, HONORS: Shamus Award, best first novel, 1994, for *A Drink before the War;* finalist for L.L. Winship/PEN New England Award, and Anthony Award for Best Novel, both 2002, both for *Mystic River.*

WRITINGS:

MYSTERY NOVELS

A Drink before the War, Harcourt (Orlando, FL), 1994.
Darkness, Take My Hand, Morrow (New York, NY), 1996.
Sacred, Morrow (New York, NY), 1997.
Gone, Baby, Gone, Morrow (New York, NY), 1998.
Prayers for Rain, Morrow (New York, NY), 1999.
Mystic River, Morrow (New York, NY), 2001.
Shutter Island, Morrow (New York, NY), 2003.

Writer, director, and producer of the film *Neighborhoods.*

ADAPTATIONS: The film rights to *Prayers for Rain* were purchased by Paramount Pictures. *Mystic River* was adapted for film by Warner Brothers in 2003.

SIDELIGHTS: "There was never any doubt in Dennis Lehane's mind that he was going to be a writer," stated *January* editor Linda Richards following her interview with the author. "It wasn't much a matter of 'if' as much as 'how' and 'when.'" The son of working-class Irish immigrants, Lehane grew up in Boston during the 1970s and 1980s "with a sense that life was hard and unfair and you just tried your best," he told *Publishers Weekly* interviewer Louise Jones. "Your children were your life and you did all you could for them." By age twenty, Lehane—a dedicated reader since childhood—was writing stories but did not submit them "because my stories didn't meet my high standards," he said to Jones. After graduating from college in 1988, Lehane entered the M.F.A. program in creative writing at Florida International University. From there it was just a few years until Lehane's first mystery novel was published. In fact, he bucked the stereotype of the typical starving artist: "My publishing career is such a fluke. I got to it faster than I expected. I have no publishing horror stories," he told Jones.

Lehane garnered several admiring reviews for his debut. The author's voice, "original, haunting and straight from the heart, places him among that top rank of stylists who enrich the modern mystery novel," noted a *Publishers Weekly* writer. Numerous other critics remarked that Lehane's hard-edged style, ambiguous characters, and unresolved endings combine to create some of the best in modern mystery writing. The main characters in most of his novels are Patrick Kenzie and Angela Gennaro, two young, cynical detectives based in Boston where they grew up together. Their debut in *A Drink before the War* showed "plenty of promise," according to Emily Melton in *Booklist*. *New York Times Book Review* critic Marilyn Stasio felt that the novel was marred by "a lot of cornball cliches and puerile private-eye humor," but she admitted that Lehane "has some honest things to say about racial and class warfare in working-class neighborhoods. . . . This is good, serious stuff, but it's not easy to reconcile it with the flippant style."

Darkness, Take My Hand was the next novel featuring Patrick and Angie, and it drew rave reviews from numerous critics. In this story, the detectives search for a brutal rapist and killer with connections to their own past. Melton described it in *Booklist* as "an explosive story that is at once gut-wrenchingly violent and achingly melancholy. . . . In a series of heart-stopping climaxes that grow ever more terrifying and bloody, Patrick and Angie lose nearly everything. Lehane's perfectly crafted plot leers, teases, taunts, and lulls, scattering bits of humor and heartbreak among the soul-chilling episodes of death and destruction. A tour de force from a truly gifted writer." *People Weekly*'s Pam Lambert was also enthusiastic, calling the book a "crackling thriller." She added, "Lehane's plotting is heart-poundingly suspenseful. However, even it is topped by the novels' subtler attractions: a sense of place as palpable as the pungent tang of garlic in the North End air, haunting characters and a gracefully elegiac style that lingers long after you've closed the covers."

Sacred is "another gritty and surpassingly entertaining mystery" that proves Lehane "belongs in the big leagues," in the opinion of a *Publishers Weekly* reviewer. The writer pointed out Patrick's "smart and often funny narration" as one of the strengths of the book and commented that "for most of the novel, the punishing pace and internal plot logic perform in perfect tandem." Lambert gave her approval to *Sacred* in her *People* review, calling the book a "dark maelstrom of a mystery." She admitted that in her opinion, the book lacks the "terrible beauty" of *Darkness Take My Hand,* but concluded that it "still crackles with enough suspense to make for many a midsummer night's screams."

The detectives search for a little girl kidnapped by a child pornography ring in Lehane's fourth novel, *Gone, Baby, Gone.* Karen Anderson, a reviewer for *Library Journal,* described it as "a tense, edge-of-your-seat story about a world that is astoundingly cruel and unbearably violent to its most innocent members." And Lambert, in another *People Weekly* assessment, called *Gone, Baby, Gone* a "chilling, masterfully plotted tale into that dark place where men try to play God and everyone gets hurt."

As 1999's *Prayers for Rain* begins, Patrick and Angie, having gone through a romance and a breakup, have turned their separate ways. Patrick works alone in Dorchester, while Angie has signed on for security work in a high-tech firm. But she is tempted away from the corporate life to help Patrick solve the mystery of a former client who has apparently leaped to her death off the Customs House Tower. Reviewing the work for *Booklist,* Wes Lukowsky commented: "Lehane has worked his way into the top echelon of crime writers."

Following five Kenzie/Gennaro stories, Lehane decided to "give those characters a rest," as Adam Dunn put it in a *CNN* report. He turned his attention to a new kind of writing: the stand-alone novel. *Daily Telegraph* reporter Michael Carlson noted that it is "exciting" to see such a departure: "Critics tend to devalue 'series' novels. . . . Recurring characters may be fine for Mark Twain or Anthony Powell, but for detective writers they are seen as just another genre shortcut." Lehane's resulting work, *Mystic River,* is set in working-class Boston, like his mystery series. But, according to Carlson, absent of the trappings of the detective tale, the novel "brings the neighbourhood into bleaker focus."

Reviewing *Mystic River* for *USA Today,* Carol Memmott wrote: "In every generation, a handful of writers of detective fiction set the pace for the rest. . . . [F]ew can match [Lehane's] capacity for capturing human emotion and our capability to do evil. . . . His ability to create crystal-clear portraits of humanity and then place them in the darker side of life is a writer's true gift." The story opens in 1975 when two eleven-year-old boys witness a third boy, their friend, bullied into a car and driven off by two strange men. Twenty-five years later, the lives of the three boys cross paths again: Sean is a burned-out cop; Jimmy is an ex-con whose teenage daughter is murdered; and Dave, who suffered abuse at the hands of the strange men in the car, "makes readers aware that he is a ticking time bomb," according to Dunn. Sean is assigned to investigate the murder; the prime suspect is Dave. The author, said Stasio in a *New York Times Book Review* piece, "spares nothing in his wrenching descriptions how a crime in the neighborhood kills the neighborhood, taking it down house by house, family by family." *Newsweek*'s Malcolm Jones lauded Lehane's "near-perfect pitch when it comes to capturing the rage that fomented racial war in the '70s and today fuels the resentment of working-class residents being driven out of [their neighborhoods] by skyrocketing property taxes and rents." Like all Lehane's books, added Jones, *Mystic River* "shimmers with great dialogue and a complex view of the world."

The plot of *Shutter Island*, described by Joanne Wilkinson in *Booklist* as a "blistering page turner," revolves around a virtually impossible escape of an inmate from a federal institution for the criminally insane on the small Shutter Island in the outer harbor of Massachusetts and two U.S. Marshalls who go to investigate. Wilkinson commented: "A master of the adroit psychological detail, Lehane makes the horrors of the mean streets pale in comparison to the workings of the human mind."

In her *January* interview, Richards commented on Lehane's use of the Irish-American dialect in *Mystic River.* The author responded that "in immigrant cultures, particularly Irish which is a very storytelling culture, a very musical culture . . . there's a certain rhythm to the language." He credited his parents with imparting their verbal gifts, saying: "My only gift as a writer—the only thing I was given, everything else I worked for—was an ear. I always had a good ear. I could always write dialog."

Of his method of writing, Lehane once commented: "I barely have a writing process. I have tried to force myself to write every day, keep a journal, and so on, but all that seems to do is make me self-conscious. I tend to write best in big bursts after long periods of silence. During those bursts, I usually write sixteen hours a day, day in and day out, until the battery runs dry. I don't recommend this process, but it's the only one that's ever worked for me."

BIOGRAPHICAL AND CRITICAL SOURCES:

PERIODICALS

Book, March, 2001, Adam Dunn, "A Good Place to Die," p. 52.
Booklist, November 15, 1994, Emily Melton, review of *A Drink before the War,* p. 582; July, 1996, Emily Melton, review of *Darkness, Take My Hand,* p. 1809; April 15, 1999, Wes Lukowsky, review of *Prayers for Rain,* p. 1481; May 1, 2001, Bill Ott, review of *Mystic River,* p. 1599; April 1, 2003, Joanne Wilson, review of *Shutter Island,* p. 1355.
BookPage, February, 2001, review of *Mystic River,* p. 10.
Boston Herald, March 4, 2001, review of *Mystic River,* p. 65.
Daily Telegraph (London, England), May 26, 2001, Michael Carlson, review of *Mystic River.*
Entertainment Weekly, February 16, 2001, review of *Mystic River,* p. 90.
Esquire, February, 2001, review of *Mystic River,* p. 38.
Globe and Mail (Toronto, Ontario, Canada), June 12, 1999, review of *Prayers for Rain,* section D, p. 19; February 17, 2001, review of *Mystic River,* section D, p. 13.
Houston Chronicle, March 11, 2001, Martha Liebrum, "Murder Reconnects Boyhood Pals in Lehane Thriller," p. 15.
Kirkus Reviews, May 15, 1999, review of *Prayers for Rain,* p. 757.
Library Journal, June 15, 1997, Ahmad Wright, review of *Sacred,* p. 98; July, 1998, Karen Anderson, review of *Gone, Baby, Gone,* p. 137; June 15, 1999, Wilda Williams, review of *Prayers for Rain,* p. 108.
Newsweek, February 19, 2001, Malcolm Jones, "Mean Street Makeover," p. 58.
New Yorker, February 19, 2001, review of *Mystic River,* p. 223.
New York Times Book Review, December 11, 1994, Marilyn Stasio, review of *A Drink before the War,* p. 38; July 25, 1999, Marilyn Stasio, review of *Prayers for Rain,* p. 20; February 18, 2001, Marilyn Stasio, review of *Mystic River,* p. 25.
Observer (London, England), April 1, 2001, review of *Mystic River,* p. 16.

People, July 22, 1996, Pam Lambert, review of *Darkness, Take My Hand,* p. 30; August 25, 1997, Pam Lambert, review of *Sacred,* p. 38; August 10, 1998, Pam Lambert, review of *Gone, Baby, Gone,* p. 43; March 19, 2001, Pam Lambert, review of *Mystic River,* p. 45.

Publishers Weekly, October 10, 1994, p. 65; May 27, 1996, p. 67; May 26, 1997, p. 69; May 10, 1999, review of *Prayers for Rain,* p. 61; June 21, 1999, Louise Jones, "Dennis Lehane: Hard-Boiled in Boston," p. 40.

Washington Post Book World, August 8, 1999, review of *Prayers for Rain,* p. 3; February 25, 2001, review of *Mystic River,* p. 4; March 4, 2001, review of *Mystic River,* p. 9.

ONLINE

Amazon.com, http://www.amazon.com/ (May 19, 2002), author interview.

Bookreporter, http://www.bookreporter.com/ (August 22, 2004), Joe Hartlaub, review of *Mystic River.*

CNN.com, http://www.cnn.com/ (January 30, 2001), Adam Dunn, "Author Dennis Lehane Plumbs Depths of Human Misunderstanding in *Mystic River.*"

Dennis Lehane Web site, http://www.dennislehane books.com/ (August 22, 2004).

January, http://www.januarymagazine.com/ (May 19, 2002), Linda Richards, author interview.

USA Today, http://www.usatoday.com/ (September 24, 2003), Carol Memmott, review of *Mystic River.*

*   *   *

LEONARD, Elmore 1925-
(Elmore John Leonard, Jr.)

PERSONAL: Born October 11, 1925, in New Orleans, LA; son of Elmore John (an automotive executive) and Flora Amelia (Rive) Leonard; married Beverly Cline, July 30, 1949 (divorced, May 24, 1977); married Joan Shepard, September 15, 1979 (died, January 13, 1993); married Christine Kent, August 19, 1993; children: (first marriage) Jane Jones, Peter, Christopher, William, Katherine Dudley. *Education:* University of Detroit, Ph. B., 1950. *Religion:* Roman Catholic.

ADDRESSES: Agent—Michael Siegel, Michael Siegel & Associates, 11532 Thurston Circle, Los Angeles, CA 90049.

CAREER: Writer, 1967—. Campbell-Ewald Advertising Agency, Detroit, MI, copywriter, 1950-61; freelance copywriter and author of educational and industrial films, 1961-63; head of Elmore Leonard Advertising Company, 1963-66. Producer of film *Tishomingo Blues,* 2002. *Military service:* U.S. Naval Reserve, 1943-46.

MEMBER: Writers Guild of America West, Authors League of America, Authors Guild.

AWARDS, HONORS: Hombre named one of the twenty-five best western novels of all time by Western Writers of America, 1977; Edgar Allan Poe Award, Mystery Writers of America, 1984, for *LaBrava;* Michigan Foundation of the Arts Award, 1985; Hammett Prize, International Association of Crime Writers, 1991, for *Maximum Bob;* Mystery Writers of America Grand Master Award, 1992; Honorary Ph.D., Florida Atlantic University, 1996, University of Detroit Mercy, 1997, and University of Michigan, 2000.

WRITINGS:

WESTERNS

The Bounty Hunters (also see below), Houghton (Boston, MA), 1953.

The Law at Randado (also see below), Houghton (Boston, MA), 1955.

Escape from Five Shadows (also see below), Houghton (Boston, MA), 1956.

Last Stand at Saber River (also see below), Dell (New York, NY), 1957, published as *Lawless River,* R. Hale (London, England), 1959, published as *Stand on the Saber,* Corgi (London, England), 1960.

Hombre (also see below), Ballantine (New York, NY), 1961.

Valdez Is Coming (also see below), Gold Medal (New York, NY), 1970.

Forty Lashes less One (also see below), Bantam (New York, NY), 1972.

Gunsights (also see below), Bantam (New York, NY), 1979.

The Tonto Woman and Other Western Stories, Delacorte (New York, NY), 1998.

Elmore Leonard's Western Roundup #1 (contains *The Bounty Hunters, Forty Lashes less One,* and *Gunsights*), Delta (New York, NY), 1998.

Elmore Leonard's Western Roundup #2 (contains *Escape from Five Shadows, Last Stand at Saber River,* and *The Law at Randado*), Delta (New York, NY), 1998.

Elmore Leonard's Western Roundup #3 (contains *Valdez Is Coming* and *Hombre*), Delta (New York, NY), 1999.

CRIME NOVELS

The Big Bounce, Gold Medal (New York, NY), 1969, revised edition, Armchair Detective, 1989.
The Moonshine War (also see below), Doubleday (New York, NY), 1969.
Mr. Majestyk (also see below), Dell (New York, NY), 1974.
Fifty-two Pickup (also see below), Delacorte (New York, NY), 1974.
Swag (also see below), Delacorte (New York, NY), 1976, published as *Ryan's Rules,* Dell (New York, NY), 1976.
Unknown Man, No. 89, Delacorte (New York, NY), 1977.
The Hunted (also see below), Dell (New York, NY), 1977.
The Switch, Bantam (New York, NY), 1978.
City Primeval: High Noon in Detroit (also see below), Arbor House (New York, NY), 1980.
Gold Coast (also see below), Bantam (New York, NY), 1980, revised edition, 1985.
Split Images (also see below), Arbor House (New York, NY), 1981.
Cat Chaser (also see below), Arbor House (New York, NY), 1982.
Stick (also see below), Arbor House (New York, NY), 1983.
LaBrava (also see below), Arbor House (New York, NY), 1983.
Glitz, Arbor House (New York, NY), 1985.
Bandits, Arbor House (New York, NY), 1987.
Touch, Arbor House (New York, NY), 1987.
Freaky Deaky, Morrow (New York, NY), 1988.
Killshot, Morrow (New York, NY), 1989.
Get Shorty, Delacorte (New York, NY), 1990.
Maximum Bob, Delacorte (New York, NY), 1991.
Rum Punch, Delacorte (New York, NY), 1992.
Pronto, Delacorte (New York, NY), 1993.
Riding the Rap, Delacorte (New York, NY), 1995.
Out of Sight, Delacorte (New York, NY), 1996.
Cuba Libre, Delacorte (New York, NY), 1998.
Be Cool (sequel to *Get Shorty*), Delacorte (New York, NY), 1999.
Pagan Babies, Delacorte (New York, NY), 2000.
Tishomingo Blues, Morrow (New York, NY), 2002.
Mr. Paradise, Morrow (New York, NY), 2004.
A Coyote's in the House, Morrow (New York, NY), 2004.

OMNIBUS VOLUMES

Elmore Leonard's Dutch Treat (contains *The Hunted, Swag,* and *Mr. Majestyk*), introduction by George F. Will, Arbor House (New York, NY), 1985.
Elmore Leonard's Double Dutch Treat (contains *City Primeval: High Noon in Detroit, The Moonshine War,* and *Gold Coast*), introduction by Bob Greene, Arbor House (New York, NY), 1986.
Three Complete Novels (contains *LaBrava, Cat Chaser,* and *Split Images*), Wings Books (New York, NY), 1992.

SCREENPLAYS

The Moonshine War (based on Leonard's novel of the same title), Metro-Goldwyn-Mayer, 1970.
Joe Kidd, Universal, 1972.
Mr. Majestyk (based on Leonard's novel of the same title), United Artists, 1974.
High Noon, Part 2: The Return of Will Kane, Columbia Broadcasting System, 1980.
(With Joseph C. Stinson) *Stick* (based on Leonard's novel of the same title), Universal, 1985.
(With John Steppling) *52 Pick-Up* (based on Leonard's novel of the same title), Cannon Group, 1986.
(With Fred Walton) *The Rosary Murders* (based on the novel by William X. Kienzle), New Line Cinema, 1987.
Desperado, National Broadcasting Corporation, 1988.
(With Joe Borrelli) *Cat Chaser* (based on Leonard's novel of the same title), Viacom, 1989.
(With Quentin Tarantino) *Jackie Brown* (based on Leonard's novel *Rum Punch*), Miramax, 1997.

Also author of filmscripts for Encyclopædia Britannica Films, including *Settlement of the Mississippi Valley, Boy of Spain, Frontier Boy,* and *Julius Caesar,* and of a recruiting film for the Franciscans.

OTHER

When the Women Come out to Dance (short fiction), William Morrow (New York, NY), 2002.

Contributor to books, including *The Courage to Change: Personal Conversations about Alcoholism,* edited by Dennis Wholey, Houghton (Boston, MA), 1984.

Contributor of stories and novelettes to *Dime Western, Argosy, Saturday Evening Post, Zane Grey's Western Magazine,* and other publications.

ADAPTATIONS: The novelette *3:10 to Yuma* was filmed by Columbia Pictures, 1957; the story "The Tall T" was filmed by Columbia, 1957; *Hombre* was filmed by Twentieth Century-Fox, 1967; *The Big Bounce* was filmed by Warner Bros., 1969, and 2004; *Valdez Is Coming* was filmed by United Artists, 1970; *Glitz* was filmed for television by NBC; *Get Shorty* was filmed by MGM/UA, 1995; *Touch* was filmed by Lumiere, 1996; *Out of Sight,* directed by Steven Soderbergh, screenplay by Scott Frank, was filmed by Universal, 1998; *Tishomingo Blues* was adapted for film in 2002; *Karen Sisco* (based on characters from *Out of Sight*) was developed for television by ABC, 2003; screen rights to the novella *Tenkiller* were purchased by Paramount, 2002; *Be Cool* was planned for a film by MGM, 2005. Many of Leonard's novels have been adapted as audiobooks, including *Mr. Paradise,* Harper Audio, 2004.

SIDELIGHTS: Elmore Leonard had been hailed as one of the top crime novelists of the late twentieth century, carrying on the tradition of the early pulp novelists into the next century. With dozens of bestselling crime novels to his credit, Leonard has earned acclaim for imbuing his thrillers with dark humor, moral ambivalence, and a unique prose style that reflects the anxious realities of modern life. Dubbing the novelist the "mastermind behind darkly comic bestsellers" like *Get Shorty, Glitz,* and *Out of Sight,* Rob Brookman maintained in a *Book* critique that Leonard combines "whip-smart prose with a seemingly inexhaustible cast of sleazeballs, scam artists and out-and-out psychopaths." While noting that Leonard began his career as a noir writer, Bill Ott explained the author's evolution, writing in *Booklist* that "Happily-ever-aftering, unimaginable in real noir, remains a tempting if hard-won possibility in Leonard's world." Leonard's novels, according to Ott, characteristically offer readers "a violent, hard-boiled, streetwise brand of romantic comedy, usually starring a hero and heroine who . . . find their way out of an outlandish mess."

In the early 1980s Leonard began to receive the kind of attention from reviewers befitting an author whom Richard Herzfelder in *Chicago Tribune* called "a writer of thrillers whose vision goes deeper than thrill." While the plots of Leonard's books remain inherently action-packed and suspenseful, he also earns praise, to quote *Washington Post Book World* critic Jonathan Yardley, "for accomplishments rather more substantial than that of keeping the reader on tenterhooks." These accomplishments, which Yardley described as raising "the hard-boiled suspense novel beyond the limits of genre and into social commentary," led critics previously inclined to pigeonhole Leonard as a crime or mystery novelist to dispense with such labels in their assessments of his work. In the process, several critics have chosen to mention Leonard's name alongside those of other writers whose literary works transcend their genre, among them Ross Macdonald and Dashiell Hammett. "Leonard is one of our finest humorists, especially when he is not trying to be funny," explained Bruce DeSilva in *New York Times Book Review.* "We laugh because we recognize people we know and sometimes, though it can be hard to admit, something of ourselves in the flawed, very real people of his hard-boiled crime novels."

Leonard began his career in the early 1950s as a writer of western stories for magazines. His first sale was the novelette *Apache Agent* to *Argosy* magazine for $90. He eventually turned his hand to novels in the genre, publishing five of them while pursuing a career as an advertising copywriter for a firm in Detroit. Copywriter was not an occupation much to Leonard's liking. "He says matter-of-factly that he hated the work," noted Bill Dunn in a *Publishers Weekly* interview, "but it allowed him precious time and a steady paycheck to experiment with fiction, which he did in the early morning before going off to work." Leonard told Dunn: "Sometimes I would write a little fiction at work, too. I would write in my desk drawer and close the drawer if somebody came in."

By the early 1960s the western genre had already peaked in popularity, and Leonard found that the market for his fiction had dried up. For several years he wrote no fiction at all, devoting his time to freelance copywriting, primarily for Hurst gear shifters, a popular feature in hot rod cars. He also wrote industrial films for Detroit-area companies and educational films for Encyclopædia Britannica at a thousand dollars apiece. Finally in 1965, when his agent sold the film rights to his last western novel, *Hombre,* for ten thousand dollars, Leonard had the financial leeway to write fiction again. This time he focused on the mystery-suspense genre. As he told Gay Rubin of *Detroiter:* "I began writing westerns because there was a market for them. Now of course there is an interest in police stories . . . suspense, mystery, crime."

Despite the shift in genre, Leonard's fiction has remained in many ways the same. In both his western and crime fiction there is an overriding interest in seeing that justice is done, as well as the world-weary recognition that justice is a very ambiguous concept. Leonard's prose, lean and hard, has consistently been of the same high quality. And his gunfighters and urban detectives approach their work with the same glib, wisecracking attitude. Writing in *Esquire,* Mike Lupica claimed that despite their apparent diversity, all of Leonard's main characters are essentially the same, but "with a different name and a different job. . . . They have all been beat on by life, they all can drop a cool, wise-guy line on you, they are all tough, don't try to push them around."

Leonard's first crime novel, *The Big Bounce,* was rejected by some eighty-four publishers and film producers before being published as a paperback original by Gold Medal. Unsure about his switch to crime writing because of the trouble he had selling the book, Leonard turned again to westerns, publishing two more novels in the genre. But when the film rights to *The Big Bounce* were sold for $50,000, Leonard abandoned the western genre almost completely, penning only an occasional short story here and there. Since making that decision, all of his subsequent novels have enjoyed both hardcover and paperback editions and have been sold to Hollywood; in fact, *The Big Bounce* was reproduced by original purchaser Warner Brothers in 2004. In *Film Comment,* Patrick McGilligan wrote: "Now there are as many Leonard stories being filmed in Hollywood as there were options left. . . . On the cusp of the millennium, after nearly fifty years in the field, Leonard finds himself the modernist crime writer of choice for all the hip young filmmakers."

The typical Leonard novel, Michael Kernan explained in *Washington Post,* is distinguished by "guns, a killing or two or three, fights and chases and sex. Tight, clean prose, ear-perfect, whip-smart dialogue. And, just beneath the surface, an acute sense of the ridiculous." Leonard has said on several occasions that he has been less influenced by other crime writers than by such writers as Ernest Hemingway, John Steinbeck, and John O'Hara. Their lean, unadorned writing style and ability to remain in the background of their stories appealed to Leonard. As he told Charles Champlin of *Los Angeles Times:* "I became a stylist by intentionally avoiding style. When I go back and edit and something sounds like *writing,* I rewrite it. I rewrite constantly, four pages in the basket for every one that survives." The result impressed Ken Tucker of *Village Voice,* who called Leonard "the finest thriller writer alive primarily because he does his best to efface style."

Many of Leonard's crime novels feature lower-class, somewhat desperate characters hoping to make fast money with a big heist or quick scam. They "fall into crime," according to Tucker, "because it's an easier way to make money than that tedious nine-to-five." George Stade, in *New York Times Book Review,* called Leonard's villains "treacherous and tricky, smart enough to outsmart themselves, driven, audacious and outrageous, capable of anything, paranoid—cunning and casually vicious—and rousing fun." Dick Roraback, in *Los Angeles Times Book Review,* claimed that "it is the mark of the author's craft that his characters do not seem to be created, 'written.' They simply are there, stalking, posturing, playing, loving, scheming, and we watch and listen and are fascinated. And appalled, yes, or approving, but always absorbed. They never let us off the hook."

Although he had been writing critically acclaimed crime novels for a decade, and his work was being adapted for the screen, Leonard had only a small cadre of fans until the early 1980s, when his novels began to attract the attention of a larger audience. With the novel *Stick* in 1982, Leonard suddenly found he had risen to the status of bestselling writer. One sign of this sudden success can be seen in the agreeable change in Leonard's finances that year. The paperback rights for *Split Images* earned him $7,000 in 1981; the rights for *Stick,* a year later, earned $50,000. Then, in 1983, *LaBrava* won an Edgar Allan Poe Award from the Mystery Writers of America as the best novel of the year. Leonard's next novel, *Glitz,* hit the bestseller lists in 1985.

Leonard's popularity continued to increase throughout the 1990s. In *Get Shorty* he drew on his years of experience as a screenwriter to create an intricate story full of inside jokes about the seamy underbelly of Hollywood. The protagonist is Chili Palmer, a Miami loan shark who travels to California in pursuit of a man. He is also being pursued, and in the course of the action, he becomes entangled with a third-rate producer, a washed-up actress, and several cocaine dealers. Writing in *Los Angeles Times Book Review,* Champlin applauded the accuracy of Leonard's portrait of the movie business, calling it "less angry than *Day of the Locust* but not less devastating in its tour of the industry's soiled follies and the gaminess beneath the grandeurs." Even more sweeping praise came from Whitney Balliett in *New Yorker,* who declared that, "Book by book . . . the tireless and ingenious genre novelist Elmore Leonard is painting an intimate, precise, funny, frightening, and irresistible mural of the American underworld. . . . Leonard treats [his characters] with the understanding and the detailed attention that Jane Austen gives her Darcys and Emma Woodhouses."

The publication of *Maximum Bob* in 1991 spurred reviewers on to even greater superlatives. Praising Leonard as "the greatest living writer of crime fiction," Barry Gifford announced in *New York Times Book Review* that with *Maximum Bob* "Leonard confirms . . . his right to a prominent place in the American *noir* writers' hall of fame. . . . Nobody I've ever read sets up pace, mood and sound better." The title character is a Florida judge whose nickname comes from his fondness for the electric chair. Having tired of his wife, who believes she is possessed by the spirit of a girl eaten by an alligator one hundred and thirty years before, the judge attempts to drive her out of his life so that he can pursue another woman. Thus begins the story, described by Robert Carver in *New Statesman & Society* as "a murder chase in reverse, where the killing hasn't yet happened, so you keep trying to guess both victim and perpetrator." Carver asserted that "this is a brilliant, funny, hugely enjoyable black comedy." Clifford Irving remarked in *Los Angeles Times Book Review* on the profound aspects of the humor found in *Maximum Bob*, stating that Leonard, "like any true comic, has a melancholy view of the world and its primitive denizens. Without moralizing, he is telling us—no, he is showing us—how rotten life is in the heartland of the USA. In *Maximum Bob*, more than ever, he is the great delineator of the macho redneck, the professional thug, the semi-mindless street-wise slob who kills and maims and rapes because it's part of the American mystique of violence and seems like fun. . . . Leonard's prose, in its way, is as good as anything being written in this country."

Laudatory remarks continued with the publication of *Rum Punch* in 1992. The novel inspired Ann Arensberg to write in *New York Times Book Review:* "I didn't know it was possible to be as good as Elmore Leonard. . . . Outpacing the classic hard-boiled novel, leaving the British detective novel in the dust, Elmore Leonard has compressed *Rum Punch* into almost pure drama, as close to playwriting as novel writing can get (and get away with)." *Washington Post Book World* contributor Michael Dirda called the book "as unputdownable as anyone could wish," as well as "a novel about growing old, about the way that time changes us, about the old dream of starting over again and its cost."

Discussing Leonard's 1993 offering, *Pronto*, Teresa Carpenter lamented the fact that "somewhere along the line, it became fashionable to discuss Elmore Leonard in terms formerly reserved for the likes of [French novelist Gustave] Flaubert." The critic readily admitted in *New York Times Book Review* that Leonard's books often "make insightful observations on contemporary culture" and "contain sharply drawn portraits of characters on the fringe of society." Other reviewers also contin-

ued to find much more than simple fun in Leonard's books. "Leonard is a literary genius," Martin Amis stated simply in his *New York Times Book Review* assessment of *Riding the Rap*, adding that the novelist "possesses gifts—of ear and eye, of timing and phrasing—that even the most indolent and snobbish masters of the mainstream must vigorously covet."

Out of Sight further cemented Leonard's reputation. The novel captures the "street, the savor and savvy, slyness and swagger of the talk that's talked on street corners and in bars, at taped-off crime scenes and in prison yards," wrote Annie Gottlieb in *Nation*. In *Out of Sight*, twenty-nine-year-old U.S. Marshall Karen Sisco—clothed in a $3,500 Chanel suit—runs into escaping convict Jack Foley. Jack reminds Karen of Harry Dean Stanton in the movie *Repo Man:* as she explains both men appear to be "real guys who seemed tired of who they were, but couldn't do anything about it." As Karen and Jack get together, cop and criminal, romance ensues in a quirky, convoluted plot that involves Foley's hit on the house of an ex-junk bond trader who supposedly has millions hidden inside. Writing for *New York Times Book Review*, Christopher Lehmann-Haupt called *Out of Sight* "an absorbing story full of offbeat characters, funny incidents, vivid locales, [and] dialogue that jumps off the page."

In *Cuba Libre* Leonard reaches for a broader audience than those he attracted with his crime novels and westerns, by combining elements of both genres. Set in Cuba around the time of the Spanish-American War, *Cuba Libre* combines adventure, history, and romance with the requisite nefarious goings-on. In a move worthy of one of his novels, Leonard arranged to have *Cuba Libre* published on the one hundredth anniversary of the sinking of the U.S.S. *Maine*. In *Cuba Libre*, Ben Tyler is a cowboy of the bank-robbing kind; in his vigilantism, he only robs banks that contain the money of people who owe him money. When he grows tired of robbing banks, Tyler joins his friend Charlie Burke in a scheme to export horses to Cuba. They arrive in Havana just as the Spanish-American War breaks out, and suddenly these petty thieves are embroiled in the larger conflict. A *Kirkus Reviews* critic noted that the "three-cornered conflict"—the heroes and the sugar baron whose price they must meet, the U.S. government and Spain, and the American capitalists's interests in Cuba—"is nothing more than a classic Leonard scam writ large," with the small scam dovetailing smoothly into the larger "scams" of the political powers. Lehmann-Haupt, in *New York Times*, found the novel "unusually rich in period atmosphere," primarily because Leonard is "as always, so uncannily at home with the slang and terminology of the times." Also writing in *New York Times Book Review,* Pico Iyer criticized the lack of character development in the novel: "With so much plot . . . there is almost no room for character or emotion." Lehmann-Haupt stressed, however, that the novel is a political satire, though "Leonard is too good a story teller to let . . . political views shape his characters."

Be Cool is a sequel to *Get Shorty* and once again features dubious Hollywood mogul Chili Palmer. Always in search for film plots, Chili decides to help a struggling young singer make it in the music industry, just to see whether or not her story would make a good movie. In short order, Chili discovers that he has run afoul of the girl's previous manager, the Russian mafia, and a gang of rap artists. To quote Anthony Wilson-Smith in *Maclean's,* "The world that Leonard sketches has remained unchanged—a place where moral ambiguity abounds, and sudden, shocking violence is never more than a flick of the page away. *Be Cool,* like *Get Shorty,* skewers the pretensions of the entertainment industry." A *Publishers Weekly* reviewer noted that Chili "remains a compulsively appealing character, . . . retaining his immaculate cool in lethal situations," while in *Booklist* David Pitt suggested that the novel "reaches a level of comic surrealism that its predecessor only approached." And Lehmann-Haupt, in his *New York Times* review, commended *Be Cool* as "thoroughly entertaining," adding that while the "plot wrinkles involve a very inside knowledge of the music industry," "Leonard seems to have mastered it."

In the opening scenes of *Pagan Babies,* the central character, Terry Dunn, contemplates a ruthless massacre that occurred before his eyes while he said his first Mass in a small church in Rwanda. Five years have passed since the massacre of his congregation, and Dunn has done little in that time except drink whiskey. When the opportunity arises to seek revenge on the murderers, however, Dunn shows his true colors: he is a petty criminal who fled America to avoid arrest for tax fraud, and he has no problem doing some murdering of his own. This tact necessitates Dunn's rapid return to his hometown of Detroit, where, with the help of an ex-convict comedienne, he concocts new and more audacious scams. An *Economist* reviewer deemed *Pagan Babies* "one of Mr. Leonard's funniest books, with a typically colourful cast of oddballs." De Silva likewise commended the novel for its "fast pace, crackling dialogue and dark ironies." In *New York Times Book Review,* Janet Maslin wrote: "The pieces of this crime tale begin falling into place so handily that Mr. Leonard might as well have hung a 'Virtuoso at Work' shingle on his door."

Noting that Leonard "is the only A-list crime fiction writer who doesn't rely on a series hero," *Booklist* critic Bill Ott nonetheless praised the author for providing another in a long line of fascinating if slightly hardened protagonists in *Tishomingo Blues.* The novel finds high-diver Dennis Lenahan working at a Mississippi resort when he spots a murder from atop his eighty-foot ladder. Immediately conspicuous to the murderer, Dennis wants to mind his own business, but he soon finds himself caught up in a sea of events that involve not only the murderer and his status as witness: Civil War re-enactors, an aggressive newscaster, and the murderer's seductive and all-too-willing wife. "As usual, Leonard's characters walk onto the page as real as sunlight and shadow," praised a *Publishers Weekly* reviewer, adding that in *Tishomingo Blues* "the dialogue is dead-on, the loopy story line strewn with the unexpected." Calling the novel "as full of pitch-perfect patter, bare-knuckle verbal sparring and whiplash one-liners as anything he has written," an *Economist* contributor noted that "the real pleasure of *Tishomingo Blues* is its diverse voices"; in *New Yorker* a contributor begged to differ, writing that Leonard's "hurtling plot twists keep coming, right up to the perfect rip of a finish."

In an online interview for the *Mr. Showbiz* Web site, Leonard said that his literary tastes and aspirations were laid down in childhood when he read the Book-of-the-Month Club offerings his mother bought. "I read a lot of them," he said. "I was intimidated by most of the novels because I thought that they were just too big and heavy, and had too many words in them. I still feel that way about most novels—that they have way too many words in them." The author who has said that he always tries "to leave out the boring parts" in his work is a disciplined practitioner of his craft. He writes every day of the week, longhand, sitting at a desk in the corner of his living room. "The satisfaction is in doing it," he told the *Mr. Showbiz* interviewer. "I'm not writing for notoriety; I'm writing to satisfy myself."

BIOGRAPHICAL AND CRITICAL SOURCES:

BOOKS

Contemporary Literary Criticism, Thomson Gale (Detroit, MI), Volume 28, 1984, Volume 34, 1985, Volume 71, 1992.

Dictionary of Literary Biography, Volume 173, *American Novelists since World War II,* Thomson Gale (Detroit, MI), 1996.

Geherin, David, *Elmore Leonard,* Continuum (New York, NY), 1989.

PERIODICALS

American Film, December, 1984.

Armchair Detective, winter, 1986; spring, 1986; winter, 1989.

Atlantic, June, 1998, Francis X. Rocca, review of *Cuba Libre,* p. 111.

Book, March-April, 2002, Rob Brookman, interview with Leonard, p. 28.

Booklist, November 1, 1998, David Pitt, review of *Be Cool,* p. 452; December 1, 2001, Bill Ott, review of *Tishomingo Blues,* p. 604; November 1, 2002, Keir Graff, review of *When the Women Come out to Dance,* p. 452; November 15, 2003, Bill Ott, review of *Mr. Paradise,* p. 548.

Boston Globe, July 30, 1992, p. 80; November 14, 1993, p. 7.

Chicago Tribune, February 4, 1981; April 8, 1983; December 8, 1983; February 7, 1985.

Christian Science Monitor, November 4, 1983; March 12, 1997.

Commentary, May, 1985, pp. 64, 66-67.

Detroiter, June, 1974, Gay Rubin, interview with Leonard.

Detroit News, February 23, 1982; October 23, 1983.

Economist (US), June 19, 1999, review of *Be Cool,* p. 4; October 14, 2000, "New Thrillers-Hit Men," p. 106; February 23, 2002, reveiw of *Tishomingo Blues.*

Entertainment Weekly, September 22, 2000, Bruce Fretts, review of *Pagan Babies,* p. 68; January 9, 2004, Rebecca Ascher-Walsh, review of *Mr. Paradise,* p. 84.

Esquire, April, 1987, pp. 169-74.

Film Comment, March-April, 1998, Patrick McGilligan, "Get Dutch," p. 43.

Globe and Mail (Toronto, Ontario, Canada), December 14, 1985.

Kirkus Reviews, November 15, 1997, p. 1665; November 15, 2001, review of *Tishomingo Blues,* p. 1571; October 15, 2002, review of *When the Women Come out to Dance,* p. 1497; November 1, 2003, review of *Mr. Paradise,* p. 1290.

Knight-Ridder/Tribune News Service, September 20, 2000, Chauncey Mabe, review of *Pagan Babies,* p. K2148; September 27, 2000, Marta Salij, "Elmore Leonard Reaches beyond Familiar Setting," p. K3888; October 4, 2000, Marta Salij, "Elmore Leonard: A Mob Mentality," p. K7276.

Library Journal, January, 2002, Karen Anderson, review of *Tishomingo Blues,* p. 153.

Los Angeles Times, June 28, 1984; May 4, 1988; January 26, 1998.

Los Angeles Times Book Review, February 27, 1983; December 4, 1983; January 13, 1985; August 30, 1987, pp. 2, 8; April 23, 1989, p. 14; July 29, 1990, p. 9; August 4, 1991, pp. 2, 9; October 24, 1994, p. 8; May 14, 1995, p. 1.

Maclean's, January 19, 1987; March 16, 1998, Brian Bethune, review of *Cuba Libre,* p. 63; March 29, 1999, Anthony Wilson-Smith, "The Master of Crime: Elmore Leonard's 35th Novel Shows Him at the Top of His Form," p. 70.

Nation, December 4, 1995, Annie Gottlieb, review of *Out of Sight,* p. 724.

New Republic, November 13, 1995, p. 32; January 26, 1998.

New Statesman & Society, October 11, 1991; November 13, 1992.

Newsweek, March 22, 1982; July 11, 1983; November 14, 1983; April 22, 1985, pp. 62-64, 67.

New Yorker, September 3, 1990, pp. 106-7; October 23, 1995, p. 96; September 30, 1996; January 12, 1998; January 26, 1998; February 11, 2002, review of *Tishomingo Blues,* p. 86.

New York Times, June 11, 1982; April 28, 1983; October 7, 1983; October 29, 1983; April 26, 1985; May 2, 1988; July 25, 1991, p. C18; September 23, 1993, p. C18; May 11, 1995; August 15, 1996; February 15, 1996; January 18, 1997; June 7, 1997; February 14, 1997; December 24, 1997; January 22, 1998, Christopher Lehmann-Haupt, "Viva la Genre! Elmore Leonard Visits Old Havana;" February 11, 1999, Christopher Lehmann-Haupt, "Get Musical: Chili Palmer's Latest Movie Idea;" September 7, 2000, Janet Maslin, "'New Elmore Leonard?' 'Yeah. You Know. Punks.'"

New York Times Book Review, May 22, 1977; September 5, 1982; March 6, 1983; December 27, 1983; February 10, 1985, p. 7; January 4, 1987, p. 7; July 29, 1990, pp. 1, 28; July 28, 1991, p. 8; August 16, 1992, p. 13; October 17, 1993, p. 39; May 14, 1995, p. 7; September 8, 1996; January 22, 1998; February 8, 1998; September 20, 1998, Charles Salzberg, review of *The Tonto Woman,* p. 24; February 21, 1999, Kinky Friedman, "The Palmer Method," p. 10; September 17, 2000, Bruce DeSilva, "Turned Collar."

New York Times Magazine, November 16, 1997.

People, January 26, 2004, Steve Dougherty, review of *Mr. Paradise,* p. 43.

Publishers Weekly, February 25, 1983; June 15, 1990, p. 55; June 10, 1996, p. 84; November 16, 1998, review of *Be Cool,* p. 52; December 10, 2001, review of *Tishomingo Blues,* p. 48; January 21, 2002, interview with Leonard, p. 52; February 3, 2003, review of *Tishomingo Blues* (audio version), p. 24;

November 24, 2003, review of *Mr. Paradise,* p. 42; April 5, 2004, review of *Mr. Paradise* (audio version), p. 22.

Sun-Sentinel (South Florida), September 20, 2000, Chauncey Mabe, review of *Pagan Babies.*

Time, May 28, 1984, pp. 84, 86; February 24, 1997; August 18, 1997; January 12, 1998.

Times Literary Supplement, December 5, 1986, p. 1370; November 30, 1990, p. 1287; September 27, 1991, p. 24; October 30, 1992, p. 21; November 5, 1993, p. 20.

Tribune Books (Chicago, IL), April 10, 1983; October 30, 1983; April 9, 1989, pp. 1, 4; May 21, 1995, p. 5.

TV Guide, August 1, 1998, Lawrence Grobel, "Get Elmore!," p. 23.

Village Voice, February 23, 1982, Ken Tucker.

Wall Street Journal, January 29, 1998.

Washington Post, October 6, 1980; February 6, 1985.

Washington Post Book World, February 7, 1982; July 4, 1982; February 20, 1983; November 13, 1983; December 28, 1986, p. 3; August 23, 1987, pp. 1-2; May 1, 1988; July 14, 1991, pp. 1-2; July 19, 1992, p. 2.

ONLINE

Elmore Leonard Home Page, http://www.elmore leonard.com/ (April 25, 2004).

Mr. Showbiz, http://mrshowbiz.go.com/ (October 19, 2000), Rick Schultz, interview with Leonard.

Random House Web site, http://www.randomhouse.com/ (October 19, 2000), biographical information and reviews.

Salon.com, http://www.salon.com/people/ (September 28, 1999), Sean Elder, interview with Leonard.

*   *   *

LEONARD, Elmore John, Jr.
See LEONARD, Elmore

*   *   *

LESIEG, Theo.
See GEISEL, Theodor Seuss

*   *   *

LESSING, Doris 1919-
(Doris May Lessing, Jane Somers)

PERSONAL: Born October 22, 1919, in Kermanshah, Persia; daughter of Alfred Cook Taylor (a farmer) and Emily Maude McVeagh; married Frank Charles Wisdom, 1939 (marriage dissolved, 1943); married Gottfried Anton Nicholas Lessing, 1945 (marriage dissolved, 1949); children: (first marriage) John (deceased), Jean; (second marriage) Peter. *Politics:* "Left-wing."

ADDRESSES: Agent—c/o Jonathan Clowes Ltd., 10 Iron Bridge House, Bridge Approach, London NW1 8BD, England.

CAREER: Writer. Worked as a nursemaid, a lawyer's secretary, a Hansard typist, and a Parliamentary Commissioner's typist while living in Southern Rhodesia, 1924-49.

MEMBER: National Institute of Arts and Letters, American Academy of Arts and Letters, Modern Language Association (honorary fellow), Institute of Cultural Research.

AWARDS, HONORS: Somerset Maugham Award, Society of Authors, 1954, for *Five: Short Novels;* shortlisted for the Booker McConnell Prize, 1971, for *Briefing for a Descent into Hell,* 1981, for *The Sirian Experiments: The Report of Ambien II, of the Five,* and 1981, for *The Good Terrorist;* Prix Medici Award for work translated into French, 1976, for *The Golden Notebook;* Austrian State Prize for European Literature, 1981; German Federal Republic Shakespeare Prize, 1982; Australian Science Fiction Achievement Award (Ditmars) nomination, 1982, for *The Sirian Experiments;* W.H. Smith Literary Award, 1986, Palermo Prize, 1987, and Premio Internazionale Mondello, 1987, all for *The Good Terrorist;* Grinzane Cavour award (Italy), 1989, for *The Fifth Child;* honorary degree, Princeton University, 1989, and Harvard University, 1995; distinguished fellow, University of East Anglia, 1991; XI Annual International Catalunya Award, James Tait Black Memorial Book Prize, University of Edinburgh, and *Los Angeles Times* Book Prize, all 1995, all for *Under My Skin;* National Book Critics Circle Award nomination for biography/autobiography, 1998, for *Walking in the Shade;* International IMPAC Dublin Literary Award nomination, 2000, for *Mara and Dann;* David Cohen British Literary Prize, 2001; Asturias Prize for literature, Prince of Asturias Foundation, 2001; named Companion of Honour, Royal Society of Literature, 2001.

WRITINGS:

FICTION

The Grass Is Singing, Crowell (New York, NY), 1950, reprinted, Perennial Classics (New York, NY), 2000.

This Was the Old Chief's Country (stories), M. Joseph (London, England), 1952.

Five: Short Novels, M. Joseph (London, England), 1955.

Retreat to Innocence, M. Joseph (London, England), 1956.

Habit of Loving (stories), Crowell (New York, NY), 1958.

The Golden Notebook, Simon & Schuster (New York, NY), 1962, with an introduction by the author, HarperPerennial (New York, NY), 1994.

A Man and Two Women (stories), Simon & Schuster (New York, NY), 1963.

African Stories, M. Joseph (London, England), 1964, Simon & Schuster (New York, NY), 1965.

Briefing for a Descent into Hell, Knopf (New York, NY), 1971.

The Temptation of Jack Orkney and Other Stories, Knopf (New York, NY), 1972, published as *The Story of a Non-Marrying Man and Other Stories,* J. Cape (London, England), 1972.

The Summer before the Dark, Knopf (New York, NY), 1973.

The Memoirs of a Survivor, Random House (New York, NY), 1975.

Stories, Knopf (New York, NY), 1978, published in two volumes as *Collected Stories I: To Room Nineteen* and *Collected Stories II: The Temptation of Jack Orkney and Other Stories,* J. Cape (London, England), 1978.

(Under pseudonym Jane Somers) *The Diary of a Good Neighbor* (also see below), Knopf (New York, NY), 1983.

(Under pseudonym Jane Somers) *If the Old Could. . .* (also see below), Knopf (New York, NY), 1984.

The Diaries of Jane Somers (contains *The Diary of a Good Neighbor* and *If the Old Could. . .*), Random House (New York, NY), 1984.

The Good Terrorist, Knopf (New York, NY), 1985.

The Fifth Child, Knopf (New York, NY), 1988.

The Doris Lessing Reader, Knopf (New York, NY), 1989.

The Real Thing: Stories and Sketches, HarperCollins (New York, NY), 1992, published as *London Observed: Stories and Sketches,* HarperCollins (London, England), 1992.

Love, Again, HarperCollins (New York, NY), 1996.

Mara and Dann: An Adventure, HarperFlamingo (New York, NY), 1999.

Ben, in the World (sequel to *The Fifth Child*), HarperCollins (New York, NY), 2000.

The Sweetest Dream, HarperCollins (New York, NY), 2002.

The Grandmothers: Four Short Novels, HarperCollins (New York, NY), 2004.

"CHILDREN OF VIOLENCE" SERIES

Martha Quest, M. Joseph (London, England), 1952.

A Proper Marriage, M. Joseph (London, England), 1954.

A Ripple from the Storm, M. Joseph (London, England), 1958.

Landlocked, Simon & Schuster (New York, NY), 1966.

The Four-Gated City, Knopf (New York, NY), 1969.

"CANOPUS IN ARGOS: ARCHIVES" SERIES

Re: Colonized Planet Five, Shikasta, Knopf (New York, NY), 1979.

The Marriage between Zones Three, Four, and Five, Knopf (New York, NY), 1980.

The Sirian Experiments: The Report of Ambien II, of the Five, Knopf (New York, NY), 1981.

The Making of the Representative for Planet Eight, Knopf (New York, NY), 1982.

Documents relating to the Sentimental Agents in the Volyen Empire, Knopf (New York, NY), 1983.

Canopus in Argos: Archives (contains *Re: Colonized Planet Five, Shikasta; The Marriage between Zones Three, Four, and Five; The Sirian Experiments: The Report of Ambien II, of the Five; The Making of the Representative for Planet Eight;* and *Documents Relating to the Sentimental Agents in the Volyen Empire*), Vintage (New York, NY), 1992.

NONFICTION

Going Home, drawings by Paul Hogarth, M. Joseph (London, England), 1957, with a new afterword, HarperPerennial (New York, NY), 1996.

In Pursuit of the English: A Documentary, Simon & Schuster (New York, NY), 1961, reprinted, 1996.

Particularly Cats, Simon & Schuster (New York, NY), 1967, revised edition published as *Particularly Cats—And Rufus,* Knopf (New York, NY), 1991.

A Small Personal Voice: Essays, Reviews, Interviews, Random House (New York, NY), 1975.

Prisons We Choose to Live Inside, Harper (New York, NY), 1987.

The Wind Blows away Our Words, Random House (New York, NY), 1987.

African Laughter: Four Visits to Zimbabwe, HarperCollins (New York, NY), 1992.

Under My Skin (autobiography), HarperCollins (New York, NY), 1994.

Walking in the Shade: Volume Two of My Autobiography, 1949-1962, HarperCollins (New York, NY), 1997.

Time Bites (essays), HarperCollins (New York, NY), 2004.

PLAYS

Mr. Dollinger, produced in Oxford, England, 1958.

Each in His Own Wilderness, produced in London, England, 1958.

The Truth about Billy Newton, produced in Salisbury, England, 1961.

Play with a Tiger (produced in London, England, 1962; produced in New York, NY, 1964), M. Joseph (London, England), 1962.

Also author of a libretto based on *The Making of the Representative for Planet Eight,* for an opera by Philip Glass.

OTHER

Fourteen Poems, Scorpion Press, 1959.

The Old Age of El Magnifico, Flamingo (London, England), 2000.

ADAPTATIONS: *The Memoirs of a Survivor* was adapted into a film and released in 1983; *The Grass Is Singing* was adapted into a film by Michael Raeburn and released as *Killing Heat* in 1984. *The Diary of a Good Neighbour* was adapted and directed by René Féret as the film *Rue du Retrait,* France, 2001.

SIDELIGHTS: Doris Lessing, whose long career as a novelist, short story writer, and essayist began in the mid-twentieth century, is considered among the most important writers of the modern postwar era. Since her birth in 1919 in Britain's sphere of influence in Persia (now Iran), Lessing has traveled widely, in geographical, social, political, psychological, and literary terms. These travels, as expressed in her writing, offer readers insights into life at distant outposts of the British Empire and at its core. Through her books—including novels and short-story collections—one can encounter people buffeted by personal, historical, and political forces, and can explore the major issues of the age: racism, communism, feminism, terrorism, and the destruction of the environment. "Lessing has written prolifically on everything from British colonialism . . . to

the failure of ideology," commented Gail Caldwell in the *Boston Globe,* adding that during her long career the versatile author has "taken on the apocalyptic potential of a futuristic, Blade Runner London, the perils of the color bar in Africa, [and] the life of a young girl growing up on the veld."

Lessing's wide-ranging literary appetite is one of the defining characteristics of her work; another is her style. "The Lessing sentence is blunt," explained Philip Hensher in the *Spectator,* "quickly veering from concrete facts to abstract nouns, tempted briefly by the possibilities of rhapsody, but always turning back to the urgency of the urban demotic. . . . Its cadences are punchy. . . . she loves the grand, dramatic force of words like wisdom, and the vivid simplicity of the names of colours." "Critics have found it extremely hard to categorize Lessing," observed Fiona R. Barnes in the *Dictionary of Literary Biography,* "for she has at various stages of her life espoused different causes and been labeled over again."

In 1924 Lessing's father took the family to Southern Rhodesia (now Zimbabwe), hoping to make a fortune growing corn and tobacco and panning for gold. The family found little fortune on its new farm, located in a remote corner of the Rhodesian bush not far from the border with Mozambique. However, in her years growing up in the African wild, her stays in convent and government schools, and her brief career as a secretary and homemaker, Lessing found a wealth of literary inspiration. As Mark Mathabane noted in the *Washington Post Book World,* "The formidable problems of racial, social and economic injustice besieging the region of her formative years, its wondrous beauty and unfulfilled promise, left a permanent imprint on her. They molded her artistic temperament, politics and loyalties and made of her a highly original and activist writer." In 1949 Lessing left Africa behind for London, the heart of the British empire. She also left behind most of her family: her brother, her two failed marriages, and her two children from her first marriage. With her son from her second marriage, she embarked on a new life in London as a writer. Her first novel, *The Grass Is Singing,* was published the following year.

Like many of the novels and short stories that would follow its debut, *The Grass Is Singing* deals with settings, characters, and issues very close to its author's experience of Rhodesian society and its government's apartheid policies. The central character of the novel is Mary Turner, the wife of a farmer in the African bush, whose affair with an African servant ends in her murder. "Mary Turner is a strange, sad woman, suffering under the burden of obligations imposed upon her as a white woman by the sad, strange conventions of a colonial settler society," explained K. Anthony Appiah in the *New Republic,* the critic going on to add that "the novel is intensely humane in its attentiveness to the minutest details of the mental life of this central character." In the opinion of *New York Review of Books* contributor J.M. Coetzee, this book represents "an astonishingly accomplished debut, though perhaps too wedded to romantic stereotypes of the African for present-day tastes." At the time of Lessing's debut in 1950, however, Appiah observed, "reviewers pronounced her the finest new novelist" since World War II.

Lessing's major and most controversial novel is *The Golden Notebook,* first published in 1962, wherein she brilliantly explores, as a *New Statesman* reviewer noted, what it is like to be "free and responsible, a woman in relation to men and other women, and to struggle to come to terms with one's self about these things and about writing and politics." Lessing once explained that the work is "a novel about certain political and sexual attitudes that have force now; it is an attempt to explain them, to objectivize them, to set them in relation with each other. So in a way it is a social novel, written by someone whose training—or at least whose habit of mind—is to see these things socially, not personally." In its structure, the novel is really two novels, divided in four sections and "The Golden Notebook." Lessing split it into four parts in order to "express a split person. I felt that if the artist's sensibility is to be equated with the sensibility of the educated person, then it is logical to use different styles to express different kinds of people." She felt that the "personality is very much what is remembered; [the form] enabled me to say to the reader: Look, these apparently so different people have got so-and-so in common, or these things have got this in common. If I had used a conventional style, the old-fashioned novel, . . . I would not have been able to do this kind of playing with time, memory and the balancing of people. . . . I like *The Golden Notebook* even though I believe it to be a failure, because it at least hints at complexity."

After her initial flourishing as a writer, during which time she explored the Africa of her youth from her new home in London, Lessing turned away from the land of her past and toward new settings: inner space and outer space. *Briefing for a Descent into Hell* is a novel of ideas based on her interest in the views of British psychiatrist R.D. Laing. In subsequent novels, Lessing has continued to produce work critiquing modern society.

In contrast to the realism that marked her earlier novels, Lessing's work of the late twentieth century—particularly her science-fiction series "Canopus in Argos: Archives"—would take startling new forms. In the five "Canopus" books she explores the destruction of life brought about by catastrophe and tyranny. Paul Schlueter in the *Dictionary of Literary Biography* noted that in this series Lessing's "high seriousness in describing earth's own decline and ultimate demise is as profoundly apocalyptic as ever."

Following her foray into science fiction, Lessing again surprised readers and critics by publishing two novels under a pseudonym, Jane Somers. *The Diary of a Good Neighbor* and *If the Old Could. . .* contain typical Lessing themes: relations between women, the question of identity, and psychological conflict. Though Lessing was able to get the "Somers" books published in both England and the United States, they were generally ignored by critics and did not sell well. Lessing finally admitted that the works were her creation, saying that she had used the pseudonym to prove a point about the difficulties facing young writers. Without adequate marketing and publicity, noted Lessing, books by unknown writers are generally doomed to oblivion.

More recent fiction by Lessing includes *The Good Terrorist,* a satirical novel about romantic politics; *The Fifth Child,* a 1998 novel about a violent, antisocial child who wreaks havoc on his family and society; and *Love Again,* a reflection on the agonies and insufficiency of romantic love. Commenting on *Love Again* in the *New Yorker,* Brooks Appelbaum maintained that the book is "really about the sawdust sensation of knowing that one's darkest despair and brightest ecstasy have been felt and expressed before, and better; and that ultimately, their expression doesn't help." The book's protagonist, an older woman, dissects "her love and grief with the ruthless precision of a forensic pathologist" in passages that "radiate the analytical purity that has always been Lessing's greatest strength."

A sequel to *The Fifth Child* published over ten years later, *Ben, in the World* continues the story of middle-class Britisher Ben Lovatt, who has been treated as an outsider since birth due to his primitive, savage physique. Now eighteen, the muscular but apelike Ben looks much older than his age; with little education and fearful of society, he nonetheless flees his uncaring family for Brazil, where he attempts to come to terms with his savage spirit in a harsh world. Noting that the novel's plot borders on "bathetic melodrama," a *Publishers Weekly* contributor nonetheless commended

Lessing for her efforts to show "how intellectuals acting in the name of art or science cruelly exploit simple people who can't defend themselves." Viewing the novel more positively in her *Christian Century* review, Trudy Bush called Lessing's approach a "fresh twist" on a traditional theme, and added that readers of *Ben, in the World* will never again "see those who are radically different from themselves in quite the same way."

Considered a semi-autobiographical novel, Lessing's *The Sweetest Dream* takes place during the 1960s and focuses on Julia, a widow living in a house in Hampstead who takes in her daughter-in-law and young grandsons after her son abandons his family in favor of the Communist Party. Due to the young mother's generosity, Julia's house is soon second home to a host of interesting characters, some of whom take advantage of the situation. In another part of the novel, a fictional African nation called Zimlia suffers through decolonization, and another political fiction is discredited as the new leaders show themselves to be as ruthless as their colonial predecessors were. In its examination of political systems gone awry and what *Booklist* contributor Donna Seaman dubbed the "sweet utopian dream of communism that went so nightmarishly wrong," Lessing's novel maintains what *New Criterion* contributor Paul Hollander called "a compelling focus on the timeless tension between idealistic social-political aspiration and the dark side of human failure. . . . As Lessing shows, 'the sweetest dream' . . . will likely continue to haunt and elude us." Calling Lessing "one of the great imaginative fantasists of our time," *Spectator* reviewer Hensher praised *The Sweetest Dream* as "loose, absorbing, urgent" in its focus on "the future of society and personal responsibility." Seaman praised the the work as "a realistic tour de force," adding that "the force of Lessing's vast knowledge and wisdom and the vigor and vision of her imagination and conviction are felt on every page."

The Grandmothers, Kirkus Reviews claimed, demonstrates that the "84-year-old author . . . still boasts a range and power few writers half her age can muster." In the title story Lessing explores a relationship between two women and their sons which if not taboo is extremely unusual. Digby Durrant wrote in the *Spectator* that "Lessing thinks the only sin committed by the grannies was to be discovered." "In 'A Love Child,' an ex-soldier longs to know the child he is sure he fathered on a brief reprieve from the horrors of World War II," Amy Ford observed in *Library Journal*, adding that Lessing is in top form in these stories. "In 'Victoria and the Staveneys,' a poor black child longs for a room of her own," Hazel Rochman noted in *Booklist*. Al-

though she found the stories too lengthy, she was struck by "beautiful individual sentences [that] stop you with their startling insight." "The Reason for It" describes a future society in decline from the viewpoint of a leader, much in the manner of *The Memoirs of a Survivor* or the *Canopus in Argos* series. Claire Messud writing in the *New Statesman* commented that "Lessing has cultivated a briskness, an impatience with certain niceties of narrative: years pass in a single sentence, characters are sketched swiftly, almost hastily, and their most radical alterations are recorded in a few words. This conversational brusqueness is not displeasing."

Lessing has also produced nonfiction tomes, including *The Wind Blows away Our Words,* about war in Afghanistan during the 1980s. A nonfiction work and two volumes of autobiography marked her eventual return to her African homeland and to the preoccupations of her youth. After leaving Southern Rhodesia in 1949, Lessing had returned only once, in 1956, an experience she recounts in *Going Home.* After this first homecoming, the white minority government blocked any future returns because of Lessing's criticism of apartheid. It was not until the 1980s, after years of civil war and thousands of deaths brought the black majority to power in the newly christened Zimbabwe, that Lessing could return. In *African Laughter: Four Visits to Zimbabwe* she chronicles her trips to southern Africa in 1982, 1988, 1989, and 1992. On one level, this book offers the keen observations of a new nation's growing pains through the eyes of someone not an insider but not an outsider. She sees first a country trying to come to terms with the outcome of a long and bloody civil war based on race. In subsequent trips, she finds exuberance, corruption, and finally decline. "One is oneself fixed in the beam of Lessing's penetrating gaze from the first moments of the book," wrote Appiah.

In *African Laughter,* according to Mathabane, "Lessing gives us one of the most penetrating and evenhanded critiques of Zimbabwe as a new nation." Her "portrait is without stereotype or sentimentality," the critic added, "and free of the overbearing shadow of South Africa and its larger-than-life problems of apartheid." For Appiah, however, Lessing's insights into the changes taking place in Zimbabwe are not complete because, as a white woman, she is unable to get inside the hearts and minds of blacks. "Lessing shows us only the exterior of the black Zimbabweans," he pointed out, "but still we are in her debt for what that view teaches us about what is happening in Zimbabwe." In Appiah's final analysis, "What we learn from this book, then, is not so much the political history of Zimbabwe in its first dozen years, but the psychic history of Southern Rhodesia, the inner history of the white settlers and what has become of them: the best of this book is the white man's story."

Under My Skin, the first volume of Lessing's autobiography, follows the writer from her birth in 1919 to 1949, the year she left Southern Rhodesia for London and her life as a single mother and aspiring writer. She recounts her very early years in Persia, the railway journey across a chaotic Soviet Russia, the promising voyage to Africa, and the years in the bush and in convent school. She also describes the lives of the Taylor family, their fellow whites, and the African majority around them. *Under My Skin* "is not so much a recollection of her early life in Southern Rhodesia as a dissection of it," commented Martha Duffy in *Time;* "The chapters on childhood are marvelously, sometimes frighteningly, detailed." Roberta Rubenstein commented in Chicago's *Tribune Books* that "*Under My Skin* makes for compelling reading because of Lessing's vivid reconstructions of decisive experiences and significant people of her childhood. Throughout, she juxtaposes descriptions of events that occurred in her youth—before she was capable of fathoming them—with her current unsentimental judgments of them." Although this is autobiography, it is Lessing, true to her strengths as an observer and writer. Duffy concluded: "Set down in blunt, fluent prose, it is the same mix of the practical and the speculative that marks all her writing. And, alas, the same lack of humor. But if that is a flaw, it also ensures the author's total engagement with any subject she tackles. That is what one reads Doris Lessing for: unsparing clarity and frankness." *Walking in the Shade,* the second Lessing autobiography, covers life in London from her arrival in 1949 to the publication in 1962 of *The Golden Notebook,* which secured her reputation as a major postwar English writer. Much of the book deals with Lessing's love/hate relationship with the Communist Party, which she joined in 1952—"the most neurotic act of my life," she once wrote—and stuck with it for nearly twenty years despite deep misgivings. "Her . . . description of the Cold War years, the potent mixture of arrogance, emotionalism and naivety that kept her and others tied to the Party line, long after they knew it was nonsense, will not be bettered," wrote Anne Chisholm in the *Times Literary Supplement.* The book also recounts Lessing's disastrous love affairs, her struggles as a single mother with little money in grim, tattered postwar London, her writing habits, her relatively rapid entry into the city's intellectual circles, and her perceptions of the famous—and eccentric—who moved in those circles. Chisholm found the book to be "not Lessing's best-written or best-constructed book; it is repetitive, and the more gossipy sections have a perfunctory air, as if added under pressure from her publishers. But

even its flaws testify to her seriousness of purpose." *Walking in the Shade* is "stingingly self-mocking," according to Claudia Roth Pierpont in the *New Yorker;* it "is about the admission of colossal, sickening error and defeat." But "it is surely Lessing's ability to hold fast to her goal even as she records every stumble and collapse along the way which has made her work of near-inspirational value to so many."

According to Mathabane, "whatever her subject, Lessing is a surefooted and convincing storyteller. Her work possesses a universality, range and depth matched by that of few other writers in our time." As Schlueter remarked of her career, Lessing's "work has changed radically in format and genre over the years, . . . and she has been more and more willing to take chances fictionally by tackling unusual or taboo subjects. . . . And while it is commonplace to note that Lessing is not a stylist, that she is repetitive, and that her fiction too easily reflects her own enthusiasms at particular moments, . . . the fact remains that she is among the most powerful and compelling novelists of our century."

BIOGRAPHICAL AND CRITICAL SOURCES:

BOOKS

Arora, Neena, *Nayantara Sahgal and Doris Lessing: A Feminist Study in Comparison,* Prestige Books/Indian Society for Commonwealth Studies (New Delhi, India), 1991.

Barr, Marleen and Smith, Nicholas D., editors, *Women and Utopia: Critical Interpretations,* University Press of America (Lanham, MD), 1983.

Bertelsen, Eve, editor, *Doris Lessing,* McGraw-Hill, 1985.

Bigsby, C.W.E., *The Radical Imagination and the Liberal Tradition,* Junction Books, 1981.

Bloom, Harold, editor, *Doris Lessing,* Chelsea House Publishers (Philadelphia, PA), 2003.

Brewster, Dorothy, *Doris Lessing,* Twayne Publishers, 1965.

Brigg, Peter, *The Span of Mainstream and Science Fiction: A Critical Study of a New Literary Genre,* McFarland & Co. (Jefferson, NC), 2002.

Bücher, Britta, *A Wordless Statement: Die Rolle der Darstellung in Doris Lessings Space-fiction,* Peter Lang (New York, NY), 2002.

Budhos, Shirley, *The Theme of Enclosure in Selected Works of Doris Lessing,* Whitston Pub. Co. (Troy, NY), 1987.

Cederstrom, Lorelei, *Fine-tuning the Feminine Psyche: Jungian Patterns in the Novels of Doris Lessing,* Peter Lang (New York, NY), 1990.

Christ, Carol P., *Diving Deep and Surfacing: Women Writers on Spiritual Quest,* Beacon Press (Boston, MA), 1980.

Contemporary Literary Criticism, Thomson Gale (Detroit, MI), Volume 1, 1973, Volume 2, 1974, Volume 3, 1975, Volume 6, 1975, Volume 10, 1979, Volume 15, 1980, Volume 22, 1982, Volume 40, 1986.

Dandson, Cathy N., and E.M. Brown, editors, *The Lost Tradition: Mothers and Daughters in Literature,* Ungar (New York, NY), 1980, pp. 207-216.

Dictionary of Literary Biography, Thomson Gale (Detroit, MI), Volume 15: *British Novelists, 1930-1959,* 1983, Volume 139: *British Short Fiction Writers, 1945-1980,* 1994.

Dictionary of Literary Biography Yearbook: 1985, Thomson Gale (Detroit, MI), 1986.

Draine, Betsy, *Substance under Pressure: Artistic Coherence and Evolving Form in the Novels of Doris Lessing,* University of Wisconsin Press (Madison, WI), 1983.

Ezergailis, Inta, *Woman Writers, the Divided Self: Analysis of Novels by Christa Wolf, Ingeborg Bachmann, Doris Lessing and others,* Bouvier Verlag Herbert Grundmann (Bonn), 1982.

Fahim, Shadia S., *Doris Lessing: Sufi Equilibrium and the Form of the Novel,* St. Martin's Press (New York, NY), 1994.

Fishburn, Katherine, *The Unexpected Universe of Doris Lessing: A Study in Narrative Technique,* Greenwood Press (Westport, CN), 1985.

Galin, Müge, *Between East and West: Sufism in the Novels of Doris Lessing,* State University of New York Press (Albany, NY), 1997.

Gardiner, Judith Kegan, *Rhys, Stead, Lessing, and the Politics of Empathy,* Indiana University Press (Bloomington), 1989.

Greene, Gayle, *Doris Lessing: The Poetics of Change,* University of Michigan Press (Ann Arbor, MI), 1994.

Hite, Molly, *The Other Side of the Story: Structures and Strategies of Contemporary Feminist Narrative,* Cornell University Press (Ithaca, NY), 1989.

Holmquist, Ingrid, *From Society to Nature: A Study of Doris Lessing's "Children of Violence,"* Gothenburg Studies in English, 1980.

Ingersoll, Earl G., editor, *Doris Lessing: Conversations,* Ontario Review Press (Princeton, NJ), 1994.

Ingersoll, Earl G., editor, *Putting the Questions Differently: Interviews with Doris Lessing, 1964-1994,* Flamingo (London, England), 1996.

Kaplan, Carey and Rose, Ellen Cronan, editors, *Doris Lessing: The Alchemy of Survival,* Ohio University Press (Athens, OH), 1988.

Knapp, Mona, *Doris Lessing,* Frederick Ungar, 1984.

Kums, Guido, *Fiction, or The language of Our Discontent: A Study of the Built-in Novelist in Novels by Angus Wilson, Lawrence Durrell, and Doris Lessing,* Peter Lang (New York, NY), 1985.

Laurenson, Diana, editor, *The Sociology of Literature: Applied Studies,* University of Keele Press (Newcastle on Tyne, England), 1978.

LeFew-Blake, Penelope, *Schopenhauer, Women's Literature, and the Legacy of Pessimism in the Novels of George Eliot, Olive Schreiner, Virginia Woolf, and Doris Lessing,* Edwin Mellen Press (Lewiston, NY), 2001.

Martinson, Deborah, *In the Presence of Audience: The Self in Diaries and Fiction,* Ohio State University Press (Columbus, OH), 2003.

Michael, Magali Cornier, *Feminism and the Postmodern Impulse: Post-World War II Fiction,* State University of New York Press (Albany, NY), 1996.

Myles, Anita, *Doris Lessing: A Novelist with Organic Sensibility,* Associated Publishing House (New Delhi, India), 1991.

Perrakis, Phyllis Sternberg, *Spiritual Exploration in the Works of Doris Lessing,* Greenwood Press (Westport, CN), 1999.

Pickering, Jean, *Understanding Doris Lessing,* University of South Carolina Press (Columbia, SC), 1990.

Pratt, Annis, Dembo, L. S., editors, *Doris Lessing: Critical Studies,* University of Wisconsin Press (Madison, WI), 1974.

Rigney, Barbara H., *Madness and Sexual Politics in the Feminist Novel: Studies in Brontë, Woolf, Lessing, and Atwood,* University of Wisconsin Press (Madison, WI), 1978.

Robinson, Sally, *Engendering the Subject: Gender and Self-Representation in Contemporary Women's Fiction,* State University of New York Press (Albany, NY), 1991.

Rose, Ellen Cronan, *The Tree outside the Window: Doris Lessing's Children of Violence,* University Press of New England (Hanover, NH), 1976.

Rowe, Margaret Moan, *Doris Lessing,* St. Martin's Press (New York, NY), 1994.

Rubenstein, Roberta, *The Novelistic Vision of Doris Lessing: Breaking the Forms of Consciousness,* University of Illinois Press (Urbana), 1979.

Sage, Lorna, *Doris Lessing,* Methuen, 1983.

Saxton, Ruth, and Jean Tobin, editors, *Woolf and Lessing: Breaking the Mold,* St. Martin's Press (New York, NY), 1994.

Schlueter, Paul, *The Novels of Doris Lessing,* Southern Illinois University Press (Carbondale, IL), 1973.

Seiler-Franklin, Carol, *Boulder-Pushers: Women in the Fiction of Margaret Drabble, Doris Lessing, and Iris Murdoch,* Peter Lang (New York, NY), 1979.

Seligman, Dee, *Doris Lessing: An Annotated Bibliography of Criticism,* Greenwood (Westport, CT), 1981.

Shapiro, Charles, editor, *Contemporary British Novelists,* Southern Illinois University Press (Carbondale, IL), 1964.

Short Story Criticism, Volume 6, Thomson Gale (Detroit, MI), 1990.

Singleton, Mary Ann, *The City and the Veld: The Fiction of Doris Lessing,* Bucknell University Press (Lewisburg, PA), 1977.

Sprague, Claire, and Tiger, Virginia, *Critical Essays on Doris Lessing,* G.K. Hall (Boston, MA), 1986.

Sprague, Claire, *Rereading Doris Lessing: Narrative Patterns of Doubling and Repetition,* University of North Carolina Press (Chapel Hill), 1987.

Taylor, Jenny, editor, *Notebooks, Memoirs, Archives: Reading and Rereading Doris Lessing,* Routledge & Kegan Paul (Boston, MA), 1982.

Thorpe, Michael, *Doris Lessing's Africa,* Evans Bros (London, England), 1978.

Whittaker, Ruth, *Doris Lessing,* St. Martin's Press (New York, NY), 1988.

Yelin, Louise, *From the Margins of Empire: Christina Stead, Doris Lessing, Nadine Gordimer,* Cornell University Press (Ithaca, NY), 1998.

Yuknavitch, Lidia, *Allegories of Violence: Tracing the Writing of War in Twentieth-century Fiction,* Routledge (New York, NY), 2001.

PERIODICALS

America, December 7, 1996, p. 25.

Antioch Review, fall, 1996, p. 493.

Ariel, July, 1995, p. 176.

Belles Lettres, summer, 1993, p. 30.

Book, May, 2001, p. 86; January-February, 2002, Penelope Mesic, review of *The Sweetest Dream,* p. 63.

Booklist, November 15, 2001, Brad Hooper, review of *The Grass Is Singing,* p. 555; December 1, 2001, Donna Seaman, review of *The Sweetest Dream,* p. 605; November 15, 2003, Hazel Rochman, review of *The Grandmothers,* p. 548.

Boston Globe, July 29, 1992, p. 62; October 16, 1994, p. B18; November 13, 1994, p. B1.

Choice, April, 1995, p. 1298; October, 1995, p. 292; March, 1997, p. 1167.

Christian Century, December 13, 2000, Trudy Bush, review of *Ben, in the World,* p. 1313.

Christian Science Monitor, December 9, 1992, p. 13; November 17, 1994, p. 14.

Critique, spring, 2002, p. 228.

Economist (United Kingdom), December 22, 2001, review of *The Sweetest Dream,* p. 117.

Frontiers, June, 2001, Roberta Rubenstein, "Feminism, Eros, and the Coming of Age,", pp. 1-20.

Globe and Mail (Toronto, Ontario, Canada), November 24, 1984; April 6, 1985; December 21, 1985; August 6, 1988.

Hudson Review, spring, 2001, Alan Davis, review of *Ben, in the World,* p. 141.

Kirkus Reviews, October 15, 2003, review of *The Grandmothers,* p. 1246.

Library Journal, February 1, 2002, Beth Anderson, review of *The Sweetest Dream,* p. 131; November 15, 2003, Amy Ford, review of *The Grandmothers,* p. 100.

London Review of Books, April 22, 1993, p. 22.

Los Angeles Times, March 1, 1983; July 6, 1983; May 10, 1984; January 14, 1988; June 25, 1992, p. E12; October 20, 1994, p. E8; December 8, 1994, p. E1.

Los Angeles Times Book Review, March 1, 1981; March 21, 1982; February 10, 1985; October 13, 1985; October 20, 1985; March 27, 1988; April 6, 1988; November 1, 1992, p. 2; September 5, 1993, p. 6.

Maclean's, January 9, 1995, p. 66; April 15, 1996, p. 64.

Modern Fiction Studies, summer, 1975; spring, 1980; spring, 1996, p. 194.

Modern Language Quarterly, March, 1974.

Nation, January 11, 1965; January 17, 1966; June 13, 1966; March 6, 1967; November 7, 1994, p. 528; May 6, 1996, p. 62; October 13, 1997, p. 31.

New Criterion, March, 2003, Paul Hollander, review of *The Sweetest Dream,* pp. 71-76.

New Republic, June 28, 1993, p. 30.

New Statesman, April 20, 1962; November 8, 1963; October 31, 1997, p. 43; October 1, 2001, Stephanie Merriman, review of *The Sweetest Dream,* p. 83; December 8, 2003, Claire Messud, review of *The Grandmothers,* p. 52.

Newsweek, October 14, 1985.

New York, October 26, 1992, p. 96.

New Yorker, June 10, 1996, p. 88; November 17, 1997, p. 108; February 18, 2002, Louis Menand, review of *The Sweetest Dream,* p. 193.

New York Review of Books, December 22, 1994, p. 51; April 18, 1996, pp. 13-15.

New York Times, October 21, 1972; October 23, 1979; March 27, 1980; January 19, 1981; January 29, 1982; March 14, 1983; April 22, 1984; October 5, 1984; October 23, 1984; July 14, 1985; September 17, 1985; March 30, 1988; June 14, 1988; June 16, 1992, p. C16; November 2, 1994, p. C1.

New York Times Book Review, March 14, 1971; May 13, 1973; June 4, 1978; November 4, 1979; March 30, 1980; January 11, 1981; February 2, 1982; April 3, 1983; September 22, 1985; January 24, 1988; April 3, 1988; April 12, 1992, p. 13; October 18, 1992, p. 13; November 6, 1994, p. 1; April 21, 1996, p. 13; September 14, 1997, p. 16.

Partisan Review, spring, 2002, Anthony Chennells, review of *The Sweetest Dream,* p. 297.

Publishers Weekly, September 19, 1994, p. 47; May 29, 2000, review of *Ben, in the World,* p. 46; January 21, 2002, review of *The Sweetest Dream,* p. 63; November 17, 2003, review of *The Grandmothers* p. 40.

San Francisco Review of Books, number 3, 1992, p. 25.

Spectator, October 31, 1992, p. 38; October 22, 1994, p. 48; April 20, 1996, p. 42; October 18, 1997, p. 55; September 1, 2001, Philip Hensher, review of *The Sweetest Dream,* p. 33; November 15, 2003, Digby Durrant, review of *The Grandmothers,* p. 51.

Time, October 1, 1984; October 7, 1985; November 21, 1994.

Times (London, England), March 19, 1981; June 2, 1983; August 12, 1985; October 7, 1985.

Times Literary Supplement, November 23, 1979; May 9, 1980; April 17, 1981; April 2, 1982; June 3, 1983; September 13, 1985; May 8, 1987; October 17, 1987; April 22, 1988; December 18, 1992, p. 8; December, 2, 1994, p. 11; April 5, 1996, p. 27; December 5, 1997, p. 6.

Tribune Books (Chicago, IL), October 30, 1979; April 27, 1980; January 24, 1982; September 29, 1985; January 31, 1988; March 20, 1988; July 26, 1992, p. 3; January 3, 1993, p. 3; October 23, 1994, p. 1.

USA Today, December 1, 1994, p. D9.

Village Voice, January 4, 1973; October 2, 1978.

Washington Post, September 24, 1984; October 1, 1984; October 24, 1984; June 11, 1992, p. B2; December 29, 1994, p. C1.

Washington Post Book World, October 21, 1979; November 4, 1979; April 6, 1980; January 25, 1981; March 21, 1982; April 24, 1983; September 22, 1985; March 20, 1988; April 19, 1992, p. 15; January, 10, 1993, p. 5; October 16, 1994, p. 14; March 31, 1996, p. 7.

Women's Review of Books, March, 1995, p. 11; October, 1996, p. 11; November, 1997, p. 5.

World Literature Today, spring, 2002, Charles P. Sarvan, review of *The Sweetest Dream,* pp. 119-120.

World Literature Written in English, November, 1973; April, 1976.

ONLINE

Doris Lessing Web site, http://www.dorislessing.org/ (August 3, 2004).

LESSING, Doris May
   See LESSING, Doris

*   *   *

LESTER, Julius 1939-
   (Julius Bernard Lester)

PERSONAL: Born January 27, 1939, in St. Louis, MO; son of W.D. (a minister) and Julia (Smith) Lester; married Joan Steinau (a researcher), 1962 (divorced, 1970); married Alida Carolyn Fechner, March 21, 1979; children: (first marriage) Jody Simone, Malcolm Coltrane; (second marriage) Elena Milad (stepdaughter), David Julius. *Ethnicity:* Black. *Education:* Fisk University, B.A., 1960.

ADDRESSES: Office—University of Massachusetts, Judaic Studies, Herter Hall, Amherst, MA 01003. *E-mail*—jbles@concentric.net.

CAREER: Newport Folk Festival, Newport, RI, director, 1966-68; New School for Social Research, New York, NY, lecturer, 1968-70; WBAI-FM, New York, NY, producer and host of live radio show *The Great Proletarian Cultural Revolution,* 1968-75; University of Massachusetts, Amherst, professor of Afro-American studies, 1971-88, professor of Near Eastern and Judaic studies, 1982—, acting director and associate director of Institute for Advanced Studies in Humanities, 1982-84; Vanderbilt University, Nashville, TN, writer-in-residence, 1985. Professional musician and singer. Host of live television show *Free Time,* WNET-TV, 1971-73. Lester's photographs of the 1960s civil rights movement have been exhibited at the Smithsonian Institution and are on permanent display at Howard University.

AWARDS, HONORS: Newbery Honor Book citation, 1969, and Lewis Carroll Shelf Award, 1970, both for *To Be a Slave;* Lewis Carroll Shelf Award, 1972, and National Book Award finalist, 1973, both for *The Long Journey Home: Stories from Black History;* Lewis Carroll Shelf Award, 1973, for *The Knee-High Man and other Tales;* honorable mention, Coretta Scott King Award, 1983, for *This Strange New Feeling,* and 1988, for *Tales of Uncle Remus: The Adventures of Brer Rabbit;* University of Massachusetts Distinguished Teacher's Award, 1983-84, and Faculty Fellowship Award, 1985; National Professor of the Year Silver Medal Award, 1985, and Massachusetts State Professor of the Year and Gold Medal Award for National Professor of the Year, both 1986, all from Council for Advancement and Support of Education; chosen distinguished faculty lecturer, 1986-87; Coretta Scott King Award, 2006, for *Day of Tears: A Novel in Dialogue.*

WRITINGS:

(With Pete Seeger) *The Twelve-String Guitar As Played by Leadbelly,* Oak (New York, NY), 1965.

Look Out Whitey! Black Power's Gon' Get Your Mama!, Dial (New York, NY), 1968.

To Be a Slave, Dial (New York, NY), 1969; thirtieth anniversary edition, illustrated by Tom Feelings, Dial (New York, NY), 1998.

Black Folktales, Baron (New York, NY), 1969.

Search for the New Land: History As Subjective Experience, Dial (New York, NY), 1969.

Revolutionary Notes, Baron (New York, NY), 1969.

(Editor) *The Seventh Son: The Thoughts and Writings of W.E.B. Du Bois,* two volumes, Random House (New York, NY), 1971.

(Compiler, with Rae Pace Alexander) *Young and Black in America,* Random House (New York, NY), 1971.

The Long Journey Home: Stories from Black History, Dial (New York, NY), 1972, reprinted, Puffin Books (New York, NY), 1998.

The Knee-High Man and Other Tales, Dial (New York, NY), 1972.

Two Love Stories, Dial (New York, NY), 1972.

(Editor) Stanley Couch, *Ain't No Ambulances for No Nigguhs Tonight* (poems), Baron (New York, NY), 1972.

Who I Am (poems), Dial (New York, NY), 1974.

All Is Well: An Autobiography, Morrow (New York, NY), 1976.

This Strange New Feeling, Dial (New York, NY), 1982.

Do Lord Remember Me (novel), Holt (Orlando, FL), 1984, reprinted, Arcade (New York, NY), 1998.

The Tales of Uncle Remus: The Adventures of Brer Rabbit, Dial (New York, NY), 1987.

More Tales of Uncle Remus: The Further Adventures of Brer Rabbit, His Friends, Enemies, and Others, Dial (New York, NY), 1988.

Lovesong: Becoming a Jew (autobiography), Holt (Orlando, FL), 1988.

How Many Spots Does a Leopard Have? and Other Tales, illustrated by David Shannon, Scholastic (New York, NY), 1989.

Falling Pieces of the Broken Sky (essays), Arcade (New York, NY), 1990.

Further Tales of Uncle Remus: The Misadventures of Brer Rabbit, Brer Fox, Brer Wolf, the Doodang, and Other Creatures, illustrated by Jerry Pinkney, Dial (New York, NY), 1990.

The Last Tales of Uncle Remus, illustrated by Jerry Pinkney, Dial (New York, NY), 1994.

And All Our Wounds Forgiven (adult novel), Arcade (New York, NY), 1994.

John Henry, illustrated by Jerry Pinkney, Dial (New York, NY), 1994.

The Man Who Knew Too Much: A Moral Tale from the Baile of Zambia, illustrated by Leonard Jenkins, Clarion (New York, NY), 1994.

Othello: A Retelling, Scholastic (New York, NY), 1995.

Sam and the Tigers: A New Telling of Little Black Sambo, illustrated by Jerry Pinkney, Dial Books (New York, NY), 1996.

How Butterflies Came to Be, Scholastic (New York, NY), 1997.

Shining, illustrated by Terea Shaffer, Silver Whistle (San Diego, CA), 1997.

Black Cowboy, Wild Horses: A True Story, illustrated by Jerry Pinkney, Dial Books (New York, NY), 1998.

From Slave Ship to Freedom Road, illustrated by Rod Brown, Dial (New York, NY), 1998.

When the Beginning Began: Stories about God, the Creatures, and Us, illustrated by Emily Lisker, Silver Whistle (San Diego, CA), 1999.

What a Truly Cool World, illustrated by Joe Cepeda, Scholastic (New York, NY), 1999.

Uncle Remus: The Complete Tales (reprint in one volume of works originally published separately 1987-1994), illustrated by Jerry Pinkney, Phyllis Fogelman Books (New York, NY), 1999.

Albidaro and the Mischievous Dream, illustrated by Jerry Pinkney, Phyllis Fogelman Books (New York, NY), 2000.

The Blues Singers: Ten Who Rocked the World, illustrated by Lisa Cohen, Jump at the Sun/Hyperion (New York, NY), 2001.

When Dad Killed Mom, Silver Whistle (San Diego, CA), 2001.

Ackamarackus: Julius Lester's Sumptuously Silly Fantastically Funny Fables, illustrated by Emilie Chollat, Scholastic (New York, NY), 2001.

Why Heaven Is Far Away, illustrated by Joe Cepeda, Scholastic (New York, NY), 2002.

Pharaoh's Daughter: A Novel of Ancient Egypt, Silver Whistle (San Diego, CA), 2000.

Let's Talk about Race, illustrated by Karen Barbour, HarperCollins (New York, NY), 2004.

Day of Tears: A Novel in Dialogue, Jump at the Sun/ Hyperion (New York, NY), 2005.

Contributor of essays and reviews to numerous magazines and newspapers, including *New York Times Book Review, New York Times, Nation, Katallagete, Democ-*

racy, National Review, New Republic, Reform Judaism, Commonweal, and *Village Voice.* Associate editor, *Sing Out,* 1964-70; contributing editor, *Broadside of New York,* 1964-70. Lester's books have been translated into seven languages.

SIDELIGHTS: Julius Lester is "foremost among . . . black writers who produce their work from a position of historical strength," wrote critic John A. Williams in the *New York Times Book Review.* Drawing on old documents and folktales, Lester fashions stories that proclaim the heritage of black Americans and "attempt to recreate the social life of the past," noted Eric Foner and Naomi Lewis in the *New York Review of Books.* Lester's tales are more than simple reportage. Their purpose, as the reviewers pointed out, is "not merely to impart historical information, but to teach moral and political lessons." Because he feels that the history of minority groups has been largely ignored, Lester intends to furnish his young readers with what he calls "a usable past" and with what the Foner and Lewis called "a sense of history which will help shape their lives and politics."

Lester has distinguished himself as a civil-rights activist, musician, photographer, radio and talk-show host, professor, poet, novelist, folklorist, and talented writer for children and young adults. His characters fall into two categories: those drawn from Afro-American folklore and those drawn from black or Judaic history. The former are imaginary creatures, or sometimes animals, such as *The Knee-High Man's* Mr. Bear and Mr. Rabbit; the latter are real people, "ordinary men and women who might appear only in . . . a neglected manuscript at the Library of Congress," according to William Loren Katz in the *Washington Post Book World.* Critics find that Lester uses both types of characters to reveal the black individual's struggle against slavery.

Black Folktales, Lester's first collection of folk stories, features larger-than-life heroes—including a cigar-smoking black God—shrewd animals, and cunning human beings. While some of the characters are taken from African legends and others from American slave tales, they all demonstrate that "black resistance to white oppression is as old as the confrontation between the two groups," said Williams. Most reviewers applaud Lester's view of Afro-American folklore and praise his storytelling skills, but a few object to what they perceive as the antiwhite tone of the book. Zena Sutherland, writing in the *Bulletin of the Center for Children's Books,* called *Black Folktales* "a vehicle for hostility. . . . There is no story that concerns white people in which they are not pictured as venal or stupid or both."

Lester also deals with white oppression in his second collection of folktales, *The Knee-High Man and Other Tales.* Although these six animal stories are funny, *New York Times Book Review* critic Ethel Richards suggested that "powerfully important lessons ride the humor. In 'The Farmer and the Snake,' the lesson is that kindness will not change the nature of a thing—in this case, the nature of a poisonous snake to bite." A *Junior Bookshelf* reviewer pointed out that this story—as well as others in the book—reflects the relationship between owner and slave. While pursuing the same theme, Lester moves into the realm of nonfiction with *The Long Journey Home: Stories from Black History,* a documentary collection of slave narratives, and *To Be a Slave,* a collection of six stories based on historical fact. Both books showcase ordinary people in adverse circumstances and provide the reader with a look at what Lester calls "history from the bottom up." *Black Like Me* author John Howard Griffin, writing in the *New York Times Book Review,* commended Lester's approach, saying that the stories "help destroy the delusion that black men did not suffer as another man would in similar circumstances," and Eric Foner and Naomi Lewis applauded the fact that "Lester does not feel it is necessary to make every black man and woman a super-hero." *New York Times Book Review* contributor Rosalind K. Goddard recommended Lester's writing as both lesson and entertainment writing, "These stories point the way for young blacks to find their roots, so important to the realization of their identities, as well as offer a stimulating and informative experience for all."

In *Lovesong: Becoming a Jew,* Lester presents the autobiographical story of his conversion to the Jewish faith. Beginning with his southern childhood as the son of a Methodist minister, following his years of atheism and civil rights activity, and ending with his exploration of many faiths, *Lovesong* concludes with Lester's embrace of Judaism in 1983. Discussing the book in a *Partisan Review* article, David Lehman remarked that the author relates his experiences with "conviction and passion."

With *How Many Spots Does a Leopard Have?* Lester drew from folktales of both the African and Jewish traditions to write new stories in a modern language. "Although I am of African and Jewish ancestry," Lester writes in his introduction to the collection, "I am also an American. . . . I have fitted the story to my mouth and tongue." Assessing the collection in the *Los Angeles Times Book Review,* Sonja Bolle called the stories "so lively they positively dance."

Lester's books often retell traditional folk tales, turning familiar stories on end while presenting them in a contemporary setting with morals intact and appropriate for today's youth. His "Uncle Remus" series has taken the "almost impenetrable phonetic transcription of the dialect" of Harris's telling and made it, according to Mary M. Burns of *Horn Book,* "more accessible through Lester's translations into Standard English. Moreover, the tales no longer suffer from the stereotyped image of Uncle Remus, which confirmed black inferiority."

In *Othello: A Retelling,* Lester tackles Shakespeare in a "re-imagining" that retains the questions about perceptions, race, and the nature of love and friendship central to the bard's original play, while modernizing the characters and adding psychological depth to make the story more appealing to today's youth.

Sam and the Tiger is a "hip and hilarious retelling" of the Little Black Sambo story, according to a *Publishers Weekly* reviewer. *John Henry* is a retelling of the popular American legend with a focus on Henry's African-American heritage. In *Black Cowboy, Wild Horses,* Lester evokes the legendary stature of real cowboy Bob Lemmons and the majesty of the Wild West.

Lester's first adult novel, *And All Our Wounds Forgiven,* is a powerful, disturbing, and controversial revisitation of the civil rights movement. Wilfred D. Samuels writing for the *African American Review,* called this fiction an attempt by Lester to "demythologize" civil rights leader Dr. Martin Luther King, Jr.

In Lester's *Shining* a young girl named Shining, growing up in a tribal society, is rejected by the women of the tribe for her refusal to speak and sing. However, after conveying a message through a "wordless song of forgiveness" that she has absorbed their culture, "Shining goes on to become designated successor to The One, a regal deity charged with guarding all souls living and dead," according to a critic for *Kirkus Reviews.* Shining's song shows her people "that she has been listening to them all along, hearing their joys, sorrows, and fears," continued the reviewer. Lester offers a preface at the beginning of *Shining* stating that through the book, he was able to, according to the *Kirkus* reviewer, "explore his own relationship with music and listening."

Lester created a funky and playfully outlandish view of Heaven in *What a Truly Cool World.* Presenting a mythical view of the afterlife in contemporary terms, Lester describes a God who walks around in slippers, has a wife named Irene, and a secretary named Bruce.

Lester published a delightful sequel, *Why Heaven Is Far Away,* in which the people of earth are being overwhelmed by snakes.

When the Beginning Began is a fusion of Lester's mixed heritage, blending the irreverence of the African-American storytelling tradition he admired and learned from his father and the imaginative inquiry of Judaism's midrashim, stories that extend and interpret bible stories. Ilene Cooper of *Booklist* called this "a reverent, wise, witty, and wonderfully entertaining book, handsomely produced."

From Slave Ship to Freedom Road is a vividly illustrated historical narration of the reality of slavery. *Pharaoh's Daughter* is a historically rich retelling of Moses—Lester-style. *Albidaro and the Mischievous Dream* is the story of what happens in a world where teddy bears in dreams tell children they can do anything they want.

Ackamarackus: Julius Lester's Sumptuously Silly Fantastically Funny Fables has been well received by the critics, generating numerous positive reviews. Wendy Lukehart of the *School Library Journal* described *Ackamarackus* as a "riotous collection" of six tales, each "featuring irrepressible animals, laugh-out-loud descriptions, alliterative language, turns of phrase that dance off the tongue, and two pithy morals brimming with wisdom and wit."

Lester continued to prove his versatility and dexterity as an writer in *When Dad Killed Mom,* a psychological mystery for young adults. A reviewer for *Publishers Weekly* described this book as "subtly and credibly done," a mystery that explores the murder and the complex feelings of the two child protagonists as they deal with the death of their mother at their father's hand. "In the end, they are learning to make new lives for themselves and to somehow live with their losses, though their lives have been forever altered," wrote Paula Rohrlick in *Kliatt.* Rohrlick continued, Lester "succeeds in creating some suspense," and though it's "not a cheerful read," Lester weaves "an engrossing story."

The Blues Singers brings Lester back to his musician roots with the creation of this picture book in tribute to the blues and ten great performers of this rich music. The book unfolds through historically rich profiles of jazz greats such as Bessie Smith, Muddy Waters, and B.B. King told in anecdotal style through a fictional grandfather storytelling for his granddaughter.

Lester once talked about goals as a writer and his belief that his main purpose as a writer is to educate. Lending credence to this position is the fact that much of his work has been either historical sketches or historically based fiction, all with his unique twist, often offering an insider view of the African-American experience. It is in his work for children and young adults that this author best demonstrates his purpose. "What children need are not role models," Lester told an audience of the New England Library Association in a speech reprinted in *Horn Book*, "but heroes and heroines. A hero is one who is larger than life. Because he or she is superhuman, we are inspired to expand the boundaries of what we had thought was possible. We are inspired to attempt the impossible, and in the attempt, we become more wholly human. . . . The task of the hero and heroine belongs to us all. That task is to live with such exuberance that what it is to be human will be expanded until the asphyxiating concepts of race and gender will be rendered meaningless, and then we will be able to see the rainbow around the shoulders of each and every one of us, the rainbow that has been there all the while."

BIOGRAPHICAL AND CRITICAL SOURCES:

BOOKS

Authors and Artists for Young Adults, Volume 12, Thomson Gale (Detroit, MI), 1994.

Chevalier, Tracy., *Twentieth-Century Children's Writers,* 3rd edition, St. James Press (Chicago, IL), 1989.

Children's Literature Review, Thomson Gale (Detroit, MI), Volume 2, 1976, Volume 41, 1997.

Contemporary Black Biography, Volume 9, Thomson Gale (Detroit, MI), 1995.

Krim, Seymour, *You and Me,* Holt, 1972.

Page, James A., and Jae Min Roh, compilers, *Selected Black American, African, and Caribbean Authors,* Libraries Unlimited (Littleton, CO), 1985.

St. James Guide to Young Adult Writers, 2nd edition, St. James Press (Detroit, MI), 1999.

Schomburg Center Guide to Black Literature, Thomson Gale (Detroit, MI), 1996.

Silvey, Anita, editor, *Children's Books and Their Creators,* Houghton Mifflin (Boston, MA), 1995.

Spradling, Mary Mace, *In Black and White,* 3rd edition, Thomson Gale (Detroit, MI), 1980.

PERIODICALS

African American Review, spring, 1998, Nikola-Lisa, W., review of *John Henry: Then and Now,* p. 51; spring, 1997, Wilfred D. Samuels, review of *And All Our Wounds Forgiven,* p. 176.

American Visions, December, 1998, review of *Black Cowboy, Wild Horses,* p. 35.

Black Issues Book Review, May, 2001, review of *Pharaoh's Daughter,* p. 82; September, 2001, Khafre Abif, review of *The Blues Singers: Ten Who Rocked the World,* p. 76.

Bloomsbury Review, March, 1995, review of *The Man Who Knew Too Much,* p. 27.

Booklist, February 15, 1994, review of *The Last Tales of Uncle Remus,* p. 1081; June 1, 1994, review of *John Henry,* p. 1809; January 15, 1995, review of *The Last Tales of Uncle Remus,* p. 861; October 14, 1994, Hazel Rochman, review of *The Man Who Knew Too Much,* p. 4342; February 15, 1995, review of *John Henry,* p. 1069, 1094; February 15, 1995, Ilene Cooper, review of *Othello: A Retelling,* p. 1074; April 1, 1995, review of *John Henry,* p. 1411; November 1, 1995, audio book review of *To Be a Slave,* p. 494; March 15, 1996, review of *Othello,* p. 1282; March 15, 1996, review of *Othello,* p. 1294; June 1, 1996, review of *Sam and the Tigers,* p. 1722; June 1, 1996, review of *The Tales of Uncle Remus,* p. 1727; January, 1997, review of *Sam and the Tigers,* p. 768; April 1, 1997, review of *Sam and the Tigers,* p. 1296; February 15, 1998, review of *From Slave Ship to Freedom Road,* p. 1009; May 1, 1998, Michael Cart, review of *Black Cowboy, Wild Horses,* p. 1522; January 1, 1999, review of *From Slave Ship to Freedom Road,* p. 783; February 15, 1999, review of *From Slave Ship to Freedom Road,* p. 1068; February 15, 1999, Ilene Cooper, review of *What a Truly Cool World,* p. 1076; March 15, 1999, review of *From Slave Ship to Freedom Road,* p. 1297; March 15, 1999, audio book review of *John Henry,* p. 1319; April 15, 1999, Shelley Townsend-Hudson, review of *When the Beginning Began: Stories about God, the Creatures, and Us,* p. 1529; October 1, 1999, Ilene Cooper, review of *When the Beginning Began,* p. 372; April 1, 2000, Ilene Cooper, review of *Pharaoh's Daughter,* p. 1474; July, 2000, Hazel Rochman, review of *From Slave Ship to Freedom Road,* p. 2025; September 15, 2000, Hazel Rochman, review of *Albidaro and the Mischievous Dream,* p. 246; February, 2001, Grace Anne A. DeCandido, review of *Ackamarackus: Julius Lester's Sumptuously Silly Fantastically Funny Fables,* p. 1056; May 14, 2001, review of *When Dad Killed Mom,* p. 83; June 1, 2001, Stephanie Zvirin, review of *The Blues Singers,* p. 1870; February 15, 2002, Patricia Austin, audio book review of *To Be a Slave,* p. 1038; September 15, 2003, Paul Shackman, audio book review of *Further Tales of Uncle Remus,* p. 253.

Book Report, February 15, 2001, review of *Othello,* p. 38; September 1, 2001, review of *The Blues*

Singers, p. 77; October 1, 2002, John Green, review of *Why Heaven Is Far Away*, p. 345

Book Talker, September, 1990, Pamela A. Todd, review of *How Many Spots Does a Leopard Have?*, p. 5.

Book World, September 3, 1972, William Loren Katz, review of *Long Journey Home*, p. 9.

Bulletin of the Center for Children's Books, April, 1969, Zena Sutherland, review of *To Be a Slave*, pp. 129-130; February, 1970, Zena Sutherland, review of *Black Folktales*, p. 101; October, 1994, Elizabeth Bush, review of *John Henry*, p. 54; November, 1994, review of *The Man Who Knew Too Much*, p. 92; March, 1995, review of *Othello*, p. 241; July, 1996, review of *Sam and the Tigers*, p. 378; February, 1998, review of *From Slave Ship to Freedom Road*, p. 212; May, 1998, review of *Black Cowboy, Wild Horses*, p. 327; February, 1999, review of *What a Truly Cool World*, p. 207; April, 1999, review of *When the Beginning Began*, p. 285; March, 2001, review of *Ackamarackus*, p. 268; May, 2001, review of *The Blues Singers*, p. 342; May, 2001, review of *When Dad Killed Mom*, p. 342.

Catholic Library World, March, 1997, review of *John Henry*, p. 14.

Children's Book and Play Review, May, 2001, review of *Albidaro and the Mischievous Dream*, p. 13.

Children's Book Review Service, December, 1994, review of *John Henry*, p. 43; February, 1995, review of *The Man Who Knew Too Much*, p. 76; November, 1996, review of *Sam and the Tigers*, p. 26; May, 1998, review of *From Slave Ship to Freedom Road*, p. 119.

Children's Bookwatch, February, 1995, review of *The Man Who Knew Too Much*, p. 5; June, 2001, review of *Ackamarackus*, p. 4.

Christian Century, July 20, 1988, Douglas Stone, review of *Lovesong*, p. 682.

Dissent, winter, 1989, p. 116.

Early Childhood Education Journal, spring, 1997, review of *Sam and the Tigers*, p. 176; fall, 1997, review of *John Henry*, p. 48.

Emergency Librarian, September, 1995, review of *Othello*, p. 58; September, 1996, review of *Othello*.

English Journal, January, 1996, review of *Othello*, p. 89.

Entertainment Weekly, January 28, 1994, review of *The Last Tales of Uncle Remus*, p. 70.

Essence, August, 1989, p. 98; July, 1991, p. 100.

Horn Book, October, 1972, review of *The Knee-High Man and Other Tales*, p. 463; June, 1975, review of *Who I Am*, p. 198; August, 1982, review of *This Strange New Feeling*, pp. 414-415; July-August, 1987, Mary M. Burns, review of *The Tales of Uncle Remus*, pp. 477-478; September-October, 1988, Mary M. Burns, review of *More Tales of Uncle Remus*, pp. 639-40; January-February, 1990, review of *How Many Spots Does a Leopard Have?*, p. 79; July-August, 1990, Elizabeth S. Watson, review of *Further Tales of Uncle Remus*, p. 478; May, 1994, review of *The Last Tales of Uncle Remus*, p. 341; November-December, 1994, Ann A. Flowers, review of *John Henry*, p. 739; fall, 1994, review of *The Last Tales of Uncle Remus*, p. 342; January, 1996, audio book review of *To Be A Slave*, p. 105; September, 1996, review of *Sam and the Tigers*, p. 536; July-August, 1998, Lauren Adams, review of *Black Cowboy, Wild Horses*, p. 477; March, 1999, Margaret A. Bush, review of *What a Truly Cool World*, p. 196; July, 1999, review of *When the Beginning Began*, p. 476; January, 2000, review of *Uncle Remus: The Complete Tales*, p. 61; July, 2000, review of *Pharaoh's Daughter*, p. 460; May 1, 2001, Deborah Z. Porter, review of *When Dad Killed Mom*, p. 330; November-December, 2002, Joanna Rudge Long, review of *Why Heaven Is Far Away*, p. 735.

Hungry Mind Review, summer, 1995, review of *Othello*, p. 41; spring, 1998, review of *From Slave Ship to Freedom Road*, p. 45.

Instructor, November, 1995, review of *The Last Tales of Uncle Remus*, p. 51; May, 1998, review of *Sam and the Tigers*, p. 62.

Interracial Books for Children Bulletin, 1975, Barbara Walker, review of *Who I Am*, p. 18.

Journal of Adolescent and Adult Literacy, October, 1997, review of *Sam and the Tigers*, p. 161.

Journal of Reading, May, 1995, review of *Othello*, p. 687.

Junior Bookshelf, February, 1975.

Kirkus Reviews, January 1, 1994, review of *The Last Tales of Uncle Remus*, p. 70; May 1, 1994, review of *And All Our Wounds Forgiven*, p. 581; October 15, 1994, review of *John Henry*, p. 1410; October 15, 1994, review of *The Man Who Knew Too Much*, p. 410; March 15, 1995, review of *Othello*, p. 386; August 1, 1996, review of *Sam and the Tigers*, p. 1154; November 15, 1997, review of *From Slave Ship to Freedom Road*, p. 1709; May 1, 1998, review of *Black Cowboy, Wild Horses*, p. 661; December 15, 1998, review of *What a Truly Cool World*, p. 1799; April 15, 1999, review of *When the Beginning Began*, p. 631; April 1, 2001, review of *The Blues Singers*, p. 499; April 1, 2001, review of *When Dad Killed Mom*, p. 500; October 1, 2003, review of *Shining*, p. 1226.

Kliatt, May, 1998, review of *Othello*, p. 14; May 1, 2001, review of *When Dad Killed Mom*, p. 12; July, 2003, Paula Rohrlick, review of *When Dad Killed Mom*, p. 24.

Language Arts, October, 1995, review of *John Henry,* p. 437.

Learning, November, 1996, review of *Sam and the Tigers,* p. 29.

Library Journal, January 1, 1975, Deborah H. Williams, review of *Who I Am,* p. 54.

Library Talk, November, 1994, review of *John Henry,* p. 23; May, 1995, review of *The Man Who Knew Too Much,* p. 52; September, 1995, review of *John Henry,* p. 43.

Los Angeles Times Book Review, January 31, 1988; January 27, 1991, p. 8; January 22, 1995, review of *John Henry,* p. 8; December 8, 1996, review of *Sam and the Tigers,* p. 19; March 25, 2001, review of *Ackamarackus,* p. 6; July 8, 2001, review of *The Blues Singers,* p. 12; December 2, 2001, review of *The Blues Singers,* p. 15; December 2, 2001, review of *Ackamarackus,* p. 16.

Magpies, March, 1997, review of *Sam and the Tigers,* p. 27.

Nation, June 22, 1970.

New Advocate, summer, 1990, p. 206; summer, 1995, review of *John Henry,* p. 209.

New Yorker, November 18, 1996, review of *Sam and the Tigers,* p. 98.

New York Review of Books, April 20, 1972, Eric Foner and Naomi Lewis, review of *Long Journey Home,* pp. 41-42.

New York Times, December 7, 1998, review of *Black Cowboy, Wild Horses,* p. E7; August 12, 2001, Peter Keepnews, review of *The Blues Singers,* p. 24; December 22, 2002, Sandy MacDonald, review of *Why Heaven Is Far Away,* p. 18.

New York Times Book Review, November 3, 1968, John Howard Griffin, review of *To Be a Slave,* p. 7; November 9, 1969, John A. Williams, review of *Black Folktales,* p. 10; October 11, 1972, Anatole Broyard, review of *Two Love Stories,* p. 41; July 23, 1972, Rosalind K. Goddard, review of *Long Journey Home,* p. 8; February 4, 1973, Ethel Richards, review of *The Knee-High Man and Other Tales,* p. 8; September 5, 1982; February 17, 1985; February 9, 1986, review of *To Be a Slave,* p. 32; May 17, 1987, p. 32; January 31, 1988, Joel Oppenheimer, review of *The Soul That Wanders,* p. 12; January 14, 1990, review of *How Many Spots Does a Leopard Have?,* p. 17; August 12, 1990, p. 29; August 7, 1994, review of *And All Our Wounds Forgiven,* p. 14; June 19, 1994, review of *The Last Tales of Uncle Remus,* p. 28; November 13, 1994, Jack Zipes, review of *John Henry,* p. 30; April 23, 1995, review of *Othello,* p. 27; November 10, 1996, review of *Sam and the Tigers,* p. 34; August 12, 2001, review of *The Blues Singers,* p. 24.

Parents, December, 1994, review of *John Henry,* p. 24.

Parents Choice, 1994, review of *John Henry,* p. 18; September, 1995, review of *Othello,* p. 14.

Partisan Review, Volume 57, number 2, 1990, pp. 321-325.

Plays, October, 1998, review of *Black Cowboy, Wild Horses,* p. 64.

Publishers Weekly, October 20, 1969, review of *Black Folktales,* p. 60; January 19, 1970, review of *To Be a Slave,* p. 83; June 5, 1972, review of *Long Journey Home,* p. 140; August 7, 1972, review of *The Knee-High Man and Other Tales,* p. 50; August 28, 1972, review of *Two Love Stories,* p. 259; March 20, 1987, Mary M. Burns, review of *The Tales of Uncle Remus,* p. 80; February 12, 1988, Barry List, "PW Interviews: Julius Lester," pp. 67-68; October 27, 1989, review of *How Many Spots Does a Leopard Have?,* p. 68; September 14, 1990, review of *Falling Pieces of the Broken Sky,* p. 115; May 2, 1994, review of *And All Our Wounds Forgiven,* p. 282; July 18, 1994, review of *To Be a Slave,* p. 31; September 4, 1994, review of *John Henry,* p. 108; November 7, 1994, review of *The Man Who Knew Too Much,* p. 241; March 20, 1995, review of *Othello,* p. 62; August 5, 1996, review of *Sam and the Tigers,* p. 441; December 1, 1997, review of *From Slave Ship to Freedom Road,* p. 54; April 6, 1998, review of *Black Cowboy, Wild Horses,* p. 78; November 23, 1998, review of *To Be a Slave,* p. 69; January 4, 1999, review of *What a Truly Cool World,* p. 89; February 1, 1999, review of *The Tales of Uncle Remus,* p. 87; March 22, 1999, review of *When the Beginning Began,* p. 89; November 8, 1999, review of *Uncle Remus: The Complete Tales,* p. 70; December 13, 1999, review of *From Slave Ship to Freedom Road,* p. 85; October, 2000, review of *Albidaro and the Mischievous Dream,* p. 81; February 12, 2001, Sally Lodge, "Working at His Creative Peak," p. 180; March 5, 2001, review of *Ackamarackus,* p. 79; May 14, 2001, review of *The Blues Singers,* p. 81; May 14, 2001, review of *When Dad Killed Mom,* p. 83; June 30, 2003, review of *When Dad Killed Mom,* p. 82.

Quill & Quire, December, 1989, Susan Perren, review of *How Many Spots Does a Leopard Have?,* p. 24.

Reading Teacher, February, 1994, review of *Long Journey Home,* p. 410; November, 1995, review of *John Henry,* p. 238; December, 1995, review of *John Henry,* p. 329; March, 1999, review of *From Slave Ship to Freedom Road,* p. 628; April, 1999, review of *Black Cowboy, Wild Horses,* p. 761; November, 1999, review of *Black Cowboy, Wild Horses,* p. 250; November, 1999, review of *From Slave Ship to Freedom Road,* p. 254; May, 2001, review of *Sam and the Tigers,* p. 812; October, 2001, review of *Pharaoh's Daughter,* p. 186.

School Librarian, May, 1988, Irene Babsky, review of *The Tales of Uncle Remus,* p. 72.

School Library Journal, May, 1969, Evelyn Geller, "Julius Lester: Newbery Runner-Up"; September, 1976, Kathryn Robinson, review of *All Is Well,* p. 146; April, 1982, Hazel Rochman, review of *This Strange New Feeling,* p. 83; April, 1987, Kay McPherson, review of *The Last Tales of Uncle Remus,* p. 99; June-July, 1988, Kay McPherson, review of *More Tales of Uncle Remus,* p. 92; November, 1989, Kay McPherson, review of *How Many Spots Does the Leopard Have?,* p. 99; May, 1990, Kay McPherson, review of *Further Tales of Uncle Remus,* p. 99; January, 1994, review of *The Last Tales of Uncle Remus,* p. 124; November, 1994, review of *John Henry,* p. 98; December, 1994, review of *The Man Who Knew Too Much,* p. 124; April, 1995, Margaret Cole, review of *Othello,* p. 154; August, 1996, review of *Sam and the Tigers,* p. 126; December, 1996, review of *Sam and the Tigers,* p. 30; February, 1998, review of *From Slave Ship to Freedom Road,* p. 119; November, 1997, review of *Sam and the Tigers,* p. 41; June, 1998, review of *Black Cowboy, Wild Horses,* p. 113; August, 1998, review of *Black Cowboy, Wild Horses,* p. 43; April, 1999, review of *What a Truly Cool World,* p. 102; May, 1999, review of *When the Beginning Began,* p. 139; June, 2000, Barbara Scotto, review of *Pharaoh's Daughter,* p. 148; November, 2000, Julie Cummins, review of *Albidaro and the Mischievous Dream,* p. 126; March, 2001, Wendy Lukehart, review of *Ackamarackus,* p. 214; May, 2001, Francisca Goldsmith, review of *When Dad Killed Mom,* p. 155; June, 2001, review of *The Blues Singers,* p. 138; December, 2001, review of *The Blues Singers,* p. 47.

Social Education, April, 1995, review of *John Henry,* p. 216; April, 1995, review of *The Last Tales of Uncle Remus,* p. 216; April, 1997, review of *Sam and the Tigers,* p. 5; May, 1999, review of *Black Cowboy, Wild Horses,* p. 8; May, 1999, review of *From Slave Ship to Freedom Road,* p. 7; October, 2002, Miriam Lang Budin, review of *Why Heaven Is Far Away,* p. 118; October, 2002, Bonnie Bolton, audio book review of *The Tales of Uncle Remus: The Adventures of Brer Rabbit,* p. 87.

Time, September 9, 1996, review of *Sam and the Tigers,* p. 72.

Times Literary Supplement, April 3, 1987.

Tribune Books (Chicago, IL), February 26, 1989, p. 8; February 11, 1990, p. 6; November 13, 1994, review of *John Henry,* p. 6; April 29, 2001, review of *Ackamarackus,* p. 8; July 1, 2001, review of *When Dad Killed Mom,* p. 2.

Village Voice, September 17, 1996, review of *Sam and the Tigers,* p. 49.

Voice of Youth Advocates, June, 1995, review of *Othello,* p. 96; April, 1998, review of *This Strange New Feeling,* p. 43; February, 1999, review of *From Slave Ship to Freedom Road,* p. 412; June, 1999, Kathleen Beck, review of *When the Beginning Began,* p. 134; February, 2001, review of *Pharaoh's Daughter,* p. 399; August, 2001, review of *The Blues Singers,* p. 225; October, 2001, review of *Voice of Youth Advocates,* p. 280.

Washington Post, March 12, 1985.

Washington Post Book World, September 3, 1972; February 14, 1988; December 4, 1994, review of *John Henry,* p. 21; February 11, 1996, review of *And All Our Wounds Forgiven,* p. 12; June 7, 1998, review of *Black Cowboy, Wild Horses,* p. 8.

ONLINE

Children's Literature, http://www.childrenslit.com/ (November 22, 2003), "Julius Lester."

Houghton Mifflin Education Place, http://www.eduplace.com/kids/hmr/ (November 22, 2003), "Julius Lester."

KidsReads, http://www.kidsreads.com/ (November 22, 2003), Shannon Maughan, review of *Ackamarackus.*

Once upon a Lap, http://wildes.home.mindspring.com/OUAL/int/ (November 22, 2003), reprint of interview with Lester.

Rutgers University, http://scils.rutgers.edu/ (March 28, 1999), "Julius Lester."

* * *

LESTER, Julius Bernard
See LESTER, Julius

* * *

LETHEM, Jonathan 1964-
(Jonathan Allen Lethem)

PERSONAL: Born February 19, 1964, in New York, NY; son of Richard Brown (an artist) and Judith Frank (an activist) Lethem. *Education:* Attended Bennington College, 1982-84.

ADDRESSES: Agent—Richard Parks Agency, 138 East 16th St., No. 5B, New York, NY 10003.

CAREER: Writer. Brazen Head Books, New York, NY, bookseller, 1977-80; Gryphon Books, New York, bookseller, 1982-84; Pegasus Books, Berkeley, CA, bookseller, 1985-90; Moe's Books, Berkeley, bookseller, 1990-94.

AWARDS, HONORS: Theodore Sturgeon Memorial Award, third place, and Nebula Award finalist, both 1991, both for novella "The Happy Man"; best first novel, *Locus* magazine, 1994, for *Gun, with Occasional Music;* World Fantasy Award for Best Collection, World Fantasy Convention, for *The Wall of the Sky, the Wall of the Eye: Stories;* National Book Critics Circle Award for Fiction, 1999, for *Motherless Brooklyn; New York Times* Editor's Choice, 2003, for *The Fortress of Solitude;* MacArthur Fellowship, John D. and Catherine T. MacArthur Foundation, 2005.

WRITINGS:

Gun, with Occasional Music (novel), Harcourt (San Diego, CA), 1994.
Amnesia Moon (novel), Harcourt (San Diego, CA), 1995.
The Wall of the Sky, the Wall of the Eye: Stories, Harcourt (San Diego, CA), 1996.
As She Climbed across the Table (novel), Doubleday (New York, NY), 1997.
Girl in Landscape (novel), Doubleday (New York, NY), 1998.
Motherless Brooklyn, Doubleday (New York, NY), 1999.
(Editor) *The Vintage Book of Amnesia: An Anthology,* Vintage Books (New York, NY), 2000.
This Shape We're In, McSweeney's Books (San Francisco, CA), 2001.
(Author of introduction) Paula Fox, *Poor George,* W.W. Norton (New York, NY), 2001.
The Fortress of Solitude, Doubleday (New York, NY), 2003.
Men and Cartoons: Stories, Doubleday (New York, NY), 2004.
The Disappointment Artist and Other Essays, Doubleday (New York, NY), 2005.

Contributor of short fiction to periodicals, including *Interzone, Journal Wired, Asimov's Science Fiction,* and *Pulphouse.*

SIDELIGHTS: Jonathan Lethem has gained a reputation as a writer whose works cross the borders of many literary genres. For example, his novel *Girl in Landscape* "exists somewhere in the previously uncharted interstices between science fiction, western, and coming-of-age novels," noted Elizabeth Gaffney in a *Publishers Weekly* profile of the author. And of the short story collection *The Wall of the Sky, the Wall of the Eye,* a *Publishers Weekly* reviewer commented that, "Although Lethem is claimed by the science fiction community as one of its own [his] work is really extra-genre, in the manner of Borges or William Burroughs."

Lethem once explained that "Everything I write is informed by genre traditions, which I love deeply. At the same time, I don't think I've written without straining against genre boundaries, and I've often violated them outright. I think my work reveals traces of an extremely eclectic reading history, and my narrative is also particularly informed by film. But my dearest models are nearly all twentieth-century Americans pursuing high art through popular forms: Shirley Jackson, Philip K. Dick, John Ford, Charles Willeford, George Herriman, and Patricia Highsmith, for instance." To Gaffney he expressed his disdain for the tendency to pigeonhole writers by genre and his sympathy for those "who had embattled careers because of genre prejudice, something I've had the good fortune to be spared. I sort of feel [science fiction writer] Philip K. Dick died for my sins."

Lethem's debut novel, *Gun, with Occasional Music,* brought him comparisons to Philip K. Dick as well as to crime novelist Raymond Chandler. In *Gun,* which combines futuristic and hard-boiled motifs, the hero is Conrad Metcalf, a Private Inquisitor or P.I., as detectives are known in Lethem's twenty-first-century society. Only P.I.s and the police are licensed to ask questions in this somewhat constricted world of the near-future; uttering one query in the course of everyday conversation will net the average citizen points on his or her "karma card." Lethem creates other bizarre elements in his vision of the next century: the government hands out drugs with names such as Acceptrol, Forgettol, and Regrettol to keep the citizenry under control. And, a disastrous experiment called "evolutionary therapy" has turned children into "babyheads"— overevolved, cynical humans who pass their lives in bars, while drinking, smoking, and speaking a language that only they can understand. In a botched attempt to replace the population doomed to "babyhead" status, animals have been genetically altered, but this too has gone awry, and some of the talking creatures have been given quasi-human status.

Gun, with Occasional Music begins as Metcalf is hired by a doctor to investigate the physician's wife. However, the practitioner is murdered and a peripheral character is wrongly accused. In trying to uncover the real perpetrator, Metcalf encounters some nefarious characters and an obvious cover-up, possibly involving the authorities and some underworld criminal elements. A trenchcoat-clad kangaroo named Joey Castle, in the employ of mobsters, proves especially troublesome. Metcalf's questions eventually lead to his imprisonment—six years in cold storage. When he awakens, Metcalf manages to solve the mystery by connecting the remaining clues, even though all memory has now been officially outlawed. In a *Newsweek* review, Malcolm Jones, Jr., called *Gun, with Occasional Music* "an audaciously assured first novel" and termed Lethem's storyline "merely an excuse for nailsplitting dialogue between the wisecracking Metcalf and a gaudy array of nemeses." Jones also praised Lethem's blend of science fiction and mystery, asserting that "Lethem conflated the two genres to fabricate a future that is frightening and funny and ultimately quite sad." A contributor to *Axcess* called the novel "a classy science fiction mystery that bristles with wit and imagination, turning both genres on their heads and inside out."

Amnesia Moon, Lethem's second novel, steers away from the conventions of noir mysteries to present a dystopic vision of the United States. Focusing on a character named Chaos, the narrative unfolds as a road trip. In search of his past identity—he was once known as Everett Moon—Chaos travels across post-apocalyptic America with a companion named Melinda. In each town they visit along their journey to San Francisco, the pair encounter a type of madness endemic to that locale, "with mass symptoms ranging from an imaginary blinding green mist to an obsession with luck," according to Carl Hays in *Booklist*. Lethem portrays "each stop on Chaos's journey with care . . . bringing to life all the horror and confusion inherent in his future world," remarked a contributor to *Publishers Weekly*. In a *Newsweek* review of *Amnesia Moon*, Jones stated that Lethem has emerged from the "shadow" of such influences as Dick to "deliver a droll, down-beat vision that is both original and persuasive."

Girl in Landscape is the story of Pella, a thirteen year old coping with the death of her mother and her family's move from a nearly uninhabitable Earth to a planet just being settled by humans. Her father, a politician, is trying to create a civilization in which humans coexist peacefully with the planet's earlier residents, the "archbuilders," of whom only a few are left. He meets an antagonist in Ephram Nugent, a settler who is prejudiced against the arch-builders but is drawn to Pella. Ephram is "a maverick John Wayne-type character," according to Gaffney in *Publishers Weekly;* indeed, she reported,

one of Lethem's influences was "his obsession with the John Ford film *The Searchers,* in which the John Wayne character tries to rescue a young girl who has been abducted by Indians." She quoted Lethem as saying, "It's an obsessive quest, and he's an anti-heroic, racist, angry figure. I wanted to explore what it was like to have your sexual coming-of-age watched over by this bullying man." A *Publishers Weekly* reviewer opined that *Girl in Landscape* "affectingly chronicles Pella's tumultuous journey through puberty and loss and the knock-about society of children thrown together by their home-steading parents." *Library Journal* contributor Starr E. Smith deemed the novel "well constructed and plotted" but thought it "breaks no new literary ground stylistically."

In his 1999 novel *Motherless Brooklyn* Lethem presents readers with a work of crime fiction not quite like any other. As a *Publishers Weekly* contributor noted, "Hard-boiled crime fiction has never seen the likes of Lionel Essrog, the barking, grunting, spasmodically twitching hero of Lethem's gonzo detective novel that unfolds amidst the detritus of contemporary Brooklyn." Lionel has Tourette's syndrome, a condition that causes uncontrollable verbal outbursts accompanied by a twisting of the language in startling, original ways. When his boss, small-time mobster Frank Minna is killed while Essrog and his coworkers in Minna's detective agency wait outside a meeting for him, the twitching minion sets out to solve the murder. Lethem takes full artistic advantage of Essrog's illness by making him the novel's narrator. As pointed out by Frank Caso in *Booklist,* Essrog's "description of the investigation—complete with Tourette tics and observations—is a tour de force of language." Starr E. Smith, writing in *Library Journal,* noted that the novel's "plot twists are marked by clever wordplay, fast-paced dialog, and nonstop irony."

After the appearance of his fifty-five-page story titled *This Shape We're In,* Lethem's next novel appeared in 2003. *The Fortress of Solitude* is a coming-of-age novel based on Lethem's own experience growing up as a white boy in a multiracial neighborhood. The story focuses on Dylan Ebdus and Mingus Rude. The white Dylan and the black Mingus grow up together in a tough environment, where Dylan learns from Mingus about life on the streets, complete with gang turf wars and graffiti. In adulthood, Mingus becomes a criminal and crack addict who ends up in prison while Dylan, who has gone to college, is a failed music journalist. Yet the bond between the two remains, not in any small part due to the bizarre fact that a vagrant gave Dylan a magic ring when he was a boy. Growing up together, the two boys shared the ring, which enabled them to fly and fight crime. Other powers of the ring include the ability to breathe underwater and to become invisible. Although the boys only use the ring sparingly, it ultimately comes into play when Dylan tries to get the ring to Mingus so he can use it to escape from jail.

In *Entertainment Weekly* Mark Harris described *The Fortress of Solitude* as "a flawlessly evoked, original, and vividly imagined (or is it remembered?) account of two boys, white and black, growing up in not-yet-gentrified Brooklyn in a decade of both freedom and urban rot." *Commentary* contributor Sam Munson was less engaged by the novel, especially the character of Dylan. "Dylan remains without shape," Munson maintained, "and so, for all of Lethem's strenuous protestations, does the world he inhabits." Max Watman had a similar objection in his *New Criterion* review, commenting that "Lethem wants it both ways: he wants to write a big novel and still be quirky—and I think he should be able to. I do not think he's done it. He has foiled his ambition with low metaphors, and he has foiled his fun with ambition. He has evaded his characters, and rested on their interactions, their society." Nevertheless, other reviewers gave the novel abundant praise. Writing in the *New Statesman*, Peter Bradshaw called *The Fortress of Solitude* "maddeningly readable and utterly baffling" and noted that, although "At the end, I didn't believe a man can fly. . . . Lethem's writing certainly does."

In addition to novels, Lethem has continues to broaden his writing to include a volume of short stories as well as essays. Nevertheless, as noted by Steven Zeitchik in *Publishers Weekly,* "there are some common threads, especially the shimmering chasm between reality and memory, between things as they were and as we wanted them to be." As Lethem explained to Zeitchik, "If you look at my books, they all have this giant howling missing center. Language has disappeared, or someone has disappeared, or memory has disappeared. I'm usually writing around a void."

BIOGRAPHICAL AND CRITICAL SOURCES:

PERIODICALS

Axcess, Volume 2, number 3, review of *Gun, with Occasional Music,* p. 106.

Book, September-October, 2003, Jerome V. Kramer, "Home Boy: Motherless Brooklyn's Jonathan Lethem Returns to the Street Where He Grew up for His New Novel, *The Fortress of Solitude,*" p. 58, and Don McLeese, review of *The Fortress of Solitude,* p. 77.

Booklist, August, 1995, Carl Hays, review of *Amnesia Moon,* p. 1933; September 1, 1996, p. 69; July, 1999, Frank Caso, review of *Motherless Brooklyn,* p. 1895; June 1, 2003, Keir Graff, review of *The Fortress of Solitude,* p. 1710.

Commentary, November, 2003, Sam Munson, review of *The Fortress of Solitude,* p. 68.

Entertainment Weekly, April 11, 1997, p. 81; September 19, 2003, Mark Harris, review of *The Fortress of Solitude,* p. 89.

Kirkus Reviews, January 1, 1994, p. 23.

Library Journal, February 15, 1994, p. 188; April 1, 1998, Starr E. Smith, review of *Girl in Landscape,* p. 123; July, 1999, Starr E. Smith, review of *Motherless Brooklyn,* p. 133; July, 2003, Nathan Ward, review of *The Fortress of Solitude,* p. 123.

Locus, July, 1995, pp. 23, 52.

New Criterion, November, 2003, Max Watman, review of *The Fortress of Solitude,* p. 59.

New Leader, July-August, 2003, Evan Hughes, review of *The Fortress of Solitude,* p. 27.

New Statesman, January 19, 2004, Peter Bradshaw, review of *The Fortress of Solitude,* p. 51.

Newsweek, April 18, 1994, Malcom Jones, Jr., review of *Gun, with Occasional Music,* pp. 62-63; October 2, 1995, Malcom Jones, Jr., review of *Amnesia Moon,* p. 92; September 15, 2003, Malcom Jones, "Books: The Next Jonathan?," p. 13.

People, Kyle Smith, review of *The Fortress of Solitude,* p. 55.

Publishers Weekly, January 17, 1994, pp. 414, 416; November 7, 1994, p. 41; June 12, 1995, review of *Amnesia Moon,* p. 44; July 15, 1996, p. 54; February 9, 1998, review of *Girl in Landscape,* p. 71; March 30, 1998, Elizabeth Gaffney, "Jonathan Lethem: Breaking the Barriers between Genres," p. 50; August 6, 1999, review of *Motherless Brooklyn,* p. 57; October 25, 1999, Judy Quinn, "Lethem's Leap," p. 20; June 16, 2003, review of *The Fortress of Solitude,* p. 47; September 15, 2003, Steven Zeitchik, "A Brooklyn of the Soul," p. 37.

Time, October 11, 1999, Nadya Labi, review of *Motherless Brooklyn,* p. 90; September 15, 2003, Lev Grossman, review of *The Fortress of Solitude,* p. 77.

*   *   *

LETHEM, Jonathan Allen
See LETHEM, Jonathan

LEVI, Primo 1919-1987
(Damiano Malabaila)

PERSONAL: Born July 31, 1919, in Turin, Italy; died from a fall during an apparent suicide attempt, April 11, 1987, in Turin, Italy; son of Cesare (a civil engineer) and Ester (Luzzati) Levi; married Lucia Morpurgo (a teacher), September 8, 1947; children: Lisa, Renzo. *Education:* University of Turin, B.S. (summa cum laude), 1941. *Religion:* Jewish.

CAREER: Chemist and author. SIVA (manufacturing company), Settimo, Turin, Italy, technical executive, 1948-77. *Wartime service:* Partisan in Italian Resistance, 1943; imprisoned in Auschwitz concentration camp, 1943-45.

AWARDS, HONORS: Premio Campiello (Venice, Italy), 1963, for *La Tregua,* and 1982, for *Se non ora, quando?;* Premio Bagutta (Milan, Italy), 1967, for *Storie Naturali;* Premio Strega (Rome literary prize), 1979, for *La chiave stella;* Premio Viareggio, 1982, for *Se non ora, quando?;* co-recipient (with Saul Bellow) of Kenneth B. Smilen fiction award, Jewish Museum (New York, NY), 1985; *Present Tense*/Joel H. Cavior literary award, 1986, for *The Periodic Table.*

WRITINGS:

Se questo e un uomo, F. de Silva (Turin, Italy), 1947, fifteenth edition, Einaudi (Turin, Italy), 1975, translation published as *If This Is a Man,* Orion Press (New York, NY), 1959, published as *Survival in Auschwitz: The Nazi Assault on Humanity,* Collier (New York, NY), 1961 (also see below), new edition, 1966, published as *If This Is a Man,* Bodley Head (London, England), 1966.

La tregua, Einaudi (Turin, Italy), 1958, eighth edition, 1965, translation published as *The Reawakening* (also see below), Little, Brown (Boston, MA), 1965, published as *The Truce: A Survivor's Journey Home from Auschwitz,* Bodley Head (London, England), 1965.

(Under pseudonym Damiano Malabaila) *Storie naturali* (short-story collection), Einaudi (Turin, Italy), 1967, translation published in *The Sixth Day and Other Tales,* 1990.

(With Carlo Quartucci) *Intervista Aziendale* (radio script), Radiotelevisione Italiana, 1968.

Vizio di forma (short-story collection), Einaudi (Turin, Italy), 1971, translation published in *The Sixth Day and Other Tales,* 1990.

Il sistema periodico, Einaudi (Turin, Italy), 1975, translation by Raymond Rosenthal published as *The Periodic Table,* Schocken (New York, NY), 1984.

Abruzzo forte e gentile: Impressioni d'occhio e di cuore, edited by Virgilio Orsini, Di Cioccio (Sulmona, Italy), 1976.

Shema: Collected Poems, Menard (London, England), 1976.

La chiave a stella (novel), Einaudi (Turin, Italy), 1978, translation by William Weaver published as *The Monkey's Wrench,* Summit Books (New York, NY), 1986.

(Editor) *La ricerca della radici: antologia personale,* Einaudi (Turin, Italy), 1981, translation by Peter Forbes published as *The Search for Roots: A Personal Anthology,* Allen Lane (London, England), 2001, Ivan R. Dee (Chicago, IL), 2002.

Lilit e altri racconti (short-story collection), Einaudi (Turin, Italy), 1981, translation by Ruth Feldman published as *Moments of Reprieve,* Summit Books (New York, NY), 1986.

Se non ora, quando? (novel), Einaudi (Turin, Italy), 1982, translation by William Weaver published as *If Not Now, When?,* introduction by Irving Howe, Summit Books (New York, NY), 1985.

(Translator) Franz Kafka, *Il processo,* 1983.

L'altrui mestiere, Einaudi (Turin, Italy), 1985, translation by Raymond Rosenthal published as *Other People's Trades,* Summit Books (New York, NY), 1989.

Sommersi e i salvati, 1986, translation by Raymond Rosenthal published as *The Drowned and the Saved,* Summit Books (New York, NY), 1988.

Survival in Auschwitz [and] *The Reawakening: Two Memoirs,* Summit Books (New York, NY), 1986.

Racconti e saggi, La Stampa (Turin, Italy), 1986, translation by Raymond Rosenthal published as *The Mirror Maker: Stories and Essays,* Schocken (New York, NY), 1989.

Autoritratto di Primo Levi, Garzanti (Milan, Italy), 1987.

The Collected Poems of Primo Levi, translation by Ruth Feldman and Brian Swann, Faber & Faber (Winchester, MA), 1988.

(With Tullio Regge) *Dialogo,* Princeton University Press (Princeton, NJ), 1989.

The Sixth Day, and Other Tales (includes *Storie naturali* and *Visio di Forma*), translation by Raymond Rosenthal, Viking Penguin (New York, NY), 1990.

Conversazione con Primo Levi, Garzanti (Milano, Italy), 1991.

L'ultimo Natale di guerra (short-story collection), edited by Marco Belpoliti, Einaudi (Turin, Italy), 2000.

The Voice of Memory: Interviews 1961-1987, edited by Marco Belpoliti and Robert Gordon, translation by Robert Gordon, New Press (New York, NY), 2001.

L'asimmetria e la vita: articoli e saggi, 1955-1987 (personal narrative), edited by Marco Belpoliti, Einaudi (Turin, Italy), 2002.

SIDELIGHTS: The suicide of Italian author Primo Levi at age sixty-eight was more than a shocking event. It was a definitive gesture by one of modern history's witnesses, a writer who had reportedly grown increasingly despondent over the fading significance of the Holocaust from generation to generation. Levi—an Italian Jew and concentration-camp survivor—was considered one of the premier chroniclers of the hellish conditions endured by his people during World War II, and his 1947 work *Se questo e un uomo,* translated into English as *If This Is a Man* and *Survival in Auschwitz: The Nazi Assault on Humanity,* remains one of the most compelling accounts of the Nazi legacy.

In a profile of Levi for *New Republic,* David Denby noted that the writer was the product of a family "with substantial roots in the tolerant soil of northern Italy. Thoroughly assimilated, Levi's family, like most Italian Jews, did not speak Yiddish but an eccentric and seemingly contradictory mixture of the Piedmontese dialect . . . and bits of Hebrew." Trained as a chemist, Levi found his career goals restricted by Italy's emerging Fascist government. With war looming in the late 1930s, Levi and his peers reacted by withdrawal.

When Germany's Nazi troops took over Italy, Levi could no longer afford to be passive. He joined the partisans in 1943, a move that, as Levi later wrote in *The Periodic Table,* was doomed to failure: "We were cold and hungry, the most disarmed partisans in the Piedmont, and probably the most unprepared." Betrayed and arrested, Levi revealed his Jewish heritage to his interrogators, "partly out of fatigue, but partly out of a sudden surge . . . of haughty pride." He was sentenced to Auschwitz concentration camp.

As a *Haftling*—a prisoner—with the number 174517 tattooed on his arm, Levi was set to work at a rubber factory connected with the concentration camp. He spent a year at labor, experiencing firsthand the definitive catastrophe of twentieth-century humanity. Release came in January of 1945 with the arrival of Soviet Army tanks. Levi was one of only three Italian partisans to survive.

Though he had not aspired to be a writer before his internment, Levi was compelled to tell the story of the millions who perished. In 1947 he published *Survival in Auschwitz: The Nazi Assault on Humanity.* This work, according to *American Journal of Sociology* contributor W.J. Cahnman, is "literally a report from hell: the detached, scientific, unearthly story of a man who descended to the nether word at Auschwitz and returned to the land of the living." Indeed, the themes of this book have been compared by some scholars to Dante's depiction of hell in his epic *The Inferno.* Survival, in Levi's experience, means learning from prisoners shrewd in the ways of accommodation and appropriation in the prison camps. In Denby's view, Levi "becomes almost vivacious in describing these schemes, the complexity of which . . . can be startling. The inmates of Auschwitz . . . had no chance of surviving if they merely obeyed the rules and ate what was given them."

In the end, *Survival in Auschwitz* "turns out to be, of all things, a book about the forms of civilization," declared Denby. "Levi describes the system of death and survival in the camp but he also presents a variety of relationships—economic, spiritual, fraternal and even cultural—that can only be called the contours of a social world." Indeed, Levi's "lack of personal bitterness is almost unnatural, especially when it is realised that he wrote so soon after the German retreat brought him his freedom," noted G.F. Seddon in the Manchester, England *Guardian.* "Levi's more outstanding virtue is his compassionate understanding of how in these conditions men cease to be men, either give up the struggle or in devious ways win it, usually at the expense of their fellow men." In an interview with a *Los Angeles Times* contributor, Levi defended his scientific approach to recounting the horrors of the Holocaust: "It was my duty not to behave as a victim, not to wail and weep, but to be a witness, to give readers material for judgment. This is Divine Law, to be a witness, not to overstate or distort but to deliver and furnish facts. The final judge is the reader."

Sergio Pacifici pointed out in *Saturday Review* that, like *Survival in Auschwitz,* Levi's *The Reawakening,* which chronicles the author's return to Italy, is more than an intimate and accurate diary. "It is a plea for self-restraint and generosity in human relations that may well be heeded in our own critical times," Pacifici said. "Levi's lucid and wise reflections on the nature of man deserve more than a mere hearing. *The Reawakening* must take its honored place next to Carlo Levi's *Christ Stopped at Eboli,* Andre Schwartz-Bart's *The Last of the Just,* and *The Diary of Anne Frank.*"

After the successful publication of his first two memoirs, Levi continued to write about the Jewish Holocaust in a variety of works, including two award-winning novels, *La chiave a stella*—published in English as *The Monkey's Wrench*—and *Se non ora, quando?*—translated as *If Not Now, When?* Toward the mid-1980s, however, Levi became progressively despondent over what he felt was a general disregard for the immense suffering and loss Jews had experienced during World War II. For reasons not clearly understood, Levi ended his life in 1987 when he jumped down a stairwell in his native town of Turin, Italy. Levi's friend, Italian newspaper editor Lorenzo Mundo, told Steve Kellerman of *New York Times* that, during the months preceding his death, Levi "would come to visit me and his face looked so discouraged and helpless. He kept saying he was tired, physically and mentally. And he was terribly pessimistic about the destiny of the world and the fate of the spirit of man."

Following Levi's death a number of his works were translated into English, among them *The Collected Poems of Primo Levi, The Mirror Maker: Stories and Essays, The Sixth Day and Other Tales, Other People's Trades,* and *The Drowned and the Saved.*

Other People's Trades presents over forty essays on a variety of diverse scientific and personal subjects ranging from insect behaviors to computers to the patterns of human memory. Critics have praised the impressive range of knowledge, insight, and originality evidenced by these essays, often noting that the volume provides insight into Levi as a talented writer apart from his role as a witness of the Holocaust. Christopher Lehmann-Haupt in *New York Times* noted that "the prevalent themes of these essays are the behavior of matter, its independence of human desires and the extent to which we project our fears onto the behavior of animals that are more or less indifferent to us." Leonard Michaels, writing in *New York Times Book Review,* emphasized the sense of alienation that characterizes Levi's contemplation of the universe and humankind's relationship to the cosmos.

The Sixth Day and Other Tales surprised many readers who were familiar with Levi's nonfiction; the volume contains fantastical short fables that reveal the influence of futurism and surrealism. Writing in Chicago's *Tribune Books,* Constance Markey argued that Levi's fiction is weak in comparison with his nonfiction writings about the Holocaust. She commented, "Rich in imagination, Levi is nonetheless uncomfortable with fiction, not to mention comedy." Richard Eder noted in *Los Angeles Times* the limitations of Levi's short fiction, but also praised the stories as imaginative vehicles of social commentary that suggest both the influence of Levi's experience of the Holocaust and his scientific training.

The Mirror Maker combines both essays and stories, many of which Levi wrote during the last twenty years of his life for the Turin newspaper *La Stampa.* Like *Other People's Trades,* the volume focuses on a variety of scientific topics and also contains stories that reveal Levi's interest in science fiction and the fantastic. Discussing *The Mirror Maker* in *Sewanee Review,* Gabriel Motola commented that "Levi's most engaging stories and essays remain those that address ethical and moral questions raised by political considerations and by his literary readings and scientific studies."

The Voice of Memory, Interviews 1961-1987 includes thirty-six newspaper, journal, radio, and telvision interviews given by Levi. In addition to discussions about the Holocaust, these interviews also cover many of Levi's other interests. A translation of a 1981 work, *The Search for Roots* is an anthology of thirty short excerpt from various works Levi collected and edited. Writers represented include Homer, Jonathan Swift, and T.S. Eliot. As noted by Gene Shaw in *Library Journal,* the excerpts focus on four primary themes that interested Levi: "salvation through laughter, our unjust suffering, our stature as human beings, and salvation through knowledge." Hazel Rochman, writing in *Booklist,* commented that "Most readers will be less interested in the selections themselves than in what Levi says about each of them and what they reveal about his life."

Levi's possible suicide remains the subject of speculative discussion, and many critics have examined his later writings in hopes of finding evidence of the author's motivation to kill himself. Critics such as Isa Kapp and Michiko Kakutani, for example, have perceived a note of darkness and pessimism concerning the human condition in some of the later pieces included in *The Mirror Maker.* Kapp, writing in *New York Times Book Review,* suggested that "Levi had many reasons for faith in humanity, for feeling himself lucky. Yet perhaps he imagined that the impact of his warnings, of his moral force, was evaporating." Richard Eder, writing in *Los Angeles Times Book Review,* noted that Levi "wrote of life as an immortal principle, not an immortal possession. The stubborn radiance of his notion of what it means to be human is universally accessible but individually transient. It is because the mortal Levi, with whatever depressions and despairs he may have possessed, could write as he did that what he wrote is so valuable."

BIOGRAPHICAL AND CRITICAL SOURCES:

BOOKS

Camon, Ferdinando, *Conversations with Primo Levi,* Marlboro Press (Marlboro, VT), 1989.

Contemporary Literary Criticism, Thomson Gale (Detroit, MI), Volume 37, 1986, Volume 50, 1988.

Hughes, H. Stuart, *Prisoners of Hope: The Silver Age of the Italian Jews, 1924-1974,* Harvard University Press (Cambridge, MA), 1983, pp. 55-85.

Levi, Primo, *The Periodic Table,* Knopf (New York, NY), 1996.

Patruno, Nicholas, *Understanding Primo Levi,* University of South Carolina Press (Columbia, SC), 1995.

Rosenfeld, Alvin H., *A Double Dying: Reflections on Holocaust Literature,* Indiana University Press (Bloomington, IN), 1980, pp. 37-61.

Rudolf, Anthony, *At an Uncertain Hour: Primo Levi's War against Oblivion,* Menard (London, England), 1990.

Short Story Criticism, Volume 12, Thomson Gale (Detroit, MI), 1993.

Sodi, Risa B., *A Dante of Our Time: Primo Levi and Auschwitz,* P. Lang (New York, NY), 1990.

Thomson, Ian, *Primo Levi: A Life,* Holt (New York, NY), 2003.

PERIODICALS

American Journal of Sociology, May, 1960, W.J. Cahnman, review of *Survival in Auschwitz,* pp. 638-639.

American Scholar, winter, 1990, p. 142.

Booklist, January 1, 2002, George Cohen, review of *The Voice of Memory, Interviews 1961-1987,* p. 901; April 15, 2002, Hazel Rochman review of *The Search for Roots: A Personal Anthology,* p. 1376.

Christian Science Monitor, May 27, 1965, p. 9.

Commentary, October, 1985, pp. 41-47.

Georgia Review, summer, 1986, pp. 576-579.

Guardian (Manchester, England), April 22, 1960; February 12, 1965.

Hudson Review, summer, 1986, pp. 329-333.

Isis, June, 1986, pp. 330-332.

Library Journal, May 1, 2002, Gene Shaw, review of *The Search for Roots,* p. 102.

Listener, April 14, 1977, pp. 491-492.

London Review of Books, December 19, 1985, p. 23.

Los Angeles Times Book Review, May 31, 1987, p. 11; June 17, 1990, p. 3; May 14, 1993, p. 8.

Nation, August 3-10, 1985, pp. 86-88.

New Leader, November 26, 1984, pp. 16-17.

New Republic, July 28, 1986, pp. 27-33; May 11, 1987, p. 42.

New Statesman, March 19, 1960, p. 410; August 20, 1971, pp. 245-46.

New Statesman & Society, October 19, 1990, p. 32.

New Yorker, May 11, 1987, pp. 31-32.

New York Review of Books, January 17, 1985, pp. 8, 10; March 28, 1985, pp. 14-17.

New York Times, November 29, 1984, p. C21; April 12, 1987, p. 42; May 22, 1989, p. C18; December 12, 1989, p. C23; August 7, 1999, Diego Gambetta, "Primo Levi's Plunge: A Case against Suicide," p. A15.

New York Times Book Review, November 7, 1965, p. 85; December 23, 1984, p. 9; October 12, 1986, pp. 1, 40-41; July 5, 1987, p. 5; May 7, 1989, p. 14; February 4, 1990, p. 15.

Observer (London, England), January 26, 1965; December 21, 1986, p. 21; April 19, 1987, p. 23; October 22, 1989, p. 49; November 11, 1990, p. 67.

Partisan Review, winter, 1989, pp. 21-23.

PN Review, Volume 14, number 1, 1987, pp. 15-19.

Publishers Weekly, February 22, 1985, p. 151; May 11, 1990, p. 246.

Saturday Review, January 2, 1960, p. 23; May 15, 1965.

Scientific American, February, 1985, pp. 23, 27.

Sewanee Review, summer, 1990, Gabriel Motola, review of *The Mirror Maker: Stories and Essays,* pp. 506-514.

Stand, summer, 1991, pp. 74-83.

Technology Review, April, 1990, p. 77.

Tel Aviv Review, winter, 1990, pp. 149-165.

Times Literary Supplement, April 15, 1960; December 3, 1982; March 9, 1990, p. 248; November 23, 1990, p. 1271.

Tribune Books (Chicago, IL), July 5, 1990, Constance Markey, review of *The Sixth Day and Other Tales.*

Vanity Fair, January, 1988, pp. 78-84, 94.

Voice Literary Supplement, March, 1986, pp. 10-14.

Washington Post Book World, December 30, 1984, p. 7; May 19, 1985, pp. 3, 14.

World Literature Today, winter, 1977, p. 75; winter, 1983, pp. 83-84; spring, 1983, pp. 265-266.

OBITUARIES:

PERIODICALS

Chicago Tribune, April 13, 1987.

Cincinnati Post, April 14, 1987.

Detroit Free Press, April 12, 1987.

Fresno Bee, April 12, 1987.

International Herald Tribune, April 13, 1987.

Los Angeles Times, April 12, 1987.

New York Daily News, April 12, 1987.

New York Times, April 12, 1987; April 14, 1987.

Time, April 20, 1987.

Times (London, England), April 13, 1987.

Wall Street Journal, April 13, 1987.
Washington Post, April 12, 1987.

*   *   *

LEVIN, Ira 1929-

PERSONAL: Born August 27, 1929, New York, NY; son of Charles (a toy importer) and Beatrice (Schlansky) Levin; married Gabrielle Aronsohn, August 20, 1960 (divorced, January, 1968); married Phyllis Finkel, 1979 (divorced, 1981); children: (first marriage) Adam, Jared, Nicholas. *Education:* Attended Drake University, 1946-48; New York University, A.B. (philosophy and English), 1950.

ADDRESSES: Home—New York, NY. *Agent*—Harold Ober Associates, 425 Madison Ave., New York, NY 10017.

CAREER: Novelist and playwright. *Military service:* U.S. Army, Signal Corps, 1953-55.

MEMBER: Dramatists Guild (council member, 1980—), Authors Guild, Authors League of America, American Society of Composers, Authors and Publishers.

AWARDS, HONORS: Edgar Allan Poe Awards, Mystery Writers of America, 1953, for *A Kiss before Dying,* and 1980, for *Deathtrap;* Antoinette Perry Award nomination for best play, 1978, for *Deathtrap;* Bram Stoker Award for lifetime achievement, Horror Writers of America, 1997; Grand Masters Award, Mystery Writers of America, 2003, for a lifetime of great work.

WRITINGS:

NOVELS

A Kiss before Dying, Simon & Schuster (New York, NY), 1953, reprinted, ImPress Mystery (1999).

Rosemary's Baby (also see below), Random House (New York, NY), 1967, reprinted, with new afterword by the author, New American Library (New York, NY), 2003.

This Perfect Day (also see below), Random House (New York, NY), 1970.

The Stepford Wives (also see below), Random House (New York, NY), 1972, reprinted, with introduction by Peter Straub, Perennial (New York, NY), 2002.

The Boys from Brazil, Random House (New York, NY), 1976.

Three by Ira Levin (contains *Rosemary's Baby, The Stepford Wives,* and *This Perfect Day*), Random House (New York, NY), 1985.

Sliver, Bantam (New York, NY), 1991.

Son of Rosemary: The Sequel to Rosemary's Baby, Dutton (New York, NY), 1997.

PLAYS

No Time for Sergeants (adapted from the novel by Mac Hyman; first produced on Broadway, 1955; produced on the West End, 1956), Random House (New York, NY), 1956.

Interlock (first produced on Broadway, 1958), Dramatists Play Service (New York, NY), 1958.

Critic's Choice (first produced on Broadway, 1960; produced in London, England, 1961), Random House (New York, NY), 1961.

General Seeger (first produced on Broadway, 1962), Dramatists Play Service (New York, NY), 1962.

Drat!, The Cat!, with music by Milton Schafer, first produced on Broadway, 1965.

Dr. Cook's Garden: A Melodrama (first produced on Broadway, 1967), Dramatists Play Service (New York, NY), 1968.

Veronica's Room (first produced on Broadway, 1973), Random House (New York, NY), 1974.

Deathtrap (first produced on Broadway, 1978), Random House (New York, NY), 1979.

Break a Leg (first produced on Broadway, 1979), Samuel French (New York, NY), 1981.

Cantorial (first produced off-Broadway, 1988), Samuel French (New York, NY), 1990.

Also author of scripts for the television series *Clock, Lights Out,* and *U.S. Steel Hour.*

ADAPTATIONS: A Kiss before Dying was filmed by United Artists in 1956 and again in 1991; *No Time for Sergeants* was filmed by Twentieth Century-Fox in 1959; *Critic's Choice* was filmed by Warner Bros. in 1962; *Rosemary's Baby* was filmed by Paramount in 1968; *Dr. Cook's Garden* was filmed by the American Broadcasting Companies, Inc. (ABC) in 1970; *The Stepford Wives* was filmed by Columbia in 1975 and by Paramount Pictures in 2004; *The Boys from Brazil* was filmed by Twentieth Century-Fox in 1978; *Deathtrap* was filmed by Warner Bros. in 1982; *Sliver* was filmed by Paramount in 1993. *Rosemary's Baby* was recorded on audio cassette and released by Random Audiobooks, 1986; *Footsteps,* an unproduced play, was adapted as a TV film by the Columbia Broadcasting System, Inc. (CBS) television network, 2003.

SIDELIGHTS: In his plays and novels, Ira Levin exhibits "a continuing preoccupation with dark matters," James Lardner stated in the *Washington Post Book World.* Levin's first novel, *A Kiss before Dying,* is a murder mystery; *Rosemary's Baby* is a horror novel, as are *This Perfect Day* and *The Stepford Wives; The Boys from Brazil* is a thriller about the resurgence of a Nazi underground; and Levin's most successful play, *Death- trap,* is a mystery comedy. Despite his dark themes, Levin's many popular successes have shown him to be "a professional writer with an ear attuned to the elusive tempo of the times," as Robert Lima wrote in *Studies in American Fiction.*

Levin decided at the age of fifteen that he wanted to be a writer. After completing high school at the prestigious Horace Mann school, he studied for two years at Drake University, and then transferred to New York University. During his final year, he entered a screen-play writing contest for seniors sponsored by the CBS television network. Although his half-hour teleplay won him only a 200 dollar runner-up prize, the National Broadcasting Company, Inc. (NBC) television network offered him 400 dollars for the script, which they turned into an episode for *Lights Out.* When Levin graduated, his father agreed to support him for two years while he pursued his passion for writing; if in that time he had not succeeded, Levin agreed, he would defer to his father's goal for him, which was to join him in the toy business. In 1953, Levin was drafted into the Army and was based in Queens, New York. During that time, he wrote and produced training films for the U.S. government. His career as a television writer began in the early 1950s, and he contributed to some of the era's top programs.

His first novel, a mystery titled *A Kiss before Dying,* appeared in 1953 to rave reviews. The novel is told in three parts: the first from the point of view of the supposed killer of a young girl; the other two from the points of view of the girl's two sisters as they attempt to track down the killer. Writing in the *Chicago Sunday Tribune,* Drexel Drake described *A Kiss before Dying* as a "remarkably constructed story depicting an inconceivably vicious character in episodes of chilling horror." Anthony Boucher of the *New York Times Book Re-*

view maintained that "Levin combines great talent for pure novel writing—full bodied characterization, subtle psychological exploration, vivid evocation of locale— with strict technical whodunit tricks as dazzling as anything ever brought off." James Sandoe of the *New York Herald Tribune Book Review* was moved to call *A Kiss before Dying* "the most striking debut of the year." The Mystery Writers of America organization awarded the novel an Edgar Allan Poe Award as the best first novel of 1953.

It was fourteen years before Levin issued another novel. With the success of his stage adaptation of Mac Hyman's *No Time for Sergeants* in 1955, which ran for more than 700 performances on Broadway and launched the career of actor Andy Griffith, Levin devoted many years to writing exclusively for the theater. But in 1967, he returned to the novel form with *Rosemary's Baby,* the story of a young couple in the clutches of a modern cult of devil-worshippers. The Satanists want Rosemary, the young wife, to give birth to the son of the Devil, hoping that the child may "overcome the influence of God's son, Christ," Lima explained. But Rosemary is a recently lapsed Catholic who may be only hallucinating the devil-worshippers out of religious guilt. She is unsure whether she is truly threatened or merely fantasizing her danger. "One by one, untoward events happen," a writer for *Time* reported. "Dark signs and other-worldly hints occur; black candles, 'tannis root' or Devil's fungus, missing articles of clothing." "The delicate line between belief and disbelief is faultlessly drawn," wrote Thomas J. Fleming in the *New York Times Book Review.* "We are with [Levin] entirely, admiring his skill and simultaneously searching out possible, probable and improbable explanations of how he is going to extricate his heroine."

The setting for the novel, a gloomy Manhattan apartment building, is based on a building where Levin once lived. It "had a laundry room kind of like the one in the book," Levin explained to a writer for *Publishers Weekly.* "I would never let my wife go down there alone." Other details in the book are based on items from the daily newspaper. For the time period covered in the novel, some nine months during 1965 and 1966, Levin worked appropriate newspaper stories into *Rosemary's Baby* to make it more realistic. Coincidentally, Pope Paul VI's visit to New York occurred at the same time that Rosemary would have conceived her baby, so Levin worked it into his story. "The contrast between the Papal visit and what was happening to Rosemary produced some highly effective and quite unexpected drama," according to the *Publishers Weekly* article.

Critical appraisal of *Rosemary's Baby* was generally favorable. Barbara Nelson of *Library Journal,* for example, compared Levin's writing in the novel to the work of Shirley Jackson. Both authors, she claimed, suggest a "veneer of normality with hideous evil forces busy just beneath the surface." Peter Corodimas of *Best Sellers* also praised the novel, calling it "an exercise in sheer terror and tight craftsmanship" that is "superb." Fleming, however, ultimately judged *Rosemary's Baby* to be "just another Gothic tale" because of its literal resolution. But in her conclusion, Nelson contended that Levin "suspends disbelief so effectively that the unwary reader may well be converted to belief in the supernatural."

Levin's next two novels, *This Perfect Day* and *The Stepford Wives,* have similarly chilling premises. In *This Perfect Day,* a huge subterranean computer regulates all human behavior. In *The Stepford Wives,* the wives in a suburban community are turned into obedient robots. Alex Keneas of *Newsweek* stated that, in *This Perfect Day,* Levin "knows how to handle plot, twisting here and turning there, so that his story breezes along. . . . For a quick couple of hours it takes you away." Speaking of *The Stepford Wives,* Webster Schott of *Saturday Review* complained that it "is written with a grade school vocabulary, a high school version of syntax, and a best-selling author's understanding of what mass audiences want." But Martin Levin of the *New York Times Book Review* found a "broad current of humor beneath the horrific surface of this little ambush of Women's Lib, life, and the pursuit of happiness."

The Boys from Brazil, Levin's next novel, postulates a Nazi underground in South America led by the infamous Josef Mengele, the doctor who performed hideous experiments on prisoners at the Auschwitz concentration camp. Mengele's experiments with cloning lead him to attempt to clone Adolf Hitler and thereby restore the Nazi movement. He clones ninety-four babies from Hitler's genes and places the children with parents similar in age and occupation to Hitler's own parents, hoping that at least one of the children will grow up with Hitler's driving ambition for political power. In his review of *The Boys from Brazil,* the critic for the *New Yorker* claimed that "the writing is smooth and suspense-inducing, the characters are wafer-thin but plausible, and Mr. Levin once again proves himself to be an author who can tell a fairly farfetched, silly story with surprising grace."

Many of the characters in the novel are based on actual people. Mengele, for example, is the real doctor from Auschwitz who was long rumored to be hiding in South America. And the novel's hero, Yakov Liberman, who

tracks down fugitive Nazis and exposes the cloning plot, is based on the actual Nazi hunter Simon Weisenthal. This use of actual people as fictional characters drew criticism from R.Z. Sheppard of *Time.* Sheppard felt that "the turning of Josef Mengele into a mad scientist from the pages of a 1940s comic book requires more than a suspension of disbelief. It also requires a suspension of taste. Exploiting such a monster for entertainment and profit is enough to give evil a bad name." However, most reviews of *The Boys from Brazil* judged it to be an entertaining novel. Valentine Cunningham of *New Statesman,* for example, felt that "the plot unfolds utterly enthrallingly to make a superior read in this genre." And Gary Arnold of the *Washington Post* called it "a snappy pop entertainment synthesis of accumulating suspense, detective work, pseudoscientific speculation and historical wish fulfillment." Writing in *Newsweek,* Peter S. Prescott admitted that a Levin novel "is like a bag of popcorn: utterly without nutritive value and probably fattening, yet there's no way to stop once you've started."

The idea for *The Boys from Brazil* came from a newspaper article on cloning in which Hitler and Mozart were given as examples of the wide range of cloning possibilities. "Needless to say," Lardner observed, "Levin never gave much thought to a novel about the cloning of Mozart." Levin's ideas for books and plays "are not so much born as incubated," Alfred Gillespie wrote in *People.* A story idea is first jotted down in one of his many notebooks and will, over a period of years, be added to and mulled over until it coalesces into a complete plot. The process of writing, too, takes time. Levin admits to being a slow writer. *Drat!, The Cat!* took ten years to reach the stage; *Rosemary's Baby* was six years in the making; and *Deathtrap* took six years from initial idea to full production.

Levin's playwriting efforts since his initial success with *No Time for Sergeants* have been only moderately fruitful. Besides *No Time for Sergeants,* only *Critic's Choice* enjoyed a substantial run on Broadway. The folding of *Drat!, The Cat!* after only a week, Levin told Gillespie, "succeeded only in sending me back to novels." There was a break in this run of bad luck when Levin returned to the stage in 1978 with *Deathtrap,* a comedy mystery involving Sidney Bruhl, a failed playwright who toys with the idea of murdering a young playwright and stealing his play. Filled with twists and turns that keep the audience guessing as to the protagonist's real intentions, *Deathtrap* ran on Broadway for over four years—from February 26, 1978, to June 27, 1982— making it the fourth-longest-running play in Broadway history at that time.

The play's structure—"as convoluted as an artichoke," Richard F. Shepard wrote in the *New York Times*—has garnered the most critical attention. Levin succeeds in turning inside-out many cliché mystery situations so that the audience is always surprised by the unexpected. A psychic character, neighbor to the Bruhls, even predicts various plot twists in advance, but her predictions only serve to mislead the audience. According to Walter Kerr of the *New York Times,* Levin "engages us all in an open-handed, evening-long game of hide-and-seek. . . . [He] has brazenly opted for revealing all, showing us the naked machinery, inviting us to compete in putting the pieces into the jig-saw. And surprised us anyway. The sheer cockiness of his method compounds our delight." Sylvie Drake of the *Los Angeles Times* called the play "two hours of escapist fun, a roller-coaster ride through convolutions of plot and psyches."

Deathtrap provides as many laughs as chills, following in the tradition of *Arsenic and Old Lace* and other Broadway thrillers. Sidney Bruhl's witty remarks about the writer's life and the writing of mysteries are a running commentary on the play itself. "All the way through," Shepard remarked, "[*Deathtrap*] is laughing at itself and perhaps at the genre on which it is a take-off, although at its moment of murder it wipes the smile off your face." Levin, Lardner wrote, "is after laughs as well as screams. . . . *Deathtrap* is capable of generating both responses, sometimes all but simultaneously." Speaking to Gillespie, Levin defends the thriller tradition in theater. "Thrillers are satisfying deep down," Levin says, "because they give you the chance to deal safely with violence and murder. . . . They're horror stories with happy endings." *Deathtrap,* too, has a happy ending. In addition to its record-breaking run on Broadway, the play was performed by four national touring companies, was made into a film, and won an Edgar Allan Poe Award.

Levin's next two plays, *Break a Leg* and *Cantorial,* were less successful, and again he returned to the novel, this time with the 1991 thriller *Sliver,* so named because the action takes place in a high-rise apartment in Manhattan built in a sliver of space between two other buildings. The main characters in the tale are a thirty-nine-year-old divorcée who has recently moved into the building—and who is being observed there through an elaborate series of hidden cameras—and her rich and apparently charming lover. "No species is as curious—and as prurient—as the human race," Carolyn See commented in the *Los Angeles Times.* "*Sliver* is about this phenomenon." *New York Times* reviewer Christopher Lehmann-Haupt noted that Levin "plots cleverly, even

scaring us into thinking he has revealed the identity of his madman . . . too early in the story." Writing for *Washington Post Book World,* suspense author Peter Straub pronounced the novel to be "as pointed, slim and nasty as its title promises" and adds that it "serves as a reminder that we can always use another new novel by this careful and painstaking writer—he's too parsimonious by half." Straub further noted, "Right up to the conclusion, Levin's people keep surprising us with their refusal to conform to the roles and attitudes the conventional thriller would assign them."

On October 12, 2003, Levin's unproduced play *Footsteps* premiered as a television movie on CBS starring Candice Bergen, Bug Hall, and Bryan Brown. Ray Richmond of the *Hollywood Reporter.com* described the play as "an original suspense thriller with abundant twists and turns that recalls the 1960s classic 'Wait Until Dark.'" A biographer for *Intercourse with the Dead* Web site noted that Levin once told Mervyn Rothstein of the *New York Times* that he believed his early, unsatisfactory relationship with his father influenced his writing. Levin commented: "I finally did work out a very good relationship with my father, but it was rough growing up. We had a lot of conflict, and I think it surfaced in many of my works."

BIOGRAPHICAL AND CRITICAL SOURCES:

BOOKS

Contemporary Literary Criticism, Thomson Gale (Detroit, MI), Volume 3, 1975; Volume 6, 1976.
Fowler, Douglas, *Ira Levin,* Starmont House, 1988.

PERIODICALS

Best Sellers, April 15, 1967, Peter Corodimas, review of *Rosemary's Baby.*
Chicago Sunday Tribune, October 25, 1953, Drexel Drake, review of *A Kiss before Dying.*
Christian Science Monitor, September 27, 1972; September 14, 1978.
Library Journal, April 15, 1967, Barbara Nelson, review of *Rosemary's Baby.*
Los Angeles Times, March 29, 1979; February 18, 1991, p. E6.
Nation, April 3, 1989, p. 463.
New Republic, June 20, 1981.
New Statesman, April 16, 1976, Valentine Cunningham, review of *The Boys from Brazil.*

Newsweek, April 17, 1967; March 16, 1970, Alex Keneas, review of *This Perfect Day;* November 5, 1973; February 23, 1976, Peter S. Prescott, review of *The Boys from Brazil.*

New York, September 8, 1997, p. 135.

New Yorker, November 21, 1953; November 5, 1973; March 8, 1976, review of *The Boys from Brazil.*

New York Herald Tribune Book Review, October 18, 1953, James Sandoe, review of *A Kiss before Dying.*

New York Magazine, November 12, 1973.

New York Times, October 25, 1953; March 5, 1978; April 30, 1979; August 17, 1981; June 8, 1982; April 23, 1985; February 12, 1989, p. 28; May 16, 1990; February 25, 1991, p. C20.

New York Times Book Review, April 30, 1967, Thomas J. Fleming, review of *Rosemary's Baby;* October 15, 1972; March 14, 1976, Thomas J. Fleming, review of *The Boys from Brazil;* March 31, 1991, William H. Banks, Jr., review of *Sliver,* p. 16; October 5, 1997, James Polk, review of *Son of Rosemary,* p. 23.

People, May 15, 1978, Alfred Gillespie, review of *The Boys from Brazil.*

Publishers Weekly, May 22, 1967; July 3, 1987, p. 38; December 21, 1990, p. 45; June 1, 1992, p. 26; June 12, 1995, p. 23; August 25, 1997, p. 47.

Saturday Review, April 15, 1967; October 7, 1972.

Studies in American Fiction, autumn, 1974, Robert Lima.

Time, June 23, 1967; November 12, 1973; February 23, 1976, R.Z. Sheppard, review of *Boys from Brazil.*

Village Voice, November 8, 1973.

Washington Post, October 5, 1978; July 22, 1979; July 26, 1979.

Washington Post Book World, February 15, 1975; February 10, 1991, Peter Straub, review of *Sliver,* p. 6.

ONLINE

Hollywood Reporter.com, http://www.hollywood reporter.com/ (October 10, 2003), Ray Richmond, review of *Footsteps.*

Intercourse with the Dead, http://www.intercoursewith thedead.com/ (August 4, 2004), Ira Levine biography.

*   *   *

LEVON, O.U.
   See KESEY, Ken

LEYNER, Mark 1956-

PERSONAL: Born January 4, 1956, in Jersey City, NJ; son of Joel (a lawyer) and Muriel (a real estate agent; maiden name, Chasan) Leyner; married Arleen Portada (a psychotherapist; marriage ended); married second wife, Mercedes; children: Gabrielle. *Education:* Brandeis University, B.A., 1977; University of Colorado, M.F.A., 1979. *Religion:* Jewish.

ADDRESSES: Agent—Amanda Urban, International Creative Management, 40 W. 57th St., New York, NY 10019.

CAREER: Panasonic Co., Secaucus, NJ, advertising copywriter, 1981-82; Brooklyn College of the City University of New York, Brooklyn, NY, lecturer in English, 1982; lecturer, Jersey City State College, 1982-84; freelance copywriter, 1984-88; freelance writer and novelist, 1989—. Columnist for *Esquire;* writer for MTV's *Liquid Television;* creator of audio series *Wiretap,* 2002—.

WRITINGS:

I Smell Esther Williams and Other Stories, Fiction Collective (New York, NY), 1983.

(Editor with Curtis White and Thomas Glynn) *American Made,* Fiction Collective (New York, NY), 1986.

My Cousin, My Gastroenterologist, Fiction Collective (New York, NY), 1989.

Et Tu, Babe, Harmony Books (New York, NY), 1992.

Tooth Imprints on a Corn Dog, Harmony Books (New York, NY), 1995.

The Tetherballs of Bougainville, Harmony Books (New York, NY), 1997.

Contributor of stories, articles, plays, and poems to magazines, including *Fictional International, Esquire, Mississippi Review, Rolling Stone, Semiotexte,* and *Between C and D.*

ADAPTATIONS: My Cousin, My Gastroenterologist, I Smell Esther Williams and Other Stories, and *Et Tu, Babe* were all released as sound recordings (read by the author) by Dove Audio in 1990, 1991, and 1992 respectively.

SIDELIGHTS: "By turns imaginative, verbose, and iconoclastic, Mark Leyner is a humorist and experimentalist who tackles the often ridiculous products of postmodern culture and squeezes new hybrids out of them, ranging from military academies of beauty to weight-loss camps for terrorists to custom-built designer electric chairs," wrote Roy C. Flannagan in the *Dictionary of Literary Biography.* Leyner's novels and short story collections to date—*I Smell Esther Williams and Other Stories, My Cousin, My Gastroenterologist, Et Tu, Babe, Tooth Imprints on a Corn Dog,* and *The Tetherballs of Bougainville,*—depict a warped, gonzo world in which literally anything can happen, and usually does. "I feel like I'm living a writer's life at warp speed," Mark Leyner told *Boston Globe* contributor Joseph P. Kahn. "In three years I've gone from being a fringe avant-gardist to a cult object to mainstream novelist." Jonathan Yardley, writing in the *Washington Post Book World,* observed that reading Leyner's books "is like watching a blend of *Saturday Night Live* and *Monty Python;* they have the energy and insouciance of high-risk, off-the-wall performance." "When you have been called America's best-built comic novelist by *The New York Times,* personal trainer to pop-culture heavyweights everywhere," Kahn argued, "you are liable to say, do and write almost anything."

Leyner began his writing career as a poet at his New Jersey high school. When he moved on to Brandeis University, he began experimenting with using poetic techniques in fiction. "I thought, 'Wouldn't it be wonderful to have the kind of fiction that was as dense with imagery and dense with excitement and pleasure as poetry is,'" Leyner commented to *Los Angeles Times* contributor Irene Lacher, "'and have a kind of fiction that didn't have all kinds of dumb transitional pages where you're getting people off a plane to a hotel?'" Leyner's first venture into this type of prose was *I Smell Esther Williams and Other Stories,* which "was written in graduate school" at the University of Colorado, Kahn explained, "and is regarded today by its author rather like an old prom date who rebuffed his advances in the back seat of her father's convertible."

Leyner's second book, *My Cousin, My Gastroenterologist,* was published in 1989 and established him as a favorite of the collegiate undergraduate literati. "That manic volume of surreal prose poetry," wrote Lacher, "offered cameo appearances from the Pope's *valet de chambre* and Nazi filmmaker Leni Riefenstahl—not to mention such unlikely inventions as Le Corbusier-designed jeans and the fearfully sexually over-mature Joey D., who at 4 1/2 revved a tricycle with a turbocharged V-8 engine." Lacher went on to explain, "Leyner is regarded as the Writer for the MTV Generation, the spiritual stepson of William Burroughs and Lenny Bruce, only with a high-tech sheen."

The author noted in a clip reprinted in *Harper's* magazine that he supported himself "by doing advertising copywriting" while working on *My Cousin, My Gastroenterologist.* The novel's success allowed Leyner to devote himself full-time to writing and also gave him a theme for his next book, *Et Tu, Babe.* "The novel (using the term in the loosest imaginable sense)," stated Yardley, "is about 'the most intense and, in a certain sense, the most significant young prose writer in America.' His name is Mark Leyner." The character Leyner, who in many respects resembles the author Leyner, is obsessed with self-promotion. He has even gathered a group of enthusiasts, called Team Leyner, to assist him in his publicity stunts. *New York Times* reviewer Michiko Kakutani wrote, "The reader learns of such bizarre phenomena as weight-loss camps for terrorists; penile-growth hormones; medical cheese sculptures (sculptures of human organs, made of mozzarella and havarti), interactive computerized laser-video players that insert Mr. Schwarzenegger as the actor in any movie . . . and 'visceral tattoos,' that is, tattoos inscribed on people's internal organs with radioactive isotopes."

"I figured Team Leyner would reach some kind of apogee in the middle of the book, when it would be most powerful," Leyner told *Bloomsbury Review* interviewers John and Carl Bellante. "The Leyner character would be at his most megalomaniacal. His delusions of grandeur would be full-blown. Then gradually, the Team Leyner minions, personnel, and staff would start deserting him." In the end the Leyner character is left alone, and finally even he vanishes—mourned in passing by such celebrities as Connie Chung and Carl Sagan. "If the world is a leopard-print cocktail lounge on the Titanic," declared Carol Anshaw in the *Village Voice Literary Supplement,* "Leyner is at the piano, noodling out 'My Way.'" "Mr. Leyner," concluded *New York Times Book Review* contributor Lewis Burke Frumkes, "is a very funny man who has written a very twisted book."

Leyner's 1995 collection of short stories, *Tooth Imprints on a Corn Dog,* continues his exploration through the manic world he perceives around him. "*Tooth Imprints,*" explained Kristan Schiller in the *New York Times,* "is based on occurrences in Mr. Leyner's life . . . spun into surreal tales that satirize the media-crazed, image-obsessed society he beholds—and accepts." "The results are intermittently hilarious," Kakutani stated in the *New York Times,* "but also silly and highly sophomoric." The work "lacks the abrasive, experimental edge of his previous fiction," observed Jonathan Bing in *Publishers Weekly,* but "it nevertheless exhibits all the whimsy, irreverence and biting satire of his best work. The protagonist is still, much of the time, Mark Leyner; yet his persona is gentler, more circumspect, given to tender reflections about the pressures of fatherhood and professional freelancing." Rick Marin argued in a *Newsweek* review of *Tooth Imprints* that though the novel is "Leyner's most accessible opus to date, it is emphatically not for everyone. Then again, what good book is?"

Leyner returned to Team Leyner with his 1997 title, *The Tetherballs of Bougainville,* "the most unified of Leyner's books in terms of its formal structure and theme," according to Flannagan. The same critic went on to note that the "book satirizes the conventional bildungsroman, complete with adolescent antihero (the thirteen-year-old 'Mark Leyner'), the death-exile of the father (who, in Leyner's twisted version, refuses to die), and the rites of sexual initiation with an older woman." Written as autobiography, screenplay and movie review, *The Tetherballs of Bougainville* twists three familiar narrative forms into the story of Mark Leyner, a thirteen-year-old, who waits in a New Jersey prison to witness his father's execution. It just so happens that this junior high schooler is on deadline to turn in a screenplay for which he has already been awarded the $250,000-a-year-for-life Vincent and Lenore DiGiacomo/Oshimitsu Polymers America Award.

When his father's years of PCP ingestion save him from the lethal injection, all is not lost, for the female warden overseeing the execution only has eyes for young Mark. Infatuation turns into an extended and athletic sexual romp in this "gonzo parody of a wannabe writer's coming-of-age," as Paula Chin described the novel in *People.* Taking up the publishing theme, Trevor Dodge, writing in *Review of Contemporary Fiction,* concluded that this novel "is both postmodern product and parody, a full-blown riot in the coffers of the New York publishing industry and a testament to Leyner's whipsmart comedic genius." Chin however was less positive in her evaluation, finding that *Tetherballs* "may give you a few chuckles, but it gets tiresome pretty quickly." Other critics had higher praise for *The Tetherballs of Bougainville.* Writing in *Entertainment Weekly,* A.J. Jacobs noted that "you don't read Leyner for the plot. The plots just there so he has a place to hang his hilarious, postmodern prose poetry—a mixture of pop-culture references, brand names, scientific mumbo jumbo, and zeitgeist-skewering satire." Similarly, *Booklist*'s Joanne Wilkinson dubbed the same novel a *twisted comic tale,* further commenting that Leyner "turns in his funniest, most inventive novel yet." For *Library Journal*'s Michele Leber, the book is "impressively researched satire," and for a *Publishers*

Weekly contributor Leyner presented himself as "jaw-slackeningly inventive." The same critic concluded that Leyner "is one of our most talented comic writers," and that he is at "his horny, hip, encyclopedic best" in *The Tetherballs of Bougainville.*

Mark Leyner commented: "My work isn't animated by a desire to be experimental or post-modernist or aesthetically subversive or even 'innovative'—it is animated by a desire to craft a kind of writing that is at every single moment exhilarating for the reader; where each phrase, each sentence is an event. That's what I'm trying for, at least. This, I think, is what gives my work its peculiar shape and feel—it's because I want every little surface to shimmer and gyrate that I haven't patience for those lax transitional devices of plot, setting, character, and so on, that characterize a lot of traditional fiction. I'm after the gaudiness, self-consciousness, laughter, encoded sadness of public language (public because language is the sea in which all our minds swim).

"I don't feel part of any artistic movement or 'ism.' But I feel linked to artists who launched their careers reading billboards aloud in the back seats on family trips, who spent their formative Saturday mornings cemented to their television screens with Crazy Glue, who grew up fascinated by the rhetoric of pentecostal preachers, dictators, game show hosts, and other assorted demagogues, who were entranced by the outlandishly superfluous chatter of baseball announcers filling air-time during rain delays, and who could never figure out the qualitative difference between Thackeray's *Vanity Fair* and E.C. Segar's *Popeye the Sailor.*

"I said in an article once that we need a kind of writing that the brain can dance to. Well, that's the kind of writing I'm trying to write—thrashing the smoky air of the cerebral ballroom with a very American ball-point baton."

BIOGRAPHICAL AND CRITICAL SOURCES:

BOOKS

Contemporary Literary Criticism, Volume 92, Thomson Gale (Detroit, MI), 1996.
Dictionary of Literary Biography, Volume 292: *Twenty-First Century American Novelists,* Thomson Gale (Detroit, MI), 2004, pp. 222-230.

PERIODICALS

Bloomsbury Review, July/August, 1993, pp. 5-7.

Booklist, March 1, 1995, George Needham, review of *Tooth Imprints on a Corn Dog,* p. 1179; October 15, 1997, Joanne Wilkinson, review of *The Tetherballs of Bougainville,* p. 388.

Boston Globe, November 9, 1993, p. 29.

Entertainment Weekly, October 9, 1992, Margot Mifflin, review of *Et Tu, Babe,* p. 54; March 17, 1995, Margot Mifflin, review of *Tooth Imprints on a Corn Dog,* p. 84; November 7, 1997, A.J. Jacobs, review of *The Tetherballs of Bougainville,* p. 80; April 26, 2002, Noah Robischon, "Wired for Weird."

Harper's, July, 1990, pp. 43-44.

Library Journal, September 1, 1997, Michele Leber, review of *The Tetherballs of Bougainville,* p. 218.

Los Angeles Times, November 6, 1992, pp. E1, E4.

Los Angeles Times Book Review, October 11, 1992, p. 6.

Newsweek, March 27, 1995, Cheech Marin review of *Tooth Imprints on a Corn Dog,* p. 68.

New York Times, October 13, 1992, p. C17; February 19, 1995, p. J13; March 7, 1995, p. C18.

New York Times Book Review, September 27, 1992, p. 14; April 23, 1995, p. 12.

People, April 24, 1995, Eric Levin, interview, p. 27; April 24, 1995, Nancy Jo Sales, review of *Tooth Imprints on a Corn Dog,* pp. 27-28; November 10, 1997, Paula Chin review of *The Tetherballs of Bougainville,* pp. 41-42.

Publishers Weekly, March 16, 1990, Penny Kaganoff, review of *My Cousin, My Gastroenterologist,* p. 65; August 24, 1992, review of *Et Tu, Babe,* p. 61; January 30, 1995, review of *Tooth Imprints on a Corn Dog,* p. 85; March 6, 1995, pp. 44-45; July 21, 1997, review of *The Tetherballs of Bougainville,* p. 181.

Review of Contemporary Fiction, fall, 1995, Steven Moore, review of *Tooth Imprints on a Corn Dog,* pp. 246-247; spring, 1998, Trevor Dodge, review of *The Tetherballs of Bougainville,* pp. 226-227.

San Francisco Review of Books, winter, 1992, p. 40.

Time, October 12, 1992, John Skow, review of *Et Tu, Babe,* p. 90.

Village Voice Literary Supplement, November, 1992, pp. 25-27.

Washington Post Book World, October 4, 1992, Jonathan Yardley, review of *Et Tu, Babe,* p. 3.

ONLINE

Team Leyner: The Unofficial Mark Leyner Links Page, http://www.spesh.com/leyner/ (July 26, 2004).

*   *   *

LIEBER, Stanley Martin
See LEE, Stan

LINDBERGH, Anne Morrow 1906-2001
(Anne Spencer Morrow Lindbergh)

PERSONAL: Born 1906, in Englewood, NJ; died February 7, 2001, in Passumsic, VT; daughter of Dwight Whitney (former U.S. ambassador to Mexico) and Elizabeth Reeve (Cutter) Morrow; married Charles Augustus Lindbergh, Jr. (an aviator; first pilot to fly from New York to Paris), May 27, 1929 (died August 26, 1974); children: Charles Augustus III (died, 1932), Jon Morrow, Land Morrow (son), Anne Spencer (died, 1993), Reeve (daughter), Scott. *Education:* Smith College, B.A., 1928.

CAREER: Writer. Former director, Harcourt Brace Jovanovich (publishers), San Francisco.

AWARDS, HONORS: Cross of Honor, U.S. Flag Association, 1933, for part in survey of trans-Atlantic air routes; Hubbard Gold Medal, National Geographic Society, 1934, for work as copilot and radio operator in flight of 40,000 miles over five continents; honorary M.A., Smith College, 1935; honorary LL.D., Amherst College, 1939, University of Rochester, 1939.

WRITINGS:

North to the Orient (travel), Harcourt (New York, NY), 1935.

Listen! The Wind (travel), Harcourt (New York, NY), 1938.

The Wave of the Future (essay), Harcourt (New York, NY), 1940.

The Steep Ascent (novel), Harcourt (New York, NY), 1944.

Gift from the Sea (essays; also see below), Pantheon (New York, NY), 1955, twentieth-anniversary edition, with an afterword by the author, Vintage (New York, NY), 1975, reprinted, Random House (New York, NY), 1995.

The Unicorn and Other Poems, 1935-1955, Pantheon (New York, NY), 1956.

Dearly Beloved (novel), Harcourt (New York, NY), 1962, reprinted, Chicago Review Press (Chicago IL), 2003.

Earth Shine (nonfiction), Harcourt (New York, NY), 1969.

Christmas in Mexico: 1972, Harcourt (New York, NY), 1971.

Bring Me a Unicorn: Diaries and Letters of Anne Morrow Lindbergh, Harcourt (New York, NY), 1972.

Hour of Gold, Hour of Lead: Diaries and Letters of Anne Morrow Lindbergh, 1929-1932, Harcourt (New York, NY), 1973.

Locked Rooms and Open Doors: Diaries and Letters of Anne Morrow Lindbergh, 1932-1935, Harcourt (New York, NY), 1974.

The Flower and the Nettle: Diaries and Letters of Anne Morrow Lindbergh, 1936-1939, Harcourt (New York, NY), 1976.

War Within and Without: Diaries and Letters of Anne Morrow Lindbergh, 1939-1944, Harcourt (New York, NY), 1980.

(Author of introduction) James D. Newton, *Uncommon Friends: Remembering Thomas Edison, Henry Ford, Harvey Firestone, Alexis Carrel, and Charles Lindbergh,* 1987.

(Author of introduction) Antoine de Saint-Exupery, *Wartime Writings, 1939-1944,* Harcourt (New York, NY), 1990.

SIDELIGHTS: While Anne Morrow Lindbergh is widely respected as an author of philosophical novels and essays, she is even better known for having lived "a life that most scenario writers would hesitate to invent," observed Glendy Culligan in *Saturday Review.* The dramatic events of Lindbergh's life, including her marriage to aviation pioneer Charles A. Lindbergh, her participation in early experimental flights, the notorious abduction and murder of their first child, and a successful career as an author, have made best sellers of her published diaries and letters.

Lindbergh was born into "what may have been the closest knit nuclear family in modern history," noted Jane Howard in the *Washington Post Book World.* Her father, Dwight Morrow, was at various times a partner to banker J.P. Morgan, an ambassador, and a U.S. senator. Her mother, Elizabeth Cutter Morrow, was a poet, a trustee of Smith College, and a crusader for equal education for women. The Morrows' wealth and status ensured that their children, all daughters, were well educated and well traveled at an early age. It also produced a "haze of insulation which permeated our early years," an "indefinable sense of isolation from the world," notes Lindbergh in the introduction to the first volume of her diaries, *Bring Me a Unicorn: Diaries and Letters of Anne Morrow Lindbergh.* She explains, "No matter what we read or where we traveled we were enclosed in the familial circle, confined, although also enriched, by the strong family bonds and strictly defined child-parent roles."

"Only in college did I begin to realize how much I resembled the 'sheltered Emelye' of Chaucer's Knight's Tale, enclosed in a walled garden," Lindbergh contin-

ues. Her years at Smith College were important for discovering the existence of a world beyond her sheltered circle, but her preoccupation with her family was still dominant. In 1927 she eagerly anticipated spending Christmas with her relatives in Mexico, where her father was then U.S. ambassador. When Anne heard that America's hero, Charles A. Lindbergh, would also be visiting the embassy as part of a good-will tour, she was unimpressed, admitting only "a little annoyance" at "all this public-hero stuff breaking into our family party." Meeting Charles swept away her indifference, however, and before the Christmas holiday was over, she admitted that she was hopelessly in love with him. He returned her feelings, and after several months, the couple announced their engagement. By that time, Anne realized that her fiancé's celebrity status would forever rule out the secluded life she preferred, but it made no difference. "Don't wish me happiness," she wrote to a friend. "I don't expect to be happy, but it's gotten beyond that. . . . Wish me courage and strength and a sense of humor—I will need them all."

The first years of the Lindberghs' marriage are covered in the second volume of her published diaries and letters, *Hour of Gold, Hour of Lead: Diaries and Letters of Anne Morrow Lindbergh, 1929-1932.* Anne learned the skills necessary to serve as Charles' copilot, navigator, and radio operator, and the newlyweds spent most of the early days of their marriage in the air. The hysterical hero-worship Charles had inspired since his solo New York-Paris flight in 1927 was only intensified by his marriage to Anne and their subsequent adventures together. "To millions around the world—reading of the Lindberghs flying everywhere in their own Lockheed Sirius seaplane, looking at photographs of the 'perfect'-looking couple ('the lone eagle and his mate') landing in Siberia, China, Japan—the Lindberghs seemed to enjoy the greatest possible good fortune that a young couple could have," wrote Alfred Kazin in his *New York Times Book Review* article on *Hour of Gold, Hour of Lead.* The image of perfection was completed in 1930 by the birth of their first child, Charles A. Lindbergh III. But on March 1, 1932, the illusion was shattered. That evening, when Anne went upstairs to check the child before retiring, she found his crib empty; the baby had been kidnaped.

Weeks passed in frantic investigations and negotiations. Over twelve thousand people wrote to describe dreams they had had envisioning the exact location of the missing child. Al Capone and other crime bosses offered their help. Reporters, photographers, and state troopers laid siege to the Lindberghs' New Jersey residence. Newspapers had extras ready at every hour, prepared to announce the baby's safe return. But on May 12, 1932, his body was found in a ditch not far from the Lindbergh home. "Rarely has a personal tragedy had such public reverberations and consequences," stated Kazin. "A whole simplistic 'American' idea of life died with the Lindbergh baby."

The parents' anguish over the loss of their baby was exacerbated by the relentless public exposure to which they were subjected. "The contrast between the Lindbergh character and the Lindbergh case is painful and ominous in its interest," noted Kazin. "Both the Lindberghs have always been intensely private persons, with an austere, restrained, glowingly creative sense of life. Their laconic self-confidence (old American style) hardly prepared them for the hideous absurdity (contemporary American style) of their public anxiety and laceration. . . . Their natural sensitiveness was intensified, after the kidnaping, by armies of reporters, photographers, marauders, publicity seekers, vandals who drove by the house just long enough to kill a dog, shakedown artists of every kind who tried to cash in on the case."

Lindbergh's diary *Locked Rooms and Open Doors: Diaries and Letters of Anne Morrow Lindbergh, 1932-1935* details the family's recovery from their trauma. The diary depicts Charles as an invaluable source of support for Anne. He urged her to begin writing the story of their daring 1931 survey flight to the Orient via the Arctic Circle, and he later convinced her to assist him in a five-month flight exploring the Atlantic for commercial air routes. Although reluctant to leave her new baby, Jon, born in August, 1932, Anne welcomed the solitude of flight. "Flying was normal life for us," she explains in her introduction to *Locked Rooms.* "The project lifted us out of the aftermath of crime and turned the publicity that surrounded us to a constructive end—the advance of air travel. . . . For me, the trip was the nearest approximation to 'a life of our own' that could then be found. It meant more freedom, more privacy with my husband, and more contact with people in natural surroundings. . . . All these factors were restoring." Reviewers have characterized Lindbergh's account of these years in *Locked Rooms and Open Doors* as many variations on a theme of anguish. *Locked Rooms and Open Doors* "is an autobiography of being imprisoned in bad dreams, great demands, self-doubt, and painful fatigue," commented Catharine R. Stimpson in the *New York Times Book Review.*

Lindbergh's engrossing personal life during this time—as she and her husband recovered from their loss and struggled to continue on with their aviation work,

Lindbergh was beginning to publish her writing even as their family continued to grow—takes over the majority of this volume of the journal. Thus the greater world beyond the private one is largely left unexplored here. "She lived on the sharp edge of history, as observer, actor, and symbol; but the energy for analysis of the great forces of the present seems to have been blunted or deflected," Stimpson observed. By contrast, *The Flower and the Nettle: Diaries and Letters of Anne Morrow Lindbergh, 1936-1939,* Lindbergh's next volume of published journals, takes as its main theme the encroaching war in Europe as the Lindbergh's witness firsthand the growing power of Hitler and the German military.

The Lindberghs' sought some relief from the relentless encroachments of reporters, well-wishers, and crazies whose interest in the couple surged once again with their return to the United States and the onset of the trial of their baby's alleged kidnapper, Bruno Hauptmann. Privacy and safety began to seem impossibilities in the United States, so after the trial and the publication of Anne's book *North to the Orient,* the couple took their baby and fled to a self-imposed exile in England and Europe. Anne described these experiences in *The Flower and the Nettle.*

They found a welcome peace in England. Charles again encouraged Anne to pursue her writing, and she began work on the story of their Atlantic flight, which was published as *Listen! The Wind.* Reviews of *North to the Orient* had been strongly favorable, Edward Weeks writing in *Atlantic Bookshelf:* "One's first impression of the book is that Anne Lindbergh writes so well that she must not stop." Publication of *Listen! The Wind* solidified her reputation as critics emphasized that Lindbergh's elegant, graceful prose gives the book an importance that goes far beyond its historical significance. *Listen! The Wind* "is a record of technical achievement, a record historically valuable; in Anne Lindbergh's hands it becomes literature," enthused Katherine Woods in the *New York Times Book Review.* In *Books,* William Soskin called the author "one of the finest writers in America, one who has emerged to an artistry which the most meticulous of critics cannot challenge."

After two years in England, punctuated by several flights and the birth of another son, the Lindberghs moved to France. World War II was by now brewing in Europe. Politically, Charles was an isolationist who believed for many reasons that the United States should not become involved in a foreign conflict. When the U.S. government asked him to quietly investigate the growth of the German air force, however, he willingly complied. The American press questioned his frequent, unexplained visits to Germany and began to paint a new picture of their former hero as a possible Nazi sympathizer. When Hitler invaded Czechoslovakia in 1939, the Lindberghs returned to the United States—and to a new public ordeal, as they were publicly reviled as traitors for their isolationist stance.

Lindbergh's account of these years in letters and journals is collected in *The Flower and the Nettle,* in which a sense of personal happiness and contentment is commingled with growing dread of the approaching political calamity spreading through Europe. Lindbergh's social position meant that during these years she met some of the most powerful people in Europe, and her account of their opinions and attitudes during this period is considered a valuable addition to the historical record. Of greater interest, according to Elizabeth Johnston Lipscomb in the *Magill's Literary Annual,* is Lindbergh's own character. "Through the flowing, unobtrusive prose of her diaries and her letters to close friends and relatives, she shows her intense awareness of her natural surroundings, her sensitivity to the people around her, her self-doubt, her courage, her humor, her acute judgment of others, and, above all, her dedication to her responsibility to her family, her work, and herself."

With war fever mounting, isolationism was popularly considered tantamount to treason. The individualistic Charles was not ashamed of his stance, but it quickly earned him the titles of anti-Semite and pro-Nazi. Although Anne only partly agreed with his position, she felt obliged to support it. Her 1940 book *The Wave of the Future* was, according to Joseph P. Lash in the *New York Times Book Review,* her "effort to build a bridge between her husband's position and her own. . . . In it she argues for staying out of the war and concentrating on domestic reform because, among other reasons, Italy, Germany, and Russia, whatever their flaws, are symptoms of a new world struggling to be born." Anne's style was once again generally praised by critics such as Clare Boothe who, in *Current History and Forum,* deemed it "clear, chiseled, cadenced—almost classic." But, stated Lash, "people Lindbergh cared about damned the widely-read book as a plea for appeasement and a condonation of totalitarianism, . . . a lyrical and silver-coated exposition of the views expressed by Charles."

Strangers threatened new disasters for the Lindbergh children as retribution for their parents' politics. Old friends, alienated by the isolationist issue, spoke publicly against them. When Charles offered his services to

the Roosevelt administration he was turned down. He then offered his services to private companies involved in the war effort; of these, only the Ford Motor Company in Detroit was powerful enough to defy the Roosevelt administration's disapproval and accept Lindbergh's offer of help. "I have had three big things to fight against in my life," wrote Anne at the time. "The first was just sorrow (the kidnapping case), the second was fear (the flights), and the third is bitterness (this whole war struggle). And the third is the hardest."

The stress brought by wartime issues did not keep Anne from writing, however. Indeed, Charles "pressed her, almost fiercely, to write and was angry when household chores or children intervened. . . . To make sure she had a quiet place to work, he pitched a tent above the beach at Martha's Vineyard, set up a trailer behind their house outside Detroit," explained *Washington Post Book World* contributor Katherine Winton Evans. "Almost all our quarrels," wrote Anne in 1941, "arise from this passionate desire to see me freed to fulfill what there is in me." Lindbergh's account of these and other experiences during the early 1940s may be found in the diaries and letters collected under the title *War Within and Without: Diaries and Letters of Anne Morrow Lindbergh, 1939-1944.*

In 1944 Anne Lindbergh's first novel was published as *The Steep Ascent,* and was well received by critics. "It would be a pity if those who were disturbed by Mrs. Lindbergh's last book *The Wave of the Future* were to ignore this one because of it," cautioned Amy Loveman in *Saturday Review.* "For they would lose in so doing one of the most beautifully written, sensitive, and lovely volumes which has appeared since those earlier ones which were akin to it, *North to the Orient* and *Listen! The Wind.*" Like those books, *The Steep Ascent* tells of a perilous flight made by a woman and her husband. "As always there is the exquisite delicacy of expression, the talent for the right word, the right phrase, and the descriptions that are acute observations of the passing scene filtered through the screen of personality. . . . To the beauty which her earlier books had there is added excitement in this one," declared Loveman. "As an adventure story it is keen and exciting," affirmed *New York Times Book Review* contributor Beatrice Sherman, "but it is much more than that. Its charm and grace are rooted in the fabric of the author's mind and in the fruit of her philosophy."

Following *The Steep Ascent, Gift from the Sea* was to become one of Lindbergh's most enduring works, a book that has remained in print since its first edition. It is a collection of essays with the central theme of "the tremendous and ever-encroaching problem of how to maintain an inner serenity in the midst of the distractions of life, how to remain balanced, no matter what forces tend to pull one off center; how to be the still axis within the revolving wheel of relationships and activities," as Sara Henderson Hay wrote in *Saturday Review*. Each essay takes the form of a meditation on a seashell, and Elizabeth Gray Vining noted in the *New York Times Book Review* that *Gift from the Sea* "is like a shell itself, in its small and perfect form, the delicate spiraling of its thought, the poetry of its color, and its rhythm from the sea, which tells of light and life and love and the security that lies at the heart of intermittency." Although it "deals with the essential needs, gifts, obligations and aspirations of woman as distinct from those of man, it is in no sense merely what is sometimes slightingly called a woman's book. A sensitive, tensile, original mind probes delicately into questions of balance and relationship in the world today, and the result is a book for human beings who are mature or in search of maturity, whether men or women." *Gift from the Sea* is also considered an important feminist document from an era during which little if any dissent was voiced regarding the proper role for women in American life. Lindbergh's struggle with maintaining a sense of self while dedicating the majority of her waking hours in service to children, husband, social obligations, and career, is a precursor to the public ruminations of women decades later on the trials and tribulations of "having it all."

The Unicorn and Other Poems was Lindbergh's next published work. "There are many beautiful lyrics here," praised Robert Hillyer in the *New York Times Book Review*. "The reader will be well rewarded who joins the poet in this garden by the mortal sea whence, from time to time, rifts in the clouds show flashes from immortality." But *Saturday Review* poetry editor John Ciardi's review stood in strong disagreement. "As a reviewer not of Mrs. Lindbergh but of her poems I have, in duty, nothing but contempt to offer," Ciardi wrote. "I am compelled to believe that Mrs. Lindbergh has written an offensively bad book—inept, jingling, slovenly, illiterate even, and puffed up with the foolish afflatus of a stereotyped high-seriousness, that species of esthetic and human failure that will accept any shriek as a true high-C." A month after Ciardi's review appeared, *Saturday Review* editor Norman Cousins reported: "Ciardi's review of Anne Morrow Lindbergh's *The Unicorn and Other Poems* has produced the biggest storm of reader protest in the thirty-three-year history of *The Saturday Review*. Hundreds of readers have hastened to tell us of their pointed disapproval of Mr. Ciardi's review; four

have written in his support. . . . There are few living authors who are using the English language more sensitively or with more genuine appeal than Lindbergh. There is in her books a respect for human responses to beauty and for the great connections between humankind and nature that gives her work rare distinction and that earns her the gratitude and loyalty of her readers, as the present episode makes clear."

Lindbergh's audience was considerably widened when publication of her diaries began in 1972. The public was eager to read the inside story on the celebrated couple, and the diaries sold briskly. Lindbergh had at first been reluctant to expose her personal papers. "William Jovanovich, who was my husband's publisher as well as mine, knew that I kept diaries and told me I should publish them," she explained in a *New York Times Book Review* interview with Carol Lawson. "But I wrote them because I *had* to, not to get them published." An autobiography was considered as a means of preserving Lindbergh's sense of privacy, but it was finally decided that the original journals would be published. She explains her decision in the introduction to *Locked Rooms:* "When one has processed and packaged part of one's life in books, as I have, it is fair to ask, Why not leave it in that form? Why go back to the imperfect raw material of the diaries? Why publish the grimy minutiae of preparing for a trip; the tedium of long hours of work, the reluctant early risings; the exasperations of cold feet and dusty clothes; the irrational night terrors, lost tempers, and depressions? Because, after sixty, I think, one knows the ups and downs that life holds for everyone, and would like—a last chance—to see and present, truthfully and not glamorized, what happened."

Her decision to print the original journals and letters won the approval of readers and reviewers alike. According to Glendy Culligan of *Saturday Review*, the "letters and diaries achieve both spontaneity and art, thanks in part to her style, in part to a built-in plot and a soul-searching heroine worthy of a Bronte novel. In only one respect does Mrs. Lindbergh fail to meet her own standard of candor. When she introduces herself as 'this quite ordinary person' any reader with a long memory is bound to smile."

BIOGRAPHICAL AND CRITICAL SOURCES:

BOOKS

Lindbergh, Anne Morrow, *North to the Orient,* Harcourt (New York, NY), 1935.

Lindbergh, Anne Morrow, *Listen! The Wind,* Harcourt (New York, NY), 1938.

Lindbergh, Anne Morrow, *Bring Me a Unicorn: Diaries and Letters of Anne Morrow Lindbergh,* Harcourt (New York, NY), 1972.

Lindbergh, Anne Morrow, *Hour of Gold, Hour of Lead: Diaries and Letters, 1929-1932,* Harcourt (New York, NY), 1973.

Lindbergh, Anne Morrow, *Locked Rooms and Open Doors: Diaries and Letters, 1932-1935,* Harcourt (New York, NY), 1974.

Lindbergh, Anne Morrow, *The Flower and the Nettle: Diaries and Letters, 1936-1939,* Harcourt (New York, NY), 1976.

Lindbergh, Anne Morrow, *War Within and Without: Diaries and Letters, 1939-1944,* Harcourt (New York, NY), 1980.

Lindbergh, Reeve, *No More Words: A Journal of My Mother, Anne Morrow Lindbergh,* Simon & Schuster (New York, NY), 2001.

Mayer, Elsie F., *My Window on the World: The Works of Anne Morrow Lindbergh,* Archon, 1988.

Saint-Exupery, Antoine de, *A Sense of Life,* translated by Adrienne Foulke, Funk & Wagnalls (New York, NY), 1965.

Vaughn, David Kirk, *Anne Morrow Lindbergh,* Twayne (Boston, MA), 1988.

PERIODICALS

Atlantic, November, 1995, p. 121.
Atlantic Bookshelf, October, 1935.
Books, October 16, 1938.
Chicago Tribune, April 4, 1980.
Commonweal, September 7, 1956, pp. 568-570.
Current History and Forum, November 7, 1940.
Horn Book, September-October, 1994, p. 589.
Magill's Literary Annual, 1977, pp. 294-298.
National Review, May 12, 1972, pp. 528, 530.
Newsweek, April 11, 1955.
New Yorker, March 21, 1974.
New York Times, September 9, 1956; October 12, 1969; February 21, 1970; April 20, 1974; April 29, 1980; August 2, 1980.
New York Times Book Review, October 16, 1938; November 3, 1940; March 19, 1944, p. 3; March 20, 1955, p. 1; September 9, 1956; June 10, 1962, pp. 6, 23; February 27, 1972; March 4, 1973, pp. 1, 10; March 24, 1974, pp. 28, 30; April 20, 1980; June 15, 1980; January 15, 1995, p. 25.
Saturday Review, October 15, 1938; March 18, 1944; February 2, 1955; January 12, 1957, pp. 54-57; February 16, 1957, pp. 22-25, 54-55; June 9, 1962; March 4, 1972, pp. 72-75.

School Library Journal, April, 1994, p. 128.
Time, September 17, 1956; June 8, 1962; March 11, 1974.
Times Literary Supplement, February 26, 1971; August 11, 1972.
Washington Post Book World, March 10, 1974; April 27, 1980.

OBITUARIES:

PERIODICALS

Chicago Tribune, February 8, 2001, sec. 2, p. 11.
Los Angeles Times, February 8, 2001, p. A1, A28.
New York Times, February 8, 2001, p. A26.
People, February 26, 2001, "The Hero's Wife: Playing Second Lead in Her Husband's Storied Life, Anne Morrow Lindbergh Created a Compelling Role of Her Own," p. 103.
Times (London, England), February 9, 2001.

* * *

LINDBERGH, Anne Spencer Morrow
See LINDBERGH, Anne Morrow

* * *

LIVELY, Penelope 1933-
(Penelope Margaret Lively)

PERSONAL: Born March 17, 1933, in Cairo, Egypt; daughter of Roger Low (a bank manager) and Vera Greer; immigrated to England, 1945; married Jack Lively (a university teacher), June 27, 1957; children: Josephine, Adam. *Education:* St. Anne's College, Oxford, B.A. (with honors), 1956. *Hobbies and other interests:* Gardening, landscape history, talking, listening.

ADDRESSES: Agent—David Higham Associates, 5-8 Lower John St., Golden Square, London W1F 9HA, England.

CAREER: Writer.

MEMBER: Society of Authors, PEN, Royal Society of Literature (fellow).

AWARDS, HONORS: Children's Spring Book Festival Award, *Book World,* 1973, for *The Driftway;* Carnegie Medal, and Hans Christian Andersen Award list, both 1973, both for *The Ghost of Thomas Kempe;* Whitbread Award, 1976, for *A Stitch in Time;* Booker-McConnell Prize shortlist, 1977, for *The Road to Lichfield,* and 1984, for *According to Mark;* Southern Arts Literary Prize, 1978, for *Nothing Missing but the Samovar and Other Stories;* Arts Council of Great Britain National Book Award, 1979, for *Treasures of Time;* Whitbread Award shortlist and Booker-McConnell Prize, both 1987, both for *Moon Tiger;* honorary D.Litt., Tufts University, 1990, and Warwick University, 1998; honorary fellow, Swansea University, 2002; Order of the British Empire, 1989, for contributions to literature; Commander of the British Empire, 2002; *The Ghost of Thomas Kempe, The House in Norham Gardens, A Stitch in Time,* and *Fanny's Sister* were all *Horn Book* honor books; *The House in Norham Gardens* was an American Library Association Notable Book.

WRITINGS:

FOR CHILDREN

Astercote, illustrated by Antony Maitland, Heinemann (London, England), 1970, Dutton (New York, NY), 1971.

The Whispering Knights, illustrated by Gareth Floyd, Heinemann (London, England), 1971, Dutton (New York, NY), 1976.

The Wild Hunt of Hagworthy, illustrated by Juliet Mozley, Heinemann (London, England), 1971, illustrated by Robert Payne, Pan Books (New York, NY), 1975, published as *The Wild Hunt of the Ghost Hounds,* Dutton (New York, NY), 1972, illustrated by Jeremy Ford, Puffin Books (New York, NY), 1984.

The Driftway, Heinemann (London, England), 1972, Dutton (New York, NY), 1973.

The Ghost of Thomas Kempe, illustrated by Antony Maitland, Dutton (New York, NY), 1973.

The House in Norham Gardens, Dutton (New York, NY), 1974.

Boy without a Name, illustrated by Ann Dalton, Parnassus Press (Berkeley, CA), 1975.

Going Back, Dutton (New York, NY), 1975.

A Stitch in Time, Dutton (New York, NY), 1976.

The Stained Glass Window, illustrated by Michael Pollard, Abelard-Schumann (London, England), 1976.

Fanny's Sister, illustrated by John Lawrence, Heinemann (London, England), 1976, new edition, illustrated by Anita Lobel, Dutton (New York, NY), 1980.

The Presence of the Past: An Introduction to Landscape History, Collins (London, England), 1976.

The Voyage of QV66, illustrated by Harold Jones, Heinemann (London, England), 1978, Dutton (New York, NY), 1979.

Fanny and the Monsters, illustrated by John Lawrence, Heinemann (London, England), 1979, enlarged edition, 1983.

Fanny and the Battle of Potter's Piece, illustrated by John Lawrence, Heinemann (London, England), 1980.

The Revenge of Samuel Stokes, Dutton (New York, NY), 1981.

Fanny and the Monsters and Other Stories (contains *Fanny's Sister, Fanny and the Monsters,* and *Fanny and the Battle of Potter's Piece*), Puffin Books (New York, NY), 1982.

Uninvited Ghosts and Other Stories, illustrated by John Lawrence, Heinemann (London, England), 1984, Dutton (New York, NY), 1985.

Dragon Trouble, illustrated by Valerie Littlewood, Heinemann (London, England), 1984, Barron's (New York, NY), 1989.

A House Inside Out, illustrated by David Parkins, Deutsch (London, England), 1987, Dutton (New York, NY), 1988.

Debbie and the Little Devil, illustrated by Toni Goffe, Heinemann (London, England), 1987.

Judy and the Martian, Simon & Schuster (London, England), 1992.

The Cat, the Crow, and the Banyan Tree, illustrated by Terry Milne, Candlewick Press (Cambridge, MA), 1994.

Good Night, Sleep Tight, Candlewick Press (Cambridge, MA), 1995.

Two Bears and Joe, Viking (New York, NY), 1995.

One, Two, Three, Jump!, M.K. McElderry Books (New York, NY), 1998.

In Search of a Homeland: The Story of the Aeneid, illustrated by Ian Andrews, Delacorte Press (New York, NY), 2001.

Also author of *The Disastrous Dog.* Contributor to children's magazines, including *Horn Book* and *Junior Bookshelf.*

ADULT FICTION

The Road to Lichfield, Heinemann, (London, England), 1977, Penguin (New York, NY), 1983.

Nothing Missing but the Samovar and Other Stories, Heinemann (London, England), 1978.

Treasures of Time, Heinemann (London, England), 1979, Doubleday (Garden City, NY), 1980.

Judgement Day, Heinemann (London, England), 1980, Doubleday (New York, NY), 1981, reprinted, Grove Press (New York, NY), 2003.

Next to Nature, Art, Heinemann (London, England), 1982, Penguin (New York, NY), 1984.

Perfect Happiness, Heinemann (London, England), 1983, Dial Press (Garden City, NY), 1984.

Corruption and Other Stories, Heinemann (London, England), 1984.

According to Mark: A Novel, Beaufort Books (New York, NY), 1984.

Pack of Cards (short stories, including "Nothing Missing but the Samovar" and "Corruption"), Heinemann (London, England), 1986, Penguin (New York, NY), 1988.

Moon Tiger, Deutsch (London, England), 1987, Grove Weidenfeld (New York, NY), 1988.

Passing On, Deutsch (London, England), 1989, Grove Weidenfeld (New York, NY), 1990.

City of the Mind, HarperCollins (New York, NY), 1991.

Cleopatra's Sister, HarperCollins (New York, NY), 1993.

Heat Wave, HarperCollins (New York, NY), 1996.

The Five Thousand and One Nights, Fjord Press (Seattle, WA), 1997.

Beyond the Blue Mountains, Viking (New York, NY), 1997.

Spiderweb, HarperCollins (New York, NY), 1999.

The Photograph, Viking (London, England), 2001, Viking (New York, NY), 2003.

OTHER

Boy Dominic (television play; three episodes), Yorkshire TV, 1974.

Time out of Mind (television play for children), BBC-TV, 1976.

(Author of introduction) Ivy Compton-Burnett, *Father and His Fate,* Oxford University Press (New York, NY), 1984.

(Author of introduction) Ivy Compton-Burnett, *Manservant and Maidservant,* Oxford University Press (New York, NY), 1987.

(Author of introduction) Edith Wharton, *The Age of Innocence,* Virago (London, England), 1988.

(Author of introduction) Lewis Carroll, *Alice in Wonderland,* Everyman (London, England), 1993.

Oleander, Jacaranda: A Childhood Perceived (memoir), HarperCollins (New York, NY), 1994.

(Author of introduction) Willa Cather, *My Antonia,* Everyman (London, England), 1996.

(Author of introduction) *The Mythical Quest,* British Library (London, England), 1996.

A House Unlocked (memoir), Viking (New York, NY), 2001.

Also contributor to books, including *My England,* Heinemann (New York, NY), 1973. Contributor of short stories and articles to periodicals, including *Encounter, Vogue, Cosmopolitan, Good Housekeeping, Literary Review,* and *Quarto.* Reviewer for newspapers and author of television and radio scripts. Many of Lively's writings have been translated into other languages.

ADAPTATIONS: Several of Lively's books have been adapted as audiobooks, including *House Inside Out,* Chivers Press, 1988. *The Ghost of Thomas Kempe* was adapted for television by ABC-TV, 1979.

SIDELIGHTS: Penelope Lively, author of more than forty books for children and adults, has distinguished herself as a writer of both juvenile and adult books in a career spanning over thirty years. She has won such prestigious awards as the Booker-McConnell Prize and the Whitbread Award. *Publishers Weekly* contributor Amanda Smith considered Lively "one of England's finest writers," and added that her novels are "characterized by intelligence, precision and wit." Sheila A. Egoff, in her *Thursday's Child: Trends and Patterns in Contemporary Children's Literature,* wrote that Lively "has an uncannily accurate and honest recall of what it is like to be a child in a world made for adults." As to her adult fiction, a *Times Literary Supplement* reviewer commented that Lively conveys "a prose that is invariably as precise as it is unostentatious."

Lively began writing children's books while raising her two children, Josephine and Adam. Writing stories for children was a convenient way to express her interests. Lively's first published novel, *Astercote,* explored her fascination with deserted medieval villages. Although the book was criticized for its lack of living characters and convincing dialogue, reviewers also found it intriguing and exciting. Lively published two subsequent juvenile novels, *The Whispering Knights* and *The Driftway. The Driftway* follows Paul and his tag-along sister as he runs away from his stepmother and a charge of shoplifting. He comes across an old road which has been used for thousands of years by various travelers. These travelers have left messages from the past, which Paul is able to see and interpret with the help of a cart-driver named Bill. Margery Fisher, editor of *Growing Point,* explained that each "interlude reflects part of

Paul's situation and brings him a step nearer to understanding himself and his family." The characters from the past make him aware that "there is more than one point of view to every story, and he takes the first steps away from the morbid self-absorption of childhood towards feeling sympathy for others," concluded a *Times Literary Supplement* reviewer. Some writers such as John Rowe Townsend felt that the point of the story is weakened because the book as a whole lacks a strong storyline—the reader never does find out what happens to Paul and his sister. However, *Junior Bookshelf* contributor Aneurin R. Williams expressed her belief that, overall, "Lively writes well, exceeding by far the style and effect of" her earlier work. *The Driftway* won the Children's Spring Book Festival Award in 1973.

Lively's best-received juvenile book, *The Ghost of Thomas Kempe,* offers a light approach to the coming-of-age theme. The author uses one of her favorite devices in this book: the ghost. The purpose of Thomas Kempe's character, explained Lively in *Junior Bookshelf,* is to explore "the memory of places and the memory of people, and the curious business that we are all of us not just what we are now but what we have been." Putting this another way, *Children's Literature in Education* contributor Judith Armstrong wrote that this book "is concerned with different aspects of the same person, the person [James] might have been, or might still become, had he not encountered the ghost of his potential self." The story involves a boy's visitation by the spirit of a sorcerer from Stuart England. At first, the ghost seems only mischievous, but slowly becomes more and more menacing. James learns through the ghost what wickedness is, and is only able to put Kempe to rest by learning to recognize and cope with the wickedness within himself. Many critics agreed that *The Ghost of Thomas Kempe* is a well-written children's book. David Rees, author of *The Marble in the Water: Essays on Contemporary Writers of Fiction for Children and Young Adults,* felt that the book is of such high quality because for the first time "the author is completely sure of her own abilities, and the writing has a positiveness that derives from the author's pleasure in her awareness of these abilities."

Rees had even higher praise for *A Stitch in Time,* Lively's Whitbread Award winner. "*A Stitch in Time* is probably Penelope Lively's most important and memorable book," he declared. "Not only is its exploration of the significance of history and memory more profound than in any other of her novels, but the unfolding of the story is very fine." As *Times Literary Supplement* reviewer Ann Thwait noted, the story does not have a great deal of plot action, since most of this action oc-

curs unobtrusively within the mind of Marie, the main character. Marie, who is spending her vacation with her parents in an old Victorian house in Lyme Regis, discovers a sampler made in 1865 by a girl named Harriet. The sampler provides a link to the past which Marie senses through such things as the squeaking of a swing and the barking of a dog, neither of which exist near the house at the present; they are only echoes of the past. The tension in the story lies in Marie's suspicion that something tragic has happened to Harriet, a belief supported by the lack of any pictures in the house of Harriet as an adult. Though the mystery is eventually solved, the real message of the book is summarized by the owner of the old house when he sagely remarks: "Things always could have been otherwise. The fact of the matter is that they are not." This declaration, explained Terry Jones, a contributor to *Children's Literature in Education,* "finally ends Maria's 'vague imaginings' and completes one part of her education. . . . She leaves the Regency house determined to acquire 'some new wisdom about the way things are.' She grows, and the reader grows with her."

"*The Voyage of QV66* (1978) is a radical departure from all of Lively's earlier books," contended Alan McLay in the *Dictionary of Literary Biography.* At some unspecified time in the future, a cataclysmic event has wiped out the earth's human population. Animals have taken the place of humans, taking on speech and other human skills. For this tale, Lively has brought together six animals, including Pal, the dog, and Stanley, the monkey, to take a voyage to London in the boat *QV66.* In following the animals along their journey, the book "views human nature and civilization from a wry, ironic perspective," noted McLay. He continued, "Readers are invited to laugh at the ways in which the animals imitate human behavior but are also exposed to the caustic comments made about humans, especially their habits of eating animals and killing one another with sharp sticks." In the end, the six voyagers find that the world has not changed; animals have simply replaced humans in carrying out the same human follies. Even so, as McLay pointed out, "The little group of animals on the QV66 . . . represents the virtues of friendship, loyalty, and community and offers hope for the future."

Lively continued to write children's books throughout the 1980s, including such titles as *The Revenge of Samuel Stokes, Uninvited Guests and Other Stories,* and *A House Inside Out.* In 1993, she published another tale of animals who carry on like people. *The Cat, the Crow and the Banyan Tree* portrays two friends, the cat and the crow, who live beneath the banyan tree, where they spend their time telling stories to each other. Critics have described the tales told by cat and crow as whimsical, imaginative, delightful, but potentially confusing for children. A reviewer for *Publishers Weekly* observed that "Lively's narrative percolates with rhythm" and focuses interestingly on the process of storytelling itself.

Although she continued to write for children, in the late 1970s, after writing children's books for almost a decade, Lively decided it was time to change her primary focus. "I began to feel that I was in danger of writing the same children's books over and over again," she explained in *Publishers Weekly*. "More than that, I'd exhausted the ways in which I could explore my own preoccupations and interests within children's books." In writing for an older audience, the author has maintained her interest in the past and memory, but has followed a different approach. Her adult characters consider memory "in the context of a lifetime rather than in the context of history," explained Lively in *Horn Book*. These later works no longer deal with how the past can teach one to mature so much as how it can change one's perspective or philosophy of life.

Lively's first novel for adults, *The Road to Lichfield*, is a complex tale about what happens to a married history teacher named Anne Linton when her conceptions about her childhood family life are suddenly altered. While going through her dying father's papers, she discovers that he was involved in an affair similar to her own extramarital relationship. "As everything in her life swings and changes, her father dies, her love is choked off, and only the road [between her present life in Cuxing and her childhood memories of Lichfield] remains permanent," summarized Jane Langton in the *Dictionary of Literary Biography*. "There is nothing very original about the plot" of *The Road to Lichfield*, noted John Mellors in the *Listener*, but the "book is lifted out of the ordinary by the author's treatment of her two main themes: continuity and memory."

In Lively's Booker-McConnell Award-winning story *Moon Tiger*, the "true center is no less than history itself—the abiding backdrop across which mere human beings flutter," said Anne Tyler in the *New York Times Book Review*. It is "the transitoriness of all human happiness and indeed of all human life" which is the concern of a respected historian, Claudia Hampton, as she considers her life from the vantage point of her deathbed, explained Francis King in a *Spectator* article. In this book, a complex interweaving of flashbacks takes the reader on a voyage through the dying historian's life, including a sojourn in World War II Egypt, where Claudia finds brief happiness with a tank commander,

who is later killed in action. "Her image for their love," wrote Richard Eder of the *Los Angeles Times Book Review*, "is the moon tiger—a spiral coil of punk that burns slowly through the night beside their bed to keep away mosquitoes and that leaves only ash in the morning."

Parallel to this image are the last lines of the book in which Claudia passes away: "The sun sinks and the glittering tree is extinguished. The room darkens again. . . . And within the room a change has taken place. It is empty. Void. It has the stillness of a place in which there are only inanimate objects; metal, wood, glass, plastic. No Life." The denouement marks the end of, in Eder's words, Claudia's "long postponed search for herself." For some critics, like Martha Duffy of *Time* magazine, the flashbacks involved in her search become "overdrawn" after a while. However, many reviewers concurred with *Times Literary Supplement* contributor J.K.L. Walker, who wrote: "Lively's ingenious, historically informed handling of [the story] is a considerable achievement and Claudia Hampton herself a formidably reflective and articulate protagonist." It is a tale told from the most widely encompassing perspective possible for a human being, a study of one character's entire lifetime memory and how she regards it. Writing in the *New York Times Book Review*, Jay Parini commented: "In that inventive re-creation of life in Egypt during World War II, an evocative mixture of memory and desire, Ms. Lively established herself as a novelist of the first rank." Although Lively bases most of *Moon Tiger* upon the memory of a single character, exploring this favorite subject in depth, the author admitted to herself in *Horn Book*: "I don't imagine that I am ever going to find the answer to the questions prompted by the workings of memory; all I can do is pose these questions in fictional form and see what happens."

Aisling Foster, in the *Times Literary Supplement*, viewed Lively's novel *Heat Wave* as "all about the power of love: protective maternal love, promiscuous sexual love, the nurturing love of Mother Nature and our love of animals and countryside which is both benign and exploitative." Set in the English countryside, the novel explores themes that have interested Lively in past works: history in the context of the present, and myth versus reality. The main protagonist is Pauline, a fifty-five-year-old freelance copy-editor who worries that her daughter will repeat her own mistakes. "Most importantly," commented a reviewer in *Publishers Weekly*, Lively "creates a convincing picture of obsessive sexual love tainted by jealousy and misery, and of the kind of maternal love that carries its own implacable mandates." While all this transpires, England is in the grip of some uncharacteristic weather. "The tension mounts as temperatures rise," observed Donna Seaman in *Booklist,* "but Lively keeps cool as she leads us to a surprise denouement—her impeccable prose delectably restrained, her humor neat and vicious, and her articulation of emotional states keen and vivifying." "The novel makes clear," in the estimation of *People*'s Joanne Kaufman, "that Lively knows well the topography of the human heart."

In *A House Unlocked* Lively explores her memories of her ancestral home Golsoncott in Somerset, England, which was originally bought by her grandparents in 1923. In 1995 the family had to sell the house after Lively's aunt died, and as Lively told Robert McCrum in the *Observer,* "My children and I were all heartbroken." They spent a great deal of time reminiscing about the house, until Lively realized "that I had this memory house and would never lose it." However, the book considers the loss of the house, and is an elegy to the era that the house embodied, as well as to the people who lived in it. A *Publishers Weekly* reviewer wrote that the book "unlocks more than the house and its century."

In the *Dictionary of Literary Biography,* Ruth P. Feingold remarked, "Over the course of her career Penelope Lively has produced an astonishing quantity of well-crafted, sometimes brilliant work. . . . The structural complexity of her texts is matched by their intellectual and moral rigor: seldom possessed of neat resolutions, her adult novels in particular tend to illustrate her view that 'I have never come to terms with life, and I wouldn't wish anyone else to do so; if fiction is to help at all in the process of living, it is by illuminating its conflicts and ambiguities.'"

BIOGRAPHICAL AND CRITICAL SOURCES:

BOOKS

Children's Literature Review, Volume 7, Thomson Gale (Detroit, MI), 1984.

Contemporary Literary Criticism, Thomson Gale (Detroit, MI), Volume 32, 1985, Volume 50, 1989.

Dictionary of Literary Biography, Thomson Gale (Detroit, MI), Volume 14: *British Novelists since 1960,* 1983, Volume 161: *British Children's Writers since 1960,* 1996, Volume 207: *British Novelists since 1960, Third Series,* 1999.

Egoff, Sheila A., *Thursday's Child: Trends and Patterns in Contemporary Children's Literature,* American Library Association (Chicago, IL), 1981.

Ellis, Alec, and Marcus Crouch, editors, *Chosen for Children: An Account of the Books Which Have Been Awarded the Library Association Carnegie Medal, 1936-1975,* 3rd edition, American Library Association (Chicago, IL), 1977.

Moran, Mary Hurley, *Penelope Lively,* Twayne (New York, NY), 1993.

Rees, David, *The Marble in the Water: Essays on Contemporary Writers of Fiction for Children and Young Adults,* Horn Book (Boston, MA), 1980, pp. 185-198.

St. James Guide to Children's Writers, 5th edition, St. James Press (Detroit, MI), 1999.

Townsend, John Rowe, *A Sounding of Storytellers: New and Revised Essays on Contemporary Writers for Children,* Lippincott (New York, NY), 1979.

PERIODICALS

Belles Lettres, spring, 1992, pp. 26-29.

Booklist, March 15, 1994, p. 1322; June 1, 1995, p. 1787; August, 1996, p. 1854; February 15, 1998, p. 1027; October 15, 2000, Karen Harris, review of *Spiderweb,* p. 471; March 1, 2002, Donna Seaman, review of *A House Unlocked,* p. 1084.

Book Report, March, 2002, review of *In Search of a Homeland,* p. 69.

Books for Keeps, November, 2001, review of *In Search of a Homeland,* p. 27; January, 2002, review of *The Driftway,* p. 22.

Bulletin of the Center for Children's Books, June, 1999, review of *One, Two, Three, Jump,* p. 358.

Chicago Tribune Book World, August 9, 1981; May 15, 1988.

Children's Bookwatch, January, 2002, review of *In Search of a Homeland,* p. 1.

Children's Literature, number 18, 1990, pp. 53-67.

Children's Literature in Education, summer, 1978, pp. 59-66; autumn, 1981.

Children's Literature Quarterly, winter, 1984-85, pp. 157-64; fall, 1985, pp. 114-16.

Encounter, May, 1981.

Globe and Mail (Toronto, Ontario, Canada), November 14, 1987; October 6, 2001, review of *A House Unlocked,* p. D23.

Growing Point, July, 1972; July, 1973.

Horn Book, June, 1973; August, 1973; February, 1978; April, 1978; March, 1999, p. 164; fall, 1999, review of *One, Two, Three, Jump,* p. 237.

International Fiction Review, January, 2001, Nora Foster Stovel, review of *Spiderweb,* p. 115.

Journal of the Short Story in English, autumn, 1989, pp. 103-111.

Junior Bookshelf, September, 1972; June, 1974.

Kirkus Reviews, February 1, 1999, review of *Spiderweb,* p. 170; February 1, 2002, review of *A House Unlocked,* p. 161.

Library Journal, November 1, 1997, p. 130; October 1, 1999, Richard Oloizia, review of *Spiderweb,* p. 160; April 1, 2002, Ravi Shenoy, review of *A House Unlocked,*p. 129; April 1, 2003, review of *The Photograph,* p. 498.

Listener, August 4, 1977.

Los Angeles Times Book Review, April 17, 1988; April 25, 1999, review of *Spiderweb,* p. 23.

New Statesman, May 8, 1987, p. 23; October 2, 1987, p. 31; April 23, 1993, p. 33; June 3, 1994, p. 44; January 20, 2003, Amanda Craig, review of *The Photograph,* p. 51.

New Statesman and Society, April 12, 1991, p. 35.

New Welsh Review, spring, 1990, pp. 36-38.

New Yorker, November 18, 1991, p. 134; June 14, 1993, p. 99.

New York Times Book Review, April 17, 1988, p. 9; May 21, 1989, p. 13; February 11, 1990, p. 12; February 17, 1991, p. 7; September 1, 1991, p. 6; April 25, 1993, p. 7; June 12, 1994, p. 32; March 19, 1995, p. 19; June 11, 1995, p. 43; March 3, 1996, p. 25; April 11, 1999, review of *The Road to Lichfield* and *Pack of Cards and Other Stories,* p. 40.

Observer, April 25, 1993; November 14, 1999, review of *Spiderweb,* p. 15; August 26, 2001, review of *A House Unlocked,* p. 16.

People, July 25, 1994, p. 26; January 13, 1997, p. 28.

Publishers Weekly, November 13, 1987; February 12, 1988, p. 71; March 25, 1988, pp. 47-48; February 3, 1989, p. 97; May 21, 1989; December 1, 1989, p. 48; November 23, 1990, p. 56; February 11, 1990; June 21, 1991, p. 53; February 8, 1993, p. 76; March 7, 1994, p. 61; March 14, 1994, p. 73; April 10, 1995, p. 61; July 1, 1996, p. 41; May 26, 1997, p. 68; February 1, 1999, review of *Spiderweb,* p. 72; March 15, 1999, review of *One, Two, Three, Jump,* p. 56; March 4, 2002, review of *A House Unlocked,* p. 67.

School Library Journal, February, 1988, p. 73; May, 1994, p. 99; June, 1995, p. 91; February 1, 1999, review of *Spiderweb,* p. 72; March 15, 1999, review of *One, Two, Three, Jump,* p. 56; July, 1999, review of *One, Two, Three, Jump,* p. 76.

Spectator, November 22, 1980; May 23, 1987; September 1, 2001, review of *A House Unlocked,* p. 35.

Time, May 2, 1988, p. 86.

Times (London, England), October 30, 1987.

Times Educational Supplement, September 10, 1999, review of *The House in Northam Gardens,* p. 31.

Times Literary Supplement, July 14, 1972; April 6, 1973; July 16, 1976; November 21, 1980; May 23, 1986; October 17, 1986; May 15, 1987; April 7, 1989; April 23, 1993; May 24, 1996, p. 27; November 9, 2001, review of *A House Unlocked,* p. 25.

Wall Street Journal, April 2, 1999, review of *Spiderweb,* p. W7.

Washington Post Book World, August 2, 1981; September 13, 1988.

Woman's Journal, December, 1999, review of *Spiderweb,* p. 18.

ONLINE

Observer, http://www.observer.co.uk/ (August 26, 2001), Robert McCrum, interview with Lively.

Penelope Lively Web site, http://www.penelopelively.net/ (May 28, 2003).

*   *   *

LIVELY, Penelope Margaret
   See LIVELY, Penelope

*   *   *

LODGE, David 1935-
   (David John Lodge)

PERSONAL: Born January 28, 1935, in London, England; son of William Frederick (a musician) and Rosalie Marie (Murphy) Lodge; married Mary Frances Jacob, May 16, 1959; children: Julia, Stephen, Christopher. *Education:* University College, London, B.A. (with first class honors), 1955, M.A., 1959; University of Birmingham, Ph.D., 1967. *Religion:* Roman Catholic. *Hobbies and other interests:* Tennis, television, cinema.

ADDRESSES: Office—Department of English, University of Birmingham, Birmingham B15 2TT, England. *Agent*—Curtis Brown Ltd., 28-29 Haymarket, London SW1Y 4SP, England.

CAREER: British Council, London, England, assistant, 1959-60; University of Birmingham, Birmingham, England, lecturer, 1960-71, senior lecturer, 1971-73, reader, 1973-76, professor of modern English literature, 1976-87, professor emeritus, 1987—. Visiting associate professor, University of California, Berkeley, 1969. *Military service:* Royal Armoured Corps., 1955-57.

AWARDS, HONORS: Harkness Commonwealth fellowship, 1964-65, for study and travel in the United States; *Yorkshire Post* fiction prize and Hawthornden Prize, both 1975, for *Changing Places: A Tale of Two Campuses;* Royal Society of Literature fellowship, 1976; Henfield writing fellow, University of East Anglia, 1977; Whitbread Award for fiction and for book of the year, 1980, for *How Far Can You Go?;* Sunday Express Book of the Year, 1989, for *Nice Work;* Royal Television Society award for best drama serial and Silver Nymph for best mini-series screenplay, Monte Carlo International TV Festival, both 1990, for *Nice Work.*

WRITINGS:

CRITICISM

Language of Fiction, Columbia University Press (New York, NY), 1966.

Graham Greene, Columbia University Press (New York, NY), 1966.

The Novelist at the Crossroads and Other Essays on Fiction and Criticism, Cornell University Press (Ithaca, NY), 1971.

Evelyn Waugh, Columbia University Press (New York, NY), 1971.

The Modes of Modern Writing: Metaphor, Metonymy and the Typology of Modern Literature, Cornell University Press, 1977.

Modernism, Antimodernism, and Postmodernism, University of Birmingham, 1977.

Working with Structuralism: Essays and Reviews on Nineteenth- and Twentieth-Century Literature, Routledge (Boston, MA), 1981.

Write On: Occasional Essays, Secker & Warburg (London, England), 1986.

After Bakhtin: Essays on Fiction and Criticism, Routledge (London, England), 1990.

The Art of Fiction: Illustrated from Classic and Modern Texts, Secker & Warburg, 1992, Viking (New York, NY), 1993.

The Practice of Writing: Essays, Lectures, Reviews, and a Diary, Secker & Warburg (London, England), 1996.

Consciousness and the Novel: Connected Essays, Harvard University Press (Boston, MA), October 2002.

NOVELS

The Picturegoers, MacGibbon Kee, 1960, new edition, Penguin (London, England), 1993.

Ginger, You're Barmy, MacGibbon, Kee, 1962, Doubleday (New York, NY), 1965, reprinted with a new introduction by the author, Secker & Warburg (London, England), 1982.

The British Museum Is Falling Down, MacGibbon, Kee, 1965, Holt (London, England), 1967, reprinted with a new introduction by the author, Secker & Warburg (London, England), 1981.

Out of the Shelter, Macmillan (Basingstoke, England), 1970, revised edition, Secker & Warburg (London, England), 1985, revised edition with an introduction by the author, Penguin (New York, NY), 1989.

Changing Places: A Tale of Two Campuses, Secker & Warburg (London, England), 1975, Penguin, 1979.

How Far Can You Go?, Secker & Warburg (London, England), 1980, published as *Souls and Bodies,* Morrow (New York, NY), 1982.

Small World: An Academic Romance, Secker & Warburg (London, England), 1984, Macmillan (Basingstoke, England), 1985.

Nice Work, Secker & Warburg (London, England), 1988, Viking (New York, NY), 1989.

Paradise News, Secker & Warburg (London, England), 1991, Viking (New York, NY), 1992.

Therapy, Viking (New York, NY), 1995.

Home Truths: A Novella, Secker & Warburg (London, England), 1999, Penguin (New York, NY), 2000.

Thinks, Viking (New York, NY), 2001.

Author, Author, Viking (New York, NY), 2004.

EDITOR

Jane Austen's "Emma": A Casebook, Macmillan (Basingstoke, England), 1968.

(And author of introduction) Jane Austen, *Emma,* Oxford University Press, 1971, revised edition, Macmillan (Basingstoke, England), 1991.

Twentieth-Century Literary Criticism: A Reader, Longman (London, England), 1972.

George Eliot, *Scenes of Clerical Life,* Penguin (New York, NY), 1973.

Thomas Hardy, *The Woodlanders,* Macmillan (Basingstoke, England), 1974.

Henry James, *The Spoils of Poynton,* Penguin (New York, NY), 1987.

Modern Criticism and Theory: A Reader, Longman, 1988, revised by Nigel Wood, Longman, 1999.

PLAYS

(With Malcolm Bradbury and James Duckett) *Between These Four Walls,* produced in Birmingham, England, 1963.

(With James Duckett and David Turner) *Slap in the Middle,* produced in Birmingham, England, 1965.

The Writing Game: A Comedy (produced in Birmingham, England, 1990, and Cambridge, MA, 1991), Secker & Warburg (London, England), 1991.

OTHER

About Catholic Authors (juvenile), St. Paul Press, 1958.

(Author of introduction) *The Best of Ring Lardner,* Dent, 1984.

Martin Chuzzlewit (television mini-series; based on the novel by Charles Dickens), British Broadcasting Corporation (BBC), 1994.

Contributor to *The State of the Language,* edited by Leonard Michaels and Christopher Ricks, University of California Press (Berkeley, CA), 1980. Also contributor of articles and reviews to *Critical Quarterly, Tablet, Times Literary Supplement, New Republic, New York Times Book Review, New York Review of Books,* and *Encounter.*

ADAPTATIONS: Nice Work was adapted by the BBC as a television mini-series in 1989; *The Writing Game* was adapted for television, 1996.

SIDELIGHTS: David Lodge is known to general readers as a novelist whose works, while often treating serious themes, are "exuberant" and "marvelously funny," in the words of *New York Times Book Review* contributor Michael Rosenthal. The settings and characters of Lodge's novels reflect his own life experiences, including a childhood in wartime London, a stint in the British Army, study as a graduate student, and work as a university professor. His Roman Catholic upbringing has profoundly influenced his fiction as well. "Most of his novels have at least some Catholic statement in them," noted Dennis Jackson in *Dictionary of Literary Biography,* and "one of the recurrent themes in Lodge's stories is the struggle of his Catholic characters to reconcile their spiritual and sensual desires."

Lodge began work on his first published novel while completing his service in the British Army. Published in 1960 as *The Picturegoers,* this book describes a group of Catholics living in a dingy London suburb and the changes they experience over the course of a year. The thoughts and dreams of over a dozen characters are revealed through their reactions to the films they watch regularly in the crumbling local cinema, focusing most sharply on Mark Underwood, a thoughtful young literature student who has fallen away from the church. While finishing school, Mark boards with the Mallory family and becomes enamored of Clare Mallory, a former convent novice. As he attempts to seduce her, she attempts to reawaken his faith. In an ironic conclusion, Clare, having fallen in love with Mark, offers herself to him, but he rejects her to join the priesthood. Some reviewers fault the book as disconnected and overburdened with characters, but "for a first novel, *The Picturegoers* is eminently lively and readable," believed Jackson. Lodge's "alternation of diction, tone, and rhythm as he shifts from . . . the inner thoughts of one character to those of another seems particularly impressive." In addition, "a lot of it is quite funny," wrote Maurice Richardson in *New Statesman.*

An "act of revenge" is Lodge's description of his next book, wrote Jackson. *Ginger, You're Barmy* grew out of the author's years in the army, an experience he bitterly resented. The tedium, brutality, and dehumanizing atmosphere of life in the service are evoked with a "total recall" that is "unnerving," according to *New Statesman* contributor Christopher Ricks. The novel's tension is provided by the contrast between the narrator, Jonathan Browne, and his friend, Mike "Ginger" Brady. Jonathan is a cynical intellectual, a former university student who concentrates on living through his two-year hitch with as little trouble as possible. Mike, on the other hand, is a passionate, idealistic fighter who eventually becomes involved with the Irish Revolutionary Army. Ultimately, Jonathan betrays Mike, stealing his girlfriend and playing a key part in his arrest. Critics have noted similarities in style and subject matter between Lodge's novels and Graham Greene's, and Lodge later acknowledged that he had modeled *Ginger, You're Barmy* after Greene's *The Quiet American.*

Some reviewers, while conceding that Lodge has portrayed army life convincingly, felt that *Ginger, You're Barmy* is plagued by stereotypes and a predictable storyline. "The story has been told so often that merely to tell it again is not enough," maintained Chad Walsh in *Washington Post Book World.* But Thomas P. McDonnell countered in a *Commonweal* review: "Some reviewers have passed off *Ginger, You're Barmy* as the same old thing about life in the army, but it is a much better book than they are readers. They are certainly unknowing in the ways of military life if they do not realize that extreme regimentation all but forces a reversion to types. . . . They have missed, certainly, that it is a beautifully written book, and that its marvelously controlled first-person orientation lifts it out of the mere melodrama that they were no doubt expecting to read in just another book about life in the army. . . . Mostly, I think, they have missed . . . a poignancy in crisis and denouement, no less, that you will be hard put to find anywhere in the reams of overblown nihilism which passes for fiction today."

Lodge followed *Ginger, You're Barmy* with *The British Museum Is Falling Down,* a book which "represented a real development in his career as a writer of fiction," according to Jackson. It was the first of the highly comic, satiric novels which were to become his trademark, and it embodies one of Lodge's recurring themes, that of the sincere Catholic struggling with the difficulties imposed on him by the rigid doctrines of his church—specifically, the complexities of the unreliable "rhythm" method of birth control, the only form of contraception permitted to Catholics. The novel details one day in the life of Adam Appleby, a harried graduate student who has already fathered three children while using the rhythm method. When Adam awakes that day, his wife Barbara confides that she may again be pregnant, sending Adam out into a day of pandemonium much like Leopold Bloom's in James Joyce's *Ulysses.* "Like Leopold Bloom, Adam—because of the domestic and academic pressures he is facing—becomes increasingly disoriented as his day progresses, and his perceptions of life around him become increasingly phantasmagoric," wrote Jackson.

After a day of countless mishaps, hallucinations, and anxious telephone calls to Barbara, Adam returns home to make love to his wife. Immediately thereafter, their "day of alarm [is] clinched by the arrival of her period," noted *Commonweal* contributor Paul West. The book concludes with a long, one-sentence monologue by Barbara (patterned after Molly Bloom's in *Ulysses*). West reported that this "night-reverie . . . twists the preceding comedy by the tail, gives it a depth and resonance." Lodge's skillful blend of humor and thoughtful discourse was also praised by Jackson, who wrote: "*The British Museum Is Falling Down* is unceasingly and vigorously funny. . . . Yet throughout the book serious undertones give emphasis and point to the author's general levity. His comic and satiric treatment of the current Catholic indecision over family planning is not a frontal attack on the church itself but rather a good-natured tickling meant to evoke laughter and a serious new consideration of the effect of the Catholic ban on artificial contraception on couples such as the Applebys."

A strong Joycean influence is again evident in Lodge's fourth novel, *Out of the Shelter.* This story of a young man's maturation opens with a stream-of-consciousness narrative inspired by the beginning of Joyce's *Portrait of the Artist as a Young Man.* The plot follows Timothy Anderson through his childhood in London during the Blitzkrieg to his coming of age on a summer holiday in postwar Germany. Jackson judged this to be Lodge's least successful novel, pointing out that "the book lacks intensity; it has no sharply drawn conflict or dramatic tension, and, for most of the story, the only real suspense has to do with this question of how and when Timothy will learn about sex." Nevertheless, *Times Literary Supplement* critic Christopher Hawtree found that "Timothy's development is chronicled with a fine sense of pace, the tone of the narrative reflecting his changing attitudes," and Philip Howard called *Out of the Shelter* "a charming period piece, heavy with nostalgia for vanished childhood" in the London *Times.*

In 1969, immediately after finishing *Out of the Shelter,* Lodge and his family traveled to the United States, where the author was to be a visiting professor for two terms at the University of California in Berkeley. It was a time of unrest on campuses everywhere, and Lodge's American stay was punctuated by student strikes and sometimes-bloody altercations between students and National Guardsmen. Although student protests were also occurring in England, they were of a much milder nature. Lodge's fascination with the differences between the two cultures led to his fifth novel, *Changing Places: A Tale of Two Campuses.* Eliciting positive responses from almost all reviewers, *Changing Places* won two major prizes and boosted Lodge's popularity considerably.

A university exchange program provides the premise for *Changing Places.* Aggressive, flamboyant Morris Zapp leaves his post at the State University of Euphoria (a thinly disguised Berkeley) to trade places with timid, unambitious Philip Swallow from the dreary University of Rummidge in the English Midlands. Eventually they exchange cars, homes, and wives as well. Prior to the switch, both Zapp and Swallow have suffered from failing marriages and stagnating careers, but each finds a new identity and flourishes in his new surroundings. Neil Hepburn wrote in *Listener* that Zapp and Swallow's parallel stories provide "a series of reflections, both on and of the two worlds—reflections on symmetry, on the novel as a reflection of reality, on the way real troubles like Vietnam and the Prague Spring are reflected in unreal ones like student unrest, on narrative techniques and literary styles . . . and, finally, on America and England as reflections of each other. No funnier or more penetrating account of the special relationship is likely to come your way for a long time."

Zapp and Swallow appear again in *Small World: An Academic Romance,* another "campus novel" and one of Lodge's best-selling books. In *Small World,* they are only two of the many characters who jet around the globe from one academic conference to another in search of glory, romantic trysts, and the UNESCO chair of literary criticism—a job with virtually no responsibilities and a $100,000 tax-free salary. Rosenthal wrote in the *New York Times Book Review:* "[This] exuberant, marvelously funny novel demonstrates [that] no one is better able to treat the peripatetic quality of current academic life than the British writer David Lodge. . . . Despite the novel's breathless pace, profusion of incident and geographic scope, Mr. Lodge never loses control of his material. His deliberately outrageous manipulation of character and event is entirely successful."

While *Changing Places* cemented Lodge's reputation as a popular novelist in England, it was only the first of his books to attract much notice in the United States. Widespread attention in America did not come to Lodge until the publication of his sixth novel, *How Far Can You Go?,* which appeared in the United States under the title *Souls and Bodies.* Jackson believed that *How Far Can You Go?* represents a "circling back over thematic grounds covered in [Lodge's] earlier novels," now handled in a more accomplished fashion by the mature novelist. As in *The Picturegoers, The British Museum Is Falling Down,* and *Out of the Shelter,* the focus is on the sexual and religious evolution of a group of English Catholic characters, treated in a comic fashion. The changes that Lodge's characters experience over the book's twenty-year time span present "a panoramic view of the vast changes effected inside the church during the era spanning the 1950s up to Pope John Paul II's installation in the late 1970s," wrote Jackson.

Lodge uses a large cast of characters to illuminate the many aspects of a Catholic upbringing in *How Far Can You Go?* Some critics disliked what they saw as a collection of stereotypes, but Le Anne Schreiber pointed out in the *New York Times:* "By drafting his characters . . . into service as prototypes of every variant of Catholic experience, the author does at times lose something vital, but, in recompense, we get a very thorough crash course in modern Catholicism, including an introduction to process theology, the charismatic movement and the debates over priestly celibacy and the ordination of women. . . . Mr. Lodge has written a book full of his own energy, intelligence, wit, compassion and anger."

To incorporate explications of Catholic doctrine, Lodge also uses narrative asides and other unconventional fictional devices in *How Far Can You Go?* Some critics find these intrusive, such as Paul Theroux, whose *New York Times Book Review* article indicated that the book is best when Lodge "forgets he is a Professor of Modern English literature, ditches the arch tone and all the mannerisms and begins to believe in these characters." Others felt that Lodge's narrative musings give his book added depth and power. Nicholas Shrimpton explained in a *New Statesman* piece: "*How Far Can You Go?* is at its best at those moments when an intimate link is established between theological debate and personal life. The real hero of the novel is the pill, and Lodge's picture of these couples struggling to come to terms with it hovers delicately between tragedy and farce."

Lodge's next campus novel, *Nice Work,* is set in Rummidge, England, in 1986 and centers on Robyn Penrose, a temporary university literature teacher who is in search of a permanent teaching position. The year 1986 is deemed "Industry Year," and Penrose has been chosen by the university vice-chancellor to visit Vic Wilcox, the manager of a local engineering firm, once a week to learn more about the world of work. Vic, wrote Hilary Mantel in the *New York Review of Books,* "is a repository of ridiculous prejudices at which Lodge invites us to laugh, as elsewhere he invites us to laugh at Robyn's pretensions, at her equally naive world view." Anthony Quinn further commented on the contrast between the two characters in *New Statesman & Society,* stating that "Robyn is erudite and sophisticated, a justice-for-all idealogue, yet she's also snobbish and doctrinaire. Vic is a hard-headed, *Daily Mail*-reading chauvinist whom we ought to dislike, but beneath his boorishness lurks a gruff sort of chivalry." While some critics faulted *Nice Work,* calling the plot, as Quinn stated, "a convenient device for a face-off between two disparate ideologies," others applauded its humor and even-handed treatment of two contradictory personalities.

Writing about *Paradise News,* Lodge's next novel, Susan Miron of the *Christian Science Monitor* stated, "Lodge's fascination with the complex social rift between classes, between men and women, and between Americans and the British continues." The work centers on Bernard Walsh, a former Catholic priest and now a theology teacher, who receives a telephone call from his long-lost aunt Ursula asking him to come to Hawaii, where she is dying of cancer. Bernard travels with his father, who, while on the island, gets hit by a car driven by a middle-aged woman named Yolande. By the end of the novel, Yolande and Bernard become involved and Bernard's father reconciles with his sister. Bette Pesetsky observed in the *New York Times Book Review* that Lodge "bravely uses coincidence and contrivance to tie up loose ends. And just under the surface of the spirited and often comic adventures of his travelers he runs an undercurrent of understanding about their longings for the perfection of paradise." Michael Dirda of *Washington Post Book World* also noted that Lodge "persistently takes on some of the grimmest of subjects, . . . death, the loss of faith, sexual dysfunction, and unhappy families being unhappy in their own ways."

"Like his characters, Lodge is searching for faith and his religion," wrote John Podhoretz in *New Republic.* "We have grown so accustomed to those highly praised novels in which adolescents discover sexual freedom, irrational violence wreaks its consequences on a wise but hapless hero, and the struggle of life is reduced to a battle between superego and id, that a good novel about a few people merely trying to *get by* may seem a rather small achievement. If so, then perhaps we have lost sight of the value and purpose of fiction. . . . The modern popular novel has devoted itself to the body alone; Lodge joins an honorable and great tradition by restoring the primacy of the soul in fiction."

The novel *Therapy* was released in 1995. The tale is of Tubby Passmore, a successful television writer, who pursues a number of types of therapy, among them cognitive therapy, acupressure, and aromatherapy, to allay his depression. Paula Chin for *People* wrote "Lodge infuses nearly every page with his relentless intelligence and dry wit." James Bowman for *National Review* ended his critique with "This is a wonderful novel." In *Home Truths,* a novella published in 2000, Lodge "skewers the media's voracious relationship with celebrity culture at the same time it examines a writer's responsibility to his talent," according to a critic for *Publishers Weekly.*

Ralph Messenger and Helen Reed are the British academics whose destinies collide at the fictitious University of Gloucester in Lodge's 2001 novel *Thinks.* A *Publishers Weekly* reviewer praised its "gentle satire, vigorous intelligence, sometimes ribald humor and a perspicacious understanding of the human condition." An *Atlantic Monthly* critic called the work "a smart, seductive novel of ideas." *Author, Author,* released in 2004, portrays the novelist Henry James as he struggles to achieve literary recognition. Lodge focuses on James's rivalry with his friend George du Maurier, whose novel *Trilby* took the world by storm in the 1890s when James's novels were largely ignored.

Lodge's works of literary criticism include *After Bakhtin: Essays on Fiction and Criticism* and *The Art of Fiction: Illustrated from Classic and Modern Texts.* The first work is more academic and, as Lee Zimmerman noted in *San Francisco Review of Books,* "moves from 'fairly long broad-ranging exercises in Bakhtinian criticism' to more or less Bakhtinian studies of particular texts and authors illustrative of developments in the novel between the nineteenth and twentieth centuries." The latter work, according to Hilary Mantel in the *Spectator,* "is a kind of readers' handbook, a book about literary criticism for the not-too-critical." Critical reaction to *After Bakhtin* was generally favorable, with Zimmerman observing that if "Lodge hasn't completely solved the 'puzzle' at the heart of Bakhtin's thought, in my view, he has produced a provocative and engaging piece of work—'critical theory and all that' at its unpedantic best." Reviewers also praised *The Art of Fiction: Illustrated from Classic and Modern Texts,* albeit for different reasons. This work, noted Mantel, "can be seen as a brave attempt to build a bridge between today's reader and today's writer—whose interests, sometimes, seem irreconcilable. It is almost jargon-free, and it is entertaining, wise and well-organized."

In 1996, *The Practice of Writing: Essays, Lectures, Reviews, and a Diary* was released. Composed of essays culled from lectures, essays, and the like, Lodge writes about how writers write. It is not a work of criticism, but it does contain reviews of some authors, such as Vladimir Nabokov, Kingsley Amis, Anthony Burgess, and Graham Greene. W.M. Hagen for *World Literature Today* related that he had to "remind myself to take notes for this review. David Lodge writes criticism like the good novelist he is." A critic for *Publishers Weekly* wrote, "The . . . book . . . should be required reading in any creative writing class not bogged down in dogma. . . . Here is a collection that is both engaging and useful."

Consciousness and the Novel: Connected Essays, published in 2002, summarizes Lodge's views on consciousness research and how the human psyche is refracted by the imagination in specific literary works. Ulrich Baer, reviewing for *Library Journal,* faulted the novelist for a lack of originality and for reworking terrain and arguments "overly familiar from his previous studies. Lodge's prose is perfectly pleasant to read but neither particularly elegant nor sufficiently idiosyncratic to engage a reader fully."

Regarding his career as a novelist and a literary critic, Lodge once noted: "I've always maintained the two careers more or less in tandem, and I've tried to write a novel and a book of criticism alternately over the last twenty years. It grew out of the fact that my interest in writing was triggered by reading, as with most people, and getting some pleasure and satisfaction out of criticism as well as writing my own work and then wanting to continue the study of literature. All along I think I saw my literary career as a writer-critic, alternating and combining both types of discourse. As I get older, in a way I find creative writing more interesting, more of a challenge, more unpredictable—and more anxiety-making, but in the end, more satisfying."

BIOGRAPHICAL AND CRITICAL SOURCES:

BOOKS

Contemporary Popular Writers, St. James Press (Detroit, MI), 1997.

Dictionary of Literary Biography, Volume 14: *British Novelists since 1960,* Thomson Gale (Detroit, MI), 1983.

PERIODICALS

Atlantic Monthly, April, 1996, p. 119; June, 2001, review of *Thinks,* p. 104.

Christian Science Monitor, April 14, 1992, p. 13.

Commonweal, November 26, 1965; September 30, 1966; June 16, 1967.

Critique, summer, 1994, p. 237.

Economist, July 17, 2004, review of *Author, Author,* p. 80.

Encounter, August-September, 1980.

Globe & Mail (Toronto, Canada), September 8, 1981; July 7, 1984.

Guardian Weekly, December 2, 1990, p. 29.

Library Journal, July, 2002, Ulrich Baer, review of *Consciousness and the Novel,* p. 80.

Listener, February 27, 1975; May 1, 1980; March 29, 1984.

London Review of Books, September 29, 1988, p. 11.

Modern Fiction Studies, summer, 1982.

Modern Language Review, October, 1972.

Month, February, 1970.

National Review, August 14, 1995, James Bowman, review of *Therapy,* p. 54.

New Republic, April 7, 1982, pp. 37-38.

New Statesman, July 30, 1960; November 9, 1962; December 17, 1971; December 9, 1977; May 16, 1980; June 26, 1981; August 13, 1982.

New Statesman & Society, September 23, 1988, p. 37; November 1, 1999, James Hopkin, review of *Home Truths,* p. 54; December 16, 2002, review of *Consciousness and the Novel,* p. 112.

Newsweek, December 28, 1981.

New York Herald Tribune, July 25, 1965.

New York Review of Books, August 10, 1995, p. 24.

New York Times, January 1, 1982; March 8, 1985; July 8, 1993, p. C17.

New York Times Book Review, January 31, 1982; March 17, 1985; July 23, 1989, p. 1; April 5, 1992, p. 6; July 15, 1995, p. 9.

Novel: A Forum on Fiction, winter, 1972.

Observer (London, England), March 18, 1984.

People, August 14, 1995, Paula Chin, review of *Therapy,* p. 30.

Publishers Weekly, October 28, 1996, review of *The Practice of Writing,* p. 64; April 3, 2000, review of *Home Truths,* p. 59; June 4, 2001, review of *Thinks,* p. 58.

Punch, March 21, 1984.

San Francisco Review of Books, January, 1990, p. 23.

Spectator, March 25, 1966; May 3, 1980; July 31, 1982; April 7, 1984; October 10, 1992, p. 29; November 30, 2002, review of *Consciousness and the Novel,* p. 62.

Tablet, October 3, 1970.

Time, April 15, 1985; August 7, 1995, Martha Duffy, review of *Therapy,* p. 71.

Times (London, England), March 22, 1984; April 4, 1985; June 29, 1985.

Times Literary Supplement, February 14, 1975; May 2, 1980; June 26, 1981; March 23, 1984; May 31, 1985; September 23, 1988, p. 1040; August 10, 1990, p. 839; October 23, 1992, p. 23.

Voice Literary Supplement, May, 1992, pp. 31-32.

Washington Post Book World, February 7, 1982; March 3, 1985; April 5, 1992, p. 4.

World Literature Today, autumn, 1991, p. 780; winter, 1993, p. 181; autumn, 1997, W.M. Hagen, review of *The Practice of Writing,* p. 795.

Yale Review, December, 1966; December, 1977; January, 1993, p. 148.

*   *   *

LODGE, David John
    See LODGE, David

*   *   *

LOGAN, Jake
    See SMITH, Martin Cruz

LONG, David 1948-

PERSONAL: Born March 6, 1948, in Boston, MA; son of John H., Jr. (a lawyer) and Jean (a cellist; maiden name, Dimond) Long; married Susan Schweinsberg (a medical librarian), December 19, 1969; children: Montana (son), Jackson. *Education:* Albion College, B.A., 1970; Hartford Seminary Foundation, M.A., 1972; University of Montana, M.F.A., 1974.

ADDRESSES: Office—c/o Author Mail, Scribner, Simon & Schuster, 1230 Avenue of the Americas, New York, NY 10020.

CAREER: Writer, 1974—. Flathead Valley Community College, adjunct instructor, 1976-83; University of Montana, adjunct professor, 1990-99; Pacific University, faculty in M.F.A. program, 1999—. Visiting writer, University of Idaho, 1996, University of North Carolina at Greensboro, 1996. Consultant and workshop instructor for the Montana State Office of Public Instruction, 1975-81; member of advisory panel for Poets and Writers in Schools Program, Montana Arts Council, 1980-83, 1989; manuscript consultant for University of Illinois Press, 1983—and University of Missouri Press, 1989; member of board of trustees of Hockaday Center of the Arts, Kalispell, MT, 1983-88 and Hellgate Writers, Missoula, MT, 1993-96; judge or literature panelist for North Dakota Arts Council, 1984, Montana Arts Council, 1984, Loft McKnight Fellowships, 1988, Idaho Commission on the Arts, 1988, Oregon Arts Commission, 1988, Lewis-Clark College, 1995, Arizona State University, 1995.

AWARDS, HONORS: Award for fiction, St. Lawrence University, 1983, for *Home Fires;* O. Henry Award, for short story "Blue Spruce," 1992; Creative Writing Fellowship, National Endowment for the Arts, 1993-94; best books of the year designation, *Publishers Weekly,* 1995, and Richard and Hinda Rosenthal Foundation Award, American Academy of Arts and Letters, 1996, both for *Blue Spruce.*

WRITINGS:

Early Returns (poems), Jawbone (Waldron Island, WA), 1981.
Home Fires (short stories), University of Illinois Press (Urbana, IL), 1982.
The Flood of '64 (short stories), Ecco Press (New York, NY), 1987.
Blue Spruce (short stories), Scribner (New York, NY), 1995.
The Falling Boy (novel), Scribner (New York, NY), 1997.
The Daughters of Simon Lamoreaux, Scribner (New York, NY), 2000.
Purgatorio, Houghton Mifflin (Boston, MA), 2005.

Contributor to magazines, including *Antaeus, Montana: Magazine of Western History, Poets and Writers, Publishers Weekly,* and *Sewanee Review.* Founding editor of *CutBank.* Long's stories have appeared in numerous anthologies, including *Writers of the Purple Sage: Contemporary Western Writings,* Viking (New York, NY), 1984; *New American Stories: Writers Select Their Favorites,* New American Library (New York, NY), 1987; *The Graywolf Annual Four: Short Stories by Men,* Graywolf Press, 1988; *Best of the West: New Stories from the Wide Side of the Missouri,* Gibbs Smith/Peregrine Smith Books, 1988; *The Last Best Place: A Montana Anthology,* Montana Historical Society Press (Helena, MT), 1988; *Voices Louder than Words: A Second Collection,* Random House (New York, NY), 1991; *New Writers of the Purple Sage,* Viking, 1992; *Prize Stories 1992: The O. Henry Awards,* Doubleday (New York, NY), 1992; *Best of the West 5,* W.W. Norton (New York, NY), 1992; *The Portable Western Reader,* edited by William Kittredge, Viking, 1997; and *Love Stories from the New Yorker,* edited by Roger Angell, Random House, 1997.

SIDELIGHTS: David Long has won much critical acclaim for both his novels and his short-story collections. The majority of his tales are set in western Montana—a harsh land that serves as a backdrop to bleak, gritty lives. Here, "happiness is nonexistent or referred to exclusively in the past tense," related David Brooks in an *American Book Review* piece on Long's second story collection, *The Flood of '64.* In the story "Compensation," a woman, who was abused in her youth, and her husband, who was debilitated by a horrible accident years before, find that love is not enough to overcome their deep personal wounds. In "Solstice," a wife-beating man is stunned when his spouse finally leaves him one bitterly cold night.

As Long once explained: "If I have a theory of fiction, it's that something of consequence must be at stake in a story; people must make choices and live with their decisions. Most of the stories in *The Flood of '64* were triggered by an event in the daily paper or a document I stumbled across—I have an intense curiosity for family letters and oral histories. A number of the stories take place in the years between my father's birth (1909) and my own (1948). If there's a common thread to my fiction, it's that ordinary life is interrupted by moments of extraordinary beauty and sadness, that whatever holds us together is fragile and must be looked after lovingly."

"Long is very good at confronting the more dismal vistas in life with an unflinching stare," affirmed Brooks. "Moreover, he is skillful in presenting plots in which unfortunate incidents take certain, crushing steps towards the protagonists. The reader is led to marvel at the fragility of the most mundane lives." Despite this praise, Brooks was ultimately critical of *The Flood of '64*, complaining that "there's enough grief and existential malaise here to have it subtitled 'High Noon and No Exit.' While it would be unfair to ask Long to lighten up a little, his style can turn into an oppressive experience in itself." *New York Times Book Review* contributor Greg Johnson did not share Brooks's view. Johnson found that Long's bleak stories "are remarkable for their affirmative endings. Though he is hard on his characters, Mr. Long highlights the quicksilver moments of humor, insight and compassion that make living worthwhile in such a barren world."

Long offers a similar vision in his award-winning fiction collection *Blue Spruce*. Most of the stories included here are set in and around the fictional town of Sperry, Montana, just south of the Canadian border. Again, readers are made to feel the icy blasts of air coming down from Alberta and to see the desolate beauty of the Rocky Mountains. In "Perfection," a high-school girl is witness to a brutal murder; in the title story, two sisters-in-law struggle for control of the family home in the wake of a suicide. "Each story engages you enough that you wish it wouldn't end so soon," claimed Ann Fisher in a *Library Journal* review. Paja Faudree expressed an opinion similar to Johnson's, writing in *Voice Literary Supplement* that "despite the dark vision of much of this work, these stories never result in despair, but rather in a rugged optimism."

"Long is a sensitive writer and, in a phrase that here and there astonishes, more than that," observed Richard Eder in the *Los Angeles Times*. Long was published as a poet before he turned to short stories, and other critics have also singled out the quality of his language as one of his greatest strengths. According to *New York Times Book Review* writer Lisa Sandlin, the tales in *Blue Spruce* "explore how we nourish the 'crimp' in ourselves—habits of meanness and fear—and how we manage to expand. Some of the stories explode into be-

ing, but most require the reader's patient orientation as relationships and consequences shape themselves. All are written in a beautiful, fine-cut prose . . . that shines and surprises." *Tribune Books* writer Michael Upchurch pointed to Long's great feeling for his protagonists as an essential element in the success of his fiction. "Whether he's portraying a tough old bird, like the sister-in-law [in *Blue Spruce*], or a teenager, like the young girl in *Perfection*, his sympathy is frank and deep. Indeed, he has a shrewd affection for almost all his characters, whatever their failings."

"Long will restore your faith in the short story," assured George Needham in his *Booklist* assessment of *Blue Spruce*. Upchurch was equally enthusiastic about the collection, saying, "The best tales . . . are unostentatious on the surface, but their interior richness merits close scrutiny. At times they feel almost like novels in miniature as they trace—with subtle economy and engagingly quiet wit—the effect of smalltown scandal, family bonds or betrayals and individual ambitions over the years. The writing is spare but poetic; the mood is one of genial sympathy and occasional regret." Upchurch concluded: "Long himself has stated his admiration for John Cheever, Joyce Carol Oates, William Trevor and other masters. It's no exaggeration to say that the best work in *Blue Spruce* places Long among such company."

With 1997's *The Falling Boy*, Long made what may perhaps prove to be a permanent shift to longer fiction. Remarking on his novel debut, he explained that *The Falling Boy* "is set in Sperry, Montana, in the 1950s and early 1960s. It's the story of a café owner, Nick Stavros, and his four daughters, especially Olivia, the third-born, and her marriage." The novel hinges around Olivia's marriage to construction worker Mike Singer, and Singer's eventually attraction to Olivia's older sister. Praising the novel as "finely crafted," *Library Journal* contributor David Sowd maintained that *The Falling Boy* stands as one of the most "honest and unflinching moral examination[s] of marital infidelity" written in the late twentieth century. A *Publishers Weekly* contributor concurred, dubbing the novel "a keenly observed and poignantly accurate portrait of the human condition" that is both "unpretentiously profound" and "memorable." "Long is a writer of extraordinary sensitivity and grace," added *Booklist* reviewer Dennis Dodge, hailing the short-story writer-turned-novelist as "an important talent."

In both *The Falling Boy* and the 2000 novel *The Daughters of Simon Lamoreaux*, Long exhibits "an affinity for describing sibling relationships, particularly among sisters," maintained a *Publishers Weekly* reviewer. In the author's second novel, he tells the story of Miles Fanning, a man haunted by the disappearance, over two decades ago, of his high-school girlfriend. Contacted by the missing woman's younger sister, Julia, Fanning is forced to confront the emotions that have haunted him throughout a subsequent marriage, and also works to solve the mystery as a way of healing his own psyche. In *Booklist* Bonnie Johnson praised *The Daughters of Simon Lamoreaux* as "a captivating story about the healing potential of love in the face of tragedy" as well as a compelling mystery, while the *Publishers Weekly* reviewer hailed Long's second novel as "richly suggestive," its "narrative sensitively exploring the ironies of unfulfilled lives."

Commenting on his writing in general, Long once stated: "I've tried to break down the clichés about Montana." Despite any literary trends to the contrary, he continues to employ "affirmative endings" in his work, noting: "It's the job of fiction writers to describe change, which is often difficult or painful (even falling in love is traumatic), but I have a strong desire to redeem my characters, to let them find, or at least sense, a way out of their messes."

BIOGRAPHICAL AND CRITICAL SOURCES:

PERIODICALS

American Book Review, March, 1988, p. 17.
Bloomsbury Review, May, 1995, p. 18.
Booklist, February 15, 1995, p. 1059; June 1, 1997, Dennis Dodge, review of *The Falling Boy,* p. 1660; April 15, 2000, Bonnie Johnston, review of *The Daughters of Simon Lamoreaux,* p. 1524.
Boston Globe, April 30, 1995, p. B16.
Detroit News/Free Press, May 7, 1995.
Gentlemen's Quarterly, June, 1994, p. 98.
Georgia Review, winter, 1995, p. 950.
Glimmer Train Stories, fall, 1995, pp. 119-137.
Library Journal, February 1, 1995, p. 102; May 15, 1997, David Sowd, review of *The Falling Boy,* p. 103; April 15, 2000, Robert E. Brown, review of *The Daughters of Simon Lamoreaux,* p. 123.
Los Angeles Times, November 25, 1982; March 9, 1995, p. E6.
Los Angeles Times Book Review, April 19, 1987, p. 3.
New Yorker, November 12, 1990, p. 46; December 9, 1991, p. 46.
New York Times Book Review, July 5, 1987; April 23, 1995, p. 26.

Ploughshares, fall, 1995, pp. 236-237.
Publishers Weekly, January 16, 1995, p. 435; June 26, 1995, p. 83; April 28, 1997, review of *The Falling Boy,* p. 47; March 27, 2000, review of *The Daughters of Simon Lamoreax,* p. 49.
Tribune Books (Chicago, IL), March 26, 1995, p. 5.
Voice Literary Supplement, April, 1995, p. 16.

*   *   *

LOOS, Anita 1893-1981

PERSONAL: Born April 26, 1893, in Sisson, CA; died August 18, 1981, of a heart attack, in New York, NY; daughter of Richard Beers (a theatrical producer and newspaper editor) and Minnie Ellen (Smith) Loos; married Frank Palma, Jr., June, 1915 (marriage annulled one day later); married John Emerson (an actor, director, and playwright), 1919 (died March 8, 1956); children: one adopted daughter. *Education:* Attended high school in San Francisco, CA.

CAREER: Writer, 1912-81.

MEMBER: Dramatists Guild.

AWARDS, HONORS: Vanity Fair magazine award for "Red-headed Woman."

WRITINGS:

(With John Emerson) *How to Write Photoplays,* McCann (New York, NY), 1920.
(With John Emerson) *Breaking into the Movies,* McCann (New York, NY), 1921.
"Gentlemen Prefer Blondes": The Illuminating Diary of a Professional Lady (also see below; story collection), Boni & Liveright (New York, NY), 1925.
"But Gentlemen Marry Brunettes" (story collection), Boni & Liveright (New York, NY), 1928.
A Mouse Is Born (novel), Doubleday (New York, NY), 1951.
No Mother to Guide Her (novel), McGraw (New York, NY), 1961.
A Girl Like I (autobiography), Viking (New York, NY), 1966.
(Author of foreword) Dody Goodman, *Women, Women, Women,* Dutton (New York, NY), 1966.

(Translator and adaptor) Jean Canolle, *The King's Mare* (also see below), Evans Brothers (London, England), 1967.

(With Helen Hayes) *Twice Over Lightly: New York Then and Now,* Harcourt (New York, NY), 1972.

Kiss Hollywood Good-by (autobiography), Viking (New York, NY), 1974.

Cast of Thousands (autobiography), Grosset & Dunlap (New York, NY), 1977.

The Talmadge Girls: A Memoir, Viking (New York, NY), 1978.

San Francisco: A Screenplay (also see below), edited by Matthew J. Bruccoli, Southern Illinois University Press (Carbondale, IL), 1979.

Fate Keeps On Happening: Adventures of Lorelei Lee and Other Writings, Dodd (New York, NY), 1984.

Contributor to *Reader's Digest, New York Times Magazine, Woman's Home Companion, Saturday Review,* and *Harper's.*

PLAYS

(With John Emerson) *The Whole Town's Talking,* produced on Broadway at Bijou Theatre, 1923.

(With John Emerson) *The Fall of Eve,* produced on Broadway at Booth Theatre, 1925.

(With John Emerson) *Gentlemen Prefer Blondes* (based on their book of the same title), produced in New York, NY, at Times Square Theatre, 1926, musical adaptation (with Joseph Fields), produced on Broadway at Ziegfield Theatre, 1949.

(With John Emerson) *The Social Register,* produced in New York, NY, at Fulton Theatre, 1931.

Happy Birthday (produced on Broadway at Broadhurst Theatre, 1946), Samuel French (New York, NY), 1948.

Gigi (based on the novel by Colette; produced in New York, NY, at Fulton Theatre, 1951), Random House (New York, NY), 1952, revised edition, 1956.

Cheri (based on the novels *Cheri* and *The End of Cheri* by Colette), produced on Broadway at Morosco Theatre, 1959.

LIBRETTOS

The Amazing Adele (based on the play by Pierre Barrillet and Jean-Pierre Gredy), produced in Philadelphia, PA, at Shubert Theatre, 1955.

Gogo Loves You, produced in New York, NY, at Theatre de Lys, 1964.

Something about Anne (based on the play *The King's Mare* by Jean Canolle), produced in London, England, 1966.

SCENARIOS FOR SILENT FILMS

The New York Hat, American Biograph, 1913.

The Power of the Camera, American Biograph, 1913.

A Horse on Bill, American Biograph, 1913.

A Hicksville Epicure, American Biograph, 1913.

Highbrow Love, American Biograph, 1913.

A Hicksville Romance, American Biograph, 1913.

A Fallen Hero, American Biograph, 1913.

A Fireman's Love, American Biograph, 1913.

A Cure for Suffragettes, American Biograph, 1913.

The Suicide Pact, American Biograph, 1913.

Bink's Vacation, American Biograph, 1913.

How the Day Was Saved, American Biograph, 1913.

Fall of Hicksville's Finest, American Biograph, 1913.

The Wedding Gown, American Biograph, 1913.

Yiddish Love, American Biograph, 1913.

Gentlemen and Thieves, American Biograph, 1913.

Pa Says, American Biograph, 1913.

The Widow's Kids, American Biograph, 1913.

The Lady in Black, American Biograph, 1913.

His Hoodoo, American Biograph, 1913.

The Deacon's Whiskers, Reliance Mutual, 1913.

His Awful Vengeance, Reliance Mutual, 1913.

All for Mabel, Reliance Mutual, 1913.

The Fatal Deception, Reliance Mutual, 1913.

For Her Father's Sins, Reliance Mutual, 1913.

Unlucky Jim, Kornick, 1913.

All on Account of a Cold, Kornick, 1913.

The Saving Grace, Cinemacolor, 1913.

A Narrow Escape, Cinemacolor, 1913.

Two Women, Cinemacolor, 1913.

The Wall Flower, Lubin, 1913.

A Bunch of Flowers, American Biograph, 1914.

When a Woman Guides, American Biograph, 1914.

The Road to Plaindale, American Biograph, 1914.

The Meal Ticket, American Biograph, 1914.

The Saving Presence, American Biograph, 1914.

The Suffering of Susan, American Biograph, 1914.

Where the Roads Part, American Film Manufacturing, 1914.

His Rival, American Film Manufacturing, 1914.

The Chieftain's Daughter (Some Bull's Daughter), Reliance Mutual, 1914.

The Fatal Dress Suit, Reliance Mutual, 1914.

The Girl in the Shack, Reliance Mutual, 1914.

His Hated Rival, Reliance Mutual, 1914.

A Corner in Hats, Reliance Mutual, 1914.

Nearly a Burglar's Bride, Reliance Mutual, 1914.

The Fatal Curve, Reliance Mutual, 1914.

The Million-Dollar Bride, Reliance Mutual, 1914.

A Flurry in Art, Reliance Mutual, 1914.

Nellie, the Female Villain, Reliance Mutual, 1914.

The Gangsters of New York, Reliance Mutual, 1914.

The Tear on the Page, American Biograph, 1915.

The Cost of a Bargain, American Biograph, 1915.

Pennington's Choice, Metro Pictures, 1915.

Sympathy Sal, Reliance Mutual, 1915.

Mixed Values, Reliance Mutual, 1915.

A Corner in Cotton, Quality Pictures, 1916.

Wild Girl of the Sierras, Fine Arts-Triangle, 1916.

Calico Vampire, Fine Arts-Triangle, 1916.

Laundry Liz, Fine Arts-Triangle, 1916.

French Milliner, Fine Arts-Triangle, 1916.

The Wharf Rat, Fine Arts-Triangle, 1916.

The Little Liar, Fine Arts-Triangle, 1916.

Stranded, Fine Arts-Triangle, 1916, also released by Sterling Pictures, 1927.

The Social Secretary, Fine Arts-Triangle, 1916, also released by Tri-Stone Pictures, 1924.

His Picture in the Papers, Fine Arts-Triangle, 1916.

The Half-Breed, Fine Arts-Triangle, 1916.

American Aristocracy, Fine Arts-Triangle, 1916.

Manhattan Madness, Fine Arts-Triangle, 1916.

The Matrimaniac, Fine Arts-Triangle, 1916.

The Americano, Fine Arts-Triangle, 1917.

In Again, Out Again, Artcraft Pictures, 1917.

Wild and Wooly (based on a story by H.B. Carpenter), Artcraft Pictures, 1917.

Down to Earth (based on a story by Douglas Fairbanks), Artcraft Pictures, 1917.

(With John Emerson) *Reaching for the Moon,* Artcraft Pictures, 1917.

(With John Emerson) *Let's Get a Divorce* (based on the play *Divorçons* by Victorien Sardou), Famous Players-Lasky, 1918.

(With John Emerson) *Hit-the-Trail Holiday* (based on the play by George M. Cohan), Famous Players-Lasky, 1918.

(With John Emerson) *Come On In,* Famous Players-Lasky, 1918.

(With John Emerson) *Good-Bye, Bill,* Famous Players-Lasky, 1918.

(With John Emerson) *Oh, You Women!,* Famous Players-Lasky, 1919.

(With John Emerson) *Getting Mary Married,* Marion Davis Film Co., 1919.

(With John Emerson) *A Temperamental Wife,* Constance Talmadge Film Co., 1919.

(With John Emerson) *A Virtuous Vamp* (based on the play *The Bachelor* by Clyde Fitch), Joseph M. Schenck, 1919.

(With John Emerson) *Isle of Conquest* (based on the novel *By Right of Conquest* by Arthur Hornblow), Select Pictures, 1919.

(With John Emerson) *In Search of a Sinner,* Joseph M. Schenck, 1920.

(With John Emerson) *The Love Expert,* Joseph M. Schenck, 1920.

(With John Emerson) *The Branded Woman* (based on the play *Branded* by Oliver D. Bailey), Joseph M. Schenck, 1920.

(With John Emerson) *The Perfect Woman,* First National, 1920.

(With John Emerson) *Two Weeks* (based on the play *At the Barn* by Anthony Wharton), First National, 1920.

(With John Emerson) *Dangerous Business,* First National, 1921.

(With John Emerson) *Mama's Affair* (based on the play by Rachel Barton Butler), First National, 1921.

(With John Emerson) *Woman's Place,* Joseph M. Schenck, 1921.

(With John Emerson) *Red Hot Romance,* Joseph M. Schenck, 1922.

(With John Emerson) *Polly of the Follies,* First National, 1922.

(With John Emerson) *Dulcy* (based on the play by George S. Kaufman and Marc Connelly), Joseph M. Schenck, 1923.

(With John Emerson) *Three Miles Out* (based on a story by Neysa McMein), Kenma, 1924.

(With John Emerson) *Learning to Love,* First National, 1925.

Publicity Madness, Fox Film, 1927.

(With John Emerson) *Gentlemen Prefer Blondes* (based on the play by Loos), Paramount, 1928.

Author of unproduced screenplays for silent films, including *He Was a College Boy, Queen of the Carnival, The Mayor-Elect, The Making of a Masher, Path of True Love, A Girl like Mother, The Mother, The Great Motor Race, A No Bull Spy, A Balked Heredity, A Blasted Romance, Mortimer's Millions, A Life and Death Affair, The Sensible Girl, At the Tunnel's End,* and *How to Keep a Husband,* all for American Biograph; *The Deadly Glass of Beer, The Stolen Masterpiece, The Last Drink of Whisky, Nell's Eugenic Wedding, The School of Acting, A Hicksville Reformer, The White Slave Catchers, The Style Accustomed, The Deceiver, How They Met, The Burlesque, The Fatal Fourth, The Fatal Fingerprints,* and *Wards of Fate,* all for Reliance Mutual; *The Earl and the Tomboy,* for Lubin; *Heart that Truly Loved,* for Pictorial Review; and *Mountain Bred,* for Mabel Normand.

Also author of *The Telephone Girl and the Lady.* Also author of title cards for the silent films *Macbeth,* Lucky Film Producers, 1916, and *Intolerance,* D.W. Griffith, 1916.

SCREENPLAYS

(With John Emerson) *The Struggle,* United Artists, 1931.

Red-Headed Woman (based on the novel by Katherine Brush), Metro-Goldwyn-Mayer, 1932.

(With Elmer Harris) *The Barbarian* (based on the story by Edgar Selwyn), Metro-Goldwyn-Mayer, 1933.

(With Howard Emmett Rogers) *Hold Your Man,* Metro-Goldwyn-Mayer, 1933.

(With John Emerson) *The Girl from Missouri,* Metro-Goldwyn-Mayer, 1934, released in England as *100 Per Cent Pure.*

Biography of a Bachelor Girl, Metro-Goldwyn-Mayer, 1935.

(With Frances Marion and H.W. Haneman) *Riffraff,* Metro-Goldwyn-Mayer, 1935.

San Francisco (based on a story by Robert Hopkins), Metro-Goldwyn-Mayer, 1936.

Mama Steps Out, Metro-Goldwyn-Mayer, 1937.

(With Robert Hopkins) *Saratoga,* Metro-Goldwyn-Mayer, 1937.

(With Jane Murfin) *The Women* (based on the play by Clare Booth), Metro-Goldwyn-Mayer, 1939.

Susan and God (based on the play by Rachel Crothers), Metro-Goldwyn-Mayer, 1940, released in England as *The Gay Mrs. Trexel.*

(With Edwin Justin Mayer and Leon Gordon) *They Met in Bombay* (based on a story by Franz Kafka), Metro-Goldwyn-Mayer, 1941.

Blossoms in the Dust (based on a story by Ralph Wheelwright), Metro-Goldwyn-Mayer, 1941.

(With S.K. Lauren) *When Ladies Meet* (based on the play by R. Crothers), Metro-Goldwyn-Mayer, 1941.

I Married an Angel (based on the musical by Vaszary Janos, Lorenz Hart, and Richard Rodgers), Metro-Goldwyn-Mayer, 1942.

(With others) *The Pirate,* Metro-Goldwyn-Mayer, 1948.

Also author of unproduced screenplays, *The Great Canadian* and *Alaska,* for Metro-Goldwyn-Mayer; also author of dialogue for *Blondie of the Follies,* Metro-Goldwyn-Mayer, 1932.

ADAPTATIONS: *Gentlemen Prefer Blondes* was filmed by Twentieth Century-Fox in 1953 and was adapted as a musical entitled *Lorelei* in 1974; *But Gentlemen Marry Brunettes* was filmed as *Gentlemen Marry Brunettes* by United Artists in 1955; *Happy Birthday* was adapted for television in Italy and the United States.

SIDELIGHTS: "I really never consider myself as a writer," Anita Loos once commented to Matthew J. Bruccoli in *Conversations with Writers II.* "I'm just a girl out there trying to get a fast buck." In a career spanning some six decades, Loos wrote over 150 screenplays and scenarios, as well as popular Broadway plays and books of memoirs. But she was always "indissolubly linked" with her best-selling story collection *Gentlemen Prefer Blondes: The Illuminating Diary of a Professional Lady,* as Alden Whitman noted in the *New York Times.* Adapted as a play, two musicals, and two movies, and translated into fourteen languages, *Gentlemen Prefer Blondes* established Loos's reputation as a writer of sparkling satire. Asked by Roy Newquist of *Palm Springs Life* whether she minded "being so closely identified" with the one book, Loos replied: "Heavens no, not as long as those lovely royalty checks keep coming in."

Loos began her career as a child actress in her father's theatrical company in San Francisco. By the time she was ten years old, her stage earnings were a vital cash source for her financially unstable family. Loos admitted on several occasions that her father's business often kept him away from home for long periods, usually in the company of other women. John Fitzgerald of the *Detroit News* quoted Loos explaining: "My mother was refined . . . my father was a charming tramp."

While still in her teens Loos became interested in the then-new medium of silent films, which were at first shown between live acts at local theatres. Believing that she could write a silent film as good as the ones shown in her father's theatre, Loos submitted the scenario for *The New York Hat* to D.W. Griffith's American Biograph Company, copying the company's address from a film canister. Griffith accepted the scenario and Loos received twenty-five dollars for her work. The resulting film featured prominent stars Lillian Gish, Dorothy Gish, Mary Pickford, and Lionel Barrymore.

Between 1912 and 1916 Loos wrote at least 100 scenarios for the silent films, usually for American Biograph but, when a particular idea did not seem strong enough to Griffith, for other film companies as well. The exact number of Loos' silent films, the years they were released, and the production companies that made them, are questions that will never be answered definitively. Few records were kept by those in the business; many films, particularly the very short films, were never registered for copyright; and others were later lost through either haphazard storage or deliberate destruction for the silver nitrate content of the film itself. And to many people in the silent film world, the business was nothing but a transitory craze not to be taken too seriously. "We . . . looked on them as a fad that would soon lose public interest," Alden Whitman quoted Loos explaining.

Specializing in writing "slapstick comedies and romantic melodramas," as Thomas Grant noted in the *Dictionary of Literary Biography,* Loos emerged as one of the luminaries of the silent film world. She wrote for such stars as Mabel Normand, Mae Marsh, Marian Davies, Francis X. Bushman, Constance Talmadge, Norma Talmadge, and Douglas Fairbanks, and worked with the legendary director D.W. Griffith. She also wrote the title cards for Griffith's *Intolerance,* one of the silent screen's classic films. Yet, despite her position in the industry, Loos never went to see any of her films. She told Bruccoli: "I never paid any attention to any of them. They were a job and I'd get them done." In 1916 Loos became the sole writer for Douglas Fairbanks after the success of the satirical film *His Picture in the Papers.* The film introduced a new element to the silent film genre: satirical title cards which were meant to contrast ironically with the action on the screen. Together with her future husband, director John Emerson, Loos and Fairbanks shaped the Fairbanks screen persona into one of the most popular and lucrative characters in the cinema industry. Speaking of Loos's writing for these early films, Joanne Yeck of the *Dictionary of Literary Biography* reported that she "introduced satire to the silent film. Her dialogue cards were bright with sharp wit, exposing her real talent for verbal comedy."

In 1919 Loos married Emerson and the two went on to collaborate on a number of films and plays. It was only years later, in her autobiography *Kiss Hollywood Good-by,* that Loos confessed that her husband's "'collaboration' consisted of glancing over my morning's work while he was eating breakfast in bed." By the late 1920s the couple had done well enough to leave screenwriting and move to Europe. Loos's movie fame allowed her entrance to European high society, and she was soon a regular at the country houses of royalty. Numbered among her friends were Ernest Hemingway, Gertrude Stein, Aldous Huxley, H.G. Wells, and F. Scott Fitzgerald. But Loos's European lifestyle came to an abrupt end with the stock market crash of 1929; Emerson had invested the couple's money in the market and lost it all. In 1931 Loos returned to the United States to be-

come a screenwriter with Metro-Goldwyn-Mayer at a salary of $3,500 a week.

During the 1930s Loos worked with Irving Thalberg, the head of MGM studios and the man Loos later claimed taught her all about the "talkies." Her first film for the studio was *Red-Headed Woman,* the story of a young vamp who breaks up a marriage. Thalberg had already had several writers try their hand at the script, including F. Scott Fitzgerald but not one had been able to render the story in the ironic manner Thalberg wanted. He thought that Loos might be able to treat the story's sexual slant humorously. Loos did. The resulting script catapulted lead actress Jean Harlow to instant fame. But the film, because of "its lighthearted view of sex," as Yeck reported, also ran afoul of the religious community. *Red-Headed Woman,* Yeck wrote, "started the national protest of women's clubs and church groups that eventually culminated in the formation of the Breen Office," a censorship group that was to set the "acceptable" standards for the film industry for years to come. Writing in *Kiss Hollywood Good-by,* Loos noted that the film outraged many people because "our heroine, the bad girl of whom all good husbands dream, ended her career as many such scalawags do, rich, happy, and respected, without ever having paid for her sins."

In 1936 Loos wrote *San Francisco* for MGM, a film inspired by her close friend Wilson Mizner. Loos and Robert Hopkins, who wrote the original story for the film, had known Mizner for many years. Mizner had worked in gambling houses, sold nonexistent Florida real estate, and engaged in a score of other fraudulent operations before finally opening a legitimate business, the Brown Derby Restaurant in Hollywood. His notorious past, colorful anecdotes, off-color remarks, and unfailing charm made Mizner a favorite with many among the Hollywood set, including W.C. Fields. After Mizner's death in 1933, Loos and Hopkins wrote *San Francisco,* as Loos explained in *Kiss Hollywood Good-by,* "to the glory of Wilson Mizner and the Frisco all three of us knew when we were kids." In the film, Blackie Norton, played by Clark Gable, is a Barbary Coast gambler in the San Francisco of the turn of the century who is inspired to go straight after the great earthquake of 1906. The story is partly based on Mizner's own career as a gambling house operator. *San Francisco,* Yeck reported, was "by far the most commercially successful film Thalberg ever produced." Loos admitted in *Kiss Hollywood Good-by* that "it became one of MGM's most durable hits."

Although she enjoyed great success as a writer for Hollywood films, Loos is best known for *Gentlemen Prefer Blondes,* a book she later adapted as a play, a musical, and for the screen. The story of an uneducated and naive young flapper who uses her charms to coax expensive gifts from her "gentlemen friends," the idea for *Gentlemen Prefer Blondes* apparently came to Loos during a cross-country train ride in the early 1920s. One of her fellow passengers was a blond Broadway actress on her way to Hollywood for a screen test. Over the course of the journey, the men on the train fawned over her while Loos, a brunette, steamed. Her resentment took shape as a series of loosely linked satirical short stories written in diary form. But on other occasions Loos claimed that she wrote *Gentlemen Prefer Blondes* because her friend H.L. Mencken had been infatuated with a particularly brainless blond and she wanted to show him his mistake.

Whatever the source of *Gentlemen Prefer Blondes,* Alden Whitman maintained that "Loos seldom permitted precise facts to spoil a good story, so the true origins of her book are in doubt." The stories were first published in *Harper's Bazaar* and immediately caused sales of the magazine to quadruple. The story proved popular when published in book form in 1925; since its first appearance there have been some eighty-five editions of *Gentlemen Prefer Blondes* and the book has even been translated into Chinese.

The book follows beautiful Lorelei Lee on a tour of Europe with her friend Dorothy. Lorelei's inane observations about European society and culture, and her frankly materialistic attitude toward sexual relations, form the basis of the comedy. "As a fictional character," Grant wrote, "Lorelei harks back to an earlier comic stereotype, the malaprop-inclined, misspelling rustic busybody." Fitzgerald noted that Loos "gave the world neither blonds nor gentlemen but managed to make both shimmer through the eyes of one diamond-loving Lorelei Lee." Perhaps the book's most famous line is Lorelei's observation that "kissing your hand may make you feel very good but a diamond lasts forever." In the course of her European tour Lorelei acquires a number of both kisses and diamonds, including a $7,500 tiara from an English nobleman. She ends the book safely ensconced on Park Avenue, the wife of a wealthy man. "Lorelei's stunning progress from small-town girl to metropolitan socialite," Grant remarked, "makes her story seem like an urban version of the familiar American tall tale, a delightfully improbable yarn perfectly suited to the 1920s era of excess."

Critical response to *Gentlemen Prefer Blondes* was enormously favorable. George Santayana, William Faulkner, James Joyce, Edith Wharton, H.L. Mencken, and Aldous Huxley were among those who recommended it. Years later, Peter S. Prescott of *Newsweek* could still note that *Gentlemen Prefer Blondes* "remains one of the great American comic novels."

The adaptations of the book also proved successful. Loos's stage version of 1926 ran on Broadway for 201 performances. A 1949 musical version enjoyed a run of 740 performances and launched the career of actress Carol Channing. The popular song "Diamonds Are a Girl's Best Friend" is from this play. In 1974 yet another Broadway adaptation appeared under the title of *Lorelei.* Loos also wrote a silent film version of *Gentlemen Prefer Blondes* which was produced in 1928; a later film, featuring Marilyn Monroe as Lorelei, appeared in 1953.

Loos followed *Gentlemen Prefer Blondes* with a sequel, *But Gentlemen Marry Brunettes,* recounting the romantic misadventures of Lorelei's girlfriend Dorothy. Lorelei, who has married successfully, assists Dorothy in her quest to enter Manhattan society. But Dorothy's eventual marriage to a rich polo player comes only after a series of trials, including a marriage to a cocaine addict who is killed by mobsters. One of the novel's high points, according to Grant, is a scene in which the two women visit the Algonquin Hotel and acidly comment on the circle of writers and journalists who frequented the hotel bar in the early 1920s. "Loos's portrayal of the Algonquin wits," Grant wrote, "has become established wisdom. She was one of their first critics, and one of the most accurate." Other reviewers, such as the *New Republic* critic, found that, like its predecessor, *But Gentlemen Marry Brunettes* contains "that wonderful mixture of canned, naive sentiment and equally naive, but extremely business-like gold-digging."

In 1946 Loos returned to the Broadway stage with *Happy Birthday,* a comedy set in a Newark saloon and starring her old friend Helen Hayes. Revolving around an inhibited librarian who finally opens up after a few drinks at the local tavern, *Happy Birthday* ran for 564 performances on Broadway. Speaking to Bruccoli about the play, Loos explained the basis of its plot: "I had this old maid go into a bar and get tight, and in the process of getting tight she regenerates her whole life." Later Loos stage efforts included two popular adaptations of novels by the French writer Colette: *Gigi* in 1951, and *Cheri* in 1959.

Beginning in the 1960s Loos began to publish a series of memoirs about her long career as a writer for Hollywood and Broadway. Written in a chatty, informal style, these books are peppered with lively anecdotes and reminiscences about the many famous people she knew. Grant explained that Loos's memoirs chronicled "her own long, lucrative career and the dazzling times in which she worked." In her review of *A Girl Like I*, Sister M. Gregory of *Best Sellers* found that the "book is more than an autobiography; it is an intriguing bit of Americana that mirrors the brash confidence, rugged independence and changing mores of a rapidly growing, prosperous country." Speaking of *Kiss Hollywood Goodby*, Joel Sayre of the *New York Times Book Review* remarked that if the book reached the best-seller lists, it would be because of Loos's "marvelous, casual putting forth of bizarre doings and sayings." Writing in the *Christian Science Monitor*, Guernsey Le Pelley called the same book "a jolly adventure in trivia. . . . But along with all the flotsam are many delectable and interesting tidbits, which make the book bouncy and largely enjoyable. Also [the book] holds up a mirror of unintended satire to that demi-Disneyland called Hollywood." In similar terms, Richard Lingeman of the *New York Times*, reviewing *Cast of Thousands*, warned that "one should not regard [Loos's] witty, determinedly surface view of life as the sign of a superficial mind. Actually, Miss Loos is a sharp-eyed chatterbox, who lets fly some quick cynical shafts."

Loos died of a heart attack on August 18, 1981, in New York City. Despite the many successes of her long career, she always maintained a cavalier attitude towards her work. Though *Gentlemen Prefer Blondes* firmly established her, she said of the story, "I had no thought of its ever being printed. My only purpose was to make Henry Mencken laugh which it did." Speaking of her career to Fitzgerald, she said: "I did it for the money and it was the easiest money I ever made." When questioned by Bruccoli about whether *Gentlemen Prefer Blondes* had obscured "the range of your other work," Loos replied: "I think *Gentlemen Prefer Blondes* is the range of my work. I think everything else I do is just earning a living." Perhaps one reason for her adamant refusal to place much value on her writings is revealed in a remark Loos made to Fitzgerald in the last interview she gave. "It was all so easy," she said. "It didn't seem to mean anything."

Critical evaluations of Loos's career usually stress the impressive range of genres in which she excelled. Her silent film work includes some of that genre's finest examples and introduced depth and subtlety to the medium. Her later films and plays feature sparkling, witty dialogue that ensures their lasting humor and audience appeal. And her character Lorelei Lee is, Grant believed, "a true American original. . . . So memorable

[that she] ought to earn her inventor a place as one of the important minor figures among twentieth-century American humorists." Enid Nemy of the *New York Times Book Review* summed up Loos in this way: "The keenness of her eye never faltered, and for something like six decades she sliced neatly through the gauze that surrounds glamour and fame."

BIOGRAPHICAL AND CRITICAL SOURCES:

BOOKS

Authors in the News, Thomson Gale (Detroit, MI), Volume 1, 1976.

Beauchamp, Cari, and Mary Anita Loos, editors, *Anita Loos Rediscovered: Film Treatments and Fiction by Anita Loos*, University of California Press (Berkeley, CA), 2003.

Carey, Gary, *Anita Loos: A Biography*, Knopf (New York, NY), 1988.

Conversations with Writers II, Thomson Gale (Detroit, MI), 1978.

Dictionary of Literary Biography, Thomson Gale (Detroit, MI), Volume 11: *American Humorists, 1800-1950*, 1982, Volume 26: *American Screenwriters*, 1984, Volume 228: *Twentieth-Century American Dramatists, Second Series*, 2000.

Dictionary of Literary Biography Yearbook, 1981, Thomson Gale (Detroit, MI), 1982.

Loos, Anita, *A Girl Like I*, Viking (New York, NY), 1966.

Loos, Anita, *Kiss Hollywood Good-by*, Viking (New York, NY), 1974.

Loos, Anita, *Cast of Thousands*, Grosset & Dunlap (New York, NY), 1977.

PERIODICALS

AB Bookman's Weekly, September 14, 1981.
Akron Beacon Journal, September 8, 1974.
Atlantic, October, 1960.
Best Sellers, October 1, 1966.
Boston Transcript, November 25, 1925.
Canadian Review of American Studies, spring, 1976.
Chicago Tribune, August 2, 1961; August 20, 1981.
Christian Science Monitor, September 18, 1974.
Detroit News, August 30, 1981.
Literary Review, November 21, 1925.
New Republic, June 13, 1928; August 10, 1974.
New Statesman, May 19, 1928.
Newsweek, August 31, 1981; December 17, 1984.

New York Times, April 29, 1918; September 23, 1918;
    October 27, 1919; January 23, 1922; February 23,
    1925; December 27, 1925; January 16, 1928; May
    20, 1928; December 11, 1935; March 2, 1935;
    January 13, 1936; June 27, 1936; July 23, 1937;
    September 22, 1939; July 12, 1940; June 27, 1941;
    July 4, 1941; September 5, 1941; July 10, 1942;
    August 19, 1981.
New York Times Book Review, May 6, 1951; August 18,
    1974; March 23, 1977; November 27, 1984; De-
    cember 30, 1984.
New York Tribune, December 27, 1925.
Palm Springs Life, October, 1974.
Publishers Weekly, September 4, 1981.
Saturday Review, June 9, 1928; September 24, 1966.
Time, August 31, 1981.
Times Literary Supplement, February 23, 1967.
Tribune Books (Chicago), November 26, 1978.

* * *

LORDE, Audre 1934-1992
(Rey Domini, Audre Geraldine Lorde)

PERSONAL: Born February 18, 1934, in New York,
NY; died of liver cancer November 17, 1992, in Chris-
tiansted, St. Croix, U.S. Virgin Islands; daughter of Frederic Byron (a real estate broker) and Linda Gertrude
(Belmar) Lorde; married Edwin Ashley Rollins (an attorney), March 31, 1962 (divorced, 1970); children:
Elizabeth, Jonathan. *Education:* Attended National University of Mexico, 1954; Hunter College (now Hunter
College of the City University of New York), B.A.,
1959; Columbia University, M.L.S., 1961. *Politics:*
"Radical." *Religion:* Society of Friends (Quaker).

CAREER: Mount Vernon Public Library, Mount Vernon, NY, librarian, 1961-63; Town School Library, New
York, NY, head librarian, 1966-68; City University of
New York, lecturer in creative writing at City College,
1968, lecturer in education department at Herbert H.
Lehman College, 1969-70, associate professor of English at John Jay College of Criminal Justice, beginning
1970, professor of English at Hunter College, Thomas
Hunter Professor, 1987-88. Distinguished visiting professor, Atlanta University, 1968; poet-in-residence, Tougaloo College, 1968. Lecturer throughout the United
States. Founder of Kitchen Table, Women of Color
Press.

MEMBER: American Association of University Professors, Harlem Writers Guild, Sisterhood in Support of
Sisters in South Africa.

AWARDS, HONORS: National Endowment for the Arts
grants, 1968 and 1981; Creative Artists Public Service
grants, 1972 and 1976; National Book Award nominee
for poetry, 1974, for *From a Land Where Other People
Live;* Broadside Poets Award, Detroit, 1975; Woman of
the Year, Staten Island Community College, 1975; Borough of Manhattan President's Award for literary excellence, 1987; American Book Award, Before Columbus
Foundation, 1989, for *A Burst of Light;* Walt Whitman
Citation of Merit, poet laureate of New York, 1991;
Lambda Literary Awards, Lesbian Poetry, 1993, for *Undersong* and 1994, for *The Marvelous Arithmetics of
Distance.*

WRITINGS:

The Cancer Journals (nonfiction), Spinsters Ink (Den-
    ver, CO), 1980.
Zami: A New Spelling of My Name (fiction), Crossing
    Press (Santa Cruz, CA), 1982.
Sister Outsider (nonfiction), Crossing Press (Santa
    Cruz, CA), 1984.
A Burst of Light, Firebrand Books (Ithaca, NY), 1988.
Need: A Chorale for Black Women Voices, Women of
    Color Press (Brooklyn, NY), 1990.

POETRY

The First Cities, introduction by Diane di Prima, Poets
    Press (Ogden, UT), 1968.
Cables to Rage, Broadside Press (Detroit, MI), 1970.
From a Land Where Other People Live, Broadside
    Press (Detroit, MI), 1973.
The New York Head Shop and Museum, Broadside
    Press (Detroit, MI), 1974.
Coal, Norton (New York, NY), 1976.
Between Our Selves, Eidolon (Westport, CT), 1976.
The Black Unicorn, Norton (New York, NY), 1978.
Chosen Poems Old and New, Norton (New York, NY),
    1982.
Our Dead behind Us, Norton (New York, NY), 1986.
Undersong: Chosen Poems Old and New, Norton (New
    York, NY), 1992.
The Marvelous Arithmetics of Distance, Norton (New
    York, NY), 1993.
The Collected Poems of Audre Lorde, Norton (New
    York, NY), 1997.

Poetry anthologized in: Langston Hughes, editor, *New
Negro Poets, USA,* University of Indiana Press (Bloomington, IN), 1962; P. Breman, editor, *Sixes and Sevens,*

Breman Ltd. (London, England), 1963; R. Pool, editor, *Beyond the Blues,* Hand & Flower Press (Amsterdam, Netherlands), 1964; G. Menarini, editor, *I Negri: Poesie e Canti,* Edizioni Academia (Rome, Italy), 1969; C. Major, editor, *New Black Poetry,* International Press (Somerville, MA), 1969; T. Wilentz, editor, *Natural Process,* Hill & Wang (New York, NY), 1970; T. Cade, editor, *The Black Woman,* American Library Publishing (Sedona, AZ), 1970; and *Soul-Script,* edited by J. Meyer, Simon & Schuster (New York, NY). Contributor of poetry to periodicals, including *Iowa Review, Black Scholar, Chrysalis, Black World, Journal of Black Poetry, Transatlantic Review, Massachusetts Review, Pound, Harlem Writers' Quarterly, Freedomways, Seventeen,* and *Women: A Journal of Liberation.*

OTHER

The Audre Lorde Compendium: Essays, Speeches, and Journals, introduction by Alice Walker, Pandora (London, England), 1996.
Conversations with Audre Lorde, edited by Joan Wylie Hall, University Press of Mississippi (Jackson, MS), 2004.

Contributor of fiction, under pseudonym Rey Domini, to *Venture* magazine. Editor, *Pound* magazine (Tougaloo, MS), 1968; poetry editor, *Chrysalis* and *Amazon Quarterly.*

SIDELIGHTS: Audre Lorde was a poet, novelist, essayist, and activist of distinction. As Irma McClaurin-Allen, writing in *Dictionary of Literary Biography* noted, "Lorde is probably best known as a feminist poet; yet her contributions to the new black poetry movement cover a wide range of themes. Black pride, black love, and black survival in an urban environment are recurring motifs; and the image of the city, in all of its destructive grandeur, dominates many of her poems." A self-styled "black, lesbian, mother, warrior, poet," Lorde dedicated both her life and her creative talent to confronting and addressing the injustices of racism, sexism, and homophobia. Her poetry, and "indeed all of her writing," according to contributor Joan Martin in *Black Women Writers (1950-1980): A Critical Evaluation,* "rings with passion, sincerity, perception, and depth of feeling." Concerned with twentieth-century American society's tendency to categorize groups of people, Lorde fought the marginalization of such categories as "lesbian" and "black woman," thereby empowering her readers to react to the prejudice in their own lives. While the widespread critical acclaim bestowed upon Lorde for dealing with lesbian topics made her a target of those opposed to her radical agenda, she continued, undaunted, to express her individuality, refusing to be silenced. As she once told interviewer Charles H. Rowell in *Callaloo:* "My sexuality is part and parcel of who I am, and my poetry comes from the intersection of me and my worlds. . . . [Conservative U.S. Senator] Jesse Helms's objection to my work is not about obscenity . . . or even about sex. It is about revolution and change. . . . Helms represents. . . . white patriarchal power. . . . [and he] knows that my writing is aimed at his destruction, and the destruction of every single thing he stands for." Fighting a battle with cancer that she documented in her highly acclaimed *Cancer Journals,* Lorde died of the illness in 1992.

Born in New York City of West Indian parents, Lorde came to poetry in her early teens, through a need to express herself. Her first poem to be published was accepted by *Seventeen* magazine when she was still in high school. The poem had been rejected by her school paper, Lorde explained in *Black Women Writers,* because her "English teachers . . . said [it] was much too romantic." Her mature poetry, published in volumes including *New York Head Shop and Museum, Coal,* and *The Black Unicorn,* was sometimes romantic also. Often dealing with her lesbian relationships, her love poems have nevertheless been judged accessible to all by many critics. In Martin's words, "one doesn't have to profess heterosexuality, homosexuality, or asexuality to react to her poems. . . . Anyone who has ever been in love can respond to the straightforward passion and pain sometimes one and the same, in Lorde's poems."

While Lorde's love poems composed much of her earliest work, her experiences of civil unrest during the 1960s, along with Lorde's own confusion over her sexuality—a bisexual, she married in 1962 and had two children before divorcing and making a renewed commitment to her female lovers—created a rapid shift to more political statements. As Jerome Brooks reported in *Black Women Writers (1950-1980),* "Lorde's poetry of anger is perhaps her best-known work." In her poem "The American Cancer Society, or There Is More than One Way to Skin a Coon," she protests against white America thrusting its unnatural culture on blacks; in "The Brown Menace or Poem to the Survival of Roaches," she likens blacks to cockroaches, hated, feared, and poisoned by whites. *Poetry* critic Sandra M. Gilbert remarked that "it's not surprising that Lorde occasionally seems to be choking on her own anger . . . [and] when her fury vibrates through taut cables from head to heart to page, Lorde is capable of rare and, paradoxically, loving jeremiads."

Lorde's anger did not confine itself to racial injustice but extended to feminist issues as well, and occasionally she criticized African-American men for their role in the perpetuation of sex discrimination: "As Black people, we cannot begin our dialogue by denying the oppressive nature of *male privilege,*" she once stated in *Black Women Writers.* "And if Black males choose to assume that privilege, for whatever reason, raping, brutalizing, and killing women, then we cannot ignore Black male oppression. One oppression does not justify another."

Of her poetic beginnings Lorde once commented in *Black Women Writers:* "I used to speak in poetry. I would read poems, and I would memorize them. People would say, well what do you think, Audre. What happened to you yesterday? And I would recite a poem and somewhere in that poem would be a line or a feeling I would be sharing. In other words, I literally communicated through poetry. And when I couldn't find the poems to express the things I was feeling, that's what started me writing poetry, and that was when I was twelve or thirteen." As an adult, her primary poetic goal remained communication. "I have a duty," she stated later in the same publication, "to speak the truth as I see it and to share not just my triumphs, not just the things that felt good, but the pain, the intense, often unmitigating pain." As a mature poet, however, rather than relying solely on poetry as a means of self-expression Lorde often extracted poems from her personal journals. Explaining the genesis of "Power," a poem about the police shooting of a ten-year-old black child, Lorde discussed her feelings when she learned that the officer involved had been acquitted: "A kind of fury rose up in me; the sky turned red. I felt so sick. I felt as if I would drive this car into a wall, into the next person I saw. So I pulled over. I took out my journal just to air some of my fury, to get it out of my fingertips. Those expressed feelings are that poem."

In addition to race problems and love affairs, another important theme that runs through many of Lorde's poems is the parent-child relationship. Brooks saw a deep concern with the images of her deceased father in Lorde's "Father, Son, and Holy Ghost" which carries over to poems dealing with Africa in *The Black Unicorn.* According to Brooks, "the contact with Africa is the contact with the father who is revealed in a wealth of mythological symbols. . . . The fundamental image of the unicorn indicates that the poet is aware that Africa is for her a fatherland, a phallic terrain." Martin, however, took a different view: "Lorde is a rare creature. . . . She is the Black Unicorn: magical and mysterious bearer of fantasy draped in truth and

beauty." Further, Martin found the poet's feelings about her mother to be more vital to an understanding of her works. In many of Lorde's poems, the figure of her mother is one of a woman who resents her daughter, tries to repress her child's unique personality so that she conforms with the rest of the world, and withholds the emotional nourishment of parental love. For example, Lorde tells us in *Coal's* "Story Books on a Kitchen Table": "Out of her womb of pain my mother spat me/ into her ill-fitting harness of despair/ into her deceits/ where anger reconceived me." In *The Black Unicorn's* "From the House of Yemanja," the mother's efforts to shape the speaker into something she is not do not quench the speaker's desire for the mother's love: "Mother I need/ mother I need/ . . . I am/ the sun and moon and forever hungry." "Balled from Childhood" in *The New York Head Shop and Museum* is Lorde's depiction of the ways in which a child's hopes and dreams are crushed by a restrictive parent. After the mother has made withering replies to her child's queries about planting a tree to give some beauty to their wasteland surroundings, the child gives up in defeat, saying: "Please mommy do not beat me so!/ yes I will learn to love the snow!/ yes I want neither seed nor tree!/ yes ice is quite enough for me!/ who knows what trouble-leaves might grow!"

As Martin noted, however, Lorde's ambivalent feelings about her mother "did not make [her] bitter against her own children when circumstances changed her role from that of child to mother." *Coal* includes the poem "Now That I Am Forever with Child," which discusses the birth of Lorde's daughter. "I bore you one morning just before spring," she recounts, "my legs were towers between which/ A new world was passing./ Since then/ I can only distinguish/ one thread within runnings hours/ You, flowing through selves/ toward You."

In addition to her poetry, Lorde was noted for eloquent prose, one example of which was her courageous account of her agonizing struggle to overcome breast cancer and mastectomy, published as *The Cancer Journals.* Her first major prose work, *The Cancer Journals* discuss Lorde's feelings about facing the possibility of death. Beyond death, Martin asserted, Lorde feared "she should die without having said the things she as a woman and an artist needed to say in order that her pain and subsequent loss might not have occurred in vain." Recounting this personal transformation was, for Lorde, of primary importance; as AnaLouise Keating noted in *Journal of Homosexuality,* "For Lorde, self-expression and self-discovery are never ends in themselves. Because she sees her desire to comprehend her battle with cancer as 'part of a continuum of women's work, of reclaiming this earth and or power,' she is confident that her self-explorations will empower her readers." Her *Journals* also reveal Lorde's decision not to wear a prosthesis after her breast was removed. As Brooks pointed out, "she does not suggest [her decision] for others, but . . . she uses [it] to expose some of the hypocrisies of the medical profession." Lorde summarized her attitude on the issue thus in the *Journals:* "Prosthesis offers the empty comfort of 'Nobody will know the difference.' But it is that very difference which I wish to affirm, because I have lived it, and survived it, and wish to share that strength with other women. If we are to translate the silence surrounding breast cancer into language and action against this scourge, then the first step is that women with mastectomies must become visible to each other." Martin concluded: "*The Cancer Journals* affords all women who wish to read it the opportunity to look at the life experience of one very brave woman who bared her wounds without shame, in order that we might gain some strength from sharing in her pain."

Lorde's 1982 novel, *Zami: A New Spelling of My Name,* was described by its author as a "biomythography, combining elements of history, biography and myth," and Rosemary Daniell, in the *New York Times Book Review,* considered the work "excellent and evocative. . . . Among the elements that make the book so good are its personal honesty and lack of pretentiousness, characteristics that shine through the writing, bespeaking the evolution of a strong and remarkable character." Daniell said that, throughout the book, Lorde's "experiences are painted with exquisite imagery. Indeed, her West Indian heritage shows through most clearly in her use of word pictures that are sensual, steamy, at times near-tropical, evoking the colors, smells—repeatedly, the smells—shapes, textures that are her life."

In the late 1980s Lorde and fellow writer Barbara Smith founded Kitchen Table: Women of Color Press, which was dedicated to furthering the writings of black feminists. Lorde also became increasingly concerned over the plight of black women in South Africa under apartheid, creating Sisterhood in Support of Sisters in South Africa and providing an active voice on behalf of these women throughout the remainder of her life. Indeed, Lorde addressed her concerns to not only the United States but the world, encouraging a celebration of the differences that society instead used as tools of isolation. As Allison Kimmich noted in *Feminist Writers,* "Throughout all of Audre Lorde's writing, both nonfiction and fiction, a single theme surfaces repeatedly. The black lesbian feminist poet activist reminds her readers that they ignore differences among people at their

peril. . . . Instead, Lorde suggests, differences in race or class must serve as a 'reason for celebration and growth.'"

Lorde fought cancer for much of her later life; she was diagnosed with breast cancer in 1978 and then in 1984 with liver cancer. Opting for a non-traditional treatment for the latter, she sought help in homeopathy and also moved to the U.S. Virgin Islands for its warmer climate. She continued to work and speak publicly until her death in 1992. Among the works of her last years was the National Book Award-winning collection of essays, *A Burst of Light.* The year of her death saw publication of *Undersong: Chosen Poems Old and New* and the following year the collection *The Marvelous Arithmetics of Distance* was published. Reviewing the latter book, a contributor for *Publishers Weekly* commented that Lorde's verses "have always melded the political and lyrical worlds, the ordinary and the luminous, addressing controversial topics." For this contributor, *The Marvelous Arithmetics of Distance* "is no exception."

In 1997 *The Collected Poems of Audre Lorde* appeared, gathering work that spanned almost three decades. For *Library Journal*'s Ina Rimpau, this collection affirmed the fact that Lorde battled "passionately and urgently throughout her oeuvre" for social justice. Reviewing the same volume in *Booklist,* Patricia Monaghan noted that Lorde's "reputation has continued to grow" since her death. Though Monaghan found some "patchy sections" in the overall work, she went on to conclude that for Lorde's finest verses, "—strong, vibrant, and wild—she will continue to be sought out." Jewelle Gomez, a fellow writer, noted in *Essence* magazine at the time of Lorde's death that the writer's work in a variety of genres was "a mandate to move through . . . victimization and create independent standards that will help us live full and righteous lives. . . . She was a figure all women could use as a grounding when they fought for recognition of their worth."

BIOGRAPHICAL AND CRITICAL SOURCES:

BOOKS

Addison, Gayle, editor, *Black Expression,* Weybright & Talley (New York, NY), 1969.
Bigsby, C.W.E., editor, *The Black American Writer,* Penguin (New York, NY), 1969.
Christian, Barbara, editor, *Black Feminist Criticism: Perspectives on Black Women Writers,* Pergamon (New York, NY), 1985.

Contemporary Literary Criticism, Thomson Gale (Detroit, MI), Volume 18, 1981, Volume 71, 1992.

Dictionary of Literary Biography, Volume 41: *Afro-American Poets since 1955,* Thomson Gale (Detroit, MI), 1984.

Draper, James P., editor, *Black Literature Criticism,* Volume 2, Thomson Gale (Detroit, MI), 1992.

Evans, Mari, editor, *Black Women Writers (1950-1980): A Critical Evaluation,* Doubleday (New York, NY), 1984.

Gay and Lesbian Biography, St. James Press (Detroit, MI), 1997.

Keating, AnaLouise, *Women Reading Women Writing: Self-Invention in Paula Gunn Allen, Gloria Anzaldua, and Audre Lorde,* Temple University Press (Philadelphia, PA), 1996.

Kester-Shelton, Pamela, editor, *Feminist Writers,* St. James Press (Detroit, MI), 1995.

Kosek, Jane Kelly, editor, *Poetry Criticism,* Volume 12, Thomson Gale (Detroit, MI), 1995.

Tate, Claudia, editor, *Black Women Writers at Work,* Continuum (New York, NY), 1984.

PERIODICALS

American Book Review, October-November, 1993, p. 15.

American Poetry Review, March-April, 1980, pp. 18-21.

Booklist, August, 1997, Patricia Monaghan, review of *The Collected Poems of Audre Lorde,* p. 1871.

Callaloo, winter, 1986, pp. 192-208; 1987; winter, 1991, pp. 83-95.

Colby Library Quarterly, March, 1982, pp. 9-25.

Denver Quarterly, spring, 1981, pp. 10-27.

Essence, January, 1988; May, 1993, Jewelle Gomez, "Audre Lorde: Passing of a Sister Warrior," p. 89; March, 1999, Catherine M. Brown, "Reflections on a 'Black, Militant, Lesbian Poet'," p. 68.

Explicator, fall, 1998, Thomas Dilworth, "Lorde's 'Power'," p. 54.

Journal of Homosexuality, Volume 26, numbers 2-3, pp. 181-194.

Library Journal, August, 1997, Ina Rimpau, review of *The Collected Poems of Audre Lorde,* p. 92.

Ms., September, 1974.

Negro Digest, September, 1968.

New York Times Book Review, December 19, 1982, Rosemary Daniell, review of *Zami.*

Poetry, February, 1977.

Publishers Weekly, July 19, 1993, "The Marvelous Arithmetics of Distance: Poems, 1987-1992," p. 240.

Signs: Journal of Women in Culture and Society, summer, 1981, pp. 713-36.

ONLINE

Audre Lorde Home Page, http://www.lambda.net/~maximum/lorde.html/ (August 12, 2004).

Audre Lorde Project Web site, http://www.alp.org/ (August 12, 2004).

*   *   *

LORDE, Audre Geraldine
See LORDE, Audre

*   *   *

LOUISE, Heidi
See ERDRICH, Louise

*   *   *

LOWRY, Lois 1937-
(Lois Hammersburg Lowry)

PERSONAL: Born March 20, 1937, in Honolulu, HI; daughter of Robert E. (a dentist) and Katharine (Landis) Hammersberg; married Donald Grey Lowry (an attorney), June 11, 1956 (divorced, 1977); married; second husband's name Martin; children: Alix, Grey (deceased), Kristin, Benjamin. *Education:* Attended Brown University, 1954-56; University of Southern Maine, B.A., 1972; graduate study. *Religion:* Episcopalian.

ADDRESSES: Home—205 Brattle St., Cambridge, MA 02138. *Agent*—Wendy Schmalz, Harold Ober Associates, 425 Madison Ave., New York, NY 10017.

CAREER: Freelance writer, children's author, and photographer, 1972—.

MEMBER: Society of Children's Book Writers and Illustrators, PEN American Center, Authors Guild, Authors League of America, MacDowell Colony (fellow).

AWARDS, HONORS: Children's Literature Award, International Reading Association (IRA), Notable Book Citation, American Library Association (ALA), state children's choice awards, Massachusetts and California, 1978, for *A Summer to Die;* Children's Book of the Year citation, Child Study Association of America, and

ALA Notable Book citation, all 1979, all for *Anastasia Krupnik;* ALA Notable Book citation, 1980, and International Board on Books for Young People Honor List citation, 1982, both for *Autumn Street;* ALA Notable Book Citation, 1981, and American Book Award nomination (juvenile paperback category), 1983, for *Anastasia Again!;* ALA Notable Book Citation, 1983, for *The One-Hundredth Thing about Caroline;* Children's Book of the Year Citation, Child Study Association of America, 1986, for *Us and Uncle Fraud;* state children's choice award, New Jersey, 1986, for *Anastasia, Ask Your Analyst; Boston Globe-Horn Book* Award, Golden Kite Award, Society of Children's Book Writers and Illustrators, and Child Study Award, Children's Book Committee of Bank Street College, all 1987, all for *Rabble Starkey;* Christopher Award, 1988; Newbery Medal, ALA, National Jewish Book Award, and Sidney Taylor Award, National Jewish Libraries, all 1990, all for *Number the Stars;* Newbery Medal, 1994, for *The Giver;* Children's Choice citation, IRA/Children's Book Council, 1997, for *See You Around, Sam!*

WRITINGS:

JUVENILE NOVELS

A Summer to Die, illustrated by Jenni Oliver, Houghton Mifflin (Boston, MA), 1977.

Find a Stranger, Say Goodbye, Houghton Mifflin (Boston, MA), 1978.

Anastasia Krupnik, Houghton Mifflin (Boston, MA), 1979.

Autumn Street, Houghton Mifflin (Boston, MA), 1979.

Anastasia Again!, illustrated by Diane deGroat, Houghton Mifflin (Boston, MA), 1981.

Anastasia at Your Service, illustrated by Diane deGroat, Houghton Mifflin (Boston, MA), 1982.

Taking Care of Terrific, Houghton Mifflin (Boston, MA), 1983.

Anastasia, Ask Your Analyst, Houghton Mifflin (Boston, MA), 1984.

Us and Uncle Fraud, Houghton Mifflin (Boston, MA), 1984.

The One Hundredth Thing about Caroline, Houghton Mifflin (Boston, MA), 1985.

Anastasia on Her Own, Houghton Mifflin (Boston, MA), 1985.

Switcharound, Houghton Mifflin (Boston, MA), 1985.

Anastasia Has the Answers, Houghton Mifflin (Boston, MA), 1986.

Rabble Starkey, Houghton Mifflin (Boston, MA), 1987.

Anastasia's Chosen Career, Houghton Mifflin (Boston, MA), 1987.

All about Sam, illustrated by Diane deGroat, Houghton Mifflin (Boston, MA), 1988.

Number the Stars, Houghton Mifflin (Boston, MA), 1989.

Your Move, J. P.!, Houghton Mifflin (Boston, MA), 1990.

Anastasia at This Address, Houghton Mifflin (Boston, MA), 1991.

Attaboy, Sam!, illustrated by Diane deGroat, Houghton Mifflin (Boston, MA), 1992.

The Giver, Houghton Mifflin (Boston, MA), 1993.

Anastasia, Absolutely, Houghton Mifflin (Boston, MA), 1995.

See You Around, Sam!, Houghton Mifflin (Boston, MA), 1996.

Stay!: Keeper's Story, illustrated by True Kelley, Houghton Mifflin (Boston, MA), 1997.

Looking Back: A Book of Memories, Houghton Mifflin (Boston, MA), 1998.

Zooman Sam, Houghton Mifflin (Boston, MA), 1999.

Gathering Blue, Houghton Mifflin (Boston, MA), 2000.

Gooney Bird Green, illustrated by Middy Thomas, Houghton Mifflin (Boston, MA), 2002.

The Silent Boy, Houghton Mifflin (Boston, MA), 2003.

OTHER

Black American Literature (textbook), J. Weston Walsh (Portland, ME), 1973.

Literature of the American Revolution (textbook), J. Weston Walsh (Portland, ME), 1974.

(Photographer) Frederick H. Lewis, *Here in Kennebunkport,* Durrell (Kennebunkport, ME), 1978.

(And photographer) *Looking Back: A Photographic Memoir* (autobiography), Houghton Mifflin (Boston, MA), 1998.

Also author of introduction to *Dear Author: Students Write about the Books That Changed Their Lives,* Conari Press, 1995. Contributor of stories, articles, and photographs to periodicals, including *Redbook, Yankee,* and *Down East.*

ADAPTATIONS: Find a Stranger, Say Goodbye was made into the *Afterschool Special* "I Don't Know Who I Am," ABC-TV, 1980; *Taking Care of Terrific* was televised on *Wonderworks,* 1988; *Anastasia at Your Service* was recorded on audiocassette, Learning Library, 1984; *Anastasia Krupnik* was made into a film-strip, Cheshire, 1987; *The Giver* has been adapted for a film produced by Walden Media and directed by Vadim Perelman.

SIDELIGHTS: Lois Lowry is an award-winning author of young adult novels. Born in 1937 in Honolulu, Hawaii, Lowry's original birth name was Cena, after her Norwegian grandmother, but the elder Cena strongly objected to having her granddaughter bear that name—Lowry's name was quickly changed, and at eleven months of age, she was baptized Lois Ann. At the time of her birth, Lowry's father, a military dentist and career army officer, was stationed at Schofield Barracks near Pearl Harbor. The family separated with the onset of World War II; her father continued his duty in the military, and Lowry spent the duration of the war with her mother's family in the Amish Country of Pennsylvania. "I remember all these relatively normal Christmases with trees, presents, turkeys, and carols, except that they had this enormous hole in them because there was never any father figure," Lowry said in *Authors and Artists for Young Adults.* This deep sense of loss is "probably why I've written a terrific father figure into all of my books—sort of a fantasy of mine while growing up." Her grandmother wasn't especially fond of children, but her grandfather adored her, and Lowry escaped the absolute trauma of war under the shelter of his affection. Much later, Lowry's wartime experience inspired her fourth novel, *Autumn Street.* As an author, Lowry has often translated her life into fiction for the purpose of helping others who may have suffered under similar circumstances. She once commented that she gauges her success as a writer by her ability to "help adolescents answer their own questions about life, identity and human relationships."

Lowry's books have dealt with topics ranging from the death of a sibling and the Nazi occupation of Denmark, to the humorous antics of the rebellious Anastasia Krupnik, to futuristic dystopian societies. In her first novel, *A Summer to Die,* Lowry portrays an adolescent's struggle with her older sister's illness and eventual death. When the Chalmers family moves to the country for the summer, thirteen-year-old Meg and fifteen-year-old Molly are forced to share a room. Already jealous of her older sister, Meg becomes increasingly argumentative and resentful when her sister's recurring nosebleeds become the focus of her parents' attention. As her sister's condition deteriorates, Meg realizes that Molly is slowly dying of leukemia. For friendship, she turns to old Will Banks, a neighbor who encourages her interest in photography, and Ben and Maria, a hippie couple who invite Meg to take pictures at the birth of their child.

A Summer to Die was well received by critics. The "story captures the mysteries of living and dying without manipulating the reader's emotions, providing understanding and a comforting sense of completion," observed Linda R. Silver in *School Library Journal.* Tragically, Lowry's sympathy for Meg and Molly was drawn from life. Her older sister, Helen, died of cancer when Lowry was twenty-five. "Very little of [*A Summer to Die*] was factual," she once commented, "except the emotions." The author added, "When my mother read the book she recognized the characters as my sister and me. She knew that the circumstances in the book were very different, but the characters had great veracity for her."

Following her successful debut as a novelist, Lowry continued to explore challenging adolescent topics. She documented an adopted child's search for her biological mother in *Find a Stranger, Say Goodbye.* Although neither Lowry nor any of her children are adopted, she felt that the subject was important enough to be dealt with at length. She explained, "Maybe it's because of having watched my own kids go through the torture of becoming adults . . . that I think those kinds of issues are important and it's important to deal with them in a sensitive and compassionate way."

Memories of her childhood as well as her experiences as a parent have led Lowry to her most popular character: Anastasia Krupnik, the spunky, rebellious, and irreverent adolescent who stars in a series of books that began in 1979. "Until I was about twelve I thought my parents were terrific, wise, wonderful, beautiful, loving, and well-dressed," the author confessed. "By age twelve and a half they turned into stupid, boring people with whom I did not want to be seen in public. . . . That happens to all kids, and to the kids in my books as well." In the first book of the series, *Anastasia Krupnik,* the ten-year-old heroine faces numerous comic crises, including a crush on a boy who is continually dribbling an imaginary basketball, and the coming arrival of a baby sibling. With the passing of each crisis Anastasia gains new insight into herself; by the book's close she is prepared to move on to a new level of maturity. "Anastasia's feelings and discoveries should be familiar to anyone who has ever been ten," noted Brad Owens in the *Christian Science Monitor,* "and author Lois Lowry has a sensitive way of taking problems seriously without ever being shallow or leaning too far over into despair."

The broad audience appeal of the first "Anastasia" book prompted Lowry to write another novel featuring her diminutive heroine. "I have the feeling she's going to go on forever—or until I get sick of her, which hasn't happened yet. I'm still very fond of her and her whole family," Lowry remarked. Subsequent titles include *Anastasia Again!* and *Anastasia at Your Service,* in which a twelve-year-old Anastasia finds a summer job serving as maid to a rich, elderly woman, who turns out to be a classmate's grandmother. Anastasia must deal with the embarrassment of working for the family of a well-to-do peer. "Despite differences the girls become friends; and with the help of Anastasia's precocious brother Sam, they generate a plot that is rich, inviting, and very funny," noted Barbara Elleman in a *Booklist* review. The popular Anastasia went on to appear in numerous additional titles, including *Anastasia, Ask Your Analyst; Anastasia on Her Own; Anastasia Has the Answers;* and *Anastasia's Chosen Career.*

In 1990 Lowry received the Newbery Medal for her distinguished contribution to children's literature with *Number the Stars.* Based on a factual account, the story is set against the backdrop of Nazi-occupied Denmark. Ten-year-old Annemarie Johansen and her family are drawn into the resistance movement, shuttling Jews from Denmark into neutral Sweden. (During the Second World War this type of heroism ensured the survival of nearly all of Denmark's Jews.) Newbery Committee Chair Caroline Ward was quoted by *School Library Journal:* "Lowry creates suspense and tension without wavering from the viewpoint of Annemarie, a child who shows the true meaning of courage." The book "avoids explicit description of the horrors of war, yet manages to convey without oversimplification the sorrow felt by so many people who were forced to flee their homeland," wrote a *Children's Literature Review* critic.

Lowry received the prestigious Newbery Medal a second time for her 1993 novel *The Giver.* In this radical departure from her previous works, Lowry creates a futuristic utopian world where every aspect of life—birth, death, families, career choices, emotions, even the weather—is strictly controlled in order to create a safe and comfortable community with no fear or violence. Jonas is twelve years old and is looking forward to an important rite of passage: the ceremony in which he, along with all children his age, will be assigned a life's vocation. Jonas is bewildered when he is skipped during the ceremony, but it is because he has been selected for a unique position. Jonas will become the new Receiver, the prestigious and powerful person who holds all the memories of the community. In his lessons with the old Receiver, whom Jonas calls the Giver, Jonas begins learning about the things—memories, emotions, and knowledge—that the community has given up in

favor of peacefulness. At first, these memories are pleasant: images of snow, colors, feelings of love. But then Jonas encounters the darker aspects of human experience—war, death, and pain—and discovers that community members who are "Released" are actually being euthanized. This discovery leads Jonas to escape from the community with his young foster brother Gabriel. In an interestingly ambiguous ending, readers can decide for themselves whether the boys have safely reached "Elsewhere," been intercepted by their community's security forces, or died from hunger and exposure.

Gathering Blue, which a *Publishers Weekly* reviewer hailed as a "dark, prophetic tale with a strong medieval flavor," is a sequel, or companion piece, to *The Giver.* Rather than depicting a technologically advanced society, however, Lowry here describes a technologically primitive world in which, as she states in her author's note, "disorder, savagery, and self-interest" rule. As in *The Giver,* a child is chosen to play a special role in this society. Kira was born with a twisted leg—a condition that would normally have resulted in her being put to death as a baby. But she was somehow allowed to live. Kira sews beautifully, and is chosen to be The Threader, whose duty it is to create the robe of The Singer, a garment that depicts the history of the world and is used in the annual ritual of the Gathering. In this role, however, Kira begins to learn the dark secrets beneath her society's rules and must make a life-altering choice. Many reviewers praised the novel for its sensitive handling of serious themes. Kay Bowes in *Book Report* considered it "thought-provoking" and "challenging," while a *Horn Book* writer observed that it "shares the thematic concerns of *The Giver* . . . [but] adds a layer of questions about the importance of art in creating and, more ominously, controlling community." Ellen Fader, in *School Library Journal,* concluded that "Lowry has once again created a fully-realized world. . . . Readers won't forget these memorable characters or their struggles in an inhospitable world."

Lowry revisited the world of Anastasia and her family with *Zooman Sam.* Anastasia's little brother, Sam (also the hero of *Attaboy, Sam!* and *See You Around, Sam!*), is on the cusp of learning to read. Acquiring the skill will allow him to be someone special, he believes: specifically, the Chief of Wonderfulness. To help him along, his mother makes Sam a special "Zooman Sam" jumpsuit for him to dress up in during Future Job Day at his nursery school—there wasn't enough room on the garment to fit the word "zookeeper." With dreams of being a zookeeper, a special type of job indeed in a room full of kids dreaming of more mundane occupations, Sam finds out that his teacher will let him stand at the head of the circle and tell about a different zoo animal each day for six weeks. With his budding reading skills, Sam is delighted to take on the task and enjoys the attention that comes with it. "Lowry gets everything about Sam just right," wrote Stephanie Zvirin in *Booklist.* Roger Sutton, writing in *Horn Book,* observed that the author "spins interesting variations on her theme," and wraps the book up with "a swell (and well-prepared) surprise."

The title character in *Gooney Bird Greene* is the newest arrival to the second grade and the most eccentric person the other students have ever seen. Leaning toward flamboyant dress (a pair of cowboy boots and pajamas one day, a polka-dot shirt and tutu the next), Gooney Bird is also a master storyteller in a small package. She delights in relating tales of herself and her "absolutely true" adventures of how she flew in from China on a flying carpet, how she got her "diamond earrings" (actually gumball machine trinkets) from a noble prince, and how she got her oddball name. Encouraged by her teacher, Gooney Bird spins out her tales, prompting the other students to create and tell their own stories. In the process, the entire class—and the book's reader—learns important lessons in storytelling and constructing a compelling and believable narrative. GraceAnne A. De-Candido, writing in *Booklist,* called *Gooney Bird Greene* a "laugh-out-loud chapter book," concluding that the character's first appearance is "quite a debut." The book's message and the "cleverly titled stories could spark children's interest in writing their own stories," wrote Janet B. Bair in *School Library Journal.* Critic Peter D. Sieruta, writing in *Horn Book* observed that Gooney Bird is "not always convincing as a character, but she's a fine storyteller, and her message to her classmates—that they, too, have stories to share—is a good one."

In *Silent Boy* Lowry returns again to a more solemn setting with the story of Katy Thatcher, her physician father, and their life in a small-town New England setting during the early part of the twentieth century. Peggy Stoltz, a local girl who helps on the Thatcher farm, is Katy's best friend. Peggy has a brother, Jacob, and a sister, Nell, who works on the farm next to the Thatcher farm. Jacob is considered an "imbecile," or "touched in the head," a gentle thirteen-year-old who never speaks but has a profound ability to handle and communicate with animals. Katy knits together a tenuous companionship with Jacob and begins to sense the wonder in his affinity with animals. Katy has trouble dealing with the realities of country life, with her pending tenth birthday, and with the arrival of a new baby in her family. Nell also expects a baby after a relationship with her em-ployers' son. When Jacob disappears with Nell's unwanted and unnamed infant—and the baby turns up dead—Katy cannot believe the sensitive and gentle boy could commit an act of murder, even one that, in his mind, may have been completely acceptable or even desirable. Jacob is incarcerated in an asylum for the rest of his life, and Katy grows up to become a doctor like her father, reminiscing about Jacob and the tragedy of his life. "Lowry's graceful, lively prose is dense with historical details," remarked Gillian Engberg in *Booklist.* Ellen Fader, writing in *School Library Journal,* noted that "Lowry excels in developing strong and unique characters and in showing Katy's life in a small town that changes around her as the first telephones and auto-mobiles arrive." Lowry's story "balances humor and generosity with the obstacles and injustice of Katy's world," a *Publishers Weekly* reviewer observed, though "Jacob's story ends in a tragedy deftly foreshadowed," remarked a *Kirkus Reviews* critic.

Although Lowry's books have explored a variety of settings and characters, she finds one unifying theme among them. "All of them deal, essentially, with the same general theme: the importance of human connections," she wrote on the *Lois Lowry* home page. Lowry is a grandmother, and has experienced the joys of life as well as its deep tragedies, such as when her fighter-pilot son, Grey, was killed in a plane crash. Lowry recounts her lifetime of remembrances in *Looking Back: A Book of Memories.* More like a visit from a favorite friend than an autobiography, *Looking Back* is "much more intimate and personal than many traditional memoirs," wrote Barbara Scotto in *School Library Journal.* A *Publishers Weekly* reviewer observed that "a compelling and inspirational portrait of the author emerges from these vivid snapshots of life's joyful, sad, and surprising moments."

BIOGRAPHICAL AND CRITICAL SOURCES:

BOOKS

American Women Writers, 2nd edition, St. James Press (Detroit, MI), 2000.

Authors and Artists for Young Adults, Volume 32, Thomson Gale, (Detroit, MI), 2000.

Beacham's Guide to Literature for Young Adults, Beacham Publishing (Osprey, FL), 1990, Volume 4, 1990, Volume 6, 1994.

Chaston, Joel D., *Lois Lowry,* Twayne (New York, NY), 1997.

Children's Literature Review, Thomson Gale (Detroit, MI), Volume 6, 1984, Volume 46, 1997, Volume 72, pp. 192-206.

Dictionary of Literary Biography, Volume 52: *American Writers for Children since 1960: Fiction,* Thomson Gale (Detroit, MI), 1987, pp. 249-261.

Green, Carol Hurd, and Mary Grimley Mason, editors, *American Women Writers,* Volume 5: *Supplement,* Continuum Publishing (New York, NY), 1994.

Lowry, Lois, *Looking Back: A Book of Memories,* Houghton Mifflin (Boston, MA), 1998.

St. James Guide to Young Adult Writers, 2nd edition, St. James Press (Detroit, MI), 1999.

Silvey, Anita, editor, *Children's Books and Their Creators,* Houghton Mifflin (Boston, MA), 1995.

Something about the Author Autobiography Series, Volume 3, Thomson Gale (Detroit, MI), 1986, pp. 131-146.

PERIODICALS

Book, May-June, 2003, review of *Gooney Bird Greene,* p. 31.

Booklist, October 15, 1979, Barbara Elleman, review of *Anastasia Krupnik,* p. 354; April 15, 1980, p. 1206; September 1, 1982, Barbara Elleman, review of *Anastasia at Your Service,* p. 46; September 1, 1987, pp. 66-67; March 1, 1989, p. 1194; March 1, 1990, Ilene Cooper, review of *Your Move, J. P.!,* p. 1345; April 1, 1991, Stephanie Zvirin, review of *Anastasia at This Address,* p. 1564; April 15, 1993, p. 1506; November 1, 1997, Ellen Mandel, review of *Stay!: Keeper's Story,* p. 472; November 1, 1998, Carolyn Phelan, review of *Looking Back,* p. 490; July, 1, 1999, Stephanie Zvirin, review of *Zooman Sam,* p. 1947; September 15, 1999, review of *Looking Back,* p. 254; June 1, 2000, Ilene Cooper, review of *Gathering Blue,* p. 1896; August 2001, Elaine Hanson, review of *Gathering Blue* (audio version), p. 2142; September 1, 2002, GraceAnne A. DeCandido, review of *Gooney Bird Greene,* p. 125; April 15, 2003, Gillian Engberg, review of *The Silent Boy,* p. 1462.

Book Report, May, 1999, review of *Looking Back,* p. 73; January, 2001, Kay Bowes, review of *Gathering Blue,* p. 58.

Books for Keeps, January, 2002, review of *Gathering Blue,* p. 26.

Bulletin of the Center for Children's Books, January, 1980, Zena Sutherland, review of *Anastasia Krupnik,* p. 99; November, 1980, pp. 57-58; January, 1982, p. 90; May, 1984, Zena Sutherland, review of *Anastasia, Ask Your Analyst,* p. 169; December,

1984, p. 71; May, 1985, p. 70; October, 1988, pp. 46-47; March, 1990, Ruth Ann Smith, review of *Your Move, J. P.!,* p. 169; April, 1993, p. 257; September, 1995, Deborah Stevenson, review of *Anastasia, Absolutely,* pp. 20-21; November, 1996, p. 105; January, 1998, Janice Del Negro, review of *Stay!,* p. 165; January, 1999, Janice Del Negro, review of *Looking Back,* p. 174; September, 1999, review of *Zooman Sam,* p. 21.

Catholic Library World, September, 1999, review of *See You Around, Sam,* p. 33.

Children's Bookwatch, March, 1999, review of *Looking Back,* p. 6; December, 1999, review of *Zooman Sam,* p. 4; March, 2001, review of *Looking Back,* p. 8.

Christian Science Monitor, January 14, 1980, Brad Owens, review of *Anastasia Krupnik,* p. B6; March 1, 1985, Lyn Littlfield Hoopes, review of *Us and Uncle Fraud,* p. 65; May 1, 1987, Betsy Hearne, "Families Shaped by Love, Not Convention," pp. B3-B4.

Five Owls, April, 1989, pp. 59-60; September-October, 1993, Gary D. Schmidt, review of *The Giver,* pp. 14-15; March, 2001, review of *Gathering Blue,* p. 92.

Horn Book, August, 1977, Mary M. Burns, review of *A Summer to Die,* p. 451; June, 1978, p. 258; December, 1979, Ann A. Flowers, review of *Anastasia Krupnik,* p. 663; October, 1981, Mary M. Burns, review of *Anastasia Again!,* pp. 535-536; December, 1982, p. 650; June, 1983, p. 304; December, 1983, p. 711; June, 1984, pp. 330-331; September-October, 1985, Ann A. Flowers, review of *Anastasia on Her Own,* pp. 556-557; May-June, 1986, Mary M. Burns, review of *Anastasia Has the Answers,* pp. 327-328; July-August, 1987, Ann A. Flowers, review of *Rabble Starkey,* pp. 463-465; January, 1988, pp. 29-31; May-June, 1989, Mary M. Burns, review of *Number the Stars,* p. 371; March-April, 1990, Ethel R. Twitchell, review of *Your Move, J. P.!,* pp. 201-202; July-August, 1990, pp. 412-421; July-August, 1990, Shirley Haley-James, "Lois Lowry," profile of Lois Lowry; November-December, 1993, Patty Campbell, "The Sand in the Oyster," pp. 717-721; July-August, 1994, Lois Lowry, "Newbery Medal Acceptance," pp. 414-422, Walter Lorraine, "Lois Lowry," pp. 423-426; September-October, 1996, Roger Sutton, review of *See You Around, Sam!,* p. 597; January-February, 1998, Roger Sutton, review of *Stay!,* pp. 76-77; January, 1999, Peter D. Sieruta, review of *Looking Back,* p. 87; September, 1999, Roger Sutton, review of *Zooman Sam,* p. 613; September, 2000, Roger Sutton, review of *Gathering Blue,* p. 573; September-October, 2002, Peter D. Sieruta, review of *Gooney Bird Greene,* pp. 575-577.

Instructor, May, 1999, review of *The Giver,* p. 16; May, 1999, review of *See You Around, Sam,* p. 16; May, 2001, review of *The Giver,* p. 37.

Journal of Youth Services in Libraries, fall, 1996, pp. 39-40, 49.

Junior Bookshelf, August, 1979, Mary Hobbs, review of *A Summer to Die,* pp. 224-225; August, 1980, p. 194.

Kirkus Reviews, April 1, 1986, review of *Anastasia Has the Answers,* pp. 546-547; March 1, 1987, review of *Rabble Starkey,* p. 374; March 15, 1991, review of *Anastasia at This Address,* p. 396; March 1, 1992, p. 326; March 1, 1993, review of *The Giver,* p. 301; October 15, 1997, review of *Stay!,* p. 1584; July 15, 1999, review of *Zooman Sam,* p. 1135; March 15, 2003, review of *The Silent Boy,* p. 472.

New York Times Book Review, February 28, 1982, p. 31; April 11, 1982, p. 27; August 5, 1984, p. 14; September 14, 1986, p. 37; May 21, 1989, Edith Milton, "Escape from Copenhagen," p. 32; October 31, 1993, Karen Ray, review of *The Giver,* p. 26; January 14, 1996, Michael Cart, review of *Anastasia, Absolutely,* p. 23; October 15, 1998, review of *Looking Back,* p. 1534; February 14, 1999, review of *Looking Back,* p. 27; November 19, 2003, Elizabeth Spires, review of *Gathering Blue,* p. 57.

Observer (London, England), October 21, 2001, review of *Gathering Blue,* p. 16.

Publishers Weekly, February 21, 1986, interview with Lowry, pp. 152-153; March 13, 1987, p. 86; November 8, 1985, review of *Switcharound,* p. 60; July 28, 1997, review of *Stay!,* p. 75; August 24, 1998, review of *Looking Back,* p. 58; April 5, 1999, review of *Stay!,* p. 243; September 13, 1999, review of *Zooman Sam,* p. 85; July 31, 2000, review of *Gathering Blue,* p. 96; March 24, 2003, review of *The Silent Boy,* p. 76; March 24, 2003, Ingrid Roper, "Picturing the Turn of the 20th Century," interview with Lowry, p. 77.

Reading Teacher, March, 2001, review of *Gathering Blue,* p. 638.

School Librarian, February, 1995, pp. 31-32.

School Library Journal, May, 1977, Linda R. Silver, review of *A Summer to Die,* pp. 62-63; May, 1978, p. 77; April, 1980, Marilyn Singer, review of *Autumn Street,* pp. 125-126; March, 1981, p. 109; October, 1981, Marilyn Kaye, review of *Anastasia Again!,* p. 144; October, 1983, Kathleen Brachmann, review of *The One Hundredth Thing about Caroline,* p. 160; May, 1984, p. 82; November, 1984, p. 133; August, 1985, p. 68; February, 1986, Maria B. Salvadore, review of *Switcharound,* p. 87; May, 1986, p. 94; September, 1987, Dudley B. Carlson, review of *Anastasia's Chosen Career,* p. 180; August, 1988, Trev Jones, review of *All about Sam,* p. 96; March, 1989, Louise L. Sherman, review of *Number the Stars,* p. 177; January, 1990, p. 9; May, 1992, Marcia Hupp, review of *Attaboy, Sam!,* p. 114; October, 1996, Starr La-Tronica, review of *See You Around, Sam!,* p. 102; October, 1997, Eva Mitnick, review of *Stay!,,* p. 134; September, 1998, Barbara Scotto, review of *Looking Back,* p. 221; September, 1999, review of *Zooman Sam,* p. 193; August, 2000, Ellen Fader, review of *Gathering Blue,* p. 186; May, 2001, review of *Gathering Blue* (audio version), p. 75; November, 2002, Janet B. Bair, review of *Gooney Bird Greene,* pp. 129-130; April, 2003, Ellen Fader, review of *The Silent Boy,* pp. 164-165.

Signal, May, 1980, pp. 119-122.

Voice of Youth Advocates, August, 1985, p. 186; April, 1988, p. 26; August, 1993, p. 167; December, 1995, p. 304; April, 1999, review of *Looking Back,* p. 76; August, 1999, review of *Looking Back,* p. 164; April, 2001, review of *Gathering Blue,* p. 12.

Washington Post Book World, May 9, 1993, p. 15.

ONLINE

Books 'n' Bytes, http://www.booksnbytes.com/ (May 28, 2003), Harried Klausner, review of *Gathering Blue.*

Houghton Mifflin Web site, http://www.houghtonmifflinbooks.com/ (May 28, 2003).

Lois Lowry Web site, http://www.loislowry.com/ (May 28, 2003).

Rambles Web site, http://www.rambles.net/ (May 28, 2003), Donna Scanlon, review of *Gathering Blue.*

*   *   *

LOWRY, Lois Hammersburg
    See LOWRY, Lois

*   *   *

LUCAS, Craig 1951-

PERSONAL: Born April 30, 1951, in Atlanta, GA; son of Charles (a Federal Bureau of Investigation employee) and Eleanor (a painter; maiden name, Altmont) Lucas. *Education:* Boston University, B.A., 1973. *Hobbies and other interests:* Swimming, reading, cooking.

ADDRESSES: Office—Intiman Theatre, Seattle Center, 201 Mercer St., Seattle, WA 98109. *Agent*—Peter Franklin, William Morris Agency, 1350 Avenue of the Americas, New York, NY 10019.

CAREER: Writer. Intiman Theatre, Seattle, WA, associate artistic director. Actor in stage productions; chorus singer in Broadway musicals, including *Shenandoah,* 1975, *Rex,* 1976, *On the Twentieth Century,* 1978, and *Sweeney Todd,* 1979. Playwright-in-residence, Seattle Repertory Theatre, 1998.

MEMBER: PEN, Amnesty International, Lamda Legal Defense League.

AWARDS, HONORS: Guggenheim fellowship, 1984; George and Elizabeth Marton Award for Playwriting, 1984, Los Angeles Drama Critics Award, 1985, and DramaLogue Award for best play, 1985, all for *Blue Window;* award for best musical from Burns Mantle Theatre Yearbook, 1987, for *Three Postcards;* Rockefeller Bellagio fellow, 1988; Rockefeller grant, 1988; Outer Critics Circle Award, Obie Award for best play from *Village Voice,* and Tony Award nomination for best play, all 1990, all for *Prelude to a Kiss;* Audience Award for best dramatic film, Sundance Film Festival, 1990, for *Longtime Companion;* Yaddo Colony fellow, 1994; member of Sundance Playwrights Retreat, 2000; Obie Award for direction, 2001, for *Save or Destroyed;* New York Film Critics' Circle Award for best screenplay, 2003, for *The Secret Lives of Dentists*; PEN/Laura Pels Foundation Award for mid-career playwrights, PEN American Center, 2003; Obie Award for best American play, *Village Voice,* 2004, for *Small Tragedy;* Obie Award nomination for best book of a musical, 2005, for *The Light in the Piazza.*

WRITINGS:

STAGE PRODUCTIONS

(With Stephen Sondheim) *Marry Me a Little* (one-act musical), 1980, produced Off-Broadway, 1981.

Missing Persons (two-act), produced Off-Off-Broadway, 1981.

Alec Wilder: Clues to a Life (two-act; adapted from Alec Wilder's book *Letters I Never Mailed*), produced Off-Broadway, 1982.

Reckless (two-act; also see below), produced Off-Broadway, 1983, revised version produced Off-Broadway, 1988.

Blue Window (one-act; also see below), produced Off-Broadway, 1984.

Prelude to a Kiss (two-act; produced 1988, revised version produced Off-Broadway, 1990), New American Library/Dutton (New York, NY), 1991, published as *A Prelude to a Kiss and Other Plays* (contains *Missing Persons* and *Three Postcards*), Theatre Communications Group (New York, NY), 2000.

Reckless [and] *Blue Window: Two Plays,* Theatre Communications Group (New York, NY), 1989; revived by Manhattan Theater Club at the Biltmore Theater (New York, NY), 2004.

Credo, produced in New York, NY, 1995.

God's Heart, produced in Providence, RI, at the Trinity Repertory Company, 1995; produced in New York, NY, at the Lincoln Center, 1997.

(With Craig Carnelia) *Three Postcards* (musical; produced in 1987), Dramatists Play Service (New York, NY), 1995.

What I Meant Was: New Plays and Selected One-Acts (contains *The Dying Gaul, What I Meant Was, Unmemorable, Throwing Your Voice, Grief, The Boom Box, Bad Dream, If Columbus Does Not Figure In Your Travel Plans, Boyfriend Riff, Credo, God's Heart,* and *Drugs in America*), Theatre Communications Group (New York, NY), 1999.

The Dying Gaul (also see below), produced in Glasgow, Scotland, 1998, produced Off-Broadway, 1998.

Strangers, produced Off-Broadway at the Vineyard Theater, 2000.

(Director; coauthor with David Schuler) *This Thing of Darkness,* Atlantic Theater Company, 2002.

(With Adam Guettel) *The Light in the Piazza* (musical; based on the novel by Elizabeth Spencer), produced in Seattle, WA, at Intiman Theatre, 2003; produced in New York, NY, at the Vivian Beaumont Theater in Lincoln Center, 2005.

Small Tragedy, produced by Playwrights Horizons in New York, 2004.

Miss Julie (adapted from the play by August Strindberg), produced in New York, NY, at the Rattlesticks Playwrights Theater, 2005.

Also author, with David Schulner, of play *Savage Light.* Author of musical, *Queen.*

OTHER

(With Gerald Busby) *Orpheus in Love* (music composition; includes *"Sleep Song," "Intentional Walk,"* and *"Little Fingers"*), 1990.

Longtime Companion (screenplay; adapted from his play), Samuel Goldwyn, 1990.

Prelude to a Kiss (screenplay; adapted from his play), Twentieth Century-Fox, 1992.

Bad Dream (radio play), WBAI, 1992.

Reckless (screenplay; adapted from his play), Samuel Goldwyn, 1995.

The Secret Lives of Dentists (screenplay, based on Jane Smiley's novella The Age of Grief), Ready Made Film, 2003.

Also author of screenplay adaptation of Anne Tyler's *Saint Maybe.*

ADAPTATIONS: Blue Window was filmed and broadcast on *American Playhouse,* PBS-TV, 1987.

WORK IN PROGRESS: Adapting *The Nutcracker* for the Turner Network; a theatrical adaptation of the film *Don Juan DeMarco;* an adaptation of *The Mayor of Castro Street* for HBO.

SIDELIGHTS: Craig Lucas has gained recognition as one of the American stage's more talented and refreshing writers of recent years. As Patti Capel Swartz wrote in *Gay and Lesbian Literature,* "AIDS has greatly affected Lucas's work and his life, infusing his work with the anguish of loss that comes from the deaths of friends and lovers. . . . Lucas puts himself on the line as an openly gay man whose social and political convictions are not separate from his vision as an artist."

Lucas studied theater and creative writing at Boston University, where he befriended poet Anne Sexton. Throughout the early 1970s Sexton served as Lucas's mentor, encouraging him to develop his talents as a playwright. At Sexton's recommendation, Lucas moved to New York City in 1973 and worked menial jobs while simultaneously performing as a chorus member in various Broadway productions, including the long-running musicals *Shenandoah* and *On the Twentieth Century.* Despite maintaining a hectic schedule, Lucas also managed to continue writing. In 1980, while Lucas was appearing in Stephen Sondheim's musical *Sweeney Todd,* a friend submitted one of his unfinished works to Norman Rene, artistic director of the Production Company, which performed Off-Off-Broadway. Rene was impressed with Lucas's play, and he agreed to produce it upon its completion.

Rene also asked Lucas to develop a modest production for the Production Company's after-hours cabaret. Lucas responded with *Marry Me a Little,* a two-performer work structured around various songs by Sondheim. This piece, which concerns two lonely apartment neighbors (who never meet), was praised by *New York Times* contributor John S. Wilson as "unusually moving."

In 1981 the Production Company presented *Missing Persons,* Lucas's play that had earlier impressed Norman Rene when he read it as a work in progress. *Missing Persons* is a grim comedy about an entomologist plagued by all manner of neuroses. *Village Voice* contributor Michael Feingold described the work as one of "wit, inventiveness, and . . . sharp-eyed honesty."

Dismayed by the generally lukewarm reception accorded *Missing Persons,* Lucas worked on only one more production, *Alec Wilder: Clues to a Life,* before withdrawing from playwriting for nearly a year. He then returned to the stage with *Reckless,* an offbeat comedy about a woman who eludes an assassin hired by her husband and enters a bizarre world in which the wholesome nature of bourgeois America is rendered pathetic and deranged. In this strange land, where every day is Christmas and all communities are named Springfield, the heroine is a contestant on a game show, observes two killings, and is eventually taken in by a doctor and his disabled wife. Writing in *Contemporary Dramatists,* Alan Strachan called *Reckless* "an unusual Christmas fable" that eventually leads to "self-discovery and maturity." Feingold, in a *Village Voice* review, noted that some portions of the play are "amusing" and some are "upsetting." In 1988 Lucas revised *Reckless,* stripping it of an espionage subplot and generally diminishing its wilder aspects. This new production readily gained recognition as a grim exposé of materialist, media-mad America, and inspired further consideration of Lucas as one of the American stage's more provocative writers.

Lucas realized his first substantial success as a playwright with *Blue Window,* about the banal, alienating nature of modern life. Here several individuals—including a lesbian couple, a composer, and a skydiving teacher—prepare for, attend, and then depart from a party. This seemingly uncomplicated work, which begins as a comedy, then shifts into uneasy drama before turning tragic, won praise as a subtle, incisive portrait of people failing to connect. *New York* critic John Simon deemed Lucas "a canny manipulator of words." Strachan described *Blue Window* as "a play of dazzling technical achievement . . . *Blue Window* combines social comedy with a melancholy substrain to potent effect."

The musical *Three Postcards,* Lucas's next work, also explores the mundane interactions of shallow, lonely people. The lone characters in the play, which is set in a trendy restaurant, are the house pianist, a waiter, and a trio of neurotic women customers. Throughout much of the play's brief duration—just under ninety minutes—the characters, in often spare, disconnected speech, reveal their boredom and isolation. *Time* contributor William A. Henry described *Three Postcards* as "poignant," and he acknowledged the work as one of "serene . . . simplicity."

Lucas next wrote *Prelude to a Kiss,* a dreamy, romantic play about a relationship that undergoes a rather extraordinary change. In this play two New Yorkers, Peter and Rita, meet and marry. Immediately Peter discerns some remarkable changes in his wife's behavior. He learns that she has somehow become trapped within the body of a mortally ill old man whom she kissed at her wedding. Although Rita's condition alters significantly, the husband continues to bestow his love and affection. "Love makes Peter resourceful enough to engineer a way by which to regain Rita's soul," wrote Strachan, "and the play ends with their reunion."

Prelude to A Kiss is probably Lucas's most acclaimed work. Clive Barnes, writing in the *New York Post,* found the play "unquestionably Lucas' most successful, tightly organized and best written," and *New York Times* contributor Frank Rich, who saw the play as indirectly about Acquired Immune Deficiency Syndrome (AIDS), deemed it "a powerful, genuine fairy tale." The production won Outer Critics Circle and Obie awards for best play.

Although probably best known for his stage work, Lucas also won praise as the author of *Longtime Companion,* director Rene's film about a group of gay friends. The film begins in 1981 on the day when the *New York Times* first reported on the AIDS virus, which attacks the human immune system and leaves its victims susceptible to a variety of fatal diseases. The movie ends eight years later after several of the protagonists have succumbed to AIDS. In the film's most wrenching portions, a dying man is tended—fed, washed, and clothed—by his lover. By film's end, both men are among the AIDS dead.

Longtime Companion drew strongly favorable reviews. *Rolling Stone* contributor Peter Travers proclaimed it a "vital" work, and David Ansen, writing in *Newsweek,* deemed it "remarkable." Kevin Thomas, in a *Los Angeles Times* review, described it as "an illuminating, deeply moving experience." For Lucas, who had explained to Jan Hoffman in *Village Voice* that he longed to render homosexuals as "like everyone else," the film constituted a considerable success.

In 1995 Lucas's companion Tim Melester died from complications of AIDS. While caring for his friend during the final months of his decline, Craig experienced what he described to Sarah Schulman in *American Theatre* as "the humiliations and brutality of hospitals and people's disgust and dismissal" of AIDS victims. The pain of illness and loss, the unfair treatment by society, and the role of drugs in getting well and killing pain were all key components in Lucas's play *God's Heart.* In it, a well-to-do white couple, a crack dealer's lookout, and two lesbians—one of them terminally ill—meet in a common dream. "*God's Heart* is an outcry against the racial, class and gender division in American society, but the let's-pretend premise seems too farfetched for us to take its heartache entirely seriously," commented Lawson Taitte in the *Dallas Morning News.* A mixed reaction also came from *Variety* reviewer Robert L. Daniels, who applauded the "freshness and vitality" in *God's Heart* but found that the characters failed to "merge with clarity" in the "meandering" story.

Lucas remarked to Schulman, "none of the ugliness in the play could match some of the responses it received" from critics. He acknowledged that the play was full of weighty themes, and commented, "Trying to let all of these things steep and boil in one play did not allow me to write something elegant and neat. If I was going to call it *God's Heart,* it had to be big and uncontainable, messy and confusing and upsetting and also hopeful, with glimpses of luminous beauty. I wanted all the hope and dreams to match the frustrations and pain. I wanted people to think differently about drugs, about class, about computers. The play was meant to be ugly."

Stronger reviews came for *The Dying Gaul,* a play that revolved around a love triangle with a quirky twist. In it, Robert, a gay playwright, becomes romantically involved with bisexual film producer Jeffrey. Jeffrey is willing to produce Robert's play—as long as it is altered to feature heterosexual characters so that it will be more palatable to the general public. Jeffrey's wife Elaine has long known of and accepted her husband's dalliances, but something about his affair with Robert is more than she can tolerate. Using Internet chat rooms that she knows Robert frequents, she strikes up her own relationship with him under an assumed identity. The central theme, in the opinion of *Boston Herald* writer Terry Byrne, is "control and what that means to different people. The character who begins with the least amount of power, Elaine, the wife of a studio executive, ends up with the most power." Commenting on the use of the Internet as an important plot device, *Buffalo News* contributor Michael Kuchwara wrote, "In 'The Dying Gaul,' playwright Craig Lucas has taken one of the oldest stories in the book—the temptations of Tinseltown—and turned it into a cool and cerebral piece of cyber-sexual theater. . . . In an odd way, the computer becomes the play's fifth character, giving 'The Dying Gaul' a strange, haunting quality that glows stronger than any computer screen."

Strangers, Lucas's next play, opens on an airplane cruising from Philadelphia to Seattle. Hush, a middle-aged man, finds himself seated next to Linda, who chatters incessantly. Although Linda's talk at first seems very banal, over the course of their conversation she reveals a sordid life of drug abuse, cruelty, and exploitation. Hush's own strange past then comes out; he has spent fifteen years in prison for kidnapping a young woman and locking her in a box for months. "Hush and Linda exchange jazzy riffs. . . . [as] they try to determine who has acted more cruelly, and who is in greater need of redemption. A cloud of desperation and dread wafts over the stage," reported Brendan Lemon in *Financial Times.* Eventually, the characters end up in a remote cabin together for a strange denoument. Discussing the play with Schulman, Lucas stated that it is meant to explore the shame that remains and transforms the lives of those who have been punished or otherwise hurt. He remarked that in the play, he "tried finding a way into those ideas that didn't drive me (and the audience) away—opening the door gently enough and walking along the path with a measure of safety so that one would be too far down the path to be able to flee or deny what one was seeing and feeling."

BIOGRAPHICAL AND CRITICAL SOURCES:

BOOKS

Contemporary Dramatists, 6th edition, St. James Press (Detroit, MI), 1999.

Contemporary Literary Criticism, Volume 64, Thomson Gale (Detroit, MI), 1991.

Gay and Lesbian Literature, Volume 2, St. James Press (Detroit, MI), 1998.

PERIODICALS

Advocate, December 26, 1995, Emanuel Levy, review of *Reckless,* p. 56; May 27, 1997, Dick Scanlan, review of *God's Heart,* p. 89; July 7, 1998, Don Shewey, review of *The Dying Gaul,* p. 59; November 21, 2000, Don Shewey, review of *Stranger,* p. 96.

American Theatre, January, 2001, Sarah Schulman, "Eyes Wide Open," p. 36.

Atlanta Journal-Constitution, July 14, 2000, Wendell Brock, review of *The Dying Gaul,* p. Q4.

Back Stage, November 27, 1992, Martin Schaeffer, review of *Marry Me a Little,* p. 44; January 1, 1993, Irene Backalenick, review of *Orpheus in Love,* p. 40; November 18, 1994, Jerry Tallmer, "Songwriter Craig Carnelia Delivers New 'Postcards,'" p. 13; February 10, 1995, William Stevenson, review of *Missing Persons,* p. 38; February 16, 1996, William Stevenson, "Craig Lucas: A New Partnership for a New 'Blue Window,'" p. 19, David Sheward, review of *Blue Window,* p. 48; April 11, 1997, David Sheward, review of *God's Heart,* p. 38; June 5, 1998, Irene Backalenick, review of *The Dying Gaul,* p. 40; November 17, 2000, Elias Stimac, review of *Restless,* p. 38.

Back Stage West, May 16, 1996, Matthew Surrence, review of *Missing Persons,* p. 11; December 19, 1996, Les Spindle, review of *Blue Window,* p. 10; October 1, 1998, Edward Shapiro, review of *Blue Window,* p. 13; October 29, 1998, Les Spindle, review of *Reckless,* p. 14.

Bomb, fall, 1996.

Boston Herald, April 14, 2000, Terry Byrne, review of *The Dying Gaul,* p. 8.

Buffalo News, February 13, 1996, Michael Kuchwara, review of *Blue Window,* p. E12; June 16, 1998, Michael Kuchwara, review of *The Dying Gaul,* p. C6; January 13, 1999, Terry Doran, review of *Prelude to a Kiss,* p. D8; May 12, 2000, Richard Huntington, review of *The Dying Gaul,* p. G25.

Christian Science Monitor, December 8, 1994, Frank Scheck, review of *Three Postcards,* p. 11.

Commonweal, February 12, 1993, Gerald Weales, review of *Orpheus in Love,* p. 16.

Contra Costa Times, October 7, 2000, Pat Craig, review of *Prelude to a Kiss,* p. D3; January 22, 2001, Pat Craig, review of *Prelude to a Kiss,* p. D3.

Dallas Morning News, December 15, 1996, Lawson Taitte, review of *Reckless,* p. C1; April 7, 1997, Lawson Taitte, review of *God's Heart,* p. A21; October 20, 1998, Lawson Taitte, review of *The Dying Gaul,* p. A23.

Denver Business Journal, September 29, 2000, Brad Smith, review of *Missing Persons,* p. 31A.

Entertainment Weekly, December 1, 1995, Bruce Fretts, review of *Reckless,* p. 50; May 17, 1996, Michael Sauter, review of *Reckless,* p. 71.

Films in Review, September-October, 1992, Maria Garcia, review of *Prelude to a Kiss,* p. 340.

Financial Times, October 18, 2000, Brendan Lemon, review of *Stranger,* p. 15.

Harper's Bazaar, August, 1992, Ross Wetzsteon, "Try a Little Tenderness," p. 40.

Houston Chronicle, October 18, 1999, Everett Evans, review of *The Dying Gaul,* p. 1.

Knight-Ridder/Tribune News Service, November 24, 2000, Jay Boyar, review of *Prelude to a Kiss,* p. K3452.

Los Angeles Times, May 17, 1990; June 5, 1990; February 27, 1994; December 20, 1996, Jana J. Monji, review of *Blue Window,* p. 6; March 9, 1999, T.H. McCulloh, review of *Blue Window,* p. 6.

Milwaukee Journal Sentinel, September 12, 2000, Damien Jaques, review of *The Dying Gaul,* p. 6.

National Review, August 17, 1992, John Simon, review of *Prelude to a Kiss,* p. 45.

New Leader, December 19, 1994, Stefan Kanfer, review of *Three Postcards,* p. 39.

New Republic, October 31, 1988, pp. 28-29; August 27, 1992, Stanley Kauffman, review of *Prelude to a Kiss,* p. 34; June 19, 1995, Robert Brustein, review of *God's Heart,* p. 33.

Newsweek, May 14, 1990; July 20, 1992, David Ansen, review of *Prelude to a Kiss,* p. 69.

New York, July 30, 1984, p. 53; October 10, 1988, pp. 75, 78; March 26, 1990, pp. 87-88; May 14, 1990, pp. 125-126; September 30, 1991, John Leonard, review of *Longtime Companion,* p. 64; January 4, 1993, John Simon, review of *Orpheus in Love,* p. 51; February 13, 1995, John Simon, review of *Missing Persons,* p. 103; June 22, 1998, John Simon, review of *The Dying Gaul,* p. 60; October 30, 2000, John Simon, review of *Stranger,* p. 97.

New Yorker, September 3, 1984, pp. 78, 80; October 10, 1988, p. 85; March 26, 1990, p. 74; July 27, 1992, Michael Sragow, review of *Prelude to a Kiss,* p. 55; February 19, 1996, John Simon, review of *Blue Window,* p. 61.

New York Post, May 15, 1987; September 26, 1988; March 15, 1990; May 2, 1990.

New York Times, November 2, 1980; May 21, 1981; June 3, 1984; May 15, 1987, p. C3; May 24, 1987; June 1, 1987, p. C16; September 26, 1988, pp. C19, C22; October 29, 1988; June 25, 1989; March 11, 1990; March 15, 1990, pp. C15, C18; March 18, 1990; May 2, 1990, p. C15; May 11, 1990; June 24, 1990, p. H1; November 17, 1994, Ben Brantley, review of *Three Postcards,* p. B3; February 2, 1995, Ben Brantley, review of *Missing Persons,* p. B3; November 17, 1995, Stephen Holden, review of *Reckless,* p. B3; February 7, 1996, Vincent Canby, review of *Blue Window,* p. B3; April 7, 1997, Ben Brantley, review of *God's Heart,* p. B2; June 8, 1997, Peter Marks, review of *What I Meant Was: New Plays and Selected One-Acts,* p. 16; June 21, 1998, Vincent Canby, review of *The Dying Gaul,* p. AR4; September 20, 1998, Steven Drukman, review of *The Dying Gaul,* p. AR4; October 18, 2000, Ben Brantley, review of *Stranger,* p. E1; July 11, 2001, Bruce Weber, review of *Blue Window,* p. E1.

North American Review, March/April, 1996, review of *God's Heart,* pp. 44-48.

Observer (London, England), March 15, 1998, Nicky Agate, review of *The Dying Gaul,* p. 9.

People, July 27, 1992, Joanne Kaufman, review of *Prelude to a Kiss,* p. 16.

Rolling Stone, May 31, 1990.

San Francisco Chronicle, April 24, 1996, Ruth Stein, review of *Missing Persons,* p. E1; May 3, 1996, Steven Winn, review of *Missing Persons,* p. D5; June 13, 2001, Robert Hurwitt, review of *The Dying Gaul,* p. E4.

Sunday Times (London), March 23, 1998, Neil Cooper, review of *The Dying Gaul,* p. 20; March 29, 1998, John Peter, review of *The Dying Gaul,* p. 22.

Spectator, February 14, 1998, Sheridan Morley, review of *Blue Window,* p. 38.

Time, May 25, 1987, p. 71; July 20, 1992, Richard Corliss, review of *Prelude to a Kiss,* p. 78.

Variety, July 13, 1992, Todd McCarthy, review of *Prelude to a Kiss,* p. 41; November 21, 1994, Greg Evans, review of *Three Postcards,* p. 44; February 13, 1995, Greg Evans, review of *Missing Persons,* p. 58; May 15, 1995, Markland Taylor, review of *God's Heart,* p. 235; September 25, 1995, Leonard Klady, review of *Reckless,* p. 95; February 12, 1996, Jeremy Gerard, review of *Blue Window,* p. 92; April 14, 1997, Robert L. Daniels, review of *God's Heart,* p. 100; June 8, 1998, Robert L. Daniels, review of *The Dying Gaul,* p. 81; October 23, 2000, Charles Isherwood, review of *Stranger,* p. 59.

Village Voice, May 27, 1981; June 7, 1983; May 15, 1990; February 24, 1996.

Wall Street Journal, June 9, 1996, Donald Lyons, review of *Blue Window,* p. A12; June 3, 1998, Donald Lyons, review of *The Dying Gaul,* p. A16.

Washington Post, May 25, 1990; February 9, 2000, Lloyd Rose, review of *The Dying Gaul,* p. C1.

ONLINE

Stage & Screen, http://www.stagenscreen.com/ (September 26, 2001), Mark Glubke, "Meet Craig Lucas" (interview).

LUDLUM, Robert 1927-2001
(Jonathan Ryder, Michael Shepherd)

PERSONAL: Born May 25, 1927, in New York, NY; died of a heart attack, March 12, 2001, in Naples, FL; son of George Hartford (a businessman) and Margaret (Wadsworth) Ludlum; married Mary Ryducha (an actress), March 31, 1951 (died, 1996); married second wife, Karen, 1997; children (first marriage): Michael, Jonathan, Glynis. *Education:* Wesleyan University, B.A., 1951. *Politics:* Independent.

CAREER: Writer, 1971-2001. Actor on Broadway and on television, 1952-60; North Jersey Playhouse, Fort Lee, NJ, producer, 1957-60; producer in New York, NY, 1960-69; Playhouse-on-the-Mall, Paramus, NJ, producer, 1960-70. *Military service:* U.S. Marine Corps, 1944-46.

MEMBER: Authors Guild, Authors League of America, American Federation of Television and Radio Artists, Screen Actors Guild.

AWARDS, HONORS: New England Professor of Drama Award, 1951; awards and grants from American National Theatre and Academy, 1959, and from Actors' Equity Association and William C. Whitney Foundation, 1960; Scroll of Achievement, American National Theatre and Academy, 1960.

WRITINGS:

The Scarlatti Inheritance, World Publishing (New York, NY), 1971, reprinted, Armchair Detective Library (New York, NY), 1990.
The Osterman Weekend, World Publishing (New York, NY), 1972, reprinted, Armchair Detective Library (New York, NY), 1991.
The Matlock Paper, Dial (New York, NY), 1973.
(Under pseudonym Jonathan Ryder) *Trevayne,* Delacorte (New York, NY), 1973.
(Under pseudonym Jonathan Ryder) *The Cry of the Halidon,* Delacorte (New York, NY), 1974.
The Rhinemann Exchange, Dial (New York, NY), 1974.
(Under pseudonym Michael Shepherd) *The Road to Gandolfo,* Dial (New York, NY), 1975, reprinted under name Robert Ludlum, Bantam (New York, NY), 1982.
The Gemini Contenders, Dial (New York, NY), 1976.
The Chancellor Manuscript, Dial (New York, NY), 1977.

The Holcroft Covenant, Richard Marek, 1978.
The Matarese Circle, Richard Marek, 1979.
The Bourne Identity, Richard Marek, 1980.
The Parsifal Mosaic, Random House (New York, NY), 1982.
The Aquitaine Progression, Random House (New York, NY), 1984.
The Bourne Supremacy, Random House (New York, NY), 1986.
The Icarus Agenda, Random House (New York, NY), 1988.
The Bourne Ultimatum, Random House (New York, NY), 1990.
The Road to Omaha, Random House (New York, NY), 1992.
The Scorpio Illusion, Bantam (New York, NY), 1993.
Three Complete Novels: The Ludlum Triad, Wings Books, 1994.
The Apocalypse Watch, Bantam (New York, NY), 1995.
The Matarese Countdown, Bantam (New York, NY), 1997.
(With Gayle Lynds) *Robert Ludlum's The Hades Factor* (first novel in "Covert-One" series), St. Martin's Press (New York, NY), 2000.
The Prometheus Deception, St. Martin's Press (New York, NY), 2000.
(With Philip Shelby) *Robert Ludlum's The Cassandra Compact* (second novel in "Covert-One" series), St. Martin's Press (New York, NY), 2001.
The Sigma Protocol, St. Martin's Press (New York, NY), 2001.
The Janson Directive, St. Martin's Press (New York, NY), 2002.
(With Gayle Lynds) *Robert Ludlum's The Paris Option* (third novel in "Covert-One" series), St. Martin's Press (New York, NY), 2002.
The Tristan Betrayal, St. Martin's Press (New York, NY), 2003.
(With Gayle Lynds) *Robert Ludlum's The Altman Code* (fourth novel in the "Covert-One" series), St. Martin's Press (New York, NY), 2003.

ADAPTATIONS: The Rhinemann Exchange was adapted as a television miniseries by NBC, 1977; *The Osterman Weekend* was filmed by EMI, 1980; *The Holcroft Covenant,* directed by John Frankenheimer and starring Michael Caine, was filmed in 1985; *The Bourne Supremacy,* read by Michael Prichard, was released on cassette tape by Books on Tape, 1986; an abridged version of *The Bourne Identity,* read by Darren McGavin, was released on cassette tape by Bantam, 1987, and a television film of this title, written by Carol Sobieski, directed by Roger Young, and starring Richard Chamberlain, was broadcast in 1988; *The Icarus*

Agenda, read by Prichard, was released on cassette by Books on Tape, 1988; *The Bourne Ultimatum,* read by Prichard, was released on cassette by Books on Tape, 1990; *The Road to Omaha,* read by Joseph Campanella, was released by Random House, 1992; *The Scarlatti Inheritance* was filmed by Universal Pictures; a feature film of *The Bourne Identity,* with a screenplay by Tony Gilroy and William Blake Herron, directed by Doug Liman, and starring Matt Damon, was released by Universal Pictures in 2002; *The Bourne Supremacy,* with screenplay by Gilroy and Brian Helgeland, directed by Paul Greengrass, and starring Damon, was released by Universal in 2004. Eric Van Lustbader has authored another book featuring the Bourne character, *The Bourne Legacy,* published by St. Martin's Press in 2004.

SIDELIGHTS: Suspense novelist Robert Ludlum "has his share of unkind critics who complain of implausible plots, leaden prose, and, as a caustic reviewer once sneered, an absence of 'redeeming literary values to balance the vulgar sensationalism,'" Susan Baxter and Mark Nichols noted in *Maclean's.* "But harsh critical words have not prevented Robert Ludlum . . . from becoming one of the most widely read and wealthiest authors in the world." In fact, with sales of his books averaging 5.5 million copies each, Ludlum was "one of the most popular . . . authors [writing] in the English language," Baxter and Nichols concluded.

Authorship came as a second career for Ludlum. Having grown up in a well-to-do family in the suburbs of New York City, he left home as a teenager to pursue an acting career, then served in the Marines during World War II before going to college to study fine arts. He worked as an actor doing theater, television films, and commercial voice-overs and found success as a producer before writing his first published novel at age forty-two—he had written one novel while in his teens, but the manuscript disappeared one night when he was carousing in San Francisco. "Ludlum's acting career accustomed him to rude reviews, and he often said that his theatrical training helped him to create the complicated plots which marked his writing," observed an obituary writer in *Times* of London. His most notable theatrical production, Bill Manhoff's *The Owl and the Pussycat,* featured then-unknown actor Alan Alda, who later gained fame for his role in the television series, *MASH.* The play was performed at Playhouse-on-the-Mall in Paramus, New Jersey, the country's first theater in a shopping center, which Ludlum opened in 1960. After serving as producer at the Playhouse for ten years, Ludlum found himself bored and frustrated with the pressures of theater work. Finally, he gave in to his wife's admonition to try his hand at writing.

The Scarlatti Inheritance, Ludlum's first novel, was written around an old story idea and outline, drafted years earlier and finally fleshed out when he left the theater. Based on Ludlum's curiosity at the wealth of one group of Germans during that country's economic collapse and skyrocketing inflation following World War I, *The Scarlatti Inheritance* follows several financiers, including some Americans, who fund Hitler's Third Reich. The book set the pattern for Ludlum's career: the story of espionage and corruption became a best-seller. Criticism of *The Scarlatti Inheritance* also foreshadowed that of future works. In *Dictionary of Literary Biography Yearbook: 1982,* Patricia L. Skarda described the novel as having a "somewhat erratic pace and occasionally melodramatic characterizations" but being nonetheless "a thrilling, compelling tale"—pronouncements typical of each of Ludlum's novels.

In his next work, *The Osterman Weekend,* a television reporter is convinced by the CIA that his friends are involved in a conspiracy to control the world economy and agrees to gather evidence against them, but finds himself in over his head when his wife and children are threatened. Though several reviewers considered the book's ending disappointing, William B. Hill, writing in *Best Sellers,* noted, "If the ending is a bit weak, it is chiefly because it lets the rider down off a very high horse." Skarda pointed out that the story "exposes the inadequacies of American intelligence operations and our deepest fears that our friends cannot be trusted." Government agents again use a civilian as an investigator in a situation beyond his expertise in *The Matlock Paper.* Professor Matlock is pushed "into an untenable and dangerous situation" while snooping around campus for information on a group of crime bosses, Kelly J. Fitzpatrick related in *Best Sellers.* "The climax is effective," Fitzpatrick wrote, "and leaves the reader wondering, 'Can it be so?'" Newgate Callendar remarked in *New York Times Book Review,* "The basic situation is unreal—indeed, it's unbelievable—but a good writer can make the reader suspend his disbelief, and Ludlum is a good writer."

Trevayne and *The Cry of the Halidon,* both written under the pseudonym Jonathan Ryder, feature protagonists who discover they were hired not for their skills, but in hopes that they would be unable to uncover the truth about their employers. Andrew Trevayne, appointed to investigate spending by the U.S. Defense Department, uncovers a company so powerful that even the president of the United States is controlled by it. "There is no doubt that big business exerts an inordinate amount of pressure," Callendar observer in a *New York Times Book Review.* "But how much pressure? Who is really running the country?" Reviewing *The Cry of the Halidon,* in which a young geologist is sent to Jamaica to conduct an industrial survey and winds up in the crossfire of British Intelligence, the corporation that hired him, and various underground factions, Callendar called Ludlum's writing style "rather crude and obvious," and commented that Ludlum "is not very good at suggesting real characters, and his hero is a cutout composite of a number of sources." A reviewer for *Publishers Weekly* found that, early on in *The Cry of the Halidon,* "cleverness ceases to look like a virtue and becomes an irritant. If the writing were as rich or subtle as the plot is involved the reader might more happily stay the course . . . , but the writing is in fact rather bare."

Ludlum's final pseudonymous offering—this time writing as Michael Shepherd—was *The Road to Gandolfo,* "a strange, lurching amalgam of thriller and fantasy," in the opinion of *Library Journal* contributor Henri C. Veit. Involving the pope, the Mafia, and the U.S. Army, the book is intended to be funny, but falls short, Veit continued. A *Publishers Weekly* reviewer similarly noted that the book "comes crammed with zaniness and playful characters, but, unhappily, neither asset produces comedy or the black humor indictment of the military mind the author intended."

The Rhinemann Exchange contains "one extremely ingenious plot gimmick," according to *New York Times Book Review*'s Callendar, in which the United States and Germany arrange a trade—industrial diamonds for Germany, a weapons guidance system for the United States. Despite the author's "commonplace and vulgar style apparently much relished by his vast audience," Veit predicted in a *Library Journal* piece that the book would be a success. In a critique of the audio version of *The Rhinemann Exchange,* a *Publishers Weekly* contributor believed Ludlum fans "will find exactly what they're looking for—in a format already quite familiar." A secret with devastating consequences, described by Irma Pascal Heldman in *New York Times Book Review* as "absolutely within the realms of authenticity and fascinating to contemplate," is the key to *The Gemini Contenders.* Twin brothers, compelled by their father's deathbed wish to find a hidden vault containing a volatile document, unleash the secret on the world. Despite criticizing the plot, characters, and period detail of *The Gemini Contenders,* reviewer T.J. Binyon commented in *Times Literary Supplement* that Ludlum "has the ability to tell a story in such a way as to keep even the fastidious reader unwillingly absorbed."

In *The Chancellor Manuscript,* Ludlum returned to remaking history as he had in *The Scarlatti Inheritance.* FBI director J. Edgar Hoover's death is found to be an assassination, not the result of natural causes as was previously believed. The murder was carried out to prevent Hoover from releasing his secret files, which, *Christian Science Monitor*'s Barbara Phillips noted, "contain enough damaging information to ruin the lives of every man, woman and child in the nation." A group of prominent citizens join forces to retrieve the files but find half have already been stolen. An unsuspecting decoy is deployed, as in many other Ludlum stories, to lead the group to the thieves. The message of *The Chancellor Manuscript* is familiar to Ludlum fans, as the book "seems to justify our worst nightmares of what really goes on in the so-called Intelligence Community in Washington," Richard Freedman remarked in *New York Times Book Review.*

The Bourne Identity, which introduces a trilogy of books, follows Jason Bourne, a spy who awakens in a doctor's office with amnesia; the story is played out as a remarkable number of killers and organizations attempt to finish Bourne off before he realizes his true identity. "Some of Mr. Ludlum's previous novels were so convoluted they should have been packaged with bags of bread crumbs to help readers keep track of the plot lines," Peter Andrews mused in *New York Times Book Review.* "But *The Bourne Identity* is a Ludlum story at its most severely plotted, and for me its most effective." The second volume, *The Bourne Supremacy,* forces Bourne to face his past when his wife is kidnapped. The final story in the "Bourne" trilogy, *The Bourne Ultimatum,* finds Bourne drawn into one last battle with his arch-enemy, the Jackal. *Los Angeles Times Book Review*'s Don G. Campbell praised the third "Bourne" book as an example of "how it *should* be done," concluding that "in the pulse-tingling style that began so many years ago with *The Scarlatti Inheritance,* we are caught up irretrievably." After Ludlum's death, Eric Van Lustbader added to the Bourne series with *The Bourne Legacy,* published by St. Martin's Press in 2004.

A woman comes back from the dead and a spy in the White House threatens humanity's continued existence in *The Parsifal Mosaic.* "Certainly, millions of entranced readers tap their feet in time to his fiction, and I'm positive this new adventure will send his legions of fans dancing out into the streets," Evan Hunter remarked in *New York Times Book Review.* "Me? I must be tone-deaf." A world takeover is again imminent in *The Aquitaine Progression,* this time at the hands of five military figures. "Ludlum's hero, Joel Converse, learns of a plot by generals in the United States, Germany, France, Israel and South Africa to spawn violent demonstrations. Once the violence bursts out of hand, the generals plan to step in and take over," Charles P. Wallace wrote in *Los Angeles Times Book Review. The Icarus Agenda* features a similar plot. This time, five wealthy, powerful figures arrange the election of the next United States president. "There is a sufficient amount of energy and suspense present in *The Icarus Agenda* to remind the reader why Mr. Ludlum's novels are best sellers," Julie Johnson commented in *New York Times Book Review.* "Ludlum is light-years beyond his literary competition in piling plot twist upon plot twist," Peter L. Robertson observed in Chicago *Tribune Books,* "until the mesmerized reader is held captive, willing to accept any wayward, if occasionally implausible, plotting device."

In *The Road to Omaha,* Ludlum departs from the seriousness of his espionage thrillers with a follow-up to *The Road to Gandolfo* that continues that novel's farcical tone. The Hawk and Sam, Ludlum's heroes in *Gandolfo,* return to fight the government for a plot of land legally belonging to an Indian tribe. In a review of the audio version of *The Road to Omaha,* a *Publishers Weekly* reviewer noted, "Hardcore Ludlum fans may be taken aback at first, but they stand to be won over in the listening."

The Scorpio Illusion returned to more familiar Ludlum territory: terrorism, international intrigue, mayhem, and death. In this novel, Amaya Bajaratt, a beautiful Basque terrorist, ignites a plot to assassinate the leaders of Israel, England, France, and the United States. Supported in her plot by a secret society of assassins known as the Scorpios, Bajaratt ventures to the United States to carry out the prize murder—the assassination of the U.S. president. The killer runs into resistance in the form of Tye Hawthorne, a former Naval intelligence officer, who is the only person capable of stopping the scheme. *The Apocalypse Watch,* Ludlum's next novel, covers similar serious territory, as a well-funded group of neo-Nazis attempts to create a Fourth Reich and achieve world domination. This intricately plotted novel features Harry Latham, who infiltrates the evil group only to be implanted with a memory chip of false information about prominent supporters of the group. When Harry is killed by the neo-Nazis, his brother Drew must pick up the fight against the group. Aided by the beautiful and mysterious Karin de Vries, Drew dodges assassination attempts and thwarts the neo-Nazis' ploy for world-domination.

The key elements of Ludlum's books—corruption in high places, elaborate secret plans, and unsuspecting civilians drawn into the fray—are what kept Ludlum fans waiting for his next offering. His writing, characterized by the liberal use of exclamation points, italics, sentence fragments, and rhetorical questions, was called crude by some critics, but others acknowledged that the style is popular with millions of readers and has proven difficult to duplicate, leaving Ludlum with little copycat competition. Still, reviewers often pointed to Ludlum's use of mixed metaphors and illogical statements as serious flaws in his books. Horror novelist Stephen King, in a somewhat tongue-in-cheek review of *The Parsifal Mosaic* for *Washington Post Book World,* highlighted some of Ludlum's "strange, wonderful, and almost Zen-like" thoughts: "'We've got . . . a confluence of beneficial prerogatives.' 'What I know is still very operative.' 'I'll get you your cover. But not two men. I think a couple would be better.'"

Robert Ludlum's The Hades Factor, written with Gayle Lynds, is the first novel in Ludlum's "Covert-One" series. Lt. Col. Jonathan Smith, a doctor and former espionage operative, is involved in biomedical research concerning deadly viruses. He is warned by an old friend—now an FBI agent—that his life is in danger. Within short order, his fiancé, also a virus researcher, is dead and Smith is forced underground after sidestepping several plots to kill him. The "doomsday" virus, unleashed by a shadowy enemy, kills three people in diverse locations within the United States, and Smith amasses his own secret force of experts in computer hacking and covert operations to stop those who are behind the virus and want to kill him. "The book reads fast," wrote Randy Michael Signor in *Book,* with "characters [who] are in service to plot, and plot [that] is in service to sales." Ronnie H. Terpening liked the book more, writing in *Library Journal* that *The Hades Factor* is "a top-notch international thriller" with "devastating double-crosses, gutwrenching twists, fast-paced action, [and] pressure that ratchets up to an explosive conclusion."

In *The Prometheus Deception,* evil forces once again attempt to take over the world. Stopping them is Nick Bryson, a retired spy who is shocked to discover that the top-secret agency he worked for—the Directorate—for twenty years was a front for the Russians. The CIA turns to him for help in dismantling the organization, which is planning terrorist attacks on the West in the form of anthrax outbreaks, train derailments, and airplane explosions. Bryson comes to suspect that the attacks are not the work of the Directorate, but rather another shadowy intelligence agency, the Prometheans. As Bryson narrowly escapes many hair-raising situations, he comes to doubt everything the CIA has told him as well. A reviewer for *Publishers Weekly* wrote that Bryson "is a dynamo and lots of fun to watch in action," but thought Ludlum's concern that "technology will soon allow for surveillance on a scale that grossly infringes on personal privacy" gets drowned out by the nonstop action of the plot. David Pitt of *Booklist* commented that *The Prometheus Deception* "should keep even the most experienced readers guessing." But some reviewers found the book more substantial than that. Michael Lollar of the Memphis *Commercial Appeal* took the book's focus on privacy invasion rather seriously. "Ludlum creates a scenario in which seemingly benign mergers and acquisitions mean that a single corporation can delve into every aspect of a person's life," Lollar wrote. "Life insurance, health insurance, medical records, credit records and banking records all are merely subsidiary operations easily retrieved at corporate headquarters." Lollar concluded that by the end of the novel, readers "will be left with the chilling feeling that just because you're paranoid doesn't mean they aren't out to get you."

In *Robert Ludlum's The Cassandra Compact,* the second "Covert-One" novel, this time written with Philip Shelby, Lt. Col. Jonathan Smith returns, hot on the heels of a plot to steal the deadly smallpox virus from a decrepit Russian laboratory. In true Ludlum fashion, the conspiracy proves to be worldwide, and Smith chases the virus from Venice back across the Atlantic Ocean, and finally meets up with it in Nevada, after the space shuttle lands with several dead astronauts aboard—all victims of smallpox. A reviewer for *Publishers Weekly* noted that the plot is not as complex as some of Ludlum's previous novels, but "the cinematic chase through changing landscapes and mounting body count gives the book its rapid pace, while insider politics, tradecraft and technical wizardry lend an extra kick."

The "Covert-One" series has continued after Ludlum's death, with Lynds fleshing out his outlines in *Robert Ludlum's The Paris Option* and *Robert Ludlum's The Altman Code. The Paris Option* finds Smith on the trail of a missing French scientist and trying to avert nuclear war. A *Kirkus Reviews* contributor termed it "tops in the series," with Lynds's "cloth-of-velvet moods" balancing Ludlum's "multidimensional paranoid sensibility." *The Altman Code* deals with biological trade involving Iraq and China. Despite some unfortunate dialogue, this novel "provides plenty of action and intrigue," a *Publishers Weekly* reviewer remarked. When Ludlum died, he left behind outlines for many more novels, which his publisher said will be finished by others and released under Ludlum's name; these include five to ten "Covert-One" books and a few stand-alone titles. He also left one near-complete manuscript, *The Sigma Protocol,*

which was given a few final touches and published in 2001. In this book Anna Navarro is a government agent assigned to a top-level case concerning a plot to murder the conspirators of a long-ago plan to steal a large amount of gold. Ben Hartman is an unsuspecting businessman who uncovers the truth about his billionaire parents and the death of his twin brother in a plane crash that Ben survived. It is the kind of book "in which the hero is just about to get an explanation for what's happening when the person he's talking to is silenced by an assassin's bullet," commented Chris Barsanti in *Book.* David Pitt of *Booklist* found *The Sigma Protocol* to contain "refreshing" differences from some of Ludlum's work, although it is nevertheless full of the author's characteristic action and plot twists. Pitt complimented Ludlum for "developing a smoother style" in his later books, with "characters that felt real and dialogue that didn't sound so obviously contrived."

At the time of his death, Ludlum was "probably the world's most read writer," according to a journalist in *Economist,* with conservative estimates of 200 million copies of his books in print. He published over twenty novels in thirty years, writing at a pace of 2,000 words a day. "His apocalyptic messages were a part of the thriller tradition that dates back at least to Sherlock Holmes," *Economist* writer continued. Journalist Bob Woodward, writing in *Washington Post Book World,* summarized the media's view of Ludlum in a review of *The Icarus Agenda:* "Ludlum justifiably has a loyal following. Reviews of most of his previous books are critical but conclude, grudgingly, that he had another inevitable bestseller." In a review of *The Bourne Identity* for *Washington Post Book World,* Richard Harwood wrote, "Whether reviewers are universally savage or effusive seems irrelevant: the book is bound to be a best seller. *The Bourne Identity . . .* is already on both the national and *Washington Post* best-seller lists and the damned thing won't officially be published [for three more days]. So much for the power of the press." Despite reviewers' advice, readers voiced their approval of Ludlum in sales figures. As Baxter and Nichols noted in *Maclean's,* "For all his imperfections, Ludlum manages—by pumping suspense into every twist and turn in his tangled plots and by demanding sympathy for well-meaning protagonists afflicted by outrageous adversity—to keep millions of readers frantically turning his pages."

BIOGRAPHICAL AND CRITICAL SOURCES:

BOOKS

Bestsellers 89, Issue 1, Thomson Gale (Detroit, MI), 1989.

Bestsellers 90, Issue 3, Thomson Gale (Detroit, MI), 1990.

Contemporary Literary Criticism, Thomson Gale (Detroit, MI), Volume 22, 1982, Volume 43, 1988.

Greenberg, Martin H., editor, *The Robert Ludlum Companion,* Bantam (New York, NY), 1993.

PERIODICALS

Best Sellers, April 15, 1973, p. 41; April, 1972, p. 5.

Book, September, 2000, Randy Michael Signor, review of *Robert Ludlum's The Hades Factor,* p. 75; November-December 2001, Chris Barsanti, review of *The Sigma Protocol,* p. 69.

Booklist, April 15, 1995, Mary Frances Wilkens, review of *The Apocalypse Watch,* p. 1452; August 2000, David Pitt, review of *The Prometheus Deception,* p. 2074; September 15, 2001, David Pitt, a review of *The Sigma Protocol,* p. 164.

Christian Science Monitor, March 31, 1977, Barbara Phillips, review of *The Chancellor Manuscript,* p. 31.

Commercial Appeal (Memphis, TN), October 29, 2000, Michael Lollar, "Big Brother Scenario Relevant in Light of Technology Today," p. H1.

Kirkus Reviews, August 15, 2001, Donald Newlove, "Bob the Ghost," p. 1141; May 15, 2002, review of *Robert Ludlum's The Paris Option.*

Knight-Ridder/Tribune Service, February 22, 1995, Fred Tasker, "Robert Ludlum, Bestselling 'Storyteller,' Unfazed by Critics or Fame."

Library Journal, October 1, 1974, p. 2504; April 1, 1975, pp. 694-695; September 1, 2000, Ronnie H. Terpening, review of *The Prometheus Deception,* p. 250; October 15, 2001, Ronnie H. Terpening, review of *The Sigma Protocol,* p. 108.

Los Angeles Times Book Review, March 11, 1984, p. 3; March 23, 1986, p. 3; March 18, 1990, p. 8.

Maclean's, April 9, 1984, Susan Baxter and Mark Nichols, pp. 50-52.

New Republic, November 25, 1981, p. 38; September 20, 1982, p. 43.

New York, May 9, 1988, pp. 74-75.

New Yorker, June 20, 1988, pp. 90-92; October 2, 2000, James Surowiecki, "The Financial Page: Lessons from Ludlum," p. 62.

New York Review of Books, May 8, 1986, pp. 12-13.

New York Times, March 13, 1978, p. C19.

New York Times Book Review, January 28, 1973, p. 20; May 6, 1973, p. 41; August 4, 1974, p. 26; October 27, 1974, p. 56; March 28, 1976, p. 18; March 27, 1977, p. 8; April 8, 1979, p. 14; March 30, 1980, p. 7; March 21, 1982, p. 11; April 22, 1984, p. 14; March 9, 1986, p. 12; March 27, 1988, p. 16; June 20, 1993, p. 16.

Publishers Weekly, April 8, 1974, p. 76; February 10, 1975, p. 52; March 1, 1991, pp. 49-50; March 2, 1992; April 19, 1993, p. 48; April 17, 1995, review of *The Apocalypse Watch,* p. 37; May 29, 1995, p. 37; April 24, 2000, review of *Robert Ludlum's The Hades Factor,* p. 58; August 28, 2000, a review of *The Prometheus Deception,* p. 50; April 2, 2001, review of *Robert Ludlum's The Cassandra Compact,* p. 38; May 5, 2003, review of *Robert Ludlum's The Altman Code,* p. 198.

Times Literary Supplement, October 1, 1976, T.J. Binyon, review of *The Gemini Contenders,* p. 1260.

Tribune Books (Chicago), February 28, 1988, Peter L. Robertson, review of *The Icarus Agenda,* p. 7.

Washington Post Book World, March 23, 1980, p. 3; March 7, 1982, p. 1; February 21, 1988, p. 1.

ONLINE

Ludlum Books Web site, http://www.ludlumbooks.com/ (April 28, 2004).

OBITUARIES:

PERIODICALS

Economist, March 31, 2001, p. 1.

Guardian (London, England), March 14, 2001, John Williams, p. 22.

Independent (London, England), March 14, 2001, p. S6.

New York Times, March 13, 2001, p. A22; March 14, 2001, Douglas Martin, "Robert Ludlum, Bestselling Suspense Novelist, Dies at 73," p. A23.

Times (London, England), March 14, 2001, p. 25.

*   *   *

LYNCH, B. Suarez
See BORGES, Jorge Luis

M

MacDONALD, Anson
  See HEINLEIN, Robert A.

*   *   *

MacDONALD, John Dann
  See MacDONALD, John D.

*   *   *

MacDONALD, John D. 1916-1986
  (John Dann MacDonald)

PERSONAL: Born July 24, 1916, in Sharon, PA; died of complications following heart surgery December 28, 1986, in Milwaukee, WI; son of Eugene Andrew and Marguerite Grace (Dann) MacDonald; married Dorothy Mary Prentiss, July 3, 1937; children: Maynard John Prentiss. *Education:* Attended University of Pennsylvania, 1934-35; Syracuse University, B.S., 1938; Harvard University, M.B.A., 1939.

CAREER: Author. Worked for a time in investment and insurance. *Military service:* U.S. Army, 1940-46; served in India and Asia with Office of Strategic Services; became lieutenant colonel.

MEMBER: Mystery Writers of America (president, 1962), PEN, Authors Guild, Authors League of America, Explorers Club.

AWARDS, HONORS: Benjamin Franklin Award, 1955, for best American short story; Gran Prix de Litterature Policiére, 1964, for French edition of *A Key to the*

Suite; Pioneer Medal, Syracuse University, 1971; Grand Master Award, Mystery Writers of America, 1972; Popular Culture Association National Award for Excellence, 1978; D.H.L., Hobart and William Smith Colleges, 1978, University of South Florida, 1980; National Book Award, 1980, for *The Green Ripper.*

WRITINGS:

FICTION

The Damned, Fawcett (New York, NY), 1952.
Cancel All Our Vows, Appleton (New York, NY), 1953.
Contrary Pleasure, Appleton (New York, NY), 1954.
The Deceivers, Dell (New York, NY), 1958.
Clemmie, Fawcett (New York, NY), 1958.
Please Write for Details, Simon & Schuster (New York, NY), 1959.
The Crossroads, Simon & Schuster (New York, NY), 1959.
Slam the Big Door, Fawcett (New York, NY), 1960, reprinted, Thorndike Press (Thorndike, ME), 1987.
A Key to the Suite, Fawcett (New York, NY), 1962.
A Flash of Green, Simon & Schuster (New York, NY), 1962.
I Could Go on Singing, Fawcett (New York, NY), 1963.
Condominium, Lippincott (Philadelphia, PA), 1977.
One More Sunday, Random House (New York, NY), 1984.
Barrier Island, Knopf (New York, NY), 1986.

MYSTERY FICTION

The Brass Cupcake, Fawcett (New York, NY), 1950.
Murder for the Bride, Fawcett (New York, NY), 1951.

Judge Me Not, Fawcett (New York, NY), 1951.

Weep for Me, Fawcett (New York, NY), 1951.

The Neon Jungle, Fawcett (New York, NY), 1953.

Dead Low Tide, Fawcett (New York, NY), 1953.

All These Condemned, Fawcett (New York, NY), 1954.

Area of Suspicion, Dell (New York, NY), 1954.

A Bullet for Cinderella, Dell (New York, NY), 1955, published as *On the Make,* 1960.

Cry Hard, Cry Fast, Popular Library, 1955.

You Live Once, Popular Library, 1955.

April Evil, Dell (New York, NY), 1956.

Border Town Girl, Popular Library, 1956.

Murder in the Wind, Dell (New York, NY), 1956.

Death Trap, Dell (New York, NY), 1957.

The Price of Murder, Dell (New York, NY), 1957.

The Empty Trap, Popular Library, 1957.

A Man of Affairs, Dell (New York, NY), 1957.

The Soft Touch, Dell (New York, NY), 1958.

The Executioners, Simon & Schuster (New York, NY), 1958, published as *Cape Fear,* Fawcett (New York, NY), 1962.

Deadly Welcome, Dell (New York, NY), 1959.

The Beach Girls, Fawcett (New York, NY), 1959.

(Editor) *Mystery Writers of America Anthology,* Dell (New York, NY), 1959.

The End of the Night, Simon & Schuster (New York, NY), 1960.

The Only Girl in the Game, Fawcett (New York, NY), 1960.

Where Is Janice Gantry?, Fawcett (New York, NY), 1961.

One Monday We Killed Them All, Fawcett (New York, NY), 1961.

On the Run, Fawcett (New York, NY), 1963.

The Drowner, Fawcett (New York, NY), 1963.

End of the Tiger and Other Stories, Fawcett (New York, NY), 1966.

The Last One Left, Doubleday (New York, NY), 1967.

SEVEN (short story collection), Fawcett (New York, NY), 1971.

The Good Old Stuff: Thirteen Early Stories, edited by Martin H. Greenberg and others, Harper (New York, NY), 1982.

More Good Old Stuff, Knopf (New York, NY), 1984.

"TRAVIS MCGEE" SERIES

The Deep Blue Good-By (also see below), Fawcett (New York, NY), 1964.

Nightmare in Pink (also see below), Fawcett (New York, NY), 1964.

A Purple Place for Dying (also see below), Fawcett (New York, NY), 1964.

The Quick Red Fox, Fawcett (New York, NY), 1964.

A Deadly Shade of Gold, Fawcett (New York, NY), 1965.

Bright Orange for the Shroud, Fawcett (New York, NY), 1965.

Darker than Amber, Fawcett (New York, NY), 1966.

One Fearful Yellow Eye, Fawcett (New York, NY), 1966.

Pale Gray for Guilt, Fawcett (New York, NY), 1968.

The Girl in the Plain Brown Wrapper, Fawcett (New York, NY), 1968.

Three for McGee (contains *The Deep Blue Good-By, Nightmare in Pink,* and *A Purple Place for Dying*), Doubleday (New York, NY), 1968, published as *McGee,* R. Hale (London, England), 1975.

Dress Her in Indigo, Fawcett (New York, NY), 1969.

The Long Lavender Look, Fawcett (New York, NY), 1970, reprinted, G.K. Hall (Boston, MA), 1986.

A Tan and Sandy Silence, Fawcett (New York, NY), 1972.

The Scarlet Ruse, Fawcett (New York, NY), 1973.

The Turquoise Lament, Lippincott (Philadelphia, PA), 1973.

The Dreadful Lemon Sky, Lippincott (Philadelphia, PA), 1975.

The Empty Copper Sea, Lippincott (Philadelphia, PA), 1978.

The Green Ripper, Lippincott (Philadelphia, PA), 1979.

Free Fall in Crimson, Harper (New York, NY), 1981.

Cinnamon Skin, Harper (New York, NY), 1982.

The Lonely Silver Rain, Knopf (New York, NY), 1985.

Five Complete Travis McGee Novels, Avenel Books (New York, NY), 1985.

(With Lewis D. Moore) *Meditations on America: John D. MacDonald's Travis McGee Series and Other Fiction,* Bowling Green State University Popular Press, 1994.

Also author of *Shades of Travis McGee,* Doubleday (New York, NY).

SCIENCE FICTION

Wine of the Dreamers, Greenberg, 1951, published as *Planet of the Dreamers,* Pocket Library (New York, NY), 1953.

Ballroom of the Skies, Greenberg, 1952.

The Girl, the Gold Watch, and Everything, Fawcett (New York, NY), 1962.

Other Times, Other Worlds (short story collection), Fawcett (New York, NY), 1978.

NONFICTION

The House Guests, Doubleday (New York, NY), 1965.
No Deadly Drug, Doubleday (New York, NY), 1968.
(With John Kilpack) *Nothing Can Go Wrong,* Harper (New York, NY), 1981.
(Author of introduction) Richard Riley, *The Gulf Coast of Florida,* Skyline Press, 1984.
A Friendship (letters written to Dan Rowen, 1967-1974), Knopf (New York, NY), 1986.
Film Classic: Cape Fear, Bloomsbury (London, England), 1997.

Work has been frequently anthologized. Contributor of over five hundred short stories, some under house pseudonyms, to *Cosmopolitan, Collier's* and other magazines.

ADAPTATIONS: Film options to several of MacDonald's novels have been sold; the novelette "Taint of the Tiger" was adapted into *Man Trap,* Paramount, 1961; the novel *The Executioners* was adapted into *Cape Fear,* Universal/International, 1962, and remade in 1991 by Martin Scorsese; some thirty MacDonald stories have been adapted for television, including "Condominium," released by Operation Prime Time TV in April, 1980, and "The Girl, the Gold Watch, and Everything," released by Operation Prime Time TV in May, 1980.

SIDELIGHTS: "Most things seem a little chancy while this 20th Century ebbs away," wrote Nick B. Williams in the *Los Angeles Times Book Review,* "but of two things you may feel reasonably certain—(1) that a John D. MacDonald mystery thriller is destined to become a runaway best seller, and (2) that his protagonist, Travis McGee, will survive all bullets and all wild or wily women, remaining as fit as ever for whatever happens to him next."

Considered the heir apparent to such classic crime novelists as Dashiell Hammett and Raymond Chandler, John D. MacDonald enjoyed critical and commercial success both as the author of the "Travis McGee" series and as a serious novelist with such books as *Condominium, One More Sunday,* and *Barrier Island* to his credit. While best known for his mysteries, MacDonald produced books in a number of genres during his lifetime; his foray into science fiction, for instance, earned him praise from Raymond Carney, who remarked in the *Dictionary of Literary Biography* that in *Wine of the Dreamers* and *Ballroom of the Skies* MacDonald "avoids entrapment by the various plots he creates. His writing depends on his ability to deploy and negotiate the intersecting technologies of law, bureaucracy, history, and memory more deftly and humanely than the best of his readers."

MacDonald began his career by writing mysteries for the "pulp" magazines popular in the 1940s and 1950s, and he soon graduated to paperback novels. Of the author's early days, Francis M. Nevins, Jr., related in *Clues:* "Several of MacDonald's earliest pulp crime stories were set in the China-Burma-India locales in which he had served during the war as an officer in the [Office of Strategic Services], but before long [his editor] persuaded him to take off his pith helmet and start writing about the United States. From then on the vast majority of his stories took place in postwar America. Indeed MacDonald portrayed more vividly and knowledgeably than any other crime writer the readjustment of American business from a war footing to a consumer-oriented peacetime economy which would soon be spewing out megatons of self-destructing plastic junk and incurring the wrath of the later MacDonald and his beach bum-philosopher-adventurer hero Travis McGee."

In 1962, after he had published a score of successful novels, MacDonald was approached by Fawcett Books senior editor Knox Burger to develop a new detective series. As the author later told Toronto *Globe and Mail* writer Patrick Hynan, he was not thrilled by the idea "because I didn't want to be locked into something that I would find hard to get out of if I didn't like it." However, MacDonald agreed to write three novels featuring a character then called Dallas McGee. While writing the first "McGee" book, *The Deep Blue Good-By,* MacDonald learned of President John F. Kennedy's assassination. Convinced that the word "Dallas" had been given a bad resonance in the public subconscious by the slaying, he changed McGee's first name to Travis, after the California air force base.

The immediate acceptance of the "McGee" books led to some twenty more—all distinguishable by their rainbow array of titles, from *Nightmare in Pink* to *The Green Ripper, The Scarlet Ruse,* and *Cinnamon Skin.* The McGee character was embraced by literary scholars and mystery buffs alike. Described by the author as a knight-errant, and by the character himself as a "salvage expert," Travis McGee is a year-round resident of Florida, where he lives on his houseboat, *The Busted Flush,* which he won in a poker game. McGee rents himself out on occasion as a private detective, abetted by his friend Meyer, an economist by trade, who once had a houseboat, *John Maynard Keynes,* named for the noted English economist.

In his adventures McGee is endangered by all manner of professional killers, amateur psychopaths, and everyday villains, but his fans can rest assured that their hero will emerge unscathed. "Travis McGee can always *get* results, and that one ability probably sets him apart from most of us," found Wister Cook in a *Clues* article. "McGee's life is violent, simple and neat—in its broad outlines not one with which we can make much sympathetic identification. His nemeses do not return to haunt him another year, as ours do. For he survives beating, shooting, and bombing; he comes back to smash heads, terrorize and kill; he oversees the violent deaths of his principal antagonists. He calls himself a salvage man, and by the end of each novel he has indeed saved something important—a life, a reputation, a fortune, a friendship. Presiding over the action and ultimately controlling it, he achieves success—within the term as he defines it. He gets money, romance, self-esteem."

But McGee's life is not always satisfying. He is also a man tormented by what he sees as the decline of America in general, and his beloved Florida in particular. In his railings against the "junk" culture of fast food, bad television, and gross commercial overdevelopment, the detective is a stringent social critic, and MacDonald devotes much of each novel to chronicling modern ills as McGee sees them. "We cannot conclude just yet, however, that in his aversions Travis McGee is just like you and me," stated Cook. "We could, actually, make the case that McGee's concern for the general trashiness of everyday consumer life is merely window-dressing: it gives him a kind of spurious depth while filling the empty spaces between beatings, bombings, stabbings and shootings." But to *Clues* critic Edgar W. Hirschberg, McGee's musings serve a more important purpose. Although he acknowledged that the salvage expert's internal monologues often "stop the action dead," Hirschberg went on to say that "what these speculations do accomplish is to provide you with a much deeper and broader understanding of why McGee does what he does than you otherwise would have. Like his recent progenitors in the hard-boiled detective genre . . . he is a knight-errant riding into a crime-infested world, righting the few wrongs he can do anything about. But he does a lot more thinking about the people who commit them . . . than most fictional detectives do, and his penchant for speculations about the social evils which are the real reason why he never lacks employment adds substantial depth and significance to MacDonald's work, both as a teller of tales about violence and detection and as a serious novelist."

Women, as consorts, victims, and villains, play an important role in McGee's life. Scarcely a novel goes by without the detective involving himself with any number of obliging women; many of them, however, end up dead by story's end. In *Free Fall in Crimson,* drugs and pornography highlight the making of a film in Iowa, sending McGee to the Midwest and into an expected romantic foray. "The sex—steamy, but not unpleasantly graphic—and the violence and the violent death seem by now ritualistic, and in some perplexing way comforting in their predictability rather than arousing," declared *Los Angeles Times Book Review* critic Charles Champlin. John Leonard, writing in the *New York Times,* saw in this novel an opportunity for the author to allow his lady-killer hero "to raise his consciousness. Instead of the usual machismo rubbish of wounded bird and tender muscle and stifled sob, there are women in [*Free Fall in Crimson*] who might actually be able to cope with New York—two of them, only one of whom sleeps with McGee."

One critic who does not appreciate MacDonald's portrayal of female characters is Barbara Lawrence. In a *Clues* article, Lawrence decried McGee as "responsible for much of the suffering endured by the women, particularly psychological suffering. For McGee has such personal magnetism and attraction that women proposition him before the introductions are completed. An endless train of women bed down with McGee, and at first reading, it appears that this great lover truly admires and respects women. . . . But a closer examination of the novels belies this assumption and shows that he intensely dislikes successful women and has no use for any woman until she is totally submissive to him. He humiliates them and occasionally physically abuses them." MacDonald once answered this charge by responding that McGee "does not dislike successful women intensely or to any other degree. He wants no woman totally submissive to him. He neither humiliates nor abuses women." Rather, the author suggested, the misinterpretation lies with "readers who believe they see proof of their pre-prejudices in whatever they come upon."

In fact, violence toward women is only one aspect of the total picture of McGee's savage world. Champlin pointed out that the detective "has been kicked, hammered, beaten, flayed, drugged, immersed, stabbed, jabbed, bent, thrown, and shot at so often he has more entry and exit signs than a shopping mall. He has spent more time unconscious than most men have spent waking." *Time*'s John Skow compared McGee to "a Robin Hood among chattel rustlers who steals loot back from thugs and swindlers and returns it, minus a 50 percent commission, to the widows and orphans from whom it was taken."

Most critics have agreed that, the appeal of sex and violence not withstanding, the real pleasure of a "McGee" mystery lies in MacDonald's crisp, hard-hitting prose style. In his study of the author, *John D. MacDonald,* David Geherin called his subject "a gifted storyteller. . . . Neither as byzantine as Ross Macdonald's nor as loose and desultory as Raymond Chandler's, MacDonald's plots are well-woven, artfully constructed arrangements of action sequences. They are neither needlessly complex nor do they exist simply to obscure the identity of the villain until the final chapter. A master at creating and sustaining mystery, suspense, tension, and drama, MacDonald understands all the tricks of readability; turning the pages in one of his novels is always a pleasure, never a duty."

In a review of *Cinnamon Skin, Washington Post* critic Jonathan Yardley said that one of MacDonald's "most admirable qualities as a novelist is that he almost unfailingly manages to deliver precisely the pleasure that his readers anticipate—a quality too-little noticed and remarked upon among writers whose principal business it is to entertain. But also as usual, MacDonald provides a good deal more than mere diversion. He is a tinkerer in the grand old American tradition, a man who loves to learn how things work and a writer who loves to pass that knowledge along to his readers. . . . He also takes pleasure in tracking the continuing emotional adventures of Travis McGee, the loner who would love to be a husband and father except that he couldn't stand it." And Skow defended the author against the stereotype of mystery novels as empty escapism; in MacDonald's examinations of his hero's complex character, Skow remarked, "let no man say that this is escapist claptrap. MacDonald offers something far more profound, the claptrap of no way out."

The series' final installment, 1985's *The Lonely Silver Rain,* was published a year before the author's death. In this novel, critics noted glimpses of a hero who was finally showing signs of old age. The plot revolves around a drug ambush that leaves three people dead on board a stolen yacht. When the family of one of the victims has the owner of the yacht murdered in retaliation, McGee springs into action to defend the yacht-owner's attractive widow. During the course of the novel, he survives a bloody drug war involving the Mafia and Peruvian drug lords. In between musings on the decadence surrounding him in south Florida, McGee ponders his aging body and the surprising discovery that he has a college-age daughter. Summing up the "Travis McGee" series and MacDonald's many virtues, *New York Times Book Review* contributor Robin W. Winks characterized the author as "spare, wryly amusing, [and] conveying a sense of moral outrage that is calculated to precisely the right nuance. He writes to be read, bought and remembered, and he believes what he says."

In 1977 MacDonald took one of his ongoing "Travis McGee" themes and developed it into a non-mystery work that eventually attained best-seller status. *Condominium,* according to Stephen Zito, "is a brief against the rape of Florida." In a *Washington Post Book World* piece, Zito explained that the author "writes with outrage about what the developers and quick-buck artists have done to his adopted state where condominiums litter the white beaches, freeways cut across the wilderness, the air and water is fouled, and there is a cheapening and coarsening of life everywhere."

"Essentially a cautionary tale, *Condominium* is intimately concerned with the balance of nature and thus with death," noted Knox Burger in the *Village Voice.* "The story concerns the developers and the inhabitants of a high-rise building designed for retired people. Badly designed. It is set on piles driven into the fragile subsurface of a sandy island just off the west coast of Florida. After numerous convincing portents, a hurricane blows in and washes everything away." The novel received mixed reviews, with the negative notices focusing on the contention that in this book MacDonald, as Michael Mewshaw put it in *New York Times Book Review,* "seems to have lost sight of what he learned from the detective genre—economy, taut structure and pace." However, critic John Leonard, while not a fan of the "McGee" series, did have praise for *Condominium.* "Those who know [MacDonald] only through the [mystery novels] are missing him at his story-telling best," stated Leonard in the *New York Times.* "Outside the series and its formulas, the wounded women and the macho rubbish, he breathes. His appetite [for issues] is enormous." "*Condominum* is, in many ways, a remarkable achievement," added Zito. "In a novel peopled by perhaps 25 major characters, MacDonald has structured a book which is compulsively readable and coherent, building from the small disturbances of domestic life to the hurricane which comes with the force of the Apocalypse."

MacDonald also takes on religious hypocrisy with *One More Sunday.* A behind-the-scenes look at the corruption rampant in the popular Church of the Eternal Believer, *One More Sunday* was compared to a classic of the genre, *Elmer Gantry,* by Yardley in a *Washington Post* piece. MacDonald's work, in Yardley's opinion, "is no mere knee-jerk [criticism] of the evangelicals. He realizes that they can often be ruthlessly exploitive—

'they rope in their supporters by playing on their fears and on their hatred and their loneliness'—but he is also quick to acknowledge that they seek, out of whatever motive, to fill a genuine longing among their followers."

Moving from evangelical corruption to white-collar crime, MacDonald produced *Barrier Island* in 1986 to praise from *Los Angeles Times Book Review* writer Stephen Vizinczey. Explaining that the story is about a "fraudulent deal in the making"—an unspoiled island off the coast of Mississippi is about to be purchased and resold to the government at an unfair profit—Vizinczey remarked that MacDonald "has the gift of moral vision, which is to say he portrays actions in the light of their consequences. This is an almost revolutionary approach in an age when every other book or film is romanticizing cruelty and unscrupulousness by concentrating on the charm of criminals rather than their crimes, and by making villains sympathetic and their victims repellant. In 'Barrier Island' there is never any doubt who hurts whom and how. Nor are readers conned into loving the sort of characters who endanger their survival."

With the acclaim for his non-mystery novels reflecting the acclaim for his Travis McGee series, MacDonald made the case for Geherin that he was a writer of worth. As Geherin concluded in his book about the author, "Whether for the sake of convenience one categorizes his works as mysteries, adventures, or thrillers, it is clear that such labels are inadequate in conveying the full extent of his accomplishment. By creating a substantial body of thoughtful and provocative entertainment for an enormously diverse and widespread audience, MacDonald has justly earned for himself the right to be considered a serious American novelist worthy of the highest distinction."

BIOGRAPHICAL AND CRITICAL SOURCES:

BOOKS

Contemporary Literary Criticism, Thomson Gale (Detroit, MI), Volume 3, 1975, Volume 27, 1984, Volume 44, 1987.

Dictionary of Literary Biography, Volume 8: *Twentieth-Century American Science-Fiction Writers,* Thomson Gale (Detroit, MI), 1981.

Dictionary of Literary Biography Yearbook: 1986, Thomson Gale (Detroit, MI), 1987.

Geherin, David, *John D. MacDonald,* Unger, 1982.

Landrum, Larry, Pat Browne, and Ray B. Browne, editors, *Dimensions of Detective Fiction,* Popular Press, 1976, pp. 149-161.

MacDonald, John D., *One More Sunday,* Random House (New York, NY), 1984.

PERIODICALS

Armchair Detective, spring, 1980.

Booklist, May 1, 2001, Bill Ott; Brad Hooper, review of *A Tan and Sandy Silence,* p. 1600.

Chicago Tribune Book World, June 27, 1982; November 27, 1983.

Clues, spring, 1980; fall-winter, 1985; spring-summer, 1986; spring-summer, 1990.

Detroit News, June 7, 1981.

Fort Lauderdale News/Sun-Sentinel, February 15, 1987.

Globe and Mail (Toronto, Ontario, Canada), February 25, 1984; May 5, 1984.

Long Island Newsday, December 29, 1986.

Los Angeles Times, December 29, 1986.

Los Angeles Times Book Review, May 4, 1980; April 19, 1981; July 4, 1982; March 4, 1984; April 28, 1985; June 1, 1986.

New Republic, June 26, 1975.

Newsweek, March 10, 1975; April 22, 1985, p. 61.

New Yorker, April 29, 1985, p. 134.

New York Times, January 1, 1974; April 5, 1977; April 17, 1981; August 3, 1983; March 12, 1985; December 29, 1986.

New York Times Book Review, January 6, 1974; February 23, 1975; March 27, 1977; October 7, 1979; May 3, 1981; August 22, 1982; April 8, 1984; March 17, 1985, p. 14.

Publishers Weekly, July 29, 1983; January 18, 1985, p. 64.

Time, December 3, 1973; July 4, 1977; October 15, 1979; April 27, 1981; February 16, 1987.

Times (London, England), August 9, 1984.

Times Literary Supplement, May 28, 1976; February 10, 1978.

Village Voice, April 11, 1977; October 4, 1983.

Washington Post, June 23, 1982; July 15, 1983; March 14, 1984; December 29, 1986.

Washington Post Book World, March 27, 1977; September 10, 1978; May 17, 1981; September 9, 1984; March 24, 1985.

OBITUARIES:

PERIODICALS

Chicago Tribune, December 30, 1986.
Detroit Free Press, December 29, 1986.

Detroit News, December 29, 1986.
Los Angeles Times, December 29, 1986.
New York Times, December 29, 1986.
Publishers Weekly, January 9, 1987.
Time, January 12, 1987.
Times (London, England), January 2, 1987.
Washington Post, December 29, 1986.

*   *   *

MACKAY, Shena 1944-

PERSONAL: Surname rhymes with "reply"; born 1944, in Edinburgh, Scotland; married Robin Brown (divorced); children: three daughters. *Education:* Attended Tonbridge Girls Grammar School and Kidbrooke Comprehensive School.

ADDRESSES: Home—15 Fortis Green Ave., London N2, England. *Agent*—c/o Author Mail, Moyer Bell, 549 Old North Rd, Kingston, RI 02881-1220.

CAREER: Writer, 1959—. Also worked as honorary visiting professor in writing, Middlesex University.

MEMBER: Royal Society of Literature.

AWARDS, HONORS: Fawcett fiction prize for *Redhill Rococo;* Scottish Arts Council Book Award, 1991, for *Dunedin;* Booker Prize short list, 1996, for *The Orchard on Fire;* Orange Prize for Fiction nomination, and Whitbread Award shortlist for best novel, both 2003, both for *Heligoland.*

WRITINGS:

NOVELS

Dust Falls on Eugene Schlumberger [and] *Toddler on the Run* (also see below), Deutsch (London, England), 1964.
Music Upstairs, Deutsch (London, England), 1965.
Dust Falls on Eugene Schlumberger, Panther Books, 1966.
Toddler on the Run, Simon & Schuster (New York, NY), 1966.
Old Crow, J. Cape, 1967, McGraw (New York, NY), 1968, Moyer Bell (Wakefield, RI), 1999.

An Advent Calendar, J. Cape (London, England), 1971, Moyer Bell (Wakefield, RI), 1997.
A Bowl of Cherries, Harvester Press (Brighton, Sussex, England), 1984, Moyer Bell (Wakefield, RI), 1992.
Redhill Rococo, Heinemann (London, England), 1986.
Dunedin, Heinemann (London, England), 1992, Moyer Bell (Wakefield, RI), 1993.
The Orchard on Fire, Heinemann (London, England), 1995, Moyer Bell (Wakefield, RI), 1996.
The Artist's Widow, J. Cape (London, England), 1998, Moyer Bell (Wakefield, RI), 1999.
Heligoland, J. Cape (London, England), 2003.

SHORT STORIES

Babies in Rhinestones and Other Stories, Heinemann (London, England), 1983.
Dreams of Dead Women's Handbags, Heinemann (London, England), 1987, Moyer Bell (Wakefield, RI), 1994.
The Laughing Academy, Heinemann (London, England), 1993.
The World's Smallest Unicorn: Stories, J. Cape (London, England), 1999, Moyer Bell (Wakefield, RI), 2000.

EDITOR

Such Devoted Sisters, Virago (London, England), 1993, Moyer Bell (Wakefield, RI), 1994.
Friendship, Orion (London, England), 1998.

SIDELIGHTS: Scottish author Shena Mackay's novels about middle-class life in Great Britain have been praised for their dark humor and stylish prose. To quote Brigid Brophy in *Listener,* Mackay's talent "is to put the ruth back into ruthless rhymes. . . . Her novels are visions of universal anguish composed in short, sharp reels." A *Times Literary Supplement* reviewer lauded Mackay for "extrapolating vividly-observed ordinariness into alarming and exuberant fantasy," a feature of many of her novels and stories. *Publishers Weekly* contributor Michele Field explained that "Mackay's signature is recognizable from book to book: a sense of menace below the check-pattern of middle-class life; a subliminal eroticism charging everything . . . and a very sharp definition of time and place, of brand names and domestic manners—altogether, as if Harold Pinter were taking you through the contents of his kitchen cupboards." The critic went on to cite Mackay for the "peculiar mix of hilarity, surrealism and gloom that animate the commonplace world of her books."

Mackay was born in Edinburgh but moved south to England while she was still a youngster. She began writing when she was fifteen years old, and by the age of twenty-seven she had finished five novels—without the benefit of a college education. Her first book, a collection of two short novels, was published when she was twenty. After such early promise, she took a long hiatus from writing between 1971 and 1983. Since then, however, she has released a significant body of work, including a novel, *The Orchard on Fire,* which was shortlisted for the Booker Prize.

Mackay displays a dour take on the world. Many of her characters live in poverty and are emotionally damaged as well. It is this very dreariness that appeals in the author's work, however. A *Publisher's Weekly* reviewer noted, for instance, that Mackay "is a poet in spirit who happens to write paragraphs about ordinary lives that turn out never to be quite ordinary." In *New Statesman and Society,* Judy Cooke observed that "Mackay's keen ear for dialogue is complemented by the precision of her descriptive writing. She can evoke a mood or point up a meaning with one or two carefully chosen images. . . . She has a great talent for comedy in the English tradition."

The darkly humorous *An Advent Calendar,* for instance, begins with a butcher's assistant who accidentally slices off his finger and grinds it with meat that is later sold to another unfortunate character. The grim tone of the novel is heightened by the fact that its events take place during the Advent season leading up to Christmas. In *A Bowl of Cherries* the central character reminisces about a time when she was sick and her mother brought her a bowl of cherries—only to sit and eat them all herself. "Mackay's writing—adroit, intelligent and evocative—is a joy," declared Walter Satterthwait in a *New York Times Book Review* appraisal of *A Bowl of Cherries.* "Almost casually, she tosses off images that are striking in their precision and their lyrical use of the commonplace" and creates "a lovely book, entertaining, insightful and, in the end, deeply satisfying."

Mackay's best-known title is *The Orchard on Fire,* a harrowing tale of childhood in a small village in Kent. Eight-year-old April lives with her struggling parents, who have come to the village to run a tea shop. Despite her budding friendship with red-haired Ruby Richards, April finds herself in troubling circumstances when she becomes the object of unwanted attention from the wealthy Mr. Greenidge. In the *New York Times Book Review,* Roxana Robinson stated: "The novel satisfies on many levels. Ms. Mackay's characters are both con-

vincing and wonderfully varied. She also demonstrates perfect pitch. . . . 'The Orchard on Fire' is an intensely domestic novel, but this is not a limitation. The book's touching and somber drama arises from much larger elements: love, loyalty, courage, sex, fear and oppression. Ms. Mackay explores them all with clarity, elegance and power." A *Publishers Weekly* correspondent commended *The Orchard on Fire* as "a finely wrought and touching novel," animated by "the throb of real life among blue-collar families."

Mackay has also published several short-story collections, most notably *Dreams of Dead Women's Handbags.* According to Katharine Weber in the *New York Times Book Review,* the collection "includes further evidence of Ms. Mackay's startling precocity, but it also displays the more recent, elegant work of a developed writer who has continued to fine-tune her distinctive voice over an unusually broad range." The critic continued: "There is perhaps a touch of Ms. Mackay's Scottish origins in her poetic and melodic language. Her descriptive precision and imagination are matched by a talent to surprise."

In the *The Artists Widow,* Mackay weaves together the story of Lyris, widow of successful artist John Crane, and an assortment of people who gather together for a showing of John Crane's last work before he died. Lyris, a painter herself, is concerned about the loss of her own creativity. Nathan, her grandnephew, is a despicable and boorish conceptual artist. Other characters include Clovis, a middle-aged bookseller, and Zoé, a beautiful young filmmaker who approaches Lyris about doing a film about forgotten women artists. As the talented and "wannabes" mix, Mackay "explores the issues of artistic creativity, moral values and friendship," wrote a *Publishers Weekly* reviewer. The reviewer added, "She writes in language as quick and lethal as a snake's tongue." Ann H. Fisher, writing in *Library Journal,* commented that "Mackay . . . has written a wonderful, very funny, and insightful novel."

In her collection *The World's Smallest Unicorn,* Mackay presents eleven stories about what a *Publishers Weekly* contributor described as "life's odd pots." Her stories include tales about a writer who visits a home for retired clowns, a man who returns to London to find a family he is no longer familiar with, and a woman who develops an unnatural fear of meeting the daughter of a friend. A *Booklist* contributor noted that the author "has an eye for the small moment and quirky detail, which helps define her characters," while in *Publishers Weekly* a critic commented that the stories comprising *The*

World's Smallest Unicorn "capture a wide range of voices, settings and styles within finely tuned tales bearing one commonality: their excellent surprise endings."

Mackay combines a series of stories to the tell the tale of Rowena Snow in *Heligoland,* which made the short list for the prestigious Whitbread Award. Beginning with Rowena as a child in a baby carriage, the stories progress through the woman's life as she is orphaned, ends up in a boarding school, and, as an adult, takes on the role of housekeeper in a place called Nautilus, once the home of a bohemian community. Now lived in by two fading eccentrics, poet Francis Campion and Celeste Zylberstein, the widow of a man of letters, the architecturally unique house soon has another boarder in Gus Crabb, an antiques dealer. For the first time in her life, Rowena seems on the verge of happiness as she instills a new sense of vitality within the decaying domain of Nautilus. Writing in the *Independent,* Stevie Davies felt that while Mackay's book is "shaped as a myth of renewal" it does not work on a "narrative level." Nevertheless, Davies went on to note, *Heligoland*'s "twin strengths lie in its sensitive treatment of Rowena and in the lyricism that lifts the creaky plot to something bizarrely beautiful, a technique which displays its own artificiality, like literary enamelling." *Guardian* contributor Peter Bradshaw commented of the book that "The writing is superb, and of that unassuming, un-worked-up kind that comes only from an author whose gentle mastery of language is quite beyond showy displays of technique." In the London *Telegraph,* Jane Shilling also praised *Heligoland* as "a slender, intelligent fiction written in ravishing prose that combines richness with translucency, luminous affection for human strangeness with an anatomist's precision."

BIOGRAPHICAL AND CRITICAL SOURCES:

PERIODICALS

Best Sellers, March 1, 1968.
Booklist, September 15, 1994, p. 114; September 15, 1996, p. 220; October 15, 1997, p. 388; November 1, 2000, Mary Ellen, review of *The World's Smallest Unicorn,* p. 519.
Books and Bookmen, September, 1967.
Guardian, March 1, 2003, Peter Bradhsaw, review of *Heligoland.*
Illustrated London News, July, 1967.
Independent (London, England), March 1, 2003, Stevie Davies, review of *Heligoland.*

Library Journal, September 15, 1993, p. 104; August, 1994, p. 136; October 1, 1996, p. 127; September 1, 1997, p. 224; June 15, 1999, p. 109; June 15, 1999, Ann H. Fisher, review of *The Artist's Widow,* p. 109.
Listener, June 15, 1967; July 8, 1971.
New Statesman, June 12, 1964; July 2, 1971; October 21, 1983, p. 27; February 14, 1986, p. 27; August 28, 1987, p. 21.
New Statesman and Society, July 10, 1992, p. 34; July 30, 1993, Judy Cooke, review of *The Laughing Academy,* p. 39.
Newsweek, January 17, 1966.
New York Times Book Review, February 25, 1968; January 17, 1993, p. 11; December 18, 1994, p. 7; November 3, 1996, p. 11; December 14, 1997, p. 22; July 18, 1999, p. 16.
Observer Review, June 11, 1967.
Publishers Weekly, September 21, 1992, p. 74; August 16, 1993, p. 86; August 22, 1994, p. 42; September 12, 1994; August 12, 1996, review of *The Orchard on Fire,* p. 62; December 2, 1996, Michele Field, "Shena Mackay: The Menace of the Domestic," p. 36; July 14, 1997, p. 62; May 10, 1999, review of *The Artist's Widow,* p. 53; September 4, 2000, review of *The World's Smallest Unicorn,* p. 82.
Saturday Review, March 2, 1968.
Spectator, July 10, 1971.
Telegraph (London, England), February 2, 2003, Jane Shilling, review of *Heligoland.*
Times Literary Supplement, June 15, 1967; July 2, 1971.

ONLINE

Contemporarywriters.com, http://www.contemporary writers.com/ (August 16, 2003), "Shena Mackay."

*   *   *

MacKINNON, Catharine A. 1946-

PERSONAL: Born October 7, 1946; daughter of George E. and Elizabeth V. (Davis) MacKinnon. *Education:* Smith College, B.A. (magna cum laude, with distinction), 1969; Yale University, J.D., 1977, Ph.D., 1987.

ADDRESSES: Office—c/o Rita Rendell, University of Michigan Law School, 909 Legal Research, Ann Arbor, MI 48109-1210. *Agent*—Elaine Markson, 44 Greenwich Ave., New York, NY 10011.

CAREER: Lawyer, legal scholar, educator, author, consultant to city and state committees writing pornography codes, and political activist. Admitted to the bar of Connecticut State, 1978; visiting professor of law at Yale University, Harvard University, Stanford University, University of California, Los Angeles, and University of Chicago, 1980-88; assistant professor of law at University of Minnesota, 1982-84; professor of law at York University, Toronto, Ontario, Canada, 1988-90; professor of law at University of Michigan School of Law, Ann Arbor, MI, 1989—.

WRITINGS:

Sexual Harassment of Working Women: A Case of Sex Discrimination, Yale University Press, 1979.

Feminism Unmodified: Discourses on Life and Law, Harvard University Press, 1987.

(With Andrea Dworkin) *Pornography and Civil Rights: A New Day for Women's Equality,* Organizing Against Pornography (Minneapolis), 1988.

Toward a Feminist Theory of the State, Harvard University Press, 1989.

Only Words, Harvard University Press, 1993.

(With Andrea Dworkin) *In Harm's Way: The Pornography Civil Rights Hearings,* Harvard University Press, 1998.

Women's Lives, Men's Laws, The Belknap Press/ Harvard University Press (Cambridge, MA), 2005.

SIDELIGHTS: Catharine A. MacKinnon, a feminist author, activist, and legal scholar, ranks among the most original and controversial social theorists in the United States. MacKinnon broke new legal ground in the late 1970s by arguing that the sexual harassment of women in the workplace constitutes a form of sex discrimination in violation of existing civil rights statutes. MacKinnon's thesis, elaborated fully in her 1979 book *Sexual Harassment of Working Women: A Case of Sex Discrimination,* has won wide acceptance in the courtroom and become an important weapon in fighting the mistreatment of working women.

MacKinnon subsequently directed her efforts toward combatting pornography. In 1983, she and her colleague, author Andrea Dworkin, helped draft an antipornography ordinance for the city of Indianapolis, Indiana. The ordinance forbade the sexually explicit subordination of women through pictures or words as a form of sex discrimination. The ordinance was supported politically and in litigation by women of many political persuasions, as well as by grass-roots feminist organizations, scholars, civil rights activists, lawyers, and survivors of sexual assault. The Indianapolis ordinance (and a similar law MacKinnon and Dworkin drafted for Minneapolis, Minnesota, and passed twice by the city council) was opposed, however, by some legal scholars, civil libertarians, and a few feminists, who argued that it amounted to state censorship. A federal appeals court struck down the ordinance as an unconstitutional violation of free speech, a result upheld without opinion by the U.S. Supreme Court.

MacKinnon outlines her views on the pornography issue and responds to opponents in *Pornography and Civil Rights,* which she wrote with Dworkin, and in *Feminism Unmodified,* a collection of speeches delivered from 1981 to 1986. In brief, the author defines pornography as the sexual subordination of women to men; it constitutes, reinforces, and perpetuates male dominance throughout society and is thus a form of sex-based discrimination. At its most pernicious, MacKinnon maintains, pornography requires for its making—and produces through its use—rape and other acts of sexual sadism and aggression against women as well as bigotry and hatred toward women throughout society. Outlawing pornography is thus not an issue of art or morality, but one of protecting and respecting women as equals.

This thesis has drawn both criticism and support across the political spectrum. Some conservatives have opposed MacKinnon's attacks on male social and sexual dominance. Among liberals are those who question a causal link between pornography and the abuse of women. MacKinnon argues that the link between pornography and sexual inequality is indisputable and based on overwhelming empirical support. She asserts in *Feminism Unmodified* that pornographers act as the shock troops for male domination by making the female body into a thing for sexual use. Dehumanized and humiliated in a way that is sexualized, women become targets of violence and discrimination, both in pornography and in other aspects of life. Hence, MacKinnon writes, pornography—by subordinating women—is "more act-like than thought-like" and free speech concerns are misplaced. "Pornography isn't protected by the First Amendment any more than sexual harassment is," the author remarked to *New York Times Book Review* interviewer Tamar Lewin. "It's not a question of free speech or ideas. Pornography is a form of action, requiring the submission of women."

Feminism Unmodified received varying critical responses. *Nation* contributor Maureen Mullarkey, for example, criticized *Feminism Unmodified* as relying on "slogans, false premises, half-information, sinister innuendo and ad-hoc reasoning." Expressing a highly favorable opinion in the *New York Times Book Review* was political philosopher Alison Jaggar, who described the book as "an unorthodox but relentlessly consistent perspective on issues fundamental to feminism" and praised it as "passionate, brilliant, [and] polemical."

MacKinnon's contributions to feminist and social theory have by no means been limited to her opposition to pornography. The speeches in *Feminism Unmodified* also address issues of abortion, rape, women's athletics, sexual harassment, and the rights of Native American women, and *Toward a Feminist Theory of the State,* published in 1989, outlines a unified political/social/sexual theory of male domination. MacKinnon reconceptualizes equality from its traditional approach focusing on sameness and difference to an analysis of dominance and subordination.

In *Only Words,* MacKinnon tackles the issue of circumstances in which forms of expression (specifically sexually explicit words or photographs) can be considered as a form of sexual harassment and therefore banned. She makes her case through three passionate and exceptionally well-researched essays in which she argues that such forms of expression may be banned, even though protected by the Constitution. The essays attack the protection of pornography and compare it and sexual harassment with racial discrimination and abuse. A *Kirkus Reviews* critic describes MacKinnon's essays as "passionate [and] intellectually fascinating." The reviewer goes on to say that though MacKinnon's conviction sometimes causes her ideas to elide, "the ideas are original and gripping, her references are wide-ranging, her legal logic is provocative."

In Harm's Way: The Pornography Civil Rights Hearings compiles the oral testimony of victims of pornography. Cass Sunstein, reviewing this volume for *Law and Philosophy,* summarized its value as "an important addition for academics and for others to the pornography debate." *In Harm's Way,* Sunstein notes, presents both sides of the debate, including pornography opponents who are social science experts and authorities on abuse and prostitution, as well as advocates of unfettered freedom of speech.

Throughout her writings, MacKinnon attacks "liberal feminism" for limiting its objectives to helping a few women "succeed" in male terms instead of addressing the roots of male domination. She is more concerned with subverting the male-biased definitions of gender that she believes permeate society and perpetuate male supremacy in a way that damages all women. MacKinnon considers issues of race and class as integral to the social/sexual equation. As a tenured professor at the University of Michigan Law School, MacKinnon is expected by observers to remain at the forefront of legal scholarship.

BIOGRAPHICAL AND CRITICAL SOURCES:

PERIODICALS

Detroit Free Press, March 1, 1989.
Globe and Mail (Toronto), December 9, 1989.
Kirkus Reviews, July 15, 1993.
Law and Philosophy, 1997, p. 177.
Nation, May 30, 1987.
New York Times, February 24, 1989.
New York Times Book Review, May 3, 1987.
Psychology Today, September, 1987.
Time, March 10, 1986; April 17, 1989.

*   *   *

MacLEISH, Archibald 1892-1982

PERSONAL: Born May 7, 1892, in Glencoe, IL; died April 20, 1982, in Boston, MA; son of Andrew (a partner in Chicago department store of Carson, Pirie, Scott & Co.) and Martha (Hillard) MacLeish; married Ada Hitchcock (a singer), June 21, 1916; children: Kenneth (deceased), Brewster Hitchcock (deceased), Mary Hillard, William Hitchcock. *Education:* Attended Hotchkiss School; Yale University, A.B., 1915; Harvard University, LL.B., 1919.

CAREER: Poet, dramatist, lawyer, and statesman. Admitted to U.S. Supreme Court Bar, 1942. Harvard University, Cambridge, MA, instructor in constitutional law, 1919, first curator of Niemann Collection of Contemporary Journalism and adviser to Niemann fellows, 1938, Boylston Professor of Rhetoric and Oratory, 1949-62, Boylston Professor Emeritus, 1962-82; Choate, Hall & Stewart (law firm), Boston, MA, staff member, 1920-23; freelance writer in France, 1923-28; *Fortune,* New York, NY, staff member, 1929-38; U.S. Government, Washington, DC, Librarian of Congress, 1939-44, director of Office of Facts and Figures, 1941-42, assistant director of Office of War Information, 1942-43, and assistant secretary of state, 1944-45. U.S.

delegate to Conference of Allied Ministers of Education in London, 1944; chair of U.S. delegation to London conference drafting UNESCO constitution, 1945, first U.S. delegate to General Conference of UNESCO in Paris, 1946, and first U.S. member of Executive Council of UNESCO. U.S. Department of State lecturer in Europe, 1957; Simpson Lecturer, Amherst College, 1963-67. Museum of Modern Art, New York, NY, trustee, beginning 1940; Sara Lawrence College, Bronxville, NY, trustee, beginning 1949. *Military service:* U.S. Army, Field Artillery, 1917-18; served in France; became captain.

MEMBER: American Academy of Arts and Letters (president, 1953-56), National Institute of Arts and Letters, Academy of American Poets (fellow, 1966), League of American Writers (chair, 1937), National Committee for an Effective Congress Commission on Freedom of the Press, Phi Beta Kappa, Century Club (New York, NY), Tavern Club and Somerset Club (Boston).

AWARDS, HONORS: John Reed Memorial prize, 1929; Shelley Memorial Award for Poetry, 1932; Pulitzer Prize in poetry, 1933, for *Conquistador;* Golden Rose Trophy of New England Poetry Club, 1934; Levinson Prize, 1941; Commander, Legion of Honor (France), 1946; Commander, el Sol del Peru, 1947; Bollingen Prize in Poetry, Yale University Library, 1952, Pulitzer Prize in poetry, 1953, and National Book Award in poetry, 1953, all for *Collected Poems: 1917-1952;* Boston Arts Festival poetry award, 1956; Sarah Josepha Hale Award, 1958; Chicago Poetry Day Poet, 1958; Antoinette Perry ("Tony") Award in drama, and Pulitzer Prize in drama, both 1959, both for *J. B.: A Play in Verse;* Academy Award for best screenplay, Academy of Motion Picture Arts and Sciences, 1966, for *The Eleanor Roosevelt Story;* Presidential Medal of Freedom, 1977; National Medal for Literature, 1978; Gold Medal for Poetry, American Academy of Arts and Letters, 1979. M.A. from Tufts University, 1932; Litt.D. from Colby College, 1938, Wesleyan University, 1938, Yale University, 1939, University of Pennsylvania, 1941, University of Illinois, 1946, Washington University, 1948, Rockford College, 1953, Columbia University, 1954, Harvard University, 1955, University of Pittsburgh, 1959, Princeton University, 1965, University of Massachusetts, 1969, and Hampshire College, 1970; L.H.D. from Dartmouth University, 1940, and Williams College, 1942; D.C.L. from Union College, 1941, and University of Puerto Rico, 1953; LL.D. from Johns Hopkins University, 1941, University of California, 1943, Queen's University at Kingston, 1948, Carleton College, 1956, and Amherst College, 1963.

WRITINGS:

POETRY

Songs for a Summer's Day (sonnet cycle), Yale University Press (New Haven, CT), 1915.

Tower of Ivory, Yale University Press (New Haven, CT), 1917.

The Happy Marriage, and Other Poems, Houghton (Boston, MA), 1924.

The Pot of Earth, Houghton (Boston, MA), 1925.

Streets in the Moon, Houghton (Boston, MA), 1926.

The Hamlet of A. MacLeish, Houghton (Boston, MA), 1928.

Einstein, Black Sun Press, 1929.

New Found Land, Black Sun Press (limited edition), 1930, Houghton (Boston, MA), 1930.

Conquistador (narrative poem), Houghton (Boston, MA), 1932.

Before Match, Knopf (New York, NY), 1932.

Poems, 1924-1933, Houghton (Boston, MA), 1933.

Frescoes for Mr. Rockefeller's City, Day (New York, NY), 1933.

Poems, John Lane (London, England), 1935.

Public Speech, Farrar & Rinehart (New York, NY), 1936.

Land of the Free, Harcourt (New York, NY), 1938.

America Was Promises, Duell, Sloan & Pearce (New York, NY), 1939.

Actfive and Other Poems, Random House (New York, NY), 1948.

Collected Poems: 1917-52, Houghton (Boston, MA), 1952.

Songs for Eve, Houghton (Boston, MA), 1954.

Collected Poems, Houghton (Boston, MA), 1962.

The Collected Poems of Archibald MacLeish, Houghton (Boston, MA), 1963.

The Wild Old Wicked Man and Other Poems, Houghton (Boston, MA), 1968.

The Human Season: Selected Poems, 1926-72, Houghton (Boston, MA), 1972.

New and Collected Poems, 1917-1976, Houghton (Boston, MA), 1976.

New and Collected Poems, 1917-1984, Houghton (Boston, MA), 1985.

Collected Poems, 1917-1982, Houghton (Boston, MA), 1985.

PROSE

Housing America (articles from *Fortune*), Harcourt (New York, NY), 1932.

Jews in America (first published in *Fortune*), Random House (New York, NY), 1936.

Libraries in the Contemporary Crisis, U.S. Government Printing Office (Washington, DC), 1939.

Deposit of the Magna Carta in the Library of Congress on November 28, 1939, Library of Congress (Washington, DC), 1939.

The American Experience, U.S. Government Printing Office (Washington, DC), 1939.

The Irresponsibles, Duell, Sloan & Pearce (New York, NY), 1940.

The American Cause, Duell, Sloan & Pearce (New York, NY), 1941.

The Duty of Freedom, privately printed for the United Typothetae of America, 1941.

The Free Company Presents . . . The States Talking (radio broadcast, April 2, 1941), [New York, NY], 1941.

The Next Harvard, Harvard University Press (Cambridge, MA), 1941.

Prophets of Doom, University of Pennsylvania Press (Philadelphia, PA), 1941.

A Time to Speak, Houghton (Boston, MA), 1941.

(With William S. Paley and Edward R. Murrow) *In Honor of a Man and an Ideal . . . Three Talks on Freedom* (radio broadcast, December 2, 1941), [New York, NY], 1942.

American Opinion and the War (Rede Lecture at Cambridge University, Cambridge, England, 1942), Macmillan (New York, NY), 1942.

A Free Man's Books (limited edition), Peter Pauper, 1942.

Report to the Nation, U.S. Office of Facts and Figures, 1942.

A Time to Act, Houghton (Boston, MA), 1943.

The American Story: Ten Broadcasts (presented on NBC Radio, 1944, and for which MacLeish served as commentator), Duell, Sloan & Pearce (New York, NY), 1944, 2nd edition, 1960.

Martha Hillard MacLeish, 1856-1947, privately printed, 1949.

Poetry and Opinion: The Pisan Cantos of Ezra Pound, University of Illinois Press (Champaign, IL), 1950.

Freedom Is the Right to Choose: An Inquiry into the Battle for the American Future, Beacon Press (Boston, MA), 1951.

Poetry and Journalism, University of Minnesota Press (Minneapolis, MN), 1958.

Poetry and Experience, Riverside Editions, 1960.

The Dialogues of Archibald MacLeish and Mark Van Doren (televised, 1962), Dutton (New York, NY), 1964.

A Continuing Journey, Houghton (Boston, MA), 1968.

Champion of a Cause: Essays and Addresses on Librarianship, compiled by Eva M. Goldschmidt, American Library Association, 1971.

Riders on the Earth: Essays and Recollections, Houghton (Boston, MA), 1978.

Letters of Archibald MacLeish, 1907 to 1982, edited by R.H. Winnick, Houghton (Boston, MA), 1983.

Archibald MacLeish: Reflections, edited by Bernard A. Drabeck and Helen E. Ellis, University of Massachusetts Press (Amherst, MA), 1986.

DRAMA

Nobodaddy (verse play), Dunster House, 1926.

(Librettist with Nicolas Nabokoff) *Union Pacific* (verse ballet written for Federal Theatre Project [WPA]), produced on Broadway, 1934.

Panic: A Play in Verse (produced on Broadway, 1935), Houghton (Boston, MA), 1935.

The Fall of the City: A Verse Play for Radio (presented on CBS Radio, 1937, and on CBS-TV, 1962), Farrar & Rinehart (New York, NY), 1937.

Air Raid: A Verse Play for Radio (presented on CBS Radio, 1938), Harcourt (New York, NY), 1938.

The Son of Man (radio play), CBS Radio, 1947.

The Trojan Horse (verse play; presented on BBC-Radio, London, c. 1950), Houghton (Boston, MA), 1952.

This Music Crept by Me upon the Waters (verse play), Harvard University Press (Cambridge, MA), 1953.

J. B.: A Play in Verse (produced at Yale School of Drama; produced on Broadway, 1958), Houghton (Boston, MA), 1958.

The Secret of Freedom (television play), produced for *Sunday Showcase,* 1960.

Three Short Plays (includes *Air Raid, The Fall of the City,* and *The Secret of Freedom*), Dramatists Play Service (New York, NY), 1961.

The Eleanor Roosevelt Story (filmscript; produced by Allied Artists, 1965), Houghton (Boston, MA), 1965.

An Evening's Journey to Conway, Massachusetts (play; produced for NET Playhouse, 1967), Gehenna Press, 1967.

Herakles (verse play; produced, 1965), Houghton (Boston, MA), 1967.

Scratch (based on short story by Stephen Vincent Benét, *The Devil and Daniel Webster*; produced on Broadway, 1971), Houghton (Boston, MA), 1971.

The Great American Fourth of July Parade: A Verse Play for Radio, University of Pittsburgh Press (Pittsburgh, PA), 1975.

Six Plays (contains *Nobodaddy, Panic, The Fall of the City, Air Raid, The Trojan Horse,* and *This Music Crept by Me upon the Waters*), Houghton (Boston, MA), 1980.

OTHER

(Adapter) William Shakespeare, *King Lear* (sound recording; recorded from the original CBS broadcast on July 10, 1937), Radio Yesteryear (Sandy Hook, CT), c. 1975.

(Coauthor with editors of *Fortune*) *Background of War,* Knopf (New York, NY), 1937.

(Author of foreword) William Meredith, *Love Letters from an Impossible Land,* Yale University Press (New Haven, CT), 1944.

(Author of introduction) St. John Perse (pseudonym for Alexis Saint-Leger Leger), *Eloges and Other Poems,* Norton (New York, NY), 1944.

(Editor) Gerald Fitzgerald, *The Wordless Flesh,* [Cambridge, MA], 1960.

(Editor) Edwin Muir, *The Estate of Poetry,* Hogarth (Oxford, England), 1962.

(With others) *Let Freedom Ring,* American Heritage, 1962.

(Editor with E.F. Prichard, Jr., and author of foreword), Felix Frankfurter, *Law and Politics: Occasional Papers, 1913-38,* Peter Smith, 1963.

(Editor) Leonard Baskin, *Figures of Dead Men,* University of Massachusetts Press (Amherst, MA), 1968.

(Author of introduction) *The Complete Poems of Carl Sandburg,* Harcourt (New York, NY), 1970.

The Nature of Poetry: Pulitzer Prize Poet Archibald MacLeish Discusses Poetry (cassette recording), interviewed by Walter Kerr, Center for Cassette Studies, c. 1975.

(Author of foreword) Anthony Piccione, *Anchor Dragging: Poems,* Boa Editions, 1977.

The Young Soldiers: For Chorus and Orchestra, Hildegard (Bryn Mawr, PA), 1995.

Also librettist for *Magic Prison,* 1967.

ADAPTATIONS: The Fall of the City: A Verse Play for Radio was produced as a cassette recording, All-Media Dramatic Workshop (Chicago, IL), 1977; *J. B.: A Play in Verse* was produced as a sound recording, Minnesota Public Radio, 1976.

SIDELIGHTS: A poet, playwright, lawyer, and statesman, Archibald MacLeish had roots firmly planted in both the new and the old worlds. His father, the son of a poor shopkeeper in Glasgow, Scotland, was born in 1837—the year of Victoria's coronation as queen of England—and ran away first to London and then, at the age of eighteen, to Chicago. His mother was a Hillard, a family that, as *Dialogues of Archibald MacLeish and Mark Van Doren* reveals, MacLeish was fond of tracing back through its New England generations to Elder Brewster, the minister aboard the *Mayflower.* MacLeish was born in Glencoe, Illinois, in 1892, attended Hotchkiss School from 1907 to 1911, and from 1911 to 1915 studied at Yale University, where he edited and wrote for the *Yale Literary Magazine,* contributed to the *Yale Review,* and composed *Songs for a Summer's Day,* a sonnet sequence that was chosen as the University's Prize Poem in 1915. MacLeish married Ada Hitchcock in 1916. Two years later he saw service in France and published his first collection of poems, *Tower of Ivory.*

MacLeish viewed World War I as the ending of an old world and the beginning of a new one that was *sensed* rather than understood. His early poetry was his attempt to understand this new world; MacLeish would later say that his education regarding this world began not in his undergraduate years at Yale, but in years after the war at Harvard Law School. As he declared in *Riders on the Earth: Essays and Recollections,* Harvard sparked in him a sense of the human tradition, "the vision of mental time, of the interminable journey of the human mind, the great tradition of the intellectual past which knows the bearings of the future."

MacLeish's personal dilemma, and the constant theme of his early writings, was the reconciliation of idealism with reality. This theme had run through his undergraduate short stories and through his first long poem, "Our Lady of Troy," which was published in *Tower of Ivory.* In his own life, he resolved this dilemma by turning from his promising career as a lawyer to pursue the vocation for which the law courts had left him little time—that of poet. In the summer of 1923, MacLeish announced his commitment to poetry by moving from Boston with his wife and two children, into a fourth-floor flat on the Boulevard St. Michel in Paris.

The first major period of MacLeish's poetic career—some would say the only major one—thus began in the early 1920s, when he gave up the law and moved abroad, and closed in the later 1930s, when he took on a succession of "public" obligations. During these years, MacLeish's work was made up of nine longer poems or sequences of poems, accompanied by lyric meditations and statements in various forms on diverse but characteristic themes: doubt, loss, alienation, art, aging, the quest. The shorter poems, some of them very successful, have by anthologizing and other emphases become better known than the longer ones. MacLeish's collection, *New and Collected Poems, 1917-1984,* however, emphasizes the interrelation of his longer and shorter poems, as did his first major collection, *Poems, 1924-1933.*

The "other poems" of 1924's *The Happy Marriage, and Other Poems,* still late Victorian prentice-work, are often reminiscent of Edwin Arlington Robinson—whom MacLeish admired—and are justly forgotten. But the title poem, with its more complex, more contemporary subject, alternates skilled imitation of major predecessors with accents of personal authority. It could even be argued that this mixed transitional style fits, if only by chance, the protagonist's own confusion between trite attitudes and existential authenticity. By Part Four of *The Happy Marriage,* the protagonist's recognition of marital reality has found its poetic voice, what Grover Smith called in *Archibald MacLeish* "conscious symbolism; witty, almost metaphysical strategies of argument; compressed and intense implications."

The Pot of Earth tells the very different story of a very different figure, a young woman deeply affected psychologically or culturally by archetypal myths of woman's fertility and its transformative powers as seen through "the figure of the dying god whose imaginative presence is at the core of cultural vitality," according to John B. Vickery in *The Literary Impact of the Golden Bough.* Obsessed by symbolic mythical images—excessively so in the unrevised version—she dies in childbirth, sought by or seeking a death dictated by myth, the unconscious, or simple biology. To tell her moving story, MacLeish interweaves narrative and lyric forms, regular and irregular verse of great eloquence that reinforces the pathos, irony, and mystery of her fate.

Besides marking the first publication of *Einstein,* 1926's *Streets in the Moon* has some of MacLeish's best and best-known shorter poems. In "Memorial Rain"—directly—and in "The Silent Slain"—indirectly—MacLeish came to what terms he could with concerns identified in Paul Fussell's *The Great War and Modern Memory.* "The Farm" illustrates the search for New England roots that ran through MacLeish's career and his writings in prose and verse. Other poems reflect the varying expatriate moods that came together after a few years in "American Letter." And the too well known, too often misunderstood "Ars Poetica" conveys in its images, imitative form, and self-contradictions MacLeish's permanent conviction that a poem should both mean and be.

In *Einstein,* published separately in 1929, MacLeish presented a day's meditation that recapitulates the major stages in Albert Einstein's physical and metaphysical struggle to contain and comprehend the physical universe, from classical empiricism through romantic empathy to modern, introspective, analytic physics. In flexible, elaborate, evocative blank verse, with an epigrammatic literal/allegorical prose gloss, and in a rich texture of spatial imagery the poem "narrates" Einstein's quest for knowledge. To Frederick J. Hoffman in *The Twenties,* this quest is shown as "pathetic and futile," but to Lauriat Lane Jr., in an *Ariel* essay, it is "potentially tragic" and an example of "modern, existential Man Thinking."

Citing *The Hamlet of A. MacLeish,* Leslie Fiedler in *Unfinished Business* identified four appeals of the story of Hamlet to the American imagination: 1) "anguish and melancholy," 2) "the notion of suicide," 3) "the inhibitory nature of conscience," and 4) "an oddly apt parable of our relationship to Europe." This poem, MacLeish's most complex and elaborate, addresses all four subjects. Combining and contrasting what Fiedler elsewhere called signature and archetype, autobiography and myth, the work, which contains fourteen sections and a Shakespearean gloss, juxtaposes dialectically *Hamlet,* MacLeish's personal and poetic autobiographical uncertainties, and two fulfilled quests—a medieval Grail romance and tribal migrations out of the *Anabase* of Saint-John Perse, whose fulfillment only intensifies the doubts and despairs of Hamlet/MacLeish. As he recorded in *A Reviewer's ABC,* Conrad Aiken, who had found *Einstein* "a long poem which any living poet might envy, as rich in thought as it is in color and movement," labeled *The Hamlet of A. MacLeish* "a kind of brilliant *pastiche,*" although "full of beautiful things." Aiken went on, however, to pose the unanswered question of "whether [MacLeish's] 'echoes' might not, by a future generation, be actually preferred to the things they echo." Often, in MacLeish's work, such "echoes" are a form of brilliant, purposeful parody, an additional stylistic power.

As its title implies, MacLeish published *New Found Land* after he had returned to America for good. Less varied and experimental in form than the short poems of *Streets in the Moon,* the poems in the slender *New Found Land* share the moods and concerns of *The Hamlet of A. MacLeish.* Along with "American Letter," the book has one of MacLeish's most famous "international" poems, "You, Andrew Marvell," and one of his greatest regional ones, "Immortal Autumn." For Signi Falk in *Archibald MacLeish, New Found Land* reveals "a poet torn between the old world and the new."

Conquistador, too, combines the old world and the new, but by 1932, the year of the book's publication, the choice had become clear if often tragic in its outcome. In the conquerors of Central American native civilization MacLeish found a romantic, exotic history that could also serve as a myth, a metaphor, for closer, more familiar history and concerns. In Montezuma, Cortez, and Diaz the poem offers three figures—god, hero, and man—who share the reader's attention and good will and who are examined in an ironic context of human blood and natural beauty, greed for gold and sun-worship, political intrigue and heroic quest. Seeing the poem wholly through its narrator, Diaz, Allen Tate praised the poem for its "finely sustained tone," its "clarity of sensuous reminiscence," and its "technical perfection," but found in its sentimentality "one of the examples of our modern sensibility at its best; it has the defect of its qualities," as Tate recorded in *Essays of Four Decades.*

In their many interrelations, *The Pot of Earth, Einstein, The Hamlet of A. MacLeish,* and *Conquistador* form a tetralogy of four major high modernist poems. With "Elpenor"—originally "1933"—which appeared in *Poems, 1924-1933* and which has subsequently been republished under each title, MacLeish moved toward the "public speech" of the post-Depression, Rooseveltian 1930s. Both a vivid retelling and sequel to Homer and Dante, this compressed little epic populates a modern Hell in the manner of Ezra Pound's poetry and points "the way on," in MacLeish's characteristic symbolic topographical imagery, where its readers can "begin it again: start over."

Among the other new poems in *Poems, 1924-1933,* "Frescoes for Mr. Rockefeller's City" dealt with a public controversy and caused additional public excitement. Although praised by Cleanth Brooks in *Modern Poetry and the Tradition,* it has "not only ideological but functional problems," as Grover Smith declared; and some of its sections, like several of MacLeish's other public poems of the 1930s, reveal "the absence of arresting images and the slackness of the rhythm" that troubled David Luytens in *The Creative Encounter.* However, as recorded in *Literary Opinion in America,* Morton D. Zabel also found in these public poems "a signal of profitable intentions" and discovered "a very moving beauty" in the very unpublic set of lyrics, "The Woman on the Stair," in *Public Speech.*

The last of MacLeish's longer poems of the 1930s was *America Was Promises.* In an essay collected in *A Poet's Alphabet,* Louise Bogan attacked it as "MacLeish's saddest and most conglomerate attempt at 'public speech's' to date . . . political poetry, even a kind of official poetry," but Smith later reassessed it as "the most eloquent of the 'public' poems . . . much better as a poem than as a message: for once, MacLeish's adaptation of St.-J. Perse's geographic evocations seems precisely right." *America Was Promises* combines such "geographic evocations" with a quasi-allegorical, populist history of Jefferson and Man, Adams and the Aristocracy, Paine and the People. For *The Human Season: Selected Poems, 1926-1972* MacLeish cut from *America Was Promises* almost all its "official" poetry and possibly made it a much better poem.

Looking back over these first two decades of MacLeish's poetry, Karl Shapiro declared in *Essay on Rime* "a special speech is born / Out of this searching, something absolute, . . . a linguistic dream . . . an influential dialect." In this poetry, said Hyatt H. Waggoner in *The Heel of Elohim,* "The will to believe is certainly present, but so also are the vacant lights, the bright void, the listening, idiot silence"; yet in *North American Review,* Mason Wade saw in the same poetry a "moving . . . intellectual anabasis," and in *Sewanee Review* Reed Whittemore praised some of it as "Democratic Pastoral."

In 1924 *The Happy Marriage* had explored the idea that out of the union of the ideal and the real must emerge a more mature sense of individual identity. This same theme carried through MacLeish's 1926 poetic drama, *Nobodaddy,* a verse play that uses the Adam and Eve story as "the dramatic situation which the condition of self-consciousness in an indifferent universe seems to me to present." MacLeish would affirm, a few years later, that the poet's role was "the restoration of man to his position of dignity and responsibility at the centre of his world." *Nobodaddy* provided its author with the opportunity to return to humankind's origins, to explore the human condition in terms of its myths and mysteries. To MacLeish, the work was a simple and forthright play of the beginnings of human consciousness.

In the resolution of his own sense of self-consciousness, symbolized by his move to Paris in 1923, MacLeish showed a certain kinship with his character Cain. Both had found the strength necessary to sever—in Cain's words—the thick vein "that knots me to the body of the earth," and to grab control of the centers of their own worlds. *Nobodaddy* is the story of humankind attempting to make sense of the chaos of its life. It can also be read as the *apologia* for its author. And its theme of a world in which humankind is bewildered and bored, a world in which its knowledge is not matched by its understanding, is one that would run through much of MacLeish's writing during the 1920s.

When MacLeish returned from Europe in 1928 and settled in Conway, Massachusetts, he had obviously "re-viewed" America. The country's idealism, reflected especially in the philosophies of its founders, supplied him with a sense of identity and place that existential *angst* had failed to engender. The questor had reached this personal goal only to find the obvious truth that each goal is a new beginning and that his search had been only his initiation into what would be a lengthy continuing journey. While the writer was now set to move in new directions, George Dangerfield asserted in a 1931 *Books* essay that "if [MacLeish] were never to write another word, he would still be a poet of definite importance."

MacLeish's first produced stage play, *Panic: A Play in Verse,* is a variation on the Cain story set against the background of the American Depression and a generation of capitalists he felt were in the process of leaving capitalism "intellectually defenseless and unarmed." The conflict of the play is between the will of a man and a fatalistic concept of human life—dialectical materialism. McGafferty surrenders to the delphic oracle of Marxist determinism and thus falls victim to it. As the Blind Man in the play observes, the financier fails because, unlike Cain, he will not trust his own freedom.

The play was MacLeish's attempt to comprehend the real sense of panic in a country where individualism had turned into individual greed and freedom had been replaced by a failing "free enterprise." U.S. Communists found the play particularly frustrating, as MacLeish—who was on the editorial board of *Fortune*—refused to view what they took to be the imminence and inevitability of the Marxist revolution as anything more than a delphic prophecy that the crowd chorus was free to reject. Various other reviews of the production centered on the poet's attempt to create a verse line for the modern stage. Malcolm Cowley declared in a 1935 *New Republic* assessment that the play brought "a new intelligence to the theatre and [embodied] the results of the experiments made by modern poets."

In the late 1930s, speaking with the "public voice" that characterized his writings from the beginning of the decade, MacLeish wrote two verse plays for radio: *The Fall of the City,* broadcast in April, 1937, and *Air Raid,* broadcast in October, 1938. The first of these was the poet's exploration of his sense of a developing worldwide change in the commitment of human consciousness to human freedom. It was a change that MacLeish's own hero and friend, President Franklin D. Roosevelt, had addressed at his first inauguration: "We have nothing to fear but fear itself." *Air Raid* grew out of the German bombing of Guernica and Pablo Picasso's response to that slaughter through his painting, "Guernica." *Air Raid* is a play for voices dealing with the changes in the nature of war and with the alterations in the human spirit that had permitted such changes. MacLeish intended neither script to be primarily a political statement; he looked upon both as poems, as creations that explored what he perceived to be these changes rather than as attempts to persuade. Still, the closeness of MacLeish's sympathies to Roosevelt's has led Luytens to call MacLeish "the poet laureate of the New Deal."

The Trojan Horse, a verse drama first presented on the BBC in 1952, is in many ways a return to earlier decades and earlier characters. Helen of Troy had been earlier seen in a closet drama titled *Our Lady of Troy* and collected in MacLeish's *Tower of Ivory.* She had later appeared in *The Happy Marriage* as the symbol of Beauty. The Blind Man, who earlier laid the future before McGafferty in *Panic,* has the same function here. Paul Brooks, in a note accompanying the first edition of *The Trojan Horse,* tied the play to the McCarthy era, but the script was intended more generally to explore in myth the sense of deception the poet had perceived in his own century. The poetic sense of awareness itself is presented in a 1953 play, *This Music Crept by Me upon the Waters,* where Elizabeth, as did Cain before her, experiences the discovery of her own place in the cosmos.

The public voice that found its way into MacLeish's poetry in the 1930s was a reflection of the sense of public responsibility he had come to accept on his return from Paris. Harriet Monroe in a 1931 issue of *Poetry,* wrote that she has "much faith in the ability of this poet to interpret his age: he has the thinking mind, the creative imagination, the artistic equipment of beautiful words and rhythms." This voice was heard most directly in the many articles and speeches MacLeish wrote on the role of the poet and, through the political chaos of the western world in the 1930s and 1940s, on the direction he felt America should be pursuing. Much of this material has been collected in *A Time to Speak, A Time to Act,* and *A Continuing Journey.* Also, as Falk points out, MacLeish committed himself to such public offices as Librarian of Congress from 1939 to 1944, assistant director of the Office of War Information in 1942,

Assistant Secretary of State from 1944 to 1945, and chair of the U.S. delegation to the founding conference of UNESCO in 1945.

MacLeish said several times that in the long poem "Actfive," published in *Actfive and Other Poems* in 1948, he tried to come to terms with his and the world's experiences in the immediately preceding years: the challenge and suffering of World War II, the opportunities and failures of the peace, the loss of so many faiths. *Conquistador* had offered an implicit choice between god, hero, and man; "Actfive," in its three scenes, redefines and makes that choice. With the God gone, the King dethroned, and Man murdered—all in elegiac, characteristically despairing lines—the heroes of the age are then thrust forward in their emptiness through sardonically abrupt rhythms. They give way, in turn, to "the shapes of flesh and bone," in whose moving, subtly musical, indirect voices MacLeish's long involvement with Matthew Arnold is fulfilled. The result is a poetic affirmation, "humanist and existentialist," according to Luytens, for an even darker, more confused, post-Arnoldian time.

"Actfive" was MacLeish's last poem to interweave lyric statement and emblematically condensed narrative within an extended structure of feeling and idea. In the ten years from 1944 to 1954, called by Grover Smith "his second renaissance," he published over eighty short poems, half of them, apparently, written in two very creative years after he began teaching poetry at Harvard, where he was Boylsten Professor from 1949 to 1962. In style these poems, having many forms and treating a great variety of subjects, might be called neomodernist, embodying a riper, wiser Imagism, for example. But their combination of immediate, personal concern with impersonal form, image, and language is not easily labeled. Poets Hayden Carruth in *Effluences from the Sacred Cave*, Richard Eberhart in *Virginia Quarterly Review*, John Ciardi in *Atlantic*, and Kimon Friar in *New Republic* have all praised these poems.

Among the lyrics of the private world, which record recognizable and therefore meaningful experience spoken in a living, personal voice, are such fine love poems as "Ever Since," "Calypso's Island," "What Any Lover Learns," and such testaments of poetic and humanist faith as "A Man's Work," "The Two Priests," "The Infinite Reason," and "Reasons for Music," some of which also look outward to the public world. MacLeish's poetic statements of and for the world of public affairs are designed both "to lash out" and to try to "make *positive* sense of the public world," as he as-

serted in *Poetry and Experience.* "Brave New World," for example, "lashes out" in tight, cutting quatrains at the loss of Jefferson's vision of human freedom. "The Danger in the Air" and "The Sheep in the Ruins" move meditatively toward making some sense against the danger, amid the ruins. Very few of these short poems look toward Rimbaud's anti-world. For MacLeish, as for Rimbaud, the sea was the great image of the Unknown: over the sea in "Voyage West," beneath it in "The Reef Fisher." MacLeish declared in *Poetry and Experience* that "Rimbaud's anti-world was not a rejection of the *possibility* of the world"; nor were MacLeish's own few visions of that anti-world. Poems of the arable world try to make familiar yet tragic "truth of the passing-away of the world." In his *Dialogues* with Mark Van Doren, MacLeish testified how much the arable world of Uphill Farm in Massachusetts meant to him, as did "The Two Trees," "The Snow Fall," and "The Old Men in the Leaf Smoke." From Caribbean Antigua, on the other hand, probably came "The Old Man to the Lizard" and "Vicissitudes of the Creator." And the truth of the passing-away of the world took another, more direct, even more moving form in "For the Anniversary of My Mother's Death" and "My Naked Aunt."

Several volumes of MacLeish's prose—*Poetry and Experience,* a section of *A Continuing Journey,* and *Poetry and Opinion: The Pisan Cantos of Ezra Pound,* on the controversy surrounding Ezra Pound's support for Mussolini during World War II—grew out of his teaching. His two earliest collections of literary and political statements were *A Time to Speak* and *A Time to Act*—"a couple of books of speeches," as he labeled them in *Letters of Archibald MacLeish, 1907 to 1982.* Some of these prose pieces, most notoriously "The Irresponsibles," strayed dangerously close to propaganda—admittedly in a time of great public danger—and were attacked for this failing by critics like Edmund Wilson in *Classics and Commercials* and Morton D. Zabel in *Partisan Review.* In still another vein, *Champion of a Cause: Essays and Addresses on Librarianship* reprinted MacLeish's deliberately nonprofessional, nontechnical "essays and addresses on librarianship."

MacLeish's prose, for the most part, bore public witness to familiar but important ideas and beliefs. The editors of *Ten Contemporary Thinkers* included four MacLeish essays that represent well the range of his prose: "The Writer and Revolution," "Humanism and the Belief in Man," "The Conquest of America," and "The Isolation of the American Artist;" his essays and books specifically on poetry and poets eloquently and even more significantly witness to the broadly defined powers of poems to move their readers. And even the most topical of MacLeish's political essays keep their relevance. In 1949 he first published "The Conquest of America" on the dangers of mindless anti-Communism and failure to reaffirm the American "revolution of the individual." In 1980 the *Atlantic* felt obliged by events to reprint MacLeish's warning. To the end of his long life he continued, in prose and in poetry, to praise and to warn "the Republic."

Having left public life and moved to Harvard by the late 1940s, MacLeish refocused his attention from the social and political themes of the preceding two decades toward an earlier poetic interest: the place and value of man in the universe. In his longer postwar poetic works, he followed his own exhortation to invent the metaphor for the age. His series of poems collected as *Songs for Eve* returned again to the setting of *Nobodaddy* to emphasize once more the fundamental importance of self-consciousness in an indifferent universe. Despite his various attempts to find in Adam and Eve the metaphor for the age, the poet's most successful image of the human spirit appeared four years later on the stage of New York's ANTA Theatre in the character of J.B. *J. B.*'s structure, in the acting edition of the play, differs substantially from the original version published by Houghton Mifflin in 1958, but the main characters remain basically the same. J.B. comes across both the footlights and the page not as a character in a morality play—for the play, despite its early scenes, is not a morality play—but as a flesh-and-blood common man beset by sufferings to which all flesh is heir. And in J. B.'s struggle and success against an inexplicable, brutal, and unjust universe, MacLeish presented what he hoped would be the metaphor for humankind's next era. Like Job, J.B. is not answered, yet his love for Sarah affirms, in the playwrights phrase, "the worth of life in spite of life." That worth is found in a love that paradoxically answers nothing but "becomes the ultimate human answer to the ultimate human question."

After receiving a Pulitzer Prize, his third, for *J. B.,* MacLeish returned to man's quarrels with the gods in *Herakles,* first produced in 1965 and published in 1967. During the first part of the play, Professor Hoadley is drawn to Greece, the *patria* of the intellectual life, in search of the spirit of Herakles, the half-man, half-god who dared to struggle with the unanswered questions of the universe. Balancing Hoadley's search for intellectual perfection is his wife's conviction that life is a concrete reality including the human imperfection her husband would transcend. In the second half of the play, a frustrated Herakles fails to receive a sign from Apollo and angrily ascends to the temple door threatening to

answer his own oracle. But, despite the merits of his deeds, he is unable to perform the god-like act of pronouncing his own destiny. In the end, Hoadley's wife and Herakles's Megara refocus the human spirit where J.B. had earlier found it—on the day-to-day occupation of living, not in glorious myth, but in concrete reality.

If *J. B.* and *Herakles* raise still-unanswered questions, they also affirm that all questions need not be answered. MacLeish's last full-length play, *Scratch,* finds its source in "The Devil and Daniel Webster," Stephen Vincent Benet's treatment of the mythical American confrontation between man and the Devil. Alone of the final three plays, it explores questions that, because of their American roots, could move closer to resolution within the text. MacLeish felt there were three reasons that Benet's story had widened into myth: that the Republic had become full of men and women who had sold their souls "for its comforts and amenities"; that "belief in hell was reviving everywhere and that, if only love of life could be turned into contempt for living, hope into despair, the entire planet would dissolve into that cistern of self-pity where [Samuel Becket's] Godot never comes"; and that Daniel Webster's concern for Liberty and Union, or freedom and government, was as contemporary as it had ever been.

During the 1960s and 1970s, MacLeish also wrote three shorter scripts: a highly polemical television play, *The Secret of Freedom;* an "outdoor play" for the bicentennial of Conway titled *An Evening's Journey to Conway, Massachusetts;* and *The Great American Fourth of July Parade,* a verse play for radio. All three works reflect their author's continual concern for the central values of America's founders, as does his dramatic monologue, "Night Watch in the City of Boston."

MacLeish would grant a series of interviews between 1976 and 1981 that he considered an accurate reflection of his life as a poet. Published as *Archibald MacLeish: Reflections* in 1986, these interviews portray a writer who was, in the words of *Choice* reviewer J. Overmyer, "meticulous about the truth, outspoken, and delightful." Full of details about his stay in Paris, his management of the Library of Congress, his law and teaching experiences, and including many reminiscences of family and friends, MacLeish initiated the interviews, which were given to Bernard A. Drabeck and Helen Ellis, teachers from a community college near the aged poet's Massachusetts home. While noting that MacLeish's descriptions of his involvement in Washington politics contained "dramatic moments," William Pratt commented in *World Literature Today* that "nothing reverberated in his memory with the passion of Paris in the twenties, the time when he found himself as a poet and the foundation on which the rest of his distinguished public career was built." Characterizing *Reflections* as "a gifted writer's purely spoken autobiography," *New York Times Book Review* critic Robert Gorham Davis maintained that "In this genial, relaxed book we have a golden view of the candidly retrospective statesman-poet in his old age as he really was, with most pretension and all rhetoric abandoned."

Retiring from public life during his last decades, MacLeish became not so much an elder statesman as an elder of various churches: the churches of friendship, of patriotism, of poetry, of love, of death. His talks, interviews, letters, essays, and poems, and his parable-play for radio, *The Great American Fourth of July Parade*, all voice the recurring, autumnal concerns of "the human season" in a quiet, personal, "elderly" voice. Almost ninety, MacLeish died on April 20, 1982, the day after Patriot's Day.

BIOGRAPHICAL AND CRITICAL SOURCES:

BOOKS

Aarons, Daniel, *Writers on the Left*, Harcourt (New York, NY), 1961.

Aiken, Conrad, *A Reviewer's ABC*, Meridian Publishing, 1958.

Amend, Victor E., and Leo T. Hendrick, editors, *Ten Contemporary Thinkers*, Free Press of Glencoe (New York, NY), 1964.

Benson, Frederick R., *Writers in Arms*, New York University Press (New York, NY), 1967.

Bogan, Louise, *A Poet's Alphabet*, McGraw (New York, NY), 1970.

Brenner, Rica, *Poets of Our Time*, Harcourt (New York, NY), 1941.

Brooks, Cleanth, *Modern Poetry and the Tradition*, Oxford University Press (New York, NY), 1965.

Bush, Warren V., editor, *Dialogues of Archibald MacLeish and Mark Van Doren*, Dutton (New York, NY), 1964.

Carruth, Hayden, *Effluences from the Sacred Caves*, University of Michigan Press (Ann Arbor, MI), 1983.

Contemporary Literary Criticism, Thomson Gale (Detroit, MI), Volume 3, 1975, Volume 8, 1978, Volume 14, 1980, Volume 68, 1992.

Dictionary of Literary Biography Yearbook: 1982, Thomson Gale (Detroit, MI), 1983.

Donoghue, Denis, *The Third Voice*, Princeton University Press (Princeton, NJ), 1959.

Drabek, Bernard A., and Helen E. Harris, *Archibald MacLeish: Reflections*, University of Massachusetts Press (Amherst, MA), 1986.

Ellis, Helen E., Bernard A. Drabeck, and Margaret E. Howland, *Archibald MacLeish: A Selectively Annotated Bibliography*, Scarecrow Press (Metuchen, NJ), 1995.

Falk, Signi Lenea, *Archibald MacLeish*, Twayne (Boston, MA), 1965.

Fiedler, Leslie, *Unfinished Business*, Stein & Day (New York, NY), 1972.

Fussel, Paul, *The Great War and Modern Memory*, Oxford University Press (New York, NY), 1975.

Gassner, John, *Theatre at the Crossroads*, Holt (New York, NY), 1960.

Graff, Gerald, *Poetic Statement and Critical Dogma*, University of Chicago Press (Chicago, IL), 1970.

Hoffman, Frederick J., *The Twenties*, Viking (New York, NY), 1955.

Hone, Ralph E., editor, *The Voice out of the Whirlwind*, Chandler, 1960.

Literary Opinion in America, Harper (New York, NY), 1937.

Luytens, David Bulwer, *The Creative Encounter*, Secker & Warburg (London, England), 1960.

MacLeish, Archibald, *Six Plays*, Houghton (Boston, MA), 1980.

Mullaly, Edward J., *Archibald MacLeish: A Checklist*, Kent State University Press (Kent, OH), 1973.

Nemerov, Howard, *Poetry and Fiction*, Rutgers University Press (Rutgers, NJ), 1963.

Saltzman, Jack, editor, *Years of Protest*, Pegasus, 1967.

Saltzman, Jack, editor, *The Survival Years*, Pegasus, 1969.

Shapiro, Karl, *Essay on Rime*, Reynal & Hitchcock, 1945.

Slote, Bernice, editor, *Myth and Symbol*, University of Nebraska Press (Lincoln, NE), 1963.

Smith, Grover, *Archibald MacLeish*, University of Minneapolis Press (Minneapolis, MN), 1971.

Tate, Allen, *Essays of Four Decades*, Oxford University Press (New York, NY), 1970.

Vickery, John B., *The Literary Impact of the Golden Bough*, Princeton University Press (Princeton, NJ), 1973.

Waggoner, Hyatt H., *The Heel of Elohim*, University of Oklahoma Press (Norman, OK), 1950.

Wilson, Edmund, *Classics and Commercials*, Farrar, Straus (New York, NY), 1950.

Winnick, R. H., editor, *Letters of Archibald MacLeish*, Houghton (Boston, MA), 1983.

Winters, Yvor, *Uncollected Essays and Reviews*, Swallow Press, 1973.

PERIODICALS

American Literature, Volume 15, 1943; Volume 35, 1963.

American Review, May, 1934.

Ariel, July, 1984.

Atlantic, May, 1953; March, 1983, Phoebe-Lou Adams, review of *The Letters of Archibald MacLeish,* p. 116.

Books, January, 1931.

Boston Globe, April 22, 1982.

Canadian Review of American Studies, spring, 1983.

Chicago Tribune Book World, April 24, 1983.

Choice, February, 1987, p. 882.

Christian Science Monitor, November 21, 1968.

English Journal, June, 1935.

Harper's, December, 1971.

New Mexico Quarterly, May, 1934.

New Republic, March 27, 1935; December 15, 1952; July 22, 1967.

New York Times, March 2, 1971; May 16, 1971.

New York Times Book Review, August 6, 1967; January 28, 1968; July 9, 1978; January 2, 1983; August 10, 1986, p. 14; December 17, 1995, p. 39.

North American Review, summer, 1937.

Partisan Review, January, 1941; March, 1941.

Pembroke Magazine, number 7, 1976, pp. 11-27, 95-108.

Poetry, August, 1930; June, 1931; April, 1940.

Saturday Review, March 6, 1954, p. 26; January 3, 1959, pp. 22-23; May 29, 1971, p. 55.

Sewanee Review, October, 1938; July, 1940; April, 1943; October, 1953.

South Atlantic Quarterly, October, 1939.

Theater Arts, August, 1959, pp. 9-11.

University of Toronto Quarterly, October, 1940.

Variety, April 14, 1971.

Virginia Quarterly Review, autumn, 1958.

Washington Post Book World, January 21, 1968; November 3, 1968.

World Literature Today, spring, 1987, pp. 293-94.

OBITUARIES:

PERIODICALS

Chicago Tribune, April 22, 1982.

Library Journal, June 1, 1982.

London Times, April 22, 1982.

New Republic, January 24, 1983, p. 28.

Newsweek, May 3, 1982.

New York Times, April 22, 1982.

Publishers Weekly, May 7, 1982.

Time, May 3, 1982.

Washington Post, April 22, 1982.

*   *   *

MacLEOD, Alistair 1936-

PERSONAL: Born July 20, 1936, in North Battleford, Saskatchewan, Canada; son of Alexander Duncan and Christene (a teacher; maiden name, MacLellan) MacLeod; married Anita MacLellan (a homemaker), September 4, 1971; children: Alexander, Lewis, Kenneth, Marion, Daniel, Andrew. *Education:* Nova Scotia Teachers College, teaching certificate, 1956; St. Francis Xavier University, B.A., B.Ed., 1960; University of New Brunswick, M.A., 1961; University of Notre Dame, Ph.D., 1968. *Religion:* Roman Catholic.

ADDRESSES: Home—231 Curry Ave., Windsor, Ontario, Canada N9B 2B4. *Office*—Department of English, 2100 Chrysler Hall North, University of Windsor, Windsor, Ontario, Canada N9B 3P4.

CAREER: Worked variously as miner, logger, and farmhand. Schoolteacher on Port Hood Island, 1956-57; Nova Scotia Teachers College, Truro, lecturer in English, 1961-63; University of Notre Dame, South Bend, IN, lecturer in English, 1964-66; associated with English faculty, Indiana University (now Indiana University-Purdue University) at Fort Wayne, 1966-69; University of Windsor, Windsor, Ontario, Canada, professor of English, 1969—; associated with faculty, Banff School of Fine Arts, summer program, 1981-86.

MEMBER: Writers Union of Canada, Writers Federation of Nova Scotia.

AWARDS, HONORS: Selected as the Canadian participant in a Canada-Scotland writers-in-residence exchange program, 1984-85; Trillium Prize, Thomas Head Raddall Atlantic Fiction Award, and Dartmouth Book and Writing Award for Fiction, all 2000, all for *No Great Mischief;* International IMPAC Dublin Literary Award, 2001, for *No Great Mischief.*

WRITINGS:

SHORT STORIES

The Lost Salt Gift of Blood (short stories; includes "The Boat"), McClelland & Stewart (Toronto, Canada), 1976, published as *The Lost Salt Gift of Blood: New and Selected Stories,* Ontario Review Press (New York, NY), 1988.

As Birds Bring Forth the Sun and Other Stories, McClelland & Stewart (Toronto, Canada), 1986.

Island: The Collected Short Stories of Alistair MacLeod, McClelland & Stewart (Toronto, Canada), 2000.

Work represented in anthologies, including *Best American Short Stories,* 1969, 1975; *Best Canadian Short Stories; Best Modern Canadian Short Stories,* Hurtig, 1978.

PLAYS

The Lost Salt Gift of Blood, Mulgrave Road Co-Op Theatre Company, tour of twenty Maritime communities, 1982.

The Boat (based on short story), Mulgrave Road Co-Op Theatre Company, tour of Maritimes, spring, 1983, Canadian National Tour, summer-fall, 1983, and tour of England and Scotland, spring, 1984.

OTHER

No Great Mischief (novel), McClelland & Stewart (Toronto, Canada), 1999.

Author of *A Textual Study of Thomas Hardy's "A Group of Noble Dames,"* 1968. Contributor to periodicals, including *Tamarack Review, Antigonish Review, Canadian Forum, Dalhousie Review, Quarry, Fiddlehead,* and *Amethyst.* Fiction editor of *University of Windsor Review,* 1973—.

SIDELIGHTS: Short story writer and educator Alistair MacLeod is one of the "most important chronicler[s] in fiction of the landscape and folkways of Cape Breton to appear on the Canadian literary scene in recent years," declared James Doyle in the *Dictionary of Literary Biography.* Known for his concise style and "historic present" narration, MacLeod has published work in periodicals, including several pieces of poetry, and collected many of his stories into two books. As Doyle explained, "Although his creative output is small . . . [MacLeod] has earned the respect of critics and editors in both Canada and the United States, especially for his mastery of the short-story form." When in 1999 MacLeod published his first novel, *No Great Mischief,* this too was met with critical acclaim.

Born in Saskatchewan in 1936 to natives of Cape Breton Island, MacLeod moved with his family back to Nova Scotia while he was still quite young. He grew up in the small, close-knit Maritime communities which later became central to his writing. MacLeod's work recreates "the scenery and human drama of his native region," described Doyle. "Virtually all his stories are devoted to the exposition and dramatization of the folkways, socioeconomic realities, and relationships of family and community in Cape Breton." In many of his tales, MacLeod uses a form of narration in which the past is described and remembered in terms of the present. His "repeated use of [this technique] indicates that he values its aura of the old-fashioned, its suggestion of stories being swapped around a hot stove. And even the stories which don't use the technique share a tone of thoughtful nostalgia," noted Laurence Ricou in *Canadian Literature.*

MacLeod's first collection, *The Lost Salt Gift of Blood,* contains seven stories. "Initiation into adulthood, separation from family, return to the place of origin from an adult life faraway, become occasions and themes for the narrators' reflections," wrote Richard Lemm in *Atlantic Provinces Book Review.* Titles such as "The Return" and "The Road to Rankin's Point" deal with a homecoming; "In the Fall" with a family facing emotional and economic stress; while mining life is the focus of "The Vastness of the Dark." "The Boat," which was adapted for stage, concerns a father and son relationship. The narrator, a college professor, remembers his childhood, especially his deceased father, who spent his life as a fisherman. For MacLeod's characters, "a literary education is very much a two-edged sword, serving to alienate characters from their origins even as it releases them from the more gruelling demands of necessary labor," commented *Canadian Literature* contributor Colin Nicholson.

"MacLeod's writing strikes home with immediacy, intensity and poetic beauty," declared Lemm. "MacLeod's stories grow from their roots in a particular place and people to a universality of human experience and insight." Nicholson also praises the "immediacy and intensity" of Macleod's tales in *The Lost Salt Gift of Blood,* noting: "It is in the sculpting of the emotional infrastructure of any given situation that MacLeod's talent shines." Jon Kertzer, writing in *Canadian Forum,* judged that "The great merit of these stories [in *The Lost Salt Gift of Blood*] is their power and authenticity of detail. . . . The weakness of the book is a tendency to excess." Kertzer felt that "one tale ceases to dramatize and lapses into moralizing; another indulges in a poolroom melodrama; another allows its tone to become remorselessly elegiac." However, he concluded: "But at his best, MacLeod weds his characters to their locales so that each is enriched by the other."

MacLeod published a second collection, *As Birds Bring Forth the Sun and Other Stories,* ten years after *The Lost Salt Gift of Blood.* The stories in *As Birds Bring Forth the Sun and Other Stories* "recall and at the same time transcend the heart of this earlier collection," representing "a mature and complex acceptance of the problematic and ultimately tragic nature of experience," commented Janice Kulyk Keefer in *Antigonish Review.* The stories are played against the backdrop of Atlantic Canada, and include "The Tuning of Perfection," in which a seventy-eight-year-old man watches traditions die or get twisted beyond recognition. Tales of fishermen and miners are also a part of *As Birds Bring Forth the Sun and Other Stories,* as in "Vision," which presents a slice of life in a fishing town, and "The Closing Down of Summer," where the mining group leader justifies his choice of mining over a college education. In "Winter Dog" a man remembers, while waiting for news of a dying relative, the childhood pet that once saved his life. Thomas P. Sullivan praised "Winter Dog" in *Quill & Quire,* writing: "This is memory as private myth (another of MacLeod's recurring themes). The effect is hypnotic; the imagery is burned into the brain and lingers."

"Death, sexual love, and the power of the past: these are the themes that run through all the stories and unify" *As Birds Bring Forth the Sun and Other Stories,* noted David Helwig in *Queen's Quarterly,* judging that the collection has "a powerful poetic unity." "While very much aware of the hardness of life for the people he writes about, MacLeod's wise heart perceives their secret longings, admires their patient strengths, and records with great authority the small triumphs in their struggle for dignity, pride, and love," commented Jack Hodgins in *Books in Canada. American Book Review* contributor Russell Brown declared that "MacLeod is one of the best literary craftsmen in Canada, capable of conveying intense emotions in a prose that never strains for effect." All of MacLeod's previous stories, plus a few new ones, were collected in *Island: The Collected Short Stories of Alistair MacLeod,* published in 2000.

MacLeod's long-awaited first novel was published in 1999. *No Great Mischief* consists of the reflections of Alexander MacDonald, a successful orthodontist who hasn't quite lost touch with his Scottish roots in Cape Breton. The story actually begins in 1779, when a brave highlander named Calum MacDonald leaves Scotland with his family. His wife dies during the course of the Atlantic crossing, leaving Calum with a large family to care for. Rough weather and hard work are the lot of the MacDonalds for generations, but Alexander has left all that behind for a soft, prosperous life. Yet he feels the emptiness of his profession, in which he charges exorbitant fees to make wealthy people smile more perfectly. While not romanticizing more primitive days and their hardships, MacLeod's book denounces the wholesale abandonment of the past. Oliver Thomson in *Economist* wrote, "For Mr. MacLeod, assimilation that destroys the past is a terrible wrong: a denial of the language, family, and culture." Thomson recommended MacLeod as a "gifted" writer "with something provocative to say—and he says it well. He spent several years writing *No Great Mischief,* and none of that time was wasted. His storytelling is taut and lucid. His characters possess strength and depth. They linger in your mind." A.J. Anderson, writing in *Library Journal,* commented on the author's "remarkable ability to create and handle an intricate plot that goes back and forth between past and present." Much of the tale unfolds as Alexander and his older, alcoholic brother journey to Cape Breton; a *Publishers Weekly* reviewer commented, "What emanates is a loving retrieval of a people's native strategy of survival through history and across a changing landscape. . . . The overall effect is authenticity, and the lack of irony is as bracing as the cold spray of the North Atlantic."

"MacLeod—ex-miner, ex-logger, ex-farmboy, professor of English and creative writing—blends a country man's clear-eyed and unselfconscious awareness with a sometimes stunning ability to write, to succeed in virtually everything he tries," judged Sullivan. Doyle wrote in his conclusion: "The folkloric elements, as well as discursive narrative and interior rumination, are the vital means of exploring and preserving an image of life that relatively few people may have experienced in its specific detail but that is universal in its implications. . . . MacLeod is a subtle, economical, forceful writer, whose small but important output must not be overlooked."

Commenting on his deliberate working style in an interview with Theodore Sleuth for *Dolomite,* MacLeod said, "I hardly ever do drafts. I do one sentence and I get ready and I do another sentence. I think this individual sentence is as good as it's going to be and then I start my next individual sentence."

BIOGRAPHICAL AND CRITICAL SOURCES:

BOOKS

Contemporary Literary Criticism, Volume 56, Thomson Gale (Detroit, MI), 1989.

Dictionary of Literary Biography, Volume 60: *Canadian Writers since 1960,* Thomson Gale (Detroit, MI), 1987.

Reference Guide to Short Fiction, St. James Press (Detroit, MI), 1993.

PERIODICALS

American Book Review, May-June, 1988, Russell Brown, review of *As Birds Bring Forth the Sun and Other Stories,* pp. 10, 21.

Antigonish Review, summer-autumn, 1986, Janice Kulyk Keefer, review of *As Birds Bring Forth the Sun and Other Stories,* pp. 113-116.

Atlantic Provinces Book Review, December, 1982, Richard Lemm, review of *The Lost Salt Gift of Blood,* p. 9.

Books in Canada, August-September, 1986, Jack Hodgins, review of *As Birds Bring Forth the Sun and Other Stories,* pp. 12-13.

Canadian Forum, June-July, 1976, Jon Kertzer, review of *The Lost Salt Gift of Blood,* p. 51.

Canadian Literature, spring, 1978, pp. 116-118; winter, 1985, pp. 90-101.

Economist, June 17, 2000, Oliver Thomson, review of *No Great Mischief,* p. 12.

Library Journal, June 1, 2000, A.J. Anderson, review of *No Great Mischief,* p. 198.

Maclean's, November 8, 1999, John Demont, review of *No Great Mischief,* p. 88; July 17, 2000, John Bemrose, review of *Island: The Collected Stories,* p. 48.

New York Times Book Review, September 11, 1988, Louise Erdrich, review of *The Lost Salt Gift of Blood,* p. 15.

Publishers Weekly, April 3, 2000, review of *No Great Mischief,* p. 62.

Queen's Quarterly, winter, 1987, David Helwig, review of *As Birds Bring Forth the Sun and Other Stories,* pp. 1022-1024.

Quill & Quire, May, 1986, Thomas P. Sullivan, review of *As Birds Bring Forth the Sun and Other Stories,* p. 25.

Time International, May 8, 2000, Katherine Govier, "Fathers and Sons: Alistair MacLeod Plumbs the Generational Chasm That Includes Social Class and Geography," p. 57.

ONLINE

January Magazine, http://www.januarymagazine.com/ (September 21, 2000), Sienna Powers, review of *No Great Mischief.*

MADDERN, Al(an)
    See ELLISON, Harlan

*   *   *

MADHUBUTI, Haki R. 1942-
    (Don L. Lee)

PERSONAL: Born Donald Luther Lee; name legally changed, 1973; born February 23, 1942, in Little Rock, AR; son of Jimmy L. and Maxine (Graves) Lee; married Safisha L.; children: three. *Education:* Attended Wilson Junior College, Roosevelt University, and University of Illinois—Chicago Circle; University of Iowa, M.F.A., 1984.

ADDRESSES: Office—Third World Press, 7524 South Cottage Grove, Chicago, IL 60619; Department of English, Speech, and Theatre, Chicago State University, 95th St. at King Dr., Chicago, IL 60628.

CAREER: DuSable Museum of African American History, Chicago, IL, apprentice curator, 1963-67; founder, publisher, and editor, Third World Press, 1967—; Montgomery Ward, Chicago, stock department clerk, 1963-64; post office clerk in Chicago, 1964-65; Spiegels, Chicago, junior executive, 1965-66; Cornell University, Ithaca, NY, writer-in-residence, 1968-69; Northeastern Illinois State College, Chicago, poet-in-residence, 1969-70; University of Illinois, Chicago, lecturer, 1969-71; Howard University, Washington, DC, writer-in-residence, 1970-78; Morgan State College, Baltimore, MD, 1972-73; Chicago State University, Chicago, professor of English, 1984—. Director of the Institute of Positive Education, Chicago, 1969-91. Cofounder, New Concept Development Center, 1971. *Military service:* U.S. Army, 1960-63.

MEMBER: African Liberation Day Support Committee (vice chairperson, 1971-73), Congress of African People (member of executive council, 1970-74), Organization of Black American Culture, Writers Workshop (founding member, 1967-75).

AWARDS, HONORS: Distinguished Writers Award, Middle Atlantic Writers Association, 1984; American Book Award, 1991; African-American Arts Alliance, 1993; fellowships from the National Endowment for the Arts and the National Endowment for the Humanities.

WRITINGS:

UNDER NAME DON L. LEE

Think Black, Broadside Press (Detroit, MI), 1967, enlarged edition, 1969.

Black Pride, Broadside Press (Detroit, MI), 1967.

For Black People (and Negroes Too), Third World Press (Chicago, IL), 1968.

Don't Cry, Scream (poems), Broadside Press (Detroit, MI), 1969.

We Walk the Way of the New World (poems), Broadside Press (Detroit, MI), 1970.

(Author of introduction) *To Blackness: A Definition in Thought,* Kansas City Black Writers Workshop, 1970.

Dynamite Voices I: Black Poets of the 1960s (essays), Broadside Press (Detroit, MI), 1971.

(Editor, with P.L. Brown and F. Ward) *To Gwen with Love,* Johnson Publishing (Chicago, IL), 1971.

Directionscore: Selected and New Poems, Broadside Press (Detroit, MI), 1971.

(Author of introduction) Marion Nicholas, *Life Styles,* Broadside Press (Detroit, MI), 1971.

The Need for an African Education (pamphlet), Institute of Positive Education (Chicago, IL), 1972.

UNDER NAME HAKI R. MADHUBUTI

Book of Life (poems), Broadside Press (Detroit, MI), 1973.

From Plan to Planet-Life Studies: The Need for Afrikan Minds and Institutions, Broadside Press (Detroit, MI), 1973.

(With Jawanza Kunjufu) *Black People and the Coming Depression* (pamphlet), Institute of Positive Education (Chicago, IL), 1975.

(Contributor) *A Capsule Course in Black Poetry Writing,* Broadside Press (Detroit, MI), 1975.

Enemies: The Clash of Races (essays), Third World Press (Chicago, IL), 1978.

Earthquakes and Sunrise Missions: Poetry and Essays of Black Renewal, 1973-1983 (poems), Third World Press (Chicago, IL), 1984.

Killing Memory, Seeking Ancestors (poems), Lotus, 1987.

Say That the River Turns: The Impact of Gwendolyn Brooks (poetry and prose), Third World Press (Chicago, IL), 1987.

Kwanzaa: A Progressive and Uplifting African American Holiday, Third World Press (Chicago, IL), 1987.

Black Men: Obsolete, Single, Dangerous?; Afrikan American Families in Transition: Essays in Discovery, Solution, and Hope, Third World Press (Chicago, IL), 1990.

(Editor) *Confusion by Any Other Name: Essays Exploring the Negative Impact of the Blackman's Guide to Understanding the Blackwoman,* Third World Press (Chicago, IL), 1992.

(Editor) *Children of Africa,* Third World Press (Chicago, IL), 1993.

Claiming Earth: Race, Rage, Rape, Redemption, Third World Press (Chicago, IL), 1994.

GroundWork: Selected Poems of Haki R. Madhubuti, foreword by Gwendolyn Brooks and introduction by Bakari Kitwana, Third World Press (Chicago, IL), 1996.

(Editor, with Karenga) *Million Man March/Day of Absence: A Commemorative Anthology: Speeches, Commentary, Photography, Poetry, Illustrations, Documents,* Third World Press (Chicago, IL), 1996.

Heartlove: Wedding and Love Poems, Third World Press (Chicago, IL), 1998.

(Editor, with Gwendolyn Mitchell) *Releasing the Spirit,* Third World Press (Chicago, IL), 1998.

Tough Notes: A Healing Call for Creating Exceptional Black Men: Affirmations, Meditations, Readings, and Strategies, Third World Press (Chicago, IL) 2002.

Run toward Fear: New Poems and a Poet's Handbook, Third World Press (Chicago, IL), 2004.

Also author of *Back Again, Home,* 1968, and *One Sided Shootout,* 1968; editor of *Why L.A. Happened: Implications of the 1992 Los Angeles Rebellion,* 1993. Contributor to more than one hundred anthologies, including *Black Women Writers (1950-1980): A Critical Evaluation,* edited by Mari Evans, Anchor-Doubleday, 1984, and *Tapping Potential: English and Language Arts for the Black Learner,* edited by Charlotte K. Brooks and others, Black Caucus of National Council of Teachers of English, 1985. Contributor to numerous magazines and literary journals, including *Black World, Negro Digest, Journal of Black Poetry, Essence, Journal of Black History, Chicago Defender,* and *Black American Literature Forum.* Founder and editor of *Black Books Bulletin,* 1972—; contributing editor, *Black Scholar* and *First World.*

SIDELIGHTS: "Poetry in my home was almost as strange as money," Haki R. Madhubuti, originally named Donald L. Lee, related in *Dynamite Voices I: Black Poets of the 1960s.* Abandoned by his father, and bereaved of his mother at the age of sixteen, Madhubuti made his living by maintaining two paper routes and cleaning a nearby bar. Poetry was scarce in his early life, he explained in the same source, because "what wasn't taught, but was consciously learned, in our early educational experience was that writing of any kind was something that Black people just didn't do." Nonetheless, he has become one of the best-known poets of the black arts movement of the 1960s, a respected and influential critic of poetry, and an activist dedicated to the cultural unity of black Americans. "In many ways," wrote Catherine Daniels Hurst in *Dictionary of Literary Biography,* Madhubuti "is one of the most representative voices of his time. Although most significant as a poet, his work as an essayist, critic, publisher, social activist, and educator has enabled him to go beyond the confines of poetry to the establishment of a black press and a school for black children."

The literature of the Harlem Renaissance—a literary movement of the 1920s and 1930s in which the works of many black artists became popular—was not deeply felt by the majority of America's black population, Madhubuti writes. "In the Sixties, however, Black Art in all its various forms began to flourish as never before: music, theater, art (painting, sculpture), films, prose (novel[s], essays), and poetry. The new and powerful voices of the Sixties came to light mainly because of the temper of the times." The writers of this turbulent generation who worked to preserve a cultural heritage distinct from white culture did not look to previous literary traditions—black or white—for inspiration. Says Madhubuti, "The major influences on the new Black poets were/are Black music, Black life style, Black churches, and their own Black contemporaries."

An *Ebony* article on the poet by David Llorens hailed him as "a lion of a poet who splits syllables, invents phrases, makes letters work as words, and gives rhythmic quality to verse that is never savage but often vicious and always reflecting a revolutionary black consciousness." As a result, his "lines rumble like a street gang on the page," remarked Liz Gant in a *Black World* review. Though Madhubuti believes, as he declares in *Don't Cry, Scream,* that "most, if not all black poetry will be *political,*" he explains in *Dynamite Voices I* that it must do more than protest, since "mere 'protest' writing is generally a weak reaction to persons or events and often lacks the substance necessary to motivate and move people." Black poetry will be powerful, he says, if it is "a genuine reflection of [the poet] and his people," presenting "the beauty and joy" of the black experience as well as outrage against social and economic oppression.

However, some critics hear only the voice of protest in Madhubuti's work. Jascha Kessler, writing in a *Poetry* review, actually saw no poetry in Madhubuti's books. "Anger, bombast, raw hatred, strident, aggrieved, perhaps charismatically crude religious and political canting, propaganda and racist nonsense, yes. . . . [Madhubuti] is outside poetry somewhere, exhorting,

hectoring, cursing, making a lot of noise." But the same elements that grate against the sensibilities of such critics stem from the poet's cultural objectives and are much better received by the poet's intended audience, said others. "He is not interested in modes of writing that aspire to elegance," wrote Gwendolyn Brooks in the introduction of *Don't Cry, Scream.* Madhubuti writes for and to blacks, and "the last thing these people crave is elegance. It is very hard to enchant, with elegant song, the ears of a fellow whose stomach is growling," she noted. Explained Hurst, "often he uses street language and the dialect of the uneducated Black community. . . . He uses unconventional abbreviations and strung-together words . . . in a visually rendered dialect designed to convey the stress, pitch, volume, texture, resonance, and the intensity of the black speaking voice. By these and other means, Madhubuti intends to engage the active participation of a black audience accustomed to the oral tradition of storytelling and song."

Poems in *Don't Cry, Scream* and *We Walk the Way of the New World* show the activist-poet's increasing incorporation of jazz into his works. In fact, the title poem of *Don't Cry, Scream,* believed Hurst, "should be dedicated to that consummate musician, John Coltrane, whose untimely death left many of his admirers in deep mourning. In this poem (which begs to be read out loud as only the poet himself can do it), Madhubuti strains to duplicate the virtuoso high notes of Coltrane's instrumental sound." This link to music is significant for the black writer: Whereas white Americans preserve themselves or their legacy through literature, black Americans have done so in music, particularly in the blues form. Madhubuti elaborates in *Dynamite Voices I:* "Black music is our most advanced form of Black art. In spite of the debilitating conditions of slavery and its aftermath, Black music endured and grew as a communicative language, as a sustaining spiritual force, as entertainment, and as a creative extension of our African selves. It was one of the few mediums of expression open to Black people that was virtually free of interferences. . . . To understand . . . art . . . which is uniquely Black, we must start with the art form that has been least distorted, a form that has so far resisted being molded into a *pure* product of European-American culture." Numerous references to black musicians and lines that imitate the sounds of black music connect Madhubuti's poetry to that tradition and extend its life as well.

Madhubuti's poetic voice softened somewhat during the 1970s, during which time he directed his energies to the writing of political essays ("From Plan to Planet-Life

Studies: The Need for Afrikan Minds and Institutions" and "Enemies: The Clash of Races"). In addition, he contributed to the establishment of a black aesthetic for new writers through critical essays and reviews. *Dynamite Voices I,* for instance, "has become one of the major contemporary scholarly resources for black poetry," noted Hurst. Fulfilling the role of "cultural stabilizer," he also gave himself to the construction of institutions that promote the cultural independence and education of his people. In a fight against "brain mismanagement" in America, he founded the Third World Press in 1967 to encourage literacy and the Institute of Positive Education in 1969 "to provide educational and communication services to a community struggling to assert its identity amidst powerful, negative forces," he told Donnarae MacCann for an interview published in *Interracial Books for Children Bulletin.*

In the same interview, he defines the publishing goals of the Third World Press, which he founded in 1967: "We look for writers who continue to critically assess the ambivalence of being Black in America. . . . What we are trying to do is to service the great majority of Black people, those who do not have a voice, who have not made it. Black themes over the past years have moved from reaction and rage to contemplative assessments of today's problems to a kind of visionary look at the world," a vision that includes not just blacks, but all people. But the development of the black community remains its main focus, he told David Streitfield for a *Washington Post* article. "There's just so much negative material out there, and so little that helps. That's not to say we don't publish material that is critical, but it has to be constructive." As Streitfield reports, "Third World's greatest success has been with . . . Chancellor Williams' *Destruction of Black Civilization,* which has gone through 16 printings." Other articles also commended the press for breaking even for the first time in nineteen years in 1987.

When reviewing *Tough Notes: A Healing Call for Creating Exceptional Black Men: Affirmations, Meditations, Readings, and Strategies,* published in 2002, for the *Progressive,* Bakari Kitwana began: "The divide between the hip-hop generation (black people born between 1965 and 1984) and the older civil rights/Black Power generation (black baby boomers) is steadily widening. It is a divide that is as vast as the one exhibited inside white America in the 1960s. . . . The older generation usually maintains that remaining in leadership for four decades without nurturing a new generation of leadership is not a problem. The younger generation, for its part, is quick to say that the older generation failed us, while benefiting every day from the struggles

of the '50s and '60s." Kitwana believed that an excellent place for the two generations to begin an attempt to understand each other is in *Tough Notes.* Madhubuti explains in his book that the most urgent reason he wrote it was "my need to personally respond to the hundreds of letters, notes, and telephone calls I received over the years from prisoners—mainly young men seeking guidance and a kind word." In the heavily autobiographical work, he touches on subjects as wide ranging as history and identity to education to parenting in an effort to help guide the younger generation through the abyss of obstacles faced by them. "Young progressives, activists, institution-builders, intellectuals, writers, and everyday people will find tons of useful information in this blend of personal narrative and advice," commented Kitwana.

Summing up the importance of Madhubuti's work, Hurst stated that, except for Imamu Baraka (LeRoi Jones), Madhubuti is the most widely emulated black poet of all time, and his enormous influence continues to grow. "His books have sold more than a million copies, without benefit of a national distributor. Perhaps Madhubuti will even succeed in helping to establish some lasting institutions in education and in the publishing world. Whether he does or not, he has already secured a place for himself in American literature. He is among the foremost anthologized contemporary revolutionary poets, and he has played a significant role in stimulating other young black talent."

BIOGRAPHICAL AND CRITICAL SOURCES:

BOOKS

Contemporary Literary Criticism, Thomson Gale (Detroit, MI), Volume 2, 1974; Volume 6, 1976.
Dictionary of Literary Biography, Thomson Gale (Detroit, MI), Volume 5: *American Poets since World War II,* 1980; Volume 41: *Afro-American Poets since 1955,* 1985.
Madhubuti, Haki R., *Don't Cry, Scream,* Broadside Press (Detroit, MI), 1969.
Madhubuti, Haki R., *Dynamite Voices I: Black Poets of the 1960s,* Broadside Press (Detroit, MI), 1971.
Madhubuti, Haki R., *Tough Notes: A Healing Call for Creating Exceptional Black Men: Affirmations, Meditations, Readings, and Strategies,* Third World Press (Chicago, IL) 2002.
Vendler, Helen, *Part of Nature, Part of Us,* Howard University Press (Washington, DC), 1980.

PERIODICALS

Black Collegian, February-March, 1971; September-October, 1974.

Black World, April, 1971; June, 1972; January, 1974.

Chicago Sun Times, December 11, 1987.

Chicago Tribune, December 23, 1987.

Ebony, March, 1969, David Llorens.

Emerge, May, 1995; April, 1996; May, 1996.

Essence, June, 1990, p. 44; July, 1991, pp. 92-94.

Interracial Books for Children Bulletin, Volume 17, number 2, 1986.

Jet, June 27, 1974.

Journal of Negro History, April, 1971.

Los Angeles Times Book Review, March 25, 1990.

National Observer, July 14, 1969.

Negro Digest, December, 1969.

New Lady, July-August, 1971.

New York Times, December 13, 1987.

New York Times Book Review, September 29, 1974.

Poetry, February, 1973, Jascha Kessler.

Progressive, July, 2001, Bakari Kitwana, review of *Tough Notes: A Healing Call for Creating Exceptional Black Men: Affirmations, Meditations, Readings, and Strategies,* p. 41.

Publishers Weekly, January 20, 1992, p. 29; December, 1992, pp. 24-25.

Washington Post, June 6, 1971; January 17, 1988.

*   *   *

MAGUIRE, Gregory 1954-
(Gregory Peter Maguire)

PERSONAL: Born June 9, 1954, in Albany, NY; son of John (a journalist) and Helen (Gregory) Maguire; married Andy Newman (a painter), June, 2004; children: Luke, Alex, Helen. *Education:* State University of New York—Albany, B.A., 1976; Simmons College, M.A., 1978; Tufts University, Ph.D., 1990. *Politics:* Democrat. *Religion:* Roman Catholic. *Hobbies and other interests:* Painting in oils or watercolors, song writing, traveling.

ADDRESSES: Agent—(literary) William Reiss, John Hawkins and Associates, 71 W. 23rd St., Ste. 1600, New York, NY 10010; (film) Stephen Moore, Paul Kohner Inc., 9300 Wilshire Blvd., Ste. 555, Beverly Hills, CA 90212; (publicist) Paul Olsweski, HarperCollins, 10 E. 53rd St., New York, NY 10022.

CAREER: Freelance writer, 1977—. Vincentian Grade School, Albany, NY, English teacher, 1976-77; Simmons College Center for the Study of Children's Literature, Boston, MA, faculty member and associate director, 1979-87; Children's Literature New England, Inc.

(nonprofit educational charity), Cambridge, MA, founder, codirector, and consultant, 1987—. Resident at Blue Mountain Center, 1986-90 and 1995-2001; artist-in-residence, Isabella Stewart Gardner Museum, 1994, Hambidge Center, 1998, and the Virginia Center for the Creative Arts, 1999.

AWARDS, HONORS: Fellow at Bread Loaf Writers' Conference, 1978; One Hundred Best Books of the Year citation, New York Public Library, 1980, for *The Daughter of the Moon;* Children's Books of the Year citation, Child Study Children's Books Committee, 1983, and Teachers' Choice Award, National Council of Teachers of English, 1984, both for *The Dream Stealer;* Best Book for Young Adults citation, American Library Association (ALA), and Choices Award, Cooperative Children's Book Center, 1989, both for *I Feel Like the Morning Star;* Parents' Choice Award, and Children's Books of the Year citation, Child Study Committee, both 1994, both for *Missing Sisters;* Notable Children's Book citation, ALA, 1994, for *Seven Spiders Spinning;* Books for the Teen Age selection, New York Public Library, 1996, for *Oasis;* One Hundred Best Books citation, Young Book Trust (England), 1997, Editors' Choice selection, *Booklist,* 1999, One Hundred Best Books of the Year citation, New York Public Library, 1999, named to *Booklist's* Top Ten Historical Fiction for Youth, 1999, Notable Social Studies Trade Book, National Council for the Social Studies/Children's Book Council, and Choices Award, Cooperative Children's Book Center, 2000, all for *The Good Liar;* Books for the Teen Age selection, New York Public Library, 2000, for *Confessions of an Ugly Stepsister.*

WRITINGS:

FOR CHILDREN AND YOUNG ADULTS

The Lightning Time, Farrar, Straus (New York, NY), 1978.

The Daughter of the Moon, Farrar, Straus (New York, NY), 1980.

Lights on the Lake, Farrar, Straus (New York, NY), 1981.

The Dream Stealer, Harper (New York, NY), 1983, Clarion Books (New York, NY), 2002.

The Peace and Quiet Diner (picture book), illustrated by David Perry, Parents' Magazine Press (New York, NY), 1988.

I Feel Like the Morning Star, Harper (New York, NY), 1989.

Lucas Fishbone (picture book), illustrated by Frank Gargiulo, Harper (New York, NY), 1990.

Missing Sisters, Margaret K. McElderry Books (New York, NY), 1994.

The Good Liar, O'Brien Press (Dublin, Ireland), 1995, Clarion Books (New York, NY), 1999.

Oasis, Clarion Books (New York, NY), 1996.

Crabby Cratchitt, illustrated by Andrew Glass, Clarion Books (New York, NY), 2000.

Leaping Beauty: And Other Animal Fairy Tales, illustrated by Chris Demarest, HarperCollins (New York, NY), 2004.

"HAMLET CHRONICLES" SERIES; FOR YOUNG READERS

Seven Spiders Spinning, Clarion (New York, NY), 1994.

Six Haunted Hairdos, illustrated by Elaine Clayton, Clarion Books (New York, NY), 1997.

Five Alien Elves, illustrated by Elaine Clayton, Clarion Books (New York, NY), 1998.

Four Stupid Cupids, illustrated by Elaine Clayton, Clarion Books (New York, NY), 2000.

Three Rotten Eggs, illustrated by Elaine Clayton, Clarion Books (New York, NY), 2002.

A Couple of April Fools, illustrated by Elaine Clayton, Clarion Books (New York, NY), 2004.

One Final Firecracker, illustrated by Elaine Clayton, Clarion Books (New York, NY), 2005.

FICTION FOR ADULTS

Wicked: The Life and Times of the Wicked Witch of the West, Regan Books (New York, NY), 1995.

Confessions of an Ugly Stepsister, Regan Books (New York, NY), 1999.

Lost, Regan Books (New York, NY), 2001.

Mirror Mirror, Regan Books (New York, NY), 2003.

Son of a Witch (sequel to *Wicked*), HarperCollins (New York, NY), 2005.

OTHER

(Editor, with Barbara Harrison) *Innocence and Experience: Essays and Conversations on Children's Literature*, Lothrop (Boston, MA), 1987.

(Editor, with Barbara Harrison) *Origins of Story: On Writing for Children*, Margaret K. McElderry Books (New York, NY), 1999.

(Selector and author of introduction) L. Frank Baum, *A Wonderful Welcome to Oz*, illustrated by John R. Neill, Modern Library (New York, NY), 2005.

Reviewer for *Horn Book, School Library Journal,* and *Christian Science Monitor;* contributor of story "The Honorary Shepherds" to collection *Am I Blue,* 1994.

ADAPTATIONS: Confessions of an Ugly Stepsister was broadcast as a two-hour segment on the American Broadcasting Companies, Inc. (ABC) special *Wonderful World of Disney,* 2002; *Wicked* was adapted as a Broadway musical by writer Winnie Holzman and composer Stephen L. Schwartz and opened in 2003, and it has been adapted as an audiobook.

SIDELIGHTS: Gregory Maguire writes about people on the edge of crisis who manage to survive their ordeal and become stronger because of it. In forms as various as science fiction and fantasy, realistic problem novels, and rhyming picture books, Maguire explores the themes of loss, freedom, spirituality, the power of love, memory, and desire. Not one to shy away from complex plot development in his young-adult titles, the author also has a lighter side, as is evident in such titles as *Missing Sisters* and *Seven Spiders Spinning.* The former is a realistic portrait of growing up Catholic and handicapped; the latter is a broad farce about seven Ice Age spiders that have some fun in a small Vermont town. Much of Maguire's output has been for young readers, but he has also become a popular author of adult books that spoof fairy tales and fantasy stories. His best-selling *Wicked: The Life and Times of the Wicked Witch of the West* is a mature look at the land of Oz created by L. Frank Baum. The work sold so well that he created a sequel, *Son of a Witch,* in 2005.

"Maguire's talents now look unpredictable," Jill Paton Walsh wrote in *Twentieth-Century Children's Writers* in 1989, and characterized his talents as "formidable and still developing." Paton Walsh was a prescient critic: since the early 1990s Maguire has authored several more children's books as well as adult fiction and has edited writings on children's literature. While fantasy was his first inspiration, he has since expanded his genres to include realism and humor. However, through many of his stories, both light and serious, one motif often recurs: the loss of a mother.

Maguire lost his own mother when she passed away while giving birth to him. With his writer father sick at the time of his birth, Maguire and his three older siblings were sent to stay with relatives for a time; Maguire ended up in an orphanage until he was reunited with his newly remarried father. Three more children were born to his father and stepmother, and Maguire finished his childhood years in a family of seven children that was supported by his father's work as a humor columnist at the Albany *Times-Union* and science writer for the New York Health Department.

Maguire grew up in a family that cared deeply about words. In addition to writing professionally, Maguire's father was well known around Albany, New York, as a great storyteller, while his stepmother wrote poetry. Maguire wrote his first story at age five and continued writing them—some as long as a hundred pages—throughout high school and into college. In fact, he was only a junior in college when he wrote what would be his first published book, *The Lightning Time.* He had not intended the novel to be a children's novel. As Maguire explained to a reviewer for *Publishers Weekly,* "The publisher said, 'This protagonist is twelve years old. I'm sending you down to the juvenile department.' They were right."

The Lightning Time tells the story of young Daniel Rider, whose mother is away from home and in the hospital. While staying with his grandmother in the Adirondacks, he meets a mysterious female cousin and together the two struggle to keep Saltbrook Mountain free from development. There is magic lightning that allows animals to talk, a villainous developer, and plenty of eerie effects. A contributor to *Publishers Weekly* thought that Maguire handled this first novel "with professional aplomb," and Ethel L. Heins concluded in *Horn Book* that Maguire "creates tension successfully, and writes with conviction and style."

Maguire followed up the success of his first fantasy with a related title, *The Daughter of the Moon,* which features another cousin of Daniel Rider's, twelve-year-old Erikka. Again the missing-mother theme is explored, this time because Erikka's birth mother is dead and Erikka is being raised by a stepmother in Chicago. Searching for more refinement in her life, Erikka is drawn to a local bookshop as well as to a painting that an aunt has left with her. The painting is magic and Erikka can actually escape into the scene painted there, ultimately retrieving a long-lost lover of the Chicago bookshop owner. There are further subplots, resulting in a complexity that at least one critic found bogged down the novel. *Horn Book* critic Mary M. Burns, while noting that some elements of the ambitious novel did not work, nevertheless concluded that Maguire "has created a fascinatingly complex heroine and a rich collection of adult and child characters."

As the third of Maguire's early fantasy novels, *Lights on the Lake* was meant to form a trilogy of sorts. Again the protagonist is Daniel Rider, and he is once more in upstate New York at Canaan Lake. This is Maguire country; a love for New York state's Lakes region developed during the author's youth. After the one friend Daniel makes, an Episcopalian priest, leaves on a vacation, the young man suddenly finds himself living in two different dimensions, influenced by the strange mists on the lake. A poet devastated by the death of a friend soon occupies Daniel's attention, and he sees a way to help the grieving man by bridging space and time and linking the living with the dead. "The provocative theme incorporates philosophical and spiritual concepts," noted Burns in *Horn Book.* Although a reviewer for the *Bulletin of the Center for Children's Books* thought that the elements of fantasy and realism did not work together, the reviewer did concede that Maguire "has a strong potential for polished and substantive writing."

Maguire's next book, *The Dream Stealer,* was the first book where Maguire felt he had created his own form. Set in Russia, the tale incorporates several age-old motifs from Russian folktales: the Firebird, Vasilissa the Beautiful, and Baba Yaga. The story of how two children set out to save their village from the terrible wolf, the Blood Prince, *The Dream Stealer* blends magic and realism to create a "fantasy full of tension and narrative strength," according to Heins in *Horn Book.* "A first rate fantasy with blood chilling villainy countered with high humor and heroism," concluded Helen Gregory in *School Library Journal.* And Paton Walsh, writing in *Twentieth-Century Children's Writers,* called *The Dream Stealer* the work of "a writer finding his voice, and putting not a foot wrong."

Meanwhile, Maguire had taken a position at Simmons College in their fledgling program in children's literature and was earning his doctorate in American and English literature. Busy with studies and teaching as well as with the compilation of a book of essays in children's literature, Maguire did not publish his next fiction title for five years. *I Feel Like the Morning Star* is a bit of a departure in that the usual fantasy element is played down. Set in a post-atomic-war underworld, the book has a science-fiction feel, but is at heart an adventure novel about three rebellious teenagers who want to break out of their prison-like underworld colony. Roger Sutton, reviewing the novel in the *Bulletin of the Center for Children's Books,* called attention to Maguire's penchant for figurative language and detail as a quality that "mired" an otherwise suspenseful escape novel. Other reviewers, such as Jane Beasley in the *Voice of*

Youth Advocates, thought the work compelling, with Beasley noting that the "suspense builds to a 'can't-put-it-down' threshold."

The picture book *The Peace and Quiet Diner* followed, and then came *Lucas Fishbone,* an attempt at a sophisticated picture book for young adults. "Actually," Maguire once explained, "the writing in *Lucas* is some that I'm the most proud of. The story is a poetic meditation on death and the cycle of life, but somehow it never found its audience." Some critics were less than pleased, such as *School Library Journal* contributor Heide Piehler, who found the work "overwhelming and confusing," and a *Publishers Weekly* contributor who dubbed *Lucas Fishbone* "overwritten."

After the lukewarm reception accorded *Lucas Fishbone,* Maguire took another hiatus from publishing, although he continued to write his usual five pages a day. While living in London, he worked on what would become *Missing Sisters.* The story was inspired by a news report he saw on television about two brothers who were reunited after being separated at birth. Maguire took that germ of an idea with him when he returned to England. Shorter than his other books, *Missing Sisters* is also Maguire's first realistic story, employing none of the fantasy and science fiction elements of his earlier books. It is set in the 1960s and tells the story of a hearing-and-speech-impaired girl who loses the one person close to her—a Catholic nun—but also finds her own missing sister. "The storytelling is sure and steady," wrote Roger Sutton in the *Bulletin of the Center for Children's Books,* while a *Horn Book* contributor called it "an unusual and compelling picture of life in a Catholic home."

The Good Liar, first published in Ireland, is another stylistic departure for Maguire. Set in occupied France in 1942 and written in epistolary style, it tells the story of three brothers who have a fibbing contest that ultimately becomes a matter of life and death. "At once poignant and thoughtful, laced with humor," according to a reviewer for *Horn Book, The Good Liar* "offers readers an unusual perspective on history." Carolyn Phelan commented in *Booklist* that the novel "carries the conviction of memoir rather than invention."

Oasis, another young adult title, explores the effects of losing a loved one. When thirteen-year-old Hand's father dies of a heart attack, Hand's mother returns from the West Coast (where she had moved three years earlier). Hand resents that she abandoned him and suspects

that his Uncle Wolfgang may have had something to do with his father's death. But when he is able to help two immigrants the way his father would have if he had been alive, and when he discovers that his uncle is dying of AIDS, Hand begins to come to terms with his grief. According to a reviewer for *Publishers Weekly,* "Maguire steers clear of the earnest tones that often characterize YA bereavement stories." Debbie Carton, writing for *Booklist,* noted, "Complex, believable characterizations are Maguire's forte."

Maguire's largest shift in writing was the leap he made into adult fiction with *Wicked.* He first began considering writing for adults in the early 1990s, when he was living in England. "I wanted to write . . . about an evil character," Maguire explained to an interviewer for *Publishers Weekly.* In thinking of who he wanted to focus on, he stumbled onto the Wicked Witch of the West. "If to each person in life comes one moment of brainstorming genius, I just had mine, because everyone knows who she is," Maguire continued. "I wrote *Wicked* in five months." Robin J. Schwartz, in her review of *Wicked* for *Entertainment Weekly,* posited that Maguire had begun to wonder how the Wicked Witch of the West became so wicked. "Since no one had the answer," Schwartz wrote, "he did what any inventive, self-respecting writer would do—he created his own malicious character."

The Witch in Maguire's story, whom the author names Elphabra, "is not wicked; nor is she a formally schooled witch. Instead, she's an insecure, unfortunately green Munchkinlander who's willing to take radical steps to unseat the tyrannical Wizard of Oz," according to a *Publishers Weekly* reviewer. But *Wicked* is not just a retelling. An early reviewer for *Publishers Weekly* called the novel a "fantastical meditation on good and evil, God and free will." Though *Wicked*'s early public success was slow, the book became a "cult hit," according to a writer for *Entertainment Weekly,* and in 2003 an adaptation by Steven Schwartz and Winnie Holzman was launched on Broadway. The musical was an instant hit, received three Tony awards, and played to sold-out audiences for months.

Ten years after the release of *Wicked,* Maguire was inspired by fan mail from those who had seen the Broadway show to return to Oz, publishing *Son of a Witch* in 2005. This time, his main character is Liir, who believes he might be the son of the now-dead Elphabra. Liir is on a mission to find and rescue the princess Nor, whom his mother tried and failed to help. The story is definitely for adults only, containing scenes of violence, political oppression, and even a homosexual sex scene between Liir and a guardsman. "This book," as the author explained to *Advocate* writer Regina Marler, "was . . . more and more about the way governments can harness false piety in order to preserve their own power." Marler described the novel as being "even darker than *Wicked*" and a "complex and surprising sequel."

Maguire has continued to focus on an adult readership with such books as *Confessions of an Ugly Stepsister,* a combination of mystery, fairy tale, and fantasy set in seventeenth-century Holland. The story begins at a time when the country is engulfed in tulip trade, with thousands on the verge of losing fortunes invested in tulip bulbs. Among these are Margarethe and her two daughters, Iris and Ruth. Following the murder of her husband, Margarethe brings her daughters back home to begin life in the village of Haarlem. Shunned by the locals, who believe she is a witch, Margarethe eventually finds work with an artist named Schoonmaker who lives on the outskirts of town. The family eventually moves to live with the van den Meers, a business family that has made its fortunes by luring people into making tulip investments. Iris, who is charged to serve as companion to Clara van den Meer, the daughter of the household, soon realizes that there is something amiss in the household and soon all their lives are in even greater turmoil as the three women learn to deal with this latest challenge. Reviewing *Confessions of an Ugly Stepsister* for the *Tribune News Service,* Brenda Cronin praised this "arresting" novel, in particular for its "precise and inventive use of language." Cronin was especially impressed with Maguire's ability to "conjure familiar scenes with new descriptions" and his perceptive observations about human beings. Similarly, a reviewer for *Publishers Weekly* noted that Maguire is able to present "an astute balance of the ideal and sordid sides of human nature in a vision that fantasy lovers will find hard to resist."

Maguire merges his interest in children's fairy tales and adult fantasy fiction in his next publication, *Lost.* A "deftly written, compulsively readable modern-day ghost story," according to a reviewer for *Publishers Weekly, Lost* traces the adventures of American writer Winifred Rudge as she visits London to research a novel about Jack the Ripper. Planning to stay with her cousin, John, in a family-owned house that once belonged to Ozias Rudge, who supposedly served as a model for Charles Dickens's Ebenezer Scrooge, she arrives only to find that John has gone missing and no one seems to know where he has gone. As she attempts to solve the mystery, she realizes that strange, supernatural occur-

rences are transpiring, and an angry poltergeist begins to influence her investigation. "Though *Lost* reads with the pace and urgency of a thriller, it gradually becomes apparent that we are also getting a sophisticated study of a woman whose past is pushing her beyond her limits," explained Robert Plunket in *Advocate.* Margee Smith, writing in *Library Journal,* proclaimed that Maguire "makes the supernatural chillingly real."

With *Mirror Mirror,* Maguire draws inspiration from the Brothers Grimm tale of "Snow White" to create a "dark and vivid" retelling, according to Susan H. Woodcock in *School Library Journal.* Maguire sets the familiar tale in seventeenth-century Italy, under the rule of the eerie Borgias, known historically for their tendency to poison their opponents. Snow White, here named Bianca de Nevada, is taken in by the family, but when Cesare, the brother/lover of Lucrezia, begins to look too closely at the young maiden, jealous Lucrezia condemns her to death. When Bianca is rescued by dwarves, they are not the familiar fairy-tale characters, but are instead a type of hybrid creature of flesh and stone, wakened only by Bianca's presence. "Readers will be intrigued by the new story and yet curious as to how the familiar elements are brought in," commented Woodcock. A critic for *Kirkus Reviews* proclaimed *Mirror Mirror* "every bit as good as *Wicked:* wicked good, in fact."

Though Maguire's adult novels have earned him both critical and popular success in the adult market, he continues to write children's novels. His "Hamlet Chronicles," set in the town of Hamlet, Vermont, was completed with a final installment, *One Final Firecracker,* in 2005. The stories, which feature the fifth-grade class of Miss Earth and her warring factions the Tattletales (the girls) and the Copycats (the boys), have covered territory including mutant chickens, ghosts, rampant cupids, and mysterious disappearances. The series was inspired by reactions of the kids to his speaking engagements. "Over the years," Maguire explained, "I've developed a very funny presentation. The kids usually howl at my speech, but when they learn that I don't have any humorous books, they're disappointed."

Maguire set out to cure that disappointment with the first book in the "Hamlet Chronicles," *Seven Spiders Spinning,* which has been characterized as something on the order of Roald Dahl meets Mother Goose. Seven spiders from Siberia escape en route to a lab for study and make their way to Vermont, where they discover seven girls whom they focus on as their mothers. The problem is, the spiders literally have the kiss of death, and the girls dispatch several of them. There are humorous subplots galore in this "high-camp fantasy-mystery," according to a *Publishers Weekly* critic. Hazel Rochman, writing in *Booklist,* commended Maguire on the "comic brew" and noted that the book would be "the stuff of many a grade-school skit." "A lighthearted fantasy," concluded a *Kirkus Reviews* critic, "that, while easily read, is as intricately structured as a spider's web." With *One Final Firecracker,* the author brings back many of the various characters from the other installments, including aliens, cupid, mad scientists, an elephant's ghost, and a spider from the first book who seeks to give one last fatal bite in what a *Kirkus Reviews* contributor described as a "winsome, bittersweet celebration of love and loss and loyalty."

Another critic for *Kirkus Reviews* called the overall formula for the series a "relentlessly edgy and smart one, and as such, a breath of fresh air." *Commonweal* reviewer Daria Donnelly noted that her son adores the series, and quoted him as saying "This is a writer who knows how to make a kid laugh."

Beyond the "Hamlet Chronicles," Maguire also authored a collection of fractured fairy tales called *Leaping Beauty: And Other Animal Fairy Tales.* Not the same kind of retelling as his adult novels, the book still puts a spin on well-known classics such as "Goldilocks and the Three Bears," casting "Goldifox" as the hero; and the title story, a play on the familiar "Sleeping Beauty," features a cursed tadpole. *Booklist* critic Kay Weisman called the book "a delightful collection, sure to be popular with sophisticated readers."

Of his future plans as a writer, Maguire explained to a reviewer for *Publishers Weekly,* "I don't ever want to be a slave to my success, if you know what I mean. I don't want to write 'Rapunzel in Duluth' just because *Mirror Mirror* is in Tuscany." But critics will not be surprised if Maguire continues on in all his venues, creating more adult novels as well as continuing on with his works for children.

BIOGRAPHICAL AND CRITICAL SOURCES:

BOOKS

Twentieth-Century Children's Writers, 3rd edition, St. James Press (New York, NY), 1989.

PERIODICALS

Advocate, October 17, 1995, Peter Galvin, review of *Wicked: The Life and Times of the Wicked Witch of the West,* p. 56; December 25, 2001, Robert Plun-

ket, review of *Lost,* p. 67; September 27, 2005, Regina Marler, "Back to Oz: Gregory Maguire, Whose Hit Novel *Wicked* Brilliantly Inverted *The Wizard of Oz,* Returns with a Sequel, *Son of a Witch*—and This Time There's Gay Stuff!," p. 72.

Booklist, September 15, 1994, Hazel Rochman, review of *Seven Spiders Spinning,* p. 136; September 15, 1996, Debbie Carton, review of *Oasis,* p. 232; April 15, 1999, Carolyn Phelan, review of *The Good Liar,* p. 1530; January 1, 2000, review of *The Good Liar,* p. 822; December 1, 2000, GraceAnne A. DeCandido, review of *Four Stupid Cupids,* p. 706; October 15, 2001, Kristine Huntley, review of *Lost,* p. 383; April 1, 2002, Kay Weisman, review of *Three Rotten Eggs,* p. 1328; September 1, 2003, Hazel Rochman, review of *Mirror Mirror,* p. 57; June 1, 2004, Kay Weisman, review of *Leaping Beauty: and Other Animal Fairy Tales,* p. 1726.

Bulletin of the Center for Children's Literature, July-August, 1980, p. 219; February, 1982, review of *Lights on the Lake;* May, 1989, Roger Sutton, review of *I Feel Like the Morning Star,* p. 230; June, 1994, Roger Sutton, review of *Missing Sisters,* pp. 327-328.

Commonweal, April 19, 2002, Daria Donnelly, "Illuminated Manuscripts," p. 22.

Entertainment Weekly, November 17, 1995, Robin J. Schwartz, review of *Wicked,* p. 73; October 24, 2003, Jennifer Reese, "Grimm Reaper," p. 109; September 30, 2005, Gillian Flynn, review of *Son of a Witch,* p. 97.

Horn Book, October, 1978, Ethel L. Heins, review of *The Lightning Time,* pp. 517-518; June, 1980, Mary M. Burns, review of *The Daughter of the Moon;* April, 1982, Mary M. Burns, review of *Lights on the Lake,* pp. 167-168; October, 1983, Ethel L. Heins, review of *The Dream Stealer,* pp. 576-577; July-August, 1994, review of *Missing Sisters,* pp. 454-455; July, 1999, review of *The Good Liar,* p. 471; January, 2000, review of *Origins of Story: On Writing for Children,* p. 105.

Kirkus Reviews, July 15, 1994, review of *Seven Spiders Spinning,* p. 989; August, 15, 2001, review of *Lost,* p. 1154; March 1, 2002, review of *Three Rotten Eggs,* p. 339; September 5, 2003, review of *Mirror Mirror,* p. 1147; April 1, 2004, review of *A Couple of April Fools,* p. 333; May 1, 2005, review of *One Final Firecracker,* p. 542.

Library Journal, September 1, 1999, Francisca Goldsmith, review of *Confessions of an Ugly Stepsister,* p. 234; October 1, 2001, Margee Smith, review of *Lost,* p. 141.

New York Times, October 24, 1995, Michiko Kakutani, review of *Wicked,* p. C17.

New York Times Book Review, November 26, 1995, review of *Wicked,* p. 19; December 12, 1999, Gardner McFall, review of *Confessions of an Ugly Step-sister*, p. 28; December 26, 1999, Malachi Duffy, review of *Wicked*, p. 19.

People Weekly, November 3, 2003, Jason Lynch, "Every Witch Way," p. 133.

Publishers Weekly, June 5, 1978, review of *The Lightning Time*, p. 89; September, 1978, Pam Spencer, review of *I Feel Like the Morning Star*, p. 143; September 28, 1990, review of *Lucas Fishbone*, pp. 101-102; August, 1994, review of *Seven Spiders Spinning*, p. 80; August 21, 1995, review of *Wicked*, p. 45; October 28, 1996, review of *Oasis*, p. 82; March 22, 1999, review of *The Good Liar*, p. 93; August 16, 1999, review of *Confessions of an Ugly Stepsister*, p. 58; September 10, 2001, review of *Lost*, p. 60; September 15, 2003, review of *Mirror Mirror*, and Ben P. Indick, interview with Gregory Maguire, p. 42; December 1, 2003, review of *Wicked* (audiobook), p. 20; August 30, 2004, review of *Leaping Beauty*, p. 56; November 8, 2004, review of *Leaping Beauty*, p. 25; October 3, 2005, James Piechota, "Oz Struck," p. 37.

School Library Journal, September, 1978, p. 143; May, 1980, Marjorie Lewis, review of *The Daughter of the Moon*, p. 69; February, 1984, Helen Gregory, review of *The Dream Stealer*, p. 75; May, 1989, Pam Spencer, review of *I Feel Like the Morning Star*, p. 127; December, 1990, Heide Piehler, review of *Lucas Fishbone*, p. 84; May, 1996, Judy Sokoll, review of *Wicked*, p. 148; November, 1996, Renee Steinberg, review of *Oasis*, p. 108; May, 1999, Linda Greengrass, review of *The Good Liar*, p. 128; October, 2000, Eva Mitnick, review of *Four Stupid Cupids*, p. 164; March, 2002, Connie Tyrrell Burns, review of *Three Rotten Eggs*, p. 234; March, 2004, Susan H. Woodcock, review of *Mirror Mirror*, p. 249; August, 2004, Eva Mitnick, review of *Leaping Beauty*, p. 126; May, 2005, Carly B. Wiskoff, review of *One Final Firecracker*, p. 133.

Tribune News Service, December 22, 1999, Brenda Cronin, review of *Confessions of an Ugly Stepsister*, p. K2155.

Voice of Youth Advocates, June, 1989, Jane Beasley, review of *I Feel Like the Morning Star*, p. 117.

ONLINE

Gregory Maguire Home Page, http://www.gregory maguire.com/ (December 29, 2005).

*   *   *

MAGUIRE, Gregory Peter
    See MAGUIRE, Gregory

MAHFOUZ, Naguib 1911(?)-
(Naguib Abdel Aziz Al-Sabilgi Mahfouz)

PERSONAL: Name also transliterated as Nagib or Najib Mahfuz; born December 11, 1911 (some sources say 1912 or 1914), in Gamaliya, Cairo, Egypt; son of Abdel Aziz Ibrahim (a merchant) and Fatma Mostapha Mahfouz; married Attiya Allah (name also transliterated as Inayat Allah, Ateyate Ibrahim), September 27, 1954; children: Om Kolthoum, Fatima. *Education:* University of Cairo, philosophy degree, 1934; post-graduate study in philosophy, 1935-36.

ADDRESSES: Agent—c/o Donald E. Herdeck, Three Continents Press, 1636 Connecticut Ave. NW, Washington, DC 20009.

CAREER: Civil servant, journalist, and writer. University of Cairo, Cairo, Egypt, secretary, 1936-38; Egyptian Government, Cairo, bureaucrat affiliated with the Ministry of Wakfs (also called Ministry of Islamic Affairs), 1939-54, director of censorship for the Department of Art, 1954-59, director of Foundation for Support of the Cinema for the State Cinema Organization, 1959-69, consultant for cinema affairs to the Ministry of Culture, 1969-71. Affiliated with Cairo newspaper *Al-Ahram.*

AWARDS, HONORS: Egyptian State Prize, 1956, for *Bayn al-qasrayn;* National Prize for Letters (Egypt), 1970; Collar of the Republic, 1972; Nobel Prize for literature, the Swedish Academy, 1988; named to Egyptian Order of Independence and to Order of the Republic.

WRITINGS:

Hams al-junun, Maktabat Misr (Cairo, Egypt), 1939.
Abath al-aqdar, Maktabat Misr (Cairo, Egypt), 1939.
Radubis, Maktabat Misr (Cairo, Egypt), 1943, reprinted as *Rhadopis of Nubia*, translated by Anthony Calderbank, American University in Cairo Press (Cairo, Egypt; New York, NY), 2003.
Kiftah Tiba, Maktabat Misr (Cairo, Egypt), 1944.
Khan al-khalili, Maktabat Misr (Cairo, Egypt), c. 1945.
Al-Qahira al-jadida, Maktabat Misr (Cairo, Egypt), 1946.
Zuqaq al Midaqq (novel), Maktabat Misr (Cairo, Egypt), 1947, translation with introduction by Trevor Le Gassick published as *Midaq Alley*, Khayats, 1966, revised edition, Heinemann (England), 1975, Three Continents (Washington, DC), 1981.

Al-Sarab, Maktabat Misr (Cairo, Egypt), c. 1949.

Bidaya wa-nihaya, Maktabat Misr (Cairo, Egypt), 1949, translation by Ramses Awad published as *The Beginning and the End,* American University in Cairo Press (Cairo, Egypt; New York, NY), 1951.

Bayn al-qasrayn, Maktabat Misr (Cairo, Egypt), 1956, translation by William M. Hutchins and Olive E. Kenny published as *Palace Walk: The Cairo Trilogy I,* Doubleday (New York, NY), 1990.

Qasr al-shawq, Maktabat Misr (Cairo, Egypt), c. 1957, translation by Hutchins, Lorne M. Kenny, and Olive E. Kenny published as *Palace of Desire: The Cairo Trilogy II,* Doubleday (New York, NY), 1991.

Al Sukkariya, Maktabat Misr (Cairo, Egypt), 1957, translation by Hutchins and Angele Botros Samaan published as *Sugar Street: The Cairo Trilogy III,* Doubleday (New York, NY), 1992.

Al-Liss wa-al-kilab (novel), Maktabat Misr (Cairo, Egypt), 1961, translation by Le Gassick and Muhammad Mustafa Badawi published as *The Thief and the Dogs,* revised edition by John Rodenbeck, American University in Cairo Press (Cairo, Egypt; New York, NY), 1984.

Al-Summan wa-al-kharif, Maktabat Misr (Cairo, Egypt), 1962, translation by Roger Allen published as *Autumn Quail,* American University in Cairo Press (Cairo, Egypt; New York, NY), 1985.

Dunya Allah, Maktabat Misr (Cairo, Egypt), c. 1963.

The Search (originally published in Arabic as *Al-Tariq,* 1964), translation by Mohamed Islam, edited by Magdi Wahba, American University in Cairo Press (Cairo, Egypt; New York, NY), 1987, Doubleday (New York, NY), 1991.

Bayt sayyi al-sum'a, Maktabat Misr (Cairo, Egypt), 1965.

Al-Shahhadh, Maktabat Misr (Cairo, Egypt), 1965, translation by Kristin Walker Henry and Nariman Khales Naili al-Warraki published as *The Beggar,* American University in Cairo Press (Cairo, Egypt; New York, NY), 1986.

Tharthara fawqa al-Nil, Maktabat Misr (Cairo, Egypt), 1966, translation by Frances Liardet published as *Adrift on the Nile,* Doubleday (New York, NY), 1993.

Miramar (novel), Maktabat Misr (Cairo, Egypt), 1967, translation by Fatma Moussa-Mahmoud published under same title, edited and revised by Maged el Kommos and Rodenbeck, introduction by John Fowles, Heinemann (London, England), 1978, Three Continents, 1983.

Awlad haratina, [Beirut], 1967, published in serialized form, 1969, translation by Philip Stewart published as *Children of Gebelawi,* Three Continents, 1981, translation by Peter Theroux published as *Children of the Alley,* Doubleday (New York, NY), 1995.

Tahta al-mizalla, Maktabat Misr (Cairo, Egypt), c. 1967.

Khammarat al-qitt al-aswad, Maktabat Misr (Cairo, Egypt), c. 1968, translation published as *The Tavern of the Black Cat,* 1976 (contains the stories "A Vague Word," "The Defendant," "The Tavern of the Black Cat," and "Paradise of the Children").

Hikaya bi-la bidaya wa-la nihaya, Maktabat Misr (Cairo, Egypt), 1971.

Shahr al-asal, Maktabat Misr (Cairo, Egypt), 1971.

Al-Maraya, Maktabat Misr (Cairo, Egypt), 1972, translation by Allen published as *Mirrors,* Bibliotheca Islamica (Minneapolis, MN), 1977.

Al-Hubb tahta al-matar, Maktabat Misr (Cairo, Egypt), 1973.

Al-Jarima, Maktabat Misr (Cairo, Egypt), 1973.

God's World: An Anthology of Short Stories (contains "Tahta al-mazalla" [title means "Under the Bus Shelter"]), translation and introduction by Akef Abadir and Allen, Bibliotheca Islamica (Minneapolis, MN), 1973.

Al-Karnak, Maktabat Misr (Cairo, Egypt), 1974, translation by Saad El-Gabalawy published in *Three Contemporary Egyptian Novels,* York Press (Parkton, MD), 1979, also translated as *Karnak Cafe.*

Hikayat haratina, Maktabat Misr (Cairo, Egypt), 1975, translation by Soad Sobhy, Essam Fattouh, and James Kenneson published as *Fountain and Tomb,* Three Continents, 1988.

Qalb al-layl, Maktabat Misr (Cairo, Egypt), 1975.

Hadrat al-muhtaram, Maktabat Misr (Cairo, Egypt), 1975, translation by Rasheed El-Enany published as *Respected Sir,* Quartet, 1988.

Malhamat al harafish, Maktabat Misr (Cairo, Egypt), 1977, translation by Catherine Cobham published as *The Harafish,* Doubleday (New York, NY), 1994.

Hubb fawqa hadabat al-haram, Maktabat Misr (Cairo, Egypt), 1979.

Shaytan ya'iz, Maktabat Misr (Cairo, Egypt), 1979.

Nagib Mahfuz-yatadhakkar (title means "Naguib Mahfouz Remembers"), edited by Gamal al-Gaytani, Al-Masirah, 1980.

Asr al-hubb, Maktabat Misr (Cairo, Egypt), 1980.

Afrah al-qubbah, Maktabat Misr (Cairo, Egypt), 1981, translation by Olive E. Kenny published as *Wedding Song,* revised edition by Mursi Saad El Din and Rodenbeck, introduction by Saad El Din, American University in Cairo Press (Cairo, Egypt; New York, NY), 1984.

Ra'aytu fima yara al-na'im, Maktabat Misr (Cairo, Egypt), 1982.

Baqi min al-zaman sa'ah, Maktabat Misr (Cairo, Egypt), 1982.

Layali alf laylah, Maktabat Misr (Cairo, Egypt), 1982, translation by Denys Johnson-Davies published as *Arabian Nights and Days,* Doubleday (New York, NY), 1995.

Amam al-'arsh, Maktabat Misr (Cairo, Egypt), 1983.

Rihlat ibn Fattumah, Maktabat Misr (Cairo, Egypt), 1983, translation by Johnson-Davies published as *Journey of Ibn Fattouma,* Doubleday (New York, NY), 1992.

Al-Tanzim al-sirri, Maktabat Misr (Cairo, Egypt), 1984.

Al-A'ish fi al-haqiqa, Maktabat Misr (Cairo, Egypt), 1985.

Yawm qutila al-za'im, Maktabat Misr (Cairo, Egypt), 1985.

Hadith al sabah wa-al-masa, Maktabat Misr (Cairo, Egypt), 1987.

Sabah al-ward, Maktabat Misr (Cairo, Egypt), 1987.

Qushtumor, [Cairo], 1989.

Echoes of an Autobiography, Doubleday (New York, NY), 1997.

The Day the Leader Was Killed: A Novel, translated by Malak Hashem, General Egyptian Book Organization (Cairo, Egypt), 1989.

The Beggar; The Thief and the Dogs; Autumn Quail, Anchor Books (New York, NY), 2000.

Akhenaten, Dweller in Truth, translated by Tagreid Abu-Hassabo, Anchor Books (New York, NY), 2000.

Respected Sir; Wedding Song; The Search, Anchor Books (New York, NY), 2001.

Naguib Mahfouz at Sidi Jaber: Reflections of a Nobel Laureate, 1994-2001: From Conversations with Mohamed Salmawy, American University in Cairo, 2001.

Futøuwat al-'utöuf, Maktabat Misr (Cairo, Egypt), 2001.

The Cairo Trilogy, (includes *Palace Walk, Palace of Desire,* and *Sugar Street*), translated by William Maynard Hutchins, with an introduction by Sabry Hafez, Alfred A. Knopf (New York, NY), 2001.

Sih'am Dhuhn'i wa-thartharah ma'a Naj'ib Mahf'uz, D'ar Akhb'ar al-Yawm, Qit'a' al-Thaq'afah (al-Q'ahirah, Egypt), 2002.

As'atidhat'i, M'ir'it lil-Nashr wa-al-Ma'l'um'at (al-Q'ahirah, Egypt), 2002.

Hawla al-adab wa-al-falsafah, al-D'ar al-Misr'iyah al-Lubn'an'iyah (al-Q'ahirah, Egypt), 2003.

Voices From the Other World: Ancient Egyptian Tales (short stories), translated by Raymond Stock, Anchor Books (New York, NY), 2004.

Also contributor to *Modern Egyptian Short Stories,* translated with a critical introduction by El-Gabalawy, York Press, 1977. Contributor to Arabic newspapers, including *Ar-Risala* and *Al-Hilal.*

ADAPTATIONS: Sixteen of Mahfouz's novels, including *Miramar,* have been adapted for films in Egypt.

SIDELIGHTS: Naguib Mahfouz is widely regarded as Egypt's finest writer. While his works were largely unknown in English-speaking countries for most of the twentieth century, the author has nevertheless been viewed by many critics outside the Middle East as the exemplar of Arabic literature. Mahfouz was suddenly cast into the limelight in the West on October 13, 1988, when he became the first Arab writer honored with the Nobel Prize for literature. Prior to his receiving the esteemed award, only a fraction of Mahfouz's more than fifty works had been translated into English; after weeks of negotiations in the fall of 1988, however, Doubleday acquired the English publishing rights to fourteen of the Nobel laureate's books, including four titles that had never before appeared in English.

Mahfouz is credited with popularizing the novel and short story as viable genres in the Arab literary world, where poetry has been the medium of choice among writers for generations. A native of the Gamaliya quarter of Cairo, the author recreates in his writings life on the streets of urban Egypt. His prose works—which have been compared in spirit, tone, and ambience to the raw social realism of nineteenth-century novelists Honore de Balzac and Charles Dickens—reflect Egypt's volatile political history and depict the distressing conditions under which the Arab poor live.

The author established his reputation in American literary circles with the 1981 release, in English translation, of *Midaq Alley,* a novel that he had originally penned in Arabic in 1947. An evocation of life in a Cairo ghetto, *Midaq Alley* centers on Hamida, a beautiful girl who escapes the poverty, filth, and contamination of her village by becoming a prostitute for wealthy Allied soldiers. Trevor Le Gassick noted in his introduction to the English edition of the book that "the universal problems of behaviour and morality [Mahfouz] examines remain . . . the same." Gassick went on to comment, "The aspirations and tragedies of [*Midaq Alley*'s] inhabitants are witnessed with total indifference by the Alley within which the circle of life and death is forever run again."

Mahfouz is best known in the Arab world for his critically acclaimed "Cairo Trilogy," which was written in 1956 and 1957 and translated into English and published by Doubleday in the early 1990s. *Bayn al-qasrayn,* the first volume in the trilogy, was published in 1990 as *Palace Walk, Qasr al-shawq,* the second volume, was published as *Palace of Desire: Cairo Trilogy II* in 1991, and the last novel in the trilogy, *Al Sukkariya,* was published in 1992 as *Sugar Street: The Cairo Trilogy III.* John Fowles, in his introduction to Mahfouz's *Miramar,* commented on the long delay in the release of the writer's books in translation for Western readers: "Of all the world's considerable contemporary literature, that in Arabic must easily be the least known. . . . It is far from easy to translate [the Arabic language] into a pragmatic, almost purely vernacular language like English. . . . [A] linguistic Iron Curtain has kept us miserably short of first-hand information about the very considerable changes that Egypt has undergone in this century."

Mahfouz's "Cairo Trilogy" chronicles these changes in its fifteen hundred pages, tracing three generations of a middle-class Cairo family. Beginning shortly after World War I, the trilogy moves through the onset and aftermath of the 1952 military coup that overthrew King Farouk—abolishing an Egyptian monarchy—and facilitated the eventual rise of Colonel Gamal Abdel Nasser to power.

Although Mahfouz had supported Nasser's revolution at its inception, the author became disillusioned with the colonel's social, educational, and land reforms. After seven years of silence, Mahfouz began to voice his frustrations in his writings, composing the pessimistic and allegorical *Children of Gebelawi* in 1967. In thinly veiled allusions to the three monotheistic religions, the narrative relates humanity's quest for religion, beginning with Adam and Eve and ending with the last prophet (represented as the modern man of science), who is inadvertently responsible for the death of Gebelawi (God). The 1969 serialization of the novel inflamed Islamic fundamentalists and led to the banning of the manuscript's publication in book form. A new English translation of the book appeared in 1995 under the title *Children of the Alley.*

In the 1960s Mafouz abandoned the traditional realism that characterized his previous works and began to experiment. He produced shorter, sparer novels that employed many of the experimental techniques—including stream of consciousness and script-like dialogue—of modern Western literature. *The Search,* written in 1964 and published in English in 1991, tells the story of Saber, the son of a prostitute, a man filled with rage who madly searches the streets of Cairo in an attempt to find

the father he has never known. Writing in the *New York Times Book Review,* Edward Hower described the book as "a powerful psychological portrait of a young criminal. . . reminiscent of the best of George St. Simeon or Graham Greene . . . a chilling and intriguing novel." Saber conspires with one girlfriend to kill her rich husband while completely deceiving another girlfriend as to his true character. Hower felt that Mahfouz not only reveals the monstrous nature of Saber, but at the same time makes the reader empathize with him.

However, Mahfouz's departure from the realism that established his reputation has not always met with approval. According to Amitav Ghosh, writing in the *New Republic,* "When the spirit moves Mahfouz to be technically adventurous, it also tends to push him away from his accustomed material, leaving him stranded in various exotic enclaves of society." Two of Mahfouz's more experimental novels, *The Thief and His Dogs* and *Wedding Song,* Ghosh dismissed as "frankly, awful." Some critics have seen Mahfouz's shift to more experimental work as a reflection of a conservative retreat from his earlier political stance that favored sweeping changes in Egypt. Feminist critics have also faulted the portrayal of women as stereotyped in Mahfouz's later works, in contrast to the fully realized women characters of his realist period, and have seen this as a negative reaction to the feminist movement.

The 1967 publication of Mahfouz's *Miramar,* a novel released in the United States in 1983, marked the culmination of the author's disenchantment with the Nasser revolution, a revolution that, according to Fowles, merely "redistributed" Egypt's "wealth and influence . . . among a new elite." Evaluated by some critics as an unabashed attack on Nasser's political policies, *Miramar* explores the clashing values in a changing Egypt. As a reaction to the 1952 revolution, continued Fowles, *Miramar* is haunted by "despair" over the "moral failure" that tainted the newly established republic.

Miramar focuses on a peasant girl named Zohra who, after fleeing from the country to escape an arranged marriage, takes a job as a maid at Miramar, a hotel in Alexandria. Striving for independence, Zohra educates herself. Her beauty and modern ideas, however, incite intrigue, jealousy, and resentment in the residents of Miramar. Told from the points of view of five different fictional characters, the narrative presents in some Egypt in microcosm.

Many of Mahfouz's later works have taken the form of extended fables. Although *The Harafish* covers thirteen generations and several hundred years, the action of the book all seems to take place in a roughly contemporary setting. The term "harafish" in medieval Arabic refers to the poor elements of society that threaten the social order. Mahfouz's harafish are the common people who inhabit an alley in old Cairo; his protagonists are the leaders of the clan that run the affairs of the alley. The fortunes of the common people rise and fall through the generations depending on the attitudes and morality of their clan leaders.

Taking its inspiration and form directly from *A Thousand and One Nights, Arabian Nights and Days* is more a loosely connected set of tales than a novel. Richard Dyer in the *Boston Globe* found the stories in the book just as fabulous but also far more realistic than those narrated by Scheherazade. Whereas *Arabian Nights and Days* takes the Eastern classic *A Thousand and One Nights* as its model, *The Journey of Ibn Fattouma* is based loosely on a classic of Western literature, Jonathan Swift's *Gulliver's Travels*. Fattouma, a devoted follower of Islam, moves through various mythical lands, driven by a search both for truth and for an ideal woman. In Mashriq, a primitive society of moon-worshipers, Fattouma's senses are awakened by monthly bacchanalian rites. In Aman, he discovers a political tyranny reminiscent of George Orwell's *1984*. Although the land of Halba offers him complete freedom and marital bliss, Fattouma travels on, again in pursuit of a woman, to the supposedly perfect society of Gebel, where he hopes to find solutions to the problems that plague his homeland. Joseph Coates, in the *Chicago Tribune,* stated that *The Journey of Ibn Fattouma* "adds still another genre to the many [Mahfouz] had worked in a career that in Western terms had already mastered—in literary technique and history—every novel form from Sir Walter Scott through Balzac and [Henry] James and on to the Modernists, including [William] Faulkner and especially [Marcel] Proust, and in the last two decades has toyed with symbolism and postmodern playfulness." At the same time, Coates felt that comparing the book to *Gulliver's Travels* reveals vast differences in the cultural assumptions between East and West.

Mahfouz's realistic accounts of Egypt's social and political history have earned him both acclaim and condemnation, as have his more experimental and fantastic works. Islamic extremists' failed assassination attempt on Mahfouz in 1994, in which the author was stabbed, and the subsequent execution of those involved, demonstrates how significant and controversial the author's works are considered in the Arab world. Philip Stewart, as cited by Fowles, recalled the author's own assessment of his works: "In relation to European literature,

[Mahfouz] said they were 'probably, like the rest of modern Arabic literature, fourth or fifth rate.'" But according to a press release from Stockholm, Sweden, published in the *Chicago Tribune,* the Swedish Academy saw fit to honor Mahfouz as an author "who, through works rich in nuance—now clearsightedly realistic, now evocatively ambiguous—has formed an Arabian narrative art that applies to all mankind."

Mahfouz's popularity in the West has resulted in more than twenty of his books being translated into English. In 1997, Mahfouz's first nonfiction book in English was published. *Echoes of an Autobiography* contains a series of short autobiographical sketches, some as brief as two or three lines long. Abandoning chronological narrative typical of most autobiographies, Mahfouz instead provides, as pointed out by Richard Woffenden in *World Press Review,* a "fast-flowing stream of short prose pieces . . . that meander through adult nostalgia, childhood memories, dreams, parables, and allegories." Woffenden, went on to note that those who like traditional biographies might not appreciate Mahfouz's approach. Nevertheless, he added, "But if the bones of a life are passed over, the spirit is there in full." *Booklist* contributor Brad Hooper commented that the author is not only concerned with his past in this unusual autobiography but also with how people should live in the present. He added, "Each of these pieces is a brilliantly polished gem that, taken together, form an iridescent mosaic."

Mahfouz's novel *Akhenaten, Dweller in Truth* was first published in Arabic in 1985 and appeared on Western bookshelves in 2000. Set in the eleventh century B.C., the author tells the story of perhaps the most infamous pharaoh of ancient Egypt, the country's first monotheistic ruler who tried to convince his subjects of his religious vision. The story is told through the eyes of Meriamum, a young boy who seeks the truth about the pharaoh after his death. Meriamum puts together fourteen testimonies as he talks to many of Akhenaten's contemporaries, including his friends, enemies, and wife Nefertiti. The more Meriamum and the reader learn about Akhenaten, the more it becomes apparent that the truth about the "mad" king is increasingly hard to ascertain and fleeting. Brendan Dowling, writing in the *Booklist,* commented, "Mahfouz populates his engrossing novel with characters that are believably human and flawed; their conflicts with religion and politics have a timeless quality to which readers will respond." A *Publishers Weekly* contributor praised Mahfouz's ability to appropriate "to wonderful effect, the craft of the biography" in the novel. The reviewer went on to note, "The making of history, like fiction, dwells in its infinite ramifications, and Mahfouz, ever the masterly stylist, accomplishes his lesson flawlessly."

In 2001, a series of conversations and interviews that Mahfouz had over several years with an Egyptian author were published as *Naguib Mahfouz at Sidi Jaber: Reflections of a Nobel Laureate, 1994-2001: From Conversations with Mohamed Salmawy.* The book includes more than 100 short vignettes. Ali Houissa, writing in the *Library Journal,* noted, "Thematically arranged, these pieces offer insights into the way this great writer thinks and his constant concern with the human condition, a principle interest behind the characters and settings he has chosen for many of his novels."

BIOGRAPHICAL AND CRITICAL SOURCES:

BOOKS

Mahfouz, Naguib, *Midaq Alley,* Khayats, 1966, revised edition, Heinemann (London, England), 1975, Three Continents (Washington, DC), 1981.
Mahfouz, Naguib, *Miramar* (novel), Maktabat Misr (Cairo, Egypt), 1967, translation by Fatma Moussa-Mahmoud published under same title, edited and revised by Maged el Kommos and Rodenbeck, introduction by John Fowles, Heinemann (London, England), 1978, Three Continents, 1983.
Milson, Menahem, *Najib Mahfuz: The Novelist-Philosopher of Cairo,* St. Martin's Press (New York, NY), 1998.

PERIODICALS

Booklist, November 15, 1996, Brad Hooper, review of *Echoes of an Autobiography,* p. 547; March 15, 2000, Brendan Dowling, review of *Akhenaten: Dweller in Truth,* p. 1328.
Boston Globe, March 31, 1995, Richard Dyer, "Ancient Fables with Modern Morals," p. 56.
Chicago Tribune, October 14, 1988, "Egyptian Wins Nobel Prize for Literature,", p. 3; August 27, 1992, "Nobel Winner traverses a Cultural and Religious Gap" (review of *The Journey of Ibn Fattouma,* p. 3.
Economist, March 15, 1997, reviews of *Echoes of an Autobiography* and *Miramar,* p. S15.
Library Journal, June 1, 2002, Ali Houissa, review of *Naguib Mahfouz at Sidi Jaber: Reflections of a Nobel Laureate, 1994-2001: From Conversations with Mohamed Salmawy,* p. p. 148.

New Republic, May 7, 1990, Amitav Ghosh, "The Human Comedy in Cairo: The Secret, Respectable World of Naguib Mahfouz," p. 32.
New York Times Book Review, August 4, 1991, Edward Hower, review of *The Search,* p. 724.
Publishers Weekly, November 11, 1996, review of *Echoes of an Autobiography,* p. 66; February 7, 2000, review of *Akhenaten: Dweller in Truth,* p. 1328.
World Press Review, July, 1997, Richard Woffenden, review of *Echoes of an Autobiography,* p. 37.

*   *   *

MAHFOUZ, Naguib Abdel Aziz Al-Sabilgi
See MAHFOUZ, Naguib

*   *   *

MAILER, Norman 1923-
  (Norman Kingsley Mailer)

PERSONAL: Born January 31, 1923, in Long Branch, NJ; son of Isaac Barnett (an accountant) and Fanny (owner of a small business; maiden name, Schneider) Mailer; married Beatrice Silverman, 1944 (divorced, 1952); married Adele Morales (an artist), 1954 (divorced, 1962); married Lady Jeanne Campbell, 1962 (divorced, 1963); married Beverly Rentz Bentley (an actress), 1963 (divorced, 1980); married Carol Stevens, 1980 (divorced, 1980); married Norris Church (an artist), 1980; children: (first marriage) Susan; (second marriage) Danielle, Elizabeth Anne; (third marriage) Kate; (fourth marriage) Michael Burks, Stephen McLeod; (fifth marriage) Maggie Alexandra; (sixth marriage) John Buffalo. *Education:* Harvard University, S.B. (cum laude), 1943; graduate studies at Sorbonne, Paris, France, 1947-48. *Politics:* "Left Conservative." *Hobbies and other interests:* Skiing, sailing, boxing, hiking.

ADDRESSES: Home—Providence, RI. *Agent*—c/o Author Mail, Random House, 299 Park Avenue, New York, NY 10171-0002.

CAREER: Writer. Producer, director, and actor in films, including *Wild 90,* 1967, and *Maidstone: A Mystery,* 1968; producer, *Beyond the Law,* 1967; actor, *Ragtime,* 1981; director, *Tough Guys Don't Dance,* 1987. Lecturer at colleges and universities; University of Pennsylvania Pappas fellow, 1983. Candidate for democratic nomination in mayoral race, New York City, 1960 and

1969. Founder, Fifth Estate (merged with Committee for Action Research on the Intelligence Community), 1973. *Military service:* U.S. Army, 1944-46, field artillery observer; became infantry rifleman serving in the Philippines and Japan.

MEMBER: PEN (president of American Center, 1984-86), American Academy and Institute of Arts and Letters, National Institute of Arts and Letters.

AWARDS, HONORS: Story magazine college fiction prize, 1941, for "The Greatest Thing in the World;" National Institute and American Academy grant in literature, 1960; elected to National Institute of Arts and Letters, 1967; National Book Award nomination, 1967, for *Why Are We in Vietnam?;* National Book Award for nonfiction, 1968, for *Miami and the Siege of Chicago;* National Book Award for arts and letters, Pulitzer prize in letters general nonfiction, and George Polk Award, all 1969, all for *Armies of the Night;* Edward MacDowell Medal, MacDowell Colony, 1973, for outstanding service to arts; National Arts Club Gold Medal, 1976; National Book Critics Circle nomination, Notable Book citation from the American Library Association, and Pulitzer prize in letters, all 1979, and American Book Award nomination, 1980, all for *The Executioner's Song;* Emmy nomination for best adaptation, for screenplay of *The Executioner's Song;* University of Pennsylvania pappas fellow; Rose Award, Lord & Taylor, 1985, for public accomplishment; Emerson-Thoreau Medal for lifetime literary achievement from American Academy of Arts and Sciences, 1989.

WRITINGS:

NOVELS

The Naked and the Dead, Rinehart (New York, NY), 1948, reprinted, Holt (New York, NY), 1998.
Barbary Shore, Rinehart (New York, NY), 1951, reprinted, Vintage International (New York, NY), 1997.
The Deer Park (also see below), Putnam (New York, NY), 1955, with preface and notes by Mailer, Berkley (New York, NY), 1976, reprinted, Vintage International (New York, NY), 1997.
An American Dream (first published in serial form in *Esquire,* January-August, 1964), Dial (New York, NY), 1965, reprinted, Vintage (New York, NY), 1999.

Why Are We in Vietnam?, Putnam (New York, NY), 1967.
A Transit to Narcissus: A Facsimile of the Original Typescript with an Introduction by the Author, Fertig (New York, NY), 1978.
The Executioner's Song (excerpted in *Playboy,* 1979), Little, Brown (Boston, MA), 1979, reprinted, Vintage International (New York, NY), 1998.
Ancient Evenings, Little, Brown (Boston, MA), 1983.
Tough Guys Don't Dance, Random House (New York, NY), 1984, reprinted, 2002.
Harlot's Ghost, Random House (New York, NY), 1991.
The Gospel according to the Son, Random House (New York, NY), 1997.

Also author of *No Percentage,* 1941.

NONFICTION

(Author of text) *The Bullfight: A Photographic Narrative* (with recording; also see below), CBS Legacy Collection/Macmillan (New York, NY), 1967.
The Armies of the Night: History as a Novel, the Novel as History, New American Library (New York, NY), 1968.
Miami and the Siege of Chicago, New American Library (New York, NY), 1968, published as *Miami and the Siege of Chicago: An Informal History of the American Political Conventions of 1968,* Weidenfeld & Nicolson (London, England), 1969.
Of a Fire on the Moon (first appeared in *Life*), Little, Brown (Boston, MA), 1970, published as *A Fire on the Moon,* Weidenfeld & Nicolson (London, England), 1970.
King of the Hill: On the Fight of the Century, New American Library (New York, NY), 1971.
The Prisoner of Sex (first published in *Harper's*), Little, Brown (Boston, MA), 1971.
St. George and the Godfather, New American Library (New York, NY), 1972.
Marilyn: A Biography, Grosset & Dunlap (New York, NY), 1973, with new chapter, Warner (New York, NY), 1975.
The Faith of Graffiti (also see below), photographs by Jon Naar, Praeger (New York, NY), 1974, published as *Watching My Name Go By,* Matthews Miller Dunbar (London, England), 1974.
The Fight, Little, Brown (Boston, MA), 1975, reprinted, Vintage International (New York, NY), 1997.
(Editor and author of introductions) *Genius and Lust: A Journey through the Major Writings of Henry Miller,* Grove (New York, NY), 1976.

Of a Small and Modest Malignancy, Wicked and Bristling with Dots (essay; also see below), Lord John (Northridge, CA), 1980.

Huckleberry Finn: Alive at One Hundred (criticism), Caliban Press (Montclair, NJ), 1985.

How the Wimp Won the War, Lord John (Northridge, CA), 1991.

Pablo and Fernande: Portrait of Picasso as a Young Man: An Interpretive Biography, Doubleday (New York, NY), 1994, published as *Portrait of Picasso as a Young Man: An Interpretive Biography,* Atlantic Monthly Press (New York, NY), 1995.

Oswald's Tale: An American Mystery, Random House (New York, NY), 1995.

The Spooky Art: Some Thoughts on Writing, Random House (New York, NY), 2003.

Why Are We at War?, Random House (New York, NY), 2003.

PLAYS

The Deer Park: A Play (two acts; adaptation of novel *The Deer Park*; produced Off-Broadway, 1967; also see below), Dial (New York, NY), 1967.

Wild 90 (screenplay; adapted from Mailer's play *The Deer Park*), Supreme Mix, 1967.

Beyond the Law (screenplay), Supreme Mix/Evergreen Films, 1968.

Maidstone: A Mystery (screenplay; includes essay "A Course in Filmmaking"), New American Library (New York, NY), 1971.

The Executioner's Song (screenplay; adapted from book by Mailer), Film Communication Inc. 1982.

Tough Guys Don't Dance (screenplay), Zoetrope, 1987.

Strawhead (play), first produced in New York, NY), 1985.

Also author of screenplay for a modern version of *King Lear.*

COLLECTIONS

The White Negro: Superficial Reflections on the Hipster (essays; includes "Communications: Reflections on Hipsterism;" "The White Negro" first published in *Dissent* magazine, summer, 1957; also see below), City Lights (San Francisco, CA), 1957.

Advertisements for Myself (short stories, verse, articles, and essays, with narrative; includes "The White Negro," "The Man Who Studied Yoga," and "The Time of Her Time"), Putnam (New York, NY), 1959, with preface by Mailer, Berkley (New York, NY), 1976.

The Presidential Papers (also see below), Putnam (New York, NY), 1963.

Cannibals and Christians (also see below), Dial (New York, NY), 1966, abridged edition, Panther (New York, NY), 1979.

The Short Fiction of Norman Mailer (also see below), Dell (New York, NY), 1967.

The Idol and the Octopus: Political Writings on the Kennedy and Johnson Administrations (includes selections from *The Presidential Papers* and *Cannibals and Christians*), Dell (New York, NY), 1968.

The Long Patrol: Twenty-five Years of Writing from the Work of Norman Mailer, edited by Robert F. Lucid, World (New York, NY), 1971.

Existential Errands (includes *The Bullfight: A Photographic Narrative with Text by Norman Mailer,* "A Course in Filmmaking," and *King of the Hill*; also see below), Little, Brown (Boston, MA), 1972.

Some Honorable Men: Political Conventions 1960-1972 (narratives), Little, Brown (Boston, MA), 1976.

The Essential Mailer (includes *The Short Fiction of Norman Mailer* and *Existential Errands*), New English Library (London, England, 1982.

Pieces and Pontifications (essays and interviews; includes *The Faith of Graffiti* and *Of a Small and Modest Malignancy, Wicked and Bristling with Dots*), edited by Michael Lennon, Little, Brown (Boston, MA), 1982, published as *Pieces,* 1982, published as *Pontifications: Interviews,* 1982.

The Time of Our Time, Random House (New York, NY), 1998.

OTHER

Deaths for the Ladies and Other Disasters: Being a Run of Poems, Short Poems, Very Short Poems, and Turns of Prose, Putnam (New York, NY), 1962, with introduction by Mailer, New American Library (New York, NY), 1971.

Gargoyle, Guignol, False Closets (booklet; first published in *Architectural Forum,* April, 1964), privately printed, 1964.

The Pulitzer Prize for Fiction (speech), Little, Brown (Boston, MA), 1967.

Of Women and Their Elegance (fictional interview), photographs by Milton H. Greene, Simon & Schuster (New York, NY), 1980.

The Last Night: A Story (first published in *Esquire,* 1962), Targ Editions (New York, NY), 1984.

Modest Gifts: Poems and Drawings, Random House (New York, NY), 2003.

Also contributor to anthologies. Author of column "The Big Bite," for *Esquire*, 1962-63; columnist for *Village Voice*, 1956, and *Commentary*, 1962-63. Contributor to numerous periodicals, including *Harper's, Rolling Stone, New Republic, Playboy, New York Times Book Review*, and *Parade*. Contributing editor of *Dissent*, 1953-69; cofounding editor of *Village Voice*, 1955.

ADAPTATIONS: The Naked and the Dead was made into a film by Warner Bros. in 1958; *An American Dream* was adapted for film as *See You in Hell, Darling*, produced by Warner Bros. in 1966. Several of Mailer's works have been adapted as audio books.

SIDELIGHTS: When Norman Mailer's *The Naked and the Dead* was published in 1948, *New York Times* critic Orville Prescott called it "the most impressive novel about the Second World War that I have ever read." Drawing on its author's experiences in the Pacific theater during World War II, the large, ambitious book was number one on *New York Times* best-seller list for eleven consecutive weeks and the object of continuing critical admiration. Mailer, then a twenty-five-year-old literary novice, was suddenly famous and at the dawn of a prolific career in which he would loom as one of the major U.S. writers of the twentieth century. He would also continue to be measured by others as well as by himself against his 1948 success. "I had the freak of luck to start high on the mountain, and go down sharp while others were passing me," Mailer later wrote in his 1959 autobiography *Advertisements for Myself.*

In the years that followed his first success, Mailer became absorbed in proving his talent as a writer by composing that one "great" book and with developing what some would consider a notorious public personality. While living in New York City, he became part of a circle of prominent cultural figures that drew him increasingly into the public profile. In later years, as cofounding editor of *Village Voice* and as a regular contributor of nonfiction to *Voice, Dissent*, and *Esquire*, Mailer found an effective arena for his combative ego. Particularly in his nonfiction writing, in which he directly engaged contemporary issues in his own distinctive voice, Mailer's persona as public gadfly was most effectively exploited. His provocative self-portrait as philosophical "existentialist" and political "left conservative" ensured that his own personality was a continuing stage for dramatic conflict.

After publishing his second book, *Barbary Shore*, to generally unenthusiastic reviews, Mailer conceived an ambitious cycle of eight novels centering on a universal mythical hero he named Sergius O'Shaugnessy. The short story "The Man Who Studied Yoga" was designed as a prologue to the series, and *The Deer Park*, published in 1955, was to be its first installment. Three years in the making, *The Deer Park*, which Mailer later adapted for the stage, also proved to be the cycle's only volume. Primarily because of the work's overt sexuality, Mailer's original publisher refused to publish the novel, which is a study in the powers of art, sex, and money in a hedonist resort in southern California. Eventually published, *The Deer Park* earned mixed reviews, with Brendan Gill asserting in *New Yorker* that "Only a writer of the greatest and most reckless talent could have flung it between covers."

Mailer published *An American Dream* in 1965. The story of a prominent professor of existential psychology who murders his wealthy wife, the novel was a great commercial success, albeit the object of intense critical controversy. Elizabeth Hardwick described it in *Partisan Review* as "a very dirty book, dirty and extremely ugly," while John Aldridge, in *Life*, called it "a major creative breakthrough." The protagonist of *An American Dream*, Stephen Rojack, is loosely modeled after Mailer himself, reflecting the novelist's tendency to incorporate autobiographical elements within his fiction.

Another self-portrait appears in *The Armies of the Night*, a literary triumph that redeemed Mailer in the eyes of critics who were convinced he had squandered his talents in playing the part of a national celebrity. In this book, an account of a demonstration against the Vietnam War staged in front of the Pentagon in the fall of 1967, Mailer's artistic skills and his compulsive involvement in the event merge, creating a work that is more than just insightful reportage of a momentous phenomenon. *The Armies of the Night*, which won both the Pulitzer prize and the National Book Award in 1969, comically inflates Mailer's role in the proceedings to create both a bracing portrait of individual orneriness shown against a backdrop of mass social tyranny and a meditation on the relationship between self and history. Richard Gilman's review in *New Republic* applauded "the central, rather wonderful achievement of the book, that in it history and personality confront each other with a new sense of liberation."

Another autobiographical nonfiction work, *Miami and the Siege of Chicago* contains fresh observations of 1968, but lacks the rich conjunction of incident and personal style found in *The Armies of the Night*. Mailer's account of the 1972 national political conventions, *St. George and the Godfather*, was not nearly as successful as his earlier nonfiction novels. The whimsically titled novel *Why Are We in Vietnam?*, a disc jockey's violent, vulgar narrative of a bear hunt in Alaska, is an ostentatiously inventive allegory of American foreign policy.

Though Mailer had studied engineering at Harvard University, he gained a reputation as a scourge of modern technology. Nevertheless, *Life* magazine commissioned him to write a book about the first moon landing in July, 1969. Published in 1970, *Of a Fire on the Moon* is the product of months spent in Houston and Cape Canaveral, Florida, and in technical research into the space program. The National Aeronautic and Space Administration (NASA), wary of the celebrated author's antibureaucratic attitudes, denied him access to the astronauts themselves. Calling himself "Aquarius," Mailer characteristically includes himself as one of the book's main characters, this time at odds with the triumphant antisepsis of the technocrats. "I liked the book in a lot of ways," Mailer later told *New York Times Book Review,* "but I didn't like my own person in it—I felt I was highly unnecessary." Depressed over the collapse of his fourth marriage, Aquarius confesses in *Of a Fire on the Moon* that "he was weary of his own voice, own face, person, persona, will, ideas, speeches, and general sense of importance."

In 1970 Mailer found himself portrayed as the archetypal male chauvinist pig in Kate Millett's groundbreaking feminist study *Sexual Politics*. In response, he participated in a debate on feminism at New York's Town Hall and authored *The Prisoner of Sex,* which, when first published in *Harper's,* resulted in the largest sales of any issue in the magazine's history, as well as in the departure of the magazine's editorial staff, who took objection to the work's offensive language. *The Prisoner of Sex* is one of several chapters in Mailer's continuous obsession with sexuality, along with his meditation on Marilyn Monroe in *Marilyn* and *Of Women and Their Elegance.* Praising *The Prisoner of Sex* as "Mailer's best book," *New York Times* critic Anatole Broyard declared: "What Mailer has tried to do here is write a love poem." Gore Vidal disagreed in *New York Review of Books,* "There has been from Henry Miller to Norman Mailer to Charles Manson a logical progression." Vidal's cutting remark not surprisingly ignited a sensational public feud between the two novelists.

Mailer attracted further public controversy when he successfully petitioned the Utah State Prison parole board to release Jack Henry Abbott, for whose book, *In the Belly of the Beast,* he had helped find a publisher.

One month after leaving prison, Abbott killed another man, and Mailer was again sparring with the press. Mailer had first met Abbott while conducting exhaustive research for *The Executioner's Song,* a self-described "true life novel" about the life and death of Gary Gilmore, who, on January 17, 1977, became the first convict to be executed in the United States in more than a decade. Perhaps the most surprising aspect of the work is the patient self-effacement of its author. Gone from *The Executioner's Song* are the familiar "Mailerisms:" the baroque syntax, the hectoring tone, the outrageous epigrams, the startling bravura imagery, the political/metaphysical digressions, the self-conscious presence of the author in every line. Instead, Mailer's prose assumes the coloration of its huge cast of characters lawyers, policemen, doctors, journalists, relatives, friends, and victims of Gary Gilmore and immerses the reader in the alarmingly ordinary world of its main character.

Mailer's characteristic intoxication with grandiose ideas, his delight in stylistic flourishes, and his preoccupation with sex and violence are again on display in *Ancient Evenings.* George Stade in *New Republic* called *Ancient Evenings* "a new and permanent contribution to the possibilities of fiction and our communal efforts of self-discovery." In contrast, Benjamin DeMott dismissed it in *New York Times Book Review* as "pitiably foolish in conception" and "a disaster." Mailer characteristically taunted his critics with a full-page advertisement for *Ancient Evenings,* juxtaposing scathing reviews of his novel with similar attacks on Herman Melville's *Moby Dick,* Leo Tolstoy's *Anna Karenina,* Walt Whitman's *Leaves of Grass,* and Charles-Pierre Baudelaire's *Les fleurs du mal.*

During the 1980s Mailer positioned himself in the role of elder statesman of American letters. The feistiness was still there, but the aging *enfant terrible* was growing perceptibly more mellow and even courtly. After seven years in the making, Mailer's 1,310-page novel *Harlot's Ghost* was published in 1991. A study of the U.S. Central Intelligence Agency (CIA) and its function within U.S. cold war society, the novel was called by *New York Times* reporter Elaine Sciolino "a glorification of the godless, life-and-death struggle against Communism from the mid-1950s to the mid-1960s and the men and women who waged it." *Harlot's Ghost* features Hedrick "Harry" Hubbard, a CIA agent whose mentor in the agency is Hugh Tremont Montague, code named "Harlot." The novel is composed in two sections: the first, "Omega," takes place in 1983, with the discovery of Harlot's deformed corpse on a beach in Chesapeake Bay. The second, "Alpha," weighing in at over 1,200 pages, flashes back to the period between 1955 and 1963 and recounts Harry's investigations into the identity of his mentor's killer. During the flashback, Mailer takes his readers on a trip halfway around the world and gives them a crash course in twentieth-century history.

Critical reception to *Harlot's Ghost* was generally favorable, except with regard to the novel's length. Suggesting that the work should have ended in 1961, with a description of CIA operations during President John F. Kennedy's Bay of Pigs invasion, Wilfred Sheed added in his review for *New York Review of Books:* "No doubt to end the book here would be false to the facts. . . . Still, it would be good for the novel, which after all, is not a perpetual motion machine, but is designed from the outset to go a certain distance, and not a heck of a lot farther. Even a novel about the Hundred Years' War has to end sometime, but *Harlot's Ghost* runs right over the sides of the frame as the author tries to cram more and more history into a manifestly finite picture." Louis Menand was more critical of the lengthy work, writing in *New Yorker* that Mailer's ambition has destroyed his art. While praising the author's fearless examination of the Establishment during the 1960s and 1970s, Menand noted that "he has never written a book so flaccid or so unwilling to challenge and provoke as [*Harlot's Ghost*]. He has set the bar at the highest level, taken a long look, and then walked underneath it." However, reviewer Thomas R. Edwards viewed the work from a different perspective in *New Republic,* opining that *Harlot's Ghost* "advances a very imposing ideal of itself as being something like a religious epic, Mailer's *Paradise Lost,* as it were, in which the cold war would figure as the War in Heaven, the Creation, and the Fall."

Reflective of Mailer's interest in human sexuality as it relates to creativity, 1994's *Portrait of Picasso as a Young Man* sets out to uncover the inner life of the noted Spanish painter during the first thirty-five years of his life. The work, illustrated with numerous examples of Picasso's artwork, focuses on the erotic aspects of the artist's life, particularly with his relationships with female and, Mailer contends, male lovers.

Portrait of Picasso was met by a strong critical backlash upon its publication. Foremost among the criticism was the author's indulgence in artistic criticism that was either derivative or deemed to be ill-founded. "What is most disturbing about *Portrait of Picasso,* however, is not its awkward assessment of Picasso's work," contended critic Michiko Kakutani in *New York Times,* "but its even more awkward attempt to promote the notion that art redeems, that the cruelties and sins of a great artist can be rationalized, excused or glossed over." Francine du Plessix Gray, writing in *Los Angeles Times,* commented on the author's relative disregard for Picasso's artistic development in favor of an almost voyeuristic obsession with his personal relationships and dubbed *Portrait of Picasso* "an impassioned, well-meaning, but curiously tentative and wobbly work."

Mailer's fascination with violence, which was given full reign in his earlier writing, resurfaces in 1995's *Oswald's Tale: An American Mystery.* Mailer's twenty-eighth published book is a journalistic rather than quasi-fictional examination of the life of Lee Harvey Oswald, the assumed assassin of President John F. Kennedy. With characteristic obsessiveness, Mailer threw himself into the task of uncovering the truth about Oswald. With the help of investigative reporter Lawrence Schiller, Mailer went to Russia to interview those who had known Oswald for the two years he resided in that country and examine KGB files in the city of Minsk, where Oswald lived between 1959 and 1962.

While praising the workmanlike quality of *Oswald's Tale,* Thomas Powers contended in *New York Times Book Review* that by the end of the book, he was unable to be moved by Mailer's portrait of Oswald. "I admire Mailer for his effort to understand Oswald," wrote Powers, "but at some level I feel invited to place a sympathetic arm around the killer's shoulder, and I'm not about to do it. . . . He brought pain to many and happiness to none. Anger is what this makes me feel." However, John W. Aldridge cited *Oswald's Tale* as "the greatest body of information on the Oswalds yet attempted." While noting that Mailer's characteristic "sprawling" style might prove off-putting to some readers, Aldridge added that the work presents a clear, well-researched case and leaves the conclusions up to the reader. "That is the primary mission of journalism at its best, and Mailer performs it with all his customary skill and thoroughness, and a quite uncharacteristic determination to keep himself out of the story."

In 1997 Mailer published *Gospel according to the Son,* a first-person account of the life of Jesus that is closely based on the events described in the New Testament. Mailer said in an interview with *New York Times Book Review*'s Bruce Weber that he considered the project "the largest dare of all" for a writer. Kakutani assessed the novel as just another installment in Mailer's self-centered exploration of fame and infamy. In *New York Times,* Kakutani compared Mailer's Jesus to Luke Skywalker and a guest on Oprah Winfrey, elaborating that

Mailer had turned both Jesus and God "into familiar contemporary types: he has knocked them off their celestial thrones and turned them into what he knows best, celebrities." A writer for *Kirkus Reviews* assessed the novel as "generally plainspoken and sometimes plodding," but found its "occasional flashes of Mailer's pugnacious intellectual gamesmanship" praiseworthy. A *Booklist* critic lauded *Gospel* for escaping "Mailer's own image" and called the book "a provocatively imagined historical novel."

With his later books, as with his earlier ones, Mailer by turns fascinated and angered critics who contend that his fame has been as much the result of his own self-aggrandizement as his writing talent. "The sour truth," Mailer wrote in *Advertisements for Myself,* "is that I am imprisoned with a perception which will settle for nothing less than a revolution in the consciousness of our time." Few U.S. writers of the twentieth century had such magisterial aspirations, *or* such genuine claims to public attention. In his foreword to the critical anthology *Norman Mailer,* biographer and critic Harold Bloom characterized the writer as "a historian of the moral consciousness of his era, and as the representative writer of his generation." And in *London Review of Books,* Andrew O'Hagan praised the author for his courage and originality. "Mailer has been as compulsive a literary character as we've had this half-century, but he has also been among the most compelling on the page," O'Hagan contended. "He has wasted much of his talent on money-spinning inelegance, and fruitless meanderings and quests into the mysteries of sex and destiny, but he has also risked and emboldened his talent by imagining himself at the core of things."

One way Mailer managed to keep himself at the "core of things" was through his continued interest in government. His investigation into spy Robert P. Hanssen led to the 2002 publication of Lawrence Schiller's book *Into the Mirror: The Life of Master Spy Robert P. Hanssen.* In 2003 Mailer's take on the Iraq War was published as *Why Are We at War?,* echoing back thirty-six years to his novel *Why Are We in Vietnam? Why Are We at War?* includes segments of interviews, a speech, and other writtings in which Mailer pontificates about America, democracy, and the troubles he sees ahead. Writing in *Newsweek,* David Gates commented that "Mailer offers a provocative—and persuasive—cultural and intellectual frame."

In celebration of his eightieth birthday, 2003 saw the publication of Mailer's *The Spooky Art: Some Thoughts on Writing,* which contains a variety of the author's writings as well as interviews and transcripts of teaching sessions. Writing in *Commentary,* Thomas L. Jeffers noted, "Mailer's intent is to provide an 'intimate handbook' for experienced writers who, he thinks, are going to need it in the years ahead. Why? Because, he rightly argues, the serious novel got into trouble as long ago as the 1930s, when our best writers stopped trying to give America what Stendhal had given France or Tolstoy Russia—namely, a picture of an entire society and strategies for 'making it' therein; now." Although Mailer does offer writers some sound advice, such as constructing first-and third-person narratives, the book also contains its opinionated author's take on everything from actor Marlon Brando's performance in the movie *The Last Tango in Paris* to his views of contemporary novelists. *Washington Times* contributor Rex Roberts called some of the essays "tired" but also commented that "Mailer's takes on fellow novelists, from Leo Tolstoy and Mark Twain to Saul Bellow and Joseph Heller, remain fresh, full of writerly intelligence." Nathan Ward, writing in *Library Journal,* noted that "overall this is a book of rich experience that can be read around in with much pleasure and insight." As for novel-writing after age eighty, Mailer told Malcolm Jones in *Newsweek* that he planned to continue. "I'm not going to talk about that novel, because I'd talk it away. I won't even mention the subject. But I've got about 200 pages written on it, and it'll probably keep me busy for the rest of my writing years—at least. It's as ambitious as anything I've ever tackled. Writing novels is physically damaging. On the other hand, what I have is, you might say, more craft and less smoke."

BIOGRAPHICAL AND CRITICAL SOURCES:

BOOKS

Algeo, Ann M., *The Courtroom as Forum; Homicide Trials by Dreiser, Wright, Capote, and Mailer,* P. Lang (New York, NY), 1996.

Alter, Robert, *Motives for Fiction,* Harvard University Press (Cambridge, MA), 1984, pp. 46-60.

Amis, Martin, *The Moronic Inferno and Other Visits to America,* J. Cape (London, England), 1986, pp. 57-73.

Anderson, Chris, *Style as Argument: Contemporary American Nonfiction,* Southern Illinois University Press (Carbondale, IL), 1987, pp. 83-132.

Arlett, Robert, *Epic Voices: Inner and Global Impulse in the Contemporary American and British Novel,* Susquehanna University Press (Selinsgrove, PA), 1996.

Bailey, Jennifer, *Norman Mailer: Quick-Change Artist,* Harper (New York, NY), 1979.

Begiebing, Robert J., *Acts of Regeneration: Allegory and Archetype in the Works of Norman Mailer,* University of Missouri Press (Columbia, MO), 1980.

Bloom, Harold, editor, *Norman Mailer,* Chelsea House (New York, NY), 1986.

Concise Dictionary of American Literary Biography: Broadening Views, 1968-1988, Thomson Gale (Detroit, MI), 1989.

Contemporary Literary Criticism, Thomson Gale (Detroit, MI), Volume 1, 1979, Volume 2, 1974, Volume 3, 1975, Volume 4, 1975, Volume 5, 1976, Volume 8, 1978, Volume 11, 1979, Volume 14, 1980, Volume 28, 1984, Volume 39, 1986, Volume 74, 1993.

Dictionary of Literary Biography, Thomson Gale (Detroit, MI), Volume 2: *American Novelists since World War II,* 1978, Volume 16: *The Beats: Literary Bohemians in Postwar America,* 1983, Volume 28: *Twentieth-Century American-Jewish Fiction Writers,* 1984.

Dictionary of Literary Biography Documentary Series, Thomson Gale (Detroit, MI), Volume 3, 1983.

Dictionary of Literary Biography Yearbook: 1980, Thomson Gale (Detroit, MI), 1981, *1983,* 1984.

Friedman, Melvin, and Ben Siegel, editors, *Traditions, Voices, and Dreams: The American Novel since the 1960s,* University of Delaware Press (Newark, DE), 1995.

Girgus, Sam B., *The New Covenant: Jewish Writers and the American Idea,* University of North Carolina Press (Chapel Hill, NC), 1984, pp. 135-159.

Glenday, Michael K., *Norman Mailer,* St. Martin's Press (New York, NY), 1995.

Gordon, Andrew, *An American Dreamer: A Psychoanalytic Study of the Fiction of Norman Mailer,* Farleigh Dickinson University Press (Rutherford, NJ), 1980.

Guest, David, *Sentenced to Death: The American Novel and Capital Punishment,* University Press of Mississippi (Jackson, MS), 1997.

Kellman, Steven G., *Loving Reading: Erotics of the Text,* Archon (Hamden, CT), 1985.

Leigh, Nigel, *Radical Fictions and the Novels of Norman Mailer,* St. Martin's Press (New York, NY), 1990.

Lennon, J. Michael, editor, *Critical Essays on Norman Mailer,* G.K. Hall (Boston, MA), 1986.

Lennon, J. Michael, editor, *Conversations with Norman Mailer,* University Press of Mississippi (Jackson, MI), 1988.

Mailer, Adele, *The Last Party: Scenes from My Life with Norman Mailer,* Barricade Books (New York, NY), 1997.

Manso, Peter, *Mailer: His Life and Times,* Simon & Schuster (New York, NY), 1985.

Millett, Kate, *Sexual Politics,* Doubleday (Garden City, NY), 1970.

Mills, Hilary, *Mailer: A Biography,* Empire (New York, NY), 1982.

Poirier, Richard, *Norman Mailer,* Viking (New York, NY), 1972.

Rollyson, Carl, *The Lives of Norman Mailer: A Biography,* Paragon House (New York, NY), 1991.

Sorkin, Adam J., editor, *Politics and the Muse: Studies in the Politics of Recent American Literature,* Bowling Green State University Popular Press (Bowling Green, OH), 1989, pp. 79-92.

Wenke, Joseph, *Mailer's America,* University Press of New England (Hanover, NH), 1987.

PERIODICALS

American Spectator, April, 1992, p. 78.

Atlantic, July, 1971; September, 1984; May, 1995, pp. 120-125.

Book, January-February, 2003, James Schiff, review of *The Spooky Art: Some Thoughts on Writing,* p. 74.

Booklist, December 1, 2002, Brad Hooper, review of *The Spooky Art,* p. 626.

Chicago Tribune, December 20, 1982; September 21, 1987.

Commentary, April, 2003, Thomas L. Jeffers, review of *The Spooky Art,* p. 68.

Esquire, June, 1966; December, 1968; June, 1986; May, 1995, p. 142.

Gentleman's Quarterly, November, 1996, p. 332.

Journal of American Studies, December, 1987; December, 1990.

Kirkus Reviews, March 15, 1997, review of *The Gospel according to the Son.*

Library Journal, March 1, 2003, Nathan Ward, review of *The Spooky Art,* p. 90.

Life, March 19, 1965; September 24, 1965; February 24, 1967; September 15, 1967.

London Review of Books, November 7, 1991; December 14, 1995, pp. 7-9.

Los Angeles Times, September 23, 1984; May 24, 1995, p. E1; May 12, 1997, p. E1.

Los Angeles Times Book Review, December 14, 1980; July 11, 1982; April 24, 1983; August 19, 1984; October 15, 1995, pp. 2, 15.

Maclean's, December 2, 1991, p. 90; June 5, 1995, p. 69.

Modern Fiction Studies, spring, 1987.

Nation, May 27, 1968; June 25, 1983; September 15, 1984; November 6, 1995, p. 543.

National Review, April 20, 1965; November 4, 1991, p. 54; August 28, 1995, p. 42; February 12, 1996, p. 50; June 23, 1997, pp. 27-29; July 28, 1997, pp. 55-56.

New Criterion, January, 1992.

New Republic, February 9, 1959; February 8, 1964; June 8, 1968; January 23, 1971; May 2, 1983; August 27, 1984; November 25, 1991, p. 42; July 17, 1995, p. 46.

New Statesman, September 29, 1961.

Newsweek, December 9, 1968; April 18, 1983; August 6, 1984; April 24, 1995, p. 60; January 27, 2003, Malcom Jones, "You're in the Lap of History" (interview), p. 62; April 14, 2003, David Gates, review of *The Spooky Art,* p. 58.

New York, September 28, 1987; September 11, 1995, p. 80; October 16, 1995, p. 28.

New Yorker, October 23, 1948; October 22, 1955; November 4, 1991, pp. 113-119; April 10, 1995, p. 56; December 11, 1995, p. 42.

New York Review of Books, May 6, 1971; June 15, 1972; December 5, 1991, pp. 41-48; May 11, 1995, p. 52; June 22, 1995, p. 7; January 11, 1996, pp. 4-8.

New York Times, October 27, 1968; April 28, 1983; December 23, 1985; September 22, 1991, p. 28; April 25, 1995, p. B2; February 4, 1997, p. B7; April 14, 1997, p. B7; April 24, 1997, p. A21.

New York Times Book Review, May 7, 1948; September 17, 1967; May 5, 1968; October 27, 1968; January 10, 1971; February 18, 1972; October 7, 1979; September 20, 1980; December 7, 1980; June 6, 1982; January 30, 1983; April 10, 1983; July 20, 1984; July 29, 1984; April 11, 1985; September 29, 1991; April 30, 1995, pp. 1, 32; October 15, 1995, p. 16; October 6, 1996, p. 94; April 14, 1997; April 24, 1997; May 4, 1997, p. 9.

New York Times Sunday Magazine, September, 1979.

Partisan Review, spring, 1965; fall, 1965; summer, 1967; July, 1980.

People, May 30, 1983; October 5, 1987.

Publishers Weekly, March 22, 1965; October 8, 1979; March 20, 1995, p. 48; June 5, 1995, p. 34; September 11, 1995, p. 69; December 9, 2002, review of *The Spooky Art,* p. 75; March 31, 2003, John F. Baker, review of *Why Are We at War?,* p. 16.

Saturday Review, January, 1981.

Time, May 28, 1951; June 28, 1982; April 18, 1983; January 27, 1986; September 30, 1991, p. 70; May 1, 1995, p. 94; April 28, 1997, p. 75; September 29, 1997, p. 46.

Times (London, England), June 10, 1983.

Times Literary Supplement, October 3, 1968; January 11, 1980; March 6, 1981; December 10, 1982; June 10, 1983; October 19, 1984.

Tribune Books (Chicago, IL), October 7, 1979; November 30, 1980; June 13, 1982; April 10, 1983; August 5, 1984; July 14, 1985.

Village Voice, February 18, 1965; January 21, 1971.

Wall Street Journal, May 17, 1995, p. A16; October 2, 1995, p. A13; April 18, 1997, p. A16.

Washington Post, August 22, 1989.

Washington Post Book World, July 11, 1970; October 14, 1979; November 30, 1980; July 11, 1982; April 10, 1983; August 12, 1984; November 24, 1985; November 5, 1995, pp. 1, 10.

Washington Times, March 2, 2003, review of *The Spooky Art,* p. 808.

Yale Review, February, 1986.

*   *   *

MAILER, Norman Kingsley
See MAILER, Norman

*   *   *

MAKINE, Andreï 1957-

PERSONAL: Born 1957, in USSR (now Russia); immigrated to France, 1987.

ADDRESSES: Home—Paris, France. *Agent*—c/o Author Mail, Arcade Publishing, 141 Fifth Ave., New York, NY 10010.

CAREER: Author.

AWARDS, HONORS: Prix Goncourt, and Prix Medici, both 1995, and finalist for National Book Critics Circle Award for Fiction, 1997, all for *Testament français.*

WRITINGS:

La fille d'un héros de l'Union soviétique, R. Laffont (Paris, France), 1990, translation by Geoffrey Strachan published as *A Hero's Daughter,* Arcade Publishing (New York, NY), 2003.

Confession d'un porte-drapeau déchu, Belfond (Paris, France), 1992, translation by Geoffrey Strachan published as *Confessions of a Fallen Standardbearer,* Arcade Publishing (New York, NY), 2000.

Au temps du fleuve Amour, Editions du Felin (Paris, France), 1994, translation by Geoffrey Strachan published as *Once upon the River Love,* Arcade Publishing (New York, NY), 1998.

Le testament français, Mercure de France (Paris, France), 1995, translation by Geoffrey Strachan published as *Dreams of My Russian Summers,* Arcade Publishing (New York, NY), 1997.

Le crime d'Olga Arbyelina, Mercure de France (Paris, France), 1998, translation by Geoffrey Strachan published as *The Crime of Olga Arbyelina,* Arcade Publishing (New York, NY), 1999.

Requiem pour l'est, Mercure de France (Paris, France), 2000, translation by Geoffrey Strachan published as *Requiem for a Lost Empire,* Arcade Publishing (New York, NY), 2001, published as *Requiem for the East,* Sceptre (London, England), 2001.

Musique d'une vie, translation by Geoffrey Strachan published as *Music of a Life,* Arcade Publishing (New York, NY), 2002.

La terre et le ciel de Jacques Dorme, Mercure de France (Paris, France), 2003, translation by Geoffrey Strachan published as *The Earth and Sky of Jacques Dorme,* Arcade Publishing (New York, NY), 2005.

La femme qui attendait, Seuil (Paris, France), 2004.

SIDELIGHTS: Reviewing his novels, which in English translation include *Dream of My Russian Summers, Requiem for the Lost Empire,* and *Music of a Life,* critics have consistently praised Andreï Makine's insightful treatment of human consciousness, while also marvelling at his beautifully wrought prose. "One of Makine's most distinctive tricks," noted *Spectator* contributor Sam Phipps, "is the way he strips away layers of the past, freezing a fine detail or image in time and then returnign to it again and again from a different angle, each reprise conjuring a fresh nunace or revelation as the main narrative drives foreward. The effect," added the critic, "is cumulative, powerful, and somwhow meditative." Remarkably, Makine writes fiction in both his native language—Russian—and in French, the language of the country he adopted after going into self-imposed exile in the 1980s. Reviewer Anita Brookner explained this bilingualism in the *Spectator,* noting of Makine's "confident lyrical French" that "The author was raised in the brutality, the penury, and the false camaraderie of the Soviet regime. He had one link with civilisation, his French grandmother, and her stories and lessons."

Makine's early fiction quickly impressed critics due to the author's soulful approach to human development. His first novel, *A Hero's Daughter,* is a memoir focusing on a World War II veteran who learns over time that the rewards he has reaped from the Soviet government exact a heavy price from both him and his daugh-

ter. Although the work was not made available to English-language readers for over a decade after its 1990 publication, it exhibits "the seeds of the powerful social criticism that flowers in Makine's more mature novels," according to a *Publishers Weekly* contributor.

While *A Hero's Daughter* was ultimately praised by reviewers, its publication came only after many of Makine's efforts at interesting publishers failed. As Julie K.L. Dam reported in *Time* magazine, Makine "had to go to great lengths just to get published. The literati initially couldn't accept a Russian writing in French, so he rewrote his first two novels in Russian and presented the French originals as translations. He even posed as his ghost French translator." Ultimately, Makine's fourth work, *Dream of My Russian Summers,* met with critical acclaim after its publication and went on to win both the Prix Goncourt and the Prix Medici—a dual recognition no French writer had yet achieved.

Critics have praised Makine's writing on varied levels. Tobin H. Jones, writing in the *French Review,* commented that, in its original French, *Confessions of a Fallen Standard-bearer* "is a novel to read for the insights it can offer into both the construction and the inscription of cultural and social identity. It also surfaces ways of art by which the writer of contemporary fiction covers the writings of others amidst the disorientation born of conflict among opposing social and ideological structures. But most of all, this novel is one to read quite simply because it is so powerfully and sensitively written." Jones went on to note that the novel "echoes Makine's preoccupation with disillusionment seen in [*A Hero's Daughter.*] . . . In this work, Makine has created an unpretentious but poetic narrative whose power lies in its evocation of generations and the discovery of the past as a means to understand the loss of self and to create from the loss endured the foundations of a new consciousness."

As the first of Makine's works translated into English, the award-winning *Dreams of My Russian Summers* met with admiration yet again. A *New York Times* reviewer commented that "Makine employs a highly poetic voice to blend memory and imagination, merging the particular realities of Soviet life with a timeless evocation of a sensitive adolescence. Skillfully constructed and elegantly written, the novel records a series of eventful recollections that never descend to the trivial or the anecdotal." A *Publishers Weekly* reviewer remarked that the novel's portrayal of the grandmother "makes this latest installment in the great European tradition also one of the toughest and, ultimately, one of the most hopeful." Lisa Rohrbaugh, writing in *Library Journal,* expressed a similar sentiment by noting that "Makine has fashioned a deeply felt, lyrically told tale."

Anglophone reviewers were again entranced by Makine's *Once upon the River Love.* Barbara Hoffert, in a review for *Library Journal,* commented that "this delicate, beautifully rendered little work reads like a precursor to the magisterial *Dreams of My Russian Summers,*" while a *Kirkus Reviews* critic found the book only "Marginally less wonderful than *Dreams,* but that's quibbling. Let's have Makine's other fiction in English as soon as possible, please." Richard Bernstein, in a long review for the *New York Times Book Review,* explained: "Makine overdoes it in places. . . . But this is a minor fault. *Once upon the River Love* marks a further development in what is turning out to be an exciting literary career. Mr. Makine leaves us with that rare sense of having been drenched, entombed like a Siberian village under the heavy snow, in an entirely unfamiliar, exotic world, captured and held there so that it will long linger in the memory." A *Publishers Weekly* added of the book that "Makine has given American readers another unforgettable novel, which wears its exoticism on its sleeve, commands respect and defies imitation."

The more recently translated novels *The Crime of Olga Arbyelina, Requiem for a Lost Empire,* and *Music of a Life* have also been received enthusiastically by English-language readers. A *Publishers Weekly* reviewer commented that the first novel "possesses the feverish beauty of a hothouse culture in its final efflorescence." Hoffert, reviewing *The Crime of Olga Arbyelina* in *Library Journal,* reiterated her delight in Makine's fiction: "in luminous, hypnotic prose that is a bit like a drug itself, he unfolds the delicate situation between mother and son, seen as if through half-closed eyes. These passages at times seem overlong and overwrought, but the description of Russia on the verge of revolution is gripping and the ending a melancholy shock well worth the wait." *Music of a Life* proved equally as impressive, Hoffert noting that Makine's "elegant, heart-rending little gem of a work" reflects the author's characteristic themes of the power of art over politics. Noting that throughout the novel's prose "even the darkest textures are shot through . . . with light," *Review of Contemporary Fiction* contributor Laird Hunt added that Makine's story of a traveling pianist forced into exile as a result of Stalin's wartime purges is both "epic" and "powerful." Citing the novel's "graceful narrative" and "perfectly conceived and controlled" story, a *Kirkus* reviewer described *Music of a Life* as a "masterly dramatization of 'the disconcerting simplicity with which broken lives are lived.'"

First published in French in 2000, *Requiem for a Lost Empire*—published in England as *Requiem for the East*—also returns readers to twentieth-century Soviet Russia, this time in a story of three generations of military men: Nikolai, who served in and then deserted the Red Army during the Russian revolution; Pavel, who fought on the Eastern front during World War II; and the unnamed narrator, who now questions his role as a cold war spy. Noting the brutality characteristic of life in wartime Russia, Roland A. Champagne noted in *World Literature Today* that nonetheless "there is still joy in the heritage and the friendships" these men enjoy during their lives. In this novel, as well as in his other fictional portraits of life in communist Russia, Makine preserves his native country's "cultural coherence and retain[s] its continuity into the future." In *Booklist* Michael Spinella dubbed *Requiem for a Lost Empire* a "magnificent saga of horrific events rendered in masterful prose," while in *Library Journal* Hoffert noted that, like Makine's other works, the novel reflects on the themes introduced in *Dreams of My Russian Summer,* creating a book that "is both a little weightier and a little more challenging."

BIOGRAPHICAL AND CRITICAL SOURCES:

PERIODICALS

Booklist, July, 2001, Michael Spinella, review of *Requiem for a Lost Empire,* p. 1982; August, 2003, Michael Spinella, review of *A Hero's Daughter,* p. 1956.

French Review, October, 1996, Tobin H. Jones, review of *Le testament français,* pp. 147-148; March, 1998, Tobin H. Jones, review of *Confession d'un porte-drapeau déchu,* pp. 677-678.

Kirkus Reviews, June 1, 1998, review of *Once upon the River Love,* p. 763; June 15, 2002, review of *Music of a Life,* p. 831; June 15, 2003, review of *A Hero's Daughter,* p. 827.

Library Journal, June 23, 1997, p. 67; July, 1997, Lisa Rohrbaugh, review of *Dreams of My Russian Summers,* p. 126; July, 1998, Barbara Hoffert, review of *Once upon the River Love,* pp. 137-138; August, 1999, Barbara Hoffert, review of *The Crime of Olga Arbyelina,* p. 140; July, 2001, Barbara Hoffert, review of *Requiem for a Lost Empire,* p. 125; July, 2002, Barbara Hoffert, review of *Music of a Life,* p. 120; July, 2003, review of *A Hero's Daughter,* p. 124.

New Yorker, September 7, 1998, review of *Once upon the River Love,* p. 89.

New York Review of Books, November 20, 1997, Tatyana Tolstaya, "Love Story," p. 4.

New York Times, July 15, 1998, Richard Bernstein, "In a Land Where Love Had No Place," p. E10.

New York Times Book Review, August 17, 1997, review of *Dreams of My Russian Summers,* p. 8; September 6, 1998, William Boyd, "Rowing from Siberia to Brighton Beach," p. 8.

Publishers Weekly, July 7, 1997, Herbert R. Lottman, "From Russia—and France—with Love," p. 18; July 23, 1997, review of *Dreams of My Russian Summers,* p. 67; June 1, 1998, review of *Once upon the River Love,* p. 46; July 26, 1999, review of *The Crime of Olga Arbyelina,* p. 59; June 10, 2002, review of *Music of a Life,* p. 39; July 28, 2003, review of *A Hero's Daughter,* p. 80.

Review of Contemporary Fiction, spring, 2002, Jason Picone, review of *Requiem for a Lost Empire,* p. 125; spring, 2003, Laird Hunt, review of *Music of a Life,* p. 138.

Russian Life, September, 2001, review of *Requiem for a Lost Empire,* p. 52.

Spectator, December 30, 1995, Anita Brookner, "Prize-winning Novels from France," p. 32; September 1, 2001, Sam Phipps, review of *Requiem for the East,* p. 35; May 1, 2004, Digby Durrant, "Decline and Fall of a Russian Hero," p. 36.

Time, November 27, 1995, Julie K.L. Dam; September 28, 1998, John Skow, review of *Once upon the River Love,* p. 90.

Times Literary Supplement, January 19, 1996, Dan Gunn, "The Chosen Country," p. 11.

World Literature Today, winter, 2002, Roland A. Champagne, review of *Requiem for a Lost Empire,* p. 181.

*   *   *

MALABAILA, Damiano
See LEVI, Primo

*   *   *

MALAMUD, Bernard 1914-1986

PERSONAL: Born April 28, 1914, in Brooklyn, NY; died of natural causes, March 18, 1986, in New York, NY; son of Max (a grocery store manager) and Bertha (Fidelman) Malamud; married Ann de Chiara, November 6, 1945; children: Paul, Janna. *Education:* City College of New York (now City College of the City University of New York), B.A., 1936; Columbia University,

M.A., 1942. *Religion:* Jewish *Hobbies and other interests:* Reading, travel, music, walking.

CAREER: Worked for Bureau of Census, Washington, DC, 1940; Erasmus Hall High School, New York, NY, evening instructor in English, beginning 1940; Harlem High School, New York, NY, instructor in English, 1948-49; Oregon State University, Corvallis, 1949-61, began as instructor, became associate professor of English; Bennington College, Bennington, VT, Division of Language and Literature, member of faculty, 1961-86. Visiting lecturer, Harvard University, 1966-68. Honorary consultant in American letters, Library of Congress, 1972-75.

MEMBER: National Institute of Arts and Letters, American Academy of Arts and Sciences, PEN American Center (president, 1979-81).

AWARDS, HONORS: Partisan Review fellow in fiction, 1956-57; Richard and Hinda Rosenthal Foundation Award, and Daroff Memorial Award, both 1958, both for *The Assistant;* Rockefeller grant, 1958; National Book Award in fiction, 1959, for *The Magic Barrel,* and 1967, for *The Fixer;* Ford Foundation fellow in humanities and arts, 1959-61; Pulitzer Prize in fiction, 1967, for *The Fixer;* O. Henry Award, 1969, for "Man in the Drawer," and 1973; Jewish Heritage Award of the B'nai B'rith, 1977; Governor's Award, Vermont Council on the Arts, 1979, for excellence in the arts; American Library Association Notable Book citation, 1979, for *Dubin's Lives;* Brandeis University Creative Arts Award in fiction, 1981; Gold Medal for fiction, American Academy and Institute of Arts and Letters, 1983; Elmer Holmes Bobst Award for fiction, 1983; Mondello prize (Italy), 1985; honorary degree from City College of the City University of New York.

WRITINGS:

NOVELS

The Natural, Harcourt (New York, NY), 1952, with introduction by Kevin Baker, 2003.

The Assistant, Farrar, Straus (New York, NY), 1957, with introduction by Jonathan Rosen, 2003.

A New Life, Farrar, Straus (New York, NY), 1961.

The Fixer, Farrar, Straus (New York, NY), 1966.

The Tenants, Farrar, Straus (New York, NY), 1971, with introduction by Aleksandar Hemon, 2003.

Dubin's Lives, Farrar, Straus (New York, NY), 1979, with introduction by Thomas Mallon, 2003.
God's Grace, Farrar, Straus (New York, NY), 1982.

SHORT STORIES

The Magic Barrel (includes "The Magic Barrel" and "The First Seven Years"), Farrar, Straus (New York, NY), 1958, with introduction by Jhumpa Lahiri, 2003.
Idiots First (includes "Idiots First" and "The Maid's Shoes"), Farrar, Straus (New York, NY), 1963.
Pictures of Fidelman: An Exhibition (includes "The Last Mohican," "A Pimp's Revenge," and "Glass Blower of Venice"), Farrar, Straus (New York, NY), 1969.
Rembrandt's Hat (includes "The Silver Crown" and "Man in the Drawer"), Farrar, Straus (New York, NY), 1973.
Two Fables, Banyan Press (Pawlet, VT), 1978.
The Stories of Bernard Malamud, Farrar, Straus (New York, NY), 1983.
The People, and Uncollected Stories, edited by Robert Giroux, Farrar, Straus (New York, NY), 1989.
Bernard Malamud: The Complete Stories, edited and introduced by Robert Giroux, Farrar, Straus (New York, NY), 1997.

OTHER

A Malamud Reader, edited by Philip Rahv, Farrar, Straus (New York, NY), 1967.
Talking Horse: Bernard Malamud on Life and Work, edited by Alan Cheuse and Nicholas Delbanco, Columbia University Press (New York, NY), 1996.

Contributor to *Writing in America,* edited by John Fisher and Robert B. Silvers, Rutgers University Press (Rutgers, NJ), 1960. Contributor of short stories to various magazines, including *American Preface, Atlantic, Commentary, Harper's, New Threshold,* and *New Yorker.* Contributor of articles to *New York Times* and *New York Times Book Review.*

A collection of Malamud's manuscripts and other papers is housed at the Library of Congress.

ADAPTATIONS: The Fixer was filmed by John Frankenheimer for Metro-Goldwyn-Mayer, 1969. *The Angel Levine* starred Zero Mostel and Harry Belafonte and was adapted by William Gunn for United Artists, 1970. *The Natural,* starring Robert Redford, Robert Duvall, Glenn Close, and Kim Basinger, was directed by Barry Levinson for Tri-Star Pictures, 1984. *The First Seven Years* was filmed by Gigantic Pictures, 1997. *A New Life* and *The Assistant* were both optioned for films.

SIDELIGHTS: Esteemed twentieth-century novelist and short story writer Bernard Malamud grew up on New York's East Side where his Russian-Jewish immigrant parents worked in their grocery store sixteen hours a day. Malamud attended high school and college during the height of the Depression. His own and his family's experience are clearly echoed in his fiction, much of which chronicles, as Mervyn Rothstein declared in *New York Times,* "simple people struggling to make their lives better in a world of bad luck." Malamud's writings were also strongly influenced by classic nineteenth-century American writers such as Nathaniel Hawthorne, Henry David Thoreau, Herman Melville, and Henry James. In addition, Malamud's works reflected a post-Holocaust consciousness in addressing Jewish concerns and employing literary conventions drawn from earlier Jewish literature.

The first major period of Malamud's work extended from 1949 to 1961 when he was teaching composition at Oregon State College. Producing three novels and a collection of short stories during this period, he won several fiction prizes, including the National Book Award. Each of the first three novels features a schlemiel figure who tries to restore a Wasteland to a Paradise against a Jewish background. The setting varies in the novels, but in the short fiction it is most often the East Side of New York. "The Prison" portrays a small New York grocery store based on that of Malamud's parents, in which a young Italian, Tommy Castelli, is trapped. Similarly "The Cost of Living"—a predecessor of *The Assistant*—and "The Bill" both present the grocery store as a sort of prison. As Leslie and Joyce Field observed in *Bernard Malamud: A Collection of Critical Essays,* "In Malamud's fictional world, there is always a prison," and in an interview with the Fields given a decade before his death, the author noted: "Necessity is the primary prison, though the bars are not visible to all." Beneath most Malamudian surfaces would lie similar moral and allegorical meanings.

Malamud's first novel, *The Natural,* would serve, as Earl R. Wasserman declared in *Bernard Malamud and the Critics,* "the necessary reference text for a reading of his subsequent fiction." The 1952 work is a mythic novel, based on the Arthurian legends, in which the

Parsifal figure, Roy (King) Hobbs, restores fertility to the Fisher King, Pop Fisher, the manager of a baseball team called the Knights. Pitcher Roy appears as an Arthurian knight modeled in part on Babe Ruth, but his character also probably is drawn from Chretién de Troye's medieval tale, *Lancelot of the Cart,* featuring a Lancelot who is most often unhorsed and frequently humiliated. As Peter L. Hays noted in *The Fiction of Bernard Malamud,* "Like Lancelot, Malamud's heroes are cut to ribbons in their quests for love and fortune."

The novel's title is baseball slang for a player with natural talent, but it can also mean, as it did in the Middle Ages, an innocent fool. As Philip Roth commented in *Reading Myself and Others,* this is "not baseball as it is played in Yankee Stadium, but a wild, wacky game." Roy thinks of himself as "Sir Percy lancing Sir Maldemer, or the first son (with a rock in his paw) ranged against the primitive papa." Even more Freudian is Roy's lance-like bat, Wonderboy, which droops when its phallic hero goes into a slump and finally splits at the novel's conclusion.

In an echo of the Black Sox scandal of 1919, Roy is bribed to throw the pennant game by evil-eyed Gus Sands, whose Pot of Fire nightclub and chorus girls wielding pitchforks suggest hell itself. Though there are few obvious Jewish traces in *The Natural,* the prank Roy plays on Gus is a retelling of a Yiddish prankster tale, with the challenge by the prankster, the foil or victim's reaction, and the retort or prank—here Roy's pulling silver dollars out of Gus's ears and nose. Yet Roy's success is only temporary. As Glenn Meeter noted in *Bernard Malamud and Philip Roth: A Critical Essay,* "From the grail legend also we know that Roy will fail; for the true grail seeker must understand the supernatural character of his quest, and Roy does not." In the end Roy, defeated, throws his bribe money in the face of Judge Banner, who is a dispenser of "dark wisdom, parables and aphorisms which punctuate his conversation, making him seem a cynical Poor Richard," as Iska Alter remarked in *The Good Man's Dilemma: Social Criticism in the Fiction of Bernard Malamud.* This dramatic scene, and others in Malamud's work, accords with the statement he once made that his novels were akin to plays.

Other influences are also clearly at work in Malamud's first novel. *The Natural* contains significant references to birds and flowers and steady reminders of the passage of the seasons. The simplicity of this pastoral style at its best allowed the presentation of complex ideas in a natural way. A second influence, as Malamud himself

acknowledged, is cinematic technique. For example, there are quick, movie-like changes of scene—called jump cuts—when Roy and Memo Paris are tricked into sleeping with each other. In addition, the portrayal of Roy has a Chaplinesque quality of humor to it. Though Malamud would never again write non-Jewish fiction, *The Natural* served as a treasure house of reusable motifs and methods for all his subsequent work.

In 1954 Malamud published one of his greatest short stories, "The Magic Barrel," which Sanford Pinsker, in *Bernard Malamud: A Collection of Critical Essays,* called "a nearly perfect blend of form and content." In this story, collected in the 1958 volume of the same name, the matchmaker Pinye Salzman, using cards listing eligible women and drawn from his magic barrel, tricks student rabbi Leo Finkle into a love match with Salzman's daughter, Stella, a streetwalker. In *Judaism,* Marcia Booher Gealy described the structural essence of such Hasidic-influenced stories: (1) the inward journey; (2) the older man tutoring the younger; (3) the triumph of love; (4) the reality of evil; and (5) transformation through the tale itself. This structure merges with another influence, that of nineteenth-century American romanticism, for Malamud often joined the Hasidic and Hawthornian in his fables. As Renee Winegarten commented in *Bernard Malamud: A Collection of Critical Essays,* "His magic barrels and silver crowns, whatever their seal, firmly belong in the moral, allegorical realm of scarlet letters, white whales and golden bowls."

Concerning protagonist Salzman, as Irving Howe noted in *World of Our Fathers,* "The matchmaker, or *shadkhn,* is a stereotypical Yiddish figure: slightly comic, slightly sad, at the edge of destitution." Such confidence men reappear throughout Malamud's fiction, in "The Silver Crown," for example. And Salzman shows Malamud's early perfection of a Jewish-American speech, which is neither pure Yiddish dialect nor mere literary chat, but an imaginative combination of both. Kathryn Hellerstein observed in *The State of the Language* that Yiddish speakers in Malamud's works are "elderly, static, or declining" and concluded that for Malamud, Yiddish figures serve as "a spectral presence of the constraining, delimited, stultified past."

What many critics would refer to as Malamud's finest novel, *The Assistant,* appeared in 1957. Ihab Hassan wrote in *The Fiction of Bernard Malamud,* "The Assistant,* I believe, will prove a classic not only of Jewish but of American literature." Frank Alpine, "the assistant," suggests St. Francis of Assisi, whose biography,

The Little Flowers, is Alpine's favorite book and whose stigmata he at one point seems to emulate. Like Roy in *The Natural,* Frank is a Parsifal figure who must bring fertility, or at least new life, to the Fisher King, here the grocery store owner Morris Bober. Some critics have contended that Bober may parallel philosopher Martin Buber, whose I-THOU philosophy of human relations Bober seems, however instinctively, to share, though Malamud himself denied any use of Buber in this novel.

When he stands under a "No Trust" sign, Bober also recalls Melville's novel, *The Confidence Man.* Giving food to a drunk woman who will never pay, Morris teaches Frank to have compassion for others. Yet Frank cannot control his passion for Morris's daughter, Helen. Thus when Frank saves Helen from an attempted rape, he fails the trial of the Perilous Bed, rapes her just as she is about to admit her love for him, and loses her.

Frank and Morris represent a familiar motif found throughout Malamud's works: that of the father-son pair, the schlemiel-schlimazel twins. Malamud liked these doublings and included three other father/son pairs in the novel. A favorite definition of these types is that the schlemiel spills his teacup, and the schlimazel is the one he spills it on. Norman Leer, thinking perhaps of Russian novelist Feodor Dostoevsky's *Crime and Punishment,* wrote in *Mosaic* of "the notion of the divided self, and the attraction of two characters who mirror a part of each other, and are thereby drawn together as doubles."

Another recurrent feature in Malamudian narrative, the Holocaust, remains never far from the surface, though it appears almost always in an oblique way. Morris, in despair over his luckless grocery store/prison, turns on the gas to commit suicide, a reminder of the gas chambers of the Holocaust. And here Malamud introduces from the world of fantasy a professional arsonist who is like a figure from hell—recalling the night club women and their pitchforks in *The Natural.* In *The Assistant,* at Morris's funeral, Frank halts the ceremony by falling into the open grave while trying to see the rose Helen had thrown into it. The characters in Malamud's fiction frequently dream, and in Frank's dream, St. Francis successfully gives Frank's rose to Helen.

In 1958, with the publication of his first volume of short stories, *The Magic Barrel,* Malamud received national recognition and in 1959 won the National Book Award for the collection. All the stories in the volume display Malamud's continuing debt to Hawthorne; as

Jackson J. Benson said in *The Fiction of Bernard Malamud,* both writers possessed "the ability to combine, with great skill, reality and the dream, the natural and supernatural." Thus a kinship can be perceived between Malamud's "Idiots First," "The Silver Crown," and "The Magic Barrel" and Hawthorne's short stories "My Kinsman, Major Molineux," "Young Goodman Brown," and "The Birthmark." Moreover, "The First Seven Years"— featuring Feld, a Polish immigrant shoemaker who refuses to speak Yiddish and who wants his daughter Miriam to marry a rising young suitor, Max, rather than his middle-aged but devoted helper, Sobel—is reminiscent of Hawthorne's "Ethan Brand," with its warning about "hardness of the heart." However, "The First Seven Years" was Hawthorne plus Holocaust, for Sobel had barely escaped Hitler's incinerators.

In the years from 1949 to 1961 Malamud grew in stature to become "one of the foremost writers of moral fiction in America," as Jeffrey Helterman commented in *Understanding Bernard Malamud.* Of his last work in this first period, Sheldon J. Hershinow remarked in *Bernard Malamud* that *A New Life* "is Malamud's first attempt at social satire, and much of the novel is given over to it." The novel's hero, marginal Jew Sy Levin, shows the complexity behind the names Malamud would give to practically all his major characters. In *City of Words: American Fiction 1950-1970,* Tony Tanner explained that the name Levin means the east, or light; it is also associated with lightning. Tanner wrote: "I have it direct from Mr. Malamud that by a pun on 'leaven' he is suggesting what the marginal Jew may bring in attitude to the American scene." Levin, whose fictional career resembles that of his creator, is a former high school teacher who joins the faculty at Cascadia University in Easchester, Oregon, a name that suggests a castle of ease. According to Mark Goldman, in a *Critique* review, "Early in the novel, Levin is the tenderfoot Easterner, the academic sad sack, or schlimazel of Yiddish literature, invoking nature like a tenement Rousseau." Levin, then is the schlemiel as lecturer, who teaches his first class with his fly open, then bumbles his way into an affair with coed Nadalee, a lady of the lake who has written an essay on nude bathing. As Sandy Cohen remarked in *Bernard Malamud and the Trial by Love,* "Malamud's favorite method of portraying a protagonist's struggle to overcome his vanity is to symbolize it in terms of the Grail myth. Thus Levin's journey to meet Nadalee takes on certain aspects of the grail quest." Indeed, Levin journeys "in his trusty Hudson, his lance at his side."

Later Levin makes love in the woods to Pauline Gilley; in an echo of English novelist D.H. Lawrence's *Lady Chatterley's Lover,* Pauline also has an impotent husband, Gerald Gilley, future chairman of the English Department. Against this pastoral background, complete with the passage of the seasons, Levin is also the American Adam: as Hershinow observed, "Immersed in the writings of Emerson, Thoreau, and Whitman, Levin believes wholeheartedly the metaphors about America as a New-World Garden of Eden. By going west he feels he can recapture his lost innocence and escape the past—become the New-World Adam."

This major love affair is also Hawthornian: as Paul Witherington noted in *Western American Literature,* "Levin's affair with Pauline matures in Hawthorne fashion to an inner drama of the ambiguities of paradise." In fact, Levin sees himself as "Arthur Dimmesdale Levin, locked in stocks on a platform in the town square, a red A stapled on his chest." From Levin's point of view, Pauline, whose love earned him his scarlet letter "A", is also the tantalizing *shiksa,* the Gentile temptress of so many Jewish-American novels, not only those of Malamud but also of Saul Bellow and Philip Roth among others. As Frederick Cople Jaher pointed out in *American Quarterly,* to Jewish men, such women seem to be "exotic insiders" and so represent "tickets of admission into American society."

At the conclusion of the novel, Gilley asks Levin why he wants to take on two adopted children and Gilley's apparently barren wife. Levin replies, "Because I can, you son of a bitch." And Levin, defeated in academe, but having impregnated the barren Pauline, whose flat breasts are beginning to swell, drives away with his new family, having agreed with Gilley never again to teach in a university. This ending, as so often in Malamud, is ambiguous, for Levin is no longer in romantic love with Pauline. Here is what *Critique* contributor Ruth B. Mandel called "ironic affirmation"—"The affirmation itself is ironic in that the state of grace is unaccompanied by paradise."

After Malamud's move back East to Bennington College, his second period—roughly 1961-1970—began, and both his stories and his next two novels took a more cosmopolitan and international direction. In *Bernard Malamud,* Sidney Richman observed that the title story in 1963's *Idiots First* is "a morality [play] *a la* Everyman in which the sense of a real world (if only the sense of it) is utterly absorbed by a dreamlandscape, a never-never-land New York City through which an elderly Jew named Mendel wanders in search of comfort and aid." Mendel is indeed a Jewish Everyman, who tries to dodge the Angel of Death (here named Ginzburg) to arrange for the future of his handicapped son, Isaac.

Another short story, "The Maid's Shoes," reveals the new subject matter and style. Professor Orlando Krantz, who plays the part of the comparatively wealthy American as Everyman, tries to give a small gift to his poor Italian maid, Rosa, but it is a gift without the understanding that the impoverished European needs: "But though they shared the same roof, and even the same hot water bottle and bathtub, they almost never shared speech." Here, failures of the heart, common to the fiction of the first period, are extended to complete failures of empathy. Furthermore, the story is no longer fantastic, as in Malamud's first period, but realistic. Of Rosa, Malamud wrote: "She was forty-five and looked older. Her face was worn but her hair was black, and her eyes and lips were pretty. She had few good teeth. When she laughed she was embarrassed around the mouth." Finally, the story has a single, consistent point of view instead of the omniscient point of view of the earlier stories. Yet since that omniscient narration contained Malamud's often compassionate comments that were characteristic of his first period manner, these newer stories have a bleaker cast to them.

Next to *The Assistant* in critical reputation would come *The Fixer,* winner of the Pulitzer Prize and the National Book Award in 1967. In a search for a suffering Everyman plot, Malamud had thought of several subjects—the trial of Alfred Dreyfus and the Sacco-Vanzetti case, among others—before deciding on a story he had heard from his father as a boy, that of the trial of Mendel Beiliss for ritual bloodletting and murder in 1913 in Russia. Through this story, Malamud also tried to answer the question of how the death camps in Germany had been possible. Hero Yakov Bok's last name suggests a scapegoat, and also the goat mentioned in the song chanted for the end of the Passover Seder as a symbol of Jewish survival. As Malamud once said in an interview with Christopher Lehmann-Haupt in *New York Times Book Review,* it was necessary "to mythologize—that is, to make metaphors and symbols of the major events and characters."

The novel itself covers two years, spring 1911 to winter 1913, during which Bok is imprisoned after being falsely accused of the ritual murder of a Gentile boy. Without legal counsel Bok suffers betrayal, gangrene, poison, and freezing cold, and finally turns inward to develop a sense of freedom. In prison this Everyman fixer learns through suffering to overcome, at least in part, his initial agnosticism, and his doubts of what is meant by the Chosen People. He rejects both suicide and a pardon, and accepts his Jewishness. Finally, in a dream encounter with Tsar Nicholas II, Bok shoots the Tsar. As John F. Desmond wrote in *Renascence,* "Yakov has come to understand that no man is apolitical, especially a Jew; consequently, if his chance came, as it does in the imaginary meeting with the Tsar, he would not hesitate to kill the ruler as a beginning step towards purging that society of its agents of repression and injustice, and thus strike a blow for freedom and humanity." Bok, at least in his dream, is no longer the passive, suffering servant of Isaiah portrayed in many of Malamud's first-period fictions, but one who seeks revenge. Has Bok lost more important values? The dream setting leaves the ending ambiguous, but Malamud's real subject was never so much Bok himself as those—like the Germans, other Europeans, and Americans did during the Holocaust—who either participate in, or passively observe, the treatment of Everyman as victim. As the Fields remarked, Malamud repeatedly tried to make clear, especially in this second period, that Jewish victims are Everyman as victim, for history, sooner or later, treats all men as Jews.

The final major work of this second period is *Pictures of Fidelman: An Exhibition.* As Leslie A. Field wrote in *Bernard Malamud: A Collection of Critical Essays,* "Of all the Malamud characters, early and late, one must return to Arthur Fidelman as the Malamud *schlemiel par excellence.*" The Fidelman stories appeared both separately in magazines and in two story collections from 1958 to 1969, and they were not originally thought of as a unit. But the last three stories are tightly linked, and as Robert Ducharme asserted in *Art and Idea in the Novels of Bernard Malamud: Toward "The Fixer,"* Malamud deliberately saved the last story for the book because he did not want to let readers know the ending. Three genres merge in *Pictures of Fidelman,* that of the *kunstlerroman* or artist novel, the *bildungsroman* or education novel, and the *Huckleberry Finn*-like picaresque novel, in which the main character wanders through a series of adventures. Fidelman (faith man) encounters Susskind (sweet child) in the first story or chapter, "Last Mohican." Susskind is a Jewish folktale type, a *chnorrer,* or as Goldman termed him, "a beggar with style," who wants the second of Fidelman's two suits. Rebuffed, Susskind steals the first chapter of Fidelman's book on Italian artist Giotto di Bondone. Hershinow suggested that "Susskind becomes for Fidelman a kind of dybbuk (demon) who inhabits his conscience, destroying his peace of mind." As Cohen remarked, "So Fidelman begins an active search for Susskind who begins to take on the roles of alter-ego, superego, and symbol for Fidelman's true heritage and past." Here again would be the familiar Malamud motif of the journey that changes a life.

In pursuit, Fidelman visits a synagogue, a Jewish ghetto, and a graveyard that contains victims of the Holocaust.

Both at the cemetery and in his crazy pursuit of Susskind, Schlemiel Fidelman recalls Frank Alpine in *The Assistant,* for Fidelman too is linked to St. Francis. In a dream Fidelman sees Susskind, who shows him a Giotto fresco in which St. Francis gives his clothing to a poor knight. As Sidney Richman affirmed in *Bernard Malamud and the Critics,* "In the same fashion as Frankie Alpine, Fidelman must discover that the way to the self is paradoxically through another; and the answer is heralded by a sudden alteration of the pursuit." At the end of this artistic pilgrim's progress, "against his will, Fidelman learns what the ancient rabbis taught and what Susskind has always known: Jews—that is, human beings, *menschen,* in Malamud's terms—are responsible for each other. That is the essence of being human," Michael Brown related in *Judaism.*

Fidelman learns in the next stories what makes a great artist. For example, in the fourth story, "A Pimp's Revenge," he returns his mistress, Esmeralda, to prostitution to pay for his constantly repainted masterwork, a portrait of her, first as Mother and Son, then as Brother and Sister, and finally as Prostitute and Procurer. "The truth is I am afraid to paint, like I might find out something about myself," Fidelman says. Esmeralda knows the secret: "If I have my choice, I'll take life. If there's not that there's no art." Barbara Lefcowitz argued in *Literature and Psychology,* "Where Malamud excels is in his subtle and nearly always comical juxtaposition of a neurotic character against a deeper and wider moral and historical context." Fidelman finally produces a masterpiece, but, second-rate artist that he is, can't let it alone, and mars it. The genius knows when to stop, but Everyman does not, and Esmeralda calls him a murderer.

In the final story, "Glass Blower of Venice," Fidelman tries to play artist once more, under the reluctant teaching of his homosexual lover Beppo, but at last gives up art for craftsmanship and returns to America. Fidelman, the craftsman, no longer the inadequate artist, has finally achieved the goals toward which Susskind—and later Esmeralda—pointed him. Samuel I. Bellman argued in *Critique* that "more than any other Malamudian character Fidelman is constantly growing, realizing himself, transforming his unsatisfactory old life into a more satisfactory new one." In *Bernard Malamud: A Collection of Critical Essays,* Sheldon N. Grebstein praised the juxtaposition of "the coarsely sexual and the sublimely aesthetic." Indeed, no other work of Malamud would show so much appetite for life; as Helterman argued, Fidelman "also seeks, and occasionally participates in, a richness of passion not typical of Malamud's urban heroes." The epigraph for *Pictures of Fidelman* is from Yeats: "The intellect of man is forced to choose Perfection of the life or of the work." However, the new Fidelman chooses "both."

The Tenants inaugurated Malamud's third and final period. In the works of this period the heroic structuring of the first period would vanish, as would the Wandering Jews and the Everyman motifs of the second. Beneath differing surface plots, though, a new structural likeness would appear. Before 1971 Malamud's typical Jewish characters tended to move towards responsibility rather than towards achievement; from 1971 on, they became extraordinary achievers, or *machers.*

In 1971's *The Tenants,* Harry Lesser, a minor Jewish novelist, is writing a novel about being unable to finish a novel, in a kind of infinite regression. He keeps on living in the apartment building that landlord Levenspiel (leaven game) wants to tear down; then a squatter, black writer Willie Spearmint (Willie Shakespeare), moves into the building. Willie and Harry are the kind of doubled pair (drawn from Edgar Allan Poe and Dostoevsky) that Malamud was fond of, for Harry's writing is all form, and Willie's is all vitality. Harry takes over Irene, Willie's Jewish girl; Willie burns Harry's manuscript; Harry axes Willie's typewriter; and in a final burst of over-achievement, Willie brains Harry and Harry castrates Willie. *The Tenants* "ends in a scream of language," reported Malcolm Bradbury in *Encounter.* Though the novel hints at two other possible endings—by fire, or by Harry's marriage to Irene—Levenspiel has the last word, which is *Rachmones,* or mercy.

Though *The Tenants* did little for Malamud's reputation, he continued to publish short fiction in top U.S. magazines up until his death in 1986; as he told *New York Times* critic Mervyn Rothstein near the end of his life, "With me, it's story, story, story." In Malamud's 1973 collection, *Rembrandt's Hat,* only one story, "The Silver Crown," is predominantly Jewish, in sharp contrast to his first collection, while other stories are more reminiscent of Chekhov. There is even a visit to the Chekhov Museum in "Man in the Drawer," a story that shows the fascination with achievement so dominant in Malamud's final period. Howard Harvitz, an intellectual tourist in Russia and a marginal Jew, has changed his name from Harris back to Harvitz. Hardly a creative writer himself, he is doing a piece on museums. A Russian writer, Levitansky—also a marginal Jew, but a determined achiever in spite of official opposition—intends to smuggle his stories out of Russia. Harvitz at first doesn't want this charge, but discovers that four of the stories show heroes not taking responsibility. After reading them, Harvitz timorously takes the stories out of Russia.

The 1979 novel *Dubin's Lives* took Malamud over five years to write, twice as long as any previous novel. Ralph Tyler in *New York Times Book Review* reported that Malamud referred to the work as "his attempt at bigness, at summing up what he . . . learned over the long haul." In the novel, the biographer Dubin is an isolated achiever, no mere recorder of biographical facts but a creative, even fictionalizing biographer: "One must transcend autobiographical detail by inventing it after it is remembered." Dubin is trying to write a biography of D.H. Lawrence, a writer who made passion his religion, yet was impotent. There had been a glancing counterpointing of Lawrence's career in *A New Life,* but here this motif is much enlarged; as David Levin observed in *Virginia Quarterly Review,* "The complexities of Dubin's subsequent adventures often run parallel to events in Lawrence's life."

In the kind of psychomachia, or inner struggle, which some critics saw as the essence of American fiction, Dubin, as Helterman noted, "loses his memory, his sexual powers, his ability to work, even his ability to relate to his family. At first, the only compensation for these losses is a kind of high-grade nostalgia brought about by a process called reverie." These reveries lead Dubin to a liaison with young Fanny Bick, whose first name comes from English novelist Jane Austen's heroine in *Mansfield Park,* Fanny Price; Fanny Bick is an Austen heroine with glands. Like a number of heroines in Malamud's fiction, she is significantly associated with wildflowers, fruit, and bird flights. Chiara Briganti remarked in *Studies in American Jewish Literature* that "all the female characters in Malamud's fiction share a common shallowness and common values: they all respect marriage and family life, and, whatever their past, they all seek fulfillment through a permanent relationship with a man." But Fanny breaks this stereotypical pattern, for at the end of *Dubin's Lives* she ambitiously intends to become a lawyer.

Dubin's affair in Venice, where the youthful Fanny almost immediately betrays him with their gondolier, is that of the schlemiel lover seen before in Frank Alpine and Sy Levin. Barbara Quart, in *Studies in American Jewish Literature,* saw a further problem: "While Malamud's central characters try to break out of their solitude, they appear to fear love and women as much as they long for them." But dominant among familiar motifs is the character of Dubin as the isolated overachiever, who moves his study from his country house into the barn to devote all possible energy and space to his biography. Dubin even begrudges time wasted thinking about Fanny, with whom he is genuinely in love.

Malamud's last finished novel, 1982's *God's Grace,* treats both the original Holocaust and a new, imagined Holocaust of the future. In *Immigrant-Survivors: Post-Holocaust Consciousness in Recent Jewish-American Literature,* Dorothy Seldman Bilik pointed out that the question of why God permitted the Holocaust was a central issue in Malamud's fiction for thirty years; indeed, for Malamud the Holocaust is the ultimate mark of inhumanity, and *God's Grace* treats the Holocaust not only as man's inhumanity to man, but as God's inhumanity to man. The novel is a wild, at times brilliant, at times confusing description of a second Great Flood. Calvin Cohn, a paleologist and the son of a rabbi-cantor, had been doing underseas research when the Djanks and the Druzhkies (Yanks and Russians) launched an atomic Holocaust and destroyed every other human. Calvin recalls many Biblical and literary figures: Parsifal, Romeo, Prospero, Robinson Crusoe, Gulliver, and Ahab. His Eve and Juliet is Mary Madelyn, a chimpanzee. An albino ape appears (possibly an oblique reference to Moby Dick) with other apes as Yahoos from Jonathan Swift's *Gulliver's Travels,* and the chimpanzee Buz serves as Cohn's Isaac, Caliban, and man Friday. There is even an Arthurian spear used to harpoon the albino ape.

On Cohn's Island Calvin turns into an overachiever, and even an un-Job-like defier of God, in spite of God's pillars of fire, showers of lemons, and occasional warning rocks. The foundation of *God's Grace* is Biblical in part, but also characteristically American, for it is the story of the Americanized—and reversed—Fortunate Fall. The idea conveyed by the Fortunate Fall is that Adam and Eve, driven from Paradise by eating of the tree of Knowledge, in fact obtained benefits from their fall, notably free will and a consciousness of good and evil. Cohn has treated the chimpanzees as his inferiors; as a schlemiel lecturer he has imposed his admonitions and teachings on them, rather than encouraging them to learn for themselves. He has promised but never given Mary Madelyn the marriage she has wanted, and he has prevented the marriage or mating of Buz and Mary Madelyn, which could have been just as desirable for the future gene stock as Cohn's half-chimpanzee child Rebekah. In short, over-achieving Calvin Cohn has eaten from the tree of hubris, or sinful pride, rather than knowledge.

This complex novel baffled its first reviewers; for example, Joseph Epstein wrote in *Commentary:* "Much of

the humor in the novel is of the kind known as faintly amusing, but the chimp humor, on the scale of wit, is roughly three full rungs down from transvestite jokes." Part of the difficulty in the novel is that *God's Grace* does not fall into a clear genre category; in a 1982 *Christian Science Monitor* article, Victor Howes called it "somewhat east of sci-fi, somewhat west of allegory." However, like much of Malamud's work, *God's Grace* not only reflects the Jewish Old Testament but also partakes of an American colonial genre, the Jeremiad, or warning of future disaster.

At Malamud's sudden death in the winter of 1986 he left behind him sixteen chapters of a twenty-one-chapter novel tentatively titled *The People.* The novel, which concerns the adventures of a Russian Jewish peddlar named Yozip in the American West, was included in its draft form in *The People, and Uncollected Stories,* in 1989. As Nan Robertson explained the work in *New York Times,* the schlemiel hero Yozip becomes a marshal, is kidnaped by a tribe of Native American Indians, and has a dialogue with an Indian chief about obtaining his freedom. In addition to *The People,* the collection also contains fourteen short stories written between 1943 and 1985, six of which had never before been published. While critics noted that the collection has interest for Malamud scholars, the author's decision not to collect these works was made due to their relative merits. While noting that the unfinished state of Malamud's posthumously published novel precludes any serious discussion of its merits, Jonathan Yardley commented in *Washington Post Book Review* that "Of the stories, one . . . has merit, and the apprenticework is mildly interesting for the foreshadowing it offers of Malamud's mature writing; but the world would not be the poorer had these tales been allowed to go undisturbed."

In 1998, Malamud's fifty-five short stories were published in one volume as *Bernard Malamud: The Complete Stories.* It features an introduction by Robert Giroux, Malamud's good friend and his editor throughout his career. Giroux also edited *The Complete Stories,* and his introduction is "valuable" reading, in the estimation of *America* contributor Loren F. Schmidtberger. Schmidtberger also approved of the book's organization. Placing stories in the order they were written, it allows readers to get a sense of Malamud's stylistic development over the course of his four-decade career. *The Complete Stories* also gives the dates and places of the first publication of each of the stories. Schmidtberger was enthusiastic about the quality of Malamud's work, stating, "All of the stories are a joy to read, even the early ones from non-paying magazines." He mentioned the "zaniness of imagery and situation" that marks much of Malamud's writing, and pointed out that many of the stories in the collection are "funny—not side-slappers, to be sure, but bittersweet comedies. They explore serious themes with the moral intensity of a Nathaniel Hawthorne, but they are seasoned with humor." The reviewer also praised Malamud's command of the Yiddish idiom, finding his dialog to be realistic and appealing. Although Malamud's characters are frequently struggling under painful burdens, they "are not quitters," mused Schmidtberger. They cannot always express themselves perfectly, but whatever happens, "they keep on talking. Through Malamud's art, they show us what it means to be human." Schmidtberger concluded that *The Complete Stories* proves Malamud to be "a marvelous storyteller of the first rank."

During his life, Malamud was a reclusive writer, giving few interviews. However, those he did grant provide perhaps the most illuminating commentary on his work. After his death, several collections of interviews, speeches, and lectures were published. In 1991's *Conversations with Bernard Malamud* thirty interviews transcribed from various sources represent the bulk of the public disclosure of this private literary figure. Within his brief, to-the-point responses to questions regarding his life, Malamud reflected his belief that the tale is far more important than the teller. "He was definite in asserting that to be a writer one must have talent and discipline," Daniel Walden explained in *Modern Fiction Studies*. Calling *Conversations* "an exceptionally useful book," Walden added of the late author: "What he saw in the writing act was a moral act, in constantly seeking the highest opportunities to do well. . . . Indeed, Malamud as moralist, although not as preacher, comes through the body of his work. The daring writer . . . who reinvented himself with each book, despite the occasional dark vision, never wavered from his positive [humanist] premise."

"People say I write so much about misery," Malamud once confided to Michiko Kakutani in a rare interview for *New York Times*, "but you write about what you write best. As you are grooved, so you are grieved. And the grieving is that no matter how much happiness or success you collect, you cannot obliterate your early experience." Malamud's contribution to twentieth-century literature can be seen most clearly in his greatest invention, his Jewish-American dialect, comic even at the height of tragedy. Recall Calvin Cohn, sacrificed in *God's Grace* by the chimpanzee Buz in a wild inversion of the story of Abraham and Isaac, as he reflects that God after all has let him live out his life. Cohn then asks himself—forgetting his educated speech and

reverting to the Yiddish rhythms of his youth—"Maybe tomorrow the world to come?" In such comic-serious questioning, Malamud captured the voice of the past and gave it relevance in the modern era.

BIOGRAPHICAL AND CRITICAL SOURCES:

BOOKS

Alter, Iska, *The Good Man's Dilemma: Social Criticism in the Fiction of Bernard Malamud,* AMS Press (New York, NY), 1981.

Astro, Richard, and Jackson J. Benson, editors, *The Fiction of Bernard Malamud,* Oregon State University Press (Corvallis, OR), 1977.

Avery, Evelyn G., *Rebels and Victims: The Fiction of Richard Wright and Bernard Malamud,* Kennikat (Port Washington, NY), 1979.

Baumbach, Jonathan, *The Landscape of Nightmare: Studies in the Contemporary American Novel,* New York University Press (New York, NY), 1965.

Bilik, Dorothy Seldman, *Immigrant-Survivors: Post-Holocaust Consciousness in Recent Jewish-American Literature,* Wesleyan University Press (Middletown, CT), 1981.

Bloom, Harold, *Bernard Malamud,* Chelsea House (New York, NY), 1986.

Bryant, Jerry H., *The Open Decision: The Contemporary American Novel and Its Intellectual Background,* Free Press (New York, NY), 1970.

Cohen, Sandy, *Bernard Malamud and the Trial by Love,* Rodopi (Amsterdam, The Netherlands), 1974.

Concise Dictionary of American Literary Biography: The New Consciousness, 1941-1968, Thomson Gale (Detroit, MI), 1987.

Contemporary Authors Bibliographical Series, Volume 1: *American Novelists,* Thomson Gale (Detroit, MI), 1986.

Contemporary Literary Criticism, Thomson Gale (Detroit, MI), Volume 1, 1973, Volume 2, 1974, Volume 3, 1975, Volume 5, 1976, Volume 8, 1978, Volume 9, 1978, Volume 11, 1979, Volume 18, 1981, Volume 27, 1984, Volume 44, 1987, Volume 78, 1994, Volume 85, 1995.

Dictionary of Literary Biography, Thomson Gale (Detroit, MI), Volume 2: *American Novelists since World War II,* 1978, Volume 28: *Twentieth-Century American-Jewish Fiction Writers,* 1984, Volume 152: *American Novelists since World War II, Fourth Series,* 1995.

Dictionary of Literary Biography Yearbook, Thomson Gale (Detroit, MI), 1980, 1981, 1986, 1987.

Ducharme, Robert, *Art and Idea in the Novels of Bernard Malamud: Toward "The Fixer,"* Mouton (The Hague, Netherlands), 1974.

Encyclopedia of World Biography, Thomson Gale (Detroit, MI), 1998.

Ertel, Rachel, *Le Roman juif americain: Une Ecriture minoritaire,* Payot (Paris, France), 1980.

Fiedler, Leslie, *Love and Death in the American Novel,* Criterion (New York, NY), 1960.

Field, Leslie A., and Joyce W. Field, editors, *Bernard Malamud and the Critics,* New York University Press (New York, NY), 1970.

Field, Leslie A., and Joyce W. Field, editors, *Bernard Malamud: A Collection of Critical Essays,* Prentice-Hall (Englewood Cliffs, NJ), 1975.

Helterman, Jeffrey, *Understanding Bernard Malamud,* University of South Carolina Press (Columbia, SC), 1985.

Hershinow, Sheldon J., *Bernard Malamud,* Ungar (New York, NY), 1980.

Howe, Irving, *World of Our Fathers,* Harcourt (New York, NY), 1976.

Kosofsky, Rita Nathalie, *Bernard Malamud: An Annotated Checklist,* Kent State University Press (Kent, OH), 1969.

Lasher, Lawrence M., editor, *Conversations with Bernard Malamud,* University Press of Mississippi (Jackson, MS), 1991.

Meeter, Glen, *Bernard Malamud and Philip Roth: A Critical Essay,* Eerdmans (Grand Rapids, MI), 1968.

Michaels, Leonard, and Christopher Ricks, editors, *The State of the Language,* University of California Press (Berkeley, CA), 1980.

Modern American Literature, 5th edition, Thomson Gale (Detroit, MI), 1999.

Radical Innocence: Studies in the Contemporary American Novel, Princeton University Press (Princeton, NJ), 1961.

Reference Guide to Short Fiction, 2nd edition, St. James Press (Detroit, MI), 1999.

Richman, Sidney, *Bernard Malamud,* Twayne (Boston, MA), 1966.

Roth, Philip, *Reading Myself and Others,* Farrar, Straus (New York, NY), 1975.

Salzburg, Joel, *Bernard Malamud: A Reference Guide,* G.K. Hall (Boston, MA), 1985.

Salzburg, Joel, editor, *Critical Essays on Bernard Malamud,* G.K. Hall (Boston, MA), 1987.

The Schlemiel as Metaphor: Studies in the Yiddish and American Jewish Novel, Southern Illinois University Press (Carbondale, IL), 1971.

Short Story Criticism, Volume 15, Thomson Gale (Detroit, MI), 1994.

Sio-Castineira, Begona, *The Short Stories of Bernard Malamud: In Search of Jewish Post-Immigrant Identity,* Peter Lang (New York, NY), 1998.

Solotaroff, Robert, *Bernard Malamud: A Study of the Short Fiction,* Twayne (Boston, MA), 1989.

Tanner, Tony, *City of Words: American Fiction 1950-1970,* Harper (New York, NY), 1971.

PERIODICALS

America, April 11, 1998, Loren F. Schmidtberger, review of *Bernard Malamud: The Complete Stories,* p. 22.

American Quarterly, Volume 35, number 5, 1983.

American Scholar, winter, 1990, p. 67.

Booklist, November 15, 2001, Brad Hooper, review of *The Natural,* p. 555.

Centennial Review, Volume 9, 1965; Volume 13, 1969.

Chicago Tribune Book World, February 11, 1979; September 5, 1982; October 30, 1983.

Christian Science Monitor, September 10, 1982.

Clio, winter, 2002, p. 129.

Commentary, March, 1953, Norman Podhoretz, review of *The Natural,* p. 321-323; July, 1957, p. 90; March, 1962, p. 201; October, 1982.

Commonweal, October 28, 1966.

Critique, winter, 1964-65, pp. 110-111; summer, 2000, Stephen Bluestone, "God as Matchmaker: A Reading of Malamud's 'The Magic Barrel,'" p. 403.

Detroit News, December 25, 1983.

Encounter, Volume 45, number 1, 1975.

English Journal, April, 1991, p. 67.

Essays in Literature, spring, 1988, pp. 87-101.

Georgia Review, winter, 1998, Erin McGraw, review of *The Complete Stories,* p. 743.

Hudson Review, winter, 1966-67, Robert Gorham Davis, review of *The Fixer,* pp. 663-665; spring, 1998, review of *The Complete Stories,* p. 243.

Journal of Ethnic Studies, winter, 1974.

Judaism, winter, 1979; fall, 1980.

Library Journal, May 1, 1996, p. 94.

Linguistics in Literature, fall, 1977.

Literature and Psychology, Volume 20, number 3, 1970.

Los Angeles Times Book Review, September 12, 1982; December 25, 1983; November 26, 1989.

Midstream, winter, 1961; July, 1990, p. 43.

Modern Fiction Studies, winter, 1991, pp. 752-753.

Mosaic, spring, 1971.

New England Review, spring, 2003, Ted Solotaroff, "An Evening with Bernard Malamud," pp. 27-31.

New Leader, May 26, 1969.

New Republic, November 18, 1961, p. 407; June 6, 1973, p. 32; March 24, 1979, pp. 28-30; September 20, 1982, pp. 38, 40; November 6, 1989, p. 116.

Newsweek, September 6, 1982; October 17, 1983.

New Yorker, November 8, 1982.

New York Review of Books, September 30, 1973; October 3, 1974, Philip Roth, review of *Pictures of Fidelman,* p. 26; October 9, 1997, Alfred Kazin, review of *The Complete Stories,* p. 8.

New York Times, May 3, 1969; February 2, 1979; July 15, 1980; August 23, 1982; October 11, 1983; February 23, 1985; July 15, 1985; November 14, 1989.

New York Times Book Review, August 25, 1952, Harry Sylvester, review of *The Natural,* p. 5; September 4, 1964; May 4, 1969; October 3, 1971; February 18, 1979; August 29, 1982; August 28, 1983; October 16, 1983; April 20, 1986; March 20, 1988, p. 15; November 5, 1989, p. 1; November 19, 1989, p. 7; March 18, 1986, p. 35; November 8, 1998, review of *The Complete Stories,* p. 36; December 6, 1998, review of *The Complete Stories,* p. 96.

Paris Review, spring, 1975.

Partisan Review, winter, 1962; summer, 1964; winter, 1998, Millicent Bell, review of *The Complete Stories,* p. 49.

Playboy, January, 1990, p. 31.

Polish Review, Volume 27, numbers 3-4, 1982, pp. 35-44.

Publishers Weekly, April 8, 1996, p. 49; October 4, 1999, review of *The Assistant* (audio version), p. 36.

Renascence: Essays on Values in Literature, winter, 1975.

Saturday Review, June 15, 1957, Meyer Levin, review of *The Assistant,* p. 21; May 17, 1958, Granville Hicks, review of *The Magic Barrel,* p. 16; October 12, 1963, David Boroff, review of *Idiots First,* p. 33; May 10, 1969; September 25, 1971, Joseph Catinella, review of *The Tenants,* p. 36.

Studies in American Fiction, spring, 1986, pp. 93-98; spring, 1992, Victoria Aarons, "'In Defense of the Human': Compassion and Redemption in Malamud's Short Fiction," pp. 57-58.

Studies in American Humor, 1989, pp. 104-106.

Studies in American Jewish Literature, spring, 1978; number 3, 1983; fall, 1988 (special Malamud issue).

Studies in Short Fiction, spring, 1981, pp. 180-183.

Threepenny Review, fall, 1998, review of *The Complete Stories,* p. 16.

Tikkun, March-April, 1989, p. 32.

Time, May 9, 1969; September 13, 1982; October 17, 1983; November 20, 1989, p. 106.

Times Literary Supplement, October 16, 1969; October 29, 1982; February 24, 1984; February 9, 1990.

Tribune Books (Chicago, IL), November 26, 1989.

USA Today Magazine, May, 1990, p. 95.

Virginia Quarterly Review, winter, 1980.

Washington Post, August 27, 1982.

Washington Post Book World, February 25, 1979; August 29, 1982; October 16, 1983; November 26, 1989, p. 3.

Western American Literature, August, 1975.

Western Humanities Review, winter, 1968; winter, 1970.

Writer's Digest, July, 1972; April, 1995, p. 40.

Yale Review, July, 1998, review of *The Complete Stories,* p. 150.

OBITUARIES:

PERIODICALS

Chicago Tribune, March 20, 1986.

Detroit News, March 23, 1986.

Los Angeles Times, March 19, 1986.

New Republic, May 12, 1986.

Newsweek, March 31, 1986.

New York Times, March 20, 1986.

Times (London, England), March 20, 1986.

Washington Post, March 20, 1986.

*   *   *

MALCOLM, Dan
    See SILVERBERG, Robert

*   *   *

MALOUF, David 1934-
    (George Joseph David Malouf)

PERSONAL: Surname is pronounced "Ma-*louf*"; born March 20, 1934, in Brisbane, Queensland, Australia; son of George and Welcome (Mendoza) Malouf. *Education:* University of Queensland, B.A. (with honors), 1954. *Politics:* Socialist.

ADDRESSES: Home—53 Myrtle St., Chippendale, New South Wales 2008, Australia. *Agent*—Rogers, Coleridge & White, 20 Powis Mews, London W11, England; and Barbara Mobbs, P.O. Box 126, Edgecliff, New South Wales 2027, Australia.

CAREER: University of Queensland, Brisbane, Australia, assistant lecturer in English, 1955-57; St. Anselm's College, Birkenhead, England, schoolmaster, 1962-68; University of Sydney, Sydney, Australia, senior tutor, then lecturer in English, 1968-77. Member of literature board, Australia Council, 1972-74.

AWARDS, HONORS: Grace Leven Prize for Poetry, and Australian Literature Society Gold Medal, both 1974, and James Cook University of North Queensland Award, Foundation for Australian Literary Studies, all 1975, all for *Neighbours in a Thicket: Poems;* Australian Council fellowship, 1978; New South Wales Premier's Fiction Award, 1979, for *An Imaginary Life; Age* Book of the Year Award and Award for Fiction, both 1982, both for *Fly away Peter;* Victorian Premier's Award, 1985, for *Antipodes;* New South Wales Premier's Drama Award, 1987, for *Blood Relations;* Miles Franklin Award, Commonwealth Prize for Fiction, and Prix Femina Étranger, all 1991, all for *The Great World;* Dublin/IMPAC Literary Award, 1996, *Los Angeles Times* Book Prize for fiction, and Booker Prize nomination, all 1994, all for *Remembering Babylon.*

WRITINGS:

(With others) *Four Poets: David Malouf, Don Maynard, Judith Green, Rodney Hall,* Cheshires, 1962.

Bicycle and Other Poems, University of Queensland Press (St. Lucia, Queensland, Australia), 1970, published as *The Year of the Foxes and Other Poems,* Braziller (New York, NY), 1979.

(Coeditor) *We Took Their Orders and Are Dead: An Anti-War Anthology,* Ure Smith, 1971.

Neighbours in a Thicket: Poems, University of Queensland Press (St. Lucia, Queensland, Australia), 1974.

Johnno (novel), University of Queensland Press (St. Lucia, Queensland, Australia), 1975, Braziller (New York, NY), 1978.

(Editor) *Gesture of a Hand* (anthology of Australian poetry), Holt (New South Wales, Australia), 1975.

Poems, 1975-1976, Prism (Sydney, Australia), 1976.

An Imaginary Life (novel), Braziller (New York, NY), 1978.

(With Katharine Brisbane and R.F. Brissenden) *New Currents in Australian Writing,* Angus & Robertson (North Ryde, New South Wales, Australia), 1978.

Wild Lemons (poems), Angus & Robertson (North Ryde, New South Wales, Australia), 1980.

First Things Last (poems), University of Queensland Press (St. Lucia, Queensland, Australia), 1981.

Selected Poems, Angus & Robertson (North Ryde, New South Wales, Australia), 1981.

Child's Play [and] *The Bread of Time to Come* (novellas), Braziller, 1981, *The Bread of Time to Come* published as *Fly away Peter,* Chatto & Windus (London, England), 1982, Vintage (New York, NY), 1998.

Child's Play [and] "Eustace" [and] "The Prowler," Chatto & Windus, 1982.

Harland's Half Acre (novel), Knopf (New York, NY), 1984.

Twelve Edmondstone Street (memoir), Chatto & Windus (London, England), 1985.

Antipodes (short stories), Chatto & Windus (London, England), 1985.

Blood Relations (play), Currency Press, 1988.

David Malouf: Johnno, Short Stories, Poems, Essays, and Interview (selected works), edited by James Tulip, University of Queensland Press, (St. Lucia, Queensland, Australia) 1990.

The Great World (historical novel), Chatto & Windus (London, England), 1990, Pantheon (New York, NY), 1990.

Selected Poems, Angus & Robertson (North Ryde, New South Wales, Australia), 1991.

Poems 1959-89, University of Queensland Press (St. Lucia, Queensland, Australia), 1992.

Remembering Babylon (historical novel), Pantheon (New York, NY), 1993.

Conversations at Curlow Creek, Thorndike Press (Thorndike, ME), 1997.

(With others)*The Fox and the Magpie,* Boosey and Hawkes (London, England), 1998.

A Spirit of Play: The Making of Australian Consciousness, ABC Books for the Australian Broadcasting Company, 1998.

Untold Tales (short stories), Paper Bark, 1999.

Dream Stuff (short stories), Pantheon (New York, NY), 2000.

Also author of opera librettos, including *Voss,* 1986; *La Mer de Glace,* 1991; and *Baa Baa Black Sheep,* 1993. Contributor to periodicals, including *Australian, New York Review of Books, Poetry Australia, Southerly,* and *Sydney Morning Herald.*

SIDELIGHTS: A prize-winning poet before he published his first novel, David Malouf was born and raised in Australia, lived for some years in Italy, and now resides in his native country. Many critics believe Malouf writes as comfortably about cosmopolitan Europe as he does about his childhood home, and the author's favored themes and literary devices also traverse his poetry and prose. Reviewers have praised the vivid, sensuous descriptions and evocative settings of his works, throughout which Malouf weaves an awareness of the distinct cultures and the diverse characters within them. In his poetry, short fiction, and novels such as *An Imaginary Life, Remembering Babylon,* and *The Great World,* Malouf often combines the past, present, and future to create an all-inclusive, multidirectional point of reference. Interested in dualities that repel and compel, Malouf searches, within his fiction, for perfect unities with nature.

Fleur Adcock commented in a *Times Literary Supplement* review of Malouf's 1980 poetry collection, *First Things Last,* that the author "has a strong visual consciousness with a sense of joyful absorption in the natural world which makes the overworked word 'celebration' irresistible." Malouf revels in nature's various forms—from paradisiacal gardens to wilderness, from life in the ocean to wild lemon trees—and searches for harmonies with the natural world. For example, in "The Crab Feast" the poet searches for crabs so that he can ingest, embody, and join with them. Music harmonizes with nature as well, and in the poem "An die Musik," man, music, and nature integrate: "We might have known it always: music/ is the landscape we move through in our dreams," Adcock quoted the poet.

In *First Things Last* Malouf experiments with time, creating a present contemporaneously with the past and future. As Adcock explained: "In an elegy for his father he writes of the dead being buried in the living and looking out through their eyes, as do the not yet born." And in the poem "Deception Bay" Malouf writes of his ancestors viewing the future through the eyes of the present generation. Malouf has also experimented with prose-poetry and other free-verse forms, although he generally emphasizes content more than technique. Critics have described his poetry as mature, elegant, fine, and lavish, and laud Malouf for his sensitivity and emotion. Adcock, concluding that "Malouf's powerful imagination allows a certain amount of surrealism," added that the poet "can be playful . . . but he is a serious poet concerned with serious things."

Malouf's first novel, *Johnno,* was published in 1975. Reviewing the work for *Times Literary Supplement,* Frank Pike commended the author for his resonant depiction of place and atmosphere, writing that Malouf creates "an unaffected and densely detailed evocation of a particular way of life at a particular time; urban, unspectacular." According to Pike, the novel commences "with a convincing account, finely written without fine writing, of childhood and early adolescence" in suburban Brisbane during World War II. The story follows the rocky friendship of the honorable but impressionable narrator, Dante, and Johnno, an intriguing, disturbed, fatherless youth. Dante is attracted to Johnno's fondness for carousing and heavy drinking and tries unsuccessfully to mimic his behavior. After Johnno departs for the Congo the youths meet again in Paris, but by now the narrator is warier of his old hero's unstable behavior. Afterward in Australia, Dante receives news of Johnno's death by drowning, an event that confirms Dante's early suspicions that Johnno was suicidal. Dante then receives an angst-ridden note from Johnno written prior to his death, in which he cited Dante's emotional indifference and restraint as reasons for his suicide.

In 1979 Malouf was awarded the New South Wales Premier's prize for fiction for his second novel, *An Imaginary Life,* a fictionalized account of the ancient Roman poet Ovid's mature life. From the sketchy information available on the Roman's later years, Malouf creates a life for the poet as he imagines it to have transpired following Ovid's exile from Rome in 8 A.D. The circumstances that led to Ovid's banishment are unclear; many historians hold that the poet was banished as punishment for ridiculing Emperor Augustus's wife Livia in his just-completed epic poem *Metamorphoses,* others believe he was exiled after arranging a lovers' tryst for Augustus's granddaughter Julia, and still others suspect it was Ovid's authorship of the intemperate "Art of Love" at a time when Augustus was calling for virtue in Roman society. Nonetheless, Malouf fills in the blanks to create what Katha Pollitt, writing for *New York Times Book Review,* deemed "an extraordinary novel" and "a work of unusual intelligence and imagination, at once sensuous and quirky, full of surprising images and intriguing insights."

In *An Imaginary Life* Malouf depicts an aging Ovid who, while once at the heart of pleasure-seeking Roman society, is now forced to the desolate reaches of the known world. He settles at Tomis, a grim village of one hundred huts located in what is now Romania on the Black Sea. There the barren land supports vegetation the poet cannot even identify. Malouf makes such a setting seemingly tangible through the use of prose Pollitt described as "a spare yet evocative English that captures both the bleak monochromes of Tomis and the sunny humanized landscape of Ovid's remembered Italy, without ever losing the distinctive voice, now caustic, now dreamlike, in which Ovid tells his own story." Kate Eldred, writing for *New Republic,* asserted that "Malouf shows us the mind of a great wordsmith struck dumb in his surroundings trying to adjust to a new life."

Carole Horn, reviewing *An Imaginary Life* for *Washington Post,* pointed out that "the story works on emotional and philosophical planes. Malouf maintains a fine consistency of tone, and his language is hauntingly lovely." Pollitt agreed, calling the novel "one of those rare books you end up underlining and copying out into notebooks and reading out loud to your friends." Eldred, impressed with Malouf's manipulation of time, remarked that the author "interplays the historical present, [which is] clumsy in English, with a narrative present and an anecdotal past tense, interweaving them so gracefully that the techniques aren't obvious, only the aftertaste of grandeur in certain passages, of a facile rhythm in others."

Harland's Half Acre also garnered critical praise. It opens with protagonist Frank Harland, who lives with his brothers and bemused father at Killarney, on the vestiges of what was once an expansive farm in the Australian countryside. Jim Crace, in a review for *Times Literary Supplement,* commended Malouf for his polished descriptions: the "opening chapters are . . . stunningly artful evocations of Queensland and Queenslanders. The Harland acres ('lush country but of the green, subtropical kind, with sawmills in untidy paddocks') are squandered with 'extravagant folly' through drink, gambling, debt and neglect." Hearing fantastic tales of the glory of Killarney spun by his father, Frank dreams of restoring the farm to its original grandeur as a gift to his family. Jonathan Yardley, writing in *Washington Post Book World,* called *Harland's Half Acre* "a rewarding book . . . long on intelligence and feeling" and commended the author for writing "a meditation on the subtle, mysterious relationship between life and art. . . . He has written it with great sensitivity."

Malouf's 1982 novella *Fly away Peter,* for which he won both the Book of the Year Award and a fiction award from the Australian literary journal *Age,* also takes place in Australia. After spending twelve years in England, protagonist Ashley Crowther returns to a thousand-acre plantation he inherited in his native Queensland, unsure of what to do with it or his future. Already inhabiting this land is Jim Saddler, a young man content with a simple existence among nature who spends his time observing the numerous species of birds that migrate to the local swamps. Ashley decides to make the estate a wildlife reserve and hires Jim to manage it. They befriend a nature photographer, Imogen Harcourt, and the three settle into a serene life until World War I disrupts the calm. Jim and Ashley enlist, and at the front they encounter the horrors of war.

Reviewing *Fly away Peter,* Alan Brownjohn commented in *Times Literary Supplement* that "The scenes in the trenches are much the finest . . . : men passing down the slope from fields where peasants continue to till the ground and birds continue to sing, to enter that labyrinth of mud, rats and twitching bodies from which they will never return, or never return the same." Ashley, far removed from his independent lifestyle, becomes disillusioned and concludes that men are as cogs in machines: indistinct and replaceable. Imogen, still in Australia, thinks the fighting is absurd and senseless and concludes that a purpose is not necessary in life. David Guy in *Washington Post Book World* wrote that Imogen "understands that the life of men should be as Jim's once was, like the life that the birds lead. 'A life wasn't *for* anything. It simply was.'" For his part, Jim reacts to the war by cultivating a tranquil plot of land in an attempt to reclaim the innocence he left behind in Australia.

Malouf made Italy the setting for his next novella *Child's Play,* a first-person narrative told by a young terrorist preparing to assassinate an internationally acclaimed author. *Times Literary Supplement* reviewer Peter Kemp described the work as "surreally hard-edged," adding that "the world *Child's Play* projects is one where details have a hallucinatory vividness and patterns stand out with stark clarity: only significance remains creepily opaque." Guy praised Malouf's depiction of the brilliant, influential writer as "masterful" and added that the novelist again employs the concept of a simultaneous past, present, and future. Guy explained that in his preparation the terrorist envisions the near and distant future and his own place in history: "Already he sees the photographs of the piazza where the assassination will take place as those of a historic site; he imagines it in newsprint and news photograph, media which distort and deaden an event but also in some ways create it; he sees himself as the hand of fate toward which a life's work has been leading, as a figure in the writer's biography." *Child's Play* prompted the critic to conclude: "Malouf is something of a primitive narrator, rough around the edges, but he is also a deeply serious writer, not to be taken up lightly . . . [and] a genuine artist."

"Eustace" and "The Prowler," the two short stories bound with *Child's Play,* take place in Australia. They, like *Child's Play* and the novel *Johnno,* focus on society's fascination with elusive, sordid characters and demonstrate the author's preoccupation with the interaction of opposites. "Conformity, community, security are repeatedly set against anarchy, loneliness, danger," Peter Kemp observed in *Times Literary Supplement.* "Obsessively, [Malouf's] work juxtaposes order and disturbance, light and dark. Those positives and negatives can unexpectedly change places. And always in Malouf's stories the powerful attraction between seemingly opposed poles is used to generate some shock effects." Also focusing on disparities is Malouf's 1985 collection of thirteen short stories, titled *Antipodes*. These tales follow Australian immigrants and the problems they encounter in their attempts to assimilate into their adopted culture, while also examining the tribulations of Australians who travel to Europe as well. Other short fiction by Malouf has been collected in the volumes *Untold Tales* and *Dream Stuff*. The nine stories in *Dream Stuff* were described by *Library Journal* contributor Rebecca Miller as "beautiful and often brutal" tales that focus on "a precarious world" wherein "the imagination, through dreams, is the only thing that can face down the losses of life."

Malouf's 1990 novel *The Great World* is an epic spanning some seventy years. The novel examines the intertwined lives of two Australians, Vic Curran and Digger Keen, in a structure "juxtaposing scenes of past and future as a kind of continuous present," noted Ray Willbanks in *World Literature Today*. The two men are first drawn together in 1942 as prisoners of the Japanese during World War II. They survive three and a half years of brutal captivity together in Malaya and Thailand, where they are assigned to a work gang laboring in construction of the infamous Bangkok-Rangoon Railway and are encamped in an abandoned amusement park, "The Great World." *New York Review of Books* critic Ian Buruma described *The Great World* as a "superb" work containing "one of the most horrifying and vivid descriptions of the death railroad camps I have read. The rotting wounds, the maddening fevers, the casual sadism of the Japanese and Korean guards, the terror of cholera, of giving in to fate, of becoming what in Auschwitz camp jargon was called a *Musulman,* a doomed man already in the grip of death." Elizabeth Ward, writing in *Washington Post Book World,* noted that their experience results in "a profound alteration in these men's sense of reality," and "both carry the horror of their memories—dormant but never dead, like malaria—permanently." Even more, perhaps, than the physical abuse and deprivation is their loss of identity, Malouf told *Observer* reviewer Ed Thomason: "Everything was taken away from those POWs—their white skin, their privileges, their manhood in some kind of way. They had to find out what it was they had to hang on to, in what way you could lose things without losing them. Really, that's what the book is about—loss, in every possible meaning of the word."

Remembering Babylon, set in the 1840s, "examines the fragility of identity from within a band of 19th-century British colonials, who have scratched out a home in the Australian bush," according to Suzanne Berne in *New York Times Book Review.* The group is transformed with the arrival of Gemmy Fairley, a British-born young man who survived being thrown overboard from a British ship at age thirteen, washed up on a Queensland shore, and lived a wandering existence with the Aborigines for sixteen years before stumbling into the colony. "There's little plot," Catherine Foster observed in *Christian Science Monitor.* "Malouf roams from mind to mind of the various town residents as they react to Gemmy or try to make sense of him. Malouf generously lets us see as much of the other residents as of this gibberish-spouting character whose other, British, self slowly reemerges." Gemmy develops into a richly "multifaceted" character, "at turns human, at turns brutal," noted Berne. Within the story of *Remembering Babylon* the author "adroitly limns each of these shifting projections, sympathetically portraying the desperation of human exile with its terrors, its possibilities, its unlikely opportunities for grace." Gemmy, "a white man with Aboriginal ways, represents a primitive immigrant's worst confusion: the man in the right skin but the wrong tribe," *Time* contributor R.Z. Sheppard assessed. "He is a reminder of instincts caged but not tamed by civilization. That such a creature has much to teach can be even more upsetting."

Malouf continued to explore the contrasts between Australia and Europe in the morality tale *The Conversations at Curlow Creek,* published in 1997. This novel tells the story of two Irishmen—one a police officer, the other a criminal—during a long night of conversation set in the gloomy Australian outback during the hours before the criminal's execution. *New York Times Book Review* contributor Richard Bernstein found *The Conversations at Curlow Creek* impressive, but expressed reservations about the extent of the novel's philosophical commentary by calling the work marred by "overstuffed feeling." Brad Hooper, reviewing the novel for *Booklist,* praised it as "intellectually rigorous," while a *Kirkus* reviewer assessed it as "an audacious and deeply moving meditation . . . on freedom and identity." In *World Literature Today* Robert Ross wrote that in *The Conversations at Curlow Creek* Malouf "finds a rich source of metaphor in the Australian emptiness" and explores "the dichotomy that has long dominated Australian thinking and has underscored the search for national identity."

BIOGRAPHICAL AND CRITICAL SOURCES:

BOOKS

Hansson, Karin, *Sheer Edge: Aspects of Identity in David Malouf's Writing,* Lund University Press (Lund, Sweden), 1991.

Indyk, Ivor, *David Malouf*, Oxford University Press (Melbourne, Australia), 1993.

Neilsen, Philip, *Imagined Lives: A Study of David Malouf*, University of Queensland Press (St. Lucia, Queensland, Australia), 1990.

Nettelbeck, Amanda, *Provisional Maps: Critical Essays on David Malouf*, Center for Studies in Australian Literature (Nedlands), 1994.

Nettelbeck, Amanda, *Reading David Malouf*, Sydney University Press (Sydney, Australia), 1995.

PERIODICALS

Antipodes, December, 2000, p. 145.

Australian Literary Studies, May, 1999, Andrew Taylor, "Origin, Identity, and the Body in David Malouf's Fiction" p. 3.

Booklist, December 1, 1996, Brad Hooper, review of *The Conversations at Curlow Creek*, p. 641; May 15, 2000, Nancy Pearl, review of *Dream Stuff*, p. 1728.

Boston Globe, April 4, 1991, p. 68; October 17, 1993, p. A15.

Chicago Tribune, November 28, 1993, sec. 14, p. 6.

Christian Science Monitor, October 21, 1993, Catherine Foster, review of *Remembering Babylon*, p. 15.

Economist (U.S.), November 16, 1996, review of *The Conversations at Curlow Creek*, p. S18; May 13, 2000, p. 14.

Guardian, August 8, 1993, p. 29.

Kenyon Review, summer-fall, 2002, interview with Malouf, p. 164.

Kirkus Reviews, November 1, 1996.

Law Society Journal, February, 2002, David Gava, review of *Dream Stuff*, p. 92.

Library Journal, June 15, 2000, Rebecca Miller, review of *Dream Stuff*, p. 120.

Listener, January 9, 1986, p. 29; February 13, 1986, p. 28; April 5, 1990, p. 32.

London Review of Books, May 8, 1986, p. 19; April 19, 1990, p. 20; June 10, 1993, pp. 28-29.

Los Angeles Times, May 13, 1991, p. E3; September 23, 1994, p. A13.

Los Angeles Times Book Review, October 31, 1993, p. 3.

New Republic, May 13, 1978, Kate Eldred, review of *An Imaginary Life*.

New Statesman, May 7, 1993, p. 40.

New Yorker, August 12, 1991, p. 79; November 1, 1993, p. 131.

New York Review of Books, July 19, 1990, pp. 43-5; December 2, 1993, pp. 13-15; April 10, 1997, Gabriele Annan, review of *The Conversations at Curlow Creek*, p. 19; December 21, 2000, Clive James, review of *Dream Stuff*, p. 90.

New York Times, July 14, 1978; October 19, 1993, p. C19.

New York Times Book Review, April 23, 1978; February 10, 1985, p. 40; June 22, 1986, p. 34; July 19, 1990, pp. 43-45; March 31, 1991, p. 20; October 17, 1993, pp. 7, 52; December 5, 1993, p. 64; January 19, 1997, p. 10; January 22, 1997.

Observer (London, England), February 10, 1985, p. 26; February 2, 1986, p. 28; April 8, 1990, p. 58; May 5, 1991, p. 61; May 30, 1993, p. 63.

PMLA, October, 2002, p. 1158.

Publishers Weekly, May 1, 2000, review of *Dream Stuff*, p. 47.

Spectator, April 8, 2000, Rory O'Keeffe, review of *Dream Stuff*, p. 42.

Time, October 25, 1993, pp. 82, 84; January 3, 1994, p. 79.

Times (London), June 17, 1982; January 31, 1985.

Times Literary Supplement, April 9, 1976; September 22, 1978; January 29, 1982; May 21, 1982; October 15, 1982; June 15, 1984; February 8, 1985, p. 140; April 6, 1990, p. 375; May 7, 1993, p. 20.

Tribune Books, November 28, 1993, p. 6.

USA Today, November 19, 1993, p. D14.

Wall Street Journal, May 8, 1991, p. A10; October 25, 1993, p. A18.

Washington Post, May 12, 1978, Carol Horn, review of *An Imaginary Life;* May 2, 1982; September 26, 1984; September 23, 1993, p. D3.

Washington Post Book World, March 24, 1991, pp. 8-9; September 5, 1993, p. 9; October 31, 1993, p. 12.

World Literature Today, summer, 1991, Ray Willbanks, review of *The Great World*, p. 543; autumn, 2000, David Draper Clark, "David Malouf Chronology," p. 706; winter, 1998, Robert Ross, review of *The Conversations at Curlow Creek*, p. 201.

* * *

MALOUF, George Joseph David
See MALOUF, David

* * *

MAMET, David 1947-
(David Alan Mamet)

PERSONAL: Surname is pronounced "*Mam*-et"; born November 30, 1947, in Chicago, IL; son of Bernard Morris (an attorney) and Lenore June (a teacher; maiden name, Silver) Mamet; married Lindsay Crouse (an actress), December 21, 1977 (divorced); married

Rebecca Pidgeon (an actress), 1991; children: Willa, Zosia, Clara. *Education:* Attended Neighborhood Play-house School of the Theater, 1968-69; Goddard College, B.A., 1969. *Politics:* "The last refuge of the unimaginative." *Religion:* "The second-to-last."

ADDRESSES: Agent—Howard Rosenstone, Rosenstone/ Wender, 3 East 48th St., New York, NY 10017.

CAREER: Playwright, screenwriter, director, and producer. Marlboro College, special lecturer in drama, 1970. St. Nicholas Theater Company, Chicago, IL, founder, 1973, artistic director, 1973-76, member of board of directors, beginning 1973; Goodman Theater, Chicago, associate artistic director, 1978-79. Goddard College, artist-in-residence in drama, 1971-73; Illinois Arts Council, faculty member, 1974; University of Chicago, visiting lecturer in drama, 1975-76 and 1979; Yale University, School of Drama, teaching fellow, 1976-77; New York University, guest lecturer, 1981; Columbia University, associate professor of film, 1988. Producer of motion pictures, including *Lip Service,* 1988, *Hoffa,* 1992, and *A Life in the Theater,* 1993. Actor in motion pictures, including *Black Widow,* 1986, and *The Water Engine,* 1992. Directed *Ricky Jay: On the Stem,* 2002, and "Ricky Jay and His 52 Assistants." Has also worked in a canning plant, a truck factory, at a real estate agency, and as a window washer, office cleaner, and taxi driver. Atlantic Theater Company, chair of the board.

MEMBER: Dramatists Guild, Writers Guild of America, Actors Equity Association, PEN, United Steelworkers of America, Randolph A. Hollister Association.

AWARDS, HONORS: Joseph Jefferson Award, 1975, for *Sexual Perversity in Chicago,* and 1976, for *American Buffalo;* Obie Awards, *Village Voice,* for best new American play, 1976, for *Sexual Perversity in Chicago* and *American Buffalo,* for best American play, 1983, for *Edmond,* and for best play, 1995, for *The Cryptogram;* Children's Theater grant, New York State Council on the Arts, 1976; Rockefeller grant, 1976; Columbia Broadcasting System fellowship in creative writing, 1976; New York Drama Critics' Circle Award for best American play, 1977, for *American Buffalo,* and 1984, for *Glengarry Glen Ross;* Outer Critics Circle Award, 1978, for contributions to the American theater; Academy Award nomination for best adapted screenplay, Academy of Motion Picture Arts and Sciences, 1983, for *The Verdict,* and 1997, for *Wag the Dog;* Society for West End Theatre Award, 1983; Pulitzer Prize for

drama, Joseph Dintenfass Award, Elizabeth Hull-Warriner Award, Dramatists Guild, Antoinette Perry ("Tony") Award nomination, American Theater Wing, for best play, all 1984, all for *Glengarry Glen Ross,* Tony Award nomination for best reproduction of a play, 1984, for *American Buffalo;* Tony Award for best play, 1988, for *Speed-the-Plow;* American Academy and Institute of Arts and Letters Award for Literature, 1986; Golden Globe Award nomination for best screenplay, 1988, for *House of Games;* Writers Guild Award nomination for best screenplay based on material from another medium, 1988, for *The Untouchables.*

WRITINGS:

PLAYS

Lakeboat (one-act; produced in Marlboro, VT, 1970; revised version produced in Milwaukee, WI, 1980), Grove (New York, NY), 1981.

Duck Variations (one-act; produced in Plainfield, VT, 1972; produced Off-Off-Broadway, 1975), in *Sexual Perversity in Chicago and Duck Variations: Two Plays,* Grove (New York, NY), 1978.

Sexual Perversity in Chicago (one-act; produced in Chicago, 1974; produced Off-Off-Broadway, 1975), in *Sexual Perversity in Chicago and Duck Variations: Two Plays,* Grove (New York, NY), 1978.

Squirrels (one-act), produced in Chicago, 1974.

The Poet and the Rent: A Play for Kids from Seven to 8:15 (produced in Chicago, 1974), in *Three Children's Plays,* Grove Press (New York, NY), 1986.

American Buffalo (two-act; produced in Chicago, 1975; produced on Broadway, 1977), Grove (New York, NY), 1977.

Reunion (one-act; produced with *Sexual Perversity in Chicago,* Louisville, KY, 1976; produced Off-Broadway with *Dark Pony* and *The Sanctity of Marriage,* 1979), in *Reunion and Dark Pony: Two Plays,* Grove (New York, NY), 1979, in *Reunion, Dark Pony, and The Sanctity of Marriage: Three Plays,* Samuel French (New York, NY), 1982.

Dark Pony (one-act; produced with *Reunion,* New Haven, CT, 1977; produced Off-Broadway with *Reunion* and *The Sanctity of Marriage,* 1979), in *Reunion and Dark Pony: Two Plays,* Grove (New York, NY), 1979, in *Reunion, Dark Pony, and The Sanctity of Marriage: Three Plays,* Samuel French (New York, NY), 1982.

All Men Are Whores (produced in New Haven, CT, 1977), in *Short Plays and Monologues,* Dramatists Play Service (New York, NY), 1981.

A Life in the Theatre (one-act; produced in Chicago, 1977; produced Off-Broadway, 1977), Grove (New York, NY), 1978.

The Revenge of the Space Pandas; or, Binky Rudich and the Two Speed-Clock (produced in Queens, NY, 1977), Sergel (Chicago, IL), 1978.

(And director) *The Woods* (two-act; produced in Chicago, 1977; produced Off-Broadway, 1979), Grove (New York, NY), 1979.

The Water Engine: An American Fable (two-act; produced as a radio play on the program *Earplay,* Minnesota Public Radio, 1977; stage adaptation produced in Chicago, 1977; produced Off-Broadway, 1977), in *The Water Engine: An American Fable and Mr. Happiness: Two Plays,* Grove (New York, NY), 1978.

Mr. Happiness (produced with *The Water Engine,* on Broadway, 1978), in *The Water Engine: An American Fable and Mr. Happiness: Two Plays,* Grove (New York, NY), 1978.

Lone Canoe; or, The Explorer (musical), music and lyrics by Alaric Jans, produced in Chicago, 1979.

The Sanctity of Marriage (one-act; produced Off-Broadway with *Reunion* and *Dark Pony,* 1979), in *Reunion, Dark Pony, and The Sanctity of Marriage: Three Plays,* Samuel French (New York, NY), 1982.

Shoeshine (one-act; produced Off-Off-Broadway, 1979), in *Short Plays and Monologues,* Dramatists Play Service (New York, NY), 1981.

Short Plays and Monologues, Dramatists Play Service (New York, NY), 1981.

A Sermon (one-act), produced Off-Off-Broadway, 1981.

Donny March, produced 1981.

Litko (produced in New York, NY, 1984), in *Short Plays and Monologues,* Dramatists Play Service (New York, NY), 1981.

Edmond (produced in Chicago, 1982; produced Off-Broadway, 1982), Grove (New York, NY), 1983.

The Disappearance of the Jews (one-act), produced in Chicago, 1983.

The Dog, produced 1983.

Film Crew, produced 1983.

4 A.M., produced 1983.

Glengarry Glen Ross (two-act; produced on the West End, 1983; produced on Broadway, 1984), Grove (New York, NY), 1984.

Five Unrelated Pieces (contains *Two Conversations, Two Scenes,* and *Yes, but so What;* produced Off-Off-Broadway, 1983), in *A Collection of Dramatic Sketches and Monologues,* Samuel French (New York, NY), 1985.

Vermont Sketches (contains *Pint's a Pound the World Around, Deer Dogs, Conversations with the Spirit*

World, and *Dowsing;* produced in New York, NY, 1984;), in *A Collection of Dramatic Sketches and Monologues,* Samuel French (New York, NY), 1985.

The Shawl [and] *Prairie du Chien* (one-act plays; produced at Lincoln Center, 1985), Grove (New York, NY), 1985.

A Collection of Dramatic Sketches and Monologues, Samuel French (New York, NY), 1985.

Vint (one-act; based on Anton Chekov's short story; produced in New York, NY with six other one-act plays based on Chekov's short works, under the collective title *Orchards,* 1985), in *Orchards,* Grove (New York, NY), 1986.

(Adaptor) Chekov, *The Cherry Orchard* (produced at Goodman Theatre, 1985), Grove (New York, NY), 1987.

Three Children's Plays (contains *The Poet and the Rent: A Play for Kids from Seven to 8:15, The Revenge of the Space Pandas; or, Binky Rudich and the Two Speed-Clock,* and *The Frog Prince*), Grove (New York, NY), 1986.

The Woods, Lakeboat, Edmond, Grove (New York, NY), 1987.

Speed-the-Plow (produced on Broadway, 1988), Grove (New York, NY), 1988.

Where Were You When It Went Down?, produced in New York, NY, 1988.

(Adaptor and editor) Chekov, *Uncle Vanya,* Grove (New York, NY), 1989.

Goldberg Street (short plays and monologues), Grove (New York, NY), 1989.

Bobby Gould in Hell, produced with *The Devil and Billy Markham* by Shel Silverstein, New York, NY, 1989.

Five Television Plays: A Waitress in Yellowstone; Bradford; The Museum of Science and Industry Story; A Wasted Weekend; We Will Take You There, Grove (New York, NY), 1990.

Oleanna (also see below; produced, 1991), Pantheon (New York, NY), 1992, Dramatists Play Service (New York, NY), 1993.

(Adaptor) Anton Chekov, *The Three Sisters: A Play,* Samuel French (New York, NY), 1992.

A Life with No Joy in It, and Other Plays and Pieces (contains *Almost Done, Monologue, Two Enthusiasts, Sunday Afternoon, The Joke Code, A Scene, Fish, A Perfect Mermaid, Dodge, L.A. Sketches, A Life with No Joy in It, Joseph Dintenfass,* and *No One Will Be Immune*), Dramatists Play Service (New York, NY), 1994.

Plays—One (collection; includes *Duck Variations, Sexual Perversity in Chicago, Squirrels, American Buffalo, The Water Engine,* and *Mr. Happiness*), Methuen (London, England), 1994.

(And director) *The Cryptogram* (also see below; produced in London, 1994; produced Off-Broadway, 1995), Dramatists Play Service (New York, NY), 1995, Vintage (New York, NY), 1995.

The Old Neighborhood: Three Plays (also see below; includes *The Disappearance of the Jews, Jolly,* and *Deeny*), Vintage (New York, NY), 1998.

Boston Marriage (produced at the American Repertory Theater in Cambridge, MA, 1999, produced at Joseph Papp Public Theater, 2002), Vintage (New York, NY), 2002.

David Mamet Plays: 4 (includes *The Cryptogram, Oleanna,* and *The Old Neighborhood*), Methuen (London, England), 2002.

Dr. Faustus: A Play, Vintage (New York, NY), 2004.

Also author of *No One Will Be Immune and Other Plays and Pieces,* and *Oh Hell.*

SCREENPLAYS

The Postman Always Rings Twice (adaptation of the novel by James M. Cain), Paramount, 1981.

The Verdict (adaptation of the novel by Barry Reed), Columbia, 1982.

(And director) *House of Games* (based on a story by Mamet; produced by Orion Pictures, 1987), Grove (New York, NY), 1987.

The Untouchables (based on the television series), Paramount, 1987.

(With Shel Silverstein; and director) *Things Change* (produced by Columbia Pictures, 1988), Grove (New York, NY), 1988.

We're No Angels (adaptation of the 1955 film of the same name; produced by Paramount, 1989), Grove (New York, NY), 1990.

(And director) *Homicide* (produced by Columbia, 1991), Grove (New York, NY), 1992.

Glengarry Glen Ross (based on Mamet's play of the same title), New Line Cinema, 1992.

The Water Engine (teleplay; based on Mamet's play of the same title), Amblin Television, 1992.

Hoffa, Twentieth Century-Fox, 1992.

Texan (film short), Chanticleer Films, 1994.

(And director) *Oleanna* (based on Mamet's play of the same title), Samuel Goldwyn, 1994.

Vanya on 42nd Street (adapted from the play *Uncle Vanya* by Anton Chekhov), Film Four International, 1994.

American Buffalo (based on Mamet's play of the same title), Samuel Goldwyn, 1996.

(And director) *The Spanish Prisoner,* Sweetland Films, 1997, published in *The Spanish Prisoner and The Winslow Boy: Two screenplays,* Vintage (New York, NY), 2002.

The Edge, Twentieth Century-Fox, 1997.

Wag the Dog (based on the novel *American Hero* by Larry Beinhart), New Line Cinema, 1997.

Lansky, HBO, 1998.

(And director) *State and Maine,* Fine Line Pictures, 2000.

Lakeboat, Oregon Trail Films, 2000.

Whistle, Geisler-Roberdeau, 2000.

Dr. Jekyll and Mr. Hyde (based on the novel by Robert Louis Stevenson), 2000.

(With Steven Zaillian) *Hannibal* (based on the novel by Thomas Harris), Metro-Goldwyn-Mayer, 2001.

(And director) *Heist,* Morgan Creek Productions, 2001.

Also author of the teleplay *A Life in the Theater,* based on Mamet's play of the same title.

NOVELS

The Village, Little, Brown (New York, NY), 1994.

The Old Religion: A Novel (historical fiction), Free Press (New York, NY), 1997.

Bar Mitzvah, Little, Brown (New York, NY), 1999.

The Chinaman, Overlook Press (Woodstock, NY), 1999.

Henrietta, Houghton Mifflin (New York, NY), 1999.

Jafsie and John Henry, Free Press (New York, NY), 1999.

OTHER

Warm and Cold (children's picturebook), illustrations by Donald Sultan, Solo Press (New York, NY), 1984.

(With wife, Lindsay Crouse) *The Owl* (children's book), Kipling Press (New York, NY), 1987.

Writing in Restaurants (essays, speeches, and articles), Penguin (New York, NY), 1987.

Some Freaks (essays), Viking (New York, NY), 1989.

(With Donald Sultan and Ricky Jay) *Donald Sultan: Playing Cards,* edited by Edit deAk, Kyoto Shoin (Kyoto, Japan), 1989.

The Hero Pony: Poems, Grove Weidenfeld (New York, NY), 1990.

On Directing Film, Viking (New York, NY), 1992.

The Cabin: Reminiscence and Diversions, Random House (New York, NY), 1992.

A Whore's Profession: Notes and Essays, Faber (New York, NY), 1994.

Passover (children's picturebook), illustrated by Michael McCurdy, St. Martin's Press (New York, NY), 1995.

The Duck and the Goat (children's picturebook), illustrated by Maya Kennedy, St. Martin's Press (New York, NY), 1996.

Make-Believe Town: Essays and Remembrances, Little, Brown (Boston, MA), 1996.

True and False: Heresy and Common Sense for the Actor (essays), Pantheon (New York, NY), 1997.

Three Uses of the Knife: On the Nature and Purpose of Drama (part of the "Columbia Lectures on American Culture" series), Columbia University Press (New York, NY), 1998.

On Acting, Viking (New York, NY), 1999.

David Mamet in Conversation, edited by Leslie Kane, University of Michigan Press (Ann Arbor, MI), 2001.

(Author of foreword) Jimmy Kennedy, Maya Kennedy, and Marialisa Calta, *River Run Cookbook: Southern Comfort from Vermont,* HarperCollins (New York, NY), 2001.

Wilson: A Consideration of the Sources, Overlook Press (Woodstock, NY), 2001.

South of the Northeast Kingdom, National Geographic Society (Washington, DC), 2002.

(With Lawrence Kushner) *Five Cities of Refuge: Weekly Reflections on Genesis, Exodus, Leviticus, Numbers, and Deuteronomy,* Schocken Books (New York, NY), 2003.

Also author of episodes of *Hill Street Blues,* NBC, 1987, and *L.A. Law,* NBC. Contributing editor, *Oui,* 1975-76. Contributed to *Donald Sultan: in the Still-Life Tradition,* with Steven Henry Madoff, 1999.

ADAPTATIONS: The film *About Last Night. . . ,* released by Tri-Star Pictures in 1986, was based on Mamet's *Sexual Perversity in Chicago.*

SIDELIGHTS: David Mamet has acquired a great deal of critical recognition for his plays, each one a microcosmic view of the American experience. "He's that rarity, a pure writer," noted Jack Kroll in *Newsweek,* "and the synthesis he appears to be making, with echoes from voices as diverse as Beckett, Pinter, and Hemingway, is unique and exciting." Since 1976, Mamet's plays have been widely produced in regional theaters and in New York City. One of Mamet's most successful plays, *Glengarry Glen Ross,* earned the New York Drama Critics' Circle Award for best American play

and the Pulitzer Prize in drama, both in 1984. Critics have also praised Mamet's screenwriting; he received Academy Award nominations for best adapted screenplay for *The Verdict* in 1983, and for *Wag the Dog* in 1997.

Mamet "has carved out a career as one of America's most creative . . . playwrights," observed Mel Gussow in *New York Times,* "with a particular affinity for working-class characters." These characters and their language give Mamet's work its distinct flavor. Mamet is, according to Kroll, "that rare bird, an American playwright who's a language playwright." "Playwriting is simply showing how words influence actions and vice versa," Mamet explained to *People* contributor Linda Witt. "All my plays attempt to bring out the poetry in the plain, everyday language people use. That's the only way to put art back into the theater." Mamet has been accused of eavesdropping, simply recording the insignificant conversations of which everyone is aware; yet, many reviewers recognize the playwright's artistic intent. Jean M. White commented in *Washington Post* that "Mamet has an ear for vernacular speech and uses cliche with telling effect." Furthermore, added Kroll, "Mamet is the first playwright to create a formal and moral shape out of the undeleted expletives of our foul-mouthed time."

In his personal and creative life, Mamet has resisted the lure of Broadway, its establishment, and its formulas for success. He was born and raised in Chicago—his father was a labor lawyer. His parents divorced while Mamet and his sisters were young. The Windy City serves not only as inspiration for much of his work, but it has also provided an accepting audience for Mamet's brand of drama, especially in the early days of his career, when he worked nights as a busboy at The Second City and spent his days with the theater crowd and writing his plays. "Regional theaters are where the life is," he told Robin Reeves in *Us.* "They're the only new force in American theater since the 30s." Yet, despite Mamet's seeming indifference to Broadway and the fact that the language and subject matter of his plays make them of questionable commercial value, several of his plays have been featured on Broadway.

The first of Mamet's plays to be commercially produced were *Sexual Perversity in Chicago* and *Duck Variations. Sexual Perversity* portrays the failed love affair between a young man and woman, each trying to leave behind a relationship with a homosexual roommate. The dialogue between the lovers and their same-sex roommates reveals how each gender can brutally characterize the other. Yet, "the play itself is not another aspect of the so-called battle of the sexes," observed C. Gerald Fraser in *New York Times*. "It concerns the confusion and emptiness of human relationships on a purely physical level." *New Yorker* reviewer Edith Oliver maintained that "the piece is written with grace," and found it "one of the saddest comedies I can remember." In *Duck Variations*, two old Jewish men sit on a bench in Chicago looking at Lake Michigan. Their observation of the nearby ducks leads them into discussions of several topics. "There is a marvelous ring of truth in the meandering, speculative talk of these old men," maintained Oliver, "the comic, obsessive talk of men who spend most of their time alone, nurturing and indulging their preposterous notions." In the conversation of these men, wrote T.E. Kalem in *Time*, Mamet "displays the Pinter trait of wearing word masks to shield feelings and of defying communication in the act of communicating." *Duck Variations* reveals, according to Oliver, that Mamet is an "original writer, who cherishes words and, on the evidence at hand, cherishes character even more." "What emerges is a vivid sense of [the old men's] friendship, the fear of solitude, the inexorable toll of expiring lives," concluded Kalem.

Mamet emerged as a nationally acclaimed playwright with his 1975 two-act *American Buffalo*. "America has few comedies in its repertory as ironic or as audacious as *American Buffalo*," proclaimed John Lahr in *Nation*. Set in a junk shop, the play features the shop's owner, an employee, and a friend engaged in plotting a theft; they hope to steal the coin collection of a customer who, earlier in the week, had bought an old nickel at the shop. When the employee fails to tail the mark to his home, the plot falls into disarray and "the play ends in confused weariness," explained Elizabeth Kastor in *Washington Post*. Although little takes place, Oliver commented in *New Yorker*, "What makes [the play] fascinating are its characters and the sudden spurts of feeling and shifts of mood—the mounting tension under the seemingly aimless surface, which gives the play its momentum."

American Buffalo confirmed Mamet's standing as a language playwright. Reviewing the play in *Nation*, Lahr observed, "Mamet's use of the sludge in American language is completely original. He hears panic and poetry in the convoluted syntax of his beleaguered characters." And, even though the language is uncultivated, David Richards contended in *Washington Post* that "the dialogue [is] ripe with unsettling resonance." As Frank Rich of *New York Times* remarked, "Working with the tiniest imaginable vocabulary . . . Mamet creates a

subterranean world with its own nonliterate comic beat, life-and-death struggles, pathos and even affection."

In this play, critics also see Mamet's vision of America, "a restless, rootless, insecure society which has no faith in the peace it seeks or the pleasure it finds," interpreted Lahr. "*American Buffalo* superbly evokes this anxious and impoverished world." Its characters, though seemingly insignificant, reflect the inhabitants of this world and their way of life. "In these bumbling and inarticulate meatheads," believed Lahr, "Mamet has found a metaphor for the spiritual failure of entrepreneurial capitalism."

Since its first Chicago production in 1975, *American Buffalo* has been produced in several regional theaters and has had three New York productions. In Mamet's management of the elements of this play, *New York Times* reviewer Benedict Nightingale highlighted the key to its success: "Its idiom is precise enough to evoke a city, a class, a subculture; it is imprecise enough to allow variation of mood and feeling from production to production." Nightingale added in another article, "*Buffalo* is as accomplished as anything written for the American stage over . . . the last 20 years."

In 1979 Mamet was given his first opportunity to write a screenplay. As he told Don Shewey in *New York Times*, working on the screenplay for the 1981 film version of James M. Cain's novel *The Postman Always Rings Twice* was a learning experience. Director Bob Rafelson "taught me that the purpose of a screenplay is to tell the story so the audience wants to know what happens next," Mamet maintained, "and to tell it in pictures." He elaborated, "I always thought I had a talent for dialogue and not for plot, but it's a skill that can be learned. Writing for the movies is teaching me not to be so scared about plots." Mamet's screenplay for *The Postman Always Rings Twice* has received mixed reviews. Its critics often point, as Gene Siskel did in *Chicago Tribune*, to Mamet's "ill-conceived editing of the book's original ending." Yet, except for the ending, suggested Vincent Canby in *New York Times*, "Mr. Mamet's screenplay is far more faithful to the novel than was the screenplay for Tay Garnett's 1946 version." Thus, Robert Hatch noted in *Nation*, "Mamet and Rafelson recapture the prevailing insanity of the Depression, when steadiness of gaze was paying no bills and double or nothing was the game in vogue."

In the 1982 film *The Verdict*, screenwriter Mamet and director Sydney Lumet "have dealt powerfully and unsentimentally with the shadowy state that ideas like good and evil find themselves in today," observed Jack Kroll in *Newsweek*. The film stars Paul Newman as a washed-up lawyer caught in a personal, legal, and moral battle. "Mamet's terse screenplay for *The Verdict* is . . . full of surprises," contended Janet Maslin in *New York Times,* "Mamet has supplied twists and obstacles of all sorts." "Except for a few lapses of logic and some melodramatic moments in the courtroom," proclaimed a *People* reviewer, "[this] script from Barry Reed's novel is unusually incisive." Kroll detailed the screenplay's strong points, calling it "strong on character, on sharp and edgy dialogue, on the detective-story suspense of a potent narrative." In a *New Republic* article, Stanley Kauffmann concluded, "It comes through when it absolutely must deliver: Newman's summation to the jury. This speech is terse and pungent: the powerful have the power to convert all the rest of us into victims and that condition probably cannot be changed, but must it always prevail?"

After writing *The Verdict* Mamet began working on his next play, *Glengarry Glen Ross.* Mamet's Pulitzer Prize-winning play is "so precise in its realism that it transcends itself," observed Robert Brustein in *New Republic,* "and takes on reverberant ethical meanings. It is biting, . . . showing life stripped of all idealistic pretenses and liberal pieties." The play is set in and around a Chicago real estate office whose agents are embroiled in a competition to sell the most parcels in the Florida developments Glengarry Highlands and Glen Ross Farms. "Craftily constructed, so that there is laughter, as well as rage, in its dialogue, the play has a payoff in each scene and a cleverly plotted mystery that kicks in with a surprise hook at its ending," wrote Richard Christiansen in *Chicago Tribune.*

As in Mamet's earlier plays, the characters and their language are very important to *Glengarry Glen Ross.* In *Nation,* Stephen Harvey commented on Mamet's ability to create characters who take on a life of their own within the framework of the play: In *Glengarry,* "he adjusts his angle of vision to suit the contours of his characters, rather than using them to illustrate an idea." Mamet told Kastor of *Washington Post,* "I think that people are generally more happy with a mystery than with an explanation. So the less that you say about a character the more interesting he becomes." Mamet uses language in a similar manner. Harvey noted, "The pungency of Glengarry's language comes from economy: if these characters have fifty-word vocabularies, Mamet makes sure that every monosyllable counts." And as Kroll remarked, "His antiphonal exchanges, which dwindle to single words or even fragments of words and then explode into a crossfire of scatological buck-

shot, make him the Aristophanes of the inarticulate." Mamet is, according to *New York Times* reviewer Benedict Nightingale, "the bard of modern-day barbarism, the laureate of the four-letter word." In *New York Times Magazine,* Richard Eder remarked, "From the beginning, Mr. Mamet's most notable and noticeable quality was his extraordinary use of speech. He concentrated not upon cultivated expression but upon that apparent wasteland of middle American speech. It was the language of the secretary, the salesman, the file clerk, the telephone lineman, the small-time crook, the semiliterate college kid. It was grotesquely realistic."

For the real estate agents in *Glengarry Glen Ross,* the bottom line is sales. And, as Robert Brustein noted, "Without a single tendentious line, without any polemical intention, without a trace of pity or sentiment, Mamet has launched an assault on the American way of making a living." Nightingale called the play "as scathing a study of unscrupulous dealing as the American theater has ever produced." The Pulitzer Prize awarded to Mamet for *Glengarry Glen Ross* not only helped increase its critical standing, but it also helped to make the play a commercial success. However, unlike his real estate agents, Mamet is driven by more than money. He told Kastor, "In our interaction in our daily lives we tell stories to each other, we gossip, we complain to each other, we exhort. These are means of defining what our life is. The theater is a way of doing it continually, of sharing that experience, and it's absolutely essential."

The Cryptogram, Mamet's 1994 play, "dramatizes a child's emotional abuse in a way that no other American play has ever attempted: from the child's point of view," according to *New Yorker* critic John Lahr. The playwright draws on his personal experiences of violent outbreaks, mistrust, and betrayal that he encountered in his own family, but the play blurs such autobiographical elements between its author's fictions. Taking place in Chicago over the span of a single month during the late 1950s, the play's main character, ten-year-old John, is trying to make sense of the double message dispensed by his parents and family friends: lies and unkept promises are commonplace, yet he is expected to trust those who deceive him. "People may or may not say what they mean," Mamet explained to Lahr, "but they *always* say something designed to get what they want." Characteristically, language plays an important role in *The Cryptogram:* as its author noted, "The language of love is . . . fairly limited. 'You're beautiful,' 'I need you,' 'I love you,' 'I want you.' Love expresses itself, so it doesn't need a lot of words. On the other hand, aggression has an unlimited vocabulary."

While Mamet's own directorship of *The Cryptogram* received the traditional mixed reviews from critics due to his fractured language, *New York Times* reviewer Vincent Canby found much to praise. Calling the play "a horror story that also appears to be one of Mr. Mamet's most personal plays," Canby noted, "It's not about the sort of physical abuse we see in television docudramas, but about the high cost of the emotional games played in what are otherwise considered to be fairly well-adjusted families." *The Cryptogram* received the Obie Award from *Village Voice* for best play in 1995.

In 1994, on the heels of *The Cryptogram,* Mamet published his first novel, *The Village.* Taking place in a small, once-thriving town in New England, the novel reveals the emotional complexity of the lives of its characters. From Dick, the hardware-store owner fighting to stay in business, Manis, a local prostitute, and especially Henry, an "outsider" retired and escaping a failed marriage who wants to recapture the macho lifestyle of a century ago, Mamet captures "the flat, dark underside of the flapjack of small town life that Thorton Wilder's 'Our Town' served as the fluffy, arcing top to," according to *Tribune Books* reviewer Ross Field. While reviewers noted that the novel's characters and central idea are well conceived, the novel's dialogue caused some critics to water down their enthusiasm for the book. James McManus contended in *New York Times Book Review* that "because of the novel's design and mechanical problems, the potency of [some] scenes tends not to accumulate. For a playwright of such muscular succinctness, Mr. Mamet has a narrative prose that turns out to be weirdly precious." However, in his review for *Washington Post Book World,* Douglas Glover praised *The Village.* "Mamet's novel explores a community with its own laws, language, codes, habits and sense of honor," noted Glover. "It does so with a deft reverence for the real—Mamet's eye for detail and his ear for the rhythms of vernacular speech are incomparable—coupled with a certain difficulty of approach, an avant-garde edge."

In addition to plays and screenplays, Mamet has published several collections of essays, including *Writing in Restaurants, Some Freaks, On Directing Film, The Cabin,* and *Make-Believe Town,* the first four volumes later collected as *A Whore's Profession: Notes and Essays.* These revealing collections are packed with Mamet's fascinating thoughts, opinions, recollections, musings, and reports on a variety of topics such as friendship, religion, politics, morals, society, and of course, the American theater. "The 30 pieces collected in David Mamet's first book of essays contain everything from random thoughts to firmly held convictions," stated Richard Christiansen in his review of *Writing in Restaurants* for Chicago's *Tribune Books,* "but they all exhibit the author's singular insights and moral bearing." Christiansen pointed out that "many of the essays have to do with drama, naturally, but whether he is talking to a group of critics or to fellow workers in the theater, Mamet is always urging his audience to go beyond craft and into a proud, dignified, loving commitment to their art and to the people with whom they work."

The Cabin, published in 1992, contains twenty essays that reflect their author's macho concerns—guns, cigars, beautiful women—as well as his life as a writer. The work's structure was characterized by *Los Angeles Times Book Review* critic Charles Solomon as "a succession of scenes illuminated by an erratic strobe light: A single moment appears in harsh focus, then vanishes." We follow the author from his tumultuous childhood in "The Rake" to a description of his New Hampshire haven where he does his writing in the title essay. The two dozen essays in *Make-Believe Town* recall Mamet's love of the theater and his respect for his Jewish heritage and introduce those "appalled" by the language of his stage plays to "Mamet the thoughtful learner, teacher, the friend, the literary critic, the hunger-nature writer, the culture, press and film critic, the political commentator, the moralist and, most delightfully, the memoirist," according to *Tribune Books* critic John D. Callaway.

With his play *Boston Marriage,* Mamet departed from his more well-known use of tough male characters to portray an elegant pair of Victorian lesbians. In this comedy of manners, Anna has become the mistress of a wealthy married man in order to supplement her income, and Claire has fallen in love with a younger woman. When that young woman wonders how Anna has acquired her mother's heirloom necklace, both affairs are endangered, leading the two women to concoct a complicated scheme to get themselves out of trouble. As a reviewer remarked in *Curtain Up,* this play, rather than being a radical departure for Mamet, "is in fact just another example of his versatility."

In 2001, Mamet took on two major projects. The first was a new novel, *Wilson: A Consideration of Sources,* which examines the impact of the Internet on society. Set far in the future, *Wilson* introduces a society that has placed all books and paper archives on the Internet, destroying the original sources. When the Internet crashes, the only remaining source of information is the hard drive of Mrs. Wilson's computer. Mamet's book is composed in skewed sections as disorderly as the world he creates in it, much to the dismay of some critics.

Frank J. Baldaro wrote in *American Theatre* that *Wilson* is "an incomprehensible work that spills over with names but is devoid of characters." Baldaro disliked the novel's structure, calling it a "collage of faked bits and fragments" which "teems with incidents and anecdotes, but lacks either plot or sense—it's ultimately a literary stunt that dares to ridicule the jargon and bombast of scholarly writing, but is itself monumentally unfunny, apocalyptically cryptic and impossible to decode." A reviewer for *Publishers Weekly,* however, liked the ridicule in Mamet's work, calling it "an imitation of a scholarly work—or at least the sort of scholarly work that might be undertaken in the 24th century," concluding, "Mamet's jeu d'esprit will certainly surprise those who imagine the author of *American Buffalo* operates only in the backstreets idiom of his plays." Joseph Dewey of *Review of Contemporary Fiction* appreciated Mamet's take on the future in *Wilson:* "Mamet targets with luscious savvy and deadpan irony the limitless pretense of academics, hungry for tenure, to suture history . . . to talk their way into reasonable order."

Mamet also penned the script for *Hannibal,* the film sequel to *Silence of the Lambs.* In the script, Hannibal has escaped prison and is hiding out in Florence, Italy, as a museum curator. FBI detective Clarice Starling (played in the second movie by Julianne Moore) is reassigned to his case and proceeds to track him down. While the sequel to the original thriller was anxiously awaited by audiences, some were disappointed at the movie's lack of horror, blood, and guts. "Hannibal is more shocking, and amusing, than disturbing," wrote Brian D. Johnson in *Maclean's.* Johnson also stated that "despite some exquisite moments, *Hannibal* feels overwrought." Todd McCarthy praised the first movie, remarking in *Variety* that "the public will . . . exhibit a ravenous appetite for the continuing saga of one of contemporary literature and cinema's most fascinating villains." McCarthy admitted that the sequel was "ultimately more shallow and crass at its heart than its predecessor," but concluded that "*Hannibal* is nevertheless tantalizing, engrossing, and occasionally startling."

Writing for *Times Literary Supplement,* Andrew Hislop declared that "Mamet has been rightly acclaimed as a great dialogist and a dramatist who most effectively expresses the rhythms of modern urban American (though the poetic rather than mimetic qualities of his dialogue are often underestimated). The best writing in [*Writing in Restaurants*] comes when he muses on the details of America—and his own life." Hislop continued, "Running through the book is the idea that the purpose of theatre is truth but that the decadence of American society, television and the materialism of Broadway are un-

dermining not just the economic basis but the disciplines and dedication necessary for true theatre."

BIOGRAPHICAL AND CRITICAL SOURCES:

BOOKS

Bigsby, C.W. E., *David Mamet,* Methuen (London, England), 1985.

Bock, Hedwig, and Albert Wertheim, editors, *Essays on Contemporary American Drama,* Max Hueber (Munich, Germany), 1981, pp. 207-223.

Brewer, Gay, *David Mamet and Film: Illusion/ Disillusion in a Wounded Land,* McFarland (Jefferson, NC), 1993.

Carroll, Dennis, *David Mamet,* St. Martin's Press (New York, NY), 1987.

Contemporary Dramatists, 6th edition, St. James Press (Farmington Hills, MI), 1999.

Contemporary Literary Criticism, Thomson Gale (Detroit, MI), Volume 9, 1978, pp. 360-61; Volume 15, 1980, pp. 355-58; Volume 34, 1985, pp. 217-24; Volume 46, 1988, pp. 245-56; Volume 91, 1996, pp. 143-55.

Contemporary Theatre, Film, and Television, Volume 27, Thomson Gale (Farmington Hills, MI, 2000.

Dean, Anne, *David Mamet: Language as Dramatic Action,* Fairleigh Dickinson University Press (Teaneck, NJ), 1990.

Drama Criticism, Volume 4, Thomson Gale (Detroit, MI), 1994.

Kane, Leslie, *David Mamet's Glengarry Glen Ross: Text and Performance,* Garland (New York, NY), 1996.

Kane, Leslie, editor, *David Mamet: A Casebook,* Garland (New York, NY), 1991.

Kane, Leslie, *Weasels and Wisemen: Education, Ethics, and Ethnicity in David Mamet,* St. Martin's Press (New York, NY), 1999.

King, Kimball, *Ten Modern American Playwrights,* Garland (New York, NY), 1982.

St. James Encyclopedia of Popular Culture, St. James Press (Detroit, MI), 2000.

PERIODICALS

America, May 15, 1993, p. 16; September 23, 1995, p. 26; June 5, 1999, Richard A. Blacke, "Boy Overboard," p. 14.

American Theatre, December 1, 1999, p. 9; November, 2002, Frank J. Baldaro, review of *Wilson: A Consideration of the Sources,* p. 80; November 1, 2002, Frank J. Baldaro, review of *Wilson,* pp. 80-81; November 1, 2002, Randy Gener, "Speed the Plot: Six Playwrights Parlay Their Dramatic Themes into New Fiction," pp. 75-76; January 1, 2003, Jonathan Kalb, "Stardust Melancholy," pp. 42-49.

Back Stage, November 22, 2002, Julius Novick, review of *Boston Marriage,* p. 48.

Booklist, December 1, 1992; June 1, 1994.

Broadcasting & Cable, September 25, 2000, "CBS Teams with Mamet, Morrie Author," p. 28; September 30, 2002, "Pariah Television," p. 18.

Chicago, January, 1990, p. 65.

Chicago Tribune, January 18, 1987, p. 7; October 11, 1987; May 4, 1988; February 19, 1989; December 10, 1989.

Christian Century, September 13, 2000, James M. Wall, "Probing the Depths," p. 932.

Commonweal, December 4, 1992, p. 15.

Daily News, March 26, 1984.

Daily Variety, November 21, 2002, review of *Boston Marriage,* p. 2.

Economist (US), August 2, 2003, "Not Just a Blond Wizard; Kenneth Branagh," p. 72.

Entertainment Weekly, August 21, 1992, pp. 50-51; June 9, 1995, p. 68; July 9, 1999, review of *Lansky,* p. 82; January 12, 2001, "What to Watch," p. 61; November 16, 2001, Lisa Schwarzbaum, review of *Heist,* p. 144; December 7, 2001, "Cybertalk," p. 108; November 29, 2002, Doug Brod, review of *Glengarry Glen Ross*; December 13, 2002, Lawrence Frascella, review of *Boston Marriage,* p. 92.

Financial Times, December 5, 2001, Alastair Macaulay, review of *Boston Marriage,* p. 18; May 17, 2002, Lisa Schwarzbaum, review of *Ricky: Jay on the Stem,* p. 71.

Gentlemen's Quarterly, October, 1994, p. 110.

Georgia Review, fall, 1983, pp. 601-11.

Harper's, May, 1978, pp. 79-80, 83-87.

Hollywood Reporter, September 5, 2001, Michael Rechtshaffen, review of *Heist,* p. 2.

Insight on the News, January 9, 1995, p. 26; January 1, 2001, Rex Roberts, "Cinema Verite," p. 27.

Interview, December 1, 2000, Guy Flatley, review of *State and Maine,* p. 58.

Kirkus Reviews, April 15, 1996, p. 580.

Library Journal, January, 1991, p. 106; June 1, 1996, p. 106; March 15, 2001, Barry X. Miller, review of *State and Maine,* p. 87.

London Review of Books, July 7, 1994, p. 7.

Los Angeles Times, November 27, 1979; June 25, 1984; July 7, 1987; October 11, 1987.

Los Angeles Times Book Review, December 13, 1992, p. 3; March 6, 1994, p. 8; June 30, 1996, p. 10; July 28, 1996, p. 11.

Maclean's, December 25, 2000, Brian D. Johnson, "Holiday Escapades: Tales of self-absorbed man enjoying mid-life epiphanies dominates this season's fare," p. 148; February 19, 2001, Brian D. Johnson, "Haute-Cannibal Cuisine," p. 48; November 12, 2001, Brian D. Johnson, "A Knack for Noir," p. 53.

Modern Drama, September, 1991, Jack V. Barbara, review of *American Buffalo,* pp. 271-72, 275.

Nation, May 19, 1979, pp. 581-82; April 14, 1981; October 10, 1981; April 28, 1984, pp. 522-23; June 27, 1987, pp. 900-02; December 30, 2002, David Kaufman, review of *Boston Marriage,* p. 35.

National Review, January 18, 1993, p. 28; May 31,1999, John Simon, "Film: Pidgeon Feathers," p. 70; March 5, 2001, John Simon, "Ominous Appetites"; February 5, 2001, John Simon, "Lost and Found."

New Leader, April 16, 1984, pp. 20-21; December 14, 1992, p. 26.

New Republic, July 12, 1982, Robert Brustein, review of *Edmond,* pp. 23-24; February 10, 1986, pp. 25-26, 28; October 29, 1990, pp. 32-37; April 24, 1995, p. 46; May 24, 1999, p. 32; January 29, 2001, p. 28; April 30, 2001, p. 30.

New Statesman & Society, September 30, 1983, pp. 33, 36; July 2, 1993, p. 34; June 2, 2003, Sheridan Morley, "Norwegian Wood: Sheridan Morley on a Damp Ibsen, an Early Mamet, and Shakespeare out of His Time," p. 46.

Newsweek, February 28, 1977, p. 79; March 23, 1981; November 8, 1982; December 6, 1982; April 9, 1984, p. 109; October 19, 1987; November 9, 1992, p. 65.

New York, December 20, 1982, pp. 62, 64; June 8, 1987, pp. 68-69; March 9, 1992, p. 77; November 9, 1992, p. 72; November 30, 1992, p. 129; August 2, 1993, p. 50; October 11, 1993, p. 79; February 21, 1994, p. 52; February 12, 2001, David Ansen, "Knock, Knock. Who's There?," p. 56; November 19, 2001, Devin Gordon, review of *Heist,* p. 69.

New Yorker, November 10, 1975, Edith Oliver, review of *Sexual Perversity in Chicago,* pp. 135-36; October 31, 1977, pp. 115-16; January 16, 1978; October 29, 1979, p. 81; June 15, 1981; November 7, 1983; June 29, 1987, pp. 70-72; November 16, 1992, pp. 121-26; August 1, 1994, p. 70; April 10, 1995, pp. 33-34.

New York Post, December 24, 1985; March 26, 1984.

New York Times, July 5, 1976; March 18, 1979; April 26, 1979; May 26, 1979; June 3, 1979; October 19, 1979; March 20, 1981; May 29, 1981; June 5, 1981; February 17, 1982; May 17, 1982; June 17, 1982; October 24, 1982; October 28, 1982, p. C20; December 8, 1982; May 13, 1983; October 9, 1983, pp. 6, 19; November 6, 1983; March 26, 1984, p. C17; March 28, 1984; April 1, 1984; April 18, 1984; April 24, 1984; September 30, 1984; February 9, 1986; April 23, 1986; January 1, 1987; March 15, 1987; June 3, 1987; October 11, 1987; May 4, 1988; December 4, 1989; April 14, 1995, p. C3.

New York Times Book Review, December 17, 1989; January 17, 1993, p. 24; November 20, 1994, p. 24; April 9, 1995, p. 20; July 14, 1996, p. 17.

New York Times Magazine, March 12, 1978, Richard Eder, profile of Mamet, pp. 40, 42, 45, 47.

People, November 12, 1979; December 20, 1982; May 4, 1987.

Playboy, September, 1994, p. 78; April, 1995, p. 51.

Premiere, January, 1990, p. 108.

Publishers Weekly, November 16, 1992, p. 55; July 4, 1994, p. 52; April 8, 1996, p. 46; September 24, 2001, review of *Wilson,* p. 67; August 4, 2003, "Five Cities of Refuge: Weekly Reflections on Genesis, Exodus, Leviticus, Numbers, and Deuteronomy," p. 75.

Review of Contemporary Fiction, June 22, 2002, Joseph Dewey, review of *Wilson,* p. 224.

Sarasota Herald Tribune, August 10, 2001, Philip Booth, review of *Lakeboat,* p. 14.

Saturday Review, April 2, 1977, p. 37.

Smithsonian, June 1, 2001, Kathleen Burke, review of *River Run Cookbook: Southern Comfort from Vermont,* p. 124.

Time, July 12, 1976; April 9, 1984, p. 105; December 25, 1989, pp. 87-90; August 24, 1992, p. 69; November 2, 1992, p. 69; October 18, 1993, p. 109; August 29, 1994, p. 71; May 17, 1999, Richard Corliss, "The Winslow Boy," p. 90; December 25, 2000, Joel Stein, "David Mamet," p. 164; January 15, 2001, Richard Corliss, review of *State and Maine,* p. 138; January 29, 2001, Jess Cagle, "The Bite Stuff," p. 60; November 19, 2001, Richard Schickel, review of *Heist,* p. 143.

Times Literary Supplement, January 29, 1988; July 15, 1994, Jim McCue, review of *A Whore's Profession,* p. 21; February 16, 1996, p. 23.

Tribune Books (Chicago, IL), January 18, 1987; December 13, 1992, p. 7; May 5, 1996, p. 3.

Us, January 10, 1978, Robin Reeves, interview with Mamet.

Variety, February 24, 1992, p. 257; May 11, 1992, p. 127; August 24, 1992, p. 65; April 5, 1993, p. 185; February 7, 1994, p. 60; June 21, 1999, Markland Taylor, review of *Boston Marriage,* p. 88; August 16, 1999, Michael Fleming, "Mamet Moves into Comedy with 'Maine,'" p. 13; November 1, 1999, Charles Isherwood, review of *The Water Engine* and *Mr. Happiness,* p. 99; January 17, 2000, Robert Hofler, review of *Sexual Perversity in Chicago* and *The Duck Variations,* p. 140; February 14, 2000, Matt Wolf, review of *American Buffalo,* p. 49; March 6, 2000, Robert L. Daniels, review of *Glengarry Glen Ross,* p. 50; March 20, 2000, Charles Isherwood, review of *American Buffalo,* p. 36; April 17, 2000, Emanuel Levy, review of *Lakeboat,* p. 28; September 4, 2000, Eddie Cockrell, review of *State and Maine,* p. 19; February 5, 2001, Todd McCarthy, review of *Hannibal,* p. 37; April 16, 2001, Matt Wolf, review of *Boston Marriage,* p. 39; September 10, 2001, David Rooney, review of *Heist,* p. 62; January 7, 2002, Chris Jones, review of *Glengarry Glen Ross,* p. 53; May 13, 2002, Charles Isherwood, review of *Ricky: Jay on the Stem,* p. 32; May 26, 2003, Matt Wolf, review of *Sexual Perversity in Chicago,* p. 42; August 4, 2003, Matt Wolf, review of *Edmond,* p. 30.

Village Voice, July 5, 1976, Ross Wetzsteon, profile of Mamet, pp. 101, 103-04; May 7, 1979, Eileen Blumenthal, review of *The Woods,* p. 103.

Washington Post, May 4, 1988.

World Literature Today, summer, 1982, p. 518.

ONLINE

CurtainUp.com, http://www.curtainup.com/ (May 28, 2003), review of *Boston Marriage* and *Ricky Jay: On the Stem.*

David Mamet Review (newsletter of the David Mamet Society), http://mamet.eserver.org/ (November 20, 2003).

FilmMakers, http://www.filmmakers.com/ (November 20, 2003), "David Alan Mamet: Filmography and Credits."

Salon.com, http://www.salon.com/ (May 28, 2003), interview with Mamet.

Smithsonian Online, http://www.smithsonianmag.si.edu/ (November 20, 2003), "Book Reviews: *River Run Cookbook.*"

Sony Pictures Web site, http://www.sonypictures.com/ (November 20, 2003), "Ricky Jay."

*   *   *

MAMET, David Alan
See MAMET, David

MARA, Bernard
  See MOORE, Brian

*   *   *

MARCHBANKS, Samuel
  See DAVIES, Robertson

*   *   *

MARÍAS, Javier 1951-

PERSONAL: Born September 20, 1951, in Madrid, Spain; son of Julián Marías Aguilera and Dolores Franco Manera.

ADDRESSES: Agent—Mercedes Casanovas, Iradier 24, 08017 Barcelona, Spain.

CAREER: Writer and translator.

AWARDS, HONORS: Nelly Sachs Preis; Premio Grinzane Cavour; Premio Alberto Moravia; Premio Comunidad de Madrid; National Translation Prize, Spain, 1979, for *Tristram Shandy;* IX Premio Internacional de Novela Romulo Gallagos, 1995, for *Mañana en la batalla piensa en mi;* Prix Femina for best foreign book, 1996, Premio Fastenrath, and Premio Modello Città di Palermo, all for *Tomorrow in the Battle Think on Me;* IMPAC Dublin Literary Award, 1997, Spanish Critics National Award, and Prix L'Oeil et la Lettre, all for *A Heart So White;* Premio Ciudad de Barcelona, for *All Souls.*

WRITINGS:

Los dominios del lobo (title means "The Domains of the Wolf"), Edhasa (Barcelona, Spain), 1971.
Travesia del horizonte, 1973, Editorial Anagrama (Barcelona, Spain), 1988.
(With Felix de Azua and Vicente Molina-Foix) *Tres cuentos didacticos* (short stories), La Gaya Ciencia (Barcelona, Spain), 1975.
El monarca del tiempo, Alfaguara (Madrid, Spain), 1978.
El siglo, Seix Barral (Barcelona, Spain), 1983.
El hombre sentimental, Editorial Anagrama (Barcelona, Spain), 1986, translation by Margaret Jull Costa as *The Man of Feeling,* New Directions (New York, NY), 2003.

Todas las almas, Anagrama (Barcelona, Spain), 1989, translation by Margaret Jull Costa published as *All Souls,* HarperCollins (New York, NY), 1992.
Mientras ellas Duermen, Anagrama (Barcelona, Spain), 1990.
Pasiones pasadas, Editorial Anagrama (Barcelona, Spain), 1991.
Corazon tan blanco, Editorial Anagrama (Barcelona, Spain), 1992, translation by Margaret Jull Costa published as *A Heart So White,* Harvill (New York, NY), 1995.
Vidas escritas, Ediciones Siruela (Madrid, Spain), 1992.
Literatura y fantasma (stories), Ediciones Siruela (Madrid, Spain), 1993.
Mañana en la batalla piensa en mi, Anagrama (Barcelona, Spain), 1994, translation by Margaret Jull Costa published as *Tomorrow in the Battle Think on Me,* Harcourt Brace (San Diego, CA), 1997.
Vida del fantasma: entusiasmos, bromas, reminiscencias y canones recortados, El Pais/Aguilar (Madrid, Spain), 1995.
Mano de sombra, Alfaguara (Madrid, Spain), 1997.
Miramientos, Alfaguara (Madrid, Spain), 1997.
Seré amado cuando falte, Alfaguara (Madrid, Spain), 1999.
Cuando fui mortal (stories), translation by Margaret Jull Costa published as *When I Was Mortal,* New Directions (New York, NY), 2000.
Salvajes y sentimentales, Aguilar (Madrid, Spain), 2000.
Negra espalda del tiempo, translation by Esther Allen published as *Dark Back of Time,* New Directions (New York, NY), 2001.
A veces un caballero, Alfaguara (Madrid, Spain), 2001.
Fiebre, Alfaguara (Madrid, Spain), 2002.
Tu rostro mañana, Alfaguara (Madrid, Spain), 2002.
El monarca del tiempo, Reino de Redonda (Madrid, Spain), 2003
Harón de mon un criminal, Alfaguara (Madrid, Spain), 2003.

Translator of classic English novels into Spanish, including *Tristram Shandy,* by Laurence Stern, and works by Joseph Conrad, Robert Louis Stevenson, Wallace Stevens, William Faulkner, John Ashbery, W.H. Auden, Frank O'Hara, Isak Dinesen, Sir Thomas Brown, Thomas Hardy, and W.B. Yeats.

Author's works have been translated into over twenty languages.

SIDELIGHTS: One of the most noted novelists of his generation and the son of a well-known cultural critic in his native Spain, Javier Marías began writing fiction in 1971 at age nineteen. In addition, he has translated many English classics into Spanish, including the works of Thomas Hardy, Robert Louis Stevenson, Joseph Conrad, W.B. Yeats, and Laurence Sterne. Cited by *Nation* reviewer Ilan Stavans as heir to such writers as Marcel Proust and Jorge-Luis Borges, Marías's prose, according to the critic, can also be compared to that of American writer Henry James; he employs "the same syncopated prose and introspective inquisitiveness, and he often uses equally long, tortuous sentences." However, unlike James, the writings of Marías are composed of "disconnected segments . . . that seldom add up to a whole," creating a reading experience that proves "rewarding because he is a literary magician who understands literature as a game of mirrors."

Marías's early novel *El siglo* is a story about fate in which a father tells his son, Casaldaliga, to seek his own destiny; as the boy learns, his father has not followed his own advice. James H. Abbott, writing in *World Literature Today,* compared the "theme of chance or coincidence," which the critic maintained is "treated capriciously" in Marías's novel *Los dominios del lobo,* to the more "analytical perspective" employed in *El siglo.* Rather than follow the events of Casaldaliga's life as they occur, Marías "chooses instead the development of the protagonist's character . . . [and] search for personal destiny." The question is whether choice of destiny is possible. Abbott commented that the author "structures *El siglo* with perfect balance . . . lyrical passages . . . [and] a sense of passing time related to *El siglo* which becomes not only Casaldaliga's time but life and the world in which the reader also lives."

Ignacio-Javier Lopez, writing in *World Literature Today,* noted that Marías ranks among those Spanish novelists in his generation who have followed the lead of Juan Benet, a writer who refused to use his work as a forum for political or social commentary. Instead these writers focus on topics of a less-timely and more universal nature, notably the topic of love. Lopez cited Marías's *El hombre sentimental* as an example of "love viewed ironically and without taking the characters' passionate declarations seriously."

Marías's highly acclaimed novel *El hombre sentimental*—translated as *The Man of Feeling*—is a portrait of an aberrant artist, told through the perspective of its narrator, Leon de Napoles, an quasi-famous opera star. Infatuated with a married woman he barely knows, Napoles declares, "I need to try to destroy myself or to destroy someone else." He accomplishes both. *Review of Contemporary Fiction*'s Steven Kellman re-

marked that "Readers in the United States have been slower than those elsewhere to discover the sophisticated pleasures" of Marías's "perverse and powerful fiction." A *Kirkus Reviews* critic found *Man of Feeling* to be "a resonant enigma, deftly explored in an elusive text that's a revealing introduction to and gloss on Marías' richer, even more puzzling subsequent fiction."

Todas las almas, published in English translation as *All Souls,* is a novel based on Marías's two-and-a-half years as a lecturer in Spanish literature at Oxford University, and his concurrent romance with a married colleague. The characters include professors, whom Michael Kerrigan called in the *Times Literary Supplement* "perfect, idealized forms in their university setting," who are "haunted by the prospect of decay . . . uncomfortably aware of their own insignificance," and serve as "mute testimony to the provisional nature of literary distinction." Juan J. Liebana in *World Literature Today* called Marías's novel "a book of memories, or perhaps a belated journal. . . . A stage of his life in which he rather felt alienated from his surroundings, more the observer than the participant." Liebana wrote that *Todas las almas* is "a unique book in many ways and is full of pleasant surprises that confirm Marías's literary craft." Guy Mannes-Abbot, writing in *New Statesman & Society,* found the novel to be a "circuitous encounter with the English, their language and their quintessential institution." "Narrator and reader become engaged in metaphorical detective work to uncover a culture," the critic added, noting that the novelist includes within his work "a swirl of masterfully choreographed narrative leaps."

Marías's *Corazon tan blanco* is a story narrated in the first person. Juan, newly married at age thirty-four, is fearful for his marriage because of the circumstances of the death of his father's first wife, also his mother's sister. At the outset of the novel Juan's Aunt Teresa commits suicide after one week of marriage to his father, Ranz, and henceforth Juan feels a sense of impending doom. He sees parallels between the events of the past and scenes he has observed in his own life. Discussing the English translation of the novel, published as *A Heart So White,* a *Kirkus Reviews* contributor noted that the title and epigraph "allude openly to Macbeth's murder of Duncan, and its sinister burden of simultaneous cumulative revelation and deepening mystery. . . . The flawed, truncated nature of all human contact and efforts to reach it has rarely been given such remorseless stress." A reviewer for *Publishers Weekly* characterized the novel's tone as similar to foreplay and added that Marías's characters "tease each other—as the author teases the reader—with nibbles of information, half-divulged stories . . . to arouse a reader's curiosity the way an interrupted caress can awaken a lover's desire." Ricardo Landeira, reviewing *A Heart So White* for *World Literature Today,* called the book "truly original, intriguing, and elegantly written."

Marías's novel *Mañana en la batalla piensa en mi* earned the 1995 Romulo Gallagos Award, the Hispanic-American equivalent of the Nobel Prize for Literature. In this story, Victor, a scriptwriter in Madrid, is having an affair with Marta, a married woman. While they are together, she dies, and Victor is faced with associated problems. A *Kirkus Reviews* critic, appraising the English translation, *Tomorrow in the Battle Think on Me,* maintained that the novel's plot "spins off into amusingly unpredictable directions," while a *Publishers Weekly* contributor wrote, "Sometimes [Marías] strikes a note of genuine pathos, but just as often his musings, with their repetitions and long, long run-on sentences, become tiresome." Lisa Rohrbaugh commented in *Library Journal* that readers of *Tomorrow in the Battle Think on Me* will find that "Victor and Marta's husband share their secrets of dealing with wives and lovers in a climactic ending."

Described by *Nation* reviewer Ilan Stavans as "by far the brainiest, most emblematic, and abstruse book by Marías, as well as the most demanding," *Dark Back of Time,* originally published as *Negra espalda del tiempo,* is a self-reflective work of literary fiction that is nonlinear in its narrative and mixes fact with non-fact in a challenging yet compelling intertwining triple narrative. The book—which its author terms a "false novel"—has its basis in Marías's creation of his novel *All Souls,* which focuses on his experiences while teaching at Oxford University. In this work the author describes the reaction to his previous novel of those people who were fictionalized within its pages, their metamorphosis sometimes aided by publishing-house editors. In one narrative the author describes how some individuals fictionalized in the novel have gone on to adopt some of the characteristics of their novel characters; the second narrative focuses on British author John Gawsworth; and the third narrative follows the author's own life, including the deaths of his mother and older brother. Describing the complex work as a "stimulating and original" novel full of "wit and wisdom," *Library Journal* reviewer Jack Shreve praised *Dark Back of Time* for providing readers with "a rare insider's view of the processes of writing fiction." To John de Falbe, writing in the *Spectator,* Marías has created a novel that "resonate[s] with wonderful and beautiful clarity," a work enhanced by "his unique style—witty and mesmerising, . . . —that makes the passage between

truth and fiction fluid and convincing." Comparing Marías with Italian novelist Italo Calvino, a *Publishers Weekly* contributor noted that *Dark Back of Time* showcases both the author's "antiquarian's taste for history's minor characters" and his "ability . . . to turn a metaphysical insight into a novelist adventure."

BIOGRAPHICAL AND CRITICAL SOURCES:

BOOKS

Marías, Javier, *El hombre sentimental,* Editorial Anagrama (Barcelona, Spain), 1986, translation by Margaret Jull Costa as *The Man of Feeling,* New Directions (New York, NY), 2003.

PERIODICALS

Booklist, November 1, 1996, p. 482; October 15, 1997, p. 389.
Hispania, summer, 1993, p. 492; March, 1996, p. 84.
Kirkus Reviews, January 1, 1996, p. 18; November 1, 1996, p. 1558; September 1, 1997, p. 1332; April 15, 2003, review of *The Man of Feeling,* p. 571.
Library Journal, August, 1997, Lisa Rohrbaugh, review of *Tomorrow in the Battle Think on Me,* p. 132; August, 2004, Jack Shreve, review of *Dark Back of Time,* p. 68.
London Review of Books, April 24, 1997, p. 13.
Nation, March 19, 2001, Ilan Stavans, "The Spanish Mien," p. 32.
New Statesman & Society, October 9, 1992, Guy Mannes-Abbott, review of *All Souls,* p. 35; July 28, 1995, p. 38.
New Yorker, April 15, 1996, p. 92.
New York Times, May 21, 2000, Elizabeth Judd, review of *When I Was Mortal.*
Observer, November 1, 1992, p. 62; November 15, 1992, p. 64; November 10, 1996, p. 18.
Publishers Weekly, January 8, 1996, review of *A Heart So White,* p. 59; July 21, 1997, p. 180; March 26, 2001, review of *Dark Back of Time,* p. 64.
Review of Contemporary Fiction, spring, 2001, Ben Donnelly, review of *A Heart So White,* p. 191; fall, 2001, Alan Tinkler, review of *Dark Back of Time,* p. 2000; summer, 2003, Steven Kellman, review of *The Man of Feeling.*
Spectator, September 8, 2001, John de Falbe, review of *Dark Back of Time,* p. 37.

Times Literary Supplement, October 6, 1989, Michael Kerrigan, review of *All Souls,* p. 19; November 6, 1992, p. 21; November 15, 1996, p. 24; September 10, 1999, review of *When I Was Mortal,* p. 21.

Tribune Books (Chicago, IL), January 12, 1997, p. 2.

Washington Post Book World, July 7, 1996, p. 6.

World Literature Today, spring, 1984, James H. Abbott, review of *El siglo,* p. 242; autumn, 1988, p. 635; winter, 1991, p. 86; autumn, 1993, p. 783.

*   *   *

MARINER, Scott
See POHL, Frederik

*   *   *

MARKANDAYA, Kamala 1924-2004
[A pseudonym]
(Kamala Purnaiya Taylor)

PERSONAL: Born 1924, in India; died of kidney failure, May 16, 2004, in London, England; married Bertrand Taylor; children: Kim (daughter). *Education:* Attended University of Madras. *Religion:* Hindu-Brahmin.

CAREER: Worked briefly for a small weekly newspaper in India; immigrated to England, 1948.

MEMBER: British Society of Authors.

AWARDS, HONORS: Nectar in a Sieve was named a notable nook of 1955 by the American Library Association; National Association of Independent Schools Award, 1967.

WRITINGS:

Nectar in a Sieve, Putnam (London, England), 1954, John Day (New York, NY), 1955, reprinted, Paradigm Publishing (St. Paul, MN), 2003.

Some Inner Fury, Putnam (London, England), 1955, John Day (New York, NY), 1956.

A Silence of Desire, Putnam (London, England), 1960, John Day (New York, NY), 1961.

Possession, John Day (New York, NY), 1963.

A Handful of Rice, John Day (New York, NY), 1966.

The Coffer Dams, John Day (New York, NY), 1969.

The Nowhere Man, John Day (New York, NY), 1972.

Two Virgins, John Day (New York, NY), 1973.

The Golden Honeycomb, Crowell (New York, NY), 1977.

Shalimar, Harper (New York, NY), 1982, published as *Pleasure City,* Chatto and Windus (London, England), 1982.

Contributor of fiction and articles to Indian and British publications.

SIDELIGHTS: British author Kamala Markandaya, who was born Kamala Purnaiya in India, wrote two novels before her third, *Nectar in a Sieve,* was accepted for publication. The work, released in the mid-1950s in both England and the United States, was highly praised for its accurate picture of Indian village life. Donald Barr commented in the *New York Times* that "The basis of eloquence is knowledge, and *Nectar in a Sieve* has a wonderful, quiet authority over our sympathies because Markandaya is manifestly an authority on village life in India. Because of what she knows, she has been able to write a story without reticence or excess." Praising the novel as "a powerful book," critic J.F. Muehl noted of *Nectar in a Sieve* in the *Saturday Review* that "the power is in the content. . . . You read it because it answers so many real questions: What is the day-to-day life of the villager like? How does a village woman really think of herself? What goes through the minds of people who are starving?"

Reviewing Markandaya's *Two Virgins,* a *New Yorker* critic observed that the author "writes in a forthright, almost breakneck style that could have been paced a little less relentlessly but could not be more precise or lucid. From the minutiae of the girls' lives we learn a great deal about the fabric of life in India today. They are constantly choosing between Eastern and Western ways of looking at the world—in their school, at home, in their language, and in their attitudes toward their own ripening sexuality, of which they are both keenly aware. . . . Both their stories are fascinating and demonstrate that [Markandaya] writes as well about such universal feelings as lust, friendship, envy, and pride as she does about matters idiosyncratic to her country." Markandaya's final novel, 1982's *Shalimar*—published as *Pleasure City* in England—focuses on a "collision between rural innocence and technological sophistication, between old tradition and modern innovation," according to *Atlantic* contributor Phoebe-Lou Adams. Following the efforts of a corporation to displace a group of fisherman in order to build a seaside vacation resort called Shalimar that promises to employ numbers of residence in an impoverished Indian community. In her two main characters, the native fisherman Rikki and Tully, a local resident descended from British colonizers, Markandaya presents an alliance between "the best of India's colonial past and the hope of India's future," Adams explained. While focusing on India's future, the critic added, "she offers no polemics, no great confrontations," but instead presents "a wonderfully varied" selection of characters.

BIOGRAPHICAL AND CRITICAL SOURCES:

BOOKS

Afzal-Khan, Fawzia, *Cultural Imperialism and the Indo-English Novel,* Pennsylvania State University Press (University Park, PA), 1993.

Bhatnagar, Anil Kumar, *Kamala Markandaya: A Thematic Study,* Sarup and Sons (New Delhi, India), 1995.

Chanda, Ramesh, *Cross-Cultural Interaction in Indian English Fiction,* National Book Organisation (New Delhi, India), 1988.

Contemporary Literary Criticism, Volume 8, Thomson Gale (Detroit, MI), 1978.

Jha, Rekha, *The Novels of Kamala Markandaya and Ruth Jhabvala,* Prestige Books, 1990.

Joseph, Margaret P., *Kamala Markandaya,* Arnold-Heinemann (New Delhi, India), 1980.

Pathania, Usha, *Human Bonds and Bondages: The Fiction of Anita Desai and Kamala Markandaya,* Kanishka (Delhi, India), 1992.

Prasad, Madhusudan, *Perspectives on Kamala Markandaya,* Vimal Prakashan (Ghaziabad, India), 1984.

Varma, R. M., *Some Aspects of Indo-English Fiction,* Jainsons Publications (New Delhi, India), 1985.

Wali, S. K., *Kamala Markandaya: Nectar in a Sieve,* Printwell (Jaipur, India), 1987.

PERIODICALS

Atlantic, September, 1983, Phoebe-Lou Adams, review of *Shalimar,* p. 124.

Best Sellers, June 1, 1969; October 15, 1973.

Christian Science Monitor, May 26, 1955; October 10, 1973.

Commonweal, August 19, 1955.

Kirkus Reviews, February 1, 1955.

New Yorker, May 23, 1955; October 22, 1973.

Saturday Review, May 14, 1955; June 14, 1969.

Time, May 16, 1955.

Times Literary Supplement, Saturday 10, 1954; June 12, 1969.

*   *   *

MARKHAM, Robert
    See AMIS, Kingsley

*   *   *

MARSHALL, Allen
    See WESTLAKE, Donald E.

*   *   *

MARSHALL, Paule 1929-

PERSONAL: Born Valenza Pauline Burke, April 9, 1929, in Brooklyn, NY; daughter of Samuel and Ada (Clement) Burke; married Kenneth E. Marshall, 1950 (divorced, 1963); married Nourry Menard, July 30, 1970; children (first marriage): Evan. *Education:* Brooklyn College (now of the City University of New York), B.A. (cum laude), 1953; attended Hunter College (now of the City University of New York), 1955.

ADDRESSES: Home—407 Central Park W, New York, NY 10025. *Office*—Feminist Press, c/o Gerrie Nuccio, P.O. Box 334, Old Westbury, NY 11568; 19 University Pl., 214, New York, NY 10003; fax: 212-995-4019.

CAREER: Freelance writer and educator. New York University, currently professor of English, distinguished chair in creative writing. Worked as librarian in New York Public Libraries; *Our World* magazine, New York City, staff writer, 1953-56; lecturer on creative writing at Yale University, 1970—; Helen Gould Sheppard Professor in Literature and Culture, New York University, 1997—; lecturer on black literature at colleges and universities including Oxford University, Columbia University, Michigan State University, Lake Forrest College, and Cornell University. Teacher of creative writing at universities such as Columbia University, University of Iowa, and University of California, Berkeley.

MEMBER: PEN American Center, Authors Guild, Authors League of America, Langston Hughes Society, Zora Neale Hurston Society, W.E.B. Du Bois Society, Modern Language Association, Phi Beta Kappa.

AWARDS, HONORS: Guggenheim fellowship, 1960; Rosenthal Award, National Institute of Arts and Letters, 1962, for *Soul Clap Hands and Sing;* Ford Foundation grant, 1964-65; National Endowment for the Arts grant, 1967-68 and 1977; Creative Artists Public Service fellowship, 1974; American Book Award, Before Columbus Foundation, 1984, for *Praisesong for the Widow; Los Angeles Times* Book Award nomination, 1992, for *Daughters;* MacArthur Foundation fellowship, 1992; Black Caucus of the American Library Association Literary Award, 2001, for *The Fisher King;* Dos Passos Prize for Literature.

WRITINGS:

Brown Girl, Brownstones (novel), Random House, 1959, with an afterword by Mary Helen Washington, Feminist Press (Old Westbury, NY), 1981.

Soul Clap Hands and Sing (short stories; includes "British Guiana"), Atheneum (New York, NY), 1961.

The Chosen Place, the Timeless People, Harcourt (New York, NY), 1969.

Praisesong for the Widow (novel), Putnam (New York, NY), 1983.

Reena, and Other Stories (includes novella *Merle,* and short stories "The Valley Between," "Brooklyn," "Barbados," and "To Da-duh, in Memoriam"), with commentary by the author, Feminist Press (Old Westbury, NY), 1983, reprinted as *Merle: A Novella and Other Stories,* Virago Press, 1985.

Daughters (novel), Atheneum (New York, NY), 1991.

Language Is the Only Homeland: Bajan Poets Abroad (nonfiction), [Bridgetown, Barbados], 1995.

The Fisher King, Scribner (New York, NY), 2000.

Contributor of short stories to periodicals and to anthologies such as *Afro-American Writing 2,* edited by Richard Long and Eugenia Collier, New York University Press (New York, NY), 1972.

SIDELIGHTS: "My work asks that you become involved, that you think," writer Paule Marshall once commented in the *Los Angeles Times.* "On the other hand, . . . I'm first trying to tell a story, because I'm always about telling a good story." In her works, "history and community, shapers of the past and the present, are vital subtexts in the lives of Marshall's characters," wrote Joyce Pettis in the *Dictionary of Literary Biography.* "Just as important," Pettis continued, "Marshall explores the notion of cultural continuity through identification with African heritage and culture

as a means of healing the psychic fragmentation that has resulted from colonization and segregation. Her fiction is noted for its artistry—for finely crafted structures, fluid narrative, for language that conveys the nuances of the spoken word, and for characters that are especially complex and rich."

Marshall received her first training in storytelling from her mother, a native of Barbados, and her mother's West Indian friends, all of whom gathered for daily talks in Marshall's home after a hard day of "scrubbing floor." Marshall pays tribute to these "poets in the kitchen" in a *New York Times Book Review* essay where she describes the women's gatherings as a form of inexpensive therapy and an outlet for their enormous creative energy. She writes: "They taught me my first lessons in the narrative art. They trained my ear. They set a standard of excellence. This is why the best of my work must be attributed to them; it stands as testimony to the rich legacy of language and culture they so freely passed on to me in the wordshop of the kitchen."

The standard of excellence set by these women has served Marshall well in her career as a writer. Her novels and stories have been lauded for their skillful rendering of West Indian-Afro-American dialogue and colorful Barbadian expressions. *Dictionary of Literary Biography* contributor Barbara T. Christian believes that Marshall's works "form a unique contribution to Afro-American literature because they capture in a lyrical, powerful language a culturally distinct and expansive world." This pursuit of excellence makes writing a time-consuming effort, according to Marshall. "One of the reasons it takes me such a long time to get a book done," she explained in the *Los Angeles Times,* "is that I'm not only struggling with my sense of reality, but I'm also struggling to find the style, the language, the tone that is in keeping with the material. It's in the process of writing that things get illuminated."

Marshall indicates, however, that her first novel, *Brown Girl, Brownstones,* was written at a faster pace. "I was so caught up in the need to get down on paper before it was lost the whole sense of a special kind of community, what I call Bajan (Barbadian) Brooklyn, because even as a child I sensed there was something special and powerful about it," she stated in the *Los Angeles Times.* When the novel was published in 1959 it was deemed an impressive literary debut, but because of the novel's frank depiction of a young black girl's search for identity and increasing sexual awareness, *Brown Girl, Brownstones* was largely ignored by readers. The novel was reprinted in 1981, and is now considered a classic in the female bildungsroman genre, along with Zora Neale Hurston's *Their Eyes Were Watching God* and Gwendolyn Brooks's *Maud Martha.*

The story has autobiographical overtones, for it concerns a young black Brooklyn girl, Selina, the daughter of Barbadian immigrants Silla and Deighton. Silla, her ambitious mother, desires most of all to save enough money to purchase the family's rented brownstone. Her father, Deighton, on the other hand, is a charming spendthrift who'd like nothing better than to return to his homeland. When Deighton unexpectedly inherits some island land, he makes plans to return there and build a home. Silla meanwhile schemes to sell his inheritance and fulfill her own dream.

Selina is deeply affected by this material conflict, but "emerges from it self-assured, in spite of her scars," wrote Susan McHenry in *Ms.* Selina eventually leaves Brooklyn to attend college. Later, realizing her need to become acquainted with her parents' homeland, she resolves to go to Barbados. McHenry observed: "*Brown Girl, Brownstones* is meticulously crafted and peopled with an array of characters, and the writing combines authority with grace. . . . Marshall . . . should be more widely read and celebrated." Carol Field commented in the *New York Herald Tribune Book Review:* "[*Brown Girl, Brownstones*] is an unforgettable novel written with pride and anger, with rebellion and tears. Rich in content and in cadences of the King's and 'Bajan' English, it is the work of a highly gifted writer."

Marshall's most widely reviewed work to date is *Praisesong for the Widow,* winner of the American Book Award. The novel is thematically similar to *Brown Girl, Brownstones* in that it also involves a black woman's search for identity. This book, though, concerns an affluent widow in her sixties, Avatara (Avey) Johnson, who has lost touch with her West Indian-Afro-American roots. In the process of struggling to make their way in the white-dominated world, Avey and her husband, Jerome (Jay), lost all of the qualities that made them unique. Novelist Anne Tyler remarked in the *New York Times Book Review,* "Secure in her middle-class life, her civil service job, her house full of crystal and silver, Avey has become sealed away from her true self."

While on her annual luxury cruise through the West Indies, however, Avey has several disturbing dreams about her father's great aunt, whom she visited every summer on a South Carolina island. She remembers the spot on the island where the Ibo slaves, upon landing in America, supposedly took one look around at their new life and walked across the water back to Africa. Avey decides to try to escape the uneasiness by flying back to the security of her home. While in her hotel on Grenada awaiting the next flight to New York, Avey reminisces about the early years of her and Jay's marriage, when they used to dance to jazz records in their living room, and on Sundays listen to gospel music and recite poetry. Gradually, though, in their drive for success they lost "the little private rituals and pleasures, the playfulness and wit of those early years, the host of feelings and passions that had defined them in a special way back then, and the music which had been their nourishment," writes Marshall in the novel.

In the morning, Avey becomes acquainted with a shopkeeper who urges her to accompany him and the other islanders on their annual excursion to Carriacou, the island of their ancestors. Still confused from the past day's events, she agrees. During the island celebration, Avey undergoes a spiritual rebirth and resolves to keep in close contact with the island and its people and to tell others about her experience.

Reviewers question if Avey's resolution is truly enough to compensate for all that she and Jay have lost, if "the changes she envisions in the flush of conversion are commensurate with the awesome message of the resisting Ibos," to use *Voice Literary Supplement* reviewer Carol Ascher's words. "Her search for roots seems in a way the modern, acceptable equivalent of the straightened hair and white ways she is renouncing," wrote *Times Literary Supplement* contributor Mary Kathleen Benet, who added: "On the other hand there is not much else she can do, just as there was not much else Jerome Johnson could do. Paule Marshall respects herself enough as a writer to keep from overplaying her hand; her strength is that she raises questions that have no answers."

Los Angeles Times Book Review contributor Sharon Dirlam offered this view: "[Avey] has learned to stay her anger and to swallow her grief, making her day of reckoning all the more poignant. She has already missed the chance to apply what she belatedly learns, except for the most important lesson: What matters is today and tomorrow, and, oh yes, yesterday-life, at age thirty, age sixty, the lesson is to live." Jonathan Yardley concluded in the *Washington Post Book World:* "*Praisesong for the Widow* . . . is a work of quiet passion—a book all the more powerful precisely because it is so quiet. It is also a work of exceptional wisdom, maturity and generosity, one in which the palpable humanity of its characters transcends any considerations of race or sex; that Avey Johnson is black and a woman is certainly important, but Paule Marshall understands that what really counts is the universality of her predicament."

Reena, and Other Stories, although a collection of short stories, contains the title story, "Reena" and the novella *Merle,* adapted from the novel *The Chosen Place, the Timeless People.* The title is based on a protagonist of the novel. "Reena" is frequently anthologized, particularly in collections of writings by African-American women writers. In her introductory comments to a reissued version of *Black-Eyed Susans/Midnight Birds: Stories by and about Black Women,* Mary Helen Washington refers to its theme of cultural identity and the role of the African-American female. Dr. Washington's commentary and analysis bolster Paule Marshall's accompanying sketch for "Reena." "Reena" is autobiographical and is a continuation of *Brown Girl, Brownstones.* Marshall describes Reena as like herself "from a West Indian-American background who had attended the free New York City colleges during the forties and fifties. The theme would be our efforts to realize whatever talents we had and to be our own persons in the face of the triple-headed hydra of racism, sexism, and class bias we confronted each day."

Daughters, Marshall's 1991 novel, has been widely acclaimed. According to the author, the novel explores significant personal themes. "Ursa is a young urban woman trying to come to terms with the two worlds that shaped her. . . . Her mother is American, her father West Indian. [I] wanted to write something that was symbolic of the two wings of the black diaspora in this part of the world." Defining the role of the female—upwardly mobile, well-educated—in the black diaspora is the cog around which *Daughters* turns. In the *New York Times Book Review,* Susan Fromberg Schaeffer saw that the key for Ursa is in what she learns from those most important in her life. Ursa learns that "to be human one must be of use. To be of use, men and women must work together—and that the relationship between the sexes is far more complicated than Ursa has ever imagined." Working together involves a struggle—sometimes erupting in conflict between men and women. Ursa discovers by novel's end that she must not evade struggle/conflict toward a common goal. She learns to stop allowing love for another to becloud her judgment, as in the case of ignoring the corruption that her father, Primus, confused with success. Ursa learns that she is "hobbled by love of her father . . . and so complete is his possession of her that she needs to 'abort' him." Ursa must break free to define herself,

continue to be "useful," continue to love all humans, yet not be bogged down by that love and get off course. "Marshall shows us how . . . women can—and perhaps should—find themselves becoming men's consciences."

Marshall's novel, *The Fisher King,* published in 2000, is a multigenerational story that serves as a "wonderful rendering of the African diaspora (from Brooklyn to Paris) in its many complexities," observed Adele S. Newson-Horst in *World Literature Today.* "Set against the backdrop of a triangular relationship, *The Fisher King* at once celebrates and delineates the nuances of diaspora interactions—a reality perhaps best captured by the musical form of jazz," Newson-Horst observed. In the 1940s, widow Ulene Payne struggles to make a living, but makes whatever sacrifices are necessary to provide classical piano lessons for her talented son, Everett (also known as Sonny-Rett). Her neighbor, Florence McCullum, lives in elegance and has little trouble providing for her daughter, Cherisse, who is blessed with a wonderful singing voice and has great promise as a singer. But Sonny-Rett soon discovers that classical piano is not to his liking, and begins to play in jazz clubs, where his reputation is made and strengthened. Cherisse, too, abandons her formal singing career and accompanies Sonny to his gigs, along with her best friend, Hattie Carmichael. Soon, Sonny-Rett and Cherisse are married, and Hattie becomes manager of their business affairs. Rather than embracing their children's success in the jazz field (which was then considered a scandalous form of music), Ulene and Florence are mortified and bitterly disappointed that Sonny-Rett and Cherisse did not follow the path provided to them. To escape their parents' resentment—as well as deepening racism throughout America—Cherisse, Sonny-Rett, and Hattie move to Paris and sever ties with family and friends in the United States. Each family blames the other for the problem, and a generations-long feud begins to smolder.

At the novel's opening, it is forty years since the trio left for Europe. Sonny-Rett and Cherisse are dead, and Hattie is the parent, friend, and guardian of their grandson, who is also called Sonny. When Sonny-Rett's brother, Edgar, a successful developer, seeks to inaugurate his neighborhood music hall with a concert honoring the memory and music of his brother, he finds Hattie and Sonny in Paris and flies them in for the event. Hattie chafes at returning, but goes for Sonny's sake. Florence and Ulene find a common interest in great-grandson Sonny, who tries in his own way to reunite the fractured families. "Jazz gives the novel its pulse, but finally this is a family drama, and Marshall beautifully evokes the myriad ways that families are torn asunder when love and power intermingle," commented Bill Ott in *Booklist*. A *Publishers Weekly* reviewer observed that "Marshall writes with verve, clarity, and humor, capturing the cadences of black speech while deftly portraying the complexity of family relationships and the social issues that beset black Americans." Similarly, Maxine E. Thompson, writing on the *BookReporter* Web site, noted that "the writing itself is subtle and quiet but exciting. Marshall has an ear for dialect, and her plots are well thought out." *New York Times* reviewer Lori Leibovich remarked that the "prose is full of expert dialogue, mellifluous rhythms, and sharply drawn portraits of Sonny-Rett's loved ones." Newson-Horst called *The Fisher King* "a national treasure as much as the musical form it employs to tell the story of the diaspora."

BIOGRAPHICAL AND CRITICAL SOURCES:

BOOKS

Black Literature Criticism, Thomson Gale (Detroit, MI), 1992.

Bruck, Peter, and Wolfgang Karrer, editors, *The Afro-American Novel since 1960*, B.R. Gruener, 1982.

Christian, Barbara, *Black Women Novelists*, Greenwood Press, 1980.

Contemporary Novelists, 7th edition, St. James Press (Detroit, MI), 2001.

Coser, Stelamaris, *Bridging the Americas: The Literature of Paule Marshall, Toni Morrison, and Gayl Jones*, Temple University Press, 1995.

DeLamotte, Eugenia G., *Places of Silence, Journeys of Freedom: The Fiction of Paule Marshall*, University of Pennsylvania Press (Philadelphia, PA), 1998.

Denniston, Dorothy Haner, *The Fiction of Paule Marshall: Reconstructions of History, Culture, and Gender*, University of Tennessee Press, 1995.

Dictionary of Literary Biography, Thomson Gale (Detroit, MI), Volume 157: *Twentieth-Century Caribbean and Black African Writers, Third Series*, 1995, Volume 227: *American Novelists since World War II, Sixth Series*, 2000.

Evans, Mari, editor, *Black Women Writers, 1950-1980*, Anchor Press, 1984.

Hathaway, Heather, *Caribbean Waves: Relocating Claude McKay and Paule Marshall*, Indiana University Press (Bloomington, IN), 1999.

Herdeck, Donald E., editor, *Caribbean Writers*, Volume 1: *Anglophone Literature from the Caribbean*, Three Continents Press, 1979.

Hine, Darlene Clark, editor, *Black Women in America*, Carlson Publishing (Brooklyn, NY), 1993.

Magill, Frank N., editor, *Great Women Writers*, Holt (New York, NY), 1994.

Mainiero, Lina, editor, *American Women Writers*, Frederick Ungar Publishing (New York, NY), 1979-1982.

Melchior, Bernhard, *"Re/Visioning" the Self away from Home: Autobiographical and Cross-cultural Dimensions in the Works of Paule Marshall*, P. Lang (New York, NY), 1998.

Morgan, Janice T., and Colette T. Hall and Carol L. Snyder, editors, *Redefining Autobiography in Twentieth-Century Women's Fiction: An Essay Collection*, Garland, 1991, pp. 135-147.

Pettis, Joyce Owens, *Toward Wholeness in Paule Marshall's Fiction*, University Press of Virginia, 1996.

Shaw, Harry B., editor, *Perspectives of Black Popular Culture*, Popular Press, 1990, pp. 93-100.

Smith, Valerie, Lea Baechler, and A. Walton Litz, editors, *African American Writers*, Scribner (New York, NY), 1991.

Sorkin, Adam J., editor, *Politics and the Muse: Studies in the Politics of Recent American Literature*, Popular Press, 1989, pp. 179-205.

Spradling, Mary Mace, editor, *In Black and White*, Thomson Gale (Detroit, MI), 1980.

Wall, Cheryl A., editor, *Changing Our Own Words: Essays on Criticism, Theory, and Writing by Black Women*, Rutgers University Press, 1989, pp. 196-211.

Washington, Mary Helen, editor, *Black-Eyed Susans/ Midnight Birds: Stories by and about Black Women*, Anchor Press (New York, NY), 1989.

PERIODICALS

Black American Literature Forum, winter, 1986; spring-summer, 1987.

Booklist, July, 2000, Bill Ott, review of *The Fisher King*, p. 2008; November 1, 2001, Nancy Spillman, review of *The Fisher King*, p. 513.

Callaloo, spring-summer, 1983; winter, 1987, pp. 79-90; winter, 1997, pp. 127-141; winter, 1999, review of *Praisesong for the Widow*, p. 208.

Chicago Tribune Book World, May 15, 1983.

Christian Science Monitor, January 22, 1970; March 23, 1984.

CLA Journal, March, 1961; September, 1972.

College Language Association Journal, September, 1995, pp. 49-61.

Critical Arts, Volume 9, number 1, 1995, pp. 21-29.

Critical Quarterly, summer, 1971.

Essence, May, 1980.

Freedomways, 1970.

Journal of American Culture, winter, 1989, pp. 53-58.

Journal of Black Studies, December, 1970.

Journal of Caribbean Studies, winter, 1989-spring, 1990, pp. 189-199.

London Review of Books, March 7, 1985.

Los Angeles Times, May 18, 1983.

Los Angeles Times Book Review, February 27, 1983.

MELUS, fall, 1995, pp. 99-120.

Ms., November, 1981.

Nation, April 2, 1983.

Negro American Literature Forum, fall, 1975.

Negro Digest, January, 1970.

New Letters, autumn, 1973.

New Yorker, September 19, 1959.

New York Herald Tribune Book Review, August 16, 1959.

New York Review of Books, April 28, 1983.

New York Times, November 8, 1969; February 1, 1983; November 26, 2000, Lori Leibovich, "Books in Brief: Fiction; Sounds Good, Feels Bad," review of *The Fisher King,* p. 21.

New York Times Book Review, November 30, 1969; January 9, 1983; February 20, 1983.

Novel, winter, 1974.

Obsidian II, winter, 1990, pp. 1-21.

Publishers Weekly, January 20, 1984, pp. 90-91; August 7, 2000, review of *The Fisher King,* p. 71.

Religion and Literature, spring, 1995, pp. 49-61.

Saturday Review, September 16, 1961.

Southern Review, winter, 1992, pp. 1-20.

Times Literary Supplement, September 16, 1983; April 5, 1985.

Village Voice, October 8, 1970; March 22, 1983; May 15, 1984.

Voice Literary Supplement, April, 1982.

Washington Post, February 17, 1984.

Washington Post Book World, January 30, 1983.

World Literature Today, summer-autumn, 2001, Adele S. Newson-Horst, review of *The Fisher King,* p. 148.

World Literature Written in English, autumn, 1985, pp. 285-298.

ONLINE

Bella Stander Home Page, http://www.bellastander. com/ (February/March, 2001), interview with Marshall.

BookReporter, http://www.bookreporter.com/ (May 28, 2003), Maxine E. Thompson, review of *The Fisher King.*

Caribbean Hall of Fame Web site, http://www.sie.edu/ ~carib/ (May 29, 2003), "Paule Marshall."

Emory University Web site, http://www.emory.edu/ (May 28, 2003), "Paule Marshall."

New York University Web site, http://www.nyu.edu/ (May 29, 2003).

Voices from the Gaps, http://voices.cla.umn.edu/ (May 28, 2003), "Paule Marshall."

Writer Online, http://www.writermag.com/ (September, 2002), "Established Writers Share Their Writing Practices."

*　　　*　　　*

MARTEL, Yann 1963-

PERSONAL: Born June 25, 1963, in Salamanca, Spain; son of Emile (a civil servant) and Nicole (a civil servant; maiden name, Perron) Martel. *Education:* Attended Trent University, 1981-84 and 1986-87; Concordia University, B.A., 1985. *Politics:* "Social politics: left wing. Economic politics: confused. Overall politics: moderately nationalist—don't want to be an American." *Hobbies and other interests:* Writing, yoga, volunteering in a palliative care unit.

ADDRESSES: Home—Montreal, Quebec, Canada. *Agent*—c/o Author Mail, Harcourt Brace and Co., 15 East 26th St., New York, NY 10010.

CAREER: Author. "Odd jobs at odd places at odd times." Has worked as library worker, tree planter, dishwasher, security guard, and parking lot attendant.

MEMBER: PEN Canada.

AWARDS, HONORS: Journey Prize for the best short story in Canada, 1991, for "The Facts behind the Helsinki Roccamatios"; National Magazine Award for best short story, 1992, for "The Time I Heard the Private Donald J. Rankin String Concerto with One Discordant Violin, by the American Composer John Morton"; story selected for 1991-92 *Pushcart Prize XVI Anthology,* Best of the Small Presses; Air Canada Award, Canadian Authors Association, 1993, for "Bright Young New Thing"; short-listed, First Novel Award, Chapters/Books in Canada, 1997, for *Self;* short-listed, Governor

General's Literary Award for fiction, 2001, Hugh MacLennan Prize for Fiction, 2001, and Booker Prize, 2002, all for *Life of Pi: A Novel.*

WRITINGS:

The Facts behind the Helsinki Roccamatios and Other Stories, Knopf Canada (Toronto, Ontario, Canada), 1993, Harcourt (New York, NY), 2004.
Self, Faber and Faber (London, England), 1996.
Life of Pi: A Novel, Knopf Canada (Toronto, Ontario, Canada), 2001; Harcourt (New York, NY), 2001.

ADAPTATIONS: Fox Studios bought film rights to Martel's novel *Life of Pi* and assigned screenwriter Dean Gorgaris to the project.

WORK IN PROGRESS: A novel about a donkey and a monkey traveling across a landscape that is actually a shirt worn during the Holocaust by a Jew.

SIDELIGHTS: Yann Martel, Canadian author of fiction, "is being hailed as a remarkable voice," wrote Rosemary Goring in the Glasgow *Herald,* "the harbinger of a fresh wave of literary invention from a nation already famous for its fiction." Following in the footsteps of Margaret Atwood, Robertson Davies, and Alice Munro, Martel has earned international repute for his fiction, in particular the award-winning 2001 title, *Life of Pi: A Novel.* Born in Spain to Canadian parents, Martel grew up and has lived all over the world, including Alaska, Costa Rica, France, Mexico, Iran, Turkey, India, and Canada. His father was a diplomat and poet from the province of Quebec, one-time winner of the Governor General's Award for poetry. Martel, who began to write after studying philosophy at college, once told *CA:* "I write because it's the only way I know how to create, and to create is to live."

Martel's short story, "The Facts behind the Helsinki Roccamatios," first appeared in the *Malahat Review* and won the 1991 Journey Prize for the best Canadian short story. Two years later, Martel published that story along with three others as *The Facts behind the Helsinki Roccamatios and Other Stories,* in a collection that dealt with the final hours of a condemned man, an AIDS patient's imaginary life, and the debut of an amazing and rather bizarre symphony. A reviewer for *Quill and Quire* felt that while the title story is a "good" tale, another of the stories collected in the book, "The Time I Heard the Private Donald J. Rankin String Concerto with One

Discordant Violin, by the American Composer John Morton," is an even "better story, and one that more clearly says, This is something new." The same reviewer further compared Martel to writers such as Paul Theroux, Bruce Chatwin, Paul Auster, and Allan Gurganus. "Martel . . . writes in a way that makes a lot of other fiction look like, well, like fiction."

In 1996, Martel published his first novel, *Self,* the fictional autobiography of a young author and traveler who suddenly finds he has changed genders. The *Quill and Quire* reviewer praised the "candid, intelligent, likable, life-embracing, protean, chatty, smug, and mischievous" narrator of that work, which views the events of thirty years through a mirthful and perceptive prism. Similarly, a contributor to the Toronto *Globe and Mail* felt that Martel "wonderfully represents the child's universe in a seamless whole," calling his novel a "penetrating, funny, original and absolutely delightful exploration."

With his 2001 novel, *Life of Pi,* Martel continued his growth as a writer in a mixture of animal tall-tale and high-seas adventure that had critics comparing him to Joseph Conrad and Salman Rushdie. The narrator, Piscine Molitor Patel, known as Pi, is now a middle-aged man living in Canada. But as a youth, he lived in the Indian city of Pondicherry where his father ran the zoo. The young boy developed an encyclopedic knowledge of animal behavior, loved stories, and learned to practice three religions: Hinduism, Christianity, and Islam. When he was sixteen, Pi's parents decided to immigrate to Canada, taking along part of the menagerie with them in a Japanese cargo ship. However, when the ship sank during a storm, there were only six survivors inhabiting a lone lifeboat on that vastness of the Pacific: Pi, a rat, a female orangutan, a zebra with a broken leg, a hyena, and a four-hundred-fifty pound Bengal tiger named Richard Parker.

Life of Pi is the recounting of the fight for survival that ensued, in which Martel, via Pi, takes the reader into the food-chain politics aboard the lifeboat. The hyena manages to devour the few flies that have been buzzing around the boat, but that does not quite stave off hunger. Thereafter the hyena makes a meal of the zebra and orangutan, in that order. The Bengal tiger then eats the hyena, and makes eyes at the young human cargo. To keep himself alive, Pi feeds the tiger the rat, but he recognizes that the only way he will be able to survive in the long term is by somehow living with the tiger. He trains Richard Parker, feeds, marks out separate territories on the boat with his urine, and comes to love the tiger. When they finally land in Mexico over two hundred days later, Pi is half blind, and the tiger runs off into the jungle. Because the authorities there do not believe Pi's fantastic tale, Pi tells a version with no animals involved, and suggests that they believe the better of the two stories.

Martel's blending of fantasy and nautical lore in *Life of Pi* prompted a reviewer for the Toronto *Globe and Mail* to note that the "whole fantastic voyage carries hints of [Ernest Hemingway's] *Old Man and the Sea* and the magic realism of [Jorge] Amado and [Gabriel Garcia] Marquez and the absurdity of [Samuel] Beckett." "Ever aware of cliches, and using them to his advantage, Pi is Martel's triumph," the same reviewer further commented. "He is understated and ironic, utterly believable and pure." Similar words of praise greeted the book's English publication around the world. "If Canadian writer Yann Martel were a preacher, he'd be charismatic, funny and convert all the nonbelievers," wrote *Nation*'s Charlotte Innes. Innes commented on the postmodernist elements of the story: "multiple narrators, a playful fairytale quality. . . , realistically presented events that may be hallucinations or simply made up," even the duplicate ending at the end of the novel and the symbolism of Pi's name, as "the irrational number with which scientists try to understand the universe." Thus the author presents his readers with a "sea of questions and confusion," yet Innes felt that Martel "makes one laugh so much, and at times feel so awed and chilled, that even thrashing around in bewilderment or disagreement one can't help but be captured by his prose." *Book*'s Paul Evans called *Life of Pi* a "work of wonder," while *Booklist*'s William Hickman called it a "strange, touching novel" that "frequently achieves something deeper than technical gimmickry." In a *Publishers Weekly* review a contributor described Martel's second novel as a "fabulous romp through an imagination by turns ecstatic, cunning, despairing, and resilient," and an "impressive achievement." The same reviewer felt that Martel "displays the clever voice and tremendous storytelling skills of an emerging master." *Los Angeles Times* reviewer Francie Lin appreciated the "lightness and humor that gives it the quality of a fairy tale," and *New York Times Book Review* contributor Gary Krist thought *Life of Pi* "could renew your faith in the ability of novelists to invest even the most outrageous scenario with plausible life."

Reception of the novel in Britain was equally positive. Novelist Margaret Atwood, writing in the London *Sunday Times*, commented, "It's fresh, original, smart, devious, and crammed with absorbing lore." Through this novel, Atwood noted, "[o]ur customary picture of life is torn apart and through the rent in the canvas we see the real world. And it's a world of wonders, and there are tigers in it." London *Times* reviewer Glyn Brown felt the story was "so magical, so playful, so harrowing and astonishing that it will make you believe imagination might be the first step [in believing in God]." Allan Massie, writing in the Edinburgh *Scotsman,* observed, "The story is engaging, Pi's resourcefulness both pleasing and amusing." Massie further noted, "What makes this novel so delightful is its light-heartedness." And for Justine Jordan, writing in the London *Guardian,* the novel was "not so much . . . an allegory or magical-realist fable, but . . . an edge-of-seat adventure." *New Internationalist* reviewer Peter Whittaker called it an "astonishingly original novel," and William Skidelsky in the *New Statesman* also praised the "compelling" storytelling.

For Jane Shilling, writing in the London *Sunday Telegraph,* however, the novel was "flawed" by what she found to be the unbalanced structure of the book, yet she still found it a "fascinating novel—though as with some jewels, the flaws are arguably part of the charm." Toby Clements also had reservations in the London *Daily Telegraph,* feeling that *Life of Pi* "never really comes alive in the emotional sense. It is more a novel of proposition and conjecture, a series of narrative questions and solutions." Yet Clements added, "Despite this, *Life of Pi* is a hilarious novel, full of clever tricks, amusing asides and grand originality."

Critical acclaim also met the Australian publication of *Life of Pi,* with Rebekah Scott noting in the Brisbane *Courier-Mail* that the novel is "strange, but it draws a gleaming confidence from its strangeness." Francesca Cann found Martel's to be an "involving narrative," in a Melbourne *Herald Sun* review, and Michelle de Krester, writing in the *Weekend Australian,* felt that "what is enchanting about this novel is not the sweep of its intellectual concerns but the intensity of its imagination. Martel is a natural."

Awards committees agreed with these reviewers, and *Life of Pi* catapulted Martel's name into the first rank of international authors, earning him a short-list position on England's prestigious Booker Prize list, as well as a similar honor on Canada's list for Governor General's Literary Award for fiction, and the 2001 Hugh MacLennan Prize for Fiction.

BIOGRAPHICAL AND CRITICAL SOURCES:

PERIODICALS

Book, July-August, 2002, Paul Evans, review of *Life of Pi: A Novel,* p. 78.

Booklist, May 15, 2002, William Hickman, review of *Life of Pi,* p. 1576.

Books in Canada, May, 1993, review of *The Facts behind the Helsinki Roccamatios and Other Stories,* p. 40; June, 1997, review of *Self,* p. 4.

Canadian Forum, June, 1993, Merna Summers, review of *The Facts behind the Helsinki Roccamatios and Other Stories,* pp. 41-42; November, 1996, Christine Hamelin, "Self and Other," pp. 43-44.

Courier-Mail (Brisbane, Australia), September 28, 2002, Rebekah Scott, "Zen and the Art of Believing the Unbelievable," review of *Life of Pi,* p. M5.

Daily Telegraph (London, England), June 1, 2002, Toby Clements, "The Tiger Who Went to Sea," review of *Life of Pi,.*

Evening Standard (London, England), September 30, 2002, Alexander Linklater, "All at Sea—The Boy and the Tiger," review of *Life of Pi,* p. 49.

Financial Times (London, England), September 25, 2002, Tony Thorncroft, "Novel Lead for Canada as Booker Begins New Chapter," review of *Life of Pi,* p. 6.

Globe and Mail (Toronto, Canada), September 8, 2001, review of *Life of Pi,* p. D6; September 22, 2001, review of *Life of Pi,* p. D13; November 24, 2001, review of *Life of Pi,* p. D14.

Guardian (London, England), May 25, 2002, Justine Jordan, "Animal Magnetism," review of *Life of Pi,* p. 10.

Harper's, June, 2002, Pico Iyer, "The Last Refuge: The Promise of New Canadian Fiction," review of *Life of Pi,* pp. 77-80.

Herald (Glasgow, Scotland), June 1, 2002, Rosemary Goring, "Life Is a Voyage with This Star Sailor," review of *Life of Pi,* p. 14.

Herald Sun (Melbourne, Australia), August 10, 2002, Francesca Cann, "Pi Charts His Destiny," review of *Life of Pi,* p. W30.

Independent (London, England), June 22, 2002, Judith Palmer, "The Tiger's Tale," review of *Life of Pi,* p. 26; September 25, 2002, Boyd Tonkin, "The Finalists by Boyd Tonkin, Literary Editor," p. 5.

Independent Sunday (London, England), July 7, 2002, Robin Buss, "Adrift on the Open Sea, with Only a Tiger for Company," review of *Life of Pi,* p. 14.

Kirkus Reviews, May 1, 2002, review of *Life of Pi,* p. 613.

Knight Ridder/Tribune News Service, June 5, 2002, Charles Matthews, review of *Life of Pi,* p. K146.

Library Journal, June 15, 2002, Edward Come, review of *Life of Pi,* p. 95.

Los Angeles Times, June 16, 2002, Francie Lin, "Floating on Faith," review of *Life of Pi,* p. BR7.

Nation, August 19, 2002, Charlotte Innes, "Robinson Crusoe, Move Over," review of *Life of Pi,* pp. 25-28.

New Internationalist, August, 2002, Peter Whittaker, review of *Life of Pi,* p. 33.

New Statesman, July 29, 2002, William Skidelsky, "Novel Thoughts," p. 39.

New Yorker, August 5, 2002, review of *Life of Pi,* p. 77.

New York Times Book Review, July 7, 2002, Gary Krist, "Taming the Tiger," review of *Life of Pi,* p. 5.

Observer (London, England), May 23, 1993, review of *The Facts behind the Helsinki Roccamatios and Other Stories,* p. 71; May 26, 2002, Tim Adams, review of *Life of Pi,* p. 15.

Publishers Weekly, April 8, 2002, review of *Life of Pi,* p. 200.

Quill and Quire, April, 1993, review of *The Facts behind the Helsinki Roccamatios and Other Stories,* p. 22; April, 1996, review of *Self,* pp. 1, 28; August, 2001, review of *Life of Pi,* p. 22.

San Francisco Chronicle, September 25, 2002, "Six Finalists for Man Booker Prize," p. D2.

Scotland on Sunday (Edinburgh, Scotland), May 12, 2002, Michel Faber, review of *Life of Pi,* p. 5; August 4, 2002, Jackie McGlone, "*Life of Pi:* Animal, Vegetable, or Mineral?," p. 9; September 29, 2002, Alex Massie, "Byng's Formula Means Knowing the Value of Pi," p. 5.

Scotsman (Edinburgh, Scotland), May 11, 2002, Allan Massie, review of *Life of Pi,* p. 9.

Seattle Times (Seattle, WA), June 16, 2002, David Flood, "*Life of Pi* Is Exhilarating Castaway Tale," p. K9.

Spectator, May 18, 2002, Francis King, "Ghastly Crew," review of *Life of Pi,* p. 43.

Sunday Herald (Glasgow, Scotland), May 12, 2002, Colin Waters, "One Man and His Boat," review of *Life of Pi,* p. 9.

Sunday Telegraph (London, England), May 19, 2002, Jane Shilling, "Desert Island Zoo," review of *Life of Pi,* p. 19.

Sunday Times (London, England), Margaret Atwood, "A Tasty Slice of Pi and Ships," review of *Life of Pi,* p. 44.

Times (London, England), May 11, 2002, Glyn Brown, "Keeping the Faith," review of *Life of Pi,* p. 13.

Times Educational Supplement, December 13, 1996, review of *Self,* p. 33.

Times Literary Supplement, May 27, 1994, review of *The Facts behind the Helsinki Roccamatios and Other Stories,* p. 21; November 22, 1996, Julian Ferraro, "Male-Female Experiences," p. 24; July 19, 2002, Roz Kaveney, "Guess Who's for Dinner?," review of *Life of Pi,* p. 25.

Weekend Australian (Sydney, Australia), August 24, 2002, Michelle de Krester, review of *Life of Pi,* p. R10.

ONLINE

Random House Web site, http://www.randomhouse.ca/
(July 16, 2002), "Yann Martel."

*   *   *

MARTIN, Webber
    See SILVERBERG, Robert

*   *   *

MASON, Bobbie Ann 1940-

PERSONAL: Born May 1, 1940, in Mayfield, KY;
daughter of Wilburn A. (a dairy farmer) and Christianna
(Lee) Mason; married Roger B. Rawlings (a magazine
editor and writer), April 12, 1969. *Education:* University of Kentucky, B.A., 1962; State University of New
York at Binghamton, M.A., 1966; University of Connecticut, Ph.D., 1972.

ADDRESSES: Home—Lawrenceburg, KY. *Office*—
University of Kentucky, Department of English, 1255
Patterson Office Tower 0027, Lexington, KY 40506.
Agent—Amanda Urban, International Creative Manage-
ment, 40 West 57th St., New York, NY 10019. *E-mail*—
bamaso2@uky.edu.

CAREER: Writer. Mansfield State College, Mansfield,
PA, assistant professor of English, 1972-79; University
of Kentucky, Lexington, visiting writer-in-residence.
Mayfield Messenger, Mayfield, KY, writer, 1960; Ideal
Publishing Co., New York, NY, writer for magazines,
including *Movie Stars, Movie Life,* and *T.V. Star Parade,* 1962-63.

AWARDS, HONORS: National Book Critics Circle
Award nomination, American Book Award nomination,
PEN-Faulkner Award for fiction nomination and Ernest
Hemingway Foundation Award, all 1983, all for *Shiloh
and Other Stories;* National Endowment for the Arts
fellowship, 1983; Pennsylvania Arts Council grant,
1983; Guggenheim fellowship, 1984; American Academy and Institute of Arts and Letters Award, 1984; National Book Critics Circle Award nomination and
Southern Book Award, both 1994, both for *Feather
Crowns;* Pulitzer Prize for biography or autobiography
nomination, 2000, for *Clear Springs: A Memoir;* Southern Book Award for fiction, Southern Book Critics
Circle, both 2002, both for *Zigzagging down a Wild
Trail.*

WRITINGS:

Nabokov's Garden: A Guide to "Ada," Ardis (Ann Ar-
bor, MI), 1974.
*The Girl Sleuth: A Feminist Guide to the Bobbsey
Twins, Nancy Drew, and Their Sisters,* Feminist
Press (Old Westbury, NY), 1975.
Shiloh and Other Stories, Harper (New York, NY),
1982.
In Country (novel), Harper (New York, NY), 1985.
Spence + Lila (novel), Harper (New York, NY), 1988.
Love Life: Stories, Harper (New York, NY), 1989.
Feather Crowns (novel), Harper (New York, NY),
1993.
*Midnight Magic: Selected Stories of Bobbie Ann Ma-
son,* Ecco Press (Hopewell, NJ), 1998.
Clear Springs: A Memoir, Random House (New York,
NY), 1999.
Zigzagging down a Wild Trail (short stories), Random
House (New York, NY), 2001.
Elvis Presley (nonfiction), Penguin, (New York, NY),
2003.

Contributor of short stories to anthologies, including
Best American Short Stories, 1981 and 1983, *The Pushcart Prize,* 1983 and 1996, and *The O. Henry Awards,*
1986 and 1988. Contributor to numerous magazines, including *New Yorker, Atlantic,* and *Mother Jones;* frequent contributor to "The Talk of the Town" column,
New Yorker.

ADAPTATIONS: In Country was filmed by Warner
Brothers and directed by Norman Jewison in 1989.

SIDELIGHTS: The people and terrain of rural western
Kentucky figure prominently in the fiction of Bobbie
Ann Mason, a highly regarded novelist and short story
writer. Herself a native Kentuckian, Mason has
chronicled the changes wrought in her region by the introduction of such phenomena as television, shopping
malls, popular music, and fast-food restaurants. Her
characters often stand perplexed at the junction between
traditionalism and modernity, between permanence and
transience, between their own deep-seated need for individual expression and their obligations to family and
home. As Meredith Sue Willis noted in *Washington
Post Book World,* Mason "has a reputation as a regional
writer, but what she is really writing about is the numerous Americans whose dreams and goals have been
uplifted and distorted by popular culture." According to
David Quammen in *New York Times Book Review,*
"Loss and deprivation, the disappointment of patheti-

cally modest hopes, are the themes Bobbie Ann Mason works and reworks. She portrays the disquieted lives of men and women not blessed with much money or education or luck, but cursed with enough sensitivity and imagination to suffer regrets." Mason has also written the autobiographical *Clear Springs: A Memoir,* which was a finalist for the Pulitzer Prize, and a short biography, *Elvis Presley.*

Mason's first volume of fiction, *Shiloh and Other Stories,* established her reputation as a rising voice in southern literature. Novelist Anne Tyler, for one, hailed her in *New Republic* as "a full-fledged master of the short story." Most of the sixteen works in *Shiloh* originally appeared in *New Yorker, Atlantic,* or other national magazines, a fact surprising to several critics who, like Anatole Broyard in *New York Times Book Review,* labeled Mason's work "a regional literature that describes people and places almost unimaginably different from ourselves and the big cities in which we live." Explained Quammen: "Miss Mason writes almost exclusively about working-class and farm people coping with their muted frustrations in western Kentucky (south of Paducah, not far from Kentucky Lake, if that helps you), and the gap to be bridged empathically between her readership and her characters [is] therefore formidable. But formidable also is Miss Mason's talent, and her craftsmanship."

In an interview published in *Contemporary Literature,* Mason commented upon the fact that she seems to be read by an audience quite different from one in which her characters might find themselves. "I don't think I write fiction that's for a select group," she said. "I'm not sure a lot of people [in rural Kentucky] read my work. . . . I think a lot of people wouldn't *want* to read my work because they might find it too close to their lives. They're not interested in reading something that familiar; it would make them uncomfortable."

Most critics have attributed Mason's success to her vivid evocation of a region's physical and social geography. "As often as not," Gene Lyons reported in *Newsweek,* the author describes "a matter of town—paved roads, indoor plumbing, and above all, TV—having come to the boondocks with the force of an unannounced social revolution." In a similar vein, Emma Cobb commented in *Contemporary Southern Writers* that "along with giving voice to characters in language that reflects their backgrounds, Mason's work is important as a chronicle of the changing physical landscape of the contemporary South. Brand names and popular culture references infiltrate her characters' vocabularies

as strip-malling, chain-store spreading, and convenience-promising change sweeps into previously isolated regions. Characters try to make their way amid the changes . . . often unsure of how to proceed and struggling to articulate their feelings." While the language of Mason's characters reflects their rural background, her people do not fit the Hollywood stereotype of backwoods "hillbillies" content to let the rest of the world pass by. Tyler noted that they have "an earnest faith in progress; they are as quick to absorb new brand names as foreigners trying to learn the language of a strange country they've found themselves in." "It is especially poignant," she added, "that the characters are trying to deal with changes most of us already take for granted." Mason's Kentucky is a world in transition, with the old South fast becoming the new.

Mason often explores intensely personal events that lead to the acceptance of something new or the rejection—or loss—of something old. These adjustments in the characters' lives reflect a general uneasiness that pervades the cultural landscape; the forces of change and alienation are no less frightening because they are universal or unavoidable. The characters in Mason's fiction are caught between isolation and transience, and this struggle is reflected in their relationships, which are often emotionally and intellectually distant.

As a result, wrote *Time* critic R.Z. Sheppard, "Mason has an unwavering bead on the relationship between instincts and individual longings. Her women have ambitions but never get too far from the nest; her men have domestic moments but spend a lot of time on wheels." Mason's characters "exist in a psychological rather than a physical environment," Broyard similarly contended, "one that has been gutted—like an abandoned building—by the movement of American life. They fall between categories, occupy a place between nostalgia and apprehension. They live, without history or politics, a life more like a linoleum than a tapestry."

Other critics, while noting Mason's ability to evoke psychological states, have emphasized her skill at depicting the material details of her "linoleum" world. Tyler pointed out that readers know precisely what dishes constitute the characters' meals, what clothes hang in their closets, and what craft projects fill their spare time. Mason intones the brand names that are infiltrating her characters' vocabularies, and the exact titles of soap operas and popular songs provide an aural backdrop for the fiction's emotional dramas. Her characters' voices, according to Tyler, "ring through our living rooms." *Dictionary of Literary Biography* contributor John D. Kalb noted that "Mason is among the first to use seriously the so-called low art of popular culture as an important underpinning to her literature and the lives of her characters. While she portrays the encroaching impact of urban America on her rural occupants . . . she usually does so not as a criticism but as a means of providing an accurate and realistic depiction of the people within their changing environments. Her inclusion of these popular elements enhances the sense of meeting real people engaged in their everyday lives."

In her first novel, *In Country,* "Mason returns to this same geographical and spiritual milieu" as her short fiction, noted *New York Times* critic Michiko Kakutani, "and she returns, too, to her earlier themes: the dislocations wrought on ordinary, blue-collar lives by recent history—in this case, recent history in the form of the Vietnam War." Seventeen-year-old Samantha Hughes doesn't remember the war, but it has profoundly affected her life: her father died in Vietnam and her uncle Emmett, with whom she lives, still bears the emotional and physical scars of his service. In the summer after her high school graduation, Sam struggles to understand the war and learn about her father. "Ten years after the end of the Vietnam War," summarized Richard Eder in *Los Angeles Times Book Review,* "in the most prosaic and magical way possible, she stubbornly undertakes the exorcism of a ghost that almost everything in our everyday life manages to bury." In the novel Mason demonstrates the same concern for particulars that distinguishes her short fiction, as *Christian Science Monitor* contributor Marilyn Gardner observed: "She displays an ear perfectly tuned to dialogue, an eye that catches every telling detail and quirky mannerism. Tiny, seemingly insignificant observations and revelations accumulate almost unnoticed until something trips them, turning them into literary grenades explosive with meaning."

Detroit Free Press writer Suzanne Yeager similarly believed that the author's details contribute to the authenticity of the novel. "Mason's narrative is so extraordinarily rich with the sounds, smells and colors of daily life in the '80s that Sam and her family and friends take on an almost eerie reality." As a result, the critic added, *In Country* "becomes less a novel and more a diary of the unspoken observations of ordinary America." Jonathan Yardley, however, faulted the novel for the "dreary familiarity" of its Vietnam themes. Writing in *Washington Post Book World,* he asserted that Mason "has failed to transform these essentially political questions into the stuff of fiction; none of her characters come to life, the novel's structure is awkward and its

narrative herky-jerky, her prose wavers uncertainly between adult and teenaged voices." But other critics found Mason's work successful; *Chicago Tribune Book World* contributor Bruce Allen, for instance, said that the novel's "real triumph . . . is Mason's deep and honest portrayal of her two protagonists," especially Sam. "More than any other character in our recent fiction," the critic continued, Sam "is a real person who grows more and more real the better we come to know her—and the novel that affords us the opportunity to is, clearly, the year's most gratifying reading experience." "[Mason's] first novel, although it lacks the page-by-page abundance of her best stories," concluded Joel Conarroe in *New York Times Book Review,* "is an exceptional achievement, at once humane, comic and moving."

Mason once commented that she had been most rewarded by the reaction real Vietnam veterans had to *In Country.* "It's been personally very gratifying to hear from them, to know that they took the trouble to write to me and tell me that the book meant something to them," she said. "Most of the Vietnam vets who wrote me didn't write at length; they just seemed to say thank you. It was very moving to hear from those people."

In *Spence + Lila,* Mason's second novel, Spence and Lila are a Kentucky farm couple who have been married for over forty years. Lila's upcoming surgery is forcing them to face the prospect of being separated for the first time since World War II. Also, as in her other work, Mason looks at the changes in the larger environment as well as those in her characters' lives—as Kalb put it, "the changes of attitudes and values in the modern world that has intruded in [an] isolated haven." "The chapters alternate between Spence's and Lila's point of view, and such resonances [in their thoughts] range freely through the past and present," described *Los Angeles Times Book Review* contributor Nancy Mairs. Despite the potential for sentimentality in the story, Mason "manages to avoid the gooey and patronizing muck that is usually described as heartwarming," remarked a *Time* reviewer. "Her account is funny and deft, with plenty of gristle." Likewise, in Kalb's opinion, "*Spence + Lila* is a novel about real love—not saccharine-sweet sentimentality, but the well-aged version of love between two people who have shared a long, sometimes difficult and trying, life together."

Newsweek writer Peter S. Prescott, however, found *Spence + Lila* a "gently tedious" book saved only by Mason's skillful writing. But Kakutani, although acknowledging that the book "suffers from a melodramatic predictability absent from Ms. Mason's earlier works," thought that the author treated her subject "without ever becoming sentimental or cliched." The critic went on to praise Mason's "lean stripped-down language" and "nearly pitch-perfect ear for the way her characters speak," and added, "Mainly, however, it's her sure-handed ability to evoke Spence and Lila's life together that lends their story such poignance and authenticity." *New York Times Book Review* contributor Frank Conroy likewise commended Mason's dialogue, but admitted that "one wishes she had risked a bit more in this book, taking us under the surface of things instead of lingering there so lovingly and relentlessly." "Awkward silence in the face of ideas and feelings is a common frailty," elaborated Mairs, "but it represents a limitation in *Spence + Lila,* constraining Mason to rush her story and keep to its surface. . . . If I perceive any defect in *Spence + Lila,*" the critic continued, "it's that this is a short novel which could well have been long." "As soon as [Mason's] characters open their mouths, they come to life and move to center stage," McCorkle similarly concluded. "If there is a weakness it would be the reader's desire to prolong their talk and actions before moving to an ending that is both touching and satisfying."

Despite the author's success with *In Country* and *Spence + Lila,* "Mason's strongest form may be neither the novel nor the story, but the story *collection,*" Lorrie Moore maintained in her *New York Times Book Review* assessment of *Love Life: Stories.* "It is there, picking up her pen every twenty pages to start anew, gathering layers through echo and overlap, that Ms. Mason depicts most richly a community of contemporary lives." While Kakutani remarked that "few of Ms. Mason's characters ever resolve their dilemmas—or if they do, their decisions take place . . . beyond the knowledge of the reader," she asserted that the stories "are not simply minimalist 'slice-of-life' exercises, but finely crafted tales that manage to invest inarticulate, small-town lives with dignity and intimations of meaning." Mason's "stories work like parables, small in scale and very wise, tales wistfully told by a masterful stylist whose voice rises purely from the heart of the country," stated Judith Freeman in *Los Angeles Times Book Review.*

Reference Guide to Short Fiction contributor Laurie Clancy opined that this collection and *Shiloh* have shown Mason to be "a regional writer par excellence;" however, she cautioned, "the best of Mason's work has a gritty authenticity and dry humor, but at times the monotony and limitations of the figures she writes about seep into the prose as well." Mason, she observed, offers "little or no analysis of the characters' inner con-

sciousness," and *New York Times Book Review* critic Michael Gorra remarked on this as well, in his review of *Midnight Magic: Selected Stories of Bobbie Ann Mason,* which republished several stories from *Shiloh* and *Love Life.* This collection, he contended, "demonstrates . . . Mason's narrow range—narrow in terms of the characters and situations on which she draws; narrow too in her reliance on a tight and impersonal third-person voice. . . . I admire Bobbie Ann Mason's craft, her precise eye, the vivid dialogue that stops just short of turning down the road toward local color. But after reading so much of her uninflected prose, I can't help longing for something a bit more full throated."

Mason's third novel marked a departure from her tendency to set her fiction in present times. *Feather Crowns* is set in turn-of-the-century Kentucky and tells the story of a farm wife named Christianna Wheeler who gives birth to quintuplets. Overnight the modest Wheeler tobacco farm becomes a mecca for the curious of every stripe as people flock to see—and hold—the tiny babies. As events unfold, Christie and her husband find themselves drawn away from home as a literal carnival sideshow attraction. The book is a meditation upon fame, self-determination, and the conflict between superstition and science. *New York Times Book Review* correspondent Jill McCorkle noted that in *Feather Crowns,* "Mason's attention to the microscopic detail of everyday life is, as always, riveting. . . . Along with the authentically colorful, often humorous dialogue, there are wonderful descriptions of churning and nursing and chopping dark-fire tobacco. And always there are subtle reminders of life's fragility, our uncertainty about what lies ahead." McCorkle concluded: "Thematically, *Feather Crowns* is a rich extension of Ms. Mason's other works. . . . The life of Christianna Wheeler and her babies is memorable and complete."

Mason told *San Francisco Review of Books* that, far from being a diversion for her, *Feather Crowns* represented a new way of looking at her Kentucky culture, filtered through her grandmother's generation. "Right now it's hard to know what's going on in America and where we're all going," she said. "It's gotten so complex, with so many people and our constant awareness of everybody globally, that it's bewildering. I think there must always be stages in history when we feel this way, but in order to get our bearings today we have to go back and get a clearer sense of where we came from and what formed us. To remember what is important. I think basically that is Christie's quest in the book. . . . It's about being faced with a bewildering set of circumstances. She tries to make sense of all of it and tries to rise above it and be herself, a survivor. I think that's also the challenge for us in this part of the twentieth century."

Women's Review of Books critic Michele Clark declared that in *Feather Crowns* Mason successfully depicts a moment of epiphany for its central character. "Christie Wheeler becomes empowered through her capacity to ask questions and her ability to experience each moment of daily life to its fullest," the critic stated. "And this long, satisfying novel offers readers who are willing to slow down the same chance to see ordinary life anew." In *Los Angeles Times Book Review,* Lisa Alther called *Feather Crowns* "a brilliantly sustained and grimly humorous parable about fame in 20th-century America," adding: "Mason's stunning morality tale about the process by which . . . degradation can overtake innocent people who simply need cash or long for some excitement is extremely illuminating—and especially for anyone alive today who has ever pondered the ravages of our modern publicity juggernaut."

Having used her rural Kentucky background in fiction, Mason explored it autobiographically in *Clear Springs: A Memoir.* "She uses this memoir of growing up in the 1950s to provide a tantalizing glimpse into the origins of her fiction," noted Josephine Humphreys in *New York Times Book Review.* "And in the process of taking a close look at her own beginnings, Mason gets to the heart of a whole generation—those of us born, roughly speaking, between Pearl Harbor and television. Behind us lay an old way, unchanged (we thought) for centuries; springing up before us was a world no one had predicted or imagined." Mason makes clear that the changes in her world—something she has explored so extensively in her fiction—are neither totally positive nor completely negative, as the old days were not idyllic. She observes that on their farm, her family had "independence, stability, authenticity . . . along with mind-numbing, backbreaking labor and crippling social isolation." Commented Humphreys: "Because Bobbie Ann Mason's language is spare and her eye unsparing, she's able to handle matters that ordinarily invite sentimentality or romanticism. She can write the hard truth about home, love, loss and the terrifying passage of time." Still, remarked a *Publishers Weekly* reviewer, Mason makes the book "a loving embrace" of her roots and "a richly textured portrait of a rapidly disappearing way of life."

Mason once told Mervyn Rothstein in *New York Times:* "I basically consider myself an exile. . . . And I have been one for years. And that's what gives me the distance to look back to where I'm from and to be able to write about it with some kind of perceptiveness. . . . It seems to me that an exile has a rather peculiar sensibility—you're straddling a fence and you don't know which side you belong on." But Mason would later return to Kentucky, to live near Lexington. She has also returned to the University of Kentucky, where she was once a student, to become a writer-in-residence. When Mason published her next collection of short stories, *Zigzagging down a Wild Trail,* it also evidenced a change, with several of the eleven stories taking place outside of small-town Kentucky.

The collection earned commendations from reviewers for providing the sharp observations and precise detail that Mason is best known for. In *Atlantic Monthly,* Bill Broun noted that "Mason almost zigzags out of her depth" in the few stories that strayed into unfamiliar thematic or geographic territory. Writing for *Library Journal,* Ann H. Fisher said the collection "reflects the sadder, wiser perspective of midlife" and concluded, "Only the kindest complaint applies: the stories end too soon." In a review for *New York Times Book Review,* Walter Kirn was convinced that Mason had rescued the minimalist short story form from oblivion. Kirn felt that Mason's new stories responded to old criticisms that her work was marred by "detachment and simplemindedness." He explained, "Mason's people may still watch too much TV, drink too much beer and love too indiscriminately, but their limitations pain them. . . . they feel the pressures of the wider world and sense both its opportunities and perils."

As part of a series published by Penguin, Mason was asked to write a brief biography about the legendary singer Elvis Presley. In *Elvis Presley* Mason shows a special understanding of her subject, having grown up in roughly the same time and place as the singer, and having listened to him throughout his entire career. The biography includes familiar stories as well as the author's observations on topics including southern foods, the hiring of Colonel Tom Parker as Presley's manager because of his familiar horse-trading style, and the singer's struggle to be both a poor boy from Tupelo, Mississippi, and "the King" of rock and roll.

The biography was described by some reviewers as a good introduction for readers who were unfamiliar with the vast body of writings on the subject. Others judged that such a short biography failed to add to their understanding of Presley. In *New York Times Book Review,* Eric P. Nash said the book was filled with "twice-told tales" and that it "does not account for the meaning of [Presley's] music or why a quarter-century after his death he remains a larger-than-life figure." Often, however, reviewers welcomed Mason's insight on Elvis Presley. Ellen Emry Heltzel wrote in *Atlanta Journal-Constitution* that Mason had done "a superb job of honing pertinent facts into a plausible, well-told story." The idea that Presley had been "raised high in Highbrowland" interested *Los Angeles Times* writer Elaine Dundy, who reflected that Mason "knows firsthand how it felt to be a fan in hot-blooded youth; how it feels to be a fan for more than four decades."

BIOGRAPHICAL AND CRITICAL SOURCES:

BOOKS

Authors and Artists for Young Adults, Volume 5, Thomson Gale (Detroit, MI), 1989.
Contemporary Literary Criticism, Thomson Gale (Detroit, MI), Volume 28, 1984, Volume 43, 1987, Volume 82, 1994.
Contemporary Southern Writers, St. James Press (Detroit, MI), 1999.
Dictionary of Literary Biography, Volume 173: *American Novelists since World War II, Fifth Series,* Thomson Gale (Detroit, MI), 1996.
Dictionary of Literary Biography Yearbook: 1987, Thomson Gale (Detroit, MI), 1988.
Prenshaw, Peggy Whitman, editor, *Women Writers of the South,* University Press of Mississippi (Jackson, MS), 1984.
Reference Guide to Short Fiction, 2nd edition, St. James Press (Detroit, MI), 1999.
Short Story Criticism, Volume 4, Thomson Gale (Detroit, MI), 1990.
Wilhelm, Albert, *Bobbie Ann Mason: A Study of the Short Fiction,* Twayne, 1998.

PERIODICALS

Atlanta Journal-Constitution, January 24, 2003, Ellen Emry Heltzel, review of *Elvis Presley,* p. E1.
Atlantic Monthly, October, 2001, Bill Broun, review of *Zigzagging down A Wild Trail,* p. 130.
Chicago Tribune Book World, September 1, 1985, Bruce Allen, review of *In Country.*
Christian Science Monitor, September 6, 1985, Marilyn Gardner, review of *In Country.*
Contemporary Literature, winter, 1991, Bonnie Lyons, interview with Bobbie Ann Mason, pp. 449-470.
Detroit Free Press, October 13, 1985, Suzanne Yeager, review of *In Country.*

Library Journal June 1, 2001, Ann H. Fisher, review of *Zigzagging down a Wild Trail,* p. 220.
Los Angeles Times Book Review, September 22, 1985, Richard Eder, review of *In Country,* p. 3; June 19, 1988, Nancy Mairs, "A Well-Seasoned Love," p. 6; March 19, 1989, Judith Freeman, "Country Parables," review of *Love Life: Stories,* p. 1; October 24, 1993, Lisa Alther, "Fame and Misfortune," pp. 2, 8; January 26, 2003, Elaine Dundy, "The Rich but Unhappy Life of a King," review of *Elvis Presley,* p. R8.
Nation, January 18, 1986, Mona Molarsky, review of *In Country,* p. 242.
New Republic, November 1, 1982, Anne Tyler, "Kentucky Cameos," p. 36.
Newsweek, November 15, 1982, Gene Lyons, review of *Shiloh and Other Stories,* p. 107; August 1, 1988, Peter S. Prescott, "Bored and Bred in Kentucky," p. 53.
New York Review of Books, November 7, 1985, Diane Johnson, review of *In Country,* p. 15.
New York Times, September 4, 1985, Michiko Kakutani, review of *In Country,* p. 23; May 15, 1988, Mervyn Rothstein, "Homegrown Fiction," p. 50; June 11, 1988, Michiko Kakutani, "Struggle and Hope in the New South," p. 13; March 3, 1989, Michiko Kakutani, review of *Love Life,* p. B4.
New York Times Book Review, November 21, 1982, David Quammen, review of *Shiloh and Other Stories,* p. 7; December 19, 1982, Anatole Broyard, "Country Fiction," p. 31; September 15, 1985, Joel Conarroe, review of *In Country,* p. 7; June 26, 1988, Frank Conroy, review of *Spence + Lila,* p. 7; March 12, 1989, Lorrie Moore, "What L'il Abner Said," review of *Love Life,* p. 7; September 26, 1993, Jill McCorkle, "Her Sensational Babies," review of *Feather Crowns,* p. 7; August 9, 1998, Michael Gorra, "The New New South," review of *Midnight Magic,* p. 7; May 30, 1999, Josephine Humphreys, "Her Old Kentucky Home," review of *Clear Springs: A Memoir,* p. 5; August 19, 2001, Walter Kirn, review of *Zigzagging down a Wild Trail,* p. 9; March 2, 2003, Eric P. Nash, review of *Elvis Presley,* p. 24.
Publishers Weekly, August 30, 1985, Wendy Smith, interview with Bobbie Ann Mason, p. 424; March 15, 1999, review of *Clear Springs,* p. 34; June 25, 2001, review of *Zigzagging down a Wild Trail,* p. 43.
San Francisco Review of Books, February-March, 1994, pp. 12-13.
Time, January 3, 1983, R.Z. Sheppard, review of *Shiloh and Other Stories,* p. 88; September 16, 1985, Paul Gray, review of *In Country,* p. 81; July 4, 1988, review of *Spence + Lila,* p. 71.

Tribune Books (Chicago, IL), June 26, 1988, Michael Dorris, "Bonds of Love: Bobbie Ann Mason's Chronicle of Family Crisis Adds Up to an Affirmation of Life," p. 6; February 19, 1989, Jack Fuller, "Bobbie Ann Mason Sees Reality on Sale at Kmart," p. 1.

Washington Post Book World, September 8, 1985, Jonathan Yardley, review of *In Country;* March 26, 1989, Meredith Sue Willis, "Stories with a Sense of Place," p. 11.

Women's Review of Books, March, 1994, Michele Clark, review of *Feather Crowns,* p. 19.

*   *   *

MASON, Ernst
    See POHL, Frederik

*   *   *

MASS, William
    See GIBSON, William

*   *   *

MASSIE, Robert K. 1929-
    (Robert Kinloch Massie)

PERSONAL: Born January 5, 1929, in Lexington, KY; son of Robert Kinloch and Mary (Kimball) Massie; married Suzanne Rohrbach (a writer), December 18, 1954 (divorced, 1990); married Deborah L. Karl, 1992; children: (first marriage) Robert Kinloch, Susanna, Elizabeth; (second marriage) Christopher. *Education:* Yale University, B.A., 1950; Oxford University, B.A. (Rhodes scholar), 1952. *Hobbies and other interests:* Sailing.

ADDRESSES: Home—60 West Clinton Avenue, Irvington, NY 10533.

CAREER: Collier's, New York, NY, reporter, 1955-56; *Newsweek,* New York, NY, writer and correspondent, 1956-62; *USA-1,* New York, NY, writer, 1962; *Saturday Evening Post,* New York, NY, writer, 1962-65; freelance writer, 1965—. Princeton University, Ferris Professor of Journalism, 1977, 1985; Tulane University, Mellon Professor of Humanities, 1981. *Military service:* U.S. Naval Reserves, 1952-55; became lieutenant, junior grade.

MEMBER: Authors Guild (vice president, 1985-87, president, beginning 1987), Authors League of America, PEN, Society of American Historians.

AWARDS, HONORS: Christopher Award, 1976, for *Journey;* American Book Award nomination, American Library Association Notable Book citation, and Pulitzer Prize for Biography, all 1981, all for *Peter the Great: His Life and World.*

WRITINGS:

Nicholas and Alexandra (biography), Atheneum (New York, NY), 1967, reprinted, Ballantine Books (New York, NY), 2000.

(With Suzanne Massie) *Journey,* Knopf (New York, NY), 1975.

Peter the Great: His Life and World, Knopf (New York, NY), 1980.

(Author of introduction) Jeffrey Finestone, *The Last Courts of Europe: A Royal Family Album, 1860-1914,* Dent (London, England), 1981, Crown (New York, NY), 1983.

Dreadnought: Britain, Germany, and the Coming of the Great War, Random House (New York, NY), 1991.

The Romanovs: The Final Chapter, Random House (New York, NY), 1995.

Castles of Steel: Britain, Germany, and the Winning of the Great War at Sea, Random House (New York, NY), 2003.

Massie's works have been translated into Spanish and German.

ADAPTATIONS: Nicholas and Alexandra was adapted into a motion picture by James Goldman and Edward Bond and released by Columbia, 1971; *Peter the Great* was adapted for television as a four-part miniseries for National Broadcasting Company, Inc. (NBC), 1986, and has been recorded as an audiobook by Books on Tape.

SIDELIGHTS: A journalist turned historian, Robert K. Massie is the author of the acclaimed works *Peter the Great: His Life and World, Dreadnought: Britain, Germany, and the Coming of the Great War,* and *Nicholas and Alexandra.* As *Booklist* critic Brendan Driscoll noted of Massie in a review of the author's *Castles of Steel: Britain, Germany, and the Winning of the Great War at Sea,* Massies's major gift is a talent for creating "narrative histories so engaging that readers, losing themselves in the romance-novel story style, forget that they're reading nearly 1,000 pages of nonfiction."

Massie worked as a journalist for ten years before the circumstances of his personal life led him to the serious examination of Russian history. Soon after joining *Newsweek* as a book reviewer, Massie and his wife Suzanne discovered that their six-month-old son Bobbie suffered from hemophilia, a hereditary and incurable blood disease. Investigating his son's condition led Massie to spend many hours in the New York Public Library where he became caught up in the story of Alexei Romanov, heir of the last ruling family of Russia, who had been stricken with hemophilia through his mother, the Empress Alexandra. Familiarity with the devastating effects resulting from such a family tragedy prompted Massie to study the short, tragic reign of Alexei's father, Czar Nicholas II, from a unique perspective. Massie once commented: "When something unusual happens in your life, you are curious to see what has happened before. We were busy trying to find out how to deal with this disease, talking to a lot of other families, to doctors and social workers and people like that about hemophilia in mid-twentieth-century America. But I knew a bit of the story of the Tsarevich Alexis and I was curious to find out how his family had dealt with it, what was all this business about hypnotism and so forth."

Massie said he had no thoughts of writing a book: He was simply curious to find out what eventuated. While reading all he could find about the family, he began to notice discrepancies between accounts. "The general narrative historians swept pretty quickly by this whole business of the boy's illness with a sentence or two. I found that it was much more complicated than that. The links that even I could find, with very little background in the field, between the illness and what was happening politically were very much in evidence and were important," he commented. *Nicholas and Alexandra* was published ten years later to much critical acclaim. Robert Payne praised the book in the *New York Times Book Review:* "Massie's canvas is the whole of Russia, the Czar and Czarina merely the focal points. . . . What emerges is a study in depth of the reign of Nicholas, and for perhaps the first time we meet the actors in the drama face to face in their proper setting." The profits from *Nicholas and Alexandra,* along with royalties from the film that would later be based upon it, provided Massie with sufficient funds to help his son cope with life as a hemophiliac.

In 1975, Massie and his wife coauthored *Journey,* chronicling their young son's courage in facing his con-

dition and describing how the disease affected their own lives as parents. "The substance of the book shifts from the mastery of pain to the mastery of life, and it is done in part by a turning outward in contrast to the Romanovs' [*Nicholas and Alexandra*] secretiveness and withdrawal," commented *New York Times Book Review* critic Elizabeth Hegeman. *Journey* contains a harsh indictment of America's "pitifully inadequate health plans, the workings of hospitals and the politics of the Red Cross which, charged the Massies, places the welfare of drug companies above that of hemophilia victims," according to *Newsweek* reviewer Margo Jefferson. Hegeman echoed the authors' frustration in describing "the grotesque folly of trying to raise enough money for the Hemophilia Society through charity balls and premieres and the inadequacy of the 'patchwork' of uncoordinated charities and agencies set up to help special need groups." She added that Massie's impassioned criticism should not be construed as self-serving: "It is the statement of a father who feels guilty over using so much of the precious blood derivative *even though he pays for it,* because he has carefully thought out his connection to society and he knows that something is deeply wrong with our social policy if blood is treated as a commodity to be exchanged for money."

After completing *Journey,* Massie once again turned his attention to the lush panorama of the Russian past. Although now familiar with the time period encompassing the life of the Tsarevich, there were still many areas of history with which Massie was unfamiliar. "While I was working on *Nicholas and Alexandra,* I was giving myself a course and reading as much as I could," Massie remembered. "I was fascinated by Peter [I]. There were glimpses of his character, stories and legends about him, but I couldn't find any biography which really captured him. After thinking about it for a while, I thought I could try one." Massie made frequent trips to Russia to do research for *Peter the Great.* He was fortunate in receiving a great deal of both official and scholarly assistance from the Soviet people who continue to have great reverence for Peter as one of the greatest of Russian heroes.

Considered the architect of modern Russia, Peter the Great was an imposing figure obsessed with forcing a backward Russian society into step with seventeenth-century Europe. Off came the flowing beards, gone were the long robes with their drooping sleeves; the monarch abolished such traditional emblems of the old order in favor of a "German" style of dress that allowed for the freedom of movement necessary for an active, forward-thinking people. Peter the Great went on to establish Russia as a major power. Flooding his homeland with

Western technology through the importation of thousands of craftsmen and military personnel, raising the educational standards of his fellow Russians by setting up schools and sending young men abroad to study arts and sciences yet unknown in Russia, and defeating long-time opponent Charles XII of Sweden in the battle of Poltava in 1709, Peter crowned his growing empire with the city of St. Petersburg, capital of the new Russia and his "window into Europe," which he commanded be built upon the northern marshes bordering the Gulf of Finland.

A London *Times* critic felt that Massie's obvious admiration for his subject tends to color his view of the facts and remarked that "the urge to show Peter in the best light must spring partly from the relief of writing about a monarch who could, and did, do everything for himself, after devoting so many years to Peter's descendants who, between them, barely seemed able to tie up a ribbon or fasten a stud." John Leonard of the *New York Times* criticized Massie for the fact that "there is, in [*Peter the Great*], no thesis. . . . Peter's spotty education, his voracious curiosity, his epileptic convulsions, his talent with his hands, his ignorance of literature, his humor and his terror—all are merely reported and forgiven, like the weather." However, while noting in the *New York Times Book Review* the book's somewhat daunting length, Kyril Fitzlyon hailed *Peter the Great* as "an enthralling book, beautifully edited, with a first-rate index and excellent illustrations," and later added: "It would be surprising if it did not become the standard biography of Peter the Great in English for many years to come, as fascinating as any novel and more so than most."

"I had done enough about Russia," Massie acknowledged in an interview with Joseph A. Cincotti for the *New York Times Book Review,* "so I decided to come home from Russia by way of western Europe." End-of-the-century western Europe was the route that Massie chose to travel and the one that provided the subject for his next book, *Dreadnought*. Nine years in the writing, the book is a narrative account of Britain's retreat from "splendid isolationism" after the crisis at Fashoda, the battle that resulted in France's cessation of efforts towards building a rival colonial empire after 1898, *Dreadnought* covers the period from 1897 to August, 1914, when Britain came to France's aid in World War I. Taking its title from the name given to the heavily armored and gunned battleship H.M.S. *Dreadnought,* designed by the British to render all other navies obsolete, Massie's lengthy volume uses the naval antagonism between Britain and Germany as a point of departure. Organizing such a broad range of cataclysmic events into a comprehensive format is no easy task, and some reviewers found fault with the book's areas of concentration. Stanley Weintraub commented in the *New York Times Book Review:* "Since Massie uses the lens of the British-Germany rivalry, the picture that emerges of the European powder keg and its multiple fuses, all sputtering at different speeds, is out of focus, although dramatic nevertheless."

However, *Dreadnought* was praised for the characteristically engaging narrative style of its author. Commending Massie's sharp eye for detail and his ability to vividly portray characters, Geoffrey Moorhouse observed in the *Los Angeles Times Book Review,* "one will not forget . . . Bismarck working in his office, watched by his dog Tiras, who terrorized all visitors . . . or Lord Salisbury, who 'treated his children like small foreign powers: not often noticed, but when recognized, regarded with unfailing politeness.'" "*Dreadnought* is a saga elegantly spun out in palaces and cabinet rooms, on the decks of royal yachts and the bridges of battleships, in Europe's spas and rambling country houses," wrote Douglas Porch in *Washington Post Book World*. "Massie traces the development of naval forces and the calculations of European diplomats with clarity and humor," he added. "He has a subtle appreciation for interplay of personalities in an era when the ruling houses of England and Germany were blood relations, and their political leaders shared a strong sense of cultural communality."

In 2003 Massie completed his equally well-researched sequel to *Dreadnought*. In *Castles of Steel* he studies the rise of the German U-boats, which through their effectiveness at travelling undetected prompted advances in sonar technologies, as well as Germany and Great Britain's battle for supremacy at sea. The assumptions undergirding the initial war strategies of both sides in the war quickly proved faulty, and Massie follows the efforts of both Germany's Kaiser Wilhelm II—grandson of England's Queen Victoria and a man who believed he could quickly gain a well-mannered victory—and the British admiralty to reassess the strengths and weaknesses of their opponents. Praising Massie's work as "readable and dramatic" as well as well researched, David A. Smith noted in the *Naval War College Review* that *Castles of Steel* gives readers "a clear sense of how important the clash of British and German navies was to the war's eventual outcome, and it illustrates how Winston Churchill's dramatic description of Admiral John Jellicoe, commander in chief of the British Grand Fleet, as 'the only commander who could lose the war in an afternoon' could be an accurate one." Massie argues that it was Germany's decision to engage in unrestricted U-Boat attacks, sinking not only British battle-ships but also neutral merchant ships and passenger liners. "The tactic worked in the sense that Britain, like Germany, started to run out of food and fuel," explained an *Economist* reviewer. "But it was also in Mr. Massie's view the colossal misjudgment that ensured Germany's defeat by bringing an entirely new enemy with unlimited resources into the war: the United States." Praising Massie's history as "imposing in both size and quality," a *Publishers Weekly* contributor noted that the historian "describes his cast of characters with the vividness of a novelist."

With the collapse of communism in Russia in the early 1990s, Massie was able to continue his story of Nicholas and Alexandra. Records formerly hidden were revealed, and this new information allowed the author to complete his 1995 volume, *The Romanovs: The Final Chapter.* Beginning with the execution of the Russian royal family, Massie traces the events of the burial of their bodies in Ekaterinburg, their discovery almost half a century later, their exhumation in 1991, and the genetic analysis of the bones that determined conclusively that all seven members of the Romanov family—including the Tsarevich and Anastasia—had been executed in 1918. "Although no specialist in Russian history, and clearly dependent on translated sources, Massie tells the story with the same narrative skill that he displayed in his bestselling *Nicholas and Alexandra,*" wrote *Times Literary Supplement* contributor Orlando Figes. Characterizing the book as "a tale of jealousy . . . ; bureaucratic fighting . . . ; false claims by impostors; endless legal hearings; and quarrelling between clans of the Romanovs," Figes added that "the prize of the imperial bones has brought out the worst in all those who would gain by laying claim to them," particularly most of the few surviving members of the Romanov family. Including a thorough discussion of the sixty-five-year-long deception by a woman claiming to be the Grand Duchess Anastasia, Massie's volume also traces the fate of other members of the Romanov family, seventeen of whom were killed within days of the Tsar. Calling the work "masterful" and "enthralling," *Washington Post Book World* contributor Joseph Finder praised *The Romanovs* as "a narrative as gripping as a well-wrought murder mystery, told in vividly realized, densely atmospheric scenes, rich with moments of grim fascination." While Massie subtitled his book "The Final Chapter," Finder noted that there are still mysteries left to be solved regarding this Russian chronicle, which may find the author returning to Mother Russia yet again in the future.

BIOGRAPHICAL AND CRITICAL SOURCES:

PERIODICALS

American Spectator, December, 1989, p. 32; September, 1992, p. 65.

Booklist, September 15, 2003, Brendan Driscoll, review of *Castles of Steel: Britain, Germany, and the Winning of the Great War at Sea,* p. 178.

Economist (U.S.), January 10, 2004, review of *Castles of Steel,* p. 73.

Kirkus Reviews, September 1, 2003, review of *Castles of Steel,* p. 1114.

Library Journal, October 1, 2003, Danile K. Blewett, review of *Castles of Steel,* p. 95.

Los Angeles Times Book Review, December 8, 1991, Geoffrey Moorhouse, review of *Dreadnought,* pp. 4, 15.

Naval War College Review, spring, 2004, David A. Smith, review of *Castles of Steel,* p. 185.

Newsweek, August 28, 1967; May 26, 1975; October 20, 1980, Walter Clemons, review of *Peter the Great,* p. 90.

New York Review of Books, March 26, 1992, p. 15.

New York Times, October 7, 1980, John Leonard, review of *Peter the Great,* section C, p. 8.

New York Times Book Review, August 20, 1967, pp. 1, 26; May 11, 1975, pp. 5-6; November 10, 1991, Joseph A. Cincotti, review of *Dreadnought: Britain, Germany, and the Coming of the Great War,* pp. 7, 9, and Stanley Weintraub, review of *Dreadnought,* p. 7.

Publishers Weekly, September 22, 2003, review of *Castles of Steel,* p. 97.

Punch, April 1, 1981, pp. 534-535.

Time, November 10, 1980, pp. 107-108; November 11, 1991, p. 90.

Times (London, England), February 5, 1981.

Times Literary Supplement, April 28, 1981, p. 467; April 17, 1992, p. 10; August 9, 1996, p. 26.

Tribune Books (Chicago, IL), December 15, 1991, p. 5; December 3, 1995, p. 3.

Washington Post Book World, November 24, 1991, Douglas Porch, review of *Dreadnought,* p. 5; October 22, 1995, Joseph Finder, review of *The Romanovs: The Final Chapter,* p. 5.

*   *   *

MASSIE, Robert Kinloch
See MASSIE, Robert K.

MATHABANE, Mark 1960-

PERSONAL: First name originally Johannes; name changed, 1976; born 1960, in Alexandra, South Africa; son of Jackson (a laborer) and Magdalene (a washerwoman; maiden name, Mabaso) Mathabane; immigrated to the United States; became U.S. citizen; married Gail Ernsberger (a writer), 1987; children: two. *Education:* Attended Limestone College, 1978, St. Louis University, 1979, and Quincy College, 1981; Dowling College, B.A., 1983; attended Columbia University Graduate School of Journalism, 1984. *Religion:* "Believes in God."

ADDRESSES: Home—1320 Frazier Court, Portland, Oregon 97229. *Agent*—Fifi Oscard Agency, 110 West 40th St., New York, NY 10018. *E-mail*—mark@ mathabane.com.

CAREER: Lecturer and writer, 1985—. Appeared on talk-shows, including *Oprah, Larry King, NPR, Today Show, CNN,* and *Charlie Rose.* Contributor to the *New York Times, Washington Post,* and *USA Today.* Established the Magdalene Scholarship Fund in his mother's name to provide scholarships for children at the Bovet School in Alexandra, Johannesburg.

MEMBER: Authors Guild, Authors League of America.

AWARDS, HONORS: Christopher Award, 1986, for *Kaffir Boy: The True Story of a Black Youth's Coming of Age in Apartheid South Africa;* nominated for Speaker of the Year, National Association of Campus Activities, 1993; White House Fellow, Department of Education, 1996-97.

WRITINGS:

Kaffir Boy: The True Story of a Black Youth's Coming of Age in Apartheid South Africa, Macmillan (New York, NY), 1986, published as *Kaffir Boy: Growing out of Apartheid,* Bodley Head (London, England), 1987.
Kaffir Boy in America: An Encounter with Apartheid, Scribner (New York, NY), 1989.
(With wife, Gail Mathabane) *Love in Black and White: The Triumph of Love over Prejudice and Taboo,* HarperCollins (New York, NY), 1992.
African Women: Three Generations, HarperCollins (New York, NY), 1994.
Miriam's Song: A Memoir, Simon & Schuster (New York, NY), 2000.

Also author of *Ubuntu* (novel), 1999, and *The Last Liberal.* Contributor to *New York Times.*

ADAPTATIONS: Kaffir Boy was adapted to sound cassette, Dove Books on Tape, 1988.

SIDELIGHTS: "What television newscasts did to expose the horrors of the Vietnam War in the 1960s, books like *Kaffir Boy* may well do for the horrors of apartheid in the '80s," Diane Manuel determined in a Chicago *Tribune Books* review of Mark Mathabane's first book. In his 1986 *Kaffir Boy: The True Story of a Black Youth's Coming of Age in Apartheid South Africa,* Mathabane recounts his life in the squalid black township of Alexandra outside Johannesburg, where he lived in dire poverty and constant fear until he seemingly miraculously received a scholarship to play tennis at an American college. *Washington Post Book World* critic Charles R. Larson called *Kaffir Boy* "violent and hard-hitting," while Peter Dreyer, writing in the *Los Angeles Times Book Review,* found Mathabane's autobiography "a book full of a young man's clumsy pride and sorrow, full of rage at the hideousness of circumstances, the unending destruction of human beings, [and] the systematic degradation of an entire society (and not only black South African society) in the name of a fantastic idea." *Kafir Boy* holds sway in the public imagination until this day, frequently appearing on reading lists in classrooms across the nation. The American Library Association selected *Kafir Boy* as one of the Outstanding Books for the College Bound.

The Alexandra of *Kaffir Boy* is one of overwhelming poverty and deprivation, of incessant hunger, of horrific crimes committed by the government and citizen gangs, and of fear and humiliation. It is a township where one either spends hours at garbage dumps in search of scraps of food discarded by Johannesburg whites or prostitutes himself for a meal, and where "children grow up accepting violence and death as the norm," reflected Larson. One of Mathabane's childhood memories is of his being startled from sleep, terrified to find police breaking into his family's shanty in search of persons who emigrated illegally, as his parents had, from the "homelands," or tribal reserves. His father was imprisoned following one of these raids and was repeatedly jailed after that. Mathabane recalls in *Kaffir Boy* that his parents "lived the lives of perpetual fugitives, fleeing by day and fleeing by night, making sure that they were never caught together under the same roof as husband and wife" because they lacked the paperwork that allowed them to live with their lawful spouses. His father was also imprisoned—at one time for more than a year with no contact with his family—for being unemployed, losing jobs as a laborer because he once again lacked the proper documents.

Yet those living in the urban ghettos near Johannesburg are more fortunate than people in the outlying "homelands," where black Africans are sent to resettle. "Nothing is more pathetic in this book than the author's description of a trip he takes with his father to the tribal reserve, ostensibly so that the boy will identify with the homelands," judged Larson. "The son, however, sees the land for what it really is—barren, burned out, empty of any meaning for his generation." In *Kaffir Boy* Mathabane depicts the desolation of the Venda tribal reserve as "mountainous, rugged and bone-dry, like a wasteland. . . . Everywhere I went nothing grew except near lavatories. . . . Occasionally I sighted a handful of scrawny cattle, goats and pigs grazing on the stubbles of dry brush. The scrawny animals, it turned out, were seldom slaughtered for food because they were being held as the people's wealth. Malnutrition was rampant, especially among the children." Larson continued to note that "the episode backfires. The boy is determined to give up his father's tribal ways and acquire the white man's education."

Although Mathabane had the opportunity to get at least a primary education, he still contemplated suicide when he was only ten years old. "I found the burden of living in a ghetto, poverty-stricken and without hope, too heavy to shoulder," he confesses in his memoir. "I was weary of being hungry all the time, weary of being beaten all the time: at school, at home and in the streets. . . . I felt that life could never, would never, change from how it was for me." But his first encounter with apartheid sparked his determination to overcome the adversities.

His grandmother was a gardener for an English-speaking, liberal white family, the Smiths, in an affluent suburb of Johannesburg. One day she took her grandson to work, where he met Clyde Smith, an eleven-year-old schoolboy. "My teachers tell us that Kaffirs [blacks] can't read, speak or write English like white people because they have smaller brains, which are already full of tribal things," Smith told Mathabane, the author recalled in his autobiography. "My teachers say you're not people like us, because you belong to a jungle civilization. That's why you can't live or go to school with us, but can only be our servants." He resolved to excel in school, and even taught himself English—blacks were allowed to learn only tribal languages at the time—through the comic books that his grandmother

brought home from the Smith household. "I had to believe in myself and not allow apartheid to define my humanity," Mathabane points out.

Mrs. Smith also gave Mathabane an old wooden tennis racket. He taught himself to play, then obtained coaching. As he improved and fared well at tournaments he gained recognition as a promising young athlete. In 1973 Mathabane attended a tennis tournament in South Africa where the American tennis pro Arthur Ashe publicly condemned apartheid. Ashe became Mathabane's hero, "because he was the first free black man I had ever seen," the author later was cited as saying in the *New York Times*. After watching the pro play, he strove to do as well as Ashe. Mathabane eventually became one of the best players in his country and made contacts with influential white tennis players who did not support apartheid. Stan Smith, another American tennis professional, befriended Mathabane and urged him to apply for tennis scholarships to American schools. Mathabane won one, and *Kaffir Boy* ends with the author boarding a plane headed for South Carolina. Lillian Thomas asserted in the *New York Times Book Review* that "it is evident that [Mathabane] wrestled with the decision whether to fight or flee the system" in South Africa. The author participated in the 1976 uprisings in Soweto, another black township near Johannesburg, after more than 600 people were killed there when police opened fire on a peaceful student protest. Yet Mathabane continued to be friends with whites whom he had met at his athletic club. He also was the only black in a segregated tournament that was boycotted by the Black Tennis Association, but he participated believing that he would meet people who could help him leave South Africa. Afterward he was attacked by a gang of blacks who resented his association with whites and only escaped because he outran them.

Times Literary Supplement critic David Papineau did not find fault with Mathabane for leaving South Africa. The reviewer contended that Mathabane "does make clear the limited choices facing black youths in South Africa today. One option is political activity, with the attendant risk of detention or being forced underground. . . . Alternatively you can keep your head down and hope for a steady job. With luck and qualifications you might even end up as a white-collar supervisor with a half-way respectable salary."

In an essay in the *St. James Guide to Young Adult Writers,* Lois Rauch Gibson and Judson Knight compared *Kaffir Boy* to Richard Wright's groundbreaking memoir, *Black Boy.* They pointed out that Mathabane had discovered the latter work as a youth, which inspired him to become a writer. Gibson and Knight noted that the similarities in title are not the only parallels; other related themes include "the violence of life in the ghetto, fear and anger at whites, conflict between father and son, love of books, education as an escape, and the determination to succeed."

Mathabane continues his autobiography in *Kaffir Boy in America: An Encounter with Apartheid,* which begins with his studies at Limestone College, South Carolina, in 1978. Armed with copies of the Declaration of Independence and the U.S. Constitution, Mathabane soon learns that the United States is not the promised land after all. *Kaffir Boy in America* recounts Mathabane's determination to get a good education and the beginnings of his career as a journalist and writer. Along the way, he attempts to understand American popular culture and American attitudes about race. Writing in the *Journal of Modern African Studies,* Mwizenge S. Tembo observed that "*Kaffir Boy in America* shows the extent of the contradictions that exist in the world's leading superpower." A *Library Journal* reviewer found *Kaffir Boy in America* to be "generally well-written," but noted that "like many sequels, this one lacks the power of the original." Lorna Hahn, writing in the *New York Times Book Review,* praised Mathabane's fairness in his discussion of American attitudes toward South Africa and called *Kaffir Boy in America* "an inspiring account of a young man's self-realization and his commitment to the self-realization of others."

With *Love in Black and White: The Triumph of Love over Prejudice,* which Mathabane coauthored with his wife, the author responds to those who criticized him for his marriage to Gail Ernsberger, a white American. In chapters divided into each spouse's perspective, the book tackles the hostility that interracial marriages still face from both races. The Mathabanes discuss their initial reactions to each other when they met as graduate students in New York, their rocky courtship and secret marriage, public reaction to their marriage from blacks and whites in both New York and North Carolina, and their experiences in raising biracial children. A *Kirkus Reviews* contributor called *Love in Black and White* "a personal and candid account of what it means to break an intransigent taboo—and a heartwarming affirmation of love and commitment." Writing in the *New York Times Book Review,* Andrea Cooper found it "lively" and especially praised Mathabane's "obvious intelligence and quiet passion" and Gail Mathabane's "specific, informal and visual" treatment of the problems of marrying outside one's race.

In 1994 Mathabane published his fourth work of nonfiction, *African Women: Three Generations,* which uses the stories of his mother, grandmother, and sister to tell the larger story of what it means to grow up female and black in South Africa under apartheid and the legacy of colonialism. Under apartheid, the family lives of black women were torn apart as the men were forced to travel far from home seeking employment. The stories each woman tells recount violent beatings and abuse by husbands and lovers, desperate poverty and hunger, deaths of children, and the effects of witchcraft and Christianity on their lives. *African Women* is broken into two parts. The first, set in South Africa, tells each woman's story from her own first-person perspective, as though she had orally told her tale to Mathabane; the second part involves the reunion of the Mathabane women with their Americanized son on the *Oprah Winfrey* show. Several reviewers found it odd that Mathabane sent his American wife to South Africa to interview his relatives. Writing in *New Statesman,* Victoria Brittain said that all the women have the same voice and "it is unmistakably the voice of the son, grandson and brother, who escaped from the townships with a tennis scholarship to America, and later graduated from the Columbia School of Journalism." In the *New York Times Book Review,* Veronica Chambers questioned Mathabane's decision to tell the women's stories in his voice rather than in their own, and a reviewer for *Booklist* found the book in need of tighter editing. Several reviewers were struck by the absence of a larger social and political context for the book, so that the women's problems seem to be "boyfriends and cheating husbands," according to Chambers. Whereas the *Booklist* reviewer praised the way in which "the political is made personal in scenes of daily confrontation," Chambers wrote, "With *African Women: Three Generations,* it feels as though the well is beginning to run dry." The *Kirkus Reviews* contributor noted that *African Women* is "a worthy subject, but its treatment is marred by the author's suspect style."

One African woman in particular—the author's sister, Miriam Mathabane—is the subject of his 2000 release, *Miriam's Song: A Memoir.* Growing up in Alexandra, Miriam faced the twin traumas of apartheid and the hardships faced by women in a society "where rape is common and early unwanted pregnancies almost a certainty," according to Mary Ellen Sullivan in the *New York Times Book Review.* Though Miriam herself would be an unwed mother by age eighteen, she knew her future success would be gained through education. Against daily beatings at school, rat-infested shacks at home, and civil unrest in her township, she worked her way out of the ghetto and to the United States to study nursing. *Miriam's Song,* said Sullivan, "brings a critical chapter of South African history to life." This "riveting memoir," as Jane Drabkin described it in *School Library Journal,* should "inspire teens to pursue their own goals against all odds."

BIOGRAPHICAL AND CRITICAL SOURCES:

BOOKS

St. James Guide to Young Adult Writers, second edition, St. James Press (Detroit, MI), 1999.

PERIODICALS

Africa Today, July/September, 1996.

Atlanta Journal, February 4, 2004, Sheila Poole, *South African Youths Ignore Past,* p. F.1.

Book, July/August, 2000, Ann Collette, review of *Miriam's Song: A Memoir,* p. 81.

Booklist, February 15, 1994, review of *African Women: Three Generations;* June 1, 2000, Gillian Engberg, review of *Miriam's Song: A Memoir,* p. 1844.

Christian Science Monitor, May 2, 1986; April 25, 1994; February 21, 1995.

Emerge, June, 2000, Phyllicia Oppelt, review of *Miriam's Song,* p. 68.

Journal of Modern African Studies, December, 1990, Mwizenge S. Tembo, review of *Kaffir Boy in America: An Encounter with Apartheid.*

Kirkus Reviews, November 15, 1991, review of *Love in Black and White: The Triumph of Love over Prejudice and Taboo.*

Library Journal, April 1, 1994, review of *Kaffir Boy in America.*

Los Angeles Times Book Review, March 30, 1986, Peter Dreyer, review of *Kaffir Boy: The True Story of a Black Youth's Coming of Age in Apartheid South Africa;* May 31, 2001, review of *Miriam's Song: A Memoir,* p. SH13.

New Statesman, March 30, 1995, p. 37, Victoria Brittain, review of *African Women.*

Newsweek, March 9, 1992.

New York Times, March 2, 1987; September 24, 1987; December 14, 1997.

New York Times Book Review, April 27, 1986; August 13, 1989; February 16, 1992; July 31, 1994, Veronica Chambers, review of *African Women,* p. 25; August 13, 2000, Mary Ellen Sullivan, review of *Miriam's Song: A Memoir,* p. 15.

People, July 7, 1986.

Publishers Weekly, December 6, 1991, review of *Love in Black and White,* p. 65; March 21, 1994, review of *African Women,* p. 62.

Sage, spring, 1995.

School Library Journal, February, 2001, Jane Drabkin, review of *Miriam's Song: A Memoir,* p. 145.

Sentinel, June 27, 2001, review of *Miriam's Song: A Memoir,* p. A10.

Times Literary Supplement, August 21, 1987, David Papineau, review of *Kaffir Boy.*

Toronto Star, April 10, 2004, Jim Atkins, *Lessons from South Africa,* p. F06.

Tribune Books (Chicago, IL), April 13, 1986, Diane Manuel, review of *Kaffir Boy.*

Washington Post Book World, April 20, 1986, Charles R. Larson, review of *Kaffir Boy.*

ONLINE

Mark Mathabane Web Site, http://www.mathabane.com/./

*   *   *

MATTHIESSEN, Peter 1927-

PERSONAL: Surname is pronounced "*Math*-e-son"; born May 22, 1927, in New York, NY; son of Erard A. (an architect) and Elizabeth (Carey) Matthiessen; married Patricia Southgate, February 8, 1951 (divorced, 1958); married Deborah Love, May 16, 1963 (deceased, 1972); married Maria Eckhart, November 28, 1980; children: (first marriage) Lucas, Sara C.; (second marriage) Rue, Alexander. *Education:* Attended Sorbonne, University of Paris, 1948-49; Yale University, B.A., 1950.

ADDRESSES: Home—Bridge Lane, Box 392, Sagaponack, Long Island, NY 11962. *Agent*—Candida Donadio Associates, Inc., 231 West 22nd St., New York, NY 10011.

CAREER: Writer, 1950—; *Paris Review,* New York, NY (originally Paris, France), cofounder, 1951, editor, 1951—. Former commercial fisherman; captain of deep-sea charter fishing boat, Montauk, Long Island, NY, 1954-56; member of expeditions to Alaska, Canadian Northwest Territories, Peru, Nepal, East Africa, Congo Basin, Siberia, India, Bhutan, China, Japan, Namibia, Botswana, and Outer Mongolia and of

Harvard-Peabody Expedition to New Guinea, 1961; National Book Awards, judge, 1970. *Military service:* U.S. Navy, 1945-47.

MEMBER: American Academy and Institute of Arts and Letters, American Academy of Arts and Sciences, New York Zoological Society (member of board of trustees, 1965-78).

AWARDS, HONORS: Atlantic Prize, 1951, for best first story; permanent installation in White House library, for *Wildlife in America;* National Institute/American Academy of Arts and Letters grant, 1963, for *The Cloud Forest: A Chronicle of the South American Wilderness* and *Under the Mountain Wall: A Chronicle of Two Seasons in the Stone Age;* National Book Award nominations, 1966, for *At Play in the Fields of the Lord,* and 1972, for *The Tree Where Man Was Born;* Christopher Book Award, 1971, for *Sal Si Puedes: Cesar Chavez and the New American Revolution;* elected to National Institute of Arts and Letters, 1974; "Editor's Choice" citation, *New York Times Book Review,* 1975, for *Far Tortuga;* Brandeis Award and National Book Award for contemporary thought for *The Snow Leopard,* both 1979; National Book Award, general nonfiction, 1980, for paperback edition of *The Snow Leopard;* John Burroughs Medal and African Wildlife Leadership Foundation Award, both 1982, both for *Sand Rivers;* gold medal for distinction in natural history, Academy of Natural Sciences, Philadelphia, PA, 1985; Ambassador Award, English-Speaking Union, 1990, for *Killing Mister Watson;* John Steinbeck Award, Long Island University, Southampton, elected to Global 500 Honour Roll, United Nations Environment Programme, and designated fellow, Academy of Arts and Science, all 1991.

WRITINGS:

FICTION

Race Rock, Harper (New York, NY), 1954.
Partisans, Viking (New York, NY), 1955.
Raditzer, Viking (New York, NY), 1961.
At Play in the Fields of the Lord, Random House (New York, NY), 1965.
Far Tortuga, Random House (New York, NY), 1975.
On the River Styx, and Other Stories, Random House (New York, NY), 1989.

"WATSON" TRILOGY

Killing Mister Watson, Random House (New York, NY), 1990.

Lost Man's River, Random House (New York, NY), 1997.
Bone by Bone, Random House (New York, NY), 1999.

NONFICTION

Wildlife in America, Viking (New York, NY), 1959, revised edition, 1987.
The Cloud Forest: A Chronicle of the South American Wilderness, Viking (New York, NY), 1961.
Under the Mountain Wall: A Chronicle of Two Seasons in the Stone Age, Viking (New York, NY), 1962.
Oomingmak: The Expedition to the Musk Ox Island in the Bering Sea, Hastings House (New York, NY), 1967.
The Shorebirds of North America, paintings by Robert Verity Clem, Viking (New York, NY), 1967, published as *The Wind Birds,* illustrated by Robert Gillmor, 1973.
Sal Si Puedes: Cesar Chavez and the New American Revolution, Random House (New York, NY), 1970, published as *Sal Si Puedes (Escape if You Can),* University of California Press (Berkeley, CA), 2000.
Blue Meridian: The Search for the Great White Shark, Random House (New York, NY), 1971.
Everglades: With Selections from the Writings of Peter Matthiessen, edited by Paul Brooks, Sierra Club-Ballantine (New York, NY), 1971.
The Tree Where Man Was Born, photographs by Eliot Porter, Dutton (New York, NY), 1972, revised edition, Penguin Books (New York, NY), 1995.
Seal Pool (juvenile), illustrated by William Pene Du Bois, Doubleday (Garden City, NY), 1972, published as *The Great Auk Escape,* Angus & Robertson (London, England), 1974.
The Snow Leopard, Viking (New York, NY), 1978.
Sand Rivers, photographs by Hugo van Lawick, Viking (New York, NY), 1981.
In the Spirit of Crazy Horse, Viking (New York, NY), 1983.
Indian Country, Viking (New York, NY), 1984.
Men's Lives: The Surfmen and Baymen of the South Fork, Random House (New York, NY), 1986.
Nine-Headed Dragon River: Zen Journals 1969-1982, Shambhala (Boulder, CO), 1986.
African Silences, Random House (New York, NY), 1991.
Shadows of Africa, illustrated by Mary Frank, Abrams (New York, NY), 1992.
Baikal, photographs by Boyd Norton, Sierra Club Books (San Francisco, CA), 1992.
East of Lo Monthang, Shambhala (Boulder, CO), 1995.

Tigers in the Snow, Farrar, Straus & Giroux (New York, NY), 2000.

The Peter Matthiessen Reader, Vintage (New York, NY), 2000.

The Birds of Heaven: Travel with Cranes, Harvill Press, 2002.

End of the Earth: Voyages to the White Continent, National Geographic Society (Washington, D.C.), 2003.

Arctic National Wildlife Refuge: Seasons of Life and Land: A Photographic Journey, photographs by Subhankar Banerje, foreword by Jimmy Carter, Mountaineers Books (Seattle, WA), 2003.

(Editor and author of introduction) *North American Indians,* Penguin Books (New York, NY), 2004.

OTHER

Contributor to *The American Heritage Book of Natural Wonders,* edited by Alvin M. Josephy, American Heritage Press, 1972. Contributor of numerous short stories, articles, and essays to popular periodicals, including *Atlantic, Audubon, Conde Nast Traveler, Esquire, Geo, Harper's, Nation, Newsweek, New Yorker, New York Review of Books,* and *Saturday Evening Post.*

ADAPTATIONS: At Play in the Fields of the Lord was produced as a motion picture by Saul Zaentz, directed by Hector Babenco, starring Aidan Quinn, Tom Berenger, Tom Waits, Kathy Bates, and John Lithgow, and released by Metro-Goldwyn-Mayer, 1992; *Men's Lives* was adapted by Joe Pintauro and was performed on Long Island at the Bay Street Theater Festival on July 28, 1992. *Adventure: Lost Man's River—An Everglades Journey with Peter Matthiessen* was produced by the Public Broadcasting System (PBS) in 1991.

SIDELIGHTS: Peter Matthiessen is widely considered one of the most important wilderness writers of the twentieth century. In fiction and nonfiction alike, he explores endangered natural environments and human cultures threatened by encroaching technology. As Conrad Silvert noted in *Literary Quarterly,* Matthiessen "is a naturalist, an anthropologist and an explorer of geographies and the human condition. He is also a rhapsodist who writes with wisdom and warmth as he applies scientific knowledge to the peoples and places he investigates. Works of lasting literary value and moral import have resulted." Matthiessen also writes of the inner explorations he has undertaken as a practitioner of Zen Buddhism. His 1979 National Book Award-winning memoir *The Snow Leopard* combines the account of a difficult Himalayan trek with spiritual autobiography and contemplations of mortality and transcendence. According to Terrance Des Pres in the *Washington Post Book World,* Matthiessen is "a visionary, but he is very hardminded as well, and his attention is wholly with abrupt detail. This allows him to render strangeness familiar, and much that is menial becomes strange, lustrous, otherworldly." *Dictionary of Literary Biography* contributor John L. Cobbs noted: "In fiction and in nonfiction, Peter Matthiessen is one of the shamans of literature. He puts his audience in touch with worlds and forces which transcend common experience."

Critics contend that despite his pessimistic forecasts for the future of natural areas and their inhabitants, Matthiessen imbues his work with descriptive writing of high quality. According to Vernon Young in the *Hudson Review,* Matthiessen "combines the exhaustive knowledge of the naturalist . . . with a poet's response to far-out landscapes. . . . When he pauses to relate one marvel to another and senses the particular merging into the general, his command of color, sound and substance conjures the resonance of the vast continental space." *New York Times Book Review* contributor Jim Harrison wrote that Matthiessen's prose has "a glistening, sculpted character to it. . . . The sense of beauty and mystery is indelible; not that you retain the specific information on natural history, but that you have had your brain, and perhaps the soul, prodded, urged, moved into a new dimension." Robert M. Adams offered a similar assessment in the *New York Review of Books.* Matthiessen, Adams wrote, "has dealt frequently and knowingly with natural scenery and wild life; he can sketch a landscape in a few vivid, unsentimental words, capture the sensations of entering a wild, windy Nepalese mountain village, and convey richly the strange, whinnying behavior of a herd of wild sheep. His prose is crisp, yet strongly appealing to the senses; it combines instinct with the feeling of adventure."

Although Matthiessen was born in New York City, he spent most of his youth in rural New York state and in Connecticut, where he attended the Hotchkiss School. His father, an architect, was a trustee of the National Audubon Society, and Matthiessen took an early interest in the fascinations of the natural world. "I had always been interested in nature," he remembered in *Publishers Weekly.* "My brother and I started with a passion for snakes, and he went into marine biology, while I took courses in [zoology and ornithology] right up through college." After service in the U.S. Navy, Matthiessen attended Yale University, spending his junior year at the Sorbonne in Paris. Having realized that a writing vocation drew him strongly, he began writing short stories, one of which won the prestigious *Atlantic* Prize in 1951. His short fiction would be collected in *On the River Styx, and Other Stories,* published in 1989. Matthiessen received his B.A. degree in 1950, and after teaching creative writing for a year at Yale, he returned to Paris.

When *Race Rock* was published in 1954, Matthiessen returned to the United States, where he continued to write while eking out a livelihood as a commercial fisherman on Long Island. Reflecting on the early stages of his writing career in the *Washington Post,* Matthiessen said: "I don't think I could have done my writing without the fishing. I needed something physical, something non-intellectual." The friendships Matthiessen formed with Long Island's fishermen enabled him to chronicle their vanishing lifestyle in his book *Men's Lives: The Surfmen and Baymen of the South Fork.*

Matthiessen embarked on his first lengthy journey in 1956. Loading his Ford convertible with textbooks, a shotgun, and a sleeping bag, he set off to visit every wildlife refuge in the United States. He admitted in *Publishers Weekly* that he brought more curiosity than scientific expertise to his quest. "I'm what the nineteenth century would call a generalist," he said. "I have a lot of slack information, and for my work it's been extremely helpful. I've always been interested in wildlife and wild places and wild people. I wanted to see the places that are disappearing." Nearly three years of work went into Matthiessen's encyclopedic *Wildlife in America,* published in 1959 to high critical acclaim. A commercial success as well, *Wildlife in America* initiated the second phase of Matthiessen's career, a period of two decades during which he undertook numerous expeditions to the wild places that captured his curiosity. Since 1959, he has supported himself solely by writing.

The popularity of Matthiessen's nonfiction somewhat overshadows his equally well-received fiction. Three of his first four books were novels, and critics found them commendable and promising works. In a *New York Herald Tribune Book Review* piece about *Race Rock,* Gene Baro commented: "Mr. Matthiessen's absorbing first novel, apart from being a good, well-paced story, offers the reader some depth and breadth of insight. For one thing, *Race Rock* is a vivid but complex study of evolving character; for another, it is a narrative of character set against a variously changed and changing social background. Mr. Matthiessen has succeeded in making from many strands of reality a close-textured book."

New York Times contributor Sylvia Berkman observed that with *Race Rock,* Matthiessen "assumes immediate place as a writer of disciplined craft, perception, imaginative vigor and serious temperament. . . . He commands also a gift of flexible taut expression which takes wings at times into a lyricism beautifully modulated and controlled." Cobbs wrote in *Dictionary of Literary Biography* that although *Race Rock* "does not anticipate the experimental techniques or exotic subject matter of Matthiessen's later fiction, the novel shows the author's early concern with fundamental emotions and with the tension between primitive vitality and the veneer of civilization."

Partisans and *Raditzer,* Matthiessen's second and third novels, garnered mixed reviews. According to M.L. Barrett in the *Library Journal,* the action in *Partisans,* "notable for its integrity and dramatic quality, is realized in real flesh-and-blood characters." *New York Times* contributor William Goyen stated: "The characters [in *Partisans*] seem only mouthpieces. They are not empowered by depth of dramatic conviction—or confusion. They do, however, impress one with this young author's thoughtful attempt to find answers to ancient and serious questions." Critics were more impressed with the title character in *Raditzer,* a man Cobbs found "both loathsome and believable." In the *Nation,* Terry Southern described *Raditzer*'s anti-hero as "a character distinct from those in literature, yet one who has somehow figured, if but hauntingly, in the lives of us all. It is, in certain ways, as though a whole novel had been devoted to one of [Nelson] Algren's sideline freaks, a grotesque and loathsome creature—yet seen ultimately, as sometimes happens in life, as but another human being." Cobbs concluded: "A skillful ear for dialect and an immediacy in sketching scenes of violence and depravity saved *Raditzer*'s moral weightiness from being wearisome, and the novel proved Matthiessen's ability to project his imagination into worlds far removed from that of the intellectual upper-middle class."

At Play in the Fields of the Lord enhanced Matthiessen's reputation as a fiction writer when it was issued in 1965; the novel would increase his renown still further after it was filmed as a motion picture directed by Hector Babenco in 1992. Set in a remote jungle village in the Amazon region, the work is, in the words of *New York Times Book Review* contributor Anatole Broyard, "one of those rare novels that satisfy all sorts of literary and intellectual hungers while telling a story that pulls you along out of sheer human kinship." The story recounts the misguided efforts of four American missionaries and an American Indian mercenary to "save" the isolated Niaruna tribe. Cobbs suggested that the book shows "a virtuosity and richness that few traditional novels exhibit. There is immense stylistic facility in shifting from surreal dream and drug sequences to scrupulous realistic descriptions of tropical nature." *Nation* contributor J. Mitchell Morse voiced some dissatisfaction with *At Play in the Fields of the Lord,* claiming that Matthiessen "obviously intended to write a serious novel, but . . . he has unconsciously condescended to cheapness." Conversely, Granville Hicks praised the work in the *Saturday Review:* "[Matthiessen's] evocation of the jungle is powerful, but no more remarkable than his insight into the people he portrays. He tells a fascinating story, and tells it well. . . . It is this firm but subtle evocation of strong feeling that gives Matthiessen's book its power over the imagination. Here, in an appallingly strange setting, he sets his drama of familiar aspirations and disappointments."

Matthiessen's 1975 novel, *Far Tortuga,* presents a stylistic departure from his previous fictional works. As Cobbs described it, "the deep penetration of character and psychology that characterized *At Play in the Fields of the Lord* yields to an almost disturbing objectivity in *Far Tortuga,* an absolute, realistic reproduction of surface phenomena—dialogue, noises, colors, shapes." In *Far Tortuga* Matthiessen creates a fictitious voyage of a Caribbean turtling schooner, using characters' conversations and spare descriptions of time, weather and place. "The radical format of *Far Tortuga* makes the novel a structural tour de force and assured a range of critical reaction," Cobbs noted. Indeed, the novel's use of intermittent blank spaces, wavy lines, ink blots, and unattributed dialogue has elicited varying critical responses. *Saturday Review* contributor Bruce Allen called the work an "adventurous failure. . . . It exudes a magnificent and paradoxical radiance; but beneath the beautiful surface [it lacks] anything that even remotely resembles a harmonious whole." Most reviewers expressed a far different opinion, however. *Newsweek*'s Peter S. Prescott praised the book as "a beautiful and original piece of work, a resonant, symbolical story of nine doomed men who dream of an earthly paradise as the world winds down around them. . . . This is a moving, impressive book, a difficult yet successful undertaking." And *New York Review of Books* contributor Thomas R. Edwards felt that the novel "turns out to be enthralling. Matthiessen uses his method not for self-display but for identifying and locating his characters. . . . What, despite appearances, does *not* happen in *Far Tortuga* is a straining by literary means to make more of an acutely observed life than it would make of itself."

Killing Mister Watson details, through the linked recollections of ten individuals, life in the Florida Everglades a century ago. Basing his story on actual events, Matthiessen novelizes the life of Edgar J. (Jack) Watson, who settled in the area in 1892 and became a successful sugar-cane farmer. Tales of a dark past begin to circulate among his neighbors: tales of murder, of past wives, of illegitimate children. People are mysteriously murdered, and Watson's volatile temper and mean streak are common knowledge. Despite, or perhaps because of, his wealth, strong physical charisma, and the golden tongue of a born politician, Watson eventually becomes the object of resentment and even fear in his community; he is a man approached with submission. Eventually, Watson is killed by a group of his neighbors—shot with thirty-one bullets—upon returning to town after the hurricane of 1910. "Aggressive and gregarious, without ethics or introspection, both hugely talented and dangerously addicted to untamed power, Edgar Watson finally seems to represent great potential gone awry, or America at its worst," noted Ron Hansen in the *New York Times Book Review.* But the act of his murder remains incomprehensible: "since accounts of the man differ so radically, we are left, like the detective-historian, with more questions than answers, and with a sense of frustration," remarked Joyce Carol Oates in the *Washington Post Book World.* "The more we learn about Watson, this 'accursed' figure, the less we seem to know."

Lost Man's River picks up on the story of Edgar Watson and forms the second installment in the "Watson" trilogy. While *Killing Mr. Watson* approached the tale of the central figure through patching together many documentary sources, *Lost Man's River* retraces this forceful man's life and his death through the single perspective of his son Lucius. Lucius, an academic and self-proclaimed failure, is haunted by his father's legacy, and fifty years later he begins to research the circumstances surrounding his death and comes across a new piece of evidence. The quest leads him into a dark and complicated family past and a tragic history, which is tied, as always, to the exploitation of the wilderness. The *New York Times Book Review*'s Janet Burroway, while praising Matthiessen for his "perfect ear for the cadences of Southern speech," suggested that the complex maze of familial connections and impostures is "hard on the reader. . . . Our involvement depends very much on our sharing Lucius's determination to thread this maze, and *Lost Man's River* does not entirely persuade us to do so." However, Kit Miniclier, a critic for the *Denver Post,* commented that Matthiessen "pulls his readers through the darkness of those human souls occupying the morose, flickering light of the deep Florida Everglades." And a *Kirkus Reviews* writer described Matthiessen's accomplishment in these glowing terms: "Interweaving a lament for the lost wilderness, a shrewd, persuasive study of character, and a powerful meditation on the sources of American violence, Matthiessen has produced one of the best novels of recent years."

Matthiessen's novel *Bone by Bone,* published in 1999, completed the trilogy, with the brawling Florida planter telling his story in his own words. This time the novel also explores Watson's youth back in Civil War days with a vicious father who beats both him and his mother. "The roots of Watson's violence aren't just familial but societal, however, which is evident in the first pages of the book as the boy observes a murdered runaway slave with a mix of sorrow and cool indifference," wrote Barbara Hoffert in *Library Journal.* As Watson recounts his tale, readers see how Watson dreamed of recovering the family plantation after the Civil War and his success as a gifted planter. Also portrayed are the violence of the times and how Watson is ultimately brought down by both his own failings and the failings of those around him. A *Publishers Weekly* contributor called Watson "a monumental creation, and in bringing him and his amazing period to life with such vigor Matthiessen has created an unforgettable slice of deeply true and resonant American history." Not all reviewers praised the novel. John Skow, writing in *Time,* felt that *Bone by Bone* and its predecessor in the trilogy were "two novels too many." Hoffert, however, commented, "A rich, provocative novel, sometimes overwritten, but who cares?" Peter Filkins, writing in *World and I,* commented "that the two powers grappling for control of Bone by Bone, if not the trilogy as a whole, are history and psychology, two very different approaches to the interpretation of individual experience." Filkins went on to note, "In the end, this urge to regenerate oneself and the freedom to do so, even in its most reckless state, are at the core of both the American spirit and Matthiessen's ambitious effort to capture that spirit."

Human victims form the core of Matthiessen's later writings about the United States. In *Sal Si Puedes: Cesar Chavez and the New American Revolution,* Matthiessen chronicles the efforts of migrant worker Cesar Chavez to organize farm laborers in California. In a review for the *Nation,* Roy Borngartz expressed the opinion that in *Sal Si Puedes* Matthiessen "brings a great deal of personal attachment to his account of Chavez and his fellow organizers. . . . He makes no pretense of taking any objective stand between the farm workers and the growers. . . . But he is a good and honest reporter, and as far as he was able to get the growers to talk to him, he gives them their say. . . . Matthiessen is most skillful at bringing his people to life."

A similar sympathy for oppressed cultures provides the focus for *Indian Country* and *In the Spirit of Crazy Horse. New Republic* contributor Paul Zweig noted that the author "has two subjects in *Indian Country:* the destruction of America's last open land by the grinding pressure of big industry, in particular the energy industry; and the tragic struggle of the last people on the land to preserve their shrinking territories, and even more, to preserve the holy balance of their traditions, linked to the complex, fragile ecology of the land." According to David Wagoner in the *New York Times Book Review,* what makes *Indian Country* "most unusual and most valuable is its effort to infuse the inevitable anger and sorrow with a sense of immediate urgency, with prophetic warnings. . . . Few people could have been better equipped than Mr. Matthiessen to face this formidable task. He has earned the right to be listened to seriously on the ways in which tribal cultures can teach us to know ourselves and the earth."

The focus of *In the Spirit of Crazy Horse,* while still directed toward the historic treatment of Native Americans, is more journalistic in nature than *Indian Country.* In fact, the book itself was the subject of much press when it became the subject of a lawsuit the year after its publication. Claiming that they were libeled in the book, both an FBI agent and then-governor of South Dakota, William Janklow, sued Matthiessen and Viking, the book's publisher, for a combined forty-nine-million dollars. While the two lawsuits were eventually thrown out by a federal appeals court, the actions of the two men effectively kept the book out of circulation for several years. A reading of the work makes their efforts understandable. *In the Spirit of Crazy Horse* presents an effective indictment of the FBI and other government offices in crushing the efforts of the American Indian Movement (AIM) to recover sacred Sioux lands illegally confiscated by the U.S. government. The discovery of uranium and other mineral deposits on the land prompted federal officials to go to desperate lengths, including, Matthiessen claims, framing AIM activist Leonard Peltier for murder. *In the Spirit of Crazy Horse* was reissued by Matthiessen in 1991, after new evidence came to light further reinforcing the author's contentions.

The Snow Leopard is perhaps the book that best integrates many of Matthiessen's themes—the abundance and splendor of nature, the fragility of the environment, the fascinations of a foreign culture—with contemplations of a more spiritual sort. The book is an autobiographical account of a journey Matthiessen took, in the company of wildlife biologist George Schaller, to a remote part of Nepal. *New York Times* columnist Anatole Broyard wrote of Matthiessen: "On this voyage he travels to the outer limits of the world and the inner limits of the self. . . . When he looks in as well as outward, the two landscapes complement one another." Jim Harrison likewise noted in a review in the *Nation:* "Running concurrent to the outward journey in *The Snow Leopard* is an equally torturous inward journey, and the two are balanced to the extent that neither overwhelms the other." As part of that "inward journey," Matthiessen remembers his second wife's death from cancer and opens himself to the spiritual nourishment of Zen. Terrance Des Pres, in the *Washington Post Book World,* suggested that as a result of these meditations, Matthiessen "has expressed, with uncommon candor and no prospect of relief, a longing which keeps the soul striving and alert in us all."

The Snow Leopard elicited wide critical respect, earning a second National Book Award for general nonfiction in 1980. In the *Saturday Review,* Zweig commented that the book "contains many . . . passages, in which the naturalist, the spiritual apprentice, and the writer converge simply and dramatically." *Atlantic Monthly* contributor Phoebe-Lou Adams concluded of the work: "It is as though [Matthiessen] looked simultaneously through a telescope and a microscope, and his great skill as a writer enables the reader to share this double vision of a strange and beautiful country." As a conclusion to his review, Des Pres called *The Snow Leopard* "a book fiercely felt and magnificently written, in which timelessness and 'modern time' are made to touch and join."

Though Matthiessen writes about Zen in *The Snow Leopard* and in *Nine-Headed Dragon River: Zen Journals 1969-1982,* he still expresses reservations about offering his personal philosophies for public perusal. "One is always appalled by the idea of wearing your so-called religion on your sleeve," he told *Publishers Weekly.* "I never talked about Zen much. . . . If people come along and want to talk about Zen, that's wonderful, but I don't want to brandish it. It's just a quiet little practice, not a religion . . . just a way of seeing the world. . . . And I find myself very comfortable with it." He elaborated briefly: "Zen is a synonym for life, that's all. Zen practice is life practice. If you can wake up and look around you, if you can knock yourself out of your customary way of thinking and simply see how really miraculous and extraordinary everything around you is, that's Zen."

Matthiessen has focused his more recent writings primarily on nature and the human relationship with the surrounding environment. In *Tigers in the Snow,* the author explores the realm of the Siberian tiger while recounting a research project that began in 1990 with photographer Maurice Hornocker, director of the Hornocker Wildlife Institute. The research was conducted as a joint Russian-American venture, and Matthiessen's account of the effort to save this endangered species is accompanied by Hornocker's photographs. Edelle Marie Schaefer, writing in *Library Journal,* pointed out that the book has a "very readable, engaging text" and called it "essential reading for everyone interested in wildlife and the preservation of endangered species." *Booklist* contributor Nancy Bent noted that Matthiessen "brings his lyrical eye to an account of the plight of the Amur (or Siberian) tiger."

In *The Birds of Heaven: Travel with Cranes,* published in 2002, the author turns his focus on cranes as he journeys on five continents in search of the fifteen known species of cranes. Matthiessen discusses the growing threats to these birds' existence by an increasingly industrialized world. Nevertheless, as pointed out by a reviewer writing in *Whole Earth,* "This isn't just a litany of losses. Matthiessen celebrates scientists and conservationists struggling to save the cranes." Kevin Krajick, writing in the *Smithsonian,* commented, "The real intrigue of this, Matthiessen's twenty-eighth book, is in his evocation of people and landscapes." The reviewer went on to note, "The crane connection is not always obvious, but with Matthiessen questions of life and death are sources of eloquent meditations." *Time International* contributor Bryan Walsh said, "In addition to the marvelous flow of his prose, Matthiessen's greatest gift as a writer may be his ability to combine precise observation with a radiant sense of spiritual wonder. Despite a lifetime of globe-trotting, his remarkable talent for conveying the freshness of encounters with new places is undiminished."

Despite being in his seventies, Matthiessen showed no signs of slowing down as he traveled to Antarctica and wrote about his voyage through the islands surrounding Antarctica in *End of the Earth: Voyages to the White Continent,* published in 2003. In addition to describing the wildlife and environment that he encountered, Matthiessen also recounted much of the region's history, including stories about the pioneers and adventurers of the past who traveled to the region. Matthiessen and the crew also encountered their own adventure as they suddenly found themselves in the midst of an unrelenting hurricane that battered their ship and injured, in some way, everybody on board. A *Publishers Weekly* contributor found Matthiessen's descriptions to be "antiseptic." Donna Seaman, however, noted in *Booklist* that the author "describes with arresting lyricism the spiritual cleansing one experiences in this pristine, wind-scoured kingdom of ice." In a review in *Sports Illustrated*, Stephen J. Bodio commented, "*End of the Earth* is a splendid book, a celebration of Antarctica and an eloquent evocation of its appeal."

BIOGRAPHICAL AND CRITICAL SOURCES:

BOOKS

Contemporary Literary Criticism, Thomson Gale (Detroit, MI), Volume 7, 1977, Volume 11, 1979, Volume 32, 1985, Volume 64, 1991.

Dictionary of Literary Biography, Volume 6: *American Novelists since World War II*, second series, Thomson Gale (Detroit, MI), 1980.

Dowie, William, *Peter Matthiessen*, Twayne (Boston, MA), 1991.

Nicholas, D., *Peter Matthiessen: A Bibliography*, Orirana (Canoga Park, CA), 1980.

Parker, William, editor, *Men of Courage: Stories of Present-Day Adventures in Danger and Death*, Playboy Press, 1972.

Styron, William, *This Quiet Dust and Other Writings*, Random House (New York, NY), 1982.

PERIODICALS

Atlantic Monthly, June, 1954; March, 1971; November, 1972; June, 1975; September, 1978, Phoebe-Lou Adams, review of *The Snow Leopard*; March, 1983.

Birder's World, August, 2002, Christopher Cokinos, review of *The Birds of Heaven: Travels with Cranes*, p. 58.

Bloomsbury Review, September-October, 1990, pp. 22, 24.

Booklist, January 1-15, 1996, p. 779; February 15, 1999, Benjamin Segedin, review of *Bone by Bone*, p. 1004; December 1, 1999, Nancy Bent, review of *Tigers in the Snow*, p. 660; September 15, 2003, Donna Seaman, review of *End of the Earth: Voyages to the White Continent*, p. 179.

Chicago Tribune Book World, April 5, 1981; March 13, 1983; June 24, 1990, pp. 1, 5; July 28, 1991, pp. 6-7.

Christian Science Monitor, March 11, 1983.

Denver Post, December 7, 1997, Kit Miniclier, "Killing 'gators, running guns, smuggling drugs," review of *Lost Man's River*, p. G5.

Hudson Review, winter, 1975-76; winter, 1981-82.

Kirkus Reviews, September 15, 1997, review of *Lost Man's River*.

Library Journal, August, 1955, M.L. Barrett, review of *Partisans*; March 15, 1999, Barbara Hoffert, review of *Bone by Bone*, p. 110; January, 2000, Edell Marie Schaefer, review of *Tigers in the Snow*, p. 152.

Literary Quarterly, May 15, 1975.

Los Angeles Times, March 22, 1979; November 16, 1990, p. E4; May 30, 1991, p. E1; November 8, 1992, p. L9.

Los Angeles Times Book Review, May 10, 1981; March 6, 1983; May 18, 1986; August 24, 1986; May 14, 1989, pp. 2, 11; July 8, 1990, pp. 1, 5; July 28, 1991, p. 4; December 6, 1992, p. 36.

Maclean's, August 13, 1990, p. 59; July 22, 1991, p. 41.

Nation, February 25, 1961, Terry Southern, review of *Raditzer*; December 13, 1965, J. Mitchell Morse, review of *At Play in the Fields of the Lord*; June 1, 1970, Roy Borngartz, review of *Sal Si Puedes: Cesar Chavez and the New American Revolution*; May 31, 1975; September 16, 1978, Jim Harrison, review of *The Snow Leopard*.

New Republic, June 7, 1975; September 23, 1978; March 7, 1983; June 4, 1984; November 5, 1990, Paul Zweig, review of *Indian Country*, pp. 43-45.

Newsweek, April 26, 1971; May 19, 1975, Peter S. Prescott, review of *Far Tortuga*; September 11, 1978; December 17, 1979; April 27, 1981; March 28, 1983; August 11, 1986; June 11, 1990, p. 63.

New Yorker, May 19, 1975; April 11, 1983; June 4, 1984.

New York Herald Tribune Book Review, April 4, 1954, Gene Baro, review of *Race Rock*.

New York Review of Books, December 23, 1965; January 4, 1968; August 31, 1972; January 25, 1973; August 7, 1975, Thomas R. Edwards, review of *Far Tortuga*; September 28, 1978; April 14, 1983; September 27, 1984; January 31, 1991, p. 18.

New York Times, April 4, 1954, Sylvia Berkman, review of *Race Rock*; October 2, 1955, William Goyen, review of *Partisans*; November 8, 1965; April 23, 1971; August 24, 1978; March 19, 1979; May 2, 1981; March 5, 1983; June 19, 1986; October 11, 1986; July 7, 1990, p. A16; August 22, 1991; July 26, 1992.

New York Times Book Review, April 4, 1954; October 2, 1955; November 22, 1959; October 15, 1961; November 18, 1962; November 7, 1965, Anatole Broyard, review of *At Play in the Fields of the Lord*; December 3, 1967; February 1, 1970; November 26, 1972; May 25, 1975; May 29, 1977; August 13, 1978; November 26, 1978; May 17, 1981; March 6,

1983; July 29, 1984; June 22, 1986; May 14, 1989, David Wagoner, review of *Indian Country,* p. 11; June 24, 1990, Ron Hansen, review of *Killing Mister Watson,* p. 7; August 18, 1991, p. 3; December 6, 1992, p. 52; December 3, 1995, p. 49; November 23, 1997, Janet Burroway, review of *Lost Man's River,* p. 16.

New York Times Magazine, June 10, 1990, pp. 30, 42, 94-96.

Progressive, April, 1990, pp. 28-29.

Publishers Weekly, May 9, 1986; September 1, 1989, p. 8; November 9, 1990, p. 12; March 15, 1999, review of *Bone by Bone,* p. 47; September 1, 2003, review of *End of the Earth,* p. 79.

Saturday Review, April 10, 1954; November 6, 1965, Granville Hicks, review of *At Play in the Fields of the Lord;* November 25, 1967; March 14, 1970; October 28, 1972; June 28, 1975, Bruce Allen, review of *Far Tortuga;* August, 1978, Paul Zweig, review of *The Snow Leopard;* April, 1981.

Smithsonian, March, 2002, Kevin Drajick, review of *The Birds of Heaven: Travels with Cranes,* p. 108.

Spectator, June 13, 1981; May 23, 1992, p. 34.

Sports Illustrated, December 22, 2003, Stephen J. Bodio, review of *End of the Earth,* p. A10.

Time, May 26, 1975; August 7, 1978; March 28, 1983; July 7, 1986; July 16, 1990, p. 82; January 11, 1993, pp. 42-43; May 17, 1999, John Skow, review of *Bone by Bone,* p. 89.

Time International, March 11, 2002, Bryan Walsh, review of *The Birds of Heaven: Travels with Cranes,* p. 52.

Times Literary Supplement, October 23, 1981; March 21, 1986, p. 299; September 22, 1989, p. 1023; August 31, 1990; July 17, 1992, p. 6.

Vanity Fair, December, 1991, p. 114.

Washington Post, December 13, 1978.

Washington Post Book World, August 20, 1978; April 19, 1981; March 27, 1983; May 20, 1984; June 29, 1986; June 24, 1990, Joyce Carol Oates, review of *Killing Mister Watson,* p. 5; July 14, 1991, p. 1.

Whole Earth, spring, 2002, review of *The Birds of Heaven: Travels with Cranes,* p. 95.

Wilson Library Bulletin, March, 1964.

World and I, October, 1999, review of *Bone by Bone,* p. 276.

*   *   *

MAUPIN, Armistead 1944-
(Armistead Jones Maupin, Jr.)

PERSONAL: Born May 13, 1944, in Washington, DC; son of Armistead Jones (a lawyer) and Diana Jane (Barton) Maupin. *Education:* University of North Carolina at Chapel Hill, B.A., 1966.

ADDRESSES: Home—San Francisco, CA. *Agent*—Amanda Urban, International Creative Management, 40 West 57th St., New York, NY 10019.

CAREER: Writer. Charleston *News & Courier,* Charleston, SC, reporter, 1970-71; Associated Press, San Francisco, CA, reporter, 1971-72; Lowry Russom & Leeper, San Francisco, CA, public-relations account executive, 1973; *Pacific Sun,* San Francisco, CA, columnist, 1974; San Francisco Opera, San Francisco, CA, publicist, 1975; *San Francisco Chronicle,* San Francisco, author of serial "Tales of the City," 1976-77; KRON-TV, San Francisco, CA, commentator, 1979; *San Francisco Examiner,* serialist, 1986.Speaker on gay issues. *Military service:* U.S. Navy, 1967-70; lieutenant; served in Vietnam.

AWARDS, HONORS: Freedom Leadership Award, Freedoms Foundation, 1972; Communications Award, Los Angeles Metropolitan Elections Commission, 1989; Gay/Lesbian Book Award, American Library Association, 1990, for exceptional achievement; best dramatic serial award, Royal Television Society (United Kingdom), Peabody Award from University of Georgia, outstanding miniseries award from Gay and Lesbian Alliance against Defamation, best miniseries award from National Board of Review, all 1994, and Emmy nomination, all for *Tales of the City.*

WRITINGS:

NOVELS; "TALES OF THE CITY" SERIES

Tales of the City (previously serialized in *San Francisco Chronicle;* also see below), Harper (New York, NY), 1978.

More Tales of the City (previously serialized in *San Francisco Chronicle;* also see below), Harper (New York, NY), 1980.

Further Tales of the City (previously serialized in *San Francisco Chronicle;* also see below), Harper (New York, NY), 1982.

Babycakes (previously serialized in *San Francisco Chronicle*), Harper (New York, NY), 1984.

Significant Others (previously serialized in *San Francisco Examiner*), Harper (New York, NY), 1987.

Sure of You, Harper (New York, NY), 1989.

28 Barbary Lane (contains *Tales of the City, More Tales of the City,* and *Further Tales of the City*), Harper (New York, NY), 1990.

The Complete Tales of the City, Harper (New York, NY), 1991.

Back to Barbary Lane: The Final Tales of the City Omnibus, Harper (New York, NY), 1991.

OTHER

Maybe the Moon (novel), Harper (New York, NY), 1992.

The Night Listener, Harper (New York, NY), 2000.

Editor of *The Essential Clive Barker: Selected Fiction,* 1999. Author of introduction, Jan Struther, *Mrs. Miniver,* Harper (New York, NY), 1985, and Don Bachardy, *Drawings of the Male Nude,* Twelvetrees Press, 1985. Author of dialogue for stage productions, including *Beach Blanket Babylon, La Perichole* (opera) by Jacques Offenbach, and *Heart's Desire* (musical) by Glen Roven, 1990. Contributor to *Faber Book of Gay Short Fiction,* edited by Edmund White, Faber, 1991. Contributor to periodicals, including the *Advocate, Los Angeles Times, New York Times,* and the *Village Voice.*

ADAPTATIONS: "Tales of the City" novels were adapted into a television miniseries (six one-hour episodes) by Richard Kramer, produced by Maupin and British Television's Channel 4 in 1993 and broadcast in the United States by the Public Broadcasting Service (PBS), 1994; an additional miniseries titled *More Tales of the City* was produced for the Showtime Channel and broadcast in 1998.

SIDELIGHTS: Armistead Maupin is the creator of the popular "Tales of the City," a cycle of stories that first appeared in the mid-1970s as a serial in the *San Francisco Chronicle.* The column was collected into a series of six novels and adapted into an award-winning television miniseries. In writing the "Tales," Maupin's "intention was to take America's shifting cultural landscape and reflect it in a work that would feature a wide cross-section of characters—gay and straight, male and female, rich and poor," explained David L. Ulin in the *Village Voice.* The stories follow the fortunes of various inhabitants of a San Francisco boarding house located at 28 Barbary Lane and operated by the mysterious but maternal Anna Madrigal. The early novels focus on Mary Ann Singleton, an ingenue from Cleveland, and her best friend, Michael Tolliver, a gay man nicknamed "Mouse." Charles Solomon pointed out in the *Los Angeles Times Book Review,* "the search for love and security in an increasingly uncertain world remains at the

heart of this popular series." As the liberated 1970s gives way to the 1980s, Solomon noted, this search becomes complicated by the rise of the AIDS epidemic that comes to dominate San Francisco. The "Tales of the City" series earned Maupin comparisons to several authors, including Charles Dickens; Marcel Proust; P.G. Wodehouse; and Jan Struther, author of *Mrs. Miniver.* It has also, according to Ulin, established the author's reputation as one of the premier "social satirists of his era."

The personal journey that brought Maupin to San Francisco and his literary career as a chronicler of the region began in Raleigh, North Carolina. As a child of the South growing up in the 1950s and 1960s, he was caught up in segregation and the emerging civil rights movement. *Los Angeles Times* contributor Steven M.H. Braitman related, "He became, in his own words, an 'uptight, archconservative, racist brat' who worked for Jesse Helms for a time. He joined the Navy and served in Vietnam. President Richard M. Nixon invited him to the White House and honored him as a patriotic model Republican." Maupin once commented: "In the late '60s I was very much the young Republican jerk. I went to Vietnam because I thought it was the right thing to do. The first election I was able to vote in, I voted for Barry Goldwater. I was raised in the South and this was just the way I thought things were supposed to be. It wasn't until I got to San Francisco in '71 that my life began to change. By that time the hippie doctrine of tolerance had come to apply to gay people as well, and I began to loosen up. It was no accident that my literary drive emerged as soon as I stopped hiding my sexuality. There was this irresistible urge to tell everything I knew, to explain myself, to demystify a subject that had scared me silly for years."

In San Francisco, a city with a thriving gay community, Maupin came into his own. He told William Hamilton of the *Washington Post,* "In 1971 I discovered a town where there were not only lots of people like me but a large number of heterosexuals who were friendly to people like me, and that made all the difference. I found a society where tolerance and acceptance were valued above everything." It is this community that Maupin set out to capture in "Tales of the City." "My aim from the very beginning was to create a large framework of humanity and to place gay characters within that framework. That was what I had missed in books all along. As a gay man, when I read a novel I wanted my own kind included in a central way, the way we fit into real life," Maupin once commented. He also wanted to explore appearances and how people hide behind them. "The books are essentially about forgiveness, acceptance, and love," he explained. "I'm also fascinated by the huge gulf between the way things appear to be and the way they really are. My characters get into trouble when they stop being honest with each other. Their deceit often arises because they love each other, but that deceit becomes, invariably, their downfall. I think both those messages—of forgiveness and of the essential folly of deceit—probably come from my being gay. When you're a gay person, it's much easier to observe the gulf between truth and illusion, because you're often a part of creating it. You learn at a very early age to wear disguises. My work is about taking off those disguises."

Critical attention was slow in coming for the "Tales of the City" books, in part, Maupin believes, because the works were originally published in a California newspaper, well outside the New York publishing scene. Yet the author has earned growing recognition for his witty and compassionate insights into contemporary life. Micheline Hagan, discussing the "Tales" series in the *San Francisco Review of Books,* admired Maupin's "ability to deliver social messages through intuitive, timely portraits," particularly of gay culture in America. "His most subversive act is to write in such a matter-of-fact manner about his gay characters. . . . Acceptance is a given," noted David Feinberg in the *New York Times Book Review.*

As he was writing his six "Tales" novels, Maupin began an effort to have them adapted for the screen. More than ten years of negotiations and struggles to preserve them against alterations taught Maupin about the film and television business. During that entire time, he was unable to find an American producer who was willing to keep the stories close to their author's original intent. As Maupin told Betsy Sharkey in an interview in the *New York Times,* "One of the things that so enrages me . . . is that 17 years after this appeared in a daily newspaper, Hollywood finds it too controversial. *Tales of the City* begins with the premise that gay people are a part of life, part of the whole canvas. It is not about the trauma of being gay; it's about the great adventure of all of us interacting with each other." In the early 1990s, Maupin finally found a backer in Britain's Channel 4. Channel 4 decided to film a six-hour miniseries in San Francisco with American actors and to keep close to Maupin's original stories. The reason, coproducer Antony Root told Sharkey, was that "we consider them modern classics. They are classic not within only the gay community, as they seem to be [in America]. Literally, you find secretaries on the Underground reading them." The television miniseries first appeared on Channel 4 in 1993 then made its way across the Atlan-

tic, airing on PBS in January of 1994. *Tales of the City* was "PBS highest-rated dramatic series in a decade," reported Judith Michaelson in the *Los Angeles Times,* and it earned both a Peabody Award for excellence in television from the University of Georgia and an Emmy nomination. Despite this reception, Maupin was unable to find a U.S. producer for a television sequel.

In *Maybe the Moon,* Maupin's first novel outside the "Tales of the City" series, the author combines his interest in contemporary society with his insights into the film and television business. The novel's main character is Cady Roth, who at thirty-one inches tall was perfect for the role of Mr. Woods in an *E.T.*-like movie. Cady's problem is that she has been forbidden by the studio to reveal that she was the actress inside the costume and cannot, therefore, enjoy the fame that goes along with the role. She finds friendship and acceptance in Hollywood's gay subculture, and eventually finds love with an average-sized man. "As usual, the author's portrayals of his characters' tangled motivations, their longings and desires, are right on the mark," commented Ulin in the *Village Voice.* Yet Ulin had some reservations: "Despite its inspirational flashes, *Maybe the Moon* doesn't take shape as successfully as *Tales of the City* did." And, he concluded, "All the editorializing tends to trivialize [Maupin's] story, turning it into a snapshot rather than a reflection of the times." For a London *Observer* reviewer, however, "the zingers remain flawless", and Maupin's portrayal of the wild West Coast is filtered through his analytical East Coast mind.

In his next novel, *The Night Listener,* Maupin created a story in which the lines between fiction and reality are blurred. The novel's narrator, Gabriel Noone, has much in common with Maupin: He is an openly gay writer whose quirky vignettes of life in San Francisco have made him something of a media celebrity. Noone's radio serial, "Noone at Night," is a success, but his personal life is a shambles. His long-time companion Jess has recently left him, and in the wake of that breakup, Noone finds himself with a massive case of writer's block. Into his life comes Pete, a 13-year-old boy who has written a book about his experience of horrific sexual abuse at the hands of his parents—pedophiles who prostituted their son. In telephone conversations with Pete, Noone learns that his radio program has served as a lifeline for the troubled, AIDS-infected boy, who now lives with the doctor who rescued him. Pete in turn becomes a vital part of Noone's life, as does Pete's adoptive mother, Donna. Yet their attempts to meet in person are continually thwarted.

Throughout his life, Noone has been betrayed by those closest to him; now, he begins to have doubts about

Pete. Jess warns Noone that Pete is nothing more than an alter ego of the troubled doctor, Donna. After Pete supposedly dies from AIDS-related complications, Noone receives a final phone call from the boy, which, according to a *Kirkus Reviews* writer "will give you the creeps and move you to tears almost simultaneously." That writer noted that the postmodern underpinnings of *The Night Listener* draw attention to "Maupin's intellectual shortcomings rather than his emotional strengths, but strong storytelling, punchy humor, and a warm-hearted narrator carry the day." *Publishers Weekly*'s reviewer gave the book an even stronger endorsement, writing: "As in his earlier works, reading Maupin's prose is like meeting up with a beloved old friend; it's an easy, uncomplicated encounter filled with warmth, wisdom and familiar touches of humor. But there's pathos here as well, and sharp-edged drama with a few hairpin turns."

BIOGRAPHICAL AND CRITICAL SOURCES:

BOOKS

FitzGerald, Frances, *Cities on a Hill,* Simon & Schuster (New York, NY), 1986.
Gay & Lesbian Literature, St. James Press (Detroit, MI), 1994, pp. 253-254.
Herron, Don, *The Literary World of San Francisco,* City Lights (San Francisco, CA), 1985.
Hudson, Rock, and Sara Davidson, *Rock Hudson: His Story,* Morrow (New York, NY), 1986.
Nungesser, Lon G., *Epidemic of Courage,* St. Martin's Press (New York, NY), 1986.
Rofes, Eric E., *Gay Life,* Dolphin/Doubleday (Garden City, NY), 1986.
Shilts, Randy, *Conduct Unbecoming,* St. Martin's Press (New York, NY), 1993.
Summers, Claude J., *The Gay and Lesbian Literary Heritage,* Holt (New York, NY), 1995.

PERIODICALS

Advocate, June 23, 1987; January 12, 1993, review of *Maybe the Moon,* p. 92; December 28, 1993, pp. 71-72.
America, February 26, 1994, p. 18.
Booklist, September 15, 1992, review of *Maybe the Moon,* p. 100; December 15, 1995, review of audio version of *Further Tales of the City,* p. 717; July, 2000, Ray Olson, review of *The Night Listener,* p. 1974.

Books, January, 1993, review of *Maybe the Moon,* p. 22; January, 1994, review of *Maybe the Moon,* p. 16.
Boston Globe, November 20, 1989, p. 32.
Chicago Tribune, April 28, 1983; July 6, 1987; January 5, 1994, p. 7.
Entertainment Weekly, November 6, 1992, p. 60; January 18, 1993, p. 30; July 30, 1993, review of *Maybe the Moon,* p. 53; May 27, 1994, review of *Tales of the City,* p. 78; July 25, 1997, review of *Tales of the City,* p. 65.
Examiner (San Francisco, CA), May 4, 1986.
Frontiers 3, November, 1989, p. 18.
Guardian Weekly, February 6, 1994, review of *Maybe the Moon,* p. 28.
Hudson Review, spring, 1980, p. 146.
Kirkus Reviews, July 1, 2000, review of *The Night Listener,* p. 910.
Kliatt, May, 1995, review of audio version of *Tales of the City,* p. 52; September, 1995, review of audio version of *Further Tales of the City,* p. 54.
Lambda Book Report, January, 1993, review of *Maybe the Moon,* p. 36; September, 1993, review of *Maybe the Moon,* p. 42.
Library Journal, November 1, 1992, review of *Maybe the Moon,* p. 118; December, 1992, review of audio version of *Maybe the Moon,* pp. 208-209; March 1, 1995, review of audio version of *Tales of the City,* p. 118; September 1, 1995, review of audio version of *Further Tales of the City,* p. 224; August, 2000, Devon Thomas, review of *The Night Listener,* p. 160.
London Review of Books, March 25, 1993, review of *Maybe the Moon,* p. 21.
Los Angeles Times, July 20, 1982; November 14, 1993, p. CAL-5; April 11, 1994, Judith Michaelson, article, "'Tales' Author: PBS Is Being Pressured by Religious Right," p. F2; June 3, 1994, Jeff Kaye, brief article, "F, 2:3," p. F2; May 10, 1995, Steven M.H. Braitman, article, "He Still Has Plenty of Tales to Tell," p. E1.
Los Angeles Times Book Review, June 9, 1982; July 19, 1987; November 5, 1989, Charles Solomon, review of *Tales of the City, More Tales of the City, Further Tales of the City, Babycakes, Significant Others,* p. 20; August 8, 1993, review of *Maybe the Moon,* p. 11; February 6, 1994, review of *Tales of the City,* p. 12.
Mother Jones, November, 1989, p. 54.
Nation, December 26, 1987, p. 796.
New Statesman and Society, March 2, 1990, pp. 36, 38; March 25, 1994, p. 13.
Newsweek, October 30, 1989, p. 77.
New York, November 2, 1992, review of *Maybe the Moon,* p. 92.

New Yorker, July 21, 1986; July 28, 1986.

New York Times, February 28, 1993, Betsy Sharkey, "Maupin's 'Dream of the Future, Set in the Past,'" p. 27; January 13, 1994, p. A21.

New York Times Book Review, November 18, 1984, Jaqueline Austin, review of *Babycakes,* p. 32; October 22, 1989, David Feinberg, review of *Sure of You,* p. 25; September 30, 1990, p. 46; November 29, 1992, Norah Johnson, review of *Maybe the Moon,* p. 24; August 29, 1993, review of *Maybe the Moon,* p. 20.

Observer (London), February 11, 1990, p. 65; June 24, 1990, p. 50; February 7, 1993, review of *Maybe the Moon,* p. 54; January 16, 1994, review of *Maybe the Moon,* p. 21.

Outweek, October 29, 1989, p. 42.

People Weekly, March 5, 1990, p. 51; January 18, 1993, p. 30.

Publishers Weekly, March 20, 1987, p. 53; September 7, 1992, p. 74; November 2, 1992, review of audio version of *Maybe the Moon,* p. 32; July 5, 1993, review of *Maybe the Moon,* p. 69; December 20, 1993, review of *Tales of the City,* p. 65; August 7, 2000, review of *The Night Listener,* p. 71.

San Francisco Bay Guardian, October 11, 1989, p. 24.

San Francisco Chronicle, July 13, 1982.

San Francisco Review of Books, number 3, 1989, p. 18; fall, 1992, p. 5.

Spectator, February 10, 1990, p. 31.

Time, December 7, 1992, review of *Maybe the Moon,* p. 83.

Times (London, England), April 14, 1988.

Times Educational Supplement, December 23, 1994, reviews of *Maybe the Moon* and *Tales of the City,* p. 19.

Times Literary Supplement, April 8, 1988; March 9, 1990, p. 258; February 5, 1993, review of *Maybe the Moon,* p. 19.

TV Guide, January 8, 1994, pp. 26-28.

Village Voice, August 31, 1982, David L. Ulin, review of *Tales of the City,* p. 10; December 1, 1992, David L. Ulin, review of *Maybe the Moon,* p. 58.

Village Voice Literary Supplement, October, 1987, pp. 6-9; October, 1993, p. 25.

Voice Literary Supplement, October, 1993, review of *Maybe the Moon,* p. 25.

Washington Post, January 10, 1994, William Hamilton, interview with Armistead Maupin, p. B1.

Washington Post Book World, November 22, 1992, review of *Maybe the Moon,* p. 11.

ONLINE

Armistead Maupin Web Site, http://www.literarybent. com/ (August 4, 2004).

OTHER

Armistead Maupin Is a Man I Dreamt Up (television documentary directed by Kate Meynell), PBS, 1993.

* * *

MAUPIN, Armistead Jones, Jr.
See MAUPIN, Armistead

* * *

MAYO, Jim
See L'AMOUR, Louis

For Reference

Not to be taken from this room